LAROUSSE
Dictionary of
WRITERS

LAROUSSE

Dictionary of

WRITERS

Editor
Rosemary Goring

LAROUSSE

LAROUSSE
Larousse plc
43–45 Annandale Street, Edinburgh EH7 4AZ
Larousse Kingfisher Chambers Inc.
95 Madison Avenue, New York, New York 10016

First published by Larousse plc 1994

British Library Cataloging in Publication Data
for this book is available from the British Library

Library of Congress Catalog Card Number: 95-081846

ISBN 0-7523-0039-3

The publisher would like to thank Peter Dollard, Library Director at
Alma College, Michigan, for his invaluable assistance
in reviewing the material for this volume.

Typeset from author-generated disks by BPC Digital Data Ltd
Printed in Great Britain by Clays Ltd, St Ives plc

Contents

Contributors

Dr Colin Affleck

Stuart Bathgate

Fran Cannon

Anne Collett

Richard Cook

Dr Jo M Evans

Dr Helena Forsås-Scott

Iain Grant

Peter Graves

Allan Hunter

Dr Jeremy Idle

Robert Irwin

Mechthild Krüger

Arne Kruse

Huw Aled Lewis

Dr Christopher Little

Henry Maas

Deirdre Maclean

Heidi Macpherson

Kenny Mathieson

Julie Morris

Brian Morton

Helen E Mundler

Hayden Murphy

Jim Orton

Greig Proctor

Dr David Reid

Dr Mario Relich

Susan Rennie

Dr Anita Shanley

Dr Berthold Schoene

Martin Seymour-Smith

Alan Taylor

Gunilla Blom Thomsen

Bjarne Thorup Thomsen

Michael Thorn

Peter Whitebrook

Karina Williamson

Introduction

In many respects this dictionary is like a well-stocked bookshop. In a relatively small space it gathers together an enormous range of authors, from the familiar names of school and university English courses to some of the most neglected figures in world literature. As in a bookshop a Bloomsbury classic may be flanked by an arresting science-fiction title, which in turn is only a short distance from a quiet enclave of women's writing, where the intriguing titles of 18th-century gentlewomen peer out from the shade of their neighbours.

We hope the *Larousse Dictionary of Writers* will be used as the first place to look when trying to find out about an author, and the aim has been to cover as widely as possible the diversity of creative writers across the world, from all periods and all countries. The basis of selection has largely been confined to novelists, short-story writers, essayists, poets, playwrights, dramatists and travel writers, plus the most notable of screen and television writers. However, we also include some names that do not fall strictly into the literary camp, but whose influence on the nature of creative writing has been immense; into this category fall such psychological theorists as Freud and Jung; critics like F R and Q D Leavis; and philosophers such as Rudolf Steiner and Gurdjieff. Also included are those who have achieved a notable literary 'first', such as Hannah Adams, the earliest professional woman writer in the United States.

Although literary merit forms the basis for the majority of the entries included, it has not been the only touchstone for selection. We have, for example, included the top best-selling authors — Jackie Collins, Jeffrey Archer, Robert Ludlum — without whom no bookshop would be complete (or as profitable). Nor would it be fully stocked without the best of the genre writers — the doyens of historical novels, romances and westerns; of detective, thriller and crime fiction; and the leaders of science and fantasy fiction.

While fame and reputation have been important indicators of whom to include, we have also strayed into less familiar territory to cover writers who are known only in their own countries, largely because they have not yet been translated, but whose talent emphatically deserves a wider public. At the other end of the spectrum are those relatively minor names who, nevertheless, remain an established part of the literary firmament, and thus are given a mention.

Inevitably there is a British and American bias to our selection, but as far as possible we have tried to cover the most significant writers from every country, and to give fair attention to those from marginalized cultures or languages, such as Native Americans, Basques, Bretons and Gaels.

Within the scope of thumbnail sketches we give a brief outline of an author's life and point to what we consider are his or her most representative works. In many cases we have attempted to place a writer in context, sometimes by making reference to other writers (referred to in bold type if they also have an entry, unless their name falls within a quotation), and to give an indication of his or her major themes and style.

To help with this we have, where feasible, given rough translations of foreign-language titles. In some cases, though, to attempt even an approximate translation might misrepresent the work, and in such instances we have left well alone. Where the foreign title is a proper name, we have not repeated this; similarly, where a published English translation is identical to the original, we have simply given the date of the translation. Also, where there has been more than one English translation, we have generally cited the earliest.

Although it may seem like stating the obvious, it is worth adding that the length of an entry is not necessarily an indicator of the subject's importance. Some authors can be dealt with succinctly, while others have had such complicated or varied careers that to give a bare outline takes several lines; some writers' works need greater elucidation, others' are relatively self-explanatory.

As a pointer towards further reading, at the end of many entries we list one or two biographies or essays about the writer. This selection has been based on the works we believe are most useful, rather than necessarily those most recently published. Where no author is given for a bibliographical reference, this is because the work cited is by the writer whose entry it is attached to, and is usually an autobiography or memoir.

Reference books stand or fall by their reliability, and every effort has been made to use the most trustworthy sources. Inevitably, though, some errors will have found their way into this work and we would be most grateful for being advised of any mistakes where they occur.

In his *Life of Schiller*, Carlyle commented that there is 'no more sickening reading than the biographies of authors'. With this dictionary we hope to prove him wrong.

Rosemary Goring
May 1994

Acknowledgements

Foremost I would like to thank Martin Seymour-Smith for the advice and knowledge he has offered throughout the compilation of this book. The suggestions he has put forward have helped substantially to shape this work, and I am hugely grateful for his perspective. I would also like to thank Kenny Mathieson, Brian Morton, Jim Orton and Peter Whitebrook for being so generous with their help; likewise Dr J G D Kerr, Alan Taylor of *Scotland on Sunday*, Sally Craighead of Thins Bookshop, Edinburgh and Catherine Schwarz. Thanks are also due to Peter Dollard, Library Director at Alma College, Michigan, the staff at Auckland Central Library, the Reference Department staff at Edinburgh Central Library, Faith Pullen at the University of Edinburgh, Catherine Lockerbie of *The Scotsman* and Giles Foden at the *Times Literary Supplement*. For help with translations I am most grateful to George Davidson, Ilona Morison, Liam Roger, Berthold Schoene and Anne Seaton. Many thanks also to my colleagues at Chambers Larousse for their unfailing encouragement and wit.

A

AAKJAER, Jeppe
(1865–1930)

Danish dramatist, novelist, poet and translator (of **Burns**), born in the Jutland village bearing his name. He was most famous for his radical novel *Vredens Born* (1904, 'Children of Rage'), a vivid protest against the exploitation of farm labourers by their wealthy masters. He is now, however, chiefly remembered for his folk-like poetry.

AARESTRUP, Emil
(1800–56)

Danish poet. A graduate in medicine, he combined a successful professional career—first as a general practitioner in the Southern Isles, then as a health inspector in Odense—with a mainly private poetic production that was to break new ground for Danish erotic poetry. With only one collection, *Digte* (1838, 'Poems'), published in his lifetime, Aarestrup was largely unimpeded by the literary conventions of his day and created a poetic universe distinctive for its bold concentration on sexual desire and fulfilment. By means of a masterly, fluid verse technique, his short texts outline a world of beauty centred on nature and the female body. Although focusing on pleasure, the poems frequently contain overtones of dread and death, conveying insights into the complex nature of desire that anticipated those of **Sigmund Freud** and many modernists.

▷ K Zeruneith, *Den frigjorte. Emil Aarestrup i digtning og samtid. En biografi* (1981)

ABBAS, (Khwaja) Ahmad
(1914–)

Indian novelist, short-story writer, filmmaker and journalist, whose Muslim background, prolific output and choice of English as his literary language have tended to marginalize him in his native country. A Gandhian nationalist, Abbas has dealt sharply with the anglophile intellectual middle class, attacking it in his first collection of short stories *Not All Lies!* (1945). A sophisticated awareness of the relationship between personal and political forces is also shown in his first novel *Tomorrow is Ours!* (1943), which anticipates some of the concerns of **Salman Rushdie**'s *Midnight's Children*. In his masterpiece, *Inqilab* (1955, 'Revolution'), he creates a deracinated and culturally displaced protagonist in order to gauge the human implications of major events in Indian history, from the Amritsar massacre to the Congress's 'Quit India' resolution of 1942. Abbas has also written perceptively about Jawaharlal Nehru, his daughter Indira Gandhi, Mao Zedong, and the Maoist Naxalite revolutionaries.

▷ *I Am Not an Island: An Experiment in Autobiography* (1977)

ABBOTT, George Francis
(1887–)

American dramatist, director, producer and actor, born in Forestville, New York State. He studied drama at the celebrated 47 Workshop at Harvard, where he began writing. His first major hit came with *Broadway* (1926), the first of a number of successful melodramas, farces and musical comedies which he either co-wrote, staged, or both. He was awarded the Pulitzer Prize for Drama in 1960 for the hit musical *Fiorello!* (1959), along with co-writer **Jerome Weidman**, lyricist Sheldon Harnick (1924–) and composer Jerry Bock (1928–). He is widely regarded as an important innovator in the staging of musicals.

ABD AL-MALIK NURI
(1914–)

Iraqi short-story writer, whose *Nasid al-ard* (1954, 'Song of the Earth') shows the influence of European techniques. He is known as a gloomy and pessimistic writer.

▷ I J Boullata (ed), *Critical Perspectives in Modern Arabic Literature* (1980)

ABD-UL-LATIF
(1162–1231)

Arabian writer, born in Baghdad. He taught medicine and philosophy at Cairo and Damascus. His best-known book is a work on Egypt.

▷ T Clabert, *Latifi, oder biografische Nachtrichten von vorzuglichen turkische Dichtern* (1800)

ABDÜLLHAK HAMID TARHAN
(1852–1937)

Turkish dramatist, born in Bebek. He belonged to the Tanzimat ('Transformation') school of writers, who sought to bring Turkey into Europe. His model was **Racine**, but he had read **Shakespeare**. His bold verse plays, usually on themes from Islamic history, are genuinely stirring as well as intelligently conceived. His influence on the Turkish theatre cannot be over-estimated.

ABE Kobo
(1924–93)

Japanese novelist and playwright, born in Tokyo. He trained as a doctor, but turned to literature after graduating. Recognition in Japan came with the award of the Akutagawa Prize for *The Wall* in 1951. His international reputation is often linked with that of writers like **Junichiro Tanizaki**, **Yasunari Kawabata**, and **Yukio Mishima**, but unlike them he stands outside the great tradition of Japanese literature. His predominant theme of alienation is explored in a series of novels and plays, his early work set in the wasteland of Manchuria and post-war Japan; in later books he focused on an urban, industrialized society on the brink of explosive economic growth. His novels include *Daiyon Kampyoki* (1959, Eng trans *Inter Ice Age Four*, 1971), *Suna no onna* (1962, Eng trans *The Woman in the Dunes*, 1965) and *Mikkai* (1977, Eng trans *Secret Rendezvous*, 1980).
▷H Yamaanouchi, *The Search for Authenticity in Modern Japanese Literature* (1978)

À BECKETT, Gilbert Abbott
(1811–56)

English humorist, born in London. He was educated at Westminster and in 1841 was called to the Bar. In 1849 he became a metropolitan police magistrate. As well as writing for *Punch* and *The Times*, he was the author of *The Comic Blackstone* (1846), and comic histories of England and Rome.
▷A A'Beckett, *The A'Becketts of Punch: memoirs of fathers and sons* (1903)

ABELL, Kjeld
(1901–61)

Danish playwright, born in Ribe, the leading modernizer of 20th-century Danish drama. After graduating in Politics, and working as a scene painter and dress designer at theatres in Paris and London, he experienced his breakthrough as a playwright in Copenhagen with the activating, revue-style play *Melodien der blev v'k* (1935, 'The Melody that got Lost'). It tells the story of the liberation of Larsen, a white-collar worker who has lost his 'melody' under the constraints of a conventional working and married life—a topical theme in European literature of the 1930s. Abell broke emphatically away from the naturalistic 'drawing-room drama' in the tradition of **Ibsen** and **Bjørnson**: he placed actors

among the audience, brought the stage decorations to life, blended speech and song, and used long addresses to the audience. In *Anna Sophie Hedvig* (1939), the title hero is a mousy schoolmistress who kills her tyrannical colleague. The play makes a political statement about the need for the individual to stand up against authoritarian ideologies. This theme was developed further in *Silkeborg*, written during World War II, but first performed in 1946. After the war, Abell continued his experimentation with plays such as *Dage på en sky* (1947, 'Days on a Cloud'), *Den blå pekingeser* (1954, 'The Blue Pekinese') and *Skriget* (1961, 'The Scream').
▷*Fodnoten i støvet* (1951); F J Marker, *Kjeld Abell* (1976)

ABERCROMBIE, Lascelles
(1881–1938)

English poet and critic, born in Ashton-on-Mersey. Educated at Malvern College and Victoria University, Manchester, he became Professor of English at Leeds (1922) and London (1929), and Reader at Oxford (1935). His works include *Romanticism* (1926) and *Principles of Literary Criticism* (1932). He published several volumes of Georgian-style poetry, collected as *The Poems of Lascelles Abercrombie* (1930). A posthumous collection of *Lyrics and Unfinished Poems* appeared in 1940. A few contemporary critics have found his poetry well above the general run of the Georgians.
▷O Ellon, *Lascelles Abercrombie, 1881–1938* (1939)

ABISH, Walter
(1931–)

American novelist, short-story writer and poet, he was born in Vienna and raised in China, before moving to the USA, where he took citizenship in 1960. After teaching at Columbia University in New York for more than 10 years, he made his name with the experimental novel *Alphabetical Africa* (1974), in which the opening chapter consists only of words beginning with A, the second of words beginning with A and B, and so on until the 26th chapter, when the process reverses. A witty linguistic device allows him to explore ideas about cultural identity in the outwardly more conventional *How German Is It* (1980), in which the central character's father has been a conspirator in the 'July Plot' to kill Hitler, but who has himself been forced to betray fellow members of a terrorist group. His later *99: The New Meaning* (1990) is also experimental in form, but with a more conventional structure, as is *Eclipse Fever* (1993). Abish's short stories are collected in *Minds*

Meet (1975) and *In the Future Perfect* (1977), his verse in *Duel Site* (1970).

▷R Martin, 'Walter Abish: Perfect Unfamiliarity, Familiar Imperfections', in *Journal of American Studies*, vol 17 (1983)

ABOUT, Edmond François Valentin
(1828–85)

French journalist and novelist, born in Dieuze, in Lorraine. After schooling in Paris, he studied archaeology in Athens. On returning to Paris, he devoted himself to a literary career. He was a sceptical, crusading journalist, and founded the journal *Le XIX Siècle* ('The Nineteenth Century'). His fiction includes *Le Roi des montagnes* (1856, 'The King of the Mountains'), *Madelon* (1863), *Alsace* (1872), which cost him a week's imprisonment at the hands of the Germans, and *Le Roman d'un brave homme* (1880, 'The Story of a Good Man').

ABRAHAMS, Peter
(1919–)

South African novelist and polemicist, son of an Ethiopian father and a 'coloured' woman (ie he was then designated as 'of mixed race'). He began as a protest poet (*A Blackman Speaks of Freedom*, 1938), then graduated to novels and stories. He left South Africa at the age of 20 to become a merchant seaman, lived in England for a time, and settled in Jamaica as a journalist. His most famous, subtle and successful novel was *A Wreath for Udomo* (1956), which dealt with the problem of what would happen when newly independent Black nations were confronted with the choice between collaborating with white imperialists for financial advantage, and their moral imperative to support other liberation movements. His work is still eagerly discussed, but after *This Island Now* (1967), on a Caribbean dictatorship, he wrote less fiction. *Tell Freedom* (1954) is a moving and widely read autobiography.

▷W Cartey, *Whispers from a Continent* (1969)

ABRAMOV, Fyodor Aleksandrovich
(1920–)

Russian novelist and story-writer, born in Verkola, in the Archangel region, which forms the background to his fiction (none of which has been translated). He has steeped himself in the history and culture of his region, and his dialogue is closely modelled on peasant usage. His main theme, which nonetheless never obtrudes, is the artificial circumstances brought about by collectivization, with its unrealistic demands.

ABREU, Casimiro José Marques de
(1839–60)

Brazilian romantic poet, born near Rio de Janeiro. Doomed to die young from consumption, his ingenuous verse has charmed most modern Brazilian readers, who also admire his dramatic fragment *Camões* (1854). He has always been the 'favourite of the folk'.

ABSE, Dannie
(1923–)

Welsh writer and physician, born in Cardiff. Educated at the Welsh National School of Medicine, King's College, London and Westminster Hospital, he has been senior specialist in the chest clinic at the Central Medical Establishment, London, since 1954. His literary output includes nine volumes of poetry, two novels and half a dozen plays. His autobiographical volumes are *A Poet in the Family* (1974) and *A Strong Dose of Myself* (1982), and the autobiographical novel *Ash on a Young Man's Sleeve* (1954).

ABUL-ALA, Ahmed ibn Adullah, al-Maarri
(973–1057)

Arabic poet, born, as his name signifies, at Mararra, near Aleppo in Syria. He was blind from early childhood, and spent most of his life in seclusion in his home town. He stands apart from all other Arab poets in what has been called his atheism and harsh judgement of the world. His most famous work, *Risalat al-Ghufran* (Eng trans *The Epistle of Forgiveness*, 1943), has been compared to the *Divine Comedy* of **Dante**, who may have heard of it (even if he never read it). The story of a journey through heaven and hell, it is one of the most original and perplexing of all long Arabic poems.

▷H Baerlin, *Abdul Ala the Syrian* (1914); R A Nicolson, *Studies in Islamic Poetry* (1921)

ABU NUWAS
(c.760–c.813–815)

Arab poet, considered one of the greatest poets of the 'Abbasid period. He abandoned older, traditional forms for erotic and witty lyrics. He was a favourite at the court of the caliph Hārūn al-Raschīd in Baghdad, and figures in the *Arabian Nights*.

▷W H Ingrams, *Abu Nuwas in Life and Legend* (1933)

ABU TAMMAM, Habib ibn Aus
(807–c.850)

Arabian poet, born near Lake Tiberias, the son of a Christian. He rose to favour under the caliphs al-Ma'mūn and al-Mu'tasim as a composer of panegyrics. He travelled extensively and towards the end of his life he discovered a private library of desert poetry at Hamadhan. From this he compiled a celebrated anthology of early Arab poetry, the *Hamasu*.

▷ F Ruckert, *Hamasa oder des altesten arabischen Volkslieder gesammelt von Abu Tammam* (1846)

ACEDEVO DÍAZ, Edourdo
(1851–1924)

Uruguayan novelist, born in La Unión, in many respects 'the father of the modern Uruguayan novel'. His son, also called Edourdo (1882–1978), was himself an Argentinian novelist of some small distinction, who wrote a book on his father (1941). Acedevo Díaz, modelling himself on **Pérez Galdós**, wrote a famous and illuminating trilogy on the history of Uruguay, *Himno de Sangre* (1888–93, 'Hymn of Blood'); but his most famous book was *Soledad* (1894), an exemplary gauchesque novel about an outlawed minstrel who falls in love with a girl on a ranch. He founded the daily newspaper *El National* in 1896.

ACHARD, Marcel, originally Marcel Auguste Ferréol
(1901–74)

French playwright, a member of the Académie française, who charmed audiences in Paris and New York with his witty comedies and fantasies. His character Charlemagne, a vagabond, was first introduced in *La Vie est belle* (1918, 'Life is Beautiful'). Many plays were adapted for the American stage, eg *I Know My Love* (1949), from *Auprès de ma blonde* (1946).

ACHEBE, Chinua, originally Albert Chinualumogo
(1930–)

Nigerian novelist, poet and essayist, born in Ogidi, the son of a mission teacher. He was educated at the University College of Ibadan, and his early career was in broadcasting, but the publication of his first novel *Things Fall Apart* (1958) at once heralded the emergence of a unique voice in African literature. Set in the second half of the 19th century and presenting an unsentimentalized picture of the Ibo tribe, it has since been translated into 40 languages. Writing exclusively in English, he confirmed his early promise with four more novels, *No Longer At Ease* (1960), *Arrow of God* (1964), *A Man of the People* (1966) and *Anthills of the Savanna* (1987), which was shortlisted for the Booker Prize. An overtly political writer, he has taught at

the universities of Massachusetts and Connecticut, and at the University of Nigeria at Nsukka.

▷ D Carroll, *Chinua Achebe* (1970); G D Skillan, *The Novels of Chinua Achebe* (1969)

ACHILLES, Tatius
(?3rd century)

Greek writer. A rhetorician at Alexandria, he wrote the romance *Leucippe and Cleitophon*.

ACHILLINI, Claudio
(1574–1640)

Italian Baroque poet, born in Bologna. A minor follower of **Marino**, he is now celebrated for his almost comic bombast and convolutedness: **Manzoni** quotes him, with notable irony, in *I promessi sposi* (Chapter XXXVII).

ACHTERBERG, Gerrit
(1905–62)

Dutch poet, born in Langbroek. He is one of the few modern poets literally to have 'acted out' his deepest and most murderous impulses: on 15 December 1937 he shot and killed his landlady; he also shot at her young daughter, who was not killed. The major theme in the two collections of poetry he had already published had been his desire to be united with a beloved in death. He did not turn the gun on himself, however, but spent six years in a psychiatric hospital before marrying, and intensifying 'his earlier struggle to write'. Despite or because of this Achterberg was a major—indeed, a unique—poet, although not one who has yet attracted even adequate criticism. He is the key figure in Netherlandic poetry, whose character it is impossible to conceive without reference to him. He is the **Jungian** 'shadow', envied by all his male successors, for whom he seems to be the hero who actually murdered his beloved. His poetry opposes a fanatically close observance of traditional form—seen by the poet as the puritanical 'control' he exercised over his life after his release—to an extreme, and deliberately psychotic, violence of content. In his most famous poem, *De ballade van de gasfitter* (1953, Eng trans in *A Tourist Does Golgotha*, 1972), a series of 14 strict sonnets themselves making up a 'macrocosmic sonnet', he presents the reader with a confused gas worker whose job is to fill holes (*dichter* in Dutch, means 'poet', 'closer of holes', and 'closer to'), and who repairs gas lines even when they do not need it; he is a 'self-mocking Orpheus': 'God is the hole' which needs filling. Achterberg is a compelling poet, and one of great power, although also one of somewhat sinister humourlessness. A critic has said of what has been described as his 'masterwork', the sequence *Spel van de wilde jacht* (1957, 'Play of the Wild Chase'), that 'the definitive interpretation has not yet appeared'; the world may have to wait for this.

▷ *Odyssey*, 1 (1961)

ACKER, Kathy
(1948–)

American novelist and short-story writer, with a visceral, 'punk' approach influenced by **William Burroughs**'s drug imagery and rhetorically violent 'cut-ups'. She also draws on rock music lyrics and pornography, as in *I Dreamt I Was a Nymphomaniac: Imagining* (1974). Her first novel, *The Childlike Life of the Black Tarantula* (1975), was published under the pseudonym Black Tarantula, while *Kathy Goes to Haiti* (1978) deliberately evokes American 'teen' movies of the fifties. *Great Expectations* (1982) and *Don Quixote* (1986) recall **Jorge Luis Borges**'s 'intertextual' adaptations of literary classics. Perhaps her best work is to be found in *Blood and Guts in High School* (1984), shorter fictions of a vividness not found in the more laboured *Empire of the Senseless* (1988) and *In Memoriam to Identity* (1990).

ACKERLEY, Joseph Randolph
(1896–1967)

English author, born in Herne Hill, Kent. His post-university acquaintance with **E M Forster** resulted in his appointment as private secretary to the Maharajah of Chhokrapur, from which experience he wrote *Hindoo Holiday* (1932), an intelligent and amusing log of his five-month sojourn in India. From 1935 to 1959 he was literary editor of *The Listener*. In 1956 he published *My Dog Tulip*, eulogized by **Christopher Isherwood** as 'one of the greatest masterpieces of animal literature', and, in 1960, his only novel, *We Think the World of You*, in which an Alsatian dog plays a lead role. His other books include the autobiographical *My Father and Myself* (1968) and *My Sister and Myself; The Diaries of J R Ackerley* (1982), both published posthumously.

▷ N Braybrooke (ed), *The Letters of J.R. Ackerley* (1975)

ACKROYD, Peter
(1949–)

English novelist, biographer and critic, born in London. He was educated at Clare College, Cambridge, and Yale University, and was literary editor of *The Spectator* (1973–7), and later television critic of *The Times*. His polemical interest in Modernism is reflected in *Notes for a New Culture* (1976), *Ezra Pound and His World* (1981) and *T.S. Eliot* (1984).

His novels are erudite, playful, and complex, and draw on literary and historical sources in fulfilment of his belief that writing springs from other writing. *The Great Fire of London* (1982), for example, has modern echoes of **Dickens**, while *Chatterton* (1987) draws on the life of its subject. *English Music* (1992) is an ambitious study of English culture seen through the trance-consciousness of its narrator, while *The House of Doctor Dee* (1993) explores history through the character of the 16th-century alchemist.

ACORN, Milton
(1923–)

Canadian poet, born on Prince Edward Island. Acorn calls himself a 'revolutionary poet' and writes in craggy solidarity with the working man. He himself has worked as a carpenter, freight handler and longshoreman, and served with Canadian forces in World War II. He was one of the mainstays of the Toronto coffee-house circuit in the 1960s and was the first recipient of the Canadian Poets Award in 1970. There have been two volumes of selected poems, *I've Tasted My Blood: Poems 1956–68* (1969), and *Dig Up My Heart: Selected Poems 1952–83* (1983).

ACOSTA DE SAMPER, Soledad
(1833–1903)

Colombian historian, editor and novelist, born in Bogotá. A pioneer feminist, she edited *La Mujer* (1878–82, 'Woman'). She is most famous for her *Los piratas en Cartegena* (1885, 'Pirates in Carthage'), a vivid, capable and psychologically convincing historical novel.

ACUÑA, Hernando de
(c.1520–c.1580)

Spanish poet, soldier and diplomat of Portuguese extraction, who wrote in Spanish. He put into verse, under the title *El caballero determinado*, a translation by Charles V of a French romance, *Le Chevalier délibéré* ('The determined knight') by Olivier de la Marche (1486). Other poems, Italian in style, were published in 1591 by his widow.

▷ N Alonso Cortes, *Don Hernando de Acuña. Noticias biograficos* (1913)

ACUÑA, Manuel
(1849–73)

Mexican poet, born in Saltillo, Coahuila. His life was by all accounts unhappy, and his congenital poor health and thwarted love affairs drove him to commit suicide at an early age. He was both an avowed atheist and a literary Romantic, and his poetry is unusual for the period in its emphasis on materialism, while its dark, bitter moods contrast with the prevailing lyricism and optimism of the Romantic temperament. In addition to poetry, he also left *El Pasado* (1872, 'The Past'), a fiery play denouncing what he saw as the outrages of Christian society and religious extremism.

ADAM OF ST VICTOR
(fl.1140)

French poet. A monk of the Augustinian order, living at the Abbey of St Victor in Paris, he was one of the supreme religious poets of the period. His Latin is beautifully polished, and his *Sequentiae* ('Sequences', the common mode for the expression of religious themes at the time) are amongst the finest examples of the genre.

ADAM, Helen Douglas
(1909–)

Scottish-born American poet. Born in Glasgow, she was raised in Scotland's rural northeast, before taking up journalism in Edinburgh and London. She moved to the USA at the onset of World War II, and took citizenship in 1977. Her debut collections were two volumes of quirky lyrics about the 'Elfin Pedlar' (1923, 1924), in which dialect and archaic forms tended to mask a concern with female sexuality and its buried power. There was a long gap between *Shadow of the Moon* (1929) and *The Queen o' Crow Castle* (1958), but the later volume drew the admiration of younger poets in California (where she had settled), and *Selected Poems and Ballads* (1974) established her as a significant outsider.

ADAM, Paul Auguste Marie
(1862–1920)

French novelist and essayist, born in Paris. Among his numerous novels are *Chair Molle* (1885, 'Weak Flesh'), *Le Mystère des foules* (1895, 'The Mystery of the Masses'), *Lettres de Malaisie* (1879, 'Letters from Malaysia'), and *La Force* (1899, 'The Power'). He was co-founder of *Symboliste* and other French literary periodicals.
▷F Jean-Desthieux, *Paul Adam: le dernier des encyclopédistes* (1928)

ADAMIC, Louis
(1899–1951)

Yugoslav-born American writer, born in Blato, Dalmatia. The son of Slovene peasants, he emigrated to the USA in 1913. He served in the American army, and became naturalized in 1918. He began writing short stories in the early twenties, utilizing his experiences and personal observations in his books— as in *Laughing in the Jungle* (1932), about an immigrant. Other works include

Dynamite: the Story of Class Violence in America (1931); an autobiographical survey, *My America 1928–38* (1938); *From Many Lands* (1940); *Dinner at the White House* (1946) and *The Eagle and the Root* (1950).
▷H A Christian, *Louis Adamic: a checklist* (1971)

ADAMNAN, St
(624–704)

Scottish or Irish biographer and cleric. He was the eighth abbot of Iona, and his great literary work, which, in its day, was read right across Europe, is a biography of the first abbot, St Columba. Written in church Latin, the work is an account of Columba's childhood in Ireland, with portents of his subsequent career and instances of his miraculous powers (a field is sown and harvested in one month; a demon is driven out of a milk pail; a lump of salt, blessed by him, is found to be indestructible). There is also a lengthy account of the founding of Iona. The classic, and still the best, translation of the work is *Life of St Columba, Founder of Hy*, ed W Reeves (1874).

ADAMOV, Arthur
(1908–70)

Russian dramatist, born in Kislovodsk in the Caucasus, brought up in France and educated in Switzerland and Germany. Before turning to drama he wrote *L'Aveu* ('The Confession'), about his despair at life's meaninglessness; his first play, *La Parodie* (1950), sees two men infatuated with the same girl, Lili, who is unable to tell them apart. Further plays such as *L'invasion* (1950) and *Le Professeur Taranne* (1951) continue the themes of bad communication and loss of identity. In the words of critic Martin Esslin, his plays depict 'a senseless and brutal nightmare world'. With *Paolo Paoli* (1957) he abandoned the Absurd, and his distinctive talent, for **Brecht**ian Epic Theatre. His death from overdosing was probably suicide.
▷M Esslin, 'Arthur Adamov: The Curable and the Incurable', in *The Theatre of the Absurd* (1983)

ADAMS, Alice
(1926–)

American novelist and short-story writer, born in Virginia and raised in North Carolina, which is the setting of *Families and Survivors* (1975). Her debut novel was *Careless Love* (1966, published in the UK as *The Fall of Daisy Duke*), which established as one of her central themes the dilemmas of women in marginal social and economic positions; she moved up the social scale with *Rich Rewards* (1980). *Listening to Billie* (1978) uses the jazz singer Billie Holiday's life as a touchstone for contemporary women. In *Superior Women* (1984) she returns to her Radcliffe education, class of '46, in a latter-day (but more formulaic) version of **Mary McCarthy**'s *The Group*. The best of Adams's short stories are collected in *To See You Again* (1982), *Return Trips* (1985), and the magnificent *After You've Gone* (1989).

ADAMS, Arthur H(enry)
(1872–1936)

New Zealand journalist and writer, born in Lawrence, Otago. After *Maoriland: and Other Verses* (1899) he visited China to report the Boxer Rebellion for a Sydney newspaper. In London he wrote one novel, *Tussock Land* (1904) and more verse, *London Streets* (1906). Returning to Sydney as editor on the periodicals *Bulletin* and *Lone Hand* he championed the work of Australian playwrights. Following publication of *The Collected Verses of Arthur H Adams* (1913) he turned again to writing novels, some under the name 'Henry Henry James', with a flavour of picaresque whimsy and a sympathy for the 'under-dog'. Adams wrote several plays, the most significant of which was *Mrs Pretty and the Premier* (1914), later included in his *Three Plays for the Australian Stage* (1914).

ADAMS, Douglas Noel
(1952–)

English novelist and scriptwriter, born in Cambridge. He was educated at Cambridge, and was script editor on the popular television series *Doctor Who* (1978–80). He is best known for a sequence of novels: *The Hitch-Hiker's Guide to the Galaxy* (1979) and *The Restaurant at the End of the Universe* (1980), *Life, The Universe and Everything* (1982) and *So Long, and Thanks for All The Fish* (1984). A further novel, *Mostly Harmless*, was added in 1992. The zany, free-wheeling satire on the nature of human evolution grew increasingly dark as the sequence progressed, a mood also evident in two linked novels, *Dirk Gently's Holistic Detective Agency* (1987) and *The Long Dark Tea-Time of the Soul* (1988).

ADAMS, Hannah
(1755–1831)

American historian and memoirist, born in Medfield, Massachusetts, whose posthumous autobiography (1832) is a vital document in the history of the young republic. Adams has often been described as the first professional female author to emerge in the United States. She grew up during the independence era and published her first important book, the *Alphabetical Compendium of the Various Sects* (1784), at the age of 29. Remarkably, it

covered schisms and doctrinal disputes from the Early Fathers to the present day. Her range of scholarship was also visible in *A Summary History of New England* (1799), one of the best available accounts of the pre- and post-Revolutionary north-eastern states. Later works were more devotional, but *The History of the Jews* (1812) is rather remarkable for its bluntness.

ADAMS, Henry Brooks
(1838–1918)

American historian, born in Boston, son of Charles Francis Adams (1807–86) and grandson of John Quincy Adams, 6th President of the USA. Educated at Harvard, he acted as his father's secretary in Washington (1860–1) and England (1861–8), then worked as a journalist in Washington (1868–70) before teaching medieval and American history at Harvard (1870–7). He edited the *North American Review* (1870–6) and wrote two novels, *Democracy* (1880) and *Esther* (1884) before embarking on important historical works. *Mont Saint Michel and Chartres* (1904) is a major study of the unity of art and religion in the middle ages. He also wrote a monumental *History of the United States during the Administrations of Jefferson and Madison* (9 vols, 1870–7); and a classic autobiography, *The Education of Henry Adams* (1907), which was awarded the Pulitzer Prize in 1919.
▷ E Samuels, *The Young Adams, Adams: The Middle Years, Adams: The Major Phase*, (1948–64); L Auchincloss, *Adams* (1971)

ADAMS, Perseus, pseud of Peter Robert Charles Adams
(1933–)

South African lyric poet, born in Cape Town. Much of his work (and he has not been unduly prolific) has been inspired by the natural scene; *The Land at My Door* (1965) is an almost **Wordsworth**ian response to the South African countryside. What pressures and contradictions there are in the verse, which is free but musically structured, are not overtly political. There is, however, a didactic strain which has largely disappeared in the later *Grass for the Unicorn* (1975), a tauter and more disciplined collection, in which the line has become shorter and less deliberately musical.

ADAMS, Richard George
(1920–)

English novelist, born in Berkshire. He was educated at Worcester College, Oxford, and after wartime service in the army he worked as a civil servant with the department of the environment (1948–74). He made his name as a writer with the bestselling *Watership Down*

(1972), an epic tale of a community of rabbits. Later books have included *Shardik* (1974), *The Plague Dogs* (1977), *The Iron Wolf* (1980), *The Girl in a Swing* (1980), *Maia* (1984) and *The Bureaucats* (1985).

▷ *The Day Gone By* (1990)

ADAMSON, Robert
(1943–)

Australian poet and editor, born in Maryborough, Victoria. A proponent of the 'New Australian School', he is known for changing the direction of the Poetry Society of Australia and its *Poetry Magazine*. After a bitter dispute concerning the amount of non-Australian verse in its pages, the magazine ceased and was replaced by *New Poetry* which, under Adamson's direction, published much overseas experimental work. His own early verse was strongly centred on his own experiences of prison life and drug abuse, but some of *Canticles on the Skin* (1970) and *The Rumour* (1971) was later revised for his *Selected Poems* (1977). *Where I Come From*, also partly autobiographical, appeared in 1979.

ADCOCK, (Kareen) Fleur
(1934–)

New Zealand poet, born in Papakura, Auckland. She was educated and then (from 1963) resident in the UK, working with the Foreign and Commonwealth Office from 1963 to 1979. She writes in a lucid, mostly narrative manner, preferring invented situations to autobiographical inscape. Her poems are mostly ironic in tone, often as a means to camouflaging fear or anxiety, and thus very English, though she is most successful when writing about apparently marginal or peripheral locations: New Zealand, Ulster, the English Lakes. This detachment is evident in her (aptly titled) first collection *The Eye of the Hurricane* (1964), but also in the excellent *In Focus* (1977) and among the Wordsworthian echoes of her Lake District sequence *Below Loughrigg* (1977). Her *Selected Poems* appeared in 1983, shortly after her editorship of the influential *Oxford Book of Contemporary New Zealand Poetry* (1982), which re-affirmed links with her country of birth. She was married to the Maori poet **Alistair Te Ariki Campbell** and her sister is the novelist **Marilyn Duckworth**.

ADDISON, Joseph
(1672–1719)

English essayist and politician, born in Milston, Wiltshire, eldest son of Lancelot Addison (1632–1703), dean of Lichfield. He was educated at Amesbury, Lichfield, then Charterhouse (where one of his school fellows was **Richard Steele**), and Queen's College and Magdalen College, Oxford, of which he became a fellow. A distinguished classical scholar, he began his literary career in 1693 with a poetical address to **Dryden**. Next year appeared his *Account of the Greatest English Poets*, and a translation of the fourth book of the *Georgics*. In 1699 he obtained a pension to train for the diplomatic service and spent four years in France, Italy, Austria, Germany, and Holland, during which he wrote his *Letter to Lord Halifax*, and made notes for his *Remarks on Italy*, and his *Dialogue on Medals*. *The Campaign*, a poem commissioned by Charles Montagu, 1st Earl of Halifax to celebrate the victory of Blenheim (1704), secured for him a commissionership of Excise. As an under secretary of state (1705–8) he produced his opera *Rosamond* (1706) and in 1707 he went with Lord Halifax to Hanover. Elected to parliament for Malmesbury in (1708), he kept the seat for life. In 1709 he went to Ireland as chief secretary to Lord Wharton, the lord lieutenant, where he formed a warm friendship with **Jonathan Swift**. Returning to England in 1710 at the fall of the Whig ministry, he became a member of the Kitcat Club, and contributed to the *Tatler*, started by his friend Steele in 1709. In March 1711 he and Steele founded the *Spectator*, 274 numbers of which (those signed with one of the letters C L I O), were the work of Addison. In 1711 he purchased the estate of Bilton, near Rugby. His blank-verse tragedy *Cato* (1713) aroused such vehement party enthusiasm that it was performed for 35 nights. In the Whig interest, he attacked the Treaty of Utrecht in *The Late Trial and Conviction of Count Tariff*. After the accession of George I (1714), he became once more, for about a year, secretary to the Earl of Sunderland as lord-lieutenant of Ireland. In 1715 his prose comedy, *The Drummer*, failed. In 1716 he became a lord commissioner of trade, and married Charlotte, Countess of Warwick. In the Hanoverian cause, he issued (1715–16) a political newspaper, the *Freeholder*, which cost him many of his old friends, and he was satirized by **Pope** as 'Atticus'. In 1717 he was appointed secretary of state under Sunderland, but resigned his post, owing to failing health, in March 1718. Almost his last literary undertaking was unfortunately a paper war, on the Peerage Bill of 1719, with his old friend Steele. He was buried in Westminster Abbey.

▷ N Ogle, *The Life of Addison* (1826); P Smithers, *The Life of Joseph Addison* (1954)

ADLER, Renata
(1938–)

American novelist and journalist. She was born in Milan, where her German family had gone to escape the Nazis. Educated at Bryn

Mawr, Harvard and the Sorbonne, she joined the *New Yorker* in 1962, and served as film critic for the *New York Times* during 1968–9, a stint recorded in *A Year in the Dark* (1969); other journalism was collected in *Toward a Radical Middle* (1970), titles that perhaps reflect some of the concerns of her two novels to date. *Speedboat* (1976), which won the **Ernest Hemingway** Award, is a series of filmic scenes about loss and abandonment, linked by a compulsive need to tell stories. In technique *Pitch Dark* (1983) recalls the suggestion that to see something clearly at night one looks slightly away, not directly at it. Adler's prose is oblique but precise, as demonstrated by her investigative reporting on Watergate and her account of Vietnam commander General Westmoreland's libel litigation against CBS, *Reckless Disregard* (1986).

ADONIAS FILHO
(1915–)

Brazilian novelist, critic and librarian, born near Bahia. His novels, not quite in the top flight of modern Brazilian fiction, but notably well observed and highly respected, all deal with cocoa production in the harsh north east of the country. He is unlucky not to have found a translator, since his depiction of brutality and reckless lawlessness in such novels as *Memorias de Lázaro* (1946) is powerful and innovative.

ADUNIS, pseud of Ali Ahmed Said
(1930–)

Syrian–Lebanese poet and critic, a leading Arabic poet of his generation. He was born in Syria but left it in 1956 for political reasons, and became a Lebanese citizen. In Lebanon he has been a prominent editor and polemicist, and has translated **Saint-John Perse** into Arabic. Poetry is to him a 'leap outside established concepts'. While some regard him as the major Arabic poet of his generation, others have attacked his work, much influenced by modern French poets, as impenetrably obscure. But few deny that the best of it is characterized by a haunting visionary beauty. Poetry in translation includes *The Blood of Adonis* (1971).
▷M Badawi, *A Critical Introduction to Modern Arabic Poetry* (1975)

ADY, Endre
(1877–1919)

Hungarian poet and journalist, who changed the direction of his country's poetry, and remains its leading literary figure. Much of his poetry was polemical, and is therefore now outdated, but the best of his work, though not yet well known outside Hungary (but **Edmund Wilson** learned Hungarian to

read him), is of the highest international standard. He is certainly one of the world's great poets; no one who has taken the trouble to study him has disagreed. He went to Paris in the wake of his Jewish mistress, Adèle Brüll, 'Leda'—with whom he conducted his affair in public—and was there stimulated by Symbolist procedures (as he understood them) to break away from the prevailing Hungarian conservative poetics. But he was not an intellectual, and did not even know French well. Nonetheless, *Új versek* (1906, 'New Verses'), was the most incisive collection of poetry ever published in Hungary, and around it and Ady himself there coalesced a group of eager young radical writers such as **Mihály Babits**. By the end of the war, and the short-lived Bela Kun government, Ady was fatally ill with syphilis (one of his self-acknowledged muses) and alcoholism; but he had started something in Hungarian poetry which is still going on, and which was partially fulfilled in the tragic poetry of **Attila József**. There is a selection of his work in English in *Poems* (1969).

AESCHYLUS
(c.525–c.456 BC)

Greek tragedian, born in Eleusis, the town of the Mysteries, near Athens. He served in the Athenian army in the Persian Wars, was wounded at Marathon (490) and probably fought at Salamis (480). His first victory as a poet was gained in the dramatic competitions of 484 BC and he won 13 first prizes in tragic competitions before losing to **Sophocles** in 468 BC. He paid two visits to Sicily. During the second, he staged a new version of the *Persians*, and died at Gela. His last great success on the Athenian stage was with the *Oresteia* trilogy in 458 BC. Out of some 60 plays ascribed to him, only seven are extant: the *Persians*, the *Seven against Thebes*, the *Prometheus Bound*, the *Suppliants*, and the *Oresteia*, which comprises three plays on the murder of Agamemnon and its consequences (the *Agamemnon*, the *Choephoroe* and the *Eumenides*). He was the first great writer of tragedy and must be credited with devising its classical form and presentation. His verse is marked by the grandeur of its diction, as his thought is by the great scope of his themes (the conflict between human and divine law, free will and fate, retribution and forgiveness). Aeschylus was regarded in antiquity as the father of tragedy and the exemplar of his two great successors, Sophocles and **Euripides**.
▷G Murray, *Aeschylus: the Inventor of Tragedy* (1940); T Rosenmeyer, *The Art of Aeschylus* (1982)

AESOP

Legendary Greek author of fables. Tradition represents him as a slave in sixth-century Samos. The fables attributed to him are simple tales, often of animals, devised to illustrate moral lessons, and are probably derived from many sources. They were popularized by the Roman poet **Phaedrus** in the 1st century AD, and served as models for the verse fables of **La Fontaine** (published 1668–94).
▷B E Perry, *The Text Tradition of the Greek Life of Aesop* (1970)

AFFORD, Max
(1906–54)

Australian dramatist and scriptwriter, mainly for radio, born in Parkside, Adelaide. From 1932 he wrote for the Australian Broadcasting Commission over 50 plays and radio serials. One serial, *Hagen's Circus*, ran for 800 episodes; two others, *First Light Fraser* and *Danger Unlimited*, ran for over 600. He also adapted **Jon Cleary**'s *The Sundowners* as a serial. Three of his stage works and two radio plays were later collected in *Mischief in the Air* (1974), and he also wrote four popular thrillers between 1936 and 1942.

AFINOGENOV, Aleksandr Nikolaevich
(1904–41)

Russian dramatist, born in Skopin. At first a crude if always skilled communist 'proletcult' playwright, Afinogenov developed into one of the more interesting dramatists to come out of the Stalinist era. His *Strakh* (1930, Eng trans *Fear*, in *Six Soviet Plays*, ed E Lyons, 1934), on the subject of government interference with individual conscience and genius, did toe the Party line—but not before it had overstepped it. Further interesting plays by him are translated in *Soviet Scene: Six Plays of Russian Life* (1946, ed H Bashky), and in *Seven Soviet Plays* (1946, ed H W L Dana). He was killed in an air raid.

AGARD, John
(1949–)

Guyanese writer of children's and adult verse, resident in Britain since 1977. For several years he worked for the Commonwealth Institute as a travelling speaker, but now writes full-time. During 1993 he was writer-in-residence at London's South Bank centre. He has identified John Arlott's cricket commentary as an early influence, but the predominant strains of his children's verse, which really requires the medium of one of his extraordinarily exciting public readings to be fully appreciated, are West Indian raps and riddles. *Laughter Is An Egg* (1990) is a representative collection. His adult verse, currently overshadowed by his renown as a children's poet, is, at its best, a witty conflation of English and Caribbean idioms.

AGEE, James
(1909–55)

American novelist, poet, film critic and screen writer, born in Knoxville, Tennessee. Educated at Harvard, he worked for several magazines before being commissioned to rove the southern states with the photographer Walker Evans, an assignment that produced *Let Us Now Praise Famous Men* (1941). He became a literary celebrity and was wooed by Hollywood, for whom he wrote classic film scripts including *The African Queen* (1951) and *The Night of the Hunter* (1955). His only novel, the transparently autobiographical *A Death in the Family* (1957), was unfinished at the time of his death, and was awarded a posthumous Pulitzer Prize.
▷L Bergreen, *Agee: a Life* (1984)

AGNON, Shmuel Yosef (Shmuel Josef Czaczkes)
(1888–1970)

Israeli novelist, co-winner of the Nobel Prize for literature. Born in Buczacz, Galicia (now Poland), he went to Palestine in 1907, studied in Berlin (1913–24), then settled permanently in Jerusalem and changed his surname to Agnon. He wrote an epic trilogy of novels on Eastern Jewry in the early 20th century: *Hakhnasath Kallah* (1931, Eng trans *The Bridal Canopy*, 1937), *Ore-ah Nata Lalun* (1939, Eng trans *A Guest for the Night*, 1968) and *Tmol Shilshom* (1945, 'The Day Before Yesterday') as well as several volumes of short stories. He is considered the greatest writer in modern Hebrew, and became the first Israeli to win the Nobel Prize for literature, jointly with the Swedish author **Nelly Sachs**, in 1966.
▷A J Band, *Nostalgia and Nightmare: a study in the fiction of Agnon* (1968); S Sneh, *Schmuel Iosef Agnon* (1970)

AGUILERA MALTA, Demetrio
(1909–81)

Ecuadorean novelist, dramatist, poet, journalist and film director, born in Guayaquil into a middle-class family. He made his mark in 1930, when the so-called *Grupo de Guayaquil* brought out a story anthology in which he had eight stories. His colleagues were **Gil Gilbert**, **Gallegos Lara**, **Pareja Diez-Canseco** and **José de la Cuadra**. He was a reporter in the Spanish Civil War, and wrote two books about it, severely critical of Franco. Aguilera became one of the leading playwrights, as well as story-writers, of Ecuador. But his chief work was done in the novel:

his two masterpieces are: *Siete lunas y siete serpientes* (1970, Eng trans *Seven Serpents and Seven Moons*, 1979) and *El sequestro del general* (1973, Eng trans *Babelandia*, 1985). Both of these books appeared during the so-called 'boom' in Latin-American fiction, and both have been classified as 'magic realist'. Aguilera employed in both of them a well tried Latin-American procedure: by blurring the line between what is normally regarded as the 'real', and the allegedly 'fantastic', he was able to give his reader a glimpse of the reality of his characters' inner lives. Colonel Candelario Mariscal, a character in the first book, thus really is a crocodile as well as a rapist and murderer. The basis of the books is not 'reality' in the banal sense, but the richer reality of the inner life. Both books are as worthy of attention as the better-known ones of **García Márquez, Fuentes** and **Cortázar** (than whom Aguilera is less cerebral). *Babelandia* in particular, a mock-epic embodying both the best elements of political conscience and magic in popular culture, is a seminal book. For a long period he was forbidden to enter the USA on account of his description of its policies in Panama in the novel *Canal Zone* (1935).

▷ V Carrabino (ed), *The Power of Myth in Literature and Film* (1981)

AGUIRRE, Domingo
(1864–1920)

Basque novelist whose *Garoa* (1912), a nostalgic portrait of a village, was the best known of all Basque novels, and was even translated into Castilian, as *El helecho* ('The Fern').

AGUIRRE, Nataniel
(1843–88)

Bolivian novelist and liberal politician, whose single novel, *Juan de la Rosa* (1885), records the struggle for independence, and is the outstanding Bolivian fiction of its century.

AGUSTÍ, Ignacio
(1913–74)

Spanish (and Catalan) novelist and poet, born near Barcelona. He was the founder and editor of the weekly *Destino* (1944–58). His novels about Barcelona, of which *Maiona Rebull* (1944) is the most famous, give a conventionally realistic, competent picture of the history of the city in modern times. The series as a whole was called *La ceniza fue arból* ('The Ashes Were Once a Tree').

AGUSTINI, Delmira
(1886–1914)

Uruguayan *modernista* poet, born in Montevideo, whose erotic poems took her country by storm, and who was murdered by her estranged husband, who then killed himself.

There is still much interest in her work: her poems were collected in 1954, and then her *Correspondencia íntima* (1969, 'Intimate Correspondence').

▷ R B Amigo, *Delmira Agustini en la vida y en la poesía* (1964)

AHLGREN, Ernst, pseud of Victoria Benedictson
(1850–88)

Swedish novelist, born into a farmer's family in Scania in the south of Sweden. Besides **Strindberg**, she was considered to be the greatest talent of her time. Disappointed at not being allowed, despite her father's promise, to train as an artist, she threw herself into an ill-matched marriage to an older widower with five children. Her first novel, *Pengar* (1885, 'Money'), is a discussion of marriage and the emancipation of women based on her own experience. Her other novel, *Fru Marianne* (1887, 'Mrs Marianne'), in which a novel-reading young woman becomes a model country housewife, represents her dream of an ideal marriage, one in which literary interests and traditional women's work are combined. Benedictson's acquaintance with the leading Scandinavian critic of the time, Georg Brandes, developed into a passionate love on her part; when met with only chilly flirtation and scornful remarks about her writing, she committed suicide in a Copenhagen hotel. *Stora Boken* (3 vols, 1978–85, 'The Great Book'), published after her death, contains autobiographical fragments and is a significant document of the period she lived in and of her own struggle for personal liberation.

▷ M Sjögren, *Rep Utan Knutar* (1979)

AHLIN, Lars
(1915–)

Swedish novelist and story-writer, born in Sundsvall. Owing to his family's poverty he had to leave school at 13 in order to work. Like many Scandinavian writers, Ahlin began as a communist and a member of the group loosely called 'proletarian'. But he is not properly of this group, since he early became interested in theology—in particular in Luther and Kierkegaard. He owes a debt to his compatriot **Pär Lagerkvist** and to **Dostoyevsky**. Thus his early (and enthralling) *Fromma mord* (1952, 'Pious Murders') is reminiscent of **Georges Duhamel's** *Salavin*, in that it presents a protagonist who wants to be a saint but cannot prevent himself from damaging everyone with whom he comes into contact. In *Stora glömskan* (1954, 'The Great Forgetting') he created a memorable adolescent character called Zackarias.

▷ A Guslafson, *A History of Swedish Literature* (1961)

AHO, Juhani, pseud of **Johannes Brofeldt** (1861–1921)

Finnish novelist, dramatist and story-writer, born in Lapinlahti. He was a leading member of the Nuori Suomi ('Young Finland') movement, which was responsible for modernizing—mainly through French sources—Finnish literature in the last years of the 19th century. Although always a romantic at heart, he infused his work with a tough realism, for which it is still read and remembered today. He was much influenced by **Selma Lagerlöf**. *Panu* (1897, Eng trans 1899) is a historical novel set in 17th-century Finland. Some of his best and most vivid writing is contained in *Hellmanin herra* (1886, Eng trans *Squire Hellman and Other Stories*, 1893).
▷ G Castren, *Juhani Aho* (1922, in Finnish)

AI CHING, pseud of **Chaing Hai-Chen** (1910–)

Chinese poet, born in I-wu, Chekiang. He spent three years in Paris studying European art and poetry; on his return to Shanghai (1932) he was imprisoned (by the French) for three years as a 'radical'. In prison he wrote his first collection, *The Dyke River*. He was very popular as a patriotic (but never 'jingoist') poet during the war with Japan. In 1941 he threw in his lot with Mao, and over the succeeding years produced flat — but never abject, and sometimes brilliantly descriptive — polemic verse. Then in 1957 he was charged with being a 'rightist', and had to 'confess his faults'. In 1977 he was 'rehabilitated', whereupon he went to America. Translations are in K-Y Hsu's *Twentieth Century Chinese Poetry* (1963).
▷ J C Lin, *Modern Chinese Poetry* (1972)

AI QING (1910–)

Chinese poet, born into a wealthy land-owning family in Jinhua County, Shejiang Province. He studied painting in France (1928–31), but returned to China when the Japanese invaded, and was arrested for leftist activities and imprisoned (1932–5). His first published poem, 'Dayanhe' (1934), named after his wet-nurse, and his collection of poetry, *Ta-yen-ho* (1936), marked him out as a socially conscious writer and brought him fame; but his later work was not considered comparable. In 1941 he joined the communists at Yenan. After the communist take-over in 1949 he became associate editor, with **Mao Dun**, of the *People's Literature* journal. He was an active propagandist for communist-controlled literature, but at the time of the 'Hundred Flowers Campaign' (1956–7) he was accused of revisionism and stripped of his party membership. In 1959 he was exiled to a remote district in the desert area of Zinjiang for 17 years.

AICHINGER, Ilse (1921–)

Austrian short-story writer and novelist, born and brought up in Vienna, where she studied medicine. Her novel *Die Grössere Hoffnung* (1948) made its mark as one of the first works in German to deal with the fate of Jews under the Third Reich. Although she has also published essays, poems, radio plays (such as *Auckland*, 1968) and sketches, it is on her short stories that her reputation rests; they range in tone from the light and capricious to the dark depression of Absurdism. In 1953 she married the poet **Günter Eich**; since his death in 1972 she has lived near Salzburg.

AIDOO, Christina Ama Ata (1942–)

Ghanian story writer and poet, whose work first appeared in the magazine *Black Orpheus*. Her story 'The Message' is in *African Writing Today* (1967).

AIKEN, Conrad Potter (1889–1973)

American poet and novelist, born in Savannah, Georgia. He was educated at Harvard, where his room mate was **T S Eliot** and his contemporaries were **Robert Benchley** and Walter Lippmann. He made his name with his first collection of verse, *Earth Triumphant* (1914), followed by a string of further volumes including *Turns and Intervals* (1917), *Punch, the Immortal Liar* (1921) and *Senlin* (1925). His *Selected Poems* won the 1930 Pulitzer Prize. He also wrote short stories and novels, including *Blue Voyage* (1927), the autobiographical *Great Circle* (1933), *King Coffin*, and another autobiographical novel, *Ushant* (1952). The novelist **Joan Aiken** is his daughter.
▷ J Martin, *Conrad Aiken: a life of his art* (1962)

AIKEN, Joan Delano (1924–)

English novelist and children's writer, born in Rye, Sussex, the daughter of the poet **Conrad Aiken**. She worked for the BBC, and for the UN Information Centre, and was a sub-editor and contributor on the literary journal *Argosy*. She is best known for her many books for children, the most famous of which are the historical adventures *Wolves of Willoughby Chase* (1962) and *The Stolen Lake*

(1981). She is a prolific and imaginative writer in that medium, and uses both historical and fantastic settings to good effect. Her books for adults include romantic thrillers as well as some poetry and plays.

AIMARD, Gustave, pseud of Olivier Gloux
(1818–83)

French novelist and adventurer, known as the French **James Fenimore Cooper**, born in Paris. He sailed as a cabin boy to America, and spent 10 years of adventure in Arkansas and Mexico. He travelled also in Spain, Turkey, and the Caucasus. In Paris, he served as an officer of the Garde Mobile (1848) and organized the Francs-tireurs de la Presse (1870–1). His numerous adventure stories include *La Grande Filibuste* (1860, 'The Great Piracy') and *La Forêt vierge* (1873, 'The Virgin Forest').

AINGER, Alfred
(1837–1904)

English biographer and essayist, born in London. He was educated with **Charles Dickens**'s sons, and much influenced by him. He abandoned his family's Unitarianism for the Anglican Church, and was master of the Temple from 1894. He is best known as the biographer and editor of **Charles Lamb** and **Charles/Thomas Hood**, and also wrote a biography of **George Crabbe**. His *Lectures and Essays* were collected in 1905.

AINSWORTH, William Harrison
(1805–82)

English historical novelist, born in Manchester. He is chiefly remembered for popularizing the story of the highwayman Dick Turpin in *Rookwood* (1834) and the legend of Herne the Hunter in *Windsor Castle* (1843). A solicitor's son, he studied for the law but married a publisher's daughter and began a literary career instead. He edited *Bentley's Miscellany* (1840–2), *Ainsworth's Magazine* (1842–54) and *New Monthly Magazine*. *Rookwood* was his first major success; but he wrote no fewer than 39 popular historical romances, seven of which were illustrated by the cartoonist George Cruikshank.

AKAHITO Yamabe no
(early 8th century)

Major Japanese poet. A minor official at the Imperial Court, he seems to have kept his position largely through his poetic ability. His impression of snow-capped Mount Fuji is a famous example of his work. He is known as one of the 'twin stars'—Hitomaro being the other—of the great anthology of classical Japanese poetry known as the *Man'yōshū*

(completed in 759, 'Collection of a Myriad Leaves', translated by J L Pierson, 1929–49).

ÅKESSON, Sonja
(1926–77)

Swedish poet, born in Buttle, on the island of Gotland. Having left school early and tried a variety of jobs, she began to attend evening classes and courses in creative writing in the mid-1950s, and her first book of poetry was published in 1957. Her later collection *Husfrid* (1963, 'Domestic Peace') established her reputation, with some of the poems also winning the acclaim of the new women's movement. She combines an innovative, often colloquial, language with ready-mades from advertising and women's weeklies, creating a world which is frequently grotesque yet mellowed by a black sense of humour. She has successfully written songs and monologues for the stage, and a number of her poems have been set to music.
▷ E Lilja, *Den dubbla tungan. En studie i Sonja Åkessons poesi* (1991)

AKHMADULINA, Bella
(1937–)

Russian poet and translator (mainly of Georgian poetry), born in Moscow into a family of mixed Italian-Russian-Tatar origin. She married, but divorced, **Yevgeni Yevtushenko**. She follows in the intense and candid tradition of **Tsvetayeva**, but does not possess the latter's driven quality, and is not up to the standard established by her, by **Akhmatova** and by **Gippius**. Nonetheless, she is a minor lyric poet of high quality, who has impressed with her fine readings of her poetry, given all over Europe and in New York, and whose first collection, *Struna* (1962, 'String'), attracted much attention. Available in English translation is *Fever* (1969).

AKHMATOVA, Anna, pseud of Anna Andreeyevna Gorenko
(1888–1966)

Russian poet, born in Odessa. The daughter of a naval officer, she studied in Kiev before moving to St Petersburg (Leningrad). In 1910 she married **Nikolai Gumilev**, who at first considerably influenced her style, and with him she started the neo-classicist Acmeist movement. After her early collections of terse but lyrical poems, including *Vecher* (1912, 'Evening'), *Chokti* (1913, 'The Rosary') and *Belaya Staya* (1917, 'The White Flock'), she developed an impressionist technique. She remained as far as possible neutral to the Revolution. Her husband, from whom she had parted, was shot as a counter-revolutionary in 1921. After the publication of *Anno Domini MCMXXI* (1922), she was

officially silenced until 1940 when she published *Iz checti knig*. But in 1946 her verse, which previously had been acceptable, was banned as being 'too remote from socialist reconstruction'. She was 'rehabilitated' in the 1950s, and received official tributes on her death. Her later works include *Poema bez geroya* ('Poem without a Hero') and the banned *Rekviem* ('Requiem', Munich, 1963), a moving cycle of poems on the Stalin purges, during which her only son was arrested. *The Complete Poems of Anna Akhmatova* was published in 1993.
▷S Driver, *Anna Akhmatova* (1972)

AKILON, pseud of **P Vathalingam Akilandam** (1923–)
Tamil novelist and story writer, author of *Pon malar* (1978, Eng trans *Flower of Gold*, 1978), described as 'the most awesomely realistic and relentless analysis of a woman's self-sacrifice in fiction'.

AKINS, Zoë
(1886–1958)
American dramatist, novelist and poet, born in Humansville, Montana. Moving to New York, where she trained as an actress, in 1912 she published *Interpretations*, a collection of poetry. Later, she concentrated on writing plays. Her most popular were *Déclassée* (1919), a society melodrama; *Daddy's Gone A-Hunting* (1921), a sentimental portrayal of a failing marriage, and *The Greeks had a Word for It* (1930), a comedy about the Ziegfield showgirls. Her best plays are witty and light, but not without irony or shrewd observation of middle-class women. In 1935, Akins was awarded the Pulitzer Prize for her dramatization of **Edith Wharton**'s novel, *The Old Maid*. Among her other works are a contribution to the screen adaptation of the musical, *Showboat*, and two novels, *Forever Young* (1941) and *Cake upon the Water* (1951).

AKSAKOV, Sergei Timofeyevitch
(1791–1859)
Russian novelist, born in Ufa in Orenburg. The son of a wealthy landowner, he held government posts in St Petersburg and Moscow before a meeting with **Nikolai Gogol** in 1832 turned him to literature. His house became the centre of a Gogol cult. He wrote *Metel* (1834, 'The Blizzard'), *Semeǐnaya Khronika* (1846–56, 'A Family Chronicle'), *Detskie gody Bagrova-vnuka* (1858, 'Childhood Years of Bagrov-grandchild'). His writing shows his love of country sports and deep feeling for nature, and conveys a vivid impression of the rural, serf-owning society of the period.

▷S I Mashinksy, *Sergei Timofeyevitch Aksakov* (1973)

AKSYONOV, Vasily Pavlovich
(1932–)
Russian novelist, son of a communist official, born in Kazan, who (eventually) abandoned medicine for a literary career. His mother, Yevgeniya Ginzburg, wrote the widely-read *Krutoy marshrut* (1947, Eng trans *Journey into the Whirlwind*, 1967), an account of her husband's murder and her own incarceration in a Stalinist concentration camp. Aksyonov published the novel *Kollegi* (1960, Eng trans *Colleagues*, 1962), about doctors, and then, most notably, a study of adolescence in Moscow, and on the coast of the Baltic Sea, called *Zvyozdny bilet* (1961, Eng trans *A Starry Ticket*, 1962).

AKUTAGAWA Ryunosuke
(1892–1927)
Japanese writer, born in Tokyo, into a wealthy middle-class family, and educated there. Though an *habitué* of literary circles, Akutagawa seems not to have written anything until he was about 25, when he began to produce work prolifically. His novel *Shogun* (1922) is a liberal and (in the circumstances) quite daring counterblast to the rising tide of militarism in Japanese society. His bourgeois liberalism was to inform his other work, the best of which is available in translation as *Kappa* (1927), which is a social satire, and *Rashomon* (1916), a charming collection of stories. He thought of himself primarily as a poet and published several collections of verse. His later years were marked by a decline into a depressive mental illness—recorded in his verse collection *Koshibito* (1926)—culminating in his suicide at the age of 35.
▷N M Lippit, *Reality and Fiction in Japanese Literature* (1980)

ALABASTER, William
(1567–1640)
English poet and theologian. Educated at Westminster and Cambridge, he was the author of a Latin tragedy, *Roxana* (1632), a number of theological works (one of which was proscribed by the Inquisition) and some religious poetry written exclusively in sonnets. Strongly devotional, they are perhaps a little too earnest for the modern reader: 'Jesu, thy love within me is so main/And my poor heart so narrow of content/That within thy love my heart is wellnigh rent/And yet I love to bear such loving pain' is a typical opening passage.

ALAIN, pseud of **Émile-Auguste Chartier** (1868–1951)

French philosopher and lecturer, born in Mortagne, Normandy. He studied at the École Normale Supérieure, became a philosophy teacher, exerting a formative influence on the succeeding generation of *littérateurs*, then fought as a private in World War I. His 'Propos d'un Normand' column in the *Dépêche de Rouen* newspaper dealt with politics, education and a wide range of moral issues. His own philosophy was similarly eclectic, being influenced by most of the great western thinkers, from **Plato** to Hegel. His *Histoire de mes Pensées* (1936) explains the development of his thought. Other important works include *Les Dieux* (1934) and *Vingt Leçons sur les Beaux-Arts* (1931).
▷A Maurois, *Alain* (1950)

ALAIN-FOURNIER, pseud of **Henri-Alban Fournier** (1886–1914)

French writer, born in La Chapelle d'Angillon, the son of a country schoolmaster. He became a literary journalist in Paris, and was killed at St Remy soon after the outbreak of World War I. He left a semi-autobiographical fantasy novel, *Le Grand Meaulnes* (1913, Eng trans in the USA *The Wanderer*, 1958, in UK *The Lost Domain*, 1966), now considered a modern classic, and a few short stories, collected in *Miracles* (1924). His voluminous family correspondence was published posthumously.
▷R D D Gibson, *The Quest of Alain-Fournier* (1953)

ALAMANNI, Luigi (1495–1556)

Italian poet, born in Florence. He died at Amboise a political refugee, having been employed as a diplomat by Francis I in France. He drew heavily on classical forms in his work, the best of which is *La coltivazione* (1546, 'Farming'), a didactic poem in the style of **Virgil**'s *Georgics*.
▷H Hauvette, *Un exile florentin à la cour de France au XVIème siècle* (1903)

ALARCÓN, Pedro Antonio de (1833–91)

Spanish writer, born in Guadic. He served with distinction in the African campaign of 1859–60, and became a radical journalist. At the Restoration in 1874, however, he became a Conservative, and served as minister to Stockholm, and councillor of state. He published a vivid war diary, travel notes and poems, but is best known for his novels, particularly *Sombrero de tres picos* (1874), on which Manuel de Falla based his ballet, *The Three-Cornered Hat*.
▷R Carrasco, *Pedro Antonio de Alarcón autor dramatico* (1933)

ALAS, Leopoldo (1852–1901)

Spanish author, born in Zamora, he also wrote under the pseudonym of Clarin, meaning 'bugle'. He was Professor of Law at Oviedo, but is better known as a literary figure. He published short stories (*Cuentos morales*, 1896, 'Moral Stories'), a social drama, *Teresa* (1895), and several novels, including *La Regenta* (1884–5, 'The Regent's Wife'). He also wrote treatises on law and economics. His writing is objective, sometimes cold, but always powerful and sincere.
▷M Goyanes Baquero, *'Clarin' creador del cuento español* (1949)

ALBEE, Edward Franklin, III (1928–)

American dramatist, born in Virginia and adopted by a rich theatre-owning family. He was educated in Connecticut and then had various jobs in New York. His play *The Zoo Story* (1958) was influenced by the Theatre of the Absurd and began his attack on the complacency of the American middle class. He continued this in further one-act plays, such as *The American Dream* (1960), a hilarious parody of family life. He had an enormous success with *Who's Afraid of Virginia Woolf?* (1962), which, with caustic wit, exposes a marriage built on illusions, and then used his new-found influence to help other writers. The bizarrely plotted *Tiny Alice* (1964) was denounced as obscure by many American theatre critics—of whom Albee has a famously low opinion. *A Delicate Balance* (1966) deals with another unhappy family. Albee's interest in experimental dramatic forms is particularly evident in *Box* and *Quotations from Chairman Mao Tse-Tung* (both 1968). His later plays, such as the brilliant allegory *The Man Who Had Three Arms* (1982), again displayed great poetic intelligence and masterly dialogue, but were not commercially successful. His dramatizations include *Malcolm* (1965) and *Lolita* (1981).
▷C W E Bigsby, *Albee* (1969); G McCarthy, *Edward Albee* (1987)

ALBERTI, Rafael (1902–)

Spanish poet and dramatist, a member of the great 'Generation of '27', which included **Lorca**, **Louis Cernuda** and **Pedro Salinas**. He began as a painter, and has always alluded to painting in his poetry. He fought against

Franco and in 1939 went into exile to Argentina, and then to Rome. After Franco's death he returned to Spain as the most honoured of all its literary veterans. It is generally conceded that his supreme poetry is in his astonishing fifth collection *Sobre los ángeles* (1929, English version, *Concerning the Angels*, 1967). This work shows the influences of Surrealism and of the critical views of the Spanish critic **Ortega y Gasset**, but far transcends the genre of Surrealism in its visionary qualities and the power of its expression of the conflict between innocence and 'authenticity', and the dehumanizing effects of Positivism. But the strain—and natural anger at injustice—proved too much for Alberti, and he retreated into more simplistic communist verse. Later, however, in the bitterness of exile, his poetry once again reverted to its old and less certain self, so that his output as a whole deserves even more close study than it gets. In general he has not yet been dealt with adequately in English-language criticism. Other poetry in English translation: *Selected Poems* (1966); *The Owl's Insomnia* (1973).

ALCAEUS
(c.620–after 580 BC)

One of the great Greek lyric poets. He lived at Mytilene on the island of Lesbos, where he was a contemporary of **Sappho**. He wrote in a variety of metres, including the four-line alcaic stanza named after him and used notably (in Latin) by **Horace**. A bluff, blustering extrovert, he composed a host of drinking songs, hymns, political odes and love songs, of which only fragments now remain.

ALCÁNTARA MACHADO, Antonio de
(1901–35)

Brazilian story writer and essayist, prominent amongst the modernist group. His laconic, ironic, pointillist collection *Brás, Bexiga e Barra-Funda* (1927), named after three poor districts of São Paulo, made his reputation. *Mana María* (1936) is an unfinished novel, also about São Paulo.

ALCIPHRON
(fl.180)

Greek writer. He wrote 118 fictitious letters from ordinary people (farmers, fisherman, etc) affording glimpses into everyday life in 4th century BC Athens.

ALCMAN
(fl.c.630 BC)

Greek lyric poet. Born, according to one tradition, in Asia Minor, he lived in Sparta. He wrote six books of poems. Of one, a choral hymn, about half survives; otherwise there are only short fragments, mostly written in the Doric dialect. His subjects include animals, food, night and sleep.

ALCOTT, Louisa May
(1832–88)

American writer, and author of the children's classic *Little Women*. The daughter of the Transcendentalist Amos Bronson Alcott, she was born in Germantown, Philadelphia. She was a nurse in a Union hospital during the Civil War, and published her letters from this period as *Hospital Sketches* in 1864. In 1868 she achieved enormous success with *Little Women*, which drew on her own home experiences, and a second volume, *Good Wives*, in 1869, followed by *An Old Fashioned Girl* (1870), *Little Men* (1871) and *Jo's Boys* (1886).
▷M Saxton, *Louisa May: a modern biography of Alcott* (1977)

ALCOVER, Joan
(1854–1926)

Spanish poet, born in Palma, Majorca. Although his first writings were in the Castilian language, he is chiefly known as a poet in Catalan. He presided over a literary *salon* in Majorca, where he was known as a precise literary critic and brilliant talker. His poetry reflects the tragedy of his private life (he lost his wife and four children in rapid succession) and a deep feeling for his native landscape. He published *Poesías* (1887), *Metereos* (1901) and *Poèmes Biblics* (1919).
▷J Arus, *Tres poetas: Maragall, Alcover, Guesch* (1970)

ALCUIN
(c.735–804)

Northumbrian scholar, and adviser to Emperor Charlemagne, born in York and educated at the cloister school, of which in 778 he became master. He is also known as Albinus, and his Anglo-Saxon name is Ealhwine. In 781, returning from Rome, he met Charlemagne at Parma, and on his invitation attached himself to the court at Aix-la-Chapelle (Aachen). Here he devoted himself first to the education of the royal family, but through his influence the court became a school of culture for the Frankish empire, inspiring the Carolingian renaissance. In 796 he settled at Tours as abbot; and the school here soon became one of the most important in the empire. Till his death he still corresponded constantly with Charlemagne. His works comprise poems; works on grammar, rhetoric, and dialectics; theological and ethical treatises; biographies of several saints; and over 200 letters.
▷E M W Buxton, *Alcuin* (1922)

ALDANA, Francisco de
(1537–78)

Spanish poet of noble family from Extremadura, probably born in the kingdom of Naples. He spent his youth in Florence under the protection of the Medici. Neoplatonism was a marked influence on him, as was the paganism of **Horace** and **Virgil**. Aldana was an unusual weave of various strands; while he wrote the usual courtly verses, they were underpinned by an unabashed sensuality far removed from the rigidity of idealized love. He also wrote military, religious and erotic poetry; 45 sonnets are preserved as well as long narrative or doctrinal poems ('Fabula de Factarte' being one), and six epistles, mainly of a moral character. Although highly regarded by **Cervantes** among others, he later fell into oblivion. Aldana disappeared in the battle of Alcazarquivir, the king of Portugal's quixotic attempt to defeat the Moors.

ALDINGTON, Richard, originally Edward Godfree
(1892–1962)

English poet, novelist, editor and biographer, born in Hampshire. He was educated at London University, and in 1913 became editor of *Egoist*, the periodical of the Imagist school, to which he belonged. His experiences in World War I left him ill and bitter, and this led to his novel *Death of a Hero* (1929). As well as other novels, such as *The Colonel's Daughter* (1931), he published several volumes of poetry, including *A Fool i' the Forest* (1925) and *A Dream in the Luxembourg* (1930). At the beginning of World War II he went to the USA, where he published his *Poetry of the English-Speaking World* (1941) and many biographies, including *Wellington* (1946), which was awarded the James Tait Black Memorial Prize, a study of **D H Lawrence** (1950), a controversial and embittered study of *Lawrence of Arabia* (1955), and a study of **Robert Louis Stevenson** (1957). He married **Hilda Doolittle**, also a poet; in 1913, they were divorced in 1937. He published his autobiography, *Life for Life's Sake*, in 1940, and his correspondence with **Lawrence Durrell**, *Literary Lifelines*, appeared in 1981.
▷A Kershaw and F J Temple, *Richard Aldington: an intimate portrait* (1965)

ALDISS, Brian Wilson
(1925–)

English science-fiction writer and novelist, born in Dereham, Norfolk and educated at Framlingham College. After a career in bookselling, he embarked on a prolific career of writing with his first novel, *The Brightfount Diaries*, in 1955. He was literary editor of the *Oxford Mail* (1958–69), and had considerable success with *The Hand-Reared Boy* (1970) and *A Soldier Erect* (1971). He is best known, however, as a writer of science fiction, such as *Non-Stop* (1958, entitled *Starship* in the USA), *Hothouse* (1962), *The Saliva Tree* (1966), *The Moment of Eclipse* (1971), *Frankenstein Unbound* (1973), *Helliconia Spring* (1982), *Helliconia Summer* (1983), *Helliconia Winter* (1985) and *Dracula Unbound* (1991). His more experimental works in the genre include *Report on Probability A* (1964) and *Barefoot in the Head* (1969). He also writes graphic novels, has edited many books of short stories, and produced histories of science fiction such as *Billion Year Spree* (1973) and *Trillion Year Spree* (1986).
▷ *Bury My Heart at W. H. Smith's* (1990)

ALDRICH, Thomas Bailey
(1836–1907)

American writer, born in Portsmouth, New Hampshire. He was Editor of the *Atlantic Monthly* (1881–90), and the author of numerous short stories and novels, and several volumes of poetry. His most successful book, *The Story of a Bad Boy* (1870) was an autobiographical novel about his boyhood. *Prudence Palfrey* (1874) and *The Queen of Sheba* (1877) were more romantic. *The Stillwater Tragedy* (1880) is a detective story.
▷C Samuels, *Thomas Bailey Aldrich* (1965)

ALDRIDGE, (Harold Edward) James
(1918–)

Australian-born British journalist and writer of popular fiction, born in White Hills, Victoria. Based in England since before World War II, during which he served as a war correspondent in Europe, his first books drew upon that experience. *Signed with Their Honour* (1942) was followed by *The Sea Eagle* (1944) and *Of Many Men* (1946). Later he turned to the political turmoil in Europe and the Near East in such books as *The Diplomat* (1950) and *The Last Exile* (1961), in which his left-wing views colour the scene. A follower of the **Hemingway** school, he paid his dues in *One Last Glimpse* (1977) in which Papa (Hemingway), **Zelda** and **F Scott Fitzgerald** and other real-life characters of the period make their appearance.

ALECSANDRI, Vasile
(1821–90)

Romanian poet and dramatist, born in Bacau. He began as a Paris-educated theatre director who was obliged to create a repertory of his own as there were no plays in his own language. He wrote polite and well-crafted farces and historical dramas. Later he became interested in folk poetry, and his understanding of it produced his most vital work:

subtle nature and landscape poems of great mellifluousness. His patriotic poetry was popular.

ALEGRÍA, Ciro
(1909–67)

Peruvian novelist, born in Sartimbamba; both his parents were of the Lynch family—that of the Argentinian novelist **Benito Lynch**. Alegría had the privilege of having been taught at school by **César Vallejo**. He worked with the forbidden APRA party of Haya de la Torre until 1931, when he was imprisoned. He was forced out of his own country in 1934, and settled down to writing in Santiago de Chile. The success of *La serpiente de oro* (1935, Eng trans *The Golden Serpent*, 1943), *Los perros hambrientes* (1938, Eng trans of an excerpt in G Arciniegas, ed, *The Green Continent*, 1944) and of the novel which gave him an international reputation, *El mundo es ancho y acheno* (1941, Eng trans *Broad and Alien Is the World*, 1941), enabled him to live and work in the United States. After he returned to Peru he became an MP, with links to the Popular Action Party. *Broad and Alien is the World*, about the Native Americans, was long taken to be his best novel, and certainly it familiarized many readers all over the world with these oppressed peoples in Peru. But more recent criticism has preferred *The Golden Serpent*, and has also pointed out that the Native Americanism is anthropologically flawed—and that the real nature of Native American peoples is better conveyed in the more poetic fiction of **José María Arguedas**.
▷J Early, *Joy in Exile: Ciro Alegría's Narrative Art* (1980)

ASCH, Sholem
(1880–1957)

Jewish writer, born in Kutno in Poland, who emigrated to America in 1914 and became naturalized in 1920. His prolific output of novels and short stories, most of them originally in Yiddish but many since translated, includes *The Mother* (1930), *The War Goes On* (1936), *The Nazarene* (1939), *The Apostle* (1943), *East River* (1946) and *Moses* (1951), mostly concerned with the fate of modern Jewry. His early work includes the plays *Mottke the Thief* (1917) and *The God of Vengeance* (1918).
▷C Lieberman, *The Christianity of Sholem Asch* (1953)

ALEIXANDRE, Vicente
(1898–1984)

Spanish poet, and winner of the Nobel Prize for literature. Born in Seville, the son of a railway engineer, he suffered from renal tuberculosis in his youth, which forced him to remain in Spain after the Civil War despite his Republican sympathies. Among his early works were *Ambito* (1928, 'Ambit'), *La Destrucción o el amor* (1935, 'Destruction or Love') and *Pasión de la Tierra* (1935, 'Passion of the World'), but it was the appearance of his collected poems, *Mis Poemas Mejores*, in 1937, that established his reputation as a major poet. His later publications include *En un vasto dominio* (1962), *Presencias* (1965, 'Presences'), and *Antologia Total* (1976, 'Complete Works'). He was awarded the Nobel Prize for literature in 1977.
▷K Schwartz, *Vicente Aleixandre* (1970)

ALEMÁN, Mateo
(1547–1610 or 1620)

Spanish novelist, born in Seville. He led a disorderly, poverty-stricken life in Spain, and ultimately emigrated to Mexico in 1608. His great work is the important picaresque novel *Guzmán de Alfarache* (1599), in which the decline and ultimate repentence of a runaway boy mirrors the sinful and corrupt state of Spain.
▷E Cros, *Mateo Alemán: introduccion a su vida y su obras* (1971)

ALENCAR, José Martiniano de
(1829–77)

Brazilian novelist, born in Mecejana, Ceará. He was Minister of Justice before he retired to devote himself to fiction in 1870. He was an early 'Indianist', seeing—largely under the influence of **Chateaubriand**, but also of **Scott** and **Fenimore Cooper**—in the Brazilian Native American the apotheosis of nobility. Conversely, he attacked the commercial greed of the white man and the obscurantism of the clergy. His romantic novel *Iracema* (1865, Eng trans *Iracema, the Honey-Lips, a Legend of Brazil*, 1886) concerns a Portuguese officer who is led into purity by the example of a lovely Native American maiden.
▷D M Driver, *The Indian in Brazilian Literature* (1942)

ALERAMO, Sibilla, pseud of Rina Faccio
(1876–1960)

Italian novelist, poet and memoirist (*Dal mio diario*, 1945, 'From My Diary'), born in Alesandria. She was the lover of a number of poets, including the great **Campana** and **Cardarelli**. Always a socialist, she joined the communists after World War II. She was a woman of great but underrated gifts, whose feminist viewpoint is most poignantly evoked in *Una donna* (1906, Eng trans *A Woman at Bay*, 1908), an early and acute description of the manner in which men, while pretending to celebrate and love women, really treat them as objects; but other work shows that she understood the poignancy of those men who wanted to be exceptional. This has yet to be re-discovered in the English-speaking world. There is a moving collection of the letters between her and Campana: *Dino Campana-Sibilla Aleramo: Lettere* (1952). Her *Amo, dunque sono* (1927, 'I Love, Therefore I Am') is yet another of her remarkable books awaiting rediscovery. It has been said that 'if men really want to understand women they must read Aleramo'.

ALEXANDER, Cecil Frances, née Humphreys
(1818–95)

Irish poet and hymn writer, born in County Wicklow, the daughter of a captain in the Royal Marines, and wife of Bishop William Alexander. She published her *Verses for Holy Seasons* in 1846, and two years later her immensely popular *Hymns for Little Children*, which included the well known 'All things bright and beautiful', 'Once in Royal David's city', and 'There is a green hill far away'. She also wrote ballads on Irish history.

ALEXANDER, Sir William
(1567–1640)

Scottish poet, born in Menstrie, Clackmannanshire. He was educated at Glasgow and Leiden universities, and became a courtier to James VI in Edinburgh, and later in London, and to Charles I. He was created Earl of Stirling in 1633, and although a powerful political figure, he ultimately died in poverty. Most of his work does not appeal to modern tastes, as in the case of the tedious verse-dramas *The Monarchick Tragedies* (1603–7), his 'Elegy on the Death of Prince Henry' (1612), and the long religious poem *Doomesday* (1614). The songs, sonnets and elegies collected in *Aurora* (1604) have fared rather better, and are now the only works by which he is likely to be remembered.

ALEXANDER, William
(1826–94)

Scottish novelist, born in Chapel of Garioch, Aberdeenshire. He worked as a ploughman until losing a leg in an accident, after which he turned to journalism. He wrote a novel in racy dialect, *Johnny Gibb of Gushetneuk* (1871), a series of realistic sketches of the remote country folk and places of north-eastern Scotland, which was serialized in the *Aberdeen Free Press*, of which he later became editor.

ALEXIS, Jacques-Stéphen
(1922–61)

Haitian novelist whose *Les Arbes musiciens* (1957, 'The Musical Trees'), is the first Haitian novel to analyse in depth the national character. He was murdered at the instructions of the dictator Duvalier.

ALFIERI, Vittorio, Count
(1749–1803)

Italian poet and dramatist, born in Asti, near Piedmont. His political writings identify him as a precursor of the Risorgimento. He inherited a vast fortune at the age of 14, and travelled throughout Europe before turning his hand to writing, achieving great success with his first play, *Cleopatra*, in 1775. In Florence in 1777 he met the Countess of Albany, the estranged wife of Prince Charles Edward Stewart; after separating from her husband, she became his mistress. He wrote more than a score of tragedies, six comedies, and a 'tramelogedia', *Abele*, a mixture of opera and tragedy. His ashes, and those of his mistress, are kept in the church of S Croce, in Florence, between the tombs of Michelangelo and **Machiavelli**.
▷ G Megaro, *Alfieri: Forerunner of Italian Nationalism* (1930)

ALFRED, the Great
(849–99)

Anglo-Saxon King of Wessex, born at Wantage in Berkshire, the fifth and youngest son of King Æthelwulf. His importance within a literary context lies in his role in restoring scholarship and learning in England in the wake of the Viking invasions; through his encouragement of translation and his emphasis on idiomatic translation, he laid the foundations of English prose. A noted scholar himself, his works include translations of Gregory the Great's *Cura Pastoralis*, **Boethius**'s *De Consolatione Philosophiae*, and Augustine's *Soliloquia*, as well as works by **Bede** and **Orosius**. It has also been suggested that it was he who inspired the production of the *Anglo-Saxon Chronicle*, the earliest historical record in the English language.
▷ E S Duckett, *Alfred the Great and his England* (1961)

ALGER, Horatio, Jr
(1832–99)

American writer and clergyman, born in Revere, Massachusetts. He was educated at Harvard, became a Unitarian minister, and wrote boys' adventure stories on the 'poor boy makes good' theme, such as *Ragged Dick* (1867) and *From Canal Boy to President*

(1881). His own life was mythicized by early biographers.

▷F Gruber, *Alger: A Biography and Bibliography* (1961)

ALGREN, Nelson
(1909–81)
American novelist, born in Detroit. He moved early to Chicago, where he trained as a journalist at the University of Illinois, before becoming a migrant worker during the Depression. In Chicago again from 1935, he became a leading member of the 'Chicago school of realism'. He produced a series of uncompromising, powerful but baggy novels which include *Somebody in Boots* (1935), *Never Come Morning* (1942) and *The Man with the Golden Arm* (1949), a novel about drug addiction regarded by some as his best work. He had a transatlantic affair with **Simone de Beauvoir**, which is described in her novel *Les Mandarins* (1954) and in her autobiography.

▷M Cox and W Chatterton, *Nelson Algren* (1975)

AL-HAKIM, Tawfik
(1898–1987)
Egyptian playwright and novelist, born in Alexandria. He studied law in Cairo and Paris. One of his best novels, *Maze of Justice: Diary of a Country Prosecutor* (1947), was translated into English by Abba Eban, and originally published in 1937. **P H Newby** called this bitter comedy about the stunted lives of Egyptian peasants (*fellahin*), oppressed by bureaucrats, 'blacker than anything by Gogol or Dickens'. Al-Hakim's often astringently comic plays pioneered modern Arabic drama. English translations include *The Tree Climber* (1966), *Fate of a Cockroach and Other Plays* (1973), both translated by Denys Johnson-Davies, and *Plays, Prefaces and Postcripts* (1981, 1984), in two volumes, translated by William M Hutchins.

AL-HALLAJ, Husayn ibn Mansur
(c.858–922)
Persian mystic, born in the Iranian province of Fars, one of Islam's most famous Sufi teachers. He travelled widely in the East before settling in Baghdad. In his teaching he stressed the soul's need to attain unity with God through love. Some critics have detected Christian and Gnostic strains in his thought. A God-intoxicated man, he was alleged to have declared 'I am the Truth'. He attracted the hostility of certain Islamic jurists and politicians and was tried for heresy. After eight years in prison, he was put to death by crucifixion. His scrappy rhymed prose treatise, the *Kitab al-tawasin*, perhaps written in prison, deals with divine unity and the status of God's prophets. His *Akhbar* ('Reports') consist of anecdotes about him as well as sayings and verses by him collected by his disciples and posthumously written down.

▷L Massignon, *The Passion of al-Hallaj* (4 vols, 1982)

AL-HAMADHANI
(969–1007)
Arabic creator of the *maqamah*, the short story written out in rhymed prose. Two characters feature in his inventions, the *rawi* or narrator, and the unscrupulous wanderer or vagabond—one of the earliest representations of the trickster in post-classical literature. Al-Hamadhani's creations in the *Maqamat* (Eng trans 1913–17) played their part in the genesis of the picaresque novel.

ALI, Ahmed
(1912–)
Pakistani story writer and novelist who writes in Urdu and in English, and was in his youth a member of the Progressive Writers' Association and an active socialist. His stories, well known in India, are in Urdu; his novels, including the historical *Twilight in Delhi* (1940, about early 20th-century Delhi Muslims), and *Ocean of Night* (1964), are in English. He is also a poet, and his anthology *The Falcon and the Hunted Bird* (1950) gives some exquisite translations into English of classical Urdu poets.

ALIGER, Margarita Iosifovna
(1915–)
Russian poet, born in Odessa and educated in Moscow. She worked as a war correspondent during World War II and *Vesna v Leningrade* (1942), containing poems about the effect on the civilian population of the blockade on Leningrad, is one of the enduring poetic achievements of the war, as is *Zoya* (1942), a long poem about a Moscow schoolgirl tortured to death by the Germans. After the war she managed to tread the line between personal integrity and the expectations of the state. She wrote a patriotic hymn for the construction of the new Moscow University, but in general her territory is small-scale and sombre.

AL-JAHIZ, Abu 'Uthman 'Amr ibn Bahr al-Kinani al-Fuqaimi al-Basri
(c.776 868)
Essayist, writing in Arabic, possibly of African descent, though born in Basra, Iraq. Allegedly al-Jahiz ('the Goggle-Eyed') wrote 231 treatises, mostly of a belle-lettristic nature. His most famous work, the *Kitab al-Hayawan* ('Book of Beasts'), took as its pre-

text a debate about the respective merits of the cock and the dog. However, the work (which is full of digressions on the most bizarre subjects) was chiefly concerned to show that the Arabs' knowledge of natural history was not inferior to that of the Greeks. Other works discussed, among other subjects, rhetoric, singing slave girls, passion, cripples, the culture of bureaucrats, the superiority of blacks to whites, the respective merits of the back and the belly, Turks, misers, etiquette and cities. Al-Jahiz was a polemical and ironical stylist who rarely resisted an opportunity for intellectual clowning.

▷ C Pellat, *The Life and Works of Jahiz* (1969)

AL-KHANSA
(fl.first part of 7th century)

Arabic poet, famous for the perfection of her dirges for her dead brothers.

▷ G Gabrieli, *I tempi, la vita e il canzoniere della poetessa Al-Hansa* (1899)

ALLEN, (William) Hervey
(1889–1949)

American author, born in Pittsburg. He trained for the American navy, in which he became a midshipman. In World War I, however, he fought with distinction as a lieutenant in the army, and later (1926) published his war diary, *Towards the Flame*. His best-known novel *Anthony Adverse* (1933) sold a million and a half copies; others are *Action at Aquila* (1938), *The Forest and the Fort* (1943), *Bedford Village* (1945) and *The City of the Dawn* which was unfinished at his death. Allen also wrote a study of **Edgar Allan Poe** under the title *Israfel* (1926).

ALLEN, James Lane
(1849–1925)

American novelist, born in Kentucky. He wrote *The Kentucky Cardinal* (1895), *Aftermath* (1896), *The Choir Invisible* (1897–8), and other novels of a romantic sort, admired for their local colour.

▷ W K Bottorff, *James Lane Allen* (1964)

ALLEN, Walter Ernest
(1911–)

English novelist and critic, born in Birmingham. After working as a schoolmaster and university lecturer in the USA, he became a journalist. His first novel, *Innocence is Drowned*, was published in 1938, and he scored a considerable success with *Dead Man over All* in 1950. His other novels include *Rogue Elephant* (1946) and *All In A Lifetime* (1959). He has written several critical works, including *The English Novel—A short critical history* (1954) and *Tradition and Dream* (1964).

ALLEN, Woody, properly Allen Stewart Konigsberg
(1935–)

American screenwriter, actor, director, short-story writer and occasional jazz clarinettist. He was born in Brooklyn, New York, and launched his career as a comedian in clubs and on television, developing the self-deprecating neurosis and 'genetic dissatisfaction with everything' that were to become his stock-in-trade. He made his film debut scripting and acting in *What's New, Pussycat?* (1965). Later movie projects—often co-scripted with Marshall Brickman—were more obviously vehicles for his stand-up routines: *Bananas* (1971), *Everything You Always Wanted to Know About Sex ... But Were Afraid to Ask* (1972), *Sleeper* (1973) and *Love and Death* (1973). After *Annie Hall* (1977) and *Manhattan* (1979), his films took on a more fictive and structured aspect (in the eyes of detractors, they were simply less funny), as in *Stardust Memories* (1980), *Broadway Danny Rose* (1984), *Hannah and Her Sisters* (1986) and *Crimes and Misdemeanours* (1989). Allen's interest in modern literature and in the curiously compressed and ironic impact of contemporary culture is reflected in his books of stories and sketches: *Getting Even* (1971), *Without Feathers* (1975), *Side Effects* (1980) and *The Floating Light Bulb* (1982).

▷ E Lax, *Woody Allen* (1991)

ALLENDE, Isabel
(1942–)

Chilean novelist, born in Lima, Peru, niece and god-daughter of Salvador Allende, the former President of Chile. Several months after the overthrow of Chile's coalition government in 1973 by the forces of a junta headed by General Augusto Pinochet Ugarte, she and her family fled Chile, Isabel seeking sanctuary in Venezuela. Her first novel, *Casa de los espíritus* (Eng trans *The House of the Spirits*, 1985), arose directly out of her exile and her estrangement from her family, in particular her aged grandfather, who remained in Chile. It became a worldwide bestseller and achieved critical success, and Allende was heralded as the most exciting talent to emerge from Latin America since **Gabriel García Márquez**. In 1987 she published *De Amor y de Sombra* (Eng trans *Of Love and Shadows*, 1987), and in 1993 *El Plan infinito* (Eng trans *The Infinite Plan*, 1993).

ALLEY, Rewi
(1897–1987)

New Zealand poet, born in Springfield, Canterbury, who spent most of his working life in China. After service in World War I he returned to New Zealand but, after a failed sheep-farming venture, went to Shanghai in 1927. There he became involved in flood and famine relief work and later organized industrial co-operatives. He published 16 volumes of poetry from *Gung Ho!* (1948) to *Today and Tomorrow* (1975), mainly set in China, though one, *Poems for Aotearoa* (1972), looks back to his homeland. Alley also translated and published over 30 volumes of Maoist verse and a book on western imperialism.

ALLFREY, Phyllis Byam, née Shand
(1915–86)

Dominican poet and novelist, daughter of the Crown Attorney and descendant of generations of white settlers. Educated at home and in Europe, she lived in England as a young woman, returning to Dominica after the war with her English husband. She was prominent in public affairs, founding the Dominican Labour Party, serving as Minister for Labour and Social Affairs in the federal government (1958–62), and editing two newspapers. She published four books of poems, a novel, *The Orchid House* (1953), and many short stories. Her writings powerfully convey the steamy atmosphere, beauty and decadence, and inbred social and political life of Dominica.
▷ E Campbell, in *Fifty Caribbean Writers*, ed D C Dance (1986)

ALLINGHAM, Margery Louise
(1904–66)

English detective-story writer, and creator of the fictional detective Albert Campion. Born in London, she wrote a string of elegant and witty novels, including *Crime at Black Dudley* (1928), *Police at the Funeral* (1931), *Flowers for the Judge* (1936), *More Work for the Undertaker* (1949), *The Tiger in the Smoke* (1952), *The China Governess* (1963) and *The Mind Readers* (1965).

ALLINGHAM, William
(1824–89)

Irish poet, born in Ballyshannon, County Donegal. He was in the Irish Customs (1846–70), and in 1874 succeeded James Froude as Editor of *Fraser's Magazine*. In 1874 he married Helen Paterson (1848–1926), who, born near Burton-on-Trent, made a name by her book illustrations and water colours, and edited his *Diary* (1907), a rich recollection of Victorian literary life. His works include *Day and Night Songs* (1855), illustrated by **Dante Gabriel Rossetti** and Sir John Millais; *Laurence Bloomfield in Ireland* (1864), *Irish Songs and Poems* (1887), and *Collected Poems* (1888–93).

▷ H Kropf, *William Allingham und seine Dichtung* (1928)

ALMADA-NEGREIROS, José de
(1893–1970)

Portuguese poet and writer of fiction, born on São Tomé, off the west African (Gabon) coast. He spent most of his life in Lisbon. His minor poetry is lively, surreal, primitivistic, naive, striving always to express the joy in living. He wrote a novel, *Nome de Guerra* (1938, 'Pseudonym').
▷ *Collóquio*, 60 (1970, in Portuguese)

ALMAFUERTE, pseud of Pedro Bonifacio Palacios
(1854–1917)

Argentinian minor poet whose too often vituperative work is, mainly, spoiled by his overly self-conscious cultivation of what he considered to be bad taste. He was by profession a self-educated village schoolmaster, who did good work in his own life, but a few Argentinian critics have found in his works what they take to be innovations. His autobiography, *La hora trágica* (1906, 'The Tragic Hour'), is in parts moving; it is also packed with interesting information. His works were collected and introduced by R Brughetti in an edition of 1954 called *Obras de Almafuerte*.

AL-MALAKAI, Nazik
(1923–)

Iraqi poet and critic, whose work has been deeply influenced by European models. Her poetry is subjective, and, in Western terms, would be called 'hermetic'. However, as a nationalist poet she is more conventional. One of her best-known collections is *Li alsalah wa al-thawra* (1978, 'To Prayer and Revolution').
▷ M M Badawi, *Critical Introduction to Modern Arabic Poetry* (1975)

ALMEDINGEN, E M (Martha Edith von)
(1898–1971)

Russian-born British novelist, biographer, autobiographer and historian, born in St Petersburg. Settling in England, she became a distinguished academic historian. She was the author of over 60 books, including novels, but is best remembered for her biographies, both for adult and younger readers. These provide a highly readable and atmospheric account of Russia's turbulent history. *A Study of Emperor Paul I of Russia: 1754–1801* (1959), and *Catherine the Great: A Portrait* (1963), drawing upon letters and memoirs, are particularly vivid and politically balanced.
▷ *Tomorrow Will Come* (1941); *The Almond Tree* (1947); *Late Arrival* (1952)

ALMEIDA, Guilherme de
(1890–1969)

Brazilian minor poet, remarkable for his delicacy of touch, born in the state of São Paulo. He was active in the Brazilian avant garde, and promoted the work of many younger poets, including **Bandeira**. He made a particularly prized translation of **Villon**.

ALMEIDA, José Américo de
(1887–1976)

Brazilian novelist, born in Areia, Paraiba. Almeida was the pioneer of Brazil's northeastern novel. Called a 'liberal politician' by some, and by others 'a servant of Brazilian politics' (he served the dictator Vargas twice), his one important book is the novel *A bagaceira* (1928, Eng trans *Cane Trash*, 1978), a crude, paternalistic but vivid and in certain respects truthful account of conditions on the cane plantations in the first years of the 20th century. As readable as it is stylistically inept and melodramatic, it turned serious people's attention towards an intractable problem.
▷F Ellison, *Brazil's New Novel* (1954)

ALMEIDA, Manuel Antônio de
(1831–61)

Brazilian novelist and journalist, born in Rio de Janeiro. He is best remembered for one anti-romantic, almost picaresque novel, which few of its first readers could really appreciate. *Memórias de um Sargento de Milicias* (1854–5, Eng trans *Memoirs of a Militia Sergeant*, 1959), the story of an illegitimate boy and his rise in fortune under the tutelage of several women, is not only an invaluable source book for life in Rio at the beginning of the 19th century, but also a work of very considerable literary worth.

ALMEIDA-GARRETT, João Baptista da Silva Leitão
(1799–1854)

Portuguese author and politician, born in Oporto. He was brought up in the Azores, and was exiled after the 1820 revolt, but returned and supported Pedro I and became Minister of the Interior. A pioneer of the romantic movement and of modern Portuguese drama, he wrote the historical play *Gil Vicente* (1838), the epic *Camões* (1825), and many ballads.
▷R B Lawton, *Almeida-Garrett, L'intime contrainte* (1966)

ALMQUIST, Carl Jonas Love
(1793–1866)

Swedish author, born in Stockholm. He had a bizarrely chequered career; a clergyman and teacher, he was accused of forgery and attempted murder, and fled to the USA.

Returning to Europe, he spent the last year of his life in Bremen under the assumed name of 'Professor Carl Westermann'. A prolific essayist and philosopher, his worked ranged from Swedenborgian mysticism to social realism, and included novels, plays, poems and essays. The 17-volume series *Törnrosensbok* (1833–40, 'The Book of the Wild Rose') was an eclectic summation of his earlier vision.
▷G Balgård, *Carl Jonas Love Almqvist: samhallsvisignaren* (1973)

AL-MUWAILIHI, Muhammad
(1858–1930)

Egyptian novelist and essayist. His *Hadith Isa ibn Hisham* (1898–1902, Eng trans 1974) was one of the most important books of its time. It offered a brilliant and satirical exposé of the faults of Egyptian society, and of the British administration.

ALONI, Nissim
(1926–)

Israeli dramatist, story writer and translator, born in Tel-Aviv. He fought in the War of Independence (1947–9), lived in Paris for a few years, and began as an author with stories of his youth in Tel Aviv. Two of his plays have received much attention. The first, *Achzar mikol hamelech* (1953, 'The Cruellest Of All—the King'), deals with the problems of the young Israel by means of biblical symbolism: the story is that of the revolt of Jeroboam, and Aloni thus is able to present Israel's conflict between its religious and its secular role. The second, *Bigdai hamelech* (1961, 'The King's Clothes'), based on **Hans Christian Andersen**'s 'The Emperor's Clothes', examines revolutionary pretences in the modern world. Aloni runs a theatre group for which he has written such plays as *Arlekino* (1963, 'Harlequin'), and much topical satire.
▷*Ariel: A Quarterly Review of Literature and the Arts in Israel*, 32 (1973)

ALONSO, Dámaso
(1898–1990)

Spanish poet and philologist, born in Madrid, where he studied under Ramon Menéndez Pidal before travelling widely in Europe and America as teacher and lecturer. He became Professor of Romance Philology at Madrid University, and established his reputation as an authority on **Góngora y Argote**. He also published poetry, of which *Hijos de la Ira* (1970, Eng trans *Children of Wrath*, 1970) is the best known. It is religious in inspiration, powerful and emotional in expression.
▷E Alvarado de Ricord, *La Obra poetica di Dámaso Alonso* (1968)

AL-RUSAFI, Maruf
(1875–1945)

Iraqi Arabic poet, mystic and critic. He was a Sufi who wrote a long mystical work which cannot be published before the year 2000. His poetry, however, was not always religious, but addressed itself to social and national issues in a boldly rebellious spirit.

AL-SHARQAWI, Abd al Rahman
(1920–)

Egyptian poet, radical verse playwright and novelist. *Thar Allah* (1969, 'God's Revenge'), is typical of his stage work. His novel *Al-Ard* (1954, Eng trans *Egyptian Earth*, 1962) is regarded as a 'realistic and obviously committed view of the Egyptian peasant'.
▷H Kilpatrick, *The Modern Eygptian Novel* (1974)

ALTERMAN, Nathan
(1910–70)

Polish–Jewish Hebrew poet, dramatist and translator, who moved to Palestine in his boyhood. He was a curious writer in that, while his poetry is wild and apparently uncontrolled (a critic spoke of 'an inoccuous alcoholic element' in it), his drama, which played an important part in the Hebrew theatrical revival, was carefully conceived and planned. He translated **Molière**, **Shakespeare**'s *Othello*, and others, and wrote a number of original plays. Some of his poetry is translated in *Selected Poems* (1968).

ALTHER, Lisa, née Reed
(1944–)

American novelist, born in Kingsport, Tennessee. She was educated at Wellesley College, Massachusetts, and although the Tennessee setting of much of her work has led to her being identified as a regional writer, it is more wide-ranging than that implies. Her characteristic theme is the evolution of personal and sexual identity, which was readily evident in her often comic first novel, *Kinflicks* (1976). *Original Sins* (1981) explored the fragmentation of a group of children as they were exposed to the social, racial and sexual pressures of adult life. *Other Women* (1985) is centred on the developing relationship between a woman and her female therapist, while *Bedrock* (1990) again focuses on her persistent concern with personal development and self-awareness.

ALTIMIRANO, Ignacio Manuel
(1834–93)

Mexican novelist and editor, of pure Native American blood, born in Tixtla. He wrote initially in the Spanish *costumbrista* tradition. His unusual *El Zarco* (1901, Eng trans *Zarco the Bandit*, 1957), presents a 'white' bandit and a 'dark' hero, and is an important part of early *indigenista* literature; but it possesses little merit as a story.

ALUKO, T M
(1918–)

Nigerian novelist whose *One Man, One Wife* (1959) was the first genuine Anglophone novel to be published in Nigeria. Accused of frivolity for his later and more broadly comic work, such as *Chief the Honourable Minister* (1970), he excelled at satirizing the more absurd aspects of native life, although always depicting these within the imperialist context.
▷A Tibble, *African/English Literature* (1965)

ALVARENGA, Manuel Inâcio da Silva
(1749–1814)

Brazilian poet, born in the Minas Gerais region. He was educated in Coimbra in Portugal. He was for a long time imprisoned, although not in harsh conditions, for his sympathy with the French Revolution. His poetry is more mellifluous and well wrought than interesting in its content, but he made technical innovations.

ALVAREZ, A(lfred)
(1929–)

English literary critic and novelist, perhaps unfortunately best known for an over-publicized affair with **Sylvia Plath**, which he documented in his own powerful study of suicide and the self-destructive impulse, *The Savage God* (1971). After graduating from Corpus Christi, Oxford, he went to the USA, out of which came his first critical book, *The Shaping Spirit* (1958, published in the USA as *Stewards of Excellence*), and somewhat later the interviews and essays in *Under Pressure* (1965), which examined the different constraints imposed on writers under state capitalism and communism. The essays in *Beyond All This Fiddle* (1968) suggested a sturdy critical consciousness largely undazzled by the trendier philosophies of the time. Unfortunately, the same could not be said about Alvarez's two novels, *Hers* (1974) and *Hunt* (1978), which are shallow and predictable. He is, however, a fine literary journalist, closely associated with *The Observer* newspaper, the *New Statesman*, and with the influential Penguin Modern European Poets in Translation series.
▷I Hamilton, interview with Alvarez in *New Review* (March 1978)

ÁLVAREZ QUINTERO, Serafín
(1871–1938)
ÁLVAREZ QUINTERO, Joaquín
(1873–1944)

Spanish playwrights, both born in Utrera. These brothers were the joint authors of well over a hundred modern Spanish plays, all displaying a characteristic gaiety and sentiment, although they are sometimes accused of being a little too stagily Spanish. Some are well known in the translations of Helen and **Harley Granville-Barker**: *Fortunato*, *The Lady from Alfaqueque*, and *A Hundred Years Old* (all produced in 1928), and *Don Abel Writes a Tragedy* (1933). In addition may be mentioned *El patio* (1900), *Las flores* (1901, 'The Flowers'), *El genio alegre* (1906, 'The Happy Spirit/Genius'), and *Pueblo de mujeres* (1912, 'Nation of Women').

▷ J Losada de la Torre, *Perfil de los hermanos Alvarez Quintero* (1945); D Diaz Hierro, *Huelva y los hermanos Alvarez Quintero* (1972)

ALVARO, Corrado
(1895–1956)

Italian novelist and journalist, born in Reggio. Sometime Editor of *Il Mondo*, he was the author of several novels and collections of essays. His best novels are *I maestri del diluvio* (1935, 'The Masters of the Flood') and *L'Uomo è forte* (1934, 'The Strong Man'), both set in Soviet Russia, though he declared that his criticisms were of fascist and not communist society. The deeply-felt disparity between town and country, his own sophisticated life as a cultivated man and a vision of an impossibly idealized memory of his native south, are recurring themes in his work.

▷ L Alessandrini, *Corrado Alvaro* (1968)

ALVER, Bettl, pseud of Elisabet Lepik
(1906–)

Estonian lyrical poet. She was the wife of the poet Heiti Talvik, who was sent to Siberia and died there in 1945. She was a leading light in the *Arbujad* ('Magicians') circle of poets, which sought in the late 1930s to create a poetry independent of politics. She was silent for many years, but then began to publish again in the 1960s, when her collections sold out.

▷ W K Matthew (ed), *A Book of Modern Estonian Poetry* (1955)

AMADI, Elechi
(1934–)

Nigerian novelist and playwright, born in Aluu and educated at Ibadan. Unfashionably

resistant to anti-colonial ideology and rhetoric, Amadi returned in his fiction to a pre-European African past, detailing village life as an organic, self-sufficient system. *The Concubine* (1966) was published by Heinemann in London and, despite its striking refusal to suggest political alternatives to white rule, was a marshalling point for black writers who sought to work outside white European models. *The Great Ponds* (1969) and *The Slave* (1978) were weaker, and the more recent *Estrangement* (1986) betrays some symptoms of artificiality. Like many of his compatriots, Amadi writes dramatically rather than discursively and has created a small but significant body of work for the stage, the best of it collected in *Peppersoup, and The Road to Ibadan* (1977). His *Sunset in Biafra: A Civil War Diary* (1973) is a strong-minded account of Nigeria's national tragedy.

▷ A Niven, *The Concubine: a Critical View* (1981)

AMADO, Jorge
(1912–)

Brazilian novelist, born on a cocoa plantation in Ilhéus, Bahia. His early fictions are pervaded with social and political themes. He was imprisoned for his political beliefs in 1935 and latterly spent several years in exile, though he was a communist deputy of the Brazilian parliament (1946–7). His first novel, *O país do carnaval* (1932, 'The Country of the Carnival'), is typically a young man's and follows a youthful member of the intelligentsia seeking political answers in the wake of the revolution of 1930. His next few novels outlined his personal manifesto and highlighted the cause of various exploited groups in society. With the publication of *Gabriela, cravo e canela* (1952, Eng trans *Gabriela, Clove and Cinnamon*, 1962) he showed a marked change in style and emphasis, Technicolor supplanting black and white. This second phase of the writer's career was marked by books like *O gato malhado e a andorinha sinha* (1976, Eng trans *The Swallow and the Tom Cat*, 1982) and *Dona Flor e seus dois maridos: História moral e de amor* (1966, Eng trans *Dona Flor and Her Two Husbands*, 1969) which, while not lacking in social awareness or compassion, use irony to charming effect.

AMBLER, Eric
(1909–)

English novelist and playwright, born in London. Educated at Colfe's Grammar School and London University, he served an apprenticeship in engineering and worked as an advertising copy-writer before turning to writing thrillers, invariably with an espionage

background. He has done much to legitimize what has too glibly been dismissed as the stuff of pot-boilers. Considered by **Graham Greene** to be Britain's best thriller writer, he published his first novel, *The Dark Frontier*, in 1936. Niggardly with words and a skilful constructor of plots, he creates a world of shadows. His best-known books are *Epitaph for a Spy* (1938), *The Mask of Dimitrios* (1939), *Dirty Story* (1967) and *The Intercom Conspiracy* (1970). He has co-authored novels with Charles Rodda under the pseudonym Eliot Reed and has received the Crime Writers' Association Award four times, and the **Edgar Allan Poe** Award (1964). He has also written a number of screenplays.
▷ *Here Lies: An Autobiography* (1985).

AMES, Jennifer *see* **GREIG, Maysie Coucher**

AMICIS, Edmondo de
(1846–1908)
Italian novelist, born in Oneglia. Although he intended to pursue a career in the army, and became director of the Italia Militare, Florence, in 1867, he turned to literature and recorded his experiences as a soldier in *La vita militare* (1868, 'The Military Life'). He is chiefly remembered for his alliance with **Alessandro Manzoni** in an attempt to 'purify' the Italian language. *L'Idioma gentile* (1905, 'The Gentle Language') presents his views on this subject. His most popular work is the sentimental *Il Cuore* (1886), translated into English as *An Italian Schoolboy's Journal* and into more than 25 other languages. His interest in education is reflected in *Il romanzo d'un maestro* (1890, 'A School-teacher's Novel'), and he also travelled widely, producing several books about his adventures.
▷ V Chialant, *Edmondo de Amicis, educatore e artista* (1911)

AMIEL, Denys, pseud of **Guillaume Roche**
(1884–1977)
French playwright, best known for his collaboration with **André Obey** on the popularly-experimental *La Souriante Mme Beudet* (1921), produced in New York as *The Wife with a Smile*. This stiffly 'presentational' work (ie drawing deliberate attention to the artificial devices of the theatre) in the up-market fashion of the time, was a variation on the 'Bovary' theme, but with a 'happy ending'. It was filmed with Germaine Dermoz in 1922. Amiel wrote many more successful 'tragi-comedies of ordinary life', at which he excelled.

AMIHAI, Yehudah
(1924–)
German-born Israeli poet and novelist, born in Würzberg. He emigrated to Palestine with his family in 1936. He is thought of as having brought a much-needed 'matter-of-fact tone' into Hebrew poetry and has been much translated, eg in *Selected Poems* (1971), *Songs of Jerusalem and Myself* (1973), *Amen* (1977) and *Time* (1979).

AMIS, Sir Kingsley
(1922–)
English novelist and poet, born in London. He was educated at the City of London School and at St John's College, Oxford, and was a lecturer in English Literature at University College, Swansea (1948–61) and fellow of Peterhouse, Cambridge (1961–3). He achieved huge success with his first novel, *Lucky Jim* (1954), the story of a comic anti-hero in a provincial university; 'Jim' appeared again as a small-town librarian in *That Uncertain Feeling* (1956), and as a provincial author abroad in *I Like It Here* (1958). After the death of **Ian Fleming**, he wrote a James Bond novel, *Colonel Sun* (1968), under the pseudonym of Robert Markham, as well as *The James Bond Dossier* (1965). His later novels include *I Want It Now* (1968), *Ending Up* (1974), *Jake's Thing* (1978), *Stanley and the Women* (1984), *The Old Devils* (1986, Booker Prize), *The Folks That Live On The Hill* (1990), and *The Russian Girl* (1992). He has also published four books of poetry, and written ten non-fiction works, including one on the history of science fiction. He was married (1965–83) to the novelist **Elizabeth Jane Howard**. His son is **Martin Amis**.
▷ *Memoirs* (1991); R Rabinowitz, *The Reaction Against Experiment in the English Novel* (1967)

AMIS, Martin Louis
(1949–)
English novelist and journalist, born in Oxford, the son of **Kingsley Amis**. He was educated at Exeter College, Oxford, and acted in the film *A High Wind in Jamaica* (1965) He worked for the *Times Literary Supplement* and *New Statesman*, but has been a full-time writer since 1979. He began precociously with his first novel, *The Rachel Papers* (1973), and followed it with two more witty and pungent socio-cultural satires, *Dead Babies* (1975) and *Success* (1978). Subsequent novels include the nightmarish *Other People* (1981), *Einstein's Monsters* (1986)—a short-story collection on the theme of nuclear destruction—and *Time's Arrow* (1991), which plays with concepts of time and history.

AMMONS, A(rchie) R(andolph)
(1926–)

American poet, born in Whiteville, North Carolina. A romantic in the line of the New England Transcendentalists, but with something of **Wallace Stevens**'s agnostic insistence on the imagination as a non-transcendent sufficiency, he draws his subject-matter and his prosodic rhythms direct from nature. His first book, *Ommateum, with Doxology* (1955), wore both influences too publicly although later works were more self-possessed. *Corsons Inlet* (1965) is a major statement of his mature style, which developed in the subsequent *Tape for the Turn of the Year* (1965) and *Northfield Poems* (1966). A *Collected Poems* appeared in 1972, an updated *Selected* in 1977, and the important *Selected Longer Poems*, representing his gift for long forms, in 1980. Ammons has been Goldwin Smith Professor of English at Cornell University since 1973.
▷A Holder, *A R Ammons* (1978)

AMORIM, Enrique
(1900–60)

Passionate Uruguayan novelist, poet and story writer, born in Salta (the home town, also, of **Horacio Quiroga**). His father was of Portuguese descent, his ardently feminist mother, herself a poet, of Basque. His literary career was built up in Argentina. His compatriot, the novelist and historian of Uruguayan literature, **Mario Benedetti**, wrote of his prolific works (also praised by **Borges**): 'a writer of extraordinary fragments, of stupendous pages, of magnificent serendipity, but also of great stylistic holes, of evident structural blunders, of overstuffed chapters'. All Amorim's novels are worthy of study, but the most famous, and his own favourites, are *La carreta* (1929, 'The Cart'), *El paisano Aguilar* (1934, 'The Peasant Aguilar') and *El caballo y su sombra* (1941, Eng trans *The Horse and His Shadow*, 1943). *Coral abierto* (1955, 'The Open Yard') is a notable tale of juvenile delinquency. With some qualities in common with **Dreiser** and **Hardy**, Amorim was a great and sometimes intemperate protester against injustice; his standing is hardly secure, and perhaps never can be—but he is widely read and much loved. Many of the allegedly gloomy conclusions he draws from his depictions of landowners and peasants have been confirmed by sociologists.
▷*Books Abroad*, 34 (1960)

AMORY, Thomas
(c.1691–1788)

Irish author and eccentric, born in Dublin. He studied medicine at Trinity College, Dublin, but was wealthy enough to adopt the life of a gentleman of leisure in London, where he lived a very secluded life, and seldom went out until dark. His chief works include *Memoirs of Several Ladies of Great Britain* (1755), *A History of Antiquities, Productions of Nature* (1755), and the *Life of John Buncle* (2 vols, 1756–66), an odd combination of autobiography, fantastic descriptions of scenery, deistical theology, and sentimental rhapsody.
▷*Memoirs of the Life, Character and Writings of the Author* (1764)

ANACREON
(c.570–?c.475 BC)

Greek lyric poet, from Teos in Asia Minor. He helped to found the Greek colony of Abdera in Thrace (c.540 BC) in the face of threatened attack by the Persians. He was invited to Samos by Polycrates to tutor his son. After the tyrant's downfall, he was brought to Athens by Hipparchus, son of the tyrant Pisistratus, and later went to Thessaly. His work, which survives only in fragments, includes convivial poems in honour of love and wine, satires, dedications and epitaphs. It served as a model for the Latin lyric poets and was widely imitated by French and English poets of the Renaissance.
▷V Martin, *Quatre Figures de la Poésie Grecque* (1931)

ANAND, Mulk Raj
(1905–)

Indian novelist and critic, born in Peshawar. His early life was fraught with tragedy and familial strife and he left India for Britain, where he was beaten up for blacklegging during the General Strike (1926). His first novel, *Untouchable* (1935), was rejected by 19 publishers, the 20th agreeing to take it on if **E M Forster** would write a preface. This he did, sparking off a remarkable career for Anand which has included novels, short stories, cookery books, philosophical exegeses, tales for children and writings on art. His novels, such as *The Coolie* (1936), *Two Leaves and a Bud* (1937) and *The Village* (1939, the first of a trilogy), promote the underdog in society, his approach being that of a humanist rather than a communist. They are uneven in quality but consistent in their depiction of life in the poverty-stricken Punjab. More recently he has concentrated on an ambitious seven-volume autobiographical work of fiction, *The Seven Ages of Man*, which began with *Seven Summers: The Story of an Indian Childhood* (1951).
▷M Berry, *Mulk Raj Anand: the man and the novelist* (1971)

ANCHIETA, Padre José de
(1534–97)

Spanish (Canary Islands) Jesuit, born in Tenerife. He was educated at Coimbra in Portugal, and went to Brazil in 1553, where he played an important priestly role. He wrote a Tupi (Brazilian Native American) grammar. He is not an important poet in any of the languages he employed for his religious verse (Tupi, Latin, Spanish, Portuguese), but was a versatile man whose historical work is invaluable, notably his *Fragmentos Históricos* (1584–6), which is an important source book.
▷D L Hamilton, *A Vida e a Obras de José de Anchieta* (1942)

AN CRAOIBHIN AOIBHINN *see* HYDE, Douglas

ANDAY, Melih Cedvat
(1915–)

Turkish poet, dramatist, critic, novelist and translator (**Molière**, **Gogol**), born in Istanbul. He has served on many Istanbul papers as a cultural columnist. With other poets he initiated, just after the end of World War II, the 'Garip' ('Strange') movement in Turkish poetry: the aims were to get rid of all conventions (there was therefore a later reaction), to bring the colloquial into poetry, and to write of social concerns. But Anday, too, reacted, and his poetry became more metaphysical and less overtly left-wing. His poetry is collected as *Sözcükler* (1978, 'Words'). There are English versions in *On the Nomad Sea* (1974) and *Rain One Step Away* (1980).
▷*Books Abroad*, 39 (1965)

ANDERSCH, Alfred
(1914–)

German novelist and critic, born in Munich. Imprisoned in Dachau by the Nazis for communist activity, Andersch was closely associated with Gruppe '47—the band of disparate friends who joined together to encourage a liberal and imaginative literature in a war-torn Germany. He eventually turned his back on his communism in favour of a still liberal but individual outlook. His major novel, *Sansibar, oder, der letze Grund* (1957, Eng trans *Flight to Afar*, 1958), exemplified this change.

ANDERSEN, Hans Christian
(1805–75)

Danish author, one of the world's great storytellers. He was born in Odense, the son of a poor but educated shoemaker. After his father's death, he worked in a factory, but soon displayed a talent for poetry. At 14 he went to Copenhagen, but failed to find a job in the theatre. His writing, however, attracted the attention of influential men and, application having been made to the king, he was placed at an advanced school. In 1829 he established his reputation with 'A Walk from the Holmen Canal to the Easternmost Point of Amager', a literary satire in the form of a humorous narrative. The following year, he published the first collected volume of his poems, and in 1831 a second. A travelling pension from the king in 1833 resulted in a volume of prose sketches of a tour in the Harz mountains, *Agnete og Havmanden* ('Agnete and the Merman'), which was completed in Switzerland, and *Improvisatoren* (Eng trans *The Improvisatore; or Life in Italy*, 1845), a series of scenes inspired by Rome and Naples. In 1835 he began publishing the tiny pamphlets of fairy tales which are his greatest work; there are more than 150 of them, including 'The Tin Soldier', 'The Emperor's New Clothes', 'The Tinderbox', 'The Snow Queen', and 'The Ugly Duckling'. He also wrote *O.T.* (1836), a novel containing vivid pictures of northern scenery and manners, *Kun en Spillemand* (1837, 'Only a Fiddler'), and an autobiography *Mit Livs Eventyr* (1855, rev edn 1870), translated by **Mary Howitt** as *The True Story of My Life* (1847).
▷R Bain, *Hans Christian Andersen: a biography* (1895)

ANDERSON, Ethel
(1883–1958)

English-born Australian writer, born in Leamington, Warwickshire, and a friend of the Keynes, Darwin, and Vulliamy families and of the poet **Frances Cornford**. She married an army officer and lived for some time in India. She wrote two books of verse, *Squatter's Luck* (1942) and *Sunday at Yarralumla* (1947), some essays, and two books of short stories, *Indian Tales* (1948) and *The Little Ghosts* (1959), delicate tales based on her Indian experiences. Her best-known book, *At Parramatta* (1956), turns vignettes of Australian middle-class life in the 1850s into a microcosm of the Seven Deadly Sins. She also wrote an oratorio, *The Song of Hagar* (1958), set to music by the composer John Antill.

ANDERSON, Jessica Margaret
(c.1918–)

Australian novelist, born in Brisbane but living mainly in Sydney. Her first book, *An Ordinary Lunacy* (1963), was not written until she was 40, and her reputation was only established in 1978 with *Tirra Lirra by the River*, a winner of the **Miles Franklin** Award, in which she recounts Nora Porteous's lifelong search for herself. Stories of her Brisbane childhood contrast with sophisticated Sydney in the 1980s in *Stories from the Warm Zone and Sydney Stories* (1987) and demonstrate a command of diverse moods. In her psychological crime story *The Last Man's Head* (1970) Anderson returns to the detective genre of her first novel. A historical novel *The Commandant* (1975), based on the true story of an early commander of the Moreton Bay (later Brisbane) penal settlement, was less successful.

ANDERSON, Maxwell
(1888–1959)

American historical dramatist, born in Atlantic, Pennsylvania, the son of a Baptist minister. A verse playwright, he was in vogue in the late 1920s to the early 1940s with numerous plays which included *Elizabeth the Queen* (1930), *Mary of Scotland* (1933), *Winterset* (1935), *Key Largo* (1939) and *The Eve of St Mark* (1942). Commercially successful, his plays tended to be centred on a strong, highly-focused idea, usually in keeping with a firm commitment to democratic humanism. He also wrote screenplays, most notably that from **Erich Maria Remarque**'s novel *All Quiet on the Western Front* (1930). He won a Pulitzer Prize for *Both Your Houses* in 1933.
▷M D Bailey, *Maxwell Anderson: the playwright as prophet* (1957)

ANDERSON, Patrick
(1915–)

English poet, born in Surrey and educated at Oxford University. He is regarded by some as a Canadian writer, having lived, taught and been anthologized there. Multi-faceted, he has produced poetry such as *The Colour as Naked* (1953) with experimental verse forms and overt, dialectical intellectualism, and *On This Side Nothing* (1948), which is more interested in ordinary nature such as wind, earth and trees. *A Visiting Distance* (1976), a selection of revised and new material, engagingly covers both the interest in what he finds in his own garden and what he finds on the other side of the world; his interest in travel shows itself also in *Over the Alps* (1969), which analyses the travel writing of **William Beckford**, **Byron** and **Boswell**.

ANDERSON, Poul William
(1926–)

American science-fiction writer, born in Pennsylvania of Swedish descent. He was educated at the University of Minnesota, and published his first short story in 1947. Most of his work is 'hard' science fiction, and he is a major figure in the genre, although he has also written fantasy and adaptations of mythological subjects. Many of his books can be grouped into loose sequences, of which the most important are the Technic History series (sub-divided into the 'Nicholas van Rijn' and

'Dominic Flandry' streams), and the smaller Psychotechnic League series. His characterization, dialogue and plotting can all be perfunctory, but he is rarely less than inventive. Important titles include *Brain Wave* (1953), *The High Crusade* (1960), *Tau Zero* (1970) and *The Book of a Million Years* (1989).

ANDERSON, Robert Woodruff
(1917–)

American dramatist, born in New York. Woodruff served as an intelligence officer in the US Navy during World War II and was awarded a Bronze Star. *Come Marching Home* (1945), a play about the return of a war hero, won an Army–Navy playwriting competition, but his reputation as a dramatist in the mould of **Tennessee Williams** was established with *Tea and Sympathy* (1953), a play about a schoolboy accused of homosexuality. (Anderson turned this into a precious and unsuccessful screenplay - much better is the screenplay he produced from someone else's book for *The Nun's Story*, 1959.) Subsequent productions have shown Anderson to be more sentimental and less subtle than Williams.

ANDERSON, Sherwood
(1876–1941)

American author, born in Camden, Ohio. He left his family and his lucrative position as manager of a paint factory to devote his entire time to writing. His first novel was *Windy McPherson's Son* (1916), but his best-known work is *Winesburg, Ohio* (1919), which portrayed the 'secret lives' of marginal characters and the sensibilities of the young artist who observes them and then escapes. *Poor White* (1920) is a strongly felt account of life under industrialization.
▷I Howe, *Sherwood Anderson: A Biography* (1951)

ANDERSSON, Dan(iel)
(1888–1920)

Swedish poet and novelist. One of Sweden's foremost writers in his time, he treated religious and metaphysical themes in his novels, like the autobiographical *De tre hemlösa* (1918, 'Three Homeless Ones'). His poems about traditional charcoal-burners in *Kolarhistorier* (1914) and *Kolvakterens visor* (1915) turned them into national folk-figures.
▷G Agren, *Dan Anderssons vag* (1970)

ANDRADE, DRUMMOND DE, Carlos
(1902–87)

Brazilian poet and short-story writer, born in Itabira, Minas Gerais. He graduated in pharmacy and worked as a journalist and teacher before moving to Rio de Janeiro in 1933. By that time his first volume, *Alguma poesia* (1930, 'Some Poetry'), had appeared, forging his links with the 'modernista' group. The spare, detached and accessible verse of *Alguma poesia* was succeeded, in 1940, by the altogether more sombre *Sentimento do mund* ('Feeling for the World'), over which looms the shadow of world war. From the end of the war onwards, his political concerns came to be more explicitly expressed in his poetry. Such collections as *A rosa do povo* (1945, 'The rose of the people'), however, remain firmly on the right side of the divide between committed art and overt propaganda.

ANDRADE, Mário de
(1893–1945)

Brazilian poet and novelist, born in São Paulo. He began by studying music, but devoted himself to writing after the publication of his first book of poems in 1917. He was a leading figure in the Brazilian modernist movement, and his avant-garde poems about his native city in *Paulicéia desvairada* (1922, Eng trans *Hallucinated City*, 1968) was influential in form and subject. His major prose work was the novel *Mucanaima* (1928), a complex, opaque work about a mythical Amazonian emperor whose adventures include a visit to 20th-century São Paulo, which carried a subtitle meaning 'hero without a character'. A *Complete Works* appeared in Portuguese in 1966.

ANDRADE, Olegario Victor
(1841–82)

Argentinian popular patriotic poet—a humble official until he suddenly became famous in the late 1870s—born in Alegrete, Brazil. Using **Hugo** (to whom he devoted a poem) as his model, he exalted the superiority of the Latin races in his technically capable, but perfervid and grandiose poems—not unlike **Swinburne** at his worst—from which there is now little to rescue except a genuine vision of a unified Latin America.

ANDRADE, Oswald de
(1890–1954)

Brazilian poet, novelist, literary publicist and founder-leader of the Brazilian *Modernista* movement (an urban and avant-garde movement, in which Andrade was associated with his namesake **Mário de Andrade** and the painter Anita Malfatti). He has been described as 'the enduring playboy of Brazilian letters'. His poetry is in itself trivial, although there has been an attempt by Brazilian critics, in recent years, to rehabilitate it, on the grounds of the 'economy with which he presents the complexity of Brazil'.

▷J Nist, *The Modernist Movement in Brazil* (1967)

ANDREAS-SALOMÉ, Lou
(1861–1937)

German novelist and thinker, loved by **Nietzsche** and the lover of **Rilke** and perhaps **Freud**, born in Russia. Lou, as she is always called, was one of the greatest women of the century. She became a lay analyst after studying with Freud. She wrote shrewdly and generously of the efforts of **Ibsen** to portray women, gave a piercing account of Nietzsche, and was responsible for releasing much poetry in Rilke, whom she understood better than any other woman in his life. Her *Die Erotik* (1910) is a key text, although it has been ignored by latter-day feminists. Her psychological and religious novels are now due for revival, as are her work and thought. Her *Rainer Maria Rilke* (1928) remains a seminal work on the poet.

▷H F Peters, *My Sister, My Spouse* (1962); L Binion, *Frau Lou* (1968)

ANDRES, Stefan
(1906–70)

German Roman Catholic novelist and poet, born in the Mosel country. He first studied for the priesthood, but abandoned this for art and then writing. His best-known novel is *Wir sind Utopia* (1942, Eng trans *We Are Utopia*, 1954), about a monk who finds himself imprisoned in the monastery he had once abandoned in order to fight against Franco. This was praised by **Graham Greene**, and its attitudes have been compared to his. He continued to write thoughtful and accomplished novels until his death.

ANDREWS, Virginia
(1933–86)

American novelist, born in West Virginia. Since her death the name has become a trademark of the Virginia C. Andrews Trust. The real Andrews lived in Portsmouth, Virginia, and was the author of four melodramatic novels about the Dollengager family. The sequence began with *Flowers in the Attic* (1979), in which children have been locked away by their mother, and ends with *Seeds of Yesterday* (1984). Andrews' commercial success, combined with the unpublished work which she left at her death, led to the unprecedented posthumous use of her name in novels such as *Midnight Whispers* (1991), part of the Cutler family saga. Although some of the work now put out in her name is a revised and augmented version of something she started, other publications are only in the style of the original author.

ANDREYEV, Leonid Nikolayevich
(1871–1919)

Russian writer and artist, born in Orel. He suffered much from poverty and ill-health as a student, and attempted suicide, before taking to writing and portrait painting. He enjoyed a period of fame after the success of *Zhili-byli* (1901, 'Once Upon a Time'). His style is over-rhetorical, but his best works overcome that weakness, notably *Gubernator* (1906, Eng trans *His Excellency the Governor*, 1921). He is most famous, however, for his terrifyingly effective drama, *Tot, kto poluchaet poshchochiny* (1915, Eng trans, *He Who Gets Slapped*, 1915). He died in exile after fleeing the 1917 revolution.

▷L N Afonin, *Leonid Andreyev* (1959)

ANDRIĆ, Ivo
(1892–1975)

Serbian author and diplomat, winner of the Nobel Prize for literature, born near Travnik. He was interned by the Austrian government as a Yugoslav nationalist during World War I, and a sense of isolation haunts his writing. He joined the diplomatic service, and was minister in Berlin at the outbreak of war in 1939. His chief works, *Na Drini Ćuprija* (1945, Eng trans *The Bridge on the Drina*, 1959) and *Travnička hronika* (1945, Eng trans *Bosnian Story*, 1958), earned him the 1961 Nobel Prize for literature and the nickname 'the Yugoslav Tolstoy'.

▷E C Hawkesworth, *Andrić: a bridge between East and West* (1984)

ANDRZEJEWSKI, Jerzy
(1909–83)

Polish novelist, one of the country's most famous, who was always controversial amongst his countrymen. He began as a somewhat right-wing Catholic writer in the tradition of **Mauriac**. He became internationally famous with *Popiol i diament* (1948, Eng trans *Ashes and Diamonds*, 1968), which was made into a famous movie: it is an analysis of an unnamed Polish town and its sufferings under the Nazis, and is likely to be judged his finest novel. At first he tried to accommodate himself to the communist regime as a 'social realist', and got himself into severe trouble with such Poles as **Czeslaw Milosz**; he became critical of the regime in modernist novels such as *Ciemnósci kryja ziemie* (1957, Eng trans *The Inquisitors*, 1960), but still not in a way that satisfied everyone. Since his death his reputation has tended to fall: his work had, a critic wrote, '*longeurs* which are hard to explain away'.

ANEIRIN, or ANEURIN
(fl.late 6th century)

Ancient British poet, creator of the oldest surviving poetry composed in Scotland. He was Bard of Gododdin, the kingdom south of the Firth of Forth whose citadel was Din Eidyn (Edinburgh) until its capture by the Angles in 638, when the kingdom ended. Nennius speaks of him, together with **Taliesin**, as a poet in the Old North, while an earlier Triad speaks of him as 'Aneirin of flowing verse, prince of poets'. The great *Y Gododdin* ascribed to him describes the ill-fated expedition of a band of warriors defeated and destroyed after a march to Catterick in Yorkshire under the leadership of Mynyddawg Mwynfawr in c. AD600. It extols the martial virtues and generosity of the dead heroes, and contains one of the earliest extant references to King Arthur. Its initial composition was evidently oral and it was apparently transferred down the generations in that form for some 300 years. As a poet Aneirin proves himself a loyal follower of exceptional devotion.

▷S Turner, *A Vindication of the Genuineness of the Ancient British Poems of Aneurin, etc* (1803)

ANGEL, Albalucía
(1939–)

Colombian short-story writer and poet, born in Bogotá, one of the new wave of feminist writers to emerge in Latin America. Her fictional works tend to be experimental and, according to some critics, unusually difficult to read because of unexpected narrator changes, manipulations of structure, and verbal fireworks. Angel is also involved in film-making and journalism; she has produced a number of documentaries and written extensively on art. Her most famous work is *Estaba la pájara pinta sentada en el verde limón* ('The Painted Bird was Sitting on the Green Lemon Tree'), a female *Bildungsroman* dealing with the sexual and political awakening of the protagonist.

ANGELOU, Maya
(1928–)

American writer, singer, dancer, performer and Black activist, born in St Louis, Missouri. After the break-up of her parents' marriage, she and her brother lived with their grandmother in Stamps, Arkansas. She was raped by her mother's boyfriend when she was eight and for the next five years was mute. In her teens she moved to California to live with her mother, and at 16 gave birth to her son, Guy. She has had a variety of occupations in what she describes as 'a roller-coaster life'. In her twenties she toured Europe and Africa in the musical *Porgy and Bess*. In New York she joined the Harlem Writers Guild and continued to earn her living singing in night-clubs and performing in **Jean Genet**'s *The Blacks*. In the 1960s she was involved in Black struggles and then spent several years in Ghana as Editor of *African Review*. Her multi-volume autobiography, commencing with *I Know Why the Caged Bird Sings* (1970), was a critical and popular success, imbued with optimism, humour and homespun philosophy. She has published several volumes of verse, including *And Still I Rise* (1987), and is the Reynolds Professor of American Studies at Wake Forest University in North Carolina. In 1994 she published a collection of personal reflections, *Wouldn't take nothing for my journey now*.

ANGELUS SILESIUS, pseud (meaning 'Silesian Messenger') of **Johann Scheffler** (1624–77)

German poet, who was born and died in Breslau (Wrocław). A physician, he became a mystic through the impact upon him, in youth, of Abraham von Franckenberg, who introduced him to the works of **Jakob Böhme**. He had been brought up a zealous Protestant, but his translation of Catholic mystical works caused the Lutherans to criticize him: he was a Catholic priest by 1661. He therefore became involved in the letters and theology of the Counter-Reformation. His poetry, which had a debt to that of Daniel von Czepko, is most prized, not for its originality of thought, but for the concise and passionate expression of the manner in which the mystic (Protestant or Catholic) loves Christ—this is often stated in metaphorical, 'bride–Christ' terms. His poems were collected under the title *Der Cherubinische Wandersmann* (1674, 'The Cherubinic Wanderer').
▷J C E Flitch, *Selections from the Cherubinic Wanderer*, with introduction (1932)

ANGIOLIERI, Cecco
(c.1260–c.1312)

Italian poet, born in Siena. Nothing is known of his life except from his sonnets, the only kind of verse he wrote, which reveal a drinker, lecher and gambler with a cynical, sardonic character and a heartless wit. He attacked **Dante** in three poems.
▷F Figurelli, *La Musa Bizarra de Cecco Angiolieri* (1950)

ANGUS, Marion
(1866–1946)

Scottish poet, born in Aberdeen, the daughter of a Church of Scotland minister. She grew up in Arbroath, and later lived in Aberdeen, Edinburgh and Helensburgh. Her volumes of verse, mostly in Scots, include *The Lilt and Other Verses* (1922), *Sun and Candlelight* (1927), *The Singin' Lass* (1929) and *Lost Country* (1937). Her best-known poem is a lament for Mary, Queen of Scots, 'Alas, Poor Queen'.

ANKER, Nini Roll
(1873–1942)

Norwegian novelist and playwright, born in Molde. She became involved in the women's rights movement and in radical politics, and the conflict between feminine self-realization and the traditional feminine roles set out by the Lutheran Church is explored in *Det svake Kjøn* (1915, 'The Weaker Sex'). The 'Stampe' trilogy (1923–7) is an ambitious historical novel, while *Den som henger i en tråd* (1935, 'Hanging by a Thread') highlights the plight of women employed in the textile industry and their joint efforts to improve their situation. *Kvinnen og den svarte fuglen* (completed in 1942, published posthumously in 1945, 'The Woman and the Black Bird') is a powerful feminist–pacifist novel, underlining the need for women to play an active social and political role.
▷'Nini Roll Anker', in I Engelstad et al (eds), *Norsk kvinnelitteraturhistorie*, vol 2 (1989)

ANNENSKY, Innocenty
(1856–1909)

Russian poet, dramatist, critic, translator and classicist, born in Omsk. When **Gumilev**, **Akhmatova** and others founded the important Acmeist school of poets, they called Annensky their mentor. He really belonged to, and certainly contributed to, the Symbolist movement in Russian poetry, but when his very late first collection, *Tikiye pesni* (1904, 'Quiet Nights'), was harshly and unfairly reviewed by the leading Symbolist **Blok**, he was mortified. His own mentors were **Verlaine** and **Mallarmé**, and he brought the former's 'decadence', which was congenial to him, into Russian poetry. At his best, in his second, posthumous collection, the unique *Kiparisovy larets* (1910, 'The Cypress Chest'), he embodies the essence of fragrant decay and hopelessness. All he wrote, it has been said, is pervaded with *toska*, 'anxiety', a kind of evertremblingness in the face of his fragile circumstances; he had a weak heart, and died while on the very verge of greater success and recognition. He still seems a very 'modern' poet. His criticism was superb and penetrating, his tragedies interestingly unplayable, his translations (eg of the whole of *Euripides*) learned. The 'flawless beauty' of his lyrics, even now not well enough known outside Russia, deeply influenced **Pasternak** and have always been much loved by connoisseurs of

Russian poetry. There are English translations in: V Markov and M Sparks, *Modern Russian Poetry* (1967).

ANNO Mitsumasa
(1926–)

Japanese children's author and illustrator, born in Tsuwano. He is renowned for his visual puzzles, and his best work can be seen in *Fushigi na E* (1968, Eng trans *Topsy-Turvies: Pictures to Stretch the Imagination*, 1970) and *ABC no Hon* (1974, Eng trans *Anno's Alphabet*, 1975), which won a special Kate Greenaway Medal.

ANOUILH, Jean
(1910–87)

French dramatist, born in Bordeaux of French and Basque parentage. He began his career as a copywriter and as a gag-man in films. His first play, *L'Hermine* (1931, Eng trans *The Ermine*, 1955), was not a success, but his steady output soon earned him recognition as one of the leading dramatists of the contemporary theatre. He was influenced by the Neo-classical fashion inspired by **Giraudoux**, but his very personal approach to the re-interpretation of Greek myths was less poetic, and more in tune with the contemporary taste for artifice and stylization. Among his many successful plays are *Le Voyageur sans bagage* (1937, Eng trans *Traveller without Luggage*, 1959), *Le Bal des voleurs* (1938, Eng trans *Thieves' Carnival*, 1952), *La Sauvage* (1938, Eng trans *The Restless Heart*, 1957), *Eurydice* (1942, Eng trans *Point of Departure*, 1950), *Antigone* (1946, prod in English, New York 1946, London 1949), *Médée* (1946, Eng trans *Medea*, 1956), *L'Invitation au château* (1948, adapted by **Christopher Fry** as *Ring Round the Moon*, 1950), *L'Alouette* (1953, Eng trans *The Lark*, 1955), *Becket* (1959, first performed in London, 1961), *Pauvre Bitos* (1956, Eng trans *Poor Bitos*, 1963), *Cher Antoine* (1969, Eng trans *Dear Antoine*, 1971), *Ne Réveillez Pas Madame* (1970, 'Don't Wake Her Up'), *L'Arrestation* (1974, Eng trans *The Arrest*, 1974), *Vive Henri IV* (1977, 'Long Live Henry IV') and *La Culotte* (1978, 'The Breeches').
▷A D Fazia, *Jean Anouilh* (1972); J Harvey, *Jean Anouilh: a study in theatrics* (1964)

ANSTEY, Christopher
(1724–1805)

English writer, born in Brinkley, Cambridgeshire. He was educated at Bury St Edmunds, Eton, and King's College, Cambridge, of which he was a fellow (1745–54). In 1766 he wrote the *New Bath Guide*, an epistolary novel in verse setting out the exploits of Squire Blunderhead and his family in Bath, which achieved great popularity.
▷W C Powell, *Christopher Anstey: Bath Laureate* (1944)

ANSTEY, F, pseud of Thomas Anstey Guthrie
(1856–1934)

English writer, born in London. He studied at Trinity Hall, Cambridge, and in 1880 was called to the Bar. A whimsical humorist he wrote *Vice Versa* (1882), *The Tinted Venus* (1885), *The Brass Bottle* (1900), and many other novels and dialogues. He was on the staff of *Punch* from 1887 to 1930.
▷M J Turner, *A Bibliography of the Writings of F. Anstey, T.A. Guthrie, etc* (1931)

ANTAR, more fully l'Antarah Ibn Shaddād Al-'Absi
(6th century)

Arab poet and warrior, born of a Bedouin chieftain and a black slave somewhere in the desert near Medina, Saudi Arabia. The author of one of the seven Golden Odes of Arabic literature, and the subject of the 10th-century *Romance of Antar*, he is regarded as the model of Bedouin heroism and chivalry and by some as 'the father of knights'.
▷V E Menil, *Disputatio philologica de Antar ejusque poemate arabico Moallakah* (1814)

ANTHONY, Frank S
(1891–1927)

New Zealand writer of humorous short stories. His experiences of farming a 'section' (of government-allocated land) produced some of the earliest natural writing of New Zealand country life; his sketches of life among the dairy farmers of Taranaki were widely published in periodicals during the 1920s. Meanwhile, in the hope of developing his writing, he had moved to London, but his early death there cut short a promising career as a humorous commentator on life. None of his books was published during his lifetime; his novel *Follow the Call* was issued in 1936 by his mother, and included a short memoir. The Taranaki stories appeared in book form as *Me and Gus* in 1938. A revised edition appeared in 1951 and, with two sequels, was reissued as *The Complete Me and Gus* in 1963.

ANTHONY, Michael
(1932–)

Trinidadian novelist, born in Mayaro. His first novel, *The Games Are Coming* (1963), added a new and distinctive voice to West Indian fiction, with its finely realized culmination in a cycle race. He lived in London and Brazil before returning to Trinidad in 1970. His later novels have seemed, to many

critics, to be less vivid than the earlier, in which he recreated the Trinidad of his youth.
▷K Ramchand, *The West Indian Novel and Its Background* (1970)

ANTHONY, Piers, pseud of **Piers Anthony Dillingham Jacob**
(1934–)

English-born American science-fiction and fantasy writer. He moved to the USA as a child in 1940, and became a US citizen in 1958. He made a positive impression at the start of his career with *Chthon* (1967) and the ambitious *Macroscope* (1969), still regarded by many as his best book, and one which transcends its space-adventure framework. His later work generally focused on multi-volume sequences, some of which also addressed larger issues, as in the *Cluster* (1977–82), *Tarot* (1979–80), *Bio of a Space Tyrant* (1983–6) or *Incarnations of Immortality* (1983–90) sequences, while others were more conventional action works. He is a prolific writer and a combative commentator.
▷*Bio of an Ogre* (1988)

ANTIN, David
(1932–)

American prose poet, born in Brooklyn, New York, and educated there at City College and New York University. Antin's verbal improvisations are pure, plotless narrative, observing few of the rules of conventional storytelling and almost none of the prosodic or metaphoric organizational principles that usually distinguish lyric poetry. Early works such as *Definitions* and *Autobiography* (both 1967) suggest more formal tampering but less imaginative control than *Talking at the Boundaries* (1976), in which Antin abandons all remaining references to poetic form and writes almost entirely in unresolved or incomplete syntactic structures. A one-time science editor, he has also published on mathematics and physics.
▷S Paul, *So to Speak: Re-reading David Antin* (1982)

ANTOKOLSKY, Pavel
(1896–1978)

Russian poet and theatrical producer, born in St Petersburg. Antokolsky was a very capable and technically gifted poet who may have limited his achievement by his tendency to follow the wind. He was an actor in his youth. Competent romantic verse was succeeded by poems praising Russian industrialization; the so-called 'Thaw' under Kruschev produced poems in praise of freedom, and these were followed by ones on 'approved themes'. All he wrote was readable and skilfully executed,

and none of his 'dutiful' verse is ludicrous in the manner of some of his contemporaries.

ANTONINUS, Brother *see* **EVERSON, William**

APOLLINAIRE, Guillaume, originally **Apollinaris Kostrowitzky**
(1880–1918)

French poet, born in Rome of Polish descent. He settled in Paris in 1900, and became a leader of the movement rejecting poetic traditions in outlook, rhythm, and language. His work often reveals a basic lyricism at its roots, but its bizarre, Symbolist and fantastic elements have affinities with the Cubist school in painting. They include *L'Enchanteur pourrissant* (1909, 'The Decaying Magician'), *Le Bestiaire* (1911, Eng trans 1977), *Alcools* (1913, Eng trans 1964) and *Calligrammes* (1918). He was wounded in World War I, and during his convalescence wrote the play *Les Mamelles de Tirésias* (1918, 'The Breasts of Tiresias'), for which he coined the term 'surrealist', and the Modernist manifesto *L'Esprit nouveau et les poètes* (1946, 'The New Spirit and the Poets'.
▷P M Adema, *Guillaume Apollinaire: le malaimé* (1952); S Bates, *Guillaume Apollinaire* (1967)

APOLLONIUS RHODIUS
(b.c.295 BC)

Greek poet and literary scholar, born in Alexandria (or possibly Naucratis). A pupil of **Callimachus**, he was head of the Alexandrian library c.260–247 BC, before retiring to Rhodes. His great (and only surviving) work is the *Argonautica*, an epic poem on the Homeric model describing the voyage of Jason and the *Argo* to recover the Golden Fleece. It was much studied and admired in antiquity, its narrative of the love of Jason and Medea serving **Virgil** as a model for the story of Aeneas and Dido in Book IV of the *Aeneid*.

APTE, Hari Narayan
(1864–1919)

Indian (Marathi) novelist who introduced the novel proper into his language. Influenced by Sir **Walter Scott** and **Dickens**, he contributed readable and intelligent episodes from the history of the Maratha empire to its literature.

APULEIUS, Lucius
(2nd century)

Roman writer, satirist and rhetorician, born in Madaura, in Numidia in Africa. Educated at Carthage and Athens, he used the fortune bequeathed him by his father to travel; he visited Italy and Egypt, where it is likely that he was initiated into the mystery religion of

Isis and Osiris. The knowledge which he thus acquired of the priestly fraternities he put to use afterwards in his novel, the *Metamorphoses* (Eng trans *The Golden Ass*, 1566). Having married a wealthy, middle-aged widow, Aemilia Pudentilla, who nursed him in Alexandria, he was charged by her relations with having employed magic to gain her affections. His *Apologia*, still extant, was an eloquent speech in his defence. He settled in Carthage, where he devoted himself to literature, philosophy and rhetoric. *Metamorphoses* is a tale of adventure containing elements of magic, satire and romance, notably the story of Cupid and Psyche.

▷E H Haight, *Apuleius and his Influence* (1927)

ARAGON, Louis
(1897–1983)

French writer and political activist, born in Paris. One of the most brilliant of the Surrealist group, he co-founded the journal *Littérature* with **André Breton** in 1919. He published two volumes of poetry, *Feu de joie* (1920, 'Bonfire') and *Le Mouvement perpétuel* (1925, 'Perpetual Motion'), and a Surrealist novel, *Le Paysan de Paris* (1926, 'The Peasant of Paris'). After a visit to the Soviet Union in 1930 he became a convert to communism. Thereafter he wrote social-realistic novels in a series entitled *Le Monde Réel* (1933–51, 'The Real World'), and war poems, including *Le Crève-Coeur* (1941, 'Heartbreak') and *Les Yeux d'Elsa* (1942, 'Elsa's Eyes'), about his lifelong partner, the writer Elsa Triolet. The novel *La semaine sainte* (1958, 'Holy Week') attempted a Marxist analysis of the events of 1815. He was an important editor of left-wing publications, and an influential essayist.

▷A Hurant, *Louis Aragon: prisonnier politique* (1970)

ARANHA, José Pereira da Graça
(1868–1931)

Brazilian novelist and, at the end of his life, embracer of the avant-garde Brazilian modernist movement (the nativism of which, however, he rejected). He was born in Maranhao in the north-east of Brazil. A diplomat by profession, he maintained a European outlook throughout his life. His most important novel is *Chanaan* (1902, Eng trans, *Canaan*, 1920), about two German immigrants to Brazil who become members of a community which has settled in the interior. Whatever the worth of this still controversial novel, it succeeds in conveying the impact of the mysterious interior on the European sensibility.

▷M de L Teixeira, *Graça Aranha* (1952, in Portuguese)

ARANY, János
(1817–82)

Hungarian poet, born in Nagy-Szalonta of peasant stock. With **Sandor Petöfi** he was a leader of the popular national school, and is regarded as one of the greatest and most characteristic of Hungarian poets. He was chief secretary of the Academy from 1870 to 1879. His satire *The Lost Constitution* (1845) won the Kisfaludy Society Prize, but his chief work is the *Toldi* trilogy (1847–54), the story of the adventures of a murderously quick-tempered young peasant in the 14th century Hungarian court. He also published successful translations of **Aristophanes** and **Shakespeare**.

▷D Kevesztury, *Arany János* (1971)

ARATOR
(fl.540)

Poet, born in what is now Italy but what was then the kingdom of the Ostrogoths. He was employed at the court of King Athalric before moving to the papal Curia under Pope Vigilius. His poetry is a fine example of the epic religious tradition of the early church in which the forms and measures of classical Latin poetry are adapted and employed for exploring religious themes. Arator is recorded in church annals as having read aloud his epic account of the Acts of the Apostles in Rome in 544.

ARCHER, Jeffrey Howard, Baron
(1940–)

Bestselling British author and former parliamentarian, educated at Wellington School and Brasenose College, Oxford, where he won Blues for athletics and gymnastics. He sat as Conservative MP for the constituency of Louth from 1969 to 1974, but resigned from the House of Commons after a financial disaster that led to bankruptcy. In order to pay his debts in full he turned to writing fiction; his first book, *Not a Penny More, Not a Penny Less* (1975), based on his own unfortunate experiences in the financial world, was an instant bestseller, which he followed up with other blockbusters like *Shall We Tell the President?* (1976), *Kane and Abel* (1979), which was dramatized on television, and *First Among Equals* (1984), which was also televised. Despite critical reservations about their literary merits, his books continue to sell in vast numbers. In 1987 he wrote a thriller for the stage, *Beyond Reasonable Doubt*, and in 1988 capped his lifelong interest in the theatre by buying one outright—the Playhouse, London. In 1990 he wrote *Exclusive*, a play. He was Deputy Chairman of the Conservative Party 1985–6, but resigned following allegations over which he later cleared his name in a successful libel action against the *Daily Star*. He was made a life peer in 1992, taking the title Baron Archer of Weston-Super-Mare. Recent titles include *Honour Among Thieves* (1993) and *Twelve Red Herrings* (1994).

ARCHILOCHUS OF PAROS
(8th–7th century BC)

Early Greek lyric and elegiac poet. He was ranked by the ancients with **Homer** and **Pindar**, and **Plato** calls him 'the very wise', but much of his renown is for vituperative satire. Only fragments of his work are extant. He died in battle.

▷T Breitenstein, *Hésiode et Archiloque* (1971)

ARCHPOET, the
(d.c.1165)

German Latin poet whose career in many ways mirrors that of his contemporary and fellow satirist **Hugh Primas**. His real name is not known, but we know from his verse that he was of gentle birth and well educated, though impoverished. His one great patron was Rainald of Dassel, arch-chancellor to Emperor Frederick Barbarossa, who was impressed with his witty images and nicely turned phrases. However, after a falling-out between them (documented in verse), the archpoet disappeared into obscurity and, presumably, poverty.

ARDEN, John
(1930–)

British playwright, born in Barnsley, Yorkshire, and educated at Sedbergh School, King's College, Cambridge, and the Edinburgh College of Art. It was in Edinburgh, while he was completing his architectural training, that the College Dramatic Society produced his first play, a romantic comedy entitled *All Fall Down*, in 1955. *Live Like Pigs* (1958), with its **Rabelai**sian realism and humour, broke new ground in theatrical presentation. His aggressive awareness of the north of England is particularly evident in *The Workhouse Donkey* (1963), a caricature of northern local politics; in *Sergeant Musgrave's Dance* (1959), very much following the tradition of Brecht in its staging, the universality of the folk idiom reveals layers of political relevance beyond the simple tale of a group of soldiers returning to a northern town, bringing home with them the realities of war. In *Armstrong's Last Goodnight* (1964) the use of ballads and formal staging are particularly successful as Arden embodies contemporary political themes in a tale of the

16th-century Scottish borders. Arden has continually experimented with dramatic form and theatrical technique, both in the plays he has written alone and in the many pieces in which he has collaborated with his wife, Margaretta D'Arcy. *The Happy Haven* (1961) followed the commedia dell'arte tradition, the nativity play *The Business of Good Government* (1960) uses medieval stage techniques, *The Hero Rises Up* (1968) is a ballad opera about Nelson, and *The Ballygombeen Bequest* (1972) uses vaudeville on the theme of the political and class conflict in Ireland. Arden admits that he is not happy within the framework of the modern theatre. His plays also include *Ironhand* (1963), an adaptation of **Goethe**'s *Goetz von Berlichingen*; *Left-Handed Liberty*, commissioned in 1965 for the 750th anniversary of Magna Carta; a version of the Arthurian legend, *The Island of the Mighty* (1972), and *Vandaleur's Folly* (1978). He has also written television scripts, a volume of essays, and a novel, *Silence Among the Weapons* (1982). Since *The Island of the Mighty*, Arden has not produced a major new stage play but has written increasingly for radio, including a nine-part series, *Whose Is the Kingdom?* (1988). A second novel, *The Book of Bale*, appeared the same year, and continues Arden's theme of using early history to look closely at timeless moral issues.

▷J R Brown, *Theatre Language: a study of Arden, Osborne, Pinter and Wesker* (1972)

ARDERÍUS, Joaquín
(1890–1969)

Spanish experimental novelist, an isolated and highly original writer in whom there is now some new critical interest in Spain. He influenced many anti-Franco modernist and post-modernist novelists, such as **Juan Benet**. He wrote surrealistic and then, later, more idiosyncratic novels, such as *Yo y tres mujeres* ('I and Three Women'), a highly original and sophisticated erotic novel, and *Justo* (1929), a satire on pious official Roman Catholicism. His work was generally too difficult for it to have had commercial success, but it is now being studied as pioneering and influential.

ARENAS, Reinaldo
(1943–)

Cuban novelist, born in a small rural town in the province of Oriente, who has risen to international stature for his poetic vision of life in Castro's Cuba. Upon moving to Havana, he studied briefly at the university there and took a job at the National Library. His first book, *Celestino antes del Alba* (1967, 'Celestino Before Dawn'), is the first of five semi-autobiographical novels which describe Arena's fantastic vision of Cuba after the

Revolution. Because of the disenchantment with the Revolution expressed in his novels and also because of his homosexuality, he was placed in a re-education camp, imprisoned, and his works banned. In 1980, he left Cuba in the Mariel Boat Lift, and now lives in exile in New York, teaching and lecturing. Though mainly a novelist, he has also written brilliant short stories, a book of articles, a number of experimental theatre pieces, and is presently working on memoirs. He has won various awards, including a Guggenheim Fellowship.

ARETINO, Pietro
(1492–1557)

Italian poet, born in Arezzo, Tuscany, the illegitimate son of a nobleman named Luigi Bacci. Banished from his native town, he went to Perugia, where he worked as a bookbinder, and afterwards wandered through Italy in the service of various noblemen. In Rome (1517–27) he distinguished himself by his wit, impudence, and talents, and secured papal favour, which he subsequently lost by writing his salacious *Sonetti Lussuriosi* ('Lustful Sonnets'). He won the friendship of Giovanni de Medici and gained an opportunity of ingratiating himself with Francis I at Milan in 1524. He later settled in Venice, and again acquired powerful friends. It is said that while laughing heartily at a droll adventure of one of his sisters, he fell from a stool, and was killed on the spot. His poetical works include five witty comedies, and a tragedy of some merit.
▷F Berni, *La Vita di Pietro Aretino* (1939)

ARÉVALO MARTINEZ, Rafael
(1884–1975)

Guatemalan poet, story-writer and novelist, inventor of 'psychozoological fiction' in his tale *El hombre que paraci un caballo* (1914, 'The Man Who Looked Like a Horse'), about the legendary homosexual Colombian poet **Porfirio Barba Jacob**, born in Guatemala City. Classified as an 'extraordinary case', Arévalo has yet to be discovered and understood outside Latin America.

ARGENSOLA, Bartolomé Leonardo de
(1562–1631)
ARGENSOLA, Lupercio de
(1559–1613)

Spanish poets, born in Barbastro. They were both educated at Huesca University and both entered the service of Maria of Austria. Their poems led them to be styled the 'Spanish Horaces', but they were also official historians of Aragon. Lupercio also wrote some tragedies.
▷J A Molina, *Los Argensola* (1939)

ARGHEZI, Tudor, pseud of Ion N Theodorescu
(1880–1967)

Romanian poet, fiction-writer and translator—always the centre of violent controversy—more than once described as Romania's 'outstanding poet of the twentieth century'. He began as a monk (1899–1904), then became a communist. He was interned for part of World War II for ridiculing the Nazi ambassador to Romania. His final poetry, some of it socialist realist, is unconvincing. But earlier, as the non-intellectual but **Baudelaire**-inspired poet of the dark side of the environment, he reached major proportions. He made translations of Baudelaire and wrote fiction (1930) about his experiences in a monastery and in prison—always almost unreasoningly wild in his polemic, he got himself charged after World War I with collaborating with a German newspaper. He was, a critic wrote, 'in search of … apocalyptic visions of a putrescent world'. He was widely recognized throughout Europe, being translated by no less than **Salvatore Quasimodo** and **Rafael Alberti**; but *Selected Poems* (1976), in English, is not quite so effective at conveying his worth. At heart, and at his greatest, he is a religious poet.
▷D Micu, *The Work of Tudor Arghezi* (1965)

ARGUEDAS, Alcides
(1879–1946)

Bolivian novelist and historian, born in La Paz. As a historian and a sociologist, Arguedas exalted the European, and emphasized (too greatly, in some modern views) the influence of the environment. As a novelist, notably in *Raza de bronce* (1919, 'The Bronze Race', a radical re-working of an earlier novel of 1904, *Wata-Wara*), he was an avid defender of the Almairá Native Americans, showing them as exploited and despoiled by arrogant, greedy priests and clerks. Although its picture of the Native Americans is comprised of more fantasy than fact, the book is powerful, was influential—and was one of the first really good novels to be published in Bolivia. He wrote a rather stuffy, but invaluable, history of Bolivia (1922).
▷F Reinaga, *Alcides Arguedas* (1960, in Spanish)

ARGUEDAS, José María
(1911–69)

Peruvian novelist, born in a small provincial town. His life was spent working in literature and anthropology in order to champion the cause of the indigenous peoples of Peru. His literary works combine Quechua words and syntax with Spanish to illustrate the combination of cultures which characterizes his country. He is an important Regionalist writer, author of *Los ríos profundos* (1958, 'Deep Rivers'), a literary landmark which signalled the transition to the New Novel. His other major novels are *Yawar Fiesta* (1941, 'Yawar Festival') and *Todas las sangres* (1964, 'Everyone's Blood').

ARIBAU, Bonaventura Carles
(1798–1862)

Spanish economist and writer, born in Barcelona. He became a banker in Madrid, and was appointed director of the Mint and of the Spanish Treasury (1847). He was also decorated by the Prince Consort for his work on the industrial section of the Great Exhibition of 1851. He was editor of the *Biblioteca de autores españoles* ('Library of Spanish Writers'), and was the author of the *Oda a la Patria* (1833, 'Ode to the Motherland'), one of the earliest and best modern poems in Catalan, which had a tremendous influence on contemporary Catalan writers.

▷M de Montoliu, *Los grans personalitats de la litteratura catalana* (1936)

ARINOS, Affonso
(1868–1916)

Brazilian novelist, born in the Minas Gerais region. His books are interesting for their slight anticipations of **da Cunha**: both *Os Jagunços* and *Pelo Sertão* (both 1898) are about the backlands of the North East.

ARIOSTO, Ludovico
(1474–1533)

Italian poet, born in Reggio Emilia. He intended to take up law, but abandoned it for poetry. In 1503 he was introduced to the court of the Cardinal Ippolito d'Este at Ferrara, who employed him in many negotiations, but was extremely niggardly in his rewards. Here, in the space of 10 years, Ariosto produced his great poem, *Orlando Furioso* (1516, 'Orlando Enraged'), which takes up the epic tale of Roland (as Orlando) from the French *chansons de geste* and forms a continuation of **Boiardo**'s *Orlando Innamorato* ('Orlando in Love'). When the cardinal left Italy (1518), the duke, his brother, invited the poet to his service, and treated him with comparative liberality. In 1522 he was commissioned to suppress an insurrection in the wild mountain district of Garfagnana, an arduous task which he successfully accomplished; and after remaining there three years as governor of the province, he returned to Ferrara, where he composed his comedies, and finished *Orlando*, which appeared in a third edition, enlarged to its present dimensions, in 1532. He was buried in the church of San Benedetto, at Ferrara, where a magnificent monument marks his resting place. Besides his great work, he wrote comedies, satires, sonnets, and a number of Latin poems. Of these the sonnets alone show the genius of the poet. His Latin poems are mediocre, and his comedies, besides lacking interest, are disfigured by licentious passages.

▷C P Brand, *Ludovico Ariosto: an introduction to the Orlando Furioso* (1974)

ARISTOPHANES
(c.448–c.385 BC)

Greek comic playwright. He wrote some 50 plays, but only 11 are extant. The best-known of his earlier works, in which the satire is largely political, are *Hippeis* (424, 'Knights'), *Nephelai* (423, 'Clouds') and *Sphekes* (422, 'Wasps') (named from their respective choruses), and *Eirene* (421, 'Peace'). These were followed by *Ornithes* (414, 'Birds'), *Lysistrata* (411, 'Destroyer of Armies'), *Thesmophoriazusae* (411, 'The Women attending the Thesmophoria') and *Batrachoi* (405, 'Frogs', which contains a burlesque poetic contest between **Aeschylus** and **Euripides**). Later come *Ecclesiazusae* (392, 'Women in Parliament') and *Plutus* (388). In the last, the themes are personal, and the chorus plays only a marginal role. Aristophanes is the only writer of Old Comedy of whom complete plays survive. The objects of his often savage satire are social and intellectual pretension; the plots of his plays show a genius for comic and often outrageous invention; his humour is usually good-natured; and the verse in his choruses marks him out as a notable poet.

▷L E Lord, *Aristophanes: his plays and influence* (1925)

ARLAND, Marcel
(1899–)

French fiction writer and critic, neglected outside his own country, a member of the Académie française since 1968. He was born in Varenne-sur-Amance. From 1953, at first with Jean Paulhan, he edited *La Nouvelle Revue Française*. He was involved in the Dada movement, but abandoned it to cultivate a precise style much influenced by his friend **André Gide**. Notable amongst his works are an influential anthology of French poetry (1941), the novel *L'Ordre* (1929, 'The Order'), and, above all, his tales of his own village, in such collections as *Il faut de tout pour faire un monde* (1946, 'It Takes Everything to Make a

World'), in which adults are seen through the eyes of a sensitive teenager.

ARLEN, Michael, originally **Dikran Kouyoumdjian**
(1895–1956)

British novelist, born in Ruschuk, Bulgaria, of Armenian parents. He was educated in England and naturalized in 1922, but lived in France from 1928 until World War II, and settled in the USA after the war. He made his reputation with *Piracy* (1922), *The Green Hat* (1924), and his short-story collections, *The Romantic Lady* (1921) and *These Charming People* (1923). His last novel was *The Flying Dutchman* (1939).
▷M J Arlen, *Exiles* (1971)

ARLT, Roberto
(1900–42)

Argentinian novelist and dramatist, born in Buenos Aires of a German emigrant father and a Swiss–Italian mother. Arlt, initially reproached for his syntax (which was poor—and, worse, as they alleged, it was 'insulting'), was the most poetic of the urban realist Latin-American novelists of his century, with the exception of the Uruguayan **Juan Carlos Onetti**, who has acknowledged his own debt. Karl Arlt, 'the black father' (as Roberto called him), a professional failure, mocked his son throughout his childhood with 'sadistic machismo'; his mother was devoted to romantic pulp fiction. 'From the age of 15 to 20 I practised all the professions,' he wrote. 'They kicked me out everywhere for uselessness.' But then he taught himself to write, and started to compose 'crime spots' in the newspapers. His major work followed: four novels, and about 50 short stories. In the 1930s he devoted himself to theatre, which, although excellent, is not on such a high level. Of his work only *Los siete locos* (1929, Eng trans *The Seven Madmen*, 1984) has ever been translated. In *Los siete locos* and its sequel *Los lanzallamas* (1931, 'The Flame Throwers')—these are, with certain stories, his masterpieces—a group of madmen led by Erdosain, who seeks (like the Jewish 'false messiahs') 'holiness in sin', set out to destroy the capitalist world. The phantasmagorical world these novels conjure up can only be matched by the Argentinian political scene which formed their background: they are perhaps the blackest novels of the century. Yet Arlt's last novel, *El Amor Brujo* (1932, 'Love the Magician'), tells of frustrated love. His pieces for the newspaper *El Mundo* have been collected as *Aguafuertes* in two volumes (1950–3). His daughter Mirta edited his complete novels and stories (1963).
▷K Schwartz, *A New History of Spanish-American Fiction* (1971)

ARNÉR, Sivar
(1909–)

Swedish novelist, short-story writer and dramatist. Born near Kalmar, he studied at the University of Lund and became a schoolteacher. An early novel such as *Plånbok borttappad* (1943, 'The Lost Wallet') reflects a **Nietzsche**an nihilism, tempered, in later novels such as *Fyra som var bröder* (1955, 'The Four who were Brothers'), by the influence of woman. Several texts offer psychological analyses of marital relationships, among them *Verandan* (1947, 'The Veranda'), a book of short stories, and *Egil* (1948), a novel. His works from the 1950s often reflect a mystical search for unity; and in the novel *Tvärbalk* (1963, 'The Cross-Beam') this quest results in a subtle critique of contemporary Swedish society. He is the author of numerous successful radio dramas.
▷B Sjöberg, *Sivar Arnér—den livsbejakande nihilisten* (1993)

ARNICHES Y BARRERA, Carlos
(1866–1943)

Spanish playwright, born in Alicante. He moved while young to Madrid and there became so entrenched in the life of the capital that he was inextricably identified with it. After starting off in journalism, he turned his hand to play-writing, at first in collaboration. He excelled in the 'sainete', a short comedy or one-act farce reflecting everyday life. Originally it was an entr'acte made famous by **Ramon de la Cruz**. This kind of popular, comic work was at first rather scorned by critics but popular with audiences, who found the characters instantly recognizable. Some of the most famous works, from an output of over 300 pieces, were *El Santo de la Isidra* (1898, 'The Saint of Isidra') and *El Puñao de Rosas* (1902, 'The Bunch of Roses'), which were comedies, and *Los Caciques* (1919), a social criticism which finally won him critical acclaim. While never patronizing his audience, he maintained a common code of morality in his well-constructed slices of 'madrileño' life.

ARNIM, Achim von, real name **Karl Joachim Friedrich Ludwig von Arnim**
(1781–1831)

German writer of fantastic but original romances. He stirred up a warm sympathy for old popular poetry and folk-tales, and published over 20 volumes, mainly tales and novels, including the folk-song collections *Des Knaben Wunderhorn* (1806, 'The Boy's Magic Horn') with **Clemens von Brentano**. His writing is overtly moralistic and his most ambitious work is the unfinished novel *Die Kronenwächter* (1817, 'The Crown Minder').

His wife, Bettina (1785–1859), Brentano's sister, was as a girl infatuated with **Goethe**, and afterwards published a (largely fictitious) *Correspondence* with him, as well as 10 volumes of tales and essays.

▷H Liedke, *Literary Criticism and Romantic Theory in the Works of Achim von Arnim* (1927)

ARNIM, Bettina von, née von Brentano
(1785–1859)

German writer, sister to **Clemens von Brentano**, who was friendly with **Goethe** (who eventually severed connections with her owing to her treatment of his wife). Her books, such as one about Goethe and another about her brother, are not novels but somewhat fanciful—yet intelligent—accounts, or 'documentary' fabrications.

ARNOLD, Sir Edwin
(1832–1904)

English poet and journalist, born in Gravesend. He won the Newdigate Prize for poetry at Oxford in 1852 for his poem 'Belshazzar's Feast', taught at King Edward's School, Birmingham, and in 1856 became principal of Deccan College, Poona. Returning in 1861, he joined the staff of *The Daily Telegraph*, of which he became Editor in 1863. He wrote *The Light of Asia* (1879) on Buddhism, and other poems coloured by his experience of the East. A later volume, *The Light of the World* (1891), did not achieve the popularity of his earlier work. He also published translations from Eastern languages.

▷*Aspects of Life* (1893)

ARNOLD, Matthew
(1822–88)

English poet and critic, born in Laleham, near Staines, the eldest son of Dr Thomas Arnold of Rugby. He was educated at Winchester, Rugby, and Balliol College, Oxford. He won the Newdigate Prize with a poem on Cromwell (1843), and in 1845 was elected a fellow of Oriel College. After acting for four years as private secretary to Lord Lansdowne (1847–51), he was appointed one of the lay inspectors of schools in 1851, an office from which he retired in 1886. From 1857 to 1867 he was Professor of Poetry at Oxford. He was frequently sent by the government to inquire into the state of education on the Continent, especially in France, Germany, and Holland; and his masterly reports, with their downright statement of English deficiencies, attracted much attention in England. So, too, did his audacious application to scripture of the methods of literary criticism. In 1883 he received a pension of £250, and in the same year he lectured in the USA. He was buried at Laleham. His early volumes of poetry, *The Strayed Revelles and Other Poems* (1849), which contained 'The Forsaken Merman', and *Empedocles on Etna* (1852), which contained 'Tristram and Iseult', both failed, but he made his mark with *Poems: A New Edition* (1853–4), which contained 'The Scholar Gipsy' and 'Sohrab and Rustum', and confirmed his standing as a poet with *New Poems* (1867), which contained 'Dover Beach' and 'Thyrsis'. He published several distinguished works of criticism including *Essays in Criticism* (1865, 1888), *On the Study of Celtic Literature* (1867), *Culture and Anarchy* (1869), *St Paul and Protestantism* (1870), *Literature and Dogma* (1872), *Last Essays on Church and Religion* (1877), *Mixed Essays* (1879), *Irish Essays* (1882), and *Discourses on America* (1885).

▷L Trilling, *Matthew Arnold* (1939); M Thorpe, *Matthew Arnold* (1969)

ARP, Hans or Jean
(1887–1966)

Alsation sculptor, graphic artist and poet, born in Strasbourg, who had a command of three languages: French, German and Alsatian. He was the outstanding poet of the Dada movement, inaugurated (1916) by **Hugo Ball** in Zurich. Critic **Martin Seymour-Smith** has said of him that his poetry 'was a necessary means of expressing his essentially playful ... response to existence: childlike, spontaneous, cheerfully and mockingly aleatory in the face of a supremely confident assumption of the absurdity of everything'.

▷R W Last, *Hans Arp* (1969)

ARRABAL, Fernando
(1932–)

Spanish dramatist and novelist, born in Melilla, Spanish Morocco. His childhood was disrupted by the opposing political convictions of his parents during the Civil War. His strongly Catholic mother led him to believe that his father, who had escaped and disappeared in 1941 after being imprisoned for his Republican sympathies, was dead. He studied law in Madrid and drama in Paris in 1954, and then settled permanently in France. His first play, *Pique-nique en campagne* (1959, Eng trans *Picnic on the Battlefield*, 1964), established him in the tradition of the Theatre of the Absurd, greatly influenced by **Samuel Beckett**. He coined the term 'Panic theatre', intended to shock the senses, employing sadism and blasphemy to accomplish its aims. In *Le Cimetière des voitures* (1958, Eng trans as *The Car Cemetery*, 1969) life is seen as a used car dump, and in *Le grand cérémonial* (1965, 'The Grand Ceremonial') and *Cérémonie* *pour un noir assassiné* (1965, Eng trans *Ceremony for a Murdered Black*, 1972), ceremonial rites are used to play out sadistic fantasies. He writes in Spanish, his work being translated into French by his wife. In 1967 he was charged by a Spanish court with blasphemy and anti-patriotism, and his *Et ils passèrent des menottes aux fleurs* (1969, Eng trans *And They Put Handcuffs on the Flowers*, 1971), based on conversations with Spanish political prisoners, was eventually banned in France and Sweden while becoming his first major success in America in 1971. As well as his many plays he has published poetry—*La Pierre de la folie* (1963, 'The Stone of Stupidity') and *100 sonnets* (1966)—and novels including *Baal Babylone* (1959, Eng trans 1961).

▷A Schifres, *Entretiens avec Arrabal* (1969)

ARREOLA, Juan José
(1918–)

Mexican satirical story writer and dramatist, born in Cuidad Guzmán—one of Mexico's most unusual and original writers of his century. He was helped, in 1945, by the great French actor Louis Jouvet to obtain a scholarship so that he could study drama in Paris. He was later helped in his literary career by **Alfonso Reyes**. His best and most famous work, the much revised and unclassifiable *Confabulario* (1952, revised as *Confabulario y Varia invención*, 1954, Eng trans *Confabulario and Other Inventions*, 1964—the final Spanish revision is *Confabulario total*, 1962), consists of fables or parables, marked by a neurasthenic fear and hatred of women—a feature that has made Arreola's work unpalatable to some critics. He later became a television personality, and his work, often in the same vein as the *Confabulario*, is generally taken to have declined in power. *La feria* (1963, Eng trans *The Fair*, 1977) is a patchwork novel about his childhood in Zapotlán el Grande.

▷Y M Washburn, *Juan José Arreola* (1983)

ARTAUD, Antonin Marie Joseph
(1896–1948)

French dramatist, actor, director and theorist, born in Marseilles. A Surrealist in the 1920s, he published a volume of verse (*L'Ombilic des limbes*, 1925, 'The Umbilicus of Limbo'), and in 1927 co-founded the Théâtre Alfred Jarry. He propounded a theatre that dispensed with narrative and psychological realism but which returned instead to theatre as primitive rite, and the mythology of the human mind as expressed in dreams and interior obsessions. The function of drama was to give expression, through movement and gesture, to the inexpressible and irrational locked within the consciousness. His main theoretical work is the book, *Le Théâtre et son double* (1938, Eng trans *The Theatre and its Double*, 1958). As the creator of what has been termed the Theatre of Cruelty, his influence on post-war theatre was profound. A manic-depressive, his last years were spent in a mental institution, from where he continued to write. His *Collected Works* appeared in English in 1968–74 (4 vols).

ARTHUR, Timothy Shay
(1809–85)

American novelist and editor, born in Newburgh, New York, and educated in Baltimore. Hugely prolific, he wrote unashamedly didactic fiction, including the classic *Ten Nights in a Barroom and What I Saw There* (1854), an influential prohibitionist tract. It was dramatized (1958) by William W Pratt and became a long-running staple of popular theatre, memorable for little Mary's plangent song to her drunken father. No teetotaller himself, Arthur also wrote moralistic advice books like *Strong Drink: The Curse and the Cure* (1877, also published as *Grappling with the Monster*). He contributed to *Godey's Lady's Book* and founded what became *Arthur's Home Magazine* (1845–85), an 'improving' monthly dedicated to exposing the evils of alcoholism and gambling and reinforcing 'family values' and the sanctity of marriage. *The Three Eras of a Woman's Life* (1848, comprising *The Maiden*, *The Wife*, *The Mother*) was among his more ambitious works.

ARTMANN, H(ans) C(arl)
(1921–)

Austrian writer of the avant-garde, born in St Achatz am Walde. From 1952 to 1958 he was associated with the Wiener Gruppe, a coterie of avant-garde writers. He is a 'concrete' poet, interested in destroying old concepts and replacing them with entirely new ones; he is also a writer of dialect poems; he has been a dominant figure in Austria, but is otherwise known only in circles of experimental writers. One of his poems is translated in **Middleton** and **Hamburger**'s *Modern German Poetry 1910–1960* (1962).

ARTZYBASHEV, Mikhail Petrovich
(1878–1927)

Russian author. His liberalist novel *Sanin* (1907) had an international reputation at the turn of the century. It was translated by P Pinkerton in 1907, who also translated *Breaking Point* (1915), and with I Ohzol, *Tales of Revolution* (1918).

▷B N Lebedev, *Mikhail Artzybashev* (1908)

ARUNDEL, Honor
(1919–73)

British author of teenage fiction, born in Wales, but living for much of her adult life in Edinburgh. She was on the editorial staff of the *Daily Worker*, and stood as a communist candidate at the 1966 General Election. She wrote several plays, worked as a critic, and was married to the Scottish actor Alex McCrindle. Her first children's book, *Green Street* (1966), was written in response to her daughters' request for stories about ordinary people. Her work may seem a little dated to today's young readers, but during the late sixties and the seventies she was an important force in establishing teenage fiction as a genre. Her robust but sympathetic narratives are set in Scotland and revolve around adolescent heroines whose experiences reflect the emotional, social and moral difficulties facing girls growing up during a time of changing values.

ASH, John
(1948–)

English poet, born in Manchester and educated at Birmingham University. His early interest in the aesthetics and lifestyle of the Symbolists and Decadents has given place to an oblique and highly individual style that occasionally suggests **John Ashbery**'s poetics of omission. Ash's most important work to date is *The Branching Stairs* (1984), which demonstrates his ability to give tangible form to quite ambiguous and only intermittently specific images. Earlier collections—*The Bed* (1981) and *The Goodbyes* (1982)—were less successful because their surrealism seemed more forced and their variations of voice more mannered. In the dislocations of *The Branching Stairs*, Ash created a highly personal voice and established himself as one of the most important poets of his generation.

ASHBERY, John Lawrence
(1927–)

American poet, critic and novelist, born in Rochester, New York, the son of a farmer. Since attending Harvard, where he became close friends with the poets **Kenneth Koch** and **Frank O'Hara**, he has been associated with the highly visual, almost Abstract Expressionist language of the 'New York' school. He published his first volume, a chapbook, *Turandot and Other Poems*, in 1953, but it was not until the publication of *Some Trees* in 1956 that he began to attract critical attention. Influenced by **W H Auden**, he inspires ardent admiration and bemused antipathy in almost equal measure, and has frequently been charged with obscurity. His reputation is international and in 1976 his twelfth collection, *Self-Portrait in a Convex Mirror*, won the National Book Critics Circle Prize, the National Book Award for poetry, and the Pulitzer Prize for poetry. Other volumes include *The Tennis Court Oath* (1962), *Rivers and Mountains* (1966), *Houseboat Days* (1977) and *Shadow Train* (1982). His only novel is *A Nest of Ninnies* (1969), co-authored with **James Schuyler**.
▷D Shapiro, *John Ashbery: An Introduction to the Poetry* (1979)

ASHFORD, Daisy (Margaret Mary)
(1881–1972)

English author, born in Petersham, Surrey. She is famous for a story she wrote as a child, but wrote nothing as an adult, apparently content to run a market garden with her husband, whom she married in 1920. Thirty years previously, in 1890, when she was nine years old, she composed *The Young Visiters, or Mr Salteena's Plan*, in which Bernard Clark and Mr Salteena ('not quite a gentleman') vie for the hand of 17-year-old Ethel Monticue. Ashford discovered her imperfectly spelled manuscript in 1919, and on its publication it became both a bestseller and a talking point. The following year *The Young Visiters* became a successful play and in 1968 provided the basis of musical, albeit with a score which caused one critic to describe it as 'amiably pointless'. Other juvenile Ashford writings appeared in *DA: Her Book* (1920).
▷R M Malcolmson, *Daisy Ashford* (1984)

ASHTON-WARNER, Sylvia
(1908–84)

New Zealand novelist and schoolteacher whose account of her teaching life, *Teacher*, was at first rejected. She recast it as fiction and it appeared, to considerable acclaim, as *Spinster* (1958); through the success of that book *Teacher* finally appeared in 1963. In *Spinster* the heroine is typical of Ashton-Warner's strong feminine characters who fight against suffocating New Zealand provinciality. Other novels are *Incense to Idols* (1960), *Bell Call* (1964), *Greenstone* (1966) and *Three* (1971), a closely observed power struggle between mother and daughter-in-law, set in London. Her autobiographical *I Passed This Way* (1979) highlights a sense of alienation from her homeland.
▷L Hood, *Sylvia!: The Biography of Sylvia Ashton-Warner* (1988)

ASIMOV, Isaac
(1920–92)

Russian-born American novelist, critic and popular scientist. Born in Petrovichi, he was brought to the USA when he was three. He took a PhD in chemistry at Columbia University and his career as an academic biochemist was as distinguished and precocious as that as a science-fiction writer. In a prodigious body of work the titles that stand out include the 'Foundation' novels—*Foundation* (1951), *Foundation and Empire* (1952) and *Second Foundation* (1953); the so-called 'Robot' novels —*The Caves of Steel* (1954) and *The Naked Sun* (1957), and the short stories which form the collection *I, Robot* (1950). A leading spokesman for science fiction, he became ubiquitous on television and on the lecturing circuit as well as being an untiring contributor to newspapers and magazines. Increasingly regarded as a scientific seer, he added the term 'robotics' to the language.

▷ N Goble, *Asimov Analyzed* (1972)

ASTLEY, Thea Beatrice May
(1925–)

Australian novelist and poet, born in Brisbane, three times winner of the **Miles Franklin** Award. Her first novel, *Girl with a Monkey* (1958), was followed by *A Descant for Gossips* (1960). *The Slow Natives* (1965) became Australian 'Best Novel of the Year' and established her reputation as a satiric and iconoclastic commentator on small-town Australian life. In *A Kindness Cup* (1974) she denounces aboriginal treatment in 19th-century Queensland. A collection of wrily humorous short stories, *Hunting the Wild Pineapple* (1979), is mostly narrated by a character from *The Slow Natives*, a favourite device of Astley.

ASTURIAS, Miguel Angel
(1899–1974)

Guatemalan fiction writer and poet, winner of the Nobel Prize for literature. A law graduate from the National University, he spent many years in exile, particularly in Paris, where he studied anthropology and translated the Mayan sacred book *Popul Vuh*, written in the Quiche language, into Spanish. This was to have an enduring influence on his fiction, though his most successful novel, *El Señor Presidente* (1946, Eng trans *The President*, 1963), reveals the Indian mythical influences only obliquely. Other books included *Hombres de maíz* (1949, Eng trans *Men of Maize*, 1975) and a trilogy on the foreign exploitation of the banana trade. A difficult, experimental and ambitious writer, he flirted with 'automatic writing' as a route into the unconscious. He was awarded the Nobel Prize for literature in 1967. In the Gua-

temalan civil service from 1946, he was ambassador to France, 1966–70.

▷ R J Callan, *Miguel Angel Asturias* (1970)

ATHENAEUS
(2nd century)

Greek writer, born in Naucratis in Egypt. He lived first in Alexandria and later in Rome about the close of the 2nd century. He wrote the *Deipnosophistae* ('Banquet of the Learned'), a collection of anecdotes and excerpts from ancient authors arranged as scholarly dinner-table conversation. Thirteen of its 15 books survive more or less complete, together with a summary of the other two.

ATHERTON, Gertrude Franklin, née Horn
(1857–1948)

American novelist, born in San Francisco. Left a widow in 1887, she travelled extensively, living in Europe most of her life and using the places she visited as backgrounds for her novels—which range from ancient Greece to California and the West Indies. She was made Chevalier of the Legion of Honour for her relief work during World War I and in 1934 became President of the American National Academy of Literature. The most popular of her many novels are *The Conqueror* (1902), a fictional biography of Alexander Hamilton, and *Black Oxen* (1923), which is concerned with the possibility of rejuvenation.

▷ J H Jackson, *Gertrude Atherton* (1940)

ATTAWAY, William
(1911–)

American black 'proletarian' novelist, born in Mississippi. He wrote *Let Me Breathe Thunder* (1939), about two white tramps, and *Blood on the Forge* (1941), about black farmers trying to get jobs in Pennsylvania steel mills.

ATTERBOM, Per Daniel Amadeus
(1790–1855)

Swedish poet, born in Östergötland. A leading member of the Uppsala Romantics clustered around the revolutionary journal *Phosphorus*, he was much influenced by German aesthetic theory, particularly the writings of Friedrich Schelling. Atterbom's lyrical talent with its descriptive sensitivity and pantheistic wonder is best seen in the 40 poems of the cycle *Blommorna* (1812, 'The Flowers'). In his poetic drama *Lycksalighetens ö* (1824–7, 'The Isle of the Blessed') he dresses the conflict between beauty and duty in a cloak of myth and symbolism and, in one part, caricatures the emergent liberal ideas of the day. His *Svenska siare och skalder 1–6* (1841–55, 'Swedish Seers and Poets') was the first real study of Swedish literary history.

▷H Frykenstedt, *Atterboms livs—och världsåskådning* (1951–2)

ATWOOD, Margaret Eleanor
(1939–)

Canadian novelist, short-story writer, poet and critic, described by one commentator as 'a staunch moralist' who insists 'that modern man must reinvent himself'. Born in Ottawa, she spent her early years in northern Ontario and Quebec bush country. After graduating from the University of Toronto and Radcliffe College, she held a variety of jobs ranging from waitress and summer-camp counsellor to lecturer in English literature and writer-in-residence. Her first published work, a collection of poems entitled *The Circle Game* (1966), won the Governor-General's Award. Since then she has published several volumes of poetry, collections of short stories—*Dancing Girls* (1977) and *Bluebeard's Egg* (1987)—and *Survival* (1972), an acclaimed study of Canadian literature. She is best known, however, as a novelist. *The Edible Woman* (1969) dealt with emotional cannibalism and provoked considerable controversy within and beyond the women's movement. It was followed by *Surfacing* (1972), *Lady Oracle* (1976), *Life Before Man* (1979) and *Bodily Harm* (1982), each in some way exploring the place of mythology on an individual's life. In 1985, *The Handmaid's Tale* was shortlisted for the Booker Prize, as was *Cat's Eye* in 1989. Her most recent novel, *The Robber Bride*, was published in 1993.

▷S Grace, *A Violent Duality* (1979); J H Rosenberg, *Margaret Atwood* (1984)

AUB, Max
(1903–72)

Spanish novelist, dramatist and literary hoaxer who is somewhat isolated in the literature of his country—unsurprisingly, because he was born in Paris of a German father and a French mother, and was not taken to Spain until he was 11 years old. He had written some poetic narratives before the Civil War, but it was that event which moved him to his best work. His cycle of novels about this war (of some of which there is a French translation), *El laberinto mágico* (1943–68, 'The Magic Labyrinth'), rivals the narratives of **Arturo Barea**. His *Josep Torres Campalans* (1958) was an illustrated and well documented biography of a Catalan painter and friend of Picasso; many claimed to have known him well, but he did not exist. Full critical appreciation of Aub is yet to come. From 1939 onwards he lived and worked in

Mexico, from which he published the humorous story collection *La verdadera historia de la muerte de Francisco Franco* (1960, 'The True History of the Death of Francisco Franco'), which displeased its subject. His plays, never successful except in small theatres, were correspondingly remarkable.

AUBANEL, Théodore
(1829–86)

Provençal poet and playwright, born in Avignon. He was described by **Paul Ambroise Valéry** as the only true Provençal poet, but was disowned in his lifetime by his native region because of the sensual and carnal subject-matter of his work. He produced three volumes of poetry: *La Grenade Entr' Ouverte* (1860, 'The Ripening Pomegranite'); *Les Filles d'Avignon* ('Daughters of Avignon', 300 copies privately circulated in 1885 and quickly banned by the archbishop); and *Le Soleil d'Outre-Tombe* ('The Sun from beyond the Tomb', published posthumously in 1899). Between 1861 and 1866 he also wrote the plays *Le Rapt* ('The Abduction') and *Le Berger* ('The Shepherd'), published in 1928 and 1944 respectively. In spite of a blissful marriage (1861) to Josephine Mazon, Aubanel dealt extensively with adultery in his work; he nonetheless professed a staunch Catholicism, and died, of apoplexy, with a crucifix pressed to his chest.

AUCHINCLOSS, Louis Stanton
(1917–)

American novelist, short-story writer and critic, born in Lawrence, New York. He trained as a lawyer and was admitted to the New York Bar in 1941. He is a novelist of manners, at home with old money and a highly codified, traditional society. He has nonetheless a keen sense of intrigue. His first novel, *The Indifferent Children* (1947), appeared under the pseudonym Andrew Lee, but subsequent books have appeared under his own name, the best of them being *Pursuit of the Prodigal* (1960), *Portrait in Brownstone* (1962), *The Embezzler* (1966) and *A World of Profit* (1963). His later novels have attracted less critical acclaim.

▷C C Dahl, *Louis Auchincloss* (1986)

AUDEN, W(ystan) H(ugh)
(1907–73)

Anglo–American poet and essayist. Born in York, he was educated at Gresham's School, Holt, and Christ Church, Oxford, and was naturalized as an American citizen in 1946. In the 1930s he wrote passionately on social problems from a far-Left standpoint, especially in his collection of poems *Look, Stranger!* (1936). He went to Spain as a civ-

ilian in support of the Republican side and reported on it in *Spain* (1937), followed by a verse commentary (with prose reports by **Christopher Isherwood**) on the Sino–Japanese war in *Journey to a War* (1939). He also collaborated with Isherwood in three plays: *The Dog Beneath the Skin* (1935), *The Ascent of F6* (1936) and *On the Frontier* (1938). He collaborated with **Louis MacNeice** in *Letters from Iceland* (1937) and wrote the libretto for *Ballad of Heroes* by Benjamin Britten in 1939. He emigrated to New York early in 1939 and was appointed associate professor at Michigan University, and Professor of Poetry at Oxford University in 1956. In America he became converted to Anglicanism, tracing his conversion in *The Sea and the Mirror* (1944) and *For the Time Being* (1944). His later works include *Nones* (1951), *The Shield of Achilles* (1955), *Homage to Clio* (1960) and *City Without Walls* (1969). He is best remembered today as the 'Poet of the Thirties', for his prodigious verbal dexterity, and for his essays of literary criticism. He met his lifelong partner, Chester Kallman, in New York, but he was also married to the writer Erika Mann, daughter of the German novelist **Thomas Mann**, in 1935; his most important relationship, however, was with Kallman, his lover and collaborator. He returned to England in 1972 but divided his time between Oxford and a second home in Kirchstetten in Austria, where he died.
▷H Carpenter, *W H Auden: A Biography* (1981)

AUDIBERTI, Jacques
(1899–1965)
French poet, playwright and novelist, born in Antibes. He wrote 15 novels, some distinguished poetry, and, above all, plays. He was a Surrealist who reacted against the confusions of Surrealism, and so tried to bring a classical order into his writings—but without suppressing any of his originally unconscious impulses. He was most influenced by **Antonin Artaud** and by the latter's theories of the 'theatre of cruelty'; but he was gifted with a sense of humour, which often went unnoticed. Essentially his project was to demonstrate that human beings tend to become, in **Wyndham Lewis**'s phrase, 'hallucinated automata', if they reject or ignore their atavistic origins, instead of coming to terms with them. He may therefore be characterized as having taken a **Jung**ian approach—but he puzzled interviewers by talking to them, not about his philosophy, but about Humphrey Bogart. His most famous play is *Quoat-Quoat* (1946), in which the rescuing stone of the Mexican God is rejected by a spy who falls in love with a ship captain's daughter under sentence of death. He has fascinated certain

critics, but the time for a more general acceptance of his message lies in the future.
▷L E Pronko, *Avant-Garde* (1962); G E Wellwarth, *The Theatre of Protest and Paradox* (1964); J Guicharnaud, *Modern French Theatre* (1967)

AUEL, Jean Marie
(1936–)
American fantasy writer, born in Chicago. Her reputation rests on the sequence of novels known as *Earth's Children*, which began with *The Clan of the Cave Bear* (1980), followed by *The Valley of Horses* (1982), *The Mammoth Hunters* (1985) and *The Plains of Passage* (1990). They are a mixture of plausible anthropology and fantastic romance set in prehistoric times, and trace the story of the orphaned Cro-Magnon girl Ayla in the matriarchal Neanderthal tribe which adopts her.

AUERBACH, Berthold, originally **Moses Baruch Auerbacher**
(1812–82)
German novelist, born in Nordstetten in the Black Forest. He studied at the universities of Tübingen, Munich, and Heidelberg, and in 1836 was imprisoned as a member of the students' Burschenschaft. Destined for the synagogue, he abandoned theology for law, then law for history and philosophy, especially that of Spinoza, on whose life he based a novel of that name (1837), and whose works he translated (1841). In *Schwarzwälder Dorfgeschichten* (1843, 'Black Forest Village Tales'), on which his fame chiefly rests, he gives charming pictures of Black Forest life. Of his longer works the best known are *Barfüssele* (1856, 'Little Barefoot') and *Auf der Höhe* (1865, 'On the Summit').
▷L Stein, *Berthold Auerbach und das Judenthum* (1882)

AUERSPERG, Anton Alexander, Graf von, pseud **Anastasius Grün**
(1806–76)
Austrian poet. He was distinguished by his Liberalism and ultra-German sympathies. He was one of the German epic and lyrical poets, among whom he holds a high rank.
▷E Schatzmayer, *Anastasius Grüns Dichtungen* (1865)

AUGIER, Guillaume Victor Émile
(1820–89)
French dramatist, born in Valence. His *Théâtre complet* (1890, 'Complete Plays') fills seven volumes, and includes fine social comedies, such as *Le Gendre de M. Poirier* (1854, with Sandea, 'Mr Poirier's Son-in-Law') and *Les Fourchambault* (1878).
▷A Denoist, *Essais de critique dramatique* (1898)

AUGUSTINE, St (Aurelius Augustinus),
also known as **Augustine of Hippo**
(354–430)

The greatest of the Latin Church fathers, born in Tagaste in Numidia (modern Tunisia). His father was a pagan, but he was brought up a Christian by his devout mother, Monica. He went to Carthage to study and had a son, Adeonatus, by a mistress there. Carthage was a metropolitan centre, and he was exposed there to many new intellectual fashions and influences. He became deeply involved in Manicheanism, which seemed to offer a solution to the problem of evil, a theme which was to preoccupy him throughout his life. In 383 he moved to teach at Rome, then at Milan, and became influenced by scepticism and then by Neoplatonism. After the dramatic spiritual crises described in his *Confessiones*, he finally became converted to Christianity and was baptized (together with his son) by St Ambrose in 386. He returned to North Africa and in 395 became bishop of Hippo, where he was a relentless antagonist of the heretical schools of Donatists, Pelagians and Manicheans and champion of orthodoxy. He remained at Hippo until his death in 430, as the Vandals were besieging the gates of the city. He was an unusually productive writer and much of his work is marked by personal spiritual struggle. The *Confessiones* (400) is a classic of world literature and a spiritual autobiography as well as an original work of philosophy (with a famous discussion on the nature of time). *De civitate Dei* (413–26, Eng trans *The City of God*, 1957–72) is a monumental work of 22 books which presents human history in terms of the conflict between the spiritual and the temporal, which will end in the triumph of the City of God, whose manifestation on earth is the church.

▷ R O'Connell, *St Augustine's Confessions: an odyssey of soul* (1969); J J O'Meara, *The Young Augustine* (1954)

AUKRUST, Olav Lom
(1883–1929)

Norwegian poet. He was a schoolmaster who wrote large quantities of religious and patriotic verse. *Himmelvarden* (1916) consists of three long cycles in New Norwegian containing many passages of great lyric power. *Hamar i Hellom* (1926), of which the chief poem is *Emme*, summons the people of Norway to use the power of their great traditions to achieve present security and progress. His final collection of poems, *Solrenning*, is incomplete and was published posthumously in 1930.

▷ I Krokann, *Olav Aukrust* (1933)

AULNOY, Marie Catherine Jumelle de Barneville, Comtesse d'
(c.1650–1705)

French writer. She wrote romances of court life, but is mainly remembered for her charming fairy-tales, *Contes de Fées* (1698).

AURELIUS, Marcus Aurelius Antoninus,
originally **Marcus Annius Verus**
(121–80)

One of the most respected emperors in Roman history, the son of Annius Verus and Domita Calvilla, born in Rome. When only 17, he was adopted by Antoninus Pius, who had succeeded Hadrian and whose daughter Faustina was selected for his wife. From 140, when he was made consul, till the death of Antoninus in 161, he discharged his public duties with the utmost conscientiousness, and maintained the friendliest relations with the Emperor. At the same time he still devoted himself to the study of law and philosophy, especially Stoicism. On his accession, with characteristic magnanimity he voluntarily divided the government with his brother by adoption, Lucius Aurelius Verus, who in 161 was sent to take command against the Parthians. Despite the self-indulgence and dilatoriness of Verus, the generals were victorious, but the army brought back from the East a plague that ravaged the empire. Peaceful by temperament, Marcus Aurelius was nevertheless throughout his reign destined to suffer from constant wars, and though in Asia, Britain, and on the Rhine the barbarians were checked, permanent peace was never secured. At Athens he founded chairs of philosophy for each of the chief schools: Platonic, Stoic, Peripatetic, and Epicurean. One of the few Roman Emperors whose writings have survived, his 12 books of *Meditations* (*ta eis heauton*) record his innermost thoughts and are a unique document. They reveal his affinity with Stoicism, and show both his loneliness and the fact that he did not allow himself to be embittered by his experiences of life. His death was felt to be a national calamity, and he was retrospectively idealized as the model of the perfect Emperor.

▷ A R Bailey, *Marcus Aurelius* (1966)

AUSONIUS, Decius Magnus
(c.309–392)

Latin poet, born in Burdigala (Bordeaux), the son of a physician. He taught rhetoric there for 30 years, and was then appointed by the Emperor Valentinian I tutor to his son Gratian; he afterwards held the offices of quaestor, prefect of Latium and consul of Gaul. On the death of Gratian, Ausonius retired to his estate at Bordeaux, where he occupied himself with literature and rural pursuits. His works, which show great versatility, include epigrams, poems on his deceased relatives and on his colleagues, epistles in verse and prose, and idylls.

▷ C Aymonier, *Ausone et ses amis* (1935)

AUSTEN, Jane
(1775–1817)

English novelist, born in Steventon, Hampshire. She was the sixth of seven children of a country rector; her father was an able scholar who also served as her tutor. She spent the first 25 years of her life in Steventon, and the last eight in nearby Chawton, and did almost all her writing in those two places, writing virtually nothing in the intervening years in Bath, which appears to have been an unsettled time in her otherwise ordered and rather uneventful life. She never married, although she had a number of suitors, and wrote percipiently on the subjects of courtship and marriage in her novels. She began to write at an early age to amuse her family, and by 1790 had completed a burlesque on popular fiction in the manner of **Richardson**, entitled *Love and Friendship*, and ridiculed the taste for Gothic fiction in *Northanger Abbey*, which was written at this time, but only published in 1818. Her characteristic subject was the closely observed and often ironically depicted morals and mores of country life, and she rendered it with genius. Her best-known works in this vein are *Sense and Sensibility* (1811), *Pride and Prejudice* (1813), *Emma* (1816), and the posthumously published *Persuasion* (1817). *Mansfield Park* (1814) is a darker and more serious dissection of her chosen fictional territory, and although never as popular, is arguably her masterpiece. Modern research has seen the publication of the fragment of an unfinished novel she was writing when she died, called *Sanditon*, and some very early pieces, including *Lady Susan*, a juvenile work in epistolary form. Her own letters, although carefully filleted by her sister Cassandra after her death, are one of the few revealing documentary sources on her life. Her greatness has been clearer to subsequent generations than to her own, although Sir **Walter Scott** praised the delicate observation and fine judgement in her work, which she herself characterized as 'the little bit (two inches wide) of Ivory on which I work with so fine a Brush, as produces little effect after much labour'. If she chose a small stage for her labours, however, she worked upon it with exquisite understanding.

▷ E Jenkins, *Jane Austen: a biography* (1938); J R Liddell, *The Novels of Jane Austen* (1974)

AUSTER, Paul
(1947–)

American novelist and poet, born in Newark, New Jersey. His varied occupations have included merchant seaman, census-taker, and teacher of creative writing. He wrote his first novel, *Squeeze Play* (1982), as 'Paul Benjamin', by which time he had already produced several volumes of poetry, a selection of which appeared with some essays in *Ground Work* (1990). The cerebral mystery novels which make up *The New York Trilogy* (1985–7) were followed by *In the Country of Last Things* (1987), a nightmare vision of a society trapped in terminal social disintegration. His novels share an ironic awareness of the limitations of language in apprehending reality, but reality itself is rendered mysterious in his evocative masterpiece *The Music of Chance* (1991).

AUSTIN, Alfred
(1835–1913)

English poet, born of Catholic parents in Leeds. He was educated at Stonyhurst and Oscott College, graduated from London University in 1853, and was called to the Bar in 1857, but abandoned law for literature. He was a strong supporter of **Benjamin Disraeli**, and an ardent imperialist. He published *The Season; a Satire* (1861), *The Human Tragedy* (1862), *The Conversion of Winckelmann* (1862) and a dozen more volumes of poems, and an autobiography (1911). Between 1883 and 1893 he edited the *National Review*; in 1896 he became poet laureate, an appointment which brought him more derision than honours from the literary community.

AUSTIN, Mary
(1868–1934)

American novelist and essayist, born in Carlinville, Illinois and educated at Blackburn College. A move to California in 1888 directly influenced her writing: Indians and the western environ figure prominently in her work, and her first book, *The Land of Little Rain* (1903), won acclaim as a western classic. Subsequent work addressed women's issues as Austin became involved in the suffrage movement and other feminist causes; other themes highlighted in her work include mysticism, Christ, and 'the individual'. A prolific writer, Austin produced 200 articles and 32 books in her lifetime. She is best known for her play *The Arrow Maker* (1911).

▷ E Stineman, *Mary Austin: Song of a Maverick* (1990)

AVERY, Gillian Elise
(1926–)
English novelist, author of children's stories and sociological studies, born in Reigate, Surrey. Her adult novels include *The Lost Railway* (1980) and *Onlookers* (1983), but she is more widely known for her children's books, such as *The Warden's Niece* (1957) and *Huck and Her Time Machine* (1977). Her non-fiction work includes pioneering surveys of education and literature for young people. *Nineteenth Century Children: Heroes and Heroines in English Children's Stories 1700–1900*, written with Angela Bull, appeared in 1965, and *The Echoing Green: Memories of Victorian and Regency Youth*, in 1974. Her authoritative study of girls' independent schools in Britain, *The Best Type of Girl* (1991), vividly charts the changing social and cultural importance of girls' private schools, and confronts issues such as social class and educational privilege entirely without bias.

AVICEBRON, Arabic name **Solomon ibn Gabirol**
(c.1020–c.1070)
Jewish poet and philosopher in the Jewish 'Golden Age' in Spain, born in Malaga. Most of his prose work is lost but an ethical treatise in Arabic survives, as does a Latin translation of his most famous work, *Fons vitae* ('The Fount of Life'). This latter is a dialogue on the nature of matter and the soul, which is Neoplatonist in character, and was very influential among later Christian scholastics. His poetry became part of the mystical tradition of the Kabbalah.
▷F Brunner, *Platonisme et Aristotelisme* (1965)

AVIENUS, Rufus Festus
(fl. c.375)
Latin poet, a native of Vulsinii (Bolsena). He wrote on natural and geographical topics, and translated the *Phainomena* of Aratus of Sicyon. He also wrote a paraphrase of a description of the world, *Descriptio Orbis Terrae*.

AVISON, Margaret Kirkland
(1918–)
Canadian poet, born in Galt, Ontario and educated at the University of Toronto. She has worked as a librarian, a lecturer at the University of Toronto, and a social worker. Though she began writing in the 1950s, she did not publish her first book of poetry, *The Winter Sun*, until 1960, and has since published only two more volumes, *The Dumbfounding* (1966) and *Sunblue* (1978). She has, however, had her poems published in many periodicals. Her work has been influenced by

her conversion to Christianity and contains elements of metaphysics. In 1990 a new edition of her first two books of poetry was published, for which she received a Governor General's Award.
▷D Kent, *Margaret Avison and Her Works* (1989)

AVITUS, Alcimus Edicus
(fl.490)
Gaulish Latin poet, born into an aristocratic family in Vienne (now in France) during the decline of the Roman Empire. He became Bishop of Vienne in 490. His poetry is in the religious epic tradition of the early church, setting out religious themes in classical form.

AWDRY, W(ilbert) V(ere)
(1911–)
English author and Church of England clergyman, born in Ampfield, Hampshire, whose railway stories for young people, especially those featuring Thomas The Tank Engine, have delighted generations of small children. The first, *The Three Railway Engines*, appeared in 1945, and *Thomas, the Tank Engine*, a year later. Over 25 books followed, each based on a real experience, until *Tramway Engines* in 1972, after which Awdry's son, Christopher, succeeded to the authorship. The passing of the age of steam has done nothing to diminish the appeal of Thomas or of his friends James the Red Engine and Henry the Green Engine, even to those who have never seen a steam locomotive. Together with their drivers and porters, the engines both inhabit and represent a comforting world, one which suffers from small divisions, but which, more importantly, has its reconciliations.

AWOONOR, Kofi
(1935–)
Arguably the leading Ghanaian poet of his generation, he combines traditional forms derived from Ewe oral poetry with a use of English that frequently recalls **T S Eliot** and **Ezra Pound**. Born in Wheta and educated in Ghana, London and New York, he has studied and been closely involved in Ghanaian culture and politics. *Rediscovery* (1964) marked a double journey back into 'the tradition' of African verse and into the poet's own divided consciousness. *Night of My Blood* (1971) and *Ride Me, Memory* (1973) were more obviously aimed at an international readership. His one novel, *This Earth, Mr Brother ...* (1972), was a rather lame and prosey attempt at similar themes He has edited important anthologies of Ghanaian verse and folktales.

AXULAR, Pedro de
(b.1556)

Basque writer, born in Navarre, the most important of a group of early clerics writing in the language, and author of *Guero* (1643), a tract on the need for repentance which, while didactic and rhetorical, is also humane and readable.

▷R Gallop, *A Book of the Basques* (1930); L Michelena, *Historia de la literatura vasca* (1960)

AYALA, Francisco
(1906–)

Spanish novelist and sociologist, born in Granada, who, after serving the legal government, went into exile in 1939, but returned in 1973 when the regime made it possible. He was originally a professor of law at Madrid University. He wrote three promising early novels, much in the style of the times, but then in 1930 abandoned the form; in 1944 he took it up again, but in an entirely different spirit. His best-known books, and his best, are *Muertes de perro* (1958, Eng trans *Death as A Way of Life*, 1964) and its sequel *El fondo del vaso* (1962, 'The Dregs'), in which he rewrites for himself and his own time **Ramón Valle-Inclán**'s novel *El tirano Banderos*: the life and aftermath of the type of the paradigmatic and mad South American tyrant of that book. Ayala has written much intelligent and ironic criticism, and is a notable exposer of the evils of bureaucracy. He investigates the nature of power, and concludes that whoever has power over others is a 'usurper'.

AYCKBOURN, Alan
(1939–)

English playwright. Born in London, he began his theatrical career as an acting stage manager in repertory before joining Stephen Joseph's Theatre-in-the-Round company at Scarborough. A founder-member of the Victoria Theatre, Stoke-on-Trent in 1962, he returned in 1964 as producer to Scarborough, where most of his plays have been premiered. His first of a torrent of west-end successes was *Relatively Speaking* in 1967, and he was quickly established as a master of farce, basing his plays in traditional manner on a single idea, usually a mistake or a confusion, from which the whole plot derives. His plays often contain shrewd observation of the English class-structure, but it is in sheer mechanical ingenuity that he excels. He has made considerable experiments with staging and dramatic structure: *The Norman Conquests* (1974) is a trilogy in which each play takes place at the same time in a different part of the setting, and *Way Upstream* (1982) is set on and around a boat and necessitates the

flooding of the stage. Among his most successful farces are *Time and Time Again* (1972), *Absurd Person Singular* (1973), *Bedroom Farce* (1977) and *Joking Apart* (1979). He has written two musicals, *Jeeves* (with Andrew Lloyd Webber, 1975) and *Making Tracks* (with Paul Todd, 1981), and was a BBC radio drama producer (1964–70). His later plays, including *Woman in Mind* (1985) and *Henceforward* (1987), reflect an increasingly bleak vision of society. Ayckbourn's techniques have become simpler and his characters more complex as he reveals himself to be not only a master farceur but a savage social commentator. He is now also recognized as a distinguished director, not only of his own work, but of plays by such authors as **Arthur Miller**.

AYGI, Gennady
(1934–)

Chuvash (originally Soviet) poet and translator, born in Shaymurino in the Chuvash republic, whose early work was in Chuvash, but who from 1960 wrote his poetry in Russian. For many years this could only be circulated in *samizdat* ('do-it-yourself publishing') form, but this changed with the collapse of the USSR. Essentially his poetry is in the tradition of his mentor, **Pasternak**, but it has also been influenced by the Czech **Wolker**, and has become markedly original, especially in technique, which breaks with conventional forms. His *Stikhi 1954–1971* ('Poems') appeared in Germany in 1975, with some notes by himself, but his work is not yet available in English.

ARMAH, Ayi Kwei
(1939–)

Ghanaian novelist, born in Accra and educated at Harvard and the University of Ghana. His first major work was *The Beautyful Ones are Not Yet Born* (1968), which explored the corruption of West African politics and the alienation of young intellectuals. Later works were less pessimistic; they include *Fragments* (1970), *Are We So Blest* (1971) and *The Healers* (1979).

▷R Fraser, *Armah* (1980)

AYMÉ, Marcel
(1902–67)

French novelist, story writer and playwright, born in Joigny. Writing in the tradition of **Rabelais**, and at heart an anarchist, his first success was his comic *La Jument vert* (1933, Eng trans *The Green Mare*, 1955), an account of the goings-on in a provincial community. He was a friend to **Louis-Ferdinand Céline**, and his fiction became increasingly informed with the latter's extreme bitterness and habit of ridicule—but he retained his popular audience, since his methods were traditional: strong plot, accurate characterization, satire of all organizations of whatever persuasion. Plays such as *Clérembard* (1950, Eng trans 1952), are unrestrained in their ridicule of pretences, hypocrisies and illusions, and have been called excessive, but they were for the most part successful with audiences.

▷D Brodin, *The Comic World of Marcel Aymé* (1964)

AYRER, Jacob
(c.1540–1625)

German dramatist, one of the most prolific of the 16th century, with over a hundred plays of all kinds, including a number of *Singspiele*, or musical plays. He was a citizen of Nuremberg in 1594, and procurator in the courts of law.

▷W Kozumplik, *The Phonology of Jacob Ayrer's Language* (1942)

AYRTON, Michael
(1921–75)

English painter, sculptor, illustrator, art critic, translator and novelist. His astonishing, polymathic gifts came in part from a cultured and intellectual family which included scientists and engineers, writers and politicians. In the early 1940s, he was the youngest ever guest on BBC radio's influential *The Brains Trust*. Though a visual artist first and foremost, Ayrton was profoundly influenced by literature and mythology; he produced a huge number of now highly prized book illustrations, including **Thomas Nashe**'s *The Unfortunate Traveller*. His book *British Drawings* (1946) had an impact on the reception of the neo-Romantics. His skittish *Tittivulus, the Verbiage Collector* (1953) was a satire on bureaucracy and the critical establishment. *The Maze Maker* (1967) was a novel based on the Daedalus story, which he had also explored in sculpture and in the prose *Testament of Daedulus* (1962). A second novel, *The Midas Consequence*, was published in 1974. He translated and illustrated **Archilochos of Paros**, wrote a study of the sculptor Giovanni Pisano, and published collections of essays. *Fabrications* (1972) summed up many of his varied concerns.

▷M Yorke, in *The Spirit of Place* (1988)

AYTMATOV, Chingïz
(1928–)

Kirgiz novelist and dramatist, writing mainly in Russian, born in Sheker. Trained as a veterinarian, and always dedicated to animals and their welfare, as a writer he was described as 'the Soviet Union's most distinguished non-Russian author writing in Russian'—but he would never have used Russian had this not been made almost obligatory by Stalinist 'cultural organizers'. Thus, his first and greatest novel, *Proshchay, Gulsary!* (1966, Eng trans *Farewell, Gulsary!*, 1970), while set in Kirgizia, was published in Russian. Gulsary is the horse of a decent old-guard communist, whose losing struggle with Stalinist officials is the theme of the book. Aytmatov was attacked for ignoring the tenets of socialist realism in this and other novels, including the moving *Bely parakhod* (1970, Eng trans *The White Steamship*, 1972), about a boy who drowns himself when he perceives the nature of the world he is growing up into.

AYTON, Sir Robert
(1570–1638)

Scottish poet and courtier, born in Kinaldie, near St Andrews. He was educated at St Andrews University, studied law in Paris, and became a courtier of James VI and I in London, and was a friend of **Ben Jonson** and Thomas Hobbes. He wrote lyrics in English and Latin, and is credited with the prototype of 'Auld Lang Syne'.

▷A Johnson, *Delitiae poetarum scotorum* (1637)

AYTOUN, William Edmonstoune
(1818–65)

Scottish poet and humorist, born in Edinburgh, the son of a lawyer. Educated at The Edinburgh Academy and Edinburgh University, he was called to the Bar in 1840. He published a collection of romantic pastiches, *Poland, Homer and Other Poems* (1832), and in 1836 began a lifelong connection with *Blackwood's Magazine*, to which he contributed countless parodies and burlesque reviews. In 1845 he was appointed Professor of Rhetoric and Belles-Lettres at Edinburgh University, and in five years quintupled the number of his students. In 1849 he married a daughter of **John Wilson** ('Christopher North'). In 1852 was made Sheriff of Orkney. His works include *Lays of the Scottish Cavaliers* (1848); *Firmilian, a Spasmodic Tragedy* (1854); *Bon Gaultier Ballads* (1855), and *Poems of Goethe* (1858), conjunctly with **Theodore Martin**; *Bothwell* (1856); and *Norman Sinclair* (1861), a semi-autobiographical novel.

▷M E Weinstein, *William Aytoun and the Spasmodic Controversy* (1968)

AZEVEDO, Aluisio de
(1857–1913)

Brazilian novelist, diplomat and journalist. He was greatly influenced, in his 11 novels, by the naturalistic movement in Europe, and by **Zola** in particular. *O Homen* (1887, 'The

Man') was sensational in its time for its clear depiction of a case of sexual frustration. *O Cortiço* (1890, Eng trans *The Tenement*, 1928), about a 'Rachmanite' landlord, was vivid in its realism, and is still eminently readable and informative about Rio life in the latter part of the 19th century. All his works were reprinted in the 1950s, and have been the subject of discussion since then.

AZORÍN, pseud of **José Martinez Ruiz** (1873–1967)

Spanish novelist and critic. Born in Monóvar and educated at Valencia, he belongs to the generation of **Baroja** and **Unamuno**, and his early novel *La voluntad* (1902, 'Willpower') reflects their pessimism. His lucid essays rebelled against the prevailing florid manner, but they are uneven in their insights. His other novels include *Don Juan* (1922) and *Dona Inés* (1925).
▷L A LaJohn, *Azorín and the Spanish Stage* (1961)

AZUELA, Mariano
(1873–1952)

Mexican novelist, born in Lagos de Moreno, Jalisco. Azuela has often been called 'the Mexican novelist of the Revolution', and certainly he was the first. As a medical student and young doctor he began to write novels (his first, *María Luisa*, appeared in 1907), and by the time he joined Pancho Villa's army as a doctor had published five of them, including *Mala yerba* (1909, Eng trans *Marcela: A Mexican Love Story*, 1932). In 1916 came what many consider to be his masterpiece, *Los de abajos* (1916, Eng trans *The Underdogs*, 1929, and in *Three novels by Mariano Azuela*, 1979), which he sold for $20 to a newspaper in El Paso, Texas, where he had taken refuge. But, great novel though this account of the barbaric side of the Revolution is, the view of Azuela as having passed his peak after it is now often considered to be jejune. He remained devoted, always, to his own profession, eschewing politics, but bringing his developing satirical techniques to bear upon the political gangs (*chusma liderista*) and opportunists (*moscas*) which even now plague Mexican life. Thus, although **Reveultas** and **Yañez** have usually been taken to be the leading modernists of Mexican fiction, similar claims may be made for Azuela, especially for his book about a mad doctor and his dog, Lenin, and an underworld girl who cannot go straight: *La malhora* (1923, 'The Evil Hour'). He wrote many more novels, novellas and plays, including, in *Two Novels of Mexico* (1957), *Los caciques* (1917, 'The Bosses'), and *Las moscas* (1918, 'The Flies'), and *Las tribulaciones de una familia decente* ('Trials of a Respectable Family' with 'The Underdogs', and *La luciérnaga*, 'The Fireflies', in *Three Novels of Mariano Azuela*).
▷L Leal, *Mariano Azuela*; J S Brushwood, *Mexico in Its Novel* (1966)

B

BA JIN, pseud of Li Feigan
(1904–)

Chinese writer, born into a wealthy family in Chengdu, Sichuan. Educated in the traditional classical style in Shanghai and Nanjing, he also studied in France (1927–9), and became an enthusiastic anarchist. His major trilogy (*Family*, 1931, *Spring*, 1938, *Autumn*, 1940) attacked the traditional family system, and was immensely popular with the younger generation. Several other novels confirmed his standing as one of China's foremost patriotic writers. Although never a member of the Communist Party, he held important literary positions in the communist regime after renouncing his earlier anarchism. During the Cultural Revolution (1966–76) he was purged and punished, and compelled to do manual work. He re-emerged in 1977, and published a collection of essays about his experience, entitled *Random Thoughts* (1979).

BABEL, Isaac Emmanuilovich
(1894–?1941)

Russian short-story writer, a protégé of **Maxim Gorky**, born in the Jewish ghetto of Odessa. He worked as a journalist in St Petersburg, served in the Tsar's army on the Romanian front and, after the Revolution, in various Bolshevik campaigns as a Cossack supply officer. He is remembered for his stories of the Jews in Odessa in *Odesskie rasskazy* (1916, Eng trans *Odessa Tales*, 1924), and stories of war in *Konarmiya* (1926, Eng trans *Red Cavalry*, 1929), but also wrote plays, albeit less successfully. He was exiled to Siberia in the mid-1930s, and died in a concentration camp there in 1940 or 1941.
▷R W Hallett, *Isaac Babel* (1973)

BABITS, Mihály
(1883–1941)

Hungarian poet of the 20th-century literary renaissance. He was a schoolmaster, but devoted himself to writing from 1917. He was also a novelist and essayist, and a distinguished translator of **Dante**, **Shakespeare**, and the Greek classics.
▷M Becedek, *Babits Mihály* (1969)

BABRIUS

Greek writer of fables. Little is known of him except that he collected **Aesop**ic fables, which

he turned into popular verse. Almost all of these were thought to have been lost, but in 1841 a Greek discovered 123 of them at Mount Athos.
▷J Werner, *Questiones Babrianae* (1892)

BACCHELLI, Riccardo
(1891–1985)

Italian novelist, born in Bologna. He wrote works in a large number of different genres and mediums, but is best known for his novels, and especially his historical novels. His works include *Il diavolo al Pontelungo* (1927, 'The Devil at Pontelungo'), a humorous tale of Bakunin's efforts to introduce socialism into Italy, the three-volume family chronicle of the Risorgimento, *Il mulino del Po* (1938–40, 'The Mill on the Po'), and *Bellezza e Unamità* (1972, 'Beauty and Humanity').
▷M Saccenti, *Riccardo Bacchelli* (1973)

BACCHYLIDES
(5th century BC)

Greek poet from Iulis on the island of Ceos (Kéa) and nephew of **Simonides**. Like his contemporary, **Pindar**, he specialized in odes commissioned to celebrate victories in the great athletic contests. Early in his career he worked in Thessaly; later he was in Athens, and in the 470s accompanied Simonides to the court of Hiero I, King of Syracuse, where they became rivals to Pindar. Towards the end of his life, he spent a period of exile in the Peloponnese where, according to Plutarch, he wrote some of his best work. His poems survived only in brief fragments until the discovery in 1896 of an Egyptian papyrus containing the text of 14 victory odes and six dithyrambs (short narrative poems). Though overshadowed by Pindar, Bacchylides's work has the merits of clarity and metrical simplicity, and he was regarded by Alexandrian critics as one of the canonical lyric poets.

BACHMANN, Ingeborg
(1926–73)

Austrian poet, short-story writer and novelist. Born in Klagenfurt and educated at several Austrian universities, she was strongly influenced by Heidegger's existentialism and

Wittgenstein's positivism. Her first two volumes of poetry, *Die gestundete Zeit* (1953) and *Anrufung des großen Bären* (1956) show the imperative unsentimentality of her voice, and combine succinct philosophical precision with the lyrical playfulness of a highly suggestive, but rationally irresolvable imagery. In her prose (*Das dreißigste Jahr*, 1961, 'The Thirtieth Birthday'; *Malina*, 1971; *Simultan*, 1972, 'Simultaneous') she likewise stresses the importance of human courage and initiative. Her mytho-magical radio plays, *Die Zikaden* (1954, 'The Cicadas') and *Der gute Gott von Manhattan* (1958, 'The Good God of Manhattan'), are dream-like parables exploring the dynamics of the human mind within the order of an inexorable outside world. In one of them, God is in the dock for having tried to assassinate two lovers whose unconditional love was believed a security risk.

▷A Hapkemeyer, *Ingeborg Bachmann. Entwicklungslinien in Werk und Leben* (1990)

BACON, Delia Salter
(1811–59)

American authoress, born in Tallmadge, Ohio, sister of **Leonard Bacon**. She spent the years 1853–8 in England trying to prove the theory that **Shakespeare**'s plays were written by Francis Bacon, Walter Raleigh, **Edmund Spenser**, and others. She did not originate the idea herself, but was the first to give it currency in her *Philosophy of the Plays of Shakspere Unfolded* (1857), with a preface by **Nathaniel Hawthorne**.

▷V C Hopkins, *Prodigal Puritan: a life of Delia Bacon* (1959)

BACON, Leonard
(1887–1954)

American poet, born in Solway, New York State, brother of **Delia Bacon**. He became Professor of English at the University of California in 1910, but resigned in 1923 to concentrate on writing. His collections of poems, which are often satirical in tone and content, include *Ulug Beg* (1923), *The Legend of Quincibald* (1928), *Rhyme and Punishment* (1936), and the wartime lyrics *Days of Fire* (1943). He won a Pulitzer Prize for Poetry in 1941 for his collection *Sunderland Capture* (1940). He also wrote an autobiographical volume, *Semi-centennial* (1939).

BACOVIA, George, pseud of G Vasiliu
(1881–1957)

Romanian poet, claimed by a few critics as the country's greatest of the 20th century, and certainly one who is now more universally admired than any other. His poetry, for once

beautifully translated into English in the bilingual *Plumb* (1980), is elegant, much influenced (initially) by **Laforgue** and (later) by **Fargue**, melancholy, and as word-perfect as any modern poet's. He was a manic-depressive and an alcoholic who captured, to a sometimes almost unbearable extent, the sad but excited nature of his fugitive and poverty-stricken existence. He exercised a great influence upon his younger contemporaries; that he was able to write at all was owing to his wife, Agatha Grigorescu, who, herself a poet, fully understood him. Much has been written about his affinities to the Symbolist movement, and assuredly he was part of the Romanian Symbolist movement; but essentially he was a law unto himself.

▷M Seymour-Smith, *Who's Who in Twentieth Century Literature* (1976)

BAGE, Robert
(1728–1801)

English novelist, born near Derby and educated at a local school. Trained by his father as a papermaker, he married in 1751 and bought a papermill in Staffordshire. He studied music, French, Italian and mathematics, and joined the Derby Philosophical Society, a group of political radicals. He turned to writing only after the failure of his business in 1780, but the mixture of humour, liberal ideas and good storytelling made his six novels an immediate success. They were admired particularly by Sir **Walter Scott**. *Hermsprong, or Man as He is not* (1796), his most original work, tells of a man reared among Native Americans whose entry into English society is used to highlight the conflict between 'natural' and 'civilized' values.

▷P Faulkner, *Robert Bage* (1979); G Kelly, *The English Jacobin Novel* (1976).

BAGGESEN, Jens
(1764–1826)

Danish poet and satirical humorist, he was born in Korsør, but spent much of his life abroad and wrote extensively in German. In 1785 he launched a long-standing feud with the Romantics, though he later became a follower of **Rousseau**. He was author of *Komiske Fortaelling* (1785, 'Comical Tales') and the more emotional *Labyrinten* (1792–3).

▷L L Albertsen, *Odins mjod. En studie i Baggesens mystike poetik* (1969)

BAGLEY, Desmond
(1923–83)

English thriller writer, a leader in his field. Born in Kendal, he received an elementary education only, and worked in the aircraft industry during the war years, before moving to Africa, where his writing career developed. Moving to Johannesburg in 1950, he was film critic for the *Rand Daily Mail* for nearly five years and scripted shorts until the success of his first novel, *The Golden Keel* (1963), allowed him to concentrate on his own writing. Bagley's great strength was the interaction of character (most often a first-person narrator) and physical environment. His settings were meticulously researched and ranged from the Andes in *High Citadel* (1965, his most successful book), to Mexico in *The Vivero Letter* (1968) and Iceland in *Running Blind* (1970), which introduced his series character, Slade. Among his other novels were the atmospheric *Wyatt's Hurricane* (1966), *The Tightrope Men* (1973) and *The Snow Tiger* (1975). *Night of Error* was published posthumously in 1984 and suggested that Bagley's talent was far from exhausted.

BAGNOLD, Enid
(1889–1981)

English novelist, playwright and children's writer. Throughout her life she balanced between 'society' and the world of artists and intellectuals; **Virginia Woolf** took an instant dislike to her, and **Nancy Mitford** described her as 'a sort of fearfully nice gym mistress'. She published *Serena Blandish* (1924, an English upper-class version of **Anita Loos**'s *Gentlemen Prefer Blondes*) under the pseudonym 'A Lady of Quality' to spare her father's feelings, and based *The Loved and the Envied* (1951) on an amalgam of her life and that of Lady Diana Cooper. She is best known, however, for *National Velvet* (1935), the skilfully-told story of a girl who wins the Grand National on a piebald horse won in a raffle, the bowdlerized film version of which provided Elizabeth Taylor with her first lead role. Of her plays, only *The Chalk Garden* (1955) was a hit, and solely in New York. Her *Autobiography* (1969) is a lively, impressionistic tumble through a life lived to the full.

BAGRITSKY, Eduard, pseud of **Eduard Dzyubin**
(1895–1934)

Russian poet and translator (of **Robert Burns** and Sir **Walter Scott**), from Odessa. Although always sickly, he worked for the police in Odessa and then fought on the Persian front. He began as a Futurist poet, in the manner of such Acmeist poets as **Gumilev**, but then came more under the revolutionary influence of **Mayakovsky**. However, in his last, most original and best phase he wrote *Duma pro Opanasa* (1926, 'The Lay of Opanas'), which was in the tradition of his native Ukrania, and deliberately echoed the style of the great Ukranian poet **Taras Shevchenko**. Criticism of him by Soviet culture-clerks at first drove

him into a defiant romanticism, then, finally, when he was weak and ill, into an attempt to come to terms with them. His final work, while interesting for what it contains despite himself, hardly counts in his development.
▷M Slonim, *Soviet Russian Literature* (1977)

BAGRYANA, Elisaveta, pseud of **Elisaveta Belcheva**
(1893–)

Bulgarian poet and editor, born in Sliven. Her first collection appeared in 1927. She was an aggressive and Bohemian personality, an urgent advocate of the emancipation of women, who shocked (and enjoyed shocking) the middle classes of inter-war Bulgaria, travelling much abroad, and announcing that she had 'a husband in every country'. She wrote 'official verse' under communism, but was clearly uneasy about it, and was finally able to give it up. Unfortunately none of her vigorous verse, most of the best of it passionate love poetry, has found a translator.
▷C A Moser, *A History of Bulgarian Literature* (1972)

BAHR, Hermann
(1863–1934)

Austrian dramatist, novelist, and critic, born in Linz. He studied in Vienna and Berlin, and took a leading part in the successive literary movements of Naturalism, neo-Romanticism and Expressionism. His 'decadent' novel *Die gute Schule* (1890, 'The Good School') is highly regarded. He published social novels such as *Die schöne Frau* (1899, 'The Beautiful Woman') and comedies such as *Die gelbe Nachtigall* (1907, 'The Yellow Nightingale') and the theatrical farce *Das Konzert* (1909, 'The Concert'). He was appointed manager of the Deutsches Theater, Berlin (1903), and the Burgtheater, Vienna (1918).
▷E Widder, *Hermann Bahr: sein Weg zum Glauben* (1963)

BAÏF, Jean Antoine de
(1532–89)

French poet, born in Venice. He was a member of the Pléiade, a group of seven poets gathered around **Pierre de Ronsard**. His works include *Amours* (1552, 'Love Poems') and *Passe Temps* (in *Oeuvres en rime*, 1573, 'Pastime'), as well as translations from the Greek. He attempted to introduce blank verse into French poetry, and experimented with combinations of poetry and music.
▷M Auge-Chignet, *La vie, les idées et l'oeuvre de Jean Antoine de Baïf* (1909)

BAIL, Murray
(1941–)

Australian experimental novelist and short-story writer, born in Adelaide. The strangely titled collection *Contemporary Portraits and Other Stories* (1975) showed the way his fiction was to develop. In *Homesickness* (1980) Bail describes the interplay of a group of tourists visiting museums round the world, each museum reflecting an aspect of their existence. *Holden's Performance* (1987) is a satire playing on the name of the hero and of Australia's popular car. Bail edited *The Faber Book of Contemporary Australian Short Stories* (1988).

BAILEY, Paul Peter Harry
(1937–)

English novelist, born in London into a working-class family. He went to grammar school in London, and later to the Central School of Speech and Drama, but did not fulfil his ambition to become an actor. He turned instead to writing, and made a striking debut with *At the Jerusalem* (1967), a novel about old age and its attendant isolation and disintegration, perennial themes in his work. His spare, allusive, concentrated style is found in more expansive form in the lighter *Peter Smart's Confessions* (1977), but he returned to old age in *Old Soldiers* (1980). *Gabriel's Lament* (1986) and *Sugar Cane* (1993) are linked by theme and characters. *An Immaculate Mistake* (1990) is a memoir which focuses on growing up as a homosexual.

BAILEY, Philip James
(1816–1902)

English poet, born in Basford, Nottingham, the son of the historian of Nottinghamshire, Thomas Bailey (1785–1856). After studying at Glasgow University, he was called to the English Bar in 1840, but never practised. Associated with the 'spasmodic' school, he was the author of *Festus: a Poem* (1839), his own version of the Faust legend, which reached, greatly altered, an 11th (Jubilee) edition in 1889. His reputation was high among his contemporaries.
▷J Ward, *Philip James Bailey, author of Festus: personal recollections* (1905)

BAILLIE, Grizel, Lady, née **Hume**
(1665–1746)

Scottish poet, daughter of the Covenanter Sir Patrick Hume. In 1684 she supplied him with food during his concealment in the vault beneath Polwarth Church, and helped shelter the Covenanting scholar, Robert Baillie of Jerviswood (1634–84), whose son, George, she married in 1692. She is remembered by her songs, particularly 'And werena my heart licht I wad dee'. In 1911 her domestic notebook was published as *The Household Book*, giving a fascinating, detailed insight into the trivia of daily household management.
▷Countess Ashburnham, *Lady Grisell Baillie: a sketch of her life* (1893)

BAILLIE, Joanna
(1762–1851)

Scottish playwright and poet. Daughter of the manse of Boswell in Lanarkshire, she moved to Hampstead in 1791 and, on being revealed as the author of the anonymous *Plays on the Passions* (1798, 1802 and 1812), was welcomed into London literary society. Sir **Walter Scott** especially admired her work. Written mainly in verse, and published as scripts before they were staged, the plays, particularly 'De Montfort' and 'Basil', now seem melodramatic, but were considered to contain striking treatments of the female character. Her *Fugitive Verses* (1790) echo the rhythms of Scottish folk song. Always retiring by nature, in later life she concerned herself with religious and philanthropic projects.

BAILLON, André
(1875–1932)

Belgian novelist, undeservedly neglected outside his own country and in France. In certain respects the **Gissing** of Belgium, Baillon was born in Antwerp. Orphaned at six, he was brought up by a pious and sadistic aunt, an experience he recollected in *Le Neveu de Mademoiselle Autorité* (1932, 'Miss Authority's Nephew'). His most famous book was *Histoire d'une Marie* (1921, 'The Story of a Mary'), a classic which for some inexplicable reason went untranslated; but his greatest works were to come. Set up in Paris as a writer, with the support of his wife and of various writers including **Vildrac**, Baillon fell victim to a mysterious and terrible depression. But, before he killed himself, he left an invaluable and extraordinary record of it, in such books as the epoch-making *Délires* (1927, 'Deliriums'). The discovery in English-speaking countries of this strange writer, with his mania for precise self-analysis, can only be a matter of time. Of *Délires* a Belgian critic has written: 'as rhythmic as a logical hallucination, this strange prose poem is the summit of an art founded on concision and the ultimate limit of experience'.

BAINBRIDGE, Beryl Margaret
(1934–)

English novelist, born in Liverpool. She attended ballet school in Tring, and was a repertory actress (1949–60), then a clerk for her eventual publisher, Duckworth (1961–73). Her novels, beginning with *A Weekend* with *Claude* (1967, rev edn 1981), are marked by concision, caustic wit, and carefully turned prose. Her family provided raw material for *A Quiet Life* (1976), just as her experience working as a cellar-woman fed into *The Bottle Factory Outing* (1975). *The Dressmaker* (1973), *Sweet William* (1976) and *Injury Time* (1978) are typical works. *Young Adolf* (1978) speculates on Hitler's reputed visit to Liverpool. She has also written a number of television plays.

BAIRD, Irene
(1901–81)

Canadian novelist. She moved to Canada from England at the age of 18, working as a reporter for the Vancouver *Sun* and the *Daily Province*, then for the National Film Board, later becoming a civil servant for a time. Her novels include: *John* (1937), her first; *Waste Heritage*, written two years later, which describes the Depression; and *The Climate of Power* (1971), which describes the government bureaucracy she became familiar with as a civil servant.

BAKER, Dorothy
(1907–68)

American novelist, born in Montana, most famous for her *Young Man with a Horn* (1938), a novel based on the character of the jazz trumpeter Bix Biederbecke, and for *Cassandra at the Wedding* (1962), an outstanding study of a young college woman. She has been likened to **Hemingway**, but the comparison is facile and misleading, since her main virtue lies in her ability to characterize her female characters.

BAKER, Elliott
(1922–)

American novelist and scriptwriter, born in Buffalo, New York. His first and best novel, *A Fine Madness* (1964, subsequently filmed to Baker's own screenplay), satirizes US society's desire to normalize and 'cure' the artist of the very turbulent and anarchic drives that fuel his creative instincts. *The Penny Wars* (1968) anatomizes a rebellious but sensitive young man facing up to fascism, war and nascent sexuality, an adolescent version of the interlinked dramas of *Unrequited Loves* (1974), in which one 'Elliott Baker' enlists in the rather more expensive conflicts of the sex war. In *Klynt's Law* (1976), Baker combines elements of **Bernard Malamud**'s academic novel-of-awakening *A New Life* with the knockabout humour of *A Fine Madness*, not always successfully. In *And We Were Young* (1979) he uses a stock reunion of army comrades to explore the long-term impact of war and corroded hopes. *Viva Max* (1970) is the best known of his screenplays.

BAKER, Louisa Alice
(1858–1926)

New Zealand romantic novelist who wrote, under the pen-name 'Alien', 16 tales of sacrifice, renunciation and the sanctity of marriage. Despite the approbation of the religious press, some contemporary critics believed that Baker dwelt perhaps a little too lovingly on the 'regrettable incidents' in her narratives. Her first book was *A Daughter of the King* (1894), followed by *The Majesty of Man* (1895). The moral point of *His Neighbour's Landmark* (1907) is heightened by the 1886 eruption of Mt Tarawera. Her last book was *A Double Blindness* (1910).

BALABAKKI, Layla
(1936–)

Lebanese writer of feminist novels of social and sexual revolt; there has been interest in her work in France, where one of her novels has been translated.

BALAGUER Y CIRERA, Victor
(1824–1901)

Spanish poet, politician and historian. A leading figure of the Catalan renaissance, he wrote a *History of Catalonia*, a *Political and Literary History of the Troubadours*, and poems in both Catalan and Spanish.

BALASSI, or BALASSA, Bálint
(1554–94)

Hungarian knight, adventurer and lyric poet, born in Kékkö. He died fighting the Turkish invaders. His poetry was inspired by military heroism, his love for the idealized figure of beauty and happiness he named 'Julia', and religion. He also experimented in drama (*Credulus and Julia*). He wrote *Little Garden for Diseased Minds* (1572). He experimented with verse forms, one of which is still known as the 'Balassi stanza'.
▷S Eckhardt, *Balassa Bálint* (1941)

BALBUENA, Bernardo de
(1568–1627)

Spanish poet and prelate, born in Valdepeñas. He spent his working life in Central America, where all his poetry was written, and became Bishop of Puerto Rico in 1620. He wrote an epic on the national hero, Bernardo del Capio, in *El Bernardo o la victoria de Roncesvalles* (1624, 'Bernardo, or the Victory of Roncesvalles'), which is excellently constructed, and full of allegory.
▷J Roja Garcidueñas, *Bernardo de Balbuena* (1958)

BALCHIN, Nigel
(1908–70)

English novelist and screenwriter, born in Potterne, Wiltshire. He is best remembered for two of his several novels, *The Small Back Room* (1943) and *Mine Own Executioner* (1946). The first is an amiably satirical attack upon Civil Service bureaucracy and is based on the author's experiences while working in a government department during World War II. The second is a psychological thriller. Among Balchin's screenplays are *The Man Who Never Was* (1956), an excellent war-time espionage drama; *The Blue Angel* (1959), and *Barabbas* (1961).

BALDI, Bernardino
(1553–1617)

Italian Renaissance author, born in Urbino. He was secretary to various prelates and to the Duke of Urbino, and became abbot of Guastalla. He wrote eclogues, a didactic poem on seafaring called *La nautica* (1590), and prose dialogues.
▷ G Zaccagnini, *Bernardino Baldi nella vita e nelle opere* (1908)

BALDINI, Antonio
(1889–1962)

Italian aesthete and writer, born in Rome. *Nostro purgatorio* (1918, 'Our Purgatory') recounts his war experiences, but his most characteristic works are *Michelaccio* (1924, 'Michael'), *La dolce calamità* (1929, 'Sweet Calamity'), and *Amici allo spiedo* (1932, 'Friends on the Spit'). He was a founder of *La Ronde*, a journal dedicated to high artistic taste and stylistic refinement, and later became Editor of the *Nuova Antologia* in 1931.
▷ C di Bicse, *Antonio Baldini* (1973)

BALDWIN, Faith
(1893–1978)

American novelist, born in New Rochelle, New York. She wrote almost 100 works, mostly romantic and light novels, but also children's books and two volumes of poetry. Many were written during the Depression and World War II in the attempt to escape oppressive reality. Her early stories and serials having appeared in a variety of magazines, she was already known to a wide readership when she published her first novel, *Mavis of Green Hill*, in 1921. A string of best-sellers followed, including *Alimony* (1928), *Office Wife* (1930) and *The American Family* (1934), several of which were made into films. Her traditional, straightforward, sentimental fictions reasserted the strength of domestic US values at a time when they appeared most under threat.

BALDWIN, James Arthur
(1924–87)

American black writer, born and brought up in a poor section of Harlem, New York. After a variety of jobs he moved to Europe, where he lived (mainly in Paris) from 1948 to 1957, before returning to the USA as a civil-rights activist. His novels are often strongly autobiographical but marked by a **Flaubert**ian attention to form. *Go Tell it on the Mountain* (1954) reflects his evangelical upbringing. *Giovanni's Room* (1957) is a study of gay relationships, *Another Country* (1963) examines the sexual dynamics of American racism. Others include *Tell Me How Long The Train's Been Gone* (1968), and *Just Above My Head* (1979). His journalism has been extremely influential and controversial. *Notes of a Native Son* (1955) is an ironic response to cultural and racial politics. Other works include *The Fire Next Time* (1963), and the plays *The Amen Corner* (1955), *Blues for Mr Charlie* (1964), and *The Women at the Well* (1972).
▷ J Campbell, *Talking at the Gates: a life of James Baldwin* (1991); W J Weatherby, *James Baldwin: artist on fire* (1989)

BALE, John
(1495–1563)

English cleric and dramatist, born in Cove, near Dunwich. A Carmelite by training, he turned Protestant in 1533 and obtained the Suffolk living of Thorndon. In 1540 he had to flee to Germany. Recalled by Edward VI, he was made bishop of Ossory in Leinster. Here 'Bilious Bale' made himself so obnoxious to Catholics with his polemical writings that they attacked his house and killed five servants. On Queen Elizabeth's accession he was made a prebendary of Canterbury. He wrote a Latin history of 'British' authors (from Adam and Seth onwards!), and several plays. Most of these were in the form of traditional morality plays, but the last, *King John*, is considered the first English historical play for its realistic portrayal of the principal characters.
▷ J W Harris, *John Bale: a study in the minor literature of the Reformation* (1940)

BALL, Hugo
(1886–1927)

German poet, born in Pirmasens, near the French border, the inaugurator of the Dadaist movement at the Café **Voltaire** in Zurich. He contributed minor nonsense poems, but within a year had repudiated his activity on the grounds that it was negative and egoistic. He wrote acutely about his friend **Hermann Hesse**.

BALLANTINE, James
(1808–77)

Scottish artist and poet, born in Edinburgh. Originally a housepainter, he learned drawing under Sir William Allan, and was one of the first to revive the art of glass-painting. Two of his volumes of prose and verse, *The Gaberlunzie's Wallet* (1843) and *Miller of Deanhaugh* (1845), contain some of his best-known songs and ballads. He also wrote *Lilias Lee* (1871), a tale after the manner of **Spenser**.

BALLANTYNE, David Watt
(1924–86)

New Zealand journalist and writer, born in Auckland, who worked on the *Auckland Star* and, between 1955 and 1965, the London *Evening News* and *Evening Standard*. His first novel, *The Cunninghams*, was published in the USA in 1948. Other books include *The Last Pioneer* (1963); a biting satire on New Zealand business ethics in *A Friend of the Family* (1966); and the Gothic story of one hot summer at a beach 'on the edge of the world' in *Sydney Bridge Upside Down* (1968). Works for television include the award-winning *Passing Through* (1961). He modelled his approach on **James T Farrell**, adopting the pose of 'disinterested observer' the better to capture the minutiae of his characters' lives.

BALLANTYNE, Robert Michael
(1825–94)

Scottish author of boys' books, born in Edinburgh, a nephew of James and John Ballantyne, the printer and publisher of Sir **Walter Scott**. Educated at The Edinburgh Academy, he joined the Hudson's Bay Company in 1841, and worked as a clerk at the Red River Settlement in the backwoods of northern Canada until 1847, before returning to Edinburgh in 1848. He wrote his first stories about his experiences in Canada, with books such as *The Young Fur Traders* (1856). *Coral Island* (1858) is his most famous work, but he was a prolific writer; his other adventures included *Martin Rattler* (1859), *The Dog Crusoe* (1861) and *The Rover of the Andes* (1885). He published an autobiography, *Personal Reminiscences in Book-Making*, in 1893.

▷E Quayle, *Ballantyne the Brave* (1967)

BALLARD, J(ames) G(raham)
(1930–)

British fiction writer, born in Shanghai, China, and educated at Cambridge. He has commented that 'science fiction is the authentic literature of the 20th century, the only fiction to respond to the transforming nature of science and technology'. Until recently he was better known for his work in that genre, fashioning a series of novels at once inventive, experimental and, in several cases, bizarre. His early novels, including his first, *The Drowned World* (1962), offer a view of the world beset by elemental catastrophe, a theme also taken up in *The Drought* (1965) and *The Day of Creation* (1985). The more experimental side of his fiction is seen in the 'fragmented novels', like *The Atrocity Exhibition* (1970) and *Crash* (1973). He has been admired for his short stories, particularly those included in such collections as *The Terminal Beach* (1964), *The Disaster Area* (1967), *Vermilion Sands* (1973) and *War Fever* (1990); *Empire of the Sun* (1984), a mainstream novel which is portentously autobiographical, was shortlisted for the Booker Prize. Its sequel, *The Kindness of Women* (1991), is also autobiographical. He won the Guardian Fiction Prize in 1984 and the James Tait Black Memorial Prize in 1985.

BALMONT, Konstantin Dmitryevitch
(1867–1943)

Russian poet, translator and essayist, born in Gumische, Vladimir province, one of the greatest of the Russian symbolists. His work was coloured by the wide travelling he did during his periodic exiles, which added a vein of exoticism to his writing.

▷L L Kobuilinksy, *Russian Symbolists* (1972)

BALZAC, Honoré de
(1799–1850)

French novelist, born in Tours. He was educated at the Collège de Vendôme, and studied law at the Sorbonne. His father wished him to become a notary, but he left Tours in 1819 to seek his fortune as an author in Paris. From 1819 to 1830 he led a life of frequent privation and incessant industry, and incurred—mainly through unlucky business speculations—a heavy burden of debt, which harassed him to the end of his career. He first tasted success with *Le Dernier Chouan* (1829, Eng trans *The Chouans*, 1893), which was followed in the same year by *Le Peau de chagrin* (Eng trans *The Magic Skin*, 1888). After writing several other novels, he formed the idea of presenting in the *Comédie humaine* (1842–53, 'The Human Comedy') a complete picture of modern civilization. Among the masterpieces which form part of Balzac's vast scheme are *Le Père Goriot* (1835, Eng trans *Pere Goriot*, 1886), *Les Illusions perdues* (1837–43, 3 vols, Eng trans *Lost Illusions*, 1893), *Les Paysans* (1855, completed by his wife, Eng trans *Sons of the Soil*, 1890), *La Femme de trente ans* (1831–4, 'The Thirty-year-old Woman') and *Eugénie Grandet* (1833, Eng trans 1859) in which meticulously observed detail and imagination are the main features. The *Contes drolatiques* (1832–7,

'Droll Tales'), a series of **Rabelais**ian stories, stand by themselves. Balzac's industry was phenomenal. He worked regularly for 15 and even 18 hours a day, and wrote 85 novels in 20 years, sometimes correcting his own proofs in legendary shambolic fashion. His work did not bring him wealth; his yearly income rarely exceeded 12 000 francs, which may help account for his obsession with the workings of money in the novels. During his later years he lived principally in his villa at Sèvres. In 1849, when his health had broken down, he travelled to Poland to visit Eveline Hanska, a rich Polish lady, with whom he had corresponded for more than 15 years. In 1850, only three months before his death, she became his wife.

▷A Maurois, *Promethée, ou La vie de Balzac* (1965); Eng translation N Denny (1965); G Robb, *Balzac* (1994)

BAMM, Peter, pseud of **Curt Emmrich** (1897–1975)

German novelist, essayist and writer of miscellaneous books. He was an effective, and ironical, popular novelist, especially with *Die unsichtbare Flagge* (1962, Eng trans *The Invisible Flag*, 1936), about his experiences as a surgeon on the Russian front during World War II.

BANCHS, Enrique (1888–1968)

Argentinian poet, born in Buenos Aires. Largely a law unto himself in Argentinian poetry, Banchs was a neoclassicist writing under the direct influence of French poets such as **Valéry**; he was also indebted to French theories of 'pure poetry'. He did not publish a collection after *La Urna* (1911), consisting of 100 sonnets. Typical of him are such lines from one of these, describing the 'favourite dwelling of his soul': 'preferring lofty ruins to the waning palm of today'.

BANDEIRA, Manuel (1886–1968)

Brazilian poet, translator (**Schiller**, **Shakespeare**) and critic, born in Recife, Pernambuco. As a critic has declared, Bandeira belongs 'to two worlds—the 19th century and [Brazilian] Modernismo'. While recovering from tuberculosis in a Swiss sanatorium at Davos he met **Éluard**, which had a decisive but delayed effect on him. His first book was *A Cinza das horas* (1917, 'The Dust of the Hours'), fairly conventional in form although playfully melancholy in content. His later poetry was seldom without the fin de siècle air which he established in this volume. But

he felt the full impact of the violent and iconoclastic *Modernismo* (the Brazilian movement), and helped to usher it in with collections such as *O Ritmo Dissoluto* (1924, 'Dissolved Rhythm'). In *Libertinagem* (1930, 'Libertinism'), he found his own voice, and demonstrated his mastery of free verse—something he had always struggled to achieve. He edited important anthologies, generously promoted the work of other poets, and became the grand old man of Brazilian letters. Minor in international terms, he was perhaps his country's most fulfilled 20th-century poet.

▷S Burnshaw (ed), *The Poem Itself* (1964, poems translated and analysed in depth)

BANDELLO, Matteo (c.1485–1561)

Italian cleric and writer of *novelle* or tales, born in Castelnuovo in Piedmont. For a while a Dominican, he was driven from Milan by the Spaniards after the battle of Pavia (1525), and settling in France was in 1550 made Bishop of Agen. His 214 tales (1554–73), collected as *Novelliere*, have no over-arching narrative framework, but were used as source material by **Shakespeare**, **Philip Massinger**, and others, and are valuable (if perhaps a little unreliable) for the social history of the period.

▷K H Hartley, *Bandello and the Heptameron* (1960)

BANERJI, Bibhuti Bhusan (1894–1950)

Indian (Bengali) author of a single masterpiece (though he wrote other good fiction) made famous by Saytajit Ray's great trilogy of movies of the same title, *Pather Panchali* (1928–9, translated into English, 1969). This book, whose title means 'Chronicle of the Street', unforgettably depicts the rural Bengal of the turn of the century: it is the tale of a boy, Opu, his sister Durga (who dies), and their parents; the father, a priest and singer, is too feckless to preserve them from poverty. It is a classic by any standards, and of it **Tagore** wrote: 'it helps one to see things—trees and shrubs ... men and women ... their joys and woes'. It was essentially the story of the author's own childhood, and the movies reflect it with an authenticity almost unique in the history of the translation of books to cinema.

BANG, Hermann Joachim (1857–1912)

Danish novelist, born in Adserballe, Isle of Als. A homosexual, he wrote impressionistic novels about loneliness and failure, of which his debut *Haabløse Slaegter* (1880, 'Lost Generations') is typical. His short stories *Ekcentriske Noveller* (1885) and *Stille Eksistenser* (1886) show the influence of **Jonas Lie**.

▷H Jacobsen, *Hermann Bang. Nye studier* (1974)

BANGS, John Kendrick
(1862–1922)

American humorous writer, lecturer and editor (of *Puck*). He was the author of the farcical *A Houseboat on the Styx* (1896), which features famous characters from the past—Diogenes, **Shakespeare**, George Washington—and facetiously but agreeably follows up the absurd situations which consequently develop.

BANIM, John
(1798–1842)
BANIM, Michael
(1796–1874)

Irish novelist brothers, born in Kilkenny. John studied art at Dublin and became a miniature painter; Michael, a postmaster. Having achieved some success as a playwright when a tragedy was produced at Covent Garden in 1821, John, with the collaboration of Michael, published such novels as the *Tales of the O'Hara Family* (1826), characterized by a faithful portrayal of humble Irish folk. John's illness and poverty were alleviated by a state pension. Michael's other novels include *The Croppy* (1828) and *The Town of the Cascades* (1864).

▷P J Murray, *The Life of John Banim* (1857)

BANKS, Iain Menzies
(1954–)

Scottish novelist and science-fiction writer, born in Dunfermline. He was educated at Gourock and Greenock High Schools, and the University of Stirling. He made a major impact with his controversial first novel, *The Wasp Factory* (1984), a study of insanity which shifted between psychological acuity and grotesque fantasy. *Walking on Glass* (1985), *The Bridge* (1986) and *Canal Dreams* (1989) drew more directly on science fiction and fantasy in multi-layered narratives. *The Crow Road* (1992) incorporated familiar motifs and themes of Scottish writing, viewed from a slightly displaced perspective. He writes science-fiction novels using the name Iain M Banks, and is highly regarded within that genre. Works in this vein include *Consider Phlebas* (1987), *The State of the Art* (1989, rev edn 1991) and *Against a Dark Background* (1993). His other works include *Cleaning Up* (1987) and *Complicity* (1993).

BANKS, John
(c.1650–c.1700)

English playwright, for whom biographical details are sketchy. His brand of historical tragedy was most successful in his day, though it has been neglected ever since. His first success was *The Unhappy Favourite: Or the Earl of Essex* (1681), which ran in London for several years despite Banks's (undeserved) critical reputation as a poor writer. He may be due for a revival because, like *The Unhappy Favourite*, his other major works *Virtue Betray'd, or Anna Bullen* (1682), *The Innocent Usurper* (about Lady Jane Grey), and *Albion Queens* (1684, about Elizabeth I and Mary, Queen of Scots) all have major, and rewarding, roles for women. Banks is perhaps a victim of the political turmoil of his own time (the English Revolution and its aftermath): the last two of these plays, both about Catholics attempting to usurp the throne, were banned by the Lord Chamberlain because of their political content.

BANKS, Lynne Reid
(1929–)

English novelist, born in London. She trained at RADA and worked as an actress and journalist before turning to writing. She was widely acclaimed for *The L-Shaped Room* (1960); *The Backward Shadow* (1970) and *Two Is Lonely* (1974), complete the trilogy. The first is particularly important, and not only because the heroine, a pregnant single woman, defied the social conventions of her class and time by refusing to undergo an abortion. It is significant because it added a female perspective to other novels being published at the time, which similarly dealt with young working- and lower middle-class people coming to terms with sexuality and family life in a grim post-war Britain. Although Banks has continued to write novels, it is her earlier books which have earned her a place in literary history.

BANKS, Russell Earl
(1940–)

American novelist and short-story writer, born in Newton, Massachusetts. A native New Englander recording the lives of the deprived, Banks is nevertheless fascinated by the warmth and light of the Caribbean, celebrated in his novel, *The Book of Jamaica* (1981). Other works are set in New Hampshire, as, for example, in the short-story collection *Trailerpark* (1981), where the lives of those living in trailer vans are recorded. *Continental Drift* (1985), his finest novel, is a story of two people attempting to begin new lives: a Haitian woman resolves to emigrate to the USA, while a troubled oil-burner repair man considers moving from New Hampshire to Florida. Banks frequently uses the device of a narrator who steps back from the main action in order to confide in the reader.

BANNERMAN, Helen Brodie, née **Boog Watson**
(1862–1946)
Scottish children's writer and illustrator, born in Edinburgh, the daughter of a Free Church minister. Her husband was a doctor in the Indian Medical Service and she spent much of her life in India, where she produced the children's classic, *The Story of Little Black Sambo* (1899), the tale of a black boy and his adventures with the tigers, based on illustrated letters she had written to her children. Phenomenally popular when it first appeared, it was judged by some after her death to be racist and demeaning to blacks. She wrote several other illustrated books for children.

BANNING, Lex (Arthur Alexander)
(1921–65)
Australian poet, born in St Leonards, Sydney, of a Belgian father and Scottish/Swedish mother. He published only three collections, *Everyman His Own Hamlet* (1951), *The Instant's Clarity* (1952) and *Apocalypse in Springtime* (1956), in each of which his own spastic condition underlies his conflict between hope and disillusion.

BANVILLE, John
(1945–)
Irish novelist, born in Wexford. He became a journalist, and has been the literary editor of the *Irish Times* since 1989. He writes in a highly compacted, allusive, and poetic manner. Much of his work is concerned with the nature of the fictionalizing process itself, and is filled with oblique literary references. His first book was a story collection, *Long Lankin* (1970). His tetralogy of novels on scientific figures, *Doctor Copernicus* (1976), *Kepler* (1981), *The Newton Letter* (1982) and *Mefisto* (1986), is highly metafictional in intent. The oblique crime story *The Book of Evidence* (1989) and its successor *Ghosts* (1993) are thematically linked.

BANVILLE, Théodore Faullin de
(1823–91)
French poet and dramatist, born in Moulins. From *Les Cariatides* (1841, 'The Caryatids') to *Dans la fournaise* (1892, 'In the Furnace'),

he showed himself one of the most musical of lyricists, and one of the wittiest of parodists. The title 'roi des rimes' was given him from his ingenuity in handling the most difficult forms of verse—the medieval ballades and rondels. His *Gringoire* (1866) holds an established place in French repertory.
▷A Carel, *Histoire anecdotique des contemporains* (1885)

BARAKA, Amiri, adopted name of **LeRoi (Everett LeRoy) Jones**
(1934–)
American poet, playwright, prose writer and essayist, born in Newark, New Jersey, into a middle-class black family. His politicization took him away from the bourgeois certainties of his roots into black nationalism (he took the name 'Amiri Baraka' in 1967) and later Marxism–Leninism. Although a prolific poet and dramatist with over 50 titles to his name, his best-known work dates from the early 1960s, when his cultural and racial anger spilled out in poetry collections like *Preface to a Twenty Volume Suicide Note* (1961), *The Dead Lecturer* (1964), *Black Magic* (1967), and in plays like *The Toilet*, *Dutchman* and *The Slave* (all 1964). His other works include a volume of stories, *Tales* (1967) and a seminal study of the social significance of black music, *Blues People* (1963).
▷ *The Autobiography of LeRoi Jones/Amiri Baraka* (1984)

BARATYNSKI, Evgeny Abramovich, properly **Boratynsky**
(1800–44)
Russian lyric poet, born into a noble family. He was disgraced for his part in a theft as a cadet, but re-enlisted and served as a soldier until he was pardoned and made an officer in 1825. He resigned shortly after, and married an heiress. He wrote melancholy, tender, but pessimistic verse, at first under the overt influence of **Pushkin**, but later in more distinctive manner. His works include *Tsiganka* ('The Gypsy Girl'), *Bal* ('The Ball') and *Piroskaf* ('The Steamboat').
▷B Dees, *Evgeny Abramavitch Baratynski* (1972)

BARBA JACOB, Porfirio, pseud of **Miguel Angel Osorio Benítez**
(1883–1942)
Colombian poet, born in Santa Rose de Osos, Antioquia. Benítez was a legendary wandering figure in Latin-American literature, not unlike Baron Corvo (**Frederick William Rolfe**), but more gifted—for his haphazardly published, lyrical poetry has hardly been studied in the depth it deserves. He began in the *modernista* style established by Darío, and

used it as a framework ever afterwards; but he was never a *modernista* poet. He is the 'man who turned into a horse' of the famous story of that title by **Arévalo Martínez**. He was homosexual, had other pseudonyms, and modelled his conduct on that of various European *poètes maudits*, 'often causing scandal by his riotous behaviour'. His most famous line is: 'En nada creo, en nada' ('I believe in nothing, nothing'), from 'La reina', a translation of which may be found in the *Penguin Book of Latin American Verse* (1971, ed E Curacciolo-Trejo). His poetry was collected in *Poesías completas* (1960), and his complete works of 1962 contains his untruthful and entertaining autobiography, *La divina tragedia* ('The Divine Tragedy').

BARBAULD, Anna Laetitia, née **Aikin**
(1743–1825)

English author, born in Kibworth-Harcourt, Leicestershire. Encouraged by the success of her *Poems* (1773), she in the same year, jointly with her brother, John Aikin, published *Miscellaneous Pieces in Prose*. She married a dissenting minister, Rochemont Barbauld, in 1774, and during the next 10 years published her best work, including *Early Lessons for Children* and *Hymns in Prose for Children*. Also with her brother she began the well-known series *Evenings at Home* in 1792.
▷*A Memoir by Lucy Aikin* (1825)

BARBEY D'AUREVILLY, Jules
(1808–89)

French Romantic writer, born in St Sauveur-le-Vicomte. He was extreme in his rejection of 18th-century values. His best-known novels were *La Vieille Maîtresse* (1851, 'The Old Mistress') and *L'Ensorcelée* (1854, 'The Bewitched Woman'), and he also published poetry and literary criticism.
▷J Canu, *Barbey D'Aurevilly* (1965)

BARBIER, Henri Auguste
(1805–82)

French poet, born in Paris. He was famous for a time for satirizing prominent social types for their efforts to procure favour after the July revolution. He wrote a number of collections of poems, including *Iambes* (1831), *Il pianto* (1833), and *Lazare* (1837), and was an influence on **Victor Hugo**.

BARBIER, Paul Jules
(1825–1901)

French dramatist, born in Paris. He wrote the libretto for Offenbach's *Tales of Hoffmann*.
▷M Carré, *L'amour mouille, comédie vaudeville* (1849)

BARBOUR, John
(c.1320–1396)

Scottish poet, prelate and scholar, known as the 'father of Scottish poetry and history'. He was probably born in Aberdeen, and was Archdeacon of Aberdeen from 1357, or earlier, till his death. He studied at Oxford and Paris, and in 1372 was appointed Clerk of Audit for King Robert II. His national epic, *The Brus*, written in the 1370s and first printed at Edinburgh in 1571, is a narrative poem on the life and deeds of King Robert I, the Bruce, having as its climax the Battle of Bannockburn, and preserving many oral traditions. He also wrote two lost epics, *The Brut* (a history of the Britons) and *The Stewartis Original* (a fictitious pedigree of the kings of Scotland).
▷G Neilson, *John Barbour: poet and translator* (1900)

BARBU, Ion, pseud of **Don Barbilian**
(1895–1961)

Romanian poet who was also a gifted mathematician—he was Professor of Mathematics at the University of Bucharest. The chief initial influences upon him, as upon most modern Romanian poets, were French writers, in his case **Mallarmé**, and, to a lesser extent, **Valéry**. He was known amongst his friends and enemies as a 'priapic vandal', yet his poetry is deliberately cold and exact in its forms and expression: he called it 'passion on ice'. There are a few translations from his poems in *Modern Rumanian Poetry* (1967, ed D Caminescu).

BARBUSSE, Henri
(1873–1935)

French novelist, born of an English mother in Asnières. He fought as a volunteer in World War I, which inspired his masterpiece, *Le Feu* (1916, Eng trans *Under Fire*, 1917) in which a powerful realism is accompanied by a deep feeling for all human suffering. Other works include *Le Couteau entre les Dents* (1921, 'Knife Between the Teeth') and *Le Judas de Jésus* (1927, 'Jesus's Judas'). A noted pacifist, and an increasingly militant communist, he later settled in the Soviet Union.
▷J Duclos and J Freville, *Henri Barbusse* (1946)

BARCLAY, Alexander
(?1475–1552)

Scottish poet and author. He was most probably born in Scotland, may have studied at universities in England, France and Italy, and in 1508 was Chaplain of Ottery St Mary, Devon. Perhaps about 1511 he became a monk of the Benedictine monastery of Ely; he later became a Franciscan. His famous poem, *The Shyp of Folys of the Worlde* (1509),

is partly a translation and partly an imitation of the German *Narrenschiff* by Sebastian Brant. He also published *Egloges* (Eclogues), an early example of English pastoral verse, and a number of translations, including Sallust's *Jugurthine War*.
▷ A Koelbing, in *Cambridge History of English History*, Volume 3 (1909)

BARCLAY, John
(1582–1621)
Scottish satirical writer, the son of a Scots father and a French mother, born in Pont-à-Mousson in Lorraine. He lived in London and Rome, and wrote mostly in Latin. His principal works are *Euphormionis Satyricon* (1603–7), a picaresque satire on the Jesuits, and *Argenis* (1621), an allegorical romance set in his own time.
▷ E Bensby, in *Cambridge History of English History*, Volume 4 (1909)

BARDIN, John Franklin
(1916–81)
American writer of bizarre detective fiction, who achieves his effect through the use of abnormal psychology, narrative non-logic and sheer freakishness. Though Bardin published his last novel in 1978, the three novels which established his cult following (stronger in Britain than in the USA) were published 30 years earlier, and his writing career was virtually over by 1955. His debut was *The Deadly Percheron* (1946). Like its successors, *The Last of Philip Banter* (1947) and *Devil Take the Blue-Tail Fly* (UK 1948, USA 1967), it is mechanical in construction but distinguished by an air of almost metaphysical menace, in which the stagey conventions of European Gothic are updated and assimilated to a topical concern for the disintegration of personality. Bardin was largely self-educated and came at his curious style independently rather than by reading others. In his fifties he was a senior editor with Coronet, and later edited the American Bar Association magazine.

BAREA, Arturo
(1897–1957)
Spanish novelist and critic, born in Madrid. He is most famous for what is undoubtedly his masterpiece, the trilogy *The Forging of a rebel* (1946), which first appeared in English in a translation by his Austrian wife, Lisa Barea: *La forja* ('The Forge'), *La ruta* ('The Route') and *La llama* ('The Flame'). The English edition is the relevant one, since the Spanish, published after it, was badly put into Spanish from it. It is an unforgettable account of Barea's experiences as a child in Madrid, as soldier in Morocco, and, finally and most

memorably, of the siege of Madrid by Franco, and of the spirit of the resistance to him. Barea's novel *La raiz rota* (in Spanish 1955, after the English translation, *The Broken Root*, 1952), about an anti-fascist who visits Franco's Spain in secret, is a sound study of the tyranny, but is unsuccessful as a novel.

BARFOOT, Joan
(1946–)
Canadian novelist, born in the province of Ontario. She is a journalist in London, Ontario. She published her first novel, *Abra*, in 1978 (reissued as *Gaining Ground* in the UK, 1980). It has been followed by *Dancing in the Dark* (1982), *Duet for Three* (1985) and *Family News* (1990). Her general theme, explored in a variety of settings, is that of a woman's search for self-identity in a society which seems to offer no palatable role, and her work has attracted comparison with that of her fellow Canadian writer, **Margaret Atwood**.

BARHAM, Richard Harris
(1788–1845)
English humorist, born in Canterbury. In 1795 he succeeded to the manor of Tappington, and in 1802 he met with an almost fatal coach accident while on his way to St Paul's School, which partially crippled his right arm for life. He entered Brasenose College, Oxford (1807), was ordained (1813), and in 1821 received a minor canonry of St Paul's Cathedral. After unsuccessful attempts at novel writing, in 1837 he began his series of burlesque metrical tales under the pen-name of Thomas Ingoldsby, which, collected under the title of *The Ingoldsby Legends* (3 vols, 1840–7), at once became popular for their droll humour, fine irony and esoteric learning. His lyrics were published in 1881.
▷ W G Lane, *Richard Harris Barham* (1968)

BARKE, James
(1905–58)
Scottish novelist, born in Torwoodlee, Selkirk. He retired from his position as chief cost accountant with a ship-building company to devote himself to writing. His novels include *The World his Pillow* (1933), *Major Operation* (1936) and *The Land of the Leal* (1939), but he is chiefly remarkable for his devoted research on the life of **Robert Burns**, resulting in a five-volume cycle of novels (1946–54) collected as *The Immortal Memory*, an edition of *Poems and Songs of Robert Burns* (1955) and the posthumous *Bonnie Jean*, about Burns and Jean Armour.
▷ Moira Burgess, *The Glasgow Novel, 1870–1970* (1972)

BARKER, A(udrey) L(ilian)
(1918–)

English novelist and short-story writer, born in Beckenham, Kent. A former producer for the BBC, she published *Innocents*, her first volume of short stories, in 1947. The book won the first **Somerset Maugham** Award. Her other collections include *Elements of Doubt* (1992), a book of ghost stories. A writer whose work is distinguished by compassionate insight into private sadnesses, her novels include *Apology for a Hero* (1950), *A Case Examined* (1965) and *A Source of Embarrassment* (1974). *John Brown's Body* (1969) was shortlisted for the Booker Prize.

BARKER, George Granville
(1913–91)

English poet, novelist, playwright and scriptwriter, born in Loughton, Essex. He lived much abroad, in the USA and Italy. Throughout a long, prolific career from 1933 he suffered by association with **Dylan Thomas**, and by the inference that he was a member of the pre-war New Apocalyptics. He was, however, a more individual poet than these associations would suggest and though often playful and self-indulgent, his best writing is energetic and eloquent. His publications culminated in the stout *Collected Poems* (1987). *Street Ballads* was published posthumously in 1992.
▷M H Fodaski, *George Barker* (1969)

BARKER, Howard
(1946–)

English dramatist. His first play, *Cheek*, was produced at the Royal Court Theatre in London in 1970. He has written over 20 plays, and his themes are ambitiously large-scale: the nature of history, the degradation of political morality and the need to re-shape society according to finer values. His plays include *Stripwell* (1975), *The Hang of the Gaol* (1978), *Victory* (1983), *Crimes in Hot Countries* (1983), *The Power of the Dog* (1984), *The Castle, Downchild* (both 1985), *Possibilities* (1988) and *Golgo* (1990). Some, such as *Scenes from an Execution* (1984, staged 1990) and *A Hard Heart* (1992), were written for radio and then adapted for stage. His poetry includes *The Ascent of Monte Grappa* (1991).

BARLACH, Ernst
(1870–1938)

German Expressionist sculptor, playwright, and poet, born in Wedel. He was identified with the German Expressionist school of both art and drama. While he was best known as a sculptor in wood (his work in this medium being influenced by Gothic sculpture and Russian folk-carving), his greatest achievement was his war memorial at Güstrow Cathedral, a great bronze Angel of Death, which was removed by Hitler as 'degenerate'. Barlach's plays include *Der tote Tag* (1912, 'The Dead Day'), *Der arme Vetter* (1918, 'The Poor Cousin') and *Die Sündflut* (1924, 'The Flood'). He also wrote fiction which, like his plays, is still read and studied in Germany.
▷E M Chick, *Ernst Barlach* (1967)

BARLOW, Joel
(1754–1812)

American poet and politician, born in Redding, Connecticut. His *Columbiad* (1807) is a historical review of events from the time of Columbus to the French Revolution. Other works include the would-be humorous poem, 'Hasty Pudding' (1796).
▷J Woodress, *A Yankee's Odyssey: the life of Barlow* (1958)

BARNARD, Marjorie Faith
(1897–1987)

Australian novelist, critic, historian and biographer, born in Sydney. She wrote many books in conjunction with Flora Eldershaw as 'M Barnard Eldershaw'. Best known are *A House is Built* (1929) and the anti-Utopian novel *Tomorrow and Tomorrow* (1947, eventually published in unexpurgated form as *Tomorrow and Tomorrow and Tomorrow*, 1983). Her historical writing includes *Macquarie's World* (1941) and the impressive and scholarly one-volume *A History of Australia* (1962). Her subsequent solo writings include two collections of short stories, biographies of convict-architect Francis Greenaway and Governor Lachlan Macquarie, and a critical study of her friend **Miles Franklin**. She won many prizes, including the **Patrick White** Literary Award in 1983.
▷L E Rorabacher, *Marjorie Barnard and M. Barnard Eldershaw* (1973)

BARNES, Barnabe
(c.1570–1609)

English poet and playwright, born in Durham, where his father was bishop. His career was extremely eventful: a member of the Earl of Essex's retinue, he took part in the campaign against the Duke of Parma in 1591. In 1598 he was accused of trying to murder the recorder of Berwick by poisoning his claret, but managed to avoid being sentenced. His best poetic work, mainly bucolic in tone, is to be found in *Pathenopil and Parthenope* (1594) and *A Divine Century of Spiritual Sonnets* (1595), but he is perhaps more memorable for the colourful life he led than for the quality of his work.

BARNES, Djuna
(1892–1982)

American novelist, poet and illustrator, born in Cornwall-on-Hudson, New York. She began her career as reporter and illustrator for magazines, then became a writer of one-act plays and short stories, published in a variety of magazines and anthologies. Her works, many of which she has illustrated, range from the outstanding novel *Nightwood* (1936) to her verse play *The Antiphon* (1958), both included in *Selected Works* (1962). Although little known to the general public, her brilliant literary style has been acclaimed by many critics, including **T S Eliot**.
▷A Field, *The Formidable Miss Barnes* (1973)

BARNES, Julian Patrick
(1946–)

English novelist, born in Leicester. The crisp precision of Barnes's prose is partly explained by his having worked both as a journalist and as a lexicographer on the *Oxford English Dictionary Supplement*. His intellect, wit, and love of France are reflected in *Flaubert's Parrot* (1984), his third novel, in which a retired English doctor discovers in the Museum of Rouen the stuffed parrot said to have stood upon **Flaubert**'s desk during the writing of *Un Coeur Simple*. This precipitates a meditation upon the nature of biography. Speculation upon the historical process forms the backbone of *A History of the World in $10\frac{1}{2}$ Chapters* (1989), a confection of fictional narrative, philosophical deliberation and art criticism, while *Talking It Over* (1991), written wholly in the words of its three lover-protagonists, deals with love, sorrow and emotional dignity. Barnes does not judge his characters, not even the vulgar Eastern European communist dictator or his state prosecutor, the central characters of *The Porcupine* (1992).

BARNES, Peter
(1931–)

English dramatist and author of screenplays. His only major commercial success has been *The Ruling Class* (1968), a play in which a madman inherits an earldom, believes he is God, and is only assumed to have been successfully rehabilitated when he makes a rampagingly right-wing speech in a decrepit House of Lords. His other plays have not shared its success. They include *Sclerosis*

(1965), *The Bewitched* (1974), *Laughter* (1978), *Red Noses* (1985), *Sunsets and Glories* (1990), and the screenplay *Enchanted April* (1991).

BARNES, William
(1801–86)

English pastoral poet, born in Rushay near Sturminster-Newton, the son of a farmer. After some time in a solicitor's office, he founded his own school, first in Wiltshire and then in Dorchester. He took time off to go to St John's College, Cambridge and take holy orders. He became curate of Whitcombe in 1847, and rector of Winterborne Came, Dorset, in 1862. Meantime he had become widely known—and greatly admired—for his fine idyllic poetry in the Dorset dialect, 'the bold and broad Doric of England'. His three volumes of poetry were collected in 1879 as *Poems of Rural Life in the Dorset Dialect*. He also wrote several philological works, and some poetry in standard English.
▷W D Jacobs, *William Barnes: linguist* (1952)

BARNFIELD, Richard
(1574–1627)

English poet, born in Norbury, Shropshire. He studied at Brasenose College, Oxford, and died a country gentleman. He is known for his pastoral poems like *The Affectionate Shepherd* (1594), which describes the love of Daphnis for Ganymede, and *Cynthia, with certain Sonnets* (1595).

BAROJA Y NESSI, Pío
(1872–1956)

Major Spanish writer, born in San Sebastian. He wrote more than 70 volumes of novels and essays, distinguished by an often violent humour and a vivid style in part derived from 19th-century Russian and French writers. He exercised a substantial influence upon his successors, in particular **Camilo Hosé Cela**.
▷B P Patt, *Pío Baroja* (1971)

BARRÈS, (Auguste) Maurice
(1862–1923)

French novelist and politician, born in Charmes-sur-Moselle. A member of the Chamber of Deputies (1889–93), he was an apostle of nationalism, individualism, provincial patriotism and national energy. He wrote a trilogy on his own self-analysis (*Le Culte du Moi*, 1888–91, 'The Cult of the Self'), and a nationalistic trilogy that included *L'Appel au Soldat* (1906, 'The Call to the Soldier'), and many other works, including *Colette Baudoche* (1909).

▷F Mauriac, *La rencontre avec Barrès* (1945)

BARRETO, Affonso Henriques de Lima
(1881–1922)

Brazilian mulatto novelist who sharply criticized the society of Rio de Janeiro. The most remarkable of his works is *Triste Fim de Policarpo Quaresma* (1915, 'The Sad End of Policarp Quaresma'), the story of a decent army officer, betrayed at every turn by ambitious men. (Barreto worked in the civil service and well understood treachery.) His work is now the subject of much critical enquiry and revaluation.

▷F de A Barbosa, *Vida de Lima Barreto* (1959, in Portuguese)

BARRIE, J M (Sir James Matthew)
(1860–1937)

Scottish novelist and dramatist, born in Kirriemuir, Angus, the son of a weaver. He was educated there and at Dumfries Academy, graduating at Edinburgh University in 1882. After a year and a half as a journalist in Nottingham he settled in London, and became a regular contributor to the *St James's Gazette* and *British Weekly* (as 'Gavin Ogilvy'). He wrote a series of autobiographical prose works, including *A Window in Thrums* (1889) and *The Little Minister* (1891, dramatized 1897), set in his native village disguised as 'Thrums'. From 1890 onwards he wrote for the theatre, works including the successful *Walker, London* (1892), *Quality Street* (1902) and *The Admirable Crichton* (1902), a good-humoured social satire. These established his reputation, but it is as the creator of *Peter Pan* (1904) that he will be chiefly remembered. Aware of the popular demand for dramatic sentimentality on the London stage, Barrie provided surface romance within dramatic structures which used indirect poetic methods to suggest a bleaker vision of life. He continued his excursions into faeryland in such later plays as *Dear Brutus* (1917) and *Mary Rose* (1920), and in his last play, *The Boy David* (1936), tried a biblical theme which, despite containing some of his finest writing, won no laurels in the theatre.

▷J Dunbar, *Barrie: the man behind the image* (1970); Harry Geduld, *J M Barrie* (1971)

BARRIOS, Edourdo
(1884–1963)

Major Chilean novelist and dramatist, born in Valparaíso, of a Chilean father and a Peruvian mother. Barrios, an unstable man (he was an unpopular Minister of Education in the government of the dictator Ibáñez del Campo, but also a weight-lifter, officer cadet, nitrate company accountant, academic and acrobat), was one of the earliest uncompromisingly psychological novelists of South America: his *El niño que enloqueció de amor* (1915, 'The Boy Who Went Mad for Love'), is often cited as the first novel of this kind. His avowed subject was 'the strange case', usually sexual; he was a student of the perverse. *El hermano asno* (1922, Eng trans as *Brother Ass* in *Fiesta in November*, 1942), often taken to be his best novel, is about two friars, one of whom is aware of his sexual urges, while the other is not. His attempt at a major novel, *Gran señor y rajadiablos* (1948, 'Gentleman and Hell Raiser'), set in the 19th century and written in a new, almost picaresque style, has not outlasted its initial popularity. *Los hombres de hombre* (1950, 'The Men of the Man'), seems, since it splits a man up into his component 'personalities', to have been written under the influence of **Gurdjieff** or one of his followers.

▷N J Davison, *Edourdo Barrios* (1970)

BARRY, Philip
(1896–1949)

American dramatist, born in Rochester, New York. While his first professional production, *You and I* (1923), enjoyed some success, he is now remembered for such plays as *The Philadelphia Story* (1939), a bright comedy of manners and a great hit for the actress Katherine Hepburn. *Holiday* (1929), a study of the generation gap, and *The Animal Kingdom* (1932), which transposes the conventional roles of a wife and mistress by making the latter the 'true love' and therefore more 'deserving', are much sharper satire but still, at heart, affectionate comedies. His genuinely more serious work, including the psychological dramas, *Hotel Universe* (1930) and *Here Come the Clowns* (1938), were not as successful.

BARSTOW, Stan(ley)
(1928–)

English novelist, born in Yorkshire. The mining communities of his youth provided much material for his fiction, which is firmly based in the entanglements and difficulties of everyday experience. He achieved a major success with his first novel, *A Kind of Loving* (1960), which later grew into a trilogy about its working-class protagonist Vic Brown, with *The Watchers on the Shore* (1966) and *The Right True End* (1976). *Joby* (1964) is a delicate evocation of childhood trauma; other novels include *A Raging Calm* (1968), *Just You Wait and See* (1986), *Give Us This Day* (1989) and *Next of Kin* (1991). He has also written short novels, stories, and plays for theatre, radio and television.

BARTAS, Guillaume de Salluste du
(1544–90)

French soldier, diplomat and poet, born in Montfort in Armagnac. A Huguenot, he fought in the religious wars, went on missions to the English court, and died of wounds received at the battle of Ivry. His chief poem, *La semaine* (1578, 'The Week'), gives an account of the creation, and is said to have influenced **Milton**'s *Paradise Lost*. He also wrote a biblical epic, *Judith* (1574), and an unfinished history from the birth of Christ, *La seconde semaine* ('The Second Week').
▷G Pelissie, *La vie et les oeuvres de Bartas* (1883)

BARTH, John Simmons
(1930–)

American novelist and short-story writer, born in Cambridge, Maryland. Educated at Johns Hopkins, he was a professional drummer before turning to literature and teaching. His earliest novels—*The Floating Opera* (1956), *End of the Road* (1958), *The Sot-Weed Factor* (1960) and *Giles Goat-Boy* (1966)—combined realism, formidable learning and fantastic humour in an attempt to make 'a transcension of the antithesis between the modern and the pre-modern which would revitalise fiction'. His later novels, *Letters* (1979), *Sabbatical* (1982), *Tidewater Tales* (1988) and *The Seventh Voyage of Sinbad the Sailor* (1991), are prolix and less assured.
▷C B Harris, *Passionate Virtuosity: the fiction of Barth* (1983)

BARTHELME, Donald
(1931–89)

American novelist and short-story writer, born in Philadelphia, Pennsylvania, the son of a Professor of Architecture, and brother of **Frederick Barthelme**. He worked as a journalist and magazine editor before turning to fiction. An experimentalist who rejected the traditions of the conventional novel form and was inventive in his use of language, he was associated with the mid-1960s avant-garde. The short stories in *Come Back, Dr Caligari* (1964) and *Unspeakable Practices, Unnatural Acts* (1968) are regarded as his most characteristic work; other collections include *City Life* (1970) and *Sadness* (1972) and are marked by the broader humour of the novels *Snow White* (1967) and *The Dead Father* (1975). He won the National Book Award in 1972.
▷M Couturier and R Durand, *Barthelme* (1982)

BARTHELME, Frederick
(1943–)

American novelist and short-story writer, he is the younger brother of **Donald Barthelme**.

His career has been slightly staccato. A brief stint in the 'family trade' of architecture interrupted his academic progress. His early fiction, the short-story collection *Rangoon* (1970) and the novel *War and War* (1971), were mannered and self-consciously experimental. Barthelme spent most of the seventies in advertising before re-emerging as a fiction writer with another story collection *Moon Deluxe* (1983) whose bald, uninflected prose offered a bleakly funny portrayal of the upper middle-class in America. *Second Marriage* (1984) and *Natural Selection* (1990) cover the same territory at greater length but, like his brother, Barthelme is less satisfying when he makes the jump to a full-scale novel.

BARTON, Bernard
(1784–1849)

English Quaker poet, born in Carlisle. A bank clerk in Woodbridge in Suffolk throughout his life, he was a friend of **Charles Lamb**, and his *Metrical Effusions* (1812) interested **Robert Southey**. His *Poems* (1820) include devotional lyrics in the style of **George Herbert**. A biography of him was written by **Edward Fitzgerald**, who married his daughter.
▷E V Lucas, *Bernard Barton and his Friends* (1983)

BASHO, pseud of Matsuo Munefusa
(1644–94)

Japanese poet, he took his pen-name from the banana tree, after settling down in his hermitage near Tokyo; he was born further west, near Kyoto. He was responsible for turning the 17-syllable *haiku* from a light-hearted diversion into a serious art form. He improvised long stanzaic sequences (*renga* or *renku*), modulating the mood and prosody of this most restrictive of forms with apparently intuitive brilliance. After being apprenticed to a *samurai*, he led a wandering life, partly documented in *Oku no hosomichi* ('The Narrow Road to the Deep North', Eng trans *Noboyuki Yuasa*, 1966). As well as formal elegance, Basho's verse has a modern and almost existential quality, which guaranteed him a receptive audience when his *haiku* appeared in R H Blyth's English translation (1949–52), though he had already made an impact on **Ezra Pound** and the Imagists.
▷M Ueda, *Basho* (1970)

BASILE, Giambattista, pseud of Gian Alesion Abbattutis
(1575–1632)

Italian soldier and writer, born in Naples. He is now remembered for the *Pentamerone* (1637), a collection of 50 extravagant fairy tales written in Neapolitan dialect, which were edited by Felix Liebrecht and translated by Sir **Richard Burton** (1893).

BASIR, Vaikkam
(1910–)

Indian (Malayalam) comic novelist, a Muslim with great resources and well educated in Hindu customs. He wrote *Nruppuppak-koranentannu!* (1951, 'Me Grandad 'ad an Elephant'), a tender love-story not actually featuring an elephant but haunted by the spirit of Ganesha, the elephant-headed son of Siva the Destroyer. A maddened elephant *does* figure in the pages of *A Bhagavadgita and Some Breasts* (1967). Basir is a learned, subtle and unique writer, much admired by his only living rival, **Takazi**.

BASSANI, Giorgio
(1916–)

Italian novelist and poet, born in Bologna, the son of a physician. He lived until 1943 in Ferrara, where much of his fiction is set. *Cinque storie ferraresi* ('Five Stories of Ferrara') appeared in 1956, most of them composed in the aftermath of World War II. A sensitive chronicler of Italian Jews and their suffering under fascism, he is a realist who writes elegiacally. One of the outstanding Italian novelists of the 20th century, he is at his most exquisite in *Gli Occhial d'Oro* (1960, 'The Gold-Rimmed Spectacles') and *Il Giardino dei Finnzi-Contini* (1965, 'The Garden of the Finzi-Continis').
▷G Varanini, *Bassani* (1970)

BASSO, Hamilton
(1904–64)

American novelist, born in New Orleans, most of whose books are set in the South. Outstanding amongst his novels is *The View from Pompey's Head* (1954), about a New York attorney from the South who is called back to his native town by a case, and reappraises his past. *Sun in Capricorn* (1942) was suggested by the career of the crypto-fascist governor of Louisiana, Huey Long.

BASTOS, Augustos Roa *see* ROA BASTOS, Augustos

BATAILLE, Félix Henry
(1872–1922)

French poet and dramatist, born in Nîmes. The predominant theme in his melodramatic plays is inner conflict, and especially sexual or erotic conflict, as in *Maman Colibri* (1904, 'Mother Colibri'), which enjoyed some notoriety at the time, and *La Marche nuptiale* (1905, 'The Wedding March'). A number of his works focused on well-known social scandals involving eminent figures of the day, including the composer Debussy.
▷G de Catalogne, *Henry Bataille ou le romantisme de l'instinct* (1925)

BATES, H(erbert) E(rnest)
(1905–74)

English novelist, playwright, and short-story writer, born in Rushden, Northamptonshire. He began his working life as a solicitor's clerk, provincial journalist and warehouse clerk. His first play, *The Last Bread*, and his first novel, *The Two Sisters*, appeared in 1926. In his early days he benefited from the advice of **Edward Garnett** and was later influenced by **Stephen Crane**. He is one of the greatest exponents of the short-story form. His essay in literary criticism, *The Modern Short Story*, is regarded as a classic. His best-known works are *Fair Stood the Wind for France* (1944), *The Jacaranda Tree* (1949) and *The Darling Buds of May* (1958).
▷*An Autobiography* (1969–72)

BATES, Ralph
(1899–)

English novelist, born in Swindon, who later worked at the railway factory there. Politically alert, he left for Spain in 1930, and fought with the Republican International Brigade during the Civil War. His first novel, *Sierra*, set in Spain, appeared in 1933. His finest novels, *Lean Man* and *The Olive Field*, were published in 1934 and 1936. In the first, the Englishman Francis Charing debates the morality of his 'necessary murder' of an anarchist, while the second is set during the uprising of Asturian miners. Both novels see revolutionary struggle as inevitable in the modern world. In 1937 Bates left for the USA and became Professor of English Literature at New York University. He also published a biography of Franz Schubert (1934).

BATYUSHKOV, Konstantin Nikolaievitch
(1787–1855)

Russian poet, born in Vologda. He served in the Napoleonic wars, but became insane in 1821 and was confined in an asylum for the remaining 34 years of his life. Profoundly influenced by French and Italian writers, his work was much admired by **Alexander Pushkin**. His most important work was *Ymerayushi Tass* ('The Death of Tasso').
▷I Serman, *Konstantin Batyushkov* (1974)

BAUDELAIRE, Charles Pierre
(1821–67)

French Symbolist poet, born in Paris. After an unhappy childhood quarrelling with his soldier-diplomat stepfather, Colonel Aupick,

he was sent off on a voyage to India. He stopped off at Mauritius, where Jeanne Duval, a half-caste, became his mistress and inspiration. On his return to Paris in 1843 he spent much of his time in the studios of Delacroix and Daumier, and wrote art criticisms in *Le Salon de 1845* and *Le Salon de 1846*. In 1847 he published an autobiographical novel, *La Fanfarlo*. By nature aristocratic and Catholic, he sided with the revolutionaries in 1848. His masterpiece is a collection of poems, *Les Fleurs du mal* (1857, Eng trans *Flowers of Evil*, 1909), for which author, printer, and publisher were prosecuted for impropriety in 1864, but which earned the praise of critics and was to exert an influence far into the 20th century. Later works include *Les Paradis artificiels* (1860, 'Artificial Paradises') and *Petits Poèmes en prose* (1869, 'Little Poems in Prose'). He was greatly attracted by **Thomas De Quincey** and **Edgar Allan Poe**, whose works he translated (1856–65). His Satanism, his preoccupation with the macabre, the perverted, and the horrid, and with previously proscribed areas of human experience of perversity, were essential features of his work. Having written a critical work on his literary associates **Honoré de Balzac**, **Théophile Gautier**, and **Gérard de Nerval**, published posthumously in 1880, he took to drink and opium, and was struck down with paralysis. He died in poverty.
▷H Peyre, *Connaissance de Baudelaire* (1951); E Starkie, *Baudelaire* (1957)

BAUGHAN, Blanche Edith
(1870–1958)

English-born New Zealand poet, born in London, where she had published *Verses* in 1898. Her first New Zealand work appeared in *Reuben* (1903) but she considered *Shingle-Short* (1908) to contain her first true local verse; it was followed by *Poems from the Port Hills* (1923). In a collection of short stories, *Brown Bread from a Colonial Oven*, she describes herself as chronicler of 'a phase of New Zealand life that is already passing . . .'.

BAUM, L(yman) Frank
(1856–1919)

American juvenile author, most famous for the perennially popular *The Wonderful Wizard of Oz*, which was first successful in its dramatized form (1901). Although without much strictly literary merit, this book remains a classic because of its appealing plot. It has been most famous in its movie version, starring the young Judy Garland.

BAUM, Vicki, originally Hedvig
(1888–1960)

Austrian-born American novelist, born in Vienna. After writing several novels and short

stories in German, she made her name with *Grand Hotel* (1930), which became a bestseller and a popular film. She emigrated to the USA in 1931, where her later novels incuded *Falling Star* (1934), *Headless Angel* (1948) and *The Mustard Seed* (1953).

BAUMBACH, Jonathan
(1933–)

American novelist and short-story writer, born and educated in New York City. He set the terms for his innovative fiction with an important critical work, *The Landscape of Nightmare* (1965), in which he argued that the methods of realism are insufficient to grasp contemporary reality. The protagonist of his first novel, *A Man to Conjure With* (1965), moves freely in time and becomes known in discrete, almost dream-like images which are closer to collage technique than to conventional narrative. Baumbach's conviction that character psychology cannot be conveyed in logical sequential prose is also asserted in the ironically titled *What Comes Next* (1968), while in *Reruns* (1974), his best book, he turns to the imagistic abstractions of experimental cinema and abandons narrative altogether, although only temporarily, for later books return to a more approachable, tale-spinning approach. *Babble* (1976) is a collection of stories told by the author's baby son, while in *Chez Charlotte and Emily* (1979), he transcribes husband/wife dialogues. In the eighties Baumbach turned increasingly to short fiction; 'From the Life of the President' (1982, *Seattle Review*) and 'Children of Divorced Parents' (1983, *Fiction International*) are perhaps the best.
▷J Klinkowitz, *The Life of Fiction* (1977)

BAWDEN, Nina
(1925–)

English novelist for adults and young people, born in London. Many of her adult novels delve into the domestic and emotional turbulence of the middle-classes: their friendships, marriages, divorces and the resulting expanding and contracting families. *Anna Apparent* (1972) is a study of an illegitimate child evacuee, spanning from the London blitz to her life 'as a wife and mistress, while the middle-aged narrator of *Afternoon of a Good Woman* (1976) reflects on a life of disappointment and emotional betrayal before turning to face her future with renewed resilience. *The Ice House* (1983) casts a discriminating eye on a thirty-year female friendship, with all its confidences and rivalries. The implication in her adult work that the feelings and thoughts of children are too often overlooked becomes a dominant note in her novels for younger readers. In *Carrie's*

War (1973), Carrie's response to being evacuated to Wales during World War II is sharply and sympathetically observed.

BAX, Clifford
(1886–1962)

English playwright, born in London and educated at the Slade School of Art, Heatherly Art School and in Munich. He was editor of the verse journal *Orpheus Quarterly* from 1909 to 1914. His plays are generally light entertainment; first performed was *The Poetasters of Ispahan* (1912) followed by over 50 more before *Circe* (1949). Bax shows a taste for historical settings: *Socrates* (1930) shows its pre-hemlock hero in breezy and brilliant mood; *The Rose without a Thorn* (1931) attempts to depict Henry VIII's court, and *The Immortal Lady* is set in London in the year 1716. His slangy upper-class dialogue, however, has the effect of trivializing history, and his originally popular work leaves little of lasting value.

BAXTER, James Keir
(1926–72)

New Zealand poet, dramatist and critic, born in Dunedin. He worked as a labourer, journalist and teacher and led a bohemian life until he was converted to Roman Catholicism. Subsequently he founded a religious community on the Wanganui River. He published more than 30 books of poetry, his first volume, *Beyond the Palisade* (1944), appearing when he was 18. The poems he wrote before his conversion are collected in *In Fires of No Return* (1958). Latterly he was less productive but his appointment to the Burns Fellowship at the University of Otago in 1966 inspired him, and *Howrah Bridge and Other Poems* (1961) and *Autumn Testament* (1972) are among his best work. His *Collected Poems* (1979) was edited by J E Weir who, since Baxter's death, has brought together editions of previously unpublished verse. His plays include *The Band Rotunda* (1967), *The Sore-Footed Man* (1967) and *The Temptation of Oedipus* (1967).
▷ J E Weir, *The Poetry of James Keir Baxter* (1970)

BAYBARS, Taner
(1936–)

Turkish Cypriot poet, resident in the UK, having previously served in the Royal Air Force. After a career in book production, since 1983 he has worked for the British Council. His first English-language collection, *To Catch a Falling Man* (1963), consists of brief, autobiographical images captured in vivid language that infuses them with a mysterious and sometimes sinister quality.

Susila in the Autumn Woods (1974) and *Narcissus in a Dry Pool* (1978) are progressively more complex in vision and rhetorical in approach, and are most successful when exploring his young daughter Susila's developing awareness of her surroundings. Baybars has also written a novel, *A Trap for the Burglar* (1965), and has translated three volumes of poetry from the Turkish of Nazim Hikmet.
▷ *Plucked in a Far-Off Land: Images in Self Biography* (1970)

BAYLEBRIDGE, William
(1883–1942)

Australian poet and writer, born in Brisbane, whose thoughts of mankind as a culmination of a Nietzschean life-force led him close to a totalitarian philosophy. He published his early verse privately in a series of booklets including *Songs o' the South* (1908) and *Moreton Miles* (1910), love poems set around his birthplace. The best of his early verse was collected as *Selected Poems* (1919); he later wrote a series of sonnets, *Love Redeemed* (1934). In his major work, *This Vital Flesh* (1939, Memorial Edition 1961), he attempted to establish the foundations of Australian nationalism. He travelled in Europe and the Middle East from 1908, returning to Australia after World War I, during which he is supposed to have worked for Allied Intelligence; he later published *An ANZAC Muster* (1921), essays and stories on the Gallipoli campaign. In memory of a close relative he established the Grace Leven Prize for Poetry.

BAYNTON, Barbara Janet Ainsleigh
(1857–1929)

Australian writer and socialite, born in Scone, New South Wales. Her father was a carpenter of Irish stock, and Baynton afterwards fantasized about her origins. While working as a governess she married a son of the house who later left her for one of her servants. She then married a 70-year-old retired surgeon, Thomas Baynton, and entered a life of leisure and culture. She began to write stories for the popular periodical *The Bulletin* and became a close friend of its editor A G Stephens. In search of a publisher for her stories, she visited London in 1902 and was befriended by Edward Garnett. When Baynton died in 1904, leaving her wealthy, she returned to London, made profitable investments on the stock exchange, and lived in a series of increasingly grand houses surrounded by choice antiques. She travelled frequently between England and Australia, and in 1921 married the fifth Lord Headley, from whom she soon separated. She wrote one novel, *Human Toll* (1907), and a number of short stories first collected in *Bush Studies*

(1902) and, with two more stories, as *Cobbers* (1917). In all her writing the grime and squalor of the real bush, as seen and endured by women and the underprivileged, contrasts hugely with the romanticized male 'mateship' of **Henry Lawson** and his followers.

BAZAN, Emilia Pardo *see* PARDO BAZAN, Emilia

BAZHAN, Mykola
(1904–)

Ukrainian poet, born in Kamenets-Podolski. His incisive, dramatic and strident early work was written under the influence of Futurism and of **Mayakovsky**; subjected to official criticism, he became an avowed socialist realist, and his poetry lost force.

BAZIN, René
(1853–1932)

French novelist, born in Angers. He depicted with charm and colour the life of peasant folk in the various French provinces, and in some of his novels, such as *Les Oberlé* (1901, 'The Oberlé Family'), dealt with the social problems of his time.
▷ G Duhamelet, *René Bazin, romancier catholique* (1935)

BEAGLE, Peter S(oyer)
(1939–)

American writer of fantasy fiction, born in New York City but quintessentially Californian in outlook. His best-known book is *The Last Unicorn* (1968), a love-generation fable whose overtones of **T S Eliot**'s *The Waste Land* pick up on ideas of rebirth and regeneration first explored in his underrated debut novel, *A Fine and Private Place* (1960). His second book, *I See By My Outfit* (1965), is a mild, search-for-America chronicle, reminiscent of Beat writing. Beagle has also written a notably sunny travel book, *The California Feeling* (1969), and an equally untroubled study of Hieronymus Bosch, *The Garden of Earthly Delights* (1982).
▷ R Olderman, *Beyond the Waste Land* (1977)

BEAN, Charles Edwin Woodrow
(1879–1968)

Australian journalist and war historian, born in Bathurst, New South Wales and educated at Oxford University. He was London correspondent for the *Sydney Morning Herald* and became official correspondent to the Australian Imperial Forces. Landing at Gallipoli in 1915, Bean was wounded in that campaign but stayed at the front throughout. He then accompanied the troops to France where he served until the end of the war. On being

appointed Australia's Official War Historian, Bean returned to Gallipoli in 1919 to research the campaign. He wrote a number of books including *On the Wool Track* (1910), the standard account of Australia's earlier dependence on sheep, and *Flagships Three* (1913). His memorial is the 12-volume *Official History of Australia in the War of 1914–18* (1921– 42), in which Bean takes much credit for the creation of the ANZAC legend. He wrote six of the 12 volumes and edited the others, and in 1946 published his own single-volume abridgement, *Anzac to Amiens*.
▷ K Fewster, *The Frontline Diary of C. E. W. Bean* (1983); D McCarthy, *Gallipoli to the Somme* (1983)

BEATTIE, Ann
(1947–)

American novelist, born in Washington DC, and educated at American University and the University of Connecticut. She has worked as a visiting lecturer at the University of Virginia and at Harvard University. She received a Guggenheim Fellowship in 1977 and has several novels and collections of short stories to her name, most of which focus on disaffected families or individuals. Both comic and detached, her work presents the theme of contemporary alienation in a minimalist manner. Her novel, *Picturing Will* (1990), uses photographic imagery to examine the issues her earlier novels and short stories explored through language.

BEATTIE, James
(1735–1803)

Scottish poet and essayist, born in Laurencekirk, Kincardineshire, the son of a shopkeeper. He was educated at the village school and at Marischal College, Aberdeen, and after some years as a schoolmaster in Fordoun he became a master at Aberdeen Grammar School, and then in 1760 became Professor of Moral Philosophy at Aberdeen. His overrated *Essay on Truth* (1770) attacked the philosopher David Hume, but he is chiefly remembered for his long poem, *The Minstrel* (1771–4), a forerunner of Romanticism.
▷ M Forbes, *Beattie and His Friends* (1964)

BEAUMARCHAIS, Pierre Augustin Caron de
(1732–99)

French playwright, the greatest French comic dramatist, born in Paris, the son of a watchmaker named Caron. Brought up in his father's trade, he invented, at 21, a new escapement which was pirated by a rival. The affair brought him to notice at court, where his good looks and fine speech and manners quickly procured him advancement. He was engaged to teach the harp to Louis XV's daughters, and in 1756 he married the wealthy widow of a court official, and assumed his title. Profitable speculation with Duverney, a rich Parisan banker, and another prudent marriage with a wealthy widow in 1768, increased his fortune. His first plays, *Eugénie* (1767, Eng trans *The School for Rakes*, 1769) and *Les Deux Amis* (1770, Eng trans *The Two Friends*, 1800), scored only a moderate success. The death of Duverney in 1770 involved him in a long lawsuit with his heir, Count Lablache, in the course of which he became the idol of the people, as the supposed champion of popular rights against the corrupt tribunals of the old regime. Beaumarchais appealed to the public by publishing his famous *Mémoires du Sieur Beaumarchais par lui-même* (1774–8, 'Autobiography'), a work which united the bitterest satire with the sharpest logic, and made his reputation. The same brilliant satire burns in his two famous comedies, *Le Barbier de Séville* (1775, Eng trans *The Barber of Seville*, 1776) and *La Folle Journée ou le mariage de Figaro* (1784, Eng trans *The Follies of a Day; or, The Marriage of Figaro*, 1785). The latter had a most unprecedented success; and both are still popular plays in France, but in Britain are chiefly known through Mozart's and Rossini's operatic adaptations. The Revolution cost Beaumarchais his vast fortune, and, suspected of an attempt to sell arms to the *émigrés*, he had to take refuge in Holland and England (1793).

▷ R Pomeau, *Beaumarchais, l'homme et l'oeuvre* (1956)

BEAUMONT, Francis
(c.1584–1616)

English Elizabethan dramatist, born in Gracedieu, Leicestershire, the third son of a judge, and brother of Sir **John Beaumont**. He was educated at Broadgates Hall (now Pembroke College), Oxford, and entered the Inner Temple in 1600. He soon became a friend of **Ben Jonson** and the other men of genius who met at the Mermaid Tavern, among them **John Fletcher**. With the latter, Beaumont was to be associated closely until he married Ursula Isley (1613) and retired from the theatre. They are said to have shared everything: work, lodgings, and even clothes. Their dramatic works, compiled in 1647, contained 35 pieces; another folio, published in 1679, 52 works. Modern research finds Beaumont's hand in only about 10 plays, which include, however, the masterpieces. Fletcher's verse avoids enjambment, rhyme and prose while Beaumont uses all three devices. *The Woman Hater* (1607) is attributed solely to Beaumont, and he had the major share in *The*

Knight of the Burning Pestle (1609), a burlesque of knight errantry and a parody of **John Heywood**'s *Four Prentices of London. Philaster, The Maid's Tragedy* and *A King and no King* established their joint popularity. Other works include *The Scornful Lady* and *Cupid's Revenge. The Masque of the Inner Temple* was written by Beaumont in honour of the marriage of the Elector Palatinate Frederick V and the princess Elizabeth (1613). He was buried in Westminster Abbey.

▷ W W Appleton, *Beaumont and Fletcher: a critical study* (1956)

BEAUMONT, Sir John
(1582–1627)

English poet, elder brother of **Francis Beaumont**. His best-known work is *Bosworth Field*, in which the heroic couplet makes its first appearance in English poetry.

▷ A Chalmers, in *The Works of Early English Poets* (1910)

BEAUMONT, Joseph
(1616–99)

English poet, born in Hadleigh, Suffolk. From 1663 he was master of Peterhouse, Cambridge. He wrote the long epic poem *Psyche* (1648).

▷ R Wrench, *A Biographical and Critical Sketch* (1859)

BEAVER, Bruce
(1928–)

Australian poet, born in Manly, New South Wales. His first collection, entitled *Under the Bridge* (1961), was followed by six more, the most significant of which was *Letters to Live Poets* (1969). In *Lauds and Plaints* (1974) he turned from semi-autobiographical subjects to a more outward vision. *Selected Poems* appeared in 1979, as did his return to personal themes in *As It Was*, an extended prose-poem. He received the **Patrick White** Literary Award in 1982.

BECK, Béatrix
(1914–)

Belgian (Francophone) novelist, born in Switzerland, herself daughter of a novelist, Christian Beck. She was for a time secretary to **André Gide**. In her novel *Barny* (1948) she introduces her perennial character who sees everything through the eyes of her insane mother. *Léon Morin, Prêtre* (1952, Eng trans *The Priest*, 1953), her most celebrated novel, deals in an acute manner with the theme of the 'leftist' priest. An unusual writer, Beck belongs essentially to the Catholic tradition in French literature—she has hardly had her due outside French-speaking countries.

▷H J G Godin, *The Creative Process in French Literature* (1974)

BECKE, Louis (George Lewis)
(1855–1913)

Australian writer of adventure fiction. Becke's early years under sail in the Pacific form the background for over 30 collections of 'yarns' in the style of **Melville**, whom he admired, and of **Conrad**, who admired Becke. *By Reef and Palm* (1894) set the pattern for those that followed, such as *His Native Wife* (1895), *The Ebbing of the Tide* (1896) and *Pacific Tales* (1897). Many of the stories rework popular themes of mixed love, mutiny and the degenerate white settler. Although Becke soon began to write to a pattern, all his tales show somebody who spoke from his hard-gained experience.

BECKER, Nikolaus
(1809–45)

German poet. He wrote the *Rheinlied* ('Rhine Song') ('Sie sollen ihn nicht haben', 'You shall not have it') in 1840, which prompted **Alfred de Musset**'s answer ('Nous l'avons eu, votre Rhin allemand', 'We have taken it, your German Rhine').
▷L Waeles, *Nikolaus Becker 'der Dichter des Rheinliedes'* (1896)

BECKETT, Samuel Barclay
(1906–89)

Irish author and playwright, winner of the Nobel Prize for literature, born in Dublin. He became a lecturer in English at the École Normale Supérieure in Paris and later in French at Trinity College, Dublin. From 1932 he lived mostly in France and was, for a time, secretary to **James Joyce**, with whom he shared the same tantalizing preoccupation with language, with the failure of human beings to communicate successfully mirroring the pointlessness of life which they strive to make purposeful. His early poetry and first two novels, *Murphy* (1938) and *Watt* (1953), were written in English, but not the trilogy *Molloy*, *Malone Meurt* and *L'Innommable* (translated in 1955, 1956 and 1958), or the plays *En attendant Godot* (1953, Eng trans *Waiting for Godot*, 1956), which took London by storm, and *Fin de partie* (1957, Eng trans *End Game*, 1958), all of which first appeared in French. *Godot* best exemplifies the Beckettian view of the human predicament, the poignant bankruptcy of all hopes, philosophies, and endeavours. His later works include *Happy Days* (1961), *Not I* (1973) and *Ill Seen Ill Said* (1981). He was awarded the 1969 Nobel Prize for literature. Although there were one or two increasingly short pieces in later years—*Breath* (1970) shows a heap of rubbish on the stage and has a soundtrack which consists of a single breath—he wrote very infrequently towards the end.
▷R Hayman, *Samuel Beckett* (1968); A Alvarez, *Beckett* (1973); Deirdrie Bair, *Samuel Beckett: A Biography* (1978)

BECKFORD, William Thomas
(1759–1844)

English writer and art collector, son of William Beckford, born in Fonthill, Wiltshire. In 1770 he inherited his father's fortune. As a young man of 16 he revealed remarkable intellectual precocity in his satirical *Memoirs of Extraordinary Painters*. From 1777 he spent much time on the Continent, meeting **Voltaire** in 1778, and later making a grand tour in Flanders, Germany, and Italy. In 1784 he entered parliament, but he became involved in a scandal and was excluded from society. He wrote, in French, *Vathek*, an Arabian tale of gloomy imaginative splendour modelled on Voltaire's style, which was published in France in 1787 and in an unauthorized English version in 1786. Revisiting Portugal in 1793, he settled in that 'paradise' near Cintra which **Byron** commemorates in *Childe Harold*. He returned to England in 1796, and proceeded to erect a new palace, Fonthill Abbey, designed by James Wyatt. Its chief feature was a tower, which fell in 1800, but was rebuilt (276 feet high). He lived there in mysterious seclusion until 1822, when he sold Fonthill Abbey, moved to Bath, and there built Lansdown Tower. In 1834 he published *Italy, with Sketches of Spain and Portugal* (incorporating, in modified form, *Dreams, Waking Thoughts*, and *Incident*, suppressed in 1783), and in 1835 another volume of *Recollections* of travel.
▷G Chapman, *Beckford* (1952)

BECKMANN, Gunnel
(1910–)

Swedish writer for children and teenagers, born in Falköping and educated at the University of Göteborg. For her first children's books, considered conventional and too idyllic by critics, she drew inspiration from her own large family. She came to notice with a novel for teenagers, *Tillträde till festen* (1969, *Nineteen is too young to die*, 1971), about a young girl who thinks she is going to die of leukemia. In subsequent novels she further develops the theme of women's growth towards awareness and independence. *Tre veckor över tiden* (1973, 'Three Weeks Late'), becomes a literary platform for the topical discussion of early pregnancy and abortion. In dealing with the generation gap, she manages to portray each generation sympathetically, as achieved in *Att trösta Fanny* (1981, 'Comforting Fanny'), where a shift of perspective is used and a young girl's problems with her divorced parents are reflected through the eyes of her grandmother.

BECQUE, Henry
(1837–99)

French dramatist, born in Paris. He is known for two naturalistic plays, *Les Corbeaux* (1882, 'The Crows') and *La Parisienne* (1885), both dramatic portrayals of bourgeois life and character.
▷L B Hyslop, *Henry Becque* (1972)

BÉCQUER, Gustavo Adolfo
(1836–70)

Spanish romance writer and lyric poet, born in Seville. His *Legends* are written in a weirdly musical prose, but he is best known for his troubadour love verses, although his poems in *Rimas* (1871) have been seen as crucial precursors of modern Spanish poetry.
▷R Benitez, *Bécquer, traditionalista* (1971)

BEDDOES, Thomas Lovell
(1803–49)

English poet and physiologist, born in Clifton (Bristol), eldest son of Thomas Beddoes (1760–1808). He was educated at Charterhouse and Oxford. In 1822 he published *The Bride's Tragedy*, a sombre murder drama. In 1825 he went to Göttingen to study medicine, and then led a strange wandering life as doctor and democrat, in Germany and Switzerland, with occasional visits to England. From 1825 he was engaged in the composition of a Gothic–Romantic drama in blank verse, *Death's Jest-book*, which appeared in 1850, a year after his suicide.
▷*The Letters of Thomas Lovell Beddoes* (1894); H W Donner, *Thomas Lovell Beddoes: the making of a poet* (1935)

BEDE, the Venerable, St
(c.673–735)

Anglo-Saxon scholar, theologian and historian, born near Monkwearmonth, Durham. At the age of seven he was placed in the care of Benedict Biscop at the monastery of Wearmouth, and in 682 moved to the new monastery of Jarrow in Northumberland, where he was ordained priest in 703 and remained a monk for the rest of his life, studying and teaching. His devotion to church discipline was exemplary and his industry enormous. Besides Latin and Greek, classical as well as patristic, literature, he studied Hebrew, medicine, astronomy and prosody. He wrote homilies, biographies of saints, biographies of abbots (*Historia abbatum*), hymns, epigrams, works on chronology (*De Temporum Ratione*, prompted by the debate over the date of Easter, and *De sex Aetatibus Mundi*, 'On the Six Ages of the World'), grammar and physical science (*De natura rerum*, 'On the Nature of the Universe'), and commentaries on the Old and New Testaments; and he translated the Gospel of St John into Anglo-Saxon just before his death. His greatest work was his Latin *Historia Ecclesiastica Gentis Anglorum* ('Ecclesiastical History of the English People'), which he finished in 731, and is the single most valuable source for early English history. It was later translated into Anglo-Saxon by, or under, King **Alfred**. He was canonized in 1899; his Feast day is 27 May.
▷P H Blair, *The World of Bede* (1970)

BEDFORD, (George) Randolph
(1868–1941)

Australian journalist, writer and politician, born in Camperdown, Sydney, who worked on newspapers in various towns and then in 1897, with **Norman Lindsay** established a literary and mining journal *The Clarion* through which he entered the literary circle of **Louis Esson**. He became wealthy through speculation in mining ventures, went to Europe in 1901 and, in London, published two partly autobiographical novels, *True Eyes and the Whirlwind* (1903) and *The Snare of Strength* (1905). He was a strong 'White Australia' advocate and made many unsuccessful attempts to enter politics from 1897 before being nominated to the Queensland Legislative Council in 1917; from then until 1941 he held a position in one or other of the state chambers. A character much larger than life, called 'The Man in the Big Hat', for the slouch hat which invariably covered his baldness, he had meanwhile continued to write novels including *Billy Pagan, Mining Engineer* (1911) and *The Silver Star* (1917), short stories, verse and descriptive books such as *Explorations in Civilization* (1914) on his travels in Italy.
▷*Naught to Thirty-Three* (1944, posthumous)

BEDFORD, Ruth Marjory
(1882–1963)

Australian writer, born in Petersham, Sydney. In collaboration with **Dorothea Mackellar** she wrote two novels, *The Little Blue Devil* (1912) and *Two's Company* (1914). She also produced collections of verse for children as well as stage and radio plays. *Who's Who in Verse* appeared in 1948 and, in 1952, *Think of Stephen: A Family Chronicle*, an affectionate portrait of family life in the mid-Victorian Sydney household of a past Chief Justice.

BEDFORD, Sybille, née **von Schoenebeck** (1911–)

German-born British novelist, biographer, journalist and travel writer, born in Charlottenburg, Brandenburg, now part of Berlin; by the mid-1920s she had settled in London. Her biography of **Aldous Huxley** (1973–4) is both scholarly and vivid. As a journalist, she has written penetratingly on the Auschwitz trial at Frankfurt, the *Lady Chatterley's Lover* trial and that of John Bodkin Adams, an Eastbourne doctor tried (but acquitted) of poisoning one of his patients. Several of her novels take up the themes of political and emotional family inheritance. Some are based upon her own experiences, such as *A Legacy* (1956), a study and satirical portrait of the wealthy middle-class of pre-World War 1 Germany. Echoes of her own family sound again in *Jigsaw: An Unsentimental Education*, a 'biographical novel' published in 1989.

BEER, Johann
(1655–1700)

Austrian-born German novelist and composer of music, born in St Georgen. He emigrated, with his Lutheran parents, to Regensburg. After giving up theology in order to become the court musician at Weissenfels he began to publish, under various pseudonyms (as was the fashion at that time), such as 'Jan Rebhu', a series of novels—there were 20 in all. He was a rich character, whose not very literary fiction has continued to offend certain critics, until the present, for its 'obscenity'—they were so lively that many believe he was second only to **Grimmelshausen**, to whose fictional character Simplicissimus he attributed some of his own stories. His authorship of them all was not established until 1932.
▷R Alewyn, *Johann Beer* (1932)

BEER, Patricia
(1924–)

English poet, born in Exmouth, Devon. Her work is characterized by an unhurried, West Country address and brilliantly intuitive matching of form to substance that is closer to **Thomas Hardy** than to her avowed most important influence, **W B Yeats**. Her first collections, *The Loss of the Magyar and Other Poems* (1959), *The Survivors* (1963) and *Just Like the Resurrection* (1967), were brisk and assured but lacked the personal focus of later work, a change Beer attributes to writing her autobiography, aged just over 40. *The Estuary* (1971) and *Driving West* (1975) were closer to the existential mode of the American 'confessional' poets, but **Ted Hughes**'s mythic self-plumbing was probably the most direct influence. *Selected Poems* appeared in 1980,

and was followed by a further imaginative reorganization which resulted in her finest book to date, *The Lie of the Land* (1983). Beer has also published an introduction to the Metaphysical poets (1972) and the deeply felt *Reader, I Married Him* (1974).
▷*Mrs Beer's House* (1968)

BEERBOHM, Sir (Henry) Max(imilian)
(1872–1956)

Known as 'the Incomparable Max', English writer and caricaturist, born in London, the son of a Lithuanian corn merchant, and half-brother of Sir Herbert Beerbohm Tree. He was educated at Charterhouse and Merton College, Oxford. He published his first volume of essays under the ironic title *The Works of Max Beerbohm* (1896), some of which had appeared in the *Yellow Book*. He succeeded **George Bernard Shaw** as drama critic of *The Saturday Review*, until 1910, when he married an American actress, Florence Kahn (d.1951), and went to live, except during the two World Wars, in Rapallo, Italy. His delicate, unerring, aptly-captioned caricatures were collected in various volumes beginning with *Twenty-five Gentlemen* (1896) and *Poet's Corner* (1904). Further volumes of parodying essays appeared, including *The Happy Hypocrite* (1897) and *A Christmas Garland* (1912), full of gentle humour, elegance, and rare wit, and ending with *And Even Now* (1920). His best-known work was his only novel, *Zuleika Dobson* (1912), an ironic romance of Oxford undergraduate life. His broadcast talks from 1935 were another of his singularly brilliant stylistic accomplishments. A month before his death he married Elizabeth Jungmann, who had been his late wife's greatest friend.
▷Lord Edward C D G Cecil, *Max: a biography* (1964)

BEER-HOFMANN, Richard
(1866–1945)

Austrian novelist, dramatist and poet, born in Vienna into a Jewish family. He was a prominent member of the Jungwein ('Young Vienna') circle—which included **Hofmannsthal** and **Schnitzler**—and, more sharply than any of his contemporaries, brought into German literature the influences of **Flaubert** and **Maupassant**, with *Novellen* (1903). He wrote one poem still famous in Austria: 'Schlaflied für Miriam' ('Lullaby for Miriam'). He is now best known for his plays, which include his impressive adaptation of *The Fatal Dowry* by **Philip Massinger**, *Der Graf von Charolais* (1905), and, most famous of all, and much played in the inter-war period, *Jaakobs Traum* (1918, Eng trans *Jacob's Dream*, 1946), in which he draws on the book which influenced him most of all, the Bible. After the Anschluss Beer-Hofmann's friends rescued him from Nazi wrath: he went to Switzerland and from there to New York, where he died. His finest work may well be his single novel, *Der Tod Georgs* (1900, 'George's Death'), a work transitional between the author's 'decadence' and his noble attempt to clarify the meaning of Jewishness: the use of interior monologue in this masterpiece is especially fruitful.

▷S Liptzin, *Richard Beer-Hofmann* (1936)

BEETS, Nicolaas
(1814–1903)
Dutch poet and writer, born in Haarlem. Professor of theology at Utrecht, he published under the pseudonym 'Hildebrand' *Camera Obscura* (1839), a series of quietly humorous sketches of everyday Dutch life, and *Volksliedjes* (1842, 'Little Folksongs'), a collection of simple verses.

▷J J Dupoix, *Nicolaas Beets et la littérature hollandaise* (1907)

BEHAN, Brendan
(1923–64)
Irish author, born in a slum district in Dublin, brother of **Dominic Behan**. He left school at 14 to become a house painter, and soon joined the IRA. In 1939 he was sentenced to three years in Borstal for attempting to blow up a Liverpool shipyard, and soon after his release given 14 years by a Dublin military court for the attempted murder of two detectives, but was released by a general amnesty (1946). He was in prison again in Manchester (1947) and was deported in 1952. In prison he had learned to speak Irish from fellow IRA detainees, and read voraciously. His first play, *The Quare Fellow* (1956; filmed 1962), starkly dramatized the prison atmosphere prior to a hanging. His exuberant Irish wit, spiced with balladry and bawdry and a talent for fantastic caricature, found scope in his next play, *The Hostage* (1958, first produced in Irish as *An Giall*). It is also evident in the autobiographical novel, *Borstal Boy* (1958), and in *Brendan Behan's Island* (1963).

▷D Behan, *My Brother Bernard* (1965)

BEHAN, Dominic
(1928–89)
Irish novelist and folklorist, born in Dublin, brother of **Brendan Behan**. He adapted old airs and poems into contemporary Irish Republican material, notably in *The Patriot Game*. Resentfully overshadowed for much of his life by the legend of his brother, he lived largely outside Ireland from 1947 as a journalist and singer. He ultimately settled in Scotland where for the first time he won acceptance in his own right as a writer, and

as an Irish and Scottish nationalist. His only novel, *The Public Life of Parable Jones*, was published just before his death.

▷*Teems of Times and Happy Returns* (1961)

BEHN, Aphra, née **Amis**
(1640–89)
English writer and adventuress, born in Wye, Kent. She was brought up in Surinam, where she made the acquaintance of the enslaved negro prince Oroonoko, the subject afterwards of one of her novels, in which she anticipated **Rousseau**'s 'noble savage'. Returning to England in 1663, she married a merchant called Behn, who died within three years. She then turned professional spy at Antwerp, sent back political and naval information, but received little thanks, and on her return was imprisoned for debt. She turned to writing, as perhaps the first professional woman author in England, and wrote many coarse but popular Restoration plays, especially *The Forced Marriage* (1670), *The Rover* (1678), and *The Feigned Courtizans* (1678), and later published *Oroonoko* (1688). She was buried in Westminster Abbey.

▷G Woodcock, *The Incomparable Aphra* (1948)

BEHRMAN, Samuel Nathaniel
(1893–1973)
American playwright, screenwriter and journalist, born in Worcester, Massachusetts. The production of a sophisticated comedy, *The Second Man* (1927), made him famous but despite being tagged the American **Noël Coward** his comedies of manners foundered on the harsh realities of Depression and war. However, his anecdotal portrait of the great art collector *Duveen* (1952) and *The Worcester Account* (1954), about his boyhood, retain their freshness and are reckoned to contain his best work. He co-wrote the screenplays *Queen Christina* (1933) and *Anna Karenina* (1935) for Greta Garbo.

▷*Tribulations and Laughter: a memoir* (1972)

BEILBY, Richard Courtney
(1918–)
Australian novelist, born in Malacca (now Melaka), Malaysia. His service in Greece and Crete during World War II provided the background for his novels *No Medals for Aphrodite* (1970) and *Gunner* (1977), though his first, *The Sword and the Myrtle* (1968), is set in an earlier conflict, the Greece of 480BC at the battle of Thermopylae. *The Brown Land Crying* (1975) looks at the half-caste aborigine trapped between cultures.

BELASCO, David
(1853–1931)

American playwright, director and theatre-manager, born in San Francisco. As one of the most powerful figures on Broadway, he owned the Belasco Theatre where, from 1906 until his death, he directed numerous plays, usually heroic melodramas, which often incorporated sensational stage effects. Surprisingly, Belasco, the 'Bishop of Broadway', also found time to write—both alone and in collaboration—over 50 plays, mostly sentimental domestic and historical dramas. *Hearts of Oak* (with James A Herne) appeared in 1879, and the Civil War play, *The Heart of Maryland*, in 1895. As an author, though, he is chiefly remembered for writing *Madame Butterfly* (with John L Long, 1900), and *The Girl of the Golden West* (1905). Both were transformed into operas by Puccini, the former becoming one of the composer's most celebrated works, the latter one of his most neglected.
▷L L Marker, *David Belasco* (1975)

BELL, J(ohn) J(oy)
(1871–1934)

Scottish journalist and humorous writer. He is best known for his *Wee MacGreegor* (1902), an amusing, poignant evocation of boyhood in Glasgow in the days before World War I. Dramatized in 1911, it has been described as Scotland's equivalent of *Huckleberry Finn* and *Just William*. It is still in print.
▷*Do You Remember?* (1934)

BELL, Julian
(1908–37)

English poet, born in London, the elder son of the art historian and critic Clive Bell and the painter Vanessa Bell. In 1930, while still at Cambridge University, he published his first collection, *Winter Movement*, which was generally highly praised, although his aunt, **Virginia Woolf**, confided to her diary that 'for all his admirable good sense & observation & love of country life, he is no poet ... Common sense and Cambridge are not enough.' Although editing *We Did Not Fight* (1935), a volume of essays written by conscientious objectors, Bell later admitted that some situations demanded force and left to fight against the fascists in Spain, where he was killed. His writings were gathered in a posthumous volume, *Julian Bell: Essays, Poems and Letters* (1938).
▷P Stansky and W Abrahams, *Journey to the Frontier* (1966)

BELL, Madison Smartt
(1957–)

American novelist, described by one reviewer as 'a writer to be admired rather than loved'. He was born on a farm in Tennessee and went to school in Nashville. After graduating from Princeton in 1979 he worked variously as sound man for a film unit, as clerk at the Franklin Library and as a freelance writer. His novel *The Year of Silence* (1987), about the disappearance of a pianist's brother, is written in the slickly uncompassionate style which has become his forte. The start of an earlier novel, *Straight Cut* (1986), is typically arresting. The first heading is 'The Day I Shot My Dog'. Bell has his followers, who enjoy the philosophical subtexts in his essentially thriller-grade fictions.

BELLAMY, Edward
(1850–98)

American novelist, born in Chicopee Falls, Massachusetts. He achieved immense popularity with his Utopian romance *Looking Backward 2000–1887* (1888), a work which predicted a new social order and influenced economic thinking in the USA and Europe. The sequel *Equality* (1897) was much less acclaimed.
▷A E Morgan, *Edward Bellamy* (1944)

BELLAY, Joachim du
(1522–60)

French poet and prose writer, born in Lire in Anjou. After his friend and fellow-student, **Pierre de Ronsard**, he was the most important member of the Pléiade. His *Deffence et Illustration de la langue françoise* (1549, 'Defense and Illustration of the French Language'), the manifesto of the Pléiade, advocating the rejection of medieval linguistic traditions and a return to classical and Italian models, had a considerable influence at the time. It was accompanied by an example in the form of a set of **Petrarch**an sonnets, *l'Olive*, dedicated to an unknown lady. He went to Rome in 1533 as secretary to his kinsman, Cardinal du Bellay, but was not a success as a diplomat, though the visit inspired more sonnets, including the collections *Les Antiquités de Rome* ('Roman Antiquities') and *Les Regrets* (1558).

BELLEAU, Rémy
(1528–77)

French poet, born in Nogent le Rotrou. He was a member of the Pléiade and published in 1556 a translation of **Anacreon** that was at first believed to be an original imitation. *Bergerie* (1565, 'Pastoral', 2nd edition 1572) is a medley of delicately descriptive prose and verse, of which *Avril* ('April') still appears in anthologies. *Amours* (1576, 'Love Poems') is a collection of poems concerned with the appearance and arcane powers of precious stones.

BELLENDEN, John

▷S Eckhardt, *Rémy Belleau, sa vie, sa 'Berg-erie'* (1917)

BELLENDEN, or BALLANTYNE, John
(d.1587)

Scottish ecclesiastic and writer, born towards the close of the 15th century. In 1508 he matriculated from St Andrews and completed his theological studies at the Sorbonne. His translations in 1533 of Boece's *Historia Gentis Scotorum*, and of the first five books of Livy, are interesting as vigorous specimens of early Scottish prose. The *Croniklis of Scotland* is a very free translation, and contains numerous passages not found in Boece, so that it is in some respects almost an original work. Bellenden enjoyed great favour at the court of James V, at whose request the translations were made. As a reward, he received considerable grants from the Treasury, and afterwards was made Archdeacon of Moray and Canon of Ross. Becoming involved, however, in ecclesiastical controversy, he went to Rome.
▷R W Chambers and W W Seton, *Bellenden's Translation of the History of Hector Boece* (1919)

BELLI, Carlos Germán
(1927–)

Peruvian poet, born in Lima, who has looked to the Spanish past, and in particular to **Quevedo**, for his inspiration. Elegant but deeply felt, his poetry is also influenced by that of **Vallejo**. Some of his poems were translated in a collection, *Carlos Germán Belli*, in 1988.
▷F Cairns, *The Poet in Peru: Alienation and the Quest for A Super-reality* (1982)

BELLIDO, José María
(1922–)

Spanish dramatist, born (a Basque) in San Sebastián. He is a trained lawyer and a linguist, most of whose plays written while Franco was in power were banned and had to appear abroad in translation—chiefly in *Modern Spanish Theatre* (1968, M Benedikt and G E Wellwarth eds) and *The New Wave Spanish Drama* (1970, ed G E Wellwarth). His *La suite fantastica*, as he calls his series of a score and more short plays (*temblores*: 'quiverings'), are a genre unto themselves: spontaneous pieces written apparently without heed to form, but in fact exceedingly skilful. They could be classed as Theatre of the Absurd. *Futbol* (1963, Eng trans *Football*, in *Modern Spanish Theatre*) did get past Franco's censors, because they did not realize that it was not about a football team but a series of strutting fascists. Bellido has also written for the commercial theatre, as in *Rubio cordero* (1970, 'Blond Lamb'); but this account of

kidnapped diplomats also has its jokes for the initiated.
▷G E Wellwarth, *Spanish Underground Drama* (1972)

BELLMANN, Carl Michael
(1740–95)

Swedish poet and writer of popular songs, born in Stockholm. In 1757 he entered banking, but had to flee to Norway six years later to escape his creditors. In 1776 he was brought back as a protegé of King Gustav III, who gave him a sinecure as secretary of the national lottery. He founded a drinking club, the *Bacci orden* or 'Knights of Bacchus', and put in verse his impressions of his friends and others. His most important collections are the *Songs of Fredman* (1790) and *Epistles of Fredman* (1791), which combine burlesque with biblical parody and minute observation of Swedish life. There is a long-standing Bellmann Society in Sweden devoted to his memory.
▷P B Austin, *Life and Songs of Carl Michael Bellmann* (1967)

BELLO, Andrés
(1781–1865)

Venezuelan poet, translator (**Byron, Hugo**), philosopher and scholar—he was also a tutor to Simon Bolívar. He lived for many years in London (1810–29), where he prepared an important edition of the poem *El Cid*. In 1829 he emigrated to Chile, where he founded the National University. His grammar of the Castilian language (1847) is a landmark. In *Filosofía del entendimiento* (1881, 'Philosophy of Understanding'), he introduced the ideas of Locke, Berkeley and Mill into Latin America. His debate with **Domingo Sarmiento**, a convinced romantic, whereas Bello was at heart a classical humanist, stimulated South American thinking. The most famous of his artificial but technically flawless poems is *La agricultura de la zona torrida* (1826, 'The Agriculture of the Torrid Zone'), part of which is translated into prose in the *Penguin Book of Latin American Verse* (1971, ed E Curacciolo-Trejo).
▷E R Monmegal, *Este otro Andrés Bello* (1969)

BELLOC, (Joseph) Hilaire Pierre
(1870–1953)

French-born British writer and poet, born in St Cloud near Paris, the son of a French barrister, Louis Belloc, and his English wife. His sister was **Marie Belloc**. The family moved to England during the Franco–Prussian war, and settled there in 1872. He was educated at the Oratory School, Birmingham, under **Newman**, and Balliol College, Oxford, but did military service in the French army. He became a naturalized British subject in 1902, and became Liberal MP in 1906, but, disillusioned with politics, did not seek re-election in 1910. Disapproving of modern industrial society and socialism, he wrote *The Servile State* (1912), advocating a return to the system of medieval guilds. He was a close friend of **G K Chesterton**, who illustrated many of his books. He is best known, however, for his delightfully nonsensical verse for children: *The Bad Child's Book of Beasts* (1896) and the *Cautionary Tales* (1907); his numerous travel books, including *Path to Rome* (1902) and *The Old Road* (1910), reconstructing the Pilgrim's Way; his historical studies *Robespierre* (1901), *Marie Antoinette* (1910), *Richelieu* (1929), *Wolsey* (1930), and *Napoleon* (1932); and his religious books, including *Europe and the Faith* (1920) and *The Great Heresies* (1938). An energetic Roman Catholic apologist, he was fearlessly, sometimes fanatically, outspoken.

BELLOC, Marie Adelaide
(1868–1947)

French-born English novelist, playwright and short-story writer, the sister of **Hilaire Belloc**. She wrote over 40 novels, mostly atmospheric, deftly-plotted crime and mystery stories, and many involving a sharp moral dilemma. The most famous is *The Lodger* (1913), in which a landlady discovers that her tenant, an outwardly dignified and respectable man, is none other than Jack the Ripper, the notorious murderer of prostitutes in the east end of London. Despite her consternation, Mrs Bunting is unable to report her discovery to the police.

BELLOC LOWNDES, Mrs *see* BELLOC, Marie Adelaide

BELLOW, Saul
(1915–)

Canadian-born American writer, winner of the Nobel Prize for literature, born in Lachine in Quebec, the son of immigrant Russian parents. He spent his childhood in Montreal; in 1924 his family moved to Chicago. He attended university there, and at Northwestern in Evanston, Illinois. He abandoned his post-graduate studies at Wisconsin University to become a writer, and his first novel, *The Dangling Man*, a study of a man in pre-draft limbo, appeared in 1944. He became an associate professor at Minnesota University, and after being awarded a Guggenheim Fellowship in 1948 travelled to Paris and Rome. Other works include *The Victim* (1947), *The Adventures of Augie March* (1953), *Henderson the Rain King* (1959), *Herzog* (1964), *Mr Sammler's Planet* (1970), *Humboldt's Gift*

(1975) and *The Dean's December* (1982). Most are concerned with the fate of liberal humanism in a violent and absurd environment which has severed the present from an intellectually and emotionally nourishing past. In 1962 he was appointed a professor at Chicago University, and in 1976 was awarded the Nobel Prize for literature.
▷M Bradbury, *Bellow* (1982); J Braham, *A Sort of Columbus: The American Voyages of Bellow's Fiction* (1984)

BELLOY, Dormont de, properly Pierre Laurent Buyrette
(1727–75)

French dramatist. He was one of the first to introduce on the French stage native instead of classical heroes. His first success, *Zelmire* (1762), was followed by *Le Siège de Calais* (1765), *Gaston et Bayard* (1771) and *Pierre le cruel* (1772).

BELY, Andrei, pseud of Boris Nikolayevich Bugayev
(1880–1934)

Russian novelist, poet and critic, born in Moscow. A leading Symbolist writer, he early met **Vladimir Soloviev**, the religious philosopher, and fell under his influence. While at Moscow University he wrote Decadent poetry which he published in *Sinfoniya (2-aya, dramaticheskaya)* (1902, 'Symphony (Second, Dramatic)'). His poetry, however, was criticized mercilessly, and his reputation rests on his prose. *Serebryany golub* (1909, Eng trans *The Silver Dove*, 1974) was his first and most accessible novel, and was followed by *Petersburg* (1916, Eng trans *St Petersburg*, 1959), his masterpiece, in which the action centres on a bomb camouflaged as a tin of sardines. The autobiographical *Kotik Letayev* (1922, Eng trans *Kotik Letaev*, 1971) is Bely's most original work, a stream-of-consciousness attempt to show how children become aware of what is going on in the world. His later novels, written after a second sojourn in Berlin (1921–3), are more overtly satirical of the pre-revolutionary Russian scene but are still highly experimental. He is regarded as one of the most important Russian writers of the 1920s.
▷J D Elsworth, *Andrei Bely* (1972)

BEMELMENS, Ludwig
(1898–1963)

American humorous memoirist, novelist and painter, born in Austria of a Belgian father and a Bavarian mother. Much of his best writing appeared in the *New Yorker*. His work has now dated, but in their day such books as *Hotel Splendide* (1941), about his years as a waiter, and *Dirty Eddie* (1947), a novel about a pig movie-star, were much read. He was at his best when he could keep sentimentality out of his irreverent writing, and concentrate on his capacity for satire.

BENAVENTE, Jacinto
(1866–1954)

Spanish dramatist, born in Madrid. He intended to enter the legal profession but turned to literature. After publishing some poems and short stories he won recognition as a playwright with his *El nido ajeno* (1893, 'The Other Nest'), which was followed by some brilliantly satirical society comedies. His masterpiece is *Los intereses creados* (1907, 'Human Concerns'), an allegorical play in the *commedia dell'arte* style. He also wrote some excellent children's plays.
▷M Penuelas, translated by K Englev, *Jacinto Benavente* (1968)

BEN-AVIGDOR, pseud of Arieh Leib Shalkovitz
(1866–1921)

Hebrew story writer, Zionist, and influential advocate of the reform of the Hebrew language, born near Vilna. He was a notable publisher (he founded Ahiahsaf, and then Tushia), who wrote stories of proletarian Jews and a long historical novel set in 15th-century Spain; his work has not found a translator.

BENCHLEY, Robert Charles
(1889–1945)

American humorist, critic and parodist, born in Worcester, Massachusetts. **E B White** and **James Thurber** thought him a finer humorist even than **Mark Twain**; he was described by **Dorothy Parker** as 'a kind of saint'. At Harvard he edited the *Lampoon* and starred in the Hasty Pudding shows. He met Parker at *Vanity Fair*; together with **Robert Sherwood**, Thurber, **George Kaufman** and Franklin D Adams, they formed the notorious Algonquin Round Table. Subsequently he worked as a drama critic for *Life* (1920–29) and the *New Yorker* (1929–40) but was fired for excessive drinking. He was at his most brilliant writing sketches, which surfaced in several collections including *20,000 Leagues under the Sea, or, David Copperfield* (1928), *From Bed to Worse* (1934) and *My Ten Years in a Quandary, and How They Grew* (1936). His humour derives from the predicament of the 'Little Man', himself writ large, beset on all sides by the complexity of existence in the modern world. A chronic worrier, minor problems (leaving a party, curing hiccoughs) assumed epic proportions. He also appeared in cameo roles in many films.
▷N W Yates, *Robert Benchley* (1968)

BENDA, Julien
(1867–1956)

French philosopher and essayist, born in Paris and educated at the university there. After initial fame writing against **Henri Bergson** just prior to World War I, he caused a sensation in 1927 with *La Trahison des clercs* ('The Treachery of the Intellectuals') in which he accuses modern thinkers of abandoning philosophical neutrality to support doctrines of class and race hatred, such as Marxism and fascism, going on to attempt to 'restore the primacy of the spiritual'. He published little during the German occupation of France but much afterwards including idiosyncratic criticisms of then fashionable thought in *Tradition du Existentialisme* (1947) and *La Dialectique Materialiste* (1948). He wrote two novels, *L'Ordination* (1911) and *Les Amorandes* (1922).
▷ *La Jeunesse d'un clerc* (1936)

BENEDETTI, Mario
(1920–)

Uruguayan novelist, short-story writer and poet, born in Paso de los Toros. His early stories, included in *Esta Mañana* (1949, 'This Morning') and *El Último Viaje y otros cuentos* (1951, 'The Last Journey and other stories'), are disciplined depictions of the frustrations of mass existence in the cities. His novels, such as *Quién de Nosotros* (1955, 'Which One of Us'), expand on that theme, but his poetry, although at times it has a political subject-matter, can also engage in more abstract notions, as is the case with the collection *Noción de la Patria* (1963, 'Concept of the Homeland'). He has written several volumes of literary criticism, lively, eclectic and opinionated, including *Literatura Uruguayo siglo XX* (1963, rev edn 1969).

BENEDIKTSSON, Einar
(1864–1940)

Icelandic poet and entrepreneur, born at Elliavatan, near Reykjavik. His mother was a fine poet; his father was a Supreme Court judge, from whom Benediktsson acquired his legal interests and nationalist sympathies. He himself became a country magistrate, but devoted many years to touring Europe, seeking capital (unsuccessfully) for ambitious industrial schemes to exploit Iceland's natural resources, notably fishing and hydroelectric power. His literary output reflected his patriotic concerns. He published five volumes of ornate poetry that harked back to the skaldic tradition of intricate metaphor and vocabulary, but which he modernized considerably.
▷S J Nordal, *Einar Benediktsson* (1971)

BENELLI, Sem
(1877–1949)

Italian dramatist, born in Prato, Tuscany. He wrote plays in prose and verse. His outstanding successes were *Tignola*, a light comedy, and *La cena della beffe* ('The Mocking Dinner'), a powerful tragedy in verse.
▷C Lavi, *Sem Benelli, il suo teatro e la sua compagnia* (1928)

BENET, Juan
(1927–93)

Spanish novelist and dramatist, a civil engineer by profession. His work, not unlike that of the French novelist **Michel Butor**, but most influenced by **Faulkner**, is immensely complex, 'hermetic' and allusive to a myriad of other writers, and for that reason has not yet been very widely read outside Spain, except by a band of critics devoted to it. But his successful novel, *Una Meditación* (1970), was translated as *A Meditation* in 1982. Benet's 'baroque prose poses substantial and sometimes insoluble problems for the reader', wrote a critic; but he added that his 'criticism [of human situations, particularly of the repressive Franco regime] is given life in a narrative that on the surface seems remote from conditions in … Spain'. As a journalist Benet was notably lucid.
▷D K Herzberger, *The Novelistic World of Juan Benet* (1977)

BENÉT, Laura
(1884–1979)

American poet and biographer, elder sister of **William** and **Stephen Benét**. She was born at Fort Hamilton, New York. Her verse, much of it written with a young readership in mind, occasionally recalls **Christina Rossetti**, but is often more robust metrically. Her most distinctive volumes are *Fairy Bread* (1921), *Basket for a Fair* (1934) and the very late *Bridge of a Single Hair* (1974), which marked a startling return to form. She also wrote literary biography for the young and a rather blowsy novel, *Come Slowly, Eden* (1942).
▷ *When William Rose, Stephen Vincent and I Were Young* (1976)

BENÉT, Stephen Vincent
(1898–1943)

American poet and novelist, born in Bethlehem, Pennsylvania. He was the son of an Army Officer and brother of **William Rose Benét**. He was educated at Yale, and had published two volumes of poetry before graduating in 1919. His college novel, *The Beginning of Wisdom*, appeared in 1921. His main subject was the nature of the American national experience and character, and his most famous explorations of it are the long

poems *John Brown's Body* (1928), on the Civil War, and *Western Star* (1943), which was part of a projected epic on American history. He wrote several volumes of evocative, well-crafted poems, including a collection, *Ballads and Poems 1915–30* (1931), and *Burning City* (1936), all of which are traditional in form. His other writings include four more novels, short stories, and two one-act folk operas.
▷C Fenton, *Stephen Vincent Benét* (1958)

BENÉT, William Rose
(1886–1950)

American poet, editor, novelist and playwright, born in Fort Hamilton, New York, brother of **Laura** and **Stephen Benét**. His main claim to fame is as a poet and he published many collections, among them *Merchants from Cathay* (1913), *Moons of Grandeur* (1920) and *The Stairway of Surprise* (1947), but his career was largely eclipsed by the success of his wife **Elinor Wylie** and his brother.
▷ *My Brother Steve* (1943)

BENGTSSON, Frans G
(1894–1954)

Swedish essayist, novelist and poet. Born at Rösjöholm in Skåne, he studied at the University of Lund. He made his debut as a poet in 1923, his verses reflecting an exclusive aestheticism which was to pervade his work. His breakthrough with the reading public came with his collections of essays, among them *Litteratörer och militärer* (1929, 'Penmen and Military Men') and *De långhåriga merovingerna* (1933, 'The Long-Haired Merovingians'). He exploits his encyclopedic knowledge with notable artistic skill and a conspicuous sense of humour, the elegant complexity of his texts influenced by British essayists. His two-volume novel *Röde Orm* (1941–5, Eng trans *The Long Ships*, 1954), which is set in the age of the Vikings, is at once scholarly and humorous and brought him considerable international fame.
▷G Hägg, 'Esteten som underhållare. Frans G. Bengtssons essäform', in *Övertalning och underhållning. Den svenska essäistiken 1890–1930* (1978)

BENJAMIN, Walter
(1892–1940)

German, Marxist, literary and cultural critic, born in Berlin, to an assimilated Jewish family; he believed himself to be a descendant of the poet **Heinrich Heine**. He was educated at the Kaiser Friedrich School, and at the Friedrich-Wilhelm Gymnasium in Thuringia. His earliest influence was the Cabbalistic tradition, which he brought to bear on the philosophical legacy of Immanuel Kant. He set out his ideas in the notoriously difficult prologue to his 1925 study of *Trauerspiel* (Eng trans *The Origin of German Tragic Drama*, 1977). This attempt to understand the 17th century from the standpoint of Germany was later followed by the so-called 'Arcades Project', which had post-Napoleonic France as its focus. Towards the end of the 1920s, Benjamin began to turn towards Marxian materialism, encouraged by his encounter with **Bertolt Brecht**: Benjamin later claimed that his best-known essay, 'The Work of Art in an Age of Mechanical Reproduction' (1936), had been deliberately written to outdo Brecht's materialism. This essay and the equally important 'Theses on the Philosophy of History' are included in a posthumous translated collection called *Illuminations* (1969), edited by Hannah Arendt. Together with the aphoristic and autobiographical writings in *Reflections* (published first in English, 1978), this effectively revived Benjamin's reputation, making him a central figure in neo-Marxist and materialist criticism, and an icon of heroic resistance against totalitarianism. In September 1940, believing that he was about to be denied asylum, he committed suicide on the Franco–Spanish border; in the words of Brecht, who composed a threnody, having encountered one impassable frontier, he willingly crossed the only passable one left available to him.

▷P Wolin, *Walter Benjamin: An Aesthetic of Redemption* (1982)

BENLOWES, Edward
(1602–76)

English religious poet. Having been brought up a staunch Roman Catholic, Benlowes scandalized his family in 1627 by changing his faith. In the eyes of some, he took another irretrievably wrong turning during the Civil War, when he became a passionate Royalist. *Theophila, or, Love's Sacrifice*, a sprawling spiritual romance completed in 1652, is his best-known work, but one with so many oddities of imagery and expression that it continues to perplex as well as intrigue scholars.

BENN, Gottfried
(1886–1956)

German poet, born in Mansfeld in West Prussia. Though the son of a clergyman he embraced the philosophy of Nihilism as a young man, but later became one of the few intellectuals to favour Nazi doctrines, although his poems were banned by the Nazis in 1938 (ironically, they were banned again by the Allies in 1945 for his earlier pro-Nazi sympathies). Trained in medicine as a venereologist, he began writing Expressionist verse that dealt with the uglier aspects of his profession, such as *Morgue* (1912). Later his outlook became more mature and his poetry

more versatile, though still pessimistic. After 1945, the cerebral, intellectually rigorous cast of his post-war poetry, and its mood of despondency in defeat, became influential and won him a place among the leading poets of the century.

▷E Buddeburg, *Gottfried Benn* (1961)

BENNETT, Alan
(1934–)

English dramatist, actor and director, born in Leeds. He came to prominence as a writer and performer in *Beyond the Fringe*, a revue performed at the Edinburgh Festival in 1960, and wrote a television series, *On The Margin* (1966), before his first stage play, *Forty Years On* (1968). Essentially a humanist, noted for his wry, self-deprecating humour, which combines a comic-tragic view of life, his subsequent plays include *Getting On* (1971, about a Labour MP), *Habeas Corpus* (1973), *The Old Country* (1977), a double bill, *Single Spies* (1988) and *The Madness of George III* (1991). He has also written much for television, including *An Englishman Abroad* (1983), *The Insurance Man* (1986), and a series of six monologues, *Talking Heads* (1988).

BENNETT, (Enoch) Arnold
(1867–1931)

English novelist, born near Hanley, Staffordshire, in the heart of 'the Potteries', the son of a solicitor. Educated locally and at London University, he became a solicitor's clerk in London, but quickly transferred to journalism, and in 1893 became assistant editor (editor in 1896) of the journal *Woman*. He published his first novel, *The Man from the North*, in 1898. In 1902 he moved to Paris for 10 years and from then on he was engaged exclusively in writing, journalistic and creative. His claims to recognition as a novelist rest mainly on the early *Anna of the Five Towns* (1902), the more celebrated *The Old Wives' Tale* (1908), and the *Clayhanger* series—*Clayhanger* (1910), *Hilda Lessways* (1911), *These Twain* (1916), subsequently issued (1925) as *The Clayhanger Family*—in all of which novels the 'Five Towns', centres of the pottery industry, feature not only as background, but almost as *dramatis personae*. He excels again with *Riceyman Steps* (1923), a picture of drab life in London, and his genial, humorous streak shows in works like *The Card* (1911), *The Grand Babylon Hotel* (1902), *Imperial Palace* (1930), and the play *The Great Adventure* (1913). *Lord Raingo* (1926) is a political novel. The play *Milestones* (1912), written in collaboration with Edward Knoblock, was much performed. He was a sound and influential critic, and as 'Jacob Tonson' on *The New Age* he was a discerning reviewer. His *Journals*, written in the manner of the

brothers **Edmond** and **Jules de Goncourt**, were published posthumously.
▷M Drabble, *Arnold Bennett: a biography* (1974)

BENNETT, Louise Simone
(1919–)

Jamaican poet, born in Kingston, and educated at Excelsior High School. She studied journalism by correspondence course before going to the Royal Academy of Dramatic Art in London in 1945. After graduating she taught drama in Jamaica, performed in theatres in Britain and America, and lectured widely on Jamaican folklore and music. She married the Jamaican actor and impresario, Eric Coverley, in 1954. Her numerous books include retellings of Jamaican folk stories and collections of her own ballads and verse monologues. Her use of Jamaican dialect and speech rhythms, humour and satirical wit for the purposes of social and political comment have made her one of the outstanding performance poets of the 20th century.
▷*Jamaican Labrish* (poetry collection, ed with introduction by R Nettleford, 1966); M Morris, in *Fifty Caribbean Writers*, ed D C Dance (1986)

BENOIT DE SAINTE-MAURE
(fl.c.1150)

French poet, born in either Sainte-Maure near Poitiers or Sainte-More near Tours. His vast romance *Roman de Troie* ('Tale of Troy') was a source book to many later writers, notably **Boccaccio**, who in turn inspired **Chaucer** and **Shakespeare** to use Benoit's episode of Troilus and Cressida.

BENSERADE, Isaac de
(1613–91)

French poet and dramatist, born in Paris. His is remembered as the librettist for Lully's ballets and as the author of a sonnet, *Job*.
▷C I Silin, *Benserade and his Ballets de cour* (1940)

BENSON, Arthur Christopher
(1862–1925)

English author, son of Edward White Benson and brother of **Edward Frederic Benson** and **Robert Hugh Benson**. He was master of Magdalene College, Cambridge, and wrote studies of **Dante Gabriel Rossetti**, **Fitzgerald**, **Walter Pater**, **Tennyson**, and **John Ruskin**, a memoir of Robert Hugh Benson, and a biography of Edward White Benson. His poems include *Land of Hope and Glory* (1902).
▷*The Diary* (1926)

BENSON, E(dward) F(rederic)
(1867–1940)

English author, son of Edward White Benson and brother of **Arthur Christopher Benson** and **Robert Hugh Benson**. He was educated at Wellington and King's College, Cambridge. After some archaeological research in Greece and Egypt (1892–95) he published several light novels including *Dodo* (1893) and *Queen Lucia* (1920) as well as three autobiographical studies of Edwardian and Georgian society.
▷*Final Edition: informal autobiography* (1940)

BENSON, Robert Hugh
(1871–1914)

English author and clergyman, son of Edward White Benson and brother of **Arthur Christopher Benson** and **Edward Frederic Benson**. Educated at Eton and Trinity College, Cambridge, he took Anglican orders but turned Roman Catholic in 1903 and rose to private chamberlain to Pope Pius X (1911). A dynamic preacher and prolific author, he wrote such novels as *Come Rack! Come Rope!* (1912).
▷A C Benson, *Hugh: memoirs of a brother* (1915)

BENSON, Stella
(1892–1933)

English novelist, poet and short-story writer, born in Much Wenlock, Shropshire. Her first novel, *I Pose* (1915), is about the suffragette movement, and contains autobiographical elements; her second, *The Poor Man* (1932), is a witty, often introspective tale. Ill health forced her to travel, and she visited Switzerland, the West Indies and California, as well as spending many years in China; some of those visits are recounted in *The Little World* (1925) and *Worlds Within Worlds* (1928). Her diary, not published until decades after her death from tuberculosis, is both a more revealing and perhaps more enduring work than her fiction.

BENTLEY, Edmund Clerihew
(1875–1956)

English journalist and novelist, born in London. He worked on the *Daily News* (1901–12) and *The Daily Telegraph* (1912–34). He is chiefly remembered as the author of *Trent's Last Case* (1913), which is regarded as a milestone in the transformation of the detective novel. A close friend of **G K Chesterton**, he originated and gave name to the type of humorous verse-form known as the 'clerihew'.
▷*Those Days* (1940)

BENTLEY, Phyllis
(1894–1977)

English novelist, born in Halifax. Love of her native Yorkshire is reflected in over 20 novels, including her first, *Environment* (1915), *Carr* (1929), and her best-known, *Inheritance* (1932). Several of her books, including *Inheritance*, are partly autobiographical, drawing on her own family experiences to present a vivid evocation of the local textile trade. Her novels are realistic and strong on character; they are also sometimes sentimental, even though sentiment was something she strove hard to avoid. Continuing the Yorkshire theme, she wrote three critical studies of the **Brontë** sisters, and in 1949 edited an edition of their works.
▷ *O Dreams, O Destinations* (1962)

BEN-ZION, Simcha, pseud of Simcha Alter Gutmann
(1870–1932)

Hebrew novelist and translator (of, for example, **Goethe**'s *Hermann and Dorothea*), born in Teleneshte, Bessarabia. The son of a very pious father, he had to educate himself in secular matters in secret. A now neglected master, his subjects are the Jews of the small towns of Bessarabia and their insoluble economic problems, their courage, and their resourcefulness.
▷ M Waxman, *A History of Jewish Literature* (1960)

BÉRANGER, Pierre Jean de
(1780–1857)

French poet, born in Paris. After a scanty education he left regular employment as a clerk at the University of Paris for an impecunious literary life in 1798. His lyrics were coloured by his politics, a curious compound of republicanism and Bonapartism, and led to spells of imprisonment in 1821 and 1828, but their vivacity, satire, and wit endeared them to the masses.
▷ E de Pompery, *Béranger: sa biographie* (1865)

BERCEO, Gonzalo de
(c.1180–c.1246)

Spanish poet, born in Verceo, the earliest known Castilian poet. He became a deacon and wrote more than 13 000 verses on devotional subjects, of which the best is a biography of St Oria. He was also the author of *Milagros de la Virgen*, a collection of legends of the Virgin's appearances on earth. His poems were not discovered and published until the late 18th century.
▷ J E Keller, *Gonzalo de Berceo* (1972)

BERCHET, Giovanni
(1783–1851)

Italian poet, born in Milan. He began by translating foreign, especially English, literature, and through his translation of *The Vicar of Wakefield* (1809) became interested in ballads. In 1816 he published a pamphlet, *Lettera semiseria di Grisostomo* ('Grisostomo's Semi-serious Letter'), which became a manifesto of the Romantic movement in Italy. In 1821 he left Italy to avoid arrest, and lived in exile, mainly in England, until the abortive Revolution of 1848. He was received in Milan with enthusiasm and made director of education, but had to flee again to Piedmont. His best-known works are *I Profughi di Parga* (1821, 'The Refugees of Parga'), *Il Romito del Cenisio* ('The Hermit of Cenisio') and *Il Trovatore* ('The Troubadour').
▷ C Rosa, *Giovanni Berchet. Studio critico biografico* (1872)

BERENT, Wacław, pseud of W Rawicz
(1873–1940)

Polish novelist and translator of **Nietzsche**. He came to prominence in the so-called 'Young Poland' period (1895–1914), in which writers reacted, on the whole in neo-romantic fashion, against the positivism of their predecessors. Berent, a marine biologist who studied in Germany, is still one of Poland's more important novelists, and one who came very early not only to modernism but also to what is now called post-modernism. His first novel, *Fachowiec* (1895, 'The Expert'), satirized positivist optimism in a poker-faced and ironic, but not romantic, manner. His relatively few novels became progressively more disillusioned with the fictional mode, until he came to disbelieve in it altogether. His novels, in particular *Żywe Kamienie* (1918, 'Living Stones'), set in medieval times, await translation into English.

BERESFORD-HOWE, Constance
(1922–)

Canadian novelist and short-story writer, born in Montreal. With the exception of the historical romance *My Lady Greensleeves* (1955), her novels deal with contemporary women, her first three: *The Unreasoning Heart* (1946), *Of This Day's Journey* (1947) and *The Invisible Gate* (1949), focusing on young women at critical stages of their worldly development. Of her later books, *A Population of One* (1977) follows a single woman's plunge into the academic world, while *Night Studies* (1985) records the dismal lives of the students and staff at an urban college of further education. Her most famous novel, however, is *A Book of Eve* (1973), in which the eponymous protagonist, a woman in her mid-sixties, leaves her husband of 40 years to start a new life alone on the other side of Montreal. Like her other novels, it is compassionate, witty and gently effective.

BERG, Leila
(1917–)

English children's writer and editor, born in Salford, Lancashire. Her *Look At Kids* (1972), illustrated with unsentimental black and white photographs of urban life, was as influential, in its way, as the Plowden report. While she was an editor for Macmillan, she launched the 'Nippers' series of primary-school readers, many of which she wrote herself. These were criticized for the stereotyped portrait they drew of working-class life and have become museum pieces of the seventies. As a story-teller her work is longer-lasting. *A Box For Benny* (1958) is still enjoyed.

BERGELSON, David
(1884–1952)

Russian (Yiddish) novelist and story writer, and one of the leaders of the Yiddish generation which followed immediately after the 'classical' period of **Scholem Aleichem**. He was born in the Ukraine into a prosperous family of timber merchants, but their fortunes declined, and he knew poverty at first hand. He differed from his predecessors in two ways: his style developed (sometimes abruptly), and he put an unforgettable emphasis upon the social decline of the period through which he lived. *Nokh alemen* (1913, Eng trans *When All is Said and Done*, 1977), features the 'first authentic heroine of Yiddish fiction'. Bergelson lived in Berlin for a while, and struggled against communist dictation of artistic creation, but eventually he submitted, returned to Russia and became a socialist realist. Yet even his fiction of that period, such as *Midas hadin* (1925, 'Full Severity of the Law'), has its power and attraction. He was executed by Stalin on a trumped-up charge after he had turned back, as well as he could, to Jewish themes. *Baym Dnieper* (1932–40, 'Along the Dnieper'), is one of the most remarkable novels written under Stalinist oppression, and awaits translation.
▷C A Madison, *Yiddish Literature* (1968)

BERGENGRUEN, Werner
(1892–1962)

German novelist, critic (eg of **E T A Hoffmann**) and poet, born in Riga (his father was a member of the German colony there, but returned to Germany early in Bergengruen's life), who fell foul of the Nazis and was expelled from the Academy of Writers in

1937. He was converted to Roman Catholicism in 1936. A conscientious, prolific, gifted and still much heeded writer (he was particularly popular after the end of World War II), he was at his best in the tradition of **Kleist** and **C F Meyer**, and it is by his historical novels that he will perhaps be best remembered, particularly for *Der Grosstyrann und das Gericht* (1935, Eng trans *A Matter of Conscience*, 1952), set in Renaissance Italy; this is a masterful and exciting allegorical arraignment of the Nazis, whose censor allowed it through. Also notable are Bergengruen's short stories, and his novels set in modern times. His poetry, although a few hymns have survived, is less effective, but has its champions.

BERGER, John Peter
(1926–)

English novelist, playwright and art critic, born in London. After studying at the Central and Chelsea Schools of Art he began his working life as a painter and a drawing teacher but soon turned to writing. His novels have a sensual awareness that is not entirely visual, but his Marxism and artistic background are ever present. Each of his novels has been well-received; they include *A Painter of Our Time* (1958), *The Foot of Clive* (1962) and *Corker's Freedom* (1964). His fame was enhanced with the publication of *G* (1972), a story of migrant workers in Europe, which won the Booker Prize; in his acceptance speech, Berger denounced the sponsors and announced that he would donate half of the prize money to the (now defunct) Black Panthers. Among his other writings the best known are *Ways of Seeing* (1972), on the visual arts, and *Pig Earth* (1979), a collection of short stories of French peasant life, and the first of the *Into Their Labours* trilogy, which was followed by *Once in Europa* (1989) and *Lilac and Flag* (1991). In 1992 he published *Keeping a Rendezvous*, a collection of essays and poems.

BERGER, Thomas Louis
(1924–)

American novelist, noted for what one critic characterized as 'bitter comedy'. Born in Cincinnati, he was educated in New York City and after military service worked as an academic librarian and editor. His sequence of novels about Carlo Reinhart spans four decades: *Crazy in Berlin* (1958) is set in occupied Germany at the end of World War II; Reinhart later studies the GI Bill (*Reinhart in Love*, 1962), and then slides inexorably through the holes in the American Dream (*Vital Parts*, 1970), before achieving a measure of chastened peace in *Reinhart's Women* (1981).

Berger's career as a novelist has been some-what overshadowed by the movie of *Little Big Man* (1964), which tended to iron out the ambiguity of his protean hero Jack Crabb and his perspective on American life from both sides of the cowboys-and-indians, success-and-failure divide. *Who is Teddy Villanova?* (1977) and *Nowhere* (1985) parody detective and spy fiction but are again concerned with the shifting nature of identity in contemporary society.

BERGGOLTS, Olga
(1910–75)

Russian poet, born in St Petersburg. She married the poet **Boris Kornilov**, who was murdered by Stalin in the Purges (1937); she was herself imprisoned. Although she had published her first book in 1934, she became well known only when she organized resistance, and made highly effective daily broadcasts in Leningrad when it was besieged by the Nazis throughout World War II. Her lyrical prose effusion *Dnevnye zvyozdy* (1959, 'Stars in Daytime'), received high praise; her poetry is workmanlike and poignant in its sincerity.

BERGMAN, Bo Hjalmar
(1869–1967)

Swedish lyric poet, born in Stockholm. He studied law at Uppsala and later became a literary critic. The pessimism of his early poetry, as in *Marionetterna* (1903, 'Puppets'), gradually gave way to the optimistic humanism of *En människa* (1908, 'A Member of the Race'), which was frequently in opposition to the growing totalitarianism of modern society. His varied output includes novels, short stories, and two volumes of memoirs.
▷K Asplund, *Bo Bergman. Manniskan och diktaren* (1970)

BERGMAN, Hjalmar Fredrik Elgérus
(1883–1931)

Swedish novelist, poet and playwright, born in Örebro, a place he frequently satirized in later life, taking revenge for the humiliation he had suffered as a stout and painfully shy youth. His work ranges from a dark psychological vision, evident in *En döds memoarer* (1918–19, 'The Memoirs of a Dead Man'), to an almost Symbolist underpinning of conventional realism, as in *Murkurells i Wadköping* (1919, Eng trans *God's Orchid*, 1924), and to the lighter comic touch of plays like *Swedenhielms* (1925, 'The Swedenhielms') and *Patrasket* (1928, 'The Rabble').
▷E Linder, translated by Catherine Djurklou, *Hjalmar Bergman* (1975)

BERGNER, Herz
(1907–)

Polish-born Australian novelist and short-story writer, who emigrated to Australia before World War I. His first stories, all originally published in Yiddish, told of the immigrant experience in Australia. The novels *Between Sky and Sea* (1946) and *Light and Shadow* (1960), and the collection of short stories *Where the Truth Lies* (1965) all won significant awards upon publication.

BERGROTH
(1886–1966)

Finnish novelist, critic and playwright, who wrote in Swedish until 1920, but then turned to Finnish. She was a student of the anthroposophy of **Rudolph Steiner**. She has received little attention from critics.

BERGSON, Henri
(1859–1941)

French philosopher, born in Paris, son of a Polish Jewish musician and an English mother, and winner of the Nobel Prize for literature. He became professor at the Collège de France (1900–24), and was a highly original thinker who became something of a cult figure. He contrasted the fundamental reality of the dynamic flux of consciousness with the inert physical world of discrete objects, which was a convenient fiction for the mechanistic descriptions of science. The *élan vital*, or 'creative impulse', not a deterministic natural selection, is at the heart of evolution, and intuition, not analysis, reveals the real world of process and change. His own writings are literary, suggestive and analogical rather than philosophical in the modern sense, and he greatly influenced such writers as **Marcel Proust** (to whom he was connected by marriage), **Georges Sorel** and **Samuel Butler**. His most important works were *Essai sur les Données Immédiates de la Conscience* (1889, Eng trans *Time and Free-will*, 1910), *Matière et Memoire* (1896, Eng trans *Matter and Memory*, 1911), and *L'Evolution Créatrice* (1907, Eng trans *Creative Evolution*, 1911). He was awarded the Nobel Prize for literature in 1927.

BERKOFF, Steven
(1937–)

English dramatist, actor and director. After studying at the École Jacques Lecoq in Paris, he founded the London Theatre Group, for whom he directed his own adaptations from the classics, including **Franz Kafka**'s *Metamorphosis* (1969), in which he himself played the role of the young man who finds himself transformed into a beetle. His own plays include *Greek* (1979), a variant of the Oedipal myth transferred to contemporary London, and *West* (1983), an adaptation of the Beowulf legend; *Decadence* (1981) counterpoints the sexual and social activities of an upper-class couple with that of a working-class woman and a private detective. Other plays and adaptations include *The Penal Colony* (1968), *The Trial* (1970), *Agamemnon* (1963), *The Fall of the House of Usher* (1974), *Sink the Belgrano* (1986) and *Brighton Beach Scumbags* (1991).

BERMANT, Chaim Icyk
(1929–)

British novelist and journalist. He was born in Breslev, Poland, and educated at rabbinical college in Glasgow. After Glasgow University and the London School of Economics he worked as an economist and television scriptwriter before publishing his first novel in 1964, *Jericho Sleep Alone*, an autobiographical account of Orthodox Jewish life in Glasgow. In *Berl Make Tea* and *Ben Preserve Us* (both 1965) he strives too hard for an ironic tone; however, his gift for compassionate observation reappears in the slight but moving *Diary of an Old Man* (1967). In *The Last Supper* (1973), he dissects the tensions and aspirations of a well-off family as it mourns the dead mother. *The House of Women* (1983) stands aside from his usual constituency and analyses another upper middle-class family without the ideological and rhetorical props they and he were accustomed to use in the more overtly Jewish books. Bermant is a close observer of British Jewry, particularly of its upper echelons; *The Cousinhood* (1971) and *The Walled Garden* (1974) are clear-sighted contributions to the sociology of religion and race.

BERNA, Paul (Jean Sabran)
(1910–94)

French children's writer, born in Hyères, and author of the classic *Le Cheval sans tête* (1955, Eng trans *A Hundred Million Francs*, 1957), set in the backstreets of Paris. He worked in administrative jobs in a bank and the Post Office but his children's books are marked by an emphasis on open-air adventure. Most of his stories involve gangs of boys and girls, usually of mixed ages, pitted against a criminal element. Unlike many adventure novels written for the young they have retained their freshness and sense of excitement.

BERNANOS, Georges
(1888–1948)

French writer, born in Paris. He did not begin to write seriously until he was 37 and had taken degrees in law and letters. A Catholic polemicist, he attacked indifference and was preoccupied with problems of sin and grace. His most memorable novels are *Sous le soleil de Satan* (1926, 'Under Satan's Sun') and *Le Journal d'un curé de campagne* (1936, 'The Diary of a Country Priest'). He also wrote a play, *Dialogues des Carmélites* (1949), and *Les grands cimetières sous la lune* (1938, Eng trans *The Fearless Heart*, 1952).

▷G Blumenthal, *The Poetic Imagination of Georges Bernanos* (1965)

BERNARD, Jean-Jacques
(1888–1972)

French novelist and dramatist, born in Enghien-les-Bains, the son of Tristan Bernard (1866–1947), humorist and playwright. Jean-Jacques was the leading exponent of the so-called 'Theatre of Silence', which drew its inspiration from the plays of **Maurice Maeterlinck**. His most famous play was *Le feu qui reprend mal* (1921, Eng trans with four more plays, in *The Sulky Fire*, 1939). In it a soldier returns from the war to a wife grown cold to him—but she remains with him out of pity. He was a classical, anti-rhetorical dramatist, whose work played well and was moderately successful. In France his most highly regarded play is *Martine* (1922, Eng trans 1927, and in *The Sulky Fire*, 1939), about a girl who is seduced and then betrayed by a slick city man. This was memorably filmed in 1944 by Jacques Remy, with a script by **Jules Supervielle**, with Nora Gregor as the unhappy but radiant girl. Bernard wrote a life of his *farceur* father, several good novels and stories, and a moving memory of those French Jews who were imprisoned in the concentration camp at Compiègne: *Le Camp de la morte lente* (1945, 'The Camp of Slow Death'). He was a dramatist whose best (earlier) plays are likely to be revived on a quite large scale.

▷M Daniels, *French Drama of the Unspoken* (1953)

BERNARD, Tristan, originally Paul
(1866–1947)

French novelist and dramatist, born in Besançon. His first success came with the novel, *Les Mémoires d'un jeune homme rangé* (1899, 'Memoirs of a Dutiful Young Man'). In the same year he wrote a comedy, *L'Anglais tel qu'on le parle* ('English as it is Spoken'), and from then on produced a number of lighthearted pieces with stock comic situations, which proved very popular, including *Daisy* (1902), *Triplipatte* (1905), *Le Petit Café* (1911, 'The Small Café') and *Le Prince Charmant* (1921, 'Prince Charming').

▷J J Bernard, *Mon père Tristan Bernard* (1955)

BERNARDES, Diogo
(1532–c.1596)

Portuguese poet, who was with King Sebastian's Moroccan expedition (1578); he was a captive in North Africa until ransomed. A distinguished and influential representative of the Renaissance period, the bulk of his work now has little appeal except to the scholar or historian. However, some of his devotional poetry is exceptional, and he is still much anthologized in his own country.

BERNARDEZ, Francisco Luis
(1900–)

Argentinian poet, who spent his youth in Spain, where he picked up a certain type of *modernista* style. Later he developed into an altogether more interesting poet, a kind of Latin-American **Claudel**, whose techniques and perfervid Catholicism he has imported into Argentinian poetry.

BERNARI, Carlo, pseud of Carlo Bernardi
(1909–)

Italian novelist from Naples, whose views were originally formed under the influence of **Croce**. He was thrown out of school for his anti-fascist attitude. A sojourn with Surrealists such as **André Breton** in Paris in 1930 did not signify a real change of direction. His most important and influential book was the novel *Tre operi* (1934, 'Three Factory Workers'), an anti-fascist study of three workers (two men and a woman), whose real hero, it has been stated, is the Neapolitan language. This, a precursor of the Italian 'neorealistic' movement, was disliked by Mussolini's censors, but not banned. Later Bernari wrote *Speranzella* (1949), a novel of Neapolitan life which won the Viareggio Prize. His journalism has been influential.

BERNART DE VENTADORN, or DE VENTADOUR)
(c.1140–c.1190)

French poet and troubadour, born in Ventadorn, who became the leading *trouvère* of his day. He served in various noble houses, notably that of Eleanor of Aquitaine (who took him to England and knighted him) and that of Count Raimon V of Toulouse. Around 45 of his long poems in Old French survive, several with the melodies to which they were originally sung. He ended his days in a monastery in the Dordogne.

BERNHARD, Thomas
(1931–90)

Austrian novelist and dramatist, born in the Netherlands but raised in Austria by his grandfather, who was a highly eccentric writer called Johannes Freumbichler. Bernhard was unique in world letters, although he had debts to, or affinities with, **Louis-Ferdinand Céline** in particular and, for the construction of his novels, to 12-tone musical theory—of which he made brilliant use. He came very close to death from a lung illness in 1949, but just survived. He was the literary scourge of an Austria which elected the ex-Nazi intelligence officer Kurt Waldheim to its presidency (for which, although no leftist or even democrat, he castigated it), and yet won virtually every prize that could be offered. His misanthropy (which concealed a wistful tenderness) is reminiscent only of Céline, as is his humour. His technique, basically consisting of interior monologues embedded within interior monologues, is very complex, yet his books are compulsively readable. They are all more or less autobiographical. *Frost* (1963), his first success, is an account, by a cantankerous writer very like Bernhard, to a young medical student, of his impressions of the mountain valley to which he has fled. In *Korrektur* (1975, Eng trans *Corrections*, 1979), the protagonist character, Roithamer, is based on the philosopher Ludwig Wittgenstein, whose nephew Paul—who went mad—Bernhard knew well. His, essentially expressionistic, drama, is less profound, but his plays acted as useful shocks to Austrian audiences, who on at least one occasion rioted in order to show their displeasure. The trilogy of autobiographical volumes, *Die Ursache* (1975, 'The Cause'), *Der Keller* (1976, 'The Cellar'), and *Der Atem* (1978, 'The Breath'), is revelatory in its explanation of what has been called his pessimism.

BERNI, or BERNIA, Francesco
(c.1497–1535)

Italian poet, born in Lamporecchio in Tuscany. In 1517 he went from Florence to Rome, where he entered successively the service of his uncle, Cardinal Bibbiena, of Ghiberti, Chancellor to Clement VII, and in 1532 of Cardinal Ippolito de Medici. This he left a year later, and went to Florence, where, refusing to poison Cardinal Salviati, he was himself poisoned. His recast or *rifacimento* of **Boiardo**'s *Orlando Innamorato* (1542) is still read in Italy in preference to the original. He played a large part in establishing Italian as a literary language.
▷A Virgil, *Francesco Berni* (1981)

BERNSTEIN, Henry
(1876–1953)

French writer of initially successful, and sensational, plays, such as *Le Voleur* (1906, 'The Thief'), a thriller with clever and topical dialogue. Later he turned to the portrayal of character, and anticipated **Galsworthy**'s play

Loyalties in *Israel* (1908), an exposure of polite anti-Semitism. He went on writing until his death, but lost favour with his boulevard audiences.

▷ B H Clark, *Contemporary French Dramatists* (1916)

BERRY, James
(1924–)

Jamaican-born poet, who moved to Britain in 1948. As an author and anthologist he has made a considerable impact on British poetry while simultaneously establishing himself as a respected authority on Caribbean culture. Collections of his own work include *Fractured Circles* (1979), *Lucy's Letters and Loving* (1982) and *Chain of Days* (1985). His anthologies include *Bluefoot Traveller: An Anthology of West Indian Poets of Britain* (1976) and *News for Babylon* (1984). He has a fine ear for speech rhythms, particularly those of the Caribbean vernacular. His own poetry, while often humorous, is compassionate and moving. He also writes for young people, his collection of stories for children, *A Thief in the Village* (1987), being especially acclaimed.

BERRY, Mary, née Seton
(1763–1852)

English dramatist and woman of letters, born in Kirkbridge in Yorkshire. Her comedy *Fashionable Friends* (1801) was played in Drury Lane, but had only small success. She held conventional opinions, but her *Journals* (edited in 1865) are of interest for the background they provide.

BERRY, Wendell
(1934–)

American poet, novelist and essayist. Growing up in Henry County, Kentucky, he quickly grasped the economic, cultural and racial contradictions of middle America. These form the substance of his finest book, *A Place on Earth* (1967, rev edn 1983) which is set in Kentucky just after World War II, but the unsentimental pastoral strain in his work is even more clearly seen in his verse, notably in *The Broken Ground* (1964), *Farming: A Handbook* (1970), *The Country of Marriage* (1973), the significantly titled *A Part* (1980) and *The Wheel* (1982). All of his verse up to that point was harvested in a *Collected Poems* (1985). *Nathan Coulter* (1960) established the retrospective style of his fiction, sustained in *The Memory of Old Jack* (1974) and *Remembering* (1988), though the latter was less focused than usual. *The Unsettling of America* (1977) gave a straightforward account of the status of US agriculture, but

completely avoided bland discursiveness or reactionary pastoralism.

▷ *The Hidden Wound* (1970)

BERRYMAN, John
(1914–72)

American poet, biographer, novelist and academic. Born John Allyn Smith in McAlester, Oklahoma, he adopted his stepfather's name at the age of 12. Educated at Columbia University and Clare College, Cambridge, he taught at Wayne State University, Harvard, Princeton, the University of Washington, the University of Connecticut, and University of Minnesota, where he was Regents Professor of Humanities (1955–72). His biography of **Stephen Crane** (1950) is rated highly but his reputation rests on his poetry. Often pigeonholed as a confessional poet he disparaged the label. His first collection, *Poems*, appeared in 1942. This was followed by *The Dispossessed* (1948) and *Homage to Mistress Bradstreet* (1956), inspired by the first New England poet, **Anne Bradstreet**, which established his reputation. His major work is his *Dream Songs*, which he began in 1955: *77 Dream Songs* (1964) won the Pulitzer Prize in 1965; *His Toy, His Dream, His Rest: 308 Dream Songs* (1968) received the National Book Award in 1969. The complete sequence was published in 1969. His other books include the novel *Recovery* (1973), which concerned alcoholism. He acknowledged his illness but could not overcome either it or his increasingly severe mental disturbances. He took his own life in Minneapolis.

▷ J Haffenden, *John Berryman* (1982)

BERSHADSKY, Isaiah, pseud of Isaiah Domachevitsky
(1872–1910)

Hebrew novelist, born in Samoscha, who wrote the first truly realistic fiction in the language. He became editor of an important periodical in Vilna. Despite the fame of his work amongst Jewish readers, and its power and psychological acumen, he has not yet found a translator.

▷ M Waxman, *A History of Jewish Literature* (1960)

BERTO, Guiseppe
(1914–78)

Italian novelist and dramatist from Mogliano Veneto, near Venice. He fought in World War II and was captured and spent 30 months as a prisoner of war in Texas. His first big success—which he wrote in captivity—was *Il cielo è rossi* (1947, Eng trans *The Sky is Red*, 1948), about the courage and recuperative powers of four children subjected to terrible bombing raids. This fulfilled all the expectations of the so-called 'neorealistic' novel: it was indebted to American novelists such as **Faulkner**, and it dealt directly with World War II. Later Berto changed direction: *Il male oscuro* (1964, Eng trans *Incubus*, 1966), is about a neurotic who seeks a cure by free association, and is written in a notably avant-garde manner.

▷D Heiney, *America in Modern Italian Literature* (1964)

BERTRAND, Aloysius *see* BERTRAND, Jacques-Louis Napoléon

BERTRAND, Jacques-Louis Napoléon
(1807–41)

French poet, more generally known as Aloysius Bertrand. He was born in Ceva, but his family later settled in Dijon (1815). He is considered a highly significant figure in the development of the French prose poem; *Gaspard de la Nuit* (1842, posthumous) was to influence **Baudelaire**, **Mallarmé**, **Rimbaud** and **Apollinaire**, with its innovative form, and treatment of quintessential Romantic themes such as heightened sensibility, the medieval and the Gothic, and the opposition of the sentimental and the grotesque. Bertrand edited and directed various periodicals between 1828 and 1831, moved to Paris in 1833 and published a volume of poetry, *La Volupté*, in 1834.

BERTRAND, Louis Marie Émile
(1866–1941)

French author, born in Spincourt. He spent some years in Algeria, which provides a setting for *Sang des races* (1898, 'Blood of the People'), *La Cina* (1900), and other realistic novels and travel books. He also wrote historical novels and biographical studies of **Gustave Flaubert** and Louis XIV.

BERTRAND DE BORN
(c.1140–c.1215)

French troubadour and political intriguer, probably born and brought up in Guyenne. His poems encouraged Prince Henry to break with his father, King Henry II of England. Then, following the death of the prince, he supported Henry II and Richard I the Lionheart against the French king, Philippe II. Principally because of his original support for Prince Henry, he is placed by **Dante**, in Canto XXVIII of the *Inferno*, among the 'sowers of schism'.

BERZSENYI, Daniel
(1776–1836)

Hungarian lyric poet, born in Heteny. Educated by his father, he won fame as a patriotic poet with his *Ode to Magyarokhoz*, inspired by the Magyar nobility's successful opposition to Napoleon on the Styrian Alps. Collections of his verse appeared in 1813 and 1830.

▷O Merenyi, *Berzsenyi Daniel* (1966)

BESANT, Sir Walter
(1836–1901)

English novelist and social reformer, brother-in-law of Annie Besant. Born in Portsmouth, he studied at King's College, London, and at Christ's College, Cambridge. After a few years as a professor in Mauritius, he devoted himself to literature. His first work, *Studies in French Poetry*, appeared in 1868. In 1871 he entered into a literary partnership with **James Rice** (1844–82), who was editor of *Once a Week*. Together they produced many novels, including *Ready-Money Mortiboy* (1872), *The Golden Butterfly* (1876) and *The Steamy Side* (1881). He himself wrote *All Sorts and Conditions of Men* (1882) and *Children of Gibeon* (1886), describing conditions in the slums of the east end of London, and other novels advocating social reform, resulting in the establishment of the People's Palace (1887) for popular recreation. He was also the author of biographical studies and works on the history of London. He was secretary of the Palestine Exploration Fund and first chairman of the Incorporated Society of Authors (1884).

▷F W Sage, *Sir Walter Besant, novelist* (1956)

BESTALL, A(lfred) E(dmeades)
(1892–1986)

English illustrator and author, born in Manderlay, Burma. Although Bestall's drawings appeared in many books, including four volumes of the *Boys and Girls Annual* (1935–6), and several issues of the *Tatler* and *Punch*, he is mainly remembered for having illustrated and written the Rupert Bear picture strip in the *Daily Express* newspaper for 30 years (1935–65), taking over from Rupert's creator, **Mary Tourtel**. He also illustrated and wrote 41 volumes of the *Rupert Bear Annual* (1936–76). Rupert's inquisitive, white furry face, red pullover and yellow check trousers and scarf are known to millions through Bestall's drawings.

▷A Bestall and G Perry, *Rupert: A Bear's Life* (1985)

BESTER, Alfred
(1913–87)

American writer, born in New York. He was educated at the University of Pennsylvania, where he studied both humanities and sciences. He won a writing competition with his first science-fiction story, 'The Broken Axiom' (1939). He wrote scripts for radio serials and comic books in the 1940s, and returned to science fiction in 1950. His first novel, *The Demolished Man* (1953), was followed by his classic *Tiger, Tiger* (1956), retitled as *The Stars My Destination* in the USA, a psychologically powerful account of a man driven by inner demons and lust for revenge in a distintegrating 25th-century world. His short stories, collected in four volumes, and novels reveal an unusual degree of psychological and formal complexity for the genre, and he is one of the most individual voices working in science fiction.

BÉSUS, Roger
(1915–)

French novelist and playwright (he wrote a single play: *Savonarole*, 1954) in the tradition of **Bernanos**, born in Bayeux. He is a Catholic, and his characters, usually Normans like himself, are souls torn apart by the battle between good and evil as seen in the novels of Bernanos or **Marcel Jouhandeau**. He is a little neglected both within and outside France (there are no translations); of his work at least *Cet Homme qui vous aimait* (1953, 'That Man You Love') deserves consideration for its psychological penetration of a lacerated Catholic soul.

BETHELL, (Mary) Ursula
(1874–1945)

New Zealand poet, born in England, who started writing in her fifties with verses describing her domestic situation in letters to English friends, published as *From a Garden in the Antipodes* (1929). Her other collections were *Time and Place* (1936) and *Day and Night: Poems 1924–1935* (1939). The posthumous *Collected Poems* (1950) was followed later by a more complete *Collected Poems* ed **Vincent O'Sullivan** (1985). Her work shows a love of nature's delicate detail and a joy in fine words.

BETI, Mongo, pseud of Alexandre Biyidi
(1931–)

French Cameroonian Francophone novelist and essayist. He published his earliest work under the name of Eza Boto. He left his country in 1959, to become a schoolteacher in Rouen; in 1972 he wrote a polemic against its government, which he considered to be the servant of French colonial interests. His first novel to gain attention, and still his best-known work, was *Le pauvre Christ de Bomba* (1956, Eng trans *The Poor Christ of Bomba*, 1971), a vigorous and ironic exposure of colonialism. Beti has since become less overtly political; yet such subtler novels as *La ruine*

presque cocasse d'un polichinelle (1979, 'The Nearly Laughable Fall of a Buffoon'), dramatize oppression and liberation in an ultimately political manner.

▷A C Brench, *The Novelists' Inheritance in French Africa* (1967); W Cartey, *Whispers from a Continent* (1969)

BETJEMAN, Sir John
(1906–84)

English poet, broadcaster and writer on architecture, born in Highgate, London. The son of a Dutch-descended manufacturer of household objects, he was educated at Marlborough College and Magdalen College, Oxford, a period covered by his blank-verse autobiography, *Summoned by Bells* (1960). Incorrigibly indolent, he left university without a degree. He marked time as a cricket master in a preparatory school and was sacked as the *Evening Standard*'s film critic before beginning to write for the *Architectural Review* and becoming general editor of the *Shell Guides* in 1934. He published the bleak 'Death in Leamington' in the *London Mercury* in 1930 and a year later his first collection of verse, *Mount Zion; or In Touch with the Infinite* appeared. Other collections include *Continual Dew; A Little Book of Bourgeois Verse* (1937), *Old Lights for New Chancels* (1940), *New Bats in Old Belfries* (1945), *A Few Late Chrysanthemums* (1954) and *Collected Poems* (1958), of which 100 000 copies were sold of the first edition. Later (but lesser) volumes are *A Nip in the Air* (1972) and *High and Low* (1976). He is the quintessential poet of the suburbs, particular, jolly, nostalgic and wary of change, preferring the countryside to the city. Inveterately self-deprecatory, he described himself as 'the **Ella Wheeler Wilcox** de nos jours', and, in *Who's Who*, as a 'poet and hack'. He was an astute and sensitive social critic, impassioned in his abhorrence of modern architecture and town planning ('Come, friendly bombs, and fall on Slough. It isn't fit for humans now'), and beneath the froth lies a poet undeniably melancholic and serious. A national institution, he succeeded **Cecil Day-Lewis** as poet laureate in 1972.

▷D Stanford, *John Betjeman: a study* (1961)

BETOCCHI, Carlo
(1899–1987)

Italian poet and editor, born in Turin and raised in Florence, whose standing has increased since his death—some have even raised him to the same status of Italy's four greatest modern poets, **Montale**, **Saba**, **Quasimodo** and **Ungaretti**. He worked as an engineer, but was always at the centre of Italian literary life, and acted for many years as editor of the Florentine magazine *Il frontispizio*. He was close personally to **Rébora**, and drew his first inspiration from the 'crepuscular' poetry of **Gozzano**. His debts to Ungaretti and other more modern Italian poets have been much exaggerated, but, a man of broad sensibilities and reading, he was indebted to English poets such as **Shelley** and **Hopkins**. Betocchi's achievement, which received belated acknowledgement with the award of the Viareggio Prize (1955), was highly original within its Italian context. His poetry, deceptively simple, is religious, supple and dedicated to the communication of primary experience: 'his work glows with an inner certainty', a critic has written. There is an English translation in *Selected Poems* (1964).

BETTI, Ugo
(1892–1953)

Italian dramatist and poet, born in Camerino. He studied law and became a judge in Rome (1930–44) and librarian of the Ministry of Justice (1944–53). His collections of verse include *Re pensieroso* (1922, 'The Meditative King'), of short stories *Caino* (1929, 'Cain') and *Le Case* (1937, 'Houses'); in the best of his plays, *La Padrona* (1929), life appears symbolically in the person of a cynical, masterful and attractive woman. His own profession was not spared in *Corruzione al Palazzo di Giustizia* (1944, Eng trans *Corruption in the Palace of Justice*, 1957), and *La fuggitava* (1953, 'The Fugitive').
▷G Moro, *Il teatro di Ugo Betti* (1973)

BEYATLI, Yahya Kemal
(1884–1958)

Turkish poet and critic, a giant in terms of his country's literature, born in Skopje (later Yugoslavia). He was a diplomat and member of parliament. Before the modern era he gained a reputation as a neoclassical poet of great technical excellence; he remained active in Turkish literature until his death, when he was given a massive state funeral.
▷A H Tanipar, *Yayha Kemal* (1962)

BEZA, Theodorus, or THÉODORE DE BÈZE
(1519–1605)

French religious reformer, born of the noble family of De Besze at Vézelay, in Burgundy. He studied Greek and law at Orléans. He became known as a writer of witty (but indecent) verses in *Juvenilia* (1548), settled with brilliant prospects in Paris, and lived for a time in fashionable dissipation. But after an illness, he took a serious view of life, and, marrying his mistress, in 1548 went with her to Geneva, where he joined Calvin; and from 1549 to 1554 was Greek Professor at Lausanne, publishing his only important literary work, a drama on *The Sacrifice of Abraham*. In 1559, with Calvin, he founded the academy at Geneva and became Professor of Theology and first rector there. In 1563 he returned to Geneva from France, and on Calvin's death (1564) the care of the Genevese church fell upon Beza's shoulders. He presided over the synods of French reformers held at La Rochelle in 1571 and at Nîmes in 1572. His best-known work is the Latin New Testament.
▷P F Geisendorf, *Théodore de Bèze* (1949)

BEZRUC, Petr, pseud of Vladimir Vasek
(1867–1958)

Czech workers' poet and (on occasion) revolutionary, whose adopted name means 'Peter Without Hands'; he wrote only one collection, but continually revised it (for, critics say, the worse). A mild postal official by profession, his literary persona was of a rough coal-worker. His regional verse is unusually effective for what it is: a protest on behalf of the Silesian miners and peasants at the way they were being treated. There is a selection of his work by I Milner in *Silesian Songs* (1966).

BHARATI, C Subramania, pseud of C Subramania Iyer
(1882–1921)

Indian (Tamil) translator, seminal essayist, story writer and poet, his language's greatest in modern times. His work is well represented in English translation, but will undoubtedly be reappraised and rendered again. He was the sole Tamil poet of the 20th century to understand that the earlier traditions of Tamil literature must be preserved, but that mere imitation would not do. He was for the last years of his life virtually in exile at Pondicherry (controlled by the French) because of his activities on behalf of the Congress Party. Like **Hagiwara** in Japan, and other similar pioneer poets of other nations, he was the first to enrich his language with the vernacular idiom, without violating its essence. He excelled in the long poem. There are selected translations by himself, with some work composed in English, in *Agni* (1937), and others in *The Voice of a Poet* (1951) and *Selected Verse* (1958); *Poems* (1977) contains his three long poems: *Kannan pattu* (1917, 'The Krishna Songs'), *Pancali capatam* (1912, 'Panchali's Vow') and *Kuyil pattu* (1912, 'Kuyil's Song'), this last being the lyrical dream of a poet who listens to stories told to him by a cuckoo. He translated some of **Tagore** into Tamil.

BHARTRIHARI
(fl.7th century)

Hindu poet and philosopher. He was the author of three *satakas* (centuries) of stanzas on practical conduct, love, and renunciation of the world, and a Sanskrit grammarian.

▷ *The Proverbial Philosophy of Bhartrihari* (1890)

BHASA
(fl.3rd century)

Sanskrit dramatist. He was the author of plays on religious and legendary themes.

▷A D Pusalkar, *Bhasa: a study* (1940)

BHATTACHARYA, Bhabani
(1906–)

Indian (Bengali) novelist, educated in Patna and in England, who was much influenced by Gandhi, and wrote a book on him. His best-known and most powerful novel, in English, is *He Who Rides a Tiger* (1954), about an untouchable who poses as a holy man, and who finds success. Critics of an imperialist or conservative cast of mind tried to dismiss Bhattacharya as merely a 'documentary' writer, but may well have been aware of the sharpness of his indictments of British and other governmental corruption. *A Goddess Named Gold* (1960) is a later novel.

BHATTACHARYA, Birendra Kumar
(1924–)

Indian novelist from the Brahmaputra valley, whose Assamese novel *Iyanvingam* (1961) gives a powerful view of events in eastern India prior to and including World War II.

BHAVABHÛTI, surnamed 'Srî-Kantha'

A great Indian dramatist, who flourished in 730.

▷Vimla Gera, *The Mind and Art of Bhav-abhûti* (1973)

BIALIK, Chaim Nachman
(1873–1934)

Hebrew poet, the outstanding figure of his age, born in the Ukraine. After studying the Talmud and becoming a follower of **Mendele Mocher Seforim** in Odessa, he returned to his home near Zhitomir and became a wood merchant, at which he failed disastrously. **Maxim Gorky** helped him to emigrate in 1921 to Berlin, where he established the Devir publishing house. When he went to Palestine in 1924 he took this with him. His poetry is always cast in a personal form, and is often uninhibitedly erotic. He made an influential anthology of the *Aggadah* (folk poetry), and was always looked up to as the natural leader of Hebrew poetry. In translation there is the first volume (only) of *Complete Poetic Works* (1948), and a *Selected Poems* (1965). *Aftergrowth* is a selection of stories.

▷M Waxman, *A History of Jewish Literature* (1947)

BIALOSZEWSKI, Miron
(1922–)

Polish poet, playwright, memoirist, essayist, whose work resists categorization. As an essayist he is against 'aesthetic values'. His plays were performed, mainly, in his own primitive apartment. 'He is', the sympathetic but perhaps impatient **Czeslaw Milosz** comments, 'fascinated by ugly sibilants and ridiculously jarring sounds.' The following remark exactly sums up his effect upon his superiors: 'in another kind of world he would have won the Nobel prize, but then in such a world there would be no Nobel prizes, since that kind of ' 'hopeless' ' honour would be mocked'. He wishes to return to the 'hopelessness' (again) of medieval Polish. He is a poet of undignified objects, 'dusty staircases, rusty pipes, old stoves, kitchen utensils, mouldy walls'. In one of his (untranslated) plays the characters are 10 fingers intimidated by a comb above them which appears to threaten their existence. They engage in dialogue which mocks philosophical niceties. Yet it is well acknowledged that his anti-eloquent accounts of the Warsaw uprising, through which he lived, are the most poignant and potent of all. Versions of some of his poems are in Milosz's *Post-War Polish Poetry* (1965).

BICHSEL, Peter
(1935–)

Swiss story writer (writing in German), born in Olten. He was given a prize by the German literary circle, Gruppe '47, in 1965. His collection *Frau Blum den Milchmann kenneriernen* (1964, Eng trans *And Really Frau Blum Would Very Much Like to Meet the Milkman*, 1969), consists of tiny stories, as does *Kindergeschichten* (1969, Eng trans *There Is No Such Place as America*, 1970). There is a limit to the interest that can be generated by such miniscule tales, all of whose detail revolves around choice of words, but Bichsel's minimalism and his outspoken criticism of his own people are based on an intelligent and sincere appraisal of what he sees around him.

BICKERSTAFFE, Isaac
(c.1735–c.1812)

Irish playwright, born in Dublin. He was page to Lord Chesterfield, the lord-lieutenant. Later he was an officer of marines, but was dismissed from the service, and in 1772 had to flee the country. Of his numerous pieces, produced between 1760 and 1771, the best known is *The Maid of the Mill*, and he is credited with establishing the comic opera in the English theatre. His musical collaborators included Thomas Arne and Samuel Arnold.

▷P A Tasch, *The Dramatic Cobbler* (1971)

BIELER, Manfred
(1934–)

German novelist, born in Zerbst, in the former East German Republic. He left in 1967 for Munich. His greatest achievement is the picaresque comic novel *Bonifaz* (1963, Eng trans *Bonifaz, or the Sailor in the Bottle*, 1966), about a 'ridiculous man', plainly modelled after the Schweyk of **Hašek**.

BIERBAUM, Otto Julius
(1865–1910)

German novelist, editor (of the influential art magazine *Pan*, which he co-founded, and of a magazine which became the famous publishing house Insel Verlag) and poet, born in Grünberg. His verse, a mixture of the traditional and the light-modern, is now remembered mainly as an important influence upon **Brecht** and other successors of like mind.

BIERCE, Ambrose Gwinnett
(1842–1914)

American short-story writer and journalist, and the **Dr Johnson** of cynicism, compiling the much-quoted *Cynic's Word Book* (published in book form 1906), now better known as *The Devil's Dictionary*. Bierce grew up in Indiana, and fought for the Union in the Civil War, an experience that provided the material for his finest stories. He lived in Britain for three years (1872–5), writing copy for *Fun* and other magazines. He published his first books, collections of brief stories and sketches, under the pseudonym 'Dod Grile'. In 1887, he joined William Randolph Hearst's *San Francisco Examiner* to write the 'Prattle' column, which honed his already sharp style. His most important collection of stories, *Tales of Soldiers and Civilians* (1892), was published at a time of great personal turmoil, during which he divorced, and his son was killed in a gunfight. The most celebrated story, 'An Occurrence at Owl Creek Bridge', is a haunted, near-death fantasy of escape, influenced by **Poe** and in turn influencing **Stephen Crane** and **Hemingway**. Hearst used Bierce as a lobbyist, and Bierce moved to Washington, DC, continuing to work as a journalist there. In 1913 he went to Mexico to report on Pancho Villa's army at first hand. Though the date of his death has been the subject of much romantic uncertainty, it seems probable that he was killed at or shortly after the battle of Ojinaga in January 1914.
▷R O'Connor, *Bierce: A Biography* (1967)

BIERMANN, Wolf
(1936–)

German poet, singer and playwright. He grew up in Hamburg in a socialist family which emigrated to East Germany in 1953. Biermann attended Humboldt University and joined the **Brecht**ian Berliner Ensemble. His own early verse reflected Brecht's militant aesthetics. In 1965 he was censured by the East German authorities and forbidden to perform in public or publish, guaranteeing him a sympathetic audience in the West. His best-known books are *The Wire Harp* (published in English in 1968) and the later and darker *Poems and Ballads* (published in English in 1977).

BIGELOW, John
(1817–1911)

American writer and diplomat, born in Malden, New York. He was co-owner and managing editor of the New York *Evening Post* from 1850 to 1861, when he went as consul to Paris. From 1865 to 1866 he was American minister in France. In 1875 he was elected secretary of state for New York. He published a biography of **Benjamin Franklin** (1874) and edited his works. His son, Poultney (1855–1954), was an international journalist and traveller, and friend of Kaiser Wilhelm II.
▷M A Clapp, *Forgotten First Citizen* (1968)

BIGGERS, Earl Derr
(1884–1933)

American novelist and playwright, born in Warren, Ohio. He was educated at Harvard, and entered journalism as a staff writer on the Boston *Traveller*. He introduced the famous character Charlie Chan in a series of detective novels starting with *The House without a Key* (1925), continuing until *Keeper of the Keys*, which appeared a year before Biggers's death.

BIGONGIARI, Piero
(1914–)

Italian poet, translator (**Ronsard**, **Rilke**, **Conrad**) and critic, born near Pisa. He was one of the minor promoters of Hermeticism, the movement so christened by the critic Francisco Flora. His own poetry has not received a great deal of attention, but, like his first collection, *La figlia di Babilonia* (1942, 'The Daughter of Babylon'), it is programmatically hermetic, and elegantly sealed from the reader.

BIJNS, Anna
(1493–1575)

Dutch poet, from Antwerp in what is now Belgium. Bijns was a schoolteacher and a strongly religious woman who took up writing verse at the behest of the Catholic Church. Many of her poems are responses to the spread of Protestantism in the northern Netherlands, others are simply devotional, and a few are more earthly love poems. She was the first major woman poet writing in Dutch or Flemish, and is still very highly regarded in Holland and Belgium. *Schoon Ende suverlijc boecken inhoudende veel— constige refereinen* (1987) is a superb facsimile edition, with the original woodcuts and a modern commentary, of her 1528 original.

BILAC, Olavo Braes
(1865–1918)

Brazilian poet, educator and newspaper essayist, born in Rio de Janeiro. In his lush, beautifully executed, highly artificial poetry he crossed Portuguese traditionalism with French Parnassianism. Two of his poems are translated in the *Penguin Book of Latin American Verse* (1971, ed E Curacciolo-Trejo).

BILDERDIJK, Willem
(1756–1831)

Dutch poet and philologist, born in Amsterdam. Crippled as a child, he had talent and intellect, albeit marred by an egotistic, rather than unbalanced, temperament. His voluminous poetry, a blend of rhapsody and neoclassical style, ranges from light verse to epic.
▷H Bavinck, *Bilderdijk als denker en dichter* (1906)

BILLETDOUX, François
(1927–)

French actor and dramatist, born in Paris. His one unequivocal success with critics was *Thcin-Tchin* (1959, Eng trans *Chin-Chin*, 1963), about a couple of betrayed spouses who have an alcoholic affair. This touching play, which has been called both **Chekhov**ian and Absurdist, was successful in London and New York as well as Paris. His later plays, such as *Va donc chez Törpe* (1961, Eng trans *Chez Törpe*, 1963), and the **Brecht**ian exercise *Comment va le Monde, Mòssieu? Il tourne, Mòssieu!* (1964, 'How Goes the World, Mister? It Revolves, Mister!'), have been described variously, as 'pretentious', 'didactic', 'crude' and 'curiously haunting'.
▷J Guicharnaud, *Modern French Theatre* (1967)

BILLINGER, Richard
(1893–1965)

Austrian poet, born in St Marienkirchen. He was the author of collections of lyrics, as well as novels coloured by peasant life in Upper Austria.

BILLINGS, Josh, pseud of Henry Wheeler Shaw
(1818–85)

American humorous writer, born in Lanesboro, Massachusetts. A land agent in Poughkeepsie, New York, he published facetious almanacs and collections of witticisms, relying heavily on deliberate misspelling. The first of these was *Josh Billings, His Sayings* (1866).
▷C Clemens, *Josh Billings, Yankee Humorist* (1932)

BINCHY, Maeve
(1940–)

Irish novelist, playwright and short-story writer, born in Dublin and educated at University College, Dublin. She worked as a teacher and part-time travel writer before joining the *Irish Times* in 1969, later becoming the paper's London correspondent. She has had plays staged in Dublin and won awards in Ireland and Prague for her TV play *Deeply Regretted By* (1979). Her collections of short stories include observations on the lives of Londoners in *Victoria Line, Central Line* (1987) and Dubliners in *Dublin 4* (1982). Her novels include *Light a Penny Candle* (1982), *Firefly Summer* (1987) and *The Copper Beech* (1992). Binchy excels at exploring the private ambitions, joys and anguish of ordinary individuals and families and at evoking everyday life in small communities. Her writing is memorable for its strong female characters and for the depiction of friendships between women.

BINYON, (Robert) Laurence
(1869–1943)

English poet and art critic, born in Lancaster. On leaving Oxford, where he won the Newdigate Prize for poetry, he took a post in the British Museum printed-books department and from 1913 to 1933 was in charge of Oriental prints and paintings. His study *Painting in the Far East* (1908) was the first European treatise on the subject. *Japanese Art* followed in 1909, while other titles, such as *Botticelli* (1913) and *Drawings and Engravings of William Blake* (1922), show the wide range of his cultural interests. Meanwhile he had achieved a reputation as a poet untouched by *fin de siècle* ideas, but strongly in the tradition of **Wordsworth** and **Matthew Arnold**. Beginning with *Lyric Poems* (1894), he issued volumes at intervals up to his *Collected Poems* (1931). His *Odes* (1901) contains some of his best work, challenging comparison with major poets, especially 'The Sirens' and 'The Idols'. He also wrote plays—*Paris and Oenone, Attila, Arthur*—which had successful runs, and his one-act pieces are frequently performed by amateurs. He translated **Dante**'s *Divine Comedy* into terza rima (1933–43), and this discipline shows in his later work. He was Norton Professor of Poetry at Harvard in 1933–4. The poet of affecting melancholy and imaginative reflection, he is forever himself commemorated in his elegy 'For the Fallen' (set to music by Elgar), extracts from which adorn war memorials throughout the British commonwealth.

▷ *A Laurence Binyon Anthology* (1927)

BION
(fl.c.100BC)

Greek poet from Phlossa near Smyrna. He lived in Sicily and wrote 'bucolic' (pastoral) poems traditionally associated with those of **Theocritus** and **Moschus**. His best-known and only substantial extant work (attributed to him in a *Lament for Bion* written by one of his followers) is the 98-line *Lament for Adonis*, a highly emotional elegy in hexameters describing the grief of Aphrodite at the death of her lover. Apart from the *Lament*, only 17 of Bion's pastoral poems have survived, and nothing is known of his life.

BIOY CASARES, Adolfo
(1914–)

Argentinian writer, born in Buenos Aires. His first novel, *Prólogo* (1929, 'Prologue'), established the surreal and metaphysical game-playing with genre forms which has informed his work. He met **Jorge Luis Borges** in 1932, and they collaborated on the stories in *Seis problemas para Don Isidro Parodi* (1942, Eng trans *Six Problems for Don Isidro Parodi*, 1981), writing as 'H Bustos Domecq'. His best-known book is *La invención de Morel* (1940, Eng trans *The Invention of Morel*, 1964), centred upon a search for immortality. A supernatural intervention is at the heart of his novel *El sueño del los héroes* (1954, Eng trans *The Death of the Heroes*, 1973). Other titles include *Plan de evasión* (1945, Eng trans *A Plan for Escape*, 1975) and *Dormir al sol* (1973, Eng trans *Asleep in the Sun*, 1978).

BIRD, Robert Montgomery
(1806–54)

American author, born in Newcastle, Delaware and originally trained as a physician. As well as two successful tragedies, he wrote *Calavar, a Mexican Romance* (1834), *Nick of the Woods* (1837), and other novels.

▷ M M Bird, *The Life of Robert Montgomery Bird* (1945)

BIRGITTA, or BRIDGET, St
(c.1303–c.1373)

One of Sweden's earliest authors. Born in Finsta, Uppland, she was married at the age of 13, gave birth to eight children, and gained considerable political insight through travel and service at the Swedish court. She undertook several pilgrimages, to Trondheim (1338), Santiago de Compostela (1341), and Palestine (1372). Widowed in 1344, she subsequently moved to Rome. Her monastery at Vadstena in Sweden was founded towards the end of her life, and she was canonized in 1391. Her numerous revelations were recorded by her confessors and published in Latin after her death as *Revelationes coelestes* (there is also a 14th-century translation into Swedish). They are characterized by vivid realistic detail and an abundant imagery, frequently inspired by her experiences as a mother, and the *Revelationes* enjoyed a huge international reputation.

▷ 'Själen är av långt bättre natur än kroppen. Om Birgitta av Vadstena', in E Møller Jensen (ed), *Nordisk kvinnolitteraturhistoria*, vol I, *I Guds namn* (1993)

BIRNEY, Earle
(1904–)

Canadian poet, born in Calgary, North West Territories (now Alberta). He was educated at the universities of British Columbia and Toronto. He won the Governor General's Award for two volumes of his poetry, *David* (1942) and *Now is Time* (1945). A collection of his poems was published in 1975, and another, *Ghost in the Wheels* (1977), includes a selection of his work from 1920–76, but neither is definitive, as Birney refutes the notion of poetic finality, often revising extensively with every new imprint: poetry, he observes, is 'an oral entertainment and a visual notation'; a notation which it would seem must reflect the fluidity and mutability of spoken language. In addition to poetry, Birney has written plays, novels, short stories and essays, and is literary editor of a number of Canadian periodicals.

▷ J David (ed), 'Earle Birney Issue' of *Essays on Canadian Writing* (1981); *Perspectives on Earle Birney* (1981)

BIRO, Val (Balint Stephen Biro)
(1921–)

Hungarian-born British illustrator and author for children, born in Budapest. Although Biro's illustrations have brightened many books and dust-jackets, it was not until 1966 that he created his own children's character, that of a vintage car named Gumdrop, modelled on his own 1926 Austin. He made his first appearance in *Gumdrop: the Adventures of a Vintage Car* (1966), and has reappeared in numerous books since, including *Gumdrop Finds A Friend* (1973), in which the car, his owner Mr Oldcastle and his new friend Horace, foil a gang of desperate smugglers.

BIRRELL, Augustine
(1850–1933)

English politician and writer, born in Waver-tree, Liverpool. Educated at Amersham and Trinity Hall, Cambridge, he was called to the Bar in 1875 and was Liberal MP for West Fife (1889–1900) and Bristol North (1906–18). He was President of the Board of Education (1905–7) and put through the 1906 Education Act, was chief secretary for Ireland (1907–16), and founded the National University of Ireland (1908); he resigned after the Easter Rising of 1916. He was the author of delightful volumes of essays, *Obiter Dicta* (1884–7) and *More Obiter Dicta* (1924), whose charm and unobtrusive scholarship inspired the verb 'to birrell' meaning to comment on life gently and allusively, spicing good nature with irony. He also wrote biographies of **Charlotte Brontë** (1887), **William Hazlitt** (1902), and **Andrew Marvell** (1905) for the English Men of Letters series.
▷ *Things Past Redress* (1937)

BISHOP, Elizabeth
(1911–79)

American poet, born in Worcester, Massachusetts. A graduate of Vassar College, she was noted for the precision, elegance and imaginative power of her verse, which often evokes images of nature. She received a Pulitzer Prize for each of her first two collections, *North and South* (1946) and *Cold Spring* (1955). She lived in Brazil from 1952 to 1967, and taught at Harvard from 1970. A *Complete Poems* was published in 1979.
▷ A Stevenson, *Elizabeth Bishop* (1966)

BISHOP, John Peale
(1892–1944)

American poet, fiction writer and essayist, born in Charles Town, West Virginia. He was managing editor of *Vanity Fair* after World War I but joined the exodus of American literati to Paris in 1922. In debt to the 17th-century metaphysical poets, his collections include *Green Fruit* (1917), *Now with His Love* (1933) and *Minute Particulars* (1936). His *Collected Poems* was published in 1948. A year before he died he was appointed consultant in comparative literature at the Library of Congress.
▷ E C Spindler, *John Peale Bishop: a biography* (1980)

BISSETT, bill
(1939–)

Canadian poet, who spells his name in lower case, born in Halifax, Nova Scotia, and educated at Dalhousie University and the University of British Columbia. He is primarily associated with the 'West Coast 60s', the non-conformity of his spelling and grammar and his graphic poetics reflecting his rejection of social restraint and his celebration of the imaginative freedom of the individual. His first collection was *we sleep inside each other all* (1966). Later works include *Selected poems: nobody owns th earth* (sic, 1971) and *beyond even faithful legends* (1980). He has experimented with visual and oral poetic representation, developing a sound poetry that has a mesmeric, meditative effect and an orthographic approach in which line ending is determined by visual rather than rhythmic measure.

BITZIUS, Albert, pseud of **Jeremias Gotthelf**
(1797–1854)

Swiss author, born in Morat, in Freiburg canton. He studied at Berne, and in 1832 became pastor of Lützelfluh, in Emmenthal, and wrote many novels of Swiss village life, including *Käthi* (1847) and *Uli der Knecht* (1841, Eng trans *Ulric, the Farm Servant*, 1885).
▷ C Guggisberg, *Albert Bitzius* (1935)

BIZCARRONDO, Indalecio
(1831–76)

Basque poet, born in Donostiarra. He used the pseudonym 'Villinch'. He had little education, and so his spontaneity was never impeded. He died in an accident, and his collections of wry, satirical poetry only appeared long after his death.
▷ *El Dia* (1931)

BJELKE-PETERSEN, Marie Caroline
(1874–1969)

Danish-born Australian writer of romantic novels, born in Jagtvejen, Copenhagen. She went to Tasmania with her parents in 1891 and, after some early writing, received attention for her *The Captive Singer* (1917) which was followed by *The Immortal Flame* (1919), *Jewelled Nights* (1924) and much more in a similar vein of romantic religiosity. The latter title was filmed in 1925, starring the Australian actress Louise Lovely, with location scenes shot in Tasmania. Subsequently Bjelke-Petersen's romances became very popular in the USA for their florid style.

BJØRNEBOE, Jens Ingvald
(1920–76)

Norwegian novelist, playwright, poet and essayist, born in Kristiansand. Educated as a painter, he was for many years a teacher at the **Rudolph Steiner** School in Oslo. A main topic throughout his authorship is to unveil and attack authoritarian figures wherever they are to be found; in court, church, prison and school. He does this by consciously using starkly contrasting characters, as in *Jonas* (1955, Eng trans *The Least of These*, 1959), a harsh attack on the Norwegian school system, and in his plays, which in their form show the marked influence of **Brecht**. His main work is usually considered to be the trilogy referred to as *The History of Bestiality*, of which the first volume is *Frihetens øyeblikk* (1966, Eng trans *Moment of Freedom*, 1975). Here Bjørneboe deals—in minute and often nauseating detail—with the problem of evil throughout history.

▷ J Garton, *Jens Bjørneboe—Prophet without Honour* (1985)

BJØRNSON, Bjørnstjerne Martinius
(1832–1910)

Norwegian writer and statesman, winner of the Nobel Prize for literature, born in Kvikne in Österdalen, the son of a pastor. Educated at Molde, Christiania (now Oslo) and Copenhagen, he was a playwright and novelist of wide-ranging interests, a lifelong champion of liberal causes and constantly active politically as a Home Ruler and republican. His first successful drama was *Mellem Slagene* (1856, 'Between Blows'), about the Norwegian civil wars. An ardent patriot, he sought to free the Norwegian theatre from Danish influence and revive Norwegian as a literary language; he worked as a newspaper editor simultaneously with being director of Bergen's Ole Bull theatre (1857–9) and of the Oslo Theatre (1863–7), where he recreated Norway's epic past in saga-inspired dramas such as *Kong Sverre* (1861) and his trilogy about the pretender *Sigurd Slembe* (1862). He was named Norway's national poet, and his poem, *Ja, vi elsker dette landet* (1870, 'Yes, We Love This Land of Ours') became the national anthem. His other major works include the novel *Fiskerjenten* (1868, 'The Fisher Girl'), the epic poem *Arnljot Gelline* (1870), and his greatest plays, *Over Evne I and II* (1893, 1895, 'Beyond One's Powers'), about a clergyman capable of working miracles but incapable of responding to his wife's love. He was awarded the 1903 Nobel Prize for literature.

▷ O Anker, *Bjørnstjerne Bjørnson: the man and his work* (1955)

BJORNVIG, Thorkild
(1918–)

Danish poet, translator (**Rilke**) and critic, born in Århus, Jutland. Influenced by **T S Eliot** and Rilke, he has been thought of as Denmark's 'foremost stylist'. He was the joint editor of one of the country's most important post-war magazines, *Heretica* (1948–50). He also wrote a revealing study of his friend **Karen Blixen**. His poetry is dense and complex, and perhaps a little more concerned with developing procedures than with making statements. Many have found his first volume, *Figur og ild* (1947, 'Figure and Fire') his most urgent.

BLACK, William
(1841–98)

Scottish novelist, born in Glasgow. Educated at the Glasgow School of Art, he moved to London as a journalist and was a war correspondent during the Austro–Prussian War (1866) and the Franco–Prussian War of 1870–1. An early member of the 'Kailyard School', his first success was *A Daughter of Heth* (1871), followed by a succession of stereotypical novels, usually with Highland settings involving an outsider marrying into the community. The landscape and natural phenomena of the region are evoked in colourfully overwritten prose.

▷ Sir Thomas Reid, *William Black, novelist* (1902)

BLACKMORE, Richard Doddridge
(1825–1900)

English novelist, born in Longworth, Berkshire. Educated at Blundell's School, Tiverton, and Exeter College, Oxford, he was called to the Bar at the Middle Temple in 1852, and practised for a while, but poor health made him take to market gardening and literature in Teddington. After publishing several collections of poetry, he found his real bent in fiction. *Clara Vaughan* (1864) was the first of 15 novels, mostly with a Devonshire background, of which *Lorna Doone* (1869) is his masterpiece and an accepted classic of the West Country. Other novels include *The Maid of Sker* (1872), *Alice Lorraine* (1875) and *Tommy Upmore* (1884).

▷ K G Budd, *The Last Victorian* (1960)

BLACKWOOD, Algernon Henry
(1869–1951)

English novelist, born in Kent. He was educated at Wellington and Edinburgh University before working his way through Canada and the USA, as related in his *Episodes before Thirty* (1923). His novels, which reflect his taste for the supernatural and the occult, include *John Silence* (1908), *The Human Chord* (1910), *The Wave* (1916), *Tongues of Fire* (1924), and a volume of short stories, *Tales of the Uncanny and Supernatural* (1949).

BLACKWOOD, Caroline Maureen
(1931–)

Irish writer, born into an aristocratic family in Northern Ireland. An occasional journalist and the co-author (with Anna Haycraft, alias

Alice Thomas Ellis) of a cookery book, *Darling, You Shouldn't Have Gone to So Much Trouble* (1980), she is best known for her complex and often psychologically disturbing novels. *The Stepdaughter* (1976) examines the convoluted relationship between a stepdaughter and a woman whose husband has recently left her, and who discovers that the girl was not, after all, his child. *The Fate of Mary Rose* (1981) is a dark study of the effect of murder on a small rural community. Her characters sometimes appear more than a little eccentric, yet many are genuinely searching for redemption, such as the criminal posing as a disabled charity worker in *Corrigan* (1984), in many ways Blackwood's most haunting book.

▷ M Crosland, *Beyond the Lighthouse: English Women Novelists in the Twentieth Century* (1981)

BLAGA, Lucien
(1895–1961)

Romanian poet and dramatist (translator of **Shakespeare**'s *Richard III* and **Goethe**'s *Faust*) who, unusually in his context, found his initial inspiration in German rather than French poetry: in **Rilke** and **Stefan George**. He was by profession a philosopher. His ironic poetry was metaphysical in style, based on a complex philosophical system in which the 'paradise' of Aristotelian logic was contrasted with an exploration of the 'Luciferian' elements in a 'topography of mysteries'. He would not conform to the socialist realism of the communist regime, and devoted the last years of his life to translation. Now he is much read and discussed.

BLAIR, Robert
(1699–1746)

Scottish poet and preacher, born in Edinburgh. Educated at Edinburgh University, in 1731 he was ordained minister of Athelstaneford, East Lothian. He is best known as the author of *The Grave* (1743), a blank-verse poem which heralded the 'churchyard school' of poetry. The 1808 edition was finely illustrated with rare imaginative power by **William Blake**.

▷ W Row, *The Life of Mr Robert Blair* (1848, ed T McCrie)

BLAIS, Marie-Claire
(1939–)

Francophone Canadian novelist and poet. She wrote her first novel at 18; *La Belle Bête* (1959, Eng trans *Mad Shadows*, 1960) was a sometimes nightmarish portrayal of a stultified childhood in her native Quebec, though the actual location was, typically, ambiguous. *Tête blanche*, which followed (1960), was

more conventional, but *Une saison dans la vie d'Emmanuel* (1965) returned to the darkly lyrical strain. **Edmund Wilson** gave Blais's career a significant boost with a sensitive appreciation in his pioneering *O Canada* (1967). In the later sixties, she published a further sequence of novels with an autobiographical theme: *Manuscrits de Pauline Archange* (1968), *Vivre! Vivre!* (1969, published together as *The Manuscripts of Pauline Archange*, 1970) and *Les Apparances* (1970, Eng trans *Dürer's Angel*, 1976). Later novels have concentrated on the theme of gay and lesbian sexuality, and include the very fine *Les Nuits d'underground* (1978, Eng trans *Nights in the Underground*, 1979). Her verse was published in *Pays voilés* (1963) and *Existences* (1964, translated and collected as *Veiled Countries/Lives*, 1984).

▷ E Wilson, *O Canada: An American's Notes on Canadian Culture* (1967)

BLAKE, William
(1757–1827)

English poet, painter, engraver, and mystic, born in London, the son of an Irish hosier. In 1771 he was apprenticed to James Basire, the engraver, and after studying at the Royal Academy School he began to produce watercolour figure subjects and to engrave illustrations for magazines. His first book of poems, *Poetical Sketches* (1783), was followed by *Songs of Innocence* (1789) and *Songs of Experience* (1794), which include some of the purest lyrics in the English language and express his ardent belief in the freedom of the imagination and his hatred of rationalism and materialism. His mystical and prophetical works include the *Book of Thel* (1789), *The Marriage of Heaven and Hell* (1791), *The French Revolution* (1791), *The Song of Los* (1795), *Vala* and many others, which mostly have imaginative designs interwoven with their text, printed from copper treated by a peculiar process, and coloured by his own hand or that of his wife, Catherine Boucher. Among his designs of poetic and imaginative figure subjects are a superb series of 537 coloured illustrations to **Edward Young**'s *Night Thoughts* (1797) and 12 to **Robert Blair**'s *The Grave* (1808). Among the most important of his paintings are *The Canterbury Pilgrims*, which the artist himself engraved; *The Spiritual Form of Pitt guiding Behemoth* (now in the National Gallery); *Jacob's Dream*; and *The Last Judgment*. Blake's finest artistic work is to be found in the *21 Illustrations to the Book of Job* (1826), completed when he was almost 70, but unequalled in modern religious art for imaginative force and visionary power. At his death he was employed on the illustrations to **Dante**. He is also known as a wood engraver. During his life he met with little encouragement from the public; but **William Hayley**, John Flaxman, and Samuel Palmer were faithful friends, and by John Linnell's generosity he was in his last days saved from financial worry. All through his life he was upheld by the most real and vivid faith in the unseen, guided and encouraged—as he believed—by perpetual visitations from the spirit-world.

▷J Bronowski, *Blake and the Age of Revolution* (1960); John Beer, *Blake's Visionary Universe* (1969)

BLANCHOT, Maurice
(1907–)

French novelist and essayist, born in Paris. A precursor of the *nouveau roman*, he has written works both of fiction and criticism which espouse an essentially absurdist view of existence. His novels include *Thomas l'Obscur* (1941, rev edn 1950), *L'Arret de Mort* (1948, 'Death Sentence') and *Le dernier Homme* (1957, 'The Last Man'). *L'Espace Littéraire* (1955, 'Literary Space') and *Le Livre a venir* (1959, 'The Book to Come') express his critical outlook on literature in general and the novel in particular. *The Sirens' Song* (1982) and *The Gaze of Orpheus* (1981) are English translations of his essays.

BLANCO FOMBANA, Rufino
(1874–1944)

Venezuelan novelist, politician, publisher (of Latin-American classics in Madrid, while he was in exile) and castigator of North American colonialism. He was imprisoned by the dictator Gómez, and had to leave the country until his death (1935). Called 'mediocre' by critics attached to North American policy towards Venezuela, Blanco Fombana's novels such as *El hombre de oro* (1916, 'The Golden Man'), unfavourably portraying the ruling elite in Venezuela, have also been found excellent—for example, by **Gabriel García Márquez**. *La mitra en el mano* (1927, 'The Mitre in the Hand'), is a novel that offended many Roman Catholics by the outspoken manner in which it portrayed the rise of a crooked and ambitious priest. He was a valuable literary critic, and edited the letters of Bolívar.

BLANCO WHITE, Joseph
(1775–1841)

Spanish poet, editor, writer and, initially, Catholic priest, born in Seville, the son of an Irishman who had practically become a Spaniard. White lost his faith and moved to England to edit a Spanish paper, *El Español* (1810–14), which was intended to stir up feeling against the French, who were then in Spain. He was the author of the famous poem so admired by **Coleridge**, and still in most school anthologies, 'Sonnet to Night' (1828). White became an Anglican priest and an intimate of **Newman** and Pusey, who learned much from him. He ended as a unitarian. His prose writings have recently been revived by **Juan Goytisolo** and much praised for their understanding of the Moors in Spain. His important and fascinating *Autobiography* appeared in 1845.

BLAUMANIS, Rudolfs
(1863–1908)

Latvian author, born in Latvia, but who died in a Finnish sanatorium of the great scourge of the Baltic of that period, tuberculosis. At first a businessman, whose few writings had been in German, he started to write in Latvian in the early 1890s while working on a Riga newspaper. At the time of his death he had become a leading writer, prized for his delicate stories, poems and rural comedies.

▷V Kalve, *Latvian Literature* (1954)

BLEASDALE, Alan
(1946–)

English dramatist, born in Liverpool. His television play *The Blackstuff* (1980), and the ensuing television series *The Boys From the Blackstuff* (1982), about a group of unemployed Liverpudlians, were an enormous success, and established his reputation for hard-hitting social dramas with a blackly comic, even surreal, edge. *The Monocled Mutineer*, a television series set during World War I, followed in 1986 but was less well received. He enjoyed another success with *GBH* (1990), a TV drama about corruption in local politics. He has written several stage plays, including *Are You Lonesome Tonight?* (1985), a respectful musical about Elvis Presley, and *On The Ledge* (1993), a savage social drama about life in high-rise flats in Liverpool.

BLESSINGTON, Marguerite, née Power, Countess of
(1789–1849)

Irish journalist, novelist, literary hostess and adventuress, born at Knockbrit, County Tipperary. She abandoned her husband, to whom she was sold at 14 by her dissolute father, and when her spouse fell to his death from a window, married the Earl of Blessington, with whom she had been living for some time. After his death from apoplexy in 1829, she became one of Mayfair's most vivacious hostesses, a prolific author, and dreadful debtor. Her entertaining *Journal of Conversations with Lord Byron* appeared in 1832; two travel books, *The Idler in Italy* and *The Idler in France*, followed in 1839 and

1841. She also produced several inter-mittently engaging three-volume novels of upper middle-class manners, and edited such annual publications as *The Keepsake* and the *Book of Beauty*, volumes containing decorous social advice for young ladies.

BLEST GANA, Alberto
(1830–1920)

Chilean novelist, born in Santiago de Chile. His father was Irish. Despite his poor, often cliché-ridden style and his failure to achieve the stature of his avowed master, **Balzac**, he deserves to be called a master within the context of his country's novel. After a false start with some romantic novels, he published *Martín Rivas* (1862, Eng trans 1918), set in Santiago. He wrote little after 1886, when he took up diplomatic posts abroad—he was Chile's ambassador to both France and England—until 1904, when he published his best novel, *Los transplantados* ('The Trans-planted'), about a Chilean girl deceived into marrying an impoverished aristocrat, and taking her own life as a consequence.

BLICHER, Steen Steensen
(1782–1848)

Danish poet and novelist, born in Jutland near Viborg, which forms the background of much of his work. He became a teacher and clergyman, was unhappily married, and took a great interest in the social and spiritual problems of his day. His collection *Traek-fuglene* (1838, 'The Migratory Birds'), ranks among the purest of Danish lyrical poetry, with its pervasive note of resignation and sorrow. His short stories, often in dialect, such as 'E Bindstouw', are among the gems of Danish literature.
▷H P B Poulsen, *Steen Steensen Blicher* (1952)

BLIGHT, (Frederick) John
(1913–)

Australian poet, born in Unley, Adelaide. His *A Beachcomber's Diary* (1963) and *Beach-combing Days* (1968) gave him a reputation as 'a poet of the sea'. His complex lyrics cap-ture the landscape and people of his adopted Queensland, such as *The Old Pianist* (1945) and *The Two Suns Met* (1954), but his verse is not restricted to concrete imagery; in *Pa-geantry for a Lost Empire* (1977) he explores themes such as urban life and the dis-appointments of age. His *Selected Poems* (1976) won a National Book Council award, and other recognition includes the **Patrick White** Literary Award in 1976.

BLIND HARRY
(fl.1440–92)

Scottish poet, said to have been blind from birth but that assertion has been challenged on the grounds of the pictorial vigour and precise topographical description in his work. He lived by telling tales, and from 1490 to 1492 was at the court of James IV, where he received occasional small gratuities. His major known work is the *Wallace*, on the life of the Scottish patriot William Wallace, written in rhyming couplets. The language is frequently obscure, but the work is written with vigour, and sometimes breaks into poetry. The author appears to have been fam-iliar with the metrical romances, and rep-resents himself as being indebted to the Latin Life of Wallace by Master John Blair, Wal-lace's chaplain, and to another by Sir Thomas Gray, parson of Liberton. The poem attri-butes to its hero some of the achievements of Robert Bruce, and contains many mistakes or misrepresentations, but much of the narrative can bear the test of historical criticism.

BLISH, James Benjamin
(1921–75)

American science-fiction writer, born in New York. He was educated at Rutgers Univer-sity, where he studied microbiology, and later read zoology at Columbia University, but gave up to concentrate on writing. He was active in the science-fiction fan community in his youth, but his writing, while very centrally of the genre, is marked by an unusual serious-ness of purpose. His best work includes the 'Okie' stories, collected as *Cities in Flight* (1970), in which mankind seeks a future among the stars, and the metaphysical 'After Such Knowledge' trilogy. His interest in 'soft' sciences is also reflected in the biological and genetic themes of *The Seedling Stars* (1957). He wrote a number of novelizations in the *Star Trek* series, and was an important critic and theorist as well as practitioner of science fiction.
▷D Ketterer, *Imprisoned in the Tesseract: The Life and Work of James Blish* (1988)

BLIXEN, Karen, Baroness, pseud Isak Dinesen
(1885–1962)

Danish story-teller and novelist, born in Rungsted. She was educated at home and in France, Switzerland and England and she adopted English as her main literary lang-uage, translating some of her most important works back into Danish. In 1914 she married her cousin, Baron Bror Blixen Finecke, from whom she contracted syphilis. Their life on an unproductive coffee plantation in Kenya is recounted in *Den Afrikanske Farm* (1937,

Eng trans *Out of Africa*, 1938), which was also the basis of a Hollywood film. After her divorce and the death of her lover Denys Finch-Hatton in a plane crash, she returned to Denmark and began writing the brooding, existential tales for which she is best known. Like the singer in 'The Wide-Travelling Lioness' (*Seven Gothic Tales*, 1934, Danish translation, 1935) they are usually concerned with identity and personal destiny, and are markedly artistocratic in spirit. This is confirmed in *Winter's Tales* (1942), *Last Tales* (1957) and *Anecdotes of Destiny* (1958) 'Babett's Feast' (1950), also successfully filmed, shows a lighter side to her artistic nature.
▷J Thurman, *Isak Dinesen: the Life of a Storyteller* (1982)

BLOCH, Jean-Richard
(1884–1947)

French novelist, playwright and critic. A polemicist for communism, his reputation is based on his novel *Et Compagnie* (1918, '& Co.'), which belongs to the school of realistic writing derived from **Émile Zola** and **Pierre Hamp**.
▷P Abraham, *Les trois frères* (1971)

BLOCH, Robert Albert
(1917–92)

American writer of suspense and science fiction, whose authorship of *Psycho* (1959) has largely been eclipsed by Alfred Hitchcock's auteurism. Bloch's early work was influenced by the highly mannered macabre tone of **H P Lovecraft**, but gradually became more relaxed and paced. His first novel, *The Scarf* (1947, also published as *The Scarf of Passion*, 1948), was the chillingly plain monologue of a serial strangler. He published no more books until *The Kidnapper* (1954), another impressively internalized tale of violence. *Psycho* established his reputation and has retained its power to shock, even though its effects work more slowly than Hitchcock's heart-stopping *coups de cinema*. In the sixties, Bloch continued to explore criminal and aberrant minds, with a style now unashamedly tailored to a movie audience. *Psycho II* (1982) was inevitably a disappointment, and *American Gothic* (1974) and *The Night of the Ripper* (1984) seemed to return to Lovecraftian material without the elaborate word-play.

BLOEM, Jacobus Cornelis
(1887–1966)

Dutch poet and critic, born in Oudshoorn. His pessimistic and well-made poetry, reminiscent of **Housman**, is treated with great respect in Holland. Rather too much the craftsman at the expense of breadth of theme,

Bloem was a gifted essayist and exponent of the work of other Dutch poets.

BLOK, Alexander Alexandrovich
(1880–1921)

Russian poet, born in St Petersburg. In 1903 he married the daughter of the famous chemist, Mendeleyev. His first book of poems, *Stikhi o Prekrasnoy Dame* (1904, 'Songs about the Lady Fair'), was influenced by the mysticism of **Vladimir Soloviev**, a **Tolstoyan** vision of reality beyond appearances, where truth is embodied in ideal womanhood. In *Nochnye Chasy* (1911, 'Nocturnal Hours') the ideal has given way to the realism of city squalor. He welcomed the 1917 Revolution and in 1918 wrote two poems, *Dvenadtsat* (Eng trans *The Twelve*, 1920), a symbolic sequence of revolutionary themes, and *Skify* ('The Scythians'), an ode, inciting Europe to follow Russia. He was soon disillusioned, however, and suffered greatly in the hard times which followed the Revolution. Other works include the romantic verse drama *Roza i Krest* (1922, 'The Rose and the Cross').
▷A Ashukin, *Aleksandr Blok* (1923)

BLOOM, Ursula
(20th century)

English novelist, born in London. Whether published under her own name or the pseudonym Deborah Mann, her output tends to be traditional, written from the viewpoint of a particular female character; it often verges on mainstream romance, but is informed by a more subtle sensibility than generally typifies the genre. *A Woman Called Mary* (1966), originally published under the pseudonym, is a version of the Gospel events through the eyes of Mary Magdalene. The 1976 publication *The Turn of Life's Tide* ('Madeleine would never forget the mixed emotions of that strange day when her husband died') is a contemporary account of one woman's reaction to bereavement.

BLOOMFIELD, Robert
(1766–1823)

English poet, born in Honington, near Bury St Edmunds, the son of a farm worker. A shoemaker's apprentice, he wrote *The Farmer's Boy* in a garret. Published in 1800 with the assistance of Capell Lofft, it proved very popular. He subsequently published *Rural Tales* (1802) and *Wild Flowers* (1806), was given a small allowance by the Duke of Grafton, but half-blind, died in poverty.
▷W Wickett and N Duval, *The Farmer's Boy* (1971)

BLOUET, Paul, pseud **Max O'Rell**
(1848–1903)
French author, born in Brittany. He served in the Franco–German war and fought against the Commune, being severely wounded. In 1873 he went to England as a newspaper correspondent, and was French master at St Paul's School (1876–84). From 1887 he lectured in Britain, the USA, and the British colonies. His works include *John Bull et son île* (1883, Eng trans *John Bull and his Island*, 1884) and *Un Français en Amérique* (1891, Eng trans *A Frenchman in America*, 1891)— both translations published under the author's pseudonym.

BLOY, Léon Marie
(1846–1917)
French author, born in Périgeux. He wrote novels, essays, and religious and critical studies with a strong Roman Catholic bias, containing bitter castigation of political and social institutions. This made him unpopular in his day but has contributed to the revival of interest in his works in the second half of the 20th century. His *Le Désespéré* (1886, 'The Desperate Man') and *La Femme pauvre* (1897, 'The Poor Woman') are autobiographical; other books include *Le Pélerin de l'absolu* (1914, 'On a Pilgrimage to the Absolute'). His journal, which relates the spiritual and mystical conversions of his later life, was published in 1924.
▷R Heppenstall, *Léon Bloy* (1953)

BLUEBUSH see **BOURKE, John Philip**

BLUM, Léon
(1872–1950)
French statesman, several times socialist prime minister of his country, who began his career as a literary critic of some influence. Blum was born in Paris into a Jewish family. He worked on magazines with **Proust** and most of the other leading authors and editors of his day. He wrote a play, *La Colère* (1902, 'Anger'), and as a theatre critic took up the cause of contemporary theatrical innovators. His *Nouvelles Conversations de Goethe avec Eckermann* (1901, 'New Conversations Between Goethe and Eckermann'), published anonymously, was his most influential work. In it he elevated the role of the non-creative critic, as a fruitful synthesizer of ideas. After World War I he turned to political writings. His literary importance lay in his transmission, to French writers, of the humanist ideas of Lucien Herr (librarian at the École Normale), who had helped convert Blum's mentor **Jean Jaurès** to socialism.

BLUME, Judy
(1938–)
American novelist. Perhaps the most controversial and certainly the most popular contemporary American writer for teenagers, she was born in New Jersey. Her first published book was *The One in the Middle is the Green Kangaroo* (1969), but her third book, *Are You There, God It's Me, Margaret* (1970), brought acclaim for her candid approach to the onset of puberty and for her natural, if unsubtle, style. As with subsequent books, attempts were made to restrict its circulation. Her explicitness brought her into conflict with parents, but she has a remarkable rapport with her readers and dares to confront subjects which previously were ignored. Her books include *Then Again, Maybe I Won't* (1971), *It's not the End of the World* (1972), *Deenie* (1973), *Blubber* (1974) and *Forever* (1975).

BLUNCK, Hans Friedrich
(1888–1961)
German novelist, poet and folklorist, born in Altona. After studying law he was successively propagandist, university official and farmer. Steeped in the folklore of the North German plain, Blunck's writings lent colour to the racial theories of National Socialism. His poetical works include *Sturm überm Land* (1915, 'Storm Over the Land'), *Der Wanderer* (1925, 'The Wanderer'), *Erwartung* (1936, 'Expectation'), and his novels *Werwendes Volk* (1933) and *Die Urvätersaga* (1934, 'Saga of the Forefathers'). He published his autobiographical *Unwegsame Zeiten* ('Pathless Times') in 1953.
▷C Jenssen, *Hans Friedrich Blunck* (1935)

BLUNDEN, Edmund Charles
(1896–1974)
English poet and critic, born in London. His family soon moved to Kent, and he was educated at Christ's Hospital and Queen's College, Oxford. He served in France in World War I and won the MC. He was Professor of English Literature at Tokyo (1924–7), fellow of Merton College, Oxford, from 1931, joined the staff of the *Times Literary Supplement* in 1943, returned to the Far East and from 1953 lectured at the University of Hong Kong. He was professor at Oxford from 1966 to 1968. A lover of the English countryside, he is essentially a nature poet, as is evident in *Pastorals* (1916) and *The Waggoner and Other Poems* (1920), but his prose work *Undertones of War* (1928) is perhaps his best. Other works include *The Bonadventure* (1922), on his visit to America, a biography of Leigh Hunt, and books on **Charles Lamb**

103

and **Keats**. He also edited **John Clare**, **Christopher Smart**, **Shelley**, **Keats** and **Collins**.

BLUNT, Wilfrid Scawen
(1840–1922)

English poet and traveller, born in Petworth, Sussex. Educated at Stonyhurst and Oscott, he served in the diplomatic service (1859–70), and published his first volume of poems, *Sonnets and Songs by Proteus* (1875). He travelled in the Near and Middle East, espoused the cause of Arabi Pasha and Egyptian nationalism (1882), stood for parliament and was imprisoned in 1888 for activity in the Irish Land League. While in prison, he wrote the sonnet sequence *In Vinculis* (1899). He wrote fierce political verse and charming love poems, and bred Arab horses. In 1858 he married Lady Anne Isobel Noel, who shared his travels and love of Arab horses.
▷M J Reinehr, *The Writings of Wilfrid Scawen Blunt* (1940)

BLY, Robert
(1926–)

American poet, critic, translator and editor, born in Madison, Minnesota. As a critic he is caustic, but his targets are legitimate. For a man so aware of foreign literature (he has translated **Pablo Neruda**, **Knut Hamsun** and **Selma Lagerlöf**, among others), his poetry is surprisingly American in tone and locale, often dealing with the space and silences of his home state. His first collection was *Silence in the Snowy Fields* (1962), followed by *The Shadow-Mothers* (1970), *Sleepers Joining Hands* (1972) and *Talking All Morning* (1980). In 1991 he published a controversial study of maleness and its discontents, called *Iron John*.
▷H Nelson, *Robert Bly: An Introduction to the Poetry* (1984)

BLYTON, Enid Mary
(1897–1968)

English children's author, born in London. She trained as a Froebel kindergarten teacher, then became a journalist, specializing in educational and children's publications. In 1922 she published her first book, *Child Whispers*, a collection of verse, but it was in the late 1930s that she began writing her many children's stories featuring such characters as Noddy, the Famous Five, and the Secret Seven. She edited various magazines, including *Sunny Stories* and *Pictorial Knowledge* for children, and *Modern Teaching*, and was part-author of *Two Years in the Infant School*. She identified closely with children, and always considered her stories highly educational and moral in tone, but has recently been criticized for racism, sexism and snobbishness, as well as stylistic inelegance and over-simplicity. She published over 600 books, and is one of the most translated British authors. Her works also include school readers and books on nature and religious study.
▷B Stoney, *Enid Blyton: a biography* (1974)

BOBROWSKI, Johannes
(1917–65)

German short-story writer, novelist and poet, born in Tilsit and brought up in Memel (now Sovetsk and Klaipeda respectively, both in Lithuania). The land of his youth saw the harmonious intermingling of ethnic groups, and the bulk of his work expresses a longing for that past. A soldier on the eastern front during World War II, he was captured by the Soviets and remained a prisoner of war until 1949, when he went to live in East Berlin. His novels *Levins Mühle* (1964, 'Levin's Mill') and *Litauische Klaviere* (1966, 'Lithuanian Pianos') are both examinations of that intractable problem, the nature of German nationalism.

BOCAGE, Manoel Barbosa du
(1765–1805)

Portuguese lyric poet, born in Setubal. He served in the army and the navy, sailed in 1786 to India and China, returning to Lisbon in 1790, where, recognized as a poet, he joined the literary coterie *Nova Arcadia*, only to be expelled from their number in 1794 for his unorthodox views. He was jailed for anticlericalism in 1797, and released two years later after 'treatment' at the hands of the Inquisition. He is essentially a romantic, but his sonnets are classical in form. He often satirizes, as in *Pina de Talião* ('Talião's Pine Cone').
▷R Correia, *Bocage: cronica dramatica e grotesca* (1965)

BOCCACCIO, Giovanni
(1313–75)

Italian writer, born in Tuscany or Paris. He was the illegitimate son of a merchant of Certaldo, who launched him on a commercial career. He soon abandoned commerce and the study of canon law, and at Naples (1328) he turned to story-writing in verse and prose, mingled in courtly society, and fell in love with the noble lady whom he made famous under the name of Fiammetta. Until 1350 he lived alternately in Florence and Naples, producing prose tales, pastorals, and poems. The *Teseide* ('Book of Theseus') is a graceful version in *ottava rima* of the medieval romance of Palamon and Arcite, which was partly translated by **Chaucer** in the *Knight's*

Tale. The *Filostrato*, likewise in *ottava rima*, deals with the loves of Troilus and Cressida, also in great part translated by Chaucer. After 1350 he became a diplomat entrusted with important public affairs, and a scholar devoted to the cause of the new learning. During this period, in which he formed a lasting friendship with **Petrarch**, he visited Rome, Ravenna, Avignon, and Brandenburg as Florentine ambassador. In 1358 he completed his great work, the *Decameron*, begun some 10 years before. Boccaccio selected the plots of his stories from the floating popular fiction of the day, and especially from the *fabliaux* which had passed into Italy from France, the matter being medieval, while the form is classical. Boccaccio's originality lies in his consummate narrative skill, and in the rich poetical sentiment which transforms his borrowed materials. For some time he held a chair founded to expound the works of **Dante**, on whose *Divina Commedia* he produced a commentary. During his last years he lived principally in retirement at Certaldo, and would have entered into holy orders, moved by repentance for the follies of his youth, had he not been dissuaded by Petrarch. He wrote in Latin an elaborate work on mythology, *De genealogia deorum gentilium* ('The Genealogies of the Gentile Gods'), and treatises such as *De claris mulieribus* ('Famous Women') and *De Montibus* ('On Mountains').

▷V Branca, *Boccaccio: the man and his works* (1976)

BOCCAGE, Marie Anne Fiquet du, née Le Page
(1710–1802)

French poet, born in Rouen. Her *Paradis terrestre* (1748, 'Earthly Paradise'), an imitation of **Milton**, and *La Colombiade* (1756), gave her an exaggerated fame, perhaps on account of their author's great beauty, but her letters to her sister, written while travelling through England, Holland, and Italy, have historical interest.

BOCK, Jerry see ABBOTT, George Francis

BODELSEN, Anders
(1937–)

Danish novelist and journalist, born in Copenhagen, where he later attended university. A prolific author, he has put the suspense novel firmly on the literary agenda as a forum for social, psychological and moral investigation, and his skill in depicting the climate of post-war Denmark has secured him large audiences. The thriller *Tænk på et tal* (1968, 'Think of a Number') gave him his popular breakthrough and has been filmed and translated into many languages. It elegantly narrates the story of a bank clerk who aims to cheat a bank robber, thus raising the question of who is the victim and who is the culprit—a theme central in Bodelsen's crime fiction. He frequently focuses on the paradoxical attachment and similarity between the hunter and the hunted, the blackmailer and the blackmailed, as in, for example, *Pengene og livet* (1976, 'Money and Life') and *Mørklægning* (1988, 'Blackout'). A 'state-of-the-nation' novelist, Bodelsen has frequently chosen to set his novels in the Denmark of the 1960s and beyond, but has also taken on all decades from the 1930s onwards, and even reflected on the future, with the science-fiction novel *Frysepunktet* (1971, 'Freezing Point').

BODENHEIM, Maxwell
(1893–1954)

American poet and novelist. After moving to Chicago and then New York, he was jailed for desertion from the army, and later was suspected of Communist Party membership. He never fulfilled his potential, though his verse is often powerful and his fiction powerfully advocated. Supporting Modernism in his criticism of the early 1920s, he wrote in a highly coloured style that combined strong images with a genuine feel for social problems. *Introducing Irony* (1922) was a collection of stories and poems; *Against This Age* and *The Sardonic Arm* (both 1923) marked his peak as a poet. Later, he managed to write a novel a year, the best of them being *Ninth Avenue* (1926), *Georgie May* (1928), the story of a run-down prostitute, and *Slow Vision* (1934), a much under-rated novel of the Depression which was to be his last prose book. He experimented with jazz forms in verse, but his *Selected Poems, 1914–1944* (1946) shows little tendency to fall prey to literary fashions. Inactive long before his death, he became a personage rather than a creator, and Sam Roth's ghosted *My Life and Loves in Greenwich Village* (1954) fed the myth posthumously. In February 1954, Bodenheim and his third wife were murdered.

▷J B Moore, *Bodenheim* (1970)

BODENSTEDT, Friedrich Martin von
(1819–92)

German writer, born in Peine in Hanover. He lived for a while in Moscow, travelled in the Middle East, was a professor at Munich University (from 1854) and director of the Meiningen court theatre (1867–73). He translated into German many Russian, English, and Persian texts, and published poetry. His best-known work is *Lieder des Mirza Schaffy*

(1851, 'Songs of Mirza Schaffy'), alleged to be a translation from the Tartar.

BODTCHER, Ludvig Adolph
(1793–1874)

Danish poet, born in Copenhagen. He lived for 11 years in Rome, where he associated with Danish artists, especially the sculptor Bertel Thorvaldsen. He was a graceful minor romantic poet, whose work in *Digte* (1856, 'Poems') is still read.

BOETHIUS, Anicius Manlius Severinus
(c.480–524)

Roman philosopher and statesman, sometimes described as 'the last of the Roman philosophers, the first of the scholastic theologians'. Born of a patrician Roman family, he studied at Athens and there gained the knowledge which later enabled him to produce the translations of and commentaries on Aristotle and Porphyry that became the standard textbooks on logic in medieval Europe. He became consul in 510 during the Gothic occupation of Rome and later chief minister to the ruler Theodoric; but in 523 he was accused of treason and after a year in prison at Pavia was executed. It was during his imprisonment that he wrote the famous *De consolatione philosophiae*, in which Philosophy personified solaces the distraught author by explaining the mutability of all earthly fortune and demonstrating that happiness can be attained only by virtue, that is by being like God. The *Consolation* was for the next millennium probably the most widely read book after the Bible.
▷H H Patch, *The Tradition of Boethius* (1935)

BÖEX, Joseph and Séraphin *see* ROSNY

BOGAN, Louise
(1897–1970)

American poet and short-story writer, born in Livermore, Maine. She began writing in high school and first published a collection of verse, *Body of this Death*, in 1923. She published comparatively few works, but enough of sufficient quality to be considered a 'poet's poet'. Her writing is a sometimes erotic celebration of, and often disillusioned lament for, romantic love. Her two marriages and other relationships with men led her to believe that love almost always ends in acrimony and betrayal. While editions of her collected poetry were published in 1941 and 1954, *The Blue Estuaries* (1968) is the definitive volume, all 105 poems having been selected by the author herself as those by which she wished to be remembered.
▷*Journey Around My Room* (ed R Limmer, 1980)

BÖHME, Jakob
(1575–1624)

German mystical writer and alchemical thinker, born near Görlitz. For many years a cobbler, he exercised as incalculable an influence on literature—in particular on **Goethe**, and on romantic thinkers such as Hamann, Hegel, Schelling and, later, **Jung**—as he did on the course of individualistic religion. Isaac Newton too studied his writings. He has been called both dualist and pantheistic, and there are, quite certainly, profoundly gnostic elements in his wild but seminal thinking. He was therefore persecuted, and from 1618 forbidden to publish (that is, to circulate his writings). He is the chief heir of **Meister Eckhart**, and of Paracelsus. Creation, for Böhme, arises from 'Nothing', which directs its will to 'Everything'. He regarded God, 'Nichts' and 'Ungrund' ('Nothing' and 'bottomlessness'), as possessing both love and anger, and therefore as containing the seeds of both good and evil: God dwells in nature as the soul lives in the body of man. Man's character is determined by the map of the heavens at the time at which his body is formed. His style (like that of Jung) is, because he dealt in paradoxes, obscure and even confused, but vigorous and spiritually provocative. His influence is most directly seen in the poetry of **Angelus Silesius**. All his writings have been translated, some of them many times.
▷S Hobhouse, *Jakob Böhme, His Life and Teaching* (1950)

BOIARDO, Matteo Maria, Count of Scandiano
(?1441–1494)

Italian poet, born in Scandiano, a village at the foot of the Lombard Apennines. He studied at Ferrara, and in 1462 married the daughter of the Count of Norellara. He lived at the court of Ferrara on intimate terms with Dukes Borso and Ercole; by the latter he was employed on diplomatic missions, and was appointed governor in 1481 of Modena, and in 1487 of Reggio. As an administrator he was distinguished for his clemency, and opposition to capital punishment. Boiardo has been called the 'Flower of Chivalry'. His early lyric poems in *Canzoniere* were inspired by a woman, Antonia Caprara, whom he met in 1469. His fame rests on the unfinished *Orlando Innamorato* (1486), a long narrative poem in which the Charlemagne romances are recast into *ottava rima*. His other works comprise Latin eclogues, a versification of **Lucian**'s *Timon*, translations of **Herodotus**, the *Ass* of Lucian, and the *Golden Ass* of

Apuleius, and a series of sonnets and *Canzoni* (1499).
▷G Reichenbach, *Matteo Maria Boiardo* (1929)

BOILEAU, or BOILEAU DESPRÉAUX, Nicolas
(1636–1711)

French poet and critic, born in Paris. He studied law and theology at Beauvais, but as a man of means devoted himself to literature. His first publications (1660–6) were satires, some of which got him into trouble. In 1677 the king appointed him, along with **Racine**, official royal historian. *L'Art poétique* ('The Art of Poetry'), imitated by **Pope** in the *Essay on Criticism*, was published in 1674, along with the first part of the clever serio-comic *Lutrin* ('Lectern'). Between 1669 and 1677 he published nine epistles, written, like his satires, on the Horatian model. In his last years he returned to Auteuil. His works include several critical dissertations, a collection of epigrams, a translation of Longinus's *On the Sublime*, a *Dialogue des héros de roman* ('A Conversation between the Heroes of Novels'), and a series of letters (many to Racine). His influence as a critic has been profound. He set up good sense, sobriety, elegance, and dignity of style as the cardinal literary virtues.
▷J E White, *Nicolas Boileau* (1969)

BOISROBERT, François de Métel, Sieur de
(1592–1662)

French dramatist, translator and professional buffoon, born in Caen. He was employed by the French prelate and statesman Cardinal Richelieu to provide entertainment at court. The author of the play *La Belle Plaideuse* (1654, 'The Beautiful Litigant'), which provided **Molière** with a scene, he was also—like **Corneille**—one of Richelieu's *cinq auteurs*, employed by the Cardinal to put his own ambitious theatrical theories into practice, and an original member of the Académie française.

BOITO, Arrigo
(1842–1918)

Italian composer and poet, born in Padua. He studied at the Milan Conservatory. His first important work was the opera *Mefistofele* (1868), which survived its initial failure and later grew in popularity. Thereafter he concentrated mainly on writing libretti, the best-known of which are those for Verdi's *Otello* and *Falstaff*. Another opera, *Nerone*, written in 1916, was not produced till 1924.
▷P Nardi, *Vita di Arrigo Boito* (1944)

BOJER, Johan
(1872–1959)

Norwegian novelist, playwright and short-story writer, he grew up in a poor rural family at Orkdalsøyra, and though he maintained great affection for that background, he became a lifelong progressive. *Den store hunger* (1916, Eng trans *The Great Hunger*, 1918) holds up technological development as the key to survival, but then recognizes the need for a supra-rational dimension to life. His novels of the 1920s recount the struggles of the rural poor; *Den siste viking* (1921, Eng trans *Last of the Vikings*, 1923) is the best, but *Vor egen stamme* (1924, Eng trans *The Emigrants*, 1925) and *Folk ved sjøen* (1929, Eng trans *Folk by the Sea*, 1931) are almost equally strong. The use of dialect established him as an important national figure.
▷C Gad, *Johan Bojer: The Man and His Works* (1974)

BOKER, George Henry
(1823–90)

American poet, playwright, and diplomat, born in Philadelphia. He won belated recognition for his 400 sonnets and for *Francesca da Rimini* (1855), a romantic verse tragedy and the best American play before the Civil War. His propaganda for the North secured him the post of minister to Turkey (1871–5) and Russia (1875–8).
▷E S Bradley, *George Henry Boker: poet and patriot* (1927)

BOLAND, Eavan
(1944–)

Irish poet and critic, born in Dublin and educated there, in London and in New York. From *New Territory* (1967) onwards she became a poetic commentator on the 'frail compasses and trenchant constellations' that she sees as constituting suburban Irish lives in the style-conscious second half of the 20th century. Her experience of motherhood lent deep emotion to *Night Feed* (1982) and her subsequent combination of intellectualism and feminism led to the award-winning *Outside History* (1990), which represented a significant step forward for women writing from within a male-dominated Irish culture.

BOLD, Alan
(1943–)

Scottish poet, biographer, critic and editor, born in Edinburgh. He was educated at Broughton High School, where he showed signs of the rebelliousness which was to mark his early poetry, and went on to Edinburgh University. After a variety of jobs, including journalism, he became a full-time writer in 1967. A prolific writer and anthologizer, he has been a particularly influential commentator on **Hugh MacDiarmid**, and his biography of the poet won the McVitie Scottish Writer of the Year Award in 1989. He has published several volumes of poetry in both English and Scots, including *In this Corner: Selected Poems 1963–83*, which traces the development in his work from an initial angry humanism into a more cooly-observed scrutiny of the natural world and of the society which surrounds him. He is a trenchant and combative literary commentator.

BOLDREWOOD, Rolf, pseud of Thomas Alexander Browne
(1826–1915)

Australian novelist, born in London. His family emigrated to Australia in 1830. He was educated in Sydney, and became a squatter in Victoria. After a series of misadventures and some years as an inspector of goldfields, he started writing serials for Australian periodicals in order to pay his debts. One, 'The Squatter's Dream' (1875), echoed Boldrewood's own misfortunes and was published as *Ups and Downs* (1878, rev edn *The Squatter's Dream*, 1890). His success was confirmed by *Robbery Under Arms*, the bushranging adventure with which his name is permanently associated. Serialized in the *Sydney Morning Herald* in 1882, it was not published until 1888 (rev edn 1889). There followed in the next 20 years a considerable number of novels in similar vein, set in Australia or New Zealand, many written from personal experience, among which were *A Colonial Reformer* (1890), *A Sydney-Side Saxon* (1891) and *A Romance of Canvas Town* (1898).
▷ A Brissenden, *Rolf Boldrewood* (1972)

BOLGER, Dermot
(1959–)

Irish novelist and playwright, born in Dublin, the city which provides the background to much of his work. His first novel, *Night Shift* (1986), was quickly followed by *The Woman's Daughter* (1987), *The Journey Home* (1990) and *Emily's Shoes* (1992). His plays include *The Lament for Arthur Cleary* (1989). Bolger is in the forefront of younger Irish writers who, rather than present Dublin as a place of amiable eccentrics and affable rogues, portray it as a mean, often violent city, corrupted and degraded by drugs and by political and criminal rivalries. In his work it appears as a place where love and compassion are coarsened, thriving only in those tenacious enough to overcome the odds against them.

BOLITHO, Hector
(1898–1974)

New Zealand biographer, novelist and historian, who moved to England at the age of 24, having struck up an acquaintance with the then Prince of Wales. Self-characterized as 'second-rate', he was an unofficial 'court biographer' who wrote more than a score of polite accounts of royalty, of which the most successful was the pallid and inaccurate *Edward VIII: His Life and Reign* (1937). He was selected by the daughter of **Rudyard Kipling** to write his 'official' biography, but could not abide her terms. His novels include *Solemn Boy* (1927).

BOLITHO, William, pseud of William Bolitho Ryall
(1890–1930)

South African author, a much-prized—and still reprinted—writer on crime, famous for his acerbic and ironic style. He served in World War I, and his health was shattered by it. *Murder for Profit* (1926) studies mass murderers. His wife Sybil Bolitho told his as well as her own story in her novel *My Shadow As I Pass* (1931).

BÖLL, Heinrich
(1917–85)

German writer, winner of the Nobel Prize for literature, born in Cologne. He served as an infantryman in World War II before becoming a full-time writer. His first novel, *Der Zug war pünktlich* (Eng trans *The Train was on Time*, 1956), was published in 1949. A trilogy, *Und sagte kein einziges Worte* (1953, Eng trans *Acquainted with the Night*, 1954), *Haus ohne Hüter* (1954, Eng trans *The Unguarded House*, 1957) and *Das Brot der frühen Jahre* (1955, Eng trans *The Bread of our Early Years*, 1957), depicting life in Germany during and after the Nazi regime, gained him a worldwide reputation. His later novels, characteristically satirizing modern German society, included *Gruppenbild mit Dame* (1971, Eng trans *Group Portrait with Lady*, 1973) and *Die vorlorene Ehre der Katherina Blum* (1974, Eng trans *The Lost Honour of Katherina Blum*, 1975). He also wrote a number of plays, and a volume of poems. He was awarded the 1972 Nobel Prize for literature.
▷ J H Reid, *Heinrich Böll: withdrawal and re-emergence* (1973); Charlotte W Ghurye, *The Writer and Society: studies in the fiction of Günter Grass and Heinrich Böll* (1976)

BOLT, Carol
(1941–)

Canadian playwright, born in Winnipeg, Manitoba, and educated at the University of British Columbia, Vancouver. A prolific writer, she has written over 20 plays, including three for television, and is noted for her frequent collaborations with other writers.

Her plays combine an understanding of Canadian life and culture with musical comedy, mythic characters, and epic romance. Much of her work is overtly political, though she also writes for children. Her best-known works are *Buffalo Jump* (1972), a play about the riots which occurred during the Depression, and *Red Emma: Queen of Anarchists* (1973), about Emma Goldman, a New York anarchist.

BOLT, Robert Oxton
(1924–)

English playwright, born in Manchester. He was educated at Manchester University, and worked as a schoolmaster until the success of his first play, *Flowering Cherry* (1957), a domestic drama about a frustrated insurance salesman. His best-known work is *A Man For All Seasons* (1960), a play about the moral courage of Sir Thomas More in refusing to recant on his beliefs, even to save his life. His writings are generally politically overt, and often return to the theme of the private conscience in conflict with public demands. Other historical works include *Vivat! Vivat! Regina* (1970), about Elizabeth I and Mary, Queen of Scots, and *State of Revolution* (1977), on Lenin, Trotsky, and the fate of the Russian Revolution. He wrote the screenplay for the film *Lawrence of Arabia* (1962). The conventional formal aspects of his work have made him more popular with theatre-goers than with critics.

BOMBAL, María Luisa
(1910–80)

Chilean novelist, born in Viña del Mar. She spent much of her youth in Paris, and acquired a degree from the Sorbonne. Back in Chile, she fell in love with the aviator Eugolio Sánchez; but he did not love her, and so, after failing to kill herself, she shot him. Luckily she did not kill him, and under the wing of **Neruda** and other friends, she was able to get to Buenos Aires. There she wrote her first and most famous novel, *La última niebla* (1935, Eng trans *House of Mist*, 1947—but this is taken from a re-working of the original). This, and her second book, *La amortajada* (1938, Eng trans *The Shrouded Woman*, 1948), have been said to have marked a turning point in Latin-American fiction: hallucinated, often unintelligible, they are (or have been taken to be) the first truly feminist books in Chilean literature. **Borges** greatly admired the second of them, about a corpse which can hear what is going on around it. She was in the news again in 1940, when she took a pistol shot at her husband—who was alleged to have been intent on killing her—but missed. She became involved in the film world, wrote a few more stories (collected in *New Island*, 1982), and on the death of her second husband, a French financier, returned to Chile, where she died in near poverty. Chronic alcoholism prevented her from carrying out many of the projects she had planned. The degree of her achievement has not yet been decided: the charge that she did little more in her novels than render, in words, some notion of the cinematic achievement of Luis Buñuel, is hard to counter; unlike Buñuel, she displayed no sense of humour. However, feminists have pointed to her as a great writer.

▷M I Adams, *Three Authors of Alienation* (1975)

BONALD, Louis Gabriel Ambroise, Vicomte de
(1754–1840)

French writer. He emigrated to Heidelberg during the French Revolution and wrote *Théorie du pouvoir politique et religieux* (1796, 'Theory of Political and Religious Power'), advocating the system of monarchy and prophesying the return of the Bourbons. He was appointed by Napoleon Minister of Instruction in 1808, in 1815 ennobled by Louis XVIII. His son, Louis Jacques Maurice (1787–1870), became Archbishop of Lyons in 1839, and Cardinal in 1841.

▷M H Quinlan, *The Historical Thought of the Vicomte de Bonald* (1953)

BOND, Edward
(1934–)

English dramatist and director, born in London. A left-wing writer whose work uses a variety of metaphors for the corruption of capitalist society, his first play, *The Pope's Wedding*, was given a Sunday night reading at the Royal Court Theatre, London, in 1962 and aroused great controversy. *Saved* (1965) achieved notoriety through a scene in which a baby in a pram is stoned to death. Both of these plays were set in contemporary England, although later plays such as *Narrow Road to the Deep North* (1968) use historical themes to look at broad contemporary issues. Other plays include *Lear* (1971), a reworking of **Shakespeare**'s play; *The Fool* (1976), based on the life of the 'peasant poet', **John Clare**; *The Woman* (1978), in which the characters are drawn from Greek tragedy; *The Worlds* (1979); a trilogy, *The War Plays* (1985); and, for television, *Olly's Prison* (1992).

BOND, (Thomas) Michael
(1926–)

English author of children's books, born in Newbury, Berkshire, who worked for many years as a BBC cameraman. He is the creator of several fictional animal characters, each of which appears in a series of stories. The adventures of Thursday, an orphan mouse, are recorded in *Here Comes Thursday* (1966), and others, while Olga da Polga, a guinea-pig, features in *The Tales of Olga da Polga* (1971), and further stories. Bond's most popular creation, however, is Paddington Bear, a small bear so named because he was discovered at Paddington Station. He wears a sou'wester, wellington boots and a duffle-coat, from a toggle of which hangs a luggage label bearing the words, 'Please look after this bear'. Hapless, vulnerable and good-natured, Paddington has so far been the hero of almost 40 stories since his first appearance in *A Bear Called Paddington* (1958); his enormous popularity shows no sign of waning.

BONER, Ulrich
(1300–49)

Swiss writer of fables. A Dominican friar in Bern from 1324, his *Edelstein* ('Precious Stone'), a collection of fables and jokes, was one of the first German books printed, in 1461.
▷ J J Oberlin, *Bonerii gemma* (1782)

BONNARD, Abel
(1883–1968)

French poet, novelist, and essayist, born in Poitiers. He won the National Poetry Prize with his first collection of poems, *Les Familiers* (1906, 'The Familiars'). He took up the psychological novel with *La Vie et l'amour* (1913, 'Life and Love'), and later published travel books and collections of essays. He was Minister of Education in the Vichy government (1942–4), fled to Spain and was sentenced to death in his absence (1945). He returned to France (1958) and was banished (1960).
▷ R Brasillach, *Abel Bonnard* (1971)

BONNEVILLE, Nicholas de
(1760–1828)

French writer. He was appointed president of a Paris district during the French Revolution (1789). A student of English and German literature, he translated **Shakespeare**, founded several newspapers, and wrote a history of modern Europe (1792).

BONTEMPELLI, Massimo
(1878–1960)

Italian novelist, playwright and journalist, born in Como. He was one of the most important of European writers, but his achievements have been passed over except in his own country. His as yet untranslated novel *La scacchiera davanti allo specchio* (1922, 'The Chess Board Before the Mirror'), bids fair to be regarded as one of the first novels of magical realism, although that term, outside painting (in which connection it was coined, by Franz Roh, in 1925—it was also coined, independently, by Bontempelli in his critical work of 1938, *L'avventura novecentista*, 'Twentieth Century Adventure'), is too often employed as applying only to German or Latin-American novels. Later Bontempelli wrote the majestic and neglected novels *Il figlio di due madri* (1929, 'The Son of Two Mothers') and *Vita e morte do Adria e suoi figli* (1930, 'The Life and Death of Adria and Her Two Sons'), both again in the 'magical realist' mode. He usually went along with fascism, although unhappily, and initially acted as a propagandist for it; but he was suspended from the party for two years from 1938, and he refused to accept a university chair offered to him after its occupier had been deprived of it because he was a Jew. But when he was elected a senator on a communist ticket after World War II, he was not able to take it up owing to his past. His Pirandellian play *Nostra Dea* (1925, 'Our Goddess') is notable.
▷ F Tempesti, *Bontempelli* (1974, in Italian)

BONTEMPS, Arna Wendell
(1902–73)

American writer and educator, born in Louisiana, associated with the so-called Harlem Renaissance. His work delves into the history and folklore of Afro-Americans: a jockey in *God Sends Sunday* (1931, later dramatized as *St Louis Woman*, 1946, in collaboration with **Countee Cullen**); slave uprisings in the very fine *Black Thunder* (1935) and *Drums at Dusk* (1939), the latter set in Haiti. In *Father of the Blues* (1941) Bontemps edited W C Handy's compositions; he later collaborated with **Langston Hughes** on *The Poetry of the Negro* (1949) and *The Book of Negro Folklore* (1958). His characteristic tone is rational, tending to mildness, and he was largely repudiated in the black nationalist atmosphere of the 1960s.
▷ R A Bone, *The Negro Novel in America* (1958)

BOON, Louis Paul
(1912–79)

Belgian (Flemish) novelist, poet, journalist and painter, born in Aalst (where he lived for most of his life), one of the outstanding writers of his day. He was the first Dutch-language author—he made a point of sticking to Flemish dialect—to employ the set of techniques first practised by **John Dos Passos** in the trilogy *U.S.A.*. Another powerful influence was that of **Louis Ferdinand Céline**, this time in the delivery of streams of bitter, colloquial invective. But he was highly original, and *Kapellekensbaan* (1953, Eng trans *Chapel*

Road, 1972), which brilliantly interweaves and counterpoints three separate tales, tells the story of the rise and fall of Belgian socialism in imaginative terms. *Abel Gholaerts* (1944) is an interesting autobiographical novel in which the author refers to the unhappy life of the painter Van Gogh.

▷ R P Meijer, *Literature of the Low Countries* (1971)

BOOTH, Martin
(1944–)

English poet and critic, born in Lancashire. He trained and worked as a teacher, but has managed to produce a substantial body of verse and of highly intelligent literary journalism, of which *Driving Through the Barricades: British Poetry 1964–1984* (1985) is the most developed example. He has tended to work best in longer or cycle forms, particularly where dream-like displacements of time are involved. This was evident in collections like *The Crying Embers* (1971) and his eleventh book, *Coronis* (1973), but his interest in the imaginative pull of the past reached its peak with *The Knotting Sequence* (1977) and *Winter's Night, Knotting* (1979), named after his home village in Bedfordshire, and *The Cnot Dialogues* (1979), named after its founder. In later work, he devises a historical perspective which differs sharply from that of **Geoffrey Hill** and other guardians of the national mythology. Recent collections include a sequence inspired by America, *Looking for the Rainbow* (1983). Booth has also edited an important textbook anthology of *Contemporary British and North American Verse* (1981), which bears witness to his instincts as a teacher.

BOOTHBY, Guy Newell
(1867–1905)

Australian novelist, born in Adelaide, where he was sometime secretary to the mayor. His early work included librettos for two operas to music by Cecil Sharp, the folk-song collector, and *On the Wallaby* (1894), an account of a journey across Australia with his brother. His first novel, *In Strange Company* (1894), was a mélange of espionage and revolution in a South American state, and set the style for his melodramatic fiction; within the next 10 years he had published over 50 novels of adventure, often in exotic settings. His third book introduced the sinister Dr Nikola, a Mephistophelian character who appeared in several of his tales.

BOOTHE, Clare, also known by her married
name of **Clare Boothe Luce**
(1903–87)

American writer, socialite and wit, born in New York City. Married to the millionaire publisher Henry Luce at 20, she was made associate editor of *Vogue* (1930), was elected to the House of Representatives as a Republican in 1942, was American Ambassador to Italy (1953–7) and was the author of several Broadway successes, including *The Women* (1936) and *Kiss the Boys Goodbye* (1938).

▷ A P Hatch, *Clare Boothe Luce: ambassador extraordinary* (1956)

BOPP, Raul
(1898–)

Brazilian poet, known mainly for his 'cannibalist' poem *Cobrata Norato* (1931, 'Norato the Snake'): 'the equivalent of the tragedy of fever', it is a lively and brilliant trip through the jungle—a true tour de force.

BORATYNSKY, Yevgeni
(1800–44)

Russian poet, born in Mara, regarded as the outstanding member of the so-called 'Pushkin Pléiade'—he was thought of by critics as **Pushkin**'s leading rival. His name, wrongly spelled as 'Baratynsky', has passed into common usage and is thus often found in many dictionaries and indices. He was a precise, aristocratic, philosophical poet, with an astringent quality which was never truly popular in his own day, but which is now increasingly valued. A few of his poems are translated into prose in the *Penguin Book of Russian Verse* (1965, ed Dimitry Obolensky).

▷ R Poggioli, *Poets of Russia* (1960)

BORCHARDT, Rudolf
(1877–1945)

German poet and essayist, born in Königsberg, and living most of his life in Italy. Borchardt was an outstanding speaker whose reputation rests predominantly on his criticism, essays, translations and anthologies. As a poet he has been described as a revolutionary conservatist, because of his attempt to reanimate everyday speech by using archaic forms—the result is a poetry as extravagantly formal as **Swinburne**'s, whose work Borchardt translated in *Swinburne Deutsch* (1919). *Jugendgedichte* (1913) contains some of Borchardt's most enduring verse.

BORCHERT, Wolfgang
(1921–47)

German short-story writer, playwright and poet, born in Hamburg. Conscripted in 1941, Borchert, not the most compliant of Wehrmacht soldiers, was imprisoned on several occasions under the Third Reich, and the privations he suffered in prison contributed to his early death. The quest for meaning in an apparently God-forsaken world underlies both his stories, such as the collection *Die Hundeblume* (1947, 'The Dogflower'), and his only play, *Draussen vor der Tür* ('Outside in front of the Door'), which was premiered the day after his death.

BORDEAUX, Henri
(1870–1963)

French novelist, born in Thonon. He studied law before he took to writing novels concerned with the defence of family life, often with a Savoy background, such as *La Peur de vivre* (1902, 'Fear of Living'), *Les Roquevillard* (1906), and *La Maison* (1913, 'The House').

▷E Mariotte, *L'Enigme de la vie* (1909)

BORDEWIJK, Ferdinand
(1884–1965)

Dutch poet, fiction writer and playwright, born in Amsterdam. One of Holland's finest writers of the 20th century, he did not find himself until middle age, when he produced *Blokken* (1931, 'Blocks'), one of the most chilling and prophetic of all depictions of totalitarian societies, and worthy to rank with **Orwell**'s *1984* and the *We* of **Zamyatin**. Before that he had written decadent poetry and stories influenced by **Poe** and **Couperus**, but these had not attracted more than cursory attention. *Bint* (1934), a similar novel about a fascistic school, employs staccato techniques imported from the last phase of German Expressionism. *Karakter* (1938, Eng trans *Character*, 1966) develops his gifts still further: in this variation on the theme of *The Ordeal of Richard Feverel* by **George Meredith**, a father destroys his son by trying to educate him by psychoanalytical methods.

▷R P Meijer, *Literature of the Low Countries* (1978)

BOREL (D'HAUTERIVE), Petrus
(1809–59)

French poet, translator (of **Defoe**'s *Robinson Crusoe*) and novelist, self-styled 'the Lycanthrope' (werewolf) on the grounds that 'man was a wolf to man'; he was born in Lyons. One of the least distinguished in the French misanthropic tradition which ran through **Vallès** and culminated in the great **Céline**, Borel became a leader of the ultra-romantic post-1831 Revolution group (its average age was 20) called 'Bousingo', after the wide-brimmed hat its members affected (*bousingo* is derived from the English word 'booze'). Another leader was **Gautier**, but, while he went on to better things, Borel produced sensationalist horror novels of no merit, and some bad poetry of hatred—although this is not, however, technically poor. He made some amends by joining the colonial service in Algeria; then, having been dismissed for inefficiency, became Mayor of Blad-Touaria.

▷E Starkie, *Petrus Borel* (1954)

BOREMAN, Yokutiel
(1825–90)

Hebrew novelist, born in Russia, whose books, written in a highly ornate and rhetorical style, deal with the pogroms, and are said to be brilliantly plotted. Unfortunately, as yet untranslated they are lost to English-speaking readers, for whom they would have been full of fascinating information, unobtainable elsewhere.

▷M Waxman, *A History of Jewish Literature* (1960)

BORGEN, Johan
(1902–79)

Norwegian novelist, playwright, critic and journalist, born in Oslo into a protective, bourgeois family—a milieu he later used as setting for the novel *Lillelord* (1955, Eng trans 1982), which was to become his literary breakthrough. One of Norway's most significant writers of this century, Borgen is also a very innovative and experimental playwright and novelist. Some of his plays are examples of early abstract theatre. In his novels and short stories he rather consistently concentrates on the existential conflict between psychological identity and social participation. The theme is given an experimental form in the novel *Jeg* (1959, Eng trans *The Scapegoat*, 1992).

▷R Birn, *Johan Borgen* (1974)

BORGES, Jorge Luis
(1899–1986)

Argentinian writer, born in Buenos Aires. He was educated there and at Geneva and Cambridge. From 1918 he was in Spain, where he was a member of the avant-garde Ultraist literary group, returning to Argentina in 1921. His first book of poems, *Fervor de Buenos Aires*, was published in 1923. He continued publishing poems and essays, and in 1941 appeared the first collection of the intricate and fantasy-woven short stories for which he is famous. Later collections include *Ficciónes* (1944 and 1956, Eng trans in US *Ficciones*, 1962, Eng trans in UK *Fictions*, 1965), *El Aleph* (1949, Eng trans *The Aleph and Other Stories 1933–1969*, 1970 (US); 1973 (UK)), *La Muerta y la Brújula* ('Death and the Compass', 1951) and the verse collection *El Hacedor* (1960, Eng trans *Dreamtigers*, 1963). Some stories from *El Aleph* appear in the collection of translations, *Labyrinths* (1962). He became director of the National Library in 1955, after losing his sight. His last book was *Atlas* (1986), written in collaboration with his companion, Maria Kodama, whom he married a month before his death.

▷J M Cohen, *Jorge Luis Borges* (1973); J Sturrock, *The Ideal Fictions of Jorge Luis Borges* (1977)

BORGESE, Giuseppe
(1882–1952)

Italian critic, novelist, political activist and teacher, born near Palermo, Sicily. His career began with his *Storia della critica romantica in Italia* (1905, 'History of Romantic Criticism in Italy'). This was directly influenced by **Croce**, who praised it highly. Borgese coined the term 'Crepusculari' ('twilight' poets) to describe **Gozzano**, **Moretti**, and others, discovered **Tozzi**, and encouraged many other major writers, such as **Moravia**. His chief novel is the prophetic and Pirandellian *Rubè* (1921, Eng trans 1923), about an anti-hero torn between the two extremes of fascism and communism. He left Italy, refusing to sign an oath of loyalty to Mussolini as all academics were required to do, and went to the USA to teach (1931–47). He repudiated Croce, but it has been well said that 'although he sided with the classicists, he continued to be an irrepressible romantic'.

▷S Pacifici, *The Modern Novel from Capuana to Tozzi* (1973)

BORROW, George Henry
(1803–81)

English author, born in East Dereham, Norfolk, the son of an army recruiting officer. He went to school at the High School in Edinburgh and at Norwich Grammar School (1816–18), and for the next five years was articled to a firm of solicitors. He turned to literature, and edited six volumes of *Celebrated Trials and Remarkable Cases of Criminal Jurisprudence* (1825). Already an accomplished linguist, from 1825 to 1832 he travelled on foot through England, France and Germany, studying the languages of the countries he visited. As an agent for the Bible Society he visited St Petersburg (1833–5), Portugal, Spain, and Morocco (1835–9). In 1840 he married a well-to-do widow, Mary Clarke, and settled down on a small estate of hers at Oulton, near Lowestoft, where, after travels in southeastern Europe (1844), a tour in Wales (1854), and a residence of some years in London, he ended his days a lonely man, sensitive to criticism. He wrote numerous books in which romantic fiction and autobiography often overlapped: *The Zincali or an Account of the Gypsies of Spain* (1840); *The Bible in Spain* (1843), which was an instant success as a travel book; *Lavengro* (1851) and its sequel, *The Romany Rye* (1857), novels

about his own gypsy life (the word 'Lavengro' means 'word-master'); *Wild Wales* (1862); and *Romano Lavo-Lil, or Word-book of the English-Gypsy Language* (1874).

▷M D Armstrong, *George Borrow* (1950)

BOSBOOM-TOUSSAINT, Anna Louisa Geetruida
(1812–86)

Dutch novelist, born in Alkmaar. Her first novels were able and readable imitations of **Scott**. Her later novels were on contemporary themes: *Majoor Frans* (1874, Eng trans 1885) seems to be her only novel which reached an English-speaking audience.

BOSCO, Henri
(1888–1976)

French regionalist novelist and minor poet, born in Avignon, and throughout his work identified with the countryside of Provence. A classics teacher by profession, he did not publish his first novel until he was 36; and became famous only in 1945, when he published *Le Mas Théotime* (Eng trans *The Farm Théotime*, 1947), almost a detective story in form (although the murder in it is accidental), but far more artistic than most detective stories. He had a feeling for mysteries hidden beneath the surface, and produced more novels at this high level of accomplishment, including *Un Rameau de la nuit* (1950, Eng trans *The Dark Bough*, 1955).

▷R T Sussex, *Henri Bosco, Poet-Novelist* (1966)

BOSTOCK, Gerald
(1942–)

Australian aboriginal poet and playwright, born in Grafton, New South Wales, who, after serving with the army in South-East Asia, became involved in the history of aboriginals. He set up the Black Theatre in Sydney where his play *Here Comes the Nigger*, calling for aboriginal nationalism, was produced in 1976. He has worked in film and co-produced *Lousy Little Sixpence* (1983), a documentary of the exploitation of aboriginal labour in the early 1900s. *Black Man Coming* (1980) is a powerful collection of poetry on the same themes.

BOSWELL, James
(1740–95)

Scottish writer and biographer of **Dr Johnson**, born in Edinburgh, the eldest son of a judge, Lord Auchinleck. He was educated privately in Edinburgh and at the University of Edinburgh. He then studied civil law at Glasgow, but his true goal was literary fame and the friendship of the famous. At the age of 18 he

began to keep an astonishingly frank and self-probing journal. In spring 1760 he ran away to London and turned Catholic. To discourage such religious fervour, Lord Eglinton, a London-based friend of Boswell's father, saw to it that Boswell became more of a libertine than ever and he reverted to his original faith. Young Boswell hobnobbed with the young Duke of York, with **Sheridan**'s father, made plans to join the army, and skilfully resisted all attempts to lure him into matrimony. He first met Dr Johnson on his second visit to London, on 16 May 1763, at Tom Davies's bookshop in Russell Street. By the following year they were on such cordial terms that Johnson accompanied him as far as Harwich. Boswell was on his way to Utrecht to continue his legal studies, but stayed only for the winter and then toured Germany, France, Switzerland, and Italy. By an astounding process of literary gatecrashing he introduced himself to **Voltaire** and **Rousseau**. From Rousseau he procured an introduction to Paoli, the hero of Corsica, whom he 'Boswellized' in *Account of Corsica* (1768), which had an immediate success and was translated into several languages. Boswell had many love affairs. There was the serious and high-minded affair with 'Zélide' of Utrecht, and liaisons with the Irish Mary Anne Montgomery, and with numerous others in London, Rome and elsewhere, including a disreputable episode with Rousseau's mistress, Thérèse Le Vasseur. He finally married in 1769 a cousin, Margaret Montgomerie, a prudent, amiable woman who put up with his shortcomings. He returned from the Continent in 1766, was admitted advocate, then in 1773 was elected to Johnson's famous literary club, and took the great doctor on a memorable journey to the Hebrides. A major literary enterprise (1777–83) was a series of 70 monthly contributions to the *London Magazine* under the pseudonym 'The Hypochondriak'. After Johnson's death appeared *The Journal of the Tour of the Hebrides* (1785). Its great success made Boswell plan his masterpiece, the *Life of Samuel Johnson* (1791), of which *The Journal* served as a first instalment. Meanwhile Boswell had entered the Inner Temple and had been called to the English Bar in 1786. He hardly practised, however, except to publish anonymously *Dorando, a Spanish Tale* (1767), a thinly disguised summary of a topical case which, at the time of publication, was still *sub judice*. Boswell's wife died in 1789, leaving him six children, and his drinking habits got the better of him. His work is that of a conscious artist, a born journalist, and a biographical researcher. The discoveries of Boswell's manuscripts, at Malahide Castle in Ireland in 1927 and at Fettercairn House in Scotland in 1930, which have been assembled by Yale University, are proof of his literary industry and integrity.
▷I Finlayson, *The Moth and the Candle: a life of James Boswell* (1985)

BOTELHO GOSÁLVEZ, Raúl
(1917–)

Bolivian novelist and critic, born in La Paz. He fought in the disastrous Chaco War, and later showed his solidarity with the Aymara Indians by going to live amongst them for a year. He became a diplomat, then a politician, and even served as interim president (1979) under a military junta which was returning the country to democratic rule. *Altiplano* (1945), his most powerful novel, deals in great and profound detail with the plight of a whole community left to its fate in the Bolivian highlands. Botelho Gosálvez has written much about **Jaimes Freyre**, whose example he believes to have been vital not only to Bolivia but also to Latin America.
▷J S Guevara, *La cien obras capitales de la literature boliviana* (1975)

BOTEV, Hristo
(1847–76)

Bulgarian poet who was educated in Odessa, where he picked up the progressive ideas of the Russian intelligentsia. Just as Hungary has its Petofi (killed in battle against Russians) and Romania its **Mihail Eminescu** (died mad), so Bulgaria has its Botev: like them, he was a poet-revolutionary who perished young. He died fighting the Turks in the abortive rising at Mount Vola, Vratsa. Mostly he wrote polemical journalism; but his few poems, based on folk song and celebrating the tradition of the *haydutin*, or guerrillas, vividly catch and preserve the spirit of Bulgarian romantic independence.
▷C Manning and R Smal-Stocki, *The History of Modern Bulgarian Literature* (1960)

BOTTO, Ján
(1829–81)

Slovak nationalist poet whose work will doubtless gain even more attention in the new republic. He brought the influences of Serbian and, especially, Polish epic and folk poetry to bear on Slovak poetry: his masterpiece, *Smrt' Jánosikva* (1862, 'Jánosik's Death'), is probably untranslatable, since it builds on Slovak folk elements that cannot be transferred to another language. Jánosik is the Slovak Robin Hood figure.

BOTTOME, Phyllis
(1884–1963)

American novelist and biographer, born in Rochester, Kentucky. She travelled extensively, both during her formative years and later, after her marriage, and her novels reflect the differing environments in which she found herself. *The Dark Tower* (1916), for example, derives from her work with the Ministry of Information in London during World War I, while *Old Wine* (1925) examines life in Vienna, where her husband was working at the time of writing. *The Mortal Storm* (1937) is based upon her experiences in Munich during the early thirties, when she observed the Nazis take political power. She had earlier (1934) written an anti-war novel, *Private Worlds*. She is also the author of several biographical studies and a biography of the Austrian psychiatrist, *Alfred Adler: Apostle of Freedom* (1939).

▷ *Search for a Soul* (1947); *The Challenge* (1952); *The Goal* (1962)

BOTTOMLEY, Gordon
(1874–1948)

English poet and playwright, born in Keighley, Yorkshire. His interest in Celtic folklore emerged in much of his work, including his first collection of verse, *The Mickle Drede* (1896). He is best remembered for his *Poems of Thirty Years* (1925) and his collections of plays, including *King Lear's Wife and Other Plays* (1920), which, although they mostly constituted an unhappy blend of poetry and rhetoric, won critical approval. His poetry anticipated Imagism.

▷ *Poet and Painter: the correspondence of Gordon Bottomley and Paul Nash* (1955)

BOTTRALL, (Francis James) Ronald
(1906–)

English poet of diverse interests. His work has ranged very widely, experimenting with most of the major prosodic types. His early poetry was published in *The Loosening* (1931), *Festivals of Fire* (1934) and *The Turning Path* (1939) and attracted the attention of **T S Eliot** and **G S Fraser**. He began to develop a new and more allusive voice after the war, beginning with *Farewell and Welcome* (1945), but reaching a new level of sophistication and confidence in *The Palisades of Fear* (1949) and in his best book, *Adam Unparadised* (1954). There have been three important collections: *The Collected Poems* appeared in 1961; *Poems 1953–1973* (1974) was complementary, and *Against a Setting Sun* (1984) brought his work up to date.

▷ G S Fraser, *The Modern Writer and His World* (1953)

BOUCICAULT, Dion(ysius Lardner)
(?1820–1890)

Dramatist and actor, born in Dublin. He was educated at University College School, London. He scored an early success on the London stage with *London Assurance* (1841), a comedy written under the pseudonym 'Lee Morton'. He adapted a number of French plays into English, then emigrated to the USA in 1853, where his successful melodramas included *The Colleen Bawn* (1860) and *The Octoroon* (1861). He was a major figure in the theatre of his day, but his reputation is now much diminished.

▷ R G Hogan, *Dion Boucicault* (1969)

BOUILHET, Louis
(1821–69)

French poet and dramatist, born in Cany in Seine Inférieure. He is best known as a lifelong friend of **Gustave Flaubert**. In his *Fossiles* (1856), he attempted to use science as a subject for poetry and also wrote on historical subjects. Of his many plays, *Madame de Montarcy* (1856) and *Conjuration d'Amboise* (1866, 'The Amboise Conspiracy') met with success.

BOULLE, Pierre
(1912–94)

French novelist and short-story writer, born in Avignon. He is best known in the English-speaking world as the author of two novels which subsequently, and—at least in box-office terms—successfully, became films: *Le Pont Sur la Rivière Kwai* (1952, Eng trans *The Bridge on the River Kwai*, 1954), the tale of a group of Allied soldiers held prisoner by the Japanese; and *La Planete des Singes* (1959, Eng trans *Planet of the Apes*, 1963), an allegory of oppression and racial hatred set on a future Earth in which chimpanzees have become the dominant species. Not nearly so well known as the two novels, his short stories—particularly the collections *Contes de l'Absurde* (1953, 'Tales of the Absurd') and *E = MC2* (1957), which were translated jointly as *Time Out of Mind* (1966)—tend to be lighter, more subtle expressions of his gentle, humane humour.

BOURDET, Édouard
(1887–1945)

French playwright, born in Saint-Germain-en-Laye. He administered the Comédie-Française from 1936 until 1940. He was a highly skilled popular dramatist, who managed to treat serious subjects, such as homosexuality, without trivializing them. *La Prisonnière* (1926, 'The Captive'), is a quite serious study of lesbianism. He also wrote in a lighter and more farcical vein. **Louis Bromfield** adapted his satirical *Les Temps difficiles* (1934) as *Times Have Changed* (1935).

BOURGES, Elémir
(1852–1925)
French novelist who is now more studied by
critics than read, but whose grandiloquent
works continue to arouse interest. After
neglect, he is coming to be appreciated for
his anticipations of modernist techniques—a
kind of prose **Mallarmé**, who was his friend.
He had few other literary connections
(although he had a correspondence with
Paule Régnier). He reacted against such naturalists as **Zola**, and, much influenced by the
English Elizabethan dramatists, and by **Shelley**, **Goethe** and Wagner, he tried, in such
massive volumes as *Le Crépuscule des dieux*
(1884, Eng trans *The Chains of Destiny*, 1928),
to present a less degraded picture of man; this
novel has been called 'one of the masterpieces
of symbolist fiction'. *La Nef* (1904–22), 'The
Ship'), is a huge two-part closet play or prose-
poem, fascinating but weighed down by its
erudition and operatic earnestness.

BOURGET, Paul
(1852–1935)
French poet, essayist and novelist, born in
Amiens. He first wrote striking verse: *La Vie
inquiète* (1875, 'The Anxious Life'), *Edel*
(1878), and *Les Aveux* (1881, 'Confessions').
His *Essais* (1883) indicated his true strength;
the second series, *Nouveaux Essais de psychologie contemporaine* (1886, 'New Essays
on Contemporary Psychology'), was a subtle
inquiry into the causes of pessimism in
France. His first novel, *L'Irréparable* (1884),
was followed by a steady stream of works
which placed him in the front rank of modern
French novelists. *L'Étape* (1902, 'The Halt-
ing-Place') marked the crystallization of his
talent. His works after 1892 showed a marked
reaction from realism and scepticism towards
mysticism.
▷ G Bennoville, *Paul Bourget* (1936)

BOURJAILY, Vance Nye
(1922–)
American novelist, raised in Ohio. His first
novel, *The End of My Life* (1947), like the
later *The Violated* (1958), was a conventionally autobiographical account of the
collapse of liberal values in the face of war;
it drew on Bourjaily's experience as an ambulance driver in the Mediterranean theatre. In
The Hound of Earth (1955), he focused on a
character troubled by his role in developing
the atomic bomb. *Confessions of a Spent
Youth* (1960) established him as a wry commentator on the making of the counter-
culture. He continued the thread in *The Man
Who Knew Kennedy* (1967), a latter-day version of **Sinclair Lewis**'s *The Man Who Knew
Coolidge* (1928), and in the romping *Brill*

Among the Ruins (1971). Later novels have
been less successful, perhaps because too self-
consciously targeted on cultural change, but
Old Soldier (1990) was a welcome return to
form, a 'green' book written without cant
or editorializing. During the fifties, Bourjaily
also edited the short-lived but influential journal *Discovery* (1953–5), which very accurately
named the contenders for literary fame in the
second half of the decade.

BOURKE, John Philip, pseud **Bluebush**
(1857–1914)
Australian bush poet, born in Nundle, New
South Wales. His vigorous verse descriptions
of the Western Australian gold diggings in
the 1890s and of the outback earned him the
praise of A G Stephens, editor of the *Bulletin*;
After Bourke's death Stephens edited a collection of his verse in *Off the Bluebush: Verses
for Australians, West and East* (1915).

BOUTENS, Pieter
(1870–1943)
Dutch poet, translator and classicist, born
on the island of Walcheren. He was initially
associated with De Nieuwe Gids, the 'Men of
the Eighties', the individualistic Dutch poetic
movement which took its bearings from contemporary French poets such as **Verlaine**. His
later poetry is elaborately Symbolist, somewhat cold, perfectly rendered, and artificial.
▷ H J Grierson, *Two Dutch Poets* (1936)

BOWEN, Elizabeth Dorothea Cole
(1899–1973)
Irish novelist and short-story writer, born in
County Cork, the daughter of a wealthy barrister and land-owner, and brought up in
Dublin. Educated in England at Downe
House School in Kent, she married in 1923
and in the same year published her first collection of short stories, *Encounters*, followed
by *Anne Lee's* (1926). Her first novel, *The
Hotel* (1927), began a string of delicately-
written explorations of personal relationships, of which *The Death of the Heart* (1938)
and *The Heat of the Day* (1949), a war story,
are the best known. She was also a perceptive
literary critic, and published *English Novelists*
(1942) and *Collected Impressions* (1950).
▷ J Brooke, *Elizabeth Bowen* (1952); A E
Austin, *Elizabeth Bowen* (1971)

BOWEN, John Griffith
(1924–)
English playwright, television scriptwriter
and novelist, born in Calcutta, India.
Athough also writing novels and stage plays

during the 1950s and 1960s, Bowen's association since 1960 with such successful television series as *The Power Game*, *The Guardians* and *The Villains* resulted in his becoming widely-known as an author for the small screen. His most successful stage plays remain *After the Rain* (1966; adapted from his 1958 novel of the same title) and *Little Boxes* (1968). Both are sympathetic studies of human nature. The second piece comprises two one-act plays, one of which, *Trevor*, deals with a young lesbian couple who attempt to keep their relationship secret from their respective parents.

BOWERING, George
(1938–)

Canadian poet, novelist, essayist and academic, born in British Columbia. Bowering set himself up as an arch-enemy of the confessional school, saying that he would rather read baseball scores than personal poetry which is too disclosing. It has been said, quite accurately, that his own work 'has more tone than taste'. He is exceptionally prolific, in both prose and verse, and correspondingly uneven. The size of his bibliography is matched by his ego: 'I was all those things that other poets always are on the dust jackets before they became poets,' he has boasted.

▷G Bowering, (Introduction to) *Touch: Selected Poems* (1971)

BOWLES, Jane Auer
(1918–73)

American fiction writer and playwright. For many years she suffered from acute ill-health and her literary output was consequently slim. An original writer, she has been linked with **Gertrude Stein** whose influence is apparent but not destructive. *In the Summer House* (1953), a play, is her most accessible work. Her *Collected Works* appeared in 1967. She married **Paul Bowles** in 1939.

▷I Finlayson, in *Tangier: the city of the dream* (1991)

BOWLES, Paul Frederick
(1910–)

American novelist, composer, poet, travel writer and translator, born in New York City. After studying at the University of Virginia, he went to Europe in 1931 to study music with Aaron Copland in Paris, and became a composer and music critic. He did not devote himself to writing until after World War II. His first novel, *The Sheltering Sky*, set in Morocco, appeared in 1949 and was immediately influential, sparking off an American literary exodus to Tangier, of which he became a resident in 1952. He wrote three

other novels, *Let It Come Down* (1952), *The Spider's House* (1955) and *Up Above the World* (1966), as well as several collections of short stories, including *Pages from Cold Point* (1968) and *Midnight Mass* (1981). He was married to the writer **Jane Bowles**.

▷*Without Stopping* (1972)

BOWLES, William Lisle
(1762–1850)

English clergyman and poet, born in King's Sutton vicarage, Northamptonshire. Educated at Winchester and Trinity College, Oxford, he became vicar of Bremhill in Yorkshire and prebendary of Salisbury in 1804, and later chaplain to the Prince Regent (1818). In his poetry he was a forerunner of the Romantic movement in English poetry. His *Fourteen Sonnets, written chiefly on Picturesque Spots during a Journey* (1789), published anonymously, had **Coleridge**, **Wordsworth** and **Robert Southey** among their enthusiastic admirers. His best poetical work is *The Missionary of the Andes*. In 1806 he published an edition of **Pope**, and an opinion which he expressed on Pope's poetical merits led to a memorable controversy (1809–25) in which **Thomas Campbell** and **Byron** were his antagonists.

▷G Gilfillan, *A Critical Dissertation by the Rev. Geo Gilfillan* (1855)

BOYD, James
(1888–1944)

American novelist, born in Pennsylvania and raised in North Carolina. His fiction delves back into the historical past. *Drums* (1925) is set in the War of Independence, and *Marching On* (1927) during the Civil War. He was not a localist, or a 'historical novelist' in any conventional sense, but used the past as a point of entry for examining contemporary issues and tensions. Other novels, less well known, include the very fine *Roll River* (1935) and *Bitter Creek* (1939). A collection of verse was published after his death.

BOYD, Martin à Beckett
(1893–1972)

Australian novelist and poet, born in Lucerne, Switzerland, son of Arthur Merric Boyd. Brought up in Melbourne, he lived for much of his life in Britain. After World War I he tried journalism for a time. His first three novels, *Love Gods* (1925), *Brangane: A Memoir* (1926) and *The Montforts* (1928) appeared under a pseudonym, 'Martin Mills', as did his fourth, *Dearest Idol* (1929), for which he adopted the name 'Walter Beckett'. Thereafter he acknowleged his authorship and produced his best work, to be seen in what is now referred to as the Langton tetralogy: *The Cardboard Crown* (1952), *A Difficult Young Man* (1955), *Outbreak of Love* (1957) and *When Blackbirds Sing* (1962). He wrote two autobiographies; the earlier, *A Single Flame* (1938) was superceded by *Day of My Delight: An Anglo-Australian Memoir* (1965) in which he casts light on his fiction and its characters, and on the multi-talented Boyd family.

▷ B Niall, *Martin Boyd* (1974)

BOYD, William Andrew Murray
(1952–)

Scottish novelist, born in Ghana, West Africa. He was educated at Gordonstoun School, and at the universities of Nice, Glasgow and Oxford. He lectured in English at Oxford (1980–3) and wrote television criticism for the *New Statesman*, before concentrating on fiction. His first book was the novel *A Good Man in Africa* (1981), which drew on the experiences of his formative years, and introduced the character of Morgan Leafy, a minor diplomat in an insignificant West African state who keeps boredom at bay by resorting to sex and alcohol. For this Boyd was hailed for his comic touch and likened to **Kingsley Amis**. His next book was a collection of stories, *On the Yankee Station* (1981), in which Leafy reappeared; then came *An Ice-Cream War* (1982), set in East Africa during World War I. In *Stars and Bars* (1984) the tone is conspicuously lighter as Henderson Dores, an English art expert, grapples with the shock of the New World. In *The New Confessions* (1987) Boyd introduced another memorable character, John James Todd, a Scottish filmmaker. *Brazzaville Beach* marked a return to Africa and the theme of conflict—professional, personal and political—as Hope Clearwater, an idealist anthropologist, studies a colony of apes against a backdrop of civil unrest and academic backstabbing. He has also written a number of screenplays and adaptations; another novel, *The Blue Afternoon*, appeared in 1993.

BOYE, Karin Maria
(1900–41)

Swedish poet and novelist, born in Gothenburg. She studied at Uppsala University and worked for a time as a teacher and journalist. In 1925 she abandoned Christianity in favour of the socialist *Clarté* group, but seems to have been more directly affected by psychoanalytic ideas than by Marxism. Sexually ambivalent, she was profoundly concerned about the relationship between instinct and social convention. Much of her poetry appeared in the modernist journal *Spektrum* which she founded and edited from

1931, and in which she also published translations of **T S Eliot**. Her collections include *Moln* (1922, 'Cloud'), *För trädets skull* (1935, 'For the Tree's Sake') and the posthumous *De sju dödssynderna* (1941, 'The Seven Deadly Sins'), published after her suicide. Despite the lyrical simplicity of this last volume, Boye had for some time been profoundly depressed about the rise of totalitarianism; this concern is explored in her novels *Kris* (1934, 'Crisis') and *Kallocain* (1940). She committed suicide.

▷ M Adenius and O G H Lagercrantz, *Karin Boye* (1942)

BOYESEN, H(jalmar) H(jorth)
(1848–95)

Born and raised in Scandinavia, he is, after **Ole Rølvaag**, the most important Norwegian–American writer. He first visited the USA in 1869, and was persuaded to stay by **William Dean Howells**'s enthusiasm for his novel *Gunnar* (1874), which first appeared in the *Atlantic Monthly*. Boyesen wrote ground-breaking *Essays on Scandinavian Literature* (1895) which, along with the autobiographical *Boyhood in Norway* (1892), written for teenagers, helped shape American awareness of Nordic culture. Later in his career, he wrote realistic but somewhat schematic novels of modern life: *The Mammon of Unrighteousness* (1891), *The Golden Calf* (1892) and *The Social Strugglers* (1893) reflect an outsider's view of American materialism.

BOYLAN, Clare
(1948–)

Irish novelist and short-story writer and journalist, born in Dublin. Her first novel, *Holy Pictures*, appeared in 1983 and her first collection of short stories, *A Nail on the Head*, later the same year. They share a common theme in loss of innocence and the human capacity for self-deception. *Holy Pictures* looks at the adult world through the eyes of two young Catholic sisters, Nan and Mary Cantwell, while in *Black Baby* (1988), an elderly Irish woman finds her way of life unexpectedly revived when she offers shelter to a young and vivacious black woman.

BOYLE, John, 5th Earl of Cork and of Orrery
(1707–62)

Irish writer, son of Charles Boyle, the 4th Earl. An intimate of **Swift**, **Pope** and **Dr Johnson**, he is remembered more by his rancorous *Remarks on the Life and Writings of Dr Jonathan Swift* (1751) than by an excellent translation of the *Letters of Pliny* (1751).

BOYLE, Kay
(1902–92)

American novelist, short-story writer, poet and essayist. Born in St Paul, Minnesota, she was brought up and educated in the USA, studying music and architecture, then lived in Europe for 30 years as part of the literary expatriate fraternity of Paris's Left Bank in the 1920s and latterly as the *New Yorker*'s foreign correspondent (1945–53). Influenced by **Henry James**, she has used her experience of expatriation most effectively in *Plagued by the Nightingale* (1931) and *Generation Without Farewell* (1960), but her novels are generally inferior to her stories, which are amassed in several volumes including *The Smoking Mountain* (1951). Her poems, indebted to **William Carlos Williams** and **Pádraic Colum**, were collected in 1962.
▷S W Spanier, *Kay Boyle: Artist and Activist* (1986)

BOYLESVE, properly **Tardivaux, René**
(1867–1926)

French novelist, born and brought up in La Haye-Descartes. He studied in Paris, and established his reputation as a portrayer of provincial life with *Le Parfum des îles Borrommées* (1898, 'The Scent of the Borrommee Islands') and *Mademoiselle Cloque* (1899).
▷A Bourgeois, *La vie de Boylesve* (1910)

BOZIĆ, Mirko
(1919–)

Croatian novelist and playwright, born in Sinj. He was a lawyer; then, in 1943, he joined Tito's partisans. He was active in the Croatian National Theatre in Zagreb, but his finest work is the novel *Kurlani* (1952, 'The Kurlans'), about peasants living in his native Dalmatia.

BRAATEN, Oskar
(1891–1939)

Norwegian dramatist and novelist, born into a poverty-stricken family in the slums of Oslo, in which two of his best novels are set: *Ulvehiet* (1919, 'The Wolf's Lair') and *Matilde* (1920). His folk comedy, *Ungen* (1911, 'The Child') was a huge success, as was his lively play about Oslo factory girls, *Den store barnedåpen* (1925, 'The Great Christening').
▷A Lind, *Oskar Braaten* (1962, in Norwegian)

BRACE, Gerald Warner
(1901–78)

American novelist, teacher and critic, born in Islip, New York. Brace published his first book, *The Islands*, in 1936 while a professor at Boston University. Although he went on to greater academic eminence and published

a further 10 perceptive novels, many critics believe he has not been given the recognition he deserves. *The Department* (1968) in particular is an excellent novel of academic life, written in the unobtrusively effective prose for which Brace is noted.
▷*Days That Were* (1976)

BRACKEN, Thomas
(1843–98)

Irish-born New Zealand poet, born in County Monaghan. His work is characterized by a sentimental Victorian attachment to nature and was written primarily for a readership 'back home', as in his *Lays of the Land of the Maori and Moa* (1884), *Lays and Lyrics: God's Own Country and Other Poems* (1893) and *Musings in Maoriland* (1890); this last was dedicated to his friend Lord **Alfred Tennyson** and bore a preface by the New Zealand governor-general. Regarded in his day as the 'poet laureate' of his adopted land, he wrote the words to New Zealand's national song 'God Defend New Zealand', and was perhaps at his best in the 'public' verse of the time. *Not Understood* (1905) went through many editions, the last as recent as 1956; the title poem, '...we wonder/Why life is life: and then we fall asleep/Not understood' has entered folk memory.

BRACKENRIDGE, Hugh Henry
(1748–1816)

Scottish-born American author of the satirical romance *Modern Chivalry*, he grew up near Campbeltown in Kintyre, Argyll, and emigrated to the USA in 1753, receiving an education at what became Princeton University. He was admitted to the Philadelphia Bar in 1780, and founded the newspaper *Tree of Liberty*, before moving to Pittsburgh to practise. His main literary achievement, *Modern Chivalry*, was originally published in four volumes between 1792 and 1797, extended (perhaps with contributions from other hands) in 1804–5, and then revised in 1815. Loosely modelled on *Don Quixote*, it recounts the adventures of Captain John Farrago and his Irish servant Teague O'Regan. Loose, episodic and shapeless, it hardly qualifies as a novel, but was nonetheless brilliantly written and remains an important source of social commentary on pre-Jeffersonian America. *Father Bembo's Pilgrimage to Mecca* (1770) was a fictional collaboration with **Philip Freneau** who also contributed to the epical *A Poem on the Rising Glory of America* (1772). Brackenridge also wrote political discourses and legal miscellanies.
▷C M Newlin, *The Life and Writings of Hugh Henry Brackenridge* (1932)

BRADBURY, Malcolm Stanley
(1932–)

English novelist, literary critic and university teacher. Born in Sheffield, he graduated from University College, Leicester, before taking undergraduate courses in London and the USA. Since 1965, he has taught at the University of East Anglia. Promoted to a professorship in 1970, he is a pioneer of American Studies in the UK, and also of the university's much-discussed creative writing programme, which he founded with **Angus Wilson**. His first novels, *Eating People is Wrong* (1959) and *Stepping Westward* (1965), established a satirical style which nonetheless contained the germ of a darker, more fabulatory approach. This began to surface in *The History Man* (1975, subsequently adapted for television), in which Bradbury's essential subject, the slow collapse of liberal humanism, received its definitive expression. *Rates of Exchange* (1983) was set in the imaginary Iron Curtain country of Slaka and was more experimental in tone. His most recent novel is *Dr Criminale* (1992). Of his literary criticism, *The Social Context of Modern English Literature* (1971) and *Possibilities: Essays on the State of the Novel* (1973) are perhaps the most important.
▷J Haffenden, *Novelists in Interview* (1985)

BRADBURY, Ray(mond Douglas)
(1920–)

American writer of science fiction, born in Waukegan, Illinois. An avid reader of sensational fiction and comics, he began early to contribute to pulp magazines, graduating to better quality magazines and short-story anthologies. While he has written notable novels—*Fahrenheit 451* (1953), *Dandelion Wine* (1957) and *Death is a Lonely Business* (1985)—he is primarily a short-story writer and has created some of the finest examples in the genre: 'The Day It Rained Forever', 'R Is for Rocket' and those included in *The Martian Chronicles* (1950). A prolific writer, he ranges widely and has been the recipient of numerous awards.
▷J L Garci, *Ray Bradbury humanista del futuro* (1971)

BRADDON, Mary Elizabeth
(1835–1915)

English novelist, born in London. She attained fame with a Victorian thriller, *Lady Audley's Secret* (1862), the story of a golden-haired murderess. Of some 75 popular novels, perhaps the best is *Ishmael* (1884). Her *The Doctor's Wife* (1864) is an adaptation of the theme of **Flaubert**'s *Madame Bovary*.

BRADDON, Russell Reading
(1921–)

Australian author, playwright and film and television scriptwriter, born in Sydney, the great-grandson of Sir Edward Braddon, premier of Tasmania (1894–9). Educated at Sydney University, during World War II he was a prisoner of the Japanese for four years, at the notorious Changi Jail, Singapore, and worked on the Burma Railway. His experiences were published as *The Naked Island* (1952, dramatized 1961) and *End of a Hate* (1958). A string of popular novels followed, including *End Play* (1972, filmed 1976) and *The Year of the Angry Rabbit* (1964, filmed as *Night of the Lepus*, 1972), but he is perhaps best known for his biographies, such as those of wartime hero Leonard Cheshire, *Cheshire VC* (1954) and the resistance heroine *Nancy Wake* (1956).

BRADFORD, Barbara Taylor
(1933–)

English novelist, born in Leeds. After working as a journalist specializing in interior design, she left for the USA, where she now lives. Her early publications, books of domestic advice such as *How to Solve Your Decorating Problems* and three volumes of *How to be a Perfect Wife*, appeared during the 1960s and 70s. She is internationally known, though, for such bestselling novels of money and romance as *A Woman of Substance* (1979), a heady, rags to riches story taking Emma Harte from obscurity in Yorkshire to a new life as the founder of a retail empire. *Hold the Dream* (1985) and *To Be the Best* (1988) continue the saga. Bradford writes about strong, adaptable, sexy women who triumph in a man's world because of their intellect and indomitable spirit.

BRADFORD, Roark
(1896–1948)

American author and newspaperman, born in Lauderdale County, Tennessee, near the Mississippi. He wrote about Blacks in his first collection, *Ol' Man Adam an' His Chillun* (1928), drawn from his contributions to the New York *World*. This was turned by **Marc Connelly** into the famous and successful play *Green Pastures*. Bradford continued in this vein, regarded by many as patronizing, in further collections.

BRADFORD, William
(1590–1656)

American colonist and religious leader, one of the Pilgrim Fathers, born in Austerfield near Doncaster. A nonconformist from boyhood, he joined a separatist group in 1606 and went with them to Holland in 1609, seeking

freedom of worship. In Leiden he became a tradesman and read widely. One of the moving spirits in the Pilgrim Fathers' expedition to the New World in 1620, he sailed on the *Mayflower*, signed the Mayflower Compact, and in 1621 took over from John Carver as elected governor of Plymouth colony. He was re-elected governor 30 times between 1622 and 1656, and guided the fledgling colony with exemplary fairness and firmness. He wrote a *History of Plimmoth Plantation* (completed c.1651, printed in 1856), a long descriptive poem (1654), a letter-book (1624–30) and a *Dialogue between some young men born in New England and sundry ancient men that came out of Holland*.
▷ B Smith, *Bradford of Plymouth* (1951)

BRADLEY, Edward, pseud Cuthbert Bede
(1827–89)
English author and clergyman, born in Kidderminster. He was educated at Durham University. His facetious description of Oxford undergraduate life in *Adventures of Mr Verdant Green* (1853–7) was the first and most popular of 26 works. He was also an illustrator, and drew for *Punch* as well as his own works.

BRADSTREET, Anne, née Dudley
(1612–72)
English-born American Puritan poet, born probably in Northampton. In 1628 she married a Nonconformist minister, Simon Bradstreet (1603–97), who later became Governor of Massachusetts. In 1630 they emigrated to New England. Her first volume of poems, *The Tenth Muse lately sprung up in America*, written in the style of *Phineas Fletcher*, was published by her brother-in-law in London in 1650 without her knowledge. She is considered the first English poet in America.
▷ E W White, *Anne Bradstreet: the tenth muse* (1971); Wendy Martin, *An American Triptych: Anne Bradstreet, Emily Dickinson, Adrienne Rich* (1986)

BRADY, Edwin James
(1869–1952)
Australian journalist, poet and writer, born in Carcoar, New South Wales. Early work on the wharves around Sydney led to a strong bond with the sailing fraternity, and it is for his sea ballads that he is especially remembered. His first collection of verse was *The Ways of Many Waters* (1899); other collections were *Bush-land Ballads* (1910), *Bells and Hobbles* (1911) and *Wardens of the Seas* (1933). His travels around Australia are recounted in *The King's Caravan: Across Australia in a Wagon* (1911), and a journey down the Murray River in *River Rovers* (1911). His

other writings include books for children, short stories and the tale of his Irish father's experiences in the American Civil War.
▷ *Life's Highway*, published posthumously in the quarterly journal *Southerly* (1952–5)

BRAGA, Rubem
(1913–)
Brazilian humorous writer, publisher and translator. Braga is a minor writer who takes an irreverent look at Brazilian life. He is best known for his *chrônicas*, short pieces which take a whimsical look at life in Rio de Janeiro.

BRAGG, Melvyn
(1939–)
English novelist and television arts presenter, born in Carlisle and educated at Wadham College, Oxford. Bragg's skill as a novelist only emerged fully with his third book, *Without a City Wall* (1968), which sets the oppositions of city (London) and country (Cumberland), centre and periphery, in terms of a powerful sexual struggle. The same themes emerge strongly in *The Silken Net* (1974), but *The Nerve* (1971), written at the time of his first wife's death, powerfully internalizes them and avoids many of the other books' tendency to schematicism. Perhaps more comfortable with set-pieces and images than straight prose, he has been an effective collaborator on film and television projects, notably with Ken Russell. Until a controversial television adaptation of his own *A Time to Dance* (1990) reawakened interest in his fiction, Bragg was better known as the front man (since 1978) of the South Bank Show, made by London Weekend Television, where he has also been Head of Arts. Previously, he was presenter of the BBC's *Second House* (1973–7) and the books programme, *Read All About It* (1976–7).

BRAINE, John Gerard
(1922–86)
English novelist, born in Bradford. He was educated at St Bede's Grammar School and had various jobs, including service in the Royal Navy, before following his mother's profession of librarian. In 1951 he went to London to become a full-time writer, but returned north the same year, after his mother's death in a road accident. He then spent 18 months in hospital suffering from tuberculosis, and it was during this period of enforced rest that he began to write his first successful novel, *Room at the Top*. He went back to library work until the publication of the book in 1957, and its success enabled him to embark again on a full-time career as a novelist. The theme of aggressive ambition

and determination to break through rigid social barriers identified him with the 'angry young men' of the 1950s. His novels include *Life at the Top* (1962), a sequel to *Room at the Top*, *The Jealous God* (1964), *The Crying Game* (1964), *The Queen of a Distant Country* (1972), *The Vodi* (1959), *Stay with Me Till Morning* (1968), *Finger of Fire* (1977) and *One and Last Love* (1981).

▷ J W Lee, *John Braine* (1973)

BRAITHWAITE, Edward Kamau
(1930–)

West Indian poet and historian, born in Bridgetown, Barbados. Described as 'one of the finest living poets of the Western hemisphere', he made his reputation with the three long poems reprinted together in 1973 as *The Arrivants: A New World Trilogy*. Each of the three — *Rights of Passage* (1967), *Masks* (1968) and *Islands* (1969) — analyses a different aspect of West Indian blacks' dispossession and their attempts to reconstitute an African-cum-Caribbean culture. His historical researches, for works such as *The Folk Culture of the Slaves of Jamaica* (1970), have complemented his creative output, which has continued with *Mother Poem* (1977) and *Sun Poem* (1982), both celebrations of his home island.

▷ L Brown, 'The Cyclical Vision of Braithwaite' in *West Indian Poetry* (1978)

BRAITHWAITE, William Stanley Beaumont
(1878–1962)

Black American poet and editor, born in Boston. He was well known for his annual *Anthology of Magazine Verse* (1913–29). His own verse, full of what **Conrad Aiken** called 'chaste, romantic awe', is no longer much read.

BRAMAH, Ernest, pseud of Ernest Bramah Smith
(1868–1942)

English short-story writer and novelist. Little is known about his life beyond the fact that he was born and educated in Manchester and worked on the land—a period covered in *English Farming and Why I Turned It Up* (1894)—before turning to journalism. He was **Jerome K Jerome**'s secretary, and worked on Jerome's *Today* magazine. In 1895 and 1896, he edited the London journal *The Minster*. He is known primarily for the Kai Lung stories, elegant chinoiseries which enjoyed a vogue but are now little read; the first of these, *The Wallet of Kai Lung* (1900), is perhaps the best. In 1914 Bramah unveiled the detective Max Carrados, who featured in four collections of stories: *Max Carrados* (1914), *The Eyes of*

Max Carrados (1923), *The Specimen Case* (1924) and *Max Carrados Mysteries* (1927), also in one novel, *The Bravo of London* (1934). What distinguishes Carrados from any other fictional detective is that he is blind. His manservant Parkinson acts as his Watson, making up the sensory deficit as the plots demand.

▷ W White, 'A Bramah Biographer's Dilemma', in *American Book Collector*, vol 15 (1965)

BRANCATI, Vitaliano
(1907–54)

Italian novelist, dramatist and journalist, born in Pachino, Sicily. At first an ardent fascist and an adherent of the proto-fascist **Gabriele D'Annunzio**, he broke with the Party in 1934 when they objected to a novel he had written (he claimed to have broken with them a year earlier, 'privately', but some doubted this). Later he certainly moved over to the left, but also—and more decisively—switched from praise of the brutal man of action to biting criticism of him and of his motives. His first novel to signify his new direction was *Gli anni perduti* (1935, 'The Lost Years'); in *Don Giovanni in Sicilia* (1942, 'Don Giovanni in Sicily'), he reached his main theme: homosexuality and impotence posing as heterosexual boastfulness—*gallismo*, as he called it. His best novel is reckoned to be *Il bell'Antonio* (1949, Eng trans *Bell'Antonio*, 1978), again about a man doomed to a (this time figurative) impotence. In his final years Brancati was beset by many difficulties, and, perhaps rightly, felt that he had failed to do full justice to his gifts.

BRAND, Dionne
(1953–)

Trinidadian-born poet, now settled in Canada, where she has worked as a teacher and counsellor in the black community. Her poems, which have been described by one critic as 'heavy stuff', are longer than most contemporary poems and attempt to deal with a wider perspective than the purely personal. *Chronicles of the Hostile Sun* (1984) is an example of her attempt to write historical verse of immediate urgency. It reflects a period of residency in Grenada, where she stayed up to the moment of the US invasion. *Sans Souci* (1989) contains short stories.

▷ D Cumberdance (ed), *Fifty Caribbean Writers* (1986)

BRAND, Max, pseud of Frederick Schiller Faust
(1892–1944)

American novelist and short-story writer, born in Seattle. An orphan by 13, he had a nomadic youth as an agricultural worker, then paid his own way through university. In 1918 he became a Western writer, contributing stories to around two dozen pulp magazines using almost as many pseudonyms. The following year his first novel, *The Untamed*, appeared under the Brand name. Other notable works in a prolific career include *Trailin'* (1919, a tale of Oedipal conflict), and *Destry Rides Again* (1930). A classicist and a Europhile, he regarded the West of which he wrote as dirty and brutish. He spent more than a decade (1926–37) in a Florentine villa, and died in Italy, where he was serving as a war correspondent with the US 88th Infantry Division.

▷ R Easton, *Max Brand: The Big Westerner* (1970)

BRANDAO, Raúl
(1867–1930)

Portuguese novelist, memoirist and playwright. He began under the influence of **Zola** as a simple naturalist, but later wrote more complex novels, such as his last, and perhaps most powerful of all, *Pobre de pedir* (1931, 'Reduced to Begging'), a vivid picture of poverty and brutality redeemed only by the compassion which pervades all his work.

BRANNER, H(ans) C(hristian)
(1903–66)

Danish novelist, short-story writer and playwright, born in Ordrup. A former actor and publisher, he wrote a number of psychologically realistic novels, beginning with *Legetøj* (1936, 'Toys'), which expressed his fears about fascism. Later works were less socially grounded and bear the mark of French existentialism: *Drømmen om en kvinde* (1949, 'A Woman's Dream'), and the later *Ingen kender Natten* (1955, 'Nobody Knows the Night'), which returns to the Nazi occupation for its material. His ability to capture the inner life was also evident in the **Joyce**an short stories of *To Minutters Stilhed* (1944, 'Two Minutes of Silence'), and his remarkable plays for radio.

▷ T L Markey, *Hans Christian Branner* (1973)

BRANT, Sebastian
(1458–1521)

German poet and humanist, born in Strasbourg. He studied and lectured at Basel. His *Narrenschiff* (1494, 'Ship of Fools'), an important vernacular satire on the follies and vices of his times, is not very poetical, but is full of sound sense and good moral teaching, and enjoyed immense popularity. It was translated into English by **Alexander Barclay** and Henry Watson, both in 1509. His other

writings include biographies of the Saints and translations from Latin texts.

▷ E H Teydal, *Sebastian Brant* (1967)

BRANTENBERG, Gerd
(1941–)

Norwegian novelist, born in Oslo. She studied at Oslo University, and had her first novel published in 1973: *Opp alle jordens homofile* (Eng trans *What Comes Naturally*, 1986) explores the complexities of being lesbian in Oslo in the 1960s, the humorous style tackling conventional prejudices head on. *Egalias døtre* (1977, Eng trans *The Daughters of Egalia*, 1985) exposes the absurdities of patriarchal society by inverting its norms, and has enjoyed considerable international success. *Favntak* (1983, 'Embraces') depicts lesbian love, while *Sangen om St. Croix* (1979, 'The Song of St Croix'), *Ved fergestedet* (1985, 'At the Ferry Crossing') and *For alle vinder* (1989, 'To the Winds') is a realist trilogy focusing on differences of class and sex.

▷ J Garton, 'Gerd Brantenberg', in *Norwegian Women's Writing 1850–1990* (1993)

BRANTÔME, Pierre de Bourdeilles, Seigneur de
(c.1540–1614)

French soldier and author, born in Périgord. He was educated at Paris and at Poitiers. In his sixteenth year he was given the abbacy of Brantôme, but he never took orders, and spent most of his life as a courtier and soldier. In 1561 he accompanied Mary, Queen of Scots to Scotland, and in 1565 he joined the expedition sent to Malta to assist the Knights of St John against the sultan. He served in Italy under the Maréchal de Brissac, in Africa under the Spaniards, and in Hungary as a volunteer against the Turks. He was made chamberlain to Charles IX and Henri III, and fought against the Huguenots. He was injured after a fall from a horse in about 1594, and he began to write his memoirs, and from then on lived in retirement. His works, first published in 1665–6, comprise *Vies des grands capitaines* ('Lives of the Great Captains'), *Vies des dames galantes* ('Lives of the Lady Courtesans') and *Vies des dames illustres* ('Lives of the Illustrious Ladies'), and provide a detailed picture of the Valois court. Their literary merit and historical interest are considerable. Their matter is often of the most scandalous nature, but they give a wonderfully vivid picture of his times.

▷ R D Cottrell, *Brantôme: the writer as portraitist of his age* (1970)

BRASCH, Charles Orwell
(1909–73)

New Zealand poet, critic and editor, born in Dunedin. In 1947 he established *Landfall*, a periodical of art, literature and politics, and was its editor for 20 years, exercising great influence on the form and direction of contemporary New Zealand poets. In 1962 he edited a selection of verse, *Landfall Country: Work from Landfall, 1947–1961*. His own verse is collected in *The Land and the People* (1939), *Disputed Ground: Poems 1939–1945* (1948), *The Estate* (1957), which collected poems written after 1945, *Ambulando* (1964), *Not Far Off* (1969) and the posthumous *Home Ground* (1974), ed Alan Roddick, who also edited *Collected Poems* (1984).

▷*Indirections: A Memoir 1909–1947* (1980), ed J Bertram

BRASILLACH, Robert
(1909–45)

French novelist and journalist, born in Perpignan. His early work includes studies of **Virgil**, **Corneille**, and the French revolutionary André Chenier. His fascist sympathies became increasingly evident as the 1930s wore on, and his novel *Les Sept Couleurs* (1939, 'The Seven Colours') has as its hero a man who becomes a Legionnaire, an admirer of Hitler, and finally one of Franco's soldiers. Under the German occupation, as editor of the fascist weekly *Je Suis Partout* ('I Am Everywhere'), Brasillach demanded the summary execution of imprisoned communists. With the liberation of the city, he was arrested—most other fascist writers had long since fled the capital—and sentenced to death as a collaborator. His trial became a focus for the debate on how collaborators should be treated in post-war France. Forty-five writers, including **Albert Camus**, signed a plea for clemency; others, among them **Simone de Beauvoir**, refused to lend their names to the appeal. The sentence was not commuted, and Brasillach was killed by firing squad.

BRATHWAITE, Errol Freeman
(1924–)

New Zealand novelist, born in Clive, Hawkes Bay. His service during World War II with the Royal New Zealand Air Force provided themes for his first novels, *Fear in the Night* (1959) concerning a crashed aircrew trapped behind Japanese lines, *An Affair of Men* (1962) and *Long Way Home* (1964). Next came a trilogy of historical novels on the New Zealand Land Wars of the 1860s: *The Flying Fish* (1964); *The Needle's Eye* (1965) and *The Evil Day* (1967). He has written topographical books including *Companion Guides* to the North and South Islands: *New Zealand and its People* (1974) and *The Beauty of New Zealand* (4 vols, 1974–82).

BRAUN, Lili, née von Kretschmann
(1865–1916)

German socialist authoress and feminist, born in Halberstadt. She married the socialist writer and politician Heinrich Braun (1854–1927). Her best-known book is *Im Schatten der Titanen* (1908, 'In the Shadow of the Titans'), and she is known for her novel *Liebesbriefe der Marquise* (1912, 'Love Letters of the Marquis'), and her *Memoiren einer Sozialistin* (1909–11, 'Memoirs of a Woman Socialist').

▷J Vogelstein, biographical note in *Gesammelte Werke* (1923)

BRAUTIGAN, Richard
(1935–84)

American fabulist and poet. Born in Tacoma, Washington, he is identified strongly with the Far West sensibility and hippy ethos of writers like **Ken Kesey**. Rejecting social fiction, Brautigan wrote brief surreal fantasies, outwardly naive, but often laden with unexpected cultural references. His finest work, *Trout Fishing in America* (1967), masquerades as a 'how-to' book; Brautigan's search for the ideal trout stream is, however, a purely rhetorical one, in which Trout Fishing in America becomes a verbal cipher or 'character' that can be placed in any context. Brautigan interweaves references to literary pastoral, American materialism and waste, and political totalitarianism; the 'novel' is also a satirical gloss on *Moby-Dick*. Other books include *In Watermelon Sugar* (1964), *A Confederate General from Big Sur* (1965) and the best of his verse collections, *The Pill Versus the Springhill Mine Disaster* (1968). After *The Abortion: An Historical Romance* (1971) he increasingly satirized popular literary genre and his books became marked by a dark thread of melancholy and loneliness. He committed suicide.

▷M Chénetier, *Richard Brautigan* (1982)

BRAZIL, Angela
(1868–1947)

English writer of girls' school stories, born in Preston. She was a governess for some years before beginning to write tales. She never married, and lived with her brother and sister, describing her adult self as 'an absolute schoolgirl'. Her stories of school life are heavily moralistic, and are notable for their healthy realism. Her best books include *The New Girl at St Chad's*, *A Fourth Form Friendship* and *Captain Peggie*.

BRECHT, Bertolt Eugen Friedrich
(1898–1956)

German playwright and poet, born in Augsburg, perhaps Germany's greatest dramatist.

He studied medicine and philosophy at Munich and Berlin Universities, and served briefly as a medical orderly in 1918. He won the **Kleist** Drama Prize in 1922 for his first two Expressionist plays, *Trommeln in der Nacht* (1922, Eng trans *Drums in the Night*, 1966), and *Baal* (1922, Eng trans 1964), followed by *Mann ist Mann* (1926, Eng trans *A Man's a Man*, 1964) with its clownish, inhuman soldiery. He was keenly interested in the effects produced by combining drama and music, and consequently collaborated with Kurt Weill, Eisler and Dessau in his major works. It was the *Dreigroschenoper* (1928, Eng trans *The Threepenny Opera*, 1958), an adaptation of **John** Gay's *Beggar's Opera* in a sham Victorian London setting, with music by Kurt Weill, that established Brecht's reputation. A Marxist, he regarded his plays as social experiments, requiring detachment, not passion, from the observing audience. To achieve this, he introduced the 'epic' theatre, where the audience is required to see the stage as a stage, actors as actors, and not the traditional make-believe of the theatre. Thus, to prevent the audience from identifying themselves with a principal actor, the camp-following title character in *Mutter Courage und ihre Kinder* (1941, Eng trans *Mother Courage and her Children*, 1961) is deliberately made to muff her lines, and *Puntilla* (1940) is given an increasingly ugly make-up. With Hitler's rise to power in 1933, Brecht sought asylum in Denmark, Sweden, and Finland, journeyed across Russia and Persia, and in 1941 settled in Hollywood. His abiding hatred of Nazi Germany found expression in a series of short, episodic plays and poems collected under the title of *Furcht und Elend des dritten Reiches* (1945, 'Fear and Loathing under the Third Reich'), and *Der aufhaltsame Aufstieg des Arturo Ui* (1957, Eng trans *The Resistible Rise of Arturo Ui*, 1976). He denied membership of the Communist Party before a Senate sub-committee on un-American activities in 1946, and in 1948 accepted the East German government's offer of a theatre in East Berlin. The *Berliner Ensemble* was founded, producing under his direction his later plays, such as *Der kaukasische Kreidekreis* (1947, Eng trans *The Caucasian Chalk Circle*, 1948), and *Der gute Mensch von Sezuan* (1943, Eng trans *The Good Woman of Setzuan*, 1948), as well as touring in Western Europe, and visiting London shortly after his death with Helene Weigel, his widow, as the company's leading actress. Although apparently antipathetic towards the East German anti-communist uprising in 1953 and a recipient of the Stalin Peace Prize (1954), he proved as artist and thinker to be an embarrassment to the East German authorities. His opera *Lukullus* (1932–51), in which the Roman general has

to account for his deeds before a tribunal-of-the-shadows, was withdrawn by order after the first night. *Galileo* (1938) underlined the moral that, however much the intellect may be oppressed, truth will out.
▷ M Esslin, *Bertolt Brecht* (1969); K Volker, *Bertolt Brecht: a biography* (1979)

BREDERODE, or BREDERO, Gerbrand Adriaenz
(1585–1618)

Major Dutch poet and dramatist, who was also a painter, born in Amsterdam. He is best known for his strident hatred of affectation, his lyrical poetry, and his stage comedies. *Spaanschen Brabander* (1618) is his play based on the great anonymous Spanish picaresque novel *Lazarillo de Tormes* (1554), which he sets in a vibrant Amsterdam.
▷ J A N Knuttel, *Bredero* (1949, in Dutch)

BREMER, Fredrika
(1801–65)

Swedish novelist, born near Åbo in Finland, and brought up near Stockholm. Her stories *Teckningar utur hvardagslifvet* (1828, 'Scenes from Everyday Life') were immediately successful and helped bring about realistic family fiction in Sweden; *Familjen H* (1831, 'The H Family'), and *Hemmet* (1839, 'The Home') developed the strain considerably. Novels like *Hertha* (1856) and *Fader och dotter* (1858, 'Father and Daughter') express her interest in female education and political emancipation, ideas she had absorbed on visits to Britain and the USA. She travelled widely elsewhere in Europe and the Levant and published two volumes of impressions.
▷ E Ehrnach, *Fredrika Bremer* (1955)

BRENAN, Gerald
(1894–1987)

English travel writer, Hispanophile and novelist, born in Malta, the son of an officer in an Irish regiment. After an itinerant boyhood he debunked with a donkey, drifting his way across Europe to the Balkans and back again. He went to Spain and settled in Yegen, an isolated village which became the focus of his classic *South from Granada* (1957). This was preceded by his best-known book, *The Spanish Labyrinth* (1943), still regarded as one of the most profound and perceptive studies of modern Spain. Other books include two volumes of memoirs, *A Life of One's Own* (1962) and *Personal Record* (1974), *The Literature of the Spanish People* (1951) and a novel, *Thoughts in a Dry Season* (1978).

BRENNAN, Christopher John
(1870–1932)

Australian poet, academic and critic, born in Sydney of a Catholic family. Intended for the priesthood, after entering Sydney University he turned to the classics and philosophy. Going to Berlin University in 1892 to read philosophy, he was distracted by the exciting social and cultural life, and by French Symbolist poetry, which influenced his future writing. Returning to Sydney University in 1894, he was appointed Associate Professor of German Literature in 1920, but his intemperate and iconoclastic nature led to his dismissal five years later. He published only a select number of volumes of verse, the best of which was written before 1900 and issued as *Poems* (1913). The sequence of verse, 'The Wanderer' suggests the torment of Brennan's own life. A later collection was *A Chant of Doom and Other Verses* (1918). Some of his verse was published posthumously, and his criticism appeared mainly in journals, but he is also known for his co-editing of the standard college anthology *From Blake to Arnold* (1900), which contains much of his critical work.

▷ J P McAuley, *Christopher Brennan* (1973)

BRENNER, Joseph Chaim
(1881–1921)

Hebrew novelist, story writer and translator (of **Dostoyevsky**'s *Crime and Punishment*), born in the ghetto in Novi Malini, Bulgaria. He studied in a Talmudic College (Yeshivah), then served in the Russian army, but in 1905 moved to London, where he lived in poverty as editor of a Hebrew periodical. He became a Zionist, and settled in Palestine in 1908—he died in the Arab riots in Jaffa. His novels and stories are very harshly realistic, but—as is so often the case with the Jewish writers of this era—unavailable in English translation.

▷ M Waxman, *A History of Jewish Literature* (1960)

BRENTANO, Clemens von
(1778–1842)

German poet, novelist and dramatist, born in Ehrenbreitstein. After a somewhat irresponsible early life, he became a Roman Catholic in 1818 and withdrew to the monastery of Dülmen, near Münster (1818–24), where he recorded the revelations of the nun, Anna Katharina Emmerich. Thereafter he led a restless life, and showed plain signs of derangement some years before his death. In his earliest poems the peculiarities of the Romantic school are carried to excess. His dramatic productions, the best of which is *Die Gründung Prags* ('The Founding of Prague'), are characterized by great dramatic power, and a wonderful humour. He was mostly successful in his novellas, particularly in the *Geschichte vom braven Kasperl* ('Tale of Honest

Kasper'), and with his brother-in-law **Achim von Arnim** he edited *Des Knaben Wunderhorn* ('The Boy's Magic Horn'), a collection of folk songs.

▷ J B Heinreise, *Clemens von Brentano* (1878)

BRENT-DYER, Elinor M(ary)
(1894–1969)

English author of the 'Chalet School' girls' stories, born in South Shields. Educated at Leeds University, she became a schoolmistress, and later headmistress of the Margaret Roper Girls' School in Hereford. Her first schoolgirl novel, *Gerry Goes to School*, appeared in 1922, inaugurating her 98 titles. Her fourth book, *The School at the Chalet* (1925), established her famous series by showing the 24-year-old Madge Bettany's successful attempt to found an English school in the Austrian Tyrol, to which Austrian as well as English parents were attracted. Centred on Jo Bettany, Madge's younger sister, the series sought to evangelize against English parochialism and xenophobia. Perhaps the best single title was *The Chalet School in Exile* (1940), a horrific if judicious account of the school's flight from Nazi rule with a grimly realistic depiction of homicidal persecution of Jews. Later stories were set in the Channel Islands, in Wales, and in the Bernese Oberland: the inevitable decline was offset for many years by the creation of another memorable character, the impetuous and gloriously frank Mary-Lou Trelawney. The final book in the series, *Prefects of the Chalet School*, was published posthumously in 1970.

BRENTON, Howard
(1942–)

English dramatist, born in Portsmouth. He wrote for fringe theatre companies during the late 1960s, and was resident dramatist at the Royal Court Theatre, London, from 1972 to 1973, where his play *Magnificence*, dealing with urban terrorism, was staged. *The Churchill Play* (1974), a bleak look at a future Britain governed by hard-liners using troops to brutalize trade unionists, was produced at the Nottingham Playhouse. *Weapons of Happiness* (1976) became the first new play to be produced at the National Theatre's recently-opened South Bank building. *The Romans in Britain* was premiered at the National Theatre in 1980, and *The Genius*, on the nuclear arms race, at the Royal Court in 1983. He has also collaborated with **David Hare** on a number of projects, the most outstanding being *Pravda* (1985), a furiously ebullient satire on the cravenness of the national press. He has also written a political thriller, *Diving for Pearls* (1989).

BRETON, André
(1896–1966)

French poet, essayist and critic, born in Tinchebray, Normandy. In 1916 he joined the Dadaist group and was co-founder of the Dada magazine *Littérature* (1919), and collaborated with Philippe Soupault to write *Les Champs magnétiques* (1920, 'Magnetic Fields'), which was described as 'an experiment in automatic writing'. In 1922 he turned to Surrealism, and in 1924 he published his first Surrealist manifesto (he developed his ideas more fully in 1930 and 1942) and *Le Poissonsoluble* ('Solublefish'), and became Editor of *La Révolution surréaliste*. His major novel, *Nadja*, which mingles the irrational and the everyday, was published in 1928 (Eng trans 1960). In 1930 he joined the Communist Party for a time. He spent the war years in the USA. His writings also include *Qu'est-ce que le surréalisme?* (1934, Eng trans *What is Surrealism?*, 1936), and he continued his highly personal, poetic exploration of Surrealism and the unconscious in his post-war writings.
▷ M A Caws, *André Breton* (1971)

BRETON, Nicholas
(c.1555–c.1626)

English poet, born in London, the son of a merchant, and stepson of **George Gascoigne**. Educated at Oxford, he became a prolific writer of all kinds of verse, prose and pamphlets. His best-known poem is *The Passionate Shepheard* (1604). His prose *Wits Trenchmour* (1597) is a fishing idyll on which **Izaak Walton** drew for *The Compleat Angler*. He also wrote a prose romance, *The Strange Fortune of Two Excellent Princes* (1600), and a collection of character observations, *Fantasticks* (1626).
▷ G A Tannenbaum, *Elizabethan Bibliographies* (1937)

BRETÓN DE LOS HERREROS, Don Manuel
(1796–1873)

Spanish dramatist. He is the author of some 150 plays, most of which are social comedies concerned with middle-class manners and mores, in which caricature rather than character is portrayed. Many of his works were translations and adaptations. He also wrote poetry, and was a popular figure in his day.
▷ G le Gentil, *La poète Manuel Bretón de los Herreros* (1903)

BREWSTER, Elizabeth
(1922–)

Canadian poet, born in Chipman, New Brunswick, she has been a university teacher of English. Her poems are quiet, meditative, and, in her own words, attempt to dramatize 'the struggle to lead a human rational life in a world which is increasingly inhuman and irrational'. Her *Selected Poems 1944–84* appeared in two volumes in 1985.
▷ *Canadian Literature* (Autumn, 1974)

BŘEZINA, Otakar, properly Václav Jebavý
(1868–1929)

Czech poet, born in Pocatky. He was a school-teacher, and lived as a bachelor recluse in a small country town. His work, which consists of five books of poems and one of philosophical essays, attempted an ambitious synthesis of philosophical and mystical elements. He was a leading exponent of a richly evocative Symbolism in Czech poetry in his collections *Vrěy od pólô* (1897, 'Polar Winds'), *Stavitelé chramu* (1899, 'Temple Builders'), *Ruce* (1901, 'The Hands'), and others.
▷ P Selver, *Otakar Březina: a study in Czech literature* (1921)

BRICKHILL, Paul Chester Jerome
(1916–91)

Australian author, born in Melbourne. Educated at Sydney University, he worked in journalism before serving with the Royal Australian Air Force during World War II. Shot down in North Africa, he was for two years a prisoner-of-war in Germany, in Stalag Luft III from which the intrepid escape was made, later described by him in *The Great Escape* (1951, filmed 1963). His first published book, *Escape to Danger* (1946), collected many stories of prison-camp life. He went on to become the most successful non-fiction writer of the post-war period, with *The Dam Busters* (1951, filmed 1956), *Escape—or Die* (1952), and the story of the legless air ace Douglas Bader, *Reach for the Sky* (1954, filmed 1956).

BRIDGES, Robert Seymour
(1844–1930)

English poet and critic, born in Walmer, Kent. Educated at Eton and Corpus Christi College, Oxford, he then studied medicine at St Bartholomew's Hospital and practised until 1881. At university he met **Gerard Manley Hopkins**, with whom he became friendly, arranging for the posthumous publication of his poems in 1918. His first collection, *Poems*, appeared in 1873, and was followed by *The Growth of Love* (1876), a sequence of sonnets which was a popular success. He followed this with two long poems, *Prometheus the Firegiver* (1883) and *Eros and Psyche* (1885), but for the next decade he concentrated on plays and wrote eight, only one of which was

performed in his lifetime. He made important contributions to criticism, with studies of **Milton** (1893) and **Keats** (1895), and wrote poems set to music by Charles Parry, as well as *A Practical Discourse on Hymn Singing* (1901). In 1912 he published his *Collected Poems* to wide public acclaim and in 1913 he was surprisingly appointed poet laureate, and produced *The Spirit of Man* (1916), an idiosyncratic anthology of prose and verse designed to lift the nation's spirits during World War I. After the war, he published *October and Other Poems* (1920) and, in his 85th year, *The Testament of Beauty*, a long poem in four parts whose philosophy is expressed in its title.
▷L P Smith, *Robert Bridges: recollections* (1931)

BRIDIE, James, pseud of **Osborne Henry Mavor**
(1888–1951)

Scottish dramatist, born in Glasgow, son of the pioneering electrical engineer Henry Mavor. He qualified as a doctor at Glasgow University and became a successful general practitioner and consultant. Always interested in theatre, he seized his chance when the Scottish National Players produced his *Sunlight Sonata* in 1928 under the pseudonym of Mary Henderson. After that, he wrote a stream of plays, among them *The Anatomist* (1931), *A Sleeping Clergyman* (1933), *Mr Bolfry* (1943) and *Dr Angelus* (1947). He served in both world wars in the Royal Army Medical Corps and after the second he became Head of the Scottish Committee of CEMA. He founded the Citizens' Theatre in Glasgow in 1943.
▷H Luyben, *James Bridie: clown and philosopher* (1965)

BRIEUX, Eugène
(1858–1932)

French dramatist and Academician, born in Paris of poor parents. He experienced many of the social evils which his powerful, didactic plays, leavened by wit, expose. His works include *L'Engrenage* (1894, Eng trans *The Evasion*, 1896) and *Maternité* (1903, Eng trans *Maternity*, 1907). His attack on the judiciary in *La Robe Rouge* (1900, 'The Red Dress'), and his use of the effects of syphilis in *Les Avariés* (1901, Eng trans *Damaged Goods*, 1914), both aroused public controversies.
▷W H Scheifley, *Brieux and contemporary French society* (1917)

BRIGGS, Raymond (Redvers)
(1934–)

English children's illustrator and author, born in London, the son of a milkman. His early publications were conventional, such as *Midnight Adventure* (1961), but in 1966 his *Mother Goose Treasury* appeared with over 900 pictures, and his talent for eccentric comedy was established, winning him the Kate Greenaway Medal. *Father Christmas* (1973), another distinctive work, uses the comic-strip format, featuring a grumpy, expletory Santa, reluctantly braving the wintry elements. For this he was awarded his second Greenaway Medal. *Fungus the Bogeyman* (1977) brought him love and loathing, and *The Snowman* (1979) enchanted adults and children alike. A provocative as well as an entertaining artist, his anxiety for the future well-being of the planet is expressed in *When the Wind Blows* (1982), while *The Tin Pot Foreign General and the Old Iron Woman* (1983) was an attack on the political manipulation of the Falklands War. In 1992 he was awarded the Kurt Maschler Award for *The Man*.

BRIGHOUSE, Harold
(1882–1958)

English playwright, born near Manchester, one of the first 20th-century English authors to write plays that were both popular and set beyond the metropolitan and country-house world of the fashionable and wealthy. Brighouse was working at a local cotton mill when Annie Horniman (the heiress of the tea empire) took over the Manchester Gaiety Theatre in 1908. He was one of several hopefuls who answered her call for new writers, and between 1909 and his death he completed over 70 plays, many of them amiably folksy one-act comedies set in Lancashire. Some of the full-length plays, such as *Lonesome-Like* (1911) and *The Odd Man Out* (1912), might profitably be revived today, but are overlooked, Brighouse's reputation depending, unfortunately, on only one play, *Hobson's Choice* (1915). In this work, the pragmatic and determined Maggie Hobson, supposedly on the shelf at 30, coerces the talented but timid bootmaker Willie Mossop into marriage, makes him her business partner and successfully takes over her domineering father's boot and shoe business. Highly popular at the time, it is frequently revived.

BRINK, André
(1935–)

South African novelist, short-story writer, playwright, critic and translator, born in Vrede, Orange Free State. An Afrikaaner dissident, he has produced a prodigious body of work of uneven quality and has, almost single-handedly, contemporized Afrikaans novel writing. He emerged as a writer in the 1950s but it was not until his seventh novel, *Kennis van die aand* (1973)—which he later translated into English as *Looking on Darkness* (1974)—was banned by the South African authorities that he began to attract international attention. Relating the story of a coloured actor who makes good in London and returns to South Africa to confront the apartheid regime, it won the author admiration, though more for his courage than his style. Subsequent books have been criticized for their sentimentality and sensationalism but the best—*Rumours of Rain* (1978), *A Chain of Voices* (1982) and *States of Emergency* (1988)—are powerful narratives which highlight conditions in South Africa without resorting to propaganda. He received the Martin Luther King Memorial Prize and the French Prix Medicis Étranger in 1980, has thrice won the CNA Award, South Africa's most prestigious commendation, and has twice been runner-up for the Booker Prize.

▷ *Pot Pourri: Skatse uit parys* (1962)

BRINSMEAD, Hesba Fay
(1922–)

Australian writer, born in Bilpin, Blue Mountains, New South Wales. The author of award-winning fiction, she was one of the first writers of 'transitional' books which give adult perspectives within an adolescent frame of reference. Her first work, *Pastures of the Blue Crane* (1964), achieved immediate success, winning two awards and becoming a popular television series in the 1970s. Many of her adolescent romances are set in country areas, such as the Tasmania of *Season of the Briar* (1965), but she is aware of the social and racial tensions which affect young people, as in *Beat of the City* (1966). *Longtime Passing* (1971) won the Children's Book of the Year Award, and was followed by *Longtime Dreaming* in 1982.

BRITTAIN, Vera Mary
(1893–1970)

English writer, born in Newcastle-under-Lyme. After studying at Oxford she served as a nurse in World War I, recording her experiences with war-found idealism in *Testament of Youth* (1933). As well as writing a number of novels, she made several lecture tours in the USA, promoting feminism and pacifism. In 1925 she married George Catlin, Professor of Politics at Cornell, and wrote the sequels, *Testament of Friendship* (1940) and *Testament of Experience* (1957). Her daughter is the English politician Shirley Williams.

▷ V Brittain and J S Reid (eds), *Selected Letters of Winifred Holtby and Vera Brittain* (1960)

BRITTING, Georg
(1891–1964)

German poet, born in Regensburg. He was severely wounded during World War I and afterwards settled in Munich. He wrote one novel, *Lebenslauf eines dicken mannes, der Hamlet hieß* (1932), a bizarre adaptation of the Hamlet story. His poetry, as found in the collections *Michael und das Fräulein* (1927) or *Der bekränzte Weiher* (1937, 'The Garlanded Pond'), is marked by colourful vocabulary and a precise technique.

BRIZEUX, Julien Auguste Pélage
(1803–58)

French poet, born in Lorient. Much of his work, including a translation of **Dante**'s *Divina Commedia*, was influenced by Italian styles, but his verse also incorporated the folklore and dialect of Britanny.

▷ C Levigne, *Brizeux et ses oeuvres* (1898)

BROCH, Hermann
(1886–1951)

Austrian novelist and essayist, born in Vienna. He spent his early adult life working in his father's textile business and was over 40 when he went to Vienna University to study philosophy and mathematics. When the Nazis invaded Austria in 1938 he was imprisoned, but influential friends, including **James Joyce**, obtained his release and facilitated his emigration to America in 1940, where he remained until he died in abject surroundings. He is regarded as one of the greatest German writers of the 20th century, though he was a reluctant writer and his books reward only readers with perseverance. His masterpiece is *The Death of Virgil* (1946). Other notable books include *The Sleepwalkers* (3 vols, 1931–2), *The Unknown Quantity* (1935) and *The Spell*, published posthumously and first translated into English in 1987.

▷ D C Cohn, *The Sleepwalkers: elucidations* (1966)

BROCKES, Barthold Heinrich
(1680–1747)

German poet, translator (**Pope, James Thomson**) and politician (he was Senator of Hamburg and then Mayor of Ritzbüttel, but more to do people a favour than out of ambition). He was born in Hamburg. Both Handel and Telemann set to music his somewhat florid verses, written in the Baroque manner. Most of his poetry is pedestrian, though it is technically adept; he was also a keen observer of the natural scene, adding to German poetry what one critic has called 'a new world of exact perception'.

▷ A Brandl, *Barthold Heinrich Brockes* (1878, in German)

BROD, Max
(1884–1968)

Austrian novelist, biographer, essayist, poet and dramatist, born in Prague. He became a Zionist and emigrated to Palestine (Israel) in 1939, where he became the literary director of the Habimah Theatre in Tel Aviv. Although he is known in the English-speaking world as the long-time friend, editor and biographer of **Franz Kafka**, he was a versatile and prolific writer in his own right. His work includes novels on religious and social themes, plays, autobiographical writings, and literary criticism.

▷M Pazi, *Max Brod, Werk und Persön-lichkeit* (1970)

BRODBER, Erna
(1940–)

Jamaican novelist, born in St Mary and educated at the University of West Indies. She is a respected sociologist/social historian and has published extensively in these fields. Her fiction draws on this knowledge and gives a strong sense of the importance of oral history in transmitting traditional wisdom and an appreciation of African ancestry. Her first novel, *Jane and Louisa Will Soon Come Home* (1981), is a semi-autobiographical prose-poem centring on the character Nellie's search for identity. In both this work and in *Myal* (1989), a lyrical, amusing novel which scrutinizes the educational and religious institutions derived from a colonial past, the acceptance of the varied strands of a multi-racial past is shown to be essential for the renewal of individual and society.

▷E O'Callaghan, 'Engineering the Female Subject: Erna Brodber's *Myal*', in *Kunapipi*, Vol XII, No.3 (1990)

BRODERICK, Damien
(1944–)

Australian science-fiction writer, born in Melbourne, whose *The Dreaming Dragons: A Time Opera* (1980) was runner-up for the international **John W Campbell** Award in 1981. With *The Judas Mandala* (1982, rev edn 1990), *Transmitters* (1984), *The Black Grail* (1986), *Striped Holes* (1988) and *The Sea's Furthest End* (1993) it comprises the thematically cross-linked *Faustus Hexagram* sequence. Short-story collections are *A Man Returned* (1965) and *The Dark Between the Stars* (1991). He has edited anthologies of Australian science fiction and writes critically on science and fiction; *The Lotto Effect* (1992) is a study of parapsychology, and recent titles are *Reading by Starlight: The Semiotics of Modern and Postmodern Science Fiction* (1994) and *The Architecture of Babel: Discourses of Literature and Science* (1994). His novels have been translated into German, Portuguese and Polish.

BRODKEY, Harold Roy
(1930–)

American short-story writer and novelist, born in Staunton, Illinois. Originally called Harold Weintraub, he took his name from the family who adopted him. His debut as a short-story writer, *First Love and Other Sorrows* (1957), led to widespread belief that he was an author of substantial promise. His output since, however, has been sparse to say the least: a gap of almost 30 years followed before his next collection, *Women and Angels*, appeared in 1985. His novel *The Runaway Soul*, also some three decades in the making, appeared in 1991; like the rest of his writing it contains a strong autobiographical thread, but is strangely devoid of vitality and verve.

BRODSKY, Iosef
(1940–)

Russian poet, translator and critic, winner of the Nobel Prize for literature, born in Leningrad, who was tried as a 'social parasite' in 1964, and sent into exile. Although he was hardly known to general readers in Russia, his poetry circulated in *samizdat* form, and various critics and poets interceded on his behalf. His cause was taken up in the USA, but in 1972 he was expelled from Russia. In 1977 he became an American citizen, and in 1987 he was awarded the Nobel Prize. He has latterly written in English and translated his own Russian poems into English; but it is for his earlier poetry that he is most valued. Often dismissed in contemporary Russia as merely a charming minor voice, he is a scholarly poet, who introduced into Russian poetry the influences of the English metaphysical poets, of **Yeats** and **Eliot**, and of his personal mentor, **W H Auden**. He is, after **Seferis**, perhaps the best of the European synthetic poets—that is, highly artificial, ornate, earnest, mannerist, learned, unspontaneous. His collections include *Stikhotvoreniia i Poemy* (1965, 'Longer and Shorter Poems'), and *Uraniia: Novaia Kniga Stikhov* (1985, 'Urania: A New Book of Poems', later reissued in English as *To Urania: Selected Poems 1965–1985*, 1988). His translations of **Donne** and **Marvell** into Russian are particularly prized. There are English translations of his work in *Selected Poems* (1973) and *Less Than One* (prose essays, 1980).
▷*A Part of Speech* (1979)

BRÓDY, Sándor
(1863–1924)

Hungarian novelist, story writer, dramatist and journalist, born in Budapest. He was extremely influential and popular in Hungarian literature for many years, but now has his sharp (mainly academic) detractors, who accuse him of sentimentality and indulgence in mediocre writing. However, he possessed a remarkable vitality, and what he took from his two chief mentors, the historical novelist **Mór Jókai** and **Zola**, was worth adopting. His stories about Rembrandt were translated in 1928; and one of his greatest stories, 'The Jest', is translated in *Hungarian Short Stories* (1962).

BRØGGER, Suzanne
(1944–)

Danish novelist, critic and playwright, born in Copenhagen, who spent long periods abroad as a child and adolescent; among her major literary influences are writers such as **Anaïs Nin** and **Henry Miller** as well as **Karen Blixen**. Her first book, *Fri os fra kærligheden* (1973, Eng trans *Deliver Us from Love*, 1977), characteristically transcends the conventional genres to formulate a critique of marriage and the nuclear family which culminates in a celebration of the free unfolding of female eroticism. *Creme Fraiche* (1978) is a fictive autobiography focusing on erotic exploits, while *Brøg* (1980, 'Brew'), a collection of articles and essays, demonstrates the scope of her cultural criticism. The ambitious novel *JA* (1984, 'YES') opens up new perspectives on *Creme Fraiche*; and the play entitled *Efter Orgiet* (1991, 'After the Orgy') offers a critical view of the 'sexual liberation' of the 1960s.
▷M Schack, 'Suzanne Brøgger', in T Brostrøm and M Winge (eds), *Danske digtere i det 20. århundrede*, vol V (1982)

BROME, Richard
(c.1590–1652)

English dramatist, of whom little is known except that he had been in his earlier days servant to **Ben Jonson**, and that he wrote as many as 24 popular plays, the best being *The Northern Lass* and *The Jovial Crew*.
▷R J Kaufman, *Richard Brome, Caroline playwright* (1961)

BROMFIELD, Louis
(1896–1956)

American novelist, born in Mansfield, Ohio, the son of a farmer. Educated at Cornell Agricultural College and Columbia University, he joined the French army in 1914, was awarded the *Croix de Guerre*, and returned to journalism in America. His novels include *The Green Bay Tree* (1924), *Early Autumn* (1926, Pulitzer Prize), *The Strange Case of Miss Annie Spragge* (1928), *The Rains Came* (1937), *Until the Day Break* (1942), *Colorado*

(1947), and *Mr Smith* (1951). His short stories include *Awake and Rehearse* (1929), and his plays *The House of Women* (1927).
▷D D Anderson, *Louis Bromfield* (1964)

BRONTË, originally Brunty or Prunty,

The name of three sisters, **Anne, Charlotte** and **Emily**, remarkable in English literary history, born in Thornton, Yorkshire. They were the daughters of Patrick Brontë (1777–1861), a clergyman of Irish descent and his Cornish wife, Maria (1783–1821), and sisters of Maria and Elizabeth, who both died in childhood, and Branwell (1817–48), a brother who squandered his many talents. The family moved to Haworth, now part of Keighley, in 1820 when their father became rector there. After the mother's death from cancer, her sister came to look after the children. Their childhood, spent in the sole companionship of one another on the wild Yorkshire moors, was happy enough. Branwell's 12 toy soldiers inspired them to construct two fantasy worlds of their own, *Gondal* and *Angria*, which contained all the exotic places and was peopled by all the great figures they had read about. Incidents in these were described by the children in verse and prose in rival collections of notebooks. Such escapism did not prepare them for their harsh schooling at Cowan Bridge, but Roe Head, their second school, proved more amenable. Branwell's debts caused them to leave home and find employment, but they always returned to their beloved Haworth.
▷W Gerin, *The Brontës* (1973–4)

BRONTË, Anne, pseud Acton Bell
(1820–49)

She went as governess to the Inghams at Blake Hall in 1839 and to the Robinsons at Thorpe Green (1841–5), a post she had to leave because of Branwell's unfortunate love for Mrs Robinson. She shared in the joint publication, under pseudonyms, of the three sisters' *Poems* (1846), only two volumes of which were sold. Her two novels, *Agnes Grey* (1845) and *The Tenant of Wildfell Hall* (1848), although unsuccessful at the time, show a decided talent, if less vivid than that of her sisters.
▷W Gerin, *Anne Brontë* (1959); *The Brontës* (1973–4)

BRONTË, Charlotte, pseud Currer Bell
(1816–55)

She returned in 1835 to her old school, Roe Head, as teacher, but gave up this post and two others, both as governess. Back at Haworth, the three sisters planned to start a school of their own and, to augment their qualifications, Charlotte and Emily attended the Héger Pensionat in Brussels (1842). Their plans foundered, however, and Charlotte returned to Brussels as an English teacher (1843–4) and formed an unreciprocated attachment to the married M Héger, whom she later scornfully satirized in *Villette* (1852). Her chance discovery of Emily's remarkable poems in 1845 led to the abortive joint publication, under pseudonyms, of the three sisters' *Poems* (1846). This provoked them all to novel-writing. *The Professor*, which did not achieve publication until Charlotte's death, dwells on the theme of moral madness, possibly inspired by Branwell's degeneration. It was rejected by her publisher, but with sufficient encouragement for her to complete her masterpiece, *Jane Eyre* (1847). This in essence, through the master-pupil love relationship between Rochester and Jane, constituted a magnificent plea for feminine equality with men in the avowal of their passions. It was followed in 1849 by *Shirley*, a novel set in the background of the Luddite riots. By now her brother and two sisters were dead, and she was left alone at Haworth with her father. *Villette*, founded on her memories of Brussels, was published in 1853. She married her father's curate, Arthur Bell Nicholls, in 1854 and died during pregnancy in the following year, leaving the fragment of another novel, *Emma*. Two stories, *The Secret* and *Lily Hart*, were published for the first time in 1978.

▷E Gaskell, *The Life of Charlotte Brontë* (1860); W Gerin, *The Brontës* (1973–4)

BRONTË, Emily Jane, pseud Ellis Bell
(1818–48)

In 1837 she became a governess in Halifax. She attended the Héger Pensionat in Brussels with Charlotte and in 1845 embarked upon a joint publication of poems after the discovery by the latter of her *Gondal* verse, including such fine items as *To Imagination*, *Plead for Me*, and *Last Lines*. Her single novel, *Wuthering Heights* (1847), an intense and powerful tale of love and revenge set in the remote wilds of 18th-century Yorkshire, has much in common with Greek tragedy, and has no real counterpart in English literature.

▷W Gerin, *Emily Brontë: a biography* (1971); *The Brontës* (1973–4)

BROOKE, Frances
(1723–89)

English novelist and playwright. After establishing herself in the literary circles of London, she spent five years in Canada and she is primarily recognized as the author of 'Canada's first novel', *The History of Emily Montague* (1769). Set in Quebec during the 1760s, the novel explores the differences of a 'woman's place' in England and Canada, the complexity of French–English relations, and details many features of the pioneer settler's life in Canada. In addition to three novels, she wrote and staged a number of dramatic works, edited her own periodical, *The Old Maid*, and translated a number of texts from Italian and French. Her work has been reassessed in the light of more recent gender studies.

▷L McMullen, in R Lecker, J David and E Quigley (eds), *Canadian Writers and Their Work: Fiction Series: Vol.1* (1983)

BROOKE, Henry
(c.1703–1783)

Irish dramatist and novelist, born in Rantavan, County Cavan. He became the friend of **Pope** and married his cousin and ward. His poem *Universal Beauty* (1735) is supposed to have suggested Erasmus Darwin's *Botanic Garden*. His novel, *The Fool of Quality* (1766), is the only one of his numerous works to have retained some reputation.

▷C H Wilson (ed), *Brookiana* (1804)

BROOKE, (Bernard) Jocelyn
(1908–66)

English novelist, poet and amateur botanist, born in Kent. After running away from boarding school twice he settled at Bedales before going to Worcester College, Oxford, emerging without distinction. He tried various occupations before joining the family wine firm. During World War II he enlisted in the Royal Army Medical Corps, and re-enlisted after the war; but the army in peacetime was not to his liking and following the critical success of *The Military Orchid* (1948) he bought himself out and thereafter devoted himself to writing. He followed this with the second and third parts of the overtly autobiographical trilogy (known subsequently as *The Orchid Trilogy*), *A Mine of Serpents* (1949) and *The Goose Cathedral* (1950), the former drawing heavily on his obsession with pyrotechnics. His works also include two volumes of poetry, *December Spring* (1946) and *The Elements of Death* (1952); a **Kafka**esque novel, *The Image of a Drawn Sword* (1950), and botanical books.

BROOKE, Rupert Chawner
(1887–1915)

English poet, born in Rugby. Educated at King's College, Cambridge, he travelled in Germany and visited the USA and Tahiti. He died a commissioned officer on Skyros on his way to the Dardanelles and was buried there. His *Poems* appeared in 1911, *1914 and Other Poems* in 1915, after his death. If lacking the insight of a maturer poet, his poetry was characterized by a youthful, self-probing honesty, a fresh perception, a gentle lyricism and comedy. These, together with his handsome appearance and untimely death, made him a favourite poet among young people in the inter-war period.

▷C Hassall, *Rupert Brooke, a biography* (1972)

BROOKE-ROSE, Christine
(1926–)

British experimental novelist and literary critic, she was born in Geneva to a Swiss-American mother and English father, and has lived much of her life in France. Her fiction draws heavily on the *nouveau roman*, but with a quirkiness that is quintessentially English. Early novels like *The Languages of Love* (1957) are reminiscent of **Ivy Compton-Burnett** and it was only with her fifth novel *Out* (1964) that she began to experiment with a version of **Alain Robbe-Grillet**'s 'dogmatic realism'. *Such* (1966) captures a three-minute flow of consciousness in a man who is being revived following a heart seizure. *Thru* (1975) is more playful, but it was to be Brooke-Rose's last novel for nearly a decade. She broke her silence with *Amalgamemnon* (1984), a novel about a university teacher who is made redundant; written entirely in unresolved tenses, it has a shimmering, uncertain quality that is appropriate to a theme also taken up in the computer fantasy *Xorandor* (1986), in which a computer begins to address two young children, and continued in *Verbivore* (1990) and *Textermination* (1991). Brooke-Rose's criticism includes *A Grammar of Metaphor* (1958) and *A Rhetoric of the Unreal* (1981). She was married to the novelist **Jerzy Peterkiewicz**.

BROOKNER, Anita
(1928–)

English novelist and art historian, born in London. An authority on 18th-century painting, she was the first woman Slade Professor at Cambridge University (1967–8), and has been a reader at the Courtauld Institute of Art since 1977. She is the author of *Watteau* (1968), *The Genius of the Future* (1971) and *Jacques-Louis David* (1981). As a novelist she was a late starter, but in eight years (1981–8) she published as many novels, elegant, witty and imbued with cosmopolitan melancholy. Invariably, her main characters are women, self-sufficient in all but love. By winning the Booker Prize, *Hôtel du Lac* (1984) has become her best-known novel and is regarded by many as her most accomplished. Her other titles include *Family and Friends* (1985) and *Friends from England* (1987).

BROOKS, Gwendolyn
(1917–)

American poet and novelist, born in Topeka, Kansas, and brought up in the slums of Chicago. An active writer from an early age, she was 13 when her first poem was published. She has taught English in a number of colleges, and was Publicity Director of the NAACP (National Association for the Advancement of Colored People) for a time in the 1930s. Her first collection, *A Street in Bronzeville* (1945), chronicles the cares of city-dwelling black Americans, while *Annie Allen* (1949) traces the growth to maturity of a black woman amid the spiritual and social ills of her race and earned her a Pulitzer Prize, of which she was the first black winner. Subsequent works in both poetry and prose have focused on the life and politics of the USA's black community, and have been increasingly radical in tone, as in *Riot* (1969) and *Blacks* (1987). Other works include the novel *Maud Martha* (1953), about one woman's growing personal and political maturity; *Report From Part One* (1972), an autobiography, may be said to account for the same process in Brooks herself.

▷G E Kent, *A Life of Gwendolyn Brooks* (1990)

BROOKS, Van Wyck
(1886–1963)

American author and critic, born in Plainfield, New Jersey. His major achievement was the thesis, first expressed in *The Wine of the Puritans* (1909), that the Puritan tradition had held back free creative expression in America. In related vein, he wrote biographical studies of **Mark Twain** (1920), **Henry James** (1925) and **Ralph Waldo Emerson** (1932), attacked American materialism, and won the Pulitzer Prize with his *Flowering of New England* (1936).

▷W Wasserstrom, *Van Wyck Brooks* (1968)

BROPHY, Brigid Antonia
(1929–)

English novelist, essayist and critic, born in London. Her first novel, *Hackenfeller's Ape*, appeared in 1953, revealing her social, ethical and philosophical concerns, and especially her opposition to vivisection. Other novels, such as *The Finishing Touch* (1963) and *In Transit* (1969), look at lesbianism and transsexuality, while in *Palace Without Chairs* (1978), the lesbian life-force bursts through a bleak Absurdist nightmare. Brophy describes her novels as 'baroque'. Her critical works include *Mozart the Dramatist: A New View of Mozart, His Operas and His Age* (1964), studies of Aubrey Beardsley (1968), censorship (1972) and a vivacious defence of the work of **Ronald Firbank** (*Prancing Novelist*, 1973).

▷'A Case Historical Fragment of Autobiography', in *Baroque-'n'-Roll and Other Essays* (1987)

BROWN, Carter, pseud of **Alan Geoffrey Yates**
(1923–85)

English-born Australian thriller writer, born in London, who served in the Royal Navy during World War II and moved to Australia in 1948. It is estimated that he wrote an average of six books a year, novels of horror, romance, science fiction and westerns, under a variety of names. In 1950 he began writing a series of 'hard-boiled' thrillers, aimed at the US market, under the pseudonym Carter Brown, which he estimated in the mid-1980s to have reached over 150 titles. An Australian radio series *The Carter Brown Mystery Theatre* ran between 1956 and 1958.

▷ *Ready When You Are, CB* (1983)

BROWN, Charles Brockden
(1771–1810)

American novelist, born of Quaker ancestry in Philadelphia. He was the first professional American writer making use of English models in a highly distinctive way. *Wieland* (1798), *Ormund* (1799) and *Jane Talbot* (1804), among many others, are Gothic romances, full of incident and subtle analysis, but extravagant in style.

▷A Axelrod, *Charles Brockden Brown: an American tale* (1983)

BROWN, Frederic William
(1906–72)

American novelist and journalist, born in Cincinnati, Ohio. He worked mainly in the science-fiction and detective genres, and brought an unusual degree of humour to his work in them. His first success was with a detective novel, *The Fabulous Clipjoint* (1947), followed by his science-fiction novel, *What Mad Universe* (1949). Other novels include *Martians, Go Home* (1955), on a comic invasion theme, and *The Mind Thing* (1961). He is best known for his short stories, and several of them, such as 'Etaoin Shrdlu' (1942) and 'Arena' (1944), are regarded as idiosyncratic classics of the science-fiction genre.

BROWN, George Douglas
(1869–1902)

Scottish writer, born in Ochiltree, Ayrshire, the illegitimate son of a farmer. Educated at the village school and Ayr Academy, he went to Glasgow University and Balliol College,

Oxford, on a scholarship. He settled in London as a journalist, published a boys' adventure book, *Love and Sword* (1899), but made his name, under the pseudonym 'George Douglas', with *The House with the Green Shutters* (1901), a powerfully realistic novel and an antidote to the 'Kailyard School'. He died of pneumonia before he was able to complete two other novels.

▷F R Hart, *The Scottish Novel* (1978)

BROWN, George Mackay
(1921–)

Scottish poet, novelist and short-story writer, born in Stromness, Orkney, the 'Hamnavoe' of his stories and poems. Suffering from tuberculosis, he was unable to work when he left school. In 1957 he went to Newbattle Abbey College, where **Edwin Muir** was warden. Encouraged in his poetry by his mentor and fellow-Orcadian, Brown was introduced by Muir to a London publisher. His first collection was *The Storm* (1954), followed five years later by *Loaves and Fishes*. Though illness prevented him from completing the course at Newbattle, he went on to Edinburgh University where he did postgraduate work on **Gerard Manley Hopkins**. In 1964 he returned to Stromness, and he has since rarely left it. A prolific and easily identifiable writer, his best work is ruggedly elemental, drawing on old sea yarns, myths, Scandinavian sagas and the folklore of Orkney. His conversion to Catholicism in 1961 brought into relief his concern with religion. A lyrically intense, poetic writer, his popularity lies in his stories and novels. Published in 1967, *A Calendar of Love*, a collection of stories, was the first trickle in what has become a dam-burst of fiction. *A Time to Keep* (1969), widely regarded as his best collection of stories, is the closest he comes to confronting contemporary life. His first novel was *Greenvoe* (1972), which describes the last days of an island community on 'Hellya' in the 1960s. *Magnus* (1973), its unconventional successor, is more a meditation on the eponymous saint than a novel, but is no less effective. His *Selected Poems* were published in 1991.

▷R Fulton, *Contemporary Scottish Poetry* (1974)

BROWN, Harry
(1917–86)

American novelist and dramatist, born in Portland, Maine. He worked for the *New Yorker*, and then, after joining the army, for *Yank* magazine. His greatest success was his war novel *A Walk in the Sun* (1944), made into a film by Lewis Milestone. Thereafter he worked in Hollywood, wrote more fiction—which was adjudged of less account—and devoted himself to film work and to hunting, his grand passion. His verse, collected in *The Beast in his Hunger* (1949) and elsewhere, attracted little attention.

BROWN, John
(1810–82)

Scottish physician and essayist, born in Biggar, Lanarkshire. He attended the High School of Edinburgh and studied medicine at Edinburgh University. He wrote *Horae subsecivae* (1858–61, 'Leisure Hours') and *John Leech and other Papers* (1882). Humour and pathos are the chief features of his style, as exemplified in his essay on the human nature of dogs in 'Rab and his Friends' and 'Pet Marjorie', an essay on the child writer **Margaret Fleming**.
▷J Brown (jr) and D W Forrest (eds), *Letters of Dr John Brown* (1907, with a biographical note by E McLaren)

BROWN, Oliver Madox
(1855–74)

English author and artist, born in Finchley, son of Ford Madox Brown. At 12 he painted a watercolour of considerable merit. In 1871 he wrote his first novel, *Gabriel Denver*, reprinted in his *Literary Remains* (1876) under its first title *The Black Swan*. He died of food poisoning.
▷J H Ingram, *Oliver Madox Brown* (1893)

BROWN, Sterling A(llen)
(1901–89)

American poet and critic, born in Washington DC. Brown was an authority on the literature of his fellow blacks, edited several anthologies and wrote about fiction and drama as well as poetry. He made full use of folk imagery and black idiom in his own work. *A Collected Poems* was published in 1980.

BROWN, Thomas
(1663–1704)

English satirist, born possibly in Shifnal or, more probably, Newport, Shropshire. As a student at Christ Church, Oxford, he produced his famous extempore adaptation of **Martial**'s 33rd epigram, 'Non amo te, Sabidi', at the demand of Dr John Fell, the dean: 'I do not love thee, Dr Fell'. After teaching at Kingston-on-Thames, he settled in London, where he made an uncertain living by writing scurrilous satirical poems and pamphlets, and published *Amusements Serious and Comical* (1700). He was buried in the Westminster cloisters near his friend, Mrs **Aphra Behn**.

BROWN, Wayne Vincent
(1944–)

Trinidadian poet, educated at the University of the West Indies and Gregory Fellow in Poetry at the University of Leeds. His first volume of poetry, *On the Coast* (1972), which won the Commonwealth Prize for Poetry, was dedicated to **Derek Walcott** and the diaspora of the Caribbean people. The title poem declares: '… I am an orphaned islander,/in a winter/of bays. I have no home.' Yet the home of memory is Caribbean sun and sea.

BROWN, William Hill
(1765–93)

American novelist and essayist, born in Boston. Related to the Mather dynasty of Puritan divines, Brown can hardly be said to have followed in his forebears' footsteps. He has been called the first American novelist, on the basis of *The Power of Sympathy* (1789), a fictional treatment of a scandal affecting the family of the poet Sarah Wentworth Morton. While Brown was alive the book was thought to have been written by Morton, whose husband was implicated in the scandal. Brown died at the age of 28, the victim of a local epidemic. He had been a prolific contributor to magazines, using the pseudonyms Pollio and The Yankee. A number of works appeared after his death, including *West Point Preserved* (1797), a drama based on the life of Major André.

BROWN, William Wells
(c.1816–1884)

American writer, born into slavery in Kentucky. He was raised in St Louis, but after gaining his freedom, helped runaway slaves in Ohio. He achieved fame with his autobiographical *Narrative of William W Brown, a Fugitive Slave* (1847), and became a leading black advocate of abolition. He published a collection of poems, *The Anti-Slavery Harp* (1848), and an account of his travels in Europe, but is best known for his novel *Clotelle; or, The President's Daughter* (1853), the story of an illegitimate mulatto girl born to President Jefferson's housekeeper. It was published in London, and subsequently appeared in the US (1864) with all references to the president omitted. His other works were a play, *The Escape* (1858), and an account of the history and culture of *The Black Man* (1863), later expanded as *The Rising Son* (1874).

BROWNE, William
(1591–1643)

English pastoral poet, born in Tavistock, Devon. Educated at Exeter College, Oxford, he entered the Inner Temple, and was then tutor to Robert Dormer, the future Earl of Carnarvon. His finest poetry is to be found in the three-volumed *Britannia's Pastorals* (1613–52) and in the *Inner Temple Masque* (1615).

▷F W Moorman, *William Browne; his Britannia's Pastorals and the pastoral poetry of the Elizabethan age* (1897)

BROWNING, Elizabeth, née Barrett
(1806–61)

English poet, born in Coxhoe Hall, Durham, wife of **Robert Browning**. She spent her girlhood mostly on her father's estate, at Hope Hill in Herefordshire. At 10 she read **Homer** in the original, and at 14 wrote an epic on *The Battle of Marathon*. In her teens she developed a tubercular complaint that damaged her spine, and was an invalid for a long time. The family ultimately settled in 50 Wimpole Street, London, in 1837. Her *Essay on Mind, and Other Poems*, was published in 1826 when she was 19. In 1833 she issued a translation of **Aeschylus**' *Prometheus Bound*. This was succeeded by *The Seraphim, and Other Poems* (1838), in which volume was republished the fine poem on **William Cowper**'s grave. When she was staying at Torquay, her brother and a party of friends were drowned there in a boating expedition, and the shock confined her for many years to the sickroom. In 1844 appeared *Poems*, which contained 'The Cry of the Children', an outburst against the employment of young children in factories. In 1845 she first met Robert Browning, six years her junior, who freed her from her sickroom and a possessive father by marrying her the following year. They settled in Pisa (1846), and then Florence (1847), where their son Robert was born in 1849. They became the centre of a brilliant literary circle there. The *Poems* of 1850 contained an entirely new translation of the *Prometheus Bound*. In *Casa Guidi Windows* (1851) she expressed her sympathy with the regeneration of Italy. *Aurora Leigh* (1856) is a long narrative poem into which all the treasures of its writer's mind and heart have been poured. In *Poems before Congress* (1860) she again manifested her interest in Italian freedom. Her so-called *Sonnets from the Portuguese* (published in the *Poems* of 1850) are not translations at all, but express her own love for the country ('my little Portuguese' was Browning's pet name for her). Her *Last Poems* were published the following year.

▷D Hewlett, *Elizabeth Barrett Browning* (1953)

BROWNING, Robert
(1812–89)

English poet, and husband of **Elizabeth Browning**, born in Camberwell, the only son of a Bank of England clerk. He attended lectures briefly at University College, London and then travelled abroad. *Pauline*, a dramatic poem, written at the age of 20, was published anonymously in 1833. He made a visit to St Petersburg (Leningrad), and on his return *Paracelsus* (1835) won him some recognition in literary circles; but *Sordello* (1840) was a failure. He wrote several dramas and dramatic poems, which were published as 'Bells and Pomegranates' in *Dramatic Romances and Lyrics*, which also contained 'My Last Duchess' 'Soliloquy of the Spanish Cloister', 'The Pied Piper of Hamelin', 'Home Thoughts from Abroad', and many other familiar and much loved poems. In 1846 he married Elizabeth Barrett, and with her settled first in Pisa (1846) and then in Florence (1847); their son, Robert Barrett (1849–1912), who became a sculptor, was born there. In 1855 he published *Men and Women*, which contained such poems as 'Fra Lippo Lippi', 'Childe Roland to the Dark Tower Came', and 'Andrea del Sarte'. After the death of his wife (1861) he settled permanently in London with his son. His masterpiece, *The Ring and the Book*, published in four volumes (1868–9), is an epic dealing searchingly with passions of humanity, and has for its basis the narrative of a murder by an Italian count, as related by the various persons concerned. Browning's poetry is distinguished by its depth of spiritual insight and power of psychological analysis; and he invented new kinds of narrative structure which have taken the place of the epic and the pastoral. In his play, *Pippa Passes* (1841), for example, a girl's song binds together a variety of scenes. His other chief works are *Dramatis Personae* (1864), *Fifine at the Fair* (1872), *The Inn Album* (1875), *Pacchiarotto* (1876) and *Asolando* (1889).

▷A Maurois, *Robert and Elizabeth Browning* (1955); T E F Blackburn, *Robert Browing: a study of his poetry* (1973)

BRU, Hedin, pseud of Hans Jacob Jacobsen
(1901–)

Faeroese novelist, story writer and translator, whose language resembles Icelandic. He was born in Skálavik. Bru has also translated **Shakespeare**'s works into Faeroese, making brilliant use of old dialects. His leading novel, about the Faeroes in the 1930s, is the richly comic and ironic *Fedgar á fero* (1940, Eng trans *The Old Man and his Sons*, 1970).

BRUCE, Mary Grant
(1878–1958)

Australian novelist, born in Sale, Victoria. She began writing as a child, but moved to Melbourne in 1898 where she ran the 'Children's Page' of the *Leader* weekly newspaper, in which some of her stories were serialized as *A Little Bush Maid* and later published in book form in 1910. In a long career she published a book nearly every year until 1942, as well as much short fiction and numerous contributions to newspapers and periodicals. Though she is considered today mainly as a children's writer, her novels were at the time widely read by adults and were so reviewed. Her fame lies mainly in the *Billabong* series of novels of Australian pastoral life and their heroine Norah Linton, perhaps the first Australian female character drawn in an unpatronizing and realistic light.

BRUCKNER, Ferdinand, pseud of Theodor Tagger
(1891–1958)

Austrian dramatist and poet who made his reputation under his given name as an expressionist poet in Berlin, where he was also a theatrical director, and where he edited a journal, *Marsyas*; he was born in Sofia while his mother was en route from Constantinople to Vienna. Wishing to make a new start with his play *Krankheit der Jugend* (1926, 'Sickness of Youth'), which was more serious than anything he had attempted hitherto, he circulated it anonymously. It was a success, and he commenced writing under a pseudonym, chosen because it combined his admiration for a dramatist, Ferdinand Raimund, and for the composer Anton Bruckner. He did not reveal his true identity for many years. When Max Reinhart produced *Die Verbrecher* (1928, 'The Criminals'), he became well known. This play, technically very brilliant, with three plots presented simultaneously, blames society for individual crimes. The more conventional *Elizabeth von England* (1930, 'Elizabeth of England'), again technically brilliant, had long runs in various capitals, and established him as a leading international dramatist. In 1933 he left Germany in protest against the Nazis, and lived in France and New York until 1947. On his return he played a large part in the West German post-war revival; he wrote well-constructed plays, some of them in turgid verse, but failed to re-establish himself. He had been caught by Hitler at the height of his powers, and never regained them.
▷H F Garten, *Modern German Drama* (1964)

BRUNET, Marta
(1897–1967)

Chilean novelist of Catalan extraction, born in Chillán. A sickly child, she was cured by a long series of mystical experiences. A traditional writer in the *costumbista* (regional) style, she gradually acquired popularity with her tales of rural life. Her chief work is the novel *Soledad de la sangre* (1948, 'Lonely Blood'). She died in Montevideo, where she had been serving as Chilean cultural attaché.

BRUNHOFF, Jean de
(1899–1937)

French writer and illustrator of children's books, born in Paris. His creation Babar the Elephant is one of the most enduring and, to some, endearing characters of 20th-century children's literature. The pachyderm possessed of a peculiarly Gallic charm and hauteur made his debut in *L'Histoire de Babar, le petit elephant* (1931, Eng trans *The Story of Babar the Little Elephant*, 1934), which de Brunhoff both wrote and illustrated. *Les Voyages de Babar* ('Babar's Travels') came out in France in 1932, and three years later in Britain, but the books' relative success in the UK meant that the English versions were being published first by the time of *Babar and Father Christmas* (1940, French edition 1941). He wrote seven Babar books in all, three of which were published posthumously. His son, Laurent de Brunhoff, continued the success of the stories after World War II.

BRUNNER, John Kilian Houston
(1934–)

English science-fiction writer, born in Preston Crowmarsh, Oxfordshire. He was educated at Cheltenham College, served in the RAF (1953–5), and worked as a book editor (1956–8). He had written over 30 science-fiction adventure novels by 1968, but his work was becoming increasingly serious in tone and experimental in form, as in *Squares of the City* (1965), based on a chess game. His major works in this new phase, which placed him among the most significant voices in the genre, are four dystopian visions of future chaos, *Stand On Zanzibar* (1969), *The Jagged Orbit* (1969), *The Sheep Look Up* (1972) and *The Shockwave Rider* (1975). The most important of his later books are *The Crucible of Time* (1983), *The Tides of Time* (1984) and *Children of the Thunder* (1989).

BRUNTON, Mary, née Balfour
(1778–1818)

Scottish novelist, born in Orkney, the daughter of an army officer. In 1798 she married the Reverend Alexander Brunton, whom she called 'my companion and instructor', and they settled in the parish of Bolton, East Lothian. Between 1803 and her death she lived in Edinburgh where her husband was minister of the Tron Kirk and Professor of Oriental Languages at Edinburgh University. She made her name with her first novel *Self Control* (1810), which she dedicated to her close friend **Joanna Baillie**, and which **Jane**

Austen called an 'elegantly written work, without anything of nature or probability in it'. Her next novel was *Discipline* (1814). Both were so-called improving works, very popular in their day, and she was included in the school of 'improver-satirists' along with **Susan Ferrier** and Elizabeth Hamilton. After a visit to England in 1815 she planned a series of domestic sketches on middle-class manners, but only one, *Emmeline* (1819), was completed before her death in childbirth.

BRUST, Alfred
(1891–1934)
German playwright from East Prussia whose *Der singende Fisch* (1922, 'The Singing Fish'), about a man's spirit becoming divorced from his body, made a sensation when Max Reinhart produced it. *Die Wolfe* (Eng trans *The Wolves*, in *Seven Expressionistic Plays*, 1968), part of a trilogy of 1924, depicts a woman being killed just as she is about to be sodomized by a wolf. Brust also wrote comedies, and exercised some short-lived influence.

BRUTUS, Dennis Vincent
(1924–)
South African poet, exiled in the USA and UK. He was born in Salisbury, Rhodesia, and educated at Witwatersrand University in Johannesburg. Despite committed opposition to the South African system (he was jailed for 18 months on the notorious Robben Island) he insists that anti-apartheid protest is simply one element among many in what is essentially lyric poetry. Few poets confronted with political violence have been able to invest it with such chastened calm. His first volume, *Sirens, Knuckles, Boots* (1963), expresses something like **W B Yeats**'s 'terrible beauty'. The prison poems in *Letters to Martha* (1968) are without rancour. Later in his career, Brutus began to take up the postcolonial cause of other Third World nations, and in *Salutes and Censures* (1982) to examine large-scale environmental and disarmament issues. In 1983, following a forceful campaign on his behalf, he avoided deportation from the USA.
▷D Herdeck, *African Authors* (1973)

BRYANT, William Cullen
(1794–1878)
American poet and journalist, born in Cummington, Massachusetts. He graduated in law and practised in Great Barrington, Massachusetts, from 1816, but in 1817 the majestic blank verse of *Thanatopsis* appeared. He continued to practise at the Bar until 1825, but more and more turned to journalism in both prose and verse, becoming co-owner and Editor of the New York *Evening Post* in 1829. The paper was Democratic, but, having anti-

slavery views, assisted in 1856 in forming the Republican party. Bryant's public addresses and letters to his paper on his visits to Europe and the West Indies were published in book form as *Letters of a Traveller* (1850), and he also published volumes of his poetry.
▷P Godwin, *A Biography of Willian Cullen Bryant* (1883)

BRYHER, pseud of **Annie Winnifred Ellerman**
(1894–1983)
English novelist, poet and autobiographer, born in Margate, the daughter of a rich shipping owner. Lover and protector of the American poet **Hilda Doolittle** (HD), Bryher helped to bring psychoanalysis to Great Britain, and to arrange for HD's analysis with **Freud**. She made two marriages of convenience. Her novels and poetry were interesting but lacked the robustness to stand the test of time, although her autobiographies *The Heart to Artemis* (1962) and *The Days of Mars 1940–1946* (1972) are illuminating.
▷N Riley-Fitch, *Sylvia Beach and the Lost Generation* (1983)

BRYUSSOV, Valery Yakovlevich
(1873–1924)
Russian poet, critic, editor and translator, born in Moscow. He was one of the leaders of the Russian Symbolist movement which looked to France for its inspiration. Like **Konstantin Balmont**, his best work was done before 1910, but unlike him his technique remained unimpaired to the last. He translated many of the major modernist writers in Europe, including **Paul Verlaine**, **Stéphane Mallarmé**, **Maurice Maeterlinck** and **Gabriele D'Annunzio**. He became an enthusiastic Bolshevist in 1917 and worked tirelessly for that cause until his death. His best-known prose works are the two novels *Ognennyy Angel* (1907–8), which provided the basis of Prokofiev's opera *The Fiery Angel*, and *Altar pobedy* (1911–12, 'The Altar of Victory').

BUBER, Martin
(1878–1965)
Austrian religious philosopher, mystic, folklorist and novelist, born in Vienna, who has had an immense—although often subterranean—influence on European and American literature. This influence has arisen from his famous 'I–Thou' philosophy, and from his reworkings into a modern idiom of Hasidic tales, collected in English translation in *The Legend of the Baal-Shem* (1955), *Tales of Rabbi Nachman* (1956), and elsewhere. His earlier thinking was much influenced by his radical reinterpretation of **Nietzsche**: man must respond creatively to the challenge made to him by God. He found, in *Ich und*

Du (1922, Eng trans *I and Thou*, 1958), that an I–Thou rather than an I–It relationship could exist between human beings: 'There is no "I" except he responds to his "Thou"'. But I–It is the 'ordinary' currency of science, politics and economics. His only novel, persistently underrated, is *Gog and Magog* (1943, in Hebrew translation, English translation *For the Sake of Heaven*, 1945—original German text, 1949), about the Hasidic world in Napoleonic times.

▷R Horwitz, *Buber's Way to 'I and Thou'* (1978); M Seymour-Smith, *Who's Who in Twentieth Century Literature* (1976)

BUCHAN, John, 1st Baron Tweedsmuir
(1875–1940)

Scottish author and statesman, born in Perth, the son of a Free Church minister. He was educated at Hutcheson's Grammar School and Glasgow University and at Brasenose College, Oxford, where he won the New-digate Prize for Poetry in 1898. In 1901 he was called to the Bar and became Private Secretary to Lord Milner, High Commissioner for South Africa. He returned in 1903 to become a director of Nelson's the publishers. During World War I he served on HQ staff until 1917, when he became Director of Information. He wrote *Nelson's History of the War* (1915–19), and became President of the Scottish History Society (1929–32). He was MP for the Scottish Universities (1927–35), and was raised to the peerage in 1935, when he became Governor-General of Canada. In 1937 he was made a Privy Councillor, and Chancellor of Edinburgh University. Despite his busy public life, Buchan wrote over 50 books, beginning with a series of essays, *Scholar Gipsies* (1896). His strength as a writer was for fast-moving adventure stories, which included *Prester John* (1910), *Huntingtower* (1922) and *Witch Wood* (1927). He became best known, however, for his spy thrillers featuring Richard Hannay: *The Thirty-Nine Steps* (1915), *Greenmantle* (1916), *The Three Hostages* (1924), and others. He also wrote biographies, including *Montrose* (1928) and *Sir Walter Scott* (1932).

▷J Adam Smith, *John Buchan* (1965)

BUCHAN, George
(c.1506–1582)

Scottish scholar and humanist, born near Killearn, Stirlingshire. Because of straitened family circumstances he attended the local grammar school, but at the age of 14 was sent by an uncle to study Latin at the University of Paris. He returned to Scotland in 1523, and did service in the army of the Duke of Albany (the future King James V). Thereafter he was enrolled at St Andrews as a poor stud-ent, before returning to Paris, where he taught at the College of Sainte Barbe (1528–37). In 1537 King James appointed him tutor to one of his illegitimate sons, the future Earl of Moray, but he was soon charged with heresy at St Andrews after writing *Franciscanus*, a satirical poem about friars, which offended Cardinal Beaton. He fled to France, where he taught at Bordeaux (1539–42), with Montaigne as one of his pupils, and wrote two tragedies in Latin, *Jeptha* and *Baptistes*. In 1547 he went to teach at Coimbra in Portugal, where he was arrested by the Inquisition as a suspected heretic. During his confinement (1547–53) he made a Latin paraphrase of the Psalms, which was published in 1566 with a dedication to Mary, Queen of Scots. He returned to Scotland in 1561 and was appointed classical tutor to the 19-year-old queen, despite his acknowledged leanings towards Protestantism. The queen awarded him a handsome pension, and in 1566 he was appointed Principal of St Leonard's College at St Andrews. He abandoned the queen's cause after the murder of Lord Darnley in 1567, and charged her with complicity in a scurrilous pamphlet, *Ane Detectioun of the Duings of Mary Quene* (1571). In 1567 he was elected Moderator of the newly-formed General Assembly of the Church of Scotland, and was later appointed Keeper of the Privy Seal of Scotland, and tutor to the four-year-old King James VI of Scotland (1570–8). He proved a hard taskmaster, ensuring that the king learned his classics thoroughly. Buchanan's main works were *De juri regni apud Scotos* (1579), an attack on the divine right of monarchs and a justification for the deposition of Mary, and a monumental but unreliable history of Scotland, *Rerum scoticarum historia* (20 vols), which he completed shortly before his death.

▷I D McFarlane, *Buchanan* (1981)

BUCHANAN, Robert Williams
(1841–1901)

English poet, novelist and playwright, born in Caverswall, Staffordshire. He was educated at Glasgow High School and University, where his closest friend was **David Gray**, with whom he set out for London in 1860. They found life hard in London and success came too late for Buchanan. He is noted for his attack in the *Spectator* on **Algernon Charles Swinburne**, whom he called unclean, morbid and sensual, and on the pre-Raphaelites under the pseudonym of 'Thomas Maitland' in another article entitled 'The Fleshly School of Poetry' (1871). *London Poems* (1866) was his first distinct success. He also wrote many now-forgotten novels and plays.

▷A Walker, *Robert Buchanan, the poet of modern revolt* (1901)

BÜCHNER, Georg
(1813–37)

German dramatist and pioneer of Expressionist theatre, born in Goddelau near Darmstadt. He studied medicine and science, became involved in revolutionary politics and fled to Zürich where he died of typhoid at the age of 24. His best-known works are the poetical dramas *Dantons Tod* (1835, Eng trans *Danton's Death*, 1958) and *Woyzeck* (1837, Eng trans 1979, of which he left many unfinished manuscript versions), the true story of an uneducated and mentally-backward army private who killed his girlfriend in a fit of jealousy. It was used by Alban Berg as the basis for his opera *Wozzeck*. His sister Louise (1821–77) was also a poet and novelist.

▷ R Hauser, *Georg Büchner* (1974)

BUCK, Pearl S, née **Sydenstricker**
(1892–1973)

American novelist, winner of the Nobel Prize for literature, born in Hillsboro, West Virginia. The daughter of Presbyterian missionaries, she lived in China from childhood, went to the USA for her education, but returned to China as a missionary and teacher in 1921. She married another missionary, John Lossing Buck, in 1917, and divorced in 1934. Her earliest novels are coloured by her experiences while living in China. *The Good Earth* (1931) was a runaway bestseller. In 1935 she returned to America, and most of her output after that date was concerned with the contemporary American scene. She was awarded the 1938 Nobel Prize for literature. Her other novels on China include *Sons* (1932), *A House Divided* (1935), *Dragon Seed* (1942) and *Imperial Woman* (1956), and amongst other works are *What America Means to Me* (1944) and *My Several Worlds* (1955).

▷ T F Hariss, *Pearl S Buck* (1969, 1971)

BUCKERIDGE, Anthony
(1912–)

English author of schoolboy fiction, born in London. Buckeridge created the characters of Jennings and Darbishire while a master at a boys' preparatory school. His first book, *Jennings Goes to School*, appeared in 1950, and by the time *Jennings at Large* was published in 1977, there were 23 in the series. The inferior *Jennings Again* followed in 1991. Jennings, an impulsive natural leader, and his great friend, the bespectacled, logical, retiring Darbishire, are 11-year-old third formers at Linbury Court Preparatory School in Sussex. The stories are zestful, full of incident and are the finest schoolboy fiction since **Richmal**

Crompton's *Just William* series. Buckeridge also had a muted success with his Rex Milligan stories (1953–61).

BUCKLER, Ernest
(1908–)

Canadian novelist, born in Dalhousie. Buckler has written many books, stories and radio plays, but is most famous for one novel, his first, *The Mountain and the Valley* (1952). This is a rich study of a doomed, artistic boy, set in Nova Scotia's Annapolis Valley, distinguished less by its plot than by the intricate and convincing picture it gives of country life in its setting. Buckler's second novel, *The Cruellest Month* (1963), again set in Nova Scotia, fared less well at the time of its publication, but has never been forgotten. *The Rebellion of Young David* (1975) is a collection of stories.

▷ G M Cook (ed), *Ernest Buckler* (1972); A Young, *Ernest Buckler* (1976)

BUCKLEY, Vincent
(1925–88)

Australian poet, critic and editor of Irish descent, born in Romsey, Victoria; a strong Catholic faith and emotional ties to his 'source-country' coloured much of his writing. His first book of verse was *The World's Flesh* (1954); he published five more volumes before *Selected Poems* in 1982. His critical work includes *Essays in Poetry: Mainly Australian* (1957) and a study of **Henry Handel Richardson** (1961). Between 1958 and 1964 he edited *Prospect*, a quarterly journal, and was poetry editor of the *Bulletin* (1961–3). He published his memoirs *Cutting Green Hay* in 1983, telling of his lifelong involvement with Irish Catholic and Republican movements, themes evinced strongly in *The Pattern* (1979), a series of poems which link Irish history with the 'Troubles' of today and with the country life. In *Late-Winter Child* (1979) he turned to intensely personal matters in celebrating the birth of his daughter.

BUCKLEY, William F(rank), Jr
(1925–)

American journalist, novelist and freelance conservative. Having served in the military and the Central Intelligence Agency, he dedicated himself to combating creeping liberalism in American life. In 1955, he founded *National Review*, an influential conduit for conservative ideas. He has taught at the New School for Social Research (1967–8) and stood as Conservative Party candidate for the mayoralty of New York City, a campaign detailed in *The Unmaking of a Mayor* (1966). *Up From Liberalism* (1959) was a strong statement of his political position, but his most effective writing has been in a syndicated gad-fly column called 'On the Right'. He brings the same acerbity to a television show, *Firing Line*. In 1976, Buckley introduced his fictional CIA hero, Blackford Oakes; the plot of *Saving the Queen* was part conventional thriller and part elaborate revenge for English snobbism (which Buckley had experienced as a public schoolboy; it was controversial for a sex scene involving the reigning Queen of England. Later Oakes novels, *Stained Glass* (1978), *Who's On First?* (1980) and *Marco Polo, If You Can* (1982) were subtler and more ambiguous in their portrayal of Cold War camaraderie.

▷ *Overdrive: a Personal Documentary* (1983)

BUCKSTONE, John Baldwin
(1802–79)

English comedian, actor-manager and playwright, born in Hoxton. He played at the Surrey, Adelphi, Drury Lane, and Lyceum theatres, mostly as a comedian, and visited the USA in 1840 and then played at the Haymarket, where he was actor-manager (1853–78). He wrote 150 pieces for the stage, including *Luke the Labourer* (1826), *Married Life* (1834) and *The Flowers of the Forest* (1847).

BUDGELL, Eustace
(1686–1737)

English writer, born in Exeter. He was a cousin of **Joseph Addison**, and contributed miscellaneous essays to the *Spectator*. He was the butt of **Pope**'s mockery in *The Dunciad*. After losing a fortune in the South Sea Company collapse (1720) he degenerated to a Grub Street writer. He drowned himself in the Thames.

▷ *A Vindication of Eustace Budgell Esq, by William Wilson* (1733)

BUDRYS, Algis (Algirdas)
(1931–)

Lithuanian–American science-fiction novelist and short-story writer, born in Konigsberg, Germany. An infant refugee, he moved with his family to the USA, and publicized the plight of his Baltic homeland throughout the long night of Soviet rule. *Who?* (1958), the book which made his reputation, is concerned with the dehumanizing effect of the Cold War. *Rogue Moon* (1960), superficially a genre action novel, but more deeply philosophical than this, is the best work to come out of his first period. *Michaelmas* (1977), which followed a decade of silence, has as its central hero one Laurent Michaelmas, the unacknowledged legislator, the secret president of the world. In its contention that great

power need not corrupt it is a profoundly optimistic book.

BUECHNER, (Carl) Frederick
(1926–)

American novelist and Presbyterian clergyman, born in New York City. After graduating from Princeton University, he taught English at Lawrenceville School, New Jersey, and worked in a Harlem employment office before studying at Union Theological Seminary. After his ordination he taught and later headed the religion department at Phillips Academy in New Hampshire, leaving to write full-time in 1967. Religion plays an inevitably powerful role in his fiction, providing the underlying moral and philosophical structure that is missing from the early *A Long Day's Dying* (1950), an elaborate and somewhat overwrought story of sexual deception. *The Final Beast* (1965) and *The Entrance to Porlock* (1970) are religious romances, and *Lion Country* (1971), perhaps his most characteristic novel, examines the state of the contemporary church. Buechner's sermons have been published in several volumes.

▷ *The Sacred Journey* (1982)

BUERO VALLEJO, Antonio
(1916–)

Spanish playwright, born in Guadalajara, who was sentenced to death (for being a medical aide to the forces of the legal government) by Franco, but 'exonerated' in 1945. He thus spent six years in prison. He did well, under Franco's censorship, to present well-made and successful plays on humane themes. His plays were not often produced, but with **Alfonso Sastre** he nevertheless dominated the Spanish theatre during the Franco years. He has not been a conventional dramatist, since he eschews 'happy endings' and wooing of audiences in search of easy pleasure. Influenced by the earlier plays of **Gerhart Hauptmann**, he mixes the naturalism of the latter with playful surrealism and attention to Spanish legend. His play *La tejedora de sueños* (1952) is translated as *The Dream Weaver* in *Masterpieces of Modern Spanish Theatre* (1967, ed Robert W Corrigan), together with his own notes.

BUKOWSKI, Charles
(1920–94)

German-born American poet, short-story writer and novelist, born in Andernach. As befits an underground writer, his world is one frequented by low lifers which he evokes, as one critic has said, in 'words nailed to the page'. His pared style, revealing an affinity with **Hemingway**, has been employed to effect in four novels, half a dozen collections of short stories and many volumes of verse. A cult figure who did not achieved popular success, he had a sardonic sense of humour and a liking for long titles, such as *Play the Piano Drunk Like a Percussion Instrument until the Fingers Begin to Bleed a Bit* (1979).

▷H Fox, *Charles Bukowski: a biographical study* (1968)

BULATOVIĆ, Miodrag
(1930–)

Yugoslav (Montenegran) fiction writer, born near Bijelo Polje. His father was a forest ranger whom, when Bulatović was 11, he saw murdered by a relative over a land dispute. Bulatović was in the 1960s and 1970s the best-known and most translated in the West of the Yugoslav younger writers. He was influenced as much by **Beckett** and **Joyce** as by native writers. He lived in Belgrade, but then moved to Slovenia. His novels, such as *Crveni petao leti prema nebu* (1959, Eng trans *The Red Cockerel*, 1962) and *Rat je bio bolji* (1970, Eng trans *The War Was Better*, 1972), reflect his belief that 'dislocation is the norm' and that the world is 'far worse' than even Beckett saw it.

BULGAKOV, Mikhail Afanas'evich
(1891–1940)

Russian novelist and dramatist, born in Kiev. His father was a professor of divinity, and he studied at Kiev Theological Academy and Kiev University, and practised as a country doctor for a short time. He settled in Moscow in 1921, and began a stormy association with the Moscow Art Theatre when he adapted part of his novel *Belaya gvardiya* (1925, Eng trans *The White Guard*, 1971) for the stage in 1926. His political attitudes in that play, and in others like *Beg* (1928, 'The Flight'), brought him much criticism, and only a personal appeal to Stalin restored him to some favour. He gained success with a play (1930) about **Molière**, on whom he wrote an imaginative biography. He described his tribulations with the theatre in *Tetralnyi roman* (1965, Eng trans *Black Show, a Theatrical Novel*, 1967). His masterpiece is the novel *Master i Margarita* (1966, Eng trans *The Master and Margarita*, 1967), a remarkable multi-level fantasy. Although he died in obscurity with much of his work unpublished, his posthumous reputation has flourished.

BULGARIN, Thaddeus
(1789–1859)

Russian author and journalist. He was a zealous supporter of reaction and of absolutism. His best novel is *Ivan Vyzhigin* (1829).

▷E von Reinthal and H Clemenz, *Bulgarin, Memoiren* (1859–60)

BULL, Olaf Jacob Martin Luther
(1883–1933)

Norwegian poet and bohemian, born in Christiania (now Oslo). He rejected his family's robustly altruistic Christianity in favour of a life of wandering and self-examination. His poetry, from the early *Digte* (1909, 'Poems') onwards, combines a strongly Romantic and quasi-Symbolist treatment of great themes like love and the natural world, with Bull's interest in the creative act itself. His style is compacted, almost private, but highly varied. He found his true voice early but continually experimented with styles. Among his more important later collections were *De hundrede år* (1928) and *Oinos og Eros* (1930). Still little-known outside Norway and France, he posthumously won the admiration of the American poet **Robert Bly**.

▷T Greiff, *Olaf Bull: Taper og seirer* (1952)

BULLEN, Frank Thomas
(1857–1915)

English writer. He was a sailor till 1883, and made notable additions to the literature of the sea, including *Cruise of the Cachalot* (1898). He also wrote *Recollections* (1915).

▷ *With Christ at Sea: a religious autobiography* (1900)

BULLETT, Gerald
(1893–1958)

English author, born in London. Educated at Jesus College, Cambridge, from 1914 his published work included fiction, poems, essays, biographies, anthologies, children's books, literary criticism, and plays. His novels include *The Pandervils*, *The Jury* and *The Snare of the Fowler*.

▷ *Modern English Fiction: a personal view* (1926)

BULLINS, Ed
(1935–)

American playwright, fiction writer and cultural activist. Born in Philadelphia, he was educated largely in California and became involved in ghetto drama projects in San Francisco, acting as a cultural adviser for the Black Panthers. Between 1968 and 1973, he edited the journal *Black Theatre*. His first major play was *Clara's Old Man* (1965), followed by *In Wine Time*, *A Son, Come Home* and his best-known work, *The Electronic Nigger*, all from 1968. Many of his plays are linked into a huge cycle about the lives of American blacks in the 20th century, projecting forward to the year 1999. Despite this, Bullins's approach has been markedly different from that of **Amiri Baraka** (Leroi Jones), attempting to work (just) within realist conventions. His angry 'Dynamite Plays' fall outside the cycle and are more ephemeral. He has also written a novel, *The Reluctant Rapist* (1973).

BULWER-LYTTON, Edward George Lytton, 1st Baron Lytton
(1803–73)

English novelist, playwright, essayist, poet and politician, born in London. He was the youngest son of General Earle Bulwer (1776–1807) by Elizabeth Barbara Lytton (1773–1843), the heiress of Knebworth in Hertfordshire. He took early to poetry and in 1820 published *Ismael and other Poems*. At Trinity Hall, Cambridge (1822–5) he won the Chancellor's Medal for a poem upon 'Sculpture', but left with only a pass degree. His unhappy marriage (1827), against his mother's wishes, to the Irish beauty Rosina Wheeler, ended in separation (1836), but called forth a marvellous literary activity, for the temporary estrangement from his mother threw him almost wholly on his own resources. His enormous output, vastly popular during his lifetime, but now forgotten, includes *Eugene Aram* (1832), *The Last Days of Pompeii* (1834) and *Harold* (1843). Among his plays are *The Lady of Lyons* (1838), *Richelieu* (1839) and *Money* (1840), and his poetry includes an epic, *King Arthur* (1848–9). MP for St Ives (1831–41), he was created a baronet in 1838, and in 1843 he succeeded to the Knebworth estate and assumed the surname of Lytton. He re-entered parliament as member for Hertfordshire in 1852, and in the Derby government (1858–9) was colonial secretary. In 1866 he was raised to the peerage. His son Edward (1831–91) was a successful diplomat and minor poet.
▷J Campbell, *Edward Bulwer-Lytton* (1986)

BUNIN, Ivan Alexeievich
(1870–1953)

Russian author, winner of the Nobel Prize for literature, born in Voronezh. He wrote lyrics and novels about the decay of the Russian nobility and of peasant life, and the disintegration of traditional rural patterns of life under the pressure of a changing world. They include *Derevnia* (1910, Eng trans *The Village* 1923), *Gospodin iz San-Frantsisko* (1914, Eng trans *The Gentleman from San Francisco*, 1922), his best-known work, which has the vanity of all things earthly as its theme, and the autobiographical *The Well of Days* (1933, trans 1946). He lived in Paris after the Russian Revolution, and received the 1933 Nobel Prize for literature. His work belongs in the great Russian realist tradition of **Turgenev**, **Tolstoy** and **Chekhov**.
▷A Poggioli, *The Art of Ivan Bunin* (1953)

BUNTING, Basil
(1900–85)

English poet, born in Northumberland. His career was one of neglect, and until the publication of *Loquitur* (1965) **Ezra Pound** seemed to be his sole aficionado. That, however, encouraged the growth of a cult following and Bunting attracted more admirers with his long poem, *Briggflatts* (1966). He assisted **Ford Madox Ford** with *The Transatlantic Review* in Paris but he largely shunned literary society. His admirers have included **Piers Paul Read**, **Henry Tomlinson**, **Hugh MacDiarmid** and **Robert Creeley**, but he has a greater following in the USA than in Britain despite attempts to revive interest. His *Collected Poems* appeared in 1968.
▷R Guedalla, *Basil Bunting: a bibliography of works and criticism* (1973); 'Basil Bunting Issue', *Poetry Information* (1978)

BUNTLINE, Ned, pseud of E Z C Judson
(1823–86)

American dime novelist (he more or less invented the genre) and organizer of the anti-Catholic Know-Nothing Party, who (with Prentiss Ingraham) helped to invent the largely fictitious exploits of 'Buffalo Bill' (ie, William Cody), himself a noted liar and showman. But Judson's own life really was an incredible one: after killing the husband of his mistress in a duel, he was actually lynched, being rescued only at the last minute; dismissed from the Union army for drunkenness, he afterwards claimed to have been a colonel, Chief of Scouts for the Army of the Potomac. Hymn-writer and temperance preacher, he wrote a 600-page novel in less than three days.
▷J Monaghan, *The Great Rascal* (1952)

BUNYAN, John
(1628–88)

English writer and preacher, born in Elstow near Bedford, son of a 'brasever' or tinker. In 1644 he was drafted into the army, in June 1645 he returned to Elstow, and there about 1649 married a poor girl who brought with her two books which had belonged to her father, the *Plain Man's Pathway to Heaven* and the *Practice of Piety*. About this time Bunyan began to experience those deep religious experiences which he has described so vividly in his *Grace Abounding* (1666). In 1653 he joined a Christian fellowship which had been organized by a converted royalist major, and about 1655 he was asked by the brethren to address them. This led to his preaching in the villages round Bedford; and in 1656 he was brought into discussions with the followers of George Fox, which led to his first book, *Some Gospel Truths Opened* (1656), a vigorous attack on Quakerism. To this Edward Burrough, the Quaker, replied, and Bunyan replied in *A Vindication of Gospel Truths Opened* (1657). In November 1660 he was arrested while preaching in a farmhouse near Ampthill. During the 12 years' imprisonment in Bedford county jail which followed, Bunyan wrote *Profitable Meditations* (1661), *I Will Pray with the Spirit* (1663), *Christian Behaviour* (1663), *The Holy City* (1665), *The Resurrection of the Dead* (1665), *Grace Abounding* (1666) and some other works. He was released after the Declaration of Indulgence of 1672, under which he became a licensed preacher, and pastor of the church to which he belonged. In February 1673, however, the Declaration of Indulgence was cancelled, and on 4 March, a warrant, signed by 13 magistrates, was issued for his arrest. Brought to trial under the Conventicle Act, Bunyan was sent to prison for six months in the town gaol. It was during this later and briefer imprisonment that he wrote the first part of *The Pilgrim's Progress*. When first issued in 1678 it contained no Mr Worldly Wiseman, and many passages were added in the second and third editions (1679). It is essentially a vision of life recounted allegorically as the narrative of a journey. There followed the *Life and Death of Mr Badman* (1680), the *Holy War* (1682), and *The Pilgrim's Progress, Second Part* (1684), containing the story of Christiana and her children. Bunyan became pastor at Bedford for 16 years until his death after a ride through the rain from Reading to London. He was buried in Bunhill Fields, the *Campo Santo* of the Nonconformists.

▷ R Sharrock, *John Bunyan* (1954)

BÜRGER, Gottfried August
(1747–94)

German lyric poet and writer of ballads, born in Molmerswende, near Halberstadt, the son of Lutheran pastor. In boyhood he displayed no inclination to study, but showed a relish for verse. In 1764 he began to study theology, but in 1768 he migrated to Göttingen, and entered on a course of jurisprudence. His life there was wild and extravagant, and he might have sunk into obscurity but for the friendship which he happily formed with **Johann Heinrich Voss**, the two **Stolbergs**, and others. He studied closely the ancient and modern classics and translated Percy's *Reliques*. His most important work lay in reviving the ballad tradition, and he wrote many, including *Lenore* (1774), which was translated (*William and Helen*, 1797) by Sir **Walter Scott**. He married unhappily three times, speculated unwisely, and although a favourite poet of the German nation, he was left to earn his livelihood by translations and similar hackwork.

▷ W A Little, *Gottfried August Bürger* (1974)

BURGESS, Anthony, pseud of **John Anthony Burgess Wilson**
(1917–93)

English novelist, critic and composer, born in Manchester into a Catholic family of predominantly Irish background. His grandfather was a publican and his father ran a tobacconist's shop. His mother was of Scottish extraction, a singer and dancer, who died in the influenza epidemic of 1919. Educated at the Xaverian College, Manchester, he did odd jobs before going to the University of Manchester where he studied language and literature. He also taught himself music, and composed a large number of works. In World War II he served in the Royal Army Medical Corps and entertained the troops with his compositions and piano-playing. He married in 1942, and after the war he taught in England before going to Malaya in 1954 where he trained teachers. He wrote his first novel, *A Vision of Battlements*, in 1953, but it was not published until 1965. In the far east he wrote the three novels which became *The Long Day Wanes: Time for a Tiger* (1956), *The Enemy in the Blanket* (1958), and *Beds in the East* (1959). Invalided out of the Colonial Service with a suspected brain tumour, he was given a year to live and wrote five novels in a year to provide for his prospective widow. But it was she who died first. In 1968 he married the Contessa Pasi and, beleaguered by death duties, went to live abroad, where he spent the rest of his life, first in Italy, latterly in Monte Carlo and Switzerland. Among his many novels are his dark and violent vision of the future, *A Clockwork Orange* (1962), *Inside Mr Enderby* (1963), *Napoleon Symphony* (1974), *Earthly Powers* (1980), *Kingdom of the Wicked* (1985) and *Any Old Iron* (1989). He was fascinated by language, as his various works of exegesis demonstrate. He also wrote biographies, books for children, and libretti.

▷ *Little Wilson and Big God* (1987); *You've Had Your Time* (1990)

BURKE, Edmund
(1729–97)

Irish essayist and politician, born in Dublin. A political writer of enormous influence, Burke began as a liberal and defender of the rights of minorities and the oppressed, but, with with advent of the French Revolution, became alarmed, and wrote the famous, and rigidly conservative, *Reflections on the Revolution in France* (1790), a vital document in modern conservatism. But Burke's greatest work, which influenced Kant and many others, is the earlier essay *A Philosophical Enquiry into the Origin of our Ideas of the Sublime and the Beautiful* (1756), a profound investigation into its subject. **Oliver Goldsmith**'s comment upon him cannot be bettered: 'Who, born for the Universe, narrowed his mind/And to party gave up what was meant for mankind'. Burke remains one of Britain's greatest literary critics and aestheticians, and his political theory, although flawed by its shortness on facts and its excess of rhetoric, is still potent.

▷T W Copeland, *Our Eminent Friend Edmund Burke* (1949)

BURKE, Kenneth Duva
(1897–1992)

American philosopher, critic, poet, and 20th-century Renaissance mage. Born in Pittsburgh, he was educated in Ohio and at Columbia University in New York City. He served as music critic for *The Dial* and *The Nation* during the 1920s, but gradually developed critical-theoretical constructs which put heavy emphasis on 'rhetoric' as a means of revealing psychological, literary and cultural motives. His most important criticism is contained in *Counterstatement* (1931), *The Philosophy of Literary Form* (1941), *A Grammar of Motives* (1945) and *A Rhetoric of Motives* (1950). He gave currency to the expression 'failure of nerve' to describe the intellectual climate that followed the collapse of utopian and chiliastic hopes when fellow-travellers began to retreat towards the US political centre in the 1950s. Burke's verse was collected in 1968. He also wrote short fiction, notably *The White Oxen* (1924), and a single, experimental novel, *Towards a Better Life* (1932), which he revised nearly 35 years after first publication.

▷M E Brown, *Kenneth Burke* (1969)

BURKE, Thomas
(1886–1945)

English writer, born in London. He is best known for his *Limehouse Nights* (1916), but he was the author of about 30 books, mostly on aspects of London or about inns. These include *Nights in Town* (1915), *The Streets of London* (1941) and *The English Inn* (1930). He also made a fine reconstruction of the Thurtell and Hunt case in *Murder at Elstree* (1936). He published an autobiography, *The Wind and the Rain*, in (1924).

▷*Son of London* (1946)

BURNAND, Sir Francis Cowley
(1836–1917)

English dramatist and journalist. He was called to the Bar in 1862, but the success of some early dramatic ventures altered his plans. He helped to start *Fun*, but in 1863 left that paper for *Punch*, of which he was Editor (1880–1906). He wrote many burlesques, including *Black-Eyed Susan* (1866) and *Cox and Box*, with music by Arthur Sullivan (1867).

▷*Records and Reminiscences* (1917)

BURNETT, Frances Eliza, née Hodgson
(1849–1924)

English-born American novelist, born in Manchester, the daughter of a manufacturer. In 1865 she emigrated with her parents to Knoxville, Tennessee, turning to writing to help out the family finances. She married Dr Swan Moses Burnett in 1873 (divorced in 1898). There is speculation that her second marriage was made under the threat of blackmail; an unhappy alliance, it did much to cloud her later life. Her first literary success was *That Lass o' Lowrie's* (1877). Later works included plays and her most popular story *Little Lord Fauntleroy* (1886), *The One I Knew Best of All* (1893, autobiographical), *The Little Princess* (1905) and *The Secret Garden* (1909), still one of the best-loved classics of children's literature. In her lifetime she was rated one of America's foremost writers, and was a friend of **Henry James**.

▷A Thwaite, *Waiting for the Party: a life of Frances Hodgson Burnett* (1974)

BURNEY, Fanny, originally Frances, later Madame D'Arblay
(1752–1840)

English novelist and diarist, daughter of Charles Burney, born in King's Lynn. She educated herself by reading English and French literature and observing the distinguished people who visited her father. By 10 she had begun her incessant scribbling of stories, plays, and poems; on her 15th birthday, in a fit of repentance for such waste of time, she burned all her papers, but she could not forget the plot of *Evelina*, her first and best novel, published anonymously in 1778, which describes the entry of a country girl into the gaieties of London life. Her father at once recognized his daughter's talent, and confided the secret to Mrs Thrale, who, as well as **Dr Johnson**, championed the gifted young authoress. *Cecilia* (1782), though more complex, is less natural, and her style gradually declined in *Camilla* (1796) and *The Wanderer* (1814). She was appointed a second Keeper of the robes to Queen Charlotte in 1786, but her health declined; she retired on a pension and married a French émigré General d'Arblay, in 1793. Her *Letters and Diaries* (1846) show her skill in reporting dramatically. As a portrayer of the domestic scene she was a forerunner of **Jane Austen**, whom she influenced.

▷M E Adelstein, *Fanny Burney* (1968)

BURNINGHAM, John
(1936–)

English illustrator and writer for children, born in Farnham, Surrey, and educated at A S Neill's Summerhill and the Central School for Arts and Crafts, London. Popular and amusing, he draws children with round, cherubic faces which belie their highly-aware resourcefulness as seen in, say, *The Shopping Basket* (1982), where young Stephen fools a number of talking animals who try to rob him of his groceries. Distinctions include illustrating **Ian Fleming**'s *Chitty Chitty Bang Bang* (1964) and receiving the Kate Greenaway Award for *Borka* (1964) and *Mr Gumpy's Outing* (1970).

BURNS, Alan
(1929–)

English writer of experimental fiction. He was born in London; after Merchant Taylor's School, he served articles in Middle Temple and was called to the Bar in 1956, practising as a barrister until 1959, when he became legal manager at Beaverbrook Newspapers. He was the first Henfield Fellow in Creative Writing at the University of East Anglia in 1971, having published his first novel, the bleak *Europe after the Rain*, in 1965. It was followed by *Celebrations* (1967) and *Babel* (1969), a violent collage owing something to **William Burroughs**'s 'cut-up' technique but rather more to the nihilism of **J G Ballard**. Many readers took *The Angry Brigade* (1973) at face value, believing that the reminiscences of a group of alienated urban guerrillas were transcriptions of actual interviews; in fact the 'documentary' aspect was entirely fictional. In 1977, Burns moved to the USA, where he taught at the University of Minnesota. After a break of nearly a decade, he returned to fiction with *The Day Daddy Died* (1981). In 1993 he became Head of Creative Writing at Lancaster University.

BURNS, John Horne
(1916–53)

American novelist. Born in Massachusetts; he was educated at Phillips Academy and Harvard. During World War II he served in Italy and North Africa, an experience that strongly influenced his first and best novel *The Gallery* (1947), one of a group of works published around this time that explored the ambiguous nature of US values on a world stage. It was followed by *Lucifer with a Book* (1949), which drew on his pre-war job in a boys' boarding school. *A Cry of Children* (1952), completed in the year before his death,

suggested that he was working towards a new, more sophisticated vision.

BURNS, Robert
(1759–96)

Scottish poet, born in Alloway near Ayr, the son of a farmer. His education, begun at a school at Alloway Mill, and continued by a tutor called John Murdoch, was thoroughly literary. Among early influences were the popular tales, ballads and songs of Betty Davidson, an old woman who lived with the poet's family. He read **Allan Ramsay**, and began to write a little. Acquaintance with sailors and smugglers broadened his outlook, and his interest in women made him a kind of rural Don Juan. The death of Burns's father in 1784 left him to try to farm for himself. Burns's husbandry at Mossgiel near Mauchline went badly; the entanglement with Jean Armour (1767–1834) began; and out of his poverty, his passion, his despair and his desperate mirth, came the extraordinary poetic harvest of 1785. To this year belong the 'Epistle to Davie', 'Death and Dr Hornbook', 'The Twa Herds', 'The Jolly Beggars', 'Halloween', 'The Cotter's Saturday Night', 'Holy Willie's Prayer', 'The Holy Fair', and 'The Address to a Mouse'. The next year produced yet more excellent work, though much of the verse is satirical. 'The Twa Dogs' is a masterpiece of humour, and 'The Lament' and 'Despondency' are fine works. In this year there was abundant trouble with Jean Armour, and there was a love episode involving 'Highland Mary' (Mary Campbell) and her subsequent death. Looking about for money to emigrate to Jamaica, Burns published the famous Kilmarnock edition of his poems (1786). Their fame spread, and with the money he received he decided to leave Scotland for good. He was just about to sail when the praises and promises of admirers induced him to stay in Scotland. That winter he went to Edinburgh and was greeted with acclaim. On returning to the country, he 'fell to his old love again', Jean Armour; then, after a Highland tour, went back to Edinburgh, and began the epistolary flirtations with 'Clarinda' (Agnes Maclehose). By this time James Johnson had set about publishing his *Scots Musical Museum*, which contains all that is briefest and brightest of Burns. He contributed an astonishing number of the most beautiful, tender, passionate and vivacious songs in any language, chiefly adapted to old Scottish airs, and moulded now and then on old Scots words. In 1788 he married Jean Armour. He took a lease of Ellisland farm, on the Nith, above Dumfries, and next year became an excise officer. 'Tam o'Shanter' (1790) was written in one day; by this time Ellisland had proved a failure. Burns left his farm, withdrew to Dumfries, flirted with the French Revolution, drank, wrote songs, expressed opinions then thought radical, and made himself unpopular with the local lairds. However, in 1795 he turned patriot again. He died of endocarditis consequent on rheumatic fever, and is buried in Dumfries. His humble origin and his identification with the Scottish folk tradition, which he rescued, refurbished and in part embellished, are factors that help to explain his unwaning popularity as the national poet of Scotland.

▷ C Carswell, *The Life of Robert Burns* (1930)

BURROUGHS, Edgar Rice
(1875–1950)

American popular author, creator of Tarzan, born in Chicago. He served in the US cavalry and fought against the Apache Indians but was discharged when it was discovered he was under age. Thereafter he had several colourful occupations before he took to writing, his aim being to improve on the average dime novel. *Tarzan of the Apes* (1914) was his first book to feature the eponymous hero, the son of a British aristocrat, abandoned in the African jungle and brought up by apes. It spawned many sequels, films (Tarzan played, most memorably, by Johnny Weismuller), radio programmes and comic strips, making Burroughs a millionaire.

▷ R A Lopoff, *Edgar Rice Burroughs, master of adventure* (1965)

BURROUGHS, William S(eward)
(1914–)

American author, born to a wealthy family in St Louis, Missouri. He graduated from Harvard in 1936 and wandered throughout the USA and Europe. In 1944 he became a heroin addict while doing odd jobs in New York. In 1953 he published *Junkie*, an account of this experience, and his novels *The Naked Lunch* (1959) and *The Soft Machine* (1961) established him as a leading figure of the Beat movement, though one who stood somewhat apart. Intensely interested in the juxtaposition of apparently random ideas and observations, his later work is concerned with innovations in the novel form, such as the techniques of 'cut-up' and 'fold-in', in which words and phrases are either cut out and pasted together or formed by cross-column reading. Other works include *The Experimentor* (1960, with Bryon Gysin), *The Ticket that Exploded* (1962), *The Yage Letters* (1963, with **Allen Ginsberg**), *Dead Fingers Talk* (1963), *Nova Express* (1964), *The Wild Boys* (1971), *Exterminator!* (1973), *The Last Words of Dutch Schultz* (1975), *Ah, Pook is Here* (1971) and *Cities of the Red Night* (1981). He has lived mainly abroad, in Tangier and Paris. His autobiography appeared in 1973.

▷ E Mottram, *The Algebra of Need* (1971)

BURTON, Sir Richard Francis
(1821–90)

English linguist, explorer, travel writer, diplomat and adventurer, born in Torquay. A flamboyant character, largely self-educated, he won a place at Oxford, where he began (without the benefit of a tutor) to study Arabic. He is said eventually to have mastered approximately 30 languages, many with various tributaries of dialect. While in India, he contributed to government reports, often masquerading as a native in order to gather information. Commissioned by the Foreign Office to search for the sources of the Nile, he was one of a party which, in 1858, discovered Lake Tanganyika. His most important books include *First Footsteps in East Africa* (1851), *The Pilgrimage to Al-Medinah and Meccah* (1855) and *The Lake Region of Central Africa* (1860). His most famous and enduring work is his translation of *The Arabian Nights* (1885–8).

▷ Lady Burton, *Life of Sir Richard Burton* (1893)

BURTON, Robert
(1577–1640)

English writer and clergyman, author of the *Anatomy of Melancholy*, born in Lindley, Leicestershire. Educated at Nuneaton, Sutton Coldfield, and Brasenose College, Oxford, in 1599 he was elected a student of Christ Church. In 1616 he was presented to the Oxford vicarage of St Thomas, and about 1630 to the rectory of Segrave. Both livings he kept, but spent his life at Christ Church, where he died. The first edition of *Anatomy of Melancholy*, written under the pseudonym 'Democritus Junior', appeared in quarto in 1621. Four more editions in folio were published within the author's lifetime, each with successive alterations and additions; the final version of the book was the sixth edition (1651–2). One of the most interesting parts is the long preface, 'Democritus to the Reader', in which Burton gives indirectly an account of himself and his studies. This strange book is a vast and witty compendium of Jacobean knowledge about the 'disease' of melancholy, gathered from even the most out-of-the-way classical and medieval writers, as well as folklore and superstition.

▷ B Evans, *The Psychiatry of Robert Burton* (1944)

BURY, Lady Charlotte Susan Maria
(1775–1861)

Scottish novelist, youngest child of the 5th Duke of Argyll, born in London. She married in 1796 Colonel John Campbell (d.1809), and in 1818 the Rev Edward John Bury (1790–1832). She briefly became lady-in-waiting to Princess Caroline of Wales (1809). Beautiful and accomplished, she published 16 novels, including *Flirtation* and *Separation*, and was reputedly the anonymous author of the spicy *Diary illustrative of the Times of George IV* (1838).

BUSCH, Frederick Matthew
(1941–)

American novelist and short-story writer. He was born in Brooklyn, educated largely at Columbia University, and has worked as a college professor. His fiction is remarkably of a piece, largely concerned with the relationships of fathers and sons, with an unusual awareness of both roles. *I Wanted a Year Without Fall* (1971) is perhaps the best example of this, but the best known is *The Mutual Friend* (1978), a semi-documentary study of episodes in **Charles Dickens**'s life, in which the aftershocks of childhood traumas and oedipal fears are explored. His prose is rhythmic, occasionally terse and ironic, his style demanding but rewarding. Other novels include *Take This Man* (1981), *Sometimes I Live in the Country* (1986) and *Harry and Catherine* (1990). *Domestic Particulars* (1976) is a family chronicle cast in the form of a short-story collection. *When People Publish* (1986) brings together the best of his essays.

BUSCH, Wilhelm
(1832–1908)

German cartoonist and writer, born near Hanover. He worked as an illustrator for the comic weekly *Fliegende Blätter* (1859–71), and wrote satirical verse-stories with his own illustrations, such as *Max und Moritz* (1865, the prototypes for Rudolph Dirks' *Katzenjammer Kids*), and *Herr und Frau Knopp* (1876). He also wrote serious poetry, but is remembered for his 'non-sense' works.

▷F Bohme, *Wilhelm Busch, Leben, Werk, Schicksal* (1958)

BUSI, Aldo
(1948–)

Italian novelist and translator, born and educated in Montichiari, west of Verona. His fiction is lively, funny and fantastical. He remains best known to an English-speaking readership for *Vita standard di un venditore di collant* (1985, Eng trans *The Short Life of a Temporary Pantyhose Salesman*, 1988), but in Italy he is highly regarded as an interpreter of English and American literature. He has translated work by **John Ashbery** and **Christina Stead**, and has prepared an Italian version of **Lewis Carroll**'s *Alice's Adventures in Wonderland*.

BUSTA, Christine, pseud C Dimt
(1915–87)

Austrian poet, born in Vienna, where she worked as a librarian. Her collections, which include *Jahr um Jahr* (1950), *Lampe und Delphin* (1955) and *Unterwegs zu älteren Feuern* (1965), all display a deep but lightly rendered religious belief. In her subject-matter and traditional craftsmanship she is similar to the English poet, **Ruth Pitter**. Busta also wrote for children.

BUTLER, Guy
(1918–)

South African poet and critic who pursued an academic career in his native country, but was opposed to its policies until the early 1990s. Although somewhat neglected outside South Africa, he is often regarded as the most considerable poet writing in it: his poetry appears to be old-fashioned, but, it has been said, often takes risks 'with rhyme, rhythm, intricate verse and image patterns, colloquialisms, cliché, plain statement, or rhetorically splendid utterance'. He has written plays, a novel and much useful criticism. The most representative volume is *Selected Poems* (1989).

▷M van Wyk Smith and D Maclennan (eds), *Olive Schreiner and After: Essays on South African Literature in Honour of Guy Butler* (1983)

BUTLER, Robert Olen
(1945–)

American novelist, born in Granite City, Illinois. His educational qualifications include an MA in playwriting from the University of Iowa. He served in Vietnam from 1969 to 1972, an experience which re-emerges in his fiction. He edited *Energy Users News* from 1975 to 1985, then joined the faculty of McNeese State University at Lake Charles in Louisiana, where he teaches creative writing. His first novel was *The Alleys of Eden* (1981), and he published four more in the ensuing decade, along with the short-story collection *The Deuce* (1989). His most successful novel to date is *A Good Scent from A Strange Mountain* (1992), which was awarded the Pulitzer Prize in 1993. It was followed by *They Whisper* (1994), a novel about sexual obsession, set in Vietnam.

BUTLER, Samuel
(1835–1902)

English author, painter and musician, born in Langar Rectory, near Bingham, Nottinghamshire. He was educated at Shrewsbury and St John's College, Cambridge. Always quarrelling with his clergyman father, he gave up the idea of taking orders and became instead a sheep farmer in New Zealand. Passages from his *A First Year in Canterbury Settlement* (1863) reappeared in *Erewhon* (1872), a Utopian satire in which many of the conventional practices and customs are reversed. For example, crime is treated as an illness and illness as a crime, and machines have been abolished for fear of their mastery over men's minds. The dominant theme of its supplement, *Erewhon Revisited* (1901), is the origin of religious belief. Butler was greatly influenced by Charles Darwin's *Origin of Species*, and accepted the latter's theory of evolution, but not of natural selection. He returned to Britain in 1864, and from then on lived in London. For a time he studied painting, and his picture *Mr Heatherley's Holiday* is in the Tate Gallery. In a series of writings he tried to revive the 'vitalist' or 'creative' view of evolution, as in *Luck or Cunning* (1886), in opposition to Darwin's doctrine of natural selection. He loved music, especially Handel's, and composed two oratorios, gavottes, minuets, fugues, and a cantata. In his later years he turned to scholarship and published translations of the *Iliad* (1898) and the *Odyssey* (1900). His essay *The Humour of Homer* (1892) is a remarkable piece of literary criticism. He is best known, however, for his autobiographical novel *The Way of All Flesh*, published posthumously in 1903, a work of moral realism on the causes of strife between different generations which left its mark on **George Bernard Shaw** and much 20th-century literature.

▷ *The Life and Letters of Dr Samuel Butler* (1856); P N Furbank, *Samuel Butler* (1948)

BUTLER, Sir William Francis
(1838–1910)

Irish soldier and author, born in Suirville, Tipperary. He joined the British army in 1858, and served in Canada from 1867 to 1873, where his experiences provided the material for his popular book, *The Great Lone Land* (1872). He served on the Red River expedition (1870–1), on the Ashanti expedition (1873), in the Sudan (1884–5), and in South Africa (1888–99). He published biographies of Gordon and Sir Charles Napier, and several travel books. In 1877 he married Elizabeth Southerden Thompson (1850–1933), a battle-painter, born in Lausanne, who made her reputation with the *Roll Call* (1874) and *Inkermann* (1877).

▷ *Remember Butler* (1967)

BUTOR, Michel Marie François
(1926–)

French writer, born in Mons-en-Baroeul. He taught in Egypt, England, Greece, Switzerland and the USA, and in French universities. He is 'professor extraordinaire' at the University of Geneva. He came to the fore in the 1950s, together with **Alain Robbe-Grillet**, **Nathalie Sarraute**, **Claude Simon** and others who were known collectively as the New Novelists. His novels include *Passage de Milan* (1954), *L'emploi du temps* (1956, Eng trans *Passing Time*, 1960), *Degrés* (1960, Eng trans *Degrees*, 1961 (US); 1962 (UK)), *Le génie du Lieu* (1960, 'The Spirit of the Place') and *Mobile* (1963), which extended the experimental nature of his texts. He wrote a series of critical volumes under the title *Répertoire 1–4* (1960–74), and other critical and nonfiction works, and is also known as a writer of poetry and drama, and has collaborated with the Belgian composer Henri Pousseur in an opera, *Votre Faust* (1968). His later fiction includes *Matière de rêves* (4 vols 1975–7, 'The Stuff of Dreams') and *Vanité: Conversation dans les Alpes-Maritimes* (1980, 'Vanitas: A Conversation in the Alpes-Maritimes').

▷ M C Spencer, *Michel Butor* (1974)

BUYSSE, Cyriel
(1859–1932)

Belgian (Flemish) novelist and dramatist, born in Nevele; he was a close friend of **Maurice Maeterlinck**, Belgium's foremost writer of the period. At first he represented the naturalist strain in Flemish literature, with such novels as his first, *Het recht van de sterkst* (1893, 'The Law of the Strongest'), about a farmer's struggle for survival. Later the tone of his work deepened, and in *De Schandpaal* (1928, 'The Pillory'), there is psychological penetration as well as his naturally pessimistic attitude. His plays include *Het gezin Van Paemel* (1903, 'The Van Paemel Family'), a sombre work about the struggle between peasants and aristocrats.

▷ S Lilar, *The Belgian Theatre Since 1890* (1962)

BUZO, Alexander
(1944–)

Australian playwright, born in Sydney, who first came to notice with *Norm and Achmed* (1968) through prosecutions for obscenity which followed its first productions. *Rooted* was produced in 1969 and was the first of his plays to receive an overseas production. In more serious vein, Buzo was awarded the Australian Literature Society's Gold Medal for *Macquarie* (1972), a study of an early governor of New South Wales, and *Tom* (1972). His plays cast a wry light on human affairs where the Australian setting is merely incidental to the drama, though a more exotic backdrop, a tropical seaport, is the setting of *Makassar Reef* (1978). Buzo's interest in the tools of his trade has resulted in three entertaining books, *Tautology* (1981), *Tautology Too* (1982), and *Glancing Blows: Life and*

Language in Australia (1987). His first novel, a humorous detective story, *The Search for Harry Allfay*, was published in 1985.

BUZZATI, Dino
(1906–72)

Italian novelist and short-story writer, born in the mountainous north-east of Italy, an area which inspired the remote, mysterious settings of much of his work. After university in Milan, he became a journalist on the *Corriere della Sera*, and continued to work for the paper, as reporter, critic and Africa correspondent, throughout his literary career. His first novellas were reminiscent of Nordic myths, and his great novel, *Il deserto dei tartari* (1940), has a mystic, allegorical power in its story of a lieutenant stationed in a border fort, awaiting a Tartar attack that never materializes. A sense of the surreal and the macabre haunts his best work, notably the short stories collected in *Sessanta racconti* (1958), which won the Strega Prize for Literature. His later writing ranged widely, from a science-fiction novel to a comic-strip version of *Orpheus and Eurydice*.

B V *see* THOMSON, James

BYARS, Betsy Cromer
(1928–)

American children's novelist, born in Charlotte, North Carolina. She began to write in the 1960s but had no great impact until *The Summer of the Swans* (1970), the story of a girl and her retarded brother, which was awarded the **Newbery** Medal. Specializing in kitchen-sink drama—contemporary realism—she produced a number of popular novels, at times perceptive and inventive, at others predictable and reminiscent of soap opera. Her titles include *The Eighteenth Emergency* (1973), *Goodbye, Chicken Little* (1979) and *The Animal, The Vegetable, and John D Jones* (1982).

BYATT, A(ntonia) S(usan)
(1938–)

English novelist and critic, born in Sheffield, elder sister of **Margaret Drabble**. She taught with Westminster Tutors (1962–5), and at the Central School of Art and Design (1965–9) before joining the extra-mural faculty at Uniersity College London (1971); she has subsequently been senior lecturer in English. In 1965 she published *Degrees of Freedom*, the first full-length study of **Iris Murdoch**'s novels, whose philosophical style has influenced her own; in 1976 she added a shorter monograph, *Iris Murdoch*. Highly respected as a critic, she made her reputation as a novelist with her third novel, *The Virgin in the*

Garden (1978). This was followed by *Still Life* (1985), and in 1990 she won the Booker Prize with *Possession* (1990), in which two young academics research the lives of a fictitious mid-Victorian poet, Randolph Henry Ash, and his contemporary, Christabel LaMotte. An excellent example of her style, it is part literary detective story, part romance, part a satirical comedy of English and American academia. Byatt has also written on **Ford Madox Ford** and on 18th- and 19th-century poetry: *Unruly Times: Wordsworth and Coleridge in their Time* (1970). Her interests extend to art and art history, literary and social history, and philosophy, all of which feature in her novels.

BYNNER, (Harold) Witter
(1881–1968)

American poet, playwright and translator, the nephew of a once-popular novelist, Edwin Lassetter Bynner. He grew up in Brooklyn, New York, and was educated at Harvard, to which he wrote a celebrated *Ode* (1907; as *Young Harvard*, 1925). After graduation, he made his way as an editor and playwright, before travelling and researching in the Far East, where he became a passionate propagandist for oriental life and culture; *The Jade Mountain* (1929) is an account of his travels. His other well-known book is *Journey With Genius* (1951), a memoir of his stay at Taos, New Mexico, with **D H Lawrence**, who anticipated the compliment by including Bynner as a character in *The Plumed Serpent* (1926). Bynner's main claim to fame, however, is an elaborate poetic hoax in which, with Arthur Davis Ficke, he published a volume called *Spectra* (1916) under the names 'Emmanuel Morgan' and 'Anne Knish', a book of supposed 'poetic experiments' that were then talked into brief vogue by glowing reviews from him and Ficke. The deception lasted somewhat longer than the 'Ern Malley' stunt in Australia, which shared many of its sincere critical motives. Sadly, Bynner's own verse, particularly those in *New Poems* (1960), have been much undervalued as a result.

BYRNE, Donn, pseud of Brian Oswald Donn-Byrne
(1889–1928)

Irish–American novelist and short-story writer, born in Brooklyn. He was educated at Dublin, the Sorbonne, and at Leipzig. A cowpuncher in South America and garage hand in New York, his works include *Messer Marco Polo* (1921) and *Hangman's House* (1926).

▷T McCauley, *Donn Byrne, Bard of Armagh* (1929)

BYRNE, John
(1940–)

Scottish dramatist and stage designer, born in Paisley. He had designed plays for the 7:84 Theatre Company before writing his first play, *Writer's Cramp*, produced at the Edinburgh Festival Fringe (1977). *The Slab Boys* (1978), concerning the lives of the employees of a carpet factory, grew into a trilogy with *Cuttin' A Rug* (1980) and *Still Life* (1983). Other plays include *Normal Service* (1979) and *Cara Coco* (1982). He wrote the highly acclaimed *Tutti Frutti* (1987), a BBC Scotland television series about an ageing pop group, and followed it with the less universally-acclaimed *Your Cheatin' Heart* (1989). He returned to writing for the stage in 1992 with *Colquhoun and MacBryde*, a play based on the lives of two Scottish artists. He has designed stage sets for most of his own work and many other productions.

BYRON, George Gordon, 6th Baron Byron of Rochdale
(1788–1824)

English poet of Scottish antecedents, born in London, son of the irresponsible and eccentric Captain 'Mad Jack' Byron (1756–91) and Catherine Gordon of Gight, Aberdeen, a Scottish heiress. His grandfather was admiral John Byron. His first 10 years were spent in his mother's lodgings in Aberdeen, her husband having squandered her fortune in France. Byron was lame from birth, and the shabby surroundings and the violent temper of his foolish, vulgar and deserted mother produced a repression in him which explains many of his later actions. In 1798 he succeeded to the title on the death of 'the wicked lord', his great-uncle. He was educated at Aberdeen Grammar School, then privately at Dulwich and at Harrow School, proceeding to Trinity College, Cambridge, in 1805, where he read much, swam and boxed, and led a dissipated life. An early collection of poems under the title of *Hours of Idleness* was reprinted with alterations in 1807 and was 'savagely cut up' by the *Edinburgh Review* in 1808. Byron replied with his powerful Popian satire *English Bards and Scotch Reviewers* (1809), and set out on his grand tour, visiting Spain, Malta, Albania, Greece, and the Aegean, returning after two years with 'a great many stanzas in Spenser's measure relative to the countries he had visited', which appeared under the title of *Childe Harold's Pilgrimage* in 1812 and were widely popular. This was followed by a series of oriental pieces such as the *Giaour* (1813), *Lara* (1814), and the *Siege of Corinth* (1816). During this time he dramatized himself as a man of mystery, a gloomy romantic figure, derived from the popular fiction of the day and not

least from *Childe Harold*. He became the darling of London society, and lover of Lady Caroline Lamb, and gave to Europe the concept of the 'Byronic hero'. In 1815 he married an heiress, Anne Isabella Milbanke, who left him in 1816 after the birth of a daughter, Ada (later Countess of Lovelace). He was also suspected of a more than brotherly love for his half-sister, Augusta Leigh, and was ostracized. He left for the continent, travelled through Belgium and the Rhine country to Switzerland, where he met **Shelley**, and on to Venice and Rome, where he wrote the last canto of *Childe Harold* (1817). He spent two years in Venice and met the Countess Teresa Guiccioli, who became his mistress. Some of his best works belong to this period, including *Beppo* (1818), *A Vision of Judgment* (1822), and *Don Juan* (1819–24), written in a new metre (ottava rima) and in an informal conversational manner which enabled him to express the whole of his complex personality. He gave active help to the Italian revolutionaries and founded with Leigh Hunt a short-lived journal, *The Liberal*. In 1823 he joined the Greek insurgents who had risen against the Turks, and died of marsh fever at Missolonghi. His body was brought back to England and buried at Hucknall Torkard in Nottingham. His reputation declined after his death despite the championship of **Matthew Arnold**. On the continent his influence was far-reaching both as the creator of the 'Byronic hero' and as the champion of political liberty, leaving his mark on such writers as **Victor Hugo**, **Paul De Musset**, **Giacomo Leopardi**, **Heinrich Heine**, **José de Espronceda**, **Alexander Pushkin**, and **Mikhail Lermontov**.
▷P Quennell, *Byron* (1934–51)

BYRON, H(enry) J(ames)
(1834–84)

English actor, prolific comic dramatist and occasional editor of humorous papers, born in Manchester. Byron notched up over 150 works, liberally laced with puns and borrowing themes from opera, contemporary political and social events, mythology and even children's stories. The dominant dramatic form of his day was melodrama and burlesque, and Byron enjoyed a considerable reputation, especially during the mid-1850s until the late 1860s, by writing burlesques of popular melodrama, of which *The Maid and the Magpie* (1858), *Blue Beard from a New Point of View* (1860), and *Ali Baba or, The Thirty-Nine Thieves* (1863), are among the more notable examples. A comedy, *Our Boys* (1875), ran for four years at the Vaudeville Theatre in London.
▷J Davis, *Plays by H. J. Byron* (1984)

BYRON, Robert
(1905–41)

English writer on travel and architecture, Byzantinist and aesthete. Born in Wiltshire, he was educated at Eton and Merton College, Oxford, where he collected Victoriana. A visit to Mount Athos led to *The Station* (1928), which was followed by *The Byzantine Achievement* (1929) and *The Appreciation of Architecture* (1932). He is best-remembered, however, for his vivacious and erudite travelogues, which include *First Russia, Then Tibet* (1933) and *The Road to Oxiana* (1937), a minor masterpiece conceived as a collection of diary jottings. Typically aggressive in its assertions, it is suffused with humour and sensibility, and won *The Sunday Times* Literary Award. A combative personality, his life was infused with passionate antagonisms and furious enthusiasms. He died during World War II when his ship was torpedoed.

C

CABALLERO, Fernán, pseud of Cecilia Francesca de Arrom
(1797–1877)

Spanish novelist, born in Morges in Switzerland. She was the daughter of Nikolaus Böhl von Faber (1770–1836), a German merchant in Spain. She spent most of her childhood in Germany, but returned to Spain in 1813. She wrote on the history of Spanish literature and introduced in Spain the picturesque local-colour novel. The first of her 50 romances was *La Gaviota* (1849, 'The Seagull'); others include *Clemencia* (1852), *Un servilón y un liberalito* (1855, 'A Groveller and a Little Liberal') and *La Familia de Alvareda* (1856). She also collected Spanish folk tales.
▷L H Klibbe, *Fernán Caballero* (1973)

CABALLERO CALDERON, Eduardo
(1910–)

Colombian writer, politician and diplomat. He ran the daily newspaper *El Tiempo* in Bogotá (1939–43), besides being a diplomat in Peru, Argentina and Spain before finally becoming a permanent representative of UNESCO. His first novels are vivid, descriptive reminiscences with a strong Creole element, a feel for colloquial speech and brutal scenes, with titles such as *Siervo Sin Tierra* (1954, 'Slave without Land') and *Manuel Pacho* (1964). His best-known work is *El Cristo de Espaldas* (1953, 'Christ with His Back Turned'), about the moral crisis of a young rural priest involved in political conflict.

CABANILLOS, Ramón
(1873–1959)

Spanish poet and dramatist writing in Galician, born in Cambados, Pontreveda. He was one of the foremost Gallegan poets of the 20th century, and also one of the most original and wide-ranging. Gallegan poetry is as much (or more) Portuguese as Spanish, and thus partakes far more of the *saudade* (nostalgic longing). But Cabanillos was influenced by the Spanish–American *modernismo*, and expanded the horizons of his poetry. He was in his way a brilliant figure who deserved, like **Eduardo Pondal**, a wider exposure than his minority language enabled him to gain.

CABELL, James Branch
(1879–1958)

American novelist and critic, born in Richmond, Virginia. He made his name with his romance *Jurgen* (1919), the best known of a sequence of 18 novels, collectively known as *Biography of Michael*, set in the imaginary medieval kingdom of Poictesme and written in an elaborate, sophisticated style showing the author's fondness for archaisms. He also published a book of criticism, *Preface to the Past* (1936).
▷C van Doren, *James Branch Cabell* (1926)

CABLE, George Washington
(1844–1925)

American author, born in New Orleans. At the age of 19 he volunteered as a Confederate soldier. After the war he earned a precarious living in New Orleans, before taking up a literary career in 1879. In 1884 he went to New England. His Creole sketches in *Scribner's* made his reputation. Among his books are *Old Creole Days* (1879), *The Grandissimes* (1880, this is his finest work, a profound study of colour and caste in New Orleans at the time of the Louisiana Purchase), *The Silent South* (1885), *Bylow Hill* (1902), *Kincaid's Battery* (1908) and *Lovers of Louisiana* (1918).
▷A Turner, *George Washington Cable: biography* (1956)

CABRAL DE MELO NETO, João
(1920–)

Brazilian poet and dramatist, born in Recife, Pernambuco. Cabral de Melo Neto is the leading poet of the group, known as 'the generation of '45', which first decisively reacted away from Brazilian *modernismo*. He took as his initial models **Jorge Guillén**, **Nicanor Parra** (in his capacity as deliberate 'anti-poet'), whose first collection had appeared in 1937, a cluster of Brazilian poets such as **Bandeira**, **Oswald de Andrade** and **Carlos Drummond de Andrade**—and, above all, the folk poetry and ballads of his own northeastern area of Brazil. Later he incorporated some of the techniques of the concrete poetry into his own work, but without accepting any of the trivial programmes of the concretists. His plays have been well received; there are translations of his work by **Elizabeth Bishop** in *An Anthology of Twentieth Century Brazilian Poetry* (1972). He has been the most widely imitated of the poets of his generation.
▷M Bandeira, *A Brief History of Brazilian Literature* (1958)

CABRERA INFANTE, Guillermo
(1929–)

Cuban-born British novelist, born in Gibara. Educated at Havana University, he emigrated to England in 1966. He is known chiefly for his fiction, particularly *Three Trapped Tigers* (1971), a highly experimental work, *A View of Dawn in the Tropics* (1978) and *Infante's Inferno* (1984), set in Havana during the 1940s and 1950s, which skilfully blurs the distinction between autobiography and fiction, in the process demythologizing the Don Juan legend in Hispanic culture. He translated **James Joyce**'s *Dubliners* into Spanish (1972), and has also written journalism, and, writing under the name Guillermo Cain, film criticism (collected in *A Twentieth Century Job*, 1991) and screenplays.

CADALSO VASQUEZ, José de
(1741–82)

Spanish writer, born in Cadiz. By profession an army officer, he wrote as a hobby. He is best known for his prose satire *Los eruditos a la violeta* (1772, 'The Scholars and the Violet'), which ridicules pedantry, and *Cartas marruecas* (1774, 'Moroccan Letters'), a work of social criticism in epistolary form. He was killed at the siege of Gibraltar.
▷R P Sebold, *Colonel Don José Cadalso* (1971)

CAEDMON
(7th century)

Anglo-Saxon poet, the earliest Christian English poet known by name. According to **Bede**, he was an unlettered herdsman who in his old age received a divine call in a dream to sing of the Creation. He then became a monk at Whitby under the rule of St Hilda, where he turned other biblical themes into vernacular poetry. But the original hymn of the Creation, a mere nine lines long, is the only extant poem that can be attributed to him with any certainty.
▷E Dobbie, *The MSS of Caedmon's Hymn and Bede's Death Song* (1937)

CAESAR, Gaius Julius
(100–44BC)

Roman general, statesman and historian. Caesar, by intrigue and bribery, got himself into a powerful position in Rome in 59; he spent the next nine years in Gaul. After winning a civil war (49–45) he became supreme ruler, but was assassinated in 44. His literary fame rests on his *Commentaries on the Gallic War* (Eng trans 1930), in seven books, and *On the Civil War* (Eng trans 1921), in three books. His style is famously straightforward and gripping, and guilefully clever at seeming objective (which it is not). He was a noted orator.
▷F E Adcock, *Caesar as a Man of Letters* (1956)

CAHAN, Abraham
(1860–1951)

Jewish–American novelist, born in Russia. He emigrated to the USA in 1882, and took up journalism as a career. He was the editor of the socialist newspaper the *Jewish Daily Forward* for many years. He wrote a number of works in Yiddish, but his best-known books are in English, and deal with the process of Americanization of Jewish immigrants. *Yekl: A Tale of the New York Ghetto* (1896) was the first of these, but his most celebrated and influential book was *The Rise of David Levinsky* (1917), which described the psychological and human price of assimilation, and remains a classic treatment of its subject. He wrote also *The Imported Bridegroom and Other Stories* (1898) and an *Autobiography* in five volumes (1916–36).

CAIN, James M(allahan)
(1892–1977)

American thriller writer, born in Annapolis, Maryland. Often associated with **Dashiell Hammett** and **Raymond Chandler**, his earliest ambition was to emulate his mother and become a professional singer. Music remained his favourite recreation and it forms the background of some of his stories. He tried various jobs, was a reporter for many years and also taught journalism, but he always hankered after 'the great American novel'. After moving to California he found the style which is his hallmark. It first emerged in *The Postman Always Rings Twice* (1934), in which an adulterous couple murder the woman's husband but betray each other, then in *Serenade* (1937), *Mildred Pierce* (1941), *Double Indemnity* (1943) and *The Butterfly* (1947). Several of his stories were filmed with what Cain described as 'legendary success', but the script credits went to others.
▷R Hoopes, *Cain: the biography* (1982)

CAINE, Sir (Thomas Henry) Hall
(1853–1931)

English novelist, born in Runcorn. He trained as an architect, and became secretary to **Dante Gabriel Rossetti** from 1881 to 1882, and later published *Recollections of Rossetti* (1882). He wrote a number of popular novels, many of them set in the Isle of Man, including *The Shadow of a Crime* (1885), *The Deemster* (1887), *The Bondman* (1890), *The Scapegoat* (1891), *The Manxman* (1894), *The Eternal City* (1901) and *The Prodigal Son* (1904). He also wrote a *Life of Christ* (1938), and published an early autobiography, *My Story* (1908).

▷C F Kenyon, *Hall Caine, the man and the novelist* (1901)

CAKS, Aleksandrs, pseud of **Aleksandrs Cadarainis**
(1901–50)
Innovatory and controversial Latvian poet and short-story writer. He studied medicine in Moscow, served in the Latvian Red Guards in the Revolution, then settled in Riga as a teacher. His highly dramatic, effective but somewhat inchoate early collections, influenced by **Mayakovsky**, broke with the pastoral traditions of Latvian poetry and caused scandal amongst both left and right elements by its frequent allusions to sexuality and drink. He later fell foul of the Soviet authorities; his poetry suffered through his unconvincing attempts to become a socialist realist. His death was passed over in silence, but he was 'rediscovered' in Latvia in 1966 and now has his rightful place as his country's leading modernist, who inspired poets both inside and outside Latvia. Poetry in translation includes *Let's Get Acquainted* (1973) and *Selected Poems* (1979).

CALDERÓN DE LA BARCA, Pedro
(1600–81)
Spanish dramatist, born of a prestigious family in Madrid. After schooling under the Jesuits, he studied law and philosophy at Salamanca (1613–19), and during 10 years' service in the Milanese and in Flanders saw much of men and manners that he afterwards utilized. On Vega Carpio's death in 1635 he was summoned by Philip IV to Madrid, and appointed a sort of master of the revels. In 1640 the rebellion in Catalonia made him return to the army; but in 1651 he entered the priesthood, and in 1653 withdrew to Toledo. Ten years later he was recalled to court and to the resumption of his dramatic activity, receiving, with other preferments, the post of chaplain of honour to Philip; and he continued to write for the court, the church, and the public theatres till his death. Castilian and Catholic to the backbone, Calderón wrote with perfect fidelity to the Spanish thought and manners of his age. His *autos sacramentales*, outdoor plays for the festival of Corpus Christi, number 72, and have been divided into seven classes—biblical, classical, ethical, 'cloak and sword plays', dramas of passion, and so forth; the finest of them is *El divino Orfeo* ('Divine Orpheus'). Of his regular dramas 118 are extant.

▷E W Hesse, *Calderón* (1967)

CALDWELL, Erskine
(1903–87)
American author, born in White Oak, Georgia. He worked amongst the 'poor whites' in the southern states, where he absorbed the background for his best-known work *Tobacco Road* (1932), of which the dramatized version by Jack Kirkland (1933) had a record run in New York. Other books include *God's Little Acre* (1933), *Sure Hand of God* (1947), *A Lamp for Nightfall* (1952), *Love and Money* (1954) and *Close to Home* (1962).

CALDWELL, (Janet) Taylor
(1900–85)
English-born American novelist, born in Manchester, of Scots descent. She moved with her family to the USA in 1906. Her debut, *Dynasty of Death* (1938), is the saga of a family of armaments manufacturers. It and its many sequels, such as *The Eagles Gather* (1940) and *Dear Glorious Physician* (1959), were bestsellers, impressing the reader by an accumulation of detail rather than by literary merit.

CALISHER, Hortense
(1911–)
American novelist and short-story writer, born in New York City. Her milieu is New York and her characters are usually drawn from the upper middle-class. A powerful and precise writer, her novels—*The New Yorkers* (1969), *Queenie* (1971), *The Bobby-Soxer* (1986)—though frequently of novella length are less successful than stories like 'In Greenwich There Are Many Gravelled Walks', which aspire to classic status.

▷*Herself* (1972)

CALLAGHAN, Morley Edward
(1903–90)
Canadian novelist, short-story writer and memoirist, born in Toronto of Irish descent. One of Canada's premier novelists, he was educated at Toronto University, and when a cub reporter on the Toronto *Daily Star* was befriended by **Ernest Hemingway**. They met up again in Paris, where his boxing prowess earned him Hemingway's respect, and he wrote about his time there in one of his most appealing books, *That Summer in Paris* (1963). He had been called to the Bar in 1928, but Hemingway encouraged him to renounce law for literature and helped him get some of his stories published in expatriate literary magazines. In terms of publication, Callaghan's career was strikingly uneven, periods of productivity mirrored by prolonged silence. His first novel was *Strange Fugitive* (1928) and his first collection of stories *A Native Argosy* (1930). From the late

1920s to the late 1930s he wrote six novels, finishing with *More Joy in Heaven* (1937). He returned to Toronto in 1929. His later novels include *The Loved and the Lost* (1951), *The Many Colored Coat* (1960), *A Fine and Private Place* (1975) and *A Time for Judas* (1983).
▷A Conron, *Morley Callaghan* (1966)

CALLIMACHUS
(c.305–c.240 BC)

Hellenistic poet, grammarian and critic, of Alexandria, born in Cyrene in Libya. He became head of the Alexandrian library, and prepared a catalogue of it, in 120 volumes. He wrote numerous prose works and plays which have not survived, a number of *Hymns*, and a long elegiac poem, the *Aitia*. He excelled in the smaller forms, and some 60 of his epigrams are included in the Greek Anthology, to which he is one of the most distinguished contributors.
▷G Capovilla, *Callimaco* (1967)

CALLOW, Philip
(1924–)

English poet, novelist and biographer, born in Birmingham, whose recurring literary theme is family relationships and the emotional chasms between the sexes. His early trilogy, *Going to the Moon* (1968), *The Bliss Body* (1969), and *Flesh of Morning* (1971), which was republished as *Another Flesh* in 1989, examines the developing maturity of a young boy in the English Midlands, his adolescent drifting, his adult love affairs and gradual acceptance of his own nature. Among his more recent works, *Some Love* (1991) is a sharply-observed study of the relationship between a young, suspicious 14-year-old boy and a 30-year-old woman disenchanted by men. Callow's first collection of poetry was *The Turning Point*; later collections include *New York Insomnia and Other Poems* (1984). He has also written studies of **D H Lawrence** and Vincent van Gogh.

CALPRENÈDE, Gautier des Costes de la
(1610–63)

French author, officer of the guards and royal chamberlain of France. He wrote tragedies, tragi-comedies, and the clever but tedious 'heroic romances', *Cléopâtre*, *Cassandre*, and others.

CALPURNIUS SICULUS, Titus
(fl.mid 1st century)

Latin pastoral poet. He is best known for his seven surviving Eclogues.

CALVERLEY, Charles Stuart
(1831–84)

English poet and parodist, born in Martley, Worcestershire, the son of a clergyman. He was educated at Marlborough, Harrow, Oxford and Cambridge. In 1858 he was elected a fellow of Christ's College, Cambridge, and in 1865 called to the Bar, and settled in London. A fall on the ice in the winter of 1866–7 put an end to a brilliant career and his last years were spent as an invalid. One of the most gifted men of his time, he is remembered as a skilful parodist in his two little volumes, *Verses and Translations* (1862) and *Fly Leaves* (1872). His translation of **Theocritus** (1869) shows at once his scholarship and his mastery of English verse.
▷R B Ince, *Calverley and the Cambridge Wits of the 19th Century* (1929)

CALVINO, Italo
(1923–85)

Italian novelist, essayist and journalist, born in Santiago de las Vegas, Cuba, of Italian parents. He grew up in San Remo on the Italian Riviera and was educated at the University of Turin. In 1940 he was forced to join the Young Fascists. He was a reluctant participant in the Italian occupation of the French Riviera, but in 1943 he was able to join the Resistance, and until 1945 he was with the Partisan forces fighting the Nazis in Liguria. Throughout the 1940s he wrote for the communist paper *L'unità* and later he succeeded **Cesare Pavese** at Einaudi, the Turin-based publishers. His first novel, *Il sentiero dei nidi di ragno* (1947, Eng trans *The Path to the Nest of Spiders*, 1956), was dubbed Neorealist, but he became increasingly interested in fantasy, folk-tales and the nature of narrative. During the Cold War years of the 1950s he wrote three fantastic 'historical' novels, collectively titled *I nostri antenati* (1960, Eng trans *Our Ancestors*, 1980). A complete translation of his *Fiabe Italiane* (1956) was published as *Italian Folktales* in English in 1980. Regarded as one of the most inventive of the European modernists, he combined fantasy and surrealism with a hard, satirical wit and his later books are complex and profound. Seminal titles are *Le città invisibili* (1972, Eng trans *Invisible Cities*, 1974), *Il castello dei destini incrociati* (1973, Eng trans *The Castle of Crossed Destinies*, 1977), *Si una notte d'inverno un viaggiatore* (1979, Eng trans *If on a Winter's Night a Traveller*, 1981) and *Palomar* (1983). In 1973 he won the prestigious Italian literary award, the Premio Feltrinelli.
▷J Cannon, *Calvino: writer and society* (1981)

CAMBRIDGE, Ada
(1844–1926)

English-born Australian novelist and poet, born in Norfolk, the second of 10 children, her father was a gentleman farmer and she was educated privately. By the time she met and married George Cross at the age of 26, she had published short stories, poems and a book of hymns. They left almost immediately for Australia where her husband was to be a missionary priest, and settled eventually in Melbourne. In 1873 she began contributing to the *Australian* which, between 1875 and 1886, serialized nine novels, of which three were subsequently published: *In Two Years' Time* (1879), *A Mere Chance* (1882) and *The Three Miss Kings* (1891). A woman with a strong sense of class, her writing called attention to women's social position and encouraged them to think for themselves. She wrote 18 novels and attracted a wide English readership but was modest about her success, regarding herself fortunate to have been the first in the field. **Jane Austen** is the most obvious influence, and her best work is to be found in *A Marked Man* (1890), *The Three Miss Kings* (1891), *Not All In Vain* (1892), *Fidelis* (1895) and *Materfamilias* (1898).
▷ *Thirty Years in Australia* (1903); *The Retrospect* (1912)

CAMERON, (John) Norman
(1905–53)

Scottish poet and translator, born in Bombay. He published only three volumes of his own verse, and financed himself by working in the colonial service (Nigeria, 1929–31); as an advertising copywriter (1933–9), and as a writer of government propaganda during World War II. He lived for a time in Deya, Majorca, home also to **Robert Graves**. His second book, *Work In Hand* (1942), was a joint effort with Graves and Alan Hodge. He was, however, by no means a follower of Graves, having early formed his own formal, introspective vision, as is shown in *The Winter House and Other Poems* (1935). *Forgive Me, Sire* (1950) is restrained, almost repressed, in its narrowness of subject matter. His *Complete Poems* was published in 1985.

CAMOENS, or CAMÕES, Luis de
(1524–80)

Portuguese poet, born in Lisbon. He studied for the church as an 'honourable poor student' at Coimbra, but declined to take orders. His *Amphitriões* ('The Host') was acted before the university. Returning to Lisbon, probably in 1542, he fell in love with Donna Caterina Ataide, who returned his affection; but her father was against the marriage, and

the poet had to content himself with passionate protestations in his *Rimas*—short poems after the model of the Italians. He was banished from Lisbon for a year, and joining a Portuguese force at Ceuta, served there for two years, losing his right eye because of a splinter. In 1550 he returned to Lisbon, where for the next three years he seems to have led a somewhat discreditable life; and having been thrown into prison for his share in a street brawl, was released only on his volunteering to go to India. At Goa (1553–5) he engaged in two military expeditions, but his bold denunciations of the Portuguese officials at length led to an honourable exile in a lucrative post at Macao (1556). Returning to Goa (1558) he was shipwrecked and lost everything except his poem, *Os Lusiadas* ('The Lusiads'). At Goa he was thrown into prison through the machinations of his former enemies; but at length, after an exile of 16 years, he returned to Portugal to spend the remainder of his life at Lisbon in poverty and obscurity. In 1572 he published *Os Lusiadas*, which had an immediate and brilliant success, but did little for the fortunes of its author, who died in a public hospital. In *Os Lusiadas* he did for the Portuguese language what **Chaucer** did for English and **Dante** for Italian, as well as making himself the interpreter of the deepest aspirations of the Portuguese nation. The Portuguese regard it as their national epic, while modern readers have learned to value its lyrical as well as its epic aspects.
▷ W Freitas, *Camoens and his Epic: a Historic, Geographic and Cultural Background* (1963)

CAMPANA, Dino
(1885–1932)

Major Italian poet from Marradi near Florence. He was for the last 12 years of his life a patient in a mental hospital, a victim of the manic-depression which had dominated his life. He earned his living in many ways, and was often jailed as a tramp. But he was almost inordinately gifted as an incantatory and visionary poet, and his *Canti Orfici* (1914, Eng trans *Orphic Songs*, 1968), was fully recognized as a work of genius by Giovanni Papini, Ardengo Soffici (who lost the original manuscript, so that Campana had to reconstruct it from memory) and eventually by most other readers of poetry in Italy. His poetry was later collected, still under the title of his only publication. His work is highly original, influenced initially by **D'Annunzio**, but also anticipating every mode in Italian literature throughout the 20th century, inspired, frenzied, mostly coherent at a deeply visionary level. All his writing, including articles, was edited in *Opere e contributi* (2 vols, 1973).

CAMPBELL, Alistair Te Ariki
(1925–)

New Zealand poet and playwright, born in Rarotonga, Cook Islands, whose first collection of verse, *Mine Eyes Dazzle: Poems 1947–49* (1950, rev edns 1951, 1956) received immediate attention. His Polynesian ancestry responds to the pulse of land and sea, as in *Sanctuary of Spirits: Poems* (1963) and *Blue Rain: Poems* (1967). His later verse closely identifies with Maori myth and history, and his search for his Cook Islands roots is reflected in *The Dark Lord of Savaiki* (1980) and *Soul Traps: A Lyric Sequence* (1985). *Collected Poems, 1947–1981* came out in 1981. Much of his radio drama is unpublished; it brings out personal concerns through themes of mental illness or racial conflict.
▷ *Island to Island* (1984)

CAMPBELL, David Watt
(1915–79)

Australian poet, born on a remote station near Adelong, New South Wales. After serving with distinction in the Royal Australian Air Force in World War II, he returned to farming and in 1964 became poetry editor of the *Australian* newspaper. His first book of verse was *Speak with the Sun* (1949), much in the Australian ballad tradition, followed by *The Miracle of Mullion Hill* (1956). *Poems* (1962) turns more to universal themes and includes the pastoral sequence of 12 poems, 'Cocky's Calendar', which ranks alongside the best of the English 18th-century tradition. Four further volumes were followed by his last book, *The Man in the Honeysuckle* (posthumous, 1979). He edited two anthologies, *Australian Poetry* (1966) and *Modern Australian Poetry* (1970), and wrote short stories and translations of Russian poetry. He received the **Patrick White** Literary Award in 1975.

CAMPBELL, George
(1916–)

Jamaican poet, born in Panama and educated in Jamaica and New York. His *First Poems* (1945) had enormous influence on the generation of Caribbean poets that includes **Edward Kamau Brathwaite**—who describes him as 'one of the most important figures in the transition from colonial apprenticeship to a sense of the autochthonous and its expression'—and **Derek Walcott**, who acknowledges the exhilarating impact of *First Poems* in *Another Life* (1973). Campbell's poetry celebrates the land and people of the Black Caribbean, demanding a humane and multicultural perspective.

CAMPBELL, John Wood, Jr
(1910–71)

American science-fiction writer and editor, born in Newark, New Jersey. He graduated in physics from Duke University in 1932. A science-fiction fan from the earliest days of the genre, he rivalled **E E 'Doc' Smith** in the galactic adventure stories known as 'space opera' in the early 1930s. From 1934 he published most of his fiction under the pseudonym 'Don A Stuart', and wrote little more after 1937. His chief claim to fame, though, was as the hugely influential editor of the magazine *Astounding Stories* (later *Astounding Science Fiction*, and still later *Analog*, 1937–71). The first decade of his editorship is remembered as a 'golden age' in which he discovered and encouraged a stable of writers who became major figures in the genre, including **Asimov**, **Del Ray**, **Heinlein**, **Van Vogt** and **Kuttner**.

CAMPBELL, (Ignatius) Roy Dunnachie
(1901–57)

South African poet, translator and critic, born in Durban, but who lived most of his life in Great Britain, and died in a car crash in Portugal. Campbell was a boisterous figure, given—as his biographer demonstrates—to lying about his exploits; the work of his middle and later period is badly flawed by over-aggressiveness or delight in violence. The consensus now, however, is that he wrote a few powerful lyrics which will outlast his self-spoiled reputation. He was an outdoors man, and much of his best poetry celebrates this. An effective satirist of apartheid and all sorts of pretension in his youth in his native South Africa, he later became the apotheosis of right-wing Catholicism, and even gave out that he had fought for Franco in the Spanish Civil War (which he had not). His defence of Franco in the long, maladroit poem *Flowering Rifle* (1939) greatly harmed his reputation, and it has not gained admirers even from the right. Among his great poems is the comparatively long 'Tristan da Cunha', written when he was a young man; many of his shorter lyrics have been anthologized. His books of poetry include *The Flamingo Terrapin* (1924), *The Wayzgoose* (1928), *Adamastor* (1930), *The Georgiad* (1931), *Mithraic Emblems* (1936), and *Flowering Rifle* (1939).
▷ *Collected Poems*, 3 vols (1949–60); *Light on a Dark Horse* (1951, autobiography); P Alexander, *Roy Campbell* (1982)

CAMPBELL, Thomas
(1777–1844)

Scottish poet and journalist, born and educated in Glasgow, the eleventh child of a tobacco merchant who was ruined by the American War of Independence. In 1797 he went to Edinburgh to study law, but was increasingly drawn to the reading and writing of poetry. *The Pleasures of Hope*, published in 1799, ran through four editions in a year. During a tour on the Continent (1800–1) he visited Hohenlinden, only just missing the battle there, fell in with the prototype of his 'Exile of Erin' at Hamburg, and sailed past the batteries of Copenhagen. In 1803 he married and settled in London, having refused the offer of a professorship at Wilna, and resolved to adopt a literary career. He contributed articles to *The Edinburgh Encyclopaedia*, and compiled *The Annals of Great Britain from George II to the Peace of Amiens*. In 1809 *Gertrude of Wyoming* appeared; in 1818 he visited Germany again, and on his return he published his *Specimens of the British Poets* (1819). In 1820 he delivered a course of lectures on poetry at the Surrey Institution, and from 1820 to 1830 he edited *The New Monthly Magazine*, contributing 'The Last Man' and other poems. He was buried in Westminster Abbey. 'Hohenlinden', 'Ye Mariners of England' and 'The Battle of the Baltic' are among his best-known poems.
▷W Beattie, *Life and Letters of Thomas Campbell* (1849)

CAMPBELL, William Wilfred
(1860–1919)

Canadian poet, born in Kitchener, Ontario. An Anglican clergyman, he joined the Canadian civil service in 1891. He was author of *Lake Lyrics* (1889) and other volumes of poetry, and was editor of the *Oxford Book of Canadian Verse* (1906).
▷C Klinck, *William Campbell, a study in late provincial Victorianism* (1942)

CAMPHUYSEN, Dirck Rafaelsz
(1586–1627)

Dutch religious poet and painter, born in Gorinchem. He studied painting, then became a priest, but was dismissed because of his Arminianism, for which he was persecuted. Thereafter he lived in poverty, making a meagre living as a flax dealer. Translations of his poetry are in *Batavian Anthology* (1824).
▷L A Rademaker, *Dirck Camphuysen* (1898, in Dutch)

CAMPION, Thomas
(1567–1620)

English poet and composer, one of the world's great song-writers. He was by profession a doctor. He wrote a treatise, *Observations in the Art of English Rhyme* (1602), which seemed to disparage rhyme; but his own songs use rhyme. Judged as poetry, his songs are slight; judged as songs, they are paramount.
▷M Kastendieck, *England's Musical Poet: Thomas Campion* (1938)

CAMPO, Estanislao del
(1834–80)

Argentinian *gaucho* poet, soldier and journalist, born in Buenos Aires. The *gaucho* poets were not nomadic cowboys, but city men who aped their dialect for sophisticated purposes—until the masterpiece of **José Hernández**, *Martín Fierro*, which was a real tribute. It is significant that his most famous and successful poem, *Fausto* (1866), angered Hernández for its mockery of its gaucho protagonist, who, having witnessed the opera *Faust*, believes he has seen a real instance of black magic. It, and Campo's other skilful and sometimes superficially amusing verse, are now of more historical than intrinsic interest.

CAMPOAMOR, Ramón de
(1817–1901)

Spanish poet, born in Navia. He studied medicine, almost became a Jesuit, and ultimately chose a career in politics and literature. He enjoyed some success during his lifetime, but his work is now neglected. His short, epigrammatic poems, including those in *Doloras* (1858, 'Laments'), *Pequeños poemas* (1871, 'Little Poems') and *Humoradas* (1890), represent his most significant literary contribution, but he also wrote larger poems, including *El drama universal* (1869, 'The Universal Drama') and *El tren expreso* (1874, 'The Express Train').
▷V Gaos, *La Poética de Campoamor* (1955)

CAMUS, Albert
(1913–60)

French writer, winner of the Nobel Prize for literature, born in Mondovi, Algeria, the son of a farm labourer. He studied philosophy at Algiers and, interrupted by long spells of ill-health, became actor, schoolmaster, playwright and journalist there and in Paris. Active in the French Resistance during World War II, he became co-editor with **Jean-Paul Sartre** of the left-wing newspaper *Combat* after the liberation until 1948, when he broke with Sartre and 'committed' political writing. Having earned an international reputation with his Existentialist novel, *L'Étranger* (1942, Eng trans *The Outsider*, 1946), 'the study of an absurd man in an absurd world', he set himself in his subsequent work the aim of elucidating some values for man confronted with cosmic meaninglessness. The essays *Le Mythe de Sisyphe* (1942, Eng trans *The Myth of Sisyphus*, 1955), concerning suicide, and *L'Homme révolté* (1951, Eng trans *The Rebel*, 1954), on the harm done by surrendering to ideologies, the magnanimous letters to a German friend (1945), a second masterpiece *La Peste* (1947, Eng trans *The Plague*, 1948), in which the plague-stricken city Oran symbolizes man's isolation, were followed by a return to extreme ironical pessimism in *La Chute* (1956, Eng trans *The Fall*, 1957). *Le Malentendu* (1945, Eng trans *Cross Purpose*, 1947) and *Caligula* (1938, Eng trans 1947) are his best plays. His political writings are collected in *Actuelles I* (1950, 'Chronicles of Today I') and *II* (1953). He was awarded the 1957 Nobel Prize for literature. He died in a car accident.

▷P Thody, *Albert Camus 1913–1960* (1962); H Lottman, *Camus: a biography* (1979)

CANETTI, Elias
(1905–)

Bulgarian writer, winner of the Nobel Prize for literature, born in Rutschuk, Bulgaria, into a community of Spanish-speaking Jews. In his formative years he moved between England, Switzerland, Austria and Germany. Since 1938 he has lived in Britain. The works for which he is best known are his novel on the growth of totalitarianism, *Die Blendung* (1935–6, Eng trans *Auto-da-Fé*, 1946), and a speculative study of the psychology of mass behaviour, *Masse und Macht* (1960, Eng trans *Crowds and Power*, 1962). His autobiographies, *Die gerettete Zunge: Geschichte einer Jugenol* (1977, Eng trans *The Tongue Set Free*, 1979) and *Die Fackel im Ohr* (1980, Eng trans *The Torch in my Ear*, 1982), have emphasized the origins of and inspiration for his life's work. He was awarded the Nobel Prize for literature in 1981.

▷D Barnouw, *Canetti* (1979)

CANNING, Victor
(1911–86)

English author of suspense thrillers, mostly with an espionage background. Born in Plymouth, he served in the Royal Artillery during World War II. His first book, and first use of a series character, was *Mr Finchley Discovers His England* (1934), a mild and slightly ironic novel with overtones of **H G Wells**. Other Finchley books followed, but it was with *The Chasm* (1947) that Canning discovered his forte for fast-paced action leavened with dry humour. In *The Whip Hand* (1965) he introduced the private investigator and intelligence operative Rex Carver, who figured in four subsequent novels. A hugely prolific author, Canning's plots are as varied

as his settings and he scrupulously avoided formulaic situations. He also wrote short stories and drama. During the 1930s he sometimes published under the pseudonym Alan Gould.

CANSINOS-ASSÉNS, Rafael
(1883–1964)

Spanish novelist, translator (the complete works of **Dostoyevsky**), editor (*Cervantes*, which he founded in Madrid) and critic, born in Seville. He was Spain's best informed critic about other literatures; charges that he was 'excessively anecdotal' ignore the sheer amount of good reading he was able to recommend, and with great authority. As a novelist he was in many ways a small edition of his friend **Valle-Inclán**, at his best when at his most brief, as in *El eterno milagro* (1918, 'The Eternal Miracle'). His *La nueva literatura* (1917–27) remains invaluable. He was the leading expert on the contribution of the Sephardic Jews to Spanish literature, as seen in *España y los judios españoles* (1919, 'Spain and the Spanish Jews').

▷S Robles, *La novela corte en España* (1952)

CANTH, Minna, née Ulrika Vilhelmina Johnsson
(1844–97)

Finnish playwright and feminist, born in Tampere. She began writing at 40 after an intensive course of self-education in literary and social history. Her reading, and her experience as the single parent of seven children, turned her into a radical. A powerful exponent of the Realist school, her best-known plays are *Työmiehen vaimo* (1885, 'A Working-class Wife') and *Kovan onnen lapsia* (1888, 'The Hard Luck Kids'). Later she turned to psychological dramas about women, such as *Anna Liisa* (1895), which recalls **Tolstoy** and some elements of **Ibsen**.

▷G von Frenckell-Thesleff, *Minna Canth* (1943)

CANTÙ, Cesare
(1804–95)

Italian historian and novelist, born in Brivio in the Milanese territory. Imprisoned as a liberal in 1833, he described the sorrows of a prisoner in a historical romance, *Margherita Pusterla* (1838). As well as his monumental history of the world, *Storia universale* (35 vols, 1836–42, 'A History of the World'), he wrote a multitude of works on Italian history and literature, as well as lighter works, and *Manzoni: Reminiscinze* (2 vols, 1883, 'Manzoni: Reminiscences').

▷G Grabinski, *Cesare Cantù* (1896)

CAO YU, pseud of **Wan Jiabao** (1910–)

Chinese playwright, born in Tianjin. The most significant 20th-century dramatist in China, he studied western literature at Qinghua University (1930–4), where he was profoundly influenced by **Ibsen** and **George Bernard Shaw** to attack the corruption of traditional society. His best-known work, *Thunderstorm*, was staged in 1935; his other major plays are *Sunrise* (1935), *Wilderness* (1936), *Metamorphosis* (1940), *Peking Man* (1940) and *Family* (1941), adapted from the novel by **Ba Jin**. He toured the USA in 1946, and after the foundation of the People's Republic in 1949 he was appointed to numerous official posts. In 1979 he wrote the play *The Consort of Peace*.

ČAPEK, Josef (1887–1945)

Czech writer and painter, born in Schwadonitz, elder brother of **Karel Čapek**. His early literary works, written in collaboration with his brother, include the allegorical *Ze života hmyzu* (1921, Eng trans *The Insect Play*, 1923). From such anxious visions of the future he progressed to a philosophy of sceptical humanism which found expression in his novel, *Stin Kapradiny* (1930), and in his essays. He died in Belsen.
▷J Peirha, *Josef Čapek* (1961)

ČAPEK, Karel (1890–1938)

Bohemian novelist and playwright, brother of **Josef Čapek**. He was born in Malé Svatoňovice, and educated in Prague, Paris and Berlin. He worked as a journalist and, in the early twenties, as stage director at the Vinograd Theatre in Prague. Several early works, including the novel *Zářivé hlubiny* (1916, *The Shining Depths*), were collaborations with his brother, but he came to international attention with the play *R.U.R.* (1920), a satirical vision of a dehumanized post-industrial society. The brothers later collaborated on *Ze života hmyzu* (1921, now best known as *The Insect Play*, 1923), which has a similar theme, as does the late novel *Válka s mloky* (1937), written as Czech independence was increasingly threatened by Nazi expansionism. Karel also wrote *Věc Makropulos* (1922), which formed the basis for his countryman Leoš Janáček's 1925 opera *The Makropulos Affair*. His style is dense, allusive and very Slavic, not always translating effectively, but his ideas and the robotic world of *R.U.R.* are still compelling.
▷W E Harkins, *Karel Čapek* (1962)

CAPOTE, Truman (1924–84)

American author, born in New Orleans of Spanish descent. He spent much of his childhood in Alabama. He won several literary prizes while at school in New York but showed little ability in other subjects. His short story 'Miriam', published in the magazine *Mademoiselle*, was selected for the **O Henry** Memorial Award volume in 1946. *Other Voices, Other Rooms* (1948), his first novel, revealed his talent for sympathetic description of small-town life in the deep South and centres on the (homo)sexual awakenings of a young boy. *The Grass Harp* (1951) is a fantasy performed against a background of the Alabama of his childhood. Other works are *Breakfast at Tiffany's* (1958), which was highly successful as a film, *In Cold Blood* (1966), a 'non-fiction novel' about a murder in Kansas; latterly he published a collection of short pieces, *Music for Chameleons* and the long-promised but unfinished novel *Answered Prayers*.
▷W L Nance, *The Worlds of Truman Capote* (1970); Gerald Clarke, *Capote: a biography* (1987)

CAPPS, Ben(jamin Franklin) (1922–)

American writer of Westerns, born in Texas, the son of a cowboy. Capps was most successful in the 1960s, winning the Spur Award and other prizes for *The Trail to Ogallala* (1964). *A Woman of the People* (1966), about a white girl captured and raised as an Indian by the Comanches, is regarded by Capps' admirers as an American classic. Since then his work has been too seriously historical to capture the popular audience of the genre. *The Heirs of Franklin Woodstock* (1989), set in present-day Texas, examines the death of the frontier spirit.

CAPUANA, Luigi (1839–1915)

Italian novelist, story writer, poet and critic, born in Mineo (Catania), Sicily. He was a leading figure in Italian letters, and an important predecessor of **Pirandello**. He began as a folklorist and philological scholar, then graduated to drama critic in Rome (1864). In 1901 he published his major novel, *Il marchese di Roccaverdina* ('The Marquis of Roccaverdina'), which has its origins in its author's liaison with an illiterate Sicilian girl who bore him children. This book is Italy's worthy naturalist version of the *Crime and Punishment* of **Dostoyevsky**, was influenced by it, and has a plot resembling it. Capuana's short novels and criticism are also notable.

The former have been collected in *Racconti* (1973–4).

▷ V Traverso, *Luigi Capuana* (1968)

CAPUS, (Vincent Marie) Alfred
(1858–1922)

French writer, born in Aix-en-Provence. He left engineering for journalism, and became political editor of *Le Figaro*. He wrote *Qui perd gagne* (1890, 'The Loser Wins') and other novels, but is best remembered for his comedies of the Parisian bourgeoisie such as *La Veine* (1901, 'Luck').

▷ E Quet, *Alfred Capus* (1904)

CARAGIALE, Ion Luca
(1852–1912)

Romanian dramatist and short-story writer of Greek extraction who, owing to his quarrelsome and satirical nature, did not receive his full due in his lifetime. He removed himself and his family to Berlin, where he died, in 1904. **Mateiu Caragiale** was his illegitimate son. The communist regime favoured his work, pretending that it was Marxist in spirit. The Romanian theatre was lifeless in his day: he put life into it with ironic comedies such as *O scrisoare pierduta* (1884, Eng trans, with other plays, *The Lost Letter*, 1956), in which the bourgeois are mocked but in which the underlying theme of the human perils of 'modernization' remains potent. His sketches, usually very short, are unparalleled in their piercing accuracy and professionalism.

CARAGIALE, Mateiu
(1885–1936)

Romanian novelist and poet, illegitimate son of the famous dramatist **Ion Caragiale**, whose work was until quite recently largely unrecognized, even in his own country. *Remember* (1921)—the title is in English, but there is as yet no translation—is a strange story about the victimization of a homosexual, but bears signs of influence from 'decadent' French writers such as **Huysmans**. His masterpiece, *Craii de Curtea Veche* (1926–8, 'Knights of the Round Table'), however, is wholly original. It is said to have been in part inspired by his dislike of his father's 'straightforwardness', but this may be an oversimplification: his father, as an ironist, was hardly straightforward. It portrays, with great power and subtlety, a mad world of utterly degenerate aristocrats in a twilit Bucharest where East jostles with West. **Kafka**, could he have read it, would have revelled in it; but it is quintessentially Romanian. **Ion Barbu** was almost alone in his immediate recognition of its greatness.

CARCO, Francis, pseud of François Carcopino-Tusoli
(1886–1958)

French author, born in Nouméa in New Caledonia. He first gained recognition with his volume of poems *La Bohème et mon coeur* (1912, 'Bohemia and My Heart'), and added to his reputation with a series of novels chiefly set in Paris's Latin Quarter. He wrote a colourful account of his early life in *De Montmartre au Quartier latin* (1934, 'From Montmartre to the Latin Quarter').

▷ S Weiner, *Francis Carco, career of a literary Bohemian* (1952)

CARDARELLI, Vincenzo, pseud of Nazareno Calderelli
(1887–1959)

Italian poet, critic and editor, born in Corneto Tarquinia (now Tarquinia). He was an influential and useful critic, always opting for a commonsense approach (in the theory-ridden Italian context), and insisting that form alone could not make good poetry: it had to have something interesting to say. He was an editor at *La ronda* (which he founded in Rome together with **Bacchelli** and **Cecchi**), and of the weekly *La fiera letteraria*. He was an active opponent of both the Futurist movement and of Hermeticism when it became a school (after the critic Flores had named it as one). His poetry, modelled on that of **Petrarch** and **Leopardi**, is unusually coherent for its time, and is chiefly meditative and concerned with the passage of time.

▷ N J Perella, *Midday in Italian Literature* (1979)

CARDENAL, Ernesto
(1925–)

Nicaraguan poet, born in Granada. He was educated at the University of Mexico and Columbia University, New York. Later he became a Franciscan priest, and ran a small religious commune in the remote hinterlands of the country. His religious beliefs were a compound of Catholicism, native Indian myth and Buddhist precepts, and he was influenced by Jose Coronel Urtecho, an older Nicaraguan poet, and the American poet-priest **Thomas Merton**. His poetry is distinctly modernist in form and rhetorical in tone, and reflects both his religious and radical political commitments. He has published numerous collections, including *Epigramas: Poemas* (1961, 'Epigrams: Poems'), *Oracion por Marilyn Monroe* (1965, Eng trans *Marilyn Monroe*, 1975) and *Salmos* (1967, Eng trans *Psalms of Struggle and Liberation*, 1981). He also wrote a number of prose works, mainly on spiritual subjects.

CARDUCCI, Giosuè
(1835–1907)

Italian poet, winner of the Nobel Prize for literature, born in Valdicastello Pisa province, the son of a physician. In 1860 he became Professor of Italian literature at Bologna, and set a new standard in scholarship. In 1876 he was returned to the Italian parliament as a Republican, and in 1890 was nominated a senator. He published several volumes of verse, and was considered Italy's national poet for his patriotic vision of a revived Italy. He was awarded the Nobel Prize for literature in 1906.
▷J C Bailey, *Carducci* (1926)

CAREW, Jan
(1924–)

Guyanese novelist, who wrote vividly and with vigour of his own country, in *Black Midas* (1958) and *The Wild Coast* (1958), and of Harlem in *The Last Barbarian* (1961). He has also written outspoken travel books, such as *Moscow Is Not My Mecca* (1964).

CAREW, Thomas
(1595–1639)

English Cavalier poet, born in West Wickham, the son of a successful lawyer. He studied at Merton College, and entered the Inner Temple to study law in 1612. Between 1613 and 1616 he visited Holland as secretary to the ambassador, but was dismissed for slandering his employers. After three years in London he went to France in 1619–24, again as secretary to the ambassador. Afterwards he rose into high favour with Charles I. A friend of **Ben Jonson** and **John Donne**, he wrote polished lyrics in the Cavalier tradition, particularly the love poem 'Rapture'.

CAREY, Henry
(c.1690–1743)

English poet and musician, born in Yorkshire, believed to have been an illegitimate son of a member of the Savile family. He published his first volume of poems in 1713. He wrote innumerable songs, witty poems, burlesques, farces, and dramatic pieces, sometimes composing the accompanying music. His best-known poem is 'Sally in our Alley'.

CAREY, Peter
(1943–)

Australian novelist, born in Bacchus Marsh, Victoria. He attended Geelong Grammar School before beginning a career as an advertising copywriter, after which he lived for a spell in London. His first book, *The Fat Man in History* (1974), was a collection of short stories, and he was quickly regarded as an innovative force in Australian writing, breaking free from the mould of realism to experiment with modes as diverse as Absurdism, Surrealism, science fiction and fable. His next book, *Bliss* (1981), explored the advertising world. In 1985 he published *Illywhacker* (Australian slang for a trickster or conman), an imaginative tour de force which was shortlisted for the Booker Prize. He won the Booker Prize with *Oscar and Lucinda* (1988), an exuberant novel constructed on a Victorian scale, in which a compulsive gambler and a Sydney heiress fascinated with the manufacture of glass are bizarrely united. In 1991 he published *The Tax Inspector*.

CARLETON, William
(1794–1869)

Irish novelist, born in Prillisk, County Tyrone, of peasant birth, the youngest of 14 children. He became a tutor and writer in Dublin, contributing sketches to the *Christian Examiner*, republished as *Traits and Stories of the Irish Peasantry* (1830). A second series (1833) was just as well received. In 1839 he published a long novel, *Fardorougha the Miser*, which was followed by *The Black Prophet* (1847), about the Famine, *The Tithe Proctor* (1849), *The Squanders of Castle Squander* (1852), *The Evil Eye* (1860), and others.

CARLETON, Will(iam McKendree)
(1845–1912)

American poet, born in Hudson, Michigan. He graduated at Hillsdale College, Michigan, and wrote *Farm Ballads* (1875), *City Ballads* (1885) and other works.
▷B Kiely, *Poor Scholar: a study of the works and days of Will Carleton* (1947)

CARLYLE, Thomas
(1795–1881)

Scottish historian, essayist and sage, born in Ecclefechan, Dumfriesshire, the son of a stonemason (and later farmer). Brought up in a strictly Calvinist and Secessionist home, he was educated at Ecclefechan village school, Annan Academy and Edinburgh University, where he studied arts and mathematics. He then spent a year studying for the Secessionist Church in Edinburgh, but turned to teaching instead, initially at Annan Academy and then in Kirkcaldy (1816–18), where he met the revivalist minister Edward Irving, who became a lifelong friend. He moved back to Edinburgh in 1818 to study law, but turned to private tutoring. He wrote several articles for Sir David Brewster, Editor of the *Edinburgh Encyclopaedia*, and immersed himself in the study of German literature, publishing his first major essay, on **Goethe**'s *Faust*, in the

New Edinburgh Review (1822). He translated Legendre's *Elements of Geometry* from the French, and wrote an ambitious *Life of Schiller*, which was published in instalments in *The London Magazine* from October 1823 and in book form in 1825. His major work during this period was his translation of Goethe's *Wilhelm Meister*, which was published in 1824 and earned him the acquaintance of **Coleridge, Hazlitt, Thomas Campbell** and other literary figures in London. In 1825 he moved to the farm of Hoddam Hill in Dumfriesshire, where he prepared a four-volume collection of translations of various writers, *German Romance* (1827). In 1826 he married Jane Baillie Welsh, and settled in Edinburgh, where he wrote articles for Francis Jeffrey in the *Edinburgh Review*. However, in 1828 he moved to the estate of Craigenputtock, near Dumfries, which Jane had inherited. There he wrote articles for the *Edinburgh Review*, and a *History of German Literature* (subsequently published in a series of essays). He also wrote his first major work on social philosophy, *Sartor Resartus*, which was published in instalments in *Fraser's Magazine* in 1833–4; it was produced in book form in the USA in 1836 with an introduction by **Ralph Waldo Emerson**, who had visited Carlyle at Craigenputtock. It was partly a satirical discourse on the value of clothes by 'Professor Teufelsdröckh', and partly a semi-autobiographical discussion of creeds and human values. In 1834 the couple moved to London, where Carlyle spent the rest of his life. Here he completed his romantic history of *The French Revolution* (1837), despite the accidental burning of the manuscript of most of the first volume by John Stuart Mill's maidservant. He was now established as a man of letters, and engaged in a series of lectures, collected as *On Heroes, Hero Worship and the Heroic in History* (1841), which foreshadowed his advocacy of the view that a strong hero-figure as a nation's leader was the best remedy for society's ills. On this theme of strong, benevolent autocracy as the best form of protection of freedom he also wrote an important essay on *Chartism* (1839), and a major political essay, *Past and Present* (1843). In 1845 he published *Oliver Cromwell's Letters and Speeches*, which revolutionized contemporary attitudes to the Protector and his dictatorship. Another collection of essays, *Latter Day Pamphlets* (1850), highlighted his increasingly right-wing political attitudes, with their emphasis on duty, obedience and punishment. His most ambitious work was then published: a six-volume *History of... Frederick the Great* (1858–65), a compelling portrait of the practical autocrat as a heroic idealist. In 1866 Carlyle was installed as Lord Rector of Edinburgh University. His

wife died suddenly at this time, and he wrote little more except for a minor work, *The Early Kings of Norway* (1875). He edited and published his wife's letters and diaries in 1883, having already written an anguished memoir of her in his *Reminiscences* (1881). He refused an honour from **Disraeli**, and was buried at his own wish in Ecclefechan, not Westminster Abbey.

▷ J A Froude, *Thomas Carlyle: a history of his life* (1884)

CARMAN, (William) Bliss
(1861–1929)

Canadian poet, born in Fredericton, who left Canada as a student to study at Harvard, and later became a journalist in New York. His first volume, *Low Tide on Grand Pré*, appeared in 1893, after which he produced three books in collaboration with **Richard Hovey**. Carman's other books include *April Airs* (1916), *Far Horizons* (1925) and *Sanctuary* (1929). He also translated the lyrics of **Sappho** in 1904 and published several volumes of essays. Carman was considered an accessible and popular poet, although he appears less highly regarded now than he was during his lifetime.

CARMAN, Dulce
(1883–1970)

New Zealand author of popular romantic fiction, originally for periodicals, whose first book was *The Broad Stairway* (1924). Throughout her work (more than 20 books) the themes are generally simple; mixed blood, inheritance and the integration of Maoris into the Paheka (white settler) way of life are treated sympathetically but naively. Typical titles are *Neath the Maori Moon* (1948), *The Tapu Tree* (1954), *The Wailing Pool* (1961) and *The Maori Gateway* (1963).

CARMEN SYLVA, pseud of Elisabeth, Queen of Romania
(1843–1916)

The daughter of Prince Hermann of Wied Neuwied, she married King (then Prince) Carol I of Romania in 1869. Her only child, a daughter, died in 1874, and out of her sorrow arose her literary activity. Two poems, printed privately at Leipzig in 1880 under the name 'Carmen Sylva', were followed by *Stürme* (1881, 'Storms'), *Leidens Erdengang* (1882, Eng trans *Pilgrim Sorrow*, 1884), *Pensées d'une reine* (1882, 'Thoughts of a Queen'), *The Bard of Dimbovitza* (1891), *Meister Manole* (1892), and other works. In the war of 1877–8 she endeared herself to her people by her devotion to the wounded.

CARMI, T, pseud of **Charmi Charny**
(1925–)
American-born Israeli poet, educated at
Yeshiva University and Columbia University, New York, afterwards at the Sorbonne
in Paris. He emigrated to Israel in 1947 and
began to write poetry that combined literary
elements from the sacred tradition with
demotic speech. His first collection, *Mum
Vahalom* ('Tainted Vision'), appeared in
1951. During the fifties he worked in literary
journalism and publishing, later (1971–4)
editing the influential *Ariel*. *Nehash Hanehoshet* (1961) was the first to be translated
into English (by **Dom Moraes** as the *Brass
Serpent* in 1964); a *Selected Poems*, translated
by Stephen Mitchell, appeared in London in
1976. Five years later, Carmi made an even
greater impact on English-speaking readers
and on international understanding of his cultural tradition when he edited the *Penguin
Book of Hebrew Verse* (1981). He has adapted
plays by **Shakespeare**, **Brecht**, **Christopher
Fry**, **Tom Stoppard** and others.

CARNER, Josep
(1884–1970)
Catalan poet and essayist. He was born in
Barcelona, and pursued a career as a diplomat until the advent of the Franco dictatorship, which he opposed. His masterpiece is
the long narrative poem on the Jonah-and-the-Whale theme, *Nabí*, containing such magnificent lines as 'Goodbye, though, great clusters of greed and punishment!' Carner has
not been translated, but it is often said that
he is worth learning Catalan for. If any single
man is responsible for the miraculous Catalan
linguistic reintegration, then it is Carner,
whose collected works were published in
1968. He died in exile in Brussels.
▷A H Terry, *Catalan Literature* (1972)

CARO, José Eusebio
(1817–53)
Colombian poet, born in Ocaña, his country's
outstanding representative of liberalism and
romanticism. His son Miguel (1843–1909),
also a writer, became President of Colombia.
He was at first influenced by **Byron**, but then
became a devout Christian. His poetry is now
more valued for its technical proficiency than
for its content.

CAROSSA, Hans
(1878–1956)
German writer and physician, born in Tölz.
A doctor in Bavaria, he became prominent
with *Eine Kindheit* (1922, 'A Childhood'), the
first of an autobiographical sequence which
also includes *Rumänisches Tagebuch* (1924,

'Romanian Journal'), a war diary, and *Verwandlungen einer Jugend* (1928, 'Transformations of a Youth'), which consciously
echoed the life-affirming example of his literary master, **Goethe**. He wrote several
novels, such as *Doktor Bürgers Ende* (1913,
'The End of Dr Bürger'), *Das Jahr der
schönen Täuschungen* (1941, 'The Year of
Beautiful Deceits') and *Ungleiche Welten*
(1951, 'Different Worlds'), and some poems.
▷A Haveis, *Hans Carossa* (1935)

CARPENTIER, Alejo
(1904–80)
Cuban novelist, born in Havana. For many
years he lived in France and Venezuela but
he returned to Cuba after the revolution and
served in several official government posts,
though some critics find the political messages in his novels at best ambiguous. One
of the major Latin-American writers of this
century, his numerous books include *El siglo
de las luces* (1962, Eng trans *Explosion in a
Cathedral*, 1963), *El reino de este mundo*
(1949, Eng trans *The Kingdom of this World*,
1957) and *Los pasos perdidos* (1953, Eng trans
The Lost Steps, 1956).
▷R Gonzalez Echevarria, *Carpentier: the pilgrim at home* (1977)

CARR, Emily
(1871–1945)
Canadian 'autobiographical' writer, and
painter, born in Victoria, British Columbia.
She studied painting in San Francisco, London and Paris, and is best known for her
representations of the West Coast Indian and
British Columbian forest; her first book of
short stories, *Klee Wyck* (1941), related her
impressions of the West Coast Indians, and
won a Governor General's Award. It was
followed by a number of further 'autobiographical' writings, including *The Book of
Small* (1942), *The House of All Sorts* (1944)
and *Growing Pains* (1946). Selections from
Carr's journals were published posthumously
as *Hundreds and Thousands* (1966). She has
been described as a 'Canadian cultural icon',
and her writings have been used extensively to
write further biography, but they have been
neglected as literary texts in their own right.
▷S H Elderkin, 'Recovering the Fictions of
Emily Carr', *WLWE*, 17:2 (1992/3)

CARR, J(ames) L(loyd)
(1912–)
English novelist and publisher, born at
Carlton Miniott, Yorkshire. A former
teacher, wartime Intelligence Officer and
headmaster (from 1951 to 1967, of a school
in Northamptonshire), Carr's first novel, *A
Day in Summer*, appeared in 1964. He has

since published several novels casting a wry, sympathetic, often quirky and sometimes sorrowful eye on everyday life and personal tragedy. Titles include *How Steeple Sinderby Wanderers Won the FA Cup* (1975) and *The Battle of Pollocks Crossing* (1985). His finest work is the elegiac *A Month in the Country* (1980), set in a north of England village in the summer of 1920; in it Carr sensitively examines the relationship of two survivors of World War I: Birkin, who arrives to restore a wall painting in the local church, and Moon, an enigmatic character camping in the adjacent field.

CARR, John Dickson
(1905–77)

American novelist, born in Uniontown, Pennsylvania, an exponent of detective fiction during its so-called 'golden age', the 1930s and 40s. The author of over 70 novels, Carr pioneered the 'locked room' mystery, the principles of which are described in his first book, *It Walks By Night* (1929). The room in which the murder was committed had 'no secret entrances; the murderer was not hiding anywhere in the room; he did not go out by the window; he did not go out by the ... door ... Yet a murderer *had* beheaded his victim there'. Carr's finest novel is perhaps *The Hollow Man* (1931), featuring his most enduring detective, Dr Gideon Fell, a portly, learned, rather dandyish Edwardian figure, partly modelled on **G K Chesterton**. Under the name Carter Dickson, he wrote over 20 novels in which the detective is the more buffoonish Sir Henry Merrivale.

CARRASQUILLA, Tomás
(1858–1940)

Colombian novelist, born in Santodomingo, Antioquia. His racy, lively work, done for his own satisfaction rather than for that of the public, is distinguished by its lack of pompous moralizing and its profound insight into human beings represented as animals—he is one of the most important of all the many South American novelists, the substance of whose work has not yet been translated into English. His first book was *Frutos de mi tierra* (1896, Eng trans *Fruits of My Earth*, 1972), in which, within its framework of city men outsmarting innocent provincials, he develops his technique. His novels include the historical *La marquesa de Yolombó* (1926, 'The Marquesa of Yolombo'), and the long *Hace tiempos* (1935–6, 'Waiting'), which he dictated during a period of blindness and which is his greatest—but still most neglected—novel. It is now gradually being understood that a few of the characteristics of his writings which have been taken as faults—

digressions, apparent anachronisms, didacticisms—probably concealed a superior art. His collected works appeared in 1958.

▷K L Levy, *Vida y obras de Tomás Carrasquilla* (1958)

CARRERA ANDRADE, Jorge
(1903–78)

Ecuadorean poet, born in Quito. Called 'one of the most original Latin-American poets of the 20th century', and certainly one of the best known, Carrera Andrade was a diplomat by profession. His first poetry was in the *modernista* vein of **Darío**, but he soon broke with this 'world of artificial paradises', and his first collection, *Estanque inefable* (1922, 'Ineffable Pond'), consisted of mostly rural poems. He helped to found the Ecuadorean Socialist Party in 1926. In a long career as a diplomat, much of it spent abroad, Carrera Andrade absorbed the influences of **Pound**, **Williams** (who described his poetry as a 'sad pleasure but a great one') and French poets such as **Valéry**; he also adapted the Japanese haiku into Spanish. His poetry has been translated in *To the Bay Bridge* (1941), *Visitor of Mist* (1950), *Secret Country* (1946), and in (the most substantial) *Selected Poems* (1972). His *Reflections on Spanish American Poetry* appeared in the USA in 1972.

▷A Flores, *The Literature of Spanish America* (1966–9)

CARRIÈRE, Jean-Claude
(1931–)

French writer, actor and director, born in Colombières-sur-Orbes. An association with comedy director Pierre Étaix brought his first involvement with the cinema as co-director of the short films *Rupture* (1961) and *Heureux Anniversaire* (1961, 'Happy Anniversary'). *Le Journal D'Une Femme De Chambre* (1964, 'The Diary of a Chambermaid') was the first of six films he wrote in collaboration with Luis Buñuel that revealed a dry, dark humour and ability to dissect the social and sexual hypocrisies of the middle-classes. Their subsequent collaborations include *Belle De Jour* (1967), *Le Charme Discrèt De La Bourgeoisie* (1972, 'The Discreet Charm of the Bourgeoisie') and *Cet Obscur Objet Du Désir* (1977, 'That Obscure Object of Desire'). A prolific scenarist whose work is often laced with a sense of anti-authoritarianism and irony, his many screenplays include *The Tin Drum* (1979), *Danton* (1982), *The Unbearable Lightness Of Being* (1988) and *Cyrano De Bergerac* (1990). A novelist, he has also written for television and the theatre, most notably for Peter Brooks's company.

CARROLL, Lewis, pseud of **Charles Lutwidge Dodgson**
(1832–98)

English writer, nonsense versifier and mathematician, born in Daresbury, near Warrington, the third of 11 children. His pseudonym derived from his first two names: Lutwidge is the same as Lutwig, of which Lewis is the anglicized version, and Carroll is a form of Charles. Throughout his childhood, with his siblings he invented and played many board games, acrostics and other puzzles. He was educated at Rugby and Christ Church, Oxford, where he lectured in mathematics after 1855 and took orders in 1861. *Alice's Adventures in Wonderland* (1865), his most famous book, had its origin in a boat trip which he made with Alice Liddell and her sisters, Lorina and Edith, the daughters of the Dean of his college, Henry George Liddell, 'all in the golden afternoon' of 4 July 1862. Originally he intended calling it *Alice's Adventures Underground*. A sequel, *Through the Looking-Glass and What Alice Found There*, appeared in 1871. Illustrated by Sir John Tenniel, both are superficially similar: in each Alice meets a succession of fantastic characters (Tweedledee and Tweedledum, the White Rabbit and the March Hare, Humpty-Dumpty), and each ends grandly, one with a trial, the other with a banquet. Each has been translated into many languages and there have been innumerable editions, many illustrated by distinguished artists. Their success among Victorian children was doubtless due to the fact that Carroll eschewed moralizing. His other works include *Phantasmagoria and other poems* (1869), *The Hunting of the Snark* (1876), *Rhyme? and Reason?* (1883) and *Sylvie and Bruno* (1889 and 1893). Of his mathematical works *Euclid and his Modern Rivals* (1879) is still of interest. He was also a pioneer photographer, and took many portraits of young girls with whom he seemed to empathize particularly. *The Diaries of Lewis Carroll* appeared in 1953, and an edition of his letters in 1979.
▷D Hudson, *Lewis Carroll: a biography* (1952)

CARROLL, Paul Vincent
(1900–68)

Irish playwright, born in County Louth, who established his name when the Abbey Theatre put on his *Shadow and Substance* (1937). This was followed by *The White Steed* (1939). After these successes his career went rather into decline, and he became overshadowed by his compatriot **Sean O'Casey**. With **James Bridie** he founded the Glasgow Citizens' Theatre (1943). *Shadow and Substance*, his acknowledged masterpiece, memorably portrays Irish bigotry.

▷P Kavanagh, *The Story of the Abbey Theatre* (1950)

CARRUTH, Hayden
(1921–)

American poet and critic, born in Waterbury, Connecticut. Carruth's reputation as an editor and critic has sometimes overshadowed his eminence as a poet. He published his first collection, *The Crow and the Heart 1946–1959*, in 1959, and has published steadily since. His *Selected Poems* appeared in 1986. But while his supporters point to the precision and vitality of his verse, others contend that the body of his work is inconsistent. All are agreed, though, that his most powerful poetry draws upon personal experience. *The Bloomingdale Papers* (1975) is a long poem written during the 1950s while Carruth was confined to a mental hospital as a consequence of alcoholism and a nervous breakdown; one of his more personal compositions, it is also one of his more profound.

CARSTAIRS, John Paddy, real name **John Keys**
(1914–70)

British novelist, film director, filmscript writer and artist. He studied art at the Slade School, and painted several light-hearted landscapes in various media. His best-known novel is *Love and Ella Rafferty* (1947).
▷*Honest Injun, a light hearted autobiography* (1942)

CARSWELL, Catherine Roxburgh, née **Macfarlane**
(1879–1946)

Scottish novelist and critic, born in Glasgow, the daughter of a merchant. Educated at the Park School, Glasgow, and in Frankfurt-am-Main, she became a socialist after reading Robert Blatchford at the age of 17, and went on to study English at Glasgow University. Her first marriage was annulled after her husband attempted to kill her. She married fellow journalist and critic Donald Carswell in 1917. She made her reputation as a dramatic and literary critic for the *Glasgow Herald* from 1907 to 1915 but lost this position when she wrote a review of **D H Lawrence**'s banned novel *The Rainbow*. Lawrence encouraged her to complete her autobiographical novel of Glasgow life *Open the Door* (1920), a work depicting a young woman's escape from the confinement of a middle-class, Calvinistic Glasgow family. Lawrence also encouraged her to emphasize Burns's passionate nature in her *The Life of Burns* (1930). She hoped to bring **Robert Burns** 'out of the mist they loved to keep about him', but the work was unfavourably received by Burns scholars in

Scotland. She also wrote biographies of Lawrence, *The Savage Pilgrim: A Narrative of D.H. Lawrence* (1932), and Boccaccio, *The Tranquil Heart* (1937), but is best remembered as a critic.

▷ *Lying Awake: an unfinished autobiography* (1952)

CARTER, Angela Olive, née Stalker
(1940–92)

English novelist and essayist, born in Eastbourne. Educated at Bristol University, she taught Creative Writing in England, the USA and Australia, and lived in Japan for two years, an experience recorded in *Nothing Sacred* (1982). Her fiction is characterized by imaginative use of fantasy, surrealism, genre pastiche, vibrant humour and psychological symbolism. Novels include *The Magic Toyshop* (1967), *Heroes and Villains* (1969), *The Passion of New Eve* (1977), *Nights at the Circus* (1985) and *Wise Children* (1991), while her stories are collected in *Fireworks* (1974), *The Bloody Chamber* (1979), *Black Venus* (1985) and *American Ghosts & Old World Wonders* (1993). *The Sadeian Woman* (1979) is a feminist reinterpretation of the Marquis de Sade. She also wrote poetry, tales for children, radio plays, and translated fairy tales. She wrote the screenplay for the film *The Company of Wolves* (1984) with **Neil Jordan**.

CARTER, Martin Wylde
(1927–)

Guyanese poet, born in Georgetown, British Guiana, and educated at Queen's College, Georgetown. He spent some time in prison for anti-colonial activities, which resulted in *Poems of Resistance* (1954). After Guyana became independent, he was prominent in the Forbes Burnham government as Minister of Public Information and Broadcasting. His frequent theme is the burning desire for liberation. In 'The Great Dark' he highlights the dilemma of the poet up against the fact that words alone cannot bring about a better world, 'caught as I am/in the great dark of the bright connection of words'. His principal collections include *Poems of Succession* (1977) and *Poems of Affinity* (1980).

CARTLAND, Dame (Mary) Barbara Hamilton
(1901–)

English popular romantic novelist, born in Edgbaston, Birmingham, and step-grandmother of Diana, Princess of Wales. She published her first novel, *Jigsaw*, in 1923, and has since produced well over 400 bestselling books, mostly novels of chaste romantic love designed for women readers, but also including biographies and books on food, health

and beauty, and several volumes of autobiography. She earned a place in the *Guinness Book of Records* for writing 26 books in the year 1983. An ardent advocate of health foods and fitness for the elderly, she has championed causes like the St John's Ambulance Brigade and the provision of camp-sites for Romany gipsies. She was appointed DBE in 1991.

▷ *The Years of Opportunity, 1939–1945* (1948)

CARTWRIGHT, William
(1611–43)

English playwright, poet, and preacher, born in Northway, near Tewkesbury. He preached at Oxford, and wrote plays such as *The Royal Slave*, which was performed at Oxford before Charles I in 1636, and a play ridiculing Puritans, *The Ordinary*. He was one of the group of young playwrights known as the 'sons' of **Ben Jonson**.

▷ A Chalmers, 'A Life', in *The Works of Early English Poets* (1810)

CARVALHO, Vicente
(1866–1924)

Brazilian poet, born in São Paulo. Carvalho was a traditional poet, a so-called 'Parnassian', who wrote one collection that has remained in print: *Poemas e Canções* (1906, 'Poems and Songs'). He is seldom included in anthologies of Brazilian poetry in translation.

▷ M Bandeira, *A Brief History of Brazilian Literature* (1958)

CARVER, Raymond
(1939–88)

American poet and short-story writer, born in Clatskanie, Oregon. He married at 18 and struggled for many years to provide for a young family and further his career as a writer. He also fought against chronic alcoholism. His first published story, 'Pastoral', was accepted by the *Western Humanities Review*. His collections include *Will You Please Be Quiet, Please?* (1976), *What We Talk About When We Talk About Love* (1981) and *Cathedral* (1983). Both his fiction and his poetry are remarkable for their spare narratives, focusing on a society of the lower and middle classes and dealing with people in a state of transition: couples breaking up, people between jobs, between sleeping and wakefulness. He wrote no novels. He was a Guggenheim Fellow in 1979 and was twice awarded grants by the National Endowment for Arts. He taught at the University of Iowa, the University of Texas and the University of California. Other books include *Fire: Essays, Poems, Stories* (1984), and books of poems: *Where Water Comes Together with Other*

Water (1985) and *Ultramarine* (1985). *In A Marine Light: Selected Poems* and *Elephant and Other Stories* appeared in the year he died.

CARY, Alice
(1820–71)

American poet and novelist, born in Cincinnati, Ohio, and sister of Phoebe Cary, another noted poet, with whom she worked closely. She was first published in her early teens and went on to produce three volumes of poetry: *Lyra* (1852), *Poems* (1855) and *Ballads, Lyrics, Hymns* (1866). Abandoned or alienated women often figure in her poetry and a sense of despair pervades much of her work. In addition to her poetry, Cary wrote novels, sketches, and children's books. She is best remembered for her 'Clovernook' series of sketches (1852), which focus on farming communities. She and Phoebe established a literary salon which gained attention from many of the leading literary personalities of the era.

CARY, (Arthur) Joyce Lunel
(1888–1957)

English novelist, born in Londonderry of English parents. He was educated at Tunbridge Wells and Clifton College and later studied art in Edinburgh and Paris, graduating (1912) at Oxford. He then served with the Red Cross in the Balkan war of 1912–13 and was decorated by the King of Montenegro. In 1913 he joined the Nigerian Political Service and fought in a Nigerian regiment in World War I. War injuries and ill-health dictated his early retirement after the war to Oxford, where he took up writing. Out of his African experiences emerge such novels as *Aissa Saved* (1932), *African Witch* (1936) and *Mister Johnson* (1939), a high-spirited, richly humorous study of a native clerk. In 1941 he was awarded the James Tait Black Memorial Prize for *The House of Children*, and established himself with the trilogy, *Herself Surprised* (1940), *To be a Pilgrim* (1942) and *The Horse's Mouth* (1944), which explores the art world in memorably comic fashion. These were followed by *Moonlight* (1946) and *A Fearful Joy* (1949), and a later trilogy on the life of Chester Nimmo, a politician, *Prisoner of Grace* (1952), *Except the Lord* (1953) and *Not Honour More* (1955), and finally an unfinished novel with a religious theme, *The Captive and the Free* (1959).
▷W Allen, *Joyce Cary* (1953)

CASA, Giovanni della
(1503–56)

Italian author and prelate, born near Florence. He was appointed archbishop of Benevento in 1544. He is remembered for stylish lyric verse, and *Il Galateo ovvero De' Costumi* (1558, 'The Book of Etiquette or of Good Manners').
▷M Richter, *Giovanni della Casa in Francia nel seculo XVI* (1966)

CASACCIA, Gabriel
(1907–80)

Paraguayan novelist, dramatist and story writer, second in importance in his country only to **Roa Bastos** (who has called him 'a founding father'). He was born in Itacurubi, into an Italian immigrant family called Bibolini (which name he dropped when he began to publish in 1930). He studied law and then served the government until the end of the Chaco War, when he left Paraguay for Posadas (1935) in Argentina. From 1951 he lived in Buenos Aires, where he died. His stories— for example those collected in *El pozo* (1947, 'The Well')—have been compared to those of **Kafka**. But his novels, with *La babosa* (1952, 'The Slug') and *Los exiliados* (1966, 'The Exiles') outstanding amongst them, represent, as Roa Bastos has written, the foundations 'of the modern Paraguayan narrative'. He is unlucky to have escaped the attention of translators.
▷*Journal of Inter-American Studies and World Affairs* (1, 1970)

CASAL, Julián del
(1863–93)

Cuban poet, born in Havana. For most of his brief life—he suffered from tuberculosis—he lived in seclusion, modelling himself on the French Parnassian poets, such as **Heredia**, who influenced him immensely. In his context he is a precursor of *modernismo*, and he met **Darío** himself during his last year. His *fin de siècle* mood and his high accomplishment made a deep impression on his contemporaries and immediate successors. Two poems are translated in the *Penguin Book of Latin American Verse* (1971, ed E Curacciolo-Trejo).

CASEY, Gavin Stodart
(1907–64)

Australian novelist and short-story writer, born in Kalgoorlie, Western Australia. He published two collections, *It's Harder for Girls* (1942) and *Birds of a Feather* (1943). In the laconic and alcoholic mateship style of **Henry Lawson**, his tales draw much on his experiences as a newspaper reporter in the Kalgoorlie goldfields during the Depression, and were later reissued as *Short Shift Saturday and Other Stories* (1973). As a journalist he worked in New York and then returned to Canberra and Sydney where he wrote a couple of humorous books. More substantial novels were *City of Men* (1950), a family saga of the West Australian goldfields; the conflict of half-caste aborigines and white inhabitants of a small town were dealt with in *Snowball* (1962) and *The Man Whose Name was Mud* (1963), again set in the goldfields.

▷D Casey, *Casey's Wife* (1982)

CASIA, or IKASIA
(fl.first half of 9th century)

Byzantine author of verse epigrams, born into a prestigious family. She spent most of her life in a convent, and was known for her harsh tongue.

CASONA, Alejandro, pseud of Alejandro Rodriguez Alvarez
(1903–65)

Spanish dramatist, who began as a poet, and then became director of the Teatro del Pueblo ('Theatre of the People') in 1931; he was born in the Asturias. His plays of the 1930s, grouped together as *teatro de evasión* ('theatre of evasion'), were influential—and, later, in the 1950s, were played all over eastern Europe. He fled to Buenos Aires in 1939, having angered the Falangists with his *Nuestro Natacha* (1936, 'Our Natacha'), about a reforming woman educator. He was allowed to return to Madrid in 1962. His famous and sarcastic *Prohibido suicidarse en primavera* (1937, 'It is forbidden to commit suicide in spring') is translated in *Masterpieces of Modern Spanish Theatre* (1967, ed Robert W Corrigan).

CASSILL, R(onald) V(erlin)
(1919–)

American novelist and short-story writer, born in Cedar Falls, Iowa. Educated at Iowa University, where he later taught creative writing, he published *Eagle on the Coin*, his first novel, in 1950. Cassill is a moralist with an instinctive sense of narrative, whose recurring themes are the nature of power and love, and the relationship between the private individual and the public event. *A Taste of Sin* (1956), *The President* (1964) and *Labors of Love* (1980) are representative works.

CASSOLA, Carlo
(1917–90)

Italian novelist from Rome. While still a student, Cassola already took up an anti-fascist position; after the fall of Mussolini he became a member of the extreme left. His early, almost minimalist stories of 1942 attracted some attention because they harked back to the 'crepuscular' tone of some 50 years earlier, and because by implication they rejected fascist and Futurist rhetoric. Two novels, *Fausto e Anna* (1952, rev edn 1958, Eng trans 1960) and *La ragazza di Bebo* (1960, Eng trans *Bebo's Girl*, 1962), were considered to be 'neorealistic' because they dealt with World War II and because they reflected the influence of such Americans as **Hemingway** and **Faulkner**. His best novel has long been considered to be *Il taglio del bosco* (1950, Eng trans *The Cutting of the Woods*, 1960), which had its source in the author's grief over the loss of his wife in 1949. In his later work, generally thought to be somewhat inferior, Cassola tried to widen his range to include a fuller treatment of female characters.

▷*Italica 54* (1977)

CASTELLANOS, Juan de
(1522–1607)

Spanish poet, born in Alanís, Seville. He led the life of a soldier until, after taking holy orders, he settled down as prebendary of Tunja, in Colombia, amongst the Chubcha Indians. He is famous for the long epic *Elegías de Varones Illustres e Indias*, about the Spanish conquest and the conquistadores. It is an imitation of the *La Araucana* of **Alonso de Ercilla**, and, while of great interest, is markedly inferior as poetry. It is to be found in Castellanos's *Obras completas* (1953, 'Complete Works').

CASTELLANOS, Rosario
(1925–74)

Mexican poet, novelist, story writer and translator, born in Mexico City, one of the great Latin-American writers of her century. Her early work, described by one influential critic, perhaps not insignificantly, as 'insubstantial and feminine', was in fact full of promise and interest; but she did not develop her full powers until *Poemas 1953–5* (1957), published at the height of her close involvement with the Native Americans of Chialas, where she had spent her childhood and adolescence: her theme, that in such conquered and suffering peoples lies the only residue of hope in a world 'civilized' in the name of barbarism, is movingly expressed. Several of these works are translated in *The Selected Poems of Rosario Castellanos* (1988). Many of her novels and stories have been translated, including *Balún-canán* (1957, Eng trans *The Nine Guardians*, 1958), about the break-up of the old ways under the impact of the reforms of Lázaro Cárdenas. Rosario Castellanos, on a visit to Israel, was electrocuted while trying to change a light bulb.

▷M Allgood, *A Rosario Castellanos Reader* 1988; D Meyer and M F Olmos (eds), *Contemporary Women Authors of Latin America: Introductory Essays* (1983)

CASTELLI, Ignaz Franz
(1781–1862)

Austrian poet, born in Vienna. He wrote *Kriegeslieder für die österreichische Armee*

(1809, 'War Songs for the Austrian Army'), which was banned by Napoleon.

CASTELO BRANCO, Camilo, Visconde de Correia Botelho
(1825–90)

Portuguese novelist. An illegitimate child whose love of literature and longing for adventure grew from his reading, he became one of the most important of modern Portuguese novelists, with a deep understanding of the life of his people. His work ranges from romances like *Mysterios de Lisboa* (1958, 'The Mysteries of Lisbon'), to closely observed, imaginative interpretations of the everyday Portuguese scene, such as *The Crime of Father Amara*. He was created viscount for his services to literature in 1885. He committed suicide.

▷ A Pimentel, *O Torturado de Seide* (1921)

CASTI, Giambattista
(c.1721–1803)

Italian poet, born in Prato, Tuscany. He took holy orders, but in 1764 went to Vienna, where he became poet laureate. On Joseph II's death he returned to Florence, and in 1798 went to Paris. He wrote the *48 Novelle galanti* (1793), and *Gli animali parlanti* (1802, 'The Talking Animals'), a political satire.

▷ H van den Bergh, *Giambattista Casti, l'homme et l'oeuvre* (1951)

CASTIGLIONE, Baldassare, Count
(1478–1529)

Italian courtier and writer, born near Mantua. In 1505 he was sent by the Duke of Urbino as envoy to Henry VII of England, who made him a knight, and was later Mantuan ambassador at the papal court in Rome (1513–24). Thereafter he was papal nuncio for Pope Clement VII in Spain, from 1524. His chief work, *Il Cortegiano* (1528, 'The Courtier'), is a manual for courtiers, in dialogue form, and was translated into English by Sir Thomas Hoby in 1561. His Italian and Latin poems are models of elegance. His Letters (1769–71) illustrate political and literary history.

▷ J Cartwright, *Baldassare Castiglione, his life and letters* (1908)

CASTILHO, António Feliciano de
(1800–75)

Portuguese poet and translator, blind from the age of six, born in Lisbon. His soft, perhaps somewhat vacuous, neo-classical poetry still has a place in Portuguese poetry today. He was and is a controversial figure, since he became a virtual dictator in Portuguese letters. He made smooth translations of many classics, including one of Goethe's *Faust*, which he took from a French version, and which bears no resemblance to the German original. His authority was finally broken by younger writers, in particular Quental: de Castilho had shown his preference for a long ultra-romantic poem called *D. Jaime* (by Thomaz Ribiero) over the *Lusiades* of Camoens, and in the so-called *Questão Coimbra* (Coimbra Dispute), of 1865, a complex pamphlet-row between younger and older poets about the virtues of romanticism, Quental tore him to pieces.

▷ A F G Bell, *Portuguese Literature* (1922)

CASTILLEJO, Cristóbal de
(c.1490–1550)

Spanish poet, born in Ciudad Rodrigo. It is thought he became a Cistercian monk in 1515, later going into the service of the Archduke Ferdinand, which allowed him to travel throughout Spain and Europe on court business. However, although a monk, he was apparently not celibate and his poetry was often dedicated to women. In fact his first poetry to be printed (1573) had to be amended to avoid trouble with the Inquisition. His works were divided into three categories: those dealing with love ('de amor'), with conversation ('de conversación y pasatiempos'), and with morals and devotion ('de morales y de devoción'). Outstanding in the former is the 'Sermón de Amores' (1542) about one who loves and is not loved, and the bittersweetness of requited love. The 'Beatus Ille' is one of the best of the second category. He also wrote a misogynistic piece entitled the 'Dialogo de Mujeres' (1544, 'Dialogue of Women'). Castillejo's talent lay in successfully fusing medieval and Renaissance thought, adapting it to traditional moulds and forms of expression. His best poetry is considered as skilled as that of Garcilaso de la Vega.

CASTRO ALVES, Antônio de
(1847–71)

Brazilian poet, born in Muritiba, Bahia, the chief representative of *Condoreira* (a style symbolic of the condor's grandeur of flight). His life was as ultra-romantic as his poetry, which, influenced by that of Hugo, celebrated his loves and his fervent hatred of the slave trade. His degree of literary merit has been the subject of controversy; but his sincerity and burning resentment of injustice have endeared him to many modern readers. His best verse is direct and simple.

▷ F P de Barros, *Poesia e vida de Castro Alves* (1962)

CASTRO, Eugenio de
(1869–1944)

Portuguese poet, born in Coimbra. He became Professor of Portuguese literature in his native town and travelled widely in Europe. In Paris he became interested in Symbolism, and introduced that movement to Portuguese writing in his poetry, beginning with *Oaristos* (1890). Although derided at first, his work eventually became influential, although his own later work reflected a return to more classical forms, and a growing fascination with folklore.

CASTRO, Guillén de
(1569–1631)

Spanish dramatist, born in Valencia. He commanded a Neapolitan fortress, but later lived in Madrid, and died in poverty. His early works were romantic comedies, before he turned to epic subjects, notably in *La Mocedades del Cid* (c.1600), which formed the basis for **Corneille**'s *Le Cid*. His other works include a realistic play about an unhappy marriage, *Los mal cascados de Valencia*, and dramatizations of works by **Cervantes**.

▷ W E Wilson, *Guillén de Castro* (1973)

CASTRO, Rosalía de
(1837–85)

Spanish poet and novelist, born in Santiago de Compostela. Her earliest works, such as the poetry collection *La Flor* (1857, 'The Flower'), were written in Spanish, but it is on her later volumes in Galician that her fame rests. *Cantares Gallegos* (1863, 'Galician Songs') and the later *Follas Novas* (1880, 'New Leaves') place her among the most significant poets of the 19th century. Her novels, written in Spanish, brought her to the attention of a wider public; they include *La Hija del Mar* (1859, 'The Daughter of the Sea') and *Ruinas* (1867, 'Ruins'). Despite the currently perilous position of Galician—it receives official support, but the number of mothertongue speakers is declining—de Castro's reputation as a poet appears secure.

CATALÀ, Victor, pseud of Caterina Albert i Paradís
(1869–1966)

Catalan writer. Born in L'Escala, a fishing village near the Catalan French border, Català published her first book, the poetry collection *El Cant del Mesos* ('Song of the Months'), in 1901. She followed this with several volumes of short stories and, in 1905, the psychological novel *Solitud*, a richly atmospheric story of a young bride's experiences and growing self-awareness in an isolated hermitage in the Pyrenees. Although continuing to write and publish—including a second novel, *Caires Vius* ('Living Aspects'), in 1907—Català largely withdrew from the public eye after the success of her first novel.

Unpublished during the Francoist suppression of Catalan writing, her work suffered critical neglect for many years, but she has recently begun to reattract attention as a pioneer of modernist literature, and her writing has been translated into many languages.

CATHER, Willa Sibert
(1873–1947)

American fiction writer, poet and journalist, born on a farm near Winchester, Virginia. Her formative years were spent in Nebraska, and after university there (1891–5), her career began with a well-written but not significant volume of poetry, *April Twilights* (1903). She moved to New York as Editor of *McClure's* magazine (1906–12). After her first novel, *Alexander's Bridge* (1912), she wrote three novels dealing with immigrants to the USA: *O Pioneers!* was published in 1913 and *The Song of the Lark* two years later. The third, *My Ántonia* (1918), is generally regarded as her best book. A homosexual who wrote primarily about independent women, she was a prolific writer, and other novels include *Death Comes for the Archbishop* (1927) and *One of Ours* (1922), which won the Pulitzer Prize.

▷ P C Robinson, *Willa: the life of Cather* (1983)

CATLIN, George
(1796–1872)

American artist and author, born in Wilkes-Barre, Pennsylvania. He studied law, but soon turned to drawing and painting. During 1832–40 he was studying the Native Americans of the Far West, everywhere painting portraits (470 full length) and pictures illustrative of life and manners, now in the National Museum at Washington. He spent eight years in Europe with a Far West show; travelled (1852–7) in South and Central America; and again lived in Europe until 1871. His works include *Manners of the North American Indians* (2 vols, 1841), *The North American Portfolio* (1844), and *Last Rambles in the Rocky Mountains* (1868).

▷ R Plate, *Palette and Tomahawk: the story of George Catlin* (1962)

CATO, Dionysius
(?4th century)

Traditional name of the Roman author of a volume of 164 moral precepts in Latin hexameters, known as *Dionysii Catonis disticha de moribus ad filium* ('Couplets on Morals, to his Son'), which was a great favourite during the Middle Ages. An English version by Benedict Burgh was printed by **William Caxton** before 1479.

▷Plutarch, *Life of Cato* in *Works*, D Wyttenbach (ed) (1795–1830)

CATO, Nancy Fotheringham
(1917–)

Australian novelist, poet and short-story writer, born in Adelaide. Her prime achievement is the trilogy of historical novels set along the banks of the Murray River, which forms a continuous counterpoint to her narrative. *All the Rivers Run* (1958) was followed by *Time, Flow Softly* (1959) and *But Still the Stream* (1962). These were later rewritten and published in 1978 under the title *All the Rivers Run* and became a popular television series. *Forefathers* (1983) follows the fortunes through seven generations of three interlinked families. Other significant novels are *North-West by South* (1964), on the last years of Arctic explorer Sir John Franklin, and a fey historical novel *Lady Lost in Time* (1985). She has also published poetry, a book for children, and, in *Mister Maloga* (1976, rev edn 1993), the biography of an aboriginal missionary.

CATS, Jacob
(1577–1660)

Enormously popular Dutch poet and statesman, born in the Hague. A lawyer by training, he was at various times the Dutch ambassador to England. Vader Cats ('Father Cats') was a homely Calvinist, whose often wildly unconventional poetry more or less ignored the Renaissance. He was a rich man through his ownership of drainage works in both Holland and England. He was not, as has been frequently emphasized by critics, a great poet—but he was much read. Although fussy and, by today's standards, often absurdly didactic, he was above all a born storyteller.
▷G Derudder, *Un poète néerlandais, Cats, sa vie et ses Oeuvres* (1898)

CATULLUS, Gaius Valerius
(c.84–c.54 BC)

Roman lyric poet, born in Verona, the son of a wealthy and well-connected family. He lived mainly in Rome, where he settled about 62 BC, and in his villas at Tibur and Sirmio. He began to write verses when a boy of 16. In Rome he became friendly with **Cicero**, the Metelli, Hortensius, and probably **Lucretius**; and in Rome he met 'Lesbia', a married woman to whom he addressed verses unequalled in the lyric poetry of passion. A final rupture seems to have happened in 57BC, and in that year he accompanied the governor, Memmius, to his province of Bithynia. A fiery, unscrupulous partisan, he assailed his enemies, including **Caesar**, with equal scurrility and wit. His extant works comprise 116

pieces (though three are spurious), many of them extremely brief, while the longest contains only some 400 lines. But in this body of poetry, there are, besides the magnificent love poems, graceful, playful verses of society, fierce, satiric poems, elaborate descriptive and mythological pieces (some of them adapted from the Greek), and the strange, wild, imaginative *Attis*. The text depends on a single manuscript discovered in the 14th century at Verona, inaccurately transcribed and subsequently lost.
▷K Quinn, *Catullus, an interpretation* (1972); and other works by Quinn

CAUSLEY, Charles
(1917–)

English poet and children's writer, whose close ties with his home town of Launceston in Cornwall provide him with a unique, rooted point of view on the world. His naval war experiences inspired his early verse, and *Farewell, Aggie Weston* (1951) broods on loss and innocence with the force of traditional ballad. His poetry has gradually become more conversational in style, yet his meditations on family memories, life, landscape and legend are far from simplistic. In his *Collected Poems 1951–1975* (1975) verse for adults sits easily beside that intended for children, both revealing the compassion and humour that make him a genuinely popular poet.
▷H Chambers (ed), *Causley at 70* (1987)

CAUTE, (John) David
(1936–)

English novelist and author of non-fiction, born in Alexandria, Egypt. In 1959 he published his first novel, *At Fever Pitch*, based upon his own adventures as an infantryman in the former Gold Coast, Africa, and thereafter for several years combined a career as a writer with that of an academic. His books deal with the relationship between the West, East and the Third World. His novel *The Decline of the West* (1966), a portrait of a fictional African state in turmoil during the years following independence, is both his most ambitious and most controversial. Among his non-fiction titles are *Under the Skin: The Death of White Rhodesia* (1983), his observations of the last days of white rule in Rhodesia and the nation's emergence as Zimbabwe.

CAVAFY, Constantine, pseud of Konstantínos Pétron Kaváfis
(1863–1933)

Greek poet, born in Alexandria, Egypt, of a Greek merchant family. After his father's death in 1872 he was taken by his mother to

England for five years, and apart from three years in Istanbul (1882–5) he spent the rest of his life in Alexandria, where he worked as a civil servant, making it the setting, either physical or symbolic, of much of his poetry. His work tends to diverge into the erotic—in which he was one of the first modern writers to deal explicitly with homosexuality—and the historical, in which he recreates the world of Greece and Alexandria in the Hellenistic period. His view of life is essentially tragic. His first book, containing 14 poems, was privately published when he was 41, and reissued five years later with an additional seven poems. He published no further work during his lifetime, preferring to distribute his work among his friends, but in recent years he has come to be regarded as one of the finest and most influential modern Greek poets. Some of his early verse was written in English, but it was not until the 1950s that his work became available in English translation. His best-known poems are, perhaps, his earlier ones, such as *I Polis* ('The City') and *Perimenondas tous Varvarous* ('Waiting for the Barbarians'). His work has been translated into English as *Poems* (1951) and *Complete Poems* (1961).
▷ R Liddell, *Cavafy: a critical biography* (1974)

CAVALCANTI, Guido
(c.1240–1300)

Italian poet, and friend of **Dante**. He married a Ghibelline, and was banished by the Guelfs. He returned to Florence only to die within the year. His works, which included ballads, sonnets and *canzoni*, were translated by **Dante Gabriel Rossetti** and **Ezra Pound**. He is said to have been a studious man, if also an eccentric one, and much of his poetry reflects that intellectualism, although he is also vividly aware of the emotional depths of his usual subject, love.
▷ A Ribera, *Guido Cavalcanti* (1911); Ezra Pound, 'Cavalcanti', in *Literary Essays* (1954)

CAVENDISH, Margaret
(?1624–1674)

English author of poetry, plays, biography and miscellanea. She was a Maid of Honour at the court of Charles I and became the Duchess of Newcastle on her marriage in 1645. She spent the ensuing 15 years of the English Civil War with her exiled husband in Europe, and on her return suffered the ridicule of society for her eccentricities of behaviour and dress. Her *Poems and Fancies* (1653) contains charming fairy verses, and both her autobiography and the *Life* of her husband show restraint and good sense. Her later

poetry is doggerel, her philosophy is pompous and naive, and **Pepys** described one of her plays as 'the most ridiculous thing that was ever wrote'.
▷ V Woolf, 'The Duchess of Newcastle', in *The Common Reader* (1938)

CAXTON, William
(c.1422–c.1491)

English printer and translator, born in Kent, important because he was the first English printer. He learned his craft in Europe, and set up his own press at Westminster in 1476, and from it issued about 100 books, including editions of **Chaucer**, **Gower** and his own translations from the French, which included a book by **Christine de Pisan**. His own prose was not outstanding, being somewhat over-elaborate and rambling; but it did contribute something to the 15th-century style. He was responsible, too, for the edition of **Malory** generally known until 1934.
▷ W Blades, *The Life and Typography of Caxton* (1861–3)

CAYROL, Jean
(1911–)

French Catholic novelist, poet, critic and film scriptwriter, from Bordeaux. He began with minor Surrealist poems. His later work is influenced by his experiences in a German concentration camp, where he was sent as a member of the wartime resistance. Much influenced by Emmanuel Mounier's Personalism—a Catholic movement blending **Bergson**ism with left-wing aspirations and proto-existentialism—his many novels and poems deal with problems of identity and guilt. Of them, *L'Espace d'une nuit* (1954, Eng trans *All in a Night*, 1957), and *Les Corps étrangers* (1959, Eng trans *Foreign Bodies*, 1960), have appeared in English. Because of his awareness of the limitations of language, he was regarded as on the edge of the *nouveau roman*, but is distinguished from it by his religious feelings. He has collaborated in films with the director Alain Resnais.

CECCHI, Emilio
(1884–1966)

Italian poet, critic, translator and essayist from Florence, who exercised a decisive influence upon the course of his country's poetry and prose. He introduced the essay, as a form, into this literature. His early attempts at poetry were a failure, but his critical work, influenced by **Croce** but always wary that Croce's idealism might undermine literature-as-history, and in particular *Peschi rossi* (1920, 'Goldfish'), succeeded (it has been asserted) in 'approximating the polyphonic essence of reality'. The short newspaper essays of *Peschi rossi* had an enormous influence, and encouraged Italians not to be afraid of making subjective investigations of reality. He based his style on that of two Englishmen, **Charles Lamb** and **Thomas De Quincey**. Those who have responded to his work include **Cesare Pavese** and **Elio Vittorini**.

CECCHI D'AMICO, Suso, originally Giovanna Cecchi
(1914–)

Italian screenwriter, born in Rome, the daughter of **Emilio Cecchi**. A student at Rome and Cambridge, she worked as a journalist and translator before writing the screenplay of the film *Mio Figlio Professore* (1946). An active figure in the school of Italian neorealism that flourished after the war, she contributed to the screenplays of *Ladri Di Biciclette* (1948, 'Bicycle Thieves') and *Miracolo A Milano* (1950, 'Miracle in Milan'), but found some of her best opportunities working in collaboration with director Luchino Visconti, especially on a number of elegant literary adaptations, including *Il Gattopardo* (1963, 'The Leopard'), *Lo Straniero* (1967, 'The Stranger') and *L'Innocente* (1976, 'The Innocent'). Dedicated to indigenous Italian storytelling, she has provided many of her country's leading film-makers with expertly crafted and structured screenplays, tailored to the specific sensibility of the director. Among her finest work is *Salvatore Giuliano* (1961), *Jesus of Nazareth* (1977) and *Oci Ciornie* (1987, 'Dark Eyes').

CECH, Svatopluk
(1846–1908)

Czech novelist, poet, dramatist and satirist, born in Ostredek. He travelled widely, and was one of the leaders of the humane resistance to Austrian tyranny. His chief work, still as topical today as it was when it was written, is the novel *Hanuman* (1884, Eng trans 1894), about a civil war amongst apes. His poetry, much of it consisting of epics, was highly thought of in its day, but is not so much read now. He punished the bourgeoisie of his own country in a series of fine satirical novels, *The Excursions of Mr Broucek* (1886–92), two of which inspired Janáček to his famous 1917 opera.

CÉITINN, Séthrún
(1570–c.1650)

Irish poet and historian, born in County Tipperary. His chief work is a defensive outline of Irish history, *Foras Feasa ar Éirinn*: although a masterpiece of Gaelic prose, it has little value as a chronicle. A few of his eloquent poems are remembered.

CELA, Camilo José
(1916–)

Spanish novelist, winner of the Nobel Prize for literature, born in Iria Flavia, La Coruña. He attended Madrid University and served in Franco's forces; his work is frequently interpreted as an eloquent, aggressive, idiosyncratic reaction to that error of judgement. He has been the dominant novelist in Spain for over 40 years. His first novel, *La familia de Pascual Duarte* (1942, Eng trans *The Family of Pascual Duarte*, 1946), appeared in 1942 and was banned, having stunned readers with its seemingly gratuitous violence. The range of his work is vast and varied but he is best known for *La Colmena* (1951, Eng trans *The Hive*, 1953), which recreates daily life in Madrid in the aftermath of the Spanish Civil War with great sensitivity and feeling for the plight of ordinary people. Others worthy of note are *Viaje a la Alcarría* (1948, Eng trans *Journey to the Alcarria*, 1948) and *San Camilo 1936* (1970). Eccentric, even scatological, he is a candid, combative protagonist who says what he thinks regardless of popularity. A member of the Spanish Royal Academy, he holds a plethora of honorary doctorates. In 1989 he was awarded the Nobel Prize for literature.
▷ D W MacPheeters, *Camilo José Cela* (1963)

CELAN, Paul, pseud of Paul Ancel or Antschel
(1920–70)

One of the greatest modern poets of the German language, born into the Jewish community at Czernowitz in Romania. He studied there and in France. His parents were murdered by the Nazis, but he survived a labour camp, later becoming a lecturer in German literature in Paris and taking French nationality. His second collection of poems, *Mohn und Gedächtnis* (1952, 'Poppy and Memory'), immediately established his reputation. It includes his most famous poem, 'Todesfuge' ('Death Fugue'), a beautiful and horrible evocation of the concentration camps. *Sprachgitter* (1959, Eng trans *Speech-Grille*, 1971) and *Die Niemandsrose* (1963, 'The No-One's Rose') reflect his ambiguous attitude to the Jewish God. The flowing lines and vivid images of his early work, influenced by the French Surrealists and **Yvan Goll**, later gave way to increasingly difficult and concentrated poems as Celan struggled to communicate the horror of his wartime experiences. He committed suicide by drowning himself in the Seine.
▷ J Glenn, *Paul Celan* (1973)

CELAYA, Gabriel, pseud of Rafael Múgica Celaya
(1911–90)

Spanish poet and publisher (he founded *Norte*), who remained in Spain after 1939, and whose voice was muted for many years. He was prolific (over 50 books); the best of his poems, some of which, written in the 1930s, were calculatedly Absurdist or Surrealist, concern the woman, Amparo Gastón, who changed his pessimistic view of the world. He was regarded as Spain's leading 'social poet' of the Franco years; but his final poems, again 'absurdist' in form, return to pessimism.

▷ *Encounter*, 12, 2 (1959)

CÉLINE, Louis-Ferdinand, pseud of L F Destouches
(1894–1961)

French novelist, born in Paris, the son of a poor clerk and a lace seamstress. His education was rudimentary and he had various jobs until 1912, when he joined the cavalry. In the first year of World War I he was wounded in the head and shell-shocked in an action for which he was decorated. The suffering, both mental and physical, caused by his wounds dogged him to the end of his days. He was invalided out of the military, took a medical degree, worked as a staff surgeon at the Ford plant in Detroit and later ministered to the poor of Paris, the experience of which, he acknowledged, was invaluable to his literary endeavours. His first novel, *Voyage au bout de la nuit* (1932, rev edn 1952, Eng trans *Journey to the End of Night*, 1934), brought international acclaim, and his reputation was enhanced by the publication of his second novel, *Mort à Crédit* (1936, Eng trans *Death on the Installment Plan*, 1938). His use of the demotic and his insights into life among the lower classes have influenced many writers, among them **Jean-Paul Sartre**, **William Burroughs** and **Henry Miller**. In the late 1930s he was a declared anti-semite, and after the liberation of France (1944) he fled to Denmark. He was tried and sentenced to death *in absentia* but this was later reversed and he spent his last years in France, suffering from partial paralysis and tinnitus, and close to insanity. His final novels, *D'un Château à L'Autre* (1957, Eng trans *Castle to Castle*, 1968) and *Nord* (1960, Eng trans *North*, 1972), are ranked with his best.

▷ D O'Connell, *Céline* (1976)

CELSUS, Aulus Cornelius
(1st century)

Roman writer. He compiled an encyclopedia on medicine, rhetoric, history, philosophy, war, and agriculture. The only extant portion of the work is the *De Medicina*, one of the first medical works to be printed (1478).

▷ N Scalinci, *La Oftalmiatria di Aulo Cornelio Celso* (1940)

CENDRARS, Blaise, originally Frédéric Louis Sauser
(1887–1961)

Swiss novelist, poet and traveller, born in Chaux-de-Fonds, Switzerland. His mother was a Scot, and he regarded himself as a cosmopolitan. When he was 15 he ran away from home to work for a jewel merchant with whom he travelled through Russia, Persia and China. He later described this journey in a long poem, *Transsibérien* (1913). In 1910 he met **Guillaume Apollinaire**, by whom he was much influenced. He wrote his first long poem in America, *Pâques à New York* (1912, 'Easter in New York'), which, with *Transsibérien* and his third and last long poem, *Le Panama ou Les Aventures de mes Sept Oncles* (written in 1918, published as *Panama; or the Adventures of my Seven Uncles* in 1931 in a translation by **John Dos Passos**), was important in shaping the spirit of modern poetry. He was careless with the truth and was fond of apocryphal stories, but he did lose an arm fighting for the French Foreign Legion in World War I. A reluctant writer, his poetry is not particularly memorable but his best novels—*La Confession de Dan Yack* (1927–9; 1946; Eng trans *Antarctic Fugue*, 1948), *Moravagine* (1926, Eng trans 1969) and *L'Or* (1925, Eng trans *Sutter's Gold*, 1926)—are less well known than they ought to be.

▷ M A Caws, *The Inner Theatre of Recent French Poetry* (1932)

CENTLIVRE, Susannah, née Freeman
(c.1667– c.1723)

English dramatist, born probably in Holbeach, Lincolnshire. She was first married at 16 and twice widowed. In 1700 she produced a tragedy, *The Perjured Husband*, and subsequently appeared on the stage in Bath in her own comedy, *Love at a Venture* (1706). In 1706 she married her third husband, Joseph Centlivre, head cook to Queen Anne at Windsor. Her 18 plays also included *The Gamester* (1705), *The Busybody* (1709) and *A Bold Stroke for a Wife* (1717).

▷ J H Bowyer, *The Celebrated Mrs Centlivre* (1952)

CERNUDA, Luis
(1902–67)

Spanish poet and critic, and, according to many critics, the greatest of all the famous 'Generation of '27', which included **Lorca** and **Rafael Alberti**. Cernuda is also highly prized as, with **Cavafy** and **Sandro Penna**, one of the great homosexual poets of the 20th century. An anti-Francoist, he escaped from Madrid in 1938 and moved, first to Britain, as a Professor of Spanish Literature at Glasgow

University, then to America; he died in Mexico City. His poetry, as well as being as explicitly homosexual as it could be at the time he wrote it, is soaked in his Andalusian origins, and has all the sad and beautiful virtues of Mediterranean art: in it, bitterness at his fate is counterpointed with a sense of the impermanence of beauty; but he had a rare ability to express beauty. His project was to find 'dignity' in a fate he deplored: he had had a fierce and *macho* militaristic father, lucidly omnipresent in his developing poetry, as a symbol of the unavoidable, unlovable hostility of reality. All his 11 collections were finally published as *La realidad y el deseo* (1964, 'Reality and Desire'). He ended in a courageous but, paradoxically, affirmative vision of absolute disgust with the world. His first teacher and mentor was **Pedro Salinas**. 'The public', he wrote: 'I do not know what it is.' In English translation are: *The Poetry of Luis Cernuda* (1971) and *Selected Poems of Luis Cernuda* (1977).

▷D Harris, *Luis Cernuda: A Study of the Poetry* (1973)

CERVANTES SAAVEDRA, Miguel de
(1547–1616)

Spanish novelist, and author of *Don Quixote*, born in Alcalá de Henares, the son of a poor medical practitioner. In 1569 he published his first known work, a collection of pieces on the death of the queen. He then travelled to Italy in the service of Cardinal Giulio Acquaviva, and enlisted as a soldier. At the battle of Lepanto a gunshot wound maimed his left hand. After further service against the Turks in Tunis, he was returning to Spain in 1575 when the galley he sailed in was captured by Algerian corsairs, and with his brother Rodrigo and others he was carried into Algiers, where he remained in captivity for five years, during which he made four daring attempts to escape. In 1580 he was ransomed by the efforts of Trinitarian monks, Algiers traders, and his devoted family. Finding no permanent occupation at home, he drifted to Madrid, and tried a literary career. In 1584 he married Catalina de Salazar y Palacios (1565–1626). The marriage was childless, but Cervantes had an illegitimate daughter, Isabel de Saavedra (c.1585–1652). His first important work was *La Galatea* (Eng trans 1867), a pastoral romance, printed at Alcalá in 1585. For some years he strove to gain a livelihood by writing plays, of which two only, *La Numancia* (1784, Eng trans 1870) and *El trato de Argel* (1798, Eng trans *The Commerce of Algiers*, 1870), have survived. In 1587 he became commissary to the fleet at Seville. In 1594 he was appointed as collector of revenues for the kingdom of Granada; but in 1597, failing to make up the sum due to the treasury, he was sent to prison in Seville, released on giving security, but not reinstated. Local tradition maintains that he wrote *Don Quixote* in prison at Argamasilla in La Mancha. In September 1604 leave was granted to print the first part of *Don Quixote*, and early in January 1605 the book came out at Madrid. It was immediately popular, though **Lope de Vega** wrote sneeringly of it; but instead of giving his readers the sequel they asked for, Cervantes busied himself with writing for the stage and composing short tales, or 'exemplary novels' as he called them, which came out as *Novelas Ejemplares* (Eng trans *Exemplary Novels*, 1972) in 1613. His *Viage al Parnaso* (1614), a poem of over 3000 lines in *terza rima*, reviews the poetry and poets of the day. In 1614 a pseudonymous writer brought out a spurious second part of *Don Quixote*, with an insulting preface, which served to spur Cervantes to the completion of the genuine second part (1615). While it was in the press he revised his various plays and interludes, and a little before his death, he finished the romance of *Persiles y Sigismunda* (1617, Eng trans *The Travels of Persiles and Sigismunda*, 1619). For *Don Quixote*, Cervantes ranks as one of the great writers of the world; though it is the most carelessly written of all great books, it is widely regarded as being the genuine precursor of the modern novel, as well as a great comic epic in its own right.

▷W Byron, *Cervantes, a biography* (1978); Manuel Duran, *Cervantes* (1974)

CÉSAIRE, Aimé Fernand
(1913–)

West Indian poet and playwright, born in Basse-Point, Martinique. One of the best-known poets and playwrights in the Third World, his reputation is based largely on two plays, *La Tragédie du roi Christophe* (1963, Eng trans *The Tragedy of King Christophe*, 1970) and *Une Tempête: Adaptation pour un théâtre negre* (1969), an original adaptation of **Shakespeare**'s *The Tempest* for black actors. He is also noted for a long poem, the *Cahier d'un retour au pays natal* (1947, Eng trans *Notebook of a Return to my Native Land*, 1969), and for a biography of the Haitian revolutionary, Toussaint L'Ouverture (1960, rev edn 1962). A militant Marxist and anti-colonialist, he played a large role in rallying decolonized Africans in the 1950s.

▷L Kesteloot and B Kotchy, *Césaire: l'homme et l'oeuvre* (1973)

CHACEL, Rosa
(1898–)

Spanish novelist and poet, born in Valladolid. Having spent much time in Italy, she was almost unknown in Spain until 1970, when her novel *La sinrazón* (1960, 'The Wrong'), was reprinted in Barcelona. Now she is recognized as one of the more important novelists of her age. She has continued to live in Brazil. Her first novel *Estación, ida y vuelta* (1930, 'Station, Round Trip'), was more original than it seemed at that time: it was influenced by **Ortega y Gasset**, but anticipated the French *nouveau roman* far more clearly than apparently similar contemporaneous novels by such as **Francisco Ayala**. However, her insistence upon examining the inner life of her characters, at the apparent expense of the outer, only gave an impression of the 'dehumanization' then fashionable in Spanish fiction. *Memorias de Leticia Valle* (1945, 'Memoirs of Leticia Valle'), is a tour de force in which a young girl relates the effects upon her of her sexual attractiveness to her male teacher. It is a novel which has annoyed male critics, as it was perhaps intended to do, and, were it translated (a critic has suggested), might become a 'woman's *Lolita*'.

CHAGAS, António das, Frei, monastic name of **António da Fonseca Soares**
(1631–82)

Portuguese poet, religious writer and moralist, born in Vidigueira. In his early life Chagas was violent and swaggering: after fighting in the Wars of the Restoration he had to flee to Brazil because he had killed a love-rival in a duel. He even earned himself the nickname of 'Captain Daisy'. In 1663, some years after he had returned to military life in Portugal, he suddenly became a Franciscan monk, and soon became famous for his 'hell-fire' sermons preaching identification with Christ. But both his fervent *Gongorista* poetry written as a soldier (he committed much of it to the flames) and his prose *Cartes Espirituals* (1684–7, 'Spiritual Letters'), his main work written towards the end of his life, are informed by the same ardour and self-knowledge, so that, despite some artificialities typical of the time, almost everything he wrote reads genuinely.
▷A F G Bell, *Portuguese Literature* (1922)

CHAMBERLAIN, Houston Stewart
(1855–1927)

English-born German author and propagandist, son of an admiral. He settled in Dresden in 1885, and in 1908 he moved to Bayreuth and married, as his second wife, Eva, daughter of Richard Wagner, and wrote in German on music, Wagner, Kant and philosophy. A committed supporter of the dogmas of Aryan supremacy, he was naturalized as a German in 1916.
▷W Vollrath, *Houston Stewart Chamberlain und sein britisches Erbgut* (1939); and other works by Vollrath

CHAMBERLAYNE, William
(1619–89)

English poet. He practised as a physician at Shaftesbury, Dorset, and fought as a royalist at Newbury. His works are *Love's Victory, a Tragi-Comedy* (1658), and *Pharonnida, An Heroick Poem* (1659) in five books of rhymed couplets, recounting the adventures of the knight Argolia in quest of his beloved, Pharonnida.
▷G Saintsbury, *Minor Poets of the Caroline Period* (1905)

CHAMFORT, Sébastien-Roch Nicolas
(1741–94)

French writer. He made an entrance into the literary circles of Paris, and lived for years 'by his wit, if not by his wits'. He joined the Jacobins at the outbreak of the French Revolution (1789), but his remarks on the Terror brought him into disfavour. Threatened with arrest, he tried to commit suicide and died after several days' suffering. His works include tales, dramas, *éloges*, brilliant maxims and even more admirably observed anecdotes (published posthumously in 1795), which attack the corruption of the period.
▷P J Richard, *Aspects de Chamfort* (1959)

CHAMISSO, Adelbert von (Louis Charles Adelaide de)
(1781–1838)

French-born German poet and biologist, born in Champagne. The French Revolution drove his parents to Prussia, and he served in the Prussian army (1798–1807). In Geneva he joined the literary circle of **Madame de Staël** and later studied at Berlin. In 1815–18 he accompanied a Russian exploring expedition round the world as naturalist, and on his return was appointed Keeper of the Botanical Garden of Berlin. In 1819 he was the first to discover in certain animals what he called 'alternation of generations' (the recurrence in the life cycle of two or more forms). He wrote several works on natural history, but his fame rests partly on his poems, still more on his quaint and humorous *Peter Schlemihls wundersame Geschichte* (1813, 'Peter Schlemihl's Remarkable Story'), the story of a man who sells his shadow to the Devil for earthly rewards. His lyrical verses *Frauenliebe und Frauenleben* ('Women's Life and Women's Love') are now best known in Schumann's song-cycle.
▷C A Lentzner, *Chamisso: a sketch of his life and work* (1893)

CHAMPFLEURY, assumed name of **Jules Fleury-Husson**
(1821–89)

French author, born in Laon. He wrote several early pieces for the theatre, and a number of novels in Realist style, inspired by the example of Courbet in painting. He became head of the Porcelain Museum in Sèvres, and published important studies on the history of caricature, literature, art and pottery, and a manifesto, *Le réalisme* (1857).

▷ E de Mirecourt, *Champfleury* (1891)

CHAMSON, André
(1900–83)

French novelist, born in Nîmes. His early novels were realistic tales of life in the Cévennes, often dealing with the Huguenot traditions which were a part of his own family. An anti-fascist activist in the 1930s, he fought in the Resistance during World War II. His later novels illustrate this social and political commitment; they include *La Galère* (1939, 'The Galley'), *La Neige et la Fleur* (1951, 'The Snow and the Flower') and *La Superbe* (1967, 'The Superb'). He was elected to the Académie française in 1956.

CHANDLER, Raymond
(1888–1959)

American novelist, born in Chicago. He was brought up in England from the age of seven, educated at Dulwich College and in France and Germany, and worked as a freelance writer in London. In 1912 he went to California, and served in the Canadian army in France, and in the RAF during World War I. After a variety of jobs, during the Depression he began to write short stories and novelettes for the detective-story pulp magazines of the day. On such stories he based his subsequent full-length 'private eye' novels, *The Big Sleep* (1939), *Farewell, My Lovely* (1940), *The High Window* (1942) and *The Lady in the Lake* (1943), all of which were successfully filmed. Chandler himself went to Hollywood in 1943 and worked on film scripts. He did much to establish the conventions of his genre, particularly with his cynical but honest anti-hero, Philip Marlowe, who also appeared in such later works as *The Little Sister* (1949), *The Long Goodbye* (1953) and *Playback* (1958).

▷ P Knight, *Down these Mean Streets a Man Must Go: Chandler's Knight* (1963)

CHANG, Eileen, originally Chang Ai Ling
(1920–)

Taiwanese (originally Chinese) novelist, the leading writer of a branch of Chinese literature-in-exile. She left China in 1952, for Hong Kong, and later became domiciled in the United States, and taught (as a virulent anti-communist) in several universities. At first she made her living from women's romances (they have been praised for their 'intimate boudoir realism'). *The Rice Sprout Song*

(1954), which she translated herself into English in 1955, is about peasants being asked for more than they can pay towards the Korean War effort. She has not attracted the attention of serious critics, but had many admirers in the 1960s and 1970s.

CHANNING, William Ellery
(1780–1842)

American clergyman, born in Newport, Rhode Island. He graduated at Harvard in 1798, and in 1803 was ordained to the Congregational Federal Street Church in Boston, where his sermons were famous for their 'fervour, solemnity, and beauty'. He was ultimately the leader of the Unitarians. In 1822 he visited Europe, and made the acquaintance of **Wordsworth** and **Coleridge**. Among his Works (6 vols, 1841–6) were his *Essay on National Literature*, *Remarks on Milton*, *Character and Writings of Fénelon*, *Negro Slavery*, and *Self-culture*.

▷ R Hudspeth, *Ellery Channing* (1973)

CHAPELAIN, Jean
(1595–1674)

French poet and critic. An original member of the Académie française (1634), he had a high reputation as a critic, as well as considerable political influence, firstly with Richelieu, and later with Colbert. He also wrote *La Pucelle* (1656, 'The Maid of Orleans'), a poem in 24 long cantos on Joan of Arc, which was savaged by **Nicolas Boileau**.

▷ G Colas, *Un poète protecteur des lettres au XVI siècle* (1912)

CHAPMAN, George
(c.1559–1634)

English dramatist, born near Hitchin, Hertfordshire. He is thought to have had a university education, possibly at Oxford. He began to make a reputation in Elizabethan literary circles with his poems *The Shadow of the Night* (1594), and in 1595 saw the production of his earliest extant play, the popular comedy *The Blind Beggar of Alexandria*. His next comedy, *All Fools*, printed in 1605, was probably produced in 1599. In 1598 he wrote a continuation of **Christopher Marlowe's** *Hero and Leander*. After partial translations from the *Iliad* in 1598 and 1610, the complete translation of *The Iliads of Homer, Prince of Poets*, appeared in 1611. Having finished the *Iliad*, he set to work on the *Odyssey* (1616), followed (about 1624) by the minor works. He joined **Ben Jonson** and **John Marston** in the composition of *Eastward Hoe* (1605), in which slighting references to the Scots earned the authors a jail sentence, and in 1606 published a graceful comedy, *The Gentleman Usher*. In 1607 appeared the tragedy *Bussy*

d'Ambois, and in 1613 *The Revenge of Bussy d'Ambois*. *The Conspiracie* and *Tragedie of Charles, Duke of Byron* (1608) are also undramatic, but are full of fine poetry. His other plays are *The May Day* (1611), *The Widow's Tears* (1612) and *Caesar and Pompey* (1631). Two posthumous tragedies (1654), *Alphonsus* and *Revenge for Honour*, bear his name, but it is doubtful that he wrote them. *The Ball*, a comedy, and *The Tragedie of Chabot* (1639) were the joint work of Chapman and **James Shirley**. Among Chapman's nondramatic works are the epic philosophical poem *Euthymiae & Raptus* (1609), *Petrarch's Seven Penitentiall Psalmes* (1612), *The Divine Poem of Musaeus* (1616) and *The Georgicks of Hesiod* (1618).
▷C K Spivack, *George Chapman* (1967)

CHAPONE, Hester, née **Mulso**
(1727–1801)
English essayist, born in Twywell, Northamptonshire. One of the 'blue-stocking' circle associated with Elizabeth Montagu, she published verse stories and wrote for the *Rambler* (No. 10), *Gentleman's Magazine* and other magazines; she is chiefly remembered for her *Letters on the Improvement of the Mind* (1772).
▷*An Account of Her Life and Character drawn up by her family* (1807)

CHAR, René
(1907–88)
Prolific French poet, born at L'Isle-sur-Sorgue, Vaucluse. He was educated in Avignon and Marseilles, and fought with the Resistance during the war. Originally associated with Surrealism, he rejected the movement's more doctrinaire aspects but drew from it a lasting belief in human individuality and the need to protest against convention. An admirer of Heraclitus, he attempted to register the flux of experience, particularly the sunny landscape and culture of the Mediterranean. In his most representative collection, *Fureur et Mystère* (1948, 'Madness and Mystery'), he claims a hermetic, almost magical role for poetry. His war journal *Feuillets d'Hypnos* (1946, Eng trans *Leaves of Hypnos*, 1973) was dedicated to **Camus**, whose emphasis on protest and southern neo-classicism he shared. Char's later work was more directly concerned with social issues, but still retains its essentially irrational emphasis.
▷M A Caws, *René Char* (1977)

CHARBONNEAU, Robert
(1911–67)
French–Canadian poet, novelist and critic, noted for his irony and in particular for his use of French techniques in such novels as

Les désirs et les jours (1948, 'Desires and Days'). The novelist who has mainly influenced him is François Mauriac.
▷M B Ellis, *Robert Charbonneau et la création romanesque* (1948)

CHARDONNE, Jacques, pseud of **Jacques Boutelleau**
(1884–1968)
French writer, born in Barbezieux. He wrote domestic novels mainly set in his native Charente, among them *Claire* (1931), *Les Destinées sentimentales* (1934–6, 'Sentimental Destinies') and *Romanesques* (1937). He also wrote essays, and a chronicle of the French collapse in 1940.
▷G Chardonne, *La Vie de Jacques Chardonne et son art* (1953)

CHARLWOOD, Don(ald Ernest Cameron)
(1915–)
Australian writer, born in Hawthorn, Melbourne, who served in the Royal Australian Air force during World War II. He achieved immediate success with *No Moon Tonight* (1956), his experiences in bombing sorties over Germany. He returned to this period of his life in a collection of partly autobiographical short stories, *Flight and Time* (1979). His other books include a history of Australian air-traffic control, in which the author worked from 1945, and two books of nautical history, *Wrecks and Reputations* (1977) and *Settlers under Sail* (1978). *The Long Farewell* (1981), based on authentic diaries, celebrates the spirit of 19th-century immigrants who made the long sea voyage to Australia.

CHARTERIS, Leslie, pseud of **Leslie Charles Bowyer Yin**
(1907–93)
British-born American crime story writer, born in Singapore, the son of an English mother and a Chinese father. Educated at Cambridge, he was author of a series of books featuring a criminal hero, Simon Templar, 'the Saint', starting with *Meet the Tiger* (1928) and *Enter the Saint* (1930). He moved to the USA in 1932 and worked in Hollywood as a screenwriter. He was naturalized in 1941.
▷W O G Lofts and D J Adley, *The Saint and Leslie Charteris* (1979)

CHARTIER, Alain
(c.1390–c.1440)
French writer and courtier, born in Bayeux. He was secretary to Charles VI and VII and went on diplomatic missions to Germany, Venice and Scotland (1425–8). His much imitated poem, *La belle dame sans merci* (1424,

'The Beautiful Woman with no Mercy'), is a piece of escapism in the midst of his pre-occupation with the plight of France in the Hundred Years War. This forms the back-cloth of his two best works, the *Livre des quatre dames* (1415–16, 'Book of Four Women'), in which four ladies on the day after Agincourt weep for their lost lovers, and the prose *Quadrilogue invectif* (1422, 'A Debate Between Four People, Containing Invective'), a debate apportioning the blame for France's ills between the people and the nobility. He also showed skill in handling the *ballade* and other lyrical forms.

▷ D Delaunay, *Étude sur Alain Chartier* (1876)

CHARYN, Jerome
(1937–)

American novelist, born and educated in New York City, where he later taught at City College and City University. Since 1980 he has been lecturer in creative writing at Princeton University, New Jersey. His first three novels, *Once Upon a Droshky* (1964), *On the Darkening Green* (1965) and *Going to Jerusalem* (1967), were episodic picaresques, mostly concerned with rebellion against conformity, but containing elements of fantasy. *American Scrapbook* (1969) portrayed a Japanese family's internment during World War II, while *Eisenhower, My Eisenhower* (1971) reimagines New York as Bedlam and converts his customary Jewish characters into gypsies. In 1975, Charyn (whose brother is a New York police inspector) introduced his fictional detective Isaac Sidel in *Blue Eyes*, the first of a tetralogy, continuing with *Marilyn the Wild*, *The Education of Patrick Silver* (both 1976), *Secret Isaac* (1978), published in the UK as *The Isaac Quartet* (1984). In the mid-eighties, he returned to the style of the earlier books with *War Cries over Avenue C* (1985).

CHASE, James Hadley, pseud of René Raymond
(1906–85)

English novelist, born in London. He is a prolific author of mystery stories, almost all of which have an American setting derived from copious second-hand research, since he has rarely visited that country. He adopted the manner of the American 'hard-boiled' school, and had an immediate success with his first novel, *No Orchids for Miss Blandish* (1939), and continued in a similar vein. He has employed a number of different detectives in various series, but their hallmark is always an intricate plot, and a fast-moving, harshly realistic narrative.

CHASE, Mary Coyle
(1907–81)

American playwright, born in Colorado. She is chiefly remembered as the author of the play *Harvey* (1944), a comedy about a drunk whose closest companion is a huge, invisible rabbit. It won her a Pulitzer Prize for Drama in 1945, and was made into a highly successful film in 1950. She wrote a number of other plays, including *Now You've Done It* (1937), *Mrs McThing* (1952) and *Cocktails with Mum* (1974). She also wrote several books for children, in which field she should not be confused with the novelist and children's writer Mary Chase (1887–1973) of Maine, an academic who also achieved a considerable reputation as a writer of popular fiction.

CHASE, Mary Ellen
(1887–1973)

American novelist and essayist, born in Blue Hill, Maine. From 1936 until her retirement she taught English literature at Smith College. Her best-known, accomplished novels are *Mary Peters* (1934) and *Silas Crockett* (1935). They are in the regional, or 'local colour', tradition established by such writers as **Sarah Orne Jewett** and **Mary Wilkins Freeman**. *Silas Crockett* is set in the Maine herring industry, and vividly depicts the misery caused by the inhumanely handled introduction of steam-ships. *A Goodly Fellowship* (1939) is autobiographical.

▷ P Westbrook, *Mary Ellen Chase* (1965)

CHASSIGNET, Jean-Baptiste
(c.1580–c.1635)

French poet, author of *Le Mespris de la vie et consolation contre la mort* (1594), a series of 434 sonnets, together with a number of other poems, which together constitute an argument (which can be inferred from the title of the work) that life and death are inseparable, that life should be lived bearing death in mind, and that death, when it comes, should be welcomed. The argument is based on Christian doctrine, and much of the imagery in this highly rhetorical but attractive work is drawn from the bible.

CHATEAUBRIAND, François René, Vicomte de
(1768–1848)

French writer and statesman, born of a noble Breton family in St Malo. He served for a short time as an ensign, and in 1791 sailed to North America, spending eight months in the travels recounted in his *Voyage en Amérique* (1827, Eng trans *Travels in America*, 1828). Returning to France, he married, but immediately joined the army of the émigrés, and was left for dead near Namur. From 1793

to 1800 he lived in London, teaching and translating. In 1797 he published an *Essai sur les Révolutions* ('Essay on Revolutions'). *Atala* (Eng trans 1802), an unfinished Romantic epic of Native American life (1801), established his literary reputation; and *Génie du christianisme* (1802, Eng trans *The Beauties of Christianity*, 1813), a vindication of the Church of Rome, raised him to the foremost position among the French men of letters of the day. In 1803 he was appointed secretary to the embassy in Rome, where he wrote his *Lettres sur l'Italie* ('Letters about Italy'), and in 1804 was sent as envoy to the little republic of Valais. But on the murder of the Duc d'Enghien, Chateaubriand refused to hold office under Napoleon. He set out for the East in 1806, visited Greece, Palestine and Egypt, and returned to France in 1807. Two years later he issued *Les Martyrs*, a prose epic of Diocletian's persecutions. From 1814 to 1824 he gave support to the Restoration monarchy. He was made a peer and minister, and in 1822-4 was ambassador extraordinary at the British court. Disappointed in his hope of becoming Prime Minister, from 1824 to 1830 he figured as a Liberal. On the downfall of Charles X he went back to the Royalists. During the reign of Louis-Philippe he occupied himself in writing his celebrated *Mémoires d'outre-tombe* ('Memoirs from Beyond the Grave'). Parts of this eloquent autobiography appeared before his death and were translated as *Memoirs* in three volumes in 1848; the whole, in six volumes, not till 1902. His writings also include the *Itinéraire de Paris à Jerusalem* (1811, Eng trans *Travels in Greece, Palestine, Egypt and Barbary*, 1812); *Les Natchez* (1827, Eng trans *The Natchez*, 1827), a prose epic dealing with Native American life; and two works of fiction, *René* (1802, Eng trans *René: A Tale*, 1813) and *Les Aventures du dernier des Abencérages* (1826, Eng trans *The Last of the Abencérages*, 1826), a tale of 16th-century Spain.
▷G Painter, *Chateaubriand: a biography* (1977)

CHATEAUBRIANT, Alphonse de
(1877-1951)

French novelist, associated particularly with the regions of Basse-Bretagne and La Brière. Born in Rennes, the son of a family particularly gifted in art and music, he won the Prix **Goncourt** with *Monsieur des Lourdines* in 1911. In spite of his Christian convictions, as revealed in the *Écrits de l'autre rive* (1950), Chateaubriant was an active supporter of Hitler's ideology, spending periods in Germany prior to World War II, openly collaborating with the Germans during the Occupation and editing the pro-Nazi journal *La Gerbe*. After the war he was exiled, and he ended his days in the monastery at Kitzbühel, Austria. Despite this retreat into mysticism towards the end of his life, Chateaubriant's work more typically reflects a belief in man's ability to redeem himself through the successful accomplishment of his dreams and aspirations.

CHATTERJEE, Bankim Chandra
(1838-94)

Indian writer, born in Katalpura, Bengal. One of the most influential figures in 19th-century Indian literature, his novels include *Durges Nandini* (1864) and *Anandamath* (1882), a novel of the Sannyasi rebellion of 1772, from which the Nationalist song *Bande Mataram* ('Hail to thee, Mother'), was taken.
▷M Lala Dasa, *Bankim Chatterjee, prophet of the Indian Renaissance* (1938)

CHATTERJI, Sarat Chandra
(1876-1936)

Indian (Bengali) novelist, most of whose fiction has been translated into English. He is thought of by the Indian public as being the greatest novelist of the continent; he was hardly that, by the highest literary standards, for he could be sentimental, and his plots were often highly artificial. But, rather like **Upton Sinclair** in the United States, he deserved his great popularity: like **Dickens**, he was appalled by poor living conditions; he was one of the first Indian writers to draw attention to the plight of women, and his style was unaffected. His feeling for women is well seen in the most famous of his many novels, *Srikanta*, part of which was translated in 1922. From a literary viewpoint, his finest work in translation is contained in a selection of stories: *The Eldest Sister* (1950).

CHATTERTON, Thomas
(1752-70)

English poet, born in Bristol. His father, a sub-chanter in the cathedral, and master of a charity school, died before the boy was born. The mother, a poor schoolmistress and needlewoman, brought up her son and his sister beneath the shadow of St Mary Redcliffe, where their forefathers had been sextons (more probably masons) since the days of Queen Elizabeth. He was a scholar of Colston's bluecoat hospital (1760-5), and then was apprenticed an attorney. Fascinated from boyhood by antiques, he wrote and published pseudo-archaic poems purporting to be the work of a 15th-century Bristol Monk, Thomas Rowley, a friend of a historical figure, a merchant called William Canynge.

In 1769 he sent a history of painting in England, allegedly by Rowley, to **Horace Walpole**, who was only temporarily deceived. He was released from his apprenticeship in 1770 and left for London, where he worked on innumerable satires, essays and epistles, and a burlesque opera, *The Revenge*. But later that year he poisoned himself with arsenic. His 'Rowley' poems, although soon exposed as forgeries, are considered to have genuine talent, and he became a romantic hero to later poets. His story was dramatized by Alfred de Vigny in 1835.

CHATWIN, Bruce
(1940–89)

English writer and traveller, born in Sheffield. He worked at Sotheby's as an expert on modern art for eight years until he temporarily went blind. To recuperate, he went to Africa and the Sudan. He was converted to a life of nomadic asceticism and began writing beguiling books which defy classification, combining fiction, anthropology, philosophy and travel. They include *In Patagonia* (1977), which won the Hawthornden Prize and the **E M Forster** Award of the American Academy of Letters; *The Viceroy of Ouidah* (1980); *On The Black Hill* (1982), winner of the Whitbread Award for the best first novel; *The Songlines* (1987), and *Utz* (1988), a novella which was shortlisted for the Booker Prize.

CHAUCER, Geoffrey
(c.1345–1400)

English poet, the son of John Chaucer, a vintner and tavern keeper in London, perhaps the John Chaucer who was deputy to the king's butler. In 1357 and 1358 he was a page in the service of the wife of Lionel, Duke of Clarence; he would seem to have been presently transferred to King Edward III's household. In 1359 he served in the campaign in France, and was taken prisoner at 'Retters' (Rethel), but was soon ransomed, the king contributing £16 towards the required amount. He returned home in 1360. In 1367 the king granted him a pension. He is described as 'our beloved yeoman', and as 'one of the yeomen of the king's chamber', and in 1368 he was one of the king's esquires. In 1369 he first appeared as a poet, with his *Book of the Duchess*, on the death of John of Gaunt's wife. In 1370 he went abroad on the king's service; in 1372–3 on a royal mission to Genoa, Pisa, Florence; in 1376, abroad again; in 1377, to Flanders and to France; in 1378, to Italy again. Meanwhile in 1374 he was appointed comptroller of the Customs and Subsidy of Wools, Skins, and Tanned Hides in the port of London; in 1382,

comptroller of the Petty Customs; and in 1385 he was allowed to nominate a permanent deputy. In 1374 the king granted him a pitcher of wine daily; and John of Gaunt conferred on him a pension of £10 for life. In 1375 he received from the crown the custody of lands that brought him in £104. In 1386 he was elected a knight of the shire for Kent. The following writings certainly belong to the period 1369–87: *The Parliament of Fowls, The House of Fame, Troilus and Cressida* and *The Legend of Good Women*; also what ultimately appeared as the Clerk's, Man of Law's, Prioress's, Second Nun's and Knight's Tales in the *Canterbury Tales*. Chaucer's earlier writings, including his translation of part of the *Roman de la Rose*, followed the current French trends, but the most important influence acting upon him during this middle period of his literary life was that of Italy. Much of his subject-matter he derived from his great Italian contemporaries, especially from **Boccaccio**, but it was the spirit, not the letter of these masters which he imitated. The crowning work of the middle period of his life is *Troilus and Cressida*—a work in which his immense power of human observation, his sense of humour, and his dramatic skill are lavishly displayed. *The Legend of Good Women* has an admirable prologue, but was never finished. His next great subject was the *Canterbury Tales*. But about the end of 1386 he lost his offices, possibly owing to the absence abroad of John of Gaunt, and fell upon hard times. In 1389 he was appointed clerk of the King's Works, but this did not last and he fell into debt. In 1394 King Richard II granted him a pension of £20 for life; but the advances of payment he applied for, and the issue of letters of protection from arrest for debt, indicate his condition. On the accession in 1399 of Henry IV, John of Gaunt, he was granted a pension of 40 marks (£26 13s 4d), and his few remaining months were spent in comfort. After his death he was laid in that part of Westminster Abbey which through his burial there came afterwards to be called the Poets' Corner. His greatest achievement is the Prologue (1387) to the *Tales*, which, as a piece of descriptive writing, is unique. Chaucer was the first great poet of the English race, and he established the southern English dialect as the literary language of England. Many works have been ascribed to Chaucer, and were long printed in popular editions, that are certainly not his—eg, *The Court of Love, Chaucer's Dream, The Complaint of the Black Knight, The Cuckoo and Nightingale, The Flower and the Leaf*, and much of the extant *Romaunt of the Rose*.

▷D S Brewer, *Chaucer* (1973, 3rd edn); I Robinson, *Chaucer and the English Tradition* (1972)

CHAUDHURI, Nirad C
(1897–)

Indian writer, born in Kishorganj, Bengal, and educated at Calcutta University. A prolific writer on Indian topics, he is best-known for *The Autobiography of an Unknown Indian* (1951), which chronicles his rural childhood and early life as a student during the British Raj. **V S Naipaul** hailed it as possibly 'the one great book to come out of the Indo-English encounter'. Acutely perceptive about the English, *A Passage to England* (1959) is an amusing account of his first visit to that country. *Thy Hand, Great Anarch! India 1921–1952* (1987) is a further, and probably final, instalment of epic autobiography.

CHAYEFSKY, Paddy (born Sidney)
(1923–81)

American stage and television playwright, born in New York City. He is best known for *Marty* (1953, television) and *The Bachelor Party* (1954, screenplay), sensitive and affecting plays about ordinary people.
▷J M Clun, *Chayevsky* (1976)

CHAZAL, Malcolm de
(1902–)

French prose-poet living in mysterious isolation in Mauritius, who was discovered by **André Breton** and was put forward as an exponent of genuine Surrealism. His *Sens Plastique* (1948, 'Plastic Sense') excited Paris. His *La Bible du mal* (1952, 'Evil Bible'), published in St Louis, has been compared to **Blake**. All his work is about the sexual act: for him, nothing else exists.
▷A Breton, *La Clé des champs* (1953)

CHÉDID, Andrée
1921–)

French novelist, poet and dramatist, of Lebanese origin, born in Cairo. She is mainly notable for her expressions of eastern myths in western, rationalistic forms. She moved to Paris in 1946. She has published many volumes of poetry, and her novels *Le sixième jour* (1960) and *Le sommeil délivré* (1976) have been translated into English as, respectively, *The Sixth Day* (1962) and *From Sleep Unbound* (1983). Her play *Bérénice d'Egypt* was published in 1968. *The Sixth Day* was filmed.

CHEEVER, John William
(1912–82)

American short-story writer and novelist. Born in Quincy, Massachusetts, he began telling stories when he was eight or nine. He sold his first story, 'Expelled', to *The New Republic* after he was thrown out of Thayer Academy in South Braintree, Massachusetts, at the age

of 17. By the time he was 22 the *New Yorker* was accepting his work and for years he contributed a dozen stories a year to it. His first collection of stories was published in 1943 when he was in the army. After the war he taught freshman English and wrote scripts for television, but in 1951 a Guggenheim Fellowship allowed him to devote his attention to writing, and a second collection, *The Enormous Radio and Other Stories*, came out in 1953. His first novel, *The Wapshot Chronicle* (1957), won the National Book Award and its sequel, *The Wapshot Scandal* (1964), was awarded the Howell's Medal for fiction. A steady stream of novels and stories followed, many of them focusing on the isolation and discontent of contemporary American life. Invariably funny and ironic, sad and sophisticated, these include *Bullet Park* (1969), *The World of Apples* (1973), *Falconer* (1977) and *The Stories of John Cheever*, winner of the Pulitzer Prize and the National Book Critics Award in 1979.
▷*The Journals* (1990); S Cheever, *Home Before Dark* (1984)

CHEKHOV, Anton Pavlovich
(1860–1904)

Russian author, born in Taganrog, the son of an unsuccessful shopkeeper and the grandson of a serf. He studied medicine at Moscow University and qualified as a doctor in 1884. As a student, he had written articles for various comic papers, and his first book, *Pëstrye Rasskazy* ('Motley Stories'), appearing in 1886, was successful enough for him to think of writing as a profession. He continued to regard himself as a doctor rather than a writer, though he practised very little except during the cholera epidemic of 1892–3. His magazine articles led to an interest in the popular stage of vaudeville and French farce, and, after the failure of his first full-length play, *Ivanov* (1887, Eng trans 1912), he wrote several one-acters, such as *Medved* (1889, Eng trans *The Bear*, 1909) and *Predlozheniye* (1889, Eng trans *A Marriage Proposal*, 1914). In 1892 he settled on a farm estate at Melikhovo. His next full-length plays, *Leshy* (1889, Eng trans *The Wood Demon*, 1926) and *Chayka* (1896, Eng trans *The Seagull*, 1912), were also failures and Chekhov had decided to concentrate on his stories (which had introduced him to his admired **Tolstoy** and **Maxim Gorky**) when Nemirovich-Danchenko persuaded him to let the Moscow Art Theatre revive *Chayka* in 1898. Produced by Stanislavsky, who revealed its quality and originality, its reception encouraged him to write for the same company his masterpieces: *Dyadya Vanya* (1896, Eng trans *Uncle Vanya*, 1912), *Tri Sestry* (1901, Eng trans *The Three Sisters*, 1916) and *Vishnyovy Sad* (1904, Eng trans *The Cherry Orchard*, 1908). Meanwhile he continued to write short stories. In 1891 he wrote *Ostrov Sakhalin* (1895, 'Saghalien Island'), after a visit to a penal settlement which had a considerable effect on subsequent criminal legislation. In 1897 tuberculosis forced him to live either abroad or at Yalta in the Crimea. In 1900 he was elected fellow of the Moscow Academy of Science, but resigned when his fellow-member, Gorky, was dismissed by order of the tsar. In 1901 he married the actress Olga Knipper, who for many years after her husband's death was the admired exponent of female parts in his plays. Chekhov is perhaps the most popular Russian author outside his own country. His stories have strongly influenced many writers, and his plays are firmly established in the classical repertoires of Europe. His technique is impressionistic—almost *pointilliste*. In all his work he equates worldly success with loss of soul. It is the sensitive, hopefully struggling people, at the mercy of forces almost always too strong for them, who are his heroes. For this reason his work, though presenting a convincing picture of Russian middle-class life at the end of the 19th century, has a timeless quality, since it reflects the universal predicament of the 'little man'. Among his many short stories, the following are outstanding: *Step* ('The Steppe'), *Khoristka* ('The Chorus Girl'), *Duel* ('The Duel'), *Palata No. 6* ('Ward No 6'), *Dushetska* ('The Darling'), *Dama s sobachkoï* ('The Lady with the Dog') and *V ovrag'e* ('In the Ravine'). The bulk of his stories were translated in 13 volumes by Constance Garnett (1916–22).

▷ E J Simmons, *Chekhov: a biography* (1962)

CHÊNEDOLLÉ, Charles-Julien Lioult de
(1769–1833)

French poet, born in Vire. While living in Hamburg during the Revolution, he was a close friend to both **Rivarol** and **Klopstock**. Later he became a friend to **Constant de Rebecque**, and joined the circle of **Madame de Staël**. He became famous for his gigantic didactic poem *La Génie de l'Homme* (1807, 'The Genius of Man'). He is transitional between neo-classicism and romanticism. **Sainte-Beuve** introduced his collected works of 1864.

▷ L de Samie, *Chênedollé* (1922, in French)

CHÉNIER, (Marie) André
(1762–94)

French poet, born in Constantinople, the third son of the French consul-general and a Greek woman. At three he was sent to France, and at 12 was placed at the Collège de Navarre, Paris, where Greek literature was his special subject. At 20 he entered the army, and served for six months in Strasbourg; but

disgusted with military life, returned to Paris and to strenuous study. To this period belong his famous idylls *Le Mendiant* ('The Beggar') and *L'Aveugle* ('The Blind Man'). His health giving way, he travelled in Switzerland, Italy and the Greek Islands. In 1786 he returned to Paris and began several ambitious poems, most of which remained fragments. The most noteworthy are *Suzanne, L'Invention* and *Hermès*, the last being an imitation of **Lucretius**. In 1787 he went to England as secretary to the French ambassador, but in 1790 he returned to Paris to find himself in the ferment of the Revolution, which at first he supported; but alarmed by its excesses he mortally offended Robespierre by political pamphlets supporting liberal monarchism. He was thrown into prison, and six months later was guillotined on 25 July—three days before the end of the Reign of Terror. Almost nothing was published in his lifetime, but the appearance of his collected poems in 1819 made a notable impression on subsequent French poetry.

▷ V Loggins, *André Chénier, his life, death and glory* (1965)

CHÉNIER, Marie-Joseph Blaise
(1764–1811)

French republican playwright, born in Constantinople. He studied at the Collège de Navarre in Paris before embarking on a military career at the age of 17. Active in the overthrow of the Ancien Régime, he saw theatre as a political weapon, publishing, in 1789, a pamphlet entitled *De la liberté du théâtre en France*. He was a successful tragedian, the period between 1791 and 1794 yielding *Jean Calas* (c.1791), which transmutes a celebrated contemporary episode of religious fanaticism into political terms, *Henri VIII* (1791), *Caius Gracchus* (1792), *Fénelon* (1793) and *Timoléon* (1794), as well as some poetry and prose. A man of irascible temperament, Chénier voted his own brother, André, to the scaffold in 1794.

CHERBULIEZ, Charles Victor
(1829–99)

Swiss-born French novelist and critic, born in Geneva. At Paris, Bonn and Berlin, he studied first mathematics, then philology and philosophy, after which he lived in Geneva as a teacher. In 1864 he went to Paris to join the staff of the *Revue des Deux Mondes*, writing under the pseudonym of G Valbert. He was elected to the Académie française in 1881. His novels include *Le Roman d'une honnête femme* (1866, 'The Story of an Honest Woman'), *Meta Holdenis* (1873), *Samuel Brohl et Cie* (1877, 'Samuel Brohl & Co.'), *L'Idée de Jean Têterol* (1878, 'Jean Teterol's Idea'), *Noirs et rouges* (1881, 'Blacks and Reds'), *La Vocation* du Comte Ghislain (1888, 'Count Ghislain's Calling') and Le Secret du précepteur (1893, 'The Tutor's Secret'). He also wrote many literary and political articles in the Revue des Deux Mondes.

CHERBULIEZ, Joel
(1806–70)

Swiss novelist and critic, born in Geneva, the son of a prosperous bookseller. He succeeded to his father's business, and edited the Revue critique from 1833. His Lendemain du dernier jour d'un condamné (1829, 'The Day After a Condemned Man's Last Day') was a clever burlesque on **Victor Hugo**'s well-known tour de force, while his Genève (1867) was a solid contribution to the history of the city.

CHERNYSHEVSKI, Nikolai Gavrilovich
(1828–89)

Russian critic and novelist. A follower of the French socialists, he wrote on political, economic and social matters such as Nihilism, and saw his literary works in a utilitarian light. A spokesman for the radical intelligentsia, he was imprisoned in Siberia from 1862 to 1883 for revolutionary activities. His Esteticheski otnoshenia iskusstva k deistvitelnosti ('Aesthetic Relationship between Art and Reality') deals with his theory of the place of art in life, and his propagandist novel, Shto delat'? (1864, 'A Vital Question', also known as 'What Is To Be Done?'), was written during imprisonment, and is said to have in part provoked **Dostoyevsky**'s Zapiski iz podpol'ya ('Notes from Underground').
▷F B Randall, Nikolai Gavrilovich Chernyshevsky (1967)

CHESNUTT, Charles Wadell
(1858–1932)

American novelist and short-story writer, born in Cleveland, Ohio, where his family had taken refuge to escape the prejudice against free blacks in their native South. After the Civil War, they returned to North Carolina, where he was educated. He worked as a school teacher and a journalist, and came to national attention with two successful volumes of short stories on the issue of colour, The Conjure Woman (1899) and The Wife of His Youth (1899). He was an accomplished writer in this form, but his three subsequent novels dealing with racial issues were less successful. The Marrow of Tradition (1901), about the struggles facing black and white half-sisters, is the best of them. He also wrote regular essays and reviews in various journals.

CHESSEX Jacques
(1934–)

Swiss (Vaudois) novelist, poet and critic, whose work expresses his reaction to a very strict Calvinistic upbringing by a father who eventually killed himself. He has written much poetry, but his most important book is La Confession du Pastor Burn (1967, 'The Confession of Pastor Burn'), which has been compared, for the power of its self-analysis, to the work of **Constant de Rebecque**. He has written illuminatingly of the Vaud people, and of Swiss literature. For his novel L'Ogre (1973), whose subject is an overwhelming father (representing, a critic has suggested, the whole of the Vaud people), he received the Prix **Goncourt**.

CHESSMAN, Caryl Whittier
(1921–60)

American convict-author, born in St Joseph, Michigan. He was sentenced to death in 1948 on 17 charges of kidnapping, robbery and rape, but was granted eight stays of execution by the governor of California amounting to a record period of 12 years under sentence of death, without a reprieve. During this period he conducted a brilliant legal battle from prison, learnt four languages and wrote the bestselling, autobiographical books against capital punishment Cell 2455 Death Row (1954), Trial by Ordeal (1955) and The Face of Justice (1958). His ultimate execution provoked worldwide criticism of American judicial methods.

CHESTERTON, G(ilbert) K(eith)
(1874–1936)

English critic, novelist and poet, born in London. He was educated at St Paul's School and studied art at the Slade School, which he never practised professionally, although he contributed illustrations to the novels of his friend **Hilaire Belloc**. His first writings were for periodicals, and all through his life much of his best work went into essays and articles in The Bookman, The Speaker, The Illustrated London News, and his own G.K's Weekly, which was born in 1925 of the New Witness inherited from his brother a few years earlier. Tremendous zest and energy, with a mastery of paradox, a robust humour and forthright devotion characterize his entire output. He became a Roman Catholic in 1922, but this decision is clearly foreshadowed in his works, the best of which were published before that date. His two earliest books were the collections of poetry The Wild Knight and Greybeards at Play (both 1900); the works which followed include The Napoleon of Notting Hill

(1904), liberal and anti-Imperialist in outlook, also brilliant studies of **Robert Browning** (1903), **Dickens** (1906) and **Robert Louis Stevenson** (1907); and the provocative *Heretics* (1908) and *Orthodoxy* (1908). The amiable detective-priest Father Brown, who brought Chesterton popularity with a wider public, first appeared in *The Innocence of Father Brown* (1911). Soon after his conversion Chesterton published his well-known Life of St Francis of Assisi, also one of St Thomas Aquinas (1933). His *Collected Poems* appeared in 1933, and his *Autobiography* posthumously in 1936. An ebullient personality, with a figure of **Johnson**ian proportions, absent-minded but quick-witted, he will go down as one of the most colourful and provocative writers of his day. His brother, Cecil Edward (1879–1918), wrote anti-liberal books and started, with Hilaire Belloc, the anti-bureaucratic paper *New Witness* in 1912. He married Ada Elizabeth Jones, journalist and writer, who pioneered the Cecil Houses for London's homeless women.
▷P Braybrooke, *Gilbert Keith Chesterton* (1922); and other works by Braybrooke

CHETTLE, Henry
(c.1560–?1607)

English dramatist and pamphleteer, born in London, the son of a dyer. A printer by trade, he turned to writing when his printing-house failed. He edited **Robert Greene**'s *Groat's-worth of Wit* (1592), and in 1593 published a pamphlet, *Kind Harts Dreame*, apologizing for Greene's attack on **Shakespeare**. He wrote a picaresque romance, *Piers Plainnes Seven Yeres Prentiship* (1595), and from 1598 turned to writing plays for Philip Henslowe's Rose Theatre in Bankside, especially *The Tragedy of Hoffman* (1602). He collaborated on many others, including *Robin Hood, Patient Grisel, The Blind Beggar of Bednal-Green* (with **John Day**) and *Jane Shore*. He also wrote an elegy for Queen Elizabeth, *England's Mourning Garment* (1603).
▷H Jenkins, *The Life and Work of Henry Chettle* (1934)

CHEVALLIER, Gabriel
(1895–1969)

French novelist, born in Lyons. He won wide acclaim with his *Clochemerle* (1934, Eng trans 1936), an earthy satire on petty bureaucracy in a vividly evoked French town, after a series of less successful psychological novels. Other books include *La Peur* (1930, 'Fear'), *Clarisse Vernon* (1933), *Sainte-Colline* (1937), *Les Héritiers Euffe* (1945, 'The Euffe Inheritance'), *Le Petit général* (1951, 'The Little General') and *Clochemerle Babylone* (1954).

CHEYNEY, Peter, pseud of **Reginald Shorthouse Cheyney**
(1896–1951)

English crime writer in a hard-boiled US idiom. His first novel, *This Man is Dangerous* (1936), introduced the FBI man Lemmy Caution, a character with some of the characteristics of **Mickey Spillane**'s Mike Hammer. Other series included Alonzo MacTavish (who featured in **Leslie Charteris**-style short stories), and the American private investigator Slim Callaghan, who first appeared in *The Urgent Hangman* (1938). Cheyney also wrote a group of tense wartime spy thrillers, beginning with *Dark Duet* (1942) and always featuring 'dark' in the title. His style here was dry, precise and unaffected. Cheyney also wrote under the name Harold Brust.
▷M Harrison, *Peter Cheyney, Prince of Hokum* (1954)

CHIABRERA, Gabriello
(1552–1637)

Italian poet, born in Savona. Educated at Rome, he served Cardinal Cornaro, but was obliged to leave for revenging himself upon a Roman nobleman. An enthusiastic student of Greek, he skilfully imitated **Pindar** and **Anacreon**, while his *Lettere Famigliari* ('Family Letters') introduced the poetical epistle into Italian.
▷E N Girardi, *Esperienza e poesia di Gabriello Chiabrera* (1950)

CHIARELLI, Luigi
(1884–1947)

Italian playwright, born in Trani. A journalist who took to the stage, he had his first play, *Vita intima* ('Inner Life'), performed in 1909. His great success was *La Maschera e il volta* (1916, 'The Mask and the Face'), a farcical comedy translated into nearly every European language.
▷M Lo Vecchio O Musti, *L'Opere di Luigi Chiarelli* (1942)

CHILD, Lydia Maria
(1802–80)

American social campaigner, essayist and novelist, born in Watertown, Massachusetts. A committed campaigner for social and political reform, Child was editor of the *National Anti-Slavery Standard* and published many essays on political and social issues. Her *The History of the Condition of Women in Various Ages and Nations* (1835) suggested women's equal capacity in the workplace, and *An Appeal in Favor of that Class of Americans*

CHILDERS, Erskine

Called Africans (1833) was particularly influential for the abolitionist cause. She published several novels, including *Hobomok* (1824), describing the conflict between the Puritans and Native American tribes in Massachusetts Bay Colony, *The Rebels* (1825), a romance set during the American revolution, *Philothea* (1836), set in Ancient Greece at the time of Pericles, and *A Romance of the Republic* (1867), a 19th-century story which dramatized her anti-slavery convictions.
▷W S Osborne, *Lydia Maria Child* (1980)

CHILDERS, (Robert) Erskine
(1870–1922)

Anglo-Irish writer and nationalist, born in London. Educated at Haileybury and Trinity College, Cambridge, he was a clerk in the House of Commons from 1895 to 1910. He served as a volunteer in the 2nd Boer War (1899–1902). A skilled yachtsman, in 1903 he wrote a popular spy novel about a German invasion of Britain, called *The Riddle of the Sands*. In 1910 he devoted himself to working for Irish Home Rule, and used his yacht, the 'Asgard', to bring German arms to the Irish volunteers in 1914. Nonetheless he served in the Royal Navy in World War I. In 1921 he became a Sinn Fein member of the Irish parliament for County Widelow and Minister for Propaganda. He opposed the treaty that established the Irish Free State, joined the IRA, but was captured by the Free State authorities and executed. One of his sons, Erskine Hamilton Childers (1905–74), became the 4th President (1973–4).
▷A F B Williams, *Erskine Childers: 1870–1922* (1926)

CHIVERS, Thomas Holley
(1807/9–1858)

American poet, mystic and dramatist who finally became mad, but was reckoned by himself and some others as a potent influence on **Poe**, with whom he carried on a running quarrel over mutual charges of plagiarism. He was the son of a wealthy Georgian plantation owner. His biographer said that he possessed 'great genius but no talent', and that was, indeed, his unhappy fate. His most solid achievement was the invention of a machine which shredded fibre from silkworm cocoons. His poems, in one of which he compares his heart to a broken egg, are laughable and yet, in their aspirations, deeply touching. His chief philosophical work was *Search After Truth: or, A New Revelation of the Psycho-Physiological Nature of Man* (1848).
▷S F Damon, *Thomas Holley Chivers: Friend of Poe* (1930)

CHOCANO, José Santos
(1875–1934)

Grandiloquent Peruvian poet, bigamist and murderer, supporter of Pancho Villa and then advisor to and apologist for the Guatemalan dictator Estrada Cabrera (the president of the *El presidente* of **Asturias**), almost executed on the latter's downfall, and finally assassinated on a Santiago tram by a madman. He spent the years 1925–7 in prison in his own country, for murdering a young critic, Edwin Elmore, who had failed to agree with him—and then left Peru in disgrace. Yet Chocano, born in Lima, was a gifted poet, whose achievement has been hailed by many—and who may have influenced **Neruda**. Though not a *modernista* poet, he introduced—as an arch opportunist—*modernismo* to Peru, and at one point his reputation rivalled that of **Darío** himself. At his best, as in *Oro de indias* (1940, 'Gold of the Indies'), Chocano is a genuinely autochthonous poet, with full sympathy for the Native Americans, who helped turn Latin-American poetry away from European models and towards its mysterious interior. Some of his poems are translated in *Spirit of the Andes* (1935), and in the *Penguin Book of Latin American Verse* (1971, ed E Curacciolo-Trejo).
▷L A Sanchéz, *Aladino* (1960)

CHODOROV, Edward
(1904–)

American stage manager, dramatist and director, brother of **Jerome Chodorov**. His first play, *Wonder Boy* (1931), written with Arthur Barton (1904–36), satirized Hollywood. *Kind Lady* (1934) was a memorable chiller about a woman kidnapped in her own home by macabre villains.

CHODOROV, Jerome
(1911–)

American playwright and screenwriter, born in New York, brother of **Edward Chodorov**. Although Chodorov was a prolific and efficient author of light comedies on his own account, writing such plays as *Three Bags Full* (1966) and *A Community of Two* (1974), and such screenplays as *Two Girls on Broadway* (1939) and *Happy Anniversary* (1959), he is mainly known for his collaborations with Joseph Fields. These include *Anniversary Waltz* (1954). Their most famous collaboration, and the work for which Chodorov will probably be best remembered, is their adaptation of their own play, *My Sister Eileen* (1940), as the book for the musical, *Wonderful Town*, for which the score was composed by Leonard Bernstein. He also successfully adapted **Eudora Welty**'s *The Ponder Heart* (1956) for the stage.

CHOPIN, Katherine ('Kate'), née
O'Flaherty
(1851–1904)
American novelist, short-story writer and
poet, born in St Louis, Missouri. The daughter of an Irish immigrant and a French–Creole
mother, she was well educated at the Sacred
Heart convent, made her 'debut' in society
and married Oscar Chopin, a Creole cotton
trader from Louisiana. It was a happy
marriage, scarred only by business failure.
After her husband died of swamp fever (1882)
she returned with their six children to St Louis
where she began to compose sketches of her
life in 'Old Natachitoches', such as *Bayou
Folk* (1894) and *A Night in Acadie* (1897).
This work gives no indication of the furore
she aroused with the publication of a realistic
novel of sexual passion, *The Awakening*
(1899), which was harshly condemned by the
public. Thereafter she wrote only a few poems
and short stories. Interest in her work was
revived by **Edmund Wilson**, and she has since
been embraced by feminists as a *fin de siècle*
iconoclast bravely articulating the plight of
the 'lost' woman.
▷P Seyersted, *Kate Chopin, a critical biography* (1969)

CHOQUETTE, Robert
(1905–)
French–Canadian poet and novelist, born in
the USA. **A J M Smith** has spoken of his
'boldness' and 'ability to create on a large
scale': he cultivated, Smith suggested, a
poetry 'that was to be at once national and
filled with energy and thought'. Choquette
has written much for radio and television. His
chief mentor is **Hugo**, and in *Suite marine*
(1953), an immense poem about the sea, he
has created what Smith called 'a long and
beautifully sustained poem'. *La Pension Le-
blanc* is the best of his novels.
▷A J M Smith, *The Oxford Book of Canadian
Verse* (1960)

CHORELL, Walentin
(1912–)
Versatile Finland–Swedish dramatist and
novelist, who has written all kinds of plays,
from farces to high tragedies. They are often
performed throughout Scandinavia and Germany. His *Madame* (1952) deals with the fantasies of a retired prima donna; the impressive
Gräset (1958) treats the theme of incest.

CHOROMÁNSKI, Michal
(1904–72)
Polish novelist who was born and brought up
in Russia, and lived there for the first 20 years
of his life. He started as a translator of Polish

works into Russian, and also put much Russian poetry into Polish. His best novels,
highly anticipatory of modernist techniques
(as is much Polish writing), are his earlier
ones, chief of which is *Zazdość i medycyna*
(1932, Eng trans *Jealousy and Medicine*,
1946), about a surgeon who relieves himself
of his jealousies in the course of a phantasmal
operation.

CHRÉTIEN DE TROYES
(d.c.1183)
French poet and troubadour, born in Troyes,
in Champagne, and author of the earliest
romances dealing with the King Arthur
legend. The greatest of the French medieval
poets, he was a member of the court of the
Countess Marie de Champagne, daughter of
Louis VII, and to whom he dedicated his
metrical romance of courtly love, *Yvain et
Lancelot*. His other romances were *Érec et
Énide* (c.1160), *Cligès* (c.1164), and the unfinished *Perceval, ou Le Conte du Graal* (c.1180,
'Percival, or the Story of the Holy Grail'). His
works enjoyed huge popularity throughout
medieval Europe.
▷U T Holmes, *Chrétien de Troyes* (1970)

CHRISTENSEN, Inger
(1935–)
Danish poet, novelist and essayist. Born in
Vejle, she trained as a teacher, and had her
first book of poetry published in 1962. Her
modernist texts locate the individual within
structures that he or she simultaneously creates and is created by; her use of language
and form highlight the inclusion of her own
works in this process. The novel *Evighedsma-
skinen* (1964, 'The Eternity Machine') is a
modern version of the story of Christ, while
her second novel, *Azorno* (1967), employs an
elaborate series of experiments to explore the
borderline between fiction and reality. *Det*
(1969, 'It') is a book of poetry which has
been characterized as a poetic drama. The
magnificent poetic structure of *Alfabet* (1981,
'Alphabet') focuses on creativity and annihilation, adding a prominent ecological dimension. She was elected a member of the Danish
Academy in 1978.
▷I Holk (ed), *Tegnverden. En bog om Inger
Christensens forfatterskab* (1983)

CHRISTIANSEN, Sigurd Wesley
(1891–1947)
Norwegian novelist and dramatist. His first
book was published in 1915, but his great
breakthrough came in 1931 with the novel *To
levende og en død* (Eng trans *Two Living and
One Dead*, 1932), first prize-winner in an
important Scandinavian competition. This
novel, easier than most of his other works,

189

focuses on the ethical values recurrent in all Christiansen's writing. Although he is not an overtly Christian author, his typical themes, such as freedom versus responsibility and guilt, are often linked to Christian ethics. Intensive soul-searching for motives behind our actions is a hallmark of what is regarded as his greatest work, the trilogy *Drømmen og livet* (1935, 'Dream and Life'), *Det ensomme hjertet* (1939, 'The Lonely Heart') and *Menneskenes lodd* (1945, 'Man's Destiny'), dating from 1935 to 1945.

▷ E Kielland, *Sigurd Christiansen i liv og diktning* (1952)

CHRISTIE, Dame Agatha Mary Clarissa, née Miller
(1890–1976)

English author, born in Torquay. Under the surname of her first husband (Colonel Christie, divorced 1928), she wrote more than 70 classic detective novels, featuring the Belgian detective, Hercule Poirot, or the village spinster, Miss Jane Marple. In 1930 she married Sir Max Mallowan (1904–1978), the noted archaeologist. Between December 1953 and January 1954, she achieved three concurrent West End productions, *The Spider's Web*, *Witness for the Prosecution* and *The Mousetrap*, which continued its record-breaking run into the 1990s. Her best-known novels are *The Mysterious Affair at Styles* (1920), first featuring the Belgian detective Poirot; *The Murder of Roger Ackroyd* (1926); *Murder at the Vicarage* (1930), introducing Miss Marple; *Murder on the Orient Express* (1934); *Death on the Nile* (1937); *And Then There Were Nine* (1941) and *Curtain* (1975), in which Poirot met his end. She also wrote under the pen-name 'Mary Westmacott'.

▷ R Barnard, *A Talent to Deceive* (1975)

CHRISTINE DE PISAN
(c.1364–1431)

French poet, born in Venice. She was daughter of an Italian who was court astrologer to Charles V. Brought up in Paris, in 1378 she married Étienne Castel, who became the king's secretary, but died in 1389. Left with three children and no money, she was obliged to call upon her literary talents and between 1399 and 1415 produced a number of brilliant works in both prose and verse, including a biography of Charles V for Philippe, Duke of Burgundy; *Cité des dames* ('City of Women'), a translation from **Boccaccio**; and *Livres des trois vertus* ('Books of the Three Virtues'), an educational and social compendium for women. Her love poems have grace and charm, but lack depth. Christine is noteworthy for her defence of the female sex, hitherto a target for satirists. Saddened by the misfortunes of the Hundred

Years War she withdrew to a nunnery in about 1418 but lived to write in celebration of Joan of Arc's early successes in 1429.

▷ E M D Robineau, *Christine de Pisan. Sa vie, ses oeuvres* (1883)

CHRISTOPHER, John, pseud of Samuel Youd
(1922–)

English novelist and science-fiction writer, born in Knowseley, Cheshire. A hugely prolific writer, he has published a few novels, including his first, *The Winter Swan* (1949), under his real name. He has since emerged under several pseudonyms, including Peter Nichols, Peter Graaf, William Godfrey and Hilary Ford. He is best known as John Christopher, writing science fiction for adults and children. *No Blade of Grass* (1956) is a particularly highly regarded adult novel of fantasy. For young people, *The Tripods Trilogy* (1967–8) imagines that the consequences of an alien invasion and domination of Earth might be an imposed feudal society; *The Sword Trilogy* (1970–2) suggests that a series of natural disasters might precipitate a similar outcome, while *The Fireball Trilogy* (1981–6), considers a Europe governed by the Roman Empire.

CHUDLEIGH, Lady Mary, née Lee
(1656–1710)

English poet and essayist, born in Winslade, Devon. In 1674 she married George Chudleigh, who became baronet in 1691. Though confined to what she called the 'rough and unpolished life' of Devon, she read widely and corresponded with other writers. The influence of the feminist, Mary Astell, is apparent in her best-known work, *The Ladies Defence* (1701), a spirited verse-debate exposing male prejudices and the deficiencies of female education. She also published *Poems on Several Occasions* (1703) and *Essays upon Several Subjects in Verse and Prose* (1710).

▷ M Ferguson, (ed), *First Feminists: British Women Writers 1578–1799* (1985)

CHUKOVSKY, Korney, pseud of Nikolay Vasilyevich Korneychuk
(1882–1969)

Russian translator (**Whitman, Defoe, Dickens** and many others), critic and children's writer, born in St Petersburg. As a young man he lived in London, where he picked up an extensive knowledge and understanding of English literature. He was the leading editor and critic of **Nekrasov**.

CHUMACERO, Ali
(1918–)

Minor Mexican poet of a highly intellectual cast. One of his most impressive poems, 'Losa del Desconocido' ('Gravestone of an Unknown Man'), is translated in J M Cohen (ed), the *Penguin Book of Spanish Verse* (1956).

▷R Xirau, *Poetas de México y España* (1962)

CHURCH, Richard
(1893–1972)

English novelist, poet and essayist, born in London. Until the age of 40 he financed his writing by working as a civil servant. This and subsequent periods of his life form the subject of his two autobiographical volumes, *Over the Bridge* (1955) and *The Golden Sovereign* (1957). *The Porch* (1937) was among the best received of his novels, and won the Femina Vie-Heureuse Prize. He also wrote for children. His poetry, as represented in *Collected Poems* (1948), is well disciplined and restrained in both form and content. Applauded as a polished craftsman in a more genteel era, he is wholly out of favour in our own age, in which the absence of rough edges appears to be regarded by some with suspicion and disdain.

CHURCHILL, Caryl
(1938–)

English dramatist. Her first play was *Light Shining* (1976), about the Levellers. Her greatest commercial success has been *Serious Money* (1987), satirizing the world of the young, get-rich-quick City financial brokers. Other plays include *Cloud Nine* (1979), *Top Girls* (1982), *Fen* (1983) and *Softcops* (1984), all of greater dramatic quality than *Serious Money*.

CHURCHILL, Charles
(1731–64)

English satirical poet, born in Westminster, the son of a curate. He was educated at Westminster School and went on to John's College, Cambridge, but ruined his academic career with a clandestine marriage at the age of 17. With his father's help he was ordained priest in 1756, and at his father's death in 1758 succeeded him as curate of St John's, Westminster. But after a bankruptcy, a formal separation from his wife and a course of unclerical dissipation, he gave up the church (1763). His *Rosciad* (1761) had already made him famous and a terror to actors. *The Apology* (also 1761) was a savage onslaught on his critics, particularly **Tobias Smollett**. In *Night* (1762) he lengthily replied to criticisms of his life. *The Ghost* (1762) ridiculed **Dr Johnson** and others in over 4000 lines. He next helped John Wilkes in the *North Briton*, and heaped ridicule upon the Scots in *The Prophecy of Famine* (1763), an admirable satire. For *The Epistle to Hogarth* (1763) the artist retaliated

with a savage caricature. Other works include *The Candidate* (1764), *Independence* (1794), and, unfinished, *The Journey* and the masterly *Dedication*. He died suddenly on a visit to Wilkes in France. He lacked the chief essential of true satire, a real insight into the heart of man, but possessed volubility in rhyming, boisterous energy, and an instinctive hatred of wrong.

▷W C Brown, *Poet, rake and rebel* (1953)

CHURCHILL, Sir Winston
(1875–1965)

British statesman and writer, born in Blenheim Palace, and awarded the Nobel Prize for literature. This was grossly out of proportion to his merits as a writer, but, like **Caesar**, he was one of the select few soldier-statesmen who have had the gift of the written gab, although his finest efforts are the radio speeches he gave to the British people during the war with Hitler. His novel *Savrola* (1900) is of no account, but *Marlborough* (1933–8), written while he was out of office and the Nazis were being appeased by his party, is a valuable biography. His history of World War II, in six volumes (1948–54), is his best single work, written as it is from the inside.

CHURCHILL, Winston
(1871–1947)

American historical novelist, born in St Louis, Missouri. His works include *Richard Carvel* (1899) and *The Crisis* (1901), and show a significant insight into the workings of political life which Churchill knew at first hand as New Hampshire delegate to the Republican National Convention (1904) and Progressive Party candidate for governorship (1912).

▷R W Schneider, *The Life and Thought of Churchill* (1976)

CHURCHYARD, Thomas
(1520–1604)

English soldier of fortune and writer, born in Shrewsbury. He served in Scotland, Ireland and the Low Countries under the Earl of Surrey and published many verse and prose pieces, the best-known being *The Legend of Shore's Wife* (1563, in *A Mirror for Magistrates*), and *Worthiness of Wales* (1587).

CHUTE, Anthony
(d.?1595)

Elizabethan poet, author of *Beawtie Dishonoured* (1593), largely plagiarized from **Thomas Churchyard**'s *Legend of Shore's Wife*. He was patronized by **Gabriel Harvey** and assailed by **Thomas Nashe** the satirist.

CIARDI, John
(1916–85)

American poet, translator (his version of the Divine Comedy of **Dante**, 1954–61, is one of the most highly esteemed of its time—'a shining deed in a bad age'), teacher and editor (of the poetry in the *Saturday Review*), born in Boston. Influenced mostly by **Yeats** in his own poetry, he aimed to steer a course between the 'Baroque' and ordinary 'poesy', being most successful in his lighter, colloquial vein.

▷ *As If, Poems New and Selected* (1955)

CICERO, Marcus Tullius
(106–43 BC)

Roman orator, statesman, and writer, born in Arpinum in Latium, of a wealthy family. At Rome he studied law and oratory, Greek philosophy, and Greek literature. He saw military service in the war of 90–88 BC under Pompeius Strabo, the father of Pompey the Great. His first important speech, in his twenty-sixth year, was the successful defence of a client against a favourite of the dictator Sulla. After a two-year stay in Athens and Rhodes, he was elected quaestor (76), and obtained an appointment in Sicily; at the request of the Sicilians he undertook his successful impeachment of the corrupt governor Gaius Verres in 70. In 63 he was consul, and foiled the plot of Catiline by carrying out the Senate's order to execute five of the conspirators. Hailed as 'father of his country' Cicero was for a brief space the great man of the day, but the tide soon turned. Faced with prosecution for the summary execution of the conspirators, he was condemned to exile. Though recalled in 57, he was no longer a power in politics, where the overriding question was the mounting rivalry between Pompey and **Caesar**. On the outbreak of the Civil War he joined Pompey's army in Greece, but after the defeat at Pharsalus (48) threw himself on Caesar's mercy. In 46–44 he wrote most of his chief works on rhetoric and philosophy, living in retirement and brooding over his disappointments. In 43, after Caesar's death, his famous speeches against Mark Antony, the *Philippics*, were delivered, and cost him his life. As soon as Antony, Octavian and Lepidus had leagued themselves in the triumvirate, they proscribed their enemies, and Cicero's name was on the fatal list. Old and feeble, he fled to his villa at Formiae, pursued by the soldiers of Antony, and was overtaken as he was being carried in a litter. With calm courage he put his head out of the litter and bade the murderers strike. He was in his sixty-fourth year. As orator and pleader Cicero stands in the first rank; of his speeches the most famous are those against Verres and Catiline. As a politician, though in the end defeated, he was one of the outstanding figures of the late Republic. He is best remembered as an essayist and letter-writer, especially for his essays *De Senectute* ('On Old Age') and *De Amicitia* ('On Friendship'). His voluminous correspondence is one of the principal sources of knowledge of the politics of his time, and his prose style was a model for the orators of the next four centuries.

▷ D Stockton, *Cicero: a political biography* (1971)

CICOGNANI, Bruno
(1879–1972)

Italian novelist, story writer and playwright, born in Florence into a family with literary connections (**Carducci, D'Annunzio**). He began in the high-romantic, decadent manner of D'Annunzio, but developed his own style in his psychological novels of Florentine life, in which he excelled in the portrayal of female characters: *La Velia* (1922) and *Villa Beatrice* (1931) are typically rich, precise masterpieces. His autobiographical works are often taken to be even better than these two novels; *L'omino che a spento i fochi* (1937, 'The Little Man Who Has Put Out the Fires') recollects his youth. His most successful play was *Yo, el rey* (1949, 'I, the King').

CISNEROS, Sandra
(1954–)

Mexican–American novelist and short-story writer, born and brought up 'rat poor' in Chicago. She was educated at Iowa University before returning home to work as an educator and arts administrator in the Latino community. In 1984 she published *The House on Mango Street*, a series of stories linked through the consciousness of a young girl. This was followed by a poetry collection, *My Wicked Ways* (1987), and another short-story collection, *Woman Hollering Creek* (1991). The foremost talent in a new wave of US Latina authors, her writing conveys the sensory textures of Chicano life with precise, prismatic brilliance, her polyphonic style capturing the *barrio*'s many diverse voices with vibrant immediacy.

CLARE, John
(1793–1864)

English peasant poet, born in Helpstone, near Peterborough, the son of a poor labourer. Though almost without schooling, he studied **James Thomson**'s *Seasons*, and began to cultivate verse writing as well as gardening. After serving in the Northamptonshire militia (1812–14), in 1817 he published *Proposals for Publishing a Collection of Trifles in Verse* at his own expense, but got no subscribers. It led, however, to the publication of his *Poems*

Descriptive of Rural Life (1820), which had a good reception; but though the Marquis of Exeter and other patrons secured him £45 a year, he continued to live in poverty, and went insane. His other published works were *Village Minstrel* (1821), *The Shepherd's Calendar* (1827) and *Rural Muse* (1835). He was committed to an asylum in Epping in 1837, and later in Northampton in 1841, where he died.

▷ J W Tibble and A Tibble, *John Clare: a life* (1972)

CLARETIE, Jules, properly **Arsène Arnaud** (1840–1913)

French novelist, born in Limoges. While a schoolboy in Paris he published a novel, and soon became a leading critic and political writer. His short story *Pierrille* (1863) was praised by **George Sand**. His novels also were generally popular. During the Franco–German war he sent a series of remarkable letters to the *Rappel* and *Opinion nationale*, and acquired the materials for a later series of bright and vigorous anti-German books of a historical character. He first made a hit on the stage with his Revolution plays, *Les Muscadins* (1874), *Le Régiment de Champagne* (1877) and *Les Mirabeau* (1878); in 1885 he became director of the Comédie Française.

▷ G de Cherville, *Jules Claretie* (1883, in French)

CLARÍN, pseud of **Leopoldo Alas y Ureña** (1852–1901)

Spanish novelist, critic and short-story writer, born in Zamora. In his teens he moved to Oviedo, where he studied law, eventually (1883) becoming a professor. His criticism, although lapsing on occasion into legalistic prolixity, brought a much-needed rigour to the Spanish literary scene of the late 19th century. Short-story volumes such as *Cuentos Morales* (1896, 'Moral Tales') display his mature style—more relaxed and less verbose—to best advantage. In the English-speaking world he is now known almost exclusively as the author of *La Regenta* (1884), an epic account, influenced by *Madame Bovary*, of the suffocating effect of small-city life on an intelligent, frustrated young woman.

CLARK, Charles Manning Hope (1915–91)

Australian historian and writer, born in Burwood, New South Wales, the son of a vicar. Educated at Melbourne and Oxford universities, in 1949 he became the first Professor of Australian History at the Australian National University, where he popularized the study of Australian history with his collections *Select Documents in Australian History* (1950–5) and *Sources of Australian History* (1957). Clark was never far from the centre of controversy on political issues, and his strong republican views colour his six-volume *A History of Australia* (1962–88). Although criticized by academics, it remains a considerable achievement and was successfully abridged into one volume by Michael Cathcart in 1993. His partly autobiographical fiction *Disquiet and Other Stories* (1969) was republished with additional material as *Manning Clark: Collected Short Stories* in 1986. He also wrote a contentious biographical essay *In Search of Henry Lawson* (1978). The first volume of a projected autobiography, *The Puzzles of Childhood*, was published in 1989, followed in 1990 by *The Quest for Grace*, a very personal odyssey 'in search of the unknowable'.

CLARK, Eleanor (1913–)

American novelist, non-fiction and short-story writer, born in Los Angeles, California and educated at Vassar College. She worked for a publishing firm and the US Office of Strategic Services before devoting herself to writing. She has twice received a Guggenheim Fellowship. In the 24 years between *The Bitter Box* (1946), her first novel, and *Baldur's Gate* (1970), her second, Clark wrote essays and longer non-fiction work, dominated by the themes of tradition, ecology, and the quest for values; *The Oysters of Locmariaquer* won the National Book Award for Non-Fiction in 1965. She has also published a collection of short stories and a children's book.

▷ Eleanor Clark issue of *The New England Review* (Winter 1979)

CLARK, John Pepper (1935–)

Nigerian poet, playwright and critic who, since his collection *State of the Union* (1985), has signed himself J P Clark Bekederemo. In 1964 he published an angry attack upon the America he knew, *Their America*; his Parvin Scholarship at Princeton was terminated on account of it. His lyrical poetry has been called over-diffuse even by his admirers, but plays, such as *Song of a Goat* (1961), have received more praise. His selected poems are in *A Decade of Tongues* (1981).

▷ R M Wren, *John Pepper Clark* (1984)

CLARK, Mavis Thorpe (?1912–)

Australian writer of books for older children, born in Melbourne. Educated at the Methodist Ladies College there, she attracted attention with *The Brown Land was Green* (1956), the story of a pioneer family, which became a long-running serial on ABC radio, as did *Gully of Gold* (1958) and *They Came South* (1963). *The Min-Min* (1967) was Australian Children's Book of the Year. Australian settings are also prominent in such novels as *Spark of Opal* (1968) and *Iron Mountain* (1970). Later titles include *Young and Brave* (1984), *No Mean Destiny* (1986) and *Soft Shoe* (1988). She has also written a biography of *John Batman* (1962), the founder of Melbourne, and *Paster Doug* (1965), the autobiography of Sir Douglas Nicholls, the first aborigine to be knighted and to become a state governor.

CLARK, Walter van Tilburg
(1909–71)

American novelist and short-story writer. Born in East Orland, Maine, he moved to Nevada in childhood and was educated there before returning to New England. While teaching English (and basketball) at Cazenovia High School in New York City, he wrote his first and best novel, *The Ox-Bow Incident* (1940), a tense Western with an unmistakable allegorical subtext about the rise of fascism. Clark's belief that liberalism is powerless in the face of mob violence and charismatic leadership anticipates the themes of **Mailer**'s post-war *The Naked and the Dead*. Clark's next novel, *The City of Trembling Leaves* (1945, republished as *Tim Hazard*, 1951), was a disappointment, but his skill returned with *The Track of the Cat* (1949), a **Faulkner**-influenced account of a panther hunt, with an obsessive psychological undercurrent. Clark's short stories were collected in *The Watchful Gods* (1950), after which he published nothing more.

▷M Westbrook, *Walter van Tilburg Clark* (1969)

CLARK, Arthur C(harles)
(1917–)

English writer of science fiction, born in Minehead, Somerset. He worked in scientific research before turning to fiction: he was a radar instructor in World War II, and originated the idea of satellite communication in a scientific article in 1945. A prolific writer and an unashamed entertainer, his themes are exploration—in both the near and distant future—and man's position in the hierarchy of the universe. His first book was *Prelude to Space* (1951) and while he is credited with some of the genre's best examples—*Rendezvous with Rama* (1973), *The Fountains of Paradise* (1979)—his name will always be associated first with *2001: A Space Odyssey* (1968), which, under the direction of Stanley Kubrick, became a highly successful film. He emigrated to Sri Lanka in the 1950s.

CLARKE, Austin
(1896–1974)

Irish poet and dramatist, born in Dublin where he was educated at the Jesuit Belvedere College and University College. He spent 15 years in England as a book reviewer and journalist before returning to Dublin in 1937. *The Vengeance of Fionn*, the first of 18 books of verse, was published in 1917. Like other earlier verse, it is markedly influenced by **W B Yeats** and his obsession with Irish mythology, but he shook this off and developed into a technically accomplished poet, sharply satirical, and critical, of Irish attitudes. *Collected Poems* was published in 1974. He was also a noted playwright and an adherent of verse drama which he promoted through the Dublin Verse-Speaking Society which he formed in 1941. His plays, drawing heavily on Irish legend, were collected in 1963. His first novel, *The Bright Temptation* (1932), was banned in Ireland until 1954. *Twice Round the Black Church* (1962) and *A Penny in the Clouds* (1968) are autobiographical.

CLARKE, Gillian
(1937–)

Welsh poet, born in Cardiff and educated at the city's University College. Her earliest collections of poems, *Snow on the Mountain* (1971) and *Sundial* (1978), were followed by the more widely-read *Letter from a Far Country* (1982). *Selected Poems* followed in 1985, then *Letting in the Rumour* (1989). She was editor of *The Anglo-Welsh Review* from 1976 to 1984, and since 1987 has been Chair of the Welsh Academy.

CLARKE, Marcus
(1846–81)

Australian novelist, born and educated in London. Collapse of the family fortunes having sent him to Australia where relatives had held high office, he contributed to the Melbourne press while working first as a bank clerk and then on sheep stations. As with many of his books, his first novel, *Long Odds* (1860), began life as a serial. He visited Tasmania to study its convict past; the subsequent articles were worked up into *Old Tales of a Young Country* (1871), and formed the basis for his best-known book, *His Natural Life* (1874, rev edn as *For the Term of His Natural Life*, 1882, under which title it was filmed and is now best known). Further financial problems were abated by his writing for the stage and contributing on various topics to newspapers and journals. He died destitute; most of his ephemeral work was subsequently collected in *The Selected Works of Marcus Clarke* (1890), and three books of

Australian tales published in 1896–7.

▷B Elliott, *Marcus Clarke* (1958)

CLARKE, Thomas Ernest Bennett
(1907–89)

English screenwriter and novelist, born in Watford, Hertfordshire. A graduate in law from Cambridge University, he lived in Australia and Argentina before returning to England, working as a reporter for the *Daily Sketch* and writing a series of novels, including *Go South—Go West* (1932) and *Cartwright Was A Cad* (1937). The wartime drama *For Those In Peril* (1944) marked his first work for the screen and he soon became one of the key creative figures at Ealing Studios, writing across a range of genres and creating a series of films that reflected the traditional English character with whimsical humour and affection. His best-known credits include *Hue and Cry* (1946), *Passport To Pimlico* (1948), *The Blue Lamp* (1949) and *The Lavender Hill Mob* (1951), for which he received an Oscar. His work away from Ealing was less distinctive, although he provided a notable adaptation of **D H Lawrence**'s *Sons and Lovers* (1960) for the cinema.

▷ *This Is Where I Came In* (1974)

CLAUDEL, Paul
(1868–1955)

French poet, essayist and dramatist, born in Villeneuve-sur-Fère. Now regarded as one of the major figures in French Catholic literature, it was long before he was recognized, even by his countrymen. He joined the diplomatic service and held posts in many parts of the world. This experience, with the early influence of the Symbolists, adds quality and richness to his work. His dramas, of which the most celebrated are *L'Annonce faite à Marie* (1892, 'The Annunciation'), *Partage de Midi* (1905, Eng trans *Break of Noon*, 1960), *L'Otage* (1909, Eng trans *The Hostage*, 1917) and *Le Soulier de satin* (1921, Eng trans *The Satin Slipper*, 1931), have a Wagnerian grandeur and, in many cases, an anti-Protestant violence that make them too strong for popular taste. He wrote memorable poetry—*Cinq Grandes Odes* (1910, Eng trans *Five Great Odes*, 1967) and *Corona benignitatis anni dei* (1915, Eng trans *Coronal*, 1943)—and the libretti for two operas: *Jeanne d'Arc au bûcher* (1943, 'Joan of Arc at the Stake') by Honegger and *Christophe Colomb* (1929, Eng trans *Christopher Columbus*, 1930) by Milhaud. His later writings were mainly devoted to biblical exegesis.

▷H A Waters, *Paul Claudel* (1970)

CLAUDIAN (Claudius Claudianus)
(4th–5th century)

The last of the great Latin poets. He came from Alexandria to Rome in AD 395, and obtained patrician dignity by favour of Stilicho, whose fall (408) he seems not to have long survived. A pagan, he wrote first in Greek, though he was of Roman extraction. Several epic poems by him, including *The Rape of Proserpine*, panegyrics on Honorius, Stilicho and others, invectives against Rufinus and Eutropius, occasional poems, and a Greek fragment, *Gigantomachia*, are still extant.

▷J H E Crews, *Claudian as Historical Authority* (1908)

CLAUDIUS, Matthias
(1740–1815)

German poet and editor (of the *Der Wandsbecker Bote*, a local newspaper), born in Reinfeld, into the family of a pastor. He studied law and theology at Jena. He is often called the father of popular (serious) German journalism, and is famous for his euphemism for death: 'Freund Hein'. The part of his poetry that is not falsely hearty is perhaps as good as uninspired poetry can be: pastoral, simple, good-hearted.

▷I Rüttenhauer, *M. Claudius* (1952, in German)

CLAUS, Hugo Maurice Julien
(1929–)

Belgian dramatist, fiction writer, poet, and film-maker, writing in Dutch. He was born in Bruges and worked as a farm labourer, house painter and actor before turning to full-time writing. His essential subject is the conflict of the natural world with abstract reason. This is evident in his fine first novel *De metsiers* (1950, published in the USA as *The Duck Hunt*, 1965, in the UK as *Sister of Earth*, 1966), one of only a few of his works known in English, and also in the brilliant play *De dans vande reiger* (1962, 'The Heron's Dance', later adapted as a screenplay, 1966). His most remarkable poem is the long *Het teken van de hamster* (1979, 'At the Sign of the Hamster'). Claus wrote the libretto for the collaborative opera *Reconstructie* (1969), composed by Louis Andriessen, Reinbert de Leeuw, Misha Mengelberg, Peter Schat, and Jan van Vlijmen. He has won the Belgian State Prize for drama three times (1955, 1967, 1973) and for poetry (1971).

▷B Kooijman, *Hugo Claus* (1973)

CLAUSSEN, Sophus Niels Christen
(1865–1931)

Danish poet, born in Heletoft, the son of a farmer and rural politician. He gave up law to concentrate on journalism and writing and lived for many years in France, where he came into contact with the symbolists, later translating **Baudelaire**, as well as **Heine** and **Shelley**. His best-known poem, 'Rejseminder' ('Recollections of a Journey'), establishes the characteristic tone of erotic reverie which runs through *Naturbørn* (1887, 'Children of Nature'), his first book. Later works were less realistic in detail and the poems in *Djaevlerier* (1904, 'Demonism') are overtly Symbolist and psychological. His complete works were published in seven volumes in 1910.

▷E Frandsen, *Sophus Claussen* (1950)

CLAVELL, James du Maresq
(1924–)

Australian-born American novelist, film producer and director, born in Sydney. Now based in New York, his work in film includes scripting the epic war movies *The Great Escape* (1960, from the book by **Paul Brickhill**) and *633 Squadron* (1963). He served during World War II and was a prisoner-of-war in Changi Jail, Singapore. The clash of East and West runs through his Asian Saga, which covers three and a half centuries, beginning in the year 1600 with *Shogun* (1975), *Tai-Pan* (1966) and *Gai-Jin* (1983). *King Rat* (1962), *Noble House* (1980) and *Whirlwind* (1986) bring the story up to the year 1979. Clavell has also published an edition of Sun Tzu's 4th-century BC classic, *The Art of War*.

CLAYTON, Richard Henry Michael *see* HAGGARD, William

CLEARY, Jon Stephen
(1917–)

Australian novelist, born in Sydney, who served in the Middle East and New Guinea during World War II. His first book after the war was a collection of short stories, *These Small Glories* (1946). This was followed by *You Can't See Round Corners* (1947), which had won a newspaper competition the year before, the story of deserter and small-time crook Frankie McCoy and his descent into murder in wartime Sydney. *The Sundowners* (1952), set in the depressed Australia of the 1920s, was his first big success, and was followed by over 40 novels, of which some of the best known are *The Climate of Courage* (1954, filmed as *Naked in the Night*, 1963), *The Commissioner* (1966, filmed as *Nobody Runs Forever*, 1968) and *High Road to China* (1977, filmed 1982). Cleary's well-constructed plots and detailed research of settings lend themselves admirably to the large screen. In *The High Commissioner* Cleary introduced the character of Scobie Malone, a hybrid from **Dashiell Hammett**'s Sam Spade school, who returns in five other books including *Helga's Web* (1970, filmed as *Scobie Malone*, 1975) and *Babylon South* (1989).

CLELAND, John
(1709–89)

English novelist, born in London. He was educated at Westminster School, and after a spell in the consular service and in the East India Company, followed by vagrant travel in Europe, he published in 1750 a pornographic novel, *Fanny Hill, or the Memoirs of a Woman of Pleasure*, a bestseller in its time which achieved a second *succès de scandale* on its revival and subsequent prosecution under the Obscene Publications Act in 1963. He also wrote *Memoirs of a Coxcomb* (1751), and *The Surprises of Love* (1764).

▷W H Epstein, *John Cleland: images of a life* (1974)

CLEMO, (Reginald) Jack (John)
(1916–91)

English poet, born in St Austell, Cornwall. The earlier poems, collected in *The Clay Verge* (1951) and *The Map of Clay* (1961), are largely descriptive of the Cornish clay-mining landscape. After he lost his sight in 1955, his work increasingly involved itself with an inner vision of sacramental love and suffering. Clemo pointed to the influence of **Francis Thompson** and **D H Lawrence**, but his rejection of bland nature mysticism and his preoccupation with original sin set him apart from the English Romantics. Nothing made a more immediate impact on his verse than the gospel rhythms of American evangelists like Billy Graham. With *The Echoing Tip* (1971), which followed his marriage, the sexual element in his verse becomes less prominent and in *Broad Autumn* (1975) he develops a more abstract and philosophical vision. The term is appropriate because Clemo always rejected interpretations based solely on his physical handicap.

▷*Confession of a Rebel* (1949); *The Marriage of a Rebel: A Mystical Erotic Quest* (1980)

CLEVELAND, John
(1613–58)

English Cavalier poet, born in Loughborough, Leicestershire, son of a poor clergyman who was ousted by parliament from the living of Hinckley in 1645. In 1627 he entered Christ's College, Cambridge, graduated BA four years later, and then moved to St John's College, where he was elected to a fellowship in 1634 and lived nine years as 'the delight and ornament of the society'. He vigorously opposed Cromwell's election to the Long Parliament for Cambridge, and was for his loyalty himself ejected from his fellowship in 1645. He joined the Royalist army, and was appointed judge advocate at Newark, but was obliged to surrender with the garrison. In 1655 he was arrested at Norwich, but was released by Cromwell, who could admire the courageous manliness of the poor poet's letter addressed to him. In 1656 he published a volume containing 36 poems—elegies on Charles I, Strafford, Laud and Edward King, and also some stinging satires. Cleveland now went to live at Gray's Inn, where he died. In 1677 was published, with a short Life, *Clievelandi Vindiciae*. Extremely popular as a poet in his day, he is little read now.

▷B Morris, *John Cleveland, 1613–1658: a bibliography* (1967)

CLIFF, Michele
(1946–)

Jamaican writer, whose family left Jamaica to live in New York when Cliff was three years old. She has called her work a 'search into the diasporic experience'. In *Claiming An Identity They Taught Me To Despise* (1980) she charted a personal and political history in a miscellany of prose and poetry. She is a 'mixed blood Jamaican' and in both the novels *Abeno* (1984) and *No Telephone To Heaven* (1987) there is a light-skinned heroine, Clare Savage. Her poetry is included in the Caribbean anthology *Creation Fire* (1989, ed Espinet).

CLIFT, Charmian
(1923–69)

Australian novelist and essayist, born in Kiama, New South Wales, and associated with the novelist **George Johnston**, whom she married in 1947. They travelled to London and then, with their three children, lived in Greece for 10 years, providing the setting for much of Clift's best writing. She wrote three novels in collaboration with Johnston, *High Valley* (1949), *The Big Chariot* (1953) and *The Sponge Divers* (1955). Her own work included two novels, *Walk to the Paradise Gardens* (1960) and *Honour's Mimic* (1964), and accounts of their life in Greece in *Mermaid Singing* (1956) and *Peel me a Lotus* (1959). Johnston later edited two collections of Clift's essays, *Images in Aspic* (1965) and *The World of Charmian Clift* (1970).

CLOSSON, Herman
(1901–)

Belgian playwright, born in Brussels. His drama, deriving from that of his compatriots **Maeterlinck** and **Crommelynck**, deals with the notion of greatness. Thus, in *William ou La Comédie de l'aventure* (1938, 'William, or the Comedy of Adventure'), **Shakespeare** is tempted into sacrificing a play for the sake of slaking his lust in a fantastic modern setting. Other plays, which treat the same theme, include ones about Joan of Arc, Cesare Borgia and Godefroy de Bouillon.

▷D Grossvogel, *20th Century French Drama* (1961)

CLOUGH, Arthur Hugh
(1819–61)

English poet, born in Liverpool, the son of a cotton merchant who emigrated to Charleston, USA, in 1823. The boy was sent back to England in 1828 and entered Rugby, where he became Dr Thomas Arnold's most promising pupil and where he began his friendship with **Matthew Arnold**. Though he only got a 'second' at Balliol College, Oxford, in 1841, he was elected a fellow of Oriel College and there lived through the crisis which resulted in **Newman**'s conversion to Rome. His own difficulties with the Thirty-nine Articles led to his resignation in 1848. He became for a time principal of the new University Hall, attached to University College, Gower Street, which had a Unitarian bias little to Clough's liking ('the Sadducees', he called them). On his dismissal from University Hall he obtained an examinership in the education department. Before taking up that appointment he spent some months in Boston, Massachusetts, where he met the Boston Brahmins. Financial worries added to his religious troubles; in the year he got his fellowship at Oriel his father became a bankrupt. He seems not to have enjoyed much of a family life before his marriage to Blanche Smith in 1854. The last years of his short life were relatively happy. He enjoyed not only the friendship of the great Victorians, **John Ruskin**, Arnold and **Thomas Carlyle**, but also of distinguished Americans of the Boston connection. At Oriel he was the self-confident leader of a group, Members of the Decade, and conducted reading parties in vacations to the Lakes and to Scotland. The latter resulted in a 'Long-vacation pastoral' called *The Bothie of Tober-na-Vuolich* (1848), which delighted those of his friends whom it did not outrage. His only other long poems were *Amours de voyage*, written in Rome in 1849; and *Dipsychus*, 1850, both published posthumously. Arnold hesitated for 10 years to write his commemorative poem *Thyrsis*. The two-volume *Correspondence* published in 1957 shows that Clough's dilemma was not confined to the Thirty-nine Articles (to which after all he subscribed) but to the whole of what is now called the Establishment. He followed the revolutionary doctrines of **George Sand**, called himself a republican, disliked class distinction ('your aversion, the Gentleman') and the capitalist system. He left two more long poems, *Mari Magno* and *Adam and Eve*, unfinished.

▷W V Harris, *Arthur Hugh Clough* (1970); Evelyn B Grenberger, *Arthur Hugh Clough* (1970)

CLUNE, Frank (Francis Patrick)
(1893–1971)

Australian writer of biography, history and adventure, born in the dockside district of Woolloomooloo, Sydney, of Irish extraction. His early life was one of travel and adventure at sea, in Europe and America. He served with the Australian Imperial Forces in World War I and was wounded at Gallipoli. A vagabond life followed, and marriage, then a career in accountancy. At the age of 40, while recuperating from an ulcer, he decided to write the story of his early years; this was published as *Try Anything Once* (1933, which includes a hilarious account of his brief career with a touring opera company) and Clune was launched into a writing career. He wrote over 60 books, often in collaboration with P R ('Inky') Stephensen, and became one of Australia's bestselling writers. Of popular appeal, Clune's work such as *Rolling down the Lachlan* (1935), *Wild Colonial Boys* (1948) and *Ben Hall the Bushranger* (1947) aroused interest in stories of Australian history.
▷ *Try Nothing Twice* (1946); *Korean Diary* (1955); B Adamson, *Francis Clune, author and ethnological anachronism* (1944)

COATES, Robert M(yron)
(1897–1973)

American novelist, short-story writer, journalist, travel writer and art critic, born in New Haven, Connecticut. Although critically well-regarded for his atmospheric novels, such as *The Eater of Darkness* (1929), and books including *Hour after Westerly and other Stories* (1957), Coates is more widely known for the accounts of his Italian travels. *Beyond the Alps* (1961) and *South of Rome* (1965), are considered among the most lucid, evocative and informed volumes of travel writing.

COATSWORTH, Elizabeth (Jane)
(1893–1986)

American novelist, poet and writer for children. She grew up in Buffalo, New York, and spent much of her life in New England, which is the main setting for her work. Her best-known book is *The Cat Who Went to Heaven* (1930), a prize-winning piece of children's fiction and perhaps her best prose work. Her adult novels, *Here I Stay* (1938) and *The Trunk* (1941), tend to lack its imaginative freedom, but something of this is captured in the verse, notably in *Fox Footprints* (1923), *Country Poems* (1942) and *The Creaking Stair* (1942), which might be compared with the work of **Ruth Pitter** in England. Her understanding of country ways is evident in the non-fiction *Country Neighbourhood* (1944). In a long life, she published well over 60 books.
▷ *Personal Geography* (1976)

COBBETT, William
(1763–1835)

English writer and champion of the poor, born in Farnham, Surrey, the son of a small farmer. In 1784 he enlisted in the 54th Foot, taught himself to read and write, and served as sergeant-major in New Brunswick (1785–91), meanwhile studying rhetoric, geometry, logic, French and fortification. He bought his discharge in 1791, and brought charges of corruption against several of his officers, but went to France when he was not even called to give evidence at the court-martial. After mastering the language he sailed for America (1792). In Philadelphia he taught English to French refugees, opened a bookshop and published a paper called *Porcupine's Gazette* (1797–9). Under the pseudonym 'Peter Porcupine' he wrote fierce onslaughts on Joseph Priestley, **Tom Paine** and the native Democrats. Twice he was prosecuted for libel, and in 1800 he returned to England. The Tories welcomed him with open arms and in 1802 he started his weekly *Cobbett's Political Register*, which, with a three-months' break in 1817, continued till his death. Tory at first, he altered its politics in 1804, till at last it became the most uncompromising champion of Radicalism. He initiated the publication of *Parliamentary Debate* (1806, later taken over by Luke Hansard) and *State Trials* (1809). A great lover of the country, he purchased a model farm at Botley in Hampshire. He got two years in Newgate (1810–12) for his strictures on flogging in the army. In 1817 money muddles and dread of a second imprisonment drove him once more across the Atlantic and he farmed in Long Island, published a *Grammar of the English Language* (1819) and, in 1819, ventured back to England. Botley had to be sold, but he started a seed-farm at Kensington and stood unsuccessfully for parliament in 1821 and 1826. In 1831 he defended himself against a charge of sedition, and in 1832, after the First Reform Bill, he entered parliament as member for Oldham. His celebrated *Rural Rides* (1830), a delightful picture of a vanishing world, were reprinted from the *Register*. He also published a savage *History of the Reformation* (1824–7), *The Woodlands* (1825), *Advice to Young Men* (1830), and 40 or 50 more works.
▷ G D H Cole, *The Life of Cobbett* (1924)

COBBING, Bob
(1920–)

English sound and concrete poet, born in Enfield, Middlesex, who rejects conventional verse in favour of diagrammatized forms, phonetic 'choreography' and improvisational contexts with jazz musicians and dancers. Cobbing has worked as a civil servant, farmer, teacher and publisher; most of his work has appeared under his own Writers Forum imprint, which he established in 1963. From a huge output, the most effective and representative collections are *Sound Poems: An ABC in Sound* (1965), *The Five Vowels* (1974) and *Bob Cob's Rag Bag* (1977). A festival favourite, alone and with his group abAna, much of his work has been recorded. *Concerning Concrete Poetry* (1978, with Peter Mayer) was the latest in a group of nondiscursive manifestos. His interest in printing technique and electronic synthesis by no means negates his essentially simple, even primitive, approach.

▷P Mayer (ed), *Bob Cobbing and Writers Forum* (1974)

COBLENTZ, Stanton A
(1896–1981)

American poet and writer, born in San Francisco. He was a popular poet of some skill and merit, whose best work is gathered in *Garnered Sheaves: Selected Poems* (1949).

COCKBURN, Alison or Alicia, née Rutherford
(1713–94)

Scottish poet, born in Selkirkshire. In 1731 she married Patrick Cockburn, an advocate, and for over 60 years she was a leading figure in Edinburgh society. Of her lyrics, the best known is the exquisite version of 'The Flowers of the Forest' ('I've seen the smiling of Fortune beguiling'), which commemorates a wave of calamity that swept over Ettrick Forest, and was first printed in 1765. In 1777 she discerned in **Walter Scott** 'the most extraordinary genius of a boy'; in 1786 she made **Robert Burns**'s acquaintance.

▷*Letters and Memoirs of Her Own Life* (1900)

COCTEAU, Jean
(1889–1963)

French poet, playwright and film director, born in Maisons-Lafitte, near Paris. Success came early with *La Lampe d'Aladin* (1909, 'Aladdin's Lamp'), and he exploited it. He postured and preened and ran the gamut of experience, first a spectacular conversion to Roman Catholicism through Jacques Maritain; a derisive repudiation of his mentor; recourse to opium; and search for salvation through solitude. Nevertheless he had astonishing success with whatever he touched. He figured as the sponsor of Picasso, Stravinsky, Giorgio de Chirico and the musical group known as *Les Six*, in complete accord with the Surrealist and Dadaist movements. He was actor, director, scenario writer, novelist, critic, artist, and all of his work was marked by vivacity and a pyrotechnic brilliance. He was elected to the Académie française in 1955. Significant works are his novels *Le Grand Écart* (1923, Eng trans *The Grand Escort*, 1925), *Thomas l'Imposteur* (1923, Eng trans *Thomas the Imposter*, 1925), *Les Enfants terribles* (1929, Eng trans *Enfants Terribles*, 1930), and plays: *Les Mariés de la Tour Eiffel* (1921, Eng trans *The Eiffel Tower Wedding Party*, 1963), *Orphée* (1926, Eng trans *Orpheus*, 1933) and *L'Aigle a deux têtes* (1946, Eng trans *The Eagle has Two Heads*, 1948). His films include *Le Sang d'un poète* (1930, 'The Blood of a Poet'), *La Belle et la bête* (1945, 'Beauty and the Beast'), *Orphée* (adapted from his play, 1949) and *Le Testament d'Orphée* (1960).

▷F Brown, *An Impersonation of Angels: a biography of Cocteau* (1968)

COETZEE, J(ohn) M(ichael)
(1940–)

South African novelist, born in Cape Town. The political situation in his native country provides him with the base from which to launch his allegories and fables, attacking colonialism and demythologizing historical and contemporary myths of imperialism. His first work of fiction was *Dusklands* (1974), followed by *In the Heart of the Country* (1977), *Waiting for the Barbarians* (1980), *Life and Times of Michael K* (1983), for which he was awarded the Booker Prize, and *Foe* (1986).

COFFEY, Brian
(1905–)

Irish poet, born in Dun Laoghaire, County Dublin; he studied with the French Catholic philosopher Jacques Maritan in Paris. A professor of philosophy in the USA for most of his life, Coffey reached a general public with his consistently experimental verse with *Selected Poems* (1971). A deep questioning of freedom, both personal and ethical, informs all his work and is seen to best effect in *Poems and Versions 1929–1990* (1991).

COFFEY, Brian *see* KOONTZ, Dean R(ay)

COFFIN, Robert Peter Tristram
(1892–1955)

American writer, born in Brunswick, Maine. He graduated from Bowdoin College in 1915, was a Rhodes Scholar at Oxford, and became Professor of English at Wells College in Aurora, New York State, in 1921, while also running two farms in Maine. He was a prolific author, but was best known for his robust pastoral poetry, collected in several volumes, beginning with *Golden Falcon* (1929). He won the Pulitzer Prize for Poetry in 1936 for *Strange Holiness* (1935), and a *Collected Poems* was published in 1948. He also wrote novels, biography, the autobiographical volume *Lost Paradise* (1934), and collections of essays ranging from literary criticism to family reminiscences and sketches of rural Maine life.

COHAN, George M(ichael)
(1878–1942)

American playwright, actor and theatre manager, born in New York. Among his plays, which were highly popular at the time, are *Johnny Jones* (1904) and *The Song and Dance Man* (1923). His songs include 'Over There', one of the best-loved numbers of American servicemen. Cohan is best known to a later generation through the 1942 film *Yankee Doodle Dandy*, in which he was played with grinning gusto by James Cagney. The autobiography *Twenty Years on Broadway* (1925) recalls his time atop the seething heap of New York's theatre world.

COHEN, Leonard Norman
(1934–)

Canadian poet, novelist and singer, whose work is valued strictly in that order in his native country, the opposite order almost everywhere else. Though his background is Jewish, he grew up in the predominantly Catholic city of Montreal, and the title of his first collection, *Let Us Compare Mythologies* (1956), offers an indication of how he has moved between traditions. *The Spice-Box of Earth* (1961) and *Flowers for Hitler* (1964) both examine aspects of the Jewish experience, but increasingly in the context of a Christianity somewhat eroticized and frequently ironic. A novel, *The Favorite Game* (1963), was written in London; *Beautiful Losers* (1966) was in the same verbosely surreal line. His recording contract with Columbia began with *The Songs of Leonard Cohen* in 1968, the same year as his *Selected Poems* appeared. Later volumes such as *The Energy of Slaves* (1972) seemed to document a rather thoughtful mid-life crisis, but with *Book of Mercy* (1984) Cohen began again to write lyrics with the strong metre and imagery of the Psalms and marked by his personal vision of redemption.
▷S Scobie, *Leonard Cohen* (1978)

COHEN, Matt(hew)
(1942–)

Canadian novelist, born in Kingston, Ontario, and educated in Ottawa and Toronto. He lectured in religion for two semesters at McMaster University, Hamilton, Ontario,

before the publication of his short novel *Korsoniloff* (1969), the diary of a self-divided academic whose very existence is a problem in philosophy. *Johnny Crackle Sings* (1971) is also concerned with self-awareness; its drug-taking rock-star hero has become an artefact, image rather than substance. Cohen takes up the theme again in his best book, *The Disinherited* (1974), which tackles a more generous social and temporal range than its predecessors. Later books are weaker, though *The Sweet Second Summer of Kitty Malone* (1979) has a gentle elegiac quality which, though different from Cohen's usual manner, is highly effective. His short stories are collected in *Night Flights* (1978) and *The Expatriate* (1981); later stories appeared in *Café le dog* (1983, published in the USA as *Life on This Planet*, 1985).

COIMIN, Mícheál
(1688–1760)

Irish poet from County Clare. He wrote of **Ossian** even as **Macpherson** was working in Scotland, and his *Laoidh Oisin ar Thir na nóg* was translated as *Lay of Oisin in the Land of Youth* in 1896.

COKAYNE, Sir Aston
(1608–84)

English minor poet, playwright and translator. The best-known of his very slight works is his version of the *Diana* of **Montemayor**.
▷ *Poems by Sir Aston Cokayne* (1877); *Dramatic Works* (1965)

COLCORD, Lincoln (Ross)
(1883–1947)

American poet, novelist and mariner. Colcord was born at sea but settled in Maine, where he studied engineering and began to write. His first major work was a novel, *The Game of Life and Death* (1914), which merits comparison with **Dana**'s equally autobiographical *Two Years Before the Mast*. In the following year, with American involvement in World War I looming, he published the long poem *Vision of War*. His other notable novel was *An Instrument of the Gods* (1922).

COLEGATE, Isabel Diana
(1931–)

English novelist, born in Lincolnshire. Between 1952 and 1957 she worked as a literary agent. Her first novel, *The Blackmailer*, appeared in 1958, since when she has written several interlinked works, of which the most ambitious is the *Orlando* trilogy: *Orlando King* (1968), *Orlando at the Brazen Threshold* (1971) and *Agatha* (1973). These trace the rise of Orlando King, from his adoption by a Cambridge don, to his appointment as a Cabinet Minister at the outbreak of World War II, and eventually to his retiral in Italy. Colegate's most notable novel, *The Shooting Party* (1980), dealing with tragic events at a country house in the autumn of 1913, is a perceptive, affectionate but critical study of a social class whose lives were to be altered by war and its consequences.

COLERIDGE, Hartley
(1796–1849)

English writer, eldest son of **Samuel Taylor Coleridge**, born in Clevedon, Somerset. He was brought up by **Robert Southey** at Greta Hall, and educated at Ambleside school and Merton College, Oxford. His scholarship was great but unequal; his failures to win the Newdigate filled him with 'a passionate despondency'; and he forfeited an Oriel College fellowship by intemperance. He spent two years in London, tried taking pupils at Ambleside, occasionally writing for *Blackwood's Magazine*, lived for some time at Grasmere, and then went to live at Leeds with a publisher, for whom he wrote biographies, published under the titles of *Biographia Borealis* (1833) and *Worthies of Yorkshire and Lancashire* (1836). He subsequently lived at Grasmere, with two short intervals of teaching at Sedbergh. Provided for by an annuity, he continued to write poetry, and edited **John Ford** and **Philip Massinger**. His days were spent in fitful study, lonely reverie, and wanderings over the Lake Country, with occasional bouts of intemperance. His poetry is graceful, tender and sincere.

▷ Earl Griggs, *Hartley Coleridge, his life and work* (1929)

COLERIDGE, Samuel Taylor
(1772–1834)

English poet, son of a vicar of Ottery St Mary, Devon. The youngest of a very large family, he had an unhappy childhood, and was educated at Christ's Hospital and went to Jesus College, Cambridge, to study for the church. His university career was interrupted in 1793 by a runaway enlistment in the 15th Dragoons, from which he was rescued by his family. On a walking tour in 1794 he met **Robert Southey** at Balliol College, Oxford, with whom he shared Romantic and revolutionary views. Together they planned a 'pantisocracy' or communist society on the banks of the Susquehanna, in Pennsylvania, but the idea came to nothing. In 1795 he married Sarah Fricker, a friend of Southey's, while her sister Edith married Southey. He had contributed some verses to the *Morning Chronicle* in 1793, and now he wrote, with Southey, a historical play, *The Fall of Robespierre*. He now became immersed in lecturing

and journalism in Bristol, interspersed with itinerant preaching at Unitarian chapels. The Bristol circle provided Coleridge with generous friends, notably Joseph Cottle the bookseller, who published his first book of poems, *Poems on Various Subjects* (1796), which contained the 'Ode to France'. In 1797 the Coleridges moved to a cottage at Nether Stowey, Somerset, and later that year met **William** and **Dorothy Wordsworth**. The result was momentous for English poetry—from their discussions emerged a new poetry which represented a revulsion from neo-classic artificiality and, as a consequence, the renovation of the language of poetry. *Lyrical Ballads* (1798), which opened with Coleridge's 'Ancient Mariner' and closed with Wordsworth's 'Tintern Abbey', was thus in the nature of a manifesto. A visit to Germany with the Wordsworths (1798–9) followed. German philosophy and criticism influenced him greatly and he published translations of **Schiller**'s *Piccolomini* and *Wallenstein*. In 1800 he moved to Keswick and for a time, with the Wordsworths at Grasmere and Southey already resident at Keswick, it looked as if a fruitful career was opening out for him, but his moral collapse, due partly to opium, made the next few years a misery to him and his friends. His 'Ode to Dejection' (1802) is both a recantation of Wordsworth's animistic view of Nature and a confession of failure. From then on his association with Wordsworth was strained; his relations with Dorothy continued only through her devotion to him. He had a sojourn in Malta as secretary to the Governor from 1804 to 1806. In 1809 he began a weekly paper, *The Friend*, which ran for 28 issues and was published as a book in 1818. In 1810 he finally broke with Wordsworth and settled in London, where he engaged in various activities, including miscellaneous writing and lecturing at the Royal Institution (his lectures on **Shakespeare** alone are extant). He also wrote a play, *Remorse* (1813), which had a mild success at Drury Lane. In 1816 he published 'Christabel' and the fragment, 'Kubla Khan', both written in his earlier period of inspiration. He had long relinquished the idea of renewing that inspiration and resigned himself, as he indicates in the close of 'Dejection', to philosophical speculation. His critical writing in these middle years is important also as the finest 'creative' criticism in the language, collected in *Biographia Literaria* (1817), *Aids to Reflection* (1825) and *Anima Poetae* (edited from his notebooks, 1895). He was a gifted poet and a writer of theological and politico-sociological works which have a relevance even today.

▷ J L Lowes, *The Road to Xanadu* (1927); T D Campbell, *Samuel Taylor Coleridge: a narrative of the events of his life* (1894)

COLET, Louise

COLET, Louise
(1810–76)

French poet, born in Aix-en-Provence and resident in Paris after marriage to Hippolyte Colet, a violin professor at the Conservatoire there. Her florid, passionate poetry, often on the theme of love's earth-shaking powers, is collected in *Fleurs du Midi* (1836), *Poesies* (1844) and *Ce qui est dans le coeur des femmes* (1852). She won the poetry prize of the Académie française four times, though according to some she had more beauty than writing talent. Infamous for violent behaviour and affairs with prominent writers such as **Flaubert** and **Alfred de Musset**, she gave the details in *Lui, roman contemporain* (1851, 'Him, A View of Him') which, in the words of critic Marilyn Gaddis Rose, involves 'skilful counterpointing of the personal and professional dilemmas of two women of letters in the 19th century'.
▷ M Bood and S Grand, *L'indomptable Louise Colet* (1986)

COLETTE, Sidonie-Gabrielle
(1873–1954)

French novelist, born in Saint-Sauveur-en-Puisaye. Her early novels, the *Claudine* series, were published by her first husband, Henri Gauthier-Villars, under his pen-name 'Willy'. After their divorce in 1906 she appeared in music-halls in dance and mime, and out of this period came *L'Envers du music-hall* (1913, Eng trans *Music-Hall Sidelights*, 1957). Her work is characterized by an intense, almost entirely physical preoccupation with immediate sense experiences. Her novels include *Chéri* (1920, Eng trans 1929), *La Fin de Chéri* (1926, Eng trans *The Last of Chéri*, 1932), *La Chatte* (1933, Eng trans *The Cat*, 1936) and *Gigi* (1944, Eng trans 1953). She married Henri de Jouvenel in 1912, and in 1935, Maurice Goudeket.
▷ J Richardson, *Colette* (1983)

COLIN MUSET
(b.c.1210)

French poet, from Champagne, of whom little is known except his poetry, from which he earned his living as a jongleur. He was a producer of light, happy verse, refreshingly free of the artifice beloved by so many of his contemporaries. Whereas they all discuss courtly love, Muset is content to talk of real emotions and real pleasures, souring this tone only with the occasional outburst against the cruelty and greed of his rich patrons. Around 15 of his poems survive, all of them short, some with their original simple musical settings.

COLLETT, (Jacobine) Camilla, née Wergeland
(1813–95)

Norwegian novelist, born in Kristiansand. She grew up in a much stricter environment than her brother, the poet **Hendrik Arnold Wergeland**, and in adult life she became a passionate champion of women's rights. Her novel *Amtmandens døttre* (1855, 'The Magistrate's Daughters') is notable for its sympathetic portrayal of young women trapped by stultifying convention. *I den lange naetter* (1862, 'Through the Long Nights') is an insomniac's pillow-book, reconstructing childhood scenes. Her occasional pieces were published in three volumes of *Sidtse blade* (1868, 1872, 1873).
▷ A Collett, *Camilla Colletts livshistorie* (1911)

COLLIANDER, Tito
(1904–)

Finland–Swedish novelist and biographer (Ilya Repin), born in St Petersburg; he taught religion (Greek Orthodox) and art in schools, finally becoming a professor and writing a book about the problems of faith and everyday life (1951). His novels, none of which has been translated, trace mystical quests; they somewhat resemble those of **Mauriac**, but are less melodramatic and the viewpoint is Greek Orthodox.

COLLIER, Jeremy
(1650–1726)

Anglican Church historian and controversialist, born at Stow, Cambridgeshire, and educated at Ipswich and Cambridge. A nonjuring bishop who opposed William and Mary, he was fierce in his polemics, which resulted in prison spells and temporary exile abroad as a political 'outlaw'. His *Ecclesiastical History of Great Britain* (1708–14) has considerable scholarly merit. He is best known, however, for *A Short View of the Immorality and Profaneness of the English Stage* (1698), a devastating attack on Restoration dramatists. Replies by **Dryden**, **Congreve**, **Vanbrugh** and others were generally considered to be ineffective. Collier's strictures did much ostensibly to reform, but actually tame, comic drama in the 18th century.
▷ Sister Rose Anthony, *The Jeremy Collier Controversy* (1937)

COLLIER, John, known as 'Tim Bobbin'
(1708–86)

English poet, born in Urmston, near Manchester, the son of the curate of Stretford. From 1729 he was usher or master of a school at Milnrow, near Rochdale. His rhyming satire, *The Blackbird*, appeared in 1739, and his *View of the Lancashire Dialect* (in humorous dialogue) in 1775.

▷J P Briscoe, *The Literature of Tim Bobbin* (1872)

COLLIER, Mary
(c.1690–c.1763)

English poet, born near Midhurst, Sussex to poor parents, she was taught to read at home. After her parents' death she earned her living by washing, brewing and field-work, later as housekeeper in Hampshire. Her best-known poem, 'The Woman's Labour' (1739), written in retort to **Stephen Duck**'s slighting reference to women's work in 'The Thresher's Labour', is forthright in expression and full of realistic detail. Labouring women, she protested, work even harder than men, for 'when we home are come,/Alas! we find our work has just begun'. She also published *Poems on Several Occasions* (1762). *The Thresher's Labour and The Woman's Labour*, ed M Ferguson was published in 1985.

▷D Landry, *Muses of Resistance* (1990)

COLLINS, Jackie
(1937–)

Bestselling English novelist, born in London. Expelled from school at 15, she moved to Hollywood in search of fame as a film actress. Instead, she has made a career out of writing fiction about the Hollywood set. Since the publication of her first novel, *The World is Full of Married Men*, in 1968, that career has been one of uninterrupted success. *The Stud* (1969) and *The Bitch* (1972) were both subsequently filmed starring her older sister, Joan Collins. *Hollywood Wives* (1983) is perhaps the archetypal Collins novel, being an engaging amalgam of young love, ageing lust, sex, shopping, glamour, grime, violence, drugs and rock'n'roll. And more sex. By 1994 she had sold in excess of 170 million copies of her books worldwide.

COLLINS, (William) Wilkie
(1824–89)

English novelist, elder son of the artist William Collins (1788–1847), born in London. He was educated partly at Highbury, but from 1836 to 1839 was with his parents in Italy. After his return he spent four years in business, and then was called to the Bar, but gradually turned to literature, his *Life* of his father (1848) being his earliest production. His first work of fiction was a novel about the fall of Rome, *Antonina* (1850). With *Basil* (1852) he turned his attention to mystery, suspense and crime. His best work was written in the 1860s when he produced *The Woman in White* (1860), *No Name* (1862), *Armadale* (1866) and *The Moonstone* (1868).

His popularity with the reading public declined after 1870, and his later novels, often driven by pressing social issues, are more uneven in quality.

▷K Robinson, *Wilkie Collins: a biography* (1951); William H Marshall, *Wilkie Collins* (1950)

COLLINS, William
(1721–59)

English poet, born in Chichester, the son of a hatter. He was educated at Winchester and Magdalen College, Oxford, but having been pronounced 'too indolent even for the army', and dissuaded from entering the church, as the sole alternative he came to London to make a living by literature. During this period he spent an inheritance, in advance of receiving it, and was forced to live on credit, reduced at times to the greatest straits; **Dr Johnson** once rescued him from the bailiffs by obtaining an advance from a bookseller on the promise of Collins to translate the *Poetics* of Aristotle. It was during this period, however, that he wrote his *Odes*, upon which his fame rests. They attracted no notice at the time of publication (1747), and were little valued even by **Thomas Gray** and Dr Johnson. On the death of an uncle in 1749, Collins inherited £2000, which enabled him to retire to Chichester, and apparently to pursue a regular course of study. It was about this time that he met **John Home**, the author of *Douglas*, and gave him his 'Ode on the Superstitions of the Highlands', a poem in which, says **James Lowell**, 'the whole Romantic School is foreshadowed'. His mental health broke down after a visit to France, and he died insane.

▷P L Carver, *The Life of a Poet: a biographical sketch* (1967)

COLLYMORE, Frank Appleton
(1893–1980)

Barbadian poet and story writer, educated at Combermere School, where he taught from 1910 to 1958. As founder and editor of the long-running literary magazine *Bim* from 1942 to 1975 he was a major force in the rise of modern West Indian literature. His short stories, published in *Bim* between 1942 and 1971, show a gift for strong characterization and insight into the dark recesses of the mind. He published five books of poems, notable chiefly for their evocation of the sea and Caribbean landscape and for a vein of social satire too seldom indulged. *Collected Poems* was published in 1959.

▷E Baugh, in *Fifty Caribbean Writers*, ed D C Dance (1986)

COLMAN, George, 'the Elder'
(1732–94)

English playwright and manager, born in Florence, the son of the English envoy. He was educated at Westminster and Oxford, and called to the Bar in 1755. In 1760 his first piece, *Polly Honeycombe*, was produced at Drury Lane with great success; next year came *The Jealous Wife*, and in 1766 *The Clandestine Marriage*, written in conjunction with Garrick. In 1767 he purchased, with three others, Covent Garden Theatre, and held the office of manager for seven years, until he sold his share. In 1776 he purchased the Haymarket Theatre from **Samuel Foote**, but was paralysed by a stroke from 1785.
▷ E R Page, *George Colman the Elder* (1935)

COLMAN, George, 'the Younger'
(1762–1836)

English playwright, son of **George Colman 'the Elder'**. He was educated at Westminster, Oxford and Aberdeen. During his father's illness he acted as manager of the Haymarket and on his death the patent was transferred to him. As Examiner of Plays from 1824 he showed himself both arrogant and excessively precise. In industry he rivalled his father, and he made money by his *John Bull, Iron Chest, Heir at Law* and other comedies, and by songs like 'Mynheer Van Dunck'. He wrote *Random Records of My Life* (1830).
▷ J F B Collins, *George Colman the Younger* (1946)

COLOMB, Catherine
(1899–1965)

Swiss (Vaudois) author of three novels which have been described as 'inexplicably neglected'. Paramount is *Les esprits de la terre* (1953, 'The Spirits of the Earth'), which deals with a leading family of wine-growers, and which fruitfully and convincingly employs such techniques as deliberate suppression of story-line and time-condensation; Colomb, claims a critic, 'possessed insights denied to the most of the "new novelists" '.

COLOMBO, John Robert
(1936–)

Canadian poet, translator, editor, journalist and sometime television personality ('Colombo's Quotes' series, 1978), born in Kitchener, Ontario. He is nationally known as the 'Master Gatherer' for his 'compilations of Canadiana' and has 'chosen not to live the life of the poet'. The essence of his poetry, much of it in free verse, has been summed up in his own lines: 'What is immensely important here is life itself: man/feeding on the world'. He has published more than 30 collections, including *Selected Poems* (1982).
▷ *Canadian Literature* (Summer, 1966)

COLONNA, Vittoria
(1490–1547)

Italian poet from Marino. Born into a noble Roman family, she married the Marquis of Pescara, but saw little of him. The arranged marriage turned into one of love-in-absence, and on his death in battle at Pavi (1525), she devoted her life to good causes. Her religious thinking was profound, as were her objections to corruption in her church. She inspired her friend Michelangelo to some of his finest poetry. Her own lyric poetry—**Petrarch**an in style—is of the first order, and deserves even more extended study than it has already had. Many translations are included in M F Jerrold's *Vittora Colonna* (1906, reprinted 1969).

COLUM, Pádraic
(1881–1972)

Irish poet and playwright, born in County Longford, the son of the warden of a workhouse. He was educated at a school in Longford, and worked as a railway clerk in Dublin. He became a leader of the Irish literary revival, and wrote plays for the Abbey Theatre including *Broken Soil* (1903, later called *The Fiddler's House*), *The Land* (1905) and *Thomas Muskerry* (1910). He published his first collection of poems, *Wild Earth*, in 1907. In 1916 he was co-founder of the *Irish Review*. From 1914 he lived in the USA, where he and his wife (Molly Maguire) taught comparative literature at Columbia University. He published two studies on Hawaiian folklore (1924 and 1926), the result of government-sponsored research. He wrote several further volumes of verse, including the lyric *She Moved Through the Fair*. His novel *The Flying Swans* (1957) was followed by the memoir *Our Friend James Joyce* (1958).
▷ Z R Brown, *Pádraic Colum* (1970)

COLUMBA, St, also known as Colmcille ('Colm of the Churches')
(521–97)

Irish apostle of Christianity in Scotland. According to his 7th-century biographer, Adomnán, he studied under St Finnian at Clonard with St Ciaran. In 546 he founded the monastery of Derry. In 561, however, he was accused of having been involved in the bloody Battle of Cuildreimhne, for which he was excommunicated and sentenced to exile. In 563, accompanied by 12 disciples, he set sail to do penance as a missionary, and found haven on the Hebridean island of Iona, where he founded a monastery that became the mother church of Celtic Christianity in Scotland. A formidably energetic administrator, he organized his monastery on Iona as a school for missionaries, and played a vig-

orous role in the politics of the country. Although he spent the last 34 years of his life in Scotland, he visited Ireland on occasions, and towards the end of his life he founded the monastery of Durrow in Ireland. He was renowned as a writer; he wrote hymns, and is credited with having transcribed 300 books with his own hand; but he was also revered as a warrior saint, and his supernatural aid was frequently invoked for victory in battle. He died on Iona and was buried in the abbey.
▷W D Simpson, *The Historical St Columba* (1927, rev edn 1963)

COLUMBAN, or COLUMBANUS, St
(543–615)

Irish missionary, 'the younger Columba', born in Leinster. He studied under St Comgall at Bangor in Down, and c.585 went to Gaul with 12 companions, and founded the monasteries of Anegray, Luxeuil and Fontaine in the Vosges country. His adherence to the Celtic Easter involved him in controversy; and the vigour with which he rebuked the vices of the Burgundian court led to his expulsion in 610. After a year or two at Bregenz, on Lake Constance, he went to Lombardy, and in 612 founded the monastery of Bobbio, in the Appenines, where he died. His writings, all in Latin, comprise a monastic rule, six poems on the vanity of life, 17 sermons and a commentary on the Psalms (1878).
▷C W Dispham, *Columban, Saint, Monk and Missionary* (1903)

COLUMELLA, Lucius Junius Moderatus
(1st century)

Roman writer on agriculture, born in Gades (Cadiz) in Spain. He wrote *De Re Rustica* (12 books), on arable and pasture lands, the culture of vines and olives, the care of domestic animals, and arboriculture. Book 10 (on gardening) is written in hexameters as an addendum to **Virgil**'s *Georgics*.
▷S Hedberg, *Contamination and Interpolation: a study of the 19th century MSS* (1968)

COMBE, William
(1741–1823)

English writer and adventurer, born in Bristol, renowned as the creator of *Dr Syntax*. The illegitimate son of a wealthy London alderman, he inherited a fortune in 1762 and led the life of an adventurer and spent much time in debtors' jails. Educated at Eton and Oxford, he wrote metrical satires like *The Diaboliad* (1776), but made his name with his three verse satires on popular travel-books. Illustrated with cartoons by Thomas Rowlandson, they recounted the adventures of a

clergyman schoolmaster on his holidays (based on William Gilpin), in *Dr Syntax in search of the Picturesque* (1809), *The Second Tour of Dr Syntax in search of Consolation* (1820) and *The Third Tour of Dr Syntax in search of a Wife* (1821). He also wrote the text for Rowlandson's *Dance of Death* (1815–16), *Dance of Life* (1816) and *Johnny Quae Genus* (1822), and for *The Microcosm of London* (1808).
▷H Hamilton, *Doctor Syntax: a silhouette of William Combe Esq* (1969)

COMFORT, Alex(ander)
(1920–)

English biologist, gerontologist, social critic, poet and novelist of anarchist sensibilities, born in London. He is probably now best known for his 'gourmet guides' to lovemaking, *The Joy of Sex* (1972) and *More Joy of Sex* (1973). Educated at Trinity College, Cambridge, and at the London Hospital, he was lecturer in physiology (1945–51) and director of research on the biology of ageing (1966–73) at University College, London. In 1974 he started lecturing in psychiatry at Stanford University, California. His *Barbarism and Sexual Freedom* (1948) and *Sexual Behaviour in Society* (1950, revised as *Sex in Society*, 1963) were notable contributions to a libertarian understanding of sexuality, which functioned in dialectical opposition to the life-denying violence he observed in his war poems: *Elegies* (1944), *The Song of Lazarus* (1945), and *The Signal to Engage* (1947). After a gap of more than a decade, *Haste to the Wedding* (1962) signalled a more affirmative sensibility, and *All But a Rib* (1973) partially documented his reaction to the women's movement.
▷A E Salmon, *Alex Comfort* (1978)

COMPTON-BURNETT, Dame Ivy
(1892–1969)

English novelist, born in London. She graduated in classics from the Royal Holloway College, London University, and published her first novel, *Dolores*, in 1911. A prolific writer, her rather stylized novels have many features in common; they are often set in upper-class Victorian or Edwardian society, for example, and the characters usually belong to a large family, spanning several generations. She was noted for her skilful use of dialogue, not because the language is appropriate to character but because it conveys the secret thoughts and understanding of the characters. Her works include *Pastors and Masters* (1925), *Brothers and Sisters* (1929), *Parents and Children* (1941), *Mother and Son* (1955, James Tait Black Memorial Prize), *A Father and his Fate* (1957), *The Mighty and their Fall* (1961) and *A God and His Gifts* (1963).

▷H Spurling, *Ivy Compton-Burnett* (2 vols, 1984–5)

CONDON, Richard
(1915–)

American novelist, born in New York City. He worked as a film-industry publicist for 21 years (1936–57), and saw service in the US merchant navy, before embarking on a literary career. He made his reputation with his second novel, *The Manchurian Candidate* (1959). It and *Winter Kills* (1974) are both political intrigues set amidst the paranoia of the Cold War. *Prizzi's Honor* (1982) was the first of a trilogy about the Prizzi crime family and their struggle to stay ahead of their rivals. Like the former two novels, it was subsequently filmed; Condon himself wrote the 1985 screenplay with Janet Roach. He describes himself as 'a professional entertainer'; his sales figures, sustained over more than 30 years, suggest he is a highly successful one.

CONGREVE, William
(1670–1729)

English dramatist and poet, born in Bardsey near Leeds. He was educated in Ireland at Kilkenny School and Trinity College, Dublin, where he was a fellow student of **Jonathan Swift**. In London he entered the Middle Temple to study law, but never practised. His first publication was *Incognita, or Love and Duty Reconciled* (1692), a novel of cross-purposes and disguises which was written in a fortnight. His translation of the eleventh satire of **Juvenal** came out soon after in **Dryden's** *Juvenal and Persius*. In January 1693 his comedy *The Old Bachelor*, produced under Dryden's auspices, with the celebrated Anne Bracegirdle as heroine, achieved brilliant success at a time when the theatre had been suffering a slump. His second comedy, *The Double Dealer* (November 1693), was in every way stronger than *The Old Bachelor*, but the satire on the heartless sexual morals of the time was aimed too directly at the theatre's best customers, and it failed to please. *The Mourning Muse of Alexis* (1695), a poetic dialogue on the death of Queen Mary II, wife of William III, was full of artificial conceits. *Love for Love*, generally regarded as Congreve's stage masterpiece, was first produced in 1695. It is more satirical, more vital, and stronger in feeling than its predecessors; it also has a more coherent plot and truer characterization. In 1697 his only tragedy, *The Mourning Bride*, appeared, best remembered for the two overworked quotations 'music hath charms to soothe the savage breast' and 'hell hath no fury like a woman

scorned'. He was next occupied busily in the famous **Jeremy Collier** controversy, defending the morality of the new stage (1698). His last play, *The Way of the World*, was produced in 1700, but was not a success. He wrote no more for the stage, apart from the words of a masque of *The Judgment of Paris*, set to music by John Eccles for a musical competition in 1701, and the undistinguished libretto of *Semele*, also to the music of Eccles, but later used by Handel. He was now almost blind owing to cataracts, but his support of the Whig party brought him a few sinecures which enabled him to live comfortably, writing occasional poems, until his death after a coach accident. He was buried in Westminster Abbey.

▷E Goss, *The Life of William Congreve* (1888); M E Novak, *William Congreve* (1971)

CONLEY, Robert J
(1940–)

American writer, born in Cushing, Oklahoma. Of Cherokee descent, Conley has drawn inspiration for his work from Cherokee history and contemporary life. His first published work, *Twenty-one Poems* (1975), was followed by the short narrative history, *Adawosgi: Swimmer Wesley Snell, a Cherokee Memorial* (1980). The poems in *The Rattlesnake Band and Other Poems* (1984) and stories that comprise *The Witch of Goingsnake and Other Stories* (1988) are overlaid with a characteristically dark vision of the potential of evil to blight human life. Conley has also written westerns with a Native American slant; *Back to Malachi* (1986), for example, depicts the life of Cherokee outlaws in Indian Territory in the 19th century. He has recently begun a series of historical novels depicting pre-contact Cherokee life in the Southeastern US, beginning with *The Way of the Priests* and *The Dark Way* (1993).

CONNELL, Evan S(helby)
(1924)

American novelist, short-story writer and poet, born in Kansas City and educated at the University of Kansas, but for long a resident of California. He is celebrated for two elegiac novels, *Mrs Bridge* (1959) and its companion piece *Mr Bridge* (1969), elegant studies of repressed gentlefolk, set against the Great Depression. *The Patriot* (1960) is more straightforwardly realistic, being the semi-autobiographical account of a young naval airman during World War II. *The Diary of a Rapist* (1966) is less gratuitous than the title suggests and considerably more insightful. His story collections include *St Augustine's Pigeon* (1980), while his calm, philosophical poetry can be found in *Notes from a Bottle Found on the Beach at Carmel* (1963), a minor classic of American writing, and *Points for a Compass Rose* (1973).

CONNELLY, Marc(us Cook)
(1890–1980)

American dramatist, born in McKeesport, Pennsylvania. As a journalist who took to the theatre, he achieved several outstanding successes in collaboration with **George Kaufman**, including *Dulcy* (1921), *To the Ladies* (1922), the amusing 'expressionist' *Beggar on Horseback* (1924) and *Hunter's Moon* (1958). His greatest individual success was *Green Pastures* (1930), adapted from Negro stories of the Deity and a Negro heaven, which won the Pulitzer Prize.

▷ P T Nolan, *Marc Connelly* (1969)

CONNOLLY, Cyril Vernon
(1903–74)

English author and journalist. Educated at Eton and Oxford, he contributed to the *New Statesman* and other periodicals and wrote regularly for *The Sunday Times*. He was founder/editor of *Horizon* (1939–50) and briefly literary editor of *The Observer*. His only novel was *The Rock Pool* (1936). Among his works are *Enemies of Promise* (1938), which included a look at the prevailing literary scene and an autobiographical fragment, *The Unquiet Grave* (1944), miscellaneous aphorisms and reflections, and various collections of essays. Inclined to sloth and prey to fitful depressions, his potential was greater than his achievement.

CONON (also QUESNES) DE BETHUNE
(d.1220)

Northern French trouvere poet. He was an important historical figure in his own right; born into the royal house of Flanders, he became one of the leaders of the Fourth Crusade. He was hugely influential in the literary development of northern France, being one of the first poets writing in the dialect of the area to gain popular acceptance elsewhere. His retort to the French queen when she mocked his northern French is famous: *Encore noe soit ma parole françoise/Si la puet on bien entendre en françois* (roughly: 'If you understand it/Then it's French enough for me').

CONRAD, Joseph, originally Jozef Teodor Konrad Nalecz Korzeniowski
(1857–1924)

Polish-born British novelist, born in Berdichev, in the Polish Ukraine, now in the USSR. His father was a revolutionary of literary gifts—he translated **Victor Hugo**'s *Les Travailleurs de la mer*—who was exiled to Vologda in 1862. In 1878 Joseph joined an English merchant ship and was naturalized in 1884 when he gained his certificate as a master. In the 10 years that followed, he sailed between Singapore and Borneo, and this gave him an unrivalled background of mysterious creeks and jungle for the tales to follow. There was also an interlude in the Belgian Congo which provided exotic colour for his *Heart of Darkness*, one of his three finest novellas, the others being *Youth* and *Typhoon*. In 1896 he married and settled at Ashford in Kent, where he lived in seclusion for the rest of his days. Conrad's first novel was *Almayer's Folly* (1894), and then followed *An Outcast of the Islands* (1896), *The Nigger of the Narcissus* (1897), *Lord Jim* (1900), *Nostromo* (1904), *The Secret Agent* (1907) and *Under Western Eyes* (1911), before *Chance* (1914) made him famous. It was only then that *Lord Jim* was recognized as a masterpiece. Perhaps the short story was his true medium—*Tales of Unrest* (1898), *Youth* (1902) and *Twixt Land and Sea* (1912). His semi-autobiographical *The Mirror and the Sea* and his *Personal Record* testify to his high artistic aims. He also wrote *Victory* (1919), but his later works, *The Arrow of Gold* (1919) and *The Rescue* (1920), owed their popularity largely to his earlier work.

▷ J Baines, *Joseph Conrad: a critical biography* (1960)

CONROY, Frank
(1936–)

American novelist and autobiographer. He was born in New York City, and educated there and at Haverford College, from which he graduated in 1958. His first book was *Stop-Time* (1965), a dreamlike memoir of his own adolescence: its exploration of the boundaries of fiction and non-fiction won the admiration of **Norman Mailer**, the most vocal exponent of the 'non-fiction novel' and Mailer's imprimatur helped foster Conroy's career. He has not been a prolific writer, however. A collection of stories, *Midair*, appeared in 1985, and a novel, *Body & Soul*, in 1993. Currently director of the Writers' Workshop at the University of Iowa, Conroy previously taught at George Mason and Brandeis Universities, and at the Massachusetts Institute of Technology (MIT).

CONSCIENCE, Hendrik
(1812–83)

Flemish novelist, born in Antwerp. From 1866 he was director of the Wiertz Museum. His *Phantazy* (1837), a fine collection of tales, and his most popular romance, *De Leeuw van Vlaenderen* (1838, 'The Lion of Flanders'), earned him a place as the father of the Flemish novel. His series of pictures of Flemish life, beginning with *Hoe man schilder wordt*

(1843, 'How to become a Painter'), carried his name over Europe.

▷ F Joster, *Hendrik Conscience* (1917)

CONSTABLE, Henry
(1562–1613)

English poet, the son of Sir Robert Constable of Newark. At 16 he entered St John's College, Cambridge, turned Catholic, and went to Paris. He was pensioned by King Henri IV, and seems to have been employed in confidential missions to England and Scotland. In 1592 he published his *Diana*, a collection of 23 sonnets; a second edition in 1594 containing 76, some by his friend, Sir **Philip Sidney**, and other poets. His other poems included a set of *Spiritual Sonnets*, first published in 1815.

▷ G A Wickes, *Henry Constable: poet and courtier* (1954)

CONSTANT DE REBECQUE, Henri Benjamin (Benjamin Constant)
(1767–1830)

French author and politician, born of French Huguenot ancestry in Lausanne. Educated at Oxford, Erlangen and Edinburgh, he settled in Paris in 1795 as a publicist. He entered the Tribunate in 1799, but was banished from France in 1802 for denouncing the despotic acts of Napoleon. After travelling in Germany and Italy with **Madame de Staël**, he settled at Göttingen. On Napoleon's fall in 1814 he returned to Paris; during the Hundred Days became one of Napoleon's councillors, though previously he had styled Napoleon a Genghis Khan; and after the second restoration of the Bourbons wrote and spoke in favour of constitutional freedom. He was returned to the Chamber of Deputies in 1819, and became the leader of the liberal Opposition. He wrote *De la religion* (5 vols, 1824–31); but more important is a remarkable psychological novel, *Adolphe* (1816), about a passionate love affair which ends in tragedy. His correspondence appeared in 1844, his *Oeuvres politiques* ('Political Works') in 1875, his Letters to Madame Récamier and his family in 1882–8, and his *Journal intime* ('Personal Diary') in 1895. *Cahier rouge* (1907, 'Red Notebook') contains a vivid account of his youth.

▷ P L Leon, *Benjamin Constant* (1930)

CONSTANTIN-WEYER, Maurice
(1881–1961)

French novelist, memoirist and biographer, who settled for a time in Canada. One of his 46 books became a success: *Un Homme se penche sur son passé* (1928, Eng trans *A Man Scans his Past*, 1929), achieved considerable popularity in France and in the USA. This was an account of his Canadian wanderings and his establishment of a horse and cattle ranch in Manitoba (1912). He wrote plays and many film scripts, and *A Man Scans his Past* was made into a Franco–German movie in 1958; but his work is now forgotten.

CONWAY, Hugh, pseud of **Frederick John Fargus**
(1847–85)

English novelist, born in Bristol, where he was an auctioneer in succession to his father. He took his writing name from the school frigate *Conway*, where he was a student for a time, but was not allowed to fulfil his ambition of joining the navy. He wrote clever newspaper verse and tales, but his greatest success was the melodramatic *Called Back* (1883), also popular as a play. Other works include *A Life's Idyll and other Poems* (1879), and the novels *Dark Days* (1884), *A Family Affair* (1885) and *Living or Dead* (1886).

▷ 'A Sketch of the Author's Life', included in *Called Back* (1885)

COOK, David
(1940–)

English novelist and television scriptwriter, born in Preston, Lancashire. His first novel, *Albert's Memorial*, appeared in 1972, since when Cook has acquired a reputation as the author of sympathetic and sensitive studies of vulnerable, decent people, written in delicate, flexible prose. His best-known work is *Walter* (1978), a thoughtful novel about a mentally impaired northerner. The film version was commissioned by and shown on the first evening's broadcasting of Channel Four Television in 1982. *Winter Doves* (1979) is a sequel to *Walter*.

COOK, Eliza
(1818–89)

English poet, daughter of a London tradesman. She contributed to magazines from an early age, and issued volumes of poetry in 1838, 1864 and 1865. She wrote *Eliza Cook's Journal* (1849–54), much of it republished as *Jottings from my Journal* (1860).

COOKE, or COOK, Ebenezer
(c.1667–c.1732)

American poet and satirist, he was one of the first observers of the colonial scene from an explicitly American point of view. He is believed to have been born in London and to have visited Maryland in the mid-1690s and later, before settling finally in Dorchester County sometime after 1710. He worked as a receiver-general and land-agent, and was later an attorney. His most important work is *The Sot-Weed Factor* (1708), a title later

appropriated by the novelist **John Barth**. Cooke's raucous couplets about a British tobacco merchant and his first contact with colonial 'civilization' were full of bombast, deflationary wit and some bile. The later *Sotweed Redivivus* (1730) was more conventional and didactic. Nothing is known about Cooke after 1731, when his compilation *The Maryland Muse* was published.
▷E H Cohen, *Ebenezer Cooke: The Sotweed Canon* (1975)

COOK-LYNN, Elizabeth
(1930–)

American writer, born in Fort Thompson, South Dakota. A member of the Crow Creek Sioux tribe and brought up on the reservation, Cook-Lynn's work focuses on the northern plains landscape and culture of the Lakota/Dakota people of North and South Dakota. She has published to date two collections of poetry—*Then Badger Said This* (1983) and *Seek the House of Relatives* (1985); the prose collection *The Power of Horses and Other Stories* (1990) and, most recently, the novel *From the River's Edge* (1991). She is also the founding editor (1985–) of the Native American literary magazine, *Wicazo-Sa Review*.

COOKSON, Catherine Ann
(1906–)

English popular novelist, born in Tyne Dock, County Durham. Her fiction is set in the north-east of England and is replete with tragedy, exploitation and romance. The author of more than 40 books, including the Mallen trilogy and the Tilly Trotter series, she is a favourite among habituées of the public library. She was made a DBE in 1993 for her charitable services in the north-east.
▷*Our Kate* (1969)

COOLIDGE, Susan, pseud of Sarah Chauncy Woolsey
(1835–1905)

American children's writer and literary critic, born in Cleveland, Ohio. She wrote the *Katy* books (*What Katy Did*, 1872, et seq) and other stories for girls, in an easy natural style, free from contemporary sentimentality.
▷Biographical sketch by 'EDWG' in *Last Verses* (1906)

COOMARASWAMY, Ananda
(1877–1947)

Ceylon-born Indian author and scholar. He was a leader of the 20th-century cultural revival in India, especially in the field of art.
▷R Livingston, *The Traditional Theory of Literature* (1962)

COONEY, Ray(mond)
(1932–)

English dramatist, director and producer, born in London. He made his debut as an actor in *Song of Norway* (1946), and appeared in several stage comedies and farces in the 1950s and 1960s. Best known as an author and director, his own first play, a farce, *One for the Pot*, appeared in 1961, and was followed by many others, including *Chase Me Comrade* (1964), *Move Over, Mrs Markham* (1969), *Two Into One* (1981), *Run for your Wife* (1983) and *Wife Begins at Forty* (1986). In 1983 he created the Theatre of Comedy, based at the Shaftesbury Theatre, London.

COOPER, Edmund
(1926–82)

English science-fiction novelist and short-story writer, born in Marple, Cheshire. From his first novel, published in the USA as *Deadly Image* and in the UK as *The Uncertain Midnight* (1958), until his final book, *A World of Difference* (1980, a collection of stories), Cooper was respected as a leading stylist of science fiction. Several of his works consider the form of a post nuclear world as a dark age through which society may have to pass before a new and perhaps more morally responsible civilization evolves.

COOPER, Giles Stannus
(1918–66)

Irish playwright and actor, born in Carrickmines, County Dublin. Although Cooper wrote several stage plays, his sensitivity to the voice and the use of sound resulted in his becoming an exceptional author for radio. His themes of the shortcomings of society, woven into largely naturalistic plays, caught the tenor of the times. *Mathry Beacon* (1956) and *Unman, Wittering and Zigo* (1958) are considered to be his best work. He died after a fall from a moving train near Surbiton, Surrey. In 1978, the annual Giles Cooper Awards for best radio scripts was inaugurated by the BBC and Methuen publishers.

COOPER, James Fenimore
(1789–1851)

American novelist, born in Burlington, New Jersey. His father, a wealthy Quaker and Federalist member of Congress, moved to Cooperstown, New York, then in a wild frontier region of great natural beauty. Cooper entered Yale College in 1803, but was expelled during his third year for a prank. In 1806 he shipped as a common sailor, and in 1808 entered the navy as midshipman. He rose to the rank of lieutenant, but in 1811 resigned his commission and married Susan, a sister of Bishop De Lancey of New York,

and settled down as a country gentleman. His first novel, *Precaution* (1819), was a failure; and the 32 which followed it were of uneven quality. The best were the stories of the sea and of Red Indians—*The Spy* (1821), *The Pilot* (1823), *The Last of the Mohicans* (1826), *The Prairie* (1826), *The Red Rover* (1827), *The Bravo* (1831), *The Pathfinder* (1840), *The Deerslayer* (1841), *The Two Admirals* (1842), *Wing-and-Wing* (1842) and *Satanstoe* (1845). His other writings include a scholarly *Naval History of the United States* (1839), and *Lives of Distinguished American Naval Officers* (1846). After visiting England and France, he was American consul at Lyons (1826–9), and then travelled in Switzerland and Italy till 1831. His later years were much disturbed by literary and newspaper controversies and litigation.
▷ S Railton, *Cooper: a study of his life and imagination* (1978)

COOPER, Jilly
(1937–)

English novelist and author of miscellaneous and humorous non-fiction, born in Hornchurch, Essex. Since the appearance of her first book, *How To Stay Married*, in 1969, she has been hugely prolific, specializing initially in cocktail-and-horsey social humour, such as *Jolly Super* (1971) and *Men and Super Men* (1972). Following a series of romantic novels, including *Emily* (1975) and *Prudence* (1978), Cooper published *Riders* (1985), her first huge bestseller, a sensational tale of sex, party-life and horses, dashing young men and highly-charged women. Other similarly raunchy and popular entertainments followed, entitled *Rivals* (1988), *Polo* (1991) and *The Man Who Made Husbands Jealous* (1993).

COOPER, Susan Mary
(1935–)

English writer, born in Burnham, Buckinghamshire. A former journalist for *The Sunday Times* (1956–63), she is best known for her award-winning children's fantasy series *The Dark is Rising*, published in five volumes between 1965 and 1977. Each of the novels in the series focuses on the struggle between the forces of good and evil, personified as Light and Dark. Other works include the realistic wartime novel *Dawn of Fear* (US 1970, UK 1972) and (for adults) the novel *Mandrake* (1964). She is the recipient of the Boston *Globe-Horn* Book Award (1973) and the Newbery Medal (1976).

COOPER, Thomas
(1805–92)

English Chartist and poet, born in Leicester. Apprenticed to a shoemaker at Gainsbor-

ough, he taught himself Latin, Greek, Hebrew and French, and at 23 turned schoolmaster and Methodist preacher. He became leader of the Leicester Chartists in 1841, and got two years for sedition in Stafford jail. Here he wrote *The Purgatory of Suicides*, a poem in the Spenserian stanza, and *Wise Saws and Modern Instances* (both 1845). He published two novels, *Alderman Ralph* (1853) and *The Family Feud* (1854), and in 1855 became a Christian lecturer.
▷ R J Conklin, *Thomas Cooper the Chartist, 1805–1892* (1935)

COOPER, William, pseud of Harry Summerfield Hoff
(1910–)

English satirical novelist, born in Crewe. After a spell as a schoolmaster in Leicester, he joined the civil service and during the late 1950s became Personnel Consultant to the Atomic Energy Research Authority. His fifth book, *Scenes from Provincial Life* (1950), tracing the early career of the lower middle-class anti-hero Joe Lunn, had an enormous impact and in retrospect is considered one of the most important of the 'angry' novels depicting provincial life in post-war Britain. Lunn reappears in *Scenes from Metropolitan Life* (written during the 1950s but not published until 1982), *Scenes From Married Life* (1961) and *Scenes from Later Life* (1983).

COORNHERT, Dirck Volkertz
(1522–90)

Dutch poet, translator (**Cicero**, **Seneca**) and dramatist, born in Amsterdam, who was also an engraver and theologian. Both in his poetry and his theology he strongly opposed the cruelties of Calvinism.
▷ R M Jones, *Spiritual Reformers of the 16th and 17th Centuries* (1914)

COOVER, Robert Lowell
(1932–)

American novelist, short-story writer and playwright, born in Iowa and educated at the universities of Indiana and Chicago. His first novel was *The Origin of the Brunists* (1966), a claustrophobic and overheated fable about the emergence of a chiliastic religious sect around a mining accident; it won Coover the **William Faulkner** Award. His interest in the construction of mythical and fictive systems developed with *The Universal Baseball Association Inc., J. Henry Waugh, Prop.* (1968). Coover's next novel exploded controversially: a phantasmagorical account of the execution of Julius and Ethel Rosenberg, *The Public Burning* (1977) received considerable publicity for its use of Richard Nixon as a (realistically) scatological narrator. Despite the fuss, the novel was a failure. Coover's best book remains his vivid collection of short stories, *Pricksongs and Descants* (1969), and in particular 'The Magic Poker', which rewrites *The Tempest* as a fable about the imagination. In the eighties and after, he has turned to elegant, reflexive forms which draw on literary pornography (*Spanking the Maid*, 1981) and baroque extensions of popular iconography (*Pinocchio in Venice*, 1991). Some of his plays were published in *A Theological Position* (1972).

▷J Cope, *Robert Coover's Fictions* (1986)

COPE, Wendy
(1945–)

English poet, born in Erith, Kent and educated at Oxford University. After 15 years as a primary-school teacher in London, she became a freelance writer. Cope has a talent for parody and for light-hearted demolitions of men; these gifts unite in her versions of male authors such as **Ted Hughes** or **Philip Larkin**. She is a little less cruel to **T S Eliot** in 'Limericks on The Wasteland'. The titles *Making Cocoa for Kingsley Amis* (1986) and *Men and their Boring Arguments* (1988) are fair indications of her approach. She has less tonal subtlety than **Stevie Smith** but more boisterous fun.

COPIĆ, Branko
(1915–)

Bosnian novelist, story writer and poet, born in Hasani. He was a Tito partisan. Ćopić is one of the most popular of Yugoslav writers since World War II. In his well-known novels dealing with the takeover of peasant land by communists in the Bosnian district of Bosanska Krajina, he managed to achieve—despite his declared 'commitment'—a remarkable degree of objectivity. His comic peasant character Nikoletina Bursaca—first introduced in *Dozivljaji Nikoletina Bursaca* (1956)—became a national folk hero. He has been Yugoslavia's leading children's writer, but his work has not yet attracted a translator.

COPPARD, A(lfred) E(dgar)
(1878–1957)

English short-story writer and poet, born in Folkestone. His schooling ceased when he was nine, and after being an office boy, then an accountant, he became a professional writer in 1919. In 1921 he published *Adam and Eve and Pinch Me*, and soon became celebrated for his tales of country life and character. His prose is remarkable for its detailed observation and poetic quality. Other volumes of stories include *The Black Dog* (1923), *The Field of Mustard* (1926) and *Lucy in Her Pink Jacket* (1954). His *Collected Poems* appeared in 1928.

▷*It's Me, O Lord!* (1957); J Schwartz, *The Writings of A.E. Coppard* (1931)

COPPÉE, François
(1842–1908)

French poet, born in Paris. For three years a war-office clerk, he soon turned to poetry, and with *Le Reliquaire* (1866, 'The Reliquary') and *Les Intimités* (1867, 'Intimacies') gained the front rank of the 'Parnassiens'. Later volumes of poetry were *Les Humbles* (1872), *Le Cahier Rouge* (1874, 'The Red Notebook'), *Olivier* (1876, his one long poem), *Les Récits et les Élégies* (1878, 'Stories and Elegies') and *Contes en vers* ('Stories in Verse'). His earliest dramatic poem, *Le Passant* (1869, 'The Wayfarer'), owed much to Sarah Bernhardt, and was followed by *Deux Douleurs* (1870, 'Two Sadnesses'), *L'Abandonnée* ('The Abandoned Woman'), *Le Luthier de Crémone* (1876, 'The Lute Maker from Cremona'), *La Guerre de Cent Ans* ('The Hundred Years War'), *Madame de Maintenon* (1881), *Severo Torelli* (1883), *Les Jacobites* (1885), *Le Pater* (1890), *Pour la couronne* (1895, 'For the Crown'). He won fame in yet another field with his *Contes en prose* ('Prose Tales'), *Vingt Contes nouveaux* ('Twenty New Tales'), and *Contes rapides* ('Brief Tales'). He wrote a novel about religious conversion, *La Bonne Souffrance* (1898, 'The Healthy Pain'), after he became a Catholic.

▷L Le Meur, *La vie et l'oeuvre de François Coppée* (1932)

CORBET, or CORBETT, Richard
(1582–1635)

English poet and prelate, the son of a gardener in Ewell, Surrey. He was educated at Westminster School then passed to Oxford, and in 1620 was made Dean of Christ Church. In 1624 he was consecrated Bishop of Oxford, and in 1632 translated to Norwich. His *Certaine Elegant Poems* (1647) reflects the jovial temper of the man. His longest piece is *Iter Boreale*, a holiday tour of four students; the best and best known is the *Faeries' Farewell*. His other volume of poems, *Poetica Stromata* (1648), was also published posthumously.

▷J E V Crofts, *A life of Bishop Corbett* (1924)

CORBIÈRE, Tristan, pseud of Édouard Joachim
(1845–75)

French poet, born in Coat-Congar, Finistère. Corbière— often bracketed with **Laforgue**— is a poet of great importance and influence. He was largely unknown until **Verlaine** brought him to the attention of the public.

CORELLI, Marie

His collection *Amours Jaunes* (1873, 'Yellow Loves') was an acknowledged influence upon **T S Eliot**. His bitter early work reflected the landscape of Brittany, and represented a powerful reaction against the excesses of romanticism. His later, ironic, poetry—which reads as if it had been written at least 50 years after its time—has been unduly neglected in France, but not elsewhere. There are good translations in *Selections from Les Amours Jaunes* (1954).
▷F C Burch, *Tristan Corbière* (1970)

CORELLI, Marie, pseud of Mary Mackay
(1855–1924)
English popular romantic novelist, born in London, the illegitimate child of Charles Mackay, a journalist, and Ellen Mills, a widow whom he later married as his second wife. She was educated by governesses and trained as a pianist, but though accomplished her métier was writing, to which she devoted herself from 1885. *A Romance of Two Worlds* (1886) marked the beginning of an unprecedented career as a bestseller. A sentimental self-righteous moralist, lacking self-criticism or a sense of the absurd, she was the writer that critics loved to hate. Later in a prolific career she refused reviewers access to her latest books, but her aficionados included Gladstone and **Oscar Wilde** and her readership was immense. Her novels include *Thelma* (1887), *Barabbas* (1893), *God's Good Man* (1904), *The Devil's Motor* (1910), *Eyes of the Sea* (1917) and *The Secret Power* (1921).
▷E Bigland, *Marie Corelli, the woman and the legend* (1953)

CORINNA
(fl.c.500BC)
Greek poet of Tanagra in Boeotia. Her poems, which survive in little beyond substantial fragments of two long pieces, are lyrical narratives derived from Boeotian legends. The titles of others are known, and include *The Return of Orion, Iolaus* and *Seven against Thebes*. The two extant poems, written in short, octosyllabic lines and five- or six-line stanzas, describe a singing contest between the mountain gods of Cithaeron and Helicon, and the marriages of the daughters of Asopus. According to tradition, Corinna taught **Pindar** in his youth and later competed against him in poetic contests.

CORKERY, Daniel
(1878–1964)
Irish cultural leader, born in Cork. Educated at University College, Cork, he was Professor of English there from 1931 to 1947. He published a collection of short stories, *A Munster Twilight* (1917), depicting ethnic and class division in Irish life, and a novel, *The Threshold of Quiet* (1917). He made a great attack on the literary historians who saw Ireland in terms of the 18th-century 'Big House', in his *The Hidden Ireland* (1925). He profoundly influenced new Irish writers such as **Frank O'Connor** and **Sean O'Faolain** and his love of the Irish language was the basis of his literary evangelism, as revealed in his *The Fortunes of the Irish Language* (1954). He also wrote *Synge and Anglo-Irish Literature* (1931) and several plays. He was elected to the Irish Senate in 1951.

CORMAN, Cid
(1924–)
American poet and editor, best known for his editorship of the **Pound**-influenced magazine *Origin*, which was amongst the earliest to publish the work of **Robert Creeley**, **Charles Olson** and others. He is a very prolific poet, author of over 70 collections in various styles (eg Beat, 'Japanese', 'projectionist'), none of which has yet engaged the attention of critics.
▷'Cid Corman Issue' of *Madrona* (Seattle, December 1975)

CORNEILLE, Pierre
(1606–84)
French dramatist, born in Rouen, where he tried to obtain a barrister's practice. In 1629 he removed to Paris, where his comedy *Mélite* (1629, Eng trans *Melite*, 1776), already performed at Rouen, proved highly successful. It was followed by *Clitandre* (1630), *La Veuve* (1634, 'The Widow'), *La Galerie du Palais* (1632, 'The Palace Gallery'), *La Suivante* (1633, 'The Lady's Maid') and *La Place Royale* (1633). In these early pieces intricate and extravagant plots are handled with ingenuity, but the writer's poetic genius flashes out only in occasional verses. For a time Corneille was one of Richelieu's 'five poets', engaged to compose plays on lines laid down by the cardinal; among the pieces thus produced were *Les Tuileries* (1635), *L'Aveugle de Smyrne* (1638, 'The Blind Man of Smyrna') and *La Grande Pastorale* (1639, 'The Great Pastoral'). Corneille, however, was too independent to retain Richelieu's favour. *Médée* (1635, 'Medea') showed a marked advance on his earlier works; and in 1636 *Le Cid* (Eng trans *The Cid*, 1637) took Paris by storm. Richelieu ordered his literary retainers to write it down; but adverse criticism was powerless against the general enthusiasm. *Horace* (1640, Eng trans *Horatius*, 1656), founded on the story of the Horatii, and *Cinna* (Eng trans *Cinna's Conspiracy*, 1713), appeared in 1640; *Polyeucte* (Eng trans *Polyeuctes*, 1655), a noble tragedy, in 1642; and *La Mort de Pompée* (Eng trans *Pompey the Great*, 1664) in 1643. *Le Menteur* (1643, Eng

trans *The Mistaken Beau; or, The Liar*, 1685) entitles Corneille to be called the father of French comedy as well as of French tragedy. *Théodore* was brought out in 1645, and *Rodogune* (Eng trans 1765) in 1646. Between 1647—when he was made an academician—and 1653 Corneille produced *Héraclius* (1646 or 1647, Eng trans *Heraclius, Emperor of the East*, 1664), *Don Sanche d'Aragon* (1649), *Andromède* (1649), *Nicomède* (1651, Eng trans *Nicomede*, 1671), and *Pertharite* (1651). These pieces, of which the last was damned, show a decline in dramatic and poetic power; and Corneille occupied himself with a verse translation of Thomas à Kempis's *Imitatio Christi, L'Imitation de Jésus-Christ* (1651). He returned to the stage in 1659 with *Œdipe*, which was followed by *La Toison d'or* (1660, 'The Golden Fleece'), *Sertorius* (1662), *Sophonisbe* (1663), *Othon* (1669), *Agésilas* (1666), *Attila* (1667) and *Tite et Bérénice* (1670). In 1671 he joined **Molière** and Quinault in writing the opera *Psyché*. His last works were *Pulchérie* (1672) and *Suréna* (1674, Eng trans *Surenas*, 1969). After his marriage in 1640 he lived habitually in Rouen until 1662, when he settled in Paris. During his later years his popularity waned before that of **Racine**, whose cause was espoused by **Nicolas Boileau** and the king. A master of the Alexandrine verse form, he concerned himself with moral and mental conflict rather than physical action.

▷P J Yarrow, *Corneille* (1963)

CORNEILLE, Thomas
(1625–1709)

French playwright, brother of **Pierre Corneille**, born in Rouen. He was a dramatist of merit, his tragedies—*Camma* (1661), *Laodice* (1668), *Pyrrhus* (1690), *Bérénice* (1657), *Timocrate* (1656), *Ariane* (1672), *Bradamante* (1696), and others—being in general superior to his comedies. He also wrote a verse translation of **Ovid**'s *Metamorphoses*.

▷D Collins, *Thomas Corneille, protean dramatist* (1968)

CORNFORD, Frances Crofts
(1886–1960)

English poet who lived most of her life in Cambridge. A grand-daughter of Charles Darwin, she wrote delicate poems of an intensely personal nature, often about favourite landscapes or minute incidents with companions. Her work has been much neglected, possibly because it can seem sentimental, but she is often capable of the sublime expression of emotional states. Her *Collected Poems* appeared in 1956.

CORRAZINI, Sergio
(1886–1907)

Italian 'crepuscular' poet, usually bracketed with the more gifted **Gozzano**. His poems,

influenced by **Laforgue**, are similarly bitter, sad and witty. He died of tuberculosis.

▷F Donini, *Vita e poesia de Sergio Corrazini* (1949)

CORRÊA GARÇÃO, Pedro Antonio
(1724–72)

Portuguese neo-classical poet, who was born in Lisbon. He became the leading member of the Arcádia Lusitana group (founded 1756), which aimed to free Portuguese poetry from foreign influences and restore the purity of the language. Under the name Córidon Erimanteu, he wrote many essays on his art. His master was **Horace**. He died in prison, for reasons which are not entirely clear.

▷T Braga, *A arcádia lusitana* (1898)

CORREIA, Raimundo
(1860–1911)

Brazilian poet, influenced by the French Parnassian poets and praised by the great **Machado de Assis**, who recognized in his poetry anguished yearnings after more than just the usual perfection of form. He was both subtle, as distinct from the facility of **Bilac**, and intense.

CORRIS, Peter
(1942–)

Australian writer of adventure novels, born in Stawell, Victoria. Although trained as a historian, and sometime literary editor of the defunct weekly *National Times*, his early addiction to the American 'hard-boiled' school of thrillers led to writing pastiches of **Raymond Chandler**. In *Cliff Hardy* (*The Dying Trade*, 1980, et seq) he created an antipodean Philip Marlowe and, like Marlowe and Chandler, both character and author matured over the years. Corris has created other pivotal characters, the most imaginative of whom is Richard Browning, a failed Australian actor who, upon his death, is found to have left a series of tape recordings of his adventures. Recent titles are *Browning PI* (1992) and *Browning Battles On* (1993), which takes the hero to an army training course in World War II and to an encounter with actor Peter Finch. The Browning titles are characterized by historicity—the last two titles each have six pages of textual notes.

CORSO, Gregory Nunzio
(1930–)

American poet, born in New York City. He had a difficult and violent childhood, and spent three years in jail for attempted robbery in his teens. He became friendly with **Allen Ginsberg**, and is associated with the Beat Poets in both style and content, although his rage against the 'hung-up' state of US society is tempered with a sardonic, irreverent humour. His first poems appeared in *The Vestal Lady of Brattle* (1955), and he has published many subsequent volumes, including *Gasoline* (1958) and *Elegiac Feelings American* (1970). Later works like *Ankh* (1971) and *Earth Egg* (1974) reflect a fascination with Egypt and Eastern religion. Other books include a novel, *The American Express* (1961).

CORTADA, Joan
(1805–68)

Catalan novelist who wrote romantic historical novels modelled on those of Sir **Walter Scott**.
▷ *Hispanic Review*, XIII (1945)

CORTÁZAR, Julio
(1914–84)

Argentinian/French writer, born in Brussels. He grew up in Argentina, where he was educated. From 1935 to 1945 he taught in secondary schools in several small towns and in Mendoza, Argentina. From 1945 to 1951 he was a translator for publishers, then moved to Paris where he lived until his death, writing and freelancing for Unesco. He is one of the most widely recognized Spanish–American writers outside the Spanish-speaking world, owing this particularly to the filming of *Hopscotch* (*Rayuela*, 1963, Eng trans 1966), and of a short story, 'Blow-Up' (from *Blow-Up and Other Stories*, 1968), by the Italian director Michelangelo Antonioni. Others of his novels which have been translated include *Los premios* (1960, Eng trans *The Winners*, 1965) and *62: modelo para armar* (1968, Eng trans *62: A Model Kit*, 1972).
▷ S Boldy, *The Novels of Cortázar* (1980)

CORVO, Baron *see* ROLFE, Frederick William

CORY, William Johnson
(1823–92)

English poet, born in Torrington, Devon. Educated at Eton and King's College, Cambridge, he was assistant-master at Eton from 1845 to 1872, when he inherited an estate, assumed the name of Cory, and moved to London. He was author of a book of anonymously published poems, *Ionica, Poems* (1858, enlarged 1891), and wrote the 'Eton Boating Song' in 1865. His *Letters and Journals* were published in 1897.
▷ F C Mackenzie, *William Cory, a biography* (1950)

COSBUC, Gheoghe
(1866–1918)

Romanian poet and translator, born in Cosbuc. He was the son of the village priest.

He edited a Bucharest periodical with **Ion Caragiale** and others, and later became one of the most influential of all 19th-century Romanian editors. He in no way anticipated modernism, but was a popular (although intellectual) peasant poet who regarded the village as the proper foundation of national life.

ĆOSIĆ, Dobrica
(1921–)

Serbian novelist and political activist, born in Velika Drenova. He was active as a partisan during World War II, a period recounted in his first novel *Daleko je sunce* (1951, Eng trans *Far Away in the Sun*, 1963). His second novel *Koreni* (1954, 'Roots') examined Serbia's slow independence from the Ottoman Empire, while the three-volume *Deobe* (1961–3, 'Partitions') returned to the period of World War II. After the war, Ćosić served as a communist representative in the Yugoslav parliament, but in 1968 he was expelled from the central committee of the Serbian League of Communists. In the years that followed, he wrote his major work, the four-volume *Vreme smrti* (1972–9), which was published in an English-language abridgement as *A Time of Death*, *Reach to Eternity* and *South to Destiny* (1978–81) and then in full as *This Land, This Time* (1983). A controversial figure, he explores his nation's history with vivid directness.

COSTA, Cláudio Manuel da
(1729–89)

Brazilian poet, born in the Minas Gerais district. His suicide over a complex political issue—he had implicated others in an anti-Portuguese conspiracy—cut short a poetic career which had, ironically, been closely based on Portuguese models. Thus he was an 'Arcadian' poet who took a pseudonym (Glauceste Satúrnio) for his highly artificial pastoral poetry. He had wanted to break with his 'European' style, but was never able to do so decisively. However, he remains one of the two great *mineiro* lyrical poets, the other, **Alvarenga**, falling short of him.

COSTA I LLOBERA, Miguel
(1854–1922)

Catalan (Mallorcan) poet, priest and writer, one of the major figures in the earlier history of the Catalan revival. After travel in Italy and the acquirement of a classical style he won (1902) the title of *mestre en gai saber* ('master troubadour') for his excellence. His poetry, although finely made and technically influential, is somewhat artificial. He was translated into several European languages by other priests, too serene in their faith to discern the disturbing elements in human nature as portrayed in his work.

COSTER, Charles de
(1827–79)

Belgian storyteller, born in Munich. He studied at Brussels. His most famous work, the prose epic *La Légende et les Aventures Héroiques, Joyeuse et Glorieuses d'Ulenspiegel* (1866, Eng trans *The Legend of the Glorious Adventures of Tyl Ulenspiegel*, 1918), took 10 years to write.

▷H Liebrecht, *La vie et le rêve de Charles de Coster* (1927)

COTTIN, Sophie, née Risteau
(1770–1807)

French writer. At 17 she married a Parisian banker, who left her a childless widow at 20. For comfort she turned to writing, wrote verses and a lengthy history, and romantic fiction. She had already written *Claire d'Albe* (1799) and *Mathilde* (1805) when, in 1806, she wrote her most successful work, *Élisabeth, ou les exilés de Sibérie*, ('Elisabeth, or the Siberian Exiles').

▷L C Sykes, *Madame Cottin* (1949)

COTTON, Charles
(1630–87)

English writer, born at his father's estate of Beresford in Staffordshire. His father was a warm friend of **Ben Jonson**, Selden, **John Donne** and other illustrious men. The boy travelled on the Continent, and early wrote verses which were circulated privately. In 1656 he married his cousin Isabella, half-sister of the regicide John Hutchinson (1615–64). Though a sincere loyalist, he seems to have lived securely enough under the Commonwealth, and the decay of his father's estate was due mainly to unprosperous lawsuits. In 1664 he issued anonymously his burlesque poem, *Scarronides, or the First Book of Virgil Travestie*, added to in later editions in grossness as well as in bulk. Later works are his *Voyage to Ireland in Burlesque* (1670), *Burlesque upon Burlesque* (1675), *Planter's Manual* (1675), and a treatise on fly-fishing contributed in 1676 to the fifth edition of Walton's *Compleat Angler*. He also published a masterly translation of **Montaigne**'s *Essays* (1685).

▷E R Miner, *The Cavalier Mode from Honson to Cotton* (1973)

COTTRELL, Dorothy
(1902–57)

Australian-born writer of popular fiction and short stories, born in Picton, New South Wales. Crippled by polio at the age of five she was subsequently confined to a wheelchair. Her early years were spent on the Queensland station of relatives where, in 1922, she married an American employed there. Her first novel, *The Singing Gold*, an unsophisticated tale set in rural Queensland, was serialized in the US *Ladies Home Journal* before publication in 1928. This enabled the Cottrells to move to the USA, where despite her severe handicap she lived an active life and travelled extensively. She was much in demand as a journalist and short-story writer, and her work was published regularly in the *Saturday Evening Post*. A mystery novel, *The Silent Reefs* (1953), was set in her beloved Caribbean and later filmed. Although championed by Dame **Mary Gilmore** she was much criticized by Australian feminist writers for moving to the USA and becoming a lucrative author, though which was the greater offence is not clear.

COUCH, Sir Arthur Quiller
(1863–1944)

English writer, born in Bodmin, in Cornwall. He was educated at Clifton College and Trinity College, Oxford, where he was a lecturer in classics (1886–7). After some years of literary work in London and in Cornwall, where he lived from 1891, he became Professor of English Literature at Cambridge (1912). He edited the *Oxford Book of English Verse* (1900) and other anthologies, and published volumes of essays, criticism, poems, and parodies, among them *From a Cornish Window* (1906), *On the Art of Writing* (1916), *Studies in Literature* and *On the Art of Reading* (1920). He is also remembered for a series of humorous novels set in a Cornish background, written under the pseudonym 'Q'.

▷B Willey, *The Q Tradition* (1946)

COUPER, John Mill
(1914–)

Australian poet, born in Dundee, Scotland. His four published volumes are *East of Living* (1957), which includes an extended section on the drowning of the crew of Flinders's ship *The Investigator*, *The Book of Bligh* (1969), dealing with the *Bounty* mutiny and its aftermath, *In from the Sea* (1974) and *The Lee Shore* (1979). His preoccupation with seafaring themes suggests his sense of isolation in his adopted land.

COUPERUS, Louis
(1863–1923)

Dutch poet and novelist, born in The Hague. He was largely brought up in Batavia, in the Dutch East Indies, and lived in Italy. His naturalistic first novel, *Eline Vere* (1889, Eng trans 1892), was a success, and he went on to write several more, including novels set in the Dutch East Indies, and a powerful, fatalistic tetralogy of life in the Hague, *Dr Adriaan* (1901-4, Eng trans *The Books of the Small Souls*, 1914).

▷ W J Simons, *Louis Couperus* (1963)

COURAGE, James Francis
(1903-63)

New Zealand writer, born in Christchurch, who lived in London from his mid-twenties and wrote a number of books, usually with a theme of obsessive love. His first novel, *One House*, was published in 1933, but the second, *The Fifth Child*, set in New Zealand, did not appear until 1948. In *The Young Have Secrets* (1954) the author revisits, in the guise of an 18-year-old, the Christchurch of his youth. He returned to England for the setting of his last two novels, *A Way of Love* (1959), a homosexual love story, and *The Visit to Penmorten* (1961). **Charles Brasch** collected a number of his shorter pieces in *Such Separate Creatures: Stories* (1973).

COURTELINE, Georges, pseud of **Georges Moinaux**
(1860-1929)

French dramatist, born in Tours. A humorous journalist who turned to the stage, he wrote satirical comedies, many of them one-acters, including *Boubouroche* (1893), *Un Client sérieux* (1897, 'A Serious Client') and *Le Commissaire est bon enfant* (1900, 'The Commissioner is Good Natured'). He also published novels, such as *Le Train de 8ʰ47* (1888, 'The 8:47 Train', dramatized 1909) and *Messieurs les Ronds-de-cuir* (1893, 'The Pen Pushers').

▷ P Bournecque, *Le théâtre de Georges Courteline* (1969)

COURTHOPE, William John
(1842-1917)

English poet and critic, born in South Malling vicarage, near Lewes. He was educated at Harrow School and Corpus Christi College and New College, Oxford, where he was Professor of Poetry (1895-1901). In 1892-1907 he was first civil service commissioner. Among his critical works are *Addison* (1883), *Pope* (1889) and *History of English Poetry* (6 vols, 1895-1909). He also published some charming verse in *Paradise of Birds* (1870) and *The Country Town* (1920), and a satire on women's rights, *Ludibria Lunae* (1869).

▷ J W Mackail, *William J Courthope, 1842-1917* (1919)

COUTO, Rui Ribeiro
(1898-1963)

Brazilian novelist and poet. A leading member of the group which promoted Brazilian Modernism, his poetry has been respected without being much discussed. He wrote many competent novels. Titles include *O jardin das Confidêcias* (1921, 'The Burden of Confidences').

COUVREUR, Jessie, née Huybers
(1848-97)

Australian novelist and short-story writer, born in Highgate, London, of Dutch-French stock. She arrived with her family in Hobart, Tasmania in the early 1850s. She married a gambler and womanizer, Charles Fraser, but in 1883 instituted divorce proceedings. She returned to Europe where she married Auguste Couvreur, member of the Belgian parliament (1864-84) and journalist. On her husband's death (1894), she took over as Belgian correspondent for the London *Times*. Her first and best-known novel, *Uncle Piper of Piper's Hill* (1889), was followed by *In Her Earliest Youth* (1890), *The Penance of Portia James* (1891) and *Not Counting the Cost* (1895). *A Fiery Ordeal* (1897) drew more on her marital experiences. Unlike many of her Australian contemporaries, Couvreur wrote not of the land but of the city, families and social divisions. Distinctly English in style, her works give a vivid picture of Australian middle-class life in the latter half of the 19th century.

COUZYN, Jeni
(1942-)

South African-born Canadian poet. She was educated at the University of Natal, taught in Rhodesia and London, and has been a full-time writer since 1968. She took Canadian citizenship in 1975. Her first volume, *Flying* (1970), described her South African background, and documented the psychological impact of exile on everyday perceptions and relationships. *Monkeys' Wedding* (1972, rev edn 1978) was much less oblique and by no means as successful. *Christmas in Africa* (1975), *House of Changes* (1978) and *The Happiness Bird* (1978) turn again to South Africa for much of their imagery, but also include poems which develop a consciousness coloured by science fiction and technological fantasy. With exceptionally balanced irony, Couzyn explores female sexuality as if it were an alien excrescence, but in her most assured collection, *A Time to be Born* (1981), she has come to terms with the world and her own identity within it, a situation reflected in her selection of work for *The Bloodaxe Book of Contemporary Women Poets* (1984). In that same year an expanded edition of her fine selected poems, *Life By Drowning* (originally published 1983), also appeared.

COVERDALE, Miles
(1488–1568)

English Protestant reformer and biblical scholar, born in Yorkshire. He studied at Cambridge, was ordained priest at Norwich in 1514, and joined the Augustinian Friars at Cambridge, where he was converted to Protestantism. He lived abroad from 1528 to 1534 to escape persecution; and in 1535 published in Zürich the first translation of the whole Bible into English, with a dedication to Henry VIII. The Prayer Book retains the Psalms of this translation, and many of the finest phrases in the Authorized Version of 1611 are directly due to Coverdale. In 1538 he was sent by Thomas Cromwell to Paris to superintend another English edition of the Scriptures. Francis I had granted a licence, but during the printing an edict was issued prohibiting the work. Many of the sheets were burned, but the presses and types were hastily carried over to London. Grafton and Whitchurch, the noted printers of that day, were thus enabled to bring out in 1539, under Coverdale's superintendence, the 'Great Bible', which was presented to Henry VIII by Cromwell. The second 'Great Bible', known also as 'Cranmer's Bible' (1540), was also edited by Coverdale, who on Cromwell's fall found it expedient to leave England. While abroad he married and acted as Lutheran pastor in Rhenish Bavaria. In March 1548 he returned to England, was well received through Cranmer's influence, and in 1551 was made bishop of Exeter. On Mary I's accession he was deprived of his see, but was allowed to leave the country, at the earnest intercession of the King of Denmark, whose chaplain, Dr Macchabaeus (MacAlpine), was Coverdale's brother-in-law. Returning to England in 1559, he did not resume his bishopric, but in 1564 he was collated by Grindal to the living of St Magnus, near London Bridge, from which he resigned from growing Puritan scruples about the liturgy in 1566.
▷ J F Mozley, *Coverdale and His Bibles* (1953)

COWARD, Sir Noël Pierce
(1899–1973)

English actor, dramatist, and composer of light music, born in Teddington. At the age of 14 he appeared in *Peter Pan*, and thereafter in other plays, including many of his own. His first play, *I'll Leave It to You* (1920), was followed by many successes, including *The Vortex* (1924), *Hay Fever* (1925), *Private Lives* (1930), *Blithe Spirit* (1941), *This Happy Breed* (1943) and *Nude With Violin* (1956), all showing his strong satiric humour and his unique gift for witty dialogue. He wrote the music for, among others, his operetta *Bitter Sweet* (1929) and his play *Cavalcade* (1931),

and for a series of revues, including *Words and Music* (1932), with its 'Mad Dogs and Englishmen', *This Year of Grace* (1928) and *Sigh No More* (1945). He produced several films based on his own scripts, including *In Which We Serve* (1942), *Blithe Spirit* (1945) and *Brief Encounter* (1945). He published two autobiographies, *Present Indicative* (1937) and *Future Indefinite* (1954).
▷ S Morley, *A Talent to Amuse* (1969)

COWLEY, Abraham
(1618–67)

English poet, born in London, the seventh and posthumous child of a stationer. Attracted to poetry by **Spenser**'s *Faerie Queen*, he wrote excellent verses at 10, and at 15 published five poems. From Westminster School he proceeded in 1637 to Trinity College, Cambridge, and while there wrote, among many other pieces, a large portion of his epic the *Davideis*, its hero David, which was published with a reprint of his first book, *The Mistress*, and a number of other poems, in 1656. During the Civil War he was ejected from Cambridge (1644) but studied at Oxford for another two years. In 1646 he accompanied or followed the queen to Paris, was sent on Royalist missions, and carried on her correspondence in cipher with the king. He returned to England in 1654 and in 1655 was arrested, released on £1000 bail, and took the Oxford MD (1657). On Oliver Cromwell's death he returned to Paris, but went home to England at the Restoration, and received a comfortable provision.
▷ J G Taaffe, *Abraham Cowley* (1972)

COWLEY, Hannah
(1743–1809)

English playwright and poet, one of the first exponents of the comedy of manners. The daughter of a Devonshire bookseller, her first play, *The Runaway* (1776), was written in a fortnight, and produced by David Garrick at Drury Lane. Before retiring to Devon in 1801, she rapidly produced 13 works for the stage, the most successful being *The Belle's Stratagem* (1780), which was frequently revived, notably by Henry Irving in 1881, with Ellen Terry as Letitia. She also wrote long narrative verses (1780–94) and, under the pseudonym Anna Matilda, carried on a sentimental, poetic correspondence in the *World*.

COWLEY, Malcolm
(1898–1989)

American writer, critic and editor, born in Belsano, Pennsylvania. His father was a doctor, which enabled him to attend Harvard, though he had to struggle to make a living as a neophyte writer in New York and

Paris. The experience of hardship, however, proved useful when he came to write *Exile's Return* (1934), about the illustrious group of American writers who convened in Paris after World War I. He returned to the theme with *A Second Flowering: Works and Days of the Lost Generation* (1973), and *The Dream of the Golden Mountains: Remembering the 1930s* (1980). He also published a volume of poetry, *Blue Juniata* (1929), and several volumes of essays. Long associated with *The New Republic* as literary editor (1929–44), and responsible for recognizing the talent of **John Cheever**, he is credited with resuscitating the career of **William Faulkner** by editing a Viking Portable selection of his work (1949).
▷ *Think Back on Us* (1967)

COWPER, Richard, originally **John Middleton-Murry**
(1926–)

English science-fiction novelist, born in Bridport, Dorset, son of the critic **John Middleton-Murry**. Although he has written some novels under the name of Colin Middleton-Murry, it is as Richard Cowper that he is most widely known. His first novel, confidently entitled *Breakthrough* (1967), led to many highly-regarded books, of which *The Road to Corlay* (1978) is perhaps the most acclaimed. Set in the future, it imagines a Britain governed by a totalitarian church, against which the Cult of the White Bird, led by a young man called Thomas, represents the only concerted opposition. This premise allows Cowper to consider serious political and moral themes within the context of a fast-paced narrative.

COWPER, William
(1731–1800)

English poet, son of the rector of Great Berkhamstead, Hertfordshire. He was educated at Westminster School, where Warren Hastings and the poet **Charles Churchill** were contemporaries. In 1752 he took chambers in the Middle Temple and was called to the Bar in 1754. He made no attempt to practise, but showed signs of mental instability. In 1763 he tried to commit suicide when he was offered the sinecure job of a clerkship in the House of Lords, involving a formal examination. Cured temporarily from his breakdown, he was received into the household of a retired evangelical clergyman, Morley Unwin, who with his wife Mary contrived to make the poet's stay at Huntingdon happy. On the death of Mr Unwin his widow removed with her children to Olney, in Buckinghamshire, which was henceforth to be associated with the name of Cowper. Unfortunately the curate of Olney, John Newton, was precisely the person to undo the work of tranquillizing the sick man. His gloomy piety, imposed on the

poet, eventually caused a recurrence of his malady (1773), but the fruit of their association was the *Olney Hymns* (1779), to which Cowper contributed some hymns which are still favourites. In 1779 Newton accepted a charge in London and his absence was at once reflected in a restoration of the poet's spirits. Mrs Unwin suggested to him the writing of a series of moral satires which were published in 1782 (*Poems*) along with some occasional pieces which show the lighter side of his talent. Further to engage him in literary activity, Lady Austen now appeared on the scene (1781) as the occupant of Newton's vicarage. It is not known why her friendship with the poet was interrupted two years later, but *The Task*, published in 1785, came from her suggestion. Cowper's cousin, Lady Hesketh, took her place as literary director (1786), but Cowper seems to have exhausted himself as a creative poet and now turned only to translations—of **Homer**, which was not successful (1791), **Milton's** Latin poems and some French and Italian translations. His genius, however, was still apparent in the short or occasional piece: 'On Receiving My Mother's Picture', 'To Mary' and 'Yardley Oak' (1791). Out of the darkest period, after Mrs Unwin's death in 1796, comes the wonderful, if tragic, 'Castaway'. The lighter side of Cowper's genius—the comic ballad 'John Gilpin', 'Table Talk', and the burlesque opening of *The Task*, a long poem on rural themes—should not be overlooked, but he is generally regarded as the poet of the evangelical revival and as the precursor of **Wordsworth** as a poet of Nature.
▷ Lord David Cecil, *The Stricken Deer* (1933)

COXE, Louis O(sborne)
(1918–)

American poet and critic, born in Manchester, New Hampshire, and educated at Princeton. His first book, *The Sea Faring and Other Poems*, was published in 1947. A major volume, *The Last Hero and Other Poems*, appeared in 1965. Among Coxe's other works are *Billy Budd* (1951), a three-act play based upon the novel of the same name by **Herman Melville** (written in conjunction with a university friend, Robert Chapman), and a highly-praised critical work on **Chaucer** (1963).

COZZENS, James Gould
(1903–78)

American writer, born in Chicago. He published his first novel, *Confusion* (1924), while a student at Harvard at the age of 19. He fought with the American air force in World War II, and on his release from service wrote the Pulitzer Prize-winning *Guard of Honour* (1948). Among his other works are *S.S. San*

Pedro (1931), *Ask Me Tomorrow* (1940), *The Just and the Unjust* (1942), *By Love Possessed* (1958) and *Children and Others* (1965).

▷M Bruccoli, *Cozzens: a new acquist of true experience* (1979) and *Cozzens: a life apart* (1983)

CRABBE, George
(1754–1832)

English poet, born in Aldeburgh on the Suffolk Coast, son of a 'salt-master' and warehousekeeper. His father's violence was offset by his mother's piety. Two of his three brothers perished at sea. His schooling was irregular, but he managed to pick up enough surgery in a nine month's course in London to enable him to set up poorly as a surgeon in Aldeburgh. This was not his chosen career, for he had already published *Inebriety, a Poem* in 1775 and *The Candidate*. He ventured into the literary world in London in 1780, but lived in poverty, unrelieved by appeals to various patrons of letters, until a favourable answer from **Edmund Burke** changed the course of his life. As the guest of Burke at Beaconsfield, he met the noted men of the day, published *The Library* (1781), and patronage flowed in. He was ordained in 1782 and the next year was established in the Duke of Rutland's seat at Belvoir with the prospect of various livings to follow his chaplaincy there. After his marriage to Sarah Elmy (1783) he spent happy years in charges in Suffolk (1792–1805); returned to Muston in Leicestershire; and finally settled in Trowbridge, Wiltshire. In 1783 *The Village*, a harshly realistic poem about village life sponsored by Burke and **Dr Johnson**, brought him fame. Twenty-four years passed before *The Parish Register* (1807) revealed his gifts as a narrative poet. He followed this with *The Borough* (1810), a collection of 24 tales in letter-form (which were later to form the basis of Benjamin Britten's opera, *Peter Grimes*). *Tales* followed in 1812, showing no decline in his powers of narrative and character-drawing. *Tales of the Hall* (1819) concluded this remarkable output of narrative genius. Crabbe's manner suited all tastes—he is still read because of his veracity and his masterly genre painting of humble and middle-class life. His strict moralism—the miseries of the poor are due to sin and insobriety—seems strange to the modern reader, but the grim stories of madness as in 'Sir Eustace Grey' (*Parish Register*) and the comic wooing in 'The Frank Courtship' (*Tales*), show his craft at its best.

▷T E Krebbel, *Life of George Crabbe* (1972)

CRACE, Jim (James)
(1946–)

English novelist and journalist, born in London, whose austere, literary prose has brought him considerable acclaim. His first novel, *Continent*, appeared in 1986, followed two years later by *Gift of Stones*. Both look at the nature of narrative and story-telling, mythology, history and change. In the latter book, these themes are interwoven through a love story. The ironically entitled *Arcadia* (1992) presents a disturbing vision of the modern city.

CRADDOCK, Charles Egbert, pseud of Mary Noailles Murfree
(1850–1922)

American writer, born in Murfreesboro, Tennessee. She published short stories in the *Atlantic Monthly* from 1878, published as *In the Tennessee Mountains* (1884), and thereafter became a prolific novelist of mountain backwoods life.

▷E Parks, *Charles Egbert Craddock* (1941)

CRAIK, Dinah Maria, née Mulock
(1826–87)

English novelist, born in Stoke-upon-Trent. Settling in London at 20, she published *The Ogilvies* (1849), *Olive* (1850), *The Head of the Family* (1851) and *Agatha's Husband* (1853). Her best-known novel was *John Halifax, Gentleman* (1857). Her short stories were collected as *Avillion* (1853), and *Collected Poems* appeared in 1881. She also wrote essays, children's stories, and fairy tales. In 1865 she married George Lillie Craik, nephew of George Lillie Craik, a partner in the publishing house of Macmillan, and was assigned the benefits of a Civil List pension awarded in 1864 to less well-off authors.

CRANE, (Harold) Hart
(1899–1932)

American poet, born in Garrettsville, Ohio. He had little formal education and resisted attempts to place him in the business world, but worked as an advertising copywriter in New York before he found a patron who gave him the wherewithal to travel and devote himself to poetry. An alcoholic and homosexual, given to troughs of shame and remorse, he placed a heavy burden on his friends' tolerance and wallets. Nevertheless he managed to publish two volumes—*White Buildings* (1926) and the long, symbolic *The Bridge* (1930)—variously hailed as masterpieces and unintelligible. Crane is now recognized as one of America's major poets, having much in common with **Walt Whitman**. Returning to America from Mexico, where he had attempted unsuccessfully to write an epic poem on Montezuma, he drowned himself by leaping from a steamboat into the Caribbean.

▷J Unterecker, *Voyager: a life of Crane* (1969)

CRANE, Nathalia, pseud of Clara Ruth Abarbanel
(1913–)

American poet. A mysterious one-off in American literature, she published her first collection of verse, *The Janitor's Boy* (1924) at the age of 11; it was widely thought to have been written by an adult. Later works evoked the same surreal blend of simplicity and precocious understanding: certainly there were no more elements of doggerel than in the jogtrot, hymn-book rhythms of **Emily Dickinson**, who by the time Crane was publishing, was enshrined as a major American poet. Crane also wrote a visionary poem of the Children's Crusade, called *The Sunken Garden* (1926).

CRANE, Stephen
(1871–1900)

American writer and war correspondent, born in New Jersey. He worked as a journalist in New York before publishing his first novel, *Maggie: A Girl of the Streets* (1893). His reputation, however, rests on *The Red Badge of Courage* (1895), which relates vividly the experiences of a soldier in the American Civil War. (The surreal verse of *The Black Riders* dates from the same year.) He had no personal experience of the war but *The Red Badge of Courage* was received with acclaim, in particular for its psychological realism. He never repeated its success but was lionized by literary London (befriended by **Joseph Conrad** and meeting **H G Wells**) before succumbing to tuberculosis in Baden Baden.
▷R W Stallman, *Crane: a biography* (1968)

CRAPSEY, Adelaide
(1878–1914)

American poet of advanced leanings and entirely posthumous reputation. She was born in Brooklyn, New York, the daughter of an eccentrically brilliant clergyman. Educated at Vassar College and in Rome (where she investigated classical archaeology), she spent the remainder of her brief life as a teacher in a girls' school. Almost all of her work was written on her deathbed, using metrical forms resembling **Ezra Pound**'s neo-classical and quasi-oriental experiments, but which were developed parallel to his and were not influenced by them. A collection of *Verse* (1915) and an ambitious but unfinished *Analysis of English Metrics* (1918) are the only publications of this remarkable figure.

CRASHAW, Richard
(c.1613–49)

English religious poet, born in London, the only son of the Puritan poet and clergyman William Crashaw (1572–1626). From Charterhouse he proceeded in 1631 to Pembroke Hall, Cambridge, and c.1636 became a fellow of Peterhouse College. In 1634 he published a volume of Latin poems, *Epigrammatum Sacrocorum Liber* (2nd edn 1670), in which occurs the famous line on the miracle at Cana: '*Nymphas pudica Deum vidit et erubuit*' (the modest water saw its God and blushed). His Catholic leanings prevented him from receiving Anglican orders, and in 1643 he lost his fellowship for refusing to take the Covenant. He went to Paris and embraced Catholicism, and in 1646 published his *Steps to the Temple*, republished at Paris in 1652, under the title *Carmen Deo Nostro*, with 12 vignette engravings designed by Crashaw. Soon afterwards he was introduced by John Cowley to Queen Henrietta Maria, who recommended him at Rome; and in April 1649 he became a subcanon at Loretto, but died four months afterwards.
▷M Praz, *Richard Crashaw* (1945)

CRATINUS
(c.484–c.419 BC)

Greek comic poet. Next to Eupolis and **Aristophanes**, he best represents the Old Attic comedy. He limited the number of actors to three, and was the first to add to comedy the interest of biting personal attack; even Pericles did not escape his pen. Of his 21 comedies, nine of which obtained the first public prize, on one occasion beating Aristophanes' *Nephelai* ('Clouds'), only some fragments are extant.

CRAWFORD, F(rancis) Marion
(1854–1909)

American novelist, born at Bagni di Lucca, Italy. After an extensive education in the USA and Europe and working as a journalist in India, he became a bestselling writer with the exotic *Mr Isaacs, A Tale of Modern India* (1882); thereafter he spent most of his life in Italy, where many of his more than 40 romantic and historical novels are set. Italian aristocratic society provided the subject-matter for the 'Saracinesca' series: *Saracinesca* (1887), *Sant' Ilario* (1889), *Don Orsino* (1892) and *Corleone* (1897). Meanwhile, in *The Novel: What It Is* (1893) Crawford set out his creed as a romantic novelist, who wrote to entertain rather than to improve his readers. His books are certainly not bereft of ideas, but despite his immense contemporary popularity, only his ghost stories, such as 'The Upper Berth' (1885) and 'The Screaming Skull' (1908) are widely read now.
▷J Pilkington Jr, *Francis Marion Crawford* (1964)

CRAWFORD, Isabella Vallancy
(1850–87)

Irish-born Canadian poet and short-story writer. An emigrant to Canada West from Dublin in 1858, Vallancy Crawford was one of 13 children of whom only three survived infancy. Earnings from her writing became the only source of support for her mother and herself after her father's death. She produced a range of periodical literature, including many short stories of which a number of selections have been published. However, it is her poetry that has earned her critical recognition, although only one volume, *Old Spookses' Pass, Malcolm's Katie and Other Poems* (1884), was published during her lifetime. In her poems she imbues the Canadian landscape with a mythic significance, imaging the forces of good, evil and love in a symbolic language specific to her Canadian pioneer experience; she was described by Northrop Frye as having 'the most remarkable mythopoeic imagination in Canadian poetry'. A revival of critical interest in her poetry during the 1970s—principally inspired by **James Reaney**'s admiration for her work—culminated in the important Crawford Symposium of 1977 (collected papers published in Ottawa, 1979).

CREASEY, John
(1908–73)

English crime and espionage writer, who used no less than 25 pseudonyms (male and female), of which J J Marric was perhaps the best known. Born in Southfields, Surrey, he was educated in London, and wrote full-time from 1935, two years after the first Department Z thriller was published. An astonishingly prolific writer, Creasey's better-known series characters were Inspector Roger West, the Hon Richard Rollison ('The Toff') and the former jewel thief John Mannering (better known as 'The Baron'). The Marric novels (1955, 1976, posthumous) all concern Commander George Gideon of Scotland Yard, and bear his name in their titles. With more than 550 novels to his credit, Creasey's work was variable in quality but was usually tightly plotted, with a skilful use of secondary narrative, and rarely muddied by abstract thought. His total sale of books is something around 70 million worldwide. Creasey stood for parliament as a Liberal candidate in 1950, and four times as a member of the All Party Alliance, which he had founded in 1967.
▷ R E Briney and J Creasey, 'A John Creasey Bibliography', in *Armchair Detective* (October 1968)

CRÉBILLON, Claude Prosper Jolyot de
(1707–77)

French novelist, younger son of **Prosper Jolyot de Crébillon**, born in Paris. After writing a number of slight pieces for the stage, he acquired great popularity as an author of elegant but licentious stories with satirical undertones aimed at the fashionable society in which he moved. In 1740 he married an Englishwoman called Lady Stafford. The indecency of his *Le Sopha, conte moral* ('The Sofa—a moral tale') having offended Madame de Pompadour, he was banished from Paris for five years, but on his return in 1755 was appointed in succession to his father as official literary censor, despite his reputation.
▷ P P Brooks, *The Novel of Worldliness* (1969)

CRÉBILLON, Prosper Jolyot de
(1674–1762)

French dramatist, born in Dijon. He studied in Paris for the law. His tragedy of *Idoménée* was successfully produced in 1703. It was followed by *Atrée et Thyeste* (1707), *Électre* (1709), and *Rhadamiste et Zénobie* (1711), his masterpiece. After writing several other pieces, Crébillon fell into neglect and produced nothing for over 20 years. He was then pushed forward as a dramatic rival to **Voltaire** by Madame de Pompadour, elected to the Academy, awarded a pension of 1000 francs, and appointed royal censor and a royal librarian. His *Catilina* was brought out with great success in 1748. Among his other works were *Xerxès*, *Sémiramis* (1717), *Pyrrhus*, and *Le Triumvirat*. His son was the novelist **Claude Prosper Jolyot de Crébillon**.
▷ P Le Clerc, *Voltaire and Crébillon Père* (1973)

CREEKMORE, Hubert
(1907–66)

American poet and novelist, whose work was deeply influenced by his Southern upbringing: raised in Mississippi, he had a powerful awareness of the social forces at work there, and the strong pressure of the past. His main achievement is a novel, *The Chain in the Heart* (1953), which is one of the best accounts (by a white author) of Afro-American life. He had a great interest in world literature, prompted partly by a search for the underlying mythologies and experiences that bind apparently disparate cultures.

CREELEY, Robert
(1926–)

American poet, born in Arlington, Massachusetts. Appointed to the faculty at Black Mountain College in North Carolina, he was linked with the Black Mountain school of poets. In the mid-1950s he moved to California, where he mixed with prominent Beat writers like **Jack Kerouac** and **Allen Ginsberg**. His poems, characterized by dense syntax and abrupt endings, have appeared in numerous collections including *If You* (1956), *The Whip* (1957), *For You: Poems 1950–60* (1962), *St Martin's* (1971) and *The Collected Poems of Robert Creeley, 1945–75* (1982). He has written one novel, *The Island* (1963); other prose appears in *The Collected Prose of Robert Creeley: A Story* (1984).

▷M Novik, *Robert Creeley, an inventory* (1973)

CRESSWELL, (Walter) D'Arcy
(1896–1960)

Expatriate New Zealand poet and writer of eccentric and archaic tastes, whose verse reflects his predilection for earlier times. Born in Christchurch, his first collections were published in London as *Poems (1921–1927)* (1928) and *Poems 1924–1931* (1932), but the best of his poetry is perhaps *Lyttelton Harbour* (1936). *The Letters of D'Arcy Cresswell* (1971) and *Dear Lady Ginger: An Exchange of Letters between Lady Ottoline Morrell and D'Arcy Cresswell* (1983) were edited by **Helen Shaw** and cast an explanatory light on his affectations.

▷ *The Poet's Progress* (1930); *Present Without Leave* (1939)

CRETIN, Guillaume
(d.1525)

French poet, born in Paris. Between Coustellier's edition of the poems in 1723 and the modern *Oeuvres Poétiques* (1932, ed Kathleen Chesney), Cretin's work received scant attention. A leader of the school of *Rhetoriqueurs* Cretin gave his name to the vogue of 'Cretinism'—the art of saying nothing in the most complicated of measures. Derided as one aspect of medievalism's last stand, Cretin's work has only recently been looked at afresh. The final decade of his life was the most productive, bringing him several royal prizes for 'ballades' and 'chants-royeaux'. A mysterious affair of mutual court animosity clouded the end of his life.

CREWS, Harry Eugene
(1935–)

American novelist, born in Georgia and temperamentally of the South, writing in a grotesque style marked by bizarre humour. His first novel, *The Gospel Singer* (1968) was followed by a succession of novels, including *The Hawk Is Dying* (1973), *The Gypsy's Curse* (1974), *A Feast of Snakes* (1976) and *All We Need of Hell* (1987). Crews has also written vivid journalism, much of it concerned with the vagaries of life below the Mason–Dixon line. A compilation of his *Esquire* columns was published as *Blood and Grits* (1979).

▷ *A Childhood: The Biography of a Place* (1978)

CRISTOFER, Michael, originally **Michael Procaccino**
(1945–)

American playwright and actor, born in New Jersey. His most familiar plays are *Black Angel* (1976), *The Shadow Box* (1977, Pulitzer Prize) and *The Lady and the Clarinet* (1980), all of which portray people at the point of emotional crisis. The first deals with three terminally ill patients and their responses as life slips away from them, while the second examines the life of a former Nazi officer in hiding many years after World War II. *The Lady and the Clarinet* is a more humorous piece, a vivacious look at the hopes and fears in the love-life of an American career woman.

CRNJANSKI, Milos
(1893–)

Serbian poet, novelist and dramatist, born in Csongrád, Hungary. He was forced to fight for the Austro–Hungarian army in World War I, and his experiences turned him into a militantly right-wing pacifist; his views might be compared to those of the English novelist **Henry Williamson**. He stayed out of Yugoslavia until 1965, when he was able to return to Belgrade as a revered national figure. His bold lyrical poetry much influenced Serbs, and his long novel *Seobe* (1929–62, 'The Migrations') has been much admired as a masterful account of the 18th-century Serbs in Vojvodina, and one of the most significant Yugoslav novels of the 20th century. His critical study of the sonnets of **Shakespeare** is famous.

▷A Kadic, *Contemporary Serbian Literature* (1964); T Eekman, *Thirty Years of Yugoslav Literature 1945–1975* (1978)

CROCE, Benedetto
(1866–1952)

Italian critic and philosopher who, though he wrote nothing creative, had an enormous influence on Italian and even on European literature. He has been compared to **Montaigne** in his capacity as an educator. His impact in Britain was felt through the historian and philosopher R G Collingwood. His notions that history is the story of liberty and that liberty is the highest value—rather than his Hegelian idealism—have proved exemplary, even if he has angered those both to the left and the right of him.

▷C Sprigge, *Benedetto Croce, Man and Thinker* (1952)

CROCKETT, Samuel Rutherford
(1860–1914)

Scottish popular novelist, born in Little Duchrae, Kirkcudbright, of tenant-farming stock. Paying his way by journalism and travelling tutorships, he attended Edinburgh University and New College, Edinburgh. Becoming a Free Church minister in Penicuik, he wrote sardonic congregational sketches, of which 24, collected as *The Stickit Minister* (1893), brought immediate fame; this was consolidated in 1894 by *The Raiders*, *The Lilac Sunbonnet* (a seemingly innocent love story which ridiculed narrow religious sects) and two novellas. Resigning the ministry in favour of full-time writing in 1895, he wrote a variety of books, from tales of Covenanting and medieval Scotland, to European historical romances and (often sensational) stories of mining, industrialism and Edinburgh slums. His posthumous works include one detective and one theological science-fiction novel.
▷I M Donaldson, *Life and Work of Samuel Rutherford Crockett* (1989)

CROFTS, Freeman Wills
(1879–1957)

Irish author of detective fiction, born in Dublin. He abandoned a career as Chief Assistant Engineer on the Belfast and Northern Counties Railway in 1929 in order to concentrate on his writing and, later, moved to England. Crofts wrote 35 novels, of which 24 feature the doggedly methodical, unassuming, courteous and wry Inspector (later Superintendent) French of Scotland Yard. He made his first appearance in *Inspector French's Greatest Case* (1925), a tale of diamonds stolen from a Hatton Garden safe, beside which lies a dead body. Other notable French novels include *The Starvel Tragedy* (1927) and *The Hog's Back Mystery* (1933), books which also capture the atmosphere of London, from raffish criminal haunts, offices and shops to commonplace suburban streets and domestic interiors.

CROKER, John Wilson
(1780–1857)

Irish politician and essayist, born in Galway, the son of the surveyor-general of Irish customs. Educated at Trinity College, Dublin, in 1800 he entered Lincoln's Inn, and in 1802 was called to the Irish Bar. Two satires on the Irish stage (*On the Present State of the Irish Stage*, 1804) and on Dublin society (*Intercepted Letters from Canton*, 1804) proved brilliant hits; so did his *Sketch of Ireland Past and Present* (1807), a pamphlet advocating Catholic emancipation. Elected MP for Downpatrick in 1807, in 1809 he helped

to found the *Quarterly Review*, to which he contributed 260 articles. He was rewarded with the lucrative secretaryship of the Admiralty (1809–30) for his warm defence of Frederick, Duke of York in the case of Mary Anne Clarke. After 1832, he refused to re-enter parliament and would not even take office under Peel, his old friend (1834). He fell out with Peel over the repeal of the Corn Laws (1846). Among the 17 works that he wrote or edited were his *Stories for Children from English History* (1817), which suggested the *Tales of a Grandfather*; the *Suffolk Papers* (1823); his edition of **James Boswell**'s *Life of Johnson* (1831); and *Essays on the Early French Revolution* (1857). He is better remembered for his attack on **Keats**, and **Thomas Macaulay**'s attack on him (Macaulay 'detested him more than cold boiled veal'); and as the originator of the term Conservative, a founder of the Athenaeum Club, and the 'Rigby' of **Benjamin Disraeli**'s *Coningsby*.
▷M Brightfield, *John Wilson Croker* (1940)

CROKER, Thomas Crofton
(1798–1854)

Irish antiquary and folklorist, born in Cork. From 1818 to 1859 he was a clerk at the Admiralty. As a boy of 14 he had begun to collect songs and legends of the Irish peasantry and in 1818 he sent **Thomas Moore** nearly 40 old Irish melodies. In 1825 he published anonymously his *Fairy Legends and Traditions of the South of Ireland*, a work which charmed Sir **Walter Scott** and was translated into German by the brothers **Grimm** (1826). A second series followed in 1827. Of nearly 20 more works the best were *Researches in the South of Ireland* (1824), *Legends of the Lakes* (1829), *The Adventures of Barney Mahoney* (1832) and *Popular Songs of Ireland* (1839).

CROLY, George
(1780–1860)

Irish poet, romance-writer, biographer and Anglican preacher, born in Dublin. Educated at Trinity College, he took orders in 1804, and went to London in 1810, in 1835 becoming rector of St Stephen's, Walbrook. From 1817 he published some 40 works, the best-known of which is the weird romance of *Salathiel* (1829), based on the legend of the Wandering Jew. Other titles include the tragedy *Cataline* (1822), the satirical *May Fair* (1827), and a romance of the French revolution, *Marston* (1846).
▷R Herring, *A Few Personal Recollections* (1861)

CROMMELYNCK, Fernand
(1888–1970)

Major Belgian playwright and novelist, born in Paris of a French mother and a Belgian

father. His first real success was *Le Cocu magnifique* (1921, Eng trans *The Magnificent Cuckold*, 1966), which was produced in Paris by Lugné-Poë. In it a husband, based on the character of Kitely in **Ben Jonson**'s *Every Man in his Humour*, seeks to be certain that he has cause for jealousy, and thus reveals his perversity. This was followed by the profound farce *Tripes d'or* (1930, 'Golden Tripes'), a study of greed so powerful that it has shocked even the dramatist's admirers. After 1934 Crommelynck suddenly ceased to be productive, confining himself to a mystery novel and to a few film-scripts. But he had left an ineradicable mark on the theatre with six explosive and entirely original plays.
▷D Grossvogel, *20th Century French Drama* (1961)

CROMPTON, Richmal, original surname **Lamburn**
(1890–1969)

English writer, and author of the *Just William* books, born in Bury, Lancashire. She was educated in Lancashire and Derby and at Royal Holloway College, London. An honours graduate in classics (1914), she taught for some years, but was struck down with poliomyelitis in 1923. She published 50 adult titles thereafter but she is best known for her 38 short-story collections (and one novel, *Just William's Luck*) about the perpetual schoolboy, the 11-year-old William Brown. Children loved the judicious deliberation with which William's incursions and imitations are described in their reduction of ordered adult life to chaos.

CRONEGK, Johann Friedrich Reichsherr von
(1730–57)

German poet, verse dramatist and editor of his own periodical, *Der Freund*, born in Ansbach into the family of a Prussian general. He died young, of smallpox. His classical tragedies, written in Alexandrines, were influenced by **Edward Young** and by French models, and played a small but decisive part in the development of German drama. He was a close friend of **Gellert**.
▷W Gensel, *Cronegk* (1894, in German)

CRONIN, A(rchibald) J(oseph)
(1896–1981)

Scottish novelist, born in Cardross, Dunbartonshire. He graduated in medicine at Glasgow in 1919, but in 1930 abandoned his practice as a result of a breakdown in his health, and turned to literature. He had an immediate success with his brooding and melodramatic autobiographical novel *Hatter's Castle* (1931). Subsequent works include

The Citadel (1937), *The Keys of the Kingdom* (1941), *Beyond this Place* (1953), *Crusader's Tomb* (1956) and *A Song of Sixpence* (1964). The medical stories in his Scottish novels formed the basis of the popular radio and television series *Dr Finlay's Casebook* in the 1960s, and again in 1993. Towards the end of his life he lived largely in the USA and Switzerland.
▷*Adventures in Two Worlds* (1952)

CRONIN, Bernard
(1884–1968)

English-born Australian writer and journalist, born in Ealing, Middlesex. He wrote about 30 light novels under various pseudonyms, and some one-act plays, mainly for radio. The novels, based on his earlier experiences as a station-hand in Victoria and Tasmania, include *The Coastlanders* (1918), *Salvage* (1923) and *The Sow's Ear* (1933). In 1920 he founded the 'Derelicts' Club for indigent authors and artists, which later became the Society of Australian Authors.

CROSS, Zora
(1890–1964)

Australian novelist and poet, born in Brisbane. Experiencing a series of affairs and an unconsummated marriage, she wrote frank poems about sexuality, physical love and motherhood which were published as *A Song of Mother Love* (1916), *Songs of Love and Life* (1917) and *The Lilt of Life* (1918). She settled into a *de facto* relationship with editor **David McKee Wright**, by whom she had two daughters and, after his sudden death in 1928, she supported her family by journalism and acting. Her novels, little regarded now, include *Daughters of the Seven-Mile* (1924) and, much later, *This Hectic Age* (1944), in which a girl from the bush adjusts to the pace of life in Sydney. Her poetry, though, shows a true gift, as in *Elegy on an Australian Schoolboy*, published in 1921, on the death of her younger brother in World War I.

CROTHERS, Rachel
(1878–1958)

American playwright, born in Bloomington, Illinois. A feminist, in 1910 she published *A Man's World*, an attack upon moral double standards, the heroine of which proclaims herself 'a natural woman because I am a free one'; at the time this was considered an extremely important work. *Ourselves* (1913) looked at the problem of prostitution. Crothers succeeded where many playwrights fail, managing to combine polemic with box-office success, although she increasingly veered towards lighter work, as in *As Husbands Go*

(1932), which contrasts English and American marriages; and while *When Ladies Meet* (1932) recalls her earlier, sharper tone, it is also outwardly a comedy.

▷L C Gottlieb, *Rachel Crothers* (1979)

CROUSE, Russel
(1893–1966)

American playwright, producer and journalist, born in New York. He is best remembered for a series of collaborations with Howard Lindsay (1889–1968), including *Life With Father* (1939) and *Life With Mother* (1948), both adapted from books by **Clarence Day**, and the comedies *The Great Sebastians* (1956) and *Tall Story* (1959). Their most important work was *State of the Union* (1945), a political satire about a presidential candidate which won the Pulitzer Prize for Drama in 1946. He also wrote a number of musical shows with other collaborators, and some non-fiction.

CRUICKSHANK, Helen Burness
(1886–1975)

Scottish poet, born in Hillside, Angus. Educated at Montrose Academy, in 1903 she joined the Civil Service in London. After her return to Edinburgh in 1912 her home became a centre for Scottish writers. She contributed poems to **Hugh MacDiarmid**'s *Scottish Chapbook* and *Northern Numbers* and the two became friends. She was secretary to Scottish PEN between 1927 and 1934, and a teacher and confidante to writers such as **Lewis Grassic Gibbon**. Her poems were first published in 1934 in *Up the Noran Water* and five more collections appeared in 1954, 1968, 1971, 1976 and 1978. She wrote both in English and a dialect Scots that drew on her Angus heritage. Her work is marked by an economy of language and variety of forms, including prose-poetry and blank verse. In 1971 she was awarded an Honorary MA from Edinburgh University for her contributions to Scottish literature. **Hugh MacDiarmid** complimented her in a radio tribute as a 'catalyst' to the Scottish Renaissance.

CRUZ, Ramón de la
(1731–94)

Spanish dramatist, born in Madrid, where he spent his life. Although he began very much in the traditional neo-classicist mould, translating works by **Racine** and **Voltaire**, and even *Hamlet*, he broke with this tradition by turning to the popular portrayal of life in Madrid as encapsulated in the 'sainete', a short play or farce. He had also composed many 'zarzuelas' (light operas) and adapted a play by **Molière**. However, he believed that drama consisted of imitating life, and wrote colourful pieces doing just that. His 'sainetes' (of which he wrote over 400) were published in 10 volumes (1786–91). They originated a strong tradition, of which **Carlos Arniches** was to become the main inheritor.

CRUZ, Sor Juana Inés de la
(1648–95)

Mexican feminist, poet and playwright, born in San Miguel Nepantle, Amecameca, not far from Mexico City. A woman of legendary beauty, she has affinities with **Christine de Pisan**. Like Christine, she became celebrated for her scholarship at an early age, and was invited by the wife of the Viceroy of Mexico to live at the court. At the age of 19 disgust, probably prompted by shock at the ways of men (she may have had a love affair) and by the frivolity of court life, led her to enter the Carmelite Order. But the artificial rigour of this life, too, revolted her, and she returned to court. A year later she joined the Hieronymite convent (in which she remained), in Mexico City, on account (she declared) of her 'total lack of matrimonial ambition' and of her wish to 'live alone, in order to have no interruption to my freedom and my study'. When instructed by a bishop, an officer of the Inquisition, to give up learning as 'unbefitting to a woman' she issued the stately *Respuesta* (1691), the *Response*, a key document in the history of feminism. With consummate irony, she pointed out that she wrote secular poetry and drama only because, as a woman, she was incapable of religious devotion—and that merely artistic heresy was not punishable by the Pope. Her own sardonic, parodic, highly erotic, and mystical poetry, especially the 'Primero sueño' ('First Dream'), is individualistic and 'modern'. Her poems about male stupidity, in particular 'Rendonillas' ('Verses'), have hardly been forgiven, and have not been translated ('Stupid men, who accuse/women unreasonably/without seeing that you are the cause/of that very thing you blame ...'). In one of her plays she demonstrates that her Catholicism was but skin-deep: she explains the Aztec rite of eating the Corn God as a Satanic parody of the Communion. With Christine, **Sappho**, **Laura Riding** and **Emily Dickinson**, she is amongst the greatest and least understood of all writers. She sold all her books, scientific equipment and musical instruments, in order to care for the poor, and died of the plague while ministering to them.

▷A Reyes, *The Position of America* (1950); E A Chávez, *Sor Juana de la Cruz* (1970)

CRUZ E SOUSA, João da
(1861–98)

Brazilian poet, born in Desterro (now Florianópolis), a son of slaves. It was the slave-owner who, noticing his unusual abilities, sent him to school. But, understandably, Cruz e Sousa could never transcend his sense of inferiority at being black. He spent a desperate life: his wife went mad and two of his children died in childhood. He was first influenced by **Baudelaire** and by **Anthero de Quental**, but essentially remained a disciple of **Olavo Bilac**, the Brazilian poet he admired most of all, possibly to his detriment (for he was more intrinsically gifted). He has been ranked with **Mallarmé**, but criticism has, in general, been rather more cautious.

ČSIKY, Gregor
(1842–91)

Hungarian dramatist, born in Pankota, Vilagos. A Professor of Theology at Temesvar seminary, he published some tales from religious history ('Photographs from Life'), and in 1875 a comedy, *Jaslot* ('The Oracle'), which was a success. Other plays followed, including comedies like *Mirkány Kariar and Anna* (1883), and tragedies—*Janus* (1877), *A Mágusz* (1878, 'The Magician') and *Theodora*. He also translated **Sophocles**, **Plautus** and **Molière** into Hungarian, as well as several English plays. *Az Ellenallhatatlan* ('The Irresistible'), which won a prize from the Hungarian Academy, typifies his talent for a direct, fresh approach to his subject.
▷G Hefedus, *Csiky Gregor* (1953)

ČSOKONAI VITÉZ, Mihály
(1773–1805)

Hungarian poet, born in Debrecen, Hungary. He was Professor of Poetry at the university there until his way of life lost him the post. His fame persists, however, chiefly through his lyrics, which are based on old Hungarian folksongs. Among his works are the drama *Tempefoi* (1793), the poems *Magyar-Musa* (1797) and *Dorottya* (1804), a mock-heroic poem.
▷V Julow, *Csokonai Vitéz Mihály* (1975)

CSOKOR, Franz Theodor
(1885–1965)

Austrian playwright who began writing in the expressionist vein, but had his popular successes in the traditional realm, with such plays as *3 November 1918* (1936), a cleverly rendered spectacle of the final dissolution of the Habsburg army. He continued to produce well-made plays until within a few years of his death.

CUADRA, José de la
(1903–41)

Ecuardorean novelist, poet and story writer, born in Guayaquil. After making his mark with early poems and stories, and qualifying

as a lawyer, de la Cuadra became a member, with **Aguilera Malta**, **Gil Gilbert**, and others, of the epoch-making, left-wing Grupo de Guayaquil, whose motto was 'Reality and nothing more than reality'. He became a university teacher, held posts in the provincial government of the Guayas, and shortly before his premature death was appointed a magistrate. His most famous work is a novel, *Los Sangurismos* (1934, 'The Sangurismos'), a brilliantly violent book; but the best Ecuadorean opinion has it that his finest work lies in the short stories he wrote from the collection *Horno* (1932, 'Furnace') onwards. However, the bitter novel he left unfinished, *Los monos enloquecidos* (1951, 'The Maddened Monkeys'), contains some of his best work.
▷A Flores, *The Literature of Spanish America* (1966–9)

CUADRA, Pablo Antonio, known as PAC
(1912–)

Nicaraguan poet, born in Managua, but brought up in his parents' native city of Granada (Nicaragua), for long Nicaragua's most distinguished man of letters. He was among the leading members of the Vanguardia movement, and was associated with its first manifesto (1931). His first collection, *Poemas nicaragüense* (1934, 'Nicaraguan Poems'), published in Santiago de Chile, was, according to a critic, 'the first book in the vernacular in central America'. He welcomed the Sandanista revolution, but was quick to denounce its excesses, and for a time went to live in Austin, Texas. His poetry was translated by **Thomas Merton**: *El jaguar y la luna* (1959, Eng trans *The Jaguar and the Moon*, 1974). Other works include *Cantos de Cifar y del Mar Dulce* (1971, Eng trans *Songs of Cifar and the Sweet Sea*, 1979) and selected translations in *the Birth of the Sun* (1987).
▷T Merton, *Emblems of a Season of Fury* (1963)

CUEVA, Juan de la
(c.1550–1610)

Spanish poet and dramatist, born in Seville. He wrote a number of rather undistinguished poems, but is regarded as an important figure in the development of Spanish drama. He is known especially for his use of new metrical forms, and for his introduction of historical material and overtly political themes into the drama.
▷R F Glenn, *Juan de la Cueva* (1973)

CULLEN, Countee
(1903–46)

American Black poet, born in New York. A leader of the so-called Harlem Renaissance,

he began his literary career with *Color* (1925), a book of poems in which classical models such as the sonnet are used with considerable effect. He published several subsequent volumes of verse, and a novel *One Way to Heaven* (1932), and collaborated with **Arna Bontemps** in the play *St Louis Woman* (1946).
▷M Perry, *A bio-bibliography* (1971)

CUMBERLAND, Richard
(1732–1811)
English playwright, born in the lodge of Trinity College, Cambridge, maternal grandson of Dr Richard Bentley. From Bury St Edmunds and Westminster School he went to Trinity College, Cambridge, and was a fellow at 20. Becoming private secretary to Lord Halifax in 1761, he gave up his intention of taking orders. He was secretary to the board of trade from 1776 to 1782. Thereafter he retired to Tunbridge Wells, where he wrote farces, tragedies, comedies, pamphlets, essays and two novels, *Arundel* (1789) and *Henry* (1795). Of his sentimental comedies the best are *The Brothers* (1769), *The West Indian* (1771), *The Fashionable Lover* (1772), *The Jew* (1794) and *The Wheel of Fortune* (1795). He was caricatured by **Richard Brinsley Sheridan** in *The Critic* as Sir Fretful Plagiary.
▷S T Williams, *Richard Cumberland* (1917)

CUMMINGS, E(dward) E(stlin), self-styled as e e cummings
(1894–1962)
American writer and painter, born in Cambridge, Massachusetts. Educated at Harvard, he is celebrated for his verse characterized by typographical tricks and eccentric punctuations, signed 'e e cummings', starting with his first volume *Tulips and Chimneys* (1924). His best-known prose work, *The Enormous Room* (1922), describes his wartime internment—brought about by an error by the authorities—in France. He also wrote a travel diary, a morality play, *Santa Claus* (1946), and a collection of six 'non-lectures' delivered at Harvard entitled *i* (1953). He studied art in Paris, and a collection of his drawings and paintings was published in 1931.
▷N Friedman, *The Growth of a Writer* (1964)

CUMMINS, Maria Susanna
(1827–66)
American writer, born in Salem, Massachusetts. Her first novel, *The Lamplighter* (1854), was a moralistic fable about a Boston orphan and won considerable success. Cummins also contributed to *Atlantic Monthly*.

CUNHA, Euclydes da
(1866–1909)
Brazilian writer, born in Rio de Janeiro province. His coverage, as a journalist, of the Canudos rebellion (1896), resulted in the exuberantly written classic *Os Sertões* (1902, Eng abridged trans *Rebellion in the Backlands*, 1944). The book has become essential reading, because da Cunha was able to write with deep sympathy of the backland rebels (*sertanejos*), mestizo cowboys, who held the Brazilian troops at bay at Canudos for the best part of a year. They were led by a religious fanatic, Antônio Conselheiro (Antonio the Counsellor), into whom da Cunha, in his incidental criticism of the government of President Barros, showed remarkable insight. This was all the more extraordinary because he was himself the intellectual victim of Spencerian misconceptions about 'backward' peoples. No book, even by **Gilberto Freyre**, has been more influential in Brazil or Latin America. The author, a man in whom there was 'more than a touch of the pathologic', and who, with **Machado de Assis**, is Brazil's greatest writer of the modern era, was shot down in the street at Santa Cruz, by an enraged army officer.
▷P Putnam, *Marvellous Journey* (1948)

CUNNINGHAM, Allan
(1784–1842)
Scottish poet and writer, born in the parish of Dalswinton, Dumfriesshire. His father was neighbour of **Robert Burns** at Ellisland and Allan, as a boy, was present at the poet's funeral. At 10 he was apprenticed to a stonemason, but he continued to pore over songs and stories. His first publications were his sham-antique verse and prose contributions to Cromek's *Remains of Nithsdale and Galloway Song* (1810). He already knew **James Hogg**, and through him he made the acquaintance of Sir **Walter Scott**, with whom 'Honest Allan' was always a great favourite. He moved to London, and became one of the best-known writers for the *London Magazine*, as well as manager of Francis Chantrey's sculpture studio (1815–41). Among his works were *Traditional Tales of the English and Scottish Peasantry* (1822), *Songs of Scotland, Ancient and Modern* (1825), *Lives of the most Eminent British Painters, Sculptors, and Architects* (6 vols, 1829–33), and *Life of Wilkie* (3 vols, 1843).
▷D Hogg, *The Life of Allan Cunningham* (1875)

CUNNINGHAM, E V *see* FAST, Howard Melvin

CUNNINGHAM, James Vincent
(1911–85)
American poet, critic and academic. His poetry was influenced by that of **Yvor Winters**, and, unusually, he eventually became more highly thought of, as a poet,

than his avowed master. He wrote witty, intellectual, incisive and always interesting—if somewhat cold—poetry, and his *Collected Poems and Epigrams* (1971) is a much respected volume. *Collected Essays* appeared in 1977.

▷ E B Hungerford, *Poets in Progress* (1962)

CUNNINGHAME GRAHAM, Robert Bontine
(1852–1936)

Scottish writer and politician, the grandson of the songwriter Robert Cunninghame Graham, born in London. He was educated at Harrow and from 1869 was chiefly engaged in ranching in the Argentine, until he succeeded to the family estates in 1883. In 1879 he married a Chilean poet, Gabriela de la Belmondiere. He was Liberal MP for North-West Lanarkshire (1886–92) and was imprisoned with John Burns, the socialist leader, for 'illegal assembly' in Trafalgar Square during a mass unemployment demonstration in 1887. He was the first President of the Scottish Labour Party in 1888. He travelled extensively in Spain and Morocco (1893–8), where an incident described in his *Mogreb-El-Acksa* (1898) inspired **George Bernard Shaw**'s *Captain Brassbound's Conversion*. He wrote a large number of travel books, but is best known for his highly individual, flamboyant essays and short stories, notably the much-anthologized 'Beattock for Moffat', collections of which are entitled *Success* (1902), *Faith* (1909), *Hope* (1910), *Charity* (1912) and *Scottish Stories* (1914). He was elected the first President of the National Party of Scotland in 1928, and of the Scottish National Party in 1934. **Joseph Conrad** and **William Henry Hudson** were among his close literary friends. He died in Argentina, where he was known as 'Don Roberto'.

▷ A F Tschiffely, *Don Roberto: Tornado Cavalier* (1937)

CUREL, François de
(1854–1928)

French dramatist, born in Metz into a family of aristocrats which had taken to industry. His first plays were presented at the Théâtre Libre, where they became critically celebrated. However the public never really took to anything of his except the long-forgotten comedy *L'Âme en folle* (1919, 'Soul in Folly'). Yet, a curious and enigmatic case, he remains admired. What seemed strained to contemporary critics in such plays as *La Figurante* (1896, 'The Stand-In')—commissioned by Bernhardt, who appeared in it—has seemed daring and proto-modernistic to later commentators. He has been called a 'dramatist's dramatist'. His strength lay in

analysis of strange psychological states; but he disturbed some critics' susceptibility to mysticism. His last and perhaps his most interesting play, *Orage mystique* (1927, 'Mystic Storm'), actually attempts to communicate with the dead. His very early *Les fossiles* ('The Fossils') is translated in *Contemporary European Plays I* (1931, ed Benfield Pressey).

▷ E Braunstein, *François de Curel et le théâtre d'idées* (1962)

CURNOW, (Thomas) Allen Munro
(1911–)

New Zealand poet and critic, born in Timaru, Canterbury, whose preoccupation with New Zealand's past and its quest for national identity is central to all his writing. His first verse was published as *Valley of Decision: Poems* (1933). *Sailing or Drowning* (1943) includes the poem 'Landfall in Unknown Seas', a commission from the Department of Internal Affairs to mark the 300th anniversary of Tasman's discovery of New Zealand; it was set to music by New Zealand composer Douglas Lilburn. Key collections are *Poems: Jack without Magic* (1946) and *At Dead Low Water and Sonnets* (1949). Major contributions were his editing of the anthology *A Book of New Zealand Verse 1923–45* (1945, rev edn 1951) and of the *Penguin Book of New Zealand Verse* (1960). His *Collected Poems 1933–1973* was published in 1974 and *Selected Poems, 1940–1989* in 1990. He has also written verse satire under the pen-name 'Whim-Wham', and four verse plays, including *The Axe: A Verse Tragedy* (1949), which in allegorical form treats of the introduction of Christianity to Polynesia.

CURROS ENRÍQUEZ, Manuel
(1851–1908)

Major Spanish poet, the political conscience of his people, writing in Galician. He was born in Celanova, Orense. He is counted as the equal in his literature to **Rosalía de Castro** and **Eduardo Pondal**. His lively and anti-clerical, liberal-minded poetry caused him to go into exile to Cuba, where he died. His most famous poem is the long *O Divino saitete* (1888, 'The Divine Bait'), about a journey he took to Rome with a friend.

CURTIS, George William
(1824–92)

American writer, born in Providence, Rhode Island. After four years in Europe (1846–50) he joined the staff of the New York *Tribune*, and was one of the editors of *Putnam's Monthly* from 1852 to 1869. He began the 'Editor's Easy Chair' papers in *Harper's Monthly* in

1853, and became principal leader-writer for *Harper's Weekly* on its establishment in 1857. A novel, *Trumps* (1862), and most of his books appeared first in these journals.

▷W Payne, *Leading American Essayists* (1910)

CURTIS, Jean Louis, pseud of Louis Lafitte
(1917–)

French novelist who wrote in traditional modes, entirely ignoring the *nouveau roman*. Initially an English teacher, he was a wartime pilot. His greatest success was his substantial, sympathetic but acid portrait of a town in occupied south-west France, *Les Forêts de la nuit* (1947, Eng trans *The Forests of the Night*, 1950). He continued to write sharp analyses of life in post-war Paris, of which *Gibier de Potence* (1949, Eng trans *Lucifer's Dream*, 1952), was filmed by Roger Richebé in 1951, with the legendary Arletty as one of the stars.

CURTIS, Tony
(1946–)

Welsh poet, born in Carmarthen and educated at University College, Swansea, and Goddard College, Vermont. He has published four collections of verse, a collection of prose-poems and short stories, two volumes of critical essays, and has edited several anthologies. A senior lecturer in English at the Polytechnic of Wales, he was Chair of The Welsh Academy from 1984 to 1987. In 1984 he won first prize in the National Poetry Competition.

CURWOOD, James Oliver
(1878–1927)

American writer, born in Owosso, Michigan. He was the author of popular novels of outdoor life, such as *The Courage of Captain Plum* (1908), *The Grizzly King* (1917) and *The Alaskan* (1923).

▷ *Son of the Forests, an autobiography* (1930)

CUSACK, (Ellen) Dymphna
(1902–81)

Australian author, born in Wyalong, New South Wales. Educated at Sydney University, she trained as a teacher. The first of her 12 novels, *Jungfrau*, was published in 1936 and dealt frankly, for its time, with sexual issues. This was followed in 1939 by *Pioneers on Parade*, written jointly with **Miles Franklin**. Illness forced her to retire from teaching in 1944, but in 1948 she won the (Sydney) *Daily Telegraph* novel competition with *Come In Spinner*, written in collaboration with **Florence James**; its outspoken handling of adultery and abortion delayed its publication until

1951. The story of the intertwined lives of a group of women in wartime Sydney, and the effects of the absence of their menfolk and the presence of American servicemen, it was an immediate success, but the full text was not published until 1988. Cusack wrote nine other novels and eight plays, which illustrate her preoccupation with social and political disadvantage. They have been translated into over 30 languages, and her plays have been broadcast by the BBC and the ABC. She edited and introduced *Caddie, the Story of a Barmaid* (1953, filmed 1976).

CYNDDELW BRYDYDD MAWR
(fl.1155–1200)

Welsh court poet, the most important of the 12th century. He wrote boldly and in demanding techniques, and had undergone a training so arduous that it would make a modern poet abandon his craft in desperation. His poetry is particularly notable for its vivid and brutal descriptions of battles.

▷J Lloyd-Jones, *The Court Poets of the Welsh Princes* (1848)

CYRANO DE BERGERAC, Savinien
(1619–55)

French writer and dramatist, born in Paris. As a soldier, in his youth he fought more than a thousand duels, mostly on account of his monstrously large nose. His works, often crude, but full of invention, vigour, and wit, include a comedy, *Le Pédant joué* (1654, 'The Pedant Outwitted') and the satirical science fantasy *Histoire comique des états de la lune et du soleil* (Eng trans *Voyages to the Moon and the Sun*, 1923). He was the subject of **Edmond Rostand**'s play, *Cyrano de Bergerac* (1897).

▷E Harth, *Cyrano de Bergerac and the politics of modernity* (1970)

CZECHOWICZ, Józef
(1903–39)

Polish poet who was born in Lublin—and died there as a result of a Nazi bomb. He was a leading poet in the inter-war *Awangarda* (Vanguard) movement. In his complex poetry ruralism and a strong affinity to folklore clashed with urban sophistication, often with surprising and powerful results. In his 'catastrophism' he influenced **Czesław Milosz**.

CZEPKO VON REIGERSFELD, Daniel
(1605–60)

German Lutheran poet, who spent much of his life in imperial service (and was ennobled for it). He was deeply influenced by **Jakob Böhme** and by his own friend the mystic

Abraham von Frankenberg. His poetry, most of which was not actually published until 1930—but which was known to and imitated by **Angelus Silesius**—used that of **Opitz** as its model, but is appealingly simple and sincere.

His mystical *Sextenta Monodisticha Sapienta* (1647) is his greatest achievement.

▷W Milch, *Daniel von Czepko* (1924, in German); R Pascal, *German Literature in the 16th and 17th Centuries* (1968)

D

DABIT, Eugène
(1898–1936)

French novelist, born in Paris, son of a labourer. He left school early and did menial jobs without thought of becoming a writer. After war service, during which he read avidly, he studied writing, and published his first, most famous novel, *L'Hôtel du Nord* (1929), based on his observations of the goings-on in a 'hotel' (really a doss-house) which his parents ran in the 1920s. Translated under the same title in 1931, it won the Prix de Roman Populiste, and in 1938 was turned into the classic movie by Marcel Carné, with a script by **Jacques Prévert**. For once the film did justice to the book. A critic wrote that 'it neither smudges nor varnishes its reality. It gives you a barefaced, simple truth'. It still possesses this stark quality, and is a classic of fiction as well as of the screen. In France there is now a revival of interest in Dabit's work, which includes more novels, and a diary. He died of typhoid while touring Soviet Russia in the company of **André Gide**.

DABYDEEN, David
(1956–)

Guyanian-born British poet, novelist and historian, who emigrated to England in 1969, and whose books have established him as a leading interpreter of the black experience. His first volume of poems, *Slave Song* (1984), is a vivid and lyrical evocation of slavery on Guyanese sugar plantations, while a novel, *The Intended* (1991), examines a young boy attempting to make sense of his Guyanese heritage while growing up in a London slum. *Hogarth's Blacks: Images of Blacks in Eighteenth Century English Painting* (1985) is a provocative and invigorating account of English perceptions of other races.

DACH, Simon
(1605–59)

German lyrical poet and playwright, born in Memel. He and other quiet poets formed what became known as Der Königsberger Dichterschule ('the Königsberg School', c.1625–1650), to whose meetings **Martin Opitz**, the chief influence on the circle, was a visitor. Some of Dach's hymns became famous.
▷J Julian, *A Dictionary of Hymnology* (1892)

DADIÉ, Bernard
(1916–)

Ivory Coast Francophone novelist, poet and playwright. He served the government of Senegal, and set up a theatre there; then he returned to his own country to become Minister of Culture. His novel *Climbié* (1956, Eng trans 1971) is about an African whose acceptance of white rule turns into hatred for it. But his plays, although untranslated, remain his most outstanding work, especially *Monsieur Thôgô-gnini* (1970), a wild **Jarry**-like farce, and *Iles de tempète* (1973, 'Stormy Islands'), perhaps the finest of all works dealing with the slave Toussaint L'Ouverture, who became ruler of Haiti.
▷A C Brench, *Writing in French from Senegal to Cameroon* (1967)

DAFYDD AP GWILYM
(c.1315–c.1370)

Welsh poet and bard, born near Aberystwyth, often hailed as the greatest of Welsh poets. Of noble birth, he was well educated and obviously well read—he introduced many elements of the European mainstream into Welsh verse and, by virtue of the quality of his poetry, brought Welsh verse into the European mainstream. A poet in the wandering bard tradition, he was a lover of nature and natural things, and seems to have spent much of his time roaming the countryside; his verse is set in forests and peopled with birds and animals as well as the usual star-crossed lovers. He is sometimes credited with having invented the *cywydd* form of verse, and he was certainly responsible for its becoming the dominant form in Welsh verse after his time.
▷R Loomis (ed), *Dafydd ap Gwilym: The Poems, Translation and Commentary* (1982); T Parry, *History of Welsh Literature* (1955)

DAFYDD NANMOR
(fl.1460–80)

Welsh poet and bard of the school known as *Beirdd yr Uchelwyr* ('Poets of the Gentry'), writing in their favoured forms, the *awdl* and *cywydd*. He idolized the civilized aspects of life (not natural beauty, as was the norm in Welsh bardic poets) and social values. His poems tend to be inspired by people and their doings and are set firmly in the social world.

DAGERMAN, Stig
(1923–54)

Swedish novelist, poet and dramatist who, like his great compatriot **Karin Maria Boye**, killed himself at the height of his powers. He is still much read, and rightly treated as a major European writer. He was one of the leading members of the *fyrtiota-listerna*, the 'Forties Group', which included the poet **Erik Lindegren**. *Ormen* (1945, 'The Snake') was one of the most powerful first novels to appear in the 20th century: its theme—fear, modern angst—is precisely that which in the end he could not resist; his suicide, like **Cesare Pavese**'s in Italy, became legendary amongst his countrymen. He was influenced by **Kafka**, but not damagingly so, and also (more significantly) by the Norwegian novelist **Tarjei Vesaas**. Perhaps his best work is seen in the story collection *Nattens lekar* (1947, Eng trans *The Games of Night*, 1960), where humour modifies terror. Other work in English includes *Bränt Barn* (1948, Eng trans *A Burnt Child*, 1950).
▷A Gustafson, *A History of Swedish Literature* (1961)

DAGLARCA, Fazil Hüsnü
(1914–)

Turkish poet, born in Istanbul, and regarded, upon the death of **Hikmet**, as his successor in stature. He was an army officer from 1935 until 1950, when he retired with the rank of captain. After that he ran a famous bookshop in Istanbul (1959–72). He was a prolific writer, producing 60 collections of verse by 1980. His first book, issued on the day he became a career officer, and containing conventional verse, was called *Havaya cizilen dünya* (1935, 'A World Sketched on Air'). Since that time he has experimented in every possible genre of poetry (including that of the patriotic epic, the comic, the juvenile and the erotic), but has never been attached to any particular school: like **Whitman**, he 'contains multitudes'. He has always been a militant socialist realist, and often used the window of his bookshop as a notice-board, to the discomfort of most Turkish governments. His most engaging work is the 'neo-mystical' cycle *Mevlana'da olmak* (1958, 'Voyage— Alive in Mevlana') on the great Sufi master (and poet) **Jalal ad-din Rumi**. His poems have been translated (not always well) in *Our Vietnam War* (1967), *Songs of Algeria* (1961), *Selected Poems* (1969) and *The Bird and I* (1980).
▷Y N Nayir, *Daglarca: Critical Approaches, Interviews, Selected Poems* (1974)

D'AGUIAR, Fred(eric)
(1960–)

Guyanese poet, born in London and brought up in Guyana. Already he is established as one of the leading poets of his generation. D'Aguiar has compared writing poems with the childhood game of chasing fireflies and trying to catch on to them before their lights fade or dart away. *Mama Dot* (1985) and *Airy Hall* (1989) were both concept collections, containing many Mama Dot ... and Airy Hall ... titles. The first reflected the poet's Guyanese upbringing, whereas the second collection was coloured by his work as a psychiatric nurse in England. He edited the black section of Paladin's *The New British Poetry* anthology (1988).

DAHL, Roald
(1916–90)

British children's author, short-story writer, playwright and versifier, born in Llandaff, Glamorgan, of Norwegian parentage. His first stories were based on his wartime experiences in the RAF and were collected in *Over to You* (1946). Subsequent collections achieved enormous popularity and include *Someone Like You* (1954), *Kiss, Kiss* (1960) and *Switch Bitch* (1974). Plot was paramount to Dahl and when he began to run short of good ones he turned to writing books for children. He is among the most popular children's authors of all time but many parents, teachers and librarians disapprove of his anarchic rudeness and violence. *Charlie and the Chocolate Factory* (1964) is his best-known book and was successfully filmed. Others include *James and the Giant Peach* (1961), *The Enormous Crocodile* (1978), *The BFG* (1982), *Matilda* (1988) and *Esio Trot* (1990). *The Minpins* and *The Vicar of Nibbleswick* were published posthumously in 1991. He also wrote the screenplays for *You Only Live Twice* (1967) and *Chitty Chitty Bang Bang* (1968), and a number of his stories were adapted for television as *Tales of the Unexpected*.
▷ *Boy* (1984); *Going Solo* (1986)

DAHLBERG, Edward
(1900–77)

American novelist, poet and critic, born in Boston; at the age of 26, he settled in Europe. There, he wrote his first and semi-autobiographical novel, *Bottom Dogs* (1929), describing a depressing slum childhood. A later work, *Those Who Perish* (1934), deals with the effect of Nazi doctrine upon Jewish Americans. Dahlberg's writing also encompassed essays on contemporary society and literature, collected under such titles as *The Flea of Sodom* (1950) and *Alms for Oblivion* (1964). His poetry includes the collection *Cipango's Hinder Door* (1965).
▷ *Because I was Flesh* (1964)

DAHLGREN, Karl Fredrik
(1791–1844)
Swedish poet and humorist, born at Stensbruk in Ostergötland. He studied at Uppsala, and from 1815 was a preacher at Stockholm. His works—novels, tales, poems, dramas—fill five volumes (1847–52).

DAILEY, Janet
(1944–)
American writer of romantic and popular fiction. Born on a farm in Iowa, Dailey worked as her husband's secretary until she was 30. Since then she has produced books at the rate of a dozen a year, claiming that '150 pagers' take her 9 days, and '350 pagers' between 30 and 45 days. A strict writing schedule, the assignment of research to her husband Bill, and the publication of a fanzine *Janet Dailey Newsletter* have helped to maintain her prodigious output and success. She has written a novel for every state in the US (the Americana series) and also found time to compose lyrics for Country and Western songs. At its best, as in the Calder series which began with *This Calder Sky* (1981), Dailey's world is a blockbustering evocation of American grit.

DA LENTINO, Giacomo
(13th century)
Italian lyric poet at the court of Frederick II. He was born in Lentino, near Syracuse. **Dante** thought of him as the foremost Sicilian poet (see *Purgatorio*, XXIV, 55–60), but his substantial work does not survive in Sicilian, since scribes (insensitively) modernized it. Inheriting the traditions of *fin'amor* ('courtly love') from the troubadours, Da Lentino saw its concepts as grown hollow from overuse, and sought to revivify it. His development of the sonnet was his greatest technical achievement.
▷E Langley (ed), *The Poetry of Giacomo Da Lentino* (1915)

DALEY, Victor James William Patrick
(1858–1905)
Irish-born journalist and lyric poet, born in Navan, County Meath, who settled in Australia at the age of 20; he had intended to go to Adelaide but by mistake landed in Sydney. Daley wrote as 'Creeve Roe' and was considered one of the 'Celtic Twilight' school, but received high praise from John Archibald of the *Bulletin*, which printed much of his work. The only book published before his early death from tuberculosis was *At Dawn and Dusk* (c.1898), which gave its name to a bohemian club where Daley mingled with such writers as **Henry Lawson** and **Norman Lindsay**. After his death appeared *Poems*

(1908), *Wine and Roses* with a memoir by A G Stephens (1911) and, later, a selection of his radical verse, *Creeve Roe* (1947).

DALIN, Olof von
(1708–63)
Swedish poet, essayist and historian, born in Vinberg. The son of a minister, he became a tutor to the aristocracy and later, between 1751 and 1756, to the future King Gustav III. He was the most influential literary figure of the Swedish Enlightenment, compiling a monumental history of Sweden (1747–62). He also published a personal newspaper, *Then swänska Argus* (1732–4), in the tradition of **Joseph Addison**'s and **Richard Steele**'s *Tatler* and *Spectator*; influenced by **Jonathan Swift**, it achieved enormous influence and popularity and is regarded as the foundation stone of modern Swedish prose. Among his other works were a verse tragedy, *Brynilda* (1738), and a brilliant prose allegory, *Sagan om hästan* (1740, 'The Story of the Horse'), which is his finest imaginative work.
▷K J Warburg, *Olof Dalin* (1884)

DALLAS, Ruth
(1919–)
New Zealand poet and writer for children, born in Invercargill. Her first collection of verse, *Country Road and Other Poems, 1947–52* (1953), indicated both her direction and her style—the simple unaffected observation of nature. It was followed by *The Turning Wheel* (1961) and *Day Book: Poems of a Year* (1966). Her *Collected Poems* was published in 1987. Her style lends itself admirably to her writing for younger readers, which includes the quartet *The Children in the Bush* (1971), *The Wild Boy in the Bush* (1971), *The Big Flood in the Bush* (1972) and *Holiday Time in the Bush* (1983), set around a single-parent family in the author's own Southland (the southern part of South Island) in the 1890s.

DALLEY, John Bede
(1876–1935)
Australian journalist and writer, born in Rose Bay, Sydney. Retiring from the legal profession after falling from a horse, he began writing for the *Bulletin* where, by 1911, he was chief leader writer and a contributor of verse and short stories. Satirical novels of upper-class Sydney life followed; the best known was *Max Flambard* (1928), but in the same year he also published *No Armour* and, in 1930, *Only the Morning*.

DALY, (John) Augustin
(1838–99)
American dramatist and manager, born in Plymouth, North Carolina. After a career as

233

a drama critic, he went into management, opening the Fifth Avenue Theatre, New York, in 1869, and his own theatre, Daly's, in 1879, with the company of which he visited London in 1884. In 1893 he opened the London Daly's with Ada Rehan in *The Taming of the Shrew*. He wrote and adapted nearly a hundred plays, of which the best was *Horizon* (1871), though the most popular were melodramas such as *Under the Gaslight* and *Leah the Forsaken*. He was chosen by **Tennyson** to adapt *The Foresters* for the stage in 1891.
▷M Felheim, *The Theatre of Augustin Daly* (1956)

DAM, Niels Albert
(1880–1972)

Danish novelist and story writer, born near Århus, Jutland. He had been writing for some 50 years before he received his due recognition. His books, slightly reminiscent of **Simenon**, and most of them dealing with crime, culminated in the novel *Morfars By* (1956, 'Grandfather's Town'), which presents the fantastic and timeless mythology of a small parish. Danes hailed him as a major modernist writer when he published his stories in *Mid moder og hendres sonner* (1969, 'My Mother and her Sons'): they were, a critic suggested, 'violent metaphysical bids to escape his sense of absolute fatedness'.

DAMPIER, William
(1652–1715)

English naval trader, travel writer and pirate, born near Yeovil. He is reputed to have been on the voyage during which Alexander Selkirk, the model for Robinson Crusoe, was sent—by his own request—into arid exile on the island of Juan Fernández. His own accounts of what he found on his travels are exhaustive and true to life. *A New Voyage Round the World* (1697) contains one of the first pieces of writing about Australia, including an unflattering assessment of its aboriginal inhabitants: 'the Hodmadods of Monomatapa, though a nasty People, yet for wealth are Gentlemen to these'. The voyage upon which that book was based had been in 1688, aboard the *Cygnet*. In 1699 he again explored the west coast of Australia, and published his findings in *A Voyage to New Holland* (1703–9).

DANA, Richard Henry, Sr
(1787–1879)

American poet and prose writer, born in Cambridge, Massachusetts. He was educated at Harvard, and admitted to the Bar at Boston in 1811. In 1818 he became associate editor of the *North American Review*, to which

he contributed. His *Dying Raven* (1821), *The Buccaneer* (1827) and some others of his poems were warmly praised by critics, but his best work was in criticism.

DANA, Richard Henry, Jr
(1815–82)

American author and lawyer son of **Richard Henry Dana**. While a student at Harvard, he shipped as a common sailor, and made a voyage round Cape Horn to California and back, which he described in *Two Years before the Mast* (1840). After graduating in 1837 he was admitted to the Massachusetts Bar in 1840, and was especially distinguished in maritime law. Among his works are *The Seaman's Friend* (1841) and *To Cuba and Back* (1859). He also edited Wheaton's *International Law*, and was a prominent free-soiler and Republican.
▷R Gale, *Dana* (1969)

DANCOURT, Florent Carton
(1661–1725)

French dramatist, actor and court favourite. He became devout in his old age, which he spent in retirement in the country. He excelled in depicting the stupidity of the peasantry and the follies of the bourgeoisie. His best-known comedy is *Le Chevalier à la mode* (1687, 'The Fashionable Knight').
▷J LeMaître, *Le Théâtre de Dancourt* (1882)

DANE, Clemence, pseud of **Winifred Ashton**
(1888–1965)

English novelist and playwright, born in Blackheath, London. Her novels included *Regiment of Women* (1917), *Legend* (1919), *Broome Stages* (1931) and *The Flower Girls* (1954), the last two dealing with theatrical families. Many of her plays achieved long runs, including *A Bill of Divorcement* (1921); the ingenious reconstruction of the poet's life in *Will Shakespeare* (1921); the stark tragedy of *Granite* (1926); *Call Home the Heart* (1927); and *Wild Decembers* (1932), about the **Brontës**.

DANIEL, Arnaut
(fl.late 12th century)

Provençal poet, born at the Castle of Rebeyrac, in Périgord, of poor but noble parents. He became a member of the court of Richard C'ur de Lion and was esteemed one of the best of the troubadours, particularly for his treatment of the theme of love. He introduced the sestina, the pattern of which was later adapted by **Dante** and **Petrarch**.
▷E Pound, in *Literary Essays* (1954)

DANIEL, Samuel
(1562–1619)

English poet, the son of a music-master, born near Taunton. He entered Magdalen Hall, Oxford, in 1597, but left it without a degree. He was sometime tutor at Wilton to William Herbert, son of the Earl of Pembroke, afterwards at Skipton to Anne Clifford, daughter of the Earl of Cumberland. In 1604 he was appointed to read new plays; in 1607 became one of the queen's grooms of the privy chamber, and from 1615 to 1618 had charge of a company of young players at Bristol. He then retired to a farm which he possessed at Beckington, in Somerset. Daniel was highly commended by his contemporaries, although **Ben Jonson** described him as 'a good honest man...but no poet'. **Coleridge**, **Charles Lamb** and **William Hazlitt** all praised him. His works include sonnets, epistles, masques and dramas; but his chief production was a poem in eight books, *A History of the Civil Wars between York and Lancaster*. His *Defence of Ryme* (1602) is in admirable prose.
▷C Seronsy, *Samuel Daniel* (1967)

D'ANNUNZIO, Gabriele
(1863–1938)

Italian writer, adventurer and political leader, born in Pescara. He began as a journalist on the *Tribuna* in Rome, but made his name as a poet with several volumes of poetry, starting in 1879 with *Primo vere*. During the 1890s he wrote 'Romances of the Rose', a trilogy of novels with **Nietzsche**an heroes, *Il Piacere* (1889, Eng trans *The Child of Pleasure*, 1898), *L'Innocente* (1892, Eng trans *The Intruder*, 1898) and *Il Trionfo della morte* (1894, Eng trans *The Triumph of Death*, 1896). *Le Vergini delle rocce* (1896, Eng trans *The Maidens of the Rocks*, 1898) is one of a 'Lily' trilogy; *Il Fuoco* (1900, Eng trans *The Flame of Life*, 1900) is the first of a 'Pomegranate' series. Elected a parliamentary deputy (1897–1900), he became notorious for his passionate affair with the actress Eleonora Duse, for whom he wrote several plays, including *La Città morta* (1898, Eng trans *The Dead City*, 1900), *La Gioconda* (1899, Eng trans *Gioconda*, 1901), *Francesca da Rimini* (1901, Eng trans 1902) and *La figlia di Jorio* (1904, Eng trans *The Daughter of Jorio*, 1907). *Le Martyre de St Sébastien* (1911) is a mystery play set to music by Debussy. Grace, voluptuousness and affection characterize this apostle of a new Renaissance. An enthusiastic patriot, he urged Italian entry into World War I, and served as a soldier, sailor and finally airman. In 1916 he lost an eye in combat in the air, and in 1918 carried out a sensational aerial reconnaissance over Vienna. In 1919 he seized and held Fiume, despite the Allies, and ruled as dictator until he was removed by the Italian government (1920). He became a strong supporter of the Fascist Party under Mussolini.
▷P Julian, *D'Annunzio* (1973)

DANTAS, Julio
(1876–1962)

Portuguese dramatist, poet and short-story writer, born in Lagos. In his light lyrical poems and stories he displayed considerable talent, but his heavier work, such as historical dramas, attempted under the influence of the Norwegian and French schools, was less successful. His *A ceia dos cardeais* (1902) was translated by H A Saintsbury as *The Cardinal's Collation* (1927).
▷J Dias Cancho, *Julio Dantas* (1922)

DANTE, in full Dante Alighieri
(1265–1321)

Italian poet, born in Florence, a lawyer's son of the noble Guelf family. He was baptized Durante, afterwards abbreviated to Dante. According to his *La Vita Nuova* (c.1292, Eng trans *The New Life*, 1861), he first set eyes on his lifelong love, Beatrice Portinari (c.1265–90), at the age of nine in 1274. There is no evidence that she returned his passion; she was married at an early age to one Simone de' Bardi, but neither this nor the poet's own subsequent marriage interfered with his pure and Platonic devotion to her, which intensified after her death. The story of his boyish but unquenchable passion is told with exquisite pathos in *Vita Nuova*. Shortly after, Dante married Gemma Donati, daughter of a powerful Guelf family. In 1289 he fought at Campaldino, where Florence defeated the Ghibellines, and was at the capitulation of Caprona. He was registered in one of the city guilds—that of the Apothecaries—being entered as 'Dante d'Aldighieri, *Poeta*'. In 1300, after filling minor public offices, and possibly going on some embassies abroad, he became one of the six priors of Florence, but for only two months. It was towards the 'White Guelfs', or more moderate section, that his sympathies tended. As prior, he procured the banishment of the heads and leaders of the rival factions, showing characteristic sternness and impartiality to Guelf and Ghibelline, White and Black, alike. In 1301, in alarm at the threatened interference of Charles of Valois, he was sent on an embassy to Rome to Pope Boniface VIII. He never returned from that embassy, nor did he ever again set foot in his native city. Charles espoused the side of the *Neri* or Blacks, and their victory was complete. He was banished from Florence in 1309 and sentenced to death in absentia. From then on he led a wandering life, first in Verona, in Tuscany, in the Lunigiano, near Urbino, and then Verona again. He eventually settled in Ravenna (1318),

where for the most part he remained until his death. He was buried with much pomp at Ravenna, where he still lies, restored in 1865 to the original sarcophagus. Dante had seven children, six sons and one daughter, Beatrice, a nun at Ravenna; but his family became extinct in the 16th century. His most celebrated work is the *Divina Commedia* (Eng trans *Divine Comedy*, 1847), begun around 1307, his spiritual testament, narrating a journey through Hell and Purgatory, guided by **Virgil**, and finally to Paradise, guided by Beatrice. It gives an encyclopedic view of the highest culture and knowledge of the age, all expressed in the most exquisite poetry. The *Divina Commedia* may be said to have made the Italian language, which was before so rude and unformed that Dante himself hesitated to employ it on such a theme, and is said to have begun his poem in Latin. The next most important work is the fragment called the *Convivio*, or *Banquet*, which takes the form of a commentary on some of the author's *canzoni*, or short poems, of which there are only three, though the work, if completed, would have contained 14. The *De Monarchia* (in Latin) expounds Dante's theory of the divinely intended government of the world by a universal pope. Another unfinished work, *De Vulgari Eloquentia*, discusses the origin of language, the divisions of languages, and the dialects of Italian in particular. *Canzoniere* is a collection of short poems, *canzoni*, sonnets, etc; and, finally, there are a dozen epistles addressed mainly to leading statesmen or rulers. There are also some *Eclogues* and other minor works, as well as several of doubtful authenticity.
▷ E Auerbach, *Dante, Poet of the Secular World* (1961); W Anderson, *Dante the Maker* (1980)

DANZIGER, Paula
(1944–)
American writer of fiction for children, a teacher before she turned to fiction. *The Cat Ate My Gymsuit* (1974) began a succession of knowing but light-hearted novels aimed at early adolescents. Titles such as *Can You Sue Your Parents For Malpractice?* (1979) and *The Divorce Express* (1982) hint at the contradictory combination of earnestness and offbeat humour which typify her work—and, as these characteristics are so common in adolescents, explain its success.

DA PONTE, Lorenzo, originally Emanuele Conegliano
(1749–1838)
Italian poet, born in Ceneda near Venice of Jewish parents. He was converted to Roman Catholicism and became Professor of Rhetoric at Treviso until political and domestic

troubles drove him to Vienna, where as a poet to the Court Opera he wrote the libretti for Mozart's operas *The Marriage of Figaro* (1786), *Don Giovanni* (1787) and *Così fan Tutte* (1790). In London he taught Italian and sold boots; in 1805 he moved to New York, where he sold liquor, tobacco and groceries and ended up as Professor of Italian literature at Columbia College from 1825.

DARÍO, Rubén, pseud of Felix Rubén García Sarmiento
(1867–1916)
Nicaraguan poet. He lived a wandering life as a journalist, full of amours and diplomatic appointments, and died of pneumonia. He inaugurated the Spanish American modernist movement with his major works, *Azul* (1888) and *Prosas Profanas* (1896, Eng trans *Prosas Profanas and Other Poems*, 1922), showing Greek and French (Parnassian and Symbolist) influence, which gave new vitality to Spanish poetry.
▷ C D Watland, *Poet-Errant: a Biography of Darío* (1965)

DARK, Eleanor, née O'Reilly
(1901–)
Australian novelist, daughter of **Dowell O' Reilly**, born and educated in Sydney. Employed briefly as a stenographer, she married a general practitioner in 1922 and a year later moved to Katoomba in the Blue Mountains. Her earliest writings, short stories and verse, were contributed from 1921 to various magazines, mostly under the pseudonym 'Patricia O'Rane' or 'P. O'R'. *Slow Dawning*, her first novel, was completed in 1923 but she had to wait until 1932 to see it published. Her other novels include *Prelude to Christopher* (1934), *The Little Company* (1945), *Lantana Lane* (1959) and the trilogy, *The Timeless Land* (1941), *Storm of Time* (1948) and *No Barrier* (1953), which charts the early years of European settlement of New South Wales. A writer of ideas, and a committed socialist and feminist, she was awarded the Australian Literature Society's Gold Medal in 1934 and 1936, and in 1978 received the Australian Society of Women Writers' Alice Award.
▷ H Anderson, *A Handlist of Books* (1954)

DARLEY, George
(1795–1846)
Irish poet and mathematician, born in Dublin. Educated at Trinity College, Dublin, from c.1822 he lived in London, and worked on the staff of the *London Magazine*. He published a volume of verse, *The Errors of Ecstasie* (1822) and a collection of prose stories, *Labours of Idleness* (1826). He also wrote a

pastoral drama, *Sylvia* (1827) and the unfinished poem *Nepenthe* (1835). He wrote essays on dramatic criticism, and also published mathematical textbooks.

▷A Leventhal, *George Darley, 1795–1846* (1950)

DARUSMONT, Frances *see* WRIGHT, Frances

DARWALL, Mary, née Whateley
(1738–1825)

English poet, born at Beoley, Worcestershire, daughter of a gentleman farmer, and scantily educated. From 1760 she kept house for her brother in Walsall, then married the vicar of Walsall (1766), with whom she ran a printing press. After his death in 1794 she moved to Wales. Her *Original Poems on Several Occasions* (1764), published with help from the poet **William Shenstone**, shows her accomplished in a range of styles, from graceful lyrics and pastoral and meditative poetry to lively satirical verse, often self-mocking, sometimes briskly feminist.

▷A Messenger, in *Bulletin of Research in the Humanities* (1986)

DARWISH, Mahmud
(1942–)

Palestinian poet, whose stark writing voices the desperation and alienation of the Palestinian people. He was born in the village of al-Birweh, near the Carmel mountains, which was erased from the Israeli map, but which Darwish successfully brought to the world's notice: 'I am a native of the Carmel,/A mountain which the evening melts down into kisses'. The author of 11 volumes of poetry and three of prose, he has won the Lotus Prize (1969), the Mediterranean Prize (1980) and the Lenin Prize (1982). One of the foremost representatives of the angry new voice of the Arab world, his outstanding collections in translation are *Victims of a Map* (1984) and *Sand and Other Poems* (1986).

DAS, Kamala
(1934–)

Indian (Malayalam) poet and novelist. She writes her poetry in English and most of her prose in her own language (eg *My Story*, 1976, translated by herself—one of the most important Indian autobiographies ever written). Kamala Das is generally regarded as the best of all Indian poets now writing in English; her novel, *Alphabet of Lust* (1977), is also a very remarkable work from an Indian woman who has been much criticized by members of her own sex in her own country for 'departing from traditional norms'. Her

poetry is sensuous, deeply felt and technically very finely accomplished.

▷D Kohli, *Kamala Das* (1975)

DASS, Petter
(1647–1707)

Norwegian poet and pastor, linked to the people and nature of Northern Norway, where he achieved heroic stature and became a figure of legend. Dass's songs and poems were spread orally and in manuscript form and had a tremendous common appeal. His poetry is characterized by an ornamental Baroque style, but more typically a Renaissance interest in the concrete, especially the relationship between people and their environment. His best-known work, *Nordlands Trompet* (1739, Eng trans *The Trumpet of Nordland*, 1954), is full of humour and love for his people and shows an intimate knowledge of the northernmost areas of Norway.

▷H Midbøe, *Petter Dass* (1947)

D'AUBIGNÉ, Théodore Agrippa
(1552–1630)

French soldier and scholar, born near Pons in Saintonge. Of noble family, but poor, he distinguished himself as a soldier in 1567 in the Huguenot cause, and was appointed vice-admiral of Guienne and Brittany by King Henri IV. His severe and inflexible character frequently embroiled him with the court; and after Henri's assassination (1610) he withdrew to a life of literary activity in Geneva, leaving a worthless son, Constant. His *Histoire universelle, 1550–1601* (1616–20, 'World History') was burned in France by the common hangman. His biting satire is shown in his *Aventures du baron de Foenestée* (1617) and in his *Confession catholique du Sieur de Sancy* (1660, 'The Catholic Confessions of the Sieur de Sancy'). His grand-daughter was Madame de Maintenon.

DÄUBLER, Theodor
(1876–1934)

German poet, born in Trieste. Only a few of his shorter poems are read now, but he is still deservedly studied in universities. An unhappy man, and always a wanderer, he was a misfit in the army and subsequently felt himself to be one elsewhere. His vast 30 000-line epic *Das Nordlicht* (1912, rev edn 1922, 'The Northern Lights'), is based on an all but inaccessible mystical system involving the earth's wish to join the sun. But this has passages of beauty, and he wrote a handful of expressionistic poems of higher quality.

DAUDET, Alphonse
(1840–97)

French writer, born in Nîmes. After being educated at the Lyons Lycée he became an usher at Alais; but, when only 17, he set out for Paris with his older brother, Ernest (1837–1921), who became a journalist and novelist of some mark, and both obtained appointments as clerk or private secretary in the office of the Duke of Morny. Alphonse's poem *Les Amoureuses* (1858, 'The Lovers') was followed by theatrical pieces (written partly in collaboration), *La Dernière Idole* (1862, 'The Last Idol'), *L'Oeillet blanc* (1865, 'The White Carnation'), *Le Frère aîné* (1868, 'The Elder Brother'), *Le Sacrifice* (1869) and particularly *L'Arlésienne* (1872, 'A Woman from Arles', with music by Bizet). His best-known work is his series of sketches and short stories of Provençal life, originally written for *Le Figaro*, especially *Lettres de mon moulin* (collected 1869, 'Letters from my Mill'), *Robert Helmont* (1874), *Contes du lundi* (1873, 'Monday Stories') and the charming extravaganza of *Tartarin de Tarascon* (1872), continued in *Tartarin sur les Alpes* (1885) and *Port Tarascon* (1890). *Le petit chose* (1868, 'Young What's His Name') is full of pathos and of reminiscences of his own early struggles. He also published long naturalistic novels, on the social conditions of the day, such as *Fromont jeune et Risler aîné* (1874, 'Fromont Junior and Risler Senior'), *Jacks* (1876), *Le Nabab* (1877, 'The Nabob') and *Numa Roumestan* (1881). In *L'Évangéliste* (1883) the Salvation Army was introduced; *Sapho* (1884) is a tale of the infatuation of a young man for a courtesan; and in *L'Immortel* (1888, 'The Immortal One') all the author's powers of ridicule are turned against the Académie française. His wife, Julia Allard Daudet (1845–1940), also published poetry.
▷R H Sherard, *Alphonse Daudet* (1894)

DAUDET, Léon
(1867–1942)

French writer and political activist, son of **Alphonse Daudet**. He studied medicine but turned to journalism, and in 1899 helped to found the right-wing royalist newspaper *Action française*, of which he became editor in 1908. He sat in the Chamber of Deputies from 1919 to 1924. In 1925 his son was assassinated and subsequently he spent some time in Belgium as a political exile. He wrote several novels, but is best remembered for his numerous memoirs and critical works, especially *Le Stupide XIXe siècle* (1922, 'The Stupid 19th Century').
▷J Marque, *Léon Daudet* (1971)

DAUTHENDEY, Max
(1867–1918)

German poet, philosopher, dramatist and novelist, a frustrated painter and a solitary and wandering man, born in Würzburg. His works run to nine volumes. Some have said that his poetry is so exotic as not to be poetry; but, although his elaborate theories of life and art are forgotten, it still has a few champions, who point to its 'orgiastic' qualities.
▷H G Wendt, *Max Dauthendey: Poet-Philosopher* (1936)

DAUMAL, René
(1908–44)

French poet and essayist, born in Boulzicourt, Ardennes. At the age of 20 he became co-founder (with Roger Gilbert-Lecomte and the Czech painter Joseph Sima) of the group and magazine *Le Grand Jeu* ('The Great Game'). The move necessitated a formal break with the surrealists, with whom, however, he retained a similarity of attitude towards art. Both *Contre-ciel* (1936, 'Counterheaven'), a collection of poetry, and *La grande beuverie* (1939, 'The Great Binge'), a fantasy, display Daumal's interest in the unconscious and its untapped potential; so too does his enthusiasm for the work of the Armenian mystic **Gurdjieff**, who had settled in France in the 1920s. Suffering from tuberculosis, he refused treatment, allowing himself to die—in the interest, or so it was claimed, of 'self-exploration'. His poems were collected by his wife and published as *Poésie noire, poésie blanche* in 1954.

D'AVENANT, Sir William
(1606–68)

English poet and playwright, born in Oxford, the son of an inn-keeper. His father kept the Crown, a tavern at which **Shakespeare** used to stop on the way between London and Stratford, thereby giving rise to the rumour that D'Avenant was Shakespeare's illegitimate son. At the age of 12 he wrote an 'Ode in Remembrance of Master Shakespeare', not printed, however, until 1638. After a short period of study at Lincoln College, Oxford, he became page to Frances, Duchess of Richmond; next he joined the household of the aged poet, **Fulke Greville**, Lord Brooke. In 1628 he turned to writing for the stage. During the next 10 years he produced many plays, including *The Cruel Brother* (1630) and *The Wits* (1636). In 1638, at the request of the queen, Henrietta Maria, he was appointed poet laureate in succession to **Ben Jonson**. About the same time he lost his nose through an illness, a calamity which exposed him to public ridicule. Later he became manager of Drury Lane Theatre. During the Civil War he was knighted by King Charles I for his gallantry at the siege of Gloucester (1643). In 1650 he was imprisoned in the Tower for two years, where he completed his epic, *Gondibert* (1651). He is considered to have been the founder of English opera with his *Siege of Rhodes* (1656), and opened a theatre, the Cockpit, in Drury Lane in 1658.

▷A Harbege, *Sir William D'Avenant, 1606–1668* (1935)

DAVENPORT, Guy (Mattison, Jr)
(1927–)

American writer of fiction and literary criticism, whose works often seem to fall between the two categories, being concerned with real or historical people and written in a deliberately naive and uncontrived prose. *Tatlin!* (1974) is a short-story collection headed by a tale about the Russian Constructivist; Leonardo appears in *Da Vinci's Bicycle* (1979); other historical characters include **Kafka** and **Pound**, about whom Davenport has also written a critical study (1983). In *Eclogues* (1981), his most distinctive volume, Davenport reintroduces Adriaan van Hovendaal from *Tatlin!* and explores his coming to terms with the non-Constructivist, non-absurd world of everyday reality; in doing so he creates a utopian vision derived from Fourier's concept of Harmony in which art plays the purest and most fundamental part. Davenport has translated **Archilochos of Paros**, **Sappho** and other classical writers and written an indexed guide to the *Iliad* and *Odyssey* (1967).

DAVICO, Oskar
(1909–)

Serbian poet and fiction writer, a teacher by profession, who was in 1932 sentenced to five years in prison for his communism. In 1941 he was interned in Italy for the same reasons, but escaped in the following year to join Tito. He made his reputation in 1929 with a set of prose poems much in the style of the French surrealists, whom he had met and studied in Paris. Later, as a result of his sufferings in the war, his poetry matured, and he wrote a powerful, if somewhat over-**Joyce**an novel, *Pesma* (1952, Eng trans *The Poem*, 1959), about the division between the intellectual and the active attitude to World War II.

DAVIDSON, Donald
(1893–1968)

American poet, critic and academic, a leading member of the Fugitive Group of poets which included **Ransom** and **Allen Tate**. He was born in Campbellsville, Tennessee. He was influential on the extreme conservative side (whereas **Robert Penn Warren** represented the liberal wing) of the so-called 'Southern Agrarian' programme advocated by this group in the manifesto *I'll Take My Stand* (1930). His poetry, taut and well-made but seldom linguistically inspired, was not as widely read as that of his colleagues.

DAVIDSON, John
(1857–1909)

Scottish poet, novelist and dramatist, born in Barrhead, Renfrewshire, the son of an Evangelical minister. Educated at the Highlander's Academy, Greenock, where he became a pupil-teacher (1872–6), and Edinburgh University, he became an itinerant teacher in Scotland. He had started to write in 1885 (four verse dramas and a couple of novels), and in 1889 moved to London where, among other works, he wrote *Fleet Street Eclogues* (1893) and *Ballads and Songs* (1894). **T S Eliot** later acknowledged a debt to the urban imagery and colloquialism of 'Thirty Bob a Week'. He wrote prolifically in the last years of his life, including a series of blank-verse *Testaments*, several other verse dramas, short stories and prose sketches. He eventually committed suicide by drowning himself at Penzance.

▷J Townsend, *Davidson, poet of Armageddon* (1961)

DAVIDSON, Lionel
(1922–)

English crime and espionage writer. Born in Hull, he served in Royal Navy submarines during the war and then worked as a magazine journalist until 1959. A highly original writer who has managed to avoid a formulaic approach, his first novel, *The Night of Wenceslas* (1960), was a superior spy thriller set in Czechoslovakia and was much praised for its settings, even though Davidson had never been there. Its successor was more exotic still, in all but the straightforwardness of narrative; *The Rose of Tibet* (1962) was hailed as 'pure' adventure. Later novels, such as *A Long Way to Shiloh* (1966, published in the USA as *The Menorah Men*) and *Smith's Gazelle* (1971), introduced an element of philosophical, almost mystical, quest; *Making Good Again* (1968) and *The Sun Chemist* (1976) explore aspects of modern Jewish life and politics, centring on the Holocaust. Davidson has also written juvenile fiction under the pseudonym David Line.

DAVIE, Donald Alfred
(1922–)

English poet, born in Barnsley and, after wartime naval service, educated at Cambridge. His first book was *Purity of Diction in English*

Verse (1952), a critical study that retrospectively reads like a manifesto for his own clear, rational prosody and thought and was taken as such by the Movement poets. His first important collection was *Brides of Reason* (1955), influenced by English Augustan poetry, morally robust and hostile to the excesses of **Dylan Thomas**; the only modernist poet to whom he claimed allegiance was **Pound**, on whom he later wrote *Poet as Sculptor* (1964) and *Pound* (1975). Though Davie was drawn to Pound's ear, it was sometimes suggested that he was attracted to his ultraconservative politics. In 1964, he became Professor of English and then Pro-Vice-Chancellor at the new University of Essex (1964–8), presiding over a stormy outbreak of student radicalism; *Essex Poems* (1969) documents his pessimistic reactions. Similar upheavals awaited him in the USA, at Stanford University (1968–78), and later at Vanderbilt University in Nashville. *The Shires* (1974) and *In the Stopping Train* (1977) were his finest achievement to date, autobiographical but disciplined. His collections include *The Battered Wife* (1985).

▷ G Dekker, *Donald Davie and the Responsibilities of Literature* (1984)

DAVIES, Hubert Henry
(1876–1917)

English playwright, born in Woodley, Cheshire. He was a journalist in San Francisco, returned to England in 1901, and disappeared in 1917. His plays included *Cousin Kate* (1903) and *The Mollusc* (1907).

DAVIES, Idris
(1905–53)

Welsh poet, born in Rhymney, Gwent. He left school at 14 to become a miner in the pit where his father worked. He later took a correspondence course and went on to study at Loughborough College and Nottingham University, qualifying as a teacher. He published three volumes of verse, his work fired with anger and indignation at the social injustices that he had witnessed. From 1932 to 1951 he worked as a school-teacher, in the East of London and (after World War II) in Rhymney Valley.

▷ I Jenkyns, *Idris Davies* (1972)

DAVIES, Sir John
(1569–1626)

English poet and statesman, born in Tisbury, Wiltshire. Educated at Winchester School, Queen's College, Oxford, and the Middle Temple, he was called to the Bar in 1595. Entering politics, he was returned to parliament for Corfe Castle and after the death of Elizabeth found favour with James I, who

sent him to Ireland as solicitor-general. Three years later he was made Irish attorney-general and knighted. In Ireland he supported severe repressive measures and took part in the plantation of Ulster. He returned to the English parliament in 1614, representing Newcastle-under-Lyme, and practised as king's serjeant in England. He had been nominated chief justice a month before his death of apoplexy. In 1622 he collected in one volume his three chief poems—*Orchestra, or a Poeme of Dancing* (1596); *Nosce Te Ipsum* (1599), a long didactic piece on the soul's immortality; and *Hymns to Astraea* (1599), a collection of clever acrostics on the name Elizabeth Regina.

▷ M Seeman, *Sir John Davies, sein Leben und seine Werke* (1813)

DAVIES, Rhys
(1901–78)

Welsh novelist and short-story writer, born in the Rhondda Valley. After attending Porth County School he worked in offices and shops in London, soon establishing a reputation with his short stories and his first novel, *The Withered Root* (1927), which, typically, sets puritanical religion against the urges of sexuality. Of his 17 novels the most popular was *The Black Venus* (1944), dealing with the conflict between traditional practices and Anglicizing modernity in a Welsh village. Described as 'a Welsh Chekhov', he was particularly distinguished and prolific as a short-story writer, describing in an objective but ironic, humorous and poetic manner the lives of ordinary Welsh people, often women. Other stories are set in Europe and England; his collections include *Boy with a Trumpet* (1949) and *The Chosen One* (1967).

▷ R L Mégroz, *Rhys Davies: A Critical Sketch* (1932)

DAVIES, (William) Robertson
(1913–)

Canadian novelist, playwright, essayist and critic, born in Thamesville, Ontario. Educated in Canada and Balliol College, Oxford, he has taught, acted (he was Sir William Tyrone Guthrie's literary assistant) and been a journalist, was Editor of the *Examiner* (Peterborough, Ontario) from 1942 to 1963 and a professor of English at the University of Toronto (1960–81). His first novel was *Tempest-Tost* (1951), the first of 'The Salterton Trilogy', but he is best known for 'The Deptford Trilogy'—*Fifth Business* (1970), *The Manticore* (1972) and *World of Wonders* (1975). This work evolved from his earlier books set in Salterton, an imagined Ontario city, patently Kingston, which is dominated by its old families, Anglican Church, military school, university, and belief in the virtues of

England and the English. He is now a writer of international repute; *What's Bred in the Bone* (1985) was shortlisted for the Booker Prize.

DAVIES, William Henry
(1871–1940)

English poet, born in Newport, Monmouthshire, the son of a publican. Emigrating to the USA at the age of 22, he lived partly as a tramp and partly as a casual workman until the loss of a leg whilst 'jumping' a train caused him to return to England, where he began to write and lived the life of a tramp and pedlar in order to raise sufficient money to have his poems printed by a jobbing printer. A copy of this first work, *A Soul's Destroyer*, came into the hands of **George Bernard Shaw**, who arranged for its regular publication in 1907. The success of this book was consolidated by *The Autobiography of a Super-tramp* (1908). He continued to publish volumes of poems and lyrics, gathered in the *Collected Poems* (1943), two novels, and the prose *Adventures of Johnny Walker, Tramp* (1926). He continued his autobiography with *Beggars* (1909), *The True Traveller* (1912), *A Poet's Pilgrimage* (1918), *Later Days* (1925), and the posthumously published *Young Emma* (1980).

▷L Hocley, *W H Davies* (1971)

DAVIN, Dan
(1913–90)

New Zealand novelist and short-story writer, born in Otago. He was educated at Otago and Oxford universities, served in several units, including Intelligence GHQ, during World War II, then went into publishing. His novels, which fall firmly within the realist tradition, include *Cliffs of Fall* (1945), *The Sullen Bell* (1956) and *Brides of Price* (1972). The first and last are set in his homeland; *The Sullen Bell* examines the condition of the expatriate New Zealander. *Crete* (1953), part of the New Zealand Official War History, is an understated, at times quietly poetic, account of the battle for control of that island.

DAVIS, Harold Lenoir
(1896–1960)

American novelist, poet and cattle-herder, born in Douglas County, Oregon. He is remembered for his vividly debunking novel *Honey in the Horn* (1935), about Oregon pioneers, which won a Pulitzer Prize. His later work dealt in an enlightened and knowledgeable manner with the great outdoors. *Team Bells Woke Me* (1953) collected expertly constructed stories.

DAVIS, Jack Leonard
(1918–)

Australian author, born in north-western Western Australia, one of the most respected aboriginal writers. He published a book of verse, *The First-Born*, in 1970 and was then for some years joint editor of an aboriginal journal *Identity*. A second volume, *Jagardoo: Poems from Aboriginal Australia*, appeared in 1978 and was followed by the plays *The Dreamers* (1982) and *Kullark* (1979), which both treat of the problems of aborigines in contemporary white society. In 1993 he published the verse collection *Black Life*.

DAVIS, Owen
(1874–1956)

American playwright, born in Maine. He graduated from Harvard University in 1893, and began his writing career by attempting serious verse tragedy for the stage. He turned to a more profitable career producing popular melodramas, literally by the hundreds, which are now largely forgotten. He returned to serious drama as well, and was awarded the Pulitzer Prize for Drama for *Icebound* in 1923. He also adapted novels for the stage, including **F Scott Fitzgerald**'s *The Great Gatsby* (1926) and **Edith Wharton**'s *Ethan Frome* (1936), and wrote an autobiography, *I'd Like To Do It Again* (1931).

DAVIS, Rebecca (Blaine) Harding
(1831–1910)

American novelist, who lived for most of her life in Philadelphia, and was one of the pioneers of realistic fiction. Such books as *Margaret Howth* (1862) are marred by the moral tone then obligatory, but their real purpose is proto-naturalistic: to explore the underbelly of urban life. *Waiting for the Verdict* (1868) shocked many by its affirmative treatment of Blacks. 'Come right down here with me,' she told her readers, 'here into the thickest of the fog and mud and effluvia'.

DAVIS, Richard Harding
(1863–1916)

American novelist, newspaper correspondent and dramatist, the son of **Rebecca Harding Davis**, born in Philadelphia. He was known as 'the Beau Brummell of the Press', and was a dashing dandy and an often unscrupulous correspondent; but, although essentially superficial, he was also a master storyteller, whose fiction can still be read with pleasure: *Van Bibber* (1892), sketches about a New York socialite, and, above all, the novel *Soldiers of Fortune* (1897), are modelled on the formula established by **Anthony Hope** in *The Prisoner of Zenda*, and worthy of it.

DAVISON, Frank Dalby

DAVISON, Frank Dalby, properly **Frederick Douglas**
(1893–1970)
Australian novelist and short-story writer, born in Hawthorn, Melbourne, whose reputation was established in three different genres. Firstly, his novels of considerable empathy with wild animals, in *Man-Shy: A Story of Men and Cattle* (1931), where the heroine is a heifer who escapes from a round-up and at the end becomes matriarch of a herd of wild cattle, and *Dusty* (1946), in which a kelpie-dingo crossbreed, after living and working with man, succumbs in time to its primitive instincts. Secondly, his short stories and especially *The Wells of Beersheba* (1933), an epic of the Australian Light Horse in Palestine during World War I. Lastly, his massive novel *The White Thorntree* (1968), which took Davison 22 years to write; in four sections he describes the search for sexual happiness and the frustrations of a family in middle-class Sydney.

DAVISON, Peter
(1928–)
American poet, born in New York. He is a publisher by profession. His poetry is precise and well crafted, 'even' and 'gem-like'; the long poem *Dark Houses* (1971) elaborates on his father, whose presence is recaptured in Davison's autobiography, *Half-Remembered* (1973).
▷ *Praying Wrong: New and Selected Poems 1957–1984* (1984); G Rotella, *Three Contemporary Poets of New England* (1983)

DAWE, Bruce
(1930–)
Australian poet and short-story writer, born in Geelong, Victoria. Dawe's writings show an unwilling acceptance of the fact that life is short, brutal and, to a large extent, pointless. Despite this, they are shot through with a wry acceptance of fate; the laconic forms of Australian speech bring to life the human tragi-comedy of which he writes. His best stories were collected in *Over Here, Harv!* (1983). His verse has won many awards, and includes *Beyond the Subdivisions* (1968), *Condolences of the Season* (1971) and *Sometimes Gladness: Collected Poems 1954–1978*, of which a new edition taking the poems up to 1982 was published in 1983. Dawe received the **Patrick White** Literary Award in 1980.

DAWE, (William) Carlton Lanyon
(1865–1935)
Australian-born British writer of popular novels of adventure and romance. He published three early volumes of verse, *Sydonia and Other Poems* (1885), later incorporated

in *Love and the World and Other Poems* (1886) and *Sketches in Verse* (1889), and a novelette *Zantha: and the Old Piano* (1886) before moving to London in the early 1880s. There he wrote *The Golden Lake; or the Marvellous History of a Journey through the Great Lone Land of Australia* (1891) and *Mount Desolation* (1892), followed by over 70 novels, many with Australian settings. He was an accomplished story-teller and his novels offered good entertainment to the users of the circulating libraries of the period; they included society romances and crime mysteries such as *The Mandarin* (1899), *The Grand Duke: a Novel* (1905), *The Plotters of Peking* (1907), *The Crackswoman* (1914) and *The Woman with Yellow Eyes* (1917). From 1931, with *Leathermouth* he began a series of tales featuring the extraordinary Colonel Leathermouth, ending with *Live Cartridge* (1937).

DAWSON, Jennifer
(1931–)
English novelist. Educated at St Anne's College, Oxford, she subsequently worked in publishing, education, and as a social worker in a psychiatric hospital, an experience which—the latter part at least—significantly influenced her first novel, *The Ha-Ha* (1961). A novel of madness, it has been much admired for its vivid reconstruction of schizophrenia and for its grasp of the social implications of schizophrenic perceptions and language. Subsequent novels, *Fowler's Snare* (1962), *The Cold Country* (1965), *Strawberry Boy* (1976) and *A Field of Scarlet Poppies* (1979), have explored similar ideas, but without the crispness of delivery found in some of Dawson's short stories, collected in *Hospital Wedding* (1978).

DAY, Clarence
(1874–1935)
American humorist, whose *Life With Father* (1935) was a popular success; its successor *Life With Mother* (1936) was posthumous. As a play (1939) the former, a fairly conventional but capable portrait of a naively angry man, set records. Day wrote for the *New Yorker* for many years, and helped to set its famous tone.

DAY, Dorothy
(1897–1980)
American writer and radical social reformer, born in Brooklyn, New York. A life-long socialist, she worked in the New York slums as a probationary nurse. Converted to Catholicism in 1927, she co-founded the monthly

Catholic Worker in 1933, drawing on her earlier experience as a reporter on Marxist publications like *Call* and *The Masses*. Under the influence of the French itinerant priest Peter Maurin (1877–1949), she founded the Catholic Worker Movement, whose Depression work was described in her *House of Hospitality* (1939). A pacifist and a fervent supporter of farm-worker unionization in the 1960s, she helped turn her church's attention to peace and justice issues. Other works include the autobiographical novel *The Eleventh Virgin* (1924) and *On Pilgrimage: the Sixties* (1972).
▷ *The Long Loneliness* (1952)

DAY, John
(1574–?1640)

English Jacobean dramatist, born in Norfolk. He studied at Caius College, Cambridge, and is mentioned in Henslowe's *Diary* in 1598 as an active playwright, and collaborated freely with **Henry Chettle**, **Thomas Dekker**, and others. His works, privately printed by Arthur Henry Bullen in 1881, include a graceful comedy, *Humour Out of Breath*, and *The Parliament of Bees*, an allegorical masque.

DAY, Thomas
(1748–89)

English writer and barrister, born in London. Educated at Charterhouse and Corpus Christi College, Oxford, he formed a close friendship with Richard Lovell Edgeworth. In 1765 he entered the Middle Temple, in 1775 was called to the Bar, but never practised. A disciple of **Rousseau**, he brought up an orphan and a foundling, one of whom, he presumed, would become his wife. That scheme miscarried; and he proposed first to Honora and next to Elizabeth Sneyd. She sent him to France to acquire French graces but on his return she laughed at him. Finally in 1778 he married an appreciative heiress, Esther Milnes, and spent 11 happy years with her, farming on philanthropic and costly principles in Essex and Surrey, until he was killed by a fall from a colt he was breaking in. He wrote a long children's tale, *The History of Sandford and Merton* (3 vols, 1783–9), a didactic novel in which the poor but virtuous Harry Sandford is a constant example to the rich, spoiled, but essentially good Tommy Merton. He wrote another moral tale, *The History of Little Jack* (1788), and a long poem, *The Dying Negro* (1773).
▷ M Sadler, *Thomas Day, an English disciple of Rousseau* (1928)

DAY-LEWIS, Cecil
(1904–72)

Irish poet, critic and detective-story writer, born in Ballintubbert, County Leix. He was

educated at Sherborne School and Wadham College, Oxford, and published his first verse in 1925, *Beechen Vigil and Other Poems*. He made his name as a lyric poet with *Transitional Poems* (1929), and during the 1930s, with **W H Auden** and **Stephen Spender**, became associated with left-wing causes, and also wrote literary criticism in *A Hope for Poetry* (1934). He became a member of the Communist Party, which he renounced in 1939. During World War II he worked in the Ministry of Information, and then published *Poetry for You* (1944) and his major critical work, *The Poetic Image* (1947). He became Professor of Poetry at Oxford (1951–6) and at Harvard (1964–5), and published his last critical work, *The Poetic Impulse* (1965). He made notable translations of **Virgil** and St Valery, and was appointed poet laureate in 1968. Under the pseudonym of 'Nicholas Blake' he wrote a score of sophisticated detective novels. His autobiography, *The Buried Day*, was published in 1960. *The Poems of C. Day Lewis 1925–72* appeared in 1977.
▷ S Day-Lewis, *Cecil Day-Lewis: a biography* (1990)

DAZAI Osamu
(1909–48)

Japanese writer, born into a wealthy family from Tsugaru. He went to Tokyo to study, and started writing there, embracing the Japanese naturalist aesthetic and producing a string of deeply introspective, delicate novels. He also became involved with the underground left, joining the (proscribed) Communist Party, though he was forced, publicly, to renounce his Marxism and quit the party after being arrested by the Kempeito (secret police). This experience and that of the war left him deeply scarred, eventually leading to his suicide, but is not reflected in much of his writing, perhaps because of the political pressure put on him by the fascist regime. *The Setting Sun* and *No Longer Human* are, however, both about Japan's loss of the war, which affected him deeply, and are both available in translation.

DEAMER, (Mary Elizabeth Kathleen) Dulcie
(1890–1972)

New Zealand journalist, poet, playwright and novelist, born in Christchurch. In 1907, at 17, she won a short-story competition run by the Australian magazine *Lone Hand*. This was collected, with other stories, in *In the Beginning: Six Studies of the Stone Age* (1909, reprinted, with illustrations by **Norman Lindsay** as *As It Was in the Beginning*, 1929). Dulcie Deamer then joined a theatrical touring company, married the business manager and, when her husband died, sent their six children home to New Zealand to be brought up by her mother. She toured China, Burma and India with another company and then settled in Sydney in the early 1920s. Her poems and novels dealt mainly with mythology and with classical times; an early book of verse, *Messalina* (1932), contained portraits of classical and historic women. Another collection of poems was *The Silver Branch* (1948). Her novels include *The Suttee of Safa: A Hindoo Romance* (1913), *The Street of the Gazelle* (1922) and *The Devil's Saint* (1924). One of her plays, *Easter*, a morality play, was included in *Best Australian One-Act Plays* (1937). Known in the Sydney of the 1920s and 1930s as the 'Queen of Bohemia', her frenetic and heterosexual lifestyle has caused her to be shunned by some modern feminist commentators, but she did much to encourage literate women of her time.

DE AMICIS, Edmondo
(1846–1908)

Italian novelist and journalist. He became famous for his *La vita militare* (1868, 'The Military Life'), sketches recalling his service against the Austrian tyrant. But his enduring book, still to be found in most Italian bookshops and schools, is *Cuore* (1886, Eng trans *Heart: A School Boy's Journal*, 1895), a sentimental, philistine, almost **Kipling**esque, but none the less appealing and not quite unrealistic novel of academic life.

DEANE, John F
(1943–)

Irish poet, fiction writer and publisher, born on the Gaelic-speaking Achill Island. He resigned as a teacher to found and develop a National Poetry Society, Eigse Eireann/ Poetry Ireland, in 1978; in 1985 he founded *The Dedalus Press*. In *The Stylized City* (1991), his seventh collection of poems, he developed a spiritual and meditative quality that has pervaded all his subsequent work. A prolific and enthusiastic interpreter of the work of other authors, through the Dedalus Press he has introduced illuminating editions of the work of, among others, the Romanian **Marin Sorescu** and Swedish poet **Tomas Tranströmer**. His fictions, *Free Range* (1994), are gentle unravellings of vulnerable 'souls' earthed in bitter, wracked bodies. His contribution to Irish literature is that of a generous, contemplative writer rather than a controversial one, though as a publisher he has certainly broken new ground.

DEANE, Seamus
(1940–)

Irish poet, critic and anthologist, born in Derry. Educated in Belfast and at Cambridge,

he became a Fulbright lecturer at Berkeley (1966–8) before returning to Ireland to become Professor of Modern English and American Literature at University College Dublin; in 1971 he became co-director of the Field Day Theatre Company, a post he held until 1993. His three-volume *Field Day Anthology of Irish Writing* was published in 1991. Of his own work, *Gradual Wars* (1972) was one of the first poetry collections to address the political unrest in Ireland since the late 1960s. Five subsequent collections and several volumes of essays, including the important *Heroic Styles: The Tradition of an Idea* (1985), made him spokesman for a questioning attitude that was often glibly dismissed as 'revisionist'. His critical analysis and declared 'desire to locate the Irish experience' in a European context make him a cultural commentator of singular importance.

DE BEAUVOIR, Simone
(1908–86)

French novelist, feminist, autobiographer and essayist, born in Paris and educated at the Sorbonne, where she later lectured. She will undoubtedly be remembered chiefly for the enormous impact made by her famous book *Le Deuxième Sexe* (1949, Eng trans *The Second Sex*, 1953), which despite its alleged shortcomings as a feminist tract, remains authoritative for its intelligence and the sheer weight of its case. It inspired many women to salutary writings and actions and has caused many of them to refer to its author as 'the mother of us all'. She was also a notable novelist (in particular in *Les Mandarins*, 1954, Eng trans *The Mandarins*, 1956) and a supreme autobiographer, as in *Memoires d'une jeune fille rangée* (1954, Eng trans *Memoirs of a Dutiful Daughter*, 1959). She was the lifelong companion of **Jean-Paul Sartre**.
▷ R D Cottrell, *Simone de Beauvoir* (1975)

DEBELYANOV, Dimcho
(1887–1916)

Bulgarian poet, the leading Symbolist of his time, who was killed fighting in Greece. He wrote in the tradition of **Hristo Botev**, but infused his poetry (of which there is comparatively little) with the spirit of the French symbolists. Like Hungary's **Ady**, he brought to the literature of his language the right foreign influence just when it was needed, but without violating it. His haunting work, which has not been translated, finds mystical significance in the relations between all phenomena—a significance alluded to in **Baudelaire**'s famous sonnet beginning 'Nature is a living temple . . .'.

▷C Manning and R Smal-Stocki, *The History of Modern Bulgarian Literature* (1960)

DE BOISSIÈRE, Ralph Anthony Charles
(1907–)

Trinidadian-born Australian novelist, born and educated in Port-of-Spain. Having worked as a clerk in commerce, he moved to Australia in 1947, taking citizenship there in 1970. His writing career has been intermittent and his output slow. *Crown Jewel* (1952) is a realistic portrait of working-class activity in pre-war Trinidad, while *Rum and Coca-Cola* (1956) covers the war years, when thousands of US servicemen arrived on the island, and replaces the social and political emphasis of its predecessor with a more psychological approach. *No Saddles for Kangaroos* (1964) is set in de Boissière's adoptive country and is much less perceptive. He also wrote the music for his own play, *Calypso Isle* (1955).

DE CAMP, L(yon) Sprague
(1907–)

American science-fiction and fantasy writer, born in New York City. His first book was a textbook on patents. He was one of the stable of writers associated with **John W Campbell** and *Astounding Science Fiction* magazine, and became an equally valued contributor to its sister publication *Unknown*, turning his attention to fantasy in the process. Notable titles include *Lest Darkness Fall* (1941), a time-travel story set in 6th-century Rome, and *The Wheels of If* (1948), an alternate world story. Both of these subjects were united in his *Incomplete Enchanter* sequence, written with Fletcher Pratt, one of a number of such collaborators, including his wife, Catherine A Crook. *Rogue Queen* (1951) is the most highly regarded novel in his *Viagens Interplanetarisas* sequence, which began in 1949. He also wrote a large number of fantasy and sword and sorcery adventure novels, and biographies of **H P Lovecraft** and Robert E Howard, whose *Conan the Barbarian* series he continued.

DECHEPARE, Bernard
(fl.mid 16th century)

Basque priest who wrote the first known book in the language, *Linguae Vasconum primitiae* ('Primitive Basque Language'), printed in 1545.
▷R Gallop, *A Book of the Basques* (1930); L Michelena, *Historia de la literatura vasca* (1960)

DEEPING, (George) Warwick
(1877–1950)

English novelist, born in Southend. He qualified as a doctor, but devoted himself to writing. It was not until after World War I,

in which he served, that he gained recognition as an author with his bestseller, *Sorrell and Son* (1925), which was later filmed. Other novels include *Old Pybus* (1928) and *Roper's Row* (1929). In his stories, all sentimental, good breeding is represented as the cardinal virtue.

DE FILIPPO, Eduardo
(1900–92)

Italian dramatist, theatre director and actor. He was born in Naples and grew up in the theatre, acting with a family troupe. He formed the Teatro Umoristico with his brother and sister (1931–44), before founding Il Teatro di Eduardo in 1945, by which time he had already written or adapted more than 25 plays. *Natale in casa Cupiello* (1931, rev edn 1942) was revived in London in 1982 as *Ducking Out*. Unlike the work of his fellow-countrymen **Luigi Pirandello** and **Dario Fo**, there is nothing stylized about de Filippo's drama and as a result its understated approach often does not translate easily. *Questi fantasmi!* (1946) was staged as *Too Many Ghosts* in Oxford in the late fifties (subsequently published as *Oh, These Ghosts*, 1971), and *Filumena Marturano* (1946) has enjoyed English-language success as *The Best House in Naples* (1956, USA) and *Filumena* (1977, UK). De Filippo uses Neapolitan dialect as a personal, almost private, language of expression and though his use of farce is internationally recognizable, some of his most telling speech simply does not translate.
▷M Mignone, *Eduardo de Filippo* (1984)

DEFOE, Daniel
(1660–1731)

English author and adventurer, born in Stoke Newington, London, the son of a butcher. He appears to have travelled widely on the Continent before setting up in the hosiery trade in London in 1683. He took part in Monmouth's rebellion and joined William III's army in 1688. Up to 1704 he strenuously supported the king's party and earned William's favour with his satirical poem *The True-born Englishman* (1701), an attack on xenophobic prejudice. In Queen Anne's reign he ran into trouble with his famous satire *The Shortest Way with the Dissenters* (1702), the irony of which at first deceived the High Church party, but which eventually cost him a ruinous fine, the pillory and imprisonment during the Queen's pleasure. In Newgate prison he managed to continue his pamphleteering on such questions as 'occasional conformity' and wrote a mock-pindaric *Hymn to the Pillory*. In 1704, after his release, he founded a newspaper, *The Review*, which is of importance in the history of journalism. Appearing thrice weekly up to 1713, it aimed at being an organ of commercial interests, but also expressed opinions on political and domestic topics, thus initiating the modern lead article. The 'Scandal Club', one of its features, anticipates the *Tatler* and *Spectator*. As well as writing *The Review* single-handed, he wrote, among much pamphleteering, the astonishingly vivid ghost story *The Apparition of One Mrs Veal*, allegedly, like so many of his fictions, a true account of an actual happening. After 1704 his political conduct becomes highly equivocal. He undertook various secret commissions for the Tory minister Harley, including dubious dealings with the Scottish commissioners for Union in 1706–7. On Harley's fall in 1708 he supported Nottingham's ministry and he again changed his coat on the return of Harley in 1710. On the accession of the House of Hanover in 1714 he tried to justify his career as a double-agent in his *Appeal to Honour and Justice* (1715). He now turned to the writing of fiction which was all passed off as actual history. In 1719–20, at the age of nearly 60, he published his best-known work, *Robinson Crusoe*. Among the other six fictions—the *Journal of the Plague Year* (1722) seems to have had a source in an actual diary—the most vivid is *Moll Flanders* (1722), which is still one of the best tales of low life. He did not repeat this triumph in *Roxana* (1724). *Memoirs of a Cavalier* and the brilliant (but uneven) *Captain Singleton* (both in 1720), along with *Captain Jack* (1722), make up an extraordinary outpouring of creative writing in these few years. He continued to write with unabated vigour, including a three-volume travel book (*Tour through the Whole Island of Great Britain*, 1724–7), *The Great Law of Subordination Considered* (1724), *The Complete English Tradesman* (1726), *Plan of the English Commerce* (1728) and *Augusta Triumphans, or the Way to make London the Most Flourishing City in the Universe* (1728). A writer of astonishing versatility, and the founder of British journalism, he published more than 250 works. He was buried in Bunhill Fields, Islington.

▷B Fitzgerald, *Defoe, a History of Conflict* (1954); P Rogers, *Defoe: the critical heritage* (1972)

DE FOREST, J(ohn) W(illiam)
(1826–1906)

American novelist and historian. He was born in Humphreysville (now Seymour), Connecticut, and after elementary education lived abroad, in Syria, Italy and France, returning to the USA in 1856 to make his way as a writer. Among his early books were travelogues of his European years, but his first significant work was the notably unromantic *History of the Indians of Connecticut*

from the Earliest Known Period to 1850 (1851), which debunked prevailing myths. His first published novel was *Seacliff* (1859), a mystery which may have had an impact on **Henry James**. Further literary effort was prevented by the outbreak of the Civil War, in which De Forest served as an officer. He sent battlefield sketches to *Harper's Monthly*, many of which were gathered in the posthumous *A Volunteer's Adventures* (1946). His main fictional achievement came with *Miss Ravenel's Conversion from Secession to Loyalty* (1867) which, despite its romantic trappings, is nonetheless notably clinical and clear-sighted. After the war, De Forest worked for a time in the Freedmen's Bureau in South Carolina. *Kate Beaumont* (1872) and *Honest John Vane* (1875) are the best of his remaining novels; others are melodramatic and formulaic.

▷J F Light, *J W De Forest* (1965)

DE GROEN, Alma Margaret
(1941–)

New Zealand playwright, born in Foxton, Manawatu, but resident in Australia. Her first play, *The Sweatproof Boy*, was published in 1969, followed by *The Joss Adams Show* (1970) and *The After-Life of Arthur Cravan* (1972). Her best-known play was *Going Home* (1977), centred on a group of expatriate Australians coming to terms with an alien way of life. *Chidley* (1977) deals with the Victorian eccentric and would-be sex reformer William Chidley, and her later work includes *The Rivers of China* (1985).

DEHMEL, Richard
(1863–1920)

German poet, born in Wendisch-Hermsdorf, Brandenburg, a forester's son. He worked for an insurance company, then served on the front line in World War I, where he was awarded the Iron Cross. He wrote intellectual verse showing the influence of **Nietzsche**, and in which he practised rigorous self-discipline, although he does succumb to the temptation of an over-rhetorical didacticism. His best-known collection is *Weib und Welt* (1896, 'Woman and World').

▷E Ludwig, *Richard Dehmel* (1913)

DEIGHTON, Len (Leonard Cyril)
(1929–)

English thriller writer, born in London. He became, variously, an art student, a railway plate-layer and a BOAC steward. His first novel, *The Ipcress File* (1962), was written when he was 33 and became a bestseller, as have almost all his books. Flip, entertaining and exciting, along with **John Le Carré**, **Graham Greene** and **Eric Ambler** he has been responsible for taking the spy novel out of the genre ghetto into mainstream literature. Notable titles are *Funeral in Berlin* (1965), *Only When I Larf* (1968) and the *Game, Set and Match* trilogy: *Berlin Game* (1984), *Mexico Set* (1985) and *London Match* (1986). It was followed by another trilogy, *Spy Hook* (1988), *Spy Line* (1989) and *Spy Sinker* (1990). He also writes cookery books.

DEKEN, Aagje ('Agatha')
(1741–1804)

Dutch novelist, born in the northern Netherlands, best known for her friendship with **Elisabeth Wolff-Bekker**. Deken grew up in an orphanage in Amsterdam and became a domestic servant. Her friendship with Wolff led to a literary collaboration which resulted most successfully in *Sara Burgerhart* (1782), an edifyingly didactic novel, written in the epistolary style of **Richardson**'s *Clarissa*. Deken and Wolff settled at Trevoux in France, returning to the Hague in 1798. Wolff's last poem, *To A Friend*, articulated the wish that she might die before Deken. She did; but only by a few weeks.

DEKKER, Eduard Douwes, pseud
Multatuli
(1820–87)

Dutch government official and writer, born in Amsterdam. He served for many years in the Dutch civil service in Java, and in his novel *Max Havelaar* (1860), and in many bitter satires, he protested against the abuses of the Dutch colonial system.
▷G Bron, *Multatuli* (1958)

DEKKER, Thomas
(c.1570–?1632)

English dramatist and pamphleteer, born in London. Around 1598 he was employed by Philip Henslowe to write plays, and in 1600 published two comedies, *The Shoemaker's Holiday, or the Gentle Craft*, and *The Pleasant Comedy of Old Fortunatus*. His next play (with **John Marston**) was *Satiromastix* (1602), which held up to ridicule **Ben Jonson**, who had castigated Dekker in *The Poetaster* (1601). In 1603 he published a pamphlet, *The Wonderful Year*, which gives a heartrending account of the plague. To the same date belongs the tract, *The Bachelor's Banquet*, in which he describes with gusto the ills of henpecked husbands. His most powerful writing is seen in *The Honest Whore* (Part I, written with **Thomas Middleton**, in 1604; Part II, which was his own work, was written in 1605, and appeared in 1630). In 1607 he published three plays written in conjunction with **John Webster**, the *Famous History of Sir Thomas Wyat*, *Westward Ho!* and *Northward Ho!*.

The pamphlet *Bellman of London* (1608) gives a lively account of London vagabonds; and he pursued the subject in *Lanthorn and Candlelight* (1608). In *The Gull's Hornbook* (1609) the life of a town gallant is racily depicted. He also published a devotional work, *Fowre Birds of Noahs Ark* (1609). The excellent comedy, *The Roaring Girl* (1611), was written partly in collaboration with Middleton. From 1613 to 1616 he was mostly in prison for debt. With **Philip Massinger** he composed the *Virgin Martyr* (1622). *The Sun's Darling*, licensed in 1624, but not printed until 1656, was written in conjunction with **John Ford**. A powerful tragedy, *The Witch of Edmonton* (1623), was written with Ford and **William Rowley**. In 1637, he republished his *Lanthorn and Candlelight* as *English Villainies*. He was also the author of masques and entertainments.
▷G R Price, *Thomas Dekker* (1969)

DELAFIELD, E M, pseud of **Edmée Elizabeth Monica Dashwood**, née **de la Pasture**
(1890–1943)

English novelist, born in Llandogo, Monmouth. She began work as a nurse during World War I, and then became a civil servant, and served as a magistrate. She married in 1921, and was the prolific author of novels which took a mildly but affectionately satirical look at the mores of genteel provincial life. Her best-known works are the series which began with *Diary of a Provincial Lady* (1930). It ran to several more 'Provincial Lady' volumes, and was successfully adapted as a film.
▷*A Note By the Way* (1933)

DE LA MARE, Walter
(1873–1956)

English poet and novelist, born in Charlton in Kent, of Huguenot descent. Educated at St Paul's Choir School, he went to work for the Standard Oil Company in 1890, and wrote in his spare time. He retired on a state pension in 1908 to take up full-time writing. The promise of his first book of verse, *Songs of Childhood* (1902, by 'Walter Ramal'), his prose romance *Henry Brocken* (1904), his children's story *The Three Mulla Mulgars* (1910) and his novel of the occult *The Return* (1910) was fulfilled in his volumes of poetry *The Listeners* (1912), *Peacock Pie* (1913) and *The Veil* (1921), in the fantastic novel *Memoirs of a Midget* (1921), and in books of short stories such as *On the Edge* (1930). Romanticist and musician in words, De la Mare has delighted children and grown-up readers alike by the delicate enchantments and humour of his *Märchen* world. In 1953, he published a new volume of lyrics, *O Lovely England*. He was buried in St Paul's

DELANEY, Shelagh

Cathedral. A *Complete Poems* was issued in 1969.

▷L Clark, *Walter de la Mare* (1960)

DELANEY, Shelagh
(1939–)

English playwright and screenwriter, born in Salford, Lancashire. Having left school at 16, Delaney completed her first and still best-known play a year later. *A Taste of Honey*, produced in London in 1958, is the story of a young white girl's abrasive home life and her pregnancy following a casual affair with a black sailor. It was immediately seen as part of a young, 'angry' movement dealing realistically with working-class, provincial life, and which included the playwrights **John Osborne** and **Arnold Wesker**. None of Delaney's more recent writing has achieved equal critical acclaim or notoriety. Among her later work is the screenplay for *Dancing with a Stranger* (1985), a film depicting the fraught life of Ruth Ellis, who murdered her lover and became the last woman to be hanged in England.

DELANO, Alonzo
(c.1802–1874)

American humorist and historian, born in Aurora in New York State. His most valuable collection of sketches, about the California of the prospectors, is *Life on the Plains and Among the Diggings* (1954).

DELANY, Samuel Ray
(1942–)

American science-fiction writer and literary theorist, born in New York City. He has held a number of academic posts. He was married to the poet **Marilyn Hacker** (1961–80), and used her poems in some of his novels. He is the most boldly experimental of science-fiction writers, and his early books are imaginative twists on genre themes. They reflect his growing fascination with language and the nature of the fiction-making process itself, notably in *Babel-17* (1966), *The Einstein Intersection* (1967) and *Nova* (1968). The massive, self-referential *Dhalgren* (1975) divided his admirers. Other important works include *Triton* (1976), the short stories in *Driftglass* (1971), *Tales of Neveryon* (1979) and several critical works on the language of science fiction.

▷*The Making of Light on Water* (1988)

DE LA ROCHE, Mazo
(1885–1961)

Canadian novelist, born in Newmarket, Ontario. She wrote *Jalna* (1927), the first of a series of novels about the Whiteoak family.

Whiteoaks (1929) was dramatized with considerable success. Her autobiography, *Ringing the Changes*, was published in 1957.

▷G Hendrik, *Mazo de la Roche* (1970)

DELAVIGNE, Jean François Casimir
(1793–1843)

French dramatist, satirist and lyricist, born in Le Havre. He became popular through his *Messéniennes* (1818, 'Messenians'), satires upon the Restoration. *Les Vêpres siciliennes* (1819, 'Sicilian Vespers'), a tragic piece, was followed by *L'École des vieillards* (1820, 'The School of Old People') and *Les Comédiens* (1821, 'The Actors'), *Louis XI*, (partly based on *Quentin Durward*, 1833) and *La Fille du Cid* (1839, 'The Daughter of El Cid').

▷F Vaucheux, *Casimir Delavigne* (1893)

DELDERFIELD, R(onald) F(rederick)
(1912–72)

English playwright, journalist and novelist, born in London. A hugely prolific and popular author, he wrote a variety of plays between 1944 and 1962, and several historical novels. He is best remembered, however, for his epic romantic novels set in England, such as *There Was A Fair Maid Dwelling* (1960, published in the USA as *Diana*), in which a Cockney falls in love with a wealthy beauty. *God Is An Englishman* (1970) and *To Serve Them All My Days* (1972) are similarly well-plotted, well-paced novels with a vivid sense of time and place.

▷*For My Own Amusement* (1968); *Overture For Beginners* (1970)

DELEDDA, Grazia
(1875–1936)

Italian writer and winner of the Nobel Prize for literature. She moved to Rome after her marriage in 1900, but her work in the next 20 years focused on peasant stories of her native Sardinia. They won her a considerable reputation for the lyricism and intensity of novels like *Cenere* (1904, 'Ashes'), *L'edera* (1908, 'Ivy'), *Marianna Sirca* (1915) and *La madre* (1920, 'The Mother'). Her later books left the Sardinian setting, but were similar in style. The posthumous *Cosima* (1937) is autobiographical. She won the 1926 Nobel Prize for literature.

▷N Zoja, *Grazia Deledda, saggio critica* (1939)

DELIBES, Miguel
(1920–)

Spanish novelist, journalist, critic and hunter of small animals. He was born in Valladolid, where he was intimately involved with the newspaper *El Norte de castilla*. He found much favour with the public with such humorous books as *Diario de un cazador* (1955, 'Diary of a Hunter'); but his finest novel is often considered to be his third: *El camino* (1950, Eng trans *The Path*, 1961), narrated by a boy who does not want to go to school in the city. There are two views of the immensely prolific Delibes: that he has wasted his gifts by superficial experimentation and that he is a major writer awaiting recognition by critics. What is not in doubt is his skill.

▷J Daiz, *Miguel Delibes* (1971)

DELILLE, Jacques
(1738–1813)

French poet, born near Aigues-Perse in Auvergne. His verse translation of **Virgil**'s *Georgics* (1769) was very popular, and was praised by **Voltaire**. After holding a canonry at Moissac, he was presented by the Comte d'Artois with the abbacy of Saint-Severin. *Les Jardins* (1782, 'The Gardens'), a didactic poem, was generally accepted as his masterpiece. The Revolution compelled Delille to leave France. He travelled in Switzerland and Germany, then in London spent 18 months translating *Paradise Lost*. After his return to France in 1802 he produced a translation of Virgil's *Aeneid* (1804), and volumes of verse in *L'Imagination* (1806), *Les Trois Règnes de la nature* (1809, 'The Three Reigns of Nature') and *La Conversation* (1812). During his life he was regarded by his countrymen as the greatest French poet of the day, and was even declared the equal of Virgil and **Homer**; but his fame was short-lived.

▷E Guitton, *Jacques Delille, 1738–1813* (1974)

DeLILLO, Don
(1936–)

American novelist, born in New York City and educated at Fordham University in the Bronx. His characteristic concerns are the paranoia and obsessive sub-cultural codes entailed by existence within very large, suprahuman systems. DeLillo's first book, *Americana* (1971), is a road narrative of the sort associated with early **Thomas Pynchon** and the Beats. *End Zone* (1972) is an American football novel with an allegoric–linguistic undercurrent contrasting verbal and actual performance. *Great Jones Street* (1973) concerns a self-probing drop-out rock-star, Bucky Wunderlick. In the ambitious *Ratner's Star* (1976), a novel about the creation of fictions, DeLillo attempts a synthesis of **Lewis Carroll**, **Laurence Sterne** and science fiction. Subsequent works, *Players* (1977), *Running Dog* (1978) and *The Names* (1982), were less ambitious, but *White Noise* (1985) was a

comic masterpiece centred on a mid-west professor of Hitler Studies whose family is affected by an environmental catastrophe that mirrors the toxic effects of fear and angst. Two later novels have explored aspects of fame and infamy. In *Libra* (1988) he probed the psyches of Lee Harvey Oswald and Jack Ruby. In *Mao II* (1991) the syntax is uninflected, Warholian, devoid of conventional 'meaning', and captures the narrow self-definitions of a media-haunted society.

DeLISSER, H(erbert) G(eorge)
(1878–1944)

Jamaican novelist, born in Falmouth, Jamaica. From 1904 to 1942 he was editor of the *Daily Gleaner* newspaper. His political conservatism is reflected in his novels, which are very much escapist entertainment, though accurate about racial tensions in Jamaica. His best-known, and most lasting, novel is *Jane's Career* (1914), originally published as *Jane: A Story of Jamaica* (1913). A pioneering work in Caribbean fiction, it chronicles the adventures of a young countrywoman who persistently manoeuvres her way up the social scale. Often reprinted also is *The White Witch of Rosehall* (1929), a historical pot-boiler.

▷F Birbalsingh, 'The Novels of H. G. DeLisser', in *Passion & Exile: Essays in Caribbean Literature* (1988)

DELIUS, Anthony
(1916–)

South African poet, novelist and dramatist. He co-founded and became editor of the newspaper the *Saturday Post* (later the *Evening Post*); he was also parliamentary correspondent of the *Cape Times*. He has carried on the tradition early established in South Africa, before they all left for Europe, by **William Plomer**, **Roy Campbell** and **Laurens van der Post** (the latter two became members of the right only long afterwards). Delius's satire of accepted-attitudes, a critic has said, 'acts like a paint-stripper'. *Black South-Easter* (1966), on the other hand, a symbolic voyage around the Cape on a windy night, could be considered to be the most sonorous long poem produced in its country since World War II. *Border* (1976) is a novel.

DELL, Ethel Mary
(1881–1939)

English novelist, born in Streatham. As a writer of light romantic novels she enjoyed a tremendous vogue in the years between the wars. Her books include her enormously successful first novel, *The Way of an Eagle* (1912), *The Lamp in the Desert* (1919), *The Black Knight* (1926) and *Sown Among Thorns* (1939).

DELL, Floyd
(1887–1969)

American novelist, playwright and social critic. He was born in Barry, Illinois, and educated there and in Davenport, Iowa, where he worked in journalism. After four years at the Chicago *Evening Post*, latterly (1911–13) as editor, he moved to New York. Increasingly interested in liberal and left-wing ideas, he became managing editor of *The Masses* (1914–17) but was arraigned under sedition laws for pacifist articles; the journal was relaunched as *The Liberator* (1918–20) with Dell as associate editor. His most important novel was his first, *The Moon-Calf* (1920). The young writer-hero Felix Fay, a version of Dell himself, also appears in a sequel, *The Briary-Bush* (1921). However, Dell's best and most revealing books are *Intellectual Vagabondage* (1926), billed as an 'apology' for the intelligentsia, and his autobiography *Homecoming* (1933). He published no more books after the mid-30s, but continued to work as an editor for the New Deal's Works Progress Administration in Washington, DC.

▷ *Homecoming* (1933); J E Hart, *Floyd Dell* (1971)

DELLA CASA, Giovanni
(1503–56)

Florentine poet, diplomat, moralist and divine, born (probably) in Mugello. He ended his ecclesiastical career as Secretary of State to the Vatican. His troubled, sexually anxious lyrics, distinguished by daring technical innovations, were praised by **Tasso**, and were amongst the finest of his century. His *Galateo ovvero de' costumi* (1558, Eng trans *Galateo, of Good Manners and Behaviour*, 1576, modern edn 1914) is a remarkable and subtle exercise in human pragmatics.

▷ *Publications of the Modern Language Association*, 41 (1926)

DELLA VALLE, Federico
(c.1560–c.1628)

Italian dramatist and poet, born near Asti in Piedmont. He was an embittered court laureate who worked for Spaniards, and who came to an almost gnostic view of existence. He wrote his four tragedies while at the court in Turin. They were rediscovered by **Croce**, who saw in them the spirit of the Baroque entering into Rennaissance humanism. Two, *Judit* and *Ester*, are from biblical subjects; *La reina di Scozia* is about Mary, Queen of Scots. They abound in pathos and psychological subtleties, and glow with their author's love of God, despite his view of existence as a living hell.

▷ B Croce, *Nuovo saggi sulla letteratura italiana del Seicento* (1931)

DELONEY, Thomas
(c.1550–1600)

English balladist and writer of fiction. Nothing is known of his birthplace or education, although his works suggest familiarity with Latin and French. A London silk-weaver, he wrote a number of ballads, but is best known for his stories in pamphlet form, such as *Jack of Newbury*, *Thomas of Reading* and *Gentle Craft* which, with their lively dialogue and characterization, are seen as a forerunner of the novel proper.

▷ R Howarth, *Two Elizabethan Writers of Fiction: Thomas Nashe and Thomas Deloney* (1956)

DELORIA, Ella
(1889–1971)

American linguist, ethnologist and novelist. Born at White Swan on the Standing Rock Sioux reservation in South Dakota, Deloria grew up in a family where traditional Dakota (Sioux) culture merged with Episcopal Protestantism. A graduate of Columbia University, she worked for several years in collaboration with the anthropologist, Franz Boas, gathering material on the Dakota language and culture she was passionate to preserve. These researches led to the publication of *Dakota Texts* (1932), a bilingual collection of traditional stories, *Dakota Grammar* (1941) and *Speaking of Indians* (1944), a description of Dakota culture written for the popular market. Her novel, *Waterlily*, written in the 1940s but unpublished until 1988, is set in the 19th century before White impingement on Dakota culture; more than simply an ethnographic record, it vividly dramatizes the everyday life of the Dakotas from the often-overlooked perspective of the women of the tribe. Deloria also compiled a Dakota–English dictionary and translated several oral narratives and autobiographies.

DEL RAY, Lester, pseud of Filipe San Juan Mario Silvio Enrico Alvarez-del Ray
(1915–93)

American science-fiction writer and editor, born in Clydesdale, Minnesota. He spent two years in college, then was a sheet metal worker before becoming a literary agent. He published his first science-fiction story in 1938 and went on to become a major figure in the mainstream of the genre. His writing is notable for its craftsmanship in plotting and thematic ingenuity. His most important science-fiction novels are *Police Your Planet* (1956, as 'Erik Van Rhin') and *The Eleventh Commandment* (1962). Almost half of his novels were written for children. He used several pseudonymns, including 'Philip St John' and 'Kenneth Wright'. He was science-fiction editor at Ballantine Books (1977–91) and encouraged many new writers.

DELVIG, Anton Antonovitch, Baron von
(1798–1831)

Russian poet, born in Moscow. He studied with **Alexander Pushkin** at the Tsarskoé Sélo school and became Keeper of the public library at St Petersburg. From 1825 to 1831 he published the miscellany *Severnye tsvety* ('Flowers from the North').
▷L Koehler, *Anton Antonovitch Delvig: a Classicist in the time of Romanticism* (1970)

DE MARCHI, Emilio
(1851–1901)

Italian novelist, born in Milan. Before he began to write, De Marchi was a teacher who read and imbibed **Manzoni**, as well as **Scott** and **Gogol**. Short stories were followed by the novels *Il capello del prete* (1888, 'The Priest's Hat') and *Dimitrio Pianelli* (1890, Eng trans 1905, 1977), the latter containing a memorable description of the boredom and horror of office work for a sensitive individual. Stylistically he is exemplarily plain. His later work is not quite as good.
▷S Pacifici, *The Modern Italian Novel from Manzoni to Svevo* (1967)

DE MENA, Juan
(1411–56)

Spanish poet and prose writer. Born in Cordoba, he was orphaned very young, educated in Salamanca and Florence, and came to be considered one of the most highly cultured men of his epoch. He was married, possibly twice, but had no children, and held a series of royal appointments under Juan II with the protection of Alvaro de Luna. Along with his close friend the **Marques de Santillana**, he developed the verse form called *arte mayor*, the first polished vernacular poetic form in Spanish. His most renowned work is the *Laberinto de la fortuna* (1444), also known as *Las trescientas*, but he is also remembered for *La coronación* (1438, published 1499), a laud to his friend the Marques; the *Iliada romanzada* (1442), a translation of the famous epic; and his lyric and cancioneril poetry.
▷M R Lida de Malkiel, *Juan de Mena, poeta del prerenacimiento español* (1950)

DE MORGAN, William Frend
(1839–1917)

English Pre-Raphaelite ceramic artist and novelist, son of the mathematician and logician Augustus De Morgan, born in London. He studied art at the Academy Schools, and started as a designer of tiles and stained glass, but became interested in pottery, and in 1871 established a kiln in Chelsea, where he turned out glazed ware in beautiful blues and greens. These won much praise in artistic circles but made little money. In 1905 he abandoned pottery and, at the age of 65, he began writing novels in a whimsical **Dicken**sian manner, like *Joseph Vance* (1906), *Alice-for-Short* (1907) and *Somehow Good* (1908). His wife, Evelyn Pickering (1855–1919), whom he married in 1887, was a Pre-Raphaelite painter, and completed his last two unfinished novels after his death, *The Old Madhouse* (1919) and *The Old Man's Youth* (1921).
▷F Seymour, *A Post Victorian Realist* (1920)

DENEVI, Marco
(1922–)

Argentinian novelist and playwright, reclusive but prize-winning and prolific. He was born in Sáenz Peña, the son of an Italian immigrant. Until 1954 Denevi worked in a bank. An avid reader of **Wilkie Collins**, he wrote the novel *Rosaura a las diez* (1954, 'Rosaura at Ten O'Clock'), which deals with the mysterious murder, apparently by a timid picture-restorer, of his young girl bride. This was filmed, televised, dramatized, and became a bestseller (but was not translated into English). *Ceremonia secreta* (1960, Eng trans *Secret Ceremony*, 1961), also won prestigious prizes, as have successive novels and plays. It remains surprising that this very able writer, not unlike his compatriot **Cortázar**, is not better known in English-speaking countries.
▷D A Yates, 'Prologue' to *Secret Ceremony* (1961)

DENHAM, Sir John
(1615–69)

Irish poet, born in Dublin, the only son of an Irish judge of English birth. He was educated in London and at Trinity College, Oxford. He studied law at Lincoln's Inn, and was called to the Bar in 1639. At the outbreak of the Civil War he was high-sheriff of Surrey, and immediately joined the king. He fell into Sir William Waller's hands on the capture of Farnham Castle, and was sent as a prisoner to London, but he was soon freed and went to Oxford. In 1641 he produced *The Sophy*, a historical tragedy of the Turkish court which was performed to great applause at Blackfriars; and in 1642 he published a long poem, *Cooper's Hill*, a topographical description of the scenery around Egham, which **Pope** imitated in his *Windsor Forest*. In 1648, being discovered in the performance of secret services for Charles I, he fled to Holland and France. In 1650 he collected money for the young king Charles II from the Scots resident in Poland, and several times visited England on secret service. At the Restoration he was appointed surveyor-general of works, and in 1661 created a Knight of the Bath. He was a better poet than architect, but he had Christopher Wren as his deputy. He was buried in Poet's Corner in Westminster Abbey.

▷B O'Hehir, *Harmony from discords: a life of Sir John Denham* (1968)

DENNERY, Adolphe Philippe
(1811–99)

French playwright, born in Paris. He was clerk to a notary, but from 1831 produced 133 dramas, vaudevilles and plays, the most successful being *Marie Jeanne* (1845). He also wrote the libretti for Gounod's *Le Tribut de Zamora* (1881) and Massenet's *Le Cid* (1885). He was the creator of the Norman wateringplace, Cabourg.

DENNIS, C(larence Michael) J(ames)
(1876–1938)

Australian poet and journalist, born in Auburn, South Australia. After some experience of journalism in Adelaide he moved to Melbourne and lived by contributing light verse to many periodicals, including the Sydney *Bulletin*. His poems were collected as *Backblock Ballads and Other Verses* (1915); some featured the larrikin Bill and reappeared as *The Songs of a Sentimental Bloke* in 1915. They were immediately popular and were repeated in *The Moods of Ginger Mick* (1916). The two books were reprinted many times and the 'Trench' pocket editions were the favoured reading of Australian troops during World War I. Within the next five years Dennis published as many books, each of them in his individual style of prose-poetry which captured the vernacular working-class speech of the cities. The fashion passed; in 1922 Dennis returned to journalism and was for some time 'Staff Poet' on the Melbourne *Age*, contributing a daily column over the next 16 years.

DENNIS, John
(1657–1734)

English critic and playwright, born in London. He was educated at Harrow and Caius College, Cambridge. After a tour through France and Italy, he took his place among the wits and men of fashion, and produced biting criticism to support the Whigs. He wrote nine plays, but had little success with them, including a satire, *A Plot and No Plot* (1697), and *Rinaldo and Armida* (1699). **Pope**'s *Essay on Criticism* (1711) contained a contemptuous allusion to another play,

Appius and Virginia (1709), answered by Dennis the next month in *Reflections Critical and Satirical*, which triggered a long feud. Among his critical works are *The Grounds of Criticism in Poetry* (1704) and *An Essay on the Genius and Writings of Shakespeare* (1712).

▷H G Paul, *John Dennis, his life and criticism* (1911)

DENNIS, Nigel Forbes
(1912–89)

English novelist and playwright, best known for his second book, *Cards of Identity* (1955), in which he comically satirizes the infringements of modern society upon the individual by means of a relatively conventional country-house plot. Born in Bletchingley, Surrey, Dennis was educated in Rhodesia and Germany. In 1935 and 1936 he was Secretary of the National Board of Review of Motion Pictures in the USA, later working as Assistant Editor on *New Republic* (1937–8), and as book reviewer on *Time* (1940–59), before returning to Britain as joint Editor of *Encounter* (1967–70) and book reviewer on the *Sunday Telegraph* (1961–82). His first novel was *Boys and Girls Come Out to Play* (1949), his third and last, was *A House in Order* (1966), which again concerns the preservation of identity under constraint. Dennis also wrote several plays, including an adaptation (1956) of *Cards of Identity* and *August for the People* (1961).

DE PISAN, Christine
(1361–c.1430)

French lyrical and didactic poet, critic, military theorist, biographer and feminist, born in Venice, daughter of the physician to Charles V of France. Beautiful, gifted and learned, she was at 15 happily married to Étienne de Castel, a royal secretary; but he died when she was 25, and, with two or three children to support, she became the first woman of substance to earn a living by writing. In a pedantic age, she had, alone, to defend her sex from the dominating, and misogynistic, Aristotelian ethos which was expressed in many major works, but not least in the *Roman de la Rose* of **Jean de Meung**, which she savagely attacked, thus initiating the first *Querelle* in French literature: the *Querelle des femmes* ('Women's Quarterly'). She wrote some of the most breathtaking love poetry in any language, including the *ballade* whose refrain is 'Vostre douceur me meine dure guerre' ('Thought of your sweetness wreaks havoc in me')—'a personal note is occasionally sounded', commented a professor, but there are hundreds of such lines in her poetry.

The most profound of her many long works is the 23 000-line octosyllabic *Livre la mutation de fortune* ('Book of the Mutations of Fortune'), an ironic allegory which employs erudite patriarchal techniques to undermine patriarchy. Some of her works were translated by **Caxton** (eg *The Book of Faytes of Arms and of Chivalrye*, modern edn, 1932). The revival of interest in her from a feminist viewpoint is now well under way. In the last years of her life she retired, with her daughter, to a convent.

▷A Kemp-Welch, *Of Six Medieval Women* (1903)

DE QUINCEY, Thomas
(1785–1859)

English critic and essayist, born in Manchester, the son of a merchant. He was educated at Manchester Grammar School, where he proved an apt pupil. In 1802 he ran away from school and wandered in Wales, and then to London, where he lived with a young prostitute called Ann. (He described this episode in his *Confessions of an English Opium-eater*, 1822.) Reclaimed from this wandering he spent a short time at Worcester College, Oxford. It was here that he became addicted to opium. A visit to his mother in Bath brought him into contact with **Coleridge**, then resident in Bristol, and through him with **Robert Southey** and **Wordsworth**. When these poets settled at the Lakes, De Quincey visited them there and, after a brief sojourn in London (which enabled him to make the acquaintance of **Charles Lamb**, **William Hazlitt** and others of the 'Cockney' school), he went to stay in Grasmere in 1809. In 1816 he married Margaret Simpson, by whom he had three daughters and five sons, two of the latter distinguishing themselves as soldiers. De Quincey now set up as an author. Except for *The Logic of Political Economy* (1841) and an unsuccessful novel, his whole literary output, including the *Confessions*, consisted of magazine articles. The *Confessions* appeared as a serial in *The London Magazine*, 1821, and at once made him famous. Visits to London varied his existence at the Lakes, but in 1828 the lure of the Edinburgh literary scene drew him to the northern capital, where he lived and worked till his death in 1859. For 20 years he lent distinction to *Blackwood's Magazine*, *Tait's Magazine* and, occasionally, *The Quarterly*, with articles like *Murder Considered as one of the Fine Arts* (1827), *Lake Reminiscences* (1834–40), the fantasies *Suspiria De Profundis* (1845) and *Levana and Our Ladies of Sorrows* (1845), and the 'Dream Fugue' at the end of *The English Mail-Coach*, and *Vision of Sudden Death* (1849).

▷H S David, *Thomas De Quincey* (1964); J S Lyon, *Thomas De Quincey* (1969)

DERÈME, Tristan, pseud of **Phillippe Huc**
(1889–1941)

French poet of the *fantaisiste* school. His works include *La Verdure dorée* (1922, incorporating eight previous collections of poems, 'The Gilded Foliage'), and *L'Enlèvement sans clair de lune* (1924, 'Kidnapping without Moonlight').

▷H Martineau, *Tristan Derème* (1927)

DERLETH, August
(1909–71)

Prolific ('a dazzling fount of energy') American novelist, biographer and poet, born in Sauk City (the Sac Prairie of his fiction), Wisconsin. In some years he produced over 20 titles, some of them near to pulp: 'I enjoy myself and thank God nobody takes me seriously,' he once exclaimed. Modelling himself on **Balzac**, he set out to write, more soberly, the history of his native city in his Sac Prairie saga, of which he published many volumes. *In Re: Sherlock Holmes: Adventures of Solar Pons* (1944), and its successors, introduce an enjoyable reincarnation of the famous detective.

DE ROBERTO, Federico
(1861–1927)

Italian novelist, journalist and critic, born in Naples. A friend to **Boito** and **Giacosa**, he began as a member of the Scapigliatura movement ('the shirtless ones', rooted in Milan and Turin, who advocated a vague bohemianism but also challenged the too-soft romantic assumptions of their time), but then turned for inspiration to **Verga**, whom he took as the model for his stories. His greatest work is the long novel *I Vicerè* (1894, Eng trans *The Viceroys*, 1962), which traces the history of a family, the Uzedas (descendants of Spanish viceroys), against the background of the Risorgimento. For many years this novel lay in the shadow of the then great Verga, but modern criticism rightly sees it as a masterpiece, and one of the paramount novels of its century. It lies firmly behind the achievement of **Lampedusa**.

▷S Pacifici, *The Modern Italian Novel from Manzoni to Svevo* (1967)

DE ROO, Anne
(1931–)

New Zealand writer for children. Her diverse output includes historical novels such as *Traveller* (1979) and *Because of Rosie* (1980) and tales of adventure, as in her first book *The Gold Dog* (1969), *Moa Valley* (1969) and *Scrub Fire* (1977). Other titles are *Boy and the Sea Beast* (1971), *Cinnamon and Nutmeg* (1972), *Mick's Country Cousins* (1974), and two related books, *Jackie Nobody* (1983) and *The Bat's Nest* (1986).

DÉROULÈDE, Paul
(1846–1914)

French politician and poet, born in Paris. A fervid nationalist, and the author of patriotic verses, his writings called for revenge on Germany, and he was active in the campaign against Dreyfus. In 1900 he was exiled for 10 years for sedition, but returned in 1905.

▷ 'H Galli' (ed), *Paul Déroulède raconté par lui-même* (1900)

DEROZIO, Henry Louis Vivian
(1809–31)

Eurasian poet and patriot, born in Calcutta. At 19 he had published two books of poems and was lecturing on English history and literature at the Hindu College, Calcutta. In the next four years he had translated de Maupertuis, lectured on philosophy, written a critique on Kant and edited four journals. He became involved in local politics, and instigated so much freethinking and social rebelliousness that he was dismissed from the College a few months before he died. Much of his verse is imitatively ornamental, but some of his sonnets put him among the lesser Romantics.

▷ E W Madge, *Henry Derozio, the Eurasian poet and reformer* (1965)

D'ERRICO, Ezio
(1892–1973)

Italian novelist, painter, thriller-writer and dramatist, born in Agrigento. He is now somewhat neglected. His avant-garde play *La foresta* (1959, 'The Forest') is a memorable contribution to the literature of terror, in this case that of the technological nightmare created by people who try to compensate for their lack of wisdom by creating over-sophisticated pseudo-scientific schemes.

DERY, Tibor
(1894–1977)

Hungarian novelist, playwright and short-story writer, born in Budapest. A Communist between the wars, he became disillusioned after Hungary was reduced to being a satellite state of the USSR. His best work, *Niki: The Story of a Dog* (1956), is set in and around Budapest just before the 1956 uprising; a sentimental but effective novel, it brought international acclaim for its author. Sentenced to nine years' imprisonment after the crushing of the 1956 revolt, he was eventually 'rehabilitated'. Notable among his later works are *The Portuguese Princess* (1967), a short-story collection, and *The Man With One Ear*

(1975), a cheerfully defiant novel about a libidinous old lecher.

DERZHAVIN, Gavril Romanovich
(1743–1816)

Russian poet, born in Kazan. In 1762 he entered the army as a private, but rose to officer rank, was transferred to the civil service, and later to governorships. In 1791 he became Secretary of State, in 1800 Imperial Treasurer, and in 1802 Minister of Justice. He published a wide-ranging variety of original and imaginative lyric poetry on many subjects, both personal and public, and is considered one of Russia's greatest poets.

▷ A V Zapadov, *Gavril Romanovich Derzhavin* (1958)

DESAI, Anita, née Mazumdar
(1937–)

Indian novelist, born in Mussoorie, Uttar Pradesh, the daughter of a Bengali father and a German mother. She was educated at Delhi University, and her works include novels for adults and children and short stories. *Clear Light of Day* (1980) and *In Custody* (1980) were both shortlisted for the Booker Prize and *The Village by the Sea* won the *Guardian* Award for children's fiction in 1982. In 1988 she published *Baumgartner's Bombay*, the grim story of a German expatriate adrift in India.

DESANI, Govindas Vishnoodas
(1909–)

African-born American novelist, born in Nairobi, Kenya. He went to Britain in 1926 and from 1928 was a correspondent for the *Times of India*, Reuters, and Associated Press. In the late 1930s he was a lecturer on antiquities for Bombay Baroda and Central India Railway and later lectured in England before becoming a broadcaster during World War II. From 1952 to 1966, pursuing a dual interest in yoga and meditation, he visited Buddhist and Hindu monasteries. Throughout the 1960s he filed a provocative column with the *Illustrated Weekly for India*. He has been an American citizen since 1979. His prose-poem *Hali* (1950) and some uncollected stories notwithstanding, his claim to posterity is dependent on *All About H. Hatterr* (1948). It reprinted the week after publication, then was neglected for several decades before being resurrected as a modern classic and placed on a pedestal alongside **James Joyce** and **Flann O'Brien**.

DE SAN PEDRO, Diego
(?1437–?1498)

Spanish prose writer. The *alcaide* of the castle of Peñafiel in Castilla in the middle of the

15th century, he is the most important of the writers of the courtly-love narrative genre known as the *novela sentimental*. He wrote *Tratado de amores de Arnalte e Lucenda*, an early courtly love narrative; poems for the *cancioneros*, *Las siete angustias de Nuestra Señora* (?1534); and *La pasión trovada* (1496, 'The Poetic Passion'). His most important work, and the best example of *novela sentimental* in Spanish, is *Cárcel de amor* ('Prison of Love'), published in 1499. This complex work begins as an allegorical novel, becomes an epistolary love story, and ends as a treatise on the goodness of women; it is one of the crowning achievements of 15th-century Spanish prose.

▷K Whinnom, *Diego de San Pedro* (1974)

DESBORDES-VALMORE, Marceline
(1786–1859)

French poet, born in Douai. She was admired by **Paul Verlaine**, who identified a musicality in her verse akin to his own, and is considered a significant early exponent of *vers libre*. From childhood she pursued a theatrical career, appearing in her hometown and in Brussels, and eventually at the Opéra-Comique in Paris. She gave up singing around 1803, and began to devote herself seriously to poetry. Her main themes are domestic, as the titles of her collections show—*Contes et scenes de la vie de famille* ('Tales and Scenes of Family Life') and *Petits Flamands* ('Flemish Children'), for example—with much reference to romantic love and children. She also wrote one short novel, *Domenica*, published in 1885 within a collection of verse entitled *Scènes Intimes* ('Private Scenes'), and based on her experiences of life and art in bohemian circles.

DESCHAMPS, Eustache, called Morel
(c.1345–c.1406)

French poet, born in Vertus in Champagne. He was brought up by Machaut, who may have been his uncle and who probably taught him his craft. A soldier, a magistrate, a court favourite and a traveller in Italy and Hungary, he held important posts in Champagne, but after his patron, Charles V, died, his possessions were ravaged by the English. He composed 1175 lyrics, besides *Le Miroir de mariage* ('The Mirror of Marriage'), a long poem satirizing women, two dramatic works, and several poems in the then current fashion, deploring the miseries of the Hundred Years War.

▷A Sarradin, *Eustache Des Champs. Sa vie et ses oeuvres* (1879)

DESMARETS, Jean, Sieur de Saint-Sorlen
(1596–1676)

French writer. A protégé of Richelieu, he was the author of many volumes of poetry and critical works, notably *Comparaison de la langue et la poésie française avec la grecque et la latine* (1670, 'Comparison of French Language and Poetry with Greek and Latin'). His play *Les Visionnaires* (1637) was a great success, and he also wrote two verse epics and a novel on biblical and classical themes. He was the first Chancellor and co-founder of the Académie française, and a protagonist in the ancients versus moderns controversy.

DESMASURES, Louis
(1515–74)

French dramatist and translator, born in Tournai. He became converted to protestantism in 1550, and finally had to leave France in 1562. He translated **Virgil's** *Aenead*, but is most famous for his trilogy of plays on David (1563), which are important as very early examples of French proto-tragedy, and as propaganda for Desmasures's cause.

DESNICA, Vladen
(1905–67)

Dalmatian novelist, story writer, dramatist, essayist and translator (writing in Croatian), born in Zadar. Desnica, a lawyer until he became a full-time writer, wrote essays and did translations before World War I; only in the last 15 years of his life did he become prominent. His reputation rests on two novels and a handful of stories, of which the novel *Proljéca Ivana Galeba* (1957, rev edn 1960, 'The Springs of Ivan Galeb') is paramount. This story of a man confined to a hospital bed, piecing his past life together as he hovers between life and death—but denied emotion in the process—is one of the outstanding psychological studies in Croatian literature. Its failure to find a translator has puzzled many critics. It is a static, yet extreme book: the over-cerebral nature of Galeb's ponderings points desperately to a need for emotion and goodwill in a world into whose nature Desnica saw only too clearly, and which, only about a quarter of a century after his death, collapsed into violent and malign chaos.

▷M Vaupotić, *Contemporary Croatian Literature* (1966)

DESNOS, Robert
(1900–45)

French poet, novelist and cinema critic, born in Paris, and deported by the Nazis to con-

centration camps for the part he had played in the resistance to them: he died, weakened by starvation, of typhus at the notorious Terezin camp in Czechoslovakia. He was one of the most formidable and substantial of all the Surrealist poets, although much of his work has a deceptively playful surface. He is particularly famous for his poems for children, and for his writings on the cinema, which were collected in *Cinéma* (1966). The claim that he was a major poet of the 20th century is not a light one, but requires better investigation than it has so far had outside France. He has been attacked for abandoning Surrealism in favour of 'moralization' in his later work; but that attack has been challenged on the grounds that it misunderstands the profundity of his irony (which is, however, fully acknowledged in the earlier, more oneiric work). **André Breton** himself said of him that he had 'gone further than any of us into the unknown'. His works in translation include *22 Poems* (1971) and *The Voice* (1972).
▷M A Caws, *The Poetry of Dada and Surrealism* (1970)

DES PÉRIERS, Bonaventure
(c.1500–1544)

French writer, born in Autun. He was a member of the court of men of letters assembled by **Margaret of Angoulême**. In a dialogue, *Cymbalum mundi* (1537), under the pretence of attacking the superstitions of the ancients, he satirized the religious beliefs of his own day. The book raised a storm of indignation, against which Margaret was powerless to shield him; and rather than fall into the hands of his persecutors he is said to have killed himself. His *Nouvelles Récréations et joyeux devis* (1558, 'Novel Recreations and Delightful Talks') consists of 129 short stories, both comic and romantic. Des Périers has often been attributed with the chief authorship of Margaret's *Heptameron*.
▷J Nodier, *Bonaventures Des Périers* (1867)

DESPORTES, Philippe
(1546–1606)

French poet, born in Chartres, who was Henri III's court poet before succeeding **Ronsard**, with whom he had been associated, as 'prince of poets'. Opinions about him are divided: on the one hand he is said to have debased and enfeebled the style established by the Pléiade (Ronsard and six others) by 'prettifying' imitations from the Italians; on the other he is praised for his fluency and mastery of versification. The consensus is that he pleased a superficial public, but lacked learning or substance. His great enemy was the infinitely more gifted **François de Malherbe**.
▷G Brereton, *An Introduction to the French Poets* (1956)

DESSÌ, Guiseppe
(1909–77)

Italian novelist, born near Cagliare, in Sardinia. His first novel, *San Silvano* (1939), was influenced by **Joyce** and **Proust**. His best-known work, *Paese d'ombre* (1972, Eng trans *The Forests of Norbio*, 1975), is historical, and traces the life story of a man who lived from the time of the Risorgimento until the first part of the 20th century. Dessì was trying to do for Sardinia what **De Roberto** and **Lampedusa** had done for Sicily, and in large part he succeeded, although his book has not been regarded as of that quality. *Il disertore* (1961, Eng trans *The Deserter*, 1962), is an ironic novel about a coward and deserter who is accidentally decorated for bravery. Despite the translations of his work, Dessì has not yet received due credit, outside Italy, for his achievement.

DESTOUCHES, Philippe, originally Néricault
(1680–1754)

French playwright, born in Tours. He wrote 17 comedies, initially in the manner, but without the talent, of **Molière**. They include *Le Philosophe marié* (1727, 'The Married Philosopher') and *Le Glorieux* (1732, 'The Boaster'), his masterpiece. He spent six years in England as a diplomat from 1717 to 1723, and adapted **Addison**'s play *The Drummer* as *Le Tambour nocturne* (1733).
▷J Hankiss, *Destouches, l'homme et l'oeuvre* (1918)

DE TABLEY, Lord (John Byrne Leicester Warren)
(1835–95)

English poet and dramatist, born in Cheshire. He never achieved popularity, but became briefly well-known at his death. His verse, interesting for its anticipation of the decadent, fin de siècle style, was uninspired ('Time goes, old girl, time goes') and mostly imitative of **Tennyson**; but there are a few melancholy lyrics containing precise natural descriptions.
▷*Collected Poems* (1903); G B Taplin, *The Life, Works and Literary Reputation of Lord de Tabley* (1946)

DEUTSCH, Babette
(1895–1982)

American poet, novelist and critic, born in New York City. She published *Banners*, her first collection of poems, in 1919, the title piece celebrating the initial achievements of the Russian Revolution. Russia became a special interest for her. She translated **Alexander Blok**'s *The Twelve* with a Russian scholar she later married, and continued to translate from both Russian and German. Her *Epistle to Prometheus* (1931) is an ambitious, book-length poetic interpretation of human history. Her collected poems appeared in 1969. Her work is noted for its perceptive preoccupation with love, war and desolation, and the historical place and fate of women. Among Deutsch's novels is *A Brittle Heaven* (1926), an autobiographical tale of a writing mother, while her criticism includes the highly regarded *Poetry in Our Time* (1952).

▷ J Gould, *American Women Poets* (1980)

DEVAL, Jacques, pseud of **Jacques Boularan**
(1894–1972)

French boulevard playwright and novelist, best known for *Tovarich* (1933, 'Comrade'). A clever and witty comedy based on the theme of aristocrats forced into service—in this case White Russians in Paris—it ran, in the adaptation by **Robert Emmet Sherwood** (1936), for more than a year on Broadway and in London, and in more than 200 other cities. Deval, who served in the US army during World War II, wrote many other successful, superficial plays. One of his novels, the spy romance *Marie Galante* (1931), was presented on the stage in 1934 with music by Kurt Weill; it appeared as an American movie, featuring Spencer Tracy, in the same year.

DEVANEY, James Martin, journalistic pseud **Fabian**
(1890–1976)

Australian poet, short-story writer and journalist, born in Sandhurst (later Bendigo), Victoria, who spent much of his early life travelling the country, writing and teaching on outback stations. His love of the 'bush' and an observant eye enabled him to contribute nature notes for over 20 years to a Brisbane newspaper. His lyric poetry was first collected in *Fabian* (1923). Five collections followed, from which he selected *Poems*, published in 1950. He wrote some novels, including *The Currency Lass: A Tale of the Convict Days* (1927) and *Washdirt* (1946), a tale of the gold-rush days in his native Bendigo. Devaney cared for the poet **John Shaw Neilson** in Neilson's last years, wrote his biography, *Shaw Neilson* (1944), and edited a collection of Neilson's unpublished verse in 1946.

DEVANNEY, Jean
(1894–1962)

New Zealand-born novelist, born in Ferntown, South Island, who moved to Australia in 1929. Before leaving New Zealand she had published a book of short stories and four novels, one of which, *The Butcher Shop* (1926), had the distinction of being banned in Australia, New Zealand *and* Nazi Germany. Like many with her radical social beliefs, she visited the Soviet Union in the 1930s, but her continual challenging of authority caused her to be expelled from the Communist Party. However, her proletarian sympathies, as in *Sugar Heaven* (1936), the story of industrial action in the Queensland canefields (later translated into Russian), never faltered.

▷ *Points of Departure*, ed C Ferrier (1986)

DE VERE, Aubrey Thomas
(1814–1902)

Irish poet, born in Curragh Chase, County Limerick, the son of Sir Aubrey De Vere (1788–1846). Educated at Trinity College, Dublin, he became a friend of **Newman**, **Wordsworth** and **Tennyson**. In addition to many volumes of poems he published poetical dramas on Alexander the Great (1874) and Becket (1876), *Essays on Poetry* (2 vols, 1887), and works on Irish ecclesiastical politics and literary criticism.

DEVLIN, Denis
(1908–59)

Irish poet, born in Greenock, Scotland, and educated in Dublin, Munich and Paris; he served as a diplomat for much of his life. A skilled translator, his own work did not get its deserved respect and attention until the publication of *Collected Poems* (1964) and the more comprehensive *Collected Poems of Denis Devlin* (1989). His assimilation of Christian iconography into cosmopolitan settings has given him an important place in European verse-making.

DE VRIES, Peter
(1910–)

American novelist, born in Chicago of Dutch immigrant parents. He was educated at Dutch Reformed Calvinist schools but rebelled against their puritanism. He was the editor of a community newspaper in Chicago before working as a vending-machine operator, toffee-apple salesman, radio actor, furniture mover, lecturer to women's clubs, and associate editor of *Poetry*. In 1943 he lured **James Thurber** to Chicago to give a benefit lecture for *Poetry* and Thurber subsequently encouraged him to write for the *New Yorker*. This he did, later joining the editorial staff, and latterly restricting his contribution to captions for cartoons. A satirist in his mentor's mould, he plays with words like **S J Perelman** and is an inveterate (and inventive) punster and epigrammatist. He has written more than 20 novels, though none has eclipsed the reception of his first, *The Tunnel of Love* (1954).

DEYSSEL, Lodewijk van, pseud of **Karel Joan Lodewijk Alberdinck Thijm**
(1864–1952)

Dutch novelist, editor and critic, born in Amsterdam. His advocation of **Zola** led him to write the naturalistic novel *Een liefde* (1887, 'A Life'). Later he turned against naturalism and wrote an influential polemic against it (1891). He wrote essentially mystical prose poetry, and became Holland's most important critic, surveying virtually the whole of the lowlands culture in the 11 volumes of his *Verzamelde opstellen* (1922–3).
▷ H G M Prick, *Lodewijk van Deyssel* (1964, in Dutch)

DE ZAYAS Y SOTOMAYOR, Mariá
(1590–?1660)

Spanish poet, novelist and playwright. Born in Madrid but brought up in Naples, she was one of the most dynamic and imaginative women writers of her time. One of the strongest defenders of women's rights of the century, she has been cited in modern times as one of the most effective pre-modern feminists. Though she was greatly praised in her day as a poet by such writers as **Lope Félix de Vega Carpio** and Castillo Solórzano, she is most famous for her short stories, which draw on the traditions of the Spanish picaresque novel, the pastoral novel and the work of **Boccaccio**. Her two most important books are *Novelas amorosas y ejemplares* (1637, 'Exemplary and Amorous Novels', published in Zaragoza, where she lived for a large part of her life), and *Desengaños amorosos, parte segunda del sarao y entretenimientos honestos* (1647, 'Disenchantments of Love, the Second Part of the Party and Entertainment'). It is not clear when she died, and she may have spent the last years of her life in reclusion in a convent.

DHONDY, Farrukh
(1944–)

English novelist, television editor and writer for children, born in Poona, India. Since his first collection of stories for children, *Come To Mecca* (1978), he has proven his versatility by working in a variety of media in different roles. *The Siege of Babylon* (1978) was a children's novel about a botched robbery, but since then he has increasingly written for an older audience. *Bombay Duck* (1990), his first novel for adults, set in London, Edinburgh, Delhi and Bombay, was a rich mixture of old myths and new. As a commissioning editor for Channel 4 television, he has played a central role in encouraging writing talent from, in particular, Britain's black and Asian communities.

DHU AL-NUN AYYUB
(1908–)

Leading Iraqi novelist, a professor of physics and chemistry, whose *Duktur Ibrahim* (1939, 'Doctor Ibrahim') analyses a Western intellectual to devastating effect; *Wa ala al-dunya al-salam* (1972, 'Farewell to the World') depicts struggles in his own country in the preceding decade. He was in exile in Vienna between 1954 and 1958 for political reasons, and wrote about this in a number of short stories, which were well thought of.

DIAMOND, I A L, originally **Itek Dommnici**
(1920–88)

Romanian-born American screenwriter. An immigrant to America in 1929, he graduated from Columbia University in New York and displayed sufficient promise to secure a contract as a junior writer at Paramount Studios (1941–3). He first received screen credit as the writer of the minor musical thriller *Murder In The Blue Room* (1944). His subsequent work comprised a string of generally undistinguished broad comedies and musicals before he embarked on a 25-year collaboration with the writer-director Billy Wilder (1906–) on *Love In The Afternoon* (1957). Together, they created witty, incisive classics of contemporary American cinema, including the uproarious farce *Some Like It Hot* (1959), bittersweet romantic comedies such as *The Apartment* (1960) and *Avanti!* (1972), and such cynical explorations of modern morality as *Kiss Me Stupid* (1964) and *The Fortune Cookie* (1966). He received the Writer's Guild Laurel Award in 1979 and collaborated a final time with Wilder on *Buddy, Buddy* (1981).

DIAPER, William
(1685–1717)

English poet, born in Bridgwater, Somerset, of a poor family. After graduating from Balliol College, Oxford, he entered the church and held various country curacies but was never ordained priest, remaining poverty-stricken despite efforts by **Swift** to help him. He published translations of classical authors, and pastoral verse: *Nereides: or, Sea-Eclogues* (1712, with mermen instead of shepherds), and *Dryades* (1712). Delicate observation of the natural world enlivens their conscious classicism. His *Brent* (posthumously pub-

lished, 1727) anticipates **George Crabbe** in its anti-pastoral realism and satirical bite.
▷*Complete Works*, ed with life and critical introduction by D Broughton (1951)

DIAZ DEL CASTILLO, Bernal
(?1492–1584)

Spanish historian, one of the more colourful of the *cronistas* of the Spanish conquest, who began as a soldier in the army of the conquistador Cortés in the attack on the Aztecs. Noted for its combination of character and anecdote, his *Historia Verdadera de la Conquista de la Nueva España* (abridged Eng trans *The Discovery and Conquest of Mexico*, 1956) gives a more human view of the conquest than other official histories. One of the main goals of his work was to correct the errors of earlier historians. His down-to-earth style is almost gossipy, full of digressions, stories, and repetitions reminiscent of the *novelas de caballería* and the epic romances.

DICK, Philip K(indred)
(1928–82)

American writer of science fiction, born in Chicago, Illinois. Educated at Berkeley High School, he worked as a record store manager and as a radio announcer. His career had two distinct phases; the first, from 1952 to 1955, remarkable for a profusion of short stories, the second, starting in 1962, notable for a torrent of novels. Despite a penchant for modish titles—*Do Androids Dream of Electric Sheep?* (1968) and *Galactic Pot-Healer* (1969), the story of a master-potter who has never thrown his own pots—he was not so much interested in technological gimickry and space-age jargon as in his characters. A spare and humorous writer, he received the Hugo Award in 1963.

DICKENS, Charles John Huffam
(1812–70)

English author, born in Landport, then a little suburb of Portsmouth. His father was John Dickens, a clerk in the navy pay office, and at that time attached to Portsmouth dockyard. In 1814 he was transferred to London, and in 1816 to Chatham, where, already a great reader, he got some schooling. In 1821 the family fell into trouble; reforms in the Admiralty made his father redundant and they had to leave Chatham, and moved to London, where they took a small house in Camden Town. But the father was soon arrested for debt in 1824 and sent to the Marshalsea prison with his whole family, apart from Charles, who was sent to work in a blacking factory at Hungerford Market, where, with half a dozen rough boys, he labelled the blacking bottles. Not only were his

days passed in this wretched work, but the child was left entirely to himself at night, when he had four miles to walk to his lonely bedroom in lodgings in Camden Town. On Sundays he visited his parents in the prison. On his father's release they all went back to Camden Town, and the boy was sent again to school, an academy in the Hampstead Road, for three or four years, after which he worked for a solicitor as an office boy (1827). Meantime, however, his father had obtained a post as reporter for the *Morning Herald*, and Charles decided also to attempt the profession of journalist. He taught himself shorthand; and he visited the British Museum daily to supplement some of the shortcomings of his reading. In 1828 he became a reporter of debates at the House of Commons for the *Morning Chronicle*, but at that time he was only interested in being an actor. It was not until 1835 that he succeeded in getting permanent employment on the staff of a London paper as a reporter and in this capacity he was sent around the country. Meanwhile in December 1833, the *Monthly Magazine* published a sketch 'Dinner at Poplar Walk', under the pen-name 'Boz' (the nickname of his younger brother, Augustus Moses). Other papers followed, but produced nothing for the contributor except the gratification of seeing them in print. He soon made an arrangement to contribute papers and sketches regularly to the *Evening Chronicle*, continuing to act as reporter for the *Morning Chronicle*, and getting his salary increased. The *Sketches by Boz* were collected and published early in 1836, the author receiving £150 for the copyright; he later bought it back for 11 times that amount. In the last week of March of that year appeared the first number of the *Pickwick Papers*; three days afterwards he married Catherine, the daughter of his friend George Hogarth, Editor of the *Evening Chronicle*. She bore him seven sons and three daughters between 1837 and 1852, three of whom predeceased him; in 1858 husband and wife separated. Success having definitely come his way, Dickens for the rest of his life allowed himself scant respite. In fulfilment of publishers' engagements he produced *Oliver Twist* (1837–9), which appeared in *Bentley's Miscellany*, and which Dickens edited for a time, *Nicholas Nickleby* (1838–9), *Master Humphrey's Clock*, a serial miscellany which resolved itself into the two stories, *The Old Curiosity Shop* (1840–1) and *Barnaby Rudge* (1841). From then on a great part of Dickens's life was spent abroad; especially notable were his visits to America in 1842 and 1867–8, his stay in Genoa in 1844–5 and in Lausanne in 1846, and his summers spent in Boulogne in 1853, 1854, and 1856. Meanwhile there came from his pen an incessant stream:

DICKENS, Monica Enid

American Notes (1842), *Martin Chuzzlewit* (1843), *The Christmas Tales—A Christmas Carol, The Chimes, The Cricket on the Hearth, The Battle of Life, The Haunted Man* and *The Ghost's Bargain* (1843, 1846 and 1848); *Pictures from Italy* (1845), *Dombey and Son* (1846–8), *David Copperfield* (1849–50), *Bleak House* (1852–3), *A Child's History of England* (1854), *Hard Times* (1854), *Little Dorrit* (1855–7), *A Tale of Two Cities* (1859), *The Uncommercial Traveller* (1861), the Christmas numbers in *Household Words* and *All the Year Round, Great Expectations* (1860–1), *Our Mutual Friend* (1864–5) and *The Mystery of Edwin Drood* (1870, unfinished). To this long roll must be added public readings (1858–70), both in Britain and in America, private theatricals, speeches, innumerable letters, pamphlets, plays, the running of a popular magazine—first (1850) called *Household Words* and then (1859) *All the Year Round.* The scale of his achievement seems all but unrepeatable in the history of English fiction. He is the most widely known English writer after **Shakespeare**, and no other novelist has managed to find both popular success and critical respect on such a lavish scale. The breadth, perception and sympathy of his writing, his abiding concern with social deprivation and injustice, his ability to conjure up memorable characters in a few paragraphs (many of which have found an almost independent, semi-mythical status in the broader cultural consciousness), and the comic genius which permeates even his most serious works, have all ensured that he continues to find a receptive audience, both for the books themselves and in film and stage adaptations of his work. He died suddenly at Gadshill, near Rochester (the place he had coveted as a boy, and purchased in 1856), and was buried in Westminster Abbey.

▷J Butt and K Tillotson, *Dickens at Work* (1957); J Carey, *The Violent Effigy* (1973); P Ackroyd, *Dickens* (1990)

DICKENS, Monica Enid
(1915–92)

English novelist and author of non-fiction, born in London and a great-grand-daughter of **Charles Dickens**. After a disrupted education and her presentation at court as a débutante, she produced a series of semi-autobiographical novels. These include *One Pair of Feet* (1942), deriving from her nursing training in the early years of World War II, and *My Turn to Make the Tea* (1951), from her days as a junior reporter on a local newspaper. She developed in her writing a compassion for human problems such as alcoholism, the subject of *The Heart of London* (1961), and child abuse, which she examined in *Kate and Emma* (1964). For 20 years she was a popular columnist for *Women's Own* magazine.

▷*An Open Book* (1978)

DICKEY, James Lafayette
(1923–)

American poet and novelist. Born in Georgia, he was alleged to be President Jimmy Carter's favourite writer of verse, sharing with him an intense concern for the fragile harmony of nature and human enterprise. This is the substance of much of his verse from the first collection *Into the Stone* (1960), *Drowning with Others* (1962, republished in part as *The Owl King,* 1977) and *Helmets* (1964). Dickey's wider fame depends on his one novel, *Deliverance* (1972), a **Hemingway**esque rite of passage set against the damming and flooding of a wild valley. It was successfully filmed by John Boorman. Later poetry collections emphasized Dickey's deep narrative urge: *The Zodiac* (1976), *The Strength of Fields* (1977), whose title poem was written for Carter's inauguration, the remarkable *Head-Deep in Strange Sounds: Free Flight Improvisations from the UnEnglish* (1979) and *Falling, May Day Sermon and Other Poems* (1981). Dickey's poems have been collected in three volumes: *Poems, 1957–1967* (1967), *The Achievement of James Dickey* (1968) and *The Central Motion: Poems 1968–1979* (1983). The *Self-Interviews* (1970) are just that.

▷B Weigl and T R Hummer (eds), *The Imagination as Glory* (1984)

DICKINSON, Emily Elizabeth
(1830–86)

American poet, born in Amherst, Massachusetts, the daughter of an autocratic lawyer who became a Congressman. She was educated at Amherst Academy and Mount Holyoke Female Seminary in South Hadley. She spent her whole life in the family home at Amherst. A mystic by inclination, she withdrew herself at 23 from most social contacts and lived an intensely secluded life, writing in secret over a thousand poems. All but one or two of these remained unpublished until after her death, when her sister Lavinia brought out three volumes between 1891 and 1896 which were acclaimed as the work of a poetic genius. Further collections appeared, as *The Single Hound* (1914) and *Bolts of Melody* (1945). Her lyrics, intensely personal and often spiritual, show great originality both in thought and in form, and have had considerable influence on modern poetry.

▷C G Wolf, *Emily Dickinson: a biography* (1986)

DICKINSON, Goldsworthy Lowes
(1862–1932)

English academic, essayist and poet, born in London and educated at King's College, Cambridge, of which he became a fellow in 1887. He taught classics and political science, among other subjects, writing books on these topics and on international peace (he played a part in the founding of the League of Nations); his *The Greek View of Life* (1896) was a popular introduction to Ancient Greece. According to **W H Auden**, Dickinson had 'little talent' for poetry, a view borne out by *Poems* (1896) and other volumes. More successful were his *Letters from John Chinaman* (1901), a critique of Western ways, written in poetic prose and the fantasy *The Magic Flute* (1920). His autobiography, published in 1973, deals frankly with his homosexuality.
▷ E M Forster, *Goldsworthy Lowes Dickinson* (1934)

DICKINSON, Peter Malcolm de Brissac
(1927–)

African-born British writer of detective fiction and other novels, born in Livingstone, Zambia. Educated at Eton College and Cambridge, he writes with the same solid Englishness demonstrated by his series detective Superintendent James Pibble, who appeared in Dickinson's first detective novel *Skin Deep* (1968, published in the USA as *The Glass-Sided Ants' Nest*), and five others. His best novel is perhaps *The Poison Oracle* (1974), which deals with environmental menace within the context of a murder mystery. Between 1952 and 1969, Dickinson was an assistant editor at *Punch*, and his prose style occasionally evinces the heavy-handed polysyllabic irony the magazine once favoured. At his best, though, he is an intelligent literary technician with a gift for subtle, multi-faceted plotting.

DICKMANN, Max
(1908–)

Argentinian novelist and translator (**Dos Passos**, **Faulkner**), born in Buenos Aires. 'The most tenacious upholder of socially conscious realism in 20th-century Argentinian literature', he had his greatest success with *Madre América* (1935), a novel in the style of Dos Passos; but it was not translated. He was a member, with **Arlt**, of the Boedo group of writers who favoured proletarian fiction in the Scandinavian manner, in contrast to the Florida group of **Borges** who favoured verse and European literature in general. His work attracted less and less critical attention, and he exiled himself to the mountains, publishing nothing after 1968; more recently critics have

started to point out what a 'widespread impact' his fiction in fact had, and it is now being re-read and re-appraised for its bitterness and honesty.
▷ N Lindstrom, *Jewish Issues in Argentine Literature from Gerchunoff to Szichman* (1989)

DIDEROT, Denis
(1713–84)

French writer, born in Langres in Champagne, the son of a master cutler. Trained by the Jesuits at home and in Paris, he refused to become either a lawyer or a physician, and was thrown upon his own resources, and worked as tutor and bookseller's hack (1734–44). In 1743 he married a young seamstress, who contrived to bring about a temporary reconciliation between father and son; but the marriage was not happy, and he had many love affairs. His *Pensées philosophiques* (1796, Eng trans *Philosophical Thoughts*, 1916) was burned by the parlement of Paris in 1746, and in 1749 he was imprisoned for his *Lettre sur les aveugles* (1749, Eng trans *An Essay on Blindness*, 1750). In 1748 he had published his first novel, *Les Bijoux indiscrets* (Eng trans *The Indiscreet Toys*, 1749). The bookseller Le Breton now invited him to edit an expanded translation of Ephraim Chambers's *Cyclopaedia* (1727) with d'Alembert. In Diderot's hands the character of the work was transformed. He enlisted nearly all the important French writers of the time as contributors, and, in place of a compendium of useful information, produced a work of propaganda for the *philosophe* party. For some 20 years he retained his post in spite of dangers and drawbacks. The sale of *Encyclopédie* was again and again prohibited, and its editor ran a constant risk of imprisonment or exile. D'Alembert abandoned him in despair in 1758. But his marvellous energy, his varied knowledge, and his faculty of rallying his fellow workers, enabled him to carry his vast undertaking to a successful conclusion. The first volume of the *Encyclopédie, ou Dictionnaire Raisonné des Sciences, des Arts et des Métiers* ('Encyclopaedia, or Critical Dictionary of Sciences, Arts and Trades') appeared in 1751; the 35th and last in 1776. In his later years he was rescued from financial difficulties by Catherine the Great of Russia, to whom in 1773 he paid a five-month visit. He died of apoplexy. One of the most prolific and versatile of writers, he was a novelist and a dramatist, a satirist, a philosopher, a critic of pictures and books, and a brilliant letter writer. His works also include *Pensées sur l'interprétation de la Nature* (1753, 'Thoughts on the Interpretation of Nature'), and two novels: *La Religieuse* (1796, Eng trans *The Nun*, 1797), an exposure of convent life; and

the **Laurence Sterne**-like *Jacques le Fataliste et son Maître* (1796, Eng trans *James the Fatalist and his Master*, 1797). In *Le Neveu de Rameau* (1821, Eng trans *Rameau's Nephew*, 1897), an imaginary conversation between the author and a parasite, the follies of society are laid bare with sardonic humour and piercing insight. His plays were somewhat unsuccessful examples of melodrama, the best efforts being two short pieces: *La Pièce et le prologue* (1820, 'The Play and the Prologue') and *Est-il bon? Est-il méchant?* (1784, 'Is He Good? Is He Bad?', not produced until 1913). His letters to Sophie Volland form the most interesting section of his voluminous correspondence. As a critic he stood far in advance of his contemporaries, and anticipated the Romanticists. His *Salons* (not published until 1957–67, in 4 vols), remarks on pictures exhibited, are the earliest example of modern aesthetic criticism.
▷L G Crocker, *The Embattled Philosopher: a biography of Diderot* (1954, rev edn 1966); other works by Crocker; P France, *Diderot* (1974)

DIDION, Joan
(1934–)

American writer, born in Sacramento, California. She was educated at the University of California at Berkeley (1952–6) and married the writer **John Gregory Dunne** in 1964. From 1956 to 1963 she was associate feature editor of *Vogue* in New York and has worked and written for the *Saturday Evening Post*, *Esquire*, and *National Review*. Her columns were published as *Slouching Towards Bethlehem* (1968) and *The White Album* (1979). Her novels portray contemporary social tensions in a laconic style that has aroused much admiration. *Run River* (1963) was her first novel, but she is best known for *A Book of Common Prayer* (1977), set in a banana republic devoid of history, and *Democracy* (1984), about the long and amorous affair between a politician's wife and Jack Lovett, a man who embodies everything her ambitious husband is not.
▷B Morton, *The Princess in the Consulate: the novels of Joan Didion* (1980)

DIGBY, Kenelm Henry
(1800–80)

English writer, born in Ireland, the youngest son of the Dean of Clonfert. Educated at Trinity College, Cambridge, he published a survey of medieval customs, *The Broad Stone of Honour* (1822), with additional volumes in 1828–9 and 1877, which was influential in the 19th-century cult of medievalism. Converted to Roman Catholicism, he published *Mores Catholici* (1831–42) and other works, including poetry.

▷K G Huston, *Sir Kenelm Digby: a checklist* (1969)

DIKTONIUS, Elmer
(1896–1961)

Finland–Swedish modernist poet, born into a Swedish-speaking family in Helsinki at a time when Finland was still part of the Russian tsar's realm. In the Civil War following Finnish independence in 1917, he sided with the Finnish Red militia. His social and political passion was linked to his broad view of life: his intentions to become a composer thwarted, he turned away from music to the written word as an instrument of expression. He was bilingual, and wrote poetry as well as prose in both Swedish and Finnish. His first collection of poems and aphorisms, *Min dikt* (1921, 'My poetry'), showed the influence of **Nietzsche** and of **Edith Södergran**, the figurehead of Finland–Swedish modernism. The powerful and daring stanzas of his programmatic poem *Jaguaren* ('The Jaguar'), in the collection *Hårda Sånger* (1922, 'Hard Songs'), demonstrates with a tremendous energy his desire to break with the literary norms and lifestyle of the past. The collection *Stark men mörk* (1930, 'Strong but Dark') marks the end of this period: in his later poems revolutionary idealism gave way to a more peaceful emphasis, on nature and the 'small things' in life. Sadly, Diktonius's creative power was lost prematurely: he spent the last few years of his life in a mental hospital.
▷G C Schoolfield, *Elmer Diktonius* (1985)

DILLARD, Annie
(1945–)

American essayist, poet and fiction writer, born in Pittsburgh, Pennsylvania and educated at Hollins College, where she received both her BA and MA. She has worked as a contributing editor at *Harpers* magazine and as an adjunct professor at Wesleyan University, and has contributed to such diverse publications as *Atlantic Monthly* and *Sports Illustrated*. Her work often concentrates on the search for the spiritual in the natural environment, and in 1974 she won a Pulitzer Prize for her collection of essays entitled *Pilgrim at Tinker Creek*. She has won a number of other awards, including a Washington Governor's Award in 1978 and a Guggenheim Foundation Grant (1984–5).
▷C Rainwater and W Scheick (eds), *Contemporary American Women Writers: Narrative Strategies* (1985)

DILLON, George
(1906–68)

American poet, translator and editor (of *Poetry*, 1937–50), born in Jacksonville, Florida. With the mellifluous collection *The*

Flowering Stone (1931) he won a Pulitzer Prize; but thereafter he concentrated, for the most part, on translation: eg his rendering of *Flowers of Evil*, by **Baudelaire**, with **Edna St Vincent Millay**, published in 1936, and his well thought of *Three Plays* (1961) of **Jean Racine**.

DIMT, C *see* **BUSTA, Christine**

DINESEN, Isak *see* **BLIXEN, Karen, Baroness**

DING LING, pseud of **Jiang Bingzhi**
(1904–86)

Chinese novelist and short-story writer, born in Linli County, Hunan Province. A radical feminist, her father died when she was three and her mother flouted tradition by enrolling in school and becoming a teacher. Jiang was educated at Beijing University, where she attended left-wing classes and started publishing stories of rebelliousness against traditional society, such as *The Diary of Miss Sophia* (1928), which dealt candidly with questions of female psychology and sexual desires, *Birth of an Individual* (1929), and *A Woman* (1930). She joined the League of Left-Wing Writers in 1930 and became editor of its official journal. She joined the Communist Party in 1932, and after a spell of imprisonment, escaped to the communist base at Yenan, where she became a star attraction for Western journalists. Her outspoken comments on male chauvinism and discrimination at Yenan led to her being disciplined by the party leaders, until her novel, *The Sun Shines over the Sanggan River* (1948), about land-reform, restored her to favour. In 1958, however, she was 'purged', and sent to raise chickens in the Heilongjiang reclamation area known as the Great Northern Wilderness (Beidahuang). She was imprisoned (1970–5) during the Cultural Revolution, but rehabilitated by the party in 1979, and published a novel based on her experiences in the Great Northern Wilderness, *Comrade Du Wanxiang* (1979).

DINGELSTEDT, Franz von
(1814–81)

German poet and novelist, born in Halsdorf, near Marburg. He began writing as a journalist and satirical novelist and poet with radical views, and published the novels *Die neuen Argonauten* (1839, 'The New Argonauts') and *Unter der Erde* (1840, 'Under the Earth'), but then converted to establishment views. He was royal librarian at Württemberg from 1843 to 1850, and director of the court theatres at Munich, Weimar and Vienna. He

wrote stories, novels and plays, but is best remembered for his work as director of these theatres.
▷M Sauerlandt, *Franz von Dingelstedt* (1854); and other works by Sauerlandt

DINIS, Julio, pseud of **Joaquim Guilherme Gomes Coelho**
(1839–71)

Portuguese novelist, a lecturer in medicine, who was born and died—of tuberculosis—in Oporto. Often ignored as dull and guilty of idealizing the rural people in whose lives he was most interested, certain critics still find him a 'demure chronicler of quiet scenes' with 'an originality which so often eludes those who most furiously pursue it', and even as having a 'touch of Jane Austen'. However, the chief influences upon him were **Dickens**, **Thackeray** and **Balzac**. Certainly such novels as *Uma Familia Inglesa* (1868, 'An English Family'), while in certain respects over-optimistic about human nature, are punctuated with shrewd psychological insight and uncanny anticipations of the technique of interior monologue.
▷A F G Bell, *Portuguese Literature* (1922)

DINIZ DA CRUZ E SILVA, Antonio
(1731–99)

Portuguese poet, born in Lisbon. He took a law degree at the University of Coimbra in 1753, and became a founder member of the *Arcadia Lusitana*, a society dedicated to the revival of national poetry. He wrote the epic poem, *O Hyssope* (1774), and *Odes Pindaricas* (published posthumously in 1801), lyrics which earned him the title of the 'Portuguese Pindar'. His later life was spent in Brazil.

DIOGENES LAERTIUS
(3rd century)

Greek writer, whose *Lives of the Greek Philosophers*, in 10 books, gives a second-hand account of the principal Greek thinkers, but provides much information not otherwise available, as well as extracts from the work of writers which has not survived in other forms.

DIONYSIUS OF HALICARNASSUS
(1st century BC)

Greek critic, historian and rhetorician. From 30 BC he lived and worked in Rome. He wrote, in Greek, *Rōmaïkē Archaeologia*, a history of Rome down to 264 BC, a mine of information about the constitution, religion, history, laws and private life of the Romans. Of its 20 books, only the first nine are complete. He also wrote a number of valuable critical treat-

ises on literature and rhetoric, particularly *On the Arrangement of Words.*
▷ S F Bonner, *The Literary Treatises of Dionysius* (1939)

DIOP, Birago
(1906–90)

Francophone Senegalese veterinary surgeon who went into the diplomatic service, but then returned to care for animals. He was both a poet and a story writer, and in the last capacity became the greatest transcriber from the *griots* (oral storytellers) of his continent. His narrator was the Wolof, Amadou Koumba, a real *griot*; a selection of his incomparable and profound animal tales is translated in *Tales of Amadou Koumba* (1966).

DI PRIMA, Diane
(1934–)

American poet, playwright and novelist. Born in New York City and educated in Pennsylvania, between 1961 and 1963 she co-edited the poetry journal *Floating Bear* with LeRoi Jones (later known as **Amiri Baraka**), continuing as sole editor until 1969. With her first husband Alan Marlowe, she founded the New York Poets Theatre in 1961, the year of her second poetry collection, *The Monster.* Di Prima writes in many voices, the exotic and marvellous in her first book, *This Kind of Bird Flies Backward* (1958) and in *The New Handbook of Heaven* (1963); the directly personal in *Poems for Freddie* (1966, reprinted as *Freddie Poems*, 1974); the socially committed in *Revolutionary Letters* (1968). Since 1973, di Prima has worked on the *Loba* cycle, a self-defining work-in-progress that examines aspects of femininity in a physical, emotional and mythic way. Related works include *Brass Furnace Going Out: Song, After an Abortion* (1975). Her novel, *Memoirs of a Beatnik* (1969), is a comic performance.

DISCH, Thomas Michael
(1940–)

American science-fiction writer and poet, born in Des Moines, Iowa. His first novel, *The Genocides*, appeared in 1965, but he earned a reputation as a writer of serious intent and disturbingly dark vision with *Camp Concentration* (1968), a political allegory set in a near-future USA, but reflecting the repression of anti-war protests of the day. That dark, pessimistic vision is also evident in *Mankind Under the Leash* (1966) and in several volumes of stories, the most important of which is *Getting Into Death* (1973, rev edn 1976). The novel *On Wings of Song* (1979) is more optimistic in tone. He has also written mainstream and horror novels, stories for children, and several volumes of poetry,

including *The Right Way to Figure Plumbing* (1971), *Burn This* (1982) and *Dark Verses and Light* (1991).

DISRAELI, Benjamin, 1st Earl of Beaconsfield
(1804–81)

British novelist and statesman, born in London. He was the eldest son of the Jewish writer **Isaac D'Israeli**, but his father, after a quarrel with his synagogue, had him baptized in 1817. He was educated at a private school in Walthamstow, and was articled as a solicitor. His first novel, *Vivian Grey* (1826), in which he imbued the youthful hero with much of his own arrogant demeanour and quick wit, was a great success. Elected to parliament in 1837, he became the head of the radical 'Young England' group of Tory MPs. As Chancellor of the Exchequer, he was responsible for the passage of the Reform Bill through parliament in 1867, and was twice prime minister at periods of great political ferment at home and abroad. As a writer, he is an important Victorian novelist, and followed his early success with a satirical work, *The Voyage of Captain Popanilla* (1827), and a society novel, *The Young Duke* (1831). He continued to write while establishing his parliamentary career, producing a string of novels which included *Contarini Fleming* (1832), *Alroy* (1833), *Ixion in Heaven* (1833), *The Infernal Marriage* (1834), *Henrietta Temple* (1837) and *Venetia* (1837), a novel about **Shelley** and **Byron**. His best-known and most politically influential novels are the 'state of the nation' trilogy of the 1840s, *Coningsby, or, The New Generation* (1844), *Sybil, or The Two Nations* (1845) and *Tancred, or The New Crusade* (1847). His periods of office inevitably slowed down his writing, but he went on to publish two more novels, *Lothair* (1870) and *Endymion* (1880), and left another, *Falconet*, unfinished at his death. He claimed that 'works are my life', and neatly symbolized that claim by taking the title 1st Earl of Beaconsfield on his elevation to the peerage in 1876, having originally invented it in his first novel.
▷ W Meynell, *Benjamin Disraeli: An Unconventional Biography* (1927); A Maorois, *The Life of Disraeli* (1928); M Komroff, *Disraeli* (1963)

D'ISRAELI, Isaac
(1776–1848)

English writer, born in Enfield, the son of a Jewish merchant of Italian descent, and father of **Benjamin Disraeli**. In 1801 he became a British subject. Although he had wished to be a creative writer, and published one or two novels, his *forte* was in literary illustrations of persons and history, as in his

Curiosities of Literature (1791–1834), *Calamities of Authors* (1812) and a commentary on Charles I (1831). **Byron** was an admirer of his work.

▷J Ogden, *Isaac D'Israeli* (1969)

DITLEVSEN, Tove
(1918–76)

Danish poet, novelist and short-story writer, whose autobiographical *Gift* (1971) was a shockingly frank portrayal of the author's sexual and marital problems and her drug addiction; the Danish word '*gift*' for 'married' also means 'toxin' or 'poison'. The same concerns are also explored in *Vilhelms Vaerelse* (1973, 'Vilhelm's Place'), which exposes a catastrophic marriage to the cold light one associates with Swedish film director Ingmar Bergman. Ditlevsen grew up in a working-class district of Copenhagen and came to attention with *Pigesind* (1939, 'A Young Girl's Mind'), a sequence of frank and probing lyrics which she continued a decade and a half later with *Kvinesind* (1955, 'A Woman's Mind'). Though often unsettling in their directness, her works retain an essential warmth and humanity, and a great sense of place.

▷ *Tove Ditlevsen om sig selv* (1975)

DIXON, Richard Watson
(1833–1900)

English poet, born in Islington. He studied at King Edward's School, Birmingham, Pembroke College, Oxford, and became a canon of Carlisle in 1874 and vicar of Warkworth in 1883. A member of the Pre-Raphaelite circle with Edward Burne-Jones and **William Morris**, and a teacher and supporter of **Gerard Manley Hopkins**, he wrote seven volumes of poetry and a *History of the Church of England* (6 vols, 1877–1902).

▷A Sambrook, *A Poet Hidden* (1962)

DIXON, Thomas
(1864–1946)

American novelist, born in North Carolina, but best known for his novels about the Reconstruction era, in which he expounded extreme and often violent segregationist views. Though he wrote more than 20 novels, the most celebrated is *The Clansman* (1905), part two of a trilogy begun with *The Leopard's Spots* (1902) and concluded with *The Traitor* (1907). Dixon dramatized it himself, but it received its widest dissemination (not necessarily in a context Dixon could have approved) as the basis of the Ku Klux Klan scenes in D W Griffiths's classic motion picture *The Birth of a Nation* (1914). Dixon himself experimented with film-making, attracted by its propagandist potential.

DJALSKI, Ksaver Sandor, pseud of **Ljubo Bratić**
(1854–1935)

Croatian novelist and story writer, born in Gredice. He was a prolific realist, much underrated outside his own country. An ardent nationalist, deeply influenced by **Balzac** and—less usually—by **Turgenev**, he moved, in his chronicles of the Croatian society (of all levels) of the end of the 19th century, from a bleak but refined pessimism to a mysticism which has seldom been well understood or appreciated. There is a translation of one of his stories in the *Slavonic and East European Review* (XVIII, 25, 1939), but otherwise his fine and subtle fiction cannot be as widely read as it deserves. He was an uneven writer, but at his best, as in the tales of *Pod starim krovovima* (1886, 'Under Old Roofs'), he was worthy to stand beside even **Senoa**.

DJORDIJIĆ, Ignjac
(1675–1737)

Dalmatian Jesuit (latterly Benedictine) poet, who is important as the last true representative of what is known as 'Dalmatian' or 'Dubrovnik' or 'Ragusan' (Dubrovnik was formerly called Ragusa) literature. This had grown up almost entirely because of Italian influences; but, while the 14th-century men knew Italian, the women did not—and so the men began to write in their own vernacular in order to impress the women. Djordijić wrote original religious poetry, much of which is also about love, just at the time when his literature went into decline owing to the opening up of Atlantic trade and the decline in the prosperity of Dubrovnik.

DJURHUUS, Jens H O
(1881–1948)

Faroese poet, whose *Yrkingar* (1914, 'Poems'), is the first individual collection to be published in Faroese. The poems have been said to be 'worthy, gloomy and tedious'.

DOBELL, Sydney Thompson
(1824–74)

English poet, born in Cranbrook, Kent. He worked with his father as a wine merchant in London and Cheltenham, but lived for some time in the Scottish Highlands and abroad, and became a passionate advocate of oppressed nationalities. His dramatic poem, *The Roman* (1850), was written in sympathy with Italian aspirations for unity, and he also wrote sonnets on the Crimean War (1855) and *England in Time of War* (1856). His chief works were in the style of the so-called Spasmodic School, caricatured by **William**

DÖBLIN, Alfred

Aytoun, appearing under the pseudonym Sydney Yendys.

▷ E Jolly (ed), *Life and Letters of Sydney Thompson Dobell* (1878)

DÖBLIN, Alfred
(1878–1957)

German novelist, born in Stettin. He grew up in Berlin, studied medicine at Berlin and Freiburg, and practised as a doctor and psychiatrist in Berlin from 1911. He published stories in the revolutionary expressionist journal *Der Sturm*, and a collection in 1913. He liked to work on a broad scale, however, as in the epic novels *Die drei Sprünge des Wang-Lun* (1915, 'The Three Leaps of Wan Lung'), an account of a failed rebellion set in 18th-century China, the satirical fantasy *Wadzek's Kampf mit der Dampfturbine* (1918, 'Wadzek's Fight with the Steam Machine'), *Wallenstein* (1920), and the futuristic *Berge Meere und Giganten* (1924, Eng trans *Giganten*, 1932). His masterpiece is *Berlin Alexanderplatz* (1929, Eng trans *Alexanderplatz Berlin*, 1931), the story of a hapless reformed criminal named Franz Biberkopf in the dark underworld of Weimar Germany. It is a modernist classic, and was influenced by the example of **James Joyce**. His socialist sympathies and Jewish background forced him to leave Germany for France in 1933, and he became a French citizen in 1936. He continued to write ambitious works in which the individual is in contention with huge and often deterministic social and historical forces, as in the novels *Pardon wird nicht gegeben* (1935, Eng trans *Men Without Mercy*, 1937) and the *Amazonas-Trilogie* (1937–47, 'The Amazon Trilogy'), as well as the later trilogy *November 1918* (1948–50). He fled to the USA in 1940, escaping through the Iberian peninsula in a hazardous journey described in *Shicksalreise* (1949, 'Fateful Journey'). He converted to the Roman Catholic faith in 1941, and returned to Germany in 1945, where he was a co-founder of the Academy of Science and Literature in 1949. He moved to France in 1951, but his last years were afflicted by illness, and he died in a nursing home in Baden-Württemberg. His last novel was *Hamlet oder Die lange Nacht nimmt ein Ende* (1956, 'Hamlet, or the Long Night is Ended').

DOBRACZYNSKI, Jan
(1910–)

Polish novelist and literary critic. He is a Catholic who writes novels on religious themes, notably in *Wybráncy gwiazd* and *Listy Nikodema* (1948–52, Eng trans *The Letters of Nicodemus*, 1958). Critics not of the Catholic faith have tended to ignore him.

DOBSON, Henry Austin
(1840–1921)

English poet, born in Plymouth. He was educated at Beaumaris, Coventry, and Strasbourg as a civil engineer like his father, but from 1856 to 1901 was a board of trade clerk. His earliest poems, published in 1868 in *St Paul's Magazine*, were followed by *Vignettes in Rhyme* (1873), *Proverbs in Porcelain* (1877), *At the Sign of the Lyre* (1885), *The Story of Rosina* (1895) and *Collected Poems* (1897, rev edns 1902, 1909, 1913). Often in rondeau, ballade or villanelle form, these poems are marked by rare perfection. In prose he published monographs of **Henry Fielding** (1883), **Richard Steele**, Thomas Bewick (and his pupils), **Horace Walpole**, Hogarth, **Oliver Goldsmith**, **Fanny Burney** and **Samuel Richardson** (1902); and *Eighteenth Century Vignettes* (1892–6), *Four Frenchwomen* and other collections of graceful and erudite essays.

DOBSON, Rosemary de Brissac
(1920–87)

Australian poet, born in Sydney, granddaughter of **Austin Dobson**. She worked for some years with the Australian publishing firm Angus & Robertson and married Alec Bolton, then its London editor. Her poems reflect her love of antiquity and a keen, painterly, eye, and her fascination with manuscripts and fine printing, as seen in 'The Missal'. Her first collection was *In a Convex Mirror* (1944); her second, *The Ship of Ice*, won an award in 1948. Later books were *Child with a Cockatoo* (1955) and *Cock Crow* (1965); selections of her verse were published in 1973 and 1980. She edited the feminist anthology *Sister Poets* (1979), in which year she received the **Robert Frost** Prize; in 1984 she won the **Patrick White** Literary Award.

DOCTOROW, E(dgar) L(awrence)
(1931–)

American novelist, born in New York City. He was educated at Bronx High School of Science, Kenyon College and Columbia University. From 1960 to 1964 he was editor of the New American Library and has held teaching posts in several colleges and universities. His first novel was *Welcome to Hard Times* (1961), followed by *Big as Life* (1966) and *The Book of Daniel* (1971), based on the story of the Rosenbergs, who were executed for spying. *Ragtime* (1975) is generally regarded as his tour de force, in which he recreates the atmosphere of the Ragtime era with wit, accuracy and appealing nostalgia. It was filmed in 1981. Later books include *Loon Lake* (1980) and *The World's Fair* (1986).

DODERER, Heimito von
(1896–1966)

Austrian 'monumental' novelist, born near Vienna. More unequivocally unhappy about the collapse of the Habsburg empire than **Joseph Roth** or **Robert Musil**, and less subtle than either, he became a fervent Nazi, welcomed the Anschluss, and fought in World War II, as he had in World War I (when he was a prisoner in Siberia). One of his key themes he expressed in the word *Menschwerdung*, 'becoming human', a notion he invented during his Nazi period. In his fiction he continually looked back to the old Austria of the Habsburgs, a period he regarded as historically superior. His claim to fame lies solely in his *Die Strudlhofstiege* (1951, 'The Strudlhof Steps') and *Die Dämonen* (1956, Eng trans, *The Demons*, 1961). The earlier novel is a shorter 'prelude' to the ambitious longer *Die Dämonen*. There are two views of these long, intricately constructed, and sometimes ponderously humorous examinations of Viennese life: that they are relatively neglected masterpieces, and that they have been overrated. They are almost excessively influenced by **Musil**, **Proust** and, above all, by his friend the Austrian writer and painter **Alfred Paris von Gütersloh**. The critical tendency now seems to be veering towards the latter view; but a minority of readers remain devoted to him.

DODGE, Mary Elizabeth, née Mapes
(1831–1905)

American writer, born in New York. She married William Dodge, a lawyer, in 1851, and after his death in 1858 turned to writing books for children, notably *Hans Brinker; or, The Silver Skates* (1865), which became a children's classic. From 1873 she was the editor of *St Nicholas Magazine*.

DODSLEY, Robert
(1703–64)

English playwright, born in Mansfield, Nottinghamshire. He was apprenticed to a stocking weaver, but, probably ill-treated, ran away and became a footman. He spent his spare time reading, and in 1732 published *A Muse in Livery*. His *Toy Shop*, a dramatic piece, was through **Pope**'s influence acted at Covent Garden in 1735 with great success. With his profits, and £100 from Pope, he set up as bookseller, but still continued to write bright plays, including *The King and the Miller of Mansfield* (1737), *The Blind Beggar of Bethnal Green* (1741) and *Rex et Pontifex* (1745), which were collected as *Trifles* (1745). In 1738 he bought *London* from the yet unknown **Dr Johnson** for 10 guineas. Other famous authors for whom he published

included Pope, **Edward Young**, Akenside and **Oliver Goldsmith**, and he founded the *Annual Register* with **Edmund Burke** in 1759. With a tragedy, *Cleone* (1758), acted at Covent Garden with extraordinary success, he closed his career as a dramatist. He is chiefly remembered for his *Select Collection of Old Plays* (12 vols, 1744–5) and his *Poems by Several Hands* (3 vols, 1748; 6 vols, 1758).

DOMETT, Alfred
(1811–87)

English-born New Zealand politician, journalist and poet, born in London. He was a friend of **Robert Browning**, who eulogized him in 'Waring'. Praised by **Tennyson**, his work was among the first to use New Zealand scenery and Maori myths, evoked in typically **Wordsworth**ian verse. In *Ranolf and Amohia: A South-Sea Day-Dream* (1872, rev edn 1883) he uses the classic devices of shipwreck, unrequited love and alienation, but the delicate detail is crushed beneath his political and philosophical digressions. He also published *Flotsam and Jetsam* (1877). An early settler in Nelson and its MP from 1855, he was involved in moves toward self-government and became premier of New Zealand briefly in 1862–3 during the Land Wars.
▷ *The Diary of Alfred Domett, 1872–1885* (1953)

DOMINGEZ DE MARGO, Hernando
(c.1602–1656)

Colombian poet, born in Bogotá. He was a Jesuit in Lima, but is thought to have left the order towards the end of his life, in order to become a priest in Guatavita. His claim to fame is his *Gongorist* epic *Poema heroico de San Ignacio Loyola* (1666), in which he ignores the famous asceticism in favour of an interest in South American matters.

DONALDSON, Stephen
(1947–)

American fantasy writer and short-story writer, born in Cleveland, Ohio, who endured countless rejections from publishers before his first book was finally accepted. Thereafter he became increasingly popular with each volume of the six-novel series *The Chronicles of Thomas Covenant* (1977–83), in which the titular character, who suffers from leprosy, is called on to save the Land, a utopian fantasy world, from the forces of evil. *The Mirror of Her Dreams* (1986) and its sequel *A Man Rides Through* (1988) are similar in theme to the Covenant chronicles, telling of a protagonist transported from our world—in this case, modern-day New York—to a fantastic realm which requires saving.

DONLEAVY, J(ames) P(atrick)
(1926–)

American-born Irish author, born in Brooklyn, New York, of Irish parents. After serving in the American navy during World War II, he studied microbiology at Trinity College, Dublin, and became a friend of **Brendan Behan**. While living on a farm in Wicklow he began painting, then wrote his first novel, *The Ginger Man*, published in 1955. Picaresque, bawdy, presenting an apparently totally irrational hero, it was hailed as a comic masterpiece. The novels, plays and stories that followed are on the same theme, that of his own 'dreams and inner desires', and have been described as paler versions of *The Ginger Man*. He became an Irish citizen in 1967 and among his other works are *A Singular Man* (1963), *Meet My Maker, The Mad Molecule* (short stories, 1964), *The Beastly Beatitudes of Balthazar B* (1968), written as a play in 1981, *The Onion Eaters* (1971), *A Fairy Tale of New York* (1973, a novel written from the play of 1960), *The Destinies of Darcy Dancer, Gentleman* (1971), *Schultz* (1980) and *Are you Listening, Rabbi Low?* (1987).

DONN, Robb
(1714–78)

Scottish poet, from Strathmore in Sutherland, where he quickly developed a reputation for his spontaneously composed Gaelic verse. He was illiterate, and spoke a very broad dialect of Gaelic, so the fact that a considerable quantity of his poetry has survived is a testament to his poetic gifts. He composed verse in the traditional Gaelic forms—he made love songs, praise songs, elegies and satires—and was renowned for his wit, achieving considerable standing in north Highland Gaelic society.
▷I Grimble, *The World of Robb Donn* (1979)

DONNAY, Maurice
(1859–1945)

French dramatist, born in Paris. His brittle *fin-de-siècle* comedy *Amants* (1895, 'Lovers') achieved considerable popularity, as did *Lysistrata* (1893), an adaptation of **Aristophanes**. Later successes in that vein included *La douloureuse* (1897, 'The Sad Woman') and *L'autre danger* (1902, 'The Other Danger'). His more serious works engaged with social problems, and were felt to be daring at that time in dealing with subjects like the marriage between Jew and gentile in *Le retour de Jérusalem* (1903, 'The Return from Jerusalem').
▷P Bathille, *Maurice Donnay. Son oeuvre* (1931)

DONNE, John
(?1572–1631)

English poet, born in London, the son of a prosperous ironmonger, but connected through his mother with Sir Thomas More. Though a Catholic, he was admitted to Hart Hall, Oxford, and later graduated at Cambridge, where his friendship with Sir Henry Wotton began. He decided to take up law and entered Lincoln's Inn in 1592. After taking part in the 2nd Earl of Essex's two expeditions to Cadiz in 1597 and the Azores in 1598 (reflected in his poems 'The Storm' and 'The Calm'), he became (1598) secretary to Sir Thomas Egerton, Keeper of the Great Seal, whose justice he celebrated in his fourth satire. His daring pieces and brilliant personality pointed to a career as notable as that of his great contemporary Francis Bacon, but his secret marriage to Egerton's niece, Anne More, caused him to be dismissed and thrown into prison. Having turned Protestant, he lived at Mitcham in Surrey, but still sought favour at the Court with an eye to employment. The work he undertook under the direction of Thomas (later Bishop) Morton was a religious polemic against the Catholics. He had already written his passionate and erotic poems, *Songs and Sonnets*, his six *Satires*, and his *Elegies*, but published no verse until 1611, when his *Anniversarie* appeared, a commemorative poem for Elizabeth Drury, daughter of his benefactor, Sir Robert Drury, whose house in the Strand offered hospitality to the poet when in London. A second *Anniversarie* followed, really a 'meditatio mortis' displaying his metaphysical genius at its best. His religious temper is seen in more lyrical form in the *Divine Poems*, some of which certainly date from before 1607. These, like most of his verse, were published posthumously but his pieces circulated widely among learned and aristocratic friends. How difficult his journey to the Anglican faith was may be judged from the satirical 'Progresse of the Soule' (1601). This ugly unfinished poem is antiheretical, but also sceptical in a disturbing way. Donne's hesitation over some 10 years to take orders is variously explained as due to a Hamlet-like indecision, or to a sense of unworthiness because of his profligate youth, or to his still having an eye on civil employment. He now courted the distinguished ladies of the time, in verse letters of laboured but ingenious compliment, among them Mrs Herbert and the Countess of Bedford. More injurious to his name was a splendid piece for the marriage of the king's favourite, Robert Carr, to the divorced Countess of Essex: a scandalous poem for a scandalous wedding. In Funeral poems, of which the first and second *Anniversaries* are the most brilliant, he also paid court to the great. His prose works of this period include *Pseudo-Martyr* (1610), which is an acute polemic against the Jesuits. More interesting is his *Biothanatos*, which discussed the question of suicide, towards which, as he says in his preface, 'I have often...a sickly inclination'. He decides that suicide is permissible in certain cases, a conclusion at variance with that affirmed in his third *Satire*, but confirmed in a letter to his friend Sir Henry Wotton. King James VI and I encouraged him to go into the Church (1614), and promoted him, after several charges, to the deanship of St Paul's in 1621 when he relinquished his readership at Lincoln's Inn. Several of his sermons are still extant. In this middle period of his life he accompanied his patron, Sir Robert Drury, to France and Spain. In 1619 and 1620 he was in Germany, where he preached one of his noblest sermons before the exiled Queen Elizabeth of Bohemia, King James's daughter. Donne's creative years fall into three periods: from 1590 to 1601, a time of action, marked by passion and cynicism; from his marriage to his ordination in 1614, a period of anguished meditation and flattery of the great; and the period of his ministry, which includes two sonnet sequences, *La Corona* and *Holy Sonnets*, the latter containing (no. xvii) an anguished tribute to his wife, who died in 1617. Also of this period are the fine 'Hymne to God, the Father', 'To God My God, in my Sicknesse', and 'The Author's Last Going into Germany'.

▷R C Bald, *John Donne: a life* (1920); J B Leishman, *The Monarch of Wit* (1951)

DONNELLY, Ignatius
(1831–1901)

American politician and writer, born in Philadelphia. After qualifying for the Bar in 1852, he moved to Minnesota in 1856, later becoming Radical Republican Congressman (1863–9). He became identified with reform, editing the *Anti-Monopolist* and later the *Representative*, and was for several years President of the State Farmers' Alliance in Minnesota, a forerunner of the Populist party. As a prophet of reform his most enduring legacy is a horrific novel, *Caesar's Column* (1891), predicting tyranny and oppression. His powerful imagination and realism on the pitfalls ahead of reform were tarnished by his anti-semitism for which US Populism as a whole has been somewhat unjustly blamed. His *Atlantis, The Antediluvian World* (1882) was a highly popular development of the idea of a former continent drowned under the Atlantic Ocean. His *The Great Cryptogram* (1888) sought to prove Francis Bacon had

written the plays usually attributed to **Shakespeare** and had hidden ciphered messages in the plays declaring his authorship.

▷M Ridge, *Ignatius Donnelly: portrait of a politician* (1962)

DONOSO, (Yanez) José
(1928–)

Chilean novelist, born in Santiago. He attended the University of Chile and spent two years at Princeton on a Doherty Foundation Fellowship (1949–51). In his time a longshoreman, teacher, editor and journalist, with his first collection of short stories he won Chile's Municipal Prize in 1951, and in 1962 received the **William Faulkner** Foundation Prize for Chile, for his novel *Coronación* (1957, Eng trans *Coronation*, 1965). His work reflects urban life and its complications, madness, opulence and decay, and several novels have been translated into English: *El obsceno pájaro de la noche* (1970, Eng trans *The Obscene Bird of Night*, 1973); *Tres novelitas burguesas* (1973, Eng trans *Sacred Families*, 1977 (US); 1978 (UK)); and *Casa do Campo* (1978, Eng trans *A House in the Country*, 1984).

▷A C Polar, *Donoso: la destruccion de un mundo* (1975)

DOOLITTLE, Hilda, known as H D
(1886–1961)

American imagist poet, born in Bethlehem, Pennsylvania, the daughter of a professor of Astronomy. She was educated at Gordon School, the Friends' Central School in Philadelphia, and Bryn Mawr College (1904–6). She lived in London from 1911 and married **Richard Aldington** in 1913. After their divorce in 1937, she settled near Lake Geneva. Her many volumes of poetry include *Sea Garden* (1916), *The Walls do not Fall* (1944), *Flowering of the Rod* (1946) and *Helen in Egypt* (1961). She also wrote several novels, notably *Palimpsest* (1926), *Hedylus* (1928), *Bid Me to Live* (1960) and *Tribute to Freud* (1965).

▷*The Gift* (1982)

DORN, Ed(ward Merton)
(1929–)

American poet, born in Illinois. He studied with **Charles Olson** at Black Mountain College, but has tended to write in a more relaxed, idiomatic style that is often more reminiscent of the rhythms of prose typical of **Hemingway**. His multi-part *Gunslinger* (1968–75) is a brilliant amalgam of narrative, pure sound and theory, skating over a bewildering range of subjects with a jokey self-confidence that is far removed from the interior 'confessional' mode that still dominated American verse at the time. A *Collected Poems* was published in 1982, bringing together the best of his other work. *What I See in the Maximus Poems* (1960) was a perceptive study of Olson's work, and there are reminiscences of Black Mountain in *Views* (1980).

▷D Wesling, *Internal Resistances: The Poetry of Ed Dorn* (1985)

DORST, Tankred
(1925–)

German dramatist, born in Sonnenberg in Thuringia. He is an experimental playwright, who has done much work for marionettes. Influenced by **Brecht** and **Kafka**, he was successful with *Die Kurve* (1960, Eng trans *The Curve*, in *The New Theatre of Europe 3*, 1968), an Absurdist drama which plays brilliantly, and *Freiheit für Clemens* (1962, Eng trans *Freedom for Clemens*, in *Postwar German Theatre*, 1967, ed G E Wellworth), about a prisoner who does not desire release.

DOS PASSOS, John Roderigo
(1896–1970)

American novelist, playwright, travel writer and poet, born in Chicago. The grandson of a Portuguese immigrant, he was educated at Choate and Harvard. In 1916 he went to Spain to study architecture but was caught up in World War I and served in the US Medical Corps. Thereafter he lived in the USA but travelled widely on journalistic assignments. In middle age he led a simple life on Cape Cod and later he and his wife moved to his father's farm at Spence's Point, Virginia, where he had spent summers as a boy. He had a precocious start as an author, publishing *One Man's Initiation* in 1917 when he was 21. The fiercely anti-war *Three Soldiers* (1921) confirmed his talent and in *Manhattan Transfer* (1925) his confidence and ambition grew, its rapid narrative transitions and collectivist approach foreshadowing the monumental *U.S.A.* trilogy: *The 42nd Parallel* (1930), *1919* (1932) and *The Big Money* (1936). A digressive, dynamic epic, it consists of a mishmash of newsreel footage, snatches of popular songs, brief but vivid sketches of public figures and prose-poetry. He also wrote three plays. An anti-capitalist, Dos Passos wrote a second trilogy, *District of Columbia* (1939–49; 1952), less radical in its criticism of the free-enterprise system. His later work continued the trend towards conservatism. *The Best Times* (1966), his last book, was a reminiscence of his boyhood and early manhood.

▷V S Carr, *Dos Passos: a life* (1984)

DOSTOYEVSKY, Fyodor Mikhailovich
(1821–81)

Russian novelist, born in Moscow, the second son of a physician's seven children. His mother died in 1837 and his father was murdered by his serfs a little over two years later. After leaving a private boarding school in Moscow he studied from 1838 to 1843 at the Military Engineering College at St Petersburg, graduating with officer's rank. His first published short story was 'Bednye Lyudi' (1846, Eng trans 'Poor Folk', 1887), which gained him immediate recognition. In 1849 he was arrested and sentenced to death for participating in the socialist 'Petrashevsky circle', but was reprieved and sent to Siberia, where he was confined in a convict prison at Omsk until 1854. From this experience grew *Zapiski iz myortvovo doma* (1861–2, Eng trans *Buried Alive; or, Ten Years of Penal Servitude in Siberia*, 1881). In 1861 he began the review *Vremya* ('Truth') with his brother Mikhail and he spent the next two years travelling abroad, which confirmed his anti-European outlook. In 1864 he published *Zapiski iz podpol'ya* (Eng trans *Notes from Underground*, 1918), whose estranged, frustrated hero prefigures the central characters of later works. At about this time he met Mlle Suslova, the model for many of his heroines, and succumbed to the gaming tables. He fell heavily into debt but was rescued by Anna Grigoryevna Smitkina, whom he married in 1867. They lived abroad for several years but he returned to Russia in 1871 as editor of *Grazhdanin*, to which he contributed his 'Author's Diary'. Like **Dickens**, Dostoyevsky was both horrified and fascinated by the Industrial Revolution, and his fiction is dark with suffering caused by poverty and appalling living conditions, crime and the exploitation of children. He is second only to **Tolstoy**. His novels—*Prestupleniye i nakazaniye* (1867, Eng trans *Crime and Punishment*, 1886), *Idiot* (1869, Eng trans *The Idiot*, 1887), *Besy* (1872, Eng trans *The Possessed*, 1913) and *Brat'ya Karamazovy* (1880, Eng trans *The Brothers Karamazov*, 1912)—were and are profoundly influential, and their impact on **Robert Louis Stevenson**'s *Dr Jekyll and Mr Hyde* (1886), among many others, is conspicuous.

▷J Frank, *Dostoevsky: I—The Seeds of Revolt, 1821–1848; Dostoevsky: II—The Years of Ordeal* (1976–83)

DOUGHTY, Charles Montagu
(1843–1926)

English travel writer and poet, born at Theberton Hall in Suffolk, the son of a clergyman, and educated at Caius College, Cambridge. Out of two years' travel and hardship in Arabia (1875–7) slowly grew his masterpiece of

philological virtuosity, *Travels in Arabia Deserta* (1888), written in austere, didactic prose. He also wrote epic poems and plays, including *The Dawn in Britain* (1906) and *Mansoul* (1923).
▷ D Hogarth, *The Life of Charles M Doughty* (1928)

DOUGLAS, Lord Alfred Bruce
(1870–1945)

English poet, son of the 8th Marquis of Queensberry. He wrote a number of brilliant sonnets, collected in *In Excelsis* (1924) and *Sonnets and Lyrics* (1935). He is remembered for his association with **Oscar Wilde**, to which his father objected, thereby provoking Wilde to bring the ill-advised libel action which led to his own arrest and imprisonment. He wrote two books on Oscar Wilde, and *The Autobiography of Douglas* (1929).
▷ R C Cooke, *Bosie: the story of Lord Alfred Douglas* (1963)

DOUGLAS, Gavin
(1798–1843)

Scottish poet and prelate, born at Tantallon Castle, East Lothian, the third son of Archibald, 5th Earl of Angus. Educated at St Andrews and possibly Paris for the priesthood, from 1501 to 1514 he was Dean or Provost of the Collegiate Church of St Giles, Edinburgh. After the Battle of Flodden (1513), Douglas's nephew, the 6th Earl of Angus, married the widowed queen, Margaret Tudor. Through her influence Douglas obtained the bishopric of Dunkeld (1515), but was imprisoned under an old statute for receiving bulls from the pope and was not consecrated until more than a year later. On the fall of Angus in 1521, the bishop fled to England to seek the aid of Henry VIII, but died suddenly of the plague in London. His works include *The Palice of Honour*, presumably written in 1501, an allegory of the life of the virtuous man, and a magnificent translation of **Virgil**'s *Aeneid*, with prologues, finished about 1513, the first version of a Latin poet published in English. He may also have written *King Hart*, an allegory about the control exercised by the heart in human personality and behaviour.

DOUGLAS, George *see* BROWN, George Douglas

DOUGLAS, Keith Castellain
(1920–44)

English poet, perhaps the only one from the World War II era to approach the critical eminence of **Rupert Brooke** or **Wilfred Owen** from that of World War I. Born in Kent, he began publishing verse in magazines during his teens, but it was the encouragement of

his tutor **Edmund Blunden** at Merton College, Oxford, that helped shape his distinctively clear-sighted approach. In 1943, Blunden arranged for the publication of a slim *Selected Poems*, using verses sent back from the Western Desert, where Douglas was serving with a tank regiment; it was the only book Douglas saw published in his lifetime. On 6 June 1944, following the D-Day landings in Normandy, he was killed by a shell fragment. It was his faintly surreal and bluntly un-optimistic memoir of the fighting in the Western Desert, *Alamein to Zem Zem* (1946), that began to establish a posthumous reputation which only became secure two decades after his death when **Ted Hughes**, an admirer, introduced an important selection. The *Complete Poems* appeared in 1979, edited by Desmond Graham.

DOUGLAS, Lloyd C(assel)
(1877–1951)

American Congregationalist minister, born in Indiana, who wrote world-wide bestsellers of immense readability and almost, according to every serious literary critic, incredible psychological bathos. He did not turn to fiction until he was past 50, when he wrote *Magnificent Obsession* (1929), about a Christian eye-surgeon, later immortalized in Douglas Sirk's deliberately high kitsch movie, starring Rock Hudson. Many have agreed with the famous judgement of an *Atlantic Review* critic, who spoke of his 'spiritual fascism'; others see him as 'harmless', and put him in the tradition of **Harold Bell Wright**. *The Robe* (1942) and *The Big Fisherman* (1948) are historical novels set in scriptural times; both were phenomenally successful.

DOUGLAS, (George) Norman
(1868–1952)

Scottish novelist and essayist, born in Tilquhillie, Deeside. His mother was part-German and he was educated at Uppingham School and at Karlsruhe, and joined the Foreign Office in 1894. He served in St Petersburg before settling in Capri in 1896, where his circle embraced **Compton Mackenzie**, **Ouida** and **D H Lawrence**. His first book, *Unprofessional Tales* (1901), was co-authored with his wife and published under the pseudonym 'Normyx', but *Siren Land* (1911) first attracted critical attention. An account of his travels in southern Italy, it is an exotic collage of anecdote, philosophy and myth. *Old Calabria* (1915) garnished his reputation and is a minor classic. Other travel books are *Fountains in the Sun* (1912), *Alone* (1921) and *Together* (1923). Of his novels, the most famous is *South Wind* (1917). Set in Nepenthe (Capri) among a floating population of expatriates, it is an unapologetic celebration of hedonism to which its author was a happy convert. *Looking Back* (1933) is an unusual autobiography, in which he recalls his life and his friends by taking up their calling cards and describing them one by one, at length or tersely, depending on his mood.

▷ R D Lindeman, *Norman Douglas* (1965)

DOUGLAS-HOME, William
(1912–92)

Scottish playwright, born in Edinburgh, and educated at Eton and Oxford. He was the author of a number of plays, principally lighthearted comedies, the best-known of which are *Now Barabbas* (1947), *The Chiltern Hundreds* (1947), *The Thistle and the Rose* (1949) and *The Reluctant Debutante* (1955).

▷ *Half-Term Report: an autobiography* (1954); *Mr. Home, pronounced Hume* (1979)

DOUGLASS, Frederick
(1817–95)

American writer, born into slavery in Maryland. He escaped to Massachusetts in 1838, where he was employed as a lecturer by anti-slavery societies, and wrote his most famous book, the autobiographical *Narrative of the Life of Frederick Douglass* (1845). He travelled to England and Ireland, but returned to America to buy his freedom, thus banishing his fear of recapture, and set up a campaigning anti-slavery newspaper, *North Star*. He was actively involved in political life, and held a number of appointments after the Civil War. In addition to a revised version of his *Narrative* (1892), he wrote two more autobiographical books, *My Bondage and My Freedom* (1855) and *The Life and Times of Frederick Douglass* (1881).

DOVE, Rita Francis
(1952–)

American poet, born in Akron, Ohio. She is Professor of English at the University of Virginia. Her first book was *Ten Poems* (1977). *The Yellow House On The Corner* (1980) contained a sequence of poems told from the point of view of negro slaves, and historical figures have recurred throughout her work. She was awarded the Pulitzer Prize for Poetry in 1987 for *Thomas and Beulah* (1986), in which she re-created the lives of her grandparents from courtship to death. Other collections include *Museum* (1983), *The Other Side of the House* (1988) and *Grace Notes* (1989). *Fifth Sunday* (1985) is a collection of short stories.

DOWLING, Basil Cairns
(1910–)

New Zealand poet, born in Southbridge, Christchurch, whose verse shows a lyricism

and a romantic response to his natural surroundings. His early work was published by **Allen Curnow**'s Caxton Press in *A Day's Journey* (1941), *Signs and Wonders* (1944) and *Canterbury and Other Poems* (1949), evoking the pastoral qualities of his own South Island. After a break, *Hatherley, Recollective Lyrics* was published in 1968, followed by *A Little Gallery of Characters* (1971), *Bedlam* (1972) and *The Unreturning Native* (1973).

DOWSON, Ernest Christopher
(1867–1900)

English poet. Born in London and brought up largely in France, he studied at Oxford, then helped his fairly unbusinesslike father in managing the unwelcome inheritance of a dry dock in Limehouse, but spent more time in literary activity. His friends at the time included **Lionel Johnson**, **Arthur Symons**, **Oscar Wilde** and **Yeats**. From 1894 writing became his livelihood. His *Verses* appeared in 1896 and *Decorations* in 1899; he also published stories, a verse play and translations, and collaborated on two novels, but despite all this work he was usually short of money. He was for years in love with the young daughter of a Polish restaurateur, but she turned him down and married the waiter. From 1895 Dowson lived mostly in France, but returned to London in 1899 and died of tuberculosis at the age of 32. His poems, on which the influence of **Verlaine** and the 'decadents' is marked, are notable for finely judged vowel sounds and metre. The two best known, 'Vitae summa brevis' (1896) and 'Cynara' (1891), have contributed several stock phrases to English: 'days of wine and roses', 'gone with the wind' and 'I have been faithful to thee, Cynara! in my fashion'.

▷ *Letters* (1967, D Flower and H Maas eds); M Longaker, *Ernest Dowson* (1944, rev edn 1968)

DOYLE, Sir Arthur Conan
(1859–1930)

Scottish writer of detective stories and historical romances, nephew of the caricaturist Richard Doyle. Born of Irish parentage in Edinburgh, he was educated at Stonyhurst and in Germany, and studied medicine at Edinburgh. Initial poverty as a young practitioner in Southsea and as an oculist in London coaxed him into authorship. His debut was a story in *Chambers Journal* (1879), and his first book introduced that prototype of the modern detective in fiction, the superobservant, deductive Sherlock Holmes, his good-natured doctor friend Dr John Watson, and the whole apparatus of detection mythology associated with Baker Street. *The Adventures of Sherlock Holmes* were serialized in the *Strand Magazine* (1891–3). They

were so popular that when Conan Doyle, tired of his popular creation, tried to kill off his hero on a cliff, he was compelled in 1903 to revive him. The serials were published as books with the titles *The Sign of Four* (1890), *The Hound of the Baskervilles* (1902), etc. Conan Doyle, however, set greater stock by his historical romances, *Micah Clarke* (1887), *The White Company* (1890), *Brigadier Gerard* (1896) and *Sir Nigel* (1906), which have more literary merit, and are underrated. A keen boxer himself, *Rodney Stone* (1896) is one of his best novels. *The Lost World* (1912) and *The Poison Belt* (1913) are essays into the pseudo-scientifically fantastic. He served as a physician in the 2nd Boer War (1899–1902), and his pamphlet, *The War in South Africa* (1902), correcting enemy propaganda and justifying Britain's action, earned him a knighthood (1902). He used his detective powers to some effect outside fiction in attempting to show that the criminal cases of the Parsee Birmingham lawyer, Edaljee (1903), and alleged murderer Oscar Slater (1909) were instances of mistaken identity. He also wrote on spiritualism, to which he became a convert in later life.
▷ H Pearson, *Conan Doyle: His Life and Art* (1943); O D Edwards, *The Quest for Sherlock Holmes* (1982)

DOYLE, Charles
(1928–)

New Zealand poet, primarily of the city and the suburbs, but responsive to natural surroundings as in his 'Starlings and History'. *A Splinter of Glass* (1956) was followed by *The Night Shift: Poems on Aspects of Love* (1957) in which he was joined by **James Keir Baxter**, **Colin Johnson** and **Kendrick Smithyman**. Other work was collected in *Distances* (1963, poems of exile), *Messages for Herod* (1965) and *A Sense of Place: Poems* (1965). He edited an important anthology, *Recent Poetry in New Zealand* (1965), which presented 'work in progress' of 13 of his contemporaries including Baxter, Johnson and the newcomer **C K Stead**. He has also written criticism and studies of **R A K Mason** (1970) and James Keir Baxter (1976).

DOYLE, Sir Francis Hastings Charles, 2nd Bart
(1810–88)

English poet, born in Nunappleton near Tadcaster. Educated at Eton and Christ Church, Oxford, he was called to the Bar, held offices in the customs, and from 1867 to 1877 was Professor of Poetry at Oxford in succession to **Matthew Arnold**. He published his two series of Oxford lectures in 1869 and 1877. His verse collections of 1834 (enlarged 1840) and 1866, are unmemorable save for

such ballads of British military fortitude as 'The Loss of the *Birkenhead*' and 'The Private of the Buffs'.
▷ *Reminiscences and Opinions* (1886)

DOYLE, Roddy
(1958–)

Irish novelist, born in Dublin. For 14 years he worked as a teacher (of geography and English) in a community school in Kilbarrack, a deprived area in north Dublin—the 'Barrytown' of his novels. An early novel, *Your Granny's a Hunger Striker* (1982), took an irreverent approach to the issue of 'ghetto politics'. *The Commitments* (1988), *The Snapper* (1990) and *The Van* (1991) spoke for communities denied a media voice, their comic style acting as a vehicle for Doyle's clear understanding of the plight of the deprived. The Booker Prize-winning *Paddy Clarke Ha Ha Ha* (1993), narrated through the sense and senses of a 10-year-old boy, similarly exhibits the inherent tragedy that underlines all comedy. A 'failed dramatist' in his own estimation, Doyle has inherited by popular acclaim the status of **O'Casey** and **Brendan Behan** in his native city.

DRABBLE, Margaret
(1939–)

English novelist, born in Sheffield. Her elder sister is the novelist **A S Byatt**. The family was bookish; her father was a barrister, then a circuit judge, and, in retirement, a novelist. Her mother was an English teacher. She was educated at the Mount School, York (the Quaker boarding school where her mother taught), and Newnham College, Cambridge. She married the actor Clive Swift, acted for a short time herself, then turned to writing. Divorced from her first husband in 1972 (after having three children), she married the biographer **Michael Holroyd** in 1982. Often mirroring her own life, her novels concentrate on the concerns of intelligent, often frustrated middle-class women. *A Summer Bird-Cage* (1963), *The Garrick Year* (1964), *The Millstone* (1965), *Jersualem the Golden* (1967), *The Needle's Eye* (1972), *The Ice Age* (1977), *The Middle Ground* (1980) and the trilogy comprising *The Radiant Way* (1987), *A Natural Curiosity* (1989) and *The Gates of Ivory* (1991) are among her titles. She was the editor of the 5th edition of the *Oxford Companion to English Literature*, and has written a biography of **Arnold Bennett** (1974).
▷ V G Myer, *Margaret Drabble: Puritanism and Permissiveness* (1974)

DRACHMANN, Holger Henrik Herholdt
(1846–1908)

Danish writer and artist, born in Copenhagen of a German family. A visit to London inspired him to revolutionary solidarity with the working class, particularly the exiled Communards, but his early poetry is mainly lyrical and subjective. Later volumes such as *Sange ved havet* (1877, 'Seaside Verses') and *Ranker og roser* (1879, 'Vines and Roses') are less conventional in form and feeling and anticipate important elements of Danish modernism. His novel *Derovre fra graensen* (1877, 'Over the Border') is nationalistic and somewhat conventional, anticipating **Jonas Lie**'s stories of respectable middle-class families. Drachmann was also an accomplished sea painter.

▷ J Ursin, *Holger Drachmann. Liv og vaerker* (1953)

DRAGÚN, Osvaldo
(1929–)

Argentinian playwright, considered by many to be the best of his generation. With no formal training, Dragún helped develop the 'New Realism' School of Argentine plays. Influenced by **Brecht**, **O'Neill** and **Valle-Inclán**, his works have won world-wide praise. Using a combination of political activism, humour, the absurd, and fantasy, his plays have progressed from portrayals of urban exploitation (*Historias para ser contadas*, 1956, 'Stories to be Told', *El Jardin del infierno*, 1959, 'Garden of Hell') to the sentimental (the sainete *Amoretta*, 'Little Love') and sublime (*Heroica de Buenos Aires*, 1966, 'Epic of Buenos Aires'). A motive force behind the Teatro Abierto festival in Buenos Aires, which stages 21 plays in 7 days, he has also lived and worked in Cuba (1961–3) and Spain (1967–72).

DRAKE-BROCKMAN, Henrietta
(1901–68)

Australian novelist and playwright, born in Perth, whose travels in the outback influenced much of her writing. Her novels, *Blue North* (1934) and *Sheba Lane* (1936), are set around the pearling town of Broome in the state's far north-west, and *The Wicked and the Fair* (1957) is based on the wreck of the Dutch ship *Batavia* on that coast in 1629. A collection of short stories, *Sydney or the Bush*, was published in 1948. Her first play was *The Man from the Bush* (1934) and four more were collected as *Men Without Wives, and Other Plays* (1955). The impact of Australia's harsh environment on character, and the theme of sacrifice, runs through much of her work, which often has a heavily romantic flavour.

DRAYTON, Michael
(1563–1631)

English poet, born in Hartshill near Atherstone, Warwickshire. He became a page in a wealthy household and spent the rest of his life in the households of patrons. His earliest work was *The Harmony of the Church* (1591), a metrical rendering of scriptural passages, which gave offence to the authorities, and was condemned to be destroyed. In 1593 he published a volume of eclogues, *Idea, the Shepherd's Garland*, which afterwards underwent considerable revision, and the first of his 'historical legends' in verse, *Piers Gaveston*. His first important poem, *Mortimeriados* (1596), recast in 1603 as *The Barons' Wars*, has some fine passages. *England's Heroical Epistles* (1597) has more polish and is more even than many of Drayton's other works. *Poems, Lyric and Pastoral* (c.1606) contains some of his most familiar poems, including the *Ballad of Agincourt* and *Fair Stood the Wind for France*. The first 18 'songs' or books of Drayton's greatest work, *Polyolbion*, were published in 1613, with annotation by John Selden, and the complete poem, the product of vast learning and the labour of years, appeared in 1622. In it he aimed at giving 'a chorographical description of all the tracts, rivers, mountains, forests, and other parts of Great Britain'. In 1619 he collected in one volume all the poems (except *Polyolbion*) which he wished to preserve. In 1627 he published a new volume of miscellaneous poems, among them the whimsical and delightful *Nymphisdia, the Court of Fairy*, a triumph of ingenious fancy. His last work, *The Muses' Elysium* (1630), contains some pastoral poems of finished elegance. His only surviving play is *The First Part of Sir John Oldcastle* (1600). He was buried in Westminster Abbey.

▷ J A Berthelot, *Michael Drayton* (1967)

DRDA, Jan
(1915–70)

Czech dramatist and novelist, born in Pribram. He began as a fine storyteller, but degenerated into an official communist writer, so that his reputation amongst many people depended entirely on his earliest work, and on a collection of stories he wrote about resistance to the Nazis—but published before the Stalinist takeover.

DREISER, Theodore Herman Albert
(1871–1945)

American novelist, born in Terre Haute, Indiana. The eleventh and penultimate child of a poor Catholic German immigrant father, he was brought up on the breadline and left home at 15 for Chicago. He did odd jobs before becoming a highly successful journalist and wrote *Sister Carrie* (1900), a powerful and frank treatment of a young working girl's climb towards worldly success. The publisher, fearful of accusations of obscenity, was diffident in its promotion and it flopped commercially. Dreiser next wrote *Jennie Gerhardt* (1911) on a similar theme, which established him as a novelist. There followed the first parts of a trilogy about Frank Cowperwood, a power-hungry business tycoon: *The Financier* (1912), *The Titan* (1914) and *The Stoic* (published posthumously in 1947). *The Genius* was published in 1915 and 10 years later came *An American Tragedy* (1925), based on a real-life murder case, which, despite reservations about its author's leaden prose, has survived as a classic. His best works have been admired by **Saul Bellow** and other notable writers.

▷R Lingeman, *Dreiser: At the Gates of the City, 1871–1907* (1986), and subsequent volumes

DREWE, Robert
(1943–)

Australian journalist and novelist, born in Melbourne. Sometime literary editor of the national newspaper, the *Australian*, he has twice won the Walkley Award for journalism. His first novel, *The Savage Crows* (1976), concerned George Robinson, the early 19th-century Protector of the Aborigines. Another novel followed and then two collections of short stories, *The Body Surfers* (1983) and *The Bay of Contented Men* (1989), which portray and parody the hedonistic Australian beach culture.

DREZEN, Youenn
(1899–)

Breton poet, dramatist, translator and novelist, whose books have become classics in their minority language; he began as a journalist. He has translated Greek tragedies and English and Spanish classics into Breton. *Chant à l'Ouest* is an epic poem about the Celts; however, his acknowledged masterpiece, written before he devoted himself to the theatre, is the novel *Notre-Dame des Carmélites* (1941). His chief aim has been to elevate Breton literature.

DRIEU LA ROCHELLE, Pierre
(1893–1945)

French novelist and political essayist, whose literary reputation has only recovered very slowly from his association with fascism and from his advocacy of collaboration during the Vichy period. Drieu fought with the French army during World War I—an experience recounted in *La comédie de Charleroi* (1934)—and became convinced that modern France was irretrievably decadent. This led him to flirt with Surréalisme and then with Third Period Communism before he discovered his intellectual niche on the far right.

His novel *Gilles* (1939) gives intermittent hints of his political convictions and these were not fully revealed or understood until his *Journal secret* was posthumously published in 1961. Having declared himself in support of collaborationism, Drieu was appointed editor of an important journal of literature and ideas, the *Nouvelle Revue Française*, a post he held until 1943. Following the Liberation, he took his own life, and his name was the target of dismissive obloquy until the early sixties when it became possible to see beyond his wartime derelictions and understand the complexities of his ideas and seriousness of his intellectual wanderings.

▷R Soucy, *Fascist Intellectual* (1979)

DRINKWATER, John
(1882–1937)

English poet, dramatist, and critic, born in Leytonstone. He was an insurance clerk who had already published several volumes of poems when he achieved an immediate theatrical success with his play *Abraham Lincoln* (1918), which he followed with *Mary Stuart*, *Oliver Cromwell* (both published in 1921), *Robert E. Lee* (1923) and a comedy, *Bird in Hand* (1927). His first volume of poems appeared in 1903, and he also wrote critical studies of **William Morris**, **Algernon Charles Swinburne** and **Byron**, and of lyric poetry. He was one of the founders of the Pilgrim Players and became manager of the Birmingham Repertory Theatre. He published two volumes of an unfinished autobiography, *Inheritance* (1931) and *Discovery* (1932).

▷G Matthews, *John Drinkwater: a lecture* (1925)

DRIVER, C(harles) J(onathan)
(1939–)

South African-born British novelist, he was educated at the University of Cape Town and later at Trinity College, Oxford, having had his South African passport revoked. His political activity in the Cape (he served as President of the desegregationist National Union of South African Students in 1963–4) forms the background to his first novel, *Elegy for a Revolutionary* (1969), whose themes are made more subtle and universal in the much stronger *Send War in Our Time, O Lord* (1970), a significant exploration of the white liberal dilemma. His later works, *Death of Fathers* (1972) and *A Messiah of the Last Days* (1974), maintain an interest in political activity within confined groups (an English public school, an anarchist collective); perhaps because he *has* worked as a teacher, the former is more convincingly portrayed. Driver has also published short fiction and some verse, including *I Live Here Now* (1979), which further documents his reactions to English society.

DRIZIC, Marin
(1520–67)

Dalmatian (Ragusan) dramatist, born in Ragusa (Dubrovnik). His comedies, such as *Dundo Maroje* (1550), about a miser, are similar in type to those of **Plautus**, were immensely popular in their own time, and have been successfully played since. He was one of the most influential of all those who played a part in the Serbo–Croatian literature which developed alongside that of Renaissance Italy.

DROST, Aarnout
(1810–34)

Dutch novelist and theologian, born in Amsterdam. The romantic historical novel for which he is best known is *Hermingard van de Eikenterpen* (1832). His short stories were collected in *Schetsen en verhalen* (1835–6).

DROSTE-HÜLSHOFF, Annette Elisabeth, Baroness von
(1797–1848)

German poet, born in Westphalia. Commonly regarded as Germany's greatest woman writer, she led a retired life and from 1818 to 1820 wrote intense devotional verses, eventually published as *Geistliche Jahre* in 1851. She wrote in a more restrained and classical style than that of most of her contemporaries, especially in her ballads and lyrics, though her long narrative poems, notably *Das Hospiz auf dem Grossen Sankt Bernard* (1838, 'The Hospice on the Great Saint Bernard') and *Die Schlacht im Loener Bruch* ('The Battle in the Loener Marsh'), were influenced by **Byron**. She also wrote a novella, *Die Judenbuche* (1841, 'The Jew's Beech-tree').
▷C Heselhaus, *Annette von Droste-Hülshoff. Werk und Lebel* (1971)

DROZ, Antoine Gustave
(1832–95)

French novelist, born in Paris. He was grandson of Jean Pierre Droz (1746–1823), an engraver of medals. He had devoted himself to art until he had his first and greatest success with *Monsieur, Madame, et Bébé* (1866, Eng trans *Papa, Mamma and Baby*, 1887). Later came *Entre nous* (1867, 'Between Ourselves'), *Les Étangs* (1876, 'The Ponds'), *L'Enfant* (1885, 'The Child'), and others.

DRUMMOND, William, of Hawthornden
(1585–1649)

Scottish poet, born in Hawthornden, near Roslin, Midlothian, the son of a courtier to King James VI and I. He was educated at the High School of Edinburgh, graduated MA at Edinburgh in 1605, studied law at Bourges and Paris, and on his father's death in 1610 became Laird of Hawthornden. Devoting his life to poetry and mechanical experiments, he was on the point of marrying Euphemia Cunningham of Barns when she died on the eve of their wedding (1615). He took a mistress, by whom he had three children, and married Elizabeth Logan of Restalrig in 1630. He had to subscribe to the National Covenant of 1638 but witnessed its triumph with a sinking heart that not even the most sarcastic verses could relieve. His death was hastened by grief for Charles I's execution. Drummond enjoyed the friendship of **Ben Jonson** who paid him a memorable visit in 1618–19, and Drummond's *Notes* of their talk form a charming chapter of literary history. His chief works are the pastoral lament *Tears on the Death of Moeliades* (ie Prince Henry, 1613); *Poems, Amorous, Funereall, Divine, Pastorall in Sonnets, Songs, Sextains, Madrigals* (1614); *Forth Feasting* (1617); and *Flowers of Sion* (1623). In prose he wrote *A Cypress Grove* (1630) and a *History of the Five Jameses*. He also wrote a *History of Scotland 1423–1524*, posthumously published in 1655.
▷F R Fogle, *A Critical Study of William Drummond of Hawthornden* (1952)

DRUMMOND DE ANDRADE *see* **ANDRADE, DRUMMOND DE**

DRUON, Maurice, pseud of **Maurice Kessel**
(1918–)

French novelist, whose reputation lies somewhat uneasily between the popular and the sub-critical. He has been in the Académie française since 1966. *Les Grandes familles* (1948–51, Eng trans *The Curtain Falls*, 1959), on the theme of a declining family, won the Prix **Goncourt**. After this he embarked on a series of historical novels, most of which have been translated; these are worthy popular literature on the grand scale, but have attracted little serious critical attention.

DRURY, Allen Stuart
(1918–)

Patriotic American novelist and journalist, born in Houston, Texas. Drury worked as Washington correspondent for the *New York Times* and *Readers Digest* before publishing his melodramatic novel *Advise and Consent* (1959), which was based on his experience of political intrigue. It won a Pulitzer Prize in 1960 and was made into a film, directed by Otto Preminger (1962). In 1971 he published a photographic encomium to the Nixon administration, calling the new president a 'decent man' surrounded by equally 'decent and worthy men'.

DRUTEN, John van
(1901–57)

English-born American playwright, born in London. He became famous with the production of his play *Young Woodley* in 1928, which was first produced in the USA after falling foul of the British censor. After several years and considerable success, he was granted American citizenship in 1944. *The Voice of the Turtle*, his most successful play with an American setting, was produced in 1943 and his adaptation of sketches by **Christopher Isherwood**, *I Am A Camera*, in 1951.
▷ *The Way to the Present* (1938).

DRYDEN, John
(1631–1700)

English poet, born at the vicarage of Aldwinkle All Saints, Northamptonshire, where his maternal grandfather was rector. He was educated at Westminster School under Richard Busby and at Trinity College, Cambridge, where he stayed until 1657. Going up to London in that year he attached himself to his cousin Sir Gilbert Pickering, Cromwell's chamberlain, in the hope of employment, which he might well have expected since on both sides his people were parliamentarians. His *Heroic Stanzas*, in quatrains, on the death of Cromwell (1658), was soon followed by his *Astrea Redux* (1660), celebrating the Restoration in heroic couplets, which was to be his staple measure even in the plays which soon poured from his pen for the amusement of 'a venal court'. The first of these 'heroic' verse plays to take the public taste was *The Indian Emperor* (1665), dealing with the conquest of Mexico by Cortes and his love for the emperor's daughter, and the last was *Aurungzebe* (1676). In 1663 he married Lady Elizabeth Howard, eldest daughter of the Earl of Berkshire. In 1667 he published *Annus Mirabilis, The Year of Wonders, 1666*, which established his reputation, and he was appointed poet laureate in 1668 following Sir **William D'Avenant**, and historiographer royal in 1670. Meanwhile he was turning out a series of comedies for the stage, including *The Rival Ladies* (1664, in rhymed verse), and culminating with *Marriage-à-la-Mode* (1673). He used blank verse for *All for Love* (1678), his best play and not unworthy to be placed beside **Shakespeare**'s *Antony and Cleopatra*. His adaptation of another of Shakespeare's plays, *Troilus and Cressida*, the following year, was by comparison a failure. Adaptation was a means of keeping up with the demands of the theatre on his service; he had already adapted *The Tempest* in 1670; **Milton**'s *Paradise Lost* (as *The State of Innocence*,

1677); and **Thomas Corneille**'s *The Mock Astrologer* (1668). He wrote a series of important critical essays as prefaces to his plays, including his charming *Essay of Dramatic Poesy* (1668), and the *Defence of the Epilogue* (to that popular play *The Conquest of Granada*, 1670). In 1680 he began a series of satirical and didactic poems, starting with the most famous, *Absalom and Achitophel* (1681), and followed by *The Medal* (1682) and *Mac-Flecknoe* (1684), written some years before, which did much to turn the tide against the Whigs. To this era also belong the didactic poem *Religico Laici* (1682), which argues the case for Anglicanism, and the much finer *The Hind and the Panther*, marking his conversion to Rome in 1685. A place in the Customs (1683) was his reward for his political labours. At the Revolution of 1688 he lost the poet laureateship and took to translation as a means of living. Of these his fine translation of **Virgil** was most profitable, that of **Juvenal** and **Persius** was prefaced by a *Discourse Concerning the Origin and Progress of Satire*, which had all his old ease and urbanity. His final work, published in 1699, was *Fables, Ancient and Modern* which, with its paraphrases of **Chaucer**, **Ovid** and **Boccaccio**, has delighted generations of readers. These works are only the most outstanding of a lifetime's industry. Dryden is transitional between the metaphysical poets of the school of **John Donne** and the neo-classic reaction which he did so much to create.
▷ C Ward, *A Life of John Dryden* (1961); G Wasermann, *John Dryden* (1964)

dsh *see* HOUEDARD, Dom Sylvester

DU BARTAS, Guilliaume de Salluste
(1544–90)

French poet from Gascony, effusive and thus eccentric-seeming to his contemporaries. Feeling divinely inspired (he has been compared to **Claudel**), he told the story of creation in *La Semaine* (1578), an enormously learned poem studded with marvellous images but as a whole quite unreadable. This was put into a crabbed, metaphysical English by **Joshua Sylvester**, who received nothing but obscurity for his immense pains. Yet du Bartas, who was famous throughout Europe in his times, is a rewarding poet in patches, 'a barbarous curiosity ... [his] is the only verse which ... provides anything approaching a counterpart to the prose of Rabelais'.

DUBILLARD, Roland
(1923–)

French story writer and playwright (and actor under the name of Grégoire), who writes Absurdist plays in a deceptively realistic, conventional style (not unlike the *One-Way Pendulum* of **N F Simpson**; but sometimes his inconsequential dialogue recalls that of **Pinter**). His best-known play is *Le Maison d'os* (1962, 'The House of Bones'), an allegory about death. The title of his essay *Méditation sur la difficulté d'être en bronze* (1972, 'Meditation on the Difficulty of Being in Bronze'), is characteristic.

▷J Guichardnaud, *Modern French Theatre* (1967)

DUBOIS, W(illiam) E(dward) B(urghardt)
(1868–1963)

American Black writer and editor, born in Great Barrington, Massachusetts. He studied at Fisk University, Tennessee, and at Harvard, where his doctoral thesis was on the suppression of the African slave trade. He was Professor of Economics and History at Atlanta University (1897–1910). He was co-founder of the National Association for the Advancement of Coloured People (1909), and edited its magazine, *Crisis* (1910–34), but later disassociated himself from the Association, finding it too conservative. He wrote a number of important works on slavery and the colour problem, including *The Souls of Black Folk* (1903), *John Brown* (1909), *The Negro* (1915), *Black Reconstruction* (1935) and *Colour and Democracy* (1945). He also wrote novels, including *The Dark Princess* (1928) and *Worlds of Color* (1961). A passionate advocate of radical Black action and an early supporter of the suffragette movement—which he tried to link with the struggle for black rights—he joined the Communist Party in 1961, and moved to Ghana at the age of 91, where he became a naturalized citizen just before he died.

▷*Autobiography* (1968)

DU CAMP, Maxime
(1822–94)

French poet, novelist and journalist, born in Paris. He travelled in the East, including a trip to the Near East with **Flaubert**. He wrote books on Paris and was a founder of the *Revue de Paris* (1851). His other writings include *Souvenirs littéraires* (1882–3, 'Literary Recollections'), and several novels.

DUCASSE, Isidore Lucien, pseud Comte de Lautréamont
(1846–70)

French writer of fantasy—a major influence on the Surrealist movement. Born in Montevideo, Uruguay, the son of a consular officer, he returned to France for his education, studying at both Pau and Tarbes. In 1868, the first instalment of his sensational masterpiece

Les Chants de Maldoror was published under a pseudonym borrowed from the title of a novel by **Eugène Sue**; it seems, however, that the printer refused to distribute the pamphlets, either because he was shocked by their contents or because he had not been paid. *Les Chants de Maldoror* first appeared in Belgium and Switzerland, where the author believed he would find a more sympathetic audience for his 'poetry of revolt'. Violent and perverse in the extreme, *Les Chants de Maldoror* transcends the human realm altogether, combining systematic blasphemy and sexual obscenity with a lyrical and hallucinatory cast of language that exercised an enormous influence on later writers like **André Breton** and **Alfred Jarry**. Shortly before his premature death, Ducasse published a volume of prose *Poèmes* (1870, under his own name) which, though less well known, confirm his wayward genius.

▷P Zweig, *Lautréamont: The Violent Narcissus* (1972)

DUCIĆ, Jovan
(1871–1943)

Serbian poet and critic, born in Trebijne. He left for the USA in 1941, and died in Gary, Indiana. He was always much influenced by the example of the French Parnassian and Symbolist poets whom he met as a young man in Paris. *Plave legende* (1908, 'Blue Legends') was an immensely popular collection of exquisite if somewhat artificial prose poems. He had initially followed in the footsteps of **Vojislav Ilić**, a lesser poet but a potent influence; he was the leading poet in the *Moderna* movement in Serbian poetry. He never really gave up his 'decadent' view of 'art for art's sake', and has been much criticized for it; but he remains the Serbian decadent poet par excellence, and not least for his fine technique.

DUCIS, Jean François
(1733–1816)

French poet and playwright, born in Versailles. His own tragedies are regarded as mediocre and he is best known for his adaptations of **Shakespeare** for the French stage, which he completed from earlier French versions, since he knew no English. They did help popularize Shakespeare in France, despite wild inaccuracies, and such liberties as allowing Othello to discover his mistake and spare Desdemona.

▷C Kueln, *Verben Ducis in seinen Bezegung zu Shakespeare* (1875)

DUCK, Stephen
(1705–56)

English ploughman-poet and scholar, born in Charlton in Wiltshire of humble parents. A self-educated farm-labourer, his verses came to the attention of Queen Caroline, who awarded him a pension and made him a Yeoman of the Guard in 1733. He published *Poems on Several Occasions* in 1736. He took holy orders in 1746 and was made rector of Byfleet in 1752, but committed suicide by drowning.

▷ R Davis, *Stephen Duck, the Thresher Poet* (1926)

DUCKWORTH, Marilyn Rose
(1935–)

New Zealand novelist, born in Otahuhu, Auckland, sister of **Fleur Adcock**. She was an early protégée of Hutchinson's pioneering 'New Authors' imprint with *A Gap in the Spectrum* (1959, 1985). Three others followed: *The Matchbox House* (1960), *A Barbarous Tongue* (1963) and *Over the Fence is Out* (1969). There was then a 15-year break before *Disorderly Conduct* (1984), with a background of the New Zealand rugby riots of 1981, and four more novels: *Married Alive* (1985), *Rest for the Wicked* (1986), *Pulling Faces* (1987) and *A Message from Harpo* (1989). Her themes are predominantly feminist, focusing on the manner in which her heroines cope with challenge.

DUDEK, Louis
(1918–)

Leading Canadian poet, born in Montreal, who has been both an academic and a publisher (Contact Press, DC Books). He has been called 'Canada's most important—that is to say consequential—modern voice'. At first deeply influenced by the Imagist movement and its poets (in particular **Pound**), he later made one of the most notable efforts to liberate Canadian poetry from its British influences. Most celebrated, after his earlier lyric poetry, are his long poems, such as *En Mexico* (1958), in which 'Pound is both hero and villain'. His *Collected Poetry* appeared in 1971; *Infinite Worlds* (1988) is the 'quasi-definitive' edition, edited by Robin Blaser.

▷ F Davey, *Louis Dudek and Raymond Souster* (1980)

DUDINTSEV, Vladimir
(1918–)

Russian novelist, born in Kupyansk, in the province of Kharkov. He is famous for only one book: *Ne khlebom yedinym* (1956, Eng trans *Not By Bread Alone*, 1957), the story of an inventor whose liveliness is stultified by bureaucrats and careerists. It became well known when subjected to attack by Soviet culture-clerks; it is not well written, but is full of energy.

DUFFY, Carol Ann
(1955–)

Scottish poet, born in Glasgow, considered one of the leading woman poets of her generation. It has been said of her that she writes love-poems 'as if she were the first one to do so'. Much influenced by the dramatic monologues of **Robert Browning**, but also—though not too obviously—by **Laura Riding**, she is striking in her use of a kind of toughened and good-natured whimsicality in her verse. Her collections include *Standing Female Nude* (1985) and *The Other Country* (1990). In 1993 she won the Whitbread Award for poetry for her collection *Mean Time*.

▷ *Bête Noir*, 6 (1989)

DUFFY, Maureen Patricia
(1933–)

English novelist, poet and dramatist, born in Worthing, Sussex. After attending university in London and five years' employment as a schoolteacher, she published her first novel in 1962, *That's How It Was*, which deals with the relationship between a mother and her illegitimate daughter. One of her most notable novels, *The Microcosm* (1966), looks at lesbian life through the eyes of three women. She has written novels set in the past, the present day, and the future, blending realism and fantasy, her subjects ranging from sexual and social themes to animal rights and the moral issues resulting from scientific progress. Her characters are often at the margins of society, hungry for affection. Her critical work includes *The Erotic World of Faery* (1972), a **Freud**ian analysis of English literature, and *The Passionate Shepherdess: Aphra Behn 1640–1689* (1977), an excellent study.

▷ J Rule, *Lesbian Images* (1975)

DU FRESNE, Yvonne
(1929–)

New Zealand novelist and short-story writer, born in Takaka of Danish Huguenot descent, the influence of which comes through in her novels, *The Book of Ester* (1982), in which the central character searches for her roots, and *Frédérique* (1987). Her short stories, in *Farvel* (1980) and *The Growing of Astrid Westergaard* (1985) show a Danish girl growing up in a New Zealand farming community, reliving the past history of her ancestors in her play.

DUGAN, Alan
(1923–)

American poet, born in Brooklyn, New York City. He was educated at Queen's College in New York, and served in World War II. In 1971 he became staff member for poetry at the Fine Arts Work Center in Provincetown, Massachusetts. His first book of poems was privately printed, and was followed by *Poems* (1961), which won him the Pulitzer Prize for Poetry in 1962. Subsequent works include *Poems 2* (1963), *Sequence* (1976), *Poems 6* (1989), as well as a *Collected Poems* (1969) and *New and Collected Poems* (1983). His terse, rather bleak poems are alleviated by an understated humour, and are directly rooted in experience.

DUGGAN, Alfred
(1903–64)

English historical novelist and biographer, writing for young people. Born in Buenos Aires, Argentina, he published *Knight With Armour*, his first novel, in 1950. While continuing to write fiction, he extended his range to biography in such books as *Thomas Beckett of Canterbury* (1952) and *Julius Caesar: A Great Life* (1955), both of which were praised for the clarity with which they presented social, moral and political issues. Duggan also wrote a series of *Look at ...* books, including *Look at Castles* (1960) and *Look at Churches* (1961). *Growing Up in the Thirteenth Century* (1962) describes the possible experience of young people in a feudal society.

DUGGAN, Eileen
(1894–1972)

New Zealand poet whose first verse, *Poems*, appeared in 1922. A collection of the same title in 1937 had an effusive introduction by **Walter de la Mare** and, like her next two books, *New Zealand Poems* (1940) and *More Poems* (1951), was published in London where her writing was identified with the Georgian school. She also wrote a collection of verse for children, *New Zealand Bird Songs* (1929).

DUGGAN, Maurice
(1922–74)

New Zealand writer, born in Auckland, who wrote excellently crafted short stories which employ melancholy motifs of movement, transition and loss. *Immanuel's Land* (1956) was followed by further titles in 1965 and 1970 and *Collected Stories* (ed **C K Stead**, 1981). Similar in mood is his work for children, as in his classic fantasy *Falter Tom and the Water Boy* (1958) and *The Fabulous McFanes* (1974).

DU GUILLET, Pernette
(?1520–1545)

French poet. Born in Lyons to a noble family, she was a well-educated woman, familiar with several European and Classical languages. She was married to the poet **Maurice Scève**

in 1536, and proved a considerable inspiration to his work. She died when she was only 25, probably as a result of an outbreak of plague, and the manuscripts of her poems were discovered after her death. Scève entrusted Antoine du Moulin with their publication, and *Rymes de gentile et vertueuse Dame D Pernette du Guillet* appeared in 1545. The collection was augmented for a second edition in 1552. Du Guillet's poetry, consisting of epigrams, songs and elegies, combines a marked originality with a rigorous technical control, and its content clearly reflects her erudition.

DUHAMEL, Georges
(1884–1966)

French novelist and poet. He originally studied medicine and worked as an army surgeon in World War I. This provided the background for *La Vie des martyrs* (1917, 'Life of the Martyrs') and *Civilisation* (1918, awarded the Prix **Goncourt**. Many of his 50 volumes of vigorous, skilful writing have been translated. They include *Salavin* (1920–32), *Le Notaire du Havre* (1913, Eng trans *News from Le Havre*, 1934), the first of the 10 parts of *Chronique des Pasquier* (1933–44, Eng trans *The Pasquier Chronicles*, 1937–45) and *Positions Françaises: Chronique de l'année 1939* (1940, Eng trans *Why France Fights*, 1940). He edited *Mercure de France*.
▷ *Light on My Days*, translation of two volumes of autobiography (1948)

DULEY, Margaret
(1894–1968)

Canadian novelist, born in Newfoundland. Duley had to curtail drama studies in London because of World War I and on her return to Canada became an active suffragette. She wrote for money and her novels—*The Eyes of the Gull* (1936), *Cold Pastoral* (1939), *Highway to Valour* (1941)—are mainly about female experience in harsh Newfoundland settings.
▷ A Feder, *Margaret Duley: Newfoundland Novelist* (1983)

DUMAS, Alexandre, in full, Alexandre Dumas Davy de la Pailleterie, known as 'Dumas père'
(1802–70)

French novelist and playwright, born in Villers-Cotterets, the son of General Alexandre Davy-Dumas and Marie Labouret, daughter of a tavern keeper and small landowner. After an idle youth, he went to Paris in 1823 and obtained a clerkship in the bureau of the Duc d'Orléans and spent some years writing. A volume of short stories and a couple of farces, however, were his only production when, at

27, he became famous for his *Henri III* (1829), performed at the Théâtre Français, which revolutionized historical drama. In 1831 he did the same for domestic tragedy with *Antony*, failed in verse with *Charles VII chez ses grands vassaux* ('Charles VII visits his Great Vassals'), and scored a tremendous success with *Richard Darlington*. In 1832 he carried the romantic 'history' to its culmination in *La Tour de Nesle* (in collaboration with Gaillardet). In that same year he fell ill with cholera, went to Switzerland to recuperate, and wrote for the *Revue des Deux Mondes* the first of his famous and delightful *Impressions de voyage* ('Travelling Impressions'). He was a prodigious worker, who would, after months of writing, refresh himself with a round of travel, and he always published his experiences, as in *En Suisse* (1833–7, Eng trans *Adventures in Switzerland*, 1960), *Le Midi de la France* (1840), and *Le Caucase* (1859, Eng trans *Adventures in Caucasia*, 1962). But it was as a storyteller that he gained enduring success. He worked with about 90 collaborators in all and disagreed violently with some of them. He borrowed indiscriminately, and brought to his borrowings his own immense and radiant personality. Still, it is undeniable that his thefts were many and flagrant. Edward Trelawny's *Adventures of a Younger Son*, for instance, appears in his collected works, and it is said that he was with difficulty restrained from signing a book of the *Iliad* which someone else had turned into prose. He decided to put the history of France into novels, and his earliest attempt was *Isabelle de Bavière* (1836, Eng trans *Isabel of Bavaria*, 1846). It was followed by *La Salle d'Armes* (1838, Eng trans *Pauline*, 1844), *Acté* (1839, Eng trans 1904), *Othon l'archer* (1840, Eng trans *Othon the Archer*, 1860)—and others all on different lines. Then he turned again to the historical vein in *Le Chevalier d'Harmenthal* (1843, Eng trans *The Château d'Harmental*, 1856) and *Ascanio* (1843, Eng trans *Francis I*, 1849). In the following decade he wrote outstandingly. In 1844, with a number of digressions into new provinces such as *Cécile* (Eng trans *Cecile*, 1904), *Fernande* (Eng trans 1904), *Amaury* (Eng trans 1854), *Le Comte de Monte-Cristo* (Eng trans *The Count of Monte Cristo*, 1846), there appeared *Les Trois Mousquetaires* (Eng trans *The Three Musketeers*, 1846). In 1845, *Vingt ans après* (Eng trans *Twenty Years After*, 1846), *La Fille du régent* (Eng trans *The Regent's Daughter*, 1847), and *La Reine Margot* (Eng trans *Margaret de Navarre*, 1845); in 1846, *La Guerre des femmes* (Eng trans *Nanot*, 1847), *Le Chevalier de Maison-Rouge* (Eng trans *Marie Antoinette*, 1846), *Le Bâtard de Mauléon* (Eng trans *The Bastard of Mauleon*, 1849),

La Dame de Monsoreau (Eng trans *Chicot the Jester*, 1857), and *Les Mémoires d'un médecin* (Eng trans *Memoirs of a Physician*, 1847); in 1848, *Les Quarante-cinq* (Eng trans *The Forty-Five Guardsmen*, 1848) and the beginnings of *Le Vicomte de Bragelonne* (Eng trans *The Vicomte de Bragalonne*, 1857) which was finished in 1850; and in 1849, *Le Collier de la reine* (Eng trans *The Queen's Necklace*, 1855). The next two years witnessed productions as varied as *La Tulipe noire* (1850, Eng trans *Rosa; or, The Black Tulip*, 1854) and *Le Trou de l'enfer* (1850–1, Eng trans *The Mouth of Hell*, 1906), and *La Femme au collier de velours* (1851, Eng trans *The Woman with the Velvet Necklace*, 1894). The historical masterpiece *Olympe de Clèves* (Eng trans *Olympe de Cleves*, 1894) came in 1852; between that year and 1854 he wrote the 10 delightful volumes of *Mes Mémoires* (Eng trans *My Memoirs*, 1907–9), with *Ange Pitou* (1853, Eng trans 1907) and *La Comtesse de Charny* (1855, Eng trans *The Countess of Charny*, 1858). Other achievements in the romance of French history were *Ingénue* (1854, Eng trans *Ingenue*, 1855), *Les Compagnons de Jéhu* (1857, Eng trans *Roland of Montreval*, 1860), *Les Louves de Machecoul* (1859, Eng trans *The Laste Vendee*, 1894) and *Les Blancs et les bleus* (1867–8, Eng trans *The Polish Spy*, 1869), with which the sequence ended. The list is incomplete, and reference can only be made in passing to the rest of his work during this period, such as drama (the great historical novels were also dramatized—the *Mousquetaires* cycle supplied at least three plays—as also were *Monte-Cristo* and others), history, *causerie*, journalism, etc. Dumas took a conspicuous part in the July Days; in 1837 he received the red ribbon; in 1842 he married Mlle Ida Ferrier, from whom he promptly separated. In 1855 he went for two years into exile at Brussels; from 1860 to 1864 he was helping Garibaldi in Italy, and conducting and writing a journal, and in 1886 he produced the last but one of his plays. By this time the end was near; he sank under his work. He had gone through a series of fortunes, and he left Paris for the last time with only a couple of napoleons in his pocket. He went to his son's villa in Dieppe, and stayed there until his death.

▷F H Gribble, *Dumas, Father and Son* (1930); R Todd, *The Laughing Mulatto* (1939)

DUMAS, Alexandre, known as **'Dumas fils'** (1824–95)

French writer, illegitimate son of **Alexandre Dumas**, born in Paris when his father was only 22 years old. He was soon legitimized, and at 16, after a course of training at the Institution Goubaux and the Collège Bourbon, he left school for the world of letters and the society to which his father, then almost at his peak, belonged. He was basically respectable, however, and having sown some wild oats settled down to serious work. He started in fiction and succeeded and went on to drama. He took to theorizing about art, morals, politics, and even religion, and was successful. His novels—from *La Dame aux camélias* (1848, Eng trans *The Lady with the Camelias*, 1856) to *L'Affaire Clémenceau* (1864, Eng trans *Wife Murder; or, The Clémenceau Tragedy*, 1866)—are all readable, and the former was a great success in dramatic form (1852). His essays, speeches, letters, and prefaces generally are brilliant. Of his 16 plays, *Le Demi-Monde* (1855, Eng trans *Le Demi-Monde*, 1921), *Le Fils naturel* (1856, Eng trans 1879), *Les Idées de Mme Aubray* (1867, Eng trans 1965), *Une Visite de noces* (1871, 'A Wedding Party'), *Monsieur Alphonse* (1873, Eng trans 1874) and *Denise* (1885, Eng trans 1885) are masterpieces. Other famous dramas in which he had a share are *Le Supplice d'une femme* (1865, 'The Torture of a Woman'), whose chaotic original is due to Émile de Girardin; *Héloïse Paranquet* (1866), in collaboration with Durantin; and *Les Danicheff* (1876, Eng trans 1876). He may have assisted **George Sand** in preparing several of her works for the stage, and he completed and produced his father's *Joseph Balsamo* (1878).

▷ F H Gribble, *Dumas, Father and Son* (1930)

DU MAURIER, Dame Daphne
(1907–89)

English novelist and short-story writer, daughter of the actor-manager Sir Gerald Du Maurier. She wrote a number of highly successful period romances and adventure stories, many of which were inspired by Cornwall, where she lived, including *Jamaica Inn* (1936), *Rebecca* (1938), *Frenchman's Creek* (1942) and *My Cousin Rachel* (1951), several of which have been filmed. Her short story, 'The Birds' (published in *The Apple Tree*, 1952), became a classic Hitchcock movie. Later books included *The Flight of the Falcon* (1965), *The House on the Strand* (1969), *The Winding Stair*, a study of Francis Bacon (1976), *The Rendezvous and other Stories* (1980), and a volume of memoirs, *Vanishing Cornwall* (1967).

▷ *Growing Pains: The Shaping of a Writer* (1977, published in the USA as *Myself When Young*); M Forster, *Daphne du Maurier* (1993)

DU MAURIER, George Louis Palmella Busson
(1834–96)

French-born British artist, cartoonist and novelist, born in Paris. He was the grandson of émigrés who had originally fled to England at the Revolution; in 1851 he went to London himself and studied chemistry, but returned to Paris to study art there and in Antwerp and Düsseldorf. Back in England he made his name as an illustrator, with new editions of **William Makepeace Thackeray**'s *Esmond* and his ballads, **John Foxe**'s *Book of Martyrs*, and stories in periodicals like *Once A Week* and the *Cornhill Magazine*. Finally he joined the staff of *Punch* (1864–96), where he became best known as a gentle satirist of middle- and upper-class society (some of his illustrations were collected as *English Society at Home*, 1880). He also wrote and illustrated three novels, *Peter Ibbetson* (1891), *The Martian* (1897), and the phenomenally successful *Trilby* (1894), the story of a young singer under the mesmeric influence of another musician, Svengali.

▷ D Whiteley, *George du Maurier: his life and work* (1948)

DUNBAR, Paul Laurence
(1872–1906)

American poet, born in Dayton, Ohio, the son of escaped Negro slaves. He gained a reputation with *Lyrics of Lowly Life* (1896), many of which were in dialect. He published several other volumes of verse, and four novels. His *Complete Poems* appeared in 1913.

▷ A Gayle Jr, *Oak and Ivy: a biography of Dunbar* (1971)

DUNBAR, William
(c.1460–c.1520)

Scottish poet, probably born in East Lothian. He seems to have studied at St Andrews University from 1475 to 1479. He became a Franciscan novice, and diligently visited every significant town in England. He preached at Canterbury but later left the order. He appears next to have been secretary to some of James IV's numerous embassies to foreign courts. In 1500 he obtained a pension from the king, and the following year visited England, probably with the ambassadors sent to arrange the king's marriage to Margaret Tudor, daughter of Henry VII. Early in 1503, before the queen's arrival, he composed in honour of the event his most famous poem, *The Thrissil and the Rois*, perhaps the happiest political allegory in English literature. It now seems that he lived chiefly about court, writing poems and sustaining himself with the vain hope of Church preferment. In 1508 Walter Chepman printed seven of his poems—the earliest specimen of Scottish typography. He visited the north of Scotland in May 1511, in the train of Queen Margaret, and his name disappears altogether after the Battle of Flodden (1513). He was certainly dead by 1530. He reached his highest level in his satires, *The Twa Marriit Wemen and the Wedo* and *The Dance of the Sevin Deadly Synnis*. His *Lament for the Makaris* is a masterpiece of pathos.

▷J Baxter, *William Dunbar, a biographical study* (1952)

DUNCAN, Robert Edward, originally **Edward Howard Duncan**
(1919–)

American poet, born in Oakland, California. He was adopted by Theosophists in 1920 and named Robert Edward Symmes. Educated at the University of California, he was editor of *Experimental Review* (1938–40) and *Phoenix and Berkeley Miscellany* (1948–9). Aligned with the 'Black Mountain' poets, and influenced by **George Barker** and **Ezra Pound**, he wrote in a style that emphasized natural forms and processes. His collections include *Heavenly City, Earthly City* (1947), *The Opening of the Field* (1960), *Roots and Branches* (1964) and *The Years as Catches* (1966). His 1944 essay, 'The Homosexual in Society', is an important document in the development of gay cultural politics.

▷*The Truth and Life of Myth: an essential autobiography* (1968)

DUNCAN, Sara Jeanette (Janet)
(1861–1922)

Canadian novelist, columnist and travel writer, born in Ontario. When she joined the *Toronto Globe* in 1886 she became the first woman to work in the editorial department of a Canadian newspaper. Using the pseudonym Garth Grafton she wrote columns for other newspapers. In 1888 she undertook a round-the-world trip with a friend, Lily Lewis, which resulted in her first full-length book, *Round the World by Ourselves* (1890). After her marriage to Everard Cotes, a museum curator in Calcutta, she spent the next 25 years in India. Her fiction, whether specifically about India, as in *The Simple Adventures of a Memsahib* (1893), or about generally paternalistic habits of mind, as in *The Imperialist* (1904), a book about small-town life in Ontario, contains acute observation of colonial attitudes.

▷M Fowler, *Redney: The Life of Sarah Jeanette Duncan* (1983)

DUNLAP, William
(1766–1839)

American playwright, born in Perth Amboy, New Jersey. Initially a painter, who was commissioned to make portraits of George and Martha Washington, he was the first American to make the theatre his only profession, and as a dramatist and manager he dominated the American stage in the 20 years from 1790 to 1810. Following *The Father; or, American Shandyism* (1789), a comedy of manners, he wrote almost 70 plays, many of them very quickly, several being adaptations of foreign dramas. Among his more successful plays, *André* (1798), based upon an incident during the American War of Independence, is considered the first tragedy to be wholly derived from American history. Dunlap was an innovative but only intermittently successful manager, and in 1805 he was declared bankrupt. Six years later he left the theatre and returned to his previous career as an artist. He is also the author of such books as *A History of the Rise and Progress of the Arts of Design in the United States* (1834).

▷O Coad, *William Dunlap* (1917)

DUNN, Douglas Eaglesham
(1942–)

Scottish poet, born in Inchinnan, Renfrewshire. He was educated at Renfrew High and Camphill schools, Paisley, before attending the Scottish School of Librarianship and Hull University, where he was employed in the library simultaneously with **Philip Larkin**, who became a friend and mentor. His first collection of poems, *Terry Street* (1969), articulates contempt and warmth in almost equal measure for the working-class suburb of Hull where he was then living. The two subsequent collections—*The Happier Life* (1972) and *Love or Nothing* (1974)—rather disappointed readers who had been drawn to *Terry Street* by its bleak humour and tacky glamour. In *Barbarians* (1979), however, he echoed and extended that first collection, and has subsequently demonstrated that he is one of Britain's finest contemporary poets, technically accomplished and artistically ambitious. He returned to Scotland in 1984. *Elegies* (1985), his sixth collection, is his best-known. Written on the death of his first wife, it is a moving valediction, emotionally raw but tightly controlled. It won the Whitbread Prize. *Secret Villages*, a collection of stories, was published in 1985, and his *Selected Poems: 1964–1983* in 1986. A new collection of poems, *Northlight*, appeared in 1988, and another, *Dante's Drum-kit*, in 1993. He edited *Scotland: An Anthology* (1991) and *The Faber Book of Twentieth Century Scottish Verse* (1992). He has been Professor of English at St Andrews University since 1991.

DUNN, Max
(1895–1963)

Irish-born journalist and poet, born in Dublin, who settled in Australia in the early 1920s after serving in World War I. He published a number of books of verse between *Random Elements* (1943) and *The Mirror and the Rose* (1954), and a collection of his translations from the Chinese was issued as *The City of Wide Streets* in 1952.

DUNN, Nell (Mary)
(1936–)

English novelist and playwright, born in London and educated at a convent school. She is known principally for her early, vivid, terse, documentary-style accounts of working-class life, set mainly in the south-London areas of Battersea and Clapham. Her first book was a collection of short stories, *Up The Junction* (1965), but her best-known work is probably the screenplay *Poor Cow* (1967, with Ken Loach), in which the heroine Joy, a young mother, takes jobs as a barmaid, model and factory-worker while her unloved husband languishes in prison. A play, *Steaming* (1981), looks at the lives of a group of women who meet regularly at a women's Turkish bath, and follows their campaign to prevent its closure.

DUNNE, Finley Peter
(1867–1936)

American humorist, born in Chicago. He worked as a journalist there, and was editor of *Chicago Journal* (1897–1900). With his creation of the Chicago Irish philosopher-bartender 'Mr Dooley' he became from 1900 the exponent of American–Irish humorous satire on current personages and events, in *Mr Dooley in Peace and War* (1898) and many other books.
▷ E J Bander, *Mr Dooley and Mr Dunne: The Literary Life of a Chicago Catholic* (1981)

DUNNE, John Gregory
(1932–)

American novelist, movie writer and journalist, born in Connecticut. He is the husband of novelist **Joan Didion**, with whom he has collaborated on several screenplays. His crime novels, *True Confessions* (1977) and *Dutch Shea Jr* (1982), are marked by a particularly strong moral sense, shaped by Irish Catholicism, which is perhaps most clearly seen in the Dunne–Didion film version of *True Confessions* (1981), in which Robert de Niro starred as a priest. The same concerns re-emerge in later books like *The Red, White and Blue* (1986) and the much acclaimed *Harp* (1989). Like his wife, Dunne is an acute observer of the Californian scene, but he brings an east-coast detachment to his accounts of Hollywood (*The Studio*, 1969), and the gambling industry (*Vegas*, 1974).
▷ *Quintana and Friends* (1978)

DUNNETT, Dorothy, née Halliday
(1923–)

Scottish novelist, born in Dunfermline and educated at James Gillespie's High School for Girls in Edinburgh. She began her career with the Civil Service as a Press Secretary in Edinburgh. A recognized portrait painter since 1950, she has exhibited at the Royal Academy and is a member of the Scottish Society of Women Artists. She has used her maiden name for a series of detective novels, starting with *Dolly and the Singing Bird* (1968), but her best-known works comprise a series of historical novels, including *Game of Kings* (1961) and *Checkmate* (1975). Featuring the fictional Scottish mercenary Francis Crawford of Lymond, these novels continue the Scottish tradition of historical romance. In 1986 she embarked upon a second historical series, this time featuring the house of Charetty and Niccoló.

DUNSANY, Edward John Moreton Drax Plunkett, 18th Baron
(1878–1957)

Irish novelist, poet and playwright, born in London. Educated at Eton and Sandhurst, he succeeded to the title in 1899, served in the 2nd Boer War with the Coldstream Guards, and thereafter settled in Ireland at Dunsany Castle in County Meath. In World War I he was an officer of the Inniskilling Fusiliers. By World War II, he was Byron Professor of English Literature in Athens, and was associated with the Irish revival led by **Yeats** and **Lady Gregory**. His literary works are highly poetic and imaginative. They began in 1905 with the mythological novel *The Gods of Pegana*, with illustrations by his frequent collaborator, S H Sime. His 'Jorkens' stories, beginning with *The Travel Tales of Mr Joseph Jorkens* (1931) were popular, while *The King of Elfland's Daughter* (1924) is his best-known work of fantasy. At W B Yeats's invitation he wrote many plays for the Abbey Theatre, including *The Glittering Gate* (1909) and *The Laughter of the Gods* (1919). These, and other works for theatre, enjoyed considerable popularity in both Britain and the USA. His verse is contained in *Fifty Poems* (1930) and *Mirage Water* (1939). He also wrote an autobiographical series: *Patches of Sunlight* (1938), *While the Sirens Slept* (1944), *The Sirens Wake* (1945) and *To Awaken Pegasus* (1949).
▷ M Amory, *Lord Dunsany* (1972)

DUNSTAN, (John) Keith
(1925–)

Australian journalist and writer, born in Melbourne. His satirical articles on the Australian way of life and its players have been collected into such books as *Wowsers* (1968), *Knockers* (1972) and *Sports* (1973). *Ratbags* (1979) brings together a notorious bilker of taxi-drivers, a state premier, a world-famous pianist and a self-made prince in a cross-section of Australia's eccentrics. Dunstan was President of the Bicycle Institute of Victoria between 1974 and 1978.

DUPONT, Pierre
(1821–70)

French popular poet and songwriter, born in Lyons, the son of a blacksmith. He moved to Paris, and enjoyed popular success as the writer of patriotic songs. He wrote knowledgeably about peasant life in books such as *Le chant des ouvriers* (1848, 'The Workmen's Song').

DURACK, Dame Mary
(1913–)

Australian author, born into a pioneering Western Australian family in Adelaide. *Kings in Grass Castles* (1959) is the saga of the Durack family from 19th-century Ireland to the time of Patsy Durack, one of Australia's greatest landowners, who died in 1898. *Sons in the Saddle* (1983) brings the story up to modern times. Other historical works include *The Rock and the Sand* (1969) and the play *Swan River Saga* (1975). She has also written a number of books for children, some with illustrations by her younger sister, Elizabeth Durack (1916–). Her libretto for the opera *Dalgerie*, with music by Australian composer James Penberthy, is based on her own novel *Keep Him My Country* (1955) and was produced at the Sydney Opera House in 1973.

DURAN, Augustín
(1793–1862)

Spanish poet and critic. He compiled a collection of literature in the Spanish ballad tradition, *Romancero general* (1828–32), and the critical work *Discurso sobre . . . la decadencia del teatro antiguo* (1828, 'Discourses on . . . the decline of classical theatre').

DURAS, Marguerite, pseud of Marguerite Donnadieu
(1914–)

French novelist, born in Indo-China. She studied law and political science at the Sorbonne in Paris. During World War II she took part in the Resistance at great risk to herself as a Jewess. She is considered one of the great European writers of the 20th century. Her books include the semi-autobiographical *La Douleur* (1985, Eng trans 1986) and *L'Amant* (1984, Eng trans *The Lover*, 1985, Prix **Goncourt**), novels like *Un Barrage contre le Pacifique* (1950, Eng trans *The Sea Wall*, 1952 (US); 1953 (UK)), *Le Vice-Consul* (1966, Eng trans *The Vice Consul*, 1968) and *Détruire, dit-elle* (1969, Eng trans *Destroy, She Said*, 1970), film scripts like *Hiroshima Mon Amour* (1960, 'Hiroshima My Love'), and a number of plays, including *La Musica* (1965, Eng trans *The Music*, 1966).
▷A Cismaru, *Duras* (1971)

DURBRIDGE, Francis Henry
(1912–)

English crime novelist and playwright, born in Hull and educated at Birmingham University. He has on occasion conceded authorial credits to his fictional detective Paul Temple, who figured in a long and popular drama series on radio (and later, less successfully, on television). Temple's Watson was his wife Steve, who brought fragrant charm and unerring social antennae to their cases, which were firmly rooted in a professional middle-class milieu. The first of the Temple stories was 'novelized' from radio scripts as *Send for Paul Temple* (1938), and the character was still active in the 1970s.

DURCAN, Paul
(1944–)

Irish poet, born in Dublin; he graduated from University College Cork in 1973 in History and Archaeology. His poems, which have won the **Patrick Kavanagh** Award for Poetry (1974) and the Whitbread Poetry Prize (1990), are direct statements of commitment to a relentless humanist standpoint. The obliquity of some references in *O Westport in the Light of Asia Minor* (1975) eased into a more confessional, conversational style in *Teresa's Bar* (1976) and *Jesus and Angela* (1988), while a more meditative and reflective tone is present in the autobiographical *Daddy, Daddy* (1990) and the politically-informed *A Snail in my Prime* (1993). The loose long line structure he assimilated from the American Beats and the Russian Modernists often conceals the craft and passion that is the emotional trademark of all his work.

DURCYCH, Jaroslav
(1886–1962)

Czech novelist and poet, a doctor by profession, who was born in Hradec Králové and died in Prague. He was a conservative

Catholic, but one of liberal sympathies, always a spokesman for the proletariat; his drama and poetry failed, but his massive, fantastic and powerful historical novel *Bloudeni* (1929, Eng trans *The Descent of the Idols*, 1935) is the finest of all fiction about the Thirty Years War and the enigmatic Wallenstein. His untranslated *Rekviem* (1930, 'Requiem') continues the story.

D'URFÉ, Honoré
(1567–1625)

French novelist, born in Marseilles. He fought in the religious wars of France and later settled in Savoy. His great work *Astrée* (1607–27), a pastoral romance, though now not much read in its entirety for pleasure, is of crucial importance in the history of the French novel. Drawing on the examples of **Montemayor** and **Guarini**, he provided his grateful 17th-century readers with a model for courtship and conversation. The work was completed by his secretary, Baro, after his death.
▷ O C Revre, *Honoré d'Urfé* (1910); M Seymour-Smith, *Introduction to Fifty European Novels* (1979)

D'URFREY, Thomas
(1653–1723)

English dramatist and songwriter, born in Exeter of Huguenot ancestry. He was a nephew of **Honoré d'Urfé**, author of the famous romance of *Astrée*. He soon became a prolific playwright, his comedies especially being popular. Among these were *The Fond Husband* (1676), *Madame Fickle* (1677) and *Sir Burnaby Whig* (1681). In 1683 he published his *New Collection of Songs and Poems*, which was followed by a long series of songs, collected as *Wit and Mirth, or Pills to Purge Melancholy* (6 vols, 1719–20). Meanwhile he had written some plays, which were criticized as being immoral by Jeremy Collier. His fortunes declined as his comedies ceased to please.
▷ R S Forsyte, *A Study of the Plays* (1916)

DURRELL, Lawrence George
(1912–90)

English novelist, poet, travel writer and playwright, born in Julundur, India. He lived in India until he was 10, when his family moved back to England. He took numerous odd jobs—in night clubs, as an estate agent and in the Jamaica police—and once said he had been driven to writing 'by sheer ineptitude'. He convinced his family that life would be more congenial in a warmer climate and they moved to Corfu until the outbreak of World War II. He moved to France in 1957 but travelled widely as a journalist and in the service of the Foreign Office. His first novel was *Pied Piper of Lovers* (1935) and his second, *Panic Spring*, appeared two years later under the pseudonym Charles Norden, so woeful were the sales of its predecessor. He made his name with the 'Alexandria Quartet'—*Justine* (1957), *Balthazar* (1958), *Mountolive* (1958) and *Clea* (1960)—a complex, interlocking series set in Egypt, remarkable for its sensuous language, intrigue and devious plotting, the nature of modern love being its central topic. He followed this with a two-novel sequence, *Tunc* (1968) and *Nunquam* (1970). The *Avignon Quincunx—Monsieur* (1974), *Livia* (1978), *Constance* (1982), *Sebastian* (1983) and *Quinx* (1985)—is also conceived on a grand and elaborate scale. His generous output includes travel books, *Prospero's Cell* (1945) and *Bitter Lemons* (1957), verse (*Collected Poems, 1931–1974*), comic sketches, criticism, plays and a children's novel, *White Eagles Over Serbia* (1957). His long friendship with **Henry Miller** is recorded in their correspondence published in 1988. His brother, the naturalist Gerald Durrell, has written several popular books about his experiences, including the bestselling memoir, *My Family and Other Animals* (1956), in which he described his family's time in Corfu as like living 'in one of the more flamboyant and slapstick comic operas'.
▷ J Unterecker, *Lawrence Durrell* (1964)

DÜRRENMATT, Friedrich
(1921–90)

Swiss author, born in Konolfingen, Bern, the son of a pastor; he studied there and at Zürich and turned from painting to writing. The theme which recurs in all his work is that life is a calamity which has to be accepted for what it is but without surrender. His novels include the detective story *Der Richter und sein Henker* (1952, Eng trans *The Judge and his Hangman*, 1954), *Der Verdacht* (1953, Eng trans *The Quarry*, 1961 (US); 1962 (UK)), *Die Panne* (1956, Eng trans *A Dangerous Game*, 1960), and his plays *Romulus der Grosse* (1949, Eng trans *Romulus*, 1961) and *Die Ehe des Herrn Mississippi* (1952, Eng trans *The Marriage of Mississippi*, 1958), which established his international reputation. *Ein Engel kommt nach Babylon* (1953, Eng trans *An Angel Comes to Babylon*, 1962) is a parable in which an angel brings chaos instead of happiness, and *Der Besuch einer alten Dame* (1956, Eng trans *The Visit*, 1958) describes the return of an old lady to her native village to revenge herself on a seducer. Other plays include *Die Physiker* (1962, Eng trans *The Physicists*, 1963), *Play Strindberg: Totentanz nach August Strindberg* (1969, Eng trans *Play Strindberg: The Dance of Death*, 1972), *Porträt eines Planeten* (1970, Eng trans *Portrait of a Planet*, 1973), and a novel, *Der Sturz* ('The Fall'), published in 1971.

▷ M B Peppard, *Dürrenmatt* (1969)

DUTT, Michael Madhu Sudan
(1824–73)

Indian poet, born in Sagandari, Bengal. He absorbed European culture, became a Christian and wrote poetry and drama in English and Bengali, such as the plays *Sarmishtha* (1858), *Padmavati* (1859), and the blank verse epics *Tillotama* (1860) and *Meghanad-Badha* (1861).

▷ H M Das Gupta, *Studies in Western Influence on 19th Century Bengali Poetry* (1935)

DUTT, Toru
(1856–77)

Indian poet who wrote in English. She died at 21, her promise almost wholly unfulfilled. She had a gift for retelling Hindu tales in English verse. Her poems are collected in *A Sheaf Gleaned from a French Field* (1976) and *Ancient Ballads and Legends of Hindustan* (1882).

▷ H Das, *Life and Letters of Toru Dutt* (1921)

DUTTON, Geoffrey Piers Henry
(1922–)

Australian poet, novelist, critic and editor, born in Kapunda, South Australia. After service during World War II he travelled overland back to Australia and became engaged in publishing. His verse collections include *Night Flight and Sunrise* (1944), the prizewinning *Antipodes in Shoes* (1958) and *A Body of Words* (1977). Other work includes his novels *The Mortal and the Marble* (1950), *Tamara* (1970) and *Queen Emma of the South Seas* (1976), based on the real life of a Samoan–American woman who founded a trading empire in the South Pacific. He has also written critical studies of **Patrick White** (1961) and **Walt Whitman** (1961), three historical biographies of pioneering Australians, as well as art appreciation, short stories (*The Wedge-Tailed Eagle*, 1980), and books for children. His work as a scholarly and enthusiastic editor has produced the acclaimed *The Literature of Australia* (1964, rev edn 1976) and representative anthologies of Australian verse.

DUUN, Olav
(1876–1939)

Norwegian novelist, born in Tosnes. He worked as a farmer and fisherman before training as a teacher, and the experience gave him a profound feeling for the lives of rural Norwegians. Between the wars he became an important exponent of the new 'national language', *Landsmål* (later known as *Nynorsk*

or New Norwegian), for which he was twice shortlisted for the Nobel Prize, but which has thwarted international translation and recognition of his work. Immensely prolific, his major fictional achievement is the massive six-volume *Juvikfolke* (1918–23, 'The People of Juvik'), which asserts human indomitability in the face of large-scale natural forces.

▷ A Overland, *Olav Dunn* (1955)

DWYER, James Francis
(1874–1952)

Australian novelist, born in Camden Park, New South Wales, who began his writing career while in prison on a forgery charge by sending pieces to a weekly magazine. On release he started in journalism, but in 1906 left for London and New York, where his short stories found a ready outlet in *Collier's* and *Harper's Bazaar*. He wrote 10 adventure novels beginning with *The White Waterfall* (1912). In search of material he travelled to Europe, North Africa and Asia, and settled in Pau, France. He escaped back to the USA after the German invasion but returned to Pau in 1945.

▷ *Leg Irons on Wings* (1949)

DYER, Sir Edward
(c.1545–1607)

English poet and diplomat, born in Sharpham Park, Somerset. He studied at Balliol College or Broadgates Hall, Oxford, and became a courtier. He was a friend of Sir **Fulke Greville** and Sir **Philip Sidney**; the latter wrote a song in praise of their friendship, while Dyer commemorated Sidney's death in a moving elegy. Only half a dozen of his poems have survived, of which the best known is 'My Mind to Me a Kingdom is'.

▷ R M Sargent, *At the Court of Queen Elizabeth: the life and hymns of Sir Edward Dyer* (1935)

DYER, George
(1755–1841)

English writer, **Charles Lamb**'s friend, born in London. From Christ's Hospital he went to Emmanuel College, Cambridge, taking his BA in 1778. In 1792 he settled in Clifford's Inn, London, and, with 'poems' and a vast mass of hack work, produced the *History of the University of Cambridge* (1814) and *Privileges of the University of Cambridge* (1824). He contributed 'all that was original' to Valpy's classics (141 vols, 1809–31), and became totally blind soon after his life's work was done.

▷ *The Poet's Fate* (1797)

DYER, John
(1699–1757)

Welsh poet and painter, born in Llanfynydd parish, Dyfed. Educated at Westminster School, he abandoned law for art, and in 1725 published his most successful work, *Grongar Hill*, notable for its warmth of feeling, simplicity and exquisite descriptions of landscape. The poem, which advocates a 'quiet in the soul', was inspired by the scenery of the valley of the river Towy in Carmarthenshire, and was written while he was an itinerant painter. In 1750 he published *The Ruins of Rome*, and was ordained the following year. Thereafter he held various livings in Leicestershire and Lincolnshire. His longest work, *The Fleece* (1757), a didactic poem, is praised by **Wordsworth** in a sonnet.

▷ 'The Poems of John Dyer' and 'The Life of John Dyer' in Dr S Johnson, *The Lives of the English Poets* (1779–81)

DYGASINSKI, Tomasz Adolf
(1839–1902)

Polish novelist who began writing late in life. He has affinities with **Kipling**, who eventually influenced him, and with **Zola**. His novels, none of which has been translated into English, are concerned with the humanly pessimistic implications of Darwinism, in which he believed.

DYGAT, Stanislaw
(1914–78)

Polish novelist, born in Warsaw. He spent most of World War II in a Nazi camp. His novels, of which *Podróz* (1958, 'Journey') is perhaps the most celebrated, are humorous and ironical in a typically Polish manner.

DYK, Viktor
(1877–1931)

Czech political poet, playwright and novelist, born in Psovska, near Melnik. Imprisoned by the Austrians, he became National Democratic MP in the new Czech parliament in 1919. His poetry began as one of protest tinged with nihilism, but ended with an acceptance of death. He wrote epics, historical plays and some less distinguished prose. He ended as a leading right-wing opponent to the regime.

DYSON, Edward
(1865–1931)

Australian writer, mainly of short stories, born in Morrison, Ballarat, Victoria. He is best known for his classic tale 'A Golden Shanty' in which Chinese fossickers keep returning to take bricks from a goldfields pub, the puzzled proprietor of which finally discovers that the bricks are made of gold-bearing clay. Dyson's stories appeared as *Below and On Top* (1898), *Fact'ry 'Ands* (1906) and *Benno and Some of the Push* (1911); he also published two novels which are merely a sequence of episodes in similar vein. A collection of his verse, *Rhymes from the Mines and Other Lines*, appeared in 1896, and the best of his stories were selected and introduced by **Norman Lindsay** as *The Golden Shanty: Short Stories* in 1963.

E

EARLE, John
(c.1601–1665)

English prelate, born in York. In 1641 he became tutor to Charles II, then Prince of Wales, and also served him as chaplain during his exile in France. He became Bishop of Worcester (1662), and of Salisbury (1663). In 1628 he published anonymously *Microcosmographie*, a set of witty character sketches and epigrammatic essays.

EASTLAKE, William
(1917–)

American novelist, born in New York City. His service in World War II provided him with the material for his best-known novel, the fantasy *Castle Keep* (1965), about a handful of American soldiers in a 10th-century castle in whose defence they die; this was filmed in 1969 by Sydney Pollack. Eastlake has also written many short stories, and the novel *Bronco People* (1958), set in New Mexico.

EBERHART, Richard Ghormley
(1904–)

American poet, born in Minnesota, and the author of almost 30 collections. Among the most notable are *A Bravery of Earth* (1930), *Reading the Spirit* (1936), *The Quarry* (1960) and *Fields of Grace* (1972). His *Selected Poems 1930–1965* won a Pulitzer Prize in 1966, and *Collected Poems 1930–1976* a National Book Award in 1977. A traditional, lyrical, reflective writer, deliberating upon the natural world and the cycles of life and death, Eberhart's writing has been acclaimed as being in the romantic tradition of **Blake**, **Wordsworth** and **Whitman**. He is considered to be one of the most important of 20th-century American poets. Since 1972, he has been Honorary President of the Poetry Society of America.

EBERS, Georg Moritz
(1837–98)

German Egyptologist and novelist, born in Berlin. Lecturer (1865) and professor (1868) at Jena, he visited the East in 1869, and from 1870 to 1889 was Professor of Egyptology at Leipzig. He discovered and published (1875) the celebrated hieratic medical *Papyrus Ebers*, and wrote on biblical sites in Goshen,

Sinai and Egypt. He is best known as the author of numerous historical novels based on ancient Egypt.
▷ H R A Gosche, *Georg Ebers der Forscher und Dichter* (1887)

EBERT, Karl Egon
(1801–82)

Bohemian poet, born in Prague. His poems include the national epic *Vlasta* (1829).

EBNER-ESCHENBACH, Marie, née von Dubsky
(1830–1916)

Austrian dramatist and writer of novellas. She was born at Castle Zdislawitz in Moravia, into the nobility, into which she also married. Somewhat stagestruck, she failed with her first writing ventures, which were in the form of drama; but her regional *novellen*, starting with her first success, *Ein Spätgwborener* (1874), much influenced by **Turgenev**, were amongst the most skilful and well observed of their time. The best of her tales include *Das Gemeindekind* (1887, Eng trans *The Child of the Parish*, 1887) and *Unsühnbar* (1890, Eng trans *Beyond Atonement*, 1892).

EÇA DE QUEIROS, José Maria de
(1845–1900)

Major Portuguese novelist, a towering figure in his country's fiction, who is still much neglected—and persistently underrated, in the European terms in which he should be considered. He was born in Lisbon, and died in a bitter Parisian exile. Although essentially a 19th-century figure, Eça established realism in the Portuguese novel. His point of departure was **Zola**, but he soon developed his own direction, which was more akin to that of his true master, **Flaubert**: to analyse what was humanly wrong with the society of his own country. His profound self-study, as the sadomasochistic writer Ega, in one of his masterpieces, *Os Maias* (1888, Eng trans *The Maias*, 1965), which has incest as its main theme, has in particular not had its due. However, no one has questioned that he is Portugal's finest prose stylist. *O Crime do Padre Amero* (1876, Eng trans *The Sin of Father Amaro*, 1962) depicts clerical 'immorality' in a bourgeois setting; *O primo Basilio* (1878, Eng trans *Cousin Basilio*, 1958) is a variation on the theme of Flaubert's *Madame Bovary*. Eça's *Cartas de Inglaterra* (1903, Eng trans *Letters from England*, 1970), provides an invaluable outsider's view of Victorian England.

▷ M Seymour-Smith, *Introduction to Fifty European Novels* (1979)

ECHEGARAY Y EIZAGUIRRE, José
(1833–1916)

Spanish dramatist, born of Basque descent in Madrid, and joint winner of the Nobel Prize for literature in 1904. He taught mathematics, held portfolios in various ministries (1868–74), then won literary fame by many plays in prose and verse. His plays are usually on simple themes, but with elaborate plot twists and rhetorical passages, and some incorporate social comment, as in his masterpiece, *El gran Galeoto* (1881, 'The Great Galeoto'). He returned to politics as Minister of Finance (1905), and to science as Professor of Physics, Madrid University (1905).

▷ J Mathias, *Echegaray* (1970)

ECHERUO, Michael Joseph Chukwudalo
(1937–)

Nigerian poet, born in Umunumo and educated at Port Harcourt, Ibadan, and Cornell University, New York. An expert on **Joyce Cary**, about whom he has written two critical monographs (1973, 1979), Echeruo is himself very much concerned with the cultural confrontation of Europe and Africa. This is the substance of his main collection, *Mortality* (1968), which documents aspects of his experience as an African in the USA. *Distanced* (1975) is a more philosophical but also more lyrical collection. Echeruo's academic career progressed from the University of Nigeria, Nsukka (1961–74) to the University of Ibadan (1974–80); since 1981 he has been Vice-Chancellor of Imo State University at Owerri.

▷ *Poets, Prophets and Professors* (1977)

ECHEVERRIA, Estaban
(1805–51)

Argentinian poet, novelist, essayist, socialist and critic, born in Buenos Aires. From 1826 until 1830 he lived in Paris, where he absorbed the essence of European romanticism, which he later introduced to his country. He died in exile because of his opposition to the terrible dictator General Juan Manuel de Rosas. The novela *El matadero* (1871, Eng trans *The Slaughter House*, 1959), written in about 1840, is one of the earliest of the great Latin-American anti-dictator documents; here the country is shown as an abattoir run by insane butchers. He is Argentina's key romantic poet; part of his famous poem 'La cautiva'

('The Captive') is translated in the *Penguin Book of Latin American Verse* (1971, ed E Curacciolo-Trejo).

ECKERMANN, Johann Peter
(1792–1854)

German author, born in Winsen in Hanover. He studied at Göttingen. The publication of his *Beiträge zur Poesie* (1823, 'Contributions on Poetry') led to his move to Weimar, where he assisted **Goethe** in preparing the final edition of his works. He achieved fame by his *Gespräche mit Goethe in den letzten Jahren seines Lebens, 1823–32* (1836–48, Eng trans of part as *Conversations with Goethe*, 1839).

▷ E Hitschman, *Johann Peter Eckermann, eine psychoanalytische-biographische Studie* (1933)

ECKHART, Johannes, known as Meister Eckhart
(c.1260–1327)

German Dominican mystic, born in Hochheim in Thuringia, of a noble family. One of the most famous teachers of his time, he was eventually prosecuted for heresy, but died before the matter had been settled. His works—seldom in authentic texts—are difficult to interpret, and have been variously understood. Like **Böhme**, he was rediscovered by 19th-century romantic thinkers who were ignorant of theological history. Orthodox scholarship now likes to claim him as an eccentric descendant of Aristotle, Aquinas and the schoolmen; but it seems that, despite his denials to the Pope, he was a sound heretic. He was certainly a pantheist, and to some extent (though less than Böhme), one of a gnostic temper. His influence is to be found in Kant, Hegel and in German romantic poetry. The poets, however, though ignorant of his theology, could be claimed to have understood the essence of his thinking better than the scholars. He wrote in both Latin and the German vernacular.

▷ J M Clark (ed), *The Great German Mystics* (1949); *Meister Eckhart: An Introduction* (1957, with translations); F E Copleston, *A History of Philosophy*, vol iii (1953)

ECO, Umberto
(1932–)

Italian novelist and semiotician, born in Alessandria in Piedmont. A student of philosophy at Turin University, he was awarded a doctorate for his thesis on St Thomas Aquinas. He taught at Turin (1956–67), and was appointed Professor of Semiotics (the study of signs in all realms of culture) at the University of Bologna in 1971. Imbued with a 'taste and passion' for the Middle Ages, he undertook a prolonged study of the commentary of Beatus of Liébana, an 8th-century saint, on the Book of Revelation and of 11th-century illuminations, all of which bore fruit in *The Name of the Rose* (1980). A suspense story set in a medieval monastery, centring on the criminal investigation of Brother William of Baskerville, an English Franciscan, it is indebted to **Arthur Conan Doyle**'s Sherlock Holmes stories, despite having been described as 'a completely semiotic book'. It was an international bestseller and was successfully translated to celluloid in a film of the same name directed by Jean-Jaques Arnaud. *Foucault's Pendulum*, his second novel, was published in 1989.

EDEN, Dorothy
(1912–82)

New Zealand writer of suspense and historical novels, the best known of which is probably *Bride by Candlelight* (1954). Early books, such as her first, *Singing Shadows* (1940), had a New Zealand setting. A move to London in the 1950s inspired contemporary themes such as Nazi Europe in *The Shadow Wife* (1968), and a spy plot in *Waiting for Willa* (1970). Her Gothic romances, mainly Victorian in period, ranged from England and Ireland to South Africa and to the China of the Boxer Rebellion. With her fortieth and last book, *An Important Family* (1982), she returned to her home province of Canterbury.

EDGAR, David
(1948–)

English dramatist, born in Birmingham. He studied drama at Manchester University before becoming a journalist in Bradford, and wrote several plays for touring fringe theatre companies before deciding to write for the stage full time. *Destiny* (1976), a large-scale play looking at the roots of fascism in British society, was produced by the Royal Shakespeare Company. His eight-hour adaptation of **Dickens**'s *The Life and Adventures of Nicholas Nickleby* for the RSC (1980) brought his work to a massive audience. *Maydays* (1983), the first contemporary play to be presented by the RSC at the Barbican Theatre in London, was similarly ambitious. *Entertaining Strangers* (1985), which is set in mid-19th-century Dorchester, counterpoints the commercial ambitions of the owner of a brewery with the fury of a fundamentalist preacher, against the backdrop of industrialization and a cholera epidemic. Other works include *The Shape of the Table* (1990), which charts the negotiations between a communist government and the forces acting against it in the autumn of 1989, a television documentary *Civil War* (1991), a radio play *A Movie Starring Me* (1991), and several adaptations, including *The Strange Case of Dr Jekyll and Mr Hyde* (1991).

EDGELL, Zee
(1940–)

Belizean novelist. Educated at the University of the West Indies, she worked as a journalist in Jamaica before travelling abroad. She has held posts in education and public service at home and abroad and spent a year in Somalia working for UNICEF. Her commitment to feminist issues is evident in her novels, which emphasize the resourcefulness of women in the face of difficult situations. In *Beka Lamb* (1982), for example, the adolescent heroine, who has grown up in Belize, a matriarchal society influenced by the Catholic Church and beset by political tensions, works hard to overcome her faults. In *In Times Like These* (1991), the central character returning to Belize with her illegitimate twins shows moral courage in confronting the complex web of personal relationships and political intrigue.

EDGEWORTH, Maria
(1767–1849)

Irish novelist, eldest daughter of the inventor and educationist Richard Lovell Edgeworth, born in Blackbourton, Oxfordshire. After being educated in England, she returned to Edgeworthstown in County Longford, Ireland in 1772 to act as her father's assistant and governess to his many other children. With her father, and to illustrate his educational ideas, she published *Letters to Literary Ladies* (1795), *The Parent's Assistant* (1796) and *Practical Education* (1798). In 1800 she published her first novel, *Castle Rackrent*, which was an immediate success, followed by *Belinda* in 1801. She was praised by Sir **Walter Scott** and was lionized on a visit to London and the Continent, where she turned down a proposal of marriage from the Swedish Count Edelcrantz for the sake of her father. The next of her 'social novels' of Irish life was *The Absentee* (1809), followed by *Ormond* (1817). All her works were written under the influence of her father, which may have inhibited her natural story-telling talent. After her father's death (1817) she did little more writing apart from a late novel, *Helen* (1834), but devoted herself to looking after the family property, and 'good works'. She is also remembered for children's stories.
▷P H Newby, *Maria Edgeworth* (1950)

EDMOND, Lauris
(1924–)

New Zealand poet and novelist, born in Dannevirke. Her first verse, *In Middle Air*, was published in 1975. Her second collection, *The Pear Tree* (1977), was written after the death of her daughter; death and transience are major themes in her work, as in *Seasons and Creatures* (1986) and *Summer near the Arctic Circle* (1988). *Selected Poems* appeared in 1984, as did her only novel to date, *High Country Weather. Hot October, an Autobiographical Story* was published in 1989. She has compiled *Women at War*, which draws on written memoirs and oral history, edited the letters of New Zealand poet **A R D Fairburn**, and written some unpublished plays.

EDSCHMID, Kasimir, pseud of Eduard Schmid
(1890–1966)

German expressionist prose writer, author of short stories, novels and influential essays, born in Darmstadt. He was one of the earliest spokesmen for Expressionism (he remains its most coherent expositor) and in his own prose aimed, initially, for effects both shocking, vitalist and ecstatic. *Die achatnen Kugeln* (1920, 'The Agate Balls'), is an ironic *Bildungsroman* on the theme of a rich heiress's education through living amongst beggars and whores. Later, after celebrating **Byron**'s incestuous feelings in *Lord Byron* (1929, Eng trans 1930), he became more darkly satirical. His later work, after he had been forbidden by the Nazis to publish, is more straightforward. His Diary, *Tagebuch 1958–1960* (1960) is an illuminating work.

EDWARDS, Amelia Ann Blandford
(1831–92)

English novelist and Egyptologist, born in London. She was the author of *My Brother's Wife* (1855), *Debenham's Vow* (1869), *Lord Brackenbury* (1880), and other romantic novels. She was founder of the Egyptian Exploration Fund, and contributed papers on Egyptology to the principal European and American journals, and wrote *A Thousand Miles up the Nile* (1877) and *Pharaohs, Fellahs, and Explorers* (1891).
▷K S MacQuoid, *Amelia Blandford Edwards* (1897)

EDWARDS, Hugh
(1878–1952)

English novelist, born in Gibraltar of a naval family. He was in army service in India and Africa until he was invalided out before World War I. He wrote five novels, one of which is a minor classic, often reprinted: *All Night at Mr Stanyhurst's* (1933), a historical novel which conceals a tale within a tale; 'its rapport with the late eighteenth century is uncanny', wrote a critic, 'every word counts, the final effect is hauntingly poetic'. It was greatly admired by **Graham Greene**.

EDWARDS BELLO, Joaquín
(1887–1968)

Chilean novelist and essayist, born in Valparaíso, a descendant of **Andrés Bello**. Edwards Bello was, in his first phase, one of Chile's foremost naturalist novelists, writing under the direct influence of **Zola** (he had been educated in Europe). His savage *El inútil* (1910, 'The Useless One'), about the downfall of a Chilean in Paris, obliged him to leave Chile. Later, in *El roto* (1920, 'The Debauchee'), his chief work, he set his horrendous tale of the 'lower depths' in Chile itself, and included statistics of alcoholism and tuberculosis in Santiago. But he was not a subtle writer, nor one of much psychological penetration.

EEDEN, Frederik Willem van
(1860–1932)

Dutch novelist, dramatist, translator, poet and critic, born in Haarlem. He was a pioneering psychiatrist who had studied under Charcot in Paris, and who later became aware of **Freud**. He translated much of **Tagore**'s work, was more widely read in foreign literatures than any of his contemporaries, and probably holds more appeal for the modern reader than almost all of them. During his life he founded two communes, and was a friend to **Upton Sinclair**. He was one of the leading members of De Nieuwe Gids, 'The Men of the Eighties', the Dutch group which swept away the cobwebs of literary conventions which had outstayed their usefulness. His two chief works are the novels *De kleine Johannes* (1887–1906, Eng trans *Little Johannes*, 1895) and *Van de koele meren des doods* (1900, Eng trans *The Deeps of Deliverance*, 1902). The first, tracing the development of a boy's soul, foreshadows his own conversion to Roman Catholicism (1922); the second, his finest work of all, is a case-study based on one of his own patients, a woman who sank into drug addiction and prostitution, but was cured by religious understanding. His drama was popular in its time.

EEKHOUD, Georges
(1854–1927)

Belgian poet, novelist and translator (of **Webster** and **Marlowe**), born in Antwerp. At first associated with the socialistic group Jeune Belgique, Eekhoud broke decisively away from it in 1893, when he felt that it was adopting as its ideal a 'Parnassian' cult of objectivity. Taking **Zola** as his inspiration he began to write naturalistic novels in which, however, he expressed a genuine love and respect for criminals and outcasts. Despite some tiresome fin de siècle affectations, his fiction remains interesting and readable, but

it is now neglected. In *Escal-Vigor* (1899, Eng trans *Strange Love*, 1933) he deals boldly (for that time) with his homosexuality; *La Nouvelle Carthage* (1888, Eng trans *The New Carthage*, 1917) memorably castigates 'urban progress' as carried out by hypocritical or misguided bureaucrats. The posthumous *Le Terroir incarné* (1928, 'The Terror Incarnate'), one of his most impressive and powerful works, is the most concise expression of his zestful and indignant philosophy—and it makes clear why he broke away from Jeune Belgique.
▷ G Turquet-Milnes, *Some Modern Belgian Writers* (1916)

EGAN, Pierce
(1772–1849)

English sporting writer, born in London. A London journalist, he was the author of many works, including *Boxiana; or Sketches of Antient and Modern Pugilism* (1812–13). He achieved fame with his description of the life of a 'man about town', *Life in London*, published in serial form in 1820 and as a book in 1821, with coloured illustrations by the brothers Cruikshank. In 1824 he launched a weekly sporting journal *Pierce Egan's Life in London*, incorporated into *Sporting Life* in 1859. His son, 'Pierce the Younger' (1814–80), was also a journalist and writer, and published dozens of 'cheap' novels.
▷ J Reid, *Bucks and Bruisers: Pierce Egan and Regency England* (1971)

EGERTON, Sarah, née Fyge, later Field
(1670–1723)

English poet, born in London, daughter of a well-born physician. She left home in disgrace after publishing a lively feminist polemic, *The Female Advocate* (1686), and married an attorney who died early. Her second marriage to the Rev Thomas Egerton, a widower of 50, was unhappy. She wrote conventional elegies on **Dryden** (1700), but her more original *Poems on Several Occasions* (1703) contains passionate accounts of her loves, marriages and sufferings, and spirited satire against tyrannical husbands and female prudes.
▷ *The Female Advocate* in *Satires on Women*, (1976, ed F Nussbaum); J Medoff, in *Tulsa Studies in Women's Literature*, 1 (1982)

EGGE, Peter Andreas
(1869–1959)

Norwegian novelist, born in Trondheim. Of humble peasant stock and too poor to pursue his education, he was discovered by **Knut Hamsun**, who arranged for the publication of his first novel, *Common People* (1891). His first real success was with *The Heart* (1917), which is a serious and penetrating study of marriage between two dissimilar personalities, and *Hansine Solstad* (1926), a delicate, sympathetic description of a woman wrongfully accused of theft in her youth, whose supposed crime dogs her through life. Egge also wrote plays in which he followed **Ibsen** in creating drama from defects of character.
▷ C M Woel, *Peter Egge* (1929)

EGGLESTON, Edward
(1837–1902)

American writer and pastor, born in Vevay, Indiana. He was a Methodist minister in Minnesota, and editor of journals like *Little Corporal, National Sunday School Teacher* and *Hearth and Home*. He also wrote several classic novels, among them *The Hoosier Schoolmaster* (1871), which was based on his brother's experience as a small-town teacher, *The Circuit Rider* (1874), on his own as an itinerant minister, and *The Graysons* (1888), in which Abraham Lincoln was a central character.
▷ W P Randel, *Eggleston, author of 'The Hoosier Schoolmaster'* (1946)

EGLITIS, Anslavs
(1906–)

Latvian poet and prolific writer of fiction, in exile in America, whose work has not been much translated—with the exception of the well-regarded story 'The Best Seller', in *Texas Quarterly* (Autumn 1960).

EGUREN, José María
(1874–1942)

Peruvian poet and translator (**Wilde, Baudelaire**), born in Lima, the natural predecessor to **César Vallejo**. He was also a painter. It was his country childhood that enriched his imagination. He offered discerning Peruvian readers a quiet and modest alternative to the 'trumpet solos' of the publicist **Chocano**, and gradually the best critics, including José Carlos Mariátegui and **González Prada**, recognized his genius as one of remarkable originality. There are translations of his poetry in the *Penguin Book of Latin American verse* (1971, ed E Curacciolo-Trejo) and in *Latin-American Poetry* (1942).
▷ J C Mariátegui, *Siete ensayos* (1952); I Goldburg, *Studies in Spanish-American Literature* (1920)

EHRENBURG, or ERENBURG, Ilya Grigorievich
(1891–1967)

Russian writer, born in Moscow. In 1908 he was imprisoned for revolutionary activities, but escaped to Paris, where he worked as a journalist until 1917, when he returned to

Russia, but went back to Paris as a correspondent. Among his best works are *The Extraordinary Adventures of Julio Jurenito* (1921), a satire on the aftermath of World War I, *The Fall of Paris* (1941) and *The Storm* (1947), both novels about World War II, and *The Thaw* (1954), a novel about the period of de-Stalinization. He published his memoirs *People, Years, Life* in six volumes from 1960 to 1966.

EHRENSTEIN, Alfred
(1886–1950)

Austrian poet and story writer, born in Vienna of Jewish descent. After studying philosophy, he became a prolific writer of fiction, essays and of the expressionist poetry for which he is now best remembered. His political ideas were revolutionary, and he left Germany in 1932 and died in New York. Most of his poetry of protest, as has been said, 'seems thin today', but a few notable exceptions still crop up in anthologies.
▷C Middleton and M Hamburger (eds), *Modern German Poetry 1910–1969* (1962)

EICH, Gunter
(1907–72)

German poet and writer of *hörspielen* (radio plays)—this has become a highly developed art in his country, and he was one of the pre-Nazi pioneers of it—who was born in Lebus on the Oder. He was married to Ilse Aichinger. He was associated with the literary circle Gruppe '47, and his poetry, amongst the most notable produced by his generation, was influential in the early post-Nazi days for its relentless examination of the Nazi past; however, by mood and habit he was a mystical poet maintaining the tradition of Angelus Silesius. His most famous and successful radio play was *Träume* (1950, 'Dreams'). In English translation are *Journeys* (1968) and *Selected Poems* (1971).
▷*Encounter 30*, 3 (1963)

EICHENDORFF, Joseph, Freiherr von
(1788–1857)

German poet, novelist and critic, born near Ratibor, into a noble family. He studied law and became a government official. He is regarded as one of the most important Romantic lyricists writing in German, and his poems were set by a number of composers, including Schumann and Mendelssohn. They reveal his profound veneration for the divine gifts of natural beauty. His novels include the idyllic *Aus dem Leben eines Taugenichts* (1826, Eng trans *Memoirs of a Good-for-Nothing*) and *Das Marmorbild* (1826, 'The Marble Statue').

▷L R Radner, *Eichendorff: the spiritual geometer* (1970)

EKELÖF, (Bengt) Gunnar
(1907–68)

Swedish poet. A leader of the post-war modernists, he is considered one of the most significant Swedish poets of this century. Much influenced by the French Symbolists, he published his first book of poetry, *Sent på jorden* ('Late Arrival on Earth'), in 1932, followed by *Dedikation* (1934, 'Dedication'), *Sorgen och stjärnan* (1936, 'Sorrow and the Star') and *Färjesång* (1941, 'Ferry Song'). *En Mölnaelegi* (1960), which is concerned with the nature of time, was translated into English (*A Mölna Elegy*, 1979), as were his *Selected poems* (1966) and *Guide to the Underworld* (1967).
▷S Karlsson and A Liffman, *En bok om Gunnar Ekelöf* (1956)

EKELUND, Vilhelm
(1880–1949)

Swedish poet and essayist. A Symbolist and early modernist, his works include poetry such as *Stella Maris* (1906), and volumes of essays inspired by Nietzsche, including *Classical Ideal* (1909).
▷S Ahlstrom, *Vilhelm Ekelund* (1940)

EKMAN, Kerstin
(1933–)

Swedish novelist. Born in Risinge, Östergötland, she worked as a teacher and in the film industry before emerging as a successful writer of thrillers. Her tetralogy tracing feminine patterns of civilization within the framework of a Swedish railway town, *Häxringarna* (1974, 'The Witches' Circles'), *Springkällan* (1976, 'The Spring'), *Änglahuset* (1979, 'House of Angels') and *En stad av ljus* (1983, 'City of Light'), established her as one of Sweden's leading contemporary novelists, its carefully researched realist elements mingling with mythical and symbolic dimensions which become particularly prominent in the final volume. *Rövarna i Skuleskogen* (1988, 'The Robbers in the Skule Forest') is a vivid and far-reaching critique of civilization, while *Händelser vid vatten* (1993, 'Events by Water') explores issues of culture and memory in an isolated community in the north of Sweden. She was elected a member of the Swedish Academy in 1978, but the failure of the Academy to express its support for Salman Rushdie following the death sentence placed on him by Iranian fundamentalists persuaded her to leave it in 1989.
▷M Schottenius, *Den kvinnliga hemligheten. En studie i Kerstin Ekmans berättarkonst* (1992)

EKWENSI, Cyprian Odiatu Duaka
(1921–)

Nigerian novelist. After attending college in Ibadan and in Ghana, he trained as a pharmacist in London and lectured on the subject in Lagos for 10 years before moving into broadcasting as head of features. He was later director of the Nigerian Ministry of Information and Head of Information Services at Enugu. His first novel was *People of the City* (1954, rev edn 1963), a powerful account of the problems of urbanization in Africa, a theme he returned to in *Jagua Nana* (1961), the story of a Lagos prostitute. In *Burning Grass* (1962), the nomadic life of Fulani herders becomes a wider symbol of social conditions in post-colonial Africa, as does the big game hunt in *Beautiful Feathers* (1963). In *Iska* (1966) and *Survive the Peace* (1976) he tackles the corruption and tribalist violence of modern Nigerian politics, culminating in the latter book, with its ironic title, set in the aftermath of the Biafran civil war. He has also written children's books.
▷E Emenyona, *Cyprian Ekwensi* (1974)

ELIN, Pelin, pseud of Dimitur Ivanov
(1877–1949)

Bulgaria's greatest story writer, and an editor and children's author, born in Baylovo. He wrote little in the last 25 years of his life, but remained active in literary circles. In his many writings he depicted the peasantry (*shopi*) of the country around Sofia, where he lived, with a loving detachment and always with a large dose of psychological realism. He was less artificial than any of his contemporaries, and his rural tales are still read and loved; his collected work was published in Bulgaria in 1958–9 and took up 10 volumes. He also wrote plays. He had the approval of the communist government, but did not like socialist realism, and declared that the emotions of men, and not machines, should determine literature. One of his stories is contained in *The Peach Thief and Other Bulgarian Stories* (1968).
▷C Manning and R Smal-Stocki, *The History of Modern Bulgarian Literature* (1960)

ELIOT, George, pseud of Mary Ann or Marian Evans
(1819–80)

English novelist, born on Arbury Farm in Astley. In her father, Robert Evans, a Warwickshire land agent, a man of strong character, were seen many of the traits transferred by his daughter to Adam Bede and Caleb Garth. She lost her mother, whom she loved devotedly, in 1836, and soon afterwards took entire charge of the household. Masters came from Coventry to teach her German, Italian and music—of the last she was passionately fond throughout her life. She was also an immense reader. In 1841 her father moved to Coventry, and there she met Charles Bray, a writer on the philosophy of necessity from the phrenological standpoint, and his brother-in-law, Charles Hennell, who had published in 1838 a rationalistic *Inquiry concerning the Origin of Christianity*. Under their influence she rejected her earlier evangelical Christianity. In 1844 she took on the laborious task of translating Strauss's *Leben Jesu* (published in 1846). After her father's death in 1849 she travelled on the Continent with Mr and Mrs Bray; returning to England in 1850 she began to write for the *Westminster Review*. She became assistant editor in 1851, and the centre of a literary circle, two of whose members were Herbert Spencer and George Henry Lewes. She translated Feuerbach's *Essence of Christianity* (1854), the only book that bore her real name. Gradually her intimacy with Lewes grew, and in 1854 she formed a liaison with him which lasted until his death in 1878. In July 1854 she went abroad with him, staying three months in Weimar, where he was preparing for his *Life of Goethe*. After a longer stay in Berlin, they returned and lived first in Dover, then in East Sheen, then in Richmond. In 1856 she attempted her first story, 'The Sad Fortunes of the Rev. Amos Barton', the beginning of the *Scenes of Clerical Life*. It came out in *Blackwood's Magazine* in 1857, and at once showed that a new author of great power had risen. 'Mr Gilfil's Love Story' and 'Janet's Repentance' followed quickly. Her first novel, *Adam Bede* (1859), had an enormous success. *The Mill on the Floss* (1860), *Silas Marner* (1861), *Romola* (1863) and *Felix Holt* (1866) appeared next in succession. Her first poem, *The Spanish Gypsy* (1868), was followed next year by *Agatha*, *The Legend of Jubal* and *Armgart*; and in 1871–2 appeared *Middlemarch*, generally considered her greatest work. After that came *Daniel Deronda* (1876), her last great novel. After the death of Lewes, she was coaxed to write *Impressions of Theophrastus Such* (1879), a volume of somewhat miscellaneous essays. She fell in love again with a banker 20 years her junior, John Walter Cross (died 1924), a friend of long standing whom she married in May 1880. She died a few months later, and was buried in Highgate Cemetery, in the grave next to that of Lewes. As a novelist, George Eliot will probably always stand among the greatest of the English realist school; her pictures of farmers, tradesmen, and the lower middle-class, generally of the Midlands, are hardly surpassed in English literature.
▷G S Haight, *George Eliot* (1968); F R Leavis, *The Great Tradition* (1948)

ELIOT, T(homas) S(tearns)
(1888–1965)

American-born British poet, critic and dramatist, and winner of the Nobel Prize for literature, born in St Louis, Missouri. After four years at Harvard (1906–10, where the chief influence upon his development was that of Irving Babbitt with his 'selective' humanism and his resistance to modern trends) he spent a year in Paris, attending lectures and improving his command of the French language. He returned to Harvard to study philosophy for three years. He had distinguished teachers, such as Josiah Royce and **George Santayana**, and, for a time, Bertrand Russell. A travelling scholarship from Harvard took him to Merton College, Oxford, for a year, where he worked on a doctoral dissertation on F H Bradley, and read **Plato** and Aristotle under H H Joachim. Persuaded by **Ezra Pound**, to whom he had shown his poems, he remained in England where he lived from then on (1911), taking up naturalization in 1927. After teaching for a term in High Wycombe, and for a year at Highgate Junior School, he worked for eight years in Lloyds Bank before becoming a director of the publishing firm of Faber. The enthusiastic support of Pound led to the publication of Eliot's first volume of verse, *Prufrock and Other Observations* (1917). He was introduced by Bertrand Russell into the Bloomsbury Circle, where the quality of his work was immediately recognized. His next two small volumes, *Ara vos prec* (1920) and the more important *The Waste Land* (1922), were published by Leonard and **Virginia Woolf** at the Hogarth Press. *The Hollow Men*, which followed in 1925, gave more excuse for regarding Eliot at that point as a cynical defeatist. *The Waste Land* had appeared in the first number of *The Criterion*, a quarterly review which Eliot edited from 1923 to 1939. *The Criterion* aimed at impartiality in presenting opposed political philosophies and is indispensable for a study of ideas, political and religious, between the wars, as well as for the literary developments, both here and abroad during that period. In 1927, the year in which he became a British subject, Eliot was baptized and confirmed, having been raised as a Unitarian. The publication of a volume of essays *For Lancelot Andrewes* (1928) gave his first public statement of his adherence to the Anglo-Catholic movement within the Church of England. *Ash Wednesday* (1930) is the first fruit of this new sacramental attitude. The religious plays *The Rock* (1934) and *Murder in the Cathedral* (1935) which followed sealed his reputation as the poet who had revived the verse play in the interests of Catholic devotion. His later dramas, *The Cocktail Party* (1950), *The Family Reunion* (1939), *The Confidential Clerk*

(1954) and *The Elder Statesman* (1958), were to aim at being West End successes rather than sacred plays in church precincts, but Catholic doctrine inspired all these plays, sometimes to the embarrassment of critics and audience alike. Before this incursion into the theatre world he produced his greatest work, *Four Quartets* (1944), which, despite its obscurity, is one of the greatest philosophical poems in the language. The most rewarding is probably the last, *Little Gidding*. Eliot's critical work consists of literary criticism, such as *The Sacred Wood* (1920, on Jacobean dramatists), the admirable *Homage to Dryden* (1924), *The Use of Poetry and the Use of Criticism* (1933), *Elizabethan Essays* (1934) and *On Poetry and Poets* (1957). When writing or lecturing on literature generally he could be very provocative, as in his *Modern Education and the Classics* (1934), where he said that the Classics were to be studied not for their own sake but as a buttress for the Faith; and in *After Strange Gods* (1934), where he tries to stretch some great writers on the Procrustean bed of 'Christian Sensibility'. In social criticisms, as in *The Idea of a Christian Society* (1939) and *Notes Towards the Definition of Culture*, he is hierarchal and undemocratic. The new poetry, as announced by Ezra Pound, **T E Hulme** and Eliot, was to be related to modern life and expressed in modern idiom, preferably in free verse. Rhetoric and romantic clichés were to be avoided. In his late essay 'Milton II', in *On Poetry and Poets*, he confessed that he and his friends had insisted over much on these ideas and this was a sort of recantation for his abuse of **Milton**. But critics today have no doubt of the salutary effect of their crusade and of Eliot's poetry as having justified it. In 1948 he was awarded the Nobel Prize for literature.
▷M Grant, *T S Eliot: the critical heritage* (2 vols, 1982); P Ackroyd, *Eliot: a life* (1984)

ELISABETH, QUEEN OF ROMANIA
see **CARMEN SYLVA**

ELISIO, Filento, 'Arcadian' pseud of Padre Manuel do Nascimento
(1734–1819)

Portuguese poet and translator, born in Lisbon. Nascimento got his 'Arcadian' name from the future Marquesa de Alorna, poet, to whom he had taught Latin. But he was a member of the opposing, neo-classical group (a *dissidente*): the Grupo da Ribeira das Naus. He is almost as famous for his escape from the Inquisition (1777–8), on the fall of his protector Pombal. He had been accused of atheism for not believing in the literal truth of the Flood. He was prolific (some 750 000 lines in a long lifetime), and highly artificial (**Horace** was his main model), but exceedingly influential upon his successors, mostly on account of what he showed could be done with Portuguese in poetic forms.

▷C Olavo, *O vida amargurada de F. Elisio* (1944)

ELISSAMBURU, Jean-Baptiste
(1828–91)

Basque lyric poet, regarded as a worthy contemporary of **Indalecio Bizcarrondo**.

▷R Gallop, *A Book of the Basques* (1930); L Michelena, *Historia de la literatura vasca* (1960)

ELKIN, Stanley Lawrence
(1930–)

American author and academic, born in Brooklyn, New York. He was educated at the University of Illinois, where he took a PhD. While his stories in *Criers and Kibitzers, Kibitzers and Criers* (1966) have their champions, and *The Living End* (1979)—three stories about heaven and hell—is his most widely read book, he is pre-eminently a novelist. *Boswell* (1964), about a professional wrestler obsessed with death and greatness, marked his debut and was followed by *A Bad Man* (1967), *The Dick Gibson Show* (1971) and *The Franchiser* (1976), all fixated with modern America. *George Mills* (1982) and *The Magic Kingdom* (1985) are set, respectively, in Sultanic Turkey and contemporary St Louis.

▷P Bailey, *Reading Stanley Elkin* (1985)

ELLIOTT, George Paul
(1918–80)

American novelist, story writer and poet, born in Knightstown, Indiana. He was a professor at Syracuse University for most of his life. His poetry is lyrical and straightforward. The most impressive of his novels was *David Knudsen* (1962), about the son of one of the scientists who invented the bomb used at Hiroshima: he has to rid himself of his 'radiation sickness', which stands for his aggressive scientism. Stories were collected in *Among the Dangs* (1962) and *An Hour of Last Things* (1969).

ELLIOTT, Sumner Locke
(1917–1991)

Australian novelist and playwright, born in Sydney. His mother, Sumner Locke (1881–1917), who died soon after his birth, wrote popular stories of 'selection' life (on government-allocated land). Elliott became an actor and wrote several plays, of which *Rusty Bugles* (1948) achieved great success and some notoriety when its realistic army language was heavily censored. By that time he had left for the USA, where he settled, becoming a US citizen in 1955. He was in demand

as a scriptwriter for NBC and CBS television and his play *Buy Me Blue Ribbons* was produced on Broadway in 1951. His semi-autobiographical novel *Careful, He Might Hear You* (1963) deals with the traumatic experiences of his own childhood and the battle for his custody. It was translated into many languages and became a successful film in 1983. *Water under the Bridge* (1977) is a complex and untidy novel set in inner Sydney, from the opening of Sydney Harbour Bridge in 1932 to the early 1950s.

ELLIS, Alice Thomas, pseud of Anna Margaret Haycraft
(1932–)

English novelist, born in Liverpool and brought up in Wales. She studied at Liverpool School of Art, and was a postulant at a convent in Liverpool, but married in 1956. Her novels include *The Sin Eater* (1977), a bitterly sharp comedy of manners involving English, Irish and Welsh characters of differing religious faiths. Subsequent novels are similarly satirical, sometimes dark, and reveal a sympathy for religious belief and the nuances of love and loathing. In *The Other Side of the Fire* (1983) several women confront a variety of emotional catharses. *The Clothes in the Wardrobe* (1987), *The Skeleton in the Cupboard* (1988) and *The Fly in the Ointment* (1989), comprise a trilogy about contemporary life.

ELLIS, Edward Sylvester
(1840–1916)

American novelist and historian, born in Geneva, Ohio. He was amongst the most successful—under various pseudonyms—of the 'dime novelists': *Seth Jones* (1860), Number 8 of Beadle's Dime Novels, a frontier tale about a man who disguises himself as a hunter, sold almost half a million copies. An inaccurate history of the United States which he wrote sold all over the country.

ELLIS, George
(1753–1815)

British satirist and poet, born in Grenada, West Indies, the son of a planter. He won early popularity with his *Poetical Tales by Sir Gregory Gander* (1778), and contributed satires on Pitt and others to the Whig *Rolliad*, though later he was co-founder with George Canning of the Tory *Anti-Jacobin*. A friend of Sir **Walter Scott**, he edited *Specimens of Early English Poets* (1790) and *Specimens of Early English Romances in Metre* (1805).

ELLISON, Harlan Jay
(1934–)

American science-fiction writer, essayist, critic and editor, born in Cleveland, Ohio.

ELLISON, Ralph Waldo

His outspoken, pugnacious attitudes and willingness to tackle taboo subjects like sex and drugs have made him a controversial figure in science-fiction circles. His best work has been in short-story form, and significant collections include *I Have No Mouth, and I Must Scream* (1967, rev edn 1983), *The Beast That Shouted Love at the Heart of the World* (1969, rev edn 1984), *Deathbird Stories* (1975), and the massive retrospective *The Essential Ellison* (1987). He is an acerbic critic of film and television, and an influential editor, notably in the ground-breaking *Dangerous Visions* anthologies (1967, 1972). He has written several novels, screenplays, and television scripts.
▷ *All the Lies That Are My Life* (1989)

ELLISON, Ralph Waldo
(1914–94)

American novelist, born in Oklahoma City, Oklahoma. Bookish as well as musical, he studied music at Tuskagee Institute and served during World War II in the US Merchant Marine. He met **Richard Wright** in 1937, through whom he became aware of social and racial injustice, and who encouraged him to write. His early work appeared in *New Challenge* magazine. *Invisible Man* (1952), his only completed novel, is the quest of a nameless black man, travelling from South to North, in search of a personal and racial identity. Allusive but highly original and ingenious, it had a seminal influence on other black writers and won the National Book Award. He was Albert Schweitzer Professor in the Humanities at New York University (1970–9). He published two books of essays, *Shadow and the Act* (1964) and *Going to the Territory* (1986), but the long-awaited second novel never appeared.
▷ R Dietze, *Ellison: the genesis of an artist* (1982)

ELLMANN, Richard
(1918–87)

American biographer and academic, born in Detroit, Michigan. He graduated from Yale University and after the war he lived in Dublin for a year, where he wrote his first book, *Yeats; the Man and the Mask* (1948). Some 10 years later came his masterful biography of **James Joyce**, now accepted as one of the pinnacles of 20th-century biography, as much for its elegant composition as its astute judgement and erudition. A professor at Northwestern University, Illinois, until 1968, he moved to Oxford in 1970 as Goldsmiths' Professor of English Literature, where he remained till his death. His biography of **Oscar Wilde** (1987), a 20-year labour of love, was published posthumously to universal acclaim. Selected essays were published under the title, *a long the riverrun* in 1988.
▷ *Literary Biography: inaugural lecture* (pamphlet, 1971)

ELMSLIE, Kenward Gray
(1929–)

American poet, playwright and librettist, born in New York. His verse has something of the surrealized illogic of **John Ashbery** and other 'New York School' writers, but in collections like *The Champ* (1968), *Circus Nerves* (1971) and, in particular, *Tropicalism* (1975), he is closer to the lushly musical imagery of **Wallace Stevens**. He has also acknowledged the impact of the great American songwriters on his work. Elmslie received the **Frank O'Hara** Award in 1971. He has adapted works by figures as disparate as **Henry James** and **Truman Capote** for the stage. His only novel is *The Orchid Stories* (1973). He wrote librettos for *Miss Julie* (1965), *Lizzie Bordern* (1965) and others.

ELSKAMP, Max
(1862–1931)

Major Belgian poet and engraver, described by a critic as being of 'agonised sensibility', born in Antwerp, which he seldom left. His high stature is recognized in Belgium, but not yet elsewhere. He was carefully read, valued and assimilated by **Apollinaire** and **Verhaeren**, but can still be dismissed by English critics as a 'pious dilettante', a lesser **Verlaine**. A responsible innovator, he was uninterested in fame, and only published his poems in a trade edition when he was approaching 40. His accompanying engravings are as important to the poems as are those of **Thomas Hardy** to his earlier poems. He is, essentially, a religious poet—his contemplation shot through and through with erotic longing—over-prolific, puzzling, but authentically devout and completely original. The poems of his last years are his most fascinating (eg in *Aegri Somnia*, 1924, 'A Sick Man's Dreams') and suggestive. A reliable collected edition of his poems was published in 1967.

ELSSCHOT, Willem, pseud of **Alfons de Ridder**
(1882–1960)

Belgian (Flemish) novelist and gifted and graceful minor poet, born in Antwerp, who began, with *Villa des Roses* (1913)—a novel about life in a Paris pension—in the naturalist style of **Zola**. After a period of silence he changed his style drastically, to become a major whimsical satirist and parodist. He was better known in Holland, where his work was rediscovered by the Forum group in the early 1930s, than in his native Belgium. Three of his best novels have been translated as *Three Novels* (1963): *Lijmen* (1924, *Soft Soap*), *Het been* (1938, *The Leg*) and *Het dwaalicht* (1946, *Will O' the Wisp*). These, together with *Kaas* (1933, 'Cheese'), have in them more than a touch of the genius of that great Uruguayan dissector of urban anguish **Juan Carlos Onetti**. As the director of an advertising agency, Elsschot put his own experiences of mendacious publicity to brilliant use. He is particularly noted for his realistic and witty approach to all kinds of literary pretension— but this attitude has cost him the neglect of all but the most discerning critics.

▷F Smits, *Willem Elsschot* (1952, in Dutch)

ÉLUARD, Paul, pseud of Eugène-Emile Paul Grindel
(1895–1952)

Major French poet, born in Saint-Denis. Éluard was from almost the beginning of his career as a poet a leading member of **André Breton**'s Surrealist group, and was also involved with the Dada movement. But he developed into France's leading 20th-century love poet. His chief Surrealist poetry is in *Les Dessous d'une vie ou la pyramide humaine* (1926, 'The Underbelly of Life or the Human Pyramid'); this contains many 'automatic' and dream poems. Throughout World War II, in the course of which he had to hide in a mental hospital and pretend to be one of the patients, Éluard was in the Resistance; after it he was a member of the Communist Party. His poetry changed, to become more direct and idiomatic; it was much concerned with his second wife Nusch, and with her tragic death. Much of the earlier poetry had similarly been concerned with his first wife Gala, whom he lost to the Surrealist Salvador Dali. English translations include: *Thorns of Thunder* (1936); *Selected Writings* (1951); *Last Love Poems* (1980).

▷P Nugent, *Paul Éluard* (1974)

ELYTIS, Odysseus, pseud of Odysseus Alepoudelis
(1911–)

Greek poet and winner of the Nobel Prize for literature, born in Heraklion, Crete. Educated at Athens University and at the Sorbonne, Paris, he has worked in broadcasting and as a critic of art and literature. His pseudonym is said to combine the three most prevalent themes in his work: Greece, hope and freedom. He was deeply influenced by the surrealists, both French and Greek, and his career as a poet began in the 1930s. His early poems exude a love of Greece, sun and life, but after war experience in Albania a natural *joie de vivre* is set against violence and the imminence of death. His greatest achievement is *To axion esti* (1959, Eng trans

The Axion Esti, 1974), a long, optimistic poem which took 14 years to write. In 1979 he was awarded the Nobel Prize for literature.

▷I Ivask, *Elytis: analogies of light* (1980)

EMBIRIKOS, Andreas
(1901–75)

Greek poet and novelist, born in Braila, in Romania, but resident for most of his life in France and England. He burst on to the Greek literary scene in 1935 with *Ipsikaminos* ('Furnace'), a collection of poetry that baffled and offended contemporary critics; a citation from the French Surrealist André Breton on its front page served to locate the work in a genre then unknown in Greece. His next two collections, the titles of which translate as 'The Vibrations of the Necktie' and 'The Appearance of Angels in a Steam Engine', were in the same vein, but were published only in literary journals. Embirikos then turned to prose, anticipating the 'automatic writing' of **Kerouac** and the American 'Beat' writers, and developing a style that mixed formal Greek *Katharevousa* and clichés culled from magazines and newspapers. In his later career he discovered **Freud** and moved away from the unbridled Surrealism of his earlier works: *Endochora* ('Hinterland'), a novel published in 1945, saw him coming to terms with Freud's acceptance of sexual instinct, and his next two books, *Argo* and *Zemphyra*, displayed an unbridled eroticism that had them censored.

EMECHETA, (Florence Onye) Buchi
(1944–)

British novelist, born near Lagos, Nigeria. She was educated at the Methodist Girls' High School, Lagos, and the University of London, and has worked as a teacher, librarian and social worker. She moved to England with her student husband in 1962 and has since lived in London with her five children. Writing of marriage as a battle of the sexes, her novels are powerful social documents, graphic in their depiction of man's inhumanity to woman (she separated from her husband). Relevant titles are *In the Ditch* (1972) and *Second-Class Citizen* (1974), which were later published together as *Adah's Story* (1983), *The Bride Price* (1976), *The Slave Girl* (1977), *The Joys of Motherhood* (1979), *Double Yoke* (1982) and *The Rape of Shavi* (1983). *Gwendolen* (1989) focuses on the cultural isolation of a young Caribbean immigrant. She has also written children's stories and television plays.

▷*Head Above Water* (1986)

EMERSON, Ralph Waldo
(1803–82)

American poet and essayist, born in Boston of a long line of ministers. He graduated at

Harvard in 1821, and after teaching at different places, became in 1829 pastor of the Second Church (Unitarian) in Boston, and married his first wife, Ellen Louisa Tucker (d.1832). In that year he preached views on the Lord's Supper which were disapproved of by the majority of his congregation; this led him finally to resign his pulpit. In 1833 he went to Europe, and visited **Thomas Carlyle** at Craigenputtock, next year beginning that 38 years' correspondence which shows the two men with all their characteristics, different as optimist and pessimist, yet with many profound sympathies. In 1834 he moved to Concord and the following year married his second wife, Lydia (Lidian) Jackson (1802–92). In 1836 he published a prose rhapsody entitled *Nature*, which, like his earlier poems, was read by few, and understood by fewer still, but which contains the germs of many of his later essays and poems. It was followed by 'The American Scholar', an oration delivered at Harvard University. These two publications, the first in the series of his collected works, strike the keynote of his philosophical, poetical and moral teachings. The 'address before the Divinity Class, Cambridge, 1838', which follows them, defined his position in, or out of, the church in which he had been a minister. A plea for the individual consciousness (as against all historical creeds, bibles, churches) for the soul of each man as the supreme judge in spiritual matters, it produced a great sensation, especially among the Unitarians, and much controversy followed in which Emerson took no part. In 1849 he revisited England to lecture on *Representative Men* (published in 1850). His *English Traits* appeared in 1856, *The Conduct of Life* in 1860, *Society and Solitude* in 1870, *Letters and Social Aims* in 1876. The idealist or transcendentalist in philosophy, the rationalist in religion, the bold advocate of spiritual independence, of intuition as a divine guidance, of instinct as a heaven-born impulse, of individualism in its fullest extent, making each life a kind of theocratic egoism—this is the Emerson of his larger utterances. For him nature was a sphinx, covered with hieroglyphics, for which the spirit of man is to find the key.
▷G W Allen, *Emerson: a biography* (1981)

EMINESCU, Mikhail
(1850–89)
Romanian poet, born in Ipoteşti. He studied at Czernowitz, Vienna and Berlin, and worked as a librarian, then editor, but eventually suffered a mental collapse in 1883 which left him with recurring bouts of madness until his death. He wrote lyric verse which was widely read and translated after his death. His works were collected in four volumes in 1939; his masterpiece is generally felt to be the long poem *Luceafărul* (1883).
▷G Calinescu, *Mikhail Eminescu* (1965)

EMPSON, Sir William
(1906–84)
English poet and critic, born in Howden, Yorkshire. He was educated at Winchester and Magdalene College, Cambridge, where he studied mathematics and literature. His first work of criticism was his university dissertation, published as *Seven Types of Ambiguity* (1930). From 1931 to 1934 he was Professor of English Literature in Tokyo, and at Peking (1937–9 and 1947–53), having been in the meantime with the BBC's Far Eastern Service. In 1953 he became Professor of English Literature at Sheffield University. His other critical works included *The Structure of Complex Words* (1951) and *Milton's God* (1961). *Collected Poems*, noted for wit, concentration and complexity of thought, was published in 1955.
▷R Gill, *William Empson, the man and his world* (1974)

ENCINA, or ENZINA, Juan de la
(c.1469–c.1534)
Spanish dramatist and poet, born near Salamanca. He was successively secretary to the first Duke of Alva, musical director in Pope Leo X's chapel at Rome, and prior of León in Spain. Besides his *Cancionero* (1496, 'Songbook'), he wrote in 1521 a poetical account of his pilgrimage to Jerusalem. His fame rests on 14 dramatic poems, 7 of which were the first secular poems to be dramatized in Spain (1492).
▷J R Andrews, *Juan Del Encina* (1959)

ENCKELL, Raabe
(1903–74)
Leading Finland–Swedish poet, dramatist, critic, essayist and painter, born in Tammela. He was an enthusiastic, even rather naive, supporter of every kind of modernism in his early years; but his finely crafted work is more highly technically accomplished than significant for its content. He is a versatile showman, capable of great charm. He has been called a 'humanist never unaware of the fragility of his emotional and aesthetic world'.
▷L Ekelund, *Raabe Enckell* (1974, in Swedish)

ENDO Shusako
(1923–)
Japanese novelist and short-story writer, born in Tokyo. After his parents divorced, he and his mother converted to Roman Catholicism. He graduated in French literature

from Keio University, then studied for several years in Lyons. He has gained wide recognition in the West and, although he is considered by some Japanese to be un-Japanese, has won many literary awards. In 1981 he was elected to the Nihon Geijutsuin, the Japanese Arts Academy. His books include *Silence* (1966), *The Sea and Poison* (1972), *Wonderful Fool* (1974), *Volcano* (1978), *When I Whistle* (1979) and *Stained Glass Elegies* (1984). Inveterately a moralist, he is often labelled 'the Japanese Graham Greene'.

ENGEL, Johann Jakob
(1741–1802)

German writer, born in Parchim. He intended to follow his father as a Lutheran pastor, but instead became a teacher. He wrote a number of plays, mainly in the comic manner of **Gotthold Lessing**, but is best known for the novel *Herr Lorenz Stark* (1795), and popular philosophical books, including the four-volume *Der Philosoph für die Welt* (1775–1803, 'The World's Philosopher').
▷C Schroeder, *Johann Jakob Engel* (1897)

ENGEL, Marian
(1933–85)

Canadian novelist, born in Toronto and educated at McMaster University and McGill University. She worked as a teacher in Canada and the USA and lived for a time in London and Cyprus. Her first novel, *No Clouds of Glory*, was published in 1968. She chaired the Writers' Union of Canada in 1973–4, and won a Governor General's Award for *Bear* in 1976; her most famous novel, it explores the complex relationship between a woman and a bear, intertwining myth and reality. Her last book, *The Tattooed Woman*, was published posthumously.
▷G Gibson, *Eleven Canadian Novelists* (1973)

ENGLE, Paul Hamilton
(1908–91)

American poet, novelist and critic, born in Cedar Rapids, Iowa. Among his collections of poetry are *Worn Earth* (1932) and *American Song* (1951), while his novels include *Always the Land* (1941) and *An Old-Fashioned Christmas* (1964). Although his writing is formal, elegant and accessible, he is best remembered as a penetrating critic and an inspirational teacher. His courses in literature and writing at the University of Iowa gave confidence to many aspiring authors.

ENGLISH, Isobel
(1925–)

English novelist and short-story writer, born in London. Although she has written comparatively few books, she was quickly established as a considered, sensitive chronicler of middle-class manners and anxieties. Her first novel, *The Key That Rusts* (1954), records a doomed love affair between the narrator's married step-brother and another woman; *Every Eye* (1956) follows a woman's journey across Europe, as she relives various past experiences. Later novels, including *Four Voices* (1961), and a collection, *Life After All and Other Stories* (1973), use a similar technique of observed and interior narrative.

ENGLISH, Thomas Dunn
(1819–1902)

American physician, lawyer and ballad-writer whose memory survives in his poem 'Ben Bolt'. This was a popular song during the Civil War, but gained worldwide prominence when **George Du Maurier** introduced it in *Trilby*. He was also the author of more than 50 now-forgotten plays.

ENNIUS, Quintus
(c.239–169 BC)

Roman poet, born in Rudiae in Calabria, and probably of Greek extraction. He is said to have served in the wars, and returned from Sardinia to Rome with Cato the Elder. Here he taught Greek, gained the friendship of Scipio Africanus, and attained the rank of Roman citizen. He introduced the Greek hexameter into Latin, using it in his *Annals*, which became the model for Latin epic poetry. His style, though rough, is striking. In addition, he wrote satires, didactic verse, epigrams and numerous plays. Only fragments of his works survive.
▷O Skutsch, *The Annals of Quintus Ennius* (1953)

ENQUIST, Per Olov
(1934–)

Swedish playwright and novelist. His best-known work for the theatre is a collection of three plays published in 1981 under the collective title *Triptych*, comprising *Lesbian Night* (about **August Strindberg** and his wife), *To Phaedra* and *The Life of the Slow-Worms* (about **Hans Christian Andersen**). His major novel is *The Legionaries* (1968), a controversial documentary account of the expulsion of Baltic refugees to Russia from Sweden after World War II.
▷A Landsmanis, *De misstolkade legionärerna* (1970)

ENRIGHT, D(ennis) J(oseph)
(1920–)

English poet, critic and literary journalist, he was born in Leamington, Warwickshire, and educated at Downing College, Cambridge, and the University of Alexandria, where he taught English (1947–50) and published his first collection of verse, *Season Ticket* (1948). His academic career continued east of Suez with appointments in Japan, Thailand and Singapore, interspersed with periods in Birmingham and Berlin. He was Honorary Professor of English at the University of Warwick from 1975 to 1980. University life figures in the novel *Academic Year* (1955), but Enright seems to have remained aloof from intellectual fashion and academic politics, carving out his own humanistic course. A *Collected Poems* appeared in 1981, suggesting a sensibility influenced by the 'Movement' poets of the fifties (**Larkin**, **Amis**, **Tom Gunn**), but more expansive and continental. Enright is the editor of *The Oxford Book of Death* (1983), a valuable anthology that wholly avoids morbidity.
▷ *Memoirs of a Mendicant Professor* (1969)

ENRÍQUEZ GÓMEZ, Antonio, properly Enríquez de Paz
(1602–c.1662)

Spanish playwright and poet, born in Segovia, the son of a baptized Portuguese Jew. In 1636 he fled to France to escape the Inquisition, and became major-domo to Louis XIII. He wrote comedies, a mystic poem, an epic, *El sansón nazareno* (1656) and a picturesque satirical novel in both prose and verse, *El siglo pitagórico* (1644, 'The Pythagorean Century'). Later he professed the Jewish faith, and in 1660 his effigy was burned at a Seville auto-da-fé.

ENZENSBERGER, Hans Magnus
(1929–)

German poet, born in Kaufbeuren and educated at Nuremberg, Freiburg and Hamburg. He saw service with the militia towards the end of World War II and worked as an editor for the Suddeutsche Rundfunk at the end of the fifties, the period when his first significant poetry was published in *verteidigung der wölfe* (1957). He lived for a period in Norway (1961–6), but has since lived in Germany, first in Berlin and later in Munich. The first English translations of his work were made by **Michael Hamburger** and appeared in 1966. Owing something to **Georg Trakl**, **Gottfried Benn** and, above all, **Brecht**, Enzensberger has developed a radical, international and epic style which attained its most distinctive expression in the long-form poem *Der Untergang der Titanic* (1978, translated by the poet as *The Sinking of the Titanic*, 1980), which opposes the reifications of industrial society with the blind forces of nature and instinct. *Die Gedichte* (1983, 'Poems') was published by Suhrkamp, Frankfurt, for whom he has acted as editor since 1960. Enzensberger has translated a wide range of British, American, Scandinavian, Latin-American and Russian literature, and like **Günter Grass**, has been a commentator on European unification.
▷ R Grimm, *Über Enzensberger* (1984)

EÖTVÖS, József, Baron
(1813–71)

Hungarian author and statesman, born in Budapest. He became an advocate in 1833, but soon devoting himself to literature, published a work on prison reform, and the novels, *A Karthausi* (1838–41, 'The Carthusian'), *A Falu Jegyzöje* (1845, Eng trans *The Village Notary*, 1850) and others. In the revolution of 1848 he was Minister of Public Instruction, holding this post again under Andrássy in 1867–71 after three years of exile.
▷ D Jones, *Five Hungarian Writers* (1966)

'EPHELIA'
(fl.1679)

The unidentified author of *Female Poems on Several Occasions* (1679), born in London, by her own account, to well-connected parents who died young. Her poems show the frank eroticism typical of Restoration love-songs. Among others published under her name is a political broadside, *Advice to his Grace* (1681), warning the Duke of Monmouth against 'mad ambition'. Attempts to identify her as the daughter of the poet **Katherine Philips** have not been substantiated, and it remains possible that 'Ephelia' was the pseudonym of a group of male poets.
▷ *Poems by Ephelia*, ed with critical essay by M E Mulvihill (1993); G Greer, et al (eds), *Kissing the Rod* (1988)

EPICHARMUS
(c.540–450 BC)

Greek poet, born in Cos or Syracuse, who wrote 35 or more comedies performed in Syracuse. Only fragments of his works survive.
▷ L Berk, *Epicharmus* (1964)

EPIMENIDES
(6th century)

Semi-legendary Cretan poet and priest, traditionally credited with a *Theogony*.
▷ H Demoulin, *Epimenides de Crète* (1901)

ERASMUS, Desiderius
(c.1466–1536)

Dutch humanist and scholar, one of the most influential Renaissance figures, born in Rotterdam. Educated by the Brethren of the Common Life at Deventer, he joined an Augustine monastery at Steyn near Gouda in 1487, and was ordained a priest in 1492. But he was already reacting against scholasticism and was drawn to the Humanists. He studied and taught in Paris, and later in most of the cultural centres in Europe, including Oxford (1499) and Cambridge (1509–14), where he was Professor of Divinity and of Greek. He travelled widely, writing, teaching and meeting Europe's foremost intellectuals (including John Colet and Thomas More, while in England), and was the very model of a cultivated and dedicated scholar. He published many popular, sometimes didactic, works like *Adagia* (1500, Eng trans *Proverbs or Adages*, 1569), *Enchiridion Militis Christiani* (1503, Eng trans *Manual of a Christian Knight*, 1533), and the famous *Encomium Moriae* (1511, Eng trans *In Praise of Folly*, 1549). He also published scholarly editions of classical authors and the Church Fathers, and edited the Greek New Testament (1516). He became strongly critical of the pedantries and abuses of the Catholic Church and his *Colloquia familiaria* (1518, Eng trans *The Colloquies*, 1965) helped prepare the way for Martin Luther and the Reformation; but he also came to oppose the dogmatic theology of the Reformers and specifically attacked Luther in *De Libero Arbitrio* (1523, Eng trans *Discourse on the Freedom of the Will*, 1961). Despite these controversies he enjoyed great fame and respect in his last years, which he spent in Basle. The story of his father's life forms the theme of **Charles Reade**'s *The Cloister and the Hearth*.
▷ J M Sowards, *Desiderius Erasmus* (1975)

ERBA, Luciano
(1922–)

Italian poet. His brief political education was conducted in the anti-fascist cells of wartime Milan, his native city, after which he was forced to flee to Switzerland in 1944. He taught in France before returning to Milan; he has subsequently held academic positions in Bari, Trieste, Bologna, Padua and Verona, as well as in the USA. A member of the 'Fourth Generation', he rejected literalism and a committed stance in favour of a highly condensed style that infuses everyday experience with epiphanic significance, but which is nonetheless broadly pessimistic and consciously disillusioned. Erba has not been highly prolific, and has not gained wide appreciation in the English-speaking world, though a significant selection of his work

appeared in *The New Italian Poetry* (1981, ed L R Smith). His most important volumes are *Il bel paese* (1956, 'The Beautiful Land'), *Il male minor* (1960) and *Il nastro de Moebius* (1980, 'The Moebius Strip'), for which he won the Viareggio Prize. He is an expert on **Cyrano de Bergerac** and, along with other French authors, has translated him into Italian.

ERBEN, Karel Jaromir
(1811–70)

Czech poet and Slavonic folklorist, born in Miletin. In 1851 Erben became archivist of the city of Prague. His ballad collection *Kytice* (1853, 'The Garland') is deservedly regarded as one of Europe's greatest transformations of popular ballad material into sophisticated literary form. The 12 ballads, with their emphasis on the grim and irrational elements in folk belief are, as critics have frequently pointed out, far from being mere 'echoes'. *101 Slavonic Fairy-Stories and Tales in their Original Tongues* (1864) and *Popular Czech Songs and Rimes* (1862–4) preserve some of his work in English translation.

ERCILLA Y ZÚÑIGA, Alonso de
(1553–c.1595)

Spanish poet, born in Bermeo on the Bay of Biscay. He entered the service of Philip II, and accompanied him in 1554 to England on the occasion of his marriage to Queen Mary I. Shortly after, he joined the expedition against the Araucanians in Chile whose amazing heroism inspired his monumental epic poem, *La Araucana* (1569–89, Eng trans 1945). An unfounded suspicion of his complicity in an insurrection nearly led to his execution. Fearing for his life, he returned to Spain, but Philip treated him with indifference so he made a tour through Europe, and for some time was chamberlain to the Emperor Rudolf II. In 1580 he returned to Madrid, where he lived in poverty till his death.
▷ J T Medina, *Vida de Ercilla* (1948)

ERCKMANN-CHATRIAN
(1822–99)

The compound name of two French writers—Lorrainers both, Émile Erckmann (1822–99), born in Phalsbourg, and Alexandre Chatrian (1826–90), born in Abreschwiller. Their literary partnership dates from 1848, but they had little success until the publication of *L'Illustre Docteur Mathéus* (1859, Eng trans *The Illustrious Dr Mathéus*, 1872). *Le Fou Yégof* (1862, Eng trans *The Great Invasion of 1813–14; or, After Leipzig*, 1870) is one of a series of novels, to which also belong *Histoire d'un conscrit de 1813* (1864, Eng trans *The Conscript: A Tale of the French War of 1813*, 1865), *Waterloo* (1865, Eng trans 1865) and

Le Blocus (1867, Eng trans *The Blockade*, 1869). Well-known plays by them are *Le Juif polonais* (1869, Eng trans *The Polish Jew*, 1871), *L'Ami Fritz* (1864, Eng trans *Friend Fritz*, 1873), *Les Rantzau* (1882, Eng trans *The Rantzaus*, 1882) and *La Guerre* (1872, Eng trans *War*, 1872). After the annexation of Alsace-Lorraine to Germany, a strong anti-German feeling was shown in several of their books—the best of these is *L'Histoire du plébiscite* (1872, Eng trans *The Story of the Plébiscite*, 1872). They had quarrelled over money just before Chatrian died.

ERDMAN, Nikolai Robertovich
(1902–70)

Russian playwright, born in Moscow, where he became involved in political cabaret at an early age. His first play, *Mandat* (Eng trans *The Mandate*, 1975), achieved great popularity when produced by Meyerhold in 1925. This ideological farce satirized the bourgeoisie who were trying desperately to adapt to communism. It was followed by another satire, *Samoubiytsa* (1928, Eng trans *The Suicide*, 1979). Among its many targets was the Soviet system, so it is not surprising that Stalin banned it during rehearsals in 1932, ending the theatrical career of 'our new Gogol', as **Gorky** called him. It seems that he may have been exiled to Siberia for writing political fables, but he later found work as a film scenarist.

▷M Hoover, 'Nikolai Erdman: A Soviet Dramatist Rediscovered', in *Russian Literature Triquarterly*, no 2 (Winter 1972)

ERDRICH, Louise
(1954–)

American novelist, short-story writer and poet, who grew up in North Dakota of mixed Chippewa, French and German descent. Her work is centrally concerned with themes of cultural identity (usually seen from a female perspective), and much of it is set in her native state. Her first books were *Jacklight* (1984), a collection of poems, and the lyrical, multi-narrator novel, *Love Medicine* (1984), which traces the history of two Native American families across three generations. The later novels *Beet Queen* (1986), *Tracks* (1988) and *The Bingo Palace* (1994) continue the story of these families and their white neighbours back to the early 1900s. Erdrich has since published another poetry collection, *Baptism of Desire* (1989), and *The Crown of Columbus* (1991), a fictional exploration of the continuing impact of Columbus's voyage on Native American culture (written with her husband Michael Dorris).

ERENBURG, Ilya
(1891–1967)

Russian novelist and journalist, famous for his reportage of World War II, born in Kiev.

A versatile writer, a born survivor, he was susceptible to many currents of thought, from Roman Catholic mysticism to communism. He lived in Paris, returned to Russia after the advent of communism, went back into exile, returned again to Russia for the war, acted as an apologist for Stalin—and was finally a leader in the Thaw, from which he took the name of his novel *Ottepel* (1954, Eng trans *The Thaw*, 1955). The best of his prolific fiction is the early *Neobychayne pokhozdeniya Khulio Khuretino* (1922, Eng trans *The Extraordinary Adventures of Julio Jurentino*, 1930), in which he satirized the contemporary world.

▷V Alexandrova, *History of Soviet Literature* (1963)

ERI, Vincent Serei
(1936–)

Papua New Guinean novelist, author of the first significant novel from that country. He was born in Moveave and educated by Catholic missionaries and at the University of Papua New Guinea, Port Moresby. He has held various government offices both at home and in Australia. Eri's novel *The Crocodile* (1970) describes the period of colonialism and concerns the opposition of traditional values with modernity. The crocodile itself is a totem of power, magic, and both fertility and death, and the novel concludes ambiguously, its central character precariously balanced between worlds.

ERINNA
(4th century BC)

Greek poet (mistakenly believed in antiquity to have lived in the 7th century), born on the island of Telos. Though she died at the age of only 19, she won fame for her epic, *The Distaff*, on the joys of childhood. Only four lines of this and a handful of epigrams survive of her work.

▷C Latte, *Erinna* (1953)

ERNST, Paul
(1866–1933)

German author of short stories, novels, drama and poetry, born in Elbingerode. Ernst once carried great weight in his literature, but his stock has fallen in favour of other writers. He began as a naturalist and Marxist, but ended up as a grand old man of Nazi letters for his (not unusual) misinterpretation of the 'superman' of **Nietzsche** as a Hitler-like being. He now reads as an over-solemn, ponderous writer; but at one time his vast epics and what he called his 'meta-tragedies' were popular and respected. However, some of his hundreds of short tales (usually grouped within a framing story) are spoken of as classics in the genre; they are quite unpretentious, and do not partake of any of the grandiosity of what he believed was his chief work.

ERSKINE, John
(1879–1951)

American novelist, born in New York City and educated to PhD level at Columbia University, where he later taught. He also taught at Amherst College and pursued his musical interests as a pianist for the New York Philharmonic. He wrote over 45 books, the best-known of which is the satirical *The Private Life of Helen of Troy* (1925), which became a bestseller. In addition to his early novels, which often retold famous legends in humorous ways, he wrote four autobiographical books, each concentrating on a different aspect of his life, and was a well-known critic and semi-biographical novelist.

ERTEL, Aleksandr Ivanovich
(1855–1908)

Russian novelist, born in Voronezh, who is prized in particular for his novel *Gardeniny, ikh dvornya, priverzhentsy i vragi* (1888, 'The Gardenins, Their House, Adherents and Enemies'), which was praised by **Tolstoy**, under whose influence it was, in part, written. He had perhaps a deeper and more realistic approach to Russia's peasant problems than any of his contemporaries, was a master of dialogue, and may well not be the merely 'minor writer' he has been considered by critics. He was regarded as the spokesman for the 'populist intelligensia', but later became interested in religion.

ERTZ, Susan, pseud of Mrs Ronald McCrindle
(c.1894–1985)

American novelist, born in Walton-on-Thames. She was the author of many popular novels including *Madame Claire* (1922) and *The Prodigal Heart* (1950).

ERVINE, St John Greer
(1883–1971)

Irish playwright and author, born in Belfast. In 1900 he emigrated to London, where he wrote novels and plays. From 1915 to 1916 he was manager of the Abbey Theatre, Dublin, where his first plays, *Mixed Marriage* (1911) and *Jane Clegg* (1914), were produced. After World War I, in which he served with the Dublin Fusiliers and lost a leg, he won a high reputation as a drama critic, working on *The Observer* and the *Morning Post*, and for the BBC (1932). His most successful plays are perhaps *Anthony and Anna* (1926), *The First Mrs Fraser* (1929) and *Robert's Wife* (1937); other publications include seven novels and several biographies.
▷ *Some Impressions of My Elders* (1922)

ESPINA, Antonio
(b.1894)

Spanish novelist, biographer, poet and essayist, born in Madrid. Espina's novels, the better known of which is *Luna de copas* (1929, 'Moon of Hearts'), were much influenced by the literary theories of **Ortega y Gasset**, and have often been compared to the fiction of **Jarnés** and **Arderíus** (with the latter of whom he founded a left-wing review, *Nuevo España*). He has written lively biographies, and his best book is reckoned to be *Luis Candeles, el bandido de Madrid* (1929, Eng trans in *Great Spanish Short Stories*, 1932). He is generally reckoned to have 'spread his talents in too many directions', but his book on **Ganivet** (1942) is regarded as one of the best on this enigmatic character. He also wrote on **Quevedo** and **Cervantes**. An anti-Francoist, he spent 10 years in prison (1937–46), then went to Mexico, and was finally allowed to return to Spain in 1955.

ESPINEL, Vicente de
(1551–1624)

Spanish writer, born in Ronda. He served as a soldier in France and Italy, meeting with some of the adventures related in his *Relaciones de la vida del Escudero Márcos de Obregón* (1618, Eng trans *The History of the Life of the Squire Marcos de Obregon*, 1816), a book largely drawn upon by **Lesage** for his *Gil Blas*. After his return to Spain he took holy orders. He also published a volume of poems (1591) and a translation of the *Ars Poetica* of **Horace**. He was, if not the inventor, the improver of the 10-line stanza, and is credited with adding the fifth string to the guitar.
▷ G Haley, *Vicente Espinel e Marcos de Obregon* (1959)

ESPINOSA, Pedro de
(1578–1650)

Spanish poet, born in Antequera, a centre for artists and poets. Initially he wrote love poetry, mainly inspired, it is said, by the poet Cristobalina Fernández de Alarcón. Disillusioned at his failure to win her, Espinosa retired to a hermitage. He became a priest and entered the service of an Andalusian grandee. He continued writing poetry, both secular and religious, such as 'Soledad de Pedro de Jesús' ('Solitude of Pedro de Jesús'), often describing nature with scientific precision, but he is chiefly remembered for his anthology of contemporary poetry, *Las Flores de Poetas Ilustres* (1605, 'The Flowers of Famous Poets'), with more than 200 compositions mainly by Andalusian poets. This book is often regarded as the beginning of the baroque period in Spanish poetry.

ESPRONCEDA, José de
(1808–42)

Spanish poet and revolutionary, born in Almendralejo in Estremadura. He travelled widely in Europe, partly to escape persecution for his liberalism, and partly in pursuit of Teresa Marcha, who is commemorated in his unfinished poem *El Diablo mundo* (1841, 'The Devil of the World'). He wrote romantic poems in the **Byronic** manner, and is considered by some the greatest lyricist of his time.
▷J Casalduero, *Espronceda* (1961)

ESQUIROS, Henri Alphonse
(1814–76)

French poet and politician, born in Paris. He published poems and romances. For his *Évangile du peuple* (1840, 'The People's Gospel'), a democratic commentary on the life of Jesus, he was fined and imprisoned; this inspired his *Chants d'un prisonnier* (1841, 'A Prisoner's Songs'). His *Vierges folles* ('Foolish Virgins'), *Vierges martyres* ('Virgin Martyrs') and *Vierges sages* (1841–2, 'Wise Virgins') showed more of his socialistic sympathies. After the revolution he became a member of the Legislative Assembly, but the *coup d'état* of 1851 drove him to England, where he gathered the materials for his *L'Angleterre et la vie anglaise* (1860–9, Eng trans *The English at Home*, 1861), *Cornwall and its Coasts* (1865, written in English) and *Religious Life in England* (1867, written in English). In 1870 he was administrator of Bouches-du-Rhône, and was sent to the National Assembly (1871) and the Senate (1875).

ESSON, Louis
(1879–1943)

Australian playwright, born in Edinburgh, and considered the first to create a corpus of native Australian plays. Influenced by the nationalistic atmosphere of Dublin's Abbey Theatre, in 1922 he joined with **Vance Palmer** in establishing the Pioneer Players in Melbourne, where his 'bush' plays were regularly performed. Collections of his plays include *The Time is Not Yet Ripe* (1912) and *Dead Timber and Other Plays* (1920). Later works were edited by his widow as *The Southern Cross and Other Plays* (1946) and *The Woman Tamer* (1976). Two collections of verse were *Bells and Bees* (1910) and *Red Gums* (1912). Other writings were collected after his death into an anthology, *Ballads of Old Bohemia* (1980). Esson was perhaps at his best in his short plays such as *Dead Timber*

(1911), *The Drover* (1919) and *Andenagora* (1937).

ESSOP, Ahmed
(1931–)

Indian novelist, living in South Africa. As a young man he wrote verse under the name Ahmed Yousuf. He took his degree at the university in Pretoria and has taught at senior school level in Johannesburg, where his first two novels were published. *The Visitation* (1980) is concerned with double selves and with the hypocrisy that sustains respectable society. *The Emperor* (1984) is more forcefully satirical though ultimately less satisfying, and Essop's best work is probably to be found among the stories in *The Hajji* (1978), which are finely judged studies of human vanity and pretensions.

ESTANG, Luc, pseud of Lucien Bastard
(1911–91)

French Catholic novelist, critic and literary editor (of the magazine *La Croix*, 1940–55). He began as a poet; his main province (although he continued to publish verse) soon became the practice of fiction in the passionate and rebellious tradition established by **Georges Bernanos**, upon whom he wrote illuminatingly. He is best known outside France for his powerful novel *Le Bonheur et le salut* (1961, Eng trans *The Better Song*, 1961), the story of a man weighed down with guilt.

ESTAUNIÉ, Édouard
(1862–1942)

French novelist, whose work is now somewhat overlooked by readers, born in Dijon and educated by Jesuits. He thought himself neglected, and certainly his sales were small; but he was always, and still is, held in high estimation by discerning critics. In reaction to his pious and strict education, he first became a 'perplexed positivist' (as critics called him), and wrote in the naturalist style of **Zola**. *L'Empreinte* (1895, 'The Imprint') is one of the most quietly deadly of all indictments of Jesuit teachers as they were in his childhood. Gradually and doubtingly he returned to his old faith, in subtle and grave novels which were certainly read and digested by such writers as **François Mauriac**. Although his novels were put into other languages, he has yet to find an English translator.

ESZTERHAS, Joe
(1944–)

Hungarian-born American screenwriter. A former journalist, his first filmed screenplay was for the trade union drama *F.I.S.T.* (1978)

and his work has tended to alternate between explorations of political and social issues, such as white supremacy in *Betrayed* (1988) and Nazism in *The Music Box* (1989), and more overtly commercial entertainment like *Jagged Edge* (1985) and *Sliver* (1993), which blend murder, sexual shenanigans and a shoal of red herrings before moving towards an often predictable surprise revelation in the film's final reel. Among the highest-paid screenwriters in Hollywood, he was rumoured to have received $3 million for writing the controversial adult thriller *Basic Instinct* (1992).

ETCHAHOUNIA, Pierre Topet d'
(1786–1862)

Major Basque poet, born in Etchahounia in the French Basque provinces. He is famous for having cursed his father for forbidding him to marry a poor girl: 'God curse Gaztelondo Topet and all those who fall in love with poor girls!' is now proverbial. He beat up the rich (and allegedly unfaithful) woman whom he did marry, killed a man for sleeping with her (although he had not done so), was refused permission to live at home, and spent much of his life as a beggar and travelling bard. His trenchant poetry, free from ecclesiastic and pious cant, often questioning the existence of God, is the best there is in the Basque language. It survives only because it is easily memorable: his family burned it on a bonfire as soon as he died. It was collected in *Le Poète Pierre Topet, dit Etchahun, et ses oeuvres* (1946). **Chamisso** told his story most memorably.

ETHEREGE, Sir George
(?1635–1691)

A Restoration dramatist, he was born probably in Maidenhead. Secretary to the ambassador at Constantinople from 1668 to 1670 or 1671, he married a wealthy widow, and in 1685 was sent to be resident at the Imperial court at Ratisbon. He varied the monotony of this banishment with coursing, drinking, play, flirtation with actresses and correspondence with **Thomas Middleton**, **Dryden** and Betterton. He seems to have died in Paris. In English literature he is founder of the comedy of intrigue. He sought his inspiration in **Molière**, and out of him grew the legitimate comedy of manners and the dramatic triumphs of **Richard Brinsley Sheridan** and **Oliver Goldsmith**. His three plays are *The Comical Revenge or, Love in a Tub* (1664); *She Would if She Could* (1668); and *The Man of Mode or, Sir Fopling Flutter* (1676)—all highly popular in their day.
▷D Underwood, *Etherege and the 17th-century Comedy of Manners* (1957)

ÉTTIENE, Frank
(1936–)

Haitian writer, who wrote the first novel in Creole, *Disaffection* (1975): 'a dead end in itself, perhaps, but a very important one', wrote a critic. It was greatly influenced by **Jacques Roumain**, founder of the Haitian Communist Party, whose final novel had abounded in Creolisms.

EUCKEN, Rudolph Christoph
(1846–1926)

German writer, born in Aurich, Ostfriesland, winner of the Nobel Prize for literature. He was educated at the University of Göttingen, where he studied philosophy, and worked firstly as a schoolteacher, and later as a professor at the universities of Basle and Jena. His family were Lutheran, but he developed as a freethinker and idealist. His numerous books were all philosophical works, the most influential of which was *Der Sinn und Wert des Lebens* (1908, Eng trans *The Meaning and Value of Life*, 1916), but he was awarded the Nobel Prize for literature in recognition of his 'earnest search for truth' and 'idealistic philosophy of life'.

EURINGER, Richard
(1891–1953)

German novelist and writer on flying, born in Augsberg, whose books influenced other writers on flying, particularly **Gerd Gaiser**. A pilot in World War I, he became an ardent Nazi and a 'Reichscultursenator'. But such novels as *Fliegerschule 4* (1929, 'Flying School 4') were efficient, authentic and well thought out.

EURIPIDES
(484 or 480–406 BC)

Greek dramatist, regarded, with **Aeschylus** and **Sophocles**, as one of the three great tragedians. He brought a new style to tragedy and the treatment of traditional mythology. Of about 80 of his dramas whose titles are known, 18 survive complete. He won the tragic prize only five times, and he died at the court of Archelaus, King of Macedonia. He did not take much part in public life; in politics he was moderate, approving of a democracy, but not of demagogues. The names and probable order of his surviving plays are: *Alcestis* (438 BC, Eng trans 1930), *Medea* (431 BC, Eng trans 1959), *Hippolytus* (428 BC, Eng trans 1959), *Andromache* (425 BC, Eng trans 1957), *Hecuba* (424 BC, Eng trans 1959), *Supplices* (423 BC, Eng trans 1957), *Heraclidae* (416 BC, Eng trans *Heracles*, 1959), *Troades* (415 BC, Eng trans *The Women of Troy*, 1954), *Helena* (412 BC, Eng trans 1951), *Phoenissae* (410 BC, Eng trans *The Phoenician Women*,

1959), *Orestes* (408 BC, Eng trans 1959); the *Bacchae* (405 BC, Eng trans 1954) and *Iphigenia Aulidensis* (405 BC, Eng trans *Iphigenia in Aulis*, 1959) were put on the Athenian stage only after the author's death; and it is uncertain to what period belonged the *Ion* (Eng trans 1937), *Heracles Furens* (Eng trans *The Madness of Heracles*, 1969), *Iphigenia Taurica* (Eng trans *Iphigenia in Tauris*, 1953), *Electra* (Eng trans 1950), and *Cyclops* (Eng trans 1957), whilst it is doubtful whether the *Rhesus* (Eng trans 1959) is genuine. He is notable for highlighting unusual opinions and portraying socially marginal characters. Sophocles, who deemed him 'the most tragic of poets', also commented that while he himself showed people as they ought to be, Euripides portrayed them as they are. Fascinated by the dark side of human nature and the conflicts this engenders, and believing that passion is often at the root of tragedy, Euripides's skill as a playwright is of the highest order; he can construct plots which are exciting beyond anything attempted by his predecessors, and he has an unerring instinct for 'situation'. But in his desire to get on to the situation as rapidly as possible, he substitutes a bald prologue for a proper exposition, and instead of working out the dénouement, makes a *deus ex machina* cut the knot of the situation. To the same end he sacrifices consistency in character. His popularity increased after his death; his plays were revived more frequently than those of **Aeschylus** or **Sophocles** and the number that have survived is greater than both of theirs put together.

EUSDEN, Laurence
(1688–1730)

English poet, born in Spofforth. He became poet laureate in 1718, but not on account of his poetic genius, merely because he had celebrated the marriage (1717) of the Duke of Newcastle (who was responsible for nominations for the position). He wrote little of value, was lampooned by **Pope**, who placed him in the realms of dullness in *The Dunciad*, and died rector of Coningsby, Lincolnshire.

EVANS, Augusta, later Augusta Wilson
(1835–1909)

American novelist, born in Columbus, Georgia, who from 1868, the date of her marriage, wrote under her married name of Wilson. *St Elmo* (1866) attracted more ridicule than praise, but this story of the prudish Edna Earle's 'taming' of the supposedly **Byronic** St Elmo, written with much pretentious erudition, became a bestseller. It offers good example of how 'unwholesome and eminently forgettable trash' can sweep a nation—but only for a short time.
▷W P Fidler, *August Evans* (1951)

EVANS, Caradoc, pseud of David Evans
(1878–1945)

Welsh short-story writer and novelist, born in Llanfihangel-ar-Arth, Dyfed. He spent much of his childhood at Rhydlewis, but left home in 1893, working as a shop assistant in Carmarthen, Barry, Cardiff and finally London. While in London, he attended evening classes and eventually found employment as a journalist in 1906. His collections of short stories, *My People* (1915), *Capel Sion* (1916) and *My Neighbours* (1919), savagely exposed the hypocrisies, lust and greed of the Chapel-going people of his native West Wales. His play, *Taffy* (1923), was in similar vein and in his own time he was vilified by the Welsh as a traitor for his assaults on many cherished aspects of the Welsh way of life, from Nonconformity and the Eisteddfod to the integrity and intelligence of the common people.
▷T L Williams, *Caradoc Evans* (1970)

EVANS, Donald
(1884–1921)

American poet, who had a small influence upon **Wallace Stevens**. Evans was a Greenwich Village decadent, well known in his lifetime, who tried to write in the tradition of **Fargue**, and who killed himself. His poetry is now virtually forgotten. His final collection was entitled, characteristically, *Ironics* (1919). He had, a contemporary said, 'a genius for exquisite masks of cynicism', 'in graceful defiance of society'. It has been asserted that he also influenced **E E Cummings**.

EVANS, George Essex
(1863–1909)

Australian poet. Born in London, he went to Australia in 1881 and settled in Queensland. After teaching in country areas he turned to journalism and wrote on agricultural matters. His first book was a long narrative poem, *The Repentance of Magdalene Despar* (1891). It was followed by *Loraine and Other Verses* (1898), *The Secret Key and Other Verses* (1906) and *Queen of the North* (1909). At his best and strongest when writing of the Australian countryside which he came to love, he also wrote ceremonial verse such as 'An Ode for Commonwealth Day', 'An Australian Symphony' and a sentimental favourite, 'The Women of the West'. *The Collected Verse of George Essex Evans* was published in 1928.

EVANS, Matilda Jane, pseud Maud Jeanne Franc
(1827–86)

English-born Australian novelist and writer of moral tales for children under her pseudonym. Born in Peckham Park, Surrey, she emigrated to Australia in 1852, opening a school and later becoming a deaconess in the Baptist Church. She wrote many novels and short stories, all with a high moral tone and aimed primarily at adolescents. Her first novel was *Marian: Or, The Light of Someone's Home* (1861), which was followed by 14 more, including *Vermont Vale: Or, Home Pictures in Australia* (1866) and *Minnie's Mission: An Australian Temperance Tale* (1869). They were popular for many years as Sunday School prizes.

EVANS, Theophilus
(1693–1767)

Welsh historian, born in Newcastle Emlyn. He was an Anglican priest. The style of his histories and sermons is bold and assertive; *A History of Modern Enthusiasm* (1752, rev edn 1757), in English, is a striking example of his contempt for Methodism, which he believed was, if secretly, a Romish sect. His marvellous history of Wales, *Drych y Prif Oesoedd* (1740) is often regarded as a work of epic proportions, abounding in striking metaphors.

EVELYN, John
(1620–1706)

English diarist and author, born of wealthy parentage in Wotton, near Dorking. He was brought up in Lewes (1625–37), then entered Balliol College, Oxford, and in 1640 the Middle Temple. He witnessed Strafford's trial and execution, and in November 1642 joined the king's army for three days. The Covenant being pressed on him, he travelled for four years on the Continent. In Paris in 1647 he married the ambassador's daughter, Mary Browne (1635–1709), and in 1652 settled at Sayes Court, Deptford. He spent a lot of time at court after the Restoration and acted on public committees and from 1685 to 1687 was one of the commissioners of the privy seal. From 1695 to 1703 he was treasurer of Greenwich Hospital and was a prominent fellow of the Royal Society. In 1694 he removed to his brother's at Wotton. Evelyn, as active and intelligent as he was honest and God-fearing, was yet neither sage nor hero. He was always active in Church affairs and was especially prominent in the rebuilding of St Paul's Cathedral. He dealt with a multitude of subjects. Of his three dozen works the chief are *Fumifiguim, or the Inconvenience of the Air and Smoke of London dissipated* (1661); *Sculptura, or the Art of Engraving on Copper* (1662); *Sylva, or a Discourse of Forest-trees* (1664); and the delightful *Diary* (discovered in an old clothes-basket at Wotton in 1817), covering the years 1641–1706 and containing vivid portraits of his contemporaries.
▷ B Saunders, *Evelyn and His Times* (1970)

EVERSON, William
(1912–)

American poet, born in Sacramento, California. A religious, contemplative man, he was for 18 years a Roman Catholic monk in a Dominican order, and produced several collections of poetry under the name of Brother Antoninus. These include *The Crooked Lines of God: Poems 1949–1954* (1959) and *The Last Crusade* (1969). Other volumes, under the name of Everson, include *X War Elegies* (1943) and *The Veritable Years: Poems 1949–1966* (1978). In both guises, as Everson and Brother Antoninus, the poet deliberates in sometimes confessional, sometimes sensual, verse upon man's search for moral and spiritual values in an uncertain, violent world.

EWALD, Johannes
(1743–81)

Danish Romantic poet and dramatist, born in Copenhagen, and writer of the Danish national anthem. At the age of 15 he ran away from home to fight in the Seven Years War (1756–63), then turned his attention to writing. He was one of the first Danish poets to use national legends and myths as material, as in his biblical drama *Adam og Eva* (1769), the historical drama *Rolf Krage* (1770) and the lyrical drama *Balders Död* (1773). He also wrote an operetta, *Fiskerne* (1779, 'The Fishermen'), which contains the song 'King Kristian stood by the lofty mast', which is now the Danish national anthem.
▷ L Labe, *Johannes Ewald* (1943)

EWART, Gavin Buchanan
(1916–)

Scottish poet, educated at Cambridge, who worked as an advertising copywriter for nearly 20 years. His main poetic model was the lean-limbed style of **Auden**. His first collection of verse appeared when he was just 23, but he only fully found his stride with the distinctive *Londoners* (1964) and the tellingly titled *Throwaway Lines* (1966). He uses the rhythms and recurrent obsessions of demotic forms—limericks in particular—to create a heavily stressed and usually rhymed verse that is robustly Anglo-Saxon. Many of the poems are sexual or scatological, mixing obscenity with lightly-worn learning and often revealing a depth of feeling under their nonsensical skittishness. Perhaps the most distinctive and individual collection is *Or Where a Young Penguin Lies Screaming* (1977). A *Collected Ewart* appeared in 1980, as did *The Penguin Book of Light Verse*, which he edited with obvious relish. He has continued to produce 'little ones'.

EWERS, J(ohn) K(eith)
(1904–78)

Australian writer of fiction, history and literary criticism, born in Subiaco, Perth. His first novel was *Money Street* (1933), followed by *Fire on the Wind* (1935) based on his family's experiences in a bushfire. He wrote for children in *Tales from the Dead Heart* (1944) and *Written in Sand* (1947), retellings of aboriginal myths. *With the Sun on My Back* (1953) was a prize-winning account of his travels in northern Australia, and he wrote one of the first studies of Australian literature in *Creative Writing in Australia* (1945). His *I Came Naked*, poetic reflections on life, was produced in a limited edition in 1976.

EWING, Julianna Horatia, née Gatty
(1841–85)

English writer for children, daughter of Margaret Gatty (1809–73), also a children's writer. Born in Ecclesfield, Yorkshire, she soon began to compose nursery plays, which are said to have suggested to her mother the starting of *Aunt Judy's Magazine* (1866), which she later edited, publishing in it many of her charming stories, such as *Jackanapes*. Her numerous books included *A Flat Iron for a Farthing* (1870), *Lab-lie-by-the-Fire* (1873) and *Daddy Darwin's Dovecot* (1881). Her *The Brownies and Other Tales* (1870) provided the name by which the junior section of the Girl Guide movement is known.

▷G Avery, *Mrs Ewing* (1961)

EYVINDUR, known as Skáldaspillir (The Plagiarist), properly Eyvindur Jónsson
(d.c.990)

Norwegian court poet of the Viking Age. Born of a noble family, he was a devoted follower of King Haakon I, 'the Good' of Norway, whom he eulogized in his *Hákonarmál*. He later wrote a eulogy in praise of Earl Haakon of Norway (*Haleygjatal*), and an *Íslendingadrápa* about Icelanders.

F

FABRE, Ferdinand
(1830–98)

French novelist, born in Bédarieux. He was educated for the priesthood, but took to writing novels instead, in which he created vivid portrayals of country priests. He wrote *L'abbé Tigrane, candidat à la papauté* (1873, Eng trans *The abbé Tigrane. Candidate for the papal chair*, 1876) and other stories of rustic life in Cévennes.

FABRE D'ÉGLANTINE, Philippe François Nazaire
(1750–94)

French dramatist, poet, and revolutionist, born in Carcassonne. He wrote *Le Philinte de Molière* (1790), a sequel to Molière's *Le Misanthrope*. A member of the National Convention, he devised some of the new names of months for the Revolutionary Calendar, but, having fallen out of favour with Robespierre, was eventually guillotined.
▷ L Jacob, *Fabre d'Églantine, chef des Fripons* (1946)

FADEYEV, Aleksandr Aleksandrovich,
pseud **Bulgya**
(1901–56)

Russian novelist of the socialist realism school. He was deeply influenced by **Tolstoy**, and wrote *Razgrom* (1926, Eng trans *The Rout*, 1929), set in the Russian civil war, and *Molodaya gvardiya* (1945, Eng trans *The Young Guard*, 1962), portraying Russian resistance against the Germans in World War II. As general-secretary of the Soviet Writers' Union (1946–55) he mercilessly exposed any literary 'deviationism' from the party line but became a target himself and, compelled to revise the last-named work (1951), took to drink and finally shot himself.
▷ V M Ozerov, *Aleksandr Aleksandrovich Fadeyev* (1960)

FAGUNDES VARELA, Luis Nicolau
(1841–75)

Brazilian poet, a typically romantic and Bohemian figure in whose work all the main trends of romanticism may be found. He never entirely escaped from the European models which had initially inspired him, but his elegies for his wife and son ('Cântico do Calvario') are moving and deservedly

famous. His most interesting and enduring work was written in collaboration with his sister: *Anchieta ou o Evangelho das Selvas*, a long religious poem.
▷ A Soares-Amora, *Grandes Poetas Românticos do Brasil* (1949)

FAGUNWA, Daniel O
(c.1910–1963)

Nigerian writer in Yoruba. A chief, he died in a boating accident. When the Anglophone novels of **Amos Tutuola** became famous worldwide, many Nigerians felt that Tutuola owed too large a debt to the former's four Yoruba novels, which were popular in Nigeria, but, naturally enough, unknown elsewhere. **Wole Soyinka**'s *Hunter's Saga* (1968) is an adaptation from Fagunwa's 1939 novel of the same title (in Yoruba). His books, of which the first, *Forest of a Thousand Demons* (1938), was translated in 1968, began a remarkable literary account of the Yoruba cosmogony.

FAINLIGHT, Ruth Esther
(1931–)

American poet, she was educated in England and in 1959 married the novelist **Alan Sillitoe**, with whom she has occasionally collaborated. Most of her work is premised on a refusal to subordinate 'life', with its compromises and hesitations, to 'art'; she refuses to deal in absolutes, calling on fairy tales and popular mythology to demonstrate the merits of adaptation without compromise. This approach lies behind her first completely individual volume, *Cages* (1966), and the aptly titled *To See the Matter Clearly* (1968). Fainlight seems to have gone through periods of quiet re-assessment and even abnegation at the start of successive decades, but returned to impressive form with *The Region's Violence* and *Twenty One Poems* (both 1973) and *Climates* and *Fifteen to Infinity* (both 1983). In the latter pair, her perceptiveness is strikingly heightened and a strong-lined metre reinforces her growing philosophical resonance. She has published one collection of short stories, *Daylife and Nightlife* (1971).

FAIRBAIRNS, Zoë Ann
(1948–)

English novelist, journalist and pamphleteer, who has written on the Campaign for Nuclear

Disarmament, women's issues, and the consequences of bad housing. Her concern for the state of contemporary society is also the central theme of her fiction. *Live as Family* (1968) and *Down: an Exploration* (1969), both deal with the individual's relationships with class and the community. *Stand We at Last* (1983) is perhaps her most important novel, a family saga spanning the years from the mid-19th century to the present day, and written from a feminist perspective. *Closing* (1987) returns to the modern era to look at the life of women in what the author considers an exploitative society.

FAIRBURN, A(rthur) R(ex) D(ugard)
(1904–57)

New Zealand poet and artist, born in Auckland. An extrovert lyricist, he was a commanding figure from the 1930s to the 1950s. His early verse was published as *He Shall Not Rise* (1930), followed by *Dominion* (1938), a long poem showing the effects of the Depression and the influence of **T S Eliot**; it was later included in *Three Poems* (1952). His *Poems 1929–1941* (1943) was reissued with other short material as *Strange Rendezvous* (1952). His *Collected Poems* came out in 1966. He was poetry editor of the *Year Book of the Arts in New Zealand* (1945–51). His prose was noted for its satire, hiding a strong vein of national pride, as in *We New Zealanders: An Informal Essay* (1944). A posthumous selection was issued in 1967 as *The Women Problem and Other Prose*.
▷ *The Letters of A R D Fairburn* (1981)

FAIRFAX, James Griffyth
(1886–1976)

Australian lyric poet and journalist, born in Sydney and descended from John Fairfax of Warwick (1804–77), founder of the *Sydney Morning Herald*. James Fairfax's first collection was *The Gates of Sleep and Other Poems* (1906). Other books of verse include *The Troubled Pool* (1911), *The Horns of Taurus* (1912) and *The Temple of Janus: a Sonnet Sequence* (1917). He served with the Australian forces in the Middle East in World War I, of which his impressions are recorded in *Mesopotamia: Sonnets and Lyrics at Home and Abroad, 1914–1919* (1919). After the war he entered the British parliament for Norwich Town (1924–9). His cousin, John Fitzgerald Fairfax, served in World War II and was a war correspondent in the South Pacific (1944–6). He published a number of books: a life of his distinguished ancestor *The Story of John Fairfax* (1941), elegant essays in *Run o' Waters* (1948) and some fine lyric verse in *A Drift of Leaves* (1952).

FAIZ, Faiz Ahmed
(1905–90)

Pakistani poet, who to some extent became the 'national poet' of his newly created country. But he was a communist (he received the Lenin Prize in 1962) who incurred the wrath of its governments: they put him in prison for plotting to overthrow them, which in some sense he had (although the charges were probably trumped up). He wrote some verse in Punjabi because he was in favour of fuller recognition of the minority languages of Pakistan. He wrote much dreary Marxist verse, but possessed qualities which put him far above the usual proponents of such material: he was a master of technique in his main language, Urdu, and was a remarkable love poet. *Poems by Faiz* (1971) is bilingual.

FALCÃO, Cristóvão
(1515–53)

Portuguese poet, born in Pertalegre. He led an adventurous life, which apparently included imprisonment for an affair he had, aged 14, with the 12-year-old Maria Brandão—for which she was sent to a convent. It has, however, been suggested on the one hand that Falcão did not exist, and on the other (and more plausibly) that his friend **Bernardim Ribeiro** invented him in the poem *Trofas de Crisfal* (1554), published as by Falcão. However, the consensus now is that Falcão is to be 'regarded as an inspired imitator of Ribeiro whom he never personally knew'. *Trofas* is a 900-line eclogue of great distinction, containing 'passionate *saudade* and sentimental grief...mystic visions...simplicity ...love of Nature'.
▷ A Bell, *Portuguese Literature* (1922)

FALCONER, William
(1732–69)

Scottish poet and seaman, born in Edinburgh. A barber's son, he went to sea, and was soon shipwrecked off Greece, this voyage forming the subject of his long poem, *The Shipwreck* (1762). He then entered the royal navy, being appointed purser on the frigate *Aurora* in 1769, which foundered with all hands near Capetown. His *Demagogue* (1764) is a satire on Wilkes and Marlborough, and he was also author of the *Universal Marine Dictionary* (1769).

FALK, Johann Daniel
(1768–1826)

German writer and philanthropist, born in Danzig (Gdansk, Poland). He founded the 'company of friends in need' for helping destitute children, and established the Falk Institute at Weimar. Of his writings the best known are his satirical works like *Der Mensch* (1795, 'The Man'), and a study on **Goethe**.

FALKEBERGET, Johann Petter, originally Lillebakken
(1879–1967)

Norwegian novelist, born in Nordre-Rugel. A miner from the age of eight, and the son of a miner, he wrote realistic novels of working-class life in his area. His first novel was *Svarte Fjelde* (1907, 'Black Mountains'). He also wrote *Den fjerde nattevakt* (1923, 'The Fourth Night-Watch'), and two trilogies, *Christianus Sextus* (1927–35) and *Nattens brød* (1940–59, 'Night's Bread').

FALLADA, Hans, pseud of Rudolf Ditzen
(1893–1947)

German writer, born in Greifswald. He achieved international fame with his novel of German social problems, *Kleiner Mann, Was Nun?* (1932, Eng trans *Little Man, What Now?*, 1969) in which a devoted young couple struggle against the hardship of rampant inflation and unemployment. *Wolf unter Wölfen* (1937, Eng trans *Wolf Among Wolves*, 1938) is a tragic novel of post-World War I Germany. Several important works appeared posthumously, including *Der Trinker* (1950, Eng trans *The Drinker*, 1952).
▷H Schulder, *Hans Fallada, humanist and social critic* (1970)

FALLON, Padraic
(1905–74)

Irish poet, born in Athenry, County Galway. He worked for 40 years as a customs official, before retiring to England where he died. Neglected for most of his lifetime, the posthumous publication of his *Collected Poems* (1990) established him as a remarkable chronicler of an aesthetic and religious fusion, in which the central dilemma is: 'much is man and/not enough'. His quiet, authoritative tone is allied to a craftsmanship that gives his poems a universal integrity much stronger than their Catholic themes might at first suggest.
▷D Davie, in D Dunn (ed), *Two Decades of Irish Writing* (1975)

FALLON, Peter
(1951–)

Irish poet and publisher, born in Germany and educated in Dublin. In 1970 he founded The Gallery Press, one of the most important Irish publishers of the latter part of the 20th century. His early work, *The First Affair* (1974), was prompted by the pop-orientated metropolitanism prevalent at the time. However, in 1982 he went to live on a farm in County Meath, and subsequent collections,

Winter Work (1983), *The News and Weather* (1987) and *Eye to Eye* (1992), demonstrate a sensitive and evocative understanding of rural values and pieties. Such work bears complimentary comparison with that of **Patrick Kavanagh**, while the selected poems *News of the World* (1994), for example, show him still utilizing the breath line and minimalist techniques of such admired American writers as **Charles Olson** and **Gary Snyder**.

FALUDY, Gyorgy
(1913–)

Hungarian poet and translator, who left Hungary after 1956 and settled in Canada. He translated **Villon** into Hungarian, wrote graceful and skilled lyrics, and a well-regarded autobiography, *My Happy Days in Hell* (1962).

FANGEN, Ronald
(1895–1946)

Norwegian novelist and dramatist, born in Kragero. He made an immediate sensation with a strident expressionistic play, but established himself more enduringly with such novels as *Duel* (1932, Eng trans 1934). His earlier work is humanistic, but he later became a member of the Oxford Movement, and turned to a somewhat simplistic Christianity. His *En lysets engel* (1945, Eng trans *Both are My Cousins*, 1949) is a memorable novel about a quisling. He was killed in an air crash.

FANSHAWE, Sir Richard
(1608–66)

English poet and translator, born in Ware. He fought on the Royalist side, and became an MP on the accession of Charles II. He was the first to translate the *Lusiads* of **Camoens** (1655). His original poetry is of little account. His wife Ann's *Memoirs* (complete edition 1829) is a fulsome tribute, with some of his letters.
▷*Annual Bulletin of the Modern Humanist Research Association*, xlii (1938)

FANTHORPE, U(rsula) A(skham)
(1929–)

English poet, educated at Oxford and the University of London Institute of Education, where she obtained a teacher's diploma. Since the mid-70s, though, she has worked as an admissions clerk in a Bristol hospital. Her characteristic style, already evident in *Side Effects* (1978), her first collection, is discreetly gossipy, and there is a touch of **Betjeman** or possibly **Larkin** in her ironically polite evasions. In writing of the natural or the wider human scene, she is quizzical, but still capable of genuine wonder. Later volumes are *Four Dogs* (1980), *Standing To* (1982) and *Voices Off* (1984). A major selection appeared in 1986.

FARGUE, Léon-Paul
(1876–1947)

French poet, anecdotist and literary journalist, born in Paris, and paramount interpreter of that city's streets, bars and railway stations (he was known as the 'the Paris stroller'). In his quiet way, Fargue, a much respected major-minor poet, sought and achieved perfection in his melancholy aspiration to recapture an irretrievable past. In that way, if in no other, he resembles **Marcel Proust**. He began in the Symbolist manner, but soon developed his own method, which was to reproduce as exactly as he could the nuances of his own superb conversation. He was a close friend to, and in many ways is the poetic counterpart of, the composer Erik Satie. Some of the best of his enchanting journalism is collected in *Lantern Magique* (1942, Eng trans *Magic Lantern*, 1946). His major work was contained in long prose-poems; essentially, in their precise cadences, they are poems: these express his unique belief that 'poetry is the only dream that one must not dream', and his desire to discover the universe within his beloved Paris. Many exquisite shorter poems are to be found in translated anthologies of French verse.
▷ L R Schub, *Léon-Paul Fargue* (1973)

FARIA, Otavio de
(1908–)

Brazilian novelist who set out to create a **Balzac**ian picture, a 'Tragedia Burguesa' ('Bourgeois Tragedy'), but from an individualistic viewpoint, of the middle classes of his country. Perhaps somewhat neglected by translators and critics alike, the vast patchwork of this cycle has been consistently interesting, well observed and intelligent.

FARIA Y SOUSA, Manuel de
(1590–1649)

Portuguese poet, born near Pombeiro. He went to Madrid c.1613, and from 1631 to 1634 was secretary to the Spanish embassy in Rome. He wrote on Portuguese history and on **Camoens**, and left approximately 200 Portuguese sonnets, 12 eclogues, and three treatises on poetry.

FARJEON, Eleanor
(1881–1965)

English writer, born in Hampstead. She led a richly imaginative fantasy life as a child, described in her autobiographical *A Nursery in the Nineties* (1935). She wrote fantasies and children's stories, beginning with her successful first novel, *Martin Pippin in the Apple Orchard* (1916), and collaborated with her brother Herbert in *Kings and Queens* (1932) and the play *The Glass Slipper* (1944). There is an annual Eleanor Farjeon Award for outstanding service to children's literature.
▷ D Blakelock, *Eleanor, a portrait* (1966)

FARMER, Philip José
(1918–)

American science-fiction and fantasy writer, born in Indiana. A fan from an early age, he began writing comparatively late, and published his first novel in 1952. He is an idiosyncratic figure in the genre hierarchy, and his work is marked by an unusually frank treatment of sexuality, often in tandem with other biological themes. The defining characteristics of his later work are its zany humour and his penchant for creating overarching literary structures which draw not only on his own works but also on the inventions and characters of other writers. His best-known works are the *Riverworld* series (from 1965), and the less well-defined aggregation of stories sometimes known as the 'Wold Newton' series, which postulates the creation of a small group of mutant supermen, manifest as fictional characters like Tarzan and Doc Savage.

FARNOL, John Jeffery
(1878–1952)

English author, born in Aston. He lived from 1902 to 1910 in the USA as a scene painter. His first successful novel was *The Broad Highway* (1910), and he went on to establish a reputation for romantic adventure stories in a period setting, such as *The Amateur Gentleman* (1913), *The Geste of Duke Jocelyn* (1919) and *Peregrine's Progress* (1922).
▷ E French, *Jeffrey Farnol* (1964)

FARQUHAR, George
(c.1677–1707)

Irish playwright, born in Londonderry, possibly in 1677 (but he is said to have fought at the Boyne). Educated at Trinity College, Dublin, he became an actor in a Dublin theatre, but proved an indifferent performer. The accidental wounding of a fellow actor so shocked him that he quitted the boards, and shortly after received a commission in a regiment stationed in Ireland. His first comedy, *Love and a Bottle* (1698), proved a success. His *Constant Couple* (1700) met with an enthusiastic reception, and he wrote a sequel, *Sir Harry Wildair* (1701). In 1703 he produced *The Inconstant*, founded on **John Fletcher**'s *Wild Goose Chase*. Having married in the same year, he fell into pecuniary difficulties, and died in poverty. During his last illness he wrote the best of his plays, *The Beaux' Stratagem* (1707), and died while its wit and invention were making the town roar with delight. *The Recruiting Officer* had been produced with success in 1706. Farquhar is one of the best of the comic dramatists, and has on the whole more variety and character than any of his compeers.

▷E Rothenstein, *George Farquhar* (1967)

FARRAR, Frederic William
(1831–1903)

English clergyman and writer, born in Bombay. He was ordained in 1854, taught at Harrow, became Headmaster of Marlborough (1871–6), Honorary Chaplain to Queen Victoria (1869–73), and later became a chaplain-in-ordinary. He was made a canon of Westminster and Rector of St Margaret's in 1876, Archdeacon of Westminster in 1883, Chaplain to the House of Commons in 1890, and Dean of Canterbury in 1895. His theological writings were many, but he is chiefly remembered for the bestseller *Eric, or Little by Little* (1858), one of several school stories that he wrote.

▷*My Object in Life* (1883)

FARRELL, J(ames) G(ordon)
(1935–79)

English novelist, born in Liverpool. His early works, such as *The Lung* (1965), were realistic novels set in the present day. He found his proper metier, however, in the historical novel. *Troubles* (1970) is set in Ireland after World War I, and has obvious analogies to the current disturbances. *The Siege of Krishnapur* (1973), set in Hindustan in 1857, won him the Booker Prize, while *The Singapore Grip* (1978) is about the Japanese capture of Malaysia in World War II. Together these novels display his major theme—the slow, at times painful, at others absurd, decline of the British Empire. Farrell drowned in a fishing accident in Ireland.

FARRELL, James T(homas)
(1904–79)

American novelist, short-story writer, critic and essayist, born in Chicago. He paid for his own education at the University of Chicago (1925–9) and lived in Paris in the early 1930s. A lapsed Catholic and a naturalist in the mould of **Émile Zola**, he owes most to the style of **Sherwood Anderson**. His first novel was *Young Lonigan* (1932), which began the *Studs Lonigan* trilogy of life on Chicago's South side, realistically and graphically expressed. The other volumes were *The Young Manhood of Studs Lonigan* (1934) and

Judgement Day (1935). An accomplished study of defeat (the hero dies aged 29), it was a landmark in American fiction. This was followed by a five-novel sequence centred on Danny O'Neill (1936–53), and another trilogy, on Bernard Clare (1946–52). He published more than 50 novels in all.

▷A M Wald, *Farrell: the revolutionary socialist years* (1978)

FARRÈRE, Claude, pseud of Frédéric Charles Pierre Édouard Bargone
(1876–1957)

French novelist, born in Lyons. He was a naval officer (1899–1919) who turned to writing. He made his name with novels of the exotic and tales of travel and adventure. Works include *Fumée d'opium* (1904, 'Smoking Opium') and *Les condamnés à mort* (1920, 'Those Condemned to Death').

▷M Revon, *Claude Farrère* (1924, in French)

FARROKHZAD, Forugh
(1935–67)

Iranian poet, major in her context, born in Tehran. She began writing classical poetry at 14, was unhappily married at 16, and soon lost her child to the custody of her brutal husband in a travesty of a divorce case. She was killed in a car accident. Her first two collections (both 1955) were both entitled *Asir* ('The Captive'): the second caused a scandal, since she confessed to sensual feelings for a man, not admitted by women in her country except in private. But the discerning recognized a new and bright talent. She wrote in a subtle and well-cadenced free verse, and is cherished as a major modernist poet.

▷E W Fernea and B Q Bezirgan, *Middle Eastern Muslim Women Speak* (1977)

FARSON, James Negley
(1890–1960)

American author, born in Plainfield, New Jersey. He trained as a civil engineer but moved to England and went from there to Russia, where he had an export business and where he witnessed the 1917 revolution. From then on he led an adventurous life as airman, sailor and journalist, which is reflected in his varied works. These include *Sailing Across Europe* (1926), *Seeing Red* (1930), *Bomber's Moon* (1941) and *A Mirror for Narcissus* (1957).

▷*The Way of a Transgressor* (1935)

FARWELL, George
(1911–76)

English-born Australian writer, radio broadcaster and actor, born in Bath. Settling in Australia in 1936 he wrote of the country, which he travelled extensively, in *Land of Mirage* (1950) and *Vanishing Australians*

(1961), and in his biographies of Ned Kelly, Edward Ogilvie and Charles Sturt. A selection of his writings was published as *Farwell Country* (1977).

▷ *Rejoice in Freedom* (1976)

FAST, Howard Melvin
(1914–92)

Immensely prolific American novelist, playwright and political commentator; he also wrote crime fiction under the pseudonym E V Cunningham. Born in New York City, Fast came of age in the radical 1930s and was drawn into its prevailing left-wing atmosphere, expressing his solidarity in a sequence of historical novels, *The Unvanquished* (1942), *Citizen Tom Paine* (1943) and *Freedom Road* (1944), whose contemporary relevance was transparently obvious. His allegiance to Popular Front communism eventually led to his being imprisoned for 'contempt of Congress' in 1947, and to his blacklisting by Hollywood, but he later recanted in a much-quoted account of writers' dealings with the Party, called *The Naked God* (1957); *Being Red* (1990) was written in a more indulgent political climate and one in which the American Left was firmly established in the academic curriculum. His best-known book is *Spartacus* (1951); it was initially published privately, and owed its success to the absence of preachy ideological speeches, and to a powerful Hollywood adaptation. With slightly ironic timing, Fast was awarded the Stalin Peace Prize in 1953.

FAULKNER, William
(1897–1962)

American novelist and winner of the Nobel Prize for literature, born near Oxford, Mississippi. His school career was undistinguished and he was rejected by the US army when America entered World War I, but he became a pilot in the Canadian Flying Corps. Later he attended Mississippi University and did odd jobs. While working in New Orleans he met **Sherwood Anderson**, who offered to recommend his first novel, *Soldier's Pay* (1926), to a publisher on condition that he did not have to read it. Other novels followed but their sales were unremarkable. In 1929, the year of his marriage, he took a job as a coal-heaver and while on night-work at a local power station is said to have written *As I Lay Dying* (1930) in just six weeks, working between midnight and 4am. *Sanctuary* (1931) was intended as a pot-boiler and was more successful commercially, but it had a profound impact on **Jean-Paul Sartre** and **Albert Camus**. However, it is novels like *The Sound and the Fury* (1929), *Light in August* (1932), *Absalom, Absalom!* (1936), *The Hamlet* (1940) and *Intruder in the Dust* (1948) that account

for his high reputation. In *Sartoris* (1929) he first describes the decline of the Compson and Sartoris families, indicative of the Old South, and the rise of the nouveau riche Snopeses, who dominate the later trilogy *The Hamlet* (1940), *The Town* (1957) and *The Mansion* (1959). Like most of the earlier books, these are set in and around Jefferson in the imaginary Yoknapatawpha County. A rare deviation is *A Fable* (1954), a reworking of Christ's Passion, set on the Western Front which, though ambitious, is accounted a noble failure. The tone of the novels is invariably sombre and elegiac but the prose sings like lyric poetry and Faulkner is revered as one of the modern masters of the novel. He was awarded the 1949 Nobel Prize for literature.

▷ J Blotner, *Faulkner: a biography* (2 vols, 1974)

FAUSET, Jessie Redmon
(1882–1961)

Black American novelist, born in New Jersey. She was the first Black woman to become a member of Phi Beta Kappa. She was associated with **William Dubois** and became a co-editor of his magazine *Crisis*. Her four novels all deal with problems of race; the best is probably *The Chinaberry Tree* (1931), whose oblique theme is the necessity for Black women not to try to become White; but its predecessor, *Plum Bun* (1929), which contrasts two sisters, one of whom tries to pass as White in Greenwich Village while the other accepts her heritage in Harlem, runs it a close second. She has more recently been accused of an illiberal, defeatist attitude; but her work undoubtedly served its cause well.

FAVART, Charles Simon
(1710–92)

French dramatist, born in Paris, the son of a pastrycook. He began writing comic opera, and the success of his first production, *Deux Jumelles* (1734), obtained for him financial backing which enabled him to continue with this genre. He married in 1745 Marie Justine Benoîte Duronceray (1727–72), a talented actress of the Opéra-Comique with whom he pioneered a new realism in costume. At the end of 1745 the Opéra-Comique, which he was directing, was obliged to close, and the Favarts went to Flanders with a company of actors attached to Marshal de Saxe, who made an unscrupulous attempt to procure Mme Favart as his mistress. When she fled from him he took out *lettres de cachet* against her husband, who had to remain in hiding until 1750, when the marshal's death put an end to the persecution, and Favart was able to return to Paris and write more comic operas. Among the best out of more than a hundred are *Les amours de Bastien et Bastienne* (co-written with his wife, 1753, 'The Loves of Bastien and Bastienne'), *Ninette à la cour* (1755, 'Ninette at Court') and *Les Trois Sultanes* (1776, 'The Three Sultans' Wives').

▷E Maddelen, *Goldoni e Favart* (1889)

FAY, András
(1786–1864)

Hungarian poet, playwright and novelist. He lived in Budapest, and was a pioneer of the social novel. He also wrote a set of fables in the manner of **Aesop** which achieved great success.

FAZEKAS, Mihály
(1766–1828)

Hungarian poet, a botanist by profession, born in Debrecan. His poems were of great simplicity, influencing and anticipating **Petöfi**. His peasant epic in hexameters, *Lüdas Matyi* (written in 1804, published in 1815), is his most famous work, and was successfully filmed in Hungary (by Kálmán Nádasdy and L Radony) in 1950.

FEARING, Kenneth Flexner
(1902–61)

American poet and novelist, born in Oak Park, Illinois, and educated at Wisconsin University. He published his first collection, *Angel Arms*, in 1929. Subsequent volumes include *Dead Reckoning: A Book of Poetry* (1938); *Stranger at Coney Island and Other Poems* (1949) and *New and Selected Poems* (1956). Fearing's writing reflects his belief that an increasingly mechanized society results in an erosion of human compassion and decency. His novels, which include *The Big Clock* (1946), are considered less important than his poetry.

FEDERMAN, Raymond
(1928–)

French-born American novelist and saxophonist. He was born in Paris and emigrated to the USA in 1947, where he spent three years as a jazz musician and took citizenship in 1953. He took a degree at Columbia University and a doctorate at UCLA. After teaching at Santa Barbara, he switched coasts and since 1968 has been based at the State University of New York, Buffalo. His first full-length fiction, *Double or Nothing* (1971), is an autobiographical *Bildungsroman* marked by the authorial digressions and revisions which also dominate *Take It or Leave It* (1976), a title that reflects Federman's capricious approach. His bilingual *The Voice in the Closet* (1979) considered the Holocaust, introducing as characters both the novelist himself and his transcultural idol

Beckett, on whose work Federman wrote persuasively in *Journey to Chaos* (1965). *The Twofold Vibration* (1982) is a hybrid of Beckett and science fiction; Federman asked that it be considered 'exploratory' rather than 'experimental' fiction, but the latter tag has stuck unmercifully. *Smiles on Washington Square* (1985) demonstrates the phrase's redundancy.

▷J Klinkowitz, in *Literary Disruptions* (2nd edn 1980)

FEDIN, Konstantine
(1892–1977)

Russian novelist, story writer and critic, born in Saratov. Fedin ended up as a toady of the Stalinist establishment, a persecutor of 'subversive' writers; but he had been a gifted writer, who in 1921 had left the Communist Party under the influence of the Serapion Brothers, that group of independent spirits who wished to keep art clear of politics. His first and certainly best novel, *Goroda i gody* (1924, Eng trans *Cities and Years*, 1962), reflected his experience of internment in Germany throughout World War I: it deals with the problem of maintaining individual integrity in revolutionary struggle. By the 1930s, however, Fedin had chosen the route of what Trotsky called the 'fellow traveller': the writer who is not of the Party but essentially with its aims. His last truly independent book was an autobiography much concerned with **Gorky**, whom he had known: *Gorki sredi nas* (1943–4, 'Gorky Amongst Us'). For this he was officially reprimanded. His massive trilogy, *Pervye radosti*, *Neobyknovennoye* and *Kostyor* (1945–62, Eng trans *Early Joys*, 1948, *No Ordinary Summer*, 1950 and *The Conflagration*, 1968), although facile, is as good as obligatory socialist-realist fiction can be, and offers indispensable information about Russia between 1910 and World War II.

▷J Blum, *Konstantine Fedin* (1967)

FEIBLEMAN, Peter S
(1930–)

American novelist and dramatist, born in New York but brought up in New Orleans. For eight years he worked as an actor in Spain and elsewhere; he had studied drama at the Carnegie Institute. He is best known for his first novel, *A Place Without Twilight* (1958), about a New Orleans Black girl whose skin is 'twilight'. He dramatized this for Broadway in 1961. Later novels have not met with such a good reception.

FEIKEMAN, Feike *see* **MANFRED, Frederick**

FEINSTEIN, Elaine
(1930–)
English novelist, poet, critic and translator, born in Bootle, Lancashire, and educated at Cambridge. During the 1960s she was a lecturer in English literature at Essex University. *The Circle* (1970), her first novel, deals with a woman's simultaneous craving for emotional independence and her desire to be insulated by marriage. Subsequent books have also examined the female experience, *The Amberstone Exit* (1972), for example, confronting the trauma of birth and motherhood. *The Survivors* (1982), on the other hand, derives partly from the history of her own family, and looks at the fate of early 20th-century Jewish refugees from Russia. Feinstein has also translated several Russian women poets and written an authoritative biography of **Marina Tsvetayeva**, *A Captive Lion* (1987).

FEITH, Rhijnvis
(1753–1824)
Dutch poet, born in Zwolle. He became mayor there in 1780. He wrote some sentimental love novels, and the lyrical *Oden en Gedichten* (1796–1810, 'Odes and Poems'). Of his tragedies, the best known are *Thirza* (1784), *Johanna Gray* (1791), and *Ines de Castro* (1793). He published a collection of criticism, *Brieven* (1784–94, 'Letters').

FELINSKI, Alojzy
(1771–1820)
Polish poet and playwright who wrote in the style of the French neo-classicists: his *Barbara* (1813, staged in Warsaw in 1817), which created a sensation, is especially admired for the 13-syllable metre of its lines, and is still regarded as a great drama.

FELIPE, León, pseud of **León Felipe Camino**
(1884–1968)
Spanish poet and translator (of **Whitman**), born in Tábora, Zamora. He was originally a pharmacist, but took to a wandering life in his early middle age. His virulent and highly colloquial denunciations of Franco led some critics to suppose that his poetry was essentially one of declamation; this proved a premature judgement, for his *Obras completas* (1963, 'Complete Works') revealed him to be a poet no more or less declamatory than his master, Whitman—and sometimes as subtle. He has been described by a conservative critic as 'too blunt in his directness'; but one of different persuasion, while conceding his occasional 'prosiness', and convinced by his almost biblical humaneness rather than by his theoretical politics, asked, 'can one be too blunt?' His style was wholly original in its Spanish context, and his subtleties and ironies were not always appreciated by critics who saw him as a necessarily crude red.
▷ *TriQuarterly*, 16 (1970)

FÉNELON, François de Salignac de la Mothe
(1651–1715)
French prelate and writer, born in the château de Fénelon in Périgord. At 20 he entered the seminary of St Sulpice in Paris, and was ordained in 1675. After some time spent in parochial duties, he became director of an institution for women converts to the Catholic faith in 1678. Here he wrote *Traité de l'éducation des filles* (1678, Eng trans *The Education of Young Gentlewomen*, 1699), urging a more liberal education for women, and criticizing the coercion of Huguenot converts. At the revocation of the Edict of Nantes (1685) he was sent to preach among the Protestants of Poitou. From 1689 to 1699 he was tutor to Louis XIV's grandson, the young Duke of Burgundy, and as such he wrote the *Fables* (first collected in parallel translation as *Twenty-Seven Tales and Fables, French and English*, 1729), *Dialogues des Morts anciens et modernes* (1713, with augmented posthumous editions, Eng trans *Fables and Dialogues of the Dead*, 1723), *Abrégé des vies des anciens Philosophes* (pub 1726, Eng trans *The Lives and Most Remarkable Maxims of the Antient Philosophers*, [sic] 1726), and *Les Aventures de Télémaque* (1699, Eng trans *The Adventures of Telemachus*, 1699). He had been presented by the king to the abbey of St Valéry (1694) and to the archbishopric of Cambrai (1695). He had formed in 1687 the acquaintance of the celebrated quietist mystic, Madame Guyon, and, convinced of the unfairness of the outcry against her, he advised her to submit her book to Jacques Bossuet, who condemned it. Fénelon acquiesced, but refused to join in any personal condemnation. Fénelon composed his own *Explication des maximes des saints sur la vie intérieure* (1697, Eng trans *The Maxims of the Saints Explained*, 1698) in defence of certain of Madame Guyon's doctrines. A fierce controversy ensued, and in the end the pope condemned the *Maximes des saints*. Fénelon's *Télémaque* was considered by the king a disguised satire upon his court and from then on Fénelon was strictly restrained within his diocese. From this date he lived almost exclusively for his flock, but in the revived Jansenistic dispute he engaged earnestly on the side of orthodoxy. His works are voluminous, and on a variety of subjects.
▷ P Janet, *Fénelon, une biographie* (1892)

FENOGLIO, Beppe
(1922–63)

Italian story writer, born in Alpa, to working-class parents. He left much unpublished at his early death, and this has proved hard to edit. He fought for 18 months with the partisans in the latter part of World War II, and his chronicle of it provided him with the material for his first book, *I ventitrè giorni della città di Alba* (1951, 'The 23 Days of the City of Alba'). It is written in a startling and not always effective mixture of dialect, regular Italian, and even English. His best-known and most vivid book is *Il partigiano Johnny* (1968, 'Johnny the Partisan').

FENTON, James
(1949–)

English poet, born in Lincoln. A highly thought of, intellectual poet, who has deliberately set himself apart from the mainstream, Fenton publishes little. He is mainly a political and satirical rather than a 'personal' poet, who makes a virtue out of reticence. He wrote some sharply satirical poems in collaboration with John Fuller, in *Partingtime Hall* (1987); his own main collections are *Terminal Moraine* (1972) and *The Memory of War and Children in Exile: Poems 1968–83* (1983).

FERBER, Edna
(1887–1968)

American writer, born in Kalamazoo, Michigan. She was the author of numerous novels and short stories, including *Dawn O'Hara* (1911), *Gigolo* (1922), *So Big* (1924, Pulitzer Prize), *Cimarron* (1929) and *Saratoga Trunk* (1941). She is probably best remembered as the writer of *Show Boat* (1926), which inspired the musical play of that name. She also wrote plays with **George Kaufman**, such as *Dinner at Eight* (1932) and *Stage Door* (1936).
▷J G Gilbert, *Edna Ferber: a biography* (1978)

FERGUSON, Sir Samuel
(1810–86)

Irish poet and Celtic scholar, born in Belfast. Called to the Irish Bar in 1838, he was appointed in 1867 the first Deputy Keeper of Irish Records. As President of the Royal Irish Academy he gave a powerful impetus to the study of early Irish art. His spirited poems were published as *Lays of the Western Gael* (1865), *Congal* (1872), *Poems* (1880) and *The Forging of the Anchor* (1883). His edition of the *Leabhar Breac* appeared in 1876; his *Ogham Inscriptions* in 1887.
▷A Dearing, *Sir Samuel Ferguson, Poet and Antiquarian* (1931)

FERGUSSON, Robert
(1750–74)

Scottish poet, born in Edinburgh, the son of a solicitor's clerk. He was educated at the High School of Edinburgh and of Dundee, and at St Andrews University, where he excelled. He was employed in the commissary office in Edinburgh, contributing poems to Ruddiman's *Weekly Magazine* from 1771, which gained him local fame. His company was much sought and convivial excesses permanently injured his health. Following an awakening of religious interest, inspired by a meeting with the minister John Brown, he fell into deep depression, and was reduced to insanity by a fall downstairs. He died in a public asylum. He was a major influence on and inspiration to **Robert Burns**, who placed a headstone on his grave in 1789. He left 33 poems in Scots, and 50 poems in English. Essentially an Edinburgh poet, his most famous poem is *Auld Reekie* (1773), tracing a day in the life of the city. Other major and well-known poems are *Elegy on the Death of Scots Music*, *The Daft Days* (his first published poem), *Hallow Fair*, *To the Tron Kirk Bell*, *Leith Races* and the satirical *The Rising of the Session*.
▷A Law, *Robert Fergusson and the Edinburgh of his Time* (1974)

FERLINGHETTI, Lawrence
(1919–)

American poet and publisher, born in Yonkers, New York. He studied at the University of North Carolina, Columbia University, and the Sorbonne, and served in the US Naval Reserve (1941–5). He worked for *Time* magazine in New York, then moved to San Francisco in 1951, where he became a prime mover in the so-called 'San Francisco Renaissance'. He was co-founder of the City Lights Bookstore, which acted as a meeting place, cultural forum and publishing house for radical poets. His own work made a major contribution to Beat poetry and beyond, beginning with *Pictures of the Gone World* (1955) and *A Coney Island of the Mind* (1958). He has published over 40 books of poetry, including *Endless Life: The Selected Poems* (1981), two novels, and a number of plays.
▷N Cherkassky, *Ferlinghetti: A Biography* (1979)

FERMOR, Patrick Michael Leigh
(1915–)

English travel writer of English and Irish descent. Expelled from King's School, Canterbury, he set out in 1933 on a leisurely walk from Rotterdam to Constantinople. *A Time of Gifts* (1977) recounted the journey as far as Hungary; *Between the Woods and the Water*

(1986) took it to its terminus. Both have been praised for their incisive grasp of the mood of pre-war Europe, and few doubted the veracity of his account despite its being more than 40 years in gestation. Later he spent an adventurous war in Albania, Greece and Crete where, disguised as a shepherd, he lived for two years organizing the Resistance and the capture and evacuation of the German commander, General Kreipe. Among his other books are *The Traveller's Tree*, about the West Indies, which won the Heinemann Foundation Prize in 1950; *Mani* (1958), which was awarded the Duff Cooper Memorial Prize; and *Three Letters from the Andes* (1991), vivid accounts of a journey in the early 1970s.

▷ *A Time to Keep Silent* (1953)

FERNANDEZ, Lucas
(1474–1542)

Spanish dramatist, born in Salamanca. His *Farsas i églogas al modo y estilo pastoril y catellano* ('Religious Plays and Pastoral Poems') consists of three secular plays, three religious plays, and a pastoral sung dialogue—he was a musician, and taught music in Salamanca. One of these plays depicts the conversion of Dionysius the Areopagite to Christianity, and is the first of its kind.

FERNANDEZ, Pablo
(1930–)

Cuban poet, who returned to Cuba after the Castro Revolution, but then fell foul of the regime. After his first collected edition (1962), his poetry became more concentrated and self-critical. Two of his poems are translated in the *Penguin Book of Latin American Verse* (1971, ed E Curacciolo-Trejo).

FERNANDEZ FLOREZ, Wenceslao
(1885–1964)

Spanish novelist and essayist, born in La Coruña. A lifelong Franco supporter, his view of life was harsh, bitter and yet sentimental. His great success was *Las siete columnas* (1926, Eng trans *The Seven Pillars*, 1934). His work is not now so much heeded, although in its time it was much appreciated.

FERNÁNDEZ DE LIZARDI, José Joaquín
(1776–1827)

Mexican novelist and journalist, known as 'El Pensador Mexicano' ('The Mexican Thinker'), after a periodical he founded and edited. He wrote the first Latin-American novel proper, the enlightened and picaresque *El Periquillo Sarniento* (1816), an attack on the manners and morals of his time which has been underestimated outside Mexico.

▷ J R Spell, *The Life and Works of José Fernández de Lizardi* (1931)

FERNÁNDEZ MORENO, Baldomero
(1886–1950)

Argentinian poet, born in Buenos Aires into a Spanish family. A doctor by profession, he lived in Spain during most of the 1890s. His poetry, more Spanish than Argentinian in inspiration, has often been compared to that of **Antonio Machado**. The best of his poetry, which set out to please no one, least of all himself, has a distinguished melancholy, not unlike that of **Hardy** or **Housman**: 'There is nothing to compare with this moment/Of the morning, uncertain and solitary/When your bedsheet is your shroud …'.

▷ E Carilla, *Genio y figura de Baldomero Fernández Moreno* (1973)

FERNANDEZ RETEMAR, Roberto
(1930–)

Cuban poet, editor and critic, born in Havana. He has played an active role in Cuba's literature after the Revolution. His first collection, *Elegía como un himno* ('Elegy Like a Hymn') appeared in 1950. Since then he has won many prizes. Two poems are translated in the *Penguin Book of Latin American Verse* (1971, ed E Curacciolo-Trejo).

FERRARI, Paolo
(1822–89)

Italian dramatist, born in Modena. He wrote many excellent comedies, including *Goldoni* (1852) and *Parini e la satira* (1857, 'Parini and the Lampoon'). In 1860 he became Professor of History at Modena, and afterwards at Milan.

▷ N de Belli, *Il Teatro di Paolo Ferrari* (1922)

FERRÉ, Rosario
(1940–)

Puerto Rican poet and narrator, one of the most expressive in Spanish America. Part of an important emerging group of Puerto Rican authors, she was born in Ponce, and studied at Wellesley, Manhattanville College, receiving her PhD from the University of Maryland in 1986. She founded and edited the influential literary journal *Zona de Carga y Descarga* (1972–5). A regular contributor to newspapers, Ferré also writes short stories, poetry, essays and translations.

FERREIRA, Antonio
(1528–69)

Portuguese poet, born in Lisbon. He studied law at Coimbra, and became a judge in Lisbon, where he spent his life. A contemplative man who had little time for the popular Iberian subjects of war and commerce, he turned to classical models for his inspiration, and introduced a classical style into Portuguese verse and drama, earning the title 'The Portuguese Horace'. His best-known work is the two-act historical tragedy on classical lines, *Inês de Castro* (1587).

▷ A Roig, *Antonio Ferreira, études sur sa vie et son oeuvre* (1970)

FERREIRA DE CASTRO, José Maria
(1898–1974)

Portuguese novelist, born in Oliveira de Azeméis. He emigrated to Brazil when he was 13 years old, and worked on a rubber plantation and then as a journalist. He achieved success with *Emigrantes* (1928, Eng trans *Emigrants*, 1962), and then won international acclaim for *A selva* (1930, Eng trans *Jungle*, 1935), a searing indictment of conditions on the rubber plantations. A later novel, *A Lã e a Neve* (1947, 'Wool and Snow'), examines, in his usual harsh style, the relationship between the shepherds of Covilhã and the voracious textile operatives who then exploited them. *A Missão* (1954, Eng trans *The Mission*, 1961) contains three short novels.

▷ A Gabral, *Ferreira de Castro* (1940, in Portuguese)

FERRIER, Susan Edmonstone
(1782–1854)

Scottish novelist, born in Edinburgh, the tenth child of a lawyer who became principal clerk to the Court of Session under Sir **Walter Scott**. With the death of her mother in 1797 she took over the running of the house, and looked after her father until his death in 1829. Her first work, *Marriage* (1818), a novel of provincial social manners, was followed by *The Inheritance* (1824) and *Destiny* (1831), a Highland romance. She enjoyed a close friendship with Scott, who was for a time credited by some with the authorship of her books. Following the publication of these works she was converted to evangelical Christianity, and became a member of the Free Church, concentrating on charitable works rather than on writing. Towards the end of her life she lived in relative seclusion, her eyesight failing badly.

▷ A Grant, *Susan Ferrier of Edinburgh* (1957)

FET, Afanásy, pseud of Afanásy Shenshin
(1820–92)

Russian romantic poet, born on an estate in the Orlov district, of a German mother and a Russian father. Fet was the poet through whose works many Russian children were introduced to poetry. He is often described as 'illegitimate' because his parents' foreign marriage was not recognized in Russia: ('Foeth', transformed to 'Fet', was his mother's

name). He was not quite the great poet he has often been made out to be, but one very melodious about 'nature and love', and valuable for his expression of the essentially unexamined theme of anxiety about being alive. His early life was unhappy: he was rejected by his muse 'Yelena', who then killed herself. But he made a rich marriage in 1856, and seemed to prosper, even though he was proscribed by radicals for his reactionary views (in fact the product of naivety rather than thought). He translated **Horace, Goethe** and **Schopenhauer** (whose attitudes much affected him), became depressed, tried to kill himself, and suddenly died. His reputation grew after his death, and his influence on such more important poets as **Blok**, was decisive—his historical, as distinct from his intrinsic, importance is thus major. There are English translations in the *Penguin Book of Russian Verse* (1965, ed Dimitry Obolensky).

FEUCHTWANGER, Lion
(1884–1958)

German writer, born in Munich. He won a European reputation with the 18th-century historical novel *Jud Süss* (1925), presenting an elaborately detailed picture of the lives, sufferings and weaknesses of central European Jewry, and the 14th-century tale *Die hässliche Herzogin* (1923), which as *The Ugly Duchess* (1927) was a great success in Britain. During World War I he was interned in Tunis. His thinly disguised satire on Hitler's Munich putsch, *Erfolg* (1930, 'Success'), earned him the hatred of the Nazis. In 1933 he fled to France, where in 1940 he was interned by the German army, but escaped to the USA. He also wrote numerous dramas, and collaborated with **Bertolt Brecht** in a translation of **Christopher Marlowe**'s *Edward II*. His later works included detailed part-biographies of Goya (1952) and **Rousseau** (1954).

▷ L Boettche and P G Krohn, *Lion Feuchtwanger* (1960)

FEUILLET, Octave
(1821–90)

French novelist, born in Saint Lô. He was one of **Dumas**'s literary assistants. From 1848 he published in the *Revue des deux mondes* a series collected in *Scènes et proverbes* and *Scènes et comédies* (1853–6). He wrote many popular novels and plays, including the sentimental novel *Roman d'un jeune homme pauvre* (1858, Eng trans *The Romance of a Poor Young Man*, 1859), which remains his most famous work.

▷ A Greuwe, *Die Literatur den Krinolin* (1974)

FÉVAL, Paul Henri Corentin

FÉVAL, Paul Henri Corentin
(1817–87)

French novelist, born in Rennes. His many novels include *Les Mystères de Londres* (1844, 'The Mysteries of London') and *Le Bossu* (1858, 'The Hunchback'); some of his novels had an extraordinary success when dramatized.

▷A Delaigue, *Un homme des lettres* (1898)

FEYDEAU, Ernest Aimé
(1821–73)

French novelist. He was a stockbroker and an archaeologist, and achieved a notorious success with his novel *Fanny* (1858). His stories depict the worst features of society in the time of the Empire. *Sylvie* (1861) is a novel of more than ordinary power.

FEYDEAU, Georges Léon Jules Marie
(1862–1921)

French dramatist, the son of **Ernest Aimé Feydeau** and a prostitute. His name is synonymous with French bedroom farce. He wrote his first play, *Le Tailleur pour Dames* (1886, Eng trans *A Gown for his Mistress*, 1969), when he was 24 and subsequently maintained a prolific output. His characters are Parisian bourgeois couples seeking diversion from each other; his farces, therefore, rely on the twin themes of adultery and the chase. Among his plays are such enduring (and rather endearing) classics as *Le Dindon* (1896, Eng trans *Paying the Piper*, 1972), *La Dame de chez Maxim* (1899, 'The Lady from Maxim's'), *L'Hôtel du libre Échange* (1899, Eng trans *Hotel Paradiso*, 1957) and *Une Puce à l'oreille* (1907), produced as *A Flea in Her Ear* (trans by **John Mortimer**) at the National Theatre in 1965.

▷A Shenkan, *Georges Feydeau* (1972)

FIACC, Padraic, real name **Joseph O'Connor**
(1924–)

Irish poet, born in Belfast; he was brought up and educated in New York, but returned to the city of his birth in 1946. His first collection, *By the Black Stream* (1969), announced a Republican voice couched in transatlantic idiom. His important and sadly prophetic *The Wearing of the Black: An Anthology of Contemporary Ulster Poetry* (1974) was largely neglected. Subsequent collections of his own work, *Nights in the Bad Place* (1977) and *Missa Terribilis* (1986), have a tragically valedictory and somewhat bitter tone. However, *The Selected Padraic Fiacc* (1979) gives a fuller picture, of a humanist at odds with his surroundings, understanding, but helpless in the face of, the escalating violence he sees around him.

FIBIGER, Mathilde
(1830–72)

Danish novelist. Born in Copenhagen, she worked as a governess. Her fame rests on her first novel, *12 Breve til Clara Raphael* (1851, '12 Letters to Clara Raphael'): boldly asserting feminine integrity and independence on the basis of Romanticism, liberalism and religious convictions, the novel provoked a major controversy but subsequently became a seminal text for the women's movement in Denmark. Her second novel, *En Skizze efter det virkelige Liv* (1852, 'Sketch from Real Life'), was an attempt to appease her readership, but *Minona* (1854), defending the role of feminine eroticism, was attacked as being immoral. Finding it increasingly hard to support herself as a writer, she became Denmark's first woman telegraphist (1863).

▷T Andersen and L Busk-Jensen, *Mathilde Fibiger—Clara Raphael. Kvindekamp og kvindebevidsthed i Danmark 1830–1870* (1979)

FICKE, Arthur (Davison)
(1883–1945)

American poet and critic, born in Iowa. He is now best-remembered for a brief but enduring encounter with **Edna St Vincent Millay**, and for his involvement in the 'Spectra' hoax. This was a rather earnest protest (his accomplice was the poet Witter Bynner) against the Imagists and Vorticists. Ficke was blusteringly anti-modernist. He liked Japanese art and wrote two books about it. *Sonnets of a Portrait Painter* (1914) was his main collection of poetry.

FIDLER, Kathleen
(1899–1980)

English author of books for children, born in Coalville, Leicestershire. Her first volume, *The Borrowed Garden*, appeared in 1944. Her most popular novels, however, proved to be those about the chirpy Brydon family, whose adventures feature in 17 books, from *The Brydons at Smuggler's Creek* (1946) to *The Brydons Go Canoeing* (1963). She is also the creator of the Dean family, whose exploits fill nine books, from *The Deans Move In* (1953) to *The Deans' Dutch Adventure* (1982). Her other books include *Stories From Scottish Heritage* (3 vols, 1951) and the *True Tales of ...* series, collections of historical stories from various regions of Britain. In 1982 the annual Kathleen Fidler Award was instituted for new novel-writing for children of 8 to 11 years old.

FIEDLER, Leslie A(aron)
(1917–92)

Controversial American literary critic, whose essay 'Come Back to the Raft Again, Huck

Honey!', reprinted in *An End to Innocence* (1955), adumbrated his belief that US literature had been dominated by suppressed homoerotic agenda. This notion was taken further in his most important critical work, the hugely influential and still debated *Love and Death in the American Novel* (1960). The argument was less assured in *The Stranger in Shakespeare* (1972), in which the commonplace perception that the plays are haunted by women, blacks and Jews was pushed to absurd lengths. A charismatic teacher at the State University of New York in Buffalo, Fiedler attempted to share his students' lifestyle and values; one of the pitfalls, a conviction for marijuana possession, was documented in *Being Busted* (1970). His novels—*The Second Stone* (1963), *Back to China* (1965) and *The Messengers Will Come No More* (1974)—were less compelling than his short fiction; the best of the collections are *The Last Jew in America* (1966) and *Nude Croquet* (1969). Other critical works include *No! In Thunder* (1960), a typically forceful discussion of classical American literature and *What Was Literature?* (1982), the latter suggesting a diminution of his powers.

FIELD, Eugene
(1850–95)

American writer, born in St Louis, Missouri. He became a journalist at 23, and from 1883 was a columnist with the *Chicago Morning News*, achieving a reputation as humorist and poet with his column 'Sharps and Flats'. He wrote the well-known nursery lullaby 'Wynken, Blynken, and Nod' and the sentimental 'Little Boy Blue', and published several books of children's verse.
▷S Thompson, *The Life of Eugene Field* (1927); and other works by Thompson

FIELD, Nathan
(1587–c.1620)

English actor and dramatist, born in London. He was educated at St Paul's school and in 1600 became one of the children of the Queen's Chapel. He was one of the comedians of the Queen's Revels (1604–13) and various other troupes. As a playwright he collaborated with **Francis Beaumont** and **John Fletcher**, and with **Philip Massinger** in the latter's *The Fatal Dowry* (c.1618, published 1632) and wrote two comedies, *A Woman is a Weathercocke* (1612) and *Amends for Ladies* (1618).
▷R F Brinkley, *Nathaniel Field, actor-playwright* (1928)

FIELDING, Henry
(1707–54)

English novelist, born at Sharpham Park, near Glastonbury in Somerset, the son of an

army lieutenant and a judge's daughter, and brother of **Sarah Fielding**. He was educated privately, then at Eton. He fell in love with a young heiress at Lyme Regis, attempted to abduct her and was bound over to keep the peace. He went to London and in 1728 published a satirical poem, *The Masquerade*, and a comedy, *Love in Several Masques*. Thereafter he studied at the University of Leiden (1728–9), before returning to London, and in the space of eight years he wrote 25 dramatic pieces: light comedies, adaptations of **Molière**, farces, ballad operas, burlesques (including *Tom Thumb*), and a series of satires attacking Sir Robert Walpole and his government. This last prompted the introduction of the Theatrical Licensing Act of 1737 and effectively ended Fielding's career as a playwright and as a theatre manager (he had formed his own company, and was running the Little Theatre, Haymarket). He now turned to the law and was admitted as a student at the Middle Temple; he was called to the Bar in 1740, but did not shine on the circuit on account of disabling gout. While still a student he turned to journalism and became editor of *The Champion* (1739–41). Incensed by the publication of **Samuel Richardson**'s prudish *Pamela* in 1740, he ridiculed it in a pseudonymous parody, *An Apology for the Life of Mrs Shamela Andrews* (1741). In 1742 came *The Adventures of Joseph Andrews and his Friend, Mr Abraham Adams*. Three volumes of *Miscellanies* (including *The Life of Jonathan Wild the Great*) followed in 1743. *The History of Tom Jones, a Foundling* was probably begun in the summer of 1746 and completed towards the end of 1748. In the interim he caused a scandal by marrying Mary Daniel, the maid of his first wife, Charlotte Craddock (d.1744). He was made a justice of the peace for Westminster and Middlesex in 1748 and campaigned vigorously against legal corruption, and helped his half-brother, Sir John Fielding (1721–80) to found the Bow Street Runners as an embryo detective force. In 1749 *The History of Tom Jones, a Foundling* was published to public acclaim, though its reception by some literary luminaries was unenthusiastic. **Samuel Johnson** called it vicious and there were those who held it responsible for two earth tremors that shook London shortly after its publication. But it endures as one of the great comic and picaresque novels in the English language, and **Coleridge** thought the plot one of the three most perfect ever planned. He followed it with *Amelia* in 1751. In 1752 he was heavily involved with *The Covent Garden Journal*, which contains some of his most acerbic satire. During his last years, however, illness overtook him. He was still ardent in his fight against corruption but at the age of 45 he could not move without the help of crutches. He died in Lisbon where he had gone in search of better health.

▷F H Dudden, *Henry Fielding* (2 vols, 1952); I P Watt, *The Rise of the Novel* (1957)

FIELDING, Sarah
(1710–68)

English novelist and translator, born in East Stour, Dorset, sister of **Henry Fielding**. Her most popular novel was *The Adventures of David Simple in Search of a Faithful Friend* (1744), a romance dealing with four young people, rejected by their families and society, in which the author's sympathy is clearly with the young women struggling to make an independent and respectable living. A sequel, *Familiar Letters Between the Principal Characters in David Simple*, appeared in 1747, together with a second edition of the first book. They are ambitious, progressive works and to these two volumes **Henry Fielding** contributed prefaces. A friend of **Samuel Richardson**, she wrote the first study of his *Clarissa* in 1749. She published several other works, including a translation of **Xenophon**'s *Memorabilia and Apologia* in 1762.

FIERSTEIN, Harvey Forbes
(1954–)

American playwright and actor, born in Brooklyn, New York. An art student at the Pratt Institute, he entered showbusiness as a female impersonator in gay nightclubs. A gravelly-voiced, overweight figure at this time, he made his dramatic debut as an asthmatic lesbian cleaning-woman in the Andy Warhol play *Pork* (1971) and appeared frequently in off-Broadway productions before writing his own plays, such as *In Search Of The Cobra Jewels* (1973), *Freaky Pussy* (1975) and *Flatbush Tosca* (1975), a transvestite version of the opera. In 1976 he wrote and acted in *The International Stud*, the first of three bittersweet, semi-autobiographical plays covering the life of sardonic, incurably romantic New York drag queen Arnold Beckoff and his search for respect, a loving boyfriend and domestic bliss. Premiered on Broadway as *Torch Song Trilogy* (1982), it won Tony awards for Best Play and Best Actor; Fierstein also wrote and starred in the film adaptation (1988). He won a further Tony for the book of the long-running Broadway musical *La Cage Aux Folles* (1983) and has also written the plays *Spookhouse* (1984), *Safe Sex* (1987) and *Legs Diamond* (1989).

FIGUEROA, John Joseph Maria
(1927–)

Jamaican poet, born in Kingston, Jamaica, and educated at Holy Cross College, Worcester, Massachusetts. He was a distinguished educator, latterly with the Open University, and edited *Caribbean Voices* (1971). His poetry is notable for its sensuous treatment of the Caribbean landscape, broad cross-cultural references, and a Christian religious sensibility. **Derek Walcott** best described the distinctive quality of his verse: 'more than Roman Catholic in themes, positively Roman in manner'. *Ignoring Hurts* (1976) and *The Chase* (1992) both include poems from his earlier collections, *Blue Mountain Peak* (1943) and *Love Leaps Here* (1962).

FIKRET, Tevfik
(1857–1915)

Turkish poet, born in Istanbul. Learned in French language and literature, he became editor of the magazine *Servet-i Funan*, which was so vital in opening up the European traditions to Turkish writers. He was the principal writer of the Edebiyat-i Cedide, or New Literature movement—opposed to a recalcitrant Sultan (well and angrily punished by Fikret in his poetry), and to stultification—which had grown from the earlier Tanzimat (Transformation) movement. He helped to adapt the sonnet to Turkish poetry, and experimented with many European forms. Essentially, he carried on and perfected the work started by **Abdüllhak Hamid Tarhan**, and was notable for the way in which his poetry remained essentially Turkish in character even while making use of Western models.

▷T S Halman, *Modern Turkish Literature* (1980)

FILICAIA, Vincenzo da
(1642–1707)

Italian lyric poet, born in Florence. He studied there and at Pisa, and held a post under the Grand-Duke of Tuscany. He is remembered for his patriotic sonnets, and his ode on the liberation of Vienna from the Turks (1684).

▷G Caponi, *Filicaia e son opere* (1901)

FINCH, Robert
(1900–)

Canadian poet, born in Freeport, Long Island, New York and educated at the University of Toronto. He has worked as a lecturer of French, a writer-in-residence, and a painter (with exhibitions in New York and Paris). He twice received a Governor General's Award (1947 and 1962). His work, at times satirical, frequently employs complex imagery: the poems in his collection *Acis in Oxford* (1961), for example, were inspired by Handel's oratorio *Acis and Galatea*, and the collection *Dover Beach Revisited and Other*

Poems (1966) takes its inspiration from **Matthew Arnold**'s poem and the events of World War II.

FINDLATER, Jane
(1866–1946)

Scottish novelist, born in Lochearnhead, Perthshire, daughter of a Free Church minister, and sister of **Mary Findlater**. She had a great success with her first novel, *The Green Graves of Balgowrie* (1896), an 18th-century fiction based on family papers. It was followed by *A Daughter of Strife* (1897), *Rachel* (1899), *The Story of a Mother* (1902) and *The Ladder to the Stars* (1906). In collaboration with her sister she wrote the novel *Crossriggs* (1908) and other works.
▷ E MacKenzie, *The Findlater Sisters* (1964)

FINDLATER, Mary
(1865–1963)

Scottish novelist, born in Lochearnhead, Perthshire, daughter of a Free Church minister, and sister of **Jane Findlater**. She wrote several novels of her own, including *Betty Musgrave* (1899) and *The Rose of Joy* (1903), a volume of *Songs and Sonnets* (1895), and collaborated with her sister on the novel *Crossriggs* (1908) and other works.
▷ E Mackenzie, *The Findlater Sisters* (1964)

FINDLEY, Timothy
(1930–)

Canadian playwright and novelist, born in Toronto and educated at St Andrew's College and Jarvis Collegiate as well as at the Royal Conservatory of Music, and the Central School for Speech and Drama in London. He worked as an actor and a Hollywood scriptwriter before turning to full-time writing in 1962. He chaired the Writers' Union of Canada in 1977–8 and has received over 10 special awards, including a Governor General's Award (1977). He is best known for his novel *The Wars* (1977), an account of a Canadian officer in World War II whose experiences lead him to treason and suspected madness.
▷ Timothy Findley issue of *Canadian Literature* (Winter 1981)

FINE, Anne
(1947–)

English novelist, born in Leicester and educated at Warwick University. Primarily a writer for children and teenagers, she started with such titles as *The Summer-House Loon* (1978), but made her reputation with *Goggle Eyes* (1989, published in the USA as *My War with Goggle Eyes*), a moving but witty account of a young girl coming to terms with her divorced mother's new boyfriend. This won the Carnegie Medal, as did *Flower Babies* (1993), while *Madame Doubtfire* (1987, published in the USA as *Alias Madame Doubtfire*, 1988) was turned into a successful Hollywood movie in 1994. A two-edged writer, whose characters often combine wisdom with a faint degree of malice, Fine has also written a disturbing and powerful adult novel about obsessive love, *The Killjoy* (1986).

FINEMAN, Irving
(1893–)

Popular American Jewish novelist, an engineer by profession, who wrote the fictionalized biography of Henrietta Szold, founder of Hadassah. *Ruth* (1949) was a version of the Bible story, while *Jacob* (1941) was autobiographical. *Fig Tree Madonna* (1951) was a successful play.

FINLAY, Ian Hamilton
(1925–)

Scottish artist, poet and writer, born in the Bahamas to Scottish parents who returned to their native country when he was a child. He spent a brief period at Glasgow School of Art before World War II. In the 1950s he began his career as a writer, and became increasingly concerned with the formal qualities of individual words; his writings of the early 1960s played a leading part in the foundation of the 'concrete poetry' movement. Since then the major theme of his art has been the relationship between words and images. In 1966 he moved, with his wife, to a farmhouse near Dunsyre in the Pentland Hills, later named 'Little Sparta', and began to transform the grounds into an original modern conception of a classical garden, with sculptures and stone inscriptions carefully placed within the landscape. Like his prints, posters and other works, these are produced in collaboration with a number of skilled craftsmen. He also designed the garden at Stockwood Park, Luton, another monument to classical culture.

FINLAYSON, Rod(erick David)
(1904–92)

New Zealand writer and one-time champion rifle shot, born in Devonport, Auckland, whose short stories are in the 'tale-teller' mode rather than the sketches of character or place of earlier writers; he depicts a realistic Maori rather than a 'noble savage'. His collections include the first, *Brown Man's Burden* (1938, rev edn 1973), and *Sweet Beulah Land* (1942). His novels are *Tidal Creek* (1948) and *The Schooner comes to Atia* (1952). *Other Lovers* (1976) includes the novellas 'Frankie and Lena' and 'Jim and Miri'. He also wrote a historical novel for younger readers, *The*

Springing Fern (1965), and published a study of **D'Arcy Cresswell** in 1972.

FIRBANK, (Arthur Annesley) Ronald
(1886–1926)

English novelist, born in London, the son of a wealthy company director. Educated at Uppingham and Cambridge, where he was converted to Roman Catholicism, in 1909 he left university without taking a degree and travelled extensively in Spain, Italy, the Middle East and North Africa. Sunstroke as a child left him delicate and although he acquired friends he was by nature solitary, invariably unaccompanied on his frequent visits to the theatre. A homosexual, he cultivated eccentricity such as the palm tree in his apartment which he employed a gardener to water twice a day. His novels (written on piles of blue postcards) are slight but innovative and anticipate **Evelyn Waugh**, **Anthony Powell**, **Ivy Compton-Burnett** and others. In 1905 he published a volume containing two short stories, *Odette d'Antrevernes*, and several novels followed, among them *Vainglory* (1915), *Valmouth* (1919) and *Prancing Nigger* (1924), inspired by a visit to Haiti. None made much of an impact though the **Sitwells** championed him. His last complete work before his premature death from a disease of the lungs, *Concerning the Eccentricities of Cardinal Pirelli* (1926), is quintessential Firbank, the dialogue witty and inconsequential, the hero meeting his end while in ardent pursuit of a choir boy.
▷M Berkowitz, *Ronald Firbank* (1970)

FIRDAUSI, or FERD(A)USI, pseud of Abu-'l Kasim Mansur
(c.935–c.1020)

Persian poet, born near Tús in Khorasan. When he was about 60 he spent some years at the court of Mahmud of Ghazni, where he wrote his masterpiece the *Shah Náma* ('Book of Kings'). When this was finished in 1008, the poet, receiving 60 000 silver dirhams instead of the promised 60 000 gold dinars, fled from Ghazni, leaving behind him a scathing satire on the sultan. Mahmud at length sent the 60 000 gold dinars to Firdausi at Tus, just as his remains were being carried to the grave. The *Shah Nama*, based on actual events from the annals of Persia, is for the most part composed of mythological and fanciful incidents. He also wrote a number of shorter pieces, kasidas and ghazals. His *Yusuf u Zulaykha* is based on the story of Joseph and Potiphar's wife.
▷H T Anklescriz, *Firdausi* (1934)

FIRENZUOLA, Agnolo
(1493–1548)

Italian author, born in Florence. He became Abbot of Prato, where he wrote the rather worldly tales in *Ragionamenti* (1525), and paraphrased the *Metamorphoses* of **Apuleius**. He was absolved of his vows in 1526 and spent 11 years in silence, but returned to writing in the last decade of his life, including religious works.

FISCHART, Johann
(c.1545–1590)

German satirist, whose **Rabelais**ian works lash with inexhaustible humour the corruptions of the clergy, the astrological fancies and other follies of the time. *Flöhhatz, Weibertratz* (1573) is outrageously comic and original. Essentially different are *Das glückhafft Schiff von Zürich* (in verse, 1576, 'The Lucky Ship of Zurich') and his spiritual songs.
▷A Hauffer, *Fischart* (1921)

FISHER, Roy
(1930–)

English poet and jazz pianist, born in Handsworth, Birmingham, and educated at the University of Birmingham. In 1982, Fisher left the Department of American Studies, University of Keele, where he had taught for 10 years, in order to write full-time. His verse combines a clear-eyed registration of detail with an almost improvisational freedom of voice. This was evident as early as his first volume *City* (1961), the subsequent *Ten Interiors with Various Figures* (1966) and *The Memorial Fountain* (1967) and the striking *Nineteen Poems and an Interview* (1975), which is a valuable source regarding his artistic priorities. *The Thing About Joe Sullivan* (1978) is a remarkable, unified sequence. A collected *Poems 1955–1980* appeared in 1980. Fisher has also written a number of unusual prose poems, including *Metamorphoses* (1970) and *The Cut Pages* (1971).
▷D Davie, in *Thomas Hardy and British Poetry* (1972)

FISHER, Vardis Alvero
(1895–1968)

American novelist, born in Annis, Idaho, into a Mormon family. Many of his novels are set in his own region. Best known is the autobiographical tetralogy about Vridar Hunter: *Tragic Life* (1932), *Passions Spin the Plot* (1934), *We Are Betrayed* (1935) and *No Villain Need Be* (1936). Chiefly interesting here is the section in the last novel dealing with Fisher's experiences as a teacher of English at the Mormon University of Utah. *The Testament of Man* (1943–60) is even more ambitious, and contains 12 novels. *Children of God* (1939), about the early Mormons, won him the Harper Prize Novel Award. Fisher's fiction is always interesting, although sometimes badly accomplished, and his relative critical neglect is not altogether deserved; however, it may not be unconnected with the rather hysterical anti-communism of his later years, and with his grandiose claims for his *Testament of Man* series.

▷ *Time* (12 August, 1946)

FISHTA, Gjergj
(1871–1940)

The best-known Albanian writer of the interwar period. He was a Franciscan friar who, almost alone and unaided, ushered a native modern literature into Albania. He was educator, politician, editor, translator, playwright, poet, novelist. The intrinsic value of his work, judged by international standards, is not more than highly competent and vigorous, and he ended, owing to his Catholic conservatism, as a member of the extreme right. Thus his direct influence has been felt mostly by Albanian writers in exile.

FITCH, (William) Clyde
(1865–1909)

American dramatist, born in Elmira, New York, whose first play, the melodrama *Beau Brummell* (1890), became a vehicle for the popular and dashing actor, Richard Mansfield. During the following 20 years, Fitch went on to write over 60 Broadway plays. The earliest, such as *Nathan Hale* (1899), were based upon incidents in American history, but by far the most popular were his later society melodramas. These were well-plotted and often gently satirized the self-styled New York aristocracy. They include *The Girl with the Green Eyes* (1902) and *The Woman in the Case* (1909). Many of his plays were conceived with specific star actors in mind and were written extremely quickly, *The Truth* (1906) supposedly written in a gondola on the Grand Canal in Venice.

FITZBALL, Edward, originally Ball
(1792–1873)

English popular dramatist. He won outstanding popularity in the 1820s for his countless fantastically staged and highly intricate melodramas. He looted his material where he chose and took wild liberties with originals, such as his *The Flying Dutchman* (1827), derived from John Howison's haunting story, *The Pilot*, from **James Fenimore Cooper**'s *The Red Rover* (1829) and from **Edward Bulwer-Lytton**'s *Paul Clifford* (1835). His *Jonathan Bradford* (1833), based on a famous murder case, ran for 260 nights at the Surrey Theatre. He wrote a vivid autobiography, *Thirty-Five Years of a Dramatic Author's Life* (1859), which is an invaluable

source for 19th-century English theatre history.

FITZGERALD, Edward
(1809–83)

English scholar and poet, born near Woodbridge, Suffolk, the translator of **Omar Khayyám**. A country gentleman by birth and inclination, he was educated at King Edward VI School in Bury St Edmunds and Trinity College, Cambridge, where he developed close literary friendships with **Thackeray**, **Thomas Carlyle** and **Tennyson** (who dedicated his poem *Tiresias* to him). He had a brief and unsuccessful marriage, wrote poetry, and in 1851 published *Euphranor: A Dialogue on Youth* (a comment on English education), followed by a book of aphorisms, *Polonius: A Collection of Wise Saws and Modern Instances* (1852). After studying Spanish privately, he published blank-verse translations of six plays by **Calderón de la Barca** in 1853. An interest in Persian poetry led him to publish, anonymously, a translation of *Salámán and Absál*, an allegory by Kami (1856). In 1859 he published, anonymously at first, his free poetic translation of quatrains from the *Rubáiyát of Omar Khayyám* (4th rev edn, 1879). He also translated **Aeschylus** and **Sophocles**, and two more plays by Calderón, and left a host of delightful letters, edited and published after his death.

▷ J Richardson, *Edward Fitzgerald* (1960)

FITZGERALD, F Scott (Francis Scott Key)
(1896–1940)

American novelist, born in St Paul, Minnesota. He was educated at Newman School, New Jersey, and Princeton, where one of his contemporaries was **Edmund Wilson**. He enlisted in the US army in World War I but never left America. He married **Zelda Fitzgerald**, and in 1920 published his first novel, *This Side of Paradise*, based on his experience at Princeton. He captured the spirit of the 1920s ('The Jazz Age'), especially in *The Great Gatsby* (1925), his best-known book. Other novels include *The Beautiful and the Damned* (1922) and *Tender is the Night* (1934). His short stories were equally notable, published in *Flappers and Philosophers* (1920), *Tales of the Jazz Age* (1922), *All the Sad Young Men* (1926) and *Taps at Reveille* (1936). He lived the strenuous life of a playboy in Europe and America, during which time his wife grew increasingly mentally unstable. He described his own problems—and those of his generation—in an influential essay, 'The Crack Up' (1935). Himself driven by debts and alcoholism, Fitzgerald wrote short stories for popular journals, notably the *Saturday Evening Post*; in the same spirit he went to Hollywood in 1937 as a scriptwriter, where he wrote a final, unfinished novel about a Hollywood producer, *The Last Tycoon* (1941).

▷A Mizener, *The Far Side of Paradise* (1951, rev edn 1965); M Bruccoli, *Some Sort of Epic Grandeur: a biography of Fitzgerald* (1981)

FITZGERALD, Penelope Mary
(1916–)

English novelist and biographer, born in Lincoln and educated at Oxford. Her biographies include *Edward Burne-Jones* (1975) and *Charlotte Mew and her Friends* (1984). The vivid evocation of period, place and character for which her biographies are noted also distinguishes her elegant, intricately-constructed fiction. *The Bookshop* (1978) conjures up the enclosed world of a small Suffolk community, with all its rivalries and in-fighting, while *Offshore* (1979), which won the Booker Prize, deals with a group of people living on barges on the River Thames. This is a novel born of salutory experience: Penelope Fitzgerald had herself, with her family, lived on a Thames barge, which sank. *The Gate of Angels* (1990) is a love story set in Cambridge in 1912.

FITZGERALD, R(obert) D(avid)
(1902–87)

Australian poet, born in Hunters Hill, Sydney, nephew of the poet John Le Gay Brereton (1871–1933). Trained as a surveyor, he spent five years in Fiji and returned to Australia to take up a position in government service. His first published poems were privately printed in *The Greater Apollo: Seven Metaphysical Songs* (1927), followed by *To Meet the Sun* (1929). A further collection, *Moonlight Acre*, appeared in 1938. His *Essay on Memory*, a long philosophical poem, appeared in 1938 and won the *Sydney Morning Herald* Sesquicentenary Prize in that year. An extensive historical narrative poem *Between Two Tides* was published in 1952, and a collection of his prose appeared in 1976 as *Of Places and Poetry*.

FITZGERALD, Zelda, née Sayre
(1900–48)

American novelist and painter, born in Montgomery, Alabama; she married **F Scott Fitzgerald**. She published a poor novel, *Save Me the Waltz* (1932), which has been occasionally somewhat over-valued by critics who believe that her husband scotched her talent. However, other prose fragments are of interest, as are many of her paintings.
▷N Milford, *The Life of Zelda Fitzgerald* (1970)

FITZMAURICE, George
(1877–1963)

Irish playwright, born in County Kerry. He drew on the life and language of his mother's farming family for his hard-hitting rural comedies, but also wrote powerful poetic folk drama which remained unappreciated until after his death. His best-known work, *The Country Dressmaker* (1907), was a huge success at the Abbey Theatre in Dublin under **Yeats**'s regime. A combination of critical incomprehension and the playwright's retiring nature allowed his work to be almost forgotten until a series of revivals at the Abbey in the 1970s, and the republishing of his works in *The Plays of George Fitzmaurice* (1970).

FLANNER, Janet
(1892–1978)

American literary journalist and novelist, born in Indianapolis. She was Paris correspondent of the *New Yorker* under the name Genêt. A leading member of the eventually influential coterie of (mostly) homosexual women (they included **Natalie Barney**, **Mina Loy** and **Djuna Barnes**) who lived in Paris between the wars, Flanner's 'Letters from Paris' to the *New Yorker* still provide the most articulate guide to all but their sexual affairs. They were edited as *Paris Letters* (1966–71) in two volumes. Her now neglected feminist novel, *The Cubical City* (1926), about Paris, attacks sexual puritanism and stuffiness.
▷I Drutman (ed), *Janet Flanner's World: Uncollected Writings, 1932–1975* (1979); S Weinstock, *Women of the Left Bank* (1986)

FLAUBERT, Gustave
(1821–80)

French novelist, born in Rouen, the son of a doctor. He studied law reluctantly at Paris, where his friendship with **Victor Hugo**, **Maxime du Camp**, and the poet **Louise Colet**, his lover from 1846 to 1854, stimulated his already apparent talent for writing. When barely past his student days he was afflicted by an obscure form of nervous disease, which may have been to some extent responsible for the morbidity and pessimism which characterized his work from the very beginning. These traits, together with a violent hatred and contempt for bourgeois society, are revealed in his first masterpiece, *Madame Bovary* (1857, Eng trans 1881), a painful but powerful tragedy of an unhappy bourgeois wife who seeks solace in dreams of ideal love, and squalid affairs. The book achieved a *succès de scandale* after it had been condemned as immoral and its author prosecuted, albeit unsuccessfully, but it has held its place among the classics. His second work, *Salammbô* (1862,

Eng trans 1886), dealt with the struggle between Rome and Carthage and is rather overweighted with archaeological detail. *L'Éducation sentimentale* (1869, Eng trans *Sentimental Education*, 1896) was less effective, but in 1874 appeared the splendid *La Tentation de St Antoine* (Eng trans *The Temptation of St Anthony*, 1895), the masterpiece of its kind. *Trois contes* (1877, Eng trans *Stories*, 1903) reveals his mastery of the short story and foreshadows **Guy de Maupassant**, whom he influenced. After his death appeared *Bouvard et Pécuchet* (1881, Eng trans *Bouvard and Pecuchet*, 1896), which had not received his final revision. His correspondence with **George Sand** was published in 1884. He brought a new awareness of form, structure and aesthetic detachment to the novel.

▷ E Starkie, *Flaubert: the making of the novelist* (1967)

FLECKER, James Elroy
(1884–1915)

English poet, born in Lewisham. Educated at Uppingham, he studied Oriental languages at Trinity College, Cambridge, then entered the consular service. He was posted first to Constantinople and then to Beirut. He wrote two posthumously published verse dramas, *Hassan* (staged 1923) and *Don Juan* (1925), and published several volumes of rich verse, *The Bridge of Fire* (1907), *The Golden Journey to Samarkand* (1913) and *Old Ships* (1915). His *Collected Poems* appeared in 1947.

▷ G E Hodgson, *James Elroy Flecker* (1925)

FLECKNOE, Richard
(c.1600–c.1678)

Irish poet, and probably a priest. After travelling (1640–50) in Europe, Asia, Africa and Brazil, he went to London, where he took part in the wars of the wits, wrote five plays, and published *Short Discourse on the English Stage* (1664), which provoked **Dryden** to caricature him as 'MacFlecknoe' in his satire on **Thomas Shadwell**, and inspired a good-humoured lampoon by **Andrew Marvell**.

FLEISCHMAN, (Albert) Sid(ney)
(1920–)

American children's author, and writer of westerns and TV scripts, born in Brooklyn. In his teens he worked as a night-club magician, before becoming a journalist. He is preoccupied with frontier-life in the decades of westward expansion, and many of his books are given a historical setting, backed-up by meticulous but lightly-worn research. They tell tall stories about strange characters. *Chancy and the Grand Rascal* (1966) is typical. Fleischman has been called the 'American Leon Garfield' and, as with **Leon Garfield**,

the finer points of his work are more often appreciated by adults than by children.

FLEMING, Ian Lancaster
(1908–64)

English novelist, born in London, brother of **Peter Fleming**. Educated at Eton and Sandhurst, he studied languages at Munich and Geneva universities, worked as a foreign correspondent with Reuters in Moscow (1929–33), and then as a banker and stockbroker (1933–9). During World War II he was a senior naval intelligence officer, and was then the foreign manager of *The Sunday Times* (1945–59). His varied career gave him the background for a series of 12 novels and seven short stories featuring Commander James Bond, the archetypal, suave British secret service agent 007, starting with *Casino Royale* (1953) and including *From Russia with Love* (1957), *Dr No* (1958), *Goldfinger* (1959), *Thunderball* (1961) and *The Man with the Golden Gun* (1965). They sold millions of copies world-wide, and have been turned into highly successful films.

▷ J Pearson, *The Life of Ian Fleming* (1966)

FLEMING, Margaret
(1803–11)

Scottish child author, born in Kirkcaldy, Fife. She was distantly related to Sir **Walter Scott**, who referred to her as 'Pet Marjorie', and she was the theme of an exquisite essay by Dr **John Brown**. She wrote poems and a three-volume diary.

FLEMING, May Agnes
(1840–80)

Canadian writer of romantic fiction, born in Portland, New Brunswick. She was Canada's first bestselling novelist and, writing three novels a year, earned an annual income of $15 000. She began publishing under a pseudonym, Cousin May Carlton, but after her wedding in 1865 (the result of a whirlwind romance) she used her married name. Her romantic fantasies about teachers, seamstresses and other poor women achieving prosperity in propitious marriages went against the grain of her own life. She left her alcoholic husband and, when she died at an early age of Bright's disease, he found that she had excluded him from her will.

FLEMING, Paul
(1609–40)

German lyric poet, born in Hartenstein. The first German to use the sonnet form, he is best known for his lyrical and religious poetry in *Geistliche und weltliche Poemata* (1642, 'Spiritual and Worldly Poems'). His love poems, inspired by Elsabe Niehus, are unusually sincere and direct in feeling and expression for their time.

▷H Pyritz, *Paul Fleming deutsch Liebeslyrik* (1943)

FLEMING, (Robert) Peter
(1907–71)

English travel writer and journalist, born in London, the brother of **Ian Fleming**. Educated at Eton and Christ Church, Oxford, he took a stop-gap job in the Economic Advisory Council before being appointed assistant literary editor of *The Spectator*. In 1932 he read an advert in *The Times* for members to make up an expedition to explore rivers in Central Brazil and ascertain the fate of Colonel Percy Fawcett who had disappeared without trace in 1925. It provided the colourful copy which surfaced in *Brazilian Adventure* (1933), a landmark in travel literature and an immediate bestseller. In a similar vein are *One's Company* (1934) and *News From Tartary* (1936), an account of 'an undeservedly successful attempt' to travel overland from Peking to Kashmir.

▷D Hart-Davis, *Peter Fleming, a biography* (1986)

FLEMING, W(illiam) M(ontgomerie)
(1874–1961)

Australian parliamentarian and children's author, born in Avon Plains, Victoria. At 27 he became the youngest member of the NSW legislative assembly, and was a member of the Australian federal parliament (1913–22). Many of his short stories and poems appeared in the *Bulletin* and *Sydney Morning Herald*, and were collected in *Bunyip Says So* (1923) and *The Hunted Piccaninnies* (1927), based on aboriginal animal folk tales. His only adult novel, *Broad Acres* (1939), became a radio serial the following year.

FLETCHER, Giles
(?1588–1623)

English poet, brother of **Phineas Fletcher**, and cousin of **John Fletcher**. He was educated at Westminster School and Trinity College, Cambridge. A classical scholar, he became reader in Greek language at Cambridge, and in 1619 became rector of Alderton in Suffolk. His chief work is his long **Spenser**ian allegorical poem *Christ's Victory and Triumph* (1610).

FLETCHER, Giles, the Elder
(1546–1611)

English poet, politician' and diplomat, who came to the attention of Queen Elizabeth's ministers after a successful political career and was sent on overseas missions to Germany and Russia. The second of these trips was later to lead to his book *Of the Russe Commonwealth* (1591), one of the first pieces of travel writing in English. He also produced a volume of poetry, *Licia* (1593). He was head of a literary family—his sons **Giles** and **Phineas Fletcher** were both poets, and his nephew was **John Fletcher**, the playwright.

FLETCHER, John
(1579–1625)

English dramatist, closely associated with **Francis Beaumont**, born in Rye, Sussex, the third son of that dean of Peterborough who disturbed the last moments of Mary, Queen of Scots. He came of a literary family, being the nephew of **Giles Fletcher**, the elder and cousin of the **Spenser**ian poets **Giles** and **Phineas Fletcher**. All that we know of him, apart from his work for the theatre, is that he entered Benet (now Corpus) College, Cambridge, and that he died of the plague in 1625. The problem of disentangling his own plays from those on which he collaborated with Beaumont, **Philip Massinger**, **William Rowley** and **Shakespeare**, is very difficult but three or four certainly of his own devising are outstanding and the collaboration with Beaumont yielded some memorable plays. The best of his own plays are *The Faithful Shepherdess*, which ranks as a pastoral with **Ben Jonson**'s *Sad Shepherd* and **Milton**'s *Comus; The Humorous Lieutenant*, acted in 1619, and *Rule a Wife and Have a Wife* (1624), on the favourite theme of conjugal mastery. Of the 10 or so plays on which he collaborated with Beaumont the best known are *The Knight of the Burning Pestle* (attributed mainly or possibly solely to Beaumont), *Philaster* (1610), a romantic comedy, *A King and No King* (1611) and *The Maid's Tragedy* (1611), generally accounted their best work. Collaboration with Shakespeare probably resulted in *Two Noble Kinsmen*, a melodramatic version of **Chaucer**'s *Knight's Tale*, and *Henry VIII* (or insertions therein). A vein of tender poetry in Fletcher and his relaxed type of versification are useful evidence in disentangling his various collaborations.

FLETCHER, John Gould
(1886–1950)

American poet and essayist, born in Little Rock, Arkansas. He followed the Imagists while living in London and Paris (1908–33), but later turned to American subjects and became a leading spirit of the Southern Agrarian movement, contributing to *I'll Take My Stand* (1930). He won the Pulitzer Prize in 1939 for his *Selected Poems*. *South Star* (1941) contains a verse history of his native state. He published his autobiographical *Life is my Song* in 1937.

▷E B Stephens, *John Gould Fletcher* (1967)

FLETCHER, Phineas
(1582–1650)

English poet, brother of **Giles Fletcher**, cousin of **John Fletcher**, and son of **Giles Fletcher, the Elder**, Queen Elizabeth's minister in Germany and Russia, and an occasional poet. He was educated at Eton and Cambridge, and in 1621 became rector of Hilgay in Norfolk. His *Purple Island, or the Isle of Man* (1633), contains an elaborate description of the human body viewed as an island, the bones being its foundations, and the veins its rivers.

FLINT, Frank Stewart
(1885–1960)

English poet and translator, born in London. A civil servant in the Ministry of Labour, he made important contributions to the Imagist movement in *Cadences* (1915). His poetry in *In the Net of Stars* (1909) and *Otherworld* (1920) is more lyrical and romantic. A brilliant linguist, he also produced many translations.

FLODOARD OF RHEIMS
(c.893–966)

French annalist and divine, he was Canon of Rheims, which had become a major centre of learning during the Carolingian Empire, and taught there in the library. Flodoard's annals, which cover the years 919–66, are an important historical source for information on western Europe in the period, and are particularly vivid in their account of the Norse invasions of the Northern French coasts.

FLORENCE of WORCESTER
(fl.1100)

English chronicler. A monk at the abbey of Worcester, he was the first in a series of English monastic historians in the 12th and 13th centuries, the greatest of whom was William of Malmesbury. Florence's Latin *Chronicle* is an important historical source for late Saxon and early Norman England, and drew heavily on the *Anglo-Saxon Chronicle*, a version of which was kept at Worcester.

FLORIT, Eugenio
(1903–)

Cuban poet and critic, born in Madrid of a Spanish father and a Cuban mother, but who spent most of his life as a teacher in the USA. His poetry, in the manner of his mentor **Jiménez**, was admired by **Alfonso Reyes**. He has made valuable comment on the work of **Neruda**, **Lorca** and many other Spanish poets. His *Obras Completas* ('Complete Works') were published in three volumes, 1982–5.
▷M D Servodedio, *The Quest for Harmony: The Dialectics of Communication in the Poetry of Eugenio Florit* (1979)

FO, Dario
(1926–)

Italian dramatist and actor, born in San Giano, Lombardy. He began his career as a stage designer and author of comic monologues, and from 1959 to 1968 ran a small theatre company in Milan with his wife, the actress Franca Rame. His reputation as a comic author was established before the abolition of stage censorship in 1962 allowed him to align himself openly with the political left in plays attacking government corruption and bureaucracy. His international fame rests primarily upon *Morte accidentale di un anarchico* (1970, Eng trans *Accidental Death of an Anarchist*, 1979), in which a political prisoner falls from a window while in police custody, and the frenetic *Non si paya, no si paya* (1974, Eng trans *Can't Pay, Won't Pay*, 1981), a protest against taxation which achieved popularity in Britain during the heated debate over the Poll Tax. Both use traditional techniques of farce in order to propound a socialist point of view.
▷P Puppa, *Il Teatro di Fo* (1978); Tony Mitchell, *Dario Fo* (1984)

FOGAZZARO, Antonio
(1842–1911)

One of Italy's leading novelists of the 19th century, born in Vicenza. A music lover, he was tutored by a poet, and his first works were poetic—but they were unsuccessful. His first novel, rather in the style of English 'sensation' fiction, and indebted to **Wilkie Collins**, was *Malombra* (1881, Eng trans *The Woman*, 1907), and is still quite as readable and interesting as the best of that genre. But his masterpiece appeared in 1888: *Piccolo mondo antico* (Eng trans *The Patriot*, 1906), tells the story of a Venetian of the first part of the 19th century, contrasting him with his wife: his Christian faith is great, but he is weak, her faith is weak, but she possesses an iron will. This is one of the great novels of its time, second only to **Manzoni**'s *I promessi sposi*. None of Fogazzaro's other novels matches this, but all contain remarkable passages. He was a faithful son of his Church, which repaid him by putting most of his work on the forbidden list.
▷T Gallerati-Scott, *The Life of Antonio Fogazzaro* (1922, reprinted 1972)

FOIX, J V
(1893–1987)

Catalan Surrealist or 'superrealist', and, simultaneously, traditionalist, who ended up as the grand old man of Catalan letters. He had long been a Catalan nationalist. He ran his family's pastrycook business, but kept this strictly separate from his literary activities.

The consistently humorous nature of his enterprises has eluded most of his foreign critics. Most of his work is ostensibly based on an early poetic diary he wrote between 1911 and 1920—but some of this was actually written after 1920. Much of *Gertrudis* (1927), poetic fragments to a destructive but creative female figure invented by Foix, is highly traditional in form, although modernist in content. *Sol i de dol* (1936, 'Alone and In Mourning'), a collection of sonnets, is similarly strict and classical in form. He ended by being called 'the Master of Sarri ', the place of his birth. His project was, essentially, to rediscover the past by seeking out the future; he is a difficult writer, but has been found to be a rewarding one.

FOLLAIN, Jean
(1903–71)

French poet, born in a village near Canisy. A lawyer, he was appointed judge in 1951. He was killed in a car accident. His poetry, in which he often seeks the universal in the re-creation of his own Norman childhood, has debts to **Fargue** and, above all, to **Guillevic**. He received many prizes, and is particularly well translated and explicated in *Contemporary French Poetry* (1965).

FOLLETT, Ken(neth Martin)
(1949–)

English crime and adventure novelist, whose bankability reached staggering heights in the early 1990s. Follett, though, imbibed socialism with his free school milk in Cardiff and has donated enormous sums to the Labour Party (for whom his second wife, Barbara, works as an image consultant). He has claimed that his politics are at least subliminally detectable in adventure stories like *Storm Island* (1978, published in the USA as *Eye of the Needle*), *The Key to Rebecca* (1980) and *The Man from St. Petersburg* (1982), each of which contains a mild revisionist subtext. For a writer in this genre, Follett is notably enlightened in his treatment of women characters, who are given purposeful, strong parts and are rarely treated as victims or comforters.

FOLZ, Hans
(c.1450–before 1515)

German Meistersinger, born in Worms. He settled in Nürnberg as a barber-surgeon, and became prominent as an advocate of the extension of Meistergesang by the use of new 'Töne', of which he himself provided 27. His obscene songs are particularly notable.

FONTANE, Theodor
(1819–98)

German poet and novelist, born in Neuruppin. He worked in the family chemist's business until in 1849 he turned to literature in Berlin. Periods of residence in Britain between 1855 and 1859 as a newspaper correspondent led to ballads such as *Archibald Douglas* and *Die Brücke am Tay* ('The Tay Bridge'), and other British-flavoured pieces. He was a war correspondent in 1866 and 1870–1, and became the secretary of the Prussian Royal Academy of Arts. He wrote his first novel, *Vor dem Sturm* (1878, 'Before the Storm'), at the age of 56; it is considered by many to be his best. It is set against the events of the Franco-Prussian war in 1812–13, but he turned to the subject of the position of women in German society in *L'Adultera* (1882, Eng trans *The Woman Taken in Adultery*, 1979) and *Effi Briest* (1895, Eng trans 1967), among others. His appraisal of social mores extended into the realms of politics and power in *Die Poggenpuhls* (1896, Eng trans *The Poggenpuhl Family*, 1979) and *Der Stechlin* (1898, 'Stechlin'). His novels influenced **Thomas Mann**.

▷A R Robinson, *Fontane: an introduction to the man and his work* (1976)

FONTANES, Louis, Marquis de
(1757–1821)

French writer and politician, born in Niort. In 1777 he went to Paris, where he acquired a reputation for his melancholy, introspective poems, among which are *Le Cri de mon coeur* (1778, 'The Cry of my Heart'), *Le Verger* (1788, 'The Orchard'), a metrical translation of **Pope**'s *Essay on Man* (1783), and an imitation of **Thomas Gray**'s *Elegy*. He supported the Revolution, but later criticized it, and was the prime founder of the *Mercure de France* in 1799. In 1804 he was made President of the Corps Législatif. In 1810 he entered the senate, and was raised to the peerage by Louis XVIII.

▷A Wilson, *Fontanes. Un essai biographique* (1929)

FONTENELLE, Bernard le Bovier de
(1657–1757)

French author, born in Rouen. A nephew of **Corneille**, he began his literary career in Paris. In the great quarrel of Moderns versus Ancients, he sided with the Moderns, assailing the Greeks and their French imitators, and receiving in return the satiric shafts of **Boileau**, **Racine**, **Rousseau** and **La Bruyère**. After the failure on the stage of his *Aspar*, he produced an imitation of **Lucian**, *Nouveaux Dialogues des morts* (1682, Eng trans *New*

Dialogues of the Dead, 1683), and the 'precious' *Lettres Diverses de Monsieur le Chevalier d'Her...* (1687, Eng trans *Letters of Gallantry from Monsieur le Chevalier d'Her...*, 1687). In 1697 he was made secretary to the Académie des Sciences, of which he later was president. He died in Paris in his hundredth year. He had attempted almost every form of literature—idylls, satires, dialogues, critical essays, histories and tragedies. His *Entretiens sur la pluralité des mondes* (1686, Eng trans *A Discourse on the Plurality of Worlds*, 1687) and *Histoire des oracles* (1686, Eng trans *The History of the Oracles*, 1688), are considered his best works.

FONVIZIN, or FON-VIZIN, Denis Ivanovich
(1745–92)

Russian dramatist, born in Moscow. He wrote in the tradition of **Molière** and **Holberg** (whom he had translated), but in a thoroughly and successfully Russian style. His masterpiece is *Nedorosl* (1782, Eng trans *The Minor*, in *Masterpieces of the Russian Drama*, ed G Z Patrick and G R Noyes, 1933). He wrote many indignant political works, reminiscent of **Voltaire**. In his last years he could not speak properly, owing to the effects of a stroke. Another play by him, *The Choice of a Tutor*, is translated in *Five Russian Plays* (1916, ed C E Beechofer).
▷H Rogger, *National Consciousness in Eighteenth Century Russia* (1960)

FOOTE, Samuel
(1720–77)

English wit, playwright and actor, born in Truro. His brilliant mimicry of prominent people led to legal proceedings being taken against him on several occasions. His plays, which include *Taste* (1752) and *The Minor* (1760), were mainly political satire, and have not stood the test of time.
▷M M Belden, *The Dramatic Works of Samuel Foote* (1929)

FOOTE, Shelby
(1916–)

American novelist and historian, born in Greenville, Mississippi. His second novel, *Follow Me Down* (1950), which gives a multiple view of a violent murder, established his name. *Shiloh* (1952) is a historical novel, dealing with the Civil War. Foote is now even better known for his detailed history, *The Civil War: A Narrative* (1958–74), than for his novels.
▷*Mississippi Quarterly* (October, 1971)

FORBES, (Joan) Rosita
(1893–1967)

English writer and traveller, born in Swinderby, Lincolnshire. Having visited almost every country in the world and particularly Arabia and North Africa, she used her experiences as the raw material for exciting travel books, including *The Secret of the Sahara-Kufara* (1922), *From Red Sea to Blue Nile* (1928), *The Prodigious Caribbean* (1940), *Appointment in the Sun* (1949) and *Islands in the Sun* (1950).
▷*Gypsy in the Sun* (1967)

FORD, Ford Madox, originally Ford Hermann Hueffer
(1873–1939)

English novelist, editor and poet, born in Merton, Surrey, the son of Francis Hueffer, the music critic of *The Times* and grandson, on his mother's side, of the Pre-Raphaelite painter Ford Madox Brown. Brought up in pre-Raphaelite circles, he published his first book when he was only 18, a fairy story entitled *The Brown Owl* (1891), and a novel, *The Shifting of the Fire*, appeared the following year. In 1894 he eloped with and married Elsie Martindale, presaging a life of emotional upheaval. He met **Joseph Conrad** in 1898 and they co-authored various works including *The Inheritors* (1901) and *Romance* (1903). He founded the *English Review* in 1908, which he edited for 15 months and in which he published **Thomas Hardy, H G Wells, D H Lawrence** and **Wyndham Lewis** among others. In 1924, while living in Paris, he was founder-editor of the *Transatlantic Review*, which gave space to **James Joyce, Ezra Pound, Gertrude Stein** and the young **Ernest Hemingway**. He wrote almost 80 books in a hectic career but is best remembered for three novels: *The Fifth Queen* (1906), *The Good Soldier* (1915) and *Parade's End*, the title he gave to what is often known as the Tietjens war tetralogy: *Some Do Not* (1924), *No More Parades* (1925), *A Man Could Stand Up* (1926) and *Last Post* (1928).
▷A Mizener, *The Saddest Story* (1972)

FORD, Jesse Hill, Jr
(1928–)

American novelist and short-story writer. Born in Troy, Alabama, he worked in public relations and technical journalism before his first novel, *Mountains of Gilead* (1961), was published. *The Liberation of Lord Byron Jones* (1965) is the story of a black funeral parlour owner who is 'set free' from the contradictions of his colour and from an unfaithful wife when he is murdered by her white policeman lover. The novel's success was fostered by a Hollywood film. The *Feast of Saint Barnabas* (1969) also deals with racial violence and is perhaps more clearly imagined and executed, reflecting the virtues of Ford's fine short stories, which were collected as *Fishes, Birds, and Sons of Men* (1967). He has also written a play, *The Conversion of Buster Drumwright* (1964), which was adapted as a musical two decades later.

FORD, John
(c.1586–c.1640)

English dramatist, born in Ilsington, Devon. He studied for a year at Oxford and entered the Middle Temple in 1602. He was expelled for debt but readmitted. He was greatly influenced by **Robert Burton**, whose *Anatomy of Melancholy* (1621) turned Ford's dramatic gifts towards stage presentation of the melancholy, the unnatural and the horrible in *The Lover's Melancholy* (1629), *'Tis Pity She's a Whore* (1633), *The Lady's Trial* (1639), etc. He also wrote a masterful chronicle play, *Perkin Warbeck* (1634). Ford often collaborated with **Thomas Dekker**, **William Rowley** and **John Webster**.
▷D Anderson, *John Ford* (1972)

FORD, Richard
(1796–1858)

English travel writer, born in Winchester. After studying at Trinity College, Oxford, he was called to the Bar, but never practised. He spent the years 1830–4 in riding tours in Spain, and wrote the popular and characterful *Handbook for Travellers in Spain* (1845), followed by *Gatherings from Spain* (1846). He introduced the British public to the works of Velazquez.
▷B Ford, *Richard Ford en Sevilla* (1963)

FORD, Richard
(1944–)

American novelist, born in Jackson, Mississippi. He graduated from the University of California, Berkeley, with an MA in 1970, and taught English at Williams College, Massachusetts, and Princeton University. His first novel was *A Piece of My Heart* (1976), followed by *The Ultimate Good Luck* (1981). Both subjected their respective protagonists to a journey of internal discovery. His best novel is *The Sportswriter* (1986), in which he creates a memorable character in the wary Frank Bascombe. A harsh, uncompassionate realist, Bascombe has renounced fiction for sports writing, which teaches him that 'there are no transcendent themes in life'. *Rock Springs* (1987) is a collection of stories, while *Wildlife* (1990) is a short novel about the disintegration of a family. He edited the *Granta Book of the American Short Story* (1991).

FORESTER, C(ecil) S(cott)
(1899–1966)

British writer, born in Cairo. He studied medicine, but turned to writing full-time after the success of his first novel, *Payment Deferred* (1926). He also wrote *The African Queen* (1935, which was made into a successful film), *The General* (1936) and *The Ship* (1943). He is best known for his creation of Horatio Hornblower, a British naval officer in the Napoleonic era whose career he chronicled in a series of popular novels, starting with *The Happy Return* (1937) and *Ship of the Line* (1938, James Tait Black Memorial Prize). He also wrote biographical and travel books and collaborated with C E Bechofer Roberts on a play about Nurse Edith Cavell.
▷C Parkinson, *The Life and Times of Hornblower* (1970)

FORSSELL, Lars
(1928–)

Swedish poet, essayist and playwright. He has been well known throughout Scandinavia since the early 1950s. His poetry is continuously experimental, sometimes fashionable and superficial, but at others, as in *F C Tietjens* (1954), an exercise in **Pessoan** ingenuity, more profound and self-searching. His play *Krönigen* (1956) was translated as *The Coronation* in 1963; he has translated **Pound** and **T S Eliot** into Swedish.

FORSTER, E(dward) M(organ)
(1879–1970)

English novelist and critic, born in London. He was educated at Tonbridge School, where he was miserable, and King's College, Cambridge, where he revelled in the 'Bloomsbury circle' of G E Moore, G M Trevelyan and **Lowes Dickinson**, whose biography he wrote in 1934, and with whom he founded the *Independent Review* in 1903. In his novels he examined with subtle insight the pre-1914 English middle-class ethos and its custodians the civil service, the church and the public schools. An indictment of the latter is embodied in *The Longest Journey* (1907), and a period in Italy provided the background for *Where Angels Fear to Tread* (1905) and *A Room with a View* (1908). *Howards End* (1910) was written after he had been tutor in Nassenheide (1905). But it is in his masterpiece, *A Passage to India* (1924), that he puts English values and Indian susceptibilities under his finest scrutiny. The spiritual tensions of two clashing civilizations are resolved in the strange symbolism of the Malabar Cave. He was awarded the James Tait Black Memorial and Femina Vie Heureuse prizes for the latter in 1925. His Indian experiences as secretary to the Maharajah of Dewas Senior (1921) he described in *The Hill of Devi* (1953). Collections of short stories include *The Celestial Omnibus* (1914) and *The Eternal Moment* (1928); collections of essays, *Abinger Harvest* (1936) and *Two Cheers for Democracy* (1951). His Cambridge Clark lectures,

Aspects of the Novel (1927), expressed his literary aesthetics as firmly opposed to Aristotle. He was elected a fellow of King's College, Cambridge in 1946. *Marianne Thornton* (1958) is a domestic biography. In 1951 he collaborated with Eric Crozier on the libretto of Britten's opera, *Billy Budd*. His novel *Maurice* (written 1913–14), on the theme of homosexuality, was published posthumously in 1971.

▷J Beer, *The Achievement of E M Forster* (1962); N Beauman, *Morgan: a biography of E. M. Forster* (1993)

FORSTER, Margaret
(1938–)

English novelist, biographer and critic, born in Carlisle and educated at Oxford. Her early novels include the topical *Georgy Girl* (1965), depicting the emotional and sexual freedoms and dangers suddenly confronting young women in a liberated decade. In her later novels, each with a strong sense of character and social context, she has looked at the problems of middle-aged married women (*Marital Rites*, 1981), and adolescent children (*Private Papers*, 1986). Her biographies include a sympathetic *Elizabeth Barrett Browning* (1988), while its companion novel, *Lady's Maid* (1990), speculates intriguingly upon the life of Browning's maid, Wilson. In 1993 she published an excellent and authoritative biography, *Daphne du Maurier*.

FORSYTH, Frederick
(1938–)

English author of suspense thrillers, born in Ashford, Kent. Educated at Tonbridge School, Kent, he served in the Royal Air Force and later became a journalist. His reputation rests on three taut thrillers, *The Day of the Jackal* (1971), *The Odessa File* (1972) and *The Dogs of War* (1974), meticulously researched, precisely plotted nail-biters.

FORT, Paul
(1872–1960)

French poet, born in Reims. He settled in Paris, where in 1890 he founded the 'Théâtre des Arts' to present a wide range of European drama and recitals of Symbolist poetry. He is best known for his popular *Ballades françaises* (1st vol 1897, 'French Ballads'), which eventually numbered 17 volumes, and in which he brought poetry closer to the rhythms of everyday speech. He also wrote several plays, founded and edited the literary magazine *Vers et Prose* (1905–14), and wrote *Histoire de la poésie française depuis 1850* (1927, 'History of French Poetry since 1850').

▷A Lowell, *Six French Poets* (1915)

FORTIGUERRA, Niccolo
(1674–1735)

Italian poet and prelate. He was bishop and papal chamberlain to Clement XI, and is remembered for his satirical epic, *Il Ricciardetto* (1738).

FOSCOLO, Ugo
(1778–1827)

Italian author, born in Zante. He was educated at Spalato (Split) and Venice. His bitter disappointment when Venice was ceded to Austria found vent in the *Lettere di Jacopo Ortis* (1802, Eng trans *Letters of Ortis*, 1818). Believing that France was destined to liberate Italy, he served in the French armies, but, no longer fooled by Napoleon's intentions, he returned to Milan, and published in 1807 his best poem, *I Sepolcri* (1807, Eng trans *The Sepulchres*, 1820). He translated **Laurence Sterne**'s *Sentimental Journey*, and wrote two tragedies, *Ajace* and *Ricciarda*. In 1809 he was for a few months Professor of Eloquence in Pavia. After 1814, when the Austrians entered Milan, he finally sought refuge in London. There he published his *Saggi sul Petrarca* (1847, 'Essays on Petrarch'), *Discorso sul testo del Decamerone* (1828, 'Discourse on the text of the *Decameron*'), *Discorso sul testo di Dante* (1825, 'Discourse on the text of Dante'), and various papers in the *Quarterly Review* and *Edinburgh Review*. His last years were embittered by poverty and neglect, and he left a long poem, *Le Grazie* (1848, 'The Graces'), incomplete on his death.

▷L Fabiani, *Ugo Foscolo* (1972)

FOSTER, David
(1944–)

Australian writer, born in Sydney, he studied as a scientist and worked in the USA before devoting himself to writing. His work is overlaid with a pseudo-scientific vocabulary which hides a quirky sense of humour and fantasy. In *Moonlite* (1981) he relates a patriarchal society on a Scottish isle to an allegory of the colonization of Australia. *The Empathy Experiment* with D K Lyell (1977) is 'straight' sci-fi, and *The Adventures of Christian Rosy Cross* (1986) is a parable, or parody, of the Rosicrucian faith as portrayed by its hero the Comte de Rosencreutz. *Testostero: A Comic Novel* (1987) is a laboured reworking of **Carlo Goldoni**'s comedy 'The Venetian Twin'.

FOUQUÉ, Friedrich Heinrich Karl, Baron de la Motte
(1777–1843)

German writer and soldier, of Huguenot ancestry. He served as a Prussian cavalry officer in 1794 and 1813. The interval between these campaigns was devoted to literary pursuits, and the rest of his life was spent in Paris and on his estate at Nennhausen, and after 1830 in Halle. He published a long series of romances, based on Norse legend and old French poetry, his masterpiece being the fairy-tale *Undine* (1811).

FOWLES, John Robert
(1926–)

English novelist, born in Leigh-on-Sea. Educated at Bedford School, Edinburgh University and New College, Oxford, where he studied French, he served in the Royal Marines (1945–6). Thereafter he taught in schools in France, and in Greece (1951–2) and London. An allusive and richly descriptive writer, his first novel was *The Collector* (1963), still perhaps his most sensational, in which he probes the reasons why a young man of one class 'collected', incarcerated and dissected the girl, from another class, whom he thought he loved. *The Magus* (1965, rev edn 1977) is the book which made his name. Drawing on his own experience, it is set in the 1960s on a remote Greek island. It is a disturbing and much-imitated yarn about an English school-teacher, his bizarre experiences, and his involvement with a master trickster. *The French Lieutenant's Woman* (1969), however, exceeded it in popularity, in large part due to the film version with Meryl Streep in the title role. Later books—*Daniel Martin* (1977), *Mantissa* (1982) and *A Maggot* (1985)—suffered a critical backlash but underlined his willingness to experiment, as well as the fecundity of his imagination. He also published a collection of short stories, *The Ebony Tower* (1974). An essay on the significance of nature in his work, originally written in 1979, was re-issued as *The Tree* (1992), and was followed by *Tessera* (1993), which he describes as 'a piece of juvenilia'.

FOX, Paula
(1923–)

American writer of fiction for children and adults, born in New York. Fox's children's books concern characters who remain confused and ill-at-ease for longer than is usual in juvenile fiction. *The Slave Dancer* (1973) is her most powerful narrative story. Set in 1840, it tells the nightmarish tale of a boy being kidnapped into slavery in New Orleans. In similar vein, the earlier *How Many Miles to Babylon* (1967) is the story of a small black boy who is seized by older children. Fox's adult novels tend to be less dramatic, concerned with suburban domestic themes. *Desperate Characters* (1970) was turned into a movie by **Frank D Gilroy**.

FOX, William Price
(1926–)

American humorist and short-story writer, born in Illinois. He remains best known for *Southern Fried* (1962), a collection of stories set in South Carolina, where he grew up. The book has achieved the status of a classic of American humour. Despite significant endorsements for his later fiction—*Dixiana Moon* (1981) was praised by **Kurt Vonnegut** and **John D Macdonald**—Fox has not enjoyed wide critical acclaim. His stories, which usually involve petty crime, are told in a conventional style, refreshingly free of subtext and complexity.

FOXE, John
(1516–87)

English martyrologist, born in Boston in Lincolnshire. At 16 he entered Brasenose College, Oxford, and was fellow of Magdalen 1538–45. During the reign of Mary I he lived on the Continent, where he met Knox, Grindal and Whittingham. On Elizabeth's accession he received a pension and a prebend of Salisbury (1563), but lived chiefly in London and was debarred from further preferment because of his objection to wearing the surplice. He published numerous controversial treatises and sermons, as well as an apocalyptic Latin mystery play called *Christus Triumphans* (1556). His best-known work is his *History of the Acts and Monuments of the Church*, popularly known as *Foxe's Book of Martyrs*, the first part of which was published in Latin at Strasbourg in 1554 (Eng trans 1563). Written in vivid English prose, it is a history of the English Protestant martyrs from the 14th century to his own day.

FRAME, Janet Paterson
(1924–)

New Zealand novelist and short-story writer, born in Dunedin. She was educated at Otago University Teachers Training College. Her first book was a collection of short stories, *The Lagoon: Stories* (1952), which she followed five years later with a novel, *Owls Do Cry*. Having spent much time in psychiatric hospitals after severe mental breakdowns, her novels walk a tight-rope between danger and safety, where the looming threat of disorder attracts those it frightens. Honoured in her homeland but only belatedly receiving international recognition, key books are *Scented Gardens for the Blind* (1963), *A State of Siege* (1966), *Intensive Care* (1970) and *Living in the Maniototo* (1979). *The Adaptable Man*, first published in 1965, was reprinted in 1993. Her short stories were collected in *The Reservoir and Other Stories* (1966) and in *You Are Now*

Entering the Human Heart (1983). *The Carpathians* was published in 1988. Some early verse is collected in *The Pocket Mirror* (1967). The background to her work is implicit in three volumes of autobiography, *To the Island* (1983), *An Angel at my Table* (1984) and *The Envoy from Mirror City* (1985).

FRAME, Ronald
(1953–)

Scottish novelist and short-story writer, born in Glasgow. Educated there and at Oxford, he has been powerfully dedicated to overturning the rugged proletarianism which has dominated writing from and about his native city. His earliest novel, *Winter Journey* (1984), won the first **Betty Trask** Award, a prize given to the best 'romantic fiction' of the year. This rather misleadingly pigeonholed Frame, whose work was subsequently felt to be rather too bourgeois and perfumed for 1980s tastes. However, in the collections *A Long Weekend With Marcel Proust* (1986) and *A Woman of Judah* (1988) and the novel *Sandmouth People* (1987) he established a strongly distinctive vision—arguably derived from **Dickens**—in which personality is artifice and coincidence dominates. Despite their odd, 'period' dressing, *Penelope's Hat* (1989) and *Bluette* (1990) were convincingly postmodern. In 1988, his play *Paris* won the **Samuel Beckett** Prize. Later novels have been less successful, but there are signs of a new direction and a less textured prose style.

FRANC, Maud Jeanne *see* EVANS, Matilda Jane

FRANCE, Anatole, pseud of Anatole François Thibault
(1844–1924)

French writer and winner of the Nobel Prize for literature, born the son of a Parisian bookseller. He began his literary career as a publisher's reader, 'blurb' writer and critic, and published his first volume of stories, *Jocaste et le chat maigre* ('Jocasta and the Thin Cat'), in 1879 and then his first novel, *Le Crime de Sylvestre Bonnard* (1881). He had married in 1877 after being appointed Keeper at the Senate Library, a position he was to lose in 1891 because of a literary quarrel with Leconte de Lisle. Under the literary patronage of Madame de Caillavet, whose love affair with him brought about his divorce (1893), he poured out a number of graceful, lively novels, critical studies and the like, such as the Parnassian *Le Livre de mon ami* (1885, 'My Friend's Book'), a picture of childhood happiness, which stands in strong contrast to the later satirical, solipsistic and sceptical works such as *Les Opinions de Jérôme Coignard* (1893). Another remarkable collection

of short stories was published under the title *Balthasar* (1889), and his vast classical knowledge found expression in *Thaïs* (1890). The Dreyfus case (1896) stirred him into politics as an opponent of church and state and champion of internationalism. His *Îsle des pingouins* (1908, 'Isle of Penguins'), in which the evolution of mankind is satirically treated, was followed by *Les Dieux ont soif* (1912, 'The Gods are Thirsty'), a fable about the Terror, and *La révolte des anges* (1914, 'The Angels' Revolt'), a satire on Christianity and theology. He was awarded the Nobel Prize for literature in 1921.
▷R Virtanen, *Anatole France* (1968); J Roujon, *La vie et les opinions d'Anatole France* (1925)

FRANCIS, Dick (Richard Stanley)
(1920–)

English jockey and author, born in Surrey, a highly successful example of a top-class sportsman who became a writer on his own subject. He turned professional at the age of 28, and was on the point of winning the 1956 Grand National when his horse Devon Loch collapsed 50 yards from the winning post. He retired the following year and became a racing correspondent with the *Daily Express*. He also began writing popular thrillers with a racing background which won him the Golden Dagger Award of the American Crime Writers' Association in 1980. He has written over 30 novels since publishing his autobiography.
▷*The Sport of Queens* (1957 and subsequent revisions)

FRANCO, Veronica
(1546–91)

Italian poet and 'courtesan', a woman who had learned much about men, and was not uncritical of them. She was born and died in Venice, and had her portrait painted by Tintoretto. Her poetry, while ostensibly **Petrarchan**, is notably erotic and abounds in the unusual. Her *terza Rima* (1575) was edited in 1912. She has not yet been sufficiently studied for her original qualities.

FRANK, Anne
(1929–45)

German Jewish concentration-camp victim, born in Frankfurt-am-Main. She fled from the Nazis to Holland in 1933 with her family, and after the Nazi occupation of Holland hid with her family and four others in a sealed-off office back-room in Amsterdam from 1942 until they were betrayed in August 1944. She died in Belsen concentration camp. The lively, moving diary she kept during her concealment was published as *Het Achterhuis*

(1947, Eng trans *The Diary of Anne Frank*, 1952), was dramatized in 1958, filmed in 1959, and Anne Frank became a symbol of suffering under the Nazis. Her name was given to villages and schools for refugee children throughout western Europe.

▷E Schnabel, *The Footsteps of Anne Frank* (1959)

FRANK, Bruno
(1887–1945)

German author, born in Stuttgart. He wrote historical novels, such as *Die Fürstin* (1915, 'The Princess'), *Aus vielen Jahren* (1937, 'From Many Years') and *Die Tochter* (1943, 'The Daughter'), in a style reminiscent of **Thomas Mann**. His lyric poetry is also noteworthy. Of Jewish descent, he fled the Nazi regime and went to Beverly Hills in California. His *Der Reisepass* (1937, 'The Travel Pass') was directed against National Socialism.

FRANK, Leonhard
(1882–1961)

German poet and novelist, born in Würzburg. His novel *Die Räuberbande* (1914, 'The Gang of Robbers') describes the adventures of a gang of roguish boys. He fought in World War I and conceived a horror of war which led to his strongly pacifist *Der Mensch ist gut* (1917, 'Man is Good'). *Die Ursache* (1915, 'The Cause') attacked the repressive educational system in Germany, while *Der Bürger* (1924, 'The Citizen') is about the deadening effect of bourgeois society on the spirit. His *Karl und Anna* (1928), also a war story, was successfully turned into a play. He left Germany and went to live in Hollywood, where he wrote several books, including *Von drei Millionen drei* (1932, 'From Three Million and Three'), and the autobiographical novel *Links wo das Herz ist* (1952, 'On the Left, Where the Heart Is').

▷C French and H Jobs, *Leonhard Frank: 1882–1961* (1962)

FRANK, Waldo David
(1889–1967)

American novelist and journalist, born in Long Branch, New Jersey. He co-edited *The Seven Arts* (1916–17) and later wrote novels and other works coloured by mysticism and expressionism, including *City Block* (1922), *The Unwelcome Man* (1917), *The Rediscovery of America* (1929) and the play *New Year's Eve* (1939).

▷P J Carter, *Waldo Frank* (1867)

FRANKAU, Gilbert
(1884–1953)

English novelist, born in London, father of **Pamela Frankau**. A son of Julia Frankau, who wrote under the name of 'Frank Danby', writing came easily to him. His early works were great successes and he continued to write best-sellers, for he was, above everything, a professional writer, with a flair for anticipating popular taste. Of his many best-sellers, the following are notable: *One of Us* (1912), *Peter Jackson, Cigar Merchant* (1919), *Men, Maids and Mustard-Pots* (1923), *World without End* (1943).

▷*Gilbert Frankau's Self-Portrait: a novel of his own life* (1940)

FRANKAU, Pamela
(1908–67)

English novelist, daughter of **Gilbert Frankau**. In her early novels such as in *The Marriage of Harlequin* (1927), her first novel, she epitomized the era of the 'bright young things'. Like her father, a true professional, she outgrew this phase and her later novels were serious in intent. Typical are *The Willow Cabin* (1949) and *A Wreath for The Enemy* (1954). *The Offshore Light* (1952) was written under the pseudonym Eliot Naylor.

▷*I Find Four People* (1935)

FRANKL, Ludwig, Ritter von Hochwart
(1810–93)

Austrian poet of Jewish origin, Professor of Aesthetics at the Vienna Conservatory (1851). He established the first Jewish school in Jerusalem (1856). He wrote epics, ballads, satirical poems, many of which have been translated.

▷Biographical note in *Moderne Klassiker* (1852)

FRANKLIN, Benjamin
(1706–90)

American statesman and scientist, youngest son and 15th child of a family of 17, born in Boston, Massachusetts. He was apprenticed at 12 to his brother James, a printer, who started a newspaper, the *New England Courant*, in 1709. When James was imprisoned by the speaker of the Assembly for his outspoken criticism, Benjamin assumed the paper's management. The two brothers later fell out and Benjamin drifted to Philadelphia, where he secured work as a printer. During 1724–6 he worked for 18 months in London, before returning to Philadelphia to establish his own successful printing house, and in 1729 he purchased the *Pennsylvania Gazette*. A year later he married Deborah Read, by whom he had two children. He also had an illegitimate son, William. In 1732 he began *Poor Richard's Almanac*, which attained an unprecedented circulation. In 1736 Franklin was appointed Clerk of the Assembly, in 1737 Postmaster of

Philadelphia, and in 1754 Deputy Post-master-General for the Colonies, being elected and re-elected a member of the Assembly almost uninterruptedly until his first mission to England. In 1746 he began his renowned researches in electricity and most famously its relationship with lightning, which made him an FRS. In 1757 he was sent to England to insist upon the right of the province to tax the proprietors of land held under the Penn charter for the cost of defending it from the French and Native Americans. In 1764 he was again sent to England to contest the pretensions of parliament to tax the American colonies without representation. The differences, however, between the British government and the colonies became too grave to be reconciled by negotiation, and in 1775 Franklin returned to the USA, where he participated actively in the deliberations which resulted in the Declaration of Independence. To secure foreign assistance in the war Franklin was sent to Paris in 1776. His skill as a negotiator and his personal popularity, reinforced by the antipathy of French and English, favoured his mission, and on 6 February 1778, a treaty of alliance was signed, while munitions of war and money were sent from France. On 3 September 1783, his mission was crowned with success through Britain's recognition of the independence of the United States. Franklin was US minister in Paris till 1785, when he returned to Philadelphia, and was elected President of the state of Pennsylvania, a post to which he was twice re-elected. He was also a delegate to the convention which framed the constitution of the USA. In 1788 he retired from public life.
▷C van Doren, *Benjamin Franklin* (1939); R W Clark, *Benjamin Franklin: a biography* (1983)

FRANKLIN, (Stella Marian Sarah) Miles, pseud Brent of Bin Bin
(1879–1954)

Australian novelist, born in Talbingo, near Tamut, New South Wales. Known to her family as Stella, she was a fifth-generation Australian, her great-great-grandfather having been a convict in the First Fleet. She was the eldest of seven children and spent her first 10 years at a farm in the bush country, described in *Childhood at Brindabella* (1963). Later the family moved downmarket to a district fictionalized in *My Brilliant Career* (1901) as Possum Gully. Eventually they settled in a Sydney suburb. Having flirted with nursing she turned to journalism, became involved in the feminist movement, wrote *My Brilliant Career*, and emigrated in 1906 to the USA, where she worked as secretary to the Women's Trade Union League. Moving to England in 1915, despite a deep aversion to

war, she helped with the war effort, serving with the Scottish Women's Hospital at Ostrovo, in Macedonia. In 1932 she returned permanently to Australia, where the 'Brent of Bin' series, starting with *Up the Country* (1928), made the pseudonymous author the subject of much speculation. Her best work appeared under her own name, including the early autobiographical novels *All That Swagger* (1936) and *My Career Goes Bung* (1946), and a collection of essays on Australian literature, *Laughter, Not for a Cage* (1956). The annual Miles Franklin awards are now among Australia's most prestigious literary prizes. The popularity of her novels, and the filming of *My Brilliant Career*, have tended to obscure the considerable contribution which she made to the social and professional development of Australian women.
▷M F Barnard, *Miles Franklin* (1967)

FRANKO, Ivan
(1856–1916)

Ukrainian novelist, poet and scholar, born near Drogobych. **Shevchenko** apart, he was the leading writer of his time in the Ukraine. His fiction, of which there are good examples in *The Boa Constrictor and Other Stories* (1957), is influenced by **Zola**, but, its socialist tendencies apart, is richly observant of rural and urban customs. His poetry, not major but skilful and widely read, passed through all the modes of the time, from neo-Romantic to Symbolist. The poem *Moysey* (1905, Eng trans *Moses*, 1938), is said to be 'a jewel of Ukrainian literature'. There is a *Selected Poems* in translation (1948).
▷*Ukrainian Quarterly* (1945–60, passim)

FRANZOS, Karl Emil
(1848–1904)

Austrian novelist, born of Jewish parentage in Podolia on the Austro–Russian border. His themes and settings were taken from Galicia, the Bukovina, south Russia and Romania; his novels, which contain vivid pictures of life among Jews and peasants, include *Aus Halbasien* (1876, 'From Asia Minor'), *Die Juden von Barnow* (1877, 'The Jews of Barnow'), *Ein Kampf ums Recht* (1882, 'A Struggle over the Law') and *Der Pojaz* (1905, 'The Pojaz').

FRASER, George MacDonald
(1925–)

English historical novelist, who grew up in Carlisle and Glasgow. Trained as a journalist, he was Deputy Editor of the *Glasgow Herald* in 1968–9, but following the success of his first novel *Flashman* (1969) he left to become a full-time writer. In this and subsequent novels, starting with *Royal Flash* (1970),

Fraser turned the bully of **Fielding**'s *Tom Brown's Schooldays* into a representative figure of the English caste system and of imperial values, contrasting him in a parallel sequence of books with the more down-to-earth McCauslan. Flashman also appears as an old man in such otherwise unrelated books as *Mr American* (1980), though these too tend to be concerned with Britain's role in a changing world and the responsibilities of the ruling class. Fraser has written effectively for the screen, scripting the James Bond film *Octopussy* (1983) and a 1987 adaptation of the life of Casanova. His war experiences fuelled the surprisingly lyrical and elegiac *Quartered Safe Out Here* (1992).

FRASER, G(eorge) S(utherland)
(1915–80)

Scottish poet, literary critic and university teacher. He was born in Glasgow, but his family moved to Aberdeen and he was educated at St Andrews University. He came to prominence in 1941 when he wrote an introduction to *The White Horseman*, an anthology of prose and verse of the so-called 'New Apocalypse' movement, which emphasized turbulently romantic imagery over the quieter classicism and plain speech of a previous generation. It was, on the face of it, an unlikely affiliation for the quiet, almost schoolmasterly Fraser, and his own verse was less enthusiastically exotic; it is collected in *Poems of G S Fraser* (1981). Fraser spent many years abroad, mostly in Egypt and Eritrea, working as a staff writer for the Ministry of Information, and many of his most moving poems take the form of an exile's letters home. Perhaps his most significant book, however, is *The Modern Writer and His World* (1953, rev edn 1964), in which he argues that 'modernity' was a question of attitude rather than of historical period.
▷*A Stranger and Afraid: Autobiography of an Intellectual* (posthumous 1983)

FRAYN, Michael
(1933–)

English dramatist, journalist and humorist, born in London. A journalist by training, he has published a number of comic novels, among them *The Tin Men* (1965), and *Towards the End of the Morning* (1967), about the newspaper business. His stage plays include *Alphabetical Order* (1975), set in the library of a provincial newspaper; *Clouds* (1976), about two rival journalists in Cuba; *Noises Off* (1982), a frenetic farce about putting on a frenetic farce; and *Benefactors* (1984), a piece about middle-class mores. His finest play is *Make and Break* (1980), a satirical look at the lives of salesmen at a foreign trade fair. He also wrote the script for the

film *Clockwise* (1986), and is a translator of **Anton Chekhov**.

FRÉCHETTE, Louis Honoré
(1839–1908)

'Canadian laureate', born in Lévis, Quebec. He was called to the Bar, and elected to the Dominion parliament in 1874. He published prose works and plays, and his poems *Mes loisirs* (1863), *La voix d'un exil* (1867), which attacked Canadian politics, and others, were 'crowned' by the Académie française.
▷M Dugas, *Un romantique canadien* (1934)

FREDERIC, Harold
(1856–98)

American novelist, born in Utica, New York. After a poverty-stricken youth, he became a journalist and was in 1884 appointed European correspondent of the *New York Times*. He wrote *Seth's Brother's Wife* (1887), *The Return of the O'Mahony* (1892) and others, novels depicting his own background, but his best work is *The Damnation of Theron Ware* (1896), about the intellectual awakening of a young minister.
▷A Briggs, *The Novels of Harold Frederic* (1969)

FREDRO, Count Aleksander
(1793–1876)

Polish memoirist, poet and major comic dramatist (in brilliant verse), born in Suchorów. He fought in the Napoleonic wars, and then returned to farming on his estate. One notable work is the recreation of his Napoleonic years, *Trzy po trzy* (1877, 'Three On Three'), modelled on **Laurence Sterne**'s *Tristram Shandy*. His comedies were of very high quality until he was silenced by a spiteful review by an envious poetaster, whereupon, over-sensitively, he wrote more plays, but would not allow them to be performed. A few of them have been translated, for example, *Dami i huzary* (1825, Eng trans *Ladies and Hussars*, 1925).
▷J Krzyzanowski, *Polish Romantic Literature* (1930)

FREELING, Nicolas
(1927–)

English crime novelist, born in London, who worked throughout Europe as a cook. He is best known as the creator of the Dutch detective, Inspector Van der Valk. He first appeared in *Love in Amsterdam* (1962), and solved many cases over the subsequent decade until the author killed him off in *A Long Silence* (1972). Van der Valk considers crime as being not so much an aberration, but part of the natural fabric of life. This emerges most absorbingly in *Criminal Conversation* (1965), a case in which a banker accuses a neurologist of murder and in which the characters' personalities and motives are studied in depth. Although Van der Valk has been revived in the occasional short story, he has not been wholly resuscitated. Other policemen have taken his place, but Freeling remains justly famed for the earlier novels.

FREEMAN, John
(1880–1929)

English poet, born in London. He rose from clerk to become secretary and director of an insurance company (1927). His *Stone Trees* (1916) and other volumes of poetry made his reputation. He won the Hawthornden Prize with *Poems New and Old* in 1920 and wrote studies of *George Moore* (1922) and *Herman Melville* (1926).
▷G Freeman and Sir John Squires (eds), *John Freeman's Letters* (1936)

FREEMAN, Mary E Wilkins
(1852–1930)

American novelist and story writer, born in Randolph, Massachusetts. Her schooling was interrupted by poor health. In her youth she acted as secretary to the elder **Oliver Wendell Holmes**. Her 238 stories about New England life, not unlike those of Mrs **Gaskell** in *Cranford*, made an important contribution to American regional, or 'local colour', fiction. Paramount amongst these are the 24 tales in *A New England Nun* (1891). She was not so happy in the novel form, but in her late collection of tales *Edgewater People* (1918) she recaptured all her old skill and pathos.

FREILIGRATH, Ferdinand
(1810–76)

German poet and democrat, born in Detmold. He abandoned commerce for literature, but became a protagonist of German democracy and his writings became more and more political. He was obliged to seek refuge in Belgium and Britain for his *Glaubensbekenntnis* (1844, 'Confession of Beliefs'). He returned to Germany in 1848 and became leader of the Democratic party. He was again expelled after a trial for his poem *Die Toten an die Lebenden* (1848, 'The Dead and the Living'), and returned to London in 1851. He translated many English classics into German. He lived in Stuttgart from 1868, and published his *Neue Gedichte* ('New Poems') in 1870.
▷H Eulenberg, *Ferdinand Freiligrath* (1948)

FRENAUD, André
(1907–)

French poet, born in Burgundy, who became impelled to write when he found himself a German prisoner-of-war in 1940. His manner was much influenced by the surrealists, but he is essentially a poet in search of small joyful facts with which he can defeat his own guilty pessimism. His early work was often about the miseries of a France occupied by Nazis. *La Sainte face* (1948, 'The Holy face') and *Il n'y a pas de paradis* (1962, 'There is no Paradise') collected earlier poems. He is represented in the *Penguin Book of French Verse* (1975, ed A Hartley).

FRENCH, Alice, pseud Octave Thanet
(1850–1934)

American short-story writer and novelist. French was born in Massachusetts but lived mainly in Arkansas and Iowa, the states which form the backdrop for her 'local colour' fiction. She was a prolific contributor to national literary magazines and her short stories were, and still are, better regarded than her longer fiction. *Stories of a Western Town* (1893) contains work in her typical vein. French was interested in workers' rights, but advocated co-operatives rather than unions. She was a staunch defender, against editors' objections, of the Arkansan idioms used in her dialogue.

FRENCH, Marilyn
(1929–)

American novelist and feminist scholar, born in New York and educated at Hofstra College and Harvard University. Her first work of fiction was *The Women's Room* (1977), a massive bestseller which, with sympathy and balance, traces its heroine's development from 1950s housewife to emancipated 1970s woman. Her two subsequent novels, *The Bleeding Heart* (1980) and *Her Mother's Daughter* (1987), have brought a strong feminine philosophy to bear on the social and moral dilemmas of the late 20th century. She has examined the female role in literature and society in *Shakespeare's Division of Experience* (1981), *Beyond Power: On Women, Men, and Morals* (1985) and *The War Against Women* (1992).

FRENEAU, Philip Morin
(1752–1832)

American sailor and poet, born in New York. Having written satirical verse in the pre-revolutionary period, he commanded a privateer in the American War of Independence, was captured by the British, and wrote *The British Prison Ship* (1781). He also wrote a number of shorter poems, including 'The Indian Burying Ground' and 'The Wild Honeysuckle'.
▷P M Marsh, *Freneau: Poet and Journalist* (1967); and other works by Marsh

FRENSSEN, Gustav
(1863–1945)
German novelist, born a carpenter's son in Barlt in Holstein. He studied for the church but turned to writing and attracted attention by his *Jörn Uhl* (1901), a novel of peasant life. *Hilligenlei* (1906, 'Holy Land'), a life of Jesus Christ set in a Germanic background, aroused much controversy.
▷W Johnson, *Gustav Frenssen. Art und Ahnen* (1934)

FRÈRE, Maud
(1923–79)
Belgian novelist, born in Brussels. Her first stories were for children, in *Vacances secrètes* (1956, Eng trans *Secret Holiday*, 1957). She then graduated to psychological novels of some substance, including *Guido* (1965).
▷M Pierson-Piérard, *Maud Frère* (1960, in French)

FREUCHEN, Lorentz Peter
(1904–57)
Danish novelist, born in Nykobing. He was an expert on Inuit (Eskimo) life and a leading explorer of Greenland, where his adventurous but stylistically undistinguished novels, such as *Nordkaper* (1929, Eng trans *The Sea Tyrant*, 1932), are set.

FREUD, Sigmund
(1856–1939)
Austrian neurologist who founded psychoanalysis, born in Freiburg, Moravia. The fragment *On Nature* by **Goethe** was instrumental in converting him from legal to medical studies. Although, like **Jung**, he was not himself a creative writer, his influence upon modern literature (and art of all kinds) has been, like that of his one-time associate Jung—who broke away from him—profound and incalculable. He did not, as is so often asserted, 'discover' the unconscious mind; but he provided the first plausible model of the manner—not always as pleasant as the authorities of his time liked—in which it might work. There is hardly a major writer of the 20th century who has not been in some way touched by his theories, the chief one of which was the so-called Oedipus Complex, which propounded that a son is in unconscious conflict with his father for the possession of his mother (or, in a modified form, for his mother's love). His masterpiece is *Die Traumdeutung* (1900, 'The Interpretation of Dreams'). His collected works in translation were issued in 24 volumes between 1953 and 1964.
▷F H Hoffmann, *Freudianism and the Literary Mind* (1945)

FREYRE, Gilberto de Mello
(1900–87)
Brazilian writer and intellectual. He was educated in Rio de Janeiro and in Texas and New York City. After working as a journalist in his native city of Recife (1927–30), he moved to an academic career and came to prominence with a large-scale historical work, *Casa-grande & Senzala* (1933, Eng trans *The Masters and the Slaves*, 1946), which altered previous thinking about colonial Brazil and its relations with Europe. The book won him the Felippe d'Oliveira Award (1934), the first of many prestigious prizes and honorary doctorates. Freyre was hugely prolific, publishing more than 50 books. His poetry and fiction are not highly regarded, but his impact on Brazilian consciousness is immeasurable.
▷D de Melo Menezes, *Gilberto Freyre* (1944, in Spanish)

FREYTAG, Gustav
(1816–95)
German novelist and playwright, born in Kreuzburg in Silesia. From 1839 to 1847 he was *Privatdozent* of German at Breslau University. A deputy to the North German Diet, he attended the Prussian crown prince in the Franco-German campaign (1870). His comedies and other plays, such as *Die Valentine* (1846) and *Die Journalisten* (1853), proved brilliant successes, but his greatest achievement is *Soll und Haben* (1855, Eng trans *Debit and Credit*, 1858), a realistic novel of German commercial life. It was followed by *Die Verlorene Handschrift* (1864, Eng trans *The Lost Manuscript*, 1865), and the series (1872–81) called *Die Ahnen*, ('The Ancestors'). He set down his dramatic theories in *Technik des Dramas* (1863, 'Technique of Drama').
▷H Lindau, *Gustav Freytag* (1907)

FRIDEGÅRD, Jan
(1897–1968)
Swedish novelist, born in Uppland, one of the many working-class writers of the first half of the century. His *Lars Hård* (1935–6) was an outstanding and controversial work. Its eponymous hero is an asocial but thin-skinned cynic whose path leads through personal degradation to salvation brought about by love and religious understanding. Fridegård achieved considerable popularity with his historical novels; a number of his other works reflect his spiritualist beliefs.
▷E Schön, *Jan Fridegård, Proletärdiktaren och folkkulturen* (1978)

FRIED, Erich
(1921–90)
Austrian poet, novelist and translator (notably of **T S Eliot**, **Dylan Thomas** and

Shakespeare), who emigrated to London in 1938 and remained there for the rest of his life. He was born in Vienna, and his parents perished in the Holocaust. His earlier poetry was politically 'unengaged', fashionably modernistic in its techniques, and doggedly optimistic; but he later switched to a more purposeful poetry of engagement. He will probably be best remembered for his fine translations.

FRIEDMAN, Bruce Jay
(1930–)

American novelist. In *Stern* (1962) he mined the same territory as **Philip Roth**'s *Portnoy's Complaint*, creating a funny and often trenchant account of American–Jewish hang-ups. *A Mother's Kisses* (1964) is in very similar vein, but *The Dick* (1971) marked a change of pace and tone, as well as subject-matter, and is considerably underrated. His most recent novel is *Tokyo Woes* (1985). Friedman has also written short stories, collected in *Far from the City of Class* (1963) and *Let's Hear It for a Beautiful Guy* (1984).

FRIEL, Brian
(1929–)

Irish playwright and short-story writer, born in Omagh. His first play, *This Doubtful Paradise* (1959), was produced in Belfast. His first major success was *Philadelphia, Here I Come!* (1964), a play about emigration and the relationship between a man and his son. Friel's writing is poetic, sometimes ironic, always compassionate and poignant. He often concentrates upon the relation between people, language, custom and the land, these forming the principal theme of his most important plays, *Translations* (1980), and the enormously successful *Dancing at Lughnasa* (1990), both of which are set in County Donegal. The first looks at a group of English soldiers anglicizing Celtic placenames in order to make new maps in 1883, while the second, set in 1936, concentrates on the sad, isolated but resiliently optimistic lives of the five adult Mundy sisters. With actor Stephen Rea, Friel was a co-founder of the Field Day Theatre Company (1980). His short-story collections include *A Saucer of Larks* (1962) and *The Diviner: Brian Friel's Best Short Stories* (1983).
▷U Dantanus, *Brian Friel* (1988)

FRIEL, George
(1910–75)

Scottish novelist, born in Glasgow, where he lived and worked throughout his life. Educated at St Mungo's Academy and Glasgow University (the only one of seven children to go to university), he trained as a teacher at Jordanhill College, Glasgow. When war broke out he served in the RAOC and then returned to teaching, a profession he grew to loathe and distrust, although he always retained his concern for children. His experiences at the chalkface are at the heart of *Mr Alfred M.A.* (1972), which has been described as 'one of the great Scottish novels'. The story of the eponymous teacher's disillusionment and downfall, betrayed by one of his wretched girl pupils, it eloquently and ironically depicts a society and an education system in a state of disintegration, the result of a breakdown in communication. Other novels include *The Bank of Time* (1959), *The Boy Who Wanted Peace* (1964), *Grace and Miss Partridge* (1969) and *An Empty House* (1975).

FRIIS MOLLER, Kai
(1888–1960)

Danish minor poet, critic and, mainly, translator (**Kipling**, **Baudelaire**, and many others). He was born and died in Copenhagen. He is said to have been feared, as a literary journalist, for his sarcasm.

FRISCH, Max Rudolph
(1911–91)

Swiss novelist and playwright, born in Zürich. In 1933, forced by economic circumstances to abandon the study of German literature at Zürich University, he became a journalist. Later he trained as an architect, but not before publishing *Blätter aus dem Brotsack* (1940, Eng trans *Leaves from a Knapsack*, 1942), while serving with the Swiss frontier guard. In 1958 he became the first foreigner to be awarded the **Büchner** Prize of the German Academy for language and poetry. His bibliography is extensive but as a novelist he is chiefly known outside German-speaking Europe for the novels *Stiller* (1954, Eng trans *I'm Not Stiller*, 1958), and *Homo Faber* (1957, Eng trans 1959) and *Der Mensch erscheint im Holozän* (1979, Eng trans *Man in the Holocene*, 1980). He has had international success as a playwright after being a disciple of **Bertolt Brecht** in the 1940s, *Biedermann und die Brandstifter* (1953, Eng trans *The Fire Raisers*, 1962) and *Andorra* (1961, Eng trans 1962) having become modern stage classics.
▷U Weisstein, *Frisch* (1967)

FRISCHLIN, Phillipp Nikodemus
(1547–90)

German dramatist and humanist writer, born in Balingen. His life was made difficult by his ardent temperament and his sharply satirical tongue, and he died while trying to escape from a castle in which he had been imprisoned for telling the truth too scurrilously. A good Latinist, he wrote plays in that language; he

also translated five plays by **Aristophanes** into Latin. Only one surviving play is in German.
▷D F Strauss, *Nicodemus Frischlin* (1856, in German)

FRISHMAN, David
(1862–1922)

Hebrew writer of short fiction, poet, editor, translator (of **Goethe**, **Shakespeare**, **Tagore**, and many other eminent writers) and critic, born in Zguerzsh, near Łodz. Some of the stories of this brilliant and versatile scholar deal with ghetto life; his posthumous *Bimidbar* (1923) is a series of tales based on episodes in the Pentateuch, and represent his genius at its most profound.
▷M Waxman, *A History of Jewish Literature* (1960)

FRÖDING, Gustav
(1860–1911)

Swedish poet, born in Alstern near Karlstad. He studied at Uppsala and became a schoolmaster and journalist, but suffered bouts of mental illness. He is considered the greatest Swedish lyric poet, often compared to **Robert Burns**, combining dialect and folksong and homespun philosophy in his portrayal of local characters, as in *Guitarr och dragharmonika* (1891, 'Guitar and Harmonica'), *Nya dikter* (1894, 'New Poems') and *Räggler å paschaser* (1896, 'Drops and Fragments'). The gentle humour of his earlier poems later turned to a tragic quest for the Holy Grail.
▷J Landquist, *Gustav Fröding, en biografi* (1956)

FROMENTIN, Eugène
(1820–76)

French novelist and painter, born in La Rochelle. Visits to Algeria and the Near East provided him with abundant material for his paintings, which betray the influence of Delacroix. His three travel books also provide vivid pictures of the Algerian scene. But he is best known as the author of *Dominique* (1862, Eng trans 1932), a nostalgic autobiographical novel, and *Les Maîtres d'autrefois* (1876, Eng trans *Masters of Past Time*, 1948), written during a tour of Belgian and Dutch art galleries, which contains some brilliant art criticism.
▷A R Evans, *The Literary Art of Eugène Fromentin* (1964)

FROST, Robert Lee
(1874–1963)

American lyric poet, 'the voice of New England', born in San Francisco, the son of a New England father and Scottish mother. He studied at Dartmouth College and Harvard, but did not graduate from either.

Betweeen 1899 and 1912 he worked as a teacher, cobbler and poultry farmer. He spent the years 1912 to 1915 in Britain, where he made contact with **Edward Thomas** and **Ezra Pound** and was encouraged by **Rupert Brooke**, **Lascelles Abercrombie** and **Wilfrid Gibson**. Pound's review of *A Boy's Will* (1913) and *North of Boston* (1914) helped bring Frost an international reputation, and he returned to the USA in triumph after Britain became involved in World War I. He became Professor of English at Amherst (1916) and cofounded the Bread Loaf School of English at Middlebury College. He was Professor of Poetry at Harvard from 1939 to 1943 before returning to Amherst (1949–63). His verse, which was seen as quintessentially New England, aimed to capture the 'abstract vitality of our speech'. Though ostensibly pastoral, it was never narrowly regionalist and was marked by a tragic vein, often overlooked but memorably defined by **Lionel Trilling** at Frost's 85th birthday dinner when the critic controversially talked of Frost's 'terrifying' vision. He was awarded the Pulitzer Prize in 1924, 1931 and 1937, and received a US senate citation of honour in 1950. His standing with the American establishment was secured when he read 'The Gift Outright' at John F Kennedy's inauguration. A *Complete Poems* (to date) appeared in 1949; all the extant verse was collected and edited by Edward Connery Latham two decades later, following posthumous editions of the letters (1964) and the prose (1966). Poems such as 'The Death of the Hired Man', 'Stopping by Woods on a Snowy Evening' and 'Out, Out' are among the most anthologized in American literature.
▷W H Pritchard, *Frost: a literary life reconsidered* (1984)

FRUG, Simon Samuel
(1860–1916)

One of the earliest Yiddish poets, born in southern Russia. He helped to create a viable Jewish poetry, but his best work remains his earliest, written before 1888, in Russian.

FRUGONI, Carlo
(1692–1768)

Italian poet, born in Genoa, laureate at the courts of the Farnese and the Bourbons. He wrote an abundance of pleasant, skilful, empty verse, absurdly over-praised in its time, and now the object of a peculiar scorn. He himself suspected it of being of small worth. He was bitterly attacked by **Alfieri**, and one of his apologists called him 'the uncorrupted father of corrupted children'.

FRUGONI, Francesco
(c.1620–c.1686)

Italian Baroque poet and prose writer, born in Genoa, whose chief work is his series of 12 stories called *Del cane di Diogene* (1689), describing the barkings of a dog against all the peoples and customs, of all times, of whom Frugoni could think. This massive work has not yet had the attention it deserves, although **Croce** wrote about it, and Frugoni is often omitted from dictionaries in favour of his inferior namesake **Carlo Frugoni**.

FRY, Christopher Harris
(1907–)

English dramatist, born in Bristol, educated at Bedford Modern School. He combined being a schoolmaster with a love of the stage, which became a full-time occupation on his appointment as Director of Tunbridge Wells Repertory Players (1932–6). In 1940 he became Director of the Playhouse at Oxford, having in the meantime written two pageant-plays, *Thursday's Child* and *The Tower*, and also *The Boy with a Cart*, a charming rustic play on the subject of the Sussex saint, Cuthman. After service in the Non-Combatant Corps during World War II he began a series of outstanding plays in free verse, often with undertones of religion and mysticism, including *A Phoenix too Frequent* (1946), *The Lady's not for Burning* (1949), *Venus Observed* (1950), *A Sleep of Prisoners* (1951), *The Dark is Light Enough* (1954), *Curtmantle* (1962) and *A Yard of Sun* (1970). He has also produced highly successful translations of **Jean Anouilh** and **Jean Giraudoux**.
▷D Stanford, *Christopher Fry* (1954)

FUCHS, Daniel
(1909–93)

American novelist and short-story writer. He grew up in New York City and used his background to great effect in the sequence of novels known collectively as *The Williamsburg Trilogy*, first published in that form in 1972. It comprises *Summer in Williamsburg* (1934), *Homage to Blenholt* (1936) and *Low Company* (1937), which was unaccountably 'translated' as *Neptune Beach* on its publication in the UK (1937). The stories are bleak, though not without humour, and tap into the same transatlantic link that saw the French Existentialists find common cause with the work of **John Dos Passos** and with **Faulkner**'s 'potboiling' *Sanctuary*. In 1971 Fuchs returned to fiction with a satiric portrayal of California in *West of the Rockies*. His short stories were collected in *The Apathetic Bookie Joint* (1979).

FUCINI, Renato, pseud Neri Tanfucio
(1843–1921)

Italian writer, born in Monterotondo, near Pisa, the son of a country doctor. He studied agriculture and engineering in Pisa, and became city engineer in Florence. He had a bright wit which found outlet in dialect verse, published as *Cento Sonetti* (1872, 'A Hundred Sonnets'). When Florence ceased to be a capital city he lost his post and retired to the country. *Le veglie di Neri* (1884, 'The Vigils of Neri'), a collection of tales, is his best-known work. *All'aria aperta* (1897, 'In the Open') is reckoned the best modern collection of Italian humorous novellas. He also wrote books for children, and personal anecdotes.
▷ *Renato Fucini* (1943)

FUENTES, Carlos
(1928–)

Mexican novelist and playwright, born in Panama City. While very young he travelled extensively as his father changed diplomatic posts. Educated at the Colegio Frances Morelos, his graduate studies took him to the National University of Mexico and the Institut des Hautes Études Internationales in Geneva, which led to a career in international affairs. A secretary of the Mexican delegation to the International Labor Organization, he eventually became cultural attaché to the Mexican Embassy in Geneva (1950–2) and press secretary to the United Nations Information Centre, Mexico City. He served as the Mexican ambassador to France (1975–7), and has held a variety of teaching posts. An energetic cultural promoter, writer of articles and reviewer, he has published prolifically since his first collection of fantastic, myth-inspired short-stories, *Los dias enmascarados* ('The Masked Days') in 1954. Many of his novels have been published in English, among them *Terra nostra* (1975, Eng trans 1976 (US); 1977 (UK)), regarded as his masterpiece, the culmination and synthesis of his novel-writing practice and thought on the identity and destiny of Spain and Latin America.
▷D de Guzman, *Carlos Fuentes* (1972)

FUGARD, Athol
(1932–)

South African dramatist and theatre director, born in Middleburg, Cape Province, and educated at Port Elizabeth Technical College and Cape Town University. After leaving university in 1953 he worked as a seaman and journalist before becoming a stage manager and settling firmly into a theatrical career in 1959 as actor, director and playwright. Since 1965 he has been director of the Serpent Players in Port Elizabeth, and in 1972 co-founded the Space Experimental Theatre, Cape Town. His plays are set in contemporary South Africa, but his presentation of the bleakness and frustration of life for those especially on the fringes of society raises their political and social deprivation to the level of universal human tragedy. His work has met with official opposition; *Blood Knot* (1960), portraying two coloured brothers, one light- and one dark-skinned, was censored, and some of his work has only been published and produced abroad. His plays include *Boesman and Lena* (1969), *Statements After an Arrest under the Immorality Act* (1972), *Sizwe Banzi is Dead* (1973), *Dimetos* (1976) and *A Lesson from Aloes* (1979). He has also written film scripts and a novel, *Tsotsi* (1980). Fugard has become increasingly popular in Britain, and later plays, *Master Harold and the Boys* (1982), *The Road to Mecca* (1984) and *A Place with the Pigs* (1987), have been staged at the National Theatre. The latter play veers away from the South African themes of his earlier work, being inspired by a newspaper story about a Red Army deserter who hid in a pigsty for over 40 years.

FUKAO Sumako
(1893–1974)

Japanese poet, born into an old but declining samurai family in Hyogo. A close friend of **Akiko Yosano**, she was extremely open, by Japanese standards, to foreign influences, modelling herself at one point on **Colette**. Her verse, full of intense, personal, sometimes erotic themes, underwent a severe change of style after Japan's defeat in 1945, when she began to be motivated by social *angst*, and a despair at the state of the country. She never recovered her previous good spirits; though she lived to see Japan's rise to economic prosperity, her poetic response to this was to complain in verse about the cost in damage to the environment and the erosion of the rights of the individual.

FULDA, Ludwig
(1862–1932)

German playwright, born in Frankfurt am Main. He is less important for his plays—deriving from **Ibsen**, **Hauptmann** and others—than for the form of the fairy-play, which he developed in *Der Talisman* (1893), which is an adaptation of 'The Emperor's Clothes' by **Hans Christian Andersen**. He greatly influenced another much more substantial dramatist, **Yevgeny Shvarts**.

FULLER, Charles H, Jr
(1939–)

American playwright, born in Philadelphia, and noted for his sensitive, unbiased but unflinching exploration of relationships, especially those between blacks and whites, and between blacks and a white-dominated bureaucracy. Among his most successful plays are *The Brownsville Raid* (1976), based upon a true incident in 1906, in which an entire US Army regiment was honourably discharged after none of the 167 black soldiers admitted inciting a riot on Brownsville, Texas. The Pulitzer Prize-winning *A Soldier's Play* (1981) is also set in the army, this time in a barracks in Louisiana during World War II, and deals with the aftermath of the murder of an unpopular sergeant. Fuller is co-founder and co-director of the Philadelphia Arts Theater.

FULLER, Henry Blake
(1857–1929)

American poet, critic and novelist, born in Chicago. His work is now somewhat underrated. His first novel, published under the pseudonym of 'Stanton Page', was a romantic tale set in Italy; but his *The Cliff Dwellers* (1892) was the first true 'city novel' in American literature. **Edmund Wilson** thought him superior to **William Howells**. Certainly his naturalism, which was taken up by **Norris**, **Dreiser** and **Farrell**, was far more thoroughgoing than that of Howells. The title 'cliff dwellers' describes the denizens of skyscrapers, and the novel itself savagely depicts the ugly fruitlessness of the quest for wealth and wealth alone. The European romances with which he interspersed his serious books are far less good, but *On the Stairs* (1918), once again depicting squalid materialist struggles, and the posthumous *Not on the Screen* (1930), a satire on the film industry as well as a story of Chicago, are both excellent realistic novels. A minor poet himself, he helped make *Poetry Chicago*, for a time, the most important poetry magazine in the world.
▷C Van Vechten, *Henry Blake Fuller* (1929); C M Griffin, *Henry Blake Fuller: A Critical Biography* (1939)

FULLER, Roy Broadbent
(1912–91)

English poet and novelist, born in Oldham. He went to school in Blackpool, trained as a solicitor, and spent his professional career as a solicitor with building societies. His first collection of poetry, *Poems*, appeared in 1939 and was, he fully admitted, very strongly influenced by **W H Auden**. His experience of war in the Royal Navy (1941–5) prompted *The Middle of a War* (1942) and *A Lost Season* (1944). This saw the development of the note of characteristic self-criticism which was to become an integral part of his later poetry. His traditionalist attitude kept him apart from the strong current of neo-Romantic revival initiated by **Dylan Thomas** after the war, but his *Brutus's Orchard* (1957) and *Collected Poems* (1962) established him as a major poet, and his later works include *Buff* (1965), *Song Cycle from a Record Sleeve* (1972), *An Old War* (1974), *From the Joke Shop* (1975) and *Retreads* (1979). His novels show great skill in observation and intricacy of plot, and include *Second Curtain* (1953), *The Ruined Boys* (1959), *The Perfect Fool* (1963) and *The Carnal Island* (1970). He was Professor of Poetry at Oxford 1968–73, and *Owl and Artificers* (1971) is a stimulating and entertaining collection of his lectures. He also published the autobiographical *Souvenirs* (1980), *Vamp Till Ready* (1982), *The Strange and the Good* (1989) and *Spanner and Pen* (1991).

▷A E Austin, *Roy Fuller* (1979)

FULLERTON, Mary Eliza
(1868–1946)

Australian poet, novelist and journalist, born in Glenmaggie, Victoria, who wrote under various names. As 'Alpenstock' she contributed to contemporary journals. In her own name she published three books of verse and wrote a series of novels: *Two Women* (1923), *The People of the Timber* (1925) and *A Juno in the Bush* (1930). Encouraged by **Miles Franklin** she published two more collections of her verse under the pseudonym 'E' in the belief that it would not receive recognition under a female name. *Moles Do So Little with their Privacy* (1942) was followed by *The Wonder and the Apple* (1946).

FURPHY, Joseph
(1843–1912)

Australian writer, who described himself as 'half bushman and half bookworm'. Born in Yering, Yarra Valley, Victoria, of hard-working and well-read Irish emigrant parents, he worked as a farmer and a bullock-driver before moving to Shepparton, Victoria, in 1883. There he worked at the iron-foundry which had been established by his elder brother. This security enabled him to contribute, under the name 'Tom Collins', a series of articles to the *Bulletin* magazine, and to write a 1220-page manuscript, *Such is Life: Being Certain Extracts from the Diary of Tom Collins*. After much revision and abridgment, this novel was published in 1903. Some excised sections were published after his death as *Rigby's Romance* (1921, rev edn 1946) and *The Buln-Buln and the Brolga* (1948). His reputation, however, rests on his one major work with its credo 'Temper, democratic; bias, offensively Australian', which encapsulated his hard-working philosophy and marked a move away from the common romantic concept of Australia's pioneering days. *The Poems of Joseph Furphy* was published posthumously in 1916.

▷M Franklin, *Joseph Furphy* (1944)

FUSSENEGGER, Gertrud
(1912–)

Austrian novelist and poet, born in Pilsen. She has not attracted much critical attention, but *Die Brüder von Lasawa* (1948, 'The Brothers von Lasawa'), which is typical of her historical novels, is a vivid and worthy tale of the Thirty Years War.

FUTABATEI Shimei
(1864–1909)

Japanese novelist, born in Edo (Tokyo), and of enormous historical importance as he was the first writer of Japanese fiction to attempt to make the written word as intelligible as the spoken, in contrast to his predecessors and his near-contemporary **Izumi**, who wrote in a form of literary Japanese far removed from everyday speech. *Ukigumo* (1887, 'Drifting Clouds') broke new ground in being composed in the vernacular. Futabatei was also the first translator into Japanese of the works of **Gogol** and **Turgenev**, again employing vernacular language.

▷M G Ryan, *Japan's First Modern Novel* (1967)

G

GABORIAU, Émile
(1835–73)

French writer of detective fiction, born in Saujon in Charente-Inférieure. He is credited with inaugurating the *roman policier* in France. He had already contributed to some of the smaller Parisian papers, when he leapt to fame with *L'Affaire Lerouge* (1866), featuring his detective Lecoq. It was followed by *Le Dossier 113* (1867), *Monsieur Lecoq* (1869), *Les Esclaves de Paris* (1869, 'Slaves of Paris'), *La Corde au cou* (1873, 'Rope Around the Neck'), and several others.

GABRYELLA see ZMICHOWSKA, Narcyza

GACE BRULÉ
(b.c.1160)

French troubadour poet, in the Provençal tradition. Little is known of his life. His poems, almost 70 of which survive, deal, conventionally, with courtly love, but are distinguished from those of his contemporaries by a slightly more melancholic air than is found elsewhere.
▷H P Dyggve, *Gace Brulé, Trouvere Champenois* (1951)

GADDA, Carlo Emilio
(1893–1973)

Italian novelist from Milan, who worked throughout his active life as an engineer. In his early days he was associated with the group of writers who published in the Florentine avant-garde magazine *Solaria*— these included **Vittorini** and **Montale**. He had published many fragments of his first, and extraordinary novel, *Quer pasticciaccio brutto de via Merulana* (1957, Eng trans *That Awful Mess on the Via Merulana*, 1965), before the whole appeared. It is a unique novel in many ways: in its use of dialect, in its adaptation (almost beyond recognition) of techniques invented or employed by **Dos Passos**, **Joyce** and other modernists, and in its strange plot, which concerns a police officer's failure to solve a murder case. *La cognizione del dolore* (1963, rev edn 1970, Eng trans *Acquainted With Grief*, 1969) is set in a South America which is recognizably Italy; *Eros e Priapo (Da furore a cenere)* (1967, 'Eros and Priapus (From Frenzy to Ashes)') is a profound analysis of Italian fascism. When Gadda was charged with obscurity, he claimed the same of reality—and remains one of the most substantial and critically well explored of modernist writers.
▷R M Adams, *After Joyce: Studies in Fiction after Ulysses* (1977)

GADDIS, William
(1922–)

American novelist, born in New York City. He was educated at Harvard University, worked for the *New Yorker* (1946–7), lived and travelled abroad, and freelanced as a speech and filmscript writer from 1956 until the 1970s. He has written three novels: *The Recognitions* (1955), a densely allusive post-Christian epic about art, forgery, money and magic; *JR* (1976), about an 11-year-old ragged capitalist operating from pay phones and post-office money orders; and *Carpenter's Gothic* (1985), in which a Vietnam War veteran works as a media consultant for a fundamentalist preacher. An ambitious satirist, he is one of America's most prominent contemporary novelists. He won the National Book Award in 1976.
▷S Moore, *A Reader's Guide to William Gaddis's The Recognitions* (1982)

GÁDONYI, Géza
(1863–1922)

Hungarian novelist, poet and dramatist, born in Agárd, who lived a hermit-like existence in Eger. He owed his initial popularity to cheap but skilfully written and humorous crime books; but *Az én falum* (1898) was in a different class from all that had preceded it, being a vivid if socially uncontroversial portrait of rural life. Following this he wrote three historical novels, which are still read, including *A láthatatlan ember* (1902, Eng trans *Slave of the Huns*, 1969), about Attila's Huns. His work, unusually, became more interesting as he grew older and more mystical. *A bor* (1902) is a good stage comedy of village life.

GAINES, Ernest J(ames)
(1933–)

Black American novelist, whose powerful writing draws heavily on his childhood in rural Louisiana. His work might be characterized as post-**Faulkner**, written from the other side of the racial fence. His first novel, *Catherine Carmier* (1964), had something of the hysteria inherent in Faulkner's, and other white Southerners', approach to miscegenation. Gaines came to wider prominence with his third book, the remarkable *Autobiography of Miss Jane Pittman* (1971), which focused on a centenarian black woman whose life and troubles encapsulated the history of the Afro–American people since Emancipation. It was subsequently made into a successful film. In his most ambitious book, *A Gathering of Old Men* (1983), Gaines revived the multiperspectival style favoured by Faulkner to tell the story of a violent stand-off between white racists and a black man accused of murdering a Cajun farmer.

GAISER, Gerd
(1908–76)

German novelist and painter, born in Oberriexingen, Württemberg, who served as a fighter pilot throughout World War II. He has been accused by certain critics of continuing the fascist spirit under concealed forms; another view is that he merely remained extremely conservative, as well as critical of the Federal Republic and its 'economic miracle'. Sometimes, certainly, he sounds, in his archaic and heroic descriptions of dream-like trances of emotional elitism, like a late expressionist writer of Nazi persuasions. Of his novels, one in particular stands out: *Die sterbende Jagd* (1953, Eng trans *The Falling Leaf*, 1956). This describes the deterioration of morale in, and destruction of, a Nazi fighter squadron towards the end of World War II. This depiction of life in the air—although it owed something to another airforce writer, *Reichskultursenator* and Nazi Richard Euringer—had never been done before.
▷B Keith-Smith (ed), *Essays in Contemporary German Literature* (1966)

GALCZYNSKI, Konstanty
(1905–53)

Polish poet, born in Warsaw. He became well known when he started to contribute short poems to the magazine *Kwadryga*, and became a member of the literary group named after it. He was taken prisoner by the Nazis when they seized Poland, and set to forced labour—an experience that may have contributed to the heart attack from which he prematurely died. He could not satisfy the communists, and his efforts to please them, although embarrassing to him—even if possibly ironic—were not successful. His poetry at its best set out to please no one, rather the contrary, and he is one of Poland's most original talents, a writer of a uniquely grotesque and mocking poetry. Titles include

Zaczurowana dorozka (1948, 'The Enchanted Coach'). However, he remains little read, and hardly translated, outside Poland.
▷C Milosz, *The History of Polish Literature* (1969)

GALE, Norman
(1862–1942)

English minor poet, editor and memorable writer on the pleasure of cricket. He edited a very early selection (1901) from the poetry of **John Clare**, and was thus a (now forgotten) pioneer, with **Arthur Symons**, in the rehabilitation of this major poet. Gale's *Collected Poems* appeared in 1914.

GALE, Zona
(1874–1938)

American novelist, story writer and dramatist, born in Portage, Wisconsin. Her earliest, regional stories, and her first novel, *Romance Island* (1906), were marred by excessive sentimentality, but at the same time so acutely observed that it was evident that she was already a writer of unusual and delicate powers. She was scorned and disliked for her increasing pacifism and feminism; but, with the novel *Birth* (1918), in which she anticipated **Duhamel**'s *Salavin*, the iron finally entered her soul; she dramatized this in 1924 as *Mr Pitt*. Meanwhile, with *Miss Lulu Bett* (1920), appearing in the same year as (and artistically superior to) **Sinclair Lewis**'s *Main Street*, she became famous. Her dramatization of it won her a Pulitzer Prize (1921). Always mystical, she turned to **Gurdjieff** and to Orage, who was teaching the latter's ideas in New York; this strengthened her later work, such as the autobiographical *Portage, Wisconsin* (1928), the story collection *Yellow Gentians and Blue* (1927) and the novel *Papa le Fleur* (1933), now neglected and too hastily written off, giving it a new psychological accuracy and confidence. She became an avid supporter of La Follette's Progressive Party. The title of the biography of her by her fellow-Wisconsin author **August Derleth** is singularly appropriate: *Still, Small Voice* (1940).

GALLAGHER, Tess
(1932–)

American poet, born in Port Angeles, Washington, and educated in Seattle (where one of her teachers was **Theodore Roethke**) and in Iowa City. Her Irish ancestry was explored in her third collection, *Under Stars* (1978), which lacks the sheer force of its predecessor *Instructions to the Double* (1976). Her characteristic tone at this period was elegiac, but without undue sentimentality, and she favoured a strong, syllabic style that registers physical sensation and emotion vividly but without sentimentality and may still have owed something to Roethke. *Portable Kisses* and *On Your Own* both appeared in 1978, the year that Gallagher—twice divorced—began living with the short-story writer **Raymond Carver**, whom she married shortly before his death. *Willingly* (1984) demonstrates her ability to create 'voices' which are rhetorically individual and far removed from the prevailing 'confessional' mode of the previous generation in American verse.

▷ Interview in *Ironwood* (October 1979)

GALLANT, Mavis
(1922–)

Canadian short-story writer and novelist, born in Montreal. Her father was English, her mother German–Russian–Breton, and she spent her childhood going from school to school, 17 in all, which made education 'virtually impossible'. Living entirely by writing, she contributes mainly to the *New Yorker* from her home in Paris. She has written two novels, *Green Water, Green Sky* (1959) and *A Fairly Good Time* (1970), several collections of short stories, and a diary of the 1968 street troubles in Paris.

GALLEGOS, Rómulo
(1884–1969)

Venezualan novelist, born in Caracas. In his country's first democratic elections (1948) Gallegos became President, but his liberalism displeased the military and certain powerful elements in the United States, and he was deposed within a few months. He lived in exile until 1958, when he was welcomed back as an honoured hero. He published a collection of stories in 1913, and in 1920 his first novel, *El último Solar* ('The Last of the Solars'), a lively and pessimistic account of corrupt politicians, failed idealism, and decadent artists. Then in 1929 he published his most famous novel, and the only one to have been translated; *Doña Bárbara* (Eng trans 1931). This is about a barbaric cattle rancher, Doña Bárbara, and her encroachments on the land of her neighbour. This made Gallegos so famous that the dictator, **Goméz**, bribed him with a senate seat—it would have meant death to refuse, so Gallegos accepted, but then used his health as an excuse not to attend sessions of the senate before, in 1931, fleeing Venezuela for a voluntary exile of four years, until Gomez died. He wrote more capable novels, but *Doña Bárbara* remains his greatest.

▷ L Dunham, *Rómulo Gallegos: vida y obra* (1957)

GALLICO, Paul William
(1897–1976)

American novelist and short-story writer, born in New York City. Having graduated from Columbia University, Gallico became a journalist before publishing his first novel, *The Adventures of Hiram Holliday*, in 1939. He is mainly remembered, however, for his shorter works, especially the hugely successful *The Snow Goose*, (1941). Set on the Essex marshes on the eve of Dunkirk, it is the poignant story of a young girl and a lonely, crippled man who care for an injured Canada Goose. Other popular Gallico stories which continue his theme of love and faith, include *The Small Miracle* (1951), and the popular Mrs Harris series, about a redoubtable London char-lady. In 1969 Gallico published *The Poseidon Adventure*, later turned into a successful film.

GALLUS, Gaius Cornelius
(c.70–26 BC)

Roman poet, born in Forum Julii (Fréjus) in Gaul. He lived in Rome and was a friend of **Virgil**. Appointed prefect of Egypt by Augustus, he was recalled and banished, and committed suicide. He was considered the founder of the Roman love elegy, from his four books of elegies upon his mistress 'Lycoris' (in reality the actress Cytheris). Only part of one line of his verse survives.

▷ J P Boucler, *Gaius Cornelius Gallus* (1966)

GALSWORTHY, John
(1867–1933)

English novelist, playwright and winner of the Nobel Prize for literature, born in Coombe, Surrey. Educated at Harrow and New College, Oxford, he was called to the Bar in 1890, but chose to travel and set up as a writer. He met **Joseph Conrad** and they became lifelong friends. He published his first book, a collection of short stories, *From the Four Winds*, in 1897, under the pseudonym John Sinjohn. In 1906 he had a success with his first play, *The Silver Box*, and in the same year published *The Man of Property*, the first in his celebrated *Forsyte Saga* series (the others were *In Chancery*, 1920, and *To Let*, 1921). In these novels is recorded a departed way of life, that of the affluent middle class which ruled England before World War I. The class is criticized on account of its possessiveness, but there is also nostalgia, for Galsworthy, as a man born into that class, could appreciate its virtues. This nostalgia deepens in what was collectively entitled *A Modern Comedy* (1929), which includes *The White Monkey* (1924), *The Silver Spoon* (1926) and *Swan Song* (1928). In this second cycle of the Saga the post-war generation is under scrutiny, but not without the author's appreciation of their plight in an age in which their world had crashed. Among his other novels are *The Island Pharisees* (1904), *The Country House* (1907), *Fraternity* (1909) and

The Patrician (1911). He was also a prolific playwright, and produced more than 30 plays for the London stage. They best illustrate his reforming zeal, and also his sentimentality. *Strife* (1909) shows employers and men locked in a four-month struggle, which ends through the death of the strike-leader's wife. *Justice* (1910) helped to achieve its object of humanizing the penal code. *The Skin Game* (1920) attempts to hold the scales between the aristocratic Mr Hillcrist and the rich parvenu Hornblower, but the latter is so vulgar that sympathies are tipped against him. Technically these plays are first-rate theatre but are marred, especially in the later ones, *A Bit o' Love* (1915) and *Loyalties* (1922), by the parsimony of the language in dialogue which did well enough in the novels but makes the plays appear rather bare. He won the Nobel Prize for literature in 1932.

▷D Holloway, *John Galsworthy* (1968)

GALT, John
(1779–1839)

Scottish novelist and Canadian pioneer, born in Irvine, Ayrshire, the son of a sea-captain. Educated at Greenock Grammar School, he became a junior clerk in a local merchant's firm in 1796. After contributing to local journals, he moved to London in 1804 and set up in business as a merchant. The venture was not a success, and from 1809 to 1811 he travelled for his health's sake in the Levant, where he met **Byron**. On his return he published *Letters from the Levant* and other accounts of his travels. He busied himself in various business posts, and wrote a number of school textbooks under the pseudonym 'Rev T Clark'. He then started to write novels for *Blackwood's Magazine*. *The Ayrshire Legatees* appeared in 1820, followed by *The Steam-Boat* in 1821. Its successor, *The Annals of the Parish* (1821), is his masterpiece, in which the description of events in the life of a parish minister throws interesting light on contemporary social history. He produced in quick succession *Sir Andrew Wylie* (1822), *The Provost* (1822) and *The Entail* (1823). His historical romances were less successful. He went to Canada in 1826, founded the town of Guelph, and played a prominent part in organizing immigration, but returned ruined in 1829, and produced a new novel, *Lawrie Todd* (1830), followed by *The Member* (1832), on corruption in politics. He also wrote a *Life of Byron* (1830) and an autobiography (1834). In his depiction of life in small towns and villages Galt has few rivals. He possesses rich humour, genuine pathos and a rare mastery of Scottish dialect.

▷I Gordon, *John Galt: a life of a writer* (1972)

GÁLVEZ, Manuel
(1887–1962)

Argentinian novelist and poet, born in Paraná into a Spanish family. Educated by Jesuits, he went to Buenos Aires and there founded a literary review and became an inspector of schools. His first books were pallid collections of *modernista* poetry. Like **Maurras**, he was deaf, and also like Maurras, he was politically reactionary—although his Catholicism was genuine, whereas the atheist Frenchman's was political. But he had begun as a socialist, was learned, interested in social issues, and never essentially illiberal—his main fault has been said to lie in his 'religious bigotry'. His master, too, was the liberal **Benito Pérez Galdós**, although his avowed ambition was to achieve for Argentinian society what **Balzac** achieved for French. In his prolific fiction he does not succeed in reconciling the various impulses that move him—naturalist zest, Catholic piety, authoritarian irritability, but he is always interesting. It is to be regretted that his inferior *Miercoles santo* (1930, Eng trans *Holy Wednesday*, 1934) should be available in English but that his tensest and finest novel, *El mal metafísico* (1917, 'Metaphysical Evil'), a psychological study of an unfortunate at odds with society, should not. He wrote a panoramic three-part novel about the war with Paraguay, and a life of Rosas.

GAMA, José Basilio da
(1740–95)

Brazilian poet, born in São José do Rio das Mortes in Minais Gerais province. He became a Jesuit novice, was expelled along with the rest of the Society in 1760, returned to Portugal, and there abandoned it. Pombal, virtual ruler of Portugal, suspected him of Jesuitry, and he therefore incorporated into the epic poem *O Uraguai!* (1769), on the Portuguese–Spanish war against the Native Americans, many attacks on the Jesuits. He was not able to be sincere in his expression, but it seems that his sympathy with the Native Americans was genuine, and that he deserves his reputation of being the first poet to introduce them into Brazilian poetry.

▷D M Driver, *The Indian in Brazilian Literature* (1942)

GAMBOA, Federico
(1864–1939)

Mexican novelist and dramatist, born in Mexico City. One of Mexico's leading naturalists, he began by translating from the French, and thus got to know the novels of **Zola** very well. His earlier fiction was crude and sensationalist, but it became subtler, and *Santa* (1903), 'Saint', although on the almost too well-worn naturalist theme of prostitution, deserved its status as Mexico's first bestseller. He went on to write several more novels and plays of the same type. He is now remembered as a good storyteller rather than as a precursor of the more important novelists of Mexico.

GANIVET, Angel
(1865–98)

Spanish essayist, novelist and thinker. He was almost equal in importance to, but not as well recognized outside his own country as, **Miguel Unamuno** (with whom he had an important and eventually published correspondence) in the formation of the 'Generation of '98'. Ganivet's was a divided personality: on the one hand strict and ethical, on the other adventurously promiscuous. Knowing that he had syphilitic paralysis, he drowned himself in the Dvina in Riga, where he was Spanish consul. His profoundly argued *Idearium español* (1897, Eng trans *Spain: An Interpretation*, 1946), analyses Spain as sick with *aboulia*—lack of will, chronic apathy, fixed ideology. (The term was coined by Unamuno, from whom Ganivet gained much of his inspiration.) His two semi-autobiographical novels, provocative and still neglected outside Spain, are *La conquista del reino de maya por el último conquistador español Pío Cid* (1897, 'The Conquest of Maya's Kingdom by the Last Spanish Conquistador Pío Cid'), and *Los trabajos del indefatigable creador Pío Cid* (1898, 'The Labours of the Indefatigable Creator Pío Cid'). He commented on **Ibsen** and other playwrights, and even wrote an Ibsenite play, *El escultor de su alma* (1904, 'The Sculptor of his Soul').
▷H Ramsden, *Angel Ganivet's 'Idearium español': A Critical Study* (1967)

GANN, Ernest K(ellogg)
(1910–)

American novelist, born in Nebraska, best known as the author of *The High and the Mighty* (1953, screenplay 1954), the story of passengers in a plane set to crash into the Pacific. An earlier novel, *Island in the Sky* (1944), had been about the survivors of a plane crash and, like the better-known book, was made into a film starring John Wayne. Gann's other novels include *Blaze of Noon* (1946) and *Band of Brothers* (1973). He has written the non-fiction *The Black Watch: America's Spy Pilots and their Planes* (1989).
▷*Fate is the Hunter* (1961); *A Hostage to Fortune* (1978)

GAOS, Vicente
(1919–)

Spanish poet and critic. Born in Valencia, he studied philosophy and literature at the University of Madrid, and has spent a substantial amount of time in North American universities teaching Spanish literature. His criticism includes *La poética de Campoamor* (1955, 'The Poetry of Campoamor'), an annotated version of *Don Quijote* (1967), and *Temas y problemas del la literatura española* (1979, 'Themes and Problems of Spanish Literature'). The 1940s and 50s were his most productive period as a poet: it was then that he wrote *Arcangel de mi noche* (1944), awarded the Adonais Prize, and *Profecia del recuerdo* (1956), considered to be his best collection. Together with **José Luis Hidalgo** and José Hierro, he was a member of the influential group of poets contributing to the poetry journal *Proel* in Santander.

GARBORG, Arne Evenson
(1851–1924)

Norwegian writer, born in Jaeren. He rejected his agricultural background and became a rural schoolmaster, working subsequently as a journalist and junior civil servant. The conflict precipitated his father's suicide. Garborg later lost his government post when he published *Mannfolk* (1886, 'Men'), in which he passionately argued that economic and social pressures drove respectable young Norwegians into the arms of prostitutes. He wrote a cycle of lyric poems, *Haugtussa* (1895, 'The Hill Innocent'), and a series of realistic novels, such as *Bondestudenter* (1883, 'Peasant Students'), *Fred* (1890, 'Peace') and *Traette Maend* (1891, 'Tired Men'). He was a leader in the movement to establish a new Norwegian literary language (*Landsmål*, 'country language') based on western country dialects (later called *Nynorsk*, 'New Norwegian'), and from 1877 edited the periodical *Fedraheimen*, which provided him with a mouthpiece for his lifelong attack on Lutheran theology.
▷R Thesen, *Arne Garborg og det norske folket* (1944)

GARCÍA GUTIÉRREZ, Antonio
(1813–84)

Spanish dramatist, born in Chiclana. He ran away from medical studies to become a soldier. His first success, *El trovador* (1836, 'The Troubadour'), provided Verdi with his opera *Il Trovatore* (1853). His romantic theatre, although there is some deliberately sensational trash in his 50 plays, was, at its best, as in *Juan Lorenzo* (1865), exceedingly skilful, written in a clever mixture of prose and verse, and with sure and unusually acute portrayals of women.
▷N B Adams, *The Romantic Drama of García Gutiérrez* (1922)

GARCÍA LORCA, Federico
(1898–1936)

Spanish poet and playwright, born in Fuente Vaqueros. He was assassinated on the orders of the Nationalist Civil Governor early in the Spanish Civil War at Granada. His gypsy songs, which include *Canciones* (1927, Eng trans 1976) and *Romancero Gitano* (1928 and 1935, Eng trans *Gypsy Ballads*, 1963), probably his best and most widely read poetry, reveal a classical control of imagery, rhythm and emotion. He is best known for his powerful dramatic tragedies, which deal with elemental themes in a striking fashion. The best of these plays are *Bodas de Sangre* (1933, Eng trans *Blood Wedding*, 1947), *Yerma* (1934, Eng trans 1947) and *La Casa de Bernarda Alba* (first performed in 1945, Eng trans *Bernarda Alba*, 1947). The elegiac poems in *Llanto por la meurta de Ignacio Sánchez Mejías* (1935, Eng trans *Lament for the Death of a Bullfighter and Other Poems*, 1937) have been seen as a foreshadowing of his own death.
▷I Gibson, *The Death of Lorca* (1973)

GARCÍA MÁRQUEZ, Gabriel
(1927–)

Colombian novelist, winner of the Nobel Prize for literature, born in Aracataca. Educated at a Jesuit school, he studied law and journalism at the National University of Colombia, Bogotá. He was a journalist from 1950 to 1965, when he devoted himself to writing. One of Latin America's most formative and formidable writers, celebrated for his craft as well as his rhetorical exuberance and fecund imagination, he is a master of 'magic realism', the practice of rendering possible events as if they were wonders and rendering impossible events as if they were commonplace. Spinning from one fantastic, hyperbolic happening to another, his fictions are carried along in a torrent of narrative. *Cien años de soledad* (1967, Eng trans *One Hundred Years of Solitude*, 1970) is the novel by which he is best known in the western world, a vast, referential 'total' novel charting the history of a family, a house, a town, from edenic, mythic genesis through the descent into history of war, politics, and economic exploitation to annihilation at a moment of apocalyptic revelation. It is one of the great novels of the 20th century. Many others have subsequently been translated, including *El otoño del patriarca* (1975, Eng trans *The Autumn of the Patriarch*, 1976), *Crónica de una muerte anunciada* (1981, Eng trans *Chronicle of a Death Foretold*, 1982) and *El amor en los tiempos del coléra* (1985, Eng trans *Love in the Time of Cholera*, 1988). He was awarded the Nobel Prize for literature in 1982.

▷V Llosa, *Gabriel García Márquez, historia de un deicidio* (1971)

GARCIA TERRÉS, Jaime
(1924–)

Minor Mexican poet and critic, who in his collections has adopted a style less indigenous than European. He has been perhaps better known outside Mexico for his left-wing affiliations than for his poetry. His chief volume is *Los reinos combatientes* (1961, 'The Combatant Kingdoms').

GARCILASO DE LA VEGA
(1503–36)

Spanish poet and soldier, born in Toledo. He fought bravely in the wars of Charles V, and died of a wound received near Fréjus. Although he was not a prolific writer, his work is carefully crafted and polished, and his language is impetuous but deeply musical. He introduced the **Petrarch**an sonnet into Spain, and wrote odes in imitation of **Virgil**.
▷D Castanian, *El Inca Garcilaso de la Vega* (1969)

GARDAM, Jane
(1928–)

English novelist and short-story writer, born in Coatham, Yorkshire, who worked as a journalist and editor. Many of her books consider the relation of people to the landscape, and to emotional change. Her novel *God on the Rocks* (1978) is set before World War II in a seaside town in northern England and depicts a young woman growing to maturity. It was shortlisted for the Booker Prize. *Crusoe's Daughter* (1985) surveys the life of Polly Flint in her lonely cottage by the sea from 1904 until the mid-1980s, and is partly a homage to **Defoe**'s *Robinson Crusoe*.

GARDNER, Erle Stanley
(1889–1970)

American crime novelist, born in Malden, Massachusetts. He was educated at Palo Alto High School, California, studied in law offices and was admitted to the Californian Bar, where he became an ingenious lawyer for the defence (1922–38). A hugely prolific writer, he dictated up to six or seven novels simultaneously to a team of secretaries and used a number of pseudonyms. His best-known creation is the lawyer-sleuth Perry Mason, hero of 82 courtroom dramas, who first appeared in *The Case of the Velvet Claws* (1933); subsequent titles used the 'Case of' formula. With a little help from Della Street, his faithful secretary, and private eye Paul Drake, Mason frequently defied the rulebook in his quest to clear his client's name. With the late Raymond Burr playing Perry Mason, the books enjoyed enhanced popularity when they were made into a long-running television series. He also wrote a series of detective novels featuring the District Attorney Doug Selby ('the DA').

▷A Johnston, *The Case of Erle Stanley Gardner* (1947)

GARDNER, Isabella
(1915–81)

American poet, born in Newton, Massachusetts, who worked in the theatre and published nothing until after her third marriage in 1947. Her husband, whom she divorced 10 years later, encouraged her writing and her first collection, *Birthdays from the Ocean*, appeared in 1955. Other volumes include *The Looking Glass* (1961), *West of Childhood: Poems 1950–65* (1965) and *That Was Then: New and Selected Poems* (1980). The theme of this last book is death, often in tragic circumstances. Yet although her recurring subjects include the failure of love, an underlying resilience and optimism for life pervade the elegiac fabric of her writing. Much admired by **Sylvia Plath**, she was the recipient of the first **Walt Whitman** Citation of Merit in 1981.

▷J Gould, *Modern American Women Poets* (1984)

GARDNER, John Champlin, Jr
(1933–82)

American novelist and literary theorist. In the 1970s, Gardner engaged in a number of public debates with **William Gass**, in which Gardner bore a standard for literary fiction as a repository for the thoughtful examination and restitution of social values; *On Moral Fiction* (1978) was the most complete statement of his position. This was already evident in his fiction, starting with *Resurrection* (1966), the hefty *Sunlight Dialogues* (1972), the pastoral *Nickel Mountain* (1973), and *October Light* (1976), which had a more sombre quality; nonetheless, 'light' and the idea of enlightenment were the dominant themes of his fiction. His stories were collected in *The King's Indian* (1974). Like his namesake, **John Edmund Gardner**, with whom he was occasionally (and hilariously) confused, he showed an interest in the mentality of evil; *Grendel* (1971) is a remarkable reworking of *Beowulf* from the monster's point of view. This also reflected his academic interest in early English literature, particularly **Chaucer** and the *Gawain* poet. He was killed in a motorcycle accident.

▷G Morris, *A World of Order and Light: John Gardner's Fiction* (1984)

GARDNER, John Edmund
(1926–)

English crime and espionage novelist. He began with a series of books spoofing imitators of **Ian Fleming**'s James Bond—Gardner described his own series character Boysie Oakes as a 'counter-irritant'—and found himself invited by the Fleming estate to use the Bond name, in such titles as *Licence Renewed* (1981), *For Special Services* (1982) and *Role of Honour* (1984). Oakes had appeared as early as 1964 (within months of Fleming's death) in *The Liquidator*. Though primarily an entertainer, Gardner is deeply interested in the effects of crime: on the victims, on those that seek to protect them, and on the perpetrators. This is behind the Derek Torry books, which began with *A Complete State of Death* (1969, published in the USA as *The Stone Killer*, 1973), and it explains the impulse to bring back Sherlock Holmes's greatest adversary in *The Return of Moriarty* (1974) and *The Revenge of Moriarty* (1975). Unexpectedly, perhaps, Gardner's degree from Cambridge was in theology and for a period in the mid-50s he was in holy orders.

▷*Spin the Bottle: The Autobiography of an Alcoholic* (1964)

GARFIELD, Leon
(1921–)

English novelist, born in Brighton, the author of adventure novels for children, most of which have 18th-century settings. His first, *Jack Holborn* (1964), was intended for adults but his publisher suggested it should be altered with a younger readership in mind. Its grim, exciting, convoluted narrative is fairly typical of Garfield's novels, the best of which are *Smith* (1967), *Black Jack* (1968) and *John Diamond* (1980), which won the Whitbread Award. A cycle of 12 short novels, *Garfield's Apprentices* (1976–8), skilfully evokes the lives of 18th-century London apprentices. He has successfully adapted **Shakespeare** stories for children and, with Edward Blishen, won the Carnegie Medal for *The God Beneath the Sea* (1970), a retelling of Greek mythology.

GARIOCH, Robert, pseud of Robert Garioch Sutherland
(1909–81)

Scottish poet, born in Edinburgh. Educated at the Royal High School, Edinburgh, and Edinburgh University, he spent most of his professional career as a teacher in Scotland and England. He made his literary debut in 1933 with the surrealistic verse play *The Masque of Edinburgh* (published in expanded form in 1954). His first publications, *Seventeen Poems for Sixpence* (1940), in which he collaborated with **Sorley MacLean**, and *Chuckies on the Cairn* (1949), were hand-printed. His later work included *Selected Poems* (1966), *The Big Music* (1971), *Dr Faust in Rose Street* (1973) and *Collected Poems* (1977). He favoured the Scots language, in which he wrote in various styles and moods, from the colloquial to the literary. He translated into Scots works as diverse as **Pindar**, **Hesiod**, **George Buchanan**'s Latin plays *Jeptha* and *Baptistes*, Anglo-Saxon elegies, and the poems of the 19th-century Italian dialect poet Giuseppe Giacchino Belli. His prose works included *Two Men and a Blanket* (1975), an account of his experience in prisoner-of-war camps during World War II. Garioch particularly acknowledged the influence of **Robert Fergusson** on his poetry, perhaps most clearly seen in his sonnet on Fergusson's grave, his *To Robert Fergusson* and *The Muir*.

GARLAND, (Hamilton) Hamlin
(1860–1940)

American writer, born in West Salem, Wisconsin. He often interrupted his schooling to help his father farm in Iowa, but in 1884 went to Boston to teach and finally to write. In short stories such as the collections *Main Travelled Roads* (1887) and *Prairie Folks* (1892), in verse and in novels, he vividly, often grimly, described the farmlife of the Midwest. *Rose of Dutcher's Coolly* (1895) was an important forerunner of the 1920s 'revolt from the village'. *A Daughter of the Middle Border* (1921), the sequel to his autobiographical novel *A Son of the Middle Border* (1917), won the Pulitzer Prize. *Crumbling Idols* (1894) was a collection of essays, setting out Garland's theories of 'veritism'.
▷ J Holloway, *Hamlin Garland: a biography* (1960)

GARNER, Alan
(1934–)

English novelist, whose fantasy writing for young readers powerfully blends the mystical and the realistic. Born into a working-class family in Alderley Edge, near Manchester, he left to study classics at Oxford University, but returned to the area to write. Local history, myth and landscape feature strongly in his novels. His first, *The Weirdstone of Brisingamen* (1960), and its sequel, *The Moon of Gomrath* (1963), are ambitious adventure tales where the mythical past intrudes into the lives of two children, Colin and Susan. Garner's subsequent works are emotionally complex and mysterious. *The Owl Service* (1967) won both the Carnegie Medal and the Guardian Award, and *The Stone Book Quartet* (1976–8) is a vibrant celebration of family and heritage told through a day in the life of a child from each of four generations of the Garner family.
▷ N Philip, *A Fine Anger. A Critical Introduction to the work of Alan Garner* (1981)

GARNER, Helen
(1942–)

Australian writer, born in Geelong, Victoria, who taught in Melbourne schools until being dismissed for answering frankly her pupils' questions on sex. Her adult fiction appeals strongly to adolescents, today's problems being examined in a clear-sighted and nonjudgemental manner. *Monkey Grip* (1977) deals sympathetically with the subculture of drug addiction; it won the National Book Award in the same year and was filmed in 1981. Two novellas, *Honour* and *Other People's Children* (both 1980), handle lightly the interplay of adult characters with the legacy of the 'swinging sixties' in Australia. *The Children's Bach* (1984) is a highly regarded treatment of stress in middle-class suburban family life. *Postcards from Surfers* (1985) is a collection of short stories on disparate themes, but with a pervasive Australian atmosphere.

GARNETT, David
(1892–1981)

English novelist, son of **Edward Garnett**, born in Brighton. He studied botany at the Royal College of Science. His first book, *Lady into Fox* (1922), won both the Hawthornden and the James Tait Black Memorial Prize. *A Man in the Zoo* (1924) and *The Sailor's Return* (1925) were also successful, as were several other novels. Literary adviser to the Nonesuch Press (1923–32) and literary editor of the *New Statesman* (1932–4), he joined the RAF in 1939, and used his experience to write *War in the Air* (1941).
▷ *The Golden Echo: memoirs 1892–1914* (1915)

GARNETT, Edward
(1868–1937)

English writer and critic, son of **Richard Garnett**. As a publisher's reader he fostered the careers of many literary figures, including **Joseph Conrad**, **John Galsworthy** and **D H Lawrence**. He was the author of the set of critical essays *Friday Nights* (1922). He also wrote plays, including *The Breaking Point* (1907) and *The Trial of Jeanne d'Arc* (1912). His wife, Constance, née Black (1862–1946), was a distinguished translator of Russian literature.
▷ H E Bates, *Edward Garnett* (1950)

GARNETT, Eve
(20th century)

English children's author and illustrator, born in Worcestershire. She studied at the Royal Academy of Art and has combined life as an author with her work as a professional artist, which has included a commission for murals at Children's House, Bow, and an exhibition at the Tate in 1939. Her name as an author rests upon *The Family from One End Street* (1937, Carnegie Medal), one of the first attempts to present working-class family life sympathetically in children's fiction. This book and its sequel, *Further Adventures of the Family from One End Street* (1956), remain popular.
▷ *First Affections* (1982)

GARNETT, Richard
(1835–1906)

English writer and bibliographer, born in Lichfield. He was Keeper of printed books at the British Museum (1890–9), and author of verse, critical works and biographies, including *Shelley* (1862), *Carlyle* (1883) and *The Age of Dryden* (1895). His best-known original work is his collection of tales on pagan themes, *Twilight of the Gods* (1888). His son was **Edward Garnett**.
▷ H Cordier, *Le Docteur Richard Garnett* (1906)

GARNIER, Robert
(1534–90)

French poet and playwright, born in Maine. He was the most distinguished of the predecessors of **Corneille**. His *Oeuvres complètes* (2 vols, 1923, 1949, 'Complete Works') include eight masterly tragedies, of which perhaps the best are *Antigone* (1580) and *Les Juives* (1583, 'The Jewesses').
▷ M Mouflard, *Robert Garnier: 1545–1590* (1961)

GARRETT, George Palmer, Jr
(1929–)

American poet, novelist and author of screenplays, born in Orlando, Florida. His first publication was a collection of poetry, *The Reverend Ghost* (1957), but his best-known work is a novel, *Death of the Fox* (1971). This is not only a historical novel in which the central character is Sir Walter Raleigh, but a meditation on the historical process itself, and is considered by critics to be his finest work. Garrett is a prolific and wide-ranging author whose screenplay credits rather bizarrely include *Frankenstein Meets the Space Monster* (1966).

GARRIGUE, Jean
(1914–72)

American poet, born in Evansville, Indiana. His first volume, *The Ego and the Centaur*, appeared in 1947; other collections include *The Monument Rose* (1953) and *New and Selected Poems* (1967). Garrigue's love and travel poetry in particular have been acclaimed for their technical poise and richness of language. The exuberant, closely observed *A Water Walk by the Villa D'Este* (1959), is considered one of her finest books.
▷ M A Shea (ed), *Jean Garrigue* in *Twentieth Century Literature*, 29 (1983)

GARSHIN, Vsevolod Mikhailovich
(1855–88)

Russian author, born in Bachmut. He wrote short stories, greatly influenced by **Tolstoy**, but without his breadth, including *Krasnyi Tsvetok* (1883, 'The Red Flower'), which is set in a lunatic asylum, and *Signal* (1912, 'The Signal'). He served in the Turkish war, and was wounded and invalided home in 1878; his story about a wounded soldier, *Chetyre Dnya* (1877, Eng trans *Four Days*, 1912), was a huge success. His work is narrow but emotionally intense. A melancholic, he eventually committed suicide.
▷ N Byelyaev, *Garshin* (1938)

GARTH, Sir Samuel
(1661–1719)

English physician and poet, born in Bowland Forest, Yorkshire. He was physician in ordinary to George I, and physician-general to the army. A member of the Kit-Cat Club, he is remembered for his burlesque poem, 'The Dispensary' (1699), a satire on uncharitable apothecaries and physicians. 'Claremont' (1715) is a topographical poem in the manner of **Pope**'s 'Windsor Forest'. He also edited a composite translation of **Ovid**'s *Metamorphoses*, published in 1717.
▷ H W Cushing, *Dr Garth the Kit Kat poet, 1661–1718* (1906)

GASCAR, Pierre, pseud of **Pierre Fournier**
(1916–)

French novelist, born in Paris. He found himself imprisoned in a concentration camp in the Ukraine for almost the entire duration of World War II, and the novel he based on this experience, *Le Temps des Morts* ('The Time of the Dead'), won him the Prix **Goncourt** in 1953. The theme of man's potential for cruelty and inhumanity is continued in *Les Bêtes* ('The Beasts'), a collection of short stories published in 1953, and in *La Barre de Corail* (1958, 'The Coral Reef'). He is known particularly for *Le Fugitif* (1961, 'The Fugitive'), set in Germany after the war; other novels include *Les Chimères* (1969, 'The Chimeras'), *L'Arche* (1971), *Dans la forêt humaine* (1976, 'In the Human Forest'), *Le Règne végétal* (1981, 'Vegetable Kingdom') and *Le Fortin* (1983, 'The Fort').

GASCOIGNE, George
(c.1525–1577)

English poet and dramatist, born in Cardington in Bedfordshire. He studied at Trinity College, Cambridge, entered Gray's Inn, wrote poems, and sat in parliament for Bedford (1557–9), but was disinherited for his extravagance. He married **Nicholas Breton**'s widowed mother (to improve his finances), but, still persecuted by creditors, served in Holland under the Prince of Orange (1573–5). Surprised by a Spanish force and taken prisoner, he was detained for four months. He then settled in Walthamstow, where he collected and published his poems. He translated in prose and verse, from Greek, Latin and Italian. *The Complaynt of Phylomene*, a verse narrative in the style of **Ovid**, was begun in 1563. *The Supposes* is from the *I Suppositi* of **Ludovico Ariosto**; *Jocasta* (1566, with Francis Kinwelmersh), practically a translation from Dolce's *Giocasta* (based on the *Phoenissae* of **Euripides**), is the second tragedy in English blank verse; *The Glasse of Government* (1575) is an original comedy. *The Steele Glas* is the earliest blank-verse satire; and in the *Certayne Notes of Instruction on Making of Verse* (1575) there is the first considerable English essay on the subject. To this zealous experimenter English literature owes a deep debt, though much of his work is hopelessly tedious.
▷ L T Prouty, *George Gascoigne, Elizabethan Courtier, Soldier and Poet* (1942)

GASCOYNE, David Emery
(1916–)

English poet, born in Harrow and educated at Regent Street Polytechnic, London. He became famous as England's 'only surrealist' at the age of 19. His poems, often dealing with violence, music and night, can be sometimes solipsistically neurotic yet at other times are very much concerned, at least when he was writing in the 30s, with European politics, as in *Roman Balcony* (1932) and *Man's Life is this Meat* (1936). His best work transcends the sloganizing or avant-garde and embraces existential fears of death and loneliness with unusual bravery. A provocative critic in his *Short Survey of Surrealism* (1936), he praises Dada ('a spit in the eye of the world'), Dali, and de Sade ('the first reasoned socialist') and contends that 'the surrealist attitude is totally in accord with ... dialectical materialism'. *Poems 1937–42* (1942) and *Night Thoughts* (1956) turn away from Surrealism towards a

calmer mood without abandoning much of his earlier substance.
▷ M Rémy, *David Gascoyne, ou l'urgence de l'inexprimé* (1984)

GASKELL, Mrs Elizabeth Cleghorn, née Stevenson
(1810–65)

English novelist, born in Cheyne Row, Chelsea, London. Her father was in succession teacher, preacher, farmer, boarding-house keeper, writer and Keeper of the records to the Treasury. She was brought up by an aunt in Knutsford—the Cranford of her stories— and grew up well-adjusted and beautiful. She married in 1832 William Gaskell (1805–84), a Unitarian minister in Manchester. Here she studied working men and women, and made important contributions to what came to be known as the 'Condition of England' novel. In 1848 she published anonymously *Mary Barton*, followed by *The Moorland Cottage* (1850), *Cranford* (1853), *Ruth* (1853), *North and South* (1855), *Round the Sofa* (1859), *Right at Last* (1860), *Sylvia's Lovers* (1863), *Cousin Phillis* (1865) and *Wives and Daughters* (1865). As well as her novels she wrote *The Life of Charlotte Brontë* (1857).
▷ M Allott, *Elizabeth Gaskell* (1960)

GASKIN, Catherine Majella Sinclair
(1929–)

Irish writer of historical romances, born in Dundalk. Gaskin grew up in Australia and was educated in Sydney. She published her first two novels, *This Other Eden* (1945) and *With Every Year* (1947), while still in her teens. *Sara Dane* (1955) was her first big success and became a television series. Her books are entertainments, which she thinks 'an honourable enough motive'.

GASS, William H(oward)
(1924–)

American novelist, born in Fargo, North Dakota. He was educated at Ohio Wesleyan University, Delaware, and Cornell University. A philosopher and literary critic, as well as novelist, he derives from and is allied with the *symbolistes*, New Critics and the structuralists. His aesthetic theories are set out in *Fictions and the Figures of Life* (1970) and in subsequent years he engaged in public debate with fellow novelist **John Gardner**, a defender of 'moral fiction'. His novels are *Omensetter's Luck* (1966), and *Willie Masters' Lonesome Wife* (1971), an essay-novella; Gass's stories are collected as *In the Heart of the Heart of the Country* (1968). His massive autobiographical novel, *The Tunnel*, has been in progress for more than 20 years.

▷A Saltzman, *The Fiction of William Gass: The Consolations of Language* (1986)

GATSOS, Nikos
(1915–)

Greek Surrealist poet, author of the celebrated *Amorgas* (1943), which contains the famous line, 'one lost elephant is always worth more than the quivering breasts of a girl'. It has been called the 'most substantial Surrealist poem ever to be written'. The best English translation is to be found in *Six Poets of Modern Greece* (1960).

GATTI, Armand
(1924–)

French playwright, greatly concerned with revolutionary politics. Born to a poor immigrant family, he was deported at the age of 17 to a labour camp in Germany. He later became active in the movement for the decentralization of the theatre in France, but was also concerned with international politics: *Un Homme seul* (1969, 'A Man Alone') is based on an incident in the Chinese civil war, and *La Naissance* ('The Birth') addresses the struggle for independence in Guatemala. Another of his major interests was the creative response of the individual to his or her environment, *Les treize soleils de la rue St-Blaise* ('The Thirteen Suns of St-Blaise Street') being the fruit of an interchange of ideas among members of an audience at the Théâtre de l'Est in Paris.

GATTO, Alfonso
(1909–76)

Italian poet from Salerno, usually classed along with **Quasimodo** and others as 'hermetic' (a term originally employed by the critic Francisco Flora to describe the 'closed' poetry of **Onofri**). His poetry became more open when, after he had served time in prison for his anti-fascist views, he joined the partisans and became a communist (until 1951). His most admired poetry is contained in his collection *La madre e la morte* (1960, 'Mother and Death'): lucid and more accessible than his earlier poetry, these poems are full of pathos and a sense of death. He was killed in a car accident. There are English translations in C L Golino, *Contemporary Italian Poetry* (1962)

GAUNT, Mary
(1861–1942)

Australian traveller and writer, born in Chiltern, Victoria, who later lived in England and Italy. She wrote a considerable number of novels, some set in Australia such as her first, *Dave's Sweetheart* (1894). *Kirkham's Find* (1897) was an early feminist novel; his find is 'pure gold'—the very independent Phoebe. *The Uncounted Cost* (1910) was banned by London circulating libraries because the fallen heroine did *not* pay the price. Other novels, *As the Whirlwind Passeth* (1923) and *Joan of the Pilchard* (1930), have historical backgrounds. Her books achieved wide sales and she indulged her love of sailing and travel; her travel books include *Alone in West Africa* (1912) and *A Woman in China* (1914).

GAUTIER, Théophile
(1811–72)

French poet and novelist, born in Tarbes. From painting he turned to literature, and became an extreme 'romanticist'. In 1830 he published his first long poem, *Albertus*, in 1832 the striking *Comédie de la mort* ('The Comedy of Death'). His poetry reached its height in *Émaux et camées* (1856, 'Enamels and Cameos'). In 1835 appeared his celebrated novel, *Mademoiselle de Maupin*, with its defiant preface. He wrote many other novels and masterly short stories—*Les Jeunes-France* (1833), *Fortunio* (1838), *Une Larme du diable* (1839, 'A Tear from the Devil'), *Militona* (1847), *La Peau de tigre* (1852, 'The Tiger's Skin'), *Jettatura* (1857), *Le Capitaine Fracasse* (1863), *La Belle Jenny* (1865, 'Beautiful Jenny'), *Spirite* (1866), and others. His theatrical criticisms were collected as *L'Histoire de l'art dramatique en France* (1859, 'A History of the Theatre in France'); his articles on the Salon form perhaps the best history of the French art of his day. *Caprices et zigzags* (1852, 'Whims and Zigzags'), *Constantinople* (1853, Eng trans *Constantinople of To-day*, 1854), *Voyage en Russie* (1867, Eng trans *A Winter in Russia*, 1874) and *Voyage en Espagne* (1850, Eng trans *Wanderings in Spain*, 1851) contain delightful travel sketches. Other works were an enlarged edition of his *Émaux et camées* (1872); *Les Grotesques* (1844), on 16th- and 17th-century writers; *Honoré de Balzac* (1858); *Ménagerie intime* (1869), a kind of informal autobiography; *Histoire du romantisme* (1872, 'A History of Romanticism'); and the posthumous works, *Portraits et souvenirs littéraires* (1875, 'Literary Portraits and Recollections') and *L'Orient* (1877). Most of his works were translated in 24 volumes by F C de Sumichrast and Agnes Lee (1900–3). His daughter Judith Gautier (1845–1917) wrote novels, plays, poems and translations.
▷R Grant, *Théophile Gautier* (1975)

GAVIN, Catherine
(1907–)

Scottish novelist, born in Aberdeen and educated at its university, where she lectured in history before working as a war correspondent and then journalist for *Time*. A writer of factually sound historical fiction, she often involves spying and romance in her stories. In the 1930s she twice stood as a Conservative candidate for Parliament, and in her writing shows a devoted fascination for great men, such as Admiral Jellicoe in *The Devil in Harbour* (1968) or Napoleon in *The French Fortune* (1991).

GAWAIN Poet, the
(fl.c.1380)

Anonymous English poet, presumed author of *Cleanness*, *Patience*, *Pearl* and—the Arthurian masterpiece after which he is named—*Sir Gawain and the Green Knight*. All four poems, written in the same north-of-England dialect, are found together in a manuscript dating from around 1200. Each of the shorter poems has an explicitly religious theme: *Cleanness* discusses spiritual purity with reference to several biblical episodes; *Patience* is the retold tale of Jonah and the whale; and *Pearl* is a dream-poem of the afterlife. *Gawain* itself is a richer, longer, less overtly didactic work: the story of one of King **Arthur**'s knights and a threatening stranger who comes to Camelot, it can be read as a straightforward adventure or as a quest for spiritual knowledge; either way it is one of the most remarkable works in the history of English poetry.

GAY, John
(1685–1732)

English poet, born in Barnstaple, Devon, into a prosperous Nonconformist family. Educated at Barnstaple Grammar School, he was apprenticed to a silk-mercer in London, but soon returned home and became a writer. In 1708 he published his first poem, *Wine*, and in 1711 a pamphlet on the *Present State of Wit*. Appointed secretary to the Duchess of Monmouth (1712), in 1713 he dedicated to **Pope** the georgic *Rural Sports*. In 1714 he published *The Fan* and *The Shepherd's Week*, and accompanied Lord Clarendon, envoy to Hanover, as secretary. When the duchess died he wrote a poem on the newly-arrived Princess of Wales. *What d'ye Call It?* (1715) was called 'a tragi-comi-pastoral farce'. *Trivia*, a clever picture of town life, came next; and later he bore the blame of *Three Hours after Marriage* (1717), a play which he had written with Pope and Arbuthnot. In 1720 he published his poems by subscription, clearing £1000; but this and some South Sea stock vanished in the crash of 1720. In 1724 he produced *The Captives*, a tragedy, and in 1727 the first series of his popular *Fables*. But his greatest success was *The Beggar's Opera* (1728), set to music by Pepusch, the outcome of a suggestion made by **Jonathan Swift** in 1716. Its popularity was extraordinary; it ran

62 nights, and by the 36th, Gay had netted over £700; immediately he started on a sequel, *Polly*, which was prohibited, but which in book form brought in £1200. After this he lived chiefly with the Duke and Duchess of Queensberry, the kindest of his many patrons. He wrote another opera, *Achilles* (produced posthumously in 1733). He was buried in Westminster Abbey.
▷P M Sparks, *John Gay* (1965)

GEE, Maggie
(1948–)

English novelist, born in Poole, Dorset. After graduating from Oxford, she was creative writing fellow at the University of East Anglia (1982). Her novels are vividly contemporary and reveal a profound concern for the political and environmental issues of our time. The earlier fiction is experimental and dark: *Dying, In Other Words* (1983) begins with the death of a woman who later becomes the apparent narrator. Both this and *The Burning Book* (1983) are powerful in post-nuclear imagery. Although *Light Years* (1985) is apparently more optimistic, in that a disintegrating marriage is repaired, *Grace* (1988) returns to confront the nuclear issue in the accounts of an anti-nuclear campaigner and the detective shadowing her. *Where Are The Snows* (1991) considers obsessive love. In 1994 she published *Lost Children*, about family bonds and the price of secrecy.

GEE, Maurice Gough
(1931–)

New Zealand novelist, born in Whakatane and educated in Auckland. Between 1967 and 1976, the year of his fourth novel *Games of Choice*, he worked as a librarian, writing fiction in his spare time. Thereafter his work gained enormously in sophistication and resonance. *Plumb* (1978), *Meg* (1981) and *Sole Survivor* (1983) all concern the Plumbs, and are extremely perceptive about the tensions and contradictions of family life. Gee's understanding of children is evident in his juvenile writing—*The World Around the Corner* (1980), *The Halfmen of O* (1982), *The Priests of Ferris* (1984) and *Motherstone* (1985)—of which he is a major practitioner, and it carries over into his adult writing in *The Burning Boy* (1990), a haunting study of a brutally scarred youth and the woman who tries to bring him out of his emotional isolation.
▷D Hill, *Introducing Maurice Gee* (1981)

GEIBEL, Emmanuel von
(1815–84)

German poet, born in Lübeck. He studied at Bonn, and was tutor (1838–9) in Athens to

359

the family of the Russian ambassador. He made many translations from the Greek, Spanish and Italian authors, and with **Paul Heyse** founded the Munich school of poetry, which emphasized harmony and form. He also wrote plays in classical form.

▷C L Leimbach, *Emmanuel von Geibel. Des Dichters Leben und Werke* (1877)

GEIJER, Erik Gustav
(1783–1877)

Swedish poet and historian, born in Ransäter in Värmland. He studied at Uppsala and was appointed Professor of History there in 1817. A founder of the Gothic Society and its journal, *Iduna*, in 1811, in which he published much of his best poetry, he had a profound influence on both literature and historiography in Sweden, promoting a Romantic aesthetic. His works included *Impressions of England* (1809–10, Eng trans 1932) and a *History of the Swedish People* (1832–6), both of which are included in *Samlade Skrifter* (13 vols, 1849–82). He was also the first to make a full Swedish translation of a **Shakespeare** play, *Macbeth* (1815).

▷S Stolpe, *Geijer. En essay* (1947)

GELBER, Jack
(1932–)

Controversial American playwright, whose powerful study of drug addiction, *The Connection* (1959), adopted and Americanized devices associated with **Brecht**. Early productions sustained the premise that the 'actors' were actual users, bribed to perform with real doses of heroin. The play also featured live on-stage jazz performances. Perhaps inevitably, nothing else of Gelber's has ever received as much attention. *The Apple* (1961) was thought to be rambling and wordy, a too self-consciously Americanized version of **Luigi Pirandello**'s *Sei personaggi in cerca d'autore*. The later *Square in the Eye* (1965) was quite simply too conventional, a straightforward proscenium piece about a would-be artist. *Rehearsal* (1976) was a partial return to a more experimental mode. Gelber has also written a novel, *On Ice* (1964), which usefully documents the kind of social and artistic context out of which he emerged.

GELLERT, Christian Fürchtegott
(1715–69)

German poet and moralist, born in Hainichen, Saxony. He was educated at Leipzig, and in 1751 became a professor there. He was a prolific writer of stories and fables, and two of his comedies, *Das Los in der Lotterie* (1746, 'The Lottery Ticket') and *Die kranke Frau* (1747, Eng trans *The Sick Wife*, 1928), were popular favourites. His moralistic novel

Leben der schwedischen Gräfin von G- (1747–8, Eng trans *The History of the Swedish Countess of Guildenstern*, 1757) shows the influence of **Samuel Richardson**.

▷L Spriegel, *Der Leipziger Goethe und Gellert* (1934)

GELLHORN, Martha Ellis
(1908–)

American journalist, travel writer and fiction writer. She was born in St Louis, Missouri, and educated at Bryn Mawr College. She became a foreign correspondent for *Collier's Weekly*, covering the Spanish Civil War, the invasion of Finland, and the European theatre in World War II. She almost certainly saw more violent action than her relentlessly macho first husband, **Hemingway**, her marriage to him neatly coinciding (1940–5) with the wider hostilities, and proving appropriately stormy. Her interest in human conflict remained undimmed and she continued to report on wars in Java (1946), Vietnam (1966), the Middle East (1967) and Central America (1983–5). Her earlier reportage was collected in *The Face of War* (1959). Her first novel, *What Mad Pursuit*, had appeared exactly 25 years earlier, followed by others— *A Stricken Field* (1940), *Liano* (1948) and *The Wine of Astonishment* (1948)—which suggested that her instincts were journalistic rather than strictly literary. For that reason, the short stories in *The Trouble I've Seen* (1936), *The Honeyed Peace* (1953), *Two by Two* (1958) and *The Weather in Africa* (1978) are much stronger, marked by acute observation, sympathy for the weak or oppressed and moral straightforwardness.

▷*Travels with Myself and Another* (1979)

GELLIUS, Aulus
(c.123–c.165)

Latin author, born probably in Rome, where he practised law. He studied philosophy in Athens, and there began to collect the material for *Noctes Atticae* ('Attic Nights'), a collection of dinner-table conversations on literature, history, law, antiquities and miscellaneous subjects. The value of *Noctes Atticae* is chiefly in the numerous quotations it gives from Greek and Roman books which would otherwise be completely unknown.

GEMS, Pam (Iris Pamela)
(1925–)

English dramatist, born in Hampshire. Among her best-known plays are *Piaf* (1978) and *Camille* (1984), portraying women as victims in worlds ruled by men. Although she had written several radio, television scripts and stage plays before the mid-1970s, it was her *Dusa, Stas, Fish and Vi* which brought her widespread recognition when it was staged in London in 1975. A look at the lives of four contemporary women, it was a courageous piece of feminist drama. She also wrote *The Danton Affair* (1986), dealing with the conflict between Danton and Robespierre, and a musical stage adaptation of the 1930 film *The Blue Angel* (1991).

GENET, Jean
(1910–86)

French author, born in Paris. At the age of seven months his mother gave him to the Hospice des Enfants Assistés in Paris and two days later he went to foster parents. He showed a religious temperament as a child and served as an altar boy in the local church, but later turned to crime and spent many years in reformatories and prisons, in France and abroad, for theft, male prostitution, and other crimes. He began to write in 1942 in Fresnes prison where he was serving a life sentence after 10 convictions for theft. His first novel, *Notre-Dame des fleurs* (1944, Eng trans *Our Lady of the Flowers*, 1949), created a sensation. In it he first portrayed his world of homosexuals and criminals, evoking in a characteristically ceremonial and religious language his view of a universe of violence and betrayal, prison and inevitable death. Later novels include *Miracle de la rose* (1946, Eng trans *Miracle of the Rose*, 1965), *Pompes funèbres* (1947, Eng trans *Funeral Rites*, 1969) and *Querelle de Brest* (1947, Eng trans 1966). In 1948 he was granted a pardon by the President after a petition by French intellectuals. The book *Saint Genet* (1952, Eng trans 1963), by **Jean-Paul Sartre**, widened his fame among the French intelligentsia. Several plays, including *Les Bonnes* (1946, Eng trans *The Maids*, 1954), *Les Nègres* (1958, Eng trans *The Blacks*, 1960) and *Les Paravents* (1961, Eng trans *The Screens*, 1962), and poems such as *Les Condamnés à mort* (1942, 'Those Condemned to Death'), *Chants Secrets* (1947, 'Secret Songs') and *La Galère, la parade, un chant d'amour* (1947, 'The Galley-ship, the Parade, the Love Song'), share the criminal underworld setting and profoundly pessimistic outlook of the novels, expressed in ritualistic and mystical style. On release from prison he was associated with revolutionary movements in many countries. He wrote an autobiography, *Le Journal du voleur* (1949, Eng trans *Thief's Journal*, 1954).
▷Jean-Paul Sartre, *Saint-Genet: actor and martyr* (1963)

GENLIS, Stéphanie Felicité Ducrest de St Aubin, Comtesse de
(1746–1830)

French writer, born in Champcéri near Autun. At the age of 16 she married the Comte de Genlis, and in 1770 was made lady-in-waiting to the Duchess of Chartres, to whose husband, Orléans 'Égalité', she became mistress. She wrote four volumes of short plays entitled *Théâtre d'education* (1779) for her charges, the royal children, including the future King Louis-Philippe, and nearly a hundred volumes of historical romances and 'improving' works. Her *Mémoires* (1825) contain interesting social comments on the period.
▷J Hammond, *Keeper of Royal Secrets* (1913)

GEORGE, Stefan
(1868–1933)

German poet, born in Büdesheim near Bingen. He edited (1892–1919) *Blätter für die Kunst*, a journal devoted to the work of a group of advanced poets and writers to which he belonged, and wrote lyric verse in *Hymnen* (1890, 'Hymns'), *Der siebente Ring* (1907, 'The Seventh Ring') and *Der Stern des Bundes* (1914, 'The Federal Star'), which shows the influence of the French Symbolists and the English pre-Raphaelites. He also translated the works of **Baudelaire**, **Shakespeare** and **Dante**. His poems, dispensing with punctuation and capitals, are an expression of mood, conveying an impression rather than a meaning. In *Das neue Reich* (1928, 'The New Reich') he advocated a new German culture, not in accord with that of the Nazis.
▷E K Bennett, *A Critical Study* (1954)

GERARD, Edwin Field, originally Gerhard
(1891–1965)

Australian poet of German extraction, born in Yunta, South Australia, who changed his name at the start of World War I and joined the Australian Imperial Force in 1915. He served at Gallipoli and later in the Middle East; his verses on war themes appeared in such periodicals as the *Bulletin* under the names 'Gerardy' or 'Trooper Gerardy'. These were published as *The Road to Palestine and Other Verses* (1918) and *Australian Light Horse Ballads and Rhymes* (1919). His later ballads, in a nostalgic 19th-century style, have not been published in book form.

GERCHUNOFF, Alberto
(1883–1950)

Argentinian novelist and journalist, born, of Russian Jewish parents, in Proskurov, Ukraine. In 1889 the family moved to Argentina under a scheme devised by Baron Hirsch, a Jewish philanthropist. But Gerchunoff's father was murdered by a drunkard, and he grew up as a 'peasant' in Rajil (Entre Rios), and then as a poor boy in Buenos Aires, doing all kinds of menial jobs. He became editor of

the leading newspaper *La Nación*. Of his many realist novels and collections of sketches, the most famous and important is *Los gauchos judios* (1910, Eng trans *The Jewish Gauchos of the Pampa*, 1955), a vivid picture of the immigrant Jews, based on his time in Rajil. He wrote books on **Heine** and Spinoza.
▷ *Hispanic American Historic Review* (34–5, 1955)

GERHARDIE, or GERHARDI, William Alexander
(1895–1977)

English novelist, born of English parents in St Petersburg, where he was educated. He served in the British Embassy at Petrograd (1917–18), later with the military mission in Siberia, before going to Worcester College, Oxford, where he wrote a lively study of **Anton Chekhov** (1923) and *Futility: A Novel on Russian Themes* (1922). In 1925 came *The Polyglots*, his most celebrated novel, described by **Anthony Powell** as 'outstanding... particularly in the rare gift of making child characters come alive'. Among his later novels only *Of Mortal Love* (1936), a love story blending humour, pathos and tenderness, and admired by **Edwin Muir** and others, stands comparison with his early fiction. *Memoirs of a Polyglot*, his autobiography, was published in 1931, a biographical history of *The Romanoffs* in 1940, and *God's Fifth Column*, an idiosyncratic account of the years 1890–1940, appeared posthumously in 1981.
▷ D Davies, *William Gerhardie: a life* (1990)

GERSHON, Karen, pseud of Karen Lowenthal
(1923–92)

German-born poet, who emigrated to Great Britain in 1938, and went to Israel in 1969. She wrote in English. Her poems first appeared in *Quarto* magazine, a broadsheet edited by **James Reeves**. Her first collection did not appear until 1966, when it attracted some notice for its moving descriptions of her plight as a refugee—her parents died in Hitler's camps.
▷ *Legacies and Encounters: Poems 1966–1971* (1972)

GERSHWIN, Ira see RYSKIND, Morrie

GERSTÄCKER, Friedrich
(1816–72)

German writer and traveller, born in Hamburg. He worked his way through the USA, South America, Polynesia and Australia, and wrote colourful adventure stories, collected in *Mississippi-Bilder* (1847, Eng trans *Western Waters*, 1864).
▷ *Gerstaecker's Travels* (1854)

GESSNER, Salomon
(1730–88)

Swiss pastoral poet, who also painted and engraved landscapes, born in Zürich, where he was a bookseller. *Daphnis* (1754), a sentimental bucolic, was followed two years later by a volume of *Idyllen* ('Idylls') and by *Inkel und Yariko* ('Inkel and Yariko'). His *Tod Abels* (1758, 'Abel's Death'), a type of idyllic heroic prose poem, had the greatest success. His landscape paintings are all in the conventional classic style, but his engravings are of real merit. In 1772 he published a second volume of *Idyllen* and a series of letters on landscape painting.
▷ R Zuerchner, *Salmon Gessner, 1730–1788* (1968)

GEZELLE, Guido
(1830–99)

Flemish poet, born in Bruges. Ordained in 1854, he was for 28 years a curé in Courtrai. He published many volumes of lyrical verse, wrote on philology and folklore, founded literary magazines, and is regarded as the founder of the West Flemish school; he inaugurated a revival in the use of Flemish as a literary language.
▷ K de Busschere, *Guido Gezelle* (1959)

GHELDERODE, Michel de, previously Adhemar Martens
(1898–1962)

Belgian dramatist, born in Ixelles. He studied art and music and these interests influenced his writing, as did Flemish folklore and history, in which he was steeped from childhood, the puppet theatre, Elizabethan drama, and Catholic tradition. Although Flemish, he spoke and wrote in French. Between 1927 and 1930 he wrote plays for the Flemish Popular Theatre, including *Barabbas* (1928, Eng trans 1960), which portrays the horror of Christ's last days, and *Pantagleize* (1929, Eng trans 1957), a tragic farce about an absurdly innocent poet. *Fastes d'Enfer* (1929, Eng trans *Chronicles of Hell*, 1960) is one of his grotesque and violent evocations of medieval Flanders, while *Les Aveugles* (1933, Eng trans *The Blind Men*, 1960) is a dramatization of Breughel's satirical painting. A recluse, Ghelderode became internationally famous after controversial productions of his cruel but poetic plays in Paris in the late 1940s.
▷ R Beyen, *Michel de Ghelderode ou la hantise du masque* (1971)

GHIL, René
(1892–1925)

French Symbolist poet, born in Tourcoing in the Flemish part of France. The all-pervading influence upon his verse was that of

Mallarmé, but he evolved his own 'scientific' conception of poetry, explained in *Traité du verbe* (1886, 'Treatise on the Word'), and illustrated it with *Légendes d'âmes et de sang* (1885, 'Legends of Soul and Blood'). He claimed that all words had their analogues in colours and in music. He had a few faithful adherents in his own time, but is now generally regarded as a worthy curiosity who tried but failed to give to poetry the status of a science.

▷M Raymond, *From Baudelaire to Symbolism* (1950)

GHOSE, Manmohan
(1869–1924)

Indian Anglophone poet, a brother to the underrated mystic **Aurobindo Ghose**, born in Bhagalopore. He was educated in England, and lived there until he was 25. From 1902 until 1921 he was Professor of English at Presidency College, Delhi. He was a friend to **Stephen Phillips** and **Laurence Binyon**, and wrote pleasant Edwardian verse somewhat in the style of the latter, but without its distinction. Collections of his work include two volumes of *Selected Poems* (1969 and 1974).

GHOSE, Sri Aurobindo
(1872–1950)

Indian poet and mystic, almost always known as Aurobindo, who was the most distinguished of all Indians who wrote poetry in the English language. 'He is often', a critic aptly wrote, 'dismissed unread'. He was educated in England, was unjustly imprisoned by the British for 'terrorism', had a vision of Vishnu while incarcerated, went to Pondicherry, founded an *Ashram*, and lived there in meditation for the rest of his life. His enormous verse epic, *Savitri* (final version, 1954), of 24 000 lines, is now hardly read in Great Britain, and even his more modest, and less archaic, *Last Poems* (1952) is hardly known. Yet these last poems, even if they are not in fact 'like the best of 17th-century Metaphysical poetry' (as has been stated), are remarkable. He regarded his philosophy as an expression of original Vedanta, and he has been taken seriously by serious thinkers, though not of the West. His *Letters* (1949) contain stimulating statements about literature.

▷S Radhakrishnan and C A Moore (eds), *A Source Book in Indian Philosophy* (1957)

GHOSE, Sudhin Nath
(1899–)

Indian Anglophone novelist who has lived in Europe and England. His pleasant, lightweight novels, such as *Cradle of the Clouds*

(1951), render an accurate picture of Calcutta and its surroundings.

GHOSE, Zulfikar
(1935–)

Indian-born American poet and novelist, born in Sialkot (now in Pakistan). He was educated at Keele University and became cricket correspondent of *The Observer* (1960–5), before moving to the USA. The verse in *The Loss of India* (1964) looks back affectionately at the past and peers uncertainly into the future, as does that of *Jets of Orange* (1967), although in the latter volume there is an increasing sense of detachment. His elegant, intellectual, deliberate and meditative style, and the richness of his experience of various cultures, gains even greater authority in such novels as *The Native* (1972), *The Beautiful Empire* (1975) and *A Different World* (1979). Together, these comprise *The Incredible Brazilian* trilogy, a magical realist history of Brazil seen through the eyes of a reincarnated character named Gregorio. Ghose's essays of literary criticism include *The Fiction of Reality* (1984).

▷*Confessions of a Native-Alien* (1965)

GIACOMO, Salvator di
(1860–1934)

Neapolitan writer. He wrote novels and plays, and songs and lyrics in dialect. He was librarian in the National Library in Naples and also compiled several historical and bibliographical works.

▷L Russo, *Salvator di Giacomo* (1921)

GIACOSA, Giuseppe
(1847–1906)

Italian dramatist, born in Colleretto-Parella, Piedmont. He was a successful practitioner of various types of play, ranging from historical dramas and comedies in verse to contemporary social problem pieces. Representative of the former are *Il Conte Rosso* (1880, 'Count Rosso') and *La Contessa di Challant* (1891, 'The Countess of Challant'). His social problem plays include *Resa a discrezione* (1888, 'The Surrender of Discretion'), *Tristi amori* (1887, 'Sad Loves'), *Diritti dell' anima* (1894, 'Rights of the Soul'), *Come le foglie* (1900, 'Like the Leaves') and *Il piu forte* (1904, 'The Strongest'). He was not a radical, but emphasized bourgeois ideals of decency, homely virtues and established institutions. Consequently, his plays are not performed in modern repertory, though *Come le foglie*, his best piece, dealing with the disintegration of a wealthy family, has been filmed. With Luigi Illica he also collaborated on the libretti for *La Bohème, Madame Butterfly* and *Tosca*.

GIARDINELLI, Mempo
(1947–)

A very influential Argentinian writer, he has written widely across such genres as the crime novel, experimental novel and poetry. He was born in Resistencia, in the province of Chaco, and because of the political situation in Argentina moved to Mexico in 1976, only returning to Argentina after the restoration of democratic government in the 1980s. His novels *El cielo con las manos* (1981, 'Touching the Sky With Your Hands') and *La revolución en bicicleta* (1980, 'The Revolution on Bicycle') are representative of the style of Post-Boom writers; his novel *Luna Caliente* (1989, 'Hot Moon') won the Premio Nacional de Novela in Mexico in 1983.

GIBBON, Lewis Grassic, pseud of James Leslie Mitchell
(1901–35)

Scottish novelist, born on the farm of Hillhead of Seggat, Auchterless, Aberdeenshire. His father was a farmer and he was educated at the local school before attending Mackie Academy, Stonehaven, which he left after a year to become a newspaper reporter. Stirred by the promise of the Russian Revolution he became a member of the Communist Party. In 1919 he moved to Glasgow where he was employed on the *Scottish Farmer*, but his career in journalism was curtailed when he was dismissed for fiddling expenses. He attempted suicide, returned home and decided to enlist. He spent three and a half years with the Royal Army Service Corps in Persia, India and Egypt. In 1923 he left the army but poverty drove him to join up again, this time in the Royal Air Force, where he served as a clerk until 1929. His first published book was *Hanno, or the Future of Exploration* (1928) and others followed rapidly: *Stained Radiance* (1930), *The Thirteenth Disciple* (1931), *Three Go Back* (1932) and *The Lost Trumpet* (1932). *Sunset Song*, his greatest achievement, was published in 1932, the first of his books to appear under his pseudonym. Written in less than two months it was published under his mother's name as the first in a projected trilogy of novels, *A Scots Quair*, on the life of a young girl called Chris Guthrie. The second volume, *Cloud Howe*, appeared in 1933 and the third part, *Grey Granite*, in 1934. An unfinished novel, *The Speak of the Mearns*, was published in 1982. He also wrote a biography of the Scottish explorer, Mungo Park (1934), and published *The Conquest of the Maya* (1934).
▷D Young, *Beyond the Sunset* (1973)

GIBBONS, Stella Dorothea
(1902–89)

English writer, born in London. She worked as a journalist and later began a series of successful novels. She also wrote poetry and short stories, but her reputation rests on *Cold Comfort Farm* (1933), a light-hearted satire on the melodramatic rural novels such as those written by **Mary Webb**, which won the Femina Vie Heureuse Prize, and established itself as a classic of parody.

GIBBS, Wolcott
(1902–58)

American short-story writer and critic, whose most effective device was the ironic squib. He was born in New York City and it is hard to imagine him anywhere else. For much of his career he was closely associated with the *New Yorker* as desk editor and drama critic, and the best of his work is definitive of the magazine's urbane wit and intelligence; his one play, *Season in the Sun* (1950), contains a lively portrait of *New Yorker* editor Harold Ross. Early pieces of writing were collected in *Bed of Neuroses* (1937), which anticipates **Woody Allen**, and which was partly reprinted in a late publication *More in Sorrow* (1958)— a book which summarized Gibbs's lofty tolerance of human frailties.

GIBRAN, or JIBRAN, Kahlil
(1883–1931)

Lebanese mystical writer, poet and artist, born in Bisharri in the Lebanese mountains, but resident, from 1912, in New York. Early on he discovered a spiritual affinity with **William Blake**, especially as expressed in his drawings, and later on with **Nietzsche**'s work. Among his earliest works is *al-Ajnihah al-mutakassirah* (1911, Eng trans *Broken Wings*, 1922), in which he liberated Arabic from its archaic, classical roots and replaced it with the language of nature, allegory, metaphor and symbolism. Best-known for *The Prophet* (1923), written in English, Gibran's books have sold more than 20 million copies worldwide, and his poetry has been translated into more than 20 languages. By writing his later works in English, notably *Jesus the Son of Man* (1928) and *The Garden of the Prophets* (1934), Gibran was assured of a much wider readership and of a place among the great thinkers and artists of his time.
▷M Naimy, *Kahlil Gibran: His Life and His Work* (1965)

GIBSON, Wilfrid Wilson
(1878–1962)

English poet and playwright, born in Hexham. He was educated privately, and from 1902 wrote numerous volumes of verse, starting with *Urlyn the Harper and Other Songs*, on the plight of ordinary people faced with industrial change. Later volumes included *The Island Stag* (1947). He also wrote plays, including *Daily Bread* (1910) and a collection of verse plays, *Within Four Walls* (1950). A realist, he was concerned with everyday matters, particularly industrial poverty.

▷J Gawsworth, *Ten Contemporaries* (1932)

GIBSON, William
(1914–)

American playwright, born in New York. He is best known for *The Miracle Worker* (1960), his play about **Helen Keller**, which began life as a TV script in 1957, and then became the much-watched film (1962), starring Anne Bancroft. Other work includes the two-hander, *Two For The See-saw* (1958), a romantic interlude between a lawyer and a girl suffering from ulcers, and *Golda* (1977), about the Israeli leader, Golda Meir. Gibson will also go on record for having thought up the title *The Butterfingers Angel, Mary and Joseph, Herod the Nut, and the Slaughter of 12 Hit Carols in a Pear Tree* (1975).

GIBSON, William Ford
(1948–)

American science-fiction writer, resident in Canada since 1968. His work is associated with the 'Cyberpunk' genre of contemporary science fiction, generally set in run-down, near-future urban locations where technology defines the environment but is not, as in traditional science fiction, the point of the story. His most successful books are the ground-breaking 'Neuromancer' trilogy, comprising *Neuromancer* (1984), *Count Zero* (1986) and *Mona Lisa Overdrive* (1988), in which the protagonist seeks escape from physical alienation in 'Cyberspace', an infinitely complex virtual reality construction. His other books include the short-story collection *Burning Chrome* (1986) and *Virtual Light* (1993).

GIDE, André Paul Guillaume
(1869–1951)

French novelist, writer, diarist, man of letters and winner of the Nobel Prize for literature, born in Paris. His father, who died when Gide was 11, was Professor of Law at the Sorbonne. An only, lonely child, Gide had an irregular upbringing and was educated in a Protestant secondary school in Paris, and privately. A devotee of literature and music, he embarked on his career by writing essays, then poetry, biography, fiction, drama, criticism, memoirs and translation. He wrote more than 50 books in all, and came to be regarded as the grand old man of French literature. By 1917 he had emerged as the prophet of French youth and his unorthodox views were the subject of much debate. Though he married his cousin in 1892, he was bisexual with a strong physical attraction towards men. His international reputation rests largely on his stylish novels in which there is a sharp conflict between the spiritual and the physical. Significant titles are *L'Immoraliste* (1902, Eng trans *The Immoralist*, 1930), *La Porte étroite* (1909, Eng trans *Strait is the Gate*, 1924), *Les Caves du Vatican* (1914, Eng trans *The Vatican Swindle*, 1925), *La Symphonie Pastorale* (1919, Eng trans *Two Symphonies*, 1931) and *Les Faux-monnayeurs* (1926, Eng trans *The Counterfeiters*, 1927, rev edn 1950, *The Coiners*). He was a founder of the magazine *La Nouvelle Revue Française*, and kept up a voluminous correspondence, as well as being a critic of French bureaucracy at home and in the African colonies. His *Journals*, covering the years from 1889 to 1949, are trenchant, witty and self-revealing, and an essential supplement to his autobiography, *Si le grain ne meurt* (1920–1, Eng trans *If It Die . . .*, 1935). In 1947 he was awarded the Nobel Prize for literature.

▷G D Painter, *Gide: a critical biography* (1968); R H S Crossman, in *The God That Failed* (1950)

GIJSEN, Marnix, pseud of Jan-Albert Goris
(1899–)

Belgian (Flemish) novelist, poet, dramatist and critic, a diplomat by profession, born in Antwerp. For long regarded as the most important living author in the Flemish–Dutch language, he has also written in English and French. He was at one time a delegate to the United Nations, and went on to even greater diplomatic placings; yet his mature writings show no signs of this dual career, and he has referred to himself as the 'Euro-American homunculus'. He retired in 1968. He first emerged as a poet, much influenced by the third phase of German Expressionism; his ironic, elegant fiction began to appear after World War II: *Het boek van Joachim van Babylon* (1947, Eng trans *The Book of Joachim of Babylon*, 1951) and *Klaaglied om Agnes* (1951, Eng trans *Lament for Agnes*, 1957) are the best known. In the first he presents the biblical Susanna as a modern wife; the second is an autobiographical story about the woman whom he loved in his youth. The most revealing book by this interesting and vital confessional writer, a Catholic who turned agnostic in revulsion at the intolerance of his church, is *De leejaren van Jan-Albert Goris* (1975, 'Jan-Albert Goris's Years of Apprenticeship').

▷R P Meijer, *Literature of the Low Countries* (1978); M Gijsen, *Belgian Letters* (1946)

GIL GILBERT, Enrique
(1912–73)

Ecuadorean story writer, novelist and poet, born in Guayaquil, and one of the famous Guayaquil Group. Always fiery, he left school when he quarrelled with his uncle, the headmaster, over his communism, which was to be lifelong. He was a close friend to **Aguilera Malta**. Throughout his life he suffered from persecution from various governments, and an event of 1970, when he was tortured, shortened his life. His manuscripts were burned in the streets and, later, one of his novels was destroyed by sadistic prison guards. He wrote six books of fiction, of which the most famous is *Nuestro Pan* (1941, Eng trans *Our Daily Bread*, 1943), a capable public service novel about the exploitation of rice workers.
▷*Hispania* (February, 1940)

GIL POLO, Gaspar
(c.1535–1591)

Spanish poet, born in Valencia. He continued **Jorge de Montemayor**'s *Diana* in his *Diana enamorada* (1564, 'Diana in Love'), which was very popular throughout Europe, and was used by both **Cervantes** and **Shakespeare** as a basis for a plot. It marks a stage in the history of the novel.

GIL Y CARRASCO, Enrique
(1815–46)

Spanish poet and major novelist in the tradition of Sir **Walter Scott**, born in Villafranco del Bierzo, Léon. His *El señor de Bembibre* (1844) has been described both as 'the culminating work of the Romantic historical novel, beyond all question', and as 'the best historical novel in [Spanish] literature'. Well documented, it is still much read for its superb descriptions of Gil's native region, as well as for its well-told story of a frustrated love affair. Gil's poetry is seen at its best in his elegy (1842) for his close friend **Espronceda**. Unlike his romantic contemporaries, he excelled in the tender nature lyric ('La violeta', 1839, is one of his most famous poems). He died in Berlin of tuberculosis soon after accepting a diplomatic post there.
▷D G Samuels, *Enrique Gil y Carrasco: A Study in Spanish Romanticism* (1939)

GILBERT, Kevin
(1933–93)

Australian activist and writer, born in Condoblin, New South Wales, who adopted the culture of his part-aboriginal mother. While serving a life-sentence for murder he learned to read and write, later becoming Australia's first 'aboriginal' playwright. He was paroled in 1971 and in that year his play *The Cherry Pickers* was produced. Two collections of his verse have been published, *End of Dreamtime* (1971) and *People are Legends* (1978).

GILBERT, William
(1804–89)

English novelist, born in Bishopstoke. He abandoned the East India Company's service for the study of surgery, and that in turn for literature. His 30 works, published from 1858 onwards, include the delightful *King George's Middy* (1869), a biography of Lucrezia Borgia, and several **Defoe**-like novels.
▷*The Doctor of Beauweir: an autobiography* (2 vols, 1869)

GILBERT, Sir William Schwenck
(1836–1911)

English parodist and librettist of the 'Gilbert and Sullivan' light operas, born in London. He studied at King's College, London, and became a clerk in the privy-council office (1857–62). Called to the Bar in 1864, he failed to attract lucrative briefs and made his living from magazine contributions to *Punch* and *Fun*, for which he wrote much humorous verse under his boyhood nickname 'Bab', which was collected in 1869 as the *Bab Ballads*. He also wrote a Christmas burlesque, *Dulcemara, or The Little Duck and The Great Quack* (1866), and *The Palace of Truth* (1870), which both made a hit on the stage, followed by *Pygmalion and Galatea* (1871). But it is as the librettist of Sir Arthur Sullivan's (1842–1900) light operas that he is best remembered. Their famous partnership, begun in 1871, scored its first success with *Trial by Jury* under D'Oyly Carte's able management at the Royalty Theatre, London, in 1875. The same jibing, ludicrously topsy-turvy wit, beautifully accentuated by Sullivan's scores, pervaded the procession of light operas that followed, from *The Sorcerer* (1877), *HMS Pinafore* (1878) and *The Pirates of Penzance* (1879) to *The Gondoliers* (1889) and *The Grand Duke* (1896), which played first at the Opéra Comique and from 1881 in the newly-built Savoy Theatre. It was a carpet in the Savoy, considered too costly by the ever-argumentative Gilbert, that touched off a quarrel between him and Sullivan. They created only three more pieces before Sullivan's death and Edward German's efforts to fill the gap in *Fallen Fairies* (1909) proved unsuccessful.
▷H Pearson, *Gilbert: his life and strife* (1957)

GILCHRIST, Ellen Louise
(1935–)

American short-story writer and novelist, born in Vicksburg, Mississippi. Her only debt to **Faulkner**, with whom she was (pointlessly)

compared, is that she renders her settings and characters with such unmediated presence as to seem almost possessed by them. Her first collection of stories, *In the Land of Dreamy Dreams* (1981), established her distinctive manner which depends almost entirely on dialogue, with very little linking narrative. *The Annunciation* (1983) was far more discursive, its characters and situations somewhat stereotyped, and suggested that Gilchrist's gift was for the shorter form. Later story collections include *Victory over Japan* (1984, National Book Award), *Drunk with Love* (1986) and *Light Can Be Both Wave and Particle* (1989). A second novel, *The Anna Papers*, also appeared in 1989; three fictions of intermediate length were collected in *I Cannot Get You Close Enough* (1990).
▷ *Falling Through Space* (1988)

GILDER, Richard Watson
(1844–1909)

American editor and poet, born in New Jersey, who was a maker of literary opinion in the last quarter of the 19th century. He was an editor of both *Scribners* and *Century* magazines. His verse, once highly regarded, and his opinions, for all their temporary influence, are now forgotten or abhorred—he once refused to receive **Robert Louis Stevenson** when he was passing through New York, because he had heard (untrue) rumours about his 'private life'. His sister Jeanette (1849–1916) took **Thomas Hardy** to account for obscenity.

GILL, Brendan
(1914–)

American novelist and book reviewer, born in Hartford, Connecticut, who worked for many years on the *New Yorker*, having joined it on graduation (1956) from Yale. He has a light touch, and such novels as his first, *The Trouble of One House* (1950), an unsentimental study of a dying woman, offered sophisticated *New Yorker* readers exactly what they desired. The comic *The Day the Money Stopped* (1957) was adapted by Gill and **Maxwell Anderson** as a successful Broadway play.

GILLETTE, William Hooker
(1853–1937)

American actor and playwright, his most famous role was Sherlock Holmes, in a stage adaptation written in collaboration with **Conan Doyle**. Gillette was born in Hartford, Connecticut, and polished his suave delivery at the Monroe School of Oratory, a branch of Boston University. His first major success

was *The Professor* (1881), which was mounted at Madison Square Garden, and contained the lineaments of his Holmes characterization. The later *Held by the Enemy* (1886) and *Secret Service* (1895) played a significant role in revising and reconciling northern attitudes to the Civil War. Gillette retired after World War I, but cornered the market in lucrative comebacks and revivals. The best of his dramas were collected and edited by Rosemary Cullen and Don Wilmeth (1983) and they stand up surprisingly well.
▷ D Cook, *Sherlock Holmes and Much More* (1970)

GILLIATT, Penelope
(1932–)

English film and theatre critic, novelist and screenwriter, born in London. She has written a handful of novels, including *The Cutting Edge* (1978), which describes the relationship between two brothers, and six collections of short stories, including *Splendid Lives* (1977), a sympathetic study of a fleet of eccentrics. She was nominated for an Oscar for her screenplay for *Sunday Bloody Sunday* (1971), a highly topical piece dealing with the triangular relationship between a middle-aged man and woman and their shared, younger male lover. Her profiles of film-makers, several of which appeared in the *New Yorker*, are considered among the best of their kind.

GILMAN, Caroline Howard
(1794–1888)

American editor, memoirist and poet, born in Massachusetts. She went with her husband, a New England Unitarian minister, to the South, where she wrote a number of accounts of their life there, including *Recollections of a Southern Matron* (1838). From 1832 she edited *The Rose Bud*, one of the first US weekly publications for juveniles. Her *The Poetry of Travelling in the United States* (1838) is remarkable for its reconciliatory attitude and its emphasis on the universally shared and superior (though she does not say so) morality of women.

GILMAN, Charlotte Anna, née Perkins
(1860–1935)

American feminist and writer, born in Hartford, Connecticut. Brought up by her mother, she was educated at Rhode Island School of Design. She married a painter, Charles Stetson, in 1884, but separated in 1888, divorcing in 1894. Moving to California, she published her first stories, most memorably 'The Yellow Wall-Paper' (1892) and a collection of poetry, *In This Our World* (1893). She lectured on women's issues, as well as wider social concerns, and in 1898 wrote *Women and*

Economics, now recognized as a feminist landmark. In 1902 she married her cousin George Gilman, a New York lawyer. She founded, edited and wrote for the journal *Forerunner* (1909–16). Her later works include *The Man-made World* (1911) and *His Religion and Hers* (1923). She commited suicide on being told that she was suffering from incurable cancer.

▷ *The Living of Charlotte Perkins Gilman: An Autobiography* (1935)

GILMORE, Dame Mary Jean
(1865–1962)

Australian poet and author, born in Cotta Walla, near Goulburn, New South Wales. She moved with her family to Wagga Wagga, New South Wales, at the age of 10. Her early teaching career in the mining town of Broken Hill gave her an abiding interest in the labour movement. She became the first woman member of the Australian Workers' Union and, in 1896, joined William Lane's Utopian 'New Australia' settlement in Paraguay, South America. There she met and married a shearer, William Gilmore, and they returned to Australia in 1902, to settle in Sydney from 1912 onwards. Her socialist sympathies were now harnessed to campaigning for the betterment of the sick and the helpless, through the women's column which she edited for over 20 years in the Sydney *Worker* newspaper, but also in her six volumes of poetry. *Marri'd and Other Verses* (1910) was followed by *The Passionate Heart* (1918), *The Wild Swans* (1930) and the radical *Battlefields* (1939). Selected verse was published in 1948 (rev edn 1969) and in her 89th year she published her last collection, the more tranquil *Fourteen Men* (1954). A further *Selected Poems* came out in 1963. Her reminiscences *Old Days: Old Ways* (1934) and *More Recollections* (1935) illustrate her lifelong efforts to preserve early Australian traditions and folklore. She was created DBE in 1937, and William Dobell's controversial portrait of her was unveiled on her 92nd birthday in 1957. A collection of tributes to Dame Mary was published in 1965, and an edition of her letters in 1980.

▷ W H Wilde, *Three Radicals* (1969)

GILROY, Frank D(aniel)
(1925–)

American playwright and writer of screenplays, born in the Bronx. Gilroy's first play, *Who'll Save the Plowboy?* (1962), was about a soldier with doubts about the military life, and his second, the Pulitzer Prize-winning *The Subject was Roses* (1964), focused on the conflict between a returning soldier and his Irish–American family. Subsequent Broadway productions were failures and Gilroy has since concentrated on TV and the cinema. *Desperate Characters* (1971), his best screenplay, and directed by Gilroy for his own company, is a well-realized suburban drama based on **Paula Fox**'s novel, and set in New York's east side.

GINSBERG, Allen
(1926–)

American poet, born in Newark, New Jersey. Brought up in a Jewish community, his father was also a poet and his mother was a left-wing Russian emigrant. He was educated at Columbia University. A homosexual and drug experimentalist, he was born of the Beat movement and was friendly with **Jack Kerouac**, **William Burroughs** and others. *Howl and Other Poems* (1956), his first book, was a *succès de scandale*. The title poem was named by Kerouac because it seemed to him to release from some primal level of human consciousness 'the pent-up rage and frustrations of the inner being'. Whether this was so or not, it launched Ginsberg on a high profile career as public performer and icon of the counter-culture. Numerous collections have appeared including *Kaddish and Other Poems* (1961), *The Gates of Wrath: Rhymed Poems, 1948–52*, and *First Blues: Rags & Harmonium Songs 1971–74* (1975). Despite his initial anti-establishment stance, he has won honours and awards. His *Journals* were published in 1977.

▷ E Mottram, *Ginsberg in the 60s* (1972)

GINZBURG, Natalia
(1916–)

Italian author, born in Palermo into a liberal Jewish family who resisted the rise of fascism in the 1930s. Her first husband died in a Nazi prison, and she was forced to leave her home in Turin and live in a small town in the Abruzzi. Her first novel, *La strada che va in città* (1942), was written there and evokes a striking sense of an enclosing environment. Her spare, deceptively simple prose communicates the inarticulacy and emotional deprivation of her female protagonists. Domestic life remains her subject in her more light-hearted family memoir *Lessico famigliare* (1963), which won the Strega Prize, and in her later novels and plays which reveal how the break-up of the restrictive family unit has had little beneficial effect on the female condition.

▷ C S Bowe, 'The Narrative Strategy of Natalia Ginzburg', in *Modern Language Review*, 68 (1973)

GIONO, Jean
(1895–1970)

French novelist, born in Manosque, Provence, where many of his works are set. He fought in World War I and consequently became a pacifist; he was imprisoned for a time at the start of World War II as a result of this stance. The central character of his early works, such as the semi-auto-biographical *Jean le Bleu* (1933), is often a beneficent Nature, to which mere humans are secondary. His later novels, or chroniques, such as *Le Hussard sur le Toit* (1951), express a deepening distaste for the modern world, especially for the urban and the industrial.

GIOVANNI, Nikki, née Yolande Cornelia Giovanni, Jr
(1943–)

American poet, educated at Fisk University, an important location in the development of Black consciousness. Though her earlier work, *Black Judgement, Black Feeling, Black Talk* (both 1968) and *Poem of Angela Yvonne Davis* (1970), was closely associated with the radical and quasi-separatist mood of the 1960s, her later verse became more intro-spective and personal, more akin to the work of **June Jordan** and **Alice Walker**, with whom she conducted a significant debate, published as *A Poetic Equation* (1974). An encounter the year before with **James Baldwin**, *A Dialogue* (1973), was even more influential. Giovanni's more recent collections include the lyrical *Cotton Candy on a Rainy Day* (1978) and *Those Who Ride the Night Winds* (1983). Like Jordan, she has also written successfully for children.
▷*Gemini: An Extended Autobiographical Statement of My First Twenty-Five Years of Being a Black Poet* (1971)

GIPPIUS, or HIPPIUS, Zinaida Nikolayevna
(1869–1945)

Russian poet, novelist and critic (under the names of 'Anton the Extreme', and 'Comrade Herman'), born in Belev, Tula. After she went into exile (1919) she spelled her name 'Hip-pius', and she is sometimes known under it. She was married to **Merezhkovski**, who was more popular in his time, but who was infi-nitely less gifted. It took some time for Gip-pius's very high merits as a poet to become widely acknowledged, since in her capacity as a critic she poured deserved scorn on many now forgotten writers, who nevertheless bequeathed their hatred of her sharp and 'very partisan' pen to others. In fact, Gippius not only played a paramount part in freeing Russian poetry from a prosody it had outworn, but also was one of the best woman poets of the 20th century. She and her husband, weary of the Orthodox Church and its hypocrisy, founded a new mystical faith, a compound of the ideas of **Dostoyevsky, Solo-viev**, and others. Yet with this apparently out-landish mysticism she combined an extreme wit and a mordant sensibility. She had wel-comed the February Revolution of 1917, but rejected the Bolsheviks on account of their godlessness. Her memoirs *Zhivye litsa* (1925, 'Living Faces') deserve to be read not as eccentric outpourings, but as sober proph-ecies of the fall of Stalinism; even more wis-dom may be gleaned from the English translation of selections from her diaries, *Between Paris and St Petersburg* (1975). But paramount are her pellucid love lyrics and her religious poetry. *Moy lunny drug* (1925, 'My Moonlight Friend') is the most evocative of all portraits of **Blok**. There are English translations of her work in *Selected Works of Zinaida Gippius* (1972) and *Intellect and Ideas in Action: Selected Correspondence* (1972).
▷O Maslenikov, *The Frenzied Poets: Andrey Biely and the Russian Symbolists* (1952); V Zlobin, *A Difficult Soul: Zinaida Gippius* (1980)

GIRALDI, Giambattista, surnamed Cynthius, Cinthio, Centeo, or Cinzio
(1504–73)

Italian writer, born in Ferrara. He was Pro-fessor of Natural Philosophy at Florence and then of *belles lettres*. Later, he held the chair of rhetoric at Pavia. He is the author of nine plays in imitation of **Seneca**, of which *Orbec-che* (1541) is regarded as the first modern tragedy on classical lines to be performed in Italy. His *Ecatommiti* (published in 1565) is a collection of tales that was translated into French and Spanish and gave **Shakespeare** his plots for *Measure for Measure* and *Othello*.
▷P R Horne, *The Tragedies of Giambattista Giraldi* (1962)

GIRARDIN, Delphine de, née Gay
(1804–55)

French writer, born in Aix-la-Chapelle, first wife of Émile de Girardin. A fashionable figure, graced by beauty, charm and wit, she was acclaimed by the outstanding literary men of the period. She contributed *feuilletons* to her husband's paper under the pseudonym of the Vicomte Charles de Launay, elegant sketches of society life, and wrote some poetry, plays and novels, of which *Le Lorg-non* (1831, 'The Eyeglasses') is the best.
▷L Séché, *Muses romantiques* (1910)

GIRAUD, Albert
(1860–1929)

Belgian poet, born in Louvain. He would now be almost unknown had Schönberg not set the lyrics of his *Pierrot Lunaire* (1884) to famous (and once notorious) music. Too artificially haughty to have been a major poet, Giraud's work was well-made and genuinely melancholy, but it is for its style and not its content that it is now read.

▷R Frickx and M Joiret, *La Poésie française de 1880 à nos jours* (1976)

GIRAUDOUX, (Hippolyte) Jean
(1882–1944)

French writer, born in Bellac in Limousin. After a brilliant academic career and extensive travel, he joined the diplomatic service and became head of the French Ministry of Information during World War II, until his affiliations became suspect. As a poet and novelist, steeped in symbolism, much affected by psychoanalytic theories, he pioneered an Impressionistic technique in literature, exemplified particularly in *Provinciales* (1909), *Simon le Pathétique* (1918), and the reflection of his war experiences, *Retour d'Alsace, août 1914* (1916, 'Return from Alsace in August 1914'). His plays, for which he is chiefly remembered and in which he remains essentially a poet, are mainly fantasies based on Greek myths and biblical lore, satirically treated as commentary on modern life. They include *La Folle de Chaillot* (1945, Eng trans *The Madwoman of Chaillot*, 1949), *La Guerre de Troie n'aura pas Lieu* (1935) and *Pour Lucrèce* (1953). The last two were translated as *Tiger at the Gates* (1955) and *Duel of Angels* (1958) by **Christopher Fry**. He also wrote literary criticism, some short stories, and two film scripts.

▷L LeSage, *Giraudoux: his life and works* (1959)

GIRONELLA, José María
(1917–92)

Spanish novelist from Girona, in Catalonia, who began as a poet and who tried to emulate **Benito Pérez Galdós**. He was a sturdy, digressive, documentary realist (but critics accused him of lack of impartial documentation), whose tetralogy *Los cipreses creen en Dios* (1953, Eng trans *The Cypresses Believe in God*, 1955), *Un milión de muertos* (1961, Eng trans *One Million Dead*, 1963), *Ha estallado las paz* (1966, Eng trans *Peace After War*, 1969) and *Condenados a vivir* (1971, 'Condemned to Live'), created much controversy owing to its partiality towards the repressive Franco regime (for which, as a young man who had just given up studying for the priesthood, he fought). He took a more liberal approach later in his career, and opposed censorship. But his view of the Civil War is no longer accepted as an adequate one. His account of his grave mental illness of the early

1950s is contained in the selection *Phantoms and Fugitives* (1964).

▷R Schwartz, *José María Gironella* (1972); *Hispania*, 42 (1958)

GIRRI, Alberto
(1919–)

Argentinian poet and translator whose poetry is (notably) composed in European rather than in Latin-American styles. He may be called a 'hermetic' poet, but the general tendency of his work is obvious: its very restraint, elegant and ironic, calls attention to his passionate humanism. His distinguished poems speak for their themes rather than for themselves. There are English translations in the *Penguin Book of Latin American verse* (1971, ed E Curacciolo-Trejo).

GISSING, George Robert
(1857–1903)

English novelist, born in Wakefield, Yorkshire, the son of a pharmacist who imbued him with a love of literature. On his father's death Gissing was sent to boarding school, where he earned a scholarship to Owens College (now the University of Manchester). From there he won another scholarship to the University of London but before he could take it up he became enamoured of Marianne ('Nell') Harrison, thought to have been a prostitute, from whom he contracted venereal disease. Intent on transforming her into a seamstress, he stole from coat-pockets in his college, for which he was sentenced to a month's hard labour and expelled from college. He was packed off to America in disgrace, where he came close to starvation, but while in Chicago he wrote a melodramatic tale of English life which was bought by the *Chicago Tribune*. He subsisted by writing for a spell but he returned to England in 1877, met up again with Harrison in London and started his first novel, *Workers in the Dawn* (1880), which predicts disaster when two such people marry. Ignoring his own sound advice he married Nell in 1879. Doggedly productive, he fed the circulating libraries with three-decker novels which appeared with almost annual regularity: *The Unclassed* (1884), *Isabel Clarendon* (1886), *Demos* (1886), *Thyrza* (1887), *A Life's Morning* (1888) and *The Nether World* (1889), one of the most graphic accounts of Victorian poverty ever written. His industry, however, was not financially rewarding and the couple struggled until Nell died in 1888. Now better off, he travelled on the continent and turned his thoughts to more middle-class matters. The result was his finest fiction: *The Emancipated* (1890), *New Grub Street* (1891), a grim rebuke to all aspiring

authors, *Denzil Quarrier* and *Born in Exile* (both 1892), *The Odd Women* (1893), *In the Year of the Jubilee* (1894), *Eve's Ransom* and *Sleeping Fires* (both 1895), *The Paying Guest* (1896) and *The Whirlpool* (1897). Late in 1890 he met Edith Underwood, of a similar background to Nell, and they married in 1891. They had two sons and many rows and separated in 1897. His latter years were slightly more prosperous and happy than his earlier ones. In Paris in 1898 he met a Frenchwoman, Gabrielle Fleury, with whom he moved to the south of France for the sake of his lungs. He wrote several books in his final five years: a notable critical biography of **Dickens** (1898), a travel book, *By the Ionian Sea* (1900), and *The Private Papers of Henry Ryecroft* (1902), a spoof autobiography that was instantly successful. Few writers have stuck at their vocation with Gissing's single-mindedness. He lacked the sense of humour that made Dickens a favourite but he never shirked from depicting the unpalatable and few have caught so memorably the drudgery of day-to-day existence. His *Commonplace Book* was published in 1962 and *The Diary of George Gissing, Novelist* appeared in 1982.
▷ G Tindall, *The Born Exile* (1974)

GIUSTI, Giuseppe
(1809–50)

Italian poet and political satirist, born near Pistoia. In a brilliant series of elegantly crafted satirical poems he mercilessly denounced the enemies of Italy and the vices of the age. He was elected to the Tuscan chamber of deputies in 1848.
▷ S Horner, *The Tuscan Poet* (1928)

GJELLERUP, Karl Adolph
(1857–1919)

Danish novelist and theologian, born in Roholte, who rather unexpectedly received the 1917 Nobel Prize, which he shared with **Pontoppidan**. His work, influenced by Buddhist philosophy, has failed to last and, as he settled in Germany (1892), may be regarded as more German than Danish.
▷ P A Rosenberg, *Karl Gjellerup, Der Dichte und Denker* (1921–2)

GLANTZ, Margo
(1930–)

Mexican novelist and writer, born in Mexico City. She earned her doctorate in literature at the Sorbonne in Paris. Her interest lies in language and repression, and the role of women in subversion of patriarchy and of language itself. Her most famous work is *Las mil y una calorias* ('The Thousand and One Calories'), which is subtitled 'a dietetic novel'.

GLANVILLE, Brian Lester
(1931–)

English novelist and sportswriter, perhaps best known for his authoritative and intelligent soccer articles in *The Sunday Times*. Glanville published his first novel, *The Reluctant Dictator* (1952), when he was only 21, and has since continued to write underrated fiction, by no means exclusively with sporting backgrounds. Only in *The Dying of the Light* (1976), perhaps his most profound novel, does sport take on a symbolic character; even here, though, it is rendered with convincing detail. The most straightforward of the footballing novels, *The Rise of Gerry Logan* (1963), is probably his best-known book, but it gains much of its power from Glanville's ability to capture the coded language and gesture of distinct social groups, something he has also done to great effect in short-story collections like *The King of Hackney Marshes* (1965) and, with a Jewish central character, in the novel *A Second Home* (1965). Glanville's sports books for young readers have the same uncompromising and uncondescending manner as his adult writing.

GLAPTHORNE, Henry
(1610–c.1644)

English dramatist, born in Whittlesey. Between 1629 and 1643, he wrote a few poems and some plays, including *Albertus Wallenstein*; *Argalus and Parthenia*, a poetical dramatization of part of the *Arcadia*; *The Hollander* and *Wit in a Constable* (comedies); and *The Ladies Privilege*. *The Lady Mother* was also attributed to him.
▷ Memoir by M H Shepherd in *Plays and Poems of Henry Glapthorne* (1874)

GLASGOW, Ellen Anderson Gholson
(1874–1945)

American novelist, born in Richmond, Virginia. She was best known for her stories of the South, including *The Descendant* (1897), *The Voice of the People* (1900), *Virginia* (1913), and *In This Our Life* (1941, Pulitzer Prize). *Barren Ground* (1925) is a more optimistic and progressivist narrative.
▷ L W Wagner, *Ellen Glasgow: beyond convention* (1982)

GLASKIN, Gerald Marcus
(1923–)

Australian writer of novels, short stories and non-fiction, born in Perth. After service in World War II he received attention for his novel *A World of Our Own* (1955) on the problems of ex-servicemen returning to civilian life. Many novels followed, including *A Lion in the Sun* (1960), and a book on

Australia's 'empty north', *The Land that Sleeps* (1961).

GLASPELL, Susan
(1882–1948)

American writer, born in Davenport, Iowa. She was the author of novels, including *Fidelity* (1915), *Brook Evans* (1928) and *The Fugitive's Return* (1929), also of plays, among them *Trifles* (1917) and *Alison's House* (1930), based on the life of **Emily Dickinson**, which won a Pulitzer Prize.
▷A Waterman, *Susan Glaspell* (1966)

GLASSCO, John
(1909–81)

Canadian poet, novelist, translator and editor, born in Montreal. Glassco has probably been most widely read in his capacity as author of the elegant pornographic classic variously known as *The English Governess* (1960), or *Under the Birch*, or *Harriet Marwood, Governess*, which he wrote as 'Miles Underwood', and which is written with great literary panache, humour and irony. But he was a gifted elegiac poet, a fine technician and author of a number of beautiful and deservedly prized poems such as 'Deserted Buildings Under Shefford Mountain'. He translated the *Journal* and the *Complete Poems* of **Hector de Saint-Denys Garneau**. His *Selected Poems* appeared in 1971. His completion of the novel *Under the Hill* by Aubrey Beardsley (1959) was regarded as a brilliant tour de force.
▷*Time* (2 December, 1974); *The Canadian* (21 February, 1976)

GLASSOP, Lawson
(1913–66)

Australian journalist and war correspondent, born in Lawson, Blue Mountains, New South Wales, whose reputation rests solely on his reportage-style novel *We Were the Rats* (1944), which described, in vivid and accurate soldiers' language, episodes of the North African war. It was banned in New South Wales until 1961 when an expurgated edition was published. A sequel, *The Rats in New Guinea* (1963), was less successful. Glassop also wrote a novel and a book for children.

GLATSTEIN, Jacob
(1896–1971)

Polish Yiddish poet and critic, born in Lublin; he emigrated to the USA just before World War I, and died in New York, where he had made his living as a leading Yiddish journalist. He travelled to Warsaw in 1909 to show his work to the master **Peretz**, who endorsed his promise. After he arrived in New York, at the age of 18, Glatstein felt discouraged, and started to write poetry in English. This short period turned out to be a useful one, for he came under the influence of **Tagore**, whose mysticism stayed with him. He then met a number of Yiddish poets, and, together with Nokhem Minkoff (1893–1958) and Aaron Glanz-Leyeles (1889–1966), he established the In Zikh movement—it derived its name from the Yiddish magazine, and meant 'within the self'. It was in part an expressionistic reaction against the dynamic, and more politically oriented, earlier group called Die Yunge ('The Young'). But Glatstein was never dogmatic, and he helped to introduce a carefully cadenced free verse into Yiddish poetry. His own poetry, vital, sharply ironic, true to his inner self, all of it with his personal signature etched into it, is paramount in the Yiddish (and Jewish) poetry of the 20th century. It is to be found in competent translation in *Poems* (1970) and *The Selected Poems of Jacob Glatstein* (1972). Two autobiographical volumes, about his return to Poland in the mid-1930s to see his dying mother, are outstanding: *Ven yash iz geforn* (1938, Eng trans *Homeward Bound*, 1969), and *Ven yash iz gekumen* (1940, Eng trans *Homecoming at Twilight*, 1962).
▷*Commentary* (January 1972); J R Hadda, *Yankev Glatstein* (1980)

GLAZAROVÁ, Jarmila, née Podivinská
(1901–)

Czech novelist, born in Malá Skála. A country doctor's wife, her early novels, already socialist in tone, dealt with the hard lives of the peoples of Moravia and Czech Silesia and, competently if not profoundly, with the problems of women. Later she became the communist government's cultural attaché to Moscow and a member of parliament. Little she wrote after 1948 has any literary value, although *Leningrad* (1950) won a State Prize.

GLEIG, George Robert
(1796–1888)

Scottish novelist and historian, born in Stirling, the son of the Bishop of Brechin. He studied at Glasgow and Balliol College, Oxford, joined the army, and served in the Peninsular War (1813) and in North America (1814). He took orders (1820), and became Chaplain-General of the army (1844) and Inspector-General of military schools (1846). He wrote *The Subaltern* (1825) and other novels, and books on military history and biographies of Wellington and Warren Hastings.
▷W Walker, *Life of George Robert Gleig* (1892)

GLEIM, Johann Wilhelm Ludwig
(1719–1803)

German poet, born in Ermsleben near Halberstadt. He held religious and political offices, and was the leader of the 'Anacreontic' school of lyric poets, celebrating the joys of wine, love and friendship, as in *Lieder* (1745, 'Songs') and *Lieder nach dem Anakreon* (1766, 'Anacreontic Songs'). His patriotic *Lieder eines Preussischen Grenadiers* (1758–78, 'Songs of a Prussian Grenadier') contributed to the war poetry of the age of Frederick II, the Great.

GLEN, Esther
(1881–1940)

New Zealand journalist and writer for children. Aware of the lack, she started writing a children's supplement for the family newspaper, the Christchurch *Sun*, and later for the *Press*. Her first novel for younger readers was *Six Little New Zealanders* (1917), followed by its sequel *Uncles Three at Kamahi* (1926). Although she only wrote four books—the others were *Twinkles on the Mountain* (1920) and *Robin of Maoriland* (1929)—her influence on New Zealand children's writing was considerable, and in 1945 the New Zealand Library Association established the annual Esther Glen Award for distinguished contributions to the genre.

GLEN, William
(1789–1826)

Scottish poet, born in Glasgow. He spent most of his life in the West Indies. His only volume of poems and songs, *Poems Chiefly Lyrical*, published posthumously in 1815, contains the popular Jacobite lament, 'Wae's me for Prince Charlie'.

GLOAG, Julian
(1930–)

English novelist. His first book, *Our Mother's House* (1963), revolving around a clandestinely buried parent, gained wider currency through a film adaptation starring Dirk Bogarde. Gloag's later books were less elegant and original but also more profound. *A Sentence of Life* (1966) is a curiously affirmative murder story, as is *A Woman of Character* (1973), which is notable for its attempt to convey distinctively female concerns. Other novels include *Sleeping Dogs Lie* (1980) and *Blood for Blood* (1985).

GLOVER, Denis James Matthews
(1912–80)

New Zealand poet, publisher and printer of fine books, born in Dunedin. His Caxton Press was established in 1933, and brought out prose and poems from the country's leading contemporary writers. After his return from naval service in World War II, recounted in his book of reminiscences *Hot Water Sailor* (1962), he immediately published **Allen Curnow**'s anthology *A Book of New Zealand Verse 1923–45* (1945), which made an immediate impact on New Zealand writers. His own verse first appeared in *Several Poems* (1936) and *Thirteen Poems* (1939), and is collected in *The Wind and the Sand: Poems 1934–44* (1945), *Enter without Knocking: Selected Poems* (1964, enlarged edn 1971), and *Selected Poems* (1981, with an introduction by Allen Curnow). His wartime experiences are further narrated in *D-Day* (1944).

GLÜCK, Louise Elisabeth
(1943–)

American poet, born and educated in New York. Though her first verses were obviously influenced by **Robert Lowell** and other male poets, she has developed a distinctively female perspective, most noticeably in her reworking of the story of King David's concubine Abishag the Shunamite in *The House on the Marshland* (1975). In the seventies she gradually modulated the staccato contractions of her debut collection *Firstborn* (1968) in favour of more varied and expressive rhythms that sometimes recall **Rilke** and even **Heinrich Heine**. Later collections include *Teh* (1976), *Descending Figure* (1980) and *Ararat* (1990).

GLYN, Elinor, née Sutherland
(1864–1943)

British popular novelist, born in Jersey, Channel Islands. She married in 1892. She began writing with *The Visits of Elizabeth* (1900), but found fame with *Three Weeks* (1907), a book which gained a reputation for being risqué. She kept her public enthralled with such books as *Man and Maid* (1922), *Did She?* (1934) and *The Third Eye* (1940). Nonsensical, faulty in construction and ungrammatical, her novels were nevertheless avidly read. She went to Hollywood (1922–7), where 'it' (her version of sex appeal) was glamorized on the screen.
▷ *Romance Adventure* (1936)

GODBER, John (Harry)
(1956–)

English playwright, born in Upton, Yorkshire. He studied at Bretton Hall College and Leeds University, and worked as a drama teacher, before becoming artistic director of the Hull Truck Theatre Company in 1984. His plays, which are mostly comedies, deal with working-class characters, usually in the contexts of sport, as in *Up 'n' Under* (1984), about Rugby League players, or entertainment, as in *Bouncers* (1984), which is set in a discotheque. *Teechers* (1987) draws on his experience of education. Godber believes strongly in physical theatre, but he also has the ability to convey deep emotion without sentimentality. He has written scripts for popular television programmes such as *Brookside*, as well as the series *The Ritz* (1987).

GODDEN, (Margaret) Rumer
(1907–)

English novelist, poet and children's author, born in Eastbourne, Sussex. She lived for many years in India, a country and culture which provide the backdrop to much of her fiction. Her third novel and first major success, *Black Narcissus* (1939), describes the struggles of nuns attempting to found a mission in the Himalaya region. Her first book for children was *The Dolls' House* (1947). She frequently writes from the point of view of a young person, most notably in *The Greengage Summer* (1958), a delicate story of love and deception set in the Champagne area of the Marne. Highly regarded for the atmospheric lucidity of her prose, Godden's most recent books include *Coromandel Sea Change* (1991), a love story set in southern India.
▷ *A Time to Dance, No Time to Weep* (1987); *A House with Four Rooms* (1989)

GODFREY, Dave
(1938–)

Canadian poet and writer of fiction, born in Toronto. Godfrey has played in a jazz band and worked in university English departments in Ghana and in Canada. His time spent in Africa resulted in *The New Ancestors* (1967), a fictional consideration of the background to the revolution of 1966. Not everyone felt the novel gave a fair picture of politics in Ghana, but it won a Governor General's Award. His earlier collection of short stories, *Death Goes Better with Coca-Cola* (1967), portrayed what Godfrey has described as 'a certain reticence in Canadian society'.
▷ G Gibson, *Eleven Canadian Novelists Interviewed* (1973)

GODWIN, Francis
(1562–1633)

English prelate and author, born in Hannington, Northamptonshire, the son of Bishop Thomas Godwin (1517–90). Educated at Oxford, he became rector of Sampford,

Bishop of Llandaff (1601) and of Hereford (1617). His eight works include *A Catalogue of the Bishops of England* (1601), but he is best known for his science-fiction romance, *Man in the Moon or a Voyage Thither, by Domingo Gonsales* (1638), used as a source by Bishop John Wilkins, **Cyrano de Bergerac** and **Jonathan Swift**.

GODWIN, Gail
(1937–)

American novelist and dramatist, born in Alabama. Her first novel was *The Perfectionist* (1970), but her most famous and highly regarded has been *The Odd Woman* (1974), a well-made and suspenseful study of an introspective college instructor who, although intelligent and aware, cannot prevent herself from over-idealism in her affair with an over-cautious academic. *Dream Children* (1976) is a collection of her stories.
▷ A Z Mickelson, *Recent American Fiction by Women* (1979)

GODWIN, William
(1756–1836)

English political writer and novelist. Born at Wisbech, he passed his boyhood at Guestwick in Norfolk. After three years at Hindolveston day school, three more with a tutor at Norwich, and one as usher in his former school, in 1773 he entered Hoxton Presbyterian College; in 1778 he left it as pure a Sandemanian and Tory as he had gone in. But during a five years' ministry at Ware, Stowmarket and Beaconsfield, he turned Socinian and republican, and by 1787 was a 'complete unbeliever'. Meanwhile he had taken up writing. The French Revolution gave him an opening, and his *Enquiry Concerning Political Justice* (1793) brought him fame and a thousand guineas, and captivated **Coleridge**, **Wordsworth**, **Robert Southey**, and later and above all **Shelley**, who became his disciple, son-in-law and subsidizer. It was calmly subversive of everything (law and 'marriage, the worst of all laws'), but it deprecated violence, and was deemed caviare for the multitude, so its author escaped prosecution. His masterpiece, *The Adventures of Caleb Williams* (1794), was designed to give 'a general review of the modes of domestic and unrecorded despotism'; unlike most novels with a purpose, it is really a strong book. In 1797 he married Mary Wollstonecraft, who was pregnant by him; but she died soon after the baby was born. Four years later he married Mrs Clairmont, who had two children already, and a third was born of the marriage. So there were poor Fanny Imlay (1794–1816), who died by her own hand; **Mary Wollstonecraft Shelley** (née Godwin); Charles Clairmont; 'Claire' Clairmont (1797–

1879), the mother by **Byron** of Allegra; and William Godwin (1803–32). A bookselling business long involved Godwin in difficulties, and in 1833 he was glad to accept the sinecure post of yeoman-usher of the Exchequer. His tragedy, *Antonio* (1800), was hopelessly damned. The best of his later prose works are *The Enquirer* (1797) and *St Leon* (1799).

▷F K Brown, *The Life of William Godwin* (1926)

GOES, Albrecht
(1908–)

German poet and novelist, a Lutheran pastor's son, who himself became a pastor (until he resigned from his ministry in 1953 in order to devote his time to writing) and was a chaplain to the army in Russia during World War II. His graceful poetry is in the tradition of his fellow pastor and native of Württemberg, **Eduard Mörike**; but his finest work, praised by **Martin Buber**, is in the harrowing novel *Das Brandopfer* (1954, Eng trans *The Burnt Offering*, 1956), about the humane wife of a butcher who takes over his business when he is called up, and is instructed to supply meat to Jews, who gradually disappear. Goes is an art critic, and was known for many years as a mediator between East and West Germany, and as a broadcaster about Nazi crimes, which he insisted must not be forgotten.

▷E W Rollins and H Zohn (eds), *Men of Dialogue: Martin Buber and Albrecht Goes* (1969)

GOETHE, Johann Wolfgang von
(1749–1832)

German poet, dramatist, scientist and court official, born in Frankfurt-am-Main. He was educated privately and studied reluctantly for his father's profession, law, at Leipzig (1765–8), but a love affair with Käthchen Schönkopf inspired his first two plays, *Die Laune des Verliebten* (1767, 'The Lover's Feelings') and *Die Mitschuldigen* (1769, 'The Guilty Parties'), which was, however, not staged until 1787. After a protracted illness he continued his law studies at Strasbourg from 1770, where he came under the influence of **Johann Herder**, the pioneer of German Romanticism. He read **Oliver Goldsmith**'s *Vicar of Wakefield* and dabbled in alchemy, anatomy and the antiquities. Another love affair, with Friedericke Brion, inspired 'Röslein auf der Heide' and several fine lyrics. In 1771 he qualified, returned to Frankfurt, became a newspaper critic and captured the thwarted spirit of German nationalism in that early masterpiece of *Sturm und Drang* drama, *Götz von Berlichingen mit der eisernen Hand* (1772, trans by Sir **Walter Scott** as *Goetz of Berlichingen with the Iron Hand*, 1799), which

in the person of the chivalrous robber-knight whose values had outlived his age, epitomized the man of genius at odds with society. *Faust* was begun, and Goethe followed up his first triumph with his self-revelatory cautionary novel, *Die Leiden des jungen Werthers* (1774, Eng trans *The Sorrows of Werther*, 1780), which mirrored his hopeless affair with Charlotte Buff, a friend's fiancée. Werther is made to solve the problem of clashing obligations by nobly and romantically committing suicide. Goethe himself, however, 'saved himself by flight'. *Clavigo* (1774), a Hamlet-like drama, followed in the same vein, based on **Beaumarchais**' *Mémoires*. Lili Schönemann inspired the love lyrics of 1775. In the autumn he surprisingly accepted the post of court-official and privy councillor (1776) to the young Duke of Weimar. He conscientiously carried out all his state duties, interested himself in a geological survey, and taken in hand, emotionally, by the young widow, Charlotte von Stein, exerted a steadying influence on the inexperienced duke. His 10-year relationship with Charlotte did little to help his development as a creative writer, valuable as his 'anchor' might have seemed to him psychologically. In 1782 he extended his scientific researches to comparative anatomy, discovered the intermaxillary bone in man (1784), and formulated a vertebral theory of the skull. In botany he developed a theory that the leaf represented the characteristic form of which all the other parts of a plant are variations, and made foolish attempts to refute Newton's theory of light. He wrote a novel on theatrical life, *Wilhelm Meisters Theatralische Sendung*, not discovered until 1910 (1911, Eng trans *Wilhelm Meister's Theatrical Mission*, 1913), which contains the enigmatic poetry of Mignon's songs, epitomizing the best in German romantic poetry, including the famous 'Nur wer die Sehnsucht kennt' ('Only He Who Knows Yearning'). His visits to Italy (1786–8 and 1790) cured him of his emotional dependence on Charlotte von Stein and contributed to a greater preoccupation with poetical form, as in the severely classical verse version of his drama, *Iphigenie* (1789, Eng trans *Iphigenia in Tauris*, 1793), and the more modern subjects *Egmont* (1788) and *Tasso Torquato* (1790, Eng trans 1980). His love for classical Italy, coupled with his passion for Christiane Vulpius, whom he married in 1806, found full expression in *Römische Elegien* (1782–9, Eng trans *Roman Elegies*, 1793). From 1794 dates his friendship with **Schiller**, with whom he conducted an interesting correspondence on aesthetics (1794–1805) and carried on a friendly contest in the writing of ballads which resulted on Schiller's part in *Die Glocke* and on Goethe's in the epic idyll *Hermann und*

Dorothea (1798, Eng trans 1801). They wrote against philistinism in the literary magazine *Horen*. Goethe's last great period saw the prototype of the favourite German literary composition, the *Bildungsroman* in *Wilhelm Meisters Lehrjahre* (1795, Eng trans *Wilhelm Meister's Apprenticeship* and *William Meister's Travels*, 1824–7), continued as *Wilhelm Meisters Wanderjahre* (1821). *Wilhelm Meister* became the idol of the German Romantics, of whom Goethe increasingly disapproved. He disliked their enthusiasm for the French Revolution, which he satirized in a number of works, including the epic poem *Reineke Fuchs* (1794, Eng trans *Reynard the Fox*, 1886), based on a medieval theme, and the drama *Die natürliche Tochter* (1803, 'The Natural Daughter'), and their disregard for style, which he attempted to correct by example in his novel *Die Wahlverwandtschaften* (1809, Eng trans *Elective Affinities*, 1960) and the collection of lyrics, inspired by Marianne von Willemer, *Westöstlicher Divan* (1819, 'Western-Eastern Divan'). But his masterpiece is his version of **Christopher Marlowe**'s drama of *Faust*, on which he worked for most of his life. Begun in 1775, its first part was published after much revision and Schiller's advice in 1808 (produced 1819, Eng trans *Faustus*, 1821), and the second part in 1832 (both parts trans 1838). The disillusioned scholar, Faust, deserts his 'ivory tower' to seek happiness in real life, makes a pact with Satan, who brings about the love-affair, seduction and death of Gretchen, an ordinary village girl, and subtly brings Faust by other such escapades to the brink of moral degradation. Part one is generally regarded as one of the classics of world literature. Goethe took little part in the political upheavals of his time. Yet Napoleon made a point of meeting him at the congress of Erfurt (1803), and Goethe in 1813 kept aloof from the *Befreiungskriege* ('Wars of Liberation'), having identified Napoleon with the salvation of European civilization. A towering influence on German literature, Goethe was buried near Schiller in the ducal vault at Weimar.

▷J P Eckermann, *Gespräche mit Goethe* (1836); G H Lewes, *The Life of Goethe* (1906)

GOGARTY, Oliver St John
(1878–1957)

Irish poet and memoir-writer, born in Dublin. Also a playwright, politician and surgeon, this polymath knew **James Joyce** and was the model for 'stately, plump Buck Mulligan' in *Ulysses*. He was a senator of the Irish Free State from its foundation in 1922 until 1939, in which year he moved to the USA. His garrulous, witty prose is at its best in *As I Was Going Down Sackville Street* (1937) and *Tumbling In The Hay* (1939). It is on these volumes, rather than the *Collected Poems* (1952), that his lessened reputation now rests.

GOGOL, Nikolai Vasilievich
(1809–52)

Russian novelist and dramatist, born in Sorochinstsi in Poltava. In 1829 he settled in St Petersburg, and in 1831–2 published his first major work, *Vechera na khutore bliz Dikanki* ('Evenings on a Farm near Dikanka'), followed by two collections of short stories, *Mirgorod* (1835, Eng trans 1928) and *Arabesques* (1835, Eng trans 1982) which contained some of his finest stories, like *Shincl'* ('The Overcoat'), *Nevsky Prospect*, and *Zapiski symashedshevo* ('The Diary of a Madman'), which introduce a nightmarish world of his fantastic imagination, exemplifying his irrational fears, frustrations and obsessions. In 1836 he brought out his play, *Revizor* (Eng trans *The Inspector-General*, 1892), the best of Russian comedies, a wild and boisterous satire exposing the corruption, ignorance and vanity of provincial officials. He left Russia for Italy in 1836, and in Rome wrote the first part of *Myortvye dushi* (1842, Eng trans *Dead Souls*, 1854), one of the great novels in world literature. It deals with an attempt by small landowners to swindle the government by the purchase of dead serfs whose names should have been struck off the register. His later work shows increasing obsession with his own sinfulness and he burnt many of his remaining manuscripts, including the second part of *Myortvye dushi*. He returned to Russia in 1846.

▷H Troyat, *Nikolai Gogol* (1971)

GOLD, Herbert
(1924–)

American novelist, born in Cleveland, Ohio, and educated at Columbia University and at the Sorbonne. Though rarely grouped with them and considered to be a more 'popular', journeyman writer, Gold shares with **Bellow** and **Malamud** a profound concern for the identity problems and cultural expectations of the Jewish American male. Perhaps his most important book is the autobiographical *My Last Two Thousand Years* (1972), which underlines how often he has mined painful personal experience for his novels; *Fathers* (1967) and *Family* (1981) are both subtitled 'a novel in the form of a memoir', recalling **Mailer**'s similar hybrids. Notable among his other novels are *The Prospect Before Us* (1954), *Salt* (1963), *Swiftie the Magician* (1974) and *He/She* (1980), which demonstrates his ability to render convincing female characters.

GOLD, Michael
(1893/4–1967)

American radical novelist, playwright and journalist, he was born Itzok Granich or Granitz—sometimes given as Irwin or Irving—in New York City. He spent a year at New York University and at Harvard, but claimed that his real education had taken place in the slums of the Lower East Side. An early play, *Down the Airshaft* (1916), attempted to capture this environment. He spent two years in Mexico, which sharpened his social conscience and converted him to communism. On his return, he began writing for the left-wing *Liberator*, for which his essay 'Towards Proletarian Art' (February 1921) became one of the defining texts of American proletarianism. In 1926 he co-founded *New Masses*, a descendant of *Liberator* and *Masses*, committed to the aggressive revolutionism of Stalin's 'Third Period'. His journalism was as violent as his politics were apocalyptic; he famously attacked **Hemingway**, whom he considered to be excessively detached from everyday reality, and the popular **Thornton Wilder**, whose work espoused what Gold dubbed 'The Gospel of the Genteel Christ'. Ironically, his own fiction was gentler and almost lyrical; the semi-autobiographical *Jews Without Money* (1930) is centred on an unexpectedly pastoral idyll in Central Park. Gold's sketches of US workers were collected in *120 Million* (1929) and his earlier essays for the *Daily Worker*, with whom he was to be a columnist until shortly before his death, appeared as *The Hollow Men* (1941). Gold's reputation has revived with a fresh interest in American proletarianism.

▷ J Pyros, *Michael Gold: Dean of American Proletarian Writers* (1979)

GOLDBERG, Leah
(1911–70)

Lithuanian poet, critic and university teacher, writing in Hebrew. She settled in Palestine from 1935, and became well known as the translator of classics such as **Tolstoy**'s *War and Peace* into Hebrew. She was one of the most prized of the lyrical poets of Israel, but little of her work has been translated.

GOLDFADEN, Avraham
(1840–1908)

The father of the modern Yiddish theatre, born in the Ukraine. He founded the first modern Yiddish theatre at Jassy, in Romania, in October 1876. Professional to his fingertips—actor, song-writer, producer, manager—he wrote some lively plays, including *The Witch* (1879). His plays are still produced

in Hebrew in Israel, and his *Shulamit* (1880) was revived in New York in 1951.

▷ C Madison, *Yiddish Literature* (1968)

GOLDING, Louis
(1895–1958)

English novelist and essayist. His best-known work is *Magnolia Street* (1932), the story of a typical street in a provincial city whose inhabitants were Jews on one side, Gentiles on the other.

▷ *The World I Knew* (1940)

GOLDING, Sir William Gerald
(1911–93)

English novelist and winner of the Nobel Prize for literature, born in St Columb Minor, Cornwall. He was educated at Marlborough Grammar School and Brasenose College, Oxford, where—after first taking examinations in botany, zoology, chemistry and physics—he revolted against science and transferred to English literature, devoting himself to Anglo-Saxon. After five years at Oxford he published his first book, *Poems* (1934), a rarity which he later disowned. He spent the next five years working in small theatre companies, as an actor, director and writer, and in 1958 he adapted the short story 'Envoy Extraordinary' for the stage as *The Brass Butterfly*. He married in 1939 and spent the war years in the Royal Navy. From 1945 to 1961 he was a teacher of English and philosophy at Bishop Wordsworth's School, Salisbury, a career he detested. He gained international celebrity with *The Lord of the Flies* (1954), which has become a classroom classic. A chronicle of the increasingly tribal and primitive activities of a group of schoolboys shipwrecked on a desert island in the wake of a nuclear war, Golding said that it arose from his five years' war service, and 10 years of teaching small boys. *The Inheritors* (1955) was his second novel and in theme and tone it is the blood-brother of its predecessor, human malevolence surfacing through mobatrocity and in the arena of power. Next came *Pincher Martin* (1956), *Free Fall* (1959), *The Spire* (1964) and *The Pyramid* (1967). There was a gap of 12 years before *Darkness Visible* (1979), during which he wrote short stories, a film script and aborted novels. In later years he returned to his old productivity. With *Rites of Passage* (1980), the first of a trilogy about a 19th-century voyage from England to Australia, he won the Booker Prize. *Close Quarter* (1987) was its sequel and the trilogy closed with *Fire Down Below* (1989). His only other novel was *The Paper Men* (1984). In 1983 he was awarded the Nobel Prize for literature.

▷ M K Weeks and I Gregor, *William Golding: a critical study* (1967)

377

GOLDMAN, William
(1931–)

American novelist and author of film screenplays, born in Chicago. Since his first novel, *The Temple of Gold* (1957), Goldman has written several books, including *Marathon Man* (1974) and *The Color of Light* (1984), the latter the story of Chubb Fuller and his attempts to be a responsible, honourable man in contemporary society. Goldman, though, is more widely known through his screenplays, a form of which he is a modern master. *Marathon Man*, the terse, thrilling story of a Nazi who emerges from hiding to claim a cache of diamonds in New York, was memorably filmed to his own script in 1976. Other Goldman screenplays include *Butch Cassidy and the Sundance Kid* (1969), *All the President's Men* (1976) and *A Bridge Too Far* (1977). He has also written one of the finest memoirs of the film business, *Adventures in the Skin Trade: A Personal View of Hollywood and Screenwriting* (1983).

GOLDONI, Carlo
(1707–93)

Italian dramatist, born in Venice. He studied for the law, but his heart was set on writing plays. A tragedy, *Belisario* (1732), proved a success; but he soon discovered that his forte was comedy, and he decided to write for the Italian comic stage. He spent several years in wandering over north Italy, until in 1740 he settled in his birthplace, where for 20 years he poured out comedy after comedy. He wrote no fewer than 250 plays in Italian, French and the Venetian dialect. He was greatly influenced by **Molière** and the *commedia dell' arte*, although many of his subjects are derived from direct observation of daily life. His best-known plays are *La locandiera* (1753, Eng trans *La Locandiera (The Mistress of the Inn)*, 1912), *I rusteghi* (1760, Eng trans *The Boors*, 1961), which provided the plot for *The School for Fathers* produced in London in 1946, and *Le baruffe chiozzote* (1762, Eng trans *The Squabbles of Chioggia*, 1914). In 1762 he undertook to write for the Italian theatre in Paris, and was attached to the French court until the revolution. He published his *Mémoires* in 1787 (Eng trans *Memoirs*, 1814).
▷H Taylor, *Goldoni: a biography* (1914)

GOLDSCHMIDT, Meïer Aron
(1819–87)

Danish journalist and novelist, born in Vordingborg of Jewish parentage. He founded a satirical periodical, *Corsaren*, in 1840. His best-known novels are *En Jøde* (1845, Eng trans *Bendixen the Jew*, 1852, and as *The Jew of Denmark*, 1952), and *Hjemløs* (1853, Eng trans *Homeless*, 1857). They are acutely psychological and relate characters to social pressures in a distinctively 'modern' way. He also wrote his autobiography (1877).
▷M Brøndstadt, *Meier Godschmidt* (1965)

GOLDSMITH, Oliver
(?1730–1774)

Irish playwright, novelist and poet, born in Pallasmore, County Longford, Ireland, the son of the curate of Kilkenny West. Educated at local schools and Trinity College, Dublin, he was rejected for the church, and thereupon started for America, but got no farther than Cork. He was next equipped with £50 to study law in London: this disappeared at a Dublin gaming-table. In 1752 he went to Edinburgh to study medicine, and stayed there nearly two years, but was more noted for his social gifts than his professional acquirements. He drifted to Leiden, again lost at play what money he had, and finally set out to make the 'grand tour' on foot, living on his wits and as a flute-playing 'busker', returning penniless in 1756. For a time he practised as a poor physician in Southwark, then was proofreader to **Richardson**, and next an usher in Dr Milner's 'classical academy' at Peckham. Ralph Griffiths of the *Monthly Review* retained him for a few months and in February 1758 appeared his first definite work, a translation of the Memoirs of Jean Marteilhe, a persecuted French Protestant. He next wrote an *Enquiry into the Present State of Polite Learning in Europe* (1759), which attracted some notice, and better days dawned for Goldsmith. He started and edited a weekly, *The Bee* (1759), and contributed to *The Busy Body* and *The Lady's Magazine*. Then came overtures from **Tobias Smollett** and **John Newbery** the bookseller. For Smollett's *British Magazine* he wrote some of his best essays; for Newbery's *Public Ledger* he wrote the *Chinese Letters* (1760–71; republished as *The Citizen of the World*). In 1764 the 'Literary Club' was founded, and he was one of its nine original members. His anonymous *History of England* was followed by *The Traveller*, a poem which gave him a foremost place among the poets of the day. *The Vicar of Wakefield* (1766) secured his reputation as a novelist. *The Good Natur'd Man*, a comedy (1768), was a moderate success. But he again escaped from enforced compilation of histories with his best poetical effort, *The Deserted Village* (1770). Three years afterwards he achieved high dramatic honours with *She Stoops to Conquer*. A year later he died of a fever. He was buried in the Temple Churchyard, and the club erected a monument to him in Westminster Abbey. In the year of his death were published the unfinished rhymed sketches called *Retaliation*, and in 1776 *The Haunch of Venison*.

▷S Gwinn, *Oliver Goldsmith* (1935); G S Rousseau, *Oliver Goldsmith: the critical heritage* (1974)

GOLDSWORTHY, Peter
(1951–)

Australian writer, practitioner in medicine, and amateur of music, which activities all figure in his writing. He was born in Minlaton, South Australia. His short stories are published as *Archipelagoes* (1982), *Zooing* (1986) and *Bleak Rooms* (1988). *Little Deaths*, a novella and nine short stories, was published in 1993. In his first novel, *Maestro* (1989), a Middle European émigré music teacher lives above a down-at-heel hotel in Darwin. A teenage pupil fantasizes about his past, and eventually comes to terms with adult responsibilities. A second novel, *Honk if You are Jesus* (1992), is a sophisticated romp around bio-ethics, *in vitro* fertilization, and American 'god-botherers'. His verse has been published as *Readings from Ecclesiastes* (1982), which won the Commonwealth Poetry Prize, and *This Goes with This* (1988). *This Goes with That: Selected Poems* was published in 1991.

GOLL, Yvan
(1891–1950)

French–German poet, novelist and playwright. Born of Jewish parents in St Dié, Alsace-Lorraine and brought up bilingually, he distinguished himself as a European pacifist. To avoid conscription in Germany, he emigrated to Switzerland in 1914 where he started writing Expressionistic poetry. Disillusioned by the political inefficiency of Expressionism, he returned to France in 1919, where he was among the first to proclaim Surrealism as the poetic mode of the future. His life was overshadowed by exile and emigration, and his poetry haunted by images of homelessness and restless itineration. In his three *Livres de Jean sans Terre* (1936–9), he both celebrates and deplores his personal destiny, using a poetic self-mythicization. Goll's love poetry, mostly written with his wife Claire in the form of poetic dialogues (*Poèmes d'Amour*, 1925; *Poèmes de Jalousie*, 1926; *Poèmes de la Vie at de la Mort*, 1927), expresses his quest for a refuge in poetry, in love, or in the simple physical closeness of lovers. From 1939 to 1947 he lived in New York, then returned to Europe, and began his poetic masterpiece, *Traumkraut* (1951), a volume full of unforgettable images of life and love and death. He died of leukaemia.

▷P G Pouthier, *Yvan à Claire — Yvan an*

Claire — Yvan to Claire. Studien zur Thematik und Symbolik der 'Clairelyrik' Yvan Golls (1988)

GOMBROWICZ, Witold
(1904–69)

Polish novelist, one of the major writers in his language this century. He was born in Maloszyce, studied law and economics in Warsaw and Paris, and spent most of his working life as a bank employee in Argentina, where he had gone on a visit on the eve of World War II. Beginning with the short stories in *Pamietnik z okresu dojrzewania* (1933, 'A Recollection of Adolescence'), his work is much concerned with patterns of sexual and psychological dependency, and it is clear from Gombrowicz's journal, published as *Dziennik, 1953–1966* (3 vols, 1957–66), that many of the complexes and inhibitions portrayed are his own. The slightly pathological tone of the early stories largely disappears in his best books, *Ferdydurke* (1937, Eng trans 1961) and *Pornografia* (1960, Eng trans 1966), which sustain a certain ironic distance from their vulnerable characters and claustrophobic situations. *Trans-Atlantyk* (1953) is a more conventional account of the Polish community in Argentina. A collected works, *Dziela zebrane* (11 vols 1969–77) began to appear in the year of his death; the strange *Opetani* (1973, Eng trans *Possessed, or The Secret of Myslotch*, 1980) was published posthumously.

▷E Thompson, *Gombrowicz* (1979)

GOMEZ DE AVELLANEDA Y ARTEAGA, Gertrudis
(1814–73)

Cuban Romantic poet, playwright, and novelist, important for her anti-slavery stance, for her erotic poetry, for her prolific theatrical production, and for her early feminism. After being educated by her parents in Cuba, she travelled to Europe in the 1830s. In Spain she was widely praised for her work, and took part in some of the most important literary tertulias (organized literary conversations) of her day. She was nominated to enter the Spanish Royal Academy but was rejected because of her gender.

GÓMEZ DE LA SERNA, Ramón
(1888–1963)

Spanish novelist, biographer, aphorist, critic, humorist and dramatist, born in Madrid—he died in Buenos Aires, where he had fled to escape the barbarities of the 1939 dictatorship. Gómez is an odd man out in Spanish literature: often called 'the Spanish Chesterton', he was even more gifted, and certainly bolder. He is most famous for one of the least important, although always delightful, parts of his work: his invention of the *greguería* (1909), a pithy aphorism which seeks to rearrange petty reality so that it recovers its original lack of triviality, for example, 'Within her wristwatch the time was so tiny that she never had enough of it for anything'. *Some greguerías* (1944) is an English selection from about a score of volumes of these. His way of writing and characterizing people had much in common with that of **Ramón Valle-Inclán** (on whom he wrote a book, 1944): he used the gestures, physical peculiarities and behaviour of his subjects in order to define their essence. He famously achieved this task—always without malice—on behalf of **Wilde**, **George Bernard Shaw**, Goya, El Greco and many others. His fiction has been seriously underrated since his death: in *Rebeca!* (1936, 'Retreat'), he portrays himself in erotic search of a figment of his own invention; recognizing that reality is 'more productive', he marries a Jewish wife—Gómez himself did this. *Cinelandia* (1923, Eng trans *Movieland*, 1930), is one of the funniest novels ever written about the pretensions of Hollywood. The richest work of this now neglected writer is probably *Automoribundia* (1948, 'Autodeathography'), one of his many autobiographical works, all of which deal uninhibitedly—and with a candour that shocked his contemporaries—with his inner life.

▷R Cardona, *Ramón: A Study of Gómez de la Serna and His Works* (1957)

GONÇALVES DIAS, António
(1823–64)

Brazilian poet, dramatist and translator, Brazil's paradigmatic romantic, born in Maranhão. He suffered the unfortunate fate of being drowned within sight of his native town, which contributed to his high reputation. He went to Coimbra to study law, but there became enamoured of poetry, in which he showed great technical skill. His intense patriotism, sympathy with both Native Americans and Blacks—he was himself of Native American and Negro as well as white blood, and could therefore identify with all three races—and ability for direct lyrical expression made him the Brazilian national poet *par excellence*. He was one of the first poets whose so-called 'Indianism' was genuine rather than merely exotic and decorative.

GONCHAROV, Ivan Alexandrovich
(1812–91)

Russian novelist, born in Simbirsk. He graduated from Moscow University (1834), and led an uneventful life in the civil service, punctuated by a trip of Japan, which he described in *Freget Pallada* (1858, Eng trans *The Frigate Pallas: Notes on a Journey*, 1965). He wrote three novels, the most important being *Oblomov* (1857, Eng trans 1915), one of the greatest and most typical works of Russian realism. Neither *Obyknovennaya istoriya* (1847, Eng trans *A Common Story*, 1894) nor *Obryv* (1870, Eng trans *The Precipice*, 1916) attains the same heights.

▷V Sechkarov, *Ivan Goncharov: his life and works* (1974)

GONCOURT, Edmond de
(1822–96)
GONCOURT, Jules de
(1830–70)

French novelists, born in Nancy and Paris respectively. Primarily artists, in 1849 they travelled across France making watercolour sketches and taking notes of everything they saw. Their important work began when, after collaborating in studies of history and art, especially Japanese art, they turned to writing novels. Their subject was not the passions but the manners of the 19th century, combined with a sense of the enormous influence of environment and habit upon man. The first of their novels, *Les Hommes de Lettres* (1860, 'The Men of Letters'; new edn as *Charles Demailly*, 1868), was followed by *Soeur Philomène* (1861, Eng trans *Sister Philomène*, 1890), *Renée Mauperin* (1864, Eng trans 1864 (US); 1887 (UK)), *Germinie Lacerteux* (1865, Eng trans 1887), *Manette Salomon* (1867), and *Madame Gervaisais* (1869), their greatest novel. After Jules's death, Edmond published the extraordinarily popular *La Fille Élisa* (1878, Eng trans *Elisa*, 1959), *La Faustin* (1882, Eng trans 1902) and *Chérie* (1885, 'Darling'). The interesting *Idées et Sensations* (1866, 'Ideas and Sensations') had already revealed their morbid acuteness of sensation, and *La Maison d'un artiste* (1881, 'An Artist's House') had shown their love for *bric-à-brac*. In the *Lettres de Jules de Goncourt* (1885) and in the *Journal des Goncourt* (9 vols, 1888–96) they revealed their methods and their conception of fiction. Various translations have been made of the de Goncourts' journals and letters, including *The Journal of the De Goncourts* (1908); *Paris Under Siege, 1870–1871* (1969); and *Edmond and Jules de Goncourt, with letters and leaves from their journals* (1894). Edmond, in his will, founded the Académie Goncourt to foster fiction with the annual Prix Goncourt.

▷R B Grant, *The Goncourt Brothers* (1972); A Billy, *La vie des Frères Goncourt* (1956)

GÓNGORA Y ARGOTE, Don Luis de
(1561–1627)

Spanish lyric poet, born in Córdoba. He studied law, but in 1606 took orders and became a prebendary of Córdoba, and eventually chaplain to Philip III. His earlier writings are elegant and stylish. His later works, consisting for the most part of longer poems, such as *Soledades* (Eng trans *The Solitudes*, 1931), *Polifemo* (Eng trans *Polyphemus and Galatea*, 1977) and *Piramo y Tisbe* ('Pyramus and Thisbe'), are written in an entirely novel style, which his followers designated the *stilo culto*. A major figure in his own day, he had fallen into disregard until the 20th century, but his reputation has been fully restored.

▷D W and V R Foster, *Góngora* (1973)

GONZAGA, Tomás António, pseud Dirceu
(1744–1809)

Portuguese poet, born in Oporto of an English mother and Brazilian father. He studied for the law, and was sent to Vila-Rica in 1782 where he met the 'Marília' of his verses. He was exiled to Mozambique for his revolutionary activities. There he married a rich mulatta and became a leading citizen of Mozambique. His *Marília de Dirceu* (1792) contains the best verses in the Arcadian tradition apart from **Manoel Bocage**, and they are considered masterpieces of the Mineiro school.

GONZÁLEZ, Angel
(1925–)

Spanish poet, born in Oviedo. He reached maturity at a time when Spanish poetry was at a low ebb: of the members of the great 'Generation of '27' **Lorca** had been murdered, and the rest were in exile (with the exception of **Aleixandre**, too ill to leave Spain)—of the next generation, **Hernandez**, too, had been killed. Spanish poetry was in a doldrums from which it has by no means yet recovered. Of the younger poets (rather hopefully called the 'Generation of '50'), González is one of the more outstanding and intelligent. As if in reaction to his rich heritage, he wrote deliberately prosaic poetry, saying in effect, 'there is no time for any rich indulgence now'. This was apparent in his first and best collection, *Áspero mundo* (1956, Eng trans *Harsh World*, 1977).

▷E A Llorach, *Angel González, poeta* (1969, in Spanish)

GONZÁLEZ DE ESLAVA, Fernán
(1534–c.1601)

Mexican playwright, born in Spain. He wrote 16 allegorical plays, or *coloquios*, which are of historical importance as demonstrating the sort of drama required by commissioning ecclesiastical authorities to commemorate various events.

GONZÁLEZ MARTÍNEZ, Enrique
(1871–1932)

Major Mexican poet, whose single sonnet, 'Tuércele el cuello al cisne' ('Let us twist this

swan's neck'), signalled the end of the Latin-American *modernismo* movement. He was born in Guadalajara, and was by profession a physician, later a diplomat. Himself initially a *modernista* poet, he turned away from the exotic in his later poetry, which has been neglected in favour of his famous sonnet. There are two translations in the *Penguin Book of Latin American Verse* (1971, ed E Curacciolo-Trejo).

GONZÁLES PRADA, Manuel
(1848–1918)

Peruvian poet and social critic, born in Lima, and one of the most powerful influences upon Peru's greatest poet, **César Vallejo**, and also upon the founder of the Peruvian Socialist Party, José Carlos Mariátegui. He succeeded **Ricardo Palma** as Head of the National Library. He was among the first in Peru to emphasize the importance of the Native American, and thus also influenced **José María Arguedas**. He was a noted enemy of the Church and its hierarchy. His poetry, which is important, but much of which appeared posthumously because of his reluctance to publish it, stands somewhat apart from his political activity (with the exception of the anti-clerical *Minísculas*, 1901). His manner is *modernista*, but the content of his poems transcends this, reflecting both his extreme originality, his mastery of form, and his essential anarchism.

▷L A Sánchez, *Don Manuel* (1930, in Spanish)

GOODE, Arthur Russell *see* RUSSELL, Arthur

GOODGE, W(illiam) T(homas)
(1862–1909)

English-born Australian writer of humorous verse and tales, born in London. He arrived in Sydney aged 20 and for some years tramped the outback, a period which produced material for yarns and poems which later appeared in the *Bulletin* magazine. His tall tales of the 'Gimcrack Club' and of outback heroes were not collected in book form, but the best of his verse was published as *The Great Australian Adjective* (1965), the title of his most famous poem.

GOODMAN, Paul
(1911–72)

American sociological journalist, poet, fiction writer and libertarian psychoanalyst. He was born and educated in New York. He co-wrote *Communitas* (1947), an influential tract on urban utopics, with his elder brother Percival and developed his very American strain of social anarchism in a later book about *Gestalt*

Therapy (1951). In 1960 he published *Growing Up Absurd*, which argued that US society offered only meretricious consolations and no substantial goals to its youth. The book was an instant success and established Goodman as a beneficent father- (or perhaps uncle-) figure to the youthful subculture of the 1960s. A novel *The Empire City* (1959) gathered themes from both *Communitas* and *Growing Up Absurd*; though it has some features in common with **Tom Wolfe**'s *The Bonfire of the Vanities*, it fatally lacks the wit. Goodman was more comfortable with short fiction, producing three fine volumes: *The Facts of Life* (1945), *The Break-Up of Our Camp* (1949) and *A Visit to Niagara* (1961). His collected stories were published as *Adam and His Works* (1968). *Collected Poems* appeared posthumously in 1974.
▷ K Widmer, *Paul Goodman* (1980)

GOODRICH, Frances *see* HACKETT, Albert

GOOGE, Barnabe
(1540–94)

English poet, born in Alvingham in Lincolnshire. He studied both at Cambridge and Oxford, travelled on the Continent, and became one of the gentlemen-pensioners of Queen Elizabeth. His best works are a series of eight *Eclogues, Epytaphes and Sonnets* (1563), which are one of the earliest examples of the pastoral form in English, and his *Cupido Conquered*.

GORBANEVSKAYA, Natalya Evgen'evna
(1936–)

Russian poet. She was born in Moscow and took her degree in Leningrad, having been expelled from Moscow University. A period of hospitalization as a result of acute vertigo attacks prefigured a more sinister committal in a state psychiatric hospital a decade later (1970–2), after she had engaged in anti-Soviet activities, including the founding of a *samizdat* journal and protest against the invasion of Czechoslovakia; the latter event was documented in her book *Polden'* (1970, published in the UK as *Red Square at Noon*, 1972). Shortly after her release she emigrated to France. Gorbanevskaya's work is known in the West through Daniel Weissbort's 1972 translation, which probably contained more of her poems than had been officially published in the Soviet Union up to that time. Her verse is highly musical and lexically playful, to a degree that renders 'translation' problematic. She also uses a rather personal and highly flexible symbolic system in which external states—cold, snow and ice—take on and shed significance with bewildering speed.

Since moving to France, she has edited a new journal, *Kontinent*.

GORDIMER, Nadine
(1923–)

South African novelist, winner of the Nobel Prize for literature, born in Springs, Transvaal. She was educated at a convent school, and at the University of the Witwatersrand, Johannesburg. One of the world's premier novelists in English, her work is rooted in South Africa, where she has continued to live. Her first book was a colleccon of short stories, *Face to Face* (1949), followed by another collection, *The Soft Voice of the Serpent* (1952). In 1954 she married, as her second husband, Reinhold Cassirer, a Jewish refugee from Nazi Germany. The previous year she had published her first novel, *The Lying Days*, in which a white girl triumphs over the provincial narrowness and racial bigotry of her parents' mining village existence, though she too has to come to terms with the limitations of her social background. This recurrent theme dominated Gordimer's early books, such as *Occasion for Loving* (1963) and *The Late Bourgeois World* (1966). Apartheid, and her characters' reaction to it, is ever present in her fiction, most powerfully in *The Conservationist* (1974), joint winner of the Booker Prize. Other important titles are *A Guest of Honour* (1970), *Burger's Daughter* (1979), *July's People* (1981) and *A Sport of Nature* (1987), in which a self-possessed white girl is transformed into a political activist intent on returning Africa to the rule of the Africans. Much fêted, she has received many awards, including the Malaparte Prize from Italy, the **Nelly Sachs** Prize from Germany, the Scottish Arts Council's **Neil Gunn** Fellowship and the French international award, the Grand Aigle d'Or. She was awarded the 1991 Nobel Prize for literature.
▷ R H Haugh, *Nadine Gordimer* (1974)

GORDON, Adam Lindsay
(1833–70)

Popular Australian poet, born in Fayal in the Azores where his mother's father had a plantation. He completed his education in England but vanished to Australia after a series of reckless adventures and had a brief career in the South Australian Mounted Police. He was a skilled horseman and established a livery stable in Victoria. There he received severe head injuries in a riding accident and then lost his money when the stable burned down. The subsequent death of his infant daughter precipitated a mental breakdown and his suicide. He is remembered for ballads that reflect his interest in horses: 'The Sick Stockrider', 'How We Beat the Favourite' and 'The Ride From the Wreck'. Much of his best work is collected in *Sea Spray and Smoke Drift* (1867, reissued 1876 with preface by **Marcus Clarke**) and *Bush Ballads and Galloping Rhymes* (1870). He is the only Australian poet honoured in the Poets' Corner of Westminster Abbey. His poem 'The Swimmer', with its undertones of suicide, was set as the last song in Elgar's *Sea Pictures*.

GORDON, Caroline
(1895–1981)

American novelist, born in Todd County, Kentucky and educated at Bethany College. She worked as a high school teacher and a reporter as well as a literary critic—her support for the New Criticism school of thought is reflected in her *How to Read a Novel* (1957). The agrarian Old South provides the backdrop for most of her novels: her first, *Penhally* (1931), set on a Kentucky plantation, was closely followed by *Alek Maury, Sportsman* (1934), and *None Shall Look Back* (1937), a fictionalized account of a confederate general's life. In 1947 she converted to Catholicism, which increasingly influenced her later work.
▷Caroline Gordon issue of *Southern Quarterly* (Spring 1990)

GORDON, Giles Alexander Esme
(1940–)

British short-story writer, novelist and literary agent. He was born and educated in Edinburgh, and worked in publishing for a decade (1962–72), before becoming one of the most respected literary agents on the London scene. His first collection of short stories, *Pictures from an Exhibition*, appeared in 1970 and his first novel, *The Umbrella Man*, in 1971, and he continued to produce high-quality fiction throughout the seventies. Among his most ambitious works are *About a Marriage* (1972) and *100 Scenes from Married Life* (1976), both of which concern a couple whose ups and downs are presented in the manner of a British **Updike**. The essay *Book 2000: Some Likely Trends in Publishing* (1969) is mostly prescient, but his backing for the strand of 'experimental fiction' represented by the late **B S Johnson** has turned out to be one of his less successful bets. In 1993, he published a name-dropping but engaging volume of memoirs, *Aren't We Due a Royalty Statement?*

GORDON, Mary Catherine
(1949–)

American novelist, born in Long Island, New York, and educated at Barnard College and Syracuse University. She worked as a teacher in a community college and as a lecturer at Amherst College. Her work is strongly influenced by both her feminism and her Catholicism. Her first novel, *Final Payments* (1978), presents a protagonist who accepts the role of caring for her bedridden father, and finds herself both liberated and frightened by his death. Gordon has to date written four novels, two collections of short stories, and a book of essays, in addition to various uncollected fiction, and has twice received the Janet Kafka Prize (1979 and 1982).
▷D Cooper-Clark (ed), *Interviews with Contemporary Novelists* (1986)

GORDON, Yehudah Leib
(1830–92)

Hebrew poet, novelist, translator (**Byron** and others) and essayist, born in Vilna, who wrote under his initials, YLB. He was the leading poet of the Haskalah movement ('the Enlightenment': the effort of Jews, in the late 18th and 19th centuries, to acquire European culture). He was the most popular Jewish poet of his time. His poetry on biblical themes influenced the entire course of Jewish poetry. He was imprisoned by the Russians, and contracted an illness from which he died prematurely.
▷A B Rhine, *Leon Gordon* (1920)

GORDONE, Charles
(1926–)

American playwright, born in Cleveland and brought up in Indiana. He was the first black playwright to win a Pulitzer Prize, for *No Place To Be Somebody* (1969), subtitled 'A Black-Black Comedy', a play in three acts about a black criminal dealing in an underworld dominated by whites. As an actor Gordone starred in his own one-man miscellany, *Gordone Is Muthah* (1970), and has been active in support of the employment of black actors.

GORE, Catherine Grace Frances, née Moody
(1799–1861)

English novelist, born in East Retford, Nottinghamshire. She was a prolific and immensely popular writer of novels, mainly of fashionable life in the manner of the 'silver fork' school. They include *Mothers and Daughters* (1831), *Mrs Armytage* (1836) and *The Banker's Wife* (1843). She also wrote three plays, and short stories.

GORKY, Maxim, pseud of Aleksei Maksimovich Peshkov
(1868–1936)

Russian novelist, born in Nizhniy Novgorod. He was successively pedlar, scullery boy, gardener, dock hand, tramp and writer, a restless nomadic life he described brilliantly in his autobiographical trilogy, *Detstvo* (1913–14, Eng trans *My Childhood*, 1915), *V lyudakh* (1915–16, Eng trans *In the World*, 1918) and *Moi universitety* (1922, Eng trans *My University Days*, 1923). He first achieved fame with his story *Chelkash* (1895), followed by others in a romantic vein, glorifying the unusual, with vividly drawn characters, mostly tramps and down-and-outs. *Foma Gordeyev* (1899, Eng trans 1902) marks his transition from romanticism to realism. In 1902 he produced his best-known play, *Na dne* (Eng trans *A Night's Lodging*, 1905; better known as *The Lower Depths*, 1912). Involved in strikes and imprisoned in 1905, he lived abroad until 1914 and then engaged in revolutionary propaganda. From 1922 to 1928 he lived abroad again on account of his health, but then returned, a whole-hearted supporter of the Soviet regime. He sponsored 'social realism' as the official school in Soviet literature and art.

▷ R Hare, *Maxim Gorky, romantic realist and conservative revolutionary* (1962); Dan Levin, *The Stormy Petrel: the life and work of Maxim Gorky* (1965)

GOROSTIZA, José
(1901–79)

Major Mexican poet, born in Villahermosa, Tabasco. Writing in the metaphysical tradition established by **Sor Juana Inés de la Cruz**, as well as in that of European poets such as **Valéry**, Gorostiza was the leading member of the group which published in the magazine *Contemporáneos* (1928–31), an avant-garde vehicle which reflected the nihilistic themes then being pursued in European, especially French, poetry. He has written comparatively little, but nonetheless has the reputation of being the most distinguished 'philosophical' poet of modern Mexico; often called a 'nihilist', it is more true to say that he explores reality from an initially nihilist point of view. His masterpiece, *Muerte sin fin* (1929, 'Death Without End'), 'the most important Mexican poem to appear up to that time', is a lyrical meditation on the question of God or Nothingness.

GÖRRES, Johann Joseph von
(1776–1848)

German writer, born in Koblenz. In 1812 Koblenz became the literary centre of the national movement. Denouncing absolutism with great vigour, he angered the Prussian government, and had to flee the country (1820). In 1827 he was made Professor of Literature at Munich, where he devoted himself to literature and controversial theology. His chief work was his *Christliche Mystik* (1842, 'Christian Mysticism').

▷ J N Sepp, *Görres* (1873)

GORTER, Herman
(1864–1927)

Dutch poet, born in Wormerveer, the son of a prominent journalist. He was an important figure in modern Dutch literature. His lushly **Keats**ian poem *Mei* (1889, 'May'), influenced by the Persephone of **Albert Verwey**, as well as by the work of **Willem Kloos** and Jacques Perk, was taken as a final model, by the so-called 'Men of the Eighties', of what the new poetry should be. In the next decade Gorter's poetry matured into something more refined and enigmatic: the strange, almost hermetic poems of this period—Verwey described them as 'sensitivist'—are included in *De school der poëzie* (1897, 'The School of Poetry'). These are his most interesting and rewarding work, and repay examination today. But the poet felt that the introspection involved in this type of composition was driving him into madness, and so became a student (and translator) of Spinoza, and, soon after that, a Marxist. But his epic *Pan* (1916), supposed to excite everyone into hurrying up the process of dialectical materialism, instead puzzled them: they found it as hermetic as ever. Gorter met Lenin and visited Russia, became disillusioned, and ended as an often illuminating but theory-bound critic, writing about poets such as **Shelley** and **Dante** from a Marxist perspective; on leaving the Communist Party in 1921 he became, perhaps prophetically, an early 'Eurocommunist'.

GOSSE, Sir Edmund William
(1849–1928)

English poet and critic, born in London, son of Philip Henry Gosse. He was educated privately, and became assistant librarian in the British Museum (1867–75), then translator to the Board of Trade (1875–1904) and finally librarian to the House of Lords (1904–14). He was an eminent man of letters in his day, and moved in influential circles; his personal friends included **Swinburne**, **Hardy**, **Stevenson** and **Henry James**. His reputation as a critic was damaged after attacks on his accuracy and scholarship by Churton Collins in 1885, an incident which troubled him throughout his life. He initially regarded himself as a poet, and published several works, including *On Viol and Flute* (1873) and *Collected Poems* (1911). His *Studies in the Literature of Northern Europe* (1879), and other critical works, first introduced **Ibsen** to English-speaking readers. He also wrote on **William Congreve** (1888), **John Donne** (1899), Jeremy Taylor (1904), Sir Thomas Browne (1905), **Algernon Charles Swinburne** (1917) and **François de Malherbe** (1920), although his special field was *Seventeenth-century Studies* (1883). He is best remembered for his masterpiece *Father and Son* (1907), a classic biographical study

of his relationship with his father which is also a reflection of their times and social milieu.
▷A Thwaite, *Edmund Gosse, a literary landscape* (1984)

GOSVAMI, Kisori Lal
(1865–1932)

Popular Hindi novelist, who wrote crude and sensationalist romances, but who had some small but definite interest in character, which lifted his works above the genre.

GOTLIEB, Phyllis
(1926–)

Canadian poet and science-fiction writer, born in Toronto. Gotlieb's poetry has been gathered in *The Works: Collected Poems* (1978). Her outstanding single collection was *Ordinary, Moving* (1969), which explored her Jewish childhood and background in a lively mosaic of telephone numbers, playground rhymes and the like. More recently she is known primarily for her science fiction. *Sunburst* (1964), still considered by many to be her best novel, is narrated by a 13-year-old who manages to triumph over a group of mutant children. Her trilogy about cats who possess the secrets of the past ended with *The Kingdom of the Cats* (1985) and featured a pair of crimson felines.

GOTTFRIED VON STRASSBURG
(fl.1200)

German poet. He wrote the masterly German version of the legend of *Tristan and Isolde*, based on the Anglo-Norman poem by **Thomas**. He is also noteworthy as an early exponent of literary criticism, having left appraisals of the work of poets of the period.
▷M S Bates, *Gottfried von Strassburg* (1971)

GOTTSCHALL, Rudolf von
(1823–1909)

German writer, born in Breslau. A keen Liberal, he produced two volumes of political verse (1842–3). From 1864 he lived in Leipzig and edited *Brockhaus'sche Blätter* and *Unsere Zeit*. He also wrote a comedy entitled *Pitt und Fox* (1854, 'Pitt and Fox'), tragedies and historical novels.
▷M Brasch, *Ein literarisches Portrait* (1893)

GOTTSCHED, Johann Christoph
(1700–66)

German writer, born in Judithenkirch near Königsberg. In 1730 he became Professor of Philosophy and Poetry at Leipzig, and in 1734 of Logic and Metaphysics. He laboured to improve his mother-tongue as a literary vehicle, and to reform the German drama by banishing buffoonery and raising the style and tone. He founded the Leipzig school of

acting and criticism, introducing French classical principles. But he became pedantic and vain, and showed a petty jealousy of all literary authority save his own, opposing Bodmer and **Gotthold Lessing**. His drama, *Der Sterbende Cato* (1732, 'The Dying Cato'), notwithstanding its immense success, is sadly barren.
▷W Rieck, *Johann Christoph Gottsched* (1972)

GOTZ, Johann Nikolaus
(1721–81)

German poet and pastor from Worms, whose **Anacreon**tic poetry was written in close imitation of the more gifted **Johann Gleim** and **Johann Uz**.

GOUDGE, Elizabeth (de Beauchamp)
(1900–84)

English writer of fiction for adults and whimsically religious books for children. She was born in Wells, Somerset. After attending Reading University's Art Department she worked for several years as a teacher of design and handicrafts. Her first novel was *Island Magic* (1934) but she waited 10 years before producing the bestselling *Green Dolphin Country* (1944), a historical romance set in New Zealand. After that her popularity, especially in libraries, remained steady. *The Little White Horse* (1946), for children, won the Carnegie Medal.

GOULD, Alan
(1949–)

Australian poet, born in London of Icelandic descent, a heritage which is reflected in his verse. His first collection was *Icelandic Solitaries* (1978), and the prize-winning *Astral Sea* (1981) derives much from Icelandic sagas. *The Passing of the Hours* followed in 1984. *The Man who Stayed Below* (1984) is his first novel, a study of the doom-laden captain of a sailing clipper on the Melbourne–London run. *The Enduring Disguises* (1988) contains three novellas.

GOULD, Nat(haniel)
(1857–1919)

English journalist and novelist of 'The Turf', born in Manchester. After working on provincial and London newspapers, he visited Australia in 1884 and became racing editor of the Sydney *Referee*. For that paper he became a successful tipster under the name 'Verax', and also published two serials, the second of which, 'With the Tide', was later published as *The Double Event* (1891). Two years later this was dramatized by George Darrell and staged in Melbourne with 20 horses in the 'cast'. Through the great success of this melodrama Gould's subsequent books became popular both in Australia and England. He returned to England in 1895 and from that time wrote over 130 novels, mainly thrillers of racing or other sporting plots, but also of the theatre, which was one of his delights. He wrote three volumes of autobiography, *On and Off the Turf in Australia* (1895), *Town and Bush* (1896) and *The Magic of Sport; Mainly Autobiographical* (1909).

GOURMONT, Rémy de
(1858–1915)

French poet, novelist and critic, born in Bazoches-en-Houlme, Normandy. Having been dismissed from his post at the Bibliothèque Nationale Paris, because of an allegedy pro-German article in *Mercure de France*, of which he was a co-founder, he lived the life of a recluse. His creative work—poetry and novels in the Symbolist manner—is cerebral and stylistic, betraying a *fin de siècle* obsession with words as sound more than as sense. But his evaluative and critical work, which includes *Le Livre des masques* (1896–8, 'The Book of Masques') and *Promenades philosophiques* (1905–9, 'Philosophical Excursions'), is clear-sighted and individualistic, exhibiting scholarship and intellectual curiosity. His novels include *Sixtine* (1890) and *Un Cœur virginal* (1907, Eng trans, by **Aldous Huxley**, *A Virgin Heart*, 1921).
▷ J de Gourmont, *Souvenirs de Rémy* (1924)

GOVER, Robert
(1929–)

American novelist, born in Philadelphia. A few of his books have appeared under the pseudonym of 'O Govi'; another, *Victor Versus Mort*, has appeared, undated, only in Portuguese. His best-known novel is his first: *One Hundred Dollar Misunderstanding* (1962), the first of a trilogy, which traces the relationship between a white man and a 13-year-old black prostitute. The sequels are *Here Goes Kitten* (1964) and *J C Saves* (1968). A writer who puts sex to the fore in all of his novels, he has been described by one critic as 'at times an accomplished satirist'.

GOVONI, Corrado
(1884–1965)

Italian poet and novelist, born in Tamara, Ferrara. He passed through the gamut of all the mainstream Italian movements: initially, a friend to Sergio Corrazzini, he wrote in the style of the 'twilight' poets, the Crepuscolari; then he was an adherent of the Futurists; finally he associated himself with the group around the Florence magazine *La voce*. Like **Willem Elsschot** and **Thomas Hardy** he illustrated much of his verse with sketches and

designs which were an integral part of them. He is particularly remembered for his passionate lament for his son Aladino, who was murdered by Nazis in 1944, in his volume *Aladino: lamento su mio figlio morto* (1946, 'Aladino: Lament for My Dead Son'). Although a minor poet, he was greatly admired by **Eugenio Montale** and, latterly, by **Primo Levi**. There are English translations in C L Golino (ed), *Contemporary Italian Poetry* (1962).

GOWER, John
(c.1325–1408)

English poet, born into a wealthy family in Kent. He spent most of his life in London, and had contacts with the court in the service of Richard II and Henry IV. He was a personal friend of **Chaucer**, and wrote *Speculum Meditantis*, in French verse, which was discovered at Cambridge only in 1898. Other works include the *Vox Clamantis*, elegiacs in Latin (1382–4), describing the rising under Wat Tyler; and the long poem entitled *Confessio Amantis*, written in English, perhaps in 1383. There are extant also 50 French ballads, written by Gower in his youth. The *Confessio Amantis* comprises a prologue and eight books, and largely consists of over a hundred stories taken from **Ovid**'s *Metamorphoses*, the *Gesta Romanorum*, and medieval histories of Troy. He was blind from about 1400.
▷ J A Burrows, *Ricardian Poetry: Chaucer, Gower, Langland and the Gawain Poet* (1971)

GOYEN, (Charles) William
(1915–83)

American novelist and short-story writer from Texas, he is unmistakably 'Southern' in his instinct for slightly baroque situations, but is also rather more quietly philosophical and lyrical than most of those writers who are saddled with that label. *The Faces of Blood Kindred* (1960) is his only stereotypically 'Southern' book. His first novel, *The House of Breath* (1950), is incidentally reminiscent of **Truman Capote**'s precocious *Other Voices, Other Rooms*, which appeared two years earlier, but it signally failed to excite the public. Goyen's reputation has remained somewhat restricted. *The Fair Sister* (1963) is a reworking of a short story about a female evangelist. *Come the Restorer* (1974) is more broadly comic. Goyen's final work was the posthumous *Arcadio* (1984), a strange novel about a hermaphrodite. He also wrote plays, some of them based on his novels and stories.

GOYTISOLO, Juan
(1931–)

Spanish novelist and critic, born in Barcelona. He was associated with progressive, anti-Franco writers in his early career, when he co-founded the group 'Turia' with **Ana María Matute** and others. Then in 1957, unlike his brother **Luis Goytisolo**, he left Spain for Paris, where he worked for the publisher Gallimard. His early novels, such as *Juegos de manos* (1954, Eng trans *The Young Assassins*, 1959), were more or less straightforwardly realistic; later, influenced both by his ambisexuality and by the Arabic elements in Spanish literature, he became a determined and highly influential modernist and postmodernist, of international stature. His two best-known novels are *Reivindicación del conde Don Julian* (1970, Eng trans *Count Julian*, 1974), and *Juan sin tierra* (1976, Eng trans *John the Landless*, 1977), essentially a 'deconstruction' of the official history of Spain in the period 1939–64.

▷ J Ortega, *Juan Goytisolo* (1972, in Spanish)

GOYTISOLO, Luis
(1937–)

Spanish novelist, born in Barcelona, the brother of the more internationally known and translated **Juan Goytisolo**. He is a publisher by profession, whose work has been somewhat unfairly overshadowed by that of his more ambitiously experimental brother. His best works are *Recuento* (1973, 'Inventory') and *Los verdes de mayo hasta el mar* (1976, 'The Green of May to the Sea'), both of them explorations of the creative process.

GOZZANO, Guido
(1883–1916)

Italian poet, born near Turin, who, after 12 years of suffering, died of tuberculosis. He was among the first and most important of the poets styled by **Borgese** as Crepusculari (the others were Sergio Corazzini, **Marino Moretti**, Carlo Chiave, Carlo Vallini—to whom Borgese first applied the term—and Fausto Maria Martini): this quiet, anti-rhetorical, self-mocking 'twilight' poetry arose in the first instance as an inevitable reaction to the *Sturm und Drang* of **D'Annunzio** and his many bombastic followers. It also gave an approving nod in the direction of **Pascoli**. The mood can be found elsewhere, in such American poets as **Robinson** and **T S Eliot** (who was aware of Gozzano through Pound), and has persisted, both in Italian poetry and, again, elsewhere, as in **James Reeves**. The tone is that of the ill (perhaps wryly syphilitic), world-weary, cynical ex-dandy and aesthete. But while Gozzano is typical, he was also a major poet, and has been virtually endorsed as such since **Montale** catalogued his virtues. His most famous poem is 'Totò Merùmeni', certainly the original for Eliot's 'Prufrock'. His genius has in its quiet way

dominated the 20th century. There are English translations in *The Man I Pretend To Be* (1981, contains a translation of Montale's pioneer essay).

GOZZI, Count Carlo
(1720–1806)

Italian dramatist, born in Venice. He wrote *Tartana* (1757), a satirical poem against **Carlo Goldoni**; a very popular comedy, *Fiaba dell' amore delle tre Melarance* (1761, Eng trans *The Love of Three Oranges*, 1949); and several similar 'dramatic fairy-tales', the best-known, from **Schiller's** translation of it, being *Turandot* (Eng trans *Turandot, Princess of China*, 1913). His brother, Count Gasparo (1713–86), edited two journals in Venice, and was press censor there. Among his works are *Il mondo morale* (1760, 'The Moral World') and *Lettere famigliari* (1755).

▷ E Borghesani, *Carlo Gozzi e l'opera sua* (1904)

GRABBE, Christian Dietrich
(1801–36)

German dramatist, born in Detmold. He lived an irregular, highly neurotic life, and died of tuberculosis and alcoholism. A precursor of Realism, he wrote powerful tragedies on the lives of *Don Juan und Faust* (1822), *Kaiser Friedrich Barbarossa* (1829) and *Napoleon* (1831).

▷ A Bergmann, *Christian Dietrich Grabbe* (1954, in German); and other works by Bergmann

GRACE, Patricia
(1937–)

New Zealand novelist and short-story writer, born in Wellington. She was one of the first published Maori writers, producing a collection of short stories, *Waiariki*, in 1975, followed by her novel *Mutuwhenua: The Moon Sleeps* (1978) on cultural conflicts in a mixed marriage. Next came *The Dream Sleepers and Other Stories* (1980), a further novel, *Potiki* (1986), with its emphatic Maori viewpoint of Paheka (white settler) standards, and *Electric City and Other Stories* (1987). She treats the Maori culture and community in realistic narrative and deals much with the significance of their extended family relationships.

GRACIAN, (y Morales) Baltasar
(1601–58)

Spanish philosopher and writer, born in Belmonte, Aragon. He entered the Jesuit order in 1619 and later became head of the College at Tarragona. His early works such as *El Héroe* (1637, Eng trans *The Hero*, 1652),

El Político (1640, 'The Politician'), *El Discreto* (1646, Eng trans *The Compleat Gentleman*, 1729) and *Oráculo manual y arte de prudencia* (1647, Eng trans *The Courtier's Manual Oracle and the Art of Prudence*, 1685) are all heavily didactic guides to life. He set out his literary ideas on *conceptismo*, the art of conceited writing, in *Agudeza y arte de ingenio* (1642, 'Subtlety and the Art of Genius'). He is best known, however, for his three-part allegorical novel, *El Criticón* (1651, 1653, 1657, 'The Critic'), in which civilization and society are portrayed through the eyes of a savage.

▷ A Coster, *Baltasar Gracian* (1958)

GRACQ, Julien, pseud of Louis Poirier
(1910–)

French novelist, critic and translator (of **Kleist**'s *Penthesilea*), who studied with the influential philosopher Alain, and went on to become a history teacher. His fiction arises, essentially, from his understanding of the mythology of the Middle Ages. He learned much from the surrealists and from their precursors, such as **Lautréamont**, but his methods do not resemble theirs, even though **Breton** (upon whom he wrote a book, *André Breton*, 1948) hailed him as a new white hope on the appearance of his haunting first book, *Au Château d'Argol* (1939, Eng trans *The Castle of Argol*, 1951). His reputation was made, however, with *Un Beau Ténébreux* (1945, Eng trans *A Dark Stranger*, 1949), about a young man who refuses the love of an enigmatic woman. Gracq, an outspoken critic of the literary establishment, declined the Prix **Goncourt** awarded him for *La Rivage des Syrtes* (1951, 'By the Shores of Syrtes'), an exploration of the Grail Myth avowedly reminiscent of the fiction of **Ernst Jünger**. His masterpiece, *Un Balcon en forêt* (1958, Eng trans *Balcony in the Forest*, 1959), draws on his war experiences in the Ardennes. *La Presqu'ile* (1970, 'The Peninsula'), contains three stories set in the Middle Ages. His style is unparalleled in modern times for its richness.

GRAF, Oscar Maria
(1894–1967)

German novelist and poet. He was born in Berg in Bavaria, the son of the village baker, but left home at 16 to become an anarchist. Always an outspoken, bold and highly individualistic man, he feigned insanity in order to escape service in World War I, since he had been given an unreasonable order. When the Nazis put his name on a list of recommended books, he wrote an open letter, 'Burn Me Too'; in 1938 he ended up in New York, where he remained—but he could not become a US citizen until 1958 because he refused to sign the clause which would require him to bear arms on behalf of US politicians. He wrote many novels and stories, most of them describing rural life and the threat of totalitarianism; the most moving is *Bolwieser* (1932, Eng trans *The Station Master*, 1933). His poetry and his 'Utopian' novels are less successful. His masterpiece was first published in English, *The Life of My Mother* (1940), and only later in German. Its title defines it.

▷ S K Johnson, *Oskar Maria Graf: The Critical Reception of His Prose Fiction* (1979)

GRAHAM, Harry
(1874–1936)

English writer of light verse, whose *Ruthless Rhymes for Heartless Homes* (1909) was for many decades one of the most popular collections. **Geoffrey Grigson** wrote of his acrid verses: 'They are the ruthless vesicles of the Galsworthy age, the nasty contradictions, in effect, of the kind vesicles of A.A. Milne'. Graham published *More Ruthless Rhymes* in 1930.

GRAHAM, W(illiam) S(ydney)
(1918–90)

British poet, born in Greenock. Graham had a never-ending fascination with the fracture and failure of communication. His prosody was tough and highly rhythmic, drawing on Anglo-Saxon and Celtic forms. Both his personality and literary output were affected by medication given for psychological problems. He spent most of his life outside Scotland, largely in the far south-west of England. *The Voyages of Alfred Wallis* (1948)—the title relates to the naive painter—marked a significant maturation of his style; the adjectives that had adorned his earlier volumes, *Cage without Grievance* (1942) and *The Seven Journeys* (1944), fell away like autumn leaves. Graham's great achievement was *The Nightfishing* (1955), a long poem comparable with **MacDiarmid**'s 'On a Raised Beach', and influenced by **Joyce** and **Marianne Moore**. He then remained virtually silent for 15 years, returning with *Malcolm Mooney's Land* (1970), a further meditation on the relationship between language and reality; Graham once asked, rhetorically, 'What is the Language Using Us For?'.

▷ T Lopez, *The Poetry of W S Graham* (1989)

GRAHAME, James
(1765–1811)

Scottish poet, born in Glasgow. He studied law at Glasgow University and was called to the Bar, but was forced to give up his career because of ill-health. He took Anglican orders in 1809 and became a curate in Shipton, Gloucestershire and later Sedgefield,

Durham. He wrote a dramatic poem, *Mary, Queen of Scots* (1801), but most of his poetry was evocative of the quiet Scottish countryside, particularly *The Sabbath* (1804) and *The Birds of Scotland* (1806), with an introduction that made it 'popular ornithology'. Christopher North (**John Wilson**) thought highly of him, but he was not rated by **Byron**.
▷Memoir in *The Sabbath* (1839, 9th edn)

GRAHAME, Kenneth
(1859–1932)

Scottish children's writer, born in Edinburgh, the son of an advocate. He was brought up in Inverary, Argyll, until 1864, and then by his grandmother in Cookham Dene, Berkshire. He was educated at St Edward's School, Oxford, and in 1876 entered the Bank of England as a gentleman clerk. He became its secretary in 1898 and retired for health reasons in 1908. His early work consisted of collected essays and country tales, *Pagan Papers* (1893), *The Golden Age* (1895) and *Dream Days* (1898), which revealed a remarkably subtle, delicate and humorous sympathy with the child mind. In 1908 he published his best-known work, *The Wind in the Willows*, originally written in the form of letters to his son Alastair, and repeatedly revised before publication. Despite its quaint and unforgettable riverside characters, Rat, Mole, Badger and Toad, it did not at first win acclaim, critics such as **Arthur Ransome** dismissing it as inferior to his previous work. Gradually, however, its popularity grew, and within a few years of Grahame's death it had become a children's classic.
▷P Green, *Kenneth Grahame* (1959)

GRAINGER, Dr James
(1721–66)

Scottish poet, born in Duns and educated in Edinburgh, where he took a degree in medicine. After an undistinguished career in the army, he returned to Edinburgh to practise medicine, and turned to writing to supplement his income, producing poems (largely paeans to nature, especially the Grampians), essays and a volume of combined critical works and medical musings, but meeting with little success. He is chiefly remembered for *Sugar Cane* (c.1760), a long poem describing his subsequent experiences as a plantationer in the West Indies.

GRANADA, Fray Luis de
(1504–88)

Spanish religious writer, born in Granada of humble origin and probably orphaned very young. Protected by the Count of Tendilla whom he served as a page, he joined the Dominican order and studied in Valladolid, where

he had the greatest theologians of the day as his teachers. He became a priest in Cordoba, where he flourished under Juan de Avila, the greatest theologian of his age. Later he fell into disfavour with Philip II through neutrality over his claim to the throne in Portugal. He wrote three books in prose, sacred works on prayer, meditation and moral guides: *El Libro de Meditacion y Oracion* (1552, 'The Book of Meditation and Prayer'), *Guía de Pecadores* (1556, 'Guide for Sinners') and *Introduccion del Símbolo de la Fé* (1582–5, 'Introduction to the Symbol of Faith'), in which he considers the natural beauties of creation and the excellence of Christianity. He was the most famous sacred orator of his day, and his sermons were used as models until the 18th century.

GRAND, Sarah, pseud of Frances Elizabeth Bellenden McFall, née Clarke
(1854–1943)

British novelist, born of English parentage in Donaghadee, Ireland. At the age of 16 she married an army doctor, D C McFall (d.1898). In 1923 and from 1925 to 1929 she was Mayoress of Bath. Her reputation rests on *The Heavenly Twins* (1893) and *The Beth Book* (1898), in which she skilfully handles sex problems. Her later works, including *The Winged Victory* (1916), are advocacies of feminine emancipation.

GRANT, Anne, née MacVicar
(1755–1838)

Scottish poet and essayist, born in Glasgow, the daughter of an army officer. She lived in North America as a child (1758–68). In 1779 she married the Rev James Grant, minister of Laggan. Left a widow in 1801, she turned to writing and published *Poems* (1803), *Letters from the Mountains* (1806), *Memoirs of an American Lady* (1808) and *Superstitions of the Highlanders* (1811). In 1810 she moved to Edinburgh, where she mixed in the best literary circles, and in 1825 received a pension of £50 through the influence of Sir **Walter Scott**.

GRANT, James
(1822–87)

Scottish novelist and historical author, born in Edinburgh. After a childhood in Newfoundland and military service, he published a long series of novels and histories, that were illustrative mainly of the achievements of Scottish arms abroad. Among his many works are *The Romance of War* (1845), his first novel; *Adventures of an Aide-de-Camp* (1848); *Bothwell* (1854); *Frank Hilton, or the Queen's Own* (1855); *British Battles on Land*

and Sea (1873); and a classic history of his native city, *Old and New Edinburgh* (1880).

GRANT, Robert
(1852–1940)

American novelist, born in Boston, and a member of its patrician class. A supposedly liberal judge (and in the matter of divorce he was so), he helped to send the communists Sacco and Vanzetti to execution for a crime which he knew they had not committed. He wrote mostly light romances and adventure stories, but *The Chippendales* (1909) was praised for the picture it gave of the frivolous, turn-of-the-century Boston.
▷ *Fourscore* (1934)

GRANVILLE-BARKER, Harley
(1877–1946)

English actor, playwright and producer, born in London. As an actor, he was distinguished by his appearance in **Shaw** plays—he played Marchbanks in *Candida* in 1900. In 1904 he became co-manager of the Court Theatre with Vedrenne, and there followed a four-year season that was a landmark in the history of the British theatre. First performances in England of plays by **Maeterlinck**, **Arthur Schnitzler**, **Gerhart Hauptmann**, **W B Yeats**, **John Galsworthy**, **John Masefield** and George Bernard Shaw were performed in circumstances that set new standards of acting and design. In 1907 he left the Court and continued his success with a series of **Shakespeare** plays at the Savoy. He retired from the stage in the early 1920s. Barker wrote several plays, including *The Marrying of Ann Leete* (1902), *The Voysey Inheritance* (1905), *Waste* (performed privately in 1907, publicly in 1936) and *The Madras House* (1910). With William Archer he devised a scheme for a national theatre. He was married first to Lillah McCarthy and then to Helen Huntington Gates, with whom he made the standard translations of plays by **Gregorio Martínez Sierra** and the **Álvarez Quintero** brothers. His prefaces to Shakespeare's plays (4 vols, 1927–45) are valuable for their original criticism and ideas on production.

GRASS, Günter Wilhelm
(1927–)

German novelist, born in Danzig (Gdansk, Poland). He was educated at Danzig Volksschule and Gymnasium. Having trained as a stonemason and sculptor, he attended the Academy of Art, Düsseldorf, and the State Academy of Fine Arts, Berlin. He served in World War II and was held as a prisoner-of-war. He has worked as a farm labourer, miner, apprentice stonecutter and jazz musician, and was a speech-writer for Willy Brandt when he was Mayor of West Berlin. *Die Blechtrommel* (1959, Eng trans *The Tin Drum*, 1962) was the first of the novels that have made him Germany's greatest living novelist. Ostensibly the autobiography of Oskar Matzerath, detained in a mental hospital for a murder he did not commit, it caused a furore in Germany because of its depiction of the Nazis. Intellectual and experimental in form, theme and language, his books consistently challenge the status quo and question our reading of the past. A prolific playwright, poet and essayist, he excels in fiction. Important books are *Katz und Maus* (1961, Eng trans *Cat and Mouse*, 1963), *Hundejahre* (1963, Eng trans *Dog Years*, 1965), *Örtlich betäubt* (1969, Eng trans *Local Anaesthetic*, 1970), *Der Butt* (1977, Eng trans *The Flounder*, 1978), *Das Treffen in Telgte* (1979, Eng trans *The Meeting at Telgte*, 1981), *Die Ratten* (1987, Eng trans *The Rats*, 1987) and *Unkenrufe* (1992, Eng trans *The Call of the Toad*, 1992). He has illustrated many of of his own book jackets.
▷ K Miles, *Günter Grass* (1975)

GRAU, Jacinto
(1877–1958)

Spanish playwright, born in Barcelona, who left Spain after Franco's victory to live in Buenos Aires. His powerful and profound plays never had the attention they deserved, but a substantial number of good critics have recognized him as a major writer. He was unpopular with those who had power in the Spanish theatre because of his consistent and sarcastically conducted struggle against commercialization—he was mostly produced outside Spain. His richly prophetic work is now being re-examined by the critics of his own country. He wrote, first, formal tragedies, but then moved to the form of farce, in which framework he presented tragic themes. His work has not yet been translated, but *El señor de Pygmalión* (1921, 'Mr Pygmalion'), was seen in Paris and Prague in the early 1920s; his plays are now gradually being revived. His greatest works are probably his last, *En el infierno se est án mudando* (1958, 'Moving Day in Hell') and—the best of all the modern plays on the Don Juan theme—*El burlador que no se burla* (1930, 'The Seducer Who Does Not Seduce').

GRAU, Shirley Ann
(1929–)

American novelist, born in New Orleans and educated at Tulane University; she taught creative writing at the University of New Orleans in 1966–7. Her short stories began appearing in magazines such as the *New Yorker* and *The Saturday Evening Post* as early as 1954. Her first book, *The Black*

Prince and Other Stories (1955), was highly acclaimed. In 1965 she won a Pulitzer Prize for her novel *The Keepers of the House*, which tells the story of a mixed race family whose members are related to the Klan. She has been termed a 'regional writer' because of her concerns with the South and race relations.

GRAVES, Alfred Perceval

(1846–1931)

Irish writer and educationist, born in Dublin. An inspector of schools in England, he wrote much Irish folk verse and songs, including 'Father O'Flynn', and an autobiography, *To Return to All That* (1930). A leader of the Celtic revival, he helped to found the Irish Literary Society in London.

▷ *To Return to All That* (1930)

GRAVES, Richard

(1715–1804)

English author, born in Mickleton. Educated at Pembroke College, Oxford, he became a fellow of All Souls, Oxford, in 1736, and also rector of Claverton, near Bath. Of his great output, only his novel *The Spiritual Quixote* (1772), a comic tilt at changing Methodist views which satirizes the evangelical preacher George Whitefield, is remembered. His other novels, though little read, contain well-observed portraits of the social conditions of his age.

▷ F Kilvert, *Richard Graves of Claverton* (1858)

GRAVES, Robert von Ranke

(1895–1985)

English poet, novelist, essayist and critic, born in London and educated at Charterhouse. He joined up in 1914 and his first poetry—*Over the Brazier* (1916), *Fairies and Fusiliers* (1917)—was published during the conflict. Poems by him also appeared in the popular anthology *Georgian Poetry*, but he did not discover his distinctive voice until 1924, when his war-shattered nerves had experienced the delights and disillusions of married love. A year later he met **Laura Riding** with whom he went into exile to Majorca on the proceeds of his autobiography, *Goodbye to All That* (1929), and a hack Life of T E Lawrence. He lived, travelled and collaborated with Riding until 1939, returned to England for World War II, but returned to settle permanently in Majorca with his second wife, Beryl Hodge, in 1946. His best poetry, written between about 1928 and 1943, is pellucid, tender and evocative, far closer to the Metaphysical Poets than the Victorians. Generally regarded as the best love poet of his generation, he has a broad-based bibliography. His historical novels, like *I, Claudius* (1934), *Claudius the God* (1934) and *The Golden Fleece* (1945), are confident and imaginative reconstructions. *The White Goddess* (1948) is his most significant non-fiction title, its credo being that real poets get their gift from the Muse. His interest in myth prompted *Greek Myths* (1955) and *Hebrew Myths* (1963).

▷ M Seymour-Smith, *Robert Graves' Life and Work* (1983)

GRAY, Alasdair James

(1934–)

Scottish novelist, painter and playwright, born in Glasgow. He was educated at Whitehill Secondary School and Glasgow School of Art. Painting was his first vocation and he came late to novel writing; *Lanark*, his first novel, was published in 1981. A gargantuan effort, it is a phantasmagoric exploration of modern city life related by Duncan Thaw, in which science fiction is counterbalanced by stark realism, the setting being a place called Unthank, palpably Glasgow. In *1982, Janine* (1984), the hero—if he can be called that—is a divorced, alcoholic, insomniac supervisor of security installations who is telling his story to the mirror in a dismal Borders' hotel. Like others of Gray's works it is erotically charged and very funny. *Unlikely Stories, Mostly* (1983), a collection of stories, demonstrated his versatility, and with *The Fall of Kelvin Walker* (1985), Gray showed that he was adept at social satire, the story being that of a Scotsman on the make in the media who gets his comeuppance. Wickedly inventive and typographically unconventional, his hallmark is a debunking of Received Pronunciation, a hilarious example of which is to be found in *Something Leather* (1990), typically described by the puckish author as 'the first British fiction since the *Canterbury Tales* to show such a wide social range in such embarrassing sexual detail'. Other books include *Old Negatives* (1989), a collection of poems, and *McGrotty and Ludmilla* (1990), 'the Aladdin story set in modern Whitehall'. *Poor Things*, a rich parody of Victorian thrillers, appeared in 1992.

GRAY, David

(1838–61)

Scottish poet, born in Merkland, near Kirkintilloch, Dunbartonshire, the son of a handloom weaver. He studied divinity at Glasgow University, but took to poetry and in 1860 moved to London with **Robert Buchanan**, although he died of consumption the following year. His only collection of poetry was *The Luggie and Other Poems*, published posthumously in 1874. Its title piece is a long

lyrical poem in praise of the stream near his birthplace, written in the manner of **James Thomson**'s *The Seasons* (1730). It also contained 'In the Shadows'.
▷A V Stuart, *David Gray, Poet of the Luggie* (1961)

GRAY, John Henry
(1866–1934)

English poet, born in London. Converted to Roman Catholicism in 1890, he was educated (after work as an apprentice metal turner) at London University and Scots College, Rome, being ordained as a priest in 1901. A member of the **Wilde** circle in the nineties, he befriended **Paul Verlaine**. His first poetry volume, *Silverpoints* (1893), contains translations of French contemporaries as well as original verse. *Poems* (1931) has moments comparable to **Gerard Manley Hopkins** but has otherwise much that is unadventurously pious or neo-Georgian. He edited editions of **Thomas Campion** and **John Suckling** in 1896.
▷Father Brocard Sewell (ed), *Two Friends: John Gray and André Raffalovitch: Essays Biographical and Critical* (1963)

GRAY, Oriel
(1921–)

Australian playwright for stage, television and radio, born in Sydney. She originally worked with the Sydney New Theatre, and her communist sympathies resulted in a series of plays based on exploitation and oppression. In 1955 *The Torrents* shared first prize in the Playwrights Advisory Board competition with **Ray Lawler**'s *Summer of the Seventeenth Doll*, but was not published until 1988. Two of her plays did achieve independent life: *Drive a Hard Bargain* (1960) and *The Golden Touch* (1965).
▷*Exit Left: Memoirs of a Scarlet Woman* (1985)

GRAY, Simon
(1936–)

English dramatist, director and novelist, born on Hayling Island. He has written novels and several television plays, but is best known as a stage dramatist. His first play, *Wise Child*, was produced in 1967. Subsequent plays include *Butley* (1971); *Otherwise Engaged* (1975); *The Rear Column* (1978); *Quartermaine's Terms* (1981); *The Common Pursuit* (1984); and *Melon* (1987). He was a lecturer in English Literature at Queen Mary College, London for 20 years, and many of his plays are set in the world of academics, publishers, or academics who publish. His best television play is *After Pilkington* (1987), a wry thriller set in Oxford. He has also published books about the process of staging a play, *An Unnatural Pursuit* (1985) and *How's That for Telling 'Em, Fat Lady?* (1988).

GRAY, Thomas
(1716–71)

English poet, born in London. His father, Philip Gray, was of so violent and jealous a temper that his wife, Dorothy Antrobus, was obliged to separate from him. It was mainly through her efforts that Gray was sent to Eton (1727) and afterwards to Peterhouse, Cambridge (1734). At Eton he met **Horace Walpole**, whom in 1739 he accompanied on the grand tour. They spent two and a half years in France and Italy, but quarrelled at Reggio and parted. Walpole afterwards returned to blame himself, and the breach was healed within three years. Gray returned to England in September 1741. In 1742 he wrote his *Ode on a Distant Prospect of Eton College*, and had begun the *Elegy Written in a Country Churchyard* in Stoke Poges, Buckinghamshire. In the winter he went back to Cambridge, took his bachelorship in civil law, and took up residence in Peterhouse. This was perhaps the happiest period of his life; he wrote letters and enjoyed the company of his friends. The *Ode on Eton College* was printed in 1747 and the *Elegy* was printed in February 1751. His mother died in 1753, and was buried at Stoke Poges, with an epitaph from her son's pen on her tombstone. In 1750 he began the *Pindaric Odes*; the *Progress of Poesy* was finished in 1754; *The Bard*, begun at the same time, in 1757. He moved to Pembroke College, where he spent the remainder of his life quietly in scholarly seclusion. His two Pindaric odes were printed in 1757, and put their author at the head of living English poets. The laureateship was offered to him in 1757, but he declined. From 1760 he devoted himself to early English poetry; later he made studies in Icelandic and Celtic verse, which bore fruit in his Eddaic poems, *The Fatal Sisters* and *The Descent of Odin*—genuine precursors of Romanticism. In 1768 he collected his poems in the first general edition, and accepted the professorship of history and modern languages at Cambridge. He was now comparatively rich, and enjoyed an enviable reputation. He was buried beside his mother at Stoke Poges.
▷R Cremer, *Thomas Gray, a biography* (1955)

GRAZZINI, Anton Francesco, 'Il Lasca'
(1503–84)

Italian author of comedies, poet and novelist, born in Florence. His nickname means 'The Roach'. His comedies give a lively picture of Florence, and his poetry was admired in its time for its humour and skill. His best work, in the tradition of **Boccaccio**, is his unfinished

Le cene (edited in 1882, 'The Suppers'), a series of tales within a frame. **D H Lawrence** translated one: *The Story of Doctor Manente* (1929).

▷R J Rodin, *Anton Francesco: Poet, Dramatist and Novelliere 1503–1584* (1970)

GREEN, Anna Katherine
(1846–1935)

American detective-story writer, born in Brooklyn. She began her writing career with well-turned and well received verse, no longer read today. Her father was a trial lawyer, and *The Leavenworth Case* (1878) was the first crime fiction to be written by a woman. The style of this well plotted and exciting novel—it was successfully dramatized, and she married one of the actors—now seems awkward, but is no worse than that of **Agatha Christie**; it was successfully reprinted in 1934. Green wrote more of the same, including *The Doctor, His Wife, and the Clock* (1895).

GREEN, Anne
(1899–1989)

American novelist and translator, born in Savannah, Georgia, and sister to one of France's most distinguished novelists and diarists, **Julien Green**; she translated some of his work into English. She described their early upbringing in a now underrated volume of reminiscences, *With Much Love* (1948). Her skilful and sardonic novels, also underrated—perhaps in part because of her brother's fame—include *The Selbys* (1930) and *The Old Lady* (1947).

GREEN, Henry, pseud of Henry Vincent Yorke
(1905–73)

English novelist, born in Tewkesbury, Gloucestershire, and brought up in his family home in the West Country. Educated at Eton and Oxford, he became managing director in his father's engineering company in Birmingham, but pursued a parallel career as a novelist. While still an undergraduate he published *Blindness* (1926), the story of a clever and artistic boy who, blinded in a senseless train accident, turns to writing with powers extraordinarily heightened by his affliction. A contemporary of **Anthony Powell** and **Evelyn Waugh**, his second novel, *Living* (1929), gave a unique insight into life on the factory floor in Birmingham. An elliptical writer and highly stylized, like **Ivy Compton-Burnett** he relies heavily on dialogue, plot being conspicuous by its absence. Partial to terse and sophisticated titles such as *Party Going* (1939), *Caught* (1943), *Loving* (1945), *Back* (1946), *Concluding* (1948), *Nothing* (1950)

and *Doting* (1952), his influence and reputation extended far beyond the literary cognoscenti, and his writing was much admired in Europe. *Pack My Bag: A Self Portrait* (1940) is autobiographical.

GREEN, Julien
(1900–)

French novelist, born of American parents in Paris. Educated partly in the USA, he was bilingual, and became a convert to Catholicism. He began a successful series of psychological studies in a melancholy vein, written in French but later translated, with *Mont-Cinère* (1925, Eng trans as *Avarice House*, 1927 (US); 1928 (UK)). His other works include *Adrienne Mesurat* (1927, Eng trans *The Closed Garden*, 1928), *Léviathan* (1929, Eng trans *The Dark Journey*, 1929), which won the Harper Prize Novel contest, and *Moïra* (1950, Eng trans *Moira*, 1951). For details of his life, see his *Journals* I, II and III (1938–46) from a continuing series (the first eight *Journals* were translated in two vols as *Journal 1928–66* in 1969; other translations of the *Journals* exist), and *Memories of Happy Days* (1942) and *Memories of Evil Days* (1976) (both written in English).

▷G S Burne, *Julien Green* (1972)

GREEN, Matthew
(1696–1737)

English poet. Brought up in a strict Dissenting family, he worked at the Custom House throughout his short career. *The Grotto*, a poem on Queen Caroline's grotto at Richmond, was printed in 1733; manuscripts of other poems were published posthumously by his friend Richard Glover, but only *The Spleen* (1737) won lasting acclaim. A light-hearted essay in octosyllabic verse commending simple rural life as a cure for melancholy, it is a witty and original variant of the Horatian 'retirement' genre made popular by **John Pomfret**.

▷H R Smith, in *Notes and Queries*, 199 (1954)

GREEN, Paul E(liot)
(1894–1981)

American playwright, born on a farm at Lillington, North Carolina. He grew up with an intimate knowledge of the conditions and experiences of black employees, and his early short plays, produced by the Carolina Playmakers, confront the problems of poor blacks and whites. His first full-length piece, *In Abraham's Bosom* (1926), produced in New York, portrays the attempt of an illiterate black man to found a school for black children; he is eventually lynched. This received a Pulitzer Prize. Later works include *The Field God*

GREEN, Roger Lancelyn

(1927), dealing with religious intolerance, and *Johnny Johnson* (1936), a vigorous anti-war play with music by Kurt Weill. In 1937 Green wrote *The Lost Colony*, the first of a series of 15 dramas of American history designed to be performed in large open-air amphitheatres.
▷V S Kenny, *Paul Green* (1971)

GREEN, Roger (Gilbert) Lancelyn
(1918–)

English writer for children, actor, and biographer, born in Norwich. He is best known for his adaptations of classical and Old English stories, such as *King Arthur and his Knights of the Round Table* (1953) and *Heroes of Greece and Troy* (1960). Abridged and at times lacking in the gamey flavours of the originals, they are nonetheless skilfully retold, and have acted as invaluable introductions for several generations of schoolchildren. His biography of C S Lewis (1974; written with Walter Hooper) is one of several studies he has written on some of the most important names of modern children's literature.

GREENBERG, Uri Zvi
(1896–1981)

Hebrew poet, born in Galicia of a noted Hasidic family, who also, in his earlier life, wrote in Yiddish. He went to Palestine in 1924. His wrathful, nationalistic and sometimes wildly polemical poetry, much influenced by the Bible, has not been much translated. He believed in the establishment of a Jewish state on both sides of the Jordan, but is most famous for his poems—powerful lamentations—about the Holocaust.

GREENE, Asa
(1789–c.1837)

American humorist, bookseller and physician. As a novelist he revelled in burlesque narratives and delighted in comical titles. *The Life and Adventures of Dr. Dodimus Duckworth* (1833) is a mock-heroic biography of a fellow New Englander and *Travels in America, by George Fibbleton Esq., Ex-Barber to His Majesty the King of Great Britain* (1833) was a genial spoof on the recently-published travelling experiences of Mrs Trollope.

GREENE, (Henry) Graham
(1904–91)

English novelist, short-story writer, essayist, playwright and biographer, born in Berkhamsted. He was educated at Berkhamsted School where his father was headmaster, a factor which made his schooldays difficult. In *A Sort of Life* (1971), the first of two autobiographies (*Ways of Escape*, the second volume, appeared in 1980), he recounts how he played Russian roulette and of how, aged 13, he tried to cut open his leg with a penknife. He went to Balliol College, Oxford, and while there published *Bubbling April* (1925), a collection of verse. He became a Roman Catholic in 1926 and took up journalism as a career with *The Times*. He married in 1927, but was later separated from his wife, although they never divorced. *The Man Within* (1925), like its two immediate successors—*The Name of Action* (1930), *Rumour at Nightfall* (1932)—made little impression and he subsequently disowned them though he later allowed the first to be included in the Collected Edition. *Stamboul Train* (1932) was his first fully successful novel. Like many of his subsequent novels it is sombrely romantic, fusing tragedy and comedy in a peculiar no-man's land that critics christened 'Greeneland'. *It's a Battlefield* (1934) and *England Made Me* (1935) are likewise 'entertainments', an almost derogatory epithet that Greene first fastened to *Stamboul Train*. A prolific writer, he wrote a great number of novels, stories, plays and biographies as well as film criticism. He was the film critic for *Night and Day*, and was partly responsible for its demise when the magazine was successfully sued after he had accused Twentieth Century Fox of 'procuring' Shirley Temple 'for immoral purposes'. His career as 'a Catholic novelist' began with *Brighton Rock* (1938), a thriller which asserts that human justice is inadequate and irrelevant to the real struggle against evil. A recurring theme in his work, this is explored in his other 'Catholic' novels—*The Power and the Glory* (1940), *The Heart of the Matter* (1948) and *The Quiet American* (1955)—whose unorthodoxy often led him into controversy with the church's hierarchy. Other notable novels include *The Third Man* (1950, filmed by Carol Reed), *The End of the Affair* (1951), *Our Man in Havana* (1958), *A Burnt-Out Case* (1961), *The Comedians* (1965), *Travels With My Aunt* (1969), *The Honorary Consul* (1973), *The Human Factor* (1978), *Doctor Fischer of Geneva* (1980), *Monsignor Quixote* (1982) and *The Captain and the Enemy* (1988). The multifarious settings reflect his wanderlust and his fascination with uncomfortable countries—Argentina, the Congo, Mexico, Vietnam—as well as his seeming disregard for his personal safety. He settled in a modest flat in Antibes in 1966, where he lived for the rest of his life. In 1982, he broke his relative seclusion by publishing an incendiary pamphlet, *J'Accuse*, which brought him into conflict with the local authorities in Nice. He also published travel books: *Journey Without Maps* (1936), *The Lawless Roads* (1939) and *In Search of a Character: Two African Journals* (1961). The *Collected Essays* appeared in 1969; the *Collected Stories* in 1972. His plays include *The*

Living Room (1953), *The Potting Shed* (1957) and *The Complaisant Lover* (1959). *A World of My Own—A Dream Diary* appeared in 1992. Few modern writers have his range and power, critical acclaim and popular success; he is cited often by his peers as the greatest novelist of his time, although there are dissenting voices from that judgement, including that of **Anthony Burgess**.

▷J A Atkins, *Graham Greene* (1957, rev edn 1966)

GREENE, Robert
(1558–92)

English dramatist, born in Norwich and educated at Cambridge. He wrote a stream of plays and romances. The latter are often tedious and insipid, but they abound in beautiful poetry. One of them, *Pandosto*, supplied **Shakespeare** with hints for the plot of *The Winter's Tale*. The most popular of his plays was *Friar Bacon and Friar Bungay*. As Greene helped to lay the foundations of the English drama, even his worst plays are valuable historically. After his death appeared the pamphlet entitled *The Repentance of Robert Greene, Master of Arts*, in which he lays bare the wickedness of his former life. His *Groat's Worth of Wit bought with a Million of Repentance* contains one of the few authentic contemporary allusions to Shakespeare.

▷W H Chapman, *William Shakespeare and Robert Greene: the evidence* (1912)

GREENWOOD, Walter
(1903–74)

English writer, born in Salford. His novel *Love on the Dole* (1933), inspired by his experiences of unemployment and depression in the early 1930s, made a considerable impact as a document of the times and was subsequently dramatized. He also wrote other novels with a social slant, and several plays.

▷ *There Was a Time* (1967)

GREGORY, Horace
(1898–1982)

American poet, anthologist, translator (**Catullus**, **Ovid**) and critic, born in Milwaukee, Wisconsin. He was married to the poet Marie Zaturenska, with whom he wrote the estimable *A History of American Poetry 1900–1940* (1946). His poetry, a little flat and lacking in inspiration, but well-crafted and thoughtful, is in *Collected Poems* (1964) and *Another Look* (1976). He wrote useful critical works on **Dorothy Richardson** and **Amy Lowell**.

▷ *Spirit of Time and Place: The Collected Essays* (1973); 'Gregory Issue' of *Modern Poetry Studies* (1973)

GREGORY, Isabella Augusta, Lady, née Persse
(1852–1932)

Irish playwright, born in Roxborough, County Galway. After her marriage in 1880 to Sir William Henry Gregory (1817–92), Governor of Ceylon (1872–7), she became an associate of **W B Yeats** in the foundation of the Abbey Theatre in Dublin, and the Irish players. For these she wrote or translated around 40 short plays, the best of which are *Spreading the News* (1904) and *The Rising of the Moon* (1907). She was a leading figure in the Irish literary revival of the period, and her home at Coole Park was a focus for that movement. She also wrote Irish legends in dialect, possessed a wide knowledge of Irish folklore which emerges in much of her work, and translated **Molière**.

▷A Saddlemayer, *In Defence of Lady Gregory* (1966)

GREIG, Maysie Coucher, properly Jennifer Greig Smith
(1901–71)

Australian journalist and writer of romantic fiction, born in Sydney. She moved to England in 1920, writing short stories and serials for London newspapers. Her first book, *Peggy of Beacon Hill* (1920), was later filmed, and was followed by nearly 200 novels. Until the 1950s she was one of the mainstays of the circulating libraries under her own name and as Jennifer Ames.

GRENFELL, Julian Henry Francis
(1888–1915)

English poet. Educated at Eton and Balliol College, Oxford, he was killed in World War I. He is remembered for his fine war poem 'Into Battle' which was published in *The Times* in 1915 and is much favoured by anthologists.

▷V Meynell, *Julian Grenfell* (1917)

GRESSET, Jean-Baptiste-Louis
(1709–77)

French poet and playwright, born in Amiens. He was the eldest of nine children, two of whom were to become nuns, and one of his first poems was inspired by the death of his sister Marguerite in an Augustine order, at the age of 15. Gresset joined the Jesuits when he was 17, becoming a teacher but also finding time to devote to his literary concerns. His poetry in the 1730s was marked by religious themes, sometimes treated satirically: *Ver-Vert* (1734) caused the Jesuits to send him to La Flèche for a penitential period. He was also the author of several plays, including a tragedy, *Édouard* (1740); a drama, *Sidney*, first performed in 1745; and a comedy, *Le*

Méchant (1747), which remained for some years in the repertoire of the Comédie-Française.

GREVILLE, Charles Cavendish Fulke
(1794–1865)

English diarist. He was educated at Eton and Christ Church, Oxford, and became private secretary to Earl Bathurst, and was clerk of the privy council (1821–59). His position gave him particular access for studying court and public life, which is reflected in his noted *The Greville Memoirs* (1875–87), and also in his *Letters* (1924) and *The Greville Diary* (1927).

GREVILLE, Sir Fulke, 1st Baron Brooke
(1554–1628)

English poet and courtier, born in Beauchamp Court, Warwickshire. He was educated at Shrewsbury and Jesus College, Cambridge. A friend of Sir **Philip Sidney** and a favourite of Queen Elizabeth, he held many important offices, including Secretary for Wales (1583–1628) and Chancellor of the Exchequer (1614–21). He was created baron in 1620. He wrote several didactic poems, over a hundred sonnets, and two tragedies, including *The Tragedy of Mustapha* (1609), printed in 1633. His best-remembered work is his *Life of the Renowned Sir Philip Sidney* (published 1652) with its vivid pictures of contemporary figures. He died a tragic death, murdered by an old retainer who thought himself cut out of his master's will.
▷R A Rebholz, *The Life of Fulke Greville* (1971)

GRÉVILLE, Henry, pseud of Alice Durand, née Fleury
(1842–1902)

French novelist, born in Paris. She accompanied her father to St Petersburg in 1857, and wrote Russian society novels.

GREVIN, Jacques
(1538–70)

French Renaissance poet and playwright, born in Clermont en Beauvaisis. He studied in Paris. His *Théâtre*, published in 1561, marks an important stage in the restoration of ancient tragic and comic forms to French drama, anticipating the Neo-Classical period. He also wrote some circumstantial dramas, including *Hymne à Monseigneur le Dauphin*, written for the occasion of his marriage to Mary Stuart on 24 April 1558. However, Grevin is better remembered for his poetry (which was admired by **Pierre de Ronsard** among others): *L'Olimpe* (1560) comprises love sonnets, satires, pastoral works and odes. Around 1562 he abandoned poetry in order to concentrate on medicine, but he died eight

years later, aged 32, after a period of service as physician to Marguerite de France, Duchess of Savoie, in Turin, leaving a wife and probably a daughter.

GREY, Francis William
(1860–1939)

English novelist, playwright and poet, born and educated in England. He moved to Ottawa to teach at the university there. He is best known for *The Cure of St Philippe: A Story of French–Canadian Politics* (1899) in which an intrusive, ironic Trollopian narrator tells in Victorian style the story of a parish in French Canada, involving small-town church and election business. The novel is one of the best of its kind. In comparison, his historical and religious plays are overly didactic, and his poetry in *Love Crucified and Other Sacred Verse* (1902) is undistinguished. He returned to Britain to live in Edinburgh for the last years of his life.

GREY, Zane
(1875–1939)

American novelist, born in Zanesville, Ohio. He began his working life as a dentist, but after a trip out west in 1904 turned out 'westerns' with machine-like regularity, totalling 54 novels and an overall sale estimated at more than 12 million copies. His best known, *Riders of the Purple Sage*, sold nearly two million copies. His hobby of big-game fishing off the coasts of Australia and New Zealand was utilized in such books as *Tales of Fishing* (1919). His success was due to the 'escapist' lure of his simple adventure plots and attractive, authentic settings.
▷C Jackson, *Zane Grey* (1973); J Kerr, *Man of the West* (1957)

GRIBOYEDOV, Aleksander Sergeyevich
(1795–1829)

Russian writer and diplomat, born in Moscow. He wrote *Góre ot Umá* (1824, Eng trans *The Misfortune of Being Clever*, 1914, also trans as *Góre ot Umá*, 1857), a comedy in rhymed iambics, which satirizes the contemporary Moscow society so aptly that it has provided household phrases for the Russian people. Involved in the Decembrist Revolt, he was, however, cleared, and in 1828 became Russian ambassador to Persia. He was killed in an anti-Russian demonstration at the embassy in Teheran.
▷V N Orlov, *Griboyedev* (1954); and other works by V N Orlov

GRIEG, (Johan) Nordahl Brun
(1902–43)

Norwegian poet and dramatist, born in Bergen. He studied at Oslo and Oxford, and spent much of his youth travelling, mirrored in his volumes of early poetry such as *Rundt Kap det Gode Haab* (1922, 'Round the Cape of Good Hope') and *Norge i våre hjerter* (1925, 'Norway in our Hearts'). His novel, *Skibet gaar videre* (1924, 'The Ship Sails On'), crystallized his experiences on a voyage to Australia as an ordinary seaman and was the model for **Malcolm Lowry**'s *Ultramarine*. A committed anti-fascist, he wrote dramas about national freedom, as in *Vår aere og vår makt* (1935, 'Our Honour and Our Might') and *Nederlaget* (1937, 'Defeat', about the Paris Commune of 1871). During World War II he joined the Resistance, escaped to London, and broadcast his patriotic verses back to his homeland. His plane was shot down over Berlin in 1943.

▷ F J Hallund, *Nordahl Grieg. En dikter og hans tid* (1962)

GRIER, Eldon Brockwill
(1917–)

Canadian poet, born in London. Grier began as a painter, working for a time in Mexico (the subject of some of his best poems) as Diego Rivera's plasterer. He married an artist, Sylvia Tait, in 1953, and taught at the Montreal Museum of Art. It was not until his mid-thirties, when he contracted tuberculosis, that he 'quite inexplicably' wrote his first poems. The work he has produced since then—*Selected Poems 1955–1970* (1971), *The Assassination of Colour* (1978)—shows the influence of his background in painting. He has been called, rather predictably, a 'verbal colourist'.

GRIERSON, Constantia, née Crawley
(c.1705–1732)

Irish poet, born in Graiguenamanagh, County Kilkenny, to poor country people. Mainly self-educated, she was already proficient in classical languages and Hebrew when she went to Dublin around 1721. In 1726 she married George Grierson, a bookseller, for whom she corrected editions of **Virgil**, **Terence** and **Tacitus**. **Swift** described her as 'a woman of uncommon learning' and commended her poems. She wrote learned philosophical poetry, but also had a talent for easy, natural expression in more personal verse.

▷ *Poems by Eminent Ladies*, ed G Colman and B Thornton (1755); A C Elias, in *Swift Studies*, 2 (1987)

GRIFFIN, Gerald
(1803–40)

Irish novelist, born in Limerick. He wrote for local journals and went to London in 1823 to make a career in literature. He failed as a dramatist, but was more successful with collections of short stories of southern Irish life like *Holland Tide* (1826) and *Tales of the Munster Festivals* (1827). His novel, *The Collegians*, on which **Dion Boucicault**'s drama *Colleen Bawn* is founded, was published anonymously in 1829. In 1838 he burned his manuscripts and entered a monastery.

▷ *The Dead March Past* (1940)

GRIFFITHS, Trevor
(1935–)

English dramatist, born in Manchester. His first plays, *The Wages of Thin* (1969) and *Occupations* (1970) were staged in his native Manchester. In 1973, *The Party* was staged by the National Theatre; set in May 1968, the play revolves around a discussion of left-wing politics, with Laurence Olivier, in his last stage role, playing the central character of John Tagg, an eloquent Glaswegian Trotskyist. *Comedians* (1975) is the story of a group of young apprentice comedians learning their craft under the guidance of an ageing comic. Other plays include *Real Dreams* (1986), a typically angry political piece, and *The Gulf Between Us* (1992), which tackles the issues of the Gulf War in the style of a dream play.

GRIGOROVICH, Dmitri
(1822–99)

Russian novelist, born in Simbirsk. He knew every Russian writer of account—he had been a student with **Dostoyevsky**—and his memoirs *Literaturnye vospominaniya* (1929) are a vital source book. His first narratives were written under the influence of the critic Belinski's 'natural school', and protested against social inequality. *Anton Goremyka* (1947) influenced **Turgenev** in its intimate portraiture of the Russian peasant. *The Cruel City* (1891) collects stories, while *Rybaki* (1853, Eng trans *The Fisherman*) was his best-known novel in English-speaking countries.

GRIGSON, Geoffrey Edward Harvey
(1905–85)

English poet, critic and editor, born in Pelynt, Cornwall. The founder of the influential magazine *New Verse* (1933–9), he published several volumes of precisely-observed and tersely expressed verse, gathered in *Collected Poems, 1924–62* (1963). A later *Collected Poems* included his subsequent work in the period 1963–82, and was followed by *Montaigne's Tree* (1984). He was an often outspoken literary critic; erudite, eclectic and idiosyncratic, his was a refreshing anti-establishment voice.

▷ *The Crest on the Silver* (1950)

GRILLPARZER, Franz
(1791–1872)

Austrian dramatic poet, born in Vienna. He was in the imperial civil service from 1813 to 1856. He first attracted notice in 1817 with a tragedy, *Die Ahnfrau* ('The Ancestress'), followed by *Sappho* (1818, Eng trans 1820), *Das goldene Vlies* (1820, Eng trans *Medea*, 1879), *Des Meeres und der Liebe Wellen* (1831, Eng trans *Hero and Leander*, 1938), *Der Traum ein Leben* (1834, Eng trans *A Dream is Life*, 1946), and others. He wrote lyric poetry and one excellent prose novel, *Der arme Spielmann* (1848, 'The Poor Musician'), the only one of his works set in the Vienna of his own day.

▷ J Nadler, *Franz Grillparzer* (1952)

GRIMALD, Nicholas
(1519–62)

English poet and playwright, born of Genoese ancestry in Huntingdonshire. He studied at Christ's College, Cambridge, and became Ridley's chaplain, but recanted under Queen Mary I. He contributed 40 poems to Tottel's *Songes and Sonettes* (1557), known as *Tottel's Miscellany*, and translated **Virgil** and **Cicero**. He also wrote two Latin verse tragedies on religious subjects.

▷ L R Merrill, *The Life and Poems of Nicholas Grimald* (1925)

GRIMM, Jacob Ludwig Carl
(1785–1863)
GRIMM, Wilhelm Carl
(1786–1859)

German folklorists and philologists, born in Hanau in Hesse-Kassel. They both studied at Marburg. In 1808 Jacob became librarian to Jérôme Bonaparte, King of Westphalia, and published a work on the Meistersingers (1811). In 1812 the brothers published the first volume of the famous *Kinder und Hausmärchen* (*Grimm's Fairy Tales*, first translated as *German Popular Stories*, 1823)—a work which formed a foundation for the science of comparative folklore. The second volume followed in 1815; the third in 1822. In 1829 the two moved to Göttingen, where Jacob became professor and librarian, and Wilhelm under-librarian (professor 1835). They were among the seven professors dismissed in 1837 for protesting against taking the oath of allegiance to the King of Hanover. In 1841 the brothers received professorships in Berlin, where they commenced the compilation of the massive *Deutsches Wörterbuch* (1854–1961, 'German Dictionary'). As a philologist, Jacob Grimm published *Deutsche Grammatik* (1819, 'German Grammar'), perhaps the greatest philological work of the age. His *Deutsche Rechtsalterthümer* (1828, 'German Legal Antiquities') and *Deutsche Mythologie* (1835, Eng trans *Teutonic Mythology*, 1883–8) dealt with German usages in the Middle Ages and the old Teutonic superstitions. He also published *Geschichte der deutschen Sprache* (1848, 'History of the German Language') and *Reinhart Fuchs* (1834, 'Reynard the Fox'). He also formulated 'Grimm's Law' of sound changes, an elaboration of earlier findings by the Swedish philologist Ihre and the Danish scholar Rask, but an important contribution to the study of philology. Wilhelm's chief independent work was *Die deutsche Heldensage* (1829, 'The German Heroic Myth').

▷ H Gerstner, *Die Brüder Grimm* (1974)

GRIMMELSHAUSEN, Hans Jacob Christoffel von
(c.1622–1676)

German novelist, born in Gelnhausen in Hesse-Kassel. He served on the imperial side in the Thirty Years War (1618–48), led a wandering life, but ultimately settled down in Renchen near Kehl, where he became a senior civil servant of the town. In later life he produced a series of remarkable novels. His best works are on the model of the Spanish picaresque romances. The sufferings of the German peasantry at the hands of the lawless troopers who overran the country have never been more powerfully pictured than in *Der Abenteuerliche Simplicissimus Teutsch und Continuatio* (1669, Eng trans *Simplicissimus the Vagabond*, 1924). It was followed by *Trutz Simplex* (1669, Eng trans *Mother Courage*, 1965), *Der seltzame Springinsfeld* (1670, Eng trans *The Singular Life Story of the Heedless Hopalong*, 1981), *Das wunderbarliche Vogelnest* (1672, 'The Amazing Bird's Nest'), and others.

▷ K Negus, *Grimmelshausen* (1974)

GRINGOIRE, or GRINGORE, Pierre
(c.1475–1538)

French poet and dramatist, born in Caen. While taking the chief roles in a theatrical society he was active in the production of pantomime farces, and is one of the creators of the French political comedy. He attacked the enemies of Louis XII and thus found cover for his comments on the vices of the nobility, the clergy and even the pope himself. In later life he was a herald to the Duke of Lorraine, and wrote religious poetry. His works include the famous *Mystère de Monseigneur Saint Loys* (c.1524). Gringoire figures in **Victor Hugo**'s *Notre Dame*, and in a play by **Théodore Banville**.

▷ E Bardel, *Gringoire* (1925)

GRIPE, Maria
(1923–)

Swedish writer of novels for children and young adults, brought up in Örebro and educated at Stockholm University. The recipient of numerous national and international awards, among them the **Hans Christian Andersen** Medal in 1974, she has seen her books translated into more than 20 languages. The breakthrough came with her ninth novel, *Josefin* (1961), about a lonely young girl, struggling to cope with the puzzling and frightening world of the grown-ups around her; as in Gripe's five later novels about the young boy Elvis Karlsson (1972–9), events are told strictly from the child's point of view. These novels remained within the confines of realism, but in later books Gripe incorporates supernatural elements within a realistic frame, eg in the fairy-tale *Glasblåsarnas barn* (1964, 'The Glass-blower's Children'), and in *Tordyveln flyger i skymningen* (1978, 'The Chafer Flies at Dusk'), in which past and present, natural and supernatural are skilfully interwoven. In *Skuggan över stenbänken* (1982, 'The Shadow across the Stone Bench'), the first of a series of 'shadow' novels set at the turn of the century, she further develops this style, blending the realistic with elements of a classical horror story. She works in close conjunction with her illustrator husband, Harald Gripe.
▷G Fagerström, *Maria Gripe, hennes verk och hennes läsare* (1977)

GROSSI, Tommaso
(1791–1853)

Italian poet, born in Bellano on Lake Como. He studied law at Padua and practised at Milan. His first poem, *La Prineide* (1814, 'The Prineide'), was a battle poem in the Milanese dialect. There followed several historical romances, the most notable of which is *Marco Visconti* (1834, Eng trans 1836) and the epic poem for which he is best known, *I Lombardi alla prima crociata* (1826, 'The Lombards on their First Crusade'), which Verdi used for his opera *I Lombardi*.
▷E Flori, *Scorci e figure del romanticismo* (1938)

GROSSMAN, Edith (Howitt) Searle
(1863–1931)

New Zealand writer of four novels, all of a moralistic cast heightened by symbolism. Her first, *Angela: A Messenger*, was published in 1890, as Edith Searle, soon followed by *In Revolt* (1893). Its sequel appeared 14 years later—*The Knight of the Holy Ghost* (1907)—and then came the more prosaic *The Heart of the Bush* (1910), which pleaded for mutual understanding in marriage. She also wrote verse for the short-lived *Zealandia*. Despite the religious overtones of her work she was a militant feminist who preached, among other things, a more honest approach to sexual matters, and was one of the first female graduates from the then University of New Zealand.

GROSSMITH, George
(1847–1912)

English humorist, actor and writer, born in London. For several years he was a police court reporter on *The Times*. In 1870 he became a singer and entertainer, creating several leading roles in the premieres of comic operas by **Gilbert** and Sullivan. He published his *Reminiscences of a Clown* in 1888, and *Piano and I* in 1910. He is best remembered, though, for his collaboration with his brother Weedon Grossmith on *The Diary of a Nobody*, serialized first in *Punch* and published in book form in 1892. An imaginary journal of domestic life in Holloway, London, it records the life of the amiable, over-dignified and often ridiculous city clerk Mr Pooter, striving to better himself culturally and socially but who, unwittingly, becomes the butt of numerous jokes he fails to understand.
▷T Joseph, *George Grossmith* (1982)

GROTH, Klaus
(1819–99)

German poet, born in Heide in Holstein. A schoolteacher, in 1866 he became Professor of German Language and Literature at Kiel. His masterpiece, *Quickborn* (1852), is a series of poems in Low German (*Plattdeutsch*) dealing with life in Dithmarshen. Some of his work is in High German, and he published children's tales and short stories.
▷H Siercks, *Klaus Groth* (1899)

GRUFFYDD, William John
(1881–1954)

Welsh poet, scholar, editor (of *Y Llenor*) and critic, born in Bethel. He went to Oxford and read in Classics. Later he became a professor at the University of Cardiff. His poetry, neither profound nor major, but well crafted, was notably influenced by that of **Thomas Hardy**. His criticism and anthologies were influential.

GRYPHIUS, or GREIF, Andreas
(1616–64)

German lyric poet and dramatist, born in Glogau, Silesia. He travelled in Holland, France and Italy, studying medicine and astronomy, and returned to his native town. His early misfortunes led him to the 'all is vanity' theme of his lyrics, expressed in deep gloom, collected under the title *Sonn-und-Feiertagssonette* (1639, 'Sonnets for Sundays and Holidays'). His dramas mainly concern martyrdom and include *Leo Armenius* (1650), *Catharina von Georgien* (1657) and *Papinianus* (1659). But he also wrote the charming pastoral, *Die geliebte Dornrose* (1660, Eng trans *The Beloved Hedgerose*, 1928), the comedies *Herr Peter Squentz* (1663, Eng trans *Absurda Comica, or Master Peter Squentz*, 1964), which resembles the Bottom scenes in **Shakespeare**'s *A Midsummer Night's Dream*, and *Horribilicribrifax* (1663), satirizing the Thirty Years War. He was indirectly influenced by Shakespeare and **Joost van den Vondel**.

▷H Becker, *Andreas Greif, poet between epochs* (1973)

GUARESCHI, Giovanni
(1908–68)

Italian journalist and writer, born in Parma. He became editor of the Milan magazine *Bertoldo*. After World War II, in which he was a prisoner, he returned to Milan and journalism, but it was *Mondo piccolo 'Don Camillo'* (1950, Eng trans *The Little World of Don Camillo*, 1951) which brought him fame. These stories of the village priest and the communist mayor with their broad humour and rich humanity have been translated into many languages, and have been followed by *Mondo piccolo 'Don Camillo e il figliol prodigo'* (Eng trans *Don Camillo and the Prodigal Son*, 1952) and others. He illustrated his books with his own drawings.

▷ *Diario clandestino, 1943–1945* (1949)

GUARINI, Giovanni Battista
(1538–1612)

Italian poet, born in Ferrara. He was entrusted by Duke Alfonso II with diplomatic missions to the pope, the emperor, and was sent to Venice and Poland. His chief work was the famous pastoral play, *Il Pastor Fido* (1585, 'Fido the Shepherd'), really an imitation of **Torquato Tasso**'s *Aminta*.

▷V Russi, *Battista Guarini ed il Pastor Fido* (1885)

GUERARD, Albert Joseph
(1914–)

American novelist and critic, born in Houston, Texas. He is better known as a critic (he has written influential books on **Conrad** and **Hardy**), and his novels may not yet have received their full critical due. He did intelligence work in France during World War II, and this forms the background for *Maquisard: A Christmas Tale* (1945). *Night Journey* (1950), a more substantial novel, was often

compared by reviewers—and not inappropriately—to **George Orwell**'s *1984*. Set in a future Europe divided between the dictatorship of the East and the so-called Democracy of the West, it memorably tries to rescue, from the realistically presented chaos, a notion of idealistic socialism.

GUÉRIN, Charles
(1873–1907)

French Symbolist poet, born in Lunéville. He travelled in Germany and Italy and periodically stayed in Paris. His work is confined to a few collections, including *Le Cœur solitaire* (1898, 'The Lonely Heart') and *L'Éros funèbre* (1900, 'Eros in Mourning'). A later series, *L'Homme intérieur* (1906, 'The Inner Man'), echoed his late conversion to the Catholic faith.

▷ Joseph B Hanson, *Le Poète Charles Guérin* (1935)

GUÉRIN, Eugénie de
(1805–48)

French writer, born in the château of Le Cayla (Tarn), sister of **Georges Guérin**, to whom she was devoted. She is chiefly known for her *Journal* (1855), which is imbued with mysticism, but she also wrote poems and edited her brother's papers.

GUÉRIN, Georges Maurice de
(1810–39)

French poet, born in the château of Le Cayla (Tarn), brother of **Eugénie de Guérin**. He entered the community of Lamennais at Le Chesnay in Brittany. He followed his master in his estrangement from Rome, and, going like him to Paris (1833) to try journalism, became a teacher at the Collège Stanislas. He married a rich Creole lady in November 1838, and died of consumption. His *Reliquiae*, including the *Centaur* (a kind of prose poem), letters and poems, were published in 1860.

▷V W Brooks, in *The Malady of the Ideal* (1913)

GUERRA, Tonino (Antonio)
(1920–)

Italian screenwriter, born in Sant' Arcangelo, Romagna. A poet and novelist, he first wrote for the cinema as a collaborator on the script for *Uomini E Lupi* (1956, 'Men and Wolves'). *L'Avventura* (1960, 'The Adventure') began a lengthy partnership with director Michelangelo Antonioni that resulted in a series of elliptical works seeking to convey a melancholic search for self-awareness and the futility of meaningful communication between men and women. Their most notable films together include *La Notte* (1961, 'The Night') and *Deserto Rosso* (1964, 'Red

Desert'). Declaring that his writing reveals a 'different face' for each of his collaborators, he has brought a poetic sensibility to a vast range of work that often laments the passing of an earlier age or the loss of a more traditional set of values. He has received Oscar nominations for his contribution to the screenplays for *Casanova '70* (1965), *Blow-Up* (1966) and *Amarcord* (1973). He has worked extensively with some of the most distinguished film-makers in contemporary European cinema, and a selection of his finest scripts would include *Cadaveri Eccellenti* (1976, 'Illustrious Corpses') for Francesco Rosi, *La Notte Di San Lorenzo* (1981, 'The Night of San Lorenzo') for the Taviani brothers, *Landscape In The Mist* (1988) for Theo Angelopoulos and *Stanno Tutti Bene* (1990, 'Everybody's Doing Fine') for Guiseppe Tornatore.

GUERRAZZI, Francesco Domenico
(1804–73)

Italian writer and politician, born in Leghorn. He had won a great reputation by his patriotic and political fictions when, on the Grand Duke of Tuscany's flight (1849), he was proclaimed dictator in spite of his disinclination for a republic. On the duke's restoration he was condemned to the galleys, but ultimately permitted to select Corsica as his place of banishment. Restored to liberty by later events, he sat in the parliament of Turin (1862–5). His chief works of fiction are *La Battaglia di Benevento* (1827, 'The Battle of Benevento'), *L'Assedio di Firenze* (1836, 'The Siege of Florence') and *Isabella Orsini* (1844).
▷P Miniati, *Francesco Domenico Guerrazzi* (1927)

GUEST, Barbara
(1920–)

American abstract poet, born in Wilmington, North Carolina, and educated at the University of California, Berkeley. She married (briefly) into the British aristocracy, but has otherwise pursued a career utterly removed from convention and only slightly reminiscent of Anglophile/phobe predecessors such as **Hilda Doolittle** ('HD'), about whom Guest wrote *Herself Defined: The Poet H.D. and her World* (1984). Her own verse is highly chromatic, drawing something from **Wallace Stevens** but often influenced by fine art rather than other poets. Titles like *The Location of Things* (1960) and *The Blue Stairs* (1968) confirm the Stevens connection, but later books are more vividly and personally observed; they include *Moscow Mansions* (1973), *The Countess from Minneapolis* (1976) and *The Türler Losses* (1979). Guest has written one novel, *Seeking Air* (1978).

GUEVARA, Antonio de
(1490–1545)

Spanish prelate and writer. A Dominican, he became Bishop of Mondoñedo and confessor of Charles V. He used in his book on Marcus Aurelius the exalted style which anticipated the euphuism of **John Lyly**. His *Epistolas familiares* (1541–3, Eng trans *The Familiar Epistles of Anthony de Guevara*, 1574) were also very popular in an English version.
▷E Grey, *Guevara, a forgotten author* (1973)

GUEVARA, Luis Vélez de
(1570–1644)

Spanish dramatist. He wrote many plays in the style of **Lope de Vega**. His novel *El Diablo cojuelo* (1641, 'The Limping Devil') was used as the model for **Alain Le Sage**'s *Diable boiteux*.
▷F E Spencer and R Schevil, *The Dramatic Works of Luiz Vélez de Guevara* (1937)

GUEVARA, Miguel de, Frey
(c.1578–1640)

Mexican Augustinian monk who included a famous sonnet, 'No me mueve, mi Dios, para querete' ('Do not move me, my God, to love thee'), in his papers; it was therefore attributed to him, but it has been shown that he did not write it.
▷C M Huff, *The Sonnet 'Ne me mueve, mi Dios': its Theme in Spanish Tradition* (1948)

GUILHEM IX, Duke of Aquitaine, Count of Poitou
(1071–1126)

The earliest known and perhaps the first of the Provençal troubadours, 'sworn enemy to all that is modest and sacrosanct', 'a vehement lover of women', and one of the most extraordinary figures in European literature—he has been found the more so, no doubt, because of the influence upon him of mystical Sufic poetry, which, with its gnostic overtones, is often not understood by modern critics. The establishment in his territory (richer than those of the King of France) of the proto-Catharist mystical order of Fontrvrault, offers the key to the understanding of a man who, on the one hand, sacrificed an army of 60 000 men in a pointless crusade (1101), and on the other perhaps 'invented' *amour courtois* ('courtly love') and who was, according to a contemporary, 'one of the most courtly men in the world'. He left 11 poems whose high quality no one has doubted: five are capably and amusingly obscene, one is an exercise, and the rest are exquisitely cryptic.
▷*Romanische Forschungen*, LXXIII (1961); R R Bezzola, *Les Origines de la littérature courtoise en occident* (1944–62)

GUILLÉN, Jorge
(1893–1984)

Spanish poet, born in Valladolid. The first edition of his important work *Cántico*, published in 1928, was a collection of 75 poems. By the edition of 1950, following his flight to the USA and his establishment in a teaching post at Wellesley, that number had risen to 334. *Cántico* consists of what the author terms 'pure poetry'—verse stripped of the prosaic, the explanatory or the merely functional. His other major work is *Homenaje* (1967, 'Homage'), which includes translations as well as original poems; the breadth and quality of the learning displayed confirmed his standing as a major poet. His critical works include the 1961 volume, published in English, *Language and Poetry*.

GUILLÉN, Nicolás
(1902–89)

Major Cuban poet, born in Camagüey. His poetry is famous for its relating of Negro to Latin-American themes: he was the first to recognize that the Black presence on his island was not merely exotic. He became Cuba's best-known poet, celebrated even by the illiterate. Much of his poetry is political, as was natural from a man who for many years was a leading member of the Communist Party of Cuba. He received a state funeral. There are two volumes of his poetry in translation: *Man-Making Words* (1972) and *The Great Zoo* (1972).
▷ L V Williams, *Self and Society in the Poetry of Nicolás Guillén* (1982)

GUILLEVIC, pseud of Eugène Guillevic
(1907–)

French poet from Carnac, in Brittany. His first small collection, *Requiem*, appeared in 1938. Although from the war years onwards a committed communist (and active in the resistance), Guillevic is above all a poet of objects and shapes: he wants to express 'things' ideas of themselves ... their philosophy of themselves in an alien world peopled by ... men'. Thus a kind of religious sense pervades his dialectical materialism, and creates a tension which has fascinated many translators. 'The reader', wrote one of his translators, 'is hypnotized out of himself to find himself.' Available in English translation are *Guillevic* (1968, 1969) and *Selected Poems* (1974).

GUILLOUX, Louis
(1899–1980)

French novelist, born in Brittany. His first publication, *Sang noir* (1935, Eng trans *Bitter Victory*, 1936), established his reputation as a philosophical novelist who was able to create rounded characters; set on his home territory, it is a study of an intellectual—reminiscent, in many respects, of Roquentin in **Sartre**'s subsequent work *La Nausée*—who is disgusted by his surroundings but apparently unable to act to improve his lot. *La Maison du peuple* (1937, 'The People's House') received praise for its portrayal of poverty, while *Jeu de patience* (1949, 'Game of Patience') is the portrayal of a small town and its life throughout the cataclysms of the first half of the century.
▷ V Brombert, *The Intellectual Hero* (1960)

GUIMARÃES, Afonso Henriquez da Costa
(1870–1921)

Brazilian poet, born in Ouro Prêto, in the province of Minas Gerais. He wrote under the name 'Alphonsus de Guimaraens'. He was influenced by the slightly earlier Brazilian poet **João Cruz e Sousa**, and his poetry is written in a distinctly Symbolist manner inherited from him. It is characteristically concerned with devoutly-held religious preoccupations, which often spill over into mysticism. He published a number of collections of poems in his lifetime, while others appeared posthumously. A *Complete Works* was published in Portuguese in 1960.

GUIMARAES, Bernardo
(1825–84)

Brazilian poet and novelist, born in Minas Gerais. He graduated in law, and worked, none too successfully, as a judge and schoolteacher, before moving to Rio de Janeiro and practising journalism (1858–61). He is best known for the novel *A escrava Isaura* (1875, 'Isaura the Slave Girl'), which at the time was a powerful anti-slavery tract, and has recently been made into a television soap opera. His progressive politics also found expression in *O ermitao de Muquem* (1866, 'The Hermit of Muquem'), the titular character of which is part-Indian. Guimaraes remains important in the development of a distinctly Brazilian school of novel-writing. His poems, too, have had an influence; his *Poesias completas* was published in 1959.

GUIMARÃES ROSA, João
(1908–69)

Brazilian novelist and story writer, one of the most important Latin-American writers of his century, born in Cordisburgo, Minas Gerais. He qualified and practised as a doctor, but became a diplomat in 1932. The chief area of his concern was that of **Euclydes da Cunha**: the backlands of Brazil, in the north of Minas Gerais. His greatest affinities are not with any other Brazilian writer but with the Peruvian **José María Arguedas**, who deeply admired him: both men tried to write in a 'native' form of their own European language—to revitalize its tired and 'civilized' complacency. *Sagarana* (1946 rev edn 1958, Eng trans 1966) collects nine 'parables of the sertão', some of them about animals, which often behave, a critic has said, 'in a markedly totemistic way' (eg an ass rescues his drunken master from drowning). His masterpiece is *Grande Sertão: veredas* (1956, rev edn 1958), for which its translators chose the title *The Devil to Pay in the Backlands* (1968). This is a monologue by a bandit, Riobaldo, and tells a magical story of how the speaker entered into a bargain with the devil, and fell into homosexual love with Diadorim, an angel who finally turns out to be a woman, the daughter of the friend whose murder he has been trying to avenge. Of all the Brazilian novelists of such high calibre only the more accessible **Graciliano Ramos** has had similar power.

GUIMERÁ, Ángel
(1849–1924)

Catalan poet and dramatist, born in Santa Cruz, Tenerife. His work falls into three periods, of which the first and third—for the most part, historical plays—show the influence of the French Romantics. His middle period owes its preoccupation with contemporary life to **Ibsen**. He is regarded as the greatest Catalan dramatist. His most famous play is *Terra Baixa* (1896, 'Lowlands'), on which D'Albert based his opera *Tiefland*.
▷J Minack, *Guimerá* (1959)

GÜIRALDES, Ricardo
(1886–1927)

Argentinian novelist, poet and editor, born in Buenos Aires. Güiraldes is one of the most important figures in his country's literature. With the young **Borges**, and others, he founded the leading periodicals *Martin Fierro* and *Proa*. He lived between Buenos Aires and Paris (where he died prematurely, of Hodgkin's Disease), and was thus in touch with European influences. His masterpiece is *Don Segundo Sombra* (1926, Eng trans 1935), the story of a childhood on a gaucho ranch, whose triumph is its style: an elegant blend of literary Argentinian, much influenced by his friend **Larbaud**, and the vernacular. It is just the kind of book one might expect of a man who said, towards the end of his suffering, 'I aim to master myself and to enter the path that will conduct me to the goal of a better self'—he had become an adherent of Vedanta. In 1932 his record of his search, *El sendero* ('The Way'), was published.
▷G Previtali, *Ricardo Güiraldes and Don Segundo Sombra* (1963)

GUIRAUT DE BORNELH
(c.1165–1220)

Provençal troubadour, born in Excideuil, and the leading poet of Limousin-Périgord. Although the poetry of his contemporary **Bernard de Ventadorn** is nowadays usually preferred, it was Guiraut who was hailed as the master in his time, and who was later praised by **Dante**. Like Bernard, he was of humble origin. Fifty of his songs are extant.
▷H J Chaytor, *The Troubadours of Dante* (1902)

GUIRAUT RIQUIER
(c.1254–1292)

Provençal troubadour—the last major one— born near Narbonne of modest parentage. By his time the poetry of *amour courtois* ('courtly love'), or, more properly, *fin'amor*, had run its course. The last of his 89 extant poems are more religious than amorous.
▷J Anglade, *Le Troubadour Guiraut Riquier* (1905)

GUITRY, Sacha
(1885–1957)

French actor and dramatist, who was born in St Petersburg. He wrote nearly a hundred plays, mostly light comedies, many of which have been successfully performed in English. The son of the actor-manager Lucien Guitry (1860–1925), he first appeared on the stage in Russia with his father's company. His first appearance in Paris was in 1902, still under his father's management. He went to London in 1920 with *Nono*, a play written when he was 16. It starred the second of his five wives, the enchanting Yvonne Printemps. He also wrote and directed several delightful films, including *Le Roman d'un tricheur* (1936, 'The Tale of a Cheat') and *Les Perles de la couronne* (1937, 'The Pearls in the Crown').
▷J Harding, *Sacha Guitry, the last boulevardier* (1968)

GUITTONE D'AREZZO
(1230–94)

Italian poet and moralist, born near Arezzo. As a young man he wrote love poetry in the style of the Provençal troubadours; then in 1265 he became a monk, joining an order known as 'the merry friars' ('frati godenti') and the content (though hardly the style) of his work changed. He was persistently criticized by **Dante**, perhaps jealous of his fame and standing, as 'vulgar' and, no doubt, because Dante's own early style had been learned from that of Guittone. He left 50 *canzoni*, 251 sonnets, eight verse epistles, and some vital letters. A very few have preferred him to Dante. He was an esoteric master of the gnostic mysteries of *fin'amor*—the proper name for 'courtly love'—and his apparent obscurities have hardly yet been elucidated. There are some able translations by Joseph Tusiani in *The Age of Dante: An Anthology of Early Italian Poetry* (1974).

▷V Moleta, *The Early Poetry of Guittone d'Arezzo* (1976)

GULLBERG, Hjalmar
(1898–1961)

Swedish poet and translator (**Sophocles, Aristophanes** and other classical writers), born in Malmö, the bastard son of a rich man; his mother left him to foster-parents. Rather like **Graves** in England, he was fully aware of but eschewed modernist techniques in favour of a generally ironic mode of expression in tight traditional forms. He had at his best an affinity with **San Juan de la Cruz**, whom he also translated. One of his most intense (and humorous) sequences is *Kärlek i tjugonde seklet* (1933, 'Love in the Twentieth Century'). He achieved a high position in his nation's regard, and this was enhanced when, after many years of silence, he published the famous *Dödsmask och lustgård* (1952, 'Death Mask and Paradise'). In the grip of a progressive and crippling paralytic illness, his last collection was *Ögon, läppar* (1959, 'Eyes, Lips'), mostly written in tribute to the woman who cared for him. His work is well represented in the volume translated by J Moffett: *'Gentlemen, Single, Refined,' and Selected Poems 1937–1959* (1979). This important poet has been seriously neglected outside Scandinavia, in part owing to postwar Swedish critics' too hasty dismissal of him as 'middlebrow'.

▷C Fehrman, *Hjalmar Gullberg* (1968)

GUMILEV, Nikolai Stepanovich
(1886–1921)

Russian poet, a leader of the Acmeist school which revolted against Symbolism. His exotic and vivid poems include *Kolchan* (1915, 'The Quiver'), with some fine verses of war and adventure, and *The Pyre* and *The Pillar of Fire*, which contain his best pieces. He also wrote criticism and translated French and English poetry. He was shot as a counterrevolutionary. His wife was the poet **Anna Akhmatova**.

▷L I Strekhobsky, *Craftsman of the Word* (1949)

GUNDULIĆ, Ivan
(1589–1638)

Ragusan poet, the leading figure of the golden age of the Serbo–Croatian literature which flourished alongside that of the Italian Renaissance. His model was **Tasso**, whose *La Gerusalemme liberta* ('Jerusalem Liberated')

he always intended to translate, but did not. His two chief works, amongst many others, were the pastoral play *Dubravka* (published in 1837), and the epic poem *Osman* (published in 1826), part of which is missing. The latter, celebrating the victory of the Poles over the Turkish Sultan Osman—thus establishing a pan-Slavic Christianity—is said to be amongst the greatest works of its time in any language.

GUNN, Neil Miller
(1891–1973)

Scottish novelist, born in Dunbeath, Caithness, the son of a fisherman. Educated at the village school, and privately in Galloway, he passed the Civil Service examination in 1907, and moved to London. He was in the Civil Service until 1937, from 1911 as an officer of customs and excise in Inverness and elsewhere in Scotland. After writing a number of short stories, his first novel, *Grey Coast* (1926), was immediately acclaimed, and was followed by *The Lost Glen* (serialized in 1928) and the even more successful *Morning Tide* (1931). Other works include a historical novel on the Viking age, *Sun Circle* (1933), *Butcher's Broom* (1934), *Highland River* (1937, James Tait Black Memorial Prize), *Wild Geese Overhead* (1939), *The Silver Darlings* (1941), and the contrasting war-time novels *Young Art and Old Hector* (1942) and *The Green Isle of the Great Deep* (1944). Gunn was at his best when describing the ordinary life and background of a Highland fishing or crofting community, and when interpreting in simple prose the complex character of the Celt. His last novels were *The Well at the World's End* (1951), *Bloodhunt* (1952) and *The Other Landscape* (1954). *The Atom of Delight* (1956) is a philosophical autobiography.

▷F R Hart and J B Pick, *Neil M Gunn: a Highland life* (1981)

GUNN, Thom(son) William
(1929–)

English poet, born in Gravesend. He attended University College School, London, and, following national service, read English at Trinity College, Cambridge. His first collection, *Fighting Terms* (1954), labelled him a 'Movement' poet. He moved to the USA in 1954 where he has lived ever since. His second book, *The Sense of Movement* (1957), is overtly existentialist; his third, *My Sad Captains* (1961), is more contemplative. Subsequent volumes—*Touch* (1967), *Moly* (1971) and *Jack Straw's Castle* (1976)—were not universally well-received, but he is undoubtedly one of the major poets of the second half of the century. His *Selected Poems 1950–1975* were published in 1979, and *The Passages of Joy*, in which he writes frankly about his homosexuality, appeared in 1982. *The Man with Night Sweats* (1992) included a series of elegies on men who had died 'before their time' as a result of AIDS. *Collected Poems* was published in 1993.

▷A Bold, *Thom Gunn and Ted Hughes* (1976)

GUNNARSSON, Gunnar
(1889–1975)

Icelandic novelist, born in Fljótsdalur, East Iceland, who wrote all his major works in Danish before re-writing them in Icelandic. At the age of 18 he went to Denmark to seek fame and fortune. His first novel, *Af Borgslægtens Historie* (1920, Eng trans *Guest the One-Eyed*, 1920), was the first Icelandic work to be turned into a feature film. A prolific writer, his acknowledged masterpiece was the autobiographical novel, *Kirken paa Bjerget* (5 vols, 1923–8, Eng trans *Ships in the Sky* and *The Night and the Dream*, 1938).

▷E O Gelsted, *Gunnar Gunnarsson* (1926)

GUNTER, Archibald Clavering
(1847–1907)

English-born American novelist (and engineer, broker and chemist). *Mr Barnes of New York* (1887), published by himself when it was turned down by publishers, became an overnight bestseller. It is a ridiculous novel, presenting an American who is able to meet every possible eventuality—he is a crack shot, an expert lover, and even a skilled surgeon; but it remains compulsively readable, for Gunter had the storyteller's gift; it now reminds its readers not only of **James Thurber**'s Walter Mitty but also of **Upton Sinclair**'s Lanny Budd (Barnes is an international trouble-shooter). *Fresh the American* (1881) was a play about an American millionaire.

GÜNTHER, Johann Christian
(1695–1723)

German poet, born in Strugan in Silesia. He lived a somewhat dissolute life, and died in poverty, rejected by his family. His poetry has a surprising range, and is unusually direct in language and emotional expression for that period. He wrote love lyrics notable for their sensitivity and their lack of affectation, as well as satires, political poems, religious poems, student songs and drinking songs.

GUNTHER, John
(1901–70)

American author and journalist, born in Chicago. He was a foreign correspondent for the *Chicago Daily News* and for NBC. He established his reputation with the bestselling *Inside Europe* (1939), followed by a series of similar works, in which firsthand material is blended with documentary information to present penetrating social and political studies. Other books include the autobiographical *Death Be Not Proud* (1949) and *A Fragment of Autobiography* (1962).

GURDJIEFF, George
(c.1865–1949)

Armenian novelist and thinker, born in or near Kars. His *Beelzebub's Tales to His Grandson* (1949) circulated in manuscript during his lifetime, but was not published until after his death. A modern Christian gnostic, Gurdjieff synthesized an extraordinary and profound system—to which his novel is a non-literary and deliberately shocking guide—which influenced many writers, including **Kipling**, **Ouspensky**, **Mansfield**, **Aldous Huxley**, **Priestley** and many others.

▷J Moore, *Gurdjieff* (1992)

GURNEY, Ivor
(1890–1937)

English composer and poet, born in Gloucester. He became a chorister in Gloucester Cathedral in 1900, and then a pupil of the organist, Sir Herbert Brewer. At the Royal College of Music he studied compositon under Stanford. On military service in France during World War I he was wounded and gassed and, after spending much time in hospital, published two collections of poems: *Severn and Somme* (1917) and *War's Embers* (1919). After the war he returned to the Royal College of Music to study with Vaughan Williams and in 1920 published his first songs, *5 Elizabethan Songs*, before returning to Gloucester. He suffered increasingly from depression, eventually entering a mental hospital from which he was transferred to a London hospital, where he died of tuberculosis. An instinctual writer of both music and poetry rather than a skilled craftsman, his songs are considered his most important work; he remained largely uninfluenced by the contemporary folk-song movement, looking rather to Elizabethan music and the German classics for inspiration.

GUSTAFSON, Ralph
(1909–)

Canadian poet, story writer and essayist, born in Lime Ridge, Québec, one of the most versatile of the Canadian poets of the older generation. **A J M Smith** has said of him that he has improved, and become more original, since he developed away from his early romanticism, through his love for **Hopkins** and **Donne**, and into his later and more subtly

allusive and elliptical style. His *Collected Poems* appeared in 1987 in two volumes.
▷W Keitner, *Ralph Gustafson* (1979)

GUSTAFSSON, Lars
(1936–)

Swedish novelist and philosopher, born in Västerås and educated in Uppsala. His doctoral thesis, *Språk och lögn* (1978, 'Language and Lies'), explored the problem of language as a barrier between experience and understanding, much influenced by Wittgenstein. He takes a mystical stance and is much drawn to arcane and gnostic systems. His major literary work is a series of novels under the general title of *Sprichorne i muren* (1971–83, 'Cracks in the Wall'). His collected verse was published in 1981; an English selection appeared 10 years earlier.

GÜTERSLOH, Albert Paris von, pseud of Albert Conrad Kiehtreiber
(1887–1973)

Austrian painter and novelist, born in Vienna, who was highly influential—in particular on the novelist **Heimito von Doderer**—as a practitioner of Expressionism. He worked as a stage designer for Max Reinhardt, but was also a professor of fine arts, until the Nazis forced him to work in a factory. The most extraordinary of his baroque novels, and one which is still studied and admired, is *Soone und Mond* (1962, 'Sun and Moon'), which is, simultaneously, a massive allegory of Austria as it tottered from grand empire to shabby and always menaced republic, and a 'huge gloss on the perennially puzzling parable of the Unjust Steward'. He started this major work as early as 1935. Gütersloh was certainly one of those few writers who rose above the generally moribund state of Austrian letters between the wars.

GUTHRIE, A(lfred) B(ertram)
(1901–91)

American novelist, born in Bedford, Indiana, but brought up in Montana. He went to live in Kentucky, and his first successful novel, *The Big Sky* (1947), is about a mountain man, of the 1840s, from that state. In his major novels, *The Big Sky*, *The Way West* (1949) and *These Thousand Hills* (1956), he tries to recreate the reality of the Frontier—a reality which had all too soon become, in the 20th century, the cheaply exploited myth of dime novels and low-budget westerns. He was probably less artistically successful than the other novelist, in a similar innovatory tradition, who emerged at about the same time, **Walter Van Tilburg Clark**; but Guthrie's achievement, despite stylistic lapses and a falling off in later novels, such as *Arfive*

(1971), has yet to be assessed. With Jack Sher, he wrote the screenplay for the classic movie *Shane* (1951).
▷T W Ford, *A B Guthrie, Jr* (1968)

GUTHRIE, Ramon
(1896–1973)

American poet, born in New York. Guthrie studied at the Sorbonne during the 1920s and became a professor of French in New Hampshire. His first significant collections appeared when Guthrie was already approaching old age—*Graffiti* (1959) and *Asbestos Phoenix* (1968)—and his most highly-regarded work was published just a few years before his death. *Maximum Security Ward* (1970) is about a sick old man summoning up all his powers of imagination, memory and wit to overcome a sense of desolation.

GUTIÉRREZ GONZÁLEZ, Gregorio
(1826–72)

Colombian poet, born in Ceja del Tambo, Antioquia, whose manners he celebrated in his famous bucolic poem *Memoria sobre el cultivo del maíz en Antioquia* (1868, 'Memories Concerning the Cultivation of Maize in Antioquia'). Gutiérrez González is a homely humorist who naturalizes his source, the *Georgics* of **Virgil**, in the interests of Antioquia's beauties and customs. The poem is still readable.

GUTIÉRREZ NÁJERA, Manuel
(1859–95)

Mexican poet and story writer, born in Mexico City. Educated in a French school, he was mainly influenced by French models, such as **Verlaine** and the symbolists. His versification has been praised as achieving the most pleasing qualities in Spanish for 'perhaps a century' before him. He drank heavily, was haunted by his ugliness, and yet was never able to express himself with real power—only with mellifluousness. His prose sketches are delicate but void of true meaning. He is reckoned to have been an important precursor of *modernismo*.
▷B G and J L Carpenter, *Manuel Gutiérrez Najera* (1966)

GUTZKOW, Karl Ferdinand
(1811–78)

German author, born in Berlin. He was influenced by the French Revolution of 1830, and for his *Wally die Zweiflerin* (1835, 'Doubting Wally') got three months' imprisonment as a champion of the 'Young Germany' movement. He next became a journalist, and in 1847 director of the Court Theatre at Dresden, having meanwhile written many dramas, the most successful being *Richard Savage* (1839) and *Zopf und Schwert* (1844, 'Pigtail and Sword'). Among his romances is *Die Ritter vom Geiste* (1850–2, 'The Knights of the Spirit').

▷ E W Dubert, *Karl Gutzkow und seine Zeit* (1968)

GUZMAN, Martín Luis
(1887–1976)

Mexican novelist, editor and journalist, born in Chihuahua. With **Azuela**, Guzmán was the most important novelist of the revolution, all the events of which he recorded in his fiction. Originally a lawyer, he became a supporter of Madero, and then, after the latter's assassination, private secretary to Pancho Villa. Later, a revolutionary who could not abide revolutionaries, he abandoned Mexico for New York and Madrid—but finally returned in 1936. *El águila y la serpiente* (1928, Eng trans 'The Eagle and the Serpent', 1930), though not quite achieving the literary quality of the fiction of Azuela, became the most famous of all Mexican novels of the Revolution. Partly autobiographical, it tells of his own participation. *La sombra del caudillo* (1929, 'In the Shadow of the Leader'), his best novel, deals with the dominance of Obregón. His *Memorias de Pancho Villa* (1938–51, Eng trans *Memoirs of Pancho Villa*, 1965) is certainly a novel, but is told in the authentic voice of the illiterate caudillo.

▷ J S Brushwood, *Mexico in its Novel* (1970);

W M Langford, *The Mexican Novel Comes of Age* (1971)

GWYNN, Stephen Lucius
(1864–1950)

Irish biographer and literary historian, born in Dublin into a scholarly family, grandson of William Smith O'Brien. Educated in Dublin and at Brasenose College, Oxford, he became a schoolmaster and then a journalist in London (1896–1904). He moved into Irish nationalist politics as MP for Galway (1906–18), and later wrote a fine memoir of his leader, *John Redmond's Last Years* (1919). His wife became a Roman Catholic and their sons prominent Roman Catholic intellectuals. His literary output was prodigious, his *Masters of English Literature* (1904) proving one of the great best-sellers of all time. Perhaps his most remarkable work is *Experiences of a Literary Man* (1926), a great record of the meaning of life in the midst of literature.

GYP, pseud of the **Comtesse de Mirabeau de Martel**
(1849–1932)

French novelist, born in the château of Koëtsal in Brittany. She wrote a series of humorous novels, describing fashionable society, of which the best known are *Petit Bob* (1868, 'Little Bob') and *Mariage de Chiffon* (1894, 'Chiffon Marriage').

▷ *Sac à papier, correspondence with Trois Étoiles* (1886)

H

HAAVIKKO, Paavo
(1931–)

Finnish poet, fiction writer and playwright. He was born in Helsinki, the son of a prosperous businessman. His first job was in the property market, but he began publishing in his early twenties and was immediately hailed as one of the most significant Finnish poets to emerge since the war. His earlier work appeared in *Runot 1951–1961* (1962), which was superseded by another collection in 1974. A concern with Finnish independence runs through his work, sometimes cast in a rather dense and enigmatic form. His best-known work is a quasi-allegorical story, 'Lumeton Aika' ('Before the Snow'), about a future invasion and suppression of national identity. His plays include *Ratsumies* (1974, 'The Horseman'), which the composer Aulis Sallinen made into an opera, with a libretto by Haavikko. Like **T S Eliot**, he draws on contemporary realities—most often, business—to support mythic examinations of human motivation and progress. Haavikko's poetry was first translated into English by **Anselm Hollo** (1974).
▷H Sihvo, *Soutu Bysanttiin* (1980)

HABIB of Isfahan, Mirza
(c.1854–1897)

Persian translator, born in Chahar Muhal. His chief achievement was a rather odd (but brilliant) one: he put into Persian the English *Adventures of Hajjii Baba of Isahan*, by James Morier, in 1906. This is said to have exercised considerable political influence.
▷H Kamshad, *Modern Persian Prose Literature* (1966)

HABINGTON, William
(1605–54)

English poet, born in Hindlip, Worcestershire. His father, Thomas (1560–1647), an antiquary, was imprisoned, and his uncle, Edward (?1553–1586) executed, for complicity in Babington's plot. He was educated at St Omer and Paris, and married Lucy Herbert, daughter of the first Lord Powis. He immortalized her in his *Castara* (1634), a collection of metaphysical lyrics which are uneven in quality but contain some pieces of considerable charm. He also wrote *The*

Historie of Edward the Fourth (1640), and a play, *The Queen of Aragon* (1640).
▷K Allott, introduction and commentary to *The Poems of William Habington* (1948)

HACKER, Marilyn
(1942–)

American poet and editor, born and educated in New York City. In 1961 she married the science-fiction writer **Samuel R Delany**, with whom she edited the little magazine *Quark* (1969–70); she has also been associated with *City Magazine* (1967–70), *Little Magazine* (1977–80) and, since 1980, *13th Moon*. Her early verse was privately printed, and her first commercially published volume was *Presentation Piece* (1970), in which she combines rich, metaphysical imagery and form with disturbingly direct and frank subject-matter, much concerned with death and sexual experimentation. Later collections—*Separations* (1976), *Assumptions* (1980) and *Taking Notice* (1980)—are not so powerful, though they are technically more polished. Hacker won a National Book Award in 1975.

HACKETT, Albert
(1900–)

American playwright and actor, born in New York. He wrote in collaboration with his wife, Frances Goodrich (1891–1984), and they are best remembered for their highly successful stage adaptation of *The Diary of Anne Frank* (1955), which won them a Pulitzer Prize in 1956. Their other stage works include *Western Union, Please* (1939) and *The Great Big Doorstep* (1942). They were also very successful screenwriters, and their many credits include such Hollywood favourites as *The Thin Man* (1934), *Easter Parade* (1948) and *Seven Brides for Seven Brothers* (1954).

HACKS, Peter
(1928–)

German dramatist, poet and critic, born in Breslau (Wrocław, now in Poland). He is often regarded as Germany's leading dramatist of the post-war era. Essentially a disciple of **Bertolt Brecht**, he left West for East Germany in 1955. From 1960 to 1963 he directed the Deutches Theater, but after that the communists actively discouraged his increasingly critical attitude towards them: they claimed that he lacked a sense of reality. For a time he had to support himself by writing historical plays and translations of classics. Possibly the best of his many and diverse plays, which draw upon any precedent which happens to suit him (**Aristophanes**, Greek myth, **Shakespeare**), are *Moritz Tassow* (1961), about a rebellious pig-keeper (in verse) and the comic and satirical tour de force about **Goethe** and Charlotte von Stein: *Ein Gespräch im hause Stein über den abwesenden Herrn von Goethe* (1976, 'A Conversation in the Stein Household about the Absent Mr Goethe').

▷ J R Scheid, *'Enfant Terrible' of Contemporary East German Drama: Peter Hacks in his Role as Adaptor and Innovator* (1977).

HACOHEN, Shalom
(1772–1845)

Hebrew poet and dramatist, born in Poland. He was one of the earliest members of the Haskalah ('Enlightenment') movement: the 18th- and 19th-century Jews who sought to acquire European culture. He wrote successful verse plays while living in Germany and then in Austro-Hungary.

▷ M Waxman, *A History of Jewish Literature* (1960)

HADEWIJCH
(mid-13th century)

Dutch mystic and poet. She wrote poetry and devotional prose in the tradition of St Bernard, and was one of the key mystics of her time. Nothing is known of her life. Some of her letters are translated in *Medieval Netherlands Religious Literature* (1965), by E Colledge.

HÁFIZ, pseud of Shams ed-Dín Muhammed
(d.c.1388)

Persian lyrical poet, born in Shíráz. From the charming sweetness of his poetry he was named by his contemporaries *Chagarlab*, or 'Sugar-lip'. His *ghazals* are all on sensuous subjects—wine, flowers, beautiful damsels—but they also possess an esoteric significance to the initiated, and his name is a household word throughout Iran. Háfiz, like nearly all the great poets of Persia, was of the sect of Súfi philosophers, the mystics of Islam. His tomb, two miles northeast of Shíráz, has been magnificently adorned by princes, and is visited by pilgrims from all parts of Iran.

▷ G M Wickens, 'Hafez', in *Encyclopaedia of Islam* (1971, rev edn)

HAFIZ IBRAHIM
(1871–1932)

Egyptian poet and translator (of **Hugo**'s *Les Misérables*), called 'the poet of the Nile', born on a Nile boat. He was Egypt's leading classical Arabic poet, famous for his skilled and sonorous obituaries, such as his well-known one for Queen Victoria. He is of mainly historical importance, not being much read for pleasure today.

▷ *Middle Eastern Affairs* (1952)

HAFSTEIN, Hannes (Pétursson)
(1861–1922)

Icelandic politician and poet, born at Möðruvellir in the north of Iceland, the first Icelandic premier under Home Rule (1904–7, 1912–14). He studied at Reykjavík and Copenhagen University, where he became a brilliant lawyer. He returned to Iceland in 1887 a fervent nationalist with a growing reputation as a lyric poet, and became leader of the independence party in the campaign for Home Rule from Denmark. In his premiership he brought about large improvements in education, health care and commerce, and inaugurated a telephone and telegraph system. In his poetry he was one of the early proponents of realism in Icelandic literature.

HAGEDORN, Friedrich von
(1708–54)

German poet, born in Hamburg. In 1733 he became secretary to the 'English Court' trading company at Hamburg, and wrote satirical, narrative and 'society' verse, much of it dedicated to a cheerful, optimistic outlook on life. His fables were popular in his own day.

▷ C J Schmid, *Biographie der Dichter* (1879)

HAGEDORN, Hermann
(1882–1964)

American biographer, editor and poet, born in New York. Much of his writing and editing was devoted to Theodore Roosevelt, whom he admired beyond idolatry. He also wrote a biography of Albert Schweitzer. His verse—which has not lasted—was conventional, somewhat in the mould of the more popular side of **Rudyard Kipling**.

▷ *The Hyphenated Family* (1960)

HAGELSTANGE, Rudolf
(1912–84)

German religious poet and novelist, born in Nordhausen. Hagelstange began his career as a journalist before being conscripted in 1940. His *Venezianisches Credo* (1945), an eloquent sonnet sequence, had earlier been passed round secretly as an underground condemnation of Nazism. *Ballade vom verschütteten Leben* (1952, Eng trans *Ballad of the Buried Life*, 1962), about two German soldiers trapped in a shelter at the end of the war, has been acclaimed as one of the most powerful long poems of the century. Other poetry is collected in *Gast der Elemente Zyklen und Nachdichtungen 1944–72* (1972, 'Guest of the Elements').

HAGGARD, Sir (Henry) Rider
(1856–1925)

English novelist, born in Bradenham Hall, Norfolk, the son of a lawyer. Educated at Ipswich grammar school, he went to Natal in 1875 as secretary to Sir Henry Bulwer, and next year accompanied Sir Theophilus Shepstone to the Transvaal. He returned in 1879 (finally in 1881) to England, married, and settled down to a literary life. His *Cetewayo and his White Neighbours* (1882) pleased the Cape politicians, but attracted no attention elsewhere. *King Solomon's Mines* (1885) made him famous, and was followed by *She* (1887), *Allan Quatermain* (1887), *Eric Bright-eyes* (1891), *The Pearl Maiden* (1903), *Ayesha: The Return of She* (1905) and many other stories. Other publications include *Rural England* (1902) and *The Days of My Life* (1926).
▷ M Cohen, *Rider Haggard* (1960)

HAGGARD, William, pseud of Richard Henry Michael Clayton
(1907–)

English novelist, born in Croydon, Surrey. Employed by the Civil Service in London, he served with the Indian Army during World War II. One of the finest exponents of the spy and suspense novel, Haggard's most popular character is Colonel Charles Russell of the Security Executive, a high-level branch of British Intelligence, who features in over 20 novels after his first appearance in *Slow Burner* (1958). A stiff-upper-lipped patriot, he is an autocrat, motivated more by duty than principle, and intensely suspicious not only of left-wingers but also of all intellectuals. Other novels, such as *The Diplomatist* (1987), feature as hero the black Englishman, Willy Smith.

HAGIWARA Sakutaro
(1886–1942)

Japanese poet, born into a wealthy rural family living and farming on the Kanto plain. His work, however, is strongly associated with Tokyo and is fondly regarded by its citizens. He was the first Japanese poet to make extensive use of free verse. His two best collections of verse, *Tsuki ni Hoeru* (1917, Eng trans *Howling at the Moon*, 1978) and *Aoneko* (1923, 'Blue-Cat'), are full of introspective, quiet portraits of tiny, often very dark, aspects of life in Tokyo. He was an admirer of **Edgar Allan Poe**, and his verse reflects this in its themes and mood. His prose writings, mainly deeply pretentious musings on literary theory, are incomprehensible.

HAHN-HAHN, Ida, Countess
(1805–80)

German novelist, born in Tressow in Mecklenburg-Schwerin. She wrote society novels influenced by the 'Young Germany' movement, before turning Catholic and founding a convent in Mainz (1854).
▷ E I Schmid Juergens, *Ida Gräfin Hahn-Hahn* (1933)

HAICÉAD, Pádraigín
(1600–54)

Irish poet, born in Tipperary. He was a Dominican monk. He has been compared to **Céitinn** for his patriotism and eloquence. He played a part in the battle against Cromwell, but was obliged to flee to Louvain—where he had been ordained—when the latter prevailed.

HAILEY, Arthur
(1920–)

English-born Canadian popular novelist, born in Luton. He became a naturalized Canadian in 1947. He has written many bestselling blockbusters about disasters, several of which enjoyed a new lease of life when filmed. Indicative titles include *Hotel* (1965), *Airport* (1968) and *Wheels* (1971).

HALAS, Frantisek
(1901–49)

Usually regarded as the greatest of the 20th-century Czech poets, born in Brno. 'Halasism' was a term of opprobrium amongst the clerks in charge of Czech communist culture. He had welcomed the Stalinist takeover, but then died feeling betrayed (he referred to his 'whored up dreams'). He began as a proletarian poet, but soon, after a brief period during which he was a part of the Czech inter-war 'poetist' movement—an optimistic, playful affair, in defiance of the realities which threatened Czechoslovakia—adopted an extreme 'subjectivism'. The two individual poets who most influenced him were **Rilke** (himself eventually a Czech, though writing in German), and the father of Czech poetry, **Karel Mácha**. His most characteristic collection, *Staré zeny* (1935, Eng trans *Two Women*, 1947), expresses his anxiety and his view of the human predicament as something essentially tragic, which yet might be overcome by true hope. Poetry in translation includes: *Our Lady Bozena Nemcová* (1944) and *A Garland of Children's Verse* (1968).
▷ A French, *The Poets of Prague* (1969)

HALDEMAN, Joe (Joseph William)
(1943–)

American science-fiction writer, born in Oklahoma City. He served as a combat engineer in the Vietnam War, and was severely wounded in action. His first novel, *War Year* (1972), was set in Vietnam, but his experiences there are also reflected in much of his science fiction, beginning with *The Forever War* (1974). *Mindbridge* (1976) was more experimental in form than in content. *All My Sins Remembered* (1977) is notable for its cogent portrait of a man attempting to create internal order from the chaos around him, while the *Worlds* trilogy (1981–92) treats a similar theme, albeit with a female protagonist and a more wide-ranging canvas. He has written a number of other novels and stories, but is not prolific.

HALE, Edward Everett
(1822–1909)

American essayist, biographer and fiction writer, born into a distinguished Boston family. After Harvard he became a journalist and Unitarian clergyman, finally becoming Chaplain to the US Senate. His philanthropical and political writings include *Letters on Irish Immigration* (1852); among his biographical works is *Franklin in France* (1887–8); and he wrote two fascinating volumes of autobiography, *A New England Boyhood* (1893) and *Memories of a Hundred Years* (1902). There is a strongly moralistic tone to his writing, particularly in his many works for children, but he could also be humorous, as in the story 'My Double and How He Undid Me' (1859). His varied fiction is now almost forgotten, apart from the famously patriotic 'The Man Without a Country' (1863), which many were convinced was a factual account.
▷J Holloway, *Edward Everett Hale: A Biography* (1956)

HALE, Nancy
(1908–90)

American novelist and critic, wife of the scholar Fredson Bowers, and grand-daughter of **Edward Everett Hale**. She was born in Boston. Her novels and stories are lively and amusing, but her chief work is *A New England Girlhood* (1958).

HALE, Sarah Josepha, née Buell
(1788–1879)

American writer, born in Newport, New Hampshire. In 1828 she became Editor of the *Ladies' Magazine*, Boston. She wrote a novel, *Northwood* (1827), and a book of *Poems for Our Children* (1830), which contained 'Mary had a Little Lamb'.
▷R Finley, *The Lady of Godey's* (1931)

HALÉVY, Léon
(1802–83)

French writer, brother of Jacques Halévy, born in Paris. He became Professor of Literature at the Polytechnic School. He wrote the introduction to Saint-Simon's *Opinions* (1825), also histories, poetry, fables, novels, dramatic poems, and translations of such works as *Macbeth* and *Clavigo*. His most important books are his *Résumé de l'histoire des juifs* (1827–8, 'Short History of the Jews'), *Poésies européennes* (1837, 'European Poetry'), and *La Grèce tragique* (1845–61, 'The Tragedy of Greece').

HALÉVY, Ludovic
(1834–1908)

French playwright and novelist, son of **Léon Halévy**, born in Paris. In 1861 he became secretary to the Corps Législatif. With **Henri Meilhac** he wrote libretti for the best-known operettas of Offenbach, and for Bizet's *Carmen*, and produced vaudevilles and comedies. His *Madame et Monsieur Cardinal* (1873) and *Les petites Cardinal* (1880) are delightful sketches of Parisian theatrical life. *L'Invasion* (1872) contained his personal recollections of the war. His charming *L'Abbé Constantin* (1882) was followed by *Criquette* (1883, Eng trans 1891), *Deux Mariages* (*Un mariage d'amour*, 1880, Eng trans *Marriage for Love*, 1890); and *Un grand mariage* (1883, 'A Grand Marriage'), *Princesse* (1884) and *Mariette* (1893).
▷*Carnets* (1935)

HALEY, Alex Palmer
(1921–92)

American novelist and biographer, born in Ithaca, New York state, and brought up in North Carolina. He worked as a coastguard for 20 years from 1939, turning to writing only with the publication in 1965 of *The Autobiography of Malcolm X*, Haley co-authoring the book after the assassination of the black activist. *Roots*, published in 1976, was a phenomenal success, being adapted for television and winning a Pulitzer Prize the following year. Beginning with the life of Kunta Kinte, an African who was enslaved and taken to America, this novel—or, to use Haley's preferred term for his realism, 'faction'—documented the history of black Americans; its essentially optimistic approach rendered it accessible to a large white audience.

HALIBURTON, Hugh, pseud of **James Logie Robertson**
(1846–1922)

Scottish poet, born in Milnathort, Kinross. He became a student-teacher in Haddington, East Lothian, and later studied at Edinburgh. He became the first English master at Edinburgh Ladies' College, later Mary Erskine's School (1876–1913). In the guise of a shepherd in the Ochil Hills, 'Hugh Haliburton', he published *Horace in Homespun: A Series of Scottish Pastorals* (1886) and *Ochil Idylls* (1891). He also wrote essays, and produced editions of several Scottish poets.

HALIBURTON, Thomas Chandler
(1796–1865)

Canadian writer and jurist, born in Windsor, Nova Scotia. He was called to the Bar in 1820, and became a member of the House of Assembly, chief justice of the common pleas (1828), and judge of the supreme court (1842). In 1856 he retired to England, and from 1859 to 1863 was Conservative MP for Launceston. He is best known as the creator of Sam Slick, a sort of American Sam Weller, in newspaper sketches collected between 1837 and 1840 as *The Clockmaker, or Sayings and Doings of Samuel Slick of Slickville*, continued as *The Attaché, or Sam Slick in England* (1843–4). Other works include *Traits of American Humour* (1843) and *Rule and Misrule of the English in America* (1850).
▷ V Chittick, *Thomas Chandler Haliburton* (1924)

HALIDE EDIB, (Adivar)
(1884–1964)

Turkish novelist, dramatist and politician, born in Istanbul, and educated at the American College for Girls there. She published her first novel in 1909. In 1919 she became, together with her husband, a leading supporter of Kemal Attatürk—but later they had to go into exile on account of their opposition to his policies. During this period she wrote several books on Turkish affairs in English. Her novels are competent studies of educated women and their problems, and include *Atesten Gömlek* (1922, Eng trans *The Daughter of Smyrna*, 1938) and (in English) *The Clown and his Daughter* (1935).

HALIFAX, Charles Montagu, 1st Earl of
(1661–1715)

English statesman and poet, a nephew of the Parliamentary general, the Earl of Manchester, born in Horton, Northamptonshire. From Westminster he passed in 1679 to Trinity College, Cambridge. He held high political office, including Chancellor of the Exchequer and Prime Minister, and was responsible for

setting up the Bank of England. His most notable poetical achievement was a parody on **Dryden**'s *The Hind and The Panther*, entitled *The Town and Country Mouse* (1687), of which he was joint author with **Matthew Prior**.

HALIKARNAS BALIKÇISI, pseud of **Cevat Sakir**
(1886–1973)

Turkish novelist, 'The Fisherman of Halicarnassus', born in Istanbul. He attended Oxford in the early years of the 20th century, and was later imprisoned for 'sedition'. An enterprising man, he was famous as a translator, journalist and a tourists' guide to the Aegean coast. His popular novels, such as *Deniz Gurbetçileri* (1969, 'Exiles of the Sea'), are based on his vast knowledge of the coast.

HALL, Basil
(1788–1844)

Scottish travel writer, born in Edinburgh. A naval officer (1802–23), he wrote popular works on Korea, Chile, Peru and Mexico and *Travels in North America* (1829). He also wrote novels and short stories. He died insane.
▷ *The Midshipman* (1862)

HALL, Donald (Andrew)
(1928–)

American poet and editor, born in New Haven, Connecticut. He was educated at Harvard and Oxford, and pursued an academic career alongside his writing and editing. In addition to editing many anthologies, he was poetry editor of *Paris Review* (1953–62). His highly crafted but sometimes rather academic poems made creative use of established forms. His first important book was *Exiles and Marriages* (1955). Other significant collections include *The Alligator Bride: Poems New and Selected* (1969), *Kicking the Leaves* (1978) and *The Twelve Seasons* (1983). The increasing expansiveness of his later work is most fully evident in the rural sequence *The One Day* (1988). His other works include books for children, literary criticism, and a prose memoir, *String Too Short to Be Saved* (1961), which he later adapted as the verse drama *The Bone Ring* (1987).

HALL, Oakley Maxwell
(1920–)

American writer of popular fiction for the mystery, crime and Western markets. For 20 years he was Director of Programs in Writing at the University of California (Irvine) and he has published a book on *The Art and Craft of Novel Writing* (1989). His recent fiction includes *Lullaby* (1982), *The Children of the Sun* (1983) and *Apaches* (1986). He also wrote the libretto for an opera based on **Wallace Stegner**'s *Angle of Repose*.

HALL, (Marguerite) Radclyffe
(1886–1943)

English writer, born in Bournemouth. She began as a lyric poet with several volumes of verse, some of which have become songs, but turned to novel writing in 1924 with *The Forge* and *The Unlit Lamp*. Her *Adam's Breed* (1926) won the Femina Vie Heureuse and the James Tait Black Memorial prizes, but her best-known book, *The Well of Loneliness* (1928), which embodies a sympathetic approach to female homosexuality, caused a prolonged furore and was banned in Britain for many years.
▷U V Troubridge, *The Life and Death of Radclyffe Hall* (1961)

HALL, Rodney
(1935–)

English-born Australian writer and critic, born in Solihull, Birmingham. He was poetry editor of the *Australian* (1967–78) and has published a number of books of verse, beginning with *Penniless till Doomsday* (1962). His *Selected Poems* appeared in 1975. Novels include *The Ship on the Coin* (1972) and *Just Relations* (1982), a hallucinatory tale of the small township 'Whitey's Falls', where most of the inhabitants are geriatric and inter-related. Hall's other contribution has been the editing of important anthologies: *Impulses in Australian Poetry* (1968, with **Thomas Shapcott**), *Australian Poetry* (1970) and *The Collins Book of Australian Poetry* (1981).

HALL, Roger Leighton
(1939–)

English-born New Zealand playwright, born in Woodford Wells, Essex. His *Glide Time* (1976), a satirical look at office life, was a success upon first production, as was *Middle-Age Spread* (1977), a tragi-comedy of mid-life crises which had a successful London West End season. He wrote the book for a musical, *Footrot Flats* (1983), based on the newspaper comic strip, and *The Hansard Show* (1986). Later essays in more serious vein were less successful, and *Conjugal Rites* (1990) signalled a return to domestic farce.

HALL, Willis
(1929–)

English dramatist, born in Leeds. His early work was written for radio; his first stage success was *The Long and the Short and the Tall* (1958), dealing with the members of a

British military patrol lost in the Malayan jungle in 1942. Hall followed this with the short plays *Last Day in Dreamland* and *A Glimpse of the Sea* (both 1959), both set in a seaside resort. He has since collaborated extensively with **Keith Waterhouse**, notably on *Billy Liar* (1960), derived from the latter's novel about a north-country Walter Mitty, and on the farce, *Say Who You Are* (1965). *Saturday, Sunday, Monday* (1973) and *Filumena* (1973), based on plays by **Eduardo de Filippo**, were both enormous successes.

HALLE, Adam de la
(c.1235–1287)

French poet and composer, born in Arras, nicknamed 'le bossu d'Arras', 'the Hunchback' (although he was not misshapen). He followed Robert II of Artois to Naples in 1283. He was the originator of French comic opera, with *Le Jeu de Robin et de Marion* ('A Play about Robin and Marion'), and the modern comedy of the half-autobiographical composition called *Le Jeu Adan ou de la feuillée* ('A Play about Adam'). He also wrote poems in medieval verse forms.
▷T Nisard, *Adam de la Halle* (1867)

HALLECK, Fitz-Greene
(1790–1867)

American poet, born in Guilford, Connecticut. He became a clerk in New York, and in 1832 private secretary to John Jacob Astor; in 1849 he retired to Guilford on an annuity left him by Astor. He published numerous poems, including the long mock-**Byron**ic poem, *Fanny* (1819), a satire on the literature, fashions and politics of the time.
▷N F Adkins, *Fitz-Greene Halleck* (1930)

HALLGRÍMSSON, Jónas
(1807–45)

Icelandic lyric poet, born in Hraun in the north of Iceland, the most important innovator in modern Icelandic poetry. He attended the Latin School at Bessastaðir, where he read deeply in classical and Old Icelandic literature, and then studied law at Copenhagen University before turning to natural history and literature. As a student he and his friends founded the periodical *Fjölnir* (1835–47), which added inspiration to the independence movement led by Jón Sigurðsson. His poetry brilliantly combined fervent nationalism—as in 'Ísland' (1835), with which *Fjölnir* was launched—and intensely lyrical romanticism, and he is still the best loved of all Icelandic poets. His collected poems were first published in 1847; an English edition appeared in 1930.
▷T V Gislason, *Jónas Hallgrimsson* (1903)

HALLIWELL, David
(1936–)

English actor, director and playwright, born in Brighouse, Yorkshire. Halliwell has written many plays, but is best-known for his first, produced in the UK as *Little Malcolm and His Struggle Against the Eunuchs* (1965) and in the USA as *Hail Screwdyke* (1966). This anarchic piece captured the contemporary mood of antagonism against authority among many young people, particularly those in further education.

HALPER, Albert
(1904–)

American novelist and story writer, born in Chicago. A latter-day naturalist, with great sympathy for the working classes of whose bitter lives he wrote, Halper has been underrated by most literary critics. *The Golden Watch* (1953) is evocative of the pre-World War I years in Chicago. *This is Chicago* (1952) is an influential anthology of stories about the city. His autobiographical *Good-bye, Union Square* (1970), recalling his first big success, *Union Square* (1933), contains a wealth of significant detail. His style is not elegant, but it has drive and power.

HAMBURGER, Michael Peter Leopold
(1924–)

German-born poet and translator, he has lived since 1933 in the UK. He published his first ground-breaking translation of **Hölderlin** in 1943, while still a student. Hamburger served in the Royal Army Education Corps during the war, and after it became a university teacher in London and Reading. During the late sixties and seventies he held visiting professorships at a number of US campuses, having established an international reputation for his versions of poets, mostly but not exclusively German, who had hitherto been unknown or under-appreciated in English, such as **Georg Trakl**, **Günter Grass** and **Nelly Sachs**. Hamburger's own poetry combines sensuousness and intellectual force; his critical book *The Truth of Poetry* (1969) is indirectly revealing about the 'tensions' underlying his own work. The *Travelling* sequence (1972, 1975, 1976) and *Palinode* (1977) trace his artistic itinerary, confirming that the stylistic associations he has contracted with other poets are subordinated to his own vision. A *Collected Poems 1941–1983* was published in 1984, following an important essay collection on German literature, *A Proliferation of Prophets* (1983).
▷*A Mug's Game: Intermittent Memoirs 1924–1954* (1973)

HAMEIRI, Avigdor, pseud of Emil Feuerstein
(1887–1970)

Hungarian Hebrew poet, translator (of **Stefan Zweig**, **Max Brod**, and others), editor, novelist and journalist, born in Bereg in the Carpathian section of Russia. He was the one Jewish writer to be influenced by, and to have affinities with, the 'father of Hungarian literary modernism', **Endre Ady**. He fought in World War I, and was taken prisoner by the Russians. He settled in Palestine in 1921, and eventually became the co-editor of the 'Jewish Hansard', the *Divrei Knesset*. His best-known work is *Hashigaon Hagadol* (1929, Eng trans *The Great Madness*, 1954), one of the most impressive and terrible novels written about World War I.
▷M Waxman, *A History of Jewish Literature* (1960)

HAMILTON, Edmond
(1904–77)

American writer of science fiction, born in Ohio. Hamilton started writing in the 1920s, contributing to the pulp magazines under a range of pseudonyms. It was largely through Hamilton's work for *Weird Tales and Amazing Stories* that certain basic sci-fi concepts (galactic civilizations, cosmic radiation) took hold. His lasting fictional creation was the tritely-named Captain Future. Hamilton's wife, Leigh Brackett, also wrote science fiction.

HAMILTON, Patrick
(1904–62)

English novelist, born in Hassock, Sussex. His gift was the rendition of a particular brand of English middle-class existence, marked by reticence, fear and sublimated desire. *Craven House* (1926) was his first novel, but it was with *Rope* (1929) and *Gaslight* (both filmed by Alfred Hitchcock) that he became well known. Apart from *Hangover Square* (1940), his most substantial achievement was the 'Gorse' trilogy: *The West Pier* (1951), *Mr Stimpson and Mr Gorse* (1953) and *Unknown Assailant* (1955).
▷S French, *Patrick Hamilton* (1994)

HAMILTON, William
(c.1665–1751)

Scottish poet, of Gilbertfield, near Glasgow, born in Ladyford, Ayrshire. An army officer like his father, he turned to writing and collecting verse. He was the friend and correspondent of **Allan Ramsay**, with whom he exchanged a series of *Familiar Epistles*. His most notable poem is the mock heroic *Last Dying Words of Bonny Heck*, about a greyhound. In 1772 he published an English translation of **Blind Harry**'s *Wallace*.

HAMILTON, William
(1704–54)

Scottish poet, born in Bangour, West Lothian. Educated at the High School of Edinburgh, and Edinburgh University, he contributed romantic songs and ballads to **Allan Ramsay**'s *Tea-table Miscellany* (1724). He joined in the Jacobite Rising of 1745, and on its collapse escaped to Rouen, but was permitted to return in 1749 and to succeed to the family estate of Bangour. The first collection of his poems was edited by Adam Smith in 1748. He is best known for his ballad, 'The Braes of Yarrow'.

HAMMERSTEIN, Oscar II
(1895–1960)

American librettist. He was the author of a large number of musical plays, often in collaboration with the composer Richard Rodgers (1902–79), of which the most popular were *Rose Marie* (1924), *Desert Song* (1926), *Music in the Air* (1932), *Oklahoma!* (1943), *Carmen Jones* (1943), *The King and I* (1951) and *The Sound of Music* (1959). He shared a Pulitzer Prize in 1950 with Rodgers and co-writer Joshua Logan (1908–88) for *South Pacific* (1949).

HAMMETT, (Samuel) Dashiell
(1894–1961)

American crime writer, born in St Mary's County, Maryland. He grew up in Philadelphia and Baltimore and left school at 14. He was a messenger boy, newsboy, clerk, time keeper, yardman, machine operator, and stevedore before joining the Pinkerton Detective Agency as an operator. World War I ruined his health, and interrupted his sleuthing but he took it up again on his discharge. He served his literary apprenticeship in magazines like *Black Mask*, writing stories as hard and multi-faceted as diamonds. His four best novels—*Red Harvest* (1929), *The Dain Curse* (1929), *The Maltese Falcon* (1930) and *The Glass Key* (1931)—made the scarred ex-detective a celebrity in Hollywood and New York, where he met **Lillian Hellman**, with whom he lived for the rest of his life; but he had already taken to the bottle and never equalled his first literary successes. *The Thin Man* (1934), written in a brief period of sobriety in **Nathanael West**'s mismanaged hotel, has an inflated reputation largely because it was made into a popular film, as were all of Hammett's novels. Drinking and gambling excessively, he made a living scriptwriting. He enlisted during World War II but was discharged with emphysema, but he continued to drink immoderately until 1948 when an attack of delirium tremens turned him to temperance. Politically a radical, he was anti-McCarthy and served a six-month jail sentence for his sympathies. A collection of short stories, *The Big Knockover and Other Stories* (1966), appeared posthumously. Original, unsentimental and an acute social observer, he is the father of the hard-boiled school of detective fiction.

▷D Johnson, *Dashiel Hammett: a life* (1983)

HAMMOND INNES, Ralph
(1913–)

English novelist, born in Horsham, Sussex. A former journalist, he published his first novel, *The Doppelganger*, in 1937. He has since written over 30 books and become established as one of the most prominent authors of adventure fiction. Mystery, suspense and romance play their part in his novels, in which the recurring theme is the struggle between man and nature, and the effect of man's actions upon the natural world. Possibly his most famous title is *The Mary Deare* (1956, published in the USA as *The Wreck of the Mary Deare*), dealing with a sea captain's struggle to save his ship after it runs aground on a treacherous reef in the English Channel. Not only has it become one of the most popular of sea stories, its comparatively slender plot gives scope for some of Hammond Innes's finest descriptive writing.

HAMP, Pierre, pseud of Pierre Bourillon
(1876–1962)

French author, born in Nice of humble parentage. He was in every sense a self-made and self-educated man, and brought to bear in his novels a realism bred of firsthand experience. Among his works are *Marée fraîche* (1908, 'Fresh-Caught Fish'), *Le Rail* (1912), *Les Métiers blessés* (1919, 'The Injured Trades'), *Le Lin* (1924, 'Flax') and *La Laine* (1931, 'Wool'), his novels of industrial life forming a cycle which he called *La Peine des hommes* ('The Suffering of Men').

HAMPOLE, Richard Rolle de
(c.1290–1349)

English hermit and poet, the 'Hermit of Hampole' (near Doncaster), born in Thornton in Yorkshire. He was sent to Oxford, but at 19 became a hermit. He wrote English lyrics and religious books in Latin and English, and translated and expounded the Psalms in prose. However, *The Pricke of Conscience (Stimulus Conscientiae)* is no longer thought to be by him.

▷F Comper, *The Life of Richard Rolle* (1928)

HAMPTON, Christopher
(1946–)

English dramatist, born in the Azores and educated at Oxford. His first play, *When Did You Last See My Mother?* (1964), led to his appointment as the Royal Court Theatre's first resident dramatist. The Court produced all his earlier plays, including *Total Eclipse* (1968), *The Philanthropist* (1970), *Savages* (1973), set in Brazil, and *Treats* (1976). His finest play is considered to be *Tales From Hollywood* (1982), but his most commercial success has been *Les Liaisons Dangereuses*, a penetrating study of sexual manners, morality and responsibility, adapted from the novel by **Pierre Laclos**, which was staged in 1985 and filmed in 1988. *White Chameleon* was staged at the National Theatre in 1991. He has made many adaptations and translations, including the serialization of Oswald Wynd's *The Ginger Tree* for television in 1989.

HAMSUN, Knut, pseud of Knut Pedersen
(1859–1952)

Norwegian novelist, winner of the Nobel Prize for literature, born in Lom in Gudbrandsdal. He had no formal education, and spent his boyhood with his uncle, a fisherman on the Lofoten Islands. He worked at various odd jobs, including shoemaking, coal-mining and teaching, and twice visited the USA (1882–4, 1886–8), where he worked as a streetcar attendant in Chicago and a farmhand in North Dakota. He sprang to fame with his novel *Sult* (1890, 'Hunger'), followed by *Mysterier* (1892, 'Mysteries') and the lyrical *Pan* (1894). His masterpiece is considered *Markens grøde* (1917, 'Growth of the Soil'), which was instrumental in his award of the 1920 Nobel Prize for literature. His last novel was the unfinished *Ringen slutlet* (1936, Eng trans *The Circle is Closed*, 1937), which reflected the emotional breakdown and therapeutic breakthrough of the 1920s. A recluse during the inter-war years, he lost popularity during World War II for his Nazi sympathies and support of the Quisling regime, for which he was imprisoned in 1948, but his reputation has been largely rehabilitated.
▷R Ferguson, *The Life of Knut Hamsun* (1987)

HAN SUYIN
(1917–)

Chinese-born English novelist, born Elizabeth Chow in Peking, the daughter of a Belgian mother and a Chinese railway engineer. She studied medicine at Yenching, Brussels and London, where after the death in the civil war of her husband, General Tang, she completed her studies. She then practised in

Hong Kong which, with its undercurrents of pro-Western and anti-Western loyalties, Old China versus the New, White versus Yellow, provided the background for her first partly-autobiographical novel *A Many Splendoured Thing* (1952) which, in the love affair of an emancipated Chinese girl and an English journalist, symbolizes the political and ideological climate of the British colony. It was made into a film in 1955. In 1952 she married an English police officer in Singapore, where she practised in an anti-tuberculosis clinic. Her other novels include *Destination Chungking* (1953), *And the Rain my Drink* (1954), *The Mountain is Young* (1958) and *Four Faces* (1963). She also wrote a semi-autobiographical and historical trilogy, *The Crippled Tree* (1965), *A Mortal Flower* (1966) and *Birdless Summer* (1968), and two volumes of contemporary Chinese history, *The Morning Deluge* and *The Wind in the Tower* (1972).

HANDKE, Peter
(1942–)

Austrian dramatist and novelist. Trained as a lawyer, his plays are obscure and the subject of some controversy. His first play, *Publikumsbeschimpfung* (1966, Eng trans *Offending the Audience*, 1970), presents four people who speak randomly and insult the audience. The titles of his other plays are intriguing, such as *Das Mündel will Vormund sein* (1696, Eng trans *My Foot My Tutor*, 1971), *Der Ritt über den Bodensee* (1971, Eng trans *A Ride Across Lake Constance*, 1972), *Wünschloses Unluck* (1972, Eng trans *A Sorrow Beyond Dreams*, 1975 (US); 1976 (UK)) and *Kaspar* (1968, Eng trans *Kaspar*, 1969). His novels include *Die Angst des Tormanns beim Elfmeter* (1970, Eng trans *The Goalie's Anxiety at the Penalty Kick*, 1972 (US); 1977 (UK)) and *Die linkshändige Frau* (1976, Eng trans *The Left-Handed Woman*, 1978 (US); 1980 (UK)).
▷J Schlueter, *The Plays and Novels of Peter Handke* (1981)

HANKA, Václav
(1791–1861)

Czech scholar, poet and forger of medieval poetic manuscripts—apparently he committed his forgeries in order to enrich Czech culture. He succeeded in passing off his epics and lyrics, and they were duly praised by scholars as genuine; but eventually, in a cause célèbre of the 1880s, they were exposed. He was inspired by **Chatterton**, and was expert at his dubious job (in which he was aided by others).

HANKIN, St John
(1869–1909)

English dramatist, born in Southampton. After writing theatre criticism for various journals, and humorous sequels to well-known plays for *Punch*, success came with his second play, *The Return of the Prodigal* (1905), an inversion of the biblical parody in which a worthless son pesters his socially ambitious family for money. Other plays include *The Cassilis Engagement* (1907) and *The Last of the de Mullins* (1909), a drama of an unmarried mother who opens a hat shop. Later that year, Hankin committed suicide by drowning himself in a river in Wales. His plays have almost vanished from the repertoire, but his theatrical achievement was to bridge the gap between the wit of **Oscar Wilde** and the social polemic of **Bernard Shaw**.

HANLEY, James
(1901–85)

Irish novelist and short-story writer, born in Dublin. He grew up in Liverpool, and first went to sea in 1914, plunging himself into a period of hard work and licentious living. *Boy* (1931), one of his first novels, is the life of a young shipworker, with episodes clearly drawn from Hanley's own experiences. *The Furys* (1935) details the travails of the poor Fury family around the time of the General Strike. His short-story collections include *People are Curious* (1938). His gritty, unremitting realism, along with his frank treatment of sex, was capable of causing outrage in his day; now, however, much of his writing seems prolix and relatively artless.
▷ *Broken Water* (1937)

HANRAHAN, Barbara
(1939–)

Australian novelist and printmaker, born in Adelaide, whose novels have a particular ability to convey a sense of place and time. Her first book, *The Scent of Eucalyptus* (1973), is a memoir of her childhood, and was continued in *Kewpie Doll* (1984). Novels include the Gothic *The Albatross Muff* (1977) and *The Frangipani Gardens* (1980). Frequently using a younger female as observer of adult behaviour, she contrasts genteel attitudes with the seamier underside of society.

HANSBERRY, Lorraine Vivian
(1930–65)

American playwright, born in Chicago, educated at the University of Wisconsin and the first black woman to have a play produced on Broadway. This was *A Raisin in the Sun* (1959), a semi-autobiographical account of the emotional and racial problems faced by a black family attempting to move into a neighbourhood traditionally dominated by whites. It was enormously successful and became the basis for *Raisin*, a musical, in 1973. Other plays include *The Sign in Sidney Brustein's Window* (1964), about a community of mixed racial and religious background in Greenwich Village, New York.

HANSEN, Martin Alfred, pseud of Jens Alfred Martin Hansen
(1909–55)

Danish novelist. He came from farming stock, worked on the land and as a teacher, but after 1945 devoted himself to writing. His early novels deal with social problems in the 1930s (*Nu opgiver han*, 1935, 'Surrender'; *Kolonien*; 1937, 'The Colony'). He developed a more profound style in *Jonathans Rejse* (1941, 'Jonathan's Journey') and *Lykkelige Kristoffer* (1945, 'Lucky Christopher'), outwardly picaresque novels but in reality closely related to his work for the Danish underground press during the Occupation. With *Løgneren* (1950, 'The Liar'), a psychological novel intended first for broadcasting as a serial, he reached a wider public. In 1952 came his most original work, the metaphysical *Orm og Tyr* ('The Serpent and the Bull'). Other writings include *Torne-busken* (1946, 'The Thorn Bush', short stories).
▷ C M Woel, *Martin Alfred Hansen. Liv og digtning* (1959)

HANSFORD JOHNSON, Pamela
(1912–81)

English novelist, playwright and critic. Born in London to theatrical parents, her background provided what **Margaret Drabble** has called 'a peculiar vantage point for an unprejudiced insight into a wide range of behaviour'. She left school at 18, working in a bank and as a book reviewer. For a short time in the early 1930s she was engaged to be married to **Dylan Thomas**. Her first novel, *This Bed Thy Centre* (1935), was set in working-class south London, and her many subsequent novels, such as the tragi-comical *The Unspeakable Skipton* (1958), are observant of both the world of her youth, and of society in the sixties and seventies, and range from the comic to the morally insightful. Her critical works include writings on **Thomas Wolfe** and **Proust**. In 1950 she married the novelist **C P Snow** and they collaborated on many literary projects.
▷ I Linbdblad, *Pamela Hansford Johnson* (1982)

HANSSON, Ola
(1860–1925)

Swedish poet and novelist, born in Hönsinge. Having acquired a name with his naturalistic lyric poetry, he left Sweden for Germany in

1890 in the face of negative criticism and public apathy on the publication of his erotic volume, *Sensitiva amorosa* (1887). Thereafter he wrote mostly in German, much influenced by **Nietzsche**, concentrating on the kind of moral anarchism he sketched out in *Parias* (1890, 'Pariahs'). The verses in *Ung Ofegs visor* (1892, Eng trans *Young Ofeg's Ditties*, 1893) are cool and accomplished.

▷O Friesen, *Kylfverstenen, Af von Friesen och Hansson* (1909)

HARDING, Lee
(1937–)

Australian science-fiction writer and editor who also writes for adolescents, born in Colac, Victoria. His first novel, *The Displaced Person* (1979), won the Childrens' Book of the Year Award in 1980. He has written a number of science-fiction novels, and edited the anthologies *Beyond Tomorrow* (1975), *An Encounter with Science Fiction* (1976, with **Ursula Le Guin**) and *Rooms of Paradise* (1978).

HARDWICK, Elizabeth
(1916–)

American essayist, critic and novelist, born in Lexington, Kentucky. She established her literary reputation by writing essays for the *Partisan Review*. Her first novel, *The Ghostly Lover* (1945), describes the relationship between a white woman and her black servant during the era of racial segregation, while the second, *The Simple Truth* (1955), again scrutinizes prejudice and versions of the truth, this time within the legal system and the judiciary. Equally as important as her novels are her collections of essays, ranging across a wide variety of cultural and political issues, but with a keen sensitivity to moral values and human worth. They are collected in *A View of My Own* (1962), *Seduction and Betrayal: Women and Literature* (1974) and *Bartleby in Manhattan* (1983). She was also, in 1963, a founding editor of the *New York Review of Books*. For some time she was married to **Robert Lowell**.

▷D Pinckney, *Paris Review, Writers at Work*, 7th series (1986)

HARDY, Alexandre
(c.1570–c.1631)

French dramatist, born in Paris. His over 500 melodramatic pieces are largely lifted from Spanish authors, but he reduced the role of the chorus in French drama.

▷K Garsche, *Hardy als Barockdramatiker* (1971)

HARDY, Frank
(1917–)

Australian radical novelist and short-story writer, whose writings are filled with his burning anger at injustice and a love of the 'underdog'. He was born in Koroit, Victoria. His first book, *Power without Glory* (1950), immediately made his name. Thinly disguised as fiction, it tells of the less than legal activities of a Melbourne millionaire of the period, and resulted in a libel action which Hardy won. The story of the trial is told in *The Hard Way* (1961). Hardy's true strength is the short story, where his fondness for the larrikin character is evident; the best are collected in *It's Moments Like These* (1972) and *The Great Australian Lover* (1972). He also wrote a scathing account of a strike by aboriginal stockmen in *The Unlucky Australians* (1968).

HARDY, Thomas
(1840–1928)

English novelist, poet and dramatist, born in Upper Bockhampton, near Dorchester, the son of a stonemason. As a boy he learned to play the fiddle and was bookish. He was educated locally and at 16 was articled to an architect. At 22 he went to London to train as an architect, and returned home in 1867 to pursue his chosen profession, but he had already begun his first novel, *The Poor Man and the Lady*, which was never published. There is speculation that around this time he met and fell in love with Tryphena Sparks, to whom he was related. The nature of their relationship is unclear but in 1868 he was sent to St Juliot, Cornwall, where he met Emma Gifford, whom he married in 1874. By then he had published four novels—*Desperate Remedies* (1871), *Under the Greenwood Tree* (1872), *A Pair of Blue Eyes* (1873), and *Far From the Madding Crowd* (1874). The marriage was not idyllic but, ironically, when Emma died in 1912 Hardy was moved to write some of the most moving love poems in the language. A flood of novels continued to appear, vibrant, brooding descriptive passages providing the backdrop to potent tragicomedies. Among the most durable are *The Return of the Native* (1878), *The Mayor of Casterbridge* (1886) and *Tess of the D'Urbervilles* (1891). Though Hardy was held in high esteem, critics carped at his seemingly inbred pessimism, and both *Tess* and *Jude the Obscure* (1895) were attacked virulently; thereafter Hardy turned his attention to poetry which he had always regarded as superior to fiction. His first collection, *Wessex Poems*, appeared in 1898; his last, *Winter Words*, in 1928, the year of his death. After Emma's death he married Florence Dugdale and lived in Dorset, much visited by aficionados and the literati. *The Dynasts*, a gargantuan drama in blank verse, occupied him for many years and was published in three instalments between 1904 and 1908. A biography published initially in two parts in 1928 and 1930 is thought to have been largely dictated by Hardy to Florence though it appeared under her name.

▷E Hardy, *Thomas Hardy, a critical biography* (1954); I Howe, *Thomas Hardy* (1968)

HARE, David
(1947–)

English dramatist, director and film-maker, born in Bexhill, and one of the finest playwrights of his generation. He graduated from Cambridge and was active in fringe theatre for many years, co-founding Portable Theatre in 1968 and Joint Stock in 1974. He succeeded **Christopher Hampton** as resident dramatist and literary manager of the Royal Court Theatre, London, 1967–71, and at Nottingham Playhouse in 1973. *Slag* was staged in 1970, *The Great Exhibition* in 1972, and *Knuckle* in 1974, but the best of his early works is *Teeth 'n' Smiles* (1975), a commentary on the state of modern Britain. His plays often have linked films, such as *Plenty* (1978), with the complementary television film *Licking Hitler* (1978), and *The Secret Rapture* (his major play to date) and the complementary political film *Paris by Night* (1989). His other television films are *Dreams of Leaving* (1980), and *Saigon ... Year of the Cat* (1983). He wrote and directed his first feature film, *Wetherby*, in 1985.

HÄRING, Georg Wilhelm Heinrich, pseud Willibald Alexis
(1798–1871)

German writer, born in Breslau. He wrote the historical romance *Walladmor* (1823–4), professedly as by Sir **Walter Scott**, a fraud that led to its translation into several languages (into English, very freely, by **Thomas De Quincey**, 1824). It was followed by *Die Geächteten* (1825, 'The Outlaws'), *Schloss Avalon* (1827, 'Castle Avalon'), and books of travel, sketches and dramas.

▷P K Richter, *Willibald Alexis, als Literatur und Theaterkritiken* (1931)

HARINGTON, Sir John
(1561–1612)

English courtier and writer, born in Kelston near Bath. From Cambridge he went to the court of his godmother, Queen Elizabeth. His wit brought him into much favour, which he endangered by the freedom of his satires. In 1599 he served under Essex in Ireland, and was knighted by him on the field, much to the

queen's displeasure. To strengthen his amazing application to King James VI and I for the office of Chancellor and Archbishop of Ireland he composed in 1605 *A Short View of the State of Ireland*, an interesting and singularly modern essay. He is remembered as the metrical translator of **Ludovico Ariosto**'s *Orlando Furioso* (1591); his other writings include **Rabelai**sian pamphlets, epigrams, *The Metamorphosis of Ajax* (1596), containing the earliest design for a water closet, and a *Tract on the Succession to the Crown*.

▷T Rich, *Harington and Ariosto* (1940)

HARJO, Joy
(1951–)

American poet, born in Tulsa, Oklahoma. Of mixed Creek, Cherokee and French descent, Harjo often draws on Native American history and mythology in her work. She has published four collections of poetry: *The Last Song* (1975), *What Moon Drove Me to This?* (1980), *She Had Some Horses* (1983), *Secrets from the Center of the World*, with Steven Strom (1989) and, most recently, *In Mad Love and War* (1990). A saxophone player, she often incorporates music in public readings of her poems.

HARLAND, Henry, also writing as Sidney Luska
(1861–1905)

American novelist and short-story writer, born in New York, not, as he claimed, in St Petersburg. After brief attendance at Harvard Divinity School and working as a clerk, he turned to writing sentimental melodramatic novels about Jewish immigrants to the USA, such as *My Uncle Florimund* (1888). Then, in 1890, he went to Britain and came under the influence of **Henry James**. Harland is best known for having founded, in 1894, the infamous quarterly *The Yellow Book*, which became one of the leading influences on turn-of-the-century tastes and aesthetics. His best-known fiction, *The Cardinal's Snuff Box* (1900), if anything looks backward to the 19th century rather than forward to the 20th; it is as light and skittish as the title suggests.

▷K Beckson, *Henry Harland* (1978)

HARNESS, Charles L(eonard)
(1915–)

American science-fiction writer, born in Colorado City, Texas. He worked as a mineral economist for much of the 1940s before becoming a patent attorney. His small body of work, which began with *Flight Into Tomorrow* (1953, also known as *The Paradox Men*), has perhaps found a more appreciative audience amongst his peers (such as **Brian Aldiss** and **Michael Moorcock**) than with the reading public at large. *The Ring of Ritornel* (1968), like *Flight Into Tomorrow*, is set in a technocratic tyranny; *The Catalyst* (1980) in a world where bureaucracy has stifled invention. Harness uses these settings to examine, respectively, the rise and fall of civilizations, and the nature of creativity. His best work represents the genre at its most thoughtful, disciplined and inventive.

HARNICK, Sheldon *see* ABBOTT, George Francis

HARPUR, Charles
(1813–68)
Australian poet, born in Windsor, New South Wales, described as 'the grey forefather of Australian poetry'. Harpur made use of traditional, ornate 18th-century English verse patterns, with an overlay of pastoral Australian imagery, in an attempt to create an appropriate colonial style. The little of Harpur's verse that was published during his lifetime, at the expense of Harpur or his friends, is in *Thoughts, a Series of Sonnets* (1845), *The Tower of the Dream* (1865) and a few small pamphlets. His reputation as a poet was not helped by the first posthumous collection, *Poems* (1883), in which the editor excised Harpur's expressions of his personal radicalism and his strong sense of injustice not only for personal misfortunes but also for the social inequalities of 19th-century Australia. Although regularly featured in anthologies, it was only in 1984 that a reasonably complete edition of Harpur's verse, with critical material, was published as *The Poetical Works of Charles Harpur*.

HARRINGTON, (Edward) Michael
(1928–)
American social commentator, born in St Louis, Missouri. He is best known for his massive and strongly advocated study of poverty in the USA, *The Other America* (1962), the title of which coined a phrase that became part of the language and of political rhetoric. A new edition was deemed relevant in 1970, and in 1984, as Reaganomics began to bite, Harrington published a work with an even more pessimistic title, *The New American Poverty*. He remains a rare example of a social scientist who writes well, conveying passion without undue histrionics.
▷ *The Long Distance Runner* (1988)

HARRIS, Frank James Thomas
(1856–1931)
Irish writer and journalist, born, according to his autobiography, in Galway, but according to his own later statement, in Tenby. He ran away to New York at the age of 15,

became a bootblack, a labourer building Brooklyn Bridge, and a worker in a Chicago hotel, but in 1874 embarked upon the study of law at the University of Kansas. About 1876 he returned to England and entered the newspaper world. Perhaps the most colourful figure in contemporary journalistic circles, an incorrigible liar, a vociferous boaster, an unscrupulous adventurer and philanderer, with an obsession with sex which got his autobiography *My Life and Loves* (1923–7) banned for pornography, he nevertheless had a considerable impact on Fleet Street as Editor of the *Fortnightly Review*, *Saturday Review*, *Vanity Fair* and of the *Evening News*, which became under his aegis a pioneer in the new cult of provocative headlines and suggestive sensationalism. He is also remembered for his *Contemporary Portraits* (1915–30), a series of profiles, interesting but distorted by personal prejudice, as well as biographies of **Oscar Wilde** (1920) and **George Bernard Shaw** (1931), some novels, short stories and plays, and two original but not particularly scholarly works on **Shakespeare**.

HARRIS, Joel Chandler
(1848–1908)
American author, born in Eatonton, Georgia. He was in turn printer, lawyer and journalist on the staff of the Atlanta *Constitution* (1876–1900). His *Uncle Remus* (1880) made him internationally famous, at once to children and to students of folklore. Later works are *Nights with Uncle Remus* (1883), *Mingo, Daddy Jake, Aaron in the Wildwoods, Sister Jane, Tales of the Home Folks, Plantation Pageants, Minervy Ann* (1899), and a history of Georgia (1899).
▷ P M Cousins, *Joel Chandler Harris: A Biography* (1968)

HARRIS, (Theodore) Wilson
(1921–)
British novelist, born in New Amsterdam, British Guiana (now Guyana). He was educated at Queen's College, Georgetown and worked as a surveyor. In 1959 he moved to London. He is one of the pre-eminent Caribbean writers, his masterpiece being *The Guyana Quartet* (1960–3); starting with a poetic exploration, it evolves into a composite picture of Guyana, its various landscapes and racial communities. Later works include *The Waiting Room* (1967), *The Tree of Life* (1978) and *Carnival* (1985).

HARRISON, Harry (Henry Maxwell)
(1925–)
American science-fiction writer and editor, born in Connecticut. His original surname was Dempsey, but was changed by his father

as a child. He has travelled widely, and lived in a number of countries. He was an illustrator, mainly of comics, before turning to writing. Much of his most popular work is marked by a sharp sense of humour and a liking for pastiche, as in the multi-volume adventure sequence *The Stainless Steel Rat* (from 1957), featuring his memorable creation Slippery Jim DeGriz. His more serious achievements include *Make Room, Make Room* (1966), a fraught meditation on over-population, and the *Eden* trilogy (1984–8).

HARRISON, Jim (James Thomas)
(1937–)

American novelist, novella-writer and poet, born in Grayling, Michigan and educated at Michigan State University. He writes a rugged, outdoors fiction which has inevitably been compared with **Hemingway** In fact Harrison has little of Hemingway's softness of touch and simple lyricism. But the early novels, especially *Wolf* (1971) and *Farmer* (1976), were promising. His recent detour into the realm of the novella, which began with *Legends of the Fall* (1979) and continued in 1991 with *The Woman Lit by Fireflies*, has resulted in a rather intense gloominess. His many volumes of poetry have not been much seen outside the USA.

HARRISON, Keith
(1932–)

Australian-born academic, poet and critic, born in Melbourne. His books include *Points in a Journey* (1966), *Songs from the Drifting House* (1972) and *A Town and Country Suite* (1980). He is now resident in North America.

HARRISON, Tony
(1937–)

English poet, whose background in working-class Leeds and subsequent education in the classics create a social tension which has proved his most fruitful theme. The desire to give a poetic voice to those who have historically lacked one informs much of his work, and he deliberately intrudes vernacular speech into traditional poetic forms. He has gained international recognition for his verse translations and adaptations for the theatre, notably of the York Mystery Plays and the Greek tragedies. He has also explored the possibilities of poetry on television with an effective broadcast of his poem *V* (1985), a denunciatory journey through modern British life.

HARROWER, Elizabeth
(1928–)

Australian novelist, born in Sydney, who lived in London during the 1950s. Her novels vary in place and time, but all emphasize the mutual dependence of the weak on the strong, of the female on the male, and all rely on the darker side of human relationships for their drive. The motifs of her first novel, *Down in the City* (1957), are repeated in *The Long Prospect* (1958) and *The Catherine Wheel* (1960). *The Watch Tower* (1966), undoubtedly the best of her writing to date, refines the tensions and conflicts of her earlier works. Harrower's novels are not Australian but international.

HARSANYI, Zsolt
(1887–1943)

Hungarian writer of skilled best-sellers based on the lives of various eminent people such as Liszt, Rubens and Galileo. Many, for example *The Lover of Life* (1942), were translated into English; they are not now much read.

HARSDÖRFFER, Georg Philipp
(1607–58)

German poet and translator (of Italian and Spanish pastorals), born in Nürnberg into a rich patrician Protestant family. His socially ingratiating and over-ornate work has led to his being described as a dilettante, and to a certain extent this is deserved; but more recent critics point to his intelligence and good-heartedness, and emphasize that his attempts to popularize culture were sincere.

HART, Moss
(1904–61)

American dramatist and director, born in the Bronx, New York. He began his career as office boy to the impressario Augustus Pitou, to whom he sold his first play, *The Beloved Bandit*, when still a teenager. His second, *Once in a Lifetime* (1930), was successfully produced after extensive re-writing by **George S Kaufman**. Although he continued to write on his own, his most successful work was always to be collaborative. With Kaufman he wrote several plays, the most popular being the wry comedies *Merrily We Roll Along* (1934), *You Can't Take It With You* (1936) and *The Man Who Came to Dinner* (1939), described by one critic as 'a merciless cartoon' of the critic Alexander Woollcott's 'bad manners, shameless egoism, boundless mischief, and widely assorted friendships'. Hart is also remembered for writing the sketches for the Irving Berlin revue, *As Thousands Cheer* (1933), and the book for the Kurt Weill/**Ira Gershwin** musical, *Lady in the Dark* (1941). ▷ *Act One: An Autobiography* (1959)

HARTE, (Francis) Bret(t)
(1836–1902)

American author, born in Albany, New York. He went to California in 1854, and became a compositor in San Francisco. Sketches of his experiences among the miners attracted much attention. He was secretary of the US Mint in San Francisco (1864–70) and during this period wrote some of his most famous poems, among them 'John Burns of Gettysburg' and 'The Society upon the Stanislau'. In 1868 he founded and edited the *Overland Monthly*, to which he contributed, among others, *The Luck of Roaring Camp* and *The Outcasts of Poker Flat* (both 1870). He was American consul at Krefeld (1878–80) and at Glasgow (1880–5), and then lived in London until his death.

▷R O'Connor, *Bret Harte, a biography* (1966)

HARTLEY, L(eslie) P(oles)
(1895–1972)

English writer, born near Peterborough. His early short stories, *Night Fears* (1924) and *The Killing Bottle* (1932), established his reputation as a master of the macabre. Later he transferred the **James**ian power of 'turning the screw' to psychological relationships and made a new success with such novels as his trilogy *The Shrimp and the Anemone* (1944), *The Sixth Heaven* (1946) and *Eustace and Hilda* (1947), and also *The Boat* (1950)—among his finest work—and *The Go-Between* (1953). Later novels include *A Perfect Woman* (1955), *The Hireling* (1957) and *My Sister's Keeper* (1970).

▷A Mulkeen, *Wild Thyme, Winter Lightning: the symbolic novels of L. P. Hartley* (1974)

HÄRTLING, Peter
(1933–)

German novelist and essayist, born in Chemnitz. For much of his writing life the inability to return to his roots has fuelled his fiction, which has been obsessed with the relationship between history and memory, particularly in the trilogy which culminated in *Das Familienfest oder Das Ende einer Geschichte* (1969, 'The Family Party, or the end of a Story'), in which a fictitious historian explores a fire from which he had escaped in his youth. Prior to the re-unification of Germany his work had become despairingly nihilistic. He has expressed strong views on children's literature and writes for children himself. With the playwright **Rolf Hochhuth**, Härtling has also edited the work of the cyclical novelist, Otto Flake.

HARTMANN VON AUE
(c.1170–1215)

German poet of the Middle High German period, who took part in the Crusade of 1197. The most popular of his narrative poems is *Der arme Heinrich* (c.1195, 'Poor Heinrich'), which, based on a Swabian tradition, is utilized in **Henry Longfellow**'s *Golden Legend*. *Erec* (c.1180–5) and *Iwein* (c.1200) are both drawn from the Arthurian cycle, and closely follow **Chrétien de Troyes**. In *Gregorius* (c.1188), he relates how worldly passion is expiated by religious faith. The songs are mainly love songs.

HARTNETT, Michael
(1941–)

Irish poet, born in Newcastle West, County Limerick. He is a prolific poet in both Gaelic and English, although in 1975, in response to political events in Ireland, he announced with *A Farewell to English* that he would no longer write poems in that language. At that stage his original work *Anatomy of A Cliché* (1968) and his 'transcreations' *Gypsy Ballads* (1973, from the Spanish) and *Tao: A Version of the Chinese Classic of the Sixth Century* (1971) had established him with a reputation for elegant experimentation. The next decade was mainly devoted to translations from other Gaelic writers, before he returned to writing original English poems with the two-volume *Collected Poems* (1984–5). These reinstated him as one of Ireland's most intense observers of implosive emotional politics. In 1990 he was awarded the American Ireland Literary Award, and in 1993 he published *Haicéad*, the first substantial translation of **Pádraigín Haicéad** (c.1600–1654).

HART-SMITH, William
(1911–90)

English-born Australian–New Zealand poet, born in Royal Tunbridge Wells, Kent. He went with his parents to New Zealand, and thereafter moved between Australia (serving with the Australian army in World War II) and New Zealand before returning to Auckland, where he died. He is considered an Australian poet as it was there that he discovered his talent and most of his significant work has been published, including his first, *Columbus Goes West* (1943). His work shows a sympathy with nature and primitive cultures, both aborigine and Maori, and has been likened favourably to the best of **D H Lawrence**'s verse. *Selected Poems 1936–84* (1985) brings together the finest of his work.

HARTZENBUSCH, Juan Eugenio
(1806–80)

Spanish dramatic poet, born in Madrid. He was director of the national library (1862), and wrote 69 plays in all, of which the medieval *Les amantes de Teruel* (1836, Eng trans *The Lovers of Teruel*, 1938) is the best. He translated **Schiller**, and wrote some poetic fables.

HARVEY, Gabriel
(c.1550–1630)

English poet, born in Saffron Walden, the son of a rope-maker. Educated at Christ Church, Cambridge, he became a fellow of Pembroke Hall. Although he was cantankerous and arrogant, he became **Edmund Spenser**'s friend. He published some satirical verses in 1579, and attacked both **Robert Greene** and **Thomas Nashe**. He claimed to be the father of the English hexameter.
▷W Schrickx, *Shakespeare's Early Contemporaries* (1956)

HARWOOD, Gwen, properly **Gwendoline Nessie**
(1920–)

Australian poet and librettist, born in Taringa, Brisbane. Originally a student and teacher of music, Harwood did not publish her first book of verse, *Poems*, until 1963. *Poems, Volume Two* followed in 1968, and then *Selected Poems* (1975) and *The Lion's Bride* (1981). During that period she wrote librettos for leading Australian composers: Larry Sitsky's operas *The Fall of the House of Usher* (1965), *Lenz* (1972) and *The Golem* (1979), as well as James Penberthy's *Choral Symphony* and Ian Cugley's *Sea Changes*. Much of her poetic work, appearing originally under a number of pseudonyms, is suffused with physical or emotional pain. Harwood has received the **Robert Frost** Award (1977) and the **Patrick White** Literary Award (1978). *Blessed City* was the Melbourne *Age* Book of the Year for 1990.

HARWOOD, Harold Marsh
(1874–1959)

English dramatist, born in Eccles, Lancashire. He served as an army physician during World War I, and married in 1918 Fryn Tennyson Jesse, the author with whom he collaborated on many light plays. He was best known for his political play, *The Grain of Mustard Seed* (1920). He managed the Ambassadors Theatre, London (1920–32).

HARWOOD, Lee
(1939–)

English poet, born in Leicester and educated at Queen Mary College, London. He worked at a variety of jobs while developing a poetic style which is fragmentary, surreal—he has translated and written about **Tristan Tzara**—

but also extremely direct and simply registered. It has become more so as the years have gone by, as seen in the verses in collections like *Title Illegible* (1965), *The Man With Blue Eyes* (1966) or *The Beautiful Atlas* (1969). *H.M.S. Little Fox* (1975) is a linked, romantic sequence; *Notes of a Post Office Clerk* (1976) documents a life in which straightforward communication is of the essence, but is also somewhat problematic. A selected poems, entitled *Crossing the Frozen River*, appeared in 1988.
▷A Kingsley Weatherhead, *The British Dissonance* (1983)

HASAYN, Taha
(1889–1973)

Major Egyptian novelist, story writer, critic and setter and keeper of standards, born in Maghagha. He was blind from early in his life. He obtained the first PhD to be granted in Egypt from the new University at Cairo, for his thesis (1915) on the Arabic poet **Ahmed ibn Abdullah Abul-Ala**. From 1950 until 1952 he was Minister of Education in the government of Mustafa al-Nahass (overthrown by General Neguib), a lapse that was soon forgiven in recognition of his work for education in his country. His autobiography, *Al-Ayyam* (1925–67, Eng trans *An Egyptian Childhood*, 1932, *The Stream of Days*, 1948, *A Passage to France*, 1976), is both a classic account of how the blind react to sound, and an important record of the progress (and regress) of an unhappy country. It helped, as a critic wrote, to mould 'the sensibilities of two generations'. The novel *Shjarat al-bus* (1944, 'The Tree of Misery'), and the stories collected in *Al-Muadhdhabun fi al-ard* (1949, 'The Sufferers on Earth') are the reflections of an essentially humane and liberal sensibility on a grotesquely unjust social system.
▷P Cacchia, *Taha Husayn: His Place in the Egyptian Literary Renaissance* (1956); D Semah, *Four Egyptian Literary Critics* (1974)

HAŠEK, Jaroslav
(1883–1923)

Czech novelist and short-story writer, born in Bohemia. A compulsive and accomplished hoaxer and practical joker who despised pomposity and authority, he is best known for the novel *Dobrý voják Švejk* (1912, Eng trans with two of its sequels as *The Good Soldier Schweyk*, 1930; complete version 1973), a brilliantly incisive satire on military life. The character of Schweyk, an irresponsible and undisciplined drunkard, liar, scrounger and Philistine, is widely thought to be at least partly autobiographical in inspiration. In 1915 he deserted the Austrian Army (Austria ruled Czechoslovakia at the time) and crossed over to the Russian side. Charac-teristically, however, he managed to make satirical attacks on both regimes.

▷C Parrott, *The Bad Bohemian: the life of Hašek* (1978)

HASENCLEVER, Walter
(1890–1940)

German dramatist and poet, born in Aachen. He wrote the lyrical poems *Der Jüngling* (1913, 'The Youngster') and *Tod und Aufer-stehung* (1916, 'Death and Resurrection'), and pioneered German Expressionism with his father–son drama *Der Sohn* (1914, 'The Son'). He later wrote a series of comedies, including *Ein besserer Herr* (1927, 'A Better Gentleman'), and film scripts. A pacifist, he committed suicide in a French internment camp.

▷P J Cremers, *Walter Hasenclever* (1922)

HASHIMOTO Osamu
(1948–)

Japanese novelist. Like **Haruki Murakami**, Hashimoto has achieved enormous success in Japan by breaking away from the accepted norms of realistic fiction, introducing a new and invigorating way of writing into Japanese fiction. In Hashimoto's case, it was the stud-ent underground movement of the 1970s and left-wing politics which gave rise to these fresh insights, his first novel, *Peach Bottom Girl* (Eng trans 1977), launching him to popu-lar success, at least with a young audience. He is a wicked parodist, often turning Japanese cultural conventions on their head, but, per-haps because of this, has yet to gain a repu-tation outside Japan.

HASLUCK, Nicholas
(1942–)

Australian writer of short stories, novels and verse, born in Canberra. The former are col-lected in *The Hat on the Letter 'O'* (1978), the title story of which exemplifies Hasluck's quirky and sometimes enigmatic writing. His first novel, *Quarantine* (1978), is in the end inconclusive and unsatisfying, but *The Bellar-mine Jug* (1984), despite its complex plot, won the Melbourne *Age* Fiction Award for that year. It casts back to the mutiny of the Dutch ship *Batavia* off the coast of Western Aus-tralia in 1629, and forward to the overthrow of Sukarno in Indonesia. *Offcuts: From a Legal Literary Life* (1993) is a collection of acute essays and articles reflecting his varied interests.

HAUCH, Johannes Carsten
(1790–1872)

Danish writer, born in Fredrikshald (Halden). He was lecturer in natural sciences

at Sorø (1824–46), and in 1846 was appointed Professor of Northern Literature at Kiel. The Holstein revolution (1848) drove him to Copenhagen, where he became Professor of Aesthetics. He wrote historical tragedies, lyri-cal poems, tales and romances.

▷K Galster, *Carsten Hauchs Barndom og Ungdom/Manndom og Alddom* (1930, 1935)

HAUFF, Wilhelm
(1802–27)

German novelist, born in Stuttgart. He stud-ied at Tübingen, was a tutor, then editor of a paper. His fairy tales and short stories are admirable for their simplicity and playful fancy—*Die Bettlerin vom Pont des Arts* (1826, Eng trans *The Beggar-Girl of the Pont-des-Arts*, 1844) and *Phantasien im Bremer Rat-skeller* (1827, Eng trans *The Wine-Ghosts of Bremen*, 1889) in particular. *Lichtenstein* (1826, Eng trans 1846) is an imitation of Sir **Walter Scott**.

HAU'OFA, Ep'li
(1939–)

The first Tongan writer to achieve an inter-national reputation, he was born in Papua New Guinea, educated in Fiji and Australia, and has since worked in both places as a teacher. Between 1978 and 1981 he served as deputy chamberlain to the King of Tonga, before returning to academic life. His literary reputation depends on *Tales of the Tikongs* (1983), a collection of wryly satirical short stories about life in the South Pacific. Hau'ofa has written about development issues and contributed a text to *Our Crowded Islands* (1977), a photographic survey of Fiji by Randy Thaman.

HAUPTMANN, Gerhart
(1862–1946)

German dramatist and novelist, winner of the Nobel Prize for literature, born in Ober-salzbrunn, Silesia. He studied sculpture in Breslau and Rome before settling down in Berlin in 1885. His first play, *Vor Son-nenaufgang* (1889, Eng trans *Before Dawn*, 1909), introduced the new social drama of **Ibsen**, **Émile Zola** and **August Strindberg** to Germany, but Hauptmann alleviated the extreme naturalism with a note of compassion. *Einsame Menschen* (1891, Eng trans *Lonely Lives*, 1898), for example, in which a man is torn between his love for two women, a young girl student and his plain, self-effacing wife, portrays the wife, not the student, as the heroine. *Die Weber* (1892, Eng trans *The Weavers*, 1899) deals with the broader setting of the Silesian weavers' revolt of 1844 and introduces a new theatrical phenomenon, the collective hero. *Florian Geyer* (1896, Eng trans 1894), a historical play, marks a transition to a strange mixture of fantasy and naturalism maintained in other such outstanding works as *Hanneles Himmelfahrt* (1893, Eng trans *Hannele*, 1894), *Die Versunkene Glocke* (1896, Eng trans *The Sunken Bell*, 1898), *Fuhrmann Herschel* (1898, Eng trans *Drayman Herschel*, 1913) and *Rose Bernd* (1903, Eng trans 1913). His later plays in a variety of styles offer no advance, although the comedies *Der Biberpelz* (1893, Eng trans *The Beaver Coat*, 1912) and *Der rote Hahn* (1901, Eng trans *The Conflagration*, 1913), were later adapted and revised by **Bertolt Brecht** to suit the East German communist censorship. His novels include *Der Narr im Christo: Emmanuel Quint* (1910, Eng trans *The Fool in Christ: Emmanuel Quint*, 1911) and *Atlantis* (1912, Eng trans 1912). He was awarded the Nobel Prize for literature in 1912.

▷C F W Behl, *Hauptmann: his life and work* (1958)

HAUSOFER, Albrecht
(1903–45)

German poet and dramatist who was shot as a member of the group which tried to assassinate Hitler. His plays on classical themes were disguised criticisms of the Hitler regime. His sonnets written in prison, *Moabiter Sonette* (1946, Eng trans *Moabit Sonnets*, 1978), are his most moving work.

HAVEL, Vaclav
(1936–)

Czech dramatist and statesman, born in Prague, where he was educated at the Academy of Dramatic Art. He began work as a stagehand at the Prague *Theater Na zábradlí* ('Theatre on the Balustrade'), becoming resident writer there from 1960 to 1969. His work includes *Zahradní slavnost* (1963, Eng trans *The Garden Party*, 1969), *Spiklenci* (1970, 'The Conspirators') and *Audience* (1976, Eng trans *Temptation*, 1976). Deemed subversive, he was frequently arrested, and in 1979 was imprisoned for four and a half years. He was again imprisoned in February 1989, but was released three months later. In December 1989, after the overthrow of the Czechoslovakian Communist Party, he was elected President by direct popular vote. He oversaw the peaceful division of Czechoslovakia into separate Czech and Slovak states in 1992, and retained political office in the new Czech state.

▷M Goetz-Stankiewicz, *The Silenced Theatre: Czech dramatists without a stage* (1979)

HAVLICEK BOROVSKY, Karel
(1821–56)

Czech poet, epigrammatist, satirist, editor and critic, born in Borová. One of his country's great anti-clerical liberals and patriots, he founded, in 1848, the first Czech daily newspaper; he fought the Austrian tyranny until, effectively, it murdered him: exiled to the Tyrol, he was released only when he was dying of tuberculosis. His posthumously published unfinished attack on the established Catholic Church and on the Austrian tryanny, *Krest sv Vladimira* (1876, Eng trans *The Conversion of St Vladimir*, 1930), is still stingingly exemplary.

HAWES, Stephen
(c.1475–1525)

English allegorical poet, born probably in Aldeburgh, Suffolk. He was attached to the court from 1502 as groom of the chamber to Henry VII. His chief work is the allegory, *The Passetyme of Pleasure* (1509), dedicated to the king. He also wrote *The Example of Virtue* (1504), *The Conversion of Swearers* (1509), an attack on blasphemy, and *A Joyful Meditation* (1509), a celebration of the coronation of Henry VIII.

▷W Murison, *Stephen Hawes* (1908)

HAWKER, Robert Stephen
(1803–75)

English poet, born in Plymouth. He was educated at Pembroke College, Oxford, and won the Newdigate Prize for poetry in 1827. In 1834 he became vicar of Morwenstow, on the Cornish coast, where he shared many of the superstitions of his people as to apparitions and the evil eye. His poetry includes *Tendrils* (1821), the Cornish ballads in *Records of the Western Shore* (1832–6), *Reeds Shaken with the Wind* (1843) and *The Quest of the Sangraal* (1864), the first part of a projected Arthurian epic. His best-known ballad is *The Song of the Western Men*, with its refrain 'And shall Trelawny die?', based on an old Cornish refrain. Twelve hours before his death he was admitted to the Roman Catholic Communion.

▷M F Burrows, *Robert Stephen Hawker* (1926)

HAWKES, John Clendennin Burne, Jr
(1925–)

American novelist and short-story writer, he writes disturbing plotless fictions in which sexual aberration, social and cultural devastation and violence are married in a cool and almost playful way. His first book was a novella, *Charivari* (1949), followed by *The Cannibal* (1949), a bleak story of post-war Germany, and a pair of short novels called

HAWKESWORTH, John

The Goose on the Grave, and *The Owl* (1954). His critical, if not commercial, breakthrough came with *The Lime Twig* (1961), which resembles a surreal version of *Brighton Rock*, and *Second Skin* (1964), a darkly exotic fantasy. Nothing written since has had quite the same power, though Hawkes has continued to write highly individual fictions, including *The Blood Oranges* (1971), *The Passion Artist* (1979), *Adventures in the Alaskan Skin Trade* (1985) and *Whistlejacket* (1988). The earlier short stories and novellas were collected in an aptly titled collection, *Lunar Landscapes* (1969).

▷ P O'Donnell, *John Hawkes* (1982)

HAWKESWORTH, John
(c.1715–1773)

English author, born in London. In 1744 he succeeded **Dr Johnson** on the *Gentleman's Magazine*. In 1752 he started, with Johnson and others, *The Adventurer*, half of whose 140 numbers were from Hawkesworth's pen. He published a volume of fairy tales (1761), wrote a play, *Edgar and Emmeline* (1761), edited **Jonathan Swift**, and prepared the account of Captain Cook's first voyage, which formed volumes two and three of Hawkesworth's *Voyages* (3 vols, 1773).

HAWTHORNE, Julian
(1846–1934)

American novelist, born in Boston, the son of **Nathaniel Hawthorne**. His work, although fluently written, does not stand comparison with his father's; nor was it very successful. The 'Gothic' and Swedenborgian *Garth* (1877) is the most interesting of his novels. He also wrote the disappointing *Nathaniel Hawthorne and His Wife* (1884).

HAWTHORNE, Nathaniel
(1804–64)

American novelist and short-story writer, born in Salem, Massachusetts, the son of a merchant captain, who died when the boy was only four years old. He and his mother lived in straitened circumstances. At the age of 14 he went with her to a lonely farm in the woods of Raymond, Maine, and there became accustomed to solitude. He began his first novel at Bowdon College, graduating in 1825, but progress was slow. After his return to Salem he shut himself away for 12 years 'in a heavy seclusion', writing tales and verses. In 1828 he published anonymously his first novel, *Fanshawe*, which was unsuccessful. Continuing to contribute to annuals and magazines, he edited in 1836 a short-lived periodical. Meanwhile some of his short stories had gained such favourable notice from the London *Athenaeum* that in 1837 a volume

of them, *Twice-told Tales*, was published. His genius, however, was not yet appreciated in his own country. In 1839 the historian George Bancroft, then collector of the port of Boston, appointed him weigher and gauger in the custom-house, a post he held until 1841. He then joined for a year the Brook Farm idyllic, semi-socialistic community near Boston. Meanwhile he wrote and published a series of simple stories for children from New England history: *Grandfather's Chair*, *Famous Old People* and *Liberty Tree* (1841). Moving to Concord, Massachusetts, he issued *Biographical Stories* (1842) for children, and brought out an enlarged edition of the *Twice-told Tales* (1842). He wrote sketches and studies for the *Democratic Review*, which formed the *Mosses from an Old Manse* (1846). The *Review* failed; and, as he lost all his savings at Brook Farm, he was forced to accept a place in the custom-house again—this time as surveyor in Salem. By the time his contract had finished he had completed (1850) *The Scarlet Letter*, still the best-known of his works. At Lenox, Massachusetts, he then entered upon a phase of remarkable productiveness, writing *The House of the Seven Gables* (1851), *Wonder Book* (1851), *The Snow Image* (1852) and *The Blithedale Romance* (1852), which drew upon the Brook Farm episode. He settled in Concord in 1852, and wrote a campaign biography of his old schoolfriend, President Franklin Pierce, and on Pierce's inauguration became consul at Liverpool (1853–7). He completed *Tanglewood Tales* in 1853, as a continuation of *Wonder Book*. A year and half spent in Rome and Florence, beginning in 1858, supplied him with the materials for *The Marble Faun* (1860), published in England as *Transformation*. Returning to Concord, he wrote for the *Atlantic Monthly* the brilliant papers on England collected as *Our Old Home* (1863). He began a new romance, based on the idea of an elixir of immortality, which remained unfinished at his death. With little faculty for poetry, Hawthorne had a singular command over the musical qualities of prose. Although exceptionally fitted for conveying subtleties of thought and fantasy, his style is invariably clear and strongly marked by common sense. Hawthorne was only gradually recognized in his own country.

▷ H James, *Hawthorne* (1879); F Crews, *The Sins of the Fathers* (1966)

HAY, George Campbell, pseud Deòrsa Caimbeul Hay
(1915–84)

Scottish poet, born in Argyll, the son of **John Macdougall Hay**. He wrote poetry in English, Scots, and in Gaelic under the name Deòrsa Caimbeul Hay. Educated at Oxford, he served in North Africa and the Middle East during World War II, an experience which left him a semi-invalid. The immediate post-war years were productive in poetic terms, however. Writing under the name Deòrsa Caimbeul Hay he published his first Gaelic collection, *Fuaran Slibh* in 1947. This was followed by *Wind on Loch Fyne* (1948), a volume of his English and Scots poems (the latter are rather fewer in number), and a second, more assured Gaelic collection, *O na Ceither Airdean* (1952). While his poetry is concerned with the landscape and people of Scotland, it is informed by a poetic and linguistic sensibility which lifts it beyond the parochial. His later work appeared alongside poets like **Sorley MacLean** in *Four Points of a Saltire* (1970) and **Derick Thompson** in *Nuabhàrdachd Ghàidlig* (1976). His incomplete long poem *Mochtàr is Dùghall*, written during the war, was published in 1982, and explores the poet's experiences of the Arab world.

▷ In *Four Points of a Saltire* (1970)

HAY, Gyula
(1900–75)

Hungarian playwright, born in Abony. He was involved with the Kun government, and lived in Germany and Russia (as a then card-carrying communist). When the communists came to power in Hungary they soon put him in prison—finally he went to live in exile in Switzerland. A leading dramatist in his country, and a serious one, his first success—some think it his best play—was *Isten, császár, paraszt* (1932, 'God, Emperor, Peasant'), staged by Max Reinhardt. It is about the confrontation between King Sigismund and Jan Huss. A later play deals with Atila. He was one of the most accomplished dramatists of the century in the technical sense. His *Geboren 1900* (1971, Eng trans *Born 1900*, 1982) is an invaluable and lively record.

HAY, Ian, pseud of **Major-General John Hay Beith**
(1876–1952)

Scottish novelist and dramatist, born in Manchester, the son of a cotton merchant. He was educated at Fettes College, Edinburgh and St John's College, Cambridge, and became a language master at his old school. He served in World War I, and was awarded the Military Cross. His light popular novels, *Pip* (1907), *A Safety Match* (1911) and *A Knight on Wheels* (1914), were followed by the war books *The First Hundred Thousand* (1915), *Carrying On* (1917) and *The Last Million* (1918). Many novels and comedies followed, the best known of the latter being *Tilly of Bloomsbury* (1919) and *Housemaster* (1936). He was director of public relations at the War Office (1938–41).

HAY, John Macdougall
(1881–1919)

Scottish novelist, born in Tarbert, Loch Fyne, in Argyll. He took an arts degree at Glasgow University and proceeded to teaching posts at Stornoway and then Ullapool. There he was crippled by rheumatic fever and left teaching to become a minister in the Church of Scotland. He returned to university in 1905 and graduated five years later, helping to support himself in the meantime with reviews for Glasgow and London magazines. At his second parish, Elderslie, near Paisley, he wrote and published his first and most successful novel, *Gillespie* (1914). A realistic novel in the tradition of **George Douglas Brown**'s *The House with the Green Shutters*, its protagonist is characterized by cunning and ambition with which he nearly ruins his town (based on Tarbert). The novel was highly praised by **Thomas Hardy** and by American critics. Hay's second novel, *Barnacles* (1916), and his poetry, *Their Dead Sons* (1918), were not as successful. His son is the poet **George Campbell Hay**.

▷ F R Hart, *The Scottish Novel* (1978)

HAY, William Gosse
(1875–1945)

Australian writer, born in Burnside, South Australia, whose mother was related to Sir **Edmund Gosse** and to William Gosse (1842–81), the English-born explorer who 'discovered' Ayers Rock. Hay's first novels, set in a fictionalized Australia, were *Stifled Laughter* (1901), *Herridge of Reality Swamp* (1907) and *Captain Quadring* (1912). His mother and sister were lost on a ship returning to England and Hay retreated to Tasmania, the setting for his last books, which were published between 1919 and 1937. His only other completed work was *An Australian Rip Van Winkle* (1921). His novels had a Gothic element, introduced, according to Hay, to 'raise Australian literature ... to her tragic and ballad-like history'; his use of historicity lifts his work above the melodrama of his contemporaries and ranks him with **Thomas Love Peacock** and Sir **Walter Scott**.

HAYASHI Fumiko
(1903–51)

Japanese writer, born into a family of itinerant gypsy-like peddlars. Hayashi's childhood was deeply unstable, and left her with an overwhelming desire for security, which turned her into a workaholic, and fostered a hedonism which led her into the Tokyo bohemian set of the 1930s. Her first book, *Horoki*, was closely drawn from her childhood experiences and those of Tokyo, and was hugely successful. It was the first of an enormous number of works (well over 200). Her best, and bleakest, is *Ukigumo* ('Drifting Cloud'), which was written in the aftermath of collapse and defeat in 1945 (she had been a war correspondent in China and South-East Asia for *Mainichi Shimbun* from 1937 to the end of the war), and is an extremely powerful tale of doomed love amid the superbly evoked ruins of a nation utterly destroyed.

HAYCOX, Ernest
(1899–1950)

American writer of Westerns, born in Portland, Oregon. Often made into films, his tales have some small sense of historical truth. Typical is *Starlight Rider* (1933).

HAYDEN, Robert E(arl)
(1913–80)

American poet, born in Detroit, Michigan, and brought up by foster parents. From 1936 to 1940 he worked as a researcher for the Federal Writers' Project. He published his first collection, *Heart-Shape in the Dust*, in 1940. His stature as one of the most important of modern American poets was confirmed in 1966 on the publication of *Selected Poems*. This reveals a profound and compassionate insight into the Afro–American experience, recorded in work of authoritative formal elegance, in which the historical and the personal appear fused in an original voice. Hayden became the first black poet to be invited to take up the prestigious office of Consultant in Poetry to the Library of Congress. His *Collected Poems* appeared posthumously in 1985.

HAYES, Alfred
(1911–85)

English-born American novelist, who was raised in New York. He also wrote plays, poems and screenplays (Rossellini's *Paisan*, 1946). His greatest successes were *The Girl on Via Flaminia* (1949), a love story, and the terse and, in a stylistic sense, **James**ian *In Love* (1953).

HAYKAL, Muhammad Husayn
(1888–1956)

Egyptian novelist, whose *Zaynab* (1913), written in France and published under a pseudonym, was the first truly realistic novel to be published in Egypt. A whole school of fiction developed from this, in certain ways making possible Egypt's first great writer of novels, **Naguib Mahfouz**.

HAYLEN, Leslie Clement
(1899–1977)

Australian politician, journalist and writer, born in Amungla, Canberra, whose novels

were originally serialized in *Australian Women's Weekly* and then on radio; the first of these was *The Game Darrells* (1933). Of his many plays, two were published; *Two Minutes' Silence* (1933) is an anti-war drama, later filmed, and *Blood on the Wattle* (1948) deals with the Eureka Stockade revolt of 1854.

▷ *Twenty Years' Hard Labour* (1969)

HAYLEY, William
(1745–1820)

English poet and writer, born in Chichester. He was a prolific writer and, although his work was held up to scorn by **Byron**, a popular one. His most ambitious works are *The Triumphs of Temper* (1781) and *The Triumphs of Music* (1804), while **Blake** illustrated his *Ballads founded on Anecdotes of Animals* (1805). He also wrote essays, plays, and biographies of **Milton**, Romney and his friend **Cowper**. Another friend, **Southey**, rather damningly suggested that 'everything about that man is good except his poetry'.

▷ W T Le Viness, *The Life and Work of William Hayley* (1945)

HAYNE, Paul Hamilton
(1830–86)

American poet, biographer and editor, born in Charleston, South Carolina, friend of **Henry Timrod** and member of the Russell's Bookstore Group of chivalric Southern writers. Hayne has been called the 'last literary cavalier'. Although his health was too frail to fight for the Confederates in the Civil War, his fervidly romantic martial poems achieved considerable renown. In Britain his admirers included **Swinburne** and **Tennyson**. *The Battle of Charleston Harbor* is his best-known poem. *Poems* (1855) and *Sonnets and Other Poems* (1857), both appearing before the Civil War, contain elegant and reflective nature verse.

▷ K H Becker, *Paul Hamilton Hayne: His Life and Letters* (1951)

HAYS, Mary
(1760–1843)

English essayist, novelist and polemicist, born in Southwark, London, the daughter of Rational Dissenters. In *Cursory Remarks* (1791), which appeared under the pseudonym of 'Eusebia', she proclaimed her support for a deity but denounced the practices of the established church. *Letters and Essays* (1793) discusses politics and feminism. *Memoirs of Emma Courtney* (1796) describes, in fictional form, a similar quest for knowledge and reason, yet the heroine is rejected by the man she loves and resorts to marrying a man for whom she has little feeling. Two years later, Hays published an anonymous *Appeal to the*

Men of Great Britain in Behalf of the Women, a robust tract calling for increased intellectual and financial independence for women.

HAYWOOD, Eliza, née Fowler
(c.1693–1756)

English novelist, born in London. After being deserted by her husband, she became an actress and wrote a number of scandalous society novels, in which the characters resembled living persons so closely, the names being thinly concealed by the use of asterisks, as to be libellous. **Pope** denounced her in *The Dunciad*. She issued the periodical *The Female Spectator* (1744–6) and *The Parrot* (1747). Her works include *Memoirs of a Certain Island adjacent to Utopia* (1725) and two 'straight' novels, *The History of Betsy Thoughtless* (1751) and *The History of Jemmy and Jenny Hessamy* (1753).

HAZAZ, Chaim
(1899–)

Hebrew novelist and dramatist, born in the Ukraine. He left Russia in 1917, and finally went to Palestine in 1931. His fiction deals mainly with Yemenite Jews, amongst whom he lived; the epic *Yaish* (1947–52), in particular, about a mystic, has been described as having 'almost classical status'. He wrote a vivid play on the subject of the 'false messiah', Sabbatai Tsevi, in 1950. Only *Mori Said* (1940) was translated (under that title, 1956).

HAZLITT, William
(1778–1830)

English essayist, born in Maidstone, Kent, the son of a Unitarian minister, who moved to Boston, Massachusetts, in 1783, and to Wem in Shropshire in 1787. At the age of 15 the boy was sent to Hackney College to study for the ministry, but had abandoned the notion when in 1796 he met **Coleridge**, and by him was encouraged to write *Principles of Human Action* (1805). Having tried portrait painting, he published in 1806 his *Free Thoughts on Public Affairs*, in 1807 his *Reply to Malthus*, and in 1812 he found employment in London on the *Morning Chronicle* and *Examiner*. From 1814 to 1830 he contributed to the *Edinburgh Review* and his *Round Table* essays and *Characters of Shakespeare's Plays* appeared in 1817. Between 1818 and 1821 he delivered at the Surrey Institute his lectures on *The English Poets, English Comic Writers*, and *Dramatic Literature of the Age of Elizabeth*. His marriage with Sarah Stoddart in 1808 proved a failure and they were divorced in Edinburgh in 1822. His essays in the *London Magazine* were later republished in his *Table Talk* (1821) and *Plain Speaker* (1826). A passion for Sarah Walker, the daughter of

a tailor with whom he lodged, found expression in the frantic *Liber Amoris* (1823). In 1824 he married a charming widow with £300 a year, who travelled with him to Italy, but left him for ever on the return journey. His *Spirit of the Age, or Contemporary Portraits* appeared in 1825, and his *Life of Napoleon Bonaparte* between 1828 and 1830. His last years darkened by ill-health and money difficulties, he died with the words, 'Well, I've had a happy life'. He was a deadly controversialist, a master of epigram, invective and withering irony. His style ranges from lively gossip to glowing rhapsody; the best of his work is in his later collections of essays.
▷P Howe, *The Life of William Hazlitt* (1922); S Jones, *William Hazlitt* (1982)

HAZZARD, Shirley
(1931–)

Australian-born American novelist, born and educated in Sydney. Her first book, *The Evening of the Holiday*, was published in 1966. Between 1952 and 1962 she worked in New York at the United Nations, an organization she was to satirize in her second novel, *People in Glass Houses* (1967). She later published a factual exposé of the UN in *Defeat of an Ideal* (1973). Other novels are *The Bay of Noon* (1970) and *The Transit of Venus* (1980), which charts the turbulent emotional involvements of an Australian woman in sophisticated America; this book established her as a major contemporary writer. Many of her short stories have appeared in the *New Yorker* magazine; some are collected in *Cliffs of Fall* (1963).

H D see DOOLITTLE, Hilda

HEAD, Bessie
(1937–86)

South African-born Botswanian novelist. Born in Pietermaritzburg, she worked as an agricultural labourer in Botswana, of which she became a citizen. The central character of her first novel, *When Rain Clouds Gather* (1968), repeats her escape from apartheid to the relative, but still compromised, freedom of Botswana. Later books—*Maru* (1971), *A Question of Power* (1974) and *A Bewitched Crossroad* (1984)—document different aspects of the same basic situation, always concentrating on the fine line between heroism and self-reliance on the one hand, and abject cultural surrender on the other. *The Collector of Treasures* (1977) was a transcription of native folk tales.
▷C Heywood, *Aspects of South African Literature* (1976)

HEAD, Richard
(c.1637–1686)

English hack-writer, born in Ireland. He is best known as the author of part one of *The English Rogue* (1665–71), the other three parts being by the bookseller Francis Kirkman.

HEANEY, Seamus Justin
(1939–)

Irish poet and critic, born in Castledawson, County Derry, in Northern Ireland. Educated at St Columba's College, Londonderry, and Queen's College, Belfast, he lectured there (1966–72) before becoming a full-time writer. An Ulster Catholic, the violence in the North so disturbed him that he moved to the Republic in 1972, and taught at Caryfort College, Dublin, from 1975. He made his debut as a poet in *Eleven Poems* (1965). Redolent of the rural Ireland in which he grew up, his work seems nurtured by the landscape, lush, peaty and, to an extent, menacing. One of the greatest modern poets writing in English, he is regarded as a worthy successor to **W B Yeats**. Significant collections are *Death of a Naturalist* (1966), *Wintering Out* (1972), *North* (1975), *Bog Poems* (1975), *Stations* (1975), *Field Work* (1979), *Station Island* (1984) and *The Haw Lantern* (1987). *Selected Poems 1965–75* appeared in 1980, and *New Selected Poems 1966–87* in 1990. A new volume, *Seeing Things*, appeared in 1991, along with his first play, *The Cure at Troy*, a translation of **Sophocles**'s *Philoctetes* for the Field Day Theatre Company in Dublin. *Sweeney's Flight* (1992) is Heaney's version of the Irish odyssey of Mad Sweeney.

HEARN, (Patricio) Lafcadio Tessima Carlos
(1850–1904)

Irish–Greek novelist, journalist and travel writer, born in Greece. He was educated in France and England, and emigrated to the USA in 1869, where he set about a writing career. He was hampered by his partial blindness and a morbid sense of inferiority, and caused a scandal through his relationship with a mulatto woman. His writings of the period include the novel *Chita* (1889), set on the Gulf Coast of Louisiana, a volume of stories translated from **Gautier** (1882), the Negro-French proverbs collected in *Gombo Zhèbes* (1885), and many newspaper sketches of Creole life. In 1890 he travelled to Japan, where he settled, became a Japanese citizen, took the name Koizumi Yakumo, and wrote a series of books about Japanese life and manners.

▷P Murray, *A Fantastic Journey* (1993)

HEARNE, John
(1926–)

Canadian-born Jamaican novelist; he has also written thrillers as John Morris, in collaboration with Morris Cargill. After military service in the RAF, Hearne studied at Edinburgh University and took a postgraduate degree in London before working as a teacher and moving to Jamaica. His first novel, *Voices under the Window* (1955), was distinctive for its portrayal of a developing professional middle class in the West Indies and remains Hearne's most read work. Later books also focused on intellectuals, often politically motivated, as in *Stranger at The Gate* (1956) and *Autumn Equinox* (1959), but almost always perceived as belonging to white society by virtue of their social and cultural aspirations. Hearne stopped writing literary fiction for nearly two decades, concentrating on espionage stories which reminded many readers that James Bond's original stamping ground had been Jamaica (or 'Cayuna', in Hearne's books); however, in 1981 he returned to more serious work with *The Sure Salvation*, a powerful psychological allegory about the Atlantic slave trade.

HEATH, Roy A(ubrey) K(elvin)
(1926–)

Guyanese novelist, born in what was then called British Guiana. He moved to London in the late 1950s, working as a teacher before becoming a barrister in 1964. He has called himself 'a chronicler of Guyanese life in this century': *A Man Come Home* (1974) deals with the working class, while *From the Heat of the Day* (1979) is concerned with the middle-class Armstrong family. His works are realistic studies of the quotidian struggle for a better life, blended with folk myths of obeah, the local version of voodoo. Social cohesion and a rich physical life are to the fore in his work, at times to the detriment of individual characterization. More recent works, such as *The Shadow Bride* (1988), tend to be better balanced in this regard.

HEAVYSEGE, Charles
(1816–76)

English-born Canadian poet, novelist and dramatist, born in Huddersfield. He went to Canada in 1853, became a journalist in Montreal, and wrote competent fiction and drama. He wrote *Sonnets* (1855) and a narrative poem, *Saul: A Drama* (1857). He is well represented in **A J M Smith**'s *Oxford Book of Canadian Verse* (1960).

HEBBEL, Friedrich
(1813–63)

German dramatist, born in Wesselburen in Dithmarshen. He studied in Hamburg from

1835 and after stays in Heidelberg, Munich, Copenhagen, settled in Vienna (1846). His only contemporary play is *Maria Magdalena* (1842, Eng trans 1914), his favourite settings being of a legendary, historical or biblical character, as in *Herodes und Mariamne* (1849, Eng trans *Herod and Mariamne*, 1914) and his masterpiece, the *Nibelungen* trilogy (1855–60, Eng trans *The Nibelungs*, 1921). Hebbel constantly portrayed the inherent Hegelian conflict between individuality and humanity as a whole.
▷T Campbell, *The Life and Works of Friedrich Hebbel* (1919)

HEBEL, Johann Peter
(1760–1826)

German poet and storyteller in Alemannic (and sometimes in German), born in Basel. He was a priest who became a headmaster, and, ultimately, Prälat, the highest office in the Evangelical Church in Germany. His simple poetry was much loved by **Goethe**, **Rilke**, **Kafka** and many others, but was for long underestimated by critics. His standing in German literature has aptly been compared to that of **Burns** in British literature.
▷A Altwegg, *Johann Peter Hebel* (1935, in German)

HÉBERT, Anne
(1916–)

French–Canadian poet, novelist, playwright and story writer, born in Sainte-Catherine-de-Fossambault, near Québec. She is cousin to **Hector de Saint-Denys Garneau**, and he personally influenced her early poems. The harsh, bright, dry 'nun-like' poems of her first collection, *Les Songes en équilibre* (1942, 'Dreams in Equilibrium'), immediately attracted attention, and won a prize. Her extreme hardness of approach produced in **Edmund Wilson** 'a mortal chill'. She is highly praised in France, where one critic called her 'one of the greatest contemporary poets' in her language. Her play *Le Temps sauvage* (1963, 'The Savage Time'), about an over-possessive mother, was successful, as was her rather more conventional novel *Kamouraska* (1970, Eng trans 1973), based on a real-life case of murder.
▷ *Selected Poems of Saint-Denys-Garneau and Anne Hébert* (1962); P Pagé, *Anne Hébert* (1965, in French)

HECHT, Anthony Evan
(1923–)

American poet, born in New York City. His first volume, *A Summoning of Stones*, appeared in 1954. Hecht's early verse was noted as being rather traditional, its style tending to the ornate, even courtly, but his poetry gradually became increasingly austere, *The Hard Hours* (1967) representing the more ascetic seam of his writing. He subsequently returned to a greater complexity. *Millions of Strange Shadows* (1977) is perhaps his most representative collection, in which lyricism combines with technical mastery.

HECHT, Ben
(1894–1964)

American writer, born in New York. Starting as a journalist in Chicago, he wrote novels, plays and filmscripts. From 1946 he was dedicated to the Zionist cause and vilification of Britain as in *A Flag is Born* (1946). His plays include *The Front Page* (1928), and his screenplays include *Wuthering Heights* (1939), *Spellbound* (1945) and *Notorious* (1946).
▷ *A Child of the Century* (1955)

HECKO, Frantisek
(1905–60)

Slovak novelist, born in Suchá nad Parnou. His *Cervené vino* (1948, 'Red Wine') was one of the best novels ever written about Slovak village life; but by the time of *Drevená dedina* (1951, 'The Wooden Village') he had fallen prey to socialist realism, and his sense of obligation destroyed the sharpness of his observation.

HEDENVIND-ERIKSSON, Gustav
(1880–1967)

Swedish novelist and short-story writer, born in Jämtland. An inspirational figure among the working-class writers of the first half of the century, he spent many years as a navvy. His writing often presents events in a wide historical perspective, as in, for example, *De förskingrades arv* (1926, 'The Inheritance of the Dispossessed'), which tells the story of the industrialization of northern Sweden. The figure of the navvy as an examplar of worker solidarity and as a free, migrating spirit is central in his books, as is the spirit of his home province. There is a strong element of myth and folktale in his writing, particularly in the short fiction of *Jämtländska sagor* (1941, 'Jämtland Tales').
▷Ö Lindberger, *Gustav Hedenvind-Eriksson* (1945)

HEIBERG, Gunnar Edvard Rode
(1857–1929)

Norwegian dramatist and director, born in Christiania (now Oslo). As artistic director of the Bergen Theatre, he staged the first performances of **Ibsen**'s *Vilbarden* (*The Wild Duck*) and *Rosmensholm*. His own first play, *Tante Ulrikke* (1884), was in the same socially aware vein. He wrote expressionist plays in

the radical and rational tradition of Norwegian literature, such as *Balkonen* (1894, 'The Balcony') and *Kjaerlighetens Tragedie* (1904, 'The Tragedy of Love').
▷ E Skavlan, *Gunnar Heiberg* (1950)

HEIBERG, Johan Ludvig
(1791–1860)

Danish playwright, son of Peter Andreas Heiberg, and the creator of vaudeville in Denmark. He wrote a series of enormously popular musical comedies, of which his masterpiece was *Nej!* (1836, 'No!'). His romantic play *Elverhøj* (1828, 'Hills of the Elves'), is considered a classic. He was married to the actress Johanne Luise Heiberg, and later became director of the Theatre Royal in Copenhagen (1849–56). He also wrote on philosophy and was significant as an interpreter of Hegel.
▷ M Borup, *Johan Ludvig Heiberg* (1947)

HEIDENSTAM, (Karl Gustav) Verner von
(1859–1940)

Swedish writer, winner of the Nobel Prize for literature, born in Olshammer. He lived in southern Europe and the Middle East (1876–87), and published his impressions in a volume of poetry, *Vallfart och Vandringsår* (1888, 'Pilgrimage and Years of Wandering') which, together with his programmatic work, *Renässans*, inspired a literary renaissance in Sweden and established him as the leader of the new romantic movement of the 1890s. He published several further volumes of poetry, including *Endymion* (1889), the epic *Hans Alienus* (1892), *Dikter* (1895, 'Poems'), and *Ett folk* (1897–8, 'One People'). In later years he turned to historical fiction, as in *Karolinerna* (1897–8, 'The Carlists') and *Folkungaträdet* (1905–7, 'The Tree of the Folkungs'). Though he was a friend of **Strindberg**, their relationship soured into bitter antagonism and rivalry. He was awarded the 1916 Nobel Prize for literature.
▷ H Kamras, *Den unge Heidenstam* (1942)

HEIJERMANS, Herman
(1864–1924)

Dutch dramatist and novelist, born in Rotterdam to a Jewish family. He first became well known as a newspaper columnist: after a false start in business, he began to contribute sketches of Dutch life to *Der Telegraaf*. He went on to become Holland's foremost dramatist, becoming internationally famous with *Op Hoop van Zegen* (1901, Eng trans *The Good Hope*, 1912), produced in 1900, a naturalistic sea drama which led to improvements in the fishing trade. This played in London with great success, with Ellen Terry in a

leading role. His novels, stories and one-acters were also very popular, since he had the capacity to create character within a short compass. The best-known Dutch playwright since **Vondel**, his like has not been seen again in modern Dutch theatre.
▷ S L Flaxman, *Herman Heijermans and his Dramas* (1954)

HEILBRUN, Carolyn, pseud **Amanda Cross**
(1926–)

American essayist and novelist, using her pseudonym for her fiction. Born in New Jersey, Heilbrun began her career as an academic at Columbia University, and served on the editorial board of *Signs*, a feminist journal. Her critical books include a study of *The Garnett Family* (1961) and *Reinventing Womanhood* (1979), a book about the androgynous. She describes her mannered detective novels featuring Kate Fansler, English professor and amateur sleuth, as social comedies in the mould of **Dorothy L Sayers**. Several of them, such as *The James Joyce Murder* (1967), have a literary theme. *Poetic Justice* (1970) is about **Auden**.
▷ M T Reddy, *Sisters in Crime: Feminism and the Crime Novel* (1988)

HEIN, Piet, pseud **Kumbel**
(1905–)

Danish poet, designer and inventor. His poems include several collections of aphoristic *Gruk* (10 vols, 1940–9, 'Grooks'). He defined the 'super-ellipse' (a special curve) and used it for architectural and design purposes; he also devised the 3D Soma Cube. From 1969 to 1976 he lived in Britain. His pseudonym is an Old Norse word for a gravestone.
▷ *Kumbelslyre* (1950)

HEINE, Heinrich
(1797–1856)

German poet and essayist, born of Jewish parents in Düsseldorf. At the age of 17 he was sent to Frankfurt to learn banking, and next tried trading on his own account in Hamburg, but soon failed. In 1819 he went to Bonn; there, and at Berlin and Göttingen, he studied law, taking his doctor's degree in 1825. But his mind was fixed on poetry. In Berlin in 1821 he published *Gedichte* ('Poems'), which was an immediate success. A second collection, *Lyrisches Intermezzo* ('Lyrical Intermezzo'), appeared in 1823. The first and second volumes of the prose *Reisebilder* ('Pictures of Travel') were published (1826–7) and *Das Buch der Lieder* (1827, rev edn 1844, Eng trans *Book of Songs*, 1856) created excitement throughout Germany. In 1825 he became a Christian to secure the rights of German citizenship, but only alienated the esteem of his own people. His revolutionary opinions remained insuperable hindrances to his official employment in Germany. When his enthusiasm was roused by the July revolution in Paris, he went there in 1831, going into a voluntary exile from which he never returned. After 1825 he travelled in England and Italy; he worked on newspapers in Bavaria; and he wrote two more volumes of *Reisebilder* (1830–1, all four vols Eng trans *Pictures of Travel*, 1855). The July revolution seems to have awakened a seriousness in Heine. He turned from poetry to politics, and assumed the role of leader of the cosmopolitan democratic movement. One of his chief aims was to make the French and the Germans acquainted with one another's intellectual and artistic achievements. From this came the *Französische Zustände* (1833, Eng trans *French Affairs*, 1889), first printed in the *Allgemeine Zeitung; De l'Allemagne* (1835), the French version of *Die Romantische Schule* (1836, Eng trans *The Romantic School*, 1882); and *Philosophie und Literatur in Deutschland* ('Philosophy and Literature in Germany'), part of the miscellaneous writings entitled *Der Salon* (4 vols, 1835–40). His ambiguous attitude and his attack on Ludwig Börne brought down upon him the enmity of his revolutionary compatriots. On the eve of a duel, which his book on Börne, *Ludwig Börne: Eine Denkschrift* (1840, Eng trans *Ludwig Börne: Portrait of a Revolutionist, 1881*) ultimately cost him, he married Eugénie Mirat ('Mathilde', d.1883), a Paris *grisette*, with whom he had been living for seven years. From 1848 he was confined to bed by spinal paralysis. He lingered on in excruciating pain, borne with heroic patience. During these years he published *Neue Gedichte* (1844, revised 1851, Eng trans *New Poems*, 1910) and *Deutschland Ein Wintermärchen* (1844, Eng trans *Germany: A Winter's Tale*, 1944); a satirical poem, *Atta Troll: Ein Sommernachtstraum*, the 'swansong of romanticism' (1847, Eng trans *Atta Troll and Other Poems*, 1876); a collection of poems, *Romanzero* (1851, Eng trans *Romancero*, 1905); and three volumes of *Vermischte Schriften* (1854, 'Various Writings'). Many of his poems were set to music, most notably by Schubert and Schumann.

▷ H Spencer, *Heinrich Heine* (1982)

HEINESEN, William
(1900–91)

Faroese novelist, short-story writer and poet, born in Tórshavn; he wrote in Danish and was a member of the Danish Academy. He made his debut with *Arktiske Elegier og andre Digte* (1921, 'Arctic Elegies and Other Poems'), in which the cycle of nature is the central theme. *Blaesende Gry* (1934, 'Windy Dawn'), his first novel, is a love story set against a period of declining traditions in Faroese society. In *Den sorte Gryde* (1949, 'The Black Pot') he satirized the boom period enjoyed by the Faroese fishing industry during the British wartime occupation. *De fortabte Spillemaend* ('The Lost Minstrels'), published a year later, is a piece of magical realism written long before that term became current; it is a paean to life and joy and a diatribe against ideology and mediocrity. Heinesen's sane and humane voice and his wonderful talents as a storyteller have made him one of the most significant Scandinavian writers of the century.

▷ W Glyn Jones, *Faerø og kosmos. En indføring i William Heinesens forfatterskab* (1974)

HEINLEIN, Robert Anson
(1907–88)

American science-fiction writer, born in Missouri. He served as a naval officer, then studied physics, before turning to writing in 1939. Much of his early work falls into his 'Future History' scheme, although he largely abandoned it after 1950. He made the breakthrough into 'mainstream' publishing with a series of science-fiction stories for children, beginning with *Rocket Ship Galileo* (1947), and established himself as one of the two or three most important practitioners of the 'hard' science-fiction genre. The harsh, hectoring militarism of *Starship Troopers* (1959) caused great controversy. The oddly whimsical fantasy *Stranger in a Strange Land* (1961) is his best-known work, although not his most typical. His later science-fiction novels tended to become mired down in that same hectoring manner, to the detriment of the action. *The Moon Is A Harsh Mistress* (1966) is the best of them.

HEINRICH VON MELK
(12th century)

German poet about whom little is known. Two well-known Early Middle High German poems are attributed to him: *Von des tödes gehugde* and *Das Priesterleben*. The first is a sermon with a grim passage on the physical details of death; the second castigates the clergy for their sinfulness. Heinrich seems to have been a nobleman who sought seclusion at the Abbey of Melk in Lower Austria. He is associated with the very ascetic Cluniac Reform movement.

HEINRICH VON NEUSTADT
(12th century)

German poet, a physician, of whom little is known beyond the fact that he lived and practised in Vienna. He wrote the romance *Apollonius von Tyrland*, a vast poem in Middle

High German, based on a Latin poem and on Byzantine material, and a quite different allegorical devotional poem, *Von Göttes Kukunft* ('On The Coming of God'), which is concerned with the making of a perfect man.
▷ M O'C Walshe, *Medieval German Literature* (1962)

HEINSE, Johann
(1746–1803)

German romance writer and poet, born in Thuringia. His verse was admired by **Goethe**, although its overt sensuality and lasciviousness shocked him. He wrote several novels in a similarly unrestrained vein, including *Ardinghello* (1787) and the partly autobiographical *Hildegard von Hohenthal* (1795–6).
▷ R Terras, *Wilhelm Heinses Ästetik* (1972)

HEISSENBUTTEL, Helmut
(1921–)

German novelist, radio playwright, avantgarde poet and essayist, born in Rüstringen. Like **William Burroughs**, he produces 'collages', 'cut-ups' and other similarly arranged material. His poetry comes near to being 'concrete', without ever quite reaching that status. His most substantial work is the novel *Projekt Nr 1, D'Alemberts Ende* (1970, 'Project No 1, The End of D'Alembert'), a vastly complex 'cut-up'—statistics, stream-of-consciousness monologues, and other material—which questions the very existence of 'individuality'. He has been described as a 'neo-Dadaist'.
▷ R A Burns, *Commitment, Language and Reality* (1975).

HEKTOROVIĆ, Petar
(1487–1572)

Dalmatian poet, born in Hvar. Educated in Italy, Hektorovic wrote the most original Serbo–Croatian work of his time, a fishing eclogue, *Ribanje i ribarsko prigovaranie*, which he published in Venice in 1568. It contains folk-songs, and improves upon the artificiality of its Italian models.

HÉLINAND DE FROIDEMENT
(?1160–?1229)

French *trouvère*, Cistercian monk and scholar, born near Beauvais. Much of his work is lost, but *Vers de la mort* (1194–7, 'Poetry of Death') influenced the later form, the *danse macabre*. The form of the poem is known by his name, and was much imitated.

HELIODORUS
(fl.3rd and 4th century)

Greek romance writer and Sophist, born in Emesa in Syria. One of the earliest Greek novelists, he was the author of *Aethiopica*, which narrates in poetic prose, at times with almost epic beauty and simplicity, the loves of Theagenes and Chariclea.

HELLAAKOSKI, Aaro
(1893–1952)

Finnish poet, critic and geologist, born in Oulu. Regarded as a leading precursor of modernism, he first wrote ardent lyrics, but later came under the influence of French poetry, in particular that of **Apollinaire**: the result was an apocalyptic type of poetry, Nihilist, Cubist and Symbolist. His first important collection was *Jääpeili* (1928, 'Ice Mirror').
▷ U Kupiainen, *Aaro Hellaakoski* (1953, in Finnish)

HELLENS, Franz, pseud of Frédéric van Ermengem
(1881–1972)

Belgian writer, born in Brussels. As a polemicist he was best known for proclaiming that the French-language writers of Belgium formed an integral part of French literature. This attitude, together with the review he founded with **André Salmon**—it appeared under many names, the best-known being *Le Disque vert* ('The Green Disc')—was exceedingly influential. He wrote over a hundred volumes in every genre, from poetry to quasi-Surrealist fiction. One commentator has shrewdly noted that his work 'is more respected than admired'; yet it is deeply interesting, and as a critic Hellens has no equal in modern Belgium. He knew everyone of importance, discovered **Michaux** and **Ghelderode**—and his work undoubtedly acted as an indispensable catalyst for those more creatively gifted.

HELLER, Joseph
(1923–)

American novelist, born in Brooklyn, New York. He served in the US army air force in World War II, drawing on the experience for his black comedy, *Catch 22*, based on the simple premise that a fighter-pilot who wants to be excused duty need only ask, but by asking proves that he is sane and fit to fly. After selling slowly for some years it became an international bestseller and a byword for war's absurdity. Heller returned to the theme with a play, *We Bombed in New Haven* (1968), and produced a sequel to *Catch 22, Closing Time*, in 1994. Later books—*Something Happened* (1974), *Good as Gold* (1979), *God Knows* (1984), a fictional monologue by the biblical King David, and *Picture This* (1988)—tended to receive churlish notices but are no less satiric, and the first is an existentialist masterpiece. During the later period his output was hampered by a neurological ailment, described in the autobiographical account below.

▷ *No Laughing Matter* (with Speed Vogel, 1986)

HELLMAN, Lillian Florence
(1907–84)

American playwright, born into a Jewish family in New Orleans. Educated at New York University and Columbia University, she worked for the New York *Herald Tribune* as a reviewer (1925–8) and for M-G-M in Hollywood as reader of plays (1927–32). She was married for a time to the dramatist **Arthur Kober**, but lived for many years with the detective writer **Dashiell Hammett**, who encouraged her writing. She had her first stage success with *The Children's Hour* (1934), which ran on Broadway for 86 weeks. This was followed by *Days to Come* (1936) and *The Little Foxes* (1939), which was later adapted into a film starring Bette Davis. During World War II she also wrote the anti-fascist plays *Watch on the Rhine* (1941, winner of the Critics Circle Award) and *The Searching Wind* (1944). When she came before the Un-American Activities committee in 1952 during the Joseph McCarthy era she coined the famous phrase 'I can't cut my conscience to fit this year's fashions'. This period was described in her *Scoundrel Time* (1976). Her other plays included *The Autumn Garden* (1951) and *Toys in the Attic* (1960). Her autobiographical works included *An Unfinished Woman* (1969) and *Pentimento* (1973). A left-wing activist, and sensitive to social injustice and personal suffering, her voice was one of the most persuasive in the modern American theatre. A mercurial woman, she nurtured her animosities, and sued for libel when **Mary McCarthy** said of her that 'every word she writes is a lie, including "and" and "the"', a reference to the misrepresentations in her memoir *Scoundrel Time*. But Hellman died before the case came to court.

▷ *An Unfinished Woman* (1969); *Pentimento* (1973); *Scoundrel Time* (1976)

HELPRIN, Mark
(1947–)

Jewish–American novelist, born in New York State. He was educated at Harvard and Oxford, and served for a time in the Israeli army. His first collection of stories, *A Dove of the East* (1975), was followed by a picaresque novel, *Refiner's Fire* (1977). The potent fusion of fantasy and realism in *Ellis Island and Other Stories* (1980) was recognizably an extension of an important Jewish tradition, and emerged in even more extravagant form in his massive novel *A Winter's Tale* (1983),

a burgeoning, inventive fable of urban life. All his books are strongly moralistic in intent.

HEMANS, Felicia Dorothea, née Browne
(1793–1835)

English poet, born in Liverpool, the daughter of a merchant. Between 1808 and 1812 she published three volumes of poems, and in 1812 married an Irishman, Captain Alfred Hemans. He deserted her in 1818, and she turned to writing for a living. She produced a large number of books of verse of all kinds, love lyrics, classical, mythological, sentimental, including *The Siege of Valencia* (1823) and *Records of Women* (1828). She is perhaps best remembered for the poem *Casabianca*, better known as 'The boy stood on the burning deck', and 'The stately homes of England'.

▷ H F Chorley, *Memories of Mrs Hemans* (1837)

HEMINGWAY, Ernest Millar
(1899–1961)

American novelist and short-story writer, winner of the Nobel Prize for literature, born in Oak Park, a respectable suburb of Chicago. His father was a doctor and a keen sportsman, an enthusiasm his son was to share though he also inherited a melancholic, self-destructive personality. He was educated at grammar school and the palatial Oak Park and River Forest Township High School, where he distinguished himself only in English. His mother wanted him to become a violinist but, modelling himself on **Ring Lardner**, he was determined to become a journalist and a writer. He got a job on the *Kansas City Star* as a cub reporter where he was paid 15 dollars a week and was given a copy of the style book which told him to write in the manner of the mature Hemingway. In April 1918 he resigned and joined the Red Cross, to be hurled into World War I as an ambulance driver on the Italian front, where he was badly wounded. Returning to America he began to write features for the Toronto *Star Weekly* in 1919 and married Hadley Richardson, the first of four wives, in 1921. That same year he went to Europe as a roving correspondent and covered several large conferences. In Paris he moved easily and conspicuously among other émigré artists and came into contact with **Gertrude Stein**, **Ezra Pound**, **James Joyce** and **F Scott Fitzgerald**. *A Moveable Feast* records this time, reliving the struggle he and his new wife had to make ends meet. *Three Stories and Ten Poems* was given a limited circulation in Paris in 1923 and in 1924 he published *In Our Time*, which met with critical approval in America a year later. *The Sun Also Rises* (1926) and a volume of short stories, *Men Without Women* (1927),

HÉMON, Louis

confirmed his reputation, and in 1928, divorced from Hadley and re-married to Pauline Pfeiffer, he moved to Key West in Florida. Disentangling fact from myth in the years that followed is not easy. Drinking, brawling, posturing, big-game hunting, deep-sea fishing and bull-fighting, all competed with writing. Nevertheless the body of work is impressive, if uneven. In 1929, he published *A Farewell to Arms*, and in 1932 the wildly overrated bull-fighting book, *Death in the Afternoon*. *Green Hills in Africa* tells of tension-filled big-game hunts. Perhaps his most popular book is *For Whom the Bell Tolls*, published in 1940, about the Civil War in Spain to which Hemingway went as a journalist. Significant later titles are *Across the River and Into the Trees* (1950) and *The Old Man and the Sea* (1952). He won the Pulitzer Prize in 1953 and the Nobel Prize for literature in 1954. He cheated death on more than one occasion and had the strange pleasure of reading his own obituary twice; however, he was given to numbing depressions and shot himself in Ketchum, Idaho, after having lived for years in Cuba.
▷S Donaldson, *By Force of·Will* (1977); M Reynolds, *The Young Hemingway* (1986)

HÉMON, Louis
(1880–1913)

French novelist, born in Brest. He went to live in England, and then emigrated to Canada, where he was killed in a railway accident. His *Lizzie Blakeston* (1908) had passed without notice, but the posthumous *Maria Chapdelaine* (serial 1914, Eng trans, 1921) was a well-deserved success when published in book form in Montreal in 1916. It is a Canadian rather than a French classic, because it depicts, with lyrical and admiring fervour, the bleak lives of Canadians who live in the forests north of Montreal.

HEMON, Roparz
(1900–78)

Breton novelist, short-story writer, poet and academic. Born in Brest, he made efforts as a child and a young man to acquire the Breton language, although it was not used by his family, and wrote in Breton; he is considered one of the major literary figures of that language. He founded a Breton journal, *Gwalarn* ('North-west') in 1925, and shortly afterwards set about compiling, single-handedly, a comprehensive Breton dictionary. In 1944 he emigrated to Ireland, where he taught at the Institute for Advanced Studies, Dublin, and lived for the rest of his life. His novels include: *An Aotrou Bimbochet e Breizh* (1925, 'Monsieur Bimbochet in Brittany'); *Alanig an tri roue* (1950, 'Alan of the Three Kings'); and *Mari Vorgan* (1962). A collection of his short stories, *War ribl an hent* ('At the Roadside'),

was published in 1971, and some poetry, under the title *Barzhonegou*, in 1967.

HENDERSON, Hamish
(1919–)

Scottish folklorist, composer and poet, born in Blairgowrie, Perthshire. One of his early poetic works, 'Ninth Elegy for the Dead in Cyrenaica' (1948), won him the **Somerset Maugham** Award, but his considerable literary output has been overshadowed by his outstanding contributions to folk-song. Through his researches in the field for the School of Scottish Studies he was largely responsible for bringing great but unknown traditional singers, such as Jeannie Robertson, to the fore, thereby ensuring the survival of the Scots ballad tradition. Many of his own compositions—notably 'Freedom Come All Ye', 'Farewell to Sicily' and 'The John Maclean March'— have themselves become part of the traditional singer's repertoire. A selection of his writings, *Alias MacAlias*, appeared in 1992.
▷P Orr (ed), *The Poet Speaks* (1966)

HENEY, Helen
(1907–)

Australian writer, born in Sydney, who lived between the wars in Poland and worked in Europe for UNRRA and the Red Cross. Her novels deal mainly with the conflict of cultures, particularly of an individual in an alien group, as in *The Chinese Camellia* (1950) and *Dark Moon* (1953). She has published a biography of the Polish–Australian explorer Sir Paul Strzelecki (1961), *Australia's Founding Mothers* (1978), a study of women during the formative years of the colonies, and has edited *Dear Fanny: Women's Letters to and from New South Wales, 1788–1857* (1985).

HENLEY, Beth (Elizabeth)
(1952)

American actress, dramatist and screenwriter, born in Jackson, Mississippi. Her first major success was *Crimes of the Heart* (1978), describing a poignant, often comic reunion of three sisters, whose self-reliance and combined emotional strength enables them to overcome the effects of violence and despondency. Staged by the Actors' Theatre of Louisville in 1979, it transferred to Broadway two years later and received a Pulitzer Prize. Several plays have followed, of which the most familiar is *The Miss Firecracker Contest* (1980), which incorporates Henley's recurring theme, that of family relationships in the American deep south.
▷K Betsko and R Koenig, *Interviews with Contemporary Women Playwrights* (1987)

HENLEY, William Ernest
(1849–1903)

English poet, playwright, critic and editor, born in Gloucester. Crippled by tuberculosis as a boy, he spent nearly two years in Edinburgh Infirmary (1873–5), where he wrote several of the poems in *A Book of Verses* (1888). In Edinburgh he became a close friend of **Robert Louis Stevenson**, with whom he collaborated in four plays, *Deacon Brodie* (1880), *Beau Austin* (1884), *Admiral Guinea* (1884) and *Macaire* (1885). Other volumes of his verse, with its unusual rhymes and esoteric words, followed: *The Song of the Sword* (1892), *Collected Poems* (1898), *For England's Sake* (1900), *Hawthorn and Lavender* (1901), *A Song of Speed* (1903) and *In Hospital* (1903), which contains his best-known poem, 'Invictus'. A pungent critic, he successfully edited the *Magazine of Art*, (1882–6) and the *Scots Observer* (1889), which became *The National Observer*. He was joint compiler of a dictionary of slang (1894–1904).
▷ J Flora, *W E Henley* (1970)

HENNINGSEN, Agnes
(1868–1962)

Danish novelist and playwright. Born on the island of Funen, she married twice and gave birth to four children. Her work, depicting women in a notable range of roles, focuses on their relations to men and to eroticism. While her novel *De spedalske* (1903, 'The Lepers') defines sexuality as fundamental to all human relations, her play *Elskerinden* (1906, 'The Mistress') exposes the implications of the conventional feminine role. *Kærlighedens Aarstider* (3 vols, 1927–30, 'Love's Seasons'), in which naturalism is fused with psychological realism, asserts the significance of women's eroticism, challenges the centrality of motherhood to women's lives and underlines the impact of self-realization through work. Her eight volumes of *Erindringer* (1941–55, 'Memoirs') have won considerable acclaim.
▷ B Wamberg, *Letsindighedens pris. En bog om Agnes Henningsen* (1983)

HENRI, Adrian Maurice
(1932–)

English poet, born in Birkenhead and saddled throughout his career with the 'Mersey Sound' tag. That was the title given to *Penguin Modern Poets 10* (1967), a hugely popular paperback compilation of his work (shared with **Roger McGough** and **Brian Patten**), which went through an unprecedented two revisions (1974, 1983), and has continued to sell well. Its success prompted him to try his luck as a performer, with the multi-media Liverpool Scene group (1968–

70); *Tonight at Noon* (1968) also belongs to this period. Henri is also a painter, whose canvases have the same immediacy and Pop imagery as his verse. Clearly influenced by the Black Mountain poets—**Charles Olson**, **Robert Creeley**, **Robert Duncan**—Henri also owes a less immediately obvious debt to the autobiographical approach and magpie linguistics of **MacDiarmid**. Significantly, his most substantial work is entitled simply *Autobiography* (1971), which is searchingly honest and unaffected. *The Best of Henri* (1975) collected the work of the sixties, but he refused to go down with the decade; *From the Loveless Motel* (1980) and *Penny Arcade* (1983) are collections of later material.
▷ J Raban, *The Society of the Poem* (1971)

HENRY, O, pseud of William Sydney Porter
(1862–1910)

American writer, master of the short story, born in Greenboro, North Carolina. Brought up during the depression in the South, he settled in Austin, Texas, where he became a bank-teller. In 1894 he 'borrowed' money from the bank to help his consumptive wife and to start a literary magazine, the *Rolling Stone*, but ran away at the height of the scandal. He returned, however, in 1897 to his wife's deathbed. He was found technically guilty of embezzlement, and spent three years in jail (1898–1901), where he adopted his pseudonym and began to write short stories. His second marriage came to nothing and he roamed about the New York back streets from 1902, where he found ample material for his tales. His first of many collections was *Cabbages and Kings* (1904). His use of coincidence and trick endings, his purple phraseology and caricature have been criticized, but nothing can detract from the technical brilliance and boldness of his comic writing.
▷ D Stuart, *O. Henry: a biography* (1986)

HENRYSON, Robert
(c.1425–c.1508)

Scottish poet. He is usually designated 'schoolmaster of Dunfermline', and was certainly a notary in 1478. His work is part of the tradition of the Scottish 'makars' (as shapers of literary artifice), and his best-known poem is the *Testament of Cresseid*, a kind of supplement to **Chaucer**'s poem on the same subject. Of his 14 extant poems, *Robene and Makyne* is the earliest Scottish specimen of pastoral poetry. His other works include a metrical version of 13 *Morall Fabels of Esope the Phrygian*, possibly his masterpiece.
▷ R L Kindrick, *Robert Henryson* (1979)

HENTY, George Alfred
(1832–1902)

English novelist and journalist, born in Trumpington. Educated at Westminster and Caius College, Cambridge, he became a special correspondent for the *Morning Advertiser* during the Crimean War and for the *Standard* in the Franco–Prussian War. He was best known, however, for his 80 historical adventure stories for boys, including *With Clive in India* (1884) and *With Moore at Corunna* (1898).

▷G M Fenn, *G. A. Henty: The Story of an Active Life* (1907)

HEPPENSTALL, Rayner
(1911–81)

English novelist and critic, born in Huddersfield, Yorkshire, and who for many years was a producer for the BBC's Third Programme. He had a wide circle of artistic and literary friends, including **George Orwell**; but, although gifted, he was justifiably regarded as extremely eccentric. His first novel, *The Blaze of Noon* (1935), was followed by several more, including *The Connecting Door* (1962). Each is lucid, intriguing and casts a sceptical but sympathetic eye over human emotions and frailties. His final novel, *The Pier* (1986), is a murder story told by an elderly writer who lives in a small seaside town.

▷ *The Intellectual Part* (1963); *Portrait of the Artist as a Professional Man* (1969)

HERBERT, Sir A(lan) P(atrick)
(1890–1971)

English writer and politician. He was called to the Bar but never practised, having established himself in his twenties as a witty writer of verses, joining *Punch* in 1924. His first theatrical success with Nigel Playfair in the revue *Riverside Nights* (1926) was followed by a series of brilliant libretti for comic operas, including *Tantivy Towers* (1930), a version of Offenbach's *Helen* (1932), *Derby Day* (1932) and *Bless the Bride* (1947). He was also the author of several successful novels, notably *The Secret Battle* (1919), *The Water Gipsies* (1930) and *Holy Deadlock* (1934). In *What a Word* (1935) and many humorous articles he campaigned against jargon and officialese. From 1935 to 1950 he was Independent Member of Parliament for Oxford University, and introduced a marriage bill in the House of Commons that became law as the Matrimonial Causes Act 1938, and did much to improve divorce conditions.

▷ *My Life and Times* (1970); S Glasspool, *Sir A P Herbert: A Short Guide to his Literary Work* (1973)

HERBERT, Frank Patrick
(1920–86)

American science-fiction writer, born in Tacoma, Washington. He was a journalist before turning to full-time fiction writing. His first novel, *The Dragon in the Sea* (1956), is an acute psychological study set on a submarine, but his breakthrough came with his series of novels about the desert planet *Dune* (1965), one of the most complex and fully realized examples of an alternative world in science fiction. The five sequels were mixed in quality, but extended the premises and issues of the novel in considerable depth. Persistent themes of his work include the development of higher or artificial intelligence in human and non-human species, genetic engineering, ecology and overpopulation. Important titles include *The Green Brain* (1966), *The Santaroga Barrier* (1968) and *Hellstrom's Hive* (1973).

HERBERT, George
(1593–1633)

English metaphysical poet and clergyman, member of a distinguished Anglo–Welsh family, the son of Lady Magdalen Herbert (to whom **John Donne** addressed his *Holy Sonnets*) and brother of Lord Herbert of Cherbury. Educated at Westminster and Trinity College, Cambridge, he was elected a fellow there at the age of 22 in 1614, and Public Orator in 1619. He was MP for Montgomery in 1624–5. His connection with the court, and particularly the favour of King James VI and I, seemed to point to a worldly career, and his poems, 'Affliction' and 'The Collar', indicate the sharpness of the decision which finally directed him to the Church. In 1630, under the influence of Laud, he took orders and spent his few remaining years as the zealous parish priest of Bemerton in Wiltshire. Like his friend Nicholas Ferrar, but without Ferrar's mystical piety, he represents both in his life and works the counterchallenge of the Laudian party to the Puritans. The Church was Christ's comely bride to be decked with seemly ornament and 'The mean thy praise and glory is'. This twofold conception, along with his ideal of Christian humility and unwearying service, pervades all his writing, verse and prose alike. Practically all his religious lyrics are included in *The Temple, Sacred Poems and Private Ejaculations*, posthumously published in 1633. His chief prose work, *A Priest in the Temple*, containing guidance for the country parson, was published in his *Remains* (1652).

▷J J D Faniell, *The Life of George Herbert of Bemerton* (1902); J B Leishman, *The Metaphysical Poets* (1934)

HERBERT, William, 3rd Earl of Pembroke
(1580–1630)

English poet. He was a patron of **Ben Jonson**, **Philip Massinger** and Inigo Jones, and a lord chamberlain of the court (1615–30). He became Chancellor of Oxford University in 1617 and had Pembroke College named after him. **Shakespeare**'s 'W H', the 'onlie begetter' of the *Sonnets* has been taken by some to refer to him.
▷T Tyler, *The Herbert-Fitton Theory of Shakespeare's Sonnets* (1898); R Holzapfel, *Shakespeare's Secret* (1961)

HERBERT, Xavier
(1901–84)

Australian novelist, born in Port Hedland, Western Australia, who, after much travel, settled in the Northern Territory. He is known mainly for his first novel and his last, *Capricornia* (1938) and *Poor Fellow My Country* (1975); the intervening years were spent drifting round Australia, a period which reinforced Herbert's sympathy with the situation and the treatment of Australia's aboriginals. This is strongly evoked in his writing, and especially in the sprawling *Poor Fellow My Country*. Longer than *War and Peace*, and the longest novel then published in Australia, it remains the lasting testament of a painstaking and poignant writer.

HERBERT, Zbigniew
(1924–)

Polish poet, born in Lvov and educated at the universities of Cracow, Toruń and Warsaw, where he studied economics, law and philosophy. He was a resistance fighter during World War II. His work takes a satiric but uncynical view of Stalinism, and often calls on a quietly heroic interpretation of biblical mythology. This is noticeable in *Struma światla* (1956, 'Harmony of Light') and *Hermes, pies i gwiazda* (1957, 'Hermes, A Dog and a Star'), and is the dominant tone in the first English translation (1968), edited by **Czesław Miłosz** and Peter Dale Scott; thereafter the tone is less passive, more robustly argumentative in a way that sometimes recalls his English Metaphysical namesake, **George Herbert**. In *Pan Cogito* (1974, 'Mr Cogito') he adopts a Cartesian persona to examine his beliefs *vis-à-vis* history, and the style is stripped and rhythmic, almost discursive, but with no metaphoric entanglements. A collected poems, *Wiersze zebrane*, appeared in Warsaw in 1971, and an important English translation (made by John and Bogdana Carpenter) three years later. Herbert has also written plays and essays on art; some of the latter are reprinted in *Barbarzyńca w ogrodzie* (1962, 'Barbarian in the Garden').

HERBST, Josephine Frey
(1897–1969)

American novelist, born in Iowa, she was perhaps the best-known female exponent of US 'proletarian' fiction in the 1930s. Her fiction was closely observed (though sometimes too obsessively documentary) and showed a fine insight into the lives of working people. Her main achievement was a trilogy of novels written during the mid- to late-1930s, when Popular Front communism was being defined as 20th-century Americanism; it consists of *Pity Is Not Enough* (1933), *The Executioner* (1934), *Rope of Gold* (1939). Later works, such as *Satan's Sergeants* (1941) and *The Watcher with the Horn* (1955), were more discursive, but Herbst is still readable.

HERCULANO, Alexandre
(1810–66)

Portuguese historian and novelist, born in Lisbon. He was not only Portugal's apostle of liberal romanticism but also her first objective historian: less through his novels (such as *O Bobo*, 1843) than through his *História de Portugal* (1846–53) and cognate works, in which he took (for the first time) an objective approach—which brought down upon him the wrath of the obscurantist church. His influence on all his successors, especially on **Antonio Soares de Passos**, has therefore been salutary and wide.

HERDAL, Harald
(1900–)

Danish left-wing poet and novelist, born in Copenhagen into a slum. His love poetry is especially prized for its freedom from the socialist dogma which many critics have felt distorted his fiction; but the latter, naturalist in cast, has moments of power and authentic descriptions of working-class misery. Titles include *Digte 1929–49* (1949, 'Poems'). He also wrote a number of autobiographical works.

HERDER, Johann Gottfried
(1744–1803)

German critic and poet, born in Mohrungen in East Prussia. He studied at Königsberg, and there made the acquaintance of Kant and Hamann. In 1764 he became teacher in a school and assistant pastor in a church in Riga. Between 1766 and 1769 he wrote two works, in which he maintained that the truest poetry is the poetry of the people. In 1769 he met **Goethe** in Strasbourg. In 1770 he was appointed court preacher at Bückeburg, and in 1776 first preacher in Weimar. Herder's love for the songs of the people, for unsophisticated human nature, found expression in

HEREDIA, José María

an admirable collection of folksongs, *Stimmen der Völker in Liedern* (1778–9, 'Voices of the Peoples in Songs'), *Vom Geist der Ebraïschen Poesie* (1782–3, Eng trans *The Spirit of Hebrew Poetry*, 1833), a treatise on the influence of poetry on manners (1778), in oriental mythological tales, in parables and legends, in his version of the *Cid* (1805), and other works. The supreme importance of the historical method is fully recognized in these and a book on the origin of language (1772), and especially in his masterpiece, *Ideen zur Geschichte der Menschheit* (1784–91, Eng trans *Outlines of a Philosophy of the History of Man*, 1800), which is remarkable for its anticipations of evolutionary theories. He is best remembered for the influence he exerted on Goethe and the growing German Romanticism.
▷ H Reisiger, *Johann Gottfried Herder* (1942)

HEREDIA, José María
(1803–39)

Cuban poet, born in Santiago de Cuba, cousin of the French poet **José María de Heredia**. He was exiled to the USA for anti-government activities in 1823. He is remembered mainly for his patriotic verse and for his ode to Niagara (1824), but the earlier 'En el teocalli de Cholula' ('In the Pyramid of Cholula') is a significant philosophical poem.
▷ A Harms, *Heredia* (1975)

HEREDIA, José María de
(1842–1905)

French poet, born in Santiago de Cuba, cousin of the Cuban poet **José María Heredia**. He went at an early age to France, where he was educated. One of the Parnassians, he achieved a great reputation with a comparatively small output, his finest work being found in his sonnets, which appeared in the collection *Les Trophées* (1893).
▷ C Utrera, *Heredia* (1939)

HERFORD, Oliver
(1863–1935)

American illustrator and humorist. Herford was born in Sheffield, England, but moved to America as a child. He was educated at Antioch College, Ohio, and at art schools in London and Paris. He produced over 50 books of frothy nonsense, mainly illustrated by his own drawings. These—with titles such as *Pen and Inklings* (1893), *Rubaiyat of a Persian Cat* (1904) and *A Little Book of Bores* (1906)—satisfied a contemporary hunger for undemanding entertainment but have little lasting worth, except for bibliophiles and anthologists with space to fill.

HERGESHEIMER, Joseph
(1880–1954)

American novelist and essayist, born in Philadelphia. He studied art, but made his name with *Mountain Blood* (1915), *The Three Black Pennys* (1917), *Tubal Cain* (1918), *Java Head* (1919), *The Bright Shawl* (1922), *The Foolscap Rose* (1934) and other romantic novels and short stories about early American life.
▷ *The Presbyterian Child* (1924)

HERLIHY, James Leo
(1927–)

American novelist, short-story writer and playwright, born in Detroit. He was educated at Black Mountain College, an influential liberal arts school in North Carolina. He is best known for his novel *Midnight Cowboy* (1965), the story of a handsome but naive cowboy who forsakes his small-town life for the dark side of New York, where he forms an unlikely alliance with a crippled pickpocket. It was successfully filmed in 1967. His other novels include *All Fall Down* (1960), about the disintegration of a middle-class family, and *The Season of the Witch* (1971), in which he returned to the theme of a runaway drifter in New York, this time female. He also wrote a number of plays and two volumes of short stories.

HERMANS, Wilhelm Frederik
(1921–)

Leading contemporary Dutch novelist, critic, poet, editor, scientist and dramatist, born in Amsterdam. Until 1973 he was a professor of physical geography at Amsterdam. A somewhat self-conscious modernist, Hermans has set himself the task—reminiscent of the French atheist–existential movement—of trying to make sense of a world that seems devoid of meaning. If Hermans had a model, then this was certainly also a French one: the novelist **Louis-Ferdinand Céline**. His first novel, written after some attempts at poetry, was *Conserve* (1947), his best-known one *De tranen der acacia's* (1949, 'The Tears of the Acacias'), which is set in occupied Amsterdam. In *De god Dernkbar kamer van Damocles* (1956, Eng trans *The Dark Room of Damocles*, 1962) he attempted a more humanistic kind of novel.

HERMLIN, Stephen, pseud of Rudolf Leder
(1915–)

German poet and story writer, born in Chemnitz. He returned from exile to East Germany in 1947, and soon ran foul of the authorities for his Surrealist poems. He later turned to socialist realism in such collections as *Stalin* (1949).

HERMODSSON, Elisabet
(1927–)
Swedish writer, composer and artist. Born in Göteborg, she studied at the University of Stockholm as well as attending art school. Her work encompasses a range of media and genres, the volume *Dikt-ting* (1966, 'Poems Objects') conflating poetry and pictures. On the basis of humanist, Christian and subsequently feminist convictions she has formulated a far-reaching cultural critique to which environmental concerns are central, for example in the poems in *Mänskligt landskap, orättvist fördelat* (1968, 'Human Province, Unfairly Distributed'), in the essays in *Synvända* (1975, 'Sight Distortion'), and in the 'ecological oratorio' *Skapelse utlämnad* (1986, 'Creation Abandoned'). Her feminism first found expression in the 1970s, notably in *Disa Nilssons visor* (1974, 'Disa Nilsson's Songs'), a volume of poems set to music and illustrated by the author, and designed to offer an antithesis to the conventional image of woman presented in **Birger Sjöberg**'s popular *Fridas visor* of 1922.
▷ B I Bergsten, *'Förflytta berg till bokstäver': Utvecklingslinjer i Elisabet Hermodssons författarskap* (1989)

HERNÁNDEZ, José
(1834–86)
Argentinian poet, born near Buenos Aires. He founded the newspaper *Rio de la Plata* in 1869. He is known for his *gaucho* poetry of life on the pampas, where he had spent his early life among the cattlemen. His masterpiece is the epic *El gaucho Martín Fierro* (1872–9).

HERNÁNDEZ, Miguel
(1910–42)
Spanish poet and playwright, a goatherd's son, who was encouraged by **Juan Ramón Jiménez**, **Antonio Machado** and members of the Generation of '27 (**Lorca** and others) to publish his precise and *Gongorista* early poetry. Under the influence of **Neruda**, he became a communist, fought against Franco, and died in a prison hospital of cold, starvation and tuberculosis. His last poems, simple and direct, are of love and yearning for his little son, whom he had never seen. When his poems were first published, some of the best were omitted by the censors; now he has the reputation of yet another major poet-victim of 20th-century barbarism. His best work has been translated in *Songbook of Absences* (1972), and another selection is contained in *Miguel Hernández and Blas de Otero: Selected Poems* (1972). His poetry, sombre and rooted in the past, yet fully contemporary, is amongst the greatest and most original produced by Spain in his century. Essentially, he was the youngest and last voice of the Generation of '27, since when Spanish poetry has floundered.
▷ G Nichols, *Miguel Hernández* (1978)

HERNÀNDEZ CATÁ, Alfonso
(1885–1940)
Cuban story writer, born of a Spanish father and a Cuban mother. He was at first a follower of **Benito Pérez Galdós**, who was his mentor. His sharp, laconic tales, much influenced by Pérez Galdós and **Maupassant**, were selected and introduced by **Barrios** in 1936. He died in a plane crash.

HERNTON, Calvin C(oolidge)
(1933–)
Black American poet and social researcher, he is almost certainly best known outside the USA for a slim but passionate essay on *Sex and Racism* (UK, 1969; the earlier US version appended *in America* to the title). Though essentially a work of sociology, it reflected much of what Hernton was doing in his verse. Born in Tennessee, his educational and professional life has been marked by a steady oscillation between north and south. His main poetic achievement is *The Coming of Chronos to the House of Nightsong* (1964), a powerful bluesy rap that is too subtly mediated to be stereotyped as 'angry'; nor is it exclusively about 'the Black experience' but resonates with mythic and philosophical concerns. Hernton published a major collection, *Medicine Man*, in 1976; some of the later work reflects his important but largely neglected work on the use of marijuana. Other non-poetic works include *White Papers for White Americans* (1966) and *Coming Together: Black Power, White Hatred and Sexual Hangups* (1971), a more obviously radicalized version of the *Sex and Racism* thesis.
▷ R Berke, *Bounds Out of Bounds* (1981)

HERODOTUS
(c.485–425 BC)
Greek historian, born in Halicarnassus, a Greek colony on the coast of Asia Minor. When the colonies were freed from the Persian yoke, he left his native town and travelled in Asia Minor, the Aegean islands, Greece, Macedonia, Thrace, the coasts of the Black Sea, Persia, Tyre, Egypt, and Cyrene. In 443 BC the colony of Thurii was founded by Athens on the Tarentine Gulf, and Herodotus joined it. From Thurii he visited Sicily and Lower Italy. On his travels, he collected historical, geographical, ethnological, mythological and archaeological material for his history which was designed to record not only the wars but the causes of the wars between

Greece and the barbarians. Beginning with the conquest of the Greek colonies in Asia Minor by the Lydian king Croesus, he gives a history of Lydia, and then passes to Persia, Babylon and Egypt. In books five to nine we have the history of the two Persian wars (494–478 BC). **Cicero** called him 'the father of history'.

▷ A de Selincourt, *The World of Herodotus* (1962)

HERONDAS, or HERODAS
(3rd century BC)

Greek poet, a native of Cos or Miletus. His work *Mimiambi* ('Iambic Mimes'), pictures of Greek life in dialogue, comprising some 700 verses, was discovered on an Egyptian papyrus in 1891.

▷ F Will, *Herondas* (1973)

HERRERA, Fernando de
(c.1534–1597)

Spanish lyric poet, born in Seville. He took holy orders and was known as 'El Divino'. Many of his love poems are remarkable for tender feeling, while his odes sometimes attain the grandeur of **Milton**. He wrote a prose history of the war in Cyprus (1572), and translated Stapleton's life of Sir Thomas More from Latin.

▷ M G Randel, *The Historical Prose of Fernando de Herrera* (1971)

HERRERA Y REISSIG, Julio
(1875–1910)

Uruguayan *modernista* poet, born in Montevideo. Herrera's poetry was artificial and affected, but also perfect in its expression: he influenced the so-called ultraists—late purveyors of art-for-art's sake—and his work was eventually edited (final edition, 1958) by the leading ultraist, **Guillermo de la Torre**. He withdrew himself from society and lived in an attic—'Tower of the Panoramas'—in Montevideo until heart disease killed him. His vision of a perfect pastoral world unsullied by greed or commerce is moving, but he does not have the experience (he invented the disreputable life of a *poète maudit* for himself) to turn it into great, as distinct from undeniably exquisite, poetry.

▷ B Gicovate, *Julio Herrera y Reissig and the Symbolists* (1957)

HERRICK, Robert
(1591–1674)

English poet, born in London, the son of a goldsmith. He was apprenticed to his uncle, also a goldsmith, but went to Trinity Hall, Cambridge, at the age of 22. After graduating in 1620 he took holy orders and was presented with a living in Devon (1629), of which he was deprived as a royalist in 1647. The following year he published *Hesperides: or the Works both Humane and Divine of Robert Herrick Esq*, with a separate section of religious verse entitled *Noble Numbers*. Despite *Noble Numbers* he is the most pagan of English poets, vying with his Latin models in the celebration of imagined mistresses—Julia, Anthea, Corinna, and others. He was at his best when describing rural rites as in *The Hock Cart* and *Twelfth Night*, and in lyrical gems such as 'Gather ye rosebuds while ye may' and 'Cherry Ripe'. Youth and love and the pagan fields were his themes at a time when the west country was devastated by the Civil War. He resumed his living in his Devon parish in 1662 after the Restoration.

▷ M Chute, *Two Gentlemen: the lives of George Herbert and Robert Herrick* (1960); John Press, *Robert Herrick* (1961)

HERRICK, Robert Welch
(1868–1938)

American novelist. In his quiet and understated way, he restated the main components of the American myth: the opposition of self-reliant and morally encompassed individuals with 'society'. He viewed the USA from a somewhat privileged angle, growing up in Cambridge, Massachusetts and receiving his education at Harvard. He combined a literary career with faculty positions at MIT (1890–3) and Chicago University (1893–1923). His first book was a collection of stories, *Literary Love-Letters* (1897), followed by a novel, *The Man Who Wins* (also 1897), in which he considers the incompatability of altruistic vocation and the success ethic. Later books, including *The Web of Life* (1900), the bestselling *The Master of the Inn* (1908) and *The Healer* (1911), likewise focus on a young physician, but almost all of his protagonists confront similar dilemmas. *The Memoirs of an American Citizen* (1905), possibly Herrick's own favourite, was edited by the critic and historian Daniel Aaron in 1963. Despite Aaron's advocacy, Herrick's reputation has not revived. His writing career had virtually come to a halt when, in 1935, he was appointed secretary to the governor of the US Virgin Islands.

▷ B Nevius, *Robert Herrick: The Development of a Novelist* (1962)

HERSEY, John Richard
(1914–93)

American author, born in Tientsin, China. He was educated at Yale, and was correspondent in the far east for the magazine *Time*. *Hiroshima* (1946), the first on-the-spot description of the effects of a nuclear explosion, took over an entire issue of the *New Yorker* on August 31 1946. His novels include *A Bell for Adano* (1944), which was dramatized and filmed, *The War Lover* (1959), *The Child Buyer* (1960), *Under the Eye of the Storm* (1967) and *The Walnut Door* (1977).

▷D Sanders, *John Hersey Revisited* (1990)

HERTZ, Henrik, originally **Heyman**
(1798-1870)

Danish poet, born in Copenhagen. He published a collection of rhymed satirical letters, *Gjengangerbreve* (1830, 'Letters of a Ghost'), and several dramas, including *Svend Dyrings Hus* (1837) and *Kong Renés Datter* (1845).

▷M Brondsted, *Henrik Hertzs Teater* (1946)

HERVIEU, Paul Ernest
(1857-1915)

French dramatist and novelist, born in Neuilly. His plays included *L'Énigme* (1901), *Le Dédale* (1903, 'The Labyrinth') and other powerful pieces, which usually took family problems as their subject-matter. He also wrote a successful drama about the Revolutionary period, *Théroigne de Méricourt* (1902), which was created for the famous actress Sarah Bernhardt.

▷P Gaultier, *Maîtres de la pensée française* (1921)

HERWEGH, Georg
(1817-75)

German revolutionary poet, born in Stuttgart. In 1836 he took up journalism, but in 1839, under threat of being court-martialled for insubordination during his military service, he fled to Switzerland. There he published *Gedichte eines Lebendigen* (1841, 'Poems from One Who is Alive'), establishing him as a revolutionary poet. He was well received in Germany, but his popularity came to an end when he led an invasion of Baden (1848), his behaviour earning him criticism from all sides, and he returned to Switzerland, publishing very little before his death.

▷V Fleury, *Le poète Georg Herwegh* (1911)

HERZEN, Alexander Ivanovich
(1812-70)

Russian political thinker and writer, born in Moscow, the illegitimate son of a nobleman. He was imprisoned in 1834 for his revolutionary socialism and exiled to the provinces. In 1847 he left Russia for Paris, and in 1851 settled in London, becoming a powerful propagandist through his novels and treatises, and by the smuggling into Russia of his journal *Kolokol* (1857-67, 'The Bell'). His memoirs were published in *Byloe i dumy*

(1861-7, Eng trans *My Past and Thoughts*, 1924-7), and are his most important writings.

▷Y M Steklov, *Aleksander Hertzen* (1920)

HESIOD
(c.8th century BC)

Greek poet, born in Ascra, at the foot of Mount Helicon, the son of a sea captain. One of the earliest known Greek poets, he is best known for two works, *Opera et dies* ('Works and Days') and *Theogonia* ('Theogony'). The *Opera et dies* is generally considered to consist of two originally distinct poems, one exalting honest labour and denouncing corrupt and unjust judges; the other containing advice as to the days, lucky or unlucky, for the farmer's work. The *Theogonia* teaches the origin of the universe out of Chaos and the history of the gods. Hesiod's poetry is didactic. *Opera et dies* gives an invaluable picture of the Greek village community in the 8th century BC, and the *Theogonia* is of importance to the comparative mythologist.

▷A R Burn, *The World of Hesiod* (1966)

HESSE, Hermann
(1877-1962)

German-born Swiss novelist and poet, winner of the Nobel Prize for literature, born in Calw in Württemberg. He was a bookseller and antiquarian in Basel from 1895 to 1902, and published his first novel, *Peter Camenzind*, in 1904 (Eng trans 1961). From then on he devoted himself to writing, living in Switzerland from 1911, becoming a naturalized citizen in 1923. *Rosshalde* (1914, Eng trans 1970) examines the problem of the artist. *Knulp* (1915, Eng trans 1971) is a tribute to vagabondage. *Demian* (1919, Eng trans 1971) is a psychoanalytic study of incest, while *Narziss und Goldmund* (1930, Eng trans *Death and the Lover*, 1932) portrays the two sides of man's nature by contrasting a monk and a voluptuary. *Steppenwolf* (1927, Eng trans 1929) mirrors the confusion of modern existence, and *Das Glasperlenspiel* (1943, Eng trans *Magister Ludi*, 1949) is a Utopian fantasy on the theme of withdrawal from the world. Hesse was awarded both the **Goethe** Prize and the Nobel Prize for literature in 1946. His poetry was collected in *Die Gedichte* in 1942 (a selection, Eng trans *Hours in the Garden and Other Poems*, 1979), and his letters, *Briefe*, appeared in 1951. *Beschwörungen* (1955, 'Affirmations'), confirmed that his powers were not diminished by age. Though he disclaimed any ruling purpose, the theme of his work might be stated as a musing on the difficulties put in the way of the individual in his efforts to build up an integrated, harmonious self. All this is expressed in sensitive and sensuous language rising to the majestic and visionary.

▷ J Mileck, *Hesse: his life and art* (1978)

HETHERINGTON, John Aikman
(1907–75)

Australian journalist, war correspondent and biographer of major Australian figures including Field Marshal Sir Thomas Blamey (1954 and 1973), Dame Nellie Melba (1967) and **Norman Lindsay** (1973). He was born in Sandringham, Victoria. Collections of his biographical cameos include *Australians: Nine Profiles* (1960) and *Uncommon Men* (1965), while *Pillars of the Faith* (1966) portrays Victorian churchmen.

▷ *The Morning was Shining* (1971)

HEWETT, Dorothy Coade
(1923–)

Australian writer of poems and plays, born in Wickepin, Western Australia, whose poetry is collected in *What about the People?* (1961, a collaboration with her third husband Merv Lilley), and four other volumes including *Journeys* (1982). Little of her prolific output of plays has been published, but *This Old Man Comes Rolling Home* (1976) and *The Man from Mukinupin* (1979) deserve notice. Her first novel, *Bobbin Up* (1959), received acclaim; its story of the political and sexual awakening of a group of factory girls stands in direct line of descent from feminist writings of the 1920s and 1930s. *The Toucher* (1993) tells of an elderly novelist and her relationship with a much younger man.

HEWLETT, Maurice Henry
(1861–1923)

English novelist, poet and essayist, born in London, the son of a civil servant. He was the Keeper of land revenue records (1896–1900), and made his name with his historical romance *The Forest Lovers* (1898). He wrote several more novels on historical themes, and a trilogy of novels featuring the invented scholar-gipsy John Maxwell Senhouse. He also wrote nature sketches and several volumes of poetry; the long poem *The Song of the Plow* (1916) is perhaps his best work.

▷ L Binyon (ed), *The Letters of Maurice Hewlett. To Which is Added a Diary in Greece* (1926)

HEYER, Georgette
(1902–74)

English historical and detective novelist, born in London of partly South Slav descent. She studied at Westminster College, London, and after marriage in 1925 travelled in East Africa and Yugoslavia until 1929. By that time she had produced several well-researched historical novels from various periods, including *The Black Moth* (1921) and *Beauvallet* (1929). She risked fictional studies of real figures in crisis with books on William I, The Conqueror, Charles II, and the battle of Waterloo. However, it was not until *Regency Buck* (1935) and later novels that she really came into her own with the Regency period, on which she made herself an outstanding authority. *My Lord John* (1976), on Henry V's brother, was unfinished at her death. She also wrote modern comedy detective novels with dexterity, such as *Death in the Stocks* (1935) and *Behold, Here's Poison* (1936), and used detective and thriller plots with pace and irony in historical fiction such as *The Talisman Ring* (1936), *The Reluctant Widow* (1946) and *The Quiet Gentleman* (1951).

▷ J A Hodge, *The Private World of Georgette Heyer* (1984)

HEYM, Georg
(1887–1912)

German poet, born in Hirschberg, Silesia, and educated at the universities of Würzburg, Jena and Berlin, where he first read law at his father's command before mutinously turning to the study of Chinese. His writing is an expression of his frustration with, and rebellion against, the restrictive conventions of Prussia's middle-class establishment. In his most famous poems he deliberately focuses on those who live on the periphery of society: suicides, murderers, the mentally deranged and the physically deformed. He shows himself fascinated by the elementary, impulsive power of the demonic and the grotesque which stands in such blatant contrast to the general predictability of society. Exploding from a violently disturbing imagery and a suggestive use of colours, Heym's poetry is full of apocalyptic visions of war, death, and human alienation. He died in an attempt to rescue a friend from drowning while ice-skating. The only volume of poetry published in his lifetime, *Der ewige Tag* (1911), was soon followed by the posthumous *Umbra Vitae* (1912) and *Dichtungen* (1922).

▷ P Bridgwater, *The Poet as Hero and Clown. A Study of Heym and Lichtenstein* (1986)

HEYM, Stefan, originally **Helmut Flieg**
(1913–)

German novelist and journalist, born in Chemnitz, the son of a Jewish businessman. He fled Germany in 1937, and later served in the US army, taking part in the Normandy Landings of 1944, before settling in Munich when peace came. He moved to East Germany in 1953, since when much of his writing has been concerned with a critique of capitalism and an often ironic commentary on the deficiencies of the erstwhile Eastern bloc. *The Eyes of Reason* (1951, written in English), the tale of three Czech brothers, makes explicit Heym's support for the communist state. *Fünf Tage im Juni* (1974, 'Five Days in June') recounts the GDR workers' revolt of 1953 in a manner sharply at odds with the official version. He has recently been critical of the 'instant capitalism' which followed the fall of the Berlin Wall.

HEYSE, Paul Johann von
(1830–1914)

German writer and winner of the Nobel Prize for literature, born in Berlin. He settled in Munich in 1854. He excelled as a short-story teller, his short stories being marked by a graceful style, sly humour and frequent sensuality. These were collected in *Das Buch der Freundschaft* (1883–4, 'The Book of Friendship') and other volumes. He also wrote novels, plays and epic poems, and translations of Italian poets. He was awarded the 1910 Nobel Prize for literature.
▷ L Ferrari, *Paul Heyse und die literarische Strömungen seiner Zeit* (1939)

HEYWARD, DuBose
(1885–1940)

American novelist, poet and playwright, born in Charleston, South Carolina. His first book of poems, *Carolina Chansons* (1922), co-written with **Hervey Allen**, was followed by *Skylines and Horizons* (1924) and *Jasbo Brown* (1931). He is best known for *Porgy* (1925), a novel about black life in the waterfront district of Charleston, or rather for the dramatic adaptation he and his wife, Dorothy, made of it, which won a Pulitzer Prize on the stage in 1927 and was made into the opera *Porgy and Bess* by George Gershwin in 1935. His other novels include *Peter Ashley* (1932), a Civil War drama, and *Star Spangled Virgin* (1939), set in the Virgin Islands during the period of the New Deal.
▷ F Durham, *Du Bose Heyward: The Man Who Wrote 'Porgy'* (1954)

HEYWOOD, John
(c.1497–c.1580)

English epigrammatist, playwright and musician, born perhaps in London. After studying at Oxford, he was introduced at Court by Sir Thomas More, who was a distant cousin by marriage, and made himself, by his wit and his skill in singing and playing on the virginals, a favourite with Henry VIII and with Queen Mary I, to whom he had been music teacher in her youth. He was a devout Catholic, and after the accession of Elizabeth went to Belgium. He wrote several short plays or interludes, whose individual characters represent classes, such as the Pedlar, the Pardoner, and the like. They thus form a link between the old moralities and the modern drama. He is remembered above all, however, for his collections of proverbs and epigrams. His wearisome allegorical poem, *The Spider and the Flie*, contrasts Catholicism and Protestantism. He was the grandfather of **John Donne**.
▷ R C Johnson, *John Heywood* (1970)

HEYWOOD, Thomas
(c.1574–1641)

English dramatist, poet and actor, born in Lincolnshire, the son of a clergyman. He was educated at Cambridge, and was writing plays by 1596. In 1598 he was engaged by Philip Henslowe as an actor with the Lord Admiral's Men. Up to 1633 he had a large share in the composition of 220 plays. He was also the author of a historical poem, *Troja Britannica* (1609); an *Apology for Actors* (1612); *Nine Bookes of Various History concerning Women* (1624); a long poem, *The Hierarchie of the Blessed Angells* (1635); a volume of rhymed translations from **Lucian**, **Erasmus**, and **Ovid**; various pageants, tracts and treatises; and *The Life of Ambrosius Merlin* (1641). 24 of Heywood's plays have survived. The best is *A Woman Kilde with Kindnesse* (1607), a domestic tragedy; and with this may be coupled *The English Traveller* (1633). His work is usually distinguished by naturalness and simplicity. In the two parts of *The Fair Maid of the West* (1631), and in *Fortune by Land and Sea* (1655), partly written by **William Rowley**, he gives some spirited descriptions of sea fights. *The Rape of Lucrece* (1608) is chiefly notable for its songs; *Love's Maistresse* (1636) is fanciful and ingenious, and there is much tenderness in *A Challenge for Beautie* (1636). In *The Royall King and Loyall Subject* (1637) the doctrine of passive obedience to kingly authority is stressed.
▷ F S Boas, *Thomas Heywood* (1950)

HIBBERD, Jack
(1940–)

Australian playwright, born in Warracknabeal, Victoria. His prolific output tends often to short pieces with a satirical or abrasive tone, some of which are brought together in his *Three Popular Plays* (1976). Of his other plays, *Dimboola* (1969, published 1974) and *A Stretch of the Imagination* (1972, published 1973) are considered his best. His first novel, *Memoirs of an Old Bastard* (1989), is intended as the first of a trilogy.

HICHENS, Robert Smythe
(1864–1950)

English novelist. He studied music, but made his name as a novelist with books such as

The Green Carnation (1894), a novel about London society in the decadent manner, *The Garden of Allah* (1905), a desert romance set in North Africa, *The Call of the Blood* (1906), *The Paradine Case* (1933) and *That Which is Hidden* (1939).
▷ *Yesterday* (1947)

HICKS, Granville
(1901–82)
American literary critic and novelist. He was born in New Hampshire and came to prominence as a notably doctrinaire Marxist journalist on *New Masses*. His most important contribution to the critical debate in the 'proletarian' period of American literature was a book called *The Great Tradition* (1933), which marks out very different territory from that considered by **F R Leavis** under the same title. Hicks left the Communist Party in 1939 and turned on former comrades with the same ferocity he had once reserved for bourgeois individualists; *I Like America* (1938) was a significant pointer to this turning of his intellectual tide. He wrote several novels, but his other significant work is a closely observed memoir called *Small Town* (1946), which offers an unexpected insight into this complex and deceptive literary figure.

HIDALGO, Bartolomé
(1788–1822)
Uruguayan poet and playwright, born in Montevideo but of Argentinian parents. Although not a *gaucho* (roaming cowboy), Hidalgo was the first man to write recognizably *gauchesque* poetry. This popular 19th-century poetry, written in the dialect of the ranches, and using the cowboys' *cielito* rhythms (a four-line stanza), was in fact practised by sophisticated urban poets, either for political or satirical purposes. His octosyllabic *Diálogos* (1822, 'Dialogues') sold on the streets and cleared the way for **Lussich** and then for **José Hernandez** and his more serious *Martín Fierro*.

HIDALGO, José Luis
(1919–47)
Spanish poet and painter. Born in Torres, a village in Santander, he studied painting in Valencia and Madrid, and eventually became a talented artist. He was the leader of an important group of poets who contributed to the journal *Proel*, and to which **Vicente Gaos** and **José Hierro** also belonged. Though he only published three books of poetry in his lifetime, his work has received extensive critical attention. *Raiz* (1943, 'Roots') and *Los animales* (1944, 'The Animals') contain relatively simple poems dedicated to themes of nature and regeneration, while *Los muertos*

(1947, 'The Dead'), his most important work, reflects on ideas of death, silence and God.

HIDAYAT, Sadiq
(1903–51)
Persia's greatest writer of the 20th century, born in Teheran into a distinguished literary family. He studied in Paris in 1926, and then attempted, unsuccessfully, to train for dentistry and engineering. He was deeply versed in ancient Iranian lore, as also in foreign literatures. He translated the work of many leading European writers into his own language. He wrote short stories, parodies, novels, sketches, plays and collections of folk stories. Prodigiously gifted, he was unable to get his life into any kind of order, was an alcoholic and a drug addict, and finally gassed himself in despair in a Paris apartment. His masterpiece is the novel *Buf-i kur* (1936, Eng trans *The Blind Owl*, 1957), one of the dozen greatest works of the 20th century, in which the narrator investigates the subtle relationship between his external and his internal lives.
▷H Kamshad, *Modern Persian Prose Literature* (1966)

HIERRO, José
(1922–)
Spanish poet, born in Madrid, who grew up in Santander, where he started writing at 14. He collaborated in a magazine called *Proel*, where his first poetry was published. In post-World War II Spain there were two principal schools of poetry, known as the 'rooted' and the 'unrooted'. Hierro was regarded as the leading poet of the latter. Rather than conform to accepted views, these poets aimed to reflect their awareness of the reality and conflict around them. Hierro won the Adonais prize for 'Alegría' (1947, 'Joy') and a critics' prize for 'Cuanto Sé de Mi' (1957, 'How Much I Know of Myself'). Also well known are 'Tierra Sin Nosotros' (1947, 'Land without Us') and 'Libro de las Aluciones' (1964, 'Book of Illusions'), amongst others. Although known as a social poet, Hierro's poetry is really a medium for personal exploration; his style and language are colloquial, not formal.

HIGGINS, George V(incent)
(1939–)
American novelist, born in Brockton, Massachusetts. He was admitted to the Massachusetts Bar in 1967, but worked in newspapers before becoming a successful attorney. He has used his experience of low-life and his observation of criminals at close quarters to telling effect in a spate of acclaimed literary thrillers. *The Friends of*

Eddie Coyle (1972) was his first book and he has published many since, invariably told almost entirely in dialogue and using Boston as a backdrop. Titles include *Cogan's Trade* (1974), *Kennedy for the Defence* (1980), *Imposters* (1986), *Outlaws* (1987) and *Wonderful Years, Wonderful Years* (1988).
▷G Daldry, in *Watching the Detective* (1990)

HIGGINS, Jack, pseud of Harry Patterson
(1929–)

English thriller writer, born in Newcastle-upon-Tyne. He also writes as Martin Fallon, Hugh Marlowe and James Graham. He was educated at Roundhay School, Leeds, Beckett Park College for Teachers, and the London School of Economics. He was a teacher and college lecturer before becoming a bestselling author with the success of *The Eagle Has Landed* (1975), a tale of derring-do set during World War II in which the Germans plot to kidnap Winston Churchill.

HIGGINSON, Thomas Wentworth
(1823–1911)

American writer, born in Cambridge, Massachusetts. He was ordained to the ministry, from which he retired in 1858. Meanwhile he had been active in the anti-slavery agitation, and, with others, was indicted for the murder of a man killed during an attempt to rescue a fugitive slave, but escaped through a flaw in the indictment. In the Civil War he commanded the first regiment in the Union army raised from among former slaves. In 1880–1 he was a member of the Massachusetts legislature. His books include, as well as histories of the USA, *Outdoor Papers* (1863), *Army Life in a Black Regiment* (1870), *Oldport Days* (1873), *Common-Sense about Women* (1881), *Hints on Writing and Speech-making* (1887) and *Concerning All of Us* (1892).
▷H N Meyer, *The Colonel of the Black Regiment* (1967)

HIGHSMITH, Patricia
(1921–)

American thriller writer, born in Fort Worth, Texas. Her first novel, *Strangers on a Train* (1950), was filmed by Alfred Hitchcock. Her third, *The Talented Mr Ripley* (1955), was awarded the **Edgar Allan Poe** Scroll by the Mystery Writers of America. She creates a world which **Graham Greene** has characterized as claustrophobic and irrational, one 'we enter each time with a sense of personal danger'.
▷F Cavigalli, *Über Patricia Highsmith* (1986)

HIGUCHI Ichiyo
(1872–96)

Japanese writer whose short life is remarkable chiefly for *Takekurabe* (1896, 'Comparison of Stature'). A delicate, self-consciously artful love story, it showed great promise, especially in its use of language, but was her only substantial work of fiction. She also kept a literary journal, which was published posthumously, and a short work entitled *Nigorie* (1895, 'Muddy Stream').
▷R L Danly, *In the Shade of Spring Leaves: The life and writings of Higuchi Ichiyo, a Woman of Letters in Meiji Japan* (1982)

HIJUELOS, Oscar
(1951–)

American writer of Cuban extraction, born in New York. He grew up in a multi-ethnic neighbourhood, but retained close ties with his family's Cuban roots, which have emerged strongly in his three novels. His first book, *Our House in the Last World* (1984), revealed the influence of the Latin-American 'magic realists' on his work. He achieved a great success, and established his international reputation, with his epic, passionate, doom-laden account of the lives of two Cuban musicians in America, *The Mambo Kings Play Songs of Love* (1990), which was later filmed. A third novel, *The Fourteen Sisters of Emilio Montez O'Brien* (1993), is a colourful, sprawling, but intricately-woven story of a female-dominated Cuban–Irish family.

HIKMET, Nazim
(1902–63)

Turkish poet, dramatist and critic, born in Salonika (then Turkish, now Greek). His surname was Ran, but he did not use it. He is usually regarded as Turkey's greatest poet of the 20th century; certainly he is the only one to be really well known abroad. He was a Marxist who was sentenced, in 1938, to 25 years in jail for sedition—he was released under an amnesty in 1950, and soon fled abroad. He died in Moscow. In 1950 he and **Neruda** shared the dubious honour of receiving the Lenin Peace Prize. During the 1930s he revolutionized Turkish poetry by introducing free verse decisively into it (although he was not the first to use it). The chief influence upon him in this was **Mayakovsky**—it became popular, however, through the efforts of the Turkish poets, such as Ahmet Hasim, who imported it from France. One of his best-known poems is the epic *Seyh Bedreddin Destam* (1936, Eng trans *The Epic of Sheik Bedreddin*, 1977), dealing with the subject of a 15th-century rebel sheik. Hikmet's grandiosity (he wrote very prolifically, at enormous length, usually in 'stepped lines', and without 'blotting a line') and his tendentious and slogan-saturated work has not made it easy for all readers to accept him as a major poet, and it seems to be agreed that he is a poet despite his communism rather than because of it. But he was inventive, and could reach great heights. The best translations of his poems are by **Taner Baybars**, in *Selected Poems* (1967); other volumes include *Poems* (1954), *The Moscow Symphony* (1970), *The Day Before Tomorrow* (1972) and *Things I Didn't Know I Loved* (1975).

HILDESHEIMER, Wolfgang
(1916–)

German painter, playwright, novelist and translator (**Shaw**, **Joyce**, **Djuna Barnes**), an associate of Gruppe '47, born in Hamburg into a Jewish family. He is an Israeli citizen. He was educated in England, and was in the British army in Palestine during World War II. He achieved fame with his collection of stories *Lieblose Legende* (1952, 'Loveless Legends'), satires on bourgeois capitalism in which he employed Surrealist techniques. He then became Germany's foremost proponent of the Theatre of the Absurd, with such plays as the three collected in *Spiele in denen es dunkel wird* (1958, 'Plays in Which Darkness Falls').

▷M Esslin, *The Theatre of the Absurd* (1969)

HILL, Aaron
(1685–1750)

English poet, dramatist and speculator, born in London. He wrote *Zaire* (1736) and *Mérope* (1749, adapted from **Voltaire**), and wrote the scenario for Handel's opera *Rinaldo* (1711). He was one of **Pope**'s victims in *The Dunciad*, and replied with *Progress of Wit* (1730). He left an epic poem, *Gideon* (1749), unfinished. He had a wide circle of literary friends, and launched the bi-weekly journal *The Plain Dealer* in 1724.

▷D Brewster, *Aaron Hill, poet, dramatist, projector* (1913)

HILL, Ernestine
(1900–72)

Australian writer and traveller, born in Rockhampton, Queensland, who, from the early 1930s, criss-crossed the continent many times. These journeys resulted in her first book, *The Great Australian Loneliness* (1937), in *Australia, Land of Contrasts* (1943) and in her important collection of Northern Territory myths, legends and characters, *The Territory* (1951). She wrote on the Murray River irrigation scheme, *Water into Gold* (1937) and *Kabbarli* (1973), a memoir of Daisy Bates, the white 'grandmother' of the aborigines. Her only novel was *My Love Must*

Wait (1941), a bestselling life of circumnavigator Matthew Flinders.

HILL, Geoffrey William
(1932–)

English poet, born in Bromsgrove, Worcestershire. Educated at Keble College, Oxford, he made his career in academia. A deep, dark and densely allusive writer, brooding on death, sex and religion, his first collection of *Poems* was published by a small press in 1952. *For the Unfallen: Poems 1952–1958* (1959) marked his true emergence, since when he has become appreciated by the cognoscenti. His later collections, *Preghiere* (1964), *King Log* (1968), *Mercian Hymns* (1971), *Somewhere is Such a Kingdom: 1952–1971* (1975), *Tenebrae* (1978) and *The Mystery of the Charity of Charles Péguy* (1983), all won prestigious literary prizes. He has been a professor at Boston since 1988, and his other writings include a book of literary criticism, *The Enemy's Country* (1991).

▷V Sherry, *The Uncommon tongue: the poetry and criticism of Geoffrey Hill* (1987)

HILL, Susan Elizabeth
(1942–)

English novelist and radio dramatist, born in Scarborough, who published her first novel, *The Enclosure* (1961), while a student at London University. Her novels are strong in terms of character and atmosphere, particularly climate. A recurring theme, and one which permeates *The Albatross and other Stories* (1971) and *The Bird of Night* (1972), is a sense of malevolence, violence and despair, while *In the Springtime of the Year* (1974) vividly evokes the aftermath of bereavement, and the pain of memory and loneliness. After a long silence, she published *Air and Angels* in 1991, a love story set in India and Cambridge. *Mrs de Winter* (1993), a sequel to **Daphne du Maurier**'s *Rebecca*, is the most successful of a vogue for sequels because, as **Anita Brookner** observed, the author 'gives us a Susan Hill novel'. A stage adaptation of *The Woman in Black* (1983), a musical chiller in which a ghost takes revenge for her child's death by murdering other children, has been a longrunning success in London.

HILLERMAN, Tony
(1925–)

American mystery writer, born in Oklahoma, where he was brought up in the Native American community. He trained as an anthropologist before working as a journalist, and later taught journalism. He became Emeritus Professor of Journalism at the University of New Mexico, Albuquerque, in 1985. He is best known for his mystery novels, which are set in the Navajo and Hopi areas of New Mexico and Arizona; featuring two Navajo detectives, they draw on his knowledge of anthropology. A controversial writer, his works have aroused much debate and strong opposition from some Native American communities for their depiction of native religion and witchcraft. Titles include *Dance Hall of the Dead* (1973), *People of Darkness* (1980), *The Dark Wind* (1982), *The Ghostway* (1985), *The Thief of Time* (1988) and *Coyote Waits* (1990). He has also written essays and children's fiction.

HILLIARD, Noel Harvey
(1929–)

New Zealand novelist, born in Napier. He is the author of a tetralogy which began with *Maori Girl* (1960), the first contemporary novel to use a Maori as a central character, through *Power with Joy* (1965), to *Maori Woman* (1974) and *The Glory and the Dream* (1978). With the last, the cohesive design of the four books is shown; Maori and white settler cultures and conflicts are resolved in human relationships. A complementary novel, *A Night at Green River* (1969), stresses the same idealism in the renunciation of culture for social cohesion. His short stories are contained in *A Piece of Land* (1963), *Send Somebody Nice* (1976) and *Selected Stories* (1977).

HILLYER, Robert Silliman
(1895–1961)

American poet, teacher and critic, born in New Jersey. Hillyer was a highly conventional poet, against anything written by or after **T S Eliot**—whom, with **Pound**, he jealously, bitterly but not effectively attacked. *Poems for Music* (1947), however, a collection of what he considered to be his best lyrics, is an attractive and skilful volume in its old-fashioned way. He was also a skilled pasticheur of the 18th-century heroic couplet. He made a version of the Egyptian *Book of the Dead: Book of the Dead—The Coming Forth By Day* (1923), which is probably his most original work. He died embittered by the hostility he had aroused in opposing the award to Pound of the Bollingen Prize. As a neo-classicist he was neither as witty nor as effective as **A D Hope**, and is now virtually forgotten.

HILTON, James
(1900–54)

English novelist, born in Leigh, Lancashire. He quickly established himself as a writer, his first novel, *Catherine Herself*, being published in 1920. Many of his successful novels were filmed—*Knight without Armour* (1933), *Lost Horizon* (1933, awarded the Hawthornden Prize in 1934), *Goodbye Mr Chips* (1934) and *Random Harvest* (1941).
▷*To You, Mr Chips* (1938)

HILTON, Walter
(d.1396)

English mystic and writer. An Augustinian canon of Thurgarton, Nottinghamshire, he was the author of *The Ladder of Perfection* and possibly *The Cloud of Unknowing*, two books important in the history of English prose.

HIMES, Chester Bomar
(1909–84)

American novelist, whose later successes with Harlem-based cop thrillers overshadowed his earlier work. Himes was born in Jefferson City, Missouri, and educated in Ohio. He spent nearly nine years in prison for armed robbery and after his release worked (1938–41) on a writers project as part of the New Deal's Works Progress Administration. His first novel was *If He Hollers Let Him Go* (1945), a tough-minded account of racial prejudice in the Californian shipyards and factories. *Cast the First Stone* (1952) exorcized his prison experiences, after which he emigrated to Europe. There, his tough detective stories were welcomed as serious existential fiction. The later, satirical *Pinktoes* (1961) spoofed the French taste for literary erotica. Many appeared in Maurice Duhamel's influential *Série Noir* at Gallimard. *For Love of Imabelle* (1957) was originally a story called 'La reine des pommes' and was republished (and subsequently filmed) as *A Rage in Harlem*. On its first appearance, it gained Himes the influential Grand Prix de Littérature Policière (1958). In subsequent Harlem books, Himes developed two black detectives, Grave Digger Johnson and Coffin Ed Jones, who live up to their soubriquets handsomely but are nonetheless intensely moral figures, battling against corruption.
▷*The Quality of Hurt* (1972); S F Miliken, *Chester Himes: A Critical Appraisal* (1976)

HIND, Archie
(1924–)

Scottish novelist. Born and educated in Glasgow, he celebrated the city in his novel *The Dear Green Place* (1965), which juxtaposes the harsh reality of urban existence with a pastoral vision. Hind has not published any more novels, but has continued to work in community education projects in housing schemes and with young offenders.

HINDE, Thomas, pseud of **Sir Thomas Willes Chitty**
(1926–)

English novelist, born in Felixstowe, Suffolk. At various times, Hinde has worked as a teacher, a revenue rating officer and a personnel officer with Shell International. He published his first novel, *Mr. Nicholas*, in 1952 and has since published several others, of which *Games of Chance* (1965) is possibly his best. His works are well-crafted, well-paced, solid reads, with strongly-defined characters. Some critics compare his style to that of **Graham Greene**. In fact, Hinde once entered a competition in the *New Statesman*, to supply the first 150 words of a supposedly new Graham Greene novel. Hinde won, beating two entries sent pseudonymously by Greene himself.

HINES, (Melvyn) Barry
(1939–)

English novelist, born in Barnsley, Yorkshire. He worked for a time as a physical education teacher. His novels are all set in his native Yorkshire, and deal with working-class life across a wide spectrum of experience. He is best known for *A Kestrel for a Knave* (1974), also known as *Kes* following a successful film adaptation from his own screenplay, one of a number of collaborations with the film-maker Ken Loach. Its story about an undersized, emotionally isolated young boy's love for a pet falcon is told with craft and sensitivity. His other novels include *The Blinder* (1966), about a young footballer, *The Gamekeeper* (1975), and the industrial novel *The Price of Coal* (1979).

HINO Ashihei
(1907–60)

Japanese novelist, born in Fukuoka in the south of Japan. Initially an officer in the army, he was expelled for left-wing activities. He was, briefly, imprisoned but renounced Marx to become a patriotic, right-wing activist, rejoining the army as an enlisted soldier. He is best known for *Mugi to Heitai* (1938, 'Barley and Soldiers'), his account of his participation in the Japanese assault on Hsuchou. It paints a realistic, (but propagandistic) picture of the ordinary Japanese soldier fighting in Asia. He was officially proscribed after the war, being so closely identified with the pre-war regime, but continued to write prolifically. He laboured long and hard to produce *Kakumei Zengo* (1929), which he regarded as his life's work and is a huge, sprawling and very dull novel tracing Japan's collapse through the lives of a Fukuoka family. He committed suicide immediately after its publication, having

completed his work and being unable to bear his disgust at Japan's abject humiliation.

HIPPIUS, Zinaida *see* **GIPPIUS, Zinaida**

HITA, ARCHPRIEST OF *see* **RUIZ, Juan**

HJARTARSON, Snorri
(1906–86)

Icelandic poet, born in Borgarfjörođur. He studied art in Copenhagen and Oslo, but soon turned to writing and published a novel written in Norwegian, *Höjt flyver ravnen* (1934, 'High Soars the Raven'). He returned to Iceland in 1936 to become one of the most influential poets of his day, combining traditional and modern poetry with musical and painterly images. He published only four volumes of poetry, including the innovative *Kvaeđi* (1944, 'Poems') and the late *Haustrokkriđ Y fir mer* (1979, 'The Autumn Mist Surrounds Me'), and was awarded the Nordic Council's Literary Award for 1981.
▷S Egilson, *Ljóđmaeli Sveinbjarner Egilssonar* (1952)

HLASCO, Marek
(1931–69)

Polish story writer, born in Warsaw. All his writings caused intense controversy—his first book was burned in the streets in many towns, by order of the priest—and he went into exile, or 'defected to the west' (1958). A melancholy man, seized by a black vision of the future, he killed himself in Wiesbaden. *Pierswsky krok w chmurach* (1956, Eng trans of the title story, 'A First Step into the Clouds', in *Introduction to Modern Polish Literature*, 1964, H Gillon and L Krzyzanowski eds) enraged the orthodox, both Communist and Catholic, but made him into an idol for the young. *Cmentarze* (1958, Eng trans *The Graveyard*, 1959) was a bitter account of the results of Stalinism. Ultimately, his prose bearing too-evident traces of the influence of **Hemingway**, he ran out of true imaginative material: invention gave way to absolute disgust. But at his best, as in *The Graveyard*, and in *Nastepny do raju* (1958, Eng trans *Next Stop—Paradise*, 1959), he was a writer of great moral power.
▷ *Polish Review*, 4 (1961)

HLAVACEK, Karel
(1874–98)

Czech Symbolist poet and designer, born in Prague into a working-class family. The shortness of his writing career (he died of tuberculosis at 23) drew deserved attention to his, tragically, only partially realized gifts, and much influenced the course of Czech poetry. His poems—two small collections, *Pozde k ránu* (1896, 'Late Towards Morning') and *Mstiva kantiléna* (1898, 'Vengeful Cantilena')—so far untranslated into English, are self-consciously decadent, but also carry within them genuine and moving intimations of his doom. He has some affinities with the English **Ernest Dowson** and with the Pole **Przybyszewski** who, like **Wilde** and **Huysmans**, influenced him. The poet most closely associated with him, as 'decadent', is **Jiri Karasek ze Lvovic**. Hlavacek revolted against everything: youth, illness, social injustice, but in his melodic poetry there is far more than self-indulgence.

HO CHING-CHI
(1924–)

Chinese playwright and Communist Party activist. His most famous work is the opera *Pai mao nii* (1944, Eng trans *The White-Haired Girl*, 1954), written in collaboration with the academic Ting Yi, depicting the struggle of the peasants against feudal oppression and their eventual liberation through communism. It was based on a traditional folk-tale, and became the model for the doctrine of socialist realism as practised in China.

HO, or HUO, Xuan Hu'o'ng
(fl.c.1780–c.1820)

Vietnamese poet, whose precise identity is unknown—we know from her work that Ho is her real family name, but Xuan Hu'o'ng is a pseudonym. An educated, cultured woman, she produced some of the most sensuous, wittiest and most readable verse to come out of Asia in the 19th century. Typically, a poem by Ho will pretend to be about a harmless domestic activity (weaving or making rice cakes), which will make it seem innocent, but there is a second level of meaning, usually sex. She has been hailed as a proto-feminist, as she argues in her verse that the sexes should be more equal, and often comes out against marriage, saying that love between men and women should be freely given.

HOAGLAND, Edward Morley
(1932–)

American novelist, short-story writer and naturalist. He and his prose style have been likened to **Hemingway**, but he is much closer in temperament to **Thoreau** or **Peter Matthiessen**. Hoagland similarly combines exact observation of natural phenomena with an astonishingly vivid turn of phrase and a firm, unsentimental understanding of the 'politics' of the natural world and mankind's treatment of animals. This was dramatized in his circus novel *Cat Man* (1956) and in *The Circle Home* (1960), a successful novel about boxing. Like Thoreau, Hoagland is not out of place in the

city; he grew up in New York and regards its functioning as very little different from that of the woods or the jungle and subject to the same complex of emotions. *The Peacock's Tail* (1965) is a vivid, latter-day attempt at a proletarian novel. Hoagland's essays began to appear in book form at the end of the sixties. *The Courage of Turtles* (1971) is subtitled 'fifteen essays about compassion, pain and love', and these are his abiding themes, whether he is talking about animal communities, sex or childbirth. *Heart's Desire* (1988) collects the best of his pieces.

HOBAN, Russell Conwell
(1925–)

American writer for children, later an adult novelist, born in Lansdale, Pennsylvania. *Bedtime For Frances* (1960) was the first of several picture books about a young badger. *The Mouse and His Child* (1967) was one of his most successful works for children, but two years later he moved to England and made the switch to adult writing. Much of his subsequent work, beginning with *The Lion of Boaz-Jachin and Jachin-Boaz* (1973), has had a fantasy or science-fictional strand to it. His most acclaimed novel to date is *Riddley Walker* (1980), a post-nuclear holocaust novel written in a language which combines scraps of English with lumpy neologisms.

HOCCLEVE, or OCCLEVE, Thomas
(c.1368–1426)

English poet. He spent his life as a clerk in the privy seal office in London (1378–1425). His chief work is a free but tedious version of the *De Regimine Principum* of Aegidius Romanus, in **Chaucer**'s seven-line stanza. He also wrote *Ars Secondi Mori*; an autobiographical poem, *La Male Regla* (1406); and *Regiment of Princes* (1412).
▷ J Mitchell, *Thomas Hoccleve: a study* (1968)

HOCHHUTH, Rolf
(1931–)

German dramatist, born in Eschwege Werran. He studied history and philosophy at Munich and Heidelberg, and worked as an editor before turning to documentary drama. His main claim to fame is the controversial subject-matter of his plays. *Der Stellvertreter* (1963, Eng trans *The Representative*, 1963) accused Pope Pius XII of not intervening to stop the Nazi persecution of the Jews. It caused a furore, as did the implication in his second play, *Soldaten* (1967, Eng trans *Soldiers*, 1968), that Winston Churchill was involved in the assassination of the Polish war-time leader, General Sikorski. He also wrote a novel, *Eine Liebe in Deutschland*

(1978, 'German Love Story'), about Nazi atrocities.

▷M E Ward, *Hochhuth* (1977)

HOCHWALDER, Fritz
(1911–)

Austrian dramatist, born in Vienna, who has written thoughtful plays, both comedies and tragedies, in essentially traditional modes. He dominated post-war Austrian theatre, even though he lived in Zürich, to which he had escaped from the Nazis in 1938. The chief early influence upon him was the expressionistic German playwright **Georg Kaiser**, whose friend he became. He has written several deserved successes, including the famous and much produced *Das heilige Experiment* (1943), a depiction of the last day (16 July 1767) of the Jesuit mission in Brazil, and the powerful *Der öffentliche Anklager* (1949), about Robespierre's successor Fouquier-Tinville, who sought out the 'enemy of the people' to guillotine him—only to discover that the culprit was himself.

▷H F Garten, *Modern German Drama* (1964)

HODDIS, Jakob von, pseud of Hans Davidsohn
(1884–1942)

German expressionist poet and co-founder of *Der neue Club* (June 1910). He published the famous 'first expressionist poem', 'Weltende' (Eng trans 'World's End', in *Twentieth-Century German Verse*, 1963, ed Patrick Bridgewater) in 1911; in the following year he became mentally ill and lived in a hospital until the Nazis removed him and had him murdered. He was a minor poet whose verse does, however, possess all the qualities of the first phase of Expressionism.

▷C Middleton and M Hamburger (eds), *Modern German Poetry 1910–1969* (1962)

HODGE, Merle
(1944–)

Trinidadian novelist. Educated at University College, London, she worked as a French lecturer at the University of West Indies, Jamaica, whilst completing a doctorate on French Caribbean literature. She spent four years in Grenada working with Malcolm Bishop, leader of the Socialist Revolution, but left when the US invaded in 1983. She now works as a writer and lecturer in Trinidad. Her novel, *Crick Crack, Monkey* (1970), sensitively explores the themes of cultural ambivalence, alienation and search for identity, through the experiences of the adolescent narrator, Tee.

HODGSON, Ralph
(1871–1962)

English poet, born in Yorkshire. He became a journalist in London and published three volumes of Georgian poems with the recurring theme of nature and England: *The Last Blackbird* (1907), *Eve* (1913) and *Poems* (1917), containing 'The Song of Honour', 'The Moor', 'The Journeyman', and the polemic against the destruction of animals for feminine vanity in 'To Deck a Woman'. He lectured in Japan (1924–38), and made his home in Ohio, USA. An anthology of his works appeared as *The Skylark and Other Poems* (1958). He was awarded the Order of the Rising Sun (1938) and the Queen's Gold Medal (1954). His *Collected Poems* appeared in 1961.

▷G B Saul, in *Withdraw in Gold: three portraits of genius* (1970)

HOEL, Sigurd
(1890–1960)

Norwegian novelist, playwright and journalist, born and brought up in Nord-Odal. He began by studying science, but won a competition for Nordic short novels with *Idioten* ('The Idiot') in 1918 and thereafter worked as a literary and theatrical critic. Following a collection of short novels *Veien vi går* (1922, 'The Way We walk'), Hoel's literary career began in earnest with *Syndere i sommersol* (1927, 'Sinners in the Summer Sun'). In this novel, a group of young intellectuals attempts to live out a free concept of life, but is forced to confess its inability to change society's conservative norms; a recurring theme in Hoel's novels is the way in which varying forms of patriarchal structure bring about deceit and faithlessness, wreaking social and psychological havoc. He emphasizes the significance of childhood and adolescent experiences on one's adult life. Despite the psychological determinism of novels such as *En dag i oktober* (1931, 'A Day in October') or *Fjorten dager før frostnettene* (1935, 'A Fortnight before the Frosty Nights'), they convey one positive message: an understanding of the psyche can have a liberating effect. His most successful novel was *Møte ved milepelen* (1947, 'Meeting with the Milestone'); this, like much of his other work, was influenced by the ideas of his close friend, Wilhelm Reich.

▷R Øystein, *Sigurd Hoel. Et nærbilde* (1991); L Sverre, *Sigurd Hoels Fiction. Cultural Criticism and Tragic Vision* (1984)

HOFFMAN, Alice
(1952–)

American novelist, born in New York City and educated at Adelphi University, New

York, and Stanford University. She is regarded by many as one of the leading writers of her generation. Her first novel, *Property Of* (1977), concerns a 17-year-old entranced by the leader of a street gang involved with violence and drugs. In much of her subsequent fiction, which also considers the search for identity in a turbulent world, realism is fused with fantasy so that the everyday events about which she writes attain an almost mythical importance. *White Horses* (1982) examines a young girl's obsession for an older brother, while the austere and haunting *At Risk* (1988) deals with the effect upon her family of a young woman suffering from AIDS.

HOFFMAN, Daniel

(1923–)

American poet and critic, born in New York. He has written influential books on poets as various as **Stephen Crane**, **Robert Graves** and **Ezra Pound**, but is best known for his essentially conservative but often modernistic and playful poetry, in such collections as *Broken Laws* (1971) and in *Hang-Gliding from Helicon: New and Selected Poems 1948–1988* (1988). He writes, he has said, 'to defy desolation'.

▷ *Poetry* (Chicago, May 1989)

HOFFMANN, August Heinrich, called 'Hoffmann von Fallersleben'

(1798–1874)

German poet and philologist, and composer of the German national anthem, born in Fallersleben in Lüneburg. He was Keeper of the university library of Breslau (1823–38), and Professor of German there (1830–42). A popular writer of light lyrics, he published *Lieder und Romanzen* ('Songs and Romances') in 1841; but the publication of his *Unpolitische Lieder* ('Apolitical Songs') in 1842 cost him his chair. In 1860 he became librarian to the Duke of Ratibor at Korvei, where he died. He is best known for his popular and patriotic *Volkslieder* (1842, 'Folk Songs'), including 'Alle Vögel sind schon da' and the song 'Deutschland, Deutschland über Alles' (1841), which became the German national anthem in 1922. He also published several works on philology and antiquities, including *Horae Belgicae* (1830–62, 'Belgian Hours').

▷ K H de Raaf, *Heinrich von Fallersleben* (1943)

HOFFMANN, Ernst Theodor Wilhelm, called 'Amadeus'

(1776–1822)

German writer, music critic and caricaturist, born in Königsberg. Trained as a lawyer, he had an unsettled career until 1816, when he attained a high position in the Supreme Court in Berlin. A remarkable essay on Mozart's *Don Giovanni*, the composition of an opera (*Undine*, 1816) and the direction of the Bamberg theatre for two months (1808), testify to his real interests. He was the archpriest of ultra-German romanticism. His wit bubbled over in irony, ridicule and sarcasm, and his imagination was inexhaustible, but utterly undisciplined, wild and fantastic. His shorter tales were mostly published in the collections *Fantasiestücke* (1814, 'Fantasies'), *Nachtstücke* (1817, 'Night-time Tales') and *Die Serapionsbrüder* (1819–21, Eng trans *The Serapion Brothers*, 1886–92). His longer works include *Elixiere des Teufels* (1816, Eng trans *The Devil's Elixirs*, 1824), *Seltsame Leiden eines Theaterdirektors* (1818, 'Strange Sufferings of a Theatre Director'), *Klein Zaches, genannt Zinnober* (1819, 'Little Sachs, called Cinnaber'), and the partly autobiographical *Lebensansichten des Katers Murr* (1821–2, 'Opinions of the Tomcat Murr'). Three of his stories provided the basis for Offenbach's opera, *Les Contes d'Hoffmann* (1880, Eng trans *Tales of Hoffmann*, 1881), and also for Delibes's *Coppelia*. As a composer his most important opera was *Undine*, a precursor of the scores of Weber and Wagner. He also composed vocal, chamber, orchestral and piano works. He was an influential writer on music, notably in his reviews of Beethoven's works.

▷ H D Daemmrich, *The Shattered Self* (1973)

HOFFMEISTER, Adolf

(1902–)

Czech dramatist, poet, essayist, cartoonist and painter. He was a minor figure, given to much experimental activity, but a vigorous one, who left valuable records of the avantgarde movement. He fled from his country when the Nazis took it over, but returned to become a diplomat (Czech ambassador to France) after the 'Communist takeover. *The Unwilling Tourist* (Eng trans 1942) is about Lidice and other matters pertaining to the Nazis.

HOFMANN, Gert

(1931–93)

German novelist and dramatist, born in Limbach in Saxony. For most of his life he taught literature in various universities. He was the German equivalent of the Austrian writer **Thomas Bernhard**, upon whose methods Hofmann frankly based his own. But his work is less humorous, and puts more emphasis on the guilty German past. His major novels are *Auf dem Turm* (1982, Eng trans *The Spectator at the Tower*, 1984) and, above all, *Der Blindensturz* (1985, Eng trans *The Parable of the*

Blind, 1986), in which the influence of the Argentinian writer **Ernest Sábato** is prominent.

▷ *World Literature Today* (Spring, 1981, Summer, 1989)

HOFMANN VON HOFMANNSWALDAU, Christian
(1617–79)

German poet and translator (from Italian poetry), of noble birth, born in Breslau. A man of some substance in his native city, he became one of the leading disciples of **Martin Opitz**, and is renowned for his technical expertise. He has, however, been accused of lacking personal feeling, and being uninvolved in his themes, his bombastic style (establishing the so-called Second Silesian School) a matter of no more than skill.

HOFMANNSTHAL, Hugo von
(1874–1929)

Austrian poet and dramatist, born in Vienna into a banking family of Austro-Jewish-Italian origins. While still at school he attracted attention by his symbolic, neo-romantic poems or 'lyrical dramas' such as *Gestern* (1896, 'Yesterday'), *Der Tod des Tizian* (1901, Eng trans *The Death of Titian*, 1920) and *Leben* (1894, 'Life'), in which the transitory and elusive nature of life and its short-lived pleasures compel the quest for the world of the spirit. An emotional and intellectual crisis, a sudden awareness of the drying-up of his lyrical gifts, precipitated the *Ein Brief des Lord Chandos* (1901, 'A Letter from Lord Chandos'), an imaginary correspondence between Lord Bacon and a young Elizabethan nobleman, in which Hofmannsthal, in the guise of the latter, gives his reasons for abandoning poetry, his new hatred for abstract terms, his doubts of the possibility of successful communication. Thenceforth he devoted himself to drama, most of his works being based on that of other dramatists: *Electra* (1903), *Das gerettete Venedig* (1905, trans from **Otway**'s *Venice Preserved*), and the morality plays *Jedermann* (1911, Eng trans *The Salzburg Everyman*, 1930) and *Das Salzburger grosse Welttheater* (1922, 'The Great World Theatre of Salzburg', based on **Calderón de la Barca**'s *El gran teatro del mundo*). One of his major works is the comedy, *Der Schwierige* (1921, Eng trans *The Difficult Man*, 1963). Having renounced **Stefan George** and his circle, Hofmannsthal turned to the composer Richard Strauss, for whom he wrote the libretti for Richard Strauss's *Der Rosenkavalier* (1911, 'Knight of the Rose'), *Ariadne auf Naxos* (1912, 'Ariadne on Naxos'), *Die Frau ohne Schatten* (1919, 'The Woman without a Shadow') and others. With Strauss and Max Reinhardt, he was instrumental in founding the Salzburg Festival after World War I. His statue there was demolished by the Nazis in 1938.

HOGAN, Desmond
(1951–)

Irish novelist and short-story writer, born in County Galway. In 1976 Hogan published his first novel, *The Ikon Maker*, tracing the journey of a mother following her son from Dublin to England. Subsequent novels include *A Curious Street* (1984) and *A New Shirt* (1986). Like many others of his generation, Hogan refuses to sentimentalize Dublin, and in the latter novel especially, presents it as a city peopled by a bewildered and resentful social underclass, a place disfigured by raucous clubs and demeaned by heroin. His collection of stories, *Lebanon Lodge* (1988), again looks at the lives of outsiders and the disenchanted: Irish exiles in London; Irish–Americans in the mid-west, and travelling players. His is a tough, sometimes tragic, often ironic vision.

HOGAN, Linda
(1947–)

American writer, born in Denver, Colorado. Of Chickasaw descent, Hogan's work is often concerned with Native American culture, reflecting as well her continuing involvement with environmental issues. She has published six volumes of poetry—*Calling Myself Home* (1979), *Daughters, I Love You* (1981), *Eclipse* (1983), *Seeing Through the Sun* (1985), *Savings* (1988) and *The Book of Medicines* (1993)—and the short-story collections *That Horse* (1985), *The Big Woman* (1987) and *Red Clay* (1991). Her first novel, *Mean Spirit* (1990), is set in Oklahoma during the time of the Osage oil boom in the 1920s, and describes a series of brutal murders against a background of judicial corruption, aimed at disinheriting the Osages of their land and mineral rights. Hogan is also the co-editor of the anthology of women's short fiction, *The Stories We Hold Secret* (1986).

HOGG, James
(1770–1835)

Scottish poet and novelist, known as the 'Ettrick Shepherd', born on Ettrickhall Farm in the Ettrick Forest, Selkirkshire. As a boy he tended sheep and had only a spasmodic education. However, he inherited a rich store of oral ballads from his mother. In 1790 he became shepherd to William Laidlaw at Blackhouse in Selkirkshire, who encouraged him to write. On a visit to Edinburgh in 1801 to sell his employer's sheep, he had his *Scottish Pastorals, Poems, Songs, etc.*, printed, but without success. He was fortunate, however, in making the acquaintance of Sir **Walter Scott**, then Sheriff of Selkirkshire, who published several of Hogg's mother's ballads in the second volume of his *Border Minstrelsy* (1803). With the proceeds of *The Mountain Bard* (1803) Hogg dabbled unsuccessfully in farming, but eventually settled in Edinburgh. Another volume of poems, *The Forest Minstrel* (1810), was unsuccessful, but *The Queen's Wake* (1813) gained him cordial recognition. A bequest of a farm at Altrive Lake (now Edinhope) from the Duchess of Buccleuch enabled him to marry in 1820 and to produce in rapid succession a number of works in both verse and prose. He ended his days a well-known figure in Edinburgh society, a regular contributor to *Blackwood's Magazine*, and was the 'Ettrick Shepherd' of **John Wilson**'s *Noctes Ambrosianae*. He described himself as 'the King of the Mountain and Fairy School'. His poems of the supernatural are at their best when he avoids Gothic elaboration and relies on the suggestive understatement of the ballad style, as in his 'Kilmeny' and 'The Witch of Fife'. 'The Aged Widow's Lament' shows the influence of the Scottish vernacular tradition. His debt to **Robert Burns** is apparent in 'The Author's Address to his Auld Dog Hector' and in the riotous 'Village of Balmaquhapple'. Of his prose works, the most remarkable is *Private Memoirs and Confessions of a Justified Sinner* (1824), a macabre novel which anticipates **Robert Louis Stevenson**'s *Dr Jekyll and Mr Hyde* with its haunting 'split personality' theme. In 1834 he published his *Domestic Manners and Private Life of Sir Walter Scott*, against the wishes of Scott's family.

▷A Strout, *James Hogg: a biography* (1946)

HOLAN, Vladimir
(1905–80)

Czech poet and translator, born in Prague. Initially a member of the 'Poetist' school, he became political when Czechoslovakia was handed over to the Nazis. Then the communists repudiated his socialist-realist verse as 'decadent' and he retreated into a long silence. When he re-emerged in the 1960s, and could publish what he had written in his period of enforced silence, it was as the leading poet of his time. A critic has written that although he was 'over-prolific' and 'frequently too influenced by Eliot', his work nevertheless 'conveys a sense of loneliness and gentleness which is as impressive as it is authentic'. There is an English translation in *Selected Poems* (1971).

HOLBERG, Ludvig, Baron
(1684–1754)

Norwegian writer, born in Bergen, and considered the founder of both Norwegian and Danish modern literature. He was educated in Copenhagen and wrote a book on the history of Europe (1711), then settled in Denmark after travelling widely in Europe, largely on foot (1714–16). He published various historical and legal works, and in 1717 was appointed Professor of Metaphysics at Copenhagen University, then of eloquence (1720), and history (1730). His career as a satirist began with a comic epic, *Peder Paars* (1719), followed by a series of more than 30 classic comedies for the newly-opened Danish theatre in Copenhagen (1722–7). Thereafter he concentrated on historical books, including biographies and histories of Denmark, the Church, and the Jews. After one more satirical classic, *Niels Klims underjordiske reise* (1741, 'Niels Klim's Subterranean Journey'), he wrote only reflective and philosophical works.

▷F J Billeskev Hansen, *Holberg* (1974)

HOLCROFT, M(ontague) H(arry)
(1902–93)

New Zealand writer, critic and historian, born in Rangiora, Canterbury. He was editor of the influential periodical *The Listener* from 1949 to 1967, from which he drew *The Eye of the Lizard* (1960) and *Graceless Islanders* (1970), both reissued as *A Voice in the Village: The Listener Editorials of M H Holcroft* (1989). He wrote three novels in the late 1920s, beginning with *Beyond the Breakers* (1928), and became a prolific essayist on literature and life. *The Deepening Stream* (1940) won first prize in the New Zealand Centenary literary competition, and was followed by *The Waiting Hills* (1943) and *Encircling Seas* (1946); these were collected as *Discovered Isles: A Trilogy* in 1950. Through his essays he exercised considerable influence on his successors. He wrote a study of **Ursula Bethell** (1975) and autobiographical works including *Dance of the Seasons* (1952), *Reluctant Editor: the 'Listener' Years, 1949–67* (1969) and *The Way of a Writer* (1984).

HOLCROFT, Thomas
(1745–1809)

English playwright and novelist, born in London, the son of a shoemaker. After three years as a Newmarket stable boy, then eight years as a shoemaker, schoolmaster, and servant-secretary to Granville Sharp, in 1770 he became a strolling player. But settling in London (1778), where he became a friend of **William Godwin**, **Thomas Paine** and **Charles Lamb**, he took to writing. *Alwyn, or the Gentleman Comedian* (1780) was the first of four novels. He also wrote nearly 30 plays, mostly melodramas, of which *The Follies of a Day* (1784) and *The Road to Ruin* (1792) were the best. His eldest son, William (1773–89), robbed his father of £40 and having been found by him on an American-bound vessel, shot himself. An ardent democrat, in 1794 Holcroft was tried for high treason with Sir Thomas Masterman Hardy, John Horne Tooke and others and acquitted, but the adverse publicity reduced him to poverty and made him go abroad to Hamburg and Paris (1799–1801). His entertaining Memoirs were continued by **William Hazlitt** (1816).

▷R Baine, *Thomas Holcroft and the Revolutionary Novel* (1965)

HÖLDERLIN, Johann Christian Friedrich
(1770–1843)

German poet, born in Lauffen on the Neckar. He studied theology at Tübingen, and philosophy with Schelling and Hegel under Fichte at Jena. With a growing enthusiasm for poetry, he developed an aversion to the 'snug parsonage' for which he was intended. As family tutor in Frankfurt-am-Main (1796–8) he found in the wife of his banker-employer, Susette Gontard (the 'Diotima' of his works), the feminine embodiment of all he venerated in Hellenism. His early poetry owed far too much to **Friedrich Klopstock** and to **Schiller**, who published Hölderlin's efforts in his literary magazines, but the inspiration provided by 'Diotima' helped him to discover his true poetical self. However the commercial philistinism, which Hölderlin roundly condemned in his philosophical novel, *Hyperion* (1797–9, Eng trans 1965), and the understandable jealousy of the banker, made his stay in Frankfurt-am-Main finally impossible. During a temporary refuge at Hamburg he wrote splendid fragments for a verse drama on the death of Empedocles, elegiac odes and the magnificent elegy 'Menon's Laments for Diotima', which examines the discrepancy between the actual and the ideally possible. For a short time he tutored in Switzerland (1801), but returned to his mother at Nuertingen where he wrote 'Brot und Wein' ('Bread and Wine') and 'Der Rhein' ('The Rhine'). In July 1802, after a spell of employment by the German consul at Bordeaux, he returned in an advanced state of schizophrenia, aggravated by the news of 'Diotima's' death. For a short time he enjoyed the sinecure of court librarian to the Landgrave of Hesse-Homburg, procured for him and paid by his friend von Sinclair. After a period in an asylum (1806–7) he lived out his life in the charge of a Tübingen carpenter. It was the admiration of **Rainer Rilke** and **Stefan George** which first established Hölderlin as one of Germany's greatest poets, 80 years after his death.

▷R Ungar, *Hölderlin's Major Poetry* (1975)

HOLLAND, Josiah Gilbert
(1819–81)

American editor and novelist, born in Belchertown, Massachusetts. He became assistant editor of the Springfield *Republican* and part proprietor in 1851. In 1870, with Roswell Smith and the Scribners, he founded *Scribner's Monthly*, which he edited, and in which appeared some of his novels, including *Arthur Bonnicastle* (1873), *The Story of Sevenoaks* (1875) and *Nicholas Minturn* (1876).

▷H H Peckham, *Josiah Gilbert and his Times* (1940)

HOLLAND, Sir Richard
(c.1415–c.1482)

Scottish poet and member of the Douglas faction at the court of James II and member of the Earl of Moray's household in the north of Scotland. The facts of his life are largely unknown, though it is suggested that he moved to Shetland following the fall of the Douglas family in 1455. His only extant work is *The Buke of the Howlat* (c.1448) which exists in manuscript form and was first published by the Bannatyne Club in 1823. An alliterative poem, it allegorically recounts the behaviour and unkind fate of an owl who dresses up in the feathers of other birds to improve his appearance, but becomes so obnoxiously vain that Nature restores him to his original ugliness with the lesson that owls are always owls and doves always doves. The story of the Douglas family fall is interpolated into the plot.

HOLLANDER, John
(1929–)

American poet and critic, born in New York City. Educated at Columbia and Indiana universities, he subsequently became a lecturer at Yale. His verse is formal, intricate and often demanding, but equally, his wit, lyricism and poignancy have earned him popularity as well as critical acclaim. His works include *Movie-Going* (1962), *The Night Mirror* (1971), *Tales Told of the Fathers* (1975) and *Spectral Emanations: New and Selected Poems* (1978). His critical works include *Rhyme's Reason* (1981), an important study of poetic structure.

HOLLAR, Constance
(1880–1945)

Jamaican poet, born in Port Royal and educated locally and at London University, where she was one of the first black women students. She worked for the Jamaica Poetry League and published a poetry anthology, *Songs of Empire* (1932). In spite of the pervasive influence of English Georgian verse on her own poems (*Flaming June*, 1941), her sensitive response to Jamaican landscape and wildlife and sharp descriptive phrasing gives her poetry an individual voice.

▷J E C McFarlane, *Literature in the Making* (1956); L W Brown, *West Indian Poetry* (1978)

HÖLLERER, Walter
(1922–)

German poet, born in Sulzbach-Rosenberg, the site of the Archives for Contemporary German Literature, founded by Höllerer in 1977. He has been assiduous in his promotion of young authors and from 1954 to 1967, in his capacity as an editor of one of Germany's foremost literary journals, *Akzente*, has helped to chart the direction of post-war German literature. He is a lyrical poet, but emotion is stripped to a minimum, with an emphasis on image and symbol, as in *Der andere Gast* (1952, 'The Other Guest'). His fiction, such as *Die Elephantenuhr* (1973, 'The Elephant Clock'), tends to be heady and theoretical.

HOLLINGSWORTH, Margaret
(1940–)

English-born Canadian playwright, born in London. She won a national drama competition at the age of 18 and had plays broadcast on television and staged in London. In 1974 she took Canadian citizenship. Her one-act stage and radio plays are economical explorations of the lives of night-shift workers, retired men, and women trapped in unrewarding relationships. Her characters often sustain a dual existence, where dreams and make-believe run in tandem with mundane reality. Different ways of using language, as a means of non-communication as well as communication, are explored in plays such as *Ever Loving* (1980) and *Mother Country* (1980).

HOLLO, Anselm Paul Alexis
(1934–)

Finnish-born American poet, his father was the distinguished translator J A Hollo. Hollo was educated in Helsinki, Cedar Rapids, Iowa, and at Tübingen University. From 1958 to 1966 he worked as a programme coordinator for the BBC in London. His first poems had been published in Finnish as early as 1956, but he quickly became a cheerfully puckish figure on the British experimental scene. One typical project was the Finnish translation of John Lennon's *A Spaniard in the Works* (1966); it appeared as *Hispanjalainen Jakovainaa* (1967). Hollo's own verse had a strong oral, almost improvisational, character that developed further after he transplanted to the USA in the later

sixties. His first important collection was *Maya: Works 1959–1969* (1970). Like many of his generation, Hollo was unsettled by the decade's crumbling promise; *Spring Cleaning Greens* (1973) was a selection from his notebooks, significantly followed by the untypically ironic *Surviving With America* (1974). The next major collection was *Sojourner Microcosms* (1979), which combined new and older verse. Hollo's impact as a translator has been considerable, his work including translations of **Allen Ginsberg**, **Paavo Haavikko** and **William Carlos Williams**.

HOLM, Ann
(1922–)

Swedish writer for children, best known in Britain for the war novel *I Am David* (1965). First published in Denmark in 1963 under the title *David*, this short book is the tale of a boy—necessarily wise beyond his years—who escapes from a concentration camp and travels across Europe to the safety of Denmark. Holm's other work available in English includes *The Sky Grew Red* (1991), in which two children, one Danish, one English, try to keep Denmark out of the Napoleonic Wars. Although these books are set in times of conflict and austerity, Holm's message is one of obdurate optimism. Appealing to the idealism of youth, her implicit message is that a younger generation can heal the social and emotional wounds inflicted by the old order.

HOLM, Gro
(1878–1949)

Norwegian novelist. Born in Odda, in Hardanger, she subsequently inherited a farm in the area and ran it for many years. She emerged as a novelist comparatively late in life, and her output was not extensive; her fame rests on her trilogy about the people of Løstøl: *Sut* (1932, 'Trouble'), *Odelsjord* (1933, 'Freehold Land') and *Kår* (1934, 'Conditions'). In a terse, uncompromising style, these novels, set in a small farming community in the west of Norway, highlight the harsh economic conditions that prevailed throughout the second half of the 19th century and that resulted in large-scale emigration, particularly to the USA. The first-person narrator, who is married to a farmer and becomes the mother of six daughters, contributes a crucial feminine perspective, fundamental to the trilogy's unobtrusive but poignant critique of male traditionalism.

▷A Hageberg, 'Mannsamfunn og kvinnekår i Gro Holms *Løstølsfolket*', in *Kvinner og bøker. Festskrift til Ellisiv Steen på hennes 70-årsdag 4. februar 1978* (1978)

HOLMES, (John) Clellon
(1926–88)

American novelist, and the first journalist to use the term 'Beat Generation' to describe the aesthetic of **Jack Kerouac**, **Allen Ginsberg** and their friends. Born in Holyoke, Massachusetts, he was educated at Columbia University, and at the New School for Social Research. *Go* (published in the UK as *The Beat Boys*, 1959), was a story of rootless searching through America that paved the way for *On the Road* (1957). Holmes had met Kerouac in 1948, and the encounter had reinforced his own sense of a new social and cultural movement. Press interest in the Beats' lifestyle inspired an editor at the *New York Times* to commission an article, which appeared on 16 November 1952 as 'This is the Beat Generation'; this one occasional work overshadowed his subsequent career. *The Horn* (1958), which has a jazz background, and the more personal *Get Home Free* (1967), never received the attention given the earlier books. A collection of essays, *Nothing More to Declare*, also appeared in 1967; a later volume, *Passionate Opinions*, appeared shortly before his death and contained significant revaluations of the Beat movement. Holmes's verse, also undervalued, was collected as *Death Drag* (1979).
▷ J Tytell, *Naked Angels* (1976)

HOLMES, Oliver Wendell
(1809–94)

American physician and writer, born in Cambridge, Massachusetts. He graduated at Harvard College in 1829, and, giving up law for medicine, spent two years in the hospitals of Europe. From 1839 to 1840 he was Professor of Anatomy and Physiology at Dartmouth College, and in 1842 made the discovery that puerperal fever, which killed mothers and newborns in huge numbers, was contagious. From 1847 to 1882 he was Professor of Anatomy at Harvard. He began writing verse while an undergraduate, but 20 years passed with desultory efforts, before *The Autocrat of the Breakfast Table* (1857–8) made him famous by its fresh unconventional tone. This was followed by *The Professor at the Breakfast Table* (1858–9) and *The Poet at the Breakfast Table* (1872). *Elsie Venner* (1859–60) was the first of three novels, foreshadowing modern 'Freudian' fiction. He published several volumes of poetry, starting with *Songs in Many Keys* (1862). He also wrote *Our Hundred Days in Europe* (1887), an account of a visit made in 1886.
▷ J T Morse (jr), *Life and Letters of Oliver Wendell Holmes* (1896); E P Hoyt, *The Improper Bostonian* (1979)

HOLROYD, Michael de Courcy Fraser
(1935–)

English biographer, born in London. He studied sciences at Eton, and literature at Maidenhead Public Library. His first book was *Hugh Kingsmill: a critical biography* (1964). His two-volume life of **Lytton Strachey**, *The Unknown Years* (1967) and *The Year of Achievement* (1968), is recognized as a landmark in biographical writing. He is the official biographer of **George Bernard Shaw**, with *The Search for Love* (1988), *The Pursuit of Power* (1989) and *The Lure of Fantasy* (1991). He is married to **Margaret Drabble**.
▷ *Unreceived Opinions* (1973)

HOLSTEIN, Ludvig
(1864–1943)

Danish poet, born in Kallhave (Zealand). He is Denmark's leading nature poet of modern times, celebrated by some as a pantheistic philosopher, but by many more as the finest of all describers of the natural scene, especially that of Zealand. There are translations of a few poems in *Twentieth Century Scandinavian Poetry* (1950, ed M S Allwood).

HOLT, Kåre
(1917–)

Norwegian novelist and author for children, born in the Vestfold region on the Oslo Fjord. He began to write after World War II, during which he took part in the Resistance against the Nazi occupiers. He has written historical fiction, and novels about the modern labour movement. One of his outstanding works is his *Kapplopet* (1974, 'The Race'), dealing with the personality of the explorer Roald Amundsen.
▷ P Larsen, *Holt* (1975, in Norwegian)

HOLT, Victoria, pseud of Eleanor Alice Burford Hibbert
(1906–93)

British writer of popular historical romances, she also published as Eleanor Burford, Philippa Carr, Kathleen Kellow and (by far her best known) Jean Plaidy. Privately educated, she published her first novel under her own name in 1941, introducing 'Jean Plaidy' shortly afterwards with *Together They Ride* (1943) and 'Victoria Holt' in 1960 with *Mistress of Mellyn*. The pattern of the novels remains unchanged, consisting of insubstantial love stories and power struggles erected on a modestly researched background of historical fact. Perhaps the best known of the early Plaidy books is *The Royal Road to Fotheringay* (1955), which dramatized the life of Mary, Queen of Scots. In the 1960s (as Plaidy again), she embarked on a series of dynastic romances or 'Sagas' which confirmed the general suspicion that, whatever the ostensible period of the stories, she essentially wrote about the upper upper English middle class that was beginning to lose its role as she grew up in the aftermath of World War I.

HOLTBY, Winifred
(1898–1935)

English novelist and feminist, born in Rudston, Yorkshire. She was educated at Oxford, and served in France with the WAAC. She was a prolific journalist, and was a director from 1926 of *Time and Tide*. She wrote a number of novels, including *The Crowded Street* (1924) and *The Land of Green Ginger* (1927), but is chiefy remembered for her last and most successful, *South Riding* (1935).
▷V Brittain, *Testament of Friendship* (1940)

HOLTEI, Karl von
(1798–1880)

German actor and dramatic poet, born in Breslau. He wrote musical plays, such as *Der alte Freiherr* (1825, 'The Old Baron') and *Lenore* (1829), as well as novels and the autobiographical *Vierzig Jahre* (8 vols, 1843–50, 'Forty Years').

HOLTHUSEN, Hans Egge
(1913–)

German critic and poet from Rendsburg, who was involved in anti-Nazi movements towards the end of World War II. His sound and useful criticism, in the Christian tradition of **T S Eliot**, has been more influential than his poetry, which, however, was much read in Germany at the end of the 1940s for its mellifluous, **Rilke**-like qualities—it has been described as possessing an 'apocalyptic sense of spiritual crisis'.
▷C Middleton and M Hamburger (eds), *Modern German Poetry 1910–1969* (1962)

HÖLTY, Ludwig Christoph Heinrich
(1748–76)

German poet, born in Mariensee, Hanover. He was a co-founder of the *Göttigen Hain*, a literary coterie dedicated to promoting the national spirit in German verse. Some of his poetry is based on the Minnesänger. His range is limited, but his early death from consumption prevented development of his promise.
▷T Oberlin-Kaiser, *Ludwig Christoph Heinrich Hölty* (1964)

HOLUB, Miroslav
(1923–)

Czech poet and scientist, born in Plzeň. He took a PhD in immunology and has had a distinguished career in medicine, doing much to popularize science through his editing of the magazine *Vesmir*. His verse is informed with analytical scepticism, wryly humorous but admirably concise and cutting. He has published several collections, many of which have been translated into English. His *Selected Poems* were published in 1967; recent collections include *Sagittal Section* (1980), *Naopak* (1982) and *Interferon čilio divadle* (1982, Eng trans together as *On the Contrary*, 1982). He published a collection of essays, *The Dimension of the Present Moment*, in 1990.
▷*Zit v New Yorku* (1969, Eng trans *To Live in New York*, 1969)

HOLZ, Arno
(1863–1929)

German author and critic, born in Rastenburg, East Prussia. He started by writing lyric poetry, but is best known for his criticism. *Die Kunst, ihr Wesen und ihre Gesetze* (1890–2, 'The Nature and Laws of Art') inaugurated the German Impressionist school. *Revolution der Lyrik* (1899, 'Revolution in Lyric') rejected all metrical devices, and *Phantasus* (1898–9) was written on this theory. *Papa Hamlet* (1899) and the drama *Familie Selicke* (1890, 'The Selicke Family'), both written in collaboration with Johannes Aschaf, are influenced by **Émile Zola**.
▷W Milch, *Arno Holz* (1933)

HOME, John
(1722–1808)

Scottish clergyman and dramatist, born in Leith, Edinburgh. He graduated at Edinburgh in 1742. Fighting on the government side in the 1745 Jacobite Rising, he was taken prisoner at Falkirk (1746), but made a daring escape from Doune Castle. The next year he became minister of Athelstaneford, where he wrote the tragedy *Agis* and, in 1754, *Douglas*, founded on a Scottish ballad. Each of these was rejected in London by David Garrick, but *Douglas*, produced in the Canongate Theatre, Edinburgh (1756), met with brilliant success, and evoked the often quoted and possibly apocryphal 'whaur's yer Wullie Shakespeare noo?' from an over-enthusiastic member of the audience. It also won great popularity in London, but it gave such offence to the Edinburgh Presbytery that Home resigned his ministry (1757). The success of *Douglas* induced Garrick to bring out *Agis*, and to accept Home's next play, *The Siege of Aquileia* (1760). His other works are

The Fatal Discovery (1769), *Alonzo* (1773), *Alfred* (1778), occasional poems and, in prose, *A History of the Rebellion of 1745* (1802). He married in 1770, and in 1779 settled in Edinburgh.

▷H Mackenzie, *An account of the life and feelings of John Home* (1822)

HOMER
(8th century BC)

Greek epic poet, to whom are attributed two distinct but complementary epics, the *Iliad* (telling of the fall of Troy) and the *Odyssey* (telling of the wanderings of Odysseus on his adventurous way back to Ithaca). Nothing is known about Homer for certain (indeed, some scholars think that no 'Homer' ever existed, or that two or more poets may have been involved). The Homer of tradition seems to have lived in Ionia, directly across the Aegean from mainland Greece, and four city-states have claims to have been his birthplace: the Ionian mainland cities of Smyrna, Colophon and Ephesus, and the island of Chios. His most likely date is the second half of the 8th century BC, with the later poem, the *Odyssey*, being written about 700 BC, half a millennium after the fall of the city of Troy to an invading Mycenaean host around 1200 BC. The method of composition of the epics is also in dispute. Some scholars believe that shorter lays by earlier anonymous poets were simply combined and amended by Homer, others believe that the amalgamation of these shorter works into the majestic structure of the two great epics was an act of individual and supreme literary genius. Homer's lifetime seems to have coincided with the introduction of writing into the Greek world, and he may have utilized this new technique and committed his verses to writing, or dictated them to others. The tradition that he was blind may have little basis in fact. From the time that the *Iliad* and *Odyssey* were put into their present form in the seventh century BC, they have been regarded as the outstanding epic poems of Western literature.

▷W J Woodhouse, *The Composition of Homer's Odyssey* (1930); M I Finley, *The World of Odysseus* (1954)

HONE, William
(1780–1842)

English writer and bookseller, born in Bath. At the age of 10 he became a London lawyer's clerk, and at 20 started a book and print shop, which, however, soon failed. He struggled to make a living by writing for various papers, then started the *Traveller* (1815), and the *Reformist's Register* (1817). In December 1817 he was acquitted in three separate trials for publishing works calculated to injure public morals and bring the Prayer Book into contempt, an historic landmark in the freedom of the press. Among his later satires, illustrated by Cruikshank, were *The Political House that Jack built* (1819), *The Man in the Moon* (1820), and *The Political Showman* (1821). His obscure antiquarian interests were reflected in *Apocryphal New Testament* (1820), *Every-day Book* (1826), *Table-book* (1827–8) and *Year-book* (1829). Nonetheless, he landed in a debtor's jail, from which his friends extricated him to start him in a coffee house— also a failure. In his last years, growing devout, he became a preacher.

▷E Rickword, *Radical Squibs and Loyal Ripostes* (1971)

HOOD, Hugh John Blagdon
(1928–)

Canadian short-story writer and novelist, born in Toronto, now living in Montreal. Hood first came to notice with the early story collection *Flying A Red Kite* (1963), and has continued to work in the short form, publishing three volumes of collected stories (1978, 1989, 1991). But since *The Swing In the Garden* (1975) he has been engaged on a major serial novel, *The New Age/Le Nouveau Siècle*, set to occupy him until the year 2000. Already more than 10 volumes of this **Balzac**ian panorama have appeared.

▷K Garebian, *Hugh Hood* (1983)

HOOD, Thomas
(1799–1845)

English poet and humorist, born in London. At the age of 13 he was placed in a merchant's counting-house in the City, but, his health failing, was sent in 1815 to Dundee, to his father's relations, where he wrote for local newspapers and magazines. In 1818 he returned to London, and in 1821 was appointed sub-editor of the *London Magazine*; here he found himself in daily companionship with such men as **Bryan Waller Procter**, John Cary, **Allan Cunningham**, **Thomas De Quincey**, **William Hazlitt** and **Charles Lamb**. It was, however, the intimacy with John Hamilton Reynolds, whose sister he married in 1825, that chiefly encouraged and trained Hood's poetic faculty. Between July 1821 and July 1823 he published in the magazine some of his finest poems— 'Lycus the Centaur', 'Two Peacocks of Bedfont' and 'Ode to Autumn'. But these, issued anonymously, failed to attract notice when in 1827 he produced them and others in book form. In 1825 he published (anonymously) a volume of *Odes and Addresses to Great People* which was an instant success. In the first series of *Whims and Oddities* (1826) he exhibited his graphic talent in those 'picture-puns' of which he seems to have been the inventor. A second series appeared in 1827, followed by *National*

Tales. In 1829 he edited *The Gem*, a remarkable little 'annual', in which his *Eugene Aram* appeared. He left London for Winchmore Hill in 1829, where he began the first of the *Comic Annuals* which he produced yearly and single-handedly from 1830 to 1839. In 1834 the failure of a publisher plunged Hood into serious difficulties; and in 1835 the family went for five years to Koblenz and Ostend. During these years, struggling against tuberculosis, he wrote *Up the Rhine* (1839). He returned to England in 1840. In 1841 he became editor of the *New Monthly Magazine*, and in 1844 started a periodical of his own, *Hood's Monthly Magazine*. Meantime in the Christmas number of *Punch* (1843) had appeared 'The Song of the Shirt', and in *Hood's Magazine* there followed the 'Haunted House', the 'Lay of the Labourer', and the 'Bridge of Sighs'. His only surviving son, Tom (1835–74), published poems and humorous novels, and in 1865 became editor of *Fun*.
▷J C Reid, *Thomas Hood* (1963)

HOOFT, Pieter Cornelisz
(1581–1647)

Major Dutch Renaissance poet and playwright, born in Amsterdam. By the age of 22 he had been able, by means of extensive travels, to see the achievements of the European Renaissance for himself, and he determined to make the Netherlands another centre of this. He was aloof from politics, and cultivated the spirit of detachment he had learned from **Montaigne**. His massive prose history of his country's Wars of Independence, *Nederlandsche Historien* (1703), is a classic modelled on the example of **Tacitus**. He reacted against Calvinism in his tragedies and in his fervent poetry, initially influenced by **Petrarch** and **Ronsard**, but entirely his own. His poetry appears in translation in *Batavian Anthology* (1824), and in Weevers' *Poetry of the Netherlands in Its European Context* (1960), which is also exemplary for its appraisal of him.

HOOK, Theodore Edward
(1788–1841)

English writer, son of James Hook, born in London. Educated at Harrow School, he achieved early fame as the author of 13 successful comic operas and melodramas (1805–11). He was well known as a maker of puns and as a practical joker—his greatest performance was the Berners Street Hoax (1809). In 1812 he was appointed accountant general of Mauritius. In 1817 he was dismissed after a large deficiency was discovered in the accounts, and was later imprisoned (1823–5). Meanwhile, in 1820, he had started the Tory journal *John Bull*. He wrote a number of short stories and fashionable novels, such as

Maxwell (1830), *Gilbert Gurney* (1936) and *Jack Brag* (1837).
▷M Brightfield, *Thomas Hook and his novels* (1928)

HOPE, A(lec) D(erwent)
(1907–)

Australian poet and critic, born in Cooma, New South Wales, the son of a Presbyterian minister. Most of his childhood was spent in New South Wales and Tasmania. He graduated from Sydney University and took up a scholarship at Oxford. He returned to Australia in 1931 and was a distinguished academic, teaching English at several Australian colleges, before retiring in 1972 to concentrate on poetry. Regarded by some critics as austere, intellectual and lacking any identifiable Australian experience, he is a richly allusive poet, pre-eminent among his contemporaries. Few awards have passed him by since the appearance of his first collection, *The Wandering Isles*, in 1955. Subsequent volumes include *Poems* (1960), *A D Hope* (1963), *Collected Poems 1930–1965* (1966, expanded edn 1972), *Selected Poems* (1973), *A Late Picking* (1975), *A Book of Answers* (1978), *The Drifting Continent* (1979), *Antechinus* (1981) and *The Tragical History of Dr Faustus* (1982). One of Australia's most respected poets, his verse has also been honoured internationally with such awards as the Levinson Prize (1968) and the **Robert Frost** Award (1976). Far from being the austere figure often portrayed, he talked entertainingly on literature as 'Anthony Inkwell' in a long-running 1940s radio programme from children.
▷L Kramer, *A. D. Hope* (1979)

HOPE, Anthony, pseud of Sir Anthony Hope Hawkins
(1863–1933)

English novelist, born in London, the son of a clergyman in Clapton. Educated at Balliol College, Oxford, he was called to the Bar in 1887. He wrote several plays and novels in his spare time, and made his name as writer with a collection of sketches, *The Dolly Dialogues* (1894). But he is chiefly remembered for his 'Ruritanian' romances, *The Prisoner of Zenda* (1894; dramatized 1896) and its sequel, *Rupert of Hentzau* (1898).
▷C Mallet, *Anthony Hope and His Books* (1935)

HOPE, Christopher
(1944–)

South African novelist, poet and non-fiction writer, now resident in England. He was educated at the Christian Brothers College in Pretoria but left South Africa in 1975. The comedy in his first novel, *A Separate Development* (1981), about a boy who cannot decide whether he is black or white, can be described literally as frightful. The book was banned in South Africa. He won a Whitbread Award in 1985 for *Kruger's Alp* (1984), and *Serenity House* (1992) was shortlisted for the Booker Prize. Hope's relish for **Kafka**esque situations comes through most strongly in two non-fiction books, *White Boy Running* (1988) and *Moscow, Moscow* (1990). The vision, bleak and instructive, avoids moralizing through its sense of the comic and ridiculous.

HOPE, Laurence, pseud of Adela Florence Nicolson, née Cory
(1865–1904)

English poet, born in Stoke Bishop, Gloucestershire. She lived in India and wrote poems, influenced by **Algernon Charles Swinburne** and coloured by the Orient, among them the *Indian Love Lyrics*, some of which are best known in their musical settings by Amy Woodford Finden.

HOPKINS, Gerard Manley
(1844–89)

English poet, born in Stratford, London, the son of a prosperous marine insurance agent. He was educated at Highgate School and Balliol College, Oxford, where he was a pupil of Jowett and **Walter Pater** and a disciple of Pusey, and met his lifelong friend **Robert Bridges**. The religious ferment of the times absorbed him and finally he followed **John Henry Newman** into the Roman Catholic Church in 1866. In 1868 he became a Jesuit novice, was ordained a priest in 1877, and taught at Stoneyhurst School (1882–4). In 1884 he was appointed to the chair of Greek at University College, Dublin. None of his poems was published in his lifetime, but his friend Bridges brought out a full edition in 1918. His first and most famous poem, 'The Wreck of the *Deutschland*' (1876) used what he called 'sprung rhythm', which gave an extraordinary freshness to his best-loved poetry, such as 'The Windhover' and 'Pied Beauty'. The *Letters to Robert Bridges, The Correspondence of Gerard Manley Hopkins and Richard Watson Dixon* (1935), and the *Notebooks* (1937), set forth his ideals for poetry, and gave explanations of his experiments in prosody.
▷ A G Sulloway, *Gerard Manley Hopkins and the Victorian Temper* (1972)

HOPWOOD, Avery
(1882–1928)

American dramatist, born in Cleveland, Ohio. Hopwood was a popular playwright who achieved considerable success with his first play *Clothes* (1906), a farce built upon the tight spots a poor girl gets herself into by dressing like a rich one. Following this he had a string of 'hits'. *The Gold Diggers* (1909)—about grasping chorus-girls—has been much revamped by Hollywood, originally in the early musical *Gold Diggers of Broadway* (1929). Hopwood did not live to see this version. During the 1920s he became a heavy drinker and drowned himself in the Mediterranean. His name is remembered most for a famous whodunit *The Bat* (1920) and for the eponymous literature prizes administered by the University of Michigan.

HORA, Josef
(1891–1945)

Czech poet who claimed the mantle of **Karel Mácha**, Czechoslovakia's great romantic poet, and who was second only to **Frantisek Halas** amongst the poets of his generation. He began as a communist, but in 1929 became an ardent socialist. He spent the war years confined to his flat by severe illness, and died just as the conflict ended. His *Pracující den* (1920, 'The Working Day'), is one of the best, least doctrinaire, and warmest collections of so-called 'proletarian poetry' ever published. But in *Máchhovské variace* (1936, 'Variations on Mácha'), written when he had become more metaphysical, he surpasses even this volume. He translated the *Eugene Onegin* of **Pushkin**, who influenced him, and has ever since his death been an example and inspiration to the young.
▷ A French, *The Poets of Prague* (1969)

HORACE, Quintus Horatius Flaccus
(65–8 BC)

Roman poet and satirist, born near Venusia in southern Italy. His father was a manumitted slave who, as collector of taxes or auctioneer, had saved enough money to buy a small estate. Horace was taken to Rome and taught by the best masters. At the age of about 18 he went to Athens to complete his education; and he was still there when the murder of **Caesar** (44 BC) rekindled civil war. The same year he joined Brutus, who visited Athens while levying troops. He was present as an officer at the battle of Philippi (42 BC), and joined in the flight that followed the Republican defeat, but found his way back to Italy. His property having been confiscated, he found employment in the civil service; but poverty, he said, drove him to make verses. His earliest were chiefly satires and lampoons; but some of his first lyrical pieces made him known to **Virgil**, who about 38 BC introduced him to Maecenas, minister of Augustus and a munificent patron of art and letters. To his liberality Horace owed release from business and the gift of the farm among the Sabine Hills. From then on his springs and summers were generally spent in Rome, his autumns at the Sabine farm or a small villa at Tibur. As the unrivalled lyric poet of the time he was virtual poet laureate after the death of Virgil. The first book of *Satires*, 10 in number, appeared in 35 BC; a second volume of eight satires in 30 BC; and about the same time the small collection of lyrics known as the *Epodes*. In 23 BC he produced his greatest work, three books of *Odes*. To about the same date belong his *Epistles*. The remainder of his writings are the *Carmen Seculare*; a fourth book of *Odes*; and three more epistles, one of which, known as the *Ars Poetica*, perhaps left unfinished at his death, had a profound influence on literary criticism in the 17th and 18th centuries. Horace's lasting popularity comes chiefly from the *Odes*, in which he combines mastery of form with elegance of style. His subjects range from great matters of state to personal lyric, and he commands a variety of metre unequalled among ancient poets.

▷G Showerman, *Horace and his Influence* (1922); G Wilson, *Horace* (1972)

HORGAN, Paul
(1903–)

American Roman Catholic poet, historian, critic, essayist and, chiefly, novelist, born in Buffalo, New York. His major work is the trilogy of novels consisting of *Things as They Are*, *Everything to Live For* and *The Thin Mountain Air* (1964–77), set in Philadelphia and New Mexico. For his history of the Rio Grande, *The Great River* (1954), he was awarded a Pulitzer Prize. Horgan's style is undistinguished, but his achievement has probably been underestimated by critics. He is an authority on Lincoln, Beethoven and Stravinsky, of whom he was a friend.

HORNE, Donald Richmond
(1921–)

Australian writer, born in New South Wales, one of Australia's most original and influential writers. The author of *The Lucky Country* (1964), he became associate Professor of Political Studies at the University of New South Wales. His other books have included *The Permit* (1965), *Money Made Us* (1976), *Death of The Lucky Country* (1976), *His Excellency's Pleasure* (1977), *Right Way, Don't Go Back* (1978), *In Search of Billy Hughes* (1979), *Time of Hope* (1980), *Winner Takes All* (1981), *The Great Museum* (1984), *Confessions of a New Boy* (1985), *A History of the Australian People* (1985), *The Public Culture* (1986) and *The Lucky Country We Visited* (1987).

▷*The Education of Young Donald* (1968)

HORNE, Richard Henry 'Hengist'
(1803–84)

English writer. He was educated at Sandhurst, and served in the Mexican navy and did his share of fighting at Vera Cruz, San Juan Ulloa and elsewhere. Having survived yellow fever, sharks, broken ribs, shipwreck, mutiny and fire, he returned to England and took up writing. He was the author of the epic *Orion* (1843), which he published at the price of one farthing to show his contempt for a public that would not buy poetry. In 1852 he went to Australia as commissioner for crown lands, and became a person of consequence in Victoria and published *Australian Facts and Prospects* and *Australian Autobiography* (1859). He returned to England in 1869. Among his books are *A New Spirit of the Age* (1844), in which **Elizabeth Barrett Browning** helped him, and two tragedies, *Cosmo de' Medici* (1837) and *The Death of Marlowe* (1837).

▷A Blainey, *The Farthing Poet: Richard Hengist Horn* (1968)

HORNER, Lance
(1903–70)
ONSTOTT, Kyle
(1887–1966)

American popular novelists, specializing in heavily prurient tales of sex, sadism and miscegenation on Southern plantations. Onstott, who was a highly successful dog breeder, only contributed to *Mandingo* (1957), which was the first of the 'Falconhurst' cycle that Horner continued on his own with *Drum* (1962) and many others (all of which included the name Falconhurst in their titles). Overwrought, politically incorrect and shapeless, the books nonetheless enjoyed considerable success and have remained in print long past their apparent sell-by date.

HORNUNG, Ernest William
(1866–1921)

English novelist, born in Middlesbrough. Brother-in-law of **Arthur Conan Doyle**, he was the creator of Raffles, the gentleman burglar, hero of *The Amateur Cracksman* (1899), *Mr Justice Raffles* (1909) and many other adventure stories.

HORTATZIS, Georgias
(fl.1590)

Cretan poet and tragedian, born in Rethymno, who was the leading voice of his island when it was under Venetian occupation. He is one of the great names in the history of the post-classical theatre of Greece. Hortatziz, contemporary to the great artist Domenico Theotokopoulos (El Greco),

HORVÁTH, Ödön von

transformed what had been a local idiom into a true literary language. He must have gathered his great classical learning in Italy, probably from the University of Padua. It is known for certain that he wrote three dramatic works: *Erofili* (tragedy), *Katzourbos* (comedy) and *Gyparis* (pastoral); there are English translations of these in J Mavrogordato, *Three Cretan Plays* (1929).

HORVÁTH, Ödön von
(1901–38)

Austro–Hungarian, German-speaking dramatist, born in Fiume (now Rijeka in Yugoslavia). After being banned by the Nazis in the 1930s, Horváth's plays remained neglected in Germany until the 1950s and were almost unknown in Britain until **Christopher Hampton** began translating them during the 1970s. *Ges Chichten aus dem Wiener Wald* (1931, Eng trans *Tales from the Vienna Woods*, 1977) presents a wry and resigned picture of lower middle-class life, while *Don Juan kommt aus dem Kreig* (1936, Eng trans *Don Juan Comes Back From The War*, 1978), portrays Don Juan as a disillusioned warrior. Throughout his writing, Horváth paints a critical picture of bourgeois greed and what he suggests is the herd-like stupidity of those seduced by economic or political lures. One day during his exile in Paris, he sheltered from a storm beneath a tree in the Champs Elysées. When a branch snapped and struck him on the head, he died instantly.
▷I Huish, *A Student's Guide to Horvath* (1980)

HOSPITAL, Janette Turner
(1942–)

Australian novelist and short-story writer, born in Melbourne then brought up in Queensland. Her debut, *The Ivory Swing*, won Canada's Seal First Novel Award in 1982. She spends part of each year in Canada, and has also lived in India, the USA and Britain. She is currently based in her native city, where she teaches at La Trobe University. Her nomadic existence has informed her work: the theme of being displaced, of belonging somewhere else, looms large in, for instance, both the metaphysical thriller *Borderlines* (1985) and the aptly-named short-story collection *Dislocations* (1986).

HOSTOVSKY, Egon
(1908–73)

Czech novelist, who spent much of his life in exile—after 1948 in the USA. Much influenced by **Graham Greene**, he wrote intelligent and exciting thriller-type novels, of which *Spiknuti* (1964, Eng trans *The Plot*, 1961) is an excellent example.

HOUDAR DE LA MOTTE, Antoine
(1672–1731)

French critic, poet and playwright, who, despite his blindness and paralysis, was a considerable literary personage in his day. He believed that poetry could be expressed in prose (it has been said that this was because he could not write poetry), and has been called dull and unimaginative. But in *Inès de Castro* (1723), the most successful play of the 17th century in France, but not taken seriously today, he departed from his own theories. He was in essence a disciple of **Fontenelle**, and took the side of the moderns in the celebrated *Querelle* between ancients and moderns.

HOUEDARD, Dom Sylvester, known as dsh
(1924–92)

British poet, priest, Benedictine monk and scholar, born in Guernsey. He was the literary editor for the *New Testament Jerusalem Bible* (1967), and at his death was completing the late George Melhuish's *On Death and the Double Nature of Nothingness*. He instigated and contributed to the annual Interfaith conferences at the Samye Ling Monastery, Dumfriesshire, Scotland, and founded, with Bob Cobbing, *The Association of Little Presses* (1965). Under the lower case designation 'dsh' he published during the 1960s and 70s over 1 000 'typetracts'. *12 Nahuatl Dancepoems from the Cosmic Typewriter* (1969) combined his innovative manner of text design with the verbal vision of a 'songdrunk/bird'. *Begin Again: a book of reflections & reversals* (1975) contrasted the silent aspects of his monastic life in Prinknash Abbey, Gloucestershire, with his cosmopolitan usage of the 'multi-valued letter'. Notorious for his appearance in *The Times* (1967) advertisement for the legalization of cannabis ('vive voce the propots') and his attacks on anti-homosexual legislation throughout the 1980s ('advocate the gladguys'), he is justly famous for his work in both Concrete and Sound-Poetry.
▷S Bann (ed), *Concrete Poetry: An International Anthology* (1967)

HOUGH, Emerson
(1857–1923)

American novelist. Hough was born in Iowa and began his career by practising law in New Mexico. His early writing consisted of magazine articles on the outdoor life but not before his mid-forties, with the publication of *The Mississippi Bubble* (1902), could he go fully freelance. This book, like many others he produced, was a historical romance set in the

American West. He also wrote a popular series for boys and was energetic in journalistic support for Yellowstone National Park.

▷ L A Stone, *Emerson Hough: His Place in American Letters* (1925)

HOUGHTON, William Stanley
(1881–1913)

English dramatist and critic, born in Ashton-upon-Mersey. A disciple of **Ibsen**'s, he was a drama critic for *The Manchester Guardian* when his first play, *The Dear Departed*, was staged at the Gaiety Theatre in 1908. His plays focus on everyday Lancashire life. The best of his later works are *The Younger Generation* (1910) and his best-known play, *Hindle Wakes* (1912).

HOULT, Norah
(1898–1986)

Irish novelist. She first made her mark with the grimly naturalistic and feminist stories in *Poor Women* (1928), and followed this up with the impressive *Holy Ireland* (1935), a massive novel of Irish life. In *There Were No Windows* (1944), her last novel of real note, she told a story based on the last unhappy years of **Violet Hunt**, once companion to **Ford Madox Ford**. *Selected Stories* (1946) reprints most of her best tales. Now neglected as an author, at her best Hoult reached the level achieved by **Christina Stead** and **Henry Handel Richardson**, from whom she learned much in her youth. In such work as *Four Women Grow Up* (1940) she could be sentimental, although she was always readable and sensible; but in other books, such as *Time, Gentlemen, Time!* (1930), she was sharp and the very opposite of sentimental.

HOUSEHOLD, Geoffrey Edward West
(1900–88)

English novelist, whose inside knowledge of military intelligence and political power-broking fuels his simply but subtly crafted adventure stories. Household has suggested the influence of **Robert Louis Stevenson** and **Conrad**; readers may find links with **John Buchan** and **John Le Carré**. By far his best-known book was his second, *Rogue Male* (1939, published in the USA as *Man Hunt*, 1942), an atmospheric survivalist thriller set in the English West Country. Later books include *A Rough Shoot* (1951) and *The Courtesy of Death* (1967), but the pace curiously slackened when Houschold began to move his adventures to more exotic settings. However, he continued to write novels well into the 1980s. He also published several short-story collections, of which *The Salvation of Pisco Gabar* (1938, extended US edn 1940) stands out, and juvenile fiction, notably

The Terror of Villadonga (1936, revised for US and subsequent editions as *The Spanish Cave*, 1936).

▷ *Against the Wind* (1958)

HOUSMAN, A(lfred) E(dward)
(1859–1936)

English scholar and poet, born in Fockbury, Worcestershire, brother of **Laurence Housman**. Educated at Bromsgrove School, he won a scholarship to St John's College, Oxford, where he failed in Greats finals and entered the Patent Office. Nevertheless he became a distinguished classical scholar, and in 1892 he was appointed Professor of Latin at University College, London, and Professor of Latin at Cambridge from 1911. He published critical editions of **Manilius** (1903–30), **Juvenal** (1905) and **Lucan** (1926). He is known primarily by his poetry, notably *A Shropshire Lad* (1896), which grew to be immensely popular after an indifferent initial reception, *Last Poems* (1922), and *More Poems*, published posthumously in 1936. Eighteen more appeared in *Laurence Housman's Memoir* (1937), and his *Collected Poems* appeared in 1939. The lyrics in *A Shropshire Lad* are arranged roughly to form a cyclical poem in which an uprooted country lad recalls the innocence and pleasures but also, and more poignantly, the frustrations and local tragedies of a countryside which is only an imagined Shropshire and indeed hardly pastoral in the old sense at all.

▷ I Kilvert, *A. E. Housman* (1955)

HOUSMAN, Laurence
(1865–1959)

English novelist and dramatist, younger brother of **A E Housman**, born in Bromsgrove. He studied art at Lambeth and South Kensington, and attracted attention by his illustrations of **George Meredith**'s poem 'Jump-to-Glory Jane'. He is best known for his *Little Plays of St Francis* (1922) and his Victorian biographical 'chamber plays', notably *Angels and Ministers* (1921) and *Victoria Regina* (1937). His novels included *Trimblerigg* (1924), a satire on Lloyd George, and he also published books of verse, including *An Englishwoman's Loveletters* (1900). His autobiography, *The Unexpected Years* (1937), reveals a romantic Victorian figure, a Conservative radical who espoused pacificism and votes for women.

▷ *The Unexpected Years* (1937)

HOVEY, Richard
(1864–1900)

American poet and dramatist, born in Normal, Illinois. Hovey, in turn brilliant graduate of Dartmouth, converted Christian,

dandy and precocious poet and actor, tried, after a visit to Europe at the beginning of the 1890s, to become the American **Oscar Wilde**. He eventually became a professor of English literature at Barnard College. His best-known poetry was written in collaboration with his friend the Canadian poet **Bliss Carman** in the three collections of *Songs of Vagabondia* (1891–1901); but none of his work has lasted.
▷A H MacDonald, *Richard Hovey, Man and Craftsman* (1956)

HOWARD, Edward
(d.1841)

English novelist, a navy lieutenant. On his retirement he wrote sea stories, including *Rattlin the Reefer* (1836) and *Outward Bound* (1838).

HOWARD, Elizabeth Jane
(1923–)

English novelist, born in London and briefly an actress and a model before turning to arts administration and then writing. Her first novel, *The Beautiful Visit* (1950), set during and after World War I, looks at a young woman's attempts to escape her repressive family and to travel and write. War also features in *After Julius* (1965), which deals with the effects of a man's death at Dunkirk on his widow and daughters several years later. Subsequent novels, such as *Something in Disguise* (1969), also look at various aspects of love and marriage. Others, such as the series about the Cazalet family of which *Confusion* (1993) is the most recent, are set in the earlier years of the 20th century, and have an equally strong sense of time and place.

HOWARD, Henry, Earl of Surrey
(c.1517–1547)

English poet, son of the Duke of Norfolk. The Howards were the most powerful Catholic family in England at the time of the English Reformation under Henry VIII, and Henry Howard had to keep a low profile to avoid being caught up in the intrigue surrounding the events of that time. After a successful career as a young aristocrat, he implicated himself in a plot to further his father's cause and was imprisoned in the Tower of London, where he wrote much of his best verse. Particularly notable is his translation of parts of **Virgil**'s *Aeneid*, which is the earliest surviving example of the use of blank verse in English. His other poetry, much of it of considerable merit, is widely anthologized and was first published in 1557 in the *Miscellany* of Richard Tottel and Nicholas Grimald.

HOWARD, Richard Joseph
(1929–)

Prolific American poet, dramatist and notable translator of modern French literature (both fiction and non-fiction), born in Cleveland, Ohio. His own early work was influenced by **Auden**. He likes to write clever dramatic monologues, as in 'November 1889' from *Findings* (1971), a poem spoken by **Browning**. 'Move Still, Still So', from a more recent collection, features one of **Lewis Carroll**'s child models, speaking from her psychiatrist's couch in 1925.

HOWARD, Sir Robert
(1626–98)

English Restoration dramatist, son of the 1st Earl of Berkshire. His plays include *The Committee* (1663) and the *Indian Queen* (1664), the latter assisted by his brother-in-law, **Dryden**. His brothers Edward and James were also dramatists. He abandoned the theatre in 1668.
▷H Oliver, *Sir Robert Howard* (1963)

HOWARD, Sydney Coe
(1891–1939)

American dramatist, born in Oakland, California. After serving in World War I, he became a journalist in New York. His first stage success came in 1924 with *They Knew What They Wanted*, about the fate of a middle-aged Italian and his bride in the grape-growing district of California. It won a Pulitzer Prize. Prolific both as an original dramatist and a translator, his other plays include *The Silver Cord* (1926), dealing with maternal possessiveness, and *Yellow Jack* (1934), written with Paul de Kruiff, rather worthily recounting the research into the identification of the cause of yellow fever. Although to many Howard's might not be an instantly familiar name, his talents as the author of the screenplay of **Margaret Mitchell**'s *Gone With The Wind* (1939) have engaged millions.

HOWATCH, Susan
(1940–)

English novelist, born in Leatherhead, Surrey. She had published six novels before achieving success in 1971 with *Penmarric*, a romantic saga about three generations of a Cornish family, owners of a tin mine, and dwellers in a grand house which stands atop a cliff. Such novels as *The Rich are Different* (1977) maintained her popularity with the same formula of glamour, romance and riches until, in 1979, a BBC television adaptation of *Penmarric* introduced her to a new readership and gave her career a second wind. Her later works include a series of novels, among them *Ultimate Prizes* (1989), about the present-day Church of England.

HOWE, E(dgar) W(atson)
(1853–1937)

American journalist and novelist. He was born in the Indianan back-country, near Treaty, and brought up in Missouri, where he worked as printer's devil on his father's newspaper, the *Union of States*, followed by printing jobs throughout the prairie states. In 1873 he became publisher of the *Globe* in Golden, Colorado, and later (1877) co-founded with his brother another *Globe* in Atchison, Texas, which he edited until 1910. His most significant book, *The Story of a Country Town* (1883), is a melodramatic but vivid tale of jealousy set in the Missouri badlands. None of his later fiction has the same concentrated quality, though there are fine moments in both *An Ante-Mortem Statement* and *The Confession of John Whitlock, Late Preacher of the Gospel* (both 1891). For nearly 35 years Howe concentrated on newspaper work, travel writing, and the stolidly philosophical aphorisms gathered in *Country Town Sayings* (1911), which gained him the title of 'The Sage of Potato Hill'. That year, he established *E W Howe's Monthly* in Atchison, editing it until four years before his death. Other volumes of sayings include *Notes for My Biographer*, *Preaching from the Audience*, *Sinner Sermons* (all 1926) and *The Indignations of E W Howe* (1933).
▷ *Plain People* (1929); C Pickett, *E W Howe: Country Town Philosopher* (1968)

HOWE, Julia, née Ward
(1819–1910)

American feminist, reformer and writer, born in New York, wife of Samuel Gridley Howe. A wealthy banker's daughter, she became a prominent suffragette and abolitionist, and founded the New England Woman Suffrage Association (1868) and the New England Women's Club (1868). She published several volumes of poetry, including *Passion Flowers* (1854) and *Words for the Hour* (1857), as well as travel books and a play. She also wrote the 'Battle Hymn of the Republic' (published in *Atlantic Monthly*, 1862), and edited *Woman's Journal* (1870–90). In 1908 she became the first woman to be elected to the American Academy of Arts and Letters.
▷ L Richards, *Julia Ward Howe* (1916)

HOWELLS, William Dean
(1837–1920)

American novelist and critic, born in Martin's Ferry, Ohio. He became a compositor in a printing office from 1856 to 1861 on the staff of the *Ohio State Journal*. Stimulated by the works of **Cervantes**, **Pope** and **Heinrich Heine**, he began to write poetry which was published in the *Atlantic Monthly* (1860–1), which he later edited (1871–81). His biography of Lincoln (1860) managed to procure for him the post of US consul in Venice (1861–5). His association with *Harper's Magazine* (1886–91) made him the King of critics in America, writing an *Easy Chair* column for *Harper's* from 1900 to 1920. The 'reticent realism' of his early novels, as in the slight *Their Wedding Journey* (1872), matured in depth of feeling in *The Lady of the Aroostook* (1879) and finally gave way to **Tolstoyan** humanitarian naturalism in his masterpiece, *The Rise of Silas Lapham* (1885), a study of a flawed self-made man, and *A Hazard of New Fortunes* (1890) about the founding of a new magazine. His theories of fiction, which influenced **Mark Twain**, **Henry James** and **Oliver Wendell Holmes**, were expounded in *Criticism and Fiction* (1891). He also wrote the autobiographical *Years of my Youth* (1915) and *Literary Friends* (1900).
▷ K S Lynn, *William Dean Howells: an American life* (1971)

HOWES, Barbara
(1914–)

American poet, born in New York, and (1947–65) wife to **William Jay Smith**. She is a formal lyrical poet, but forthright within the limitations she sets for herself. *A Private Signal* (1977) is a selection from all her poetry to the date of its publication. She has been influenced by **Emily Dickinson**, old French poetry, and by **Genevieve Taggard**.
▷ L Bogan, *Selected Criticism* (1955)

HOWES, Edith
(?1874–1954)

New Zealand writer for children, whose early titles, such as *The Sun's Babies* (1910) and *Fairy Rings* (1911), indicate her style. Although publishing for overseas markets, she introduced local elements in *Where Bell-Birds Chime* (1912) and *Maoriland Fairy Tales* (1913), and was immensely popular between the wars. A teacher of science and botany, she used her stories to pass on instruction, in *The Cradle Ship* (1916) on the facts of life, and in *The Singing Fish* (1921) on equality between the sexes. Her 'real-life' books such as *Silver Island: A New Zealand Story* (1928) and *Young Pioneers* (1934) demonstrate the survival value of a knowledge of nature.

HOWITT, William
(1792–1879)
HOWITT, Mary
(1799–1888)

English educational writers, both born of Quaker stock, though in later life Mary converted to the Roman Catholic Church. In collaboration they wrote many books of popular instruction, including a book of verse *The Book of the Seasons, or, The Calendar of Nature* (1831), *Ruined Abbeys of Great Britain* and their most successful work, *A Popular History of England* (1856–64). Their prolific output covered poetry, fiction, history and social and economic issues. Howitt spent some time in Australia with his two sons and subsequently wrote *Land, Labour and Gold: Or, Two Years in Victoria* (1855) and *The History of Discovery in Australia, Tasmania, and New Zealand* (1865). The former is considered one of the most accurate, yet engaging, portraits of the Australia of the gold-rush era. His other books include *A Popular History of Priestcraft* (1833) and *Rural Life in England* (1838). Mary wrote a *Popular History of the United States*, translated **Hans Christian Andersen**'s *Improvisatore* and, in 1846, his fairy tales under the title *Wonderful Stories for Children*.

HOYLE, Sir Fred
(1915–)

English astronomer and science-fiction writer, born in Bingley, Yorkshire. He was Plumian Professor of Astronomy at Cambridge University until 1973, and an eminent espouser of the Solid State theory of the creation of the universe, which he advocated with passion in his non-fiction books, beginning with *The Nature of the Universe* (1950). He published his first novel, *The Black Cloud*, in 1957. His science fiction shows a curious disregard for scientific plausibility or accuracy, but gives free rein to his imagination, and allows him to create worlds less intractable to his political and scientific views than the real one. Most of his fiction was written in collaboration with his son, Geoffrey Hoyle (1942–).
▷ *The Small World of Fred Hoyle* (1986)

HRABAL, Bohumil
(1914–)

Czech prose writer, who did not begin to publish until he was almost 50. He first became controversial amongst Stalinist conservatives with his earliest work, in 1963; then again, amongst decent Czechs, when he gave public support to the Soviet puppet Husák (who had suppressed his writings). It soon became clear that his support was ironic, since he had unpublishable typescript material in circulation. His most famous work is still *Ostre sledované vlaky* (1965, Eng trans *Closely Watched Trains*, 1968), although this critical account of a young World War II hero is the most conventional of his books. He writes in the tradition of **Jaroslav Hašek**, but is far more deliberately sophisticated and literary. *Closely Watched Trains* became a famous movie. A further volume in English translation is *The Death of Mr Baltisberger* (1975).

HRISTOV, Kiril
(1875–1944)

Bulgarian poet, born in Stara Zagora. Although he lived most of his life in exile, he was a central figure in his country's emerging literature, as dramatist and story writer as well as poet. His lyrical poetry, of a classical kind, was uninhibited and technically well accomplished.
▷ C Manning, and R Smal-Stocki, *The History of Modern Bulgarian Literature* (1960)

HROSTWITHA (also Roswita or Hroswita or Hroswitha)
(fl.10th century)

German playwright and Benedictine nun, of Gandersheim, near Göttingen. She is the author of six comedies in Latin (*Gallicanus, Dulcitus, Callimachus, Abraham, Pafnutius,* and *Sapientia*) which are closely modelled on the work of **Terence**, but are Christian in theme. As the first known plays by a woman, they are of great historical importance. Furthermore, the verse in which they are written is lively and witty; her works are ripe for a long-overdue revival.

HSU Chih-mo
(1895–1931)

Chinese poet, critic and academic, educated in Peking and Britain. On his return to China he took up a number of academic posts, eventually becoming professor of literature at Peking University, and founding the liberal 'Modern Review' group of poets and writers. Like **Wen I-to**, he was a formalist, stressing the importance of structure and technique in verse, often, his detractors would claim, at the expense of content. Some idea of the austere beauty of his work can be gleaned from *Poems*, posthumously published in translation in Peking. He was killed in an aeroplane crash at Tsinafu.

HUBBARD, L(afayette) Ron(ald)
(1911–86)

American Scientologist and science-fiction writer, born in Tilden, Nebraska, and the inspiration behind the Church of Scientology. From the age of 16 he travelled extensively in the Far East before completing his education at Woodward Preparatory School and George Washington University. He became a professional writer of adventure stories, turning to science fiction in 1938, with such classics as *Slaves of Sleep* (1939), *Fear* (1940), *Final Blackout* (1940), *Death's Deputy* (1940) and *Typewriter in the Sky* (1940). He served in the US navy during World War II, and in 1950 published *Dianetics: The Modern Science of Mental Health*, which claimed to be pioneering in its exploration of the human mind and its detailed description of how the mind works. This was followed by *Science of Survival* (1951), which formed the basis of the Scientology philosophy which has made a significant impact on many American artists. The first Church of Scientology was founded by a group of adherents in Los Angeles in 1954; in 1955 Hubbard became the executive director of the Founding Church Washington. From 1959 to 1966 he made his base in East Grinstead in England, and resigned his position as executive director of the church in 1966. In 1982 he returned to science fiction with an epic bestseller, *Battlefield Earth: A Saga of the Year 3000*, followed by a 10-volume series under the composite title *Mission Earth* (1985–87).

▷R Miller, *Bare-Faced Messiah: the true story of L. Ron Hubbard* (1987)

HUBER, Therese
(1764–1829)

Prolific German novelist and journalist, born in Göttingen. Her father, C G Heyne, was a distinguished professor, but Huber herself had no formal education. She abandoned her first husband, Georg Foster, an explorer and travel writer, for her lover L F Huber. She obtained a divorce from Foster in 1793, a year before his death in Paris, where he had become painfully disillusioned with the realities of the French Revolution. Until his death, she published all her work under her second husband's name. Her novel *Die Familie Seldorf* (1795) is an early female *Bildungsroman*.

HUCH, Ricarda
(1864–1947)

German novelist, historian and feminist, born in Brunswick into a wealthy Protestant merchant family. She studied history at Zürich, taught at a girls' school there, travelled extensively in Italy, married (unhappily) twice, and finally settled in Munich in 1910. A neo-romantic, she rejected naturalism, and wrote novels including the semi-autobiographical *Erinnerungen von Ludolf Ursleu dem Jüngeren* (1893, 'Memoirs of Ludolf Ursleu the Younger') and *Aus der Triumphgasse* (1902, 'Out of Triumph Lane'), criticism including *Die Blütezeit, Ausbreitung und Verfall der Romantik* (1899–1902, 'The Blossoming, Spread and Decline of Romanticism'), and social and political works including *Der Grosse Krieg in Deutschland* (1912–14, 'The Great War in Germany'). She also wrote on religious themes, in *Luthers Glaube* (1915, 'Beliefs of Luther') and *Das Zeitalter der Glaubenspaltung* (1937, 'The Age of Schism'). The first woman to be admitted to the Prussian Academy of Literature in 1931, she resigned in 1933 over the expulsion of Jewish writers. She lived in Jena during World War II.

▷H Baumgarten, *Ricarda Huch* (1968)

HUCHEL, Peter
(1903–81)

German poet and editor, born in Berlin. He withdrew a planned collection of his already well regarded poetry in 1933 as a protest against the Nazi seizure of power. After World War II, in which he served and was taken prisoner on the Russian front, he became East Germany's most liberal and dignified man of letters, and courageous editor of the magazine *Sinn und Form*. Dismissed from this post as not sufficiently dedicated to socialist realism, he eventually (1971) emigrated to West Germany. He was a Symbolist poet in the tradition of **Wilhelm Lehmann** and **Oscar Loerke**, drawing his imagery from nature; but his awareness of his times and his disillusion with the policies of the East German government (whose early reforms he had welcomed) gradually penetrated into his verse; he ended as perhaps the most admired German poet of his generation.

▷J Flores, *Poetry in East Germany* (1971)

HUDSON, William Henry
(1841–1922)

American-born British author and naturalist, of Argentine extraction, born near Buenos Aires. He moved to England in 1869 and became a British subject in 1900. His early writings concerned the natural history of South America, but he is best known for his delightful account of his rambles in the New Forest in *Hampshire Days* (1903) and his romantic novel *Green Mansions* (1904). His ornithological works include *Birds in London* (1898), *Birds of La Plata* (1920), *The Book of a Naturalist* (1919), and *Rare, vanishing and lost British Birds* (1923). A bird sanctuary, containing Sir Jacob Epstein's 'Rima' sculpture, was erected to his memory in Hyde Park, London (1925).

HUERTA, Vicente García de la
(1730–87)

Spanish poet and critic, born in Zafra. He was head of the Royal Library in Madrid. His famous tragedy of *Raquel* (1778) was based upon the story of Alfonso VIII's love for the beautiful Jewess, Rachel.

HUGH PRIMAS
(fl.1150)

French Latin poet, associated mainly with the town of Orléans. A satirist, like **Walter of Châtillon**, he often employed the Goliardic measure. We know from his often clever and amusing poetry that he was not of noble birth, and that he was dogged by money troubles all his life, but his habit of attacking in verse those on whom he relied for a living could scarcely have helped him. He is thought to have died in poverty in the hospice at Orleans.

HUGHES, David John
(1930–)

English novelist, born in Alton, Hampshire and educated at Oxford. He has worked widely as a magazine editor, documentary and feature-film writer, and film critic. His books include *A Feeling in the Air* (1957), *Memories of Dying* (1976) and *The Imperial German Dinner Service* (1983), demanding fictions revealing a fascination for interior reality and the historical process. Two of his best-known books, *The Pork Butcher* (1984) and *But for Bunter* (1985), consider this theme in markedly different ways. The first examines the German destruction of a French village in retaliation for the killing of a German soldier, while in the second, an elderly man purporting to have been the model for Billy Bunter, the Fat Owl of the Remove at Greyfriars School, presents his account of 20th-century British history. At each critical turn, Bunter himself is found to have played a crucial role.

HUGHES, Hatcher
(1883–1945)

American playwright, born in North Carolina. He was a professor of drama at Columbia University. His play *Hell Bent For Heaven*, a drama set in a mountain community in North Carolina, won the Pulitzer Prize for Drama in 1924. His other works include *Wake Up, Jonathan* (1921), co-authored with **Elmer Rice**, the comedy *Ruint* (1925), which returned to a mountain community setting, and *The Lord Blesses the Bishop* (1934).

HUGHES, John
(1677–1720)

English essayist, dramatist and poet, born in Marlborough, Wiltshire. Hughes worked as a clerk in the Ordnance Office and wrote for the *Tatler* and *Spectator*. **Joseph Addison** was

an admirer of the plays, the most striking being *The Siege of Damascus*. The play excited the author too. He died on its opening night.

HUGHES, (James Mercer) Langston
(1902–67)

American poet, short-story writer and dramatist, born in Joplin, Missouri, and educated at Lincoln University, Pennsylvannia. Throughout the 1920s he was a leading figure in the Black renaissance, but his influence was belatedly recognized. *Weary Blues* (1926) was his first of several collections of verse, culminating in *Selected Poems* (1959). His memorable character, 'Jesse B Simple', first made his entrance in racy newspaper sketches and thereafter in several volumes before the publication in 1957 of *The Best of Simple*. His lyrical verse, resonant of his vast knowledge of folk culture, jazz, the blues and colloquial speech, was highly popular and made him famous, but critics were slow to take him seriously. *The Big Sea* (1940) and *I Wonder as I Wander* (1956) are autobiographical.
▷M Meltzner, *Langston Hughes* (1968)

HUGHES, Monica
(1925–)

English-born children's author, born in Liverpool. She emigrated to Canada in 1952, where she has become especially known for her understanding depiction of adolescent characters and for her science fiction. The 'Isis' trilogy, her best-known work, typifies her narrative approach: visitors from one culture (planet) to another force re-evaluation; new perspectives on life are discovered; readers are instructed. As a didactic novelist she is considered very 'suitable'.

HUGHES, Richard Arthur Warren
(1900–76)

English novelist, born in Weybridge, Surrey, of Welsh descent. He was educated at Charterhouse and Oriel College, Oxford. He wrote poetry and plays from an early age, co-founded and directed the Portmadoc (Caernarvonshire) Players (1922–5), wrote a one-act play, *The Sister's Tragedy* (1922), and a volume of verse, *Gypsy Night and Other Poems*, in the same year, followed by *Confessio Juvenis* (1925). He travelled widely in Europe, America and the West Indies, and eventually settled in Wales. He is best known for *A High Wind in Jamaica* (1929, entitled *The Innocent Voyage* in the USA), a superior adventure yarn about a family of children captured by pirates while sailing to England. In *Hazard: A Sea Story* (1938) he also drew on his experience of the sea. Of his later work, *The Fox in the Attic* (1961), and *The Wooden*

Shepherdess (1973), the first of an unfinished series covering the period from World War I to the rise of the Nazis and their aftermath, were significant.

▷P Thomas, *Richard Hughes* (1973)

HUGHES, Shirley
(1919–)

English writer and illustrator for children, born in Lancashire. She began as an illustrator of other people's works, but by 1960 she was writing her own books for young children. *Lucy and Tom's Day*, produced in that year, was the first of six volumes about those two children. There followed a number of works about Alfie, a grubby but lovable chub, including *Alfie's Feet* (1982), the comic tale of the eponymous urchin's pedal appendages. Her other works, light and gleeful, but realistic, include *Here Comes Charlie Moon* (1980).

HUGHES, Ted (Edward James)
(1930–)

English poet, born in Mytholmroyd, a mill town in West Yorkshire. When he was seven his family moved to Mexborough, Yorkshire, where his parents opened a stationery and tobacco shop. At the local grammar school he began to write poetry—bloodcurdling verses about Zulus and cowboys. He won a scholarship to Pembroke College, Cambridge, where he opted for English literature, but switched to archaeology and anthropology, which was to have a profound effect on his poetry. After graduating he had a number of colourful jobs—zookeeper, gardener, nightwatchman—and occasionally published poems in university poetry magazines. He married the American writer **Sylvia Plath** in 1956 and they settled in Cambridge where Hughes taught while Plath studied. That same year he won an American poetry competition, judged by **W H Auden**, Sir **Stephen Spender** and **Marianne Moore**, with the poems that were to form *The Hawk in the Rain* (1957). For the next few years he lived in America where he taught and was supported by a Guggenheim Foundation grant. *Lupercal* (1960), his second collection, won the **Somerset Maugham** Award and the Hawthornden Prize. In 1963 Sylvia Plath committed suicide and for the next few years no new book of adult verse emerged, though he did complete books of prose and poetry for children. *Wodwo* (1967) was his next major work, and in 1970 came *Crow*, an evocation of a mythical, symbolic bird and witness to the history of man and his destruction. Among later volumes are *Cave Birds* (1975), *Season Songs* (1976), *Gaudete* (1977), *Moortown* (1979), *The Remains of Elmet* (1979), on which he collaborated with the photographer

Fay Godwin, and *Wolfwatching* (1989). Of his books for children, the most remarkable is *The Iron Man* (1968). Drawn magnetically towards the primitive, he is a writer at one with nature, mesmerized by its beauty but not blind to its cruelty and violence. Much acclaimed and imitated, he was appointed poet laureate in 1984, and published the collection *Rain-Charm for the Duchy and other Laureate Poems* in 1992.

▷T West, *Ted Hughes* (1985)

HUGHES, Thomas
(1822–96)

English reformer and novelist, born in Uffington, Berkshire. He was educated at Rugby and Oriel College, Oxford, was called to the Bar in 1848, and became a county court judge in 1882. He was Liberal MP (1865–74), was closely associated with the Christian Socialists, supported trade unionism, and helped to found the Working Men's College, of which he was principal from 1872 to 1883, and a model settlement in Tennessee, USA. He is primarily remembered as the author of the semi-autobiographical public school classic, *Tom Brown's Schooldays* (1856), based on his school experiences at Rugby under the headmastership of Dr Thomas Arnold. The sequel, *Tom Brown at Oxford* (1861), was less successful. He also wrote a number of biographies and social studies.

▷E C Mack and W H G Armytage, *Thomas Hughes* (1952)

HUGO, Richard
(1923–82)

American poet, born in Seattle where, for 12 years, he worked for the Boeing air company. He later became Professor of English at the University of Montana. His early poems were marked by a linguistic compression akin to **Emily Dickinson** (see the 6-line poem 'Somersby' in *The Lady in Kicking Horse Reservoir*, 1973), but later work, found in *31 Letters and 13 Dreams* (1977), became more sprawlingly confessional.

HUGO, Victor Marie
(1802–85)

French poet and author, and leader of the French Romantic movement, born in Besançon, the son of a general. He was educated in Paris at the Feuillantines, in Madrid, and at the École Polytechnique. At the age of 14 he produced a tragedy; and at 20, when he published his first set of *Odes et Ballades* (1822), he had been victor three times at the Floral Games of Toulouse. In 1823 he published *Han d'Islande* (Eng trans *Han of Iceland*, 1825), a wild romance of an impossible Iceland; and followed it with *Bug-Jargal*

471

(1824, Eng trans *The Slave King*, 1833), a second set of *Odes et ballades* (1826), and *Cromwell* (1827), a play whose preface set out Hugo's poetical creed. In 1828 his *Orientales* revealed him as a master of rhythms. In 1830 came *Hernani* (Eng trans 1830)—the first of those 'five-act lyrics' of which Hugo's drama is composed. In 1831 he produced one of his best-known novels, *Notre-Dame de Paris* (Eng trans *The Hunchback of Notre-Dame*, 1833), an outstanding historical romance, and *Les Feuilles d'automne* ('Autumn Leaves'), which includes some of his best poetry and his best play, *Marion Delorme* (Eng trans *The King's Edict*, 1872). *Le Roi s'amuse* (1832, Eng trans 1843), which was banned, is superbly written, and as Verdi's opera *Rigoletto* has become universally popular. *Lucrèce Borgia* (Eng trans *Lucretia Borgia*, 1847) and *Marie Tudor* followed in 1833. In 1834 came *Claude Gueux*, which is pure humanitarian sentimentalism, and the *Littérature et philosophie mêlées* ('Literature and Philosophy Combined'), a collection of his youthful writings in prose. In 1835 came *Angelo* (Eng trans *Angelo*, ·1855), a third melodrama in prose, and the admirable *Chants du crépuscule* (Eng trans *Songs of Twilight*, 1836), and in 1836 the opera of *La Esmeralda*, by Dargomizhsky. In 1837 *Les Voix intérieures* ('Inner Voices') appeared, in which the poet's diction is held by some to have found its noblest expression, and in 1838 *Ruy Blas* (Eng trans 1860), after *Hernani* the most famous of his dramatic works. In 1840 *Les Rayons et les ombres* ('Sunlight and Shadows'), yet another collection of sonorous verse, appeared. He failed at the Théâtre Français in 1843 with the ponderous trilogy of *Les Burgraves*. During the 1840s he became involved with republican politics, and was elected to the Constituent Assembly in 1848. After the *coup d'état* he was exiled by Napoleon III, and went to Guernsey in the Channel Islands (1851–70) where he issued his satirical *Napoléon le petit* (1852, Eng trans *Napoleon the Little*, 1852). His next book of poetry, *Les Châtiments* (1853, 'The Punishments'), was followed by *Les Contemplations* (1856, 'Contemplations'), the best of his earlier poems, and perhaps his greatest poetic achievement, the *Légende des siècles* (1859, 'Legend of the Centuries'). His greatest novel, *Les Misérables* (Eng trans 1862), a panoramic piece of social history, appeared in 1862. This was followed by the extraordinary rhapsody called *William Shakespeare* (1864, Eng trans 1864), *Les Chansons des rues et des bois* (1865, 'Songs of the Street and the Forest'), the novel *Les Travailleurs de la mer* (Eng trans *Toilers of the Sea*, 1866), an idyll of passion, adventure and self-sacrifice, set in Guernsey (1866), and *L'Homme qui rit* (1869, Eng trans *By*

Order of the King, 1870), a piece of fiction meant to be historical. He returned from Guernsey to Paris in 1870, and stayed through the Commune, but then departed for Brussels, protesting publicly against the action of the Belgian government in respect of the beaten Communards, in consequence of which he was again expelled. In 1872 he published *L'Année terrible* ('The Terrible Year'), a series of poems about the war, and in 1874 his last romance in prose appeared, *Quatre-vingt-treize* (Eng trans *Ninety-Three*, 1874). In 1876 he was made a senator, and published the second part of the *Légende*. *L'Histoire d'un crime* (1877, 'The Story of a Crime') has been described as 'the apotheosis of the Special Correspondent', and *L'Art d'être grand-père* (1877, 'The Art of Being a Grandfather') contains much charming verse. His declining years produced *Le Pape* (1878, 'The Pope', a humanitarian, anticlerical, and above all theatrical, poem), more poetry in the form of *La Pitié suprême* (1879, 'The Greatest Pity'), *L'Âne* (1880, 'The Ass'), *Les Quatre Vents de l'esprit* (1881, 'The Four Winds of the Spirit'), and the play *Torquemada* (1882). He was buried in the Panthéon.

▷A Maurois, *Hugo and His World* (1966); H Peyre, *Hugo, Philosopher and Poet* (1980)

HUIDOBRO, Vicente
(1893–1948)

Chilean poet, publicist, critic, playwright, novelist and biographer, born in Santiago, and one of the most influential figures in Latin-American literature. Huidobro was a flamboyant man, who once stood for the presidency of Chile; but he was also a hugely gifted poet. He wrote in Spanish and in French. He and/or **Reverdy** (it has never been decided who preceded whom) invented the short-lived movement called creationism, which demanded that poems should grow as naturally as trees: 'Why do you sing of the rose, O poets?/Make it blossom in the poem.' Huidobro's critical thinking was first prompted by his response to the innovative side of the *modernismo* of **Darío**, and then to his reading of **Apollinaire** on cubism. It may well be that his 1916–17 visit to Spain, where he tried, 'caudillo-like', to promote cubism and creationism, was the decisive factor in the foundation of ultraism, or *ultráismo* (1919), which eventually led to the seminal essay of **Ortega y Gasset**, *The Dehumanisation of Art*. Huidobro resolutely lived out his private life in public: when he met Ximena Amuntágui, a high school student, in 1925, he announced his passion, and intention to leave his wife and children, in the nation's leading newspaper. But by 1932 and his return to Chile, he was somehow respectable, despite having

become a communist. His novels and bio-graphies are all considerable works, but it is as a lyric poet that he will be remembered: in *Altazor* (written in 1919; published in 1931, definitive text, 1981, Eng trans 1988) and *Temblor de cielo* (1928, 'Quivering Sky'), both prose poems, he wrote what many agree are the most substantial experimental poems of the century. There are many translations: *Arctic Poems* (1974); *The Selected Poetry* (1981); *The Poet is a Little God* (1990).
▷H A Holmes, *Vicente Huidobro and Cre-ationism* (1933); R de Costa, *Vicente Hui-dobro: The Careers of a Poet* (1984)

HULL, E(dith) M(aude)
(early 20th century)

English 'queen of desert romance', about whom very little is known. Her real name was Winstanley and, according to her travel book, *Camping in the Sahara* (1926), she visited Algeria when she was young. Although her life has not been conclusively documented, it is known that she married a gentleman pig-farmer in Derbyshire and wrote *The Sheikh* (1919), her first and enormously popular desert romance, while her husband was away during World War I. The story of an inde-pendent Englishwoman who refuses offers of marriage in order to travel, is captured and raped by a sheik, whom she then marries, it was transformed into film (1921) as a vehicle for Rudolph Valentino. Hull swept on to write *The Sons of the Sheikh* (1925) and *The Lion-Tamer* (1928), equally pulsating stories of exotic romance.

HULME, Keri Ann Ruhi
(1947–)

New Zealand writer of mixed Maori, Orkney and English descent, born in Otautahi, Christchurch. She achieved notice by winning the Booker Prize with her first novel, *The Bone People* (1983), a spell-binding mixing of Maori myth and Christian symbolism. After another novel, *Lost Possessions* (1985), she published a collection of short stories, *Te Kai-hau: The Windeater* (1986). Some of her verse in Maori and English is collected in *The Sil-ences Between* (1982).

HULME, T(homas) E(rnest)
(1883–1917)

English critic, poet and philosopher, born in Endon, Staffordshire. He was educated at Newcastle-under-Lyme High School, and was sent down from St John's College, Cam-bridge, for brawling. After a stay in Canada he taught in Brussels and developed an inter-est in philosophy. He joined **Ezra Pound**, **Wyndham Lewis** and Epstein as a champion

of modern abstract art, of the poetic move-ment known as 'Imagism' (his own small number of surviving poems are in that style) and of the anti-liberal political writings of Georges Sorel, which he translated. Killed in action in France, he left a massive collection of notes, edited under the titles *Speculation* (1924) and *More Speculation* (1956), which expose philistinism and attack what he con-sidered to be weak and outworn liberalism. Most of his poetry appeared in *The New Age* in 1912. He was described by **T S Eliot** as 'classical, reactionary and revolutionary'.
▷M Roberts, *T. E. Hulme* (1982)

HUME, Alexander
(c.1556–1609)

Scots poet, of whom little is known beyond his having been educated at St Andrews and having thereafter spent some time in France. He became a minister during the upheaval and turmoil caused by the Scottish Refor-mation, and his Scots poetry reflects this and Hume's own religious commitment in its preaching, sermonly tone. His best-known poem is 'Of the Day Estivall' ('Of the Summer Solstice'), in his collection *Hymnes, or Sacred Songs, wherein the richt use of poesie might be espied*, which was published in Edinburgh in 1599. There is, perhaps, a certain tension between the subtitle of the collection and its somewhat plodding content.

HUME, Fergus
(1859–1932)

English writer. Brought up in Dunedin, New Zealand, he was called to the New Zealand Bar and practised as a lawyer. He was a pion-eer of the detective story in *The Mystery of a Hansom Cab* (1887), and returned to England in 1888, where he published around 140 other detective novels, including *The Bishop's Sec-ret* (1900) and *The Caravan Mystery* (1926).

HUM-ISHU-MA *see* MOURNING DOVE

HUMPHREY, William
(1924–)

American novelist and short-story writer, born in Clarksville, Texas. After studying at Southern Methodist University and the Uni-versity of Texas at Austin, he taught in New York State and elsewhere, then spent some years in Italy. *The Last Husband and Other Stories* (1953) draws on the life of com-munities in rural Texas, addressing such themes as adolescence, male pride, and adult-ery. These themes were developed in *Home from the Hill* (1958), his most successful novel. His insight into character and nar-rative gift was demonstrated in further novels, including *Hostages to Fortune* (1984), about a writer beset by tragedy. A remark-ably vivid autobiography, *Farther Off from Heaven* (1977), reveals the roots in childhood of his fictional concerns.

▷J W Lee, *William Humphrey* (1967)

HUMPHREYS, Emyr Owen
(1919–)

Welsh novelist, poet and dramatist, born in Prestatyn, Clwyd, and educated at University College, Aberystwyth, where he read history, learned Welsh and became a nationalist. He has worked as a teacher and a BBC Wales drama producer. The author of 19 novels, he won the **Somerset Maugham** Award for *Hear and Forgive* (1952), and the Hawthornden Prize for *A Toy Epic* (1958). He has also published two collections of short stories and six volumes of verse. Some of his poems have been set to music by the composer Alun Hoddinott.

HUNEKER, James Gibbons
(1857–1921)

Influential American critic and essayist, born in Philadelphia. His writing career began with musical criticism, but he later wrote on drama, literature and art, always enthusiastically promoting the new, the exciting, and the European. Like his friend and follower **H L Mencken**, he opposed the drabness of American puritanism and portrayed the pursuit of the arts as 'a magnificent adventure'. His most popular book of essays, *Iconoclasts* (1905), dealt with dramatists such as **Ibsen** and **Shaw**. His fiction—the exotic stories of *Melomaniacs* (1902) and *Visionaries* (1905) and the sexually advanced novel *Painted Veils* (1920)—continues the work of his essays by other means, with the same relentless allusions to foreign writers, and discussion of artistic, particularly musical, concerns.

▷A T Schwab, *James Gibbons Huneker: Critic of the Seven Arts* (1963)

HUNT, E(verette) Howard
(1918–90)

American spy and detective novelist and political operative; as an adviser to Richard Nixon's re-election committee he became embroiled in the Watergate scandal in 1972. Conspiracy theorists also claim that Hunt appears on photographs of the notorious 'grassy knoll' on Dealey Plaza, Dallas, where John F Kennedy was ambushed in November 1963, and among the mysterious 'tramps' arrested subsequent to the assassination. Born in Hamburg, New York, he graduated from Brown University in 1940, and served with the Air Force (1943–6) after writing scripts for the hugely influential *March of Time* newsreels. He was recruited as a political officer after the war and saw diplomatic service in Paris, Vienna, Mexico, Tokyo and Montevideo; an impression of his career can be had from **Mailer**'s CIA novel *Harlot's Ghost* (1991). Hunt's first novel was called *Maelstrom* (1948), reissued seven years later as *Cruel is the Night*. Others included *Dark Encounter* (1950) and *The Judas Hour* (1951). He also used pseudonyms, writing as John Baxter, Robert Dietrich and David St John, and detective fiction as Gordon Davis. Following his release from prison in 1977, he resumed his writing career; his work provides a fascinating insight into the clandestine side of US politics from the end of World War II through the Bay of Pigs (in which he had a hand), to Vietnam and beyond.

▷*Undercover: Memoirs of an American Secret Agent* (1974)

HUNT, (James Henry) Leigh
(1784–1859)

English poet and essayist, born in Southgate, Middlesex, the son of an immigrant US preacher. Educated at Christ's Hospital, his first collection of poetry was privately printed as *Juvenilia* in 1801. With his brother, a printer, he edited, from 1808 to 1821, *The Examiner*, which became a focus of liberal opinion and so attracted leading men of letters, including **Byron**, **Thomas Moore**, **Shelley** and **Charles Lamb**. He was imprisoned with his brother for two years (1813–15) for a libel on the Prince Regent. *The Examiner*, however, was more a literary and social than a political forum. It introduced Shelley and **Keats** to the public—Keats' sonnet *On First Looking into Chapman's Homer* first appeared there in 1816, the year in which Hunt issued his own romance, *The Story of Rimini*. He founded and edited *The Indicator* (1819–21). In 1822 he joined Shelley in Italy with his wife and seven children to found a new quarterly, *The Liberal*. Shelley's tragic death by drowning that year forced Hunt to accept the hospitality of Lord Byron at his palace in Pisa. The association with Byron was unhappy and *The Liberal* (1822–3) was short-lived. After Byron's death in 1824, Hunt returned to England in 1825 to carry on a busy life of literary journalism, liberal politics and poetry. His house at Hampstead attracted all that was notable in the literary world, not without envy or ridicule, however, as **Dickens**' caricature of him as Harold Skimpole in *Bleak House* shows. His importance is less in his works, poetic or critical, than in his being one of those invaluable people who introduce authors to each other, but his *Examiner* is not to be dismissed, and his autobiography is a valuable picture of the times.

▷E Blunden, *Leigh Hunt* (1930)

HUNT, Violet
(1866–1942)

English novelist and biographer, born in Durham, the daughter of the painter Alfred William Hunt. Having trained as a painter, she turned to writing, her first novel, *The Maiden's Progress: A Novel in Disguise*, appearing in 1894. She was an outspoken supporter of women's suffrage and most of her 17 books, such as *Unkist, Unkind!* (1897) and *Tales of the Uneasy* (1911), deal frankly, for the time, with the psychological effects on women of sexual repression. *White Rose of Weary Leaf* (1908), in which human relationships are restricted by social conventions, is often judged to be her finest novel. Her memoirs include a rather unreliable book about the Pre-Raphaelite painters, *Those Flurried Years* (1926). Although she never married, Violet Hunt had several turbulent and well-publicized affairs, but in later life withdrew into virtual seclusion.

▷M and R Secor, *F.M.Ford and V. Hunt's 1917 Diary* (1983)

HUNTER, Evan, originally Salvatore A Lambino
(1926–)

American novelist, born in New York City. Writing under the name 'Ed McBain', he is renowned for his '87th Precinct' thrillers. He was educated in New York, served in the US navy and taught before concentrating on his career as a novelist. As Evan Hunter he is best known for *The Blackboard Jungle* (1954), about a young teacher in an inner-city high school confronted with recalcitrant students and sundry social problems. It was acclaimed for its realism and topicality.

HUNTER, Mollie
(1922–)

Scottish writer, born in Longniddry, East Lothian. Until 1960 she worked as a freelance journalist, but she is best known for her work in children's fiction, and has published 25 books of various types in this field, including fantasy and historical fiction. Her works include *Hi Johnny* (1963), *Haunted Mountain* (1972) and *A Stranger Came Ashore* (1975). She has been Writer-in-Residence at Dalhousie University in Halifax, Canada, and has lectured and written on writing for children. She has been the recipient of many major awards, including the Scottish Arts Council Literary Award (1972), the Carnegie Medal (1975) and the Arbuthnot Lectureship (1975).

HUNTER, Norman
(1899–)

English writer for children, born in London. He is best known as the begetter of Professor Branestawm, the archetypal crackpot genius, who made his debut in *The Incredible Adventures of Professor Branestawm* (1933). The professor, despite the hazardous nature of his many experiments, has enjoyed remarkable longevity; *Professor Branestawm's Crunchy Crockery* was published on the 50th anniversary of the original adventure. During a period of 21 years in South Africa Hunter produced no fiction, but his arrival back in the United Kingdom in 1970 brought a return to writing. Subsequent volumes include *Dust-up at the Royal Disco* (1975). He has also worked as a copywriter and a conjuror.

HUNTER, N(orman) C(harles)
(1908–71)

English playwright and novelist, born in Derbyshire. He served in the army before joining the BBC as a producer. He is best remembered for his play, *Waters of the Moon* (1951), in which several guests, stranded in a hotel by heavy snowfalls, are forced to come to a new understanding of each other. This and other plays, such as *A Touch of the Sun* (1958), are clearly influenced by Chekhov. His smoothly-structured, naturalistic dramas were increasingly criticized during the 1950s and 60s for their preoccupation with middle-class mores and their sentimentality, although with time they may come to be looked upon again more kindly.

HUON, Ronan
(1922–)

Breton poet who has always aimed at a minority audience, and who has written a scholarly Breton grammar. His poetry is modestly modernistic, and its reputation is high amongst readers of Breton.

HURSTON, Zora Neale
(c.1901–1960)

American black novelist, born in Eatonville, Florida. The nine secure years she spent there, described in *Dust Tracks on a Road* (1942), ended when her mother died and her father, a Baptist preacher and thrice mayor of the town, remarried. Her life from then on was 'a series of wanderings'—occasional work, interrupted education, working as a wardrobe assistant with a theatre troupe—until she enrolled as a full-time student at Baltimore's Morgan Academy. Moving to Washington DC she became a part-time student at Howard University and began to write. Influenced by her studies in cultural anthropology at Barnard College and Columbia University, she became a prominent figure in the Harlem Renaissance. A precursor of black women writers like Alice Walker and Toni Morrison, her novels include *Jonah's*

Gourd Vine (1934), *Their Eyes Were Watching God* (1937), *Moses, Man of the Mountain* (1939) and *Seraph on the Suwanee* (1948). In the 1950s she withdrew from public life, and was distanced from many contemporaries by her controversial attack on the Supreme Court's ruling on school desegregation. She argued that pressure for integration denied the value of existing black institutions. Her last years were plagued by ill-health and she died in poverty.

▷ *Dust Tracks on a Road* (1942)

HURTADO DE MENDOZA, Diego de
(1503–75)

Spanish poet and historian, born in Granada; he was one of the great Renaissance humanists. As well as Spanish, he had mastery of Arabic, Hebrew, Greek and Latin. He was an important diplomat who was entrusted with the task of arranging marriages between Henry VIII and the Duchess of Milan, and Mary Tudor with Don Luis of Portugal (he failed in both instances). It was once widely believed that he wrote the picaresque *Lazarillo de Tormes*, and, although he probably did not, he was capable of it. His fine 'indecent' poem, *Fábula de cangrejo* ('Fable of the Crab'), deservedly enjoyed long and wide circulation, as did his *jocoso* (light verse) work. But his outstanding book is his account of the Morisco rebellion of 1568–70, *La guerra de Granada* (1627, 'The Granada War'), a biting history in the style of Sallust, which spares no one. Philip II expelled him from court in 1568.

HUTCHINSON, Pearse
(1927–)

Irish poet, writing in both Gaelic and English, born in Glasgow and educated in Dublin. He moved to Spain in the 1950s to teach English in Barcelona, but returned to Dublin in 1970. His four collections in Gaelic and nine in English reveal a consistent identification with the underdog, a championing of the deprived. *The Frost is All Over* (1975) opens with the words 'to kill a language is to kill a people', and this central theme led him to important translations from the fringe European languages of Galico–Portuguese and Catalan. His *Selected Poems* (1982) portray the depth of his beliefs and demand a reader's complicity with his insistence on compassion and understanding.

HUXLEY, Aldous Leonard
(1894–1963)

English novelist and essayist, son of the editor Leonard Huxley and brother of the biologist Sir Julian Sorell Huxley, born in Godalming, Surrey. He was educated at Eton and Balliol College, Oxford, where he read English, not biology as he intended, because of an eye disease, which compelled him to settle in the warmer climate of California (1937). Some **Shelley**an poetry, literary journalism and a volume of short stories *Limbo* (1920) were followed by *Crome Yellow* (1921) and *Antic Hay* (1923), satires on post-war Britain. *Those Barren Leaves* (1925) and *Point Counter Point* (1928) were written in Italy, where he associated with **D H Lawrence**, who appears as Mark Rampion in the last named. In 1932, in his most famous novel, *Brave New World*, Huxley warned of the dangers of moral anarchy in a scientific age, by depicting a repulsive Utopia, in which Platonic harmony is achieved by scientifically breeding and conditioning a society of human robots, for whom happiness is synonymous with subordination, a much more sinister prophecy than **George Orwell**'s *1984*, which still required thought control and police terror. Despite the wit and satire, Huxley was in deadly earnest, as his essay *Brave New World Revisited* (1959) shows. An alternative possibility, of bestial individualism in the degeneration of the survivors of an atomic war, is explored in *Ape and Essence* (1948). From such pessimism Huxley took refuge in the exploration of mysticism. *Eyeless in Gaza* (1936) and *After Many a Summer* (1939, James Tait Black Prize) pointed the way to *Time must have a Stop* (1944), in which he attempted to describe a person's state of mind at the moment of, and just after, death. *The Doors of Perception* (1954) and *Heaven and Hell* (1956) describe a controversial short-cut to mysticism, the drug mescalin which reduces the 'sublime' mystical state to a mere function of the adrenal glands. In contrast, the novelette *The Genius and the Goddess* (1955) reverts to the earlier Huxley, the problems posed by the discrepancy between an extraordinary intellect and a deficiency in other human endowments. *Island* (1962) is a more optimistic utopian novel. Huxley wrote numerous essays on related topics, beginning with *Proper Studies* (1927), biographies, and a famous study in sexual hysteria, *The Devils of Louden* (1952).

▷ S Bedford, *Aldous Huxley, a biography* (2 vols, 1973–4)

HUXLEY, Elspeth Josceline, née Grant
(1907–)

English novelist, born in Kenya. In 1931 she married Gervas Huxley (1894–1971), grandson of Thomas Henry Huxley, and has written many novels and essays on her native land, its history, and its problems. Her best-known novel is *The Flame Trees of Thika* (1959), which deals with her childhood, as do

The Mottled Lizard (1962) and *Death of an Aryan* (1986, also known as *The African Poison Murders*).
▷ *Love Among the Daughters* (1968)

HUYGENS, Constantijn
(1596–1687)

Dutch poet, statesman, composer and humanist, son of the scientist Christian Huygens, born in The Hague. The recipient of a rich and pious Calvinist education, he was one of the foremost linguists of his day, having seven languages at his command. He was also one of the best-known men of his time, and was knighted by Charles I (1622) and honoured by the French King (1632). He regarded his poems as 'cornflowers': they embellished, as he saw it, his religious and political work. He admired **John Donne** (19 of whose poems he translated) and **Giambattista Marino**, and his poetry is akin to that of both, being highly emotional but also 'metaphysical'—distinguished by its many conceits and daring play on words. He has been called 'the last of the true Renaissance virtuosi'. His play *Tryntje Cornelis* (1653) is surprisingly down-to-earth. It was for long thought that Huygens did damage to his poetry by regarding it so casually; but it is now becoming apparent that this gave it 'non-literary' qualities of great interest. There are English translations in: J Bowring and H S van Dijk (eds), *Batavian Anthology* (1824); F J Warnke, *European Metaphysical Poetry* (1961).
▷ A G H Bachrach, *Sir Constantine Huygens and Britain* (1962)

HUYSMANS, Joris Karl
(1848–1907)

French novelist of Dutch origin, born in Paris. From ultrarealism, as in his *Les Soeurs Vatard* (1879, 'The Vatard Sisters'), *À vau-l'eau* (1882, 'Downstream') and *À rebours* (1884, 'Against the Grain'), he changed over to a devil-worshipping mysticism as in *Là-Bas* (1891, 'Over There'), but returned to the Roman Church with *En Route* (1892). His *L'Art Moderne* (1882) is a superb study of Impressionist painting. The decadent, aesthetic hero of *À rebours* (1884) was much admired by **Oscar Wilde** and his circle, and established Huysmans as a leading light in the decadent movement of the period.
▷ R B Baldick, *The Life of J. K. Huysmans* (1955)

HYDE, Douglas
(1860–1949)

Irish poet, folklorist, academic and politician, born in Frenchpark, County Roscommon, where his father was the Protestant rector.

Ostensibly studying law at Trinity College Dublin, he published poems under the pseudonym 'An Craoibhin Aoibhinn' ('The Agreeable Little Branch'), which he also used in his subsequent translations from the Gaelic of folktales and poems. In 1892 he became president of the National Literary Society and a year later, the year of his marriage, held a similar position in the faction-ridden Gaelic League. In 1932 he was elected first President of the Republic of Ireland and held office until 1944. In literature his most important work was *Abhran Gradh Chuige Connacht* (1893, Eng trans *Love Songs of Connacht*, 1893), though it is arguable that his essay *The Necessity for De-Anglicising Ireland* (1892), a plea for cultural autonomy, has had greater influence on consequent cultural-political attitudes.
▷ *I Believed* (1950); D Daly, *The Young Douglas Hyde: The Dawn of Irish Revolution and Renaissance* (1974)

HYDE, Robin, pseud of **Iris Guiver Wilkinson**
(1906–39)

New Zealand journalist, poet, and novelist, born in South Africa of an Anglo–Indian father and Australian mother. In *Journalese* (1934) New Zealand society in the 1930s is viewed with acute perception. Her newspaper background is evident in her novels, which often blend fact and fiction as in *Passport to Hell* (1936) and in *Nor the Years Condemn* (1938) with the real-life anti-hero and misfit James Douglas Stark. Here, and in *Check to Your King* (1936), a novelized account of Baron Charles de Thierry (the French adventurer and eccentric who sought to establish himself as Sovereign Chief of New Zealand in the 1830s), she shows her empathy with the outcast and under-dog. The autobiographical *A Home in this World* (1937) describes the social pressures which drove her to drugs and eventual suicide. She wrote three collections of verse, *The Desolate Star* (1929), *The Conquerors* (1935) and *Persephone in Winter* (1937). She visited China in 1938, a time when she produced her best work in *Houses by the Sea, and Later Poems* (1952), which also includes backward glances at the innocence of her childhood.

HYNE, Charles John Cutcliffe Wright
(1865–1944)

English traveller and author, born in Bibury. He is remembered above all as the creator of the fictional character 'Captain Kettle' in several adventure stories.

HYRY, Antti
(1931–)
Finnish writer of stories and novels, born in
Kuivaniemi. An experimentalist, he has cultivated a naively objective style which more
recently has tended towards monotony.

HYSLOP, James
(1798–1827)
Scottish poet, born in Kirkconnel, Dumfriesshire. While a shepherd he wrote the
poem 'The Cameronian's Dream' (1821).
▷Biographical sketch in *The Poems of James
Hyslop* (1887)

I

IAMBLICHUS
(2nd century)

Syrian–Greek author of a lost Greek romance, *Babyloniaca*.

IBÁÑEZ, Sara de
(1909–71)

Uruguayan poet, born in Chamberlain as Sara de Casadei, she married the poet Roberto Ibáñez in 1928. Her first collection, *Canto* (1940), had a prologue by **Neruda**, in which he praised her as 'great, exceptional and cruel'. Using strict forms, she wrote in a hermetic or Surrealist style; despite praise from many more than Neruda, eg **Carrera Andrade**, her work has been neglected in English-language surveys and anthologies.
▷D E Marting, *Women Writers of Latin America* (1987)

IBÁÑEZ, Vicente Blasco
(1867–1928)

Spanish novelist, born in Valencia. He dealt in realistic fashion with provincial life and social revolution. Notable works are *Sangre y Arena* (1908, Eng trans *Blood and Sand*, 1913), *La Barraca* (1899, Eng trans *The Cabin*, 1919) and *Los Cuatro Jinetes del Apocalipsis* (1916, Eng trans *The Four Horsemen of the Apocalypse*, 1918 (US); 1919 (UK)), which vividly portrays World War I and earned him world fame.
▷A Day, *Vicente Blasco Ibáñez* (1972)

IBARBOUROU, Juana de
(1892–1979)

Uruguayan poet, born in Melo, on the border with Brazil. She was one of the most distinguished 'wife and mother' poets of the 20th century, not unlike **Judith Wright**, but with more Latinate opportunity to express her passions (for the military man whom, as Juana Fernandéz, she married in 1914). Her poems became famous throughout Argentina and, indeed, Spanish America. She felt misunderstood, and declared: 'the adjective erotic attached itself to those poems like a fly on a pile of butcher's refuse'. But it was widely understood that no one had before published such erotic poetry in Spanish in modern times. She was named 'Juana of America' at a grand ceremony in Montevideo (1929), at which men, including poets such as **Alfonso Reyes**, broke down and wept with joy. But when she published more verse, in 1930, it

went almost unnoticed, and by the end of her life she had become prone to depression and religious devotion. More of a phenomenon, perhaps, than a writer, her early verse does have the spontaneity of complete subjectivity within a patriotic and conventional context.
▷M J de Queiroz, *La poesia de Juana de Ibabourou* (1961)

IBN 'ARABI
(1165–1240)

Arab mystic poet. His writings present in obscure language a form of pantheism.
▷R Landau, *The Philosophy of Ibn 'Arabi* (1959)

IBRAHIM, Sonallah
(1935–)

Egyptian novelist, whose candid 1968 novel, translated as *The Smell of It* (1971), about a young man's sexual frustrations in Cairo, aroused interest because it was banned. As a critic wrote, with it the Egyptian novel could be considered to have 'come of age'.

IBSEN, Henrik
(1828–1906)

Norwegian dramatist, born in Skien, the founder of modern prose drama. The son of a wealthy merchant who went bankrupt, he worked as a chemist's assistant in Grimstad (1844–50), intending to study medicine, and wrote his first play there, *Catilina*, which was rejected. He got a job in journalism in Bergen, then was given a post as stage director and resident playwright at Ole Bull's Theatre, for which he wrote five conventional romantic dramas. In 1857 he was appointed director of the Norwegian Theatre in Christiania (Oslo), having just written his first play of significance, *Kongsemnerne* ('The Pretenders'), on a historical theme from Norway's past, in the manner of **Schiller**. In 1862 he wrote *Kjaerlighedens Komedie* ('Love's Comedy'), with its satirical theme of marriage as a millstone to idealism. The theatre went bankrupt the following year, and Ibsen went into voluntary exile for the next few years, to Rome, Dresden and Munich (1864–92), and it was there that he wrote the bulk of his dramas. The dramatic poem *Brand* appeared in 1865, and gave him his first major success, as well as the award of a government pension. The existentialist *Peer Gynt* followed in 1867, and a third historical drama, *Kejser og Galilaer* ('Emperor and Galilean') in 1873. He then turned to his plays of realism and social issues, which revolutionized European drama and on which his towering reputation rests: *Samfundets støtter* (1877, 'Pillars of Society'), *En dukkehjem* (1879, 'A Doll's House'), *Gengangere* (1881, 'Ghosts'), *En folkefiende* (1882, 'An Enemy of the People'), *Vildanden* (1884, 'The Wild Duck'), *Rosmersholm* (1886), *Fruen fra havet* (1888, 'The Lady from the Sea') and *Hedda Gabler* (1890). Thereafter he returned to Norway; his last plays are characterized by a strong emphasis on symbolism, with *Bygmester Solness* (1892, 'The Master Builder'), *Lille Eyolf* (1894, 'Little Eyolf'), *John Gabriel Borkman* (1896) and *Naar vi døde vaagner* (1899, 'When We Dead Awaken'). In 1900 he suffered a stroke which ended his literary career.

▷ M Meyer, *Ibsen* (3 vols, 1967–71)

IBUSE Masuji
(1898–)

Japanese writer, born in Hiroshima into a wealthy family. He moved to Tokyo to study at Waseda University and settled there. He is a writer of rich, colourful and humorous novels of ordinary life, of which *Seikatsu no Tankyu* (1937, 'Making a Living') is the most popular in Japan. His reputation in the West, however, rests on his *Kuroi Ame* (1966, 'Black Rain'), an uncharacteristically dark work about the atomic bomb dropped on his home town.

IBYCUS
(fl.mid 6th century BC)

Greek poet from Rhegium in Italy. He lived at the court of Polycrates, tyrant of Samos, and wrote choral lyrics in Doric anticipating **Pindar**. Legend has it that he was slain by robbers near Corinth, and as he was dying he called upon a flock of cranes to avenge him. The cranes then hovered over the theatre at Corinth, and one of the murderers exclaimed, 'Behold the avengers of Ibycus!' This led to their conviction. The story is told in **Schiller**'s ballad.

▷ M Noethiger, *Die Sprache des Stresichorus und des Ibycus* (1971)

ICAZA, Jorge
(1906–78)

Ecuadorean novelist, born in Quito. Icaza was his country's most important *indigenista* novelist, and, although his most important book, *Huasipungo* (1934, Eng trans *The Villagers*, 1964), one of the most brutal novels ever written, is not as subtle or profound in its depiction of Native Americans as are the novels of Icaza's Peruvian contemporary **José**

María Arguedas, it is epoch-making in its context. Icaza began as a playwright and denouncer of abuses. Then, with the collection of stories, *Barro de la sierra* (1933, 'Mountain Clay'), Icaza began his ruthless examination of the injustices of the *latifundio* system of great landed estates. *Huasipungo* (it means 'inherited land') is rather more an indictment of governmental injustice than a convincing portrait of Native Americans, but the frequent dismissal of it on account of its too 'brutal realism' can only raise questions about the critic's own attitude, for Icaza's protest, though exaggerated, is vivid and truthful enough to transcend political questions—whatever the stature of his artistry. *En las calles* (1935, 'In the Streets') *Huasipungo*'s successor, a satirical novel, is less effective. But later works, such as the scarifying picture of city life *El chulla Romero y Flores* (1958, 'The Upstart Romero y Flores') and the trilogy *Los atrapados* (1972, 'The Trapped'), continuing Icaza's almost uniquely brutalist exploration of racial prejudice, add to his achievement. The view that Icaza's 'totally black and bleak portrayal of human brutishness fails to convince' is, paradoxically, challenged by the same critic's concession that he 'moves us by his conviction'. Director of the National Library, he is still regarded by many as Ecuador's greatest novelist—but he is far surpassed in artistry by **Aguilera Malta**.

▷ J R Spell, *Contemporary Spanish American Fiction* (1944)

IDRIESS, Ion Llewellyn
(1889–1979)

Australian author, born in Waverley, Sydney. After a wandering life as opal miner, rabbit exterminator and crocodile hunter, he served with the Australian Imperial Forces at Gallipoli and in the Near East. He then travelled widely throughout Australia and in the Pacific Islands, episodes that were to provide colour for his books, such as *Madman's Island* (1927), which was based on his own experiences while marooned. His first success was *Lasseter's Last Ride* (1931), the story of the search for a legendary lost gold reef. In the next 40 years Idriess wrote a book almost every year, of which the best known are *Flynn of the Inland* (1932), about Rev John Flynn, founder of Australia's Flying Doctor Service; *The Desert Column* (1932), based on his service with the Australian Light Horse during World War I; *The Cattle King* (1936); and *The Red Chief* (1953). His earlier experiences resulted in his being commissioned to write six 'survival' guides for the Australian Army during World War II.

▷ *The Silver City* (1957)

IDRIS, Yusuf
(1927–91)

Egypt's outstanding modern short-story writer, also a novelist and playwright, born in al-Bayrum in the Nile delta. He qualified as a doctor and became a medical inspector in 1951. He began publishing short fiction as a result of his urge to portray the poor of Cairo and the shocking conditions in which they lived. He was often imprisoned. Later he turned to journalism and to surrealistic fiction and drama. His most successful play is *Al-farafir* (1964, Eng trans *Flipflap and his Master*, 1977); but he is most valued for his stories, some of which may be found in *In the Eye of the Beholder: Tales from Egyptian Life* (1978) and in *The Cheapest Nights* (1978).
▷J Beyerl, *The Style of the Modern Arabic Short Story* (1971); M Mikhail, *Images of Arab Women* (1979)

IGLÉSIES, Ignasi
(1871–1928)

Catalan dramatist, known as the '*poeta dels humils*' ('poet of the humble'), born in San Andrés de Palomar. His plays, influenced by **Ibsen**, dealt almost exclusively with the cruel lot of working people, such as his own parents. Of these, *Els Vells* (1903, 'The Old People'), was perhaps the most affecting and well made. A critic has suggested that he is 'a first-rate topical dramatist, an acute social commentator' but consequently has little to offer 'except to his own age'.
▷R Tacis y Marca, *La literatura catalana moderna* (1937)

IGNATOW, David
(1914–)

American poet, born in Brooklyn, New York. After working at various jobs, including salesman and newspaper man, he turned to academia, and is now Professor Emeritus at York College, City University of New York. He published his first collection, *Poems*, in 1948. His recurring theme of the relation of man to his political and natural environment is expressed in lyrical, often brief poems in such works as *Facing the Tree: New Poems* (1975) and *Whisper to the Earth* (1981). His *New and Collected Poems 1970–1985* appeared in 1987. Ignatow writes from personal experience—so much so that some critics have observed that his poetry represents the transformation of autobiography into art.
▷ *The One in the Many* (1989)

IHIMAERA, Witi Tame
(1944–)

New Zealand author, born in Gisborne, who, with his collection of short stories *Pounamu, Pounamu* (1972), became the first published Maori writer in English. Other collections followed: *The New Net Goes Fishing* (1977) and *Dear Miss Mansfield: A Tribute to Kathleen Mansfield Beauchamp* (1989). In the first two, he alludes to the Paheka (white settler) fantasy *The Wizard of Oz* in his exploration of Maori identity. In his epic novel *The Matriarch* (1986) he attempts, through the life of his hero Te Kooti, to reconstruct world and New Zealand history in terms of Maori legend. With Don Long he edited *Into the World of Light* (1982), an important anthology of Maori writing. He was for some years a diplomat with the New Zealand Department of Foreign Affairs.

ILF, Ilya, pseud of **Ilya Arnoldovich Faynzilberg**
(1897–1937)
PETROV, Yevgeny, pseud of **Yevgeny Petrov Katayev**
(1903–42)

Russian satirists and comic writers. All their important writing was done in collaboration. Ilf was the son of a bank clerk, and was originally a graduate of an Odessa technical college. Petrov was the younger brother of **Valentin Katayev**, who first suggested the famous collaboration. Previous to this, both had worked as journalists on various papers, and Petrov had even been a policeman. Their account of a search for a chair in which diamonds are secreted, *Dvenadstat stulyev* (1928, Eng trans *Diamonds to Sit On*, 1930, *The Twelve Chairs*, 1961), has become a comic classic not only in Russian but also all over the world. The anti-hero, Ostap Bender, is one of the greatest—and most lovable—confidence-men in world literature. Through him the authors criticized the bureaucratic and other ridiculous aspects of the Soviet system as it was then being applied; but it reads as well today as it did then, because it mercilessly satirizes not just communism but every politician's 'plan for humanity'. Bender was murdered in *The Twelve Chairs*, but he proved so popular that he had to be resurrected in *Zolotoy telyonok* (1931, Eng trans *Little Golden Calf*, 1932, *The Golden Calf*, 1962), a less effective novel because here the two writers pursued a more obviously Marxist line—in the interval between the two books Soviet cultural policy had hardened. Thus, their third book, *Odnoetazhnaya Amerika* (1936, Eng trans *Little Golden America*, 1937), though an amusing satire, is far behind the first two. Ilf died in 1937, a victim of tuberculosis. Petrov was killed in World War II, while serving as a correspondent for *Pravda*. They wrote much else beside their three novels, mostly story-cycles, and this is collected in the five volumes of their *Sobraniye sochninenii* (1961, 'Collected Works').

ILIĆ, Vojislav

ILIĆ, Vojislav
(1860–94)

Serbian poet and dramatist, born in Belgrade. His straightforwardly lyrical poetry was widely influential in a period when poetry was going through some artifice, resulting in much of what has been called 'versified prose'. His epic and narratives are less impressive.

▷M Pavic, *Vojislav Ilić* (1963, in Serbian)

ILLYÉS, Gyula
(1902–83)

Hungarian novelist, essayist, critic, memoirist, for long regarded as his country's finest poet. His main inspiration came from his peasant origins and from his long sojourn in Paris as a student, when he made friends with **André Malraux** and briefly flirted with Surrealism. His book *Puszták népe* (1936, Eng trans *People of the Puszta*, 1967), an account of the atrocious conditions on the manorial estate upon which he was born (the son of a mechanic), awakened the conscience of the Hungarian people to the semi-feudal conditions in which they lived. He became a member of parliament in 1945, but later defied the communist government, and was even for a time silenced by it—and 'investigated' by its 'cultural' secret police. The historical plays of his final years dealt in impressive fashion with the complex and unconquerable notion of freedom. His *Once Upon a Time: Forty Hungarian Folktales* was published in England in 1964; a *Selected Poems* appeared in English in 1971.

▷T Kabdebo and P Tabori, *Tribute to Gyula Illyés* (1968)

IMMERMANN, Karl Leberecht
(1796–1840)

German dramatist and novelist, born in Magdeburg. In 1817 he entered the public service of Prussia, and served in Münster, Magdeburg and Düsseldorf. His fame rests upon his tales (*Miscellen*, 1830) and the satirical novels *Die Epigonen* (1836, 'Those who Follow After') and *Münchhausen* (1839). He also wrote plays, poetry, and autobiographical works.

▷B V Wiese, *Karl Immermann* (1969)

INCHBALD, Elizabeth, née **Simpson**
(1753–1821)

English novelist, playwright and actress, born in Bury St Edmunds, the daughter of a farmer. She ran away to go on the stage and in 1772 married John Inchbald, an actor in London. She made her debut at Bristol as Cordelia. After the death of her husband in 1779 she appeared at Covent Garden, but from 1789 made her name as a playwright and author of 19 sentimental comedies, including *The Wedding Day* (1794) and *Lover's Vows* (1798), the play which the Bertram children are acting in a famous scene in **Austen**'s *Mansfield Park*. She also wrote the novels *A Simple Story* (1791) and *Nature and Art* (1796). She was editor of the 24-volume *The British Theatre* (1806–9).

INGAMELLS, Rex, properly **Reginald Charles**
(1913–55)

Australian poet, born in Ororoo, South Australia. He was founder of the nationalistic 'Jindyworobak Club', a frustrated attempt in the late 1930s to graft a characteristically 'Australian' school of poetry on to the dying trunk of colonist writing. It did not survive the impact of World War II and the flood of writing from the USA and other cultures. Ingamells compiled a 'history' of the movement, *Jindyworobak Review 1938–48*, and a survey of its writings *The Jindyworobaks* appeared in 1979. Ingamells's own verse first appeared in *Gumtops* (1935) and *Forgotten People* (1936), followed by four other books and the epic *The Great South Land* (1951). He edited an anthology for schools, *New Song in an Old Land: Australian Verse* (1944), and the best of his own work was published as *Selected Poems* in the same year.

INGE, William Motter
(1913–73)

American playwright and novelist, born in Independence, Kansas. He was educated at Kansas University and George Peabody College for Teachers, and taught and wrote art criticism for the St Louis *Star-Times*. Outside the mainstream of American theatre, he is nevertheless important for four plays—*Come Back, Little Sheba* (1950), *Picnic* (1953), *Bus Stop* (1955) and *The Dark at the Top of the Stairs* (first produced in 1947 and revised in 1957)—in which he transforms the lives of drab people living in drab surroundings into significant dramas of human experience. He was awarded the Pulitzer Prize in 1953.

▷R B Schuman, *William Inge* (1965)

INGELOW, Jean
(1820–97)

English poet and novelist, born in Boston, Lincolnshire. She wrote devotional poetry, lyrics and ballads, of which the short poem 'High Tide on the Coast of Lincolnshire 1571', published in *Poems* (1863), is her best. Other well-known poems include 'Divided' and 'A Story of Doom' (1867). Her tales for children include *Mopsa the Fairy* (1869), and her adult novels were *Off the Skelligs* (1872),

Fated to be Free (1875) and *Sarah de Beranger* (1879).

▷ *Some Recollections of Jean Ingelow* (1972)

INGEMANN, Bernhard Severin
(1789–1862)

Danish poet and novelist, born in Thorkildstrup in Falster. He is best known for his idealized romantic historical novels *Valdemar Sejer* (1826), *Kong Erik* (1833) and *Prins Otto af Danmark* (1835), and historical poems *Waldemar the Great* (1824), *Queen Margaret* (1836) and *Holger Danske* (1837). From 1822 he lectured at the Royal Academy of Sorø, near Copenhagen and was headmaster from 1842 to 1849.

▷ C Langballe, *Bernhard Severin Ingemann* (1949)

INGRAHAM, Joseph Holt
(1809–60)

American novelist and clergyman, born in Portland, Maine. He was for some time a sailor, and then taught languages at a college in Mississippi. He published some sensational romances, such as *Pirate of the Gulf* (1836) and *Scarlet Feather* (1845); but after he was ordained to the Episcopal priesthood (1852) he wrote religious romances such as *The Prince of the House of David* (1855).

INGRAHAM, Prentiss
(1843–1904)

American soldier of fortune and novelist, son of **Joseph Holt Ingraham**. He served in Mexico, Austria, Africa and Cuba before settling in New York and writing some 700 'dime novels', many with Buffalo Bill (William Cody) as the hero. He also wrote plays, short stories and poems.

INGRAM, Anne, Viscountess Irwin, née Howard
(c.1695–1764)

English poet, daughter of the Earl of Carlisle, she grew up at Castle Howard, Yorkshire. Her first husband Richard Ingram, Viscount Irwin, died in 1721; she was married again in 1737 to Col William Douglas (d.1748). She was appointed to the Princess of Wales's court, and was familiar with leading figures in literary circles, including **Pope**, **Lady Mary Wortley Montagu** and **Horace Walpole**. She published *Castle Howard* (1732), a descriptive poem, but is better known for *An Epistle to Mr Pope* (1736), a good-humoured retort to his misogynistic *Characters of Women*. Her lively letters recording her travels abroad, life in court and city, and reflections on literature remain mostly unprinted.

▷ R Lonsdale (ed), *Eighteenth-Century Women Poets* (1989)

INNES, Michael *see* **STEWART, JIM**

INNES, Ralph Hammond *see* **HAMMOND INNES, Ralph**

IONESCO, Eugène
(1912–94)

Romanian-born French playwright, educated at Bucharest and Paris, where he settled in 1940. He pioneered a new style of drama with his short surrealistic plays, including *La Cantatrice chauve* (1950, Eng trans *The Bald Soprano*, 1956), *La Leçon* (1951, Eng trans *The Lesson*, 1958), *Les Chaises* (1952, Eng trans *The Chairs*, 1957), *Amédée* (1954, Eng trans *Amedee*, 1955), *Victimes du devoir* (1953, Eng trans *Victims of Duty*, 1958), *Le Tableau* (1955, Eng trans *The Picture*, 1968) and *Rhinocéros* (1959, Eng trans *Rhinoceros*, 1960), based on the highly personal material of his dreams, hidden desires and inner conflicts, on the **Freud**ian assumption that humanity has a dream-world in common. His contempt for realism, the robot-like deficiencies of his characters, the suggestive irrationality of their outpourings, his paradoxical view that art is the attempt to communicate an incommunicable reality, have led to criticism by disciples of social realism. His later plays include *Jeux de Massacre* (1970, Eng trans *Wipe-Out Game*, 1971), *Macbett* (1972, Eng trans 1973) and *Voyages chez les Morts ou Thème et Variations* (1980, Eng trans *Journey Among the Dead*, 1983); among many essays and other writings, he wrote the novel *Le Solitaire* (1973, Eng trans *The Hermit*, 1974 (US); 1975 (UK)).

▷ R Hayman, *Ionesco* (1972); A Lewis, *Ionesco* (1972)

IRELAND, David
(1927–)

Australian novelist, born in Lakemba, Sydney, whose work combines elements of Surrealism, anarchy, nihilism and whimsy. His first book was *The Chantic Bird* (1968), followed by *The Unknown Industrial Prisoner* (1971). His most recent was *Bloodfather* (1987) which, in its hero's turning from printing to writing, suggests elements of autobiography. The slight *Archimedes and the Seagle* (1984), in which the narrator is Archimedes, a setter or 'dogperson', is perhaps the most accessible of his writing.

IRELAND, Kevin Jowsey
(1933–)

New Zealand poet, born in Auckland. His taut, traditional verse first appeared as *Face to Face* (1963), *Educating the Body* (1967) and *A Letter from Amsterdam* (1972). He sends up his own style in *Literary Cartoons* (1977) and marked his return home from many years in England and Ireland with *The Year of the Comet: Twenty-Six 1988 Sonnets* (1987) and *Tiberius at the Beehive* (1990).

IRIARTE Y OROPESA, Tomas de
(1750–91)

Spanish poet, writer of fables, born in Orotava, Tenerife. He was the author of *Fábulas Literarias* (1782), in which a number of animals are made to speak out against the author's literary enemies; he was also a translator of **Horace**. He loved music, and wrote a long poem on the subject, as well as a poetic tribute to Haydn.

▷ R Cox, *Tomas de Iriarte* (1972)

IRVING, John Winslow
(1942–)

American novelist, born and educated in Exeter, New Hampshire, and subsequently at the universities of Pittsburgh, Vienna, New Hampshire and Iowa. His early novels, *Setting Free the Bears* (1969), *The Water-Method Man* (1972) and *The 158-Pound Marriage* (1974), established a quirky style marked by recurrent obsessions—Vienna, animals, wrestling, psychoanalysis, and bizarre relationships—but failed to achieve popular success. This changed with *The World According to Garp* (1978), a modern fairy tale about an illegitimate child, which swings between innocent affirmation and sexual violence and mutilation, and between great narrative simplicity and intertextual literariness. A huge success, it was made into a Hollywood film. This propelled Irving out of academic life into full-time fiction writing. *The Hotel New Hampshire* (1981) was also bought for the movies, but it read like a reworking of the earlier books. Its successor, *The Cider House Rules* (1985), though unmistakably from the same source, was more humane and socially engaged. In 1989 he published *A Prayer for Owen Meany*.

▷ G Miller, *John Irving* (1982)

IRVING, Washington
(1783–1859)

American writer, born in New York, the son of a prosperous hardware merchant. He studied law, but on account of his delicate health was sent in 1804 to Europe. He visited Rome, Paris, the Netherlands and London, and in 1806 returned to New York, and was admitted to the Bar. His first publication was *Salmagundi* (1808), a series of satirical essays in semi-monthly sheet in imitation of the *Spectator*, which ran for 20 issues. His first characteristically boisterous work was *A History of New York, by Diedrich Knickerbocker* (1809), a good-natured burlesque upon the old Dutch settlers of Manhattan Island. He served as an officer in the 1812 war, wrote biographies of American naval heroes, became a friend of Sir **Walter Scott** and under the pseudonym 'Geoffrey Crayon' wrote *The Sketch Book* (1819–20), a miscellany, containing in different styles such items as 'Rip Van Winkle', 'The Legend of Sleepy Hollow' and 'Westminster Abbey', which have something of his sadness at the loss of his betrothed and his brothers' fortune. Another sketch book, *Bracebridge Hall* (1822), was followed after three years' travel in France and Germany by another miscellany, *Tales of a Traveller* (1824). His stay in Spain (1826–9) produced such studies as *The History of the Life and Voyages of Christopher Columbus* (1828), *A Chronicle of the Conquest of Granada* (1829) and *Voyages of the Companions of Columbus* (1831). After leaving Spain, he was for a short time secretary to the United States Legation in London. On his return to his native city (1832) he was welcomed enthusiastically, but the criticisms by **James Fenimore Cooper** and others that he had written only about Europe resulted in *A Tour on the Prairie* (1835) and *The Adventures of Captain Bonneville, USA* (1837). He reached the height of his career when he was appointed US ambassador to Spain (1842–6).

▷ S T Williams, *The Life of Irving* (1935)

IRZYKOWSKI, Karol
(1873–1944)

Polish novelist and critic. He is most celebrated for his single novel, *Pałuba* (1903), which may be translated as 'The Old Bitch', although it means much more than that in the book, which is a kind of search for the full meaning of the term. It is an account of 'life's bashful moments' and is often said to have anticipated **Freud**. But at least one critic believes this to be impossible (*The Interpretation of Dreams* was published in 1900). However, *Pałuba* does anticipate **Proust** and many other modernist writers, and is one of the most startling novels in a literature of many startling novels. Irzykowski died of wounds he received in the Warsaw rising. That he is not internationally known, and more widely translated, has been described as 'scandalous'.

▷ *Slavonic and East European Review*, 29 (1951)

ISAACS, Jorge
(1837–95)

Colombian novelist and poet, born in Cali in Antioquia to an English Jewish father and a Spanish mother. He is most famous for his novel *María* (1867, Eng trans 1890). A journalist and diplomat, Isaacs' chief work, regarded (perhaps a little facilely) as the finest

Latin-American romantic novel, is a story, set in the Cauca valley in Antioquia, of the love between a doomed foster-child and the son of the house. Its merits lie less in its story, however, than in the descriptions of the countryside. Isaacs, who took part in the civil war of 1876 on the liberal side, was mainly influenced by French models, and his *Poesias* (1864) suffer from his over-dependence on **Lamartine**. *María* is still widely read.

ISHERWOOD, Christopher William Bradshaw
(1904–86)

English-born American novelist, born in Disley, Cheshire. He was educated at Repton and Corpus Christi College, Cambridge, studied medicine at King's College, London (1928–9), but gave it up to teach English in Germany (1930–3). His first two novels were *All the Conspirators* (1928) and *The Memorial* (1932). His best-known works, *Mr Norris Changes Trains* (1935) and *Goodbye to Berlin* (1939), were based on his experiences in the decadence of post-slump, pre-Hitler Berlin. In collaboration with **W H Auden**, a school friend, he wrote three prose-verse plays with political overtones in which by expressionist technique, music hall parody and ample symbolism, the unsavoury social climate was forcefully exposed against idealist remedies: *The Dog beneath the Skin* (1935), *The Ascent of F6* (1937) and *On the Frontier* (1938). He travelled in China with Auden in 1938 and wrote *Journey to a War* (1939). In 1939 he emigrated to California to work as script-writer for Metro-Goldwyn-Mayer and in 1946 took American citizenship. He translated the Hindu epic poem, the *Bhagavad-Gita*, with Swami Prabhavananda (1944), who also collaborated in *Shan-Kara's Crest-Jewel of Discrimination* (1947) and *How to Know God; the Yogi Aphorisms of Patanjali* (1953). The Broadway hit *I am a Camera*, and the musical *Cabaret*, were based on his earlier Berlin stories, especially *Sally Bowles* (1937). He also translated **Baudelaire**'s *Intimate Journals* (1947). Later novels include *Prater Violet* (1945), *The World in the Evening* (1954) and *Meeting by the River* (1967). He has also written several autobiographical books, and the semi-autobiographical *Lions and Shadows* (1938).
▷ *Christopher and His Kind* (1963)

ISHIGURO, Kazuo
(1954–)

Japanese-born British novelist. Originally from Nagasaki, he settled in Britain and came to notice as a student on the influential creative-writing course at the University of East Anglia. After working as a community worker in Glasgow in the late 1970s (and,

more incidentally, as a grouse beater for the Queen Mother, an experience which may have fostered his later interest in the English ruling class), he published the delicate *A Pale View of Hill* (1982), which represented a highly personal approach to modern Japanese history and society. *An Artist of the Floating World* (1988) was much more mannered, and so too, in the most positive sense, was *Remains of the Day* (1989), which shifted the setting to England for the first time. An elegiac study of a vanishing class told through the eyes of a butler, it won Ishiguro the Booker Prize and has subsequently been filmed.

ISHIKAWA Takuboku
(1886–1912)

Japanese poet, born in Iwate in the northeast of Japan, into the family of a Zen priest. He worked as a teacher and an itinerant newspaper vendor before moving to Tokyo to follow his enthusiasm for poetry, becoming the most influential poet of his day, though not commercially successful. His ascetic, disciplined, Buddhist upbringing manifested itself in his maturity in a leftish, liberal cast of mind, and occasional flirtations with anarchism. He rejected the then predominant literary theory known as Japanese naturalism, being more interested in the ideas coming out of the turmoil following the Russian revolution of 1905, as can be seen in his collections *Ichiakuno una* (1910, 'Handful of Sand') and *Kuu beshiki* (1909, 'Poems to Eat'). After a life of poverty, he died of tuberculosis at the age of 26.
▷ Y Hijiya, *Ishikawa Takuboku* (1979)

ISLA, José Francisco de
(1703–81)

Spanish satirist, born in Vidanes, northwest Spain. After joining the Jesuits, for some years he lectured on philosophy and theology in Segovia, Santiago and Pamplona, and became famous as a preacher, but still more as a humorist and satirist by his writings, especially his novel of *Fray Gerundio* (1758–70, 'Friar Gerundio'). The *Cartas de Juan de la Encina* (1732, 'Juan de la Encina's Letters') are a good example of his style. A more characteristic one is the *Dia Grande de Navarra* ('The Great Day of Navarre'). What **Cervantes** had done with the sham chivalry and sentiment of the romances, Isla strove to do in *Fray Gerundio* with the vulgar buffooneries of the popular preachers, and especially the preaching friars of the day. It was well received by all except the friars, but the Inquisition stopped the publication of the book. In 1767 he shared the fate of the Jesuits in their expulsion from Spain, and went to Bologna. He translated **Alain Le Sage**'s *Gil Blas*, which he humorously claimed to have restored to its native language.

ISLAM, Kazi Nazrul
(1899–1976)

Bengali poet, hailed as the 'Rebel Poet of Bengal' and later as the 'National Poet of Bangladesh', born into extreme poverty in the West Bengali village of Churulia. He rose to fame in the 1920s as a poet and leader of the anti-British movement in India with his poem *The Rebel*, which brought him overnight fame. He published a bi-monthly radical magazine, *Dhumketu* ('The Comet') which was virulently revolutionary and anti-British in tone, and spent 40 days on hunger-strike in jail. In the 1930s he concentrated more on composing music and songs—over 4000 songs and lyrics in all— and made a huge name also as an actor and radio personality. In 1942 he contracted a brain disease that left him bereft of his faculties, including his speech; after Partition, which he had always opposed, he lived in penury until he was brought home in honour to the newly independent state of Bangladesh and installed as the national poet. A Muslim, he married a Hindu and was a lifelong advocate of Muslim–Hindu unity; he wrote more than 500 devotional Hindu songs.

ITAPARICA, Frei Manuel de Santa María
(1704–c.1770)

Brazilian Franciscan monk and minor poet, born in Bahia. He published his poems in Lisbon in 1769; the 'Descrição' ('Description') is a poem about the Brazilian landscape based on classical modes.

IVANISEVIĆ, Drago
(1907–)

Croatian poet, translator, critic and dramatist, born in Trieste. After World War II he became drama director of the Croatian National Theatre. His poetry, his main sphere of activity, is modernistic, hermetic and owes its greatest debt to French Surrealism. Many believe that his finest collection is *Jubav*, which contains lyrics in the dialect of his home town in Dalmatia, Split.

IVANOV, Georgy
(1894–1958)

Russian poet and novelist from Kovno, who began as an associate of **Gumilev** and the Acmeist group of poets, of which he was but a minor member; he also owed much, and most fruitfully, to **Kuzmin**. Later, in exile in France, he produced more mature, chiselled, almost always 'chillingly pessimistic' poetry, and he came to be regarded as the major poet of the emigration. His prose includes

the fascinating memoirs *Peterburgsiye zimy* (1928, 'Petersburg Winters').

IVANOV, Vsevolod Vyachislavovich
(1895–1963)

Russian fiction writer, born in Semipalatinsk in Siberia. He fought for both sides in the Russian Civil War, but latterly for the Reds. He was one of the foremost members of the Serapion Brothers, a 'fellow travelling' group which aims, with varying degrees of determination, to maintain the autonomy of art from politics. His realistic *Bronepoezd 14– 69* (1922, Eng trans *Armoured Train 14–69*, 1933) made him known throughout Europe. Although his other large-scale treatments of the Revolution were widely taken to be approving, they were in fact just the opposite: Ivanov despised political activism. He was unable to pursue his true vein under Stalinism, and his writing declined into a highly competent sort of modern reportage. Some critics have extolled his vivid and well-made short stories. There is a version of his early autobiography translated under the title of *I Live a Queer Life* (1936).
▷E J Brown (ed), *Major Soviet Writers* (1973)

IVANOV, Vyacheslav Ivanovich
(1866–1949)

Russian poet and critic. He studied in Berlin and lived in Greece and Italy, where he was converted to Roman Catholicism. The publication of his first poems established him as a leading figure in the Symbolist movement, but his poetry was later enriched by a powerful strain of mysticism and his philological interests, and he wrote studies on the cult of Dionysus, on **Dostoyevsky**, **Byron** and **Nietzsche**.
▷C Tschoepel, *Vyacheslav Ivanov* (1968)

IWASZKIEWICZ, Jaroslaw
(1894–1980)

Polish poet, novelist, dramatist and storywriter, born in Kalnik (near Kiev). He was one of the founders of the important Warsaw Group, the Skamander. His poems published during the 1920s attracted much attention for their expressionist fervour and descriptions of nature. His fiction is equally vital: often autobiographical, it uses techniques not unlike those of **Dos Passos**. His collection of literary essays, *Lato w Nohant* (1936), was translated as *Summer at Nohant* (1942). A prolific writer, Iwaszkiewicz was one of the most important of the 20th century.

IZUMI Kyoka
(1873–1939)

Japanese writer, born into an artisan family in Kanazawa. He set out for Tokyo in his late teens to become a novelist. This he did, becoming the finest craftsman of the Japanese language then writing. His very traditional novels are written in a beautifully refined, highly literary form of Japanese which began increasingly to be seen as archaic as his career progressed. Despite the enormous elegance and grace of works such as *Uta Andon* (1911, 'Lantern Song'), he became an anachronism as literature assimilated a growing number of non-Japanese influences and saw the need to be accessible to its readership. His work now seems the product of a far earlier age.

J

JABAVI, Noni
(1920–)

South African Xhosa writer who married an Englishman. Her father D D T Jabavi was a famous scholar, who wrote *The Influence of English on Bantu Literature*, and was a Professor at Fort Hare University. Noni's *Drawn in Colour* (1960) describes a visit to her sister in Uganda, where she lived with her husband for a time; *The Ochre People* (1963) is about a return visit to her home. The quaint English of the latter has aroused controversy: some critics think it an obstacle, others that it is 'admirably supple'.

JABRA, Jabra Ibrahim
(1919–)

Palestinian novelist, short-story writer, poet, critic and translator, born in Bethlehem and educated in Jerusalem and Cambridge, England. Since 1948 he has worked as a cultural bureaucrat in Iraq. Fluent in English, he wrote one of his novels, *Hunters in a narrow street* (1960), in English, while his translation of part of Sir James Frazer's *Golden Bough* influenced a whole school of Arab poets. His other novels, however, have been written in Arabic. His masterpiece, *Al-Safina* (1969, 'The Ship'), features intellectual and cosmopolitan Arabs on a Mediterranean cruise ship. The complex issues raised by their debates and pessimistic outcome to their journey may remind some readers of **Thomas Mann**'s *Magic Mountain*. Also important is *Al-Bahth 'an Walid Masud* (1987, 'In search of Walid Masud'), in which the mysterious disappearance of a heroic freedom fighter furnishes a pretext for a presentation of the Palestinian predicament from multiple perspectives. All Jabra's writings make great play with myth and metaphor and are heavy with reference to both eastern and western culture. Almost certainly he is the most influential of critics writing in Arabic today.

JACCOTTET, Philippe
(1925–)

Swiss-born French poet and translator, who has consistently documented his own literary and imaginative processes in published notebooks, *Carnets/La Semaison 1954–67* (1963, 1971, published in the USA as *Seedtime*, 1977), and in such books as *L'entretien des muses: Chroniques de poésie* (1968). Educated in Lausanne, he worked as a translator there from 1946, before migrating to southern France in 1953, when he published his crucial second collection, *L'Effraie*. The poems are mostly rhymed and in conventional metres that consistently suggest a plain-speaking, unliterary manner. The work of the early sixties in *Airs* (1967) is formally more varied and adventurous, and also more distanced in tone, a tendency reinforced in later volumes. Gallimard published a substantial compilation as *Poésie 1946–1967* (1971), but it was not until 1974 that **Cid Corman** completed the first substantial English translations, which were issued as *Breathings*. Jaccottet's own translations have included works by **Thomas Mann**, **Homer**, **Robert Musil**, the complete works of **Hölderlin**, the mysterious **B Traven**'s *The Death Ship* (1967), and others. He has won several awards for his work in this field, notably the Voss Prize (1966).
▷ A Clerval, *Philippe Jaccottet* (1976)

JACKSON, Helen Maria
(1830–85)

American novelist, poet and writer for children, born in Amherst, Massachusetts, where she went to school with **Emily Dickinson**. Jackson's own poetry was grossly overvalued by **Emerson**, who acclaimed her as 'America's greatest woman poet'. In fact it is her two prose works championing the Native American cause which have survived best: the polemical *A Century of Dishonor* (1881) and the sentimental but highly popular novel *Ramona* (1884). Even so, it is the connection with Emily Dickinson which has done most to keep Jackson's name alive. The novel *Mercy Philbrick's Choice* (1876) is generally considered to contain a fictional portrait of her Amherst schoolfriend.
▷ R Odell, *A Life* (1939)

JACKSON, Shirley
(1919–65)

American writer, born in San Francisco. A masterly storyteller who wrote in the genre of the psychological Gothic, Jackson published several novels and numerous short stories, many written for the *New Yorker* and other magazines. Her collection *The Lottery* (1949) included two of her best stories: 'The Daemon

Lover', describing the desperate loneliness of a New York woman seduced by a supernaturally elusive lover, and the title story, a bleak allegorical tale in which a remote rural community enacts its annual harvest tradition of selecting a human sacrifice by lottery. Perhaps Jackson's most powerful novel is *The Haunting of Hill House* (1959), depicting a woman's psyche torn by madness, guilt and fear, and told within the conventions of a haunted-house story; the book was filmed in 1963 as *The Haunting*. Jackson managed always to describe the bizarre as if entirely natural and everyday, a prime example being *We Have Always Lived in the Castle* (1962). In contrast, she also wrote lighter, humorous sketches of domestic life, such as *Life Among the Savages* (1953) and *Raising Demons* (1957), and several stories for children.
▷J Oppenheimer, *Private Demons: the Life of Shirley Jackson* (1988)

JACOB, Max
(1876–1944)

French 'cubist' poet, clown, mystic, novelist, critic, professional astrologer, artist, visonary and monk (he converted himself to Roman Catholicism in 1915, and his 'godfather' in this process was Picasso), born in Quimper. He was *the* pivotal avant-garde figure of the 20th century. A Jew, he died in Drancy concentration camp. Always on the vital edge of various avant-garde movements, in essence he belonged to none; but each owed a massive debt to his example. He knew everybody of note. His greatness is contained in his conversation (some of it recorded in L Emié's untranslated *Dialogues avec Max Jacob*, 1956) and in his letters (*Lettres*, ed S J Collier, 1966, again untranslated) and in a single collection' of prose-poems, *Le Cornet de dés* (1917, 'The Dice Cup'). But his many mystical works, in particular *L'Homme de cristal* (1946, 'The Crystal Man'), are also seminal within their area. Available in English translation are *Drawings and Poems* (1951) and *The Dice Cup: Selected Prose Poems* (1980).
▷J M Schneider, *Clown at the Altar* (1978)

JACOB, Naomi Ellington
(1884–1964)

English actress, novelist, essayist and biographer, born in Ripon, Yorkshire. Her first novel, *Jacob Ussher*, appeared in 1926, following which the enormously industrious Jacob published almost 80 books, including two on her eightieth birthday. *The Beloved Physician* (1930) examines the fraught personal and professional life of a female doctor. Her most successful novel, however, was *Four*

Generations (1934), the fourth of her seven-volume 'House of Gollantz' saga, a huge narrative embracing many characters and several countries and a heady concoction of romance and exoticism. She also produced books of womanly advice, such as *Me—in the Kitchen* (1935) and *Me—Thinking Things Over* (1964), which are not without charm, and in 1936 published a workmanlike biography of Marie Lloyd.
▷J Norbury, *Naomi Jacob* (1965)

JACOB, Violet, née Kennedy-Erskine
(1863–1946)

Scottish poet and novelist, born in Montrose, Angus, the daughter of the laird of Dun. She married Major Arthur Otway Jacob and lived for some years in India. Although she began her writing career as a historical novelist with *The Sheep-stealers* (1902), she is best known for poems in the Angus dialect, such as *Songs of Angus* (1915), *More Songs of Angus* (1918), *Bonnie Joan* (1922) and *The Northern Lights* (1927). Her partly autobiographical *Lairds of Dun* (1931) is a standard history of her native district.

JACOBI, Johann Georg
(1740–1814)

German poet and editor (of *Iris*, which printed many of the first poems of **Goethe**), brother to the philosopher Friedrich Heinrich Jacobi, born in Düsseldorf. He was a professor of philosophy at Halle and then at Freiburg. His verse, though skilful, consists in the main of 'pseudo-Anacreontic trivialities'.

JACOBS, William Wymark
(1863–1943)

English short-story writer, born in Wapping, London. He was a post-office official (1883–99) and began writing humorous yarns of bargees and tars, most of which were illustrated by Will Owen, such as *Many Cargoes* (1896), *The Skipper's Wooing* (1897) and *Deep Waters* (1919). He also wrote macabre tales, such as his best-known story, *The Monkey's Paw* (1902).

JACOBSEN, Jens Peter
(1847–85)

Danish novelist, born in Thisted in Jutland. He studied science at Copenhagen, translated Charles Darwin and became, under the influence of Georg Brandes, the leader of the new Danish naturalistic movement. Having contracted tuberculosis in Italy, he published some beautiful poems and short stories such as 'Mogens' (1872), and also two psychological novels, *Fru Marie Grubbe* (1876) and *Niels Lyhne* (1880). Half-realist, half-dreamer, his deliberate impressionist style found many disciples, **Rainer Rilke** among them. Jacobsen's collected works were edited by Fredrik Nielsen in the early 1970s.

▷A Gustafson, in *Six Scandinavian Novelists* (1940)

JACOBSEN, Jorgen-Frantz
(1900–38)

Faroese novelist and essayist. He was a journalist in Copenhagen for a number of years, and there contracted the tuberculosis which killed him. His posthumous novel *Barbara* (1939, Eng trans 1948) has ensured his survival. It is about an Epicurian woman of the 18th-century Faroes—a legendary figure in fact—who married two priests and refused a third.

JACOBSON, Dan
(1929–)

South African-born British novelist, long resident in London. Jacobson is a highly regarded writer who has never quite received full recognition. Earlier novels such as *The Trap* (1955) and *A Dance in the Sun* (1956) dealt with South African problems; later Jacobson expanded his range, especially in his short stories (*Through the Wilderness*, 1977, is a selection), and became a writer of exquisitely observant and objective qualities, yet one with much compassion.

▷*Midstream* (1966)

JACOBSON, Howard
(1942–)

English novelist and travel-writer, born in Manchester. He has taught English at Cambridge University and at Wolverhampton Polytechnic, the latter providing the setting for his first, comic novel, *Coming From Behind* (1983), describing the life of a lecturer, Sefton Goldberg, obsessed by thoughts of failure. Subsequent novels—*Peeping Tom* (1984) and *The Very Model of a Man* (1992)—are a similar deft blending of vibrant satire, eroticism and literary sophistication. His travel books include *In the Land of Oz* (1987), while *Roots Schmoots* (1993), an investigation into the heritage of Jewishness and what it means to be a Jew in contemporary society, continues in documentary terms one of the recurring themes of his fiction, that of personal identity in a modern, fast-moving world.

JAHNN, Hans Henny
(1894–1959)

German novelist and dramatist who, a lifelong pacifist, devoted himself not only to writing but also to musical composition and organ-building. He was born near Hamburg,

the son of a shipbuilder. He was out of Germany for much of his life, in Norway and Denmark, but he returned for his last nine years. When **Oscar Loerke** awarded him the **Kleist** Prize in 1920 for his violent and expressionistic drama *Pastor Ephraim Magnus* (1919) there was a storm of controversy. This play depicts an unhinged parson who enshrines the headless corpse of his brother, and tears out his own eyes in the wish to be crucified. Although Jahnn gradually eschewed Expressionistic techniques in favour of more conventional presentation, his subject-matter remained similar. The essence of all his work, including his celebrated (but unfinished) trilogy of novels *Fluss ohne Ufer* (1949–61, Eng trans, first volume only, *The Ship*, 1961), is the conflict between perversity and sexual terror—the influence of **Freud** was decisive—and a quasi-religious wish for harmony. Jahhn, who founded his own cultural organization, never quite achieved coherence, but he remains a fascinating and, above all, powerful writer.

JAHIER, Piero
(1884–1966)

Italian poet and translator (of **Julien Green**, **Graham Greene**, **Robert Louis Stevenson**, and many others) from Genoa, a writer somewhat apart from groups and movements. His father was a protestant minister who killed himself. A railway official by profession, Piero Jahier remained aloof from fascism (being carefully watched by Mussolini's secret policemen, as an independent socialist). He was associated with the magazine *La voce*, and eventually became its director. His satirical novel *Resultanze in merito alla vita e al carattere di Gino Bianchi* (1915, 'The Outcome Concerning the Life and Character of Gino Bianchi') remains one of the most scarifying attacks on the dehumanizing effects of bureaucracy ever written. His *Con me e con gli Alpini* (1919, 'With Me and the Alpini'), a mixture of prose and verse dealing with his service with the Alpine troops, was one of Italy's most popular books of World War II. His genius may most clearly be perceived in *Ragazzo* (1919, rev edn 1939, 'Boy'), an autobiography. He anticipated the 'hermeticism' of later poets such as **Ungaretti**, but, though he contributed to many periodicals, added little of substance to his output.

▷A Testa, *Piero Jahier* (1970, in Italian)

JAIMES FREYRE, Ricardo
(1868–1933)

Bolivian poet, historian and socialist, born in Tacna. Jaimes Freyre was one of the most important in the *modernista* movement. From 1916 until 1923, and then from 1927 until his death, he lived in Argentina—but he

remained a Bolivian at heart, and served as Minister of Education and Foreign Minister (1923–7) in his country's government. He founded the *Revista de Améérica* with the key figure of the *modernista* movement, **Rubén Dario**. He held eccentric theories about rhythm, but his own technique was unerring. His famous first collection, *Castalia bárbara* (1899, 'Pagan Fountain'), is incomparably his best. Influenced in particular by **Carducci**, as well as by Spanish models and the Nordic mythology which is its subject, it conveys an icy and prophetic vision of the future, especially in 'El Canto del mal', ('Song of Evil', Eng trans in M Seymour-Smith, *Macmillan Guide to Modern World Literature*, 1986). His second collection, *Los sueños son vida* (1917, 'Dreams are Life'), shows some decline in his powers.
▷E Carilla, *Ricardo Jaimes Freyre* (1962, in Spanish)

JAKOBSDÓTTIR, Svava
(1930–)

Icelandic short-story writer, novelist and playwright. Born in Neskaupstaður, she worked as a journalist and studied in the USA and England. She became active in the Icelandic women's movement in 1970, and from 1971 to 1979 she represented the Socialist Party in the Icelandic parliament. Her first collection of short stories, *12 konur* ('12 Women'), appeared in 1965, followed in 1967 by *Veizla undir grjótvegg* ('Party beneath a Stone Wall'). Her texts, highlighting the problems of alienation in modern society and, especially, the position of women in a patriarchal system, tend to open in an atmosphere of everyday realism which alarmingly assumes Surrcalist and absurd proportions. The novel *Leigjandinn* (1969, 'The Lodger') is an allegory about oppression, the central female character representing a curtailment of freedom that is not only sexual but also political and military. *Gunnlaðar saga* (1987, 'The Story of Gunnlod') is a novel making extensive use of myth as a means of illuminating the present.
▷D Kristjánsdóttir, ' "Frihed og sikkerhed er dybest set modsætninger." Introduktion til Svava Jakobsdóttirs forfatterskab', in *Litteratur og samfund*, vol 33/34 (1981)

JAKSIC, Djura
(1832–78)

Serbian poet, dramatist and story writer, born in Srpska Crnja, Banat. He took part in the 1848 revolution, tried and failed to be a painter, and then settled down to the life of schoolmaster—and perfervid, hyperbolic romantic poet; in the latter he was unhappily half-successful. Only his lyrical poetry is now

of value, but this—at its best—has its rightful place in the Serbian canon.

JALAL AD-DIN RUMI, Mohammed ibn Mohammed
(1207–73)

Persian lyric poet and mystic, born in Balkh. He settled at Iconium (Konya) in 1226 and founded a sect. He wrote a lot of exquisite lyrical poetry, including a long epic on the Sufi mystical doctrine, *Masnavi y ma' navi*.
▷A L Aristah, *Rumi, the Persian, the Sufi* (1974)

JAMES, Brian, pseud of John Tierney
(1892–1972)

Australian short-story writer and novelist, born in Eurunderee, New South Wales, whose father taught **Henry Lawson** in his 'bush' school. Himself a teacher, James writes of the educational system in his two novels, *The Advancement of Spencer Button* (1950) and *Hopeton High* (1963). His short stories, much influenced by Lawson, appeared in the *Bulletin* and were collected as *First Furrow* (1944), *Cookabuddy Bridge* (1946) and *The Bunyip of Barney's Elbow* (1956). The best were selected by **Norman Lindsay** as *The Big Burn and Other Stories* (1965).

JAMES, C(yril) L(ionel) R(obert)
(1901–89)

Trinidadian writer, lecturer, political activist and cricket enthusiast, born in Tunapuna, Trinidad. He won a scholarship to Queens Royal College. An autodidact and a useful cricketer, he was urged to leave Trinidad for England by Constantine O'Leary and it was there that *The Life of Captain Cipriani* was published in 1929 at O'Leary's expense. James repaid the kindness by acting as his mentor's amanuensis for his newspaper column and five books. James's aim was the freedom of the black races through Marxism and revolution. For his political activities he was deported from the USA, while in Trinidad his former pupil, Eric Williams, the prime minister, put him under house arrest. Perhaps his most influential book was *The Black Jacobins: Toussaint L'Ouverture and the San Domingo Revolution* (1938). He wrote only one novel, *Minty Alley* (1936), a study of the relationship between education and working-class West Indians. *Beyond the Boundary* (1963) is in part autobiographical: it is a fusion of anecdote, report, analysis and comment, in which sport and politics are harmoniously and ingeniously conjugated.
▷Autobiographical account in *Radical America* (1970)

JAMES, Florence
(1902–93)

New Zealand writer, born in Gisborne, who went to Australia as a child, began a career in music but later moved to art, and then read philosophy. At Sydney University she met **Dymphna Cusack** with whom she wrote *Come In Spinner*. In 1948 this long novel won first prize in a competition in the Sydney *Daily Telegraph* which promised publication, but the strict indecency laws of Australia at that time meant that it was only issued after much debate in a bowdlerized version, edited by James, in 1951. A committed Quaker, she spent time in London's Holloway Women's Prison in the 1960s for her activities with the Campaign for Nuclear Disarmament. A close friend and supporter of **Christina Stead**, she worked in London for the publishing firm of Constables and helped publish younger Australian writers such as **Kylie Tennant**. With Cusack she also wrote a children's book, *Four Winds and a Family* (1947).

JAMES, George Payne Rainsford
(1799–1860)

English novelist, born in London. Influenced by Sir **Walter Scott** he wrote over a hundred historical romances, such as *Richelieu* (1829), *Danley* (1830), *Henry Masterton* (1832), *Arabella Stuart* (1844) and *The Cavalier* (1859). His habit of opening his novels with two horsemen was parodied by **Thackeray** in *Barbazure*, where he is characterized as 'the solitary horseman'. He served as a British Consul in Europe and America for many years.
▷S Ellis, *The Solitary Horseman* (1927)

JAMES, Henry
(1843–1916)

American novelist, brother of **William James**, born in New York, of Irish and Scottish stock. Until his father's death he was known as Henry James, junior; his father, Henry James (1811–82), was a well-known theological writer and lecturer, and an exponent of Swedenborg and Sandemanianism. After a roving youth in America and Europe (where he met **Ivan Turgenev** and **Gustave Flaubert**), and desultory law studies at Harvard, he began in 1865 to contribute brilliant literary reviews and short stories. His work as a novelist falls into three periods. To the first, in which he is mainly concerned with the 'international situation', the impact of American life on the older European civilization, belong *Roderick Hudson* (1875), *The American* (1877), *Daisy Miller* (1879), *Washington Square* (1880), *Portrait of a Lady* (1881), *Princess Casamassima* (1886), in which he probes the shadier aspects of European political life, and finally *The Bostonians* (1886). From 1876

he made his home in England, chiefly in London and in Rye, Sussex, where he struck up an oddly contrasted friendship with the brilliant pioneer of science fiction and self-conscious reformer of mankind, **H G Wells**, a friendship which lasted until the latter's savage attack on the Jamesian ethos in the novel *Boon* (1915). His second period, devoted to purely English subjects, comprises *The Tragic Muse* (1890), *The Spoils of Poynton* (1897), *What Maisie Knew* (1897) and *The Awkward Age* (1899). James reverts to Anglo-American attitudes in his last period, which includes *The Wings of a Dove* (1902), *The Ambassadors* (1903), possibly his masterpiece, *The Golden Bowl* (1904) and two unfinished novels. Collections of his characteristic 'long short stories' include *Terminations* (1895), *The Two Magics* (1898) and *The Altar of the Dead* (1909). James is the acknowledged master of the psychological novel, which has profoundly influenced the 20th-century literary scene. Plot is sacrificed in the interests of minute delineation of character. Many seemingly insignificant incidents, however, subtly contribute allegorically or metaphorically to the author's intentions. The outbreak of World War I brought out his pro-English sympathies. He became a British subject and shortly before his death was awarded the OM. He also wrote critical studies such as *French Poets and Novelists* (1878), and the essay 'On the Art of Fiction' (1884), travel sketches such as *The American Scene* (1906) and three volumes of memoirs, *A Small Boy and Others* (1913), *Notes of a Son and a Brother* (1914) and the unfinished *The Middle Years* (1917).
▷F O Matthiessen, *Henry James: the major phase* (1944); L Edel, *Henry James* (5 vols, 1953–72)

JAMES, M(ontague) R(hodes)
(1862–1936)

English writer of ghost stories, born in Goodnestone, Kent. Educated at Eton and Cambridge, he had a distinguished career as an archaeologist, medievalist and palaeographer, becoming Provost of King's College and then of Eton, and publishing numerous scholarly works. *Ghost Stories of an Antiquary* (1904) was followed by three more collections, all demonstrating James's technique of establishing a comfortable, everyday, contemporary setting, and then gradually introducing supernatural horror; erudite scholarly details, often invented, add an air of veracity, and evil manifestations tend to be hinted at rather than explicitly described. Among his best stories are 'Oh, Whistle, and I'll Come to You, My Lad' (1904) set, typically, in East Anglia, and 'Casting the Runes' (1911).

▷ M Cox, *M. R. James: An Informal Portrait* (1983)

JAMES, P(hyliss) D(orothy)
(1920–)

English thriller writer, born in Oxford, the eldest child of an official in the Inland Revenue. She was educated at Cambridge Girls' High School. Before World War II she worked in the theatre; during the war she was a Red Cross nurse, and also worked in the Ministry of Food. Later she was employed in hospital administration before working in the home office, first in the police department, where she was involved with the forensic science service, thereafter in the criminal law department. Since 1979 she has devoted herself to writing. *Cover Her Face*, published in 1962, was her first novel, a well-crafted, but slight detective story. She has written steadily since, many of her works featuring the superior detective who is also a minor poet, Commander Adam Dalgleish; these include *A Mind to Murder* (1963), *The Black Tower* (1975) and *Death of an Expert Witness* (1977). *A Taste for Death* (1986), a macabre, elegant and substantial story, enjoyed an international vogue and was followed by *Devices and Desires* (1989). *The Skull Beneath the Skin* (1982) featured a female private detective, Cordelia Gray. One of the new 'queens of crime', she was awarded the Crime Writers Association Diamond Dagger in 1987. She was made a life peer in 1991, and became Baroness James of Holland Park.

JAMES, William
(1842–1910)

American philosopher, elder brother of **Henry James**. William James was not a creative writer, but he exercised a vast influence both on politicians (who, like Mussolini, often misunderstood him) and on writers, such as his pupil **Gertrude Stein**, who remained ever grateful to him, and, not least, on his brother. A profound thinker with an occasionally fatal gift for popularization, he was a pioneer psychologist (influencing both branches of his subject, the behaviouristic and the introspective), who transformed the complex and obscurely expressed opinions of the philosopher Charles Sanders Pierce into the popular philosophy of pragmatism (Pierce thereupon referred to his own concept as 'pragmaticism'). James and **Bergson** were responsible for the formulation of the concept of 'stream of consciousness', a term which James himself coined. In his sympathetic *Varieties of Religious Experience* (1902) he showed himself to be a master of literary style, and simultaneously encouraged his readers, in an age of painful loss of faith, not to be afraid of religious and mystical experiences;

the essence of pragmatism was that things were to be judged in terms of their useful function, hence beliefs are true if and because they work, not vice versa.

▷ E de Bono (ed), *The Greatest Thinkers* (1976)

JAMESON, (Margaret) Storm
(1891–1986)

English novelist, born in Whitby. Her first success was *The Lovely Ship* (1927), which was followed by more than 30 books that maintained her reputation as storyteller and stylist. These include *The Voyage Home* (1930), *The Delicate Monster* (1937), *Cloudless May* (1943), *The Black Laurel* (1948), *The Hidden River* (1955), *A Cup of Tea for Mr Thorgill* (1957), *Last Score* (1961), *The Aristide Case* (1964), *The White Crow* (1968). She also wrote poems, essays, criticism and biography, and several volumes of autobiography, including *No Time Like the Present* (1933) and *Journey from the North* (1969).

▷ *The Writer's Situation* (1950)

JAMI
(1414–92)

Persian poet, born in Jam in Khorasan. Among his poems were *Yūsuf o Zalīkhā* (Eng trans *The Book of Joseph and Zuleika* by A Rogers, 1892) and *Salámán u Absál* which was translated by **Edward Fitzgerald** as *Salámán and Absál: an Allegory* (1856). He also wrote prose works.

▷ E Bertel, *Jami* (1949)

JAMMES, Francis
(1868–1938)

French writer, born in Tournay in the Pyrenees. He wrote poems of nature and religion, such as *De l'angélus de l'aube à l'angélus du soir* (1898, 'Between the Morning and the Evening Angelus Bells'), *Deuil des primevères* (1901, 'Primroses in Mourning'), *Triomphe de la vie* (1904, 'The Triumph of Life') and *Géorgiques Chrétiennes* (1911–12, 'Christian Georgics'), and prose romances such as *Le Roman du lièvre* (1903, 'The Romance of the Book').

▷ R Mallet, *Francis Jammes* (1961)

JANIN, Jules Gabriel
(1804–74)

French critic and novelist, born in St Etienne. He turned to journalism in his youth, and his dramatic criticisms in the *Journal des Débats* made his reputation as an opponent of Romanticism and advocate of a Classical revival. His strange and at least half-serious story *L'Âne mort et la femme guillotinée*

(1829, 'The Dead Donkey and the Guillotined Woman') was followed by *Barnave* (1831), half-historical novel, half polemic against the Orléans family. He also compiled a *Histoire de la littérature dramatique* (1858, 'History of Dramatic Literature').

JANOWITZ, Tama
(1957–)

American novelist and short-story writer, born in San Francisco. She made her mark with the novel *American Dad* (1981), in which a psychiatrist is overawed by his father's physical and sexual prowess. *Slaves of New York* (1986), a short-story collection, deals with the garish gallery-goers, the low-lifes and no-lifes, of modern Manhattan. *A Cannibal in Manhattan* (1987) is a subtle, blackly humorous parable which refuses to engage in overt moralizing or political point-scoring. A writer who became trendy with young readers in the late 1980s, she has the talent and the lightness of touch to avoid that generic straitjacket.

JANSSON, Tove
(1914–)

Finland–Swedish author and artist, whose Moomintroll books for children, starting with *The Magician's Hat* (1949) and illustrated by herself, are as much appreciated by adults. Set in the fantastic yet real world of the Moomins, the books emphasize the security of family life. They have reached an international audience and she has been the recipient of many literary prizes. In later years she has written a number of books such as *Sommarboken* (1972, 'The Summer Book') for adults.
▷W G Jones, *Tove Jansson* (1984)

JAPRISOT, Sébastien, anagrammatical pseud of Jean-Baptiste Rossi
(1931–)

French novelist, born in Marseilles, and educated there and at the Sorbonne. He wrote his first novel, *Les mals partis* (1948), at the age of 17 and then translated **J D Salinger**'s *The Catcher in the Rye* into French. While working in advertising, he wrote two successful crime novels, *Piège pour Cendrillon* (1962, Eng trans *Trap for Cinderella*, 1962), for which he won the Grand Prix de la Littérature Policière, and *Compartiment tueurs* (1962, Eng trans *The Sleeping Car Murders*, 1962); a later work, *La dame dans l'auto avec des lunettes et un fusil* (1966, Eng trans *The Lady in the Car with Glasses and a Gun*, 1966) was awarded the Prix d'Honneur. For most of the next decade, Japrisot worked in the film industry as a scriptwriter, returning to fiction in 1978 with *L'Été meurtrier* (Eng

trans *One Deadly Summer*, 1978). All of his novels have been adapted for the screen. In 1986 he published *La passion des femmes* (Eng trans *Women in Evidence*, 1986) and in 1991 *Un long dimanche de fiançailles* (Eng trans *A Very Long Engagement*, 1993), a remarkable story about a young disabled woman's quest for the truth about her fiancé, killed in odd circumstances during World War I.

JARDIEL PONCELA, Enrique
(1901–52)

Spanish dramatist and novelist, born in Madrid. Wishing to revolutionize drama and the novel, he collapsed under the weight of his own ambition. He was a humorist who made early contributions to the Theatre of the Absurd, and whose innovations in the novel have not yet been taken seriously enough. His most substantial work is the novel *La 'tournée' de Dios* (1932, 'The Tour of God').
▷D D Mackay, *Enrique Jardiel Poncela* (1974)

JARNÉS, Benjamín
(1888–1949)

Spanish novelist, biographer and critic, born in Codo, Saragossa. He was in a seminary from 1898 until 1908. He left Spain for Mexico at Franco's victory, but the tyranny allowed him to return to Spain to die (in Madrid) when he was infirm and could offer no threat to it. He has been called, with some justice, 'the most notable novelist of the Generation of 1927', which itself was mainly one of poets (such as **Lorca**, **Alberti** and **Cernuda**). His fiction questions the nature of reality, and mocks its readers' conventional expectations at every point. His work was suppressed by Franco's censors, but there is now a new interest in it. He wrote several quizzical biographies, including one (the best) of **Stefan Zweig**.
▷J S Bernstein, *Benjamín Jarnés* (1971)

JARRELL, Randall
(1914–65)

American poet and critic, born in Nashville, Tennessee. He served in the air force in World War II. He loved teaching and eschewed prestigious universities for unfashionable girls' colleges in the south. A potent, passionate and compassionate writer, he published several collections including *Blood for a Stranger* (1942) and *The Lost World*, published posthumously in 1966. His *Complete Poems* appeared in 1969. An uncompromising critic and merciless reviewer of bad verse, he wrote one novel, *Pictures from an Institution* (1954), an early satirical campus novel. He committed suicide, possibly as a result of his war experience.

▷K Shapiro, *Randall Jarrell* (1967)

JARRY, Alfred
(1873–1907)

French writer, born in Laval, Mayenne. He was educated at Rennes. His play, *Ubu roi* (Eng trans 1951), an attack on bourgeois conventions, was first written when he was 15; later rewritten, it was produced in 1896. In a crude parody of *Macbeth*, Ubu, the hero, symbolizes the crassness of the bourgeoisie pushed to absurd lengths by the lust for power. He wrote two sequels, *Ubu enchaîné* (1900, Eng trans *Ubu Enslaved*, 1953) and *Ubu cocu* (not published until 1944, Eng trans *Ubu Cuckolded*, 1965), and a two-act musical version of *Ubu roi* for marionettes, *Ubu sur la butte* (1901), as well as short stories and poems and other plays. He invented a logic of the absurd, which he called *pataphysique*, and his work is considered a precursor of the Theatre of the Absurd. He died an alcoholic.

▷R Shattuck, *The Banquet Years: the arts in France, 1885–1919* (1959)

JASMIN, pseud of **Jacques Boé**
(1798–1864)

Provençal poet, born in Agen. A barber by profession, he wrote homely verses in his local Gascon dialect. Among his best pieces (collected in *Las Papillôtos*, 1835, French trans *Las Papillôtos*, 1860) are the mock-heroic *Charivari* (1825); *L'Abuglo de Castèl-Cuillé* (1835, Eng trans by **Longfellow**, *The Blind Girl of Castel-Cuillé*); *Françovneto* (1840); and *La Semaine d'un Fils* (1848, 'A Son's Week').

▷J Andrieu, *Jasmin et son oeuvre* (1881)

JASTRUN, Mieczyslaw, pseud of
Mieczyslaw Agatstein
(1903–)

Polish poet and translator who, although he contributed poems to the publications of the inter-war *Skamander* group, never really belonged to any of the main movements in Polish poetry. Of Jewish origin, he was in considerable danger throughout World War II, during which he was a member of the resistance. He is an elegiac poet, who has learned much from **Rilke** (from whom he has made translations) and from the French symbolists. He would have liked to be a meditative poet without commitment, but history assigned him another course. Poland's most intellectual poet, devoted above all to **Cyprian Norwid**, he has long enjoyed high respect. Three poems are included in **Czeslaw Milosz**'s *Post-War Polish Poetry* (1965).

JÁUREGUI, José Martínez de
(1583–1641)

Spanish poet, painter, critic and translator, born in Seville, who settled in Madrid and was (essentially) a representative of the movement now known as *culturanismo*—a cultivation of extreme classical artificiality. Yet Jáuregui, characteristically, had earlier censured *culturanismo* as being excessively artificial. Jáuregui translated the *Aminta* of **Tasso** (1607) and imitated **Ovid** in *Orfeo* (1624). He wrote some memorable poetry, in particular in his vigorous re-creation of the *Pharsalia* of **Lucan**, (1684), which for some is an improvement on the original. Two of his poems are translated in J M Cohen's *Penguin Book of Spanish Verse* (1965).

JAURÈS, Jean
(1859–1914)

French socialist leader and political writer from Castres, who was assassinated. His anti-Marxist socialist ideas, many of them gained through Lucien Herr, librarian at the École Normale, had a profound influence on such writers as Charles Péguy and **Roger Martin Du Gard**; the latter dealt with them (and with Jaurès's assassination) in his epic novel *Les Thibault*.

JEAN BODEL
(c.1165–1210)

French poet and playwright, from Arras. Even if he is not a great poet, his work contrasts favourably with much medieval lyric poetry in being down-to-earth, set in the society he obviously lived in with relish. He was, however, forced to withdraw from society when he contracted leprosy, and produced his best-known poetical work, the *Congés*, as a farewell to his friends. He is also the author of *Le Jeu de Saint Nicholas*, the first French miracle play. Typically, much of its action is set in a tavern.

JEAN LEMAIRE DE BELGES
(1473–c.1515)

French poet and historian, born either in Bavai (then known as Belges) or in Belgium (hence the epithet) and educated at the University of Paris. His poetry is ponderous and portentous, full of allusion and often on classical themes, yet he was one of the first poets to employ such material to explore the Renaissance theme of humanism. His best work is to be found in *La Concorde des deux langages* (1511), a poetical debate on the relative merits of French and Italian.

▷P Spack, *Jean le Maire de Belges* (1926)

JEAN PAUL, pseud of **Johann Paul Friedrich Richter**
(1763–1825)

German novelist and humorist, born in Wunsiedel in north Bavaria. In 1781 he was sent to Leipzig to study theology, but turned to literature. He got into debt, and in 1784 fled from Leipzig, to hide in the poverty-stricken home of his widowed mother at Hof. His first literary efforts were satires which no-one would publish, until in 1783 **Johann Voss** of Berlin gave him 40 louis d'or for *Grönländische Prozesse* (1784, 'The Greenland Law-suits'). The book was a failure, and for three years Jean Paul struggled on at home. In 1787 he began to teach, and during his nine years of tutorship produced the satirical *Auswahl aus des Teufels Papieren* (1789, 'Extracts from the Devil's Papers'); the beautiful idylls *Leben des vergnügten Schulmeisterleins Maria Wuz'* (1793, 'Life of the Cheery Little Schoolteacher, Mariz Wuz), *Quintus Fixlein* (1796; trans by **Thomas Carlyle** as *Life of Quintus Fixlein*, 1827), and the *Der Jubelsenior* (1797, 'The Chairman of Revels'); grand romances, such as *Die unsichtbare Loge* (1793, 'The Invisible Lodge'), *Das Kampanertal* (1797, Eng trans *The Campaner Thal*, 1864) on the immortality of the soul; and the prose idyll, *Jean Pauls biographische Belustigungen* (1797, 'Jean Paul's Prospective Autobiographies'). *Die unsichtbare Loge* was his first literary success; but *Hesperus* (1795, Eng trans 1865) made him famous. For a few years he was the object of extravagant idolatry on the part of the women of Germany. In 1801 he married and three years later settled at Bayreuth, living there until his death. The principal works of his married life were the romances *Titan* (1800–3, Eng trans 1868), which he himself considered his masterpiece and *Flegeljahre* (1804–5, Eng trans *Walt und Vult*, 1846), *Des Feldpredigers Schmelzle Reise nach Flätz* (1809, Eng trans by Carlyle *Schmeltzle's Journey to Flätz*, 1827) and *Dr Katzenbergers Badereise* (1809, 'Dr Katzenberger's Trip to the Spa'), the best of his satirico-humorous writings; the idyll *Leben Fibels* (1812, 'Fibel's Life'); the fragment of another grand romance, *Der Komet; oder, Nikolaus Marggaf* (1820–2, 'The Comet; or, Nicholas Marggaf'); reflections on literature (*Vorschule der Ästhetik*; improved edn 1812, Eng trans *Preparatory School of Aesthetics*, 1830); another series on education (*Levana*, 1807, Eng trans 1848), a book that ranks with **Rousseau**'s *Émile*; various patriotic writings (1808–12); and an unfinished autobiography, *Wahrheit ans Jean Pauls Leben* (1826–33, 'The Truth About Jean Paul's Life'). Jean Paul stands alone in German literature. All his great qualities of imagination and intellect were made subservient to his humour, which has the widest range, moving from the petty follies of individual men and the absurdities of social custom up to the paradoxes rooted in the universe.

JEFFERIES, (John) Richard
(1848–87)

English naturalist and novelist, born near Swindon, the son of a Wiltshire farmer. He started as a provincial journalist and became known by a letter to *The Times* (1872) on the Wiltshire labourers. His first real success, *The Gamekeeper at Home* (1878), was followed by other books on rural life, including *Wild Life in a Southern County* (1879), *Hodge and his Masters* (1880), *Wood Magic* (1881), the autobiographical *Bevis: The Story of a Boy* (1882), and his last and most successful novel, *Amaryllis at the Fair* (1887). *The Story of my Heart* (1883) is a strange autobiography of inner life; *After London, or Wild England* (1885), is a curious romance of the future.
▷P E Thomas, *Richard Jefferies: his life and work* (1972)

JEFFERS, (John) Robinson
(1887–1962)

American poet and dramatist, born in Pittsburgh, whose first collection, *Flagons and Apples*, appeared in 1912. His principal themes derive from biblical stories and Greek and Roman legend, and concern the corruption of moral values and the purpose of mankind in a dark and dangerous world; they first became apparent in *Tamar and Other Poems* (1924), the title poem being based upon the Old Testament story of the rape of Tamar. In this and other works Jeffers attempted to reclaim a psychological intensity in poetic expression. Other collections include *The Women at Point Sur* (1927), *Be Angry at the Sun* (1941) and *Hungerfield and Other Poems* (1954). He also wrote a version of *Medea* (1946).

JEFFREY, William
(1896–1946)

Scottish poet, born in Kirk o' Shotts, Lanarkshire, and educated at Glasgow and Edinburgh universities. Having served in France in World War I, where he was gassed, he became a journalist for the *Glasgow Evening Times* and then the *Glasgow Herald* as theatre critic before being first published in 1921 with *Prometheus Returns and other Poems*. Scottish influences on his work include the Makars as well as border ballads; images of his native land's scenery recur in his work, as in *The Lands of Lomond* (1926), *Mountain Songs* (1928) and *The Golden Stag* (1932), though he was also capable of the very different *Fantasia in an Industrial Town* (1933). He also derives heavily from **Blake**, **Tennyson** and, more latterly, **Yeats**.

▷A Scott (ed), *Selected Poems of William Jeffrey* (1951)

JELLICOE, (Patricia) Ann
(1927–)

English dramatist and theatre director, born in Middlesborough, and the author of two important plays, *The Sport of My Mad Mother* (1956) and *The Knack* (1961). The first is an Absurdist celebration of youth and captures the wishful anarchism among the younger generation of the time. *The Knack* is less obscure, and a more successful satire of sexual conventions and expectations. During the 1970s, Jellicoe moved to Devon and has since concentrated on writing plays for amateur community productions, many intended to be acted in a promenade fashion in the open air. Plays such as *The Tide* (1980) and *The Western Women* (1984) deal with historical events, demand large casts and are notable for revealing the crucial role played by women in local affairs.

JENKINS, (John) Robin
(1912–)

Scottish novelist, born in Cambuslang, Lanarkshire, and educated at Hamilton Academy and Glasgow University. At various times an English teacher in Scotland, Afghanistan, Spain and Borneo, he has set many of his stories in these countries. A prolific writer, his works begin with *So Gaily Sings the Lark* (1950), carry on to *Willie Hogg* (1993), and fall into three main groups: those set in Scotland; those set in 'Norania', his fictional Afghanistan; and those dealing with 'Kalewentan', a far eastern sultanate. Interested in exploring human beings' moral possibilities, in those of his works set outside Scotland, such as *Dust on the Paw* (1961), he looks at the paradoxes of society's values. In his Scottish novels he concentrates on Calvinism, often dealing with characters, as in *A Would-be Saint* (1978), who are so holy that the concept of 'good' must be re-examined. His best-known novels are *The Cone-Gatherers* (1955) and *Fergus Lamont* (1979).

▷F R Hart, *The Scottish Novel* (1985)

JENNINGS, Elizabeth
(1926–)

English poet, born in Boston, Lincolnshire. A student at Oxford, she became friends with several writers who went on to form the Movement. Her early work—1953 saw the publication of her first volume, *Poems*—was confident and rational, technically tight, and displayed the influence of the Movement ethos, although she was never formally allied to that group. A nervous breakdown at the start of the 1960s appeared to rid her poetry of its repressed edge, and subsequent volumes, such as *The Mind has Mountains* (1966), are concerned far more about the emotional and spiritual life. Latterly her work has become a serene evocation of her Catholicism; *Moments of Grace* (1980) is typical in this regard. Her *Collected Poems* were published in 1967 and 1986.

JENS, Walter
(1923–)

German novelist, critic (notably of **Euripides**) and radio playwright, born in Hamburg. A well-known theological and scriptural scholar, Jens was a member of the literary circle Gruppe '47. His **Kafka**esque novel *Der Blinde* (1951) was translated as *The Blind Man* in 1954.

JENSEN, Johannes Vilhelm
(1873–1950)

Danish novelist, essayist and poet, winner of the Nobel Prize for literature, born in Farsö, Jutland, one of 10, one of whom was **Thit Jensen**. His native land and its people are described in his *Himmerlandshistorier* (1898–1910), but many of his works, such as *The Forest* and *Madama d'Ora* (1904), are based on his extensive travels in the Far East and America. In *Den Lange Rejse* (1908–22, *The Long Journey*, 1922–4) the journey traced, however, is that of man through the ages, the three constituent novels being an expression of Jensen's Darwinism. His psychological study of Kristian II of Denmark, *Kongens Fald* (1933, 'The Fall of the King'), his short prose works, *Myter* (1904–44), 14 of which were translated into English as *The Waving Rye* (1959), and his lyric poetry (1901–41), all serve to vindicate his high place in modern Scandinavian literature. He was awarded the Nobel Prize for literature in 1944.

▷E O Gelsted, *Johannes Vilhelm Jensen* (1938)

JENSEN, Thit
(1876–1957)

Danish novelist and lecturer, born in Farsø on Jutland. One of 10 sisters and brothers—one of whom was **Johannes Jensen**—she published her first novel in 1903. Early works such as *Martyrium* (1905, 'Martyrdom') and *Ørkenvandring* (1907, 'Through the Desert') are pleas for women's equality in marriage. However, her later work deals with the conflict between the demand for equality and motherhood. While the central character in *Gerd* (1918) rejects conventional feminine roles in favour of a career, the renowned MP in the sequel, *Aphrodite fra Fuur* (1925, 'Aphrodite from Fuur'), experiences a sense of fragmentation that forces her back into a more traditional existence. The theme of motherhood was subsequently explored by Jensen in a number of historical novels. Her public lectures, most famously in favour of contraception, made her a highly controversial figure.

▷L Møller Jensen, *Roser og laurbær. Om grundstrukturen i Thit Jensens kvindepolitiske forfatterskab* (1978)

JENSEN, Wilhelm
(1837–1911)

German poet and novelist, born in Heiligenhafen in north-east Holstein. He studied medicine and history at a variety of universities, and his main works, such as *Vom römischen Reich deutscher Nation* (1882, 3 vols, 'The Roman Empire of the German Nation'), are concerned with German history. In 1888 he moved to Munich where he spent most of his life. His writing includes tragedies, songs, poetry, and novels such as *Flut und Ebbe* (1877, 'Ebb and Flow') and *Aus See und Sand* (1897, 'From Sea and Sand').

▷W Birchfield, *Wilhelm Jensen als Lyriker* (1913)

JEROME, Jerome K(lapka)
(1859–1927)

English humorous writer, novelist and playwright, born in Walsall, Staffordshire, and brought up in London. Successively a clerk, schoolmaster, reporter, actor and journalist, he became joint editor of *The Idler* in 1892 and started his own twopenny weekly, *To-Day*. His magnificently ridiculous *Three Men in a Boat* (1889), the account of a boat trip up the Thames from Kingston to Oxford, established itself as a humorous classic of the whimsical. Other books include *The Idle Thoughts of an Idle Fellow* (1889), *Three Men on the Bummel* (1900), *Paul Kelver* (1902), the morality play *The Passing of the Third Floor Back* (1907), and his autobiography, *My Life and Times* (1926).

▷A Moss, *Jerome K. Jerome: his life and work* (1929)

JERROLD, Douglas William
(1803–57)

English author, dramatist and wit, born in London, the son of Samuel Jerrold, actor and manager. In 1813 he joined the navy as a midshipman, but on the close of the war he started life anew as a printer's apprentice, and in 1819 was a compositor on the *Sunday Monitor* but rose to become its dramatic critic. In 1825 he was engaged to write plays

for the Coburg Theatre, and from 1829 for the Surrey Theatre. From 1841 he was one of the original contributors to the newly-launched *Punch* magazine, writing under the pseudonym 'Q', and edited the *Illuminated Magazine* (1843–4), *Douglas Jerrold's Shilling Magazine* (1845–48) and *Douglas Jerrold's Weekly Newspaper* (1846–8). In 1852 he became Editor of *Lloyd's Weekly Newspaper*. He wrote several novels, including *The Story of a Feather* (1844), and *Cakes and Ale* (1852, essays and tales), *Punch's Letters to his Son* (1843), *Punch's Complete Letter-writer* (1845), and *Mrs Caudle's Curtain Lectures* (1846), as well as several plays, including *Black-ey'd Susan* (1829), and the comedies *The Bride of Ludgate* (1831), *The Prisoner of Ludgate* (1831), *Time Works Wonders* (1845) and *The Catspaw* (1850). *Other Times* (1868) is a selection from his political writings in *Lloyd's*. His son William Blanchard Jerrold (1826–84), succeeded his father as Editor of *Lloyd's* and also wrote novels and plays.

▷W Jerrold, *Douglas Jerrold* (1914)

JESSE, Fryn (Friniwyd Tennyson)
(1888–1958)

English novelist, dramatist and editor of several volumes of the *Notable British Trials* series, born in Chiselhurst, Kent. A greatniece of **Tennyson**, she studied painting, but during World War I took up journalism and after it served on Herbert Hoover's Relief Commission for Europe. In 1918 she married H M Harwood, the dramatist, and with him collaborated in a number of light plays and a series of war-time letters, *London Front* (1940) and *While London Burns* (1942). But she is best known for her novels set in Cornwall, such as *The White Riband* (1921), *Tom Fool* (1926) and *Moonraker* (1927), as well as *The Lacquer Lady* (1929), set in Burma and regarded by many as her best novel, and *A Pin to See a Peepshow* (1934), based on the Thompson-Bywaters murder case. She also published collected poems, *The Happy Bride* (1920), and remarkable accounts of the trials of Madeleine Smith (1927), Timothy Evans and John Christie (1958).

▷ *Sabi Pas, or I Don't Know* (1935)

JEWETT, (Theodora) Sarah Orne
(1849–1909)

American novelist, born in South Berwick, Maine. She wrote a series of sketches, *Deephaven* (1877), and a more structured fiction, *The Country of the Pointed Firs* (1896), which developed her interest in the psychology of small, out of the way places and their inhabitants. She also wrote romantic novels and stories based on the provincial life of her state, such as *A Country Doctor* (1884) and *A White Heron* (1886), and a historical

novel, *The Tory Lover* (1901). She was the first President of Vassar College (1862–4).
▷ F O Matthiessen, *Sarah Orne Jewett* (1929)

JEWSBURY, Geraldine (Endsor)
(1812–80)
English novelist, born in Measham, Derbyshire, the daughter of a businessman. From 1854 she lived in Chelsea, to be near her friend Jane Welsh Carlyle. She contributed articles and reviews to various journals, and wrote six novels, including *Zoë* (1845), *The Half Sisters* (1848), *Marion Withers* (1851) and *Right or Wrong* (1859). *A Selection from the Letters of Geraldine Jewsbury to Jane Carlyle* (1892) aroused controversy over the emotional nature of their relationship.
▷ S Howe, *Geraldine Jewsbury* (1935)

JHABVALA, Ruth Prawer
(1927–)
British novelist, short-story and screenplay writer, born in Cologne, Germany, of Polish parents. Her parents emigrated to Britain in 1939. She graduated from Queen Mary College, London University, married a visiting Indian architect, and lived in Delhi (1951–75). Most of her fiction relates to India, taking the viewpoint of an outsider looking in. Significant novels include *To Whom She Will Marry* (1955), *Esmond in India* (1958), *The Householder* (1960), *A Backward Place* (1963) and *Heat and Dust* (1975), which won the Booker Prize. Her short stories have been collected in several volumes. In association with film makers James Ivory and Ismail Merchant, she has written several accomplished screenplays, among them *Shakespeare Wallah* (1965), *A Room with a View* (1986) and *Howard's End* (1992).

JIMÉNEZ, Juan Ramón
(1881–1958)
Spanish lyric poet, winner of the Nobel Prize for literature. He was born in Moguer, Huelva, which he made famous by his delightful story of the young poet and his donkey, *Platero y Yo* (1914, Eng trans *Platero and I*, 1956), one of the classics of modern Spanish literature. He abandoned his law studies and settled in Madrid. His early poetry, impressionistic and rich in evocative imagery and sound, echoed that of **Paul Verlaine**. *Almas de Violeta* (1900, 'Violet Souls'), *Arias Tristes* (1903, 'Sad Arias') and *Jardines lejanos* (1905, 'Far-off Gardens') belong to this period. With *El silencio de oro* (1922, 'The Silence of Gold') there came a mood of optimism and a zest for experimentation with styles and rhythms. In 1936 he left Spain because of the Civil War and settled in Florida. In his last period he emerges as a major

poet, treating the major themes of life in novel sounds, illusions and styles in a subtly spun *vers libre*. He was awarded the Nobel Prize for literature in 1956.
▷ D Fogelquist, *Jiménez* (1976)

JIRÁSEK, Alois
(1851–1930)
Czech historical novelist and dramatist, born in Hronov. Throughout his life he taught history in a Prague secondary school. He is important because his nationalist novels still reflect, to a remarkable degree, the Czechs' own view of their oppressed past. His characterization is weak, but he regarded the Czech masses as his true subject. His collected works ran to 47 volumes.
▷ K Nejedlý, *Alois Jirásek* (1952)

JOCHUMSSON, Matthías
(1835–1920)
Icelandic poet and clergyman, born at Skógar in Thorskafjörður, a farmer's son. After training as a merchant in Copenhagen, he became a Lutheran pastor (1865) at various places in Iceland. Best known as a lyric poet, he drew for his inspiration on the historic traditions of the sagas and on the dramatic natural scene. He composed the words of the choral anthem written for the millennial celebrations of 1874 (*Ó, Guð vors lands*—'God of our Land') which is now the national anthem. He was regarded as unofficial poet laureate. He also wrote plays, including a historical drama about Bishop Jón Arason (1900), and translated **Byron**, **Ibsen**, and **Shakespeare**'s major tragedies.
▷ D Ostlund, *70th Birthday Essays* (1905)

JODELLE, Étienne
(1532–73)
French poet and dramatist. He was the only Parisian member of the Pléiade, and he wrote the first French tragedy, *Cléopatre captive* (1552, 'Cleopatra the Prisoner'), based on classical models. He also wrote two comedies, including *Eugène*.
▷ E H Balmas, *Un poeta del Rinascimento francesca* (1962)

JOHANNES SECUNDUS, Jan Everts, or Everaerts
(1511–36)
Dutch poet, writing in Latin, born in The Hague. He studied law at Bourges, and was secretary to the Archbishop of Toledo, the Bishop of Utrecht, and the Emperor Charles V. His famous work is *Basia*.

JOHANNES VON SAAZ

JOHANNES VON SAAZ, also known as **Johannes von Tepl** (c.1350–1415)

German author, born in Schüttwa. He wrote *Der Ackermann aus Böhmen* (c.1400, 'The Bohemian Peasant'), a classic piece of German prose in which the author, in the character of a peasant, reproaches Death for the loss of his wife, Margarete, before the heavenly Judge, but eventually accepts that God has ordained these events.

JOHN OF HOWDEN
(d.1274)

English Latin poet and canon of Howden. An important figure in his day in many ways, he followed a career in politics which led him to court, where he became clerk to Eleanor, queen to Henry III of England. He was also a gifted astronomer and astrologer. His poems are on religious themes and employ mystical imagery. They centre mainly on the Passion of Christ and that of Mary, and they represent a growing cult of mysticism and personal devotion within the late 13th-century church.

JOHNS, W(illiam) E(arl)
(1893–1968)

English aviator and writer, author of the 'Biggles' stories, born in Hertford. He served in the Norfolk Yeomanry and when commissioned in 1916, transferred to the Royal Flying Corps where he served wtih some distinction. He retired from the Royal Air Force in 1930, edited *Popular Flying* and *Flying* in the 1930s, and served in the Ministry of Information (1939–45). His wartime marriage broke up after 1918 and he lived for many years with a lady his publishers prevented him from marrying, considering that his status as a children's author forbade his divorce. His stories are rattling good flying yarns, with his World War I experiences almost bodily transferred to later periods. In World War I he had been captured and sentenced to be shot; the 'Biggles' series reflects unspoken anger at the expendability of airmen in bureaucratic thinking, while his World War II female pilot, 'Worrals', is savagely contemptuous of male self-satisfaction and hostility to acceptance of women as equals. He later tried his hand, less successfully, at space exploration stories.
▷P B Ellis and P Williams, *The Life of Captain W. E. Johns* (1981)

JOHNSON, B(ryan) S(tanley William)
(1933–73)

English experimental novelist, born in London and briefly lionized there for having brought a Continental playfulness to contemporary fiction. His first significant book, *Travelling People* (1963), is an exhaustive illustration of **James**ian 'point of view' in fiction, and is full of typographical and other estranging devices. *Albert Angelo* (1964) was relatively conventional up to a notorious intervention—'Fuck all this lying'—by the author himself. *Trawl* (1966) carried a Wittgensteinian conceit to extraordinary lengths by having holes cut in some pages: language-as-net. Johnson's most celebrated post-modernist device was his 'loose-leaf' novel *The Unfortunates* (1969), which consisted of 27 separate sections, all but the first and last of which could be read in any order the reader chose. After this, there was nowhere to go but back towards more conventional narrative; *House Mother Normal* (1971) and *Christy Malry's Own Double-Entry* (1973) are both disappointing, though the first reflects Johnson's obsessive interest in ageing, which resulted in the posthumously published *See the Old Lady Decently* (1975), a quasi-documentary account of his mother's death. Having prepared a collection of short stories with the ironic title *Aren't You Rather Young to be Writing Your Memoirs?* (1974), and despite respectful critical and commercial attention, Johnson hanged himself in a fit of recurrent depression.
▷A Burns and C Sugnet, *The Imagination on Trial* (1976)

JOHNSON, Colin *see* MUDROOROO, Nyoongah

JOHNSON, Denis
(1949–)

American novelist and poet, born in Munich and brought up in Tokyo, Manila and Washington, DC. His first novel, *Angels* (1983), is a skilfully carved slice of US low life; the book's latter section, a description of a young man's days on Death Row, is particularly well wrought. *Fiskadoro* (1985), a post-holocaust tale, is a detour in Johnson's development as a novelist, but *Resuscitation of a Hanged Man* (1991), the story of a sombre failed suicide turned private investigator, marks a return to the wit and gritty realism of his debut. His volumes of poetry include *Inner Weather* (1976); he won the **Robert Frost** Poetry Prize in 1983.

JOHNSON, Diane
(1934–)

American novelist, biographer and critic, Professor of English at the University of California. Johnson was born in Illinois and several of her novels look at Californian life from a mid-West point of view. *Burning* (1971) is an apocalyptic (and prophetic) portrait of life in Los Angeles. She has produced an authorized biography of **Dashiell Hammett**, was co-author (with Stanley Kubrick) of the screenplay for **Stephen King**'s *The Shining*, and has written, in *Lesser Lives* (1972), an account of the trials of **Thomas Love Peacock**'s daughter. *Terrorists and Novelists* (1982), a collection of reviews, is further testimony to her range and energy. *Natural Opium* (1993), a travel book written on the rebound from a messy divorce, was waspish and self-critical.

▷J Todd, *Women Writers Talking* (1983)

JOHNSON, Dorothy M(arie)
(1905–84)

American novelist, born in Iowa. She grew up in Montana. The author of two classic western stories, 'The Man Who Shot Liberty Valance' and 'A Man Called Horse' (immortalized by Richard Harris, but not published until 1984 in *The Reel West* and *The Western Hall of Fame* respectively), she was a journalist, working as a magazine editor in New York for 15 years before returning to Montana and joining the staff of a local paper. She also wrote full-length novels. *Warriors For A Lost Nation* (1969) was a biography of Sitting Bull.

JOHNSON, Eyvind Olof Verner
(1900–76)

Swedish novelist and short-story writer, joint winner of the Nobel Prize for literature, born of working-class parents in the far north of Sweden. After a number of years in mainly manual occupations he spent most of the 1920s in Paris and Berlin. His four-part *Romanen om Olof* (1934–7, 'The Story of Olof') is the finest of the many working-class autobiographical novels written in Sweden in the 1930s. He was much involved in anti-Nazi causes, and produced a number of novels, especially the *Krilon* series (1941–3), castigating totalitarianism. The same humanitarian values are evident in his later historical novels, particularly *Strändernas svall* (1946, 'Return to Ithaca'), *Drömmar om rosor och eld* (1949, 'Dreams about Roses and Fire') and *Hans nådes tid* (1960, 'The Days of his Grace'). He shared the 1974 Nobel Prize for literature with his fellow Swede, **Harry Martinson**.

▷G Orton, *Eyvind Johnson* (1972)

JOHNSON, James Weldon
(1871–1938)

American author, born in Jacksonville, Florida. He practised at the Bar there from 1897 to 1901, and in 1906 he was American consul at Puerto Cabello, Venezuela, and at Corinto, Nicaragua (1909–12). He was secretary of the National Association for the Advancement of Colored People (1916–30) and was awarded the Spingarn Medal (1925). His finest poetry is included in *God's Trombones* (1927). From 1930 he was Professor of Creative Literature at Fisk University. He wrote extensively on Black problems, and compiled collections of Black poetry.

▷E D Levy, *James Weldon Johnson: Black Leader, Black Voice* (1973)

JOHNSON, Josephine Winslow
(1910–)

American novelist and poet. She won a Pulitzer Prize with her first novel *Now in November* (1934), a celebration of unmechanized farming life, a subject she knew intimately, having grown up on a farm. (Johnson's husband eventually became editor of *Farm Quarterly*.) Other novels, written in a distinctively quiet but stylish manner, have sombre themes. *Wildwood* (1946) is about a frustrated and lonely young girl growing up in the oppressive home of relatives, and the main character of *The Dark Traveller* (1963) is a schizophrenic.

JOHNSON, Linton Kwesi
(1952–)

Jamaican-born reggae poet and performer, he has lived in Britain since the age of nine. He studied sociology at London University and holds a creative writing fellowship at Warwick University. His verdict on British culture was most succinctly expressed in the title of a 1980 book and recording, *Inglan is a Bitch*. He writes powerful, committed verse which follows the cadences of Caribbean speech and the alternately pointed and hypnotically elongated rhythmic values of reggae and dub. His distinctive style was immediately evident in *Voices of the Living and the Dead* (1974) and he became part of a revived poetry/performance movement in Britain, adopted by Michael Horovitz's New Departures road show and latterly by the Anti-Nazi League in its crusade against British racism. His most powerful work is the sombre rumble of *Dread Beat an' Blood* (1975), which is almost as effective on the page as it is on the Virgin Records album that followed.

JOHNSON, Lionel Pigot
(1867–1902)

English poet and critic, born in Broadstairs, Kent, but brought up in Wales. The son of an army officer, he was educated at Winchester and New College, Oxford, where he distinguished himself by the excellence of his work. After graduating, he moved to London, surrounded himself with books, and made a living in literary journalism. He converted to Roman Catholicism in 1891—thus becoming one of the most notable converts of this era—and fell under the spell of the Celtic Twilight, as *Poems* (1895) and *Ireland and Other Poems* (1897) testify. His most famous and frequently anthologized poem, however, is *By the Statue of King Charles at Charing Cross*. A member of the Rhymers' Club, and a friend of **Oscar Wilde** and **W B Yeats**, he was influential in his day and, a percipient critic, did much to promote an appreciation of **Thomas Hardy**. But he was an immoderate drinker and often appears tipsy and ridiculous in anecdotes. He died as a result of a fall caused by the effects of alcohol.

▷A W Patrick, *Lionel Johnson: poète et critique* (1939)

JOHNSON, Louis
(1924–88)

New Zealand poet and critic, whose first work was collected as *Stanza and Scene: Poems* (1945). A poet of the city, and a leading member of the 'Wellington Group', he attracted attention with his next two books, both published in 1951: *The Sun Among the Ruins* and *Roughshod Among the Lilies*. After *Bread and a Pension: Selected Poems* (1954) he moved to Australia where he published *Selected Poems* (1972) and *Fires and Patterns* (1975). Returning to New Zealand, his later work was published as *Coming and Going: Poems* (1982) and *Winter Apples* (1984). *Last Poems* was published posthumously in 1990. He was active in support of his fellow poets, founding, and for many years editing, the *New Zealand Poetry Yearbook*. He also edited a quarterly, *Numbers*, and his Capricorn Press published much work by his contemporaries.

JOHNSON, Pamela Hansford *see* HANSFORD JOHNSON, Pamela

JOHNSON, Pauline
(1861–1913)

Canadian poet, born on the Six Nations Reservation near Ontario. Her father was a Mohawk, while her English mother was related to **William Dean Howells**. Her earliest poems were published in magazine form in 1884, and her work was collected in several volumes, including *Canadian Born* (1903) and *Flint and Feather* (1912). From 1892 to 1909 she gave extensive public readings of her work, often dressed in Native American costume and using the name Tekahionwake. She also wrote short prose works, collected in *Legends of Vancouver* (1911) and other volumes.

▷B Keller, *Pauline* (1981)

JOHNSON, Samuel, known as **Dr Johnson**
(1709–84)

English writer, critic, lexicographer, and conversationalist, born in Lichfield, Staffordshire. The son of a bookseller, he read voraciously in his father's shop. Educated at Lichfield Grammar School and Pembroke College, Oxford, he left without taking a degree in 1731. He taught briefly at a school in Market Bosworth, and then moved to Birmingham where he did some writing. In 1735 he married a widow 20 years older then himself, Elizabeth ('Tetty') Porter, and they opened a school at Edial, near Lichfield, where one of the pupils was the future actor, David Garrick. The school failed, and in 1737, accompanied by the young Garrick, Johnson and his wife moved to London, where he finished writing a tragedy, *Irene* (not to be staged for 12 years), and earned a living writing parliamentary reports for *The Gentleman's Magazine*. In it he published (anonymously) his first poem, *London: A Poem in Imitation of the Third Satire of Juvenal* (1738). In 1744 he produced a topical and successful *Life* of his friend **Richard Savage**. Meanwhile he had been cataloguing the great library of Edward Harley, Earl of Oxford, and was able further to indulge his huge appetite for reading. In 1747 he issued a prospectus of a *Dictionary of the English Language*, which was to take him eight years to complete. During this time he published a long didactic poem, *The Vanity of Human Wishes* (1749), based on another of **Juvenal**'s satires. Garrick fulfilled a boyhood promise by producing his *Irene* at Drury Lane Theatre (1749), and Johnson himself wrote and edited, practically single-handedly, a bi-weekly periodical, *The Rambler*, which ran for 208 issues (1750–2), full of moral essays written (anonymously) by himself. In 1752 his wife died, plunging him into lasting depression. His great Dictionary appeared in 1755, which gave rise to a celebrated letter in which Johnson disdained an offer of patronage from Lord Chesterfield. Johnson was awarded an honorary degree at Oxford, but he had to continue literary hack-work to earn a living, contributing reviews for the *Literary Magazine*, and The *Idler* series of papers in *The Universal Chronicle* (1758–60). During this time his mother died, and in a week he wrote his moral fable, *Rasselas: The Prince of Abyssinia* (1759), to defray the funeral expenses. With the accession of George III in 1760, Johnson was granted a pension of £300 for life, which brought him financial security for the first time. In 1763 he met the young Scot, **James Boswell**, who would become his biographer, and with whom he would share a delightful tour of the Hebrides in 1773 (*A Journey to the Western Isles of Scotland*, 1775). In 1764

he founded the Literary Club with a circle of friends, including Joshua Reynolds, **Edmund Burke** and **Oliver Goldsmith**; later members were Boswell, Garrick and Charles James Fox. In 1765 he published his critical edition of **Shakespeare**'s plays (8 vols), with its classic Preface, and then set to work on his monumental *Lives of the Most Eminent English Poets* (10 vols, 1779–81). In that year his friend, the brewer Henry Thrale, died; his widow, Hester Thrale, who had looked after Johnson for many years, fell in love with an Italian musician, Gabriele Piozzi, and Johnson's wounded fury at their marriage in 1784 provoked a total estrangement. He died in dejection, and was buried in Westminster Abbey.
▷J Boswell, *Life of Johnson* (1791, 1799); J Wain, *Samuel Johnson* (1944)

JOHNSON, Uwe
(1934–84)

German novelist, born in Pomeranian Poland and educated in Rostock and Leipzig. He belongs to the first generation of writers to experience the post-war division of Germany as a normal fact of life rather than a novelty. He rarely wrote direct political commentary, preferring to concentrate on the moral and psychological implications of division; critics expecting—or demanding—a more realistically politicized approach were themselves deeply divided over his first published novel, *Mutmassungen über Jakob* (1959, Eng trans *Speculations about Jakob*, 1963), and it may be that lack of general understanding led him to a more straightforward narrative approach in later books. *Das dritte Buch über Achim* (1961, Eng trans *The Third Book about Achim*, 1967) is fascinating as a study of the East German attitude to sport, but Johnson's philosophical agenda are somewhat downplayed. *Zwei Ansichten* (1965, Eng trans *Two Views*, 1966) is a rather banal Cold War love story, but Johnson returned to form with the huge and hugely impressive *Jahrestage: Aus dem Leben den Gesine Cresspahl* (4 vols, 1970–83, Eng trans *Anniversaries: From the Life of Gesine Cresspahl*, 1975), in which he picks up the lives of characters from his first novel and projects them back into the Nazi years and forward into post-war exile, and represents a profound essay in historical memory. Johnson was awarded the **Raabe** Prize in 1975 and the **Thomas Mann** Prize in 1978.
▷M Boulby, *Uwe Johnson* (1974)

JOHNSTON, or JONSTON, Arthur
(1587–1641)

Scottish physician, poet and humanist, born in Caskieben, Aberdeenshire. He graduated MD at Padua in 1610, and visited many academic institutions. He practised medicine in France, and his fame as a Latin poet spread across Europe. In about 1625 he was appointed physician to King Charles I. His famous translation of the Psalms of David into Latin verse was published in Aberdeen in 1637. He edited the *Deliciae Poetarum Scotorum Hujus Aevi* (1637), an anthology of Latin poetry from Scotland, to which he also contributed notable poems. In 1637 he became Rector of King's College, Aberdeen.
▷J W L Adams, in *Scottish Poetry, a critical survey* (1955, ed J Kinsley)

JOHNSTON, (William) Denis
(1901–84)

Irish playwright, born in Dublin, the son of a Protestant liberal judge. Educated at St Andrew's School, Dublin, Merchiston Castle School, Edinburgh, Cambridge and Harvard, he joined the English (1925) and Northern Ireland (1926) bars. His impressionist play, *Shadowdance*, was rejected by Lady **Gregory** for the Abbey Theatre, then retitled *The Old Lady Says 'No'*, and became a major success at the Gate Theatre in 1929, followed by a further triumph with *The Moon on the Yellow River* (1931) and several others for the next three decades. His autobiographical *Nine Rivers from Jordan* (1953) recounted his experiences as a war correspondent. His *In Search of Swift* (1959) was an impressive argument for **Jonathan Swift**'s inability to marry Esther Johnson ('Stella') having been caused by an illegitimate half-sibling relationship. He wrote a later autobiographical work, *The Brazen Head* (1977). His daughter is the novelist **Jennifer Johnston**.
▷J Ronsley, *Denis Johnston, a retrospective* (1981)

JOHNSTON, George Benson
(1913–)

Canadian poet and translator of Old Norse sagas, born in Hamilton, Ontario, known for his solemn treatments of ridiculous subject-matter. Johnston is a fine exponent of traditional verse forms. His poems are witty and concise, and he is given to the creation of comic characters with names like Miss Knit. This, coupled with the fantastic element on display in *Ark Redivivus: Selected Poems* (1981), gives him the air of a Canadian **Lear**, as in 'And often at the droop of day/When evening grumbles in/The great dufuflu has his say/Above the braffic's din.'

JOHNSTON, George Henry
(1912–70)

Australian author and journalist, born in Malvern, Victoria. After studying commercial art, he worked as a journalist and during World War II as a war correspondent, when his syndicated dispatches from New Guinea, India and Burma, Italy and the North Atlantic were read world-wide. He wrote five books on his war experiences, published between 1941 and 1944, before returning to journalism. He worked in London as European editor of the Sydney *Sun*, then made a new home in the Greek islands with his wife and fellow-author, **Charmian Clift**, with whom he wrote three novels, and who described their life in the islands in short stories and essays. Johnston wrote a number of novels including *Monsoon* (1948), *The Cyprian Woman* (1955) and *Closer to the Sun*, which won the US Literary Guild Award in 1960. As well as short stories and plays, he achieved distinction with his semi-autobiographical trilogy *My Brother Jack* (1964), *Clean Straw for Nothing* (1969) and the unfinished *A Cartload of Clay* (1971).

JOHNSTON, Jennifer Prudence
(1930–)

Irish novelist, born in Dublin, the daughter of **Denis Johnston**, and educated at Trinity College, Dublin. In such works as *The Gates* (1973) Johnston monitors the class and religious divisions in contemporary Ireland, and the slow erosion of the Irish Protestant gentry. *How Many Miles to Babylon?* (1974), in which two childhood friends from either end of the social scale are plunged into World War I, is particularly notable for its atmospheric portrayal of life in the trenches. In *Shadows on Our Skin* (1977), Joe Logan, a Londonderry Catholic youth, dreams of becoming a poet, his schoolteacher becomes engaged to a British soldier, and Joe's brother returns from England to join the Provisional IRA. Subsequent novels, including *Fool's Sanctuary* (1987), deploy similar themes.

JÓKAI, Maurus or Mór
(1825–1904)

Hungarian novelist, born in Komárom. He was an active partisan of the Hungarian struggle in 1848. As well as dramas, humorous essays and poems, he wrote many novels and romances, including *Török világ Magyarországon* (1852, 'The Turks in Hungary'), *Egy magyar nábob* (1853, Eng trans *An Hungarian Nabob*, 1898) and its continuation *Kárpáthy Zoltán* (1862, Eng trans *The New Landlord*, 1868), *A fekete gyémántok* (1870, Eng trans *Black Diamonds*, 1896), *A jövő század regénye* (1873, 'Romance of the Coming Century'), *Egy ember a ki mindent tud* (1875, 'The Modern Midas'), *Az élet komédiásai* (1876, 'The Comedians of Life') and *A löcsei fehér asszony* (1884, 'The White Woman of Leutschau'). He was editor

of several newspapers, and conspicuous as a Liberal parliamentarian.
▷M Nágy, *Jókai* (1968)

JOLLEY, (Monica) Elizabeth
(1923–)

English-born Australian author of novels, short fiction and plays, born in Birmingham. She settled in Western Australia in 1959 and in *Five Acre Virgin* (1976) collected some of her writing between those years. It received immediate critical praise and was followed by *The Travelling Entertainer* (1979), longer pieces from the same period. Her first novel was *Palomino* (1980). *The Newspaper of Claremont Street* (1981) is the story of a small-town gossip. *Mr Scobie's Riddle* won the Melbourne *Age* Book of the Year Award in 1982. In her later books *My Father's Moon* (1989) and *Cabin Fever* (1990) she returns to her earlier years in post-war England. This partly autobiographical trilogy was completed with the elegiac *The Georges' Wife* (1993). She has also written a number of plays, mostly for radio. With her translator Françoise Cartano she won the inaugural 1993 France–Australia Award for Literary Translation for her novel *The Sugar Mother* (1988, as *Tombe du Ciel*).

JØLSEN, Ragnhild
(1875–1908)

Norwegian novelist, who studied sculpture, but also trained as a telegraphist. She was attracted to a bohemian lifestyle, and her early death appears to have been the result of an overdose. Her texts, in which folklore and dreams are prominent elements, have been described as products of the tensions between a traditional way of life on the ancient family estate and the new values prevailing in the modern industrial communities. Most notably, the fin de siècle atmosphere of her texts is coloured by a sexual outspokenness which shocked her contemporaries. In *Rikka Gan* (1904), which exploits certain features of the Gothic novel, eroticism is seen to be linked with domination and death as the heroine becomes the mistress of the new owner of Gan to preserve the farm for her family. In *Fernanda Mona* (1905), which takes as its starting-point the same setting, there are conspicuous instances of perverted sexuality. *Hollases krønike* (1906, 'The Chronicles of Hollas'), about an agricultural community, combines the everyday with the supernatural.
▷J Garton, 'Ragnhild Jølsen', in *Norwegian Women's Writing 1850–1990* (1993)

JONES, David Michael
(1895–1974)

English poet and artist, born in Kent. His father was Welsh and though he only lived

briefly in Wales he identified himself strongly with the country. After art school he served in World War I and had an abiding interest in martial matters. He became a Roman Catholic in 1921. In 1922 he met Eric Gill, the beginning of a long association. His war experience is central to *In Parenthesis* (1937), the first of his two major literary works. *The Anathemata* (1952) is likewise personal but draws heavily on his religious influences. He published a series of fragments of another large religious work as *The Sleeping Lord* (1974), but never finished it. As an artist he is less well known but his paintings, watercolours, drawings and inscriptions have a lucidity that some of his literary work lacks.
▷K Raine, *David Jones, Solitary Perfectionist* (1974)

JONES, Ebenezer
(1820–60)

English poet, born in Islington, London. He was brought up a strict Calvinist and despite long hours as a clerk completed *Studies of Sensation and Event* (1843), which were admired by **Robert Browning** and **Dante Gabriel Rossetti**. In his *Land Monopoly* (1849) he anticipated the economic theory of Henry George by 30 years.
▷T Mardy Rees, *The Neglected Poet* (1909)

JONES, Henry Arthur
(1851–1929)

English dramatist, together with **Arthur Wing Pinero** the founder of the 'realist problem' drama in Britain, born in Grandborough, Buckinghamshire. He was in business until 1878, when *Only Round the Corner* was produced at Exeter. His first great hit was a melodrama, *The Silver King* (1882). This was followed by *Saints and Sinners* (1884), *Rebellious Susan* (1894), *The Philistines* (1895), *The Liars* (1897), *The Manoeuvres of Jane* (1898), *Mrs Dane's Defence* (1900), *Mary Goes First* (1913) and other social comedies, many of which also engaged with serious social issues. He was a highly popular writer in his own day.
▷R A Cordell, *Jones and the Modern Drama* (1932)

JONES, James
(1921–77)

American novelist, born in Robinson, Illinois, the son of a dentist. Educated at the University of Hawaii, he served in the US army as a sergeant (1939–44), boxed as a welterweight in Golden Gloves tournaments, and was awarded a Purple Heart. His wartime experience in Hawaii led to *From Here to Eternity* (1951), a classic novel dealing with the period before Pearl Harbor, for which he received a National Book Award. Later work was disappointing, with the exception of *The Thin Red Line* (1962), which was a sequel.
▷F McShane, *Into Eternity—James Jones: the life of an American writer* (1985)

JONES, LeRoi *see* BARAKA, Amiri

JONES, Marion
(1934–)

Trinidadian novelist, one of the leading woman writers of her generation. *Pan Beat* (1973), her first novel, deals impressively with several middle-class marriages in Port of Spain. *J'Ouvert Morning* (1976) is about a Port of Spain family, the Grants; it has been described as 'soap-operaish' but also as a 'riveting document of a troubled society in a state of transition'.

JONES, Thomas Gwynn
(1871–1949)

Welsh poet, translator (**Ibsen**, **Goethe**'s *Faust*, and much else), scholar, critic, novelist and playwright, born in Gwyndy Uchaf, Betwsyn-rhos, Denbighshire. An industrious and learned man, who was almost entirely self-taught, he served his apprenticeship on various newspapers. His best-known novel is *John Homer* (1923). Poetry was his chief medium of expression, and he was amongst the most skilled Welsh technicians of his day, in a field in which technical accomplishment is very high. It has been declared that the psychology of his mythological poems is 'exquisitely exacting'.
▷W B Davies, *Thomas Gwynn Jones* (1970)

JONG, Erica, née Mann
(1942–)

American novelist and poet, she was born and educated in New York City, and taught college there for several years. Thrice married and divorced, she retains the name of her second husband. Approaching Jong's fiction by way of her verse helps confirm that her novels are more serious and sombre than their soft-core eroticism and mass-market appeal initially suggest. The wry and sardonic poems in *Fruits and Vegetables* (1971) and *Half-Lives* (1973) are superficially reminiscent of **Sylvia Plath** and they clearly establish Jong's Jewish background as an essential aspect of her literary personality. In 1973, she published the massively bestselling *Fear of Flying*, which was hailed as a sort of female *Portnoy's Complaint*. The novel introduced the angst-haunted Isadora Wing, and documents her search for the guilt-free 'zipless fuck' and for a degree of self-determination in her sexuality. Isadora returns in *How to Save Your Own Life* (1977) and in *Parachutes and Kisses* (1984), in which her eternal quest is renewed. In between, Jong wrote *Fanny, Being the True History of the Adventures of Fanny Hackabout-Jones* (1980), a clever, feminist send-up of 18th-century erotic novelists like **John Cleland**. Isadora also narrates *Any Woman's Blues* (1990).

JONKER, Ingrid
(1933–65)

South African poet (writing in Afrikaans), who drowned herself as a response to the cruelty of the Apartheid policy then practised by the South African government. Her poems are moving although perhaps not in themselves enduring protests against violence and evil. There is an English translation in *Selected Poems* (1968).

JONSON, Ben (Benjamin)
(1572–1637)

English dramatist, born in Westminster, probably of Border descent. He was educated at Westminster School under Camden, to whom he paid the tribute 'Camden most reverend head to whom I owe/All that I am in arts, all that I know'. After working for a while with his stepfather, a bricklayer, he volunteered for military service in Flanders before joining Henslowe's company of players. He killed a fellow player in a duel, became a Catholic in prison, but later recanted. His *Every Man in his Humour*, with **Shakespeare** in the cast, was performed at the Curtain in 1598 to be followed not so successfully by *Every Man Out of His Humour* in 1599. The equally tiresome *Cynthia's Revels*, largely allegorical, was succeeded by *The Poetaster*, which at least was salted by a personal attack on **Thomas Dekker** and **John Marston**. He now tried Roman tragedy, but his *Sejanus* (1603) and his later venture, *Catiline* (1611), are so larded with classical references as to be merely closet plays. If he was trying to show Shakespeare how to write a Roman tragedy he failed badly, but his larger intent of discarding romantic comedy and writing realistically (though his theory of 'humours' was hardly comparable with genuine realism) helped to produce his four masterpieces— *Volpone* (1606), *The Silent Woman* (1609), *The Alchemist* (1610) and *Bartholomew Fair* (1614). *Volpone* is an unpleasant satire on senile sensuality and greedy legacy hunters. *The Silent Woman* is farcical comedy involving a heartless hoax. **Dryden** praised it for its construction, but *The Alchemist* is better with its single plot and strict adherence to the unities. *Bartholomew Fair* has indeed all the fun of the fair, enlivened by his anti-Puritan prejudices, though the plot gets lost in the motley of eccentrics. After the much poorer *The Devil is an Ass* (1616), Jonson turned

or rather returned to the masque—he had collaborated with Inigo Jones in *The Masque of Blacknesse*, 1605—and produced a number of those glittering displays down to 1625 when James VI and I's death terminated his period of Court favour. His renewed attempt to attract theatre audiences left him in the angry mood of the ode 'Come leave the loathed stage' (1632). Only his unfinished pastoral play *The Sad Shepherd* survives of his declining years. Ben attracted the learned and courtly, to several of whom his superb verse letters are addressed. His lyric genius was second only to Shakespeare's. 'Drink to me only with thine Eyes' in *Volpone* (of all places) and 'Queen and Huntress chaste and fair' and 'Slow, slow fresh Fount' in the dreary stretches of *Cynthia's Revels* are but a few of these gemlike lyrics. His *Timber; or Discoveries*, printed in the folio of 1640, prove him a considerable critic with a bent towards the neoclassicism which **Cowley** and Dryden inaugurated.
▷D Riggs, *Ben Jonson, a life* (1989)

JÓNSSON, Bólu-Hjálmar
(1796–1875)

Icelandic folk-poet, born in Eyjafjörður. A man of fierce pride and temper, he lived on a peasant croft and struggled with poverty all his life, making a meagre living from woodcarving. He was also one of the most eloquent and natural of poets; his verses, whether railing against the church and authority or revelling in marvellous poetic imagery, circulated orally all over the country, and were only collected and published after his death.
▷Dð Gislason, in *Lögrétta 27* (1932)

JONSTON, Arthur *see* JOHNSTON, Arthur

JORDAN, June
(1936–)

American poet, essayist, political activist and writer for children. She was born in New York City, and educated at Barnard College and the University of Chicago. After working as assistant movie producer, she became a college teacher in Connecticut and New York; she was Professor of English at the State University of New York, Stony Brook, and is now Professor of African American Studies and Women's Studies at the University of California, Berkeley. Jordan's main literary model is **Orwell**. In 1973 she published *Poem: On Moral Leadership as a Political Dilemma*, her response to Watergate. *Things That I Do in the Dark* (1977) was a selection that for the first time made clear the extent to which her militancy was not so literal and dogmatic as to leave no room for a more oblique, metaphoric vision and a chancy, experimental prosody. In 1993 she published a volume of love poetry, *Haruko*, which touched on bisexuality and feelings of loss and was remarkable for its stoically maintained pessimism. Among Jordan's works for young people are *His Own Where—* (1971) and *Kimako's Story* (1981).

JORDAN, Neil
(1950–)

Irish film-maker and writer, born in Sligo. After reading history and literature at University College, Dublin, he worked at various jobs in London before returning home and helping to form the Irish Writers Co-operative (1974). His first collection of stories, *Night in Tunisia* (1976), earned the Guardian Fiction Prize and was followed by the acclaimed novels *The Past* (1980) and *The Dreams of the Beast* (1983). Interested in exploring cinema as a visual means of storytelling, he was given the opportunity to work as a script consultant on *Excalibur* (1981). He made his directorial debut with the thriller *Angel* (1982) and has boldly emphasized the fairy-tale and fantasy elements of such challenging works as *The Company of Wolves* (1984) and *Mona Lisa* (1986). He turned his hand to comedy with *High Spirits* (1988) and *We're No Angels* (1989), but returned to serious drama with *The Crying Game* (1992).

JÖRGENSEN, Johannes
(1866–1956)

Danish novelist and poet, born in Svendborg. He lived most of his life in Italy, in Assisi, where he became a Roman Catholic (1896), but returned to Svendborg, his birth-place, shortly before his death. He published several volumes of poetry, as well as biographies of St Francis of Assisi (1907), St Catherine of Siena (1915), and St Birgitta of Sweden (1941–3), and an autobiography, *Mit livs Legende* (Legend of my Life, 1916–28).
▷W G Jones, *Johannes Jörgensen* (1969)

JOSEPH, Jenny
(1932–)

English poet, born in Birmingham and educated at Oxford University. Variously a journalist, pub landlady, lecturer and language teacher, she was first published in the 1950s by **John Lehmann**. Her first volume, *The Unlooked-for Season*, appeared in 1960, followed by *Rose in the Afternoon* (1974), *The Thinking Heart* (1978), *Beyond Descartes* (1983) and *Collected Poems* (1992). Her poems' philosophical qualities recall **R S Thomas** and their sometimes plain diction **Philip Larkin**, but they are neither so introverted nor so depressive as his work. *Persephone* (1986), an innovative mixture of narrative prose, drama, poetry and photostory moving between Greek legend and modern analogues, won the James Tait Black Prize.

JOSEPH, M(ichael) K(ennedy)
(1914–81)

English-born New Zealand academic, novelist and poet, born in Chingford, Essex, who wrote one of the best novels to come out of World War II in *I'll Soldier No More* (1958), which deals with the war in the West and provides a grim picture of occupied Germany after 1945. It was followed by *A Pound of Saffron* (1962), a satire of power politics in Auckland University, and by two novels of a 'possible future' in *The Hole in the Zero* (1967) and *The Time of Achamoth* (1978). He returned to wartime again in *A Soldier's Tale* (1976) and there is a posthumously published historical novel *Kaspar's Journey* (1988). He wrote two collections of verse, *Imaginary Islands* (1950) and *The Living Countries* (1959); the best were collected as *Inscription on a Paper Dart: Selected Poems 1945–72* (1974), and he published a study of **Byron** in 1964.

JOSIKA, Baron Miklós von
(1794–1865)

Hungarian novelist, who introduced the historical novel into Hungarian literature, and is sometimes referred to as the Hungarian Sir **Walter Scott**, from his adherence to the romantic tradition of that writer. He was involved in the revolution of 1848, and had to live in exile in Brussels and Dresden. His best-known novel is his first, *Abafi* (1836).
▷F Szinneyi, *Josika Niklós* (1915)

JOSIPOVICI, Gabriel David
(1940–)

English novelist, dramatist and academic, born in Nice and educated in Cairo, Gloucestershire and Oxford. In 1963 he became a lecturer at Sussex University, and was appointed Professor of English in 1984. Josipovici's fiction and drama are often described as 'experimental', but the values expressed in his major critical work *The World and the Book* (1971) suggest that playfulness is in itself the moral function of fiction. Certainly, he is little interested in conventional narrative; **Beckett**, **Pinter**, and the *nouveau roman* would seem to be his main influences. *The Inventory* (1968) established his interest in things as active, but nonhuman, agents in plot, and in the idea of words-as-things. This became more overt in *Words* (1971), *Migrations* (1977) and in *The Air We Breathe* (1981), which marked a widening of his vision. Josipovici's short stories and plays were first collected in the punning *Mobius the Stripper* (1974). Of his later dramatic works the radio play *Vergil Dying* (broadcast 1979, published 1981) stands out as a remarkable feat of imagination. His other critical books include *The Lessons of Modernism* (1977) and a collection of occasional pieces, *The Mirror of Criticism* (1983).

JOTUNI, Maria
(1880–1943)

Finnish novelist, story-writer and dramatist, born in Kuopio. Her first and best work consists of realistic and humorous stories; they did not get much attention in their own time, but since then have been much admired. Her plays, unpretentious and well made, were more popular and successful.

JOUBERT, Joseph
(1754–1824)

French writer and moralist, born in Montignac in Périgord. He studied and taught at the college of Toulouse. He then went to Paris, and lived through all the fever of the Revolution. In 1809 he was nominated by Napoleon to the council of the new university. His friend **François Chateaubriand** edited a small volume from his papers, and Joubert found fame with his *Pensées* (1838, 'Thoughts'), which are in the best French tradition of **La Rochefoucauld**, Pascal, **La Bruyère** and Vauvenargues.
▷I Babbitt, *Masters of Modern French Criticism* (1912)

JOUHANDEAU, Marcel
(1888–1979)

French novelist and essayist, born in Guéret, near Limoges. A schoolteacher, the son of a butcher, he situated much of his fiction in 'Chaminadour', a version of his home town. *La Jeunesse de Théophile* (1921, 'The Early Life of Théophile'), *Monsieur Godeau Intime* (1926, 'Monsieur Godeau Intimately') and *Monsieur Godeau Marié* (1932, 'Monsieur Godeau Married') are all semi-autobiographical, while *Chaminadour* (3 vols, 1934–41) paints on a broader canvas. *Essai sur moi-même* (1946, 'Essay About Myself') continues the confessional in non-fictional form, although other volumes, such as *Confidences* (1954), deal more generally with life, treating especially of his religious views, which were summarized as 'mystique de l'enfer' ('the mystery of hell'), and stressed the continued reality of evil.

JOUVE, Pierre-Jean
(1887–1976)

French mystical poet, music critic (Mozart, Berg), translator (**Hölderlin**, **Shakespeare**) and novelist, born in Arras. He began his writing career as a poet under the auspices of the Unanimiste or Abbaye group (**Duhamel**, **Romains**, and others), but in 1928 boldly repudiated, in the preface to his collection *Noces* (1928, 'Nuptials'), all that he had written before 1925: he had experienced a 'conversion to spiritual values' (not to Catholicism, as some claimed), and thenceforth devoted himself to what he called 'the Nada theme ... borrowed from mystical Spain ... [Nada is] the right word for opening the essential door'. His poetry, as reminiscent of that of **Baudelaire** as it is of anyone, 'posits a world of seemingly irreconcilable contraries' which he 'seeks to harmonize'. Later decisive influences were those of **Freud** and (though the latter has been less noticed) **Jung**. His fiction is important but now somewhat neglected, in particular his first novel about a woman tormented by her erotic mysticism, *Paulina 1880* (1925, Eng trans 1973). In Britain he has elicited the particular admiration of **David Gascoyne**. Also available in translation is *An Idiom of Night* (selected poems, 1968).
▷M Callander, *The Poetry of Pierre-Jean Jouve* (1965)

JOUY, Victor Joseph Étienne de
(1764–1846)

French playwright, librettist and writer, born in Jouy near Versailles. Until 1797 he served as a soldier in India and at home. He wrote *L'Hermite de la Chaussée d'Antin* (1812–14, 'The Hermit of the Chaussée d'Antin') and other prose works, and a number of popular comedies, vaudevilles, comic operas and one tragedy, *Tippo-Saïb* (1813).

JOVINE, Francesco
(1902–50)

Italian novelist and story writer from Guardialfiera (Molise), Campobasso. He was by profession a school inspector. He had written a novel in the 1930s, but did not attract critical attention until he published *Signora Ava* (1942, Eng trans *Seeds in the Wind*, 1946), a historical novel about the aftermath of the Risorgimento (the title refers to a figure in a popular song). This was ignored at its publication, but interest in it developed after the end of World War II. Jovine joined the Resistance and then (1948) the communists. His most famous (just posthumous) novel was the partly autobiographical *Le terre del Sacramento* (1950, Eng trans *The Estate in Abruzzi*, 1952), set in southern Italy, against the background of Mussolini's march on Rome.
▷M Grillandi, *Francesco Jovine* (1971, in Italian)

JOYCE, James Augustine Aloysius
(1882–1941)

Irish writer, born in Dublin which, despite his long exile, provides the setting for most of his work. Educated by Jesuits at Clongowes Wood College and Belvedere College, he went to University College, Dublin. A linguist and voracious reader, he corresponded with **Ibsen**. Among other influences were **Dante**, **George Moore** and **W B Yeats**. Catholicism's bigotry distressed him and he went to Paris for a year (1902), living in poverty and writing poetry. His mother's death prompted his return to Ireland, when he stayed briefly in the Martello Tower which features in the early part of *Ulysses*; he then left Ireland with Nora Barnacle, who was to be his companion for the rest of his life. He taught English for a spell in Trieste, but had to scrounge to make ends meet. After a war spent mainly in Switzerland the couple settled in Paris. By now Joyce was the author of two books: *Chamber Music* (1907), a volume of poems, and *Dubliners* (1914), a collection of short stories that includes among other celebrated items, 'The Dead'. The stories were greeted enthusiastically, and Joyce was championed by **Ezra Pound**. The autobiographical *A Portrait of the Artist as a Young Man* appeared in instalments in *The Egoist* (1914–15). Petitioned by Yeats and Pound on his behalf, the Royal Literary Fund in 1915 made him a grant and shortly afterwards the civil list followed suit. But his health was failing, his eyesight deteriorating and he was deeply disturbed by his daughter's mental illness. In 1922 his seminal novel, *Ulysses*, was published in Paris on 2 February. It immediately provoked violent reactions, but the story of Leopold Bloom's day-long perambulation through Dublin is now regarded as epochal, a great leap forward for fiction. It was not published in the United Kingdom until 1936. Plagued by worsening glaucoma, Joyce supervised publication of *Finnegans Wake* in 1939. Much critical energy has been spent trying to analyse Joyce's work, but readers continue to delight in his word play, comedy and irrepressible power of invention.
▷R Ellman, *James Joyce* (1965)

JÓZSEF, Attila
(1905–37)

Hungarian poet, born in Budapest, his country's most distinguished poet after **Endre Ady**, and in certain important respects the latter's heir. József suffered from severe bi-polar mental illness, and ended his life by throwing himself in front of a train at Szársó. He is the poetic counterpart of the composer Bela Bartók, and should be as well known. He was of working-class origin, and began as a communist steeped in the poetry of Ady.

Then, breaking away from communism, he was successively influenced by **Villon**, Surrealism and folk poetry. His style and his rhythms are original in Hungarian poetry, and can hardly be captured in any other language. But John Bákti's *Selected Poems and Texts* (1973) is a notable attempt, with a useful introduction.

JUAN DE LA CRUZ, San, originally Juan de Yepes y Alvarez
(1542–91)

Spanish mystical poet, born in Fontiveros, Old Castille. He was canonized in 1726. In the English world he is known as St John of the Cross. A Carmelite, he joined the movement's reforming wing, and became the director of St Teresa's convent in Ávila. Persecuted by the orthodox members of his movement, he ended in banishment in a convent in Andalusia. His mystical poetry, influenced by **Garcilaso de la Vega**, describes the union of the soul with God after its spiritual and erotic journey through its 'dark night'. They were translated with some success by **Roy Campbell** (1960).
▷P Crisógono, *San Juan de la Cruz* (1929, in Spanish, translated 1958)

JUDAH BEN SAMUEL HA-LEVI
(c.1075–1141)

Spanish Hebrew poet and philosopher. A doctor by profession, he lived in various cities in Spain, including his birthplace, Tudela. His most famous prose work is *The Kuzari*, one of the greatest of medieval theological books; it is the only Jewish classic written in Platonic dialogue form. He set out for the Holy Land in the last years of his life, and travelled about the Middle East; but no one knows his exact fate. His philosophy was in itself an attack on the inadequacy of philosophy: God is known by his revelation, and his existence therefore requires no proof. Judah's poetry has become very well known, and some of it is even incorporated into the Jewish liturgy. He also wrote poems of love and friendship. Much of his work is in translation.
▷R Kayser, *The Life and Times of Jehudah Halevi* (1949)

JUHÁHZ, Ferenc
(1928–)

Hungarian poet from Bia, who, during the 1960s and 70s, achieved international status; since that time, however, Juháhz seems to have lost direction. At first an ambitious socialist realist, hungry for recognition, he broke away from this with *Óda a repüleshez* (1953, 'Ode to Fight'); later works, influenced by **Weöres** and by his reading of modernist

509

foreign poets, did not 'liberate ... the Hungarian poetic imagination', as has foolishly been claimed, but did make bold experiments, and displayed remarkably inventive gifts. His chief poem, which he has not yet bettered, is 'A szarvassá változott királyfi' ('The Boy Changed into a Stag'), in the volume *A virágok hatalma* (1956, 'The Potency of Flowers'), in which he takes his inspiration from the music of his compatriot Béla Bartok. Later work has so far been of less account. There is an English translation in *Selected Poems* (1970).

JUHASZ, Gyula
(1883–1937)

Hungarian poet, who began as a member of the *Nyugat* group which originated with **Endre Ady**. Not unlike his Romanian counterpart **George Bacovia**, he 'slipped into the background', making his living as a teacher in small schools and dedicating himself to adoration of 'Anna', an actress said to have been 'undeserving'. His poetry is polished and melancholy, word perfect, and impressionistic. He was a supporter of the 1919 communist regime, and wrote some verse, his least distinguished, expressing his dreams of a just future. He killed himself in Szeged when his hopes for this future, and for himself, finally ran out.

▷J Reményi, *Hungarian Writers and Literature* (1964)

JULIANA, or JULIAN OF NORWICH, Dame
(1342–c.1416)

English mystical writer who, after an illness in 1373, experienced *A Shewing of God's Love* (Eng trans 1958). A modest and self-critical woman, an anchoress of little book-learning, she illuminated her visions of the Passion of Christ with a serenity that has made her seem highly convincing even to sceptics of her mystical experience. Her main work is the *Revelations of Divine Love*, of which the most accessible edition is that of 1966.

▷P Molinari, *Julian of Norwich* (1958)

JUNG, Johann Heinrich, pseud Jung Stilling
(1740–1817)

German mystic and writer. He was a schoolteacher before qualifying in medicine, then he became Professor of Political Economy at Marburg (1787–1804), then at Heidelberg, and wrote semi-mystical, pietistic romances and works on political economy, as well as a charming autobiography which began with *Heinrich Stillings Jugend* ('Heinrich Stilling's Youth'), and had grown to five volumes when edited by **Goethe** (1777–1804). A sixth volume was published in 1817.

▷H Müller, *Jung Stilling* (1965)

JÜNGER, Ernst
(1895–)

German novelist, brother of the poet **Friedrich Georg Jünger**. He served in the German army in World War I, and his post-war fiction served to keep alive the spirit of Prussian militarism and, increasingly, the mystique of technological advance. Though initially an enthusiastic supporter, he was disappointed by the Nazis on their accession to power. Enlisting again, he served in France during World War II, where he became a major influence on the French right-wing. There has been considerable controversy about the intention of his novels, *Marmorklippen* (1939, 'On the Marble Cliffs') and *Heliopolis* (1949), both of which seem to extol deutero-fascist ideas, but which have also been interpreted as texts of resistance. Jünger himself complicated the issue by remaining silent on it, while continuing to write in a not dissimilar vein.

JÜNGER, Friedrich Georg
(1898–)

German poet, younger brother of **Ernst Jünger**; unlike the totalitarian idealist Ernst, he opposed Nazism quite unequivocally, and emigrated to Switzerland in 1937. The best of his somewhat classical poems is the anti-Nazi 'Der Mohn' (1934, Eng trans 'The Poppy', *Twentieth-Century German Verse*, 1963, ed Patrick Bridgewater), which was secretly circulated throughout Germany.

JUNQUEIRA FREIRE, Luis José
(1832–55)

Brazilian romantic poet who belongs to the third, 'subjectivist' phase of his country's poetry, which characterized the decade in the middle of which he died. It is his confusions rather than his conclusions which are interesting, and the title of his best-known collection is *Contradicções Poéticas* (1867, published with his complete poetry). For a time he was a Benedictine monk, but he withdrew before taking his final vows.

▷H Pires, *Junqueira Freire, sua vida, sua época, sua obra* (1929)

JUNQUEIRO, Ablio Manuel Guerra
(1850–1923)

Portuguese lyric poet and satirist, born in Freixo. He became a deputy in 1872, opposed the Braganzas (the ruling Portuguese dynasty) and was tried for *lèse majesté* in 1907. After the revolution, when a republic was established, he was minister to Switzerland

(1910). His poetry shows the influence of **Victor Hugo**, and is concerned with social and political reform, rather than more traditional subjects. His work was very popular in his own day, when he was seen as a champion of the people.

JUSSERAND, Jean (Adrien Antoine) Jules
(1855–1932)

French writer and diplomat, born in Lyons. He served in the French embassy in London from 1887 to 1890, and from 1902 to 1925 was ambassador to the USA. He wrote (in French and in English) on the English theatre, *Le Théâtre en Angleterre depuis la conquête jusqu'aux prédécesseurs immédiats de Shakespeare* (1878, 'The English Theatre from the Norman Conquest until Shakespeare's Immediate Predecessors'); a book on the early novel, *Le Roman au temps de Shakespeare* (1887, Eng trans *The English Novel in the Time of Shakespeare*, 1890); a literary history of the English people, *Histoire littéraire du peuple anglais* (1895–1909); and *Amerique jadis et maintenant* (1916, Eng trans *Americans of Past and Present Days*, 1916, Pulitzer Prize).

JUSTICE, Donald Rodney
(1925–)

American poet, born in Miami, Florida. He has taught at a number of universities. His poetry is notably well-made, and reveals a great formal concern with the nuances of language as well as emotion. His first book, *The Summer Anniversaries* (1960), has been followed by a relatively small body of work, but each has served to increase his standing. He won the Pulitzer Prize for Poetry in 1980 for his *Selected Poems* (1979). Other volumes include *Night Light* (1967), *Departures* (1973), *The Sunset Maker* (1987), which also contains stories and a memoir, and the libretto *The Death of Lucifer* (1988).

JUVENAL, Decimus Junius Juvenalis
(c.55–c.140)

Roman lawyer and satirist, born in Aquinum in the Volscian country. Almost nothing is known of his life except that he lived in Rome, was poor and was a friend of **Martial**. His 16 brilliant verse satires of Roman life and society (c.100–c.128), written from the viewpoint of an angry Stoic moralist, range from savage attacks on the vices and the extravagance of the rich to portrayals of the precarious makeshift life of their hangers-on and the hardships of the poor. Society women came under his lash in the celebrated sixth satire, and his work takes occasional swipes at Jews and other foreigners. **Dryden**'s versions of five of Juvenal's satires are amongst the best of his works. **Dr Johnson** imitated two of the most famous in his *London* and *Vanity of Human Wishes*.
▷G Highet, *Juvenal the Satirist* (1954)

JUVONEN, Helvi
(1919–59)

Finnish poet, born in Iisalmi. Strongly influenced by both **Emily Dickinson** and **Marianne Moore**, she wrote original modernist poetry, distinguished by its use of animal and plant imagery.

K

KABAK, Abraham Abba
(1881–1944)

Hebrew novelist and critic, born in Smorgon, Russia, and died in Jerusalem. He wrote a famous life of Jesus. He was one of the most prolific writers of fiction of his generation. His major work was the medieval historical trilogy *Shlomoh Molkhoh* (1928–30, Eng trans of part of it, 1973): in this account of the martyred visionary Cabalist Solomon Molcho (c.1500–1532) his mastery became fully apparent. His earlier fiction, written in Russia, deals with the harsh lot of the Jew in alien surroundings.

KAFFKA, Margit
(1880–1918)

Hungary's first major feminist woman author, who was a friend to, and influenced by, **Endre Ady**. Her life and achievement were, like those of **Apollinaire**, cut short by the influenza epidemic which swept over Europe after World War I. She has become significant to Hungarian writers in recent years, but her stories—her best work—have yet to be translated.

KAFKA, Franz
(1883–1924)

Austrian novelist, born of German Jewish parents in Prague. He graduated in law from Prague, and although overwhelmed by a desire to write, found employment (1907–23) as an official in the accident prevention department of the government-sponsored Workers' Accident Insurance Institution. A hypersensitive, almost exclusively introspective person with an extraordinary attachment to his father, he eventually moved to Berlin to live with Dora Dymant in 1923, his only brief spell of happiness before succumbing to a lung disease. His short stories and essays, including, 'Der Heizer' (1913, 'The Boilerman'), 'Betrachtungen' (1913, 'Meditations') and 'Die Verwandlung' (1916, Eng trans 'The Transformation', 1933; better known as 'Metamorphosis'), were published in his lifetime, but he refused to do the same for his three unfinished novels, which, through his friend **Max Brod**, were published posthumously and translated by **Edwin** and **Willa Muir**. They are *Der Prozess* (1925, Eng

trans *The Trial*, 1937), *Das Schloss* (1926, Eng trans *The Castle*, 1937) and *Amerika* (1927, Eng trans *America*, 1938). Literary critics have interpreted *Das Schloss* variously as a modern *Pilgrim's Progress* (but there is literally no progress), as a literary exercise in Kierkegaardian Existentialist theology, as an allegory of the Jew in a Gentile world, or psychoanalytically as a monstrous expression of Kafka's Oedipus complex, but his solipsism primarily portrays society as a pointless, schizophrenically irrational organization into which the bewildered but unshocked individual has strayed. Kafka has exerted a tremendous influence on Western literature, not least on such writers as **Albert Camus**, **Rex Warner** and **Samuel Beckett**. As *The Trial*, *Der Prozess* has been memorably filmed by Orson Welles (1962) and staged by **Steven Berkoff** (1970). A number of his other writings have been published posthumously, including *Briefe an meinem Vater* (1919, Eng trans *Letters to my Father*, 1954), *Briefe an Milena* (1952, Eng trans *Letters to Milena*, 1967) and *Briefe an Felice* (1967, Eng trans *Letters to Felice*, 1974), and his diary and other correspondence.
▷J P Stern, *The World of Kafka* (1980); A Thorlby, *Franz Kafka* (1972)

KAHN, Gustave
(1859–1936)

French Symbolist poet and essayist, self-proclaimed inventor of *vers libre*, born in Metz. Kahn was one of the first, along with **Laforgue**, to use the techniques of free verse, and was an influential theoretician of the new form of prosody, which he defended in a preface to *Premieres Poèmes* (1897), a republication of earlier work. Probably his most lasting impact was as co-founder of two important journals—*Le Symboliste* and *Vogue*. Later work appeared posthumously in *Poèmes 1921–1935* (1939).
▷J C Ireson, *L'Oeuvre poétique de Gustave Kahn* (1962)

KAILAS, Uuno, pseud of **Frans Uuno Salonen**
(1901–33)

Major Finnish poet, born in Heinola. He moved to Nice to try to cure himself of the tuberculosis which was the scourge of

Finland, but died there, still a young man. His health had been undermined when he took part in the doomed Aunus expedition in 1919, to support the independence of Russian Karelia. He introduced German expressionism to Finland with his volume of translations *Kaunis Saska* (1924). Finland's one authentic modern *poète maudit*, Kailas was manic for a whole year (1928–9, he had been misdiagnosed as schizophrenic). His style became increasingly classical as he drew nearer to death, and his last collection, *Sleep and Death* (1931), is his most powerful.

KAISER, Georg
(1878–1945)

Major German expressionistic dramatist, poet and novelist, born in Magdeburg. He wrote 78 plays, and was thus the most prolific, as he was the most influential and gifted, of the expressionist playwrights. He went into exile as soon as the Nazis took power. His own life itself had more than an 'expressionist tinge' (it included a six-month spell in jail for stealing and pawning a landlord's furniture: his defence—supposed to annoy the judges, which it did, as it now does some critics—was that he needed the money to maintain the high standards of his youth and his artistic requirement for luxuries and immunity from bourgeois pseudo-morality, and helps to explain the strident tone of his work, which lives on because the best of it transcended the expressionist movement. *Von Morgens bis Mitternacht* (1916, Eng trans *From Morn to Midnight*, 1920), originally produced by Max Reinhardt, features a non-character, The Bank Cashier, the deadness of whose inner life is exposed and revealed by presenting it in the form of fantasy: he mistakes the friendliness of a woman customer, embezzles money; has misadventures, and kills himself at midnight after a Salvation Army girl has betrayed him to the police. Other plays, such as *Gas I* and *Gas II* (1918–20) work in the same way. Later he wrote romantic dramas, and, finally, a *Hellenic Trilogy* (1948), which has been underrated. He wrote two libretti for Kurt Weill, and a now neglected novel, *Es ist genug* (1932, 'It is Enough'), about incest.

KALÉKO, Masche
(1912–)

German poet, born in Kladow who, from 1938, has lived in New York with her conductor/composer husband. She made her reputation in the 1930s, and was praised by **Thomas Mann** for her 'mocking, melodious voice', with its echo of **Heine**. Five of her poems are translated in *Twentieth-Century German Verse* (1963, ed Patrick Bridgewater).

KÁLIDÁSA
(fl.450)

India's greatest dramatist, he is best known through his drama *Sákuntala* (Eng trans 1853).
▷H H Wilson, *The Hindu Theatre* (1871)

KALLAS, Aino, née Krohn
(1878–1956)

Finnish story writer and 'prose balladeer', born in Viipuri parish; she married the diplomat Oskar Kallas in 1900, and lived with him in Estonia, whose history and customs she carefully studied. Her stories, a cross between poetry and raw, instinctive prose, deal with subjects, such as adultery, which were then 'forbidden to women'. She was fortunate in having a good and loyal translator in A Matson, who translated *Barbara von Tisenhusen* (1923, Eng trans 1925), and most of its successors. She lived in London for 12 years (1922–34) while her husband was ambassador; later she had to go into exile (1944–53) in Stockholm. Despite translations, outside Finland and Estonia she has not yet been accorded the recognition she deserves.

KALLOC'H, Yann Ber
(1888–1917)

French poet, a Breton nationalist who wrote in Breton; he was killed in World War I. He was the dominant figure in Breton literature, and has hardly been equalled except by **Tanguy Malmanche**. His richly audacious, bitter and melancholy poems were collected after his death, with a French translation: *A Genoux* (nd, 'Kneeling').

KALVOS, Andreas
(1792–1869)

Greek poet, born on Zakynthos six years before the great **Solomos**. The marriage of his aristocratic mother and humble father caused a scandal on the island, and his father abandoned his mother, taking the young Kalvos and his brother abroad. After a desultory education and peripatetic childhood, Kalvos settled in Florence, where he met the Italian poet **Ugo Foscolo**, becoming his secretary and following him into exile in Switzerland and then London. Kalvos's first writings were all in Italian; his Greek poems consist solely of two slim volumes, published simply as *Lyra* in 1824 and 1826. They contain some of the most powerful poems ever written in Greek, among them his muse on the death of **Byron** and an ode on his mother's death. Having flourished, like Solomos, during the Greek War of Independence, he retired from the fray to become a university professor in Corfu, and finally the headmaster of a girls' school in Louth in Lincolnshire, where he died.

KAMBARA Ariake
(1876–1952)

Japanese poet, from Tokyo. He began his writing career as a novelist, winning a minor literary prize in 1897 with *Daijihi*. Immediately after this he began to publish poetry which was strongly influenced by British Romantics such as **Byron**, **Keats** and **Shelley**. He also admired the French Symbolists, and advocated many of the tenets of their approach to verse composition, himself exerting a strong influence over his younger contemporaries over what turned out to be a short creative life—he gave up composition in 1908, after the publication of his seminal collection *Yumeishu*, to concentrate on criticism and editing.

KANE, Chiekh Hamidou
(1928–)

Francophone Senegalese novelist, born of a Muslim family. He differs from most other modern African writers in that his chief concern is with the conflict between Islam and European technological civilization. The partly autobiographical *L'aventure ambiguë* (1961, Eng trans *Ambiguous Adventure*, 1963) is, after the work of **Camera Laye**, probably the most substantial of its time. It tells the story of a man whose Koranic faith, and even his mysticism, is destroyed by his Parisian education; he himself chooses to die.
▷A C Brench, *The Novelists' Inheritance in French Africa* (1967); W Cartey, *Whispers from a Continent* (1969)

KANEKO Mitsuharu
(1895–)

Japanese poet, sadly unknown outside his homeland. He produced little of any lasting worth before the war (his experience of which, after an initial flirtation with extreme nationalism, turned him into something of a liberal pacifist, causing his work to be suppressed), but since then has been considered one of the leading lights of Japanese poetry.
▷H Hibbett (ed), *Contemporary Japanese Literature* (1975)

KANIN, Garson
(1912–)

American actor, novelist and playwright, born in New York. *Born Yesterday* (1946), set in Washington in World War II, is one of his most famous farces. The more serious *Smile of the World* (1949) traces the moral decline of an ambitious lawyer. *Hollywood* (1974) is an amusing and informative autobiography.

KANTARIS, Sylvia
(1936–)

English poet, born in Grindleford, Derbyshire. She spent 10 years in Australia, during which time she received a doctorate in French literature from the University of Queensland. She won the Poetry Magazine (Australia) Award in 1969 and her first volume of poetry, *Time and Motion* (1975), was published in Sydney. In 1974 she made her home in Cornwall, and in 1986 was appointed Cornwall's first 'Writer in the Community'. She has published two jointly authored collections (1983 and 1988) and a selected poems, *Dirty Washing* (1989). In her poetry, personal reflections on love and loss, comfort and despair, are imaged with warmth and wit, in a language that is described by herself as kaleidoscopic—'multifolate,/manifold with meaning'.

KARADŽIĆ, Vuk Stefanović
(1787–1864)

Serbian poet and philologist, born in Tršić. He published collections of national songs and tales, and evolved the simplified Cyrillic alphabet in order to produce literature in the vernacular, a reform which was resisted initially, especially by the Orthodox Church, but his orthography was officially adopted in 1868, having already been taken up by Serbian writers. He translated the New Testament into Serbian.
▷D Wilson, *The Life and Times of Vuk Stepanovic Karadžić* (1970)

KARAGATSIS, Michaelis, pen-name of Dimitri Rodopoulos
(1908–60)

Greek novelist and short-story writer. A prolific writer, he was hailed for his extreme realism and inventiveness of plot, and had already published four novels and two volumes of stories by 1940. His novels are concerned with a 'tragic eroticism', the characters being brought to disaster by an unquenchable erotic passion that masters them. In *Colonel Liapkin* (1933), as in *Junkermann* (1936), Karagatsis's most famous novel, the protagonists, both foreign men, come to Greece and initially prosper before being brought to ruin by their compulsive sexual desire; in *Chimera*, also published in 1936, it is a foreign woman who similarly courts disaster. Karagatsis's post-war attempts to construct a roman-fleuve around the character of Michaelis Roussis were less successful: in the event only the first three of the projected series were published. In his later years he again turned to 'erotic' writing, but after the publication of a short story, 'O Megalos Hypnos' ('The

Great Sleep'), in 1946, he received little further critical acclaim.

KARAMZIN, Nikolai Mikhailovich
(1766–1826)

Russian historian and novelist, born in Mikhailovka in Orenburg. Among his writings are *Pisma ruskovo putishestvenika* (1790–2, 'Letters of a Russian Traveller'), an account of his travels in western Europe, several novels, including *Bednaya Lisa* (1792, 'Poor Lisa') and *Natalia, boyarskaya doch* (1792, 'Natalia, the Boyar's Daughter'), and a great unfinished *Gosudarstvo rossüskovo* (1816–29, 'History of Russia') down to 1613. His influence on the literature of Russia and its development was considerable. He modernized the literary language by his introduction of western idioms and his writing as a whole reflected western thought.
▷H Nebel Jr, *Nikolai Mikhailovich Karamzin: a Russian sentimentalist* (1967)

KARAOSMANOGLU, Yakub Kadri
(1889–1974)

Turkish novelist, born in Cairo. He was a 'Young Turk', a prominent supporter of Mustafa Kemal, and served him as member of parliament and diplomat. He came to fame as a writer with his novels of the 1920s and 30s, dealing with corruption in high places and bad rural conditions. The most famous is *Yaban* (1932, 'Stranger'), an exposure of the poor conditions in the villages—this was translated into German (1934), but not into English. He was not a major novelist by international standards because he allowed his journalism to affect his style adversely, but all his fiction is highly efficient, humane and well plotted.

KARASEK ZE LVOVIC, Jiri, pseud of Josef Karasek
(1871–1951)

Czech poet, playwright and novelist. He was perhaps the leading Czech 'decadent', being influenced by **Wilde** and the earlier **Huysmans**. His works fill 19 volumes. He was an interesting writer, whose most powerful influence was the mystical Catholicism of the Middle Ages, of which he was a scholar. He was associated with **Neumann, Dyk**, and various other writers who had at different times been under the Austrian tyranny.
▷G Kahn, *Symbolistes et Décadents* (1912)

KARAVELOV, Lyuben
(1835–79)

Bulgarian story writer and revolutionary, born in Koprivshtsa. He lived most of his life abroad: in Russia, Serbia, Hungary and Romania, but died in his own country. He was influenced by *narodnik* thought in Russia, and, in particular, by **Gogol**. An ethnographer, he edited émigré revolutionary journals. His masterly stories created the prototype of the obstinate old Bulgarian peasant still known and appreciated in Bulgaria. He is a major figure in his literature, who just lived to see his aim, Bulgarian independence, realized.
▷C Manning and R Smal-Stocki, *The History of Modern Bulgarian Literature* (1960)

KARINTHY, Frigyes
(1887–1938)

Hungarian humorous writer and translator, who put some of **Jonathan Swift** into Hungarian. His best-known book is *Utázas a Kopony ám Körül* (1937, Eng trans *A Journey Round My Skull*, 1939), an extraordinary account of a brain operation he underwent, and which soon proved his undoing. He was a member of the *Nyugat* (*West*) group, whose essays in the absurd and paradoxical made him into his country's **Chesterton**.

KARLFELDT, Erik Axel
(1864–1931)

Swedish lyric poet, winner of the Nobel Prize for literature, born in Folkärna, Dalarna. He published several volumes of highly individual nature poetry reflecting the traditional language and customs of peasant life in his native province. In *Fridolins visor* (1898, 'Fridolin's Songs') he introduced a peasant character/persona who combined simplicity with deep learning; he reappeared in *Fridolins lustgård* (1901, 'Fridolin's Pleasure Garden'). Critics have not been kind to his poetry, but it proved enduringly popular with the public until it began to darken with oddly erotic volumes like *Flora och Bellona* (1918). He was secretary of the Swedish Academy from 1912. He was posthumously awarded the 1931 Nobel Prize for literature.
▷T Fogelquist, *Erik Axel Karlfeldt* (1941)

KARP, David
(1922–)

American author, born in New York of Russian–Jewish descent. He served in the American army, worked as a journalist, as a radio, TV and paperback writer, and emerged as a serious novelist with *One* (1953), an **Orwell**ian condemnation of totalitarianism. Other works include *The Day of the Monkey* (1955), on British colonialism, *All Honourable Men* (1956), *The Sleepwalkers* (1960) and *Last Believers* (1964).

KARPÍNSKI, Franciszek
(1741–1825)

Polish poet, born in Holosków. He was an impoverished aristocrat who never succeeded in obtaining a patron, but lived to a great age and was admired by those romantics who, like him, had no money with which to pay their respects. He is now generally seen as the leading lyrical poet of his age. His memoirs are a model of candour.

KARR, (Jean Baptiste) Alphonse
(1808–90)

French writer, born in Paris. His *Sous les tilleuls* (1832, 'Under the Linden Trees') by its originality and wit found its author an audience for a long series of novels, of which *Geneviève* (1838) is the best. In 1839 he became Editor of *Le Figaro*, and started the issue of the bitterly satirical *Les Guêpes* ('The Wasps'). His *Voyage autour de mon jardin* (1845, Eng trans *A Tour Around My Garden*, 1855) is his best-known book. He wrote his reminiscences, *Livre de bord* (4 vols, 1879–80, 'Logbook'). His daughter, Thérèse (1835–87), published tales and historical books.
▷L Bauthier, *Portraits du 19ième siècle* (1894)

KARYOTAKIS, Costas
(1896–1928)

Greek poet, born in Tripolis, who killed himself in Preveza. His death had a major effect on the development of Greek poetry—although not perhaps a profound one, or even one of a weight which his work, which has hardly worn well, can quite carry. But a manifestation fairly called 'Karyotakism', a literary fashion for nihilism, certainly pervaded Greek poetry for some years after his death. He was a minor civil servant who became disenchanted with everything, and who wrote well-accomplished and deeply sarcastic verses demonstrating that every effort on earth merely (for example) amuses 'the fire demons far beneath the ground ... and those who live on high'. Beyond this nihilism, there is little of interest in his work.

KASACK, Hermann
(1896–1966)

German novelist, dramatist and poet, a publisher by profession, born in Potsdam. He began as a strident expressionist poet, and always considered himself above all a poet, but his most discussed and possibly most successful work is the novel *Die Stadt hinter dem Strom* (1947, Eng trans *The City Beyond the River*, 1953), the haunting and Kafkaesque tale of a 'dead zone' occupied by dead souls. This has been a little too confidently dismissed by certain more recent critics as 'now exposed' as relying on 'nineteenth-century values that are no longer adequate'. Such critics prefer the later novel, *Fälschungen* (1953, 'Falsifications').

KASCHNITZ, Marie Luise, pseud of Marie Luise von Kaschnitz-Weinberg
(1901–74)

German poet, story writer, critic and novelist, born in Karlsruhe into an old aristocratic family. Technically proficient, her poetry developed, and became increasingly rich in psychological content; her novels, in particular *Das Haus der Kindheit* (1956, 'The House of Childhood'), are equally telling. Although the writers who have helped to form her style and method include Kafka and Beckett, her work has often been too hastily written off as over-traditional; but she is likely to have a revival.

KASPROWICZ, Jan
(1860–1926)

Polish poet, dramatist and translator (eg of Shakespeare's *Hamlet* and of plays by Aeschylus and Euripides), one of the leading members of the neo-romantic 'Young Poland' (Mloda Polska) movement which ran from the 1890s until the outbreak of World War I, and which was a reaction to the Positivism which preceded it. He was born in Szymborze into a poor peasant family. In his youth he was jailed by the Prussians for his pro-Polish activities. He was, like many Polish writers, essentially a mystic, with gnostic tendencies (he divided every aspect of the world into good and evil, and saw life as a battle-ground between them). Although he was learned and intelligent, his thought at times appears tawdry; but his best poetry is of a far higher order. Amongst his many poems, his *Hymny* (1921, 'Hymns'), written at the turn of the century, are the most important, since they combine his love of the landscape of his country with his understanding of Polish peasant songs, thus revealing what has been called his 'profoundly pagan interpretation of Christianity'. The effort of synthesis begun in the Hymns culminates in the posthumous *Mój świat* (1926, 'My World').

KASSÁK, Lajos
(1887–1967)

Hungarian poet, novelist, autobiographer and painter of working-class origins, born in a town that is today in the Czech Republic. Critics have not yet succeeded in sorting out his confusions. He began as a 'proletarian' writer, a travelling blacksmith, then became a pacifist, then a communist opposed to socialist realism. His best poetry is reminiscent of Whitman; but his most important work is his huge autobiography, *Egy ember élete* (1927–39, 'The Life of a Man').
▷*Modern Language Journal* (February 1951)

KÄSTNER, Erich
(1899–1974)

German writer, born in Dresden. He is best known for his books for children. His writing career, however, began with two volumes of verse, *Herz auf Taille* (1928, 'Heart on Waistline') and *Lärm im Spiegel* (1929, 'Noise in the Mirror'), both cleverly satirical. His novels include *Fabian: Die Geschichte eines Moralisten* (1931, Eng trans *Fabian: The Story of a Moralist*, 1932) and *Drei Männer im Schnee* (1934, Eng trans *Three Men in the Snow*, 1935). His delightful children's books, which include *Emil und die Detektive* (1928, Eng trans *Emil and the Detectives*, 1930), *Annaluise und Anton* (1929, Eng trans 1932) and *Das fliegende Klassenzimmer* (1933, Eng trans *The Flying Classroom*, 1934), gained him worldwide fame. Among his later writings is the autobiographical *Als ich ein kleiner Junge war* (1957, Eng trans *When I was a Little Boy*, 1959).
▷L Enderle, *Erich Kästner Bildbiographie* (1960)

KATAYEV, Valentin
(1897–)

Russian novelist and playwright, born in Odessa, the elder brother of Yevgeny Katayev (**Yevgeny Petrov**). A humorous and easy-going writer of the 'Odessa school'—of just such good-natured, easy-going character—Katayev came early under the influence of the (in Trotsky's phrase) 'fellow travelling' Serapion Brothers, although he did not join them. His best novel, the richly comic *Rastratchiki* (1926, Eng trans *The Embezzlers*, 1929), set against Stalin's New Economic Policy, tells of two drunks who go off with some money from a trust-fund for a good time. When cultural policy became sterner Katayev fell into line for a time: *Beleet parus odinoky* (1936, Eng trans *Lonely White Sail*, 1937) represented something of an escape for him; regarded by some as his best book, it deals with children, who were at that time allowed to be portrayed as naturally 'irresponsible' (ie not as hardline communists). Later he turned to highly original memoirs in which he combined fact, fiction and fun (often made of Soviet officialdom, but not in a way censors could put their finger on, although they reproved Katayev when they could). His stage comedies, the most famous of which is *Kvadratura kruga* (1918, Eng trans *Squaring the Circle*, 1934), offered excellent and intelligent entertainment.

KATONA, József
(1791–1830)

Hungarian playwright who wrote many now-forgotten historical dramas, including one, *Bánk Bán* (1814, 'The Viceroy'), a **Shakespeare**an drama set in 13th-century Hungary, which became a classic after his death. It was first performed in 1833, and was by mid-century regarded as the greatest of all Hungarian tragedies. It deals with a problem that beset Hungary until only recently: what attitude could be taken to an oppressive ruler? It was made into an opera by Ferencz Erkel in 1861.

KATZ, Steve
(1935–)

American author of disruptive 'novels' which confirm **Philip Roth**'s contention that the most important literary distinction is not between 'fiction' and 'non-fiction', but between the 'written' and 'unwritten' worlds. In Katz's second novel, *The Exagggerations of Peter Prince* (1968, the extra consonant is perfectly deliberate), he allows his ending to remain in what he has called the 'archive of the unwritten'. This is the underlying theme of *Stolen Stories* (1984), a much later collection of short pieces, and it emerges throughout his masterpiece *Wier and Pouce* (1984), a synoptic novel which uses the death of John F Kennedy as a symbol of betrayed hopes and dreams and then proposes that only by unfettered story-telling can we survive a world without valid dreams. His other works include *The Lestriad* (1962), which was published only in Italy, and *Moving Parts* (1977). Since the mid-70s, he has lived in Boulder, Colorado, where he teaches in the university English department.
▷J Klinkowitz, *The Life of Fiction* (1977)

KATZNELSON, Jehuda Loeb
(1847–1917)

Hebrew (and Russian) writer and scholar, born in Tchernigov, Russia. His renditions of ancient legends are outstanding, and the work he wrote on the origins of Jewish laws concerning hygiene is still consulted.

KAUFMAN, George S(imon)
(1889–1961)

American playwright, born in Pittsburgh. In collaboration with **Moss Hart** he wrote *You Can't Take it with You* (1939, Pulitzer Prize) and *The Man Who Came to Dinner* (1939). Other works include *The Solid Gold Cadillac* (with Howard Teichmann, 1953) and many musicals, some of which have been filmed.
▷S Meredith, *George S. Kaufman and his Friends* (1974), revised as *Kaufman and the Algonquin Round Table* (1977)

KAVAN, Anna
(1901–68)

English novelist and short-story writer, born in France to English parents. Originally called Helen Edmonds, she changed her name by deed poll; other attempts to erase her origin included a refusal to reveal her place of birth or her exact age. *Let Me Alone* (1930) was published under her married name, Helen Ferguson, although, confusingly, one of the characters is called Anna Kavan. She was a heroin addict for many years, and the alternation of numbness and pain which typifies that life is evident in *Ice* (1967), her best novel, a **Kafka**esque account of flight and fear in a frozen world where order has collapsed. *My Madness* (1990) contains the whole of *Ice*, as well as selections from her short stories and autobiographical writings.

KAVANAGH, Patrick Joseph
(1905–67)

Irish poet and novelist, born in County Monaghan. The son of a cobbler and smallholder he farmed before leaving for Dublin in 1939 to pursue a career as a writer and journalist. A caricature of the roistering Irish poet, perhaps his greatest achievement is *The Great Hunger* (1942), a long, angry and passionate poem which does not gloss the harsh reality of life for a frustrated Irish farmer and his sister. In *Tarry Flynn* (1948), an autobiographical novel, he depicts sensitively and convincingly the countryside where he was brought up. Kavanagh's unorthodox and virtually antisocial lifestyle in Dublin led to a savage anonymous profile (actually by another poet, Valentin Iremonger). In his libel action, *Kavanagh* v *The Leader* (1953), he was the victim of a brutal cross-examination by opposing counsel John A Costello, from which he never really recovered. Poems written in the last decade of his life when his health was failing are generally thought to be inferior, but the best are admirably direct, intelligently and wittily contemplating his sexual isolation and his attempts to overcome his academic stage-Irishness. *Collected Poems* was published in 1964, and the *Complete Poems* followed in 1972.

KAVANAGH, P(atrick) J(oseph)
(1931–)

English poet and novelist, born in Worthing, Sussex. Following the death of his first wife, Sally Phillips, in 1958, he wrote one of the 20th-century's most tender and inspiring autobiographies, *The Perfect Stranger* (1966). It was followed in 1990 with *Finding Connections*, another autobiography, tracing Kavanagh's Irish ancestors in Australia and elsewhere. A constant searching quality, fused by a devout Catholicism, informs his eight collections of poetry. *Collected Poems* (1987) gathers work from six of these and conveys an unfashionable pastoralism, given sustaining quality by Kavanagh's sure tech-

nique and his passionate involvement with his adopted Gloucestershire.

KAVERIN, Veniamin, pseud of **Veniamin Zilber**
(1902–)

Russian novelist, playwright and critic, born in Pskov, who studied under Boris Eikhenbaum and Yury Tynyanov, two of the critics whose 'formalism' made Russia's main contribution to critical theory in the 20th century, and who deeply influenced him. Formalism began as a reaction to Futurism, by tersely defining literature as 'the sum total of all stylistic devices employed in it', a slogan which could easily be accommodated by official Marxism; later it developed into something subtler, different and more independent of politics—and Kaverin to a certain extent anticipated this. He joined the 'fellow-travelling' but independent group of writers who called themselves the Serapion Brothers, and modelled himself on **Laurence Sterne**. His early and hilariously funny and deftly plotted novel about the Leningrad underworld, *Konets khazy* (1926, 'End of a Gang'), remains one of his best books; but *Khudozhnik neizvesten* (1931, Eng trans *The Unknown Artist*, 1947), about a character modelled on the restless poet **Viktor Khlebnikov**, represents the height of his achievement. Later he became involved with socialist realism, but then, in advance of the temporary Kruschev 'Thaw', began to publish more books of criticism again.
▷D G P Piper, *Kaverin* (1970)

KAWABATA Yasunari
(1899–1972)

Japanese writer and winner of the Nobel Prize for literature, born in Osaka. He was educated at Tokyo University (1920–4), reading English and then Japanese literature. In 1922 he published some short stories, *Tales to hold in the Palm of your Hand*. His first novel, *Izu no odoriko* (Eng trans *The Izu Dancer*, 1955), was published in 1925. He experimented with various Western novel forms, but by the mid-1930s returned to traditional Japanese ones. Later novels, which are typically melancholy, include *Yukiguni* (1935–47, Eng trans *Snow Country*, 1957), *Sembazuru* (1949, Eng trans *Thousand Cranes*, 1959), *Kyoto* (1962) and *Yama no oto* (1949–54, Eng trans *The Sound of the Mountain*, 1971). He won the 1968 Nobel Prize for literature, the first Japanese writer to do so. He committed suicide.
▷G B Peterson, *The Moon in the Water: on Tanizaki, Kawabata and Mishima* (1979)

KAYE, Louis, pseud of **Noel Wilson Norman**
(1901–81)

Australian writer, born in Claremont, Tasmania, whose short stories were eagerly sought by overseas magazines. He is best known for his novels which between them cover most aspects of Australian outback life, from sheep farming in *Tybal Men* (1931), through opal prospecting in *Tightened Belts* (1935), to stock droving in *Pathways of Free Men* (1935). Despite Kaye's youthful experiences in the Australian outback his stories show a tendency to adopt the style and language of the American 'western'.

KAYE, M(ary) M(argaret)
(1909–)

English novelist, born in Simla, India. A daughter of the Raj, she married into the army and subsequently travelled extensively with her husband. She is the author of several detective novels with exotic settings, written with a lively mixture of mystery and romance. *Death in Kenya* (1983) is a representative example. She is best known, however, for her bestselling historical romantic epics. *Trade Wind* (1963), set in 19th-century Zanzibar, is a story of the slave trade, while her two most famous books, *Shadow of the Moon* (1957) and *The Far Pavilions* (1978), are both set in 19th-century India.
▷ *The Sun in the Morning* (1990)

KAYE-SMITH, Sheila
(1887–1956)

English novelist, born in St Leonards, Sussex. She wrote novels mainly about fate and Sussex. In 1924 she married T P Fry, a clergyman and heir to a baronetcy, and in 1929 became a Roman Catholic. Her writings include *Sussex Gorse* (1916), *Tamarisk Town* (1919), *Joanna Godden* (1921) and *The End of the House of Alard* (1923). She was satirized by **Stella Gibbons** in *Cold Comfort Farm*.
▷ E T Hopkins, *Sheila Kaye-Smith and the Weald Country* (1925)

KAZAKOV, Yury
(1927–)

Russian story writer, born in Moscow. Writing in the tradition of **Bunin** and **Turgenev**, Kazakov has by some been regarded as old-fashioned and lacking in innovatory technique; but his quiet tales of the humble people of central Russia have been greatly prized, and may best be read in *Selected Short Stories* (1963), which has a valuable critical introduction by G Gibian, but which is in Russian.

KAZANTZAKIS, Nikos
(1883–1957)

Greek novelist, poet and dramatist, born in Heraklion, Crete. After studying law at Athens University, he spent some years travelling in Europe and Asia. He published his first novel *Toda Raba* in French in 1929 (Eng

trans 1964), but is best known for the novel *Vios kai Politeia tou Alexi Zorba* (1946, Eng trans *Zorba the Greek*, 1952) and the epic autobiographical narrative poem, *Odyseia* (1938, Eng trans *The Odyssey, a Modern Sequel*, 1958). He wrote several other novels, including *O Christos Xanastavronetai* (1954, Eng trans *Christ Recrucified*, 1954), *O Kapetan Michalis* (1953, Eng trans *Freedom or Death*, 1955) and *O Teleftaios Peirasmos* (1955, Eng trans *The Last Temptation of Christ*, 1960), and translated many literary classics into modern Greek. He spent his last decade living in Antibes, in France.
▷ P Bien, *Nicos Kazantzakis* (1968)

KAZINCZY, Ferenc
(1759–1831)

Hungarian writer, born in Érsemlyén. He published a radical journal, and was imprisoned for his membership of a Jacobin society. He was a leading figure in the Hungarian literary revival and a strong advocate of the reform of the language, and is often referred to as 'the father of Hungarian criticism'. He translated many European classics and wrote poetry, including the first sonnets in Hungarian; there are 22 volumes of his letters. He died of cholera.
▷ J Váczy, *Kazinczy Ferences Kora* (1915)

KEANE, Molly
(1904–)

Irish novelist, born in County Kildare into 'a rather serious Hunting and Fishing and Church-going family'. Her father originally came from a Somerset family and her mother, a poet, was the author of 'The Songs of the Glens of Antrim'. When young she wrote only to supplement her dress allowance, adopting the pseudonym M J Farrell. *The Knight of the Cheerful Countenance*, her first book, was written when she was 17. Between 1928 and 1952 she wrote 10 novels, including *The Rising Tide* (1937), *Two Days in Aragon* (1941) and *Loving Without Tears* (1951), drawing her material from the foibles of her own class. A spirited, impish writer, she also wrote plays, such as *Spring Meeting* (1938), *Ducks and Drakes* (1942), *Treasure Hunt* (1949) and *Dazzling Prospect* (1961). When her husband died at 36 she stopped writing for many years, but *Good Behaviour* (1981), shortlisted for the Booker Prize, led to the reprinting of many of her books and a revival of critical appreciation. *Loving and Giving* (1988) is a bleak comedy seen through the eyes of an eight-year-old girl who is a witness to the break-up of her parents' marriage and the desuetude of the family mansion.
▷ B O'Toole, in *Across a Roaring Hill: The Protestant Imagination in Modern Ireland* (1985, Gerald Dawe and Edna Longley, eds)

KEATS, Ezra Jack
(1916–83)

American illustrator and children's story-teller, born in Brooklyn. His early picture-books, for which he wrote his own text, mixed gouache and collage. In his final books the style was becoming increasingly impression-istic. He was interested in the emotional experience of young children, rather than in the purely narrative aspects of a story, and, as in *Apt. 13* (1971), was particularly good at focusing on the life of city children in high-rise apartments.

KEATS, John
(1795–1821)

English poet, born in London, the son of a livery-stable keeper. He went to school at Enfield. In 1811 he was apprenticed to a sur-geon at Edmonton, and later (1815–17) was a medical student in the London hospitals, but took to writing poetry. **Leigh Hunt**, his neighbour in Hampstead, introduced him to other young romantics, including **Shelley**, and published his first sonnets in *The Exam-iner* (1816). His first volume of poems (1817) combined 'Hymn to Pan' and the 'Bacchic procession' which anticipate the great odes to come. In 1818 he published the long mytho-logical poem *Endymion*. He returned from a walking tour in Scotland (1818), which exhausted him, to find the savage reviews of *Endymion* in *Blackwood's Magazine* and the *Quarterly*. To add to his troubles his younger brother Tom was dying of consumption, and his love affair with Fanny Brawne seems to have brought him more vexation than comfort. It was under these circumstances that he published the volume of 1820, *Lamia and Other Poems*, a landmark in English poetry. Except for the romantic poem 'Isa-bella or The Pot of Basil', a romance based on **Boccaccio**'s *Decameron*, and the first ver-sion of his epical poem, 'Hyperion', all the significant verse in this famous volume is the work of 1819, such as the two splendid romances 'The Eve of St Agnes' and 'Lamia', and the great odes—'On a Grecian Urn', 'To a Nightingale', 'To Autumn', 'On Mel-ancholy' and 'To Psyche'. In particular, 'The Eve of St Agnes' displays a wealth of sen-suous imagery almost unequalled in English poetry. In 'Lamia', the best told of the tales, he turns from stanza form to the couplet as used by **Dryden** in his romantic *Fables*. Keats's letters are regarded as equally impor-tant as his poems, and throw light on his poetical development no less than on his unhappy love affair with Fanny Brawne. It is clear that he was both attracted and repelled by the notion of the poet as teacher or prophet. Having prepared the 1820 volume for the press, Keats, now seriously ill with consumption, sailed for Italy in September 1820, reached Rome and died there attended only by his artist friend Joseph Severn. The house in which he died (26 Piazza di Spagna), at the foot of the Spanish steps, is now known as the Keats–Shelley house, a place of literary pilgrimage with an outstanding library of English romantic literature.
▷R Gittings, *John Keats* (1968)

KEDRIN, Dmitry
(1908–45)

Russian poet, born in Bogodukhovo; he was murdered by unknown attackers. He is best known for his long poem *Zodche* (1938), tell-ing of Ivan the Terrible's cruelty to his archi-tects. His verse, simple and evocative of common suffering, became popular during World War II.

KEE, Robert
(1919–)

English broadcaster and writer. After reading history at Magdalen College, Oxford, he joined the RAF and was shot down over Hol-land, spending four years in a POW camp. His first novel, *A Crowd is Not Company* (1947), reflected this experience and won him the Atlantic Award for literature. Other nov-els include *The Impossible Shore* (1949) and *A Sign of the Times* (1955). As a print journal-ist, he worked for *Picture Post* (1948–51) and was a special correspondent for *The Observer* (1956–7) and *The Sunday Times* (1957–8). Joining the BBC, he worked on *Panorama* from 1958 to 1962. He was the recipient of the Richard Dimbleby BAFTA Award (1976); his other major television work includes the series *Ireland* (1981), co-founding the breakfast programme TV-am (1983), and *Seven Days* (1984–8). His non-fiction books include *The Green Flag* (1972), *Ireland: A His-tory* (1980) and *Trial and Error* (1986).

KEILLOR, Garrison
(1942–)

American humorous writer and radio per-former, born in Minnesota. He graduated from Minnesota University in 1966, already writing for the *New Yorker*. In 1974 he first hosted the live radio show 'A Prairie Home Companion', delivering a weekly monologue set in the quiet, fictional mid-western town of Lake Wobegon, 'where all the women are strong, all the men are good-looking, and all the children are above average'. When the show closed in 1987 he was celebrated for his wry, deliberate, hypnotic storytelling. Most of his written work appears first in the *New Yorker*. Described as 'the best humorous writer to have come out of America since Thurber', his books are *Happy to be Here*

(1981), *Lake Wobegon Days* (1985), *Leaving Home* (1987), *We Are Still Married* (1989), the novel *Radio Romance* (1991), and *The Book of Guys* (1993).

KELLER, David H
(1880–1966)

American physician and writer, born in Philadelphia. He made his notoriety from his series *Sexual Education* (1929), in a day when such matters were hardly discussed; but he is prized by a few science-fiction enthusiasts for the bizarre and effective plots of his speculative novels and stories. Two of these admirers, Moskowitz and Sykera, compiled *Life Everlasting*, a collection of his best tales (1948).

KELLER, Gottfried
(1819–90)

Swiss poet and novelist, born near Zürich. He studied landscape painting at Munich (1840–2), but turned to literature. From 1861 to 1876 he was state secretary of his native canton. His chief works are *Der grüne Heinrich* (1854, Eng trans *Green Henry*, 1960), *Die Leute von Seldwyla* (1856; which includes *A Village Romeo and Juliet*), *Sieben Legenden* (1872, Eng trans with the previous work as *Seven Legends* and *The People of Seldwyla*, 1929), *Züricher Novellen* (1878, 'Zurich stories') and *Martin Salander* (1886, Eng trans 1963). He excelled as a writer of short stories, and his powers of characterization and description and his sense of humour are best illustrated in his volumes of *Novellen*.
▷J M Lindsay, *Gottfried Keller: his life and works* (1968)

KELLER, Helen Adams
(1880–1968)

American writer, born in Tuscumbia, Alabama. She became deaf and blind at 19 months, but, educated by Anne M Sullivan (Mrs Macy), she later learned to speak, graduated in 1904, and attained high distinction as a lecturer, writer and scholar.
▷ *The Story of My Life* (1902)

KELLEY, William Melvin
(1937–)

Black American novelist, whose books all begin with the letter D. He was brought up in the Bronx, but went on to Harvard, where he studied under **John Hawkes** and **Archibald MacLeish** and won the **Reed** Prize in 1960. His first novel, *A Different Drummer* (1963), was a fantasy about mass (and voluntary) black emigration from a southern state. *A Drop of Patience* (1965) took its title from *Othello* and much else from *Porgy and Bess*. The story of a blind jazz musician, it offers a

powerful study of white attitudes to black creativity. *Dem* (1967) are the whites of America, viewed with hostility but little rancour. Kelley's experimental vein resurfaced in *Dunfords Travels Everywheres* (1970), an ambitious failure. His stories were collected in *Dancers on the Shore* (1965). Kelley has been important in registering the variety and internal hierarchies of 'the black experience' in the USA.

KELLGREN, Johan Henric
(1751–95)

Swedish poet and journalist, born in Floby. He was editor from 1780 of the journal *Stockholmsposten*, where he made a reputation as a satirist. He was librarian (1780) and later secretary and literary adviser to King Gustav III, with whom he collaborated on a tragedy, *Gustav Wasa* (1782), and became a member of the newly-founded Swedish Academy in 1786. As a poet he excelled in patriotic and lyrical verse, and, although a representative of the Enlightenment, was not unsympathetic to the new ideas of Romanticism. Ek and Sjöding edited a nine-volume collected works (1923–70).
▷O Sylwan, *Johan Henric Kellgren* (1939)

KELLY, George Edward
(1887–1974)

American dramatist, born in Philadelphia, whose first successful play, *The Torchbearers* (1922), satirizes a young woman's plunge into near-amateur dramatics. Kelly came to prominence two years later with *The Show-Off*, a classic portrayal of a boaster. *Craig's Wife* (1925) is a more caustic look at female possessiveness within a loveless marriage, and won a Pulitzer Prize. Although ambitious and domineering women feature again in plays such as *Behold the Bridegroom* (1927) and *Maggie the Magnificent* (1929), none of Kelly's later plays was as well-received as his earlier work. This made him so disenchanted with the theatre that after 1931 he wrote only intermittently, his last play, *The Fatal Weakness* (1946), dealing again with a flawed marriage.

KELLY, Hugh
(1739–77)

Irish playwright, born in Killarney, County Kerry. With little formal education, he began as an apprentice staymaker before being inspired by the actors who frequented his father's pub to experience the London theatre. He went there in 1760, soon becoming a journalist, publishing his theatre criticism in a volume entitled *Thespis* (1766). His first comedy, *False Delicacy* (1768), was an overnight success despite its stock and uninspired nature and set him up as a rival to **Oliver Goldsmith**. However, after a number of other, less successful plays and work for the government as a newspaper hack, he tried a career in law which also failed. He took to drink in the 1770s and died shortly afterwards.

KELMAN, James
(1946–)

Scottish novelist, short-story writer and playwright, born in Glasgow, one of five brothers. His father was a frame maker and picture restorer. He left school at 15 to become an apprentice compositor, abandoning this two years later when his family decided to emigrate to America. However, he returned soon after and worked at various short-term jobs whose nature is clear to readers of his fiction: labouring, bus-conducting and stocking shelves in stores. For long periods he was unemployed, but he was a voracious reader and when his unemployment benefit was about to be cut he enrolled expediently at Strathclyde University. He left, nonetheless, in his third year, dissatisfied with the irrelevance of the philosophy course. In any case he was now determined to be a writer, and since 1983, with the publication of *Not Not While the Giro*, a collection of laconic stories, he has carved a niche as the spokesman for the disaffected, downtrodden and disenfranchised. Invariably, he is associated with the west of Scotland and the working class. He writes in the demotic voice and uses swear words liberally, but few deny his potency or authenticity. *The Busconductor Hines* (1984), a triumph of the mundane, confirmed his promise. *A Chancer*, the story of a small-time gambler, followed a year later. *Greyhound for Breakfast* (1987) evoked comparisons with **Chekhov** and **Beckett**, though the clipped style was quintessential Kelman. *A Disaffection*, his third novel, the story of a secondary-school teacher at odds with the system and society, found a wide audience through its shortlisting for the Booker Prize in 1989. Further stories were collected in *The Burn* (1991), and three plays are included in *Hardie and Baird & Other Plays* (1991). His fourth novel, *How late it was, how late* (1994), a witty and satirical exploration of blank-faced bureaucracy, was acknowledged by many critics to contain his best work to date.
▷I Bell, in *Planet* (1986–7)

KELTON, Elmer
(1926–)

American writer of Westerns, born in Texas. Kelton's father was a cowboy and his grandfather a ranch foreman. Kelton himself trained as a journalist and was associate editor of *West Texas Livestock Weekly* (1968–90). He maintained his two careers (agricultural

journalist and writer of fiction) for over 30 years. He has won four Spur Awards, and *The Man Who Rode Midnight* (1987) won the Western Heritage Award. He has used several pen-names. *Sons of Texas* (1990) was published under the name Tom Early.

KEMAL, Namik
(1840–88)

Turkish dramatist, novelist, poet, critic and historian, born in Tekirdagi into an aristocratic family. He soon had to flee the country as a result of his membership of a revolutionary society. In London he and other patriots published the subversive paper *Hürriyet* (1868). When he returned to Istanbul his play *Vatan* (1872) caused riots, and he was sent to Famagusta in Cyprus, from which he continued his activities. He is important as one of the first writers to break out of the stultifying literary tradition.

KEMAL, Orhan, pseud of **Mehmet Resit Ogutcu**
(1914–70)

Turkish novelist, story writer and dramatist, mostly of the oppressed lower and criminal classes, popular and much read in his own country, but so far without a translator. He was too prolific, and thus careless; his style, though direct, was distinctly rough; but his understanding of the psychopathic mentality was without parallel in his country's realist literature, and deserves to be more widely known.

KEMAL, Yashar, pseud of **Yashar Kemal Gokçeli**
(1922/3–)

Turkish novelist, perhaps the best-known internationally, he has also gained widespread sympathy as a political activist, briefly interned by the Turkish authorities for his communist activities in Istanbul. His first novel, *Ince Memed* (1955, Eng trans *Memed, My Hawk*, 1961), won the Varlik Prize and established his international reputation. A sequel *Ince Memed II* (1969) is known in English as *They Burn the Thistles* (1973); a third, as yet untranslated volume appeared in 1984. Kemal's work is marked by a profound sympathy for the peasantry of southern Turkey, and it is his solidarity with them that radiates through his best novel, *Ortadirek* (1960, Eng trans *The Wind From the Plain*, 1963), which is the first part of a trilogy completed by *Yer Demir, Gök Bakir* (1963, Eng trans *Iron Earth, Copper Sky*, 1974) and *Ölmez Otu* (1969, Eng trans *The Undying Grass*, 1977). Much of his work has been translated into English by his wife, Thilda Kemal.

KEMELMAN, Harry
(1908–)

American novelist, whose 'Rabbi' books overturn the usual urban setting for detective (and Jewish) fiction and take place in a small Massachusetts town, similar to that in which Kemelman makes his home. He was born in Boston and went to Boston University and Harvard. His professional career has been divided between writing and business. His novels all concern Rabbi David Small, a younger, Judaic Father Brown; these titles all follow the formula of the first, *Friday the Rabbi Slept Late* (1964), which won an 'Edgar', the Mystery Writers of America **Edgar Allan Poe** Award. The week cycle was completed in 1978 with *Thursday the Rabbi Walked Out*. Short stories appeared in *The Nine Mile Walk* (1967).

KENDALL, (Thomas) Henry
(1839–82)

Australian pastoral and lyric poet, born in Milton, Ulladulla, New South Wales. After early years spent in the New South Wales countryside, he settled in Sydney and contributed verse to local newspapers and journals, first collected in *Poems and Songs* (1862). After his marriage in 1868 he moved to Melbourne where a second book, *Leaves from Australian Forests*, was published in 1869. Continuing problems with debt and alcohol led to separation from his family, but friends eventually restored him to health and in 1879 he won the International Exhibition poetry competition. The next year saw publication of his third and last collection, *Songs from the Mountains*. Renowned in his day for poems such as 'Bell Birds' and 'September in Australia', his patriotic and ceremonial verse shows that Kendall was a significant poet of the colonial period, reflected in the definitive *The Poetical Works of Henry Kendall* (1966).

KENEALLY, Thomas Michael
(1935–)

Australian novelist, born in Sydney, New South Wales. He studied for the priesthood and the law and served in the Australian Citizens' Military Forces. He has taught and lectured in drama. He would like, he has said, to disown his first two novels—*The Place at Whitton* (1964) and *The Fear* (1965). His third novel, *Bring Larks and Heroes* (1967), was 'an attempt to follow out an epic theme in terms of a young soldier's exile to Australia'. *Three Cheers for a Paraclete* (1968) and *The Survivor* (1969) were 'character' studies in the English tradition, but it was the publication of *The Chant of Jimmy Blacksmith* (1972), based on the slaughter of a white family by a hitherto docile Aboriginal employee, that

marked the beginning of his mature fiction. As gifted as he is prolific, he is a born storyteller whose sympathies lie with the oppressed and the outcast. His reputation grew steadily until he published *Schindler's Ark* (1982), which tells how a German industrialist helped over 1000 Jews survive the Nazis. It was a controversial winner of the Booker Prize because it blurred the boundary between fact and fiction. It was memorably filmed, as *Schindler's List*, in 1994. Recent books include *A Family Madness* (1985), *The Playmaker* (1987), *By the Line* (1989), *Flying Hero Class* (1991) and *Woman of the Inner Sea* (1992). His writings include political commentary and travel, but later novels have been criticized for apparent haste.

▷P Quartermaine, *Thomas Keneally* (1991)

KENNAWAY, James
(1928–68)

Scottish novelist, born in Auchterarder, Perthshire, into a quiet middle-class background, the son of a solicitor and a doctor. He went to public school at Glenalmond. He did national service before going to Trinity College, Oxford, after which he worked for a London publisher and began to write in earnest. He married in 1951, and *The Kennaway Papers* (1981), edited by his wife Susan, gives an insight into his mercurial character and their turbulent relationship. *Tunes of Glory* (1956) was his first novel and remains his best known. The author himself wrote the screenplay to the successful film starring Alec Guinness and John Mills in a class confrontation set in a military barracks in Scotland. *Household Ghosts* (1961) was equally powerful, and was made into a stage-play (1967) and a film (1969) under the title *Country Dance*. Later books of note are *The Bells of Shoreditch* (1967), *Some Gorgeous Accident* (1967) and the autobiographical *The Cost of Living Like This* (1969). *Silence*, a novel, was published posthumously in 1972.

KENNEDY, John Pendleton
(1795–1870)

American novelist and social commentator. He was born and educated in Baltimore, Maryland, and saw service in the war of 1812 against the British. He subsequently entered the Maryland legislature (1820–3), and was elected to Congress in Washington as a representative from Maryland, serving two terms (1838, 1840–4). His passage in politics was eased by a substantial legacy from his uncle. In 1852, President Fillmore appointed him Secretary of the Navy. Kennedy is remembered primarily for two books, *Swallow Barn* (1832), a satirical and episodic 'Sojourn in the Old Dominion', and the later *Horse-Shoe Robinson* (1835), a more structured romance in the tradition of Sir **Walter Scott**. They were published under the pseudonym Mark Littleton. Here and in his two other fictional works, *Rob of the Bowl* (1838) and the **Swift**ian *Quodlibet* (1840), he seems to make a case for a modest balance of aristocratic values and democratic reform (*Quodlibet* is a devastating satire on Jeffersonism run amok). Kennedy's collected works were published in 10 volumes just after his death (1871–2) and included a life by Henry T Tuckerman.

▷ J V Ridgely, *John Pendleton Kennedy* (1966)

KENNEDY, Margaret Moore
(1896–1967)

English novelist, journalist and playwright, born in London, the daughter of a barrister. She was educated at Cheltenham College and Somerville College, Oxford. A historian by training, her first book was *A Century of Revolution* (1922). Thereafter she wrote novels, all of which gained a fair measure of success, particularly her second, *The Constant Nymph* (1924), and its sequel, *The Fool of the Family* (1930). She also wrote plays, notably *Escape Me Never* (1933).

▷ V Powell, *The Constant Novelist* (1983)

KENNEDY, William Joseph
(1928–)

American novelist and screenwriter, born in Albany, New York. Educated at Siena College, Loudonville, New York, he served in the US army (1950–2) before becoming a journalist and eventually a full-time writer. *The Ink Truck* (1969) is distinct from subsequent novels for it does not use the locale of his hometown as a backdrop. *Legs* (1975) is the first of the 'Albany' novels, a mixture of fact and fiction which retells the story of Legs Diamond, the notorious gangster. In *Billy Phelan's Greatest Game* (1978) Albany is as important as the two main characters, the gamester Billy Phelan and journalist Martin Daugherty. *Ironweed* (1983), his best-known novel, describes the homecoming of a fallen baseball star, now down-and-out, drunk and maudlin. Jack Nicholson made an accurate film portrayal and the book won a Pulitzer Prize. *Quinns's Book* was published in 1988.

▷ E C Reilly, *William Kennedy* (1991)

KENNEDY, X J, pseud of Joseph Charles Kennedy
(1929–)

American poet, born in Dover, New Jersey, and educated at Columbia University, New York, and the Sorbonne. After service in the US Navy, he taught at Michigan University (1956–62), where his poetic career began with the extraordinary *Nude Descending a Staircase* (1961), a brilliant collection which for sheer force of character he has not matched since. The following year Kennedy moved to the University of North Carolina (1962–3), and subsequently to Tufts University, Massachusetts, where he was promoted to Professor of English in 1973. Kennedy's reputation was consolidated by *Breaking and Entering* (1972), which was published in the UK, and by *Emily Dickinson in Southern California* (1974), a delightfully unlikely juxtaposition that manages to give a reasonable sense of the vividly metrical, simply rhymed approach which makes him such a successful poet for children. With the exception of the extraordinary *Hangover Mass* (1984) his later work has been disappointing, though a selection, *Cross Ties* (1985), reawakened interest in his work.

KENNELLY, Brendan
(1936–)

Irish poet, novelist and playwright. Born in Ballylongford, County Kerry, he has been Professor of Modern Literature at Trinity College, Dublin since the mid-1970s. A prolific author with over 30 poetry collections, five plays and two published novels to his credit he also edited the *Penguin Book of Irish Verse* (1970, 1986). The immediacy of language and accessibility of themes which is evident in his early work, *Collection One* (1966), is echoed nearly 30 years later in the fierce rhetoric of *Cromwell* (1983) and *Judas* (1991). These two works are vigorously pacifist, addressing intolerance and the subversion of language by politics.

KENNY, Maurice
(1929–)

American poet, born in Watertown, New York State, of Mohawk descent, whose work has influenced a whole generation of Native American poets. He has published over 18 collections of poetry and fiction, his poetry including *North: Poems of Home* (1979), *Kneading the Blood* (1981), *The Smell of Slaughter* (1982), *Is Summer This Bear* (1985) and *Greyhounding This America* (1986). His poems, written in a characteristic incantatory style, often celebrate the vitality of the earth and the natural world. *Blackrobe* (1982), a cycle of poems about the 17th-century Jesuit missionary priest Isaac Jogues, was nominated for a Pulitzer Prize, and *The Mama Poems* won an American Book Award in 1984. Recently, many of his poems have been collected in *Between Two Rivers: Poems 1956–1984* (1987). Kenny is a longtime resident of Brooklyn, co-edits the poetry journal *Contact/II*, and is the publisher of Strawberry

Press. *Rain and Other Fictions* was published in 1985.

KERNER, Andreas Justinus
(1786–1862)

German poet, born in Ludwigsburg in Württemberg. He became a physician at Wildbad, and settled finally in Weinsberg in 1818. He published several volumes of poetry between 1811 and 1852. He studied animal magnetism, believed in occultism, and wrote *Die Seherin von Prevorst* (1829, 'The Clairvoyant of Prevorst'), a study of a psychic case.
▷H Buttiker, *Justinus Kerner* (1952)

KEROUAC, Jack (John)
(1922–69)

American novelist, born in Lowell, Massachusetts. His parents, devout Roman Catholics, came from rural communities in the French-speaking part of Quebec, and French was spoken in the home. He did not begin to learn to speak English until he was six. His childhood was happy, but various disasters struck the stability of the family, including the death of an older brother and floods which destroyed his father's print shop and press. He was educated at Lowell High School before accepting a football scholarship at Columbia University, but he turned his back on both and spent the early years of World War II working as a grease monkey in Hartford before returning to Lowell, where he got a job as a sports journalist on the *Lowell Sun*. His major energies, however, were spent working on an autobiographical novel that was never published. In 1942 he went to Washington where he worked briefly on the construction of the Pentagon before joining the US merchant marines, subsequently enlisting in the US navy (1943). After only a month he was discharged and branded an 'indifferent character'. His life is frequently seen as a rebellion against authority but his various scrapes and outbreaks of outrageous behaviour were less the actions of a subversive than of a weak-willed conservative influenced by persuasive friends like **Allen Ginsberg**, **Gary Snyder** and Neal Cassady, whom Kerouac portrayed as Dean Moriarty in his most famous novel, *On the Road* (1957). He was identified as leader of the so-called 'Beat Generation', a label he came to regret and repudiate. *The Town and the City* (1950), his first novel, showed the scars of his reading of **Thomas Wolfe**. *On the Road* was his second. Loose, apparently structureless and episodic, it follows two friends as they weave their way across America. It has been much imitated (on film as well as in fiction) and made Kerouac a cult-hero. Later books—*The Dharma Bums* (1958), *Doctor Sax* (1959), *Big*

Sur (1962)—were even more self-indulgent as he flirted with Zen Buddhism.
▷A Charters, *Jack Kerouac: a biography* (1973)

KESEY, Ken Elton
(1935–)

American author, born in La Junta, Colorado. Associated with the 'Beat' movement, he worked as a ward attendant in a mental hospital, an experience he used to telling effect in *One Flew Over the Cuckoo's Nest* (1963), narrated by an Indian named Chief Bromden whose father was the last chief of the tribe. Filmed in 1975 by Milos Forman it won five Oscars, including that for Best Film. *Sometimes a Great Notion* (1966) sank like lead and he relinquished 'literature' for 'life'. He served a prison sentence for marijuana possession and formed the 'Merry Pranksters', whose weird exploits are described at length in *The Electric Kool-Aid Acid Test* (1967) by **Tom Wolfe**. *Sailor Song* (1990) confirmed the underlying green values of *Demon Box* (1987), a collection of stories and pieces, and returned to something like the roistering fantasy of the earlier books.
▷S Tanner, *Ken Kesey* (1983)

KESSON, Jessie, originally Jessie Grant McDonald
(1915–)

Scottish novelist, short-story writer and playwright, born in Inverness. Not knowing who her father was, she soon moved to Elgin with her mother. Estranged from many of the family, mother and daughter lived meagrely on their own resources, becoming adept at evading the Cruelty Inspector and the rent man. In her teens, however, Jessie was sent to an orphanage in Skene, Aberdeenshire. Later she entered service, settling in 1934 on a farm with her husband Johnnie, a cottar. Although she managed eventually to devote herself to writing, she worked for many years as a cinema cleaner, artists' model and a social worker in London and Glasgow. *The White Bird Passes* (1958), *Glitter of Mica* (1963), *Another Time, Another Place* (1983) and *Where the Apple Ripens* (1985) recreate faithfully, and without sentimentality, her hard early years in a farming community.

KESTEN, Hermann
(1900–)

German-born American novelist, playwright, biographer (Copernicus, Ferdinand and Isabella of Spain,) and translator (**Julien Green**, **Jules Romains**), born in Nuremberg of Jewish parents. In 1932 he wrote his anti-Hitler novel *Der Scharlatan* ('The Charlatan'), which meant that he had to leave Germany the following year. He spent the war in America, and took American citizenship. Outstanding amongst his many books is *Die Zwillinge von Nürnburg* (1947, Eng trans *The Twins of Nuremberg*, 1946), a novel about inter-war Germany.

KEY, Francis Scott
(1780–1843)

American lawyer and poet, born in Maryland, author of *The Star-Spangled Banner*. During the British bombardment of Fort McHenry, Baltimore, in September, 1814, which he witnessed from a British man-of-war, he wrote a poem about the lone American flag seen flying over the fort as dawn broke. It was published as *The Defence of Fort McHenry*, and later set to a tune by the English composer, John Stafford Smith (*To Anacreon in Heaven*). In 1931 it was adopted as the American national anthem as *The Star-Spangled Banner*.

KEYES, Daniel
(1927–)

American science-fiction writer, born in New York City. He taught English at the University of Ohio, Athens, and was briefly an associate editor of the science-fiction magazine *Marvel Science Fiction* in 1951. His reputation rests on his novel *Flowers for Algernon* (1966), originally written as a short story in 1959. It is a moving account of a man whose intelligence is artificially increased to the level of genius, but with tragic consequences, and was successfully filmed as *Charly* (1968). He did not repeat the book's success with his second novel, *The Touch* (1968), about the psychological results of a nuclear accident.

KEYES, Frances Parkinson
(1885–1970)

American novelist, born at the University of Virginia. In 1904 she married Henry Wilder Keyes, Governor of New Hampshire (1917–19), and a senator (1919–37); she made use of her position to write *Letters From a Senator's Wife* (1924), and to travel widely. *The Old Gray Homestead* (1919), her first novel, was followed by dozens of successful works, her popularity proving to be enduring. She is now best known for the murder mystery *Dinner At Antoine's* (1948), set in New Orleans during the run-up to Mardi Gras.

KEYES, Sidney Arthur Kilworth
(1922–43)

English poet, born in Dartford, Kent, and educated at Tonbridge School and Oxford University, where he co-edited *Eight Oxford Poets* (1941), which included his own work.

His first book of poems, *The Iron Laurel*, was published in 1942, and his second, *The Cruel Solstice*, in 1944 (Hawthornden Prize), after his death in action in Libya. His *Collected Poems* appeared in 1945.

▷J Guenther, *Sidney Keyes: a biographical enquiry* (1967)

KHAN, Ismith
(1925–)

Trinidadian-born American novelist, born in Port of Spain. Although Khan's novels are about Trinidad, he did not publish them until he had put a distance between his native land and himself. His first, *The Jumbie Bird* (1961), is in part autobiographical, and centres on the Khan family and its Indian roots. Khan's unusual fiction offers an interesting and valuable contrast to that of the better known **V S Naipaul**.

KHANDEKAR, Vishnu Sakharam
(1898–1976)

Indian (Marathi) novelist who was able to support himself by his writing, although he also had to work in the Indian movie industry. He was left-wing in his views, but never failed to be objective. *White Clouds* (1940) deals with Gandhi's spinning people. *Yayati* (1959, Eng trans 1978) is his major novel, a searing attack on modern materialism, cast in the form of a retelling of a celebrated episode of the *Mahabharata*.

KHARMS, Daniil, pseud of **Daniil Yuvachov**
(1905–42)

Russian poet, dramatist and critic, born in St Petersburg. He was a member (with his friend **Nicolay Zabolotsky**) of the late avant-garde group which called itself OBERIU (acronym of the Russian for Association for Real Art) which gathered itself around the officially 'pure' children's writer **Samuel Marshak** in the hope of surviving the Stalinist onslaught against individuality in art. Kharms could be said to have invented the term 'The Theatre of the Absurd' with his play *Yelizaveta Bam* (1927). He died in a Stalinist prison.

▷G Gibian, *Russia's Lost Literature of the Absurd* (1974)

KHLEBNIKOV, Velimir, pseud of **Viktor Khlebnikov**
(1885–1922)

Major Russian poet and dramatist, born in Tundutovo, in the Astrakhan province, of an ornithologist father; he studied biology as a student, and this left its mark on his poetry. Whatever the final verdict on Khlebnikov's intrinsic achievement, he was one of the most original poets of the 20th century. As well as being an arch intellectual, he was certainly half-mad, and thus spent much of his time attempting to calculate an algorithm by which he could derive the cyclic laws of history; he was on the move for the whole of his short life, and finally died of malnutrition. But he was also a genuine visionary (in a way not wholly uncommon in Russia at that dangerous time), and it is in its visionary qualities that the true value of his extraordinary poetry lies. With **Mikhail Kuzmin, Vyacheslav Ivanov** and others he did 'hatch', as has been aptly said, the Russian Futurist movement (a year behind the birth of the Italian movement of the same name, but superior to it in quality), yet in essence he was a religious poet, expressing himself in terms of Slavic mythology and pagan folk epic. Like **Laura Riding**, he wanted to redefine every word in his language; to that end he (with others) devised *zaum*, a 'transrational' language which would lead to world peace (another concern of Riding's) and to heaven on earth. His numerological eccentricities are not irrelevant to his achievement, but they are not a part of it: he was capable of coherent (if always mystical) and inspired lyrics and longer poems, all of which are now continually being restudied and reassessed by readers and critics—to some of whom the nature of the madness behind them is once again relevant. There are English translations of his work in *Smoke Train: Selected Poetry and Prose* (1976).

KHODASEVICH, Vladislaw
(1886–1939)

Russian poet, translator (of Polish and Hebrew poetry) and critic, born in Moscow; he died in exile and in poverty in Paris. His father was Polish, his mother Jewish, and he was always fascinated by Jewish culture and history. **Nabokov**, whose very earliest literary efforts he encouraged, pointed to him as 'the greatest Russian poet of our time'—he knew he exaggerated, but was thus fruitfully able to attract attention to Khodasevich's achievement. A man who, had he not been a poet of such high quality, might have been called unduly sensitive, he was certain that he stood at the end of Russian culture, and in a sense he was right. A Platonist, disgusted by the world, he tried to retreat into himself and to write of the purity he had discovered within his own mind; after his exile to Paris, in which he was helped, painlessly, in 1922, by the good offices of his friend **Gorky**, he also tried to make a success of himself as an émigré poet. But he failed, and after 1928 relapsed into a virtual silence relieved only by some exquisite critical essays. He took after, and almost worshipped, **Pushkin**, hated Futurism and everything 'modern', but was nevertheless and despite himself eminently a poet of the modern sensibility. 'Ballata', (Eng trans 'Ballad'

in the *Penguin Book of Russian Verse*, 1965, ed Dimitry Obolensky), is typical in its invocation to poetry, and shows him at his greatest.

▷V Nabokov, *Strong Opinions* (1973); S Karlinsky and A Appel (eds), *The Bitter Air of Exile* (1977)

KHVYLOVY, Mikola, pseud of Mykola Fitilov
(1893–1933)

Ukrainian story writer, critic and poet, born in Trostyanets, a village in the Kharkov province. He was a keen supporter of the Soviet presence in his country, and was the organiser of the VAPLITE group of proletarian writers. But Stalin's stupidity and bullying drove him to resistance and then to suicide. He wrote satirical stories (his best work), strident poetry and some immature criticism. Stories are translated in *Stories from the Ukraine* (1960, ed W K Matthews).

KIANTO, Ilmari
(1874–1970)

Finnish novelist and (initially) poet, born in Pulkkila. He wrote two classic novels, *Punainan viiva* (1909, 'The Red Line'), and *Ryysyrannan Jooseppi* (1924, 'Ryysyranna's Joseph'), under the combined influences of **Zola** and **Strindberg**, but wholly Finnish in conception. They describe rural poverty with a vivid humour that makes them virtually unique in the literature.

KIELLAND, Alexander L(ange)
(1849–1906)

Norwegian novelist, born in Stavanger, where he became burgomaster in 1891, having withdrawn from literary life. A follower of Georg Brandes, he was an exponent of the realist school. His stylish novels of social satire included *Garman og Worse* (1880), *Skipper Worse* (1882) and *Tales of Two Countries* (1891). He also wrote plays and short stories. Despite intense lobbying by **Bjørnson** and **Jonas Lie**, he was not awarded a state literary pension; though he returned to writing later, disappointment drove him to reject the literary world.

▷J Lunde, *Alexander Lange Kielland* (1970)

KIELY, Benedict
(1919–)

Irish novelist, story writer and critic, born near Dromore, County Tyrone, and much influenced by **William Carleton**. He was a Jesuit novitiate, but was forced to abandon this vocation owing to severe illness. He has been adjudged more skilful in the short story than in the novel, although *The Cards of the Gambler* (1953) was successful. His stories, popular with readers of the *New Yorker*, have been said to 'weave a kind of tapestry around a scarcely satiric love of humanity'. They are collected in *A Journey to the Seven Streams* (1963), *A Ball of Malt and Madame Butterfly* (1973) and elsewhere.

▷G Eckley, *Benedict Kiely* (1975)

KILLENS, John Oliver
(1916–87)

American novelist, born in Macon, Georgia, whose fictional work represents an episodic commentary on the lives and struggles of Afro-Americans. His experience as a soldier in racially segregated units during World War II led him to write *And Then We Heard the Thunder* (1962), one of the most powerful American war novels. It was Killens's second book; its predecessor, *Youngblood* (1954), is a part-sociological, part-symbolic story of racial prejudice, and advocates working-class solidarity rather than separatism as the most valid response to oppression. *'Sippi* (1967) is too obviously marked by the civil rights and Black Power rhetoric of the time, and despite Killens's ideological sophistication, is far less well argued than the essays in *Black Man's Burden* (1966). *The Cotillion* (1971) is at once more sophisticated in imaginative terms and a return to a plainer, folksier style. It was turned into an effective musical (1975) with music co-written by Smokey Robinson. His desire to understand the wider aspects of 'the black experience' led him to write *The Great Black Russian* (1988), a posthumously published novel about the mulatto **Pushkin**. Killens also wrote intelligent and unpatronizing children's books.

KILLIGREW, Anne
(1660–85)

English poet, born in London into a Royalist family connected with the Restoration theatre. She was appointed maid of honour to the Duchess of York, and painted portraits of the duke and duchess. Her *Poems* (1686), prefaced by the famous ode to her memory by **Dryden**, are mostly pious, melancholy and conventionally baroque in style. She died of smallpox.

▷A Messenger, *His and Hers: Essays in Restoration and Eighteenth-Century Literature* (1986)

KILLIGREW, Thomas
(1612–83)

English dramatist, brother of Sir **William Killigrew**, page in the household of Charles I, and afterwards a companion of Charles II in exile and his groom of the bedchamber after

the Restoration. He published in 1664 nine indifferent plays, written, he claimed, in nine different cities. The most popular of them was *The Parson's Wedding*. He was for some time manager of the king's company, and obtained permission to give female parts to women. His son, Thomas Killigrew (1657–1719), wrote a theatrical comedy, *Chit Chat* (performed 1719).

▷A Harbage, *Killigrew: Cavalier dramatist* (1930)

KILLIGREW, Sir William
(1606–95)

English dramatist, brother of **Thomas Killigrew**. He fought in the Civil War, and wrote a comedy, *Pandora*, and tragi-comedies, such as *Selindra*, *Ormasdes* and *The Siege of Urbin*.

KILMER, (Alfred) Joyce
(1886–1918)

American poet, saddled eternally with credit for writing 'Trees', a poem so over-quoted— 'I think that I will never see/A poem lovely as a tree'—and easily spoofed that it has blurred perceptions of his very real gifts. Kilmer published only three collections—*Summer of Love* (1911), the ubiquitous *Trees and Other Poems* (1914) and *Main Street* (1917)—before he was killed on the Western Front, where he was a volunteer; he was awarded a posthumous Croix de Guerre for gallantry. His wife Aline also wrote verse, notably *Candles That Burn* (1919).

KILPI, Volter
(1874–1939)

Finnish novelist, born in Kustavi. Much neglected owing to the highly individualistic style of the books he published in the last six years of his life, when he discovered his own voice, he is one of the most extraordinary writers of his period. His *Alastalon salissa* (1933, 'Alastolo's Hall'), is an often comic meditation on death, reminiscent of **Edgar Lee Masters** as well as of **Joyce**, with whose *Ulysses* it has been compared. *Kirkolle* (1937, 'On the Way to Church'), is a similar but more lyrical meditation, celebrating the moment at the expense of all else. Kilpi was deaf for most of his life, and this contributed to his hermetic style; but the posthumous *Gulliverin matka Fantomimian mantereelle* (1944, 'Gulliver's Journey to Fantomimia') achieves a new clarity.

▷J Ahokas, *A History of Finnish Literature* (1973)

KILVERT, (Robert) Francis
(1840–79)

English clergyman and diarist. He was a curate at Clyro in Radnorshire and later vicar of

Bredwardine on the Wye. His *Diary (1870–79)*, giving a vivid picture of rural life in the Welsh marches, was discovered in 1937 and published in three volumes (1938–40).

▷F Grice, *Kilvert: priest and diarist* (1975)

KINCAID, Jamaica, originally **Elaine Potter Richardson**
(1949–)

American novelist and journalist, born in St John's, Antigua. Her novels include *At the Bottom of the River* (1983) and *Lucy* (1991), the latter being the sensitive tale of a young West Indian girl who, having fled to New York, grows ever more appreciative of, and eager to return to, her own land. The book is, in part, autobiographical: Kincaid herself has made the same journey, and is currently a staff writer for the *New Yorker*. She enjoys a certain cachet among a feminist audience, and has also written a non-fictional account of her home island, *A Small Place*.

KINCK, Hans Ernst
(1865–1926)

Norwegian novelist and dramatist, born in Øksfjord. His works illustrate his deep love of nature and his interest in the lives of peasants, and include *Sneskavlen brast* (1918–19) and *Driftekaren* (1908, 'The Drover'), a verse play. *Ungtfolk* (1893, Eng trans *A Young People*, 1929) introduced the problematic question of social betterment, taken up again in *Emigranter* (1904, 'Emigrants').

▷E Beyer, *Hans Ernst Kinck* (1956–65)

KING, Francis Henry
(1923–)

English novelist, critic and short-story writer, born in Adelboden, Switzerland, but who spent much of his childhood in India before the family returned to England. After graduating from Oxford, he worked for the British Council, travelling extensively, before retiring to write full-time in 1964. His novels include *The Dividing Stream* (1951), *The Widow* (1957), and the novellas in *Flights* (1973), sensitive fiction whose outward highly-wrought delicacy is sometimes deceptive, for his writing often plunges into the decadent and the bizarre, even horrific. *Act of Darkness* (1983), for instance, is a violent murder mystery set in India, while *Voices in an Empty Room* (1984) deals with the paranormal. He has also written travel books and a short study of **E M Forster** (1978).

KING, Grace Elizabeth
(1851–1932)

American author of local-colour fiction about New Orleans. Her stories first appeared in magazines such as *Harpers* and *Century*

Magazine, and were then collected in three volumes—*Monsieur Motte* (1888), whose title story was King's first published work, *Tales of Time and Place* (1892) and *Balcony Stories* (1893). She wrote several historical novels on religious themes and one about the Reconstruction period in New Orleans, *The Pleasant Ways of St. Medard* (1916). She was also a stalwart of the Louisiana Historical Society.

KING, Henry
(1592–1669)

English poet, born in Worminghall, Buckinghamshire, and educated at Westminster School and Christ Church, Oxford. He entered the church, rising to Bishop of Chichester in 1641, and was a friend of **Jonson**, **Donne** and **Izaak Walton**. During the interregnum he was deprived of his bishopric, living in retirement from 1643 to 1660. He published sermons, elegies on Charles I, and a metrical paraphrase of the Psalms; his *Poems, Elegies, Paradoxes, and Sonnets* (1657) were published without authority. The poignant 'Exequy to his Matchless never to be forgotten Friend', written on the death of his young wife Anne in 1624, has secured his reputation as a minor but gifted Metaphysical poet.

▷*Poems*, ed with life and critical introduction by M Crum (1965)

KING, Stephen Edwin
(1947–)

American author of horror fiction, perhaps the most successful practitioner of the art since **Edgar Allan Poe**. He was born in Portland, Maine. His debut novel *Carrie* (1974)—the story of a socially and sexually repressed girl who uses the gift of psychokinesis to take revenge on her tormentors—was a bestseller, as have been most subsequent works, each book augmenting the already vast army of his followers. His short-story collections include *Skeleton Crew* (1985). In novels and stories alike, his most common theme is the irruption of the irrational, the supernatural, into the solid, semi-rural milieu of New England. Like *Carrie*, *The Shining* (1977) and *The Dead Zone* (1979) were successfully filmed. His status as a bestseller, and his popularity with young fans of horror, tend to obscure the fact that, as a storyteller, he is a consummate craftsman.

KING, William
(1663–1712)

English poet, born in London and educated at Westminster School and Christ Church, Oxford, where he took a law degree and became advocate in Doctors' Commons. In

Dialogues of the Dead (1699) he joined in the 'Battle of the Books' against Richard Bentley. Appointed judge in Ireland in 1701, later keeper of records at Dublin Castle, he spent more time writing humorous verse than on his duties. He returned to England in 1708 to live by his pen, publishing copiously: pamphlets, satires and burlesque poems, including *The Art of Cookery* (1708), an imitation of **Horace**. As **Samuel Johnson** remarked, his purpose was to be merry, and he succeeded.
▷ Dr S Johnson, *Lives of the Most Eminent English Poets* (10 vols, 1779–81); G G Williams, in *Sewanee Review*, 35 (1927)

KINGO, Thomas Hansen
(1634–1703)

Danish poet and prelate, born in Slangerup, of Scottish descent. The greatest Baroque poet in Denmark's literary history, he was Bishop of Fyn from 1677. He wrote collections of hymns (*Aandeligt sjungekor*, 1674 and 1681, 'Spiritual Chorus'; and *Vinterparten*, 1689, 'The Winter Part') and much secular and religious poetry. His complete works were published in seven volumes between 1939 and 1975.
▷ J Simonsen, *Thomas Kingo* (1970)

KINGSLEY, Charles
(1819–75)

English author, born at Holne vicarage, Dartmoor. In 1838 he entered Magdalene College, Cambridge, and took a classical first in 1842. As curate and then rector (1844) he spent the rest of his life at Eversley in Hampshire. His dramatic poem, *The Saint's Tragedy, or The True Story of Elizabeth of Hungary* (1848), was followed by *Alton Locke* (1850) and *Yeast* (1851), brilliant social novels which had enormous influence at the time. He had thrown himself into various schemes for the improvement of the working classes, and like F D Maurice was a 'Christian Socialist'. As 'Parson Lot' he published an immense number of articles on current topics, especially in the *Christian Socialist* and *Politics for the People*. *Hypatia* (1853) is a brilliant picture of early Christianity in conflict with Greek philosophy at Alexandria. *Westward Ho!* (1855) is a lifelike representation of Elizabethan England and the Spanish Main. *Two Years Ago* (1857) and *Hereward the Wake* (1866) were his later novels. In 1860 he was appointed Professor of Modern History at Cambridge; *The Roman and the Teuton* (1864) was based on his Cambridge lectures. In 1869 he resigned his professorship and was appointed canon of Chester. In 1869–70 he made a voyage to the West Indies, and on his return issued the charming account *At Last*. In 1873 he was appointed canon of Westminster and chaplain to Queen Victoria. The col-

lected works of this combative, enthusiastic and sympathetic apostle of what was called (*not* by him) 'muscular Christianity' fill 28 volumes (1879–81), and include *Glaucus* (1855), *The Heroes* (1856), *The Water Babies* (1863), *Town Geology* (1872), *Prose Idylls* (1873) and *Health and Education* (1874).
▷ S Chitty, *The Beast and the Monk* (1974)

KINGSLEY, Henry
(1830–76)

English novelist, brother of **Charles Kingsley**. He was educated at King's College School, London, and Worcester College, Oxford. From 1853 to 1858 he worked as a gold prospector in Australia, and on his return published a vigorous picture of colonial life in *Recollections of Geoffry Hamlyn* (1859). After this came *Ravenshoe* (1861), his masterpiece, followed by *Austin Elliot* (1863), and then *The Hillyars and the Burtons*, another novel of Australian life (1865). In 1869–70 he edited the *Edinburgh Daily Review*.
▷ J S D Mellick, *The Passing Guest: a life of Henry Kingsley* (1983)

KINGSLEY, Mary St Leger *see* **MALET, Lucas**

KINGSLEY, Sidney, originally **Sidney Kirschner**
(1906–)

American dramatist, born in New York City and educated at Cornell University. He won a Pulitzer Prize with his first play, *Men in White* (1933), set in a hospital, which deals with a young intern's conflicting sense of duty and search for personal happiness. His second, extremely successful drama, *Dead End* (1935), is a realistic study suggesting that poverty is the seedbed of crime. His following two plays were both failures, but *The Patriots* (1943), a historical drama recounting the formative years of American democracy, and which served as a call for national unity during World War II, restored him to critical and popular acclaim. In his later plays, *Detective Story* (1949) and *Night Life* (1962), he returned to describing tough social conditions.

KINGSMILL, Hugh, originally **Hugh Kingsmill Lunn**
(1889–1949)

English biographer and anthologist, younger brother of Arnold Lunn and Brian Lunn. Educated at Harrow, Oxford and Dublin, he became a writer, initially winning odium for iconoclasm degenerating into idleness. But after the failure of his *Matthew Arnold* (1928), he recovered himself with the satirical fantasy *The Return of William Shakespeare* (1929), produced works of art in his *Frank Harris*

(1932) and his elegant essays *The Table of Truth* and *The Progress of a Biographer* (1949). He produced excellent anthologies, such as *Invective and Abuse* (1944), *Johnson Without Boswell* (1940) and *The Worst of Love* (1931), while with Hesketh Pearson he established a delightful art-form in conversational literary journeys such as *Skye High* (1937), *This Blessed Plot* (1942) and *Talking of Dick Whittington* (1947).

▷ M Holroyd, *The Collected Hugh Kingsmill* (1964, rev edn 1971)

KINGSTON, Maxine Hong
(1940–)

Chinese–American novelist and autobiographer, born and educated in California. *The Woman Warrior* (1976) is an account of her coming to terms with the tension between two inimical cultures; though barely fictionalized, it also poses serious literary questions about narrative method and the relationship between fantasy and memory. *China Men* (1980) is in similar vein, but *Tripmaster Monkey* (1989) transfers the essential dilemmas and desires of the earlier books to a Sino–American man who considers himself to be an avatar of the sacred Monkey King.

KINGSTON, William Henry Giles
(1814–80)

English author, son of a merchant in Oporto, where he spent much of his youth. He wrote over 150 boys' adventure stories including such favourites as *Peter the Whaler* (1851) and *The Three Midshipmen* (1862).

▷ M R Kingsford, *The Life, Work and Influence of William Kingston* (1947)

KINKEL, Gottfried
(1815–82)

German poet, born in Oberkassel near Bonn. He lectured at Bonn on theology, poetry and the history of art. Involved in the revolutionary movement of 1848, he was imprisoned in Spandau (1850), from where he escaped. He taught German in London until 1866, when he was appointed Professor of Archaeology and Art at Zürich. As a poet his fame rests upon *Otto der Schütz* (1846, 'Otto the Hunter'), *Der Grobschmied von Antwerpen* (1872, 'The Blacksmith of Antwerp'), *Tanagra* (1883, Eng trans *Tanagra: an idyll of Greece*, 1893), *Gedichte* (1843–68, 'Poems'), and a drama, *Nimrod* (1857). He also wrote a history of art (1845) and monographs on **Ferdinand Freiligrath** (1867) and Rubens (1874). His first wife, Johanna (1810–58), a distinguished musician, wrote a novel, *Hans Ibeles in London* (1860), and, with her husband, *Erzählungen* (1849, 'Tales'), a collection of tales.

KINNELL, Galway
(1927–)

American poet and translator. He was born in Providence, Rhode Island, and educated at Princeton University and the University of Rochester, and has taught at campuses throughout the USA. His early work was gathered as *First Poems, 1946–1954* (1970), establishing a direct, semi-'confessional' style, with a muscular edge. *The Avenue Bearing the Initial of Christ into the New World* (1974) collected work from 1946 to 1964, a pattern of dates that suggests again that Kinnell's reputation was as slow to build as his art was deliberate, undemonstrative and carefully crafted. The title poem uses Avenue C in New York as a focus for a study of human suffering. *The Book of Nightmares* (1971) covered similar ground in a single long poem. Later books include *The Last Hiding Places of Snow* (1980) and *The Fundamental Project of Technology* (1983). He has written one novel, *Black Light* (1966), and has published many translations, most significantly his versions of **François Villon** (1965, 1977, 1982). Kinnell won the Pulitzer Prize in 1983.

▷ *Walking Down the Stairs* (interviews, 1978)

KINOSHITA Junji
(1914–)

Japanese playwright, one of the first modern Japanese dramatists. His work varies between the two extremes of intellectual, issue-based theatre and popular, accessible plays. He is best known for *Yuzuru* (1949, 'Twilight Crane'), which is based on a folk tale and is a repertory classic in Japan, being an accessible and rewarding play. *Furu* (1947, 'Wandering'), on the other hand, about the Meiji Restoration in 1868 and the subsequent political upheavals, is a superbly crafted piece of historical theatre, being particularly strong in its depiction of the mental sufferings of the protagonists. His work at its weightiest, however, tends to sacrifice theatricality for analysis, and some of it is barely possible to stage.

KINSELLA, Thomas
(1928–)

Irish poet and translator (from the ancient Irish), born in Dublin. Although highly thought of in his native country, and described there as one of Ireland's 'most original and stimulating' practitioners, Kinsella's poetry has not yet been much read outside it. More indebted to the work of English and American poets (**Auden** in particular) than to that of his Irish predecessors, Kinsella's later poetry has moved in a **Jung**ian direction, being much concerned with the notion of 'individuation'. This has led some Irish critics to declare that he has 'brooded himself to pieces'; but others point to his establishment of 'reasonably authentic myth'.

▷ *Selected Poems 1956–1968* (1973); M Harmon, *The Poetry of Thomas Kinsella* (1974)

KINSELLA, W(illiam) P(atrick)
(1935–)

Canadian novelist and short-story writer, born in Edmonton. He worked in the retail business, as a restaurateur and taxi driver in Victoria, British Columbia, before joining the English faculty at the University of Calgary, Alberta (1978–83) following the publication of his first collection of stories. *Dance Me Outside* (1977) and the later *Born Indian* (1981) and *The Moccasin Telegraph* (1983) are all concerned with a young Indian boy and his rites of passage. Based on an earlier baseball story, Kinsella's first novel was *Shoeless Joe* (1982), a fable about the betrayal and restitution of innocence; its connections to *A Catcher in the Rye* and *The Great Gatsby* are confirmed when **J D Salinger** and the historical 1919 Chicago White Sox team appear as characters. The novel was subsequently made into the movie *Field of Dreams* (1989). Kinsella's later novel—*The Iowa Baseball Confederacy* (1986), and the stories in *The Further Adventures of Slugger McBatt* (1988)—are more conventional, but collections like *The Thrill of the Grass* (1984) and *The Fencepost Chronicles* (1986) continue the line of his earlier books.

KIPLING, Rudyard
(1865–1936)

English writer and winner of the Nobel Prize for literature, born in Bombay, the son of John Lockwood Kipling (1837–1911), Principal of the School of Art in Lahore. He was educated at the United Services College, Westward Ho!, in Devon, in England, but returned in 1880 to India, where he worked as a journalist on the Lahore *Civil and Military Gazette*. His mildly satirical verses *Departmental Ditties* (1886), and the short stories *Plain Tales from the Hills* (1888) and *Soldiers Three* (1889), won him a reputation in England. He returned in 1889 and settled in London, where *The Light that Failed* (1890), his first attempt at a full-length novel, was not altogether successful. In London he met Wolcott Balestier, the American author-publisher, with whom he collaborated in *The Naulakha* (1892), and whose sister Caroline he married (1892). A spell of residence in his wife's native state of Vermont ended abruptly in 1899 through incompatibility with in-laws and locals, and the remainder of Kipling's

career was spent in England. Meanwhile he had written the brilliantly successful *Barrack Room Ballads* (1892) and *The Seven Seas* (1896), both collections of verse, and further short stories published as *Many Inventions* (1893) and *The Day's Work* (1899). The two *Jungle Books* (1894–5) have won a place among the classic animal stories, and *Stalky and Co* (1899) presents semi-autobiographical but delightfully uninhibited episodes based on the author's schooldays. *Kim* appeared in 1901, and the children's classic *Just So Stories* in 1902. The verse collection *The Five Nations* (1903) included the highly successful 'Recessional', written for Queen Victoria's diamond jubilee in 1897. Later works include *Puck of Pook's Hill* (1906), *Rewards and Fairies* (1910), *Debits and Credits* (1926), and the autobiographical *Something of Myself* (1937). Kipling's real merit as a writer has tended to become obscured in recent years and he has been accused of imperialism and jingoism, but this ignores not only the great body of his work which was far removed from this sphere, but also his own criticisms and satire on some of the less admirable aspects of colonialism. He was awarded the Nobel Prize for literature in 1907.

▷ C Carrington, *Rudyard Kipling: his life and work* (1955)

KIPPHARDT, Heinar
(1922–)

German novelist and playwright, born in Heidersdorf, Silesia. A psychiatrist until 1951, he became famous overnight with his play *In der Sache J. Robert Oppenheimer* (1964, Eng trans *In the Matter of J. Robert Oppenheimer*, 1967), a chilling re-shaping of the moral case against the American Atomic Energy Commission. This is one of the most effectively **Brecht**ian plays since Brecht. In the novel *März* (1976, 'March') he turns back to his psychiatric experience.

KIRK, Hans
(1898–1962)

Danish novelist, born into a radical, atheistic doctor's family in North Jutland. He graduated in law from the University of Copenhagen in 1922, then worked at the Danish Embassy in Paris before becoming a journalist for a Danish provincial newspaper. A communist, he came to notice with his first novel *Fiskerne* (1928, 'The Fishermen'), a collective narrative that focuses on the relationship between social class and religion in a small fishing and farming community by the Limfjord. This and the subsequent connected works *Daglejerne* (1936, 'The Day-Labourers') and *De ny Tider* (1939, 'New Times'), about the rise of the industrial working classes in Denmark, firmly established the collective novel as a popular and prestigious form in Danish literature of the 1930s.

▷C Jensen, *Folkelighed og utopi. Brydninger i Hans Kirks forfatterskab* (1981)

KIRKUP, James
(1923–)

English poet, born in South Shields, and the holder of academic posts, first at home (Leeds University, 1950–2), then, from the early 1960s, in Japan, where he became Professor of English Literature at Kyoto University. His collections include *A Correct Compassion* (1952) and *Zen Contemplations* (1978). As its title suggests, the latter—sparse, economical, unostentatious—shows the influence of Japan on his work. He has also published plays, fiction and a frank autobiography, *The Only Child* (1957).

KIRKWOOD, James
(1930–89)

American dramatist, novelist and actor, born in Los Angeles. He acted on both stage and in television, but is best known as a writer. His plays include an adaptation of *There Must Be A Pony* (1962), *UTBU (Unhealthy To Be Unpleasant)* (1965) and *PS. Your Cat is Dead* (1975, from his own novel). His other novels include *Good Times/Bad Times* (1966), *Some Kind of Hero* (1975) and *Hit Me With A Rainbow* (1980). He co-wrote the book (script) for the broadway smash-hit musical *A Chorus Line* (1975, with Nicholas Dante), for which they were awarded a Pulitzer Prize for Drama, with composer Marvin Hamlisch (1944–), lyricist Edward Kleban (1939–87) and director Michael Bennett (1943–).

KIRSANOV, Semyon
(1906–72)

Russian poet, born in Odessa. At first associated with and influenced by **Mayakovsky**, he later became a reluctantly Stalinistic poet; however, he contributed vital satirical poems in the 1956 'Thaw'.

KIRSHON, Vladimir
(1902–38)

Russian dramatist, born in St Petersburg, who vanished and was then murdered in the Purges—despite the fact that his well-made plays were all 'politically correct'. *Khleb* (1930, Eng trans *Bread*, in *Six Soviet Plays*, ed E Lyons, 1934) is typical in its supposed demonstration that wealthy farmers ('kulaks') were villainous starvers of the common people. He also wrote many film scenarios.

KIŠ, Danilo
(1935–)

Yugoslavian novelist, born in Subotica, Vojdovina, in the extreme north of the province, near the Hungarian and Romanian borders. He was educated in Belgrade, and moved to France as a teacher of Serbo–Croat. His first novel, *Mansarda; Psalam 44* ('The Garret, Psalm XLIV'), appeared in 1962, but it was the strongly autobiographical *Bašta, pepeo* (1965) which, as *Garden, Ashes* (1976), established his reputation in the West. Its impact was reinforced by *Grobnica za Borisa Davidoviča* (1976, Eng trans *A Tomb for Boris Davidovich*, 1978), a collection of short stories about the Holocaust, a subject Kiš had already explored in the brilliant *Peščanik* (1972, Eng trans *Hourglass*, 1990). Though favourably received elsewhere, *A Tomb* was greeted with charges of plagiarism in Yugoslavia, to which Kiš responded vigorously in the satirical *Čas anatomije* (1978, 'The Anatomy Lesson'). Later works incude *Enciklopedija mrtvih* (1983, Eng trans *The Encyclopedia of the Dead*, 1987).

KISFALUDY, Karoly
(1788–1830)

Hungarian dramatist, brother of the poet Sandor Kisfaludy (1772–1844). He turned his back on his noble upbringing, and lived the life of a bohemian artist. He was the regenerator of the national drama, and became famous for his *A' Tatárok Magyar Országban* (1819, 'Tartars in Hungary'). His brother's poetry continued to reflect the noble family tradition.

▷F Szinnyei, *Kisfaludy Karoly* (1927)

KITAHARA Hakushu
(1885–1942)

Japanese poet and lyricist who achieved great popular success in his day, and is still widely read. Writing in all the traditional forms, *waka*, *haiku* and free verse, Kitahara was a highly accomplished wordsmith with a spare, elegant turn of phrase, and produced intensely personal verse, much of it with a rhythmical structure which made it ideal for use as song lyrics, which partly accounts for his popularity.

KITZBERG, August
(1856–1927)

Estonian playwright and story writer, born in Halliste, Pärnumaa. His plays about country life, sometimes using folklore material, have become classics of the Estonian theatre. The most famous is *Libahunt* (1911), on a werewolf theme.

KIVI, Aleksis, originally **Stenvall**
(1834–72)
Finnish playwright and novelist, born in Nur-
mijärvi or Palojoki, the son of a poor tailor.
He managed to gain a place at Helsinki University but did not graduate. He wrote in
Finnish not Swedish, establishing the western
dialect as the modern literary language of
Finland, and is considered the father of the
Finnish theatre and novel. He wrote the first
Finnish novel, *Seitsemän veljestä* (1870, Eng
trans *Seven Brothers*, 1929), and a collection
of Finnish poems, *Kanervala* (1866). As a
dramatist he wrote rural comedies like *Num-
misuutarit* (1864, 'The Cobblers on the
Heath'), and a tragedy, *Kullervo* (1864), based
on one of the central figures in the national
epic, the *Kalevala*.
▷V Tarkiainen, *Alexis Kivi* (1950)

KIVIMAA, Kaarlo Arvi
(1904–)
Finnish poet, critic, novelist and dramatist,
born in Hartola. From 1949 he was Director
of the Finnish National Theatre. Originally
associated with the Torchbearer Group of the
1920s, his novels, poetry and drama all seek
to promote 'Europeanism', as well as to
express his melancholy appreciation of the
beauties of his country.

KIZER, Carolyn Ashley
(1925–)
American poet, born in Spokane, Washington. She was educated at Columbia University and the University of Seattle, and
founded the journal *Poetry Northwest* in
Seattle. She worked briefly for the State
Department as an adviser on Pakistan, and
has taught at a number of universities. Her
first collection, *Poems* (1959), was followed
by *The Ungrateful Garden* (1961). Subsequent
volumes include *Knock Upon Silence* (1965),
Midnight Was My Cry (1971), *Mermaids in
the Basement: Poems for Women* (1984) and
The Nearness of You: Poems for Men (1986).
She won the Pulitzer Prize for Poetry in 1985
for *Yin* (1984). Her translations from several
languages, including Urdu and Chinese, are
gathered in *Carrying Over* (1988).

KLABUND, pseud (meaning
'transformation') of **Alfred Henschke**
(1890–1928)
German poet, dramatist and novelist, born
in Crossen on the Oder. He died young of
tuberculosis, which had made him into an
invalid for much of his life. His work was
widely read in the years before his death,
which was lamented by his friend **Gottfried
Benn**. His plays were clever, his short novels
readable; his poetry, which was wide in its

range, went deeper, especially his sensual
poems and his adaptations from the Chinese.
Two of his historical novels were translated,
Pjotr (1923, Eng trans *Peter the Czar*, 1925),
and *Borgia* (1928, Eng trans 1929); but the
finest, the posthumous *Rasputin* (1929), was
not.
▷C Middleton and M Hamburger (eds),
Modern German Poetry 1910–1969 (1962)

KLEIN, A(braham) M(oses)
(1909–72)
Canadian editor, critic, essayist, translator of
Hebrew and Yiddish writers, and
accomplished author of prose and poetry,
born in the Ukraine. He lived in Montreal
from early infancy, graduating from McGill
in 1930 and the Université de Montreal law
school in 1933. He was a committed Zionist,
of which the poetry of *The Second Scroll*
(1951) is an important expression. He has
been described as 'the first contributor of
authentic Jewish poetry to the English language', and was an important influence on the
younger generation of Jewish writers based in
Montreal including **Irving Layton** and **Leonard Cohen**. *The Rocking Chair* (1948) won a
Governor General's Award, and includes the
much anthologized poem, 'Portrait of the
Poet as Landscape'.

KLEIST, Ewald
(1715–59)
German poet, born in Zeblin, near Köslin, in
Pomerania. A nobleman by birth, he studied
at Königsberg University, then joined the
Danish army in 1736. He left in 1740 and was
commissioned in the Prussian army later that
year. His poetry of the early 1740s is melancholic, reflecting his dislike of military life.
In 1749 he published, to widespread acclaim,
Der Frühling ('Spring'). A major by the beginning of the Seven Years War, he turned to
patriotic verse during that campaign. One of
his last works was the epic *Cissides und Paches*
(1759), set in ancient Greece after the death
of Alexander the Great. He died of wounds
received during the battle of Kunersdorf.

KLEIST, Heinrich von
(1777–1811)
German dramatist and poet, born in Frankfurt an der Oder. His family had a long military tradition, but he left the army in 1799 to
study, and soon devoted himself to literature.
His work is marked by a sometimes anguished struggle to come to terms with his
doubts over man's ability to shape his own
fate and destiny amid the political and personal upheavals of the age. His best plays
are still popular, notably *Prinz Friedrich von
Homburg* (1811, Eng trans *The Prince of*

Homburg, 1959), and his finest tale is *Michael Kohlhaas* (1808–10). He committed suicide.
▷W Silz, *Heinrich von Kleist* (1961)

KLINGER, Friedrich Maximilian von
(1752–1831)
German playwright and novelist, born in Frankfurt-am-Main. He was an officer in the Russian army from 1780 to 1811, and curator of Dorpat University from 1803 to 1817. The 'Sturm und Drang' school was named after one of his tragedies, *Der Wirrwarr* ('Confusion'), published as *Sturm und Drang* (1776, literally 'Storm and Stress': the phrase was adopted as the label for a major school of 19th-century German writing). He wrote several other plays and some novels.
▷M Rieger, *Friedrich Maximilian Klinger* (3 vols, 1880–96)

KLITGAARD, Mogens
(1906–45)
Danish novelist, born into a lower middle-class family. One of the most innovative of the Danish social realists of the 1930s, he came to notice with his first novel *Der sidder en Mand i en Sporvogn* (1937, 'A Man Sits in a Tramcar'). It is an atmospheric, unromantic fiction about the social and psychological downfall of a Copenhagen shopkeeper, Lundegaard, whose business goes bust in the recession years. This and subsequent works such as the everyday novel *Elly Petersen* (1941) and the montage fiction *Den guddommelige Hverdag* (1942, 'The Divine Ordinary Day'), in which Klitgaard makes clever use of documentary clips from the media, reveal the author's main preoccupations: the big city and the little man or woman in crisis. Like his German contemporary **Hans Fallada**, Klitgaard focuses on the poorly paid white-collar worker, whose dangerous attraction to the authoritarian ideologies he highlights, occasionally counterpointing a utopian hint of social insight and group solidarity.
▷J Levy, 'Mogens Klitgaard', in *Dansk digtere i det 20. århundrede*, vol 2 (1981)

KLOOS, Willem
(1859–1938)
Dutch poet, translator (**Euripides**) and critic, the central figure—with his friend **Verwey**—in the 'Movement of the Eighties'. Fired by his understanding of **Keats** and **Shelley**, he successfully challenged the didactic course of Dutch poetry. He is most famous for his early sonnets, *Het Boek van Kind en God* (1888, 'The Book of the Child and God'); but in his later life he could not maintain his inspiration, and his verse became more academic and self-consciously beautiful. As a critic he

set enduring standards for the poetry of his country.
▷K H de Raaf, *Willem Kloos, de mensch, de dichter, de criticus* (1934)

KLOPSTOCK, Friedrich Gottlieb
(1724–1803)
German poet, born in Quedlinburg. Inspired by **Virgil** and **Milton**, he began *Der Messias* ('The Messiah') as a student at Jena (1745), continued it at Leipzig (1748), and completed it in 1773. He settled in Hamburg in 1771 with a sinecure appointment, and pensions from Frederik V of Denmark (from 1751) and the Margrave of Baden. Regarded in his day as a great religious poet, he helped inaugurate the golden age of German literature. He wrote a number of plays, works on language, and a series of lyrical and highly accomplished odes.
▷G Kaiser, *Klopstock* (1962)

KLYUYEV, Nikolay
(1887–1937)
Russian poet from a family of educated peasants in the Olonets province who, although he sang praises of the Revolution (because he believed that it represented the fulfilment of God's mission to Russia), was murdered by it when they sent him to Siberia as a kulak (wealthy peasant). He was an 'Old Believer', a member of the 'Khlysty' ('God's People') sect, and he had a great influence not only upon the more sophisticated, but also more susceptible, **Blok**, but also on **Yesenin**. When he first went to Moscow he surprised everyone with his peasant dress and dedicated religiosity, taken as shameless hypocrisy by some, but as prophetic certainty by others. His early poetry, intensely folkloristic, filled with local colour, and pious, was very popular. He wandered around Russia, became disillusioned about the role of the Revolution, and was eventually arrested; **Gorky** interceded for him, but this gave him only a temporary reprieve. For long he was persona non grata in Soviet Russia, but now his important poetry is being reassessed. One of his most famous poems is his lament for Esenin's suicide, which is translated in *Poems* (1977), which has a useful and informative introduction.
▷L Trotsky, *Literature and Revolution* (1923); V Zavalashin, *Early Soviet Writers* (1958)

KNEALE, Nigel
(1922–)
Manx writer and dramatist, born on the Isle of Man. After working in a lawyer's office, he first gained attention with a collection of short stories, *Tomato Cain* (1949), which won

the **Somerset Maugham** Award. After a spell at RADA he joined the drama department of the BBC in a general capacity and progressed to writing the serial *The Quatermass Experiment* (1953): an imaginative science-fiction drama, reflecting the paranoia of the day, its immense popularity led to *Quatermass II* (1955), *Quatermass and the Pit* (1959), *Quatermass* (1978) and three feature films. His early television adaptations also include *Curtain Down* (1952), *Wuthering Heights* (1953) and *1984* (1954). His film scripts include *The Abominable Snowman* (1957), *First Men in the Moon* (1964), *The Witches* (1966) and *Halloween III* (1983). His television plays include *The Year of the Sex Olympics* (1968), *Bam! Pow! Zap!* (1969), *Beasts* (1975) and *Kinvig* (1981).

KNIGHT, Damon Francis
(1922–)

American science-fiction writer, born in Oregon. He was a member of the New York fan group The Futurians, and wrote a history of their activities. He published his first story in 1941, but made his initial impact in the genre as a critic and reviewer. His own best fiction has been in the form of short stories, notably those which he wrote in the 1950s. His stories are collected in several volumes, including *Far Out* (1961), *Off Centre* (1965) and *Turning On* (1966). His novels have rarely achieved the same standard, but the best of them include *The People Maker* (1959) and *Why Do Birds* (1992). He was a significant editor of anthologies, notably the long-running *Orbit* series, and did much to create the institutional base of contemporary science fiction.

KNOWLES, James Sheridan
(1784–1862)

Irish dramatist, born in Cork, the son of a schoolmaster and a cousin of **Richard Brinsley Sheridan**. After serving in the militia he studied medicine at Aberdeen, but took to the stage. He did not achieve distinction and subsequently opened a school in Belfast and (1816–28) in Glasgow. His tragedy, *Caius Gracchus* (1815), was first performed in Belfast. *Virginius*, his most effective play, had been a success in Glasgow before William Macready produced it at Covent Garden in 1820. As well as *William Tell* (1825), his most successful plays were *The Hunchback* (1832), *The Wife* (1833) and *The Love Chase* (1837). He appeared with fair success in many of his own pieces. About 1844 he became a Baptist preacher, drew large audiences to Exeter Hall, and published two anti-Roman Catholic works.
▷L H Meeks, *Sheridan Knowles and the theatre of his time* (1933)

KNOWLES, John
(1926–)

American novelist, born in Fairmont, West Virginia and educated at Yale University. He has been a reporter, an assistant editor of a magazine, and a writer-in-residence. In 1961 he won three special awards, including a **Rosenthal** Foundation Award and a **Faulkner** Foundation Award. His first novel, *A Separate Peace* (1959), remains his most famous; it tells the story of two boys at a boarding school in New England during World War II and their intense and ambivalent relationship. He is the author of eight other novels, including a sequel to his first entitled *Peace Breaks Out* (1981), which does not, however, live up to its predecessor.

KNOX, Edmund George Valpy, pseud Evoe
(1881–1971)

English humorous writer and parodist, brother of **Ronald Arbuthnott Knox**. He joined the staff of *Punch* in 1921 and became editor from 1932 to 1949, contributing articles under his pen-name. His best work was republished in book form and includes *Fiction as She is Wrote* (1923), *Quaint Specimens* (1925), *Folly Calling* (1932), and others.

KNOX, Ronald Arbuthnott
(1888–1957)

English theologian, writer and detective novelist, born in Birmingham, the son of an Anglican bishop and brother of **Edmund George Knox**. Educated at Eton and Balliol College, Oxford, he became a fellow and lecturer at Trinity College, Oxford, in 1910, but resigned in 1917 on his reception into the Church of Rome. He was Catholic chaplain at Oxford from 1926 to 1939. Author of numerous works of apologetics, his modern translation of the Bible, widely used by Roman Catholics, is specially noteworthy. His essays are distinguished by their satirical wit and trenchant criticism of some contemporary modes and manners. He published his autobiographical *A Spiritual Aeneid* in 1918. He also wrote several detective novels, such as *Still Dead* (1934).

KNUDSEN, Erik
(1922–)

Danish poet, born in Slagese, Zealand, who has taken a socialist and anti-American line which has much in common with such German writers as **Hans Magnus Enzensberger**. His poetry, beginning by expressing some interest in religion, has gradually eschewed this, in favour of an aggressive atheism and a belief in love as the only redeeming quality in an otherwise doomed world. His mature style is reflected in his collection *Forsog på at gå* (1978, 'Attempts to Walk').

KNUDSEN, Jacob
(1858–1917)

Danish novelist, born in Redding, a South Jutland village. He studied theology, and became a schoolteacher, then a minister, and finally a lecturer. *Den gamle Praest* (1899, 'The Old Pastor') has the unusual theme of a pastor's exhortation to a parishioner to seek redemption from an act of murder, not through giving himself up to the law, but through killing himself. *Gjaering-Afklaring* (1902, 'Fermentation-Clarification') is largely autobiographical. Knudsen has been found to be an unattractive novelist, cold and repellent, but he is one of great interest because of the nature of his subjectivity.

▷C Roos, *Jacob Knudsen* (1954, in Danish)

KOBAYASHI Takiji
(1903–33)

Japanese novelist and political activist. Born on the northern island of Hokkaido, he went to Tokyo having become a convinced Marxist. He wrote two political novels: *Toseikatsusha* (1934, 'Party Worker') and *Kani Kosen* (1929, Eng trans *The Factory Ship and the Absentee Landlord*, 1933), which depicts the grim struggle for better conditions of a group of canning factory workers. At the height of the fascist regime's power, Kobayashi was arrested by the Kempeito (secret police) in Tokyo for subversive political activities and murdered by them.

KOBER, Arthur
(1900–74)

Polish-born American dramatist, writer of newspaper sketches and screenwriter, who was brought to New York from Poland as a child of four. Many of his dialect stories set in the Bronx were published by the *New Yorker*. His best-known play is *Having Wonderful Time* (1937, a comedy about people trying to improve themselves; it became the musical *Wish You Were Here*, 1952). He was for a time married to **Lillian Hellman**.

KOCH, C(hristopher) J(ohn)
(1932–)

Australian novelist, born in Hobart, Tasmania, which features in his first novel *Boys in the Island* (1958, rev edn 1974), concerned with growing up—sooner than one wants. Making much use of symbolism and imagery, it was followed by *Across the Sea Wall* (1965, rev edn 1982) which moves between India and Australia and, again, describes the betrayal of innocence. Koch's exotic thriller *The Year of Living Dangerously* (1978) is set in a tense Indonesia just before the downfall of Sukarno in the 1960s. It became immensely popular through Peter Weir's adventure film in which symbol, in the shape of Javanese 'Wayang' puppets, once more punctuates the action. *Crossing the Gap: a Novelist's Essays* (1993) explores his experiences of Australia's Empire past and Asian future.

KOCH, Kenneth Jay
(1925–)

American poet and playwright. Though identified with the 'New York School', along with **Frank O'Hara** and **John Ashbery**, he was raised in Cincinnati and educated at Harvard. He taught at Rutgers University, New Jersey in the mid-1950s, and in 1962 joined the faculty at Columbia University. His long poem *The Burning Mystery of Anna in 1951* (1979) offers a picture of life in New York during that time. His first major work, however, was the surreal epic *Ko, or A Season on Earth* (1959), written in the same poetic form as **Byron**'s *Don Juan* and embodying the New York School's slightly cavalier approach to semantics. In 1973 he won the Frank O'Hara Prize, awarded in memory of his friend. Later collections include *The Art of Love* (1975) and *Days and Nights* (1982). *A Selected Poems* appeared in 1985. Koch has also written a considerable number of lyric plays, including *George Washington Crossing the Delaware* (1962) and *The Tinguely Machine Mystery, or The Love Suicides at Kaluka* (1965), both of which reflect some of the fine-art concerns of the New York poets. Koch has long been interested in teaching poetry to the young and to the terminally ill; he discusses the former in *Rose, Where Did You Get That Red?* (1973) and the latter in *I Never Told Anybody* (1977).
▷*John Ashbery and Kenneth Koch: A Conversation* (1965)

KOCH, Martin
(1882–1940)

Swedish novelist, born in Stockholm. Regarded as a seminal figure among the many working-class writers of the first half of the century, he was above all a moralist. In *Arbetare* (1912, 'Workers') he contrasts what he sees as the two extremes of working-class existence: the criminality of the lumpenproletariat and the morality of the organized socialist whose duty it is to lead the former out of its darkness. His finest work—for which he has been compared to **Dostoyevsky**—was *Guds vackra värld* (1916, 'God's Beautiful World'), in which he ultimately posits a vaguely Christian religiosity as an antidote to the condition of modern industrial man.

▷G D Hansson et al, *Martin Koch—tre studier* (1988)

KOCHANOWSKI, Jan
(1530–85)

Polish poet—the greatest Slavic writer of his time. Born in Sycyna, he served as a courtier, but withdrew from court life in 1570 and settled down to a farming life in Czarnolas. His earlier work had been done in both Latin and Polish, but his most important was the wholly Polish work that he did in his retired life. His famous and much valued *Piésni* (1586, Eng trans *Chants*, 1932), are the most Horatian of any truly original European writer's. His *Fraszki* (1584, 'Trifles'), brilliant epigrams, were unlike anything written in his language up to that date. The first tragedy in Polish, *Odpawa posłow greckich*, (1578, Eng trans *The Dismissal of the Greek Envoys*, 1918), was modelled on **Seneca**, and surpassed him, although it has been called 'static'. It has been said that his influence proved as vital to Polish poetry as that of **Spenser** and **Shakespeare** to English. A selection is translated (badly) in *Poems* (1908).

▷J Langlade, *Kochanowski: L'Homme, le penseur, le poète lyrique* (1932)

KOCK, Charles Paul de
(1794–1871)

French novelist, born in Passy. He produced an enormously long series of novels about Parisian life, vivacious, piquant and very readable. They were highly popular at the time, and were widely read in England. *Georgette* (1820, Eng trans 1843), *Mon voisin Raymond* (1822, Eng trans *My Neighbour Raymond*, 1903) and *L'amant de la lune* (1847, 'The Lover of the Moon') were among the most popular.

▷T Trimm, *Paul de Kock* (1877)

KOESTLER, Arthur
(1905–83)

Hungarian-born British author and journalist, political refugee and prisoner, born in Budapest. He studied pure science at Vienna and, embracing the cause of Zionism as described in *Promise and Fulfilment* (1949), worked on a collective farm in Palestine (1926). However, his idealism gradually modified by his experiences, he became a political correspondent and later scientific editor for a German newspaper group. Dismissed as a communist, he travelled in Russia (1932–3), but became disillusioned, breaking with the party finally in 1938, as described in *The God that Failed* (1950). He reported the Spanish Civil War (1936–7) for the London *News*

Chronicle, was imprisoned under sentence of death by Franco, as retold in *Spanish Testament* (1938) and *Dialogue with Death* (1942), and again by the French (1940). He escaped from German-occupied France via the French Foreign Legion, and, after a short imprisonment in London, joined the Pioneer Corps. These experiences, described in *Scum of the Earth* (1941), provided the background of his first novel in English, *Arrival and Departure* (1943). The degeneration of revolutionary idealism in Roman times under Spartacus he portrayed in *The Gladiators* (1939), which was followed in 1940 by the striking modern equivalent, *Darkness at Noon*, Koestler's masterpiece and one of the great political novels of the century. Intelligent humanism and anti-communism provide the themes for such essays as *The Yogi and the Commissar* (1945), *The Trail of the Dinosaur* (1955), *Reflections on Hanging* (1956) and *The Sleepwalkers* (1959), on the theories, lives and struggles with religious orthodoxy of Copernicus, Kepler and Galileo. *The Act of Creation* (1964), *The Ghost in the Machine* (1967) and *The Case of the Midwife Toad* (1971) were among his later works; *Bricks to Babel* (1980) is a selection from his non-fiction writings. He and his wife committed suicide together when he became terminally ill.

▷I Hamilton, *Koestler: a biography* (1982)

KOLCSEY, Ferenc
(1790–1838)

Hungarian poet, critic and orator, born in Szödemeter. He is best known as author of the Hungarian national anthem, *Himnusz* (1823, Eng trans *Hymn*, 1947), but this was not his best or most vital work. He introduced the critical essay, as a form, into his language, and he made pioneer use of ballads and folklore in his poetry. He was second only to **Ferenc Kazinczy** in reforming the Hungarian language so that it could accommodate a new type of literature. For all his efforts for his country, his own more personal poetry is extremely pessimistic.

KOLIQUI, Ernest
(1903–75)

Albanian poet and storyteller. His stories of the northern highlands of Albania, never translated, have not bettered stylistically in traditional literature; but he became embroiled with fascism and, after the war, fled to Rome.

KOLLÁR, Jan
(1793–1852)

Czech poet and Slavonic scholar, a Hungarian Slovak. He was Protestant pastor at

Pest (1813–49), and then Professor of Archaeology at Vienna. He was a proponent of a cultural Pan–Slavic union. He wrote a cycle of sonnets, which eventually rose to over 600 in number, and compiled an edition of Slovakian folk-songs.

▷A Mráz, *Jan Kollár Literarna študia* (1952)

KOLLONTAI, Alexandra Mikhaylovna
(1872–1952)

Russian feminist and revolutionary, the world's first female ambassador. Born in St Petersburg into an upper-class family, she rejected her privileged upbringing and became interested in socialism. Married to an army officer, she nevertheless joined the Russian Social Democratic Party, and for her revolutionary behaviour was exiled to Germany in 1908. In 1915 she travelled widely in the USA, begging the nation not to join World War I, and urging the acceptance of socialism. In 1917, following the Revolution, she returned to Russia, becoming commissar for public welfare. In this post she agitated for domestic and social reforms, including collective childcare and easier divorce proceedings. Although her private liaisons shocked the party, she was appointed minister to Norway (1923–5, 1927–30), Mexico (1926–7) and Sweden (1930–45), becoming ambassador in 1943. She played a vital part in negotiating the termination of the Soviet-Finnish war (1944). Her works, such as *The New Morality and the Working Class* (1918), and her collection of short stories, *Love of Worker Bees* (1923), aroused considerable controversy because of their open discussion of subjects like sexuality and women's place in society and the economy. Her autobiography, written in 1926, was not published in Russia.

KOLMAR, Gertrud
(1894–?1943)

German–Jewish poet, born in Berlin. A shy and modest loner, she was known among her contemporaries for her immense kindness. Working as a language teacher and interpreter, she was fluent in English, French, Russian and Hebrew. Later, she dedicated herself to the education of deaf-and-mute children. From 1928 she gradually withdrew from a public life, becoming a nurse to her ailing elderly parents. When most of her relatives left Germany in 1933, Kolmar stayed with her father. She is believed to have been murdered in Auschwitz; the exact date is unknown. Her poetry is of a highly individualistic kind and difficult to categorize. Using enchanting, often haunting, imagery, her work is infused with visionary melancholy, demanding protection for the vulnerable and innocent. In *Gedichte* (1917,

'Poems') she celebrates the vision of a simple female existence, while in *Preußische Wappen* (1934, 'Prussian Heraldry') she shows her fascination with historical figures.

▷K Krolow, 'Das lyrische Werk Gertrud Kolmars', in *Akzente 3* (1956)

KOLTSOV, Alexey
(1809–42)

Russian minor poet, self-taught, born in Voronezh. His imitations of folk-songs caused him to be compared to **Burns**, but **Tolstoy** believed that his genius was spoiled by getting into city company.

KØLTZOW, Liv
(1945–)

Norwegian novelist, born in Oslo, who studied at the University there. Her first novel, *Hvem bestemmer over Bjørg og Unni?* (1972, 'Who Decides What Happens to Bjørg and Unni?'), became an important text for 'second-wave' feminism, exploring as it does the social and political manipulation of women and the potential for achieving change. Her subsequent works are more markedly modernist, with fragmented narratives focusing uncertainties as to language and reality. *Historien om Eli* (1975, 'The Story of Eli') is a female *Entwicklungsroman*, the central character's shadowy identity strikingly conveyed by the language, while *Hvem har dit ansikt?* (1988, 'Who Has Your Face?') employs narrative experimentation, including the conflation of the narrator and the central character, to suggest the complexities of identity.

▷J Garton, 'The Personal is Political', in *Norwegian Women's Writing 1850–1990* (1993)

KONINGII, Abraham de
(1587–1619)

Dutch poet and dramatist, born in Belle in Flanders. He is often regarded as the most important precursor of **Vondel**. He was brought up in the *rederijker* (from the French *rhétoriqueur*) tradition, a name given to 'amateur poets' to read aloud in the Chambers of Rhetoric, but was not afraid to break out of it when he felt it would be effective.

KONOPNICKA, Maria
(1842–1910)

Polish story writer and poet, born in Suwalki. She was chiefly known as a poet, but, with a few notable exceptions, her poetry has not lasted, as it is spoiled by her excessive emotionalism and rather specious-sounding patriotism (for all that this was entirely sincere). The best of her poetry is translated in *Five Centuries of Polish Poetry* (1960). The greatest of her books was written for children: *O krasnoludkach i o sierotce Marysi* (1896, Eng trans *The Brownie Scouts*, 1947), a classic fairy-tale about a little girl and some dwarfs. But the best of her stories are of quite a different order: lacking her usual earnestness, they give incomparable shrewd and warm-hearted appraisals of women from the lower classes. They are still being published, and still being widely read. One, 'Still Life', appears in English translation in *Introduction to Modern Polish Literature* (1964, H Gillon and L Krzyzanowski eds).

▷M Kridl, *Survey of Polish Literature* (1911)

KONRAD VON WÜRZBURG
(1220–87)

German Middle High and epic burgher poet, born in Würzburg. He was supported by patrons of Basle, where he settled, and died. A well educated man, from a non-aristocratic family, he wrote all kinds of poems, from lyric to epic. A follower of **Gottfried von Strassburg**, author of *Tristan*, he also wrote shorter works, such as *Der Schwanritter*, a version of the Lohengrin legend. Highly influential, he is now better remembered for his versatility and mastery than for his originality.

▷A Moret, *Un Artist méconnu* (1932)

KONSTANTINOV, Aleko
(1863–97)

Bulgarian story writer and satirist who called himself 'the lucky one'—until his sharp and irreverent pen got him murdered. He was a senior lawyer until his innate integrity forced him into satirical humour instead. An inveterate traveller with a keen sense of the division in his country between East and West, he invented the most famous of all Bulgarian characters, Bay Ganyu (*Bay Ganyu*, 1895), a 'partisan thug' who travels about at home and abroad selling various articles. The name of Bay Ganyu is a by-word in Bulgaria, and Konstantinov himself the finest ironist his country ever produced.

▷C Manning and R Smal-Stocki, *The History of Modern Bulgarian Literature* (1960)

KONSTANTINOVÍC, Radomir
(1928–)

Serbian novelist and editor of literary journals, born in Subotica. He has modelled himself mainly upon **Beckett**—and is often compared to his compatriot and contemporary **Bulatovic**. *Exitus* (1960, Eng trans 1965) excited some interest outside Yugoslavia, but he has also been called pretentious and impenetrable.

▷ *Slavonic and East European Review*, XI, 94 (1961)

KONWICKI, Tadeusz
(1926–)

Lithuanian-born dissident writer and filmmaker. After fighting with guerrilla forces in Lithuania against both German and Russian occupation in World War II he moved to Poland, where he has made his home. His book *Mala apokalipsa* (1979, Eng trans *A Minor Apocalypse*, 1983) was banned. In the 1950s, *Przy budowie* (1950, 'At the Construction Site') was a much prized novel about the party as an engineer of souls. He was denounced in 1968. His latest book, *Wschody i zachody kziezyca* (1982, Eng trans *Moonrise, Moonset*, 1988), is about the early struggles of the Solidarity movement. His films include *Salto* (1965) and *Ostatni dzień lata* (1958, 'The Last Day of the Summer').

▷J Wegner, *Konwicki* (1973)

KOONTZ, Dean R(ay)
(1945–)

American author of bestselling formula fiction (horror, science fiction, detection), the secrets of which he attempted to pass on in *Writing Popular Fiction* (1973) and *How To Write Best-Selling Fiction* (1981). He was born in Everett, Pennyslvania, and published his first novel, *Star Quest* (1968), at the age of 23. Since then he has published in excess of 50 novels, using at least three pseudonyms, of which 'Brian Coffey' is the most widely recognized. *The Demon Seed* (1973) was a huge bestseller and it conveniently illustrates how Koontz has managed to manipulate genre and sub-generic styles in such a way as to attract the uncommitted without alienating hard-core readers. A decade later, in *Phantoms* (1983), he attempted a wholesale mythology on a scale not seen since **H P Lovecraft**.

KOPIT, Arthur L(ee)
(1937–)

American dramatist, born in New York City, and educated at Harvard, where he began writing and directing his own plays. His best-known earlier works are Absurdist, disturbing farces. *Oh Dad, Poor Dad, Mamma's Hung You in the Closet and I'm Feelin' So Sad* (1960), a dark parody of the Oedipus story, is sub-titled 'a pseudo-classical tragi-farce in a bastard French tradition'. Kopit satirizes socially ambitious middle-class America in *The Day the Whores Came Out to Play Tennis* (1965). The more serious *Indians* (1968) is set in the Wild West and attacks America's treatment of its Native American population, while *Wings* (1978) follows the fortunes of a stroke victim. The more recent *End of the World* (1984), in which a millionaire commissions a play about nuclear weapons, returns to the world of macabre comedy.

KOPS, Bernard
(1926–)

English dramatist, born in London, who worked variously as a docker, salesman, chef and waiter before devoting himself to writing full-time. As with playwrights such as **Arnold Wesker**, who also sought to portray real, Jewish working-class life on the stage, Kops deals with social and economic issues and makes a plea for tolerance, and for the accrual of intellectual rather than monetary riches. Several critics, however, have accused Kops of political naivety and sentimentality. *The Hamlet of Stepney Green* (1957) is a mordantly comic variation on the Hamlet story, in which the Hamlet-character, attempting to come to terms with the world around him, promises to carry the spirit of revolution forward. *Enter Solly Gold* (1962), in which a confidence-trickster poses as a rabbi, is a more ruthless comedy exposing social and moral hypocrisy. His more recent plays have been less successful and include *Simon at Midnight* (1985).

KORAÏS, Adamantios
(1748–1833)

Greek educator and man of letters, born in Smyrna. By profession a physician, Koraïs moved to Paris in the years of the Revolution and wrote his marvellous and indispensable account in *Koray's Letters Written from Paris 1788–1792* (Eng trans 1898). He edited classical Greek documents, and also wrote the famous *Atakta* (1828–35), the first proper lexicon in modern Greek.

KORINFSKY, Apollon
(1868–1937)

Russian minor poet and translator (of **Coleridge**'s *The Ancient Mariner*). His contemplative lyrics found great favour just before the advent of modernism, but then he fell out of vogue.

KORNBLUTH, C(yril) M
(1923–58)

American science-fiction writer, born in New York City. He is most famous for *The Space Merchants* (1953), a futuristic satire on consumer capitalism, one of four novels he wrote in collaboration with **Frederik Pohl**. *The Syndic* (1953), a solo production, is set in a utopian New York ruled by the Mafia. *Not This August* (1955) is a more conventional science-fiction work, envisaging an America in the grip of the Soviet Union. Kornbluth perhaps best suited to the short story; his most accomplished tales, such as 'The Little Black Bag', display a calm, almost quaint humanity which was a rarity in contemporary science fiction.

KÖRNER, Karl Theodor
(1791–1813)

German lyric poet, born in Dresden. He wrote plays and fiery patriotic songs such as *Leier und Schwert* (1814, 'Lyre and Sword'), which contained the *Schwert-Lied* ('Sword Song'), written shortly before his death in battle during the Napoleonic Wars, a patriotic end which served to inflate his literary reputation.
▷K Bergens, *Theodor Körner* (1912)

KORNILOV, Boris
(1907–39)

Russian poet, whose wild and alcoholic life ended when he was arrested by Stalin's secret police and murdered. He was briefly married to **Olga Berggolts**. High claims for his reflective poetry have been made by a few critics, and he was republished after the 1956 'Thaw'; but he has not yet attracted much critical attention.

KORNIYCHUK, Oleksandr
(1905–72)

Ukrainian dramatist, born in Khrystinovka. He was a socialist realist and a politician who held various high offices in Sovietized culture. He married the Polish author Wasilewska. His *Front* (1942, Eng trans *The Front*, in *Four Soviet Plays*, 1944), set on the Russo–German front, was the most sensational of his well-made, tendentious plays. For this he was hailed as a Soviet hero, and won the Stalin Prize. He wrote almost all his works in his native language, and they were translated into Russian for popular consumption. Another play available in English is *V stepyakh Ukrainy* (1942, Eng trans *Guerillas of the Ukrainian Steppes*, in *Four Soviet Plays*, 1944).

KOROLENKO, Vladimir
(1853–1921)

Russian novelist, born in Zhitomir. Returning from exile in Siberia (1879–85), he published his most famous story, *Son Makara* ('Makar's Dream'), and earned a reputation as a supporter of the underprivileged. He was involved in the Populist Movement, and opposed the Bolshevik Revolution in 1917. He is best known for his short stories, but left an important autobiography unfinished at his death.
▷M Comtet, *Vladimir Korolenko, 1853–1921: l'homme et l'oeuvre* (1975)

KOSINSKI, Jerzy Nikodem
(1933–91)

Polish-born American novelist, born in Łodz. Educated in political science at Łodz University, he taught there (1955–7) before emigrating to the USA in 1957. He wrote two

541

polemical books, *The Future is Ours, Comrade* (1960) and *No Third Path* (1926), under the pseudonym Joseph Novak. The trauma of war had rendered him (literally) speechless and his novels, particularly the quasi-autobiographical *The Painted Bird* (1965), set language at a considerable premium, espousing sexual experimentation and a radically existential morality as the basis of a brutal survivalism. Later works include *Steps* (1968), *Being There* (1971), *The Devil Tree* (1973), *Cockpit* (1975), *Blind Date* (1977), *Passion Play* (1979), *Pinball* (1982) and *The Hermit of 69th Street* (1988).

▷ P R Lilly Jr, *Words in Search of Victims* (1988)

KOTSYUBYNSKY, Mykhaylo
(1864–1913)

Ukrainian novelist and short-story writer, born in Vinnitsa. After a rebellious youth he became, with the greatest reluctance, a government official. The best-known of all his fiction is the novel *Tini zabutkh predkiv* (1911, Eng trans *Shadows of Forgotten Ancestors*, 1979), based on legends of the Hutsul region, and a masterpiece by any standards—as the late date of its translation (which has an important introduction) suggests. Most prefer *Fata Morgana* (1903–10), a more straightforward novel about a Ukrainian village in ferment. A highly intelligent man, and a great writer by international standards, Kotsyubynsky developed from a comparatively crude populist realist into an almost fully-fledged modernist, learning from **Hamsun** and **Strindberg**. *Chrysalis* (1958) selects from his stories.

▷ *Ukrainian Review*, VII

KOTZEBUE, August Friedrich Ferdinand von
(1761–1819)

German dramatist, born in Weimar. He filled various offices in the service of Russia, and was a facile writer of plays, tales, satires, historical works, etc; he was stabbed to death by a Jena student, because he had ridiculed the *Burschenschaft* movement. Besides quarreling with **Goethe**, Kotzebue satirized the leaders of the Romantic school. Among his 200 lively but superficial dramas are *Menschenhass und Reue* (1788, Eng trans *The Stranger*, 1798), *Die Hussiten vor Naumburg* (1801, Eng trans *The Patriot Father*, 1830) and *Die beiden Klingsberge* (1799, Eng trans *Father and Son*, 1814).

▷ H N Fairchild, *The Noble Savage* (1928)

KOTZWINKLE, William
(1938–)

American fantasy writer. He was born in Scranton, Pennsylvania, and educated in New Jersey and Pennsylvania. Early short stories were collected as *Elephant Bangs Train* (1971), but his first novel was *Hermes 3000* (1972). It was written in a rather formulaic science-fiction style which was formed into something far wittier and more penetrating in *Doctor Rat* (1976), his best book. *The Fan Man* (1974) was droll but lightweight and Kotzwinkle's fiction-writing began to take a back seat to screenwriting. He scripted the hugely successful *E.T.: The Extra-Terrestrial* for Steven Spielberg in 1982, and the following year 'novelized' *Superman III*. Like Spielberg, Kotzwinkle has an instinctive purchase on the dream-life of Americans.

KOVACIC, Ante
(1834–89)

Croatian novelist and radical polemicist who eventually, in part owing to his poverty, became insane. But he had been the best realistic novelist writing in his language. His finest novel, and one which ought to have been translated, was the semi-autobiographical *U registraturi* (1888, 'The Apprentice'), about a peasant boy who comes to town to serve a bad master. This combines his usual realism with elements of the picaresque and the grotesque.

KOVALEVSKAYA, Sofya Vasilyevna
(1850–91)

Russian mathematician and novelist, daughter of a Moscow artillery officer. Married to a brother of Alexander Kovalevsky, she made a distinguished name for herself throughout Europe as a mathematician. As a woman she found it impossible to obtain an academic post in Europe until finally she obtained a lectureship at Stockholm and then a professorship in 1889. She worked on Abelian integrals, partial differential equations and the form of Saturn's rings. She also made a name as a novelist, her works including *Vera Brantzova* (1895) and the novella *The Nihilist Girl* (1890), which reveal her lively gift as a storyteller. In 1878 she published her autobiography, *A Russian Childhood*.

▷ A Rakhmanova, *Sofya Kovalevskaya* (1953)

KOZLOV, Ivan Ivanovich
(1779–1840)

Russian poet, born in St Petersburg. He translated **Byron** and **Thomas Moore**. He turned to poetry at the age of 42, after going blind at the age of 30. His romantic poems include *Chernets* (1824) and *Knyaginya Natalya Dolgarukiya* (1828).

▷ G R V Barratt, *Ivan Kozlov* (1972)

KRAMER, Larry (Lawrence)
(1935–)

American novelist, playwright and author of film screenplays, born in Bridgeport, Connecticut. Kramer is a prominent spokesman for the American homosexual rights movement, although his novel *Faggots* (1978), an outspoken portrayal of promiscuous gay life in New York City, caused heated controversy both within and outside the movement. He is best known for his impassioned plays *The Normal Heart* (1985) and *The Destiny of Me* (1992), both of which address the issue of AIDS. The first piece, arguably a tract rather than a fully-fledged drama, has been produced in many countries and had an enormous impact, alerting many people to the seriousness of the disease and to how little progress had been made to combat it.

KRAMER, Theodor
(1897–1958)

Austrian minor poet who emigrated to England when the Nazis invaded his country. He wrote most of his best poetry while in his exile.

KRAMM, Joseph
(1908–)

American playwright and actor, born in South Philadelphia. He graduated from the University of Pennsylvania, and worked as a journalist for a time. He is chiefly remembered for his only successful play, *The Shrike* (1951), a drama about a man driven to attempt to commit suicide in order to be free of his insanely possessive wife. This won the Pulitzer Prize for Drama in 1952. His only other notable play is *Giants, Sons of Giants* (1962), in which the central character is another unhappy man.

KRANJCEVIĆ, Silvije Strahimir
(1865–1908)

Croatian poet, born in Senj. He reacted violently to Rome, where he was sent to study for the priesthood, and returned angrily to Zagreb; from 1893 until his death he taught, edited his periodical *Nada*, and changed the course of Croatian poetry by his example. There is controversy as to when he wrote his best poems: one school holds that this was before he was 35, but another finds his best in the late and deeply pessimistic collection *Pjesme* (1908, 'Poems').

KRASÍNSKI, Count Zygmunt
(1812–59)

Polish poet, dramatist and novelist, born in Paris. His father, General Wincenty, who married Ursula (née Princess Radziwill), fought in the Napoleonic Wars. The general educated his son well, and while he was studying law at Warsaw University he began to write fiction and verse. He was close to **Mickiewicz**, who deeply influenced him. The conflict in Krasínski stimulated by his father's eventual 'loyal' acceptance of Russian rule, and his own patriotic impulses forced him into writing works of a visionary nature—in them occurred the famous line, 'Murder will spread by electric current', incomprehensible to most of his contemporaries—which ultimately have less to do with Polish independence than with the nature of existence itself. This prominent tradition in Polish literature—that of a torn nation—was to culminate in the strange and rich works of **Micinsky**, **Witkiewisz** and, in an entirely different, less confused manner, in **Bruno Schulz**. In the play *Nieboska komedia* (1835, Eng trans *The Undivine Comedy*, 1924), really a gnostic vision, he resolved the conflict between his loyalty to his father's position and his belief in an independent Poland by envisaging a victory of the Polish people followed by their perishing in a grand realization that only Christ could save them. *Irydion* (1836, Eng trans *Iridion*, 1927), a more mature prose play, dealt, majestically, with the problem of how to avoid hatred in politics. After an unhappy affair he found a woman, Delphina Potocka, who understood him, and to her he dedicated *Przédświt* (1843, 'Pre-Dawn'), another visionary poem about the future of Poland or, perhaps, since he was so smothered by his father (who predeceased him by only one year, and who forced him to make an undesirable marriage to an heiress in 1843), of humanity itself. He remains one of the most puzzling and yet powerful—and hitherto hardly investigated—European writers of his age. The translations by Martha Walker Cook of 1875 should be ignored, since they are grossly inaccurate.

▷M M Gardner, *The Anonymous Poet of Poland: Zygmunt Krasinski* (1919); W Lenicki (ed), *Zygmunt Krasinski: Romantic Universalist* (1964)

KRASZEWSKI, Józef Ignacy
(1812–87)

Polish historical novelist and poet, born in Warsaw. He was one of the most prolific of all Polish authors, producing more than 300 works. His best-known novel is *Jermola: obrazki wiejskie* (1857, Eng trans *Jermola*, 1891), a tale of peasant life. In 1884 he was imprisoned at Magdeburg for treason.

KRAUS, Karl
(1874–1936)

Austrian critic and dramatist, and publisher and sole writer of the radical satirical magazine *Die Fackel* ('The Torch'), from 1899 to

1936. He was among the first to champion the work of the German playwright, **Frank Wedekind**. He himself wrote the apocalyptic and satirical plays, *Die letzten Tage der Menschheit* (1918, 'The Last Days of Mankind') and *Die Unüberwindlichen* (1928, 'The Unconquerable Ones'), both savage portraits of politics and social morality. He wrote several volumes of poetry, and a great deal of criticism.

▷F Filed, *The Last Days of Mankind, Karl Kraus and his Vienna* (1967)

KRETZER, Marx
(1854–1941)

German novelist, born in Posen (Poznań). Essentially a writer on social problems and working people, he has, on account of his naturalism, been called the German **Zola**. His books include *Die Betrogenen* (1882, 'The Duped', concerning poverty and prostitution), *Die Verkommenen* (1883, 'The Fallen'), *Meister Timpe* (1888) and *Das Gesicht Christi* (1897, 'The Face of Christ').

KREVE-MICKIEVICIUS, Vincas
(1882–1954)

Lithuanian poet, dramatist, playwright and essayist, who left Lithuania in 1944, after having been in hiding for four years (he had been Lithuanian Foreign Minister), and finally settled in America. He is usually known simply as 'Kreve'. He was an important figure in his country's literature, both for his stories (some are published in English translation as *The Herdsman and the Linden Tree*, 1964) and for his remarkable unfinished novel about the life of Christ, *Dangaus ir zemes sunus* (1907–63, 'Children of Heaven and Earth'). *Pagunda* (1950, Eng trans *The Temptation*, 1965) is about Stalinist duplicity and remains instructive. He wrote a few works in Russian and Polish.

▷ *Essay in English*, in *Studio baltici* (1952)

KREYMBORG, Alfred
(1883–1966)

American minor poet, editor and critic, born in New York. His first collection of poems, the imagistic *Mushrooms* (1916), attracted some attention by its attempt to achieve simplicity and directness, but he was soon eclipsed by such figures as **Pound** and **Stevens**. In his magazine *The Glebe* (1913–15) he published **Joyce** and **Aldington**. He later edited *Broom* (1921–4).

▷ *Troubadour* (1925)

KREZLA, Miroslav
(1893–1981)

Croatian dramatist, poet, novelist and, in his earlier days, attacker of the Catholic hierarchy, who dominated his literature. He served in the Austrian army, but then became a noted nationalist and communist (however, he did not join Tito in the war against Hitler); he attacked socialist realism as a mean and narrow creed. His greatest work is in drama, in particular his three-part play, in the **Ibsenite** tradition—it is untranslated—on the decline of a Croatian family, *The Glembays* (1930–2). His novel *Hravatski bog Mars* (1922, 'The Great God Mars') is a savage satire on the Austrian use of Croatian peasants as cannon fodder. *Povratak Filipa Latinovicza* (1930, Eng trans *The Return of Philip Latinovizc*, 1972) is about an artist trying to make sense of the chaos of World War II; *Na rubu pameti* (1938, Eng trans *On the Edge of Reason*, 1976) is a very powerful and ironic study of the disintegration of the life of a middle-aged lawyer owing to his sudden blurting out of the truth at a party. Krezla has been called, with justice, 'among the most neglected of the world's great writers'.

▷A Kadic, *Slavonic and East European Review*, 104 (1967)

KRIGE, Uys
(1910–87)

South African short-story writer, playwright, poet and journalist, born in the Cape Province and trained in law at Stellenbosch University. He lived in Spain between 1931 and the start of the Civil War. During World War II he was a war correspondent in Abyssinia and Egypt, and was then a POW in Italy (his escape is documented in *The Way Out: Italian Intermezzo*, 1946, rev edn 1955). His first book of Afrikaans stories, *Die Palmboom* ('The Palm Tree'), had appeared in 1940, but it was with his second, *The Dream and the Desert* (1953), that he became more widely known. The stories in it evoked a South African childhood with a dreamy irony that also emerges in his verse, for which he has stuck to Afrikaans. The most striking single collection is *Ballade van die Groot Begeer* (1960, 'Ballad of the Great Desiring'); a substantial collected poems appeared in 1985. Krige has also written a large number of original and adapted plays. Outstanding is *Die Twee Lampe* (1951, Eng trans *The Two Lamps*, 1964). A tale of generational conflict against a background of racialism and religious sectarianism (and in a swampy, treacherous setting), it struck a sizeable chord in the American South when it was translated.

▷C van Heymingen and J Berthoud, *Uys Krige* (1966)

KRISTENSEN, Tom
(1893–1974)

Danish novelist and poet, born in London to Danish parents and brought up in Copenhagen. He wrote under the shadow of World

War I and the ideological turmoil it caused. His debut collection of poetry, *Fribytterdrømme* (1920, 'Freebooter Dreams'), reveals an inclination for revolt, adventure and sensuality which is counterbalanced by the controlled form of the poems. This focus on anarchism, revolution and destruction was continued in the expressionist novel *Livets Arabesk* (1921, 'The Arabesque of Life'), but after a journey to China and Japan in 1922 Kristensen became increasingly critical of what he saw as his poetic and personal search for excitement. His self-scrutiny culminated in the semi-autobiographical novel *Hærværk* (1930, 'Vandalism'), which follows a downwardly mobile journalist and poet on a drinking odyssey through Copenhagen: the novel is a warning against soul-searching and ends on an open but sobering note. After *Hærværk*, Kristensen's poetic flow began to ebb, and he concentrated on a career as a newspaper critic and essayist.

▷J Andersen, *Dansende stjerne—en bog om Tom Kristensen* (1993)

KROENENBERGER, Louis
(1904–80)

American editor, novelist and critic, born in Ohio. He was for many years the drama critic of *Time*. His novels *The Grand Manner* (1929) and *The Grand Right and Left* (1952), owing a little to **Swinburne**'s *Lesbia Brandon*, satirize, respectively, politics and the wealthy; *A Month of Sundays* (1962) is set in a luxurious lunatic asylum. *No Whipping, No Gold Watches* (1970) is autobiographical.

KROETSCH, Robert
(1927–)

Canadian novelist and poet, born in Alberta. Kroetsch's work is set mainly in Alberta and the Northwestern territory. The early novel *But We Are Exiles* (1965) is about a crew struggling to steer their boat out of the Mackenzie river, and *The Words of My Roaring* (1966) takes a comic look at an Alberta election. *The Studhouse Man* (1969), which won a Governor General's Award, concerns the narrator's search for a mare across Alberta. *Alberta* (1968) is a work of non-fiction, published in the Travellers' Canada series. Kroetsch's poetry is best sampled in *The Stone Hammer Poems* (1973).

KROETZ, Franz Xaver
(1946–)

German playwright, born in Bavaria. He had little formal education and was unsuccessful in his ambition to become an actor. He joined the Communist Party in 1972, shortly after the production of his first play *Wildwechsel*.

The decision reflected his strong identification with the working class, but also, as in the touching *Stellerhof* (1972, Eng trans *Farmyard*, 1976) and its sequel *Geisterbahn* (1975, 'Horror Train'), with *lumpen* figures who fall outwith the scope of the competing political ideologies. This is also the subject of early pieces like *Heimarbeit* (1971, Eng trans *Homeworker*, 1974), which was the first of Kroetz's plays to be produced in the UK; *Wunschkonzert* (1973) made an impact at the 1974 Edinburgh Festival, translated as *Request Programme*. Kroetz left the Party in 1980; by that time he was, in the title of a surreal play from the following year, *Nicht Fisch nicht Fleisch* ('Neither Fish nor Flesh'), stranded between alienation and accommodation with the 'normalized' politics of the Cold War twilight. In 1982 he published a 'reader' of prose pieces and scripts which not so much clarified his position as confirmed his irresolution.

▷R W Blevins, *Franz Xaver Kroetz: The Emergence of a Political Playwright* (1983)

KROG, Helge
(1889–1962)

Norwegian left-wing dramatist, born in Christiania (now Oslo). He followed on from **Ibsen**, without adding anything important except for his absolute commitment to Marxism. Fulfilling a role not unlike that of **Shaw** in Britain, he wrote well-made, gripping plays, such as *Opbrudd* (1936, Eng trans *Break-up*, 1939), often demonstrating the superiority of women, in which he firmly believed.

KROLOW, Karl
(1915–)

German poet and translator (mainly of French and Spanish poetry), born in Hanover. In his first phase he wrote, essentially, in the tradition of **Oskar Loerke** and **Wilhelm Lehmann**; but at the same time he imported Surrealist techniques into German poetry. He had published a book during World War I, but became known just after it. In his second phase he inclined more towards an Absurdism influenced by **Hans Arp** and by modern linguistic theory; still later, he abandoned the surreal mode for a minimalist one. Many feel him to embody the mainstream of post-war German poetry. His works in English translation are *Leave Taking* (1968); *Poems Against Death* (1969).

KRÚDY, Gyula
(1878–1933)

Hungarian prose-poet, 'an isolated and enigmatic figure in modern Hungarian literature', who drank himself to an early death. He was prolific, writing 60 novels and over 3000 stories. He has become more famous since his death, but his Sinbad (*Szindbád*) novels were always popular. Sinbad is, to all intents and purposes, a portrait of himself. Krúdy has been compared to **Marcel Proust**. His best-known novel is *A vöros postakocsi* (1912, Eng trans *The Crimson Coach*, 1967), which also deals with Sinbad.

▷J Reményi, *Hungarian Writers and Literature* (1964)

KRYLOV, Ivan Andreevich
(1768–1844)

Russian writer of fables, born in Moscow. He started writing from the age of 20. Secretary to a prince, and then aimless traveller through Russia, he obtained a government post in 1806, and, settling down, wrote nine collections of fables which appeared between 1809 and 1843. He also translated **Jean de la Fontaine**'s *Fables*.

▷N Stepanov, *Ivan Andreevich Krylov* (1973)

KUDDOUS, Ehsan Abdel
(20th century)

Egyptian realistic novelist, who began as a journalist. He is best known for his novel about the Suez affair of 1956, *Don't Shut Off the Sun*. His work has not been translated into English.

KUHLMANN, Quirinus
(1651–89)

German poet and mystic (or 'religious fanatic'), born in Breslau. Married three times, he unsuccessfully attempted to convert the Sultan of Turkey; he was burned at the stake (but for political rather than religious reasons) after preaching his **Böhme**- and Quaker-influenced notion of the Kingdom of God upon Earth. He was an erotico-religious poet of immense gifts and technical ability: criticism, while admiring of his qualities, has not yet come to terms with the nature of his mysticism. He was regarded as egocentric, but, as one critic has written, 'actually he was completely selfless in his earnestness and impelled by a sense of mission so profound and enduring as to amount to obsession'. But even this unusually generous judgement fails to lay emphasis on his sense of humour, reflected in some of his bizarre and complex titles. There are a few translations of his work in *The German Lyric of the Baroque in English Translation* (1962).

▷W Dietze, *Quirinus Kuhlmann, Ketzer und Poet* (1963)

KULISH, Mykola
(1892–1937)

Ukrainian dramatist, born in Kherson. He was murdered by Stalin in a concentration camp on the grounds of his 'nationalism'. His masterpiece is *Narodny Malakhiy* (1929, 'The People's Malakhiy'). His *Patetchyna sonata* (1943, Eng trans *Sonata Pathétique*, 1975, performed in 1931), about the ill effects of the Revolution, probably spelled his doom—its success in Russian cities, including Moscow, led to its being banned. Kulish was first arrested in 1934, but managed to survive for three years.

KUMIN, Maxine
(1925–)

American poet, novelist, and writer for children, born in Philadelphia and educated at Radcliffe. Her first novel, *Through Dooms of Love* (1965), describing the clash between a radical, college-educated girl and her pawnbroker father, was directly autobiographical. As a poet Kumin has been tagged 'Roberta Frost', but she is more than the Earth Mother poet this nickname implies. Although her work is autobiographical it is not confessional in the manner of her friend and collaborator, **Anne Sexton**. Recently, as in *Nurture* (1989), which focuses on threatened species, her work has become more passionately environmental.

KUMINÍC, Evgenij
(1850–1904)

Croatian novelist, born in Berséc. His nationalistic novels, written under the influence of **Zola**, do not really transcend their message: that everything Hungarian in Croatian society was corrupt. But he was a vivid writer, particularly prized for his fictional account of his military life, *Pod puskom* (1889).

KUNDERA, Milan
(1929–)

Czechoslovakian-born French novelist, born in Brno, the son of a pianist. He was educated in Prague at Charles University and the Academy of Music and Dramatic Arts Film Faculty. He worked as a labourer and as a jazz musician before devoting himself to literature. For several years he was a professor at the Prague Institute for Advanced Cinematographic Studies. *Zert* (Eng trans, *The Joke*, 1969), his first novel, was published in 1967. After the Russian invasion in 1968 he lost his post and his books were proscribed. In 1975 he settled in France and took French citizenship. *Zert* and the stories in *Smēšné lásky* (1970, Eng trans *Laughable Loves*, 1974) are his only books to have been published in his homeland; the publication in 1979 of *Kniha smichu a zapomnēní* (Eng trans *The Book of Laughter and Forgetting*, 1980 (US); 1982 (UK)) prompted the revocation

of his Czech citizenship. Once described as 'a healthy sceptic whose novels are all anti-something', in exile he has emerged as one of the major world writers of the late 20th century. Other novels are *Zivot de jinde* (1973, Eng trans *Life is Elsewhere*, 1974), *Valčik na rozloučenou* (1976, Eng trans *The Farewell Party*, 1976 (US); 1977 (UK)), *Nesnesitelná lehkost byti* (1984, Eng trans *The Unbearable Lightness of Being*, 1984) and *Immortality* (1991). He also published a critical work, *Umění romanu* (1960, Eng trans *Art of the Novel*, 1988).
▷R Porter, *Kundera: a voice from Central Europe* (1981)

KUNERT, Günter
(1929–)

German poet, short-story writer and play-wright. Born in Berlin, he received his edu-cation in the East after the post-war division, but moved to West Germany in 1979, fol-lowing his expulsion from the Communist Party as a result of his 'negative stance' on the socialist utopia. His first collection *Weg-schilder und Mauerinschriften* (1950, 'Street-signs and Graffiti') was a bleak meditation on the late war and the present 'peace'. The tone darkened further with *Unter diesem Himmel* (1955, 'Under These Skies') and *Erinnerungen an einen Planeten* (1963, 'Memories of a Planet'), which communicated his growing sense of isolation. In 1975, when he was writer-in-residence at Warwick University, he published the prose *Der andere Planet. Ansichten von Amerika* (1974, 'The Other Planet: Views from America'), whose title echoes the **Stefan George** poem used in Schönberg's Second String Quartet: '*Ich fühle Luft von anderen Planeten*' ('I feel an air from other planets blowing'). Kunert was inhaling mysterious airs from the West and his final split with the GDR authorities swiftly followed. His career as a 'free' writer has been largely undistinguished.
▷M Krüger, *Kunert Lesen* (1979)

KUNITZ, Stanley Jasspon
(1905–)

American poet, born in Worcester, Mas-sachusetts and educated at Harvard Univer-sity. A literature academic, he taught poetry at the New School for Social Research in New York City (1950–7) and Columbia University (from 1963). His first collection of verse was *Intellectual Things* (1930). *Selected Poems 1928–1958* was awarded a Pulitzer Prize in 1959. Subsequent books include *The Testing-Tree* (1971), *The Terrible Threshold: Selected Poems 1940–1970* (1974) and *Next-to-Last Things* (1985). He has also published literary reference books.

▷G Orr, *Stanley Kunitz: an introduction to the poetry* (1985)

KUO Mo-jo
(1892–1972)

Chinese poet, academic and revolutionary, born into a bourgeois Szechuan family, he became the leading light of revolutionary literature. Kuo studied medicine in Japan, starting his writing career whilst there by translating foreign classics into Chinese from Japanese sources. He returned to China to fight in the Civil War of 1925, as a result of which his work was banned by the nationalist *Kuomintang*. His early work—*Nü-shen* (1921, Eng trans *The Goddesses*, 1958) was his first collection of verse—is liberal-democratic in tone, but it became increasingly didactic and polemical as he embraced communism. His play *Chu-Yuan* (1942) is a reworking of a traditional piece about a hero-poet, now with a pro-communist message grafted on to it. In 1949, immediately after the revolution, his status as grand old man of revolutionary literature was confirmed by his being appointed president of the First All China Congress of Writers and Artists.

KUPRIN, Alexander
(1870–1938)

Russian novelist. He gave up the army for literature. As a teller of short tales he ranks next to **Anton Chekhov**, although his work is uneven in quality. Those translated include *Poedinok* ('The Duel'), *Reka zhizni* ('The River of Life'), *Slavyanskaya dusha* ('A Slav Soul'), *Granatovyi braskyet* ('The Bracelet of Garnets') and *Sasha*. He left Russia and set-tled in France after the Revolution of 1917, but returned to his homeland in 1937.
▷N Loker, *Alexander Kuprin* (1978)

KUREISHI, Hanif
(1954–)

English novelist, playwright and author of film screenplays, born in Bromley, Kent, and educated at King's College, London. He attracted considerable attention with *Out-skirts* (1981), a play looking at the fate of two south-London white men who committed a savage racial attack. A recurring theme in Kureishi's work is that in the face of racial and cultural prejudice, much of which is deliberately maintained by a profiteering social class, it is almost impossible to sustain productive human relationships. In such film scripts as *My Beautiful Launderette* (1985) and more particularly *Sammy and Rosie Get Laid* (1987) and *London Kills Me* (1991) he vividly portrays British inner-city life as a cultural and moral wasteland. *The Buddha of*

Suburbia (1989) is a satirical novel about racial attitudes in south-east London.

KUSANO Shimpei
(1903–)

Japanese poet, arguably the greatest living, certainly one of the most accessible. He has achieved his enormous reputation within Japan by articulating a closeness to nature, which Japanese people like to think of as a national trait, and (a quality highly unusual in Japanese poetry) a sense of humour. This has also enabled him to acquire a reputation in the West, especially in the USA. There are English translations in *Frogs and Others*, translated by C Corman (1969).

KUSHNER, Tony
(1956–)

American playwright, born in New York City. He grew up in Lake Charles, Louisiana, and was educated at Columbia University and New York University. His plays are highly political in both content and intention, and are informed by an acute sense of historical awareness. *Yes, Yes, No, No* was produced in 1985, and was followed by several more before the appearance of his most important and controversial work to date, the two-part epic on the catastrophic effects of AIDS in New York, *Angels of America*, which won him the Pulitzer Prize for Drama in 1993. Its two parts, running to almost seven hours, are *Millenium Approaches* (1991) and *Perestroika* (1992).

KUTTNER, Henry
(1914–58)

American fantasy and science-fiction writer, born in Los Angeles. He began his writing career by contributing stories of occult fantasy to **H P Lovecraft**'s *Weird Tales* from 1936, and turned to science fiction in 1937. His stories were ingenious and often deftly humorous, a tendency which was enhanced by his marriage to the writer **C L Moore** in 1940. Much of their subsequent work was collaborative. He wrote, both by himself and with his wife, under various pseudonyms, the most important of which is 'Lewis Padgett'. He was a prolific writer, but a number of his/their stories are highly regarded. He was less successful in the novel format, but his best is *Fury* (1947). He enrolled with his wife in the University of California in 1950, after which they wrote a number of mystery stories, but very little science fiction.

KUZMIN, Mikhail
(1872–1936)

Major Russian poet, novelist, dramatist, composer and translator—still neglected (although not untranslated) outside his own country. He was born in Yaroslavl but grew up in St Petersburg. Kuzmin was an exceedingly complex, subtle-minded figure, who has not been understood by non-Russian critics. He was homosexual, and the Russians were then as intensely puritanical about homosexuality as any people in the world. Therefore, although, like so many Russians, he was essentially a mystic whose chief interests lay in Gnosticism and allied movements or schemes of thought, he was forced to pose as a decadent dandy, the **Oscar Wilde** of the North. He had another persona: as a follower of the 'Old Believers' sect—thus, he could own a waistcoat for every day of the year, and yet also act as a peasant. He was immensely erudite, and understood what he knew. After 1929 he was forbidden to publish, and only his death saved him from being murdered in the purges. He studied music under Rimsky-Korsakov, and wrote music for some of his own delicate plays. His fiction is lively and adept at dealing with homosexual (as well as heterosexual) relationships over the heads of Stalinist censors. *Krilya* (1906, Eng trans, with some poems and other prose, *Wings*, 1972) is a major novel on a homosexual theme, and caused a scandal when it appeared. His early poems consciously rejected Symbolism, and yet partook of it (thus the common association of him with the Symbolist movement is correct, yet also incorrect). He is seen at his greatest in his later poetry, which takes German Expressionism as a kind of springboard, but develops the expressionist procedures into something uniquely individual and moving. Central in Russian literature until 1929, then forgotten for too long, Kuzmin's work is now in the process of full reappraisal. There is an English translation of his work in *Selected Prose and Poetry* (1980).
▷ G Gibian and H W Tjalsma (eds), *Russian Modernism* (1976); *Slavonic Review* 34 (1975)

KYD, Thomas
(1558–94)

English dramatist, born in London. He was probably educated at Merchant Taylors' School, and was most likely brought up as a scrivener under his father. His tragedies early brought him a reputation, especially *The Spanish Tragedy* (c.1587). Kyd translated from the French (1594) a tedious tragedy on Pompey's daughter Cornelia, perhaps produced *Solyman and Perseda* (1592) and *Arden of Faversham*. He has been credited with a share in other plays, and probably wrote the lost original *Hamlet*. Between 1590 and 1593 he was in the service of an unknown lord. Imprisoned in 1593 on a charge of atheism (Unitarianism), which he tried to shift on to

Christopher Marlowe's shoulders, **Ben Jonson**'s 'sporting Kyd' died in poverty.
▷ A Freeman, *Kyd: facts and problems* (1967)

KYRKLUND, Paul Wilhelm ('Willy') (1921–)

Swedish novelist, story writer and dramatist, who was born and raised in Helsinki but later settled in Sweden. His *Twåsam* (1949, 'Twosome') showed that he was Sweden's most notable disciple of **Kafka**. A cool writer, he repels some by his creation of an ironic distance between his narrative and those he most pities.

L

LABÉ, or CHARLIEU, Louise
(c.1520–1566)

French poet, born in Parcieux, Ain. Educated in the Renaissance manner, she learned Latin and music, and was a skilled rider. In 1542 she fought, disguised as a knight, at the siege of Perpignan. In 1550 she married a wealthy rope manufacturer, Ennemond Perrin, at Lyons, and was then called 'la Belle Cordière' (the Lovely Ropemaker). In 1555 she published her *Oeuvres* ('Works'), which included 3 elegies and 23 sonnets in the **Petrarch**an manner. She also wrote a prose work, *Débat de Folie et d'Amour* (1555, 'Debate Between Folly and Love'), and was noted for her love affairs, which are reflected in her work.
▷F Zameron, *Louise Labé, sa vie et son oeuvre* (1945)

LABICHE, Eugène
(1815–88)

French playwright, born in Paris. He wrote one novel, *La Clef des Champs* (1838, 'Key of the Fields'), and was the author of over 150 skilfully observed and crafted comedies, farces and vaudevilles, which dominated the light theatre of his day in France. His *Frisette* (1846) was the original of **John Maddison Morton**'s *Cox and Box*, and his *Le Voyage de M. Perrichon* (1860) is a perennial favourite.
▷P Soupault, *Eugène Labiche, sa vie et son oeuvre* (1945)

LA BRUYÈRE, Jean de
(1645–96)

French writer, born in Paris. He was educated by the Oratorians, and was chosen to aid Jacques Bossuet in educating the Dauphin. For a time he was treasurer at Caen. He became tutor to the Duc de Bourbon, grandson of the great Condé, and received a pension from the Condés until his death. His *Caractères* (1688), which gained him a host of implacable enemies as well as an immense reputation, consists of two parts, the one a translation of Theophrastus, the other a collection of maxims, reflections and character portraits of men and women of the time. He found a powerful protector in the Duchesse de Bourbon, a daughter of Louis XIV. His *Dialogues sur le quiétisme* (1699, 'Dialogues on Quietism') were directed against **François Fénelon**. A writer rather than a thinker of any

real depth, his insight into character is shrewd rather than profound.
▷E Gosse, in *Three French Moralists* (1918)

LA CEPPÈDE, Jean de
(1550–1623)

French poet. Born in Marseilles or Aix, he grew up in Aix during a time of intense religious and political conflict, and began to write poetry at an early age. He studied law, becoming a *conseiller* in the Parlement of 1578 and rising to president of Aix's Chambre des Comptes in 1608. He benefited financially from his marriage to Madeleine de Brancas in 1585. A religious poet, he published his *Imitation des Psaumes de la Pénitence*, poems based on the psalms of David, together with *Douze Méditations* in 1594. However, he is best known for his *Théorèmes sur le sacré mystère de nostre redemption* ('Theorems on the Sacred Mystery of Our Redemption'), sonnets reputedly composed over a period of 30 years, and which were published in two volumes in 1613 and 1631 respectively. These poems draw on both Christian and secular sources in their treatment of religious conflict and the quest for harmony, in both the individual and society.

LA CHAUSSÉE, Pierre Claude Nivelle de
(1692–1754)

French playwright, born in Paris. He began writing plays after he was 40 and produced several of a sentimental nature which enjoyed great popularity. *La Comédie larmoyante* ('Tearful Comedy'), as his work was named by critics, had some influence on later writers, including **Voltaire**. Among his plays were *Le Préjugé à la mode* (1735, 'Fashionable Prejudice'), *Mélanide* (1741) and *L'École des mères* (1744, 'School for Mothers').
▷G Lanson, *Nivelle de la Chaussée et la comédie larmoyante* (1903)

LACLOS, Pierre Ambroise François Choderlos de
(1741–1803)

French novelist and politician, born in Amiens. Romantic and frustrated, he spent nearly all his life in the army but saw no active service until he was 60 and ended his career as a general. He is remembered by his one masterpiece, *Les Liaisons dangereuses* (1782,

Eng trans *Dangerous Connections*, 1784). This epistolary novel reveals the influence of **Rousseau** and **Samuel Richardson** and is a cynical, detached analysis of personal and sexual relationships, influenced by both Clauswitz and his own profound feminism. He also wrote *De l'éducation des femmes* (1785, 'On the Education of Women').

▷R Vaillant, *Laclos par lui-même* (1953)

LA COUR, Paul
(1902–56)

Danish poet, born in Zealand. His poetry is outside the mainstream, but nevertheless thoroughly modernistic in spirit. He was at first predominantly a nature poet, in the tradition established by **Jensen**; but later, in his most vital work, *Fragmenter af en Dagbog* (1943, 'Fragments of a Diary'), a kind of pantheist. The influence of this book on modern Danish poetry has been decisive.

▷P Schmidt, *Paul la Cour* (1971, in Danish)

LACRETELLE, Jacques de
(1888–1985)

French novelist, scion of a noble and literary family, born in its Burgundian château, who has failed to obtain his due outside France, despite his admission to the Académie Française in 1938. His friend **Marcel Proust** was the first decisive influence upon his versatile fiction, and his *La Vie inquiète de Jean Hermelin* (1920, 'The Restless Life of Jean Hermelin') was an immediate and deserved success. Then, with his oblique comment on the Dreyfus case, *Silbermann* (1922, Eng trans 1923), he started to write in the more 'classical' style of **André Gide**, who admired—and published—him. He followed the Silbermann theme in two more novels. *Le Bonifas* (1925, Eng trans *Marie Bonifas*, 1927), the moving tale of a rejected old maid, was in more realistic mode. *Les Haut Ponts* (1932–4, 'The Tall Bridges') was a short *roman-fleuve* about a family not unlike Lacretelle's own. His *Le Pour et le contre* (1946, 'For and Against'), an experiment in autobiography, was a failure on its publication, but will undoubtedly be reissued. *Les Vivants et leur ombre* (1977, 'The Living and Their Shadows') was a masterful and funny parody of the *nouveau roman* after its decline—it has often been taken as an actual attempt at a 'new novel', but Lacretelle's motives were clear. The work of this ceaselessly experimental and resourceful novelist is due for reappraisal.

▷D Alden, *Jacques de Lacretelle: An Intellectual Itinerary* (1958)

LA FARGE, Christopher
(1897–1956)

American novelist, born in New York, son of John La Farge, architect, and brother of the novelist **Oliver**. He wrote a novel in verse, *Each to the Other* (1939), and *The Sudden Guest* (1946), which is in prose, a selfish woman's account of the damage done by a hurricane of 1944, during which she behaved with a total lack of consideration for others—the woman, here, represents America and its foreign policy.

LA FARGE, Oliver
(1901–63)

American anthropologist and novelist, who is reckoned to have been a more powerful writer than his by no means incapable brother **Christopher La Farge**. The vivid *Laughing Boy* (1929), like *The Enemy Gods* (1937), is about Navajo Native American life. The former won the Pulitzer Prize. He wrote many studies of Native Americans. *Raw Material* (1945) is autobiographical.

▷D McNickle, *Indian Man* (1971)

LA FAYETTE, Marie Madeleine Pioche de Lavergne, Comtesse de
(1634–93)

French novelist and reformer of French romance-writing, born in Paris, daughter of the governor of Le Havre. She married the Comte de La Fayette in 1655, and in her 33rd year formed a liaison with **La Rochefoucauld** which lasted until his death in 1680. Down to her own death she still played a leading part at the French court, as was proved by her *Lettres inedites* (1880, 'Unabridged Letters'); prior to their publication it was believed that her last years were given to devotion. Her novels are *Zaïde* (1670, Eng trans *Zayde: A Spanish History*, 1678) and her masterpiece, *La Princesse de Clèves* (1678, Eng trans *The Princess of Cleves*, 1679), a study in conflict between love and marriage in the court-life of her day, which led to reaction against the long-winded romances of **Gautier Calprenède** and **Madeleine de Scudéry**.

▷M J Durry, *Madame de la Fayette* (1962)

LA FONTAINE, Jean de
(1621–95)

French poet, born in Château-Thierry in Champagne. He assisted his father, a superintendent of woods and forests. He soon devoted himself to the study of the old writers and to verse writing. In 1654 he published a verse translation of the *Eunuchus* of **Terence**, and then went to Paris, where **Friedrich Fouqué** became his patron. His *Contes et nouvelles en vers* ('Stories and Tales in Verse') appeared in four volumes, 1665–74 and in an augmented edition in 1686, his *Fables choisies mises en vers* (Eng trans *Fables*, 1804) in three volumes 1668–9, augmented 1693, and his *Amours de Psyché et de Cupidon* (Eng trans

The Loves of Cupid and Psyche, 1744) in 1669. For nearly 20 years he was maintained in the household of Mme de la Sablière. In 1684 he presented an admirable *Discours en vers* ('An Oration in Verse' on his reception by the Academy. La Fontaine was a brilliant writer and his verse, especially as found in the *Contes* and *Fables*, is lively and original.

▷ L Roche, *La vie de La Fontaine* (1913)

LAFORET DÍAZ, Carmen
(1921–)

Spanish novelist and short-story writer. Born in the Canary Islands, she studied at Barcelona University and then moved to Madrid. She achieved instant fame in 1945 with her first novel *Nada* ('Nothing'), which portrays economic and psychological depression in the wake of civil war and is based on her own arrival in Barcelona in 1939. *La isla y los demonios* (1952, 'The island and the devils'), set in the Canaries, conjures up an equally unsettling picture of family life gently simmering with neurosis and sexual frustration. In 1956 she published an ambitious but less well-received novel based on her conversion to Catholicism in 1951, *La mujer nueva* ('The new woman'). She went on to write *La insolación* (1963, 'Sunstroke'), tracing 20 years of Nationalist rule in Spain.

LAFORGUE, Jules
(1860–87)

French poet. Born in Montevideo, Uruguay, and educated largely in Paris, he was brilliantly precocious. Up to the time of his marriage, he worked as reader to the Empress Augusta of Germany. His compressed poetic career was undertaken with a level of seriousness and dedication which belies Laforgue's reputation as a dilettante or *flâneur*. In the verse published in his lifetime—*Les Complaintes* (1885), *L'Imitation de Notre-Dame la Lune* (1886) and *Le Concile féerique* (1886)—there are only hints of the qualities that would make him such an important influence on later French poets and on the younger **T S Eliot**. The verse is stylish and witty, superbly reworking popular materials, and the Pierrot poems created a new cultural role for the *commedia* figure, as passive, nihilistic and androgynous; the same anti-heroic temperament is evident in the rewritten folk materials that make up *Moralités légendaires* (1887). However, it was the mere dozen poems in Laforgue's posthumous *Les Derniers Vers* (1890) that had such an impact, validating free verse (Laforgue had translated **Whitman**) and suggesting that poetry could be as abstract or impressionist as music or painting. A *Poésies complètes* appeared in 1894, but it was not until Pascal Pia's two-volume edition of 1979 that an authoritative

text was available. His influence on French literature is almost equal to that of **Rimbaud**.

▷ M Collie, *Jules Laforgue* (1977)

LAGERKVIST, Pär Fabian
(1891–1974)

Swedish novelist, poet and playwright, winner of the 1951 Nobel Prize for literature. He studied at Uppsala and began his literary career first as a prose writer and then as an expressionist poet with *Ångest* (1916, 'Angst') and *Kaos* (1918, 'Chaos'), in which he emphasizes the catastrophe of war. Later, in the face of extremist creeds and slogans, he adopted a critical humanism with the (later dramatized) novel *Bödeln* (1933, 'The Hangman') and the novel *Dvärgen* (1944, 'The Dwarf'), which explored the problems of evil and human brutality. His novel *Barabbas* (1950) concerns the thief in whose place Christ was crucified. Man's search for God was also explored in the play *Mannen utan själ* (1936, 'The Man without a Soul'). An ideological play, *Lät människan leva* (1949, 'Let Man Live'), was a study of political terrorism in which Jesus Christ, Socrates, Bruno, Joan of Arc and an American negro appear as victims.

▷ L Sjöberg, *Pär Lagerkvist* (1976)

LAGERLÖF, Selma Ottiliaa Lovisa
(1858–1940)

Swedish novelist, the first woman winner of the Nobel Prize for literature (1909), and the first woman member of the Swedish Academy (1914). She taught at Landskrona (1885–95), and first sprang to fame with her novel *Gösta Berlings saga* (1891, 'The Story of Gösta Berling'), based on the traditions and legends of her native Värmland, as were many of her later books, such as her trilogy on the Löwensköld family (1925–8, Eng trans *The Rings of the Lowenskolds*, 1931). She also wrote the children's classic *Nils Holgerssons underbara resa genom Sverige* (1906–7, 'The Wonderful Adventures of Nils'). Although a member of the neo-romantic generation of the 1890s, her work is characterized by a social and moral seriousness, as in *Antikrists Mirakler* (1897, 'The Miracles of Anti-Christ') and *Bannlyst* (1918, 'The Outcast').

▷ V Edström, *Selma Lagerlöf* (1984)

LAGUNA, Andrés
(1499–1560)

Spanish satirist, born in Segovia, whose *El viaje de Turquía* ('Voyage to Turkey'), if it is his, circulated widely in manuscript (it was first published in 1905). He was a doctor, and is the most likely author of this lively satire—sometimes called a masterpiece—in dialogue form about a man who, captured by the

Turks, manages to pass himself off as a doctor. The work is notably influenced by **Erasmus**.

▷M Bataillon, *Erasmo y España* (1966)

LA HARPE, Jean François de
(1739–1803)

French poet and critic, born in Paris. In 1763 he produced a successful tragedy, *Warwick*, followed by others. His best-known works are, however, his critical lectures *Lycée, ou Cours de littérature* (1799–1805, 'The Study of Literature'). His *Correspondance littéraire* (1801), by the bitterness of its criticisms, rekindled fierce controversies. He supported the revolution at first, but after five months' imprisonment (1794) became a firm supporter of church and crown.

▷C A Sainte-Beuve, *Causeries de lundi* (1850–69)

LAMANTIA, Philip
(1927–)

American poet, who espouses an aesthetic of extreme Romanticism, influenced by religious experience and by drugs. Born in San Francisco, he received a rather cursory education and acquired a distinctive blend of hardboiled street awareness and arcane knowledge. He was taken up by Parker Tyler, the leading US theorist of Surrealism, who published the 15-year-old Lamantia's first verses in *View* magazine (1942), later giving him a job as assistant editor. Lamantia's first collection, *Erotic Poems*, appeared in 1946, but there was a substantial gap between it and *Ekstasis* (1959), which contains some of his most distinctive poems. Lamantia destroyed most of his early poems, though they were resurrected for the compendious *Destroyed Works: Hypodermic Light, Mantic Notebook, Still Poems, Spansule* (1962). He was experimenting with hallucinogens as early as 1954, and reading *Touch of the Marvelous* (1966) is a little like experiencing one of the European Decadents re-scripted and shot on faulty stock by B-movie genius Roger Corman. *Selected Poems 1943–1966* (1967) confirmed the significance of his instinctive assault on academicism and the Puritan mythos of **T S Eliot** and **Frost**. Two years later, inclusion in *Penguin Modern Poets 13* (1969) opened him up to British readers. Later work is less compelling and more pedestrian, but there are excellent things in *Becoming Visible* (1981).

▷P Tyler, introduction to *Touch of the Marvelous* (1966)

LAMARTINE, Alphonse Marie Louis de
(1790–1869)

French poet, statesman and historian, born in Mâcon. He was brought up on ultraroyalist principles, spent much of his youth in Italy, and on the fall of Napoleon entered the garde royale. His first volume of poems, probably his best known and most successful, the *Méditations*, was published in 1820. He was successively secretary of legation at Naples and *chargé d'affaires* at Florence. In 1829 he declined the post of foreign secretary in the Bourbon ministry of the Prince de Polignac, and with another series of poems, *Harmonies poétiques et religieuses* (1829, 'Poetical and Religious Harmonies'), achieved his unanimous election to the Academy. Lamartine, still a royalist, disapproved of the revolution of 1830. A tour to the East produced his *Souvenirs d'Orient* (1841, Eng trans *Recollections of a Pilgrimage to the Holy Land*, 1850). Recalled to France in 1833, he became deputy for Mâcon. Between 1834 and 1848 he published his poems, *Jocelyn* (1836, Eng trans 1837) and *La Chute d'un ange* (1838, 'The Fall of an Angel'), and the celebrated *Histoire des Girondins* (1846, Eng trans *History of the Girondins*, 1947–8). He did not support the Orléanist regime and he became a member of the Provisional Government (1848), and, as Minister of Foreign Affairs, its ruling spirit. In the presidential election of December 1848 he was defeated by Louis-Napoléon and when he came to power as Napoleon III Lamartine devoted himself to literature, publishing *Confidences* (1849 and 1851, Eng trans *Memoirs of My Youth*, 1849 and 1851), *Raphaël* (1849, Eng trans 1849) (both autobiographical), *Geneviève, Tailleur de pierres de St-Point* (1851, Eng trans *The Stonecutter of St Point*, 1851, a prose tale), and *Histoire de la restauration* (1850). He wrote on Joan of Arc, Cromwell, Madame de **Sévigné**, and others, and issued monthly *Entretiens familiers* ('Intimate Conversations').

▷M F Guyard, *Alphonse de Lamartine* (1956)

LAMB, Charles
(1775–1834)

English essayist and poet, born in the Temple, London, where his father was a clerk to Samuel Salt, a wealthy bencher. Educated at Christ's Hospital (1782–9), where he formed a lasting friendship with **Coleridge**, he obtained a position in the South Sea House, but in 1792 was promoted to the India House, where he remained for more than 30 years. In 1792, also, Samuel Salt died, and with a legacy from him, his own salary, and whatever his elder sister Mary (1764–1847) could earn by needlework, the family retired to humble lodgings. In 1796 the terrible disaster occurred which was destined to mould the future life of Charles Lamb. The strain of insanity inherited from their mother began to show itself in Mary, and in an attack of mania

she stabbed her invalid mother to death. Her brother's guardianship was accepted by the authorities and to this trust Lamb from that moment devoted his life. In the meantime he had fallen in love, but renounced all hope of marriage when the duty of tending his sister appeared to him paramount. Lamb's earliest poems (1795), first printed with Coleridge's in 1796–7, were prompted by this deep attachment. In 1798 Lamb and Charles Lloyd attempted a slight volume of their own (*Blank Verse*) and here for the first time Lamb's individuality made itself felt in 'Old Familiar Faces'. In 1797 he also published his little prose romance, *The Tale of Rosamund Gray and Old Blind Margaret*; and in 1801 *John Woodvil*—the fruit of that study of the dramatic poetry of the Elizabethan period, in whose revival he was to play so large a part. Meantime, Lamb and his sister were wandering from lodging to lodging, and in 1801 they moved to Lamb's old familiar neighbourhood, where they stayed for 16 years. Charles's experiments in literature had as yet brought him neither money nor reputation and so he wrote a farce, *Mr H* (1806), which failed. For **William Godwin**'s 'Juvenile Library', Charles and Mary wrote in 1807 their *Tales from Shakespeare*—Mary taking the comedies, Charles the tragedies. This was Lamb's first success. The brother and sister next composed jointly *Mrs Leicester's School* (1807) and *Poetry for Children* (1809). Charles also made a prose version of the *Adventures of Ulysses*, and a volume of selections from the Elizabethan dramatists showed him as one of the most subtle and original of critics. Three years later his unsigned articles in **Leigh Hunt**'s *Reflector* on Hogarth and the tragedies of **Shakespeare** proved him a prose writer of new and unique quality. In 1818 Lamb collected his scattered verse and prose in two volumes as the *Works of Charles Lamb*, and this paved the way for his being invited to join the staff of the new *London Magazine*. His first essay, in August 1820, 'Recollections of the old South Sea House', was signed 'Elia', the name of a foreigner who had been a fellow-clerk. The first collection of the *Essays of Elia* was published in 1823; *The Last Essays of Elia* appeared in 1833. In 1825 Lamb, who had been failing in health, resigned his post in the India House. The brother and sister were now free to wander and finally they moved to Edmonton. The absence of settled occupation had not brought Lamb the comfort he had looked for: the separation from his friends and the now almost continuous mental alienation of his sister left him companionless, and with the death of Coleridge in 1834 the chief attractions of his life were gone. In December of that year, he too died and was buried in Edmonton churchyard. His sister survived him by nearly 13 years, and was buried by his side. Lamb's place in literature is unique and unchallengeable. He is familiar through his works, which are composed in the form of personal confidences; through his many friends, who have made known his every mood and trait; and through his letters, the most fascinating correspondence in the English language.
▷ E V Lucas, *Life of Charles Lamb* (2 vols, 1905, 1921)

LAMBERT, Eric
(1918–66)
English-born Australian author, born in Stamford, Lincolnshire, who went to Australia in his teens and served with Australian forces during World War II. Befriended by **Frank Hardy**, he turned to communism in the late 1940s and in 1951 published *The Twenty Thousand Thieves*, based on his own wartime experiences; the title derives from an epithet applied to the Allied division in North Africa. Lambert portrayed the soldier as a bronzed, courageous hero and his officer as a drink-befuddled buffoon, but the book was a popular success. He wrote over 15 novels of which some, such as *The Veterans* (1954), returned to the theme of war, but none repeated his first success. He went to London in 1955 and from there reported, for a Sydney newspaper, the Hungarian uprising of 1956, which alienated him from the Australian communists. He wrote two novels on the theme of the Eureka goldfield revolt of 1854, and *Kelly* (1964), based loosely on the life of the Australian outlaw Ned Kelly.

LAMDAN, Yitzchak
(1899–1954)
Hebrew poet, born in Mlinov, Ukraine. He went to Palestine in 1920. His most famous, and still much read, poem was *Masada* (1924): this is the name of the last fortress held by the Jews against the Romans, although the poem itself is about a *halutz* Jew returning to his homeland. Another famous, and more profound, poem, is 'For the Sunset', a kind of concealed dialogue between God and Jacob.
▷ L A Yudkin, *Isaac Lamdan* (1971)

LAMMING, George Eric
(1927–)
Barbadian novelist, born in Carrington Village. He was a teacher in Trinidad and in Venezuela before going to England in 1950, where he worked as a factory labourer and hosted a book programme for the BBC West Indian Service. His first novels, with their unfamiliar background and argot, received a lukewarm reception. Beginning with *In the*

Castle of My Skin (1953), he has explored the West Indian experience in a complex and highly textured way. Of his novels, *The Emigrants* (1954) is the saddest; *Season of Adventure* (1960) articulates his own dilemma as an artist; *Natives of My Person* (1972), with its archaic vocabulary and mythic roots, is perhaps his tour de force.

▷S P Paquet, *George Lamming* (1982)

LA MOTTE, Antoine Houdar de
(1672–1731)

French poet and playwright, born in Paris. He was translator of the *Iliad* into French verse (1714). Of his other writings, perhaps the best known is the play *Inès de Castro* (1723).

▷P Du Pont, *Antoine La Motte* (1898)

L'AMOUR, Louis
(1908–88)

American writer of crude, effective Wild West novels. Born in Jamestown, North Dakota, he grew up riding and hunting in the West, and earned his living in a variety of ways— prize-fighter, tugboat deckhand, lumberjack, gold prospector and deputy sheriff. His first novel about the Wild West, *Hondo* (1953), was an instant success, and he followed it with another 80 novels, including *Hopalong Cassidy and the Riders of High Rock* (1951), *High Lonesome* (1962), *Ride the Dark Trail* (1972) and *The Iron Marshall* (1979), of which several were made into successful films. In 1984 he was awarded the Presidential Medal of Freedom.

▷*Education of a Wandering Man* (1989)

LAMPEDUSA, Giuseppe Tomasi di
(1896–1957)

Italian novelist, born in Palermo, Sicily, son of the Duke of Parma and grandson of the Prince of Lampedusa. His family had once been rich but indolence, divided inheritance and apathy had reduced its circumstances. As a youth he was wild but he turned bookish and scholarly and, despite familial disapproval, buried himself in his library where he read voraciously and eclectically in several languages. His mother, born Beatrice Mastrogiovanni Tasca, was the dominant influence in his life and it was not until she died that he felt free to embark on the novel that is his memorial, his only book, *Il Gattopardo* (1958, Eng trans *The Leopard*, 1960). Set in Sicily in the latter half of the 19th century it is a historical novel, violent, decadent and nostalgic. It was rapturously received then vilified by the Italian literary establishment, including Moravia, but has subsequently come to be regarded as one of the greatest Italian novels of the 20th century.

▷A Vitello, *I Gattopardi di Donnafugato* (1963)

LAMPMAN, Archibald
(1861–99)

Canadian poet—one of the group known as the 'Confederation Poets'; he was born in Morpeth, Canada West and spent most of his life in and around Ottawa. His poetry is attuned to the music and mystery of a 'sweet sombre land'—a natural world that allows the mind and the soul space to grow. Although his poems regularly appeared in Canadian, American and British periodicals, only one volume of his work was published during his lifetime: *Among the Millet and Other Poems* (1888). However, **Duncan Campbell Scott**, friend, fellow poet and literary executor, edited and arranged the posthumous publication of Lampman's poetry, including *The Poems of Archibald Lampman* (1900) and *At the Long Sault and Other New Poems* (1943).

▷S Djwa, 'Lampman's Fleeting Vision', in *Canadian Literature*, 55 (1973); L R Early, in R Lecker, J David and E Quigley (eds), *Canadian Writers and Their Work: Poetry Series: Volume II* (1983)

LAMPO, Hubert
(1920–)

Belgian (Flemish) novelist, born in Antwerp. An eclectic writer, he has written realistic novels of a psychological cast, historical fantasies, occult works, and criticism. *Terugkeer naar Atlantis* (1953, 'Return to Atlantis') is perhaps his most substantial work. It deals with a man's search for a new reality: he can no longer believe that his father 'died' 30 years earlier, and so looks for him. *Hélène Defraye* (1945) is, on the other hand, a straightforwardly realistic novel.

LAMPRECHT, Pfaffe
(fl.1130)

German poet and priest, from Trier. He is principally remembered as the author of the Middle High German epic life of Alexander, *Alexanderlied* (c.1130), though he is by no means responsible for all the text which has survived to the present day, as it was edited, added to and changed by any number of subsequent individuals. He is thought to be the author of an ascetic introduction to the work which (though it is not altogether consistent with the rest of the poem) warns of the worthlessness and triviality of worldly things. The poem is of little value, except historically, as one of the earliest non-religious long works in German.

LANCASTER, G B, pseud of **Edith Joan Lyttleton**
(1873–1945)

Australasian author of novels and short stories. Of Scottish–Canadian descent, born in Clyne Vale, Tasmania, and reared on a sheep station outside Canterbury, New Zealand, she lived in London between 1909 and 1925. She was a prolific author, with hundreds of short stories and 13 novels to her credit. Her first novel was *Sons o' Men* (1904) and her last *Grand Parade* (1943), the story of the colonization of Nova Scotia. She travelled extensively in Europe and North America, and only three of her novels have an identifiably Australian origin, of which the most significant is *Pageant* (1933), the tale of a Tasmanian family in which she drew extensively upon her family history. In *Promenade* (1938) she returned to a New Zealand historical theme but she was always more popular in Britain than in either of her homelands, which saw her as an 'expatriate' writer.

LANDÍVAR, Rafael
(1713–93)

Guatemalan poet and Jesuit priest, born in Santiago de los Cabelleros. After the expulsion of the Jesuits from Spanish territory he went to Italy, where he wrote, in Latin hexameters, *Rusticatio Mexicana* (1781), a lively description of Mexico in the tradition of **Virgil**.

LANDOLFI, Tomasso
(1908–79)

Italian fiction writer, critic and translator, born in Pico. As a story writer (and distinguished translator from Russian, French and German literatures) he was described as a 'hermetic': one whose 'obscurity' came from his inability to express his hatred for fascism in literary form. But he went to prison in any case. His roots were in the pessimistic **Leopardi**, but he also sought inspiration from **Kafka**, **Proust** and the Sicilian **Pirandello**. He was best in shorter forms, but the long *La pietra lunare* (1939, 'The Moon Stone'), a novel about a creature half-goat, half-woman, significantly named Gurù, is one of the strangest books published in modern Italy. *La muta* (1964, Eng trans *The Mute*, 1971), is about a man who murders a beautiful mute in order that she may be spared the horror of speech. Many have seen *Cancroregina* (1950, Eng trans *Cancerqueen*, 1971) as his most powerful evocation of his concern with the irrelevance of words: the pilot of a spaceship records his thoughts and fears, knowing that they will never be read.

In *Le due zitelle* (1946, Eng trans *The Two Old Maids*, 1961) Landolfi posits a Roman Catholic monkey, who proves himself superior to the bourgeois world. Much more appreciated in the USA than in Great Britain, Landolfi's quasi-Surrealist vision has yet to be more fully recognized. He was an influence on the final work of **Italo Calvino**. He remained aloof from all literary movements and avoided publicity.
▷ *Modern Language Notes*, 89 (1974)

LANDON, Letitia Elizabeth
(1802–38)

English popular poet and novelist, born in London, who wrote under the initials 'L. E. L.'. Her work is more important as a guide to early 19th-century taste than in itself; her most popular novel was *Ethel Churchill* (1837). She killed herself accidentally when treating herself with prussic acid.
▷H Ashton, *Letty Landon* (1951)

LANDOR, Walter Savage
(1775–1864)

English writer, born in Warwick, the son of a doctor. At 10 he was sent to Rugby, but was removed for insubordination; he was also sent down from Trinity College, Oxford, which he entered in 1793. Soon after publishing *Poems* in 1795 (which he soon withdrew), he quarrelled with his father, but was reconciled, and retired to South Wales on an allowance of £150 a year. The exotic *Gebir* (1798), a poem showing the influence of **Milton** and **Pindar**, was the occasion of his life-long friendship with **Robert Southey**; but it was a failure. On his father's death in 1805 Landor had a considerable income, but much of it went in equipping volunteers to fight Napoleon in Spain (1808). Next year he purchased Llanthony Abbey in Monmouthshire, but soon quarrelled with neighbours and tenantry alike, and had ruin staring him in the face. In 1811 he married Julia Thuillier, but the marriage was not a success and in 1814 he left her in Jersey and crossed to France. Rejoined by his wife in Tours, he went in 1815 to Italy, where he remained in Como, Pisa and Florence until 1835, with the exception of a short visit to England. *Count Julian*, lacking in all the qualities of a successful tragedy, had appeared in 1812; and to this period belongs his best-known work, *Imaginary Conversations* (i and ii, 1824–9). A second quarrel with his wife in 1835 led to his return to Bath until 1858. During these years he wrote the *Examination of Shakespeare* (1834), *Pericles and Aspasia* (1836), *Pentameron* (1837), *Hellenics* (1847) and *Poemata et Inscriptiones* (1847). In 1858 an unhappy scandal (see his *Dry Sticks Fagoted by Landor*, 1858), which involved him in an action for libel, again drove him to Italy and he lived in Florence until his death.

▷R H Super, *Landor, a biography* (1954)

LANG, Andrew
(1844–1912)

Scottish writer, born in Selkirk, nephew of the scholar William Young Sellar. Educated at The Edinburgh Academy, St Andrews and Glasgow universities and Balliol College, Oxford, he was a fellow of Merton College, Oxford (1868–74), studying myth, ritual and totemism. He moved to London in 1875 to take up journalism, and became one of the most versatile writers of his day. He specialized in mythology, and took part in a celebrated controversy with Friedrich Max Müller over the interpretation of folk tales, arguing that folklore was the foundation of literary mythology. He wrote *Custom and Myth* (1884), *Myth, Ritual and Religion* (1887), *Modern Mythology* (1897) and *The Making of Religion* (1898). He wrote a *History of Scotland* (3 vols, 1899–1904) and a *History of English Literature* (1912), and published a number of fairy books which enjoyed great popularity. He also produced studies of many literary figures, including *Books and Bookmen* (1886) and *Letters to Dead Authors* (1886), a translation of **Homer**, and several volumes of verse.

▷R L Green, *Andrew Lang, a critical biography* (1946)

LANG, John George
(1816–64)

Australian novelist, journalist and lawyer, born in Sydney, who in his teens was an outstanding Latin scholar. He went to England in 1837, read law at Cambridge but was sent down for blasphemy and completed his studies at Middle Temple. He returned to Australia in 1841 and is credited with the anonymous, and incomplete, *Legends of Australia* (1842) and thus with being Australia's first native-born novelist. He left precipitately for India in 1842 and for three years practised law in Calcutta. In 1846 he established an English-language newspaper in Meerut, northern India, which serialized some of his nine novels, including *Too Clever by Half* and *Too Much Alike* (1853–4). He travelled in Europe and had many friends in London literary circles; he contributed stories to **Charles Dickens**'s magazines *All the Year Round* and *Household Words*. His most significant fiction was *Botany Bay; Or, True Tales of Early Australia* (1859).

LANGE, Antoni
(1861–1929)

Polish poet, dramatist, critic and writer of speculative fiction. His neglected poetry is unusual, as is his novel *W czwartym wymiarze* (1912, 'In the Fourth Dimension'), which is comparable with **H G Wells**. His most famous poem is called 'Rym', in which he learnedly analyses the nature and the techniques of poetry.

LANGE, Per
(1901–)

Danish poet, born in Rungsted. An erotic and mystical writer, he was a leading figure in the mid-1920s, when he tried to overcome the chaos of the period by writing in clear-cut classical forms. *Orfeus* (1932) is his most characteristic collection.

LANGGÄSSER, Elizabeth
(1899–1950)

German Roman Catholic novelist and poet, born in Alzey, Hesse, a victim of multiple sclerosis for the last 12 years of her life. Her poetry, in the tradition of **Wilhelm Lehmann**, combines a love of nature with a zealous Catholic mysticism. But her best-known work by far is the novel *Das unauslöschliche Sigel* (1947, 'The Indelible Seal'). This, in some ways reminiscent of **Bernanos**, tells of the struggle for the soul of a Jewish convert to Catholicism between God and Satan; it is cast in surreal, almost hysterical terms, but its power transcends its pious dogmatism.

LANGHORNE, John
(1735–79)

English poet, born in Winton, Kirkby Stephen. From 1766 he was rector of Blagdon, Somerset, and was a justice of the peace from 1772. He published several volumes of poetry, and his best-known poem is 'The Country Justice' (1774). He also published an Oriental tale of the kind then fashionable, and *Genius and Valour: a Scotch pastoral* (1764). With his brother, the Rev William Langhorne (1721–72), he translated **Plutarch**'s Lives (6 vols, 1770).

▷H MacDonald, in *Essays Presented to David Nichol Smith* (1945)

LANGLAND, or LANGLEY, William
(c.1332–c.1400)

English poet, born possibly in Ledbury in Herefordshire, thought to have been the illegitimate son of the rector of Shipton-under-Wychwood in Oxfordshire. Educated at the Benedictine school at Malvern, he became a clerk, but, having married early, could not take more than minor orders, and possibly earned a poor living in London from

1362 by singing in a chantry and by copying legal documents. In that year he began the composition of his famous *Vision of William concerning Piers the Plowman*. This has great defects as a work of art, but the moral earnestness and energy of the author (or authors as has been theorized) sometimes glow into really noble poetry brightened by vivid glimpses of the life of the poorer classes.

LANGLEY, Eve
(1908–74)

Australian novelist, born in Forbes, New South Wales, whose interest centres mainly on her personal quirks, such as wearing trousers before it became usual, always carrying a gun or sheath knife, and changing her name to 'Oscar Wilde'. She moved to New Zealand in 1932 and had a short and unhappy marriage although raising three children. Back in Sydney she threw herself into the literary milieu but later lived, and tragically died, as a recluse. She wrote a number of novels of which the best are *The Pea Pickers* (1942) and its sequel *The White Topee* (1954), in which the feminine 'hero' Steve plays out her own fantasies of virginal love which possibly mirror the sexual conflicts of her author.

LANIER, Sidney
(1842–81)

American poet, born in Macon, Georgia. He was a Confederate private in Virginia, an advocate in Macon, a flute player with the Peabody Orchestra, Baltimore, and lecturer in English literature at Johns Hopkins University (1879). Among his writings are a novel, *Tiger Lilies* (1867), critical studies such as *The Science of English Verse* (1880) and *The English Novel* (1883), as well as poetry. He believed in a scientific approach towards poetry-writing, breaking away from the traditional metrical techniques and making it more akin to musical composition, illustrated in later poems such as 'Corn' and 'The Symphony'.
▷A H Starke, *Sidney Lanier* (1933)

LAO She, originally **Shu She-yu**
(1899–1966)

Chinese poet, novelist and playwright, born into a poor family in Peking. He escaped poverty by means of his academic gifts, leaving China to teach at the University of London between 1924 and 1930. The poems which he produced in this period were liberal in tone and often humorous. Once he embraced communism in the 1930s, however, all traces of humour disappeared from his work. He is, perhaps, best remembered for *Lo-t'o Hiang-tzu* (1937, Eng trans *Rickshaw Boy*, 1945), a

novel detailing and condemning the exploitation of the urban poor by the rich.

LAPINE, James Elliot
(1949–)

American playwright and director, born in Mansfield, Ohio. He studied design at the California Institute of the Arts and drama at Yale Drama School. He came to notice with the play *Table Settings* (1980), followed by his staging of the Off-Broadway musical hit *March of the Falsettos* (1981, which was followed by *Falsettoland* in 1990) and *A Midsummer Night's Dream* (1982). He wrote *Sunday in the Park with George* (1984), with music and lyrics by **Stephen Sondheim**, for which he won a Pulitzer Prize in 1985. Further collaborations with Sondheim followed, including *Into The Woods* (1987).

LARBAUD, Valéry-Nicolas
(1881–1957)

French poet, essayist, critic, translator (of some of **James Joyce**, Sir Thomas Browne, **Whitman** and others), born in Vichy. Larbaud inherited a fortune, and spent it wisely—in travel and in shrewd furtherance of the cause of good writing. Particularly illuminating are his correspondences with **Gide** and **Fargue** (1948 and 1971 respectively). For the last part of his life he was a semi-invalid, the result of a stroke he had suffered in 1935. Most vital and influential of his own varied works were his *Journal de A O Barnabooth* (1913, Eng trans *A O Barnabooth, His Diary*, 1924) and the poems of this same young American, first published as *Poèmes par un riche amateur* (1908, Eng trans *Poems of a Multimillionaire*, 1955). Although these poems owe much in form to Whitman, they are original in a manner reminiscent of **Fernando Pessoa**, inasmuch as their author presents himself under a 'heteronym'. All his fiction is substantial, and his *Journal 1912–1935* (1955) is essential reading for those who require a complete knowledge of 20th-century French literature. His life (1950) was written by G Jean Aubry, French biographer of **Conrad**, but this has not yet been translated into English.
▷M Raymond, *From Baudelaire to Surrealism* (1950)

LARDNER, Ring (Ringgold Wilmer)
(1885–1933)

American short-story writer and journalist, born in Michigan. He was a successful sports writer and newspaper columnist in Chicago, St Louis and New York, and drew on that sporting background in his first collection of stories, *You Know Me Al: A Busher's Letters* (1916), set in the world of baseball. His racy vernacular idioms and rather black, somewhat cynical humour mark him out as a distinctive voice. Story collections include *Gullible's Travels* (1917), *Treat 'Em Rough* (1918), *The Love Nest* (1926) and *First and Last* (1934). He also wrote one novel, *The Big Town* (1921), satirical verse, a satirical pseudo-autobiography, *The Story of a Wonder Man* (1927), and a musical comedy, *June Moon* (1929).

▷D Elder, *Ring Lardner* (1956)

LARIVEY, Pierre
(c.1550–1612)

French dramatist of Italian descent. As the introducer of Italian-style comedy to the French stage he foreshadowed **Molière** and **Jean Regnard**. His licentious *Comédies facétieuses* (2 vols, 1579, 1611, 'Facetious Comedies') were adaptations of existing Italian pieces.

▷L Morin, *Les trois Pierre de Larivey* (1937)

LARKIN, Philip Arthur
(1922–85)

English poet, librarian and jazz critic, born in Coventry, Warwickshire, where his father was city treasurer. He was educated at King Henry VIII School, Coventry, and at St John's College, Oxford. The Oxford of the time is evoked in his early novel, *Jill* (1946). After leaving Oxford, he took up librarianship and *A Girl in Winter* (1947), his only other novel, tells of a day in the life of a refugee librarian employed in a drab English provincial town. He eventually became librarian at the University of Hull in 1955. His early poems appeared in the anthology, *Poetry from Oxford in Wartime* (1944), and in a collection, *The North Ship* (1945). **W B Yeats**, **Thomas Hardy** and **Dylan Thomas** were then his presiding influences. He was friendly with **Kingsley Amis** who made the hero of his novel *Lucky Jim* (1954), Jim Dixon, share Larkin's antipathy towards Mozart. *XX Poems* was published in 1950 when he was in Belfast and marked the emergence of an individual 'voice'. Further collections appeared at measured intervals: *The Less Deceived* (1955), *The Whitsun Weddings* (1964) and *High Windows* (1974). *Collected Poems* was published posthumously in 1988 and became a bestseller. He also edited *The Oxford Book of Twentieth Century English Verse* (1937). The self he projected to the world from his fastness in Hull was of a xenophobic, reactionary old fogey, downcast and ill at ease in the modern world. But much of the time his tongue was firmly in his cheek and his poetry reveals a considerable talent for technique and a sure grasp of modern idiom. His articles on jazz were collected in *All What Jazz?* (1970), and his essays in *Required Writing* (1983).

▷A Motion, *Philip Larkin* (1993)

LA ROCHEFOUCAULD, François, 6th Duc de
(1613–80)

French writer, born in Paris. He devoted himself to the cause of the queen, Marie de Medici, in opposition to Richelieu, and became entangled in a series of love adventures and political intrigues, the result being that he was forced to live in exile from 1639 to 1642. About 1645 he formed a liaison wth Mme de Longueville. He then joined the Frondeurs and was wounded at the siege of Paris. In 1652, wounded again, he retired to the country. On Mazarin's death in 1661 he returned to the court of Louis XIV, and about the same time began a liaison with Mme de Sablé. A surreptitious edition of his *Mémoires*, written in retirement, was published in 1662, but as it gave wide offence he denied its authorship. His *Réflexions, ou sentences et maximes morales*, appeared in 1665. His last years were brightened by his liaison with Mme **de La Fayette**, which lasted until he died. For brevity, clearness and style the *Réflexions* could hardly be excelled. Their author was a remorseless analyst of man's character, and tracks out self-love in its most elusive forms and under its most cunning disguises.

▷W G Moore, *La Rochefoucauld* (1969)

LA ROCHEJAQUELEIN, Marie Louise Victoire
(1772–1857)

French writer, wife of the soldier Louis du Verger de Larochejaquelein. She published valuable *Mémoires* of the Napoleonic War (1815).

LARRA, Mariano José de
(1809–37)

Spanish poet, satirist and political writer, born in Madrid. As a journalist he was unequalled and he published two periodicals between 1828 and 1833, but it was as a satirist that he became well known. His stylistically masterly prose writings include *El Doncel de Don Enrique el Doliente* (1834, 'Don Enrique's Manservant'), a novel, *Macías* (1834), a play, and adaptations of French plays.

▷R B Moreno, *Mariano Larra* (1957)

LARRAMENDI, Padre Manuel de
(1690–1766)

Basque Jesuit humorist and scholar, who wrote in Castilian as well as Basque, born in Andoain, Guipúzoca. He is most famous for his Basque grammar, *Imposible vencido* (1729), and his *Diccionario trilingüe* (1736). He was amongst the first to assert that Basque was the original language of Spain (which is likely). He also liked to assert that it was one of the 75 languages which came into existence after the building of the Tower of Babel, and that it was spoken by God. He wrote a fascinating history, in Castilian, of his native province, which was not printed until long after his death (1882).

▷R Gallop, *A Book of the Basques* (1930); L Michelena, *Historia de la literatura vasca* (1960)

LARRETA, Enrique Rodríguez
(1875–1961)

Argentinian novelist, essayist, poet and playwright. Born in Buenos Aires, he received his doctorate in jurisprudence and social sciences. He travelled extensively in Europe, and from 1910 to 1918 was a diplomat for Argentina in France. He was best known as one of the 'Seis de la fama', the six most important writers in Latin America in the first decades of this century, though he was far from being that. His first novel, *Artemisa*, was published in 1896. Twelve years later he published his most important novel, *La gloria de don Ramiro* (1908, 'The Glory of don Ramiro'), which combines modern Spanish narration with highly polished archaic Spanish dialogue to create a highly interesting, 'modernist' effect. In addition to many other novels, he wrote two books of essays, several plays, and a book of 88 sonnets.

▷H Campanella, *Enrique Larreta, el hombre y el escritor* (1987)

LA SALE, or SALLE, Antoine de
(c.1398–1470)

French writer, born in Burgundy or Touraine. He lived at the courts of Provence and Flanders, and wrote *Chronique du petit Jehan de Saintré* (1456), may have written the ironic satire *Quinze joyes de mariage* (early 15th-century, Eng trans *The Fifteen Comforts of Matrimony*, 1682), and was the reputed author of *Cent nouvelles nouvelles* (1462, 'One Hundred New Tales', modelled loosely on **Boccaccio**'s *Decameron*).

▷A Bronavski, *Le petit Jehan de Saintré, une enigme littéraire* (1922)

LASKER-SCHÜLER, Else
(1869–1945)

German–Jewish poet, playwright and painter. Born in Elberfeld, Wuppertal, she was never much concerned with factual authenticity. 'I was born in Thebes, Egypt ...' is how her own account of her life begins. Apart from her drama *Die Wupper* (1909) and the

travelogue *Das Hebräerland* (1934), it is her poetry for which she is most renowned. Comprising numerous volumes of poetry from *Styx* (1902) to *Mein blaues Klavier* (1943, 'My Blue Piano'), it is marked by a completely unselfconscious mythicization of herself and her friends, climaxing in love/play poetry full of unbridled images of ardour, tenderness and passion; not without reason was she once called 'the snake charmer of love'. Conjuring up biblical or ancient oriental settings, she renames her friends and lovers, turning them into the legendary aristocracy of real and sometimes imaginary kingdoms. Her private poetic myth had its counterpart in her bohemian life style. A public assault by Nazis in 1933 made her flee to Switzerland before moving to Jerusalem in 1937.

▷S Bauschinger, *Else Lasker-Schüler. Ihr Werk und ihre Zeit* (1980)

LASKI, Marghanita
(1915–88)

English novelist and journalist, born in Manchester, niece of Harold Joseph Laski. Educated at Oxford, her first novel, *Love on the Supertax*, appeared in 1944. She wrote extensively for newspapers and reviews. Her later novels include *Little Boy Lost* (1949) and *The Victorian Chaise-longue* (1953). She also wrote a play, *The Offshore Island* (1959), as well as editing and writing various studies and critical works.

LA TAILLE, Jean de
(?1535–1608)

French dramatist and essayist, born in Bondaroy. He studied at the Collège de Boncourt in Paris before going to Orléans to study law, but once there his literary career quickly overtook his interest in the legal profession. He returned to Paris and by 1562 had published his masterpiece, *Saül le Furieux* ('Saul the Furious'), as well as *Le Negromant* ('The Necromancer') and *Les Corivaux. La Famine ou les Gabéonites* ('The Famine or the Gabeonites'), a sequel to *Saul*, appeared in 1573. He is also known for an important essay, *De la Tragédie*, on the renaissance of the classical unities in French drama. He is rarely considered without some reference to his younger brother Jacques, whose work Jean published after his death at the age of 20: this included two tragedies, *Alexandre* and *Daire* (Darius), and several poems, in both Latin and French.

LATINI, Brunetto
(c.1210–c.1295)

Florentine writer and statesman. A member of the Guelf party, he was exiled to France from 1260 to 1266, and there wrote the encyclopaedic *Li Livres dou Trésor*, a survey of

extant learning written in French. His other works include the poems *Tesoretto* and *Farolello*, and a commentary on part of **Cicero**'s *De inventione*.
▷T Sundby, *Della vita e delle opera* (1884)

LATORRE, Mariano
(1886–1955)
Chilean story writer and novelist, born in Cobquecura, into a family which was originally Basque on his father's side and French on his mother's. A librarian and teacher, he became famous as an innovator who wrote incomparably about the topography of Chile, and was his country's master of *criollismo* (the equivalent of *costumbristo*, ie regionalism). He said that Nature 'had imposed its presence' in his works. His best stories are contained in *Sus mejores cuentos* (1962, 'His Best Stories'). He also wrote a novel, *Zurzulita* (1920), dealing with the clash between town and country. A critic has said that his chief virtue is his *afán* ('desperate anxiety').
▷H Castillo, *El criollismo en la novela chilena* (1962)

LA TOUR DU PIN, Patrice de
(1911–75)
French Catholic poet whose early work was hailed by conservative critics as the grand answer, by a young poet, to the shocking confusions of Surrealism. He was encouraged by **Jules Supervielle**. His work is grandiloquent, mystical, and, some say, 'rather colourless', but it remains respected amongst its readers, and is eminently and undoubtedly worthy of consideration within the Catholic tradition established by **Paul Claudel**. His *La Vie recluse en poésie* (1938) was translated as *The Dedicated Life in Poetry* (1948).

LATTIMORE, Richmond
(1906–84)
American poet, born in China, who had perhaps the highest reputation of his generation as a translator (**Pindar**, **Homer**, **Aristophanes**, **Euripides**, **Hesiod** and others). His translation of the *Iliad* is particularly prized. His own poetic gift, though less distinguished, nevertheless contributed to his skill as a translator; it is to be found in *Poems from Three Decades* (1972).

LAUBE, Heinrich
(1806–84)
German playwright and manager, born in Sprottau in Silesia. He was one of the leaders of the 'Young Germany' movement and editor of *Die elegante Welt* ('The Elegant World'), its literary organ. He was director of Vienna's Burgtheater (1850–67), and

among his writings are works on the theatre, on historical themes, novels such as *Das junge Europa* (1833–7, 'Young Europe'), *Die Karlsschüler* (1847, 'The Boys of the Karls-School'), a drama of the young **Schiller**, and a biography of **Franz Grillparzer**.
▷M Dürst, *Heinrich Laube* (1951)

LAUDER, Sir Thomas Dick
(1784–1848)
Scottish writer, born in Fountainhall, Midlothian. He served in the Cameron Highlanders and in 1808 married the heiress of Relugas in Morayshire. He succeeded to the baronetcy in 1820, and lived at the Grange, Edinburgh, from 1832 until his death. He was Secretary to the Board of Scottish Manufacturers (1839–48), and was a proponent of the establishment of technical and art schools. He wrote two romances, *Lochindhu* (1825) and *The Wolf of Badenoch* (1827), but his best works are *An Account of the Great Morayshire Floods* (1830) and the unfinished *Scottish Rivers*, which appeared in *Tait's Magazine* (1847–9). He also compiled *Highland Rambles and Legends to Shorten the Way* (1837) and *Legends and Tales of the Highlands* (1841).

LAURENCE, Margaret, originally **Jean Margaret Wemyss**
(1926–87)
Canadian novelist of Scots–Irish descent, born in the prairie town of Neepawa, Manitoba. Her first stories appeared in the high-school paper. Aged 18, she left home to study at United College (now Winnipeg University), from which she graduated in 1947, the same year she married John Laurence, a civil engineer. His job took them to England, Somaliland and, in 1952, to Ghana, where they spent five years. *A Tree for Poverty* (1954), a collection of translated Somali poetry and folk-tales, and the travel book *The Prophet's Camel Bell* (1963), came from her East African experience. *This Side Jordan* (1960), her first novel, was set in Ghana. She moved to England in 1962 and a year later a collection of stories, *The Tomorrow-Tamer*, set in West Africa, appeared. In Penn, Buckinghamshire, she wrote her famous Manawaka series based on her home town: *The Stone Angel* (1964), *A Jest of God* (1966), *The Fire-Dwellers* (1969), *A Bird in the House* (1970) and *The Diviners* (1974). One of Canada's most potent novelists, she received Governor General Awards in 1967 and 1975, and in 1972 was made a Companion of the Order of Canada.
▷W H New, *Margaret Laurence: the writer and her critics* (1977)

LAURENTS, Arthur
(1920–)

American writer of scripts for hit musicals, such as *West Side Story* (1957). His first success was *Home of the Brave* (1945), about racial prejudice. The finest of his screenplays was for *The Snake Pit* (1948).

LAUTRÉAMONT, Comte de *see* DUCASSE, Isidore Lucien

LAVANT, Christine, pseud of Christine Habernig, née Thornhauser
(1915–)

Austrian Roman Catholic poet, born in Gross-Eding. The daughter of a miner, and partially blind and deaf from birth, she was forced to earn a living from knitting; then she built up a deserved reputation as Austria's leading lyrical mystical poet, drawing on nature and her reading of **Rilke** to gain her haunting effects.

LA VARENDE, Jean-Balthazar Marie Mallard, Comte de
(1887–1959)

French novelist and biographer. Born in the Pays d'Ouche, Normandy, he manifested a lifelong attachment to his ancestral home, the Chateau de Bonneville-Chamblanc. His work reflects an intense interest in the lives of the aristocracy, coupled with a fervent belief in its right to power and privilege. He despised what he considered to be the decadence of the bourgeoisie and, through his fiction, sought to escape into the old order. Most of his prolific output of novels is set in the early 19th century, and he often uses his own forebears as heroes. He was awarded the Grand Prix du Roman of the Académie française in 1938, for *Le Centaure de Dieu* ('God's Centaur'). His biographies include *Guillaume le Bâtard, conquérant* (1946).

LAVATER, Johann Kaspar
(1741–1801)

Swiss physiognomist, theologian and poet, born in Zürich. In 1769 he took Protestant orders. He made himself known by a volume of poems, *Schweizerlieder* (1767, 'Swiss Songs'). His *Aussichten in die Ewigkeit* (1768–78, 'Prospects of Eternity') is characterized by religious enthusiasm and mysticism. He attempted to elevate physiognomy into a science in his *Physiognomische Fragmente* (1775–8, Eng trans *Essays on Physiognomy designed to promote the knowledge and the love of mankind*, 5 vols, 1789–98). While tending the wounded at the capture of Zürich by Masséna (September 1799) he received a wound, of which he later died.
▷T Hasler, *Johann Lavater* (1942)

LAVEDAN, Henri
(1859–1940)

French dramatist, born in Orléans, author of both comedies and 'problem plays'. His most famous play, was *Le Prince d'Aurec* (1892, Eng trans *The Prince d'Aurec*, in *Three Modern Plays from the French*, 1914), about a prince who borrows money from a Jewish baron who makes financial loans to anti-Semitic aristocrats in order to become their equal; the prince ends by deciding to live an honest life, which is dealt with in an inferior sequel, *Les Deux Noblesses* (1894, 'The Two Nobilities'). Pierre Fresnay directed a movie version of Lavedan's play *Le Duel* ('The Duel') in 1939, with himself, Yvonnes Printemps and Raimu in the leading parts.

LAVER, James
(1899–1975)

English writer and art critic, born in Liverpool. He won the Newdigate Prize for verse at Oxford in 1921, and later books of verse included *His Last Sebastian* (1922) and *Ladies' Mistakes* (1933). He was Assistant Keeper, later Keeper at the Victoria and Albert Museum from 1922 to 1959. He wrote several books of art criticism, including *French Painting and the 19th century* (1937) and *Fragonard* (1956), and made a substantial contribution to the history of English costume with such books as *Taste and Fashion* (1937), *Fashions and Fashion Plates* (1943) and *Children's Costume in the 19th Century* (1951).

LAVIN, Mary
(1912–)

Irish short-story writer and novelist, born in East Walpole, Massachusetts. Her parents returned to Ireland when she was nine and she has lived there ever since. 'Miss Holland', her first short story, was published in the *Dublin Magazine* where it was admired by Lord **Dunsany**, who encouraged her and later wrote an introduction to her first collection, *Tales from Bective Bridge* (1942), which was awarded the James Tait Black Memorial Prize. Notwithstanding two early novels— *The House in Clewe Street* (1945) and *Mary O'Grady* (1950)—she has concentrated on the short story. She has published many collections, and a *Collected Stories* appeared in 1971. Further collections are *A Memory and Other Stories* (1972), *The Shrine and Other Stories* (1977) and *A Family Likeness* (1985). Her laurels include the **Katherine Mansfield** Prize and the Gregory Medal, founded by **W B Yeats** to be 'the supreme award of the Irish nation'.
▷R Peterson, *Mary Lavin* (1978)

LAWLER, Ray
(1921–)

Australian playwright, born in Melbourne, who has also worked as an actor, producer and director. His first play was *Cradle of Thunder* (1952), but it was not until his tenth, *Summer of the Seventeenth Doll* (1955), that he attracted notice. This takes its title from the collection of fairground dolls which mark the 16 summers in which Roo and his mates have holidayed from their cane-cutting jobs in Queensland and gone south to their Melbourne girlfriends 'for the mating season'. *Kid Stakes* (1975) looks back to the beginning of these relationships, and *Other Times* (1976) to the period immediately after World War II. The three plays were collected as *The Doll Trilogy* in 1978. *The Piccadilly Bushman* (1961) looks at divided loyalties, and *The Man Who Shot the Albatross* (1972, not published) concerns William Bligh of the *Bounty* and his later career as Governor of New South Wales.

LAWRENCE, D(avid) H(erbert)
(1885–1930)

English novelist, poet and essayist, born in Eastwood, Nottinghamshire, the son of a miner. With tubercular tendencies, of which he eventually died, he became, through his mother's devotion, a schoolmaster and began to write, encouraged by the notice taken of his work by **Ford Madox Ford** and **Edward Garnett**. In 1911, after the success of his first novel, *The White Peacock*, he decided to live by writing. In 1912 he eloped with Frieda von Richthofen, a cousin of the German war ace Baron Mannfred von Richthofen and wife of Ernest Weekley, a professor at Nottingham University. They travelled in Germany, Austria and Italy from 1912 to 1913, and married in 1914 after her divorce. Lawrence had made his reputation with the semi-autobiographical *Sons and Lovers* (1913). They returned to England at the outbreak of World War I and lived in an atmosphere of suspicion and persecution in a cottage in Cornwall. In 1915 he published *The Rainbow*, an exploration of marital and sexual relations, and was horrified to find himself prosecuted for obscenity. He left England in 1919, and after three years' residence in Italy, where after he produced another exploration of sex and marriage, *Women in Love* (1921), he went to America, settling in Mexico until the progress of his disease drove him back to Italy where his last years were spent. His sensitive spirit was again shocked by his further prosecutions for obscenity over the private publication in Florence of *Lady Chatterley's Lover* in 1928 and over an exhibition of his paintings in London in 1929. *Lady Chatterley's Lover* was not published in the UK in unexpurgated

form until after a sensational obscenity trial in 1961. Opinion is still divided over Lawrence's worth as a writer but there can be no doubt about his effect on the younger intellectuals of his period. He challenged them by his attempt to interpret human emotion on a deeper level of consciousness than that handled by his contemporaries. This provoked either sharp criticism or an almost idolatrous respect. His descriptive passages are sometimes superb, but he had little humour, and this occasionally produced unintentionally comic effects. His finest writing occurs in his poems, where all but essentials have been pared away, but most of his novels have an enduring strength. His other major novels include *Aaron's Rod* (1922), *Kangaroo* (1923, reflecting a visit to Australia) and *The Plumed Serpent* (1926, set in Mexico). His collected poems were published in 1928, and his *Complete Poems* in 1957. A *Complete Plays* appeared in 1965; his other writings include vivid travel narratives, essays, works of literary criticism, including *Studies in Classic American Literature* (1923), and two studies of the unconscious.

▷K Sagar, *The Life of D H Lawrence* (1980)

LAWSON, Henry Hertzberg
(1867–1922)

Australian poet and short-story writer, born in New South Wales, the son of a Norwegian sailor and gold miner. His mother Louisa Lawson (1848–1920) was a strong personality who, in 1887, founded a radical journal, *The Republican*, and, in 1888, *Dawn*, a monthly magazine of strong feminist sympathies which began the movement for women's suffrage in New South Wales. From his mother and her friends Henry acquired the radical opinions which coloured his own writing. He travelled widely in Australia and New Zealand and contributed to the *Bulletin*, but his first collection, *Short Stories in Prose and Verse*, was published by Louisa in 1894. Lawson then prepared two substantial collections, of verse in *In the Days When the World Was Wide* (1896) and stories in *While the Billy Boils* (1896). Another collection of verse and two of prose followed. Lawson then moved with his wife and son to London, where he prepared for Blackwood's Magazine a collection of his earlier stories, published as *The Country I Come From* (1901), and worked on the tales which were to appear the same year as *Joe Wilson and His Mates*. Returning to Australia in 1902, Lawson separated from his wife. His later years were marred by ill health and alcoholism. During this period, and since his death, his tales and poems have appeared in numerous editions. A definitive seven-volume edition was edited by Colin Roderick (1967–72), including not only the verse and

LAWSON, John Howard

stories, but also Lawson's letters and autobiographical writings.

▷M Clark, *In Search of Lawson* (1978)

LAWSON, John Howard
(1894–1977)

American dramatist, born in New York City. He was a politically alert man, angered by the economic and social injustice he considered was blighting the USA. His first play, *Processional* (1925), is set during a coal-mining strike in West Virginia. He wrote seven more dramas before completing *Marching Song* (1937), another play in which the workers successfully rise up against a repressive management. In Hollywood as a screenwriter, Lawson was identified as a communist and summoned before the House Un-American Activities Committee as one of the 'Hollywood Ten'. He was convicted of contempt, served a one-year prison sentence and emerged effectively blacklisted. He wrote only one more play, *Parlor Magic* (1963).

LAXNESS, Halldór Kiljan, pseud of Halldór Guðjónsson
(1902–)

Icelandic novelist, born in Reykjavík, winner of the Nobel Prize for literature in 1955. Brought up on the farm of Laxnes, near Reykjavík, he travelled widely to seek experience. After World War I he steeped himself in Expressionism in Germany, Catholicism in a monastery in Luxembourg, and Surrealism in France, before going to Canada and the USA (1927–30), where he was converted to socialism. In his fiction he explored the reality of Iceland, past and present, and rejuvenated Icelandic prose, in a series of incomparable epic novels like *Salka Valka* (1931–2), *Sjálfstætt fólk* (1934–5, *Independent People*, 1945–6), *Heimsljós* (1937–40, *World Light*, 1969) and *Íslandsklukkan* (1943–9, 'Iceland's Bell'). After World War II he continued to turn out a stream of brilliantly executed novels on Icelandic life: *Atómstöðin* (1948, Eng trans *The Atom Station*, 1961), *Gerpla* (1952, Eng trans *The Happy Warriors*, 1958), *Brekkukotsannáll* (1957, Eng trans *The Fish Can Sing*, 1966), *Paradísarheimt* (1960, Eng trans *Paradise Reclaimed*, 1962) and *Kristnihald undir Jökli* (1968, Eng trans *Christianity at Glacier*, 1972). He has also written a number of plays, and adapted some of his own novels for the stage.

▷P Hallberg, *Laxness* (1971)

LAYAMON
(fl.early 13th century)

English poet and priest at Ernley (now Areley Regis), on the Severn near Bewdley. In c.1200 he wrote an alliterative verse chronicle, the *Brut*, a history of England which was an amplified imitation of **Robert Wace**'s *Brut d'Angleterre*. It is important in the history of English versification as the first poem written in Middle English, and contains the first English versions of the stories of **Arthur**, Lear, Cymbelene and others.

▷J S P Tetlock, *The Legendary History of Britain* (1950)

LAYE, Camera
(1928–80)

Major Francophone novelist, born in French Guinea of a Malinke family. Of his generation, Laye probably had more (deserved) attention paid to him by critics than any other African novelist. 'No other novelist', it has been written, 'approached him in artistry or in psychological insight'. But some accused him of a 'lack of commitment' to the Black struggle. He grew up away from the influence of colonialism; his father was a smith, a master of both metalwork and magic. Laye was sick and weak for the last years of his life; in 1965 he left his own country in disgust, for Senegal—President Touré had him condemned to death *in absentia*. His two masterpieces are his first two novels: the autobiographical *L'Enfant noir* (1953, Eng trans *The Dark Child*, 1954), and *Le Regard du roi* (1954, Eng trans *The Radiance of the King*, 1956). The first is based on his own enchanted childhood, the second is a profound allegory about a white man's search for a king he wished to serve. Later work, such as *Le Maître de la parole* (1978, 'The Wordmaster'), is powerful in parts but weaker as a whole.

▷A C Brench, *The Novelists' Inheritance in French Africa* (1967); W Cartey, *Whispers from a Continent* (1969)

LAYTON, Irving
(1912–)

Romanian-born Canadian poet, lecturer, critic and editor, educated at MacDonald College, Quebec and McGill, Montreal. The author of some 50 volumes of poetry, Layton proclaims: 'the poet must insist on a complex, imaginative awareness and remain the sworn enemy of all dogmas and dogmatists'. His famous rebuke of Canadian torpor, 'A dull people, without charm/or ideas', is deliberately provocative, reflecting his passionate belief in the poet's role as social discomforter. He received the Governor General's Award for *Collected Poems: A Red Carpet for the Sun* in 1959; a selected volume of poetry, *A Wild Peculiar Joy*, representing the work of more than 40 years, was published in 1982 (rev edn 1989).

▷E Mandel, *The Poetry of Irving Layton*

(1981); W Francis, *Irving Layton and His Work* (1985)

LAZARUS, Emma
(1849–87)

American poet and essayist, born in New York. She published striking volumes of poems and translations, including *Admetus and other poems* (1871), *Songs of a Semite* (1882) and *By the Waters of Babylon* (1887). She also wrote a prose romance, *Alide: An Episode of Goethe's Life* (1874), and a verse tragedy, *The Spagnaletto* (1876). A champion of oppressed Jewry, she is best known for her sonnet, 'The New Colossus' (1883), inscribed on the Statue of Liberty in New York harbour.
▷H E Jacob, *The World of Emma Lazarus* (1949)

LEACOCK, Stephen Butler
(1869–1944)

English-born Canadian humorist and economist, born in Swanmore, Hampshire. Educated at the University of Toronto, he became first a teacher, later a lecturer at McGill University, and in 1908 head of the economics department there. He wrote several books on his subject, including *Elements of Political Science* (1906), *Practical Political Economy* (1910) and *The Economic Prosperity of the British Empire* (1931). But it is as a humorist that he became widely known. Among his popular short stories, essays and parodies are *Literary Lapses* (1910), *Nonsense Novels* (1911), *Behind the Beyond* (1913), *Winsome Winnie* (1920) and *The Garden of Folly* (1924). He also wrote biographies of **Mark Twain** (1932) and **Dickens** (1933). *The Boy I Left Behind Me*, an autobiography, appeared in 1946.
▷D M Legate, *Stephen Leacock: a biography* (1970)

LEAR, Edward
(1812–88)

English artist, humorist and traveller, born in London. In 1832 he was engaged by the 13th Earl of Derby to make coloured drawings of the rare birds and animals in the menagerie at Knowsley Hall (Merseyside). Under the earl's patronage he travelled widely in Italy and Greece, making landscape sketches and oil paintings which he published in several travel books, including *Sketches of Rome* (1842) and *Illustrated Excursions in Italy* (1846). He became a friend of his patron's grandchildren, whom he entertained with nonsense limericks and other verse which he illustrated with his own sketches and first published (anonymously) as *A Book of Nonsense* in 1846. Later he published *Nonsense Songs, Stories, Botany, and Alphabets* (1870), *More Nonsense Rhymes* (1871) and *Laughable Lyrics* (1876). He spent most of his latter years in Italy.
▷S Chitty, *That Singular Person Called Lear* (1988)

LEAVIS, F(rank) R(aymond)
(1895–1978)

Influential English critic who taught at Cambridge University for the whole of his life. He first learned from **I A Richards**, but developed Richards's ideas about practical and close criticism into a kind of crusade against industrialization and 'mass culture'. His chief mentors were **D H Lawrence** and **Blake**. He was notoriously ill-mannered and paranoid in style, but had been badly treated at Cambridge, and had ample justification for his prickly attitudes. Few writers who came under his influence do not owe him something, but he is now less important as a polemicist—his battle against mass culture having been lost, and his other concerns having passed into the hands of the environmentalists—than as a gifted if somewhat narrow critic who extolled **Donne**, **Hopkins** and **T S Eliot**, at the expense of **Milton**, **Swinburne** and other exponents of what he took to be musical rhetoric. The oft-repeated judgement that he was 'the most important English-speaking critic of his time' is a debatable point—chiefly because of his unwillingness to see the virtues of those poets and novelists he disliked. His wife was **Q D Leavis**, also a noted critic.
▷M Bell, *F R Leavis* (1988)

LEAVIS, Q(ueenie) D(orothy)
(1906–81)

English literary critic. Born in London, she studied at Girton College, Cambridge, under **I A Richards**. Though her powerful sociological analysis of 19th-century fiction made a substantial impact on her husband **F R Leavis**, whom she married in 1929, she has only rarely (and posthumously) received full credit for it. This is partly due to the fact that, despite writing regularly for Leavis's journal *Scrutiny*, and continuing to publish perceptive essays and papers on literary subjects, she wrote only one book, *Fiction and the Reading Public* (1932). Though by no means a doctrinaire feminist, she had a particular interest in women's writing and wrote shrewdly about the **Brontë** sisters, **Jane Austen** and **Edith Wharton**. Some of her best essays were posthumously collected.

LEAVITT, David
(1961–)

American novelist and short-story writer, born in Pennsylvania. Brought up in Northern California, and educated at Yale, he then worked for a time in publishing in New York. His first collection of stories, *Family Dancing* (1984), demonstrated both his observant interest in emotional disturbances within middle-class American families, especially those caused by cancer and homosexuality, and his cool, sometimes dryly witty style. These themes were further explored in the novels *The Lost Language of Cranes* (1986), in which a family has to deal with the homosexuality of both father and son, and *Equal Affections* (1989), which explores the history and structure of a family deeply affected by the mother's cancer. Further stories appeared in *A Place I've Never Been* (1990).

LEBENSON, Micha Joseph
(1828–54)

Hebrew (Lithuanian) poet and brilliant translator from the German (**Schiller**'s *Virgil*), born in Vilna. His father was the great Haskalah ('Enlightenment') scholar Abraham Dov Lebenson (1794–1878). He also wrote historical epic poems.

LE CARRÉ, John, pseud of **David John Moore Cornwell**
(1931–)

English novelist, born in Poole, Dorset. He was educated at Sherborne School, Berne University, and, after military service in Austria, at Oxford. He taught French and German for two years at Eton before going into the British Foreign Service as second secretary in Bonn, and consul in Hamburg, from which post he resigned in 1964 to become a full-time writer. His novels present the unglamorous side of diplomacy and espionage, a world of boredom, squalor and shabby deceit in complete contrast to the popular spy fiction of **Ian Fleming**. His settings and characters have a compelling authenticity and he questions the morality of present-day diplomacy and traditional patriotic attitudes. His first published novel, *Call for The Dead* (1961), introduced his 'anti-hero' George Smiley, who appears in most of his stories. *A Murder of Quality* appeared in 1962, followed the next year by the very successful *The Spy Who Came In From The Cold*. After *The Looking-Glass War* (1965) and *A Small Town in Germany* (1968), a departure from his usual subject and style entitled *The Naive and Sentimental Lover* (1971) was not well received, and he returned to his former world with *Tinker, Tailor, Soldier, Spy* (1974), *The Honourable Schoolboy* (1977), *Smiley's People* (1980), *The Little Drummer Girl* (1983), *A Perfect Spy* (1986), *The Russia House* (1989) and *The Secret Pilgrim* (1992), in which Smiley takes his final bow. His most recent novel is *The Night Manager* (1993). Many of his novels have been successfully filmed or televised, although the presumed end of the Cold War may have removed his most fertile subject-matter.
▷E Homberger, *John Le Carré* (1986)

LE CLÉZIO, J(ean)-M(arie) G(ustave)
(1940–)

French philosophical novelist of highly individual style. His work is dominated by tremendous mythological or elemental oppositions and can be seen to form a single, continuous cycle representing the novelist's quest for truth. His early life was markedly peripatetic. He was born in Nice, educated there and in Africa, spending a year at Bristol University in England (1958–9), and a further year in London (1960–1). After taking another degree in Aix-en-Provence, he went to Bangkok to teach at the Buddhist University (1966–7), moving on to Mexico and spending the years 1969 to 1973 living with the Embara Indians in Panama. He returned to the south of France in 1973. His first novel was *Le Procès-Verbal* (1963, Eng trans *The Interrogation*, 1964), followed by *La Fièvre* (1965, 'Fever'), *Le Déluge* (1966, Eng trans *The Flood*, 1967) and *Le Livre des fuites* (1969, Eng trans *The Book of Flights*, 1971), among others. Thereafter, English-language interest in his work declined, though he is still read and admired in France. Following the publication of *Désert* (1980), his best book for many years, he was awarded the French Academy's Prix **Morand**.
▷J Waelti-Walters, *J-M G Le Clézio* (1977)

LECONTE DE LISLE, Charles Marie
(1818–94)

French poet, born in Réunion. After some years of travel he settled down to a literary life in Paris. He exercised a profound influence on all the younger poets, headed the school called *Parnassiens*, and succeeded to **Victor Hugo**'s chair at the Academy in 1886. His early poems appeared as *Poésies complètes* (1858). Other volumes are *Poèmes barbares* (1862) and *Poèmes tragiques* (1884); and he translated many classics. His verse is marked by regularity and faultlessness of form.
▷P Flottes, *Leconte de Lisle* (1954)

LEE, (Nelle) Harper
(1926–)

American novelist, born in Alabama and educated at Alabama State University. Her only novel, *To Kill A Mockingbird* (1960), was an immediate success, and has subsequently enhanced its reputation as a modern classic. Narrated by Scout, a six-year-old white tomboy in the American south, it is centred on a trial at which Scout's father is the defence lawyer for a black man accused of raping a white woman. It won a Pulitzer Prize in 1961, and was made into a highly successful film (1962) starring Gregory Peck.

LEE, Harriet
(1757–1851)

English novelist, born in London. She wrote with her sister, **Sophia Lee**, *The Canterbury Tales*, one of which was dramatized by **Byron** and called *Werner, or, The Inheritance*. Her other novels included *Errors of Innocence* (1786), an epistolary novel, and *Clare Lennox* (1797).

▷D Punter, *The Literature of Terror* (1980); K Rogers, *Feminism in 18th century England* (1982)

LEE, John Alfred Alexander
(1891–1982)

New Zealand politician and novelist, born in Dunedin. He won the DCM in World War I in France, where he lost an arm. He was a Labour MP for many years and member of cabinet as under-secretary in the 1935 and 1938 governments, but his bitter ambition and his vindictiveness towards Prime Minister Savage hastened Savage's death and his own expulsion. He formed his own party in 1939 but lost his seat in 1943. His novels *Children of the Poor* (1934), *The Hunted* (1936) and *Civilian into Soldier* (1937) are partly autobiographical; all his serious fiction is powerful but crude socialist propaganda, written originally for serialization in his own magazine *John A Lee's Weekly*, though *The Politician* did not appear until 1987, after his death. He wrote *Socialism in New Zealand* (1938) with an introduction by Clement Attlee and published a number of accounts of his political life.

▷*The John A Lee Diaries, 1936–40* (1981)

LEE, Laurie
(1914–)

English poet and author, born in Slad, Gloucestershire. He was educated at the village school and in Stroud, Gloucestershire. He worked as a scriptwriter for documentary films during the 1940s and his travels in many parts of the world are the subject of much of his writing. A nature-poet of great simplicity, his works include *The Sun My Monument* (1944), *The Bloom of Candles* (1947) and *My Many-Coated Man* (1955). *A Rose For Winter* (1955) describes his travels in Spain, and his autobiographical books, *Cider With Rosie* (1959), *As I Walked Out One Midsummer Morning* (1969) and *I Can't Stay Long* (1975) are widely acclaimed for their evocation of a rural childhood, and of life in the many countries he has visited. *A Moment of War*

(1991) takes up from the end of *As I Walked Out*, and recounts his experiences in Spain during the Civil War.

LEE, Nathaniel
(1649–92)

English dramatist. From Westminster he passed to Trinity College, Cambridge. He failed as an actor through nervousness (1672), produced nine or 10 tragedies between 1675 and 1682, and spent five years in Bedlam (1684–9). His best play is *The Rival Queens* (1677). He wrote with **Dryden** two plays, *Oedipus* and *The Duke of Guise*.

LEE, Sophia
(1750–1824)

English writer, sister of **Harriet Lee**. She enjoyed greater success as a dramatist than her sister, notably with her play *The Chapter of Accidents* (1780; the success of which enabled her to open a girls' school in Bath), and the verse tragedy *Almeyda, Queen of Grenada* (1796). Her historical novel *The Recess* (1783–5) was a success, and she also wrote a lengthy ballad, *The Hermit's Tale* (1787). Her epistolary novel *The Life of a Lover* (1804) has autobiographical elements.

▷D Punter, *The Literature of Terror* (1980); K Rogers, *Feminism in 18th century England* (1982)

LEE, Vernon, pseud of Violet Paget
(1856–1935)

English aesthetic philosopher, critic and novelist, born in Boulogne of English parentage. She travelled widely in her youth and settled in Florence. Studies of Italian and Renaissance art were followed by her philosophical study, *The Beautiful* (1913), one of the best expositions of the empathy theory of art. She also wrote two novels and a dramatic trilogy, *Satan the Waster* (1920), giving full rein to her pacifism.

▷P Gunn, *Vernon Lee: Violet Paget, 1856– 1935* (1969)

LEEUW, Aart van der
(1876–1932)

Dutch poet and novelist, born in Delft. He is one of the more interesting of now almost completely neglected Dutch writers, having taken his inspiration from the English poet **Thomas Traherne**. The style of his novels—his best work—has been mistaken as 'romantic', but in fact he was a mystic trapped in a century inimical to his genius. He made his real mark late in his life, with the novels *Ik en mijn speelman* (1927, 'I and My Minstrel') and *De kleine Rudolf* (1930, 'Little Rudolf').

LE FANU, Joseph Sheridan
(1814–73)

Irish novelist and journalist, born in Dublin, a grand-nephew of **Richard Brinsley Sheridan**. Called to the Bar in 1839, he soon abandoned law for journalism. He began writing for the *Dublin University Magazine*, of which he became editor and proprietor (1869), and later bought three Dublin newspapers. His novels include *The House by the Churchyard* (1863), and the best-known of them, *Uncle Silas* (1864). His short stories are collected in *In a Glass Darkly* (1872), and he wrote 14 other works, remarkable for their pre-occupation with the supernatural. His *Poems* were edited by **Alfred Perceval Graves** (1896). His reputation, which had fallen into neglect, was restored by the publication of *Madam Crowl's Ghost* (1923), edited by **M R James**, and he is again recognized as an important writer in the fields of mystery, suspense and the supernatural.
▷ I Melada, *Sheridan Le Fanu* (1987)

LEFFLAND, Ella
(1931–)

American novelist and short-story writer. She was born and grew up on the West Coast, and the San Fransciso Bay area, in particular, forms the setting for much of her fiction. *Love out of Season* (1974) describes the hectic San Francisco scene of the 1960s from a woman's perspective. Some of her stories are collected in *Last Courtesies* (1980).

LE FORT, Gertrud von
(1876–1971)

German novelist and poet, born into an aristocratic, originally Huguenot, family in Minden. As a Protestant she wrote her most famous collection of poems, *Hymnen an die Kirche* (1924, Eng trans *Hymns to the Church*, 1937); then she became a Catholic, and wrote dedicated novels and poems of high competence in the interests of her new faith. Her *Die Letze am Schafort* (1931, Eng trans *The Song of the Scaffold*, 1953), formed the basis for Poulenc's well-known opera *Dialogues de Carmelites* (1956), which in turn inspired the film script by **Bernanos** on the same theme. Selected novellas are in *The Judgement of the Sea* (1962).
▷ I O'Boyle, *Gertrude le Fort: An Introduction to her Prose* (1964)

LE FRANC, Marie
(1879–1964)

French (Breton) novelist who emigrated to Canada and there published her first novel, *Grand Louis l'Innocent* (1927), which had a great success. Her work deals with simple French Canadians, whose lyrical inner lives she sought to convey.
▷ *Corymbe*, special number devoted to Marie Le Franc (1936, in French)

LE GALLIENNE, Richard
(1866–1947)

English writer, born of Guernsey ancestry in Liverpool. In 1891 he became a London journalist but later lived in New York. He published many volumes of prose and verse from 1887, when his first collection, *My Ladies Sonnets*, was published. He was an original member of the Rhymers Club with **Yeats**, **Wilde** and others. His style, that of the later 19th century, is old-fashioned, but his best books are *Quest of the Golden Girl* (1896), *The Romantic Nineties* (1926) and *From a Paris Garret* (1936).

LE GUIN, Ursula, née Kroeber
(1929–)

American science-fiction writer, born in Berkeley, California, the daughter of the anthropologist Alfred Louis Kroeber (1876–1960). She was educated at Radcliffe College and Columbia University. A prolific writer both for adults and children, she has demonstrated that it is possible to work in genre and be taken seriously as a writer. Much of her work focuses on subjective views of a universe incorporating numerous habitable worlds, each spawned by beings from the 'Hain'. Hain novels include *Rocannon's World* (1966), *Plant of Exile* (1966), *The Left Hand of Darkness* (1969) and *The Word for World is Forest* (1976). In a prodigious oeuvre for children, known as the 'Earthsea' trilogy—*A Wizard of Earthsea* (1968), *The Tombs of Atuan* (1971) and *The Farthest Shore* (1972)—she depicts a magical but threatening world where every village has its small-time sorcerer and the forces of evil are uncomfortably close. She continued this trilogy in an overtly feminist vein with *Tehanu* (1990).
▷ E C Cogell, *Understanding Ursula K. Le Guin* (1990)

LEGUIZAMÓN, Martiniano
(1858–1935)

Argentinian novelist and dramatist, born in Rosario del Tala. One play, *Calandria*, 1895, reached the stage. The collection *Recuerdos de la tierra* (1896, 'Memories of the Land'), like his play, dealt with legends such as that of the gaucho outlaw Calandria, murdered by the police. He later more or less abandoned fiction, to become a historian.

LEHMANN, Geoffrey John
(1940–)

Australian poet, editor and taxation specialist, born in Sydney. After reading German

Literature at Sydney University he practised as a solicitor and then taught commercial law. His poetry has a strong sense of times past; whether dealing with the life of his father or of a Roman general, his clear verse gives shape and life to a loved image. His first book, *The Ilex Tree* (1965, with **Les Murray**) was followed by five others including *From an Australian Country Sequence* (1973) and *Nero's Poems* (1981). His *Selected Poems* was published in 1976. As editor he has produced *Comic Australian Verse* (1972), and with Robert Gray has co-edited *The Younger Australian Poets* (1983) and *Australian Poetry in the Twentieth Century* (1991). His legal and artistic *alter ego* has written a standard work on taxation law and *Australian Primitive Painters* (1977).

LEHMANN, (Rudolph) John Frederick
(1907–87)

English poet and writer, born in Bourne End, Buckinghamshire, son of Rudolph Chambers Lehmann. He was educated at Eton and Trinity College, Cambridge, and founded the periodical *New Writing* in book format, *New Writing* (1936–41). He was managing director of the Hogarth Press with Leonard and **Virginia Woolf** (1938–46), and ran his own firm, John Lehmann Ltd, with his sister, **Rosamond Lehmann**, as co-director from 1946 to 1953. In 1954 he inaugurated *The London Magazine*, which he edited until 1961. His first publications were volumes of poetry, including *A Garden Revisited* (1931) and *Forty Poems* (1942). He also wrote a novel, *Evil was Abroad* (1938), and studies of *Edith Sitwell* (1952), *Virginia Woolf and her World* (1975) and *Rupert Brooke* (1980). He wrote his autobiography in three volumes, *The Whispering Gallery* (1955), *I am my Brother* (1960) and *The Ample Proposition* (1966). His *Poems New and Selected* appeared in 1986.
▷ *In My Own Time* (3 vols, 1969)

LEHMANN, Rosamond Nina
(1901–90)

English novelist, daughter of Rudolph Chambers Lehmann and sister of Beatrix and **John Lehmann**, born in High Wycombe, Buckinghamshire. She was educated at Girton College, Cambridge, which provided the background for her first novel, *Dusty Answer* (1927). Her novels show a fine sensitive insight into character and her women especially are brilliantly drawn. Among her other books are *A Note in Music* (1930), *An Invitation to the Waltz* (1932) and its sequel *The Weather in the Streets* (1936), and *The Echoing Grove* (1953). Her last novel was *A Sea-Grape Tree* (1970). She also wrote a play, *No More Music* (1939), and a volume of short

stories, *The Gypsy's Baby* (1946). She produced the autobiographical *The Swan in the Evening* in 1967. She later developed a belief in spiritualism, and became President of the College of Psychic Studies.
▷ G Tindall, *Rosamond Lehmann: an appreciation* (1985)

LEHMANN, Wilhelm
(1882–1968)

German poet, critic and novelist, born in Venezuela (his father was a Lübeck merchant). His influence on the modernist poets who became his successors was wide and decisive (eg on **Eich**, **Krolow** and many others); yet his own procedures were not modernist but, as a critic has pointed out, traditional in the manner of **Robert Graves** or, in particular, **Robert Frost**. He was a prisoner-of-war in England during World War I. His early work consisted of novels and stories; he did not begin to publish poems until he was over 50. He initiated, under the influence of his close friend **Oscar Loerke**, and inspired by his reading of **Goethe**, a new kind of poetry: a pantheistic and Symbolist nature poetry in which everything is to be interpreted in the light of the 'Green God' which refers man back to the nature from which he has been estranged: 'God and the world appear only to the summons of mysteriously planned syllables'. His novels and stories, less memorable, have been described as 'rhapsodically idyllic'.
▷ C Middleton and M Hamburger (eds), *Modern German Poetry 1910–1969* (1962)

LEHTONEN, Joel
(1881–1934)

Finnish poet, translator (**Stendhal** and others) and novelist, born in Saaminki. His earlier, neo-romantic work, in verse and prose, shows the influence of **Nietzsche**; but with the novel *Putkinotko* (1919), his masterpiece, a Finnish counterpart to **Goncharov**'s *Oblomov*, he came into his own. The rest of his life was spent in a series of vain attempts to defeat depression through writing, each book of the greatest interest, but ultimately he killed himself in Huopalahti.

LEIBER, Fritz Reuter, Jr
(1910–92)

American fantasy and science-fiction writer, born in Chicago. He studied psychology and physiology at the University of Chicago, and worked as an editor and a teacher. His first story, 'Two Sought Adventure' (1939), launched his sophisticated and increasingly complex *Fafhrd and the Grey Mouser* heroic-fantasy series, characters he returned to throughout his career. Other important fantasy works include *Conjure Wife* (1953) and *Our Lady of Darkness* (1977). His science fiction has generally been seen as secondary to his work in fantasy, but he has made significant contributions to the genre, notably in the short story, but also with the novels *The Big Time* (1961) and *The Wanderer* (1964).

LEINO, Eino, pseud of **Armas Eino Leopold Lönnbohm**
(1878–1926)

Finnish poet and novelist. He published his first collection, *Maaliskuun lauluja* (1896, 'Spring Songs'), aged only 18. He developed the *Kalevala* metre into a distinctive, sombrely lyrical style of his own, best exemplified in the two volumes of *Helkavirsiä* (1903, 1916, 'Whitsongs'), the second of which is shadowed by his reaction to World War I. He also wrote novels, and made fine translations of **Dante**, **Racine**, **Corneille**, **Goethe** and **Schiller**.
▷P Saarikoski, *Eino 'Leino'* (1974)

LEIRIS, Michel
(1901–90)

French anthropologist, writer and poet, born in Paris. After an early involvement with the Surrealist movement (1925–9), he joined the trans-African Dakar–Djibouti expedition of 1931 to 1933. He returned to study and take up anthropology as a profession, and went on to travel widely in Africa and the Caribbean. His writings, many of them autobiographical, as in *L'Âge d'homme* (1939, Eng trans *Manhood*, 1966) and *La règle du jeu* (4 vols, 1948–76, 'The Rules of the Game'), are marked by a consuming interest in poetry, and he combined anthropology with a distinguished career as a literary and art critic. His major works include *L'Afrique Fantôme* (1934, 'Phantoms of Africa') and *Afrique Noire: la création plastique* (1967, Eng trans *African Art*, 1968).
▷M Nadeau, *Michel Leiris et la quadrature du cercle* (1963)

LEIVICK, Halper
(1882–1962)

Yiddish poet and dramatist from Minsk who was arrested in Russia, for revolutionary activities, in 1912. He managed to escape while he was being transported to Siberia; eventually (1913) he went to New York and settled there. For a long time his mystical, strident poetry had a large following amongst readers of Yiddish; now it is falling into neglect. He wrote some 20 plays, of which the most successful was *The Golem* (1925).

LELAND, Charles Godfrey, pseud **Hans Breitmann**
(1825–1903)

American author, born in Philadelphia. He graduated at Princeton in 1845, and afterwards studied at Heidelberg, Munich and Paris. He was admitted to the Philadelphia Bar in 1851, but turned to journalism. From 1869 he resided chiefly in England and Italy, and investigated the gypsies, a subject on which between 1873 and 1891 he published four valuable works. He is best known for his poems in 'Pennsylvania Dutch', the famous *Hans Breitmann Ballads* (1871; continued in 1895). Other similar volumes gained him great popularity during his lifetime. He also translated the works of **Heinrich Heine**.
▷*Memoirs* (1893)

LELCHUK, Alan
(1938–)

American novelist, born in New York, educated at Columbia University there, and in London and at Stanford University, California. He was a member of the faculty and writer-in-residence for 15 years (1966–81) at Brandeis University, Massachusetts, and was associated with the literary journal *Modern Occasions*. Lelchuk's scandalous debut was the anarchic *American Mischief* (1973), a multifaceted novel about campus revolt, the relationship between liberalism and libertinism, and the questionable value of 'art' over 'life', whose complexities were overlooked in the furore over a scene in which **Mailer** (who sued) is assassinated in what was intended to be the most demeaning way imaginable. It was clear that Lelchuk was attempting to satirize the excesses of fellow-Jews like Mailer and **Philip Roth**, and similar themes emerged in his later books. *Shrinking: The Beginning of My Own Ending* (1978), his third novel, is a perceptive satire on the literary and psychic odysseys of the sixties, carried out as they were (Mailer and Roth again) in the full glare of media publicity. *Miriam at Thirty-Four* (1974) and *Miriam in Her Forties* (1985) tells the story of a gifted but unstable photographer who serves as a barometer of cultural obsessions and hang-ups.

LEM, Stanisław
(1922–)

Polish science-fiction writer, born in Lwów. He completed his medical studies after World War II, and began to write fiction. He is widely regarded as one of the most significant literary voices working in the science-fiction genre, and his work is characterized by great seriousness of purpose balanced by brilliant black humour and cutting satire, and a resistance to any attempts to impose absolute systems of explanation on a fluid reality. His major books include the 'Ijon Tichy' series of stories (from 1957) and the novel *Solaris* (1961). His other writings included **Borges**-like essays and imaginary reviews, and books of startling cosmological speculation.

▷ *Wysoki zamek* (1966)

LEMAÎTRE, François Élie Jules
(1853–1914)

French playwright and critic, born in Vennecy, Loiret. His articles, written first for the *Journal des débats*, were issued in book form as *Impressions de théâtre* (1888–98, 'Impressions of a Theatre-goer'), and those written for *Revue bleue* on modern French literature became *Les Contemporains* (1886–99, 'Our Contemporaries'). A masterly critic with a charming, lucid style, he also wrote *Rousseau* (1907), *Racine* (1908), *Fénelon* (1910) and *Chateaubriand* (1912). His plays and short stories are less distinguished.

LEMOINE, Sir James MacPherson
(1825–1912)

Canadian naturalist and writer, born in Quebec. He became superintendent of inland revenue at Quebec in 1858. He studied archaeology, ornithology and other sciences, wrote on Canadian history and was the first Canadian author to receive a knighthood.

LEMON, Mark
(1809–70)

English author and journalist, born in London. In 1835 he wrote a farce, followed by several melodramas, operettas, novels (the best of which is, perhaps, *Falkner Lyle*, 1866), children's stories, a *Jest Book* (1864) and essays. In 1841 he helped to establish *Punch*, becoming first joint editor (with **Henry Mayhew**), then sole editor from 1843.

▷ A A Adrian, *Mark Lemon: first editor of Punch* (1966)

LEMONNIER, Antoine Louis Camille
(1844–1913)

Belgian writer, writing in French, born in Ixelles near Brussels. He took up art criticism in 1863, and by his novels *Un Mâle* (1881, Eng trans *A Male*, 1917), *Happe-Chair* (1888) and other works, full of strong Flemish realism and mysticism, won fame as one of Belgium's leading prose writers. He wrote books on art, including *Gustave Courbet* (1878), *Alfred Stevens et son oeuvre* (1906, 'Alfred Stevens and his Work') and *L'École Belge de la peinture* (1906, 'The Belgian School of Painting').

▷ B M Woodridge, in *Le roman belge contemporain* (1930)

LENAU, Nikolaus, in full Nikolaus Niembsch von Strehlenau
(1802–50)

German poet, born in Czatad in Hungary. He studied law and medicine at Vienna. He suffered from extreme melancholy and in 1844 he became insane, dying in an asylum near Vienna. His poetic power is best shown in his short lyrics, collections of which appeared in 1832, 1838 and 1844. His longer pieces include *Faust* (1836), *Savonarola* (1837) and *Die Albigenser* (1842, 'The Albigensians').

▷ E Castle, *Nikolaus Lenau* (1902)

LENCLOS, Ninon de, pseud of Anne de Lenclos
(1620–1705)

French feminist and light poet, described by male literary historians as a 'courtesan', who was born and died in Paris. She founded a salon which favoured Jansenists, was a close friend to **Saint Evremond**, and could hold her own with **La Rochefoucauld** and the other thinkers and wits of her time.

L'ENGLE, Madeleine
(1918–)

American novelist, born in New York City and educated at Smith College, Northampton, Massachusetts and at the New School for Social Research in New York. A prolific writer for children, who also writes for adults, she imbues her work with explicitly Christian ideas and morals. Described by one critic as 'perilously near the sugary', and by another as 'one of the truly important writers of juvenile fiction in recent decades', her most popular titles include *A Wrinkle in Time* (1962, **Newbery** Medal) and *The Young Unicorns* (1968), both of which combine elements of fantasy with tough ethical concerns.

LENGYEL, Menyhért or Melchior
(1880–1957)

Hungarian dramatist who lived in America for much of his life. He scored many successes in the theatre: the most famous was *Taifun* (1909, Eng trans *Typhoon*, 1912), a romantic thriller about Japanese agents in Paris. He wrote the scenario for Bartók's ballet, *The Miraculous Mandarin*.

LENNEP, Jacob van
(1802–68)

Dutch writer and lawyer, born in Amsterdam. He achieved a great reputation for legal knowledge. His most popular works were comedies, such as *Het Dorp aan die Grenzen* (1831, 'The Village on the Frontier'). Of his novels, several, such as *De Roos van Dekama* (1836, Eng trans *The Rose of Dekama*, 1846)

and *De Pleegzoon* (1835, Eng trans *The Adopted Son*, 1847), have been translated.
▷T van Lennep, *Het Leven van Mr Jacob van Lennep* (1909)

LENNGREN, Anna Maria
(1754–1817)

Swedish poet and journalist. Born in Uppsala, she received a good education and became an accomplished translator from French and Latin. She joined the radical *Stockholms-Posten* as a journalist in 1780. She published—up to 1797 anonymously—elegant satires which renewed and invigorated Swedish journalism, and sharply observed, humorously realistic poems. The latter, superbly skilful in their handling of metre and rhyme and characterized by a simple and mercilessly precise language, convey vivid images of a broad range of contemporary life, and expose the ruling classes to an intrepid satire. A number of her poems were set to music and remain popular songs to this day.
▷'Från Smakens Tempel till Parnassen. Om Anna Maria Lenngren', in E Møller Jensen (ed), *Nordisk kvinnolitteraturhistoria*, vol I: *I Guds namn* (1993)

LENNOX, Charlotte, née Ramsay
(c.1729–1804)

British novelist and playwright, born in New York, whose early adventures inform the spirited character of her fictional heroines. Sent from New York, where her father was posted, to England when she was 15, she found herself unprovided for when her father died, and supported herself as an actress and writer. Her first novel, *The Life of Harriot Stuart* (1750), is a romantic adventure yarn, but her next and most famous work, *The Female Quixote* (1752), is a satirical romp through the life of Arabella, a young lady besotted with French romantic novels. She also wrote *Shakespeare Illustrated* (1753–4), an examination of the playwright's sources, translated many French works, and was much admired by **Samuel Johnson**, who cites her under Talent in his Dictionary.

LENORMAND, Henri René
(1882–1951)

French dramatist, born in Paris. He was the author of *Les Possédés* (1909, 'The Possessed'), *Le Mangeur de rêves* (1922, 'The Eater of Dreams'), a modern equivalent of *Oedipus Rex*, *L'Homme et ses fantômes* (1924, 'Man and his Phantoms'), and several other plays in which **Freud**'s theory of subconscious motivation is adapted to dramatic purposes. He discusses the aesthetics of his dramatic

style in *Confessions d'un auteur dramatique* (1949, 'Confessions of a Playwright').
▷P Blanchart, *Le théatre de Lenormand* (1947)

LENZ, Jakob Michael Reinhold
(1751–92)

German author, born in Livonia. He was one of the young authors who surrounded **Goethe** in Strasbourg. He first wrote two plays which were well received, *Der Hofmeister* (1774, 'The Steward') and *Die Soldaten* (1776, 'The Soldiers'). Like all the 'Sturm und Drang' poets he was a fervent admirer of **Shakespeare**, and this was expressed in his *Anmerkungen übers Theater* (1774, 'Remarks on the Theatre'). He was a gifted writer of lyrics, some of them being at first attributed to Goethe, and also wrote several novels, but of lesser quality. He suffered a mental breakdown while still young and died in poverty.

LENZ, Siegfried
(1926–)

German novelist and short-story writer, born and raised in the Masurian Lakes area of East Prussia. He studied philosophy and English literature, then worked for the newspaper *Die Welt* from 1948 before becoming a full-time writer three years later. His realist, socially committed novels display a tender, at times ponderous, concern for the individual in a dehumanizing age. *Stadtgespräch* (1963, 'Town Conversation') centres on a would-be self-sacrificing resistance leader; *Deutschstunde* (1968, 'German Lesson') analyses the relationship between a young hooligan and his policeman father; while in *Das Vorbild* (1973, 'The Example') three teachers fail to find decent role models for the young.

LEONARD, Elmore John
(1925–)

American thriller writer, born in New Orleans. He lived in Dallas, Oklahoma City and Memphis before his family settled in Detroit in 1935. During World War II he served in the US navy and afterwards studied English literature at Detroit University. Throughout the 1950s he worked in advertising as a copywriter but since 1967 he has concentrated on screenplays and novels, remarkable for their relentless pace and vivid dialogue. Regarded as the foremost crime writer in America, his books include *Unknown Man No. 89* (1977), *The Switch* (1978), *Gold Coast* (1980), *Stick* (1983), *La Brava* (1983), *Glitz* (1985) and *Touch* (1987).
▷D Geherin, *Elmore Leonard* (1989)

LÉONARD, Nicholas-Germain
(1744–93)

French minor poet and sentimental novelist, born in La Basse-Terre in Guadeloupe. His poetry, influenced by that of the then popular Swiss **Salomon Gessner**, and by the Latin poet **Tibullus**, reflects his over-sensitive temperament and the unhappiness caused to him by the failure of his first love. A diplomat, he was about to embark from France to serve in Guadeloupe when he died.

▷W M Kerby, *The Life, Diplomatic Career and Literary Activity of Nicholas-Germaine Léonard* (1925)

LEONARD, Tom
(1944–)

Scottish poet, born in Glasgow, whose phoneticized dialect verse has been the despair of 'southron' readers and the more po-faced of his compatriots; in the 1973 *Poems*, he provided an RP 'translation' in parallel text for the benefit of the former. Like **Edwin Morgan**, whom he encountered at Glasgow University in the late sixties, he is a dedicated experimenter with poetic form, attempting everything from strict metres and forms to linguistic 'found objects', complex word association to snippets of conversation heard in bus queues. His first published collection was the slim *Six Glasgow Poems* (1969), followed by *A Priest Came On at Merkland Street* (1970), *Poems* (1973) and *Bunnit Husslin* (1975). The best of his early work was collected as *Intimate Voices: Writing 1965–83* (1984). He edited *Radical Renfrew: Poetry from the French Revolution to the First World War* (1990).

LEONOV, Leonid
(1899–)

Russian novelist and dramatist, born in Moscow, the most gifted writer in his country to accept and try to accommodate himself to the Stalinist regime. From the West his works, continually sniped at by orthodox critics in the Soviet Union, have been viewed as paradigmatic of the struggle between creative individualism and Marxist–Stalinist theory. In his early novella *Konets melkogo cheloveka* (1924, 'End of a Petty Man'), written while the atmosphere was comparatively free of interference, he prophesied his creative future, but reversed the roles of writer and scientist—a scientist is persuaded by a **Dostoyevsky**an double to destroy all his research. He was initially influenced by **Leskov** and **Gogol** in his use of *skaz*, highly individualized first-person narration. Gradually he took, almost reluctantly, the direction of realism, which, as things became more difficult, turned into half-observance of socialist realism. His important novels are *Barsuki* (1924, Eng trans *The Badgers*, 1947), *Vor* (1927, Eng trans *The Thief*, 1931), about a man who cannot accept the New Economic Policy, and *Russkiy les* (1953, Eng trans *The Russian Forest*, 1966),

in which he obliquely criticized the crazed and humanly wasteful policies of Stalin. His plays, well-made psychological thrillers, generally avoided the problems he faced as a novelist. The final verdict upon him is likely to be that he was a great writer lost to Stalinist dogma.

▷E J Brown, *Russian Literature Since the Revolution* (1969)

LEOPARDI, Giacomo
(1798–1837)

Major Italian poet, born of poor but noble parentage in Recanati. At the age of 16 he had read all the Latin and Greek classics, could write French, Spanish, English and Hebrew, and wrote a commentary on Plotinus. After a short stay in Rome, he devoted himself to literature, but finding his home increasingly unbearable he began to travel and, an invalid, lived successively in Bologna, Florence, Milan and Pisa. In 1833 he accompanied his friend Ranieri to Naples, and there in constant bodily anguish and hopeless despondency he lived until his death. His pessimism was unquestionably the genuine expression of Leopardi's deepest nature as well as of his reasoned conviction. He was specially gifted as a writer of lyrics, which were collected under the title *I Canti* (1831, Eng trans *The Poems*, 1893) and are among the most beautiful in Italian literature. His prose works include the dialogues and essays classed as *Operette Morali* (1827, trans in a bilingual edn under original title, 1983), and his *Pensieri* (7 vols, 1898–1900, 'Thoughts') and letters.

▷H H Whitfield, *Giacomo Leopardi* (1954)

LEOPOLD, Jan Hendrik
(1865–1925)

Dutch Symbolist poet, born in s' Hertogenbosch. He was an early member of the 'Men of the Eighties' group, comprising **Verwey** and others. Deaf and lonely, he turned, as so many Dutchmen did at that time, to Eastern mysticism—then to Persian poetry and to the philosophy of Spinoza. He adapted ancient Sufic poetry to his own ends, and wrote technically flawless lyrics in which there is expressed much beautiful despair. Available in English translation are *The Flute* (1949) and *The Valley of Irdin* (1957).

LE PAN, Douglas
(1914–93)

Canadian poet, novelist, professor and diplomat—'man of letters and man of affairs', born in Toronto and educated at the university there and at Oxford. His first collection, *The Wounded Prince* (1948), charts a perilous voyage 'into the dark interior'—of mind and heart—in the symbolic craft of a Canadian *coureur de bois* canoe. He received the Governor General's Award for his second volume of poetry, *The Net and the Sword* (1953), and again in 1964, for a novel, *The Deserter*. *Weathering It* (1987) collects the elegant work of 40 years.

▷S C Hamilton, 'European Emblem and Canadian Image', in *Mosaic III: 2* (1970); J M Kertzer, 'The Wounded Eye', in *Studies in Canadian Literature* (1981)

LEPROHON, Rosanna
(1829–79)

Canadian novelist, born in Montreal, the mother of 13 children and the author of several novels acclaimed as some of the truest portraits of 19th-century French–Canadian life. Five of these books were serialized in the *Literary Garland* between 1847 and 1851. Her three major titles are *The Manor House of de Villerai* (1860), *Antoinette de Mirecourt* (1864) and *Armand Durand* (1868). In all three she managed to communicate the French–Canadian viewpoint to an English–Canadian audience.

▷C Gerson, *Three Writers of Victorian Canada and their Works* (1983)

LE QUEUX, William Tufnell
(1864–1927)

English mystery and espionage writer, an immensely prolific author whose backlog of manuscripts was still appearing several years after his death. Born in London, he was educated by tutors there and in Italy; he also studied painting at the Louvre and was an accomplished artist. Le Queux worked as Foreign Editor of the *Globe* (1890–3) and thereafter as a freelance writer, sending back despatches from the First Balkan War in 1912. His overseas contacts added a gloss to the story (one he did much to encourage) that he was a spy himself and his claim to have an inside track on political intrigues in the Habsburg and Hohenzollern courts gained some credence in 1914 when the outbreak of war confirmed the gloomy prognostications of quasi-fictional propaganda like *The Invasion of 1910, with a Full Account of the Siege of London* (1906). Le Queux's novels had long been anti-German, and after the invasion of Belgium he readily turned his hand to atrocity stories. After the war, he emigrated to Switzerland, where he continued writing, publishing almost 200 books—novels, short-story collections and propaganda—in his lifetime, and several more from beyond the grave.

▷N St Barbe Sladen, *The Real Le Queux* (1938)

LERMONTOV, Mikhail Yurevich
(1814–41)

Russian poet, born of Scottish extraction (Learmont) in Moscow. He attended Moscow University for a short time and then the military cavalry school of St Petersburg, where he received a commission in the guards. A poem written in 1837 on the death of **Alexander Pushkin** caused his arrest and he was sent to the Caucasus. Reinstated, he was again banished following a duel with the son of the French ambassador. Another duel was the cause of his death in 1841. He wrote from an early age, but much of his work was not published until the last years of his short life and his fame was posthumous. The sublime scenery of the Caucasus inspired his best poetic pieces, such as 'The Novice', 'The Demon', 'Ismail Bey', and others. His novel, *Geroy nashevo vremeni* (1839, Eng trans *A Hero of Our Times*, 1854), is a masterpiece of prose writing. He wrote also a romantic verse play, *Maskarad* (1842, 'Masquerade').

▷J Garrard, *Mikhail Lermontov* (1982)

LERNER, Laurence
(1925–)

South African-born British poet, novelist and critic, born in Cape Town. After a distinguished academic career in South Africa and England, he became a professor at Vanderbilt University, Tennessee. Best known as a critic, he is generally regarded as a sound, traditional, even if not adventurous, poet. *Selected Poems* (1984) is representative.

LERNET-HOLENIA, Alexander
(1897–)

Austrian playwright, novelist and poet, born in Vienna of (on his father's side) Franco–Belgian stock. He fought as a cavalry officer on the Russian front in World War I. His experience of the collapse of the Habsburg Empire, as in the case of **Joseph Roth**, was catastrophic; but he took a different and more defiantly nostalgic approach. He has been accused of being 'facile', and certainly he wrote (excellent) detective stories and other 'entertainments'; but his best works are far from facile. He was first successful as a playwright, with such brilliant comedies as *Ollapotrida* (1926, 'Nasty Hotchpotch'), which have been noted for their theatricality. Of his many and diverse novels, *Mars im Widder* (1941, 'Mars in Aries'), is a fine oblique critique of the Nazis who had just taken over his country. He was also a critic and biographer.

LEROUX, Etienne, pseud of **Stephanus Petrus Daniel Le Roux**
(1922–)

South African novelist (writing in Afrikaans), author of the 'phantasmal' trilogy *Sewe Dae by die Silbersteins* (1962, Eng trans *Seven Days at the Silbersteins*, 1967), which was praised by **Graham Greene** and other critics but has not yet found a wide audience. It is a strange but eventually rewarding novel, constructed on **Jung**ian concepts, and pessimistically implying that 'individuality' in the strictly Jungian sense is impossible in the Western world. It was followed by more novels, including *18–44* (1967).

LE SAGE, Alain René
(1668–1747)

French novelist and dramatist, born in Sarzeau in Brittany. In 1692 he went to Paris to study law, but an early marriage drove him to seek his fortune in literature. The Abbé de Lionne, who had a good Spanish library, allowed Le Sage free access to it, with a pension of 600 livres. The first fruit was a volume (1700) containing two plays in imitation of Rojas and **Lope de Vega**. In 1702 *Le Point d'honneur* ('A Point of Honour'), from Rojas, failed on the stage. His next venture (1704) was a remake of Avellaneda's *Don Quixote*. In 1707 *Don César Ursin*, from **Calderón de la Barca**, was played with success at court, and *Crispin rival de son maître* ('Crispin, His Master's Rival') in the city; but more successful was the *Diable boiteux* ('The Devil with a Limp', largely based on **Luiz Vélez de Guevara**). In 1708 the Théâtre Français accepted his work but shelved one play and rejected another, which later became his famous *Turcaret*. In 1715 *Gil Blas* (vols 1 and 2) came out, followed between 1717 and 1721 by an attempt at an *Orlando*. In 1724 came volume three of *Gil Blas*; in 1726 a largely extended *Diable boiteux*; in 1732 *Guzman de Alfarache* and *Robert Chevalier de Beauchêne*; in 1734 *Estebanillo Gonzalez*; in 1735 vol four of *Gil Blas* and the *Journée des Parques* ('The Day of the Fates'); between 1736 and 1738 the *Bachelier de Salamanque*; in 1739 his plays, in two vols; in 1740 *La Valise trouvée* ('A Suitcase Discovered'), a volume of letters; and in 1743 the *Mélange amusant*, a collection of facetiae. The death of his son (1743), a promising actor, and his own increasing infirmities, made him abandon Paris and literary life, and retreat with his wife and daughter to Boulogne, where his second son held a canonry, and he lived there until his death in his 80th year. Le Sage's reputation as a dramatist and as a novelist rests in each case on one work: on *Turcaret* and *Gil Blas* respectively. Some critics deny originality to one who borrowed ideas, incidents and tales from others as Le Sage did, but he was the first to perceive the capabilities of the picaresque novel. His delightful style makes him the prince of raconteurs, and the final effect of his work is all his own.
▷ E Lintilhac, *Alain Le Sage* (1893)

LESKOV, Nicolai Semyonovich
(1831–95)

Russian novelist and short-story writer, born in Gorokhovo, Oryol province. His parents dying when he was 17, he had a picaresque career in the provinces before becoming, aged 30, a journalist in St Petersburg. *No Way Out* (1864) and *At Daggers Drawn* (1871) met with critical disparagement, being insufficiently innovative for the mood of the time. Despite the disdain of reviewers, his work slowly accumulated a faithful general readership, who responded to his wit, narrative power and vibrant use of common speech. His first major work was the short story 'Lady Macbeth of the Mtsensk District' (1865), which was first published in **Dostoyevsky**'s periodical *Epoch*. His volumes of short stories include *Details of Episcopal Life* (1880), while his most enduring longer fiction is the novel *Cathedral Folk* (1872).

LESLIE, Sir Shane (John Randolph)
(1885–1971)

Irish writer, born in Glaslough, County Monaghan, into a conservative Irish Protestant landed family. Educated at Eton, Paris University and King's College, Cambridge, he visited Russia in 1907 and became friendly with **Tolstoy**. He was converted to Roman Catholicism in 1908 and unsuccessfully contested Londonderry in the Irish Nationalist interest in 1910. He published poems of some quality and produced a brilliant analysis of the pre-war generation in *The End of a Chapter* (1916). Under the influence of **Henry Adams** he followed it with a startling attempt at Irish geopolitics, *The Celt and the World*, intended to attract the Anglophobe Irish–Americans to the Allied cause: it influenced the young **F Scott Fitzgerald** but was otherwise forgotten and never published in Britain. He wrote impressive novels based on his boyhood and youth, *Doomsland*, *The Oppidan* and *The Cantab*, and published some useful clerical biographies, investigated the relations of George IV and Mrs Fitzherbert (from whom he was descended), and wrote cautious memoirs, as well as some good short stories with faintly chilling supernatural themes.

LÉSMIAN, Boleslaw, pseud of **Boleslaw Lesman**
(1878–1937)

Polish poet and translator (of, in particular, **Poe**), born in Warsaw; he was educated in Kiev. He was cautious in what he published, producing only three collections in Polish in his lifetime. His earliest poetry was written in Russian. Known as 'the poets' poet', and a highly original one, he was mainly influenced in his thinking by **Bergson**. His poetry

abounds in neologisms, called 'Lésmianisms' by critics in his lifetime. A cult figure, he was recognized as a major poet only after the end of World War II. To be understood, his poetry needs to be read in the context of Russian Symbolism from which he drew his initial inspiration. It is steeped in allusion to Polish folklore: 'Lésmian,' wrote a Polish critic, 'seemed to be outside the current literary fashion, a symbolist who would persist with his weird ... coinages and macabre ballads ... His originality is now undisputed.'
▷ R H Stone, *Boleslaw Lésmian: The Poet and his Poetry* (1976)

LESSING, Doris May, née **Tayler**
(1919–)
Rhodesian writer, born in Kermanshah, Iran, the daughter of a British army captain. Her family moved to Salisbury in Southern Rhodesia (now Zimbabwe), which she left at the age of 14. She continued her own education while living on the family farm by reading in European and American literature, and started to write novels. She lived in Salisbury from 1937 to 1949, where she became involved in politics and helped to start a non-racialist left-wing party. She was married twice while living in Rhodesia (Lessing is her second husband's name). Her experiences of life in working-class London after her arrival in 1949 are described in *In Pursuit of the English* (1960). She joined the Communist Party briefly, and left it in 1956, in which year Rhodesia declared her a 'prohibited immigrant'. Her first published novel was *The Grass is Singing* (1950), a study of the sterility of white civilization in Africa. *This was the Old Chief's Country* (1951), a collection of short studies, continued this theme. In 1952 *Martha Quest* appeared, the first novel in her sequence *The Children of Violence* (completed in *A Proper Marriage*, 1954, *A Ripple from the Storm*, 1958, *Landlocked*, 1965, and *The Four-Gated City*, 1969). This sequence, to a certain extent autobiographical, explores through the life story of the heroine, Martha, contemporary social and psychological problems. The theme running through the whole sequence is the ideal city where there is no violence. The city is, however, unattainable, and political and personal catastrophe is seen as inevitable. Other novels include *The Golden Notebook* (1962) and *Briefing for a Descent into Hell* (1971), both studies of so-called 'mental breakdown' and return to normality, which question the conventional definitions of 'sanity' and 'insanity'. Other collections of short stories include *A Man and Two Women* (1963), *African Stories* (1964) and *The Story of a Non-marrying Man* (1972). Latterly, in *Canopus in Argos: Archives*, a quintet of novels, she has attempted science fiction but

her commitment to exploring political and social undercurrents in contemporary society has never wavered and can be seen to potent effect in *The Good Terrorist* (1985) and *The Fifth Child* (1988).
▷ R Whittaker, *Doris Lessing* (1988)

LESSING, Gotthold Ephraim
(1729–81)
German writer, born in Kamenz in Saxony, the son of a pastor. In 1746 he started as a theological student at Leipzig. Soon he was writing plays in the French style; leaving Leipzig in debt, in Berlin he joined the unorthodox Mylius in publishing *Beiträge zur Historie des Theaters* (1750, 'Contributions to the History of the Theatre'), and independently wrote plays, translated and did literary hackwork. His chief means of support was the *Vossische Zeitung*, to which he contributed criticisms. In 1751 he went to Wittenberg, took his Master's degree, and produced a series of *Vindications* of unjustly maligned or forgotten writers, such as Cardan, Lemnius, and others. Back in Berlin, in *Ein Vademecum für Herrn S.G. Lange* (1754, 'A Handbook for Herr S.G. Lange') he displayed unrelenting hostility to pretentious ignorance and with Moses Mendelssohn he wrote an essay on *Pope, ein Metaphysiker* (1755). After writing a trio of comedies, in 1755 he produced his classic German tragedy *Miss Sara Sampson* (1755), based on English rather than French models. In 1758 he was assisting Mendelssohn and **Christoph Nicolai** with a new critical Berlin journal (*Briefe', die neueste Literatur betreffend*, 'Letters Concerning the Most Recent Literature'), in which he protested against the dictatorship of French taste, combated the inflated pedantry of the **Gottsched** school, and extolled **Shakespeare**. While secretary to the governor of Breslau he wrote his famous *Laokoon; oder, Über die Grenzen der Malerei und Poesie* (1766, Eng trans *Laocoon; or, The Limits of Poetry and Painting*, 1853), a critical treatise defining the limits of poetry and the plastic arts. The comedy *Minna von Barnhelm* (1767, Eng trans *The Disbanded Officer*, 1786) is the first German comedy on the grand scale. Appointed playwright to a new theatre in Hamburg in 1767, he wrote the *Hamburgische Dramaturgie* (1769), in which he finally overthrew the dictatorship of the French drama. The Hamburg theatre failed, and Lessing was soon in the thick of a controversy, this time with Klotz, a Halle professor, producing the *Briefe antiquarischen Inhalts* (1769, 'Letters on an Antiquarian Theme') and *Wie die Alten den Tod gebildet* (1769, 'How the Ancients Portrayed Death'). In 1769 the Duke of Brunswick appointed Lessing as Wolfenbüttel librarian; and he at once began to publish some of the

less-known treasures of the library in *Zur Geschichte und Literatur* (1773–81, 'On History and Literature'). In 1772 he wrote the great tragedy *Emilia Galotti*. Shortly before his marriage he spent eight months in Italy as companion to the young Prince Leopold of Brunswick. Between 1774 and 1778 he published the *Wolfenbüttelsche Fragmente eines Ungennanten* ('Anonymous Fragments from Wolfenbüttel'), a rationalist attack on orthodox Christianity from the pen of Reimarus which, universally attributed to Lessing, provoked a storm of refutations. The best of Lessing's counter-attacks were *Anti-Goeze* (1778) and the fine dramatic poem, *Nathan der Weise* (1779, Eng trans *Nathan the Wise*, 1868), one of the noblest pleas for toleration ever written. Later works were *Erziehung des Menschengeschlechts* (1780, 'Education of the Human Race') and *Ernst und Falk* (1778–81, Eng trans *Ernst and Falk*, 1854–72), five dialogues on freemasonry.
▷H B Garland, *Lessing, founder of modern German criticism* (1937)

LEVER, Charles James
(1806–72)

Irish novelist, born of English parentage in Dublin. He graduated from Trinity College, Dublin in 1827, and then went to Göttingen to study medicine. His most popular work, *Charles O'Malley* (1841), is a description of his own college life in Dublin. About 1829 he spent some time in the backwoods of Canada and North America, and related his experiences in *Arthur O'Leary* (1844) and *Con Cregan* (1849). He practised medicine in various Irish country towns, and in 1840 in Brussels. Returning to Dublin, he published *Jack Hinton* in 1843, and from 1842 to 1845 acted as editor of the *Dublin University Magazine*, and wrote further novels. In 1845 he again went to Brussels, Bonn, and Karlsruhe, where he published the *Knight of Gwynne* (1847), and to Florence, where he wrote *Roland Cashel* (1850). Then, completely changing his style, he wrote *The Daltons* (1852), followed by the *Fortunes of Glencore* (1857). He was appointed British vice-consul in Spezia in 1858, and continued to write, his work including *Luttrel of Arran* (1865) and three other novels in rapid succession, and some racy essays in *Blackwood's* by 'Cornelius O'-Dowd'. In 1867 he was promoted to the consulship in Trieste. Lever's work contained brilliant, rollicking sketches of a phase of Irish life which was passing away, though no doubt his caricatures created a false idea of Irish society and character.
▷E Donney, *Charles Lever: his life in his letters* (1906)

LEVERSON, Ada
(1865–1936)

English novelist and journalist, born in London. After being educated privately, she became a member of the circle which included **Max Beerbohm** and **Oscar Wilde**, whom she bravely supported during his trials in 1895. Wilde referred to her as 'The Sphinx'. Having published literary parodies in *Punch*, she contributed stories for *The Yellow Book* and, as 'Elaine', wrote over 100 columns for *The Referee*, in some of which she satirized other advice columnists. Her six novels, written between 1907 and 1916, include such titles as *Love's Shadow* (1908), *Tenterhooks* (1912) and *Love at Second Sight* (1916). Domestic stories of difficult marriages (not unlike her own to the gambler Ernest Leverson), they rely for their readability mainly on the author's wit.
▷J Speedie, *Wonderful Sphinx: The Biography of Ada Leverson* (1993)

LEVERTIN, Oscar
(1862–1906)

Swedish poet, critic and essayist. He was born in Stockholm, of a Jewish family, and studied at the University of Uppsala. From 1899 he was professor of literature at the University of Stockholm. His work focuses a conflict between emotion and reflection, with an early book of poetry such as *Legender och visor* (1891, 'Legends and Songs') employing an exuberant, complex language to convey a romanticism that includes a preoccupation with religion and the Middle Ages. His prose texts range from the brilliant pastiches of *Rococonoveller* (1899, 'Short Stories from the Rococo') to the evocative portrait essays in *Diktare och drömmare* (1898, 'Writers and Dreamers'). As a critic in the daily *Svenska Dagbladet* from 1897 he exerted a huge influence.
▷B Julén, *Hjärtats landsflykt. En Levertinstudie* (1961)

LEVERTOV, Denise
(1923–)

English-born American poet, born in Ilford, Essex, into a literary household; she was the daughter of a Welsh mother and a Russian Jewish father who became an Anglican clergyman. Educated privately, she emigrated to the USA in 1948. She was appointed poetry editor of *The Nation* in 1961. *The Double Image* (1946) was her first collection of verse and others have appeared steadily. A 'British Romantic with almost Victorian background', she has been outspoken on many issues (Vietnam, feminism, etc), and her poetry is similarly questioning. Her attachment to the 'Black Mountain' poets like **Charles Olson** and **William Carlos Williams** is palpable but her voice is distinctive. *With Eyes at the Back of Our Heads* (1959), *Relearning the Alphabet* (1970), *To Stay Alive* (1971) and *Footprints* (1972) particularly stand out.

▷L Wagner, *Denise Levertov* (1967)

LEVET, Henri-Jean-Marie
(1874–1906)

French poet and dandy, now almost forgotten, whose exotic *Cartes postales* (1900, 'Postcards') influenced **Larbaud** and **Fargue**, and are still worth reading for their quiet audacity and charm.

▷M Raymond, *From Baudelaire to Symbolism* (1950)

LEVI, Carlo
(1902–75)

Italian novelist, journalist and politician, born in Turin. He qualified as a doctor in 1923, but soon became immersed in literature and politics. He was imprisoned by the Fascists in 1935–6, then went into exile before returning to Italy to join the resistance. His most important novel, *Christ Stopped At Eboli* (1945), is set in the quasi-pagan, poverty-stricken deep south of his homeland. His non-fiction includes an examination of the Mafia and Sicily, *Words Are Stones* (1955), and a Russian travelogue, *The Future Has An Ancient Heart* (1956). He remained politically active throughout his life, and in 1963 was elected as a Communist senator.

LEVI, Primo
(1919–87)

Italian writer and chemist, born in Turin to Jewish parents. On completing his schooling he enrolled at Turin University to study chemistry for, as he wrote in *Il sistemo periodico* (1984, Eng trans *The Periodic Table*, 1984), he believed that 'the nobility of Man…lay in making himself the conqueror of matter'. During the war he fled into the mountains and formed a small guerrilla force; but he was betrayed and in December 1943 was arrested, turned over to the SS, and despatched to Auschwitz. He was one of the few to survive, partly because he contracted scarlet fever when the Germans evacuated the camp as the Russians approached. Those 10 months in Auschwitz haunted him for the rest of his life and may have prompted his suicide. His first book, *Se questo è un uomo* (Eng trans *If This Is a Man*, 1959), was completed soon after his return to Turin and was published in 1947. A graphic account of life in a concentration camp, it is written with a chemist's detached sensibility, making it all the more powerful. He continued to combine his career

as a chemist with that of a writer. His best-known book is *Il sistemo periodico*, a volume of memoirs and autobiographical reflections. One of the 20th century's most incisive commentators, his other titles include *La chiave a stella* (1978, Eng trans *The Wrench*, 1987), *Se non ora, quando?* (1982, Eng trans *If Not Now, When?*, 1985) and *Altrui mestiere* (1985, Eng trans *Other People's Trades*, 1985).

LEVIN, Ira
(1929–)

American novelist and playwright, born in New York City. *A Kiss Before Dying* (1953), a tightly plotted murder story, made his reputation and remains one of the most highly rated of post-war crime novels. His plays include *Deathtrap* (1978), but it is as a popular novelist that he is best known. The horror story *Rosemary's Baby* (1967), the science-fictional study of suburban alienation *The Stepford Wives* (1972), and the nutty Nazis novel *The Boys From Brazil* (1976) are among his most read works. All have been filmed. His best novel, however, is probably the lesser-known *This Perfect Day* (1970), in which his mastery of suspense is most expertly employed.

LEVIN, Meyer
(1905–81)

American novelist, known for his studies of Jewish life in Chicago, where he was born. His early experience as a journalist formed the backdrop to his first novel *Reporter* (1929). This was drawn a little too closely from life; a libel suit was threatened and the book had to be withdrawn. Levin went on to publish *Frankie and Johnny* (1930) and *Yehuda* (1931), about life in a Zionist commune in Palestine. In *The Golden Mountain* (1932) he retold some Hasidic folk-tales. *The Old Bunch* (1937), about immigrant children living in Chicago, was informed by personal experience.

▷*In Search* (1950)

LEVINE, Philip
(1928–)

American poet, born in Detroit. After graduating from the universities of Detroit and Iowa, he lectured at California State University at Fresno, and since 1981 has been Professor of English at Tufts University, Medford. Compassion and concern for the conditions of the working-class of both Detroit and southern California form the basis of much of his poetry, published in such collections as *Silent America: Vivas For Those Who Failed* (1965) and *5 Detroits* (1970). Subsequent volumes include *The Names of the Lost* (1976) and *One For the Rose* (1981).

A collection of *Selected Poems* appeared in 1984.

LEWALD, Fanny
(1811–89)

German novelist, born in Königsberg (now Kaliningrad). Jewish by birth, she became a Lutheran convert in 1828 to marry a young theologian, who died just before the wedding. In 1845 she met Adolf Stahr (1805–76), a Berlin critic, with whom she lived until he was free to marry in 1855. She was an enthusiastic champion of women's rights, which were aired in her early novels, *Clementine* (1842), *Jenny* (1843) and *Eine Lebensfrage* (1845, 'A Question About Life'). Her later works were family sagas, like *Von Geschlecht zu Geschlecht* (1863–5, 'From Generation to Generation') and *Die Familie Darner* (3 vols, 1887, 'The Darner Family'). She wrote records of travel in Italy (1847) and Great Britain (1852), and published an autobiography, *Meine Lebensgeschichte* (1861–3, 'The Story of my Life').

LEWES, G(eorge) H(enry)
(1817–78)

English writer, born in London, grandson of the comedian, Charles Lee Lewes (1740–1803), and companion and supporter of **George Eliot** from 1854. Educated at Greenwich and in Jersey and Brittany, he went to Germany for nearly two years in 1838, studying the life, language and literature of the country. On his return to London he started writing about anything and everything for the *Penny Encyclopaedia* and *Morning Chronicler*, later was a contributor to numerous journals, reviews and magazines, and was Editor of the *Leader* (1851–4), and of the *Fortnightly* (1865–6), which he himself founded. He was unhappily married, with a family, when he began his lifelong affair with **George Eliot**. His works include two novels, *Ranthorpe* (1847) and *Rose, Blanche and Violet* (1848), and 10 plays, but he is best known for his writings on biography, the theatre, and later the sciences. His most important work in that vein was his *Life and Works of Goethe* (1855).
▷A R Kaminsky, *George Henry Lewes as literary critic* (1968)

LEWIS, Alun
(1915–44)

Welsh soldier-poet and short-story writer, born in Cwmaman, near Aberdare. He was educated at Cowbridge School, the University College of Wales, Aberystwyth and at Manchester University. A lieutenant in the army, his first work, a volume of short stories about army life, was *The Last Inspection*

(1942), followed by a volume of poetry, *Raiders' Dawn*, in the same year. He died of gunshot wounds at Chittagong during the Burma campaign. Another volumes of verse, ironically entitled *Ha! Ha! Among the Trumpets*, was published posthumously in 1945, followed by a collection of short stories and letters, *In the Green Tree* (1948).
▷A John, *Alun Lewis* (1970)

LEWIS, C(live) S(taples)
(1898–1963)

British novelist, literary scholar and religious writer, born in Belfast. He lost his Christianity while at school, won a scholarship to Oxford in 1916, but served in World War I before entering University College in 1918. His first book of poems, *Spirits in Bondage*, was published in that year. He became a fellow of Magdalen College in 1925, where he headed an informal group of writers known as 'The Inklings', which included **J R R Tolkein** and **Charles Williams**. He was appointed to the newly created Chair of Medieval and Renaissance English at Cambridge University in 1954. He was a distinguished teacher, and wrote a number of important scholarly works, including *The Allegory of Love* (1936), on medieval poetry, and *English Literature in the Sixteenth Century* (1954). He returned to Christianity in the period 1929–31 and won a wide popular audience during World War II for his broadcast talks (collected as *Mere Christianity*, 1952) and his books on religious subjects, notably *The Screwtape Letters* (1940), in which a senior devil instructs a junior on methods of winning souls away from the true path. His most important adult novels are the science-fiction trilogy *Out of the Silent Planet* (1938), *Perelandra* (1939) and *That Hideous Strength* (1945), in which the allegorical battle for the survival of mankind is set out in distinctly religious symbolism. His series of seven books for children, collectively known as *The Chronicles of Narnia*, which began with *The Lion, The Witch and The Wardrobe* (1950) and ended with *The Last Battle* (1956, Carnegie Medal), is similarly suffused with Christian allegory and ethics, and is among the most important writing for children of the century. His other works include two slight fantasy novels, *The Great Divorce* (1945) and *Till We Have Faces* (1956).
▷*Surprised By Joy* (1955); A N Wilson, *C. S. Lewis: A Biography* (1990)

LEWIS, Janet
(1899–)

American poet, novelist and author of children's books, born in Chicago. The first of her six collections of poetry, *The Indians in the Woods* (1922), established her as a poet preferring to look back with nostalgia to a time when man appeared to be more serene, and in greater harmony with nature. Her first historical novel, *The Invasion* (1932), depicts Native Americans acclimatizing themselves to the British presence during the early 1760s. It became the first of a series, each concerned with moral dilemmas and social convention. *The Trial of Soren Qvist* (1947) is set not in the USA, but in 17th-century Jutland. Lewis's major collection of verse, *Poems Old and New*, appeared in 1981.

LEWIS, M(atthew) G(regory)
(1775–1818)

English novelist, born in London. He was educated at Westminster School and Christ Church, Oxford, and in Germany, where he met **Goethe**. In 1794 he was an attaché to The Hague and it was there he wrote *Ambrosio, or the Monk* (1796), a Gothic novel now generally known as *The Monk*, which was influenced by his formative reading of tales of witchcraft and the supernatural, and **Ann Radcliffe**'s *Mysteries of Udolpho*, and which inspired his nickname 'Monk' Lewis. Many others in a similar vein followed, including a musical drama, *The Castle Spectre* (1798). He published several volumes of verse, but his best-known poem, 'Alonzo the Brave and the Fair Imogine', appeared in *The Monk*. Concerned about the treatment of the slaves on the estates he had inherited in the West Indies, he went there in 1817, but died of yellow fever on the way home. His *Journal of a West Indian Proprietor* was published in 1834.
▷ L F Peck, *A Life of Monk Lewis* (1961)

LEWIS, Saunders
(1893–1985)

Welsh dramatist, poet and nationalist, born in Cheshire. He studied English and French at Liverpool University, and in 1924 published a study of English influences on classical Welsh 18th-century poetry, *A School of Welsh Augustans*, having become lecturer in Welsh in University College, Swansea, in 1922. He was co-founder of the Welsh Nationalist Party (later Plaid Cymru) in 1925, and became its president in 1926. He became a Roman Catholic in 1932. Imprisoned in 1936 for a token act of arson against building materials for construction of an RAF bombing school at Penyberth, he was dismissed from Swansea and made his living by journalism, teaching and farming until his appointment as lecturer (later senior lecturer) in Welsh at University College, Cardiff, in 1952. He published many essays, 19 plays in Welsh and English, poems, novels, historical and literary criticism, chiefly in Welsh. He retired from public life in

1957, but continued publishing plays, his last being *Excelsior* (1980).
▷ P Davies, *Saunders Lewis* (1950)

LEWIS, (Harry) Sinclair
(1885–1951)

American novelist, winner of the Nobel Prize for literature, born in Sauk Center, Minnesota, the son of a doctor. Educated at Yale, he became a journalist and wrote several minor works before *Main Street* (1920), the first of a series of bestselling novels satirizing the arid materialism and intolerance of American small-town life. *Babbitt* (1922) still lends its title as a synonym for middle-class American philistinism. Other titles of this period are *Martin Arrowsmith* (1925), *Elmer Gantry* (1927) and *Dodsworth* (1929). From then on he tended to exonerate the ideologies and self-sufficiency he had previously pilloried; the shift of attitude did nothing to diminish his popularity. His later novels include *Cass Timberlane* (1945) and *Kingsblood Royal* (1947). He refused the Pulitzer Prize for *Arrowsmith*, but accepted the Nobel Prize for literature in 1930, being the first American writer to receive it.
▷ M Schorer, *Sinclair Lewis: an American life* (1961)

LEWIS, (Percy) Wyndham
(1882–1957)

English novelist, painter and critic, born in Amehurst, Nova Scotia. He was educated at Rugby School and the Slade School of Art. With **Ezra Pound** he instituted the Vorticist movement and founded *Blast* (1914–15), the magazine which expounded their theories. From 1916 to 1918 he served on the Western Front, as a bombardier, then as a war artist. In the early 1930s, his right-wing sympathies were out of vogue. He emigrated to Canada at the beginning of World War II, returning to London in 1945. In 1951 he went blind. His novels, *Tarr* (1918), *The Childermass* (1928), and *The Apes of God* (1930) are powerful, vivid satires reflecting his talent as a painter; other important novels are *The Revenge for Love* (1937) and *Self Condemned* (1954), which is partly autobiographical. *The Human Age* (1955), a trilogy which was conceived with *The Childermass* and continued with *Monstre Gai* and *Malign Fiesta* (both 1955), was modelled in part on **Dante** and **Milton**, and had a projected but never written fourth part. As a writer he has been ranked by some critics alongside **James Joyce**; as a painter, he was both the foremost experimentalist of his time in British art, and a portraitist of the highest calibre. Other writings include political and critical essays, short stories, and the

autobiographies *Blasting and Bombardiering* (1937) and *Rude Assignment* (1950).
▷J Meyers, *The Enemy: a biography* (1980)

LEWISOHN, Ludwig
(1883–1955)

German-born American critic and novelist, he moved to the USA as an eight-year-old. Educated in Charleston, South Carolina, he became an academic, specializing in European (particularly German) literature and the reciprocal impact of Judaism and modern culture. His *The Spirit of Modern German Literature* (1916) is still an important source, as are his books about the Diaspora: *Israel* (1925), *The Answer: The Jew and the World* (1939), and the later *The American Jew* (1950). The best of his novels are *The Broken Snare* (1908), *Don Juan* (1923) and *The Case of Mr Crump* (1926). His last book was *In a Summer Season* (1955).
▷ *Up Stream* (1922); *Mid-Channel: An American Chronicle* (1929)

LEYDEN, John
(1775–1811)

Scottish poet and orientalist, born in Denholm, Roxburghshire, the son of a farmer. He studied medicine at Edinburgh University, and was licensed as a preacher in 1798. He wrote a book on European settlements in Africa (1799), helped Sir **Walter Scott** to gather materials for his *Border Minstrelsy*, and his translations and poems in the *Edinburgh Magazine* attracted attention. In 1803 he sailed for India as assistant surgeon at Madras, travelled widely in the East, acquired 34 languages, and translated the gospels into five of them. He accompanied Lord Minto as interpreter to Java, and died of fever at Batavia. His ballads have taken a higher place than his longer poems, especially *Scenes of Infancy* (1803). His dissertation on Indo–Chinese languages is also well known.
▷J Reith, *John Leyden* (1923)

LEZAZA LIMA, José
(1910–76)

Cuban novelist and poet. In the 1930s he was one of Cuba's leading intellectuals. Brought up against a militaristic background, he early developed asthma, an illness which was to plague him throughout his life. First known as a poet and prose poet, Lezaza Lima's acknowledged masterpiece is his novel *Paradiso* (1966, Eng trans 1974), described by one critic as a 'Bildungsroman, and a poetic summation of all the themes of [Lezaza Lima's] poetry'. This is now required reading for all students of the Latin-American novel in its middle phase. So great was this author's stature in Cuba that when confronted with

evidence of his negative sentiments about Castro's Cuba, he was left alone (although isolated).
▷R S Minc (ed), *Latin-American Fiction Today* (1980)

LI PO
(c.700–762)

Chinese poet, born in the province of Szechwan. He led a dissipated life at the emperor's court and later was one of a wandering band calling themselves 'The Eight Immortals of the Wine Cup'. Regarded as the greatest poet of China, he wrote colourful verse of wine, women and nature. It is believed that he was drowned while attempting to kiss the moon's reflection. *Li T'ai-po Chüan-chi* ('The Complete Works') were published in 3 vols in 1977. Collections of Li Po's translated work have been published in 1922 and 1973.
▷A Waley, *The Poetry and Career of Li Po* (1950)

LIBEDINSKY, Yury
(1898–1959)

Russian novelist and dramatist, born in Odessa. He is best remembered for *Nedelya* (1922, Eng trans *A Week*, 1923), the first fully 'proletarian novel'. Libedinsky was a slavish follower and even designer of official communist literature, but he was not entirely incapable, and eventually he got himself into trouble—if mainly through others' jealousy of him—with Stalin's cultural officials on charges of 'Trotskyism'. The 'characters' in *A Week* are formulaic Bolshevik types, not existing in reality; but they were very influential on later, and better, communist fiction, such as Fyodor Gladkov's *Cement* (1925, Eng trans 1929).

LICHTENBERG, Georg Christoph
(1742–99)

German aphorist, diarist, scientific writer and satirist. Born, the son of a pastor, in Oberramstadt, he was crippled in an accident in childhood. He early attracted attention by his brilliance at mathematics and science, which he studied at Göttingen University, where he became Professor of Physics. Lichtenberg, although a 'child of the Enlightenment', was essentially a deflationist of even its certainties. His ironic and exemplary writings are major, but, as has been said, they have suffered neglect because he never expressed himself in the major forms. **Goethe** called his work 'the most amazing divining rod: wherever he makes a joke, a problem is hidden'. He was Germany's **Swift**, but more akin to mysticism (he praised **Böhme**). Of the translations of his work, *The Lichtenberg Reader* (1959) is the best. His acute interpretations of the drawings of

Hogarth are translated as *Lichtenberg's Commentaries on Hogarth's Engravings* (1966).
▷J P Stern, *Lichtenberg* (1959)

LICHTENSTEIN, Alfred
(1889–1914)

German poet. He is remembered as an early expressionist whose 'Die Dämmerung' ('Dusk', Eng trans in *Twentieth-Century German Verse*, 1963, ed Patrick Bridgewater) was the second programmatically expressionist poem to appear in print, the first having been the 'World's End' of **Jakob von Hoddis**, upon which it is modelled. He was killed in action in World War I.
▷C Middleton and M Hamburger (eds), *Modern German Poetry 1910–1969* (1962)

LIDMAN, Sara
(1923–)

Swedish author, born in Missenträsk in the far north of the country. The area was the setting for her early novels such as *Tjärdalen* (1953, 'The Tar Still') and *Hjortronlandet* (1955, 'Cloudberry Land'). The support for the underdog visible in these novels became more overtly political in the 1960s after her experiences of South Africa, Kenya and Vietnam. In the highly-acclaimed series of novels beginning with *Din tjänare hör* (1977, 'Thy Servant Heareth'), she returns to her roots and takes as her theme the building of the railways of the north. She has experimented with documentary forms of writing and has also written plays.
▷J Mawby, in *Writers and Politics in Modern Scandinavia* (1978)

LIE, Jonas Lauritz Idemil
(1833–1908)

Major Norwegian novelist and poet, born in Eker near Drammen. He trained as a lawyer but abandoned law for literature; like Sir **Walter Scott**, he saw writing first and foremost as a means of paying off debt. His novels, which present realistic portayals of fisher-life in Norway, include *Den fremsynte* (1870, 'The Visionary'), *Lodsen og hans Hustru* (1874, 'Lodsen and his Wife'), *Livsslaven* (1883, 'One of Life's Slaves') and *Kommandørens Døtre* (1886, 'The Commander's Daughters'). He also wrote fairy-tales like *Trold* (1891–2, 'Trolls'), and some poetry and plays.
▷A Garborg, *Jonas Lie* (1925)

LIGNE, Charles Joseph, Prince de
(1735–1814)

Belgian soldier and writer, born in Brussels, son of an imperial field marshal whose seat was at Ligne near Tournai. In the Seven Years War (1756–63) he served at Kolin, Leuthen and Hochkirch, and in the Russo–Turkish war (1787–93) at the siege of Belgrade (1789). A skilful diplomatist, the favourite of Maria Theresa and Catherine the Great of Russia, and the friend of Frederick II, the Great, **Voltaire** and **Rousseau**, he wrote *Mélanges* (34 vol, 1795–1811), *Oeuvres posthumes* (1817, a collection of his work, published posthumously), a biography of Prince Eugène (1809), and *Lettres et Pensées* (1809, 'Letters and Thoughts').

LIHN, Enrique
(1929–88)

Chilean poet and story writer, born in Santiago, and regarded as the leading member of the so-called 'Generation of '50'. A decisive influence upon him was his meeting with the poet **Nicanor Parra** (upon whose work he wrote a book, 1952), and by 1963 with the small collection *La pieza oscura* (Eng trans, *The Dark Room and Other Poets*, 1978), he had established himself as a highly original poet, writing hauntingly and mystically about his feelings as a stranger in a world no longer familiar to him. *Agua de arroz* (1964, 'Rice Water'), contains stories of the same kind. Much has been translated: *The Endless Malice* (1969) and *If Poetry is to be Written Right* (1977). He died prematurely, of cancer.
▷*Dactylus*, 6 (1986)

LILIENCRON, Detlev von
(1844–1909)

German poet and novelist, born in Kiel. He fought in the Prussian army in 1866 and 1870. He went to America but returned to Holstein in 1882, where for a time he held a civil service post. He is best known for his lyrics, which are fresh, lively and musical. His first volume, *Adjutantenritte* ('The Adjutant's Rides'), appeared in 1883. Other volumes of verse were *Der Heidegänger* (1890, 'The Moors Walker'), *Neue Gedichte* (1893, 'New Poems') and *Gute Nacht* (1909, 'Good Night'). He also wrote novels and a humorous epic poem, *Poggfred* (1896). A selection of translations of his poems was published in 1914 as *Selected Poems*.
▷O J Bierbaum, *Detlev von Liliencron* (1892)

LILIEV, Nikolay, pseud of Nicolay Mihaylov
(1863–1960)

Bulgarian Symbolist poet, and gifted translator (for example, of **Shakespeare**), who was born in Stara Zagora and died in Sofia. He was educated in France, and helped to bring French literary influences to Bulgaria. His poetry, which owes much to **Paul Verlaine**, is musical and carefully wrought.

▷C Manning and R Smal-Stocki, *The History of Modern Bulgarian Literature* (1960)

LILLO, Baldomero
(1867–1923)

Chilean story writer, born in Lota. He was one of Chile's earliest social realists, and its first one of real account. His father, though middle-class, worked as an official in the mines, and his son thus knew the atrocious conditions in them at first hand—and better when he himself went to work for a mining company. He learnt to apply the methods of **Zola** to specifically Chilean affairs, and was a far more accomplished artist than **Blest Gana**. He achieves, a critic wrote, 'a heartrending power through physical descriptions of people distressed by oppression'. His best stories are in *Sub terra* (1904, 'Underground'); his most famous tale of all is 'La compuerto número 12', ('Hatch 12'), about a terrified child forced to work in a mine.

LILLO, George
(1693–1739)

English dramatist and jeweller, born in London of mixed Dutch and English Dissenting parentage. He wrote seven plays, including *The London Merchant, or the History of George Barnwell* (1731) and *Fatal Curiosity* (1736), both tragedies. His *Arden of Feversham*, which was published posthumously in 1759, is a weak version of the anonymous play of that title (1592). Among the first to put middle-class characters on the English stage, he had a considerable influence on European drama.
▷T Drucker, *The Plays* (1979)

LIMA, Jorge de
(1893–1953)

Brazilian Mulatto poet, novelist, translator (**Bernanos, Claudel**) and artist, born in União, Alagoas. Throughout his life he practised as a doctor, and, although he was an early adherent of (Brazilian) *Modernismo*, he is something of a law unto himself. He is sometimes regarded as Brazil's greatest poet of the century. In 1935 he became a Roman Catholic, and combined the earlier influence of Surrealism with that of **Claudel**. His best poetry, in *Essa negra Fuló* (1928, 'That Nigger Fuló'), and the remarkable *Invenção de Orfeu* (1952, 'The Invention of Orpheus'), is 'negrista', or Afro–Brazilian, and reaches somnambulatory heights above even those of **Bandeira**. His three novels, including *O anjo* (1934, 'The Angel'), are unjustly neglected. His poetry has been translated in *Anthology of Contemporary Latin-American Poetry* (1942, ed Dudley Fitts) and in *The Poem Itself* (1964, ed Stanley Burnshaw).

▷P Cavalcanti, *Vida e obra de Jorge de Lima* (1969, in Portuguese)

LINDAU, Paul
(1839–1919)

German writer, born in Magdeburg. He founded *Die Gegenwart* (1872, 'The Present') and *Nord und Süd* (1877, 'North and South'), and wrote books of travel and works of criticism. He is better known as a writer of plays and novels; the most successful of the former was perhaps *Maria und Magdalena* (1872, Eng trans 1874). The novels include *Herr und Frau Bewer* (1882), and *Berlin* (1886–7). His brother, Rudolf Lindau (1829–1910), wrote travel books and novels, and was an editor of *Revue des deux mondes* and *Journal des débats*.

LINDEGREN, Erik
(1910–58)

Swedish poet. Born in Luleå, he attended the University of Stockholm. His first major book of poetry, *Mannen utan väg* (1942, 'The Man without a Way'), gradually established him as a leading Swedish modernist, the 'exploded sonnets' with their Surrealist imagery conveying the urgency of humankind's desperate situation. The affinity between his poetry and music and pictorial art, including Swedish Surrealist painting, is apparent in his next collection, *Sviter* (1947, 'Suites'). The poems in *Vinteroffer* (1954, 'Winter Rites') draw on mythical and ritual patterns to assert the significance of art. An accomplished translator, he also wrote the libretto of the opera *Aniara* (1959), based on **Harry Martinson**'s epic poem about the space age.
▷R Lysell, *Erik Lindegrens imaginära universum* (1983)

LINDGREN, Astrid
(1907–)

Swedish children's novelist, born in Vimmerby. At 18 she had an illegitimate child who was raised by her parents; she portrayed them in *Samuel August från Seudstorp och Hanna: Hult* (1975). She established her reputation with *Pippi Långstrump* (1945, Eng trans *Pippi Longstocking*, 1954), and while she wrote at least 50 more books, including *Mästerdetektiven Blomkvist* (1946, Eng trans *Bill Bergson Master Detective*, 1951), none has eclipsed its popularity.
▷V Edström, *Astrid Lindgren* (1987)

LINDSAY, Sir David *see* LYNDSAY, David

LINDSAY, David
(1878–1945)

English novelist, born in Blackheath, London, where he spent his formative years.

Much of his childhood, however, was spent in Jedburgh with his father's relations. Intent on taking up a university scholarship, he had to abandon this avenue when his father deserted the family. Instead, he became an insurance broker, a career he pursued successfully for 20 years. After World War I he left the City and moved to Cornwall to fulfil his ambitions to be a full-time novelist. Over the next two decades he published five books. *A Voyage to Arcturus* (1920) is his most notable work. Often ghettoized as science fiction, it has been more accurately described by the critic Roderick Watson as 'an allegory of spiritual and philosophical search'. It was a powerful and original work, and **C S Lewis** was not alone in declaring it an influence. Subsequent books, including *The Haunted Woman* (1922) and *The Violet Apple*, published posthumously in 1976, demonstrate that there was depth to Lindsay's talent, though the reading public remained largely impervious to it.

▷J B Pick, C Wilson and E Visiak, *The Strange Genius of David Lindsay* (1970)

LINDSAY, Frederic
(1933–)

Scottish novelist and screen-writer, born in Glasgow. He was educated at Glasgow University, Jordanhill College, and Edinburgh University. He worked at the Mitchell Library, Glasgow (1950–4), then as a teacher (1961–6) and lecturer (1966–78), before becoming a full-time writer in 1979. His first book was a volume of poetry published in 1975, but he is best known as a novelist and screen writer. His first novel, *Brond* (1984), is a complex and multi-layered examination of the mysterious workings of the state intelligence machine; he later adapted this for television. *Jill Rips* (1987) also burrows into the world of political and business intrigue and corruption, through a powerful inversion of the Jack the Ripper story, in which male victims fall to a female killer in a fictionalized Glasgow. He published a third novel, *A Charm Against Drowning*, in 1988, and has also written for theatre and radio. Another powerful psychological thriller, *After the Stranger Came*, appeared in 1992.

LINDSAY, Harold Arthur
(1900–69)

Australian novelist and children's writer, born in Adelaide, who travelled widely through the continent and became expert on the aborigines' life in the Australian deserts. Between 1941 and 1946 he was instructor in survival techniques to soldiers in Australia and New Britain, Papua New Guinea, passing on to them the bushcraft he had learned on his travels; this he later published as *The*

Bushman's Handbook (1948). After the war he broadcast on nature topics and contributed to newspapers and periodicals. He wrote five adult novels, including *The Red Bull* (1959), which drew on his earlier experiences of forestry, and a number of novels for younger readers, mainly in collaboration with the anthropologist Norman Tindale, including the award-winning *The First Walkabout* (1954) and *Aboriginal Australians* (1963).

LINDSAY, Jack
(1900–90)

Australian poet, novelist, historian and translator. Born in Melbourne, the eldest son of artist and writer **Norman Lindsay** and brother of **Philip Lindsay**, he later mixed with Sydney's bohemians and described the era vividly in *The Roaring Twenties* (1960). His first book of verse, *Fauns and Ladies* (1923), a mock-classical collection illustrated by his father, was published in Sydney. With a friend, he founded the Fanfrolico Press for which Lindsay translated many classics and his father contributed illustrations. He left for England in 1926 where the Press prospered, to be acclaimed by collectors of fine printing and 'curiosa'. During World War II he published more verse, *Second Front* (1944), and war novels such as *We Shall Return* (1942) on Dunkirk. Later verse included *Peace is Our Aim* (1950). He achieved international respect as an historian and, in the 1960s, produced impressive critical studies of artists such as Turner and Cézanne. Well-known for historical novels such as *Light in Italy* (1941), he also wrote novels of contemporary life, such as *Rising Tide* (1953). The three volumes of his autobiography, *Life Rarely Tells* (1958), *The Roaring Twenties* and *Fanfrolico and After* (1962), capture vividly the many-faceted interests of a Renaissance Man. *Blood Vote*, his novel of the World War I anti-conscription movement, set in Brisbane, was written in 1937, mislaid by the author, rediscovered and eventually published in 1987. From the late 1930s much of his writing was informed by a naive Marxist philosophy and coloured by events of the time, such as the Spanish Civil War and the Nazi–Soviet conflict.

LINDSAY, Joan, properly Lady Lindsay
(1896–1984)

Australian writer, born Joan à Beckett Weigall, who married Sir Daryl Lindsay of the prominent literary and artistic family. Born in Melbourne, she was trained in art but turned to writing; her earlier works, largely autobiographical, were *Time without Clocks* (1962), the 'timeless clockless summers' of her married years, and *Facts Soft and Hard* (1964). The haunting Victorian period piece

Picnic at Hanging Rock (1967) was inspired by a painting and became a successful film in 1975. The disappearance of three schoolgirls on a school outing allows Lindsay to explore a favourite theme of the relationship between actual and imagined time. The final chapter of the book was held back by the publishers and not issued until after Joan Lindsay's death, as *The Secret of Hanging Rock* (1987).

LINDSAY, (John) Maurice
(1918–)

Scottish poet, critic and editor, born in Glasgow. Educated at Glasgow Academy, he trained as a musician at the Scottish National Academy of Music. Between 1946 and 1960 he worked as drama and music critic for the *Bulletin*, Glasgow. After working with Border Television (1961–7), first as Programme Controller and latterly as Chief Interviewer, he became (1967) Director of the Scottish Civic Trust, and in 1983 Honorary Secretary General of Europa Nostra. His poems reflect his concern for worldly affairs: they are short, more statements than meditations. His major works are his critical treatments of **Robert Burns** and his *History of Scottish Literature* (1977). His own poetry was first published in *The Advancing Day* (1940) and the best of his work is brought together in *Collected Poems* (1979).

LINDSAY, Norman Alfred William
(1879–1969)

Australian artist and writer, born in Creswick, Victoria, whose diverse (and now dated) novels mostly portray aspects of a **Rabelais**ian Melbourne peopled by drunken but lovable artists and disapproving clergy. They include *A Curate in Bohemia* (1913), the rollicking *A Cautious Amorist* (1932), *Age of Consent* (1938) and *The Cousin from Fiji* (1945). Some of his novels were banned in Australia until the late 1950s. His children's book *The Magic Pudding* (1918) stars hero Bunyip Bluegum, a perennial favourite with adults too. A highly respected artist, he illustrated not only much of his own work but books by contemporaries including **Hugh McCrae**, **Kenneth Slessor** and **Douglas Stewart**. His sons were **Jack** and **Philip Lindsay**.

LINDSAY, Philip
(1906–58)

Australian historian, biographer, novelist and writer for films, third son of **Norman Lindsay** and brother of **Jack Lindsay**. After publishing an early collection of verse he followed Jack to England to pursue a journalistic career, and began a long series of picaresque novels with a tale of the buccaneer

Captain Henry Morgan in *Panama is Burning* (1932). The books that followed dealt with most periods of British history including *Gentleman Harry Retires* (1936), *Pudding Lane* (1940), *The Devil and King John* (1942) and his last, *Rusty Sword* (1946). A respected medievalist, he also wrote the lives of English kings Henry V (1934) and Richard III (1939), and of Australian batsman Don Bradman (1951).
▷ *I'd Live the Same Life Over* (1940)

LINDSAY OF PITSCOTTIE, Robert
(c.1500–c.1570)

Scottish writer and historian, and minor laird from the Cupar area of Fife. Little is known about his life, but he is the originator (and author of large parts of) the *History and Chronicles of Scotland* (c.1580), a highly readable and, largely, accurate source for the history of 16th-century Scotland. It is written very elegantly, with a dry wit, an example of which is his comment on the death of James II (killed by an exploding gun at the siege of Roxburgh): 'This Prince mair curieous nor became him or the maiestie of ane King, did stand neir hand by quhen the artaillezerie was dischargeand' (he stood too close when the artillery was firing).

LINDSAY, (Nicholas) Vachel
(1879–1931)

American poet, born in Springfield, Illinois. He studied painting in Chicago and New York, and from 1906 travelled America like a troubadour, trading and reciting his very popular ragtime rhymes for hospitality. His irrepressible spirits appear in *General Booth enters Into Heaven* (1913) and *The Congo* (1914). His later volumes of verse were less successful, and, suffering from extreme depression, he returned to Springfield and committed suicide.
▷ E Ruggles, *The West-Going Heart* (1959)

LINKLATER, Eric
(1899–1974)

Scottish novelist, born in Penarth, the son of a shipmaster. His paternal ancestors were Orcadian and he spent much of his childhood on the islands, returning there in later life. He was educated at the grammar school and university in Aberdeen, and served in World War I as a private in the Black Watch. In the mid-1920s he worked as a journalist on the *Times of India*, returning to Aberdeen as assistant to the Professor of English (1927–8). A commonwealth fellowship took him to the USA from 1928 to 1930, after which he had a varied career as a broadcaster and a prolific writer of novels, popular histories, books for children (*The Wind on the Moon* was awarded the Carnegie Medal in 1944), plays and memoirs. *Juan in America* (1931), a picaresque classic, is his most enduring novel. His other novels include *White Maa's Saga* (1929), *Poet's Pub* (1929), *Laxdale Hall* (1933), *Magnus Merriman* (1934), *Juan in China* (1937), *Private Angelo* (1946), *The House of Gair* (1953), *The Ultimate Viking* (1955) and *The Voyage of the Challenger* (1972). *The Man on My Back* (1941), *A Year of Space* (1953) and *Fanfare for a Tin Hat* (1970) are autobiographical.

▷ M Parnall, *Eric Linklater: a critical biography* (1984)

LINNA, Väinö
(1920–92)

Finnish novelist of working-class background. Born in Vrjala, he worked in a factory at Tampere before starting to write. His best-known works are *Tuntematen sotilas* (1954, Eng trans *The Unknown Soldier*, 1957), a controversial novel about the Russo–Finnish war, and his trilogy *Tä ällä Pohjantähden alla* (1959–62, 'Here Under the North Star'), about Finnish independence in 1918. He gave up fiction writing in the early 1960s.

▷ N Stormbom, *Väinö Linna* (1963)

LINS DO RÊGO, José
(1901–57)

Brazilian novelist, famous author of the 'Sugar Cane Cycle', born in Pilar, Paraíba. Son of a sugar-planter family, he was brought up in a privileged atmosphere. A chronic hypochondriac (thus learned in medicine), obsessive practical joker, elaborate public insulter of his friends, he is one of the few writers, besides the inefficient **Cervantes**, to have worked as a tax inspector. The first three (and best) books of the five-novel 'Sugar Cane Cycle' were translated in one volume as *Plantation Boy* (1966). The sociological viewpoint is generally enlightened and anti-racist, but has been criticized by Marxists as following that of Lins do Rêgo's friend, **Gilberto Freyre**: the tyrannical planters are shown as granting more freedom to their serfs than the new factory tyrants, *usinas*. Later Lins do Rêgo's novels were influenced by the one novelist of his generation superior to him, **Graciliano Ramos**; it has been suggested that the greatest and best-written of his novels, never distinguished by careful writing, is *Euridice* (1947), the story of a sex killer. Also notable are *Pureza* (1937, Eng trans, *Purity*, 1948), *Fogo morto* (1943, Eng trans, *Dead Fire*, 1944), and the 'backlands novel', recalling **da Cunha**, *Os cangaceiros* (1953, 'The Outlaws').

▷ H J Maxwell, *Lins do Rêgo's Sociological Novels* (1954)

LIN YÜTANG
(1895–1976)

Chinese author and philologist, born in Changchow, Amoy. He studied at Shanghai, Harvard and Leipzig, became Professor of English at Peking (1923–6), secretary of the Ministry of Foreign Affairs (1927), lived mainly in the USA from 1936, and was Chancellor of Singapore University (1954–5). He is best known for his numerous novels and essays on, and anthologies of, Chinese wisdom and culture, and as co-author of the official romanization plan for the Chinese alphabet.

▷ *My Country and My People* (1935)

LIPPARD, George
(1822–54)

American novelist, born in Pennsylvania. He gained a reputation as the author of arresting, occasionally lurid, novels about city life and its inherent immorality, which were intended to have a reforming effect on their readers. Titles most representative of his stance are *The Quaker City: or, The Monks of Monk Hall* (1844), which won widespread popularity both in the USA and abroad, and *New York: Its Upper Ten and Lower Million* (1854). Following in his wake came a genre of 'city novel writing'. He also wrote romantic historical fiction, such as *Blanche of Brandywine* (1846) and *Legends of Mexico* (1847).

LISPECTOR, Clarice
(1917–77)

Ukrainian-born Brazilian novelist, whose reputation has been slow to develop in the English-speaking world. She was trained in law in Rio de Janeiro and spent much of her adult life abroad; her husband was in the Brazilian diplomatic service. She has been hailed as the first major woman writer to emerge from Latin America, but her concerns are neither exclusively nor narrowly feminist. Her early fiction—*Perto do coracao salvagem* (1944) and *O lustre* (1949)—is still virtually unknown in the anglophone countries and even the more direct narrative of *A maçã no escuro* (1961, Eng trans *The Apple in the Dark*, 1967) occasionally falls foul of untranslatable elements and rhythms in the original Portuguese. This is particularly true of *A paixão segundo G H* (1964, Eng trans *The Passion According to G H*, 1988). Her most popular book is *A hora da estréla* (1977, Eng trans *The Hour of the Star*, 1986), a winsome and slightly formulaic novel prepared for the press shortly before her death. Lispector also wrote short fiction, but is more effective in her longer evocations of developing consciousness.

LISSAUER, Ernst
(1882–1937)

German poet and dramatist, born in Berlin. Much of his writings had a strong nationalist flavour. *1813* (1913), a poem cycle, is a eulogy on the Prussian people in their fight to remove Napoleon from their land, as is the successful drama *Yorck* (1921) about the Prussian general. The poem *Hassgesang gegen England* (1914, 'Hate-Song against England') achieved tremendous popularity in wartime Germany with its well-known refrain 'Gott strafe England' ('God Punish England'). Other works include a play about **Goethe** called *Eckermann* (1921), poems on Bruckner, *Gloria Anton Bruckners* (1921), a critical work, *Von der Sendung des Dichters* (1922, 'The Vocation of a Poet'), and some volumes of verse.

LISTA Y ARAGON, Alberto
(1775–1848)

Spanish pre-Romantic poet, born in Seville. As a professor in Madrid he taught **Espronceda**. He was accused of teaching 'revolutionary ideas' by the authorities, and consequently co-founded the Free University of Madrid. He was associated, in the poetic 'School of Seville', with **Blanco White**. He adapted **Pope**'s *Dunciad*. But his own poetry was less important than his teaching, which was famous throughout Spain. As an *afrancesado* ('Frenchified Spaniard', ie, one who, like **Quintana** or **Meléndez Valdés**, believed that, after the Napoleonic armies entered Spain, Fernando VII should no longer reign), he was in exile in France between 1813 and 1817.

▷J C J Metford, *Alberto Lista and the Romantic Movement in Spain* (1940)

LITTLE, Jean
(1932–)

Canadian children's author, born in Taiwan. Little has been partially sighted from birth, has worked as a teacher of crippled children in Ontario, and her much-translated novels frequently feature a handicapped main character. *Mine For Keeps* (1961) was about a child suffering from cerebral palsy, and *From Anna* (1972) was about the wartime experiences of a partially-sighted German child living in Toronto. Her books are positive in tone, showing children working through difficult situations.

LITVINOFF, Emanuel
(1915)

British novelist and short-story writer, perhaps best known for the collection *Journey Through a Small Planet* (1972). Born in London, and apprenticed to the garment trade, he served with the Royal West African Frontier Force during World War II. His main fictional concern, however, is the fate of Holocaust survivors; *The Lost Europeans* (1959) is a bleak portrayal of post-war reconstruction and the uneasy *rapprochement* between exiled Jews and gentile compatriots who remained in Germany during the Third Reich. In the thriller *Falls the Shadow* (1983) he treats the same subject-matter in a more open style. For *The Man Next Door* (1968) and in many of his stories, Litvinoff switches the scene to London, but the trilogy comprising *A Death Out of Season* (1973), *Blood on the Snow* (1975) and *The Face of Terror* (1978) is concerned with a generation of young Russian idealists whose hopes are fulfilled by the Bolshevik Revolution and then shattered by the Stalinist reaction. Director of the Contemporary Jewish Library in London since the late 1950s, he has also edited the *Penguin Book of Jewish Short Stories* (1979).

LIVELY, Penelope Margaret
(1933–)

English novelist and children's author, born in Cairo, Egypt. She read history at Oxford, and a preoccupation with the relationship between the present and the past, and a vivid sense of time and place, form the central thread of much of her writing. In her children's book *The Ghost of Thomas Kempe* (1973), a present-day family is haunted by a 17th-century sorcerer, while the heroine of *A Stitch in Time* (1976) finds strange links between herself and the child who, a hundred years previously, embroidered a sampler hanging in her family's home. The adult novel *Moon Tiger* (1987) chronicles the life of intellectual, independent historian Claudia Hampton, while in *Cleopatra's Sister* (1992), a palaeontologist and a young journalist meet when the aircraft on which they are travelling is hijacked and forced to land at Callimba, a fictitious state on the north African coast. Lively has also written *The Presence of the Past: An Introduction to Landscape History* (1976).

LIVESAY, Dorothy
(1909–)

Canadian poet, born in Winnipeg, Manitoba and educated at the University of Toronto, the Sorbonne and the University of British Columbia; she has been a social worker, journalist, documentary scriptwriter, lecturer and editor. She is a poet of intense emotional impact, for whom the political is always personal: she writes of her poetry as reflecting the pull 'between community and private identity that is characteristic of being a woman'. Winner of the Governor General's Award for *Day and Night* (1944) and *Poems For People*

(1947), at her best she is a poet of rare luminosity. The collected poems of *The Two Seasons* (1972), those selected for *The Self-Completing Tree* (1986) and the collection of essays, poems, letters and reminiscences, *Right Hand Left Hand* (1977), cover the range of her work.

▷ 'Livesay Special Issue' of *A Room of One's Own*, V: 1/2 (1979)

LIVIUS ANDRONICUS
(fl. 3rd century BC)

Roman writer, known as 'the father of Roman dramatic and epic poetry', probably a Greek by birth, from Tarentum. He was taken prisoner at the Roman capture of the city and sold as a slave in Rome in 272 BC. He was afterwards freed by his master. He translated the *Odyssey* into Latin Saturnian verse, and wrote tragedies, comedies and hymns after Greek models. Only fragments are extant.

▷ S Mariotti, *Livio Andronico e la traduzione artistica* (1952)

LIVY, properly Titus Livius
(59 BC–17 AD)

Roman historian, born in Patavium (Padua), of a noble and wealthy family. He settled in Rome in about 29 BC and was admitted to the court of Augustus. He never flattered the emperor, but avowed his preference for a republic. He praised Brutus and Cassius, sympathized with Pompey, and stigmatized **Cicero**, as an accessory to the murder of **Caesar**, as having got from Mark Antony's bravoes only his deserts. Of the great Caesar himself he doubted whether he was more of a curse than a blessing to the commonwealth. Such friendship as they had for each other Livy and Augustus never lost. Livy died in his native Patavium. His history of Rome from her foundation to the death of Nero Claudius Drusus (9 BC) comprised 142 books, of which those from the 11th to the 20th, and from the 46th to the 142nd, have been lost. Of the 35 that remain, the 41st and 43rd are imperfect. The 'periochae', or summaries of the contents of each book, composed in the wane of Roman literature to catalogue names and events for rhetorical purposes, have all survived except those of books 136 and 137. But what has been spared is more than enough to confirm in modern days the judgement of antiquity which places Livy in the forefront of Latin writers. His impartiality is no less a note of his work than his veneration for the good, the generous, the heroic in man. For investigation of facts he did not go far afield. Accepting history as an art rather than a science, he was content to take his authorities as he found them, and where they differed was guided by taste or predilection.

The fame of his work comes chiefly from his vision of Rome as destined to greatness.

▷ P G Walsh, *Livy, his historical methods* (1961)

LIZARDI, Xabier de, pseud of José Maria Aguirre
(1896–1933)

Spanish–Basque poet, about whom very little is known except in the Basque provinces, where, however, he is widely regarded as having been the purest and most original lyrical poet of the 20th century.

▷ R A Gallop, *Book of the Basques* (1930)

LLEWELLYN, Richard, pseud of Richard Doyle Vivian Llewellyn Lloyd
(1907–83)

Welsh author, born in St David's, Pembrokeshire. He established himself, after service with the regular army and a short spell as a film director, as a bestselling novelist with *How Green was my Valley* (1939), a novel about a Welsh mining village. Later works include *None but the Lonely Heart* (1943), *The Flame of Hercules* (1957), *Up into the Singing Mountain* (1963), *Green, Green My Valley Now* (1975) and *I Stand On A Quiet Shore* (1982).

LLWDD, Morgan
(1619–59)

Welsh Puritan polemicist and poet, born in Cynfal Fawr. As a Puritan clergyman, he fought for the parliamentarians in the Civil War, and ended as the minister of Wrexham Parish Church. Three of his 11 works are in English; the rest are in Welsh. He was a wizard with words, a demagogue, and he believed in the imminent coming of Christ's Kingdom upon earth. His work is more interesting than much in the same tradition: he was well versed in esoteric lore, from the hermetic Books through astrology to the writings of **Jakob Böhme**, and he was a genuine mystic rather than a prophet. His fiery prose has been described as, at its best, 'unequalled in Welsh'.

▷ *Anglo-Welsh Review*, 23, 51 (1974)

LOBO, Francisco Rodrigues
(c. 1580–1622)

Portuguese writer, born in Leiria. He wrote *Primavera* (1601, 'Spring') and other remarkable prose pastorals and verse. He was drowned in the Tagus. His lyrics are of great beauty and his work holds a valuable place in the literature of his country.

▷ R Jorge, *Francisco Lobo* (1920)

LOCHHEAD, Liz
(1947–)

Scottish poet and dramatist, born in Motherwell, Lanarkshire. After studying at Glasgow School of Art (1965–70), she worked as an art teacher at Bishopbriggs High School, Glasgow, before becoming a full-time writer in 1979. A frank and witty poet, with a nice line in irony, she has published several collections, including *Dreaming Frankenstein and Collected Poems* (1984), and *True Confessions and New Clichés* (1985), a collection of songs, monologues and performance pieces. Her most powerful work has been written for the stage, where she has profitably re-worked the staples of Scottish history in *Mary Queen of Scots Got Her Head Chopped Off* (1987), literary biography (**Mary Shelley** in *Blood and Ice*, 1982), popular culture in *The Big Picture* (1988), and horror fiction in a version of **Bram Stoker**'s *Dracula* (1985), which restored the serious intent of the original, all from a thoroughly modern perspective. She translated **Molière**'s *Tartuffe* (1985) into demotic Glaswegian, and has written for radio and television. She wrote the text for the epic music theatre production *Jock Tamson's Bairns* in Glasgow in 1990.

LOCKE, Elsie Violet
(1912–)

New Zealand historian and writer for children, born in Hamilton. Her first book was *The Runaway Settlers*, in which a mother flees her husband and with her large family settles in New Zealand. *The End of the Harbour* (1968) and *Journey under Warning* (1983) again deal with events in colonial New Zealand and *A Canoe in the Mist* (1984) features the eruption of Mt Tarawera in 1886. The autobiographical *Student at the Gates* appeared in 1981.

LOCKE, William John
(1863–1930)

English novelist, born in Demerara, British Guiana (Guyana). He was educated in Trinidad and at Cambridge. He taught between 1890 and 1897 at Clifton and Glenalmond. Disliking teaching, he then became secretary of the Royal Institute of British Architects until 1907. In 1895 appeared the first of a long series of novels and plays which with their charmingly written sentimental themes enjoyed a huge success during his life in both Britain and America. *The Morals of Marcus Ordeyne* (1905) and *The Beloved Vagabond* (1906) assured his reputation. Others of his popular romances included *Simon the Jester* (1910), *The Joyous Adventures of Aristide Pujol* (1912) and *The Wonderful Fear* (1916). His plays, some of which were dramatized versions of his novels, were produced with success on the London stage.

LOCKER-LAMPSON, Frederick
(1821–95)

English writer, born in London. He came of naval ancestry, and from government service passed to the Admiralty. He left government service in 1850. *London Lyrics* (1857) revealed him as a writer of bright and clever light verse dealing with society topics. Later collections of verse were *Lyra Elegantiarum* (1867) and *Patchwork* (1879). Among his influences was the work of **Winthrop Praed**.
▷A Lampson, *An Appendix to the Rowfant Library* (1900)

LOCKHART, John Gibson
(1794–1854)

Scottish biographer, novelist and critic, born in Cambusnethan, Lanarkshire, the son of a Church of Scotland minister. He spent his boyhood in Glasgow, where at 11 he went from the high school to the college. At the age of 13, with a Snell exhibition to Balliol College, he went up to Oxford. In 1813 he took a first in classics. Then, after a visit to the Continent to see **Goethe** in Weimar, he studied law at Edinburgh, and in 1816 was called to the Bar. While still at Oxford he had written the article 'Heraldry' for the *Edinburgh Encyclopaedia*, and translated **Schlegel**'s *Lectures on the History of Literature*. From 1817 he turned increasingly to writing, and with **John Wilson** ('Christopher North') became the chief mainstay of *Blackwood's Magazine*. There he exhibited the cruelty with which he savaged other writers and the caustic wit that made him the terror of his Whig opponents. In 1819 he published *Peter's Letters to His Kinsfolk* in three volumes, a clever skit on Edinburgh intellectual society. In 1820 he married Sophia, eldest daughter of Sir **Walter Scott**, and wrote four novels—*Valerius* (1821), *Adam Blair* (1822), *Reginald Dalton* (1823) and *Matthew Wald* (1824). *Ancient Spanish Ballads* appeared in 1823, biographies of **Robert Burns** and Napoleon in 1828 and 1829, and the memoirs, *The Life of Sir Walter Scott*, his masterpiece, in 1837–8 (7 vols). In 1825 he moved to London to become Editor until 1853 of the *Quarterly Review*. In 1843 he also became auditor of the Duchy of Cornwall. His closing years were clouded by illness and deep depression; by his only daughter and her husband, J R Hope-Scott, becoming Catholic; and by the loss of his wife in 1837, and of his two sons in 1831 and 1853. The elder was the 'Hugh Littlejohn' of Scott's *Tales of a Grandfather*; the younger, Walter, was in the army. Like Scott, Lockhart visited Italy in search of health, and he too came back to Abbotsford to die. He is buried in Dryburgh Abbey beside Scott.

▷A Lang, *Life and Letters of John Gibson Lockhart* (1896)

LOCKRIDGE, Ross
(1914–48)

American novelist, the author of just one title before taking his own life at the age of 34. Lockridge was born in Bloomington, Indiana, and had taught at Indiana University and Simmons College before publication of the ambitious *Raintree County* (1948). This told about events on a single day (4th July) but, unlike **Joyce**'s *Ulysses*, it was expansive in tone and owed more to the influence of **Thomas Wolfe**. The book was hailed as a triumph. Hollywood tried to turn it into another *Gone With The Wind*, starring Montgomery Clift and Elizabeth Taylor. The film's oblivion is deserved; the novel will enjoy recurrent waves of interest.

LODGE, David John
(1935–)

English novelist and critic, born in London. His earlier novels include the realistic light comedy *The Picturegoers* (1960). In *The British Museum is Falling Down* (1965) and *How Far Can You Go?* (1980), in which Roman Catholics wrestle with the moral problems of contemporary life, he introduces various forms of literary allusion and parody. This device is perfected in comedies such as *Small World* (1984), which echoes the form of an Arthurian Romance. It is a sequel to the highly amusing *Changing Places* (1975), in which Philip Swallow, a shy English academic, changes places with his sardonic American counterpart, Maurice Zapp. The 19th-century state-of-the-nation novel provides the literary model for *Nice Work* (1988), a comedy in which an industrialist and an academic shadow each other's working lives. Lodge's criticism includes *Language of Fiction* (1961) and *Working With Structuralism* (1981).

LODGE, Thomas
(c.1558–1625)

English dramatist, romance writer and poet, born in West Ham. From Merchant Taylors' School he went to Trinity College, Oxford, and from there in 1578 to Lincoln's Inn, but led a wild life. He published a *Defence of Poetry* anonymously in 1580, and an attack on abuses by moneylenders, *An Alarum against Usurers*, in 1584, along with his first romance, *The Delectable Historie of Forbonius and Priscilla*, followed by *Scillaes Metamorphosis* in 1589. About 1588 he took part in a buccaneering expedition to the

Canaries, and wrote another romance, *Rosalynde* (1590), his best-known work, which supplied **Shakespeare** with many of the chief incidents in *As You Like It*. He went on a second freebooting expedition to South America in 1591. He wrote many other works, including *The Wounds of the Civil War* (1594) and *A Looking-glass for London and England* (with **Robert Greene**, 1594). He turned Catholic and is believed to have taken a medical degree at Avignon (1600), and to have written a *History of the Plague* (1603). Among his remaining writings are *A Fig for Momus* (1595); translations of **Seneca** (1614) and Josephus (1602); *Life of William Longbeard* (1593); *Robin the Divell*, *Wits Miserie and Worlds Madness* (1596), and a collection of poems, *Phillis* (1593).

▷W D Roe, *Thomas Lodge* (1967)

LOERKE, Oscar
(1884–1941)

German poet, novelist, writer on music and critic, born in Jungau an der Wischel (now in Poland). A publisher (S Fischer Verlag), he held important cultural posts until effectively deprived of them by the Nazis, who suspected him—he called their regime 'Das Unheil' ('the mischief'), and lived in lonely estrangement in his last years. In his poetry, which decisively influenced the late flowering of his friend **Wilhelm Lehmann**, he developed expressionist techniques (strictness of form, 'uprooted' metaphors) in the interests of what has been called a 'cosmo-centric' *Naturlyrik*. His later poems, which took into account 'the mischief', are his most profound, and may well outlast those of the more modernistic successors whom he influenced. His remaining works were edited by **Hermann Kesten**.

▷C Middleton and M Hamburger (eds), *Modern German Poetry 1910–1969* (1962)

LOESSER, Frank Henry
(1910–69)

American lyricist, born in New York. His first work on Broadway came as lyricist on *The Illustrator's Show* (1936). One of the most important American songwriters for the stage and screen, he is best known for his brilliantly colloquial songs for *Guys and Dolls* (1950), a ground-breaking musical comedy based on the stories of **Damon Runyon**, which achieved massive success on stage, and later as a film (1955). He shared the Pulitzer Prize for Drama in 1962 with writer Abe Burrows (1910–85) for the hit musical comedy *How to Succeed in Business Without Really Trying* (1961).

LOFTING, Hugh John
(1886–1947)

English children's novelist, born in Maidenhead. The 'Dr Dolittle' books (1920–53), for which he is famous (despite slurs that they are racist and chauvinistic), had their origins in the trench warfare of World War I, of which he had first-hand experience. The idea of the doctor who learns animal languages came to him from his reflections on the part that horses were playing in the war. There were a dozen Doolittle books, which he also illustrated, and though he tired of his eponymous hero—on one occasion attempting to abandon him on the Moon—his popularity with readers kept him alive. Lofting was mainly resident in the USA from 1912.

LOFTS, Norah
(1904–83)

English novelist, born in Bury St Edmunds. The author, under her own name, of historical romances such as *The Brittle Glass* (1942), she also wrote thrillers, such as *Lady Living Alone* (1944), under the pseudonym Peter Curtis. The heroine of *The Brittle Glass*, the young daughter of a Norfolk trader, is a typical Lofts protagonist, an independent woman seeking self-determination in a patriarchal world. *Madselin* (1969) depicts the clash in medieval England between the conquering Normans and oppressed Saxons, as seen through the eyes of the titular character. *Crown of Aloes* (1974) is about Queen Isabella of Spain. Although at times stereotypically romantic, Lofts' novels also have a more realistic side and a contemporary resonance, given that their protagonists are often strong, resilient women who are left to pick up the pieces in a Europe laid waste by the violence of men.

LOGAN, John
(1748–88)

Scottish poet and clergyman, born in Soutra, Midlothian. He was educated at Musselburgh Grammar School and Edinburgh University, and was appointed minister of South Leith in 1773. He wrote a successful play, *Runnemede*, in 1784, and moved to London. He is mainly remembered for his plagiarism of several poems of his friend Michael Bruce, including 'Ode to the Cuckoo', which he included in his own volume of poetry (1781).
▷J Anderson, *A Life of John Logan* (1953)

LOGAN, John
(1923–87)

American poet, academic and editor of poetry journals, born in Red Oak, Iowa, and educated at Iowa University. Logan's critical reputation has always been high, but his sometimes difficult verse has prevented him from becoming a truly popular author. His first collection, *A Cycle for Mother Cabrini*, appeared in 1955. It was followed by *Ghosts*

of the Heart (1960), *The Zig-Zag Walk* (1969) and *Poem in Progress* (1974). His *Collected Poems* appeared in 1988. He published a volume of autobiographical fiction, *The House That Jack Built*, in 1974 (rev edn 1984).

LOGAN, Joshua *see* HAMMERSTEIN, Oscar II

LOGAU, Friedrich, Freiherr von, pseud Salomon von Golaw
(1604–55)

German epigrammatic poet, born in Brockuth into a noble family. His epigrams, his only known work, written under his pseudonym, combine worldly wisdom, devout Christianity, and sharp satire. He was forgotten until revived by **Gotthold Lessing** in 1759.
▷P Hempel, *Der Kunst Logau* (1967)

LOHENSTEIN, Daniel Caspar von
(1635–82)

German poet, dramatist, translator (**Gracian**, **Marino**) and novelist, born in Nimptsch in Silesia. The son of a tax-collector, and himself a busy lawyer and city functionary of Breslau, he rose above all this to become a major writer as tragedian and as novelist. His most substantial work is the unfinished novel *Grossmüthiger Feldherr Arminius* (1689), which a few critics have interpreted as an intended repository of all essential knowledge. It is a neglected and underestimated work.
▷*German Life and Letters, XXIV* (1971–2)

LO-JOHANSSON, Ivar
(1901–91)

Swedish novelist and short-story writer, born in Sörmland, a major figure among the working-class writers of the first half of the century. In his youth he worked and travelled throughout Europe and his first books are proletarian travel-narratives based on these experiences. He was a campaigning writer who, in novels such as *Godnatt, jord* (1933, 'Goodnight, Earth') and short stories such as *Statarna* (1936–7, 'The Statare'), highlighted the conditions of farmworkers and other oppressed groups in naturalistic detail. Many of his novels had an autobiographical basis, particularly the series introduced by the warm-hearted *Analfabeten* (1951, 'The Illiterate Man'). Beginning with *Passionerna: Älskog* (1968, 'The Passions: Love'), he produced seven volumes of stories focusing on the passions that afflict humanity; they contain some of the most powerful short fiction written in Swedish.
▷M Edström, *Äran, kärleken, klassen* (1976)

LOM, Iain

LOM, Iain, Gaelic name of **John MacDonald** (1624–1710)

Gaelic poet, descended from the MacDonald chiefs of Keppoch. He was involved in the clan feuds as a staunch Catholic and bitter enemy to the Covenanters of the clan Campbell. His verse was often political, as in works such as 'L'a Inbhir L'ochaidh', in which he glories in the Royalist victory over the Marquis of Argyll, Archibald Campbell. He composed elegies and public poems in honour of the MacDonald chiefs and also wrote in support of the Jacobite cause. His poetry is in the traditional form of classical poets and is remarkable for its consistent loyalty to clan and to king. Charles II appointed him poet laureate in Scotland at the time of the Restoration. A poet of public affairs to the end of his long life, he denounced William of Orange as a 'borrowed king' and wrote a satire of the 1707 Act of Union. A collection of his poems and songs, *Orain Iain Luim*, was published in 1964.

LOMONOSOV, Mikhail Vasilievich
(1711–65)

Russian scientist and writer, born in Denisovka, near Archangel. The son of a fisherman, he ran away to Moscow in search of education, and later studied at St Petersburg and at Marburg in Germany under the philosopher Christian von Wolff. Turning to science, he became Professor of Chemistry at St Petersburg Academy of Sciences in 1745, and set up the first chemical laboratory in Russia there. In 1755 he founded Moscow University. Apart from his many works on science, he also wrote poetry on scientific and religious subjects. His writings include works on rhetoric (1748), grammar (1755) and Russian history (1766); his greatest contribution to Russian culture was his systematization of the grammar and language.
▷I Serman, *Poeticheskii stil' Lomonosova* (1966)

LONDON, Jack (John Griffith)
(1876–1916)

American novelist, born in San Francisco. He was successively sailor, tramp and gold miner before he took to writing. He used his knowledge of the Klondyke in the highly successful *Call of the Wild* (1903) and *White Fang* (1907), both about a stoical sled-dog. He used his knowledge of the sea in *The Sea-Wolf* (1904) and *The Mutiny of the 'Elsinore'* (1914). As well as pure adventure tales, he also wrote the more serious political novel *The Iron Heel* (1907), and his autobiographical tale of alcoholism, *John Barleycorn* (1913).

▷R O'Connor, *Jack London: a biography* (1964)

LONGFELLOW, Henry Wadsworth
(1807–82)

American poet, born in Portland, Maine. He graduated at Bowdoin College in Brunswick, Maine, where one of his classmates was **Nathaniel Hawthorne**. In 1826 the college trustees sent him to Europe to qualify for the chair of foreign languages, and he spent three years abroad (1826–9) before taking up the chair at Bowdoin (1829–35). He married in 1831, but his wife died in 1835. *Outre Mer*, an account of his first European tour, appeared in 1835; and *Hyperion*, which is a journal of the second, in 1839. In 1836, after another visit to Europe, when he met **Thomas Carlyle**, he became Professor of Modern Languages and Literature at Harvard, and held the chair for nearly 18 years. *Voices of the Night* (1839), his first book of verse, made a favourable impression, which was strengthened by *Ballads* (1841), which included 'The Skeleton in Armour', 'The Wreck of the Hesperus', 'The Village Blacksmith' and 'Excelsior'. *Poems on Slavery* appeared in 1842. He made a third visit to Europe in 1842, and the next year married his second wife, Frances Appleton, who died in a fire in 1861. *The Belfry of Bruges and other Poems* appeared in 1846. One of his most popular poems is *Evangeline* (1847), a tale (in hexameters) of the French exiles of Acadia. *The Golden Legend* (1851) is based on *Der arme Heinrich* of **Hartmann von Aue**. His most popular work, *Hiawatha* (1855), is based on the legends of the Redskins, using a metre borrowed from the Finnish epic, the *Kalevala. The Courtship of Miles Standish* (1858) is a story in hexameters of the early days of the Plymouth colony in Massachusetts. It was followed by *Tales of a Wayside Inn* (1863), which included 'Paul Revere's Ride', and an undistinguished translation of **Dante**'s *Divina Commedia* (1865–7). He paid a last visit to Europe in 1868–9. As a poet he was extremely popular during his lifetime and although his work lacks the depth of great poetry, his gift of simple, romantic story-telling in verse makes it still read widely with pleasure.
▷N Arvin, *Longfellow, his life and works* (1963)

LONGLEY, Michael
(1939–)

Irish poet, born in Belfast. He graduated from Trinity College, Dublin in 1963, and worked as a schoolmaster until 1970, when he became Director for Literature and Traditional Arts of the Arts Council of Northern Ireland. His first collection, *No Continuing City: Poems 1963–1968* (1969), revealed an already mature talent and a compassionate, humane voice which emerged even more strongly in *An Exploded View: Poems 1968–1972* (1973). He is a scrupulous craftsman in both free and metric verse forms, and covers a wide range of subject-matter. He writes beautifully on nature, perceptively about human relationships, and with deep feeling on the Irish situation. Later books include *Poems 1963–1983* (1985) and *Gorse Fires* (1991). He edited **Louis MacNeice**'s *Selected Poems* (1988).

LONGUS
(?3rd century)

The author of the Greek pastoral romance *Daphnis and Chloe*. He was probably a native of Lesbos.
▷ B P Reardon, *Les courants littéraires grecs* (1971)

LÖNNROT, Elias
(1802–84)

Finnish philologist and folklorist, born in Sammatti in Nyland. He studied medicine, and was district medical officer for 20 years in Kajana. As a result of his folklore researches, he was appointed Professor of Finnish at Helsingfors (now Helsinki) (1853–62). His major achievement was the collection of oral popular lays, which he organized into a long, connected epic poem of ancient life in the far north, the *Kalevala* (the shorter *Old Kalevala* in 1835, the longer version in 1849). Having standardized the national epic, he also compiled a great Finnish–Swedish dictionary (1866–80), which helped to establish a literary Finnish language.
▷ W Wilson, *Folklore and Nationalism in Modern Finland* (1976)

LONSDALE, Frederick, originally **Frederick Leonard**
(1881–1954)

British playwright, born in Jersey, the son of a tobacconist. He was known for his witty and sophisticated society comedies, among them *The Last of Mrs Cheyney* (1925), *On Approval* (1927) and *Canaries Sometimes Sing* (1929). He collaborated in operettas, including *Maid of the Mountains* (1916).
▷ F Donaldson, *Frederick Lonsdale* (1957)

LOOS, Anita
(?1893–1981)

American scriptwriter and novelist, born in California. Starting her literary career at the age of 10, when she wrote for her father's paper, she began writing film-scripts and silent-film subtitles for D W Griffith in 1912. Her comic masterpiece, *Gentlemen Prefer Blondes* (1925), with its naive, gold-digging heroine, Lorelei Lee, summed up the mood

of the Roaring Twenties. It scored a huge success as novel, musical and movie, and she became one of Hollywood's most influential screenwriters, working with her second husband, director John Emerson. She also wrote stage-plays, including *Gigi* (1952), an adaptation of **Colette**'s novel, and two gossipy Hollywood memoirs, *A Girl Like I* (1966) and *Kiss Hollywood Goodbye* (1974). Doubt has been cast on her commonly accepted birthdate by her biographer, Gary Carey, who suggests she was born in 1888.
▷ G Carey, *Anita Loos, A Biography* (1988)

LOOY, Jacobus van
(1855–1930)

Dutch story writer and painter, born in Haarlem. A typical Dutch impressionist, he recorded the dream-world of a child in his *Jacob* (1930).

LOPEZ, Vicente
(1815–1903)

Argentinian novelist and historian, born in Buenos Aires, the son of a famous statesman, Vicente Lopez y Planos. He wrote in the manner of Sir **Walter Scott**, achieving his finest novel with *La novia del hereje o La Inquisición de Lima* (1854, 'The Heretic's Fiancée, or the Lima Inquisition'), which forms a later part of the cult of the pirate introduced by **Byron**. His historical work is also important. His anger was always directed at fanatical and sadistic Roman Catholic inquisitors and torturers, and this type finds its fullest expression in the psychotic Father Andrés in *La novia*.

LÓPEZ VELARDE, Ramón
(1888–1921)

Major Mexican poet and impressionistic prose writer, born in Zacatecas. His supposedly patriotic poems to his country, although full of love for it, are also full of a subtle irony which, however, for the most part has not been perceived by critics. He was one of the greatest love poets of his age in any language, and perhaps the most ironic of all. He learned mainly from the early **Lugones** —whom he soon surpassed; from the *modernista* style fashionable when he began to write; and, above all, from **Jules Laforgue**. By 1910 he had found his own very distinctive voice: satirical, quiet, phenomenological, far ahead of his time. His posthumous prose sketches, most conveniently to be found in his complete poems, *Poesias completas* (1957) are also remarkable. His influence upon Latin-American poetry as a whole, as well as on Mexican, has been unobtrusive but absolute, and he did more, in fact, than even **González**

Martínez to bring poetry out of the *modernista* phase in which it was beginning to stultify.

▷A W Phillips, *Ramón López Velarde* (1962, in Spanish)

LOPEZ Y FUENTES, Gregorio
(1897–1966)

Mexican novelist and poet, born in Veracruz. His poems are of little account, being but pale imitations of **Darío**; but his fiction, particularly the novels *Tierra* (1933, 'Earth'), about the revolutionary leader Zapata, and *El indio* (1935, Eng trans *They That Reap*, 1937), is in a higher category, and the latter, although not 'the great Indianist classic' that it has been called, is a worthy indictment of the Mexican government's failure to protect the Native Americans and their way of life.

LORCA *see* GARCÍA LORCA

LORDE, Audre Geraldine
(1934–92)

American poet, born in New York of West Indian parents, she was proud to be black, feminist, lesbian *and* a mother of two children. From her earliest collection, *The First Cities* (1968), through to the later *Our Dead Behind Us* (1987), she singlemindedly explored themes of race and sex, using memories of her own childhood and the efforts of a light-skinned mother to 'beat me whiter every day'.

▷*Zami: A New Spelling of My Name* (1982)

LORRIS, Guillaume de
(fl.13th century)

French poet. He wrote, before 1260, the first part (c.4000 lines) of the *Roman de la Rose* (completed c.1280, Eng trans *The Romaunt of the Rose* by **Chaucer**, c.1370), which was later continued by **Jean de Meung**. Nothing certain is known of his life.

LOTI, Pierre, pseud of Louis Marie Julien Viaud
(1850–1923)

French naval officer and novelist, born in Rochefort. He entered the navy in 1869 and served in the east, retiring as captain in 1910, but was recalled to service in World War I. His voyages as a sailor and as a traveller provide the scenes for most of his writings, and from the native women of the South Sea Islands he gained his pseudonym Loti, 'Flower of the Pacific'. *Aziyadé* (1879), his first novel, was a series of pictures of life on the Bosphorus and it was followed by the very successful *Rarahu* (1880), published in 1882 as *Le Mariage de Loti* (Eng trans *Rarahu; or, The Marriage of Loti*, 1892). Semi-autobiographical, and set among the coral seas, this story of the love of an Englishman for a Tahitian girl immediately captured the imagination. Of his novels, the best known is *Pêcheur d'Islande* (1886, Eng trans *An Iceland Fisherman*, 1888), a descriptive study of Breton fisher life in Icelandic waters. Other works include *Le Roman d'un Spahi* (1881, Eng trans *The Romance of a Spahi*, 1890), *Mon Frère Yves* (1883, Eng trans *My Brother Yves*, 1884), *Madame Chrysanthème* (1887, Eng trans 1889) and *Vers Ispahan* (1904, 'Towards Ispahan').

LOUW, N P Van Wyck
(1906–70)

South African poet and radio dramatist (writing in Afrikaans), and his literature's leading practitioner until his death. He was and will remain important. Despite his prejudices about racial matters, he was not a member of the extreme right. He was influenced by **Nietzsche**, **Roland Holst** and Hendrik Marsman. *Raka* (1941, Eng trans 1941), a narrative poem on folkloric themes, is generally regarded as the best poem of its kind in Afrikaans. His most notable play is *Germanicus* (1956). There are English translations in the *Penguin Book of South African Verse* (1968, Jack Cope and Uys Krige eds).

LOUŸS, Pierre
(1870–1925)

French poet and novelist, born in Ghent. He moved to Paris, where in 1891 he founded a review called *Le Conque* to which **Mathurin Régnier**, **André Gide** and **Paul Valéry** were contributors. In this were printed his first poems, most of which later appeared in *Astarté* (1891). His lyrics, based on the Greek form which he so much admired, are masterpieces of style. Other volumes are *Poésies de Méléagre de Gédara* (1893), *Scènes de la vie des courtisanes de Lucien* (1894, 'Scenes from the Life of the Courtesans by Lucian') and *Les Chansons de Bilitis* (1894, Eng trans *The Songs of Bilitis*, 1928). In 1896 his novel *Aphrodite* (Eng trans 1906) was published with great success, and a psychological novel *La Femme et le pantin* (Eng trans *Woman and Puppet*, 1902) appeared in 1898.

▷C Farrere, *Mon Ami Pierre Louÿs* (1953)

LOVECRAFT, H(oward) P(hillips)
(1890–1937)

American science-fiction writer and poet, born in Providence, Rhode Island, where he lived all his life. Educated at local schools, he married the writer Sonia Greene in 1924 but they were divorced in 1929. A writer from

1908, he supported himself by ghost writing and as a revisionist. From 1923 he was a regular contributor to *Weird Tales*. His cult following can be traced to the 60 or so stories first published in that magazine and to what has posthumously come to be known as the 'Cthulhu Mythos', which holds that in the days before mankind the earth was inhabited by fish-like beings called the 'Old Ones' who worshipped the gelatinous Cthulhu. Not surprisingly Lovecraft had difficulty in accumulating readers but he gradually attracted a small but fanatical following in America and abroad, particularly France. In an area in which accepted literary criteria go by the board, Lovecraft was unique. Among his various collections are *The Shadow over Innsmouth* (1936), *The Outsider and Others* (1939), *Dreams and Fancies* (1962) and *Dagon and Other Macabre Tales* (1965), the posthumous volumes edited by August Derleth. His novellas included *The Case of Charles Dexter Ward* (1928), and *At the Mountains of Madness* (1931).
▷A Derleth, *H P Lovecraft: A Memoir* (1945)

LØVEID, Cecilie
(1951–)

Norwegian poet, novelist and playwright. She grew up in Bergen, studied at art college, and had her first literary text published in 1969. Her work, which often employs a collage technique and transcends the conventional notions of genre, is heavily dependent on the effects of imagery and sound, the experimental language centring on the female body. The poetic novel *Most* (1972) focuses, like so many of her subsequent works, on a female-male relationship, while *Alltid skyer over Askøy* (1976, 'Always Clouds over Askøy') traces the changing experiences of several generations of women. The novel *Sug* (1979, Eng trans *Sea Swell*, 1986), with its kaleidoscopic composition and stylistic experimentation highlights a search for feminine identity which also becomes a search for language. Linguistic boldness is also characteristic of her radio drama *Måkespisere* (Eng trans *Seagull Eaters*, 1989), first performed in 1982 and winner of the Prix Italia the following year.
▷J Garton, 'Cecilie Løveid', in *Norwegian Women's Writing 1850–1990* (1993)

LOVEIRA, Carlos
(1882–1928)

Cuban novelist and politician. He began writing when he became involved with the organization of the Cuban railway workers. His fiction is polemical but vivid and well observed. His best novel is *Juan Criollo* (1927), an undisguised critique of the independent Cuban governments.

LOVELACE, Earl
(1935–)

Trinidadian novelist, whose first novel, *While Gods Are Falling* (1965), gave one of the most vivid and memorable portraits of Port of Spain, in whose slums it is set. Its central character, Walter Castle, wants to escape from a place of such meaninglessness; Lovelace's second novel, *The Schoolmaster* (1968), is a bitter account of a place in Trinidad that might have been expected to yield 'meaning'. It was held by critics to mark an advance on the first novel, which, for all its power, was obviously influenced by **Alan Paton**. *The Dragon Can't Dance* (1979), again set in the slums, was even more vivid and accomplished, although this author's progressive message did not find universal agreement.

LOVELACE, Richard
(1618–57)

English cavalier poet, born in Woolwich, or perhaps in Holland, the eldest son of a Kentish knight. He was educated at Charterhouse and Gloucester Hall, Oxford. He found his way to court and went on the Scottish expedition in 1639. In 1642 he was imprisoned for presenting to the House of Commons a petition from the royalists of Kent 'for the restoring the king to his rights', and was released on bail. He spent his estate in the king's cause, assisted the French in 1646 to capture Dunkirk from the Spaniards, and was flung into jail on returning to England in 1648. In jail he revised his poems, including 'To Althea, from Prison', and in 1649 published his collection of poems, *Lucasta*. He was set free at the end of 1649. In 1659 his brother published a second collection of his poems, *Lucasta: Posthume Poems*.
▷C S Ker, *Richard Lovelace* (1949)

LOVER, Samuel
(1797–1868)

Irish writer, artist and songwriter, born in Dublin. In 1818 he established himself there as a marine painter and miniaturist. One of the founders of the *Dublin University Magazine*, he published *Legends and Stories of Ireland* in 1831 with his own illustrations. In 1835 he moved to London, where he wrote two popular novels, *Rory O'More* (1836) and *Handy Andy* (1842). He helped **Dickens** found *Bentley's Miscellany* and in 1844 started an entertainment, called 'Irish Evenings', which was a hit both in England and the USA (1846–8) with songs like 'The Low-Backed Car' and 'Molly Bawn'.
▷W B Samuel, *The Life of Samuel Lover* (1874)

LOWELL, Amy
(1874–1925)

American imagist poet, born into an extremely wealthy family in Brookline, Massachusetts, sister of Abbott Lowell and Percival Lowell. She travelled extensively with her parents in Europe, and bought the parental home, 'Sevenals', in 1903. She wrote volumes of *vers libre* which she named 'unrhymed cadence', starting with the conventional *A Dome of Many-coloured Glass* (1912) and *Sword Blades and Poppy Seeds* (1914). She also wrote polyphonic prose. Her other works include *Six French Poets* (1915), *Tendencies in Modern American Poetry* (1917) and a biography of **Keats** (1925).
▷F C Flint, *Amy Lowell* (1969)

LOWELL, James Russell
(1819–91)

American poet, essayist and diplomat, born in Cambridge, Massachusetts, the son of a minister. He graduated from Harvard in 1838. In 1841–4 he published two volumes of poetry, in 1845 *Conversations on the Old Poets*; and in 1843 he helped to edit *The Pioneer*, with **Nathaniel Hawthorne**, **Edgar Allan Poe** and **John Whittier** for contributors. In 1846, at the outbreak of the war with Mexico, he wrote a satiric poem in the Yankee dialect denouncing the pro-slavery party and the conduct of the government, and out of this grew the *Biglow Papers* (1848). A great many serious poems were written about 1848, and formed a third volume. *A Fable for Critics* (1848) is a series of witty and dashing sketches of American authors. In 1851–2 he visited Europe. In 1855 he was appointed Professor of Modern Languages and Literature at Harvard and went to Europe to finish his studies. He also edited the *Atlantic Monthly* from 1857, and with Charles Eliot Norton the *North American Review* (1863–7). His prose writings—*Among my Books* (1870) and *My Study Windows* (1871)—are of a very high quality. The second series of *Biglow Papers* appeared during the Civil War, in 1867. Lowell was an ardent abolitionist, and from the first gave himself unreservedly to the cause of freedom. Though he had never been a politician he was appointed in 1877 US Minister to Spain, and was transferred in 1880 to Great Britain, where he remained until 1885.
▷H E Scudder, *James Russell Lowell* (2 vols, 1901)

LOWELL, Robert Traill Spence, Jr
(1917–77)

American poet, born in Boston, Massachusetts, of a patrician New England family, the great-grand-nephew of **James Russell Lowell**. He attended St Mark's School, then Harvard, but left after two years to go to Kenyon College to study poetry, criticism and classics under **John Crowe Ransom** in what he called 'the heyday of the New Criticism'. He then attended Louisiana State University and afterwards worked briefly for a New York publisher. During World War II he was a conscientious objector and was imprisoned for six months (1944). In 1940 he married the writer **Jean Stafford** and became an ardent convert to Roman Catholicism. It was a fraught and violent liaison, Lowell being subject to periods of mental instability exacerbated by heavy drinking. His first collection was *Lands of Unlikeness* (1944), the first step towards what amounts, in the words of one critic, 'to his own exhaustive critical biography'. But it was not until the publication of his widely-acclaimed second volume, *Lord Weary's Castle* (1946), awarded the Pulitzer Prize in 1947, that he was accorded the status of a major poet. Divorced from Jean Stafford, he married the writer **Elizabeth Hardwick** but that union also faltered and he married in 1973 another writer, **Caroline Blackwood**. *Life Studies* (1959) was again intensely 'confessional', as were *For the Union Dead* (1964) and *Near the Ocean* (1967), in what was a highly productive period during which he also wrote many plays and translations. He had a high public profile during the Vietnam years, as can be gauged from *Notebook* (1968), but his personal life began to disintegrate. Rather than shrink from his problems he faced them directly in *The Dolphin* (1973), making public personal letters and anxieties, and inviting new notoriety. Latterly his poetry became increasingly obscure and monotonous, and *Day by Day* (1977), published shortly before he died, did not enhance his reputation.
▷I Hamilton, *Robert Lowell: a biography* (1985)

LOWER, Lennie
(1903–47)

Australian humorous writer, born in Dubbo, New South Wales, who wrote for various Sydney journals before publishing *Here's Luck* in 1930. Through the success of this picaresque novel his work was in demand by national periodicals, and in turn brought forth a series of books from *Here's Another* (1932) to *Lennie Lower's Annual* (1941). Essentially a writer of his time, the **C J Dennis** of the 1930s, Lower's humour relied heavily on the male chauvinist vernacular of the period and on the author's atrocious punning. A selection, *The Best of Lennie Lower*, came out in 1963.

LOWRY, (Clarence) Malcolm
(1909–57)

English novelist, born in Cheshire. He was a rebel, wanderer, and chronic alcoholic. He

left public school to sign as a deck-hand on a ship bound for China, but returned to take a degree at St Catherine's College, Cambridge. He wrote about the voyage in his first novel, *Ultramarine* (1933), but completed only one more book in his lifetime, his masterpiece *Under the Volcano* (1947), a relentlessly confessional story about the last day of an alcoholic British consul. He lived in Mexico with his first wife, and in a squatter's shack in British Columbia with his second (1940–54), where he did his most productive writing. They returned to England, where he died 'by misadventure', choking in his sleep. Posthumous publications from his mass of writings include stories, poems, letters, and three novels, *Lunar Caustic* (1963), *Dark as the Grave Wherein my Friend is Laid* (1968) and *October Ferry to Gabriola* (1970).
▷ D Day, *Malcolm Lowry* (1974); G Bowker, *Pursued by Furies* (1993)

LOY (Lowy), Mina
(1882–1966)

English playwright, poet, satirist and painter, born in London. After studying art during the early years of the century, she moved to Florence and composed a manifesto exhorting female artists to interpret Futurist ambitions from a feminist point of view. Becoming disenchanted with the movement, she wrote *The Pamperers*, an unpublished play violently attacking what she considered the Futurists' overwhelming male vanity. Moving to New York City in 1916, she married Arthur Cravan, an aspiring Dadaist, 'fugitive, forger and master of disguise', who abandoned her within months. Loy published modernist poetry in many small magazines and busied herself in a number of artistic ventures. In 1923 she published a collection, *Lunar Baedecker*, reissued, with more verses, as *Lunar Baedecker & Time-Tables* (1958). More pieces were collected posthumously as *The Last Lunar Baedecker* in 1982.
▷ V M Kouidis, *Mina Loy* (1980)

LOZEAU, Albert
(1878–1924)

Elegant and gifted French–Canadian poet who became known as the 'poet of the closed-in life', owing to his confinement, from the age of 18, to his bed with a form of spinal paralysis. He is well represented in **A J M Smith**'s *Oxford Book of Canadian Verse* (1956).

LU HSUN, or LU HSIN
(1881–1936)

Chinese writer, born in Shaohsin in Chekiang, of a family of scholars. In 1909 he became Dean of Studies at the Shaohsin Middle School and later its principal. By 1913 he was Professor of Chinese Literature at the National Peking University and National Normal University for Women. In 1926 he went as professor to Amoy University and later was appointed Dean of the College of Arts and Letters at Sun Yat-Sen University, Canton. His career as an author began with a short story, *Diary of a Madman* (1918). In 1921 appeared *The True Story of Ah Q* (Eng trans 1941). Considered his most successful book, it has been translated into many languages. Between 1918 and 1925 he wrote 26 short stories and these appear in two volumes entitled *Cry* and *Hesitation*.
▷ H Sung-k'ang, *Lu Hsun and the New Culture Movement in Modern China* (1957)

LUBRANO, Giacomo
(1619–93)

Italian Jesuit Baroque poet, born in Naples. A renowned preacher, he was a follower of **Marino**.

LUCAN (Marcus Annaeus Lucanus)
(39–65)

Roman poet, born in Corduba (Córdoba) in Spain, the nephew of the philosopher **Seneca, 'the Younger'**. He studied in Rome and in Athens, and became proficient in rhetoric and philosophy. He was recalled to Rome by the emperor Nero, who held him in high favour and made him quaestor and augur. In 60 he won the poetry competition in the first Neronia games. In 62 he published the first three books of his epic *Bellum Civile* (*Pharsalia*) on the civil war between Pompey and **Caesar**. Soon the emperor, perhaps jealous of Lucan's literary successes, forbade him to write poetry or plead in the courts. In 65 Lucan joined the conspiracy of Piso against Nero, but was betrayed and compelled to commit suicide. A precociously fluent writer in Silver Latin, the epic *Pharsalia* is all that has survived of his writing.
▷ M P O Morford, *Lucan the Poet* (1967)

LUCAS, Edward Verrall
(1868–1938)

English essayist and biographer, born in Eltham, Kent. He became a bookseller's assistant, a reporter, contributor to and assistant editor of *Punch* and finally a publisher. He compiled anthologies, wrote novels (the best of which was *Over Bemerton's*, 1908), books of travel and about 30 volumes of essays in a light, charming vein. An authority on **Charles Lamb**, he wrote a Life of him in 1905.
▷ *Reading, Writing and Remembering* (1932)

LUCAS, F(rank) L(awrence)
(1894–1967)

English critic and poet, born in Hipperholme, Yorkshire. A fellow of and former reader in English at King's College, Cambridge, he wrote many scholarly works of criticism, including *Seneca and Elizabethan Tragedy* (1922) and *Eight Victorian Poets* (1930). Among his volumes of poetry are *Time and Memory* (1929) and *Ariadne* (1932). His plays include *Land's End* (1938). He also wrote novels and popular translations of Greek drama and poetry.

LUCE, Clare Boothe *see* BOOTHE, Clare

LUCEBERT, pseud of Lubertys Jacobus Swaanswijk
(1924–)

Dutch poet, graphic artist and photographer from Amsterdam. Lucebert was the most radical member of the 'Experimentalist Group' of the 1950s, and was called by his colleagues 'Emperor of the Fifties'. He is an internationally known painter. His apparently nonsensical poems, full of word play, have been presented as having a world of their own. Later he turned more towards art.

LUCIAN
(c.117–c.180)

Greek satirist, rhetorician and writer, born in Samosata in Syria. Having learned Greek and studied rhetoric, he practised as an advocate in Antioch, and wrote and recited show speeches for a living, travelling through Asia Minor, Greece, Italy and Gaul. Having made a fortune and a name in this way, he settled in Athens, and there devoted himself to philosophy. There, too, he produced a new form of literature, the humorous dialogue. Lucian lived at a time when the old faiths, the old philosophy, the old literature, were all rapidly dissolving. Never was there a better target for satire and Lucian revelled in it. The absurdity of retaining the old deities without the old belief is brought out in such works as the *Deorum Dialogi* ('Dialogues of the Gods'), *Mortuorum Dialogi* ('Dialogues of the Dead') and *Charon*. Whether philosophy was more disgraced by the shallowness or the vices of those who now professed it, is discussed in his *Symposium, Halieus, Biōn Prasis, Drapetae* and others. The old literature had been displaced by novels or romances of adventure of the most fantastic kind, which Lucian parodies in his *Vera Historia* ('True History'). His style, which is notable for the purity of his Attic Greek, is straightforward and elegant.
▷J Bompaire, *Lucian écrivain* (1958)

LUCIE-SMITH, (John) Edward McKenzie
(1933–)

British poet, editor and writer on art and aesthetics. He was born in Kingston, Jamaica, educated at the King's School, Canterbury, and at Merton College, Oxford, where his first verses were published; his upbringing in the Caribbean forms the background to *A Tropical Childhood* (1961), vividly realized poems that somehow make a nonsense of his supposed loyalty to 'Group' values. He has admitted the influence of Victorian poets, **Robert Browning** foremost, on his longer, more dramatic forms, and *Confessions and Histories* (1964) confirms the extent of the debt. He became highly prolific, producing at least a volume a year until the mid-70s, when his poetic output faltered. His writing on the visual arts is intelligent, occasionally brilliant and thoroughly un-British. *Movements in Modern Art since 1945* (1969, published in the USA as *Late Modern*) has long been a stand-by for the educated amateur and has been regularly updated (1975, 1984). Among Lucie-Smith's many credits as editor are the Penguin books of *Elizabethan Verse* (1965) and of *Satirical Verse* (1967).

LUCILIUS, Gaius
(c.180–c.102 BC)

Roman satirist, born in Suessa Aurunca in Campania. He wrote 30 books of *Satires*, of which only fragments remain. These *saturae* (or medleys), written in hexameters, are on a mixture of miscellaneous subjects, everyday life, politics, literature, travel. Their occasionally mocking and critical tone gave the word 'satire' its modern meaning.
▷G C Fiske, *Lucilius and Horace* (1920)

LUCRETIUS (Titus Lucretius Carus)
(?94–?55 BC)

Roman poet and philosopher. His great work is his hexameter poem *De Rerum Natura* (Eng trans *On the Nature of Things*, 1937), in six books, in which he tried to popularize the philosophical theories of Democritus and Epicurus on the origin of the universe, with the special purpose of eradicating anything like religious belief, which he savagely denounces as the one great source of man's wickedness and misery. A calm and tranquil mind was his aim, the way to it being through a materialistic philosophy. His poem abounds in strikingly picturesque phrases, episodes of exquisite pathos and vivid description, rarely equalled in Latin poetry.
▷E E Sikes, *Lucretius* (1936)

LUDLOW, Fitzhugh
(1836–70)

American editor and writer, author of *The Hasheesh Eater* (1857), born in New York.

Ludlow possessed a versatile talent, working as a teacher and a lawyer in addition to his literary pursuits. His best-known book, plainly inspired by **De Quincey**, began as a magazine article entitled *Apocalypse of Hasheesh*. After publication of the expanded version he worked as a hack travel writer and reviewer. He had a collection of stories published in 1867, but narcotics were generally blamed for a muted end to his promising career.

LUDLUM, Robert
(1927–)

American writer of suspense fiction, whose understanding of history and politics in no way conflicts with narrative pace or popular taste. Following graduation from Wesleyan University, Connecticut, his first career was as an actor; he has been a full-time writer since 1969. Novels written under his own name—he has also written as Jonathan Ryder and Michael Shepherd—all follow the title formula of his first, *The Scarlatti Inheritance* (1971): typical examples include *The Matlock Paper* (1973), *The Chancellor Manuscript* (1977), *The Holcroft Covenant* (1978) and *The Parsifal Mosaic* (1982). Ludlum sees modern history in particular as a contrivance rather than a neutral record of reality and the appeal of his work lies in his exposition of how interest groups, by no means always political, construct their own versions of reality.

LUDWIG, originally Emil Cohn
(1881–1948)

German author, born in Breslau (Wrocław). He wrote some novels and plays, but made his name as a biographer of the intuitive school, with biographies of **Goethe**, Napoleon, Wilhelm II, Bismarck, Christ, Lincoln, and others, in which he assembled carefully researched sources in a manner more appropriate to fiction narrative. He lived in Switzerland, and became a Swiss citizen in 1932, but settled in the USA in 1940.

LUDWIG, Otto
(1813–65)

German novelist, playwright, critic (particularly of **Shakespeare**) and frustrated composer (he studied music with Mendelssohn and wrote a youthful opera), born in Eisfeld, Thuringia, to which he was, it has been suggested, attached 'with almost pathetic intensity'. He was of delicate constitution and led a secluded life. He was overdependent on various literary models and somewhat swaddled in theory (he was the principal advocate of the movement known as Poetic Realism, a term he coined, which tried to steer a course between realism and idealism in the interests

of a humane approach), but in his novel *Zwischen Himmel und Erde* (1856, rev edn 1862, Eng trans *Between Heaven and Earth*, 1911) he transcended his difficulties and disabilities to produce a genuinely tragic provincial tale: set within a 'frame', and therefore technically a *Novelle*, it portrays the family of a steeplejack. His plays are less successful, but made him famous.

▷G Brandes, *Main Currents in Nineteenth-Century Literature* (1901–5)

LUGONES, Leopoldo
(1874–1938)

Argentinian poet, novelist, critic, and (later) nationalistic fascist, born in Villa Maria del Rio Seco. When young he worked closely with **Rubén Darío**, and was, with **Jaimes Freyre**, one of the three most important of the *modernista* poets. He began as an anarchistic socialist and has some affinities with the Peruvian **José Santos Chocano**, having been an inveterate and over-rhetorical exhibitionist. Much of his best work, which transcends his glaring faults, is contained in his collection *Lunario sentimental* (1909, 'Sentimental Lunarium'), which imports French Symbolist and even Japanese procedures. He was very influential in Argentinian literature, both for his earlier importations from the European avant garde and then for his celebration of the Argentinian countryside. He had much political influence on the extreme right in his last years before he killed himself by taking cyanide. Some of his best poetry is translated in the *Penguin Book of Latin American verse* (1971, ed E Curacciolo-Trejo).

▷J L Borges and B Edelberg, *Leopoldo Lugones* (1955)

LUGOVSKY, Vladimir
(1901–57)

Russian poet, who fought for the Bolsheviks and who later worked with Eisenstein on the film *Ivan the Terrible* (1942–6). He was at first a Symbolist, then an Acmeist, then a Futurist, but finally became a Constructivist. Not a poet of great importance, but a pleasant and helpful man, he became popular towards the end of his life amongst those not unhappy with communist rule.

LUIS DE LEON, Fray
(?1528–1591)

Spanish writer, born in Belmonte, in Aragón, of an old Jewish family. By 1560 he had received a doctorate in theology from the University of Salamanca; a year later he began a long battle with the Dominican order by winning the Chair of St Thomas Aquinas from one of their protégés. On 27 March 1572 he was arrested by the Inquisition and jailed,

in part for his interpretation of the Hebrew tradition. He fought the accusation until 1576, when he was freed and totally absolved, and after spending many years in the reforms of his Augustinian order died in Madrigal. His life was marked by controversy and a firm belief in his own righteousness. His most important prose works are *De los nombres de Cristo* (1583, Eng trans *The Names of Christ*, 1955), *La perfecta casada* (1583, Eng trans *The Perfect Wife*, 1943), and a commentary on Job. Today, however, it is his polished and precise poetry, virtually unknown in his lifetime, which receives the most critical attention. The odes he wrote are among the most famous poetry in the Spanish language, combining the pure nature of **Horace** with the Christian elements of the poetry of **San Juan de la Cruz**. He was deeply influenced by classical models like **Virgil**, and closely followed **Garcilaso de la Vega**.
▷O Macrí, *Fray Luis de Leon: Poesias* (2nd edn, 1982)

LUNDKVIST, Artur
(1906–92)

Swedish poet, prose-writer, critic and translator, born in Skåne. He was a member of the Swedish Academy. Initially a primitivist much influenced by **Whitman** and **D H Lawrence**, and one of the earliest exponents of modernism in Sweden, he collaborated on and largely stimulated the pioneering anthology *fem unga* (1929, 'five young men'). His prose writings are of three main types: travel books; collages of poetry, prose poems, sketches and essays; and historical novels. He was above all an eclectic, who gathered his ideas world-wide, and the contents of his prodigious output (70 books) reflects his varied sources. He played a vital role in introducing contemporary international literature into Sweden, particularly that from the Anglo–American, French and Hispanic worlds.
▷C-E Nordberg, *Det skapande ögat. En färd genom Artur Lundkvists författarskap* (1981)

LURIE, Alison
(1926–)

American novelist, born in Chicago and educated at Radcliffe College, Massachusetts. Since 1968 she has taught at Cornell University, since 1976 as Professor of English, and academic life forms the backdrop to her first books, the ironically titled *Love and Friendship* (1962), *The Nowhere City* (1965) and *Foreign Affairs* (1984); the two latter novels also deal with cultural displacement, Easterners in the Far West in the first, an American in London in the second, which won Lurie the Pulitzer Prize. Her skill in using enclosed, even hermetic worlds to reflect the progress and problems of the wider culture can be gauged in *Imaginary Friends* (1967), about a chiliastic cult, and in *The War Between the Tates* (1974), set against the background of the Vietnam War. *The Truth about Lorin Jones* (1988) is a more recent novel, but Lurie has increasingly turned to non-fictional commentary, brilliantly in *The Language of Clothes* (1981), often contentiously in *Don't Tell the Grown-ups: Children's Literature* (1990).

LURIE, Morris
(1938–)

Australian writer of Polish origin, born in Melbourne, whose early work is in the **Woody Allen**-Jewish vein of adolescent humour, as in *Flying Home* (1978), which captures the rootlessness of the diaspora. Collections of short stories, of 'factional' prose pieces, and three plays followed. He is perhaps at his best in short stories, such as his collection *Outrageous Behaviour* (1984). He has since published *Madness: A Novel* (1991), but his autobiography is perhaps his most involving work.
▷*A Whole Life* (1987)

LUSKA, Sidney *see* HARLAND, Henry

LUSSICH, Antonio de
(1848–1928)

Uruguayan poet, born in Montevideo, the son of an Austrian sailor. He was a friend of **José Hernandez**, author of *Martin Fierro*, and certainly influenced him. His gaucho poetry is remarkable for its extremely accurate use of dialect.

LUYKEN, Jan
(1649–1712)

Dutch poet, born in Amsterdam. The chief influence on his life and work (which included etchings), was the German mystic **Böhme**. Some of his best poetry is translated in *Coming After: An Anthology of Poetry from the Low Countries* (1948).

LUZI, Mario
(1914–)

Italian poet, translator and scholar, once classed with the 'hermetics', born in Florence. The 'hermeticism' of such poets as **Gatto** was in part a result of the necessity on the part of writers to veil their humane attitudes from the failed novelist Mussolini's culture-police; but it was also a bid to regain the purity of the word, and Luzi, while no fascist, was devoted to the latter, as his many essays in the magazines *Il Frontespizio* and *Letteratura* testify. A scholar and teacher of French literature, the chief initial influence upon him was that of **Mallarmé**. A difficult but eloquent and rewarding writer, of very great integrity, Luzi is often regarded as the most important poet of the generation immediately following that of **Montale**. English translation: *In the Dark Body of Metamorphosis* (1975).

LUZZATTO, Moses Chayim
(1707–47)

Hebrew poet, dramatist and mystic, born in Padua, Italy, who wrote on national themes. He wrote his first play while still a boy, but only fragments of it survive. His allegorical play *Migdal* (1927), influenced by **Tasso**, has been described as marking 'the culmination of a vast dramatic literature': his style, modelled on the Bible, dominated the Hebrew language for well over a century. His Psalter was condemned as sacrilegious, and destroyed; eventually he had to flee to Amsterdam to avoid persecution. In the latter part of his life he became a devotee of Cabalism, an important follower of Isaac Luria (1534–72), and wrote a 'Second Zohar'.
▷S Ginsburg, *The Life and Works of Moses Chayim Luzzatto* (1931)

LUZZATTO, Shmuel David
(1800–65)

Italian Hebrew poet and writer, who wrote in both Hebrew and Italian, born in Trieste. At the age of 14 he planned to act as the regenerator of his nation; in 1829 he became professor at the Rabbinical College at Padua, where he died. He is regarded as one of the great Jewish scholars.
▷N H Rosenbloom, *Luzzatto's Ethico-Psychological Interpretation of Judaism* (1965); S Morais, *Italian Hebrew Literature* (1926)

LYALL, Gavin Tudor
(1932–)

English thriller writer, born in Birmingham and educated there and at Pembroke College, Cambridge. Service in the peacetime Royal Air Force (1951–3) lent a strong interest in aviation to his work, most convincingly in his first novel, *The Wrong Side of the Sky* (1961) and its successor *The Most Dangerous Game* (1963). Before turning to full-time fiction writing, Lyall worked for *Picture Post*, the BBC, and *The Sunday Times*; he married the journalist Katharine Whitehorn in 1958. In *The Secret Servant* (1980) he introduced the military intelligence operative Harry Maxim, who reflects the quintessentially English character of Lyall's imagination and values; he also appears in *The Conduct of Major Maxim* (1982). Lyall's novels are strongly plotted and well researched, without extraneous detail or mere set-dressing.

LYBECK, Mikael
(1864–1925)

Finland–Swedish poet, dramatist and novelist, born in Nykarleby. The main theme of his fiction is his hatred of religious fanaticism, plenty of which was evident in his environment. His novels, greatly influenced by those of **Kielland**, but not to their disadvantage, reach a high degree of psychological penetrativeness.

LYDGATE, John
(c.1370–c.1451)

English monk and poet, born in Lydgate, near Newmarket. He became a Benedictine monk at Bury St Edmunds. He may have studied at Oxford and Cambridge. He travelled in France and perhaps Italy, and became prior of Hatfield Broadoak (Essex) in 1423. A court poet, he received a pension in 1439, but died in poverty. Lydgate's longer works are the *Troy Book*, the *Siege of Thebes* and the *Fall of Princes*. The *Siege of Thebes* is represented as a new Canterbury tale, and was based on a French verse romance. The versification is rough, and the poem dull and long-winded. The *Troy Book* was based on Colonna's Latin prose *Historia Trojana*, and the *Fall of Princes* on **Boccaccio**. Other works include the *Daunce of Machabre*, from the French, *Temple of Glas*, a copy of **Chaucer**'s *House of Fame*, and *London Lickpenny*, a vivid description of contemporary manners in London.
▷D Pearsall, *John Lydgate* (1970)

LYLY, John
(c.1554–1606)

English dramatist and novelist, 'the Euphuist', born in the Weald of Kent. He took his BA at Magdalen College, Oxford, in 1573, and studied also at Cambridge. William Cecil, Lord Burghley, gave him some post of trust in his household, and he became vice-master of the St Paul's choristers. Having in 1589 taken part in the Marprelate controversy, he was returned to parliament for Aylesbury and Appleby (1597–1601). His *Euphues*, a romance in two parts—*Euphues, The Anatomie of Wit* (1579) and *Euphues and his England* (1580)—was received with great applause. One peculiarity of his 'new English' is the constant employment of similes drawn from fabulous stories about the properties of animals, plants and minerals; another is the excessive indulgence in antithesis. His earliest comedy was *The Woman in the Moone*, produced in or before 1583. *Campaspe* and *Sapho and Phao* were published in 1584, *Endimion* in 1591, *Gallathea* and *Midas* in 1592, *Mother Bombie* in 1594, and *Love's Metamorphosis* in 1601. The delightful songs (of doubtful

601

authorship) were first printed in the edition of 1632.

▷J D Wilson, *John Lyly* (1905)

LYNCH, Benito

(1885–1951)

Major Argentinian novelist, born in Buenos Aires. The subject of both his novels and his stories is gaucho (cowboy) life, but he does not flatter the gaucho, who, in his estimation, is dour and violent. He excelled in description, and the lack of translation of his work, especially of his great novel *El inglés de los guesos* (1924, 'The Englishman of the Bones'—'guesos' is the gaucho pronunciation of 'huesos', meaning bones), is a major literary scandal. This tells of a love affair between an English archaeologist and a simple girl; he ruins her, and she hangs herself. Lynch also excelled in his portrayals of women, whom he valued more than men. *El romance de un gaucho* (1933, 'The Romance of a Gaucho'), written entirely in gaucho slang, tells a similar story. After this Lynch abandoned the literary world.

LYNDSAY, or LINDSAY, Sir David of the Mount

(c.1486–1555)

Scottish poet, born probably at the Mount near Cupar, Fife, or at Garmylton (now Garleton), near Haddington, East Lothian. In 1512 he was appointed 'usher' of the newborn prince who became James V. In 1522 or earlier he married Janet Douglas, the king's seamstress. In 1524 (probably), during the regency of the Douglases, he lost or changed his place, but was restored to favour in 1529 when James V became king in his own right. In 1538 he appears to have been Lyon King-of-Arms. He went on embassies to the Netherlands, France, England and Denmark, and he (or another David Lyndsay) represented Cupar in the parliaments of 1540–6. For two centuries he was the poet of the Scottish people. His poems, often coarse, are full of humour, good sense and knowledge of the world, and were said to have done more for the Reformation in Scotland than all the sermons of Knox. The earliest and most poetic of his writings is the allegorical *The Dreme* (1528), followed by *The Complaynt of the King* (1529) and *The Testament and Complaynt of Our Soverane Lordis Papyngo* (1530). He wrote a satire on court life in *Ane Publict Confession of the Kingis Auld Hound Callit Bagscie* (1536). His most remarkable work was *Ane Satyre of the Thrie Estaitis*, a dramatic work first performed at Linlithgow in 1540, and revived with great success at the Edinburgh Festival; the most amusing was *The Historie of Squyer Meldrum*.

▷W Murison, *Sir David Lindsay* (1938)

LYTLE, Andrew

(1902–)

American novelist, editor and historian, born of a family prominent on both sides in Murfeesboro, in Tennessee. He was associated with the group of poets and writers who called themselves the Fugitives or Southern Agrarians (they included **Allen Tate**, **Ransom** and **Penn Warren**). He was a professor of history at various universities and edited the *Sewanee Review* (1961–73). He also practised as a farmer. It is generally conceded that his four novels have never received the critical attention they deserve. *The Long Night* (1936) is a tragedy of revenge set in the Civil War; *At the Moon's End* (1941) is historical; the powerful ghost story *A Name for Evil* (1947) is about a modern Southerner who cannot let go of his vision of the past and brings ruin to himself and to his family; *The Velvet Horn* (1957), regarded as his masterpiece, deals with a boy's rites of passage just after the Civil War. **Caroline Gordon**, for long the wife of Tate, and herself a major novelist, called this novel a 'landmark in American fiction'.

▷M E Bradford (ed), *The Achievement of Lytle* (1973)

M

MAARTENS, Maarten, pseud of **Jost Marius Willem van der Poorten Schwart** (1858–1915)

Dutch novelist, born in Amsterdam. He spent part of his boyhood in England, went to school in Germany, and studied and taught law at Utrecht University. He wrote powerful novels in English, including *The Sin of Joost Avelingh* (1889) and *God's Fool* (1893). His Letters were edited by his daughter (1930).

MAC AN BHAIRD, Eoghan Ruadh (c.1530–1610)

Irish (Gaelic) bard. He has been described as the 'professor in chief of poetry' for Red Hugh O'Donnell's battles against the English at the end of the 16th century. In 1603, however, Mac an Bhaird turned on O'Donnell, who had made peace and become Earl of Tyrconnell. Nonetheless, on the earl's death five years later Mac an Bhaird wrote the superb lamentation *A Bhean Fuair Faill ar an Bhfeart* ('O Woman That Has Found Opportunity at the Tomb'), famously if freely rendered by **James Clarence Mangan** (1803–69) as *O Woman of the Piercing Wail*. The themes of a ravaged country and a grieving nation are paramount in Mac an Bhaird's work. Some of the later poems ascribed to him by Professor Tomas O'Raghallaigh have been attributed by later scholars to others.
▷A de Blacam, *Gaelic Literature Surveyed* (1929; reprinted 1973)

MACAN T-SAOIR, Donnachadh Ban *see* **McINTYRE, Duncan Ban**

MacARTHUR, Charles (1895–1956)

American playwright, born in Pennsylvania. MacArthur was a heavy drinker and prankster. While working as a journalist in Chicago he managed to convince the Chief of Police that one **Henry Wadsworth Longfellow** had been wrongly charged with rape. During World War I he is said to have dropped empty whisky bottles over Berlin—friends suggested he might simply have leaned out of the plane and breathed over the city. He is best known for his collaborations with **Ben Hecht**: *The Front Page* (1928) for the stage, and *Barbary Coast* (1935) and *The Scoundrel* (1935) for the silver screen, plus their enduring adaptation of *Wuthering Heights* (1939).

MACAULAY, Dame (Emilie) Rose (1881–1958)

English novelist and essayist, born in Rugby, Warwickshire, the daughter of a Cambridge University lecturer in classical literature. Educated at Oxford High School and Somerville College, Oxford, where she read history, her first novel was *Abbots Verney* (1906), followed by *Views and Vagabonds* (1912) and *The Lee Shore* (1920), winner of a £1000 publishers' prize. Her later novels include *Potterism* (1920), *Dangerous Ages* (1921, which won the Femina Vie Heureuse Prize), *Told by an Idiot* (1923), *Orphan Island* (1924), *Crewe Train* (1926), *Keeping Up Appearances* (1928), *They were Defeated* (1932), *I Would be a Private* (1937) and *And No Man's Wit* (1940). After World War II she wrote two further novels, *The World My Wilderness* (1950), and *The Towers of Trebizond* (1956), which won the James Tait Black Memorial Prize. Her travel books include *They Went to Portugal* (1946), *Fabled Shore* (1949) and *The Pleasure of Ruins* (1953).
▷C B Smith, *Rose Macaulay, a biography* (1972)

MACAULAY, Thomas Babington, 1st Baron Macaulay (1800–59)

English author, born in Rothley Temple, Leicestershire, son of Zachary Macaulay (1768–1838). In 1812 he was sent to a private school at Little Shelford near Cambridge, and moved in 1814 to Aspenden Hall in Hertfordshire, from where, an exceptionally precocious boy, he entered Trinity College, Cambridge, in 1818. He detested mathematics, but twice won the Chancellor's Medal for English verse, and obtained a prize for Latin declamation. In 1821 he carried off the Craven Prize, in 1822 took his BA, and in 1824 was elected to a fellowship. He was one of the most brilliant debaters in the Cambridge Union. Called to the Bar in 1826 he had no liking for his profession but literature had irresistible attractions for him. In 1823 he became a contributor to *Knight's Quarterly Magazine*, in which appeared some of his best verses—*Ivry*, *The Spanish Armada* and

Naseby. In 1825 he was discovered by Francis Jeffrey, and his famous article on **Milton** in the August number of the *Edinburgh Review* secured him a position in literature. For nearly 20 years he was one of the most prolific and popular of the writers on the *Edinburgh Review.* In 1830 he entered parliament for the pocket borough of Calne, and in 1834, mainly for the sake of his family, impoverished by his devotion to philanthropy, he accepted the office of legal adviser to the Supreme Council of India, with a salary of £10 000, and sailed for Bengal, returning to England in 1838. In 1839 he was elected member of parliament for Edinburgh, and entered Lord Melbourne's cabinet as secretary of war. The *Lays of Ancient Rome* (1842) won an immense popularity; so too did his collected *Essays* (3 vols, 1843). His connection with the *Edinburgh Review* ceased in 1845; he had by then begun his *History of England from the Accession of James II.* In 1846 he was re-elected for Edinburgh but was defeated at the general election of 1847. In 1852 he was again returned for Edinburgh and in 1856 he retired. The first two volumes of his *History* appeared in 1848, and at once attained greater popularity than any other purely historical work. The next two followed in 1855, and an unfinished fifth volume was published in 1861. In 1849 he was elected Lord Rector of Glasgow University. In 1857 he was raised to the peerage as Baron Macaulay of Rothley. He was buried in Westminster Abbey. Macaulay has been convicted of historical inaccuracy, of sacrificing truth for the sake of epigram, of allowing personal dislike and Whig bias to distort his views of men and incidents, but as a picturesque narrator he has no rival.
▷J Millgate, *Macaulay* (1973)

MacBETH, George Mann
(1932–92)

Scottish poet and novelist, born in Shotts, Lanarkshire. He was educated at King Edward VII School in Sheffield and New College, Oxford, and was a producer of poetry programmes at the BBC (1955–76). He was associated with the informal coterie known as The Group (and was represented in *The Group Anthology,* 1963), and with performance poetry in the 1960s. He published 20 books of verse, some of it experimental in form and violent in matter, although his later work was more traditional in form. A *Collected Poems 1958–70* appeared in 1971, and was later updated as *Collected Poems 1958–82.* He also published children's books and 10 novels, the last of which was *The Testament of Spencer* (1992), which appeared shortly after his death.
▷*A Child of the War* (1987)

MacCAIG, Norman Alexander
(1910–)

Scottish poet, born in Edinburgh, the son of a chemist. His mother was born in Scalpay, Harris, and, as he wrote in 'Return to Scalpay', 'Half my thought and half my blood is Scalpay'. A poet of town and country, his formative years were spent in Edinburgh; he was educated at the Royal High School and the university, where he read classics. He became a primary school teacher, for which his friend **Hugh MacDiarmid** pronounced he had 'a real vocation', and for nearly 40 years it engaged his daylight hours. His first two collections—*Far Cry* (1943) and *The Inward Eye* (1946)—tarred him as a member of the New Apocalypse school and the label stuck 'long after it was contravening the Trades Description Act'. He disowned these poems when *Collected Poems* was published in 1985. *Riding Lights* (1955) is the first evidence of the real MacCaig, lucid, direct and richly descriptive. His distinctive voice, witty and philosophical, is heard in numerous subsequent collections including *The Sinai Sort* (1957), *A Round of Applause* (1962), *Measures* (1965), *A Man In My Position* (1969), *The White Bird* (1973), *The Equal Skies* (1980), *A World of Difference* (1963) and *Voice-Over* (1988). He was the first fellow in creative writing at Edinburgh University (1967–9), and on retiring from schoolteaching he lectured in English studies at Stirling University (1970–9). The finest Scottish poet of his generation writing in English, he was awarded the Queen's Gold Medal for Poetry in 1986. A new edition of *Collected Poems* appeared in 1990.
▷R Fulton, in *Contemporary Scottish Poetry* (1974)

MacCARTHY, Denis Florence
(1817–82)

Irish author, born in Dublin. He trained for the priesthood, but wrote poetry, much of it in a historical and patriotic vein. He also published highly-regarded translations of a number of plays by **Calderón de la Barca**, and published *Shelley's Early Life* (1872).

MAC CONMIDHE, Giolla Brigdhe Albanach
(c.1180–c.1260)

Irish court poet, born in County Tyrone. He was called 'Albanach' ('Scottish') because of his Scottish connections. He is most famous for his last poem, a lament for the King of Ulster, Brian O'Neill, who was killed at the Battle of Down in 1260. At a time when Bardic poets were almost too heavily restrained by both metrical and linguistic rules, Mac Conmidhe succeeded in leaving genuine poetry without breaking them.

▷A de Blácam, *Gaelic Poetry Surveyed* (1933)

MacCUARTA, Seamus Dall
(c.1650–1733)

Irish (Gaelic) poet, born in County Louth; he spent most of his life there and, later, in the midlands of Meath. His claim to literary fame is based on his use of '*tri rann agus amhran*', three verses in syllabic metre followed by one in song metre, the best-known example of which is the lyric *The Cuckoo's Return* (nd). This form was imported by MacCuarta from the south-east of Ulster and due to its structure has been compared to the contemporary English-language sonnet. He was revered in his lifetime, and his most famous poem, *Is Fada Me* (nd, 'Long Have I Been'), is evidence of a lovable if vulnerable man: 'I never repented as I should, but spent my life composing songs; but now that I am sick and weak, O God have mercy on Blind Jim'.

▷S Deane (ed), *Field Day Anthology of Irish Writing: Vol 1* (1991)

MacDERMOT, Thomas Henry ('Tom Redcam')
(1870–1933)

Jamaican poet and novelist, born in Clarendon of Irish parents. As journalist and editor of the *Jamaica Times* (1904–23) before retiring to England because of ill-health, he campaigned vigorously to encourage local writing, and was himself one of the fathers of modern West Indian literature. He was honoured as Jamaica's first poet laureate for his patriotic and descriptive verse, published posthumously in *Orange Valley and other poems* (1951). His novels, *Becka's Buckra Baby* (1903) and *One Brown Girl and — A Jamaican Story* (1909), were clumsy but earnest attempts to illustrate the innate worth of humble black people.

▷W A Roberts, *Six Great Jamaicans* (1952); L W Brown, *West Indian Poetry* (1978); K Ramchand, *The West Indian Novel and its Background* (1983)

MacDIARMID, Hugh, pseud of Christopher Murray Grieve
(1892–1978)

Scottish poet, pioneer of the Scottish literary renaissance, born in Langholm, Dumfriesshire. Educated at Langholm Academy, he became a pupil-teacher at Broughton Higher Grade School in Edinburgh before turning to journalism. He served with the Royal Army Medical Corps in Greece and France during World War I, and was a munitions worker in World War II. After World War I he married

Peggy Skinner and settled as a journalist in Montrose, where he also became a town councillor (1922), and edited anthologies of contemporary Scottish writing, such as *Northern Numbers* (1920–2) and *The Scottish Chapbook* (1922–3), in which he published his own early poetry. Beginning with such outstanding early lyrical verse as *Sangschaw* (1925) and *Penny Wheep* (1926), he established himself as the leader of a vigorous Scottish Renaissance by *A Drunk Man Looks at the Thistle* (1926), full of political, metaphysical and nationalistic reflections on the Scottish predicament. In his later works, however, this master of polemic, or 'flyting', increasingly allowed his poetical genius to be overburdened by philosophical gleanings in the service of a customized form of communism. Nevertheless, items such as 'The Seamless Garment', 'Cattle Shaw' and 'At Lenin's Tomb' raise these later works to a very high level. Other works include *To Circumjack Cencrastus* (1930), the two *Hymns to Lenin* (1930; 1935), *Scots Unbound* (1932), *Stony Limits* (1934), *A Kist o' Whistles* (1947) and *In Memoriam James Joyce* (1955). His numerous essays such as *Albyn* (1927) and *The Islands of Scotland* (1939) suffer from the same intellectual scrapbook tendency. Founder-member of the Scottish National Party, and intermittently an active communist, he stood as a communist candidate in 1963. He dedicated his life to the regeneration of the Scottish literary language, repudiated by his fellow Scottish poet, **Edwin Muir**, in 1936. He succeeded brilliantly by employing a vocabulary drawn from all regions and periods, intellectualizing a previously parochial tradition. In 1931 he met his second wife, Valda Trevelin, and in 1933 he went into self-imposed exile on the island of Whalsay, in Shetland. After World War II he lived in a cottage at Brownsbank, near Biggar, Lanarkshire. His autobiography was published in *Lucky Poet* (1943) and *The Company I've Kept* (1966).

▷A Bold, *Hugh MacDiarmid: a biography* (1985)

MAC DOMHNAILL, Seán Clárach
(1691–1754)

Irish poet, the leading Jacobite writer, born in County Cork, who lived in Munster. Much of his poetry supports Bonny Prince Charlie (whom he does not, by tradition, directly name), but the best of it consists of *aisling*, or 'vision' poems.

▷R O Foghludha, *Seán Clárach* (1934, in Irish)

MacDONAGH, Donagh
(1912–68)

Irish dramatist, born in Dublin, the son of **Thomas MacDonagh**. Orphaned by his father's execution in 1916 and the drowning of his mother in an attempt to plant the tricolour on an island in Dublin Bay in 1917, he was educated at Belvedere College and University College, Dublin, became a barrister in 1935 and was made a district justice in 1941. A hunchback, he won success as a writer of the exuberant *Happy as Larry* (1946), and other plays such as *God's Gentry* (1951, a study of tinker life) and *Step-in-the-Hollow* (1957). He was a highly acclaimed broadcaster, and edited with Lennox Robinson *The Oxford Book of Irish Verse* (1958), which drew criticism for its loose interpretation of Irishness. He published poems, *The Hungry Grass* (1947) and *A Warning to Conquerors* (1968), and a perceptive essay on his father, placing him in the context of the European intellectual death-wish in World War I.

▷Introduction to *The Oxford Book of Irish Verse* (1958)

MacDONAGH, Thomas
(1878–1916)

Irish poet, critic and nationalist, born to a schoolteaching family in Cloughjordan, County Tipperary. He went to Dublin, where he helped **Patrick Pearse** to found St Enda's College (1908), and published several volumes of delicate and sardonic poems, original works and translations from the Irish. In 1914 he founded the Irish Theatre with Joseph Plunkett and **Edward Martyn**. He was also an outstanding critic of English literature, and his aspirations for Irish literature derived from his deep love of English and his recognition of comparable possibilities, as may be seen by his *Literature in Ireland* (posthumous, 1916) and *Thomas Campion* (1913), and by his articles in the *Irish Review*. He took part in the Irish Volunteers, was very belatedly drawn into preparations for the Easter Rising of 1916, commanded at Jacob's Factory in the fighting, and was executed. The poet **James Stephens** impressively introduced his *Poetical Works* (1917) after his death, and **W B Yeats** wrote his epitaph in 'Easter 1916'.

▷A W and E Parks, *Thomas MacDonagh, the Man, the Patriot and the Writer* (1967)

MACDONALD, Alexander (Gaelic **Alasdair Mac Maighstir Alasdair**)
(c. 1695–c. 1770)

Scottish poet, born in Islandfinnan, where his father was minister, and educated in Glasgow. He was the foremost Gaelic literary figure of the 18th century, and his poems reflect the turbulent times in which he lived. He took part in the 1745 rebellion on the Jacobite side, and his best verse is inspired by the subsequent upheavals in and diminution of Gaelic culture. His masterwork is *Birlinn*

Chlann Raghnaill (c.1780), a long poem about the war galley of Clan Ranald, which laments the fate of Gaeldom after the '45. A translation of the poem by **Hugh MacDiarmid** was published in 1935.

MACDONALD, George
(1824–1905)

Scottish novelist, lecturer and poet, born in Huntly, Aberdeenshire, the son of a farmer. He was educated at King's College, Aberdeen, and Highbury Theological College. He became a Congregationalist pastor at Arundel, but his unorthodox views—especially his belief in purgatory, and in a place in heaven for everyone, even animals—caused conflict with his parishioners, and finally brought about his resignation. After the success of his first publication, the poem 'Within and Without' (1856), he turned to writing and lecturing, publishing the allegorical novel *Phantastes* (1858), which met with a cold reception. He followed this with a series of novels, including *David Elginbrod* (1863), *Robert Falconer* (1868) and *Lilith* (1895), confessing that he used his books as his pulpit. He is now best known for his children's books, among them *At the Back of the North Wind* (1871), *The Princess and the Goblin* (1872) and *The Princess and Curdie* (1888), but his adult works have enjoyed a revival, especially among evangelical Christians.

▷W Raeper, *George MacDonald* (1987)

MACDONALD, John *see* LOM, Iain

MACDONALD, John D(ann)
(1916–86)

American mystery writer, born in Pennsylvania. He served in the army during World War II and spent time in the East, the stimulus for his first published fiction, a short story, 'Interlude in India'. After the war he moved to Florida. His first mystery, *The Brass Cupcake*, was published in 1950. Since then his books have sold many millions of copies, the most popular being his stories of Travis McGee, all of which have a colour in their title, eg *The Deep Blue Goodbye* (1964), *The Lonely Silver Rain* (1985). Macdonald's efficient plotting has been much-admired. The chauvinist treatment of sex is par for the course in mystery writing of this period.

MacDONALD, Ross, pseud of **Kenneth Millar**
(1915–83)

American thriller writer, born in Los Gatos, California, of Canadian parentage, and raised in Ontario. He took a PhD at the University of Western Ontario, and became a college teacher. From the 1950s he lived in

southern California. One of the finest writers in the genre, his Lew Archer series, a chip off **Raymond Chandler** and **Dashiell Hammett**'s block, is sustained by tough and witty dialogue and rare intelligence. His wife **Margaret Millar**'s novels are no less intelligent and literary. Immensely popular yet academically acceptable, many of his novels have been hijacked by Hollywood. Durable titles are *The Moving Target* (1949), *The Drowning Pool* (1950), *The Barbarous Coast* (1956), *The Galton Case* (1959), *The Underground Man* (1971) and *The Blue Hammer* (1976). He also wrote as John MacDonald and John Ross MacDonald.
▷ J Speir, *Ross MacDonald* (1978)

MacEWEN, Gwendolyn
(1941–87)
Canadian poet and novelist, born in Toronto, where she was for many years a part-time children's librarian. Her first husband was the poet, **Milton Acorn**; her second a Greek singer, with whom she ran the Greek Horse, a Toronto coffee-house, during the 1970s. Her poetry is exuberant, direct and accessible. 'A Breakfast for Barbarians' begins: 'my friends, my sweet barbarians,/there is that hunger which is not for food'. She produced eight collections in all. In 1965 she received a Canada Council grant to research a historical novel in Egypt. The result was *King of Egypt, King of Dreams* (1971), an imaginative portrait of the eccentric pharaoh Akhnaton.
▷ J Bartley, *Invocations: The Poetry & Prose of Gwendolyn MacEwen* (1983)

MAC GEARAILT, Gearóid, Earl of Desmond
(d.1398)
Irish poet, a Norman nobleman who had become assimilated into his adopted country. He is said to have written the earliest Gaelic love poem, beginning, 'Bad luck to him who speaks ill of women'. He wrote in the style of the French troubadour poets.

MacGILL, Patrick
(1890 1963)
Irish navvy, novelist and poet, born in the Glenties, County Donegal. Sold into servitude by his farming parents, he escaped to go to Scotland, working as a farm-labourer and a navvy. He wrote verses, hawked them round, attracted the attention of patrons and worked on the London *Daily Express* before being adopted as secretary by Canon John Dalton of Windsor. Eventually this resulted in his brilliant, naturalistic semi-autobiographical novel of migrant navvy life,

Children of the Dead End (1914), to be followed by a powerful parallel narrative of the forcing of female Irish labour into prostitution, *The Rat-Pit* (1915). MacGill volunteered when war broke out, gave a kaleidoscopic account of the troops before embarkation (*The Amateur Army*, 1915), and followed it up well with *The Red Horizon* (1916) and *The Great Push* (1916), describing action in France in which he was wounded. He returned to Ireland as a theme with *Glenmornan* (1919), an anti-clerical but self-excoriating novel of his native parish, the comedy of economic adventures *Lanty Hanlon* (1922), the study of the impact of Sinn Féin, *Maureen* (1920), and a somewhat romanticized return to navvy-land, *Moleskin Joe* (1923), while *Black Bonar* (1928) looked at the self-made petty capitalist more savagely. MacGill married Margaret Gibbons (who published charming stories as Mrs Patrick MacGill), and went to the USA in 1930, where he declined into poverty and developed multiple sclerosis.

MACGILL-EAIN, Somhairle *see* MACLEAN, Sorley

MAC GIOLLA MEIDRE, Bryan *see* MERRIMAN, Bryan

MÁCHA, Karel Hynak
(1810–36)
Czech romantic (but also proto-existentialist) poet, still widely regarded as his country's greatest. His major and main work, the robber-romance epic *Máj* (1836, Eng trans *May*, 1932) introduced iambic verse into a language whose rhythm had hitherto been predominantly trochaic, and combined **Byron**ic with metaphysical and atheistic themes. Its opening lines are the best-known poetry in Czech. The poem is one of the first long works in· any language to reject 'the order of the Universe and the absolute', and can carry the weight of this rejection. Mácha rejects both God and the power of love, favouring instead an eternity of loneliness. A son of a poor family, he lived a wandering bohemian life (much of it actually in Bohemia), then was forced to take a post in a lawyer's office. He died of cholera in the midst of plans to marry the mother—described as a 'shallow coquette'—of his son. His masterpiece was coldly received by the professors of his day—they detected 'irregularities'—but is now very widely studied. There is little on him in English.
▷ *Slavonic and East European Review*, 15, 54 (1937)

MACHADO, Antonio
(1875–1939)

Spanish writer, born in Seville. His father was the eminent folklorist Machada y Alvarez. He wrote lyrics characterized by a nostalgic melancholy, among them *Soledades* (1903, 'Solitudes'), *Galerías y otros poemas* (1907, 'Galleries and Other Poems') and the more philosophical *Campos de Castilla* (1912, 'Fields of Castille'). His brother Manuel (1874–1947), also a poet, collaborated with him on several plays.

MACHADO DE ASSIS, Joaquim Maria
(1839–1908)

Brazilian novelist, born in Rio de Janiero. He was an epileptic, and a mulatto from a humble family background, but became a high-ranking official in the civil service. He was the co-founder of the Brazilian Academy of Letters in 1896, and its president from 1897. His novels dissect the minutiae of Brazilian upper-class life in dazzling, measured, highly discursive, and cunningly ambiguous prose. He also wrote several volumes of short stories. His principal novels are *Memórias pósthumos de Brás Cubas* (1881, Eng trans *Epitaph of a Small Winner*, 1952), *Quincas Borba* (1891, Eng trans *Philosopher or Dog?*, 1954), *Dom Casmurro* (1900, Eng trans 1953) and *Esaú e Jacó* (1904, Eng trans *Esau and Jacob*, 1966). A complete edition of his works in Portuguese was issued in 1959.
▷H Caldwell, *Machado de Assis: the Brazilian master and his novels* (1970)

MACHAR, Josef Svatopluk
(1864–1942)

Czech poet, born in Kolin. A bank official in Vienna, he was the author of satirical and political verse, known for the trilogy *Confiteor* (1887, 'I Confess'), the verse romance *Magdalena* (1893), and the epic *Warriors of God* (1897). His 9-volume *Svědomim věků* (1902–26, 'The Conscience of the Age') is a pessimistic epic of humanity's progress, or lack of it. He became Inspector General of the Czechslovak Army in 1919, having been imprisoned by the Austrians during World War I.
▷V Martinek, *Josef Svatopluk Machar* (1948)

MACHEN, Arthur
(1863–1947)

Welsh-born English novelist, born in Carleon-on-Usk. Popular with readers, but never subjected to the critical appraisal he deserves, Machen wrote such famous books as *The Great God Pan* (1894) and *The Hill of Dreams* (1907). If referred to at all, these have been described as 'escapist', but in fact they depict an inner turmoil that is very far from escapist. *Things Far and Near* (1923) is an interesting volume of recollections. He wrote many well-executed tales of the uncanny, collected in the excellent *Tales of Horror and the Supernatural* (1964).

MACHIAVELLI, Niccolò
(1469–1527)

Italian statesman, writer and political philosopher. He was born in Florence, but nothing much is known of his early life. In 1498, Savonarola's regime in Florence was overthrown, and despite his lack of political experience Machiavelli was among those who rapidly rose to power in the new republic. His reports and correspondence demonstrate a shrewd appraisal of people and events and enabled him to try out ideas he was later to develop in his political works. When the republic was dissolved in 1512, Machiavelli was dismissed from his post (the reasons are unclear), and in 1513 suffered the further disaster of arrest on the charge of conspiracy against the new regime. He was tortured, and although soon released and pardoned, was obliged to withdraw from public life and devote himself to writing. To console himself, as he explained in a famous letter to his friend Francesco Vettori, he studied ancient history, pondered the lessons to be learned from his experiences in government service, and drafted 'a little book' on the subject. That was his masterpiece, *El principe* (not published until 1532, Eng trans *The Prince*, 1560). It was intended to be a handbook for rulers, advising them what to do and what to say to achieve political success, and its main theme is that rulers must always be prepared to do evil if they judge good will come of it. Machiavelli's admirers have praised him as a political realist, his critics (historically the more numerous and vocal) have denounced him as a dangerous cynic and amoralist. He dedicated the book to the Medici, hoping to secure their sympathetic attention, but he was never offered any further political offices and spent his last 15 years as a writer. He wrote a series of *Discorsi sulla prima deca di Tito Livio*, a full-scale analysis of republican government, completed in about 1518 and published in 1531 (Eng trans *Discourses on Livy*, 1636), a treatise *Dell'Arte della guerra* (1521, Eng trans *The Art of War*, 1562), *Mandragola* (Eng trans 1940), a comic play about a seduction (completed in about 1518), and several minor literary and historical works. He died among family and friends, and was buried in Santa Croce, Florence.
▷R Ridolfi, *The Life of Machiavelli* (1963)

MacINNES, Colin
(1914–79)

English novelist and essayist. He was the son of the novelist **Angela Thirkell**, who took him to Australia as a child. After completing his education there, he returned to Britain and served in the Intelligence Corps during the war, a discipline that taught him to see through surface detail to the reality underneath. MacInnes became a perceptive commentator for a variety of liberal newspapers and journals on the sub-cultures of the 1950s. *To the Victor the Spoils* (1950), his first novel, was a definitive account of social and cultural disenchantment. It was followed by the more sanguine *June in Her Spring* (1952) and *City of Spades* (1957), one of the first books by a white writer to examine the fate of Britain's Caribbean immigrants. In 1959 he published *Absolute Beginners*, a work of raw immediacy which has become a classic statement of a society poised on the brink of major change. *Mr Love and Justice* (1960) followed, together with collections of MacInnes's journalism. Another of the minority groups for whom he spoke was the homosexual community; *Loving Them Both* (1974) was an account of gay and bisexual relationships in the post-Wolfenden era.
▷T Gould, *Inside Outsider* (1984)

MACK, Amy Eleanor
(1876–1939)

Australian naturalist and writer for children, born in Port Adelaide, the younger sister of **Louise Mack**. She was editor of the women's page of the *Sydney Morning Herald* between 1907 and 1914, where some of her stories first appeared. Her 'bushland' tales for younger children were published in *A Bush Calendar* (1909) and *Bushland Stories for Children* (1910). Five other titles appeared up to 1914 and *The Wilderness* was published in 1922. Despite, perhaps, an unfashionable anthropomorphism, her stories provide a solid background of natural history and are still popular.

MACK, (Marie) Louise Hamilton
(1874–1935)

Australian novelist, journalist and war correspondent, born in Hobart, Tasmania, sister of **Amy Mack**. Her first juvenile novel *The World is Round* appeared in 1896; the trilogy *Teens* (1897), *Girls Together* (1898) and the much later *Teens Triumphant* (1933), drew on her own school experiences. She moved to London in 1901 and wrote the popular *An Australian Girl in London* (1902); nine other adult novels include *The Red Rose of Summer* (1909) and *The Music Makers* (1914). She spent some years in Florence during which she edited the English-language *Italian Gazette* (1904–7). In 1914 she went to Belgium for the London *Daily Mail* and *Evening News* as the first woman war correspondent; her adventures were published in 1915 as *A Woman's Experiences in the Great War*.

MACKAY, Jessie
(1864–1938)

New Zealand poet of Scottish descent, born in Rakaia Gorge, Canterbury, and recognized as the first native-born poet of any merit. Her verse drew heavily on the vocabulary of Celtic and Scandinavian myth, but she was a liberal thinker and ardent feminist. She fought for the issues of the day, as in her 'Vigil, April 10, 1919' on the eve of a Prohibition referendum. Her first collections were *The Spirit of the Rangatira* (1889), *The Sitter on the Rail* (1891) and *From the Maori Sea* (1908); her last, *Vigil* (1935).
▷N F H McLeod, *A Voice on the Wind* (1955)

MACKAY, Robert, English name of Rob Donn MacAoidh
(1714–78)

Gaelic poet, born in Strathmore, Sutherland. He became a herdsman for the MacKay chief, Lord Reay. As an oral bard he became known as 'Rob Donn', describing rural life in his area and the disintegration of clan society on Strathnaver and Strathmore after the 1745 Jacobite Rising.

MACKAY, Shena
(1946–)

Scottish novelist and story writer. She published her first short novels (in one volume), *Dust Falls on Eugene Schlumberger [and] Toddler on the Run*, in 1964. In 1993 she published *Dunedin*, a novel along the lines of, and with much of the substance of, **Henry Handel Richardson**'s *The Fortunes of Richard Mahoney*. Her stories explore, with non-moralizing humour and knowing panache, the vagaries of human existence.

MacKAYE, Percy Wallace
(1875–1956)

American dramatist, born in New York City, whose first play, *The Canterbury Pilgrims* (1903), describes in blank verse the Wife of Bath's amorous stalking of **Chaucer**. He went on to write *Jeanne D'Arc* (1906), but his most successful play, *The Scarecrow* (1908), was an adaptation of *Feathertop*, a short story by **Nathaniel Hawthorne**. MacKaye also wrote hugely ambitious masques intended to be staged as public events, one of which, *St Louis* (1914), calls for 7 500 actors.

MACKELLAR, Dorothea
(1885–1968)

Australia's most often quoted poet, born in Sydney. Her fame rests solely on 'My Country', first published in the London *Spectator* in 1908. Later revised and included in her first collection *The Closed Door* (1911), its opening lines 'I Love a Sunburnt Country,/A Land of Sweeping Plains ...' evoke an emotional response from Australians the world over.

MACKENZIE, Sir (Edward Montague) Compton
(1883–1972)

English writer, born in West Hartlepool. Educated at St Paul's School and Magdalen College, Oxford, he studied for the English Bar but gave up his law studies in 1907 to work on his first play, *The Gentleman in Grey*. His first novel, *The Passionate Elopement*, was published in 1911. There followed his story of theatre life, *Carnival* (1912), which was a huge success, and the autobiographical *Sinister Street* (2 vols, 1913–14) and *Guy and Pauline* (1915). In World War I he served in the Dardanelles, and in 1917 became director of the Aegean Intelligence Service in Syria, described in his book on the Secret Service, *Extremes Meet* (1928). His considerable output included *Sylvia Scarlett* (1918), *Poor Relations* (1919), *Rich Relatives* (1921), *Vestal Fire* (1927), *The Four Winds of Love* (4 vols, 1937–45), *Aegean Memories* (1940), *Whisky Galore* (1947), *Eastern Epic, vol I* (1951) and *Rockets Galore* (1957). His monumental autobiography, *My Life and Times* (1963–71), came out in 10 *Octaves*.

MACKENZIE, Henry
(1745–1831)

Scottish writer, known as the 'Man of Feeling', born in Edinburgh, the son of a doctor. He was educated at Edinburgh University. He became a crown attorney in the Scottish Court of Exchequer (1765), and in 1804 Comptroller of Taxes. For more than half a century he was 'one of the most illustrious names connected with polite literature in Edinburgh', and a regular contributor to the *Scots Magazine and General Intelligencer*. His sentimental, but highly influential, novel, *The Man of Feeling*, was published in 1771, followed by *The Man of the World* in 1773, and *Julia de Roubigné* in 1777. He also wrote two tragedies, *The Spanish Father* (1773, but never performed), and *The Prince of Tunis* (1773). He was one of the founders of the Royal Society of Edinburgh (1783). He is also remembered for his recognition of **Robert Burns**, and as an early admirer of **Lessing** and of **Schiller**. His memoirs were published as *Anecdotes and Egotisms* (1927).

MACKENZIE, Seaforth, pseud of **Kenneth Ivo Mackenzie**
(1913–55)

Australian novelist and poet, born in Perth, whose importance was not fully recognized until long after his suicide by drowning. The first of his four novels, *The Young Desire It* (1937), remains one of the best of 20th-century accounts of the strains, homosexual and otherwise, of adolescence, and, although not as accomplished, is worthy to rank with the *Young Törless* of **Robert Musil**. Of his novels the best known is *Dead Men Rising* (1951), based on a mass break-out of Japanese prisoners-of-war from a New South Wales prison camp in 1944 which Mackenzie, as a drafted soldier, witnessed. His poems (*Selected Poems*, 1961, *The Poems of Kenneth Mackenzie*, 1972), published under his real name, are amongst the best written this century by an Australian: brilliant in natural technique, they are visionary and death-haunted.
▷ E Jones, *Kenneth Mackenzie* (1969)

MACKENZIE, Kenneth Ivo see MACKENZIE, Seaforth

MACKINTOSH, Elizabeth see TEY, Josephine

MACLAREN, Ian, pseud of **John Watson**
(1850–1907)

Scottish minister and writer, born in Manningtree, Essex. He was a Presbyterian minister in Liverpool from 1880 to 1895. His amazing success with his *Beside the Bonnie Brier Bush* (1894) gave rise to the name 'Kailyard School', and was followed by *Days of Auld Lang Syne* (1895) and others. He also wrote religious works, such as *Children of the Resurrection* (1912).
▷ W R Nicoll, *Ian MacLaren* (1908)

MacLAVERTY, Bernard
(1942–)

Irish short-story writer and novelist, born in Belfast. He was educated at Queen's University, and worked as a laboratory technician, then as a teacher in Edinburgh and on Islay. He has been a full-time writer since 1981. His best work is found in his humane, highly crafted, emotionally powerful short stories, collected in *Secrets* (1977), *A Time to Dance* (1982), and *The Great Profundo* (1987), followed by a 'Best of' selection in 1990. His first novel, *Lamb* (1980), reflected a persistent theme in his work, that of alienation and the difficulties of human contact, while *Cal* (1983) dealt more directly with guilt and the political turmoil of his native city. He has also written screenplays for both his novels, plays for radio and television, and children's books.

MACLEAN, Alistair
(1922–87)

Scottish author, born in Glasgow. He was educated at Inverness Royal Academy, Hillhead High School and Glasgow University. He served in the Royal Navy from 1941 to 1946. In 1954, while a school-teacher, he won a short-story competition held by the *Glasgow Herald*, contributing a tale of adventure at sea. At the suggestion of Collins, the publishers, he produced a full-length novel, *HMS Ulysses*, the next year, and this epic story of war-time bravery became an immediate bestseller. He followed it with *The Guns of Navarone* in 1957, and turned to full-time writing. He preferred the term 'adventure story' to 'novel' in describing his work. His settings are worldwide, including the China Seas (*South by Java Head*, 1958), Greenland (*Night Without End*, 1960), Florida (*Fear is the Key*, 1961), the Scottish islands (*When Eight Bells Toll*, 1966), a polar scientific station (*Ice Station Zebra*, 1963) and the Camargue (*Caravan to Vaccares*, 1970). As well as two secret service thrillers (written as Ian Stuart), *The Dark Crusader* (1961) and *The Satan Bug* (1962), he wrote a Western (*Breakheart Pass*, 1974) and biographies of T E Lawrence and Captain Cook. Other titles include *Where Eagles Dare* (1967), *Force Ten From Navarone* (1968) and *Athabasca* (1980). Most of his stories were made into highly successful films.

MacLEAN, Sorley, or MACGILL-EAIN, Somhairle
(1911–)

Gaelic poet, born on the island of Raasay, off Skye. He attended Raasay school and Portree High School on Skye before reading English at Edinburgh University (1929–33). He began to write while a student, and by the end of the 1930s was already an established figure on the Scottish literary scene. In 1940 he published *Seventeen Poems for Sixpence*, which he produced with **Robert Garioch**, and in 1943, after his recovery from wounds sustained during active service at El Alamein, came *Dàin do Eimhir* (*Poems to Eimhir*), which contained, among other shorter poems, many of his love lyrics addressed to the legendary Eimhir of the early Irish sagas. Influenced by the metaphysical poets as well as the ancient and later Celtic literature and traditional Gaelic song, he reinvigorated the Gaelic literary language and tradition, creating a medium capable of expressing contemporary intellectual challenge, much as his friend **Hugh MacDiarmid** was reinstating Scots as a serious literary language. A teacher and headmaster until his retirement in 1972, his major collection of poems, *Reothairt is Contraigh* ('Spring Tide and Neap Tide'),

appeared in 1977. His work has been translated and issued in bilingual editions, and has reached a wide and appreciative public all over the world. His *Collected Poems* appeared in 1991.

▷T McCaughey, in *The History of Scottish Literature* (vol 4, 1987, ed Cairns Craig)

MACLEISH, Archibald
(1892–)

American poet and librarian, born in Glencoe, Illinois. Educated at Yale and the Harvard Law School, he married Ada Hitchcock in 1916. After military service in France and his graduation from law school in 1919, he taught constitutional law briefly at Harvard College but moved to Europe in 1923 to concentrate on writing. His first book of poems, *The Happy Marriage*, was published a year later. His many works include *The Pot of Earth* (1925), *The Hamlet of A. MacLeish* (1928), and *Conquistador* (1932), winner of that year's Pulitzer Prize for poetry. For his *Collected Poems 1917–1952* he was awarded a second Pulitzer Prize as well as the Bollingen Prize and a National Book Award in 1953; and *J.B.*, a verse play, won both the Pulitzer Prize in drama and the Antoinette Perry Award for best play in 1959. He was Librarian of Congress (1939–44), Assistant Secretary of State (1944–5), co-founder of UNESCO, and Boylston Professor of Rhetoric and Oratory at Harvard University.

▷G Smith, *Archibald MacLeish* (1971)

MacLENNAN, (John) Hugh
(1907–)

Canadian novelist, born in Glace Bay, Nova Scotia—the setting of *Each Man's Son* (1951)—and educated at Dalhousie University, Oriel College, Oxford, and Princeton. While teaching classics in Montreal, he wrote *Barometer Rising* (1941), arguably the first important modern Canadian novel, at whose climax is the apocalyptic munition ship explosion which devastated Halifax, Nova Scotia, in 1917, and which MacLennan had experienced as a boy. Positively or not, it became a defining text in the development of a distinctive Canadian consciousness. *Two Solitudes* (1945) was equally successful at home, as were *The Precipice* (1948) and *The Watch That Ends the Night* (1959), both of which reflected his acute psychological grasp. *Voices in Time* (1980) looks forward to a bleak, post-nuclear future. His essays were collected as *The Other Side of Hugh MacLennan* (1978).

▷E Cameron, *Hugh MacLennan: A Writer's Life* (1981)

MACLEOD, Fiona *see* SHARP, William

MacLEOD, Mary, English name of **Màiri nighean Alasdair Ruaidh** (c.1615–1705)

Gaelic poet, born in Rodel on Harris. She first came to the MacLeod court at Dunvegan, on Skye, as a nurse and looked after several members of the family during her long life there. She depended upon the MacLeod court for favour and the leisure to write her songs, of which only 16 survive. One of these tells how she was sent away in disfavour and then later restored to Dunvegan by the new heir. Her songs and verses were composed in honour of the MacLeods and in honour of other great families such as the Mackenzies of Applecross. Her poetry, which praised the chiefs and their great generosity, is notable for its break from classical syllabic metres, being composed in the form of a freer, more spontaneous stress pattern.
▷ J Carmichael Watson, *Gaelic Songs of Mary MacLeod* (1934)

MAC LIAMMÓIR, Mícheál (Michael Wilmore) (1899–1978)

Irish actor, painter and writer, born in Cork. His family moved to London, and he became a child actor as Michael Darling in Herbert Beerbohm Tree's production of *Peter Pan*, with **Noël Coward** as Lost Boy. He studied art at the Slade School, becoming a distinguished painter and designer inspired by Beardsley, and also became a proficient multilinguist after residence abroad. With his lifelong friend Hilton Edwards, he founded the Gate Theatre Company in Dublin (1928), having toured Ireland with the **Shakespeare**an Company of Anew MacMaster. His company's work made the most of dramatic possibilities of Irish writing, drew in much European drama using his translations, adaptations, design and lighting, and offered classical material as bold in rethinking as anything in London or New York. He wrote distinguished fiction, plays and memoirs in Irish and in English, and in the 1960s his one-man shows crowned an outstanding international reputation. *The Importance of Being Oscar* (1960) magnificently realized the dramatic possibilities of **Wilde**'s life, while paying homage to his life-long beloved idol. *I Must Be Talking to My Friends* (1963, on Irish history and literature) and *Mostly About Yeats* (1970) were worthy successors. His most famous film appearance was as Iago in Orson Welles' *Othello* (1949, brilliantly described in his *Put Money in Thy Purse* 1954) and (for voice only) as the narrator in *Tom Jones* (1963).
▷ *An Irish Actor Young and Old* (1977), and other autobiographical volumes

MacMHUIRRIC, Niall (c.1637–1726)

Last of the Gaelic professional poets, whose livelihood it was to write elegies and encomiums for their patrons. He is known primarily for his two elegies composed for Allan MacDonald of Clanranaland, who died in 1715, one elegy classical and the other vernacular. His political or Jacobite poetry was written in the old style of formal bardic verse. In this he stands in contrast to the innovations of **John MacDonald** and **Mary MacLeod**. The family of MacMhuirric was the chief bardic family of Scotland. They were powerful landowners and flourished in the Highlands and Western Isles from the 13th to the 18th centuries. Niall and his predecessor Cathal MacMhuirric are two of the greatest members of the family and a selection of their work may be found in the *Red Book of Clanranaland*.
▷ D Thompson, *An Introduction to Gaelic Poetry* (1974)

MacNAMARA, Brinsley, real name **John Weldon** (1890–1963)

Irish novelist and dramatist, the son of a schoolmaster in the town of Delvin, County Westmeath in the midlands. In 1910 he joined the Abbey Players, touring with them in the USA. His novel *The Valley of the Squinting Windows* (1918) led to unprecedented scenes: the book, a satire on village life, was burned publicly in Delvin, the school was boycotted and his father was forced to leave the region (he later died prematurely in Dublin following an unresolved court case against the school's Catholic directors). His son divided his time between County Clare, where he wrote a series of novels including *The Clanking of Chains* (1920) and *The Various Lives of Marcus Igoe* (1929), and Dublin, where he produced plays for the Abbey Theatre. The most interesting of these is the grim *Look at the Heffernans* (1926). MacNamara became increasingly bitter and reactionary and in 1939 resigned as director of the national theatre following a production of **Sean O'Casey**'s 'vulgar and worthless plays' and in particular the 1935 production of *The Silver Tassie*. He died intestate in Dublin.
▷ P O Farrell, *The Burning of Brinsley MacNamara* (1990)

MacNEICE, (Frederick) Louis (1907–63)

Irish poet, born in Belfast, the son of a Church of Ireland clergyman who became a bishop. Educated at Marlborough and Merton College, Oxford, he became a lecturer in classics at Birmingham (1930–6) and in Greek

at Bedford College, University of London (1936–40). He was closely associated with the British left-wing poets of the 1930s, especially **W H Auden**, with whom he wrote *Letters from Iceland* (1937). His poetry often has a biting colloquial humour and, with his writing for radio, ranges over a vast area of contemporary experience, ideas and images. His volumes of poetry include *Blind Fireworks* (1929), *Autumn Journal* (1938), *Collected Poems* (1949), *Autumn Sequel* (1954), *Eighty-Five Poems* and *Solstices* (both 1961). He was the author of a pseudonymous novel, *Round about Way* (1932, as 'Louis Malone'), and several memorable verse plays for radio, notably *The Dark Tower* (published with other radio scripts in 1947), as well as translations of **Aeschylus** and of **Goethe**'s *Faust*. He also produced several volumes of literary criticism. A volume of autobiography, *The Strings Are False*, appeared posthumously in 1965, and his *Collected Poems* in 1966.
▷ *The Strings are False* (1965)

MACPHERSON, James
(1736–96)

Scottish poet, renowned as the 'translator' of the legendary Gaelic bard **Ossian**, born in Ruthven, Inverness-shire, a farmer's son. He was educated at King's College and Marischal College, Aberdeen, and studied for the ministry, but in 1756 became a village schoolmaster in Ruthven. In 1758 he published an epic poem, *The Highlander*, and two years later he published some fragments of Gaelic oral poetry, which he had collected and translated, as *Fragments of Ancient Poetry Collected in the Highlands of Scotland* (1870). In the introduction (by Hugh Blair) it was suggested that a great poetic epic relating to the legendary hero Fingal, as told by his son Ossian, was still extant. In 1760, Macpherson was commissioned by the Faculty of Advocates in Edinburgh to tour the Highlands in search of this material, which he published in 1762 as *Fingal: an Ancient Epic Poem in Six Books*, followed by *Temora, an Epic Poem, in Eight Books* (1763). They were received with huge acclaim, but a storm of controversy soon arose about their authenticity. Macpherson could not or would not produce any originals, and it appears that he used only about 15 genuine pieces of original verse which he altered and amended, and invented the rest to create an epic form for them. In 1763 he was appointed Surveyor-General of the Floridas, but soon returned to London and became a wealthy merchant with interests in the East India Company as agent to the Nabob of Arcot. He sat in parliament as MP for Camelford from 1780. He was buried, at his own request and expense, in Westminster Abbey.

MACPHERSON, Jay
(1931–)

English-born Canadian poet and academic. She made a reputation with *The Boatman* (1957, rev edn 1968), which contained subtle, gracefully metaphysical lyrics of an essentially literary nature, and with a core of fervent Christian feeling at its heart. Since that time she has written little, and *Welcoming Disaster* (1974), adddessed to her teddy bear, her 'glum chum', was not as well received.
▷ *Canadian Literature* (Winter, 1960)

MACPHERSON, Mary
(1821–98)

Scottish Gaelic poet, born on the Isle of Skye, who was a passionate advocate of Highland Land Reform. She was an interestingly uneven poet, the best of whose work transcends its polite intentions.

MACROBIUS, Ambrosius Theodosius
(5th century)

Roman writer and neo-Platonist philosopher, born probably in Africa. He wrote a commentary on **Cicero**'s *Somnium Scipionis*, and *Saturnalia*, a series of historical, mythological and critical dialogues in the manner of **Athenaeus**.

MADÁCH, Imre
(1823–64)

Hungarian dramatist and poet, born in Alsó-Sztregova. Regarded by some as the 'greatest philosophical poet of Hungary', his dramatic poem, eventually staged, *Az ember tragédiája* (1861, Eng trans *The Tragedy of Man*, 1933), is the nearest work to *The Dynasts* of **Thomas Hardy** in world literature (Hardy did not know it, or Hungarian). It brought Madách into contention as one of the world's great playwrights of his century, but has not yet become well-enough known outside Hungary, for all the critical work that has been done upon it. Its protagonists are Adam, optimist, Lucifer, pragmatist and Eve, enigmatic cause of both Adam's fall and his redemption.
▷S Hevesy, *Introduction to the Tragedy of Man* (1935); J Gassner, *Master of the Drama* (1940)

MAERLANT, Jacob van
(c.1235–c.1300)

Flemish didactic poet. He was the author of verse translations of French and Latin originals, including the *Roman de Troie* (c.1264, 'The Tale of Troy') and de Beauvais' *Speculum Majus* (1284), as *Spiegel Historiael*, a history of the world.

MAETERLINCK, Count Maurice
(1862–1949)

Belgian dramatist and winner of the Nobel Prize for literature, born in Ghent. He studied law at Ghent University, but became a disciple of the Symbolist movement, and in 1889 produced his first volume of poetry, *Les Serres chaudes* ('The Greenhouses'). In the same year came his prose play, *La Princesse Maleine* (Eng trans *The Princess Maleine*, 1890), and in 1892 *Pelléas et Mélisande* (Eng trans *Pelleas and Melisande*, 1894), on which Debussy based his opera. Other plays include *Joyzelle* (1903, Eng trans 1906) and *Marie-Magdeleine* (1910, Eng trans *Mary Magdalene*, 1910). *La Vie des abeilles* (1901, Eng trans *The Life of the Bee*, 1901) is one of his many popular expositions of scientific subjects, and he also wrote several philosophical works. He was awarded the Nobel Prize for literature in 1911.
▷ B Knapp, *Maurice Maeterlinck* (1975)

MAFFEI, Francesco Scipione, Marchese di
(1675–1755)

Italian dramatist, born in Verona. He fought in the War of the Spanish Succession (1703–4) under his brother Alessandro, a field-marshal. A leading reformer of Italian drama, his tragedy *Merope* (1714, Eng trans 1740) ran through 70 editions, and the comedy *Le Ceremonie* (1728) was also successful. He also wrote scholarly works, including *Verona illustrata* (1731–2).
▷ G Silvestri, *Un europeo del Settecento* (1954)

MAGALHÃES, Domingos José Gonçalves de
(1811–82)

Brazilian romantic poet, a Rio doctor who published his first collection in 1832, then went to Europe—France and Italy—and met many representatives of the romantic movement. On his return to Brazil his style changed, and he founded a magazine in order to promote romanticism. His second collection, *Poéticos e Saudades* (1836), is usually considered to have inaugurated romanticism. He wrote verse plays and epics. His importance is more historical than intrinsic: even Brazil's 'first national play', *Antonio José* (1838), written by him, is dull.
▷ J A Castelo, *Gonçalves de Magalhães* (1946, in Portuguese)

MAGINN, William
(1794–1842)

Irish writer, born in Cork. He was educated in his father's private school and at Trinity College, Dublin, and took his LL D. He taught in Cork for 10 years, and in 1823 moved to London. He was a prolific contributor to *Blackwood's Magazine*, and the *Standard*, and was the joint founder of *Fraser's Magazine* (1830). A collection of his tales was edited by Eric Partridge (1933).
▷ R S Mackenzie (ed), *Miscellaneous Writings* (1855–7)

MAGRIS, Claudio
(1939–)

Italian writer, born in Trieste. He taught German at the University of Turin (1970–8), and now lectures at Trieste University. His writing includes non-fiction works on Austro-Hungarian culture and literature, and literary criticism, including a book on the writer **Joseph Roth**. His best-known work is *Danubio* (1986, Eng trans *Danube*, 1989), a compendious account of the great central European river which is part invention, part travelogue, and part cultural, historical and literary meditation. His cerebral, playful novels include *Illazioni su una sciabola* (1984, Eng trans *Inferences from a Sabre*, 1990) and *Altro mare* (1991, Eng trans *A Different Sea*, 1993).

MAHFOUZ, or MAHFUZ, Naguib
(1911–)

Egyptian novelist and winner of the Nobel Prize for literature, born in the al-Gamaliyya old quarter of Cairo, the setting for several of his works. The youngest son of a merchant, he graduated from King Fuad I (now Cairo) University in 1934 with a degree in philosophy. An avid reader of French, British, Russian, American and Arab writers, he especially admired the critical writings of ostracized fellow Egyptians such as **Taha Husayn**. He worked in university administration and then for the government's Ministry of Waqfs, or religious foundations, and in journalism. He started writing as a boy and by 1939 had already written three novels, one of which, *Kifah Tiba* (1944, 'The Struggle of Thebes'), drew a parallel between the Hyksos invasion of ancient Egypt and the pre-war British occupation of modern Egypt. He later began work on *Al-Thulathiya* (1956–7, 'The Cairo Trilogy'), a monumental, somewhat autobiographical work, described by **John Fowles** as revealing 'the struggles and convolutions of Egyptian society with a Balzacian breadth and degree of technical innovation unparalleled in any other writer of his time'. Nevertheless, it was overshadowed by the notoriety surrounding *Awlad Haratina* (1967, Eng trans *The Children of Gebelawi*, 1981), serialized in the magazine *al-Ahram*. An allegorical work which marks a departure from his previous style and shows his disillusionment with

religion, it depicts average Egyptians living the lives of Cain and Abel, Moses, Jesus and Muhammad, and portrays the decline of five communities towards futility and nihilism. It was banned throughout the Arab world, except in Lebanon. Becoming more interested in the plight of the individual, in *Al-Liss wa-l-Kilab* (1961, 'The Thief and the Dogs'), *Al-Shahhadh* (1965, 'The Beggar'), *Tharthara fawq al-Nil* (1966, 'Chit-Chat on the Nile') and *Miramar* (1967, Eng trans 1978) he explores the fate of members of different classes in Egyptian society after the Nasserite revolution, these works affirming his tragic vision of life and universalizing the experience of his characters. Described as 'a Dickens of the Cairo cafés' and the 'Balzac of Egypt', he won the Nobel Prize for literature in 1988. His work is still unavailable in many Middle Eastern countries on account of his outspoken support for President Sadat's Camp David peace treaty with Israel. At the heart of his profound fiction is his mystical Sufism.
▷S Somekh, *The Changing Rhythm: a study of Mahfuz's novels* (1973)

MAHON, Derek
(1941–)

Irish poet, born in Belfast. He was educated at Belfast Institute and Trinity College, Dublin, and taught before turning to journalism and other writing. He was associated with the 'Northern Poets' in Belfast in the 1960s, with **Seamus Heaney** and **Michael Longley**. A poet of place, drawn to squalid landscapes and desperate situations, his acknowledged influences are **Louis MacNeice** and **W H Auden**. *Twelve Poems* was published in 1965, since when there have been a number of others including *Night-Crossing* (1968), *The Snow Party* (1975), *The Hunt by Night* (1982), *A Kensington Notebook* (1984) and *Antarctica* (1985). *Poems 1962–1978* (1979) contained some revised versions of earlier works, and a new *Selected Poems* appeared in 1991.
▷Introduction to the *Penguin Book of Contemporary Irish Poetry* (1990)

MAHONY, Francis Sylvester, pseud Father Prout
(1804–66)

Irish priest and humorous writer, born in Cork. He became a Jesuit priest, but was expelled from the order for a late-night frolic and was ordained a priest at Lucca in 1832. He moved to London in 1834 and forsook his calling for journalism and poetry, and contributed to *Fraser's Magazine* and *Bentley's Miscellany*. He is remembered as author of the poems 'The Bells of Shandon' and 'The Lady of Lee'.
▷C Kent, memoir in *Works* (1881)

MAHY, Margaret
(1936–)

New Zealand writer of children's fiction, born in Whakatane, whose books are internationally recognized: *The Haunting* (1982) won the Carnegie Medal, as did *The Changeover: A Supernatural Romance* (1984). Her work ranges from texts for picture books, through short stories, to novels for younger readers and teenagers and, in *Aliens in the Family* (1986), to science fiction. Her younger tales are full of fantasy but in *The Tricksters* (1986) and the award-winning *Memory* (1987) she adopts contemporary settings and raises current concerns.

MAIDEN, Jennifer Margaret
(1949–)

Australian poet, born in Penrith, New South Wales, who has published a number of collections of prose and verse between *Tactics* (1974) and *For the Left Hand* which appeared as a special issue of *Poetry Australia* in 1981. Both *Mortal Details* (1971) and *The Warm Thing* (1983) contain verse and prose. She has also edited anthologies of verse and written plays.

MAILER, Norman Kingsley
(1923–)

American novelist, journalist and polemicist, born in Long Branch, New Jersey. He was brought up in Brooklyn and educated at Harvard. During World War II he served in the Pacific and his first novel *The Naked and the Dead* (1948) draws heavily upon his own experience. An anti-war blast and social satire, it was a remarkable work for one so young and it became a bestseller, establishing him as a leading novelist of his generation. He maintained his antagonism towards contemporary society and mores in *Barbary Shore* (1951) and *The Deer Park* (1955) but the writing of the period documents his gradual ideological transformation from liberal socialism through Trotskyism to a species of anarchistic libertarianism which he has characterized as left conservatism, and which involves an elaborate eschatology compounded of Judaistic mythology, existentialism, and private, **Hemingway**esque obsessions about courage, sex, cancer and death. A proponent of the 'New Journalism', and one who helped define that solipsistic genre, he has created a vast body of work, impressive for its energy and its self-obsession. *Advertisements for Myself* (1959), whose own blurb admitted that 'some of the pieces are mediocre', is generally regarded as one of his more successful books. As a polemicist, campaigner and protester he was prominent throughout the 1960s, publishing

An American Dream (1965), Why Are We In Vietnam? (1967) and Armies of the Night (1968), whose subject is the 1967 protest march on the Pentagon. It won a National Book Award and the Pulitzer Prize. Subsequent books include Miami and the Siege of Chicago (1969), The Prisoner of Sex (1971), Marilyn (a pictorial life of Marilyn Monroe, 1973), The Executioner's Song (1979), a fictionalized study of the execution of convicted killer Gary Gilmore, Ancient Evenings (1983), a gargantuan historical novel, and a thriller, Tough Guys Don't Dance (1984). His most recent novel is Hamlet's Ghost (1991), an account of the CIA from the end of World War II to the assassination of John F Kennedy. He has also been active as a screenwriter, film director and actor, with such works as Maidstone (1970) and Tough Guys Don't Dance (1987).

▷ H Mills, Mailer: a biography (1982)

MAILLART, Ella Kini
(1903–)

Swiss travel writer, born in Geneva. She represented Switzerland in the·1924 Olympic Games in Paris in the single-handed sailing competition, captained the Swiss Ladies Hockey Team in 1931 and skied for her country from 1931 to 1934. In 1932 she crossed Russian Turkestan and wrote of her tribulations in both French and English. In 1934, working as a journalist for Petit Parisien, she went to Mongolia to report on the Japanese invasion and returned via Peking across Tibet and into Kashmir with Peter Fleming, described in Oasis interdites (1937, Eng trans Forbidden Journey, 1937). She worked and journeyed in Iran and Afghanistan, and then spent the war years living in an ashram in southern India under the tutelage of Sri Ramama. She was one of the first travellers into Nepal when it opened in 1949, and wrote The Land of the Sherpas (1955).

MAIS, Roger
(1905–55)

Jamaican novelist and dramatist, he worked as a journalist, civil servant and photographer. A supporter of the People's National Party and associate of Norman Manley in the 1930s and 40s, he was imprisoned for his anticolonial article, 'Now we know' (Public Opinion, 1944). Considered a pioneer of national literature, the themes of Mais's three major novels draw on his socio-political commitment to the working class and explore the inner life of the individual. The Hills were Joyful Together (1953) is a violent depiction of the sufferings of the inhabitants of a Kingston tenement yard, whilst Brother Man (1954) explores the practical difficulties of translating dreams of brotherhood to reality.

His final novel, Black Lightning (1955), set in rural Jamaica, concentrates on the complex relationship between the West Indian artist and his home community.

MAISTRE, Xavier, Comte de
(1763–1852)

French novelist, painter and soldier, born in Chambéry, brother of the political philosopher Joseph Marie, Comte de Maistre. Exiled after the French occupation of Savoy (1798), he joined the Russian army and became a general. He spent most of the rest of his life in Russia, publishing several appealing works, such as Voyage autour de ma chambre (1794, 'Journey around my Room'), describing a period of imprisonment he endured, and Les Prisonniers du Caucase (1825, 'The Prisoners of the Caucasus') and La Jeune Sibérienne (1825, 'The Young Siberian Woman').

▷ A Berthier, Xavier de Maistre (1921)

MAJEROVA, Marie, pseud of Marie Tusarová
(1882–1967)

Czech novelist from Úvaly in the Kladno mining area, and a communist from the inception of the party in 1921. She spent some years amongst anarchists in Paris, in the course of a courageous and independent life; it was this experience, and her compassion— rather than her rather naive communism— that made her into a powerful novelist. She did not please the Stalinist dictators of her country. Of her novels only Havírská balada (1938, Eng trans Ballad of a Miner, 1960) has appeared in English.

MAJOR, Clarence
(1936–)

Black American poet and novelist, born in Atlanta, Georgia, and educated in Chicago, and at the New School for Social Research, New York. In an attempt to capture the reality of the Afro–American experience, he devised a surreal approach which can be obscure as well as powerful, but which is much concerned with the artificiality of accepted social and cultural norms. His most significant verse appeared in his second collection Love Poems of a Black Man (1965), though later books such as Symptoms and Madness (1971), The Cotton Club (1972), The Syncopated Cakewalk (1974) and Some Observations of a Stranger at Zuni in the Latter Part of the Century (1989) are no less effective. Major also edited the influential anthology The New Black Poetry (1969). His fiction includes the autobiographical All-Night Visitors (1969) and No (1973), which bears comparison with Richard Wright's

Black Boy. Major's concern for the linguistic aspects of the black experience in the USA resulted in a *Dictionary of Afro-American Slang* (1970, published in the UK as *Black Slang*, 1971).

MALAMUD, Bernard
(1914–86)

American novelist, born in Brooklyn, New York, and educated at Columbia University, New York. He taught at Oregon State University (1949–61) and Bennington College (1961–86). One of the leading writers of contemporary America and among the 'urban-Jewish' Americans, he was more influenced by mainstream American writers than those ghettoized by their creed. *The Natural* (1952), his first novel, which used baseball as an extended metaphor for life, took as its starting point the mythic aspects of professional sport, and followed the fading career of the once-promising big-hitter Roy Hobbs. With *The Assistant* (1957) the mood is darker but the critical reception was warm. *A New Life* (1961) marked a new departure, from the compressed urban environment to mountainous western America, where Seymour Levin arrives at a small college to teach and analyse happiness. *The Fixer* (1966), set in Tsarist Russia, was his bleakest and most potent book, streaked with self-deprecating humour. He wrote four more novels: *Pictures of Fidelman* (1969); *The Tenants* (1971); *Dubin's Lives* (1979); and *God's Grace* (1982), a prophetic, apocalyptic allegory. He was also an accomplished short-story writer and *The Stories of Bernard Malamud* was published in 1983. He won the National Book Award twice, in 1959 and 1967, and the Pulitzer Prize in 1967.
▷J Helterman, *Understanding Malamud* (1985)

MALAPARTE, Curzio, pseud of Kurt Erich Suckert
(1898–1957)

Italian novelist and playwright, born in Prato, near Florence, to German–Italian parents. A liking for extreme politics dogged his life: in the 1920s, his attraction towards Fascism did not stretch to obeying the dictates of the Duce; in 1933 he received a five-year prison sentence, later commuted. A restless individual, he was a journalist and film-maker as well as a writer of fiction. *Kaputt*, a portrayal of a war-ravaged Europe first published in 1944, verges on nihilism, and is regarded as his best work. A later novel, *La pelle* (1949, 'The Skin'), draws on his experiences of Naples in 1944.

MALET, Lucas, pseud of Mary St Leger Kingsley
(1852–1931)

English novelist, daughter of **Charles Kingsley**. In 1876 she married the Rev W Harrison, rector of Clovelly, and as 'Lucas Malet' completed her father's *Tutor's Story* (1916) and wrote powerful novels, including *Mrs Lorimer* (1882), *Colonel Enderby's Wife* (1885), *The Wages of Sin* (1890), *The Carissima* (1896) and *Sir Richard Calmady* (1901). She became a Roman Catholic in 1899.

MALGONKAR, Manohar Dattatray
(1913–)

Indian novelist and short-story writer. A professional big-game hunter in his early twenties, he worked for the Indian government before taking a commission in the army, where he reached the rank of lieutenant-colonel. Between 1953 and 1959, he ran his own mining concern and stood as independent parliamentary candidate. His fiction is brightly coloured and romantic, with an emphasis on narrative action rather than psychological profundity. His first novel was *Distant Drum* (1960), but it was with his first British-published book, *Combat of Shadows* (1962), that he rose to prominence, fulfilling an appetite for stories of the Raj. *The Princes* (1963) and *A Bend in the Ganges* (1964) are more profound. Later novels include *The Garland Keepers* (1980) and *Bandicoot Run* (1982). Malgonkar's short fiction has been collected in a number of volumes, most notably *A Toast in Warm Wine* (1974) and *Bombay Beware* (1975). His non-fiction includes Indian social history and a perceptive study (1978) of Gandhi's assassins.
▷J Y Dayananda, *Manohar Malgonkar* (1974)

MALHERBE, François de
(1555–1628)

French poet, born in Caen. He ingratiated himself with Henri IV, and received a pension. He was an industrious writer, producing odes, songs, epigrams, epistles, translations and criticisms. He founded a literary tradition—'Enfin Malherbe vint'—and led his countrymen to disdain the richly-coloured and full-sounding verses of **Pierre de Ronsard**, and to adopt a style clear, correct and refined, but cold and prosaic.
▷R Fromilhague, *La vie de Malherbe* (1954)

MALLARMÉ, Stéphane
(1842–98)

French Symbolist poet, born in Paris. He taught English in various schools in Paris and elsewhere and visited England on several occasions. He translated **Edgar Allan Poe**'s

'The Raven' as 'Le Corbeau' (1875). In prose and verse he was a leader of the Symbolist school, revelling in allegory, obscurity, bizarre works and constructions, *vers libre* and word-music. *L'Après-midi d'un faune* ('A Faun's Afternoon'), illustrated by Manet (1876), is his best-known poem and made the wilful obscurity of his style famous. His *Les Dieux antiques* (1880, 'The Ancient Gods'), *Poésies* (1899) and *Vers et prose* (1893) were other works admired by the 'decadents'. He planned a work called his *Grand Oeuvre* which would represent the attainment of a pure poetic essence in a distilled, concentrated language, but completed only fragments of it.
▷H Mondor, *La vie de Mallarmé* (2 vols, 1941)

MALLEA, Edourdo
(1903–82)

Major Argentinian novelist, essayist and editor, born in Bahia Blanca, son of a humane and self-sacrificing country doctor who greatly influenced him. He was a key figure in the literature of his country; from 1931 he was literary editor of the newspaper *La Nación*. His ambition in his fiction was always to explore the essence of Argentina: his own statement to Angel Flores in the latter's *Spanish American Literature: The Twentieth Century* (1992) is most eloquent of this. But he was an inveterate traveller, and his books drew intelligently from European models, including **Chekhov**, **William Blake**, **Unamuno** and **Pérez de Ayala**. All he wrote is of high value — some find him a greater writer than the more politically ambiguous **Borges**. But, like Borges, he has been attacked by Marxists, most particularly by **Viñas**. Important books of his that have been translated include *Historia de una passión argentina* (1937, Eng trans *History of an Argentine Passion*, 1983) and *Todo verdor perecer* (1941, Eng trans *All Green Shall Perish and Other Novels and Stories*, 1966).
▷J H Richard, *The Writings of Edourdo Mallea* (1959); H E Lewald, *Edourdo Mallea* (1977)

MALLET, David, originally Malloch
(c.1705–1765)

Scottish poet, born near Crieff, Perthshire, the son of a schoolmaster. After a period working as the janitor at Edinburgh High School (1717–18), he studied at the university. In 1720 he became a tutor, working from 1723 to 1731 in the family of the Duke of Montrose. Living mostly in London, he changed his name 'from Scots Malloch to English Mallet'. *William and Margaret* (1723), developed from the fragment of an old ballad, gained him a reputation as a poet, which he

enhanced by *The Excursion* (1728). He also tried his hand at play-writing. *Mustapha* had a brief success in 1739; *Eurydice* (1731) and *Elvira* (1763), both tragedies, were failures. *Alfred, a Masque* (1740), was written in conjunction with **James Thomson**, and one of its songs, 'Rule Britannia', was claimed by both.

MALLET-JORIS, Françoise, pseud of Françoise Lilar
(1930–)

Belgian-born French novelist, she was born in Antwerp, and educated in the USA and at the Sorbonne. Her first novel, *Le Rempart des Béguines* (1950), appeared in the US as *The Illusionist* (1952) and in the UK as *Into the Labyrinth* (1957). Until the 1980s she was routinely translated, the translations often miscasting her vivaciously individual feminism as a sober intellectual stance rather than as a more instinctive reaction to social conditioning. Affected by existentialism, she is deeply concerned with personal authenticity, a theme that emerges strongly in *Les Mensonges* (1956, Eng trans *House of Lies*, 1957) and *L'Empire Céleste* (1958, Eng trans *Café Céleste*, 1959), for which she was awarded the prestigious Prix Femina. The autobiographical *Lettre à moi-même* (1963, Eng trans *A Letter to Myself*, 1964) traces her conversion to Roman Catholicism. Her later work is more conventional in approach. For many years she worked in publishing and as a songwriter; in 1973, she was elected President of the Académie **Goncourt**.
▷M Détry, *Mallet-Joris* (1976)

MALLIN, Tom
(1927–77)

English novelist, born in West Bromwich in the Midlands. Orphaned at four, he was educated at boarding school, and at Birmingham School of Art, winning a scholarship to the Royal Academy. Military service (1945–7) took him to the Middle East, after which he worked as a cartoonist, sculpting in his spare time. His first novel was *Dodecahedron* (1970), a remarkable debut for a 43-year-old. He published three other novels, *Knut* (1971), *Erowica* (1972) and *Lobe* (1977), all of them playful rather than 'experimental' fantasies. A fifth, *Bedrok*, was published posthumously.
▷Interview with Alan Burns in *The Imagination on Trial* (1981)

MALLOCK, William Hurrell
(1849–1923)

English novelist, born in Devon. His single famous book is the novel *The New Republic* (1877, of which it is necessary to refer to the

1975 edition by John Lucas, since this identifies the characters). *The New Republic* anticipates the New Right in its fanatic hatred of liberalism; but it is not incapable satire. It is a roman à clef in which the author ridicules such figures as **Matthew Arnold**, **Walter Pater**, T H Huxley and others. Lucas comments: 'Mallock is often outrageous, frequently silly ... But he is always readable ...'. He also describes *In An Enchanted Island* (1889), about Cyprus, as 'one of the best travel books ever written'.
▷A B Adams, *The Novels of Mallock* (1934)

MALMANCHE, Tanguy
(1875–1953)
French playwright, writing in Breton, who was an important figure in his minority literature after the early death of **Yann Ber Kalloc'h**. Most of his plays were translated into French. His masterpiece was *Gurvan le chevalier étranger* (1923, 'Gurvan, the Strange Knight'), a character about whom he wrote more plays. He has been compared both to **Claudel** and to **Synge**.

MALMBERG, Bertil
(1889–1958)
Swedish poet. Born in Härnösand, he published his first book of poetry in 1908, focusing contemporary Swedish Symbolism. From 1917 to 1926 he lived in Germany. The poems in *Orfika* (1923, 'Orphica') are characterized by elaborate metric forms which convey a far-reaching aestheticism shot through with feelings of guilt. *Dikter vid gränsen* (1935, 'Poems on the Border') is imbued with a profound, often Spenglerian pessimism, its formal expression inspired by myths and archetypes. The plainer, toned-down poems of the 1940s, for example in *Under månens fallande båge* (1947, 'Beneath the Falling Arc of the Moon'), show him as a modernist. *Åke och hans värld* (1924, 'Åke and His World') is a perceptive prose account of the development of a child.
▷I Algulin, *Tradition och modernism. Bertil Malmbergs och Hjalmar Gullbergs lyriska förnyelse efter 1940–talets mitt* (1969)

MALORY, Sir Thomas
(d.1471)
English writer. **Caxton**'s preface to Malory's masterpiece, the *Morte d'Arthur*, states that Malory was a knight, that he finished his work in the ninth year of the reign of Edward IV (1469–70), and that he 'reduced' it from some French book. It is probable that he was the Sir Thomas Malory of Newbold Revel, Warwickshire, whose quarrels with a neighbouring priory and (probably) Lancastrian politics brought him imprisonment. Of Caxton's black-letter folio only two copies now exist. An independent manuscript was discovered at Winchester in 1934. *Morte d'Arthur* is the best prose romance in English and was a happy attempt to give epic unity to the whole mass of French Arthurian romance. **Tennyson**, **Swinburne** and many others took their inspiration from Malory.
▷S Johnson, in *Lives of the Most Eminent English Poets* (10 vols, 1779–81)

MALOUF, David
(1934–)
Australian novelist, born in Brisbane. His father's family came to Australia in the 1880s from Lebanon and his mother's from London just before World War I. He was educated at Brisbane Grammar School and Queensland University, where he subsequently taught for two years. He went abroad for a decade and returned to Australia, tutoring at Sydney University before leaving for Italy. A full-time writer since 1978, an early project was the libretto for an opera of **Patrick White**'s *Voss*. Previously concentrating on poetry, his first novel was *Johnno* (1975) and in 1979 he was awarded the New South Wales Premier's Literary Award for *An Imaginary Life* (1978), which had been serialized in the *New Yorker*. Other works include the novella *Fly Away Peter* (1982) and the novels *Harland's Half Acre* (1984), *Great World* (1991) and *Remembering Babylon* (1993). *Antipodes*, a collection of stories, appeared in 1985, and some of his poetry in *Poems 1959–1979* (1992). His most recent operatic collaboration was with composer Michael Berkeley in *Baa Baa Black Sheep*, taken from **Kipling**'s autobiographical story of that title, and premiered in 1993.
▷P Neilsen, *Imagined Lives: a study of the novels of David Malouf* (1990)

MALRAUX, André
(1901–76)
French writer, born in Paris. He studied oriental languages and spent much time in China, where he worked for the Kuomintang and was active in the 1927 revolution. He also fought as a pilot with the Republican forces in the Spanish Civil War, and in World War II he escaped from a prisoner-of-war camp to join the French resistance movement. He was Minister of Information in de Gaulle's government (1945–6), then delegate from 1958 and Minister of Cultural Affairs (1960–9). He is best known for his novels, which are a dramatic meditation on human destiny and are highly coloured by his personal experience of war, revolution and resistance to tyranny. Among them are *Les Conquérants* (1928, Eng trans *The Conquerors*, 1929), *La Condition humaine* (1933, Eng trans *Man's*

Fate, 1934, winner of the Prix **Goncourt**) and *L'Espoir* (1937, Eng trans *Man's Hope*, 1938). He also wrote *La Psychologie de l'art* (1947, Eng trans *The Psychology of Art*, 1949), *Les Voix du silence* (4 vols, 1951, Eng trans in 4 vols *The Voices of Silence'*, 1953), and other books on art and museums.

▷C Malraux, *Le bruit de nos pas* (3 vols, 1965–9); A Madsen, *Malraux* (1979)

MAMELI, Goffredo
(1827–49)

Italian poet and patriot, born in Genoa. He was a volunteer in Garibaldi's forces and wrote his patriotic poem *Fratelli d'Italia* ('Brothers of Italy'), which was adopted as the Italian national anthem in 1946. He died in the defence of Rome against the French. His other poetry is undistinguished.

▷A Viviani, *Mameli* (1937)

MAMET, David
(1947–)

American dramatist, screenplay writer and film director, born in Chicago. He graduated from Goddard College in Vermont and studied acting in New York. His plays, such as *American Buffalo* (1975), *Glengarry Glen Ross* (1983) and *Speed-the-Plow* (1988), address the psychological and ethical issues that confront modern, urban society, its professional superstructure and near-criminal substructure. His other plays include *Sexual Perversity in Chicago*, and *Duck Variations* (both 1976); *Reunion*, and *The Water Engine* (both 1977); *A Life in the Theater* (1978); *Edmond* (1982); and *The Shawl* (1985). He has translated plays by **Anton Chekhov**, and his screenplays include a new adaptation of *The Postman Always Rings Twice* (1981), and *The Untouchables* (1987). He wrote and directed *House of Games* (1987), a look at seedy professional gambling, and, with Shel Silverstein, *Things Change* (1988). He published a book of essays, *Writing in Restaurants*, in 1986.

▷C W E Bigsby, *David Mamet* (1985)

MANCHESTER, William
(1922–)

American novelist, foreign correspondent and contemporary historian, born in Attleboro, Massachusetts. His magnum opus is *The Death of a President* (1967), written at the behest of the Kennedy family. A landmark in reportage, it received mixed reviews and sold in millions but has subsequently been superseded as new evidence on the assassination of President Kennedy has emerged. Manchester has also written biographies of, among others, General Douglas MacArthur (1978) and **Winston Churchill** (1984–8).

▷*Controversy* (1976)

MANDEL, Eli
(1922–)

Canadian poet and critic, born in Estevan, Saskatchewan. Mandel is a poet in the so-called 'mythopoeic' tradition recommended by the Episcopalian critic-priest Northrop Frye. It has been said of him that had 'Carl Jung written poetry, he might have written some of Mandel's poems'; the remark is helpful in pointing to the nature of Mandel's achievement, which has been described as a 'bellweather of changing poetic fashion'. His vision of the future is summed up in his well-known lines: 'Notice: there will be no further communication/lectures are all cancelled/all students are expelled/the reading of poetry is declared a public crime'.

▷*Dreaming Backwards: Selected Poems 1954–1981* (1981); *Waves*, 10, no. 4 (1982)

MANDELSTAM, Nadezhda Yaklovlevna,
née **Khazina**
(1899–1980)

Russian writer and memoirist. Born in Kiev, she studied art and, following travel in Europe, worked as a translator. In 1919 she met the poet **Osip Mandelstam** and became his companion. Her main works were memoirs of him, known in English as *Hope Against Hope* (1970) and *Hope Abandoned* (1972, Eng trans 1974). After Osip's death in 1938, she lived largely in poverty, making a scant living by giving English lessons.

MANDELSTAM, Osip
(1891–1938)

Russian poet, critic and translator, born in Warsaw. He grew up in Leningrad and attended Heidelberg University. His wife was **Nadezhda Mandelstam**. A classicist whose Russian 'sounds like Latin', he had a fierce love of Greek poetry. Three books of poems appeared during his lifetime: *Kamen* (1913, Eng trans *Stone*, 1981), *Tristia* (1922) and *Stikhotvoreniya* (1928, 'Poems'). *Sobraniye sochineniy* (1964–71, Eng trans *The Complete Poetry*, 1973) was published in 1973. Regarded by some as the greatest Russian poet of the century, his life after the revolution was filled with pessimism for the future of Russia. Arrested, exiled and rearrested, he died of a heart attack on his way to one of Stalin's camps.

▷N Struve, *Osip Mandelstam* (1982)

MANDER, (Mary) Jane
(1877–1949)

New Zealand novelist, who spent much of her writing life in England and the USA. One of the last of the 'colonial' writers, her early novels, beginning with *The Story of a New Zealand River* (1920) and *The Passionate*

Puritan (1921), glory in the building of a new liberal society in her homeland, but frustration with puritan sentiments drove her abroad. Her last New Zealand novel was *Allen Adair* (1925); *The Besieging City* (1926) is set in New York and *Pins and Pinnacles* (1928) in London.

MANDEVILLE, Bernard
(1670–1733)

Dutch-born British satirist, born in Dort in Holland. He took his MD at Leiden in 1691, and immediately settled in London in medical practice. He is known as the author of a short work in doggerel verse originally entitled *The Grumbling Hive* (1705), and finally *The Fable of the Bees* (1723). Writing in a vein of acute paradox, he affirms that 'private vices are public benefits', and that 'every species of virtue is basically some form of gross selfishness, more or less modified. The book was condemned by the grand jury of Middlesex, and was attacked by William Law the nonjuror, by Berkeley, Warburton, Hutcheson and others. Other works arguing for an improvement in the status of women are *The Virgin Unmasked* (1709), *Free Thoughts on Religion* (1720), and *A Modest Defence of Public Stews* (1724), on the condition of brothels.
▷J M Robertson, *Pioneer Humanists* (1907)

MANDEVILLE, Jehan de, or Sir John
(14th century)

The name assigned to the unknown compiler of a famous book of travels, *The Voyage and Travels of Sir John Mandeville, Knight*, published apparently in 1366, and soon translated from the French into all European tongues. It may have been written by a physician, Jehan de Bourgogne, otherwise Jehan á la Barbe, who died in Liège in 1372, and who is said to have revealed on his death-bed his real name of Mandeville (or Maundevylle), explaining that he had had to flee from his native England for a homicide. Some scholars, however, attribute it to Jean d'Outremeuse, a Frenchman. 'Mandeville' claims to have travelled through Turkey, Persia, Syria, Arabia, North Africa and India, but much of the book is a compilation from various literary sources.
▷J W Bennett, *The Rediscovery of Sir Jehan Mandeville* (1954)

MANE, Mordecai Zevi
(1860–87)

Russian Hebrew poet and essayist, born near Vilno. The son of a poor teacher, by the time of his premature death he had demonstrated his originality and independence of his contemporaries: his nature poetry, which has been compared, for the quality of 'fright' in

it, to the music of Schubert, is among the most accomplished and distinguished in the history of Russian Jewish literature.
▷M Waxman, *A History of Jewish Literature* (1960)

MANFRED, Frederick
(1912–)

American novelist, born near Doon, Iowa and educated at Calvin College, Michigan. He has worked as a salesman, a reporter, and a writer-in-residence, and has twice received a National Endowment for the Arts grant (1976 and 1983). He wrote under the name 'Feike Feikeman' until 1951. Manfred's subject-matter is the American midwest, and his work is characterized by epic and autobiographical elements. His first novel, *The Golden Bowl* (1944), concerns two generations of farmers; *Boy Almighty*, written a year later, is an account of life in a midwestern tuberculosis sanitarium. He has written over 20 novels, but has received little critical acclaim—perhaps due to the narrowly midwestern focus of his work.
▷R C Wright, *Frederick Manfred* (1979)

MANGAN, James Clarence
(1803–49)

Irish poet, born in Dublin, the son of a grocer. His life was a tragedy of hapless love, poverty and intemperance. He worked as a lawyer's clerk, and later found employment in the library of Trinity College, Dublin. There is fine quality in his original verse. Although he knew no Irish, he published English versions of Irish poems in *The Poets and Poetry of Munster* (1849), notably 'My Dark Rosaleen', 'The Nameless One' and 'The Woman of Three Cows'. He also published translations from German poets in *Anthologia Germanica* (1845).
▷D J O'Donaghue, *The Life and Writings of James Clarence Mangan* (1897)

MANGAN, (John Joseph) Sherry
(1904–61)

Radical American poet and journalist, he claimed to be a great nephew of the Irish poet **James Clarence Mangan**. Born in Lynn, Massachusetts, he graduated from Harvard in 1925 and in 1927 founded the fashionably lower-case *larus: The Celestial Visitor*, a short-lived little magazine in which he published his own verse and that of others. Gradually radicalized, he moved away from his own earlier aestheticism and collaborated on a poetry series 'Vanguard Verse' with his friend **John Wheelwright**. He also wrote international socialist propaganda under a number of Irish aliases, and was sent to Europe as a US delegate to the Fourth International.

His most important verse is collected in the volume *No Apology for Poetrie* (1934). For a period he maintained dual identities as a mainstream journalist and Trotskyist cadre, but in 1943 he was appointed *Life*'s head in Europe. Largely forgotten, he came to notice again with a revival of academic interest in the American far left that came, paradoxically, with the Reagan years.

▷A M Wald, *The Revolutionary Imagination* (1983)

MANIFOLD, John Streeter
(1915–85)

Australian poet and collector of folk-songs, born in Melbourne of a pioneering pastoral family. Educated at Cambridge University where he joined the Communist Party, he served during World War II with the British Intelligence Corps. His first collection was *Verses 1930–1933* (1933). On his return to Australia he published *Selected Poems* (1947) and *Nightmares and Sunhorses* (1961), but his interest in folk songs and ballads was evinced in *Bandicoot Ballads* (1953), followed by a number of books on folk music and verse. He is probably best known for editing the *Penguin Australian Song Book* (1964), but *Who Wrote the Ballads? Notes on Australian Folksong* (1964) is a scholarly appraisal of an important area in Australian literature. His academic interest in music is well demonstrated in two unjustly neglected earlier books, *Music in English Drama from Shakespeare to Purcell* and *Music of the Elizabethan Stage* (1964).

MANILIUS, Marcus
(fl.early 1st century)

Roman poet who wrote the *Astronomica*, a didactic poem on astrology, in five books, amounting to some 4 500 lines. Nothing is known of his life except that he was working in the reigns of Augustus and Tiberius. His writing sometimes achieves eloquence but is often weighed down by the demands of technical and mathematical instruction. The poem is of some interest as the most substantial extant work by a contemporary of **Ovid**, but chiefly because it engaged half a lifetime's attention from **A E Housman**, the outstanding Latinist of the early 20th century, whose edition appeared in 1903–30.

MANKIEWICZ, Herman Jacob
(1897–1953)

American screenwriter, born in New York. A member of the United States Marine Corps, he later worked in Europe for the Red Cross Press Service, as Isadora Duncan's publicity manager and as Berlin correspondent for the *Chicago Tribune*. Returning to the USA in 1922, he was Assistant Drama Editor for the *New York Times* (1922–6) and wrote his first screenplay for *The Road To Mandalay* (1926). A prolific writer, he was also much in demand as a script doctor and in addition was the producer of a number of films, including the Marx Brothers comedies *Horse Feathers* (1932) and *Duck Soup* (1933). A member of the Algonquin Round Table set and a frequent contributor to the *New Yorker*, he was once dubbed 'The Central Park West Voltaire' and the move to Hollywood was widely seen as the prostituting of a fine, witty literary talent. His most significant contribution to the cinema came as the co-writer of Orson Welles' *Citizen Kane* (1941), for which he received an Oscar. Other credited screenplays include *The Royal Family of Broadway* (1930), *Dinner At Eight* (1933), *It's A Wonderful World* (1939) and *The Enchanted Cottage* (1946). His brother was the writer–director Joseph L Mankiewicz (1909–93).

MANKOWITZ, (Cyril) Wolf
(1924–)

English author, playwright and antique dealer, born in Bethnal Green, London. An authority on Wedgwood, he published *Wedgwood* (1953) and *The Portland Vase* (1953), and was an editor of *The Concise Encyclopedia of English Pottery and Porcelain* (1957). Other publications include the novels *Make Me an Offer* (1952) and *A Kid for Two Farthings* (1953), and a collection of short stories, *The Mendelman Fire* (1957). Among his plays is *The Bespoke Overcoat* (1954), and his films, *The Millionairess* (1960), *The Long, The Short, and the Tall* (1961), *Casino Royale* (1967) and *The Hebrew Lesson* (1972), as well as his documentary on Yiddish cinema, *Almonds and Raisins* (1984).

MANLEY, Mary de la Rivière
(c.1672–1724)

British writer, born in Jersey, the daughter of a future governor of Jersey. After her father's death (1688) she was lured into a bigamous marriage with her cousin, John Manley of Truro, MP, who soon deserted her. She went to England, where she had a success with the publication of her letters. In 1696 she wrote two plays, *The Lost Lover* and *The Royal Mischief*. She wrote gossipy chronicles disguised as fiction, especially the scandalous anti-Whig *The New Atlantis* (1709). In 1711 she succeeded **Jonathan Swift** as editor of *The Examiner*. She wrote a fictional account of her own early struggles in *The Adventures of Rivella* (1714). Her last work was *The Power of Love, in Seven Novels* (1720).

▷*Letters Written by Mrs Manley* (1696)

MANN, Heinrich
(1871–1950)

German novelist, brother of **Thomas Mann**, born in Lübeck. He began to be described as the German **Zola** for his ruthless exposure of pre-1914 German society in *Im Schlaraffenland* (1901, Eng trans *Berlin, the Land of Cockaigne*, 1925), and the trilogy describing the three classes of Kaiser Wilhelm II's empire, *Die Armen* (1917, 'The Poor'), *Der Untertan* (1918, 'The Subject') and *Der Kopf* (1929, 'The Head'). He is best known for the macabre, Expressionist novel, *Professor Unrat* (1904, 'Professor Nonsense'), describing the moral degradation of a once outwardly respectable schoolmaster, which was translated and filmed as *The Blue Angel* (1932). He lived in France (1933–40) and then escaped to the USA. Other works include *Die kleine Stadt* (1901, 'The Little Town'), set in a small Italian town, and a remarkable autobiography, *Ein Zeitalter wird besichtigt* (1945–6, 'Exposition of an Era'). His influence is noticeable on **Jakob Wasserman** and **Lion Feuchtwanger**.
▷ R N Lina, *Heinrich Mann* (1967)

MANN, Leonard
(1895–1981)

Australian novelist and poet, born in Toorak, Melbourne. His service in France during World War I resulted in the powerful novel *Flesh in Armour* (1932), with its strong imagery of men and battles. Six more novels followed, of which the last, *Venus Half-Caste* (1963), was an early portrayal of mixed race conflict in Australia, and typified Mann's social realism. This was more muted in his verse, the first collection of which was *The Plumed Voice* (1938) followed by *The Delectable Mountains* (1944) and *Elegiac and Other Poems* (1957).

MANN, Thomas
(1875–1955)

German novelist and winner of the Nobel Prize for literature, brother of **Heinrich Mann**, born into a patrician family of merchants and senators of the Hanseatic city of Lübeck. His mother was a talented musician of mixed German and Portuguese West Indian blood. The opposition between a conservative business outlook and artistic inclinations, the clash between Nordic and Latin temperaments inherent in his own personality, and the Schopenhauerian doctrine of art being the self-abnegation of the will as the end product of decay, were to form his subject-matter. At the age of 19, without completing school, he settled with his mother in Munich, and after dabbling at the university, he joined his brother in Italy, where he wrote his early masterpiece, *Buddenbrooks: Verfall einer Familie* (1901, Eng trans *Buddenbrooks: The Decline of a Family*, 1924), the saga of a family like his own, tracing its decline through four generations, as business acumen gives way to artistic sensibilities. At the age of 25 he thus became a leading German writer. On his return to Munich he became reader for the satirical literary magazine, *Simplicissimus*, which published many of his early, remarkable short stories. The novelettes *Tonio Kröger* (1902, Eng trans 1928), *Tristan* (1903, Eng trans 1928) and *Der Tod in Venedig* (1912, Eng trans *Death in Venice*, 1925), all deal with the problem of the artist's salvation, positively in the case of the first, who resembles **Goethe**'s Werther, negatively in the last, in which a successful writer dies on the brink of perverted eroticism. World War I precipitated a quarrel between the two novelist brothers, Thomas's *Betrachtungen eines Unpolitischen* (1918, Eng trans *Reflections of a Nonpolitical Man*, 1983) revealing his militant German patriotism, already a feature of his essay on Frederick the Great (1915) and a distrust of political ideologies, including the radicalism of his brother. *Der Zauberberg* (1924, Eng trans *The Magic Mountain*, 1927) won him the Nobel Prize for literature in 1929. It was inspired by a visit to his wife at a sanatorium for consumptives in Davos in 1913 and tells the story of such a patient, Hans Castorp, with the sanatorium representing Europe in its moral and intellectual disintegration. The same year, Mann delivered a speech against the rising Nazis and exposed Italian fascism in *Mario und der Zauberer* (1930, Eng trans *Mario and the Magician*, 1930). He left Germany for Switzerland after 1933 and in 1936 delivered an address for **Freud**'s eightieth birthday. Both shared an enthusiasm for the biblical patriarch, Joseph, and Mann wrote a tetralogy of novels on his life, *Joseph und seine Brüder* (1933–43, Eng trans *Joseph and his Brothers*, 1934–44). He settled in the USA in 1936 and wrote a novel on a visit to Goethe by an old love, Charlotte Buff, *Lotte in Weimar* (1939, Eng trans 1940). His anti-Hitler broadcasts to Germany were collected under the titles *Achtung Europa!* (1938) and *Deutsche Hörer!* (1942, Eng trans *Listen Germany! Twenty-Five Messages to the German People over the BBC*, 1943; augmented edn of 55 messages, 1945). In 1947 he returned to Switzerland and was the only returning exile to be fêted by both West and East Germany. His greatest work, a modern version of the medieval legend, *Doktor Faustus* (1947, Eng trans *Doctor Faustus*, 1948), combines art and politics in the simultaneous treatment of the life and catastrophic end of a composer, Adrian Leverkühn, and German disintegration in two world wars. His last, unfinished work, hailed as Germany's greatest comic novel, *Bekenntnisse des Hochstaplers Felix Krull* (1922; 1953, Eng trans *Confessions of Felix Krull, Confidence Man,* 1955), written with astonishing wit, irony and humour and without the tortuous stylistic complexities of the *Bildungsroman,* commended itself most to English translators. Essentially a 19th-century German conservative, whose cultural landmarks vanished in World War I, he was compelled towards a critique of the artistic. Ambivalently the artist and the bourgeois fearer of bohemianism, the unpolitical man with political duties, he was a brilliant storyteller in the classical German tradition, whose subject-matter was paradoxically the end of that tradition. Other later works include *Der Erwählte* (1951, Eng trans *The Holy Sinner,* 1951), *Die Betrogene* (1953, Eng trans *The Black Swan,* 1954) and *Last Essays* (1959), on **Schiller,** Goethe, **Nietzsche** and **Anton Chekhov.**

▷ H Hatfield, *Thomas Mann* (1951)

MANNER, Eeva-Liisa
(1921–)

Finnish poet, dramatist and writer of fiction, born in Helsinki, and a leading figure in postwar modernism. Her earlier poetry was traditional, but later she turned to free verse and themes reminiscent of **T S Eliot,** and so began to attract attention.

MANNERKORPI, Juha
(1915–)

Finnish novelist, translator (**Sartre, Camus**) and poet, who was born in Ohio, USA, the son of a parson. He is a successful radio playwright in his own country. Although he is thought highly of for his terse, suggestive style, he has not produced any major work.

MANNIN, Ethel
(1900–84)

English novelist, travel and short-story writer, born in London, of Irish ancestry. Her early works include *Venetian Blinds* (1933), a novel set in working-class south London around World War I. She wrote over 40 novels, of which *Red Rose* (1941), based on the life of the anarchist Emma Goldman, most closely reflects her own concerns. Her commitment to the far left is evident in such works of non-fiction as *Women and the Revolution* (1938) and *Rebels' Ride* (1964). She travelled widely, and wrote several books on the Middle East (such as *A Lance For The Arabs,* 1963) as well as volumes on Germany, Burma and Japan.

MANNING, Olivia
(1908–80)

English novelist, born in Portsmouth, the daughter of a naval officer. Much of her youth was spent in Ireland and she had 'the usual Anglo-Irish sense of belonging to nowhere'. She trained at art school, and then went to London, and published her first novel, *The Wind Changes,* in 1937. She married in 1939 and went abroad with her husband, Reggie Smith, a British Council lecturer in Bucharest. Her experiences there formed the basis of her Balkan trilogy, comprising *The Great Fortune* (1960), *The Spoilt City* (1962) and *Friends and Heroes* (1965). As the Germans approached Athens, she and her husband evacuated to Egypt and ended up in Jerusalem. She returned to London in 1946, where she resided until her death. A prolific author, her publications include *Artist Among the Missing* (1949), *School for Love* (1951), *A Different Face* (1953), and her Levant Trilogy, comprising *The Danger Tree* (1977), *The Battle Lost and Won* (1978) and *The Sum of Things* (1980). The Balkan Trilogy and the Levant Trilogy form a single narrative entitled *Fortunes of War* which **Anthony Burgess** described as 'the finest fictional record of the war produced by a British writer'.

▷ K Dick, *Friends and Friendship* (1974)

MANNYNG, Robert, also known as Robert of Brunne
(d.c.1338)

English chronicler and poet, born in Bourne in Lincolnshire. In 1288 he entered the nearby Gilbertine monastery of Sempringham. His chief work is *Handlynge Synne* (c.1303), a free and amplified translation into English rhyming couplets of the *Manuel des Pechiez* of William of Wadington. It is a landmark in the transition from early to later Middle English, and a colourful picture of contemporary life. He also composed a rhyming translation of **Robert Wace**'s *Brut d'Angleterre,* with a translation from French of a rhyming chronicle, *The Story of Ingeland,* by the Augustinian canon, Peter Langtoft.

▷ R Crosby, *Robert Mannyng of Brunne: a new biography* (1942)

MANRIQUE, Jorge
(1440–79)

Spanish poet, born of a noble family in Paredes de la Nava. He is best remembered for his fine elegy on his father's death, *Coplas por la muerte de su padre* ('Verses for the Death of his Father'). He also wrote love-songs, satires and acrostic verses, and was killed in the Civil Wars of the period.

▷A Serraro de Hero, *Personalidad y destino de Jorge Manrique* (1966)

MANSFIELD, Katherine, pseud of **Kathleen Mansfield Beauchamp**
(1888–1923)

New Zealand short-story writer, born in Wellington, the daughter of a successful businessman. Educated at Queen's College, London, she returned to New Zealand for two years to study music, and left again for London in 1908, determined to pursue a literary career. She lived on the breadline and like a bohemian and met, married and left her first husband, George Bowden, in the space of three weeks. Finding herself pregnant (not by her husband) she was installed by her mother in a hotel in Bavaria, but she miscarried. The experience bore fruit in the stories collected in *In A German Pension* in 1911, most of which had previously appeared in *The New Age*. That same year she met **John Middleton Murry**, and thereafter her work began to surface in Murry's *Rhythm*. From 1912 the couple lived together (they did not marry until 1918), mingling with the literati, particularly **D H Lawrence**, who portrayed them as Gudrun and Gerald in *Women in Love*. In 1916, she and Murry founded the short-lived magazine *Signature*, but she began to suffer from tuberculosis which precipitated her premature death. Her first major work was *Prelude* (1917), a recreation of the New Zealand of her childhood. *Bliss, and other stories* (1920), containing the classic stories 'Je ne parle pas francais' and 'Prelude', confirmed her standing as an original and innovative writer, named in company with **Anton Chekhov** despite the backstabbing of her near-contemporary, **Virginia Woolf**. The only other collection published before her death at Fontainebleau was *The Garden Party, and other stories* (1922). Her other collections are *The Dove's Nest and Other Stories* (1923) and *Something Childish and Other Stories* (1924, published in the USA as *The Little Girl and Other Stories*, 1924). *The Letters of Katherine Mansfield*, edited by Murry, appeared in 1928 and *Katherine Mansfield's Letters to John Middleton Murry 1913–1922*, detailing the couple's stormy but tender relationship punctuated by lengthy separations, in 1951. **Vincent O'Sullivan** edited a selection, *Poems of Katherine Mansfield* (1988), and her work for the theatre was collected in *Katherine Mansfield: Dramatic Sketches* (1988).
▷A Alpers, *The Life of Katherine Mansfield* (1980)

MANTU, Saadat Hasan
(1912–55)

The leading Urdu short-story writer of his time. He was also a prolific translator. His stories, some of which are collected in *Black Milk* (1955), often led him into the law courts.

MANZONI, Alessandro
(1785–1873)

Italian novelist and poet, born in Milan of a noble family. He went to Paris from 1805 to 1807, published his first poems in 1806, married happily in 1810, and spent the next few years in writing sacred lyrics and a treatise on the religious basis of morality. But the work which gave him European fame is his historical novel, *I promessi sposi* (1827, Eng trans *The Betrothed Lovers*, 1828), a Milanese story of the 17th century, and the most notable novel in Italian literature. Despite his Catholic devoutness, he was a strong advocate of a united Italy, and became a senator of the kingdom in 1860.
▷A Colquhoun, *Manzoni and His Times* (1954)

MAO DUN, pseud of **Shen Yanbing**
(1896–1981)

Chinese writer, born in Wuzhen, Zhejiang Province. Educated at Beijing University, he became one of the foremost left-wing intellectuals and writers in China. In 1920 he was a founder-member of the Literary Research Society, and was Editor of the *Short Story Monthly* (1921–3). Moving to Shanghai, he taught a course of fiction at Shanghai College, and became editor of the Hankow National Daily. In 1926 he joined the Northern Expedition as a propagandist, but had to go underground in Shanghai as a communist activist. He wrote a trilogy of novellas, published as *Shih* (1930, 'Eclipse'), and a bestselling novel, *Ziye* (1932, 'Midnight'), about financial exploiters in the decadent Shanghai of the time. His other major works were *Hong* ('Rainbow'), and a collection of short stories in *Spring Silkworms*. In 1930 he helped to organize the influential League of Left-Wing Writers. After the communists came to power in 1949 he was China's first Minister of Culture (1949–65), and was founder-editor of the literary journal *People's Literature* (1949–53). During the Cultural Revolution he was kept under house arrest in Beijing (1966–78).
▷M Galik, *Mao Tun and Modern Chinese Literary Criticism* (1969)

MAP, or **MAHAP** or **MAPES, Walter**
(c.1137–1209)

Ecclesiastic and writer, sometimes said to have been a Welshman, probably a native of Herefordshire. Of noble stock, he studied at Paris, became a clerk to Henry II of England, went on a mission to Rome, and became canon of St Paul's and archdeacon of Oxford (1197). Although famous in his day as a writer and wit, the only work which can be attributed to him with certainty is the satirical miscellany *De Nugis Curialum* ('Of Courtier's Trifles') a collection of anecdotes and reflections, and tales gleaned from history, romance and gossip.

▷ T Wright, *Latin Poems Commonly Attributed to Walter Map* (1879)

MAPU, Abraham
(1808–67)

Hebrew novelist, born in Slobodka-Kovna. A member of the Haskalah ('the Enlightenment', the 18th- and 19th-century Jews who sought to acquire European culture), and Cabalist, he was the author of the first truly original Hebrew novel. He was so learned at a young age that he earned the rare soubriquet of 'Illuy'—a 'phenomenon'. This was justified, for, after learning several European languages, he published *Ahavat Zion* (1853, Eng trans *Amnon, Prince and Peasant*, 1887; *The Days of Isaiah*, 1902), a historical novel of the times of Isaiah; this, although influenced by French romanticism, like his second great novel *Ashmat Shomron* (1865), is vivid and wholly free from didacticism. Because of Mapu's Cabalistic involvements, both novels—and a third somewhat undervalued one, set in contemporary times—carry profound hidden meanings, which have not yet, however, been openly discussed.

▷ D Patterson, *Abraham Mapu* (1964)

MÁRAI, Sandor
(1900–)

Influential Hungarian novelist and essayist, born in Kassa. Upon the advent of communism in his country he left for exile in Italy. His *Egy polgár vallomásai* (1934, 'Confessions of a Bourgeois') is a key novel of its period. While, like **Thomas Mann**'s *Buddenbrooks*, it never sentimentalizes its subject, it finds within it no less dignity than any other kind of society. Márai felt that the most civilized values could be preserved by quiet defence of the existence of the bourgeoisie. An eclectic, he was influenced by writers as diverse as **Cocteau**, **Duhamel** and **Mallarmé**. His style became famous, and was much admired; but in later work, such as his journal, *Napló: 1957–1957* (1958) and his memoirs *Föld ... föld* (1972), his style became more precious.

MARAN, René
(1887–1960)

Caribbean-born African novelist, born in Martinique (but of Black parents from French Guinea). He wrote in French, and was perhaps the most influential of all the earlier writers of the modern African novel. Long before Colin Turnbull's *The Mountain People*

(1972) gave its famous description of the Ik of Uganda, Maran had shown imaginatively, in his masterpiece, *Batoula* (1921, translated in the following year), which won the Prix **Goncourt**, just how such a society could come into existence. This was also the first novel, as has been said, 'to portray Negroes as Negroes, and not as white men in blackface'. Maran wrote many more exotic and worthy books, but became disillusioned and could not repeat the success of his first. Ultimately he felt more concerned with Africa than with the Caribbean.

▷ W Cartey, *Whispers from a Continent* (1969)

MARC, Ausias
(1397–1459)

Catalan poet, the last great medieval writer in the language and the first major one to use only Catalan. Marc is an example of a figure of undeniably high international stature being lost to the majority of readers through linguistic ignorance. All his 128 poems, divided into cycles (of love and death) are intensely individual, and amount to a passionate and profound examination of the concept of courtly love, of which he was critical, but which he tried to purify by stripping it of formalities and hyperbole, in order to concentrate upon the precise truth. He has been translated at least twice into Castilian, but not yet into English. His influence was wide, as much on Castilian as on later Catalan poetry.

▷ A Terry, *Catalan Literature* (1972)

MARCABRU
(fl.1140)

Troubadour from Gascony, and one of the most influential. Details of his life are sketchy and have to be inferred from his songs, but he seems to have found employment in many royal houses, including that of Alfonso VII of Castile, by virtue of his great poetic and musical skill. His verse is usually about courtly love and contains highly complex language and inventive imagery. He lived a colourful life, and his memory and reputation were revered by subsequent troubadours. One version of his life story has it that he was eventually murdered by someone who objected to the way Marcabru had portrayed him in a song. There is no way of knowing whether this is true, but it is a tribute to the power of his work.

MARCEAU, Félicien, pseud of **Albert Carette**
(1913–92)

Belgian-born French writer. As Carette, Marceau served as a broadcaster in Brussels during World War II, and was sentenced to prison for it. He escaped and changed his name and nationality, becoming a successful and shrewd popular novelist and playwright. His first success was the satirical play *L'Oeuf* (1956, Eng trans *The Egg*, 1958), on the theme of society's hypocrisy. Among his many novels *Les Élans du Coeur* (1955, Eng trans *The Flutterings of the Heart*, 1957), an account of a provincial family in decline, is the most substantial. He was elected to the Académie française in 1975, amid protests during which he maintained that he had been cleared of actual Nazidom in 1962.

MARCEL, Gabriel Honoré
(1889–1973)

French existentialist philosopher and dramatist, born in Paris. He was a Red Cross Worker in World War I but made his living thereafter as a freelance writer, teacher, editor and critic. In 1929 he became a Catholic and came reluctantly to accept the label 'Christian Existentialist', partly in order to contrast his views with those of **Jean-Paul Sartre**. He emphasized the importance and possibility of 'communication' between individual people, as well as between themselves and God, but was suspicious of all philosophical abstractions and generalizations which misrepresented the freedom, uniqueness and particularity of human individuals. He was not himself a system-builder and his philosophical works tend to have a personal, meditative character, as in *Journal métaphysique* (1927, Eng trans *Metaphysical Journal*, 1952), *Être et avoir* (1935, Eng trans *Being and Having*, 1949), *Le Mystère de l'être* (1951, Eng trans *The Mystery of Being*, 1951), *Les Hommes contre l'humain* (1951, Eng trans *Men Against Humanity*, 1952) and *L'Homme problématique* (1955, Eng trans *Problematic Man*, 1967). His plays include *Un Homme de Dieu* (1925, 'A Man of God'), *Le Monde Cassé* (1933, 'The Broken World'), *Ariadne: Le Chemin de Crête* (1936, Eng trans *Ariadne*, 1952) and *La Dimension Florestan* (1956, 'The Florestan Dimension').
▷S Keen, *Gabriel Marcel* (1967)

MARCH, Auziàs
(1397–1459)

Catalan poet, born in Valencia. He was pioneer of the trend away from the lyricism of the troubadours towards a more metaphysical approach. Influenced by Italian models, he wrote chiefly on the themes of love and death.
▷A Pagès, *Auziàs March et ses prédécesseurs* (1912)

MARCH, William, pseud of W E M Campbell
(1893–1954)

American novelist and story writer, born in Mobile, Alabama. His best, and now perhaps neglected novel, is his last, *The Bad Seed* (1954), which was dramatized by **Maxwell Anderson** and played on Broadway with great success. The gripping and convincingly told story of a little girl who is a mass murderess, it is in essence a fable almost as persuasive as **William Golding**'s *Lord of the Flies*. When it was made into a movie the audience had to be assured, at the end, that it could not really be true. March also wrote *Company K* (1933) and *The Little Wife* (1935), a **Faulkner**esque novel, set in Mobile. His best stories are in *Some Like Them Short* (1939). His fiction is overdue for critical reappraisal.
▷A Cooke (ed), *A William March Omnibus* (1956, with an introduction)

MARCHWITZA, Hans
(1890–1965)

German novelist, born in Scharley in Silesia. An early member of the KPD, the communist party which was banned by the Nazis but then took power after World War II, Marchwitza's trilogy about miners, the first volume of which is *Die Kumiaks* (1934), became officially approved reading in the German Democratic Republic (the former East Germany). His work, however, has little artistic value. *Meine Jugend* (1947, 'My Youth') was an autobiographical novel.

MARDEKAR, B S
(1905–56)

Indian (Marathi) poet who was influenced by **T S Eliot**'s *Prufrock*, but who never found a worthy English translator.

MARECHAL, Leopoldo
(1900–70)

Argentinian novelist, poet, dramatist and essayist, born in Buenos Aires. Because he was one of the few writers to collaborate with Perón—and thus gain high official posts—he was for some time eschewed by critics; but the importance of his work, much of it experimental, is now more frequently canvassed. He is usually described today as of 'major significance'. He began as a socialist and an *ultraísta* poet, but turned to the novel when he could no longer, as he maintained, 'translate his life experiences into poetry'. His poetry is not now much discussed (one of his most sonorous poems is translated in *An Anthology of Contemporary Latin-American Poetry*, 1942, ed Dudley Fitts). His major work, derived from **Joyce**'s *Ulysses* and based on **Dante**'s *Inferno*, is the novel *Adán Buenosayres* (1948). This records an imaginary journey undertaken by Marechal (Adam) around Buenos Aires, and ends in a confrontation with Christ. Later works include *Heptameron* (1965). The work of Marechal, owing to lack of translations, has not yet been tested in the light of world opinion—but of his importance in Argentinian literature there can be no doubt.

▷ *Papers on French, Luso-Brazilian, Spanish-American Relations* (1970)

MARECHERA, Dambudzo
(?1954–)

Zimbabwean novelist and short-story writer of strikingly original vision, whose work is set against anti-colonial struggle and internecine conflict. Little is known about his early life and career, but he attended the University of Rhodesia in Harare (from which he was sent down in 1974 for unspecified opposition activities) and, more briefly, New College, Oxford. His first published work was *The House of Hunger* (1978, Guardian Fiction Prize), a novella and group of short stories which portray the struggle for independence as a brutal Darwinian opposition of tribalist loyalties and antagonisms. This was followed in 1980 by a novel, *Black Sunlight*, in which a press-photographer (ironically named Christian) documents a hellish slough of terrorism and violence, his cool journalistic detachment gradually unravelling as the plot descends into horror. Despite being one of the most significant figures of the highly touted new African writing 'movement' of this period, Marechera suffered disproportionately during the inevitable backlash.

▷ D Caute, *The Espionage of the Saints* (1986)

MARGARET OF ANGOULÊME, also
known as **Margaret of Navarre**
(1492–1549)

Queen of Navarre, and one of the most brilliant women of her age. The sister of Francis I of France, she married first the Duke of Alençon (d.1525) and then, in 1527, Henry d'Albret (titular King of Navarre), to whom she bore Jeanne d'Albret, mother of Henri IV of France. Margaret had from her youth a strong interest in Renaissance learning, and was much influenced by **Erasmus** and the religious reformers of the Meaux circle, who looked to her for patronage and protection. Although she remained a Roman Catholic, she was also influenced by the writings of Luther, with which she had a certain sympathy. She encouraged agriculture, learning and the arts, and her court was the most intellectual in Europe. The patron of men of letters, including the heretical poet **Clément Marot**, she herself was a prolific writer. Her works included long devotional poems published as *Le Miroir de l'âme Pécheresse* (1531, 'The Mirror of a Sinner's Soul') and *Les Marguerites de la Marguerite des princesses* (1547, 'The Daisies of Princess Marguerite'), the

shorter *Chansons religieuses* ('Religious Songs'), dramas, and the secular poem *La Coche* ('The Coach'); her last works, written at the end of her life in some mental anguish, were found and published in 1895 as *Les Dernières poésies* ('The Last Poems'). Her most celebrated work was *Heptaméron*, a collection of stories on the theme of love, modelled upon the *Decameron* of **Boccaccio**.

▷ L Febvre, *Autour de L'Heptaméron* (1944)

MARGARET OF NAVARRE *see*
MARGARET OF ANGOULÊME

MARGUERITTE, Paul
(1860–1918)
MARGUERITTE, Victor
(1866–1942)

French novelists, born in Algeria. They wrote in collaboration or separately novels and histories, many dealing with the Franco–German war period, such as the series *Une Époque* (1898–1904).

▷ S Barreaux, *Paul et Victor Margueritte* (1909)

MARIE DE FRANCE
(fl.c.1160–90)

French poet, born in Normandy. She spent much of her life in England, where she wrote her *Lais* sometime before 1167 and her *Fables* sometime after 1170. She translated into French the *Tractatus de Purgatorio Sancti Patricii* (c.1190, 'St Patricius's Treatise on Purgatory') and her works contain many classical allusions. The *Lais*, her most important work, dedicated to 'a noble king', probably Henry II of England, comprises 14 romantic narratives in octosyllabic verse based on Celtic material. A landmark in French literature, they influenced a number of later writers.

▷ H Hoepffner, *Les lais de Marie de France* (1935)

MARINETTI, Emilio Filippo Tommaso
(1876–1944)

Italian writer, born in Alexandria, one of the founders of Futurism. He studied in Paris and Genoa, and published the original Futurist manifesto in *Figaro* in 1909. In his writings he glorified war, the machine age, speed and 'dynamism', and in 1919 he became a fascist. His publications include *Le Futurisme* (1911), *Teatro sintetico futuristo* (1916, 'The Synthetic Futurist Theatre') and *Manifesti del Futurismo* (4 vols, 1920, 'Manifesto of Futurism'). He condemned all traditional forms of literature and art, and his ideas were applied to painting by Boccioni, Balla and others.

▷ W Vaccari, *Vita e tumulti di Filippo Tommaso Marinetti* (1959)

MARINKOVÍC, Ranko
(1913–)

Croatian novelist, satirist, story writer and dramatist, born on the island of Vis. He had intimate connections with the Croatian National Theatre. He published his early short stories, still regarded as the genre in which he works most effectively, in Krleža's journal *Pecat*. His best-known and most discussed work is the novel *Kiklop* (1965, 'Cyclops'), an over-complex work that yet has vivid passages, is studded with knowing literary allusions, and is remarkable for its portrait of an individual caught up in and destroyed by the toils of the city (Zagreb just before World War II).
▷A Kadíc, *From Croatian Renaissance to Yugoslav Socialism* (1969)

MARINO, or MARINI, Giambattista
(1569–1625)

Italian poet, born in Naples. He was ducal secretary at Turin, and wrote his best work, the *Adone* (1622), at the court of France. His principal gift lies in his ability to conjure up rich and evocative descriptions of nature and the external world, but he shows no great insight into the human heart. His florid hyperbole and overstrained imagery were copied by the Marinist school.
▷J V Mirollo, *The Poet of the Marvellous* (1963)

MARION, Frances, originally Frances Marion Owens
(1887–1973)

American screenwriter and novelist, born in San Francisco. A reporter with the *San Francisco Examiner*, she had worked as a commercial artist and model before arriving in Hollywood in 1913 as the protégé of director Lois Weber. A prolific screenwriter during the silent era, she was associated with actress Mary Pickford on such films as *Rebecca Of Sunnybrook Farm* (1918) and *Pollyanna* (1920). One of the first female war correspondents during the latter stages of World War I, she also directed such films as *Just Around The Corner* (1921) and *The Love Light* (1921). Adept at heart-tugging melodrama, hard-bitten adventure yarns and epic romances, she was also much praised for her skilled adaptations of *Stella Dallas* (1925), *The Scarlet Letter* (1926) and *The Wind* (1928). Surviving the transition to sound, she wrote star vehicles for the likes of Greta Garbo and Jean Harlow and received Academy Awards for *The Big House* (1930) and *The Champ* (1931). She retired from screenwriting in 1940 and subsequently wrote such novels as *Westward The Dream* (1948) and *The Powder Keg* (1954).
▷*Off With Their Heads!* (1972)

MARIVAUX, Pierre Carlet de Chamblain de
(1688–1763)

French playwright and novelist, born in Paris of a good Norman family. He published *L'Homère travesti* ('Homer Burlesqued'), a burlesque of the *Iliad*, in 1716, and from then on wrote several comedies, of which his best is *Le Jeu de l'amour et du hasard* (1730, Eng trans *Love in Livery*, 1907). His best-known novel, *La Vie de Marianne* (1731–41, Eng trans *The Life of Marianne*, 1736–42), was never finished; it is marked by an affected 'precious' style—'Marivaudage'. His numerous comedies are the work of a clever analyst rather than a dramatist. His other romances, *Pharsamon* (1737, Eng trans *Pharsamond*, 1950) and *Le Paysan parvenu* (1735–6, Eng trans *The Fortunate Villager*, 1765) are considerably inferior to *Marianne*.
▷E J H Greene, *Marivaux* (1965)

MARK, Jan(et) Marjorie
(1943–)

English author of children's books, born in Welwyn Garden City, Hertfordshire; she now lives in Norfolk, the setting of several of her quietly witty novels, including *Thunder and Lightnings* (1976) and *Handles* (1983). She has also written a science-fiction trilogy intended for older children, comprising *The Ennead* (1978), *Divide and Rule* (1979) and *Aquarius* (1982), a comparatively grim study of an exploitative society.

MARKFIELD, Wallace Arthur
(1926–)

American novelist and short-story writer, born in Brooklyn, New York, where he also attended college. Though squarely of the 'Jewish–American' school, his fiction is perhaps closer to **Woody Allen**'s prose than to **Philip Roth**'s, full of tongue-in-cheek literary allusions and cultural transvaluations. The best example comes in his first and best-known book, *To an Early Grave* (1964), which re-works Paddy Dignam's funeral in **Joyce**'s *Ulysses* in a way that also recalls **Bellow**'s *Seize the Day*. The association with Roth is stronger in *Teitelbaum's Widow* (1970), a funny-sad exploration of the Jewish Oedipus complex, but comparing Markfield's book to *Portnoy's Complaint* is not to suggest that it is derivative, merely to underline the extent to which he is conscious of the literary traditions in which he works. *You Could Live If They Let You* (1974) was taken to be a fictionalized biography of comedian Lenny Bruce; it examines the darker ramifications of Jewish humour. Markfield's stories were collected in 1977 with the modest title *Multiple Orgasms*.

▷ Markfield issue of *Review of Contemporary Fiction* (1982)

MARKHAM, Edwin, originally **Charles Edward Anson Markham**
(1852–1940)

American poet, born in Oregon and educated in California. He is now remembered chiefly for 'The Man with the Hoe' (1899), a relatively tough-minded poem (inspired by the Millet painting) about the dignity and injustices of labour. It was an immediate success on its first publication in the San Francisco *Examiner* and Markham attempted to repeat the formula in later poems such as the similarly inspired 'The Sower', which was collected in *Lincoln and Other Poems* (1901). Outwardly he was a conventional schoolmaster-poet, dedicated to muscular-Christian virtues and to democracy. However, his inner life was clearly a great deal more complex; thrice married and twice divorced, he was driven by unappeasable desires and the nightmarish fear of his own dark side, which emerges in a late poem, 'The Ballad of the Gallows Bird'. His collected poems were published in 1950, prompting a revisionist approach to his life and career.
▷ L Filler, *Edwin Markham: His Mystery and Its Significance* (1966)

MARKHANDEYA, Kamala, pseud of **Mrs Kamala Purinya Taylor**
(1924–)

Indian novelist writing in English, member of a noble family which served the princes of Madras. She married an Englishman and moved to England after an education in Mysore. Her novels have consistently gained in psychological depth. One of the best is *A Silence of Desire* (1960), about a man who is opposed to his wife's resort to a faith-healer.

MARKISCH, Peretz
(1895–1952)

Yiddish poet, novelist and dramatist, born in Polonoya; he turned from Russian to Yiddish in 1917. He left Russia in 1921, returned in 1926 to become the leading Soviet–Jewish writer, received the Order of Lenin in 1939, but was murdered by Stalin in the Jewish purges. His epic poem *Milkhome* (1928) was written in praise of Jewish heroism.
▷ A Roback, *The Story of Yiddish Literature* (1940)

MARKOOSIE, pseud of **Markoosie Patsauq**
(1942–)

Canadian Inuit writer, born in Port Harrison, Quebec. Patsauq worked for several years as a pilot in the Northwest Territories, and in state and local government in Quebec. His novel *Harpoon of the Hunter* (1970), an atmospheric retelling of an Inuit legend about a young boy's initiation to manhood, was first serialized in an Inuit newsletter and later translated by himself; it was the first piece of Inuit fiction to be published in English.

MARLOWE, Christopher
(1564–93)

English dramatist, born in Canterbury, a shoemaker's son. From the King's School there he was sent to Benet (now Corpus Christi) College, Cambridge. He graduated BA in 1583 and MA in 1587. His *Tamburlaine the Great*, in two parts, was first printed in 1590, and probably produced in 1587. In spite of its bombast and violence it was infinitely superior to any tragedy that had yet appeared on the English stage. Earlier dramatists had used blank verse, but it had been stiff and ungainly, and Marlowe was the first to discover its strength and variety. *The Tragical History of Dr Faustus* was probably produced soon after *Tamburlaine*; the earliest edition is dated 1604. *Faustus* is rather a series of detached scenes than a finished drama and some of these scenes are evidently not by Marlowe. *The Jew of Malta*, produced after 1588 and first published in 1633, is a very uneven play. *Edward II*, produced about 1590, is the most mature of Marlowe's plays. It has not the magnificent poetry of *Faustus* and the first two acts of *The Jew of Malta*, but it is planned and executed with more firmness and solidity. *The Massacre at Paris*, the weakest of Marlowe's plays, has descended in a mutilated state. It was written after the assassination of Henri III of France (1589) and was probably one of the latest plays. *The Tragedy of Dido* (1594), left probably in a fragmentary state by Marlowe and finished by **Thomas Nashe**, is of slight value. Marlowe had doubtless a hand in the three parts of *Henry VI*, and probably in *Titus Andronicus*. A wild, shapeless tragedy, *Lust's Dominion* (1657) may have been adapted from one of Marlowe's lost plays. The unfinished poem, *Hero and Leander*, composed in heroic couplets, was first published in 1598; a second edition, with Chapman's continuation, followed the same year. Marlowe's translations of **Ovid**'s *Amores* and of the first book of **Lucan**'s *Pharsalia* add nothing to his fame. The pastoral ditty, 'Come, live with me and be my love', to which Sir Walter Raleigh wrote an Answer, was imitated, but not equalled, by **Robert Herrick**, **John Donne** and others. It was first printed in *The Passionate Pilgrim* (1599), without the fourth and sixth stanzas, with the author's name, 'C. Marlowe', written below. Another anthology, Allot's *England's Parnassus* (1600), preserves a fragment by Marlowe, beginning 'I walked along a stream for pureness rare'. Marlowe led an irregular life, mingled with the rabble, and was on the point of being arrested for disseminating atheistic opinions when he was fatally stabbed in a tavern brawl. In tragedy he prepared the way for **Shakespeare**, on whose early work his influence is firmly stamped.

▷F S Boas, *Christopher Marlowe* (1940); H Levin, *The Over-Reacher* (1954)

MARMION, Shackerley
(1603–39)

English dramatist, born in Aynho, Northamptonshire. He was educated at Wadham College, Oxford, squandered a fortune, and fought in the Low Countries. He was the author of an allegorical epic, *Cupid and Psyche* (1637), and three comedies, *Holland's Leaguer* (1632), *A Fine Companion* (1633) and *The Antiquary* (1635), generally regarded as his best play.

▷G E Bentley, *The Jacobean and Caroline Stage* (1956)

MARMOL, José Pedro Crisólogio
(1818–71)

Argentinian Romantic poet and novelist, born in Buenos Aires, who is most famous for his effective diatribes against the 19th-century proto-fascist dictator of Argentina, Juan Manuel de Rosas, who imprisoned him. He owed his main inspiration to **Byron**, and several of his narrative poems are direct imitations. His most important poetic work is *Cantos del peregrino* (1847, 'Songs of the Pilgrim'). His novel *Amalia* (1844, rev edn 1851), also an attack on Rosas, was one of the most important Latin American Romantic novels. Mármol conterpoints, with subtle irony and skill, the romantic stuff of a conventional 'tragic affair' with the realistic horrors of the Rosas regime. Like Byron, he also wrote many lyrics. He was able to return to Buenos Aires with due honour after Rosas had been overthrown (1852).

▷*University of Colorado Studies*, 22, 2–3 (1935); M C Suárez-Murias, *La novela romántica en Hispanoamérica* (1963)

MARMONTEL, Jean François
(1723–99)

French author, born in Bort in the Limousin. He studied in a Jesuit college. Settling in Paris in 1745 on the advice of **Voltaire**, he wrote successful tragedies and operas, and in 1753 got a secretaryship at Versailles through Madame de Pompadour. In the official journal, *Le Mercure*, by then under his charge, he began his *Contes moraux* (1761, 'Moral Tales'). Elected to the Academy in 1763, he

became its secretary in 1783, as well as royal historian of France. His most celebrated work was *Bélisaire* (1766, 'Belisarius'), a dull and wordy political romance, containing a chapter on toleration which excited furious hostility. His uncritical *Éléments de littérature* (1787) consists of his contributions to the *Encyclopédie* (35 vols, 1751–80), to which he was the main contributor on literature. His *Mémoires d'un père* (1804, Eng trans *Memoirs of Marmontel*, 1805) include portraits of many of his contemporaries.

▷S Lenel, *Jean François Marmontel* (1902)

MARNAU, Fred
(1918–)

Austrian poet and novelist, born in Bratislava. He lived in England, and his poems appeared in bilingual editions, all translated by E O Sigler; such collections of his long-lined and rhetorical poems as are contained in *The Wounds of the Apostles* (1944) attracted some favourable attention. Later he was read only in Austria.

MAROT, Clément
(c.1497–1544)

French poet, born in Cahors. He entered the service of **Margaret of Angoulême**, Queen of Navarre. He was wounded at the battle of Pavia in 1525, and soon after imprisoned on a charge of heresy, but liberated next spring. He made many enemies by his witty satires, and in 1535 fled first to the court of the Queen of Navarre, and later to that of the Duchess of Ferrara. He returned to Paris in 1536, and in 1538 began to translate the Psalms into French, which, when sung to secular airs, helped to make the new views fashionable; but accused of heresy by the Sorbonne, he had again to flee in 1543. He made his way to Geneva, where Calvin was devoting himself to the Reformation. Marot decided not to stay there because of this and went on to Turin. His poems consist of elegies, epistles, rondeaux, ballads, sonnets, madrigals, epigrams, nonsense verses and longer pieces; his special gift lay in badinage and graceful satire.

▷C A Mayer, *Marot* (1969)

MARQUAND, John P(hillips)
(1893–1960)

American novelist, born in Wilmingon, Delaware. He was educated at Newbury Port High School, Massachusetts, and Harvard University. He served with the military, was a war correspondent and wrote advertising copy. He started as a writer of popular stories for magazines, featuring the Japanese detective Mr Moto, and later gently satirized affluent middle-class American life in a vein

similar to **Sinclair Lewis**, whom he admired, in a series of notable novels. Key titles are *The Late George Apley* (1937), *Wickford Point* (1939) and *Point of No Return* (1949).
▷M Bell, *John P Marquand: an American life* (1979)

MÁRQUEZ, Gabriel García *see* GARCÍA MÁRQUEZ

MARQUIS, Don(ald Robert Perry)
(1878–1937)

American novelist, playwright and poet, born in Walnut, Illinois. His formal education was aborted at 15 and he worked at various jobs before studying art for a spell. He had a varied career as a journalist and wrote serious plays and poems, but he became a celebrity as a comic writer with *The Old Soak's History of the World* (1924). *archy and mehitabel* (1927) and *archys life of mehitabel* (1933) follow the fortunes of Archy the cockroach who cannot reach the typewriter's shift key (hence the lower case titles) and Mehitabel, an alley cat.
▷E Antony, *O Rare Don Marquis* (1962)

MARRIC, J J *see* CREASEY, John

MARRYAT, Florence
(1838–99)

English novelist, daughter of **Frederick Marryat**, born in Brighton. She was successively Mrs Ross Church and Mrs Lean, and from 1865 published about 80 novels, as well as a drama and many articles in periodicals. She edited *London Society* (1872–6).
▷E Showalter, *A Literature of their Own* (1977)

MARRYAT, Frederick
(1792–1848)

English naval officer and novelist, the son of an MP. In 1806 he sailed as midshipman under Lord Cochrane. After service in the West Indies, he had command of a sloop cruising off St Helena to guard against the escape of Napoleon. He also did good work in suppressing the Channel smugglers, and some hard fighting in Burmese rivers. On his return to England (1826) he was given the command of the *Ariadne* (1828). He resigned in 1830, and from then on led the life of a writer. He was the author of a series of novels on sea life of which the best known are *Frank Mildmay* (1829), *Peter Simple* (1833), *Jacob Faithful* (1834) and *Mr Midshipman Easy* (1834). In 1837 he set out for a tour through the USA, where he wrote *The Phantom Ship* (1839) and a drama, *The Ocean Waif*. He received £1200 for *Mr Midshipman Easy* and £1600 for his *Diary in America* (1839), but

was extravagant and unlucky in his money matters, and eventually was financially embarrassed. *Poor Jack, Masterman Ready, The Poacher* and *Percival Keene* appeared before he settled (1843) on his small farm of Langham, Norfolk, where he spent his days in farming and in writing stories for children, including the once very popular *Children of the New Forest* (1847).
▷O Warner, *Captain Marryat* (1953)

MARS-JONES, Adam
(1954–)

English novelist, short-story writer, editor and critic, born in London and educated at Cambridge. Mars-Jones's first book, *Lantern Lecture*, a volume of short stories, appeared in 1981. Two years later, he co-edited *Mae West is Dead: Recent Lesbian and Gay Fiction*, and in 1987, in collaboration with **Edmund White**, published a second book of stories, *The Darker Proof: Stories from a Crisis*. Much of this work examines the effect of AIDS upon those close to the victims of the disease, and arose from Mars-Jones's own experience as a 'buddy', a volunteer friend to a sufferer. His discursive, sympathetic style is evident once again in the novel *The Waters of Thirst* (1993).

MARSÉ, Juan
(1933–)

Spanish novelist, born Juan Fonseca in Barcelona; his mother died at his birth, and he was immediately adopted by the Marsé family. He published his first novel, *Encarrados con un solo juguete* ('Locked in with a Single Toy'), in 1961, by which time he was mixing with other emerging writers. An opponent of the Franco regime, he exiled himself to Paris, where he knew other exiles such as **Juan Goytisolo**. Later he went into the cinema business. He began to make a reputation as an ironic critic of society with *Ultimas tardes con Teresa* (1965, 'Last Evenings with Teresa'), a novel influenced by the techniques of **Ramón Valle-Inclán**, the extraordinary Catalan Josep Pla and, mainly, the Castilian **Luis Martín-Santos**, a psychiatrist who with his single completed novel changed the direction of Spanish fiction. Like Martín-Santos, Marsé flayed the submissiveness of post-Civil War Spanish society, by means of the technique Martín-Santos called 'dialectical realism'. In *Si te dicenque caí* (1973, Eng trans *The Fallen*, 1979), whose publication in Spain was delayed, Marsé even more robustly mocked the society around him. His other translated novel, *La muchacha de las bragas de oro* (1978, Eng trans *Golden Girl*, 1981), mercilessly burlesques the memoirs of the half-repentant Falangist rector of Madrid University, Pedro Laín Entralgo.

MARSH, Dame (Edith) Ngaio
(1899–1982)

New Zealand detective novelist and theatre director, born in Christchurch. After a brief career on stage and as an interior decorator, she introduced her detective-hero Roderick Alleyn in *A Man Lay Dead* (1934), which was followed by 30 more stories ending with *Light Thickens* (1982). In theatre, she toured with the Wilkie company in **Shakespeare** during the early 1920s, and devoted much time to theatrical production in New Zealand in the 1940s and 1950s. She also wrote on art, theatre and crime fiction, as well as the libretto for a fantasy-opera *A Unicorn for Christmas* (1962) to music by New Zealand composer David Farquhar.
▷ *Black Beech and Honeydew* (1966, rev edn 1981)

MARSHAK, Samuel
(1887–1964)

Russian children's writer, poet and translator, born in Voronezh. Devoted to children, his voluminous work for them largely determined the official Bolshevik line; it was not nearly as poor as it might have been. **Nahzda Mandelstam** said of him, in her memoirs, 'he was a superb fisher of men, whether weak, susceptible ones or men of power': her husband suffered his first attack of angina pectoris while listening to Marshak expound 'the official line'. But, while a natural toady, Marshak possessed talents which lifted him above the wholly mediocre. His translations of the Sonnets of **Shakespeare**, and of other classics, are efficient—and he gave what help he could to those more gifted and less fortunate than himself. *V nachala zhinzi* (1960, 'At Life's Beginning') is his autobiography.

MARSHALL, (William) Alan
(1902–84)

Australian writer, born in Noorat, Victoria. Permanently crippled by polio at six, he went to business college and worked as an accountant before becoming a columnist for Melbourne newspapers. He travelled widely within Australia and also spent time in Asia, but it was his own story of childhood and struggle with handicap in *I Can Jump Puddles* (1955) that brought him to notice. He produced five collections of short stories between 1946 and 1975, as well as writings for children, on travel and Australian country life, and an evocation of aboriginal myths in *People of the Dreamtime* (1952). His anecdotal style thinly disguises the personal narrative,

and this best comes out in his collection *Hammers over the Anvil* (1975) where he throws away his observational manner and speaks in his own voice. *The Complete Short Stories* was published in 1977.

MARSHALL, Paule
(1929–)

American author, born in Brooklyn, New York City. Her parents emigrated from Barbados during World War I and she grew up in Brooklyn during the Depression. In 1948 she studied at Hunter College, New York City, but left prematurely because of illness. Later she graduated from Brooklyn College and worked for *Our World Magazine*. *Brown Girl, Brownstones* (1959), her first novel, is regarded as a classic of Black American literature, telling the story of the coming of age of Seling Boyce, the daughter of Barbadian immigrants living through the Depression and World War I. Later novels are *The Chosen Place* (1969), *The Timeless People* (1969) and *Praisesong for the Widow* (1983).

MARSON, Una
(1905–65)

Jamaican poet and playwright, educated at Hampton School. She trained as a social worker but was equally interested in journalism, founding and editing *The Cosmopolitan magazine*. She worked in England (1932–6), as secretary to the League of Coloured Peoples, then private secretary to Emperor Haile Selassie. She wrote the first play performed by black colonials in London (*At What a Price*, 1932). Back in Jamaica she was a dynamic figure in many fields: she founded the Save the Children Fund, the Readers' and Writers' Club, and a progressive paper, *Public Opinion*. Between 1930 and 1945 she published four books of verse, and during World War II she presented the BBC's influential 'Caribbean Voices' programme in London. By her use of jazz rhythms and Jamaican dialect in verse and her focus on issues of gender, race and identity, she pioneered a new movement in Jamaican writing in the 1940s.
▷ E Smilowitz, *Critical Issues in West Indian Literature* (1984)

MARSTON, John
(1576–1634)

English dramatist and satirist, born in Wardington, Oxfordshire, the son of a Shropshire lawyer and an Italian mother. He studied at Brasenose College, Oxford, and then studied law at the Middle Temple. Apart from *The Insatiate Countess* (which is of doubtful authorship), all his plays were published between 1602 and 1607. He then gave up play-writing, took orders in 1609, and (1616–31) was a clergyman at Christchurch, Hampshire. His first work was *The Metamorphosis of Pygmalion's Image: and Certain Satires* (1598), a licentious poem which was condemned by Archbishop Whitgift. Another series of uncouth and obscure satires, *The Scourge of Villany*, appeared in the same year. He began to write for the theatre in 1599. Two gloomy and ill-constructed tragedies, *Antonio and Mellida* and *Antonio's Revenge*, were published in 1602; in them passages of striking power stand out above the general mediocrity. A comedy, *The Malcontent* (1604), more skilfully constructed, was dedicated to **Ben Jonson**, with whom he had many quarrels and reconciliations. *Eastward Ho* (1605), written in conjunction with **George Chapman** and Jonson, is far more genial than any comedy that Marston wrote single-handed. For some reflections on the Scots the authors were imprisoned (1604). Other plays include a comedy, *The Dutch Courtesan* (1605), *Parasitaster, or the Fawn* (1606), *Sophonisba* (1606, a tragedy) and *What You Will* (1607). The rich and graceful poetry scattered through his last play, *The Insatiate Countess* (1613), is unlike anything that occurs in Marston's undoubted works, and it may have been completed by another hand.

▷A F Caputi, *John Marston, Satirist* (1961)

MARSTON, John Westland
(1819–90)

English dramatic poet, father of **Philip Bourke Marston**, born in Boston, Lincolnshire. He gave up law for literature; and in 1842 his *Patrician's Daughter* was brought out at Drury Lane by the actor William Macready. It was the most successful of more than a dozen plays, all **Sheridan-Knowles**ian, and all forgotten. He wrote a novel (1860), a good book on *Our Recent Actors* (1888), and a mass of poetic criticism.

MARSTON, Philip Bourke
(1850–87)

English poet, son of **John Westland Marston**, born in London. He became blind at the age of three. He was grief-stricken at the death of his fiancée and then of his sisters, and his friends, **Oliver Madox Brown** and **Dante Gabriel Rossetti**. He is remembered for his friendship with Rossetti, **Walter Watts-Dunton** and **Swinburne** rather than for his sonnets and lyrics—although a few of these are exquisite. *Songtide, All in All* and *Wind Voices* were the three volumes of poetry he published between 1870 and 1883. A collection of his short stories was published posthumously in 1887.

▷C C Osborne, *Philip Bourke Marston* (1926)

MARTI, José
(1853–95)

Cuban poet and rebel. Born in Havana, the son of a Spanish settler, he was continually in trouble with the Spanish authorities for his views on independence; he was eventually killed by Spaniards on the military expedition of 1895: he had been proclaimed supreme leader just before his murder. But Marti was not just a simple patriot: he had one of the best minds of his time, and intellectually stood, as has been said, 'head and shoulders above his contemporaries'. His poetry is more direct in its expression of feelings than that of his contemporaries, and his prose contains many correct prophecies about race and integration.

▷I A Schulman, *Simbolo y color en la obra de José Marti* (1960)

MARTIAL (Marcus Valerius Martialis)
(c.40–c.104)

Roman poet and epigrammatist, born in Bilbilis in Spain. He went to Rome in AD64 and became a client of the influential Spanish house of the **Seneca**s, through which he found a patron in L Calpurnius Piso. The failure of the Pisonian plot to assassinate **Cicero** lost Martial his warmest friends—**Lucan** and Seneca. He courted imperial and senatorial patronage by his verses for particular events. When the Emperor Titus dedicated the Colosseum in AD80, Martial's epigrams in *Liber Spectaculorum* ('Book of Spectacles') brought him equestrian rank; his flattery of Domitian was gross and venal. The first 12 books of the *Epigrams* began to appear in 86. Advancing years having bereft him of Domitian and his friends of the palace, in a fit of homesickness he borrowed from his admirer, the younger **Pliny**, the means of returning to Bilbilis, where he spent the rest of his life. His best work is often his most scurrilous.

▷P Nixon, *Martial and the Modern Epigram* (1927)

MARTIN, C(atherine) E(dith) M(acauley)
(1847–1937)

Scottish-born Australian novelist and poet, born on the Isle of Skye, known now mainly for her early novel of the trials of a colonial woman and wife, *An Australian Girl*, originally published anonymously in 1890. Other novels were *The Silent Sea* (1892, as by Mrs Alick Macleod), *The Old Roof-Tree* (1906) and *The Incredible Journey* (1923), a sympathetic tale of two aboriginal women in search of a kidnapped child. Her serial work 'Bohemian Born' never appeared in book form. A book of verses, *The Explorers and Other Poems*, came out in 1874 under the initials M C.

MARTIN, Claire, née **Montreuil**
(1914–)

French–Canadian novelist and translator, born in Quebec, who began her career in radio. Her books are often about the duplicities of love and triangular relationships alive with deception. This is especially so in her early work: *Doux-amer* (1960, Eng trans *Best Man*, 1983) and *Quand j'aurai payé ton visage* (1962, Eng trans *The Legacy*, 1986). She won a Governor General's Award in 1967 for her two volumes of autobiography—*Dans un gant de fer* (1965) and *La Joue droite* (1966)—in which she described an oppressive childhood in a patriarchal household. These were translated as *In An Iron Glove* (1973) and *The Right Cheek* (1975). Her own translations into French have included books by **Robertson Davies** and **Margaret Laurence**.

MARTIN, David
(1915–)

Hungarian–German novelist and poet of Jewish descent, now settled in Australia. He began writing in London in the late 1930s and became known for his novel *Tiger Bay* (1946), later a popular film. His prolific output includes novels, eight collections of verse and many books for children. He explores the sensitivities of the displaced Jew in *Where a Man Belongs* (1969) and the theme of alienation emerges frequently in other books. *My Strange Friend*, a study in autobiography, was published in 1991.

MARTIN, Sir Theodore
(1816–1909)

Scottish writer and biographer, born in Edinburgh. The well-known series of poetic parodies collected as the *Bon Gaultier Ballads* (1855), written in conjunction with **Aytoun**, were followed by verse translations from **Goethe**, **Horace**, **Catullus**, **Dante** and **Heine**. He was requested by Queen Victoria to write the life of Prince Albert (5 vols, 1874–80), and he also wrote biographies of Aytoun (1867), Lord Lyndhurst (1883) and the Princess Alice (1885). His wife, Helen Faucit (1820–98), was a well-known actress, noted for her interpretations of **Shakespeare**'s heroines. The couple were frequent visitors to the royal household.

MARTIN, Violet Florence, pseud **Martin Ross**
(1862–1915)

Irish writer, born in County Galway. She is known chiefly for a series of novels written in collaboration with her cousin **Edith Somerville**, including *An Irish Cousin* (1889) and *Some Experiences of an Irish R M.* (1908). She also wrote travel books about the Irish countryside, and two autobiographical works, *Some Irish Yesterdays* (1906) and *Strayaways* (1920).
▷M Collis, *Somerville and Ross* (1968)

MARTIN DU GARD, Roger
(1881–1958)

French novelist and winner of the Nobel Prize for literature, born in Neuilly-sur-Seine. After studying history, he qualified as an archivist before turning to writing, publishing his first novel, *Devenir* ('Becoming'), in 1909. In that same year the *Nouvelle Revue Française*, with which he had a long and fruitful association, was founded. After serving in World War I he lived as a recluse and devoted himself to writing in various forms, including novels, plays and memoirs. His novels include *Jean Barois* (1913), which deals, among other matters, with the Dreyfus affair, and *Vieille France* (1933, 'Old France'), a study of a less-than-idyllic rural life. He is best known, however, for his eight-novel series *Les Thibault* (1922–40) dealing with family life during the first decades of the 20th century. He was awarded the Nobel Prize for literature in 1937. The correspondence (1913–51) between him and **André Gide** was published in 1968.
▷D L Schak, *Martin du Gard* (1967)

MARTINEAU, Harriet
(1802–76)

English writer, sister of James Martineau, born in Norwich, the daughter of a textile manufacturer of Huguenot descent. In 1821 she wrote her first article for the (Unitarian) *Monthly Repository*, and then produced *Devotional Exercises for the Use of Young Persons* (1826), and short stories about machinery and wages. Her next book was *Addresses for the Use of Families* (1826). In 1829 the failure of the house in which she, her mother and sisters had placed their money obliged her to earn her living. In 1832 she became a successful author through writing tales based on economic or legal ideas, in *Illustrations of Political Economy*, followed by *Poor Laws and Paupers Illustrated* (1833–4), and settled in London. After a visit to the USA (1834–6) she published *Society in America* and a novel, *Deerbrook*, in 1839, followed by a second novel, *The Hour and the Man*, about Toussaint l'Ouverture. From 1839 to 1844 she was an invalid at Tynemouth but recovered through mesmerism (her subsequent belief in which alienated many friends), and made her home at Ambleside in 1845, the year of *Forest and Game-law Tales*. After visiting Egypt and Palestine she issued *Eastern Life* (1848). In 1851, in conjunction with H G Atkinson, she published *Letters on the Laws of Man's Social Nature* which was so agnostic that it gave much offence, and in 1853 she translated and condensed Comte's

Philosophie positive. She also wrote much for the daily and weekly press and the larger reviews. *An Autobiographical Memoir* was published posthumously in 1877. Her brother James Martineau (1805–1900) wrote many theological works, and also poems and hymns.

▷ V Wheatley, *Life and Work of Harriet Martineau* (1957)

MARTÍNEZ, Luis A
(1869–1909)

Ecuadorian novelist, born in Ambato. He wrote about farming, and then became an enlightened Liberal Minister of Education. His novel *A la costa: costombres ecuatoriana* (1904, 'Ecuadorean Customs') is a well-written naturalist polemic in fictional form, attacking wealthy city idlers and praising the natural life of the honest farmer. It is as relevant to modern-day Ecuador as it was to the Ecuador of 1904.

MARTINEZ ESTRADA, Ezequiel
(1895–1964)

Argentinian writer. He started off as a post-office worker but later taught literature at universities in Argentina and Mexico, continuing in Cuba, where he went after Castro's revolution, while he prepared a biography of Jose Martí, the Cuban writer and nationalist. Although he wrote widely—articles, drama, essays, stories, poetry—he is best known as a poet and essayist, with an interest in philosophy, psychology and politics. His view of contemporary Argentina is pessimistic and even bitter; although he never abandoned his political involvement, his focus changed to Third World problems. Some of his poetry collections are: *Oro y Piedra* (1918, 'Gold and Stone'), *Nefelibal* (1922), *Argentina* (1927) and *Humoresca* (1929). His most successful stories were *Tres Cuentos Sin Amor* (1956, 'Three Stories without Love'), and he also wrote a play in verse entitled *Titeres de Pies Ligeros* (1929, 'Puppets on Light Feet').

MARTÍNEZ SIERRA, Gregorio
(1881–1947)

Spanish novelist and dramatist. A theatre manager and an original and creative producer as well as publisher, he was also a prolific writer. His plays *Canción de Cuna* (1917, Eng trans *The Cradle Song*, 1934), *El Reino de Dios* (1916, Eng trans *The Kingdom of God*, 1927) and *El Sueño de Una Noche de Agosto* (1918, Eng trans *The Romantic Young Lady*, 1929) were also popular in Britain and America. Much of his writing was done in collaboration with his wife Maria, whose feminist opinions find expression in some of the plays.

▷ G Serrat, *Imager humana y literara de Gregorio Martínez Sierra* (1965)

MARTÍN GAITE, Carmen
(1925–)

Spanish novelist, one of the three most important female novelists in Spain in the latter half of the 20th century (the others are **Carmen Laforet** and **Ana Maria Matute**). Born in Salamanca, she received her doctorate from the University of Madrid, and has written scholarly works on the 18th century and literary criticism. She gained her reputation as a social realist writer and member of the Postwar Generation, but more recently has worked in psychological novels and the fantastic. Her main themes are the lives of women in society, communication, the isolation of the individual, and the deeper side of reality. She has won many literary honours, including the Premio Nadal (1959) and the Premio Nacional de Literatura (1979).

MARTÍN-SANTOS, Luis
(1924–64)

Spanish novelist, born in Larache, Morocco, who helped to revolutionize and make viable the form of the novel in his country during the Francoist period. He was a psychiatrist by profession (he directed the mental hospital at San Sebastian), whose first writings were technical—although in the light of his enormous achievement they are now interesting, especially his early work on the German philosopher Dilthey. He was killed in a car accident as fatal to Spanish literature as to himself. His only finished novel was the significantly titled *Tiempo de silencio* (1962, Eng trans *Time of Silence*, 1965—truthful imaginative exploration of reality was virtually silenced by Franco's censors), which deals with a man, Pedro, living in the sick and submissive society of Madrid in 1949, in which he cannot discover the sort of fulfilment he might naturally, as a human being, expect. This novel exposed the artistic disingenuousness of the attempts made by such pro-Francoist authors as **Gironella** to explain their hero to his liberal European critics. Its technique, which tries to reconcile subjectivity with objectivity in a manner much influenced by the psychology of Karl Jaspers, has been decisive in its effect on subsequent literature. All Martín-Santos's work is pervaded by his desire to understand and relieve mental illness, and this may ultimately prove to be even more important than his aesthetic innovations. His stories were collected in *Apólogos* (1970, 'Apologues'), and an attempt has been made to reconstruct his unfinished novel, *Tiempo de destrucción* (1975, 'Time of Destruction'), about a law student, which seems to have been even more pessimistic and savage in its criticism of post-Civil War society than his first.

▷J C Mainer (ed), Introduction to *Tiempo de Destrucción* (1975)

MARTINSON, Harry Edmund
(1904–78)

Swedish poet and novelist, joint winner of the Nobel Prize for literature, born in Jäshög in Blekinge. After a harsh childhood as a parish orphan he went to sea as a stoker in 1919 and travelled worldwide in the following decade. He made his poetic debut in 1929 along with a number of young vitalist poets but soon found an individual and quickly acclaimed voice, particularly as a nature poet with such volumes as *Nomad* (1931) and *Natur* (1934); these established his reputation as a renewer of the poetic language. During the 1930s he was married to the writer **Moa Martinson**. He came increasingly to question whether or not man possessed sufficient ethical maturity to control his own technological inventions and this led to his masterpiece, the poetic space epic *Aniara* (1956), which deals with the evacuation by rocket of a radiation-damaged earth; it was set to music as an opera by Karl-Birger Blomdahl. His account of his childhood and youth in *Nässlorna blomma* (1935, 'Flowering Nettle') and *Vägen ut* (1936, 'The Way Out') is his moving contribution to the many working-class autobiographical novels of the Swedish 1930s. His tramp novel *Vägen till Klockrike* (1948, 'The Road to Klockrike') is a worthy addition to that genre. He shared the 1974 Nobel Prize for literature with the Swedish novelist **Eyvind Johnson**. A Harry Martinson Society was founded in 1984.

▷I Holm, *Harry Martinson* (1960)

MARTINSON, Moa
(1890–1963)

Swedish novelist. Born near Norrköping to an unmarried mill-hand, she received only intermittent schooling, trained as a cold-buffet manageress, married early and gave birth to five sons. Having been widowed, she was subsequently married (1929–41) to the author **Harry Martinson**. Her political interests resulted in articles for the radical press; her first novel, *Kvinnor och äppelträd*, which uses the maternal body as its structuring principle, appeared in 1933 (Eng trans *Women and Apple Trees*, 1985). As the leading woman among the Swedish 'proletarian' writers of the 1930s, she enjoyed a huge success with her autobiographical trilogy, *Mor gifter sig* (1936, 'Mother Gets Married'), *Kyrkbröllop* (1938, 'Church Wedding') and *Kungens rosor* (1939, 'The King's Roses'). Quick-witted and sharp-tongued, she achieved a considerable reputation as a speaker; but her lasting popularity with the Swedish reading public rests on her knowledgeable yet suggestive narratives about working-class life.

▷E Witt-Brattström, *Moa Martinson. Skrift och drift i trettiotalet* (1988)

MARTORELL, Joanot
(c.1413–1468)

Catalan prose writer. His *Tirant lo Blanc* (1490, Eng trans 1984) was described by **Cervantes** in *Don Quixote* as 'the best book of its kind in the world'; but, like the poetry of **Ausias Marc** (who married Martorell's sister), its greatness was for long forgotten through linguistic ignorance, despite the fact that Catalan is easy to read for those who know romance languages. When it appeared in English in 1984 a new and delighted audience discovered it. It thus joined the hitherto closed list of 'great medieval and Renaissance classics', as its translator hoped it would. Martorell left it unfinished, and it was completed and published by Martí Joan de Galba (whose contribution was probably very slight). Ostensibly a tale of chivalrous adventure, it owed much to the Catalan mystic Ramon Llull, and is unrivalled for its psychological penetration and its erotic realism. It anticipated much of what is now taken for 'modern' (eg the existence of the unconscious mind), and its calculated mixture of farce, fantasy, onslaught upon conventional morality and effortless recognition of the dangerous relationship between love and mystical insight, makes it read very like a new work.

MARTYN, Edward
(1859–1923)

Irish playwright, now best known for his friendship with **George Moore** and **W B Yeats**. He was born in County Galway. His reaction against the main movement in Irish theatre culminated in the founding of the Abbey Theatre. He was for four years the President of Sinn Fein. His plays, now somewhat underrated, were modelled upon those of **Ibsen**; *Romulus and Remus* (1916) is memorable for its savage and not inaccurate caricatures of Moore and Yeats. *Regina Eyre* (produced in 1919, not published), which was hissed when it was performed, is a courageous and interesting variation on the *Hamlet* theme, in which he reverses the gender of the characters. His dialogue was often inept, and had he had a collaborator he might have achieved much more.

▷G Moore, *Hail and Farewell* (1911–14)

MARTYNOV, Leonid
(1905–)

Russian poet from Omsk, who graduated from the Futurist movement, and who at first wrote in the style of **Mayakovsky**. His best-known poem is the narrative *Lukomorye* (1945, 'Cove'), on the theme of never-never land, set, in his case, in a Siberia almost unknown to his contemporaries (unless they had been sent there). This effectively combines contemplative folklorism with the colloquial. Criticized by cultural officers of state, he reacted by composing a somewhat more conformist poetry which, after a long gap, brought him honours and recognition.

MARULIĆ, Marko
(1450–1524)

Dalmatian poet and classical scholar, born in Split, who achieved renown in Europe. Like the other writers of Dalmatia of his age and that following it, he studied in Italy (Padua) and based his practice on what he learned there. Much of what he wrote is in Latin, but his epic poems, on biblical themes, are in Serbo–Croat—the first literary writings in that language of known authorship.
▷ *Slavonic and East European Review*, XLI (1962)

MARVELL, Andrew
(1621–78)

English poet, born in Winestead rectory, south east Yorkshire, the son of a clergyman. He was educated at Hull Grammar School and Trinity College, Cambridge. He travelled (1642–6) in Holland, France, Italy and Spain. After a period as tutor to Lord Fairfax's daughter, when he wrote his pastoral and garden poems, he was appointed tutor to Cromwell's ward, William Dutton. In 1650 he wrote his *Horatian Ode upon Cromwell's Return from Ireland*, which also reflected the warmest sympathy for Charles I. In 1657 he became **Milton**'s assistant. In January 1659 he took his seat in parliament as member for Hull, for which he was returned again in 1660 and 1661. From 1663 to 1665 he accompanied Lord Carlisle as secretary to the embassy to Muscovy, Sweden and Denmark, but the rest of his life was devoted to his parliamentary duties, fighting against intolerance and arbitrary government. His republicanism was less the outcome of abstract theory than of experience. He accepted the Restoration while still admiring Cromwell. His writings show him willing to give Charles II a fair chance, but convinced eventually that the Stewarts must go. His last satires are a call to arms against monarchy. Though circulated in manuscript only, they were believed to endanger his life. He died due to the stubborn ignorance of his physician—a baseless rumour suggested poison. Marvell's works are divided by the Restoration into two very distinct groups. After 1660 he concentrated on politics, except when his friendship for Milton drew from

him the lines prefixed to the second edition of *Paradise Lost*. In 1672–3 he wrote *The Rehearsal Transpros'd* against religious intolerance; and in 1677 his most important tract, the *Account of the Growth of Popery and Arbitrary Government*, was published anonymously. As a poet, Marvell belongs to the pre-Restoration period, although most of his poetry was not published until 1681 as *Miscellaneous Poetry*. A subsequent volume was entitled *Poems on Affairs of State* (1689–97).
▷ P Legouis, *Andrew Marvell, poète, puritain, patriote* (1928); J B Leishman, *The Art of Marvell's Poetry* (1966)

MASAMUNE Hakucho
(1879–1962)

Japanese writer. Born in the South of Honshu, Japan's main island, he gravitated towards Tokyo in early adulthood. Masamune, of all his contemporaries, was one of those most open to western influences—he read western literature, often expressed a desire to go abroad, embraced Christianity and even described himself as 'worshipping the West'. His novels are still very Japanese in conception; like so many of his contemporaries, he was an exponent of Japanese naturalism, and his writing is introspective, realistic and full of minute descriptive detail, coming close at times to internal monologue.

MASAOKA Shiki
(1867–1902)

Japanese poet, from Ehime but living in Tokyo. Masaoke was the greatest poet of his day, working with the traditional poetic forms, especially *waka* and *haiku*, refining them and devising new ways of seeing them, to the extent that there is good reason to think of him as the originator of the modern haiku (as a concise, beautiful and above all self-sufficient expression of some idea or feeling). Some of his most beautiful and poignant verse was written in the final stages of his drawn-out and agonizing death from spinal tuberculosis. His famous poem *Drop of Ink* was composed when he was totally paralysed.
▷ 'Masaoka Shiki and Tanka Reform' in D Shively (ed), *Tradition and Modernisation in Japanese Culture* (1971)

MASEFIELD, John Edward
(1878–1967)

English poet and novelist, born in Ledbury, Herefordshire. Educated at the King's School, Warwickshire, and schooled for the merchant service, he served his apprenticeship on a windjammer and acquired that intimate knowledge of the sea which gives atmosphere and authenticity to his work. Ill-health drove him ashore, and after three years in New York he returned to England to become a writer in 1897, first making his mark as a journalist. His earliest poetical work, *Salt Water Ballads*, appeared in 1902; *Dauber* (1913) confirmed his reputation as a poet of the sea. *Nan* (1909) is a tragedy of merit. His finest narrative poem is *Reynard the Fox* (1919). Other works are *The Everlasting Mercy* (1911); *The Widow in the Bye-Street* (1912); *Shakespeare* (1911); *Gallipoli* (1916); and the novels *Sard Harker* (1924), *Odtaa* (1926) and *The Hawbucks* (1929). His plays are *The Trial of Jesus* (1925) and *The Coming of Christ* (1928). He became poet laureate in 1930. Later books included the sea-novels *Dead Ned* (1938) and *Live and Kicking Ned* (1939). His final work was *Grace before Ploughing* (1966).

▷ *So Long to Learn* (1952)

MASON, Alfred Edward Woodley
(1865–1948)

English novelist, born in Dulwich. He was educated at Oxford, became a successful actor, and subsequently combined writing with politics, as Liberal MP for Coventry (1906–10). His first published novel was *A Romance of Wastdale* (1895). The adventure novel *Four Feathers* (1902) captured the popular imagination and *The Broken Road* (1907) cemented his success. With *At the Villa Rose* (1910) he started writing detective novels and introduced his ingenious Inspector Hanaud. From then on he alternated historical adventure and detective fiction. Several of his books have been filmed.

▷ R L Green, *Alfred Mason: the adventures of a story-teller* (1952)

MASON, Bobbie Ann
(1940–)

American novelist and short-story writer, born in Mayfield, Kentucky. One of the much-hyped 'dirty realists' who came to prominence in the mid-1980s, she writes of ordinary Americans, often poor and rural, facing common problems: inter-generational strife; lack of understanding; lack of cash. Her short-story collections *Shiloh* (1982) and *Love Life* (1989) include her best work to date; the economy of her prose seems most suited to a short form. Her novels, *In Country* (1985) and *Spence + Lila* (1988), are also brief.

MASON, Bruce Edward George
(1921–82)

New Zealand playwright, born in Wellington, whose plays, beginning with *The Pohutukawa Tree* (1956, rev edn 1963), were widely produced; his *The End of the Golden Weather*

(1962, rev edn 1970) received over 500 performances in every New Zealand city. Later work was written for solo performance, often drawing on his previous writings. Four such plays were published as *Bruce Mason Solo* (1981). Three plays for television and a full-length stage play, *Blood of the Lamb* (1980), were produced after his death. His *New Zealand Drama: A Parade of Forms and a History* (1973) was written for school use but gives useful background on his plays.

MASON, F Van Wyck
(1901–78)

American popular novelist, born in Boston. He has written mysteries, adventure stories, books for juveniles and, perhaps most notably, historical novels, such as *Proud New Flags* (1951), about the navy in the American Civil War. *Cutlass Empire* (1949) is about the pirate Henry Morgan.

MASON, R(onald) A(rthur) K(ells)
(1905–71)

New Zealand poet, born in Auckland, who came to attention aged 19 with *The Beggar* (1924), which he paid to have published. Legend has it that, disappointed with the sales, he dumped the remaining copies in Waitemata harbour. *No New Thing: Poems, 1924–29* was published in 1934, *End of Day* followed in 1936 and *Recent Poems* (with work by **Allen Curnow**, **Denis Glover** and **A R D Fairburn**) in 1941. His work is collected in *This Dark Will Lighten: Selected Poems, 1923–41* (1941) and *Collected Poems* (1962, with an introduction by Curnow).

MASON, William
(1725–97)

English poet and clergyman. He was a friend of **Thomas Gray**, who had been attracted to him by his *Musaeus* (1747), a lament for **Pope** in imitation of **Milton**'s *Lycidas*. He published two poor tragedies, *Elfrida* and *Caractacus*; the *English Garden* (1772–82), a tedious poem in blank verse; and, as Gray's executor, the *Memoirs of Gray* in 1775. He became vicar of Aston, Yorkshire, in 1754, and canon of York in 1762.

▷ J W Draper, *William Mason* (1924)

MASSEY, Gerald
(1828–1907)

English mystic and poet, born near Tring. He became a Christian socialist, edited a journal, lectured, and between 1851 and 1869 published several volumes of poetry, including *Babe Christabel and other Poems* and *Craigcrook Castle*. He also wrote mystical and speculative theological or cosmogonic works, and claimed to have discovered a 'Secret Drama' in **Shakespeare**'s sonnets.

MASSIE, Allan
(1938–)

Scottish novelist, critic and journalist, born in Singapore and brought up in Aberdeenshire. Educated at Glenalmond and Cambridge, he taught in a private school before going to Italy, where he taught English as a foreign language. His first two novels—*Change and Decay In All Around I See* (1978) and *The Last Peacock* (1980)—placed him firmly in the camp of **Ronald Firbank** and **Evelyn Waugh**, but those who saw him as other than Scottish were off the mark. Although inclined to think in terms that transcend place, his sensibility is native. *The Death of Men* (1981) was a stylish thriller drawing on the kidnapping in Italy of Aldo Moro. In 1986 he turned again to Italy with *Augustus*, a historical novel purporting to be the long-lost memoirs of the maligned emperor. *Tiberius* (1990) and *Caesar* (1993) brilliantly perpetuated the conceit, drawing on his knowledge of the ancient world while convincingly filling in gaps with his imagination. *A Question of Loyalties* (1989), set in Vichy France, and *The Sins of the Father* (1991), in which the children of war criminals and victims attempt to cope with their parents' legacies, similarly demonstrate his unwillingness to allow history to remain the preserve solely of historians. In both there are no pat answers, only sympathy and a quest to interpret the past from an unconventional point of view. *These Enchanted Woods* (1993) makes comic play of the contrasting attitudes of an aggressive London speculator with the country society of rural Perthshire. As well as being a prolific novelist, Massie has written books on **Muriel Spark**, the Caesars and Lord **Byron**. He is also a respected reviewer and a columnist, with trenchant political views.

MASSINGER, Philip
(1583–1640)

English dramatist, born in Salisbury, the son of a retainer of the Earl of Pembroke. After leaving Oxford without a degree he became a playwright and was associated with Philip Henslowe, who died in 1616. In later years he wrote many plays on his own, but much of his work is mixed up with that of other men, particularly **John Fletcher**. He and Fletcher are buried in the same grave. Probably the earliest of Massinger's extant plays is *The Unnatural Combat*, a dreadful tragedy, printed in 1639. The first in order of publication is *The Virgin Martyr* (1622), partly written by **Thomas Dekker**. In 1623 was published *The Duke of Milan*, a fine tragedy, but too rhetorical. Other plays include *The Bondman* (1623),

The Roman Actor (1626), *The Great Duke of Florence* (1627) and *The Emperor of the East* (1631). **Nathan Field** joined Massinger in writing the fine tragedy *The Fatal Dowry*, printed in 1632. *The City Madam*, licensed in 1632, and *A New Way to Pay Old Debts*, printed in 1633, are Massinger's most masterly comedies—brilliant satirical studies, though without warmth or geniality. It is difficult to say how much Massinger was involved in the plays under the names of **Francis Beaumont** and Fletcher.

▷ A Dunn, *Massinger: the man and the playwright* (1957)

MASTERS, Edgar Lee
(1869–1950)

American author, born in Garnett, Kansas. A successful lawyer in Chicago, he wrote poetry, and became famous with the satirical *Spoon River Anthology* (1915), a book of epitaphs in free verse about lives of people in Illinois. He published several more collections and some novels, and returned to his first success with *The New Spoon River* (1924), attacking the new style of urban life. *Across Spoon River* (1936) is an autobiography.

▷ H W Masters, *Edgar Lee Masters: a biographical sketchbook* (1978)

MASTERS, John
(1914–1983)

British writer, born in Calcutta into a Raj family and going into the army, in India, from Sandhurst. After service during World War II in Asia, he took up full-time writing in 1948, turning out adventure stories, mainly for American magazines, and then producing a string of historical novels, many of them (including *Nightrunners of Bengal*, 1951) set in India. He also wrote extensively about World War I, producing a history, *Fourteen Eighteen* (1971), and a trilogy of novels, *Loss of Eden* (1979–80). His fiction tends to go for breadth of action rather than depth of vision, but can astonish the reader in doing so, and the nostalgia underlying much of his work is usually kept at a discreet distance.

MATAVULJ, Simõ
(1852–1906)

Serbian novelist, story writer and translator (of **Zola**, **Mérimée**, **Maupassant**), born in Belgrade. Much of his work was translated into French and Italian, but nothing into English. His semi-naturalistic depictions of the South Adriatic are anything but idealistic. He wrote six collections of stories and two novels, of which *Bakonja fra Brne* (1892) is a comic classic, set in a Catholic monastery. His true master was Maupassant.

MATHEWS, Aidan
(1956–)

Irish poet, fiction writer and playwright, born in Dublin. In 1976 he won the **Patrick Kavanagh** Award for Poetry, in 1978 the **Macaulay** Fellowship for Writing and in 1984 the Listowel Drama Award. An intellectual intensity informs his verse, particularly *Windfalls* (1977) and *Minding Ruth* (1983). His short-story collections *Adventures in a Bathyscope* (1988) and *Lipstick on the Host* (1992) and his novel *Muesli at Midnight* (1990) show an entertaining sense of the absurd, one which is almost overwhelmingly present in the surreal drama *The Diamond Body* (1985). A rejection of traditional political imperatives—as in the three-line *The Deanth of Irish* (1987): 'The tide gone out for good,/Thirty-one words for seaweed/whiten on the foreshore'—has gained him over the years a questionable reputation as 'Irish fabulist'.

MATHEWS, Harry Burchell
(1930–)

American writer of bizarre lexical fantasies. He was born in New York City and educated at Harvard and at the École Normale de Musique in Paris. In 1952 he moved to Europe, where his brand of highly literary fiction is more readily understood than in the US; he has lived there, mainly in France, ever since. He is a member of the hermetic Ouvroir de Littérature Potentielle (Oulipo). In 1960, he joined **John Ashbery**, **Kenneth Koch** and **James Schuyler** in founding the influential magazine *Locus Solus*, which was based in France. His fictional writing includes *The Conversions* (1962), *Tlooth* (1966) and his masterpiece, *The Sinking of the Odradek Stadium* (1971–5), originally published in the *Paris Review*, which concerns the correspondence between a librarian and his Thai wife. *Cigarettes* (1982) was a slighter work. Mathews's collected verse was published as *Armenian Papers* (1987).

MATHEWS, John Joseph
(1894–1979)

American writer, born in Pawhuska, Indian Territory (now Oklahoma). Of mixed Osage and French descent, Mathews studied sciences at the University of Oklahoma and Merton College, Oxford. His studies interrupted by World War I, he served for a time as a pilot in the US Air Service. After the war, he spent several years studying and working as a newspaper correspondent in Europe before returning to Pawhuska in 1929, where he began both to write and to take an active part in Osage tribal affairs, serving several years on the Tribal Council. His first important work, *Wah'Kon-Tah: the Osage and the White Man's Road*, a non-fictional account of Osage life, was published in 1932. This was followed by *Sundown* (1934), a semi-autobiographical novel describing a young mixed-blood Osage's struggle to fit in with either White or Native American worlds, and *Talking to the Moon* (1945), a lyrical, **Thoreau**-like account of the 10 years he lived in solitude on a ranch in northeastern Oklahoma. His major work, on which he spent some 30 years, was the cultural history *The Osages: Children of the Middle Waters* (1961); based on a series of interviews Mathews conducted with tribal elders, it traces the history of the Osages from traditional accounts of the creation to the mid-20th century.
▷G Bailey, 'John Joseph Mathews', in M Liberty (ed), *American Indian Intellectuals* (1978)

MATKOVIĆ, Marijan
(1915–)

Croatian dramatist, born in Karlovac. He has written many radio plays. Essentially Matković is an innovative and inventive follower of Krleža. His trilogy *The Gods Also Suffer* (1959–61) is a mocking examination of the 'personality cult'.

MATOS, Antun Gustav
(1873–1914)

Croatian poet, story writer, essayist, critic and part-time cellist who deserted from the hated Austrian army in 1898, and fled to Paris. He acted as Croatian (and to an extent Serbian) literature's **Endre Ady**, if at a less intensive pitch: he brought French procedures into what became Yugoslavia. He was most important as a critic, although his poems, the product of his closing years, are well made.

MATOS GUERRA, Gregorio de
(1623–96)

Brazilian baroque poet, influenced by **Góngora** and **Quevedo**. He was the first to depict the evils of Brazilian society in satirical verse, his most lively work. His lyrics are indifferent.

MATTHIAS, John Edward
(1941–)

American poet. He grew up in Columbus, Ohio, attended university there and in California, and spent 1966–7 in London as a Fulbright Fellow. Since then, he has taught English at the University of Notre Dame, Indiana, where he became full professor in 1980. His first verse collection, *Other Poems* (1971), marked him out as a disciple of **John Berryman** but, since the period of his Fulbright Fellowship, he has been increasingly influenced by English life and landscape, particularly that of East Anglia, and his work is closely aligned to the mystical historicism of **David Jones** and **Geoffrey Hill**. More playful than either, he often constructs poems out of elaborate linguistic conceits and transpositions, as in 'Turns' and the remarkable 'Double Derivation, Association and Cliché: From the Great Tournament Roll of Westminster' (both 1975). Later collections include *Rostropovich at Aldeburgh* (1979) and *Bathory and Lermontov* (1980), in which he experiments with historical 'rhymes' and coincidences, and the magnificent *Northern Summer* (1984), his finest work. His most recent published verse evokes **Edward Thomas**, using leys and pilgrimage routes to create a poetry of great historical focus.

MATTHIESSEN, F(rancis) O(tto)
(1902–50)

American literary critic. He was born near Pasadena, California, and grew up in Illinois. Though from a wealthy background, he quickly espoused socialism (though originally it was intermingled with Christian ideals). He studied at Yale and Harvard, and spent a year as Rhodes Scholar at Oxford. His studies of **Henry James** (1944) and **T S Eliot** (1935, rev edn 1947) are direct and perceptive. Joining the faculty at Harvard, he supported civil liberties causes and trade unionism, arguing that individualism was the bane of American life and culture: this was the underlying thrust of his masterpiece, *American Renaissance* (1941), a panoramic study of the literary environment of **Nathaniel Hawthorne**, **Ralph Waldo Emerson**, **Walt Whitman** and **Herman Melville**, that galvanized a generation of American students. At the end of World War II, Matthiessen became involved in Henry Wallace's Progressive third party movement and was widely reviled from left and right for either closet communism or 'accommodationism'. His journal *From the Heart of Europe* (1948) suggested growing introspection; two years later, Matthiessen threw himself from a hotel room window. He bequeathed his inheritance to the struggling journal *Monthly Review*; his intellectual legacy is harder to calculate, but his ideas remain of consequence in American letters.
▷W Cain, *F O Matthiessen and the Politics of Criticism* (1988)

MATTHIESSEN, Peter
(1927–)

American novelist, travel writer, naturalist and explorer, born in New York City. He has made anthropological and natural history expeditions to Alaska, the Canadian Northwest Territories, Peru, New Guinea, Africa, Nicaragua and Nepal, out of which have come a number of eloquent ecological and natural history studies, which reflect the concerns of the cultish novel *At Play in the Fields of the Lord* (1965). He won the National Book Award with the bestselling *The Snow Leopard* (1978), one man's inner story of a mystical trek across the Tibetan plateau to the Crystal Mountain to catch a glimpse of the rarest and most beautiful of the great cats. Other novels include *Race Rock* (1954), *Partisans* (1955), the superb *Far Tortuga* (1975) and *Killing Mister Watson* (1990). In recent years, Matthiessen has taken up the cause of Native Americans; *In the Spirit of Crazy Horse* (1983), an account of a 1975 shoot-out with the FBI, was delayed by litigation.

MATTO DE TURNER, Clorinda
(1854–1909)

Peruvian novelist, poet, and playwright. One of the most important Latin-American female writers of the 19th century, she occasionally wrote under the pseudonym of 'Carlota Dumont'. She is claimed by some critics as an early feminist, though she is most famous for her *Aves sin nido* (1889, 'Birds Without a Nest'); the only Indianist novel of the 19th century, it has a Romantic plot, realist detail, a strong anti-clerical message, and displays elements of *criollismo* (narratives on popular customs and language). Her other major work was *Tradiciones cuzqueñas* (1884–6, 'Traditions of Cuzco'), a development of the uniquely Peruvian genre invented by **Ricardo Palma**.
▷A Tauro, *Clorinda Matto de Turner y la novela indigenista* (1976)

MATURIN, Charles Robert
(1782–1824)

Irish dramatist and novelist, born in Dublin. Educated at Trinity College, Dublin, he became a curate in Loughrea and Dublin. He made his name with a series of extravagant novels in macabre vein that rivalled those of **Ann Radcliffe**. These included *The Fatal Revenge* (1807), *Melmoth the Wanderer* (1820), which influenced **Honoré de Balzac**, and *The Albigenses* (1824). His tragedy, *Bertram*, had a success at Drury Lane in 1816; its successors, *Manuel* (1817) and *Fredolpho* (1819), were failures.
▷W Scholten, *Charles Robert Maturin: the terror novelist* (1933)

MATUTE, Ana María
(1926–)

Spanish novelist, born in Barcelona, one of those who decided to remain in Spain after the Civil War and to denounce injustice under the eyes of the censors. She came into prominence in the 1950s and 1960s as one of a generation who had experienced the war as children: her best-known novel, the long *Los hijos muertos* (1958, Eng trans *The Lost Children*, 1965), examines just this problem in the objectivist manner then almost statutory in a Spain where little that was directly critical of the regime could appear. She has continued to explore these themes, of war and children, in a series of novels and stories upon which critical opinion is divided: one school holds that her work is, though worthy, poorly written and excessively rhetorical, the other that she is a major novelist.

▷ M E W Jones, *The Literary World of Ana María Matute* (1970); J W Díaz, *Ana María Matute* (1971)

MAUGHAM, W(illiam) Somerset
(1874–1965)

British writer, a modern master of the short story, born in Paris, of Irish origin. He was educated at King's School, Canterbury, read philosophy and literature at Heidelberg and qualified as a surgeon at St Thomas's Hospital, London. Afflicted by a bad stammer, he turned to writing in his student days and a year's medical practice in the London slums gave him the material for his first novel, the lurid *Liza of Lambeth* (1897), and the magnificent autobiographical novel, *Of Human Bondage*, eventually published in 1915. Attempts to have his plays accepted having failed, he settled in Paris and with **Laurence Housman** revived a 19th-century annual, *The Venture* (1903–4). With the success of *Lady Frederick* (1907), four of his plays ran in London in 1908. In 1914 he served first with a Red Cross unit in France, then as a secret agent in Geneva and finally in Petrograd, attempting to prevent the outbreak of the Russian Revolution. *Ashenden* (1928) is based on these experiences. He travelled in the South Seas, visiting Tahiti, which inspired *The Moon and Sixpence* (1919), in which an Englishman, Strickland, leaves his wife and stockbroking to end his life in a leper's hut. Maugham spent two years in a Scottish tuberculosis sanatorium and this again finds expression in several short stories. He then visited the Far East, writing such plays as *East of Suez* (1922) and *Our Betters* (1923). In 1928 he settled in the South of France, where he wrote his astringent, satirical masterpiece, *Cakes and Ale* (1930). A British agent again in World War II, he fled from France in 1940 with only a suitcase, and lived until 1946 in the USA where he ventured into mysticism with *The Razor's Edge* (1945). But he is best known for his short stories, several of which were filmed under the titles *Quartet* (1949), *Trio* (1950) and *Encore* (1951). The best of them, 'Rain', was originally published in the collection *The Trembling of a Leaf*

(1921). His sparse, careful prose has sometimes unjustly been mistaken for superficiality. He refused to do more than tell a story; all else is propaganda, which seriously impairs a work of art. Other works include *Catalina* (1948), *The Complete Short Stories* (3 vols, 1951), *A Writer's Notebook* (1949) and essays on **Goethe, Anton Chekhov, Henry James** and **Katherine Mansfield** in *Points of View* (1958).

▷ *Summing Up* (1938); *Strictly Personal* (1941); R Calder, *Willie: the life of Maugham* (1989)

MAUPASSANT, Guy de
(1850–93)

French novelist, born in the Norman château of Miromesnil. He was educated at Rouen and spent his life in Normandy. After a short spell as a soldier in the Franco–German war he became a government clerk, but encouraged by **Gustave Flaubert**, a friend of his mother's, he took to writing and mingled with **Émile Zola** and other disciples of Naturalism. His stories range from the short tale of one or two pages to the full-length novel. Free from sentimentality or idealism, they lay bare with minute and merciless observation the pretentiousness and vulgarity of the middle class of the period and the animal cunning and traditional meanness of the Norman peasant. His first success, *Boule de suif* (1880, 'Ball of Tallow'), exposes the hypocrisy, prudery and ingratitude of the bourgeois in the face of a heroic gesture by a woman of the streets, while *La Maison Tellier* (1881, Eng trans *The House of Madame Tellier and Other Stories*, 1959) tells with penetrating satire and humour the tale of an outing for the inmates of a provincial house of ill-repute. At the other end of the scale *Le Horla* (1887, Eng trans 1890) and *La Peur* (posthumous 1925, 'The Fear') describe madness and fear with a horrifying accuracy which foreshadows the insanity which beset de Maupassant in 1892 and finally precipitated his death. His short stories, the form in which he excelled, number nearly 300, and he wrote several full-length novels, including *Une Vie* (1883, Eng trans *A Woman's Life*, 1888) and *Bel-Ami* (1885, Eng trans *Bel-Ami*, 1891).

▷ F Steegmuller, *Maupassant* (1950)

MAUPIN, Armistead
(1944–)

American novelist, born into a 'mossbacked' Republican family in Washington DC, and brought up mainly in North Carolina. Educated at the University of North Carolina, he served in Vietnam, where he later returned to build housing for the disabled, receiving a Presidential Commendation for this work. Turning to journalism, he began to write a fictional column for the *San Francisco Chronicle*. This soon evolved into *Tales of the City* (1978) and five subsequent novels, a saga that focuses on the lovable homosexual Michael ('Mouse') Tolliver and his unconventional collection of friends as they each discover that the concept of family is broader than kin. Warm-hearted, witty and emotional, these stories gained huge popularity with straight and gay readers alike. A writer concerned with promoting tolerance, and a respected gay rights advocate, Maupin moved beyond this series in 1992 with the novel *Maybe the Moon*.

MAURIAC, François
(1885–1970)

French novelist and winner of the Nobel Prize for literature, born in Bordeaux of Roman Catholic parentage, and regarded as the leading novelist of that faith. He started as a poet, publishing his first volume of verse in 1909. In his novels, his treatment of the themes of temptation, sin and redemption, set in the brooding Bordeaux countryside, showed his art as cathartic, exploring the universal problems of sinful, yet aspiring, man. His principal novels, all translated into English, are *Le Baiser au Lépreux* (1922, Eng trans *The Kiss to the Leper*, 1923); *Génitrix* (1923, Eng trans 1930); *Thérèse Desqueyroux* (1927, Eng trans 1928; and *Le Noeud de Vipères* (1932, Eng trans *Vipers' Tangle*, 1933). Also important is his play *Asmodée* (1938, Eng trans 1939). He was awarded the 1952 Nobel Prize for literature.
▷M Alyn, *François Mauriac* (1960)

MAURICE, Furnley, properly Frank Leslie Thompson Wilmot
(1881–1942)

Australian poet, born in Collingwood, Melbourne. For the last 10 years of his life he was manager of the Melbourne University Press. He produced his early verse on a hand press; his first published work was *Eyes of Vigilance* (1920), which included his impassioned poem against war, 'To God, from the Warring Nations', which had originally appeared in 1916. He loved the country, but wrote of the town with the style and verve of the old bush poets. *Melbourne Odes* (1934) sings of city life in the 1930s depression years. His best work was edited by Percival Serle in *Poems by Furnley Maurice* (1944).

MAUROIS, André, pseud of Émile Herzog
(1885–1967)

French novelist and biographer, born in Elbeuf. He was one of a family of Jewish industrialists from Alsace who settled in Normandy after 1870. During World War I he was a liaison officer with the British army, and began his literary career with two books of shrewd and affectionate observation of British character, *Les Silences du Colonel Bramble* (1918, 'The Silences of Colonel Bramble') and *Les Discours du Docteur O'-Grady* (1920, 'The Speeches of Dr O'Grady'). His large output includes such distinguished biographies as his *Ariel* (1923), a biography of **Shelley**, *Disraeli* (1927), *Voltaire* (1935), *À la recherche de Marcel Proust* (1949, 'In Search of Marcel Proust'), and *La vie de Sir Alexander Fleming* (1959, Eng trans *The Life of Sir Alexander Fleming*, 1959). He also wrote several novels, fantasies, tales for children, and critical and philosophical essays.
▷J Suffel, *André Maurois* (1963)

MAURRAS, Charles
(1868–1952)

French minor poet and traitor, born in Martigues. A tragic figure, the deaf Maurras was for many years the leading voice in the ultra right-wing, anti-Semitic, royalist movement, Action Française. His chief claim to distinction lies in his forceful, classical and lucid style; but, for all his courage, his polemical arguments were highly emotional and prejudiced. His deafness meant that he understood little of how ordinary people lived, felt or thought. He collaborated with the Vichy government and was sentenced to life imprisonment in 1945. He is now little read, although the long introduction to *La Musique intérieure* (1925), a collection of artificial poems of little account, is moving in its loftily sad isolation from real experience.
▷M Mourre, *Charles Maurras* (1958); C H Sisson, *The Avoidance of Literature* (1986)

MAVILIS, Lorentsos
(1860–1912)

Greek poet, born in Corfu and educated on the island and then for 15 years at German universities, where he studied philosophy (particularly the work of **Schopenhauer**), Sanskrit and Indian religion. He returned to Corfu in 1893 and wrote the bulk of his slim poetic output over the next seven years. His sonnets are concerned with moral and human nobility, and he himself took part in the struggles against the Turks in Crete in 1896 and then in Epirus in the following year. He died on a battlefield outside Iannina in 1912, while he was serving as an officer in the Garibaldi Officer Corps.

MAVOR, Elizabeth Osborne
(1927–)

Scottish novelist and biographer, born in Glasgow and educated at Oxford. She has written four novels, of which the first, *Summer in the Greenhouse*, appeared in 1959. One of her recurring themes is of women attempting to come to terms with their emotions and hoping thereby to discover a sense of direction in a sometimes violently chaotic world. In *A Green Equinox* (1973) Hero Kinoull, during one short summer, suffers a series of traumatic experiences while trying to make sense of her complicated sexual life. Mavor's biographies include the intriguing *The Ladies of Llangollen: A Study in Romantic Friendship* (1971), dealing with the relationship between Lady Eleanor Butler and Sarah Ponsonby who, in 1778, shocked society by setting up a remote home together in Wales.

MAXTON, Hugh, pseud of W J McCormack
(1947–)

Irish poet and critic, born in County Wicklow. A lecturer in Modern Literature at Trinity College Dublin, he brought a new severity to analysis of Irish studies with two volumes of literary criticism, *Sheridan Le Fanu and Victorian Ireland* (1980) and *The Battle of the Books* (1987). As Hugh Maxton (after **Hugh MacDiarmid** and James Maxton), his challenging, sometimes cryptic verse fuses mid-European themes with modern Irish political and social concerns. *Jubilee for Renegades: Poems 1976–1980* (1982), *The Puzzle Tree Ascendant* (1988) and *New and Selected Poems: The Engraved Passion* (1991) show a remarkable willingness to experiment with form, and present a humane and liberating philosophy.

MAXWELL, William
(1908–)

American novelist, story writer and critic, born in Lincoln, Illinois. From 1936 he worked (eventually becoming fiction editor) for the *New Yorker* magazine, of whose values his readable and well-crafted novels might be called an enshrinement. Reacting against the protesting note to be found in the fiction of **Sherwood Anderson** and the early **Sinclair Lewis**, Maxwell found beauty and dignity in the midwestern middle-class: *They Come Like Swallows* (1937) tells of the way in which a mother's premature death affects an Illinois household, while *The Folded Leaf* (1945) is about two midwestern students who have to try to come to terms with what they are offered by their limited circumstances. Maxwell also wrote many short stories.

MAY, Thomas
(1595–1650)

English dramatist and historian, born in Sussex. He was educated at Sidney Sussex College, Cambridge, and became a member of Gray's Inn and a courtier. He wrote dramas, comedies, poems and translations of **Lucan**'s *Pharsalia* (1627), **Virgil**'s *Georgics* (1628) and **Martial** (1629). A Puritan, he was secretary and official historian to the Long Parliament, and produced a *History of the Parliament 1640–1643* (1647), and a *Breviary* (1650).

▷ A G Chester, *Thomas May: man of letters* (1932)

MAYAKOVSKY, Vladimir Vladimirovich
(1894–1930)

Russian poet and playwright, born in Bagdadi (now Mayakovsky), Georgia. The son of an impoverished Russian nobleman, he was involved in the Social Democratic movement during his youth, but when he was imprisoned for 11 months he renounced politics for art. Writing was his first love, however, and in 1912 he wrote a poem that was published in the miscellany *Poshchochina obshchestvennomu vkusu* ('A Slap in the Face of Public Taste'). An enthusiastic supporter of the Revolution in 1917, both his play *Misteriya-Buff* (1918, Eng trans *Mystery-Bouffe*, 1968) and the long poem *150 000 000* (1919–20) are masterpieces of the period. But when the Civil War ended and the New Economy Policy was introduced in 1921, he found himself at odds with the new, conservative leaders. In response he wrote *Pro eto* (1923, 'About This'), poems pre-Revolution in sentiment, and satirical plays like *Klop* (1929, Eng trans *The Bedbug*, 1960) and *Banya* (1930, Eng trans *The Bath-House*, 1966), concerned with the betrayal of the Revolution by its self-appointed officials. His fame in the former Soviet Union is dependent on three works: *Vladimir Ilyich Lenin* (1924), *Khorosho!* (1927, 'Good!') and the unfinished *Vo ves golos* (1929–30, translated into Scots by **Edwin Morgan**, 1972). Towards the end of his life he was severely castigated by more orthodox Soviet writers and critics for his outspoken criticism of the bureaucracy and his unconventional opinions on art, and was even forced to abandon the Left Front for the Arts for the reactionary Russian Association of Proletarian Writers. But he was always regarded as an outsider, and this, together with an unstable personal life, undoubtedly contributed towards his suicide.

▷ E Brown, *Mayakovsky: a poet in the revolution* (1973)

MAYHEW, Henry
(1812–87)

English author, born in London, and first joint editor of *Punch* with **Mark Lemon**. He ran away from Westminster School and collaborated with his brother Augustus (1826–75) in writing numerous successful novels such as *The Good Genius that turns Everything to Gold* (1847) and *Whom to Marry* (1848). He also wrote on many subjects, his best-known work being the classic social survey, *London Labour and the London Poor* (1851–62). Another brother, Horace (1816–72), also collaborated with Henry and was a contributor to *Punch*.

▷G S Jones, *Outcast London* (1971)

MAYKOV, Appolon
(1821–97)

Russian poet, born in Moscow into a noble family. His father was a painter and his mother was a writer. Conservative critics pronounced him the heir of **Pushkin** for his careful and chiselled poetry, but after his death he was rightly relegated to the role of skilful (and often tedious) minor poet. There are some translations of his work in John Pollen's *Russian Songs and Lyrics* (1917).

MAYNE, Jasper
(1604–72)

English playwright and poet, born in Hatherleigh, Devon. He is known as the author of two plays, *The City March* (1638) and *The Amorous War* (1648), both clearly influenced by **Ben Jonson**. The former is a satire set in London, portraying the duping of a rich uncle by an unscrupulous nephew, while the latter is a tragi-comedy dealing with love and infidelity. They are rumbustious pieces, but sprawling and cumbersome; they are forgotten now, and the more uncharitable might add that it is not without good reason. Mayne was also the author of a volume of verse, *To The Duke of York on Our Late Sea Flight* (1665).

MAYNE, Seymour
(1944–)

Canadian poet and broadcaster. Mayne was born in Montreal and in 1985 became Professor of English at Ottawa University. The titles of his collections—*Diaspora* (1977), *Abel and Cain* (1980) and *The Impossible Promised Land* (1981)—reflect the biblical and Jewish preoccupations of his verse. His work has been described as 'persistent'. He is certainly energetic and in addition to his writing and broadcasting has edited several magazines and founded two small presses.

MAZURANIĆ, Ivan
(1814–90)

Croatian poet and politician, born in Novi Vinodol. He completed the missing two cantos of the *Osman* of **Gundulic**. His epic *Smrt Smail-age Cengica* (1846, Eng trans *The Death of Smail Aga*, 1918) is often pointed to as the finest Croatian poem of its century. It tells of the 1840 execution by ambush, at the hands of the Montenegrins, of a tax-collecting Turk, but is unusual in that it gives some dignity to the greedy tyrant. Mazuranić was governor of Croatia from 1873, and was also an educational reformer.

▷*Slavonic and East European Review*, XLIV (1966)

McALMON, Robert
(1896–1956)

American writer, small-press publisher and literary socialite, long resident in Paris, a member of the 'lost generation' of **Gertrude Stein**. His own verse and prose are unimportant and characterized by what a critic called 'pathetic nihilism'; but his mediocre career and his autobiography, *Geniuses Together* (1938), are of genuine interest.

▷R E Kroll, *Robert McAlmon: Expatriate Publisher and Writer* (1957)

McAULEY, James
(1917–76)

Australian poet, critic and writer, born in Lakemba, Sydney. He spent much time during and after World War II in Papua New Guinea, where he likened the destruction there of traditional social structures to the larger upheavals of the western world. His verse, unlike that of his contemporaries, is of a classical and visionary style, and was first collected in *Under Aldebaran* (1946). Never a copious writer, his second volume, *A Vision of Ceremony*, did not appear until 1956, followed by *Captain Quiros* (1964), an epic narrative of the 16th-century Portuguese explorer of Melanesia. Not sympathetic to modern fashions, in 1955 McAuley foisted on Max Harris, unsuspecting editor of a modernistic broadsheet *Angry Penguins*, the collected works of a fictitious dead poet, 'Ern Malley', thus hastening the demise of that periodical and starting a controversy which lasted for 40 years. McAuley founded the conservative literary and political journal *Quadrant* and edited it from its inception in 1956 to 1963. He also published some books of critical writing and compiled *A Map of Australian Verse: The Twentieth Century* (1975).

McBAIN, Ed *see* HUNTER, Evan

McCARTHY, Cormac
(1933–)

American novelist, born in Rhode Island but educated in Tennessee. He began publishing in the sixties and seventies. His first novels were Gothic and grotesque stories about life in the Southern backwoods. Early books such as *Child of God* (1974) lapsed into incredible depths of depravity and violence. In more recent fiction, particularly with the epic *Blood Meridian* (1985), McCarthy has achieved a powerfully descriptive narrative style. *All the Pretty Horses* (1993), the first book in a projected trilogy, was universally greeted as his finest work.

McCARTHY, Justin
(1830–1912)

Irish politician, novelist and historian, born in Cork. He joined the staff of the *Northern Times*, Liverpool, in 1853, and in 1860 entered the reporters' gallery for the *Morning Star*, becoming its chief editor in 1864. He resigned in 1868, and devoted the next three years to a tour of the USA. Soon after his return he became connected with the *Daily News*, and contributed to the *London*, *Westminster* and *Fortnightly Reviews*. He entered parliament in 1879 for Longford. He is better known, however, as a novelist than as a politician. His novels include *Dear Lady Disdain* (1875) and *Miss Misanthrope* (1877). Other works include *A History of our Own Times* (7 vols, 1879–1905) and *The Four Georges and William IV* (4 vols, 1889–1901).
▷ *An Irishman's Story* (1904)

McCARTHY, Mary Thérèse
(1912–89)

American novelist and critic, born in Seattle, Washington, of mixed Catholic, Protestant and Jewish descent. She and her three younger brothers were orphaned as young children in 1918 and they were raised by grandparents, uncles and aunts. At the age of eight she won a state prize for an article entitled 'The Irish in American History'. She was educated at Forest Ridge Convent, Seattle, and Anne Wright Seminary, Tacoma, and graduated from Vassar College, New York in 1933. She married an actor, Harold Johnsrud, who died in a fire. She began to write book reviews for the *Nation* and the *New Republic* and was an editor for *Covici Friede* in 1936–7; from 1937 to 1948 she was an editor and theatre critic for the *Partisan Review*, during which period she wrote articles, stories and eventually novels. In 1938 she married the critic **Edmund Wilson**, but they divorced soon afterwards. In 1948 she married Bowden Bowater, whom she divorced in 1961 to marry James West, an information officer. Her voice has often been described as scathing, yet although she brought little emotional warmth to her work, she was a highly intelligent, observant novelist. Her best-known fiction is *The Company She Keeps* (1942), *The Groves of Academe* (1952) and *The Group* (1963), a bestseller about eight Vassar graduates and their sex lives. She also wrote documentary denunciations of US involvement in the Vietnam war,

in *Vietnam* (1967) and *Hanoi* (1968). Other works include *A Charmed Life* (1955), *Sights and Spectacles* (1956), the autobiographical *Memories of a Catholic Childhood* (1957) and *Cannibals and Missionaries* (1979).
▷ C Gerlderman, *Mary McCarthy* (1988)

McCLURE, James Howe
(1939–)

British crime novelist, born and educated in South Africa, on whose political and cultural situation he commented through the medium of the 'police procedural' and through the relationship of the white policeman Lieutenant Kramer and his Zulu assistant Sergeant Zondi. They first appeared in *The Steam Pig* (1971) and *The Caterpillar Cop* (1972), elegantly plotted thrillers revealing a journalist's eye for significant detail; McClure has worked for several newspapers in South Africa, and subbed for some years on the *Oxford Times* and *Oxford Mail* (1966–74). Other Kramer and Zondi novels include *The Gooseberry Fool* (1974) and *The Blood of an Englishman* (1980). McClure has also written 'ride-along' accounts of police activity in Liverpool (*Spike Island*, 1980) and San Diego (*Copworld*, 1985).

McCLURE, Michael Thomas
(1932–)

American poet, born in Marysville, Kansas, and educated there and in Arizona and California. He has taught at the California College of Arts and Crafts in Oakland since 1962. A highly prolific writer, much of his work reflects his interest in visual imagery, often of an apocalyptically violent nature and frequently combining historical characters, chiefly outlaws, in surreal juxtaposition. McClure's interest in Native American anthropology and in European post-Symbolist styles is reflected in the titles of his second and third volumes, *Peyote Poem* (1958) and *For Artaud* (1959), but it was with his fourth, the fiery *Hymns to St Geryon and Other Poems* (1959) that he emerged as an individual voice; it was the first of his collections to appear (1969) in the UK. The important prose *Meat Science Essays* (1963) appeared in Britain shorn of the notorious opening piece 'Phi Upsilon Kappa', a Lawrentian discourse on the word 'fuck'. McClure writes in a passionate upper-case telegraphese, a title like *Oh Christ God Love Cry of Love Stifled Furred Wall Smoking Burning* (1969) is representative. Later volumes are more conventionally lyrical and include *September Blackberries* (1974) and *Fragments of Perseus* (1978). McClure has also written experimental plays and appeared as an actor in two of **Norman Mailer**'s films.

McCONKEY, James Rodney
(1921–)

American novelist and academic, born in Ohio. McConkey taught at Cornell and his literary criticism includes *The Novels of E. M. Forster* (1957) and *Chekhov and our Age* (1985). Memory is a constant refrain in his fiction. *Crossroads* (1968) contains fragments of autobiography and in *The Tree House Confessions* (1979) a 50-year-old man dredges up memories of the past when visiting a treehouse built for his dead son. Memory is again at play in a recent title: *Kayo: the Authentic and Annotated Autobiographical Novel from Outer Space* (1987).

McCORD, David Thompson Watson
(1897–)

American writer of light verse. A graduate of Harvard, McCord was for a while editor of its *Alumni Bulletin*. *One At A Time* (1977) brings together work from five collections of children's and humorous verse. The earlier *Selected Poems* (1957) is amusingly annotated by McCord himself. In an extended career he has published books consistently at the rate of a volume a year since the mid-1920s. In addition to his own poetry, which displays good command of metre and rhyme, he will be remembered for *What Cheer*, an anthology of humorous verse which he edited in 1945.

McCORMACK, W J *see* MAXTON, Hugh

McCORMICK, Eric Hall
(1906–)

New Zealand cultural historian, born in Taihape. As biographer, editor and critic he contributed greatly to the recognition of New Zealand literature from 1940. He was secretary of, and later editor to, the National Historical Committee which commissioned publications to mark the centenary of European settlement in 1840. For this series he wrote *Letters and Art in New Zealand* (1940), the first critical conspectus of New Zealand writing. This was later expanded as *New Zealand Literature: A Survey* (1959). His other critical works include *Alexander Turnbull: His Life, His Circle, His Collections* (1974), on the wealthy merchant who left his library of 50 000 books to the nation; biographies of prominent New Zealand scholars, and studies of a New Zealand artist in *The Expatriate, a Study of Frances Hodgkins* (1954) and *Portrait of Frances Hodgkins* (1981). *The Inland Eye: a Sketch in Visual Autobiography* (1959) gives his personal and critical creed.

McCOY, Horace
(1897–1955)

American novelist and journalist, born in Tennessee, best-known as the author of *They Shoot Horses Don't They* (1935), his first novel. He had worked as a mechanic, salesman and taxi driver before joining the *Dallas Journal*, and publishing his first story, *Brass Buttons*, in 1927. Much of his early work was printed in detective magazines such as *Black Mask*. *No Pockets in a Shroud* (1937), about corruption beneath the surface of an apparently decent American town, *I Should Have Stayed Home* (1938), a portrait of degenerate Hollywood life, along with later books, confirmed McCoy's bleak outlook, as did the Sydney Pollack movie of *They Shoot Horses Don't They* (1969).

McCRACKEN, Esther Helen, née Armstrong
(1902–71)

English playwright and actress, born in Newcastle-upon-Tyne. From 1924 to 1937 she acted with the Newcastle Repertory Company. Her first play, *The Willing Spirit*, was produced in 1936, but it was with *Quiet Wedding* (1938) that her reputation was made as a writer of domestic comedy. Other successes were *Quiet Weekend* (1941) and *No Medals* (1944). Her first husband, Lt-Col Angus McCracken, died in action in 1943, and the following year she married Mungo Campbell.

McCRAE, George Gordon
(1833–1927)

Scottish-born Australian poet, born in Leith, Edinburgh, the eldest son of lawyer Andrew Murison McCrae, Writer to the Signet, and father of **Hugh McCrae**. He went with his mother the artist Georgiana Huntly McCrae to Australia in 1841 and developed an affection for the aborigines. He first published *Two Old Men's Tales of Love and War* (1865) and, two years later, *The Story of Balladeädro* and *Mämba, 'The Bright-Eyed'*, some of the earliest Australian poems on aboriginal themes. A selection of his varied verse was published in 1915 as *The Fleet and Convoy and Other Verses*.
▷H McCrae, *My Father and My Father's Friends* (1935)

McCRAE, Hugh Raymond
(1876–1958)

Australian artist and poet, born in Melbourne, son of **George McCrae**. He spent some time in New York and returned to make a precarious living by acting small parts in plays and films, and contributing sketches and verse to the *Bulletin*. He published much verse, often illustrated by his close friend **Norman Lindsay**. *Silvarum Libri* (1909) was reissued as *Satyrs and Sunlight* in 1911. The titles of his collections echo the world of **Norman Gale** and **Rupert Brooke**: *Colombine* (1920), *Idyllia* (1922), *Forests of Pan* (1944) and *Voice of the Forest* (1945). *The Best Poems of Hugh McCrae*, ed R G Howarth, appeared in 1961.

McCUAIG, Ronald
(1908–93)

Australian journalist and lyric poet, born in Newcastle, New South Wales. He was the writer of satirical verse for the *Bulletin* between the wars, which was privately published as *Vaudeville* (1938) and *The Wanton Goldfish* (1941), collected in *Quod Ronald McCuaig* (1946) and further cumulated in *The Ballad of Bloodthirsty Bessie* (1961). His style varied between crude cynicism and delicate 17th-century pastiches; examples of both are in *The Passionate Clerk: Selected Poems* (1992).

McCULLERS, (Lula) Carson, née Smith
(1917–67)

American novelist, born in Columbus, Georgia, where she was brought up and attended high school, graduating in 1933. Between 1934 and 1936 she went to classes at Columbia University, New York, and New York University. In 1937 she married Reeves McCullers, with whom she moved to Charlotte, North Carolina; in 1941 they moved to Greenwich Village and divorced, but were remarried in 1945, finally divorcing again in 1948. *The Heart is a Lonely Hunter*, her first book, about a deaf mute, appeared in 1940, distinguishing her immediately as a novelist of note. She wrote the best and the bulk of her work in a six-year spell through World War II. Along with **William Faulkner**, **Tennessee Williams** and **Truman Capote** she is credited with fashioning a type of fiction labelled by critics as Southern Gothic. Fusing, in her own words, 'anguish and farce', she peopled her work with grotesque characters who are expressionistic extensions of normal, universal human problems. *Reflections in a Golden Eye* appeared in 1941, followed by *The Member of the Wedding* (1946), *The Ballad of the Sad Cafe* (1951) and *Clock Without Hands*, a last ironic look at the South, in 1961.
▷ V S Carr, *The Lonely Hunter* (1975)

McCULLEY, Johnston
(1883–1958)

American popular novelist, born in Ottawa, Illinois (not in Canada, as is sometimes supposed). He is known primarily for the creation of Zorro, a mysterious nemesis with a lightning sword-blade and the ability to vanish apparently at will. McCulley wrote more than 25 Zorro stories, beginning with *The Mask of Zorro* (1924)—masks feature with disconcerting prominence in his work—and continuing through highly successful radio and television series. The prose scarcely commands serious attention, but his main character is one of the great popular creations.

McCULLOUGH, Colleen
(1937–)

Australian novelist, born in Wellington, best known for the Cleary family's saga of sex, religion and disaster, *The Thorn Birds* (1977), later produced as a televison series. Her earlier book *Tim* (1974) was also filmed, as was *An Indecent Obsession* (1981). A delicate novella, *The Ladies of Missalonghi* (1987) showed that she is capable of some fine writing, and her latest books, a series of six novels set in Ancient Rome, demonstrate a concern for historical detail.

McCUTCHEON, George Barr
(1866–1928)

Prolific American novelist, born in Indiana. McCutcheon worked for a time on his hometown paper, the *Lafayette Chronicle*, but resigned as soon as his fiction became successful. He is still best-known for his two early books, *Graustark* (1901), set in an imaginary Balkan kindgom, à la *The Prisoner of Zenda*, and *Brewster's Millions* (1902), an account of the farcical consequences of suddenly inheriting a fortune. The second of these was turned into a British film in 1935, and there have been several remakes. McCutcheon's readers were hungry for more Balkan adventure and he obliged with two sequels and other novels in similar vein. His own favourite was his single realistic novel, *Mary Midthorne* (1911).

McDONALD, Nan(cy May)
(1921–74)

Australian poet, born in Eastwood, Sydney, who for much of her life was editor for the publishers Angus & Robertson. *Pacific Sea* (1947) won the inaugural Grace Leven Prize for Poetry. Other books were *The Lonely Fire* (1954) and *The Lighthouse and Other Poems* (1959). *Selected Poems* was published in 1969. Her stoic reflections on life and suffering seem to anticipate her early death from cancer.

McDONALD, Roger
(1941–)

Australian novelist and poet, born in Sydney. Following two books of verse, *Citizens of Mist* (1968) and *Airship* (1975), he turned to fiction with *1915* (1979), a highly successful retelling of the Gallipoli campaign which was later turned into an award-winning television series. His second novel, *Slipstream* (1982), is loosely based on the exploits of pioneer aviator Charles Kingsford Smith. His third, *Rough Wallaby* (1989), is a comedy of crooked doings on and off the racetrack. A work of non-fiction, *Shearer's Hotel* (1992), is based on the writer's experiences as camp cook for itinerant shearers in the outback and won the 'Banjo' Award for non-fiction in 1993. *Water Man* (1993) describes the grip of a long-dead water diviner on an outback town.

McEWAN, Ian Russell
(1948–)

English novelist and author of screenplays and short stories, born in Aldershot, Hampshire, and educated at the universities of Sussex and East Anglia. His first books, the short-story collections *First Love, Last Rites* (1975) and *In Between the Sheets* (1978), combine elegant writing with explicit sexual imagery and themes of obsession and perversion, and drew immediate critical controversy. The novel, *The Comfort of Strangers* (1981), while still macabre has a greater psychological depth. *The Child in Time* (1987) deals sympathetically with the emotional trauma experienced by a couple whose infant daughter is stolen and never discovered. His oratorio, *Or Shall We Die?* (1983), is an impassioned outcry against nuclear arms, while the screenplay for the film *The Ploughman's Lunch* (1983) bleakly and wittily satirizes the political atmosphere under Margaret Thatcher's Conservative government. Later novels include *The Innocent* (1990), a thriller set in Germany during the 1950s, and *Black Dogs* (1992).

McFARLANE, John Ebenezer Clare
(1894–1962)

Jamaican poet, born in Spanish Town and educated at Cornwall College. He joined the civil service, rising to the rank of Financial Secretary of Jamaica. He founded the Poetry League of Jamaica in 1923, became its second poet laureate, and edited the first anthology of Jamaican poetry, *Voices from Summerland* (1929). His taste and poetic style were romantic, as shown in his narrative poems, *Beatrice* (1918), *Daphne* (1931) and *The Magdalen* (1957), and shorter *Poems* (1924); but his most valuable contribution to West Indian literature was as patron and critic.

McFEE, William Morley Punshon
(1881–1966)

English-born American novelist and short-story writer. McFee's first book, *Letters from an Ocean Tramp* (1908), reflected his experience as a ship's engineer. Later he served with the British Navy in World War I, although by this time his home was in the USA. *Aliens* (1914) and *Casuals of the Sea* (1916), his first two novels, both focused on the experiences of British families during the war. Sometimes compared to **Conrad**, merely because so much of his fiction is set at sea, McFee's narrative voice, especially in the short stories (which feature Chief Engineer Spenlove, McFee's *alter ego*) is closer to **Somerset Maugham**.

McGAHERN, John
(1934–)

Irish novelist and short-story writer, born and educated in Dublin. His first novel was *The Barracks* (1963), a highly acclaimed study of a family, set in a provincial Irish police station. Its successor, *The Dark* (1965), was no less concentrated but it also signalled the beginning of a certain claustrophobia in McGahern's writing that persisted through the short-story collection *Nightlines* (1970) and a third novel, *The Leavetaking* (1974, rev edn 1984), and virtually exhausted itself in *The Pornographer* (1979), which explores the gap between the written and unwritten worlds, the fantasy of sex and the reality of death. McGahern had worked as a primary-school teacher in Dublin from 1963 to 1970, and held a research fellowship at the University of Reading for the final two years of that period. His work of the 1980s was—with the exception of the stories in *High Ground* (1985)—less successful than his first three books, but he returned to form with *Amongst Women* (1990), the story of an elderly IRA man, which was shortlisted for the Booker Prize.

McGEE, Thomas D'Arcy
(1825–68)

Irish-born Canadian writer and politician, born in Carlingford, County Louth. Educated at a Catholic 'hedge school', he was influenced by the mass movements of the Rev Theobald Mathew and Daniel O'Connell against drink and the Union. He became Editor of the Catholic *Boston Pilot* at the age of 19, wrote fiction and supported a variety of romantic causes, returning to Ireland in 1845 where he was identified with the Young Ireland *Nation*. After the abortive rebellion of 1848 he returned to the USA, where he argued for US annexation of Canada in his New York *Nation*. He lost Catholic support by sympathy for Mazzini's anti-Papal Roman Republic, and started the *American Celt* in Boston, publishing high-flown Romantic poems and *A History of the Irish settlers in North America* (1851). He moved to Montreal in 1857, founded the *New Era* newspaper, took Canadian citizenship and became an MP in 1858, and was Minister of Agriculture

(1864–8). He was a strong advocate of Canadian Confederation. He was assassinated in Ottawa for his opposition to a threatened Fenian invasion of Canada. His literary work as poet, publicist and political thinker improved as he aged; his published works included *A Popular History of Ireland* (1862–9) and *Poems* (1869).

▷ I M Skelton, *The Life of Thomas McGee* (1925)

McGINLEY, Phyllis
(1905–78)

American (Roman Catholic) author of skilful light verse, born in Oregon. She was very widely read during her lifetime, during which she was praised by **W H Auden**; but her work has failed to last, not being quite of the order of that of **Harry Graham**, **Ogden Nash** and others of that calibre. Many of her verses appeared in the *New Yorker*. She also wrote successful and charming books for children.

McGONAGALL, William
(c.1825–1902)

Scottish poet and novelist, son of an immigrant Irish weaver. He spent some of his childhood on the island of South Ronaldsay in the Orkneys, settled with his family in Dundee at the age of 11, and became a handloom weaver with his father. In 1846 he married Jean King. He did some acting at Dundee's Royal Theatre, and in 1878 published his first collection of poems, including 'Railway Bridge of the Silvery Tay'. From then on he travelled in central Scotland, giving readings and selling his poetry in broadsheets. In Edinburgh he was lionized by the legal and student fraternity. He visited London in 1880 and New York in 1887. His poems are uniformly bad, but possess a disarming naivety and a calypso-like disregard for metre which remain entertaining. His *Poetic Gems* were published in 1890, and *More Poetic Gems* in 1962, followed by others.

McGOUGH, Roger
(1937–)

English poet, playwright and performer, born in Liverpool and associated for ever with the 'Mersey Sound', a title used for the hugely successful *Penguin Modern Poets 10* (1967, 1974, 1983), which he shared with **Adrian Henri** and **Brian Patten**. Educated at Hull University, he worked as a schoolteacher and art college lecturer; he enjoyed brief, bizarre pop success with the performing group Scaffold. McGough's characteristic stance is the lugubrious self-ironizing wit and runaway punning that John Lennon brought to Beatles interviews, with something of the same faintly adolescent desire to shock. Much more of a 'street' poet than either Henri or Patten, he uses the rhythms of speech in a curiously subversive way. This was evident in the novel-plus-poems *Frinck, A Life in the Day of, and Summer with Monika* (1967), and it saw service again in collections like *Gig* (1973), *In the Glassroom* (1976) and the superb *Waving at Trains* (1982). McGough has written many plays, often with music, and a number of funny children's books.

McGRATH, John Peter
(1935–)

English writer, director and film-maker, born in Birkenhead, Cheshire. Following National Service, he studied at St John's College, Oxford (1955–9), where his earliest plays were performed. Subsequently moving into television, he was one of the creators of the innovative police drama series *Z Cars* in 1962, and wrote such programmes as *Diary of A Nobody* (1966) before writing the film scripts *Billion Dollar Brain* (1967) and *The Bofors Gun* (1968). In 1971 he founded the 7:84 Theatre Company, which dedicated itself to the production of radical populist drama and took its name from the fact that 7 per cent of the population owned 84 per cent of the country's wealth. Artistic Director of 7:84 Scotland from 1973 to 1988, with his plays he attempted to illuminate Scottish historical struggles and explore issues vital to the current political agenda in the country. Notable works include *The Cheviot, The Stag and The Black, Black Oil* (1973), *The Game's A Bogey* (1974) and *Women in Power* (1983). As founder of Freeway Films in 1983 he has made such television drama as *Blood Red Roses* (1986) and *Border Warfare* (1988) and the film *The Dressmaker* (1988). His passionate and critical commitment to Scottish theatre is reflected in books like *The Bone Won't Break: On Theatre and Hope in Hard Times* (1990). Recent work, such as *Waiting for the Dolphins* (1991) and *The Wicked Old Man* (1992), has seen him question the changing validity of socialism in contemporary Europe.

▷ A Bold, 'The Impact of 7:84', in *Modern Scottish Literature* (1983)

McGRATH, Patrick
(1950–)

English novelist and short-story writer, born in London; he grew up near Broadmoor Hospital, where his father was Medical Superintendent for many years. Perhaps partly as a result, his writing reveals a grim, Gothic imagination, in the tradition of **Edgar Allan Poe**, spiced with mordant comedy. His first collection of short stories, *Blood and Water and Other Tales*, appeared in 1989, as did his first, macabre novel *The Grotesque*, a gripping tale involving the tense relationship between a landowner and his butler. *Spider* (1990), and the excellent and compulsive *Dr Haggard's Disease* (1993), continue to exploit psychological horror in vivid, taut, elegant prose.

McGUANE, Thomas Francis, III
(1939–)

American novelist. He was born and educated in Michigan, which is the setting of his first comic novel, *The Sporting Club* (1968). Its guying of the **Hemingway** code is equally evident in a third novel, *Ninety-Two in the Shade* (1973), which deals with big-game fishing among the Florida Keys. McGuane scripted and directed a Hollywood version of the book, having already written a screenplay for another Michigan story, *The Bushwhacked Piano* (1970, 'novelized' 1971), and for the Marlon Brando vehicle, *The Missouri Breaks* (1976). In that year, he married (and divorced) the actress Margot Kidder. Subsequent novels have been less powerful; they include *Panama* (1978), *Nobody's Angel* (1982), *Something to Be Desired* (1984) and *Keep the Change* (1989). *An Outside Chance* (1980) is a collection of essays on sport and his collected stories are contained in *To Skin a Cat* (1986).

McGUCKIAN, Medbh, née McCaughan
(1950–)

Irish poet. Born in Belfast, she received a convent education there before studying English at Queen's University. She has been a school-teacher in Belfast since 1975 and was married two years later. Her first volume, *Single Ladies: Sixteen Poems*, appeared in 1980; it has a directness that she was later to reject in favour of the denser language of *The Flower Master* (1982) and, her most important work to date, *Venus and the Rain* (1984). Despite the obvious artifice and craft of her later work, its emotional range is increasingly simple and accessible.

McGUINNESS, Frank
(1956–)

Irish playwright, born in Buncrana, County Donegal; he moved to Dublin as a teacher in the mid-1980s. An early play, *The Factory Girls* (1982, rev edn 1988), gave evidence of his ambition to give voice to the misunderstood or the misrepresented. This was given most eloquent substance in his questioning of tribalism, enforced fidelities and personal loyalties in *Observe the Sons of Ulster Marching Towards the Somme* (1985). Its questioning of the traditional nationalist/loyalist divide was followed by the blistering anger against human waste of

Carthaginians (1988), which debated the false evaluation of martyrdom that prevented dialogue in his native Ulster for much of the latter part of the 20th century.

McILVANNEY, William Angus
(1936–)

Scottish novelist and poet, born in Kilmarnock, Ayrshire, brother of sports writer Hugh McIlvanney. He was educated at Kilmarnock Academy and Glasgow University and taught from 1960 to 1975, when he took up writing full-time. His first novel was *Remedy is None* (1966), a paean to working-class values, in which a student avenges what he surmises is his mother's betrayal of his father. *A Gift from Nessus*, published two years later, developed the same theme as a travelling salesman chooses self-assertion over self-destruction. With *Docherty* (1975) McIlvanney extended his range without abandoning his roots, in the convincing story of the eponymous 'hard man', an Ayrshire miner, whose uncompromising life is seen through the eyes of his son. It won the Whitbread Award. *The Big Man* (1985) was set in similar territory and pitched Dan Scoular, a hero in his own locality, into a bare-knuckle fight where there is more at stake than money. Though he has been described by **Alan Bold** as 'a rhetorician occasionally overcome by his own verbosity', he has an enviable way with metaphor and simile and in the thrillers featuring the Glasgow detective Jack Laidlaw—*Laidlaw* (1977), *The Papers of Tony Veitch* (1983) and *Strange Loyalties* (1991)—comparisons with **Raymond Chandler** are not inappropriate. Volumes of poetry include *The Longships in Harbour* (1970) and *These Words* (1984). His short stories are collected in *Walking Wounded* (1989), and his essays and journalism in *Surviving the Shipwreck* (1991).

McINERNEY, Jay
(1955–)

American novelist, born in Hartford, Connecticut. His early posts included being a reader for Random House publishers, and working as one of the fabled fact-checkers on the *New Yorker* magazine. The latter occupation is the profession of the central character of his novel *Bright Lights, Big City* (1984), an acclaimed account of young New York professionals during the 1980s boom years. *Brightness Falls* (1992) is, as the title suggests, a companion piece or antidote to the earlier work, representing a move away from the frenzied trendies of *Bright Lights, Big City* into the real world where yuppies grow old and marriages crumble. His other works include *Ransom* (1985), being the titular character's experiences in contemporary Japan.

McINTYRE, Duncan Ban, English name of **Donnchadh Ban Macan t-Saoir** (1724–1812)

Gaelic poet, and gamekeeper of Bein-nodòrain, born in Glenorchy, Argyll. He worked as a forester, fought as a Hanoverian at Falkirk in 1746, and from 1799 to 1806 was one of the City Guard of Edinburgh. He composed a great deal of rich, celebratory nature poetry which, since he was illiterate, was written down by the minister's son at Killin and published in a collection of 1768. Some of it has been translated into English by **Hugh MacDiarmid** and **Iain Crichton-Smith**, including his long poem 'Moladh Beinn Dòbhrainn' ('The Praise of Ben Doran'). He also wrote formal occasional verse, love poems, satires and songs.

McKAY, Claude, originally **Festus Claudius** (1889–1948)

American poet and novelist, and supposed instigator of the 'Harlem Renaissance' in Afro–American writing. McKay was born in Jamaica, where he served as a policeman—an experience recounted in *Constab Ballads* (1912)—before moving to the USA and a period of study at **Booker T Washington**'s Tuskegee Institute in Alabama. During the 1920s and the early 1930s he mostly lived abroad, working on a communist newspaper in London (1919–20), before returning to New York to co-edit the *Liberator* (1921–2). His fourth and most important poetry collection, *Harlem Shadows* (1922), asserted a kind of instinctualism at odds with his socialist principles. In 1922 he moved to the new Soviet Union for a year, living in France and Tangier for the next decade before returning to New Deal America. His most important fiction was written abroad: *Home to Harlem* (1928), *Banjo* (1929) and *Banana Bottom* (1933). McKay's fiction portrayed the Afro–American as a repository of essentially non-intellectual and explicitly sexual energies. It was a view that had a major impact on both black and white reactions to his race. His autobiography, *A Long Way from Home* (1937), predated his religious conversion, but the decision was clearly anticipated in his thinking during the mid-thirties.

▷W F Cooper, *Claude McKay: Rebel Sojourner in the Harlem Renaissance* (1987)

McKENNA, Stephen (1888–1967)

English novelist, born in London. His socio-political novels of the rich upper crust, of which he was a member, are now virtually forgotten; but they were intelligent, if not penetrating, accounts of what he saw and understood in the course of a career in government posts. His only real success was *Sonia* (1917), a melodramatic but skilful chronicle of fashionable life in the first years of the 20th century. *While I Remember* (1921) is autobiographical.

McKIE, Ronald (1909–91)

Australian journalist and writer, born in Toowoomba, Queensland, who worked in Singapore and China before serving with the Australian forces in World War II. He was a war correspondent in Burma and Italy, and after the war covered the Potsdam Conference and the trial of Norwegian traitor Vidkun Quisling. His war books include an account of the Japanese invasion of Singapore, *This Was Singapore* (1942), *Proud Echo* (1953) and *The Heroes* (1960), which describes the barbaric executions of prisoners-of-war in Singapore. He wrote other books on South-East Asia, and three novels; the award-winning *The Mango Tree* (1974), a tale of Australian childhood in the early years of this century which won the **Miles Franklin** Award, *The Crushing* (1977), a tragi-comedy of social pretensions in a small Queensland sugar town, and *Bitter Bread* (1978), a study of contrasting characters in the Depression years. *We Have no Dreaming* (1988) is an autobiographical journey which takes a sympathetic look at the Australian search for identity.

McLUHAN, (Herbert) Marshall (1911–80)

Canadian writer, born in Edmonton. He studied English literature at the universities of Manitoba and Cambridge. In 1946 he became professor at St Michael's College, Toronto. In 1963, having directed two surveys into culture and communication media, he was appointed director of the University of Toronto's Centre for Culture and Technology. He held controversial views on the effect of the communication media on the development of civilization, claiming that it is the media *per se*, not the information and ideas which they disseminate, that influence society. He sees the invention of printing, with its emphasis on the eye rather than the ear, as the destroyer of a cohesive, inter-dependent society, since it encouraged man to be more introspective, individualistic and self-centred. His publications include *The Mechanical Bride* (1951), *The Gutenberg Galaxy* (1962), *Understanding Media* (1964), *The Medium is the Message* (with Q Fiore, 1967) and *Counter-Blast* (1970).

▷D Duffy, *Marshall McLuhan* (1969)

McMURTRY, Larry Jeff
(1936–)

American novelist, born in Wichita Falls, Texas, whose vision of his state's history has gone some considerable way towards establishing the generic Western as a serious contemporary form. He attended North Texas State College at Denton and then Rice University, Houston, where he later taught. In addition to academia, McMurtry has worked as a journalist and antiquarian bookseller, but Hollywood's interest in his work consolidated his reputation, often at the expense of his more strictly literary worth—*Horseman, Pass By* (1961) was successfully filmed (and re-issued, 1963) as *Hud*, and McMurtry wrote the screenplay for Peter Bogdanovich's prize-winning movie of his third novel, *The Last Picture Show* (1966). Later books also dealt with the opposition of freedom and rootedness, new and inherited values, and a kind of heroic resistance to circumstance. This was evident, among others, in *All My Friends are Going to be Strangers* (1972), the comic *Terms of Endearment* (1975), basis of a third successful film, and in *Cadillac Jack* (1982), but it was with *Lonesome Dove* (1985), the epic story of a quixotic cattle drive from Texas to Montana, that McMurtry staked his claim to greatness. Subsequent works include *Some Can Whistle* (1989), which some took to be a fragment of autobiography, and the disappointing *Buffalo Girls* (1990).
▷C D Peavy, *Larry McMurtry* (1977)

McNEILE, Herman Cyril *see* SAPPER

McNICKLE, D'Arcy
(1904–77)

American writer, born in St Ignatius, Montana, the son of an Irish–American father and Métis mother. A member of the Confederated Salish and Kutenai tribes, McNickle is known both as a historian and publicist of Native American issues and as an accomplished novelist and biographer. His early short fiction and first novel, *The Surrounded* (1936), were written while he worked as an editor in New York. Increasingly drawn to work for Native American causes, McNickle took up a post in the reformist Collier administration at the BIA, and later became programme director of the Center for American Indian History in the Newberry Library, Chicago. In his novels and short stories, McNickle presented an unromanticized view of the West and the harsh lives of those living on farms and reservations during the Depression. His many non-fiction works, such as *They Came Here First: The Epic of the American Indian* (1949) and *Indians and Other Americans: Two Ways of Life Meet* (1959), deal with Native American history and contemporary issues. He also published a biography of **Oliver La Farge**, and a children's story, *Runner in the Sun: a Story of Indian Maize* (1954). *Wind From an Enemy Sky*, his second novel, was published posthumously in 1978.
▷D R Parker, *Singing an Indian Song: a Biography of D'Arcy McNickle* (1992)

McPHERSON, James Alan
(1943–)

American novelist, born in Georgia. He graduated from both Harvard Law School and the creative writing course at the University of Iowa, and became a professor of literature, first at the University of California in Santa Cruz, and then at the University of Virginia. He is primarily known as a writer of short stories set in the south, as in his best-known book, *Elbow Room* (1977), which won a Pulitzer Prize in 1978. His other fiction includes *Hue and Cry* (1969), *A World Unsuspected* (1987) and *The Prevailing South* (1988).

MEDWALL, Henry
(1462–c.1505)

English dramatist. He wrote *Fulgens and Lucres*, the earliest extant English secular play written before 1500. Little is known of his life, but he was a chaplain to Cardinal Morton, and held various livings. His only other extant work is a morality play, *Nature*, printed in 1530.
▷P Hogrefe, *The Thomas More Circle* (1959)

MEGGED, Aharon
(1920–)

Israeli novelist who was born in Poland but was taken to Palestine at the age of six. He has become one of the outstanding Hebrew novelists. His first book, a story collection, *Ruah Yamim* (1950, 'Spirit of the Sea'), deals with the people of the kibbutz in which he lived for so long, and with the stevedores of Haifa with whom he worked. *Ha-Hai Al Ha-Met* (1967, Eng trans *The Living and the Dead*—it should be 'on', not 'and'), one of the most revealing of Israeli novels, is about a young Israeli who discovers that a 'founding father' of the state was anything but the upright person his legend insists upon: Jason Rabinowicz, the young protagonist, refuses to sanctify his old hero, and therefore is being sued for breach of contract by his publishers—his trial is a lengthy one.

MEHREN, Stein
(1935–)

Norwegian poet and essayist, who has also written novels and plays. Intellectual and particularly interested in philosophy, Mehren is preoccupied with the relationship between language and reality, between time and memory. Both in his poems, where he describes modern society's violence and alienating mass-consumption, and in his tender love poems, Mehren is a master of the art of bringing out the music and the beauty of the language.

▷P T Andersen, *Stein Mehren—en logosdikter* (1982)

MEHRING, Walter
(1896–1981)

German Dadaist poet and playwright, born in Berlin. Mehring's early satirical songs, contained in *Geschichte, Lieder und Chansons des Walter Mehring* (1929, 'Stories, Songs and Chansons of Walter Mehring') were sung at Max Reinhardt's cabaret in Berlin. His play *Der Kaufmann von Berlin* (1929, 'The Merchant of Berlin') was too scandalous and was banned. He left Germany in 1933 and, after a period of internment in France, escaped to the USA and lived at Ascona. *No Road Back* (1944) was a collection of poems and *The Lost Library* (1951) an autobiography and individual view of modern culture.

MEHTA, Ved Parkash
(1934–)

Indian writer, born in Lahore. He was one of seven children of a Hindu doctor who was an officer in the Health Services of the Indian government. Blind from the age of eight, he went to the USA for his education when he was 15 and attended the Arkansas School for the Blind at Little Rock and Pomona College, before going to Oxford and Harvard universities. While at Pomona he published his first book, the autobiography *Face to Face* (1957). He has had a distinguished career as a journalist, contributing chiefly to the *New Yorker*. Employing amanuenses he has written biographies (*Mahatma Gandhi and His Apostles*, 1977), stories, essays and portraits of India. His enduring achievement, however, is *Continents of Exile*, an acclaimed series of autobiographical books: *Daddyji* (1972), *Mamaji* (1979), *Vedi* (1982), *The Ledge Between the Streams* (1984), *Sound-Shadows of the New World* (1986) and *The Stolen Light* (1989).

MEI SHENG
(d.140BC)

Chinese poet. He is often credited with the introduction of the five-character line. For this reason he is sometimes called the father of modern Chinese poetry.

▷E von Zach, *Die chinesische Anthologie* (1958)

MEILHAC, Henri
(1831–97)

French playwright, born in Paris. From 1855 he produced a long series of light comedies—some in conjunction with **Ludovic Halévy**, and, some, including *La Belle Hélène* (1865), well known through Offenbach's music. His masterpiece is *Frou-Frou* (1869). He also collaborated with Halévy and Gille respectively in the libretti of the operas *Carmen* (1875) and *Manon* (1884).

▷F Gaiffe, *Le rire et la scène française* (1932)

MEINHOLD, Johann Wilhelm
(1797–1851)

German pastor and poet, born on the island of Usedom. He was the Lutheran pastor there and at Krummin and Rehwinkel. He published poems and dramas, but is best known for his novels *Maria Schweidler, die Bernsteinhexe* (1838, Eng trans *Maria Schweidler, the Amber Witch*, 1844) and *Sidonie von Bork, die Klosterhexe* (1847, 'Sidonie von Bork, the Nunnery Witch').

MEIRELES, Cecília
(1901–64)

Major Brazilian Catholic poet, critic, and dramatist, born in Rio de Janeiro. She was well established as a poet from 1919, when she published her first collection; but she rejected everything she had written before *Viagem* (1939, 'Voyages'). An orphan, unhappily married, her convincing rejection of the consolations of 'ordinary' experience is in itself replete with experience. Her poetry, which crosses the metaphysical and the lyrical in a fluid, dream-like manner, has been described as second only, in her century, to that of **Laura Riding**. Two representative poems are translated in the *Penguin Book of Latin American Verse* (1971, ed E Curacciolo-Trejo).

▷'Critical study' by D Damosceno, in *Obra poética* (1967, in Portuguese)

MELEAGER
(c.140–c.70 BC)

Greek poet and epigrammatist, from Gadara, in Syria. He was the author of 128 exquisite short elegiac poems and epigrams included in his anthology *Stephanos* (Garland).

▷C Redinger, *Meleagros von Gadara* (1895)

MELÉNDEZ VALDÉS, Juan
(1754–1817)

Spanish poet, born near Badajoz. He became a professor of Classics at the University of Salamanca, fought for Napoleon in the War of Independence, and held political office in Madrid. Considered the greatest lyric poet of his time, he is known for his odes, ballads and romantic verses.

▷R Froldi, *Un poeta illuminista* (1967)

MELGAR, Mariano
(1791–1815)

Peruvian *mestizo* poet and translator (**Ovid**, **Virgil**), executed (shot) during the Battle of Umachiri, and therefore a national hero. He was born in Arequipa. He introduced new forms into the poetry, and had studied the Quechua language and its poetry. He was not a romantic, but was in every sense his country's leading precursor of the movement. His poetry was burned by priests owing to its erotic content; thus they ensured that it would circulate more widely.

▷A T Azurra, *Melgar, precursor del romanticismo* (1966)

MELL, Max
(1882–1971)

Austrian playwright, novelist and poet, born in Marburg. He was overpraised by his friend **Hugo von Hofmannsthal**, which may have led to an artificially inflated reputation. But although wholly traditional and never profound, his stories achieved a high level of competence, and his verse plays were the subject of major productions in the conventional theatre. His message is a simple one of Christian piety in the medieval mode; his knowledge of Austrian folkways was deep.

MELO, Francisco Manuel de
(1608–66)

Portuguese writer, born in Lisbon. He had an arduous and hazardous life as soldier, political prisoner, and exile in Brazil, whence he returned in 1657. He wrote in both Spanish and Portuguese, and is better remembered for his critical works and his history of the Catalan wars than for his voluminous poetry.
▷E Prestage, *Don Francisco Manuel de Melo* (1922)

MELVILL, Elizabeth
(c.1580–c.1630)

Scottish Presbyterian poet renowned for her piety. She was the daughter of Christina Boswell and Sir James Melvill of Halhill, a courtier and memoirist. On her marriage to John Colville of Culcross she became Lady Culcross and has been identified as the 'M.M.' (Mistress Melvill) credited on the title page for *Any Godlie Dreame, Complyit in Scottish Meter*, published in Edinburgh in 1603. This vehement but elegant Calvinist tract was popular enough to require regular reprinting up to the end of the 19th century. More recently Melvill's work has been included in feminist anthologies, such as *Kissing The Rod* (1988, ed G Greer et al).

MELVILLE, Herman
(1819–91)

American novelist, born in New York. He became a bank clerk but, in search of adventure, joined a whaling ship bound for the South Seas. He deserted at the Marquesas and spent some weeks with a savage tribe in the Typee valley, an episode which inspired his first book, *Typee* (1846). Having been taken off by an Australian whaler, he was jailed in Tahiti as a member of a mutinous crew, but escaped and spent some time on the island. This adventure was the basis of his second book, *Omoo* (1847). *Mardi* (1849) also dealt with the South Seas, but entered the realm of satire not too successfully, so that Melville returned to adventure fiction with *Redburn* (1849) and *White Jacket* (1850), in which he drew on his experiences as a seaman on the man-of-war which brought him home from Tahiti. In 1847 he had married, and, after three years in New York he took a farm near Pittsfield, Massachusetts, where **Nathaniel Hawthorne** was his neighbour and friend. It was during this period that he wrote his masterpiece, *Moby-Dick* (1851), a novel of the whaling industry, whose extraordinary vigour and colour and whose philosophical and allegorical undertones reflecting on the nature of evil have given it a place among the classic sea stories. Later novels included *Pierre* (1852), in a symbolic vein which was not appreciated by his readers, and the satirical *Confidence Man* (1857). *Billy Budd* was published posthumously in 1924 and used as the subject of an opera by Benjamin Britten in 1950. Melville also wrote short stories, most notably 'Benito Cereno' and 'Bartleby the Scrivener', which were collected, with others, in *The Piazza Tales* (1856). Now regarded as one of America's greatest novelists, he was not so successful during his life, even *Moby-Dick* being unappreciated. After 1857, disillusioned and by then a New York customs official, he wrote only some poetry. Recognition did not come until some 30 years after his death.
▷E H Miller, *Herman Melville* (1975); C Olson, *Call Me Ishmael* (1947)

MEMMI, Albert
(1920–)

French–Tunisian academic and novelist, born in Tunisia to a French–Jewish family; Arabic was his native language, but he was later naturalized as a French citizen, and he wrote in French. He was largely responsible for instituting Maghrebian studies in France, editing an *Anthologie des ecrivains maghrébins d'expression français* in 1964, and teaching at L'École Pratique des Hautes Études in Paris. He became well-known with his autobiographical novel *La Statue de Sel* (1953,

'Pillar of Salt'), which was prefaced by **Albert Camus**; his other novels, pursuing the theme of cultural dominance, include *Agar* (1953) and *Le Scorpion* (1969). Also an essayist, he published the two parts of *Portrait d'un juif* in 1962 and 1969, *L'Homme Dominé* in 1968 and *Juifs et Arabes* in 1975. He is ranked among the greatest and most influential of Maghrebian/French writers.

MENA, Juan de
(1411–56)

Spanish poet and intellectual, born in Córdoba and educated at Salamanca and Rome. His early poetry (*La coronación*, 1438, 'The Coronation') and prose works such as his carefully constructed *Omero romançado* (c.1442), a translation of the *Ilias latina*, already display the highly Latinate style and intellectual concerns which mark his later works, and which reached their culmination in his *El laberinto de Fortuna* (1444, 'The Labyrinth of Chance'), an allegorical poem which depicts three wheels representing the past, present and future. The purpose of the poem is clearly political, being an attempt to win the support of King John II for Alvaro de Luna against the Castilian nobility.
▷M R Lida de Malkiel, *Juan de Mena, poeta del prerrenacimiento español* (1950)

MENANDER
(c.343–c.291 BC)

Greek poet, and the greatest writer of Attic New Comedy, born in Athens. His comedies were more successful with cultured than with popular audiences; but Quintilian praised him, and **Terence** imitated him closely. He wrote more than a hundred comedies, but only a few fragments of his work were known until 1906, when Lefebvre discovered in Egypt a papyrus containing 1328 lines from four different plays. In 1957, however, the complete text of the comedy *Dyskolos* (Eng trans 1960) was brought to light in Geneva.
▷O Veh, *Beitrage zu Menander Protektor* (1955)

MENCETÍC, Sisko
(1457–1527)

Ragusan poet, born in Ragusa (Dubrovnik). He was one of the earliest of the Serbo–Croat writers in the Dalmatian literature which modelled itself upon that of the Italian Renaissance. He wrote love lyrics in the style of **Petrarch**.

MENCKEN, H(enry) L(ouis)
(1880–1954)

American journalist, editor, critic and historian of language, born in Baltimore.

Mencken was a popular, readable, intelligent writer, whose great enemy throughout his life was what he called the boo-joy (bourgeois). He has been represented as a proto-fascist, but that is to miss his irony and deliberate desire to write for non-literary readers: his criticisms of democracy did not advocate dictatorship. He championed many writers, including **Dreiser** and **Sherwood Anderson**, and edited *The Smart Set* and the *American Mercury*. His *The American Language* (1919–48) is an authoritative and invaluable mine of information: *Prejudices* (1919–27) remains a readable and amusing collection of iconoclasm. He was not profound, but he was seldom foolish.

MENDELE, Mocher Seforim, pseud
(meaning 'Mendele the Bookseller', ie 'propagator of knowledge') of **Sholem Jacob Abramovitch**
(1835–1917)

Yiddish and Hebrew novelist, known as the grandfather of both modern branches of Jewish literature. With **Scholem Aleichem** and **Peretz** he may be said to have founded modern Yiddish literature. He worked all his life, from Odessa, to try to create a dignified Jewish life within Russia. His finest novel, in Yiddish, *Dos Wunshfingerl* (1889, 'The Wishing Ring'), has not been translated, but much else has, notably *Fishke, the Lame* (1869, translated in 1929 and again in 1960) and *Di Kliatche* (1873, *The Nag*, 1955). Mendele himself translated most of his Yiddish fiction into Hebrew, and thus influenced the fiction of the latter language. He also introduced the novel and the short novel into Yiddish.
▷M Waxman, *A History of Jewish Literature* (1947)

MENDÈS, Catulle
(1841–1909)

French writer, born in Bordeaux of Jewish parentage. A Parnassian, he founded the *Revue Fantaisiste* (1859), and later recorded the history of the movement in *La légende du Parnasse contemporain* (1884, 'The Legend of Le Parnasse contemporain'). He switched to Romanticism and wrote poems, novels, dramas and libretti as well as articles and criticism.
▷A Bertrand, *Catulle Mendès, une biographie critique* (1908)

MENDES, Murilo
(1902–)

Brazilian poet and diplomat, born in Minas province. He began as a Surrealist, but his later work, written under the influence of his conversion to Catholicism, has been compared to that of the Spanish poet **Antonio Machado**.

MENDES PINTO, Fernao
(c.1510–1583)

Portuguese travel writer, author of the famous and (in the 17th century) very popular *Peregrinaçam da Fernam Pinto* (1614, Eng trans *The Voyages and Adventures of Ferdinand Mendes Pinto*, 1653, abridged 1894, adapted as *The Great Peregrination*, 1949). This book, for long regarded as almost pure fantasy, describes Pinto's astonishing life and travels to China, Japan, Africa and elsewhere (including, certainly, countries he did not visit). Its prophetic importance lay in part in Pinto's shrewd and ironic use of information about supposedly 'barbaric' peoples to show up the actual barbarity and greed of 'civilized' ones. There has long been controversy about the merits of the *Peregrination*, and **Congreve** referred to its author as 'a liar of the first magnitude'; but the consensus is now that he was a great anticipator of the modern form known as 'faction', fiction based on facts—and so far the finest practitioner of it. The text of this masterpiece was undoubtedly tampered with by its earliest editors, but its essence comes through.
▷M Collis, in *The Great Peregrination* (1949)

MENDOZA, Inigo Lopez de
(fl.1450)

Spanish statesman and poet, father of Pedro Gonzalez de Mendoza and great-grandfather of Diego Hurtado de Mendoza. He was created Marquis of Santillana by John II of Castile in 1445 for his services on the field. He was a wise statesman, a sturdy patriot, and an admired poet of **Petrarch**an sonnets, lyrics, allegories and didactic poems. He left an excellent account of the Provençal, Catalan and Valencian poets, and was an early folklorist and collector of popular proverbs.
▷J Rodriguez-Puertolas, *Fray Inigo de Mendoza y sus 'Coplas de Vita Christi'* (1968)

MENON, Vallatol Narayana
(1879–1958)

Indian (Malayalam) poet, with **Takazi** and **Basir** the best-known writer in his language. He created versions of the great classical texts, the *Ramayana* and the *Rig Veda*, in Malayalam. A Sanskrit scholar, he had a profound understanding of the difficult and complex Sanskrit poetics, and his own work—in the most Sanskritized of all the Indian languages—amply displays this. He was a nationalist poet, but his patriotism expressed itself in an abiding love for the ancient India: 'it was,' wrote a critic, 'his mission to make

the classical vision part of contemporary consciousness'. The direction in his poetry is of a movement from romanticism to realism.

MENZEL, Wolfgang
(1798–1873)

German critic and historian, born in Waldenburg in Silesia. He studied at Jena and Bonn, but from 1825 lived mainly in Stuttgart, where he made a reputation as an outspoken journalist and critic. He edited magazines, and wrote poems, novels, histories of German literature and poetry, a history of the world, literary criticism and polemics.

MERA, Juan León
(1832–94)

Ecuadorian novelist and poet. Born in Ambato, he lived under and supported the repressive theocrat García Moreno. Mera had a deeply religious background, and was to experience difficulty in combining traditional Catholicism with his Romantic style of writing. His most famous novel is *Cumandá, o un drama entre salvajes* (1871, 'Cumandá, or a Drama Among the Natives'), a novel which attempts to deconstruct European stereotypes of nature, indigenous peoples, and human existence. His Romantic poetry collected in *Melodías indígenas* (1868, 'Native Melodies') is not now considered as important as his collection of Ecuadorian popular poetry *Cantares del pueblo ecuatoriano* (1892).

MERCER, David
(1928–80)

English dramatist, born in Wakefield. After studying painting at King's College, Newcastle, he moved to Europe and began to write. His first television play, *Where the Difference Begins* (1961), signalled his interest in fusing the personal and the political in work that challenged the conventions of television drama. Further plays, like *A Climate of Fear* (1962), *A Suitable Case for Treatment* (1962) and *In Two Minds* (1967), explored his fascination with mental health, psychiatry and his struggle to reconcile a belief in socialism with the repression revealed during his stays in Eastern Europe. Winner of the 1965 *Evening Standard* Award for most promising playwright, his stage work includes *Ride A Cock Horse* (1965), *Flint* (1970) and *Cousin Vladimir* (1978). His film scripts include *Morgan* (1965) and *Providence* (1977). He continued to address issues of personal alienation and the class system in later television plays like *Huggy Bear* (1976), *The Ragazza* (1978) and *Rod of Iron* (1980).

MEREDITH, George
(1828–1909)

English novelist, born in Portsmouth, the grandson of a famous naval outfitter (the 'great Mel' of *Evan Harrington*). He was educated privately in Germany and was thus able to view the English class system with detachment. In London, after being articled to a solicitor, he turned to journalism and letters, his first venture appearing in *Chambers's Journal* in 1849, the year in which he married Mary Ellen Nicolls, a widowed daughter of **Thomas Love Peacock**. This disastrous marriage gave him an insight into relations between the sexes, which appear as largely in his work as his other great interest, natural selection as Nature's way of perfecting man. His works did not bring him much financial reward and he had to rely on his articles in *The Fortnightly* and his work as a reader in the publishing house of Chapman and Hall. His prose works started with a burlesque Oriental fantasy, *The Shaving of Shagpat* (1855), followed in 1859 by *The Ordeal of Richard Feverel*, which is based on parental tyranny and a false system of private education. He did not achieve general popularity as a novelist until the delightful *Diana of the Crossways* appeared in 1885. In the meantime he wrote less successful works, such as his two novels on the Italian revolt of 1848, *Sandra Belloni* (1864) and *Vittoria* (1866). Other popular works are *Evan Harrington* (1860), which throws light on Meredith's origins; *Harry Richmond* (1871); and best of all, *Beauchamp's Career* (1875), which poses the question of class and party and is well constructed and clearly written. This cannot be said of Meredith's later major novels, *The Egoist* (1879), a study of refined selfishness, and *The Amazing Marriage* (1895). These two powerful works are marred by the artificiality and forced wit which occurs in so much of his poetry. His first volume of verse (1851) is quite unremarkable, but *Poems and Lyrics of the Joy of Earth* (1883) displays his new cryptic manner and discusses the two master themes—the 'reading of earth' and the sex duel. His masterpiece on the latter theme had appeared in 1862 when he was influenced by the pre-Raphaelite poets and painters. This is *Modern Love*, a novelette in pseudo-sonnet sequence form in which the novelist in him plays powerfully on incompatibility of temper. His 'reading of earth' is expressed cryptically in the magnificent *Woods of Westermain*, intelligibly in *The Thrush in February* and thrillingly in *The Lark Ascending*. The volume called *A Reading of Life* (1901) adds little to the record. The modern revaluation of the Victorians has enhanced the fame of this very cerebral poet.

▷L Stevenson, *The Ordeal of Meredith* (1954)

MEREDITH, Gwen(yth Valmai)
(1907–)

Australian playwright and scriptwriter especially, for over 30 years, of radio plays and serials. She was born in Orange, New South Wales. She has written very successful 'serious' stage plays, but is best known for popular serial stories on Australian radio such as *The Lawsons*, an everyday story of farming folk (1943–9), and the marathon-running *Blue Hills*, which went on air four days a week continuously between 1949 and 1976. While touching on human relationships and public concerns, neither series broached the then current standards of permissiveness.

MEREDITH, William Morris
(1919–)

American poet, librettist and anthologist, born in New York City. Meredith published his first collection, *Love Letter from an Impossible Land*, in 1944. His subsequent volumes include *Earth Walk: New and Selected Poems* (1970) and *Partial Accounts: New and Selected Poems* (1987). His verse is often wistful, sometimes ironic, always highly crafted and polished; traditional in its sense of rhyme and metre, it is noted for its subtle and precise observation of thought and feeling.
▷G Rotella, *Three Contemporary Poets of New England* (1983)

MEREZHKOVSKI, Dmitri Sergeyevich
(1865–1941)

Russian novelist, critic and poet, born in St Petersburg. He wrote a historical trilogy *Khristos i Antikhrist* (1896–1905, 'Christ and Antichrist'), and books on **Tolstoy**, **Ibsen**, and **Nikolai Gogol**. He opposed the Revolution in 1917 and fled to Paris in 1919, where he continued to write historical novels, including one on Jesus (1932–3) and another on **Dante** (1939). His wife was **Zinaida Gippius**.
▷C Bedford, *Dmitri Sergeyevich Merezhkovski and the Silver Age* (1975)

MERI, Veijo
(1928–)

Finnish novelist, born in Viipuri; he is one of Finland's most outstanding writers. His themes are almost always those of war or childhood, which he contrasts. Behind all his work is the figure of **Gogol**, whose bitter humour he has carefully adapted to modern times. Many books by him have been translated into French, but none into English.

MERILUOTO, Aila
(1924–)
Finnish poet and translator (**Harry Martinson**), born in Pieksämäki. Her first collection of 1946, *Lasimaaulaus* ('Stained Glass Window'), was hailed as a major breakthrough in Finnish lyrical poetry; but with *Portaat* (1961, 'Staircase'), under the influence of **Rilke** (a powerful presence in Finnish poetry) she became more intellectual and the straightforward voice vanished. Poems are translated in *Twentieth Century Scandinavian Poetry* (1950).

MÉRIMÉE, Prosper
(1803–70)
French novelist, born in Paris, the son of a painter. He studied law, visited Spain in 1830, and held posts under the ministries of the navy, commerce and the interior. He was appointed inspector-general of historical remains in France in 1833, and became a senator in 1853. His last years were clouded by ill-health and melancholy, and the downfall of the Second Empire hastened his death. He wrote novels and short stories, archaeological and historical dissertations, and travel stories, all of which display exact learning, keen observation, real humour, and an exquisite style. Among his novels are *Colomba* (1841, Eng trans 1856), *Mateo Falcone* (1833), *Carmen* (1847, Eng trans 1878), *La Vénus d'Ille* (1837, Eng trans *The Venus of Ille*, 1887), *Lokis* (1870), *Arsène Guillot* (1852), *La Chambre bleue* (1866, 'The Blue Room') and *L'Abbé Aubain* (1846, Eng trans *The Abbé Aubain*, 1903). His letters include the famous *Lettres à une inconnue* (1873, 'Letters to an Unknown Woman'), the *Lettres à une autre inconnue* (1875, 'Letters to Another Unknown Woman') and the letters to the bibliographer Panizzi (1881). He also wrote some plays.
▷P Léon, *Mérimée et son temps* (1962)

MERRILL, James Ingram
(1926–)
American poet, novelist and playwright, born in New York City. His first publication, *Jim's Book: A Collection of Poems and Short Stories*, appeared in 1942. A volume of 30 years of poetry, *From the First Nine: Poems 1946–1976*, was published in 1982. Although Merrill has also published two plays and two novels, he is principally known as a poet and, specifically, as 'the ouija poet'. His interest in the spirit world and use of a ouija board apparently to converse with it is recorded in a huge epic poem in three parts, collected under the title of *The Changing Light at Sandover* (1982). The mystic quality of much of his verse, dealing with the themes of loss and

lost time, has resulted in comparisons with **Yeats**.

MERRILL, Stuart Fitzrandolph
(1863–1915)
American Symbolist poet, born in Hempstead, Long Island, New York. His French poems *Les gammes* (1895), *Les quatre saisons* (1900), and others developed the musical conception of poetry, and made full use of alliteration. *Une voix dans la Foule* (1909) espouses a strongly democratic sympathy which is unmistakably American.
▷M L Henry, *Stuart Merrill, sa vie, sa oeuvre* (1929)

MERRIMAN, Bryan, anglicized version of **Bryan Mac Giolla Meidre**
(1747–1805)
Irish–Gaelic poet, born in Ennistymon, County Clare, the son of a stonemason. He became a schoolteacher and small farmer in Feakle, later (1790) marrying and settling as a mathematics teacher in Limerick. His reputation depends on a stupendous 1000-line mock-heroic epic, traditional in its use of dream-vision, but satirical and feminist in content: *Cúirt an Mheáin Oidhche* (c.1786, Eng trans as *The Midnight Court* by **Frank O'Connor** in the *Penguin Book of Irish Verse*, 1970), which has been described as 'by far the most successful sustained effort in verse in modern Irish'. It is a wild (and woundingly gross) attack on Irish Catholic puritanism, greatly and influentially praised by O'Connor, the most successful of its many translators. Imagining its author's presence at a ferocious fairy inquisition against bachelors, it lampoons sexual mores, celibacy, the clergy and male chauvinism, and all in vigorously earthy and erotic language. The poem was banned in all English translations after Irish independence, but the Irish language itself was deemed incapable of corrupting influence. Liberal Irish intellectuals have established an annual Merriman Summer School, convening in August in Clare.

MERTON, Thomas
(1915–69)
American poet and devotionist, born in France of an English father and an American mother. From 1941 he was a Trappist monk in Kentucky. His best book is perhaps the one which made him famous: the spiritual autobiography *The Seven Storey Mountain* (1948). This became a bestseller and exercised some influence upon religious thinking. He later became interested in Zen Buddhism, and wrote some of the best popular books about

it. As a poet he is respected as a minor practitioner in the tradition of **Traherne** and **Hopkins**. He was electrocuted in an accident.

MERWIN, W(illiam) S(tanley)
(1927–)

American poet and dramatist, born in New York City. He was educated at Princeton University, and was briefly a tutor to the son of **Robert Graves**, and later a translator, a playwright-in-residence, and poetry editor of *The Nation* (1962). His first book, *A Mask of Janus* (1952), was followed by a series of elegant, lyrical poems in books like *Dancing Bears* (1954) and *The Moving Target* (1967). His imagery took on a more surreal tinge with *The Lice* (1967), and subsequent books seemed more contemplative in tone, and more concerned with absence and silence. They include *Writings To an Unfinished Accompaniment* (1973) and *Selected Poems* (1988). His other works include several plays and translations; and *Regions of Memory* (1987), a collection of prose.
▷ *Unframed Originals: Recollections* (1982)

MESONERO ROMANOS, Ramón de
(1808–82)

Spanish *costumbrista* writer (local colourist, or regionalist), and editor, born in Madrid, who sometimes wrote under the pseudonym of 'El Curioso Parlante'. He was a paramount (and acknowledged) influence upon **Pérez Galdós**. His *Manual de Madrid* (1831) is full of extraordinary facts and figures about the city. He edited the weekly *Seminario pitoresco español* (1836–57), and published essays on Madrid customs and society. Writing nostalgically and in reaction to Romanticism, he defended traditional values, but in so charming and observant a way that he could not possibly be described as reactionary. He had a considerable influence, especially in disabusing Spanish readers of the prejudice that a contemporary novel could not achieve an audience. 'It was he', wrote one critic, 'more than any other contemporary writer, who opened the pages of [Spanish] literature to ordinary daily life'. His complete works, *Obras*, were published in eight volumes between 1924 and 1926.
▷ *Romanic Review*, XXI (1930)

METASTASIO, Pietro, originally Trapassi
(1698–1782)

Italian poet, born in Rome. A gift for versifying gained him a patron in Gravina, a lawyer, who educated him, and left him his fortune (1718). He gained his reputation by his masque, *The Garden of Hesperides* (1722), wrote the libretti for 27 operas, including Mozart's *Clemenza di Tito* (libretto Eng trans *The Clemency of Titus*, 1828), and became court poet at Vienna in 1729.
▷ C Burney, *Life and Letters of Metastasio* (1796)

MEUNG, Jean de, or Jean Clopinel
(c.1250–1305)

French poet and satirist. He flourished in Paris under Philip IV, 'the Fair'. He translated many books into French, and left a witty *Testament*. His great work is his lengthy continuation (18 000 lines) of the *Roman de la Rose* by **Guillaume de Lorris**, which substituted for tender allegorizing his own satirical pictures of actual life and an encyclopaedic discussion of every aspect of contemporary learning, which inspired many later authors to write in support of or in opposition to his views.

MEW, Charlotte Mary
(1869–1928)

British poet and short-story writer, whose reputation has been sustained by the critical support of those such as **Walter de la Mare** and **Thomas Hardy**, who predeceased her only briefly; the circumstances of Mew's suicide, following the death of her sister, has fostered a certain romantic cult around her. Born in London, she was essentially self-educated and her work largely concerned the problems of women in a society that provided few reliable terms of reference or role models for female individuality. Her most famous poem is 'The Farmer's Bride' (1915), a vigorous narrative about an emotionally restricted life. In the late 1970s, Mew was rediscovered by the feminist movement; her collected verse and prose, reissued by Virago Press, made a significant impact on a revisionist awareness of post-Victorian social and cultural attitudes.
▷ P Fitzgerald, *Charlotte Mew and her Friends* (1984)

MEYER, Conrad Ferdinand
(1825–98)

Swiss poet and novelist, born in Zürich. After a period during which he concentrated mainly on ballads and verse romances, he composed the epic poem *Huttens Letzte Tage* (1871, 'Hutten's Final Days') and a number of historical novels such as *Jürg Jenatsch* (1876) and *Der Heilige* (1880, 'The Saint'), in which he excels in subtle and intricate psychological situations and complex characters.
▷ H Mayne, *Conrad Ferdinand Meyer und sein Werk* (1925)

MEYNELL, Alice Christiana Gertrude, née **Thompson**
(1847–1922)

English essayist and poet, born in Barnes, London, the daughter of a scholar and a concert pianist, and sister of the battle-painter Elizabeth Butler. She spent her childhood on the Continent, and became a convert to Catholicism. Her volumes of essays include *The Rhythm of Life* (1893), *The Colour of Life* (1896) and *Hearts of Controversy* (1917). She published several collections of her own poems, starting in 1875 with *Preludes*, and anthologies of **Coventry Patmore**, of lyric poetry, and of poems for children. In 1877 she married Wilfrid Meynell (1852–1948), author and journalist, with whom she edited several periodicals.
▷A K Tuell, *Mrs Meynell* (1925)

MEYRINK, Gustav
(1868–1932)

German writer, born in Vienna. He translated **Dickens** and wrote satirical novels with a strong element of the fantastic and grotesque. Among the best known are *Der Golem* (1915, 'The Golem'), *Das grüne Gesicht* (1916, 'The Green Face') and *Walpurgisnacht* (1917, 'The Witches' Sabbath').

MHAC AN TSAOI, Máiri
(1922–)

Irish Gaelic poet, born in Dublin. She has written and translated a remarkable and singular oeuvre of 'feminist-orientated' poems and verses in Gaelic. She has always emphasized, as in *Cré na Mna Ti* (1958, 'The Housewife's Credo') for example, that it is essential to realize and utilize creativity despite the dictates of domesticity: 'like Scheherazade, you will *need* to write poetry also'. Her sense of the present being interdependent on a richly cultivated past is most in evidence in the invaluable English translations *A Heart Full of Thought* (1959).

MICHAËLIS, Karin
(1872–1950)

Danish novelist, short-story writer and journalist, born in Randers. The novel *Barnet* (1902, 'The Child') focuses on the theme of childhood, but she was to become best known for her explorations of female sexuality. *Den farlige Alder* (1910, Eng trans *The Dangerous Age*, 1912), which resulted in international fame, is an epistolary and diary novel about a menopausal woman, pinpointing the lies and dissimulation which are part of the social construction of the feminine role. Her extensive output includes the seven-volume series for children about Bibi (1929–39) and two autobiographical series, *Træt på godt og ondt* (1924–30, 'The Tree of Good and Evil') and *Vidunderlige Verden* (1948–50, 'Marvellous World').
▷S Fabricius, 'Karin Michaëlis', in *Danske digtere i det 20. århundrede*, I, Torben Brostrøm and Mette Winge (eds) (1980)

MICHAUX, Henri
(1899–1984)

Belgian poet, autobiographer, mystic, astrologer and artist (his art is not negligible), first discovered by **Franz Hellens** and then encouraged by **Jules Supervielle**. Born in Namur, he lived mostly in Paris. His most easily accessible work, and the one for which he is best known, is *Un Certain Plume* (1930, Eng trans, in part, in the usefully bilingual *Selected Writings*, 1968): this describes a Chaplin-like figure whose crazy adventures resemble surrealist narratives. He was influenced by the surrealists, but always remained his own man. The most pervasive influence upon all his writings was his 14th-century lowlands compatriot, the mystic Jan van Ruysbroeck; but he was also a humorist of nearly the calibre of **Max Jacob**, who also exercised a vital effect upon him. Much of his writing is unclassifiable, but his poetry, which often resembles in presentation the 'cubist' poetry of **Pierre Reverdy** and **Vicente Huidobro**, has long been popular amongst French-speaking readers. His autobiography, *Les Grandes Epreuves et les innombrables petites* (1966, Eng trans *The Major Ordeals of the Mind and the Countless Minor Ones*, 1974), is a classic little read outside France and Belgium; it demonstrates his critical but generous awareness of almost all the major philosophical and religious developments of the 20th century. **André Gide** issued a little book on him (based on the text of a lecture), *Découvrons Henri Michaux* (1941, 'We Discover Henri Michaux'), which is a useful if incomplete introduction. Also available in translation is *Light Through Darkness* (1964).
▷M Bowie, *Henri Michaux* (1973)

MICHENER, James
(1907–)

American novelist, born in New York. A teacher and book editor during World War II, he turned to writing following his service in the navy. *Tales of the South Pacific* (1947), which won a Pulitzer Prize, was adapted by Rodgers and Hammerstein into the musical *South Pacific* (1949). Later novels in a prolific and prodigiously successful career include *Hawaii* (1959), *Space* (1982) and *Poland* (1983). Although often lacking the light touch or insightful detail, these daunting doorsteps do impress by the sheer accumulation of information. His non-fictional output includes *The Bridge at Andau* (1956), an account of the Hungarian uprising; *Iberia* (1968), on travelling through Spain; and *Presidential Lottery* (1969), a critique of the American political system.

MICIŃSKI, Tadeusz
(1873–1919)

Polish poet, novelist, playwright and philosopher, one of the most peculiar and strangely gifted in a peculiar and strangely gifted literature. He was killed fighting the Bolsheviks. Few critics have known what to say of him, for in many of his strange poems and novels he practised a sort of Slavonic gnosticism, full of out-of-the-way learning. He offered hope only of a very special sort: it depended on the kind of knowledge gnostics insist can be used to circumvent the devil, who is equated with earthly existence. There was an early collection of poems, an extraordinary play, *W mroku złotego pałacu czyll Bazylissa Teofanu* (1909, 'In the Night of the Golden Palace or the Empress of Teophan'), which centres around a demonic empress, and two novels on gnostic themes. There is considerable new interest in him in Poland.

MICKIEWICZ, Adam Bernard
(1798–1855)

Polish poet, born near Novogrodek in Lithuania (Minsk). He published his first poems in 1822, and as founder of a students' secret society was banished to Russia (1824–9); there he produced three epic poems, glowing with patriotism. After a journey through Germany, France and Italy his masterpiece, the epic *Pan Tadeusz* (Eng trans *Master Thaddeus*, 1885), appeared in 1834—a brilliant delineation of Lithuanian scenery, manners and beliefs. After teaching at Lausanne, he was appointed Slavonic Professor at Paris in 1840, but was deprived of the post in 1843 for political utterances. He went to Italy to organize the Polish legion, but in 1852 Louis Napoleon appointed him a librarian in the Paris Arsenal. He died in Constantinople, where the emperor had sent him to raise a Polish legion for service against Russia. His body, first buried at Montmorency in France, was in 1890 laid beside that of the solider and patriot Kosciuzko in Cracow Cathedral. Mickiewicz is the national poet of the Poles, and one of the greatest of all Slav poets.
▷K Pruszynski, *Adam Mickiewicz: the life story of the greatest Polish poet* (1950)

MICKLE, William Julius
(1735–88)

Scottish poet, the son of a minister, born in Langholm, Dumfriesshire. Educated at Edinburgh High School, he failed as a brewer, and turned author in London. In 1765 he published a poem, *The Concubine* (or *Syr Martyn*), and in 1771–5 his version rather than translation of the *Lusiad* of **Camoens**. In 1779 he went to Lisbon as secretary to Commodore Johnstone, but his last years were spent in London. His ballad of *Cumnor Hall* (which suggested *Kenilworth* to Sir **Walter Scott**) is poor poetry, but 'There's nae luck aboot the hoose' ensured his immortality, even if his authorship of it has been challenged.

MIDDLETON, (John) Christopher
(1926–)

English poet and translator, born in Truro, Cornwall and educated at Merton College, Oxford. After service in the Royal Air Force, he taught English at the University of Zurich and German at the University of London, before moving to the USA (1966) as Professor of Germanic languages and literature at the University of Texas, Austin. His verse has a deceptive, fleeting quality, which is captured in the title of an important volume of essays, *The Pursuit of the Kingfisher* (1983); his poems are intense, often visionary, in a way that combines English models with the simultaneously more playful (as in the Surrealists) and intellectual tenor of the Continental traditions. In 1963 with his appearance in *Penguin Modern Poets 4*, Middleton began to attract wider attention. *Nonsequences: Selfpoems* (1965) brought this earlier period to an end. With his move to America, the verse became less interiorized, and more limber. *The Fossil Fish* (1970) and *Briefcase History* (1972) were ultra-terse, and, like the collection *The Lonely Suppers of W V Balloon* (1975), signalled his interest in that most un-English of forms: prose poetry. Later collections include *Pataxanadu* (1977) and *III Poems* (1983). Middleton has translated many modern German writers, including **Robert Walser**, **Christa Wolf** and **Gert Hofmann**.

MIDDLETON, Osman Edward
(1925–)

New Zealand short-story writer, born in Christchurch, whose work first appeared in book form in *Short Stories* (1953) and then in *The Stone* (1959), *A Walk on the Beach* (1964) and *The Loners* (1972). *Selected Stories* appeared in 1975, and two novellas, *Confessions of an Ocelot, and, Not for a Seagull*, in 1979.

MIDDLETON, Stanley
(1919–)

English novelist, born and educated in Nottingham, where he also worked as a schoolmaster from 1947 to his retirement in 1981.

Middleton's critical highwater mark was the (shared) award of the Booker Prize for his fourteenth novel, *Holiday*, in 1974. His work has been criticized for being middle-class and too deeply rooted in the anti-experimental tradition of conventional British fiction. His works are, however, highly reflexive, usually concerned with the lives of artists or teachers; they often compress time disturbingly. The best of the books are *Harris's Requiem* (1960), *Terms of Reference* (1966), *Brazen Prison* (1971) and *In a Strange Land* (1979), which returns to Middleton's favourite subject of music. His career acquired new impetus in the 1980s, presumably as a result of his retirement from school-teaching, and he has continued to publish a steady novel per year into the early nineties, most notably *After a Fashion* (1987) and *Recovery* (1988).

MIDDLETON, Thomas
(c.1580–1627)

English dramatist, probably born in London, where his father was a bricklayer. He is first mentioned in Henslowe's *Diary* in 1602, when he was engaged with **Anthony Munday**, **Michael Drayton** and **John Webster** on a lost play, *Cæsar's Fall*. First on the list of his printed plays is *Blurt, Master Constable* (1602), a light, fanciful comedy. Two interesting tracts, *Father Hubbard's Tale* and *The Black Book*, exposing London rogues, were published in 1604, to which year belongs the first part of *The Honest Whore* (mainly written by **Thomas Dekker**, partly by Middleton). *The Phœnix* and *Michaelmas Term* (both 1607) are lively comedies; even more diverting is *A Trick to Catch the Old One* (1608); and *A Mad World, My Masters* (1608), from which **Aphra Behn** pilfered freely in *The City Heiress*, is singularly adroit. *The Roaring Girl* (1611; written with Dekker) idealizes the character of a noted cutpurse and virago. Middleton was repeatedly employed to write the Lord Mayor's pageant. *A Chaste Maid in Cheapside* was probably produced in 1613, as was *No Wit, No Help like a Woman's*. *A Fair Quarrel* (1617) and *The World Lost at Tennis* (1620) were written in conjunction with **William Rowley**, as were probably *More Dissemblers Besides Women* (?1622) and *The Mayor of Quinborough*. In 1620 Middleton was appointed city chronologer, and a MS Chronicle by him was extant in the 18th century. The delightful comedy, *The Old Law*, first published in 1656, is mainly the work of Rowley, with something by Middleton, all revised by **Philip Massinger**. In the three posthumously-published plays, *The Changeling*, *The Spanish Gypsy* and *Women Beware Women*, Middleton's genius is seen at its highest. Rowley had a share in the first two and probably in the third. A very curious and skilful play is *A Game at Chess*, acted in 1624. *The Widow*, published in 1652, was mainly by Middleton. *Anything for a Quiet Life* (c.1619) may have been revised by **James Shirley**. Middleton was concerned in the authorship of some of the plays included in the works of **Francis Beaumont** and **John Fletcher**.
▷R H Barker, *Thomas Middleton* (1958)

MIHURA SANTOS, Miguel
(1905–77)

Spanish playwright, and painter and editor of humorous magazines, born in Madrid into a family of actors. His somewhat Absurdist plays, not unlike the *One Way Pendulum* of **N F Simpson**, mocked mankind's enslavement to machinery. *Tres sombreros de copa* (1932, rev edn 1952, Eng trans *Three Top Hats*, in *Modern Spanish Theatre*, 1968, M Benedikt and G E Wellwarth eds), is his best-known play, and was very popular in Franco's dreary Spain when it was reissued. A very highly skilled craftsman, Mihura lacked depth and substance.
▷R Mackay, *Miguel Mihura* (1977)

MIHYAYLOVSKI, Stoyan
(1856–1927)

Bulgarian poet, critic and editor, who spent his life punishing injustice; he was less satirical and humorous than **Aleko Konstantinov**, and more vituperative. But he made vituperation an art. A brutal pessimist, he saw no compromise between anarchy and enslavement. He has been called 'Bulgaria's **Juvenal**'. Even his scathing *Kniga za balgarskiya* (1897, 'Book of the Bulgarian People', set, provocatively, in Turkey), his most famous book, has not been translated into English.
▷C Manning and R Smal-Stocki, *The History of Modern Bulgarian Literature* (1960)

MIKSZÁTH, Kálmán
(1847–1910)

Hungarian novelist, born in Szklabonya. He was the editor of the periodical *A Hon*, owned by **Jokai**. At first he was influenced by this great historical novelist, but gradually evolved his own more realistic procedures, becoming a quirky romantic satirist of highly original qualities. He treated the decline of his own rural middle-class with sympathy but without reservation. *A jopalocok* (1882, Eng trans *The Good People of Palocz*, 1893) and *Különös hazasság* (1900, Eng trans *A Strange Marriage*, 1964) are typical of his work.
▷J Reményi, *Hungarian Writers and Literature* (1964)

MILES, Josephine Louise
(1911–85)

American poet and literary scholar. Born in Chicago she studied at the University of California, Los Angeles, and then at Berkeley, joining the faculty in 1940 (shortly after the publication of her first verse collection, *Lines of Intersection*), becoming full professor in 1952 and University Professor in 1973. Her poems are frequently concerned with the minutiae of academic life and with ideas, and are written with the deliberately awkward asymmetry of natural speech; *Prefabrications* (1955), *Civil Poems* (1966) and *Kinds of Affection* (1967) are typical. As the 1960s advanced, she was a tolerant but never passively uncritical observer of the radical student movement; *Fields of Learning* (1968) expressed a sense of quiet detachment from its attendant idolatries. In a major critical essay, *Poetry and Change: Donne, Milton, Wordsworth and the Equilibrium of the Present* (1974) and in *Working Out Ideas: Predication and Other Uses of Language* (1979), she re-examined poetry's intellectual role. Miles's *Collected Poems* (1983) provoked a belated and often apologetic reassessment of her contribution to American verse.

MILLAR, Margaret
(1915–)

American novelist and short-story writer, born in Kitchener, Canada and educated at the University of Toronto. She worked as a screenwriter for Warner Brothers and was the president of Mystery Writers of America in 1957–8. The *Los Angeles Times* voted her Woman of the Year in 1965. She is the author of over 20 novels and several short stories, mostly in the detective fiction genre—though she probes more deeply into the psychology of her characters than most crime writers. She wrote her first novel, *The Invisible Worm*, in 1941. *Beast in View* (1955) won her the Mystery Writers of America **Edgar Allan Poe** Award, as did *Banshee* nearly 30 years later, in 1983.

MILLAY, Edna St Vincent
(1892–1950)

American poet, born in Rockland, Maine. Her first poem was published when she was a student at Vassar College. Moving into Greenwich Village, then at its height as a meeting place for artists and writers, she published *A Few Figs from Thistles* (1920). In 1923 came *The Harp Weaver and Other Poems*, for which she was awarded a Pulitzer Prize. During her lifetime she was a feminist and though she was latterly dismissed as arrogant, egotistic and whimsical, the admiration of writers like **Maya Angelou** has caused her

to be re-evaluated and there has been renewed interest in her sonorous verse.
▷ N A Brittan, *Edna St Vincent Millay* (1967)

MILLER, Arthur
(1915–)

American playwright, born in New York City. He was educated at the University of Michigan but changed his mind about an intended career in journalism when he won a play-writing prize and worked for the Federal Theater project instead. His *Death of a Salesman* (1949) won the Pulitzer Prize and brought him international recognition, though *All My Sons* (1947) had already placed him in the front rank of American dramatists. *The Crucible* (1953) is probably, to date, his most lasting work, since its theme, the persecution of the Salem witches equated with contemporary political persecution, stands out of time. Other works include *A View from the Bridge* (1955), the film script of *The Misfits* (1960), *After the Fall* (1963), *Incident at Vichy* (1964), *The Creation of the World and Other Business* (1972) and *Playing for Time* (1981). His marriage to Marilyn Monroe, from whom he was divorced in 1961, and his brush with the authorities over early communist sympathies, brought him considerable publicity. Recent plays include *Danger: Memory!* (1987). During the 1980s, almost all of Miller's plays were given major British revivals and without doubt, Miller is now more popular in Britain than in America, where the apparent spurning of serious work by Broadway has made it difficult even for the voice of Miller to be heard.
▷ N Carson, *Arthur Miller* (1982)

MILLER, Henry Valentine
(1891–1980)

American writer, born in New York. His parents were German–Americans and he was brought up in Brooklyn. He rebelled against a conventional upbringing and a traditional career pattern, and after two months at the City College in 1909 took a job with a cement company. With money from his father which was intended to finance him through Cornell, he travelled in the south west and Alaska. When he returned home he went to work in his father's tailor shop but left after trying to unionize the workforce. In 1920 he became employment manager for the Western Union Telegraph Co.; in 1927 he ran a speakeasy in Greenwich Village. But in 1930 he moved to France for nine years during which time he published *Tropic of Cancer* (1934) and *Tropic of Capricorn* (1938), as well as *Black Spring* (1936). He returned to the USA in 1940 but travelled extensively both at home and abroad before settling in Big Sur, California.

He has been described as a folk hero, an ardent Bohemian whose life was his work. Though much of his fiction is autobiographical and explicitly sexual, he regarded his childhood as seminal: 'From five to ten were the most important years of my life; I lived in the street and acquired the typical American gangster spirit'. This undoubtedly helped him overcome many impecunious years and rebuffs from state censors. (American editions of the *Tropics* were not published until 1961 and 1962 respectively.) In his time, however, he became one of the most read American authors, solipsistic, surrealistic and blackly comic, empathizing with the outcast: prostitutes, hobos and artists. Important books are *The Colossus of Maroussi* (1941), a dithyrambic travel book, *The Air-Conditioned Nightmare* (1945), a bleak essay on contemporary America, and *The Rosy Crucifixion* trilogy of novels: *Sexus* (1949), *Plexus* (1953) and *Nexus* (1960). A guru of the sexually liberated 1960s, he fell foul of feminist critics in the 1970s.

▷ J Martin, *Always Merry and Bright: the life of Henry Miller* (1978)

MILLER, Hugh
(1802–56)

Scottish geologist and writer, born in Cromarty. Having lost his father at sea at the age of five, he had a rebellious school career, and was apprenticed as a stonemason at the age of 16, a trade he followed for 17 years. He developed an interest in fossils, and he devoted the winter months to reading, writing and natural history. In 1829 he published *Poems Written in the Leisure Hours of a Journeyman Mason*, followed by *Scenes and Legends of the North of Scotland* (1835). He contributed to **John Mackay Wilson**'s *Tales of the Borders* (1834–40), and to *Chambers's Journal*. He married the daughter of an Inverness businessman and worked as a bank accountant for a time (1834–9), but when he became involved in the controversy that led to the Disruption of the Church of Scotland (1843) with a ferocious open *Letter to Lord Brougham* (1839) he was invited to Edinburgh to start the anti-patronage journal *The Witness*, and became the outstanding journalist of the Disruption. He wrote a series of geological articles in *The Witness*, later collected as *The Old Red Sandstone* (1841). In 1845 he wrote *First Impressions of England* (1847). His *My Schools and Schoolmasters* (1854) is the story of his youth. A pioneer of popular science books, he combated the Darwinian evolution theory with *Footprints of the Creator* (1850), *The Testimony of the Rocks* (1857) and *Sketchbook of Popular Geology* (published posthumously, 1859).

Worn out by illness and overwork, he shot himself.

▷ P Bayne, *Hugh Miller* (2 vols, 1871)

MILLER, Jason
(1939–)

American playwright and actor, born in Long Island, New York. He was educated at the University of Scranton, Pennsylvania. His first important play was *Nobody Hears A Broken Drum* (1970), set during the American Civil War. His best-known work is *That Championship Season* (1972), a play which, in the course of a college reunion, unpeels the veneer of middle-America to reveal the greed and corruption lying beneath. It won him a Pulitzer Prize in 1973. He has pursued a parallel career as an actor, and was nominated for an Oscar for his role in the film *The Exorcist* (1973).

MILLER, Joaquin, pseud of **Cincinnatus Heine Miller**
(1839–1913)

American poet, born in Liberty, Indiana. He became a miner in California, and fought in the Indian wars. After practising law in Oregon, he edited a paper suppressed for showing Confederate sympathies. In 1866–70 he was a county judge in Oregon, and after a spell as a Washington journalist, in 1877 he settled in California as a fruitgrower. His poems include *Songs of the Sierras* (1871). He also wrote a successful play, *The Danites of the Sierras* (1877). He wrote his autobiography in *My Life among the Modocs* (1873) and *My Own Story* (new ed 1891).

▷ M M Marberry, *Splendid Poseur: Joaquin Miller, American Poet* (1953)

MILLER, Walter Michael
(1922–)

American science-fiction writer, born in Florida. He flew combat missions in World War II, and converted to Catholicism in 1947. He wrote around 40 short stories, collected in *Conditionally Human* (1962) and *The View from the Stars* (1965), many of which have been influential in the development of the genre. He is best known for his only novel, *A Canticle for Leibowitz* (1960), originally published in parts in magazine form (1955–7). One of the few serious attempts to deal with religion in a science-fiction narrative, it spans a millennium, and sets the preserving religious impulse against the destructive scientific one in a post-holocaust human civilization moving inexorably towards another catastrophe. He has reportedly been working on a sequel into the 1990s.

MILLER, William
(1810–72)

Scottish poet, born in Glasgow, known as the 'Laureate of the nursery'. He was a wood-turner by profession, having relinquished a medical career through ill-health. In 1863, urged on by his friends, he published a collection of poems which brought him some fame. Today, however, he is remembered only as the author of 'Wee Willie Winkie', one of his numerous dialect poems about children and childhood.

MILLETT, John
(1928–)

Australian poet who served in the Australian air force in Britain during World War II; his experiences resulted in *Tail Arse Charlie*, published in *Poetry Australia* in 1982, and later dramatized for radio. Earlier he had produced four collections ranging from the semi-autobiographical *Calendar Adam* (1971) to *West of the Cunderang* (1982), all characterized by vivid use of language and a keen sense of *locale*.

MILLIGAN, Spike (Terence Alan)
(1918–)

English humorist, born in Ahmadnagar, India. A singer and trumpeter before doing war service, he made his radio debut in *Opportunity Knocks* (1949) and, along with Peter Sellers, Harry Secombe and Michael Bentine, co-wrote and performed in *The Goon Show* (1951–9). His unique perspective on the world, allied to an irrepressible sense of the ridiculous and the surreal, has been expressed in all the artistic media and has left an indelible influence on British humour. On stage, he has appeared in *Treasure Island* (1961, 1973, 1974, 1975) and *The Bed-Sitting Room* (1963, 1967), which he also co-wrote. Aside from numerous television series and small roles in feature films, he has published a variety of children's books, poetry, autobiography and comic novels including *Puckoon* (1963), *Adolf Hitler, My Part in His Downfall* (1971), *The Looney: An Irish Fantasy* (1987), and the autobiographical volumes *Where Have All the Bullets Gone?* (1985) and *Peacework* (1991).

MILLIN, Sarah Gertrude
(1889–1968)

South African novelist, a candid racist whose novel *God's Stepchildren* (1924) was used by the Nazis as an anti-Semitic tract. She was capable and skilful, and because of her undoubted talents has been described as 'perhaps the most unpleasant woman writer of this century'. Wife of a judge, haunted by fear

of miscegenation, she wrote 15 other well-executed novels.

MILLS, C(harles) Wright
(1916–62)

American sociologist and academic. He was born in Waco, Texas, and joined the faculty of Columbia University, New York City. His two main contributions to social understanding were *White Collar* (1951), a critical account of the 'new', post-war middle classes, and *The Power Elite* (1956), a darker and more pessimistic study of social control by the military, politicians and corporate money. *The Causes of World War Three* (1958) suggested the direction of Mills's thought and his subsequent impact on the New Left in the USA. However, his career was drastically foreshortened: after writing the highly prescient *Listen Yankee: The Revolution in Cuba* (1960), he died aged just 46.
▷J Eldridge, *C Wright Mills* (1983)

MILMAN, Henry Hart
(1791–1868)

English poet and church historian, born in London, son of Sir Francis Milman (1746–1821), physician to George III. He was educated at Eton and Oxford, where he won the Newdigate Prize (1812). In 1816 he became vicar at Reading, from 1821 to 1831 Professor of Poetry at Oxford, and in 1849 Dean of St Paul's. His *Poems and dramatic works* (3 vols, 1839) are almost forgotten, except for a few hymns.

MILNE, A(lan) A(lexander)
(1882–1956)

English author, born in St John's Wood, London. He was educated at Westminster and Trinity College, Cambridge, where he edited the undergraduate magazine *Granta*. He joined the staff of *Punch* as assistant editor, and became well known for his light essays and his comedies, notably *Wurzel-Flummery* (1917), *Mr Pim Passes By* (1919) and *The Dover Road* (1922). In 1924 he achieved world fame with his book of children's verse, *When We were Very Young*, written for his own son, Christopher Robin. Further children's classics include the enchantingly whimsical *Winnie-the-Pooh* (1926), *Now We are Six* (1927) and *The House at Pooh Corner* (1928), memorably illustrated by E H Shepard. He wrote an autobiography, *It's Too Late Now* (1939).
▷A Thwaite, *A. A. Milne* (1990)

MILNES, Richard Monckton, 1st Baron Houghton
(1809–85)

English politician and writer, born in London. His father, 'single-speech Milnes'

(1784–1858), declined the Chancellorship of the Exchequer and a peerage; his mother was a daughter of the fourth Lord Galway. At Cambridge he was a member of the Apostles Club with many future leading literary figures like **Tennyson** and **Thackeray**. He was MP for Pontefract from 1837 until he entered the House of Lords in 1863. A patron of young writers, he befriended **David Gray**, and was one of the first to recognize **Swinburne**'s genius, and secured the poet laureateship for Tennyson (1850). He was the 'Mr Vavasour' of **Disraeli**'s novel *Tancred*. A traveller, a philanthropist, and an unrivalled after-dinner speaker, he went up in a balloon and down in a diving-bell; he was the first publishing Englishman who gained access to the harems of the East; he championed oppressed nationalities, liberty of conscience, fugitive slaves, the rights of women; and carried a bill for establishing reformatories (1846). As well as his poetry—his collected *Poetical Works* appeared in 1876—and essays, he published *Life, Letters and Remains of Keats* (1848).
▷J Pope-Hennessey, *Monckton Milnes* (1950–2)

MILOSZ, Czeslaw
(1911–)

Polish poet, novelist and essayist, winner of the Nobel Prize for literature, born in Szetejnie, Lithuania. *Trzy zimy* (1936, 'Three Winters'), his second book of poems, had established a reputation for him by the time war broke out. In 1945, after having worked for Polish Radio and a variety of underground publications, he brought out *Ocadenie* ('Rescue'), a collection primarily of war poems. Not until 1980, in which year he won the Nobel Prize for literature, was another book of his published in Poland. He spent much of the intervening 35 years in exile, first in Paris, then in California. His prose works include the novel *Zdobycie władzy* (1953, 'The Seizure of Power'). *Collected Poems 1931–1987* (1988) is a splendid summation of the career of Milosz, one of the greatest European poets of the century.

MILOSZ, Oscar-Vladislas de Lubisez
(1877–1939)

Lithuanian mystic, poet, novelist, philosopher, scientist and dramatist who wrote in French (his family, related to that of **Czeslaw Milosz**, moved to Paris when he was 11 years old). There are two views: that he was pretentious and crazy, and that he was one of the greatest poets of the 20th century. The truth lies in between: he was not pretentious, but his lush and complex work is hard to read and harder to understand—he could fairly be described as a substantial minor poet of

profound interest. After the Russian revolution he represented Lithuania as minister to France and the League of Nations. His poems are indeed almost impenetrable; but, as Marcel Raymond wrote, he sometimes sang 'as Rilke sang': an opulent integrity informs all his work, so that his reader immediately knows that his unique and erudite synthesis of music, Cabala, modern physics (he anticipated Einstein in the formulation of relativity), Swedenborg and other mystics is genuine. Available in English translation are *14 Poems* (1952) and the novel *Miguel Manera* (1919).

MILTON, John
(1608–74)

English poet, born in Bread Street, Cheapside, the son of a composer of some distinction. From St Paul's School he went up to Christ's College, Cambridge, where he spent seven not altogether blameless years, followed by six years of studious leisure at Horton which he regarded as preparation for his life's work as a poet. His apprentice work at Cambridge—apart from some poems of elegant Latin written there or at Horton—includes the splendid 'Nativity Ode', the brilliant epitaph on **Shakespeare** and 'At a Solemn Music'. The poems he wrote at Horton—*L'Allegro* and *Il Penseroso, Comus* and *Lycidas*—he also regarded as preparatory for the great poem or drama which was to be 'doctrinal and exemplary for a nation'. *Lycidas* (1637) is an excellent pastoral elegy, though it was censured for its outburst against the Laudian clergy by critics who were ignorant of the Renaissance pastoral convention. On this ominous note Milton concluded his formal education with a visit to Italy (1638–9). The fame of his Latin poems had preceded him and he was received in the academies with distinction. His Italian tour was interrupted by news of the imminent outbreak of Civil War in England. This event, into which he threw himself with revolutionary ardour, silenced his poetic outpourings for 20 years except for occasional sonnets, most of which were published in a volume of *Poems* in 1645. They range from civilities to friends to trumpet-blasts against his and the Commonwealth's detractors. Two stand out—the noble 'On His Blindness' and 'On the Late Massacre in Piedmont'. On his return to London in 1639 Milton undertook the education of his two nephews, but in 1641 he emerged as the polemical champion of the revolution in a series of pamphlets against episcopacy, including an *Apology for Smectymnuus* (1642). *Smectymnuus* was an attack on episcopacy by five Presbyterians. He was now launched on his second series of controversial pamphlets—the divorce pamphlets which were occasioned by the refusal of his 17-year-old bride, Mary Powell, daughter of a Royalist, whom he married in 1642, to return to him after a visit to her home. The first of these, *The Doctrine and Discipline of Divorce* (1643), involved him in three supplementary pamphlets against the opponents of his views on divorce, and these occasioned a threat of prosecution by a parliamentary committee dominated by the Presbyterians who were now to be reckoned his chief enemies after the episcopacy pamphlets. *Areopagitica, A Speech for the Liberty of Unlicensed Printing* (1644) was the famous vindication which is still quoted when the press is in danger. The contemporary *Tractate on Education*, a brilliant exposition of the Renaissance ideals of education, has much less appeal today. Meanwhile his wife returned to him in 1645 accompanied by her whole family as refugees after Naseby, and two years later, his father having left him enough to live on comfortably, he was able to give up schoolmastering. The execution of King Charles I launched him on his third public controversy, now addressed however to the conscience of Europe. As Latin secretary to the new council of state to which he was appointed immediately after his defence of the regicides (*The Tenure of Kings and Magistrates*, 1649), he became official apologist for the Commonwealth. As such he wrote *Eikonoklastes* and two *Defensiones*, the first, *Pro Populo Anglicano Defensio* (1650), addressed to the celebrated humanist Salmasius. The second, also in Latin, *Defensio Secunda* (1654), contains autobiographical matter and so supplements the personal matter in the *Apology for Smectymnuus*. Meanwhile, his wife having died in 1652, leaving three daughters, he married Catherine Woodcock, whose death two years later is the theme of his beautiful sonnet 'Methought I saw my late espoused Saint'. Although blind from 1652 onwards, he retained his Latin secretaryship until the Restoration (1660), which he roused himself to resist in a last despairing effort as pamphleteer. But the fire had gone out of him, and *The Readie and Easie Way*, which pointed to dictatorship, became the target of the Royalist wits. After the Restoration Milton went into hiding for a short period, and then after the Act of Oblivion (August 1660) he devoted himself wholly to poetry with the exception of his prose *De Doctrina Christiana* (which did not appear until 1823). He married his third wife, Elizabeth Minshull, in 1662 and spent his last days in what is now Bunhill Row. His wife survived him. The theme of *Paradise Lost* (completed 1665, published 1667) had been in Milton's mind since 1641. It was to be a sacred drama then; but when in 1658 his official duties were lightened so as

to allow him to write, he chose the epic form. The first three books reflect the triumph of the godly—so soon to be reversed; the last books, written in 1663, are tinged with despair. God's kingdom is not of this world. Man's intractable nature frustrates the planning of the wise. The heterodox theology of the poem which is made clear in his late *De Doctrina Christiana* did not trouble Protestant readers till modern critics examined it with hostile intent; at the same time they made him responsible for that 'dissociation of sensibility' in the language of poetry which had fatal effects on his 18th-century imitators. *Paradise Regained* (1671) ought to have appeased these critics, for its manner is quiet and grave, though not without grand rhetorical passages. The theme here is the triumph of reason over passion; Christ is more the elevated stoic than the redeemer. Resignation is the note of *Paradise Regained*, but *Samson Agonistes*, published along with it in 1671, shows the reviving spirit of rebellion, due no doubt to the rise of Whig opposition about 1670. The parallel of his own fortunes, both in the private and the public sphere, with those of Samson made Milton pour out his great spirit into this Greek play, which also became the libretto of Handel's oratorio. His last years were spent in sociable comfort in Cripplegate; he was buried next to his father in St Giles' Churchyard, Cripplegate.

▷ D Masson, *The Life of John Milton* (7 vols, 1859–80); W Parker, *John Milton* (2 vols, 1968)

MILUTINOVIĆ SARAJLIJA, Sima
(1791–1847)

Serbian poet, dramatist, would-be folk-song collector (he lacked system) and historian, born in Sarajevo. He was a paradigmatically romantic poet who led a life of adventure. His poetry is fervently patriotic, but exceedingly confused. Perhaps his most significant role was as tutor to **Petar Petrović Njegoš**, whose style he certainly influenced.

MIOMANDRE, Frances de, pseud of François Durand
(1880–1959)

French writer, born in Tours. His first book was a collection of verse, but he was best known as a novelist, and was awarded the Prix **Goncourt** for *Écrit sur l'eau* in 1908. Many of his books are set in Provence, and are characterized by detailed observation, picturesque description, and an elegant, rather old-fashioned prose style. *Direction Étoile* (1937) is one notable exception, a fantasy set on the Paris Métro. He also translated the work of a number of Spanish writers, including **Unamuno**, **Cervantes** and **Asturias**.

MIRA BAI
(c.1498–1546)

A *bhakti* poet and mystic, devoted to Krishna. She was born a Rajput princess, and was duly married to a prince before she was 20. However, even then she had already surrendered herself to Krishna and neglected her husband as a result. Mira Bai constantly had to fight against the traditional roles ascribed to women in society, the crisis coming on the death of her husband when her father-in-law insisted that she become a *sati*. She escaped to a community of bhakti devotees who supported her, eventually becoming a wandering ascetic attached to a temple in the holy city of Dwarka. Mira Bai's poetry reflects her deep love for Krishna, especially in her use of the romantic symbolism of the 'mystical marriage' between herself and her Lord. In common with other mystics Mira Bai often expresses her devotion in two contrasting ways. Firstly, in describing Krishna's beauty and the blissful experience of being in his presence; and secondly in expressing the deep pain of separation from Krishna. Mira Bai is unusual in that she cannot be placed in any particular category, her notion of Krishna encompassing both his mythological and the transcendent natures. As a result she is able to identify herself with him on the personal level and by seeing herself as being absorbed in him. Indeed, it is this that helps to explain her wide appeal.

MIRANDA, Francisco de Sá de
(1481–1558)

Portuguese poet, playwright and Renaissance humanist and moralist. He introduced the Italian style (he spent some years in Italy and Sicily in the 1520s) into his literature with his eclogue *Alexo*, of which he is one of the major exponents and formers. He helped prepare the way for **Camoens**, though was in no way his equal as a poet. He was at first a courtier; in 1532 he returned to his own estates, where he lived the life of a gentleman deeply and expressively displeased with the frivolity of all he saw about him. He wrote some poetry in Castilian, and, of all the poets of major historical importance, was perhaps the least skilled in technique; yet by sheer persistence and hard work he founded the new school which culminated in Camoens.
▷A F G Bell, *Portuguese Literature* (1922)

MIRBEAU, Octave
(1850–1917)

French dramatist, novelist, and journalist, born in Trevières (Calvados). A radical, he attracted attention by the violence of his writings. His play *Les Affaires sont les affaires* (1903, 'Business is Business') was adapted by

Sidney Grundy (1905). Other works include *Le Jardin des supplices* (1898, Eng trans *Torture Garden*, 1931) and *Le Journal d'une femme de chambre* (1900, Eng trans *A Chambermaid's Diary*, 1934).
▷M Renan, *Octave Mirbeau* (1924)

MIRÓ, Gabriel
(1879–1930)

Spanish novelist, born in Alicante; he was and still is renowned for his sensuous and evocative style. A Spanish critic called him 'a hermit drunk with sensuality'. His novel about Christ, as seen through the eyes of his contemporaries, *Figuras de la Pasión del Señor* (1917, Eng trans *Figures of the Passion of our Lord*, 1925), was condemned by his fellow Roman Catholics but established his reputation with discerning critics. The first volume of his two-part novel *Nuestre padre San Daniel* (1921) has been translated (*Our Father San Daniel*, 1930); the second volume, *El obispo leproso* (1926, 'The Leprous Bishop'), has not. This work is an unequivocal masterpiece, set in the last two decades of the 19th century, and depicting a bishop who loves life, and so is rewarded with a horrible disease—but this, it is shown with great affirmative conviction, cannot eat into his heart. The Spanish Academy of Letters refused recognition of Miró owing to his liberalism; now he is revered in Spanish letters.

MIRO, Ricardo
(1883–1940)

The national poet of the small country of Panama, born in Panama City. He worked to free Panama from Colombian rule, and after independence was declared in 1903 devoted himself to literary journalism, editing the periodical *Nuevos Ritos* ('New Rites') and founding a newspaper. His poetry helped give Panama a sense of national identity, but it has never been seriously suggested that it exports well, and he is absent from most anthologies of Latin American verse.

MIRON, Gaston
(1928–)

French–Canadian poet, born in Saint-Agathe-des-Montes, Québec. In the 1950s and 1960s he became a legendary personality in Québec and Montreal, the author of long poems which he did not care if he published or not, and with a dramatically separatist stance. The best-known of these poems was 'La Vie agonique', ('The Anguished Life'). He reached the status of 'Miron le magnifique' with the publication of the collection *L'Homme rapaillé* (1970), a collection of 57 poems on the theme of 'the present impossibility of writing a book'. He has been called the 'single most influential figure in French–Canadian literature today'. Poems are translated in *The Poetry of French Canada in Translation*, edited by **John Glassco** and published in 1970.

▷J Brault, *Miron le magnifique* (1966, in French)

MISHIMA Yukio, pseud of Hiraoka Kimitake
(1925–70)

Japanese writer, born in Tokyo. He published his first story in 1944 at the age of 19. He attended Tokyo University before becoming a civil servant and embarking on a prolific writing career which, as well as 40 novels, produced poetry, essays and modern Kabuki and Nō drama. His first major work was *Kamen no Kokuhaku* (1949, Eng trans *Confessions of a Mask*, 1958) which dealt with his discovery of his own homosexuality and the ways in which he attempted to conceal it. After many other works, notably the novels *Kinkakuji* (1956, Eng trans *The Temple of the Golden Pavilion*, 1959) and *Utage no ato* (1960, Eng trans *After the Banquet*, 1963), he wrote his great tetralogy, *Hojo no umi* (1965–70, Eng trans *The Sea of Fertility*, 1972–4), which, with a central theme of reincarnation, spanned Japanese life and events in the 20th century. Passionately interested in the chivalrous traditions of Imperial Japan, he believed implicitly in the ideal of a heroic destiny, the pursuit of an absolute ideal of beauty, and the concept of a glorious and honourable death in battle. He became an expert in the martial arts of *karate* and *kendo*, and in 1968 founded the Shield Society, a group of a hundred youths dedicated to a revival of *Bushido*, the Samurai knightly code of honour. The most extreme expression of his elitist right-wing views was in an essay *Taiyo to tetsu* (1968, Eng trans *Sun and Steel*, 1970), and in the same year he committed suicide by performing *seppuku* after a carefully-staged token attempt to rouse the nation to a return to pre-war nationalist ideals. Among his other novels are *Ai no kawaki* (1950, Eng trans *Thirst for Love*, 1969), *Shiosai* (1954, Eng trans *The Sound of Waves*, 1956) and *Gogo no eilo* (1963, Eng trans *The Sailor Who Fell from Grace with the Sea*, 1965); his plays include *Sado koshaku fujin* (1965, Eng trans *Madame de Sade*, 1967) and *Waga tomo Hitler* (1968, 'My Friend Hitler').

▷H S Stokes, *A Life of Mishima* (1974)

MISTRAL, Frédéric
(1830–1914)

Provençal poet and winner of the Nobel Prize for literature, born in Maillane near Avignon. After studying law at Avignon, he went home to work on the land and write poetry. He helped to found the Provençal renaissance movement (Félibrige school). In 1859 his epic *Mirèio* (Eng trans 1890) gained him the poet's prize of the Académie française and the *Légion d'honneur*. He was awarded a Nobel Prize for literature in 1904. Other works are an epic, *Calendau* (1861), poems *Lis Isclo d'or* (1876), a tragedy *La Reino Jano* (1890), and a Provençal–French dictionary (1878–86).

▷L Larguier, *Mistral* (1930, in French)

MISTRAL, Gabriela, pseud of Lucila Godoy de Alcayaga
(1889–1957)

Chilean poet, diplomat and teacher, winner of the Nobel Prize for literature, born in Vicuña. As a teacher she won a poetry prize with her *Sonetos de la muerte* ('Sonnets of Death') at Santiago in 1915. She taught at Columbia University, Vassar and in Puerto Rico, and was formerly consul at Madrid and elsewhere. The cost of publication of her first book, *Desolación* (1922, 'Desolation'), was defrayed by the teachers of New York. Her work is inspired by religious sentiments and a romantic preoccupation with sorrow and death, infused with an intense lyricism. Her career as a teacher led her to write a great deal of work for children, notably the songs in *Ternura* (1924); much of her children's writing is translated in *Crickets and Frogs* (1972). She was awarded the Nobel Prize for literature in 1945.

▷M Arce de Vázquez, *Gabriela Mistral: the poet and her work* (1964)

MISTRY, Rohinton
(1952–)

Canadian novelist and short-story writer, born in Bombay. He emigrated to Toronto in 1975, working in a bank for a decade while establishing himself as a writer. He has twice won the Hart House Prize (1983, 1984), for his short stories, a collection of which, *Tales From Firozsha Baag* (1987), was his first book to be published. *Such A Long Journey* (1991), his first novel, is the tale of Gustad Noble, a Zoroastrian, and his family, set during the war which resulted in the birth of Bangla Desh. It was shortlisted for the Booker Prize.

MITCHELL, (Sibyl) Elyne Keith
(1913–)

Australian writer, born in Melbourne, author of a popular children's series of novels about horses, beginning with *The Silver Brumby* (1958), followed by *Silver Brumby's Daughter* (1960) and others including *Snowy River Brumby* (1980). She also wrote *The Colt from Snowy River* (1979), a novel based on the film of **Banjo Paterson**'s poem *The Man from Snowy River* (1982), and two books on World

MITCHELL, Margaret

War I, *Light Horse: The Story of Australia's Mounted Troops* (1978) and *The Lighthorse Men* (1987). From her home on the western slopes of the Snowies she has also written *Australia's Alps* (1942) and *The Discoverers of the Snowy Mountains* (1985).

MITCHELL, Margaret
(1900–49)

American novelist, born in Atlanta, Georgia. She studied for a medical career, but turned to journalism. After her marriage to J R Marsh in 1925, she began the 10-year task of writing her only novel, *Gone with the Wind* (1936), which won the Pulitzer Prize, sold over 25 million copies, was translated into 30 languages and was the subject of a celebrated film in 1939.
▷A Edwards, *The Road to Tara* (1983)

MITCHISON, Naomi Mary Margaret, née Haldane
(1897–)

British writer, born in Edinburgh, the daughter of the physiologist J S Haldane. Educated at the Dragon School, Oxford, she won instant attention with her brilliant and personal evocations of Greece and Sparta in a series of novels such as *The Conquered* (1923), *When the Bough Breaks* (1924), *Cloud Cuckoo Land* (1925) and *Black Sparta* (1928). In 1931 came the erudite *Corn King and Spring Queen*, which brought to life the civilizations of ancient Egypt, Scythia and the Middle East. She has travelled widely, and in 1963 was made Tribal Adviser and Mother to the Bakgatla of Botswana. She has written more than 70 books, including her memoirs in *Small Talk* (1973), *All Change Here* (1975) and *You May Well Ask* (1979), among many other writings. She married the Labour MP Gilbert Richard Mitchison (1890–1970) in 1916. Since 1937 she has lived in Carradale in the Mull of Kintyre, Scotland.
▷J Benton, *A Century of Experiment* (1990)

MITFORD, Mary Russell
(1787–1855)

English novelist and dramatist, daughter of a spendthrift physician. At the age of 10 she won £20 000 in a lottery and went to school in Chelsea. As the family became more and more impoverished she had to write to earn money. Several plays were produced successfully but failed to keep the stage. Her gift was for charming sketches of country manners, scenery and character, which after appearing in magazines were collected as *Our Village* (5 vols, 1824–32). She received a civil list pension in 1837 which was increased on her father's death from subscriptions raised

to pay his debts. In 1852 she published *Recollections of a Literary Life*.
▷V Watson, *Mary Russell Mitford* (1949)

MITFORD, Nancy Freeman
(1904–73)

English writer, daughter of the 2nd Baron Redesdale and sister of Unity Mitford. She established a reputation with her witty novels such as *Pursuit of Love* (1945) and *Love in a Cold Climate* (1949), followed by *The Blessing* (1951) and *Don't Tell Alfred* (1960). After the war she settled in France and wrote her major biographies *Madame de Pompadour* (1953), *Voltaire in Love* (1957), *The Sun King* (1966) and *Frederick the Great* (1970). As one of the essayists in *Noblesse Oblige*, edited by herself (1956), she helped to originate the famous 'U', or upper-class, and 'non-U' classification of linguistic usage and behaviour. Her sister Jessica (1917–) wrote *Hons and Rebels* (1960), an autobiography that told the story of the Mitfords' unconventional childhood.
▷S Hastings, *Nancy Mitford* (1985)

MITTELHOLZER, Edgar
(1909–65)

Guyanian novelist. Born and educated in Guyana, he worked as a customs official and journalist before serving in the Navy in World War II. Settling in London in 1945, he became a full-time writer in 1952 when he received a Guggenheim Fellowship. Of mixed race origins, his unhappy personal life led to psychological illness and his eventual suicide. He wrote 22 novels, mostly set in modern Guyana, plus his autobiography, *A Swarthy Boy* (1963). One of the pioneers of Caribbean literature, his first novel, *A Morning at the Office* (1950), was acclaimed for its realistic portrayal of racial tensions in city life. His trilogy, *Children of Kaywana*, portrays Guyana's unchronicled past. Although much of his later work is flawed by excessive violence, his earlier novels are distinguished by their narrative excitement, sense of place and array of fascinating characters.
▷M Gilkes, 'Pioneers', in *The West Indian Novel* (1981)

MIYOSHI Tatsuji
(1900–64)

Japanese poet, from Tokyo. He was highly influential in the middle years of the 20th century, being the centre of a number of literary circles, though his work—long poems in blank verse with elaborate imagery—is not now so highly esteemed. His chief importance lies perhaps in his editorship of a series of literary magazines, especially *Buntai*, which

was the arena in which a number of up-and-coming writers of the 1930s cut their literary teeth.
▷D Keene (ed), *The Modern Japanese Prose Poem: An Anthology of Six Poets* (1980)

MLODÓZENIEC, Stanislaw
(1895–1959)

Polish poet prominent in the Futurist movement inspired by **Marinetti**, but more particularly a 'Polish primitivist'. He was born to peasant parents in Dobrocice. In his poetry he combined strident Futurist presentation with folkloristic themes—the latter of which are the more interesting and original. He went to London after the Russian takeover, but returned to Warsaw to die. He is well represented in *Five Centuries of Polish Poetry* (1960).

MO, Timothy
(1950–)

British novelist and journalist, born in Hong Kong of an English mother and a Cantonese father. He was educated at Oxford. Mo writes incisively but compassionately about cultural ambitions and the lack of comprehension between races. His first novel, *The Monkey King* (1978), concerns family and business affairs in Hong Kong and the Chinese mainland, while *Sour Sweet* (1982) looks at the precarious and sometimes comic fate of a family of Chinese immigrants to London, who open a restaurant and brush against the Chinese criminal fraternity. *An Insular Possession* (1986) is a more ambitious, longer work, set during the 19th-century opium wars between China and Britain, partly a novel of political intrigue, partly a comedy of manners. *The Redundancy of Courage* (1991) continues the more serious theme, charting the life of a hotel worker who becomes politically involved following the American invasion of East Timor in 1975.

MOBERG, (Carl Artur) Vilhelm
(1898–1973)

Swedish author, born in Algutsboda in Småland. He came from a family of crofters and enlisted soldiers and remained loyal to his background. His best-known work is the series of novels that deal with documentary accuracy with the 19th-century mass migration of Swedes to the USA: *Utvandrarna* (1949, Eng trans *The Emigrants*, 1951), *Invandrarna* (1952, Eng trans *Unto a Good Land*, 1957), *Nybyggarna* (1956, 'The Settlers') and *Sista brevet till Sverige* (1959, 'Last Letter to Sweden'). His unfinished *Min svenska historia 1–2* (1970–1, 'My Swedish History') looks at history from the viewpoint of the common people. He was a popular

dramatist and several of his novels, notably *The Emigrants*, have been filmed.
▷P Holmes, *Vilhelm Moberg* (1980)

MOCKEL, Albert
(1866–1945)

Belgian Symbolist poet, critic and editor, born in Ougrée. He founded *La Wallonie* (1886–93), the Symbolist review. Initially influenced by **Gorter**, he soon turned for inspiration to **Mallarmé** and to Mallarmé's French disciple **René Ghil**. His poetry is in a melodious free verse, much influenced by the Wagnerian notion of key motifs, and, as in *La Flamme immortelle* (1924, 'The Immortal Flame'), his major work, is schematic and impersonal. Today, he is much respected but not widely read.

MOE, Jørgen Engebretsen
(1813–82)

Norwegian folklorist and poet, Bishop of Christiansand (1875–81). With Peter Christian Asbjørnsen he collected and edited *Norwegian Folk Stories* (1841–4). He also published a book of Romantic verse (1850), and a children's classic, *I brønden og i kjærnet* (1851).
▷P C Asbjørnsen, *Mannen og livsverket* (1947)

MOGUEL Y URQUIZA, Juan Antonio
(1745–1804)

Basque novelist, born in Eibar, Guipúzoca. He achieved the remarkable feat of translating the *Pensées* of Blaise Pascal into Basque. His moralistic but nonetheless lively and acutely observed novel *Pero Abarca*, first published in Castilian in 1899 (in Basque in 1955), circulated widely in Basque manuscript in his lifetime. It was written in dialogue, and its protagonist, a street barber, Maisu Juan, became a legendary character.
▷R Gallop, *A Book of the Basques* (1930); L Michelena, *Historia de la literatura vasca* (1960)

MOIR, David Macbeth
(1798–1851)

Scottish physician and writer, born in Musselburgh, East Lothian, where he practised as a physician from 1817 until his death. Under his pen-name of *Delta* (δ) he contributed verses to *Blackwood's Magazine* (collected 1852), and is remembered for his humorous *The Life of Mansie Wauch, Tailor in Dalkeith* (1828).
▷Sir G Douglas, *The Blackwood Group* (1897)

MOLESWORTH, Mary Louisa, née Stewart
(1839–1921)
Scottish novelist and writer of children's
stories, born in Rotterdam. She spent her
childhood in Manchester, Scotland and Switzerland. She began writing as a novelist under
the pseudonym 'Ennis Graham', but she is
best known as a writer of stories for children,
such as *Carrots: Just a Little Boy* (1876), *The
Cuckoo Clock* (1877), *The Tapestry Room*
(1879), and the more realistic *Two Little
Waifs* (1883).
▷ R L Green, *Mrs Molesworth* (1961)

MOLIÈRE, stage name of **Jean Baptiste
Poquelin**
(1622–73)
French playwright, born in Paris, the son of
a well-to-do upholsterer. He studied with the
Jesuits at the Collège de Clermont, under the
philosopher and scientist Pierre Gassendi. He
may have been called to the Bar. His mother,
who had some property, died when he was 10
years old, and thus when he came of age he
received his share of her fortune. He declined
to follow his father's business, hired a tennis
court, and embarked on a theatrical venture
(1643) with the Béjart family and others,
under the title of L'Illustre Théâtre, which
lasted for over three years in Paris. The company then proceeded to the provinces from
Lyons to Rouen, and had sufficient success
to keep going from 1646 to 1658. Prince François de Conti took it under his protection
for a time; and when he took to Catholic
Methodism, Molière obtained the patronage
of the king's brother, Philippe d'Orléans, so
that his troupe became the servants of Monsieur. He played before the king on 24 October
1658, and organized a regular theatre, first in
the Petit Bourbon, then, on its demolition, in
the Palais Royal. In the provinces Molière
had acquired experience as a comic writer,
mostly in the style of the old farces. But he
had also written *L'Étourdi* (1655, Eng trans
The Blunderers, 1762) and *Le Dépit amoureux*
(1656, Eng trans *The Amorous Quarrel*, 1762).
As a theatre manager he had to perform tragedy as well as comedy. **Corneille**'s *Nicomède*,
with which he opened, was not a success; and
though the other great tragedian of the day,
Racine, was a personal friend of Molière's,
their connection as manager and author was
brief and unfortunate. But Molière soon realized his own immense resources as a comic
writer. *Les Précieuses ridicules* (Eng trans *The
Conceited Young Ladies*, 1762) was published
in November 1659, and every year until his
death he produced at least one of his comic
masterpieces. In the spring of 1662 he married
Armande Béjart, an actress in his own
company, probably about 19, and the youngest member of the Béjart family, of which
two other sisters, Madeleine and Geneviève,
and one brother, Joseph, had been members
of L'Illustre Théâtre. It has been suggested
that Madeleine Béjart and Molière were
lovers, that Armande was Madeleine's
daughter, even that Molière was the father of
his own wife! It is also said that Armande was
unfaithful to her husband. In August 1665
the king adopted Molière's troupe as his own
servants. In 1667 symptoms of lung disease
showed themselves. He died in his home in
the rue de Richelieu the night after having
acted as the *Malade* in the seventh performance of his last play, *Le Malade Imag-
inaire* (1673, Eng trans *Doctor Last in his
Chariot*, 1769). He was generous and amiable;
and there are insufficient grounds for the
accusations of irreligion brought against him.
The dates and titles of his other plays are:
Sganarelle (1660, Eng trans *The Picture*,
1745); *Don Garcie de Navarre* (1661, Eng
trans *Don Garcia of Navarre; or The Jealous
Prince*, 1714); *L'Ecole des maris* (1661, Eng
trans in parallel *The School for Husbands*,
1732), *Les Fâcheux* (1622, Eng trans *The
Impertinents*, 1732), *L'Ecole des femmes*
(1662, Eng trans *The School for Wives*, 1971),
La Critique de l'École des femmes (1663, Eng
trans in parallel *School for Wives criticis'd*,
1755), *Impromptu de Versailles* (1663, Eng
trans in parallel *The Impromptu of Versailles*,
1755); *Le Mariage forcé* (1664, Eng trans *The
Forced Marriage*, 1762), *La Princesse d'Élide*
(1664, Eng trans *The Universal Passion*,
1737), *Tartuffe* (partially, 1664, Eng trans
1670); *Le Festin de Pierre [Don Juan]* (1665,
Eng trans in parallel *Don John*, 1755), *L'Amour médecin* (1665, Eng trans *The Quacks*,
1705); *Le Misanthrope* (1666, Eng trans
1762), *Le médecin malgré lui* (1666, Eng trans
The Dumb Lady, 1672), *Mélicerte* (1666, Eng
trans 1755), *Le Sicilien* (1666, Eng trans *The
Sicilian*, 1732); *Tartuffe* (1667, a revised version); *Amphitryon* (1668, Eng trans 1690),
George Dandin (1668, Eng trans 1732), *L'Av-
are* (1668, Eng trans *The Miser*, 1672); *Monsieur de Pourceaugnac* (1669, Eng trans *The
Cornish Squire*, 1734); *Les Amants mag-
nifiques* (1670, Eng trans in parallel *The
Magnificent Lovers*, 1755), *Le Bourgeois
gentilhomme* (1671, Eng trans *The Citizen
Turned Gentleman*, 1672); *Les Fourberies de
Scapin* (1671, Eng trans *The Cheats of Scapin*,
1677); *La Comtesse d'Escarbagnas* (1671,
'The Countess of Escarbagnas') and *Les
Femmes savantes* (1672, Eng trans *The Female
Virtuosoes*, 1690). To this must be added part
of *Psyché* (1671), in collaboration with **Phi-
lippe Quinault** and **Corneille**, two farces, a
few court masques, and some miscellaneous
poems.
▷ J Palmer, *Molière* (1930)

MÖLLER, Poul Martin
(1794–1838)

Danish literary figure, born in Uldum. He graduated in theology at Copenhagen and later became a Professor of Philosophy, first in Oslo, and then in Copenhagen. His chief work, *En dansk Students Eventyr* ('Adventures of a Danish Student'), which he finished in 1824, but which was published posthumously, is a charming, light-hearted account of undergraduate life in Copenhagen. During a journey to China he wrote in verse nostalgically of his homeland. *Sceneri Rosenborg Slotshave* (1819–21, 'Scenes from the Garden at Rosenberg Castle') is a representative work, showing how he avoids the abstract and metaphysical, for his credo was 'all poetry that does not come from life is a lie'. He made the first Danish translation of *The Odyssey*, wrote philosophical essays and coined brilliant aphorisms.
▷F Nielson, *Om Poul Möller* (1961)

MOLNÁR, Ferenc
(1878–1952)

Hungarian novelist and dramatist, born in Budapest. He is best known for his novel *A Pál-utcai fiúk* (1907, 'The Paul Street Boys'), and his plays *The Devil* (1907), *Liliom* (1909, Eng trans 1944), which formed the basis of the musical comedy *Carousel* (1921 as a stage play; 1945 as a musical by Rodgers and **Hammerstein**; 1956 as a musical film), and *A zenélő angyal* (1930, Eng trans *Angel Making Music*, 1934), all of which have achieved success in English translation. He emigrated to the USA in 1940.
▷I Vécsei, *Molnár Ferenc* (1966)

MOMADAY, N(avarre) Scott, also known by the Kiowa name **Tsoai-talee**
(1934–)

Native American novelist and autobiographer, born in Oklahoma and raised on a reservation in the South West. He attended the University of New Mexico, Albuquerque, and Stanford University, California, where he returned as professor in 1972, having taught at other Californian campuses. Like **Ralph Ellison** in black writing, his reputation is based on one definitive text, the Pulitzer Prize-winning novel, *House Made of Dawn* (1968), which concerns the conflict between Native American and Anglo-Saxon culture. Its themes were already present in Momaday's collection of Kiowa tales, *The Journey of Tai-me* (1967, revised and commercially published as *The Way to Rainy Mountain*, 1969), and recur in his powerful memoir *The Names* (1976). However, it was not until 1989 that he wrote another full-length fiction; *The*

Ancient Child is about a half-Kiowa artist's rediscovery of his ethnic heritage.
▷A Velie, *Four American Indian Literary Masters* (1982)

MOMBERT, Alfred
(1872–1942)

German poet and contemplative who remained aloof from literary movements, but who in certain important respects anticipated Expressionism. In 1940 he was taken, as a Jew, into a concentration camp, but a friend secured his release; he died in Switzerland. Occasionally compared, perhaps over confidently, to **William Blake**, he erected a vast and unfortunately grandiose 'cosmic myth' to account for his feelings of union with nature and his belief in the transmigration of souls. But his poetry remains a quarry in which jewels may often be found. The massive mystical closet-play *Aeon* (1907–11), occasionally glowing in its authentic sense of the fulfilled inner life, is worthy if not quite a masterpiece. His late *Sfaira der Alte* (1936–42, 'Sfaira the Elder'), in which he is Sfaira the old poet, is a moving allegorical account of the struggle between himself and Nazism—he had refused to leave Germany—and is cast in a wholly pantheistic form.

MOMMSEN, Christian Matthias Theodor
(1817–1903)

German scholar and writer, born in Garding, Schleswig. He studied law in Kiel, and was briefly a newspaper editor before holding professorships at universities in Leipzig, Zurich, Breslau and Berlin. Although his writings were historical and scholarly rather than literary, their vivid and dramatic narratives brought him the Nobel Prize for literature in 1902. His most famous work was the multi-volume *Romische Geschichte* (1854–85, Eng trans *History of Rome*, 1862–86), but he wrote a number of other historical works, and edited the *Corpus Inscriptionum Latinarum*, a collection of all Latin inscriptions then extant. His *Gesammelte Schriften* ('Collected Writings') were published in Berlin (1905–13).
▷V Klosterman, *Theodor Mommsen* (1958–80)

MONRO, Harold (Edward)
(1879–1932)

English poet and anthologist, born in Brussels. After graduating from Cambridge, he travelled abroad and was involved with various progressive communities before taking up the promotion of English poetry. He founded the influential *Poetry Review* in 1912 and the Poetry Bookshop in London the following year. Generous to other poets, he published the Georgians and the Imagists; some of his own work is close to the former, including such popular pieces as the closely observed 'Milk for the Cat' (1914), but his best, least romantic and most original poems, mainly written in his later years, are bitter in tone, reflecting a loneliness related to his alcoholism and bisexuality. These include 'Strange Meetings' (1917), 'The One, Faithful ...' (1933) and 'Bitter Sanctuary' (1933). His *Collected Poems* (1933) were edited by his second wife, Alida.

▷ J Grant, *Harold Monro and the Poetry Bookshop* (1967)

MONROE, Harriet
(1860–1936)

American poet and critic, born in Chicago. In 1912 she founded the magazine *Poetry*, which was influential in publicizing the work of **Vachel Lindsay**, **T S Eliot**, **Ezra Pound** and **Robert Frost**, among others. She wrote the 'Columbian Ode' for the Chicago World's Columbian Exposition (1892), celebrating the 400th anniversary of the west's 'discovery' of America. In 1917 she edited the influential free verse anthology, *The New Poetry*. Her own work was collected in *Chosen Poems* (1935).

▷ *A Poet's Life* (1937)

MONSARRAT, Nicholas John Turney
(1910–79)

English novelist, born in Liverpool. He was educated at Winchester and at Trinity College, Cambridge, abandoned law for literature and wrote three quite successful novels, and a play, *The Visitors*, which reached the London stage. During the war he served in the navy, and out of his experiences emerged his bestselling novel *The Cruel Sea* (1951), which was filmed. *The Story of Esther Costello* (1953) repeated that success, followed by *The Tribe That Lost Its Head* (1956) and *The Pillow Fight* (1965). He settled in Ottawa, Canada, as director of the UK Information Office (1953–6) after holding a similar post in South Africa (1946–52).

MONTAGU, Lady Mary Wortley, née Pierrepont
(1689–1762)

English writer, born in London, the daughter of the Earl (later Duke) of Kingston. Mostly self-educated, she taught herself Latin and wrote poetry from childhood. In 1712 she eloped with Edward Wortley Montagu and lived in London, where she gained a reputation for wit and was on close terms with **Addison**, **Pope** and others. From 1716 to 1718 she lived in Constantinople while her husband was on embassy; the sparkling letters she wrote from Turkey were published posthumously (1763). On her return she was prominent in intellectual and court circles for 20 years, became a friend of the feminist Mary Astell, was involved in a bitter literary feud with Pope, wrote satirical verse, published political essays (1737–8) in support of Sir Robert Walpole, and campaigned successfully for the introduction of smallpox inoculation. In 1739 she travelled to Italy in vain pursuit of a young writer Francesco Algarotti with whom she had fallen in love, then stayed on the Continent until shortly before her death. As a poet and essayist she was versatile, witty and accomplished, but her letters, whether written for publication or as personal correspondence, are in a class apart for candour, intelligence, keen observation and vivid expression.

▷ *Complete Letters*, ed R Halsband (1965–7); R Halsband, *The Life of Mary Wortley Montagu* (1956)

MONTAGUE, Charles Edward
(1867–1928)

English novelist and essayist, of Irish parentage. He was on the staff of *The Manchester Guardian* from 1890 to 1925. His numerous writings include the novels *A Hind Let Loose* (1910), *Rough Justice* (1926) and *Disenchantment* (1922), an account of his experiences as a soldier in World War I.

MONTAGUE, John
(1929–)

Irish poet, born in New York and educated in Dublin, at whose University College he graduated in History and English. He has received many awards, and is a popular reader of his own work to audiences in Ireland and in the USA. He has published some 30 volumes of verse, as well as a play, a novel, a critical work, and some stories. Critical response has been generous but often imprecise, coping, as it has to, with an unusually versatile and varied corpus of work, much influenced by such American poets as **William Carlos Williams**, and with, as has been remarked, some lack of direction. It is the impact of his whole work, rather than individual poems, which has impressed critics.

▷ T D Redshaw (ed), *Hill Field: Poems and Memories for John Montague on his 60th Birthday* (1989)

MONTAIGNE, Michel Eyquem de
(1533–92)

French essayist, third son of the Seigneur de Montaigne, born at the Château de Montaigne in Périgord. As an experiment in

humanist upbringing, he spoke no language but Latin until he was six, and at the Collège de Guienne in Bordeaux he remained for seven years, boarding in the rooms of his famous teachers, George Buchanan and **Marc-Antoine de Muret**. He subsequently studied law; but from the age of 13 to 24 little is known of him, though it is certain that he was frequently in Paris, knew something of court life, and took his full share of its pleasures. He obtained a post in connection with the *parlement* of Bordeaux, and for 13 years was a city counsellor. He formed a close friendship with Étienne de la Boëtie (1530–63). He married (1565) Françoise de la Chassaigne, daughter of a fellow counsellor. A translation (1569) of the *Natural Theology* of a 15th-century professor at Toulouse was his first attempt at literature, and supplied the text for his *Apologie de Raymon Sebond* ('Apologia for Raymond Sebond'), in which he exhibited the full scope of his own sceptical philosophy. In 1571, as his two elder brothers had died, he succeeded to the family estate at Château de Montaigne, and there lived the life of a country gentleman, varied only by visits to Paris and a tour in Germany, Switzerland and Italy. There he began those *Essais* (1572–80 and 1588, Eng trans *Essays*, 1603) which were to give him a place among the foremost names in literary history. The record of his journey (1580–1), in French and Italian, was first published in 1774. Unanimously elected Mayor of Bordeaux (against his wishes), he performed his duties to the satisfaction of the citizens, and was re-elected. Despite the free expression of scepticism in his writings, he devoutly received the last offices of the church. From the very first, men like Pascal, differing completely from him in all the fundamental problems of life (as in his inconclusive philosophy, his easy moral opinions, his imperfect sense of duty), have acknowledged their debt to his fearless and all-questioning criticism, expressed mainly in haphazard remarks, seemingly inspired by the mere caprice of the moment, but showing the highest originality, the very broadest sympathies, and a nature capable of embracing and realizing the largest experience of life.
▷ D M Frame, *Montaigne* (1965)

MONTALE, Eugenio
(1896–1981)

Italian poet, winner of the Nobel Prize for literature, born in Genoa. He worked as a journalist and critic, and was an early opponent of fascism. World War I and its aftermath left him with a deep pessimism, which permeates his writing. He was the leading poet of the modern Italian 'Hermetic' school, and his primary concern was with language and meaning. His works include

Ossi di Seppia (1925, 'The Bones of Cuttlefish'), *Le occasioni* (1939, 'Opportunities'), *Finisterre* (1943, 'Finistère'), *La bufera e altro* (1956, 'The Storm and Other Things'), *Satura* (1962, Eng trans *Satura: Five Poems*, 1969) and *Xenia* (1966, Eng trans 1970). He was awarded the Nobel Prize for literature in 1975.
▷ S Ramat, *Eugenio Montale* (1965)

MONTCHRESTIEN, Antoine de
(?1575–1621)

French playwright, economist and poet (probably originally named Mauchrestien). He was orphaned at an early age, but acquired a university education as companion to two brothers, Jacques and François Thézart, whose sister Suzanne he later married. He published an edition of five tragedies in 1601, including *L'Ecossaise ou le désastre* ('Mary Queen of Scots'), which was banned following diplomatic embarrassment over its treatment of Mary Stuart's death. He worked for many years in commerce, and wrote a *Traité de l'économie politique* (1615), calling for national economic reform. He was also Governor of Chatillon-sur-Loire for a time. His poetry includes *Susane ou la Chasteté*, published in 1601. He died fighting on the rebel side in the Huguenot revolt.
▷ R Griffiths, *The Dramatic Technique of Antoine de Montchrestien* (1970)

MONTEIRO LOBATO, José Bento
(1882–1948)

Influential Brazilian essayist, satirist and children's writer, born in Taubaté, São Paulo. He created a still well known comic character, the backlands cowboy (*caboclo*) Jecá Tatú, in *Urepês* (1918) and subsequent books: it is a sympathetic but in no way uncritical portrait. In time Monteiro Lobato was jailed for his generally liberal ideas. He was also the author of much-loved children's books.

MONTEMAYOR, Jorge de
(c.1515–1561)

Spanish novelist and poet, born in Portugal. He was a musician and singer as well as a poet. He wrote the unfinished pastoral romance *Diana* (1559) in Castilian, which influenced Sir **Philip Sidney** and **Shakespeare**.
▷ J B Auraille-Arce, *La novela pastoril española* (1959)

MONTESINO, Ambrosio
(c.1448–c.1512)

Spanish poet and religious writer. Montesino was a Franciscan monk, under the protection of Ferdinand and Isabella. He later rose to become the bishop of Cerdeña and his work was favoured by the powerful Cardinal Cisneros. Under the aegis of Cisneros, Montesino issued a deluxe edition of the *Vita Christi* of Landulfo of Saxony specially commissioned by the king and queen (1503). Two of his prose works, a breviary and meditations on Saint Augustine, remain unedited. However, it is for his poems that he is best known. These are preserved in the *Cancionero de Diversas Obras* (1508, 'Songbook of Diverse Works'), in which his compositions in honour of the birth of Christ stand out.

MONTESQUIEU, Charles de Secondat, Baron de la Brède et de
(1689–1755)

French philosopher and jurist, born at the Château La Brède near Bordeaux. He became counsellor of the *parlement* of Bordeaux in 1714, and its president in 1716. He discharged the duties of his office faithfully, but, until defective eyesight hindered him, by preference devoted himself to scientific researches. His first great literary success was the *Lettres persanes* (1721, 'Persian Letters'), containing a satirical description, put in the mouths of two Persian visitors to Paris, of French society. Weary of routine work, he sold his office in 1726 and settled in Paris. He travelled for three years to study political and social institutions, visiting, among other places, England, where he remained for two years (1729–31), mixing with its best society, frequenting the Houses of Parliament, studying the political writings of Locke, and analysing the English constitution. *Causes de la grandeur des Romains et de leur décadence* (1734, 'Causes of the Greatness and Decadence of the Romans') is perhaps the ablest of his works. His monumental *De l'esprit des lois* (1748, 'The Spirit of the Laws') was published anonymously and put on the Index, but passed through 22 editions in less than two years. By the spirit of laws he means their *raison d'être*, and the conditions determining their origin, development and forms; the discussion of the influence of climate was novel. The work, which held up the free English constitution to the admiration of Europe, had an immense influence. In 1748 he published *Lysimaque*, followed in 1750 by *Défense de l'esprit des lois*, a dialogue on despotism, *Arsace et Isménie* (Eng trans 1927), a romance, and an essay on taste (*Goût*) in the *Encyclopédie* (1751–80). A member of the Académie française from 1728, he died totally blind.
▷ J Starobinksi, *Montesquieu par lui-même* (1953)

MONTGOMERIE, Alexander
(c.1545–c.1611)

Scottish poet, probably born at Hessilhead Castle near Beith in Ayrshire. He was 'maister

poet' to James VI and I. He was detained in a continental prison, and embittered by the failure of a lawsuit involving loss of a pension. Implicated in Barclay of Ladyland's Catholic plot, he was denounced as a traitor in 1597, and went into exile. His fame rests on the *Cherrie and the Slae*, published twice in 1597, and his love lyrics, especially 'To his Mistress'.
▷ R D S Jack, *Montgomerie* (1985)

MONTGOMERY, James
(1771–1854)

Scottish poet, born in Irvine, Ayrshire. The son of a Moravian pastor, he settled down, after various occupations, as a journalist in Sheffield, where in 1794 he started the *Sheffield Iris*, which he edited until 1825. In 1795 he was fined £20, and spent three months in York Castle for printing a 'seditious' ballad; in 1796 he was fined £30 and served six months for describing a riot. However, by 1832 he had become a moderate Conservative, and in 1835 accepted a pension of £150 from Peel. He died in Sheffield; his poems (4 vols, 1849) have been described as 'bland and deeply religious'.

MONTGOMERY, L(ucy) M(aud)
(1874–1942)

Canadian novelist, born in Clifton, Prince Edward Island. She qualified as a schoolteacher from Prince of Wales College, Charlottetown, and after studying at Dalhousie College, Halifax, Nova Scotia, she returned to Cavendish to care for her grandmother for 13 years. She published as her first book the phenomenally successful *Anne of Green Gables* (1908), the story of an orphan girl adopted in error for a boy by an elderly brother and sister. She followed it with several sequels, of which *Rilla of Ingleside* (1921) is an invaluable description of the impact of World War I on the island community. She married the Rev Ewan MacDonald in 1911, and moved to his manse at Leaskdale, Ontario. Her works are sometimes highly satirical; at her best she captures memorably the mysteries and terrors of early childhood, as in *Magic for Marigold* (1929), while her later works show qualities which recall **Guy de Maupassant**.
▷ H M Ridley, *The Story of Lucy Montgomery* (1956)

MONTGOMERY, Robert
(1807–55)

English preacher and poet, born in Bath, the illegitimate son of a clown. He studied at Lincoln College, Oxford; and from 1843, after some years in Glasgow, became minister of Percy Chapel, London. *The Omnipresence* of the Deity (1828) and Satan (1830) are remembered by **Thomas Macaulay**'s onslaught in the *Edinburgh Review* (April 1830).

MONTHERLANT, Henri Millon de
(1896–1972)

French novelist and playwright, born in Neuilly-sur-Seine. He was severely wounded in World War I, after which he travelled in Spain, Africa and Italy. A man of athletic interests, in his novels, as in his plays, he advocates the overcoming of the conflicts of life by vigorous action, disdaining the consolation of bourgeois sentiment. His novels, all showing his mastery of style, include the largely autobiographical *La Relève du matin* (1920, 'The Morning Relief'), *Le Songe* (1922, 'The Dream'), *Les Bestiaires* (1926, Eng trans *The Bullfighters*, 1927), *Les Jeunes filles* (1935–9, 'The Young Girls') and *L'-Histoire d'amour de la rose de sable* (1954, 'The Love Story of the Sandflower'). His plays include *La Reine morte* (1942, 'The Dead Queen'), *Malatesta* (1946), *Don Juan* (1958) and *Le Cardinal d'Espagne* (1960, 'The Cardinal of Spain').
▷H Perruchot, *Henri de Montherlant* (1959)

MONTI, Vincenzo
(1754–1828)

Italian poet, born in Alfonsine. He was professor at Pavia and official historian to Napoleon, although his political allegiances were apparently flexible, if his poems condemning the French Revolution, then welcoming the triumph of Napoleon, and finally celebrating his defeat, are anything to judge by. He wrote epics and tragedies on classical models and translated **Homer** from Latin and Italian versions rather than the original text.
▷D Chomenti Vasselli, *Vincenzo Monti nel dramma dei suoi tempo* (1968)

MOOCK, Armando
(1894–1942)

Important Chilean playwright, much of whose best work was seen in Buenos Aires. *Mocosita* (1929, 'The Youngster') and *Rigoberto* (1935) were both effective and highly popular comedies. His most serious play, however, had been the tragic (and autobiographical) *Monsieur Ferdinand Pontiac* (1922). In general, the lighter Moock's always finely made plays became, the more successful they were.

MOODIE, Susanna
(1803–85)

English novelist and poet, born in Bungay, Suffolk. After her marriage she reluctantly emigrated to Canada, where her husband took up farming with limited success. She began writing partly in order to contribute to the family income, publishing a collection of verse, *Enthusiasm and Other Poems*, in 1831. Her novels include *Mark Hurdlestone and the Gold Worshipper* (1853) and *Flora Lyndsay* (1854), sentimental light reading in which the women are strong and determined and the men weak. Her most popular non-fiction books, *Roughing It in the Bush, or Life in Canada* (1852) and *Life in the Clearings Versus the Bush* (1853), are loosely based upon her own experiences.

MOODY, William Vaughn
(1869–1910)

American dramatist and poet, born in Indiana. His plays are crucially important in the history of American theatre, because he was among the first to move from popular adaptations of French farce in order to deal realistically with wholly American subject-matter and themes. *The Great Divide* (1906, originally *A Sabine Woman*), uses the story of a woman's abduction from Massachusetts by a man from Arizona, their tempestuous association and eventual marriage, to reflect the cultural differences between a settled, inflexible society on the one hand and the wild spirit of the frontier on the other. Moody also wrote an incomplete trilogy in verse, and several volumes of poems of which *Poems* (1901), containing the much-anthologized 'Gloucester Moors', is perhaps the most representative.

MOON, Lorna, pseud of (Helen) Nora Wilson Low
(1886–1930)

Scottish short-story writer and novelist, born in Strichen, Aberdeenshire. Her father was a plasterer who worked mostly abroad. After an itinerant life he acquired the Temperance Hotel in Strichen, a haunt of commercial travellers. One, an American called Hebditch, who dealt in jewellery, married Lorna, and they left for America, where they had a child. Eventually she reached Hollywood, where she wrote scripts for Metro-Goldwyn-Mayer, who employed her on the screenplay for *Mr. Wu*, starring Lon Chaney, which was a huge success. A friend of **Frances Marion** and **Anita Loos**, she wrote for magazines in her spare time, contributing stories about Strichen, barely disguised as 'Pitouie'. Her first book, *Doorways in Drumorty* (1926), was a collection of stories; when it was published in Britain it was banned from the local library in Strichen, as was her novel *Dark Star* (1929). Wickedly and deftly puncturing her parents' social pretensions and the Nosey Parker proclivities of village life, she combined Gothic tragedy with black humour, sharpened no doubt by distance from her targets. When she died of consumption in Albuquerque, New Mexico, it made front-page news in America.

MOORCOCK, Michael
(1939–)

English novelist, whose work transcends the 'science fiction' and 'fantasy' categories into which it has often been shoe-horned. Born in Mitcham, Surrey, Moorcock became, at 17, editor of *Tarzan Adventures* and was a regular contributor to the *Sexton Blake Library*. From the mid-1960s onwards, he was editor, then publisher, of the influential SF series *New Worlds*, establishing a working routine that often required up to 15 000 words a day. He also wrote comic strips. Much of Moorcock's fiction has been organized in cycles. The 'Elric' novels began with *Stormbringer* in 1965. Perhaps his best-known sequence, starring the morally and sexually ambiguous 'Jerry Cornelius', started with *The Final Programme* (1968). Moorcock introduced 'Karl Glogauer' in *Behold the Man* (1969), a controversial re-working of the Crucifixion. A further enormous mythic cycle began with *The Eternal Champion* in 1970. Moorcock has also written in non-SF mode, but even here his work is notably open-ended. He wrote the sprawling, **Dicken**sian *Mother London* (1988) before embarking on a complex, emotionally demanding cycle, beginning with *Byzantium Endures* (1981), that will ultimately lead his anti-semitic anti-hero to the death camps.
▷ M Moorcock, with C Greenland, *Michael Moorcock: Death is no Obstacle* (1991)

MOORE, Brian
(1921–)

Irish–Canadian novelist, born in Belfast. He served with the British Ministry of War Transport during the latter stages of World War II. After the war he worked for the United Nations in Europe before emigrating to Canada in 1948, where he became a journalist and adopted Canadian citizenship. He spent time in New York before moving to California. Though he has written thrillers under the pseudonym Michael Bryan, he is best known for novels like *The Feast of Lupercal* (1957), *The Luck of Ginger Coffey* (1960), *Catholics* (1972) and *The Temptation of Eileen Hughes* (1981). Particularly admired for his portrayal of women, he won the Author's Club First Novel Award with *The Lonely Passion of Judith Hearne* (1955), though it was not, strictly speaking, his first novel. *The Great Victorian Collection* (1975) was awarded the James Tait Black Memorial Prize, and both *The Doctor's Wife* (1976) and *Black Robe* (1985) were shortlisted for the Booker Prize.
▷ H Dahlie, *Brian Moore* (1981)

MOORE, Charles Leonard
(1854–1923)

American poet from Philadelphia, whose verse was hailed in its time, but is now completely forgotten. He wrote the once celebrated 'Ode to America', sometimes still recited at Klu Klux Klan meetings.

MOORE, Edward
(1712–57)

English dramatist, born in Abingdon, Berkshire, the son of a dissenting minister. He was a draper in London who, to avoid going bankrupt, took to writing plays. The comedy *Gil Blas* (1751), based on **Le Sage**, and the prose tragedy *The Gamester* (1753), are his best-known productions. He also edited the weekly journal *The World* (1753-7).
▷ J M Caskey, *The Life and Works of Edward Moore* (1927)

MOORE, George Augustus
(1852–1933)

Irish writer, born in Ballyglass, County Mayo. He was the son of a landed gentleman in southwest Ireland who was an MP and bred horses for racing. His youth was spent partly there and partly in London. He was educated at Oscott College, Birmingham, and intended for the army, but soon became an agnostic, abandoned a military career and lived a bohemian life in London until his father's death in 1870 left him free to become a dilettante artist and writer in Paris. After 10 years of this life, **Émile Zola**'s example revealed to him his true métier as a novelist of the realist school. His importance as a writer is that in the years of relative poverty in London, from 1880 to 1892, he introduced this type of fiction into England, with *A Modern Lover* (1883), *A Mummer's Wife* (1885) and others. *Esther Waters* (1894), the last of his novels in this vein, was regarded as rather offensive, but these novels of low life, drawn from Moore's own experience of racing touts and shabby lodgings, introduced the public to a wider world than the fashionable novel of the day. During the Boer War Moore sought exile in Ireland—such was his hatred of England's wars—and this had the double effect of arousing his interest, as in *Evelyn Innes* (1898) and *Sister Teresa* (1901), in love, theology and the arts, and encouraging his preoccupation with the texture of his prose which increasingly engaged his attention. The Irish scene also helped to turn his attention away from sordid realism as in *A Drama in Muslin* (1886), and the stories in *An Untilled Field* (1903). Moore returned to England early in the century and eventually occupied a flat in Ebury Street where he wrote dialogues, essays (*Conversations in Ebury Street*, 1924)

and confessions—a sure sign that he had exhausted his experience for novel writing. He had already written *Confessions of a Young Man* (1888), but then came *Memoirs of My Dead Life* (1906) and the belated and inferior *In Single Strictness* (1926). The most famous of his works of this sort is *Hail and Farewell* in three parts (1911–14), *Ave* (1911), *Salve* (1912) and *Vale* (1914). The malicious element in this trilogy, in which he wrote about his friends and his associates in setting up the Abbey Theatre in Dublin, particularly **W B Yeats**, does not detract from his claim to be one of the great memoirists. With this prose style now perfected, Moore turned in his last phase to romanticize history, beginning with the masterpiece *The Brook Kerith* (1916), which relates an apocryphal story of Paul and Christ among the Essenes. *Héloïse and Abelard* (1921) tells the famous love story with distinction and compassion. He also wrote the mythical *Aphrodite in Aulis* (1930).
▷J Hone, *The Life of George Moore* (1936)

MOORE, John
(1729–1802)
Scottish physician and writer, father of the soldier Sir John Moore. After studying medicine and practising in Glasgow, he travelled with the young Duke of Hamilton (1772–8), and then settled in London. His *View of Society in France, Switzerland, Germany and Italy* (1779–81) was well received, but it is for the novel *Zeluco* (1789), which suggested **Byron**'s *Childe Harold*, that he is best remembered today. His other novels are *Edward* (1796), and the epistolary *Mordaunt* (1800).
▷J M S Tompkins, *The Popular Novel in England* (1932)

MOORE, Marianne Craig
(1887–1972)
American poet, born in Kirkwood, Missouri, and educated at the Metzger Institute, Carlisle, Pennsylvania, Bryn Mawr College, and Carlisle Commercial College. She taught commercial studies there, tutored privately, and was a branch librarian in New York (1921–5). She contributed to the Imagist magazine, *The Egoist*, from 1915, and edited *The Dial* from 1926 until its demise in 1929. America's most popular female poet of the 20th century, she was acquainted with seminal modernists like **Ezra Pound** and **T S Eliot**, but New York was her milieu not Paris, and she associated with the Greenwich Village group including **William Carlos Williams** and **Wallace Stevens**. She was much liked and admired by contemporaries, even those—like Eliot—at odds with her artistic beliefs. Idiosyncratic, a consummate stylist and unmistakably modern, she has supplied a much-quoted definition of the creative ideal as 'imaginary gardens with real toads in them'. Her first publication was *Poems* (1921); *Selected Poems* appeared in 1935 and *The Complete Poems* in 1968. She published *Predilections*, a collection of essays, in 1955.
▷E P Sheehy and K A Lohf, *The Achievement of Moore, 1907–1957* (1958)

MOORE, Thomas
(1779–1852)
Irish poet, born in Dublin, the son of a Catholic grocer. He was educated at Whyte's School, Trinity College, Dublin, and the Middle Temple. His translation of **Anacreon** (1800) proved a great success, followed by *Poems* (1801) and, with his musical talent as a singer, procured him admission to high society. In 1803, after being appointed registrar of the Admiralty Court in Bermuda, he arranged for a deputy and returned after a tour of the USA and Canada. In 1811 he married an actress, Bessy Dyke, and later settled in Wiltshire. Meanwhile he had published the earlier of the *Irish Melodies* (1807–34) and *The Twopenny Post-bag* (1812). In 1817 the long-expected *Lalla Rookh* appeared, for which Longmans paid him 3000 guineas; the *Irish Melodies* brought in £500 a year. Moore had 'a generous contempt for money', his Bermuda deputy embezzled £6000, and in 1819, to avoid arrest, he went to Italy and then to Paris. He returned in 1822 to Wiltshire, where he spent his last 30 years, during which he published *The Loves of the Angels* (1823), and a novel (*The Epicurean*, 1827), and wrote biographies of **Richard Brinsley Sheridan** and **Byron** and other works. In 1835 he received a pension of £300, but his last days were clouded by the loss of his two sons. In his lifetime his work was as popular as that of his friend, Byron. His poetry was light, airy, graceful, but soulless. He is best in his lyrics.
▷T de Vere White, *Tom Moore, the Irish Poet* (1977)

MOORE, Thomas Sturge
(1870–1944)
English poet, critic and wood-engraver, born in Hastings in Sussex, brother of the philosopher George Edward Moore. He is known as the author of polished verse of classical style, beginning with *The Vinedresser* (1899), verse dramas, works on Dürer and other artists, and as a distinguished designer of book-plates, including those of his friend **W B Yeats**. His *Collected Poems* appeared in four volumes between 1931 and 1933.
▷F C Gwynn, *Moore and the life of art* (1951)

MOORHOUSE, Frank
(1938–)
Australian fiction writer. He was born in
Nowra, New South Wales, and educated at
the University of Queensland, Brisbane,
before beginning his career as a journalist on
the Sydney *Telegraph*. It is not quite accurate
to describe him either as a 'short-story writer'
or as a 'novelist'—he writes what he himself
has described as 'discontinuous narratives'.
His first book, *Futility and Other Animals*
(1969), had a flavour of **Saki**, but it was in
later books, *The Americans, Baby* (1972), *The
Electrical Experience* (1974), *Conference-ville*
(1976) and *The Everlasting Secret Family*
(1980), that he unfolded an increasingly
dominant interest in sexual ambiguity and
experiment. This played a surprisingly central
role in his epic—and self-admittedly
obsessed—study of the League of Nations,
Great Days (1993), which in turn reintroduced a character who had appeared (in
old age) in some sections of the earlier *Forty-
Seventeen* (1987). Neither book is strictly a
'novel', but *Great Days* has a consistency of
narrative line that Moorhouse had not
attempted before and is much less impressive.
He has also written a variety of screenplays.

MÓRA, Ferenc
(1879–1934)
Hungarian popular novelist, poet and story
writer, born in Kiskunfélegyháza. He wrote
about the Szeged region, where he lived and
died, with intimate realism. *Aranykoporsó*
(1933, Eng trans *The Gold Coffin*, 1964) is
about the early days of Christianity; but his
finest psychological study, about a schoolmaster, *Hannibal föltamasztasa* (1924), has
not yet been translated. However, some of
the sketches in which he excelled above all
are in *Ének a búzmerzökröl* (1927), which was
translated in 1931 as *Song of the Wheatfields*.

MORAES, Dom(inic Frank)
(1938–)
Indian–Anglican poet and journalist, born in
Bombay and educated at Jesus College,
Oxford. He has written numerous non-fiction
books about India, including *Bombay* (1980);
a Time-Life publication, *Mrs Gandhi* (1980);
and a portrait of the cricketer *Sunil Gavaskar*
(1987). However, there is little distinctively
Indian about his poetry, which has been criticized for lack of cultural conviction. His
first collection, *A Beginning* (1957), won a
Hawthornden Prize, the first time one had
been awarded to a non-Anglo-Saxon poet.
Moraes broke nearly 20 years of poetic silence
in 1983 with *Absences*.
▷E Lall, *The Poetry of Encounter: Three
Indo-Anglican Poets* (1983)

MORAES VINCIUS, Mello de
(1913–)
Brazilian poet and dramatist, associated with
the second phase of Brazilian Modernism. He
was initially influenced by **Péguy** and French
mysticism; this was succeeded by a more
ironic and socially aware poetry, haunted by
various notions of time. Some of his poetry
appears in translation in the *Penguin Book of
Latin American Verse* (1971, ed E Curacciolo-
Trejo) and in John Nist's *Modern Brazilian
Poetry* (1962).

MORAND, Paul
(1889–1975)
French diplomat and writer, born in Paris. In
the French diplomatic service from 1912 to
1944, his early posts included the secretaryship of the French embassies in London
(where he was also minister plenipotentiary
in 1940), Rome and Madrid. In 1939 he was
head of the French mission of economic warfare in England, in 1943 minister at Bucharest
and in 1944 ambassador at Berne. He turned
to writing in 1920, beginning with poetry,
then publishing short stories and novels, with
a background of cosmopolitan life in post war
Europe. These include *Ouvert la nuit* (1922,
'Open All Night'), *Fermé la nuit* (1923,
'Closed at Night') and *Lewis et Irène* (1924).
He also wrote travel books, studies of cities,
and political and biographical works. Among
his later works were *Vie de Maupassant* (1942,
'Life of Maupassant'), *Journal d'un attaché
d'ambassade* (1948, 'Journal of a Diplomatic
Attaché'), *Fouquet* (1961) and *Tais-toi* (1965,
'Be Quiet').
▷B Delvaille, *Paul Morand* (1966)

MORANTE, Elsa
(1916–85)
Italian novelist, poet and short-story writer,
born and educated in Rome. Her first publication, a collection of short stories called *Il
gioco segreto* (1941, 'Secret Jest'), coincided
with her marriage to **Alberto Moravia**; they
subsequently divorced. Her second book,
Menzogna e sortilegio (1948, 'Lies and Riddles'), won the Viareggio Prize and was later
published in the USA as *House of Liars*
(1951). Its successor, *L'isola di Arturo* (1957,
Eng trans *Arturo's Island*, 1959), was a lyrical-
elegiac account of childhood and the viola-
tion of innocence. It won Morante the prestigious Strega Prize. Her greatest single
achievement, however, was *La storia* (1974,
Eng trans *History*, 1977), a large-scale,
almost **Faulkner**ian narrative about the
degeneracy of the Italian family under
fascism. Though politically engaged and consistently espousing Morante's Christian-

Marxist principles, the novel never deteriorates into a tract. Morante's verse includes *Il mondo salvato dai ragazzini e altri poemi* (1968); she also translated **Katherine Mansfield** into Italian.

▷G Venturi, *Elsa Morante* (1977)

MORATA, Olympia
(1526–55)

Italian Humanist scholar and poet, daughter of the poet and scholar Pellegrino Morato. She gave public lectures when 15; but, having in 1548 married the German physician Andreas Grundler, she followed him to Germany, became a Protestant, and died penniless, leaving numerous Latin and Greek poems, a treatise on **Cicero**, dialogues and letters.

MORATIN, Leandro de
(1760–1828)

Spanish dramatist and poet, born in Madrid. He began as a designer of jewellery, and later held official and ecclesiastical positions. He wrote a number of successful comedies influenced by French ideas and especially by **Molière**, and translated *Hamlet*. He also wrote poetry, and a history of Spanish literature. His work is carefully crafted, and reflects his belief in reason and orderly morality. His acceptance of the post of librarian to Joseph Bonaparte resulted in his exile to Paris in 1814.

MORAVIA, Alberto, pseud of Alberto Pincherle
(1907–90)

Italian novelist and short-story writer, born in Rome of middle-class parents. He spent some years in a sanatorium as a result of a tubercular infection. Before the outbreak of World War II he travelled extensively and lived for a time in the USA when out of favour with the fascist government. His first novel, *Gli indifferenti* (1929, Eng trans *The Indifferent Ones*, 1932), which achieved popular success, contains many of the ingredients of his later novels and short stories. He analyses without compassion but without explicit moral judgement the members of decadent bourgeois society in Rome, portraying in a fatalistic way their preoccupation with sex and money, their apathy, their lack of communication, the total incapability of action of even the intellectuals who acknowledge the corruption but cannot break away from it. In *La romana* (1947, Eng trans *The Woman of Rome*, 1949) many of these themes remain but his canvas has broadened to include the corruption and socio-economic problems of the working class. In *Raconti romani* (1954, Eng trans *Roman Tales*, 1956) he turns his critical eye to the corruption of the lower middle class. His works include *Agostino* (1944, Eng trans 1947), *L'amore coniugale* (1949, Eng trans *Conjugal Love*, 1951), *La ciociara* (1957, Eng trans *Two Women*, 1958), *L'attenzione* (1965, Eng trans *The Lie*, 1966), *La vita interiore* (1978, Eng trans *Time of Desecration*, 1980) and *L'uomo che guarda* (1985, Eng trans *The Voyeur*, 1986). His former wife is **Elsa Morante**.

▷K Longobardi, *Alberto Moravia* (1970)

MØRCH, Dea Trier
(1941–)

Danish novelist and artist. Having trained in graphics in Denmark, she continued her education at art colleges in Eastern Europe, and her first published books record her impressions of the Soviet Union and Poland. She made her breakthrough with *Vinterbørn* (1976, Eng trans *Winter's Child*, 1986), a collective novel set in a maternity ward at a Copenhagen hospital, and lovingly illustrated by the author. With the women's perspective predominating, the text depicts pregnancy and childbirth as radicalizing experiences, carrying with them the potential of an alternative community. The novel achieved considerable success in Denmark and abroad, and has also been made into a film. *Kastaniealleen* (1978, 'Chestnut Avenue') is a sensitive exploration of the relationships between an elderly couple and their grandchildren, while *Den indre by* (1980, 'The Inner City') highlights the problems of combining family life with an active political commitment, especially for women.

▷G Agger, 'Dea Trier Mørch', in T Brostrøm and M Winge (eds), *Danske digtere i det 20. århundrede*, vol V (1982)

MORE, Hannah
(1745–1833)

English playwright and religious writer, born in Fishponds, near Bristol, daughter of a schoolteacher. She was educated at the boarding school in Bristol run by her elder sisters, where she wrote verses at an early age. She was engaged in 1767 to a Mr Turner, who failed to marry her for six years and eventually settled £200 a year on her and left her. In 1773 she published *The Search after Happiness*, a pastoral drama for schools, and then went to London in 1774, where she joined the 'Blue Stocking' coterie of Elizabeth Montagu and her friends. She wrote two tragedies for David Garrick: *Percy* (1777) and *The Fatal Secret* (1779). Led by her religious views to withdraw from society, she retired to Cowslip Green near Bristol, where she did much to improve the condition of the poor. She published *Sacred Dramas* (1782) and a collection of religious poems in *Bas Bleu* (1786), and an essay *Estimate on the Religion*

of the Fashionable World (1790). Her moral tracts for the poor, *Village Politics by Will Chip* (1793) and *Cheap Repository Tracts* (1795–8), led to the founding of the Religious Tracts Society. She also wrote a didactic novel, *Coelebs in Search of a Wife* (1809).
▷M G Jones, *The Life of Hannah More* (1952)

MORÉAS, Jean, originally Yannis Papadiamantopoulos
(1856–1910)

Greek-born French poet, born in Athens. He wrote first in Greek, then settled in Paris (1879) and became a leader of the Symbolist school, to which he gave its name in 1886. He gradually grew interested in a return to classical and traditional forms, however, and formed a new grouping under the name École Romane, dedicated to antiquity, by 1891. His works include *Les Syrtes* (1884), *Cantilènes* (1886, 'Ballads'), *Le Pèlerin passioné* (1891, 'The Passionate Pilgrim') and *Les Stances* (1905, 'Stanzas'), the masterpiece of his classical period.
▷R Niklaus, *Jean Moréas, poète lyrique* (1936)

MORETTI, Marino
(1885–1979)

Italian poet (one of the more important, with **Gozzano**, of the Crepusculari) and novelist, from Cesenatico. Moretti was unlucky never to have attracted an English translator: had he done so, it is likely that he would now be internationally regarded as a major writer. He was a lifelong friend to **Palazzeschi**, and at times influenced by him—but at others he seemed to go in an exactly opposite direction. He also knew the great Sienese novelist **Tozzi** well. He refused a prize awarded to him by the fascists, which had been designed to obtain his support; previously he had signed the anti-Fascist manifesto of **Benedetto Croce**. It was his early poetry, along with that of Carlo Chiave, which led **Borgese** to coin the term 'crepuscular'; yet, with the exception of Casnati, Edoardo Sanguinetti and a few other critics, this has been neglected. His early novel *Il sole de sabato* (1916, 'Saturday's Sunshine'), about a poor and afflicted woman who learns, convincingly, to love through her sufferings, was a popular success. He wrote many more powerful and varied novels, and then returned triumphantly to poetry. When he died he was Italy's most neglected great writer, and undoubtedly his time is yet to come.
▷S Pacifici, *The Modern Italian Novel from Capuana to Tozzi* (1973); F Casnati, *Marino Moretti* (1952, in Italian)

MORGAN, Charles Langbridge
(1894–1958)

English author, born in Kent, the son of a civil engineer. He served in Atlantic and China waters as a midshipman (1911–13), but finding it uncongenial, resigned. He rejoined the navy in 1914 and was later interned in Holland until 1917. On repatriation he went to Oxford University, where he published *The Gunroom* (1919) on his early experiences, and became a well-known personality. In 1921, on leaving Oxford, he joined the editorial staff of *The Times*, and was their principal drama critic from 1926 to 1939. Under the pen-name of 'Menander' he also wrote for the *Times Literary Supplement* critical essays called *Reflections in a Mirror*, which were later (1944–5) collected in two series. His novels and plays show high professional competence, but lack vividness and urgency. *Portrait in a Mirror* (1929), which won the Femina Vie Heureuse Prize in 1930, is his most satisfying novel. Later works show too much preoccupation with values of the heart to the detriment of narrative sweep, and his earnestness seems unduly solemn, pompous and vaguely sentimental. Nonetheless, *The Fountain* (1932) won the Hawthornden Prize and *The Voyage* (1940) won the James Tait Black Memorial Prize. His plays are *The Flashing Stream* (1938), *The River Line* (1952) and *The Burning Glass* (1953).
▷H C Duffin, *The Novels and Plays of Charles Morgan* (1959)

MORGAN, Edwin George
(1920–)

Scottish poet and critic, born in Glasgow. His education at Glasgow University was split by service in the Royal Army Medical Corps during World War II, an option he chose as a conscientious objector. He was appointed Assistant Lecturer in English at Glasgow University in 1947, and remained there until 1980, rising to titular Professor of English in 1975. He published his first volume of poems, *The Vision of Cathkin Braes*, and a translation of *Beowulf*, in 1952. His verse from the 1950s is introspective and rather gloomy, unlike his later work, which is marked by an apparently irrepressible (although never simply naive) optimism and a readiness to embrace change. By the time of *A Second Life* (1968), he had embraced his homosexuality, and given free rein to his willingness to be influenced by developments in American (both North and South) and European arts. His wide-ranging and often formally experimental work finds room for science fiction alongside a minute observation of reality. His work is defiantly non-parochial, but has remained rooted in Glasgow, where he has continued to live, playing a maverick role in the city's cultural life. An incomplete *Collected Poems* was published in 1990, followed by a collection of his influential essays and critical writings, *Crossing The Border* (1990). A skilled translator, he collected his translations of various writers, such as **Pasternak**, **Pushkin** and **García Lorca**, in *Rites of Passage* (1976). His adaptation of **Edmond Rostand**'s *Cyrano de Bergerac* into demotic Glaswegian in 1992 was highly acclaimed.

▷R Fulton, *Contemporary Scottish Poetry* (1974)

MORGAN, (George) Frederick
(1922–)

American poet and literary journalist, born in New York City. Morgan was the founder and for many years editor of the prestigious and influential literary magazine, the *Hudson Review*, and did not publish his first collection, *A Book of Change*, until 1972, when he was 50. However, as one critic observed, he subsequently 'lost no time in catching up to his contemporaries'. His poetry is diverse both in form and subject-matter, although a recurring theme is the quest for personal values and the realization that death is daily more imminent. His *Poems: New and Selected* appeared in 1987.

MORGAN, Lady Sydney, née Owenson
(1783–1859)

Irish novelist, born in Dublin. Her father, a theatrical manager, got into financial difficulties and she supported the family, first as governess, next as author of sentimental poems and novels. In 1812 she married a surgeon, Thomas Charles Morgan (1783–1843), who was later knighted. Her works—lively novels, verse and travels—were bestsellers of their day, and include *St Clair* (1804), *The Wild Irish Girl* (1806), *O'Donnel* (1814), *Florence Macarthy* (1816), *The O'Briens and the O'Flahertys* (1827) and *Memoirs* (1862).

MORGENSTERN, Christian
(1871–1914)

German poet and philosopher. Morgenstern, first a disciple of **Arthur Schopenhauer**, then of **Nietzsche** and, finally, of the anthroposophy of **Rudolph Steiner**, wrote much 'serious poetry' but, despite the intrinsic interest of this, and the efforts of a few (on the whole old-fashioned) critics to rehabilitate it, could express himself to truest effect only in his world-famous 'nonsense poems'—the profoundest ever written in that genre. His most famous humorous poetry deals with the absurd characters Palmström and Herr von Korf (and others), and is contained in *Galgenlieder* (1905, 'Gallows Song'), *Palmström* (1910) and posthumous collections; but he

began in this vein, in 1895, with *In Phantas Schloss*, ('In Phanta's Castle'). He travelled in Norway, where he met **Ibsen**, whom, as well as **Strindberg** and **Hamsun**, he translated. His project, in which he succeeded, perhaps mainly because in comic form he could combine playfulness with religious (non-Christian) profundity, was to 'strip language of the bourgeois conventions in which we have taken refuge'. He died of tuberculosis. Works in English translation are: *The Gallows Songs* (1964); *The Gallows Songs: A Selection* (1966); *Gallowsongs* (1970).

▷E Hofacker, *Christian Morgenstern* (1978)

MORI Ogai (Rintaro)
(1862–1922)

Japanese writer, aristocrat, soldier, doctor and bureaucrat, and a towering figure in the history of the transformation of Japanese culture and society in the 20th century. Born into a samurai family in Shimane, Mori (whose given name was Rintaro) studied medicine, rising to become director of the Army Medical Corps and being influential in the introduction of western medicine. He started writing by translating European literature (one of the first to do so), then produced his own historical fiction in a style strongly influenced by the directness and accessibility of the Europeans (again, one of the first to do so). His style was to supplant traditional literary forms as practised by the likes of **Kyoka Izumi**. The best example of his fiction available in translation is *Incident at Sakai and Other Stories*.

▷R J Bowring, *Mori Ogai and the Modernisation of Japanese Culture* (1979)

MORICZ, Zsigmond
(1879–1942)

Hungarian novelist and dramatist, of peasant stock, whose plays laid the foundations of his country's modern theatre. Moricz was Hungary's leading naturalist, influenced by **Zola**, with whom he may fruitfully be compared. He is outstripped in importance in Hungarian literature only by **Endre Ady**, whose friend he became, and from whose poetry he took his original inspiration. He was the first prose writer to challenge the sentimentality of the peasant–landlord relationship, which it had suited the more conservative novelists to idealize—but Moricz saw his peasants with a clear eye, and thus anticipated such writers as **Roger Martin du Gard**, who were also to present country people as they really are. He did not spare his polite readers the full facts, erotic or otherwise, and was thus execrated. His most powerful novel is *Legy jó mindhalálig* (1920, Eng trans *Be Faithful unto Death*, 1962), about a child who struggles against the evil adult world. This is still well

MORIER, James Justinian

known and widely read in Hungary, and Moricz continues to be rightly revered there. He was a writer of international stature, each of whose works should automatically have been put into English. *A fáklya* (1917, Eng trans *The Torch*, 1931) is about an idealistic priest whose life is shattered by his parishioners.

▷ *American Slavic Review*, 4 (1945)

MORIER, James Justinian
(1780–1849)

English novelist, son of the consul at Smyrna. He turned to literature after a diplomatic career and wrote a number of travel books. His great work is that inimitable picture of Persian life, *The Adventures of Hajji Baba of Ispahan* (1824), followed by the less brilliant *Hajji Baba in England* (1828).

MÖRIKE, Eduard
(1804–75)

German poet and novelist, born in Ludwigsburg. He entered the theological seminary at Tübingen in 1822 and became vicar of Kleversulzbach in 1834, retiring in 1843. He was weak, hypochondriacal, unhappily married and lazy, yet he produced a minor masterpiece in *Mozart auf der Reise nach Prag* (1856, 'Mozart on the Journey to Prague') and many poems of delicacy and beauty with something of the deceptive simplicity of **Heinrich Heine**. These were collectively published in 1838.

▷ M More, *Mörike: the man and the poet* (1957)

MORITZ, Karl Philipp
(1756–93)

German writer, born in Hameln. He was in turn hat-maker's apprentice, actor, teacher and professor. Self-educated, he travelled in England and Italy and wrote *Reisen eines Deutschen in England* (1783, 'Travels of a German in England'), and *Reisen eines Deutschen in Italien* (1792–3, 'Travels of a German in Italy'). His autobiographical novel, *Anton Reise* (1785–90), influenced **Goethe**. He was a precursor of the German Romantic movement, delved into the past, and wrote *Versuch einer deutschen Prosodie* (1786, 'Essay on German Prosody'), which he dedicated to Frederick II, the Great.

▷ W Rose, *From Goethe to Byron* (1924)

MORLEY, Christopher Darlington
(1890–1957)

American novelist and essayist, born in Haverford, Pennsylvania. He was a Rhodes scholar at Oxford, and joined the editorial staff of Doubleday's from 1913 to 1917 and later contributed to numerous periodicals such as *Ladies' Home Journal*, the New York *Evening Post* and the *Saturday Review of Literature*. His chief works, whimsical and urbane, included *Parnassus on Wheels* (1917), and a sequel *The Haunted Bookshop* (1919), *Thunder on the Left* (1925), *Swiss Family Manhattan* (1932), *Human Being* (1932), *Streamlines* (1937), *Kitty Foyle* (1939), *The Ironing Board* (1949) and a book of poems, *The Middle Kingdom* (1944).

▷ *John Mistletoe* (1931)

MORPURGO, Rahel
(1790–1871)

Hebrew poet, who was born in Trieste, and was thus a part of the great flowering of Jewish literature which took place in the 18th and early 19th centuries. With her boldly magnificent ode dedicated to the revolutions of 1848 she well deserves her title of first Hebrew modern poet. It has been said that no woman who hopes to make a mark in poetry can afford to neglect study of her achievement. English translations of her work can be found in *Collected Poems and Letters* (1890).

MORRIS, George Pope
(1802–64)

American journalist and poet, born in Philadelphia. In 1823 he founded the *New York Mirror* (editor 1824–42), and later edited the *Evening Mirror* and the *Home Journal* (1846–64), publishing **Edgar Allan Poe**'s 'The Raven' in the former. He published many poems, including the celebrated 'Woodman, Spare that Tree!', which appeared in *The Deserted Bride* (1838).

MORRIS, Sir Lewis
(1833–1907)

Welsh poet and barrister, born in Carmarthen, and educated at the town's Queen Elizabeth Grammar School, Sherborne, and Jesus College, Oxford. His main literary works were *Songs of Two Worlds* (3 vols, 1872–5), followed in 1876 by *The Epic of Hades* and more verse and drama, largely drawing on incidents in Welsh history and mythology. In the later stages of his career he campaigned for the fostering of higher education in Wales and the establishment of a National University. In 1895 he was made knight-bachelor and thereafter entertained fruitless hopes of becoming poet laureate.

▷ D Phillips, *Sir Lewis Morris* (1981)

MORRIS, Mervyn
(1937–)

Jamaican poet, born in Kingston, and educated at the University of the West Indies and Oxford (as a Rhodes scholar). He might be described as a minimalist poet, being the master of the brief but cogent comment. His words bear a heavy burden, not least of which is the desire to maintain a variousness of perspective. A generous and careful critic and the editor of many anthologies of Caribbean poetry, he has a particular interest in overcoming the difficulties in transcribing oral, performance-based poetry. His own poems first appeared in the early 1960s in Jamaican journals and newspapers; collections include *The Pond* (1973), *On Holy Week* (1976) and *Shadowboxing* (1979).

MORRIS, William
(1834–96)

English craftsman, poet and socialist, born in Walthamstow, near London, of middle-class parents. Educated at Marlborough School and Exeter College, Oxford, he studied for holy orders, but his friendship with members of the Pre-Raphaelite Brotherhood, particularly the painter Edward Burne-Jones, aroused a deep love of Gothic architecture, and they both renounced the church. He turned to the study of architecture under George Edmund Street, but on the advice of **Dante Gabriel Rossetti** became a professional painter (1857–62). In 1859 he married a model, Jane Burden, and moved into the Red House at Bexley Heath, which he designed and furnished with the architect Philip Webb; from the ideas expressed there he founded in 1861, with the help of his pre-Raphaelite associates, the firm of Morris, Marshall, Faulkner and Company, which would revolutionize the art of house decoration and furniture in England. His literary career began with a volume of poetry, *The Defence of Guinevere, and other Poems*, in 1858, followed by *The Life and Death of Jason* (1867), a long narrative poem in rhyming couplets and the three-volumed *The Earthly Paradise* (1868–70), a collection of 24 classical and medieval tales in a **Chaucer**ian mould. He developed a passionate interest in the heroic literature of Iceland, and worked with Eiríkur Magnússon on a series of saga translations. He visited Iceland twice, in 1871 and 1873, and was inspired to write *Three Northern Love Songs* (1875) and a four-volumed epic, *The Story of Sigurd the Volsung and the Fall of the Nibelungs* (1876), regarded as his greatest work. Also at this time he published a verse morality, *Love is Enough, or The Freeing of Pharamond* (1872), a translation of **Virgil**'s *Aeneid* (1875), and a translation of **Homer**'s *Odyssey* (1887). He founded a Society for the Protection of Ancient Buildings in 1877. His experience as a master-craftsman, and his devotion to the Gothic, persuaded him that the excellence of medieval arts and crafts sprang from the joy of free craftsmen, which

was destroyed by Victorian mass-production and capitalism. He joined the Social Democratic Federation in 1883; his Utopian ideals did much to develop the philosophy of socialism, and when the Social Democratic Federation suffered disruption in 1884 he led the seceders into a socialist League. His socialist zeal inspired two prose romances, *The Dream of John Ball* (1888) and *News from Nowhere* (1891). Further prose romances concentrated more on story-telling: *The House of the Wolfings* (1889), *The Roots of the Mountains* (1889) and *The Story of the Glittering Plain* (1891), all set in the far north. His last books were a book of verse (*Poems by the Way*, 1891), and further prose romances: *The Wood beyond the World* (1895), *The Well at the World's End* (1896), *The Water of the Wondrous Isles* and *The Story of the Sundering Flood* (both published posthumously in 1897). In 1890, in a further rejection of Victorian values, he founded a publishing house, the Kelmscott Press at Hammersmith, for which he designed clear typefaces and wide ornamental borders; it produced a stream of his own works and reprints of English classics.

▷J W Mackail, *William Morris* (1899); P Henderson, *Morris, His Art, Writings and Public Life* (1967)

MORRIS, Wright Marion
(1910–)

American novelist, short-story writer and photographer, born in Nebraska and educated in Chicago and California. Throughout his career, in both his fiction and his photographic images, Morris has striven to keep alive the myth of America as a culture of newness. His first novel, *My Uncle Dudley* (1942), recounts a comic expedition from West to East; his third, *The World in the Attic* (1949), more sombrely confronts the vexed question of America's cultural 'thinness' and has an appropriately **James**ian tinge. Morris was awarded the National Book Award for *The Field of Vision* (1956), but despite other prizes he has never shaken off his critical marginality. Later novels include *Fire Sermon* (1971) and *The Fork River Space Project* (1977). He has written many books combining text and pictures, including *The Inhabitants* (1946) and *God's Country and My People* (1968). His highly visual short stories were gathered in *Green Grass, Blue Sky, White House* (1970), *Real Losses, Imaginary Gains* (1976) and other volumes. He published three volumes of memoirs, *Will's Boy* (1981), *Solo* (1983) and *A Cloak of Light* (1985).

▷G B Crump, *The Novels of Wright Morris* (1978)

MORRIS-JONES, John
(1864–1929)

Welsh scholar, translator (**Heine**, **Omar Khayyám**) and poet, born in Trefor on Anglesey. At Oxford he read mathematics. As a scholar he worked with great (as well as pedantic) zeal in the interests of purity of the language. His single collection of poems, *Caniadau* (1907), once highly regarded, is for the most part too sentimental for modern taste; but his poetry was skilfully wrought; two examples are included in the *Penguin Book of Welsh Verse* (1967).
▷ *Poetry Wales*, 15, 3 (1979)

MORRISON, Arthur
(1863–1945)

English novelist, born in Poplar, Kent, the son of an engine fitter. He became clerk to the People's Palace in Mile End Road, then a journalist on the *National Observer*, for which he wrote a series of stories published as *Tales of Mean Streets* (1894). His reputation rests on his powerfully realistic novels of London life such as *A Child of the Jago* (1896) and *The Hole in the Wall* (1902). He also wrote detective stories featuring a private investigator, Martin Hewitt.
▷ A Brome, *Four Realist Novelists* (1965)

MORRISON, Toni Chloe Anthony, née Wofford
(1931–)

American novelist, winner of the Nobel Prize for literature, born in Lorain, Ohio. She was educated at Howard University and Cornell University, and taught at Howard before moving to New York in 1965. She worked in publishing as senior editor at Random House before turning to fiction. Labelled as a black **James Joyce** or **William Faulkner**, she explores in rich vocabulary and cold-blooded detail the story of black Americans. *The Bluest Eye* (1970) focuses on the incestuous rape of an 11-year-old girl; *Sula* (1974) again confronts a generation gap, but between a grandmother and the eponymous scapegoat; *Song of Solomon* (1977) is a merciless study of genteel blacks. Her most recent novels, *Tar Baby* (1981), *Beloved* (1987) and *Jazz* (1992), formidable in their mastery of technique and courageous in their subject-matter, confirmed her as one of the most important novelists of her generation. She won a Pulitzer Prize in 1988 and the Nobel Prize for literature in 1993.

MORSZTYN, Count Jan Andrezej
(c.1613–1693)

Polish poet, translator (of **Corneille**'s *Le Cid*—a masterpiece) and courtier. Charged with high treason, in 1683, because of his close relations with the court of Louis XIV (he may have intrigued for a French king to the Polish throne), he fled to France. His master was the Italian Baroque poet **Marino**, and his poetry has some affinities with that of English metaphysical poets such as **Crashawe**. He excelled in compact forms, in elaborate and over-elaborate conceits, and in those violent and paradoxical comparisons which characterize Baroque poetry. His two collections were *Kanicula* (1647, 'The Dog Star') and *Lutnia* (1661, 'The Lute'). Some poems are well translated in *Five Centuries of Polish Poetry* (1960, B Singer and J Peterkiewicz eds). He was a fine writer of erotic (or so-called 'obscene') verse, much of it addressed to his Scottish wife, Catherine Gordon.

MORSZTYN, Zbigniew
(c.1620–c.1689)

Polish poet who, like his namesake **Count Jan Andrezej Morsztyn**, was a leading exponent of the then-prevalent Baroque school of poetry. The key to his poetry, however, lies in his belief in the 'heresy' of Arianism, or (as it is often now called) 'Polish Unitarianism': after the Jesuits succeeded in expelling the Arians from Racow in 1638 he chose exile in Prussia, and died in Königsberg. (Essentially, the Arians or Unitarians believed in the doctrines of Socinus, who rejected the Trinity in the interests of the unipersonality of God.) His *Emblemata*, in the tradition of erotic mysticism, are contained in *Muza domowa* ('The Homely Muse'), not properly edited until 1954. He owed much to **Kochanowski**.

MORTIMER, John Clifford
(1923–)

English dramatist, novelist and barrister, born in London. He was called to the Bar in 1948, participating in several celebrated civil cases, and is a constant defender of liberal values. His series of novels featuring Horace Rumpole, an amiable, late-middle-aged defence barrister and frequenter of Pomeroy's bar, has been adapted for television as *Rumpole of the Bailey*. His other novels, including *Paradise Postponed* (1985) and *Summer's Lease* (1988), are highly popular, evoking, often savagely, what Mortimer perceives as the moral decline of the English middle-class. His many plays and adaptations for the stage include *The Dock Brief* (1958), *The Wrong Side of the Park* (1960), *Two Stars for Comfort* (1962) and an autobiographical play, *A Voyage round My Father* (broadcast 1963, staged 1970), which was filmed for television in 1982 with Laurence Olivier as the father. An autobiographical volume, *Clinging to the Wreckage*, appeared in 1982. He has made notable translations, especially of **George Feydeau**, and several TV screenplays including *Brideshead Revisited* (1981), from the novel by **Evelyn Waugh**, *The Ebony Tower* (1984), from the story by **John Fowles**, and his own *Paradise Postponed* (1986). He has been twice married; his first wife was **Penelope Mortimer**.

▷J R Taylor, *Anger and After* (1962)

MORTIMER, Penelope Ruth
(1918–)

Welsh novelist, born in Rhyl, Flint, and educated at a variety of schools, and at University College, London. Her first novel, *Johanna* (1947), appeared under the name of Penelope Dimont (using her first husband's surname). Her other novels, many of which look at the female experience of life among the English professional classes, include *Daddy's Gone A-Hunting* (1958), *My Friend Says It's Bullet-Proof* (1967) and *The Handyman* (1983). Her most famous, *The Pumpkin Eater* (1962), describes a woman who imagines that pregnancy will give a direction to her life, but who is persuaded by her husband to have an abortion. She was married for more than 20 years to **John Mortimer**.

▷*About Time Too* (1993)

MORTON, John Cameron Andrieu Bingham Michael
(1893–1979)

English author and journalist. After serving in World War I he took up writing and published many books of humour, fantasy and satire, as well as a number of historical works including several on the French Revolution. From 1924 to 1975 he contributed a regular humorous column, 'By the Way', to the *Daily Express* under the name of 'Beachcomber'.

MORTON, John Maddison
(1811–91)

English dramatist, son of **Thomas Morton**, born in Pangbourne. He became a prolific writer of farces (mostly from the French), but is best remembered as the author of *Cox and Box* (1847). The rise of burlesque was his ruin and he became a 'poor brother' of the Charterhouse.

▷F Wilson, *An Epistolary Remonstrance* (1887)

MORTON, Thomas
(1764–1838)

English dramatist, father of **John Maddison Morton**, born in Durham. He abandoned Lincoln's Inn for play writing, and produced *Speed the Plough* (1798, with its invisible 'Mrs Grundy'), *The Blind Girl* (1801), *Town and Country* (1807), *School for Grown Children* (1826), and other popular plays.

MOSCHEROSCH, Johann Michael
(1601–69)

German satirical writer, poet, and translator (**Quevedo**), born in Willstädt, near Strasbourg. His *Gesichte* (1643) began with translations from Quevedo, but then continued with original work—witty and effective attacks on greed, extravagance and pretentiousness. Moscherosch was one of the chief anticipators of **Grimmelshausen**.

MOSCHUS
(fl.c.150BC)

Greek pastoral poet from Syracuse and follower of **Theocritus**, he wrote a handful of surviving short poems on the pleasures of country life and love. He is credited also with the *Europa*, a mini-epic (*epyllion*) in 166 hexameters describing the abduction of Europa by Zeus, disguised as a bull, and her voyage to Crete on his back. Moschus's style well exemplifies Alexandrian ideals for poetry: it is concise, elegant, polished and apt to concentrate on picturesque detail. **Shelley** translated two of his short poems, as well as part of the *Lament for Bion* (attributed to Moschus, but almost certainly not by him).

MOSEL, Tad George Ault, Jr
(1922–)

American dramatist, born in Steubenville, Ohio. He was educated at Amherst, Yale School of Drama, and Columbia University. His only significant success on the stage came with his dramatization of **James Agee**'s novel *A Death in the Family* as *All The Way Home* (1960), which won him a Pulitzer Prize in 1961. He also co-wrote a biography of the American actress Katherine Cornell, *Leading Lady* (1978).

MOSLEY, Nicholas (Lord Ravensdale)
(1923–)

English novelist and biographer, born in London and educated at Eton and Oxford. His earlier books, such as *Spaces of the Dark* (1951) and *Corruption* (1957), are realistic novels set during World War II. Those of his 'middle period' include *Accident* (1965), which became the basis of a memorable film, and those of his 'later period', the stylistically experimental and intellectually ambitious *Catastrophe Practice* series. This comprises five volumes, beginning with *Catastrophe Practice* in 1979, and ending with *Hopeful Monsters* (1990), and ranges back and forth across history and continents. His biographies include two definitive volumes about his father, *Rules of the Game: Sir Oswald and Lady Cynthia Mosley 1896–1933* (1982) and *Beyond the Pale: Sir Oswald Mosley and family 1933–1980* (1983).

MOSLEY, Walter

MOSLEY, Walter
(1952–)

American novelist, born in Los Angeles. His debut, *Devil in a Blue Dress* (1990), won the **John Creasey** Award for the year's best first crime novel. It and its two sequels, *A Red Death* (1991) and *White Butterfly* (1992), are narrated by the black private investigator Easy Rawlins. Although firmly within the crime genre, the trilogy also functions as a fictionalized history of black Americans since World War II. Far from being the white knight of **Raymond Chandler**'s ideal, Rawlins is continually compromised by real life; like the rest of his community, he literally cannot afford to be noble.

MOSS, Howard
(1922–87)

American poet, playwright and critic, born in New York City. He published his first collection, *The Wound and the Weather*, in 1946. It was followed by several more, including *A Winter Come, a Summer Gone: Poems 1946–1960* (1960), volumes of meticulously structured, reflective verse. His most familiar play is his first, *The Folding Green* (1958), revised and republished in 1980 as *Two Plays: The Palace at 4am and The Folding Green*. Perhaps his most significant book, however, is a critical work, *The Magic Lantern of Marcel Proust* (1962), which does much to clarify the **Proust**ian literary puzzle.

MOTION, Andrew Peter
(1952–)

English poet, born in London. He was educated at University College, Oxford, and taught at the University of Hull, where he met **Philip Larkin**. His biography of the poet, *A Writer's Life*, appeared in 1993, and won the Whitbread Award. He has worked in publishing since 1982. His early books established his concern with narrative in poetry, albeit obliquely rendered, and drew on historical as well as highly personal subjects. *Secret Narratives* (1983) and *Natural Causes* (1987) continued in that vein, but *Love—A Life* (1991), a verse anatomy of a marriage, was more direct in its statements. His novels *The Pale Companion* (1989) and *Famous for the Creatures* (1991) trace the development of the would-be writer Francis Mayne. He has written critical studies of **Edward Thomas** (1980) and Larkin (1982), and co-edited the *Penguin Book of Contemporary British Poetry* (1982).

MOTLEY, Willard
(1912–65)

American novelist, born in Chicago—one of the first of America's most eloquent Black writers. He came from middle-class Chicago,

but moved into the slums to discover what life was like there—the results were *Knock on Any Door* (1947) and *We Fished by Night* (1951), the most accomplished of his four **Zola**-like novels. The latter reveals punks and gangsters 'in the leer of the neon night', ruled over by corrupt politicians and police. His work is crude and flawed, but exceptionally powerful.

▷ *Studi Americani* (7, 1961, article in English)

MOTTRAM, Ralph Hale
(1883–1971)

English novelist, born in Norwich. He began his working life as a banker. **John Galsworthy** is the main influence in his work, as is clearly seen in his first book, *Spanish Farm* (1924), and its sequels, *Sixty-Four, Ninety-Four* (1925) and *The Crime at Vanderlynden* (1926), a trilogy of novels based on his experiences in France and Flanders during World War I.

MOURNING DOVE, or **HUM-ISHU-MA**,
English name **Christine Quintasket**
(1888–1936)

American writer. Born in a canoe on the Kootenai River in Idaho while her parents were making a ferry crossing, Mourning Dove was a member of the Colville Confederated Tribes of Eastern Washington and the first Native American woman to publish a novel: *Cogewea, the Half-Blood* (1927). Receiving little formal education, she worked for most of her life as a migrant farm labourer, travelling always with her typewriter on which she produced the stories she heard from the Okanogans with whom she lived and worked, and which formed the basis of her published collection, *Coyote Stories* (1933). Passionately concerned to record the threatened traditions and oral literature of her people, and encouraged by her friend and literary collaborator, Lucillus McWhorter, she also travelled and lectured to audiences in the east about Okanogan traditions. Her novel, *Cogewea*, describing the trials of a young mixed-blood woman ranch-hand, combines the plot of a frontier romance with descriptions of Okanogan culture and lively colloquial dialogue. Her autobiographical writings were recently collected and published as *Mourning Dove: a Salishan Autobiography* (1990, ed Jay Miller).

▷ A P Fisher, *The Transformation of Tradition: a Study of Zitkala-Sa and Mourning Dove* (1979)

MOWATT, Anna Cora
(1819–70)

American playwright and actress, best known for her social comedy, *Fashion, or Life in New York* (1845). Mowatt was of refined birth and character, and her success was seized on as proof that a woman could succeed in the theatre without compromising her standards of moral behaviour. The play was a mild and somewhat confusing satire about the marriage plans of a rich couple's daughter. On the wave of its success she formed her own company and brought it to London.

MPHAHLELE, Es'kia, originally Ezekiel
(1919–)

African novelist, short-story writer and critic. He was born in Pretoria, and (after working in a hospital for the blind) took his degree at the University of South Africa there, before completing a doctorate in the USA. He was fiction editor of the influential South African journal *Drum* (1955–7), before moving to Nigeria and the English faculty at the University of Ibadan (1957–61). Thereafter, he worked throughout Africa and in the USA before returning to his native country (1979) as Professor of African Literature at the University of Witwatersrand. Mphahlele's first book was a collection of stories, *Man Must Live* (1947), but his main achievement was a novel, *The Wanderers* (1971), which offered a bleak picture of the intellectual and emotional impact of exile, and developed ideas he had sketched out in an autobiographical volume, *Down Second Avenue* (1959). Mphahlele's introduction to the Penguin *African Writing Today* (1967) and the essays that comprise *Voices in the Whirlwind* (1972) represent a major statement in the development of African literary consciousness.
▷ N C Manganyi, *Exiles and Homecomings: A Biography of Es'kia Mphahlele* (1983)

MROZEK, Slawomir
(1930–)

Polish playwright and novelist, born in Borzecin and trained as an architect at Krakow. He worked as a cartoonist until, following the positive reception of his story collection *Slon* (1958, Eng trans *The Elephant*, 1962) and his play *Policja* (1963, Eng trans *The Policeman*, 1961) in the USA and Britain, he moved to the West (until 1972). Several of his plays were produced at the Edinburgh Festival in 1964 and struck a chord with their Kafkaesque portrayal of totalitarian absurdities. Later plays such as *Tango* (1966, published in Polish in 1973), a powerful study of family politics, and *The Prophets* (1970, published in Polish as *Testarium*, 1973) were first seen in translation. Mrozek's prose has been less widely recognized outside his native country, but *The Ugupu Bird* (1968) was a valuable selection of pieces. In 1975, he again left Poland and is now based in Paris.

MUCHA, Jiří
(1915–)

Czech novelist, born in Prague. He was imprisoned on a trumped-up charge by the communist regime. *Problémy nadporcika Knapa* (1946, Eng trans *The Problems of Lieutenant Knap*, 1945), the Czech version of which appeared after the English, consists of stories which draw on his World War II experiences as a Free Czech soldier, as does the novel *Spálaňa setba* (1948, Eng trans *Scorched Crop*, 1950); *Studené slunce* (1968, Eng trans *Living and Partly Living*, 1967) is based on his persecution by the Czech Stalinists. His father was a famous Art Nouveau painter, of whom he wrote an entertaining memoir, *Alphonse Mucha* (1966, Eng trans 1966).

MUDIE, Ian
(1911–76)

Australian poet, born in Hawthorn, South Australia, identified with **Rex Ingamells**'s 'Jindyworobak' movement. His *Corroboree to the Sun* (1941) was followed by other volumes, including *The Kingfisher* in 1970. Poems such as 'They'll Tell You About Me' are so full of Australian folk references and *patois* that they require a glossary almost as long as the verse. Formerly editor-in-chief of the renowned (now defunct) Australian publishing house of Rigby, his best verse is collected in *Selected Poems 1934–1974* (1976), although *The Blue Crane* (1959) is perhaps the most personal of his work. He edited *Poets at War* (1944), which was the first appearance between covers of many of the succeeding generation of poets, and has also written two historical books, *Riverboats* (1961) and *The Heroic Journey of John McDouall Stuart* (1968).

MUDROOROO, Nyoongah, originally Colin Johnson
(1939–)

Australian novelist of part-aboriginal descent, now writing as 'Mudrooroo Narogin', born in Beverley, Western Australia. His partly autobiographical first novel *Wild Cat Falling* (1965) tells of a half-caste's experiences on release from prison. He has since reworked the theme in *Doin' Wildcat* (1988), the story of a film production of his earlier book. He returns to the problems of mixed blood in *Long Live Sandawara* (1979), which portrays the conflicting calls of aboriginal culture and urban living. He has also written on aboriginal history and collaborated in *Before the Invasion: Aboriginal Life to 1788* (1980). *The Song of Jacky and Selected Poems* appeared in 1986 and *Master of the Ghost Dreaming* in 1991. He received the Special Award in the NSW State Literary Awards

1993 in recognition of his contribution over many years to aboriginal literature.

MUHSUM, Erich
(1878–1934)

German poet, dramatist, satirist and anarchist, one of the first victims of the Nazis. He was a minor Expressionist, many of whose activities were devoted to revolutionary politics.

MUIR, Edwin
(1887–1959)

Scottish poet, born in Deerness on the Mainland of Orkney. The son of a crofter, he left the Orkneys at 14 when his family migrated to Glasgow, where he suffered the period of drab existence described in his *The Story and the Fable* (1940), revised as *An Autobiography* in 1954. He moved from job to job, but spent much time reading **Nietzsche**, **Shaw**, **Ibsen**, **Heine** and Blatchford, and became interested in left-wing politics. In 1919 he married the novelist Willa Anderson (**Willa Muir**), with whom he settled in London, and travelled on the Continent from 1921 to 1924, where the couple collaborated in translations of **Kafka** and **Feuchtwanger**. Back in Scotland in 1925 he published his first volume of verse (*First Poems*), and then returned to France where he wrote novels, notably *The Marionette* (1927). He spent most of the 1930s in Sussex and St Andrews. On the outbreak of World War II he joined the staff of the British Council, and in 1945 returned to Prague as first director of the British Institute there, which was closed after the communist coup of 1948. He then took over the British Institute in Rome until 1950, when he was appointed warden of the adult education college at Newbattle Abbey, Midlothian. After a year as Eliot Norton Professor of Poetry at Harvard (1955–6), he retired to Swaffham Prior near Cambridge. His verses appeared in eight slim volumes—*First Poems* (1925), *Chorus of the Newly Dead* (1926, omitted from *Collected Poems*), *Variations on a Time Theme* (1934), *Journeys and Places* (1937), *The Narrow Place* (1943), *The Voyage* (1946), *The Labyrinth* (1949), *New Poems* (1949–51) and finally *Collected Poems* (1952). Further poems appeared in *The Listener* and other periodicals later. Muir's critical work includes a controversial study of John Knox, *Scott and Scotland* (1936), *Essays on Literature and Society* (1949) and *Structure of the Novel* (1928). A new *Collected Poems* was issued in 1991.
▷W Muir, *Belonging* (1968)

MUIR, Willa, née **Anderson**, pseud **Agnes Neill Scott**
(1890–1970)

Scottish novelist and translator, born in Montrose, Angus. She showed an early apti-

tude for languages as a child, speaking both her parents' Shetland dialect and English. Educated at St Andrews University, she taught classics and educational psychology in London until forced to resign when marrying the 'atheist' **Edwin Muir** in 1919. Despite her ill-health, brought on by poor medical treatment after the birth of their son Gavin in 1927, the Muirs punctuated their lives in Scotland with much travelling, and lived for short periods in Prague, Rome and the USA. They translated jointly (although often only Edwin was credited), and were influential in spreading the work of **Kafka** in the 1930s. Her essay *Women: An Enquiry* (1925) dealt with the demoralizing effects of Scottish small-town life, a subject she returned to in her novel *Imagined Corners* (1931). *Mrs Grundy in Scotland* (1936) examined the role of women in Scottish culture. She wrote a moving account of her long and creative partnership with Edwin Muir, *Belonging* (1968), and finished his project *Living With Ballads* (1965) after his death.

MUKHERJEE, Bharati
(1940–)

Indian-born American novelist, born in Calcutta. Mukherjee, who lived in Canada from 1966 until 1980 and became a Canadian citizen in 1971, has since taken up permanent residence in the USA. She now sees herself writing in the American immigrant tradition. Until her move Mukherjee's books were very much concerned with her homeland. *The Tiger's Daughter* (1972) was about a westernized Indian's return to her native country, a theme taken up in non-fiction form in *Darkness: Days and Nights in Calcutta* (1977), a book co-written with her husband, the writer Clark Blaise. Her most recent novel, *The Holder of the World* (1993), continues her stand against what she sees as the tightly-reined, miniaturist school of 'Indian' novels written in English.

MULDOON, Paul
(1951–)

Irish poet, born in Moy, County Armagh, in Northern Ireland. He was educated at Queen's University in Belfast, and worked as a radio and television producer (1973–86), then held a number of academic posts. He currently lectures at Princeton University. Early collections like *New Weather* (1973) and *Mules* (1977) revealed a precocious talent. His subsequent work built on auspicious beginnings in even more extravagant, witty and politically aware fashion in *Why Brownlee Left* (1986). His *Selected Poems 1968–1983* appeared in 1986.

MULGAN, Alan E(dward)
(1881–1961)

New Zealand writer and journalist, born in Katikati, author of *Maori and Paheka: A History of New Zealand* (1922, with A W Shrimpton), *The City of the Strait: Wellington and its Province: a Centennial History* (1939), *Literature and Authorship in New Zealand* (1943) and *Great Days in New Zealand Writing* (1962). He has also published verse, a novel and a collection of plays, travel and history.

▷ *The Making of a New Zealander* (1958)

MULGAN, John Alan Edward
(1911–45)

New Zealand writer, son of **Alan E Mulgan**. He wrote only one novel, the sprawling **Hemingway**-esque *Man Alone* (1939). Through the struggles of his war-veteran hero, Johnson, in the Depression years, he analyses and criticizes the structure of contemporary New Zealand society. The novel is important in New Zealand literature for spawning other books on the theme of the 'isolated man', alone either by virtue of his nature, race or environment. Mulgan took his own life.

▷ *Report on Experience* (1949, posthumous)

MULISCH, Harry Kurt Victor
(1927–)

Dutch novelist, born and educated in Haarlem. Mulisch grew up during World War II, which plays a major role in his work, centrally in *Het stenen bruidsbed* (1959, Eng trans *The Stone Bridal Bed*, 1962), whose subject-matter is similar to **Kurt Vonnegut**'s *Slaughterhouse Five* and which remains one of the few works by which Mulisch is known in the English-speaking world. During the 1960s, he devoted much of his time to political and cultural journalism, writing a collection of manifesto pieces, *Voer voor psychologen* (1961, 'Food for Shrinks') and a sympathetic study of the Provo libertarians, *Bericht aan de rattenkoniing* (1966, 'Briefing for King Rat'). *Twee vrouwen* (1975) was translated as *Two Women* in 1980; it differs sharply from **Alberto Moravia**'s book of the same name. A collected edition of Mulisch's stories appeared in 1977; *The Decorated Man* (1984) brought together a group of longer short stories. *De mythische formule* (1981, 'The Mythic Formula') is an important anthology of conversations.

▷ J H Caspers, N S Huisman and J G M Weck, *Mulisch* (1971)

MÜLLER, Heiner
(1929–)

German playwright, frequently dubbed 'the new Brecht'. He was born in Eppendorf, Saxony, worked as a bookseller and journalist, and at the Maxim Gorki Theatre in Berlin. His early works are dialectical variations on classical forms, including *Herakles 5* (1966) and *Philoktet* (1968, Eng trans *Philoctetes*, 1981); scenes from both reappear in *Zement* (1973, Eng trans *Cement*, 1979). After the political upheavals of 1968, Müller's drama took on a darker and more experimental tone, culminating in his versions of *Hamlet* (1977), *Die Hamletmaschine* (1978) and *Shakespeare Factory 2* (1980), which call for the overthrow of dramatic orthodoxy. Later productions strongly resemble the static tableaux and mixed-media presentations of the radical American director Robert Wilson, but even here the continuity with Müller's earlier **Brecht**ian phase is clearly discernible.

▷ D Calandra, *New German Dramatists* (1983)

MÜLLER, Wilhelm
(1794–1827)

German lyrical poet and translator (the *Faustus* of **Marlowe**), born the son of a tailor, in Dessau. He is most famous as the author of the 20-poem-cycle set by Schubert, *Die schöne Müllerin*—of which the music is always taken to be considerably superior to the fluent but rather facile verse.

▷ P S Allen, *Wilhelm Müller and the German Volkslied* (1902)

MULTATULI, pseud of **Eduard Douwes Dekker**
(1820–87)

Dutch novelist and aphorist whose pseudonym means 'I have suffered greatly', born in Amsterdam. A difficult and rebellious youth with a righteous indignation against injustice and stuffiness, he made the reverse of progress in the Dutch Colonial Service. His masterpiece, the preposterous but magnificent *Max Havelaar* (1860, Eng trans 1966), presents himself as hero · against his hypocritical, racist, smug superiors in the East Indies. For the rest of his debt-ridden life he sought and obtained notoriety, and paved the way for the 'Men of the Eighties', who finally broke with the old and decayed literary conventions. He was the liveliest prose writer in Dutch in his century. **D H Lawrence**, among others, responded positively to his rage and fervour.

MUMFORD, Lewis
(1895–1990)

American author, editor and critic, a lecturer on social problems, born in Flushing, Long Island. Influenced by the theories of Patrick Geddes, he wrote extensively on urban society and human progress; *The Culture of*

Cities (1938) and *The City in History* (1961) are perhaps the best known, but the earlier *Technics and Civilisation* (1934) was also influential. He wrote *The Story of Utopias* (1922), *The Brown Decades* (1931), *Faith for Living* (1940), *The Human Prospect* (1955), *The Myth of the Machine* (1967), *The Pentagon of Power* (1971) and other works, examining the prospects for meliorism.

▷ *My Works and Days: A Personal Chronicle* (1979)

MÜNCHHAUSEN, Karl Friedrich Hieronymus, Baron von
(1720–97)

German soldier, born in Bodenwerder, a member of an ancient Hanoverian house. He was the narrator of ridiculously exaggerated exploits, and served in Russian campaigns against the Turks. A collection of marvellous stories attributed to him was first published as *Vademecum für lustige Leute* (1781–3, 'A Handbook for Jolly Folk'); then, much expanded, in English as *Baron Münchhausen's Narrative of his Marvellous Travels and Campaigns in Russia* (1785) by Rudolf Erich Raspe. This version was then expanded again and translated into German by G A Bürger as *Wunderbare Reisen zu Wasser und zu Lande, Feldzüge und lustige Abenteuer des Freyherrn von Münchhausen* (1786, 'Amazing Travels on Water and Land, Campaigns and Amusing Adventures of Baron von Münchhausen'). The legend was again expanded by **Karl Immermann** in the 1830s, and **Walter Hasenclever** in the 1930s. *Münchhausen* is based partly on 16th-century German jokes, and is partly a satire on James Bruce and other travellers.

MUNDAY, Anthony
(1560–1633)

English poet and playwright, born in London. A stationer and actor, he wrote many poems and pamphlets (including one inveighing against theatrical performances) and plays, mostly in collaboration. Among those credited to him in whole or part are *John a Kent and John a Cumber*, *The Downfall* and *The Death of Robert, Earle of Huntington*. He reported on the activities of English Catholics in France and Italy, and was pageant writer for London.

▷ C Turman, *An Elizabethan Man of Letters* (1928)

MUNK, Kaj, born Kaj Harald Leininger Petersen
(1898–1944)

Danish playwright, priest and patriot, born in Maribo, Laaland. He studied theology at Copenhagen University, and as priest of a small parish in Jutland wrote heroic and religious plays that led the Danish dramatic revival in the 1930s. His first play was *En Idealist* (1928), followed by *Cant* (1931), *Henrik VIII* (1931), *Ordet* (1932, 'The Word') and *Han sidder ved smeltedigien* (1938, 'He Sits by the Melting-Pot'). Though he had initially admired the two fascist leaders, their aggressive expansionism and repressive methods changed his mind; during World War II he was one of the spiritual leaders of the Danish Resistance. In 1943 he wrote a patriotic drama, *Niels Ebbeson*; early in 1944 he was taken from his home by the Gestapo one night and was found murdered in a ditch near Silkeborg next morning.

▷ B N Broust, *Kaj Munk—liv og død* (1984)

MUNONYE, John Okechukwu
(1929–)

Nigerian novelist, born in Akokwa and educated at Onitsha and the University of Ibadan. After further training in London, he returned to Nigeria as an education officer. His fiction is largely concerned with the confrontation of Catholic Christianity and traditional Igbo culture. The bleak tragedy of *The Only Son* (1966) and *Obi* (1969) gradually gives way, in the last volume of the trilogy, *Bridge to a Wedding* (1978), to a more philosophically accommodating and affirmative stance, already represented in his fifth novel, *A Dancer of Fortune* (1974). He also portrayed the harrowing civil war in *A Wreath for Maidens* (1973), which is more journalistic than the others.

MUNRO, Alice
(1931–)

Canadian short-story writer and novelist, born in Wingham, Ontario, where she was brought up before attending the University of Western Ontario. She wrote short stories from an early age, waiting until she was 'ready' to write the great novel. Her only novel to date, *Lives of Girls and Women* (1971), accomplished though it is, cannot claim to be that. Her stories, however, published for many years without being collected, are recognized as among the finest of the day. They are invariably set in rural and semi-rural Ontario, the landscape of her childhood; she has published several collections, from *Dance of the Happy Shades* (1968)—winner of the Governor General's Award for Fiction—and *The Progress of Love* (1987) to *Friend of My Mouth* (1990) and *Something I've Been Meaning to Tell You* (1992).

▷ 'The Colonel's Hash Resettled', in J Metcalf, *The Narrative Voice* (1972)

MUNRO, Hector Hugh *see* SAKI

MUNRO, Neil
(1864–1930)

Scottish novelist and journalist, born in Inveraray, Argyll, the son of a farmer. He worked in a law office before taking up journalism in Glasgow, where he became Editor of the *Glasgow Evening News* (1918–27). He wrote romantic Celtic tales in *The Lost Pibroch* (1896) and *Gilian the Dreamer* (1899), and historical Highland novels in *John Splendid* (1898), *Doom Castle* (1901) and *The New Road* (1914). However, he is best known for his humorous tales about a Clyde puffer, published as *The Vital Spark* (1906) and collected as *Para Handy and Other Tales* (1931). His memoir, *Brave Days*, was published posthumously in 1931.
▷ G Blake, introduction to *The Brave Days* (1931)

MUNSHI, Kanaiyalal Maniklal
(1887–1982)

Indian (Gujarati) novelist and historian, close friend to and critic of Gandhi; he served in the Indian government after independence. One of his best books is in English: *Gujarat and its Literature* (1935). His chief literary work lies in his highly competent and readable historical novels.

MUNTHE, Axel
(1857–1949)

Swedish physician and writer, born in Oskarshamn. He practised as a physician and psychiatrist in Paris and Rome, was Swedish court physician and retired to Capri, where he wrote his bestselling autobiography, *The Story of San Michele* (1929), which has gone through endless editions since its first publication.
▷ A Andrén, *Boker om Axel Munthe* (1957)

MURAKAMI Haruki
(1949–)

Japanese novelist, born in Kobe and educated (in classics) at Waseda University. He started his career in writing by translating the works of modern American writers (**Raymond Chandler**, **Truman Capote** and **Richard Brautigan** amongst others) into Japanese, and his own highly original novels are remarkable for being more influenced by the Americans than by his Japanese predecessors—his work could not contrast more vividly with the naturalism of such writers as **Hakucho Masamune** or **Toson Shimazaki**. Wild, surreal, mystical and often extremely funny, he is now the bestselling author in Japan. Of his works available in English, *A Wild Sheep Chase* (1982) is one of the best, and is a sort of detective novel in

which a psychic detective searches for a war criminal, a woman with beautiful ears, and a supernatural sheep with a star on its back.

MURASAKI Shikibu
(c.970–c.1015)

Japanese author, responsible for the *Genji Monogatari* (Eng trans *The Tale of Genji*, 1925–35). She was a member of the Fujiwara family, one of the most powerful aristocratic dynasties in Japan, but her real name is unknown: 'Shikibu Murasaki' is a later fictive construction. Genji was the first great work in Japanese; indeed, there are many who think it still the greatest piece of literature Japan has ever produced. Complex, delicate and often sublimely beautiful, it far outclasses anything produced elsewhere in its day. Like many other aristocratic ladies in late Heian Japan, Murasaki also wrote a *Nikki* ('Diary') which, apart from being beautifully constructed, contains valuable insights into court life of the period.
▷ I I Morris, *The World of the Shining Prince* (1964)

MURDOCH, Dame Iris Jean
(1919–)

Irish novelist and philosopher. Born in Dublin of Anglo–Irish parents, she was educated at Badminton School, Bristol, and Oxford, where she was fellow and tutor in philosophy at St Anne's College from 1948 to 1963. She published a study of **Jean-Paul Sartre** (like her, both a novelist and a philosopher) in 1953 and two important but unfashionable philosophical works, much influenced by **Plato**, *The Fire and the Sun* (1977) and *The Sovereignty of the Good* (1970). These deal with the relationships between art and philosophy, and between love, freedom, knowledge and morality. She began writing novels as a hobby. *Under the Net* appeared in 1954, to be followed by more than 20 titles in the next 25 years, including such well-known works as *The Sandcastle* (1957), *The Bell* (1958), *A Severed Head* (1961), *An Unofficial Rose* (1962), *The Red and the Green* (1965), *The Nice and the Good* (1968), *The Black Prince* (1972), *The Sea, The Sea* (1978, winner of the Booker Prize), *Nuns and Soldiers* (1980), *The Good Apprentice* (1985), *The Book and the Brotherhood* (1987) and *The Message to the Planet* (1989). The popularity of the fiction derives largely from her narrative skill in controlling tangled and shifting patterns of relationships, the ironic or even startling circumstances in which the characters find themselves, and the pervasive blend of realism and symbolism. She has also written several plays, including *A Severed Head* (adapted with **J B Priestley** in 1963), *Servants* *and the Snow* (1970), *The Two Arrows* (1972) and *Art and Eros* (1980).

MURE, Sir William
(1594–1657)

Scottish poet, born in Rowallan, Ayrshire. A staunch Protestant and Royalist, he was wounded at Marston Moor (1644), but later led his regiment at Newcastle (1644). He wrote a long religious poem, *The True Crucifixe for True Catholikes* (1629), a fine version of the Psalms (1639), and some love and courtly poems. *The Cry of Blood and of a Broken Covenant* (1650) is a poem on behalf of the Covenanters' cause. He also translated parts of **Virgil**'s *Aeneid*.

MURENA, H A, pseud of Hector Alberto Alvarez
(1923–75)

Argentinian novelist, poet and critic, born in Buenos Aires. He made his first vivid impression on the reading public of Argentina—an enlightened and sophisticated one—as a pessimistic social essayist and leftist critic of leftists. His thesis was that Latin Americans suffered from guilt and insecurity because they had deliberately—out of a mixture of pride and stupidity—cut themselves off from European culture. Murena illustrated his thesis with discussions of the work of most of the great Argentinian writers, including **Arlt**, **Horacio Quiroga** and the man whose intellectual heir he was, **Estrada Martínez**. His criticism of **Borges** was the sharpest ever made. His great novel, *Las leycs de la noche* (1956, Eng trans *The Laws of the Night*, 1976), the central book of a trilogy, is reminiscent of both Arlt and **Sabato** in the extreme horror of its situations. It was Borges above all who commended his fiction to the public. His final novels, under the umbrella title of *El sueño de la razón* (he was able to publish four of a projected seven titles before his untimely death) are quite different, and are exclusively concerned with language and the parody of overvalued authors. Prophet of the end of life on earth, Murena wrote a play and many excellent and original stories; his was one of the most formidable and interesting minds of his country.
▷ *Seis novelistas argentinos de la nueva promocion* (1959)

MURET, Marc-Antoine de
(1526–85)

French humanist and poet, born in Muret near Limoges. He lectured on civil law and classics in France, but later fled on a charge of heresy to Italy, where he edited Latin authors and wrote orations, poems and commentaries.
▷ C Dejob, *Marc-Antoine Muret* (1881)

MURGER, Henri
(1822–61)

French writer, born in Paris. He began life as a notary's clerk, and, devoting his time to literature, led the life of privation and adventure described in his first and best novel, *Scènes de la vie de Bohème* (1845, Eng trans *The Bohemians of the Latin Quarter*, 1887), the basis of Puccini's opera, *La Bohème* (1896). During his later years he led a dissipated life and wrote slowly and fitfully. *Le Manchon de Francine* ('Francine's Muff') is one of the saddest short stories ever written. Other prose works are *La Vie de jeunesse* (1861, 'The Youthful Life') and *Le Pays Latin* (1861, 'Latin Country'). His poems, *Les Nuits d'hiver* (1862, Eng trans *Winter Nights*, 1923), are graceful and often deeply pathetic; several were translated by **Andrew Lang** in his *Lays of old France*.
▷ R Baldick, *The First Bohemian* (1961)

MURNER, Thomas
(1475–1537)

German Roman Catholic satirist, the most prominent of his time, born in Oberehnheim in Alsace. In 1490 he became a wandering Franciscan friar, but died as a priest in his native village. His first full-scale satire, in rhyming verse, *Die Narrenbeschwörung* (1512, 'Invocation of Fools'), is candidly, right down to its title, modelled on **Brant**. Later he excoriated Luther, whom at first he believed was on the Catholic side. A vain, difficult and quarrelsome man, he has been described as possessing an 'almost tragic genius'. But he was the only Roman Catholic—he had hoped to reform the fabric of the Church, without rocking its foundations—whose mastery of theological dispute equalled that of his opponents. Much attention has been devoted to him in Germany, but there is no good work on him in English. His understanding of the colloquial and his closeness to how the common people thought and felt gives his poetry an edge which has now been fully recognized.
▷ R Newald, *Probleme und Gestalten des deutschen Humanisimus* (1963)

MURPHY, Arthur
(1727–1805)

Irish actor and playwright, born in Clomquin, Roscommon. He was educated at St Omer. He worked as a clerk in Cork and then London from 1747 to 1751. From 1752 to 1774 he published the weekly *Gray's Inn Journal*, and so got to know **Dr Johnson**. By going on the stage he paid his debts, and entered Lincoln's Inn in 1757. In 1758 he produced *The Upholsterer*, a successful farce; in 1762 he was called to the Bar, but continued to write farces and adaptations for

the stage. His translation of **Tacitus** (1793) is excellent, unlike his *Essay on Johnson* (1792) and *Life of David Garrick* (2 vols, 1801).
▷J P Murphy, *Arthur Murphy* (1946)

MURPHY, Richard
(1927–)

Irish poet, born in Galway, but brought up in Ceylon and educated at Oxford and the Sorbonne. In the 1960s he 'retired' to the Aran Islands, later living outside Dublin and dividing his time between Ireland and Sri Lanka. His training in the Classics lends authoritative skill to such long narrative poems as *The Cleggan Disaster* (in *Sailing to an Island*, 1963) and *The Battle of Aughrim* (1968), but sometimes distracts from the lyrical assurance of the shorter poems and ballads that are a major part of *New Selected Poems* (1989).
▷M Harmon, *Richard Murphy: Poet of Two Traditions* (1979)

MURPHY, Thomas
(1935–)

Irish dramatist, born in Tuem, County Galway. He gained international repute following Joan Littlewood's London production of his *A Whistle in The Dark* (1961). In 1969 he returned to Dublin and joined the Abbey Theatre as director and author of the startlingly innovative *The Morning After Optimism* (1971). Since then *Famine* (1977), *The Gigli Concert* (1984) and *Bailegangaire* (1985) have established him as a great dramatic voice, speaking for the vulnerable and the oppressed, the vain yet emotionally imprisoned, and the aged made angry by both physical and spiritual decay. Much of his later work has come about through his creative collaboration with the Galway theatre company Druid, for whom he worked as Writer in Residence during the 1980s.
▷F O'Toole, *The Politics of Magic: The Work and Times of Thomas Murphy* (1987)

MURRAY, Charles
(1864–1941)

Scottish poet, born in Alford, Aberdeenshire. He trained as an engineer and had a successful career in South Africa, where in 1917 he became Director of Defence. His poems were written in the Aberdeenshire dialect and admirably portrayed country life and character at the turn of the century. His first major collection, *Hamewith* (1900), was his best and most characteristic. A *Complete Poems* was published in 1979.
▷C Christie, *Some Memories of Charles Murray* (1943)

MURRAY, Les (Leslie Allan)
(1938–)

Australian poet, critic and editor, born in Nabiac, New South Wales. His childhood and adolescence were spent on a dairy farm. He attended Sydney University but left in 1960 without taking a degree. He has worked as a translator but has long been a freelance writer, frequently contributing literary journalism to newspapers and magazines. His poetry, which has made him one of Australia's leading literary figures, is revered for its perceptive and pungent evocation of rural life. His verse includes *The Ilex Tree* (1965, with Geoffrey Lehmann), *The Weatherboard Cathedral* (1969), *Poems Against Economics* (1972), a verse-novel in 140 sonnets called the *Boys Who Stole the Funeral* (1980), and *The People's Otherworld* (1983), which won the Australian Literary Society's Gold Medal the following year. His *Selected Poems: the Vernacular Republic* was published in 1976 and revised as *The Vernacular Republic; Poems 1961–1981* (1982). In 1993 he received his fifth National Book Council poetry prize for *Translations from the Natural World* (1992), which also won the NSW State Literary Prize for Poetry and the Victorian Premier's Prize in the same year. His latest verse is *The Middle Sea: Book 1 of a Verse Novel in Progress*, published in the *Sydney Review* (1993). Murray compiled and edited the *New Oxford Book of Australian Verse* (1986).
▷P Nelson, *Study Notes on the Poetry of Les A Murray* (1978)

MURRY, John Middleton
(1889–1957)

British writer and critic, born in Peckham. He wrote some poetry and many volumes of essays and criticism which had a strong influence on the young intellectuals of the 1920s. In 1911 he met **Katherine Mansfield**, whom he married in 1918, and introduced her work in *The Adelphi*, of which he was founder and editor from 1923 to 1948. He also produced posthumous selections from her letters and diaries, and a biography in 1932. He edited the *Athenaeum* (1919–21). He became a pacifist and was editor of *Peace News* from 1940 to 1946. Towards the end of his life he became interested in agriculture, and started a community farm in Norfolk. His major works include critical studies on *Keats and Shakespeare* (1925), his friend *D H Lawrence* (1931), *William Blake* (1933) and *Swift* (1954). He also wrote religious works, including *To The Unknown God* (1924) and *The Life of Jesus* (1926). He published his autobiography, *Between Two Worlds*, in 1935.
▷F A Lea, *The Life of John Middleton Murry* (1959)

MUSAEUS
(5th–6th century)

Greek epic poet, author of *Hero and Leander*, which has been translated into many languages.
▷M H Jellinek, *Die Sage in der Dichtung* (1890)

MUSÄUS, Johann Karl August
(1735–87)

German writer, born in Jena. He studied theology there, and in 1770 became professor at the Weimar gymnasium. His first book (1760) was a parody of **Samuel Richardson**'s *Sir Charles Grandison, Der deutsche Grandison*; in 1778–9 he satirized **Johann Lavater** in *Physiognomische Reisen* (Eng trans *Physiognomical Travels*, 1800). But his fame rests on his German popular tales (*Volksmärchen der Deutschen*, 1782–6, Eng trans *Popular Tales of the Germans*, 1791), which claimed, falsely, to be a collection taken down from the lips of old people. Their chief note is artificial naivety, but they are a blend of satirical humour, quaint fancy and graceful writing.
▷A Richli, *Johann Musäus* (1957)

MUSCHG, Adolf
(1934–)

Swiss novelist and story writer, writing in German, born in Zollikon near Zürich (where he teaches literature at the university). His novels, such as *Abissers Grund* (1974, 'Abisser's Motive'), tend to satirize his countrymen and their middle-class habits.

MUSHANOKOJI Saneatsu
(b.1885)

Japanese novelist, playwright and critic, born into an aristocratic family. His early work was marked by a romantic liberalism—he was greatly influenced by **Tolstoy**, even going so far as to set up an 'ideal village' on the Tolstoyan model. As World War II loomed closer, however, he became increasingly right-wing, drifting off into despair and a remote isolation after the defeat in 1945.
▷T Arima, *The Failure of Freedom: A Portrait of Modern Japanese Intellectuals* (1969)

MUSIL, Robert
(1880–1942)

Austrian novelist, born in Klagenfurt. He was trained as a scientist (he invented a chromatometer) and as a philosopher. During World War I he was an officer and drew on his experience for *Die Verwirrungen des Zöglings Törless* (1906, Eng trans *Young Törless*, 1955), a terrifying, sadistic story of life inside a military academy. Memorable though it is, it is eclipsed by *Der Mann ohne Eigenschaften*

(1930–43, Eng trans *The Man Without Qualities*, 1953–60), his unfinished tour de force. Portraying a society on the brink of the abyss through the eyes of Ulrich, the man who has dispensed with conventional qualities, its narrative covers just one year, 1913–14. Plotless but dealing in interrelated facts, it is multilayered. It is widely acknowledged as one of the great novels of the century despite the confusion of final drafts which the author did not have time to tidy up before his sudden death in Geneva.
▷K Dinklage, *Robert Musil. Leben, Werk, Wirkung* (1960)

MUSKETT, Netta
(1887–1963)

English romantic and historical novelist, who published her first book, *The Jade Spider*, in 1927, and who continued writing prolifically until the 1960s. Muskett was not a wholly conventional romantic novelist, for while her books reflect a strict morality, her heroines are not necessarily paragons of virtue. For example, in *Painted Heaven* (1934) a woman who lost her fiancé, brothers and parents during World War I, attempts to find new happiness by having an illegitimate child. The result, however, is not contentment but insecurity: a 'painted heaven'. Later, Muskett looked at the conflicting work and family lives of the emerging career-women of the late 1950s.

MUSSET, (Louis Charles) Alfred de
(1810–57)

French poet and dramatist, born in Paris. After tentative study first of the law, then of medicine, he found he had a talent for writing and at 18 published a translation of **Thomas De Quincey**'s *Confessions of an Opium Eater* (*L'anglais mangeur d'opium*, 1828). His first collection of poems, *Contes d'Espagne et d'Italie* (1830, 'Tales of Spain and Italy'), won the approval of **Victor Hugo** who accepted him into his *Cénacle*, the inner shrine of militant Romanticism. But Musset had no real desire to commit himself to any particular cult; indeed he had already begun to poke gentle fun at the movement, and had indicated that he wished to 'se déhugotiser'. His first excursion into drama, *La Nuit vénitienne* ('A Night in Venice'), failed at the Odéon in 1830, and from then on he conceived an 'armchair theatre' with plays intended for reading only. The first of these, *La Coupe et les lèvres* ('The Cup and the Lips') and *À quoi rêvent les jeunes filles* ('What do Young Girls Dream Of?'), together with the narrative poem *Namouna*, were published as *Spectacle dans un fauteuil* ('Armchair Theatre') in 1832, and next year the tragi-comedies *André del Sarto* and *Les Caprices de Marianne* (1851,

'The Whims of Marianne') appeared in the *Revue des deux mondes* ('Review of Two Worlds'). Also among his *Comédies et proverbes* (1840), as these pieces were called, are *Lorenzaccio* (1834), *On ne badine pas avec l'amour* (1836, Eng trans *No Trifling with Love*, 1890) and *Il ne faut jurer de rien* (1836, 'Never Take an Oath'). *Un Caprice*, published in 1837, and several of his other 'armchair' plays were staged successfully more than 10 years later, and thus reassured he wrote *On ne saurait penser à tout* (1849, 'You Can Never Think of Everything'), *Carmosine* (1850, Eng trans 1865) and *Bettine* (1851) for actual performance. In 1833 Musset had met **George Sand**, and there began the stormy love affair which coloured much of his work after that date. The pair set out to spend the winter together at Venice, but Musset became ill, Sand became capricious, and in April the poet returned alone, broken in health and sunk in depression. His *Nuits*, from *Nuit de mai* (1835, 'A Night in May') through *Nuit de décembre* (1835, 'A Night in December') and *Nuit d'août* (1836, 'A Night in August') to *Nuit d'octobre* (1837, 'A Night in October'), trace the emotional upheaval of his love for George Sand from despair to final resignation. His autobiographical poem *Confessions d'un enfant du siècle* (1835, Eng trans *The Confessions of a Child of the Century*, 1892) is a study of the prevalent attitude of mind—the *mal du siècle*—resulting from the aftermath of revolution and the unrest of the early years of the century. *L'Espoir en Dieu* (1838, 'Hoping in God'), an expression of the soul's longing for certainty, is perhaps not altogether convincing. In 1838 he was appointed Home Office librarian. He died of heart failure.

MUSSET, Paul de
(1804–80)

French novelist and man-of-letters, brother to the dramatist **Alfred de Musset**, whose affair with **George Sand** prompted Paul de Musset's *Luis et elle* (1859). This was a thinly disguised response to Sand's own *Elle et lui* (also 1859), which dealt with the breakdown in her relationship with Paul's brother. It is as the author of a minor classic of French children's literature, the 'conte' *Monsieur le Vent et Madame la Pluie* (1860), which has been much reprinted, that Paul de Musset's name survives.

MYERS, Frederic William Henry
(1843–1901)

English poet and essayist, brother of Ernest James Myers, the son of a clergyman. A classical scholar, and a school inspector from 1872 to 1900, he wrote poems (collected 1921), essays, a book on *Wordsworth* (1881) and *Human Personality and its Survival of* *Bodily Death* (1903). He was one of the founders of the Society for Psychical Research in 1882.

MYERS, L(eopold) H(amilton)
(1881–1944)

English novelist and dramatist, born in Cambridge. As a result of a legacy, he was financially able to devote himself to writing full-time from an early age. Although he produced a verse play, *Arvat*, in 1908, he is principally remembered now for *The Near and the Far* (1929), an ambitious tetralogy of novels set in 16th-century India. Myers believed contemporary society to be spiritually and morally impoverished, and in his writing used an idealized past of the Moghul Empire to emphasize by comparison the poverty of the present.

MYKLE, Agnar
(1915–)

Norwegian novelist and short-story writer, who enjoyed a certain scandalous vogue in Britain at the beginning of the 1960s, when his two most important novels, *Lasso rundt fru Luna* (1954) and *Sangen on den røde rubin* (1956), were translated into English, as *Lasso Round the Moon* (1960) and *The Song of the Red Ruby* (1961) respectively. He grew up in Trondheim, and the restrictions of his middle-class home became one of the obsessive themes of his writing, which consistently argued in favour of eliminating social and moral restraints. His first story collection, *Taustigen* (1948, 'The Rope Ladder'), appeared when he was 35; his first novel was *Tyven, tyven, skal du dete* (1951, Eng trans *The Hotel Room*, 1963). In 1957 he was tried for obscenity following the publication of *Sangen on den røde rubin* (1956); his acquittal and that of his publisher was a significant moment in liberating modern fiction from 19th-century standards. Having written the autobiographical story of Ask Burlefot, Mykle wrote very little more and was mostly silent in his later years.

▷P Houm, *Ask Burlefot og vi* (1957)

MYRVILIS, Stratis, pseud of Stratis Stamatopoulos
(1892–1969)

Greek novelist and short-story writer, born on Mytilene. He served in the Balkan Wars and in World War I. Both his first collection of short stories, *Kokines Histories* (1915, 'Red Stories'), and his first novel, *Zoë en Tapho* (1924, Eng trans *Life in the Tomb*, 1931, 1977), were published only on Mytilene; it was not until *Zoë en Tapho* was republished in Athens in 1930 that it came to the attention of reviewers and made his reputation. A classic war tale written as the journal of a sergeant in the trenches, it earned the author comparison with **Erich Maria Remarque**. His next novel, *Dhaskala me ta Chrysa Matia* (1933, Eng trans *The Schoolmistress with the Golden Eyes*, 1964), again drew on his war memories, telling the story of a young soldier's return to Mytilene after the war; his guilt at the death of his friend in the fighting

is exacerbated when he realizes he is falling in love with his friend's young widow. Myrivilis then returned to writing short stories, revealing a surprisingly lyrical feel for nature in a collection published in 1935. His later work includes a novel, *Panaghia Ghorghona* (1949, Eng trans *The Mermaid Madonna*, 1959), and two more collections of short stories (1952 and 1959).

N

NABOKOV, Vladimir
(1899–1977)

Russian-born American novelist, born in St Petersburg. His family was wealthy and aristocratic and he was a precocious child. He attended St Petersburg's relatively progressive Tenishev School, where he was accused of 'not conforming' to his surroundings. In 1919, following the Bolshevik Revolution, his family became émigrés, and he and his brother went to Cambridge on a scholarship, where he studied Russian and French literature. When he graduated in 1922 he rejoined his family in Berlin, where his father was the victim of a senseless murder. He lived for more than 15 years in Berlin but admitted to never having mastered the language, though his first literary success was a translation of some of **Heinrich Heine**'s songs. From 1937 to 1940 he was in Paris, where he met **James Joyce**, and then emigrated to the USA where he took citizenship in 1945. He published his first novels in Berlin: *Mashenka* (1926, Eng trans *Mary*, 1971), *Korol, Dama, Valet* (1928, 'King, Queen, Knave'), *Zashita Luzhina* (1936, 'The Defense') and *Otchayanie* (1936, 'Despair'). In Paris he wrote *Soglodatai* (1938, 'The Eye') and *Priglashenie na kazn'* (1938, 'Invitation to a Beheading'). All were written in Russian, under the pseudonym V Sirin, the author himself later collaborating on English translations. In the USA he taught at Wellesley College and Cornell University, and earned distinction as a lepidopterist. Writing now in English he published many short stories and novels including *The Real Life of Sebastian Knight* (1941), *Bend Sinister* (1947), *Pale Fire* (1962) and *Ada* (1969). *Lolita* (1959) was a *succès de scandale* and brought his name before the general public, and allowed him to abandon teaching and devote himself full-time to writing. From 1959 he lived in Montreux in Switzerland. Among 20th-century novelists he is regarded for his linguistic ingenuity and dazzling intellect. **H G Wells** was his first love but his debt to **Jane Austen**, **Dickens**, **Robert Louis Stevenson** and others is acknowledged in *Lectures on Literature* (1980). He also translated **Alexander Pushkin**'s *Eugene Onegin* (1963).

▷A Field, *Vladimir Nabokov, the life and art* (1977)

NAEVIUS, Gnaeus
(c.264–c.201 BC)

Roman poet and dramatist, born probably in Campania. He served in the first Punic war (264–241 BC), and started producing his own plays in 235. A plebeian, for 30 years he satirized the Roman nobles in his plays, and was compelled to leave Rome, ultimately retiring to Utica in Africa. Fragments of an epic, *De Bello Punico* ('The Punic Wars'), are extant.
▷M Barchiesi, *Nevio epico* (1962)

NAGAI Kafu
(1879–1962)

Japanese writer, born into an aristocratic samurai family in western Japan, though he is strongly associated with Tokyo, where he lived most of his life, particularly amongst the geisha houses of the Shinbashi area. He was one of the first writers from Japan to travel extensively in the West and to open himself to western influences, being particularly affected by his experiences of French culture, and producing a new, more generally accessible kind of fiction writing. At the same time, he was deeply rooted in Japan's own traditions, and was very much saddened by the passing of the traditional way of life in old Edo (the old name of Tokyo)—one critic said that he 'closed his eyes to historical change'. His wistful nostalgia and graceful style are at their best in *Bokuto Kitan* (1936, Eng trans *A Strange Tale from East of the River*, 1965), a collection of stories set in the geisha houses and eating places of Tokyo's red light district.
▷E Scheidensticker, *Kafu, the Scribbler* (1965)

NAIDU, Sarojini, née **Chattopadhyay**
(1879–1949)

Indian feminist and poet, born in Hyderabad and educated at Madras, London and Cambridge. Known as the 'nightingale of India', she published three volumes of lyric verse: *The Golden Threshold* (1905), *The Bird of Time* (1912) and *The Broken Wing* (1915). She organized flood-relief in Hyderabad

(1908), and lectured and campaigned on feminism, particularly the abolition of purdah. Associated with Mahatma Gandhi, she was the first Indian woman to be President of the Indian National Congress, in 1925. She was imprisoned several times for civil disobedience incidents, and took part in the negotiations leading to independence. In 1947 she was appointed governor of United Provinces (now Uttar Pradesh).

▷P Sengupta, *Sarojini Naidu* (1966)

NAIPAUL, Shiva(dhar Srinavasa)
(1945–85)

West Indian novelist and prose writer, born in Port of Spain, Trinidad. The younger brother of V S Naipaul, he became noted as a writer of exceptional promise with the publication in 1970 of his first work, *Fireflies*, which won three awards. By then based in London, he augmented his success with his novel *The Chip-Chip Gatherers* (1973), which won the Whitbread Award for Fiction. He travelled widely in the USA, India and the Caribbean, and wrote an account of an African journey in *North of South* (1978). His last works—six articles and the start of a projected work on Australia—are gathered in the posthumously published *An Unfinished Journey* (1986).

NAIPAUL, V(idiadhar) S(urajprasad)
(1932–)

Trinidadian novelist. His brother **Shiva Naipaul** was also a gifted writer. Educated at Queen's Royal College, Port of Spain, he left the Caribbean for Oxford in 1950, where he took his degree. The editor of 'Caribbean Voices' for the BBC, he dabbled in journalism before his first novel, *The Mystic Masseur* (1957), was published. *Miguel Street* (1959) collected sketches depicting lower-class life in Trinidad through the eyes of a growing boy. The book which made his name was *A House for Mr Biswas* (1961), a spicy satire spanning three Trinidadian generations but focusing on its eponymous six-fingered sign-writer. Thereafter the Caribbean figured less prominently in his work, which grew steadily darker and more complex. *In a Free State* (1971) won the Booker Prize, and in 1979 he published *A Bend in the River*, a masterly re-creation of what it is like to live under an African dictatorship. As well as novels he has written several trenchant 'travel' books including *An Area of Darkness: An Experience of India* (1964) and *Among the Believers: An Islamic Journey* (1981). *Finding the Centre* (1984) is autobiographical.

▷S Kamra, *The Novels of V S Naipaul* (1990)

NAIRNE, Carolina, née Oliphant, Lady
(1766–1845)

Scottish song writer, born in Gask, Perthshire, the daughter of a Jacobite laird. In 1806 she married her second cousin, Major Nairne (1757–1830), who became Lord Nairne in 1824. She lived in Edinburgh, but travelled widely in Ireland and Europe after her husband's death. Collecting traditional airs, she wrote songs to them under the pseudonym 'Mrs Bogan of Bogan', which were published in *The Scottish Minstrel* (1821–4), and posthumously as *Lays from Strathearn*. They include the lament for Prince Charles Edward Stuart, 'Will ye no' come back again', 'The Land o' the Leal', 'Caller Herrin'', 'The Laird o' Cockpen', 'The Rowan Tree' and 'The Auld Hoose', as well as the martial setting for 'The Hundred Pipers'.

▷K Oliphant, *Jacobite Lairds of Gask* (1970)

NAKANO Shigeharu
(1902–)

Japanese poet and novelist. In his twenties and early thirties, Nakano produced a stream of Marxist poetry, until he was arrested as a subversive by the *Kempeito* (secret police). This experience turned him into a novelist. He was a leading light in the pre- and postwar Marxist underground, which was part of a continuous thread in Japanese culture, giving rise to the student underground movement of the 1970s. Nakano's writing, whilst not short on rhetoric, also displays great literary prowess.

NALÉ ROXLO, Conrado
(1898–1971)

Argentinian dramatist, story writer, novelist, children's writer, poet and humorist, of Uruguayan descent, born in Buenos Aires. He was a close friend to the great **Roberto Arlt**. His essays and stories were often signed 'Chamico'. His poetry, witty and unambitious, has been compared to that of **Heine**; he later turned to a playful, unserious Surrealism. Most highly thought of now, however, are his fantasy dramas, slightly influenced both by the plays of the *grottesco criollo* school—a kind of early Argentinian theatre of the absurd, or cruelty—and (technically) by the two popular playwrights 'Darthéz and Damel'. Most successful is his witty reworking of the Faust legend, *El pacto de Christina* (1945, 'Cristina's Pact'), in which a girl makes an agreement with the devil in return for the love of a man. His single novel, *Extraño accidente* (1960, 'Strange Accident'), has been commended for its 'audacity', and its 'strange quality and poetic depth'.

▷A Flores, *The Literature of Spanish America* (1966–7)

NALKOWSKA
(1884–1954)

Polish novelist and dramatist, born in Warsaw, the daughter of a famous geographer and his wife, who were enlightened enough to give her a sound education, and to be proud of her. She was initially associated with the so-called Positivist movement, which preceded that of the neo-romantic 'Young Poland' (Mloda Polska). Her first novel, *Kobiety* (1906, Eng trans *Women*, 1920), published when she was only 22, was well intentioned, but too closely reflected what she thought she ought, as a Positivist, to believe: however, its characterization bore sure signs that she was a woman of unusual genius, who did not pander to male notions of women. Eighteen years later she had matured beyond recognition; *Romans Teresy Hennert* (1924, 'Teresa Hennert's Affair') is a scathing account of the bourgeois attitude to 'illicit' love in Poland after World War II. She wrote at least three more excellent psychological novels, of which *Granica* (1935, 'The Boundary') is perhaps the finest. She is most famous, however, for *Medaliony* (1946, Eng trans of part of it in *Introduction to Modern Polish Literature*, 1964, H Gillon and L Krzyzanowski eds): as a member of the International Commission to Investigate Nazi Crimes, she had, early, to investigate torture and concentration camps in Poland, and in these sketches, amongst the most harrowing and ironic ever written on this subject, she reported her findings. 'Professor Spanner', about making soap from prisoners, is peculiarly memorable for its bland summaries of the good reasons advanced for this process.

NAMARA, Fernando
(1919–)

Portuguese poet, novelist and essayist, born near Coimbra. He was a country doctor until 1965 (when he decided to devote himself to writing), as his eloquent *Retalhos da vida de um medico* (1949, Eng trans *Mountain Doctor*, 1956) testifies. His realistic, psychologically penetrating and socially aware fiction includes *O trigo e o joio* (1954, Eng trans *The Fields of Fate*, 1970).

NAOGEORGUS, or NAOGEORG, Thomas, Latin name of **Thomas Kirchmair**
(1511–63)

German dramatist, classicist, poet, translator (**Sophocles** into Latin) and Lutheran preacher, born in Straubing. His *Pammachius* (1538), in Latin like his other plays, is a swingeing attack on the pope and all things papist. So is the verse epic *Regnum papisticum* (1555). *Pammachius* was performed in Cambridge in 1545, by members of Christ's College. *Mercator* (1540) is a notable Jederman (Everyman) comedy, in which salvation is seen as gained by good works.
▷F Wiener, *Naogeorgus im England der Reformationszeit* (1907)

NARAYAN, Rasipuram Kirshnaswamy
(1906–)

Indian novelist, born in Madras, south India. He was educated there and at Maharaja's College in Mysore. His first novel, *Swami and Friends* (1935), and its successor *The Bachelor of Arts* (1937), are set in the enchanting fictional territory of 'Malgudi'. Other Malgudi novels are *The Dark Room* (1938), *The English Teacher* (1945)—a thinly veiled account of his own marriage and the event that most matured and shaped his character, the early death of his beloved wife—*Mr Sampath* (1949), *The Financial Expert* (1952), *The Man-Eater of Malgudi* (1961), *The Painter of Signs* (1977) and *The Tiger for Malgudi* (1983). His novel *The Guide* (1958) won him the National Prize of the Indian Literary Academy. He has also published stories, travel books, books for children and essays, as well as *My Days: A Memoir* (1974). The best Indian novelist of his generation, his publication in Britain was brought about by **Graham Greene**.
▷C Vander, *R. K. Narayan* (1986)

NASH, (Frederic) Ogden
(1902–71)

American writer of light verse, born in Rye, New York. Educated at Harvard, he tried various occupations—teaching, editing, selling bonds, copy writing—before devoting himself to verse. Taking outrageous liberties with the English language ('I would live all my life in nonchalance and insouciance/Were it not for making a living, which is rather a nouciance'), he soon became the most popular modern versifier, frequently to be seen in the *New Yorker*, whose sophisticated tone he helped establish. No subject, however odd, inconsequential or mundane was safe from his wit. Puns, parody and pastiche—as well as alliteration—were his stock in trade, which he used to amuse as well as shock. He published many collections, including *Free Wheeling* (1931), *Hard Lines* (1931), *Parents Keep Out: Elderly Poems for Youngerly Readers* (1951), *The Private Dining Room and Other New Verses* (1953) and *Boy is a Boy* (1960). *I Wouldn't Have Missed It: Selected Poems of Ogden Nash* was published in 1983.
▷L B Axford, *An Index to the Poems of Ogden Nash* (1972)

NASHE, Thomas
(1567–1601)

English dramatist and satirist, born in Lowestoft. He studied for seven years at St John's College, Cambridge, travelled in France and Italy, and then went to London to earn a precarious living by his pen. His first work was the *Anatomie of Absurditie* (1589), perhaps written at Cambridge. He plunged into the Martin Marprelate controversy, showing a talent for vituperation which he expressed in his works. *Pierce Penilesse, his Supplication to the Divell* (1592) began the series of attacks on the Harveys (Richard Harvey had criticized Nashe's preface to **Robert Greene**'s *Menaphon*), which culminated in *Have with you to Saffron Walden* (1596), against **Gabriel Harvey**, who had by then assailed Greene's memory in *Foure Letters*. In 1599 the controversy was suppressed by the Archbishop of Canterbury. Nashe's satirical masque *Summer's Last Will and Testament* (1592) contains the song 'Spring the sweet Spring is the year's pleasant king'. *The Unfortunate Traveller* (1594) is a picaresque tale, one of the earliest of its kind. After **Christopher Marlowe**'s death, Nashe prepared his unfinished tragedy *Dido* (1596) for the stage. His own play *The Isle of Dogs* (1597), now lost, drew such attention to abuses in the state that it was suppressed, the theatre closed, and the writer himself thrown into the Fleet prison. His last work was *Lenten Stuffe* (1599), a panegyric on the red herring trade at Yarmouth.
▷M Schaluch, *Antecedents of the English Novel* (1963)

NATHAN, Robert Gruntal
(1894–1985)

American poet and novelist, born in New York City, educated at Harvard, and seven times married. His masterpiece is *Peter Kindred* (1919), a highly personalized fiction which gives an unparalleled portrayal of a social class undergoing a period of enormous change. Its lilting, almost poetic style is reproduced in *The Puppet Master* (1923) and *The Woodcutter's House* (1927), both of which are greatly underappreciated. In *The Bishop's Wife* (1928) an angel poses as an archdeacon and falls for the bishop's wife; *There Is Another Heaven* (1929) puts a converted Jew into a Calvinist heaven; and *One More Spring* (1933) offers a coy way through the economic depression. Ironically, Nathan's verse is much less compelling than his poetic prose; collections of poetry include *The Cedar Box* (1929) and *Winter in April* (1958).

NATION, Terry (Terence)
(1930–)

English television scriptwriter and novelist. Nation came to prominence as the original scriptwriter for the long-running *Doctor Who* television science-fiction series, (1963 onwards), in which the benevolent title character used an old-fashioned police telephone box, 'the Tardis', to travel through time and space. Nation also created the daleks, the Doctor's most deadly foes. These herd-like robotic creatures, shaped like pepper-pots, barking 'I obey!' or 'Exterminate!', enjoyed huge popularity and appeared in such films, based on Nation scripts, as *The Daleks: Invasion Earth 2150* (1966). Nation is also the author of *Rebecca's World* (1975), a science-fiction story for young people, and the post-nuclear catastrophe television series, *The Survivors* (1976). He has also collaborated on other series.

NAU, John-Antoine, pseud of **Antoine Torque**
(1860–1918)

French writer, born in San Francisco of French parents. He was brought up in France from the age of three, after the death of his father. As a young man he worked for a time as a sailor, and continued to travel widely. His novels utilize a variety of colourful locations which reflect that experience, as in *Cristobal le poète* (1912), which is set in Algiers, and *Thérèse Donati* (1921), which evokes the landscape and people of Corsica. He published several volumes of poetry as well as novels, and has the historical distinction of being the first recipient of the Prix **Goncourt** for his novel *Force ennemie* in 1903.

NAVARRETE, Fray Manuel de
(1768–1809)

Minor Mexican poet and Franciscan, who kept his poetry a secret from his superiors. He read widely, especially in the English preromantic school of the *Night Thoughts* of **Edward Young**, which influenced him.

NAWAL EL SAADAWI
(20th century)

Prominent and militant Egyptian doctor and novelist, born in Kafr Tahla. As a doctor she became aware of women's social and economic problems, and in her first non-fictional work in Arabic, *Women and Sex* (1972), and in her stories in *Two Women in One* (1975, Eng trans 1985), she highlighted their plight. *God Dies by the Nile* (1974, Eng trans 1985), considered a 'metaphor for the Sadat regime', further reveals how class and oppression by landlords augments their misery. Her outspokenness resulted in her losing her post as Director of Health in Cairo. In her later works, such as *She Has No Place in Paradise* (1987) and *Death of His Excellency, the Ex-Minister* (1987), all published outside Egypt, she further illustrated the impotence of the political and religious system in overcoming the influences of imperialism and colonialism.

NAZOR, Vladimir
(1876–1949)
Croatian poet, born in Postire on the island of Brač. He wrote lyrics and ballads as well as epic poems and dramatic works in a style similar to the Symbolists. His works include *Slav Legends* (1900), *Lirika* (1910, 'Lyrics'), *Carmen Vitae*, an anthology (1922), and a diary of his experiences with the Yugoslav partisans in World War II.

NEAL, John
(1793–1876)
American editor, poet, novelist and critic, born in Falmouth in Maine, who sometimes signed himself 'Jehu O'Cataract'. After going into business and failing, he qualified as a lawyer, then became editor of the *Portico*, a literary monthly published by the chauvinistic Delphian Club, from Baltimore. His melodramatic novel *Keep Cool* (1817), about a man's guilt because he has killed someone in a duel, made him famous. He wrote many more novels, including *Logan, A Family History* (1822), about an (actual) Englishman who married the Queen of Native American tribe. Neal soon after went to England, where he acted as secretary to Jeremy Bentham. His finest novel was *Rachel Dyer* (1828), about a Salem witch. His meandering *Wandering Recollections of a Somewhat Busy Life* (1869) is an invaluable source book.

NECATIGIL, Behçet
(1916–)
Turkish poet, radio dramatist and translator (**Heine, Hamsun, Böll** and others), born in Istanbul. A teacher of literature in lycées by profession, he has German connections, and has compiled a *Who's Who* of Turkish literature. He is, paradoxically, an intellectual poet whose work was entirely devoted to the expression and explanation of the lives and feelings of 'ordinary' (non-intellectual) people; as such, he is one of Turkey's most interesting and original poets of his generation.

NECHUY, pseud of **Ivan Levytsky**
(1838–1918)
Ukrainian novelist in the tradition of **Zola** and the naturalists. His novels were forbidden in Russia but he published in Polish Galicia. Once regarded as one of the greatest of his country's writers, his work has by now somewhat faded.

NEDREAAS, Torborg
(1906–)
Norwegian novelist of Jewish extraction, born in Bergen. She turned to writing late in life, after World War II. A left-wing feminist, her books highlight social life and class struggle in Norwegian urban society. Especially powerful are *Musikk fra en blå brpnn* (1960, Eng trans *Music from a Blue Well*) and *Ved neste nymåne* (1971, Eng trans *At the Next New Moon*), about a girl called Herdis growing up in Bergen between the wars. Her best stories were collected in *Stoppested* (1953, 'Stopping Place').
▷H Eriksen, *Nedreaas* (1979)

NEGRI, Ada
(1870–1945)
Italian poet, born in Lodi. She became a teacher in a small primary school, and made her literary debut with *Fatalità* (1892, 'Destiny'), a derivative and idealistic collection of humanitarian poems. Her subsequent works, nine more volumes of verse and a number of prose works, refined the political, feminist and mystical basis of her work.
▷M Magni, *L'opera di Ada Negri e la su umanita* (1961)

NEIHARDT John G(neisau)
(1881–1973)
American short-story writer, novelist and poet, born in Illinois. He lived amongst the Omaha Indians for nearly 10 years and his five-part epic, published collectively as *A Cycle of the West* (1949), deals with a tribe of Plains Indians. The cycle opened with *The Song of Hugh Glass* in 1915. Previous books had included *The Lonesome Trail* (1907), a collection of short stories featuring pioneering heroes, and *The River and I* (1910), an account of a river trip on the Missouri.

NEILSON, John Shaw
(1872–1942)
Australian poet, born in Penola, South Australia, the son of a Scottish-born poet and bushworker. His first work was published in the Sydney weekly *Bulletin* by A G Stephens, who befriended and guided Neilson, and took much of his early work. His first published collection, *Heart of Spring*, came out in 1919, followed by *Ballad and Lyrical Poems* (1923) and *New Poems* (1927). Though Nielson was uneducated and weakened by a life of hard work (sheep shearer, roadmaker, farmer), his verse couples surprising delicacy, almost naivety, with delicate imagery. *Collected Poems* appeared in 1934; later verse was published after Nielson's death in *Unpublished Poems*

(1947) and *Witnesses of Spring* (1970). The definitive edition is *The Poems of Shaw Nielson*, ed A R Chisholm (1965, rev edn 1973).

NEKRASOV, Nikolai Alexeievich
(1821–78)
Russian lyrical poet of the Realistic school, born near Vinitza, Podolia. He worked as a journalist and critic, and made his name with poems depicting the social wrongs of the peasantry, such as his unfinished narrative epic, *Komu na Rusi zhit khorosho?* (1879, Eng trans *Who Can Be Happy and Free in Russia?*, 1917). His writings have been widely acknowledged as an important influence by successive generations of Russian writers.
▷M Peppard, *Nikolai Alexeyevich Nekrasov* (1967)

NELLIGAN, Emile
(1879–1941)
Canadian poet—a controversial member of the École litteraire de Montreal—who has been described as 'the first modern Canadian poet', and a Symbolist poet of great musical sensibility. Most of his poems were composed in the five years before his incarceration in various mental institutions from 1899 to the end of his life. His most famous poem, 'Le vaisseau d'or' (1899, 'The Ship of Gold'), has been seen as a premonition of this tragic loss of self, this 'death in life': 'What of my heart's lost fate, poor derelict?/—Founded, alas! in the black gulf of Dream!' His poems were collected and edited by his friend Louis Dantin and published under the title *Emile Nelligan et son oeuvre* in 1904, but the most comprehensive edition of his work was compiled by Luc Lacourciere in 1952 (*Poesies Completes, 1896–1899*); English translations were made available by P F Widdows, *Selected Poems* (1960) and F Cogswell, *The Complete Poems of Emile Nelligan* (1983).
▷P Wyzynski, *Emile Nelligan* (1976)

NEMCOVÁ, Bozena, née Panklová
(1820–62)
Czech novelist, born in Vienna, of an Austrian father, a coachman on an estate in Bohemia, and a Czech mother. She garnered her considerable wisdom from her old grandmother, whom she lovingly and memorably portrayed in *Babicka* (1855, Eng trans *Granny*, 1962), one of the great books of the 19th century. At 17 she married unhappily—her husband, an excise man much older than her, could not reconcile his duties to his Austrian masters with her habits of thinking for herself and writing, and they parted in 1850. Beautiful, sensitive, intense, Nemcová became (almost like **George Eliot** in England)

the subject of much vulgar gossip, since she chose to have many love affairs (which were as unhappy as her marriage had been). However, she also became the first truly eminent Czech women writer—*Granny* has gone through over 300 Czech editions since it first appeared, and through many more in other Slavonic languages. She wrote many more novels and stories, some of them folk- and fairy-tales. She died prematurely, while trying to collect an edition of her works, as a result of exhaustion and disappointment. Some of her fairy-tales are translated in *The Shepherd and the Dragon* (1930).

NEMEROV, Howard
(1920–)
American poet, novelist and playwright, born in New York City. He was based in England while serving with the Royal Canadian Air Force during World War II. He has written several novels, including *The Melodramatists* (1949), but has won greater acclaim as a poet. His relatively accessible verse, in which, as he has said, he 'writes of history from the point of view of the loser', includes *The Image and The Law* (1947) and *The Next Room of the Dream* (1962). His *Collected Poems* (1977) won the National Book Award.

NÉMETH, László
(1901–75)
Hungarian novelist, dramatist, critic and translator (of **Tolstoy**'s *Anna Karenina*, reckoned to be one of the greatest translations of the 20th century), born in Nagybánya (now Baia-Mare in Romania). A medical doctor by profession, he burst on the literary scene in 1925 with his now-famous story, published in Hungary's premier literary magazine *Nyugat*, 'Horváthné meghal' ('Mrs Horvath Dies'). He wrote dramas about Galileo (1954, Act IV translated in *The Plough and the Pen*, 1963) and Gandhi. However, his best work was done in the novel: in *Iszony* (1947, Eng trans *Revulsion*, 1965), about an unhappy marriage, and *Bün* (1936, Eng trans *Guilt*, 1966). His reputation, despite the 'subtly intellectual' anti-Semitism of which he has—not altogether convincingly—been accused, has steadily grown. For many years between the wars he ran and wrote the magazine *Tanu* ('Witness'), in which he argued for what is (correctly but misleadingly) described as the 'populist' view, that Hungary had the right to choose between Soviet communism and capitalism. A resourceful man, perhaps excessively intellectual, he is a undoubtedly one of the giants of modern Hungarian literature.
▷*The Personalist*, XXXI (1950)

NENNIUS
(fl.769)

Welsh writer, reputedly author of the early Latin compilation known as the *Historia Britonum*, which purports to give an account of British history from the time of **Caesar** to towards the end of the 7th century. The book gives a mythical account of the origins of the Britons, and recounts the Roman occupation, the settlement of the Saxons and King Arthur's 12 victories. Although it contains fanciful material of doubtful historical significance, its real value lies in its preservation of material needed for the study of early Celtic literature in general, and the Arthurian Legend in particular.

▷J F Kenney, *Sources for the Early History of Ireland* (1929)

NEPOS, Cornelius
(c.99–c.24 BC)

Roman historian, a native of Pavia or Hostilia in northern Italy. He was the contemporary and close friend of **Cicero**, and **Catullus** dedicated his poems to him. His *De Viris Illustribus* ('Lives of Famous Men'), of which only some 25 (mainly Greek warriors and statesmen) survive, are written in a clear and straightforward style. He was the first to adopt the pairing of Greek and Roman soldiers and statesmen, a form later followed by **Plutarch**.

NERUDA, Jan
(1834–91)

Czech writer, born in Prague. He was brought up in poverty, an experience reflected in some of his work, notably *Povídky malostranské* (1878, Eng trans *Tales of the Little Quarter*, 1957), and became a teacher before switching to a career in journalism. He suffered from persistent ill-health. He was a disciple of Romanticism but developed into the foremost classical poet in modern Czech literature. He is also known for some excellent prose and drama.

▷M Novotný, *Zivot, Jana Nerudý* (4 vols, 1951–6)

NERUDA, Pablo, born Ricardo Eliecer Neftalí Reyes
(1904–73)

Chilean poet, winner of the Nobel Prize for literature, born in Parral in southern Chile, and educated at Santiago. He made his name with *Veinte poemas de amor y una canción desesperada* (1924, Eng trans *Twenty Love Poems and a Song of Despair*, 1969). From 1927 he held diplomatic posts in various East Asian and European countries (in Spain during the Civil War) and in Mexico from 1940. It was on his way back to Chile from Mexico

in 1943 that he visited the Inca city of Macchu Picchu, which was the inspiration of one of his greatest poems. Once settled in Chile again he joined the Communist Party and was elected to the senate in 1945. When the party was outlawed in 1948 he left to travel in Russia and China, returning in 1952. He was awarded the Stalin Prize in 1953. He was the Chilean ambassador in Paris (1970–2). His works include *Residencia en la Tierra* (I, II and III, 1933, 1935, 1947, 'Residence on Earth'), *Alturas de Macchu Picchu* (1945, Eng trans *The Heights of Macchu Picchu*, 1966), which later became part of *Canto General* (published in Mexico, 1950, Eng trans in part as *Poems from Canto General*, 1966), and *Odas elementales* (1954, Eng trans *Elementary Odes*, 1961). In 1971 he was awarded the Nobel Prize for literature. Already ill with cancer, he died of a heart attack shortly after the military overthrew the democratic socialist President Allende.

▷E Rodriguez Moregul, *El viajero immovil* (1967)

NERVAL, Gérard de, properly Gérard Labrunie
(1808–55)

French writer, born in Paris. He was greatly influenced by reading his uncle's collection of occult books as a youth. He published at the age of 20 a translation of **Goethe**'s *Faust*, expanded as *Faust, et le Second Faust* (1840), which Berlioz drew on in his *La Damnation de Faust* (1846). Desultory work, a love affair, fits of restless travel, dissipation, gloom and insanity, and death by his own hand, sum up the story of his life. Nerval wrote admirably both in prose and verse. But his travels, criticism, plays and poems are less interesting than his fantastic short tales, the *Contes et facéties* (1852, 'Stories and Jests'), the semi-autobiographical series of *Filles du feu* (1854, Eng trans *Daughters of Fire*, 1923) and *La Bohème galante* (1855, 'Gallant Bohemian Life'). He is often seen as a precursor of both the Symbolist and Surrealist movements.

▷L Cellier, *Gérard de Nerval* (1956)

NERVO, Amado
(1870–1919)

Mexican modernist writer and poet, whose prolific output fills 30 volumes and includes poetry, novels, short stories, criticism, essays and drama. Born in Tepic and educated at a parochial school where he was taught by Catholic priests, his works are imbued with a quest for truth and beauty. His first creative period, as a writer deeply involved in the Latin-American Modernist movement, was heavily influenced by French Symbolist and Parnassian poets and by other Latin-American Modernist poets. Later he developed a mature style unrelated to any school or poetic movement. His most important themes involve the search for God, the meaning of existence, mysticism, and worldly love.

NESBIT, Edith
(1858–1924)

English writer, born in London, the daughter of an agricultural chemist who died when she was three. She was educated at a French convent, and began her literary career by writing poetry, having met the **Rossettis** and their friends. In 1880 she married the Fabian journalist Hubert Bland. To help with the family finances she turned to popular fiction and children's stories about the Bastaple family, including *The Story of the Treasure Seekers* (1899), *The Would-be-Goods* (1901), *Five Children and It* (1902), *The New Treasure Seekers* (1904), *The Railway Children* (1906) and *The Enchanted Castle* (1907). She also wrote other novels, and ghost stories. After her husband's death in 1914 she married an engineer, Terry Tucker, in 1917. Her last novel was *The Lark* (1922).

▷N Streatfeild, *Magic and Magician* (1958)

NESIN, Aziz
(1915–)

Turkish story writer, novelist, dramatist and satirist, born in Istanbul. He was jailed repeatedly for his left-wing views and satirical publications. *Istanbul Boy* (1977) is a selection in English translation from his autobiography. The scourge of the establishment, he has published over 80 books, mostly of stories.

NESTROY, Johann Nepomuk
(1801–62)

Austrian dramatist, born in Vienna. He began life as an operatic singer, turned playwright and was director of the Vienna Carl-Theater (1854–60). His 60-odd plays, which include *Der böse Geist lumpazivagabundus* (1833, 'The Wicked Ghost Lumpazivagabundus'), *Einen Jux will er sich machen* (1842, 'He Wants to Play Pranks'), *Der Undbedeu tende* (1846) and *Judith und Holofernes* (1849, 'Judith and Holofernes'), are mostly elaborate jibes at theatrical sentimentality characterized by a deft play on words, thoughts and afterthoughts. They revolutionized the Viennese theatre and influenced Wittgenstein.

▷M Preisner, *Johann Nepomuk Nestroy* (1968)

NESVADBA, Josef
(1926–)

Czech writer of science fiction (one of the very few to practise this genre in his country since

Čapek), born in Prague. By profession he is a psychiatrist. He has published many novels and story collections, including *Tarzanova smrt* (1958, 'The Death of Tarzan') and *Kongres o dusi* (1968, 'Congress on the Soul'). A story by him, 'The Planet Circe', appears in *New Writing in Czechoslovakia* (1969).

NEUMANN, Stanislav Kostka
(1875–1947)

Czech poet, novelist and critic, born in Prague into a wealthy family against which he rebelled. He was imprisoned by the Austrian tyrants for advocating independence. An anarchist who finally became a convinced communist, he wrote in a free verse which was for a long time very popular, although he is less widely read today. He was essentially superficial, but the vitalist poetry of his youth, with its open praise of sensuality and its contempt for aristocratic puritanism, was bold and well expressed. He is not unlike **Felipe**, but altogether lacks the Spaniard's subtlety and power of phrase.

NEWBERY, John
(1713–67)

English publisher and bookseller, born in Berkshire, a farmer's son. He settled about 1744 in London as a seller of books and patent medicines. He was the first to publish little books for children, and he was himself—perhaps with **Oliver Goldsmith**—part author of some of the best of them, notably *Goody Two-Shoes*. In 1758 he started the *Universal Chronicle*, or *Weekly Gazette*, in which the *Idler* appeared. In the *Public Ledger* (1760) appeared Goldsmith's *Citizen of the World*. Since 1922 the Newbery Medal has been awarded annually for the best American children's book.

NEWBOLT, Sir Henry John
(1862–1938)

English poet, born in Bilston, Staffordshire. He studied at Clifton School and Oxford, became a barrister, and published a novel *Taken from the Enemy* (1892), followed by *Mordred: A Tragedy* (1895). He is best known, however, for his sea songs—*Admirals All* (1897), which contained 'Drake's Drum', *The Island Race* (1898), *Songs of the Sea*, and others. In World War I he was controller of telecommunications and an official war historian, and published *The Naval History of the Great War* in 1920.

NEWBY, Eric
(1919–)

English travel writer, born in London. He worked briefly in advertising before joining a

Finnish four-masted bark in 1938, an adventure described in *The Last Grain Race* (1956). In 1942 he was captured off Sicily while trying to rejoin the submarine from which he had landed to attack a German airfield. For some years he worked in the rag trade, which he eagerly left to take *A Short Walk in the Hindu Kush* (1958). In 1963, after some years as a fashion buyer to a chain of department stores, he made a 1200-mile descent of the Ganges, described with typical aplomb and wit in *Slowly Down the Ganges* (1966). Later he became travel editor of *The Observer*. Other significant books are *The Big Red Train Ride* (1978), the story of a journey from Moscow to the Pacific on the Trans-Siberian Railway, *Love and War in the Apennines* (1971), his autobiography, *A Traveller's Life* (1982), and *Round Ireland in Low Gear* (1987), about a wet journey on mountain bikes.

NEWBY, P(ercy) H(oward)
(1918–)

English novelist and critic, born in Crowborough, Sussex, in the house once owned by Sir **Arthur Conan Doyle**. Newby taught English in Cairo for many years and in 1949 joined the BBC, becoming Controller of the Third Programme in 1958 and Director of Radio Programmes from 1973 to 1975. Several of his novels reflect his love of Egypt, and while he does not evade the violence of the world, the predominant tone is sympathetic and often touching, as his characters attempt to discover an ethical code by which to live. *Something to Answer For* (1968) won the first Booker Prize in 1969. His other novels include *Leaning in the Wind* (1986) and *Coming in with the Tide* (1991), the latter set in south Wales at the turn of the century, and examining the lives of an ambitious builder and freethinker, and the fiercely religious woman he loves.

NEWMAN, John Henry
(1801–90)

English autobiographer, poet and religious writer. Appointed Vicar of St Mary's, Oxford, he became celebrated as a preacher and leader of the Tractarian (or Oxford) Movement, but in the early 1840s found himself drawing closer to Roman Catholicism. Converted in 1845, he became a Catholic priest and established the Birmingham Oratory. He was frequently embroiled in controversy and wrote extensively on the theological questions of the day, but is famous chiefly for the *Apologia pro Vita Sua* (1864), in which he set out the history of his religious views and defended himself forcefully against the charge of untruthfulness levelled against him by **Charles Kingsley**. This unusual autobiography established him as one of the great stylists in the history of English prose. His poem 'The Dream of Gerontius' (1865), provided the text of Elgar's oratorio, and his hymn 'Lead, kindly light' illustrates his gift for a memorable turn of phrase. Made a cardinal in 1879, Newman avoided public display and remained in Birmingham serving his congregation for the remainder of his life.
▷ M Trevor, *Newman's Journey* (1974)

NEXÖ, Martin Andersen
(1869–1954)

Danish novelist, born in a poor quarter of Copenhagen. He spent his boyhood in Bornholm near Nexö (from where he took his surname). From shoemaking and bricklaying he turned to books and teaching, and in 1906 won European fame with *Pelle Erobreren* (4 vols, 1906–10, Eng trans *Pelle the Conqueror*, 1915–17), describing poor life from within and the growth of the Labour movement. He spent considerable time abroad, an experience that fostered his sympathy for the working class; *Morten hin Røde* (1945–7, 'Morten the Red') is an uncharacteristically dull, three-volume sequence.
▷ B Houmann, *Martin Anderson Nexö og hans samtid* (1981–2)

NEZVAL, Viteslav
(1900–58)

Czech poet, novelist and dramatist, one of the most important writers of his generation, born in Biskoupky. Dedicated to the communist cause (though never to socialist realism) throughout his earlier life, for a time in the late 1940s and early 1950s he conformed to the shallow demands of his Stalinist cultural masters; but he finally abandoned this stance to complete a body of dedicated and personal work. He began as a 'proletarian' poet in the style of his friend **Jiri Wolker**, but soon became the leading light in Karel Teige's 'Poetist' movement, which advocated 'pure poetry'. When this transformed itself into Surrealism, Nezval went along, but discovered his own individual voice in doing so, producing an extraordinary and prolific body of poetry and fiction. There is currently a dearth of good translations from the poetry of Nezval.
▷ A French, *The Poets of Prague* (1969)

NGUGI wa Thiong'o, originally James T Ngugi
(1938–)

Kenyan novelist, who writes in English and Kikuyu. He was born in Kamiriithu, in the Kiambu District, and educated at University College, Kampala, Uganda, and at Leeds University. While in England, his first novel,

Weep Not, Child (1964), was published, followed by an earlier novel, The River Between (1965), which filled in more of the cultural and socio-political background to the so-called Mau Mau emergency. A Grain of Wheat (1967) contrasts the shallow optimism of the Uhuru celebration of Kenyan independence with the violence of Mau Mau. His fourth novel, Petals of Blood (1977), has a hectoring, neo-Maoist tone, and clearly cost Ngugi considerable effort to write. In 1977 he was imprisoned by the Kenyan authorities under the catch-all Public Security Act; his experience is recounted in Detained: A Writer's Prison Diary (1981). For his next book, known in English as Devil on the Cross (trans 1982), he reverted to Kikuyu; it was originally published as Caitaani Mutharaba-ini (1980) and it is clear that the incantatory style of the original is largely lost in the prosy discursive English version.

▷D Cook and M Okenimkpe, Ngugi wa Thiong'o: An Exploration of His Writings (1983)

NI TSAN, or NI ZAN
(1301–74)

Chinese landscape painter, calligrapher and poet, born in Wu-hsi (Kiangsu Province). Of the Four Great Masters of the Yuan period, he may not be the greatest, but he certainly is the purest. A passionate lover of culture and aesthetics, he nevertheless spent the last 20 years of his life travelling the lakes of the lower Yangtze river with no possessions. His solitary temperament, search for purity and an absolute spiritual certainty and technical discipline permeate his work. Instead of showing the typical development from early to mature, his work consists of a rational, austere and disembodied assemblage of expressive forms, almost reduced to signs, which constituted a radical departure from all previous traditions.

NICHOLS, Peter Richard
(1927–)

English dramatist, born in Bristol. Starting his career as an actor and schoolteacher, he wrote for television before turning to the stage with A Day in the Death of Joe Egg (1967), concerning the stress imposed upon a couple whose child is mentally handicapped. Later works include Privates on Parade (1977), a musical recalling Nichols's own days in an army concert party; Passion Play (1981), dealing with the effects of adultery, and Poppy (1983), a musical in pantomime form about the English opium trade wars with China, for which the music was written by Monty Norman. A Piece of My Mind (1987), about a disconsolate playwright, was widely seen as an autobiographical work by an

under-rated dramatist who had already threatened to retire from the theatre.
▷Feeling You're Behind (1984)

NICHOLSON, Norman Cornthwaite
(1914–87)

English poet, whose verse had the craggy quality of his native Lake District, where he continued to live throughout his life and about which he wrote several prose accounts. To the obvious literary associations of the area, he added a new awareness of its modern industrial transformation and, in the 1980s, retrenchment. His first poems were published in a volume (1943) shared with **Keith Douglas** and J C Hall, but after 1954 and The Pot Geranium Nicholson effectively gave up poetry for a decade, returning to form only with A Local Habitation (1972), which established his reputation. Later collections, such as Sea to the West (1981) documented a changed landscape. A Selected Poems 1940–1982 appeared a year later. His account of life in Millom, Cumberland, was published as Wednesday Early Closing (1975).
▷P Gardner, Norman Nicholson (1973)

NÍ CHUILLEANÁIN, Eilean
(1942–)

Irish poet, born in Cork. She was educated in Cork and then at Oxford, specializing in Renaissance English, and later became a lecturer at Trinity College Dublin. From Acts and Monuments (1972) through to The Second Voyage (1986) and in The Magdalene Sermon (1990) she lucidly doles out 'a spoonful of light on the cellar walls below' the male-orientated monopoly of Irish writing in the latter part of the 20th century. Though often judged oblique and difficult, her work is a necessary challenge to that accepted hegemony.

NICOL, Abioseh, originally **Davidson Sylvester Hector Willoughby Nicol**
(1924–)

Sierra Leonean short-story writer and poet, born in Freetown. He was educated in Sierra Leone, Nigeria and, following a period as a science teacher in Freetown, at Christ's College, Cambridge. He worked as a doctor in London in the early 1950s, and subsequently at the University Medical School, Ibadan, Nigeria. In later years he was Sierra Leone's High Commissioner in the UK and ambassador to other European countries. Nicol has also worked for the United Nations. He was encouraged to write by **Langston Hughes**, and the stories in The Truly Married Woman and Two African Tales (both 1965) are reminiscent of Hughes's more lyrical style. Public duties limited his literary output thereafter, but he has produced one volume of poetry (1967) and has written and edited a number of important studies on Third World and women's issues.

▷A Roscoe, *Mother is Gold* (1971)

NICOLAI, Christoph Friedrich
(1733–1811)

German author, bookseller and publisher, born in Berlin. A champion of the German Enlightenment, he soon distinguished himself by a series of critical letters (1756), contributed to many literary journals, and for many years edited the *Allgemeine deutsche Bibliothek* (106 vols, 1765–92, 'General Library of German Writing'). He wrote topographical works, satires, anecdotes of Frederick II, the Great, and an autobiography, recording strange apparitions and hallucinations.

NICOLAY, John George
(1832–1901)

Bavarian-born American journalist and historian, co-author of a 10-volume uncritical biography of President Lincoln, *Abraham Lincoln: A History* (1890). Nicolay was taken to America when he was six years old and grew up in Illinois. He entered journalism and in his mid-twenties was editor and proprietor of the Pittsfield Free Press. He sold the paper, became Secretary of State for Illinois and in 1860 was made Lincoln's private secretary. After the president's assassination he collaborated with his friend John Hay to produce a historical biography. The work was delayed by Nicolay's public appointments— he served as US Consul in Paris from 1865 to 1869 and, on his return, as Marshal of the Supreme Court—but the 10 volumes were finally completed in 1890.

NICOLE, Christopher
(1930–)

West Indian (Barbadian) novelist, author of more than 50 books, some published under such pseudonyms as 'Leslie Arlen' and 'Peter Grange'. His most favoured form is the historical novel, and his historical novels—for example, the 'Amyot' trilogy, (*Amyot's Cay*, 1964; *Blood Amyot*, 1964; *The Amyot Crime*, 1966)—are, like his thrillers, efficient. However, as a critic has said, echoing the consensus: 'Nicole's contribution is sometimes suggestive, but it is too superficial to fulfil its possibilities'.

NIELSEN, Morten
(1922–44)

Danish poet. In just two collections of poetry, *Krigere uden Vaaben* (1943, 'Warriors without Weapons') and *Etterladte Digte* (1945, 'Posthumous Poems'), he strikingly captures the mood in Denmark under the German occupation during World War II. On the one hand, his poems reflect the meaningless, moribund and provisional character of the war years; on the other hand, they express the heightened sense of intensity, the isolated moments of beauty and fulfilment. Nielsen was involved in the resistance against the Nazi occupation and died in a shooting accident when he was only 22. His 'letters to a friend', *Breve til en Ven*, were published in 1962.

▷T Bredsdorff, 'Morten Nielsen', in *Danske digtere i det 20. århundrede*, vol 3 (1981)

NIELSON, Niels Jorgen
(1902–45)

Danish psychological novelist, born near Sikeborg in central Jutland. The reputation of his grim novels set amongst the peasantry of his native region has steadily grown. His most successful novel was the love story *En Kvinde ved Baalet* (1933, 'A Woman by the Bonfire').

NIETZSCHE, Friedrich Wilhelm
(1844–1900)

German philosopher, scholar and writer, though really unclassifiable by conventional labels. He was born in Röcken, Saxony, son of a Lutheran pastor (who died in 1849), and proved himself a brilliant classical student at the school at Schulpforta and at the universities of Bonn and Leipzig. He was appointed Professor of Classical Philology at the University of Basel at the age of 24 and became a Swiss citizen, serving briefly as a medical orderly in 1870 in the Franco–Prussian war but returning to the university in poor health. His first book, *Die Geburt der Tragödie* (1872, Eng trans *The Birth of Tragedy*, 1909), with its celebrated comparison between 'Dionysian' and 'Apollonian' values, was dedicated to Richard Wagner, who had become a friend and whose operas he regarded as the true successors to Greek tragedy. But he broke violently with Wagner in 1876, nominally at least because he thought the Christian convictions expressed in *Parsifal* 'mere playacting' and political expediency. In 1878 he was forced to resign his university position after worsening bouts of his psychosomatic illnesses and he spent most of the next 10 years at various resorts in France, Italy and Switzerland writing and trying to recover his 'shattered health'. But in 1889 he had a complete mental and physical breakdown, a collapse that was probably syphilitic in origin, and he was nursed for the next 12 years first by his mother at Naumberg then by his sister Elizabeth at Weimar. He never recovered his sanity. In the 16 years from 1872 he had produced a stream of brilliant, unconventional works, often aphoristic or poetical in form, which have secured him an enormous, if sometimes cultish, influence in modern intellectual history. The best-known writings are: *Unzeitgemässe Betrachtungen* (1873–6, Eng trans *Thoughts Out of Season*, 1909), *Die Fröliche Wissenschaft* (1882, Eng trans *The Joyful Wisdom*, 1910), *Also Sprach Zarathustra* (1883–92, Eng trans *Thus Spake Zarathustra*, 1900), *Jenseits von Gut und Böse* (1886, Eng trans *Beyond Good and Evil*, 1907), *Zur Genealogie der Moral* (1887, Eng trans *A Genealogy of Morals*, 1897) and *Ecce Homo* (Eng trans 1911, his autobiography, completed in 1888 but withheld by his sister and not published until 1908). One cannot derive systematic 'theories' from these often highly-wrought literary works but the characteristic themes are: the vehement repudiation of Christian and liberal ethics, the detestation of democratic ideals, the celebration of the *Übermensch* (superman) who can create and impose his own law, the death of God, and the life-affirming 'will to power'. His reputation suffered when his views were taken up in a simple-minded and perverted form by the German Nazis, but he is now regarded as a major, though very individual, influence on many strands of 20th-century thought, including existentialism and psychoanalysis, and on figures as various as Jaspers, Heidegger, **Thomas Mann**, **W B Yeats**, Mannheim and Foucault.

NIEVO, Ippolito
(1831–61)

Italian novelist, poet and dramatist, born in Padua. Although little known in his lifetime, Nievo was very prolific, and wrote much prose and verse besides the work for which he is justly most celebrated today: the extraordinary, posthumous *Le confessioni d'un italiano* (1867, Eng trans *The Castle of Fratta*, 1957), known for many years as *Le confessioni di un ottuagenario* because its publisher changed its title. Nievo fought alongside Garibaldi in his 1859 campaign, but then perished in a shipwreck off Sicily. This patriotic presentation of the years which led up to the Risorgimento, presented in the guise of a diary written by a man whose life spanned the years 1775–1855, immediately became famous; later critics have seen in it remarkable anticipations of modernity, because Nievo boldly combines autobiography with historical narrative.
▷ *Italian Quarterly*, 2 (1958)

NIGEL DE LONGCHAMPS
(c.1130–c.1205)

English poet of Norman descent (he may have been related to William de Longchamps,

Chancellor under Richard I). Known as 'Wireker', he was a Benedictine monk of Christ Church, Canterbury, and was possibly born in Longchamps in Normandy. His *Speculum stultorum* (1179–80, Eng trans in *A Mirror for Fools*, 1961), is a satire on the monastic orders, with its anti-hero Burnellus, an ass who is unhappy with the size of his tail (a reference to the materialistic ambitions entertained by most priests). Gifted with a good measure of originality, he also wrote a prose complaint against the clergy, and adapted 17 Mary-legends into graceful Latin verse.
▷ F J E Raby, *Secular Latin Poetry* (1957)

NIJHOFF, Martinus
(1894–1953)

Dutch poet, critic, dramatist, translator (of **André Gide**, **T S Eliot** and **Shakespeare**) and editor, a leading figure in his literature. He is usually compared to Eliot, and this is fair inasmuch as Eliot deeply influenced him, and he was, like Eliot again, decisive in the formation of his country's critical tastes. His later poetry, deriving from the 'sensitivism' of the pre-Marxist **Gorter**, but aware of modern European currents, seeks intelligently for meaning: typical is the long poem 'Awater' from his *Nieuwe gedichten* (1934, 'New Poems'), in which the central figure is the man he is trying to understand, the representative of modern society. Nijhoff stands at the opposite pole, in Dutch poetry, to the more powerful **Achterberg**: where the latter is subjective, he tries to be objective.

NIKITIN, Ivor Savvich
(1824–61)

Russian poet, born in Voronezh. His verse veered somewhat uncertainly between imitation of folk-poetry and social protest. The long *Kulak* (1857), a realistic narrative of peasant life, was his best-known and liked poem. He was at his most talented and original when writing melancholy nature lyrics.

NILAND, D'Arcy Francis
(1919–67)

Australian author, born in Glen Innes, New South Wales. After his early years working in the bush, he went to Sydney and in 1942 married the New Zealand writer **Ruth Park**, after which he settled down to writing. Between 1949 and 1952 he won many prizes for short stories and novels, and in 1955 achieved international fame with his novel *The Shiralee* (filmed 1957). This was followed by *Call Me When the Cross Turns Over* (1957), *Gold in the Streets* (1959) and perhaps his best novel, *Dead Men Running* (1969, later an ABC serial). Niland also wrote radio and television plays, and hundreds of short stories, some of which were published in four collections between 1961 and 1966. With Ruth Park he wrote the story of their early married life and writing careers in *The Drums Go Bang* (1956).

NILSSON PIRATEN, Fritiof
(1895–1972)

Swedish novelist and short-story writer, born in Skåne. He is a storyteller in the oral tradition, whose humour and fine style have won lasting popularity and more transient critical notice. The elements of disillusion and tragedy in his writing are apparent even in his first book, *Bombi Bitt och jag* (1932, 'Bombi Bitt and Me'), and these become more marked in his later work. The collection *Historier från Färs* (1940, 'Stories from Färs') contains some of his best writing.
▷M von Platen, 'Piratens två världar', in *Biktare och bedragare* (1959)

NIMS, John Frederick
(1913–)

American poet, critic and translator (*St John of the Cross*, **Euripides**), born in Muskegon, Michigan. His poetry is well known for its clear-cut precision: a critic has compared it to 'carved, antique furniture, or to cut glass'. He writes in classical metres, and is openly Catholic; 'form,' he has unfashionably written, 'is what ... poems come into the world with, like plants and animals'. *A Local Habitation* (1985) is a collection of his essays on poetry.
▷*Selected Poems* (1985); J Dickey, *Babel to Byzantium* (1968)

NIN, Anaïs
(1903–77)

American writer, born in Paris to parents of mixed Spanish–Cuban descent. She spent her childhood in Europe until, at the age of eleven, she left France to live in the USA. Ten years later, after her marriage to Hugh Guiler, a banker, she returned to Paris, where she studied psychoanalysis under Otto Rank, became acquainted with many well-known writers and artists and began to write herself. Her first novel, *House of Incest*, was published in 1936 and was followed by volumes of criticism, among them *The Novel of the Future* (1968), and a series of novels including *Winter of Artifice* (1939), *A Spy in the House of Love* (1954) and *Collages* (1964). She also published an early collection of short stories, *Under a Glass Bell* (1944). Ultimately, however, her reputation as an artist and seminal figure in the new feminism of the 1970s rests on her seven *Journals* (1966–83). Spanning the years 1931–74 they are an engrossing

record of an era and some of its most intriguing and avant garde players, as well as a passionate, explicit and candid account of one woman's voyage of self-discovery.
▷N Scholar, *Anaïs Nin* (1984)

NISTOR, Der, pseud of Pinchas Pinie Kahonovitch
(1884–1950)

Yiddish novelist, born in Berdichev—yet another Jew murdered on Stalin's orders, in the 'hospital' of a forced labour camp. Der Nistor wrote in the Hasidic tradition, and was never (like his contemporary **David Bergelson**), a wholehearted communist. Hasidism, based on the gnostic Cabala, was mystical, ecstatic, inward-looking, and Der Nistor was essentially a Symbolist. He began with prose poems, then proceeded to his major novel cycle, *Di mishpokhe Mashber* (1939–48, 'The Family Mashber'), an ostensibly realistic novel which in fact is alive with hidden meanings in the learned Hasidic tradition. The pseudonym 'Der Nistor' means 'the occult one'. There is a translation of *Di mishpokhe Mashber* into German, and an English one is overdue.
▷A Roback, *The Story of Yiddish Literature* (1940)

NIVEN, Frederick John
(1878–1944)

Scottish novelist, born in Chile of Scots parentage. Educated at Hutcheson's Grammar School, Glasgow, and Glasgow School of Art, he travelled widely in South America and worked as a journalist (1898–1914). After World War I he emigrated to Canada. He wrote more than 30 novels, mostly set in Glasgow or Canada, including *The Lost Cabin Mine* (1908), *The Justice of the Peace* (1914) and *The Staff at Simsons* (1937). His major work was a trilogy on Canadian settlement, comprising *The Flying Years*, *Mine Inheritance* and *The Transplanted* (1935–44). He also published an autobiography, *Coloured Spectacles* (1938).

NIVEN, Larry (Laurence Cott)
(1938–)

American science-fiction writer, born in Los Angeles. He studied mathematics at Washburn University in Kansas, and has established a reputation as one of the leading writers of 'hard' science fiction, with the emphasis on technological and scientific extrapolation. He published his first story in 1964, and it began his future history series he called *Tales of Known Space*, which includes his most important work, notably the novel *Ringworld* (1970). His commercially astute collaboration with Jerry Pournelle (1933–)

713

began with the highly readable space epic *The Mote in God's Eye* (1974), and they have written a number of subsequent adventures. Outstanding amongst his recent work are collaborative works with Steven Barnes, 1952–), including *The Barsoom Project* (1988) and *Dreampark* (1991), about a huge technology development plant in the California desert, and incorporating ideas about virtual reality.

NJEGOS, Petar Petrovíc, originally Rade Tomov
(1813–51)

Montenegrin poet, born in Njegusi. He succeeded his uncle as Prince of Montenegro, which he ruled as Prince–Bishop from 1830, and so took his name from his birthplace. His extraordinary long philosophical poem, *Luca mikrokozma* (1845, Eng trans *The Rays of Microcosm*, 1953; another translation under the same title in *Harvard Slavonic Studies*, III, 1957), puts him in the forefront of the European poets of his time—and perhaps ahead of many of them. In terms of the creation of the world and Satan's revolt, it has never been adequately discussed, nor have its gnostic elements been fully analysed. The poetic drama *Gorski vjenac* (1847, Eng trans *The Mountain Wreath*, 1930), describes the struggles of the Montenegrins against the usurping Turks. Njegos looked to **Milton**, **Hugo** and others, but was a markedly original writer. He died of tuberculosis.
▷M Djilas, *Njegos, Poet, Prince, Bishop* (1966)

NOAILLES, Anna Elizabeth de Brancoven, Comtesse Mathieu de
(1876–1933)

French poet and novelist, born in Paris of Romanian and Greek descent and acclaimed as 'Princesse des lettres'. With her first book, a collection of sensual and musical poems, *Le Coeur innombrable* (1901, 'The Innumerable Heart'), written under the influence of **Francis Jammes**, she won the hearts of the French poetry-reading public. This verse has now dated, but the best of it is still worthy of attention. However, her last poems show her at her most original. A friend to **Barrès**, she was greatly disliked by some French critics, and has hardly had her posthumous due.
▷C Fournet, *Un Grande Poète française moderne: la Comtesse de Noailles* (1950)

NODIER, Charles
(1780–1844)

French writer, born in Besançan. He was persecuted for an anti-Napoleon pamphlet in 1803, and held a number of jobs, including editing a newspaper, before becoming a librarian in 1824 in Paris. His novels were widely known in his own day and he had a profound influence on the Romanticists of 1830, but only his short stories and fairy tales are remembered, such as *Les Vampires* (1820) and *Le Chien de Brisquet* (1844, 'The Dog of Brisquet').
▷J Richer, *Charles Nodier* (1962)

NOOT, Jonker Jan van der
(1539–59)

Dutch poet, born in Brecht. He led an adventurous life: as Sheriff of Antwerp he took part in an uprising in 1567, and was obliged to flee to London and thence to Germany and France. When he could return to Antwerp, it was as a poverty-stricken poet. He is regarded as the first truly Renaissance poet of his country, reflecting the influence of **Ronsard**. He was translated (via a French version) by **Edmund Spenser**.

NORDAU, Max Simon, originally Südfeld
(1849–1923)

Hungarian author and physician, born of Jewish descent in Budapest. He studied medicine and established himself as physician, first in Budapest (1878) and then in Paris (1886). He wrote several books of travel, but became known as the author of works on moral and social questions, including *Die conventionellen Lügen der Kulturmenschheit* (1883, Eng trans *Conventional Lies of Our Civilization*, 1884) and *Entartung* (1892, Eng trans *Degeneration*, 1895), and as a novelist. He was also an active Zionist leader in Europe.

NORDENFLYCHT, Hedvig Charlotta
(1718–63)

Swedish writer of poetry and prose. Born in Stockholm, she was well educated and became one of the first female Swedish authors able to make a living from her work. Her first book of poetry, *Den sörgande Turtur-Dufwan* ('The Mourning Turtle-dove'), was published in 1742, introducing a new subjectivity and a strongly feminine self-assertion. Between 1744 and 1750 she published four volumes of poetry, all under the title of *Qvinligit Tankespel* ('A Woman's Thoughts'). In 1753 she became one of the leading members of a new literary society in Stockholm (*Tankebyggarorden*, 'The Society of Thought Builders') and subsequently published works in conjunction with other members. Famous for the love poetry she wrote late in her life, she is also renowned as the author of a challenge to **Rousseau**'s misogynism, *Fruentimrets försvar* (1761, 'The Defence of Woman').

▷S G Hansson, *Satir och kvinnokamp i Hedvig Charlotta Nordenflychts diktning. Några konflikter, motståndare och anhängare* (1991)

NORDSTRÖM, Ludvig
(1882–1942)

Swedish novelist, short-story writer and Utopian, born in Härnösand. At his best in humorous, often satirical, stories of small-town life, he was less successful in such more ambitious works as the multi-volume novel *Petter Svensks historia* (1925–7, 'Peter Swede's Story'), in which he attempted to express his vision of a Utopia based on urbanization and technology. His books of social reportage such as *Lort-Sverige* (1938, 'Dirt-Sweden') prompted vigorous debate.
▷G Qvarnström, *Från Öbacka till Urbs* (1954)

NORMAN, Marsha
(1947–)

American dramatist and novelist, born in Louisville, Kentucky. She graduated from the University of Georgia and for two years worked with emotionally disturbed children. The heroine of *Getting Out* (1977), her first play to be produced, is a murderer represented as both Arlie and Arlene, a double character from whose dialogue the audience learns of her complex emotional background. Norman's best-known play is the Pulitzer Prize-winning *'night Mother* (1982), a much more naturalistic piece dealing with the relationship between a woman who is about to commit suicide and her mother. The mother and daughter theme is continued in *The Fortune Teller* (1987), a novel examining the ethics of abortion.
▷K Betsko and R Koenig, *Interviews With Contemporary Women Playwrights* (1987)

NORRIS, (Benjamin) Frank(lin)
(1870–1902)

American novelist, born in Chicago. He first studied art but later turned to journalism, and while a reporter for the San Francisco *Chronicle* (1895–6) was involved in the Jameson raid in South Africa. He was influenced by **Zola** and was one of the first American naturalist writers, his major novel being *McTeague* (1899), a story of lower-class life in San Francisco, which formed the basis for the classic movie *Greed* (1924). He also wrote the first two volumes of an unfinished 'epic of the wheat' trilogy, *The Octopus* (1901) and *The Pit* (1903). The essay *The Responsibilities of the Novelist* also appeared posthumously as did *Vandover and the Brute*, a novel whose manuscript was believed lost during the San Francisco earthquake and only published in 1914.
▷F Walker, *Frank Norris: a biography* (1932)

NORRIS, Kathleen, née Thompson
(1880–1966)

American novelist, born in San Francisco. She began writing stories and published her first novel, *Mother*, in 1911. After that she wrote many popular novels and short stories, including *Certain People of Importance* (1922) and *Over at the Crowleys* (1946).

NORTH, Christopher *see* WILSON, John

NORTH, Sterling
(1906–74)

American author, born in Wisconsin. His early work—poetry—appeared during the 1920s in publications like *The Dial* and *Harpers*. He worked in newspapers for several years, eventually becoming the literary editor of two New York papers. His most successful book, a bestseller, was the rural idyll *So Dear To My Heart* (1947), which became a Walt Disney film the following year. A comment on the film—'mainly appealing to well brought up children'—might be applied to North's work as a whole. In the 1950s and 60s he published wholesome, juvenile non-fiction, such as *Abe Lincoln, Log Cabin to White House* (1956).

NORTON, Andre (Alice Mary)
(1912–)

American science-fiction writer, born in Cleveland, Ohio. She adopted the male pseudonym when she began to write fiction for boys. *Sword In Sheath* (1949) is typical of her work for adolescents, being high on adventure and low on subtlety. Her best-known work for adults is the *Witch World* series, which, with its sword-and-sorcery trappings, is as much fantasy as science fiction. *Web of the Witch World* (1964) is a typical volume from the series. Although by no means an innovator in the field, she merits respect as a compassionate novelist who, at least in her adult work, provides an antidote to the mechanical, militaristic spirit of much male science fiction.

NORTON, Caroline Elizabeth Sarah, née Sheridan
(1808–77)

Irish writer and reformer, born in London, grand-daughter of **Richard Brinsley Sheridan**. In 1827 she married a dissolute barrister, the Hon George Chapple Norton (1800–75), and bore him three sons. She took up writing to support the family, and published a successful book of verse, *The Sorrows of Rosalie* (1829). In 1836 she separated from her husband, who brought an action of 'criminal conversation' (adultery) against Lord Melbourne, obtained custody of the children and tried to obtain the profit from her books. Her spirited pamphlets led to improvements in the legal status of women in relation to infant custody (1839) and marriage and divorce (1857). She married Sir William Stirling-Maxwell in 1877, but died soon afterwards. Her other books of verse included an attack on child labour in *Voice from the Factories* (1836), *The Dream* (1840) and *The Lady of Garaye* (1862), and she also published three novels. She was the model for **George Meredith**'s central character in his novel *Diana of the Crossways* (1885).

NORTON, Mary
(1903–92)
English children's novelist, born in Leighton Buzzard. Aiming to become an actress she joined the Old Vic Theatre Company in the 1920s, but marriage took her to Portugal, where she first began to write, and later to America. Returning to Britain in 1943, she published her first book two years later. But it was *The Borrowers* (1952), an enchanting story about tiny people living beneath the floorboards of a big house, which established her as one of the foremost children's writers of her generation, and which won the Carnegie Medal. There were four sequels, the last being *The Borrowers Avenged* (1982).

NORTON, Thomas
(1532–84)
English lawyer, MP, and poet, born in London. He was a successful lawyer and a zealous Protestant, married to a daughter of Thomas Cranmer. He translated Calvin's *Christianae Religionis Institutio* (1561). With **Thomas Sackville** he was joint author of the tragedy *Gorboduc*, which was performed before Queen Elizabeth in 1562, and has some claim to be considered the first proper English tragedy.

NORWID, Cyprian Kamil
(1821–83)
Polish author and painter, since 1901 regarded as Poland's greatest writer. After brief success as a poet in Warsaw in his youth, he had little recognition in his lifetime. He lived in New York for three years, and finally went to Paris (he was befriended there by Chopin), where he lived in poverty from 1855 until his death in a home for destitute Poles. He was ridiculed for his later poetry, which was anti-romantic and decidedly 'modern' in tone. He anticipated Symbolism, and introduced free verse into Polish poetry. His poems are highly intellectual, although they

sometimes contain vernacular expressions; they demand much effort from the reader— once again, in a 'modernist' style. His revival came in 1901, and has continued ever since. His plays are of the closet variety, but are deeply interesting. Not all of his essays and other prose, which included stories, have been preserved. Little has been translated into English, but good examples of poems are to be found in *Five Centuries of Polish Poetry* (1960). It is generally conceded that Norwid is, because of his aloof irony, a difficult writer; but no non-Pole who has studied him in depth has come away without recognizing him as both unique and of very high international stature. To Poles he is now a—to some *the*— central literary figure.
▷ *Slavonic and East European Review*, 27 (1949)

NOSAACK, Hans Erich
(1901–77)
German fiction writer, poet, critic and dramatist, from Hamburg, praised by **Jean-Paul Sartre**. His leading work, and his most accessible, is the novel *Der Fall d'Arthez* (1968, Eng trans *The d'Arthez Case*, 1971), a subtle and even prophetic work set in a state in which 'authenticity' is a treasonable crime, and whose protagonists strive, in various ways, to achieve it.

NOUVEAU, Germain
(1851–1920)
French poet, born in Pourrières. **Aragon** unwisely pronounced him, after his death, to be the equal of **Rimbaud**, whom Nouveau had met in the course of squandering a small inheritance. Under the influence of **Verlaine**, he converted to Catholicism. His poetry was hardly known until the surrealists and Aragon re-discovered it, although he had known many writers, including Jean Richpin, **Bourget** and the great **Charles Cros**. After being shipped home from the Lebanon by the French consulate, and conducting a long affair with Valentine Renault, he suffered a five-month bout of 'religious mania' (alcoholism). His poetry consists for the most part of overblown rhetoric in the style of Rimbaud, but there are occasionally inspired passages, which, together with his exotic life, gave the surrealists plenty of reason to admire him.
▷ L Forestier, *Germain Nouveau* (1971, in French)

NOVAK, Helga, pseud of **Helga Maria Karlsdottir**
(1935–)
German poet, story-writer, and writer of radio plays, born in Berlin. She lived first in

East Germany, then (from 1961 to 1970) in Iceland, and since then in her native city. She could not publish until 1965, when her first collection of satirical poems, *Ballada von der reisenden Anna* ('Ballad of Wandering Anna') appeared. Her most characteristic work is the overtly feminist and, once more, satirical, *Eines Tages hat sich die Sprechpuppe nicht mehr ausziehen lassen* (1972, 'One Day the Talking Doll Refused to be Undressed'). Translations of her work are available in *German Women Writers of the Twentieth Century* (1978).

NOVAK, Vjenceslav
(1859–1905)

Croatian novelist, poet and dramatist, influenced by **Zola**, who wrote in a naturalistic style of the harsh poverty and squalor of life on the Adriatic coast. None of his books was translated into English.

NOVALIS, pseud of Friedrich von Hardenberg
(1772–1801)

German Romantic poet and novelist, born at Wiederstadt. He was called the 'Prophet of Romanticism'. At Weissenfels (1795) he fell in love with a beautiful girl, whose early death left a lasting impression upon him, and in whose memory he wrote the prose lyrics of *Hymnen an die Nacht* (1800, Eng trans *Hymns to the Night*, 1948). He also published *Geistliche Lieder* (1799, Eng trans *Devotional Songs*, 1910). He left two philosophical romances, both incomplete, *Heinrich von Ofterdingen* (1802) and *Die Lehrlinge zu Sais* (1802, 'The Apprentices at Sais'). He died of tuberculosis.

▷F Hiebel, *Novalis* (1972, in German)

NOVO, Salvador
(1904–74)

Mexican poet, critic, translator (**O'Neill**, **Synge**) and playwright, born in Mexico City, one of the leading members of the *Contemporáneos* group, including **Gorostiza** and **Jaime Torres Bodet**. A homosexual, his affairs became legendary; but this caused him surprisingly little trouble in a distinctly *macho* society—until he took up a highly reactionary political attitude, when, in 1968, he fervently applauded the massacre of the students by President Díaz Ordaz. But a critic wrote: 'the fact that his politics were reactionary, unlike his attitude towards sexuality, does not invalidate his work, it simply determines it'. As a homosexual poet, he is not in the class of **Cernuda**, **Penna** or **Cavafy**, but his elegant and often playful irony has a distinct charm.

▷A Mangāna-Esquival, *Salvador Novo* (1971, in Spanish)

NOWAK, Tadeusz
(1930–)

Polish poet, story writer and novelist, born into a peasant family in Sikorzyce (near Dabrowa Tarmowska). He was educated in Kracow. Like so many Polish poets, his poetry is based in folk traditions; some have described him as a 'peasant surrealist'. In the 1960s he apparently gave up writing verse, to concentrate on novels and stories.

NOWRA, Louis
(1950–)

Australian playwright and novelist, born in Melbourne. Of his plays the best known are *Inner Voices* (1977), in which the central figure is Ivan, an imprisoned claimant to the Russian throne, and *Inside the Island* (published 1981 with *The Precious Woman*). He has written two novels, *The Misery of Beauty* (1976) and *Palu* (1987); the last again deals with imprisonment, this time as a political sacrifice of the wife of a New Guinea president. Nowra's autobiographical play *Summer of the Aliens* was produced in 1993 with the author as narrator; *The Temple* (1993) explores in documentary style the excesses of Australia's corporate high-flyers before the stock-market crash of the late 1980s and *Radiance* (1993) concerns three aboriginal sisters who meet again at the funeral of their mother.

NOYES, Alfred
(1880–1958)

English poet, born in Staffordshire. He began writing verse as an undergraduate at Oxford, and on the strength of getting a volume published in his final year he left without taking a degree. This book, *The Loom of Years* (1902), which was praised by **George Meredith**, was followed by *The Flower of Old Japan* (1903) and *The Forest of Wild Thyme* (1905), both of which attracted some notice. Noyes now turned to the subject of some of his most successful work—the sea, and in particular the Elizabethan tradition. *Forty Singing Seamen* (1908) and the epic *Drake* (1908) were in this vein. Having married an American, he travelled in the USA and became Visiting Professor of Poetry at Princeton (1914–23). Between 1922 and 1930 appeared his trilogy *The Torchbearers*, praising men of science. He published literary essays in *Some Aspects of Modern Poetry* (1924), a defence of traditionalism. He also wrote plays, and studies of **William Morris** and **Voltaire**. He wrote an anecdotal memoir, *Two Worlds for Memory* (1953).

NU'AYMAH, Mikhail
(b.1889)

Prolific Lebanese writer. He was born in Biskinta, at the base of the snow-capped Sannine mountains, where the simple life of the inhabitants and majestic landscape inspired his literary works, and to which he returned after 25 years' absence. Between 1902 and 1932 Nu'aymah studied and lived in Palestine, Russia, the USA and France. In Russia, along with his religious studies, he immersed himself in the works of **Gogol** and **Chekhov**, and later in the USA in those of the Transcendentalists. As a result, and together with the literary group which included **Kahlil Gibran**, he revitalized the art of Arabic fiction and literary criticism. Most notable of his translated works are *Fathers and Sons* (1917), a drama set during Ottoman times; *The Book of Mirdad* (1948), encapsulating his Sufistic notions, and *Memoirs of a Vagrant Soul* (1952).

▷N Nuaymah, *Mikhail Nuaymah* (1978, in Arabic)

NÚÑEZ DE ARCE, Gaspar
(1834–1903)

Spanish poet, dramatist and statesman, born in Valladolid. He held office in the government in 1883 and 1888, and in 1894 received a national ovation at Toledo. As a lyric poet he may be styled the 'Spanish Tennyson', and among his poems are *Gritos del Combate* (1875, 'Cries of Battle'), *Última Lamentación de Lord Byron* (1879, 'Lord Byron's Last Lamentation'), *El vértigo* (1879, 'Vertigo'), *La Pesca* (1884, 'Fishing') and *La Maruja* (1886). His plays include *La Cuenta del Zapatero* (1859, 'The Countess of Zapatero') and *El Haz de Leña* (1872, 'The Bundle of Firewood').

▷J Romano, *Gaspar Núñez de Arce* (1944)

NUTTALL, Jeff
(1933–)

British poet and controversialist, probably still best known for his polemic *Bomb Culture* (1968), very much a tract for the times. During the late 1960s, he was much involved in the performance art, politics-as-spectacle movement; he founded the mixed-media People Show in 1967, published his verse *Journals* and appeared in *Penguin Modern Poets 12* the following year. His verse is as passionately committed as **Allen Ginsberg**'s but, unlike the American's, his style did not survive the apocalyptic temper of 1968, which *Bomb Culture* helped define in the UK. Later work has been rather tired; the best of his verse is in *Poems 1962–69* (1970). Nuttall has written some fiction, most notably *Oscar Christ and the Immaculate Conception* (1968) and the overlooked *The Patriarchs: An Early Summer Landscape* (1978).

NYE, Robert
(1939–)

English novelist, poet and journalist. He grew up in London and the Home Counties, and has been closely associated with both *The Scotsman* and *The Times* as a literary reviewer, to which he brings considerable intelligence and taste, and an infectious love of poetry. He began writing verse very early and published two volumes, *Juvenilia* (1961, 1963), before toughening up his style and switching his attention largely to prose fiction. A collected edition of his verse appeared in 1992. Nye's first novel was the rather **Joyce**an *Doubtfire* (1968). *Tales I Told My Mother* (1969) is elegantly intertextual. Nye discovered his métier with *Falstaff* (1976), a novel about the original of **Shakespeare**'s character; ever since he has concentrated on semi-mythic historical characters—*Merlin* (1978), *Faust* (1980), Ralegh in *The Voyage of the Destiny* (1982), *The Memoirs of Lord Byron* (1989), and the original of Barbe-Bleue in *The Life and Death of My Lord Gilles de Rais* (1990). He is an able playwright and a notably uncondescending writer for children, but remains, chiefly, a poet.

O

OATES, Joyce Carol
(1938–)

American writer, born in Millersport, New York. She was educated at Syracuse University and the University of Wisconsin. Married in 1961, she taught English at the University of Detroit (1961–7), then was appointed Professor of English at the University of Windsor in Ontario. A hugely prolific novelist, story writer and essayist, she published her first novel,*With Shuddering Fall*, in 1964. Splintered with violence and impressive in its social scope, her fiction challenges received ideas about the nature of human experience. *Them* (1969), her fourth novel, won a National Book Award. Later novels include *Marya: A Life* (1986) and *You Must Remember This* (1989). Her interest in pugilism emerged in *On Boxing* (1987), first published in the *Ontario Review*, with which she has long had a connection.

OBALDIA, René de
(1918–)

French avant-garde playwright, novelist and poet. He was born in Hong Kong, but moved to France with his mother at an early age, and attended the Lycée Condorcet in Paris. As a naturalized Frenchman he had to serve in World War II, and spent a long period in a concentration camp. Released in 1945, he published a volume of Surrealist poetry, *Midi*, in 1949, and became a regular contributor to many literary reviews, including *Le Mercure de France* and *Le Contemporain*. He published two prize-winning novels, *Fugue à Waterloo* (1955) and *Le Centenaire* (1960), but is better known for his plays: *Génousie* (1960), *Le Satyre de la villette* (1963) and *Du vent dans les branches de Sassafras* (1965). A further volume of his poetry, *Innocentines*, appeared in 1969.

OBENG, R E
(20th century)

African writer, author of the first novel proper in English, *Eighteenpence* (1943), by a native African (published at his own expense in Ilfracombe, England), and therefore of historical importance. Much influenced by the Bible and missionaries' comforting words, it is nonetheless a genuinely pioneering book.

OBEY, André
(1892–1975)

French dramatist and novelist, born in Douai, whose first success (he had previously collaborated with **Denys Amiel**) was with *Noë* (1931, Eng trans *Noah* in *Twenty Best European Plays on the American Stage*, 1963, ed John Gassner), well described as 'histrionic theatre-poetry'. It played with success in various capital cities. **Thornton Wilder** adapted his *Le Viol de Lucrèce* (1931) as *Lucrece* (1932). A playwright boldly presentational in his techniques, he did much for the theatre in his year (1946–7) as Director of the Comédie-Française. He had many other fashionable and skilful successes.

OBLIGADO, Rafael
(1851–1920)

Argentinian poet, born in Buenos Aires. He met **Darío** and, being wealthy, was able to act as host to all the important Argentinian writers of his time—and some others. He wrote only a single collection, *Poesías* (1885, revised and enlarged 1906). This is defiant of European modes, and tries to develop national themes in the style of **Echeverria**, the chief influence upon him; but he wrote nothing of the first rank.

O'BRIEN, Edna
(1932–)

Irish novelist, short-story writer and playwright, born in Tuamgraney, County Clare. Educated at the Convent of Mercy, Loughrea, and at the Pharmaceutical College of Dublin, she practised pharmacy briefly before becoming a writer. Her dominant themes are loneliness, guilt and loss, articulated in musical prose. 'My aim', she has written, 'is to write books that in some way celebrate life and do justice to my emotions'. Among her celebrated books are *The Country Girls* (1960), *The Lonely Girl* (1962), *Girls in Their Married Bliss* (1964), *August is a Wicked Month* (1965) and *A Pagan Place* (1970). *The Collected Edna O'Brien*, containing nine novels, was published in 1978, and she has also published several collections of short stories. Recent novels include a collection of *The Country Girls Trilogy* with an epilogue (1986), and *The High Road* (1988). She has also written a number of plays and screenplays, a book of verse, *On the Bone* (1989), and some non-fiction.

▷ G Eckley, *Edna O'Brien* (1974)

O'BRIEN, (Michael) Fitz-James
(1828–62)

Irish–American writer, born in County Cork. He composed sentimental poems from an early age, including the once popular 'Loch Ina' (1845). After spending an inherited fortune in London, he arrived in New York in 1852, immediately becoming a figure in literary Bohemia. He had some success with plays, particularly *A Gentleman from Ireland* (1854), and wrote numerous poems, stories and articles. However, he is now remembered mainly for a few fantastic stories influenced by **Poe**, such as 'The Diamond Lens' (1858) and 'What Was It?' (1859); these display much imagination, employing to great effect convincing shifts from the mundane to the bizarre, and pseudo-scientific explanations. O'Brien died fighting for the Union in the Civil War.

▷ F Wolle, *Fitz-James O'Brien: A Literary Bohemian of the Eighteen-Fifties* (1944)

O'BRIEN, Flann, pseud of Brian O'Nolan
(1911–66)

Irish writer, born in Strabane, County Tyrone, the third child in a family of 12. His father working in the Customs and Excise, his early life was peripatetic but the family settled for a spell in a large house near Tullamore where Irish was the common tongue. Later they moved to Dublin and it was here that his formal education began at the Christian Brothers' school, renowned for its rigidly basic and brutally applied methods of education. In 1927 the family moved to the seaside suburb of Blackrock, where he wrote his earliest and finest books. He attended Blackrock College and University College, Dublin, studying German, Irish and English, although much of his time was frittered away at billiards or in pubs. From 1933 to 1934 he was in Germany where there is speculation (but no proof) that he married a girl called Clara who died of consumption a month later. He returned to Dublin, finished his thesis, had it rejected (it was finally accepted in 1935) and founded *Blather*, whose six editions he wrote mainly himself. On Irish radio he gave talks on literature, and published his eccentric but brilliant novel *At Swim-Two-Birds* (published four years later in 1939) and joined the Irish Civil Service, which occupied him until his premature retirement in 1953.

The death of his father and the need to supplement his salary to support his kin led him reluctantly to submit *At Swim-Two-Birds* to publishers. Its acceptance by Collins owed much to **Graham Greene**'s enthusiasm and led to the birth of the Flann O'Brien pseudonym. A year later, in 1940, came the debut of 'Myles na Gopaleen', the pseudonym under which he contributed a column to the *Irish Times* for some 20 years, and which he regarded as not so much a *nom de plume* as a *nom de guerre*. His second novel *An Béal Bocht* was published in Irish in 1941 (*The Poor Mouth*, 1973); *The Third Policeman*, written and rejected in 1940, was published posthumously in 1967. He is best known as an idiosyncratic newspaper columnist, and various anthologies appeared after his death—*The Best of Myles* (1968), *The Various Lives of Keats and Chapman and the Brother* (1976) and *Myles From Dublin* (1985).

▷ T O'Keeffe, *Myles* (1973)

O'BRIEN, Kate
(1897–1974)

Irish playwright and novelist, born in Limerick. She was educated at Laurel Hill Convent, Limerick, and University College, Dublin. At 30 she began a career in London as playwright and in 1931 she published her prize-winning *Without My Cloak*, followed by *Mary Lavelle* (1936), *Pray for the Wanderer* (1938), *The Land of Spices* (1941), *The Last of Summer* (1943), *That Lady* (1946) and *As Music and Splendour* (1958). A remarkable observer of life, she was injured by a profoundly unhappy marriage to the Dutch historian Gustaaf Johannes Renier, and her novels are best understood by appreciation of her consciousness of a lesbian sexual identity. Her work reflected deep knowledge of Ireland and Spain as may be seen from her *Farewell Spain* (1937) and *My Ireland* (1962).

▷ *English Diaries and Journals* (1943)

O'BRIEN, Richard Barry
(1847–1918)

Irish nationalist historian and biographer, born in Kilrush, County Clare. He studied at Newman's ill-fated Catholic University of Dublin, after which he was called to the Irish (1874) and English (1875) bars without practising much. He was drawn into skilful and detailed historical writing in the cause of Irish home rule, producing many detailed works whose nationalist apologetics did not greatly weaken their considerable historical value. His masterpiece, *The Life of Charles Stewart Parnell* (1898), is one of the great political biographies of all time. He was founder, chairman and (from 1906) president of the Irish Literary Society in London from 1892 to 1911.

O'BRIEN, Tim (William Timothy)
(1948–)

American novelist. Born and raised in a Minnesota prairie town, he served as a soldier in Vietnam (1969–70). On his return he studied for his doctorate in political science at Harvard and became a reporter for the *Washington Post*. His war experiences, described in his acclaimed war memoir *If I Die in a Combat Zone* (1973), strongly influence his novels. In *Going After Cacciato* (1979), which won the US National Book Award, Vietnam is the setting for an exploration of the nature of fear and courage. In *The Nuclear Age* (1986) the instinct for survival is frustrated by the fear of war and death. A thought-provoking writer with a delicate touch, O'Brien has won widespread praise both for his literary talent and for his ability to articulate the experience of Vietnam War veterans. The combination of writer and ex-soldier is most evident in *The Things They Carried* (1990), a highly personal collection of war stories.

Ó BRUADAIR, Dáibhidh (David)
(?1625–1698)

Irish Gaelic poet, recording the destruction of his culture, born in Cork into a family of some substance. He was impressively educated, but the wars and proscriptions drove his FitzGerald patrons in Kerry into danger and exile, and the poet's later verses dramatically and lyrically convey his fall from places of patronage and honour to the status of farm labourer. His work, complex and resourceful, innovative as well as traditional, offers a bridge from the earlier, assured world of the Gaelic bards to the dark dispossession of the next century. The Irish Texts Society published a bilingual edition of his surviving poems, *Duanaire Dháibhidh Uí Bhruadair* (1913–17).

Ó CADHAIN, Máirtín, anglicized name Martin Kane
(1906–70)

Irish Gaelic short-story writer and novelist, born in Spiddal, Connemara, the Gaelic-speaking area of Galway in the west of Ireland, who worked for a time as a schoolteacher. He was actively involved in the IRA and interned during World War II. In 1969 he became Professor of Irish at Trinity College Dublin. The second of five collections of short-stories, *An Braon Broghach* (1948, Eng trans 'The Hare Lip', in *The Field Day Anthology of Irish Writing*, 1991), established him as a stern critic of accepted social conventions. The novel *Cré Na Cille* (1949, 'The Clay of the Churchyard') is a commentary by the dead beneath the earth on the perfidities of the politicians in the 'fledgling Free State' on the 'uppersoil'. An unrepentant advocate of revolution, Ó Cadhain had a strong influence on subsequent generations of writers, a role which has often detracted attention from the stylish, inventive originality of his writing.
▷ *Pápéir Bhána Pápéir Bhreaca* (1969); A Titley, *Máirtín Ó Cadhain* (1975)

OCAMPO, Silvina
(1906–)

Argentinian writer, born into a wealthy family in Buenos Aires. With her sister **Victoria Ocampo** she is one of the most important women writers and poets of the first half of the 20th century in Latin America. She and her husband **Adolfo Bioy Casares** held an influential literary tertulia (conversation group) which included writers and poets like **Jorge Luis Borges**, **Maria Luisa Bombal** and **Ezequiel Martinez Estrada**. She writes dramatic and amorous poetry, as well as collections of short stories and juvenile fiction. Her titles include *Sonetos del jardin* (1948, 'Garden Sonnets') and the short-story collection *Informe del cielo y del infierno* ('Report on Heaven and Earth'). She is also an accomplished painter.

OCAMPO, Victoria
(1891–1979)

Argentinian writer, born into a rich family in Buenos Aires, the sister of **Silvina Ocampo**. She is most highly regarded as the editor and motivational force behind one of Latin America's most important literary journals, *Sur*, which combined the mission of publishing new Latin-American writers (like **Jorge Luis Borges**) and translations of major North American and European writers. Born into a wealthy family, she lived in Paris and London as a child, and learned French, English and Italian. Her literary creations are extensive, including biography (*338171 T.E.*, 1942, a biography of **T S Eliot**), essays and criticism (*Testimonios* is a 10-volume collection of these), novels, and translations.

O'CASEY, Sean
(1884–1964)

Irish playwright, born in a poor part of Dublin. He picked up whatever education he could and worked as a labourer and for nationalist organizations before beginning his career as a dramatist. His early plays, dealing with low life in Dublin—*Shadow of a Gunman* (1923) and *Juno and the Paycock* (1924)—were written for the Abbey Theatre. Later he became more experimental and impressionistic. Other works include *The Plough and the Stars* (1926), *The Silver Tassie* (1929), *Cockadoodle Dandy* (1949) and *The Bishop's Bonfire* (1955). He also wrote essays,

O CONAIRE, Pádraic

such as *The Flying Wasp* (1936). He was awarded the Hawthornden Prize in 1926. His autobiography, begun in 1939 with *I Knock at the Door*, continued through six volumes to *Sunset and Evening Star* (1954).
▷E O'Casey, Sean (1971)

O CONAIRE, Pádraic (Patrick Conroy)
(1883–1928)

Irish Gaelic writer, born in Galway and educated in Gaelic-speaking Rosmuc. He went to sea, and spent many years in the London civil service, which he left in 1913 having won prizes in 1904 and 1909 for stories in Gaelic. He won fame as a novelist, essayist, travel-writer and short-story writer of deceptive simplicity and fine construction, sometimes working in children's fiction, sometimes taking up themes of psychological complexity which worried the more puritanical elements in the Gaelic revival. His later years were spent in writing and teaching Irish, chiefly in Galway.
▷*An Crann Géagach* (1919)

O'CONNER, Elizabeth, properly Barbara McNamara
(1913–)

Australian writer, born in Dunedoo, New South Wales, who has published three novels dealing with aspects of rural life in northern Queensland: *The Irishman* (1960), *Find a Woman* (1963) and *Spirit Man* (1980). *The Irishman*, the experiences of teamster Paddy Doolan and his sons, won the **Miles Franklin** Award in 1960 and was filmed in 1978. Her two best-known works, though, are perhaps *Steak for Breakfast* (1958) and *A Second Helping* (1969), autobiographical accounts of her life on outback cattle stations, reminiscent of **Monica Dickens**'s best work.

O'CONNOR, Edwin
(1918–68)

American novelist, born in Rhode Island. By profession he was a radio announcer, writer and producer, which provided him with the material for *The Oracle* (1951), about a 'radio personality'. His most famous book, which was filmed, was *The Last Hurrah* (1956), about a crooked but warm-hearted Boston political boss; it was based on the career of the politician James M Curley. *The Edge of Sadness* (1961), a novel graver in tone, about a Roman Catholic priest, and also set in Boston, won the Pulitzer Prize.

O'CONNOR, (Mary) Flannery
(1925–64)

American novelist, born in Savannah, Georgia, whose environs she rarely left during her short life. She was educated at Peabody High School, Midgeville, Georgia, graduating in 1942. Thereafter she attended Georgia State College for Women and the University of Iowa. Brought up a Catholic and in the 'Christ-haunted' bible-belt of the Deep South, she homed in on Protestant fundamentalists who dominated the region. The characters in her work seem superficially similar to those photographed by Diane Arbus: grotesque, deformed, freakish. This to her, however, was reality, and her heightened depicton of it is unforgettable. *Wise Blood* (1952), the first of her two novels, is a bizarre tragi-comedy, and its theme of vocation is taken up again in her second, *The Violent Bear It Away* (1960). Regarded as one of the finest short-story writers of her generation, her work in that form can be found in *A Good Man Is Hard To Find and other stories* (1955, 'nine stories about original sin'), and *Everything That Rises Must Converge* (1965), affected by the pain she was suffering in the closing stages of chronic disseminated lupus. *The Habit of Being: Letters of Flannery O'Connor* was published in 1979.
▷L Getz, *Flannery O'Connor, her life and library* (1980)

O'CONNOR, Frank, pseud of Michael O'Donovan
(1903–66)

Irish writer, born in Cork. He was a member of the Irish Republican Army in his teens (1921–2), fought in the War of Independence and was imprisoned. He then worked as a railway clerk in Cork, and later a librarian in Wicklow, Cork and Dublin. Although he wrote plays and some excellent literary criticism—*Art of the Theatre* (1947), *The Modern Novel* (1956), *The Mirror in the Roadway* (1957)—his best medium was almost exclusively the short story. **W B Yeats** said of him that he was 'doing for Ireland what Chekhov did for Russia'. Representative titles include *Guests of the Nation* (1931), *Bones of Contention* (1936), *Crab Apple Jelly* (1944), *Travellers' Samples* (1956), *Domestic Relations* (1957) and *My Oedipus Complex* (1963). He also wrote two volumes of memoirs, *An Only Child* (1961) and *My Father's Son* (1969), several plays, translations of Irish verse, a novel, *Dutch Interior* (1940), the critical studies *The Lonely Voice* (1963) and *Shakespeare's Progress* (1960), and a biography of Michael Collins, *The Big Fellow* (1937).

Ó'DÁLAIGH, Donnchadh Mór
(1170–1244)

Irish poet; he was the greatest religious poet of medieval Ireland. He was described by the Four Masters (in *The Annals of the Kingdom of Ireland*, written by four monks, and completed in 1636 as a poet who never was and never would be surpassed. His most famous poem, 'Sorrowful My Pilgrimage to Loch Dearg', was translated by **Sean O'Faolain** in *With the Gaels of Wexford* (1955).

▷L McKenna, *Don Dé* (1922)

Ó DÁLAIGH, Muireadhach Albanach
(c.1180–c.1250)

Irish poet, an outstanding character of his time. Muireadhach is perhaps the only poet who has killed a tax-collector (with an axe). Owing to this indiscretion, he had to flee his home in County Sligo, and ended in Scotland (hence 'Albanach'). His poem on the death of his (probably Scottish) wife, beginning 'I was robbed of my soul last night', is one of the most famous in Irish literature.

▷R Flower, *The Irish Tradition* (1947)

O'DELL, Scott
(1898–)

American novelist, born in Los Angeles, and educated at the University of Wisconsin, Stanford University, and the University of Rome. He was a film cameraman in the 1920s, a newspaperman and a book reviewer, and served in the US Air Force in World War II. He has three adult novels to his name but is best known for his children's books, especially *Island of the Blue Dolphins* (1960), which is based on the true story of a young girl left alone on an island for several years. He has won numerous awards, including the **Newbery** Medal (1961) and the **Hans Christian Andersen** International Medal (1972).

ODETS, Clifford
(1906–63)

American playwright and actor, born in Philadelphia. In 1931 he joined the Group Theatre, New York, under whose auspices his early plays were produced. The most important American playwright of the 1930s, his works are marked by a strong social conscience and grow largely from the conditions of the great depression of that time. They include *Waiting for Lefty*, *Awake and Sing* and *Till the Day I Die*, all produced in 1935, and *Golden Boy* (1937). He was responsible for a number of film scenarios, including *The General Died at Dawn*, *None but the Lonely Heart* (which he directed), *Deadline at Dawn* and *The Big Knife*.

▷M B Gibson, *Odets, American Playwright: the years from 1906 to 1940* (1981)

Ó DIREÁIN, Máirtín
(1910–88)

Irish Gaelic poet, born on the Aran Islands. He spent most of his life as a civil servant in Dublin. He published some of his own poems during the 1940s and quickly became the leading Gaelic poet of his generation. *Dánta 1939–1979* (1980, 'Poems') established him as a writer for whom memory was of paramount importance in the elucidation of experience. In *Ómós do John Millington Synge* (nd, 'Homage to John Millington Synge') he wrote 'The book was always in your heart/You brought the words in it to Life'. This could equally be applied to his own supple encapsulation of a declining Gaelic oral culture which he dignified into a lasting literary one.

▷S Deane (ed), *Field Day Anthology of Irish Writing: Vol 3* (1991)

Ó DOMHNAILL, Maghnas
(d.1563)

Irish poet and politician, of the house of O'Donnell. He wrote love poems in the troubadour manner, as well as satires. His prose *Life* of the saint, Colum Cille, written in 1532, is his most famous single work.

O'DONNELL, Peadar (Peter)
(1893–1986)

Irish revolutionary and writer, born in Meenmore, County Donegal, the son of a small farmer. He reflected the vigorous agrarian traditions of his native Donegal and added to them a lifelong republicanism and socialism. First a teacher, then labour organizer, then guerrilla republican leader, he opposed the 1921 Anglo–Irish Treaty, was captured in Civil War fighting, and escaped after a 41-day hunger-strike. A vigorous publicist and editor of *An Phoblacht*, the official IRA newspaper, he gave (and then withdrew) qualified support for Eamon de Valera in 1932, left the IRA in 1934, fought for the Spanish Republic in 1936–7 and wrote extensively on his experiences: the novel *Storm* (1925) on the Anglo–Irish war, *The Gates Flew Open* (1934) on his imprisonment, *Salud!* (1937) on the Spanish Civil War, and *There Will Be Another Day* (1963) on his campaign against land annuities which led to the Anglo–Irish Economic War of the 1930s. His editorship of the literary monthly, *The Bell* (1946–54), was invaluable in furthering Irish writing. His finest work is *Islanders* (1927), but his last novel, *The Big Windows* (1955), is also evocative of his power in social depiction.

O'DOWD, Bernard Patrick
(1866–1953)

Australian poet and journalist, born in Beaufort, Victoria, who, while a lifelong radical and republican, managed to combine his militancy with a career in public service. He was Librarian to the Supreme Court in Melbourne for 16 years and then from 1913 a parliamentary draughtsman. In that role he edited several law books and latterly, as head of the department (1931–5), was responsible for major Victorian state legislation. Meanwhile he was writing for and publishing various radical periodicals and in 1903 published his first collection of verse, *Downward?*, which included his best-known poem, 'Australia'. There followed *The Silent Land* (1906), *Dominions of the Boundary* (1907) and *The Seven Deadly Sins* (1909). After *Alma Venus* (1921) he wrote very little; a collected edition of his verse was published in 1941.

O'DUFFY, Eimar Ultan
(1893–1935)

Irish satirical playwright and novelist, born in Dublin. Educated at Stonyhurst (Jesuit) College in Lancashire, at first he followed his father in studying dentistry at University College, Dublin, but embraced the new Irish revolutionary cultural nationalism under the influence of **Thomas MacDonagh** and Joseph Plunkett, who published and produced his first play, *The Walls of Athens*, and whose Irish Theatre also staged his *The Phoenix on the Roof* (1915). He broke with them on the Easter Rising of 1916 where, as an Irish volunteer loyal to John MacNeill, he was one of the couriers who tried to transmit the order countermanding it. His best play, *Bricriu's Feast* (1919), satirized neo-Gaelicism, and his first novel, *The Wasted Island* (1919, rev edn 1929), is a valuable source on the origins of the Rising. He was responsive to **James Joyce**'s *Ulysses*, and wrote many novels, of which the Butlerian fantasies *King Goshalk and the Birds*, *The Spacious Adventures of the Man in the Street* and *Asses in Clover* are the most noteworthy. Emigrating to England in 1925, he ultimately espoused the Social Credit philosophy of Major C H Douglas, his autobiographical *Life and Money* (1932) winning some success.

OE Kenzaburo
(1935–)

Japanese novelist, born in Shikoku and educated at Tokyo University, where he studied French literature. His earliest fiction, influenced by **Kobo Abe**, attempts to come to terms with the bleak cultural landscape of post-war Japan. His first three novels, beginning with *Shisha no Ogori* ('The Arrogance of the Dead'), were all published in 1958, but it was not until 1963 that Oe found an effective personal voice. In that year, he visited Hiroshima and witnessed the delivery of his son, who was born with a major skull abnormality. Thereafter, his writing became more personal and engaged, less dependent on second-hand Decadence, imported from France. *Kojinteki na taiken* (1964) was the first of his books to be published in English, as *A Personal Matter*

(1968). Perhaps his finest book followed in 1967; *Man'en gannen no futtuboru* (Eng trans *The Silent Cry*, 1974) concerns two brothers' search for their roots. It won Oe the **Tanizaki** Prize. Four of his short novels of the 1970s were collected in translation as *Teach Us to Outgrow Our Madness* (1977). In the 1980s he began to explore new principles of organization for his fiction, drawing on social anthropology and philosophy.

▷Y Hisaaki, *The Search for Authenticity in Modern Japanese Literature* (1978)

OEHLENSCHLÄGER, Adam Gottlob
(1779–1850)

Danish poet and playwright, born in Copenhagen. The founder of Danish Romanticism, and the greatest Danish poet of his day, he was much influenced by **Goethe** and the **Schlegel** brothers. He published his symbolic poem, *Goldhornene* ('The Golden Horns') in 1802 and a verse fantasy, *Aladdin*, in 1805. He wrote some 24 blank-verse historical tragedies, starting with *Hakon Jarl* (1807, 'Earl Hakon'), followed by *Baldur hin Gode* ('Baldur the Good') in 1808, *Palnetoke* (1809), *Correggio* (1909, written in German), and *Axel og Valborg* (1810). He later wrote a cycle of verse romances, *Helge* (1814), and *Nordens Guder* ('Gods of the North'), an epic ballad cycle based on the Norse mythology of the *Edda*. He was appointed Professor of Aesthetics at Copenhagen in 1810. In 1829 he was crowned 'king of the Scandinavian singers' by **Elaias Tegnér** at Lund, and in 1849 was publicly proclaimed as the national poet of Denmark.

▷V Andersen, *Adam Oehlenschläger* (1899–1900)

O'FAOLAIN, Julia
(1932–)

Irish novelist, born in London, daughter of **Sean O'Faolain**. A writer whose exuberant, multi-layered fiction combines aspects of the domestic novel with political, religious and historical concerns, her early work draws on her experience as a convent-educated Irish girl studying in Rome and Paris; her short-story collection, *Man in the Cellar* (1974), reveals a macabre side to her humour. Catholicism has played a strong role in her later work. *Women in the Wall* (1975) is an examination of the female role in medieval society, based around the setting-up of a convent, and the Booker-shortlisted *No Country for Young Men* (1980) puts Irish nationalism under the microscope. *The Obedient Wife* (1982) and *The Irish Signorina* (1984) explore the crisscross of different cultures and divergent ways of life, while *The Judas Cloth* (1992) is the story of a young priest, set during the reign of Pope Pius IX.

O'FAOLAIN, Sean
(1900–91)

Irish writer, born in Dublin. He was educated at the National University of Ireland, and took his MA at Harvard. He lectured for a period (1929) at Boston College, then took a post as a teacher in Strawberry Hill, Middlesex and in 1933 returned to Ireland to teach. His first writing was in Gaelic, and he produced an edition of translations from Gaelic, *The Silver Branch*, in 1938. Before this, however, he had attracted attention with a novel, *A Nest of Simple Folk* (1933). He never quite repeated its success with later novels, and from then on wrote many biographies, including *Daniel O'Connell* (1938), *De Valera* (1939) and *The Great O'Neill* (1942), this last being a biography of the 2nd Earl of Tyrone. He edited the autobiography of Wolfe Tone (1937) and published one of his own, *Vive-moi!* (1964). His *Stories of Sean O'Faolain* (1958) cover 30 years of writing and progress from the lilting 'Irishry' of his youth to the deeper and wider artistry of his maturity. A later version was published as *Collected Stories* in 1981. His daughter is the novelist **Julia O'Faolain**.
▷P A Doyle, *Sean O'Faolain* (1968)

O'FLAHERTY, Liam
(1897–1984)

Irish writer, born on Inishmore in the Aran Islands. Educated at Rockwell College, Tipperary and University College, Dublin, he fought in the British army during World War I and later wandered in North America and Latin America. He returned to Ireland in 1921 and fought on the Republican side in the Irish Civil War. He went to London in 1922 to become a writer, and published his first novels, *Thy Neighbour's Wife* (1923) and *The Black Soul* (1924). *The Informer* (1926) won the James Tait Black Prize and was a popular success. Other books, reflecting the intensity of his feeling and style, include *Spring Sowing* (1926), *The Assassin* (1928), *The Puritan* (1932), *Famine* (1937) and *Land* (1946). He also wrote three volumes of autobiography, *Two Years* (1930), *I went to Russia* (1931) and *Shame the Devil* (1934).

OFTERDINGEN, Heinrich von
(12th–13th century)

One of the famous *Minnesinger* or lyric poets of Germany, who flourished between the years 1170 and 1250.

OGILVIE, William Henry
(1869–1963)

Scottish poet, born near Kelso, who, after having admired the verse of **Adam Lindsay Gordon**, went to Australia at the age of 20 to work in Queensland. A highly skilled horseman, he worked round the State droving, mustering and breaking horses, and became a friend of Henry 'Breaker' Morant. All the while he was contributing ballads under the name 'Glenrowan' to such periodicals as the *Bulletin*. In 1898 he published his best-known book, *Fair Girls and Gray Horses*, and three years later went back to Scotland, never to return. *Hearts of Gold and Other Verses* (1903) and a compilation, *The Australian and Other Verses* (1916), were published in Australia after he left, as was another collection, *Saddle for a Throne* (1952). His verse, though sometimes over-sentimental, is the equal of other 'Bush' poets and its romanticism a welcome change from the male-oriented rhymes of **Banjo Paterson** and **Henry Lawson**. After his return to Scotland he contributed to *Punch* and *Country Life* among others and was called by **Hugh MacDiarmid** 'The Grand Old Man of Borders Song'. He was well known for his hunting verse, the best of which is in *The Collected Sporting Verse of W H Ogilvie* (1932).
▷ *My Life in the Open* (1910)

OGOT, Grace
(1930–)

Kenyan story writer, born in Central Nyanza Province. Trained as a midwife, she became a headmistress and a scriptwriter for the BBC. Her stories have a strong folkloric element and have appeared in many important magazines, such as *Black Orpheus*. One of her best known, 'Tekayo', is in *African Writing Today* (1967).

O'GRADY, Desmond
(1935–)

Irish poet, born in Limerick. He was a friend of **Ezra Pound**, and worked as a teacher in Rome, Cairo and Alexandria before retiring in the mid-1980s to Kinsale in the south of Ireland. Known since the publication of *The Dark Edge of Europe* (1967) as 'the Poet O'Grady', his appetite for the epic, the rhetorical and the 'grand' style made him a somewhat dangerous influence on succeeding generations of poets. However, *New and Selected Poems* (1978), together with his informed translations—*The Gododdin* (1977), *A Limerick Rake: Versions from the Irish* (1978) and *Ten Arab Poets* (1992)—and his consistent injection of 'linguistic glamour' into classical themes, make him an important figure in late 20th-century European literature.

Ó'GRIANNA, Séamus
(1891–1969)

Irish novelist and story writer, born in County Donegal. His **Maupassant**-like, but frequently sentimental, stories, of which there were many, were very popular, but have not attracted the attention of critics.

O'HARA, Frank
(1926–66)

American poet and art critic, born in Baltimore, Maryland. Since the publication of *A City Winter* (1952) his poetry collections were influenced by his life in New York, and are often based on autobiographical incidents. The posthumously published *Selected Poems* (1973) won a National Book Award, while *Art Chronicles* (1975) is a collection of his fine-art criticism; he was the Assistant Curator of the Museum of Modern Art, New York, when he died. His best work came when he engaged in light, conversational celebrations of his adopted city. Wilfully ephemeral, such pieces as 'Steps' ('How funny you are today New York ...') are now more valuable as records of a bygone era than as art in their own right.

O'HARA, John
(1905–70)

American novelist and short-story writer, born in Pottsville, Pennsylvania. In his fiction Pottsville becomes 'Gibbsville', the setting for *Appointment in Samarra* (1934). Its naturalistic, fatalistic account of the last three days in the life of Julian English made him almost overnight a success. O'Hara was notoriously irascible and hypersensitive. 'Brash as a young man', wrote **John Updike**, 'he became with success a slightly desperate braggart'. Two of his works—*Butterfield 8* (1935) and *Pal Joey* (1940)—became film and stage successes. His short stories are obsessed with class, social privilege and feminist issues.
▷F Farr, *John O'Hara: a biography* (1973)

O'HARA, Mary, pseud of Mary O'Hara Alsop
(1885–1980)

American novelist and children's writer, best-known for her winsome trilogy about horses, *My Friend Flicka* (1941), *Thunderhead* (1943) and *The Green Grass of Wyoming* (1946), all written on her Wyoming ranch. The Hollywood version of the first of these books, and its sequel, became two of the most popular family films of the forties. She was also a composer of piano suites.

OHNET, George
(1848–1918)

French novelist, born in Paris. Under the general title of *Les Batailles de la vie* ('The Battles of Life'), he published a series of novels, some of which went beyond one hundred editions.

Ó'HUIGINN, Tadghh Dall
(1550–91)

Irish poet, 'the greatest master of the dán díreach [the rules of Irish classical metres] that ever lived'. He was brother of a Catholic archbishop, and lived in County Sligo. The subject-matter of most of his poetry, however, was conventional: it consisted of odes to chieftains. But his two *aislings*, or vision-poems, are different and more powerful.
▷E Knott, *The Bardic Poems of Tagdh Dall* (1922–6)

O'KEEFFE, John
(1747–1833)

Irish dramatist, born in Abbey Street, Dublin, of a Catholic family. He left Ireland to work as an actor, but later returned to work under Henry Mossop at the Theatre Royal, Smock Alley, Dublin, the first Restoration theatre in either England or Ireland. Some 77 'Dramas' are listed in his *Recollections* (2 vols, 1826). Prolific but pedantic, he dined off **Richard Brinsley Sheridan**'s description of him as 'the first that turned the public taste from the dullness of sentiment ... towards the sprightly channel of comic humour'. Following the Royal Shakespeare Company's 1976 revival of his *Wild Oats* (1791) he gained a misplaced reputation as a composer-playwright; as the earlier *Tony Lumpkin in Town* (1774) shows, he was, rather, a skilful assimilator of other people's plots and sanitized versions of traditional Irish folksongs. Following an accident in 1780 he began to go blind; he received an annuity from Covent Garden in 1803, and in 1826 a pension from George IV.
▷F M Link (ed), *The Plays of John O'Keeffe* (4 vols, 1981)

OKRI, Ben
(1959–)

Nigerian novelist, poet and short-story writer, born in Minna, now living in London. His first, precocious novel was *Flowers and Shadows* (1980), but it was not until 1987, and the publication of its successor, *Incidents at the Shrine*, that he achieved recognition in the form of the Commonwealth Writers' Prize for Africa. *Stars of the New Curfew* (1988), a volume of short stories, marked time, but his career began a new stage with his third novel, *The Famished Road* (1991), which won the Booker Prize; the sequel, *Songs of Enchantment*, followed in 1993.

Ó'LAOGHAIRE, Peadar
(1839–1920)

Irish Gaelic writer and translator (he made a disastrous attempt at *Don Quixote*), born in

West Cork. A canon, he adapted ancient stories and also wrote a famous novel, *Séadna* (1904) on the Faust theme. He was the first important modern writer to employ Irish as a medium, and with *Séadna* is said to have 'put all lovers of the Irish language in his debt': even though it is unsuccessful in psychological terms, it is nonetheless a 'kind of bible with revivalists … three hundred pages of living language!'

OLBRACHT, Ivan, pseud of Kamil Zeman
(1882–1952)

Czech novelist and story writer, born in Semily. Like many Czech writers, he supported the Communist Party in the inter-war period; he became a politician after World War II. He was at first much influenced by **Maxim Gorky**; but his later main work, *Nikola Suhaj loupeznik* (1933, Eng trans *Nikola Suhav—Bandit*, 1954), the success of which he could never repeat, is far more original in its retelling of the story of a popular Robin Hood-like hero. It remains one of the peaks of Czech achievement in the novel. Some of his stories are translated in *The Bitter and the Sweet* (1967).

OLDHAM, John
(1653–83)

English satirical poet, born in Shipton-Moyne, Gloucestershire. Educated at Oxford, he became a teacher. His most enduring works are those written after the exposure of the Popish Plot. These include *A Satire Upon a Woman, Who By Her Falsehood and Scorn Was the Death of My Friend* (1678); *A Satire Against Virtue* (1679), and the four *Satires upon the Jesuits* (1681). A highly intelligent and ebullient character, Oldham wrote not only in his own boisterous, aggressive style, but also parodied that of others, including **Horace**. He died from smallpox.

OLES', Oleksander, pseud of Oleksander Kandybar
(1878–1944)

Eastern Ukrainian poet and verse dramatist, born in Verkhosuly, Sumy. His fervent poetry is still remembered. After Ukraine became part of Soviet Russia he lived abroad, and died in Prague. He has been called Ukrainia's leading exponent of neo-romanticism.

OLESHA, Yury
(1899–1960)

Russian novelist and playwright from Odessa, one of the most gifted of his generation. He 'disappeared' during the 1930s, owing to his inability to conform, and was only 'rehabilitated' towards the end of his life, when he had been reduced to but a pale

shadow of his old self. He approved of the Revolution but could not reconcile himself to its 'collective' results, and so, in his finest novel, *Zavist* (1927, Eng trans *Envy*, 1936 and *The Wayward Comrade and the Commissar*, 1960), classic by any standards, he 'sent it up', but in such a manner that some comrade-critics believed he was supporting it. It tells of the conflict between an efficient sausage-manufacturer and an irresponsible anarchist. He puts forward the undoubtedly vigorous case for the sausage manufacturer with a poker-faced, mocking irony, reserving his fiercest criticism for the anarchist. The result is certainly 'ambiguous', but the ambiguity has less to do with politics than with individualism versus life-as-organized by politicians, and *Envy* is therefore of perennial interest. After this he was unable to take his own course, but, as a historian has written, 'the problems of technology and bureaucracy described in his works are as applicable to the West as … to the Soviet Union. One can only regret the failure of history to permit Olesha a normal artistic development'. After his 'disgrace', he wrote a script for a film of *The Idiot*, by **Dostoyevsky**, and translated much Turkmenian literature into Russian. His *Tri tolstyaka* (1924, 'The Three Fat Fellows') is a superb novel for children.
▷G Struve, *Soviet Russian Literature 1917–1950* (1951)

OLIPHANT, Laurence
(1829–88)

English travel writer and mystic, born in Capetown of Scottish descent, son of the attorney-general there. His first work, *A Journey to Khatmandu* (1852), was followed by *The Russian Shores of the Black Sea* (1853). As secretary to James Bruce, 8th Earl of Elgin, he travelled to China in 1857–8, thus finding material for further books. In 1861, while acting as *chargé d'affaires* in Japan, he was severely wounded by assassins. From 1865 to 1868 he sat for the Stirling burghs. His satirical novel, *Piccadilly* (1870), was a book of exceptional promise, full of wit and delicate irony. He joined the religious community of Thomas Lake Harris in the USA, and later settled in Haifa in Palestine. His mystical views he published in 1886 in *Sympneumata* (written with his wife and advocating purity in one's sex life) and *Scientific Religion* (1888).
▷P Henderson, *Life of Oliphant* (1956)

OLIPHANT, Margaret, née Wilson
(1828–97)

Scottish novelist, born in Wallyford, Midlothian. When she was 10 years old her family moved to England. She took her name from her mother; little is known about her father,

OLIVEIRA, Antônio Mariano de

Francis Wilson, except that he once 'took affadavits' in a Liverpool customs house. Precocious, she wrote a novel when she was 16, but her first published work was *Passages in the Life of Mrs Margaret Maitland* (1849), and two years later she began her lifelong connection with the Edinburgh publishers Blackwood and *Blackwood's Magazine*, culminating in a history of the firm, which was published posthumously (1897). In 1852 she married her cousin, Frances Oliphant, an artist, but she was widowed in 1859 and found herself £1000 in debt with an extended family to support and educate. Her output was astonishing and uneven, hardly surprising in an author who wrote almost a hundred novels, the best known of which are in the group known as *The Chronicles of Carlingford*, consisting of *The Rector and the Doctor's Family* (1863), *Salem Chapel* (1863), *The Perpetual Curate*, (1864), *Miss Majoribanks* (1866) and *Phoebe Junior* (1876), which have earned her the sobriquet, a 'feminist Trollope'. She wrote novels of Scottish life, including *The Minister's Wife* (1869), *Effie Ogilvie* (1886) and *Kirsteen* (1890). Other notable works include *Hester* (1883), *Lady Car* (1889), *The Railway Man and His Children* (1891) and *Sir Robert's Fortune* (1895). She was awarded a Civil List pension in 1868, but her industry was unabated and she produced a spate of biographies, literary histories, translations, travel books, tales of the supernatural, and an autobiography (1899).
▷A L Coghill, *The Life and Letters of Mrs Oliphant* (1899)

OLIVEIRA, Antônio Mariano de, known as Alberto de Oliveira
(1857–1937)

Brazilian poet who was left untouched by Brazilian *modernismo*. He was one of the main figures to react against romanticism, which he did by turning to the French Parnassian school. He was a superb technician, but had less to say than his contemporaries **Bilac** and **Correia**.

OLIVER, Mary Jane
(1935–)

American poet (not to be confused with the Spanish writer Maria Oliver). She was born in Ohio and educated at the state university, but has spent most of her adult life in Provincetown, Massachusetts. She was awarded a Pulitzer Prize in 1984 for *American Primitive* (1983) which, like all her work, contained modest reflections on the pastoral life. She has, especially since she moved to New England, been compared with **Robert Frost**. Any malevolence to be found in her poetry is seen as ultimately friendly and controllable.

OLMEDO, José Joaquín
(1780–1847)

Ecuadorean poet and translator (of the *Essay on Man* of **Alexander Pope**), born in Guayaquil. He combined romantic matter with classical form, and in this style wrote one of the most famous Latin-American poems, *La victoria de Junín: Canto a Bolívar*, an ode to Simon Bolívar, to whom he was close friend and aide. His poetry is not much read today.

OLSEN, Ernst Bruun
(1923–)

Danish dramatist, born in Nakskov. He was originally an actor and producer, whose *Teenagerlove* (1962), on the pop industry, was an immense success throughout Scandinavia.

OLSEN, Tillie
(1913–)

American novelist, critic and short-story writer, born in Omaha, Nebraska. She did not publish her first volume of stories, *Tell Me A Riddle*, until 1962, when she was almost 50. A novel, *Yonnondio: From the Thirties*, followed in 1974 and *Silences*, a collection of essays, four years later. Her writing draws upon her own working-class experiences and identifies poverty as being the root of individual despair and political oppression. In the title story of *Tell Me A Riddle*, an elderly working-class woman looks back over her life and blames the failure of her hopes upon the pressures of being a wife and mother, while in the novel, a young woman recounts her family's journey from country to city in a disastrous attempt to find economic salvation.
▷J and R Newton (eds), *Feminist Criticism and Social Change* (1985)

OLSON, Charles John
(1910–70)

American poet. He was born in Worcester, Massachusetts, and educated at Wesleyan University, Yale, and at Harvard, where the young literary radical began to feel uncomfortable in the liberal American studies programme. During World War II, he worked as a civil liberties activist, and in 1947 published *Call Me Ishmael*, ostensibly a study of **Melville**, but one which strongly emphasizes Olson's concern for ethnic minorities and for working-class solidarity. In 1950 he published an essay called 'Projective Verse' in the magazine *Poetry New York*, in which he drew on **Whitman** and **William Carlos Williams** to advocate a poetry governed by human speech and the rhythms of breath; as a means of indicating these, the tab button and space bar of the typewriter were to become major poetic tools. From 1951 to 1956, Olson directed

Black Mountain College near Asheville, North Carolina, and became nominal head of the 'Black Mountain poets' (**Robert Creeley, Ed Dorn** etc). His most important work was *The Maximus Poems*, which appeared in several volumes during his lifetime (1953–70), but were left unfinished at his death. The sequence resembles William Carlos Williams's *Paterson* in its dramatic and lyric centring, but in later volumes it took on more of the mythological concerns of **Pound**'s *The Cantos*; the sequence as a whole was edited by George Butterick in 1983. The first important critical response had been by Ed Dorn, who published *What I See in the Maximus Poems* in 1960. Olson's shorter verse was collected as *Archaeologist of Morning* in the year of his death; *The Complete Shorter Poems* appeared in 1985.

▷G Butterick, *A Guide to the Maximus Poems* (1978)

OLSON, Elder James

(1909–)

American poet, essayist and critic, born in Chicago. Olson's first collection, *Thing of Sorrow*, appeared in 1934; a major volume, *Plays and Poems: 1948–1958*, in 1958, and *Last Poems* in 1984. His verse is strictly formal, lyrical and immensely highly crafted, with the result that he is often regarded as rather unobtrusive, a writer whose poetry is not as robust as his criticism. Certainly *The Poetry of Dylan Thomas* (1954) was a pioneering and serious attempt to grapple with this poet's output, while *Theory of Comedy* (1968) represents an orthodox Aristotelean interpretation of the nature of comedy in drama.

O'MacCAISIDE, Tomas, real name **Thomas Cassidy**

(c.1710–c.1770)

Irish Gaelic poet, born in County Fermanagh. He entered the priesthood as an Augustinian friar but, as he explains in *Eachtra an Brathar Ultaigh* (nd, 'The Spoilt Priest'), was expelled due to an alleged association with a woman; in *An Cassideach Ban* (nd, 'Cassidy the White') he argues 'All I got was the edge of the rug'. He wandered around Ireland as an 'itinerant story-teller' and bard before joining the French army in the 1730s. He deserted, was taken by '*sgiobuirigh*' (kidnappers) in Hamburg, but escaped (by 'a bird-like leap') from a third-floor window. He eventually returned to Ireland, and spent the remainder of his life there.

▷A de Blacam, *Gaelic Literature Surveyed* (1929; reprinted 1973)

Ó'MAOIL CHONAIRE, Flaithri

(1560–29)

Irish scholar, translator and priest, an expert on the work of **St Augustine**. His chief work is his adaptation of the anonymous Catalan allegorical novel *El desseoso* (1515), as *Desiderius* (1616, modern edn 1941). This is the chief devotional work in Irish of its century.

OMAR KHAYYÁM

(c.1048–c.1122)

Persian poet, mathematician and astronomer, born in Níshápūr. His father was a tent-maker, hence his surname. He was well educated, particularly in the sciences and philosophy, in his home town and in Balkh. Later he went to Samarkand where he completed a seminal work on algebra. Consequently he was invited by Seljuq sultan Malik-Sháh to make the necessary astronomical observations for the reform of the calendar, and collaborated on an observatory in Isfahan. When his patron died in 1092 he made a pilgrimage to Mecca, on his return from which he served at the court as an astrologer. In his own country and time he was known for his scientific achievements but in the English-speaking world he is indelibly associated with the collection of *robátyát*, or quatrains, attributed to him. As a poet he had attracted little attention until **Edward Fitzgerald** translated and arranged the fugitive pieces into *The Rubáiyát of Omar Khayyám*, first published anonymously in 1859. Replete with memorable sayings, they have been translated into all the world's major languages and have influenced Western ideas about Persian poetry. Though some questioned their authorship, it has been established that at least 250 *robátyát* were the work of Omar.

▷A Dashti, *In Search of Omar Khayyám* (1971)

ONDAATJE, (Philip) Michael

(1943–)

Canadian poet and novelist. He was born in Ceylon and emigrated to Canada in 1962, in the footsteps of his brother. Two decades later, he portrayed his aristocratic and eccentric relatives in the beguiling memoir, *Running in the Family* (1982), displaying the same touch of surrealism that had marked his early verse collections. The first was *The Dainty Monsters* (1967), followed by *The Man With Seven Toes* (1969) and the prize-winning sequence *The Collected Works of Billy the Kid: Left Handed Poems* (1970), which mixed documentary fact with fantasy, and involved elements of prose writing. In that same year, Ondaatje wrote a critical study of the lyricist and novelist **Leonard Cohen**, which clarified some of his own literary concerns. The collected poems of the 1960s and 70s appeared as *There's a Trick With a Knife I'm Learning to Do* (1979, published in the UK as *Rat Jelly and Other Poems*, 1980) but by this time he was turning increasingly to prose. *Coming Through Slaughter* (1976) was a dreamlike reconstruction of the life of the semi-mythical jazz cornetist Buddy Bolden. Later novels included the more conventional *In the Skin of a Lion* (1987) and the hauntingly lyrical *The English Patient* (1991), for which he shared the Booker Prize with **Barry Unsworth**. Ondaatje has directed several films and is editor of the *Faber Book of Canadian Short Stories* (1990).

O'NEACHTAIN, Seán
(c.1650–1729)

Irish Gaelic poet, born in County Roscommon, Connaught, in the west of Ireland. In 1690 he moved with his family to Dublin, where much of his subsequent life was spent combining writing poetry with a professional career as a schoolmaster in the midlands of County Meath. His work in prose and rhyme is singular in its use of bilingual and transcultural puns. In the autobiographical *Stuir Eamonn Ui Chleiri* (nd, 'The Story of Eamonn O'Cleary'), for example, '*bhui le Dia*' literally means 'thanks be to God', but it can also mean 'yellow with God'—the apostate writer is in fact giving thanks for a gift of butter. In a wooing poem to Una Ni Bhroin O'Neachtain tells her 'water will be your music while the otters and fish cleverly wrestle together'; suprisingly, she did become his wife. He died quietly, and content.
▷S Deane (ed), *The Field Day Anthology of Irish Writing: Vol 1* (1991)

O'NEILL, Alexandre
(1924–)

Portuguese poet, born in Lisbon. He was a founder of the first (1947) Surrealist group in Portugal: this provided a way for poets both to mock Salazar's steely dictatorship and simultaneously to steer clear of its philistine censors, who believed that such writers were insane and harmless purveyors of literal nonsense. He has perhaps been praised above his powers by some Portuguese critics—he has none of the profundity of **Sá-Carneiro** or **Fernando Pessoa**; but he provided humorous delight and salutary satirical abilities at a time when these were desperately needed.

O'NEILL, Eugene Gladstone
(1888–1953)

American playwright, winner of the Nobel Prize for literature, born in New York, the son of the actor James O'Neill (1847–1920).

After a fragmentary education and a year at Princeton, he took various clerical and journalistic jobs and signed on as a sailor on voyages to Australia, South Africa and elsewhere. Then he contracted tuberculosis and spent six months in a sanatorium, where he felt the urge to write plays, the first being *The Web* (1914). He joined the Provincetown Players in 1915, for whom *Beyond the Horizon* (1920; Pulitzer Prize) was written. This was followed, during the next two years, by *Exorcism* (1920), *Diff'rent* (1920), *The Emperor Jones* (1921), *Anna Christie* (1922; Pulitzer Prize) and *The Hairy Ape* (1922). *Desire Under the Elms*, his most mature play to date, appeared in 1924. He then began experimenting in new dramatic techniques; in *The Great God Brown* (1926) he used masks to emphasize the differing relationships between a man, his family and his soul. *Marco Millions* (1931) is a satire on tycoonery. *Strange Interlude* (1928; Pulitzer Prize), a marathon nine-acter, lasting five hours, uses asides, soliloquies and 'streams of consciousness'. In the same year he wrote *Lazarus Laughed*, a humanistic affirmation of his belief in the conquest of death. *Mourning Becomes Electra* (1931) is a re-statement of the Orestean tragedy in terms of biological and psychological cause and effect. *Ah, Wilderness*, a nostalgic comedy, appeared in 1933 and *Days Without End* in 1934. Then, for 12 years he released no more plays but worked on *The Iceman Cometh* (New York 1946, London 1958) and *A Moon for the Misbegotten* (1947). The former is a gargantuan, broken-backed, repetitive parable about the dangers of shattering illusions. It is impressive by its sheer weight and redeemed by O'-Neill's never-failing sense of the theatre. *Long Day's Journey into Night* (1957; Pulitzer Prize), probably his masterpiece, whose tragic Tyrone family is closely based on O'Neill's early life, *Hughie* (1964) and *A Touch of the Poet* (1957) were published posthumously. He was awarded the Nobel Prize for literature in 1936, the first American dramatist to be thus honoured.
▷L Sheaffer, *Eugene O'Neill: son and playwright* (1968); *Eugene O'Neill: son and artist* (1973)

ONERVA, L, pseud of Hilja Onerva Lehtinen
(1882–1972)

Finnish poet, novelist, biographer (of, notably, **Leino**) and translator (from French poetry), born in Helsinki. She was a leading figure in the earlier part of the century, and remained respected until her death.

ONETTI, Juan Carlos
(1909–94)

Uruguayan novelist and short-story writer, born in Montevideo. He left school early and, following a succession of menial jobs, became a full-time writer in 1939, when he began working for the magazine *Marcha*. That year saw the publication of his short novel *El Pozo* ('The Well'), now recognized as a masterpiece. He moved to Buenos Aires shortly after. His next novel, *Tierra de Nadie* (1941, 'No Man's Land'), was the first of his works to be set in a fictional fusion of Buenos Aires and Montevideo, and as such is an important landmark in the creation of a modern, urban Latin American literature. He returned to his homeland in 1954, but left 20 years later for Spain after having been imprisoned by the military government. His short-story collections include *Un Sueño Realizado y otros cuentos* (1951, 'A Dream Comes True and other stories'). He has been described as 'the greatest urban novelist of our century'.

ONO NO KOMACHI
(c.810–c.880)

Japanese poet, born, probably, in Kyoto in the classical period of Japanese literature. Like many of the other great figures of classical literature in Japan, she was a court poet, writing in a rarefied form of the vernacular—it was more common for men to write in a form of Chinese, which is why so much surviving classical Japanese literature is by women (see **Shikibu Murasaki**). She is known in Japan as one of the Six Poetic Geniuses, the supreme writer of the verse form *tanka*
▷H C McCullough, *Ise Monogatari. Tales of Ise: Lyrical Episodes from Tenth Century Japan* (1968)

ONOFRI, Arturo
(1885–1928)

Italian poet and critic, born in Rome. His later work was much influenced by his interest in the anthroposophy of **Rudolph Steiner**. He is a difficult but rewarding poet, whose work **Sanguineti** represents fully in his important anthology *Poesia italiana del Novocento* (1969–71, '20th-century Italian Poetry').

ONSTOTT, Kyle *see* HORNER, Lance

OODGEROO, Noonuccal Moongalba,
originally **Kath(leen Jean) Walker**
(1920–93)

Australian Aboriginal artist and writer, born in Brisbane, Queensland, and brought up with the Noonuccal tribe on Stradbroke Island, Queensland. From the age of 13 she worked in domestic service in Brisbane, gaining her education mainly from the libraries of her employers. She joined the Australian Women's Army Service during World War II, and afterwards became involved in aboriginal

activism. In 1964 she became the first aboriginal writer to be published, with her collection of poems *We are Going*, followed by *The Dawn is at Hand* (1966). With other works these were republished in 1970 as *My People, a Kath Walker Collection*. In 1972 she published a book of aboriginal stories, *Stradbroke Dreamtime*. She won a number of awards, including the **Mary Gilmore** Medal. She visited the USA on a Fulbright Scholarship from 1978 to 1979, lecturing on aboriginal rights, and was active on many aboriginal interest committees including the Aboriginal Arts Board. In 1985 she published *Quandamooka, the art of Kath Walker*. She also ran a Centre for Aboriginal Culture, for children of all races, on Stradbroke Island. Australian composer Malcolm Williamson has set some of her poems for choir and orchestra: *The Dawn is at Hand* was premiered in 1989. In 1988 she adopted the aboriginal name Oodgeroo of the tribe Noonuccal.

OOKA Shohei
(1909–)

Japanese diarist and novelist, famed in Japan for his vivid and chilling account of fighting and being captured by the Americans during World War II, and for his novel *Nobi* (1951, Eng trans *Fires on the Plain*, 1957), which has also achieved a reputation in the West. *Nobi* is similar in tone to **William Golding**'s *Lord of the Flies*, in that it details what happens when a society breaks down, but, unlike Golding's book, it is based on personal experience.

OPATOSHU, Josef, originally **Josef Opatofski**
(1887–1954)

Yiddish novelist, born in Mlava in Poland, and died in New York, where he had gone in 1907. Until **Isaac Bashevis Singer**, his were the most powerful historical novels in his language. Indeed, he introduced the form. His trilogy about life in 19th-century Poland, *In Pollishe velder*, is largely episodic, and is hardly a novel by Singer's standards, but is nonetheless vivid and masterful. *A tog in Regensburg* (1933, Eng trans *A Day in Regensburg* 1968), on Jewish life in 16th-century Germany, is more coherent as a single work. His complete works in Yiddish were published in 14 volumes in New York (1928–36).
▷C A Madison, *Yiddish Literature* (1968)

OPIE, Amelia
(1769–1853)

English novelist and poet, born in Norwich. Despite having espoused radical political and social opinions, marrying the painter John Opie and becoming a friend of **Mary Wollstonecraft Shelley**, Opie produced several sensational but sternly moralizing novels. These include *Father and Daughter* (1801), in which a girl's seduction results in her father's madness, and *Adeline Mowbray, or The Mother and Daughter* (1804), in which a woman lives bitterly to regret rejecting an opportunity to marry. Her final novel, *Madeline*, appeared in 1822. After the death of her husband, Opie became a Quaker, abandoned her writing and devoted much of her time to good works, including the Bible and Anti-Slavery Societies.

OPITZ, Martin, or OPITZ VON BOBERFELD
(1597–1639)

German poet, born in Bunzlau in Silesia. The founder of the Silesian school of poets, he wrote a plea for the purification of the German language in *Aristarchus sive de contemptu linguae Teutonicae* (1617, written in Latin) and other works. In 1620 he fled to Holland to escape war and the plague, but still fell victim to that terrible disease. His didactic poems are cold and formal and lacking in feeling. His works include translations from classical authors (**Sophocles** and **Seneca**), the Dutchmen Daniel Heinsius and Grotius, and from the Bible. He also wrote a prose translation of **Ottavio Rinuccini**'s *Daphne* (1627), which formed the basis of the first German opera in 1627.
▷J Gellinek, *Martin Opitz* (1973)

OPPEN, George
(1908–84)

American poet and publisher, whose career was profoundly affected by radical politics (and by the McCarthyite backlash of the 1950s). In the early 1930s, he and his wife co-founded The Objectivist Press, which published some of the most advanced poetry of the time, and took its name from **Louis Zukofsky**'s 1932 anthology; it was in this vein that Oppen wrote his first collection, *Discrete Series* (1934), which was sparse, taciturn and imagistic. His literary career was interrupted at that point. Oppen became a factory hand and union organizer in Detroit, served as an infantryman in World War II and was indicted by the House Un-American Activities Committee in 1950; he avoided prison by moving to Mexico and did not return to the US until Senator Joe McCarthy's death in 1957. He also began to write again and a second volume, *The Materials*, appeared in 1962, followed by *This in Which* (1965) and the Pulitzer Prize-winning *Of Being Numerous* (1968). A *Collected Poems* was published in 1975.

OPPENHEIM, Edward Phillips
(1866–1946)

English novelist, born in London. He had his first book published in 1887 and went on to become a pioneer of the novel of espionage and diplomatic intrigue. Among his best are *Mr Grex of Monte Carlo* (1915), *Kingdom of the Blind* (1917), *The Great Impersonation* (1920) and *Envoy Extraordinary* (1937).
▷R Standish, *The Prince of Story-Tellers* (1957)

Ó RATHAILLE, Aodhagán (Little Hugh O'Rahilly)
(1670–?1730)

Classical Irish Gaelic poet, born in Kerry on lands formerly ruled by the MacCarthy earls of Clancarty, whose memory he idolized as a descendant of their hereditary bards. His poetry embodies the great Jacobite lament for the overthrow of Catholic Gaelic Ireland, much of it realized in rich lyrical and elegant development of the *Aisling* (patriotic dreamvision). Although essentially oral, his Gaelic poems survived in part and were edited for the Irish Texts Society bilingually (1900, rev edn 1911). His death date is unknown, usual estimates being based on a poem avowedly written on his death-bed which shows not the slightest sign of diminution of powers of proficiency, intricacy, beauty or invective.
▷P Ua Duinnin, introduction to *Collected Poetry* (1900–11)

ORCZY, Baroness (Emma Magdalena Rosalie Marie Josefa Barbara)
(1865–1947)

Hungarian-born British novelist and playwright, born in Tarnaörs, the daughter of a musician. *The Scarlet Pimpernel* (1905) was the first success in the Baroness's long writing career. It was followed by many popular adventure romances, including *The Elusive Pimpernel* (1908) and *Mam'zelle Guillotine* (1940), which never quite attained the success of her early work.
▷ *Links in the Chain of Life* (1947)

O'REILLY, Dowell Philip
(1865–1923)

Australian poet and writer, born in Sydney, who worked variously as a teacher and public servant, and was for four years a member of the NSW Legislative Assembly. He published little work; his verse included *Australian Poems* (1894) and *A Pedlar's Pack* (1888) but, disappointed by poor sales, he destroyed the remaining copies. There was a novel, *Tears and Triumph*, in 1913, and a collection of short stories, *Five Corners* in 1920. The best of his work was collected in 1924 as *The Prose and Verse of Dowell O'Reilly*. In 1927 his second wife, his cousin Mollie Miles, published his courtship letters to her in *Dowell O'Reilly from his Letters*. He was the father of **Eleanor Dark**.

Ó RÍORDÁIN, Seán
(1916–77)

Irish Gaelic poet. Born into the bilingual community of Ballyvorney, County Cork, he worked as a tax-inspector until his retirement in 1965. From 1967 his pungent column in *The Irish Times* became an important focus of debate within Gaelic-speaking circles. Published from the 1940s onwards, his five collections of poems are small and slim evidence of the major influence he had on three generations of writers. His powerful, minimal verses have proved difficult to translate and appear to greatest advantage in English in Sean Dunne's *Poets of Munster* (1985).

ORIXE see ORMAECHEA, Nicolás de

ORMAECHEA, Nicolás de
(1888–1961)

Basque poet who used the pseudonym 'Orixe'. He translated the novel *Lazarillo de Tormes*, and wrote a long account in verse of the Basque people, and their history, called *Euskaldunak* (1950). It is not a great poem, but is certainly indispensable for those who wish to understand the Basque people. He was a close friend to **Lizardi**, some of whose qualities he shared.
▷R Gallop, *A Book of the Basques* (1930); L Michelena, *Historia de la literatura vasca* (1960)

ORMOND, John
(1923 90)

Welsh poet and film-maker, born in Dunvant, near Swansea, and educated at University College, Swansea. After training as a journalist he joined BBC Wales in 1957 as a director and producer of documentary films, including studies of Welsh painters and writers such as Ceri Richards, **Dylan Thomas**, **Alun Lewis** and **R S Thomas**. He himself established a reputation as a fine Anglo–Welsh poet.
▷Autobiography in M Stephens, *Artists in Wales* (1973)

ORTEGA Y GASSET, José
(1883–1955)

Spanish critic, journalist and philosopher, born in Madrid, son of a well-known novelist. Although not himself a creative writer, he had an effect greater than **Unamuno** on his country's literary practice. He studied in Germany, and picked up proto-existentialist ideas from teachers such as Hermann Cohen. He came, prophetically, to believe that

Spain's future lay in Europeanization; as a politician in the Cortes in the years immediately preceding the Civil War he made proposals which, had they been accepted, could have led to peace—the decrying of him as proto-fascist has no foundation. He left Spain between 1936 and 1946, and never lived there permanently again. Two of his seminal books are *Meditaciones del Quixote* (1914, Eng trans *Meditations on Quixote*, 1961) and *La dehumanización del arte* (1948, Eng trans *The Dehumanization of Art*, 1948). In these he brought a phenomenological attitude to bear upon literary problems, and anticipated every single modern critical concept, particularly those of structuralism and deconstruction. He early saw that critics are quite unable to eliminate subjectivity from their interpretations of texts, and made proposals to deal practically with this. His best-known work in *La rebelión de las masas* (1930, Eng trans *The Revolt of the Masses*, 1932), often mistakenly taken as a right-wing and élitist document, is a masterly analysis of the 20th-century situation, in which the masses have revolted against minorities. He corrected any possible ambiguities inherent in this book in his posthumous *El hombre y la gente* (1957, Eng trans *Man and People*, 1957). He has radically influenced the majority of Spanish writers of his time and after him.
▷J F Mora, *Ortega y Gasset* (1963); R McClintock, *Man and His Circumstances* (1971)

ORTESE, Anna-Maria
(1915–)

Italian novelist and journalist, born in Rome. Her work was praised by **Bontempelli** and **Vittorini**, who became her mentor. Her first publication (1937) was a collection of surrealistic stories. She is best known, however, for her mythic treatment of Italy's southern cities, *Il mare non bagna Napoli* (1953, Eng trans *The Bay is Not Naples*, 1955), which received the Viareggio Prize, and for *Poveri e semplici* (1967, 'Poor and Simple People'), set in Milan, which won the Strega Prize.

ORTIZ, Simon
(1941–)

American writer, born in Albuquerque, New Mexico. Ortiz grew up in Acoma in New Mexico, in a family deeply rooted in the Pueblo's religious and artistic traditions, and much of his work is concerned with the importance of cultural survival for Native American peoples, especially those of the Southwest where he has lived most of his life. His first major poetry collection, *Going for the Rain* (1976), was followed by *A Good Journey* (1977), containing poems rich in details of everyday life in Acoma. Ortiz's military experiences during the Vietnam era informed the cycle of poems that comprise *From Sand Creek: Rising in This Heart Which is Our America* (1981); set in a Colorado veterans' hospital, the poems juxtapose descriptions of the 1864 massacre of Sand Creek with accounts of military atrocities in Vietnam. Ortiz has also written many short stories, included in *Howbah Indians* (1978) and *Fightin': New and Collected Stories* (1983). *Fight Back: For the Sake of the People, For the Sake of the Land* (1980) is a mixture of poems and essays depicting the lives of Pueblos, Navajos and Whites working in New Mexico's uranium industry, and stresses the need for inter-ethnic recognition and respect. Ortiz has also written two books for children—*The People Shall Continue* (1977) and *Blue and Red* (1982). More recently, he has published *After and Before the Lightning* (1991), a collection of poems inspired by the starkly beautiful landscape and harshness of life in South Dakota where he lived for some years.

▷ A Wiget, *Simon Ortiz* (1986)

ORTON, Joe, originally **John Kingsley** (1933–67)

English dramatist, born in Leicester. After training as an actor, he turned to writing vivid, outrageous farces, beginning with *The Ruffian on the Stair* (1963) and *Entertaining Mr Sloan* (1964). Subsequent plays include *Loot* (1966), *The Erpingham Camp* (1966) and *What the Butler Saw* (1969). He was murdered by his lover, failed artist Kenneth Halliwell, who subsequently killed himself.

▷ J Lahr, *Prick Up Your Ears* (1978)

ORWELL, George, pseud of **Eric Arthur Blair**
(1903–50)

English novelist and essayist, born in Motihari in Bengal. He was educated at Eton, served in Burma in the Indian Imperial Police from 1922 to 1927 (later recalled in 1935 in the novel *Burmese Days*), and then literally went *Down and Out in Paris and London* (1933), making an occasional living as tutor or bookshop assistant. In 1935 he became a small country shopkeeper, and published two novels, *A Clergyman's Daughter* (1935) and *Keep the Aspidistra Flying* (1936). *Coming Up for Air* (1939) is a plea for the small man against big business. He fought and was wounded in the Spanish Civil War and he developed his own brand of socialism in *The Road to Wigan Pier* (1937), *Homage to Catalonia* (1938) and *The Lion and the Unicorn* (1941). During World War II, he was war correspondent for the BBC and *The Observer*, and wrote for *Tribune*. His intellectual honesty motivated his biting satire of communist ideology in *Animal Farm* (1945), which was

made into a cartoon film; and the terrifying prophecy for mankind in *Nineteen Eighty-Four* (1949), the triumph of the scientifically-perfected servile state, the extermination of political freedom by thought-control and an ideologically delimited basic language of *newspeak* in which 'thought crime is death'. Other penetrating collections of essays include *Inside the Whale* (1940) and *Shooting an Elephant* (1950); his *Collected Essays* appeared in four volumes in 1968.

▷ B Crick, *Orwell: a life* (1979)

ORZESKOWA, Eliza
(1841–1910)

Polish realistic novelist, whose notable work is mostly associated with the area around Grodno, where she was born. She was one of the most educated women of her time, largely owing to her enlightened father's library. She was associated with the 'Positivist' movement—a reaction to the 'romanticism' which had led to the failed uprisings of 1863–4—and her huge fictional output deals with 'ordinary people'; but she gradually became more idealistic. As a whole, her work, which has been undervalued until recently, may be compared to that of **Balzac**: a huge 'Polish Comedy'. She dealt with women, Jews, and—adeptly—with political censors. Novels available in English include *Meir Ezofowicz* (1878, Eng trans *An Obscure Apostle*, 1898), *Argonauci* (1899, Eng trans *The Modern Argonauts*, 1901) and *Piesn Przerwana* (1896, Eng trans *The Interrupted Melody*, 1912). Her books remain eminently readable.

OSARAGI Jiro, pseud of **Koyohiko Nojiro**
(1897–1973)

Japanese novelist, living in Tokyo, who is principally remembered as the author of a long and very popular series of historical adventure novels featuring the anti-hero Kurama Tengu. A sort of Robin Hood figure with a gift for swordplay and an extremely gloomy outlook—possibly a result of Osaragi's wartime experiences in the army—Tengu travels medieval Japan righting wrongs but not feeling very good about it. *Kikyo* is available in translation as *The Homecoming*, *Tabiji* as *The Journey*. They are, by Japanese standards, rattling good reads.

OSBORNE, John James
(1929–)

Welsh playwright and actor, son of a commercial artist. He left Belmont College, Devon, at 16 and became a copywriter for trade journals. Hating it, he turned actor (1948) and by 1955 was playing leading roles in new plays at the Royal Court Theatre. There his fourth play, *Look Back in Anger*

(1956; filmed 1958), and *The Entertainer* (1957; filmed 1960), with Sir Laurence Olivier playing Archie Rice, established Osborne as the leading young exponent of British social drama. The 'hero' of the first, Jimmy Porter, the prototype 'Angry Young Man', as well as the pathetic, mediocre music hall joker Archie Rice, both echo the author's uncompromising hatred of outworn social and political institutions and attitudes. An earlier play, *Epitaph for George Dillon*, written in collaboration with Anthony Creighton and exploring the moral problems of the would-be literary genius, was also staged in 1957. Among other works are *Luther* (1960), *Inadmissible Evidence* (1965), *Time Present* and *The Hotel in Amsterdam* (1968), and the filmscript of *Tom Jones*, which won him an Oscar. He wrote his credo in *Declarations* (1957), and two volumes of autobiography, *A Better Class of Person* (1981) and *Almost a Gentleman* (1991).

▷ S Trussler, *The Plays of John Osborne* (1969)

OSBOURNE, Lloyd
(1868–1947)

American writer, born in San Francisco. He was the son of Fanny Osbourne (née Vandegrift, 1840–1914) and stepson of **Robert Louis Stevenson**. He collaborated with Stevenson on several books, including *The Wrong Box* (1889), *The Wrecker* (1892) and *The Ebb Tide* (1894). He became American vice-consul in Samoa, and published several books of his own including *An Intimate Portrait of RLS* (1925).

▷ *Memoirs of Vailima* (1902)

O'SHAUGHNESSY, Arthur William Edgar
(1844–81)

English poet, born in London. In 1861 he began work in the British Museum, moving to the natural history department in 1863. An associate of the Pre-Raphaelites, he published *An Epic of Women* (1870), *Lays of France* (1872), *Music and Moonlight* (1874) and *Songs of a Worker* (1881). His best-known poem is 'The Music-Makers'.

OSKISON, John Milton
(1874–1947)

American novelist, short-story writer, biographer and journalist, born in Vinita, Indian Territory (now Oklahoma). Of mixed Cherokee and White descent, Oskison's Native American background was largely unknown to his readership at the time. His many short stories, written at the turn of the century and published in popular magazines, and his novels of the 1920s and 30s—*Wild Harvest* (1925), *Black Jack Davy* (1926) and *Brothers Three* (1935)—are all set in Cherokee Indian Territory, but differ in their emphases and style: whereas the stories often concentrate on Native American characters and make use of regional dialect, the novels follow the genre of the frontier romance and portray the lives of White settlers. His best novel is generally thought to be his last, a semi-autobiographical story of three mixed-blood brothers, with its theme of spiritual renewal through closeness to the land. Oskison also wrote biographies of the Texas statesman Sam Houston and the Shawnee chief, Tecumseh.

▷ D F Littlefield, Jr and J W Parins, 'Short Fiction Writers of the Indian Territory', in *American Studies 23:1* (1982)

OSSIAN, or Oisín Mac Fhinn Mhic Cumhail Mhic Tréanmóir Uí Baoisne

Legendary Gaelic bard and warrior, the son of Finn (Fingal). After many years' service in the *Fianna*, or sworn band of heroes, he departed for *Tír na n-Óg*, the land of perpetual youth, with its queen, Niamh Chinn Óir, from whom he returned after 300 years to age catastrophically and, after extended acrimony, to be converted to Christianity by St Patrick. Oral ballads, lyrics and prose ascribed to him, and a disputation supposedly recorded between Patrick and himself, were circulated in Ireland and Scotland, but the texts are probably from the 2nd century. The *Ossian* of **James Macpherson** supposes a coherence and royal status lacking in the original, since after Ossian's departure his father Fionn and his followers were finally defeated by the actual King of Ireland (or Tara), Cairbre Lifeachar, son of the Fianna's former suzerain, Cormac Mac Airt. The Fionn of Ossianic folklore had the intellectual's moral ambiguity also found in contrasting Odysseus myths: Macpherson's Fingal was of impeachable but interesting probity.

OSTROVSKY, Alexander
(1823–85)

Russian dramatist, born in Moscow. He studied law, but joined the civil service. He became director of a school of drama in 1885 and was given the task of choosing the repertoire for the Moscow Imperial Theatres. His own dramas are mainly domestic in nature, although he also looked at the darker side of official life, and his later work included historical dramas, and a fairy tale, *Snegurochka* (1873, 'Snow Maiden'), which Rimsky-Korsakov later used as the basis for his opera. His best-known play is *The Storm* (1860; Eng trans 1899).

▷ M Hoover, *Alexander Ostrovsky* (1981)

Ó SÚILLEABHÁIN, Eoghan Ruadh (Red Owen O'Sullivan)
(1748–84)

Irish Gaelic poet, born in County Kerry. He symbolizes the last phase of native Irish vernacular poetry. He was variously a teacher in proscribed Catholic ('hedge') schools, an itinerant labourer, a sailor serving with Rodney in the West Indies, a British soldier, and at all times an insatiable lover. His work followed Irish patriotic poetic traditions, and obvious parallels exist with his contemporary **Robert Burns**; and **W B Yeats**'s 'Red Hanrahan' was based on him, as is 'Owen MacCarthy' in Thomas Flanagan's *The Year of the French* (1979).
▷ D Corkery, in *The Hidden Ireland* (1924)

O'SULLIVAN, Vincent
(1937–)

New Zealand poet and critic, who has also written novels and short stories. His first verse was *Our Burning Time* (1965), followed by *Revenants* (1969). A black humour is uppermost in the series of 'Butcher' poems: *Butcher & Co* (1977) and *The Butcher Papers* (1982), and a satiric edge in *Brother Jonathan, Brother Kafka* (1980) and *The Pilate Tapes* (1986). He has also written a novel, *Let the River Stand* (1993); his short-story collections include *Dandy Edison for Lunch and Other Stories* (1981) and *The Snow in Spain* (1990), while drama includes work for radio and television in *Ordinary Nights in Ward Ten* (1984) and a stage play *Shuriken* (1983), dealing with cultural conflicts in a camp for Japanese prisoners-of-war during World War II. He is perhaps best-known for his editing of the Oxford *Anthology of Twentieth-Century New Zealand Poetry* (1970, rev edns 1976, 1987).

OSWALD VON WOLKENSTEIN
(1377–1445)

Austrian (Tyrolese) poet, a Minnesinger. Of aristocratic birth, he led an exceedingly adventurous life—he escaped from his home at the age of 10, to follow the Austrian army into Prussia, and was later imprisoned, by a trap she set for him, in the dungeon of the woman he loved. Many have enjoyed his varied work because in it 'there is more zest than discrimination', and because of his 'strongly sensual and turbulent nature' (as critics have expressed it). His directness and liveliness made him one of the most gifted German poets of his age, as well as one of the most technically accomplished. He invigorated his courtly themes with folk-song elements, and was a talented composer, many of whose melodies have survived.
▷ *London Medieval Studies for F. Norman* (1965)

OTCENÁSEKK, Jan
(1924–)

Czech novelist, born in Prague. He had a success with *Romeo a tma* (1958, Eng trans *Romeo and Juliet and The Darkness*, 1960), a wartime tale of a man's love for a Jewish girl in Nazi-occupied Prague, but his earlier *Obcan Brych* (1955), an attempt to reconcile conscience and communism, was reckoned by most to have been an over-ambitious failure.

OTERO, Blas de
(1916–79)

Spanish poet, born in Bilbao, the leading member of the so-called Generation of '36, the inferior successor to those of '98 and '27. His poetry has aptly been described as moving from the influence of **Miguel Hernández** to that of **Léon Felipe**. His poetry was more effectively lyrical than that of his contemporaries, was carefully wrought, and much respected. Poems in English translation are *Twenty Poems* (1964) and *Miguel Hernández and Blas de Otero: Selected Poems* (1972).

OTHÓN, Manuel José
(1858–1906)

Mexican poet and playwright, born in San Luis Potosí. He reacted against *modernismo*, being too mature in outlook to fall for its sugariness. In his outstanding collection *Poemas rústicos 1890–1902* (1902) he expressed his pantheistic beliefs in a manner which Mexico had never seen and will never see again. Then, in *Idilio salvaje* (1905, Eng trans 'Wild Idyll' by **Samuel Beckett** in *Translations of Mexican Poetry*, 1959), he recorded, in seven sonnets, his love for a young girl, which are amongst the great love poems of the 20th century.
▷ B Dromundo, *Manuel José Othón: su vida y su obra* (1959)

OTTLEY, Reginald Leslie
(1909–)

English-born Australian writer for children, born in London. His first book, *By the Sandhills of Yamboorah* (1965), won a New York *Herald Tribune* prize in the following year. It was followed by *The Roan Colt of Yamboorah* (1966) and the trilogy was completed with *Rain Comes to Yamboorah* in 1967. Seven other books appeared between 1968 and 1974, and a book of short stories, *Brumbie Dust*, in 1969.

OTWAY, Thomas
(1652–85)

English dramatist, born in Trotton in Sussex. From Winchester he passed in 1669 to Christ

Church, Oxford. He left the university without a degree in 1672, failed utterly as an actor, but made a fair hit with his tragedy *Alcibiades* (1675). In it the actress Elizabeth Barry made her first appearance, and Otway is said to have fallen in love with her. In 1676 Betterton accepted his *Don Carlos*, a good tragedy in rhyme. In 1677 Otway translated **Racine**'s *Bérénice*, as well as **Molière**'s *Cheats of Scapin*. In 1678–9 he was in Flanders as a soldier; in the May of the former year appeared his coarse but diverting comedy, *Friendship in Fashion*. The year 1680 yielded two tragedies, *The Orphan* and *Caius Marius*, and his one important poem, *The Poet's Complaint of his Muse*; to 1681 belongs *The Soldier's Fortune*. His greatest work, *Venice Preserved, or a Plot Discovered* (1682), is a masterpiece of tragic passion. For a time he sinks out of sight, to reappear again in 1684 with *The Atheist*, a feeble comedy, and in February 1685 with *Windsor Castle*, a poem addressed to the new king, James VII and II. He died in poverty. In 1719 a badly edited tragedy, *Heroick Friendship*, was published as his.
▷ E Rothstein, *Restoration Tragedy* (1967)

OUIDA, pseud of Marie Louise de la Ramée
(1839–1908)

English popular novelist, born in Bury St Edmunds. Her mother was English, her father a French teacher. 'Ouida' was a childish mispronunciation of 'Louise'. Educated in Paris, she settled in London in 1857. Starting her career by contributing stories to magazines, in particular to *Bentley's Miscellany* (1859–60), her first success was *Held in Bondage* (1863), shortly followed by *Strathmore* (1865), another three-decker aimed at the circulating libraries. She was soon established as a writer of hot-house romances, often ridiculed for her opulent settings, preposterous heroes and improbable plots, as well as for her ignorance of male sports and occupations. But her narratives were powerful and readers responded to her emotional energy and until her popularity waned in the 1890s she was a bestseller. From 1860 she spent much time in Italy and in 1874 settled in Florence where she lived lavishly in a style recognizable from her novels. She wrote almost 50 books, mainly novels, such as *Under Two Flags* (1867), *Folle-Farine* (1871) which was praised by **Edward Bulwer-Lytton**, *Two Little Wooden Shoes* (1874), *A Village Commune* (1881) and *In Maremma* (1882)—but also animal stories, essays and tales for children. Latterly her royalties dried up. She fell into debt, moved to Lucca in 1894, and her last years in Viareggio were spent in destitution.
▷ E Bigland, *Ouida* (1950)

OUOLOGUEM, Yambo
(c.1930–)

Mali poet, novelist, author of school textbooks, of Dogon ancestry, who was well known for his angry early poem 'When Negro Teeth Speak'. His best-known novel is *De Devoir de violence* (1968, Eng trans *Bound to Violence*, 1971); the pornographic *Les Milles et une bibles du sexe* (1969, 'The Thousand and One Bibles of Sex') has yet to find a translator.

OUSMANE, Sembene
(1923–)

Senegalese Francophone novelist and maker of films. The son of a fisherman, a militant socialist, he has been one of the most persistent and best known of his country's writers. He is not, like **Kane** or **Laye**, an elegant stylist, but—as in his first book, *Le Docker noir* (1956, 'The Black Docker'), set in Marseilles in the later 1930s—gives it to his reader hot and strong, in the tradition of **Zola**. *Les Bouts de bois de Dieu* (1960, Eng trans *God's Bits of Wood*, 1970) is generally regarded as his finest book. It is centred on the great strike of African railwaymen on the Dakar–Niger line in 1947–8, and has much of the power of Zola at his best.
▷ A C Brench, *The Novelists' Inheritance in French Africa* (1967); W Cartey, *Whispers from a Continent* (1969)

OUSPENSKY, Peter
(1878–1947)

Unorthodox but highly influential Russian philosopher (in the **Soloviev** tradition, but with more lucidity), who became a student of **Gurdjieff** in 1914, and eventually broke off relations with him in order to teach his own version of Gurdjieff's doctrine in London and America. He wrote several works of fiction, including *Strange Life of Ivan Osokin* (1947). His *In Search of the Miraculous* (1949) has been one of the most widely read religious books of the post-war period. His theories about time are behind both the 'time plays' of **Priestley** and the *Four Quartets* of **T S Eliot**.
▷ M Nicoll, *Living Time* (1949)

ØVERLAND, Arnulf
(1889–1968)

Norwegian poet, born in Kristiansund. He wrote radical poetry in volumes such as *Brød og vin* (1919, 'Bread and Wine') and *Berget det Blå* (1937, 'The Blue Rock'). A committed anti-fascist and socialist, he wrote *Den røde front* (1937, 'The Red Front'), which contained the famous warning 'You must not sleep', and circulated Resistance poetry during the German occupation of Norway, for which he was imprisoned in a concentration camp. His post-war verse was more philosophical in tone.

▷C Hambro, *Arnulf Øverland* (1984)

OVID (Publius Ovidius Naso)
(43 BC–?17 AD)

Roman poet, born in Sulmo (Solmona), in the Abruzzi, son of a well-to-do *eques*. He was trained for the law in Rome, but gave his whole energies to poetry. His first literary success was his collection of love poems, the *Amores* ('Loves'). Then came his *Heroides* ('Heroines'), imaginary love letters from ladies of the heroic days to their lords. The *Ars Amandi*, or *Ars Amatoria* ('The Art of Love'), a handbook of seduction, appeared about 1 BC, followed by the equally outrageous *Remedia Amoris* ('Cures for Love'). His second period of poetic activity opens with the *Metamorphoses*, a collection of mythological and near-magical tales in 15 books, and with the *Fasti* ('Calendar'), designed to be in 12, of which six only were completed. Midway in composition he was banished by Augustus (AD8), for some unknown reason, to Tomis (Constanza) on the Black Sea, where he died. On his way from Rome he began his third period with the elegies which he published in five books, the *Tristia* ('Sorrows'). Similar in tone and theme are the four books of the *Epistolae ex Ponto* ('Letters from the Black Sea'). His *Ibis*, written in imitation of **Callimachus**, and his *Halieutica* ('Fishing Matters'), a poem extant only in fragments, complete the list of his works. Ovid is the most voluminous of the Latin poets and master of the elegiac couplet. His style is light, elegant and varied.

▷H Fränkel, *Ovid, a Poet between Two Worlds* (1945)

OWEN, Daniel
(1836–95)

Welsh novelist, born in Mold in Flintshire. After a poverty-stricken childhood, during which his father and two of his brothers were drowned in a mining accident, he studied for the Calvinist ministry, but gave this up when he came to doubt his vocation. He wrote 'for the common man'. His major novel is *Rhys Lewis* (1885), a first-person work telling the life-story of a minister. It contains a 'gallery of the best-known characters in Welsh-language fiction', and has been called 'the greatest single step forward in the history of the Welsh-language novel'.

▷J G Jones, *The Novelist from Mold* (1976)

OWEN, Goronwy, pseud of **Goronwy Ddu o Fôn**
(1723–69)

Welsh poet, born on Anglesey. Brought up in the demanding Bardic tradition, he was ordained priest (1746) and served for a year, on Anglesey, before being 'obliged to leave'. In 1657 he sailed for America, where, after a life of disappointment (in the course of which he lost two wives) he turned, as the vicar of a parish in the heart of the Virginia tobacco country, to a careful drinking—it had once been prodigal. These lapses apart, he was, as he has been called, the 'first great poet of the Welsh middle class', in whose work 'Horace and Dafydd Nanmor mingle'.

▷S Lewis, *A School of Welsh Augustans* (1924)

OWEN, John
(c.1560–1622)

Welsh epigrammatist, born in Llanarmon, Pwllheli. Educated at Winchester, he became a jurist fellow at New College, Oxford, in 1584. He was later employed as a schoolmaster at Trelleck, Gwent, and in 1595 became headmaster of Warwick school. He published 10 books of *Epigrammata*, written in Latin, between 1606 and 1613. His epigrams were bestsellers in their day, and particularly popular on the Continent.

▷*Owen the Epigrammist* (1909)

OWEN, Wilfred
(1893–1918)

English poet, born in Plas Wilmot, near Oswestry, Shropshire, where his father worked on the railway. Educated at the Birkenhead Institute and at Shrewsbury Technical School, he worked as a pupil-teacher at Wyle Cop School while preparing for the matriculation exam for the University of London. But money was too short for him to be able to take up courses there. In 1913 he left England to teach English in Bordeaux at the Berlitz School of Languages. He was tutoring a private pupil in the Pyrenees when war was declared. He enlisted in 1915 and in 1917 suffered concussion and trench fever on the Somme. In the summer of that year he was sent to recuperate at Craiglockart War Hospital, near Edinburgh, where he introduced himself to **Siegfried Sassoon**, who suggested improvements to his poems and encouraged him. However, he was posted back to France near the end of the war where he won the MC, but was killed on the bank of the Oise-Sambre Canal, near Ors, just a week before the Armistice was signed. Only five of his poems were published while he was alive, most of them being published between the summer he arrived at Craiglockhart and the time of his death. His work was first collected in 1920 by Sassoon and reappeared in 1931 with a memoir by **Edmund Blunden**. *The Collected Poems* was published in 1963. His poetry is distinguished by its directness, realism and vivid imagery, and individual poems like 'Dulce et Decorum Est' and 'Anthem for doomed Youth' have shaped the attitude of many towards war.

▷ D S R Welland, *Wilfred Owen* (1960)

OWENSON, Sydney, Lady Morgan
(1776–1859)

Irish novelist and woman-of-letters. In her, wrote a critic, 'were met all the contradictions that identified Irish conflicts and troubles'. Her third novel, *The Wild Irish Girl* (1806), made her famous; she married the surgeon Sir Charles Morgan in 1812. She fought all her life for reconciliation of all kinds. The best of her warm, interesting but stylistically undistinguished novels is *The O'Briens and the O'Flahertys* (1827).

▷ L Stevenson, *The Wild Irish Girl* (1936); M Campbell, *Sydney Owenson* (1988)

OYONO, Ferdinand
(1929–)

Francophone Cameroon novelist, son of a devoutly Roman Catholic mother. He studied law in Paris, and became a diplomat. He was also an actor. The great strength of such satirical novels as *Une Vie de Boy* (1956, Eng trans *Houseboy*, 1966) lies in their good-tempered but accurate descriptions of life in the Cameroons under French rule.

▷ *Black Orpheus*, 2 (1958)

OZ, Amos
(1939–)

Israeli Hebrew-language writer, born in Jerusalem. At the age of 14 he went to live in a kibbutz, where he taught in the school and became a writer of international stature. His works, which deal with historical and contemporary themes of guilt and persecution, include *Makom aber* (1966, Eng trans *Elsewhere, Perhaps*, 1973), *Har ha-etsah ha-raah* (1976, Eng trans *The Hill of Evil Counsel*, 1978), *Israel* (1983, Eng trans *In the Land of Israel*, 1983) and *Menuhah nekhonah* (1984, Eng trans *A Perfect Peace*, 1985). His work has been widely translated (a process in which he has collaborated) and he has won many awards. *Mikha'el sheli* (1972, Eng trans *My Michael*, 1972), described by the *New York Times* as 'a modern Israeli *Madame Bovary*', is the book by which he is best known. *Kufsah shehorah* (Eng trans *Black Box*, 1988) appeared in 1988.

OZICK, Cynthia
(1928–)

American novelist and short-story writer, born in New York City. Educated at New York University and Ohio State University, she has said she began her first novel, *Trust* (1966), an American writer and ended it six and a half years later a Jewish one. Powerfully and originally expressing the Jewish ethos, her slight but significant oeuvre includes *The Pagan Rabbit and Other Stories* (1971), *Bloodshed* (1976), *Levitation* (1982), *The Cannibal Galaxy* (1983) and *The Messiah of Stockholm* (1987).

▷ J Lowin, *Cynthia Ozick* (1988)

P

PAGAZA, Joaquin
(1839–1918)

Mexican poet and translator (**Virgil**, **Horace**). A priest, he tried to describe Mexico's beauties in the style of Virgil. His careful poetry influenced the great **Othón**.

PAGE, P(atricia) K(athleen)
(1916–)

English-born Canadian poet, novelist and artist. An early novel, *The Sun and the Moon* (1944), was published under the name Judith Cape and as a painter Page works as P K Irwin. Her first collection of poems was *As Ten as Twenty* (1946), which showed the influence of British Thirties writing. As an assistant editor of the magazine *Preview* Page was instrumental in the development of a modernist school of poetry in Canada. After marrying the Chairman of the Canadian Film Board, who was then made a High Commissioner to Australia, Page travelled widely. Some critics have noticed her work becoming purer, more oracular—a result, it is suggested, of an interest in Sufism.

PAGE, Thomas Nelson
(1853–1922)

American novelist and diplomat, born in Hanover County, Virginia. He practised law in Richmond, wrote many stories, some in Negro dialect, the best of which were *Marse Chan* (1884) and *Ole Virginia* (1887). He became American Ambassador to Italy from 1913 to 1919.
▷H Holman, *The Literary Career of Page, 1884–1910* (1978)

PAGNOL, Marcel
(1895–1974)

French dramatist and film-script writer, born near Marseilles. His childhood in Provence informs his best work, the play trilogy *Marius* (1929, filmed in 1931), *Fanny* (1931, filmed 1932) and *César* (1936, having been filmed two years earlier), each part being a comedy of Marseilles life. He first became widely known with the memoir *Topaze* (1928), a satirical study of bourgeois bad faith, which was filmed five years later by Louis Gasneur. Provence and its warmth, both literal and human, is at the centre of *La Gloire de mon père* (1957) and his other memoirs. He became a member

of the Académie française in 1946, the first film-maker to be so honoured.

PAINE, Albert Bigelow
(1861–1937)

American editor and biographer of **Mark Twain**. Paine began his working life as the employee of a photography supply firm in Kansas. He submitted some prose sketches to *Harpers Weekly* and when they were accepted set off for New York. He published a successful book for children, *The Arkansaw Bear* (1898) and New York's theatre area was named after his play *The Great White Way* (1901). But his later career was determined by the success of his biography of Thomas Nast (1904), following which Mark Twain immediately engaged him as his secretary and official biographer. In addition to the biography (1912), Paine edited Twain's speeches and correspondence.

PAINE, Tom
(1737–1809)

English radical politician and writer, born in Thetford, Norfolk. He left school when he was only 13 and, after trying out many jobs, and much study, became an excise officer. He began to try to organize labour, and published his first pamphlet in 1772: *The Case of the Officers of Excise*; as a result of it he was dismissed. Soon after this he met **Benjamin Franklin**. In America he became editor of the radical *Philadelphia Magazine*; in the War of Independence, he fought in Washington's army. In 1887 he returned to England, where he wrote his most famous and influential work, *The Rights of Man* (Part 1, 1790, Part 2, 1792), which was, initially, a reply to the *Reflections on the Revolution in France* of **Edmund Burke**. In 1792 he was indicted for treason, and fled to France (where *The Rights* had been instantly translated). He took part in French affairs, but was imprisoned by Robespierre when he spoke (and wrote) against the execution of the French king. His release, after two years of confinement, was secured by a friend. In prison he wrote what is in fact his most substantial work: *The Age of Reason* (1794–6), an attack on the Church and (less successfully) an advocation of deism. He died in America in poverty and neglect. Paine's influence lay not in his originality of thought but in his passion and directness, which, if only very occasionally, cut through the elegance and intricacy of Burke, and cause it to look a little disingenuous. His defences of democracy have always been extremely persuasive.

▷H Pearson, *Tom Paine, Friend of Mankind* (1937); R R Fennessey, *Burke, Paine and the Rights of Man* (1963)

PAKKALA, Teuvo, pseud of T O Frosterus
(1862–1925)

Finnish dramatist and novelist, born in Oulu, who is now remembered for his plays. His fiction, although well written, has dated.

PALACIO, Pablo
(1906–47)

Ecuadorean novelist, militant socialist, translator and philosopher, born in Loja. Palacio was forgotten by readers for a decade after his death, but then rediscovered by the critic Jorge Enrique Adoum. In his works, a critic wrote in 1981, the contemporary reader 'began to rediscover the incredible profundity and modernity of the forgotten ... author. In this work, sometimes hermetic, always taciturn and hallucinated, the attentive reader finds many contemporary anxieties and obsessions'. Described by one critic as 'a character in one of Arlt's works', the syphilitic and eventually mad Palacio anticipates, in his stories in *Un hombre muerte a putapiés* (1927, 'The Man Kicked to Death'), and in his novels *Débora* (1928) and *Vida de ahorcado* (1932, 'A Hanged Life'), every modernist technique. His collected works appeared in 1964.

▷J Ruffinelli, *Critica en Marcha* (1980)

PALAMAS, Kostis
(1859–1943)

One of the greatest modern Greek poets, and for 50 years the most influential critic in the country. Born in Patras, the son of a magistrate, he was orphaned at the age of seven and brought up by an uncle in Missolonghi. In 1875 he went to Athens to study, and began to have his poems published in journals, although his first collection, *Tatraghoudhia tis Patridos Mou* ('The Songs of My Country'), did not appear until 1886. In 1889 he won the first Philadelphian Poetry Prize with his hymn to Athena, and he won again with 'Ta Matia tis Psychis Mou' ('Eyes of My Soul') the following year. The title of this second poem is taken from a very famous line by **Solomos**, and some critics have found Palamas's obvious homage to the great Greek masters too derivative. *Asalenti Zoë*, a collection published in 1904 (Eng trans *Life Immutable*, 1919), is still reckoned to be his greatest, containing 'He Phinikia' ('The Palm Tree'), one of the most famous poems in the language. Although he did not publish anything during the last 10 years of his life, his death while the country was under enemy occupation was seized upon as a potent symbol of resistance, and his funeral was attended by a huge crowd.

▷G Katsimbalis, *Bibliography of Kostis Palamas* (1975, lists more than 2 500 essays and articles written by the poet)

PALAZZESCHI, Aldo, pseud of Aldo Giurlani
(1885–1974)

Italian poet and major novelist, born in Florence. He began, with his close friend **Moretti**, as an actor, but abandoned this career when he issued (1905) a collection of verse, *I cavalli bianchi* ('White Horses'). This, a curious and interesting debut, mixed the traces of the influence of **D'Annunzio** with (more surely) those of the school of poets who had reacted against his decadent bombast, the Crepusculari (of which Moretti was a representative). For a short period (1909–14) he was associated with the Futurist movement of **Marinetti**, but he broke with it to take his own course, one unique in modern Italian letters. His chief novels are the fantastic *Il codice di Perelà* (1911, Eng trans *Perela, The Man of Smoke*, 1936), about a man actually made of smoke (and himself a reflection of Palazzeschi's own faintly homosexualized aestheticism—an early hero was **Oscar Wilde**); his majestically tragic masterpiece *Le sorelle Materassi* (1934, Eng trans *The Materassi Sisters*, 1953), apparently relatively conventional, but written in a subtle parody of regular 'realistic' prose; and *Roma* (1953, Eng trans *Rome*, 1965), a satire on 'good government'. Many of his poems, such as 'Rio Bo', are still much anthologized.

▷G Pullini, *Aldo Palazzeschi* (1965, in Italian); S Pacifici (ed), *From Verismo to Experimentalism* (1969)

PALÉS MATOS, Luis
(1898–1959)

White Puerto Rican, born in Guayama, who became his country's most distinguished negrophile modern poet. His father—like his mother, a poet and freethinker—was a rural teacher who earned a pittance; Palés's childhood was one of acute poverty. The best account of his life is given in his unfinished novel *Littoral* (published in his *Obras*, 1984, 'Works'). A melancholy man, quite lacking in literary ambition, he published only two collections in his lifetime, but his poems circulated widely in typescript. 'Palés,' wrote the editor of a critical edition of his works, 'is the indispensable initiator of Negritude in the Hispanic Antilles.' In his poetry, especially in the influential *Tuntún* (1937), he mixed Spanish with African words and phrases, sometimes neologisms, to give a 'Negro' effect.

PALEY, Grace, née **Goodside**
(1922–)

American short-story writer, born in New York City. She was educated at Hunter College, New York, and has taught in several US colleges. Her fiction has all been in the short-story form, usually set in New York, and often with Jewish settings and themes. Her sharp ear for convincingly realistic dialogue is evident in all her stories. Those in *Little Disturbances of Man* (1959) have a wider range of social settings than *Enormous Changes at the Last Minute* (1974), which are all set in the run-down world of inner-city slums, but they share a common wit, compassion, and characteristic tone of voice. Her support of the peace movement is evident in *Later the Same Day* (1985), as well as in the non-fiction *365 Reasons Not to Have Another War* (1989). Other writings include *Begin Again: New and Collected Poems* (1992), and an essay collection, *Long Walks and Intimate Talks* (1991).

PALGRAVE, Francis Turner
(1824–97)

English poet and critic, born in Great Yarmouth, eldest son of Sir Francis Palgrave. He became a scholar of Balliol College, Oxford, and fellow of Exeter College, was successively vice-principal of a training college, private secretary to George Leveson-Gower (Earl Granville), an official in the education department, and Professor of Poetry at Oxford (1886–95). His works include *Idylls and Songs* (1854), *Essays on Art* (1866), *Hymns* (1867), *Lyrical Poems* (1871), *Visions of England* (1881), and *Landscape in Poetry* (1897). He is best known as the editor of the *Golden Treasury of Lyrical Poetry* (1875); *Sonnets and Songs of Shakespeare* (1877); selections from **Robert Herrick** (1877) and **Keats** (1885); and *Treasury of Sacred Song* (1889).
▷ R H Palgrave, in *Collected Works* (1919–22)

PALLISER, Charles
(1947–)

American novelist and academic, born near Boston, Massachusetts, but who has made his home in Scotland, where he teaches at Strathclyde University. His first novel, *The Quincunx* (1989), set in Regency London, has an extremely intricate plot involving John Huffam's quest to discover the truth about his family's past, in which wealth and murder play equal parts. The research and the writing took Palliser 12 years and the result is both

a substantial and lengthy work. His second novel, *The Sensationist* (1991), the story of a disastrous contemporary love affair, is considerably shorter, and was followed by *Betrayals* (1994), a novel of 10 independent chapters, which develops his interest in literary pastiche.

PALMA, Ricardo
(1883–1919)

Major Peruvian writer, who invented a new and unique genre, the *tradición*, and is in many ways still one of Peru's chief keepers of conscience—nor can Peru be fully understood without close acquaintance with his works. The *tradición* is based on some single fact or folk belief, and then expands upon it in a kind of essay-fiction of some thousand words. His *Tradiciones peruanas* were collected in 1957, and a good selection from them was translated in 1945 as *The Knights of the Cape*. Palma was an ultra-critical lover of his country and its ways, and these ironic, racy, colloquial pieces, examples of very high art which read spontaneously, cover almost every aspect of its life—and often anticipate events which have taken place since his death. He was director of the National Library. His son, Clemente Palma (1872–1946), was himself an important writer—though somewhat neglected at present—whose *Cuentos malévolos* (1904, rev edn 1923, Eng trans *Malevolent Tales*, 1984) and *Historietas malignas* (1925, Eng trans *Malignant Tales*, 1988) are **Schopenhauer**ian *tours de force*. Ricardo Palma wrote much else besides the *tradiciones*, including vital books on Peruvian Spanish.
▷ J M Oviedo, *Ricardo Palma* (1968, in Spanish); E M Aldrich, *The Modern Short Story in Peru* (1966)

PALMER, (Edward) Vance
(1885–1959)
PALMER, Nettie (Janet Gertrude)
(1885–1964)

Australian writers, born in Bundaberg, Queensland, and Bendigo, Victoria, respectively. They worked in most genres, including novels, short stories, plays, poetry, and social and literary criticism. Vance Palmer established the Pioneer Players in Melbourne in 1922, and many of his plays were performed by that group. His *Separate Lives* (1931), *Sea and Spinifex* (1934) and *Let the Birds Fly* (1955) typify his anecdotal sketches and stories; his first serious attempt at the novel came in *Cronulla* (1924) but his best-known is *The Passage* (1930), set in a Queensland fishing village which itself develops into one of the main characters in a study of inevitable change. Palmer's political concerns show strongly in his trilogy of a power-broking union man, Macy Donovan, in a small mining community based on the copper town of Mt Isa in north-west Queensland. *Golconda* (1948), *Seedtime* (1957) and *Big Fellow* (1959) chart Donovan's climb to political power. Nettie Palmer graduated from Melbourne University, travelled and studied in Europe, and married Vance Palmer in London in 1914, creating a partnership that for nearly 40 years dominated the literary left. She was a prolific writer for contemporary journals but little of her criticism has been collected except for the ground-breaking *Modern Australian Literature 1900–1923* (1924). Her major contribution to Australian literature was in the advocacy of other, especially women, writers. She was among the first to recognize the worth of **Henry Handel Richardson** and to promote such diverse authors as **Barbara Baynton**, **Shaw Nielson** and **Katharine Susannah Prichard**.

PALMOTIĆ, Junije
(1607–75)

Ragusan poet and dramatist, who took over Italian Renaissance themes and adapted them to Ragusan (Dalmatian) settings.

PALTOCK, Robert
(1697–1767)

English lawyer and writer, born in London. He took up law and practised as an attorney at Clement's Inn. He wrote the fantasy novel *The Life and Adventures of Peter Wilkins* (1751), in which the shipwrecked hero finds himself in a distant land where people can fly by means of a silky outer skin. Its authorship remained a mystery till 1835.

PALUDAN, Jacob
(1896–1975)

Danish novelist, son of a professor of Danish literature at the University of Copenhagen, trained as a pharmacist. From a conservative stand, Paludan criticizes the Americanization of traditional European and Danish values and equates the rise of industrial mass culture with the victory of mediocrity. Paludan's debut novel *De vestlige Veje* (1922, 'The Western Roads'), about a Danish emigrant's encounter with the USA, is a denunciation of the transatlantic capitalism epitomized by New York. A master of the large-scale social realist novel, Paludan first gained a wide readership with *Fugle omkring Fyret* (1925, 'Birds around the Lighthouse'), a vivid novel about a small fishing and farming community, Sandhavn, which the commercial and political establishment, governed by a blind belief in material progress, seeks to transform into a major sea port. His subsequent works *Markerne modnes* (1927, 'The Fields Ripen') and

Jørgen Stein (1932–3), his last major piece of fiction and a canonical text in Danish literature, are classic novels of social and individual development. In two large volumes the latter presents a panorama of Denmark's transformation from 1914 to 1933, with the emphasis on the breakdown of the traditional patriarchal culture.
▷H Oldenburg, *Jacob Paludan. Historien om et venskab* (1984)

PALUDAN-MÜLLER, Frederick
(1809–76)

Danish poet. He wrote poems, dramas and romances, including the verse novel *Danserinden* (1833, 'The Dancer'), but his fame rests on *Adam Homo* (1841–9), a humorous, satiric, didactic epic about the worldly sin and moral decline of a successful man.
▷S Møller Kristensen, *Digtning og livssyn* (1959)

PANDURO, Leif
(1923–77)

Danish novelist and television dramatist, born in Copenhagen; he practised as a dentist until 1965, when he became a full-time writer. He came to notice with the witty, youthful novel *Rend mig i traditionerne* (1958, 'Sod The Traditions'), which demonstrates a linguistic energy and ingenuity reminiscent of **Salinger**'s *The Catcher in the Rye*. It views adult life and its norms through the quizzical eyes of David, a boarding-school pupil whose legs suddenly begin to perform subversive acts such as kicking the headmaster's backside or running away from school. David is admitted to a mental hospital but eventually discharged. The novel questions the validity of a sharp distinction between mental 'illness' and 'normality' and this remained one of Panduro's main preoccupations, evident also in novels such as *Den gale mand* (1965, 'The Mad Man'), *Daniels anden verden* (1970, 'Daniel's Other World') and *Høfeber* (1975, 'Hayfever'). While hyperbole and caricature are indispensable ingredients in his novels, Panduro's television plays are more naturalistic. Plays such as *Et godt liv* (1970, 'A Good Life'), *Rundt om Selma* (1971, 'Around Selma'), *I Adams verden* (1973, 'In Adam's World') and *Louises hus* (1977, 'Louise's House') set new standards for Danish television drama and achieved outstanding audience ratings: they typically depict the existential fall and subsequent awakening of an upper middle-class hero, whose psychological predicaments and social environment would be recognizable to many viewers.
▷J C Jørgensen, *Leif Panduro. En biografi* (1987)

PANFYOROV, Fyodor
(1896–1960)

Russian novelist, whose socialist-realist work, particularly *Bruski* (1931–7, Eng trans of part, *And then the Harvest*, 1920–39), was at one time widely discussed. He was criticized by **Gorky** for his poor craftsmanship, and is by now almost forgotten. *Svoimi glazmi* (1942, Eng trans *With Their Own Eyes*, 1942) held appeal during World War II.

PANNIKAR, Sardar, K M
(1895–1963)

Indian (Malayalam) statesman and ambassador, known in India for his poetry and drama, and, especially, historical novels.

PANSHIN, Alexei
(1940–)

American science-fiction writer and critic, born in Ann Arbor, Michigan. His first novel, *Rite of Passage* (1968, Nebula Award Winner), remains his best-known work: set mainly on a generation starship, it is the account of the survival tests undergone by the vessel's adolescents. The Villiers trilogy, which began with *Star Well* (1968) and continued in *The Thumb* (1968) and *Masque World* (1969), is more playful and less successful. His later works have been written in collaboration with his wife, Cory Panshin. These include the heroic fantasy *Earth Magic* (1978) and the critical study *SF in Dimension: A Book of Explorations* (1968).

PANZINI, Alfredo
(1863–1939)

Italian novelist, born in Senigallia. Like **Barrès** in France at approximately the same time, his theme for much of his fiction was 'rootlessness' and the emptiness of modern existence. Very learned in the classics, with a fine if somewhat over-elaborate and 'super-literary' style, he well understood the state of spiritual emptiness, but tended to equate it with the natural roughness and disorderliness of life, so that his appeal is to the academic, not to the common man. Yet he was popular, and such books as *Il bacio di Lesbia* (1937, 'Lesbia's Kiss') were widely read. He was adored by, and adored, Mussolini. One of his better books, *Io cerco moglie* (1920), was translated as *Wanted, A Wife* (1922).
▷S Pacifici, *The Modern Italian Novel from Capuana to Tozzi* (1973)

PAPADIAMANTIS, Alexandros
(1851–1911)

Greek novelist and writer of more than 200 'genre' tales. Born on Skiathos, the son of a priest, he was himself a cantor, and unlike his contemporaries refused to switch from *Katharevousa*, the official Greek used in church services and for official announcements, to demotic Greek. Although he later lived in Athens, almost all of his stories are set on his native island, and hark back to a golden age unspoilt by 'progress'. Those published before 1900 established his reputation, but it is his remarkable story of the gulf between human and divine justice, *Fonissa*, published in 1903 (Eng trans *The Murderess*, 1983), that has survived best; its protagonist is a 60-year-old woman, Frangogiannou, who comes to the realization that a woman's life is one of slavery, in turn to parents, husband and children, and so conceives of the idea of killing little girls to spare them their fate.

PAPATSONIS, Takis
(1895–)

Greek poet, critic and translator (of **Claudel**, **Aragon** and others), born in Athens who, although he came to poetic maturity at the time of the suicide of **Karyotakis**, reacted differently from the majority of his contemporaries to that event: instead of nihilism, romantic despair and decadence, he chose to express his religious (Catholic) faith. He was a civil servant and an expert in banking. His first poems appeared during World War I, when he was scarcely out of his boyhood, and anticipated many modernistic procedures. But he kept to his own path. His poetry has been called 'almost Surrealist'. Neglected by some, he is highly prized by others as a too-little-heeded and original religious poet.

PARDO BAZÁN, Emilia, Condesa de
(1851–1921)

Spanish writer, born of an aristocratic Galician family. Her literary vocation was formed early, then developed when the family moved to Madrid. This gave her access to the literary circles of the capital and cultivated her interest in contemporary European thought and affairs; her interests ranged over Darwinism, feminism and science, Russian and French literature. Besides her novels, she produced over 500 short stories, articles, criticism, poems and travel literature, as well as giving lectures. She was strongly influenced by the French naturalist writers, and this can be seen in her first novel, *Pascual Lopez* (1879). Her best-known books in this genre are *Los Pazos de Ulloa* (1886, 'The Manors of Ulloa') and *La Madre Naturaleza* (1887, 'Mother Nature'), both set in the rural decadence of her native Galicia. Later novels such as *La Quimera* (1905, 'The Chimera') and *La Sirena Negra* (1908, 'The Black Mermaid') are unmistakably modernist in atmosphere and psychology. Latterly she came under the influence of *fin-de-siècle* spiritualism and adopted more idealistic values. She also published works on **Zola** and naturalism, the revolution in Russia, and modern French literature. She was the first Spanish woman of note to sustain a feminist campaign, and she ran a library for women, amongst many other feminist activities.

▷M Hemingway, *Emilia Pardo Bazán. The Making of a Novelist* (1983)

PARDO Y ALIAGA, Felipe
(1806–69)

Peruvian poet, humorist and dramatist. He was born in Lima, his father having been a Spanish official. In 1840 he founded a satirical review, *El Espejo de Mi Tierra* ('Mirror of my Land'), with his pamphlet of that title attacking the new republic. His plays, poetry and essays are mainly satirical. The 'grandfather of Peruvian drama' was **Manuel Ascensio Segura**, a more substantial figure, but the exchanges between Pardo and the latter, leader of the *creolist* school of writing, form an important part of Peruvian literary history.

PAREJA DIEZ-CANSECO, Alfredo
(1908–)

Major Ecuardorean novelist, born in Guayaquil. His first novel, *La casa de los locos* (1929, 'The House of Madmen'), a savage and youthful *roman à clef* on corrupt politicians, made a sensation and sold out in a few days. But his first mature novel was *El muelle* (1933, 'The Voluptuous'), written after he had returned from a period in the United States: it is set in New York and Guayaquil at the time of the depression, and, although it reflects the author's Marxism, contains vivid and accurate portraits of both big and small business gangsters. He contributed to the book of stories, *Los que se van* (1930), brought out by the famous Grupo de Guayaquil, of which he was a member. His greatest novel is *Hombres sin tiempo* (1941, 'Men Without Time'), written as a result of his prison experiences (he, together with many others, was thrown into jail, as an MP, by the dictator Arroyo del Rio). This is influenced by **Thomas Mann**, under whose tutelage Pareja became a liberal rather than a communist. Later he became what he ironically called a 'bourgeois', prospered in business, wrote a bestseller, and was able to move with his family to Mexico. In 1951 he founded the newspaper *El Sol*. A historian as well as a novelist, he remains untranslated into English.

PARETSKY, Sarah
(1947–)

American crime writer, born in Eudora, Kansas and educated at the University of Kansas and the University of Chicago, where she received an MBA and a PhD in history. She worked for a research firm and as a marketing manager for an insurance company, before becoming a full-time writer in 1986. That same year she co-founded Sisters in Crime, an organization devoted to promoting women crime writers. Her novels feature the feisty female detective V I Warshawski (played on screen by Kathleen Turner in 1992), who faces such diverse problems as toxic waste and anti-abortionists. From these situations Paretsky looks at the nature of relationships between women, and at the line between the personal and professional as experienced by her outwardly tough but essentially warm-hearted heroine. Her most recent works include *Burn Marks* (1990) and *Guardian Angel* (1992).

PARGETER, Edith, pseud Ellis Peters
(1913–)

English novelist from Shropshire, also a highly successful crime writer under her pseudonym. Pargeter, always a prolific writer, wrote a string of quietly successful detective novels, many featuring Inspector Felse (*Fallen into the Pit*, 1951, was the first of these). Real success, however, came when she was in her sixties when, reading about a historical incident in which the relics of St Winifred were moved to Shrewsbury Abbey, she hit upon the idea of Brother Cadfael, a medieval detective. *A Morbid Taste for Bones: A Mediaeval Whodunnit* (1977, as Ellis Peters) was an instant hit, and a series was born. By no means as literary as **Umberto Eco**'s comparable *The Name of the Rose*, the Cadfael books are, nevertheless, prime examples of the sort of quintessentially English detective fiction where there is no gore and anything too unpleasant is described from a discreet distance. The period setting, though a strong selling point, is incidental. Pargeter was awarded the Crime Writers' Association Diamond Dagger Award—its highest—in 1993.

PARINI, Giuseppe
(1729–99)

Italian poet, born near Milan. He became a priest in 1754, and was professor at the Palatine and Brera schools (1769–99). He made his name as a poet by the sequence of poems called collectively *Il Giorno* (1763–1803, 'The Day'), which satirized the daily round of a young nobleman.

▷G Petronio, *Parini, storia della critica* (1957)

PARK, Ruth
(?1923–)

New Zealand-born Australian writer, born near Hamilton, and educated at Auckland university. She went to Australia in 1942 and married the author **D'Arcy Niland**. Her first success was in 1947 with the novel *The Harp in the South*, which won a newspaper competition. This story of slum life in the Surry Hills district of Sydney has been translated into 10 languages and forms a trilogy with *Poor Man's Orange* (1949) and the retrospective *Missus* (1986). *Swords and Crowns and Rings* (1977) won the **Miles Franklin** Award for its sensitive tale of an outcast of society. She created the popular books based on an ABC children's series about *The Muddle-Headed Wombat* between 1962 and 1981, and has also written novels for adolescent readers, including two set in Victorian Sydney, *Come Danger, Come Darkness* (1978) and the haunting *Playing Beatie Bow* (1980, filmed 1987). The autobiographical *A Fence Round the Cuckoo* (1992) was awarded the Foundation for Australian Literature Studies Award. A second volume of autobiography was published in 1993 as *Fishing in the Styx*.

PARKER, Dorothy, née **Rothschild**
(1893–1967)

American wit, short-story writer and journalist, born in West End, New Jersey, daughter of a clothes salesman. Her mother died when she was five and her father re-married; Dorothy could barely contain her antipathy to her stepmother and refused to address her. Her formal education ended in 1908 at the age of 14, but she was a voracious reader and, having read **Thackeray** when she was 11, decided to make literature her life. In 1916 she sold some of her poetry to the editor of *Vogue*, and was given the job of writing captions for fashion photographs and drawings. She then became drama critic of *Vanity Fair* (1917–20), where she met **Robert Benchley** and **Robert Sherwood** and formed with them the nucleus of the legendary Algonquin Hotel Round Table luncheon group. Famed for her spontaneous wit and acerbic criticism, she was at her most trenchant in book reviews and stories in the early issues (1927–33) of the *New Yorker*, a magazine whose character she did much to form. Her work continued to appear in the magazine at irregular intervals until 1955. Her reviews were collected in *A Month of Saturdays* (1971). She also wrote for *Esquire* and published poems and sketches. Her poems are included in *Not So Deep as a Well* (1930) and *Enough Rope* (1926), which became a bestseller. Her short stories were collected in *Here Lies* (1936). She also collaborated on several film scripts, including *The Little Foxes* and *A Star Is Born*. Twice married (1917 and 1933), she took her surname from her first husband. Both marriages foundered, there was a string of lacerating

love affairs, abortive suicide attempts, abortions, debts and drinking bouts, and she died alone in a Manhattan apartment with Troy, her poodle, at her side.
▷J Keats, *You Might As Well Live* (1971)

PÁRMENO, pseud of **José López Pinillos**
(1875–1922)

Spanish sensationalist novelist and playwright, born in Seville. Pármeno is a character in **Manuel Rojas**'s novel *Celestina*, suggestive of virile candour. Influenced by **Zola**, his crudely naturalistic and excessively violent novels have a certain raw power; he was unlucky in not finding an English translator, for he was readable.

PARNELL, Thomas
(1679–1718)

Irish poet and clergyman, born in Dublin. He was educated at Trinity College, took holy orders in 1700, and received the archdeaconry of Clogher (1706), and the vicarage of Finglass (1716). He also owned property in Cheshire, and he lived much in London, where his wit brought him the friendship of Harley, **Jonathan Swift** and **Pope**. After his wife's death in 1711 he took to drink, and died while on his way to Ireland. The following year Pope published a selection of his poems, the best-known of which are 'The Hermit', 'The Nightpiece on Death' and 'Hymn to Contentment'. His *Complete Poems* were first published in 1985.
▷O Goldsmith, *The Life of Parnell* (1770)

PARNICKI, Teodor
(1908–)

Polish novelist, born in Berlin and brought up in Moscow—he did not settle in Poland until he was 60—whose work is so learned, complex and subtle that it lacks what a critic has called its 'deserved international reputation'. He is Poland's most distinguished modern historical novelist, and he applied advanced modernist techniques in his revival of this form. His earlier novels took a conventionally **Freud**ian approach; but he soon matured. His untranslated later novels are interesting because they candidly take into account the inevitable subjectivity of the historian. His chosen areas of research—Rome in decline, Poland in the 11th century—are usually more or less unexplored territory. Typical of his novels—he is prolific, and each book is massive—is *Inne zcie Kleopatry* (1969, 'The Other Life of Cleopatra').

PARRA, Nicanor
(1914–)

Chilean poet, born in San Fabián de Aliceo. After the death of **Pablo Neruda** he became

Chile's leading poet (or, as he prefers to be called, antipoet). But in 1937, in a Chile dominated by Surrealism, Neruda and **Huidobro**, his first collection, *Cancionero sin nombre* (1937, 'Lyrics Without Name'), went almost unnoticed. But his second collection, *Poemas y antipoemas* (1954), although badly received, met with praise from Neruda himself. Parra, now a professor of theoretical physics, had discovered his own voice, whose intention was to create 'a poetic atmosphere of dynamic disarray'. In terms of English-language poetry, Parra's expression 'anti-poet' may perhaps best be understood as 'anti-lyrical'. By the side of Neruda or Huidobro he is a minor poet, but he has been influential on the American Beat poets, and he has in Chile a school of disciples. In common with many other writers of his century, Parra sees the world as a brutal and senseless place— Neruda and Huidobro, on the contrary, are visionary poets, for all their political beliefs— but he does so in a uniquely playful, likeable manner. There are many translations: *Poems and Antipoems* (1967), *Antipoems: New and Selected* (1985), *Emergency Poems* (1972), *Sermons and Homilies of the Christ of Elqui* (1984). For his most enthusiastic critics, he is the latest in a line of great antipoets, who include **Catullus**, **Villon** and **Quevedo**.
▷V M Valenzuela, *Contemporary Latin American Writers* (1971)

PARRA, Teresa de la
(1895–1936)
Venezuelan novelist, born into a wealthy family on an estate near Caracas, but educated in Paris. She wrote two important and well observed fictional autobiographies, *Ifigenia* (1924) and the more famous *Las memorias de Mamá Blanca* (1929, Eng trans *Mama Blanca's Souvenirs*, 1959), a witty account of the Venezualan capital and the countryside around it, as seen through the eyes of a refined Paris lady.

PARRY, Robert Williams
(1884–1956)
Welsh poet, born in Daffryn Nantlle. He won the National Eisteddfod in 1910, and was thereafter regarded as one of the country's leading poets. After the Penyberth scandal in 1936, when three prominent Welshmen (including **Saunders Lewis**) were unjustly sentenced at the Old Bailey, he began to write political satire. His sonnets of the 1930s are his most prized work; two of these are well translated in the *Penguin Book of Welsh Verse* (1967).
▷B L Jones, *Robert Williams Parry* (1972)

PARRY-WILLIAMS, Sir Thomas Herbert
(1887–1975)
Welsh poet, scholar and critic, born in Rhyddu. He won both Chair and Crown at the National Eisteddfod in 1912 and 1915. He was for most of his working life Professor of Welsh at Aberystwyth. With his kinsman **Robert Williams Parry**, he is the acknowledged master of the sonnet in the Welsh language. His best poetry is evocative of Welsh landscape, which he sees as formative of human character. He was an influential scholar of Welsh poetry. He was knighted in 1958.
▷*Poetry Wales* (1974, issue devoted to his work)

PARUN, Vesna
(1922–)
Croatian poet, born on Zlarin. She made a mark with her first and incomparably finest collection, *Zore i vihori* (1947, 'Dawns and Gales'), which paid no attention to the tenets of socialist realism, and was immediately criticized by party hacks. Forced into silence, she eventually returned to her childhood Catholicism, and wrote a less convincing and urgent poetry. Some of the love poems in *Bila sam djecak* (1963, 'I Was a Boy') are memorable.

PASÇOAES, Joaquim Teixeira de, pseud of **Joaquim Pereira de Vasconcelos**
(1877–1952)
Portuguese poet, editor and mystical nationalist, who declared, 'I was born to live beyond life', and tried to prove it with his vision of an incarnate God created by man as a result of his struggle against evil. *Saudade* is the specifically Portuguese version of **Unamuno**'s *aboulia*: apathy, lack of will, torpor, frozen ideology. Pasçoaes' poetry, after false starts, tried to define this with increasing exactitude, and he is therefore known as the *saudosista* poet *par excellence*. Egoistic, he was also crucial in the development of modern Portuguese literature. His magazine *A Águia* ('The Eagle'), which he edited from 1912 until 1916, was the gathering point for all the most gifted members of Pasçoaes's generation. His poetry is more interesting than his confused philosophy suggests: the long *Regresso ao Paraíso* (1912, 'Return to Paradise') is one of the more curious poems of its century.

PASCOLI, Giovanni
(1855–1912)
Italian poet and writer, born in San Mauro di Romagna. He was Professor of Latin at Bologna from 1907. Much of his poetry, set in the background of his native Romagna, is

of a tragic nature; his volumes of verse include *Myricae* (1891), *In Or San Michele* (1903, 'For San Michele') and *Canti di Castelvecchio* (1903, 'Songs of Castelvecchio'). *Sotto il Velame* (1900, 'Beneath the Veil') and *La Mirabile Visione* (1902, 'Heavenly Vision') are critical studies of **Dante**'s *Commedia Divina*.

▷P Mazzamuto, *Pascoli* (1966)

PASEK, Jan Chryzostom
(c.1636–c.1701)

Polish diarist, born in Rawa. A squire, he led an adventurous life, fighting invaders of Poland, but also a quiet one, buying and selling, and running his farm on what were for those days enlightened principles. He had little tolerance for the law. His memoirs in diary form, *Pamietniki* (1836), of which there is a translation in French, is an incomparable mixture of complexity and simplicity, ranging from vivid semi-fictional portraits of soldiers to lists of a peasant's proper duties. Furthermore, the book has great linguistic importance.

▷J K Heck, *Jan Chryzostom Pasek* (1902)

PASOLINI, Pier Paolo
(1922–75)

Italian critic, poet, novelist, film director and screen-writer, born and educated in Bologna. Most of his childhood was spent in Casara della Delizia, in his mother's birthplace of Friuli. He became notorious in the 1950s, principally through the publication of the first two parts of a projected trilogy, *Ragazzi di vita* (1955, Eng trans *The Ragazzi*, 1968) and *Una vita violenta* (1959, Eng trans *A Violent Life*, 1968). Superficially works of protest, they exhibit a strong thematic continuity with his early youthful poetry, portraying the timeless innocence of Friuli. His later writings did not match those of his youth, and during the 1960s and 1970s he devoted himself to directing films, many based on literary sources: *Il Vangelo Secondo Matteo* (1964, 'The Gospel According to Saint Matthew'), *Il Decamerone* (1971, 'The Decameron') and *Salò, o, Le centoventi giornate di Sodoma* (1975, 'Salo: The 120 Days of Sodom'). He was murdered as the result of a homosexual encounter with a young criminal.

▷E Siciliano, *Pasolini* (1981, in Italian)

PASTERNAK, Boris Leonidovich
(1890–1960)

Russian lyric poet, novelist and translator of **Shakespeare**, born in Moscow. He was the son of Leonid Pasternak (1862–1945), painter and illustrator of **Tolstoy**'s works. He studied law at the university, then musical composition under Scriabin, abandoning both for philosophy at Marburg. A factory worker in the Urals during World War I, he was employed in the library of the education ministry in Moscow after the Revolution. His early collections of verse, written between 1912 and 1916, were published under the title *Poverkh bar'erov* (1917, Eng trans *Above the Barriers*, 1931), followed by *Sestra moya zhizn': Leto 1917 goda* (1922, Eng trans *Sister my Life: Summer 1917*, 1967) and *Temy i variatsii* (1923, 'Themes and Variations'). Under the influence of his friend **Vladimir Mayakovsky** he wrote the political poems *Devyat'sot pyaty god* (1927, 'The Year 1905'), on the Bolshevik uprising, and *Levtenant Schmidt* (1927, 'Lieutenant Schmidt'), on the *Potemkin* mutiny. *Spectorsky* (1931) and *Vtoroye rozhdeniye* (1932, 'Second Birth') are autobiographical. Among his outstanding short stories are the collection *Vozdushnye puti* (1933, 'Aerial Ways') and particularly *Detstvo Lyuvers* (1922, Eng trans *The Childhood of Luvers*, 1945), a delicate presentation of a girl's first impressions of womanhood, and *Provest'* (1934, Eng trans *The Last Summer*, 1959), in which Pasternak's imagery is at its freshest and most unexpected. The long years under Stalin turned Pasternak into the official translator into Russian of Shakespeare, **Paul Verlaine**, **Goethe** and **Heinrich von Kleist**, but he did compose incidental verse such as *Na rannikh poezdakh* (1936–44, 'In Early Trains'). With Khrushchev's misleading political 'thaw' Pasternak caused a political earthquake with his first novel, *Doktor Zhivago* (1957, Eng trans *Doctor Zhivago*, 1958), banned in the Soviet Union. A fragmentary, poet's novel, it describes with intense feeling the Russian revolution as it impinged upon one individual, who was both doctor and poet. Its strictures on the postrevolutionary events are those not of an antiMarxist but of a communist who is disappointed that history has not conformed to his vision. Expelled by the Soviet Writers' Union, he had to take the unprecedented step of refusing the 1958 Nobel Prize for literature, and in a thoroughly self-critical letter to Khrushchev, echoed **Ovid** by his plea that exile would for him be the equivalent of death.

▷R Hingley, *Pasternak, a biography* (1983)

PATCHEN, Kenneth
(1911–72)

American poet, novelist and painter. He grew up in Ohio, and was educated at the Experimental College, University of Wisconsin, Madison, and at Commonwealth College, Mena, Arkansas. After working as an agricultural labourer and as a freelance writer, he briefly joined the editorial staff at New Directions in 1939, the year of *First Will and*

Testament, his second volume of verse. Patchen wrote in a characteristically straightforward, unmetaphorical style, using the language of speech in a dramatically direct way; *First Will* actually contained an oral playlet which anticipated his later radio play *The City Wears a Slouch Hat* (1942), one of the forgotten masterpieces of modern American writing. *Selected Poems* appeared in 1947; later volumes included *A Surprise for the Bagpipe Player* (1956), *Hurrah for Anything* (1957), which included poems and drawings, and *Doubleheader* and *Hallelujah Anyway* (both 1966). *The Collected Poems* was published in 1968. Patchen also wrote a number of novels, most notably *The Journal of Albion Moonlight* (1941) and *The Memoirs of a Shy Pornographer* (1945).
▷L Smith, *Patchen* (1978)

PATEL, Ravji
(1939–68)

Indian (Gujarati) poet, who has achieved more than any of his contemporaries—in a context in which non-fiction prose has been paramount. He was influenced by many European models, particularly **Lorca**, and his poetry will undoubtedly gain the closer international attention it deserves. His *In Memory of Hushilah*, in which he uses the forms of the traditional *marahya* in order to mock it, was translated into English in *Poetry India* (II, 2). His employment of folk-rhythms and dialects to create a new and viable Gujarati poetry has been widely admired.

PATER, Walter Horatio
(1839–94)

English critic and essayist, born in London, the son of a doctor. He was educated at King's School, Canterbury, and Queen's College, Oxford, became a fellow of Brasenose College and from then on lived the life of a scholar. His *Studies in the History of the Renaissance* (1873) shows the influence of the pre-Raphaelites with whom he associated. His philosophic romance, *Marius the Epicurean* (1885), appealed to a wider audience. His *Imaginary Portraits* (1887) and *Appreciations* (1889), followed by *Plato and Platonism* (1893), established his position as a critic, but already people were beginning to talk of his influence as being unhealthy, in the sense that he advocated a cultivated hedonism. That his neo-Cyrenaism, as it might be called, involved strenuous self-discipline hardly occurred to his critics, who found in his style alone an enervating quality. His influence on Oxford, however, was profound. He died having left unfinished another romance, *Gaston de Latour* (1896).
▷A C Benson, *Walter Pater* (1906)

PATERSON, Banjo (Andrew Barton)
(1864–1941)

Australian bush poet and balladeer, born at 'Narrambla', Orange, New South Wales, best known for his verse 'Waltzing Matilda', which he set to an old Scottish melody to become the 'unofficial' national anthem of Australia. Under the pseudonym 'The Banjo' (the name of a bush racehorse) he contributed verse to the Sydney periodical, the *Bulletin*. *Clancy of the Overflow* appeared there in 1889, and *The Man from Snowy River* the following year. By 1895 these verses and others had become so popular, and had been reprinted so widely, that they were collected as *The Man from Snowy River, and Other Verses*, the first of many such collections of his work. *Rio Grande's Last Race, and Other Verses* followed in 1902, and his popular bush character appeared in *Saltbush Bill JP, and Other Verses* in 1917. His first *Collected Verse* was published in 1923. He also wrote two novels and a collection of short stories, a book of verse for children, illustrated by **Norman Lindsay**, *The Animals Noah Forgot* (1933), and edited a pioneering collection of *Old Bush Songs* (1905).
▷C Gemmler, *The Banjo of the Bush* (1966)

PATMORE, Coventry Kersey Dighton
(1823–96)

English poet, born in Woodford, Essex. An assistant librarian at the British Museum, he was associated with the Pre-Raphaelite brotherhood whose members were much taken with his verse. The epitome of Victorian values, a father to six children and a husband to three wives, his best work is *The Angel in the House* (4 vols, 1854), a poetic treatment of married love which delighted a generation devoid of cynicism. A rabid Tory who put England's decline down to 'the disenfranchisement (in 1867) of the upper and middle classes by the false English nobles and their Jew', his conversion to Roman Catholicism after the death of his first wife may well have been responsible for the plummet in his popularity. Later works include *The Unknown Eros* (1877) and *The Rod, The Root and the Flower* (1895), a collection of religious meditations.
▷J C Reid, *The Mind and Art of Coventry Patmore* (1957)

PATON, Alan
(1903–88)

South African writer and educator, born in Pietermaritzburg. Educated at the University of Natal, he spent 10 years as a schoolteacher, first at a native school and later at Pietermaritzburg College. From 1935 to 1948 he was principal of the Diepkloof Reformatory for young offenders, where he became known for the success of his enlightened methods. From his deep concern with the racial problem in South Africa sprang the novel *Cry the Beloved Country* (1948). His other novels were *Too Late the Phalarope* (1953) and *Ah, But Your Land is Beautiful* (1981). He also wrote *Hope for South Africa* (1958), a political study written from the Liberal standpoint, *Debbie Go Home* (1961, short stories), *Instrument of Thy Peace* (1968), *Apartheid and the Archbishop* (1973), and his autobiography, *Towards the Mountain* (1981). He was national president of the South African Liberal Party from 1953 to 1960.

▷E Callan, *Alan Paton* (1968)

PATON WALSH, Jill (Gillian Honoinne Mary)

(1937–)

English children's author, born in London and educated at Oxford. She began writing when she left teaching to raise a family. Her first book was *Hengest's Tale* (1966), a rather dour historical novel set in the Dark Ages. This was followed by *The Dolphin Crossing* (1967), about two boys helping at Dunkirk, but both were significantly surpassed by *Fireweed* (1970), a novel set in the London Blitz. *Goldengrove* (1972) and its sequel *Unleaving* (1976), taking their titles from a **Gerard Manley Hopkins** poem, are considered her best work. She won the Whitbread Award for *The Emperor's Winding-Sheet* (1974), and the Smarties Prize for *Gaffer Samson's Luck* (1984). Recent works have consolidated her focus on adolescence rather than childhood. She has also written for adults.

PATSAUQ, Markoosie *see* MARKOOSIE

PATTEN, Brian

(1946–)

English poet and playwright, born in Liverpool and educated at Sefton Park Secondary, after which he worked as a reporter. With **Roger McGough** and **Adrian Henri** he shared the phenomenally successful *Penguin Modern Poets 10* (1967). Patten was, perhaps, the closest of the three to the earlier English tradition, and there are moments in the early poems, those gathered in *Walking Out: The Early Poems of Brian Patten* (1970), or in the fine sequence *Notes to the Hurrying Man* (1969), which align him with the 19th-century greats. However 'serious' he appears, relative to McGough, Patten is never academically sententious; the bizarrely titled *The Eminent Professors and the Nature of Poetry as Enacted Out By Members of the Poetry Seminar One*

Rainy Evening (1972) neatly captures his view of the literary world's pretensions. Later volumes include *The Unreliable Nightingale* (1973) and *Love Poems* (1981). In 1983, he joined McGough and Henri in an updated version of *The Mersey Sound*. He has written for the theatre and for children; *Gargling with Jelly* (1985) is a small masterpiece.

PATTEN, William Gilbert, pseud Burt L Standish

(1866–1945)

American novelist, born in Maine. He began as a writer of Westerns, using the name William West Wilder. But it was with the pseudonym Burt L Standish that he achieved huge commercial success with his stories for boys featuring an all-American lad from Yale named Frank Merriwell. The series included more than 200 titles and is said to have sold more than 10 million copies. *Mr. Frank Merriwell* (1941) was a curiously belated attempt to bring his priggish hero up against contemporary issues.

PATTERSON, H Orlando

(1926–)

Jamaican novelist and sociologist. He is the author of *Children of Sisyphus* (1965), probably the most vivid and authentic study ever made of the Rastafarian cult in fictional form—it has not yet had its due from critics. Besides important sociological studies, he has written further novels, of which *An Absence of Ruins* (1967) and *Die the Long Day* (1972), stand out.

PAULDING, James Kirke

(1778–1860)

American writer, born in Great Nine Partners (Putnam County), New York. He was a friend and associate of **Washington Irving** in *Salmagundi* (1807–8), and during the 1812 war published the *Diverting History of John Bull and Brother Jonathan*. In 1814 a more serious work, *The United States and England*, gained him an appointment on the Board of Naval Commissioners. He also wrote *The Dutchman's Fireside* (1831), *Westward Ho!* (1832), a *Life of Washington* (1835), and a defence of *Slavery in the United States* (1836). From 1838 to 1841 he was secretary of the navy.

▷A L Herold, *James Kirke Paulding: Versatile American* (1926)

PAULIN, Tom

(1949–)

British poet, born in Leeds but brought up in Belfast. He was educated at the universities of Hull and Oxford, and now lectures at Nottingham University. He is usually numbered among the Ulster Poets, and much of his writing in both poetry and prose is directly concerned with the political and social realities of life in Northern Ireland. His urban poems are hard-hitting and often violent in their preoccupations, and make skilful use of vernacular idioms. His principal collections include *A State of Justice* (1977), *The Strange Museum* (1980) and *Selected Poems 1972–1990* (1993). *The Riot Act* (1985) and *Seize the Fire* (1990) are versions of classic Greek texts with distinct contemporary resonances. He has also published essay collections, notably *Ireland and the English Crisis* (1984) and *Minotaur: Poetry and the Nation State* (1992).

PAUSTOVSKY, Konstantin
(1892–1968)

Russian novelist and memoirist, born in Moscow and brought up in Kiev. His most famous work is his six-part autobiography, *Povest o zhini* (1945–64, Eng trans *The Story of a Life*, 1964; *Slow Approach of Thunder*, 1965; *In That Dawn*, 1967; *Years of Hope*, 1968; *Southern Adventure*, 1969; *The Restless Years*, 1974). In this work, with its memories of such men as **Babel** and **Bulgakov**, Paustovsky presented what is perhaps the most 'human face' of all loyal communists, that of a man who could not be corrupted by even the worst excesses of Stalinism. It was somewhat overrated in the West, and has hardly lasted. His fiction and plays are, by contrast, run-of-the-mill.
▷G Simmonds (ed), *Soviet Leaders* (1967)

PAVESE, Cesare
(1908–50)

Italian novelist, poet, critic and translator, born in Piedmont. He was brought up in Turin where he worked for Einaudi, the publisher. Among his translations, that of **Melville**'s *Moby-Dick* (1932) is regarded as a classic. A leader of the Italian post-war Neorealist school he was politically disillusioned and sexually neurotic and he committed suicide. His poetry is slight; his finest works are novels like *La casa in collina* (1949, Eng trans *The House on the Hill*, 1961) and *La luna e i falò* (1950, Eng trans *The Moon and the Bonfire*, 1952), which express precisely and categorically his abhorrence of war and fascism.
▷D Lajolo, *Absurd Vice: a biography of Pavese* (1983)

PAYN, James
(1830–98)

English novelist, born in Cheltenham. He was educated at Eton, Woolwich Academy, and

Trinity College, Cambridge. In 1853 he published a volume of *Poems*, from 1859 to 1874 was editor of *Chambers's Journal*, and from 1882 to 1896 edited the *Cornhill*. He wrote a hundred novels, such as *Lost Sir Massingberd* (1864), *By Proxy* (1878) and *The Luck of the Darrells* (1885).

PAYNE, John Howard
(1791–1852)

American actor and playwright, born in New York. He made his debut there in February 1809, and in 1813 appeared in London. For 30 years he had a successful career as an actor and author of plays, chiefly adaptations. His play *Clari* contains the song 'Home, Sweet Home', the music being by Sir Henry Bishop. Payne was appointed American consul in Tunis in 1841.
▷G Overmeyer, *America's First Hamlet* (1957)

PAYNO Y FLORES, Manuel
(1810–94)

Mexican novelist, whose popular serialized adventure stories were well written and gave vivid pictures of the society of his times. Best known is *El fistol del diablo* (1845–6, 'The Devil's Scarf Pin'). He could be compared to **Henty**, but his range was far less wide, and he wrote for adults.

PAYRO, Roberto J
(1867–1928)

Argentinian novelist, dramatist and socialist, born in Mercedes, Buenos Aires. He was markedly anti-German, and was imprisoned by the Germans for his criticisms of them while he was working in Belgium during World War I. As a novelist his strength lay in his humorous, shrewd, and compassionate portrayal of rural life in the Argentine. He was a ruthless and effective critic of corruption. His real mentor was **Peréz Galdós**, and all his best novels owe a debt to the Spaniard. The episodic *Pago chico* (1908), about political corruption in the provinces, is less substantial than the longer, often very funny, picaresque *El casamiento de Laucha* (1906, 'Laucha's Marriage'), in which a scoundrel prospers amongst his fellow frauds. His gaucho plays were popular in their time, and his urban novel *Divertidas aventuras del nieto de Juan Moreira* (1910, 'Diverse Adventures of Juan Moreira'), again about a rogue, survives in dramatizations. Three stories are translated in *Tales from the Argentine* (1930).

PAZ, Octavio
(1914–)

Mexican poet, winner of the Nobel Prize for literature, born in Mexico City. He attended the National University of Mexico, and fought on the Republican side in the Spanish Civil War. Diplomat (he was ambassador to India in the 1960s), essayist and editor, with strong metaphysical leanings, he is best known for his poetry. His long poem, *Piedra de sol* (1957, Eng trans *Sun Stone*, 1963), is one of the most remarkable of 10 volumes that have appeared. There is also a perceptive study of Mexican character and culture, *El laberinto de la soledad* (1950, rev edn 1959, Eng trans *The Labyrinth of Solitude*, 1962). *Postdata* (1970, Eng trans *The Other Mexico: Critique of the Pyramid*, 1972), written after the student massacre and other events in 1968, revises views he had held earlier. Thereafter he emigrated to Britain. He was awarded the 1990 Nobel Prize for literature.

▷I Ivask, *The Perpetual Present: the poetry and prose of Octavio Paz* (1973)

P'BITEK, Okot
(1931–82)

Ugandan poet, writing in English. He was born in Gulu, northern Uganda, and attended the Government Training College at Mbarara (1952–4), returning to his home township as a teacher of English and religious knowledge. His first publication was *Lak tar miyo Kinyero wi lobo?* (1953), written in the Acoli language. A gifted footballer, p'Bitek was a Ugandan international. He decided to remain in England following a soccer tour and studied law at the University College, Aberystwyth, and social anthropology at Oxford, a discipline he then rejected along with the Christianity of his upbringing. He returned to Uganda for a time in 1962 and began to research folk culture and oral literature. *Song of Lawino* (1966) and its 'response' *Song of Ocol* (1970) were originally written in Acoli but translated by the poet himself. He controversially steered the Ugandan national theatre in the direction of folk arts; he was dismissed from the Cultural Centre in Kampala, and thereafter spent much of the rest of his life working in universities abroad—in Zambia, Nigeria and the US—before returning to Makerere as Professor of Creative Writing; he died shortly thereafter. Other works include collections of Acoli songs and tales, *The Horn of My Love* (1974) and *Hare and Hornbill* (1978), and an important book of essays *Africa's Cultural Revolution* (1973).

▷G A Heron, *The Poetry of Okot p'Bitek* (1976)

PEACOCK, Thomas Love
(1785–1866)

English novelist and poet, born in Weymouth, the son of a London merchant. He was a friend of **Shelley**. He entered the service of the East India Company in 1819 after producing three satirical romances, *Headlong Hall* (1816), *Melincourt* (1817) and *Nightmare Abbey* (1818). *Crochet Castle* (1831) concluded this series of satires, and in 1860 *Gryll Grange* appeared. He also published two romances, *Maid Marian* (1822) and *The Misfortunes of Elphin* (1829). The framework of his satirical fictions is always the same—a company of humorists meet in a country house and display the sort of crotchets or prejudices which Peacock, the reasonable man, most disliked: morbid romance, the mechanical sort of political economy, the 'march of science' and transcendental philosophy. The poets of the Romantic school, **Wordsworth**, **Coleridge**, Shelley, **Byron** and **Robert Southey**, are caricatured along with the Edinburgh Reviewers, who offer the extra target of being Scots.

▷M van Doren, *Thomas Love Peacock* (1911)

PEACOCKE, Isabel Maude
(1881–1973)

New Zealand writer of novels for adults and children. From 1915, with *My Cousin Phil*, to *The Good Intentions of Angela* (1937) and *Lizbett Anne* (1939), she produced 25 stories for children, young and older. The later books were among the first of their kind to establish a 'sense of place' and to set her characters in recognizable surroundings—usually her home town of Auckland. Her adult novels, however, are a late flowering of the melodramatic and moralistic Victorian novel with an emphasis on the sanctity of marriage and the benefits of resisting temptation; in *Cinderella's Suitors* (1918) her heroine eventually throws away an inheritance upon marriage, only to find that she gets the money after all as a reward for her self-denial. Four other adult novels appeared before 1929; she then returned to adult fiction in the 1940s. Her last book, *Change Partners*, was published in 1955.

PEAKE, Mervyn Laurence
(1911–68)

English author and artist, born in south China, where his father was a missionary. He was educated at Tientsin Grammar School, Eltham College and the Royal Academy Schools. While living on Sark (1933–5) and thereafter teaching at the Westminster School of Art, his reputation as an artist grew. His first book was a children's story, *Captain Slaughterboard Drops Anchor* (1939), with his own illustrations. *The Craft of the Lead Pencil* (1946), a book on drawing, was published in the same year as his first novel, *Titus Groan*, the first part of a Gothic fantasy trilogy completed in *Gormenghast* (1950) and *Titus Alone*

(1959). Another novel, *Mr Pye*, appeared in 1953, and his only play, *The Wit to Woo*, in 1957. He published two volumes of verse, *Shapes and Sounds* (1941) and *The Glassblowers* (1950), a ballad set during the blitz, *The Rhyme of the Flying Bomb*, the lighter sketches collected in *A Book of Nonsense* (1972). He illustrated several classics, notably *Treasure Island*, *The Hunting of the Snark* and *The Ancient Mariner*.

PEARCE, Philippa
(1920–)

English children's novelist and short-story writer, born in Great Shelford, Cambridgeshire. From 1945 she spent 13 years scriptwriting in the BBC's schools broadcasting department, then became an editor, first with Oxford University Press and later with André Deutsch. Her first novel, *Minnow On the Say* (1955), combines the excitement of a treasure-hunt with the relaxed, at times poetic, depiction of her home territory. Her second, *Tom's Midnight Garden* (1958), won the Carnegie Medal; a magical but credible story of time travel and nascent sexuality, it is among the most enduringly popular of post-war novels for children. Her other books include *A Dog So Small* (1962), set, again, just south of Cambridge, and *The Strange Sunflower* (1966), about a boy's dream trip to Sunflower Land.

PEARSE, Patrick Henry
(1879–1916)

Irish poet, polemicist, politician and insurrectionist, born in Dublin of an English father and Irish mother. In 1908 he founded St Endas, a school in which he promoted traditional Gaelic–Irish language and custom. He was a member of the Irish Volunteers and the more socialist-orientated Irish Republican Brotherhood. He led the Easter Rising of 1916 and was executed by the British in May of that year. Despite late 20th-century revisionism, he remains a totem for much Republican thinking in Ireland and an inspiration for the positive role of Irish heritage in education. His pamphlet *The Murder Machine* (1916), a selection of articles on Irish school practices, attacks accepted schoolroom tactics of teaching rather than educating, and presents a stimulating argument for change. His *Political Writings and Speeches* (1952) and *Poems* (1958) are evidence of his deeply felt political and social commitment: 'I speak, being full of vision/I speak to my people, and I speak in my people's name to the masters of my people ... Beware of the thing that is coming, beware of the risen people' ('The Rebel').
▷ R D Edwards, *Patrick Pearse: The Triumph of Failure* (1977)

PECHAM, or PECKHAM, John
(d.1292)

English Latin poet and Archbishop of Canterbury. A priest of the Franciscan order, he issued a codified series of rules for the clergy at the Lambeth Council of 1281. Written in church Latin, they represent a complete prescription for the way a priest should live his life, touching on love, chastity, obedience, etc. His religious poetry also reflects his conservative theology, and stresses the mystical experience of the love of Christ.

PEDRAYO, Ramón Otero
(1888–1972)

Galician writer, a member of the group centred around the Galician magazine *Non, Us*. He wrote an important book about Galician culture, *Ensaio sobre a cultura gelega* (1954, 'Essay on the Galician Culture'), which was published in Lisbon at the height of the Franco tryanny.

PEELE, George
(c.1558–1596)

English Elizabethan dramatist, born in London. He went up to Oxford in 1571, where he took his bachelor's degree in 1577 and his master's in 1579. By 1581 he had moved to London, where for 17 years he lived a roistering Bohemian life as actor, poet and playwright. He was one of those warned to repentance by **Henry Greene** in his *Groatsworth of Wit* (1592). *The Arraignment of Paris* (1584) is a dramatic pastoral containing ingenious flatteries of Queen Elizabeth. Other works include his *Farewell* to Sir John Norris on his expedition to Portugal (1589, eked out by *A Tale of Troy*), *Eclogue Gratulatory* (1589) to the Earl of Essex, *Polyhymnia* (1590), *Speeches* for the reception of Queen Elizabeth (1591), and *Honour of the Garter* (1593). The historical play of *Edward I* (1593) is marred by its slanders against Queen Eleanor. His play, *The Old Wives' Tale* (1595), probably gave **Milton** the subject for his *Comus*. *David and Bethsabe* was published in 1599.
▷ P H Cliford, *George Peele* (1913)

PÉGUY, Charles Pierre
(1873–1914)

French nationalist, publisher, and neo-Catholic poet, born of peasant stock in Orléans. He was educated at the École Normale and the Sorbonne, after which he opened a bookshop. In 1900 he founded the *Cahiers de la quinzaine* in which were first published his own works as well as those of such writers as **Romain Rolland**. Deeply patriotic, he combined sincere Catholicism with socialism and his writings reflect his intense desire for justice and truth. His most important works include *Le Mystère de la charité de Jeanne d'Arc* (1910, 'The Mystery of Joan of Arc's Charity'), *Victor Marie, Comte Hugo* (1910, 'Victor Hugo'), *L'Argent* (1912, 'Money') and *La Tapisserie de Notre Dame* (1913, 'The Tapestry of Notre Dame'). He was killed in World War I.

▷ R Rolland, *Charles Péguy* (1944)

PEKKANEN, Toivo
(1902–57)

Major Finnish novelist, dramatist and poet, born in Kotka. Until he was almost 30 he worked as a blacksmith. He was the first important Finnish 'proletarian' writer, a genre already well established in Norway and Sweden. *Lapsuuteni* (1953, Eng trans *My Childhood*, 1966), a starkly objective autobiography, is an established classic. His great Kotka saga, consisting of many volumes, has divided critics, some of whom see it as political, while others regard it as having an almost esoteric depth. His style has been well described as one of 'earnest artlessness'; his best works of fiction await translation into English.

▷ K Kare, *Toivo Pekkanen* (1952, in Finnish)

PELLICER, Carlos
(1897–1976)

Mexican poet, born in Villahermosa in Tabasco. He is most famous for his sonnets, which he began writing very early in his life; but he also wrote many poems in a pellucid free verse. He was a member of the *Contemporáneos* group, which established modern poetry in Mexico. For himself he chose to follow the traditions laid down by **Othón** and **Ramón López Velarde**, the two quintessentially Mexican, and proto-modern, poets of the generation that preceded his. Throughout his life he remained committed both to the left-wing and to a Bolivarist ideal of a union of Latin America; he went to Europe in 1937 with other Mexicans, **Paz** amongst them, to give support to the Spanish Republic. But he firmly believed that such beliefs were, as he said, 'in agreement with Christian doctrine'. In his poetry—which is unusually optimistic for a modern Mexican—it has been claimed that 'he uses landscape in such a way that through it the words are expressed'.

▷ *Southern Review* (Spring 1965)

PELLICO, Silvio
(1789–1854)

Italian writer and patriot, born in Saluzzo in Piedmont. He spent four years in Lyons, and in Milan (1810) was French tutor at the military school. His tragedies of *Laodamia* and *Francesca da Rimini* (1815) made his name, and he translated **Byron**'s *Manfred*. In 1820 he was arrested and imprisoned for two years in Venice. He was then, on a charge of Carbonarism, condemned to death, but had his sentence commuted to 15 years' imprisonment in the Spielberg near Brünn, and was released in 1830. During this time he wrote two other dramas. He published an account of his imprisonment, *Le mie Prigioni* (1833, 'My Prisons'), and subsequently numerous tragedies, poems and a catechism on the duties of man.

▷ I Rineri, *Della vita e delle opera di Silvio Pellico* (1898–1901)

PEMBERTON, Sir Max
(1863–1950)

English writer, born in Birmingham. Educated at Merchant Taylors' School and Gonville and Caius College, Cambridge, he was editor of *Chums* (1892–3) and of *Cassell's Magazine* from 1896 to 1906. He produced a succession of historical romances including *Impregnable City* (1895), *Queen of the Jesters* (1897), *The Show Girl* (1909), *Captain Black* (1911) and *The Mad King Dies* (1928). He also wrote revues and plays. He founded the London School of Journalism, and in 1920 became a director of Northcliffe newspapers, two years later publishing a biography of Lord Northcliffe (Alfred Harmsworth).

PEMBROKE, Countess of, née **Mary Sidney**
(1561–1621)

English poet and patron of the arts, born at Tickenhall near Bewdley, Worcestershire. Educated at home, she learnt Latin, French, Italian and probably Greek. She went to court in 1575 and two years later married Henry Herbert, Earl of Pembroke, her elder by 30 years. This involved her in the administration of four country estates; at the same time she maintained a close literary collaboration with her brother Sir **Philip Sidney**, which produced, amongst others, translations of the *Psalms*. She also edited his *The Countess of Pembroke's Arcadia* (1593), and wrote elegies for him; preserving his memory after his early death became her overriding concern.

▷ M P Hannay, *Philip's Phoenix* (1990)

PENA, Luis Carlos Martins
(1815–48)

Brazilian writer of comedies, who was one of the chief pioneers of his country's theatre, being the first playwright to write on Brazilian themes. His 19 comedies were almost all successful; *O Juiz de Paz na Roca* (1838, 'Justice of the Peace of the Plantation') was the first of them. His most famous play is the tragic farce *O Noviço* (1845, 'The Novice').

PENDSE, Shripad Narayan
(1913–)

Indian (Marathi) novelist, an heir to and improver on the tradition of serious fiction established by **Hari Narayan Apte**. Pendse is noted for his human and humane depiction of female characters in a male-dominated society. *Garambicha Bapu* (1952) was translated as *Wild Bapu of Garambicha* in 1969.

PENNA, Sandro
(1906–77)

Italian poet from Perugia, whose poetry dealt mainly with homosexual love, and did so more boldly and openly than any other 20th-century poet's other than **Cavafy**'s. He is thus, with **Cernuda**, valued as one of the century's most important writers of this kind. His chief preoccupation was with boys, not always a popular predilection; but in his work celebration of their beauty seems innocent and, in any case, foredoomed. His candour is therefore of a unique brand, and the lyric record which he left of his questing life—much of it spent cruising in Rome, where he lived—is an instructive one. He was greatly influenced, like **Quasimodo**, by the simplicity of the Greek lyric poets, and by his friend, early model and great encourager, the Triestine **Umberto Saba**. The tension in his poetry between the natural, which he so desperately sought, and the forbidden, gives it a highly significant aura. In him homosexuality was emphatically not a matter of 'choice'. There are English translations in: C L Golino (ed), *Contemporary Italian Poetry* (1962).
▷ *Books Abroad*, 47 (1973)

PENNANEN, Jarno
(1916–)

Finnish novelist, translator and critic, born in Tampere. Her highly charged psychological novels and stories usually deal with children or young people; she is unlucky not to have found a translator.

PEPYS, Samuel
(1633–1703)

English diarist and Admiralty official, son of a London tailor. He was educated at St Paul's School and Trinity Hall and Magdalene College, Cambridge. After the Civil War he lived poorly with his young wife, Elizabeth St Michel, whom he married in 1655, but after the Restoration, through the patronage of the Earl of Sandwich, his father's cousin, he rose rapidly in the naval service and became secretary to the Admiralty in 1672. He lost his office and was imprisoned on account of his alleged complicity in the Popish Plot (1679), but was reappointed in 1684 and in that same year became President of the Royal Society. At the Revolution (1688) he was again removed from office. The celebrated Diary, which ran from 1 January 1660 to 31 May 1669, the year his wife died and his eyesight failed him, is of extraordinary interest, both as the personal record (and confessions) of a man of abounding love of life, and for the vivid picture it gives of contemporary life, including naval administration and Court intrigue. The highlights are probably the accounts of the three disasters of the decade—the great plague (1665–6), the great fire of London (1666) and the sailing up the Thames by the Dutch fleet (1665–7). The veracity of the Diary has been accepted. It was apparently written in cipher (a kind of shorthand), in which form it remained at Magdalene College till 1825, when it was deciphered and edited.
▷ A Bryant, *Pepys* (3 vols, 1933–8)

PERALTA BARNUEVO, Pedro de
(1664–1743)

Peruvian poet and historian, born in Lima. He taught mathematics at San Marcos University in Lima, and served as Rector there. His *Lima fundada* (1732), a verse epic of Pizarro, set the Inquisition on his trail for 'endangering the Faith'. He was a pioneer of the scientific method, some of whose investigations now look ludicrous—by no means all of his *Gongoriste* conceits in his poetry are effective—but he was a deeply serious man, astronomer, engineer, and sceptic, whose efforts have now been fully appreciated.

PERCIVAL, James Gates
(1795–1856)

American poet, born in Berlin, Connecticut. He graduated from Yale in 1815, studied botany and medicine, and became Professor of Chemistry at West Point in 1824 and of geology at Wisconsin in 1854. His poems *Prometheus* and *Clio* appeared between 1822 and 1827, and *The Dream of a Day* in 1843.
▷ F Cogswell, *James Gates Percival and His Friends* (1902)

PERCY, Thomas
(1729–1811)

English antiquary, poet and churchman, author of *Percy's Reliques*, born in Bridgnorth, the son of a grocer. Educated at Bridgnorth Grammar School and Christ Church, Oxford, he became vicar of Easton Maudit in Northamptonshire (1753) and also rector of Wilby (1756). Later he was appointed chaplain to the Duke of Northumberland and George III, Dean of Carlisle (1778) and Bishop of Dromore (1782). As a man of letters his fame rests on his *Reliques of Ancient English Poetry* (1765), largely compiled from a 17th-century manuscript of medieval ballads and other material found in a house in Shifnal, Shropshire, and much 'restored' by him. Earlier he had published the first English version of a Chinese novel, *Hau Kiou Choaun* (1761, translated from the Portuguese), and *Miscellaneous Pieces translated from the Chinese* (1762). Prompted by the success of **James Macpherson**'s spurious Ossianic translations, he also published, anonymously, *Runic Poetry translated from the Icelandic language* (1763), a group of five poems actually translated from Latin versions. He later wrote a ballad of his own, *The Hermit of Warkworth* (1771).

PERCY, Walker
(1916–90)

American novelist, born in Birmingham, Alabama. He studied medicine, intending to make this his career, but had to abandon it when he contracted tuberculosis. His first novel, *The Moviegoer* (1961), won a National Book Award. A philosophical writer, his novels are firmly grounded in social observation seen from the standpoint of a liberal Catholic Southerner. *Love in the Ruins* (1971) was subtitled 'The Adventures of a Bad Catholic at a Time Near the End of the World'. He is the author of several novels, including *The Last Gentleman* (1966), *The Second Coming* (1980) and *The Thanatos Syndrome* (1987). He also wrote *Novel-Writing in an Apocalyptic Time* (1984).
▷L A Lawson and V A Kramer, *Conversations with Walker Percy* (1985)

PEREC, Georges
(1936–82)

French novelist, born in Paris. His first novel, *Les Choses* (1965), won the Prix Renaudot, and was eventually published in English, in 1990, as *Things: A Story of the Sixties*. *La Vie mode d'emploi* (1978) won the Prix Medicis, and in 1985 was voted Novel of the Decade by the Salon du Livre. Published in English as *Life: A User's Manual* (1987), it is a compendious and complicated tome, the most finely wrought work of a playful polymath. A man devoted to literary and linguistic puzzles, Perec also succeeded in writing a complete novel, *La Disparition* ('A Void'), without using the letter E. In conjunction with his burgeoning career as a writer, he worked, from 1962 until his death, as an archivist in a medical research library in Paris.

PEREDA, José Maria de
(1833–1906)

Spanish novelist, born in Polanco near Santander. His novels give a realistic picture of the people and scenery of the region where he was born and where much of his life was spent, an outstanding example being *Sotileza* (1885, 'Sublety'). Other novels are *Del tal palo tal astilla* (1880, 'Like Father, Like Son'), *Pedro Sanchez* (1883) and, perhaps his finest, *Peñas arriba* (1895, 'Up the Mountain'). He was called 'the modern Cervantes'.
▷R Gullon, *Vida de Pereda* (1944)

PERELMAN, S(ydney) J(oseph)
(1904–79)

American humorous writer, born in Brooklyn, New York City. Graduating from Brown University in 1925 he contributed to magazines until the publication of *Dawn Ginsbergh's Revenge* (1929), which had the nation in stitches and secured the author's fame. He went to Hollywood and wrote scripts for, among others, the Marx Brothers. Latterly his work found its way to the *New Yorker* (from 1931) before coming to rest between hard covers. His writing is remarkable for its linguistic dexterity and ingenuity; he took pot shots at modern sitting ducks and most sunk under a side-splitting fusillade, though somehow the entertainment and advertising industries survived. He is at his best in *Crazy Like a Fox* (1944), *Westward Ha! or, Around the World in 80 Clichés* (1948), *The Swiss Family Perelman* (1950) and *The Road to Miltown, or, Under the Spreading Atrophy* (1957). *The Most of S J Perelman* was published in 1958.
▷D Herrmann, *S J Perelman: A Life* (1986)

PÉRET, Benjamin
(1899–1959)

French poet and short-story writer, born in Rézé. A member of the Dadaists and subsequently the Surrealists, he remained faithful throughout his career to the central figure of the latter group, **André Breton**, and to such methods as automatic writing. The best of his work was collected in *Main Forte* (1946) and *Feu Central* (1947). He fought in the Spanish Civil War, and later, following the fall of France, left his homeland, along with Breton, for Mexico. In 1949 he founded the Union Ouvrière Internationale (International Workers' Union), and once listed his hobby as 'insulting priests'.

PERETZ, Isaac Leib
(1851–1915)

Polish–Yiddish writer who was born in Zamoszcz. He spent his entire life in Poland. His first stories were in Polish, then he took to Hebrew; in 1888 he published his first story in Yiddish, and soon became the central literary figure in that language. Although quintessentially Jewish, he brought a deep understanding of Russian and European literatures into his fiction. He was an aggressive, courageous, Hasidic Messianist who argued against the doctrine of 'assimilation', and got himself banned from practising as a lawyer by the Tsarist authorities for it. The painter Chagall, amongst many others, was influenced by him. He wrote popular lyric poetry, realistic tales, and some lively plays. There are many volumes of English translations, including *My Memoirs* (1965) and *The Three Canopies* (1968).

▷C A Madison, *Yiddish Literature* (1968)

PÉREZ DE AYALA, Ramón
(1881–1962)

Spanish novelist, poet and critic, born in Oviedo. He first attracted attention with his poetry when *La paz del sendero* ('The Peace of the Path') was published in 1904. A sequel volume appeared in 1916 under the title *El sendero innumerable* ('The Innumerable Path'). As a novelist he combines realism with beauty, best shown in the philosophical *Belarmino y Apolonio* (1921). Other novels include the humorous and satirical *Troteras y Danzaderas* (1913), the anti-Jesuit *A.M.D.G.* (1910), and perhaps his best, *Tigre Juan* (1924) which, with *El Curandero de su honra* (1926, 'The Saviour of his Honour'), appeared in English as *Tiger Juan* (1933). Among his works of criticism are *Máscaras* (1917, 'Masks') and *Política y Toros* (1918, 'Politics and Bulls'). He was ambassador to London from 1931 to 1936.

▷F Agustin, *Ramón Pérez de Ayala, su vida e su obras* (1927)

PÉREZ GALDÓS, Benito
(1843–1920)

Spanish novelist, born in Las Palmas, Canary Islands. He moved to Madrid as a student in 1861, and supported his family by writing. He was a prolific novelist and dramatist, and also wrote journalism, travel diaries, criticism, and memoirs. He divided his novels, which are largely naturalistic in style, into categories in the manner of **Balzac**, the principle two being the novels of contemporary Spanish life and the 46-volume historical series he called 'Episodios nacionales'. He is an acute, psychological percipient observer of life, and has been considered the greatest Spanish novelist after **Cervantes**. His best book is the novel *Fortunata y Jacinta* (1886–7, Eng trans *Fortunata and Jacinta*, 1986).

▷B J Dendle, *Galdós: the mature thought* (1980)

PERI ROSSI, Cristina
(1941–)

Uruguayan militant, iconoclastic, feminist short-story and novel writer, poet, and journalist. Her work is among the best experimental fiction written by a Latin-American writer, and tests the limits of genre, language and form. Her main interests lie in shifting literature, society, and gender roles, and both her poetry and her prose employ humour and irony to illustrate the disintegration of outdated modes of social interaction. Among her awards are the **Benito Pérez Galdós** Prize for *La rebelión de los niños* (1976, 'The Children's Rebellion') and the Ciudad de Palma Prize for *Linguística General* (1979). She has lived in exile in Barcelona since 1972.

PÉRIER, Odilon Jean
(1900–28)

Belgian poet, playwright and novelist, born in Brussels. Unique in the literature, Périer's language is quite different from that of his contemporaries: unornamented, without affectation, and apparently uninfluenced by any ideas of his time. *Notre Mère la ville* (1922, 'Our Mother the Town') celebrates Brussels. He wrote a play and a novel called *Le Passage des Anges* (1926, 'The Crossing of Angels'). He died of a heart ailment. His finest work is usually said to be *Le Citadin*, a poem in classical alexandrines about Brussels; but in fact his work, although unusual, is not of major calibre.

PERRAULT, Charles
(1628–1703)

French writer, born in Paris. He studied law, and from 1654 to 1664 had an easy life working for his brother, the receiver-general of Paris. In 1663 he became a secretary or assistant to Colbert. His poem, *Le Siècle de Louis le Grand* (1687, 'The Century of Louis XIV'), and **Nicolas Boileau**'s outspoken criticisms of it, opened up the dispute about the relative merits of the ancients and moderns. To the modern cause Perrault contributed his poor *Parallèle des anciens et des modernes* (1688–96, 'Comparison of the Ancients and the Moderns'), and his *Hommes illustres qui ont paru en France pendant ce siècle* (1696–1700, 'Great Men Who Emerged in France this Century'). His *Mémoires* appeared in 1769. All his writings would have been forgotten but for his eight inimitable fairy tales, the *Histoires ou Contes du temps passé* (1697, Eng trans *Perrault's Popular Tales*, 1888), including 'Belle au bois dormant' ('The Sleeping Beauty'), 'Le Petit chaperon rouge' ('Red Riding Hood') and 'La Barbe-Bleuc' ('Bluebeard').

▷M Soriano, *Les contes de Perrault* (1968)

PERRY, Grace
(1927–)

Australian poet and paediatrician, publisher and cattle-breeder, born in Sydney. Her medical experience is reflected in much of her verse, from the early *Red Scarf* (1963) to the verse-diary which gives the title to *Journal of a Surgeon's Wife and Other Poems* (1976), the chronicle of a doctor's wife in early colonial Australia. Her strong feeling of place emerges in *Black Swans at Berrima* (1972) and *Berrima Winter* (1974), set around her historic home town in New South Wales. Much of her work is published from the South Head Press, which she established in 1964, the year in which she founded the quarterly journal *Poetry Australia.*

PERS, Ciro de
(1599–1663)

Italian poet and dramatist (*L'umilià esaltata o vero Ester regina*, 1664), born in Castello di Pers in Friuli. He was friendly with and influenced by the Marinist, **Achillini**. He went to Malta on a diplomatic mission (1627–9), but, unfortunate with his erotic undertakings, became a Knight of Malta and withdrew into seclusion. The two main themes of his notable poetry, Marinist in style, were the misery of human existence and the ecstatically melancholy tension achieved by meditation.
▷ B Croce, *Lirici marinisti* (1910)

PERSIUS (Aulus Persius Flaccus)
(34–62)

Roman satirist, born of a distinguished equestrian family in Volaterrae in Etruria. He was educated in Rome, where he came under Stoic influence. He wrote fastidiously and sparingly, leaving at his death only six admirable satires, the whole not exceeding 650 hexameter lines. These were published by his friend Cornutus after his death. **Dryden** and others have translated them into verse.
▷ E V Marmorale, *Persio* (1956)

PERZYNSKI, Wlodzimierz
(1878–1930)

Polish dramatist and writer of fiction, born in Opaczno. His ironic plays, revealing middle-class values by means of skilful dialogue, are frequently said to have been underrated— none appears to have been translated into English. They have been compared to those of **Shaw**. His fiction, however, has dated.

PESADO, José Joaquin
(1801–61)

Minor Mexican poet, whose ornate pre-romantic poems tried to incorporate the past of the Mexican Native Americans in a Spanish traditional style.

PESSHANA, Camilo
(1867–1926)

Portuguese Symbolist poet, born in Coimbra. He lived for many years in Macao, where he died. Like Arthur Waley in England, Pesshana translated Chinese poetry into his own language—unlike Waley, he hardly knew Chinese. But the effect was similar. His carefully wrought poetry, among the best written in Portugal before that of **Pessoa**, most of it collected in *Clepsidra* (1920), had a strong influence on **Sá-Carneiro** and on Pessoa himself.

PESSOA, Fernando António Nogueira
(1888–1935)

Portuguese poet, born in Lisbon and educated in South Africa. He studied briefly at Lisbon University and worked as a commercial translator. In 1915, he founded the journal *Orfeu*. After 1914, he created four distinct 'heteronyms', each one stylistically distinct and to some extent antagonistic. There was the Symbolist 'Fernando Pessoa', the pastoral 'Alberto Caeiro', the Futurist 'Álvaro de Campos', and the elegant classicist 'Ricardo Reis'. In addition, Pessoa created many other partial heteronyms, identities proliferating towards the point where there was a new author for each and every poem. His/their complete works were published from 1952, and an English translation was prepared by Jonathan Griffin in four volumes (1974); three volumes of *English Poems* had already appeared in 1921. It has been unconvincingly suggested that, far from being a conscious literary strategy, Pessoa's heteronymity was a symptom of multiple personality disorder, and there is in his work an awkward, unresolved balance between hectic self-probing and obsessiveness on the one hand, classicist escapism on the other. But, although he did live on the edge of sanity, this is a deliberately staged conflict. His is one of the essential literary careers of the Modernist movement.
▷ G Monteiro (ed), *The Man Who Never Was* (1982)

PETER DAMIEN (or DAMIANI), St
(c.1006–1076)

Italian poet, theologian and moralist. His theological writings are amongst the most severe arguments for the monastic way of life to be found anywhere: he views all love between humans as essentially evil, even within marriage, and he cites homosexuality as evidence of demonic possession. He was initially a friend of Pope Gregory VII, but later condemned him in verse. His own works were not universally popular within the church—Pope Leo IX condemned him for his cruelty. His religious poetry reflects his stern theology.

PETERKIEWICZ, Jerzy
(1916–)

Polish novelist, poet, playwright, critic and translator, long resident in the United Kingdom. His earlier and most interesting work is in Polish, his later in English. The Polish work, mostly poetry, is expressionistic. His English novels (eg *The Knotted Cord*, 1953) were catastrophic visions of nightmare futures and pasts running concurrently. Later he settled into a more predictable Roman Catholicism, and as a critic he has veered towards the Catholic right.

PETERKIN, Julia
(1880–1961)

American novelist, born in South Carolina. The wife of a plantation manager, she became known as the leading depictor of (and spokeswoman for) the region's Gullah Blacks. *Scarlet Sister Mary* (1928), which won a Pulitzer Prize, was dramatized, with white actors (such as Ethel Barrymore) in blackface. *Black April* (1927) was also a major novel. It is likely that criticism has not yet caught up with her achievement.

PETERS, Ellis *see* PARGETER, Edith

PETERSEN, Nis
(1897–1943)

Danish poet and novelist, cousin of **Kaj Munk**, born in South Jutland. He rebelled against a strict upbringing and became a journalist, casual labourer and vagabond until he became famous for his novel of Rome in the time of Marcus Aurelius, *Sandalmagernes Gade* (1931, Eng trans *The Street of the Sandal-makers*, 1932). His later poetry is highly considered; his verse appeared in a collected edition in 1949. His adult life was haunted by alcoholism and spiritual crises.
▷J Andersen, *Nis Petersen* (1957)

PETERSON, Ralph
(1921–)

Australian scriptwriter for radio, television and film, born in Adelaide. He has written for comedians Dick Bentley, Tony Hancock and Benny Hill, and attracted attention with his play *The Square Ring*, filmed by Ealing Studios with Jack Warner, Kay Kendall and Sid James; Peterson turned this into a novel in 1954. Since returning to Australia he has written a number of award-winning plays and television serials, a novel *Greater the Truth* (1956) concerning the conflicting claims on a journalist's conscience, and a play based on

the defection of a diplomat, *The Third Secretary* (1972).

PETÖFI, Sandor
(1823–49)

Hungarian poet, born in Kiskörös. He was successively actor, soldier and literary hack, but by 1844 had made his name as a poet. In 1848 he threw himself into the revolutionary cause, writing numerous war songs. He fell in battle at Segesvár. His poetry broke completely with the old pedantic style, and, full of national feeling, began a new epoch in Hungarian literature. He also wrote a novel called *A hóhér kötele* (1846, 'The Hangman's Rope'), and translated **Shakespeare**'s *Coriolanus*.
▷L Havatny, *Igy élt Petöfi* (5 vols, 1955–7)

PETRARCH, Francesco Petrarca
(1304–74)

Italian poet and scholar. One of the earliest and greatest of modern lyric poets, he was the son of a Florentine notary, who, exiled (1302) along with **Dante**, settled in Arezzo, where Francesco was born. In 1312 his father went to Avignon, then the seat of the papal court; and there and in Bologna the boy devoted himself with enthusiasm to the study of the classics. After his father's death Petrarch returned to Avignon (1326). Being without means, he became a churchman, though perhaps never a priest, and lived on the small benefices conferred by his many patrons. It was at this period (1327) that he first saw Laura (possibly Laure de Noves, married in 1325 to Hugo de Sade; she died, the mother of 11 children, in 1348). She inspired him with a passion which has become proverbial for its constancy and purity. Now began also his friendship with the powerful Roman family of the Colonnas. As the fame of Petrarch's learning and genius grew, his position became one of unprecedented influence. His presence at their courts was competed for by the most powerful sovereigns of the day. He travelled repeatedly in France, Germany and Flanders, searching for MSS. In Liège he found two new orations of **Cicero**, in Verona a collection of his letters, in Florence an unknown portion of Quintilian. Invited by the senate of Rome on Easter Sunday, 1341, he ascended the capitol clad in the robes of his friend and admirer, King Robert of Naples, and there, after delivering an oration, he was crowned poet laureate. In 1353, after the death of Laura and his friend Cardinal Colonna, he left Avignon and his country house at Vaucluse for ever, disgusted with the corruption of the papal court. His remaining years were passed in various towns of northern Italy. Petrarch may be considered as the earliest of the great

PETRESCU, Camil

humanists of the Renaissance. He himself chiefly founded his claim to fame on his epic poem *Africa* (Eng trans 1977), the hero of which is Scipio Africanus, and his historical work in prose, *De Viris Illustribus* ('On Famous Men'), a series of biographies of classical celebrities. Other Latin works are the eclogues and epistles in verse; and in prose the dialogues, *Secretum meum* ('My Secret'), the treatises *De Otio Religiosorum* (a work about the tranquillity of the monastic life) and *De Vita Solitaria* (Eng trans *The Life of Solitude*, 1924), and his letters—he was in constant correspondence with **Boccaccio**. It is as a poet that his fame has lasted for over five centuries. His title deeds to fame are in his *Canzoniere* (Eng trans *Sonnets and Stanzas*, 1879), in the Italian sonnets, madrigals, and songs, almost all inspired by his unrequited passion for Laura. The *Opera Omnia* ('Complete Works') appeared at Basel in 1544. His Italian lyrics were published in 1470, and have since gone through innumerable editions.
▷T Bergin, *Petrarch* (1970)

PETRESCU, Camil
(1894–1957)

Romanian novelist, playwright and poet who was well known in the inter-war period as a journalist, literary editor and theatre director. His remarkable genius collapsed in his last years, as a result of his attempt to become a socialist realist and to write a long novel reflecting the Marxist view of Romanian national history. He failed to complete it, and what he left of it is of no value. His greatest novel is *Patul lui Procust* (1933, 'Procrustian Bed'), which reflects the fruitful influence of the phenomenological philosopher Husserl, upon whom he had written a book. Here he anticipated many of the techniques to be employed by **Jean-Paul Sartre**. Also remarkable is the slightly earlier novel *Ultima noapte de dragoste, initia noapte de razboi* (1930, 'The Last Night of Love, the First Night of War').

PETRESCU, Cezar
(1892–1961)

Romanian popular novelist who also wrote for children. (He was not a relative of his namesake **Camil Petrescu**.) It has been said that, despite the lack of depth of his characters, his novels 'present the most complete tableau of Romanian life in the first half of [the 20th] century'. One, *Intunecare* (1927), has been translated as *Gathering Clouds* (1957). He has also been compared, with some aptness, to **Anthony Trollope**.

PETRONIUS ARBITER
(1st century)

Latin satirical writer, and author of the *Satyricon* ('Tales of Satyrs'). He is usually supposed to be the voluptuary Gaius Petronius, whom **Tacitus** calls 'arbiter elegantiae' at the court of Nero. He was governor of Bithynia for a time. The *Satyricon* is a long satirical romance in prose and verse, of which only parts of the 15th and 16th books, in a fragmentary state, are still extant. The work depicts with wit, humour and realism the licentious life in southern Italy of the moneyed class. The favour Petronius enjoyed as aider and abettor of Nero and his entourage in every form of sensual indulgence aroused the jealousy of another confidant, Tigellinus, who procured his disgrace and banishment. Ordered to commit suicide, he opened his veins.
▷H Rankin, *Petronius the Artist* (1971)

PETROV, Yevgeny *see* ILF, Ilya and PETROV, Yevgeny

PETRY, Ann
(1911–)

American novelist and short-story writer, born in Old Saybrook, Connecticut and educated at the University of Connecticut. She moved to New York in 1938 and worked as a reporter for *Amsterdam News* and *People's Voice*. She published her first short story, 'On Saturday the Siren Sounds at Noon', in 1943, after studying creative writing at Columbia University. Social realism characterizes her work: her first novel, *The Street* (1947), is an account of slum life and domestic unrest which ends in a tragic death, while *The Narrows* (1951) focuses on an inter-racial marriage, and again has a tragic outcome. Petry was the first black woman writer to sell over a million copies of a book.
▷M Pryse and H J Spillers (eds), *Conjuring: Black Women, Fiction, and Literary Tradition* (1985)

PÉTURSSON, Hallgrímur
(1614–74)

Icelandic poet, pastor and hymn-writer, the greatest devotional poet in Icelandic literature, who struggled with poverty all his life and died afflicted with leprosy. Born in the north of Iceland, he ran away to Denmark to become a blacksmith's apprentice, but was put to school in Copenhagen by an Icelandic patron, the future bishop Brynjólfur Sveinsson, who recognized his unusual abilities. He was entrusted with the task of rehabilitating the Icelandic survivors of a Moorish pirate raid on Iceland by 'Turks' (1627), whose captives had been sold as slaves and were now in Copenhagen after being ransomed. He fell in love with one of them, a 38-year-old Icelandic woman known as Turkish-Gydda. They married in Iceland, where Hallgrímur worked as a labourer before becoming pastor of the

church at Saurbær in the west of Iceland (1651). Here he wrote his masterpiece, *Passion Hymns* (1666), a cycle of 50 meditations on the Crucifixion. One of the hymns, *Allt eins og blómstrið eina* ('Just as the one true flower') is still sung at funerals in Iceland. The new cathedral in Reykjavík, Hallgrímskirkja, is named after him.
▷M Jónsson, *Hallgrímur Pétersson* (2 vols, 1947)

PEYREFITTE, Roger
(1907–)

French novelist. He wrote one serious novel, *Les Amitiés particulières* (1945, Eng trans *Special Friendships*, 1950), about homosexuality in a school, and then devoted himself to amusing, sophisticated but often irresponsible entertainments and exposés, such as *Les Clés de Saint Pierre* (1955, 'The Keys of St Peter'), which won him a bad reputation with critics and many readers. His penchant was for collecting embarrassing facts, which he then made even more ridiculous than they actually were.

PEZOA VÉLIZ, Carlos
(1879–1908)

Chilean poet, born in Santiago. He died prematurely from injuries received in the 1906 Valparaiso earthquake. His poetry—published posthumously as *Alma chilena* (1912, 'Chilean Soul'), is simple and unpretentious, and is now receiving the attention it has always deserved. There is an excellent anthology of his prose and poetry, *Antologia* (1957), with a useful introduction (in Spanish) by N Guzmán.

PHAEDRUS, Gaius Julius
(c 15 BC–c.50 AD)

Translator and adaptor of **Aesop**'s fables into Latin verse. Born in Macedonia, he was taken to Rome at an early age and became the freedman of Augustus or Tiberius. Under Tiberius he published the first two books of his fables, but his biting though veiled allusions to the tyranny of the emperor and his minister Sejanus caused him to be accused and condemned—his punishment is unknown. On the death of Sejanus he published his third book. The fourth and fifth books belong to his last years. He was more than a reproducer of Aesop; he invented fables of his own and also borrowed from other sources.

PHILIPPE, Charles-Louis
(1874–1909)

French novelist, born in Cérilly who, ill from early youth, died young of a syphilitic infection. He is best known for his naturalistic but softened, near-sentimental portraits of a prostitute and her pimp, *Bubu de Montparnasse* (1901, Eng trans 1932), but this is not quite typical of his work as a whole, which has attracted considerable critical interest since his death. His predominantly oral and highly complex style is original and has been influential (eg on **Larbaud**, but perhaps, too, on **Céline**). Such 'populiste' authors as **Eugène Dabit** also drew upon him for inspiration and example. In his unfinished novel *Charles Blanchard* (1913) he was experimenting in a rural setting. His *Le Père Perdrix* (1903) is available in English translation as *A Simple Story* (1924). 'Philippe', a critic has written, 'achieved that marvellous art which results from the reportage of the innocent eye and the humble heart'.

PHILIPS, Ambrose
(?1674–1749)

English poet, born in Shrewsbury. He was educated at St John's College, Cambridge, and became a fellow there. A friend of **Joseph Addison** and **Richard Steele**, he did hack work for Tonson, and gained a reputation by the *Winter-piece* in the *Tatler* and six Pastorals in Tonson's *Miscellany* (1709). These were praised in the *Guardian* at **Pope**'s expense, and Pope's jealousy started a bitter feud. He was dubbed 'Namby Pamby' by either **Henry Carey** or **Jonathan Swift** for the oversentimentality of some of his poetry. Of his plays only *The Distrest Mother* (1712), based on **Racine**'s *Andromaque*, found favour with his contemporaries. He was MP for Armagh, secretary to the Archbishop of Armagh, purse-bearer to the Irish Lord Chancellor, and registrar of the Prerogative Court.
▷Dr S Johnson, *Lives of the Most Eminent English Poets* (10 vols, 1779–81)

PHILIPS, John
(1676–1709)

English poet, born in Bampton, Oxfordshire. He was the son of the Archdeacon of Shropshire, and was educated at Winchester and Christ Church, Oxford. He wrote three very popular poems: *The Splendid Shilling* (1701), a Miltonic burlesque; *Blenheim* (1705), a Tory celebration of Marlborough's great victory; and *Cyder* (1708), an imitation of **Virgil**'s *Georgics*. He has a monument in Westminster Abbey.
▷Dr S Johnson, *Lives of the Most Eminent English Poets* (10 vols, 1779–81)

PHILIPS, Katherine, née **Fowler**, pseud 'Orinda'
(1631–64)

English poet, born in London, the daughter of a merchant. Called 'the matchless Orinda', at 16 she married James Philips of

Cardigan Priory. She is the first English woman poet to have her work published (it included an address to the Welsh poet **Henry Vaughan**). She received a dedication from Jeremy Taylor (*Discourse on the Nature, Offices and Measures of Friendship*, 1659). She ran a literary salon, described in the *Letter of Orinda to Poliarchus* (1705). She translated **Corneille**'s *Pompée*, which was performed in Dublin in 1663, and the greater part of his *Horace*. Her poems, surreptitiously printed in 1663, were issued in 1667. She died of smallpox on a visit to London.

▷P W Souers, *The Matchless Orinda* (1931)

PHILLIPS, Caryl
(1958–)

British novelist and author of non-fiction, born in St Kitts, West Indies. Brought up in England, he was educated at Oxford. His first novel, *The Final Passage* (1985), looks closely and often ironically at the West Indian experience of Britain. *A State of Independence* (1986), on the other hand, is a sympathetic study of a British West Indian who, after 20 years' absence from the Caribbean, returns on the eve of independence, only to discover that he has become an outsider. A writer noted for creating narrative in an episodic, fragmented, sometimes epistolary style, his powerfully haunting novel *Crossing the River* (1993) follows the lives, in different countries and different centuries, of two brothers and a sister sold into slavery.

PHILLIPS, David Graham
(1867–1911)

American feminist novelist and journalist, born in Madison, Indiana. He played a part in the 'muckraker' movement of reform-minded journalism in the early 20th century. He also wrote powerfully in several novels in favour of the emancipation of women, notably in *The Plum Tree* (1905) and *Susan Lennox: Her Fall and Rise* (1917), and was ultimately assassinated by a lunatic who regarded his efforts in this direction as contributory to female moral depravity. Despite the identification of his name with his attacks on political servitude to capitalist interests, it is for his devoted service to the cause of women's rights that he deserves best to be remembered.

▷L Filler, *Voice of Democracy* (1978)

PHILLIPS, Jayne Anne
(1952–)

American novelist and short-story writer, born in Buckhannon, West Virginia. She first became known in the UK as part of the 'dirty realism' school of American writers. If, however, that general label is at best an inexact description, in Phillips' case it is wholly inappropriate. While her work is based in a recognizable real world, it is also—as shown by her short-story collection *Black Tickets* (1979)—impressionistic, fanciful, and at times a touch precious. *Machine Dreams* (1984), her only novel to date, is easily her most accomplished and engaging work. The story of two generations of an American middle-class family who grow up to lose their illusions and see their dreams die, it is acted out against a background of social dislocation and the Vietnam War. Her other publications include the short-story collection *Fast Lanes* (1984).

PHILLIPS, John
(1631–1706)

English writer, brother of Edward Phillips, nephew of **Milton**. He was educated by his uncle, and replied to Salmasius's attack on him, and acted as his secretary. His *Satyr against Hypocrites* (1655) was a bitter attack on Puritanism, and *Speculum Crape Gownorum* (1682) on the High Churchmen.

PHILLIPS, Stephen
(1864–1915)

English dramatist and poet, born near Oxford and related to **Wordsworth** on his mother's side. He went to school at Oundle and then studied for the Civil Service but chose in preference to become an actor and a tutor. He published several volumes of poetry and, in 1898, won a 1000-guinea prize put up by a literary weekly. Four years later his verse play *Paolo and Francesca* became a stupendous hit at St James's Theatre and the critics hailed him as the new **Sophocles**, the new **Shakespeare**. The acclaim went to his head, the royalties were squandered, his marriage failed, the critics deserted him and friends tried in vain to take him in hand. His days ended in privation.

PHILLPOTTS, Eden
(1862–1960)

English novelist, dramatist and poet, born in Mount Aboo, India. He studied for the stage in London, but turned to literature instead (1893), and made his name by realistic novels chiefly dealing with Devonshire, such as *Lying Prophets* (1896), *Children of the Mist* (1898) and *Widecombe Fair* (1913). Of his plays, *The Farmer's Wife* (1917: staged 1924) and *Yellow Sands* (1926), which he wrote with his daughter Adelaide, were perhaps the most successful. He wrote more than 250 books in all, and collaborated with **Arnold Bennett** and **Jerome K Jerome** on plays.

▷*From the Angle of 88* (1951)

PHIPSON, Joan
(1912–)

Australian writer of fiction for children, born in Warrawee, New South Wales, whose first novel, *Good Luck to the Rider* (1953), won the Children's Book of the Year Award, as did the later *The Family Conspiracy* (1962). Her books range over a variety of themes, from fantasy to adventure, and from a historical re-creation *Bass and Billy Martin* (1972) to contemporary themes of the environment and urban life.

PICARD, Louis-Benoît
(1769–1828)

French dramatist and actor-manager, born in Paris. He wrote 85 plays, of which most were comedies. One, *Le conteur* (1793, 'The Storyteller'), remained in the repertory of the Comédie Française for 40 years; and many felt that he was the best painter of society since **Molière**. His work was meticulously crafted, and often shrewdly observant of contemporary manners.

▷W Staaks, *The Theatre of Louis-Benoît Picard* (1952)

PICCHIA, Paulo Menotti de
(1892–1976)

Brazilian poet. He was associated with Brazilian Modernism, but, before that, had become well known for his *Juca Mulato* poems, expressing (and anticipating) the 'back-to-primitive-roots' aspect of Modernism.

PICHETTE, Henri
(1924–)

French verse-dramatist, half-American by birth, whose oddly Surrealist–Classical plays were much heeded when they were given expensive productions in Paris. Characteristic is *Nucléa* (1952), written in alexandrines, about the struggle between good and evil.

▷L Pronko, *Théâtre d'avant garde* (1963, in French)

PICKEN, Ebenezer
(1769–1816)

Scottish poet, born in Paisley, the son of a silk weaver. He was educated at Glasgow University, and was a teacher in Edinburgh. He published several volumes of Scots poems, including satires, descriptive verses and songs; his principal works were *Poems and Epistles* (1788), and *Miscellaneous Poems and Songs* (1813). He also published an important *Pocket Dictionary of the Scottish Dialect* (1818).

PICKTHALL, Marjorie
(1883–1922)

English poet, short-story writer and novelist, born in Gunnersby. She emigrated with her family to Toronto in 1889, but returned to England after her mother's death in 1912, where she lived until 1920, briefly residing in Canada for the last two years of her life. She is best known as a poet of visionary lyrics, a reputation based on two major collections of poetry published during her lifetime—*The Drift of Pinions* (1913) and *The Lamp of Poor Souls* (1916)—but she was also the author of over 200 short stories, and a number of novels for adults and children. Her poetry presents a gentle imagery of natural beauty, tinted with the sadness of a vague sense of loss.

PIERCY, Marge
(1936–)

American novelist and poet, born in Detroit, Michigan. She was educated at the University of Michigan, and has taught in a number of colleges. Her writing stems from strongly held political and feminist standpoints. Novels like *Going Down Fast* (1969), *Small Changes* (1973) and *Vida* (1980) are revealing documents of the emerging feminist consciousness of the 1960s and 1970s. *Woman On the Edge of Time* (1976) was a science-fiction narrative which contrasted a future utopia with the economic, environmental and gender abuses of contemporary America. Later novels include *Gone to Soldiers* (1987), set during World War II. Her poetry has utilized vernacular language and speech rhythms to good effect.

PIEYRE DE MANDIARGUES, André Paul Édouard
(1909–91)

French novelist and poet, fondly remembered in the UK for the novel that provided the singer Marianne Faithfull with her one convincing film role, *Girl on a Motorcycle*. Pieyre de Mandiargues's ninth work of fiction, *La Motocyclette* (1963, published in the USA as *The Motorcycle*, 1966, in the UK as *The Girl on the Motorcycle*, 1966), was a work of highbrow erotica. As in all the other books, it presupposes that extremes of sensation yield moral or at least psychological insights. *Le Lis de Mer* (1956, Eng trans *The Girl Beneath the Lion*, 1958) is subtler but less dramatically compelling, and his other novels and short stories too often suggest formulaic wish-fulfilment. His verse has a sensuous quality that is reminiscent of the great French cabaret singers, but with a strong infusion of Surrealist imagery, and his admiration for the *trompe l'oeil* painter Arcimboldo *Arcimboldo le Merveilleux* (1977, Eng trans *Arcimboldo the Marvellous*, 1978)—suggests a sidelight on his characteristic technique. He has also translated into French works by **Yeats, Octavio Paz** and **Yukio Mishima**.

▷D Bond, *The Fiction of André Pieyre de Mandiargues* (1982)

PILKINGTON, Laetitia, née Van Lewen
(c.1706–1750)

Irish writer, born in Dublin, daughter of an obstetrician. She was an intimate friend of **Swift** and wrote verse from an early age. In 1725 she married a minor writer, Matthew Pilkington, who deserted her. She followed him to London but he divorced her in 1738 on grounds of adultery. Jailed for debt in 1742, she later supported herself by bookselling. Her vivacious *Memoirs* (1748–54) give a candid, racy account of her life and adventures, with revealing anecdotes of **Swift, Pope** and other authors. They include her poems: usually light-hearted or satirical, she can also write with dignity and feeling about personal misfortune.

▷*Memoirs*, ed I Barry (1928); V Woolf, *The Common Reader* (1925)

PILLECIJN, Filip de
(1891–1962)

Belgian (Flemish) fiction writer. He worked in the Ministry of Education in the Belgian government under the Nazi occupation, and as a result served five years in prison for collaboration. His defence was that he had been serving Flemish interests. He wrote strange and brooding novels, combining decadence with neo-romantic elements (not altogether unlike **Gracq**): *Blauwbaard* (1931, 'Bluebeard'), in which there is a sort of gloating over the murders, is typical. His bitter experiences in World War II, and the price he paid, humanized him, and his later work was more generous in spirit. *Anvaard het leven* (1956, 'Taking Life As It Is'), for example, is a more straightforwardly realistic novel, both moving and well observed.

PILNYAK, Boris, pseud of Boris Andreyevich Vogau
(1894–1937)

Russian author, whose work was highly popular in the 1920s. He wrote novels and short stories including *Golý gok* (1922, Eng trans *The Naked Year*, 1929) and *Volga vpalaet b kaspinskoe more* (1930, Eng trans *The Volga Flows Down to the Caspian Sea*, 1932). His main theme was the effect of the Revolution on the middle classes in Russia. Despite efforts to please the ruling hierarchy, as in the anti-American novel *O-Key* (1932), his writings met with disapproval and he was arrested, charged with spying for Japan, and executed.

▷P Jensen, *Nature as Code: the achievement of Boris Pilnyak* (1979)

PILON, Jean-Guy
(1930–)

French–Canadian poet and editor, born in Saint-Polycarp, Quebec. His poetry, well represented in **A J M Smith's** *Oxford Book of Canadian Verse* (1960), is well-wrought, cosmopolitan and optimistic. He has also written a novel, *Solange* (1965).

PILCHER, Rosamunde
(1924–)

English novelist, born in Lelant, Cornwall. She worked in the Women's Royal Naval Service but, from the age of 18 when her first story was published in *Woman and Home* magazine, pursued another career as a writer, at first publishing under the pseudonym Jane Fraser. The romance *A Secret To Tell* (1955) was the first book to appear under her own name, but three decades passed before that name became more widely known with the publication of the bestselling *The Shell Seekers* (1987). A romance of a bittersweet nature, it is the story of an artist's daughter who, finding that a painting of her father's is worth a small fortune, suddenly has the financial power to become independent—to the possible detriment of her family. The success of *The Shell Seekers* was followed in 1989 by *September*.

PINDAR, Greek Pindaros
(c.518–c.438BC)

Greek lyric poet, born of an old and illustrious family in Cynoscephalae near Thebes, the capital of Boeotia. He began his career as a composer of choral odes at 20 with a song of victory still extant (*Pyth. X*, written 498 BC). He soon reached the highest rank in his profession, and composed odes for a wide range of people—for the tyrants of Syracuse and Macedon, as well as for the free cities of Greece. In his poems he gives advice and reproof as well as praise to his patrons. He wrote hymns to the gods, paeans, dithyrambs, odes for processions, mimic dancing songs, convivial songs, dirges, and odes in praise of princes. Of all these poems only fragments are extant, but his *Epinikia* ('Triumphal Odes') can be read in their entirety. They are divided into four books, celebrating the victories won in the Olympian, Pythian, Nemean and Isthmian games. They show the intense admiration of the Greeks for bodily prowess and beauty; such gifts come from the gods and are sacred. The groundwork of Pindar's poems consists of those legends which form the Greek religious literature, and

his protest against myths dishonouring to the gods shows his pious nature.
▷C M Bowra, *Pindar* (1964)

PIÑERA, Virgilio
(1912–79)

Cuban playwright, novelist, story writer and poet, born in Matanzas province, son of a surveyor; he was the most important and influential dramatist of his generation. He came to Havana at the age of 28. From 1946 until 1958, just before the advent of the Castro regime, he lived in Argentina, where, among other things, he helped translate **Witold Gombrovich**'s *Ferdiduke* into Spanish. His semi-autobiographical play *Aire frio* (1959, 'Cold Air') is one of his best known; he was most influenced by **Eugene O'Neill** and by **Ionesco**. He was very active in the theatre as a director. He was homosexual, and when the authorities began to persecute homosexuals (1971), he fell from state favour, although he was allowed to continue with his activities as a translator. He died a neglected figure, of whom there were few obituaries, but his importance is now re-emerging.
▷S Bueno, *Historia de la literatura cubana* (1963); S Menton, *Prose Fiction of the Cuban Revolution* (1975)

PINERO, Sir Arthur Wing
(1855–1934)

English playwright, born in London. He studied law, but in 1874 made his debut on the stage in Edinburgh, and in 1875 joined the Lyceum company. His first play, *£200 a Year*, appeared in 1877, followed by a series of comedies. In 1893, with *The Second Mrs Tanqueray*, generally reckoned his best, he began a period of realistic tragedies which were received with enthusiastic acclamation and made him the most successful playwright of his day, although his popularity declined sharply with the rise of a new kind of theatre. He was the author of some 50 plays which included *The Squire* (1881), *The Magistrate* (1885), *Dandy Dick* (1887) and *The Profligate* (1889) from his earlier works, and from his later *The Gay Lord Quex* (1899), *His House in Order* (1906) and *Mid-Channel* (1909).
▷C Hamilton, *The Social Plays of Arthur Wing Pinero* (4 vols, 1917–22)

PINGET, Robert
(1919–)

Swiss (French) playwright, novelist and collaborator with **Samuel Beckett** (who translated some of his plays into English); he was born in Geneva. One of his chief works is the novel, later dramatized as *Lettre morte* (1960, Eng trans in *Plays*, 1965–7), *Le Fiston* (1959, Eng trans *No Answer*, 1961). Pinget's fiction

has affinities with Beckett's, but, as is often noted, also with the world as conceived in the writings of **Henri Michaux**. While his novels, of which *L'Inquisitoire* (1962, 'The Inquisitorial'), is outstanding, resemble *nouveaux romans* in presentation, they in fact contain 'a Balzacian multiplicity of characters'.
▷V Mercier, *The New Novel: From Queneau to Pinget* (1971)

PINILLOS, Manuel
(1914–)

Spanish poet and editor (of *Ambito*, 1951–62), born in Saragossa. Out of the mainstream, he has published quiet, meditative poetry influenced less by his compatriots than by **Hölderlin** and **Rilke**.

PINSKI, David
(1872–1959)

Yiddish novelist, essayist and, primarily, playwright, born in Mohilev in the Ukraine; he lived in Europe and, from 1899, in New York; he went to Israel late in his life, in 1950. Most of his plays were translated and adapted for British and American performances. He was most influenced by **Ibsen**, but wrote plays in almost every form: comedy, allegory, biblical, realistic. He had international stature. Best known of his plays are *Di Familie Tsvi* (1905, 'The Tsvi family or The Last Jew'), and the satirical masterpiece *Der Oytser* (1906, 'The Treasure'). He was an active socialist and Zionist, and wrote many vital essays on the Yiddish drama and its future (unhappily unfulfilled).
▷C A Madison, *Yiddish Literature* (1968)

PINTER, Harold
(1930–)

English dramatist, the son of a London East End tailor of Portuguese–Jewish ancestry (da Pinta). He became a repertory actor and wrote poetry and later plays. His first London production was trounced by the critics unused to his highly personal dramatic idiom. A superb verbal acrobat, he exposes and utilizes the illogical and inconsequential in everyday talk, not to illustrate some general idea (as does **Eugène Ionesco**), but to induce an atmosphere of menace in *The Birthday Party* (1957), or of claustrophobic isolation in *The Caretaker* (1958; filmed 1963). His TV play *The Lover* (1963) won the Italia Prize. Other plays include *The Collection* (TV 1961; stage 1962), *The Dwarfs* (radio 1960, stage 1963), and *The Homecoming* (1965). His filmscripts include *The Servant* (1963) and *The Pumpkin Eaters* (1964). Later plays include *No Man's Land* (1975), and *Betrayal* (1978), the story of an adulterous relationship told in reverse chronological order. He did not produce another full-length play until *Party Time* (1991). Three short pieces, under the title *Other Voices*, were shown at the National Theatre in 1982. The subsequent plays, *One for the Road* (1984) and *Mountain Language* (1988), both about 25 minutes in length, show that while he has lost none of his ability to create quickly an atmosphere of threat, his subject-matter is now explicitly political, *Mountain Language* being a play set in a prison camp in which the guards brutalize the inmates and their visiting relatives, while *A New World Order* (1990) also has a menacing political theme. More recent filmscripts include *The French Lieutenant's Woman* (1981), from the novel by **John Fowles**. He was married first (1956–80) to the actress Vivien Merchant (1929–83); in 1980 he married the writer and biographer Lady Antonia Fraser. In 1991 he helped launch a campaign against the celebration of Columbus's 'discovery' of America.

PINTO, Fernão Mendez
(c.1510–1583)

Portuguese adventurer and writer, born near Coimbra. At the age of 27 he made his way to India, and remained for 21 years in southeast Asia, leading a life of adventure, fighting pirates, trading and going on special missions to Japan or elsewhere. He returned in 1558, and wrote an extravagant account of his adventures, *Peregrinaçao* (1614, Eng trans *The Voyages and Adventures of Fernand Mendez Pinto*, 1653).

PIONTEK, Heinz
(1925–)

German poet, critic, novelist and translator, a more lyrical and intelligible poet—who was initially influenced by **Oskar Loerke** and **Wilhelm Lehmann**—than most of his contemporaries. He has translated **John Keats** well. Some critics have accused his later poetry of being versatile to the point of facility, but this is by no means a majority opinion. His criticism is incisive and to the point.

PIOVENE, Guido
(1907–75)

Italian novelist, travel writer, journalist and critic, from a noble family of Vicenza. A novelist directly in the French moralistic tradition, and in Italy in that of **Fogazzaro**, he veered from an extreme youthful fascism (inherited from his father) to a humane Marxism—a process which he examines, with wit and candour, in the essays of *La coda di paglia* (1962, 'The Coward'). His first, epistolary, novel, *Lettere di una novizia* (1941, Eng trans

Confession of a Novice, 1951), which was successfully filmed, and which made his name, was a Pirandellian exploration of the difference between reality and illusion. But his two more mature novels, *Le furie* (1963, 'The Furies') and *Le stelle fredde* (1970, 'The Cold Stars'), were his greatest achievements. Both are fantastic works, largely autobiographical, only classifiable as 'essay novels', but interspersed with dreams and (for example) a visit from **Dostoyevsky** from the spirit-world for a conversation with the author. He has been criticized for brittleness and tediousness, and Italian opinion is still divided as to his ultimate worth.

▷ G Catalano, *Piovene* (1967, in Italian)

PIRANDELLO, Luigi
(1867–1936)

Italian dramatist, novelist and short-story writer, winner of the Nobel Prize for literature, born in Girgenti (Agrigento), Sicily. He studied philology at Rome and Bonn, becoming a lecturer in literature at Rome (1897–1922). After writing powerful and realistic novels and short stories, including *Il Fu Mattia Pascal* (1904, rev edn 1921, Eng trans *The Late Mattia Pascal*, 1923) and *Si Gira* (1916, Eng trans *Shoot!*, 1926), he turned to the theatre and quickly established his own extraordinary genre. Among his plays are *Sei personaggi in cerca d'autore* (1921, Eng trans *Six Characters in Search of an Author*, 1922), *Enrico IV* (1922, Eng trans *Henry IV*, 1922) and *Come Tu Mi Vuoi* (1930, Eng trans *As You Desire Me*, 1931). In 1925 he established a theatre of his own in Rome, the Teatro d'Arte, and his company took his plays all over Europe. Many of his later plays have been filmed. In 1934 he was awarded the Nobel Prize for literature.

▷ D Vittorini, *Luigi Pirandello* (1937)

PIRES, José Cardoso
(1925–)

Portuguese novelist, dramatist and critic, born in Pêso de Régua. He criticized the Salazar regime in various oblique ways, as in *Dinossaure excelerntissime* (1972, 'Imperial Highness, Dinosaurus I'). His most serious work is *O hósepede de Job* (1963, 'Job's Guest'), about a rural father and son trying to deal with forces they cannot control—and is thus an allegory of modern Portugal.

PIRON, Alexis
(1689–1773)

French poet, playwright and wit, born in Dijon. He wrote farces for fairground theatres, and eventually graduated to the legitimate stage, writing both tragedies and comedies. His works include the comic opera *Endriaque*

(1723) and a variety of plays, of which the extravagant satire *La métromanie* (1738) is the best known. Piron described himself as 'nothing, not even an Academician'.
▷P Chaponnière, *Piron* (1910)

PISEMSKY, Alexey
(1820–81)

Russian realist novelist and playwright, born in Kostromo province. He wrote two masterpieces, and a fine play: *Tyufyak* (1850, Eng trans *The Simpleton*, 1960), *Tysyacha dush* (1858, Eng trans *A Thousand Souls*, 1959), and the drama *Gorkaya sudbina* (1859, Eng trans *A Bitter Fate*, 1933), a peasant tragedy. Sceptical, sardonic, sarcastic, he was persistently underrated outside Russia (in which, however, he was always attacked by radicals and communist critics), until Ivy Litvinov translated his two major novels.
▷I D Ivanov, *Pisemsky* (1898, in Russian); M Slonim, *Modern Russian Literature* (1953)

PITTER, Ruth
(1897–1992)

English poet, born in Ilford, Essex, the daughter of a schoolmaster. She wrote verse from a very early age and later was encouraged by **Hilaire Belloc**. Her writing belongs to no particular school and for inspiration she has drawn mainly upon the beauty of natural things and her Christian faith. In 1955 she was awarded the Queen's Gold Medal for Poetry, having already won the Hawthornden Prize in 1936 with *A Trophy of Arms*. Other volumes include *First and Second Poems* (1927), *A Mad Lady's Garland* (1934), *Urania* (1951), *The Ermine* (1953), *Still by Choice* (1966) and *End of Drought* (1975). A *Collected Poems* appeared in 1990.
▷A Russell, *Homage to a Poet* (1969)

PIXÉRÉCOURT, René Charles Guilbert de
(1773–1844)

French dramatist, born in Nancy. Known as 'the father of melodrama', he wrote 111 plays. He had initial difficulties, but following the successful comedy *Les Petits Auvergnats* (1797, 'The Little Citizens of the Auvergne'), did not look back. He wrote all sorts of plays, but his Gothic melodramas, such as his dramatization of the *Mysteries of Udolpho* of *Mrs Radcliffe* (1797), did more than the plays of any other single writer to provide the standard fare of the 19th-century playgoer. A master-craftsman, he ably defended his own procedures. He was, wrote a modern French critic, 'superior to his work'.
▷M W Disher, *Blood and Thunder* (1949)

PIZARNIK, Alejandra
(1936–72)

Argentinian poet, whose work is characterized by mystery, surrealism, and a dreamy quality, which attempt to make reality greater than it is in normal life. She lived in Argentina and France, where she contributed to a number of literary magazines. Important themes in her work are death, the loss of innocence, nostalgia, and longing. Her works include *El deseo de la palabra* (1975, 'Desire of the Word') and *El Infierno musical* (1971, 'The Musical Hell'). She is considered one of the foremost Latin-American female poets of the 20th century.

PLAIDY, Jean *see* HOLT, Victoria

PLANCHÉ, James Robinson
(1796–1880)

English playwright, antiquary and herald, born in London of Huguenot ancestry. He was a prolific writer of burlesques and extravaganzas, such as *Amoroso, King of Little Britain* (1818), *Success; or, a Hit if you like it* (1825) and *High, Low, Jack and the Game* (1833). His best-known work is *The Vampyre; or the Bride of the Isles* (1820). He wrote the libretto for Weber's *Oberon*, and other operas. As a heraldic scholar he wrote *History of British Costumes* (1834) and other works. He was appointed Somerset Herald in 1866.
▷H Granville-Barker, *Exit Planché—enter Gilbert* (1932)

PLANTE, David Robert
(1940–)

American novelist, resident for much of his career in London. He grew up in Providence, Rhode Island, which became the basis of his later trilogy, *The Francoeur Family* (collected 1984). He was educated at Boston College and at the University of Louvain in Belgium. He taught at the English School in Rome and at schools in Massachusetts, then moved to the UK. Before receiving a measure of public and commercial recognition with the first of the autobiographical 'Francoeur' novels, *The Family* (1978), Plante had published five rather hermetic novels, which work almost musical variations on delicately registered patterns of sexual and familial relationship. Despite a darkening of tone that foreshadows the erotic violence of later books, these early novels represent different approaches to the same basic literary and philosophical issues. The 'Francoeur' novels continued with *The Country* (1981) and *The Woods* (1982). Later novels, *The Foreigner* (1984) and *The Catholic* (1985), are more extreme in their dissection of sexual identity and are as aggressively overt as the early books were reticent and veiled.

PLATANOV, Andrey, formerly **Andrey Klimentov**
(1896–1951)

Russian short-story writer, dramatist, and poet. Platanov, who was born in Voronezh, was consistently underrated in his lifetime, both inside and—more shamefully—outside his own country. Only in the last decade has his work been re-examined and reappraised. He was an electrical engineer by training, but his first writings appeared in 1917 and 1918, while he was fighting with the Bolsheviks. He remained in his profession until 1927, when he decided to dedicate his life to writing. His work became interesting and invaluable as soon as he lost his youthful enthusiasm for the Revolution, and saw the results of 'total organization from above'. His *Chevengur* (Eng trans 1978) was not even published until 1972, and then in an incomplete text (the English version is complete); nor is he mentioned in official histories. He was at heart, like **Leo Tolstoy**, a constructive anarchist, and this caused his work to be proscribed after 1931. When a few years later his work re-appeared, he had stripped it of its satirical tendencies; World War II gave him an opportunity to publish patriotic (but never poor) tales, and he regained some of his former popularity. It has now been recognized that all of his later writings are exceedingly subtle reactions to his circumstances, and nowhere more than in his style, which, the most advanced of all variations of *skaz* (idiomatic writing), combines parody of Soviet mediaspeak with inimitable rustic wisdom.
▷M Jordon, *Andrey Platanov* (1973)

PLATEN, August von, in full **Karl Georg August Maximilian Graf von Platen-Hallermünde**
(1796–1835)

German poet, born in Ansbach. He ill-advisedly joined the Bavarian army, but royal patronage secured him indefinite leave and he studied widely at Würzburg and Erlangen. A perfectionist, he frequently wrote in metrically complex foreign forms, such as the Persian ghazal (*Ghaselen*, 1821 and 1824) and the **Petrarch**an sonnet; one of his greatest achievements was the *Sonette aus Venedig* (1825, Eng trans *Sonnets from Venice*, 1923), which combine a sense of beauty and of *Weltschmerz* ('world-weariness'). He also wrote ballads, such as 'Der Pilgrim vor St Just' (1820), plays (including satires on Romanticism), and diaries, which reveal the torments caused by his homosexuality. His feelings of isolation led to self-exile in Italy (where his disastrous life ended at Syracuse),

and infused his poetry with its characteristic pessimism.
▷P Bumm, *August Graf von Platen: Eine Biographie* (1990)

PLATER, Alan Frederick
(1935–)

English dramatist, born in Jarrow-on-Tyne. Trained as an architect, his writing was first published in *Punch* (1958) and, since 1960, he has built up an enormous body of work, both originals and adaptations, reflecting his working-class origins, political beliefs and interest in jazz. A regular writer for *Z Cars* (1963–5), his many television plays include *Ted's Cathedral* (1964), *Close the Coalhouse Door* (1968) and *The Land of Green Ginger* (1974). He is also responsible for such literate and skilled screen translations as *The Good Companions* (1980), *Fortunes of War* (1987) and *A Very British Coup* (1988). Equally prolific in other media, he has contributed to *The Guardian*, and written film scripts like *The Virgin and the Gypsy* (1969) and *Priest of Love* (1980), as well as such novels as *Misterioso* (1987) and *The Beiderbecke Affair* (1985), from his television series of the same title. He received a BAFTA Writer's Award in 1989.
▷J R Taylor, *The Second Wave* (1971)

PLATH, Sylvia
(1932–63)

American poet, born in Boston, Massachusetts, the daughter of a German-born Professor of Biology and a school-teacher. Educated at Bradford High School and Smith College, where she suffered from deep depression and attempted suicide, she won a Fulbright Fellowship to Newnham College, Cambridge, in 1956, where she studied English and met and married **Ted Hughes**. After a spell of teaching in the USA they settled in England, first in London and then in Devon, but separated in 1962; a year later Sylvia committed suicide. She wrote poetry from early childhood; her first volume, *A Winter Ship* (1960), was published anonymously, but she put her name to her second volume, *The Colossus* (1960). After the birth of her second child she wrote a radio play, *Three Women* (1962), set in a maternity home. Often termed a 'confessional' poet because of the inclusion in her work of personal details about her own life and the influence of poets such as **Robert Lowell**, her earlier, highly controlled poetry gave way to an almost visionary expression and intensity, reaching its culmination in the last few days before her death. This late poetry was published posthumously in *Ariel* (1965), *Crossing the Water* (1971) and *Winter Trees* (1972). Her only novel, *The Bell Jar* (1963), about her student collapse, was published just before her death, under the

pseudonym Victoria Lucas. *Collected Poems*, edited by Ted Hughes, was published in 1982.
▷A Stevenson, *Bitter Fame* (1989)

PLATO
(c.428–c.348 BC)

Greek philosopher, indisputably one of the most important of all Western philosophers, and so enormously influential that A N Whitehead was able to characterize the subsequent history of Western philosophy as a series of 'footnotes to Plato'. He was the pupil (or at least the associate) of Socrates and the teacher of Aristotle. Plato was probably born in Athens, of a distinguished family, but little is known of his early life. Any youthful political ambitions must have withered when his friend and mentor, Socrates, was condemned to death in 399 BC by the restored democracy in Athens. Plato immortalized the story of Socrates' trial and last days in three of his dialogues: the *Apologia*, the *Crito* and the *Phaedo*, where his profound affection and respect for Socrates come through vividly. After the execution he and other disciples of Socrates took temporary refuge at Megara with the philosopher Euclides, and he then travelled widely in Greece, Egypt, the Greek cities in southern Italy (where he no doubt encountered Pythagoreans) and Sicily (where he made friends with Dion, brother-in-law of Dionysius I, the ruler of Syracuse). He returned to Athens in c.387 BC to found the Academy, which became a famous centre for philosophical, mathematical and scientific study, and over which he presided for the rest of his life. He visited Sicily again in 367 BC, at Dion's request, to try and train Dionysius II to become a philosopher–statesman, but despite a second visit in 361–60, which placed him in some personal danger, the attempt failed completely. His corpus of writings consists of some 30 philosophical dialogues and a series of *Letters*, of which the Seventh is the most important (biographically and philosophically) and only the Seventh and Eighth are likely to be genuine. The dialogues are conventionally divided into three groups—early, middle and late—though the exact relative chronology of individual dialogues is a vexed and probably insoluble problem of scholarship. The early, 'Socratic' dialogues have Socrates as the principal character, usually portrayed interrogating his interlocutors about the definition of different moral virtues (piety in the *Euthyphro*, courage in the *Laches*, and so on); their initially confident assertions are shown to be confused and contradictory and all parties end up sharing Socrates' professed perplexity. The middle dialogues show the character 'Socrates' expressing more positive, systematic views, which are taken to be Plato's own. This group

includes the most dramatic and literary of the dialogues, the *Symposium*, *Gorgias*, *Phaedo*, and *Republic*, and presents such famous Platonic doctrines as the theory of knowledge as recollection, the immortality of the soul, the tripartite division of the soul, and above all the theory of forms (or 'ideas') which contrasts the transient, material world of 'particulars' (objects merely of perception, opinion and belief) with the timeless, unchanging world of universals or forms (the true objects of knowledge). The *Republic* also describes Plato's celebrated political utopia, ruled by philosopher-kings who have mastered the discipline of 'dialectic' and studied the hierarchy of the forms, including its apex, the form of the Good. The details of this visionary state—the rigid class structure of workers, soldiers and rulers, the education of the rulers (both men and women), their communism of property and family, their totalitarian powers—have been variously idealized, attacked, misinterpreted and imitated in subsequent political theory and literature, but the *Republic* remains one of the most compelling and influential works in the history of philosophy. The third group of 'late' dialogues is generally less literary in form and represents a series of sustained and highly sophisticated criticisms of the metaphysical and logical assumptions of Plato's doctrines of the middle period. *Parmenides*, *Theaetetus* and *Sophist* in particular have attracted the interest of contemporary analytical philosophers and contain some of Plato's most demanding and original work. Taken as a whole, his philosophy has had a pervasive and incalculable influence on almost every period and tradition, rivalled only by that of his greatest pupil Aristotle, which was its principal competitor for much of the Hellenistic period, the Middle Ages and the Renaissance.
▷R M Hare, *Plato* (1982)

PLAUTUS, Titus Maccius, or Maccus
(c.250–184 BC)

Roman writer of comedies, born in Sarsina in Umbria. It is probable that he went to Rome while still young, and there learned his mastery of the most idiomatic Latin. In Rome he found employment in connection with the stage, and saved enough money to enable him to leave Rome and start in business on his own account in foreign trade. His plays show close familiarity with seafaring life and adventure, and an intimate knowledge of all the details of buying and selling and bookkeeping. He failed, however, in business, and returned to Rome in such poverty that he had to earn his livelihood in the service of a baker by turning a handmill. While thus employed he wrote three plays which he sold to the managers of the public games. The money for these enabled him to leave the mill, and he spent the rest of his life in Rome. Probably he began to write about 224 BC, and, until his death, he continued to produce comedies. His plays appear to have been left in the hands of the actors, who probably interpolated and omitted passages to suit them for the stage, and some of the prologues may have been written after his death. About 130 plays were attributed to him in the time of Aulus Gellius, who believed most of them to be the work of earlier dramatists revised and improved by Plautus. Roman critics considered most of them spurious. **Marcus Terentius Varro** limited the genuine comedies to 21; and these so-called 'Varronian comedies' are those which are now extant, the *Vidularia* ('The Rucksack Play') being fragmentary. Plautus borrowed his plots to a large extent from the New Attic Comedy, which dealt with social life to the exclusion of politics.

▷K McLeish, *Roman Comedy* (1976)

PLESHCHEYEV, Alexey
(1825–93)

Russian poet and translator (**Heine**), who was sentenced to execution along with **Dostoyevsky** as a revolutionary, and, like him, reprieved and sent to Siberia. His verse is rather insipid, and today not much read.

PLIEVIER, Theodor
(1892–1955)

German novelist, of working-class birth, born in Berlin. He fled Nazi Germany in 1933 and returned to Berlin in 1945, where he published *Stalingrad*, the first in a trilogy of grippingly realistic war novels, for which he is best-known. This and its sequels, *Moskau* (1952) and *Berlin* (1954), were best-sellers.

▷H Wilde, *Theodor Plievier* (1965)

PLINY, Gaius Plinius Secundus, known as 'the Elder'
(23–79)

Roman writer on natural history. He came of a wealthy north Italian family owning estates at Novum Comum (Como), where he was born. He was educated in Rome, and when about 23 entered the army and served in Germany. He became colonel of a cavalry regiment, and a comrade of the future emperor Titus, and wrote a treatise on the throwing of missiles from horseback and compiled a history of the Germanic wars. He also made a series of scientific tours in the region between the Ems, Elbe and Weser, and the sources of the Danube. Returning to Rome in 52, he studied for the Bar, but withdrew to Como and devoted himself to reading and authorship. Apparently for the guidance of

his nephew, he wrote his *Studiosus*, a treatise defining the culture necessary for the orator, and the grammatical work, *Dubius Sermo*. By Nero he was appointed procurator in Spain, and through his brother-in-law's death (71) he became guardian of his sister's son, **Pliny the Younger**, whom he adopted. Vespasian, whose son Titus he had known in Germany, was now emperor, and became a close friend; but court favour did not wean him from study, and he brought down to his own time the history of Rome by Aufidius Bassus. A model student, amid metropolitan distraction he worked assiduously, and by lifelong application filled the 102 volumes of manuscript which, after using them for his universal encyclopaedia in 37 volumes, *Naturalis Historia* (77), he bequeathed to his nephew. In 79 he was in command of the Roman fleet stationed off Misenum when the great eruption of Vesuvius was at its height. Eager to witness the phenomenon as closely as possible, he landed at Stabiae (*Castellamare*), but had not gone far before he succumbed to the stifling vapours rolling down the hill. His *Naturalis Historia* alone of his many writings survives. Under that title the ancients classified everything of natural or non-artificial origin. Pliny adds digressions on human inventions and institutions, devoting two books to a history of fine art, and dedicates the whole to Titus. His observations, made at second-hand, show no discrimination between the true and the false, between the probable and the marvellous, and his style is inartistic, sometimes obscure. But he supplies information on an immense variety of subjects about which, but for him, we should have remained in the dark.

▷H N Wethered, *The Mind of the Ancient World* (1937)

PLINY, Gaius Plinius Caecilius Secundus, known as 'the Younger'
(c.62–c.113)

Roman writer and orator, born in Novum Comum, the nephew and adopted son of **Pliny** 'the Elder'. He wrote a Greek tragedy in his 14th year, and made such progress under Quintilian that he became noted as one of the most accomplished men of his time. His proficiency as an orator enabled him at 18 to plead in the Forum, and brought him much practice. He served as military tribune in Syria, and was *quaestor Caesaris*, then praetor, and afterwards consul in AD100, in which year he wrote his laboured panegyric of Trajan. In 103 and 105 he was in Bithynia and, among other offices, held that of curator of the Tiber, chiefly for the prevention of floods. He married twice; his second wife, Calpurnia, is fondly referred to in one of his most charming letters for the many gifts and accomplishments with which she sweetened his rather invalid life. It is to his 10 volumes of letters that Pliny owes his assured place in literature, giving an intimate picture of the upper class in the 1st century; above all, it is from his correspondence with Trajan that we get our clearest knowledge of how even the most enlightened Romans regarded the then obscure sect of the Christians and their 'depraved and extravagant superstition'.

▷A M Guillemin, *Pliné et la vie littéraire de son temps* (1929)

PLISNIER, Charles
(1896–1952)

Belgian fiction writer and poet, born in Hainaut, who began as a militant communist and ended as a mystical Christian; but who managed to effect the transformation in a significant and convincing manner. His *Faux passeportes* (1937, Eng trans *Memoirs of a Secret Revolutionary*, 1938), five connected stories which deal with mystical militants deceived by Stalinism and bureaucracy, won the Prix **Goncourt**. His roman-fleuve *Meutres* (1939–44, 'Murders'), powerful despite its tediousness—unfortunately a much noted flaw—analyses bourgeois bad faith in the light of individual sincerity and the quest for purity. Plisnier's most profound and original novel, however, is *Beauté des laides* (1952, 'The Beauty of Ugly Women').

PLOMER, William Charles Franklin
(1903–73)

British writer, born in Pietersburg, Transvaal. He was educated at Rugby, was a farmer and trader in South Africa before becoming an author, and also lived for a while in Greece and Japan. With **Roy Campbell** he ran a South African literary review, and in World War II he served at the Admiralty. His works include the novels *Turbott Wolfe* (1926), *Sado* (1931) and *Ali the Lion* (1936); collections of short stories *I Speak of Africa* (1928) and *Paper Houses* (1929); and *Collected Poems* (1960). He edited the diaries of **Francis Kilvert** and the poems of **Herman Melville**, and wrote the librettos for several of Benjamin Britten's operas, including *Gloriana*. He also wrote the autobiographical *Double Lives* (1943).

▷W Doyle, *William Plomer* (1969)

PLUNKETT, James, originally James Plunkett Kelly
(1920–)

Irish novelist and short-story writer, born in Dublin. He is best known for the novel *Strumpet City* (1969) and its sequel *Farewell Companions* (1977). The first deals with Ireland from 1907 to 1914; the latter spans from the Easter Rising of 1916 to the end of World War II. *Strumpet City* is more successful in evoking Dublin life in the years leading up to World War I; *Farewell Companions*, perhaps because of its greater timescale and array of characters, is less able to depict individual lives—instead, the cityscape and history itself might be regarded as the central characters. *The Circus Animals* (1990) picks up where *Farewell Companions* leaves off, being set in what the author sees as the poverty, both material and spiritual, of post-World War II Dublin.

PLUTARCH, Greek **Ploutarchos**
(c.46–c.120)

Greek historian, biographer and philosopher, born in Chaeronea in Boeotia. He was in Athens in 66, studying science and rhetoric. He paid more than one visit to Rome—once representing his native town—and gave public lectures in philosophy. After travels in Greece, Asia Minor and Egypt, he settled in Chaeronea. His extant writings comprise his historical works, and those that are grouped under the general head of *Opera Moralia* ('Moral Works'). To the former belong his *Vitae* ('Lives')—the work by which he is best known. These contain a gallery of 50 portraits of the great characters of the age preceding his own. They are mostly arranged in pairs, a Greek and Roman soldier or states-man with some resemblance between their respective careers being chosen for the subject of each. Plutarch's biographies are of value particularly for the view they offer of ancient history as it was understood in antiquity. The author adheres throughout to his professed purpose—portraiture of character; he lists the most famous actions or events which distinguish the career of each subject of his biography, often using them as the basis of moral reflection. His other surviving writings, the *Moralia*, are a collection of short treatises and dialogues on religion, philosophy, science and education. Though not a profound thinker, Plutarch occupies an important place in literary history. He was much read in the Renaissance, and the translation of the *Vitae* by Sir Thomas North (1579) was the major source for **Shakespeare**'s Roman plays.

PO-CHÜ-I
(772–846)

Chinese poet under the T'ang dynasty, born in Honan, of which he became governor in 831. He was so esteemed as a lyric poet that his poems were collected by imperial order and engraved on stone tablets.

▷A Waley, *The Life and Times of Po-Chu-I* (1949)

POE, Edgar Allan
(1809–49)

American poet and story writer, born in Boston, Massachusetts. After being orphaned in his third year, he was adopted by John Allan (1780–1834), a wealthy and childless merchant in Richmond, Virginia. From 1815 to 1820 the family lived in England, and the boy went to school in Stoke Newington. The year 1826 was spent at the University of Virginia; but, offended by his dissipation and gambling debts, his patron moved him to the counting-room, from where he ran away to Boston. He published *Tamerlane and other Poems* (1827), enlisted in the US army that year, and rose to be sergeant-major in 1829. He then procured his discharge and after a year's delay his admission to West Point Military Academy (1830), but the following March he was dismissed for deliberate neglect of duty. Now he was thrown on his own resources. A third edition of his *Poems* (1831) contained 'Israfel', his earliest poem of value, and 'To Helen'. In Baltimore he won a prize in 1833 for his story 'A MS. found in a Bottle'. From then on he lived with his aunt, Mrs Clemm, and wrote for the *Saturday Visitor*. His connection with the *Southern Literary Messenger* began with his tale *Berenice* in 1835 and he went to Richmond as its assistant editor (1835–7). In 1836 he married his cousin Virginia. He left Richmond in 1837, and after a year or less in New York, of which the chief result was *The Narrative of Arthur Gordon Pym*, in 1838 he established himself in Philadelphia. Here he published *Tales of the Grotesque* and *Arabesque* (1840), was connected with Burton's *Gentleman's Magazine* (1839), and for a year (1842–3) edited *Graham's Magazine*. He won another short-story competition in 1843 with 'The Gold Bug'. In 1844 he moved to New York, and in *The Evening Mirror* (1845) published 'The Raven', which won immediate fame. In 1847 his wife died. 'The Bells', 'The Domain of Arnheim', the wild 'prose poem' *Eureka* (1848) and a few minor pieces belong to the brief remainder of his life. He attempted suicide in November 1848, and had an attack of *delirium tremens* in June 1849. Recovering, he spent over two months in Richmond, lecturing there and at Norfolk. He became engaged to a lady of means, and in September went to wind up his affairs in the north. In October he was found in a wretched condition in Baltimore, and died in the hospital. Weird, wild, fantastic, dwelling by choice on the horrible, Poe's genius was nevertheless great and genuine. His short stories show great originality, and from some of them, such as 'The Murders in the Rue Morgue', Poe emerges as a pioneer of the modern detective story. The chief charm of his poems is exquisite melody.

▷W Bittner, *Poe: a biography* (1962); D Hoffman, *Poe Poe Poe Poe Poe Poe Poe* (1972)

POGODIN, Nikolay, pseud of Nikolay Fedorovich Stukalov
(1900–62)

Soviet dramatist, born in the Don province. A socialist realist with humour and humanity, Pogodin's popular plays were on such themes as the Five-Year Plan and Lenin; he was also an exceedingly able craftsman, expert in creating gripping crowd scenes. His most famous play is undoubtedly *Kremlyovsky kuranti* (1940, Eng trans in *Soviet Scene: Six Plays of Russian Life*, 1946), the second of his Lenin trilogy.

▷V Komissarzhecsky, *Moscow Theatres* (1959)

POHL, Frederik
(1919–)

American science-fiction writer, born in Brooklyn, New York. In 1938 he became a founder-member of a group of left-wing science-fiction writers known as the Futurists, which included **Isaac Asimov** and others. He served in the air force in World War II, worked as a literary agent, and edited various science-fiction magazines (1953–69). He describes his own multifarious books as 'cautionary literature', seeing science fiction as a kind of alarm signal. Of his vast output of novels, stories and anthologies, *The Space Merchants* (1953) and *Gladiator-at-Law* (1955), both written with C M Kornbluth, exemplify his social concern and strength as a storyteller.

▷ *The Way the Future Was* (1978)

POKAGON, Simon
(1830–99)

American writer, dubbed in his day the 'Indian Longfellow', and the author of the first major novel published by a Native American. The son of the Potawotomi chief Leopold who had ceded the area on which Chicago was eventually built to the Whites, Pokagon spent much of his life trying to get compensation on behalf of his people for the loss of this land, eventually winning $104 000 from the US government. He personally distributed his pamphlet, *The Red Man's Rebuke* (later published as *The Red Man's Greeting*), printed entirely on birchbark and describing his people's land claim, at the World's Fair in Chicago in 1893, at which exhibition his people were unrepresented. Pokagon's major work, the novel *Queen of the Woods*, was published posthumously in 1899. Beginning as a woodland idyll, the novel doggedly traces the destruction of a Native American couple and their children by external forces, ending with a bleak apocalyptic vision of the destructive power of alcohol.

▷D H Dickason, 'Chief Simon Pokagon: "The Indian Longfellow"', in *Indiana Magazine of History*, 57 (1961)

POLACEK, Karel
(1892–1944)

Czech satirical novelist, who wrote particularly of the first republic. A Jew, he was murdered by the Nazis during their occupation of his country.

POLIAKOFF, Stephen
(1952–)

English dramatist. He achieved recognition with the plays *Hitting Town* and *City Sugar* (both 1975), both looking at the plight of urban young in a Britain of concrete shopping arcades and consumerism. Several plays followed on the same theme, but *Breaking the Silence* (1984), set in the aftermath of the Russian Revolution, is his finest work to date. *Coming Into Land* (1987) follows the fortunes of a Polish refugee as she tries to enter Britain. Other stage plays include *Strawberry Fields* (1977), *Shout Across the River* (1978) and *Sienna Red* (1992). His television plays include *Caught on a Train* (1980). He made his debut as a film director with *Hidden City* (1987), and both wrote and directed *Close My Eyes* (1991), based on *Hitting Town*.

POLITIS, Kosmas, pen-name of Paris Taveloudis
(1888–1974)

Greek novelist, born on Poros. He came late to prominence, and was over 40 when his first novel, *Lemonodhasos* ('Lemon Grove'), was published in 1930. *Eroica* (1938) is widely regarded as his best work; the novel is a nostalgic portrayal of youthful life on Poros. Politis himself was largely educated in Smyrna, later the scene of terrible suffering during the war with Turkey, and in his last novel, *Stou Chatzifrangou* (1963, 'At Chatzifrangos'), he describes a quarter of the town before the tragedy. His other books include *Gyri* (1946), set in the Patras district of that name.

POLIZIANO, Angelo
(1454–94)

Italian poet and humanist, often called Politian. A tutor in the household of Lorenzo d'Medici, he was the foremost Latinist of his time. But he is most famous for his poetry in the vernacular, particularly for the *Stanze*, in ottava rima, about the victory in tournament of the brother of Lorenzo Giuliano, and for *Orfeo*, the first dramatic treatment, in the form of a 'sacred representation', of a non-

Christian subject. Poliziano's poetic gifts are rated very highly, and it has been said that he conveys 'a fragile vision of love and death ... with Botticelian poignancy'. There is an English translation of *Orfeo* in: *Romanic Review*, 20 (1929); of *Stanze* in: *Delos*, 4 (1970).

▷ *Romanic Review*, 44 (1953)

POMFRET, John
(1667–1702)

English poet, born in Luton and educated at Bedford Grammar School and Queens' College, Cambridge. He was rector of Maulden, Bedfordshire (1695–1702). He published several poetical works, and his *Miscellany Poems on Several Occasions* (1702) were frequently reprinted, but *The Choice* (1700) eclipsed all the rest in popularity. Modelled on **Horace**'s Sat. II.6, it recommends a country life of 'pleasure, ease, and plenty' with no wife but a 'fair creature' nearby for company: this preference is said to have cost him promotion in the church.

▷Dr S Johnson, *The Lives of the English Poets* (1779—81)

POMPÉIA, Raul D'Avila
(1863–95)

Brazilian novelist and poet, born in Rio de Janeiro. A depressive (he killed himself) influenced by **Nietzsche**, Pompéia's chief claim to fame lies in his incomparable novel of school life, *O Ateneu* (1888, 'The Academy'), worthy to rank with **Musil**'s *Young Törless*. It is the story of a megalomaniac headmaster and of a boy's awakening into manhood, told with lucid irony and sensitivity. It is remarkable that this novel has not yet been translated. His other prose, and his poetry, has attracted much recent interest.

PONCE DE LEÓN, Luis
(1527–91)

Spanish monk, scholar and poet, born in Granada. In 1544 he entered the Augustinian order, and became Professor of Theology at Salamanca in 1561. From 1572 to 1576 he was imprisoned by the Inquisition for his translation and interpretation of the *Song of Solomon*; but shortly before his death he became general of his order. His poetical remains, published in 1631, comprise translations from **Virgil**, **Horace** and the *Psalms*; his few original poems are lyrical masterpieces.

▷W Carlos Williams, *In the American Grain* (1925)

PONDAL, Eduardo
(1835–1917)

Spanish poet (a doctor by profession), who wrote both in Galician and in Castilian. With

Rosalía de Castro and Manuel Curros Enríquez he was the leader of the Galician revival of his time; he was regarded as the romantic, Celtic voice of the movement. His sonorous, pessimistic poetry is still studied and admired.

PONGE, Francis
(1899–1987)

French poet—a title he has repudiated—and essayist, born in Montpellier. A committed communist from 1936 until after World War II, and perhaps always a dialectical materialist, he began publishing in 1926, but was virtually unknown until the mid-1940s, except to a few discerning critics such as Jean Paulhan. Of all the many avant-garde poets of France Ponge was the most sheerly phenomenological with regard to language: his project throughout his writings was to make language 'an object of scientific enquiry'. He therefore became one of the heroes of the structuralist magazine *Tel Quel*, edited by Philippe Sollers, who wrote on him (1963). He is a cerebral poet, or, rather, prose-poet (he wants to abolish the distinction), deliberately eschewing the lyricism of emotion except as an object of enquiry. His own enquiry, however, is witty, punning and frequently ironic. He invests the mundane objects he describes with great poignancy, thus mocking his own rejection of 'anthropocentric bias'. He was devoted to **Malherbe**, and wrote about him. His most accessible work is the long meditation on soap, *Le Savon* (1967, Eng trans *Soap*, 1969), actually written during the war when soap was a scarce commodity. His most characteristic work is to be found in the prose-poems of *Proêmes* (1948). He became a grand old man of French letters in his last years.

PONIATOWSKA, Elena
(1933–)

French-born Mexican writer, born in Paris. Her father was Polish and her mother was Mexican, and the family emigrated to Mexico when she was 10 years old. She is a fiercely original writer whose works include journalism (she is one of the most respected interviewers in Mexico), testimonial literature, short stories, novels (notably *Hasta no verte, Jesus mío*, 1969, 'Until I See You, dear Jesus') and literary criticism. Her most famous work is the collage *La noceh de Tlatelolco* (1971, Eng trans *Massacre in Mexico*, 1975). One of her main areas of interest is re-creating the modes of speech of the Mexican popular classes. She is a contributor to several of the best newspapers in Mexico.

PONTANO, Giovanni
(1429–1503)

Italian poet and scholar, born in Cerreto in Umbria. He served the Aragonese court at Naples, but ended his life in obscurity after having negotiated the surrender of the kingdom to France (1495), for which he was pardoned. He was, **Poliziano** apart, the foremost Latinist of his time, and founded an important tradition as the force behind the Neapolitan Academy. He wrote on all the vital subjects of his times, from morals and manners to astrology and philology, and his *Eclogues* (Eng trans 1957) and idylls were regarded highly by those who came after him.
▷ E Percopo, *Vita do Giovanni Pontano* (1938)

PONTOPPIDAN, Henrik
(1857–1944)

Danish novelist and joint winner of the Nobel Prize for literature, born in Fredericia, the son of a pastor. He trained as an engineer but turned to writing. Among his novels were *Det forjaettede land* (1891–5, Eng trans *Land of Promise*, 1896), the transparently autobiographical *Lykke-Per* (1898–1904, 'Lucky Per'), the story of a young engineer's conflict with his spiritual father, and *De dødes rige* (1912–16, 'The Realm of the Dead'). He shared the Nobel Prize for literature in 1917 with his fellow Danish novelist, **Karl Gjellerup**.
▷ K Ahnlund, *Henrik Pontoppidan* (1956)

POOLE, John
(1786–1872)

English playwright, of whom little is known, other than that his first piece, *Hamlet Travestie* (1811), helped usher in a 19th-century vogue for parodies of well-known contemporary and classical plays. A later comedy, *Paul Pry* (1825), was a huge success, partly because it provided a plum leading role for an actor-manager. It was much revived during and beyond Poole's own lifetime, although apparently frequently adjusted to suit the star of the moment.

POOT, Hubert Kornemiszoon
(1689–1733)

Dutch poet, born in Abtwoude into a family of peasants. He had some affinities with an English poet of a later age, **John Clare**, in that he began with an exaggerated respect for his contemporaries, almost all of whom were his considerable inferiors. His finest poetry, in the main consisting of nature lyrics, has the unmistakable mark of a major writer.

POPA, Vasko
(1922–)

Serbian Yugoslav, born in Grebenac and educated largely abroad, where he studied French literature and language. He served as a partisan during World War II, subsequently working as a publisher in Belgrade. His first collection, *Kora* (1953, 'Bark'), is derivative of French models and gives only intermittent signs of the folk-influenced originality of later collections. Perhaps his most important statement is the densely mythological *Sporendo nebo* (1968, 'Secondary Heaven'), which uses an elaborate 7 x 7 structure and evokes weighty philosophical agenda. An important stage in his reception abroad was Anne Pennington's translation for the Penguin Modern Poets series (1969); she also translated the later *Uspravna zemlja* (1972, as *Earth Erect*, 1973), and a substantial *Collected Poems* (1978), which documents Popa's rediscovery of native elements and the troubled history of his country.

POPE, Alexander
(1688–1744)

English poet, born in London. His father was a linen merchant who retired soon after his son was born, and the family moved to Binfield in Windsor Forest when Alexander was an infant. He was educated erratically at Catholic schools but was largely self-taught, which left gaps in his knowledge of literature. At the age of three he suffered his first serious illness and at 12 he was crippled by a tubercular infection of the spine which accounted for his stunted growth (4ft 6in). He began writing at an early age; 'Ode to Solitude' was completed in the same year as his illness. Reading and writing feverishly, he got to know members of the literati—William Walsh, Henry Cromwell, and Sir William Trumball—who acted as mentors, critics and encouragers. He wrote *The Pastorals* while a teenager and they were eventually published by Jacob Tonson in 1709. Metrically adept, they are remembered for his mastery of technique rather than their poetry. But already he had moved on and was working on the seminal work *An Essay on Criticism* (1711), whose couplets caused a stir. *The Rape of the Lock* followed in 1712 and confirmed him as a poetic force. A mock epic, this exquisite work can be enjoyed throughout as a true epic diminished to contemporary proportions. With *Windsor Forest* (1713) his popularity was further enhanced and he became a favourite in London where he was now living. **Joseph Addison** and **Jonathan Swift** were among his acquaintances and he became a member of the Scriblerus Club. His persistent ambition was to translate **Homer**, and the first instalment of the *Iliad* appeared in 1715; when completed in 1720 its genius was immediately acknowledged though it bore flimsy resemblance to the original. During this time he also issued his *Works* (1717), a pot-pourri of odes, epistles, elegies and a translation of **Chaucer**'s *The House of Fame*. He also met and befriended Lady **Mary Wortley Montagu**, a friendship which foundered after they quarrelled in 1723. Pope contemptuously dismissed her in a few lines in his *Imitations of Homer*. With the success of the *Iliad*, Pope was financially secure and was regarded as the senior figure of English letters, much sought after and revered. He bought a villa in Twickenham and lived there until his death. In 1726 he completed the *Odyssey*, following the failure of his edition of **Shakespeare** (1725) which Lewis Theobald criticized for its slip-shoddiness and poor scholarship. Pope got his revenge in *The Dunciad* (1728), a mock-heroic satire, published anonymously, whose butt is 'Dulness' in general and, in particular, all the authors whom he wanted to hold up to ridicule. It is not, however, confined to personal animus, and literary vices are likewise exposed and scorned. With Swift, **John Gay**, Lord Oxford, Arbuthnot and Bolingbroke he arranged the publication of a *Miscellany* of which three volumes appeared between 1727 and 1728. Pope's contributions included *An Epistle to Dr Arbuthnot* (published separately in 1735) and *Martinus Scriblerus peri Bathous: or The Art of Sinking in Poetry*, a satirical invective that insulted various poetasters. That and *The Dunciad* prompted a tiresome literary feud which dragged on interminably. In 1733–4 he published his *Essay on Man* and wrote *Moral Essays* (1731–5). His last years were engaged in organizing his correspondence for publication, but while this marked a new development in English literature he tinkered too much with the originals and their value as social documents was impaired. Since his death his reputation has waxed, waned and waxed again. His technical brilliance has never been in doubt, but he lacked the surface warmth that endears lesser poets to the reading public. Nor was he an attractive figure, either in manner or physique. Much of this may have been due to inconsistent health, but without his abrasive side English satire would be the poorer, for he was the sharpest and most innovative of its practitioners.

▷M Mack, *Alexander Pope, a life* (1985)

PORTA, Carlo
(1776–1821)

Italian poet, born in Milan. Writing in the dialect of Milan, he showed his insight into human character in narrative poems which are satirical and grimly realistic. These include *La Nomina del Capellan* (1819, 'The

Selection of the Chaplain') and *Disgrazzi de Giovannin Bongee* (1812, 'The Misadventures of Giovannino Bongeri').

▷H Auréas, *Carlo Porta* (1959)

PORTA, Giovanni Battista della
(1543–1615)

Italian physicist and philosopher. He wrote on physiognomy, natural magic, the steam pump, the properties of lenses, and gardening, besides several comedies.

PORTER, Anna Maria
(1780–1832)

English novelist, born in Durham, younger sister of **Jane Porter** and Robert Ker Porter. Her novel *The Hungarian Brothers* (1807), about the French Revolution, was highly successful and achieved numerous editions. She wrote several other novels, and also ballads and poems.

▷G Curia, introduction to *Walsh Colville* (1974)

PORTER, Eleanor, née Hodgman
(1868–1920)

American novelist, born in Littleton, New Hampshire. She studied music at the New England Conservatory. She married in 1892. Her first novels included *Cross Currents* (1907) and *Miss Billy* (1911). In 1913 *Pollyanna* appeared; this was an immediate success and has retained its popularity ever since. A sequel, about the 'glad child', *Pollyanna Grows Up*, was published in 1915, and two volumes of short stories, *The Tangled Threads* and *Across the Years*, appeared posthumously in 1924.

PORTER, Gene(va), née Stratton
(1868–1924)

American novelist, born on a farm in Wabash County, Indiana. She married Charles D Porter in 1886, and as Gene Stratton Porter attained great popularity with *A Girl of the Limberlost* (1909) and other stories full of sentiment and nature study.

▷J P Meehan, *The Lady of the Limberlost* (1928)

PORTER, Hal
(1911–84)

Australian novelist, playwright and poet. He reacted strongly to the prevailing provincialism and realism of Australian literature in his youth, writing elegantly fanciful fictions and richly imagistic poetry. His best-known works are *The Tilted Cross* (1961), *The Right Thing* (1971) and, perhaps his best book, the autobiographical *Watcher on the Cast Iron Balcony* (1964). *Selected Stories* appeared in 1971.

PORTER, Jane
(1776–1850)

English writer, born in Durham, sister of **Anna Maria Porter** and Robert Ker Porter, and daughter of an army surgeon. She made a great reputation in 1803 by her high-flown romance, *Thaddeus of Warsaw*, and had even more success in 1810 with *The Scottish Chiefs*, although her stage tragedy *Switzerland* (1819) was a failure. Other books were *The Pastors' Fireside* (1815), *Duke Christian of Lüneburg* (1824), *Tales Round a Winter's Hearth* (with her sister Anna Maria, 1824) and *The Field of Forty Footsteps* (1828). *Sir Edward Seaward's Shipwreck* (1831), a clever fiction, edited by her, was almost certainly written by her eldest brother, Dr William Ogilvie Porter (1774–1850).

▷ *These Were the Muses* (1924)

PORTER, Katherine Anne Maria Veronica Callista Russell
(1890–1980)

American writer, born in Indian Creek, Texas. Brought up by a grandmother near Kyle, Texas, she ran away and got married at 16, but divorced at 19. She worked as a reporter and actress, moved to Greenwich Village, and went to Mexico (1920–2) and took up Mexican causes. She had started writing at a very early age, but allowed nothing to be published until 1928, with her first collection of stories, *Flowering Judas*. Later, in Paris, she married a consular official (divorced 1938), and wrote her first novel, *Hacienda* (1934). Back in the USA she married for a third time, a professor of English, but divorced four years later. Three short novels, published as *Pale Horse, Pale Rider* (1939), were a success. *Ship of Fools* (1962), a huge allegorical novel analysing the German state of mind in the 1930s was almost universally regarded as a failure. A volume of essays, *The Days before*, appeared in 1952. *Collected Short Stories* (1965) won a Pulitzer Prize.

▷R B West, *Katherine Anne Porter* (1963)

PORTER, Peter
(1929–)

Australian poet and critic, born in Brisbane. He has lived in England since 1951, though he frequently visits Australia. He has worked as a bookseller, journalist, clerk and advertising copywriter. A difficult, clever and allusive poet, his several collections include *Words Without Music* (1968), *A Porter Folio* (1969), *The Last of England* (1970) and *The Cost of Seriousness* (1978). His *Collected Poems* (1983) confirmed him as a gifted aphorist.

He has published two excellent volumes of translation from the Latin, *Epigrams by Martial* (1971) and *After Martial* (1972), demonstrating that affection for the classics which is displayed in his poem 'On First Looking Into Chapman's *Hesiod*' (1975).

▷ R Garfit, in *British Poetry since 1960* (1972, M Schmidt and G Lindop eds)

PÔRTO ALEGRE, Manuel José de Araújo
(1806–79)

Brazilian poet and romantic critic, who collaborated with **Magalhães** in his polemic magazine *Niterói-Revista Brasiliense*. But Pôrto Alegre's own verse is so disciplined as to be regarded by most critics as classical.

PORTO-RICHE, Georges de
(1849–1930)

French dramatist, born in Bordeaux. After an early success with *La Chance de Françoise* (1889, 'Françoise's Luck'), he wrote several successful psychological plays which investigated the relationships between men and women in love (known as 'théâtre d'amour), including *L'Amoureuse* (1891, 'The Woman in Love'), *Le Vieil Homme* (1911, 'The Old Man') and *Le Marchand d'Estampes* (1917, 'The Print Seller').

POSEY, Alexander
(1873–1908)

American poet. Born near Eufala, Creek Nation Territory (now Oklahoma), the son of a Creek mother and Scots–Irish father, Posey began to write and publish poetry at university. He was appointed to several public positions in the Creek Nation, and worked between times on his farm. It was as Editor of the Eufala *Indian Journal* from 1902 (during the turbulent period following the Dawes Act allotment legislation) that Posey made his literary mark with his series of humorous topical sketches, written in the form of letters by the imaginary Creek front-porch philosopher, Fux Fixico. Posey died in a drowning accident. His poems were collected and published posthumously by his wife, Minnie Harris, in 1910.

▷ D F Littlefield, *Alexander Posey: Creek Poet, Journalist and Humorist* (1992)

POSTOLI, Foquion
(1887–1927)

Albanian writer of the 1912 'liberation' period. He wrote competent patriotic novels—the best known was *Lulja e kujtimit* (1924, 'In Defence of the Homeland')—none of which was translated.

POTGIETER, Everhardus Johannes
(1808–75)

Dutch poet and critic, born in Zwolle. An anti-romantic, he co-founded the important magazine *De Gids* in 1837. His satirical prose against the complacency of his age was salutary; but his poetry, exquisite and finely wrought, has now dated. He had a vital influence upon Dutch literature.

▷ T Weevers, *Goethe and Holland* (1949)

POTOK, Chaim (Herman Harold)
(1929–)

American novelist, born and educated in New York City, where he studied at Yeshiva University and the Jewish Theological Seminary. He was ordained as a rabbi in 1954. After teaching in seminaries, he became scholar-in-residence at Har Zion Temple in Philadelphia (1959–63) and, later, special projects editor at the Jewish Publication Society, for whom he wrote a 14-pamphlet series on *Jewish Ethics* (1964–9). In view of Potok's highly committed exploration of Judaism in modern America, it may be as well to re-label 'Jewish–American' novelists like **Philip Roth** and **Bernard Malamud** as 'post-Jewish'. His novels explore the problems of Orthodox and Hasidic communities within an aggressively secular society, but they are, if anything, more directly concerned with conflicts *within* Judaism than between Jews and WASPs. *The Chosen* (1967) charts the growing friendship between a young progressive scholar and the son of a highly traditional Hasid. In 1972 Potok published the controversial *My Name Is Asher Lev* in which the hero abandons his religious calling to become a painter, shocking his community with a work called 'Brooklyn Crucifixion'. Later works include *The Book of Lights* (1982) and *Davita's Harp* (1985); in 1990, Potok revived his troubled artist-hero in *The Gift of Asher Lev*. *Wanderings* (1978) is a scholarly but personal history of the Jews.

POTTER, (Helen) Beatrix
(1866–1943)

English author and illustrator of books for children, born in Kensington, London, into a wealthy family. The atmosphere at home was oppressively quiet and Beatrix, supervised by nurses and educated by governesses, grew up a lonely town child longing for the country. She taught herself to draw and paint, and while still quite young did serious natural history studies of fungi with the intention of making a book of watercolours. She turned to sketching pet animals dressed as human beings to amuse younger children. The original version of *The Tale of Peter Rabbit* was enclosed with a letter to her ex-governess's

777

child in 1893 and later published at her own expense, with fuller illustrations, in 1900, as was *The Tailor of Gloucester* (1902). When Frederick Warne took over publication in 1903 she had her first popular success with *The Tale of Squirrel Nutkin* (1903). In an appreciative, if gently satirical, review **Graham Greene** considered *The Roly-Poly Pudding* (1908, later changed to *The Tale of Samuel Whiskers*), to be her masterpiece. Miss Potter was not amused. In 1913, eight years after she had moved to a farm at Sawrey, near Lake Windermere (where six of her books are set), she married William Heelis, a Lake District solicitor. Thereafter she devoted herself almost entirely to farming and the new National Trust. *Johnny Town-Mouse* (1918) was her last book in the familiar style. She devised an elaborate cryptic diary whose code was broken by Leslie Linder and published as *The Journal of Beatrix Potter 1881–1897* (1966). She was the outstanding writer and artist of picture-story books of her time, and Peter the Rabbit, Jemima Puddle-Duck, Mrs Tiggy-Winkle, Benjamin Bunny and the rest have become classics of children's literature.

POTTER, Dennis Christopher George
(1935–94)

English dramatist, born in Forest of Dean. Although he wrote for the stage (*Sufficient Carbohydrate*, 1984), he was primarily a television dramatist. Following *Vote, Vote, Vote for Nigel Barton* (1965), he wrote over 25 television plays and series. *Son of Man* (1969) was the first television screenplay that depicted Christ as a man who struggled as much with his own doubts as with those opposed to his teaching. Other controversial plays include *Brimstone and Treacle* (1978), *The Singing Detective* (1986) and *Blackeyes* (1989). He was also technically innovative: *Pennies from Heaven* (1978) required the actors to mime to popular songs of the 1920s and 30s that intercut the action; *Blue Remembered Hills* (1979), a memory play, required the adult actors to impersonate children, but his technical freshness seemed a little worn in *Lipstick On Your Collar* (1993), another television drama in which music plays a central role. His novel *Ticket to Ride* (1986) was later adapted as the film *Secret Friends* (1992). He was the undisputed master of the serious television play, which he might well have been said to have invented and made his own.

POUND, Ezra Loomis
(1885–1972)

American poet and critic, born in Hailey, Idaho. Brought up in Wyncote, near Philadelphia, he graduated at Pennsylvania University in 1906, became an instructor in Wabash College in Crawfordsville, Indiana, but after four months left for Europe, travelling widely in Spain, Italy and Provence. He published his first collection of poems, *A Lume Spento* (1908), in Venice. In London later that year he met **Ford Madox Ford**, **James Joyce** and **Wyndham Lewis**, and published *Personae* and *Exultations* in 1909, followed by a book of critical essays, *The Spirit of Romance*, in 1910. He was co-editor of *Blast* (1914–15), the magazine of the short-lived 'Vorticist' movement, and London editor of the Chicago *Little Review* (1917–19), and in 1920 became Paris correspondent for *The Dial*. From 1924 he made his home in Italy. He became involved with fascist ideas and stirred up much resentment by antidemocracy broadcasts in the early stages of the war. In 1945 he was escorted back to the USA and indicted for treason. The trial did not proceed, however, as he was adjudged insane, and placed in an asylum. Three years later, a distinguished jury of his peers controversially awarded him the Bollingen Prize for *The Pisan Cantos*. In 1958 he was certified sane and released, and returned to Italy. In addition to his poetry he wrote books on literature, music, art and economics, and translated much from Italian, French, Chinese and Japanese. As a poet, of the Imagist school at the outset of his career, he was a thorough-going experimenter, deploying much curious and often spurious learning in his illustrative imagery and in the development of his themes. **T S Eliot** regarded him as the motivating force behind 'modern' poetry, the poet who created a climate in which English and American poets could understand and appreciate each other; *The Waste Land* bore a tribute to *il miglior fabbro*. *Homage to Sextus Propertius* (1919) and *Hugh Selwyn Mauberley* (1920) are among his most important early poems. His *Cantos*, a loosely-knit series of poems, appeared first in 1917, continuing in many instalments, via *The Pisan Cantos* to *Thrones: Cantos 96–109* (1959). It was intended as a vast, self-glossing purview of world culture but degenerated into an anti-Semitic rant on Poundian obsessions like usury and the redundancy of democracy; in anguish, the poet himself wrote 'the damned stuff will not cohere'. His work in the classics and Chinese poetry are discernible in their form. Apart from his life work in poetry, significant collections are *Translations of Ezra Pound* (1933) and *Literary Essays* (1954).

▷ N Stock, *The Life of Ezra Pound* (1970, rev edn 1982); H Kenner, *The Pound Era* (1971)

POURRAT, Henri
(1887–1959)

French novelist, born in Ambert in the Auvergne, where most of his work is set. His most famous books are the series of four novels under the title *Les Vaillances: farces et aventures de Gaspard des Montagnes* (1922–31), in which the daily life and customs of the Auvergne form a backdrop to a 19th-century tragedy, based on a story handed down in local tales, and narrated, in deference to the oral tradition, by a story-teller. He was dubbed 'France's Grimm' for his *Le Trésor des contes* (1948, Eng trans *A Treasury of French Tales*, 1953), which were also based on the folklore and peasant tales of the Auvergne. He was awarded the Prix **Goncourt** in 1941.

POWELL, Anthony Dymoke
(1905–)

English novelist, born in London, the son of an army officer. He was educated at Eton and Balliol College, Oxford, where he met several other young writers, including **Evelyn Waugh** and **Graham Greene**. He worked in publishing and journalism before World War II, and by 1936 had published four satirical novels, among them *Afternoon Men* (1931), *Venusberg* (1932) and *What's Become of Waring?* (1939). After the war he returned to book-reviewing, wrote a biography of John Aubrey (1948), and began the series of novels he called *A Dance to the Music of Time*—12 volumes, beginning with *A Question of Upbringing* (1951), covering 50 years of British upper middle-class life and attitudes. The light, witty, satirical tone of the pre-war novels developed, in *The Music of Time*, into an intricate and disciplined interweaving of personal relationships, ironic, humorous, and with extraordinary scope and depth of vision. He has won the James Tait Black Prize and W H Smith Literary Award. Since the completion of the cycle with *Hearing Secret Harmonies* (1975), he has published a four-volume autobiography, *To Keep the Ball Rolling* (1976–82), and two novels, *O, How the Wheel Becomes It!* (1983) and *The Fisher King* (1986), and two volumes of criticism, *Miscellaneous Verdicts* (1990) and *Under Review* (1992).
▷ B Bergonzi, *Anthony Powell* (1962)

POWERS, J(ames) E(arl)
(1917–)

American novelist and short-story writer, born in Jacksonville, Illinois and educated at Northwestern University. He has worked as an editor, a lecturer and a writer-in-residence. His special awards include an American Academy Grant (1948), a Guggenheim Fellowship (1948), three Rockefeller Fellowships, and a National Book Award in 1963 for his first novel *Morte d'Urban* (1962), which relates the tale of an initially moral priest who becomes perverted by the capitalists who

surround him. Powers began publishing short stories in the 1940s, and his subject-matter has remained constant from that time: he writes primarily about the midwest, race relations, and Catholicism.
▷ J F Hagopian, *J F Powers* (1968)

POWNALL, David
(1938–)

British playwright and novelist. He was born in Liverpool, and educated at Long Wandsworth College, Hampshire, and at Keele University. He worked in the personnel department of Ford at Dagenham, and for Anglo-American in Zambia, where his first play, *As We Lie*, was produced in 1969. He has been resident writer with theatre groups in Lancaster and London, and was founder (1975) of the Paines Plough Theatre. His first novels, *The Raining Tree War* (1974) and *African Horse* (1975), draw on an African background, satirizing the tribalism and superstition of political conflict, and the economic and cultural repercussions of colonial rule. *Light on a Honeycomb* (1978) is a remarkable portrait of an English community for the insane, using it as a symbol for wider social malaise. *Beloved Latitudes* (1981) is more inward. Pownall's careful balance of violence and humour, redemption and despair, has been likened to **Evelyn Waugh**.

POWYS, John Cowper
(1872–1963)

English novelist, poet and essayist, born in Shirley, Derbyshire, where his father was vicar; his mother was descended from **John Donne** and **William Cowper**; his brothers were **T F** and **Llewelyn Powys**. He was brought up in the Dorset-Somerset countryside and though he spent much of his later life in America, his formative years greatly influenced his work. Educated at Sherborne and Corpus Christi College, Cambridge, he taught and lectured before becoming a prolific author. Of some 50 books, his best known are his novels, particularly *Wolf Solent* (1929), *A Glastonbury Romance* (1932), gargantuan in scale, in which the myths surrounding the ancient abbey have a supernatural effect on the citizens of the town, *Weymouth Sands* (1934), *Maiden Castle* (1936) and *Owen Glendower* (1940). His reputation is the subject of much argument, but his standing is probably that of a cult author, rather than a widely recognized one.
▷ H P Collins, *John Cowper Powys, Old Earthman* (1966)

POWYS, Llewelyn
(1884–1939)

English essayist and novelist, brother of **John Powys** and **T F Powys**, born in Dorchester.

He suffered from recurrent tuberculosis which caused him to spend some years in Switzerland and in Kenya, and from which he died. From 1920 to 1925 he was a journalist in New York. His work include *Ebony and Ivory* (1922), *Apples be Ripe* (1930) and the biographical *Confessions of Two Brothers* (with his brother John, 1916), *Skin for Skin* (1925) and *The Verdict of Bridlegoose* (1926).

▷R H Ward, *The Powys Brothers* (1935)

POWYS, T(heodore) F(rancis)
(1875–1953)

English novelist and short-story writer, brother of **John** and **Llewelyn Powys**, born in Shirley, Derbyshire. He lived in seclusion and wrote original and eccentric novels of which the best known is *Mr Weston's Good Wine* (1927). Other works are *Mr Tasker's Gods* (1925), *Captain Patch* (1935) and *Goat Green* (1937).

▷H Coombes, *T. F. Powys* (1960)

PRAED, Rosa
(1851–1935)

Australian novelist, born in Bromelton, Logan River, Queensland, best known as a writer of romantic fiction under the name of Mrs Campbell Praed. The privations of her early married life on outback Queensland stations resulted in *An Australian Heroine* (1880) and *The Romance of a Station* (1889). In 1875 she left with her husband for London where she became a popular novelist and the 'Queen' of circulating libraries, mixing in literary circles which included **Oscar Wilde**. During the next 40 years she produced almost as many novels, many with an Australian setting. *Policy and Passion* (1881) dealt, as did many of the others, with the disillusion which marriage brings. She questioned the permanency of marriage in *The Bond of Wedlock* (1887), which created controversy as a play. The failure of her marriage, and the death of her four children in tragic circumstances, turned her to aspects of spiritualism and she set up house with a 'medium', Nancy Harward (1899–1927), producing a number of occult books.

PRAED, Winthrop Mackworth
(1802–39)

English poet, born in London. He was educated at Eton (where he founded the 'Etonian') and at Trinity College, Cambridge, where he twice won the Chancellor's Medal. Called to the Bar in 1829 he went on to become an MP and junior minister. A promising parliamentary career was cut short by consumption. His light, society verse, such as 'Good Night to the Season' and 'The Letter of Advice', has been likened to **Thomas Hood**

in comic vein, but the comparison flatters Praed. Yet, although he has been described rather dismissively as a 'clever punster', he nevertheless influenced several 19th-century poets, notably **Frederick Locker-Lampson**.

▷D Hudson, *A Poet in Parliament* (1939)

PRATCHETT, Terry
(1948–)

English fantasy writer, born in Beaconsfield, Buckinghamshire. He worked as a journalist, and later as a publicity officer, before becoming a full-time writer in 1987. His first book was a fantasy for children, *The Carpet People* (1971, rev edn 1992). Later books for children include the *Book of the Nomes* sequence (from 1989) and *Only You Can Save Mankind* (1992). *The Dark Side of the Sun* (1976) and *Strata* (1981) were parodies of science fiction, but his popular success was secured by the *Discworld* sequence of comic fantasy novels, which began with *The Colour of Magic* (1983).

PRATI, Giovanni
(1815–84)

Italian lyric and narrative poet, born near Trento. Court poet to the House of Savoy, he became a deputy to the Italian parliament (1862) and a senator (1876). His lyrics, which fill several volumes, include *Canti lirici* (1843, 'Lyrical Songs'), and *Canti del popolo* (1843, 'Songs of the People'). He enjoyed a popular success with the romantic poem *Edmenegarda* (1841), but later turned to a simpler form of expression.

▷P L Mannucci, *Giovanni Prati* (1934)

PRATOLINI, Vasco
(1913–89)

Italian novelist, born in Florence, usually classed as 'neorealist'. Neorealism was first defined by the critic Arnaldo Bocelli in 1930 as a sort of neo-naturalism. But it did not reach its zenith until after World War II, when Italian authors became free to write as they wished—and then it was much influenced by the busy Italian film industry. Pratolini, who came from a working-class background, was in 1936 a young fascist interested in literature, and contributing eagerly to a fascist periodical, when he met **Elio Vittorini**; the latter helped him to shed the fascism, and encouraged him to write. He made his name with the partly autobiographical *Il quartiere* (1945, Eng trans *A Tale of Santa Croce*, 1952), a skilfully written panorama of life in this Florence district in the 1930s. *Cronache di povere amanti* (1947, Eng trans *A Tale of Poor Lovers*, 1949), his masterpiece, presents a rich canvas—there are more than 50 characters—of working-class Florentine life from the rise of fascism. After the trilogy *Una storia italiana* (*Metello*, 1955, Eng trans 1968; *Lo scialo*, 1960, 'Waste'; *Allegoria e derisione*, 1966, 'Allegory and Derision'), Pratolini wrote little more. He has been criticized for his Marxism (and his popularity in the then Soviet Union), but acclaimed for his human warmth and emphasis on individual aspiration.

▷F Rosengarten, *Vasco Pratolini: The Development of a Social Novelist* (1965)

PRATT, E(dwin) J(ohn)
(1882–1964)

Canadian poet, born in Western Bay, Newfoundland. He spent his early years in small fishing villages and taught in remote island communities, then after gaining his PhD in theology from the University of Toronto (1917) joined the English department there (1920) and edited the *Canadian Poetry Magazine* from 1936 to 1942. He won Governor General's Awards for *The Fable of the Goats and Other Poems* (1932), *Brebeuf and His Brethren* (1940) and *Towards the Last Spike* (1952). *The Collected Poems of E. J. Pratt* (1958) has been described as charting the Canadian movement from a colonial to a national literature, and he is particularly renowned for narrative poetry that explores the growth of a national sense of time and space within the wider context of the world.
▷S Djwa, *E. J. Pratt: The Evolutionary Vision* (1974); Frank Davey, 'Apostle of Corporate Man' and 'Rationalist Technician', in *Canadian Literature* (43, 1970 and 61, 1974)

PREDA, Marin
(1922–)

Romanian novelist and story writer, widely thought of as the outstanding living writer of his country. Being of peasant origin, he steered a cunning and sometimes funny line between criticism of the communist regime and appearing to approve of it. Many of his colleagues hated him, especially for serving as a vice-president of the Writers' Union. His chief work is *Morometii* (1955–67), the first part of which was translated as *The Morometes* (1957). In this book his chief character, Ilie Moromete, is a philosophical peasant who delights in leading everyone up the garden path, and is in certain respects a representation of his creator, who has never seriously sought for anyone's approval.

PREMCHAND, pseud of Dhanpat Rai Srivastav
(1880–1936)

The leading Indian writer of fiction in Hindi, still unsurpassed for the picture he gives of North Indian life, born in Benares. Until 1914 he wrote mainly in Urdu; but after that he devoted himself to establishing Urdu forms, stories and novels, in Hindi. He was a follower of Gandhi, and gave up his teaching post in 1921 as a protest against British policies. He wrote more than 300 tales, as well as novels. Much is available in English, including the selection *The World of Premchand* (1969), his greatest novel, *Godan* (1935, Eng trans *The Gift of a Cow*, 1968) and *A Premchand Reader* (1962).

PRERADOVIĆ, Paula von, married name Molten
(1887–1951)

Austrian Roman Catholic poet, who was arrested in 1944 for her involvement with the anti-Nazi resistance. She wrote the words of the Austrian National anthem. Her well-respected and accomplished poetry, much of it devotional, was influenced by that of **Rainer Maria Rilke**.

PRESSBURGER, Emeric (Imre)
(1902–88)

Hungarian screenwriter, born in Miskolc. Educated at Prague and Stuttgart, he worked as a journalist in Hungary and Germany before entering the film industry. Resident in Britain from 1935, he worked on a number of projects for Sir Alexander Korda before writing the fast-moving thriller *The Spy In Black* (1939) for director Michael Powell. They subsequently formed The Archers, one of the most innovative production units in the history of British cinema. As film-makers their work embraced the notion of film as a medium to express grand emotions, poetry, fantasy and sensuality rather than the earthbound social realism that had often characterized British cinema of the period. Among their most distinctive films are *The Life And Death Of Colonel Blimp* (1943), *A Matter Of Life And Death* (1946), *Black Narcissus* (1947) and *The Red Shoes* (1948). The partnership was dissolved in 1957. Working alone Pressburger had directed *Twice Upon A Time* (1953). He subsequently wrote a number of short stories and novels, one of which was adapted into the film *Behold A Pale Horse* (1964); he re-united with Powell as the writer of the children's film *The Boy Who Turned Yellow* (1972).

PREVELAKIS, Pandelis
(1909–)

Cretan novelist, born in Rethymno, and a pupil and imitator of the great **Kazantzakis**, although much more polished in style. A student of aesthetics and art, Prevelakis made a startling debut in 1938 with *To Chronico* *mias politeias* (Eng trans *The Tale of a Town*, 1978), a love story set against the backdrop of an anonymous town in silent decay. However, critical opinion is that his best books were written after World War II. *Pantermi Crete* ('Wretched Crete'), published in 1945, was a chronicle of the uprising of 1866, and his three-volume masterpiece *O Cretikos* (1948–50, 'The Cretan') traced events from this uprising until 1910. He himself said his intention was 'to express the whole soul of the Greek people at one point of its history'.

PRÉVERT, Jacques
(1900–77)

French poet and screenwriter, born in Neuilly-sur-Seine. A shop-worker, he turned to writing after his military service and worked for *L'Argus De La Presse* and the publicity agency Damour. A member of the Surrealist movement before being expelled for irreverence, he first made his name as the author of humorous, anarchic 'song poems' about street life in Paris, collected in *Paroles* (1946, Eng trans in part *Paroles: Selections*, 1958) and *Spectacle* (1951). Active as a writer and performer with the agit-prop theatre group Octobre, he wrote the screenplay for their film *L'Affaire Est Dans Le Sac* (1932, 'It's in the Bag') and subsequently pursued a career as a screenwriter, achieving his greatest renown during a 10-year collaboration with director Marcel Carné. Together they made such atmospheric classics of fatalistic pre-war French cinema as *Quai Des Brumes* (1938, 'Port of Mists') and *Le Jour Se Lève* (1939, 'Daybreak'), as well as their masterpiece, *Les Enfants du Paradis* (1944, Eng trans 1968). In later years he collaborated with his brother, the director Pierre Prévert (1906–88), on short, animated films for children, and worked extensively for French television between 1961 and 1968.
▷J Queval, *Jacques Prévert* (1955)

PRÉVOST, Abbé (Antoine François Prévost d'Exiles)
(1697–1763)

French novelist, born in Artois. Educated by the Jesuits, at 16 he enlisted in the army, but soon returned to the Jesuits, and had almost joined the order when he was again tempted to the soldier's life. In 1720, following an unhappy love affair, he joined the Benedictines of St Maur, and spent the next seven years in religious duties and in study. But about 1727 he fled for six years, first to London, where he started to write *Histoire de Cleveland*, and then to Holland (1729–31). He issued volumes 1–4 of *Mémoires d'un homme de qualité* (Eng trans *Memoirs of a Man of Quality*, 1938) in 1728 and volumes 5–6 in 1731, *Manon Lescaut* (Eng trans 1738) forming volume 8. He employed himself in additional novels—*Le Philosophe anglais; ou, Histoire de Monsieur Cleveland, fils naturel de Cromwell* (1731–9, Eng trans *The Life and Adventures of Mr Cleveland*, 1734) and *Le Doyen de Killerine* (1735–40, Eng trans *The Dean of Coleraine*, 1742–3)—and in translations. In London again after another affair he started *Le Pour et contre* (1733–40, 'Arguments For and Against'), a periodical review of life and letters, modelled on the *Spectator*. In France by 1735, he was appointed honorary chaplain to the Prince de Conti, and compiled over a hundred volumes more. He died suddenly at Chantilly. Prévost's reputation stands securely on *Manon Lescaut*. It remains fresh, charming and perennial, from its perfect simplicity, the stamp of reality and truth throughout, and a style so flowing and natural that the reader forgets it altogether in the interest of the story.
▷J Sgard, *Prévost, romancier* (1968)

PRÉVOST, Eugène Marcel
(1862–1941)

French novelist, born in Paris. A civil engineer, he worked in a tobacco factory until 1891. From the age of 25 he wrote in his leisure hours. Of his clever novels and plays many have been translated, including *Cousine Laura* (1890, Eng trans *Cousin Laura*, 1913), *Frédérique* (1900, Eng trans 1901) and *Léa* (1900, Eng trans *Léa, a Sequel to Frédérique*, 1902).

PRICE, Reynolds
(1933–)

American novelist, born in Macon, North Carolina and educated at Duke University and Oxford. He has been a professor of English in a number of universities and in 1976 chaired the National Endowment for the Arts Literature Advisory Panel. He has received numerous awards, including a Guggenheim Fellowship (1964) and a National Book Critics Award (1987). His first novel, *A Long and Happy Life* (1962), introduces the Mustian family who appear in several of his later books. He writes of rural life in North Carolina, but his work has become increasingly more abstract, with mythic elements featuring implicitly or explicitly. *Kate Vaiden* (1986) is his most critically acclaimed novel to date.

PRICHARD, Katharine Susannah
(1883–1969)

Australian writer, born in Levuka, on Ovalau, where her father was Editor of the *Fiji Times*. She started work on a Melbourne

newspaper, for which she made a trip to London in 1908. Four years later she returned to journalism in London. In 1915 her first novel, *The Pioneers*, won the 'colonial' section of a publisher's competition and was filmed in Australia the following year. In 1916 she returned to Australia, married Captain Hugo Throssell VC and in the next 50 years produced 12 novels, many poems, plays and short stories, and an autobiography, *Child of the Hurricane* (1963). In 1920 she had become a founding member of the Australian Communist Party, and her socialist convictions coloured much of her subsequent work, especially her powerful trilogy set in the West Australian goldfields, *The Roaring Nineties* (1946), *Golden Miles* (1948) and *Winged Seeds* (1950). Her last novel, *Subtle Flame* (1967), was a study in the conflicts facing a newspaper editor. Her son, Ric Prichard Throssell, wrote the play *For Valour* (1960, published 1976), a study of the economic and personal decline of a returned war hero, closely modelled on his father, and a biography of his mother, *Wild Weeds and Wind Flowers* (1975).
▷H D Brochmann, *Katharine Susannah Prichard* (1967)

PRIESTLEY, J(ohn) B(oynton)
(1894–1984)

English novelist, playwright and critic, born in Bradford. He was educated there and at Trinity Hall, Cambridge. He had already made a reputation by critical writings such as *The English Comic Characters* (1925), *The English Novel* (1927), *English Humour* (1928), and books on **George Meredith** (1926) and **Thomas Love Peacock** (1927) in 'The English Men of Letters' series when the geniality of his novel *The Good Companions* (1929) gained him a wide popularity. It was followed by other humorous novels, though not all of equal merit, including *Angel Pavement* (1930), *Let the People Sing* (1939), *Jenny Villiers* (1947) and *The Magicians* (1954). His reputation as a dramatist was established by *Dangerous Corner* (1932), *Time and the Conways* (1937), and other plays on space-time themes, as well as popular comedies such as *Laburnum Grove* (1933), and his psychological mystery, *An Inspector Calls* (1947). Best known as a writer of novels, Priestley was also master of the essay form. He was an astute, original and controversial commentator on contemporary society—*Journey Down the Rainbow* (1955), written with his wife Jacquetta Hawkes the archaeologist, was a jovial indictment of American life; in serious vein, his collected essays, *Thoughts in the Wilderness* (1957), deal with both present and future social problems.
▷J Braine, *J. B. Priestley* (1978)

PRIETO, Jenaro
(1889–1946)

Chilean novelist, author of *El socio* (1928, Eng trans, *The Partner*), 1931), a novel worthy of **Pirandello**, in which a man invents a business partner and is then, after he 'commits suicide', hunted as his murderer.

PRIJAM, Amitra
(1919–)

Indian (Punjabi) poet, well known throughout the Indian sub-continent for her mellifluous and reconciliatory poetry.

PRINCE, F(rank) T(empleton)
(1912–)

South African-born British poet, educated at Balliol College, Oxford, and at Princeton University. He served in the Intelligence Corps during World War II, subsequently joining Southampton University, where he taught English until 1974; he later held other academic posts in Britain and overseas, including a period of three years as Professor of English at the University of the West Indies. His elegant, traditionally rhymed and metred verse first appeared in book form in 1938 with the fine *Poems*. 'Soldiers Bathing' from the 1954 volume of that name is his best-known work and one of the finest to have emerged out of World War II. The best of the earlier work was collected as *The Doors of Stone* (1963). Later volumes include *Drypoints of the Hasidim* (1975), *Afterword on Rupert Brooke* (1976) and the magnificent *Yüan Chên Variations* (1981), the latter postdating a *Collected Poems*, which appeared in 1979. Prince has also been a significant scholar of **Milton** and of **Shakespeare**'s verse.
▷A Nigam, *F T Prince: A Study of His Poetry* (1983)

PRINGLE, Thomas
(1789–1834)

Scottish writer, born in Blakelaw, Roxburghshire, the son of a farmer. He was educated at Kelso Grammar School and Edinburgh University, and in 1811 became an archivist in the Register Office. In 1817 he started the *Edinburgh Monthly Magazine*, later *Blackwood's Magazine*. In 1820 he emigrated to Cape Colony, and for three years was government librarian at Cape Town. He started a Whig paper, but it was suppressed by the governor. Returning to London in 1826 he became Secretary of the Anti-Slavery Society. He wrote *African Sketches* (1834), and published two collections of poems and lyrics, *The Autumnal Collection* (1817), and *Ephemerides* (1828).
▷W Hay, *Thomas Pringle* (1912)

PRIOR, Matthew
(1664–1721)

English poet and diplomat, born in Wimborne, Dorset, the son of a joiner. Under the patronage of Lord Dorset he was sent to Westminster School, and from there with a scholarship from the Duchess of Somerset to St John's College, Cambridge. He was first employed as secretary to the ambassador to The Hague. In Queen Anne's time he turned Tory, and was instrumental in bringing about the treaty of Utrecht (1713), for which dubious service he was imprisoned for two years (1715–17) after the queen's death. His Tory friends recouped his fortunes by subscribing handsomely to a folio edition of his works (1719). He also received a gift of £4000 from Lord Harley to purchase Down Hall in Essex. Prior was a master of neat, colloquial and epigrammatic verse. His first work, a collaboration with Charles Montagu (Lord **Halifax**), was *The Hind and the Panther Transvers' to the story of the Country and the City Mouse* (1687), a witty satire on **Dryden**'s *Hind and the Panther*. His long poem, *Alma or The Progress of the Mind* (1718), was composed in prison. The long soliloquy in couplet form, *Solomon on the Vanity of the World*, is definitely tedious. His political verse, with the exception of his brilliant burlesque of **Nicolas Boileau**'s *Épître au roi* (*An English Ballad on the Taking of Namur*), is now of historical interest only. He is best known as the poet of light occasional verse—mock-lyrics such as *A Better Answer (to Chloe Jealous)*, or charming addresses to noble children (*A Letter to the Lady Margaret Cavendish when a Child*), and, in serious vein, *Lines Written in the Beginning of Mézeray's History of France*, a favourite with Sir **Walter Scott**. His wittiest trifle is *The Secretary*, but *Jinny the Just* is also popular. He was buried in Poets' Corner in Westminster Abbey.

▷ F Bickley, *Matthew Prior* (1914)

PRISHVIN, Mikhail
(1873–1974)

Russian novelist and naturalist, born near Yelets. He was expelled from his school for rudeness to a teacher, who happened to be **Vasily Rozanov**. Arrested for Marxist activities during 1897–9, he first qualified as an agronomist. His first book, *V krayu nepuganykh* (1905, 'In the Country Where the Birds Show No Fear'), records his impressions of a Russian countryside unspoiled by human beings. Being a nature writer, he was relatively safe from Stalin's censors, and could enjoy the reputation he deserved. *Kalendar prirody* (1937, Eng trans *The Lake and the Woods*, 1952, *Nature's Diary*, 1958) and *Zhan-shen* (1933, Eng trans *Jen Sheng:*

The Root of Life, 1936) are his most representative works in translation.

▷ M Slonim, *Soviet Russian Literature: Writers and Problems 1917–1977* (1977)

PRITCHETT, Sir V(ictor) S(awdon)
(1900–)

English writer and critic, born in Ipswich. He was educated at Alleyn's School, Dulwich, and Dulwich College. After working in the leather trade he became a newspaper correspondent in France, Morocco and Spain, and in 1929 published his first novel, *Claire Drummer*. His style is witty and idiosyncratic, his themes satirical, and he is particularly interested in the 'puritan' character with its fanaticism and guilt, which he portrays with increasing humour in his novels *Nothing Like Leather* (1935), *Dead Man Leading* (1937) and *Mr Beluncle* (1951). A highly-regarded literary critic, he travelled and lectured widely, especially in the USA. Among his critical works are *The Living Novel* (1946), *Books in General* (1953), and a biography of **Honoré de Balzac** (1973), and he is the author of many volumes of short stories, a form in which he excels, and two autobiographical books, *A Cab at the Door* (1968) and *Midnight Oil* (1973). *The Complete Essays* was published in 1991.

PROCTER, Adelaide Ann, pseud Mary Berwick
(1825–64)

English poet, born in London, daughter of **Bryan Waller Procter**. In 1851 she turned Roman Catholic. By her *Legends and Lyrics* (1858–60), some of which were written for *Household Words*, she won poetical renown. Her poems included 'The Lost Chord', which was set to music by Sir Arthur Sullivan.

▷ J Janku, *Adelaide Ann Procter: ihr Leven und ihre Werke* (1912)

PROCTER, Bryan Waller, pseud Barry Cornwall
(1787–1874)

English poet, born in Leeds. After studying at Harrow with **Byron** and Peel he became a solicitor, went to London and in 1815 began to contribute poetry to the *Literary Gazette*. In 1823 he married Anne Benson Skepper (1799–1888). He had meanwhile published poems and produced a tragedy at Covent Garden, *Mirandola*, whose success was largely due to the acting of Macready and Kemble. He was called to the Bar in 1831, and from 1832 to 1861 was a metropolitan commissioner of lunacy. His works comprise *Dramatic Scenes* (1819), *Marcian Colonna* (1820), *The Flood of Thessaly* (1823) and

English Songs (1832), besides memoirs of Kean (1835) and **Charles Lamb** (1866).
▷R W Armour, *Barry Cornwall* (1935)

PROKOSCH, Frederic
(1908–89)

American novelist and poet. Born in Wisconsin, he attended Yale and King's College, London. His best-known novel is *The Asiatics* (1935), whose settings reflect Prokosch's travels; during World War II, he was the US cultural attaché in Stockholm. His novels about the war include *The Skies of Europe* (1941) and *The Conspirators* (1943). In later years, he wrote fiction based on the lives of great Europeans, Beatrice Cenci in *A Tale for Midnight* (1955) and a rather uncertain **Byron** in *The Missolonghi Manuscript* (1968). His most effective volume of poetry was *The Assassins* (1936). *Chosen Poems* (1947) gathers the best of them. A few years before his death he published *Voices* (1983), a powerful literary memoir.

PROPERTIUS, Sextus
(c.48–c.15 BC)

Roman elegiac poet, born probably in Asisium (Assisi) in Umbria. He had a portion of his patrimony confiscated after Philippi by the Triumvirs (41 BC), to reward their veterans, but he retained sufficient funds to proceed to Rome for education, and became a poet. He won the favour of Maecenas, to whom he dedicated a book of his poems, and even ingratiated himself with Augustus, whose achievements he duly celebrated. But the central figure of his inspiration was his mistress Cynthia. Propertius left Rome apparently only once, on a visit to Athens. Of his poems only the first book, devoted to Cynthia, was published during his lifetime.
▷G Luck, *The Latin Love Elegy* (1969)

PROUST, Marcel
(1871–1922)

French novelist, born in Auteuil, Paris. A semi-invalid all his life, he was cosseted by his mother, and her death in 1905, when he was 34 years old, robbed him of any desire to continue his 'social butterfly' existence. Instead he withdrew from society, immured himself in a sound-proof flat and gave himself over entirely to introspection. Delving into the self below the levels of superficial consciousness, he set himself the task of transforming into art the realities of experience as known to the inner emotional life. Despite the seemingly dilettante approach to life prior to his start on his novel, *À la recherche du temps perdu* (1913–27, 13 vols, trans by Scott Moncrieff as *Remembrance of Things Past*,

1922–31), it is evident from the various volumes which make up this title that no detail ever escaped his amazingly observant eye, and he subjected experience to searching analysis to divine in it beauties and complexities that escape the superficial response of ordinary intelligence. Thinking about the philosophy of Henri Bergson on the subconscious, his distinctions between the various aspects of time, and insistence on the truths perceived by involuntary memory, Proust evolved a mode of communication by image, evocation and analogy for displaying his characters—not as a realist would see them, superficially, from the outside, but in terms of their concealed emotional life, evolving on a plane that has nothing to do with temporal limitations. *À la recherche* started off with *Du côté de chez Swann* (1913, Eng trans *Swann's Way*, 1922), and, after a delay caused by the war, *À l'ombre des jeunes filles en fleur* (1919, Eng trans *Within a Budding Grove*, 1924), which won the Prix **Goncourt** in 1919. *Le Côté de Guermantes* (1920–1, 2 vols, Eng trans *The Guermantes' Way*, 1925) and *Sodome et Gomorrhe* (1922, 3 vols, Eng trans *The Cities of the Plain*, 1927) followed. These achieved an international reputation for Proust and an eager public awaited the posthumously published titles, *La Prisonnière* (1923, Eng trans *The Captive*, 1929), *Albertine disparue* (1925, Eng trans *The Sweet Cheat Gone*, 1930), and *Le Temps retrouvé* (1927, Eng trans *Time Regained*, 1931), each in two volumes. Apart from his masterpieces, there was also posthumous publication of an early novel, *Jean Santeuil* (1952, Eng trans 1955) and a book of critical credo, *Contre Sainte-Beuve* (1954, Eng trans *By Way of Sainte-Beuve*, 1958). A new English translation of his masterwork by **D J Enright** appeared under the title *In Search of Lost Time* in 1992.
▷G D Painter, *Proust: a biography* (2 vols, 1959–65)

PROUX, Prosper
(1811–75)

Breton poet, who made an influential anthology of Goliardic poetry, and who wrote 'hearty and often bawdy' poems, which are still read.

PROYSEN, Alf
(1914–70)

Norwegian novelist, short-story writer and balladist, born in Hedmark. His most famous creation internationally is Mrs Pepperpot, the central character of a number of short-story collections (such as *Little Old Mrs Pepperpot*, 1959). Despite being miniscule, she overcomes astonishing adversity, and is emblematic of the author's populist socialism. In his own country, Proysen's celebrity was more broadly based; he first achieved widespread popularity in 1948–9 with the publication of three satirical ballad collections (including *Musavisa*, 1949). His only novel, *Trost i Toklampa* (1950, 'Thrush in the Ceiling Light'), satirizes the idiocies of rural life, and contributed greatly to his status as the country's most popular writer since World War II.

PRUDENTIUS, Marcus Aurelius Clemens
(348–c.410)

Latin Christian poet, born in the north of Spain. He practised as a pleader, acted as civil and criminal judge, and afterwards received high office at the imperial court. A Christian all his life, he devoted himself in his later years to the composition of religious poetry. Of his poems the chief are *Cathemerinon Liber*, a series of 12 hymns (trans 1845); *Peristephanon*, 14 lyrical poems in honour of martyrs; *Apotheosis*, a defence of the Trinity; *Hamartigeneia*, on the origin of evil; *Psychomachia* (Eng trans *War of the Soul*, 1743), on the Christian Graces; and *Contra Symmachum*, against the heathen gods; and *Diptychon*, on scriptural incidents. He is the best of the early Christian verse-makers.
▷T R Glover, *Life and Letters in the 4th Century* (1901)

PRUS, Boleslaw, pseud of Aleksander Glowacki
(1847–1912)

Polish novelist, born in Hrubieszów. He belonged to the period of realism in literature which followed the unsuccessful revolt against Russian domination in 1863–4. His novels and short stories are written as social novels, mainly about common people, and include *Omylka* ('The Blunder'), *Lalka* (1887, 'The Doll'), considered to be his masterpiece, a vivid and sympathetic picture of Warsaw, and *Emancypantki* (1893, 'Emancipated Women').
▷S Malkowski, *Boleslaw Prus* (1964)

PRYS-JONES, Arthur Glyn
(1888–1987)

Welsh poet, born in Denbigh and educated at Llandovery College and Jesus College, Oxford. A teacher by profession, he edited the first anthology of Anglo–Welsh poetry, *Welsh Poets* (1917), and published six volumes of his own, including *Poems of Wales* (1923), *Green Places* (1948), *High Heritage* (1969) and *Valedictory Verses* (1978). The doyen of Anglo–Welsh writers, he was President of the Welsh Academy from 1970 until his death.

PRZYBOS, Julian
(1901–70)

Polish poet and poetic theoretician, born of a poor peasant family in Gwóznica. He was the influential leader (in Cracow) of the poetry movement known as the First Vanguard—'rationalistic and constructivist'—and as such he opposed both the Second Vanguard and the *Skamander* group. Czeslaw Milosz (originally a Second Vanguard, or 'Catastrophist' poet) has written that although his 'obsession with a poetry controlled by the will sometimes leads him to the very edge of the ridiculous ... he is recognized as one of those who contributed most to the transformation of modern Polish verse'. He insisted that poets must avoid direct expression of the feelings but create their emotional equivalent in their images. There are elements of Futurism in his earlier work. Two poems are translated in *Post-War Polish Poetry* (1965, ed Milosz).

PRZYBYSZEWSKI, Stanislaw
(1868–1927)

Polish novelist, dramatist and critic, born in Lojewo. He was educated in Germany, and lived from 1898 in Cracow, where he became Editor of *Life* and a leader of the new literary 'Young Poland' movement. His work, reflecting his 'naturalist' ideas, included *Homo Sapiens* (1901), *Matka* (1903) and the drama *Śnieg* (1903, Eng trans *Snow*, 1920).
▷S Halsztynski, *Stanislaw Przybyszewski* (1958)

PSYCHARIS, Iannis
(1854–1929)

Novelist and poet of Chiot origin, but born in Odessa and educated in Constantinople. At the age of 15 he left for Paris and Germany, eventually settling in Paris in 1885, where he taught modern Greek at the École des Hautes Études, and where he lived for the rest of his life. He was the principal catalyst for the shift in Greek poetry from the use of the archaic *Katharevousa* to demotic Greek. His book on why this change was necessary, *To Taxidhi Mou* (1888, 'My Journey'), was immediately adopted as a handbook by many Greek poets. He also attempted to introduce the 'psychological' novel into Greek literature, with works such as *Zoë ki'Agapi sti Monaxia* (1904, 'Life and Love in Solitude') and *Ta Dheo Adherfia* (1911, 'The Two Brothers'); these did not receive a warm critical reception. However, his largely autobiographical *T'Oneiro tou Gianniris* (1897, 'The Dream of Gianniris'), a lyrical depiction of some of his years as a soldier, added greatly to his reputation.

PÜCKLER-MUSKAU, Hermann, Fürst von
(1785–1871)

German travel writer, patron of the arts, dandy, personality and poet (although his early collection has been called an 'indiscretion'). He owned extensive estates at Muskau, where he was born, and at Branitz, where he died. His travel books, including *Briefe eines Verstorbene* (1830–2, Eng trans *Tour in Germany, Holland and England 1826–1828*, 1832), were written in the style of **Sterne**.

▷ E H Butler, *The Tempestuous Prince* (1929)

PUIG, Manuel
(1932–90)

Argentinian novelist, born in General Villegas. A gifted writer who wrote in both Spanish and English, he has been labelled with the 'magical realist' tag for his stylistic diversity and playful imagination. He came to attention with *La traición de Rita Hayworth* (1968, Eng trans *Betrayed by Rita Hayworth*, 1971), which made an ironic contrast of the 'gaucho' myth with a contemporary Argentine culture dominated by Hollywood and television, which Puig loved. *Boquitas pintadas* (1969, Eng trans *Heartbreak Tango*, 1973) was followed by a detective novel, *The Buenos Aires Affair* (1973). His biggest success was *El beso de la mujer araña* (1976, Eng trans *Kiss of the Spider Woman*, 1979). The story of the relationship which develops between two unlikely prisoners, it has been adapted for film and stage. The posthumous *Tropical Night Falling* appeared in 1992.

PUJMANOVÁ, Marie, née **Hennerová**
(1893–1958)

Czech novelist and poet, born in Prague. She took a conventionally Marxist view, but her trilogy of Czech life from before until after World War II, tracing the fortunes and misfortunes of two families, one working- one middle-class, effectively evokes the atmosphere of Czechoslovakia in those years, in particular the Nazi occupation.

PULCI, Luigi
(1432–84)

Italian poet, born in Padua. A protégé of Cosimo de Medici, he wrote *Il Morgante Maggiore* (1481, 'Morgante the Giant'), a burlesque epic, one of the most valuable specimens of the early Tuscan dialect. He also produced a comic novel and several humorous sonnets.

▷ A Gianni, *Pulci uno e due* (1967)

PURCHAS, Samuel
(1577–1626)

English compiler of travel books, born in Thaxted in Essex. He studied at St John's College, Cambridge, and became vicar of Eastwood in 1604, and in 1614 rector of St Martin's, Ludgate. He assisted Hakluyt in his later years. His own great works were *Purchas his Pilgrimage, or Relations of the World in all Ages* (1613) and *Hakluytus Posthumus, or Purchas his Pilgrimes* (1625), based on the papers of Hakluyt and archives of the East India company. Another work is *Purchas his Pilgrim: Microcosmus, or the History of Man* (1619).

PURDY, Al
(1918–)

Canadian poet, born in Wooler, Ontario; his lack of academic qualifications or involvement is unusual among Canadian poets. The winner of Governor General's Awards for *The Cariboo Horses* (1965) and *Collected Poems* (1986), he is the author of more than 30 volumes of poetry, in which 'an engaging conversational fluency is almost always present'. Purdy's is a poetry that gives Canadian history a landscape and a presence: 'The carving is laid aside/in beginning darkness/at the end of hunger/after a while wind/blows down the tent and snow/begins to cover him/After 600 years/the ivory thought/is still warm' ('Lament for the Dorsets', in *Wild Grape Wine*, 1968).

▷ T Marshall, *Harsh and Lovely Land* (1979)

PURDY, James Otis
(1923–)

American satirical novelist and short-story writer, much concerned with socially and sexually marginal characters and groups. He was born in Ohio, educated in Chicago and Mexico, and worked for some time as a translator and college lecturer. Early stories were privately published with the help of friends, as·*Don't Call Me by My Right Name* and *63: Dream Palace* (both 1956), and Purdy has been only slowly and rather grudgingly accepted by the US literary establishment. He has acknowledged the assistance of **Edith Sitwell** in securing a sympathetic readership. His first novel was *Malcolm* (1959), subsequently dramatized by **Edward Albee**. Like its successor, *The Nephew* (1960), it deals with a quest for information about a missing character; together they serve as a prologue to Purdy's lifelong interest in outsiders. The 'hero' of *Cabot Wright Begins* (1964) is a rapist; later books, particularly *Eustace Chisholm and the Works* (1967), have dealt with homoeroticism. The writing is vivid and vernacular and often realistically oblique in dealing with extremes of consciousness. Three novels about a disintegrating American family (1970–81) were collected as *Sleepers in Moon-Crowned Valleys* (1981). *Narrow Rooms* (1978) was strongly touted as a gay classic in the making. Purdy's verse has appeared in two volumes, *The Running Sun* (1971) and *Sunshine Is an Only Child* (1973).

▷ S D Adams, *James Purdy* (1976)

PUSHKIN, Alexander Sergevich
(1799–1837)

Russian poet, born in Moscow. His lineage was illustrious, and he attended the Lyceum at Tsarkoe Selo, in the environs of St Petersburg, where his talent for poetry first emerged. In 1817 he entered government service, but because of his liberalism was exiled in 1820 to the south. In 1824 he was dismissed and confined to his estate near Pskov, and did not return to Moscow until after the accession of Nicholas I. He married Natalia Goncharova in 1832, whose beauty attracted Baron Georges D'Anthès, a French royalist in the Russian service. Pushkin challenged him to a duel and was killed. Regarded as Russia's greatest poet, his first success was the romantic poem *Ruslan i Lyudmilla* (1820, 'Ruslan and Ludmilla'), followed by *Kavkazki plennik* (1822, 'The Prisoner of the Caucasus'), *Bakhchisarai fontan* (1826, 'Fountain of Bakhchisarai'), *Tzigani* (1827), and his masterpiece, *Evgeny Onegin* (1828, Eng trans *Eugene Onegin*, 1881), a sophisticated novel in verse that was much imitated but never rivalled. Prolific for one whose life was so short, he also wrote lyric poems, essays, the blank verse historical drama *Boris Godunov* (1825, Eng trans 1899), and, in 1830, the four 'Little Tragedies': *Motsart i Sal'eri* (Eng trans *Mozart and Salieri*, 1899), *Skupoy rytsar* (Eng trans *The Covetous Knight*, 1939), *Kamenny gost* (Eng trans *The Statue Guest*, 1899), and *Pir vo vremya chumy* (Eng trans *The Feast During the Plague*, 1946). His chilling novella of avarice and deceit, *Pikovaya dama* (1834, Eng trans *The Queen of Spades*, 1858), is one of his greatest works, its supernatural realism typifying much Russian fiction of the 19th century. He is to Russian literature what **Shakespeare** is to English.

▷ B Tomashevsky, *Alexander Pushkin* (1956–61); W Vickers, *Pushkin* (1970)

PUZO, Mario
(1920–)

American novelist, born in New York City. Educated at Columbia University, he served in the US air force during World War II and worked for 20 years as an administrative assistant in government offices at home and overseas. His first novel was *The Dark Arena* (1955), but his breakthrough came with his novel about the Mafia, *The Godfather* (1969), the epic story of Don Corleone and his extended 'family' of Sicilian immigrants who impose their will by brutal force and terror. It became a bestseller, and was filmed by Francis Coppola in 1972 with Marlon Brando playing Corleone.

PYE, Henry James
(1745–1813)

English poet, born in London. He studied at Magdalen College, Oxford. He held a commission in the Berkshire militia, in 1784 became MP for that county, and in 1790 succeeded Thomas Warton as poet laureate. In 1792 he was appointed a London police magistrate. The works of 'poetical Pye' number nearly 20, and include *Alfred: an Epic* (1801), with numerous birthday and New-Year odes, all extremely loyal and extremely dull.

PYLE, Howard
(1853–1911)

American illustrator and writer. In 1876 *Scribners Magazine* accepted some of Pyle's sketches while he was still helping in his father's leather business and on the strength of this success he moved to New York. Returning to Wilmington a few years later, he began to write children's books and a growing reputation for line-and-wash depictions of colonial life led to the opening of his own art school in 1900. His children's publications indulged a liking for medieval lore and legend, and included versions of Robin Hood and King Arthur.

PYM, Barbara Mary Crampton
(1913–80)

English novelist, born in Shropshire. She was educated at St Hilda's College, Oxford, and later worked at the International African Institute in London. Her fiction is deliberately confined within narrow bounds, characteristically exploring the tragi-comic lives of frustrated middle-class spinsters in a delicate, understated fashion. She published three novels in the 1950s, the best of which is *A Glass of Blessings* (1958), then lapsed into obscurity until, partly through the support of **Philip Larkin**, her *Quartet in Autumn* appeared in 1977. *The Sweet Dove Died* (1979) was the last book published in her lifetime, but four more novels, *A Few Green Leaves* (1980), *An Unsuitable Attachment* (1982), *Crampton Hodnet* (1985) and *An Academic Question* (1986), appeared posthumously.

PYNCHON, Thomas
(1937–)

American novelist, born in Glen Cove, New York, and educated at Cornell University. Seen by some as wilfully obscure, by others as a swashbuckling experimentalist, his sprawling, loquacious novels are ingenious, fabulous structures in which the normal conventions of the novel have been largely abandoned. Studiously avoiding public forums, he is obsessively studied and mined for autobiographical and more arcane references, of which there is no shortage. *V* (1963), a loose, episodic book, influenced by the Beats and by Pynchon's developing use of paranoia as a structural device, centres on a mysterious female principle at work in modern history. Subsequent publications include *The Crying of Lot 49* (1966) and *Gravity's Rainbow* (1973), concerning Tyrone Slothrop, lost in a surreal labyrinth but imbued with the wherewithal—in his reproductive organ—to predict exactly the sites of V-2 explosions in London. *Vineland* (1990) appeared to return to an earlier, more free-wheeling and satirical style and received mixed reviews, particularly in the UK. *Slow Learner* (1984) collected early stories and included a disarmingly straightforward introduction.

▷T H Schaub, *Pynchon: the voice of ambiguity* (1981)

789

Q

QUARLES, Francis
(1592–1644)

English poet, born in the manor house of Stewards near Romford, Essex, the son of the surveyor-general of victualling for the navy. He studied at Christ's College, Cambridge, and at Lincoln's Inn, and was successively cup-bearer to the princess Elizabeth (Queen of Bohemia) when she went to marry Elector Frederick V in Germany (1613), secretary to Archbishop Ussher (c.1629), and chronologer to the City of London (1639). He married in 1618 a wife who bore him 18 children and prefixed a touching memoir to his *Solomon's Recantation* (1645). Quarles was a royalist and churchman who suffered in the cause by having his books and manuscripts destroyed. He wrote abundantly in prose and verse. His *Emblems* (1635), in spite of many imperfections, occasionally shows a flash of poetic fire, and is his best-known work, although *Hieroglyphikes of the Life of Man* (1638) was also a popular success. Other poetical works include *A Feast of Wormes* (1620), *Argalus and Parthenia* (1629), *Divine Poems* (1630), *The Historie of Samson* (1631) and *Divine Fancies* (1632). The prose includes a book of aphorisms (*Enchyridion*, 1640) and *The Profest Royalist* (1645).
▷J Horder, *Francis Quarles* (1953)

QUASIMODO, Salvatore
(1901–68)

Italian poet, winner of the Nobel Prize for literature, born in Syracuse, Sicily. A student of engineering, he became a travelling inspector for the Italian state power board before taking up a career in literature and music. A professor of Literature at the Conservatory of Music in Milan, he wrote several volumes of spirited poetry. These reflect above all his deep interest in the fate of Italy, and his language is made particularly striking by the use simultaneously of both Christian and mythological allusions. He won the Nobel Prize for literature in 1959. His works include *Ed è Subito Sera* (1942, 'And Suddenly It Is Evening'), *La Vita non è sogno* (1949, 'Life is Not a Dream') and *La Terra impareggiabile* (1958, 'The Matchless Earth'). A collection of translated works was published as *Selected Poems* (1965).
▷P Mazzamutto, *Salvatore Quasimodo* (1967)

QUEEN, Ellery, pseud of Frederick Dannay
(1905–82)
LEE, Manfred B
(1905–71)

American writers of crime fiction, cousins, both born in Brooklyn, New York City. As businessmen they entered for a detective-story competition, and won with *The Roman Hat Mystery* (1929). From then on they concentrated on detective fiction, using Ellery Queen both as pseudonym and as the name of their detective. Others of their very popular stories are *The French Powder Mystery* (1930), *The Greek Coffin Mystery* (1932), *The Tragedy of X* (1940), *Double, Double* (1950) and *The Glass Village* (1954). They also wrote under the pseudonym Barnaby Ross, featuring the detective Drury Lane. In 1941 they founded *Ellery Queen's Mystery Magazine*.
▷F M Nevins Jnr, *Royal Bloodline: Ellery Queen, Author and Detective* (1974)

QUEIROS, Raquel de
(1910–)

Major Brazilian novelist, critic and translator, born in Forteleza, the daughter of a planter. Her early novels, written before 1940, are all remarkably mature for so young an author. In *O Quinze* (1930, 'The Year Fifteen') she outdid—even though it inspired her—the *Cane Trash* of **Almeida**. She rebelled against the patriarchal system she had seen in her youth, became involved with the left wing, and was unable to write as she wished under the dictator Vargas. Her masterpiece is *As Três Marias* (1939, Eng trans, *The Three Marias*, 1939), tracing the lives of three girls after they leave a convent school—in particular that of Maria Guta, who aborts her child rather than have it grow up in a world which would destroy it.
▷F P Ellison, *Brazil's New Novel* (1954)

QUENEAU, Raymond
(1903–76)

French novelist, poet and painter. He was born in Le Havre and educated at the Sorbonne. From 1938, he worked on *Encyclopédie de la Pléiade* and became its director for two decades (1955–75). His novels included *Le Chiendent* (1933, Eng trans *The Bark Tree*, 1968), a witty reworking of Descartes, the untranslatable, punning verse novel *Chêne et chien* (1937), *Pierrot Mon Ami* (1942, Eng trans *Pierrot*, 1950) and *Zazie dans le métro* (1959, Eng trans *Zazie*, 1960). Queneau was a founder member of OuLiPo, the hermetic Ouvroir de Littérature Potentielle, a philosophy related to the 'Pataphysical 'science of imaginary solutions'; see *La littérature potentielle* (1973). Perhaps Queneau's most famous book is the *Exercices de style* (1947, Eng trans *Exercises in Style*, 1958) which gives a multiplicity of versions of exactly the same literary 'opening'. His verse was published in *Cent mille milliards de poèmes* (1961, Eng trans *One Hundred Million Million Poems*, 1983); an English edition of his poetry appeared in 1970. He also wrote as 'Sally Mara' and published 'her' *Oeuvres complètes* in 1962.

▷ R Cobb, *Queneau* (1976)

QUENTAL, Anthero de
(1842–91)

Portuguese poet, born in Ponta Delgada in the Azores. He studied at Lisbon and Coimbra, publishing his first collection of sonnets in 1861 and his *Odes Modernas* in 1865. He followed the latter with a pamphlet, *Good Sense and Good Taste*, which exposed the view that poetry depends upon richness and vitality of ideas rather than upon technical skill with words. He lived in Paris and America from 1866 to 1871, and on his return to Portugal became a leading socialist until, after a severe nervous illness, he committed suicide.

▷ J B Carreira, *Anthero de Quental* (1948)

QUENTIN, Dorothy, properly **Madeleine Batten**
(1911–)

New Zealand writer of romantic fiction who, in 30 years, wrote an average of two novels a year. From *Brave Enterprise* (1939) to *Goldenhaze* (1969), her 59 books are mainly set in a New Zealand which, whether urban or rural, she portrays as an ideal society in a sub-American utopia—clean, bright, efficient and open, with her characters imposed on this backdrop. Only occasionally, as in *Lugano Love Story* (1960), does the scene move to England or Europe. Her books were published in London and written for her large international readership.

QUESNES DE BETHUNE *see* CONON DE BETHUNE

QUEVEDO Y VILLEGAS, Francisco Gómez de
(1580–1645)

Spanish writer, born in Madrid. His father was secretary to the queen, and his mother a lady-in-waiting. He left the University of Alcalá with a reputation for varied scholarship. The fatal result of a duel drove him in 1611 to the court of the Duke of Ossuna, Viceroy of Sicily, who made him his right-hand man, and, when promoted to the viceroyalty of Naples, chose him for Minister of Finance. Quevedo was involved in Ossuna's fall in 1619, and put in prison, but allowed to retire to the Sierra Morena. He returned to Madrid in 1623 and was one of the favourites at the court of Philip IV. In his *Política de Dios* (1626, 'Politics of God') he appealed to the king to be a king, not in name only, but in fact; in 1628 he followed up this attack on government by favourites with an apologue, *Discorso de todos los diablos, o Infierno enmendado* ('Discourse on the Devil's Death; or, Hell Reformed'). He remained, however, on friendly terms with Olivares and accepted the honorary title of royal secretary. In 1639 a memorial in verse to the king, imploring him to look to the miserable condition of his kingdom, was one day placed in Philip's napkin. Quevedo was denounced as the author, arrested and imprisoned in a convent at Leon, where he was struck down by an illness, from which he never recovered. In 1643 Olivares fell from power, and Quevedo was free to return to Madrid. He died two years later. Quevedo was one of the most prolific Spanish poets, but his verses were all written for his friends or for himself, and, except those in the *Flores* of Espinosa (1605), the few pieces published in his lifetime were printed without his consent. His poetry is therefore largely of an occasional character. About a dozen of his short pieces are extant, but of his comedies almost nothing is known. His prose is even more varied than his verse. His first book (1620) was a biography of St Thomas de Villanueva, and his last one of St Paul (1644), and most of his prose is devotional. Of his political works the *Política de Dios* is the main one. His brilliant picaresque novel, the *Historia de la Vida del Buscón Pablos* (1626, Eng trans *The Life and Adventures of Buscon the Witty Spaniard*, 1657), or, as it was called after his death, the *Gran Tacaño*, at once took its place beside Enrique Moreno Baez's *Guzmán de Alfarache*. His five *Sueños* (Eng trans *Visions*, 1640) were printed in 1627; to obtain a licence they were barbarously mutilated.

▷ O H Green, *Courtly Love in Quevedo* (1952)

QUINAULT, Philippe
(1635–88)

French playwright, born in Paris. He studied law, then began to write tragi-comedy in the 1650s, having gained some knowledge of high society—the usual setting for the genre—by working as a valet and gentleman-companion to members of the aristocracy. He presents love intrigues, using traditional devices such as disguise and double identity. Among his works are *Les coups de l'amour et de la fortune* ('The winds of love and chance'), first performed in 1655, *Le fantôme amoureux* (1656, 'The Amorous Ghost') and *Le mariage de Cambyse* (1659, 'The Marriage of Cambyse'). He is also known for his collaboration with the composer Lulli, for whose operas he provided several libretti. He gave up writing plays in 1686 because of the Church's condemnation of the theatre, and assumed an extreme piety for two years prior to his death.

QUINET, Edgar
(1803–75)

French writer and politician, born in Bourg. He studied at Strasbourg, Geneva, Paris and Heidelberg. The remarkable introduction to his translation of **Johann Herder**'s *Philosophy of History* (1825) won him the friendship of Cousin and Michelet; a government mission to Greece produced *La Grèce moderne* (1830, 'Modern Greece'). *Ahasvérus* (1833), a kind of spiritual imitation of the ancient mysteries, was followed by the less successful poems, 'Napoléon' (1836) and 'Prométhée' (1838); in his *Examen de la vie de Jésus* (1838, 'Investigation of the Life of Jesus') he argued that Strauss was too analytic, and that religion is the very substance of humanity. Appointed Professor of Foreign Literature at Lyons in 1839, he began the lectures which formed his brilliant *Du génie des religions* (1842, 'On the Genius of Religions'); then once recalled to the Collège de France in Paris, he joined Michelet in attacking the Jesuits. His lectures caused so much excitement that the government suppressed them in 1846. At the revolution Quinet took his place on the barricades, and in the National Assembly voted with the extreme left. After the *coup d'état* of 1851 he was exiled to Brussels, from where in 1857 he emigrated to Switzerland. At Brussels he produced *Les Esclaves* (1853, 'The Slaves'), and in Switzerland *Merlin l'Enchanteur* (1860, 'Merlin the Wizard'). Other works were *La Révolution religieuse au XIXᵉ siècle* (1857, 'The Religious Revolution of the 19th Century'), *Histoire de mes idées* (1858, 'History of My Ideas'), *Histoire de la campagne de 1815* (1862, 'History of the Campaign of 1815') and *La Révolution* (1865). After the downfall of Napoleon III he returned to Paris, and during the siege strove to keep patriotism alive. He sat in the National Assemblies at Bordeaux and Versailles, and aroused great enthusiasm by his speeches. His last books were *La Création* (1870), *La République* (1872), *L'Esprit nouveau* (1874, 'The Spirit of the New'), and *Le Livre de l'exilé* (1875, 'The Book of Exile').

▷A Vales, *Edgar Quinet, sa vie et son oeuvre* (1935)

QUINTANA, Manuel José
(1772–1857)

Spanish poet and advocate, born in Madrid, where his house became a resort of advanced liberals. Besides his classic *Vidas de los Españoles célèbres* (1807–34), he published tragedies and poetry written in a classical style, the best of which are his odes, ardently patriotic yet restrained. On the restoration of Ferdinand VII he was imprisoned (1814–20); but he recanted, and by 1833 had become tutor to Queen Isabella. He was crowned national poet in 1855.

▷J V Selma, *Ideario de Manuel José Quintana* (1961)

QUINTASKET, Christine *see* MOURNING DOVE

QUIROGA, Elena
(1919–)

Spanish novelist, born in Santander. She began with a regional novel, *Viento del norte* (1950, 'North Wind'), set in Galicia, but later tried to extend her range. Her most successful novel is reckoned to be *Algo pasa en el calle* (1954, 'Something is Happening in the Street'), which was influenced by **Camilo José Cela**, and is more dramatic than the rest of her work. She is respected but has not yet attracted much critical following—or many translators.

QUIROGA, Horacio
(1878–1937)

Major Uruguayan story writer and (initially) poet, one of the greatest of his generation in Latin America. He was born in Salto. His life was a chapter of horrible accidents out of which he drew his always desperate inspiration to create a new genre: the mature horror story crossed with the animal fable. Influenced by **Lugones**, **Poe** and **Chocano**, he published a collection of *modernista* poems. Quiroga's father shot himself (probably), and so did his first wife and two of his children. He himself shot and killed a friend by accident at the turn of the century, and had to flee to Buenos Aires. He was a manic-depressive, subject to strange states of anxiety, tension, agitated depression and hypomania—all of which he tried to relieve through drink. He became a cotton planter in the Chaco region of Argentina, and no writer has evoked this uncanny wilderness with more accuracy. One critic has called him 'in the last analysis maladjusted'; but another claims that he 'succeeded in releasing himself from his own death-wish', and is therefore 'one of our century's greatest depictors of the extreme situation'. He is not always seen at his best in the English-language collections *Stories of the Jungle* (1922; 1923; 1940), but his work has now generated enormous new interest, both in Spain and elsewhere. He had something

of the ability of **Carrasquilla** to see men in animals, and vice versa, but in his tales morbidity is taken to its last extreme. When he learned that he had cancer he shot himself.

▷N Jitrik, *Horacio Quiroga* (1967, in Spanish)

R

RAABE, Wilhelm, pseud **Jakob Corvinus**
(1831–1910)

German novelist, born in Eschershausen in Brunswick. He was a bookseller and student before turning to writing. Reacting against 19th-century progress and materialism, he wrote novels which were often grim, tragic and pessimistic although often alleviated by humour. They include *Der Hungerpastor* (1864, Eng trans *The Hunger-Pastor*, 1885), *Des Reiches Krone* (1870, 'Crown of the Realm') and *Meister Autor* (1871, 'Master Author').
▷H Pongs, *Wilhelm Raabe* (1958)

RABAN, Jonathan
(1942–)

English travel writer and novelist, born in Norfolk. He lectured at the University College of Wales and the University of East Anglia, and his earliest books were works of criticism, including *The Technique of Modern Fiction* (1968) and *The Society of the Poem* (1971). He wrote a study of cities in *Soft City* (1974), and turned to travel writing with *Arabia Through the Looking Glass* (1979), which established him as an important figure in the genre. His vivid style combines the colour of traditional travel narrative with a novelist's eye for telling detail and a social scientist's interest in the historical and sociological context of his experiences. Subsequent travel narratives include *Old Glory* (1981), an account of a voyage down the Mississippi, *Coasting* (1986), and *Hunting Mister Heartbreak* (1991), in which he followed the immigrant trail to America, where he now lives (Seattle). He published a novel, *Foreign Land* (1985), and edited the *Oxford Book of the Sea* (1992). *God, Man and Mrs Thatcher* (1989) is a political polemic.

RABE, David William
(1940–)

American dramatist, born in Iowa, whose preoccupation with modern American history and the Vietnam War, into which Rabe was drafted, pervades his writing. His 'Vietnam trilogy' begins with his first play, *The Basic Training of Pavlo Hummel*, and continues with *Sticks and Bones* (both 1971) and *The Orphan* (1973). In the first, a teenage soldier is killed after an altercation with another; in the second, a blinded serviceman returns home to the US, while the third is a loose modern reworking of **Aeschylus**'s *Oresteia*. However, the tautly written *Streamers* (1976) is considered his best work. Set in an army barracks in Virginia, the piece suggests that war is a natural condition of mankind. Less successful was *Hurlyburly* (1984), a satire set in Hollywood.

RABEARIVELO, Jean-Joseph
(1901–37)

Malagasy (Francophone) poet, the founder of his country's literature; he killed himself when French officials, whose relentlessness had already driven him to drugs, refused to allow him to visit France, where he had hoped to study. He never knew French perfectly but, by a mixture of luck and genius, managed to construct a poetic French which reflected the heart of Malagasy experience. He made use of popular ballad forms of Madagascar, especially the 'hain-teny' (traditional love poetry), to write hauntingly tropical poems evocative of the excited melancholy which was native to him. In English translation is *24 Poems* (1962).

RABELAIS, François
(?1494–?1553)

French satirist, said to have been born at a farmhouse near Chinon, or possibly in the town of Chinon, where his father was an advocate. At nine he was sent to the Benedictine abbey of Seuilly, and from there to the Franciscan house of La Baumette near Angers. He became a novice of the Franciscan order, and entered the monastery of Fontenay le Comte, where he had access to a large library, learned Greek, Hebrew and Arabic, and studied all the Latin and old French authors within his reach, as well as medicine, astronomy, botany and mathematics. In Fontenay he found a friend, André Tiraqueau, a lawyer and scholar; his patron, the Bishop of Maillezais, lived close by and he corresponded with Budaeus. But Franciscan jealousy of the old learning was transformed into jealousy of the new. His books were taken from him and he conceived a loathing for the convent, and fled to a Benedictine house near Orléans. Perhaps through his friend the bishop, he obtained the pope's permission (1524) to pass from the Franciscan to the Benedictine order. He stayed with the bishop for at least three years. After studying medicine at Montpellier he left in 1532 and became a physician in the hospital. Lyons was then a great intellectual centre. There he began the famous series of books by which he will for ever be remembered. In 1532 there appeared at Lyons fair a popular book, *The Great and Inestimable Chronicles of the Grand and Enormous Giant Gargantua*. It was almost certainly not by Rabelais, but to this book he wrote, in the same year, a sequel, *Pantagruel*, in which serious ideas are set forth side by side with overwhelming nonsense. In 1534 he supplied a first book of his own, a new *Gargantua*, fuller of sense and wisdom than *Pantagruel*. Both books (published under the name of Alcofribas Nasier, an anagram of François Rabelais and translated by Sir **Thomas Urquart**, 1653) had a prodigious success. Meanwhile he had begun his almanacs or *Prognostication Pantagruéline* (Eng trans *Pantagruel's Prognostication*, 1660), which he continued for a number of years; few of them survive. In 1533 he accompanied Jean du Bellay, Bishop of Paris, to Rome; in 1536 he was in Italy again with du Bellay, the latter then a cardinal. There he amused himself with collecting plants and curiosities—to him France owes the melon, artichoke and carnation. He also received permission to go into any Benedictine house which would receive him, and was enabled to hold ecclesiastical offices and to practise medicine. From 1537 (when he took his doctorate) to 1538 he taught at Montpellier. From 1540 to 1543 he was in the service of the cardinal's brother, Guillaume du Bellay, sometimes in Turin (where Guillaume was governor), sometimes in France. Guillaume died in 1543, in which year Rabelais was appointed one of the *maîtres des requêtes*. In 1546 he published his third book, this time under his own name. The Sorbonne condemned it—as it had done its predecessors—and Rabelais fled to Metz, where he practised medicine. In 1547 Francis I died; Henri II sent the French cardinals to Rome; and du Bellay summoned Rabelais there as his physician (1548). In Rome until 1549, he thereafter stayed near Paris; he received two livings from the cardinal in 1551–2, and resigned them two years later. A 'partial edition' of a fourth book had appeared in 1548, the complete book in January 1552–3 (to be banned by the theologians); and a professed fifth book, *L'Isle sonante* ('The Sweet-Sounding Island'), perhaps founded on scraps and notes by Rabelais, in 1562. The riotous licence of his mirth has made Rabelais as many enemies as his wisdom has made him

friends, yet his works remain the most astonishing treasury of wit, wisdom, commonsense and satire that the world has ever seen.
▷ M A Screech, *Rabelais* (1979)

RABEMANANJARA, Jean-Jacques
(1913–)

Malagasy poet, dramatist and statesman, born in Tamatave. He was a follower and friend of his country's greatest writer, **Rabéarivalo**. The latter was driven to death by French bureaucrats, and Rabemananjara was imprisoned by the French, but he later became a Minister of National Development in the first free government of Madagascar (1960). His poetry is modelled on that of **Senghor** and **Claudel**. His plays, particularly *Les dieux malagaches* (1947, 'The Malagasy Gods'), are more original. His later work embraces a dazzling kind of post-*négritude*.

RACINE, Jean
(1639–99)

French dramatist and poet, born in La Ferté-Milon, the son of a solicitor. He was sent to the college of Beauvais, from where he went to Port Royal in 1655. He studied hard, and discovered a faculty for verse-making and a liking for romance that perturbed his teachers. At 19, when he went to study philosophy at the Collège d'Harcourt, he appears to some extent to have exchanged the severity of his Jansenist upbringing for libertinism and the life of letters. He wrote an ode, *La Nymphe de la Seine* (1660, 'The Nymph of the River Seine'), on the marriage of Louis XIV, finished one piece and began another for the theatre, made the acquaintance of **Jean de la Fontaine**, **Jean Chapelain** and other men of letters, and assisted a cousin who was a secretary to the Duc de Luynes. In 1661 he went to Uzès in Languedoc, hoping in vain to get a benefice from his uncle, the vicar-general of the diocese. Having returned to Paris, he obtained in 1664 a gift from the king for a congratulatory ode. Another ode, titled *La Renommée aux muses* ('The Muses' Reputation'), gained him the lifelong friendship of **Nicolas Boileau**; and now began the famous friendship of 'the four'—Boileau, La Fontaine, **Molière** and Racine. His earliest play, *La Thébaïde ou Les Frères ennemis* (1664, Eng trans *The Fatal Legacy*, 1723), was acted by Molière's company at the Palais Royal. His second, *Alexandre le grand* (1665, Eng trans *Alexander the Great*, 1714), was after its sixth performance played by the rival actors at the Hotel de Bourgogne, which led to a rupture with Molière. Racine showed himself as hostile to **Corneille**. Stung by one of **Nicole**'s *Lettres visionnaires* (1666, 'Visionary Letters') condemning in accordance with Port

Royal ethics the romancer or dramatist as an *empoisonneur public* ('poisoner of the people'), he published a clever letter to the author, full of indecent personal remarks. During the following 10 years Racine produced his greatest works—*Andromaque* (1667, Eng trans *Andromache*, 1675); *Les Plaideurs* (1668, Eng trans *The Litigants*, 1715), satirizing lawyers; *Britannicus* (1669, Eng trans 1714); *Bajazet* (1672, Eng trans *The Sultaness*, 1717); *Mithridate* (1673, Eng trans *Mithridates*, 1926), produced almost at the moment of his admission to the Academy; *Iphigénie* (1675, Eng trans *Achilles; or, Iphigenia in Aulis*, 1700), a masterpiece of pathos; *Phèdre et Hippolyte* (1677, Eng trans *Phaedra and Hippolytus*, 1756), a marvellous representation of human agony; and *Bérénice* (1670, Eng trans *Titus and Berenice*, 1701). Then the *troupe du roi* introduced a rival *Phèdre*, by Jacques Pradon, which was supported by a powerful party. Whether from mortification or from alleged conversion, Racine retired from dramatic work, made his peace with Port Royal, married in June 1677, and settled down to 20 years of domestic happiness. His wife brought him money (as well as two sons and five daughters); and he had found ample profit in the drama, besides enjoying an annual *gratification* that grew to 2000 livres, at least one benefice, and, from 1677, jointly with Boileau, the office of royal historian. In 1689 he wrote *Esther* (Eng trans 1715) for Madame de Maintenon's schoolgirls at Saint-Cyr; *Athalie* (Eng trans *Athaliah*, 1722) followed in 1691. Four *cantiques spirituels* and an admirable *Histoire abrégée de Port-Royal* (1742, 'Brief History of Port-Royal') make up Racine's literary work. In his later years he somehow lost the favour of the king. In France Racine is regarded as the greatest of all masters of tragic pathos; this estimate is not inflated. He took the conventional French tragedy from the stronger hands of Corneille, and added to it all the grace of which it was capable, perfecting exquisitely its versification, . and harmoniously subordinating the whole action to the central idea of the one dominant passion.
▷L Goldman, *Racine* (1973)

RADCLIFFE, Ann, née Ward
(1764–1823)

English romantic novelist, born in London. At 23 she married William Radcliffe, a graduate of Oxford and student of law, who became proprietor and editor of the weekly *English Chronicle*. In 1789 she published the first of her Gothic romances, *The Castles of Athlin and Dunbayne*; then followed *A Sicilian Romance* (1790), *The Romance of the Forest* (1791), *The Mysteries of Udolpho* (1794) and *The Italian* (1797). She travelled much, and her journal shows how keen an eye she had for natural scenery and ruins. A sixth romance, *Gaston de Blondeville*, with a metrical tale, 'St Alban's Abbey', and a short Life, was published in 1826. Her reputation among her contemporaries was considerable. She was praised by Sir **Walter Scott**, and influenced writers such as **Byron**, **Shelley** and **Charlotte Brontë**. Her particular brand of writing found many imitators, most of them unfortunately inferior to herself, and prompted **Jane Austen**'s satire *Northanger Abbey*.
▷C F MacIntyre, *Ann Radcliffe in Relation to her Time* (1920)

RADICEVÍC, Branko
(1824–53)

Serbian romantic poet, born in Slavonski Brod. He studied law and medicine in Vienna, but most of his short life was devoted to his lyrical poetry, which became very popular. These poems were important because they were the first in the language to jettison 'poetical' decoration and to partake of natural speech. He was much affected by folk poetry and popular erotic song. He has been described as the 'founder of romantic Serbian poetry'.

RADIGUET, Raymond
(1903–23)

French novelist and poet, born in Saint-Maur. He is best known for two stories, *Le Diable au Corps* (1923, 'The Devil in the Flesh') and *Le Bal du Comte d'Orgel* (1924, 'The Count of Orgel's Ball'). Acclaimed as the 'Rimbaud of the novel', his writing is as austerely controlled as his personal behaviour was erratic and unpredictable. The nature of love is his dominant theme, comparable in his fiction to the high moral conception of love in the tragedies of **Racine**.
▷C R Goesch, *Raymond Radiguet* (1955)

RADNÓTI, Miklós
(1909–44)

Jewish Hungarian poet and translator, murdered (and thus immortalized) by the Nazis while on a forced march. He recorded his difficult childhood in the moving *Ikrek hava* (1939, Eng trans *The Month of Gemini*, 1979). His beginnings as a poet were uncertain and influenced by all kinds of French literary extremes. However, by the time that he published the collection *Jakalj csak, halalriélt* (1936, 'Man Condemned to Death, Just Keep Walking'—an uncanny anticipation of his own murder); it is clear that he was even then trying to reconcile himself to what he already seemed to know would be his fate. This inspired him to his best poetry—redolent of

humanity, and love for his wife—which is contained in the posthumous *Tajtékos ég* (1946, Eng trans *The Clouded Sky*, 1972).
▷ *Slavonic Review* (June 1965)

RADUASKAS, Henrikas
(1910–70)

Lithuanian poet whose mature later work, written in exile in America, attracted the attention of **Randall Jarrell**. He has been compared to **Osip Mandelstam**, and is often seen by Lithuanians as their finest poet yet. Some of his poems are translated in *The Green Oak: Selected Lithuanian Poetry* (1962).

RAHBEK, Knud Lyne
(1760–1830)

Danish poet, critic and editor, born in Copenhagen. He became Professor of Aesthetics at Copenhagen University, and edited several literary journals, notably *Den Danske Tilskuer* (the Danish *Spectator*). As well as poetry, he wrote many plays, songs and works on drama.
▷ A E Jensen, *Rahbek og Danske Digtere* (1960)

RAICKOVIĆ, Stefan
(1928–)

Serbian poet, translator (of **Shakespeare**) and editor, born in Nesresnica. He is a lyrical poet, some of whose work appears in translation in *New Writing in Yugoslavia* (1970, ed B Johnson).

RAIFTERI, Antoine, real name Anthony Raftery
(c.1784–1835)

Irish (Gaelic) poet, born in Lios Ard, County Mayo. At nine he was blinded by smallpox, and he later became a 'wandering bard'— 'with eyes that have no light/With gentleness that has no misery', as he wrote in *Mise Raifteri An File* (nd, 'I Am Raftery the Poet'). Such poems as *Cill Liadan* (nd, 'Killeaden', or 'County Mayo') and the tender love poem to a local beauty *Maire Ni Eidhin* (nd, 'Mary Hynes') were largely part of an oral tradition until Lady Gregory and **Douglas Hyde** collected many of them in *Love Songs of Connacht* (1893; reprinted 1903, 1979). His informed use of rhyme and speech rhythms has led to much of his work being denigrated as 'mere song'. The warm and passionate humanity pervading all his preserved work demands and deserves recognition as some of the finest poetry ever written.
▷ Lady Gregory, *Poets and Dreamers* (1903)

RAIMBAUT, Count of Orange
(c.1150–1173)

Provençal Troubadour who inherited the lands of Orange from his mother, Tiburge. Many stories were told about his exploits and early death, and one of the four women Troubadour poets, Beatrice, Countess of Die, is supposed to have addressed love poems to him. He began by writing in the difficult and deliberately esoteric *trobar clus* style, but was persuaded by his friends, who included **Guiraut de Bornelh**, to make it simpler and more straightforward.
▷ W Pattison (ed), *The Life and Works of the Troubadour Raimbaut de'Orange* (1952)

RAIMUND, Ferdinand, pseud of Ferdinand Raimann
(1790–1836)

Austrian dramatist, born in Vienna. After serving an apprenticeship to a confectioner, he became a highly successful comic actor, although his aspiration to play the great tragic parts failed. As a playwright he was a leading exponent of the Viennese *Volksstück*, the play written in local dialect; it came to take two distinct forms, the *Zauberstück* (magic farce), set in a fairyworld, and the more plebeian *Lokalstück*. Raimund was a master of the first type of play. His most famous work is *Der Verschwender* (1833, Eng trans *The Spendthrift*, 1949), about the wastrel Julius von Flottwell who is saved by his servant Valentin (a part played by the author), because he is under the protection of a fairy. Some of this still excellent and much studied play is in verse. Raimund—who suffered, like so many of the great humorists, from depression—was bitten by a dog, thinking he had contracted rabies, shot himself while on his way to Vienna to consult a doctor.
▷ J Michalski, *Ferdinand Raimund* (1968)

RAINE, Craig Anthony
(1944–)

English poet, born in Bishop Auckland, County Durham. Educated at Oxford, he lectured in several colleges there. He became poetry editor at Faber and Faber in 1981, but later returned to Oxford. His first collection, *The Onion, Memory* (1978), established a characteristic method of attempting to 'see' familiar things in new and unusual ways, which he developed in even greater depth in the 'alien' viewpoint adopted in *A Martian Sends A Postcard Home* (1979). His work is ingenious, highly wrought and rich in linguistic invention. Later collections include *A Journey to Greece* (1979) and *Rich* (1984), which revealed a greater maturity and directness, and included a prose memoir of his

childhood, 'A Silver Plate'. *1953* (1990) was
a version of **Racine**'s drama *Andromaque*.

RAINE, Kathleen Jessie
(1908–)

English poet and critic, educated at Girton
College, Cambridge, where she was subsequently a research fellow. Her first volume
of verse was *Stone and Flower: Poems 1935–
43* (1943), which was inspired by a para-
mystical appreciation of nature. This has
grown somewhat more intellectual but also
more hermetically mystical over the years;
Raine shows a profound understanding of
the symbolic imagination, and has written
persuasively about **Blake**, **Yeats**, **Hopkins** and
David Jones. In more recent years, she has
been markedly supportive of the work of
Cecil Collins, a visionary painter in the Blake
and Palmer tradition; essays include *Cecil
Collins: Painter of Paradise* (1979) and a
notable appreciation in *The Inner Journey of
the Poet* (1982), an essay collection that usefully summarized her basic aesthetic stance.
She was prolific both as critic and poet;
later volumes of verse include *The Hollow
Hill* (1965), *The Oval Portrait* (1977) and *The
Oracle in the Heart* (1980). A *Collected Poems*
appeared in 1981.
▷R J Mills, *Kathleen Raine* (1967)

RAINIS, Janis, pseud of Janis Plieksans
(1865–1929)

Latvian poet, dramatist and politician, who
was born in Tadenava, and was for a time
in exile owing to his campaigns against the
Tsarist Russians. His wife, the poet known as
Aspazija, was with him in Switzerland from
1906 until 1920 (the year of Latvian independence). His dignified, German-influenced
style made him an illustrious name in his time,
and he is still taught in schools. Some of his
verse is in *Tricolor Sun* (ed W K Matthews,
1936), and one of his plays, *Speleju, dancoju*
(1919) was translated in 1924 as *The Sons of
Jacob*.
▷V Kalve, *Latvian Literature* (1954)

RAJAGOPALACHARI, Chakrovati
(1879–1972)

Tamil (and Anglophone) Indian writer and
politician who was associated with Gandhi,
served as Nehru's deputy, and who eventually, in despair at Congress Party policies,
founded the Swatantra Party. His chief work
in English is his translation of the Tamil version of the great classical text, the *Ramayana*.
He also wrote for children. A selection of his
tales is available in *The Fatal Cart* (1946).

RAKIC, Milan
(1876–1938)

Serbian poet, a diplomat by profession,
whose output is small but is much prized for
its delicacy and precision (he was a perfectionist), somewhat in the style of the
French Parnassians. A few of his poems are
translated in Janko Lavrin's *An Anthology of
Modern Yugoslav Poetry* (1963).

RAMLER, Karl Wilhelm
(1725–98)

German poet and translator (**Horace**), born
in Kilberg. Like **Cowley**, he was taken seriously—as a 'master of form'—in his own day,
even by **Goethe**, but is now seen as devoid
of originality, and hardly has even Cowley's
reputation as a minor poet; but, though
unread now, he was a skilled craftsman.

RAMOS, Graciliano
(1892–1953)

Major Brazilian novelist, born in Quebrangulo,
Alagoas, the son of a corrupt local judge and
an unstable mother. If anyone can be considered to be the heir of the incomparable
Machado de Assis, then it must be Ramos, who
wrote the best prose of his generation. As a not
very convinced communist, he was imprisoned
by President Vargas in a concentration camp
(1936), and his experiences there (recorded in
his scarifying *Memórias do Cárcere*, 1953,
'Memories of Imprisonment') led to his early
death. He was a realistic and, most essentially,
a psychologically penetrating novelist of great
power. He took a while to discover himself: his
first novel, *Caetés* (1933), the name of a tribe
which was known to have practised cannibalism, does not display his full subtlety and
power, because its thesis, that everyone acts
only from selfishness, is rather too glibly
adhered to. But its successor, *São Bernardo*
(1934, Eng trans, *Saint Bernard*, 1940), about a
guilty plant owner, is a great novel by any
standards. *Angústia* (1936, Eng trans *Anguish*,
1940), another masterpiece, is probably the
most lucid and moving study of a sex killer
written in the 20th century: the crime is attributed to a backlander's inability to function as
a human being in a malevolent city. *Vidas sêcas*
(1938, Eng trans *Barren Lives*, 1965) abandons
the stream-of-consciousness method of its predecessor: it is the third-person narrative account of a backlander driven, finally, to the city,
and to defeat. Ramos's collected works appeared in Brazil in 1961–2.
▷B M Woodbridge, *Graciliano Ramos* (1954)

RAMSAY, Allan
(c.1685–1758)

Scottish poet, born in Leadhills, Lanarkshire.
His father was manager of Lord Hopetoun's

mines there, and his mother, Alice Bower, was the daughter of a Derbyshire mining expert. In 1704 he was apprenticed for five years to a wigmaker in Edinburgh. By 1718 he had become known as a poet, having issued several short humorous satires printed as broadsides. He had also written (1716–18) two additional cantos to the old Scots poem of *Christ's Kirk on the Green*, cheerful pictures of rustic life and broad humour. Ramsay then started business as bookseller, later adding a circulating library (1725), apparently the first in Britain. 'Honest Allan's' career was eminently prosperous, although the theatre he built in Edinburgh at his own expense (1736) was soon closed down by the magistrates. In 1740 he built himself a quaint house (the 'goose-pie') on the Castle Hill, where he spent his last years in retirement. He was buried in Greyfriars' Churchyard. Among his works are *Tartana, or the Plaid* (1718), *Poems* (collected edition published by subscription in 1721, by which it is said he realized 400 guineas—other editions in 1720, 1727, 1728), *Fables and Tales* (1722), *Fair Assembly* (1723), *Health, a Poem* (1724), *The Monk and the Miller's Wife* (1724), *The Tea-table Miscellany*, a collection of songs (4 vols, 1724–37), *The Evergreen* (1724), *The Gentle Shepherd, a Pastoral Comedy* (1725)—his best and most popular work, and *Thirty Fables* (1730).

RAMUZ, Charles-Ferdinand
(1878–1947)

Swiss writer, born in Cully near Lausanne. He wrote in French, mainly about life in his native canton of Vaud. His first book, *Le Petit Village* ('The Little Village'), appeared in 1903, and from then on he wrote prolifically. His pure prose style and fine descriptive power won him wide admiration and repute, his European popularity being somewhat tempered in Britain, though he has been translated into English—*Beauté sur la terre* (1927, Eng trans *Beauty on Earth*, 1929) and *Présence de la mort* (1922, Eng trans *The Triumph of Death*, 1946). Other writings include *Jean Luc persécuté* (1909, 'Jean Luc Persecuted') and *Besoin de grandeur* (1937, 'Need for Grandeur'). He wrote the narration for Stravinsky's *A Soldier's Tale*.
▷G Guisan, *Charles-Ferdinand Ramuz* (1967)

RAND, Ayn
(1905–82)

American conservative theorist and writer of propagandist fiction. She was born and educated in pre-revolutionary Russia but was brought to the USA as a child and seems to have overdosed rapidly on American individualism. Her Objectivist 'philosophy' was premised on enlightened selfishness and rejected altruistic welfarism in favour of aggressive self-reliance. Her four novels were little more than vehicles for these ideas. The best-known is perhaps *The Fountainhead* (1943), which was filmed starring Gary Cooper; others are *We, the Living* (1936), *Anthem* (1938) and *Atlas Shrugged* (1957). For anyone unable to absorb too much of her heated intellectual melodrama, there were briefer, cooler essays: *For the New Intellectual* (1961) and *The Romantic Manifesto* (1969). There was a strong revival of interest in Rand's work during the Reagan presidency, but this has rapidly faded.

RANDALL, James Ryder
(1839–1908)

American poet, born in Baltimore. He was first a teacher, then a journalist. His lyrics, which in the Civil War gave powerful aid to the Southern cause, include 'Maryland, My Maryland' (1861), 'Stonewall Jackson' and 'There's life in the old land yet'. A collected *Poems* appeared posthumously in 1910.

RANDOLPH, Thomas
(1605–35)

English poet and dramatist, born in Newnham near Daventry. He studied at Westminster School and Trinity College, Cambridge, where he was elected a fellow, and soon began to write, gaining the friendship of **Ben Jonson** and leading a boisterous life. He left a number of bright, fanciful poems, and six plays: *Aristippus, or the Jovial Philosopher* (1631); *The Conceited Peddler* (1631); *The Jealous Lovers* (1632); *The Muses' Looking-glass* (1632); *Amyntas, or the Impossible Dowry* (1635); and *Hey for Honesty* (1651).
▷S A and D R Tannenbaum, *Thomas Randolph* (1947)

RANSOM, John Crowe
(1888–1974)

American poet and critic, born in Tennessee. His family were Methodists and he was educated locally and at Oxford. He co-founded a little magazine called *The Fugitive* which, though short-lived (1922–5), established a pattern for the revival of post-bellum Southern literature—formal, classical, agrarian —and lent its name to a significant movement in American literature. He had a long association with Kenyon College (1937–58) and was formative in the founding of the *Kenyon Review*, which beat a drum for the New Criticism. His poetry came early in his career. *Poems About God* (1919), *Chills and Fever* (1924) and *Two Gentlemen in Bonds*

(1927) illustrate his aptitude as a balladist and elegist. Critical books include *God Without Thunder* (1930) and *The New Criticism* (1941).

▷T H Parsons, *John Crowe Ransom* (1969)

RANSOME, Arthur Mitchell
(1884–1967)

English journalist and writer of children's books, born in Leeds. His father was a history professor, and he was educated at Rugby where he was a poor scholar and—by virtue of bad eyesight—inept at games. He worked as an office boy in a publishing house before graduating to ghost-writing, reviewing and writing short stories, meanwhile living a bohemian existence. He became a reporter on the *Daily News* and, in 1919, for the *Manchester Guardian*. He was widely travelled and, having learned Russian in 1913, was sent to cover the Revolution, a welcome relief from his stormy relationship with his first wife. They divorced in 1924 and he married Trotsky's secretary, Evgenia Shelepin, with whom he fled from Russia, staying for a while in Estonia before settling in the Lake District. He had been a published author for a quarter of a century before the appearance of *Swallows and Amazons* (1930), the first of 12 perennially popular novels featuring two families of adventurous but responsible children, the Blacketts and the Walkers, who spend their school holidays revelling in the open air, free from the cramping attention of adults. Of his numerous other books, *Old Peter's Russian Tales* (1916) is worthy of note. *The Autobiography of Arthur Ransome* (1976) is interesting but unrevealing.

▷A B Shelley, *Arthur Ransome* (1960)

RAO, Raja
(1909–)

Indian novelist and short-story writer, born into the Brahmin caste in the south of the country. *Kanthapura* (1938), a novel, and the short-story collection *The Cow of the Barricades* (1947) both deal with the Indian independence movement, which he supported. His best-known work in English—and probably his best altogether—is *The Serpent and the Rope* (1960), a semi-autobiographical novel about an Indian's coming of age in France. His later, less acclaimed, novels include *The Policeman and the Rose* (1977).

RAPHAEL, Frederic Michael
(1931–)

American novelist, educated and resident in the UK. After Charterhouse School, he studied at St John's College, Oxford, an experience reflected in *The Glittering Prizes* (1976),

an autobiographical *roman à clef* which later set new standards as a television drama. Raphael's first novel was *Obbligato* (1956), about a singer; his third book was *The Limits of Love* (1960), the story of a deracinated Jew coming to terms with the lack of an informing system of belief. Raphael is a liberal agnostic, but—as in *The Glittering Prizes*—is strongly aware of how corrosive un-belief can be. *The Graduate Wife* and *The Trouble With England* (both 1962) are effective satires with a firm psychological grasp; *Richard's Things* (1973) is bolder and more abrasive. In the 1970s, Raphael seemed concerned to dramatize aspects of his own creative dilemma, but always without sentimentality and with impressive honesty. *Heaven and Earth* (1985) handled big themes without portentousness. Raphael's gift for dialogue lent itself to drama; he has written extensively for stage, screen and television, including scripts for **Hardy**'s *Far From the Madding Crowd* (1967) and **Iris Murdoch**'s *The Severed Head* (1970). Critically underpraised, he is a writer of significant intelligence; his judgements of others can be seen, for example, in *Cracks in the Ice: Views and Reviews* (1979).

RASHI, abbreviation of **Rabbi Shelomoh Izhaqi**, otherwise **Solomon Ben Isaac**
(1040–1105)

French Hebrew poet, who was born in Troyes, where he founded a Talmudic academy. His influence on Jewish thinking cannot be overestimated, for his commentaries on the Bible were read by all educated Jews throughout the Middle Ages, and beyond. Although difficult to read and understand now, his poetry is distinguished by its simplicity and its powerful devotional feeling.

▷H Hailperin, *Rashi and the Christian Scholars* (1963)

RASMUSSEN, Halfdan
(1915–)

Danish poet. He was born in Copenhagen, to a working-class family, and passed much of his early life in poverty. During World War II his first book of verse, *Soldat eller menske* (1941, 'Soldier or Man'), became an important rallying text for the Danish Resistance. The dark tone persisted after the war with *Korte skygger* (1946, 'Foreshortened Shadows') and other volumes, but increasingly he held up childhood and 'primitive' societies as alternatives to the compromised and over-intellectualized West; the war in Vietnam provided a particularly strong focus for these feelings. Rasmussen has written many volumes of verse for children—'*børnerim*' —of which perhaps the best is *Hokus Pokus* (1969, Eng trans *Hocus Pocus*, 1973). These have given him a broad and lasting appeal in Denmark.

▷ E Clausen, *Hilsen til Halfdan* (1983)

RASPUTIN, Valentin Grigorevich
(1937–)

Russo–Siberian novelist and a leading figure in the 'village' movement. He was born in Ust'-Uda, in the lakeland north of Irkutsk, where he attended university and still lives. His first novel, *Kray vozle samovo neba* (1966, 'The Land that Borders Heaven'), established him as a powerful voice in a new trans-Ural consciousness, in which young Siberian writers set themselves apart from the literary world of the cities, affirming localism over urban values, Asiatic rather than European themes and ideas. The first of his books to be translated into English was *Zhivi i pomni* (1975), which appeared as *Live and Remember* in 1978; but in 1981 the earlier *Den'gi dlya Marii* (1968, Eng trans *Money for Maria*, 1968) and *Posledny srok* (1976, Eng trans *Borrowed Time*, 1976) were collected under the general rubric *Two Village Tales*. Rasputin has written slowly and patiently, and is not prolific; however, his work significantly anticipates the de-Sovietization of Russia.

RASTELL, John
(1475–1536)

English printer, lawyer and dramatist, born in Coventry. He was called to the Bar and in 1510 set up his own printing press. Married to the sister of Sir Thomas More, he printed More's *Life of Pico*, a grammar by Linacre, the only copy of **Henry Medwall**'s play *Fulgens and Lucres*, and many law books. Himself a dramatist, his plays, printed on his own press, include *Nature of the Four Elements* (1519), *Of Gentylness and Nobylyte* ... (c.1527) and *Calisto and Meleboea* (c.1527). An ingenious deviser of pageants, he presented several of them at court. His expedition to found a settlement in the 'New Found Lands' in 1517 came to nothing through mutiny on his ship.

▷ A W Reed, *Early Tudor Drama* (1926)

RATHERIUS (RATHER) OF LIEGE
(c.887–974)

Cleric and writer, born in Liège. Ratherius became Bishop of Verona three times, losing the position repeatedly after political intrigue. He was a hugely influential man of letters in 10th-century Europe—his *Praeloquia* (collections of sermons and other writings) were to be found in every centre of learning in Christendom. His writings, often illustrated with autobiographical anecdotes, argue that believers should go out and do battle with evil, and that a strict monastic regime is the best means of preparing for this. He also complains ceaselessly about the corruption, sloth and uxoriousness of the clergy. This did little to increase his popularity and made him an easier target for those who would intrigue against him.

RATOSH, Yonathan
(1908–)

Hebrew poet, born in Russia, but who went to Palestine early, and who wrote his unique and sonorous poetry in a special dialect, a mixture of Hebrew and the extinct language Ugaritic. The 'Canaanite' group, of whom he was one, wished to embrace a semitic state, and regarded the diaspora as an 'inconsequential period in Jewish history'. The notion of a semitic state has not been popular in Israel, and for this reason many readers have been cut off from an exceedingly original and powerful poet, and author of some of the most erotic poetry of the 20th century. Titles include *Yuhud* (1952).

RATTIGAN, Sir Terence Mervyn
(1911–77)

English playwright, born in London. Educated at Harrow and Oxford, he scored a considerable success with his comedy *French Without Tears* (1936). After that, most of his works, with the possible exception of *Adventure Story* (1949), a play about Alexander the Great, were internationally acclaimed; they reveal not only a wide range of imagination but a deepening psychological knowledge. Best known are *The Winslow Boy* (1946), based on the Archer Shee case, *The Browning Version* (1948), *The Deep Blue Sea* (1952), *Separate Tables* (1954) and *Ross* (1960), a fictional treatment of T E Lawrence. He was responsible for several successful films made from his own and other works.

RATUSHINSKAYA, Irina
(1954–)

Russian poet and literary *cause célèbre*. Ratushinskaya was achieving a reputation as a skilled poet with a concern for social issues in Moscow when, in the 1970s, she began to get into trouble with the Soviet authorities who found her work distasteful. She was eventually sentenced to seven years' internal exile for anti-Soviet activities. Her cause was, however, taken up in the West, where she found fame and a market for her verse. *No I'm Not Afraid* (1986) was, for a poetry book, very successful, and was followed by further volumes, notably *Dance with a Shadow* (1992). On her release from prison camp she went to live in the West, and has since published two volumes of autobiography: *Grey is* the *Colour of Hope* (1989) and *In the Beginning* (1991).

RAU, Santha Rama
(1923–)

Indian writer, who was educated in England and married an Englishman. Her father was an ambassador. She has written autobiographical works, and one novel, *Remember the House* (1956), influenced by **E M Forster**, whose *Passage to India* she successfully dramatized (1960).

RAVEN, Simon Arthur Noël
(1927–)

English novelist and playwright, born in London and educated at Charterhouse School and King's College, Cambridge. He began to write after a period in the army. His fictional output is mostly concentrated in two large cycles: *Alms for Oblivion* (1964–75) consisted of 10 novels, beginning with *The Rich Pay Late* and ending (appropriately) with *The Survivors*. A later sequence, entitled *The First-Born of Egypt*, was commenced in 1984 with *Morning Star* and is also largely concerned with the foibles and moral hubris of the upper classes. Of the novels that stand outwith the two cycles, *Doctors Wear Scarlet* (1960) and *The Roses of Picardie* (1980), are outstanding. Raven wrote screenplays for the James Bond film *On Her Majesty's Secret Service* (1969) and the bleak hostile school story, *Unman, Wittering and Zigo* (1971). He has adapted a large number of books for television, by **Aldous Huxley** and **W Somerset Maugham**, among others.

RAVENSCROFT, Edward
(1644–1704)

English lawyer turned playwright, born in London into the family of a lawyer. He abandoned law after the enormous success of his farce, *The Citizen Turn'd Gentleman* (1672) to concentrate on writing for the stage, achieving further successes with *Scaramouch, The London Cuckolds* and his last play, *The Anatomist* (all published posthumously). His work is bawdy, often downright crude, and very funny, but if his reputation has declined since his own day, it is due in large part to the prevalence of more censorious attitudes in public life rather than to a lack of sophistication in his work. Ravenscroft drew on a remarkably eclectic set of European influences, from **Molière** to *commedia dell'arte*, and is the first successful and consistent *farceur* in the history of the British stage.

RAWLINGS, Marjorie
(1896–1953)

American novelist, born in Washington DC and educated at the University of Wisconsin,

Madison. She worked as a journalist, an editor, and a syndicated verse writer before devoting herself to full-time creative writing in 1928. She was awarded the **O Henry** Award in 1933 for her short story 'Gal Young Un'. She published her first novel, *South Moon Under*, in the same year but is best remembered for her Pulitzer Prize-winning novel *The Yearling* (1938), later filmed, which centres on a young boy's attachment to his pet fawn. Her autobiographical work *Cross Creek* (1942) heightened her reputation as a 'regionalist' writer.
▷E Silverthorne, *Marjorie Kinnan Rawlings: Sojourner at Cross Creek* (1988)

RAYHANI, Amin
(1876–1940)

Lebanese Arabic poet, who initiated the modern Arabic prose poem. Some of his work was written in English.
▷A J Arberry (ed and translator), *Modern Arabic Poetry* (1950)

RAYNOUARD, François Juste Marie
(1761–1836)

French poet and philologist, born in Brignoles in Provence. A prosperous Paris advocate, in 1791 he entered the legislative assembly. Later he joined the Girondins, and was imprisoned. His poems and tragedies were successful, and in 1807 he was elected to the Academy, of which he became permanent secretary in 1817. He was elected to the imperial legislative body in 1806 and 1811. After 1816 he wrote on the Provençal language and literature, notably his *Lexique Roman* (1838–44).

REA, Domenico
(1921–)

Italian novelist and story writer, born near Naples, the legend of whose merry exoticism he seeks to challenge in such harsh tales of poverty as *Quel che vide Cummeo* (1955, 'What Cummeo Saw'). *Una vampata di rossore* (1959, Eng trans *A Blush of Shame*, 1963) is his most substantial work.
▷L Russo, *I narratore* (1968)

READ, Sir Herbert Edward
(1893–1968)

English art historian, critic and poet, born near Kirby Moorside, Yorkshire. Educated in Halifax and at Leeds University, he became Assistant Keeper at the Victoria and Albert Museum in London (1922–31) and Professor of Fine Art at Edinburgh University (1931–3); he was Editor of the *Burlington Magazine* (1933–9), and held academic posts at Cambridge, Liverpool, London, and Harvard universities. As an art critic he revived interest in the 19th-century Romantic movement, and championed modern art movements in Britain. His broad interests extended to industrial design, and his *Art and Industry* (1936) was seminal in the development of this new discipline. He was director of the first major British design consultancy, the Design Research Unit. As a poet he wrote *Naked Warriors* (1919, based on his war experiences), and published his *Collected Poems* in 1946. His other publications include *English Prose Style* (1928), *The Meaning of Art* (1931), *Form in Modern Poetry* (1932), *Art Now* (1933), *Art and Society* (1936), *The Philosophy of Modern Art* (1952), and the autobiographical *Annals of Innocence and Experience* (1940). His son is the writer **Piers Paul Read**.

▷ H Treece, *Herbert Read* (1944)

READ, Piers Paul
(1941–)

English novelist and author of non-fiction, born in Beaconsfield, Buckinghamshire. The son of the poet and art critic Sir **Herbert Read**, he was educated at a Roman Catholic school, and published his first novel, *Game in Heaven With Tussy Marx*, in 1966. He has since become established as a mainstream storyteller, a realist whose work sympathetically deliberates moral and ethical issues. *A Married Man* (1979) is a representative work. His non-fiction books extend this interest, although rather more sensationally. *Alive! The Story of the Andes Survivors* (1974) is an account of the aftermath of an air crash in remote mountains, during which a group of athletes cannibalized fellow passengers in order to survive. *The Train Robbers* (1978) follows the prison lives and domestic intrigues of those who robbed a London–Glasgow mail train in 1963.

READE, Charles
(1814–84)

English novelist and playwright, born in Ipsden House, Oxfordshire, the youngest of eleven. After five harrowing years at Iffley, and six under two milder private tutors, in 1831 he gained a scholarship at Magdalen College, Oxford, and in 1835, having taken third-class honours, was duly elected to a lay fellowship. Next year he entered Lincoln's Inn, and in 1843 was called to the Bar, but never practised. In 1850 he first tried to write for the stage, producing about 13 dramas. Through one of these dramas he formed a platonic friendship with Mrs Seymour, a warmhearted actress, who from 1854 until her death (1879) kept house for him. His life after 1852 is a succession of plays by which he lost money, and novels that won profit and fame. These novels illustrate social injustice

and cruelty in one form or another, and his writing is realistic and vivid. They include *Peg Woffington* (1852), *Hard Cash* (1863), *Foul Play* (1869, with **Dion Boucicault**), *A Terrible Temptation* (1871) and *A Woman-hater* (1877). His masterpiece was his long, historical novel of the 15th century, *The Cloister and the Hearth* (1861).

▷ M Elvin, *Charles Reade* (1931)

READING, Peter
(1946–)

English poet, born in Liverpool. He has worked as a lecturer and as a weighbridge operator. Influenced by **e e cummings**, and much given to pastiche, Reading's most characteristic poem is *C* (1984), a 'poem of 100 proses', supposedly assembled by a terminally-ill cancer patient. In other poems Reading mixes newsprint with his own inventions, in a rather uncertain manner, and takes a high risk with the reader with ironic and occasionally disturbing strategies. There is no lyrical element in his prolific verse, even in *The Essential Reading* (1986), which has been edited by Alan Jenkins.

REANEY, James
(1926–)

Canadian playwright and poet, born in South Easthope, Ontario, and educated at the University of Toronto. He won Governor General's Awards for Poetry (1950, 1959 and 1962) and Drama (1963). The founding editor of *Alphabet*, an active member of theatre groups in London and Winnipeg, a university lecturer and a critic, he perceives himself to be 'a teacher first' and observes of his work: 'I want to tell the story of the people I live with in Southwestern Ontario'. The poetic libretto of *Twelve Letters to a Small Town* (1962) and the dramatic trilogy of *The Donnellys* (performed on a cross-Canada tour in 1975), in particular, demonstrate the success of his endeavour.

RÈBORA, Clemente
(1885–1957)

Italian poet from Milan, whose first collection, *Frammente lirici* ('Lyrical Fragments'), was published in 1913. Soon afterwards he was badly wounded while on military service; he then became interested in **Leo Tolstoy**, translating his *Happy Ever After*, and devoted himself to care of the poor, living amongst them. In 1931 he entered a religious order, the Rosminian Fathers of Domodossala, and was ordained as a priest in 1936. He had a profound influence on his friend **Carlo Betocchi**. In his final poems, in *I canti d'infermità* (1956, 'Songs of Illness'), he 'identified poetry with liturgy', 'verse had become a concrete means of expressing his love for God and his fellow man'. Because this poetry is not merely pious, but rather fully aware of the difficulties of human existence, it is still frequently anthologized and gratefully read. There are English translations in M Marchione (ed), *Twentieth-Century Italian Poetry* (1974).

REBREANU, Liviu
(1885–1944)

Romanian novelist who, with **Duiliu Zamfirescu**, developed fiction in his country. He had a wide education (in Germany and Hungary as well as in Romania). His *Ion* (1920) was an almost epic account of Transylvanian peasant life. This he followed with the poignant *Padurea spînzuratilor* (1922, Eng trans *The Forest of the Damned*, 1930), which is worthy to be ranked with **Arnold Zweig**'s *Sergeant Grischa* as an indictment of injustice, but which never gained its deserved reputation. It is dedicated to the memory of his brother Emil, judicially murdered by the Austrians on the Romanian front in 1917. *Rascoala* (1933, Eng trans *The Uprising*, 1964) is a sequel to *Ion*, a violent and moving realization of the peasant uprising of 1907.

RECHY, John Francisco
(1934–)

American novelist, born and educated in El Paso, Texas. He gained instant fame—or notoriety—with his first novel, *City of Night* (1963), a frank and unsentimental study of homosexuality in the American city. To a degree, his later fiction has been a reworking of this first book, but by no means in a negative sense. For Rechy, the gay world is morally hermetic, a freemasonry governed by rules and conventions which are the opposite, or 'night', aspect of those that apply in straight society. The almost biblical associations of the title *City of Night* (which also echoes **James Thompson**'s 'The City of Dreadful Night') is sustained in Rechy's second book *Numbers* (1967). In *This Day's Death* (1970) it appears that Rechy is debunking the **Hemingway** myth. Other novels include *Rushes* (1979) and *Marilyn's Daughter* (1988). Rechy's defiant anti-revisionism—and underlying biblical symbolism—is well represented in *The Sexual Outlaw* (1978), an account of three days in the 'sexual underground'.

REDCAM, Tom, pseud of Thomas Macdermot
(1870–1933)

West Indian poet and novelist. He has been called, and there have been few to demur, 'the unpromising colonial father of West Indian

poetry', and his work is now seldom read or referred to.

REDGROVE, Peter William
(1932–)

English poet and novelist, born in Kingston, Surrey. He was educated at Queen's College, Cambridge, worked as a scientific journalist, taught at Falmouth School of Art (1966–83), and has held a number of poet-in-residence positions. He was a founder member of The Group in the 1950s, and published his first collection, *The Collector*, in 1960. His poetry is rich in both its linguistic density and visual imagery, and he has shown a persistent fascination with dreams and the unconscious, a subject he addressed in the study *The Black Goddess and the Sixth Sense* (1987). He has published numerous collections of poems, including *The Moon Disposes: Poems 1954–1987* (1987, enlarged 1989). His other writings include seven novels, plays, stories, and some non-fiction, including *The Wise Wound* (1978), a study of the fertility cycle, co-written with his wife, Penelope Shuttle.

REDI, Francesco
(1626–97)

Italian physician and poet, born in Arezzo. He studied at Florence and Pisa, and became physician to the dukes of Tuscany. He wrote a book on animal parasites and proved by a series of experiments that maggots cannot form on meat which has been covered. His best-known poem is the dithyrambic celebration of Bacchus and the wines of Tuscany, *Bacco In Toscana* (1685). He also wrote love sonnets on the **Petrarch**an model, and more earthy poems.
▷G Imbert, *Francesco Redi, l'uomo* (1975)

REDON, Odilon
(1840–1916)

French painter and lithographer, born in Bordeaux, usually regarded as a forerunner of Surrealism because of his use of dream images in his work. He made many charcoal drawings and lithographs of extraordinary imaginative power, but after 1900 he painted, especially in pastel, pictures of flowers and portraits in intense colour. He was also a brilliant writer; his diaries (1867–1915) were published as *A soi-même* ('To Himself') in 1922, and his *Lettres* in 1923.

REED, Bill
(1939–)

Australian playwright and novelist, born in Perth. His published plays range from *Burke's Company* (1969), on the tragic last days of the Burke and Wills expedition in 1861 and its aftermath, to *Truganini* (1977), a sequence of plays which contains *King Billy's Bones* and deals with the treatment of aborigines in colonial Australia. His later novels include the Gothic horror of *Stigmata* (1980), which won the Australian Natives' Association Literary Award for that year, and a fantasy on Sydney's underworld, *Crooks* (1984).

REED, Henry
(1914–)

English poet and dramatist. He was born in Birmingham and educated at the university there. After a period in the Army and at the Foreign Office, he made his living as a freelance writer and journalist. He established a reputation with his plays for radio, particularly those concerning the mannishly modernist composer Hilda Tablet (who was probably modelled on Ethel Smyth, among others). *The Private Life of Hilda Tablet* (1945) has been broadcast several times. Reed's reputation as a poet rests not so much on his own volume, *A Map of Verona* (1947), but on a single poem, 'Chard Whitlow', which is a brilliant satire of **T S Eliot**'s ponderously philosophical 'Burnt Norton' in *Four Quartets*. It is a rare example of a parody that is almost better than the original.

REED, Ishmael Scott
(1938–)

American novelist, poet and publisher. Born in Chattanooga, Tennessee, he grew up and was educated in Buffalo, New York. After graduation, he wrote for *Empire Star Weekly* before founding his own magazine, the *East Village Other*, which was dedicated to experimental writing. In 1967, Reed published his first novel, *The Freelance Pallbearers*, which was controversial for its sarcastic treatment of black politics. In his next and best novel, *Yellow Back Radio Broke Down* (1969), Reed introduced the concept of Hoodoo, a compression of racial and cultural mythologies represented by the person of Loop Garoo; Reed's best-known poem began 'I am a cowboy in the boat of Ra'. Later novels, such as *The Last Days of Louisiana Red* (1974), *Flight to Canada* (1976) and *Reckless Eyeballing* (1986), whose title echoed the indictment of a lynch victim, are more direct in their examination of the Afro–American condition, and less confident in their linguistic and typographical radicalism. Reed's poetry appeared in *Conjure* (1972), a collection of pieces from the sixties, in *Chattanooga* (1973) and in *New and Collected Poetry* (1988).

REED, Talbot Baines
(1852–93)

English author of books for boys, born in London, the son of Sir Charles Reed (1819–

81), chairman of the London School Board. He became head of his father's firm of typefounders, and wrote books on the history of printing (such as *History of the Old English Letter-foundries* (1887). His robust, moral, but entertaining school stories first appeared in the *Boy's Own Paper*. They include *The Fifth Form at St Dominic's* (1881), *The Master of the Shell* (1887) and *Cockhouse at Fellsgarth* (1891).

REES, Leslie
(1905–)

Australian playwright and author, born in Perth. A drama critic in London during the 1930s, he then became national radio drama editor for the Australian Broadcasting Corporation until 1966. He wrote the standard *History of Australian Drama* (1973–8) and has edited a number of anthologies, including *Australian Radio Plays* (1946). His own *Sub-Editor's Room* (1937) later became the first play to appear on Australian television, and he worked with **Ruth Park** on the dramatization of her *The Harp in the South* (1949). He has written much for children, including adventure tales such as *Panic in the Cattle Country* (1974), and, for younger readers, tales of animal wildlife in *The Story of Shy the Platypus* (1944). With his wife Coralie Clarke he wrote books of Australian travel such as *Spinifex Walkabout* (1953) and *People of the Big Sky Country* (1970).
▷ *Hold Fast to Dreams* (1982)

REES, Rosemary
(1876–1963)

New Zealand writer of popular fiction, whose first book was *April's Sowing* (1924). Some 20 books followed, of which *Wild, Wild Heart* (1928), *Home's Where the Heart Is* (1935) and *Love is a Lonely Land* (1958) may be taken as typical. She also wrote the popular *New Zealand Holiday* (1933) which, however, portrayed her country as a comfortable middle-class paradise—even in the 1930s. Superficially 'moral', her plots pose no severe problems for the characters, and social issues are neatly evaded.

REESE, Lizette Woodworth
(1856–1935)

American poet and schoolteacher, born in Maryland. *A Branch of May* (1887), Reese's first collection, was welcomed for its eschewal of Victorian sentimentality in favour of a spare, aphoristic style which some have seen as the first step, in the USA, towards modern Symbolism. But although one of Reese's sonnets—'Tears'—achieved enormous popularity and was much anthologized, she was not a Movement poet, preferring to ply a craft of private passion whilst holding down a job as high-school teacher for her entire working life. In her last years she published two volumes of autobiography.

▷ *A Victorian Village* (1929); *The York Road* (1931)

REEVE, Clara
(1729–1807)

English novelist of the 'Gothic' school, born in Ipswich, the daughter of the rector of Freston. She translated **John Barclay**'s *Argenis* (1772), and wrote *The Champion of Virtue, a Gothic Story* (1777), renamed *The Old English Baron*, which was avowedly an imitation of **Horace Walpole**'s *The Castle of Otranto*. Her other novels were *The Two Mentors* (1783), *The Exiles* (1788), *The School for Widows* (1791), *Memoirs of Sir Roger de Clarendon* (1793), and *Destination* (1799). She also wrote a critical account of *The Progress of Romance* (1785).

▷ Sir Walter Scott, memoir in *Old English Baron* (1823)

REEVES, James, pseud of John Morris Reeves
(1909–78)

English poet, critic, anthologist and children's writer, born in Finchley, London. He is best known as a writer (of poetry and fiction) for children, but as a poet he gradually built up a high reputation: **Edwin Muir** made the comment that 'perfection rarely draws attention to itself'; another critic described him as a 'uniquely English crepuscular poet in the psychological tradition of Gozzano'. *The Idiom of the People* (1958), an edition of the folksongs originally collected by Cecil Sharpe, stimulated many writers, including **Anthony Burgess**. With **Martin Seymour-Smith** he wrote, among other books, *Inside Poetry* (1968), an influential book of practical criticism.

▷ *Collected Poems* (1977)

REEVES, William Pember
(1857–1932)

New Zealand politician, historian, anthologist and poet, born in Lyttelton, Canterbury, and best known for his long poem 'A Colonist in his Garden', which was included in his *New Zealand and Other Poems* (1898). He published *The Passing of the Forest* privately in 1925; with George Phipps Williams he published two collections of light verse, and with J Ward *The Book of Canterbury Rhymes* (1866, rev edn 1883), a significant early anthology of New Zealand colonial verse. He was a member of cabinet from 1891 to 1896, but in 1896 left politics, moving to London as Agent-General for New Zealand,

and in 1905 becoming New Zealand's first High Commissioner. During this time he wrote a number of books on his homeland, of which *The Long White Cloud: Ao Tea Roa* (1898, rev edn 1924) includes many incisive yet affectionate portraits of contemporary personalities.

▷ K Sinclair, *William Pember Reeves: New Zealand Fabian* (1965)

REGINALD OF CANTERBURY
(fl.1080)

French poet from Poitou, who spent most of his life as a monk at the abbey of St Augustine in Canterbury. His best-known work is *Vita Sancti Malchi*, a lengthy verse biography of the hermit St Malchus.

REGNARD, Jean François
(1655–1709)

French comic dramatist, born in Paris, the son of a rich shopkeeper. He found himself at the age of 20 the master of a considerable fortune, and set out on his travels. In his autobiographical romance, *La Provençale* ('A Woman from Provence'), he tells of his and his Provençal mistress's capture and sale as slaves by Algerian corsairs, their bondage in Constantinople, and their ransom. After wanderings as far as Lapland, he found his vocation in the success of *Le Divorce* at the Théâtre-Italien in 1688. *Le Joueur* (1696, 'The Gambler'), a hit at the Théâtre-Français, was followed by *Le Distrait* (1697, 'The Absent-minded Man'), *Le Retour imprévu* (1700, 'The Unexpected Return'), *Les Folies amoureuses* (1704, 'Follies of Love'), and his masterpiece, *Le Légataire universel* (1708, Eng trans *The Sole Heir*, 1912).

▷ A Caleme, *Jean François Regnard, sa vie et son oeuvre* (1960)

RÉGNIER, Henri François Joseph de
(1864–1936)

French Symbolist poet, novelist and critic, born in Honfleur. He studied law in Paris, and then turned to letters. His *Poèmes anciens et romanesques* (1890, 'Ancient Poems and Romances') revealed him as a Symbolist, though later he returned to more traditional versification. In both poetry and prose his style and mood were admirably suited to evocation of the past, and expressive of a melancholy disillusionment induced by the passage of time. Poetical works include *La Sandale ailée* (1906, 'The Winged Sandal'), *Vestigia flammae* (1921, 'Traces of the Flame') and *Flamma tenax* (1928, 'The Steadfast Flame'). His novels were mainly concerned with France and Italy in the 17th and 18th

centuries. Two of these are *La Double Maîtresse* (1900, 'The Double Mistress') and *Le Bon Plaisir* (1902, 'One's Pleasure').
▷E Buenzod, *Henri Régnier* (1966)

RÉGNIER, Mathurin
(1573–1613)
French satirist, born in Chartres. After taking orders he grew up dissipated and idle, obtained a canonry at Chartres, and enjoyed the favour of Henri IV. His whole work hardly exceeds 7 000 lines—16 satires, three epistles, five elegies, and some odes, songs and epigrams, yet it places him high among French poets. He is best at satires, admirably polished, but vigorous and original and giving a lively picture of the Paris of his day.
▷J Vieney, *Mathurin Régnier* (1896)

RÉGNIER, Paule
(1888–1950)
French Catholic novelist and diarist, whose remarkable achievement is now in danger of being forgotten. An illness in infancy left her hunchbacked and crippled. She was extremely sensitive and religious, and turned to literature for solace as a young woman. After an unhappy love affair with a writer (Paul Drouot) who was killed in World War II, she became a poor recluse, struggled with her doubts, and eventually killed herself. She wrote two masterpieces, one a private *Journal* (1951), kept until the night before she died. Her novel *L'Abbaye d'Evolayne* (1933, 'The Abbey of Evolayne'), about a woman who became a nun but could not keep her vows, and killed herself in front of her monk-husband, is one of the most powerful of its time.

REID, Forrest
(1875–1947)
Irish novelist and croquet player. He was born in Belfast, where he lived for most of his life. After an uncongenial job in a tea company, he belatedly became a Cambridge student (1905). His fiction expresses his obsession with boyhood, which he ascribed to 'arrested development'. *The Garden God* (1905) deals, typically, with ideal boyhood friendship, while *Apostate* (1926) nostalgically describes his own childhood. The Tom Barber trilogy—*Uncle Stephen* (1931), *The Retreat* (1936) and *Young Tom* (1944)—atmospherically relates the perceptions of an imaginative young boy, together with dream-like supernatural events that seem at times profound, at others whimsical. Reid's spiritual appreciation of the Ulster landscape and his love of animals are omnipresent in all these lucid and lyrical works.
▷B Taylor, *The Green Avenue* (1980)

REID, Thomas Mayne
(1818–83)
Irish writer of boys' stories, born in Ballyroney, County Down. In 1840 he emigrated to New Orleans, settled as a journalist in Philadelphia (1843), and served in the US army during the Mexican war (1847), where he was severely wounded. Returning to Britain in 1849, he settled down to a literary life in London. His vigorous style and hairbreadth escapes delighted his readers. Among his books, many of which were popular in translation in Poland and Russia, were *The Rifle Rangers* (1850), *Scalp Hunters* (1851), *Boy Hunters* (1853), *War Trail* (1857), *Boy Tar* (1859) and *Headless Horseman* (1866). He went back to New York in 1867 and founded the *Onward Magazine*, but returned to England in 1870.
▷J Steele, *Captain Mayne Reid* (1977)

REID, Victor Stafford
(1913–)
West Indian novelist, born and educated in Jamaica. His early novels, *New Day* (1949) and *The Leopard* (1958), were innovative in many ways, particularly in their use of language. The latter, set in Kenya, is a book to be considered alongside such as **Achebe**'s *Things Fall Apart*. But Reid, although he has written for children, and a few adult stories, has, disappointingly, not followed them up.

REINMAR VON ZWETER
(c.1200–c.1255)
German poet and Minnesinger, born into a noble family in the Rhineland but living the life of a wandering minstrel, mainly in the southern German areas, especially in and around Vienna. His Middle High German verse is moral in tone, highly rhetorical and deeply conservative, preaching the value of a well-ordered society. Some 300 poems, many with music, survive.

REIZEN, Abraham
(1875–1953)
Lithuanian Yiddish poet and story writer, born in Kojdanov; he emigrated to the USA in 1908. He achieved great popularity with his tales and simple songs, many of which were set to music. The periodical, *Di Europeishe Literatur*, which he edited from 1919, was important for the translations it carried of European books into Yiddish. By 1924 his works took up 12 volumes.

REJ, Mikolaj
(1505–69)
'The father of Polish literature' (though this title has been challenged on the grounds that he came at the end of the Polish medieval

tradition), born in Zorawno, a squire. At the age of about 40 he turned from Lutheranism to Calvinism. Poet and polemicist, a stern moralist, 'he wrote as he spoke'. Although learned in theological dispute, and widely read, he had little formal education (some schooling in Skalmierz and Cracow), and thus offers an incomparable guide to the vernacular of his time. He wrote didactic plays, verse, and homilies. Like many Poles of his time, he composed enormous epic poems. His main importance lies in his profound influence on the Polish literary language through his use of vernacular. His most famous work is *Zywot Czlowieka Poczciwego* ('Life of a Noble Man', 1568 in *Zwierzyniec*, 'The Speculum'), a 'faithful mirror of the life of an average nobleman in Poland', a sort of later Polish equivalent of **Castiglione**'s *The Courtier*.

REMARQUE, Erich Maria
(1898–1970)

German novelist, born in Osnabrück. He served in World War I, and published his famous war novel, *Im Westèn nichts Neues* (1929, Eng trans *All Quiet on the Western Front*, 1929). He lived in Switzerland from 1929 to 1939, and published *Der Weg zurück* (1931, Eng trans *The Road Back*, 1931). In 1939 he emigrated to the USA, and became a naturalized citizen. There he wrote *Flotsam* (English and German language versions, 1941), *Arc de Triomphe* (1946, Eng trans *Arch of Triumph*, 1946), *Der schwarze Obelisk* (1956, Eng trans *The Black Obelisk*, 1957) and *Die Nacht von Lissabon* (1962, Eng trans *The Night in Lisbon*, 1964).
▷ W K Pfeiler, *War and the German Mind* (1941)

REMÉNYIK, Sándor
(1890–1942)

Hungarian (Transylvanian) poet and editor, born in Kolozsvár, the chief city of Transylvania. He was in the peculiar position of being a Hungarian who was handed over to Romanian rule (1920). Two of his poems are translated into English in *Modern Magyar Lyrics* (1934, ed W Kirkconnell).

REMINGTON, Frederic Sackrider
(1861–1909)

American artist and author, known primarily for his action scenes of the American West, derived from first-hand experience as a ranchhand. Remington wrote his books—*Pony Tracks* (1895), *Crooked Trails* (1898), *The Way of An Indian* (1906) to name a few—as vehicles for his painting. His big break came when he was asked to do the drawings for Theodore Roosevelt's *Ranch Life and the Hunting Trail* (1888). This led to other commissions. In total he illustrated more than 70 books, 17 of them his own. Remington also edited the correspondence of **Owen Wister**, author of *The Virginian*.
▷ H McCracken, *Frederic Remington—Artist of the Old West* (1947); B M Vorpahl, *Frederic Remington and the West* (1978)

REMIZOV, Alexei Mikhailovich
(1877–1957)

Russian writer, born in Moscow. He lived in St Petersburg, but left Russia at the Revolution, going first to Berlin and finally settling in Paris. His writing is full of national pride and a deep love of old Russian traditions and folklore; it contains realism, fantasy and humour. His main works are the novels, *Prud* ('The Pond'), *Chacy* ('The Clock'), *Pyataya yazva* ('Fifth Pestilence') and *Krestovye syostri* ('Sisters of the Cross'), legends, plays and short stories.

RÉMUSAT, Charles François Marie, Comte de
(1797–1875)

French aristocrat, born in Paris, son of the Comte de Rémusat (1762–1823), who was chamberlain to Napoleon. Early on he developed liberal ideas, and took to journalism. He signed the journalists' protest which brought about the July Revolution (1830), was elected deputy for Toulouse, in 1836 became under-secretary of state for the interior and in 1840 Minister of the Interior. Exiled after the *coup d'état* of 1848, he devoted himself to literary and philosophical studies, until, in 1871, Thiers called him to the portfolio of foreign affairs, which he retained until 1873. Among his writings are *Essais de philosophie* (1842, 'Essays in Philosophy'); *L'Angleterre au XVIIIe siècle* (1856, 'Eighteenth-century England'); studies on *St Anselm* (1853), *Bacon* (1857), *Channing* (1857), *John Wesley* (1870) and *Lord Herbert of Cherbury* (1874); *Histoire de la philosophie en Angleterre de Bacon à Locke* (1875, 'History of English Philosophy from Bacon to Locke'); and two philosophical dramas, *Abélard* (1877) and *La Saint Barthélemy* (1878, 'Saint Bartholomew's Day').

RENARD, Jules
(1864–1910)

French novelist, playwright, diarist and socialist (he was a friend of Jean Jaurès, the French socialist leader, and Léon Blum, the future socialist prime minister, and he was the conscientious socialist mayor of his old home town of Chitry-les-Mines from 1904 until his death). He is best known for his semi-autobiographical novel *Poil de Carotte* (1894,

Eng trans 1967), about the war between a mad mother and the son she loathes. This deserves its classic stature, as does *L'Ecornifleur* (1892, Eng trans *The Sponger*, 1957), which has been misunderstood because it is as acidly critical of the 'artistic' as of the 'bourgeois' temperament. His animal pieces *Histoires naturelles* (1894, Eng trans *Natural Histories*, 1966) have been called 'dated' but are not found so by those who understand animals. Renard combined the natural suspiciousness of the countryman with the sophistication of an urban littérateur who could co-found the *Mercure de France*: as his most important work, *Journal* (1925–7, Eng trans of selections, 1964), demonstrates, he was an exceedingly complex and honest man. The manuscript of the journal was destroyed—but even the poor text we have of it shows that Renard will endure as a major, and self-questioning, writer.

RENART, Jean
(fl.early 13th century)

French writer, who treats the themes of courtly love and military heroism. The references to historical figures and events in the works now attributed to him suggest that he lived in the late 12th and early 13th centuries. Almost nothing is known about his life, but Franklin Sweetser deduces an aristocratic lineage from Renart's apparent familiarity with court circles. The fact that Renart signed only one manuscript in full (that of *Le Lai de L'Ombre*) has led to some difficulty in identifying his works, but he is now believed to be the author of the courtly romances *L'Escoufle*, *Guillaume de Dole, ou Le Roman de la Rose* ('Guillaume de Dole, or The Romance of the Rose'), and the shorter *Le Lai de L'Ombre* ('The Poem of the Shadow'). P H Beekman also ascribes to him the poems *De Renart et de Piaudoue* ('The Story of Renart and Piaudoue') and *De plait Renart de Dammartin contre Vairon son roncin* ('The Trial of Renart against his Horse').

RENAULT, Mary, pseud of Mary Challans
(1905–83)

British historical novelist, born in London. She worked in medicine before turning to writing serious novels about war and hospitals, the best of which is *The Charioteer* (1953). She found her greatest success with her eminently readable adventure novels set in ancient Greece, including a trilogy about Alexander and several retellings of the Greek myths. Best known amongst these are *The Mask of Apollo* (1966), a spy-thriller starring an extrovert actor, and *The King Must Die* (1958), a retelling, with modern psychological insights, of the story of Theseus.

▷ D Sweetman, *Mary Renault: A Biography* (1993)

RENDELL, Ruth Barbara, also writes as Barbara Vine
(1930–)

English novelist, born in London. She is established as one of Britain's finest authors of detective fiction, of which the most popular are her 'Wexford' books. Rendell's first novel, *From Doon With Death* (1964), introduces Chief-Inspector Reginald Wexford, a compassionate, humane man serving with the Kingsmarkham CID in southern England. Wexford's cases take place within a domestic, often middle-class and apparently comfortable world. In the twelfth Wexford novel, *Kissing the Gunner's Daughter* (1992), the discovery of three bodies leads him into a mire of greed, fear and obsession. These preoccupations find a darker home in the much more psychologically macabre novels Rendell writes under the name of Barbara Vine, of which *King Solomon's Carpet* (1991) is representative.

RENÉE, properly Renée Gertrude Taylor
(1929–)

New Zealand playwright, born in Napier. A strong feminist, she has been involved in drama workshops as writer and director since the mid-1960s. Her *Setting the Table* was broadcast, then produced on stage in 1981. Her first success on the professional stage was *Wednesday to Come* (1984); this became the central play of a trilogy, with *Jeannie Once* coming out in 1990 and *Pass It On* in 1986. The feminist theme is carried on in *What Did You Do in the War, Mummy?* (1982) and *Asking for It* (1983).

RENN, Ludwig, pseud of Arnold Friedrich von Golssenau
(1889–1979)

German novelist, one of the greatest chroniclers of World War I. His style in his early and greatest book, *Krieg* (1928, Eng trans *War*, 1929), was influenced by the explorer Sven Hedin. This pungent and still underrated account has long been known as inimitably superior to **Remarque**'s more facile *All Quiet on the Western Front*. Later work, especially after he turned to communism, is less important, but some of the novels repay closer investigation.

▷ W K Pfeiler, *War and the German Mind* (1941)

RESTIF (or Rétif) DE LA BRETONNE, Nicolas Edme
(1734–1806)

French writer, born in Sacy, Yonne. His many voluminous and licentious novels, such

REUTER, Christian

as *Le Pied de Fanchette* (1769, 'Fauchette's Foot') and *Le Paysan perverti* (1775, 'The Corrupted Peasant'), give a vividly truthful picture of 18th-century French life, and entitle him to be considered as a forerunner of Realism. He described his own not unsullied life in the 16-volume *Monsieur Nicolas* (1794–7, Eng trans 1930). He also wrote on social reform.

▷ C R Dawes, *Rétif de la Bretonne* (1946)

REUTER, Christian
(1655–after 1710)

German dramatist and novelist, born in Kütten in Saxony. He first attracted attention when, while a student in Leipzig, he pilloried his landlady (of the Red Lion) and her son in two comedies—Frau Muller sued him and eventually got him sent down, but is still laughed at as the hilariously vulgar Frau Schlampampe. Her son, Eustachius, was Schelmuffsky in the mock travel book *Schlemuffskys Curiose unde sehr gefärlich Reisbesreibung* (1796, Eng trans *Schlemuffsky's Curiosity*, 1962).

REUTER, Fritz
(1810–74)

German humorist, born in Stavenhagen in Mecklenburg-Schwerin. He studied law at Rostock and Jena. In 1833 he was condemned to death, as with other Jena students he had indulged in wild talk about the Fatherland, but his sentence was commuted to 30 years' imprisonment. Released in 1840, with his career spoilt and his health ruined, he tried to resume his legal studies, learned farming, and taught pupils. His rough *Plattdeutsch* (Low German) verse setting of the jokes and merry tales of the countryside, *Läuschen un Rimels* (1853, 'Anecdotes and Rhymes'), became at once a great favourite, and another humorous poem, *Reis' nah Belligen* (1855, 'The Trip to Belgium'), was equally successful, followed by a second volume of *Läuschen un Rimels* (1858) and the tragic poem *Kein Hüsung* (1858, 'No Home'). The rest of his best works, except the poem *Hanne Nüte* (1860), were all written in Low German prose. *Ut de Franzosentid* (1860, Eng trans *The Year '13*, 1873), *Ut mine Festungstid* (1862, 'During my Imprisonment') and *Ut mine Stromtid* (1862–4, 'During my Apprenticeship') made him famous throughout Germany. He lived in Eisenach from 1863 until his death.

▷ K Batt, *Fritz Reuter, Leven und Werk* (1967)

REVERDY, Pierre
(1899–1960)

French poet and critic who, together with the Chilean poet **Vicente Huidobro**, invented the concept of 'creationism'. Reverdy, who was born in Narbonne, the son of a vine-grower ruined by the disaster of 1907, at first wanted to be an artist, and throughout his life was associated with painters (including Gris, Picasso and Braque, who illustrated his last posthumous collections of prose-poems). Creationism demanded that a poem be autonomous: that it should not imitate nature, but create in its own right. From this Reverdy, in constant touch with **Apollinaire** and the painters whom Matisse had in 1908 mockingly called cubist (Picasso, Braque), developed a poetry which came to be known as itself 'cubist': essentially what this meant was that Reverdy, as he said of Picasso, 'called upon himself to learn everything afresh'. The resulting poetry, profoundly religious, but by a man who was distressed by his inability to understand God, seems disjointed and, initially, unrewarding; but the integrity and deliberateness of the poet, as he painfully tries to re-create the world in images, grow on the reader. Available in English translation is *Poems* (1968).

▷ R Greene, *The Poetic Theory of Pierre Reverdy* (1967)

REVIUS, Jacobus
(1586–1658)

Dutch poet, born in Deventer. A Calvinist parson, his devotional sonnets have been held to be amongst the best poetry ever produced by a Dutchman. His poetry is interesting to modern minds less for its author's convictions than for his concealed doubts. He helped in the translation of the Dutch Bible. There is a useful account of his work in *European Metaphysical Poetry* (1961) by F J Warnke, which includes some translations into English.

REVUELTAS, José
(1914–76)

Major novelist, playwright, essayist and political activist, born in Durango. He is regarded, with **Rulfo** and **Yañez**, as one of the founding fathers of modern Mexican fiction. In his youth he went to prison many times for organizing strikes, and his first novel, *Los muras de agun* (1941, 'The Walls of Water'), was about the penal colony at Isla Marias. Expelled from the Mexican Communist Party, he continued to work—as an anti-Stalinist—for Marxist ideals. His best-known novel outside Mexico is *El luto humano* (1943, Eng trans *The Stone Knife*, 1947), about three families who survive a failed strike at an irrigation system. His best novel is considered to be *Los errores* (1964, 'The Errors'), which embodies his criticisms of the failure of the Mexican Communist Party to live up to its ideals.

▷M R Frankenthaler, *José Revueltas: El solitario solidario* (1978)

REXROTH, Kenneth
(1905–82)

American poet, critic and father figure to the Beat Generation. Born in South Bend, Indiana, he was largely self-educated. He worked as a manual labourer during the 1920s and became a prominent figure in the libertarian movement on the West Coast during the 1930s. He was a conscientious objector during World War II, serving as a hospital orderly in San Francisco; during this time he published his first book of verse, *In What Hour?* (1940). Other volumes include *The Signature of All Things* (1950), the quest-poem *The Dragon and the Unicorn* (1952) and *In Defense of the Earth* (1956). *Collected Shorter Poems* appeared in 1967, and a volume of longer works a year later. The best of his critical writing was published in *The Rexroth Reader* (1972).
▷M Gibson, *Kenneth Rexroth* (1982)

REYBAUD, Louis
(1799–1879)

French journalist and politician, born in Marseilles. He travelled in the Levant and India and, returning to Paris in 1829, wrote for the Radical papers and edited a history of the French expedition to Egypt (1830–6). His *Réformateurs ou Socialistes modernes* (1840–3, 'Reformers, or Modern Socialists') popularized the word 'socialism'.

REYES, Alfonso
(1889–1959)

Major Mexican poet, critic, essayist, diarist and man of letters, born in Monterrey. By profession he was a diplomat, his country's ambassador to Argentina and Brazil. He was universally respected, as a creator in his own right and as a keeper of standards, and very widely influential. His poetry reflected his reading of Góngora and of other European poets, such as Mallarmé (upon whom he wrote an essential book, *Mallarmé de nosotros*, 1938, 'Mallarmé Between Ourselves'). His *Diario 1911–1930* (1960) is crucial reading for an understanding of Mexican literature in the period it covers. He spent many years in Spain, and became one of the world's leading authorities on the Golden Age of Spanish literature. *Selected Essays* (1964) is a good introductory selection. Two other important books of his about Mexico have been translated: *The Position of America* (1950) and *Mexico in a Nutshell* (1964).
▷B B Aponte, *Alfonso Reyes and Spain* (1972)

REYLES, Carlos
(1868–1938)

Major Uruguayan novelist, born in Montevideo. With Horacio Quiroga and Onetti, Reyles is the leading prose writer of his country. His first phase, after he had inherited a fortune (of which he quickly but 'disinterestedly' relieved himself) and gone to live in Spain, was wholly naturalist: his first efforts, already powerful, but flawed by theory, were based on the prescriptions of Zola. But he had also learned from the psychologically subtler Pérez Galdós, and his later fiction became more original. His atypical *El embrujo de Sevilla* (1922, Eng trans *Castanets*, 1929) is often cited as his finest novel, but, although an excellent evocation of Andalusia, this neglects his *El terruño* (1916, 'The Soil'), his most exact portrayal of a type who had turned up in his fiction from the start: the failed Nietzschean intellectual, who is contrasted with Reyles's most vital creation, the practical woman Mamagela. This is the novel most favoured by Uruguay's most outstanding critic and her modern keeper of conscience, Mario Benedetti.
▷M Benedetti, *Literatura uruguaya siglo XX* (1969); L A Menagra, *Carlos Reyes* (1957) (both in Spanish)

REYMONT, Władysław Stanisław
(1867–1925)

Polish novelist, winner of the Nobel Prize for literature, born in Kobiele Wielke, near Radon, the son of a village organist. He held a variety of jobs—wandering actor, tailor, novice monk. His first novel, *The Promised Land* (1899, Eng trans 1928), was about urban life in the industrial town of Łodz, but his masterpiece is a study of rural life, *The Peasants* (1902–9, Eng trans 1924–5), a tetralogy which was instrumental in his being awarded the Nobel Prize for literature in 1924. Other books are *The Comédienne* (1896, Eng trans 1920), and a historical trilogy, *The Year 1794* (1914–19).
▷L Budnecki, *Wladyslaw Stanislaw Reymont* (1953)

REZÁC, Václav, pseud of Václav Vonavka
(1901–56)

Czech novelist, born in Prague. His early novels were more interesting than his later ones, which were socialist realist and consequently lost power and psychological conviction.

REZNIKOFF, Charles
(1894–1976)

American poet and historian. His central subject was the lives of Jews in modern America, which forms the substance of the autobiographical, blunt and often violent *Family*

Chronicle (1969). The best of Reznikoff's verse appeared in *Inscriptions*, published a decade earlier in 1959, and working essentially the same territory. *Holocaust* (1975) contained rather discursive lyrics on the extermination of his people in Europe. His projected four-volume *Testimony*, a history of the American Diaspora, never got past the first volume (1965) and the eve of World War I. In his poetry he subscribed to Objectivism, stripping his lyrics of the inessential; this occasionally led to prosiness, as in *By the Waters of Manhattan* (1962) and the edited volume *By the Well of Living and Seeing* (1974), which appeared shortly before his death.

RHIGAS, Konstantinos
(1760–98)

Greek poet, born in Velestino. He organized the anti-Turkish revolutionary movement in Vienna, but was betrayed and shot. He is mainly remembered as a patriotic hero, but was also the author of many patriotic songs and poems, and translated works of European literature into Greek.

RHYS, Jean, pseud of Gwen Williams
(1894–1979)

British novelist, born in the West Indies. Her father was a Welsh doctor, her mother a Creole. Educated at a convent in Roseau, Dominica, she moved to England in 1910 to train at the Royal Academy of Dramatic Art, but her father's death after only one term obliged her to join a touring theatre company. At the end of World War I she married a Dutch poet, Max Hamer, and went to live on the Continent, spending many years in Paris where she met writers and artists, including **Ernest Hemingway**, **James Joyce** and **Ford Madox Ford** (the last-named in particular encouraged her writing). In 1927 she published *The Left Bank and Other Stories*, set mostly in Paris or in the West Indies of her childhood. Four novels followed, *Quartet* (originally published as *Postures*, 1928), *After Leaving Mr Mackenzie* (1930), *Voyage in the Dark* (1934) and *Good Morning Midnight* (1939); her heroines were women attempting to live without regular financial support, adrift in European cities between the worlds of wealth and poverty. After nearly 30 years she published in 1966 what was to become her best-known novel, *Wide Sargasso Sea*, based on the character of Rochester's mad wife in **Charlotte Brontë**'s *Jane Eyre*. Further short stories followed in *Tigers are Better Looking* (1968) and *Sleep It Off, Lady* (1976); an autobiography, *Smile Please*, was published posthumously in 1979.
▷P Wolfe, *Jean Rhys* (1980)

RIBAS, Oscar
(1909–)

Lusophone Angolan novelist, poet and essayist, a major figure in African literature. Born in Luanda of mixed parentage, he was blind from 1930. He is the world's leading authority on his own people, the Kimbundu, whose folk beliefs and religion he has studied through his stories, enthnographic writings and poetry.

RIBEIRO, Aquilino
(1885–1963)

Portuguese novelist, story writer and essayist who, from the beginning until the end of his career, opposed hypocrisy, corruption and tyranny. He was born in Carregal da Tabosa. When his novel *Quando os Lobos uivam* (1958, Eng trans *Where the Wolves Howl*, 1963) appeared, the police arrested him, but, horrified by the protests from abroad, hastily released him. However, the book was never available in shops. It deals with a peasants' revolt against a government afforestation scheme and the salutary revenge of a father against petty clerks for the unjust imprisonment of his son. His first book was the story collection *Jardim das Tormentas* (1913, 'Garden of Torments'). His language is so rich in the vernacular that a special glossary was compiled as a guide to it. He has been called modern Portugal's 'most rewarding writer to the outsider precisely because he is the most Portuguese'.

RIBEIRO, Bernardim
(1482–1552)

Portuguese novelist and poet of whose life little is certainly known. He is supposed, on good evidence, to have died mad—driven thus by a fatal passion—in a Lisbon hospital. It is likely that he was a 'converted' Jew, although there in no trace of more than a formal Christianity in any of his work. His main poetry consists of six eclogues. His most famous work is the plotless novel known (from its first three words) as *Menina e moça* (1554, second and augmented edition, by another hand, 1557, 'The Young Girl'). It is episodic and its text is unsatisfactory, but it is one of the most feminist of all 16th-century novels; it is a 'gentle tale of love and languishment' in which the vital Portuguese concept of *saudade* originates. *Menina e moça* emphasizes, as **Freud** was later to emphasize, that there is inherent in the sexual urge some impossibility of complete fulfilment.
▷A F G Bell, *Portuguese Literature* (1922)

RICARDO, Cassiano
(1895–1976)

Brazilian poet. He was an adherent of Brazil's Modernist movement who became associated with the 'Green-Yellow' fascist movement of Plinio Salgado, since he felt that this best fitted Brazilian aspirations. He later revised his opinions.

RICE, Elmer, originally **Elmer Reizenstein**
(1892–1967)

American dramatist, born Elmer Reizenstein in New York. He studied law and turned to writing plays. His prolific output includes *The Adding Machine* (1923), *Street Scene* (1929), which won a Pulitzer Prize, *The Left Bank* (1931), *Two on an Island* (1940) and *Cue for Passion* (1958).
▷ *Minority Report* (1963)

RICE, James
(1843–82)

English novelist, born in Northampton. He studied at Queen's College, Cambridge, drifted from law into literature, and was proprietor and editor of *Once a Week* (1868–72). From 1872 he was involved in writing novels with Sir **Walter Besant**, beginning with the successful *Ready-Money Mortiboy* (1872).
▷ J Rice, *The Autobiography of Sir Walter Besant* (1902, ed S S Sprigge)

RICH, Adrienne Cecile
(1929–)

American poet, born in Baltimore, Maryland, and educated at Radcliffe College, Cambridge, Massachusetts. Her first volume of verse, *A Change of World* (1951), was published while she was still an undergraduate, but it foreshadowed her emergence as the most forceful American woman poet since **Elizabeth Bishop** and **Sylvia Plath**. Later collections include *Snapshots of a Daughter-in-Law* (1963) and *The Will to Change* (1971). The latter took her up to the point of her husband's suicide. Thereafter, Rich began to align herself more directly with the women's movement, often dating poems as if they documented stopovers on a campaign trail. Her prose became almost as influential as her verse. *Of Woman Born* (1976) is a ruggedly unsentimental account of maternity. *On Lies, Secrets, and Silence* (1979) collected the best of her occasional prose. In *Blood, Bread, and Poetry* (1986) she aligned herself with radical lesbianism, defined in a broad non-sexual way that embraces the entire cathexis that binds woman to woman. Later verse appeared as *The Dream of a Common Language* (1978) and *A Wild Patience Has Taken Me This Far* (1981), which established her lineage from **Emily Dickinson**. *The Fact of a Doorframe* (1984) collected her poetry from 1950.
▷ M Díaz-Diocaretz, *The Transforming Power of Language* (1984)

RICH, Barnabe
(c.1540–1617)

English soldier and romance writer, born in Essex. Under the patronage of Sir Christopher Hatton he served as a soldier in France, the Low Countries and Ireland. He was the author of exaggerated tales in *The Strange and Wonderful Adventures of Don Simonides* (1581) and *The Adventures of Brusanus, Prince of Hungaria* (1592). His *Apolonius and Silla* (contained in *Riche, his Farewell to the Militarie Profession*, 1581) was used by **Shakespeare** as a source for the plot of *Twelfth Night*. He was also a prolific pamphleteer on military matters, and on Ireland.

RICHARDS, Alun
(1929–)

Welsh novelist, short-story writer and playwright, born in Pontypridd, Glamorgan. He was educated at the Monmouthshire Training College, Caerleon, and at University College, Swansea. He has published six novels, including *The Elephant You Gave Me* (1963), *A Woman of Experience* (1969) and *Barque Whisper* (1979), and two collections of short stories (*Dai Country*, 1973, and *The Former Miss Merthyr Tydfil*, 1976), often drawing on his varied experiences working as a probation officer, a sailor and a teacher. Besides editing several short-story anthologies, he has written a book about Welsh rugby, and many plays and adaptations for television, notably *The Onedin Line*.
▷ Autobiography in M Stephens, *Artists in Wales* (1971)

RICHARDS, Frank, properly **Charles Hamilton**
(1875–1961)

English children's writer, author of the 'Tom Merry', 'Billy Bunter' and other school-story series. He wrote for boys' papers, and particularly for *The Gem* (1906–39) and *The Magnet* (1908–40). After World War II he published school stories in book and play form, and his *Autobiography* (1952).
▷ M Cadogan, *The Man Behind Chums* (1985)

RICHARDS, Ivor Armstrong
(1893–1979)

English scholar and literary critic, and initiator of the so-called 'New Criticism' movement. Professor at Cambridge (1922–9), with Charles Key Ogden he developed the idea of Basic English, and in 1924 published the influential *Principles of Literary Criticism*, followed by *Science and Poetry* (1825) and *Practical Criticism* (1929). In 1939 he left Cambridge for Harvard, where he was professor (1939–63). There he taught **William**

Empson, became a friend of **Robert Lowell**, and began himself to write poetry, publishing, among other collections, *Goodbye Earth and other poems* (1958), *The Screens* (1960) and *New and Selected Poems* (1978).

▷ I P Schiller, *I A Richards's Theory of Literature* (1969)

RICHARDSON, Dorothy M(iller)
(1873–1957)

English novelist, born in Abingdon, Berkshire. After her mother's suicide in 1895 she moved to London and worked as a teacher, a clerk, and a dentist's assistant. She became a Fabian, and had an affair with **H G Wells** which led to a miscarriage and a near-collapse in 1907. Later (1917) she married a painter, Alan Odle. She started her writing career with works about the Quakers and George Fox (1914). Her first novel, *Painted Roofs* (1915), was the first of a 12-volume sequence entitled *Pilgrimage*, culminating with *Clear Horizon* (1935) and *Dimple Hill* (1938). She was the first exponent of the 'stream of consciousness' style later made famous by **Virginia Woolf**.

▷ C R Blake, *Dorothy Richardson* (1960)

RICHARDSON, H(enry) H(andel), pseud of Ethel Florence Lindesay Robertson
(1870–1946)

Australian novelist and short-story writer, born in Fitzroy, Melbourne, the daughter of an Irish immigrant doctor, who claimed descent, through her grandfather, from the ancient Irish Earls of Lindesay. After an unhappy childhood in which her father died insane, she travelled widely with her mother and younger sister and studied music with distinction at Leipzig Conservatorium, graduating with honours in 1892. She married a fellow-student, John George Robertson, and they moved to London. Her first novel, *Maurice Guest*, was published there in 1908, under her masculine-sounding pseudonym, followed by *The Getting of Wisdom* in 1910. He major work was the trilogy *The Fortunes of Richard Mahoney*; the first book, *Australia Felix* (1917), was followed in 1925 by *The Way Home*. This sold so poorly that the final book, *Ultima Thule*, was initially privately published at her husband's expense, but the three were re-published together in 1930. In *Maurice Guest* and in her later novel *The Young Cosima* (1939), a study of the interwoven lives of Liszt, Wagner and Wagner's second wife Cosima von Bülow, her deep musical sympathies are evident. She wrote some short stories, and a rather imaginative 'autobiography', *Myself when Young* (posthumous, 1948).

▷ N Palmer, *Henry Handel Richardson: a Study* (1950); V Buckley, *Henry Handel Richardson* (1970)

RICHARDSON, Jack Carter
(1935–)

American dramatist and novelist, born in New York. His first play, *The Prodigal* (1960), was an impressive re-interpretation of the Orestes–Agamemnon myth in terms of a struggle between idealism and pragmatism. His next play, *Gallows Humor* (1961), was a biting but intelligent satire on capital punishment. The rest of Richardson's career has lacked focus. The autobiographical *Memoir of a Gambler* (1979) is diagnostic.

RICHARDSON, Samuel
(1689–1761)

English novelist, born in Derbyshire, where his father, a London joiner, had apparently taken refuge after the Monmouth rebellion. He may have gone to Merchant Taylor's School. He was apprenticed to a printer, married his master's daughter, and set up in business for himself in Salisbury Court, where in the heyday of his fame (and in much enlarged premises) he received **Dr Johnson**, **Edward Young**, and the blue stockings. He was represented as the model parent and champion of women, but his three daughters seem to have had a repressed upbringing. In a letter he says that as a boy he wrote love letters for a group of young women, and this may have been the origin of his epistolary novels. In 1741 he published *Letters Written to and for Particular Friends*, generally referred to as *Familiar Letters*, which gave advice on 'how to think and act justly and prudently in the common concerns of human life'. *Pamela* (1740), his first novel, is also 'a series of familiar letters now first published in order to cultivate the Principles of Virtue and Religion', and this was the aim of all his works; but the virtue taught was of the prudential sort and the manners mean and bourgeois. After holding out for conditions against her brutal employer, Pamela, in the sequel, plays the Lady Bountiful and mingles easily in genteel life. In his second novel, *Clarissa, Or the History of a Young Lady*, Richardson depicts the high life, of which he confessed he knew little. Clarissa Harlowe in the toils of Lovelace is the main theme, but parental repression is also to be corrected. With all her charm Clarissa is too much the victim of her pride for her tragedy to be truly moving, and Lovelace is too ambiguous a character to be credible. Nevertheless, the seven volumes issued in 1748 made Richardson famous, and he was flattered by society as he took the cure at Tunbridge Wells or was visited at his fine new house, Northend. He corresponded with several society women. Fine ladies and gentlemen such as Lady **Mary Wortley Montagu**, **Horace**

Walpole and Lord Chesterfield might 'hesitate dislike', but the middle classes were enthusiastic. Richardson's third novel, *Sir Charles Grandison* (1754), designed to portray the perfect gentleman, turns on the question of divided love. Not only English bluestockings but Continental writers raved about Richardson's novels. **Denis Diderot**'s eulogy in *Le Journal étranger*, though extravagant, is sincere—his *La Religieuse* is modelled on Richardson—and **Rousseau**'s *La Nouvelle Héloïse* confesses his discipleship. Apart from its technical advantages and disadvantages, the epistolary method was a means to suggest authenticity at a time when mere fiction was frowned upon. Thus Richardson called himself the editor, not author, of his works. He was also a redoubtable correspondent.

▷A Dobson, *Samuel Richardson* (1902); I Watt, *The Rise of the Novel* (1957)

RICHEPIN, Jean
(1849–1926)

French poet, playwright and novelist, born in Medeah, Algeria. Before the appearance of his first romance in 1872 he had been *franc-tireur*, sailor and actor. His revolutionary book of poems, *La Chanson des Gueux* (1876, 'The Beggars' Song') led to a fine and his imprisonment.

▷A Zevcas, *Les Procès littéraires au XIXième siècle* (1924)

RICHLER, Mordecai
(1931–)

Canadian novelist, born in Montreal. He grew up in a Jewish working-class neighbourhood and attended Baron Byng high school and Sir George Williams College. He travelled in Europe, but returned to Canada in 1952, working for the Canadian Broadcasting Corporation before moving to England in 1959, since when he has been a professional writer. His first novel, *The Acrobats* (1954), was derivative of **Ernest Hemingway** and subsequently disowned. In 1955 he published *Son of a Smaller Hero*, about a young man endeavouring to escape the Jewish ghetto and North American society in general. It was the first of several books for which he was accused of anti-semitism. It was followed by *A Choice of Enemies* (1957), but his break-through came with *The Apprenticeship of Duddy Kravitz* (1959), about an endearing shyster. Subsequent novels—*St Urbain's Horseman* (1971), *The Incomparable Auk* (1963) and *Cocksure* (1968)—have enhanced his reputation as one of Canada's richest novelists, a bawdy humorist and vitriolic satirist.

▷V Ramraj, *Mordecai Richler* (1983)

RICHTER, Conrad Michael
(1890–1968)

American novelist and short-story writer, born in Pine Grove, Pennsylvania. After various menial jobs—farm work, clerking, and journalism—he moved to New Mexico, and the landscape of the South West made a profound impact on him. His best-known novel, *The Sea of Grass* (1937), concerns a cattle baron. The three novels that followed—*The Trees* (1940), *The Fields* (1946) and *The Town* (1950)—comprise a frontier trilogy published in collected form as *The Awakening Land* (1966). Other novels include *Always Young and Fair* (1947), *The Light in the Forest* (1953) and *The Waters of Kronos* (1960), a dreamlike elegy for a vanished America that reflects Richter's occasional sententiousness; *The Mountain on the Desert* (1955) is a leaden spiritual odyssey.

▷E Gaston, *Conrad Richter* (1965)

RICHTER, Hans Werner
(1908–)

German novelist, born in Bansin, Usedom, a Baltic island. After service in World War II, during which he was taken prisoner, Richter helped to found the literary circle Gruppe '47. His worthy fiction has been described by most critics as 'formless' and having only documentary value, but may not have had its due as humane, highly informative prose. His *Die Geschlagenen* (1949), describing the Nazis' brutal behaviour in Italy, was twice translated, as *The Odds Against Us* (1950) and *Beyond Defeat* (1961).

RICHTER, Johann Paul Friedrich *see* JEAN PAUL

RICKWORD, Edgell
(1898–1982)

English poet and critic, born in Colchester and educated at Oxford University. The youngest of the trench poets in World War I, he was influenced originally by **Siegfried Sassoon** but came to find his own voice, which involved erotic and satirical lyrics as well as Symbolist poetry. He was first published in 1921 with *Behind the Eyes*; his later collected editions of poetry (1947, 1970, 1976) found gradual favour. A socialist from boyhood, he joined the Communist Party in 1934, edited the influential *Left Review*, joined the International Union of Revolutionary Writers and became known for his unbending Far-Left orthodoxy; he left the communists, however, in the large exodus of 1956.

▷C Hobday, *Edgell Rickword: A Poet at War* (1989)

RIDGE, John Rollin, Native American name **Yellow Bird**
(1827–67)

American writer and poet. Born in Georgia, the son of a well-to-do Cherokee father and White mother, Ridge was early caught up in the violent and tragic history of his people in the mid-19th century. His grandfather, the Cherokee leader Major Ridge, having been a leading advocate for the tribe's removal to Indian Territory, the family were ever after targets for the opposing faction, and when Ridge was 12 his father was assassinated in front of him. Beset by enemies throughout his life, Ridge killed a man in a dispute in his late teens, and fled to Missouri where he tried to raise funds for a fair trial; but, his finances poor, he was soon lured by the gold rush to move to California, where he stayed the rest of his life. Meeting no luck as a prospector, Ridge turned to journalism and became a regular contributor of poems and sketches to the new literary magazine, the San Francisco *Pioneer*. His most famous work, however, was the *Life and Adventures of Joaquín Murieta* (1854), a bloodthirsty, romanticized account of the life of the Mexican bandit which established Murieta's status as a folk hero, and the first major piece of fiction published by a Native American. Ridge's collected poems were published posthumously in 1868.
▷ J W Parrins, *John Rollin Ridge: His Life and Works* (1991)

RIDGE, William Pett
(1857–1930)

English writer, born in Chatham, Kent. He was educated at the Birkbeck Institution, and worked as a civil servant for several years before turning to a career in journalism and novel-writing. He was a prolific writer, and published over 60 books in all. He is best known as an exponent of cockney humour, in works like *A Clever Wife* (1895) and *Mord Em'ly* (1898).

RIDING, Laura, née **Reichenfeld** (later **Laura Riding Gottschalk**, then, after 1941, **Laura (Riding) Jackson**)
(1901–91)

American poet, critic, story writer, novelist and polemicist. Daughter of an Austrian immigrant, she took some courses at Cornell University (and married Louis Gottschalk, a history instructor there). Her first collection of poetry, *The Close Chaplet*, appeared in England, under the imprint of the Hogarth Press, run by Leonard and **Virginia Woolf**. She was the lover (1926–9) and then the literary associate (1929–39) of **Robert Graves**, with whom she lived in Mallorca, London

and Rennes. In 1941 she married Schuyler Jackson, a minor poet and farmer, with whom she wrote a long (unpublished) study of language. It is generally agreed that her poetry is superior to her prose, which became increasingly convoluted and denunciatory of those whom she regarded as her enemies (chiefly, and notoriously, Graves himself). Her poetry is quite unlike any other poetry of this century: based, rhythmically, on a very surely-handled four-accent line, it seeks unabashedly to examine the reasons for human existence, and to establish human obligations. It has attracted the attention of many, including Graves, **Auden**, **Larkin**, **Robert Fitzgerald**, **Robert Nye**, but has never received satisfactory critical exegesis. *First Awakenings* (1992), edited by her friend Nye and assistants, adds considerably to the canon.
▷ Riding's introduction to *Collected Poems* (1938); J P Wexler, *Laura Riding's Pursuit of Truth* (1979)

RIFBJERG, Klaus
(1931–)

Danish novelist and poet, born in Copenhagen. He studied at the universities of Princeton and Copenhagen and worked as an assistant film director before becoming a full-time writer. From 1984 to 1991 he was literary director of Denmark's dominant publishing house, *Gyldendal*. Widely viewed as the modern Danish author par excellence, he has published more than 100 titles since his debut in 1956 with *Under vejr med mig selv* ('Under the Weather With Myself'), a provocatively 'premature' autobiography in poetic form. It heralded the modernistic movement in Danish poetry and was followed in 1960 by *Konfrontation* ('Confrontation'), a landmark collection of poetry exhibiting Rifbjerg's linguistic wizardry and gargantuan appetite for modern life. His almost sensual relationship to the writing process has also resulted in a string of novels. The first one, *Den kroniske uskyld* (1958, 'The Chronic Innocence'), is a highly entertaining account of two young men's disastrous sexual debuts and displays one of Rifbjerg's main preoccupations: the dangers connected with the transition from childhood to adulthood. Rifbjerg's later novels include *Anna (jeg) Anna* (1969, Eng trans *Anna (I) Anna*, 1982), in which his talent for portraying women reaches a peak, *De hellige aber* (1981, Eng trans *Witness to the Future*, 1987), about two boys who are transported forward in time, from 1941 to 1981, and *Engel* (1987, 'Angel'). Rifbjerg has been awarded numerous literary prizes.
▷ T Brostrøm, *Klaus Rifbjerg. En digter i tiden, I & II* (1991)

RIGGS, (Rolla) Lynn
(1899–1954)

American dramatist and poet, born in Clare-more, Cherokee Nation (now Oklahoma). Of Cherokee descent, Riggs never identified himself as a Native American writer and little of his work deals directly with Native American life. He is best known as the author of *Green Grow the Lilacs* (1930), the play upon which the musical *Oklahoma!* was based. In plays such as *Big Lake* (1927) and *The Cherokee Night* (1936), Riggs depicts his characters and situations with a brooding sense of tragedy and fatalism. The latter, the only one of his plays to centre on Native American characters, describes problems of cultural disintegration among the Cherokees over several generations in Indian Territory/Oklahoma. Though he made his career as a dramatist, Riggs also wrote imagist-style poetry, which he collected and published as *The Iron Dish* (1930).

RILEY, James Whitcomb
(1849–1916)

American poet, known as the 'Hoosier poet', born in Greenfield, Indiana. He made his name contributing homely dialect poems to the *Indianapolis Journal* (1877–85). He published several volumes, and is also known for his poems about children, including 'Little Orfant Annie' and 'The Raggedy Man', written as Benjamin F Johnson. Earlier in his career he had been fired from a newspaper job after forging a poem allegedly by **Edgar Allan Poe**.
▷P Revell, *James Whitcomb Riley* (1970)

RILEY, Joan
(1958–)

Jamaican novelist, working and writing in Britain, whose books explore the problems faced by different generations of West Indian immigrant women. *The Unbelonging* (1985) is about an 11-year-old girl brought to Britain to be re-united with her father. *Waiting in the Twilight* (1987) contains a retrospective view of immigrant life in the Britain of the 1950s and 1960s, while *Romance* (1988) features the archetypal presence of so much Caribbean writing—the charismatic grandmother.

RILKE, Rainer Maria
(1875–1926)

Austrian lyric poet, born in Prague. He deserted a military academy to study art history in Prague, Munich and Berlin. The spiritual melancholy of his early verse turns into a mystical quest for the deity in such works as *Vom lieben Gott und Anderes* (1900, Eng trans *Stories of God*, 1931) and *Das Stun-denbuch* (1905, Eng trans *Poems from the Book of Hours*, 1941), written after two journeys to Russia (1899–1900), where he met **Tolstoy** and was deeply influenced by Russian pietism. In 1901 he married Klara Westhoff, a pupil of Rodin, whose secretary Rilke became in Paris, publishing *Auguste Rodin* (1903, Eng trans 1919). Mysticism was abandoned for the aesthetic ideal in *Neue Gedichte* (1907, 1908, 'New Poems'). *Die Aufzeichnungen des Malte Laurids Brigge* (1910, Eng trans *Journal of My Other Self*, 1930) portrays the anxious loneliness of an imaginary poet; a key text of existentialism, it prefigured such works as **Sartre**'s *La Nausée*. In 1923 he wrote two masterpieces, *Die Sonnette an Orpheus* (Eng trans *Sonnets to Orpheus*, 1936) and *Duineser Elegien* (Eng trans *Duino Elegies*, 1939), in which he exalts the poet as the mediator between crude nature and pure form. One of the most important figures in modern European literature, his work greatly extended the range of expression and subtlety of the German language.
▷J F Hendry, *The Sacred Threshold* (1983)

RIMBAUD, (Jean Nicolas) Arthur
(1854–91)

French poet, born in Charleville, Ardennes, the son of an army captain and his stern, disciplinarian wife. After a brilliant academic career at the Collège de Charleville, he published in 1870 his first book of poems, and the same year ran away to Paris, the first stage in his life of wandering. He soon returned to Charleville, where he wrote, while leading a life of leisure, drinking and bawdy conversation, *Le Bateau ivre* (1871, Eng trans *The Drunken Boat*, 1952), which, with its verbal eccentricities, daring imagery and evocative language, is perhaps his most popular work. Soon after its publication in August 1871, **Paul Verlaine** invited Rimbaud to Paris, where they began a homosexual affair. In Brussels in July 1873 Rimbaud threatened to terminate the friendship, and was shot at and wounded by Verlaine, who was imprisoned for attempted murder. The relationship had, however, given Rimbaud some measure of stability, and from its height, the summer of 1872, date many of *Les Illuminations* (1886, Eng trans 1973), the work which most clearly states his poetic doctrine. These prose and verse poems show Rimbaud as a precursor of Symbolism, with his use of childhood, dream and mystical images to express dissatisfaction with the material world and a longing for the spiritual. In 1873 he published the prose volume *Une Saison en enfer* (Eng trans *A Season in Hell*, 1939), which symbolized his struggle to break with his past—his 'enfer' (hell); he was bitterly disappointed at its cold reception by the literary critics, burned all his manuscripts, and at the age of 19 turned his back on literature. Then began years of varied and colourful wandering in Europe and the East—in Germany, Sweden, Aden, Cyprus and Harar, as soldier, trader, explorer and gun-runner. During these years, in 1886, Verlaine published *Les Illuminations* as by the 'late Arthur Rimbaud', but the author ignored, rather than was ignorant of, the sensation they caused and the reputation they were making for him. In April 1891, troubled by a leg infection, he left Harar and sailed to Marseilles, where his leg was amputated, and where he died.

▷ E Starkie, *Rimbaud* (1961)

RINEHART, Mary
(1876–1958)

American novelist, born in Allegheny, Pennsylvania and educated at the Pittsburgh Training School for Nurses. She began by writing mysteries in order to supplement her family's income. Early success prompted her to continue writing, and she eventually, in addition to her lucrative mysteries, produced plays, popular romances, and factual articles, many of which were based on her own life experiences. She adapted her first novel, *The Circular Staircase* (1908), into a successful play, *The Bat* (1920). Her most enduring heroine was 'Tish', who was introduced in 1910 in stories for *The Saturday Evening Post* and later featured in several novels.

RINGELNATZ, Joachim, pseud of Hans Böttischer
(1883–1934)

German poet, of sharp intelligence and satirical capacity, who had been a sailor and had knocked around doing odd jobs. However, during World War I he commanded a minesweeper. His irreverent poetry is still eminently readable. He was most successful as a reciter of his own verses in cabaret.

▷ C Middleton and M Hamburger (eds), *Modern German Poetry 1910–1969* (1962)

RINGWOOD, Gwen Pharis
(1910–84)

Canadian playwright. Ringwood grew up in Alberta and attended universities in Montana and North Carolina. Her plays, which number more than 60 and include musicals, show the influence of both **Synge** and **Lorca**. The best known, *Still Stands the House* (1939), is about a time of depression and drought on the prairie. She built up a solid reputation in Canadian theatre. A *Collected Plays* was published two years before her death.

RINUCCINI, Ottavio
(1562–1621)

Italian poet. He wrote *Dafne* (1594), the first Italian melodrama, based on the earlier Greek work.

▷ E Li Gotti, *Restauri trecenteschi* (1947)

RIOU, Jakez
(1899–1937)

Breton story writer, perhaps the leading practitioner of this genre in his language in the 1930s.

RISCO, Vecente
(1874–1963)

Spanish novelist, poet and scholar, born in Orense. He wrote in Castilian mainly but wrote poetry in Galician, and was a notable leader of the Galician revival. *La puerta de paja* (1953, 'The Straw Door') was a didactic novel written with a semi-modernist technique; but it is Risco's Galician poetry that is chiefly remembered nowadays.

RISKIN, Robert
(1897–1955)

American playwright and screenwriter, born in New York City. After serving in the United States Navy during World War I, he worked as a freelance writer and later enjoyed success as a Broadway playwright, creating a number of smart, sophisticated comedies, including *She Couldn't Say No* (1926) and *Bless You Sister* (1927, with J Meehan). A screenwriter from 1931, he was under contract to Columbia, where he worked in collaboration with director Frank Capra on a succession of sparkling popular comedies that often celebrated the idealism of the common man as he triumphed over the cynicism of his corrupt masters. Winner of an Academy Award for *It Happened One Night* (1934), he received further nominations for *Lady For A Day* (1933), *Mr Deeds Goes To Town* (1936) and *You Can't Take It With You* (1938), and adapted **James Hilton**'s *Lost Horizon* (1937) for the screen. Also a producer, he created the Overseas Motion Picture Bureau in 1942. Ill health forced his early retirement, but his body of work was honoured with the Laurel Award from the Writer's Guild of America in 1954.

RIST, Johannes von
(1607–67)

German poet and dramatist, a Protestant pastor, born in Otensen near Hamburg. The leading disciple of **Opitz**, he wrote many plays, most of which have now disappeared; he is most outstanding, however, as a religious poet and many of his 600 hymns survive to the present day. He was attacked for writing vigorous secular poetry, but gave this up. His best poetry is in the style of Opitz, but heavier.

▷ J Julian, *Dictionary of Hymnology* (1907)

RITCHIE, Anne Isabella Thackeray, Lady
(1837–1919)

English writer, daughter of **Thackeray**, born in London. A close companion of her father, and well acquainted with his friends of literary and artistic note, she contributed valuable personal reminiscences to an 1898–9 edition of his works, and also wrote memoirs of their contemporaries, such as **Tennyson** and **John Ruskin**. Her novels include *The Village on the Cliff* (1867), *Old Kensington* (1873) and *Mrs Dymond* (1885).

RITSOS, Iannis
(1909–90)

Hugely influential left-wing Greek poet, dogged by family tragedy and constant oppression by a right-wing Greek government. Born into a wealthy Athenian family, he was still a boy when they were financially ruined and both his father and sister went insane. He joined the Communist Party in 1934, and worked as a lawyer's clerk, actor and dancer before being thrust into the limelight with his third collection of poems, *Epitaphios*, in 1936: his lament of a mother over her dead son, killed in a demonstration of out-of-work tobacco workers, was promptly banned by the ruling Metaxas dictatorship. Politically active during the German occupation, Ritsos was exiled from the mainland after it, and lived until 1952 on a succession of islands, including Lemnos. His books remained banned until 1954. Following the coup d'état and establishment of the junta in 1967, the poet found himself exiled again, this time to Samos, and his books were once again banned, until 1972. He was twice nominated for the Nobel Prize for literature. Many of his works were made into anthems by the musician Mikis Theodorakis, and are still powerful songs of protest for Greece's disaffected youth.

RITTER, Erika
(1948–)

Canadian playwright and stand-up comic, born in Saskatchewan. Ritter writes comedies which set independent and intelligent women at logger-heads with the urban world. She is not a 'soap-boxing' playwright and this, coupled with her authentic feel for comedy, has helped bring success at the box-office, as with *Automatic Pilot* (1980), which concerned the autobiographical routine of a female comic. *Ritter In Residence* (1987), like *Urban Scrawl* (1984), showed that she could communicate her shrewd angle on life in essay form as well as on the stage.

RIVAROL, Antoine
(1753–1801)

French writer, born in Bagnols in Languedoc. He went to Paris in 1780 where he adopted the aristocratic form 'Comte de', and worked his way into fashionable society, where he found much material for his sarcastic writings, and in 1788 set the whole city laughing at the sarcasms in his *Petit Almanach de nos grands hommes* ('Little Almanac of Our Great Men'). Emigrating in 1792, and supported by royalist pensions, he wrote pamphlets in Brussels, London, Hamburg and Berlin.

▷ A Le Breton, *Antoine Rivarol* (1896)

RIVAS, Angel de Saavedra *see* SAAVEDRA, Angel

RIVAS, Manuel Linares
(1867–1938)

Spanish playwright, now remembered chiefly for one drama, very popular in its time: *La garra* (1914, 'The Claw'), about a man destroyed by reactionaries because he sought a divorce.

RIVAUDAUD, André de
(c.1540–1580)

French dramatist, translator (of Epictetus) and poet, born in Poitou. His biblical play *Aman* (1556) has been called the 'first humanist religious tragedy', inasmuch as it conformed to classical rules. A Protestant, he attacked **Ronsard** for 'paganism'.

▷ R Lebègue, *Le Théâtre religieux en France* (1929)

RIVERA, José Eustacio
(1889–1928)

The most important Colombian novelist before **Gabriel García Márquez**, Rivera was also a poet, teacher, and lawyer. His adventurous life took him on travels throughout Colombia: to the oil fields as an inspector and to the jungle around the Orinoco and Rio Negro basins as a member of a boundaries commission. He was also a member of the National Congress. His most important work is *La Vorágine* (1924, 'The Vortex'), a pessimistic view of man's inherently violent nature and a stunning presentation of the world of the jungle. This novel marks a complete rupturing of the idealized Romantic view of nature, and deeply affected later writers like **Mario Vargas Llosa** and **Miguel Angel Asturias**. An example of his Parnassian poetry is *Tierra de Promisión* (1921, 'The Promised Land').

▷ L A Sánchez, *José Eustacio Rivera* (1957)

RIVIÈRE, Jacques
(1886–1925)

French writer and critic, born in Bordeaux. In 1919 he became the first editor of the *Nouvelle Revue Française*, as such playing a prominent part in the cultural life of post-war France. His writings include novels, essays and a justification of the Christian conception of God, *À la trace de Dieu* (1925, 'Following God').

▷ R Beaulieu, *Jacques Rivière* (1955)

RIZAL, José
(1861–96)

Filipino patriot and writer, born in Calamba, Luzon. He studied medicine at Madrid, and on his return to the Philippines published a political novel, *Noli me tangere* (1886, 'Do not touch me'), whose anti-Spanish tone led to his exile. He practised in Hong Kong, where he wrote *El Filibusterismo* (1891), a continuation of his first novel. Returning to the Philippines, he arrived just when an anti-Spanish revolt was erupting; he was accused of instigating it, and was shot.

▷ A Coates, *Rizal: Philippine Nationalist and Martyr* (1968)

ROA BASTOS, Augusto
(1917–)

Major Paraguayan novelist—the greatest his country has produced—and poet. He was born in Asunción (Paraguay), although he now lives in Toulouse. His father, often misleadingly described as a worker on a sugar plantation, was in fact a cultured man, who had taken minor orders—a once successful importer, he was forced into bankruptcy by unfair competition. As a boy of 15, Roa Bastos was made to fight in the 'despicable' Chaço War against Bolivia. He was exiled to Buenos Aires after supporting the losing side in the 1947 civil war. A man of wide culture (he spent some years in Europe, part of them in Great Britain), his interesting poetry, initially neo-*gongorista*, has been somewhat neglected. He has long been a pacificist, and thus regarded by many patriotic critics as an incurable eccentric. But both *Hijo de hombre* (1959, Eng trans *Son of Man*, 1988) and *Yo el Supremo* (1974, Eng trans *I the Supreme*, 1988) have been hailed almost everywhere as great novels. Of the first, which traces the unhappy history of his country by means of episodes related by a narrator, **Mario Benedetti** wrote that with it Roa Bastos 'placed himself firmly in the pantheon of great writers'. *I the Supreme*, about the legendary (mad, but shrewd and learned) 19th-century dictator of Paraguay, Dr Francia, is perhaps the 'dictator novel' of all 'dictator novels'. **Carlos**

Fuentes called it 'one of the milestones of the Latin-American novel', and **John Updike** felt that its 'deliberate prodigiousness . . . intimidated criticism'.

▷ D W Foster, *The Myth of Paraguay in the Fiction of Roa Bastos* (1969); D W Foster, *Augusto Roa Bastos* (1978)

ROBBE-GRILLET, Alain
(1922–)

French novelist, born in Brest. Educated in Paris, he worked for some time as an agronomist and then in a publishing house. His first novel, *Les Gommes* (1953, Eng trans *The Erasers*, 1964), aroused much controversy and with the appearance of his later ones (*Dans le labyrinthe*, 1959, Eng trans *In the Labyrinth*, 1960, etc), he emerged as a leader of the *Nouveau Roman* ('new novel') group. He uses an unorthodox narrative structure and concentrates on external reality, believing this to be the only one. He has also written film scenarios, eg, *L'Année dernière à Marienbad* (1961, Eng trans in novel form and filmed as *Last Year at Marienbad*, 1962) and essays, *Pour un nouveau roman* (1963, Eng trans *Towards a New Novel*, 1965). Other publications include the novel *Projet pour une révolution à New York* (1970, 'Project for a Revolution in New York'), *La Belle Captive* (written with René Magritte, the painter, 1976; adapted as a screenplay, 1983, 'The Beautiful Prisoner'), *Djinn* (1981, Eng trans 1982) and *Angélique ou l'enchantement* (1984, 'Angelique; or, The Enchantment').

▷ J Fletcher, *Alain Robbe-Grillet* (1983)

ROBBINS, Harold
(1916–)

American bestseller novelist, born of unknown parentage in the Hell's Kitchen area of Manhattan, New York City. At 15 he dropped out of George Washington high school, left his foster parents and eventually became an inventory clerk in a grocery store. During the Depression he showed entrepreneurial flair by buying up crops and selling options to canning companies and the canning contracts to wholesale grocers. He was a millionaire by the time he was 20, but speculation in sugar before the outbreak of World War II relieved him of his fortune. He became interested in writing in 1949. Drawing on his knowledge of street life, high finance and Hollywood, he produced a string of earthy bestsellers: *Never Love a Stranger* (1948), *The Dream Merchants* (1949), *A Stone for Danny Fisher* (1952), *79 Park Avenue* (1955) and *The Carpetbaggers* (1961), which together sold six million copies throughout the 1960s.

ROBBINS, Tom (Thomas Eugene)
(1936–)

American comic novelist, born in Blowing Rock, North Carolina. After working as a journalist and broadcaster, he published his first novel, *Another Roadside Attraction* (1971), in which Christ's mummified body, discovered in the Vatican cellars, becomes an advertising draw for a freeway hot-dog stand. In *Even Cowgirls Get the Blues* (1976) Robbins portrays the ultimate hitch-hiker, Cissy Hankshaw, to dramatize his curious view of a female-dominated America. *Still Life With Woodpecker* (1980) and *Jitterbug Perfume* (1984) both showed some signs of strain. Though often unthinkingly described as a '60s writer', Robbins's work is largely concerned with the long hangover left after the Great Society and Woodstock. It is an essentially pessimistic vision.

▷ M Siegel, *Tom Robbins* (1980)

ROBERTS, Sir Charles George Douglas
(1860–1943)

Canadian writer and naturalist, born in Douglas, New Brunswick. A graduate of Fredericton, he was professor in King's College, Nova Scotia (1885–95), and settled in New York as an editor, joining the Canadian army at the onset of World War I. An outstanding lyric poet, he wrote *Orion and Other Poems* (1880), *In Divers Tones* (1887), and other verse, a history of Canada, *Canada in Flanders* (1918), and nature studies, in which he particularly excelled, including *The Feet of the Furtive* (1912) and *Eyes of the Wilderness* (1933).

▷ W J Keith, *Sir Charles Roberts* (1969)

ROBERTS, Elizabeth Madox
(1881–1941)

American novelist and poet, born in Perrysville, Kentucky. Opinions are still divided as to her merits, but she was regarded in her day as a major novelist. Some have seen her as over-poetic and over-diffuse—as 'indeterminate'; others as transcending regionalism. Her works include *The Time of Man* (1926), about Kentucky hill-dwellers, *My Heart and my Flesh* (1927), a study of a family in decline, and *The Great Meadow* (1930), a historical novel about the settlement of Kentucky by emigrants from Virginia. Criticism has yet to assess her.

▷ H M Campbell and R E Foster, *Elizabeth Madox Roberts: American Novelist* (1956)

ROBERTS, Kate
(1891–1985)

Welsh novelist and short-story writer, born in Rhosgadfan, near Caernarfon, Gwynedd. She was educated at the University College of North Wales, Bangor. Sometimes described as 'the Welsh Chekhov', she is generally regarded as the most distinguished prose writer in Welsh this century. She was a teacher of Welsh at Ystalyfera (1915–17) and Aberdare (1917–28), and later (with her husband Morris T Williams) bought Gwasg Gee, the publishers of the newspaper *Baner ac Amserau Cymru* (later *Y Faner*), and settled in Denbigh.

▷ B Jones, *Kate Roberts* (1969)

ROBERTS, Keith
(1935–)

English author of science-fiction novels and short stories, born in Kettering, Northamptonshire. Considered one of the finest stylists of the genre, Roberts's works include *Pavanne* (1968) and *The Chalk Giants* (1975). *Molly Zero* (1980) is set 200 years hence, in a Britain governed by martial law. Molly Zero, destined to become one of the elite caste, rebels and in doing so confronts unexpected political and moral questions. Another version of future-Britain, this time a disintegrating country seen from the point of view of a resentful lavatory attendant, is the subject of the title story of *The Lordly Ones* (1986). Another story, 'The Checkout', features Anita, a modern-day witch and a familiar Roberts character.

ROBERTS, Kenneth Lewis
(1885–1957)

American novelist, essayist and dowsing expert, born in Kennebunk, Maine. After graduating from Cornell, he worked as a journalist from 1909 till 1928. He is considered one of the best historical novelists the USA has produced. *Arundel* (1930) was the first in a projected cycle presenting the history of Maine. It told the story of Benedict Arnold's expedition against Quebec and was based on careful research into journals and related papers. The series was never completed but there were two sequels, *Rabble in Arms* (1933) and *Captain Caution* (1934). Other historical novels include *Northwest Passage* (1937) and *Oliver Wiswell* (1940), about the American Revolution from the viewpoint of a loyal colonial soldier.

ROBERTS, W(alter) Adolphe
(1886–1962)

Jamaican poet and novelist, born in Kingston, son of a wealthy silk merchant. Educated privately, he was a journalist on the Jamaican *Daily Gleaner*, then in the USA from 1904, finally returning to Jamaica in 1949. His verse, *Pierrot Wounded and other poems* (1919) and *Pan and Peacocks* (1928), is graceful and accomplished in the English

ROBERTSON, Angus

aesthetic tradition, but the last four of his many novels, *Royal Street* (1944), *Brave Mardi Gras* (1946) and *Creole Dusk* (1948), set in Louisiana, and *The Single Star* (1949), set in Cuba, reflect a more realistic interest in Creole culture and West Indian independence.

ROBERTSON, Angus
(1870–1948)

Scottish Gaelic poet and novelist, born on the Isle of Skye. He wrote one historical novel and many songs; his use of language has been described as 'grotesquely overloaded', but at its best was evocative both of Skye and of the injustices suffered by a Gaelic society. His essays on Celtic themes, *The Children of the Fore-World* (1933), contain his finest work.

ROBERTSON, Elizabeth Arnot
(1903–61)

English novelist, now virtually forgotten, who scored a success with her first novel, *Cullum* (1938). She was best known for her film-criticism. Her most widely-read novel was *Four Frightened People* (1931).

ROBERTSON, Thomas William
(1829–71)

English dramatist, brother of Madge Kendal, born in Newark-on-Trent, of an old acting family. Going to London in 1848, he was an actor, prompter and stage manager, wrote unsuccessful plays, contributed to newspapers and magazines, and translated French plays. His first notable success as a dramatist was with *David Garrick* (1864) and *Society* (1865), and his next comedy, *Ours* (1866), established his fame. *Caste* (1867), *Play* (1868), *School* (1869), *M.P.* (1870)—all performed by the Bancrofts at the Prince of Wales Theatre—and also *Home* (1869) and *Dreams* (1869) were all equally successful.
▷I E Pemberton, *Life and Work of Thomas William Robertson* (1893)

ROBERTSON, Edwin Arlington
(1869–1935)

American poet, born in Head Tide, Maine. He was brought up in the town of Gardiner, Maine, which provided the background for 'Tilbury Town', the fictional New England village setting of his best poetry. He was educated at Harvard, and went to New York to find work. He made a name with an early collection of poetry, *The Children of the Night* (1897), followed by *Captain Craig* (1902), *The Town down the River* (1910), *The Man against the Sky*, which confirmed his reputation, and *King Jasper* (1935), his last work. Poems such as 'Miniver Cheevy' and 'Richard Cory' are now recognized as American classics, and are much anthologized. He was three times a Pulitzer Prize-winner, for his *Collected Poems* (1922), *The Man Who Died Twice* (1925) and *Tristram* (1927), one of his several modern renditions of Arthurian legends.
▷H Hagedorn, *Edwin Arlington Robinson* (1938)

ROBINSON, Henry Crabb
(1775–1867)

English journalist and diarist. He was articled to a Colchester attorney (1790–5), then travelled in Germany where he met **Goethe** and **Schiller**, and studied at Jena University. He joined *The Times* in 1807 as a foreign correspondent, and covered the Peninsular War as a war correspondent (1808–9)—the first of his kind. He worked as a barrister from 1813 to 1828. He knew and corresponded with many of the major literary figures of the day (**Coleridge**, **Wordsworth**, **Charles Lamb**, **William Blake**, etc), who all figure in his voluminous diaries, correspondence and reminiscences. He was one of the founders of London University (1828) and the Athenaeum Club in London.
▷E Morley, *Life and Times of Henry Crabb Robinson* (1935)

ROBINSON, Kim Stanley
(1952–)

American science-fiction writer, born in California. He published a small number of stories and an academic study of the novels of **Philip K Dick** prior to his first novel, *The Wild Shore* (1984), a sophisticated post-disaster novel set in California. *The Gold Coast* (1988) and *Pacific Edge* (1990) form a thematic trilogy with that book. He began a second major trilogy about the colonization of Mars with *Red Mars* (1992) and *Green Mars* (1993), which is intended to range over a vast 200-year timespan, encompassing the social, political and environmental issues raised on his lucidly imagined planet. He has written several other science-fiction works, including *Icehenge* (1984) and *A Short Sharp Shock* (1990).

ROBINSON, (Esmé Stuart) Lennox
(1886–1958)

Irish dramatist, born in Douglas, County Cork. His first play, *The Clancy Game*, was produced in 1908 at the Abbey Theatre, Dublin, where he was appointed manager in 1910 and then director from 1923 to 1956. Other plays include *The Cross Roads* (1909), *The Dreamers* (1915) and *The White-Headed Boy* (1920). He also compiled volumes of Irish verse, including the Irish *Golden Treasury* (1925), and edited Lady **Gregory**'s *Journals*

(1946). His autobiographical works were *Three Homes* (1938) and *Curtain Up* (1941).
▷ F O'Connor, *My Father's Son* (1969)

ROBINSON, Mary ('Perdita'), née Darby
(1758–1800)

English poet and novelist, born in Bristol, daughter of a merchant and educated at schools in Bristol and London. Her adventures and tribulations started with marriage at 16; at 17 she was imprisoned for debt with her husband and infant daughter, and published her first poems; turned actress in 1776, she was mistress of the Prince of Wales, later George IV, who deserted her in 1780. Saved from destitution by an annuity secured by Charles James Fox, she travelled to France with her lover, Col Banastre Tarleton, but from 1783 was lamed by partial paralysis. Left by Tarleton in 1792 she struggled to support her family by writing. She associated with radical intellectuals, and her poems were highly admired by **Coleridge**. Her prolific output included satirical verse, love-sonnets (*Sappho and Phaon*, 1796), a long poem on the French Revolution, *Lyrical Tales* (1800), showing affinities with the nascent Romantic movement, two plays, and several novels of sentiment and Gothic romance, including the bestselling *Vancenza* (1792).
▷ *Memoirs* (1801), ed J F Molloy (1930); M Steen, *The Lost One* (1937); R D Bass, *The Green Dragoon: the lives of Banastre Tarleton and Mary Robinson* (1957)

ROBINSON, Marilynne
(1943–)

American novelist and essayist, born in Sandpoint, Idaho and educated at Brown University and the University of Washington. Her first novel, *Housekeeping* (1980), was later filmed and has been hailed as a feminist classic; this lyrical novel focuses on the different life choices of two previously inseparable sisters. Robinson's work has been strongly influenced by the American Transcendentalists. In 1989 she published her first non-fiction book, *Mother Country: Britain, The Nuclear State, and Nuclear Pollution*. In 1982 she received both the **Hemingway** Foundation Award and the American Academy **Rosenthal** Foundation Award.
▷ E A Meese, *Crossing the Double Cross: The Practice of Feminist Criticism* (1986)

ROBINSON, Roland
(1912–92)

Irish-born Australian poet and mythologist, born in County Clare. An admirer of the verse of English nature poet **Edward Thomas**, his love of the Australian bush often shows a similar turn-of-century ripeness. Considered

the best among **Rex Ingamells**'s 'Jindyworobak' movement, Robinson's variety of output effectively distinguished him from others of that school, even in his first book *Beyond the Grass-Tree Spears* (1944). *Tumult of the Swans* (1953) won him the Grace Leven Prize in that year. A sparse collection of his verse was published in 1971 as *Selected Poems* and a further selection was edited, under the same title, in 1983. His keen interest in aboriginal life and lore was reflected in five books, from *Legend and Dreaming* (1952) to *Aboriginal Myths and Legends* (1966).
▷ *The Drift of Things* (1973); *The Shift of Sands* (1976); *A Letter to Joan* (1978)

ROCHE, Denis
(1937–)

French avant-garde novelist, born in Paris. He served on the editorial board of the influential avant-garde magazine *Tel Quel* (1963–73). He studied dentistry. His verse and prose is in effect a complex questioning of its own right to exist: its readers—of whom there have not been so many—do not 'read' but study it. Roche wishes, however, 'to lay bare the world of excrement, sexuality and death': *Louve basse* (1976, 'Low She-Wolf') is a series of 13 texts; *Notre antéfixe* (1978) is a series not of words but of photographs of the author and his lover in 40 different poses in various hotel rooms, and is described as a novel.

ROCHEFORT, Christiane
(1917–)

French novelist, born in Paris. No novel by her has made the same impact as her first, *Le Repos du guerrier* (1958, Eng trans *Warrior's Rest*, 1959). This well-written and ironically told story of a girl's submission to a sadistic alcoholic contained much scabrous detail, and won the Prix de la Nouvelle Vague.

ROCHESTER, John Wilmot, Earl of
(1647–80)

English courtier and poet, born in Ditchley, Oxfordshire. He was educated at Burford school and Wadham College, Oxford. He travelled in France and Italy, and then returned to court, where his good looks and lively wit made him a prominent figure. In 1665 he showed conspicuous courage against the Dutch. He is said to have been a patron of the actress Elizabeth Barry, and of several poets. In 1667 he married a wealthy heiress, Elizabeth Malet, and plunged into a life of debauchery, yet wrote excellent letters, satires (particularly 'A Satyr against Mankind', 1675), and bacchanalian and amatory songs and verses. Finally he was moved to repentance by Bishop Burnet. Among the best of his poems are imitations of **Horace** and **Nicolas Boileau**, *Verses to Lord Mulgrave*, and *Verses upon Nothing*.

▷V de Sola Pinto, *Rochester, Portrait of a Restoration Poet* (1935)

ROD, Édouard
(1857–1910)

Swiss writer, born in Nyon in Vaud. He studied at Lausanne, Bonn and Berlin, was professor at Geneva, and settled in Paris. Among his 30 works are *La Chute de Miss Topsy* (1882, 'Miss Topsy's Fall'), *La Course à la mort* (1885, 'The Race to Death'), *Le Sens de la vie* (1889, 'The Sense of Life'), *Le Dernier Refuge* (1896, 'The Last Refuge') and *Les Unis* (1909, 'The United').

▷C Delhorbe, *Édouard Rod* (1938)

RODARI, Gianni
(1920–)

Italian children's writer and journalist, born in Omegna (Novara). He established himself with the boys' novel *Le avventure di Cipollino* (1950, 'The Adventure of Cipollino'), which he followed up with many more psychologically convincing yarns.

RODE, Helge
(1870–1937)

Danish dramatist, poet and essayist, born in Copenhagen. He was a dominant force in literature for much of his life, chiefly as a religious thinker. A mystic and early symbolist under the influence of **Maeterlinck**, he was at his best in such dreamy verse dramas as *Kampene i Stefan Borgs Hjem* (1900, 'The Battles in the Home of Stefan Borg').

RODENBACH, Georges
(1855–98)

Belgian poet and novelist, born in Tournai. His mature poetry, turning away from **Hugo**, emulated **Mallarmé** in its Symbolist procedures—but it is not unoriginal for all that, and has not been studied outside French-speaking countries as much as it deserves. It amounts to a remarkable, dreamy, moving evocation of the mysterious region of Flanders. *Bruges-la-Morte* (1892, 'Bruges: Dead City'), a novel, has a similar effect.

▷P Maes, *Georges Rodenbach (1855–98)* (1952, in French)

RODENBERRY, Gene
(1921–91)

American scriptwriter, producer and director, born in Texas. He was a pilot before turning to writing, and has worked mainly in television. He has earned lasting fame within science-fiction circles (and beyond) as the creator of the popular *Star Trek* series which,

after a slow beginning when first screened in 1966–8, has built up a huge following in television, book and film formats. He was unable to repeat the success with several subsequent ventures in the science-fiction and horror field, but participated in the creation of *Star Trek: The Next Generation* (from 1987).

RODGERS, Richard *see* HAMMERSTEIN, Oscar II

RODGERS, W(illiam) R(obert)
(1909–69)

Irish poet and broadcaster. Born in Belfast, he was ordained as a Presbyterian minister in 1935 and served in Loughall, Co. Armagh, from 1935 to 1946. The following year he resigned and settled in London, where he made many contributions to the BBC. *Awake! And Other Poems* (1941), *Europa and the Bull* (1952) and the posthumous *Collected Poems* (1971) provide but small evidence of his work. His contagious respect for the craft of writing led to many unfinished and unpublished pieces, including the commissioned but uncompleted *The Character of Ireland* (with **Louis MacNeice**). In his largely unpublished Epilogue to this piece he wrote 'Here I come, always in at the tail-end,/A good man for a funeral or a wake:/Patient in graveyards, used to thinking long/and walking short'.

▷D Davin, *Closing Times* (1975; reprinted 1985)

RODÓ, José Enrique
(1872–1917)

Uruguayan essayist, born in Montevideo, author of the seminal *Ariel* (1900, Eng trans 1922), an immensely influential essay pleading for spiritual values to be upheld in the coming age of materialism (represented by Caliban). His attack on the United States as the materialistic state *par excellence* was prophetic. He was the foremost prose writer of the modernist movement in Latin America. His chief work, however, was his profound treatise on work and fulfilment, *Los motivos de Proteo* (1914, Eng trans *The Motives of Proteus*, 1928).

RODOREDA, Mercè
(1909–83)

Catalan writer, born in Barcelona. Beginning her career as a writer soon after the proclamation of the Spanish Republic, Rodoreda published prolifically between 1932 and 1937: five novels, plus numerous short stories in literary magazines, established her as a rising star of Catalan literature. With the end of the Spanish Civil War, however, and the suppression of the Catalan language, her books were banned and she fled to France to live in exile. Unable to write during this time, she published her first book for 20 years in 1957 (*Vint-i-dos Contes*, 'Twenty-two Stories'), followed in 1962 by her masterpiece, *La Plaça del Diamant* ('Diamond Plaza'), a stream-of-consciousness novel depicting the psychic and material horrors of the Civil War through the experiences of an ordinary Catalan woman. *Carrer de les Camèlies* ('Camellia Street'), a novel set in war-torn Barcelona in the 1940s and 50s, was published in 1966 and *La Meva Cristina i Altres Contes* ('My Christina and Other Stories') in 1967. Rodoreda returned to Spain in 1979, after Franco's death. Her books have been translated into many languages.

RODRIGUEZ, Claudio
(1934–)

Spanish poet, considered one of Spain's leading poets, his main themes being love and nature. He believes that love, in the universal sense, is poetry, and that everything in the universe should be celebrated, even suffering and death; that poetry should be cathartic and take us back to our roots so that we can view the world with innocence. His language, therefore, is brief and intense to reflect these beliefs. That his freshness and enthusiasm can still be seen in *Casi una Leyenda* (1991, 'Almost a Legend') as much as in his first book, *Don de la Ebriedad* (1953, 'Gift of Drunkenness'), speaks much for his conviction.

RODRÍGUEZ GALVAN, Ignacio
(1816–42)

Mexican poet and dramatist, born in Fizayuca. A rebel, his poetry is mostly spoilt by ultra-romantic grandiloquence. His verse plays were on colonial themes. He is not much read now, but remained important to late 19th-century critics.

ROE, Edward Rayson
(1838–88)

American clergyman and novelist, born in New Windsor, New York. He became chaplain in the volunteer service (1862–5), and afterwards pastor of a Presbyterian church in Highland Falls. The Chicago fire of 1871 furnished him with the subject of his first novel, *Barriers Burned Away* (1872), whose success led him to resign his pastorate in 1874. His other moralistic best sellers included *A Knight of the Nineteenth Century* (1877).

ROETHKE, Theodore
(1908–63)

American poet. He was born in Saginaw, Michigan, where his father grew and sold flowers, a setting that figures in many of the poems in *The Lost Son* (1948), his second and breakthrough collection. He was educated at Michigan University and Harvard and was Professor of English at Washington University from 1948. It was not until the publication of *The Waking* (1953) and the award of a Pulitzer Prize that he became widely known. He suffered from melancholia and in his work was occasionally self-indulgent; however, he wrote with a powerful rhythmic music that often yielded visionary effects. **Robert Lowell** and others of the 'Confessional' poets were influenced by him. *Words for the Wind* (1958) is a selection from his first four books; the *Collected Poems* appeared posthumously in 1968.
▷J Parini, *Theodore Roethke: an American romantic* (1979)

ROF CARBELLO, Juan
(1905–)

Spanish doctor and psychoanalyst, born in Lugo, whose ideas have been highly influential in modern Spain. He is an immensely eclectic practitioner, as influenced by **Jung** and Binswanger (from whom the Scottish psychiatrist R D Laing culled his ideas) as by **Freud**. In his *Entre el silencio y la palabra* (1960, 'Between Silence and the Word'), he examines the thinking of Kierkegaard, **Rilke** and others. This book profoundly influenced the fiction of Rof Carbello's fellow psychiatrist **Martín-Santos**.

ROGERS, Samuel
(1763–1855)

English poet, born in Stoke-Newington. He entered his father's bank, in 1784 was taken into partnership, and in 1793 became head of the firm. In 1781 he contributed essays to the *Gentleman's Magazine*, next year wrote a comic opera, and in 1786 published *An Ode to Superstition*. In 1792 appeared *The Pleasures of Memory*, on which his poetical fame was chiefly based. There followed *An Epistle to a Friend* (Richard Sharp, 1798), the fragmentary *Voyage of Columbus* (1812), *Jacqueline* (1814, bound up with **Byron**'s *Lara*), and the inimitable *Italy* (1822–8). The last, in blank verse, proved a monetary failure; but the loss was recouped by the splendid edition of it and his earlier poems, brought out at a cost of £15 000 (1830–4), with 114 illustrations by Turner and Stothard. In 1803, with £5000 a year, he retired from the bank as a sleeping partner, and settled down to bachelor life and an art collection which sold at his death for £50 000. He was quietly generous to **Thomas Moore**, as well as to some unknown writers. But despite the kindest heart he had so unkind a tongue that 'melodious Rogers' is better remembered today

by a number of ill-natured sayings than by his poetry.
▷P W Claydon, *Samuel Rogers* (1889)

ROGERS, Will
(1879–1935)

American actor, rancher and humorist, born in Native American territory in what is now Oklahoma. His wisecracks became legendary, and led to his writing of a syndicated news column from 1926; he also appeared in many movies—whose directors allowed him to ad-lib at pleasure. *Will Rogers' Political Follies* (1929) illustrates his homely liberalism and cracker-barrel philosophy. *The Autobiography of Will Rogers* (1949) was compiled by Donald Day from all his writings and sayings. He was killed in an air accident.
▷H Croy, *Our Will Rogers* (1953)

ROHMER, Sax, pseud of Arthur Sarsfield Ward
(1886–1959)

English author of mystery stories, born in Birmingham. Interested in things Egyptian, he found literary fame with his sinister, sardonic, oriental criminal genius villain, Fu Manchu, whose doings were told in many spine-chilling tales, including *Dr Fu Manchu* (1913), *The Yellow Claw* (1915), *Moon of Madness* (1927) and *Re-enter Fu Manchu* (1957).

ROIDIS, Emmanuel
(1836–1904)

Greek short-story writer and critic, born in Syros but brought up in Genoa. He was educated abroad also, before returning to Athens in 1863. He achieved scandalous success when his first book *He Papissa Ioanna* (1866, Eng trans *Pope Joan*, 1888, abridged versions 1900, 1954) was condemned by the church, and provoked rioting in Athens. His style of ironic rationalism found few champions, but the series of short stories he wrote about his childhood on Syros received a warm critical reception. His own career as a critic included the discovery of **Iannis Psycharis**, and *Ta Idola* (1893, 'The Idols'), a linguistic study firmly in favour of demotic Greek—but written in the formal *Katharevousa*.

ROJAS, Fernando de
(c.1465–1541)

Spanish novelist of Jewish descent, born in Puebla de Montalbán. He wrote most (Acts I–XXI) of one of the most influential dialogue-novels in all European literature: *La Celestina, La Tragi-comedia de Calisto y Melibea* (1502). This sardonic and mock-moral tale of how a young gentleman makes use of a bawd (Celestina) to seduce a woman of prestigious family presents many problems, textual and otherwise. In all probability the whole text is by Rojas, and in it he was obliquely referring to the enforced conversion of the Spanish Jews. It was first translated by J Mabbe in 1631; there is a version in Penguin Classics by J M Cohen (1964), with an introduction.
▷M R L Malkiel, *Two Spanish Masterpieces* (1961)

ROJAS, Manuel
(1896–1973)

Chilean novelist and short-story writer; he was born in Buenos Aires, but returned to Chile early in life. Probably the best Latin-American realist writer, his work has been described as social realism or picaresque realism. His predominant themes include the effects of the urban environment on the human spirit, the accidental connections between people, and his own life—much of his work is at least partly autobiographical. His major work is *Hijo de ladrón* (1951), an attack on life in the city and social determinism, employing and adapting techniques like interior monologue to describe cruel and happy turns of fate, friendship and family ties.
▷D Cortés, *La narrativa anarquista de Manuel Rojas* (1986)

ROJAS ZORILLA, Francisco
(1607–48)

Spanish playwright, born in Toledo. One of the best Golden Age dramatists, he is usually thought to belong to the school of **Calderón de la Barca**, with whom he collaborated, but certain of his themes were unusual for the time and peculiar to him. Chief among these was honour, often shown as tested when duty conflicts with emotion. For example, in *El Caín de Cataluña* ('Cain of Catalonia') a father has to choose between condemning his son or evading justice. Rojas's best-known drama is *Del Rey Abajo, Ninguno* ('None Lower than the King'), where the protagonist mistakes the thief for the king and cannot avenge his honour. Exact dates for his works are difficult to ascertain, but most were published between 1640 and 1645.

ROLAND HOLST, Adriaan
(1888–1976)

Dutch poet and editor, born in Amsterdam. His highly, sometimes even excessively, romantic poetry is the Dutch equivalent of that of **W B Yeats**, who greatly influenced him. He studied at Oxford, and became interested in Celtic mythology. His poetry seemed incongruous in its context, but he came to be universally respected, and in his old age won all the prizes his country could offer.

ROLAND HOLST-VAN DE SCHALK, Henriette
(1869–1952)

Dutch poet, whose progress was not unlike that of the Belgian **Charles Plisnier**, inasmuch as she progressed from communism to Christianity. She followed **Gorter**, the first influence on her fervid poetry, into communism, which she repudiated with the advent of Stalin. She was a leading feminist, and she wrote many useful biographies of people who interested her, among them **Leo Tolstoy**. But her rather careless although always burningly sincere poetry has not worn well.

ROLFE, Frederick William, styled Baron Corvo
(1860–1913)

English novelist and essayist, born in London. A convert to Roman Catholicism, his life was shattered by his rejection from the novitiate for the Roman priesthood at the Scots College in Rome; but it prompted his most famous work, *Hadrian VII* (1904), in which a comparable and obviously self-modelled 'spoiled priest' is unexpectedly chosen for the papacy, institutes various reforms and is ultimately martyred. He contributed to the *Yellow Book* in the 1890s with *Stories Toto Told Me* (afterwards republished in book form, 1895) and is also remembered for *Chronicles of the House of Borgia* and the posthumous *The Desire and Pursuit of the Whole*, published in 1934. Other novels are *Don Tarquino* (1905), and the posthumously published *Nicholas Crabbe* (1958) and *Don Renato* (1963).
▷A J A Symons, *In Quest of Corvo* (1934)

ROLLAND, Romain
(1866–1944)

French musicologist and author, winner of the Nobel Prize for literature, born in Clamecy, Nièvre. He studied in Paris and at the French School in Rome, and in 1895 gained his doctorate of letters with a thesis on early opera, *L'Histoire de l'opéra en Europe avant Lulli et Scarlatti* ('A History of Opera in Europe before Lulli and Scarlatti'). A number of dramatic works written at this time won comparatively little success. In 1910 he became Professor of the History of Music at the Sorbonne, and in the same year published *Beethoven*, the first of many biographical works including biographies of Michelangelo (1906), Handel (1910), **Tolstoy** (1911) and Gandhi (1924). His 10-volume novel cycle *Jean-Christophe*, the hero of which is a musician, was written between 1904 and

1912, and in 1915 he was awarded the Nobel Prize for literature. During World War I he aroused unpopularity by promulgating his pacifist and internationalist ideals in his writings, which were published in 1915 as *Au dessus de la mêlée* ('Above the Fray'). He lived in Switzerland until 1938, completing another novel cycle, *L'Âme enchantée* (1922–33, 'The Enchanted Spirit'), a series of plays upon the French Revolution, and a further study of Beethoven, as well as numerous pieces of music criticism. On his return to France he became a mouthpiece of the opposition to fascism and the Nazis, and his later works contain much political and social writing.
▷S Zweig, *Romain Rolland* (1929)

ROLLE OF HAMPOLE, Richard
(c.1290–1349)

English hermit, mystic and poet, born in Thornton in Yorkshire. He studied at Oxford, but at 19 became a hermit, first at Dalton and then at Hampole, near Doncaster. He wrote lyrics, meditations and religious works in Latin and English, and translated and expounded the Psalms in prose.
▷F Cooper, *Life of Richard Rolle* (1928)

ROLLENHAGEN, Georg
(1542–1609)

German dramatist and poet, born in Bernau. After some years as a schoolmaster, he became pastor at Magdeburg (1573). His *Froschmeuseler* (1595) is an adaptation of the pseudo-**Homer**ic *Batrachomyomachy*, the battle between frogs and the mice. This is a clumsy but telling and well-observed satire on the society of his time. His son Gabriel (1583–1619) was also a well-known writer of plays and an emblem book.

ROLLI, Paolo Antonio
(1687–1765)

Italian poet, editor and librettist (for Handel and Bononcini), born in Rome. In 1716 he moved to England, at the invitation of the Earl of Pembroke: there he acted as a vital link between his own and English culture. **Goethe** in particular admired his poetry, which was based on classical models such as **Virgil**. He became tutor to the children of the Prince of Wales, who later became George II. His most famous work is his monumental translation of **Milton**'s *Paradise Lost*.
▷G E Dorris, *Paolo Rolli and the Italian Circle in London 1714–1744* (1967)

ROLLS, Eric C
(1923–)

Australian poet and naturalist, born in Grenfell, New South Wales. His verse ranges from experiences of farming life in *Sheaf Tosser* (1967), through *The Green Mosaic* (1977), with recollections of tropical New Guinea, to *Miss Strawberry Verses* (1978), a collection for younger readers. His non-fiction also expresses his love of nature: *They All Ran Wild* (1969) examines the impact on Australia of the importation of the rabbit in the 19th century, and *A Million Wild Acres* (1981), a loving study of a small forest, was the Melbourne *Age* Book of the Year choice. Partly autobiographical works are *The River* (1974) and *Celebration of the Senses* (1984).

RÖLVAAG, Ole Edvart, originally Ole Pedersen
(1876–1931)

Norwegian-born American writer. Born in a small fishing community in northern Norway, Rölvaag took the name of a cove near his birthplace when he settled in America. An avid reader from childhood, the first book he read was *The Last of the Mohicans* in Norwegian, and the seeming promise of the New World led him to abandon the life of a fisherman at 20 and take up the offer of a ticket from his uncle in South Dakota. His journey and early experiences as an immigrant were described in *Amerika-Breve* (1912, 'Letters from America'). Unsuited to the harshness of life as a prairie farmer, however, Rölvaag enrolled in a local school to improve his English, went from there to university and eventually took up a teaching career at St Olaf College in Minnesota. He published six novels, all dealing with the Norwegian immigrant experience and published in Norwegian in the US. His masterwork was *Giants in the Earth*, a grimly realistic, tragic story of the personal and psychological costs of pioneer life. Published initially in Norwegian in two parts—*I De Dage* (1924, 'In Those Days') and *Riket Grundlaegges* (1925, 'Founding the Kingdom')—the two volumes were combined for the English translation in 1927, which brought Rölvaag to a greater audience, although his importance in the literature of the American West has yet to be fully recognized.

▷P Reigstad, *Rölvaag, his life and art* (1972)

ROMAINS, Jules, pseud of Louis Farigoule
(1885–1972)

French writer, born in Saint-Julien Chapteuil. After graduating in both science and literature at the École Normale Supérieure, he taught in various lycées. In 1908 his poems, *La Vie unanime* ('The Unanimous Life'), established his name and, along with his *Manuel de déification* (1910, 'A Treatise on Deification'), the Unanimist school. He remained prominent in French literature, and from 1936 to 1941 was President of the International PEN Club. His works include the books of poems *Odes et prières* (1913, 'Odes and Prayers'), *Chants des dix années 1914–1924* (1928, 'Songs of the Ten Years 1914–24') and *L'Homme blanc* (1937, 'The White Man'), the dramas *L'Armée dans la ville* (1911, 'The Army in the Town') and *Knock, ou le triomphe de la médecine* (1923, Eng trans *Doctor Knock*, 1925), his most successful play, the novels *Mort de quelqu'un* (1910, Eng trans *The Death of a Nobody*, 1914) and *Les Copains* (1913, 'The Friends'), and the great cycle *Les Hommes de bonne volonté* in 27 volumes (1932–46, partial Eng trans in 18 vols as *Men of Good Will*, 1933–40), covering the early 20th-century era of French life. He published his autobiographical *Souvenirs et confidences d'un écrivain* ('Memories and Confidences of a Writer') in 1958.

▷M Berry, *Jules Romains* (1960, in French)

ROMERO, José Rubén
(1890–1952)

Mexican novelist, born in Contija de la Paz, who wrote one of Mexico's true picaresque novels of modern times, *La vida inútil de Pito Pérez* (1938, Eng trans *The Futile Life of Pito Pérez*, 1967), a neglected masterpiece, and the key to 'the philosophical complexities' of its author's country. He joined the *Maderistas* in 1911, and had to flee the country in 1914. He was Mexico's ambassador to Cuba from 1939 until 1945, when he retired. Sketches are collected and translated in *Notes of a Villager* (1988).

RONSARD, Pierre de
(1524–85)

French poet, born in the Château de la Possonnière in Vendôme. He served the dauphin and the Duc d'Orléans as a page, and accompanied James V with his bride, Mary of Lorraine (Guise), to Scotland, where he stayed three years. Becoming partially deaf, he abandoned arms for letters, and studied under the great humanist Jean Daurat, at first with his future fellow member of the Pléiade, Jean Antoine de Baïf, at the house of his father the scholar and diplomat Lazare de Baïf, and later at the Collège de Coqueret, where du Bellay and **Rémy Belleau** joined them. His seven years of study resulted first in the *Odes* (1550), which excited violent opposition from the older national school. In 1552 appeared his *Amours* ('Love Poems'), a collection of **Petrarch**an sonnets, followed by his *Bocage* (1554, 'Grove'), his *Hymnes* (1555), the conclusion of his *Amours* (1556), and the first collected edition of his poetry (1560). He subsequently wrote two bitter reflections on the political and economic state of the country, *Discours des misères de ce temps* (1560–9, 'Discourse on the Miseries of Our Times') and *Remonstrance au peuple de France* (1563, 'Address to the People of France'), and in 1572, following the massacre of St Bartholomew, *La Franciade* ('The Hymn of France'), an unfinished epic. Charles IX, like his predecessors, heaped favours on the poet, who, despite recurrent illness, spent his later years in comfort at the abbey of Croix-Val in Vendôme. The most important poet of 16th-century France, Ronsard was the chief exemplar of the doctrines of the Pléiade, which aimed at raising the status of French as a literary language and ousting the formal classicism inherited from the middle ages. Despite the great success of Ronsard's poems in his lifetime, the classicists regained the upper hand after his death, and his fame suffered an eclipse until the 19th century, when the Romantic movement brought recognition of his true worth.

▷G Cohen, *Ronsard, sa vie et son oeuvre* (1924)

ROS, Uilleam *see* ROSS, William

ROSCOE, William
(1753–1831)

English historian, born in Liverpool. In 1769 he was articled to an attorney, and began to practise in 1774. In 1777 he published a poem, *Mount Pleasant*, and in 1787 *The Wrongs of Africa*, a protest against the slave trade. But it was his *Life of Lorenzo de' Medici* (1796) that established his literary reputation. His second great book, *Life of Leo X* (1805), like the former, was translated into German, French and Italian. He had retired from business in 1796, but in 1799 became partner in a Liverpool bank, which involved him in pecuniary embarrassment (1816–20). He also wrote poems, of which the best known is the children's classic, *The Butterfly's Ball and the Grasshopper's feast* (1807); he wrote an edition of **Pope**, and a monograph on Monandrian plants.

▷Sir C S Jones, *The Life of William Roscoe* (1931)

ROSEGGER, Peter, known until 1894 as P K (Petri Kettenfeier)
(1843–1918)

Austrian poet and novelist, born of peasant parents near Krieglach, Styria. In 1870 he published *Zither und Hackbrett* ('Zither and Chopping-board'), a volume of poems in his native dialect, and followed this with autobiographical works such as *Waldheimat* (1897, 'Home in the Woods') and *Mein Him-* *melreich* (1901, 'My Heavenly Kingdom'), and novels, including *Die Schriften des Waldschulmeisters* (1875, 'Writings of a Woodland Schoolmaster'), *Der Gottsucher* (1883, 'The Searcher After God') and *Jakob der Letzte* (1888, 'Jacob the Last'), vividly portraying his native district and its people.

ROSEN, Michael Wayne
(1946–)

English writer and performer, chiefly for children, born in Harrow, London. His ebullient delivery and accessible verse have made him a favourite with children in both performance and print, as well as leading to his frequent appearance on radio shows about books, such as *Treasure Islands* on BBC Radio 4. His humorous, quirky collections include *Quick Let's Get Out of Here* (1983), *Don't Put Mustard in the Custard* (1984) and *We're Going On A Bear Hunt* (1989). He has received several prizes for his poetry, including the Signal Poetry Award (1982) and the Smarties Award (1989).

ROSENBERG, Isaac
(1890–1918)

English poet and artist, born in Bristol, the son of Jewish émigrés from Russia. Educated at council schools in the east end of London, he was apprenticed as an engraver before studying art at Slade School. He kept poor health and went to South Africa in 1914 but returned to England the following year, enlisted in the army and was killed in action in France. He published his first collection, *Night and Day*, in 1912, and *Youth* in 1915 before the posthumous appearance of *Poems* in 1922, a selection edited by **Gordon Bottomley** and introduced by **Laurence Binyon**. Though revered by the cognoscenti, his reputation languished until the appearance in 1937 of his *Collected Works* (newly edited in 1979). His comparatively poor upbringing, highly charged vocabulary and bluntly realistic attitude to the war mark him out from other war poets.

ROSENFELD, Isaac
(1918–56)

American critic and writer of fiction. Rosenfeld was a contemporary, and at one time rival, of **Saul Bellow**. His novel *Passage From Home* (1946), set in his native Chicago, was one of the first Jewish-American novels about adolescence. It promised much, but Rosenfeld was undisciplined and dissipated his talents in literary journalism, collected in *An Age of Enormity* (1962). Having called his generation 'moral undergroundlings', he died of a heart attack, aged 38, while living in squalor in a Chicago basement.

ROSENFELD, Morris
(1862–1923)
American poet, born in Poland and heavily influenced by an Orthodox Jewish upbringing. He was sent to London when he was 20 years old to learn tailoring and four years later emigrated to the USA, where he worked in the New York ghetto. His poems, which were printed in Yiddish newspapers, gave voice to the tribulations of his fellow sweatshop workers. *Songs from the Ghetto* (1898), a translated collection, was followed 10 years later by the three-volume *Works of Morris Rosenfeld*.

ROSENTHAL, Jack Morris
(1931–)
English dramatist, born in Manchester. Educated at Sheffield University, he joined the promotions department of Granada television in 1956 and made his professional writing debut with over 150 episodes of *Coronation Street* (1961–9). A contributor to the influential satirical programme *That Was The Week That Was* (1963), he created the series *The Lovers!* (1970). A prolific writer of individual plays dramatizing real-life stories, wartime nostalgia and Jewish domestic issues, his warmly humorous television work includes *The Evacuees* (1975), *Barmitzvah Boy* (1976), *Spend, Spend, Spend* (1977), *And A Nightingale Sang* (1989) and *London's Burning* (1986), which spawned the long-running series. His film scripts include *Lucky Star* (1980) and *Yentl* (1983) in collaboration with Barbra Streisand, whilst stage work includes *Smash!* (1981) and *Our Gracie* (1983). He is married to the actress Maureen Lipman.

ROSHWALD, Mordecai Marcelli
(1921–)
American author, born in Drohobycz, Poland, and educated at the Hebrew University of Jerusalem. Roshwald's first book, *The Education of Man* (1954), was published in Hebrew. Outside of academia—Roshwald worked for many years at the University of Minnesota—he is best known as the author of the futuristic novel *Level Seven* (1959), set in an underground bunker during a nuclear showdown.

ROSNY
joint pseud of the brothers
Boëx, Joseph Henri
(1856–1940)
Boëx, Séraphin Justin François
(1859–1948)
French novelists, born in Brussels. Their vast output of social novels, naturalistic in character, includes *L'Immolation* (1887, 'The Sac-
rifice') and *L'Impérieuse Bonté* (1905, 'Pressing Kindness'), signed jointly, and after 1908, when they separated, the older Rosny's *L'Appel au bonheur* (1919, 'The Appeal to Happiness') and *La Vie amoureuse de Balzac* (1930, 'Balzac's Love Life'), and *La Courtisane passionée* (1925, 'The Passionate Prostitute') and *La Pantine* (1929, 'The Puppet') by the younger Rosny.
▷M C Poinsou, *Joseph Henri Böex* (1907)

ROSS, William, also known as **ROS, Uilleam**
(1762–90)
Gaelic poet, born in Broadford, Skye and educated at Forres, Morayshire. In his youth he became proficient in the Gaelic dialects of the Western Highlands and in playing a number of different instruments. He was soon acknowledged for his great range of pastoral and descriptive verse, which also showed considerable spirit and humour. After only a few years' employment as parish schoolmaster of Gairloch, however, he died, probably of tuberculosis, but possibly of unrequited love for a woman called Marion Ross, who is described in his *Praise of the Highland Maid*. Two volumes of his work were posthumously published: *Orain Ghae'lach* (1830) and *An dara clobhualadh* (1834).

ROSSETTI, Christina Georgina
(1830–94)
English poet, born in London, daughter of **Gabriele Rossetti** and sister of **Dante Gabriel Rossetti**. Educated at home, she was to have been a governess but she retired through ill-health which may originally have been feigned or psychosomatic. She was precocious poetically; her grandfather printed a pamphlet by her before she was in her teens. She was engaged to James Collinson, the painter, but this was broken off when he returned to the Catholic faith, Christina being a devout High Anglican. Her first lyrics, including 'An End' and 'Dream Lane', were published in the first issue of *The Germ* (1850) under the pseudonym Ellen Alleyne. *Goblin Market*, her first and best-known collection, was published in 1862, and in 1866 came *The Prince's Progress. Sing Song: A Nursery Rhyme Book*, illustrated by Arthur Hughes, appeared in 1872. By the 1880s recurrent bouts of illness had made her an invalid, but she still continued to write, later works including *A Pageant and Other Poems* (1881), *Time Flies: A Reading Diary* (1895), and *The Face of the Deep: A Devotional Commentary on the Apocalypse* (1892). Technically a virtuoso, she ranged far emotionally and imaginatively.

▷E W Thomas, *Christina Georgina Rossetti* (1931)

ROSSETTI, Dante Gabriel, in full Gabriel Charles Dante Rossetti
(1828–82)

English poet, painter and translator, son of **Gabriele Rossetti** and brother of **Christina** and William Rossetti, born in London. His father was Gabriele Pasquale Giuseppe Rossetti, a Neapolitan political refugee; his mother was Frances Mary Lavinia Polidori Rossetti, daughter of Gaetano Polidori and sister of Lord **Byron**'s physician, Dr John Polidori. The household was artistic and more Italian than English. He was educated at King's College School and attended Cary's Art Academy, having shown early his inclination towards poetry and art. There was a short spell at the Antique School of the Royal Academy before he persuaded Ford Madox Brown to tutor him, but this was short-lived. With Holman Hunt and Millais he formed the Pre-Raphaelite Brotherhood. Throughout the 1840s his poetry and painting prospered, and he completed on canvas 'The Girlhood of Mary Virgin', 'How They Met Themselves' and 'Ecce Ancilla Domini', symbolic, historical, overpowering. Like Christina, several of his poems—'The Blessed Damozel' and 'My Sister's Sleep'—had appeared in *The Germ* in 1850, the year he met Elizabeth Siddal (or Siddall), whom he married in 1860 after a fraught and prolonged courtship. Already an invalid, she died in 1862 from a surfeit of laudanum. He met **John Ruskin** in 1854 and two years later **William Morris**, whom he manifestly influenced. His wife's death, however, affected him deeply and his work took on the taint of morbidity. (He exhumed her body to retrieve manuscripts left by her side.) *The Early Italian Poets* was published in 1861, translations from 60 poets such as **Dante** and **Guido Cavalcanti**. *Poems* appeared in 1870, drawing on those he had interred with his wife, but though he replied robustly to **Robert Buchanan**'s attack on him in 'The Fleshly School of Poetry' with 'The Stealthy School of Criticism', he fell into a depression and attempted suicide in 1872. Nevertheless, *Ballads and Sonnets* with the sonnet sequence 'The House of Life' and 'The King's Tragedy' appeared in 1881. At odds with Victorian morality, his work is lush, erotic and medieval, romantic in spirit, and of abiding interest and fascination.
▷C Davies, *Dante Gabriel Rossetti* (1925)

ROSSETTI, Gabriele
(1783–1854)

Italian poet and writer, father of **Christina Rossetti**, **Dante Gabriel Rossetti** and the critic William Michael Rossetti, and sometime curator of ancient bronzes in the Museum of Bronzes at Naples. He was a member of the provisional government set up by Murat in Rome (1813). After the restoration of Ferdinand I to Naples, he joined the Carbonari secret society and greeted the constitution demanded by the patriots in 1820 in a famous ode. On the overthrow of the constitution he went to London (1824), where he became Professor of Italian at the new University of London. Besides writing poetry he was a close student of **Dante**, whose *Inferno* he maintained was chiefly political and anti-papal.
▷R D Williams, *The Rossetti Family* (1932)

ROSSNER, Judith Perelman
(1935–)

American novelist, born and educated in New York City. Her first book, *To the Precipice* (1966), established her interest in women who are no longer willing or able to accept the overdetermining pressures of society, but who are not allowed simply to choose their destinies. This was handled with heavier irony in *Nine Months in the Life of an Old Maid* (1969) and in the rather better *Any Minute I Can Split* (1972), but had its definitive statement in *Looking for Mr Goodbar* (1975), an unforgiving and ruthless exploration of female sexuality and sexual stereotyping; it was mangled by Hollywood, its psychological and psycho-social insights reduced to prurient and voyeuristic sentimentalism. Later works have included *Attachments* (1977) and *August* (1983).

ROSSO, Renzo
(1926–)

Italian novelist, born in Trieste, and originally a student of philosophy at its university. He then studied the violin. His chief work is the novel *La dura spina* (1963, Eng trans *The Hard Thorn*, 1966), a subtle novel about a pianist whose powers of interpretation are becoming eroded by his unintentionally cruel womanizing.

ROSTAND, Edmond
(1868–1918)

French poet and dramatist, born in Marseilles. He published *Les Musardises* ('Dawdlings'), a volume of verse, in 1890 but rose to fame with *Cyrano de Bergerac* (1897, Eng trans 1898; also trans by **Anthony Burgess** for the film by Jean Paul Rappeneau, 1992), *L'Aiglon* (1900, Eng trans 1900), *Chantecler* (1910, Eng trans 1910), and other plays in verse which eschewed the prevailing moods of Naturalism and Expressionism in favour of a lighter, more vivacious popular style.
▷R Gérard, *Edmond Rostand* (1935)

ROSTEN, Leo Calvin
(1908–)

American anthologist, novelist and social scientist, born in Łodz, Poland. *The Education of H*y*m*a*n K*a*p*l*a*n* (1937), a comic tale set in a night school for adult immigrants in the United States, first established his reputation as a gentle humorist. His best-known book is probably *The Joys of Yiddish* (1968); following its success, he has written a number of popular anthologies of humour, many of them dealing largely with Jewish wit. These include *O Kaplan!, My Kaplan* (1976). Some of his works were originally published under the pseudonym Leonard Q Ross; using the same name minus the Q he has also written stage plays.

ROTH, Henry
(1906–)

American novelist. He was born in Tysmenica in the Austro–Hungarian Empire, arriving in the USA as a baby. His childhood is fictionalized in *Call It Sleep* (1934), one of the classics of 20th-century American literature. It dramatizes David Schearl's awakening consciousness against the background of New York City. Though 'authentic', it is by no means a sociological documentary, and is marked by a hallucinatory inwardness which is influenced by **Joyce**. During the Depression Roth worked for the New Deal Works Progress Administration and as a teacher, later making his living as a mental hospital assistant, duck farmer and machine toolist. *Shifting Landscape*, a collection of occasional pieces, was published in 1987. He took many years to complete his long-projected second novel, the first volume of which, *Mercy Of A Rude Stream*, appeared in 1994.
▷ *Nature's First Green* (1979)

ROTH, Joseph
(1894–1939)

Austrian novelist, short-story writer and critic, brought up on the eastern frontiers of the Austro–Hungarian Empire. His father was Austrian, his mother a Russian Jew. He had a miserable life. His father left his mother before he was born, the war disrupted his education, his wife went mad, and he survived by doing menial jobs and journalism until the 1930s when, exiled in Paris, he became an alcoholic and died destitute. A prolific writer, his major themes were not dissimilar to those of **Robert Musil**. His concern for those brought up in the Austro–Hungarian Empire, however, was linked with that of the Jewish diaspora. Narratively conventional, he was a versatile and readable writer, still underrated

though more of his work has been translated in recent years. Key works are *Hiob: Roman eines einfachen Mannes* (1930, Eng trans *Job: The Story of a Simple Man*, 1931), *Radetzkymarsch* (1932, Eng trans *The Radetzky March*, 1934), *Beichte eines Mörders* (1936, Eng trans *Confessions of a Murderer*, 1938), *Hotel Savoy* (1924), *Tarabas* (1934, Eng trans 1935) and *Die Kapuzinergruft* (1938, 'Grave of the Capucins').
▷ *Juden auf der Wanderschaft* (1926, 'Wandering Jews')

ROTH, Philip Milton
(1933–)

American novelist, born in Newark, New Jersey. He attended Bucknell University as an undergraduate and received a master's degree from Chicago University where he taught (1956–8). His upbringing was Jewish, conventional and lower middle-class; he did not begin to fight the 'taboos that had filtered down to me' until he was in his late teens. An uncompromising, tough-minded writer, his portraits of Jews adept at scheming and compromise have frequently irritated rabbis and Jewish organizations. Daring to talk about abortion, masturbation and other sexual matters has led him into conflict with conservatives who have sought to restrict access to his books. His first book was *Goodbye Columbus* (1959), a collection of short stories, each obsessed with confrontations between Jews of radically different persuasions and temperaments. Two accomplished novels succeeded these—*Letting Go* (1962) and *When She Was Good* (1967) —before publication of his 'masturbation' masterpiece, *Portnoy's Complaint* (1969), made him notorious. The success of the monotone confession of Alexander Portnoy to his psychiatrist lies in the fascination of the narrator's 'voice'. Roth's prolific career has taken many turns; much more than a one-joke writer, he is constantly exploring the relationship 'between the written and the unwritten world', a distinction he finds more useful than that between imagination and reality, or art and life. Nathaniel Zuckerman, a writer, is the central presence in the trilogy of novels—*The Ghost Writer* (1979), *Zuckerman Unbound* (1981) and *The Anatomy Lesson* (1983)—and its epilogue, *The Prague Orgy* (1985), collected in *Zuckerman Bound* (1985). *The Counterlife* appeared in 1987 and the autobiographical *Patrimony* (which bore the teasing subtitle 'A True Story') in 1991. In 1993 he published the novel *Operation Shylock*. He is married to the actress Claire Bloom.
▷ *The Facts: A Novelist's Autobiography* (1988)

ROTROU, Jean de
(1609–50)

French playwright, born in Dreux. He went to Paris, qualified as a lawyer, and turned to writing plays, as well as becoming one of the five poets who worked into dramatic form the ideas of Richelieu. His first pieces were in the Spanish romantic style. Next followed a classical period, culminating in three masterpieces, *Saint-Genest* (1646), a tragedy of Christian martyrdom, *Don Bernard de Cabrère* (1648) and *Venceslas* (1647). He died of the plague. Thirty-five of his plays are still extant.

▷H Chandon, *La vie de Rotrou* (1884)

ROUGET DE LISLE, Claude Joseph
(1760–1836)

French soldier, born in Lons-le-Saunier. He wrote and composed the French national anthem *La Marseillaise* (originally *Chant de guerre pour l'armée du Rhin*, 'War Song for the Army on the Rhine') when stationed in 1792 as captain of engineers at Strasbourg. Wounded at Quiberon (1795), he left the army, and published in 1796 a volume of *Essais en vers et en prose* ('Essays in Prose and Verse'). The *Marseillaise* was made known in Paris by troops from Marseilles.

▷M Henry-Rosier, *Rouget de Lisle* (1937)

ROUMAIN, Jacques
(1907–44)

The leading figure in Haitian literature. Of an elite mulatto family, he was a poet, diplomat, essayist, editor and politician (he founded the Haitian Communist Party in 1934). His magazine *Revue Indigène* educated Haitian intellectuals. His best novel is his last: *Gouvenours de la rosée* (1944, Eng trans *Masters of the Dew*, 1947).

ROUMANILLE, Joseph
(1818–91)

French writer, born in Saint-Rémy, Bouches-du-Rhône. He taught at Avignon, his pupils including **Frédéric Mistral**. In 1847 he published *Li Margarideto*, a book of his own poems, in 1852 a volume of Provençal poems, and later many volumes of verse and prose in Provençal dialect. With Mistral and others he founded the 'Soci dou Félibrige' for the revival of Provençal literature.

▷E Ripert, *Joseph Roumainille* (1948)

ROUSSEAU, Jean Baptiste
(1671–1741)

French poet, born in Paris, the son of a shoemaker. He wrote for the theatre, and composed lampoons on the literary frequenters of the Café Laurent which started feuds leading to recriminations, lawsuits and a sentence of banishment (1712). Thereafter he lived abroad, in Switzerland, Vienna (with Prince Eugene) and Brussels. His sacred odes and *cantates* are splendidly elaborate, frigid and artificial; his epigrams are bright, vigorous and unerring in their aim.

ROUSSEAU, Jean Jacques
(1712–78)

French political philosopher, educationist and author, born in Geneva. His mother died at his birth, and he had little early family life and no formal education. In 1728 he ran away to Italy and Savoy, where he lived with Baronne Louise de Warens (1700–62) and was baptized a Catholic, and after an itinerant existence for a few years eventually became her lover and general factotum (1733–41). In 1741 he was supplanted, and moved to Paris where he began to thrive, making a living from secretarial work and music copying. There he began a lifelong association with an illiterate maidservant at his inn, Thérèse le Vasseur; by her he had five children, all of whom he consigned to foundling hospitals, despite his later proclamations about the innocence of childhood. He composed an operetta, *Les Muses Galantes* (1745, 'The Gallant Muses'), which led to correspondence with **Voltaire** and acquaintance with **Diderot**, and through that came to contribute articles on music and political economy to the *Encyclopédie*. In 1750 he made his name with a prize essay, *Discours sur les sciences et les arts* (Eng trans *A Discourse on the Arts and Sciences*, 1752), which argued that civilization had corrupted our natural goodness and decreased our freedom; and in 1752 he triumphed with a second operetta, *Le Devin du village* (Eng trans *The Cunning Man*, 1766). He was now a celebrity, and in 1754 wrote *Discours sur l'origine et les fondements de l'inégalité parmi les hommes* ('Discourse on the Origin and Causes of Inequality Among Men'), in which he attacked private property and argued that man's perfect nature was corrupted by society. He travelled restlessly first to Geneva, where he was much influenced by Calvinism, back to Paris and then to Luxembourg in 1757, and in 1758 published his *Lettre à d'Alembert sur les spectacles* (Eng trans *A Letter to M. d'Alembert*, 1759), in which he argued against the establishment of a theatre in Geneva on Puritan grounds. In 1762 he published his masterpiece, *Du contrat social* (Eng trans *A Treatise on the Social Compact*, 1764), which begins with the ringing paradox, 'Man is born free; and everywhere he is in chains'. It postulated a social contract in which every individual surrenders his rights totally to the collective 'general will', which is the sole source of legitimate sovereignty and by definition represents the common good; the aberrant can then, in the sinister phrase, 'be forced to be free' in their own interests. His text, with its slogan 'Liberté, Égalité, Fraternité' ('Liberty, Equality, Fraternity'), became the bible of the French Revolution and of progressive movements in general, though clearly the main thesis was vulnerable to totalitarian perversions. Also in 1762 he published in novel form *Émile, ou de l'éducation* (Eng trans *Emilius and Sophia; or, A New System of Education*, 1762–3), a simple romance of a child reared apart from other children as an experiment; it greatly influenced educationists like Pestalozzi and Froebel, but so outraged the political and religious establishment that he had to flee to Switzerland. He moved to England in 1766 at the invitation of David Hume and went to live at Wootton Hall near Ashbourne in Derbyshire (1766–7), where he began writing his *Les Confessions* (Eng trans *Confessions*, 1783–91), a remarkably frank if somewhat narcissistic volume of self-revelations. He became seriously unstable at about this time, quarrelled with his English friends (particularly Hume), and fled back to France in 1767 with a full-blown persecution complex. In Paris from 1770 to 1778 he completed *Les Confessions* (published 1782–9), wrote a justification of his past actions (*Rousseau, juge de Jean Jacques*, 1780, 'Rousseau, Judge of Jean-Jacques') and *Rêveries du promeneur solitaire* (1782, Eng trans *The Reveries of a Solitary*, 1927), and eked out a living as a music copyist again. He declined further, became seriously insane, and died in Ermenonville. In 1794 his remains were placed alongside Voltaire's in the Panthéon in Paris. By the time of his death he had become very much a spokesman for Romanticism in Britain and Europe.

ROUSSEL, Raymond
(1887–1933)

French fabulist. He was born in Paris to a stockbroker father and an eccentrically artistic mother. He dabbled in verse when very young and wrote his first novel, *La Doublure*, at the precocious age of 10. In 1910 he published his most important work, *Impressions d'Afrique* (Eng trans *Impressions of Africa*, 1965), a surreal fantasy about parts of the continent he had never actually visited. The book is full of non-sequiturs, quasi-documentary asides and sheer invention. It made a considerable impact on such American writers as **John Ashbery** and **Harry Mathews**, who named their experimental journal after a later book of Roussel's; *Locus Solus* was published in part in 1918, but only appeared in its entirety in 1963. Roussel was a homosexual whose heavy addiction to barbiturates is reflected in the astonishing pace and arrhythmia of his prose. In 1933, following a long build-up in which he wrote testaments and letters of farewell, he committed suicide.
▷ M Foucault, *Death and the Labyrinth: The World of Raymond Roussel* (1966)

ROUSSIN, André
(1911–)

French boulevard playwright and theatre director, born in Marseilles. He co-founded the Rideau Gris Company in his native city. He won popular acclaim for his clever if ultimately frivolous farces, such as *La Petite Hutte* (1947). This, his most famous, was adapted by **Nancy Mitford**: as *The Little Hut* (1948) it delighted London and New York audiences.

ROWBOTHAM, David
(1924–)

Australian poet, born in Toowoomba, Queensland, who worked for the Brisbane *Courier-Mail* as literary and drama critic and later as literary editor before publishing *Ploughman and Poet* (1954). This was followed by a number of books including *All the Room* in 1964, in which year he was awarded the Grace Leven Prize. Three more books preceded *Selected Poems* (1975) and *Maydays* (1980). His rather spare style has gained him a reputation abroad in literary circles.

ROWE, Elizabeth, née Singer
(1674–1737)

English poet, born in Ilchester, Somerset, daughter of a dissenting minister. She was educated at boarding school, began writing early and had poems published in magazines from 1691. Her friends included the Countess of Winchilsea, **Matthew Prior**, and Isaac Watts. In 1710 she married a scholar, Thomas Rowe, and moved to London, but after his early death in 1715 she retired in grief to Somerset where she occupied herself with charitable works and writing. Her prose epistles on moral and religious themes, *Friendship in Death* and *Letters Moral and Entertaining* (1728–32), cast in the form of sentimental romance, were admired by **Dr Johnson** and **Samuel Richardson** and remained popular until the 19th century in England and America. Her poems also were highly esteemed for their piety, tender feeling, purity of sentiment and lyrical grace.
▷ *The Poetry of Elizabeth Singer Rowe*, ed with introduction by M F Marshall (1987); H F Stecher, *Elizabeth Singer Rowe, the Poetess of Frome* (1973)

ROWE, Nicholas
(1674–1718)

English poet and dramatist, born in Little Barford, Bedfordshire. He was educated at

Westminster, was called to the Bar, but from 1692 devoted himself to literature. Between 1700 and 1715 he produced eight plays of which three were popular—*Tamerlane* (1702), *The Fair Penitent* (1703) and *The Tragedy of Jane Shore* (1714), followed by *The Tragedy of Lady Jane Grey* (1715). Lothario in *The Fair Penitent* was the prototype of Lovelace in **Samuel Richardson**'s *Clarissa* and the name is still the synonym for a fashionable rake. Rowe translated **Lucan**'s *Pharsalia* and his edition of **Shakespeare** (1709–10) at least contributed to the popularity of his author. Rowe was under-secretary to the Duke of Queensberry from 1709 to 1711; in 1715 he was appointed poet laureate and a surveyor of customs to the port of London; the Prince of Wales made him clerk of his council, and Lord Chancellor Parker appointed him clerk of presentations in chancery.

▷Dr Johnson, *Lives of the Most Eminent English Poets* (10 vols, 1779–81)

ROWLEY, William
(c.1585–c.1642)

English actor and playwright. Little is known about him, except that he collaborated with **Thomas Dekker**, **Thomas Middleton**, **John Heywood**, **John Webster**, **Philip Massinger** and **John Ford**. Four plays published with his name are extant: *A New Wonder, a Woman Never Vext* (1632); *All's Lost by Lust*, a tragedy (1633); *A Match at Midnight* (1633); and *A Shoemaker, a Gentleman* (1638).

▷C W Stock, *William Rowley* (1910)

ROWSON, Susanna Haswell
(c.1762–1824)

American dramatist, novelist, poet, essayist and actress. Born in Portsmouth, England, she moved to the USA as a child, returned to England in 1777, and went back to America in 1793. Considered by many to be America's first professional novelist, she published seven sometimes sensational novels, including *Charlotte Temple, A Tale of Truth* (1791 in the UK, 1794 in the USA), a seduction tale modelled upon **Richardson**'s *Clarissa*. It sold badly in Britain but became a huge bestseller in America. For the stage she wrote a series of social comedies, including *The Female Patriot* (1794) and *Americans in England* (1796). Keenly interested in education for women, she wrote several tracts and essays on the subject, and in 1797 left the Boston theatre where she had been acting in order to found a boarding school for girls.

▷P Barker, *Susanna Rowson* (1986)

ROY, Gabrielle
(1907–83)

French Canadian novelist, born in Manitoba, later resident in Quebec. Roy's first novel, *Bonheur d'occasion* (1945), translated as *The Tin Flute* (1947), was the first French–Canadian work to be awarded the Prix Femina. It was a realistic and compassionate novel about a slum family and a young woman's role in a society dominated by religion and the church. Subsequent novels drew on her prairie childhood and were marked by a strong and straightforward narrative style.

▷*La Détresse et l'enchantment* (1984), Eng trans *Enchantment and Sorrow* (1987); M Genuist, *La création romanesque chez Gabrielle Roy* (1966)

ROY, Jules
(1907–)

French air force officer (until 1953) and admirer of **Alfred de Vigny** and **Antoine de Saint-Exupéry**, who scored a popular success with his *La Vallé heureuse* (1946, 'The Happy Valley'), a semi-novel about his wartime air service. He began as a poet and essayist, and also wrote plays. His *Le Navigateur* (1954, Eng trans *The Navigator*, 1955) was a readable straight novel.

ROY, Namba, originally Nathan Roy Atkins
(1910–61)

Jamaican novelist. He was educated in Kingston but grew up among descendants of Maroons (escaped slaves) in Cockpit Country, where surviving African traditions of craftsmanship and oral narrative were formative influences. He joined the merchant navy in 1939, was invalided out in 1944, and settled in England with his English wife. He earned repute as a wood-carver and wrote two novels: *Black Albino* (1961), an imaginative re-creation of life in an 18th-century Maroon community, and *No Black Sparrows* (1989, posthumous), a realistic story about working-class struggles in 1930s Jamaica.

ROYDE-SMITH, Naomi
(c.1880–1964)

Welsh novelist, dramatist and biographer. In the early 1920s she held a literary salon with Rose Macauley, but never reached the latter's eminence. However, her many novels, although tending to the sentimental, were well constructed and well written. Her biography of the actress Sarah Siddons, *The Private Life of Mrs Siddons*, was published in 1933. She was married to the well-known **Shakespeare**an actor Ernest Milton.

ROZANOV, Vasili Vasilievich
(1856–1919)

Russian writer, thinker and critic, born in Vetluga, Kostroma. He became a teacher in

provincial schools. His literary studies include that of **Fyodor Dostoyevsky**'s *Grand Inquisitor*, which, published in 1894, first brought him into prominence. Though a Christian, in his prolific writings he criticized from a **Nietzsche**an standpoint the contemporary standards in morals, religion, education, and particularly the too-strict attitude towards sex, which was for him the very soul of man. Much of his work is highly introspective, and his literary reputation is firmly based on the two books of fragments and essays *Uyedinyonnoe* (1912, Eng trans *Solitaria*, 1927) and *Opavshie listya* (1913; 1915, Eng trans *Fallen Leaves*, 1929).
▷M G Kurdyumov, *Vasili Vasilievich Rozanov* (1929)

ROZDHESTVENTSKY, Robert
(1932–)

Russian poet, born in the Arday region. He writes on topical themes, always with **Mayakovsky** in mind as an exemplar, in a light and easily assimilable style. He has travelled a great deal, and this is reflected in his lively, if not particularly profound, work.

ROZOV, Victor
(1913–)

Russian playwright, born in Yaroslavl. He was at first an actor, but, wounded early in the fight against the Nazis, turned to drama. His most famous play was *Vechno zhivye* (1956, Eng trans *Alive Forever*, in *Contemporary Russian Drama*, ed F D Reeve, 1968), upon which the film *The Cranes Are Flying* (1957) was based. His plays are light in the best possible way, with skilful characterization.

RÓZEWICZ, Tadeusz
(1921–)

Polish poet (regarded as an 'anti-poet') and story writer, born in Radomsko, whose view of life, stemming from his traumatic war experiences in the resistance to the Nazis, resembles that of **Samuel Beckett**. He acquired a huge following when he published his first poems immediately after World War II. These reflected his disenchantment with the idea of the relevance of 'beautiful poetry' to life as it really is in the 20th century. Later he took to writing rather more conventional plays of the absurd, most of which were translated (eg *Gone Out*, 1969). His reputation became a little dented when he published works 'warped by party propaganda', and he was attacked by communists and Catholics alike; but he abandoned this stance after 1956, and remains important for his initial impact on the Polish literary scene with his first collection, *Niepokóv* (1945, 'Anxiety').

Later plays include *Biale malzeństwo* (1975, Eng trans *Mariage Blanc*, 1983) and *Teatr niekonsekwencji* (1979, 'The Inconstant Theatre').
▷H Vogler, *Rósewicz* [sic] (1976)

RUBENS, Bernice Ruth
(1928–)

Welsh novelist and playwright, born and educated in Wales. She trained as a teacher and was an English mistress at a boys' school in Birmingham before working for the United Nations as a documentary film-maker. Her first novel was *Set on Edge* (1960), followed by *Madame Sousatzka* (1962, subsequently filmed), *Mate in Three* (1965) and *The Elected Member* (1969, published in the USA as *Chosen People*), for which she was awarded the Booker Prize. These were more overtly Jewish in subject-matter than subsequent books, but they clearly marked out Rubens's interest in familial guilt and the psychic damage caused by withdrawn or compromised love. In later books Rubens showed an interest in marginal social and sexual types, the 'cold and chosen ones'. Later novels include *A Five Year Sentence* (1978) and *Mr Wakefield's Crusade* (1985); there is some sense that in the later eighties and early nineties she has, like **Graham Greene** and, arguably, **Iris Murdoch**, interspersed more serious novels with lighter 'entertainments'. However, *A Solitary Grief* (1991) found her at the top of her powers, being a work of genuine profundity.

RUCCELLAI, Giovanni
(1475–1525)

Italian poet, a nephew of Lorenzo de Medici. He lived in Rome and took orders. His works include the blank verse *Le Api* ('The Bees'), an instructive poem based on book four of **Virgil**'s *Georgics*. He also wrote early Italian tragedies, such as *Rosamunda* (1515) and *Oreste* (1525).
▷A Marpicati, *Saggi critica* (1934)

RÜCKERT, Friedrich
(1788–1866)

German poet and scholar, born in Schweinfurt. He studied law, philology and philosophy at Würzburg, and during the Napoleonic wars stirred up German patriotism with his *Deutsche Gedichte* (1814, 'German Poems'). After the wars he studied oriental languages, of which he became professor at Erlangen (1826–41) and Berlin (1841–8), and recast in German verse many famous books of countries of the orient. His original work includes the lyrical *Liebesfrühling* (1923, 'The Springtime of Love'), the reflective poems *Die Weisheit des Brahmanen* (1836–9, 'The Wisdom of the Brahmans'), and the personal *Kindertotenlieder* ('Songs of the Deaths of Children'), posthumously published in 1872 and set to music by Mahler in 1902.

▷H Prang, *Friedrich Rückert* (1963)

RUDD, Steele, properly **Arthur Hoey Davis** (1868–1935)

Australian humorous writer, born in Drayton, Darling Downs, Queensland. Davis, a clerk in the public service, started by writing articles on rowing under the name Steele Rudd. His famous creations Dad and Dave began life in the Sydney *Bulletin* in 1895, in a series of humorous articles on 'selection' life (on crown land allocated for tenant cultivation), which appeared in book form as *On Our Selection* in 1899, followed by *Our New Selection* (1903). The popularity of the series led to his dismissal from the public service and to his starting *Steele Rudd's Magazine* in 1904. The chronicles of the Rudd family were covered in 10 books and extended to the stage and to both silent and sound films, but the formula lost its attraction and developed into farce, losing its earlier relevance to pioneering life and to Davis's own family experiences.

RUDNICKI, Adolf (1912–90)

Polish novelist, story writer and essayist, often called the 'Jeremiah of the Warsaw ghetto'. His first novel, *Szcury* (1931, 'The Rats'), with its downtrodden 'little man' protagonist, was one of the best examples of Polish inter-war **Kafka**-influenced books. After World War II he emerged as Poland's leading chronicler of the plight of the Jews, deeply sarcastic and deliberately 'rough', yet compassionate beneath this surface. There are two selections of stories in translation: *Ascent to Heaven* (1951) and *The Dead and Living Sea* (1957).

RUDOLF VON EMS (c.1200–c.1254)

German poet and knight from Hohenems (Ems) near Bregenz in what is now Austria. His Middle High German poetry owes stylistic and formal debts to his acknowledged mentor **Gottfried von Strassburg**, though he later disavowed Gottfried in favour of a more 'worldly' style. He wrote prolifically, and on a huge range of subject-matter: Romance (*Der Gute Gerhard*), religious epic (*Josaphat und Barlaam*) and history (*Alexander*). His last, most ambitious project was a history of the world (*Weltchronik*). Though this only gets as far as the Hebrew kings, it is still some 30 000 lines long. Rudolf died in Italy, in the

service of the German King Konrad IV, defending Konrad's interests against the papacy.

RUEDA, Lope de (c.1510–1565)

Spanish dramatist, born in Seville. He became manager of a group of strolling players. A pioneer of Spanish drama, he wrote comedies in the Italian style, short humorous pastoral dialogues, known as *pasos*, a form developed by **Cervantes**, and 10 burlesques.

▷D V Otero, *Lope de Rueda* (1960)

RUFFINI, Giovanni Domenico (1807–81)

Italian writer, born in Genoa. In 1833 he joined Young Italy, and in 1836 had to flee to England. From 1875 he lived in Taggia in the Riviera. He wrote *Lorenzo Benoni: Passages in the Life of an Italian* (1853), *Dr Antonio* (1855), *Vincenzo* (1863), and other novels in English, and the libretto for Donizetti's *Don Pasquale* (1843).

▷A Linaker, *Giovanni Ruffini* (1882)

RUIBAL, (Argibay) José (1925–)

Spanish playwright and co-leader of the Underground Drama movement. He was born in Galicia, near Ponteverda, but lived in Latin America, mostly Uruguay and the Argentine, during his twenties and thirties. His early dramas were collected as *Los mendigos y seis peizas de caféteatro* (1969, title piece translated as *The Beggars*, 1969). The book was banned by the fascist government in Spain and was subsequently reissued under the more anodyne title *El mono piadoso* (1969). Ruibal's reputation established itself first in the USA, where he taught in the early 1970s at the University of New York, Albany, and the University of Minnesota, Minneapolis. His play *La máquina de pedir* (1970) was published in' the US as *The Begging Machine* in 1975 in a special issue of the journal *Modern International Drama*; in 1971, his most important play *El hombre y la mosca* (published in Spanish, 1977) was produced in upstate New York as *The Man and the Fly*. It is densely symbolic, drawing on **Góngora y Argote**, Dalian Surrealism, **Kafka** and the **Čapek** brothers, and represents the most devastating of the Underground Dramatists' attacks on the Franco regime.

▷G E Wellwarth, *Spanish Underground Drama* (1972)

RUIZ, Juan (?1283–?1350)

Spanish writer, Archpriest of Hita, of whose life nothing certain is recorded—even his name Juan Ruiz may be an invention; his *Libro de Buen Amor* ('Book of Good Love') is—along with *El Cid*—the most important long medieval Spanish poem. According to it, he was born at Alcalá de Henares, educated at Toledo, was a popular author of songs (some of which are in the book), and was archpriest of the village of Hita near Alcalá. But none of this may be true. The *Libro*, a masterwork by any standards, and a readable one, owes much to **Ovid**, to Goliardic poetry (poetry in Latin written by wandering scholars), to Latin secular drama and to the budding popular tradition as exemplified in its lyrics. Its subject is 'good love', as the title states—but it is an ironic and ambiguous work and no two scholars have ever agreed what exactly this 'good love' is; the author needed to cover his tracks, since he was producing a work in an esoteric tradition of very late courtly love (although this has been disputed). It incorporates the comic and morality tale, the sermon, the mock-autobiography and the fable. There is also much evidence of Islamic influence (perhaps absorbed from the author's alleged education in Toledo). **Chaucer** knew of it, and was influenced by it. The most scholarly edition of it was published in 1974.

▷M R L de Malkiel, *Two Spanish Masterpieces: the 'Book of Good Love' and 'The Celestina'* (1962)

RUIZ DE ALARCÓN Y MENDOZA, Juan
(1581–1639)

Spanish dramatist, born of a Spanish family in Mexico City. He studied at the University of Salamanca and probably practised law for a short time in Seville, where he took part in the literary life of the city. He returned to Mexico where he tried unsuccessfully to teach, then went back once more to Spain, where he tried to enter court life and was taunted by his contemporaries **Lope de Vega**, **Tirso de Molina** and **Quevedo** for his pretensions. He produced over 20 works, the main feature of which is their high moral tone: usually the good and just, if ordinary, man defeats the cheat and liar. His most famous play is probably *La Verdad Sospechosa* ('The Suspicious Truth'), and most of his plays deal with a moral point, eg *Las Paredes Oyen* ('Walls Have Ears') denounces gossip. Always held back by his physical defects (he was hunchbacked and knock-kneed), he envied Lope de Vega's popularity. His acute sense of inferiority (physical as well as worldly) may explain his recourse to moral rectitude. His work, however, is of high quality with sharply drawn characters and profound analysis of moral questions.

▷W Poesse, *Alarcón* (1972)

RUKEYSER, Muriel
(1913–80)

American poet, biographer, and translator, born and educated in New York. From the end of World War II until 1960 she was Vice-President of the House of Photography; technical and scientific ideas and processes play an important role in her verse. Her first collection, *Theory of Flight* (1935), reflects this most directly. In later volumes she develops a terse, imagistic style, stripped of rhetorical artifice and false emotion; collections include *Beast in View* (1944) and *Body of Waking* (1958). An important selection appeared as *Waterlily Fire* in 1962, and a full-scale *Collected Poems* two years before her death. Rukeyser also wrote biographies of Willard Gibbs (1942), Wendell Wilkie (1957) and Thomas Hariot (1971), reflecting her political interests. She also translated **Octavio Paz** and **Gunnar Ekelöf**.

▷L Kertesz, *The Poetic Vision of Muriel Rukeyser* (1980)

RULE, Jane Vincent
(1931–)

Canadian novelist and short-story writer, born in Plainfield, New Jersey, and educated in California and London. Her first novel was *Desert of the Heart* (1964), a bold study of two women tentatively approaching a lesbian relationship. Later books, such as *This is Not for You* (1970) and *Against the Season* (1971), explore similar territory, though in the latter book the range of characters is widened considerably. In *The Young in One Another's Arms* (1977) and *Contact with the World* (1980) homosexuality is used more broadly and metaphorically as an index of the estrangement felt by artists in an essentially philistine world. Typically, Rule uses a multiple narrative perspective. In 1975, she published the important study *Lesbian Images*, followed a decade later by *A Hot-Eyed Moderate* (1985), which includes essays on earlier lesbian writers such as **Marguerite Radclyffe Hall** and **Vita Sackville-West**. Her short stories are collected in *Themes for Diverse Instruments* (1975), *Outlander* (1981), a volume that also includes non-fiction, and *Inland Passage* (1985).

RULFO, Juan
(1918–)

Mexican novelist and short-story writer, born in Sayula, Jalisco. Much of his writing is based on his early life in the provinces, where his once-wealthy family were forced to flee following the loss of their fortune in the revolution. His early stories were collected in *El Llano en Llamas* (1953, *The Burning Plain*, 1956). The novel *Pedro Páramo* (1955, Eng trans 1959) is his most important work; taking as its central character an insecure and isolated man, it uses techniques such as interior monologues, along with the voices of dead peasants that linger on the air in their equally dead village, to construct a panorama of Mexican life in the early part of this century.

RUMENS, Carol
(1944–)

English poet, novelist and critic, born in London. A main theme of her poetry has been to try to give a response to the universal suffering of the 20th century: she has written, 'I believe that all the forces of the imagination should be employed to speak of their suffering'. But her love poems are also well regarded, and it has been said that she possesses 'an ability to touch the nerves underlying the domestic and the personal'. Her novel is *Plato Park* (1987), and she wrote a well-received study of **Jean Rhys** (1985).
▷ *Selected Poems* (1987)

RUNEBERG, Johan Ludvig
(1804–77)

Finnish poet, born in Jakobstaed (Pietarsaari). Writing in Swedish, his style was much influenced by his studies of Finnish folk-poetry, and he is considered the greatest poet of the national-Romantic school. He taught at Helsinki (1830–7), and at Porvoo (1837–57). He wrote several volumes of lyric verse, but his major works were *Elgskyttaråe* ('The Elk Shooters', 1832), a Norse epic, *Kung Fjalar* (1844, Eng trans *King Fjalar*, 1904), and his collection of patriotic ballads, *Fänrik Ståls Sägner* (1848–60, 'Tales of Ensign Stål', 2 vols), about Finland's war of independence (1808–9). It begins with 'Vårt land' ('Our land'), which has become the Finnish national anthem. He wrote epic poetry, notably *Hanna* (1836) and *Julquällen* (1841, 'Christmas Eve'), some plays, and edited for the Lutheran Church of Finland a Psalm Book which contained some 60 pieces of his own.
▷ T Wretö, *Johan Ludvig Runeberg* (1980)

RUNYON, (Alfred) Damon
(1884–1946)

American author and journalist, born in Manhattan, Kansas. After service in the Spanish–American war (1898) he turned to journalism and sports reporting for the *New York American* from 1911, and then feature writing with syndicated columns *Both Barrels* (1918–36) and *The Brighter Side*, from 1937. His first books were volumes of verse, *Tents*

of Trouble (1911) and *Rhymes of the Firing Line* (1912), but it was his short stories, written in a characteristic racy style, using the present tense, with liberal use of American slang and jargon, and depicting life in underworld New York and on Broadway, which won for him his great popularity. One collection, *Guys and Dolls* (1932), was adapted for a musical revue (1950). Other books include *Blue Plate Special* (1934) and *Take it Easy* (1939), and the play, with Howard Lindsay, *A Slight Case of Murder* (1935). From 1941 he worked as a film producer.
▷ T Clark, *The World of Runyon* (1978)

RUSHDIE, (Ahmed) Salman
(1947–)

British novelist, born in Bombay. His family moved to Pakistan when he was 17. He was educated at the Cathedral School, Bombay, then at Rugby in England where he experienced 'minor persecutions and racist attacks which felt major at the time'. He emigrated to Britain in 1965 and graduated from King's College, Cambridge in 1968. He worked as an actor and an advertising copywriter before becoming a full-time writer. Writing in the tradition of **James Joyce**, **Günter Grass** and the South American 'magic realists', he published his first novel, *Grimus*, in 1975, a muddled fable which sold poorly. With *Midnight's Children* (1981), a tour de force poised at the moment when India achieves independence, he emerged as a major international writer, inventive, imaginative and an intoxicating storyteller. It was awarded the Booker Prize. *Shame* (1983), a trenchant satire and a revisionist history of Pakistan and its leaders, was similarly conceived on a grand scale and was acclaimed another virtuoso performance. In *The Satanic Verses* (1988) he turned his attention towards Islam, in his familiar hyperbolic mode. The book was banned in India in 1988, and in 1989 Iran's Ayatollah Khomeini declared it blasphemous and issued a 'fatwa', or order of death, against him. Demonstrations followed and copies of the book were burned in Bradford along with effigies of the author, who was forced into hiding under police protection. Despite having to live in hiding since, he has published *Haroun and the Sea of Stories* (1990), a children's book, and a book of essays, *Imaginary Homelands* (1991). His public appearances are infrequent, and are usually part of his continuing attempt to have the fatwa revoked.

RUSKIN, John
(1819–1900)

English author and art critic, the son of a prosperous wine merchant in London.

Private tutoring took the place of schooling so that when he went up to Christ Church, Oxford in 1836, he was lacking in experience of the world. At Oxford he won the Newdigate Prize for poetry, and fancied himself as a poet until shortly after graduating, when he met Turner and discovered that his immediate task was to rescue the great painter from obscurity and neglect. *Modern Painters* (1843) was the result of this championship, which may well have embarrassed the painter. This work developed through another four volumes (1846–60) into a spiritual history of Europe with comments on every phase of morals and taste. For his task he had the advantage of frequent visits to the Continent with his parents. His marriage in 1848 to Euphemia (Effie) Chalmers Gray, who afterwards became Millais' wife, was legally annulled about the time he began his crusade on behalf of a new set of obscure or vilified painters, the pre-Raphaelite brotherhood, with which Millais was associated. *Modern Painters* and the offshoots of that great work, *The Seven Lamps of Architecture* (1848) and *The Stones of Venice* (1851–3), with its great chapter three 'On the nature of the Gothic', made him the critic of the day and something more than that, for the moral and social criticism in those works raised him into a moral guide or prophet, even though he had rejected the religious upbringing of his childhood. Following on the publication of the completed *Modern Painters* in 1860 he transferred his interest in art to the social question which had been implicit in much pre-Raphaelite painting. **Thomas Carlyle**'s attacks on utilitarianism no doubt helped, but Ruskin's resentment of the social injustice and squalor resulting from unbridled capitalism led him to a sort of Christian communism, for which he was denigrated. *Unto This Last* (1862), a protest against the law of supply and demand, was discontinued after four essays in *Cornhill Magazine* by **William Makepeace Thackeray** (1860). The contemptuous rejection of his social economics in this work, and in *Munera Pulveris* (1872), which was stopped after six essays in *Fraser's Magazine* (1862–3), was almost mortal to Ruskin. In *Sesame and Lilies* (1864–9), addressed to privileged young ladies, admonishing them on their duties, he likened his temper to that of Dean **Jonathan Swift**. In 1869 Oxford made him its first Slade Professor of Fine Art. He settled at Coniston, in the Lake District, and his incomparable vitality showed in the publication of various Slade lectures, but more memorably in *Fors Clavigera*, a series of papers addressed 'To the Workmen and Labourers of Great Britain' (1871–84), in which his social philosophy is fully discussed. Meanwhile he began to spend his fortune on such individual enterprises as

the St George's Guild, a non-profit-making shop in Paddington Street, in which members gave a tithe of their fortunes, the John Ruskin school at Camberwell, and the Whitelands College at Chelsea. His last regret was that he had not, like St Francis, denuded himself of all wealth. In 1878, in failing health, he resigned the Slade professorship, but he returned to it briefly in 1883–4. In his last work, his unfinished autobiography *Praeterita*, also published in numbers (1886–8), he reminisced quietly, all passion spent save for a final jab at the railways which disturbed rural beauty. His last years were spent at Brantwood, Coniston, his solitude being consoled by the affection of his cousin Mrs Arthur Severn and her family. His influence was profound and enduring.

▷T J Wise and J P Smart, *A Life of John Ruskin* (1893)

RUSS, Joanna
(1937–)

American science-fiction writer, born in New York City. She has been Professor of English at the University of Washington since 1977. She published her first story in 1959. Her early work was more conventional in genre terms, but the novel *Picnic on Paradise* (1968), later incorporated in *Alyx* (1976), introduced the female adventurer to centre stage, and revised genre expectations in the process. Her most important novel is *The Female Man* (1975), a complex feminist study which postulates four alternate lives for its female protagonist, before bringing them together on the utopian female planet Whileaway. Her stories are collected in several volumes, and she has also written fantasy and juvenile novels, and criticism.

RUSSELL, Arthur, properly Arthur Russell Goode
(1889–1971)

Australian writer of adventure stories for children, born in Wedderburn, Victoria. His first book, *Dream Island: an Australian Story* (1926), was followed by perhaps his best-known, *Ginger for Pluck* (1926). Other titles include *The Sky Pirates* (1947) and *Mason's Circus* (1947). Set against a realistic Australian background, often on the south coast of Victoria, his stories mix standard elements such as hidden caves, smuggling, treasure and last-minute rescue, often with the aid of a wireless. Radio was one of Goode's subjects; he was for some years technical editor of a weekly magazine for Melbourne listeners, and edited a collection *Twenty-Six Radio Stories* (1931) as well as *Twenty-Six South Sea Stories* (1936).

RUSSELL, Bertrand Arthur William, 3rd Earl Russell

(1872–1970)

Welsh philosopher, mathematician, prolific author, winner of the Nobel Prize for literature, and controversial public figure throughout his long and extraordinarily active life. He was born in Trelleck, Gwent; his parents died when he was very young and he was brought up by his grandmother, the widow of Lord John Russell, the Liberal Prime Minister and 1st Earl. He was educated privately and at Trinity College, Cambridge, where he took first-class honours in mathematics and philosophy. He graduated in 1894, was briefly British Embassy attaché in Paris, and became a fellow of Trinity in 1895, shortly after his marriage to Alys Pearsall Smith. A visit to Berlin led to his first book, *German Social Democracy* (1896), and he was thus launched on an amazingly long, wide-ranging and fertile intellectual career. His most original contributions to mathematical logic and philosophy are generally agreed to belong to the period before World War I, as expounded for example in *The Principles of Mathematics* (1903), which argues that the whole of mathematics could be derived from logic, and the monumental *Principia Mathematica* (with Alfred North Whitehead, 1910–13), which worked out this programme in a fully developed formal system and stands as a landmark in the history of logic and mathematics. Russell's famous 'theory of types' and his 'theory of descriptions' belong to this same period. Wittgenstein came to Cambridge to be his student from 1912 to 1913 and began the work that led to the *Tractatus Logico-philosophicus* (1922), for the English version of which Russell wrote an introduction. He wrote his first genuinely popular work in 1912, *The Problems of Philosophy*, which can still be read as a brilliantly stimulating introduction to the subject. Politics became his dominant concern during World War I and his active pacifism caused the loss of his Trinity fellowship in 1916 and his imprisonment in 1918, during the course of which he wrote his *Introduction to Mathematical Philosophy* (1919). He had now to make a living by lecturing and journalism, and became a celebrated controversialist. He visited the Soviet Union, where he met Lenin, Trotsky and **Gorky**, which sobered his early enthusiasm for communism and led to the critical *Theory and Practice of Bolshevism* (1919). He also taught in Peking from 1920 to 1921. In 1921 he married his second wife, Dora Black, and with her founded (in 1927) and ran a progressive school near Petersfield; he set out his educational views in *On Education* (1926) and *Education and the Social Order* (1932). In 1931 he succeeded his elder

brother, John, 2nd Earl Russell, as 3rd Earl Russell. His second divorce (1934) and marriage to Patricia Spence (1936) helped to make controversial his book *Marriage and Morals* (1932); and his lectureship at City College, New York, was terminated in 1940 after complaints that he was an 'enemy of religion and morality', though he later won substantial damages for wrongful dismissal. The rise of fascism led him to renounce his pacifism in 1939; his fellowship at Trinity was restored in 1944, and he returned to England after the war to be honoured with an OM, and to give the first BBC Reith Lectures in 1949. He was awarded the Nobel Prize for literature in 1950. He had meanwhile continued publishing important philosophical work, mainly on epistemology, in such books as *The Analysis of Mind* (1921), *An Enquiry into Meaning and Truth* (1940) and *Human Knowledge: Its Scope and Limits* (1948), and in 1945 published the bestselling *History of Western Philosophy*. He also published a stream of popular and provocative works on social, moral and religious questions, some of the more celebrated essays later being collected in *Why I am not a Christian* (1957). After 1949 he became increasingly preoccupied with the cause of nuclear disarmament, taking a leading role in CND and later the Committee of 100, and engaging in a remarkable correspondence with various world leaders. In 1961 he was again imprisoned, with his fourth and final wife, Edith Finch, for his part in a sit-down demonstration in Whitehall. His last years were spent in North Wales, and he retained to the end his lucidity, independence of mind and humour. The last major publications were his three volumes of *Autobiography* (1967–9).

RUSSELL, Eric Frank

(1905–78)

English science-fiction writer, born in Camberley, Surrey. He was the first writer from the UK to publish stories on a regular basis in US science-fiction magazines. The ingenious, often ironic short story was his most productive form. Much of his work was influenced by the outlandish pseudo-philosophical ideas of the American writer Charles Fort. His stories are collected in several volumes, including *Men, Martians and Machines* (1955), a collection of adventures featuring interplanetary explorers, which prefigures **Gene Rodenberry**'s *Star Trek* scenario, and *The Best of Eric Frank Russell* (1978). His novels, which include *Sinister Barrier* (1943, rev edn 1948) and *Sentinels From Space* (1953), are less satisfactory.

RUSSELL, George William, pseud **AE** or **A.E.**
(1867–1935)

Irish poet, painter, writer and economist, born in Lurgan, County Armagh. In 1877 the family went to Dublin, where at the Metropolitan School of Art Russell met **W B Yeats**, and, already something of a mystic, through him became interested in theosophy. This led him to give up painting, except as a hobby. Having worked first in a brewery, then as a draper's clerk, he published his first book in 1894, *Homeward: Songs by the Way*, and from then on became a recognized figure in the Irish literary renaissance. He was Editor of the *Irish Homestead* from 1906 to 1923, when it amalgamated with the *Irish Statesman*, and as editor of the latter from 1923 to 1930 he aimed at expressing balanced Irish opinion of the 1920s, although he held nationalistic sympathies. His writings include books on economics, *The Candle of Vision* (1918), which is an expression of his religious philosophy, books of essays, many volumes of verse, all expressing his mysticism, among them *The Divine Vision* (1903) and *Midsummer Eve* (1928), and a play, *Deirdre* (1907).
▷D Figgis, *A Study of a Man and a Nation* (1916)

RUSSELL, Willy (William)
(1947–)

English playwright, born in Whiston, Cheshire, who became a teacher after several years of working in industry. He is one of the most frequently performed of contemporary British dramatists, perhaps best known for the enormously popular *Educating Rita* (1979), in which a bubbly, working-class hairdresser embarks on an Open University English Literature course taught by a weary, middle-class lecturer. Combining poignant and mildly abrasive social comment with broad, sentimental humour, this is probably his most representative work. The musical *Blood Brothers* (1983) continues the formula, this time in the form of the story of two brothers who were separated at birth and brought up in different social classes. In the play *Shirley Valentine* (1986), a Liverpudlian housewife attempts to transform herself by impulsively deciding to become an independent woman.

RUTEBEUF
(c.1230–1286)

French trouvère, Champenois in origin but Parisian by adoption. He was the author of the semi-liturgical drama *Miracle de Théophile* (c.1260, a prototype of the Faust story), the *Dit de L'Herberie* ('The Tale of the Herb Market'), a monologue by a quack doctor, full of comic charlatanesque rhetoric, and also several typical stories.
▷L Chédat, *Rutebeuf* (1909)

RUTHERFORD, Mark *see* **WHITE, William Hale**

RUZZANTE, real name **Angelo Beolco**
(1502–42)

Italian dramatist and actor, born in Padua. He became famous under his stage name of 'Ruzzante'. He believed that the artist should shun grand effects in favour of the simple truths of peasant life, and most of his plays were comedies and dramas of rural life.
▷C Grabler, *Ruzzante* (1953)

RYDBERG, Abraham Viktor
(1828–95)

Swedish writer and scholar, born in Jönköping. After a hard childhood and early struggles to gain an education he worked as a journalist on the liberal newspaper *Göteborgs Handels - och Sjöfartstidning* (1855–76), and was professor at Stockholm (1884–95). He wrote historical novels, including *Fribytaren på Östersjön* (1857, 'Freebooter in the Baltic'), *Singoalla* (1857), *Den siste atenaren* (1859, 'The Last Athenian') and *Vapensmeden* (1891, 'The Armourer'), and several volumes of Bible criticism. The leading cultural figure of his day, he also wrote works on philosophy, philology and aesthetics, translated **Goethe**'s *Faust*, and published a mythological study, *Undersökningar i germanisk mytologi* (1886–9).
▷K Warburg, *Viktor Rydberg* (1900)

RYLSKY, Maksym
(1895–1964)

Ukrainian poet and translator (**Pushkin**), born in Kiev. His father, a well-known intellectual, was of Polish descent. Forced to accommodate to Stalinism, he managed nevertheless to express his own voice—and often, indeed, overstepped the socialist-realist mark; later, with the 'Thaw', he regained something of his early power. Regarded by some as the master of his language and the greatest Ukrainian poet of the mid-20th century, he has not yet, unfortunately, been translated into English.

RYSKIND, Morrie
(1895–1985)

American lyricist and sketch writer, born in New York and educated at Columbia University. He wrote sketches for *The 49ers* (1922) and *Merry Go Round* (1927), and co-wrote *Animal Crackers* (1928) with **George Kaufman**. He worked with Kaufman again on *Strike Up The Band* (1930) and *Of Thee I Sing* (1931). The latter brought him a Pulitzer Prize for Drama in 1932, shared with Kaufman and lyricist Ira Gershwin (1896–1983), a collaboration which also produced *Let 'Em Eat Cake* (1933). His other work includes screenplays, and a number of less successful musicals.

S

SAAR, Ferdinand von
(1833–1906)

Austrian dramatist, erotic poet, and, most successfully, writer of novellas, born in Vienna. He retired from a military life in order to devote himself to literature, and for many years lived in straitened circumstances. He was ultimately successful, but, at 70, fell victim to a painful cancer, and shot himself.

SAAVEDRA, Angel de, Duque de Rivas
(1791–1865)

Spanish poet, playwright, and politician, born in Córdoba. He was in exile from 1823 until 1834, when he inherited his title. Later he became a conservative prime minister. Now much of his work seems dated, but he has historical importance because for Spain he was the apotheosis of romanticism, and his play *Don Alvaro o la fuerza del sino* (1835, 'Don Alvaro or the Force of Destiny') was considered to be the Spanish equivalent of **Hugo**'s *Ernani*: 'not a single topic of romanticism is absent' from it, remarked a critic. Now it is remembered as having supplied the original for Verdi's opera *La forza del destino*. His poems were sonorous and influential, many of them being ballads in the style of Sir **Walter Scott**.
▷ G Boussagol, *Angel de Saavedra, Duc de Rivas* (1926)

SABA, Umberto, pseud of Umberto Poli
(1883–1957)

Major Italian Jewish poet from Trieste. He kept himself intact from Italian literary politics—as ferocious and partisan as in any country in the world—and wrote as he wished, eventually reaching a peak of almost unprecedented eminence. The collection to which he added throughout his life, *Canzionieri*, is a 'massive lyric autobiography', 'a type of Odyssey of man in our times'. Thus a series of lyrics became an epic, and one of the most celebrated and loved long poems of our times.
▷ J Cary, *Three Modern Italian Poets* (1969)

SABAHADDIN, Ali
(1909–48)

Turkish story writer and novelist, described by some as the best short-story writer of his time. He was born in Gümülcine in Thrace, and murdered also in Thrace—at Kirklarei—

by Turkish policemen posing as peasants; this was during the presidency of Inönü. He wrote, in his shorter fiction, of the lives of Anatolian peasants, and as such was the chief pioneer of socialist realism in the mid-1930s. His finest novel is a portrait of an Anatolian town, *Kuyucakh Yusuf* (1937). His complete works, published in 1965–6, take up seven volumes. He is one of the very few writers whose gifts transcended his submission to socialist realism, driven by not only his genius but also by the truly terrible conditions prevailing in the Anatolia of his day.

SABATINI, Rafael
(1875–1950)

Italian-born novelist, born of Italian and British parentage in Jesi. Writing in English, he first made his name as an author of historical romances with *The Tavern Knight* (1904), which he followed after he settled in England in 1905 with many other such tales, including *The Sea Hawk* (1915), *Scaramouche* (1921) and *Captain Blood* (1922), historical biographies, and a study of *Torquemada* (1913).

SÁBATO, Ernesto
(1911–)

Major Argentinian novelist and essayist, born in Rojas, a village in the province of Buenos Aires, into an Italian family. He married a woman of Russian–Jewish origin, and has had to defend himself from almost every faction in what he has called his 'ill-fated' country: from anti-Semites, Peronists such as **Marechal**, Nazis (who abounded in Argentinia) and hardline Marxists (he was himself a communist until 1934). He became a professor of theoretical physics, but was dismissed in 1944 (when Peron was already in virtual control) for having been critical of Perónism. It is not insignificant that Sábato's cat is called **Freud** or that his dog is called **Jung**, nor that he is 'very unhappy' with himself, believing that he disrupts the lives of those around him—for this is the natural ambience of a man in whose non-fiction, fiction abounds, and vice versa. But, as has been claimed, he is primarily a novelist of the inner life, and readers with a capacity for introspection are at home with him in his three monumental novels: *El túnel* (1950, Eng trans, *The Outsider*, 1950, *The Tunnel*, 1988),

Sobré héroes y tumbas (1961, Eng trans, *On Heroes and Tombs*, 1981), and *Abaddón el exterminador* (1974, Eng trans *The Angel of Darkness*, 1991). These phantasmagorias, or 'gnostic eschatologies', written in tribute to 'the powers of the unconscious', are of enormous, although always fruitful, complexity, and have been described as 'the fullest presentation of Jungian ideas in modern fiction'; but they are eminently readable. His humane non-fiction, which includes a series of dialogues with **Borges**, is seminal, and forms a guide to Argentinian and Latin-American problems.

▷H D Oberhelman, *Ernesto Sábato* (1970)

SÁ-CARNEIRO, Mário de
(1890–1916)

Portuguese poet, story writer (*Céu em fogo*, 1915, 'Sky on Fire') and critic, whose poetry is amongst the best—with that of **Pesshana**—written in the early 20th century in Portugal. He was born in Lisbon and died by poison in Paris. He was a close friend to, and deeply influenced, **Pessoa**, Portugal's greatest poet since **Camoens**. Sá Carneiro was a genuine *poète maudit*, hugely gifted, and with some affinities to **Rimbaud**. At its worst his work is flatly decadent; at its best it is inspired and has not yet gained the recognition it deserves outside Portugal (where his genius is well recognized).

▷D Wohl, *Realidade e idealidade na lirica de Mário de Sá-Carneiro* (1968, in Portuguese, revised from the original German edition of 1960)

SACCHETTI, Franco
(c.1330–1400)

Italian novelist, born in Florence. He held several diplomatic offices. He wrote *Trecento Novelle* ('Three Hundred Stories') in the style of **Boccaccio**, first printed in 1724, of which 10 are translated in **William Roscoe**'s *Italian Novelists* (1825). He also published poetry and burlesques.

▷L Caretti, *Saggio sul Sacchetti* (1951)

SACHER-MASOCH, Leopold von
(1836–95)

Austrian lawyer and writer, born in Lemberg. He wrote many short stories and novels, including *Der Don Juan von Kolomea* (1866), depicting the life of small-town Polish Jews. The term 'masochism' has been coined to describe the form of eroticism detailed in his later works.

SACHS, Hans
(1494–1576)

German poet and dramatist, born in Nuremberg, the son of a tailor. He was bred a shoemaker, and early learnt verse-making from a weaver. On finishing his apprenticeship in 1511 he travelled through Germany, practising his craft in various cities, and frequenting the schools of the *Meistersinger*. On his return to Nuremberg in 1516 he started up business as a shoemaker, becoming a master of his guild in the following year. Sachs' literary career, which resulted in the tremendous output of more than 6300 pieces, falls into two periods. In the first he celebrated the Reformation and sang Luther's praises in an allegorical tale entitled *Die Wittenbergisch Nachtigall* (1523, 'The Nightingale of Wittenberg'), while his poetical fly-sheets, numbering about 200, considerably furthered the Protestant cause. In his second period his poetry deals more with common life and manners, and is distinguished by its vigorous language, good sense, homely morality and fresh humour. His best works are *Schwänke* ('Merry Tales'); serious tales; allegorical and spiritual songs; and Lenten dramas. He was the central character in Wagner's opera *Die Meistersinger von Nürnberg* (1886, 'The Master Singers of Nuremberg').

▷H von Wendler, *Hans Sachs* (1933)

SACHS, Nelly Leonie
(1891–1970)

German-born Swedish poet and playwright, joint winner of the Nobel Prize for literature, born in Berlin of a wealthy Jewish family. Between the wars she published a book of stories, *Tales and Legends* (1921), and several volumes of lyrical poetry. With the rise of Nazi power she studied Jewish religious and mystical literature, and in 1940 escaped to Sweden through the intercession of the Swedish royal family and **Selma Lagerlöf**. After World War II she wrote plays and poetry about the anguish of the Jewish people. She was awarded the 1966 Nobel Prize for literature, jointly with the Israeli novelist **Shmuel Yosef Agnon**.

▷W A Berendon, *Nelly Sachs zu Ehren* (1966)

SACKLER, Howard
(1929–82)

American playwright, director and actor, born in New York and educated at Brooklyn College. He is chiefly remembered for the success of his play *The Great White Hope* (1968), based on the career of the black American prizefighter Jack Johnson, which was a Broadway hit, and won him a Pulitzer Prize in 1969. His other works include a volume of poems, *Want My Shepherd* (1954) and a quartet of one-act plays, gathered together as *A Few Enquiries* (1970).

845

SACKVILLE, Charles, 6th Earl of Dorset
(1638–1706)

English courtier and poet. He succeeded to the earldom in 1677, having two years before been made Earl of Middlesex. He was returned by East Grinstead to the first parliament of Charles II, and became an especial favourite of the king, and notorious for his boisterous and indecorous frolics. He served under the Duke of York (James II) at sea, but could not endure his tyranny as king and ardently supported the cause of William III. His later years were honoured by his generous patronage of **Matthew Prior**, **William Wycherley** and **Dryden**. He wrote lyrics (such as 'To all you Ladies now at Land') and satirical pieces.

▷ B Harris, *Charles Sackville* (1940)

SACKVILLE, Thomas, 1st Earl of Dorset
(1536–1608)

English poet and statesman, born in Buckhurst in Sussex, the only son of Sir Richard Sackville, Chancellor of the Exchequer. He studied law at Hart Hall, Oxford, and St John's College, Cambridge, and entered the Inner Temple and became a barrister. In 1555 he married, and in 1558 was in parliament. With **Thomas Norton** he produced the blank-verse tragedy of *Ferrex and Porrex* (later called *Gorboduc*) which in 1560–1 was acted before Queen Elizabeth, Sackville's second cousin. This work, after the style of **Seneca**, is claimed to be the earliest tragedy in English. He also wrote the verses *Induction* and *Buckingham's Complaint* for *A Mirror for Magistrates* (1563). His prodigality brought Sackville into disgrace, but he was later restored to political favour. It was he who announced Queen Elizabeth's death sentence to Mary, Queen of Scots in 1586. In 1599 he was made lord high treasurer, and in 1604 Earl of Dorset.

▷ P Bacquet, *Un contemporain de Elisabeth I* (1966)

SACKVILLE-WEST, Vita Victoria Mary
(1892–1962)

English poet and novelist, born in Knole House, Kent, daughter of the 3rd Baron Sackville. Educated privately, she started writing novels and plays as a child. In 1913 she married the diplomat Harold Nicolson, and their marriage survived despite Nicolson's homosexuality and her own lesbian affair with Violet Trefusis. Her first published works were a collection of poems, *Poems of West and East* (1917), and a novel, *Heritage* (1919). In her *Orchard and Vineyard* (1921) and her long poem *The Land*, which won the 1927 Hawthornden Prize, her close sympathy with the life of the soil of her native county is expressed. Her prose works include the novels *The Edwardians* (1930), *All Passion Spent* (1931) and *No Signposts in the Sea* (1961), an account of her family in *Knole and the Sackvilles* (1947), and studies of **Andrew Marvell** and Joan of Arc. *Passenger to Teheran* (1926) records her years in Persia with her husband. A passionate gardener at Sissinghurst, Kent, her married home, she wrote a weekly gardening column for *The Observer* for many years. She was the model for **Virginia Woolf**'s *Orlando*.

▷ M Steven, *Vita Sackville West: a critical biography* (1973)

SADE, Donatien Alphonse François, Comte de, (known as **Marquis**)
(1740–1814)

French writer, born in Paris. An army officer in the Seven Years War (1756–63), in 1772 he was condemned to death at Aix for his cruelty and unnatural sexual practices. He made his escape, but was afterwards imprisoned at Vincennes and in the Bastille, where he wrote works of sexual fantasy and perversion, including *Les 120 Journées de Sodome* (1784, Eng trans *The 120 Days of Sodom*, 1954), *Justine; ou, Les Malheurs de la vertu* (1791, Eng trans *Justine; or, the Misfortunes of Virtue*, 1954), *La Philosophie dans le boudoir* (1793, Eng trans *The Bedroom Philosophers*, 1965), *Juliette* (1798, Eng trans 1968) and *Les Crimes de l'amour* (1800, Eng trans, in part, as *Quartet*, 1963). He died in a mental asylum at Charenton. The word 'sadism', derived from his name, is used to describe the type of sexual activities which he practised.

▷ J Lély, *La vie de Sade* (1952–7)

SADEH, Pinchas
(1929–)

Israeli novelist, who 'sees life as a parable' and is somewhat out of the mainstream of his country's literature. His first novel was translated as *Life is a Parable* (1966); later work is quaintly experimental (in one book none of the characters knows any of the others) and more secure.

SÁDI, SAADI, or SA'ADI, the assumed name of **Sheikh Muslih Addin**
(c.1184–?1292)

Persian poet, highly regarded in his native land. He was a descendant of 'Alî, Muhammad's son-in-law. He studied at Baghdad, travelled much, and near Jerusalem was taken prisoner by the Crusaders, but was ransomed by a merchant of Aleppo, who gave him his daughter in marriage. The catalogue of his works comprises 22 different kinds of writings in prose and verse, in Arabic and Persian, of which odes and dirges form the predominant part. The most celebrated of his works, however, is the *Gulistan* ('Rose Garden'), a kind of moral work in prose and verse, inter-mixed with stories, maxims, philosophical sentences, puns and the like. Next comes the *Bostan* ('Orchard Garden'), written in verse, and more religious than the *Gulistan*. Third comes the *Pend-Nameh* ('Book of Instruc-tions').

▷ H Massé, *Essai sur le poète Sádi* (1919)

SADLEIR, Michael
(1888–1957)

English author and publisher, born in Oxford, a son of Sir Michael Ernest Sadler, and great-grand-nephew of Michael Thomas Sadler; he took an older form of the name to avoid confusion. Educated at Rugby and Oxford, he joined the publishing firm of Con-stable, becoming a director in 1920. As well as numerous bibliographical works—he was Sandars reader in bibliography at Cambridge in 1937—he published novels, including *Hyssop* (1915), *These Foolish Things* (1937) and *Fanny by Gaslight* (1940), and biographies, of which *Michael Ernest Sadler: a memoir by his son* (1949) and *Anthony Trollope* (1927) are noteworthy.

SADOVEANU, Mihail
(1880–1961)

Romanian novelist, born in Pascani, Molda-via. At its best, in his stories, his style was simple and unaffected, and his story-telling powers were masterly. A prolific writer, his most famous tale is *Baltagul* (1930, Eng trans *The Hatchet*, 1964), about a woman who hunts down her husband's killers. His genius for evoking the Romanian rural scene has not been matched. *Povestiri din razboi* (1906, Eng trans *Tales of War*, 1962) shows him at his best, but *Mitrea Cocor* (1949, Eng trans 1953) is a tedious essay in socialist realism, and shows his powers greatly diminished.

▷ J Steinberg, *Introduction to Rumanian Literature* (1966)

SAGAN, Françoise, pseud of Françoise Quoirez
(1935–)

French novelist, born in Cajarc in the Lot region, and educated at a convent in Paris and private schools. At the age of 18 she wrote, in only four weeks, the bestselling *Bonjour tristesse* (1954, Eng trans 1955; filmed 1958), followed by *Un Certain Sourire* (1956, Eng trans *A Certain Smile*, 1956; filmed 1958), both remarkably direct testa-ments of wealthy adolescence, written with the economy of a remarkable literary style. Irony creeps into her third, *Dans un mois, dans un an* (1957, Eng trans *Those Without*

Shadows, 1957), but moral consciousness takes over in her later novels, such as *Aimez-vous Brahms...* (1959, Eng trans 1960; filmed 1961 as *Goodbye Again*) and *La Chamade* (1966, Eng trans 1966). A ballet to which she gave the central idea, *Le Rendez-vous manqué* ('The Missed Rendezvous'), enjoyed a tem-porary *succès de scandale* in Paris and Lon-don in 1958. Her later works, including several plays, such as *Château en Suède* (1960, 'Castle in Sweden'), *Les Violons, parfois...* (1961, 'Sometimes, Violins...') and *Un Piano dans l'herbe* (1970, 'A Piano on the Grass'), and novels such as *L'Echarde* (1966, 'The Splinter'), *Le lit défait* (1977, Eng trans *The Unmade Bed*, 1978), *La Femme Fardée* (1981, Eng trans *The Painted Lady*, 1983) and *Un orage immobile* (1983, Eng trans *The Still Storm*, 1984) have had a mixed critical recep-tion.

▷ G Hourdin, *Le cas de Françoise Sagan* (1958)

SAHGAL, Nayantara
(1927–)

Anglophone Indian novelist, eloquent op-ponent and niece to Nehru, born in Allaha-bad. Her *A Situation in New Delhi* (1977) fas-cinatingly explored, with an insider's know-ledge, the dangers inherent in the power-gap left on her uncle's death. *The Day in Shadow* (1971) is an acute feminist account of modern India.

SAID FAIK
(1906–54)

Major Turkish story writer and poet, born in the Anatolian town of Adapazari. The family house he lived in became, after his death, a museum. In an unmatched colloquial Turkish he wrote of the common people of Istanbul; especially those who lived on the periphery of society. They include, in particular, fish-ermen, vagabonds and tramps. It used to be asserted by professors that his style was 'unpolished'; but it has since become appar-ent that he could only capture the very essence of those whose lives he portrays (often he speaks in their own persons) by defying lit-erary conventions. *A Dot on the Man* (1979) is a selection from his tales, most of which, however, still await a translator.

SAINT AMANT, Antoine Girard de
(1594–1661)

French poet, born in Rouen. An early exponent of French burlesque poetry, as in *Rome ridicule* (1649), he also wrote the mock heroic *Albion* (1643), the biblical epic, *Moyse sauvé* (1653, 'Moses Saved'), and an ode, *A la solitude* ('To Solitude').

▷ J Legmy, *Le poète Saint Amant* (1965)

SAINT-DENYS GARNEAU, Hector de
(1912–43)

French–Canadian poet (and painter), born in Montreal, who initiated the modern movement in French–Canadian poetry with his collection *Regards et jeux dans l'espace* (1937, 'Gazes and Games in Space'). In it he made the 'first free and unashamed use of free verse rhythms and techniques'. He suffered from a heart ailment, and wrote virtually all his poetry between 1935 and 1938. His *Poésies complètes* appeared in 1949. His cousin was the equally gifted **Anne Hébert**, also (as a child) an invalid. It is towards these two, suggests **A J M Smith** in his *Oxford Book of Canadian Poetry* (1960), that we must turn for a sense of the 'spiritual' in Canadian poetry. His *Journal* (1954, Eng trans 1962) is valued highly for its awareness of Canadian problems and for its lucid expression of its author's anguish.
▷ J Glassco (translator), *Complete Poems* (1985); E Kushner, *Saint-Denys-Garneau* (1967)

SAINT-ÉVREMOND, Charles Marguetel de Saint Denis, Seigneur de
(1610–1703)

French writer and wit, born in St Denis le Guast near Coutances. He fought at Rocroi, Freiburg and Nördlingen, was steadily loyal throughout the Fronde, but in 1661 fled by way of Holland to England on the discovery of his witty and sarcastic letter to Créqui on the Peace of the Pyrenees. He was warmly received by Charles II, and in London he spent almost all the rest of his days, delighting the world with his wit. His satire, *La Comédie des académistes* (1644, 'The Comedy of the Academy'), is masterly, and his letters to and from **Ninon de Lenclos** charming.
▷ M Willmotte, *Saint-Évremond, critique littéraire* (1921)

SAINT-EXUPÉRY, Antoine de
(1900–44)

French novelist and airman, born in Lyons. He became a commercial airline pilot and wartime reconnaissance pilot. His philosophy of 'heroic action' based on the framework of his experiences as a pilot is expressed in his sensitive and imaginative *Courrier sud* (1929, 'Southbound Mail'), *Vol de nuit* (1931, Eng trans *Night Flight*, 1932), *Terre des Hommes* (1939, Eng trans *Wind, Sand and Stars*, 1939) and *Pilote de guerre* (1942, Eng trans *Flight to Arras*, 1942); but his most popular work is *Le Petit Prince* (1943, Eng trans *The Little Prince*, 1944), a touching allegorical story of a little boy from another planet who befriends a pilot stranded in the desert. Saint-Exupéry was declared missing after a flight in World War II.
▷ C Cate, *Saint-Exupéry, his life and times* (1971)

SAINT-GELAIS, Mellin de
(?1487/?1490–1558)

French poet, born in Angoulême, and either the son or nephew of Octavien de St-Gelais, poet, and bishop of that town. Mellin was brought up in the bishop's palace and was later educated at the Collège de Poitiers, where he studied law. He then spent some time in Italy, at the universities of Bologna and Padua, ostensibly completing his legal studies, but actually preoccupied by poetry: he flourished under the great Italian poets of the day, among them **Petrarch**. He later became a steward to François I, and is believed to have acted for a time as chaplain to the Dauphin, taking holy orders at some point after 1518. His *Sanglais oeuvres de luy* ('Saint-Gelais's Works'), a poetry collection, was first published in Lyons in 1547. **Pierre de Ronsard** was among his admirers.

SAINT-JOHN PERSE, pseud of **Marie René Auguste Alexis Saint-Léger Léger**
(1887–1975)

French poet and diplomat, winner of the Nobel Prize for literature, born in St Léger des Feuilles, an island near Guadeloupe. He studied at Bordeaux, and after many adventures in New Guinea and a voyage in a skiff along the China coast he entered the French foreign ministry in 1904. He became secretary-general in 1933, was dismissed in 1940 and fled to the USA, where he became an adviser to Roosevelt on French affairs. The Vichy government burnt his writings and deprived him of French citizenship, but it was restored in 1945. Although Symbolism was an influence on his earliest verse, he had soon superceded that school and all others. His blank verse utilizes an exotic vocabulary of little-used words and is at times opaque, at times vertiginously vivid. The best known of his earlier works, which include *Éloges* (1910, 'Eulogies') and *Amitiés du prince* (1924, 'The Prince's Friendships'), is the long poem *Anabase* (1924; Eng trans *Anabasis* by **T S Eliot**, 1930). Later works include *Exil* (1942, 'Exile'), *Pluies* (1944, 'Rain'), *Amers* (1957, Eng trans *Seamarks*, 1958) and *Chroniques* (1960, Eng trans 1961). He was awarded the Nobel Prize for literature in 1960.
▷ J Champier, *Saint-John Perse* (1962)

SAINT PIERRE, Jacques Henri Bernardin de
(1737–1814)

French author, born in Le Havre. After a voyage to Martinique he served for some time in the army engineers, but quarrelled with his chiefs and was dismissed, and next year was sent to Malta, with the same result. He was greatly influenced by the writings of **Rousseau**, and he made public employment impossible by the innumerable utopian criticisms with which he deluged the ministers. With dreams of a new state to be founded on the shores of the Aral Sea, he travelled to Russia, and returned in dejection to Warsaw. He abandoned a government expedition to Madagascar at the Île de France (Mauritius), to spend there almost three years of melancholy and observation. His *Voyage à l'Île de France* (1778, 'Journey to the Isle of France') gave a distinctly new element to literature in its close portrayal of nature. His *Études de la nature* (3 vols, 1784, 'Studies of Nature') showed the strong influence of Rousseau. A fourth volume (1788) contained the popular *Paul et Virginie* (Eng trans *Paul and Mary*, 1789), the story of the love between two young people, untainted by civilization, in the natural surroundings of Mauritius. His next works were *Voeux d'un solitaire* (1789, 'A Hermit's Vows') and the novel, *La Chaumière indienne* (1791, 'The Indian Cottage'). His *Harmonies de la nature* (1796) was a pale repetition of the *Études*. Napoleon heaped favours upon him, and he lived comfortably for the rest of his days.

SAINT-POL-ROUX, pseud of Pierre-Paul Roux
(1861–1940)

French poet, dramatist and essayist, born near Marseilles and often called 'Le Magnifique'. From 1898 he lived in some seclusion in a Breton manor. Some of his life's work was destroyed after a Nazi soldier had drunkenly entered his house in order to rape his daughter; he started shooting, murdered the housekeeper, and eventually caused the old poet to die of shock. Saint-Pol-Roux began his career promisingly, as a leading disciple of **Mallarmé**; he then became a self-styled 'ideorealist', seeking to magnify reality. The surrealists championed him as one of their chief precursors, but this did not satisfy him, and he continued to produce massive dramas and poems: always interesting and inventive, preposterous, unheeding of fashion. Many of them were published after his death. Yet he wrote the libretto for Gustave Charpentier's popular *Louise* (1900), although it is usually wrongly attributed to the composer.

SAINT-RÉAL, César Vichard, Abbé de
(1631–92)

French historian, born in Chambéry. He visited London, and in 1679 returned to his birthplace as historiographer to the Duke of Savoy. He wrote *Dom Carlos* (1672) and *La*

Conjuration que les Espagnols formèrent en 1618 contre Venise (1674, 'The Spanish Conspiracy Against Venice in 1618'), early examples of the serious French historical novel.

SAINTE-BEUVE, Charles Augustin
(1804–69)

French writer, the greatest literary critic of his time, born in Boulogne-sur-Mer. His father was a commissioner of taxes who died three months before the birth of his son, leaving his wife in straitened circumstances. He attended school in Boulogne, then went to the Collège Charlemagne in Paris, and next (1824–7) took a course of medical study. One of his teachers at the Collège Charlemagne founded a literary and political paper called the *Globe*, and to it, along with Jouffroy, **Charles Rémusat**, Ampère and **Prosper Mérimée**, Sainte-Beuve became a contributor. For three years he wrote the short articles collected posthumously as *Premiers Lundis* (1874–5, 'First Mondays'). In 1827 a review praising the *Odes et Ballades* of **Victor Hugo** led to the closest relations between the poet and his critic, which lasted until broken in 1834 by Sainte-Beuve's affair with Madame Hugo. For a time he was a zealous advocate of the Romantic movement. In 1828 he published *Tableau de la poésie française au seizième siècle* ('Survey of 16th-Century French Poetry'), and in 1829 and 1830 *Vie et Poésies de Joseph Delorme* ('Life and Poems of Joseph Delorme') and *Les Consolations*, poems full of morbid feeling. In 1829 in the *Revue de Paris* he began the *Causeries* ('Chats', longer critical articles) on French literature. After the Revolution of July 1830 he again wrote for the *Globe*, now in the hands of the Saint-Simonians, but he soon fell out with his new colleagues and for the next three years he was on the staff of the *National*, the organ of extreme republicanism. From 1830 to 1836 he became a sympathetic listener of Lamennais, but with the ultra-democratic opinions of Lamennais after his breach with Rome he had no sympathy. His single novel, *Volupté* (1835, 'Voluptuousness'), belongs to this period. In 1837 he lectured on the history of Port Royal at Lausanne, and in book form these lectures contain some of his finest work. In Lausanne he produced his last volume of poetry, *Pensées d'août* (1839, 'Thoughts of August'). A journey to Italy closes the first period of his life. In 1840 he was appointed Keeper of the Mazarin Library. During the next eight years he wrote mainly for the *Revue des deux mondes*. The political confusions of 1848 led him to become Professor of French Literature at Liège, where he lectured on *Chateaubriand et son groupe littéraire* (pub 1851, 'Chateaubriand and his Literary Set'). In 1849 he returned to Paris, and began to

write for the *Constitutionnel*, producing an article on some literary subject, to appear on the Monday of every week. In 1861 these *Causeries du lundi* were transferred to the *Moniteur*, in 1867 back to the *Constitutionnel*, and finally in 1869 to the *Temps*. In 1854, on his appointment by the emperor as Professor of Latin poetry at the Collège de France, the students refused to listen to his lectures, and he was forced to resign the office. The undelivered lectures contained his critical estimate of **Virgil**. Nominated a senator in 1865, he regained popularity by his spirited speeches in favour of that liberty of thought which the government was doing its utmost to suppress. It was his special instruction that he should be buried without religious ceremony. It is by the amount and variety of his work, and the ranges of qualities it displays, that Sainte-Beuve holds such a place among literary critics. He published many other literary works, including *Critiques et portraits littéraires* (1836–9, 'Literary Portraits and Critical Essays'), *Portraits de femmes* (1844, 'Portraits of Women'), and, posthumously, *M. de Talleyrand* (1870) and *Souvenirs et indiscrétions* (1872, 'Recollections and Indiscretions').
▷A Billy, *Sainte-Beuve et son temps* (1952)

SAINTINE, or BONIFACE, Joseph Xavier
(1798–1865)

French writer. He was the author of many plays, poems and tales, the best known being the sentimental *Picciola* (1836, Eng trans *Picciola, or Captivity Captive*, 1837).

SAKI, pseud of Hector Hugh Munro
(1870–1916)

British novelist and short-story writer, born in Burma, the son of a police inspector. Educated in England at Bedford Grammar School, he returned to Burma and joined the police force in 1893, but went to London in 1896 and took up writing for *The Westminster Gazette*, and from 1902 as the Balkans correspondent for *The Morning Post*. He settled in London again in 1908. He is best known for his short stories, humorous and macabre, which are highly individual, full of eccentric wit and unconventional situations. Collections of his stories are *Reginald* (1904), *The Chronicles of Clovis* (1911), *Beasts and Superbeasts* (1914) and the posthumously published *The Toys of Peace* (1919) and *The Square Egg* (1924). His novels *The Unbearable Bassington* (1912) and *When William Came* (1913) show his gifts as a social satirist of his contemporary upper-class Edwardian world. He was killed on the Western front during World War I.
▷E M Munro, *The Square Egg* (1924)

SAKUTARO Hagiwara
(1886–1942)

The greatest of modern Japanese poets, well translated in both Graeme Wilson's selection, *Face at the Bottom of the World* (1969), and (closer to the original) *Howling to the Moon* (1978), from the collection *Tsuki ni hoeru* (1917). He was the first substantial Japanese poet to employ the colloquial, and the result was startling: all new styles, as he rightly if immodestly claimed, stemmed from *Howling to the Moon*. He has been compared to **Baudelaire** and to **Lorca**, and it is true that he was much influenced by European poetry; but he forced himself to keep his poetry quintessentially Japanese yet new; there have been few to match him in his success. As a man he was often close to madness, always neurotic (he believed that consummation of a marriage ought to take place under 'the watchful eye of the bridegroom's mother'), drank to excess, and yet is, as a critic has written, 'in certain respects … the subtlest poet of the century'.

SALA, George Augustus Henry
(1828–96)

English journalist and novelist, born in London of Italian ancestry. He studied art and drew book illustrations, but in 1851 became a contributor to *Household Words*, and later contributed to the *Welcome Guest*, *Temple Bar* (which he founded and edited 1860–6), the *Illustrated London News* and *Cornhill*. As a special correspondent of *The Daily Telegraph* he was in the USA during the Civil War, in Italy with Garibaldi, in France in 1870–1, in Russia in 1876, and in Australia in 1885. *Twice Round the Clock* (1859) is a social satire, and he also wrote novels such as *The Strange Adventures of Captain Dangerous* (1863) and *Quite Alone* (1864), many books of travel, and the autobiographical *Life and Adventures* (1895).

SALACROU, Armand
(1899–1990)

French dramatist, born in Rouen and brought up in Le Havre who, although hailed in many countries as one of the century's important playwrights, never had a real success in London or New York. This has puzzled many theatre critics, one of whom wrote: 'Salacrou's philosophy as well as his dramaturgy are in the mainstream of popular contemporary theatre'. He was also a remarkable stage technician. He was first encouraged, as a young socialist on the edge of the Surrealist and Dada groups, by **Tristan Tzara**. He made a fortune in advertising, but abandoned this for the theatre. He wrote all kinds of plays: boulevard farces, spectacle plays, dramas and 'problem plays'. A thoughtful and in no way superficial dramatist, his real concern was with what could replace true morality in the absence of a universal religious faith. His masterpiece may well be *L'Inconnue d'Arras*, (1935, 'The Unknown Woman of Arras'), a technically brilliant play about a man's reliving of his entire life in the second before he kills himself, which is frankly indebted to the *Der Vertraagde Film* ('Slow-Film') of the great Flemish writer **Herman Teirlinck**. Salacrou early said that he wanted to be 'compromised with his generation', and he always managed to disconcert critics.

▷J Guichardnaud, *Modern French Theatre* (1961)

SALDA, Frantisek Xaver
(1867–1937)

The leading Czech critic of all time, and a poet and novelist; he was born in Liberec. His own creative work is not usually more than indifferent, although well executed; but his criticism, essentially creative, taught his compatriots to view their own literature against its European background. His masterpiece in this respect is *Duse a dilo* (1913, 'Spirit and Work'). It has often been remarked that a volume of selected criticism is overdue for translation into English.

▷R Wellek, *Essays on Czech Literature* (1963)

SALINAS, Pedro
(1891–1951)

Spanish poet, playwright and critic, who was born in Madrid and died in Boston in exile from Franco. He was in many senses the chief mentor to many of the Generation of '27, which included his pupil **Cernuda**, and was not only an acute critic and teacher but also a major love poet. His aim was to purge his language of rhetoric. The earlier poetry is playful, but the later is sombre. He translated *El Cid* into good modern Spanish verse. His works in English include *Lost Angels* (1938), *Truth of Two* (1940) and *To Live in Pronouns* (1974).

SALINGER, J(erome) D(avid)
(1919–)

American novelist and short-story writer, born in New York. His father was a Jewish cheese importer, his mother Scots. Brought up 'an affluent big-city boy', he attended schools in Manhattan, but instead of going to high school in 1932 he transferred to Mac-Burney's, a private institution which he left after a year. Two years later his father enrolled him at Valley Forge Military Academy, 'Pencey Prep' of *The Catcher in the Rye*

(1951). He left school at 17, provided a dancing-partner for wealthy spinsters on a cruise liner, dabbled in writing, and went to Austria to retrace his father's footsteps. At 19 he enrolled at Ursinus College, Collegeville, Pennsylvania, where he lasted a semester before going to Columbia University where his performance was 'below average'. His constant ambition was to become a writer and after service as an infantryman in World War II he graduated from popular magazines to the *New Yorker. The Catcher in the Rye*, his first and enduringly popular novel (which sells 250 000 copies annually), made him the guru of disaffected youth. Its hero, Holden Caulfield, plays hooky from his Pennsylvania boarding-school and goes to New York, where he tries in vain to lose his virginity. Written in a slick and slangy first-person narrative, disrespectful to adults and authority, it provoked a hostile response from some critics who objected to the forthright language, iconoclasm and élitism. This did not prevent it becoming a college set text and a perennial bestseller. It was succeeded by four works about the Glasses—*Nine Stories* (1953, published in Britain as *For Esmé—With Love and Squalor, and Other Stories*), which included 'A Perfect Day for Bananafish', and contained the suicide of the brilliant Seymour Glass, who is the presiding genius of the family; *Franny and Zooey* (1961); *Raise High the Roof Beam, Carpenters* and *Seymour: an Introduction* (both 1963). Twice married and divorced, Salinger lives in rural reclusion in New Hampshire, apparently still writing and cultivating Zen philosophy.

▷I Hamilton, *In Search of J. D. Salinger* (1988)

SALKEY, Andrew
(1928–)

Panamanian playwright, poet and ficti writer, born in Colon. He graduated from University of London in 1955 and spent next 20 years working in London: he is ticularly respected for his pioneering wo a broadcaster and playwright for the and as a teacher, mentor and founding member of the Caribbean Artists' Movement. He has written much children's fiction, centred in the Caribbean, and a number of adult novels, of which *A Quality of Violence* (1959) was the first, as well as a number of short stories based on the legendary Afro-Caribbean figure of Anancy, eg *Anancy's Score* (1973) and *Anancy Traveller* (1989). His poetry includes *In the Hills Where Her Dreams Live* (1979), which received the Sri Chimnoy Poetry Prize and Casa de las Americas Poetry Prize. A symposium was held at the Commonwealth Institute in London in 1992 to celebrate the humour, compassion and Caribbean focus of his untiring and influential work.

SALMON, André
(1881–1969)

French poet, editor, novelist and art critic, born in Paris. Although only a minor figure, he was a playful and graceful poet, knew everyone of account (including many Belgian writers), and was closely associated with **Guillaume Apollinaire, Max Jacob, Franz Hellens** and the painters Braque and Picasso. *Souvenir sans fin* (1955–6, 'Endless Memories'), his autobiography, is a mine of intelligent information—and essential reading for those who wish to understand the modern period in French literature. His aim in poetry was 'to restore emotion to the impersonal'.
▷M Raymond, *From Baudelaire to Surrealism* (1950)

SALTEN, Felix, pseud of Siegmund Salzmann
(1869–1945)

Hungarian-born Austrian novelist and essayist, born in Budapest. He is known especially for his animal stories, particularly *Bambi* (1929) which, in translation and filmed by Walt Disney (1941), achieved great popularity in America and Britain. He also wrote *Florian* (1934, Eng trans *Florian: An Emperor's Horse*, 1934) and *Bambis Kinder* (1940, Eng trans *Bambi's Children*, 1940).

SALTYKOV, Michail Evgrafovich, pseud N Shchedrin
(1826–89)

Russian writer and satirist, born in Tver. He was exiled (1848–56) because of a satirical story called 'Contradictions' (1847), but later became a provincial vice-governor of Ryazen (1858–60) and Tver (1860–4). He edited with **Nikolai Nekrasov** the radical *Otechestvennye zapiski* ('Notes of the Fatherland'), and of his many books, *Gospoda Golovlevy* (1876, Eng trans *The Golloviev Family*, 1916) and *Skazki* (pub 1939, Eng trans *Fables*, 1931) are among those translated.
▷K Samine, *Saltykov-Schetchédrine* (1955)

SALVERSON, Laura Goodman
(1890–1970)

Canadian novelist, born in Winnipeg to poor Icelandic immigrants who moved to Minnesota when Salverson was 10. She married a railwayman in 1913 and led an itinerant life in the Canadian west. Not surprisingly, much of her work is about immigrant displacement. Her first novel, *The Viking Heart* (1923), concerned the mass immigration of one and a half thousand Icelanders to Canada in 1875.

The Dark Weaver (1937), a Governor General's Award winner, was strongly pacifist and feminist in tone. She could also write romantically, as in *Black Lace* (1938), a novel about piracy and dark intrigue in the reign of Louis XIV.

SAMAIN, Albert Victor
(1858–1900)

French poet, born in Lille. He was a clerk in the Prefecture of the Seine. His Symbolist poetry, though not original in subject, is delicate, fresh and musical, and was well received in his lifetime. Among his collections of verse are *Au jardin de l'infante* (1893, 'In the Infanta's Garden'), *Aux flancs de la vase* (1898, 'On the Sides of the Vase') and *Le Chariot d'or* ('The Chariot of Gold'), published posthumously.

SANCHEZ, Florencio
(1875–1910)

Uruguayan playwright and journalist. Born in Montevideo, he had no formal education, but became one of the most important and influential Latin-American playwrights of this century. His plays and sainetes (light one-act comedies), the first of which were performed in 1902, were deeply influenced by **Henrik Ibsen, Luigi Pirandello,** Roberto Bracco, **Bjørnstjerne Bjørnson,** and **Guiseppe Giacosa.** The period from 1903 to 1905 was his most productive, when he wrote *M'hijo el dotor* (1903, 'My Son the Doctor'), his most famous *La gringa* (1904), and *Baranca abajo* (1905, 'Downhill'). His favoured themes are the corruption caused by money and power, the effect of social problems on the individual, and the clash between the old and the new. *Moneda falsa* ('Counterfeit Money') is his one play in lunfardo, the dialect of Buenos Aires.

SANCHEZ, Thomas
(1944–)

American novelist, born in California. He was educated at San Francisco State University, and taught there for two years from 1967 to 1969, then spent some time in Europe. He became actively involved in political agitation on behalf of Native American causes on his return, and finished his first and best-known novel, *Rabbit Boss* (1973). It traces the disintegration of the Washo tribe and their ancient way of life through the story of a family across four generations. His later titles are *Zoot Suit Murders* (1978) and *Mile Zero* (1989).

SANCHEZ DE BADAJOZ, Garci
(c.1460–c.1526)

Spanish poet. According to tradition, he went mad from love (for whom, the legend does not say). He did, however, enjoy fame in his time as an erotic poet. His poems bear such titles as 'Lamentaciones de Amor', 'Infierno de Amor', and his parody 'Liciones de Job' ('Lessons of Job') was banned by the Inquisition, as he followed the fashion for adapting prayers to 'misas a lo profano' (masses to the profane), using erotic language. Probably his most successful poem was one entitled 'Sueño' ('Dream'), where the poet relates a vision of his own burial and the birds lament that he died of love.

SANCHEZ FERLIOSO, Rafael
(1927–)

Spanish novelist, whose *El jarama* (1956, Eng trans *The One Day of the Week*, 1962) received much attention at the time of its publication. It is an account of a Sunday outing, during which nothing happens except that someone is drowned; one critic called it 'one of the most boring works in the history of the novel ... no doubt intentionally', while a few others acclaimed it as a brilliant tour de force.

SAND, George, pseud of Amandine Aurore Lucie Dupin, Baronne Dudevant
(1804–76)

French novelist, born in Paris, the illegitimate daughter of Marshal de Saxe. Her father died when she was very young, and she lived principally at Nohant in Berri with her grandmother, Madame Dupin, on whose death she inherited the property. At the age of 18 she married Casimir, Baron Dudevant, and had two children, but after nine years left him and went to Paris with her children to make her living by literature in the Bohemian society of the period (1831). For the best part of 20 years her life was spent in the company and partly under the influence of various distinguished men. She scandalized bourgeois society with her unconventional ways and her love affairs. Her first lover was **Jules Sandeau**, from whose surname she took her pseudonym, and with whom she wrote a novel, *Rose et Blanche* (1831, 'Rose and Blanche'). She was always interested in poets and artists, including **Prosper Mérimée**, **Alfred de Musset**, with whom she travelled in Italy, and Chopin, who was her lover for 10 years. In the second decade her attention shifted to philosophers and politicians, such as Lamennais, the socialist Pierre Leroux, and the republican Michel de Bourges. After 1848 she settled down as the quiet 'châtelaine of Nohant', where she spent the rest of her life in outstanding literary activity, varied by travel. Her work can be divided into four periods. When she first went to Paris, her candidly erotic novels—*Indiana* (1832, Eng trans 1850), *Valentine* (1832, Eng trans 1900), *Lélia*

(1833, Eng trans 1978) and *Jacques* (1834, Eng trans 1847)—shared in the Romantic extravagance of the time, and declared themselves against marriage. In the next period her philosophical and political teachers inspired the socialistic rhapsodies of *Spiridion* (1838, Eng trans 1842), *Consuelo* (1842–4, Eng trans 1846), *Comtesse de Rudolstadt* (1843–5, Eng trans *The Countess of Rudolstadt*, 1847) and *Le Meunier d'Angibault* (1845, Eng trans *The Miller of Angibault*, 1847). Between the two periods came the fine novel *Mauprat* (1837, Eng trans 1847). Then she began to turn towards the studies of rustic life—*La Mare au diable* (1846, Eng trans *The Haunted Marsh*, 1848), *François le Champi* (1847–8, Eng trans *Francis the Waif*, 1889) and *La Petite Fadette* (1849, Eng trans *Little Fadette*, 1850), which are, by modern standards, her best works. The fourth period comprises the miscellaneous works of her last 20 years—some of them, such as *Les Beaux Messieurs de Bois-Doré* (1858, Eng trans *The Gallant Lords of Bois-Doré*, 1890), *Le Marquis de Villemer* (1860–1, Eng trans *The Marquis of Villemer*, 1871) and *Mlle la Quintinie* (1863), of high merit. Her complete works (over 100 vols), besides novels and plays, include the autobiographical *Histoire de ma vie* (1855, 'The Story of My Life'), *Elle et lui* (on her relations with de Musset, 1859, Eng trans *He and She*, 1900), and delightful letters, published after her death.
▷M Louise Pailleron, *George Sand* (2 vols, 1938–43)

SANDBURG, Carl
(1878–1967)

American poet, born in Galesburg, Illinois, of Swedish stock. After trying various jobs, fighting in the Spanish–American war and studying at Lombard College, he became a journalist in Chicago and started to write for *Poetry*. His verse, realistic and robust but often also delicately sensitive, reflects industrial America. Among his volumes of poetry are *Chicago Poems* (1915), *Corn Huskers* (1918), *Smoke and Steel* (1920), *Slabs of the Sunburnt West* (1922) and *Good Morning, America* (1928). His *Complete Poems* gained him the Pulitzer Prize in 1950. Interested in American folksongs and ballads, he published a collection in *The American Songbag* (1927). He also wrote a vast *Life of Abraham Lincoln* (1926–39).
▷Gay Wilson Allen, *Carl Sandburg* (1972)

SANDEAU, Jules Léonard Sylvian Julien
(1811–83)

French author, born in Aubusson. He went to Paris to study law, but soon devoted himself to letters. He co-wrote *Rose et Blanche* (1831, 'Rose and Blanche') with **George Sand**.

His first independent novel was *Madame de Sommerville* (1834) and his first success was *Marianna* (1840). His books give an accurate picture of the social conflicts of the France of his day, and he was master of the *roman de moeurs*. He became Keeper of the Mazarin Library in 1853, and librarian at St Cloud in 1859.

▷ M Silver, *Sandeau, l'homme et la vie* (1937)

SANDEL, Cora, pseud of Sara Fabricius
(1880–1974)

Norwegian author and painter, born in Oslo and brought up in Tromsø in northern Norway. She lived as a painter in Paris from 1906 until 1921 and published her first novel, *Rosina*, in 1922. In many of her novels she condemns small-town and middle-class mores; another important theme in her work is the difficulty experienced by women in achieving artistic self-realization. Her poignant and subtly ironic manner of narration conveys great psychological insight and a profound knowledge of human nature. Following *Rosina*, her writing career began in earnest with the 'Alberte' trilogy (*Alberte* (1926), *Alberte og Friheten* (1936, 'Alberte and Freedom') and *Bare Alberte* (1939, 'Just Alberte'), in which she describes a woman's experiences of power and powerlessness. In the short novel collection *Vårt vanskelige liv* (1960, 'Our Difficult Life') Sandel addresses women's longing for acknowledgement and self-determination, while a further collection, *Barnet som elsket veier* (1973, 'The Child who loved Roads'), reflects her empathy with a child's view of the world. Although her protagonists belong to the perpetually powerless, they revolt unremittingly against their oppressive environment by means of obstinacy and fantasy, and sublime optimism pervades all her writing.

▷ A H Lervik, *Menneske og miljø i Cora Sandels diktning* (1977)

SANDEMOSE, Aksel
(1899–1965)

Danish–Norwegian novelist, born into a working-class family in North Jutland. One of the most innovative, idiosyncratic and prolific Scandinavian authors of the 20th century, he experienced a resounding breakthrough with the modernist novel, *En flyktning krysser sitt spor* (1933, 'A Fugitive Crosses his own Track'), in which he immortalized the parochial and oppressive town of 'Jante', a fictitious version of his Danish birthplace Nykøbing Mors. The search for an antidote to the narrow-mindedness and ethnocentricity epitomized by 'Jante' drew Sandemose to consider the lives of North American immigrants, which he depicted in a trilogy of novels, *Ross Dane* (1928), *En*

sjømann går i land (1931, 'A Sailor Goes Ashore'), *September* (1939), and also in his debut collection of short stories, *Fortællinger fra Labrador* (1923, 'Stories from Labrador'). In 1930 he had himself become something of an immigrant, when he left Denmark for Norway, his mother's native country, and began to write in Norwegian. He then spent four years during World War II in exile in Sweden, where in 1944 he published another notable novel, *Det gångna år en dröm* ('The Past is a Dream'), a document fiction about a murder mystery. After the war, he returned to Norway.

▷ E Haavardsholm, *Mannen fra Jante. Et Portrett av Aksel Sandemose* (1988)

SANDOZ, Mari Susette
(1896/1901–1966)

American novelist and popular historian, born in Nebraska to Swiss immigrants. Her biography of her father, *Old Jules* (1935), a frontier farmer who thought writers and artists 'the maggots of society', was rejected 13 times before being finally published. Her next book, *Slogum House* (1937), was a historical novel, but her best writing is to be found in closely researched books of non-fiction. *Crazy Horse* (1942) tells the life of the Sioux chief.

SANGUINETI, Edourdo
(1930–)

Italian critic (chiefly), poet and novelist, born in Genoa. He was reckoned to be the leader of the Italian avant garde in its revolt of the 1960s, and his anthologies of poetry, which have a genuine air of authority, have been particularly influential—and useful to non-Italian students of Italian poetry. His creative work is more an illustration of his complex critical method than interesting in its own right; but his mind is fascinating, and has fascinated a generation of often puzzled readers.

SANNAZARO, Jacopo
(c.1458–1530)

Italian poet, born in Naples. He sought favour at the court there. His *Arcadia* (1485), a pastoral medley of prose and verse which drew on the example of **Boccaccio**, is full of beauty and won him considerable fame. He also wrote Latin elegies, and religious works.

▷ A Altamure, *Jacopo Sannazaro* (1951)

SANSOM, Clive
(1910–81)

English poet, anthologist and speech therapist, who moved to Tasmania at the age of 40. His verse includes *In the Midst of Death* (1940) and *The Unfailing Spring* (1943). The title poem of *The Witnesses and Other Poems* (1956) was a prize-winner in the 1951 Festival of Britain poetry competition. In Australia he published *The Cathedral* (1958), *Dorset Village* (1962) and *Return to Magic* (1969), which look back to his English heritage and religious faith. He also wrote a novel and a verse play, and compiled the two anthologies for which he is best known, *The English Heart* (1945) and *The World of Poetry* (1959).

SANSOM, William
(1912–76)

English short-story writer and novelist, whose work is marked by a strong balance of outward and internal realities. He lived in London and during the war served with the Volunteer Fire Brigade, an experience which inspired many of the stories in *Fireman Flower* (1944), perhaps his most distinctive collection. After the war he wrote *The Body* (1949), a powerful study of a fragmented personality. Thereafter, though he wrote prolifically, his skill seemed progressively less focused; his travel writing was, however, vividly done.
▷P Michel-Michot, *William Sansom: A Critical Assessment* (1971)

SANTAYANA, George
(1863–1952)

Spanish philosopher, poet and novelist, born in Madrid, and educated from 1872 in the USA. He taught at Harvard from 1889 and was professor there from 1907 to 1912, but always retained his Spanish citizenship and returned to Europe in 1912. He spent much time in England but settled in Rome in 1924 and passed his last years as the guest of a convent of nuns there. Santayana is always regarded as a very literary philosopher, and a fine stylist. He was a poet (*Sonnets and Other Verses*, 1894), a successful novelist (*The Last Puritan*, 1935) and a cultivated literary critic, aesthetician and essayist. His main philosophical works are: *The Sense of Beauty* (1896), *The Life of Reason* (1905–6), *Scepticism and Animal Faith* (1923), which is itself an introduction to the comprehensive four-volume work *Realms of Being* (1927–40), and *Platonism and the Spiritual Life* (1927). He also wrote a three-volume autobiography, *Persons and Places* (1944–53).
▷W E Arnett, *George Santayana* (1968)

SANTIĆ, Aleksa
(1868–1924)

Serbian poet and nationalist, born in Mostar. At first he followed in the footsteps of **Illic**, but he later turned to his native folk-song for inspiration. His 'The Fields of Misery' has

been translated in *Slavonic and East European Review* (XXIX, 73, 1951).

SANTILLANA, Iñigo López de Mendoza, Marqués de
(1398–1458)

Spanish scholar, soldier and poet, born in Carrión de los Condes. He led expeditions against the Moors in Spain, but is best known as a patron of the arts. Influenced by the poetry of **Dante** and **Petrarch**, he introduced their style and methods into Spanish literature. His shorter poems, especially his *serranillas* (pastoral songs), are among his best work, and he was the first Spanish poet to write sonnets. His principal prose work, *Proemio e carta a condestable de Portugal* (1449, 'Proem and Letter to the Constable of Portugal'), is a discourse on European literature of his day.
▷J Delgado, *Iñigo de Santillana* (1968)

SAPPER, pseud of **Herman Cyril McNeile**
(1888–1937)

English novelist and short-story writer, remembered chiefly for the invention of Bulldog—originally Bull-Dog—Drummond, a laddish sprig of Edwardian England. Born in Bodmin, Cornwall, McNeile was educated at Cheltenham and at the Royal Military Academy at Woolwich. He joined the Royal Engineers as a regular in 1907 and was promoted to Captain on the eve of World War I; he won the Military Cross and rose to Lieutenant Colonel before his retirement. He published five collections of short stories during the war; his first novel, *Mufti*, appeared in 1919. and a year later he introduced Drummond in an eponymous novel bearing the tellingly Hannay-ish subtitle *The Adventures of a Demobilized Officer Who Found Peace Dull*. That is essentially the formula for the Drummond books, of which there were seven between 1920 and Sapper's death. The best is unquestionably *The Female of the Species* (1928, published in the USA as *Bulldog Drummond Meets ...*, 1943), in which the hero rescues his wife from kidnap by Sapper's stock gang of low-rent, unEnglish thugs. The social and political attitudes are far more extreme than in **John Buchan**'s books and there is a blimpishness that Buchan usually avoids. There is, however, no mistaking the vigour of the storytelling. Though now little read, Sapper has a significant place in British popular culture.

SAPPHO
(b.c.612 BC)

Greek lyric poet, born on the island of Lesbos. She went into exile about 596 BC from Mytilene to Sicily, but after some years returned to Mytilene. She married Cercylas, and had a daughter, Cleis. She seems to have been the centre of a circle of women and girls, probably her pupils. Tradition represents her as homosexual because of the love and admiration she expresses in some of her poems addressed to girls. The greatest woman poet of antiquity, she wrote lyrics unsurpassed for depth of feeling, passion and grace. Only two of her odes are extant in full, but many fragments have survived. It is from her that 'lesbian' has acquired its modern meaning and the four-line sapphic stanza (used in Latin by **Catullus** and **Horace**) its name.

▷ C M Bowra, *Greek Lyric Poetry* (1961)

SARDOU, Victorien
(1831–1908)

French dramatist, born in Paris. His first efforts were failures, but through his marriage to the actress Brécourt, who nursed him when he was sick, he became acquainted with Déjazet, for whom he wrote successfully *Monsieur Garat* (1860) and *Les Prés Saint-Gervais* (1860, Eng trans *The Meadows of Saint-Gervais*, 1871). Soon he had amassed a fortune and had become the most successful European playwright of his day, and his popularity was immense in the USA. Pieces like *Les Pattes du monde* (1860, 'The World's Legs'), *Nos intimes* (1861, Eng trans *Our Friends*, 1879), *La Famille Benoîton* (1865, 'The Benoîton Family'), *Divorçons* (1880, 'Let's Get Divorced'), *Odette* (1882) and *Marquise* (1889) are fair samples of his work. For Sarah Bernhardt he wrote *Fédora* (1883, Eng trans 1883), *La Tosca* (1887, Eng trans *Tosca*, 1900), etc, and with Moreau *Madame Sans-Gene* (1893); for Irving *Robespierre* (1899, Eng trans as a novel, 1899) and *Dante* (1903, Eng trans 1903). He attempted the higher historical play in *La Patrie!* (1869, Eng trans 1915). Today his plays appear over-technical and over-theatrical, and the plot and characters shallow and rather obvious.

▷ J A Hunt, *Sardou and the Sardou Plays* (1913)

SARDUY, Severo
(1937–)

Cuban novelist and poet, considered one of the foremost Post-Boom writers in Latin America and the most famous young Cuban writer of the late 20th century. His experimental novels *De donde son los cantantes* (1967, 'From Cuba With a Song') and *Cobra* demonstrate the striking stylistic and thematic innovations for which he has been widely praised. He has also published essays, literary criticism, and two books of poetry. Living in France during the 1960s, he was on the staff of the influential journal *Tel Quel*.

SARGESON, Frank (Norris Frank Davey)
(1903–82)

New Zealand short-story writer and novelist, born in Hamilton. Through his easy use of colloquial idioms and speech patterns, he is regarded as the founder of modern New Zealand writing. He qualified as a lawyer but did not practise. In 1926 he went to Europe but returned to New Zealand two years later. He worked briefly as a market gardener, milkman, pantryman and freelance journalist, but his main energy was devoted to writing novels and short stories. He made his name with collections of short stories like *Conversations with My Uncle* (1936), *A Man and His Wife* (1940) and *That Summer and Other Stories* (1946), satirizing the provincial attitudes of his surroundings. A novel, *I Saw in My Dream* (1949), included the earlier *When the Wind Blows* of 1945. His *Collected Stories, 1935–1963* came out in 1964 and an expanded edition, as *The Stories of Frank Sargeson*, in 1973. Other novels include *Memoirs of a Peon* (1965) and *Joy of the Worm* (1969). He wrote three works of autobiography, *Once is Enough* (1973), *More than Enough* (1975) and *Never Enough!* (1977). These were collected in one volume as *Sargeson* in 1981.

▷ B Benson, introduction to *The Collected Stories of Frank Sargeson* (1964)

SARKIA, Kaarlo
(1902–45)

Finnish poet and translator (**Baudelaire**, 'The Bateau Ivre' of **Rimbaud**—a famous tour de force in the literature), born in Kiikka. He helped to bring the influence of French poetry into Finnish. Like so many Finns, he suffered from tuberculosis, and his life was considerably shortened by it. His poetry is more technically brilliant and assured than significant in content.

▷ E Tompuri, *Voice from Finland* (1947)

SARMENT, Jean, pseud of Jean Bellemère
(1897–1976)

French dramatist, poet, novelist and actor, known for such successful plays as *Le Pêcheur d'ombres* (1921, Eng trans *Fishing for Shadows*, 1940) and *Les Plus Beaux Yeux du monde* (1925, 'The Most Beautiful Eyes in the World'). The best of his proficient, bittersweet plays, influenced by **Musset** and the psychology of **Freud**, tend to be the earlier ones. He acted, with Michel Simon, in the 1934 movie **Marcel Pagnol** made of one of his own best plays: *Léopold le Bien-Aimé* (1927, 'Leopold the Well-Disposed').

SARMIENTO, Domingo Faustino
(1811–88)

Argentinian politician, educator and writer, born in San Juan, who became president of his country and wrote the most important essay of his day—*Civilización y Barbarie: La vida de Juan Facundo* (1848, 'Civilization and Barbarism: The Life of Juan Facundo'), better known simply as *Facundo*. After being arrested and condemned to death by the dictator Rosas, he fled to Chile, where he worked as a journalist and teacher. Much of his life was spent travelling the world to study educational reform. His *Facundo* is a combination of essay, novel and political treatise on the peoples of Argentina.

SAROYAN, William
(1908–81)

American playwright and novelist, born in Fresno, California. His first work, *The Daring Young Man on the Flying Trapeze* (1934), a volume of short stories, offered a hallucinatory but also strikingly sympathetic view of Depression America and was a great critical success; it was followed by a number of highly original novels and plays. *The Time of Your Life* (1939), a play, was awarded the Pulitzer Prize. Among later works are the autobiographical *My Name is Aram* (1940), *The Bicycle Rider in Beverley Hills* (1952), *The Human Comedy* (1943, a novel), *Days of Life and Death* and *Escape to the Moon* (1971), *Places Where I've Done Time* (1973), and the autobiographical *Obituaries* (1979).
▷ *Short Drive, Sweet Chariot* (1966)

SARRAUTE, Nathalie, née Tcherniak
(1920–)

Russian-born French writer, who was born in Ivanovno-Voznesenk. Her parents settled in France when she was a child. She was educated at the Lycée Fénelon and the Sorbonne, graduating in arts and law. She spent a year at Oxford (1922–3) doing graduate studies, and then studied sociology in Berlin, before establishing a law practice in Paris (1922–39). Her first book was a collection of sketches on bourgeois life, *Tropismes* (1939, Eng trans *Tropisms*, 1934), in which she rejected traditional plot development and characterization to describe a world between the real and the imaginary. She developed her theories further in her later novels: *Portrait d'un Inconnu* (1948, Eng trans *Portrait of a Man Unknown*, 1958), *Martereau* (1953, Eng trans 1959), *Le Planétarium* (1959, Eng trans 1960), *Les Fruits d'or* (1963, Eng trans *The Golden Fruits*, 1964), *Entre la vie et la mort* (1968, Eng trans *Between Life and Death*, 1969) and *Vous les entendez?* (1972, Eng trans *Do You Hear Them?*, 1973). She has also written plays, *Le Silence, suivi de Le Mensonge* (1967, Eng trans *Silence, and The Lie*, 1969), *Isma* (1970, Eng trans *Izzuma*, 1980) and *Elle*

est là (1978, Eng trans *It Is There*, 1980), and collections of essays.
▷ G R Besser, *Nathalie Sarraute* (1979)

SARRUF, Yaqub
(1852–1927)

Lebanese writer, who established himself in Egypt. His main task, as he saw it, was to popularize science; but he also wrote some popular historical fiction.

SARTON, (Eleanor) May
(1912–)

American poet and novelist, born in Wondelgem, Belgium, who emigrated with her family to the USA at the age of four, and became a naturalized citizen in 1924. Her first book, the poetry volume *Encounter in April* (1937), was followed by six more, including *Collected Poems* (1974). *The Silence Now*, a volume of new and uncollected early poems, appeared in 1989. Interspersed with these are novels such as *The Single Hound* (1938), dealing with a young English poet; *The Birth of a Grandfather* (1957), sympathetically examining the issue of growing older; and *Mrs. Stevens Hears the Mermaids Singing* (1965), looking at lesbian experience.

SARTRE, Jean-Paul
(1905–80)

French philosopher, dramatist and novelist, born in Paris. He studied at the Sorbonne with **Simone de Beauvoir** and taught philosophy at Le Havre, Paris and Berlin (1934–5). He joined the French army in 1939, was a prisoner of war in Germany (1941), and after his release became an active member of the Resistance in Paris. In 1945 he emerged as the leading light of the left-wing, left-bank intellectual life of Paris, but he eventually broke with the communists. In 1946, with Simone de Beauvoir, he founded and edited the avant-garde monthly *Les Temps modernes* ('Modern Times'). A disciple of Heidegger, he developed his own characteristic Existentialist doctrines, derived from an early anarchistic tendency, which found full expression in his autobiographical novel *La Nausée* (1938, Eng trans *Nausea*, 1949) and in *Le Mur* (1938, Eng trans *The Wall and Other Stories*, 1949), a collection of short stories. The Nazi occupation provided the grim background to such plays as *Les Mouches* (1943, Eng trans *The Flies*, 1946), a modern version of the Orestes theme, and *Huis clos* (1944, Eng trans *In Camera*, 1946; also known as *No Exit* and *No Way Out*). *Les Mains sales* (1948, Eng trans *Crime Passionnel*, 1949, under which title it was filmed) movingly portrayed the tragic consequences of a choice to join an extremist party. He

SASSOON, Siegfried Louvain

became the most prominent exponent of
Atheistic Existentialism. His doctrines are
outlined in *L'Existentialisme est un hum-
anisme* (1946, Eng trans *Existentialism and
Humanism*, 1948) and fully worked out in
L'Être et le néant (1943, Eng trans *Being and
Nothingness*, 1956). Other notable works
include the three novels which comprise *Les
Chemins de la liberté* ('Paths of Freedom'),
L'Âge de raison (1945, Eng trans *The Age of
Reason*, 1947), *Le Sursis* (1945, Eng trans *The
Reprieve*, 1947) and *La Mort dans l'âme*
(1949, Eng trans *Iron in the Soul*, 1950); the
play *Les Séquestrés d'Altona* (1959, Eng trans
Loser Wins, 1960); and a study of **Gustave
Flaubert**, *L'Idiot de la famille* (1971, Eng trans
The Family Idiot, 1982). In 1964 he was
awarded, but declined to accept, the Nobel
Prize for literature. In the late 1960s he
became closely involved in opposition to
American policies in Vietnam, and expressed
support for student rebellion in 1968. His
autobiography, *Les Mots* (Eng trans *The
Words*, 1964), appeared in 1963.
▷A C Solal, *Sartre* (1988)

SASSOON, Siegfried Louvain
(1886–1967)

English poet and novelist, born in Kent. His
experiences in World War I formed in him a
hatred of war, fiercely expressed in his *The
Old Huntsman* (1917), *Counter-Attack* (1918)
and *Satirical Poems* (1926). A semi-fictitious
autobiography, *The Complete Memoirs of
George Sherston* (1937), started with *Memoirs
of a Fox-Hunting Man* (1928; Hawthornden
Prize 1929), and continued in *Memoirs of an
Infantry Officer* (1930) and *Sherston's Progress* (1936). Truly autobiographical are *The
Old Century* (1938), *The Weald of Youth*
(1942) and *Siegfried's Journey 1916–20*
(1945). He also wrote an influential biography of **George Meredith** (1948). His later
poems, including those in *Vigils* (1935) and
Sequences (1956), are predominantly spiritual
in tone, and he became a Roman Catholic in
1957. His *Collected Poems* appeared in 1961.

SASTRE, Alfonso
(1926–)

Spanish playwright, essayist, novelist and
story writer who helped, under severe difficulties from the censorship, to found the
Grupo de Teatro Popular Realista. Born in
Madrid, he writes realistic 'problem' plays,
but in many different modes; he has expressed
his indebtedness to **Arthur Miller** and to
Sartre. But the essence of his theatre, influenced by European models as it is, may ultimately be traced to Spanish dramatists.
Together with **Buero Vallejo** he dominated
the Spanish theatre in the difficult years of the
Franco dictatorship. His plays are explicitly

critical of society, and few of them could be
performed. His *Escuadra hacia la muerte*
(1953, Eng trans *The Condemned Squad*,
1964), in which an obviously Franco-style
officer is murdered by his men, was closed
after three performances, but this merely
enhanced his reputation as an underground
writer. He later wrote in a form he described
as that of the 'complex tragedy', in which he
admits the pervasive influence of **Valle-Inclán**
(in particular), **Brecht**, and **Beckett**. *Ana Klei-
ber* (1952), a technically brilliant study of the
anti-feministic character of fascism, is perhaps the most powerful of all his plays. English translations of five plays may be found
in *The Modern Spanish Stage* (1970, ed
Marion Holt), *Masterpieces of the Modern
Spanish Theatre* (1967, M Benedikt and G E
Wellwarth eds), *The New Theatre of Europe*
(1962), *International Drama* (1968) and *The
New Wave Spanish Drama* (1970, G E
Wellwarth). He is perhaps the most gifted and
incisive of all living playwrights.
▷F Anderson, *Alfonso Sastre* (1971)

SATCHELL, William
(1860–1942)

English-born New Zealand author, born in
London. He wrote four novels of an agnostic-
philosophical cast, deploying romantic
themes against a setting of nature and myth.
After *The Land of the Lost* (1902), *The Toll
of the Bush* (1905), *The Elixir of Life* (1907)
and *The Greenstone Door* (1914), the author
produced nothing more.
▷P Wilson, *The Maorilander* (1961, rev edn
1968)

SAVAGE, Richard
(?1697–1743)

English poet, claimed to be the illegitimate
child of Richard Savage, fourth and last Earl
Rivers, and the Countess of Macclesfield. In
the dedication to his comedy *Love in a Veil*
(1718) he asserted the parentage, but in
Curll's *Poetical Register* (1719) the story is
for the first time fully given. **Aaron Hill**
befriended him, and in 1724 published in *The
Plain Dealer* an outline of his story which
brought subscribers for his *Miscellanies*
(1726). In 1727 he killed a gentleman in a
tavern brawl, and narrowly escaped the
gallows. His attacks upon his alleged mother
(now Mrs Brett) became louder and more
bitter in his poem *The Bastard* (1728). *The
Wanderer* (1729) was dedicated to Lord Tyr-
connel, nephew of Mrs Brett, who had
befriended him. Savage led a dissipated life
and the queen's pension (1732) of £50 for
a birthday ode was squandered in a week's
debauchery. On Queen Caroline's death
(1737) **Pope** tried to help him, but after about
a year he went to Bristol, was jailed for debt,

and died there. He wrote a comedy, *Love in a Veil* (1718), and *The Tragedy of Sir Thomas Overbury* (1723), and at least one notable poem, *The Wanderer* (1729). He owes his reputation mainly to **Samuel Johnson**, who wrote what is perhaps the most perfect Life in English literature, though it was later discredited.

▷S V Makover, *Richard Savage: a mystery in biography* (1909)

SAVERY, Henry
(1791–1842)

English-born Australian author, born near Bristol, where his father was a prominent banker. Savery is generally considered to be the first Australian novelist. A bankrupt, he was convicted of forgery and sentenced to death. This was commuted to transportation for life and he arrived at Hobart Town in 1825. His wife Eliza followed him, was rescued from a shipwreck, and arrived in 1828 to find her husband back in prison for debt; she left Hobart never to return. Meanwhile Henry was writing from prison for the local newspaper as 'Simon Stukeley'. His essays were published in 1829 and immediately became the subject of a libel suit. Eventually he secured his release and then, possibly with a view to his rehabilitation in society, published his autobiographical 'novel' *Quintus Servinton: A Tale Founded upon Incidents of Real Occurrence* (1830–1, 3 vols). Falling into debt once more, he returned in 1840 to the notorious Port Stanley prison where he died two years later. His reputation rests more on his primacy than on the quality of his writing, but he undoubtedly influenced **Henry Kingsley** and possibly **William Hay**.

SAVILLE, (Leonard) Malcolm
1901–82)

English author, born in Hastings, Sussex. Saville wrote over 80 books, the vast majority for young people, beginning with *Mystery at Witchend* in 1943. This book introduced the characters who became known as The Lone Pine Club, and who reappeared in *Seven White Gates* (1944), and in almost 20 subsequent volumes. Other Saville characters include the secret agent Marston Baines, who featured in several books, such as *Marston, Master Spy* (1978), and who appealed to older boys; while the 'Susan and Bill' series, beginning with *Susan, Bill and the Ivy-Clad Oak* (1954), was designed for younger readers. Saville also wrote adult books on gardening, travel and various aspects of the south of England.

SAYERS, Dorothy L(eigh)
1893–1957)

English detective-story writer, born in Oxford. Educated at the Godolphin School,

Salisbury, and Somerville College, Oxford (she took a first in modern languages), she taught for a year and then worked in an advertising agency until 1931. In 1924 she had an illegitimate son, and in 1926 married Captain Oswald Fleming. Her novels are distinguished by taste and style. Beginning with *Whose Body?* (1923) and *Clouds of Witness* (1926), she told the adventures of her hero Lord Peter Wimsey in various accurately observed milieux—such as advertising in *Murder Must Advertise* (1933) or campanology in *The Nine Tailors* (1934). Her other stories included *Strong Poison* (1930), *Gaudy Night* (1935), *Busman's Honeymoon* (1937) and *In the Teeth of the Evidence* (1939). She earned a reputation as a leading Christian apologist with two successful plays, *The Zeal of Thy House* (1937) and *The Devil to Pay* (1939), a series for broadcasting (*The Man Born to be King*, 1943) and a closely reasoned essay (*The Mind of the Maker*, 1941). A translation of **Dante**'s *Inferno* appeared in 1949 and of *Purgatorio* in 1955. *Paradiso* was left unfinished at her death.

▷F Wolcher, *Der literarische Mord* (1953); B Reynolds, *Dorothy L. Sayers, Her Life and Soul* (1993)

SAYLES, John Thomas
(1950–)

American screenwriter, novelist, actor and film-maker, born in Schenectady, New York. A dedicated sportsman, he worked at a number of jobs after his graduation from Williams College, before winning **O Henry** awards for the short stories *I-80 Nebraska, M.490– M.205* (1975) and *Breed* (1977). His novels *Pride Of The Bimbos* (1975) and *Union Dues* (1979) earned extensive praise for their wit, irony and his ear for dialect. As a screenwriter he brought a knowing humour and inventiveness to such projects as *Piranha* (1978) and *The Howling* (1980). He made his directorial debut with *The Return Of The Secaucus Seven* (1979), an examination of the sense of disillusionment that infects a reunion of 1960s college radicals, which received an Oscar nomination for Best Original Screenplay. As a writer-director, he has been committed to exploring a radical political and social agenda whilst giving voice to characters marginalized within the mainstream film arena. His most accomplished films include *Lianna* (1982), *Matewan* (1987), *City Of Hope* (1991) and *Passion Fish* (1992), for which he received a further Oscar nomination. An occasional playwright and actor, he returned to novel writing with *Los Gusanos* (1991), an epic account of Cuban exiles in Miami.

SAYONOV, Vissarion
(1903–)
Russian descriptive minor poet, born in Siberia. A socialist realist, he excels in laconic observation of nature. There are a few translations of his work in *Modern Russian Poetry* (1966, V Markov and M Sparks eds).

SCANLAN, Nelle M(argaret), properly Ellen Margaret
(1882–1968)
New Zealand journalist, foreign correspondent, social commentator and, later, author of light novels and of the bestselling *Pencarrow* tetralogy. She was born in Picton. Her first book, *Primrose Hill* (1931), was a social comedy set in London, where she moved from Washington, DC, in 1923, as were others such as *The Marriage of Nicholas Cotter* (1936). By that time she had published *Pencarrow* (1932), the first of her 'New Zealand' quartet, followed by *Tides of Youth* (1933), *Winds of Heaven* (1934) and *Kelly Pencarrow* (1939). The four books make up a dynastic saga of a 'typical' New Zealand pioneering family through the evolution of that country's society.
▷ *Road to Pencarrow* (1963)

SCARFE, Francis
(1911–86)
English poet, born in South Shields, Durham and educated at the universities of Durham, Cambridge and Paris. A lecturer in French at Glasgow University Scarfe's more permanent home was Oxford. Coming to prominence in the 1930s, he combines lyrical passion like **Dylan Thomas**'s, surrealism akin to **David Gascoyne**'s, and an apocalyptic phrase-making and balladry comparable to **Auden**'s. Never finding an original poetic voice, he nevertheless made the combination his own. His best work is found in *Inscapes* (1940) and *Poems and Ballads* (1942). His critical prose includes *Auden and After* (1942) and *The Art of Paul Valéry* (1954).

SCARRON, Paul
(1610–60)
French writer, born in Paris, the son of a lawyer. He became an *abbé*, and gave himself up to pleasure. About 1634 he paid a long visit to Italy, and in 1638 began to suffer from a malady which ultimately left him paralysed. He obtained a prebend in Mans (1643), tried physicians in vain, and, giving up all hope of remedy, returned to Paris in 1646 to depend upon letters for a living. From this time he began to pour forth endless sonnets, madrigals, songs, epistles and satires. In 1644 he published *Typhon, ou la giganto-machie* (Eng trans *Typhon: or the Wars of the Gods and the*

Giants, 1704); and made a still greater hit with his metrical comedy, *Jodelet, ou le maître valet* (1645, 'Jodelet; or, the Master-Butler'), followed by *Les Trois Dorothées* (1648, 'The Three Dorothies') and *Les Boutades du Capitaine Matamore* (1647, 'The Jests of Captain Matamore'), the plots taken from the Spanish. In 1648 appeared his *Virgile travesti* (part one, 'Virgil Burlesqued') and the popular comedy, *L'Héritier ridicule* (1653, 'The Ridiculous Heir'). One of the bitterest satires against Mazarin which he wrote for the *Fronde* probably lost him his pensions. The burlesque predominates in most of his writing, but it is as the creator of the realistic novel that he will always be remembered. *Le Romant comique* (1651–7, Eng trans *The Comical Romance*, 1665) was a reaction against the euphuistic and interminable novels of **Madeleine de Scudéry** and **Honoré d'Urfé**. The work of **Alain Le Sage, Daniel Defoe, Henry Fielding** and **Tobias Smollett** owes much to him. In 1652 he married Françoise d'Aubigné, afterwards Madame de Maintenon, who brought a hitherto unknown decorum into his household and writings.
▷ E Magne, *Scarron et son milieu* (1923)

SCARRY, Richard McClure
(1919–)
American illustrator and writer of children's books, born in Boston. He was educated at Boston Museum School of Fine Arts and served in the US army in the Mediterranean and North Africa. Didactic, detailed and scatty, his output is prolific and he is hugely popular with children tolerant of his formulaic approach. Indicative titles are *What Do People Do All Day?* (1968) and *Hop Aboard, Here We Go!* (1972).

SCÈVE, Maurice
(1510–64)
French Renaissance poet, born in Lyons. He was a leader of the *école lyonnaise*, which paved the way for the *Pléiade*, a group of poets which gathered around **Ronsard**. His most important poem is *Délie, object de plus hautte vertu* (1544, 'Delia, Object of the Highest Virtue'), on the subject of love. Other works include *La Saulsaye* (1547), and a didactic poem on the history of mankind, *Microcosme* (1563).
▷ V C Saulnier, *Maurice Scève* (1948)

SCHADE, Jens August
(1903–78)
Danish novelist and poet, born in Skive, Jutland. The major theme of his writing has been defined as 'the coincidental unity between everyday life and cosmic Eros'. The chief influences upon him were, from his own

country, **Claussen**, and from Great Britain, **D H Lawrence**. The title of the novel *Mennesker modes og sod Musik opstaar i Hjwetet* (1944, 'People Meet and Sweet Music Fills the Heart') is characteristic.

SCHAEFER, Jack Warner
(1907–)

American short-story writer and novelist, born in Cleveland, Ohio. He was educated at Columbia University, and worked as a journalist, teacher and editor. His perennial subject was the American West, but he transcends the limitations of the 'western' genre in both psychological depth and literary merit, and is its most distinguished fictional chronicler. His first novel, *Shane* (1949), remains his best known, but his other works include the lengthy novel *Monte Walsh* (1965), a realistic if rambling account of cowboy life, and a number of short stories and novellas, gathered together in *Collected Stories* (1966) and *The Short Novels* (1967). A critical edition of *Shane* was published in 1984.

SCHAEFFER, Albrecht
(1885–1950)

German poet, novelist and essayist from Elbing. He was a young member of the circle of **Stefan George**—upon whom he wrote an illuminating essay in his *Dichter und Dichtung* (1923, 'Poets and Poetry'); to some extent he always suffered from the heaviness of thought associated with that master. He left Germany for America in 1939, and died in the year of his return home. He published much religious poetry and a *Bildungsroman* in the style of **Goethe**: *Helianth* (1920–1, shortened 1929). He believed that the world had been created by the Spirit, whose medium was himself and other selected poets.

SCHAEFFER, Susan F(romberg)
(1941–)

American novelist, poet and short-story writer, born in Brooklyn, New York. She received her PhD from the University of Chicago in 1966, and has since combined her academic with her writing career, currently working as a professor of English at Brooklyn College. Her novels, of which *The Madness of a Seduced Woman* (1983) is the best known, combine some of the trappings of romance, suitably updated, with a feminist sensibility. The latter, as is shown in *Buffalo Afternoon* (1989), is often extended to empathize with men: in this novel she deals with a young soldier's experience of Vietnam, and the traumatic aftermath of the war there. *The Injured Party* (1986) is a melioristic account of domestic life, in which a woman and her husband

are reconciled after the death of the wife's ex-fiancé.

SCHAPER, Edzard
(1908–)

German novelist, essayist, dramatist and radio playwright, born in Ostrovo, Posen. He settled in Estonia in 1930, but was driven out by the Nazis and the Soviets (both of whom sentenced him to death *in absentia*, for his liberal journalism). After much travelling he eventually settled in Cologne in the early 1950s. A much respected and thoughtful Christian novelist (he moved from the Greek Orthodox Church to Catholicism in 1951), he has written both historical and contemporary novels. Two collections of stories have been translated: *Sterne über der Grenze* (1950, Eng trans *Star Over the Frontier*, 1961) and *Das Tier* (1928, Eng trans *The Dancing Bear*, 1961).
▷W Grenzmann, *Dichtung und Glaube* (1960)

SCHAUKAL, Richard
(1874–1942)

Austrian Symbolist poet, born in Brünn. He was in the Austrian civil service, and like **Hugo von Hofmannsthal** turned away from the decadence of the declining Austrian Empire to seek perfection in lyrical expression of poetic dreams in *Gedichte* (1893, 'Poems'), *Tage und Träume* (1899, 'Days and Dreams'), *Sehnsucht* (1900, 'Yearning'), and the posthumous collection *Spätlese* (1943, 'Late Harvest').

SCHEFFEL, Joseph Viktor von
(1826–86)

German poet and novelist, born in Karlsruhe. He studied law at Heidelberg, Munich and Berlin, but in 1852 went to Italy to write. His best book is *Der Trompeter von Säckingen* (1854, 'The Säckingen Trumpeter'), a romantic and humorous tale in verse. His other best-known books are the historical novel *Ekkehard* (1855), and the Lieder and student songs of *Gaudeamus* (1868).
▷J Proelss, *Scheffels Leben und Dichten* (1887)

SCHÉHADÉ, Georges
(1910–89)

Lebanese poet and dramatist. Born in Alexandria, he lived for long periods in Beirut, but made frequent visits to France. Two plays, *Monsieur Bob'le* (1952) and *La Soirée des proverbes* (1954, 'The Evening of Proverbs'), preceded *Histoire de Vasco* (1956), which won Schéhadé international fame in spite of an initially mixed critical reception, the enthusiasts praising its subtle and gentle satire while

the sceptics reduced its tragedy to pathos, rejecting its poetry and humour. *Vasco* received particular acclaim in Britain, where the play was first performed at the 1960 Edinburgh Festival by the Oxford Theatre Group. His poetry collections include *Poésies I, II* and *III* (1938, 1948, 1949), and *Anthologie du vers unique* (1977). Schéhadé's is a significant voice in the established tradition of French anti-war literature.
▷ R Baldick, Introduction to *Theatre of War* (1967)

SCHENKKAN, Robert Frederic
(1953–)

American playwright and actor, born in Chapel Hill, North Carolina. He graduated in Theatre Arts from the University of Texas in 1975, and studied acting at Cornell University. His first play was *Final Passages*, originally produced as *Derelict in Buffalo* (1982), followed by the one-act plays *Intermission* and *Lunchbreak* (both 1982). His most successful work to date, *The Kentucky Cycle* (1991–2), won him a Pulitzer Prize for Drama in 1991. His other plays include *The Survivalist* (1983) and *Tall Tales* (1988).

SCHERFIG, Hans
(1905–79)

Danish novelist, born into a liberal and affluent printer's family in Copenhagen. A simultaneously venemous and warm-hearted satirist who exposes the vices of the class-based society, his most notable novel is *Det forsømte Foraar* (1940, Eng trans *Stolen Spring*, 1986), a classic in Danish literature, about pupils crippled by an authoritarian education system and the subsequent poisoning of a hated Latin teacher, Mr Blomme. The hallmarks of Scherfig's bestseller novels are their unconventional crime plots and their ironic, pseudo-objective narration, which imitates conventional modes of speaking or writing. Masterful examples are *Den forsvundne Fuldmægtig* (1938, Eng trans *The Missing Bureaucrat*, 1988), about a civil servant in crisis who eventually finds peace in prison, and *Frydenholm* (1962), an extensive, semi-documentary novel about Denmark under German occupation during World War II, with particular focus on the unlawful arrest and internment of the members of the Danish Communist Party in 1943. Scherfig had joined the Communist Party in 1932 and remained a stalwart communist through Stalinism and the emergence of the New Left right up to his death.
▷ C E Bay (ed), *Hans Scherfig 1905–1979* (1989)

SCHICKELE, René
(1883–1940)

German Alsatian writer, born in Oberehnheim. His father was German, and his mother French. A journalist by profession, he wrote poems, plays and novels, including the trilogy of realist novels *Das Erbe am Rhein* (1925–31, 'The Inheritance on the Rhine'), and the poetry collections *Weiss und Rot* (1911, 'White and Red') and *Die Leibewache* (1914, 'The Bodyguard'). He was a pacifist, and argued in his writings for cultural unity in Europe.

SCHILLER, Johann Christoph Friedrich von
(1759–1805)

German dramatist, poet and historian, born in Marbach on the Neckar. His father was an army surgeon in the service of the Duke of Württemberg. He was educated at the grammar school in Ludwigsburg, and was intended for the church, but at the age of 13, at the personal request of the duke, was obliged to attend the latter's military academy, studying the law instead of theology, but finally qualified as a surgeon (1780) and was posted to a regiment in Stuttgart. Although outwardly conforming well, he found an outlet for his true feelings in the reading and eventually writing of *Sturm und Drang* verse and plays. His first play, *Die Räuber* (1781, Eng trans *The Robbers*, 1792), published at his own expense, was, on account of its seemingly anarchical and revolutionary appeal, an instant success when it reached the stage at Mannheim the following year. Schiller played truant from his regiment to attend the performance, was arrested but, forbidden to write anything but medical works in the future, fled and, in hiding at Bauerbach, finished the plays *Die Verschwörung des Fiesko zu Genua* (1783, Eng trans *Fiesco; or, The Genoese Conspiracy*, 1796) and *Kabale und Liebe* (1783, Eng trans *Cabal and Love*, 1795). For a few months he was dramatist to the Mannheim theatre. He next issued a theatrical journal, *Die rheinische Thalia*, begun in 1784, in which were first printed most of his play *Don Carlos* (1787, Eng trans 1798), many of his best poems, and the stories *Verbrecher aus verlorener Ehre* (1786, Eng trans *The Dishonoured Irreclaimable*, 1826) and *Der Geisterseher* (1787–9, Eng trans *The Ghost-Seer, or Apparitionist*, 1795). In 1785 he went by invitation to Leipzig and in Dresden, where **Karl Theodor Körner** was living, he found rest from emotional excitement and financial worries. Here he finished *Don Carlos*, written in blank verse, not prose, his first mature play, though it suffers artistically from excessive length and lack of unity. Amongst the finest fruits of his discussions with Körner and his circle are the poems *An die Freude* (c.1788, 'Ode to Joy'), later magnificently set to music by Beethoven in his choral symphony, and *Die Künstler* (1858, 'The Artist'). After two years in Dresden and an unhappy love affair he went to Weimar, where he studied Kant, met his future wife, Charlotte von Lengefeld, and began his history of the revolt of the Netherlands. In 1788 he was appointed Honorary Professor of History at Jena, and married, but his health broke down through overwork from writing a history of the Thirty Years War, *Geschichte des dreissigjährigen Krieges* (1793, Eng trans *The History of the Thirty Years' War in Germany*, 1799), the letters on aesthetic education, *Briefe über die ästhetische Erziehung des Menschen* (1795, Eng trans *Upon the Aesthetic Culture of Man*, 1845), and the famous *Über naive und sentimentalische Dichtung* (1795–6, Eng trans *On Simple and Sentimental Poetry*, 1884), in which he distinguishes ancient from modern poetry by their different approaches to nature. His short-lived literary magazine, *Die Horen* (1795–7), was followed by the celebrated *Xenien* (1797, 'Epigrams'), a collection of satirical epigrams against philistinism and mediocrity in the arts, in which the new friendship between **Goethe** and Schiller found mutual expression. This inspired the great ballads (1797–8), *Der Taucher* ('The Diver'), *Der Ring des Polykrates* ('The Ring of Polycrates'), *Die Kraniche des Ibykus* ('The Cranes of Ibycus'), the famous *Lied von der Glocke* (completed in 1799, 'Song of the Bell') and, under the influence of **Shakespeare**, the dramatic trilogy, *Wallenstein* (1796–9, trans by **Samuel Taylor Coleridge**, 1800), comprising *Wallensteins Lager*, *Die Piccolomini*, and *Wallensteins Tod*, the greatest historical drama in the German language. This was followed by *Maria Stuart* (1800; Eng trans *Mary Stuart*, 1801; also trans by **Stephen Spender**, 1957), a remarkable psychological study of the two queens, Elizabeth and Mary, Queen of Scots, in which the latter by her death gains a moral victory. Schiller the historian is here at odds with Schiller the dramatist. Again, in *Die Jungfrau von Orleans* (1801, Eng trans *The Maid of Orleans*, 1835), Joan of Arc dies on the battlefield and is resurrected. *Die Braut von Messina* (1803, Eng trans *The Bride of Messina*, 1837) portrays the relentless feud between two hostile brothers, and the half-legend of *Wilhelm Tell* (1804, Eng trans *William Tell*, 1825) is made by Schiller a dramatic manifesto for political freedom. There is a fragment of *Demetrius* (1804–5; published 1859), his unfinished work. He was ennobled in 1802 and fell ill in 1804.

▷ W Witte, *J C F Schiller* (1949)

SCHIMPER, Carl Friedrich
(1803–67)

German naturalist and poet, a pioneer in modern plant morphology. He was notable for his work on phyllotaxis, and in geology for his theory of prehistoric alternating hot and cold periods. Despite his talents, he failed to secure any academic post. Many of his scientific ideas were published as poems; several hundred are known.

SCHLAF, Johannes
(1862–1941)

German novelist and dramatist, born in Querfurt. He studied at Berlin and with **Arno Holz** wrote *Papa Hamlet* (1889), a volume of short stories, *Die Familie Selicke* (1890, 'The Selicke Family'), a social drama, *Peter Boies Freite* (1902, 'Peter Boie's Wooing'), and others.

▷ S Bergen, *Johannes Schlaf* (1941)

SCHLEGEL, August Wilhelm von
(1767–1845)

German writer and pioneer of the German Romantic movement, brother of **Friedrich von Schlegel**, born in Hanover. He studied theology at Göttingen, but soon turned to literature. In 1795 he settled in Jena, and in 1796 married a widow, Caroline Böhmer (1763–1809), who separated from him in 1803 and married Friedrich Schelling. In 1798 he became Professor of Literature and Fine Art at Jena, and founded with his brother the literary journal *Das Athenäum*. In 1801–4 he lectured at Berlin. Most of the next 14 years he spent in the house of **Madame de Staël** at Coppet, though he lectured on *Vorlesungen über schöne Literatur und Kunst* (3 vols, 1810, Eng trans *Dramatic Art and Literature*, 1815) at Vienna in 1808, and was secretary to the Crown Prince of Sweden (1813–14). From 1818 till his death he was Professor of Literature at Bonn. He translated 17 plays of **Shakespeare**, and also translated works by **Dante**, **Calderón de la Barca**, **Cervantes** and **Camoens**, and edited the *Bhagavad-Gita* and the *Ramayana*.

SCHLEGEL, (Karl Wilhelm) Friedrich von
(1772–1829)

German writer and critic, and pioneer of the German Romantic movement, brother of **August Wilhelm von Schlegel**, born in Hanover. He was educated at Göttingen and Leipzig, in 1798 he eloped with Dorothea (1763–1839), the daughter of Moses Mendelssohn and wife of a Jewish merchant, Simon Veit, and mother of Philipp Veit the religious painter, and next year utilized his experiences in a notorious romance, *Lucinde* (1799). He then joined his brother at Jena,

and with him wrote and edited the journal *Das Athenäum*, in the interests of Romanticism. *Charakteristiken und Kritiken* (1801, 'Characterizations and Criticisms') contains some of both brothers' best writing. He studied oriental languages at Paris (1802–4), and in 1808 he published a pioneering work on Sanskrit and Indo–European linguistics, *Über die Sprache und Weisheit der Indier* (1808, 'On the Language and Wisdom of the Indians'). In 1808 he became a Roman Catholic, and joined the Austrian foreign service; it was he who penned the Austrian proclamations against Napoleon in 1809. His best-known books are two series of lectures: *Philosophie der Geschichte* (1829, Eng trans *The Philosophy of History*, 1835) and *Friedrich Schlegels Geschichte der alten und neuen Literatur* (1815, Eng trans *Lectures on the History of Literature*, 1818). There are also English versions of his *Philosophie des Lebens* (1828, *The Philosophy of Life*, 1847) and *Über die neuere Geschichte* (1811, *A Course of Lectures on Modern History*, 1849).
▷ E Behler, *Friedrich von Schlegel* (1966)

SCHLEGEL, Johann Elias
(1718–49)

German dramatist and literary theorist, uncle of **August Wilhelm** and **Friedrich von Schlegel**, born in Meissen and educated at Leipzig University. The author of at least 14 plays, such as the tragedies *Canut* (1746) and *Hekuba* (1736) and the comedies *Der Geheimnisvolle* (1747) and *Die stumme Schönheit* (1747), Schlegel is better known for his criticism. In *Vergleichung Shakespears und Andreas Gryphs* (1741) he is the first of his countrymen to interpret **Shakespeare** sympathetically; in *Abhandlung von der Nachahmung* (1742–5) he qualifies the idea of Art as imitation of Life by stressing the selective and intensifying power of the medium involved.
▷ E M Wilkinson, *Johann Elias Schlegel: A German Pioneer in Aesthetics* (1945)

SCHMIDT, Augusto Frederico
(1906–65)

Brazilian poet and publisher. He began as a *modernista* poet, but gradually abandoned this style for a simpler, more mystical type of poetry. As a publisher he issued works by **Ramos** and other leading writers. A few of his poems are translated in the *Penguin Book of Latin American Verse* (1971, ed E Curacciolo-Trejo).
▷ J Nist, *The Modernist Movement in Brazil* (1967)

SCHNABEL, Johann Gottfried
(1692–after 1750)

German novelist and physician, born in Sandersdorf near Bitterfield. He published under the pseudonym of 'Gisander'. He served as a surgeon in the War of the Spanish Succession, and then practised in Hamburg and Stolberg. Of all the many novels which tried to emulate **Defoe**'s *Robinson Crusoe*, Schnabel's *Die Insel Felsenberg* (1731–43) was by far the most original and successful—it is still read with pleasure today. In many ways it epitomizes, although in German terms, just those individualistic and religious concerns which Defoe himself brought to British attention.
▷ F Brüggemann, *Utopie und Robinsonade* (1914)

SCHNACK, Anton
(1892–1974)

German poet, story writer and novelist, born in Rieneck. His elder brother Friedrich (1888–1973) was a well-known popular writer. His delicate novels and stories, as well as his early expressionist verse, found favour with discerning readers.

SCHNEIDER, Rolf
(1932–)

German dramatist and story-writer, born in what was Karl–Marx Stadt. He lived and worked in the former East Germany, both as an editor (of *Aufbau*) and as a radio playwright. His most notable play is a semi-documentary on the trials at Nuremberg: *Prozess in Nürnberg* (1967). Some of his stories may be read in *Brücken und Gitter* (1965, Eng trans *Bridges and Bars*, 1967).

SCHNEUR, Zalman, originally Zalman Zalkind
(1886–1959)

Hebrew and Yiddish poet and novelist, born in Sklov, Russia, into a noted Hasidic family; he died in the USA, whence he had escaped from Germany during World War I. His attitude is well summed up by the affectionate description of him as one who followed 'the style of the big I'; his friend and mentor **Bialik** said of him that he 'assailed the universe'. His earlier poetry is in Yiddish, but he discovered his own voice in his Hebrew poetry. Many readers turned to his 'Noah Pandre' stories—in *Noah Pandre* (1908, Eng trans 1936) and in *Song of the Dnieper* (1945)—as an antidote to the notion of the servile Jew in Russia: in these a butcher's son shows the despots and racists what a Jewish fist can do. His **Whitman**esque poetry is not subtle, but is often overwhelmingly powerful.

SCHNITZLER, Arthur
(1862–1931)

Austrian dramatist and novelist of Jewish origin, born in Vienna. He practised as a physician in Vienna from 1885 before he turned playwright. His highly psychological, often strongly erotic short plays and novels, executed with great technical skill, frequently underline some social problem, mostly against the familiar easy-going Viennese background. *Anatol* (1893, Eng trans 1911) and *Reigen* (1900, Eng trans *Hands Around*, 1920; better known as *La Ronde*, the title of a 1959 translation) are cycles of one-act plays linked with one another by the overlapping of one of the characters until the chain is completed by a character of the last meeting one from the first. Other notable works include *Der grüne Kakadu* (1899, Eng trans *The Green Cockatoo*, 1913), *Liebelei* (1895, Eng trans *Light-o'-Love*, 1912), *Der Weg ins Freie* (1908, Eng trans *The Road to the Open*, 1923), *Professor Bernhardi* (1912, Eng trans 1913), on anti-Semitism, and *Flucht in die Finsternis* (1931, Eng trans *Flight into Darkness*, 1931).

▷ B von Brentano, *Arthur Schnitzler* (1965)

SCHNURRE, Wolfdietrich
(1920–)

German story writer, satirist, poet, novelist and (notably) writer of *horspielen* (radio plays), born in Frankfurt am Main. He was one of the founders of the literary circle Gruppe '47, but soon resigned from it. Grotesque and tender by turns, his often memorable, and almost always laconic, work may have been neglected because of its extreme pungency and irony. He is represented in **Hamburger** and **Middleton**'s *Modern German Poetry* (1962).

SCHÖNHERR, Karl
(1867–1943)

Austrian folk dramatist, story writer and poet, born in Axams in the Tyrol. He practised as a doctor in Vienna until 1905, when he gave up medicine for literature. He is remembered chiefly for his drama. He began under the influence of **Anzengruber** and, to a smaller extent, **Werfel**. His comedies and tragedies of Tyrolese peasant life subsequently became more solid and original. Many of his plays, such as *Glaube und Heimat* (1910, 'Faith and Fireside'), are historical. *Der Weibsteufel* (1914, 'The Female Devil') is a skilfully written and powerful sex tragedy of naturalistic proportions about a woman who has her feeble husband murdered by a young hunter, whom she thereafter destroys. Schönherr wrote many more plays, some patriotic, some city comedies, and a gripping religious mystery about Judas: *Passionspiel* (1933). He was not commercially successful in the theatre in the latter half of his career.

SCHOPENHAUER, Arthur
(1788–1860)

German philosopher and essayist, born in Danzig. A radical philosopher of pessimism, besides being one of the very few philosophers who was also a great stylist, he had unbounded influence upon a host of writers, including **Friedrich Nietzsche**, **André Gide**, **Thomas Hardy**, **Thomas Mann**, the composer Richard Wagner (who exercised such an influence on French literature), and countless others. Popularly taken to have been an excessively unpleasant and vindictive man (as presented by, for example, **Bertrand Russell**), the truth is more complex—he bequeathed all he had to the relief of human suffering. Schopenhauer's beautifully and eloquently expressed tone, that life is not worth living unless the nature of what he called the Will is contemplated, chimed in exactly with both his era's loss of faith, and with its turning towards Indian religion (he drew much inspiration from the *Upanishads*). His mother Johanna Schopenhauer was herself a novelist of note, and an associate of **Goethe**. Schopenhauer also, by his insistence upon the fact that only self-denial and withdrawal from materialist aspirations can bring peace—in his terms surrender to the universal Will as distinct from the individual will—influenced many more modern thinkers, from **Rudolph Steiner** through **Buber** to **Jung**. For many he presented the only possible solution to the problem of the existence of evil in the world. The only consolation, for Schopenhauer, lies in *Mitleid*, compassion. His picture of suffering in the world, despite his insistence that his work had been dictated to him by a religious entity whose existence he denied, remains one of the most powerful of all.

▷ R Taylor (ed), *The Will to Live: Selected Writings* (1962); A S Zimmern, *Arthur Schopenhauer: His Life and Philosophy* (1932)

SCHORER, Mark
(1908–77)

American novelist, critic and biographer, born in Sauk City, Wisconsin and educated at the state university. He went on to teach at Dartmouth, Harvard, and Berkeley. His third novel, *The Wars of Love* (1953), won critical acclaim for its skilful portrayal of the complex and tragic relationships linking a one-female and three-male foursome through childhood to middle age. His short stories, collected in *The State of Mind* (1956), often concern retrospection and ambivalent nostalgia for early youth. He is best known, however, for his criticism, which includes famous essays on *Lady Chatterley's Lover* and *Wuthering Heights*, available in the collection *The World We Imagine* (1968).

SCHRADER, Paul
(1946–)

American film-maker, born in Grand Rapids, Michigan. Raised in a strict Calvinist household, he did not see his first film until in his late teens, but soon became a voracious viewer and incisive critic, whose influential writing includes *Transcendental Style In Film: Ozu, Bresson and Dreyer* (1972). A student of film at UCLA, he entered the film industry as a screenwriter, collaborating to memorable effect with director Martin Scorsese on a series of films that portrayed the hell-on-earth of contemporary urban existence, the brutality of traditional masculine values and the possibility of redemption. Their films together include *Taxi Driver* (1976), *Raging Bull* (1980) and *The Last Temptation Of Christ* (1988). He made his directorial debut with *Blue Collar* (1978), a gritty exposé of union corruption, and has also worked as a writer-director on a diverse range of films dominated by a strong visual sensibility and an emotional coldness. His work includes *American Gigolo* (1980), an examination of redemption through love, *Mishima* (1985), a stylized dramatization of the life and work of the Japanese writer, and *Light Sleeper* (1992), a convincing portrait of mid-life anxiety and the desire for change.

SCHREINER, Olive
(1855–1920)

South African author and feminist, born in Wittebergen Mission Station, Cape of Good Hope, the daughter of a German Methodist missionary and an English mother. She grew up largely self-educated and at the age of 15 became a governess to a Boer family near the Karoo desert. She lived in England (1881–9), where her novel, *The Story of an African Farm* (1883), the first sustained, imaginative work to come from Africa, was published under the pseudonym Ralph Iron. She had a fiery, rebellious temperament and a lifelong hatred of her mother; in her later works the creative artist gave way to the passionate propagandist for women's rights, pro-Boer loyalty and pacifism. These include the allegorical *Dreams* (1891) and *Dream Life and Real Life* (1893), the polemical *Trooper Peter Halket* (1897), a sociological study, *Woman and Labour* (1911), and her last novel *From Man to Man* (1926). In 1894 she married S P Cronwright, who took her name, wrote a biography of her (1924) and edited her letters (1926).
▷ S C Cronwright-Schreiner, *The Life of Olive Schreiner* (1924)

SCHUBART, Christian Friedrich Daniel
(1739–91)

German poet, born in Obersontheim in Swabia. He wrote satirical and religious poems. He was imprisoned at Hohenasperg (1777–87) by the Duke of Württemberg, whom he had offended by an epigram. He is largely remembered for his influence on **Schiller**.
▷ K M Klos, *Christian Schubart* (1908)

SCHULBERG, Budd Wilson
(1914–)

American novelist and screenwriter, born in New York City. He moved to California as a child, and was brought up in Hollywood, which became the satirically treated subject of his novel *What Makes Sammy Run?* (1941). His best-known work is the film *On the Waterfront* (1954), a hard-hitting, realist exposé of corruption on the New York docks which he turned into the novel *Waterfront* in 1955. *The Harder They Fall* (1947), about corruption in boxing, and *Everything That Moves* (1980), about the connection between gangsters and the unions, treated similar themes. *The Disenchanted* (1950) traced the decline of a writer based on **F Scott Fitzgerald**, while *Sanctuary V* (1969) entered the seamy world of Latin-American politics. His stories were collected in *Some Faces in the Crowd* (1950).
▷ *Moving Pictures: Memories of a Hollywood Prince* (1981)

SCHULZ, Bruno
(1892–1942)

Polish writer of magical short stories. He grew up in the predominantly Jewish town of Drohobycz, taught art at the local school, and was murdered there by a Wehrmacht officer during the occupation. He published only two books in his lifetime, both of which have enjoyed considerable success in English. *Sklepy cynamonowe* (1934, published in the UK as *The Street of Crocodiles*, in the USA as *Cinnamon Shops and Other Stories*, 1963) is a collection full of magical transformations and cabbalistic connections, centred on the experience of one Joseph N, who is clearly a projection of Schulz himself. A later book, *Sanatorium pod klepsydra* (1937, Eng trans *Sanatorium Under the Sign of the Hourglass*, 1978), shows Schulz bringing his unique vision to bear on wider social and philosophical questions. He was clearly still a writer of immense promise when he died.
▷ E Baur, *Die Prose von Schulz* (1975)

SCHUYLER, James Marcus
(1923–91)

American poet, novelist, playwright and art critic, born in Chicago, whose poetry unflinchingly confronts the modern middle-class environment. Collections such as *Salute* (1960) and *The Home Book: Prose and Poems*

1951–1970 (1977) look in almost obsessive detail at the minutiae of daily life. His first novel, *A Nest of Ninnies* (1969), written with **John Ashbery** who, like him, was associated with the New York school of poets, is an almost plotless attack upon what the authors consider to be the vacuousness of much middle-class life. A similar theme pervades his next novel, *What's for Dinner?* (1978), almost a third of which is set in a hospital ward for alcoholics. He won the Pulitzer Prize for Poetry in 1981 for *The Morning of the Poet* (1980). His play, *Unpacking a Trunk* (1965), written with **Kenward Elmslie**, shows a group of people describing the objects they have retrieved from a trunk.

SCHWARTZ, Delmore
(1913–66)

American poet, story writer and critic, born in Brooklyn, New York City. He was educated at New York University and made a startling debut as a poet while still a student. Writing lyrics, fiction, drama and criticism, he was associated with the *Partisan Review* group of writers as editor (1943–55), and editor of *The New Republic* (1955–7). A profound ironist, in 1960 he became one of the youngest winners of the Bollingen Prize. His collections of verse include *In Dreams Begin Responsibilities* (1938), *Shenandoah* (1941), *Vaudeville for a Princess* (1950) and *Summer Knowledge* (1959). His stories are collected in *The World is a Wedding* (1948) and *Successful Love* (1961). **Saul Bellow** memorably portrayed him in *Humboldt's Gift* (1975).
▷J Atlas, *Delmore Schwartz: the life of an American poet* (1977)

SCHWOB, Marcel
(1867–1905)

French critic, novelist, dramatist, story writer, scholar (of English, German, classical and Indian literatures, and of the criminal *argot* of **François Villon**). He was born in Chaville, of Jewish parents. He anticipated many modern notions, such as that of 'biography as a mode of fiction'; his poetic *Le Livre de Monelle* (1894, Eng trans *The Book of Monelle*, 1929), based on his friendship with a prostitute, is a remarkable book by any standards. He had wide influence, especially on **Valéry** and **Jarry**.

SCIASCIA, Leonardo
(1921–89)

Sicilian novelist, born in Racalmuto. Taking Sicily for the focus of his work, his themes embrace its society past and present which he saw as exemplifying the political, social and spiritual tensions to be found on the wider stage of Europe. A teacher and politician, he first published *Favole della dittatura* (1950, 'Fables of Dictatorship'). *Le parrocchie di Regalpetra* (1956, Eng trans *Salt in the Wound*, 1969) pointed the way ahead for his fiction and subsequent works developed his early themes. *Candido* (1977) was published in English in 1977 and in the 1980s his novels, several of which were re-translated, reached a wider English-speaking audience. These include *Il consiglio d'Egitto* (1963, Eng trans *The Council of Egypt*, 1966) and *A ciascuno il suo* (1968, Eng trans *A Man's Blessing*, 1968 (US); 1969 (UK)).
▷G Jackson, *Sciascia: a thematic and structural study* (1981)

SCOTT, Alexander
(c.1515–1584)

Scottish lyrical poet of the school of **Dunbar**. Little is known of his early life, except that he became musician and organist at the Augustinian priory of Inchmahome, in the Firth of Forth, in 1548. He had associations with the court of Mary, Queen of Scots, and in 1565 was a canon of Inchaffray in Perthshire. He bought an estate in Fife in 1567 and became a wealthy landowner. He wrote 36 short poems, either courtly love lyrics or poems offering moral advice. He is considered to be the last of the Scottish 'Makars' (15th/16th-century poets).
▷A K Scott (ed), *Poems* (1953)

SCOTT, Duncan Campbell
(1862–1947)

Canadian poet, short-story writer, literary editor and critic (known in particular for his editions of **Archibald Lampman**'s poetry and his contributions to the Toronto *Globe* column, 'At the Mermaid Inn'). He was born in Ottawa and spent much of his life as an emissary of the Canadian Department of Indian Affairs. *The Magic House* and *Labour and the Angel* were published in 1893 and 1898 respectively, but it is his third volume of poetry, *New World Lyrics* (1905), that includes many of the 'Indian poems' for which he is best known. This preoccupation with the unsettling and often tragic interaction of indigenous and settler cultures also figures prominently in subsequent volumes, and the collected *Poems of Duncan Campbell Scott* (1926).

SCOTT, Evelyn, originally Elsie Dunn
(1893–1963)

American poet and novelist, born in Tennessee. She changed her name in 1913, aged 20, having run away to Brazil with a married university Dean. After several years of hardship in South America she returned to the USA and began her career as a writer with a volume of poetry, *Precipitations* (1920), in the Imagist vein. *The Wave* (1929), a popular novel about the Civil War composed as a montage of letters, newspaper reports, army records and poetic narrative, brought her greater notice. **William Faulkner**, whom she admired, judged her pretty good 'for a woman'.

SCOTT, F(rancis) R(eginald)
(1899–1985)

Canadian poet and critic, born in Quebec. As a witty and graceful poet, both satirical and otherwise, Scott was only a moderate practitioner, but he made Canadian readers aware of **T S Eliot** and **Pound**, was an active socialist, and compiled one or two influential anthologies. Some of his best poetry is collected in *The Eye of the Needle* (1957).
▷D Pacey, *Ten Canadian Poets* (1958)

SCOTT, Gabriel
(1874–1958)

Norwegian writer of novels, short stories, poetry and drama, strongly linked to the nature and people of the south coast of Norway. As a young author he won a name as a writer of children's books, but he is now remembered best for his novel *Kilden* (1918, 'The Source'), about the life and thoughts of the mild and loving fisherman Markus. As in all his novels, Scott here advocates a mystic and pantheistic form of Christianity, based on an individualistic closeness to nature and God, and asks critical questions about the kind of fundamentalist free-church movement he saw around him.

SCOTT, John
(1730–83)

English poet and essayist, best known for his celebration of village life in *Amwell* (1776). Born in Bermondsey, the son of a Quaker linen draper, his first verses were published in *The Gentleman's Magazine*. He was acquainted with **Johnson** and the philosophical Scot, **James Beattie**.

SCOTT, Mary
(1888–1979)

New Zealand writer of light novels and the *Barbara* series (1936–54) of rural sketches which drew upon her two decades of contributions to a regional newspaper. Born in Bay of Islands, she was among the first writers consistently to use a New Zealand setting for her novels, which became very popular overseas, especially in Europe. Her first novel, *Breakfast for Six*, did not appear until 1953, and was followed by others whose titles convey the remote, homely, rural 'backblocks' life on which they are based, from *Dinner*

Doesn't Matter (1957), *Tea and Biscuits* (1961) and *Turkey at Twelve* (1968), which describes a backblocks Christmas, to her last novel *Board but No Breakfast* (1978). Between 1960 and 1965, with **Joyce West**, she wrote five crime novels, again using local settings, beginning with *Fatal Lady* and including *The Mangrove Murder* (1963) and *No Red Herrings* (1964). She also wrote a more serious novel, *The Unwritten Book* (1957), evoking the grim side of rural life and drawing upon her own experiences.
▷*Days That Have Been* (1966)

SCOTT, Michael
(1789–1835)

Scottish author, born in Cowlairs, Glasgow, the son of a merchant. Educated at Glasgow High School and University (1801–5), he went to seek his fortune in Jamaica. He spent a few years in the West Indies, but in 1822 settled in Glasgow. His vivid, amusing stories, *Tom Cringle's Log* (1829–33) and *The Cruise of the Midge* (1834–5), first appeared serially in *Blackwood's Magazine*.
▷Sir G Douglas, *The Blackwood Group* (1897)

SCOTT, Paul Mark
(1920–78)

English novelist, born in London. He served in the British army (1940–3), and in the Indian army, in India and Malaya (1943–6). The first of his 12 novels was *Johnnie Sahib* (1952), but his great achievement is *The Raj Quartet* (*The Jewel in the Crown*, 1966; *The Day of the Scorpion*, 1968; *The Towers of Silence*, 1971; *A Division of Spoils*, 1975). Set in the years 1939–47, the overlapping novels give a vivid portrait of India at the demise of the Raj. Critical acclaim came late for the author, encouraged by a popular television adaptation of the books. *Staying On* (1977), which can be seen as a coda to the *Quartet*, was awarded the Booker Prize.

SCOTT, Sarah, née Robinson
(1723–95)

English novelist, born into a well-connected family and sister of the 'bluestocking' Elizabeth Montagu, she was educated at home in Kent. She travelled widely in England, was married briefly and unhappily (1751–3) to the Prince of Wales's tutor, then lived with her friend Lady Barbara Montagu in a female community near Bath teaching poor children (1754–65). Most of her six novels are conventional tales of moral sentiment, but *A Description of Millennium Hall* (1762), her most popular work, is interesting as one of the first female Utopias; narrated through a series of personal stories, it portrays life in a caring community of women as an appealing alternative to marriage.

▷W M Crittenden, *The Life and Writings of Mrs. Sarah Scott—Novelist* (1932); E R Napier, in *British Novelists, 1660–1800*, ed M Battestin, *Dictionary of Literary Biography*, 39 (1985)

SCOTT, Tom
(1918–)

Scottish poet, born in Partick, Glasgow; as a 'mature student' he graduated from Edinburgh University in the 1950s. With encouragement from **T S Eliot** he translated poems by **François Villon** into Scots (*Seeven Poems o Maister Francis Villon*, 1953). *An Ode til New Jerusalem* (1956), *The Ship and Ither Poems* (1963) and the biographic narrative *Brand the Builder* (1975) established him as a 'maister' in the language. In English, his near epic *The Tree* (1977) and the angry humanist poem *The Dirty Business* (1986) were further evidence of his skill as polemicist and poet. *The Collected Shorter Poems* (1993) assured his status as a major figure in 20th-century Scottish writing.

SCOTT, Sir Walter
(1771–1832)

Scottish novelist and poet, born in Edinburgh, son of a Writer to the Signet and of Anne Rutherford, a daughter of the Professor of Medicine at the university. When young he contracted polio in his right leg, which lamed him for life, and was sent to his grandfather's farm at Sandyknowe to recuperate, thus coming to know the Border country which figures often in his work. Neither at the High School, Edinburgh, nor at Edinburgh University did he show much promise. His real education came from people and from books—**Fielding** and **Smollett**, **Walpole**'s *Castle of Otranto*, **Spenser** and **Ariosto** and, above all, **Percy**'s *Reliques* and German ballad poetry. He did better in his father's office as a law clerk, and became an advocate in 1792. His first publication consisted of rhymed versions of ballads by Bürger in 1796. The following year he was an ardent volunteer in the yeomanry, and on one of his 'raids' he met at Gilsland spa Charlotte Charpentier, daughter of a French émigré, whom he married in Carlisle on Christmas Eve, 1797. Two years later he was made Sheriff-Depute of Selkirkshire. The ballad meanwhile absorbed all his literary interest. *Glenfinlas* and *The Eve of St John* were followed by a translation of **Goethe**'s *Göetz von Berlichingen*. His skill as a writer of ballads led to the publication by James Ballantyne, a printer in Kelso, of Scott's first major work, *The Border Minstrelsy* (vols 1 and 2, 1802; vol 3, 1803). The *Lay of the Last Minstrel*

(1805) made him the most popular author of the day. The other romances which followed—*Marmion* (1808) and *The Lady of the Lake* (1810)— enhanced his fame, but the lukewarm reception of *Rokeby* (1811), *Lord of the Isles* (1815) and *Harold the Dauntless* (1817) warned him that he should turn his attention away from the ballad form and concentrate on writing novels. In 1811 he built his country seat, Abbotsford, near Galashiels, in the Borders. The business troubles that overshadowed his later career began when he set up a publishing firm with James Ballantyne and his brother John in the Canongate in Edinburgh. All went well at first, but along with expanding business came expanding ambitions, and when Archibald Constable with his London connections entered the scene, Scott lost all control over the financial side of the vast programme of publication, much of it hack work, on which he now embarked; hence the bankruptcy in the middle of his great career as a novelist (1826). The Waverley novels fall into three groups—first, from *Waverley* (1814) to *The Bride of Lammermoor* (1819) and *A Legend of Montrose* (1819); next, from *Ivanhoe* (1820) to *The Talisman* (1825), the year before his bankruptcy; *Woodstock* (1826) opens the last period, which closes with *Castle Dangerous* and *Count Robert of Paris* (1832), in the year of his death. The first period established the historical novel based, in Scott's case, on religious dissension and the clash of races English and Scottish, Highland and Lowland, his aim being to illustrate manners but also to soften animosities. In *Guy Mannering* (1815) his great humorous characters first appear, and are found in *Old Mortality* (1816) and *The Heart of Midlothian* (1818). His Scottish vein exhausted, he turned to England in the middle ages in *Ivanhoe*. With *The Monastery* and *The Abbot* (1820) he moved to Reformation times, where he showed a respect for what was venerable in the ancient church, a mood which might have been predicted from his harshness to the Covenanters in *Old Mortality*. This group of works is distinguished by its portrait gallery of queens and princes. The highlights in his last period are the not entirely successful *Woodstock* (1826), and *The Fair Maid of Perth* (1828), where again the ballad motif appears. He worked best on a traditional or ballad theme, as in *Proud Maisie*, but Highland themes, as in *Pibroch of Donuil Dhu* (1816), equally proved his lyric powers. He was also writing other works for the publishers, much of which was simply hack work—the editions of **Dryden** (1808), of **Swift** (1814), and the *Life of Napoleon* (9 vols, 1827). However, the *Tales of a Grandfather* (1828–30) keeps its charm, and his three letters 'from Malachi

Malagrowther' (1826) are remembered for their patriotic assertion of Scottish interests. A national figure, he helped to supervise the celebration for George IV's visit to Edinburgh in 1822. His last years were plagued by illness, and in 1831–2 he toured the Mediterranean in a government frigate. He died at Abbotsford soon after his return, and was buried in the ruins of Dryburgh Abbey. Publication of a definitive edition of the *Waverley Novels* was begun in 1993 by Edinburgh University Press. The project is scheduled to take 10 years to complete, and the texts will incorporate a mass of textual corrections, and undo the substitution and excisions of his original editors.

▷ J G Lockhart, *Memoirs of the Life of Sir Walter Scott, Bart* (10 vols, 1839); Sir Herbert Grierson, *The Life of Sir Walter Scott* (1938)

SCOTT, William Bell
(1811–90)

Scottish painter and poet, born in Edinburgh, brother of the painter David Scott and son of an engraver. While training as an engraver he also began to write poetry and had verses published for the first time in 1831. He exhibited paintings at the Royal Scottish Academy from 1834. He moved to London in 1837 and in the following year his first volume of poetry was published. He married in 1839, began exhibiting at the Royal Academy from 1842 and, in 1843, became Master of the Government School of Design in Newcastle. His major paintings were of scenes of Northumberland history which were exhibited in London and Newcastle prior to their installation (1861) at Wallington Hall, Northumberland. He moved back to London in 1864 and, in 1875, published *Poems* dedicated to his friends **Dante Gabriel Rossetti**, **William Morris** and **Swinburne**. His *Autobiographical Notes* were published posthumously in 1892.

SCOTT, Winfield Townley
(1910–68)

American poet and editor (*Providence Journal*), born in Haverhill, Massachusetts. A good craftsman, Scott worked in the tradition of **Robinson** and **Frost**, writing mostly of his native New England. His *Collected Poems* appeared in 1962.

SCRIBE, Augustin Eugène
(1791–1861)

French dramatist, born in Paris. After 1816 his productions became so popular that he established a type of theatre workshop in which numerous *collaborateurs* worked under his supervision, turning out plays by 'mass-production' methods. The best known are *Le Verre d'eau* (1840, Eng trans *A Glass of Water*, 1851), *Adrienne Lecouvreur* (1848, Eng trans 1883) and *Bataille des dames* (1851, Eng trans *The Ladies' Battle!*, 1851). Scribe also wrote novels and composed the libretti for 60 operas, including *Masaniello* (1842, Eng trans 1843), *Fra Diavolo* (1842, Eng trans 1857), *Robert le Diable* (1841, Eng trans *Robert the Devil*, 1842), *Les Huguenots* (1842, Eng trans *The Huguenots*, 1842) and *Le Prophète* (1847, Eng trans *The Prophet*, 1850).

▷ E Legouv́, *Augustin Scribe* (1874)

SCUDÉRY, Georges de
(1601–67)

French writer, born in Le Havre, brother of **Madeleine de Scudéry**. After a brief military career he wrote a number of plays which achieved some success. In 1637 his *Observations sur le Cid* led to a controversy with **Pierre Corneille**. He later wrote novels and had a small share in his sister's works, which first appeared under his name.

▷ C Clare, *Un Matamore des lettres* (1929)

SCUDÉRY, Madeleine de
(1608–1701)

French novelist, born in Le Havre, sister of **Georges de Scudéry**. Left an orphan at six, she went to Paris in 1639 and with her brother was accepted into the literary society of Mme de Rambouillet's salon. From 1644 to 1647 she was in Marseilles with her brother. She had begun her literary career with the romance *Ibrahim ou l'illustre Bassa* (1641, Eng trans *Ibrahim; or, The Illustrious Bassa*, 1652), but her most famous work was the ten-volume *Artamène, ou le Grand Cyrus* (1649–59, Eng trans *Artamenes, or the Grand Cyrus*, 1653–5), written with her brother, followed by *Clélie* (10 vols, 1654–60, Eng trans *Clelia*, 1656–61). These highly artificial and ill-constructed pieces, full of pointless dialogue, were popular at the court because of their sketches of and skits on public personages. Her last novel was *Mathilde d'Anguilon* (1667). She was satirized by **Molière** in *Les précieuses ridicules* (1659, 'The Conceited Young Ladies').

▷ C Aragonnès, *Madeleine de Scudéry, Reine du tendre* (1934)

SEAGER, Allen
(1906–68)

American novelist, autobiographer and critic, born in Michigan. He wrote several competent novels, and, more notably, a book of memoirs, *A Frieze of Girls* (1964), in which he tells of his youth in Michigan and his experiences at Oxford as a Rhodes Scholar. He wrote an early biography of **Theodore Roethke**, *The Glass House* (1968).

SEAMAN, Sir Owen
(1861–1936)

English writer. He was educated at Shrewsbury and Clare College, Cambridge, became Professor of Literature at Newcastle (1890), and was editor of *Punch* (1906–32). His parodies and verses on society which include *Paulopostprandials* (1833), *In Cap and Bells* (1889) and *From the Home Front* (1918), were very popular.

SEBASTIAN, Mihai
(1907–45)

Romanian dramatist and novelist, born in Braila, who was killed prematurely in a traffic accident. The Romanian theatre has not yet produced a dramatist of the calibre of **Caragiale**, but many pointed to Sebastian's *Ultima ora* (1945, 'The Last Hour') as one of the best comedies written since his time.

SEDAINE, Michel-Jean
(1719–97)

French poet and playwright, born in Paris. Self-educated, and a stonemason by trade, he went on to forge a prolific and varied literary career. He began by writing poetry, publishing *Poésies fugitives* ('Fleeting Poems') in 1752; the collection was considered in the main mediocre, although 'L'Épitre a mon habit' ('Letter to My Garment') was admired. Also a librettist for the opéra-comique, he enjoyed particular success with *Le Diable à quatre ou la Double Métamorphose* (1756 'The Four-part Devil'), written in collaboration with the composer Duni. Sedaine launched his career as a dramatist by providing short comic pieces for performance at the fairs of Paris; he also wrote three plays based on the fables of **La Fontaine**, *Blaise le savetier* (1759, 'Blaise the Cobbler'), *L'Huitre et les plaideurs* (1759, 'The Oyster and the Litigants') and *Le Jardinier et son seigneur* (1761, 'The Gardener and his Master'), and went on to write for Italian theatre. His *Le philosophe sans le savoir* (1765, 'The Philosopher who did not know it') is considered a masterpiece of the then-emergent *drame bourgeois*, and was much admired by **Diderot**.

SEDGWICK, Catharine Maria
(1789–1867)

American novelist and poet, born in Stockbridge, Massachusetts. She was the author of *A New England Tale* (1822), considered to be an early example of fiction addressed primarily to a female audience, and she went on to become noted for her depiction of the simple domestic virtues. Her novels are valuable historical records of American social customs, and are deceptively satirical. *A New England Tale* was intended as an attack on Calvinism and *Hope Leslie* (1927), by common consent her best book, was based upon careful research into Puritan documents. She was active in the Unitarian church and, despite the domestic settings for so much of her fiction, a staunch defender of women's right to lead a single life—a position which she argued at length in *Married or Single* (1857).

SEDLEY, Sir Charles
(1639–1701)

English courtier and poet, born probably in London. He was notorious at court for both debauchery and wit. He became an MP in 1668. He is remembered less for his plays—*The Mulberry Garden, Antony and Cleopatra, Bellamira*—than for a few songs and *vers de société*.
▷ V de Sola Pinta, *Sir Charles Sedley* (1927)

SEEDORFF PEDERSEN, Hans Hartvig Otto
(1896–1971)

Danish poet, born in Århus. He gained the same kind of popularity in Denmark as **Humbert Wolfe** did in England, for his mellifluousness and superficial charm, but he was more 'Bacchic' in his inspiration. Critics believed him to be shallow, and his verse is not now much read.

SEEGER, Alan
(1888–1916)

American poet, born in New York City. Educated at Harvard, he left the USA to settle in Paris. When war was declared in Europe in 1914, he enlisted in the French Foreign Legion and fought courageously before being killed at the Battle of the Somme. His collection, *Poems*, was published later the same year. Although unjustly neglected in favour of the English war poets, Seeger is remembered for the much-anthologized poem, 'I Have A Rendezvous With Death'.

SEFERIADES, George *see* SEFERIS

SEFERIS, George, pen-name of George Seferiadis
(1900–71)

Greek poet and diplomat, who in 1963 became the first Greek winner of the Nobel Prize for Literature. He was born in Smyrna, the son of a university professor; in 1914 his family moved to Athens, where his father became Professor of International Law at the University. Seferis studied law in Paris and London and spent the rest of his life as a diplomat, serving as the Greek Ambassador to London from 1957–62. His first collection of poetry, *Strophe* ('Turning Point'), published in 1931, was an immediate sensation: it defined the voice of a new generation, signalling a move away from the depression and narcissism that had been so fashionable. The extent of Seferis's debt to modernists such as **Pound** and **Eliot** became clear in his second collection, *Mythistorima* (1935, 'Myth History'), which contained some of the first free-verse poems in the language. His later collections include *Hemerologhia Katastromatos* ('Log Books') *I*, *II* and *III* (1940, 1944 and 1965). He was also a noted translator and worked on versions of **Valery**, Eliot, **Yeats** and Pound.

▷K K Katsimbalis, *Vivliografia* (1961)

SÉGALEN, Victor
(1878–1919)

French prose-poet, novelist and sinologist, a French Naval Officer by profession. He was born in Brest, and vanished under mysterious circumstances during an expedition to the forest of Hoelgoat. His best-known work, which certainly influenced **Claudel**, **Gide** and **Jouve** (who edited it with a preface in 1955), was the prose-poetry of *Stèles* (1912, rev edn 1914, Eng trans *Stelae*, selection, 1969; *Steles*, complete, 1987). These unique poems have been described as a 'reading' of Chinese civilization made at a time 'when it seemed to be coming to an end', and eventually became the subject of a cult. In some ways Ségalen (his first 'e' is sometimes accented, sometimes not) anticipated the work of the anthropologist Claude Lévi-Strauss.

SEGHERS, Anna, pseud of Netty Radványi, née Anna Reiling
(1900–83)

German novelist from Mainz, daughter of a Jewish antique-dealer. Her communist faith dominated her work, and led her ultimately to become a willing purveyor of socialist realism. Her later novels of the 1930s resembled her first, *Aufstand der Fischer von St Barbara* (1928, Eng trans *The Revolt of the Fishermen*, 1930), in essential content: revolution lends meaning and solidarity to hopeless and helpless individual lives. Seghers fled from Hitler in 1933 to France and Mexico, where she wrote the vastly successful (in part through the movie made by Fred Zinnermann) *Das siebte Kreuz* (1942, Eng trans *The Seventh Cross*, 1942), her best novel, and a powerful indictment of the cruelties of the Nazi regime. Her later novels, written in East Germany, are documents more or less completely convinced of the rightness of the new rulers.

SEGURA, Manuel Ascensio
(1805–71)

Peruvian dramatist, born in Lima. He wrote 14 plays, of which *La saya y el manto* (1841), satirical of politicians and their mistresses, is probably the best remembered. He very successfully redid *La Celestina* in Creole form in *Ña Catita* (1845, rev edn 1856). He played an important part in the development of Peruvian theatre.

▷I H Delgado, *Manuel Ascensio Segura y el teatro peruano* (1939)

SEIDEL, Ina
(1885–1974)

German novelist, biographer and poet from Halle an der Saale. She was a capable lyrical and narrative poet, but her chief work was done in fiction: in particular in her *Das Labyrinth* (1921, Eng trans *The Labyrinth*, 1932), an internally directed study of the inscrutable 18th-century naturalist and travel writer Georg Forster, and in *Das Wunschkind* (1930, Eng trans *The Wish Child*, 1935), an account of the Napoleonic Wars and the loss, to the reconciliatory central character, a courageous widow, of her son. This last, although in many respects dated, has acquired the status of something of a classic, especially amongst older readers.

SEIFERT, Jaroslav
(1901–86)

Czech poet, winner of the Nobel Prize for literature, brought up in a poor family in a working-class suburb of Prague. His first collection was *Město v slzáck* (1921, 'City of Tears') in which he looked back in anger at the human waste of World War I, urging a working-class revolution. In 1923 he moved to and fell under the spell of Paris and translated **Guillaume Apollinaire**. His second collection was *Samá láska* (1923, 'All Love') in which his private experience is to the fore. He was expelled from the Communist Party in 1929 and joined the Social Democrats. After Munich (1938) and the Nazi occupation his patriotism emerged in *Přílba Llíny* (1945, 'A Helmet of Earth'), in which he identifies himself with the people's grief. Most memorable are the poems which evoke the four days in May 1945 when the citizens of Prague rose against the tatters of the Nazi forces. He edited *Práce*, a trade union paper, but he was too much his own man to enjoy the trust of the Communist Party. New work was shunned and *Morový sloup* (1977, Eng trans *The Prague Column*, 1979) had to be published abroad. He was awarded the Nobel Prize for literature in 1984.

SELBY, Hubert, Jr
(1928–)

American novelist and short-story writer, born in Brooklyn, New York. He enlisted in the US Merchant Marines in 1944, but was hospitalized two years later with tuberculosis. In all, he spent nearly five years as a patient, subsequently working at a number of jobs until the publication of his controversial bestseller, *Last Exit to Brooklyn* (1964), a set of connected stories. It is a bleak, pitiless account of an urban hell, mired in violence, sexually brutalized, dependent on anodynes like alcohol and dope. In concentrating on his **Swift**ian satire and references to **Dante** and **Poe**, and on the obscenity trials which followed the book's publication, commentators often ignore Selby's concern with the effects of unemployment, strike-breaking and overcrowding. In his next book, *The Room* (1971), Selby delves painfully into the brutal fantasies and obsessions of a man in confinement. Few novels have ever concentrated so unforgivingly on a corrupt consciousness. *The Demon* (1976) concerns a sexual obsessive, while *Requiem for a Dream* (1978) suggests that 'acceptable' sops like television and food serve exactly the same psychic function as hard drugs. Selby's stories have been collected as *Song of the Silent Snow* (1986).

▷'Hubert Selby issue', *Review of Contemporary Literature* (1981)

SELLASIE, Sahle
(1936–)

Ethiopian (Chaha) author of the first book in Chaha, *Shinega's Village: Scenes of Ethiopian Life* (1964), which was translated in 1970. His fascinating detective story, *The Afersata* (1969), is in English.

SELVON, Sam
(1923–94)

Trinidadian novelist and playwright. Born and educated in Trinidad, he served in the Navy in World War II and worked as a journalist before moving to London in 1950. He became a full-time writer in 1954 and settled in Canada in 1978. He introduced a form of modified dialect in his novels in which narration of standard English is interspersed with dialogue in dialect. Novels with a Trinidadian setting, notably *A Brighter Sun* (1952), centre on the positive aspects of creolization. His trilogy: *The Lonely Londoners* (1956), *Moses Ascending* (1975), *Moses Migrating* (1983), follows the changing fortunes of Moses from the initial hardships of emigrant life in Britain. Combining mixed dialect with folk and calypso tradition, Selvon produced comedy ranging from slapstick to biting satire.

SEMPILL, Francis
(c.1616–1682)

Scottish poet, born at the ancestral home of Beltrees in Renfrewshire. Little is known of his life. He studied law, probably in Europe, and was appointed Sheriff-Depute of Renfrewshire in 1677. He was the son of **Robert Sempill** (?1595–?1665), who is well known for his poem 'The life and death of Habbie Simpson, the Piper of Kilbarchan'. Francis shared his father's gift for vernacular poetry and wrote 'The Banishment of Poverty by James Duke of Albany', in which he recounts being pursued by merciless poverty until he takes refuge in the debtor's sanctuary at the Abbey of Holyrood. His authorship is tentatively ascribed to numerous other pieces, including the poems 'Blythesome Wedding' and 'Maggie Lauder', though it is suggested that he may only have re-worked them from earlier sources. He worked in the traditional form of the *Christis Kirk* stanza which was used largely to create comic caricatures of peasant customs and rites.

▷J Paterson (ed), *The Sempill Ballads* (1849)

SEMPILL, Robert
(?1595–?1665)

Scottish poet, from the hamlet of Beltrees, Renfrewshire. A supporter of the Reformers, he spent some time in Paris, but left after the St Bartholomew's Day Massacre, and spent most of the rest of his life in Edinburgh. He was probably employed in some military capacity (he was present at the sieges of Leith and of Edinburgh), and there is evidence that he was at one point employed at court. He revived the methods of the Scottish 'Makars', started a trend for poetry in the vernacular, and invented the six-line stanza later christened the 'Standard Habbie'. He wrote *Habbie Simson*, *The Blythesome Bridal* and, possibly, *Maggie Lauder*. His father, Sir James Sempill (1566–1625), also wrote a number of poems, including the anti-Catholic *The Packman's Pater Noster* (1669). His son was **Francis Sempill**.

▷J Paterson (ed), *The Sempill Ballads* (1849)

SENANCOUR, Étienne Pivert de
(1770–1846)

French author, born in Paris. After nine years in Switzerland he returned to Paris about 1798. His fame rests on three books; *Rêveries sur la nature primitive de l'homme* (1799, 'Musings on the Primitive Nature of Man'), *Obermann* (1804) and *Libres Méditations d'un solitaire inconnu* (1819, 'Free Meditations of a Solitary Unknown'). The influence of **Goethe**'s *Werther* (1774) is persistent in his work. Senancour, neglected in his day, was appreciated by **George Sand, Charles Sainte-Beuve** and **Matthew Arnold**.

▷J Merlant, *Étienne Senancour* (1907)

SENARENS, Luis Philip
(c.1863–1939)

American 'dime novelist', born in Brooklyn, New York City. He wrote more than 1 500 books, mostly very short, under a variety of pseudonyms such as 'Noname' and 'Police Captain Howard'. His best-known work is *Frank Reade* and its successors.

SENDAK, Maurice Bernard
(1928–)

American illustrator and writer of children's books, born in Brooklyn, New York, to a family of indigent Polish immigrants. Sickly (he was often quarantined) and bookish, he attended Lafayette High School, but formal education did not appeal to him and he thrived on a diet of comics, movies and his father's Jewish folk tales. Working as a window-dresser, he encountered classic illustrators in a toy store and was subsequently introduced to and commissioned by a publisher to illustrate *The Wonderful Farm* (1951) by Marcel Aymé. For *A Hole Is To Dig* (1952) he produced humorous, unsentimental drawings and in 1956 came *Kenny's Window*, the first book he both illustrated and wrote. But it was *Where the Wild Things Are* (1963) that made him internationally famous. Exploring the fantasy world of mischievous Max in whose room grows a forest inhabited by scary monsters, it fascinated children and perturbed parents. It won the Carnegie Medal and sold hugely. After this acknowledged classic he produced another, *In The Night Kitchen* (1970). Latterly he has collaborated on operas as well as continuing to produce the distinctive, disturbing and daring books—*Outside Over There* (1981), *Nutcracker* (1981) and *Dear Mili* (1988)—that have made him the premier practitioner of his métier.

SENDER, Ramón J
(1902–82)

Spanish novelist, born in Alcolea de Cinca, Huesca. He fought in the war against Morocco (1922–4), then worked for left-wing journals such as *La Libertad* ('Freedom'). After the Spanish Civil War he eventually settled in the United States, teaching Spanish literature. His experiences informed his early fiction: *Iman* (1929) deals with an ordinary soldier's experiences of the Moroccan war, while *Contraataque* (1938, 'Counter-attack') is about the civil war. His more mature works, while retaining the compassion evident in his earlier writing, display deeper psychological

insight and originality. *Requiem por un campesino espanol* (1960, 'Requiem for a Spanish Peasant') is a later take on the upheaval caused by the civil war, while *El lugar del hombre* (1939, 'The Place of Man') examines the effect on a community of the return of a poor labourer presumed to have been murdered by two villagers 15 years previously.

SENECA, Lucius Annaeus, called 'the Younger'
(c.4 BC–c.65 AD)

Roman Stoic philosopher, statesman and tragedian, born in Cordova, Spain, the son of Seneca the Elder. He was educated in rhetoric and philosophy for a career in politics and law, which he began in Rome in 31. But in 41 he was banished to Corsica by the Emperor Claudius on a charge of adultery with the emperor's niece Julia Livilla, sister of Caligula; he spent eight years there in study and wrote the three treatises called *Consolationes*. He was recalled to Rome in 49 through the influence of Agrippina the younger, 3rd wife of Claudius and sister of Julia and became tutor to her son, the future Emperor Nero. He enjoyed considerable political influence for a while and was made consul by Nero in 57. But his moral influence waned, and though he tried to withdraw progressively from public life to devote himself to philosophy he lost favour with Nero, was denounced as a party to the conspiracy of Piso, and was ordered to commit suicide, which he did with composure and dignity. He was an eclectic Stoic, a moralist rather than a theorist, and a stylist much imitated by later essayists. His writings include: *De Ira* ('On Anger'), *De Clementia* ('On Mercy'), *De Beneficiis* ('On Generosity'), *Epistolae morales ad Lucilium* ('Moral Letters to Lucilius') and the *Apocolocyntosis divi Claudii* (literally, 'The Pumpkinification of the Divine Claudius', a scathing satire); he also wrote a number of verse tragedies which were influential in Elizabethan drama in England.

▷A L Motto, *Seneca* (1973)

SENGHOR, Léopold Sédar
(1906–)

Senegalese politician and poet. Educated in Dakar and at the Sorbonne in Paris, he taught classics in France from 1935, where he became involved with literary figures and wrote poetry advocating the concept of 'negritude' to glorify African civilization and values. After World War II he sat in the French National Assembly (1946–58) and was a leader of the Senegalese independence movement. After independence in 1960, as leader of the Senegalese Progressive Union (UPS), he became the new nation's first president. In 1976 he reconstituted the UPS as the

Senegalese Socialist Party (PS) and gradually the one-party political system which he had created became more pluralist, although the PS remained the dominant force. Senghor was consistently re-elected until his retirement in 1980, his successor being Abdou Diouf.

▷A Guibert, *Léopold Sédar Senghor* (1961)

SENOA, August
(1838–81)

Croatian poet, dramatist, critic and novelist. His work in the theatre is important because he helped to free this from German influences, but his own best work is in his historical novels. Towards the end of his life he seemed to the younger men to be too conservative, but later his work was reappraised and collected in 20 volumes (1931–5).

SERAFIMOVICH, Alexsandr, pseud of Alexsandr Serafimovich Popov
(1863–1949)

Russian novelist and story writer. The son of a Cossack officer, he was born in Nizhne-Jumoyarskaya in the Don region. Serafimovich was always a champion of the under-privileged, although he did not become a communist until 1919; his populist tales, which he began publishing as a young man, forced him into exile from 1887 until 1890. The title story of *Peski*, 'Sand', (Eng trans *Sand and Other Stories*, 1957) elicited the admiration of **Leo Tolstoy**. Serafimovich's most famous work, which earned him the dubious sobriquet of 'co-founder of Soviet literature', is his least good; it is the 'proletarian' novel *Zhelezny potok* (1924, Eng trans *The Iron Flood*, 1935) which is capable in its attempt to blend folk and even surrealistic idiom with socialist realism, but which fails because the author has set out to destroy individuality in the interests of the Stalinist 'mass'. Serafimovich influenced **Sholokhov**, and, like him, dried up in later life.

▷E J Brown, *Russian Literature Since the Revolution* (1969)

SERAFINO AQUILANO DE' CIMINELLI
(1466–1500)

Italian poet, musician and courtier, born in Aquila in the Abruzzi. He first gained a reputation by his skilled adaptations of the lyrics of **Petrarch** for singing to the lute. He was a brilliant reciter and singer of his own verse, and his poems were translated or adapted by Sir Thomas Wyatt and many other English and European poets. He was more popular than any other Italian poet at the time of his death. Posterity has seen him as artificial, just as the scholar Pietro Bembo viewed him in his own time.

SERAO, Matilde
(1856–1927)

Italian novelist and journalist, born in Patras in Greece, the daughter of a Greek father and a Neapolitan political refugee. She graduated as a teacher in Naples, worked in a telegraph office, and started writing articles for newspapers (1876–8). Her first novel of Neapolitan life was *Cuore Infermo* (1881), after which she joined the Rome newspaper *Capitan Fracassa*. She had a huge success with her next romantic novel, *Fantasia* (1882), followed by *Conquista di Roma* (1886, 'Conquest of Rome'), *Riccardo Joanna* (1887), *All' Erta Sentinella* (1889) and *Il Paese di Cuccagna* (1891).

▷A Barti, *Serao* (1965)

SERGEYEV-TSENSKY, Sergey
(1875–1958)

Russian novelist, born in Tambov province. From a Dostoyevskian passion for morbid characterization, as in *Tundra* (1902, 'The Tundra'), he developed greater simplicity of style and social sense in the massive 10-volume novel sequence, *Preobrazhenye zapiski* (1914–40, 'Transfiguration'), which won him the Stalin Prize in 1942.

▷A V Pryenkov, *Sergeyev Tsensky* (1963)

SERLING, Rod
(1924–75)

American science-fiction writer and television playwright, born in Syracuse, New York. A combat paratrooper during World War II, he attended Antioch College and began writing radio scripts before securing a radio staff job in Cincinnati. He first wrote for television in 1951 and won the first of six Emmy Awards for *Patterns* (1955). His other plays include *Requiem for a Heavyweight* (1956) and *The Comedian* (1957). He created, wrote and hosted the popular anthology series *The Twilight Zone* (1959–64), which often reflected his interest in the individual's struggle against social and political pressures, while also showing his mastery of the surprise, twist-in-the-tail ending. If the *Twilight Zone* scripts now seem creaking and hackneyed, it is partly because their ideas have been so often imitated. Sterling created, hosted and occasionally wrote the similar series *Night Gallery* (1970–3) and frequently narrated documentaries on scientific and nature subjects. The author of over 200 television plays, his few film scripts include *Seven Days in May* (1964).

SERRAILLIER, Ian Lucien
(1912–)

English author of children's fiction, nonfiction and poetry, best known for *The Silver Sword*, which, since its publication in 1956, has acquired the status of a modern children's classic. Set in World War II, it is the account of a Polish family divided by the Nazis, and of the children's attempts to escape to safety and become reunited with their family. They do so, and the book ends on an upbeat note at a newly-founded international children's village in Switzerland. Serraillier's widest influence has probably been as editor of Heinemann Educational Books' New Windmill Series. His other adventure novels include *There's No Escape* (1950) and *The Cave of Death* (1965).

SERVICE, Robert William
(1874–1958)

English-born Canadian poet, born in Preston. He went to Canada, travelled as a reporter for the *Toronto Star*, served as ambulance driver in World War I and wrote popular ballads, most notably 'The Shooting of Dangerous Dan McGrew', which appeared in *Songs of a Sourdough* (1907), and those in *Rhymes of a Rolling Stone* (1912). The alliterative urge persisted in *Ballads of a Bohemian* (1920), *Rhymes of a Rebel* (1952) and the late *Carols of a Codger* (1954). He also wrote novels, of which *The House of Fear* (1927) is the most accomplished.
▷ *Ploughman of the Moon* (1945); *Harper of Heaven* (1948)

SETH, Vikram
(1952–)

Indian poet, novelist and travel writer, born in Calcutta and educated at universities in England, the USA and China. His first poetry collection, *Mappings* (1980), was followed by *The Humble Administrator's Garden* (1985) and *All You Who Sleep Tonight* (1990). His travel book, *From Heaven Lake: Travels Through Sinkiang and Tibet*, appeared in 1983. His first novel, *The Golden Gate* (1986), although written in verse, describes the lives of the contemporary Californian professional classes. His following novel was even more ambitious. At over 1300 pages, *A Suitable Boy* (1993) is one of the longest single-volume novels in English. Set in immediate post-independence India, it is a love story which encompasses a vast number of characters and attempts a complete portrait of Indian social, political and cultural life.

SETON, Anya
(1916–)

American historical novelist, born into an east coast middle-class family but fascinated by British (especially English) history. A Seton novel—the best-known include *Dragonwyck* (1944), *Foxfire* (1951), *Katherine* (1954) and *Avalon* (1965)—is typically written with a great deal of earnest enthusiasm for the period in which it is set, be it Plantagenet England, Arthurian Cornwall or an 18th-century plantation. Historical accuracy is not the real aim, however, and Seton is more concerned with the emotional interactions between the characters (typically a shy but soon-to-blossom virgin and a rough but handsome older man). Their physical qualities are described minutely (and constantly). The packaging in which the books are sold tends to reflect these concerns admirably, placing them firmly in the low-to-middlebrow range of the women's market.

SETON, Ernest Thompson, pseud of Ernest Seton Thompson
(1860–1946)

English-born Canadian writer and illustrator of nature books. He was born in South Shields, County Durham, but early became a naturalized Canadian. He founded the Boy Scouts of America. His books on animals were instructive and popular. Among the best known are *Biography of a Silver Fox* (1909) and his autobiography, *The Trail of an Artist-Naturalist* (1940).

SETTLE, Elkanah
(1648–1724)

English dramatist, born in Dunstable. He went from Oxford to London to make a living by his pen. In 1671 he had a success with his bombastic tragedy of *Cambyses*. To annoy **Dryden**, the Earl of Rochester arranged for Settle's *Empress of Morocco* to be played at Whitehall by the court lords and ladies. In reply to Settle's attack in *Absalom Senior* (1682), Dryden scourged 'Doeg' with his scorn in the second part of *Absalom and Achitophel*, and Settle replied in *Reflections on several of Mr Dryden's Plays* (1687). He adapted *A Midsummer Night's Dream* as *The Fairy Queen* in 1692, with music by Henry Purcell. He was made poet of the City of London in 1691, and contributed pageants until 1708. He wrote short comic pieces known as 'drolls', of which only one, *The Siege of Troy* (1707), survives. He is remembered more through Dryden's scurrilous portrait than his own work.
▷ F C Brown, *The Life and Work of Elkanah Settle* (1910)

SEUSS, Dr, pseud of Theodor Seuss Geisel
(1904–91)

American author and illustrator of a profusion of children's books, born in Springfield, Massachusetts. Though his animals have been described as 'boneless wonders', there is no denying his ingenuity, particularly in early books like *And to Think that I Saw it*

on *Mulberry Street* (1937) and *The 500 Hats of Bartholemew Cubbins* (1938). He wrote the screenplay for the animated cartoon *Gerald McBoing Boing* (1950), which won several awards. In 1957 he began to write and draw a series of 'Beginner Books', intended to help teach reading, for Random House, starting with *The Cat in the Hat* (1958) and *Yertle the Turtle* (1958). By 1970, 30 million copies had been sold in America and Seuss had become synonymous with learning to read. He also wrote a bestselling book for adults, *You're Only Old Once!* (1986).
▷ M Stoffler, *Dr Seuss From Then to Now* (1986)

SÉVIGNÉ, Madame de, née Marie de Rabutin-Chantal
(1626–96)

French letter writer, born in Paris. She was orphaned at an early age and was carefully brought up by an uncle, the Abbé de Coulanges, at the Abbaye de Livry in Brittany. She married the dissolute Marquis Henri de Sévigné in 1644, but he was killed in a duel in 1651. From then on, in the most brilliant court in the world, her thoughts were centred on her children, Françoise Marguerite (b.1646) and Charles (b.1648). On the marriage of the former to the Comte de Grignan in 1669, she began the series of letters to her daughter which grew sadder as friend after friend passed away. She died of smallpox, after nursing her daughter through a long illness. Madame de Sévigné's 25 years of letters reveal the inner history of the time of Louis XIV in wonderful detail, but the most interesting thing in the whole 1600 (one-third letters to her from others) remains herself.
▷ J Aldis, *Madame de Sevigné* (1907)

SEWARD, Anna
(1747–1809)

English poet, known as the 'Swan of Lichfield', born in Eyam Rectory, Derbyshire. She lived from the age of 10 at Lichfield, where her father, himself a poet, became a canon. He died in 1790, but she continued to live on in the bishop's palace, and wrote romantic poetry. Her 'Elegy on Captain Cook' (1780) was commended by **Dr Johnson**. She bequeathed all her poems to Sir **Walter Scott**, who published them in 1810 (*Poetical Works*).
▷ J Pearson, *The Swan of Lichfield* (1956)

SEWELL, Anna
(1820–78)

English novelist, born in Yarmouth. She was an invalid for most of her life. Her only book, *Black Beauty, The Autobiography of a Horse* (1877), a work for children which was written as a plea for the more humane treatment of animals, is perhaps the most famous fictional work about horses.
▷ M Bayly, *The Life and Letters of Mrs Sewell* (1881)

SEXTON, Anne, née Harvey
(1928–74)

American poet, born in Newton, Massachusetts. A confessional poet in the mould of her teacher, **Robert Lowell**, and her friend, **Sylvia Plath**, with whom she is often bracketed, she writes frankly about her personal experiences, including a nervous breakdown. In 1948 she married Alfred Sexton and had two daughters. She taught at Boston University (1969–71) and Colgate (1971–2). *To Bedlam and Part Way Back* (1962) was her first collection of poetry; others are *All My Pretty Ones* (1962), *Live or Die* (1966), *Love Poems* (1969), *Transformations* (1971), *The Book of Folly* (1972), *The Death Notebooks* (1974), *The Awful Rowing Towards God* (1975), and the posthumously published *45 Mercy Street* (1976). The *Complete Poems* were published in 1981, seven years after she committed suicide.
▷ D W Middlebrook, *Anne Sexton: A Biography* (1990)

SEYMOUR, A(rthur) J(ames)
(1914–89)

Guyanese poet and critic. He thought of himself primarily as a love poet and the sensuousness of his verse can be sampled in the 70th birthday tribute *A J Seymour at 70* (1984, ed Ian McDonald). Much of Seymour's poetry was printed privately and a Collected Poems is overdue. He compiled the *Dictionary of Guyanese Folklore* (1975) and the *Dictionary of Guyanese Biography* (1984).

SEYMOUR-SMITH, Martin
(1928–)

English poet, literary historian (*Guide to Modern World Literature*, 1986), biographer (**Graves**, **Kipling**, **Hardy**) and humorist (*How To Bluff Your Way in Literature*, 1966, rev edn 1971), born in London. Seymour-Smith's poems (eg *Reminiscences of Norma*, 1971), alternating uneasily between the 'embarrassingly over-passionate' and the bitterly or humorously cynical, are not at all in the mainstream, and have understandably, despite the admiration of a very few (Graves, **Sisson**, **Nye**, **Reeves**—all, however, his personal friends), been passed over as irrelevant to the needs of a properly flourishing literature. As a critic he is useful and very widely read in foreign literatures, but unreliable and often, it has been felt, wilfully non-conformist: in the words of Sisson, his work 'induces some hostility as well as gratitude' because 'it

results in the rough handling of some reputations which many not un-influential persons think deserve more respect'. *Wilderness* (1994) collects later poems.
▷C H Sisson, *The Avoidance of Literature* (1978)

SHAARA, Michael Joseph, Jr
(1929–88)

American novelist, born in Jersey City, New Jersey. He graduated from Rutgers University, and served as a paratrooper before taking up an academic career as Professor of English at Florida State University, Tallahassee. That military background was a recurring theme in his fiction, which began with *The Broken Place* (1968). His most successful book was his second novel, *The Killer Angels* (1974), which recreated the battle of Gettysburg from the perspective of a group of officers in the Southern forces, and won the Pulitzer Prize for Fiction that year. His later novels were *The Herald* (1981) and *Soldier Boy* (1982).

SHADBOLT, Maurice Francis Richard
(1932–)

New Zealand biographer, novelist and short-story writer, born in Auckland. Some of his earlier work in *The New Zealanders* (1959) and *Summer Fires and Winter Country* (1963) was later used in *Strangers and Journeys* (1972), a rambling novel of contrasted families through two generations. His first novel was *Among the Cinders* (1965), followed by *The Presence of Music: Three Novellas* (1967). The best of his early work is in *This Summer's Dolphin* (1969), *An Ear of the Dragon* (1971) and *Figures in Light: Selected Stories* (1978). He has a keen sense of history as shown in his novels *A Touch of Clay* (1974) and *Season of the Jew* (1986) and, less seriously, in *The Lovelock Version* (1980), a light-hearted reworking of New Zealand history. Non-fiction includes a re-examination of the ANZAC myth in *Voices of Gallipoli* (1988).

SHADWELL, Thomas
(c.1642–1692)

English dramatist, born at Broomhill House, Brandon. He made a hit with the first of his 13 comedies, *The Sullen Lovers* (1668). He also wrote three tragedies. **Dryden**, grossly assailed by him in the *Medal of John Bayes*, heaped deathless ridicule upon him in *MacFlecknoe* ('Shadwell never deviates into sense'), and as 'Og' in the second part of *Absalom and Achitopel*. His works exhibit talent and comic force. He succeeded Dryden as poet laureate in 1689.
▷M W Alssid, *Thomas Shadwell* (1967)

SHAFFER, Peter Levin
(1926–)

English dramatist, born in Liverpool. His plays are variations on the themes of genius and mediocrity, faith and reason, and the question of whether God, if he exists, is benevolent or not. These ideas form the intellectual core of *The Royal Hunt of the Sun* (1964), *Equus* (1973) and *Amadeus* (1979). His first play was *Five Finger Exercise* (1958), followed by the comedies *The Private Ear* and *The Public Eye* (1962). *Yonadab* (1985), a story of incest and envy set in the Jerusalem of 1000 BC, was not well-received, but *Lettice and Lovage* (1987), a comedy, proved a great success. Other plays include *Black Comedy* (1965), *White Lies* (1967) and *The Battle of Shrivings* (1970). His twin brother, Anthony, also writes plays; his works include the successful thriller *Sleuth* (1970).

SHAFTESBURY, Anthony Ashley Cooper, 3rd Earl of
(1671–1713)

English moral philosopher, politician and essayist, the grandson of Anthony Ashley Cooper, 1st Earl of Shaftesbury, born in London. John Locke supervised his early education and he then attended Winchester College. He entered parliament in 1695 and sat as a Whig for Poole until 1698, succeeding as 3rd Earl in 1699 and regularly attending the House of Lords until ill-health forced him to abandon an active political life in 1702. He moved to Naples in 1711 and died there. He wrote stylish (if to a modern taste, overwrought) essays on a wide range of philosophical and cultural topics, and these are collected in three volumes under the title *Characteristicks of Men, Manners, Opinions, Times* (1711). He is usually regarded as one of the principal English deists, and he argued (both against orthodox Christianity and against Hobbes) that we possess a natural 'moral sense' and natural affections directed to the good of the species and in harmony with the larger cosmic order. He gained more favourable attention abroad, perhaps, than at home, and Leibniz, **Voltaire**, **Denis Diderot** and **Gotthold Lessing** were among those attracted by his work.
▷R L Brett, *The Third Earl of Shaftesbury* (1951)

SHAKESPEARE, William
(1564–1616)

English playwright, poet, actor, also joint-manager of a London acting company and part-owner of one of its theatres, born in Stratford-upon-Avon in Warwickshire, the eldest son of John Shakespeare, glover and wool dealer. By long-established tradition, his birthday is celebrated on 23 April, St George's Day. The register of Holy Trinity Church, Stratford, records that he was christened there on 26 April 1564. He lived for 52 years, partly in Stratford and partly in London, and died at his home in Stratford on 23 April 1616. Two days later, he was buried in the church in which he had been christened. His life turned on its Stratford–London axis: Stratford, where he grew up, where his parents, his wife and his children lived; London, where he made the theatre career that brought him fame and fortune, and from which he withdrew while still preeminent. His life can be divided into three consecutive periods. The first period, spent wholly in Stratford, included boyhood and education, early marriage and the birth of his three children. The second period began when, still a very young man, he left Stratford to work in London as an actor and playwright. It lasted for 25 years, in the course of which he became a permanent and leading member of a great acting company. For that company he then wrote plays that gave it a commanding place in the London theatre. With his principal colleagues, he was responsible for the day-to-day business management and artistic direction of the company, receiving a share of its profits in return and becoming part-owner of one of the two theatres in which it was based. On top of all that, he acted for many years, performing in his own plays and in those of other dramatists whose work was in his company's repertory. Throughout this period he had lodgings in London and he used most of his very considerable income to increase the security and status of his family in their Stratford home, spending time with them between theatre seasons. The beginning of the third period of his life was marked by his carefully-planned and gradual withdrawal from his heavy commitments in the theatre. Then, when he was in his late forties and possessed of ample means, he left London to live full time in Stratford, where he spent the remainder of his days. There is no documentary proof that he was educated at Stratford Grammar School, but the numerous classical allusions in his plays and poems were drawn from the Latin and Greek poets, dramatists, philosophers and historians closely studied by Elizabethan grammar school pupils; and John Shakespeare's civic status entitled him to send his son to Stratford's excellent school free of charge. In the winter of 1582–3, at the age of 18, he married Anne Hathaway, a farmer's daughter who lived in Shottery, near Stratford. She was 26, and pregnant by him. Having no income of their own, they lived with the elder Shakespeares. Less than six months after their wedding, their first child,

Susanna, was baptized in Stratford church. Early in 1585, Anne gave birth to twins: Hamnet, their only (and short-lived) son, and Judith, their second daughter. With a wife and three children to maintain, and still dependent on his father, Shakespeare decided to try his luck in the London theatre. Stratford was a regular touring venue for the London acting companies, and three troupes were playing there from 1583 to 1588. He must have begun to work in the theatre soon after the twins were born. There is evidence that he had written several very successful plays in 1592. The theatre impresario Philip Henslowe recorded in his diary that 'Harey the vj' played to packed houses at the Rose Theatre between March and June 1592. Clearly, he was referring to *Henry VI*; but whether to one part of that play or to all three is not plain. In the September of that year, **Robert Greene** wrote a pamphlet, *Greene's Groatsworth of Wit, Bought with a Million of Repentance*, which included a ranting and envious attack on 'an upstart crow', a 'Shake-scene'. The pun on Shakespeare's name was obvious, but Greene identified his target even more precisely by parodying a line from *Henry VI* Part 3. The three parts of *Henry VI* were not the only successes of these first seven years. He wrote two other histories (*King John* and *Richard III*); three comedies (*The Comedy of Errors*, *The Taming of the Shrew*, *The Two Gentlemen of Verona*); and a revenge-tragedy (*Titus Andronicus*). By 1592 he had tried out each of the then most popular forms of drama and made his own distinctive contributions to them. Theatre-going London was well aware that a new star had risen, its light shining as brightly as any then burning—even **Christopher Marlowe**'s. In June 1592 the theatres were closed by an outbreak of the plague and they were not allowed to re-open until the summer of 1594. While the London stages were silent, Shakespeare wrote two long narrative poems: *Venus and Adonis* (published 18 April 1593) and *The Rape of Lucrece* (published 9 May 1594). Both were dedicated to the 3rd Earl of Southampton; but no reliable information about his connection with that young patron of the arts has been discovered. In the literary and courtly circles in which they were read, the poems were highly praised for their eloquent treatment of classical subjects. The sonnets were probably in private circulation by 1598. Though they were not published until 1609, it is generally held that they were written between 1592 and 1598. The order in which he composed these 154 poems is not known; and nobody has succeeded in arranging them to tell a coherent 'story'. The temptation to read them as autobiography has been—and still is—strong, and many attempts have been made to identify the mysterious people—'young man', 'dark lady', 'rival poet'—who appear in them. Sonnet sequences were in vogue, and Shakespeare's own added considerably to his contemporary reputation. Later generations have ranked many of the individual sonnets in the collection among the world's finest poems. The language in which they treat recurrent themes—love's ecstasy and despair, implacable time, lust and its shames, separation, betrayal, fame and death—echoes that of the plays. When the theatres re-opened, Shakespeare joined the newly-formed Lord Chamberlain's Men as a 'sharer'. It was the turning point in his career. In the first years as an actor he had been a 'hired man', working for a wage. From now on, he was entitled to a share of the company's profits. Previously, too, he had been a freelance playwright and, though his work had found a ready market, he had little security. The founder of the Chamberlain's Men, James Burbage, and the other sharers, knew what they were about when they brought him into their company. They already had some of the best actors. For example, Richard Burbage, James's son, was considered to be as good a tragic and heroic actor as the great Edward Alleyn of the Admiral's Men; and Will Kempe was a very popular comic. It was with those two fellow sharers that Shakespeare, on behalf of the Chamberlain's Men, received the queen's payment for the company's performances at court during the Christmas festivities of 1594–5. By securing the exclusive services of the best playwright in London, the Chamberlain's Men were justifiably confident that they would outdo all their rivals. It is clear that Shakespeare wrote the following plays for his company between 1594 and 1598: *The Merchant of Venice*, *A Midsummer Night's Dream*, *The Merry Wives of Windsor*, *Much Ado About Nothing*, *As You Like It*, *Richard II*, *Henry IV* Parts 1 and 2 and *Romeo and Juliet*. The prodigious output of five comedies, three histories and one tragedy took the London theatre world by storm. The language and the characters of the plays captured people's imagination and entered their daily conversation: 'dull as a Justice Shallow' was a term used by a letter writer of the day; and a contemporary dramatist noted rather sourly that playgoers were talking 'pure Juliet and Romeo'. The material rewards of these triumphs enabled Shakespeare to meet the heavy expenses incurred when his father was awarded a grant of arms in October 1596. Henceforth, John Shakespeare was entitled to the style of 'Gentleman', an honour that would descend in due course to his eldest son. That style, and the heraldic display that went with it, was prized in an age of rigid social distinction; for the Shakespeares it was also

a tangible sign that the family had regained—surpassed, indeed—its former status in Stratford. Ironically, the award of honour was received little more than two months after Shakespeare's only son, Hamnet, died, aged eleven. Given the dynastic ambition common in that age and evident in Shakespeare's conduct of his worldly affairs, it was a heavy blow. Of his personal grief we have no record. The welfare of his wife and his daughters was now his main family preoccupation. In 1597 he bought New Place, a large and imposing mansion in Stratford, close by the Guild Chapel and the grammar school and a few minutes' walk from his parents' house. He spent freely on improvements to the house and garden before Anne, Susanna and Judith moved into their new home. At about this time, trouble with the owner of the site on which Burbage's playhouse (called the Theatre) stood, forced the Chamberlain's Men to move. They dismantled the Theatre and used much of its material to build a new playhouse—the Globe—on Bankside, south of the Thames. It was a bold and successful venture. Sited in the heart of London's pleasureland—dicing-houses, bear-gardens, brothels and theatres—the Globe was the finest playhouse of them all, bigger and better equipped than any of its rivals. Its huge stage, with 'cellarage' below and balcony above, provided the space and permitted the rapidity and continuity of action which the dramas of the day demanded and which Shakespeare most notably exploited in the plays he wrote for performance there. He followed the brilliant success of *Henry V* (the Globe's opener) with *Julius Caesar*, *Twelfth Night*, *Hamlet* and *Othello*. In all, he had now written 14 plays which were the exclusive property of the Chamberlain's Men, and nine before he joined them. Nor did his current successes lead to the neglect of his earlier plays. Unwilling to allow popular plays to 'fust unused', the company rang the changes on its play stock and often revived former works. Takings at the Globe far exceeded those at the Theatre. The accession of King James VI and I in 1603 brought the company new and very great benefits. He immediately conferred his own royal patronage on Shakespeare and his fellow sharers. They became the King's Men—'His Majesty's Servants'—and were granted a patent. James thought it good to see them often. Court performances had always been a prestigious and lucrative addition to their ordinary programme. They had played for Queen Elizabeth on average three times a year. Between 1603 and 1614, the King's Men averaged 13 royal command shows a year and got for each twice as much as Queen Elizabeth had paid. The darker tone of the plays that Shakespeare wrote in the early years of James

I's reign has led to speculation that it reflected some kind of personal and spiritual crisis. But nothing that is known about him amounts to a feasible 'explanation' of why he wrote a succession of 'problem plays' (or 'dark comedies') and tragedies between 1603 and 1608–9: *All's Well, Measure for Measure, King Lear, Macbeth, Antony and Cleopatra, Timon of Athens, Coriolanus* and *Troilus and Cressida*. Great popular successes at the Globe, these plays were also received with acclaim at court and when performed for wealthy and socially exclusive audiences in private halls and in the lawyers' Inns of Court. It was audiences of this kind who were now flocking to the so-called 'private theatres'. The term is misleading. Like the 'public playhouses', they were commercial enterprises. They charged much more for admission and attracted fashionable patrons willing to pay to sit in comfort, protected from the elements. Because they were roofed over, these theatres were artificially lit. Stage illusion of a kind not possible in the public theatres was an integral part of their more sophisticated entertainments. In 1608 Shakespeare's company decided to beat the opposition by joining it. The King's Men took over the most successful of the private theatres—the Blackfriars—using it for their winter seasons and performing at the Globe in the summer. They now got the best of both worlds and prospered exceedingly. Shakespeare, who had bought a share in the Blackfriars Theatre, immediately began to write plays that could be performed with equal success on two very different stages. He solved the technical problems with increasing sureness: *Pericles, Cymbeline, The Winter's Tale* and *The Tempest*. Those plays were enthusiastically received at the Blackfriars, at the Globe and at Court; and they have all held the stage to this day. Collectively known now as the 'Last Plays', they were the results of Shakespeare's characteristic urge to experiment with and make a distinctive contribution to developments in the art and craft of drama. Tragi-comedy was then all the rage and he wanted to find his own way of writing it. Meanwhile, there were signs that he was preparing to return to Stratford, where there was much to demand his attention. His parents were now dead and he was the head of the family, a position he took seriously. He had long been investing in land and tithes in and around the town. In 1607, Susanna had married a respected physician, Dr John Hall. Their daughter Elizabeth, Shakespeare's first grandchild, was born in 1608. Soon after writing *The Tempest*, he freed himself of his major commitment to his company by bringing forward **John Fletcher** to take over as the King's Men's chief dramatist. Shakespeare—whose own still very

popular plays were company property, to be staged whenever the sharers wished—could now spend more time in Stratford. By 1612 he had completed his withdrawal, leaving management in the safe hands of his 'fellows'. In a legal document that he signed while visiting London in that year, he identified himself in these terms: 'William Shakespeare of Stratford-on-Avon in the County of Warwick, gentleman of the age of 48 years'. Even so he did not quite abandon his writing. In 1613, with John Fletcher's collaboration, he wrote *Henry VIII*. In the same year, he helped Fletcher by contributing several scenes and most of one act to *The Two Noble Kinsmen*. Shakespeare died on 23 April 1616. The nature of his fatal illness is not known, but the male Shakespeares of his generation were not long-lived. Of John Shakespeare's four sons, he was the last to go. He had made provision in his will to keep the bulk of his estate intact, entailed for the benefit of his descendants. His intentions were soon thwarted. His direct line of descent ended when his grand-daughter died childless in 1670. In 1623, his monument was erected in Holy Trinity Church. A few months later, John Hemminge and Henry Condell—two of his friends and principal colleagues in the King's Men—published his collected plays in the First Folio. But for them much of his work would have been lost; and all subsequent editions of his plays have been based on the text they so diligently and lovingly established. Attempts have been made at various times to ascribe his work to other writers, but no convincing evidence of that argument has yet prevailed.

▷ E K Chambers, *A Study of Facts and Problems* (1930); S Schoenbaum, *Shakespeare's Lives* (1938); E M Tillyard, *The Elizabethan World Picture* (1943)

SHAMIR, Moshe
(1921–)

Hebrew novelist and dramatist, born in Safed, Israel, and therefore a Sabra Jew. From 1941 until 1947 he was a member of the kibbutz Mishmar. He is a 'Palmach novelist'—that is to say, one of those who fought in the striking arm of the Haganah defence forces. His novel *Melech Basar Vedam* (1954, Eng trans *The King of Flesh and Blood*, 1958), set in Hasmonean times, deals with the question of whether Israel should be a moral or a political power. *Kivsath Harash* (1957, Eng trans *David's Stranger*, 1964) is also a historical novel, about King David.

SHANGE, Ntozake, pseud of Paulette Williams
(1948–)

Black American playwright, poet and novelist, she adopted her new name in 1971, after leaving the University of Southern California. Five years later, her remarkable 'choreopoem' *for colored girls who have considered suicide/when the rainbow is enuf* (1976) was produced on Broadway, a benchmark in the articulation of black feminist consciousness in America. The piece uses female personae, identified by colour, to articulate aspects of black American history. Later works have been less startling in impact. Other plays include *A Photograph: A Study of Cruelty* (1977) and *Spell #7: A Geechee Quick Magic Trance Manual* (1979). She has also written novels—*Sassafrass, Cypress & Indigo* (1976, rev edn 1982), *Betsey Brown* (1985)—and poetry, most notably *A Daughter's Geography* (1983).

SHAPCOTT, Thomas William
(1935–)

Australian poet, editor and critic, born in Ipswich, Queensland. From *Time on Fire* (1961), for which he received the Grace Leven Prize, he has been acknowledged as one of Australia's best-known poets, not least for his involvement in the politics of writing through the Australia Council's Literature Board and the 'New Australian Poetry' movement of the 1960s–70s. For the latter, with **Rodney Hall** he edited the anthology *New Impulses in Australian Poetry* (1968) and *Australian Poetry Now* (1970). Of his own work both *A Taste for Salt Water* (1967) and *Inwards to the Sun* (1969) won the Myer Award for Poetry. His *Selected Poems* was published in 1978.

SHAPIRO, Karl Jay
(1913–)

American poet and critic, born in Baltimore, Maryland. He was educated at the University of Virginia, Charlottesville, and then clerked in a family business before completing his studies at Johns Hopkins University, Baltimore. During the interim he published his first collection of verse, *Poems* (1935). However, his first major book was written while he was in military service during World War II. *V-Letter and Other Poems* (1944) won him the Pulitzer Prize; it was followed by *Essay on Rime* (1945) and the superb *Trial of a Poet* (1947). Work of this period was strictly rhymed and formally structured. Later, Shapiro grew interested in free verse and prose poetry, drawing on the unconscious as an inspiration. The major work in this style is *The Bourgeois Poet* (1964). Shapiro was influential as a critic. Early books were concerned with prosody; later, in *Beyond Criticism* (1953, rev edn as *A Primer for Poets*, 1965), he widened his range considerably. He has written one novel, *Edsel* (1971), a campus story; it reflects his own academic career in Indiana, Nebraska, Illinois and California. Shapiro is significant for his rejection of the

Europeanism of **T S Eliot** and **Pound** in favour of a robust Americanism; his models were **Whitman, William Carlos Williams** and **Randall Jarrell**, on whom he wrote an influential study (1967).
▷J Reino, *Karl Shapiro* (1981)

SHARP, Alan
(1934–)

Scottish novelist and film-maker, born near Dundee and raised in Greenock. He left school at 14 and worked in the shipyards as an apprentice joiner. Following National Service in the army, his occupations ranged from labourer to assisting a private detective, before he began to write for BBC radio and television and completed a widely praised autobiographical novel, *A Green Tree in Gedde* (1964), which evoked his working-class background. He followed this with *The Wind Shifts* (1967) and then embarked upon a career as a screenwriter in Hollywood. Able to invest traditional genres such as the western and the thriller with trenchant resonances of issues in contemporary American life, his filmed screenplays include *The Hired Hand* (1971), *Ulzana's Raid* (1972), *Night Moves* (1975) and *The Osterman Weekend* (1983). More recently he has turned to direction with the film *Little Treasure* (1985).

SHARP, William, pseud Fiona Macleod
(1855–1905)

Scottish writer, born in Paisley, and educated at Glasgow University. After some time in Australia he settled in London (1879), working as a journalist and editor. Throughout his life he travelled widely. He published a collection of poetry, *Earth's Voices*, in 1884. He wrote books on contemporary English, French and German poets, but is chiefly remembered as the author of the remarkable series of Celtic—or neo-Celtic—tales and romances by 'Fiona Macleod'—a pseudonym he systematically refused to acknowledge. They include *Pharais* (1894), *The Mountain Lovers* (1895), *The Sin-Eater* (1895) and *The Immortal Hour* (1900).
▷ *William Sharp, a Memoir by Mrs Sharp* (1912)

SHARPE, Tom (Thomas)
(1928–)

English satirical novelist, born in London. He began his authorial career as a playwright in South Africa between 1951 and 1961, after which he returned to England. His first novel, *Riotous Assembly* (1971), ridicules corruption in a small South African town. He is more widely known, however, for his lampooning of the English academic establishment in *Porterhouse Blue* (1974), about the attempts of the fictional Porterhouse College, Cambridge, to resist modernization, and in *Wilt* (1976) and *Vintage Stuff* (1982). Henry Wilt, a lecturer at a college of further education, and the hero of the second book, reappears in two later novels. British bureaucracy and planning regulations are ruthlessly satirized in *Blott on the Landscape* (1975). Although Sharpe's humour is often vulgar, his satire is well aimed.

SHAW, Charles, pseud Bant Singer
(1900–55)

Australian writer, born in Melbourne, best known for his novel *Heaven Knows, Mr Allison* (1952), which had international success as a Hollywood film. Under the name Bant Singer he also wrote *You're Wrong Delaney* (1953) and two sequels in the 'hard-boiled' **Chandler** school of thriller fiction. In Australian style he wrote some short stories and a late flowering of the bush-ballad in *The Warrrumbungle Mare* (1943).

SHAW, George Bernard
(1856–1950)

Irish dramatist, essayist, critic, vegetarian and pamphleteer, winner of the Nobel Prize for literature, born of Irish Protestant parents in Dublin. His mother was a singing teacher in Dublin and later in London, and from her he inherited strength of character and the great love and knowledge of music so influential in his life and work. After short and unhappy periods at various schools, in 1871 he entered a firm of land-agents, disliked office routine, and left Ireland for good to follow his mother and sister Lucy, a musical-comedy actress, to London. His literary life had already begun in 1875 with a letter to the press (one of his favourite means of expression), shrewdly analysing the effect on individuals of sudden conversion by the American evangelists, Moody and Sankey. In London his early years were a long period of struggle and impoverishment, and of the five novels he wrote between 1879 and 1883, the best of which are probably *Love Among the Artists* and *Cashel Byron's Profession*, all were rejected by the more reputable publishers. An encounter (1882) with Henry George and the reading of Karl Marx turned his thoughts towards socialism, and while any direct propagation of it is absent from his plays, his faith in it and a 'kindly dislike' (if not dread) of capitalist society form the backbone of all his work. Political and economic understanding stood him in good stead as a local government councillor in St Pancras (1897–1903) and also on the executive committee of the small but influential Fabian Society, to which he devoted himself selflessly for many years (1884–1911) and for which he edited *Fabian Essays* (1889) and wrote many well-known socialist tracts. Journalism provided another lively platform for him, and it was as 'Corno di Bassetto', music critic for the new *Star* newspaper (1888–90), that he made his first indelible impact on the intellectual and social consciousness of his time. In this and in his later music criticism for *The World* (1890–4) and, above all, in his dramatic criticism for **Frank Harris**'s *Saturday Review* (1895–8), he was making his name. To this period also belong *The Quintessence of Ibsenism* (1891) and *The Perfect Wagnerite* (1898), tributes to fellow 'artist-philosophers' who, together with **John Bunyan**, **Dickens**, **Samuel Butler** and Mozart, he acknowledged had influence on his work. The rest of Shaw's life, especially after his marriage (1898) to the Irish heiress Charlotte Payne-Townshend, is mainly the history of his plays. His first, *Widowers' Houses*, was begun in 1885 in collaboration with his friend William Archer, but was finished independently in 1892 as the result of the challenge he felt to produce the newer drama of ideas he had been advocating. Into the earliest plays, which also include *Mrs Warren's Profession* (1898), *Arms and the Man* (pub 1898) and *Candida* (1897, one of the first in a long series of remarkable female portrayals), comes already the favourite Shavian theme of conversion—from dead system and outworn morality towards a more creatively vital approach to life—and this is further developed in *Three Plays for Puritans*: The *Devil's Disciple* (pub 1897), *Caesar and Cleopatra* (1901) and *Captain Brassbound's Conversion* (1900). His long correspondence with the famous Lyceum actress, Ellen Terry, was also at its peak during these years. At last Shaw was becoming more widely known, first of all in the USA and on the Continent, and then, with the important advent of the playwright-producer-actor, **Harley Granville-Barker**, in England itself, especially after the epoch-making Vedrenne-Barker Court Theatre season of 1904–7. This had been preceded by one of Shaw's greatest philosophical comedies, *Man and Superman* (1902), in which, in quest of a purer religious approach to life, Shaw advocated through his Don Juan the importance of man's unceasing creative evolutionary urge for world-improvement. Other notable plays from the early part of the century are *John Bull's Other Island* (1904), *Major Barbara* (1905), *The Doctor's Dilemma* (1906), and two uniquely Shavian discussion plays, *Getting Married* (1908) and *Misalliance* (1910). They further display Shaw's increasing control of his medium and the wide range of his subject-matter (from politics and statecraft to family life, prostitution and vaccination). Before the Joint Committee on

SHAW, Helen

Stage Censorship of 1909 he proudly proclaimed himself as 'immoralist and heretic', and insisted on the civilized necessity for toleration and complete freedom of thought. Just before World War I came two of his most delightful plays; *Androcles and the Lion* (1912), a 'religious pantomime', and *Pygmalion* (1913), an 'anti-romantic' comedy of phonetics (adapted as a highly successful musical play, *My Fair Lady* in 1956, filmed in 1964). During the war, though he later toured the front at official invitation, he created controversy and recrimination with his fearless and provocative *Common Sense About the War* (1914). After the war followed three of his greatest dramas in near succession: *Heartbreak House* (1919), an attempt to analyse in an English **Chekho**vian social environment the causes of present moral and political discontents; *Back to Methuselah* (1921), five plays in one, in which Shaw conducted a not altogether successful dramatic excursion from the Garden of Eden to 'As Far as Thought Can Reach'; and *Saint Joan* (1923), in which Shaw's essentially religious nature, his genius for characterization (above all of saintly yet very human women), and his powers of dramatic argument are most abundantly revealed. In 1925 Shaw was awarded the Nobel Prize for literature, but donated the money to inaugurate the Anglo-Swedish Literary Foundation. In 1931 he visited Russia, and during the 1930s made other long tours, including a world one with his wife in 1932, during which he gave a memorable address on political economy in the Metropolitan Opera House, New York. Greater perhaps than any of the plays written during the last years of his life are the two prose works: *The Intelligent Woman's Guide to Socialism and Capitalism* (1928), one of the most lucid introductions to its subjects, and *The Black Girl in Search of God* (1932), a modern *Pilgrim's Progress*. The later plays, except for *The Apple Cart* (1929), have scarcely received adequate public stage presentation but they continue to preach the stern yet invigorating Shavian morality of individual responsibility, self-discipline, heroic effort without thought of reward or 'atonement', and the utmost integrity. Plays such as *Too True to Be Good* (1932) and *The Simpleton of the Unexpected Isles* (1934) also show signs of sounding a newer and even more experimental dramatic note altogether. His *Collected Plays*, with their important Prefaces, was issued in seven volumes (1970–4). ▷M Holroyd, *George Bernard Shaw* (3 vols, 1989–91)

SHAW, Helen
(1913–85)

New Zealand poet and short-story writer, an early contributor to the periodical *New Zealand New Writing*. Her stories were first published in *The Orange Tree and Other Stories* (1957) and later in *The Gipsies and Other Stories* (1978). Verse includes her first volume, *Out of the Dark* (1968), *This is My Sorrow: As from Heloise to Abelard* (1981) and her last *Time Told from a Tower* (1985). She also edited a collection of **D'Arcy Cresswell**'s letters in 1983.

SHAW, Irwin
(1913–84)

American popular novelist, born in Brooklyn, who first became known with his *The Young Lions* (1948), about two American soldiers. *The Troubled Air* (1951), his best novel, dramatically analysed the situation in American radio caused by the anti-communist witch-hunting of the time. *Rich man, Poor Man* (1970), although skilful, more represented a soap-opera than a serious novel, and was made into one for television.

SHECKLEY, Robert
(1928–)

American science-fiction writer, born in New York City. He began publishing in 1952, and quickly gained a deserved reputation for witty, ingenious and highly crafted short stories, which still stand among the best the genre has to offer. His work grew more satiric and speculative in the 1960s, as exemplified in the novels *The Status Civilisation* (1960), set on a prison planet where accepted norms are reversed, and *Mindswap* (1966), in which an Earthman finds himself literally trading minds with a Martian, to unbridled satiric effect. His later works lack the sure sense of purpose of his earlier stories, although *The Alchemical Marriage of Alastair Crompton* (1978) is a strong exception, perhaps because it originated in an earlier short story. An incomplete *Collected Short Stories* appeared in five volumes in 1991.

SHEED, Wilfrid John Joseph
(1930–)

American novelist, born in London. He went to live in the USA aged 10, but returned to England to complete his education at Lincoln College, Oxford. From 1957 to 1966, he worked on *Jubilee* magazine in New York, later writing for *Commonweal* and *Esquire*. His first novel was *A Middle Class Education* (1960), a satirical attack on British public schools and universities. *The Hack* (1963) concerned a freelance theological journalist, whose career moves and ostensible principles work at some remove from each other. Later novels include *Office Politics* (1966), *People Will Always be Kind* (1973) and *Transatlantic Blues* (1978), but Sheed's most memorable work remains the 'short novel and long story' *The Blacking Factory, and Pennsylvania Gothic* (1968), which draws together his interest in the media, in guilt and acceptance, and in the damage inflicted by an uncaring upbringing. The essays in *Three Mobs: Labor, Church and Mafia* (1974) reflect some of his obsessions.

▷ *Frank and Maisie: A Memoir With Parents* (1985)

SHEFFIELD, John, 1st Duke of Buckingham and Normanby
(1648–1721)

English political leader and poet. He succeeded his father as third Earl of Mulgrave in 1658, served in both navy and army, and was lord chamberlain to James II and a cabinet councillor under William III, who in 1694 made him Marquis of Normanby. Queen Anne made him Duke of (the county of) Buckingham (1703); but for his opposition to Godolphin and Marlborough he was deprived of the Seal (1705). After 1710, under the Tories, he was Lord Steward and Lord President till the death of Anne, when he lost all power, and intrigued for the restoration of the Stuarts. Patron of **Dryden** and friend of **Pope**, he wrote two tragedies, a metrical *Essay on Satire*, an *Essay on Poetry*, and other works.

▷ J H Wilson, *The Court Wits of the Restoration* (1948)

SHELDON, Charles Monroe
(1857–1946)

American Congregationalist and novelist, born in New York. After studying theology he became pastor of a church in Topeka, Kansas. *In His Steps* (1896) tells the story of a minister, Rev Henry Maxwell, and his congregation, who become spurred into basing their every action on what Jesus would do in the same circumstances. The synopsis might not set a modern editor's eyes alight, but it became a fly-away success. Translated into more than 20 languages, and selling over six million copies, it was the biggest bestseller of its era. Little else Sheldon published, apart from his autobiography, is remembered. In his sixties he became editor of the *Christian Herald*.

▷ C M Sheldon, *His Life and Story* (1925)

SHELDON, Edward Brewster
(1886–1946)

American playwright, born in Chicago and educated at Harvard. He became most widely known as the author of *Romance* (1913), in which an elderly bishop tells the cautionary story of his youthful love for an opera singer in an attempt to prevent his grandson from marrying an actress. This rather far-fetched fable established Sheldon as a successful commercial author. He also wrote such plays as *Salvation Nell* (1908), *The High Road* (1912) and *The Garden of Paradise* (1914), the latter adapted from **Hans Christian Andersen**'s *The Little Mermaid*. Since his heyday, however, Sheldon's plays have slipped from the repertoire.

SHELDON, Sidney
(1917–)

American novelist and playwright, born in New York City. His early work includes the 1950 screenplay for *Annie Get Your Gun*, but he has since become far better known as a bestselling novelist. A Sheldon blockbuster is typically an amalgam of money, glamour, crime and grimy secrets. In *The Other Side of Midnight* (1974) a beautiful actress has to stand trial for murder; its less successful sequel, *Memories of Midnight*, was published in 1990. His other novels include *The Master of the Game* (1982) and *The Sands of Time* (1988); many have been made into TV miniseries. Sheldon himself was the creator of two TV series, *Hart to Hart* and *I Dream of Jeannie*, which he produced and directed.

SHELLEY, Mary Wollstonecraft, née Godwin
(1797–1851)

English writer, the daughter of **William Godwin** and Mary Wollstonecraft Godwin. In 1814 she eloped with **Percy Bysshe Shelley**, and married him as his second wife in 1816. They lived abroad throughout their married life. Her first and most impressive novel was *Frankenstein or, The Modern Prometheus* (1818), her second *Valperga* (1823). After her husband's death in 1822 she returned from Italy to England with their son in 1823. Her husband's father, in granting her an allowance, insisted on the suppression of the volume of Shelley's *Posthumous Poems* edited by her. *The Last Man* (1826), a romance of the ruin of human society by pestilence, fails to attain sublimity. In *Lodore* (1835) the story is told of Shelley's alienation from his first wife. Her last novel, *Falkner* appeared in 1837. Of her occasional pieces of verse the most remarkable is 'The Choice'. Her *Journal of a Six Weeks' Tour* (partly by Shelley) tells of the excursion to Switzerland in 1814; *Rambles in Germany and Italy* (1844) describes tours of 1840–3; her *Tales* were published in 1890. Two unpublished mythological dramas, *Proserpine* and *Midas*, were edited and published in 1922.

▷ E Bigland, *Mary Shelley* (1959)

SHELLEY, Percy Bysshe

SHELLEY, Percy Bysshe
(1792–1822)

English poet, born in Field Place, near Horsham in Sussex. He was educated at Syon House Academy and Eton, where he acquired the sobriquet 'Mad Shelley' for his independent spirit and was later dubbed 'Eton Atheist'. While at Eton he published *Zastrozzi* (1810), a Gothic novel. That year, with his sister Elizabeth, he produced *Original Poetry by Victor and Cazire*, and the following year another Gothic romance, *St Irvine, or, The Rosicrucian*. He attended University College, Oxford, where he read radical authors like **William Godwin** and **Paine**, and dressed and behaved in an eccentric and provocative manner. In 1811, he produced a pamphlet, co-authored with Thomas Jefferson Hogg, called *The Necessity of Atheism*, a formative declaration. Both authors were expelled. That and Shelley's elopement to Scotland with 16-year-old Harriet Westbrook caused a rift between him and his family that was never repaired. Shelley would not recant, and relinquished his right to his inheritance. He lived itinerantly for the next three years; in York, in the Lake District where only **Robert Southey** was at home, in Dublin where he advocated the repeal of the Union and Catholic emancipation, and at Lynmouth in Devon where he set up a commune of 'like spirits'. *Queen Mab* (1813) was the poetic fruit of this time but it made little impact. In London he met, befriended, subsidized and fell out with Godwin, and was close to **Thomas Love Peacock**. Despite having two children, his marriage to Harriet failed and he fell in love with Mary, the 16-year-old daughter of Godwin and Mary Wollstonecraft. Predictably they eloped, making up a *ménage à trois* with Mary's half-sister, Jane 'Claire' Clairmont. The three travelled on the continent where Shelley wrote an unfinished novella, *The Assassins* (1814), collaborated on a journal, and published *The History of a Six Weeks' Tour* (1817). Shelley returned to London, to face financial problems, and Mary gave birth to a daughter who died prematurely. The couple took a house near Windsor Great Park and he wrote *Alastor* (1816), its publication coinciding with the birth of his beloved son, William. 1816 was a traumatic year. He spent time with **Byron** at Lake Geneva, Harriet Westbrook drowned herself, and Shelley immediately married Mary. His reputation was growing. He met **Keats** and **William Hazlitt** and, having moved to Marlow in 1817, he wrote *An Address to the People on the Death of Princess Charlotte*, a fine political pamphlet. He published *The Revolt of Islam* in 1818, the year he finally left England for Italy where he was to spend the rest of his life. In Este he wrote *Julian and Maddalo* (1818), which explores his relationship with Byron, and in 1819 came the major part of *Prometheus Unbound*, his masterpiece. William's death in Rome devastated him and he moved to Tuscany, finally settling in Pisa. From the middle of 1819 to summer 1820 came an extraordinary burst of creative energy resulting in the completion of the fourth part of *Prometheus*, *The Masque of Anarchy* (1819, inspired by the Peterloo massacre), 'The Ode to the West Wind', 'To Liberty' and 'To Naples', the *Letter to Maria Gisborne* (1820) and *The Witch of Atlas*. His son Percy was born in November 1819. Still to come was *A Philosophical View of Reform* (1820), *Essay on the Devil* (1821), poems, *The Defence of Poetry* (1821) and *Swellfoot the Tyrant* (1820), a burlesque. *Adonais* (1821), an elegy and meditation on death, was inspired by the death of Keats. *Epipsychidion* (1821) was the fruit of a platonic affair with a beautiful Italian heiress locked away in a convent. Byron came to Pisa in 1821, where a bohemian group gathered. Roused by the Greek war of independence, Shelley wrote *Hellas* (1822), a verse drama. It was to be his last work. The *ménage* moved to Lerici. Mary had a miscarriage and Claire was distraught at the death of her daughter, Allegra, whom she had had by Byron. Returning from a visit to Byron and **Leigh Hunt** at Livorno in August 1822 in the schooner 'Ariel', Shelley, Edward Williams and an English boatboy were drowned when they were surprised by a sudden squall. Shelley's body was cremated at Viareggio. As much a political activist as a poet, Shelley's adventurous life and unconventional behaviour have tended to overshadow his poetry. He was revolutionary in both spheres of life, turning away from **Coleridge**'s German Romanticism and reaffirming Mediterranean values: an inspirational polemicist and a poet of genius. His *Letters* in two volumes appeared in 1964.
▷T J Hogg, *The Life of Shelley* (1858)

SHEN KUA
(1030–93)

Chinese administrator, engineer and scientist, born in Hangchow. He made significant contributions to such diverse fields as astronomy, cartography, medicine, hydraulics and fortification. As director of the astronomical bureau from 1072 he improved methods of computation and the design of several observational devices; in 1075 he constructed a series of relief maps of China's northern frontier area, and designed fortifications as defences against nomadic invaders. He surveyed and improved the Grand Canal over a distance of some 150 miles, using stone-filled gabions, wooden piles and long bundles of reeds to strengthen the banks and close gaps. In 1082 he was forced by intrigue to resign from his government posts, and occupied his last years in the writing of *Brush Talks from Dream Brook*, a remarkable compilation of about 600 observations which has become one of the most important sources of information on early science and technology.

SHENSTONE, William
(1714–63)

English poet, born near Halesowen, Worcestershire. He studied at Solihull Grammar School and Pembroke College, Oxford. In 1735 he inherited the estate of the Leasowes, and spent most of his income on 'landship gardening' to turn it into a show garden. In 1737 he published his best-known poem, 'The Schoolmistress' (revised in 1742) which, written in imitation of **Edmund Spenser**, foreshadowed **Thomas Gray**'s *Elegy*. He published *The Judgement of Hercules* in 1741. His *Pastoral Ballad* (1755) was commended by Gray and **Samuel Johnson**.
▷ A R Humphreys, *William Shenstone* (1937)

SHEPARD, Sam, originally Samuel Shepard Rogers
(1943–)

American dramatist and actor, born in Illinois. He moved to New York City and worked in the avant-garde theatre of the 1960s with one-acters. His first plays, *Cowboy* and *The Rock Garden*, were written in 1964 and produced by Theater Genesis in New York, followed by *Dog* and *Rocking Chair* (both 1965) at La Mama. *The Tooth of Crime*, a rock drama, was staged at the Royal Court Theatre, London, in 1974, followed by *The Curse of the Starving Class*, at the New York Shakespeare Festival, in 1976. He won the Pulitzer Prize with his 1978 play, *Buried Child*. He was resident playwright at the Magic Theater, San Francisco, for several years, and two of his plays were first staged there, *True West* (1979) and *Fool For Love* (1983). *A Lie of the Mind* (1985) was very successful in America. Few living American playwrights have such sensitivity for landscape and time as Shepard, and few can produce such economic theatrical intensity. He also appeared in films, and has written screenplays, including *Paris, Texas* (1984), a tale of drifting and homecoming.
▷ R Mottram, *Inner Landscapes* (1984)

SHEPHERD, Nan
(1893–1981)

Scottish novelist and critic, raised in Aberdeen, where she graduated from university in 1915. She worked until 1956 as a lecturer at Aberdeen College of Education and was a friend and correspondent of **Neil Gunn**. Her three novels, *The Quarry Wood* (1928), *The Weatherhouse* (1930) and *A Pass in the Grampians* (1933), all deal with aspects of a young woman's development in north-east Scotland. In these works she is concerned to show the way women are societized to make compromises which do not allow them to fulfil their potential. Her creative work has been largely ignored by critics. As well as writing novels she was also involved in academic research. Her last book was a non-fiction study of the mountains, *The Living Mountain* (1977).

SHERIDAN, Frances, née Chamberlaine
(1724–66)

Irish novelist and playwright, born in Dublin, daughter of an archdeacon. Educated by her brothers because of her father's disapproval of education for women, she wrote a romantic novel, *Eugenia and Adelaide*, at 15. She married the actor-manager Thomas Sheridan in 1747; they moved to London in 1754, then for reasons of health and economy to France in 1764. At **Samuel Richardson**'s urging she wrote a second novel, *Memoirs of Miss Sidney Biddulph* (1761, sequel 1767); its conservative morality and pathos, enlivened by humour and psychological realism, made it a popular success. Her son **Richard Brinsley Sheridan** borrowed incidents from it for *The School for Scandal*. She had two comedies staged by Garrick in 1763, and her intelligent, entertaining oriental tale *The History of Nourjahad* (1767) was admired and often reprinted.
▷ R L Mack, (ed), *Oriental Tales* (1992); A Lefanu (her daughter), *Memoirs of the Life and Writings of Mrs Frances Sheridan* (1824); M A Doody, in *British Novelists, 1660–1800*, ed M Battestin, *Dictionary of Literary Biography* 39 (1985)

SHERIDAN, Richard Brinsley
(1751–1816)

Irish dramatist, born in Dublin. He was grandson of **Jonathan Swift**'s friend, Thomas Sheridan, (1687–1738), and son of Thomas Sheridan (1719–88), a teacher of elocution, actor and author of a *Life of Swift*; his mother was the novelist and playwright **Frances Sheridan**. Richard Sheridan was educated at Harrow, and after leaving school, with a school-friend named Halhed wrote a three-act farce called *Jupiter* and tried a verse translation of the *Epistles of Aristoenetus*. After a romantic courtship, Richard married Elizabeth Linley in 1773. The young couple settled in London to a life much beyond their means. Sheridan now made more serious efforts at dramatic composition. On 17 January 1775 *The Rivals* was produced at Covent Garden, and after a slight alteration in the cast met with universal approval. In the same

year appeared a poor farce called *St Patrick's Day* and also *The Duenna*. In 1776 Sheridan, with the aid of Linley and another friend, bought half the patent of Drury Lane Theatre for £35000 from Garrick, and in 1778 the remaining share for £45000. His first production was a purified edition of Sir **John Vanbrugh**'s *Relapse*, under the title of *A Trip to Scarborough*. *The Critic* (1779), teeming with sparkling wit, was Sheridan's last dramatic effort, with the exception of a poor tragedy, *Pizarro*. On the dissolution of parliament in 1780 Sheridan was elected for Stafford, and he concentrated thereafter on his distinguished Parliamentary career until he was defeated in 1812. In 1792 his first wife died, and three years later he married Esther Ogle, the silly and extravagant daughter of the Dean of Winchester, who survived him. The affairs of the theatre had gone badly. The old building had to be closed as unfit to hold large audiences, and a new one, opened in 1794, was burned in 1809. This last calamity put the finishing touch to Sheridan's pecuniary difficulties, which had long been serious. He died in great poverty, but was given a magnificent funeral in Westminster Abbey.
▷ L Gibbs, *Sheridan* (1947)

SHERRIFF, R(obert) C(edric)
(1896–1975)

English playwright, novelist and scriptwriter, born in Kingston-upon-Thames. He achieved an international reputation with his first play, *Journey's End* (1929), based on his experiences in the trenches during World War I. His other plays include *St Helena* (1934), on the last years of the exiled Napoleon, and *The White Carnation* (1953), a ghost story. He also wrote several novels. He became a scriptwriter in Hollywood, and wrote the scripts for films like *The Invisible Man* (1933), *Goodbye Mr Chips* (1936), *The Four Feathers* (1938), *Lady Hamilton* (1941) and *The Dambusters* (1955).

SHERWOOD, Mary Martha, née Butt
(1775–1851)

English writer of children's books, daughter of a chaplain to George II, born in Stanford, Worcestershire. In 1803 she married Henry Sherwood and went to India with him (1805–66). Her 77 works include *Little Henry and his Bearer* (1815), and the long-popular *History of the Fairchild Family* (1818–47).
▷ N G Royde Smith, *The State of Mind of Mary Sherwood* (1946)

SHERWOOD, Robert Emmet
(1896–1955)

American playwright and author, born in New Rochelle, New York. He wrote his first play, *Barnum Was Right*, while at Harvard, and after service in World War I he became Editor of *Life* (1924–8), and a member of **Dorothy Parker**'s celebrated Algonquin Round Table. He won four Pulitzer Prizes, the first three for drama—*Idiot's Delight*, (1936), *Abe Lincoln in Illinois* (1939) and *There Shall be No Night* (1941)—and the last (1949) for his biographical *Roosevelt and Hopkins* (1949).

SHEVCHENKO, Taras
(1814–61)

Ukrainian poet and prose writer, born a serf in Kirilovka (Kiev). He showed an early interest in writing and drawing, and was taken up by a literary circle in St Petersburg, who bought his freedom in 1838. His early poems included Romantic ballads, love songs and historical subjects. He became professor at Kiev (1845), and founded an organization for radical social reforms. He was exiled to central Asia for 10 years, but was eventually freed in 1857, although kept under surveillance. He is remembered as the creator of a new Ukrainian literary language.
▷ W K Matthews, *Taras Sevchenko* (1951)

SHIGA Naoya
(1883–1971)

Japanese writer of short stories and one novel. He produced his best work during the turmoil of the run-up to the Sino–Japanese War and the rise of fascism, when he flirted, dangerously, with non-Japanese doctrines such as socialism and Christianity. He looked to the West for inspiration, but his novel *Anya Koro* (1926, Eng trans *A Dark Night's Passing*, 1976), is a distinctly Japanese and naturalist work of the kind known as *watakushi shosetsu* (I-novel). It is an internal monologue, set during a train journey, presented in a cold, sparse, unemotional (yet compelling) style.

SHILLABER, Benjamin Penhallow
(1814–90)

American humorist. He founded and edited *The Carpet Bag* (1851–3) and was the author of *The Life and Sayings of Mrs Partington* (1854), which used a popular invented character (credited for creating her lies elsewhere) as a basis for contemporary comment and satire.

SHIMAZAKI Toson
(1872–1943)

Japanese writer from Nagano in the west of Japan. Like most of his contemporaries, he espoused the literary doctrine known as Japanese naturalism, but took it a step further, writing a number of *watakushi shomei*

('I-novels'), closely narrated works in which little actually happens, the important thing being the narrator's states of mind and emotions. *Ie* (1910, 'Home') is a prime example of this esoteric, intricate, and distinctly Japanese form of writing. *Yokae mae* (1929–36, 'Before the Dawn') is an analysis of the hopes, fears and expectations of the peasantry at the time of the Meiji Restoration of 1868 seen through the eyes of a character closely modelled on Shimazaki's father. He was also a poet—his 1897 collection *Wakanashu* ('Seedlings') was an instant success, but its romantic, impressionistic verse veers between the sickly sweet and the hopelessly unfocused.

SHIRLEY, James
(1596–1666)

English late-Elizabethan dramatist, born in London. From Merchant Taylors' he passed in 1612 to St John's, Oxford, but migrated to Catharine Hall, Cambridge. He took orders, and held a living at St Albans. Turning Catholic, he taught (1623–4) in the grammar school there, but soon went to London and became a playwright. The suppression of stage plays in 1642 ended his livelihood, and he took to teaching again. The Restoration revived his plays, but brought him no better fortunes. His death was a result of the Great Fire of London. **Francis Beaumont** and **John Fletcher** and **Ben Jonson** were his models, but he has little of the grand Elizabethan manner. Most of his plays are tragi-comedies. His chief works are *Eccho* (1618), a poem on the Narcissus subject; comedies, *The Witty Fair One* (1628); *The Wedding* (1628); *The Grateful Servant* (1629); *The Example* (1634); *The Opportunity* (1634); *The Lady of Pleasure*, the most brilliant of his comedies (1635); tragedies, *The Cardinal*, to the author himself 'the best of his flock' (1641); *The Traytor* (1631), a great drama. As a masque writer he is second only to Jonson; among his best masques are *The Triumph of Peace* (1633) and *The Contention of Ajax and Ulysses* (1659, including 'the glories of our blood and state').
▷A H Mason, *James Shirley* (1915)

SHLONSKY, Avraham
(1900–73)

Hebrew poet, born in Russia, who was educated in Palestine, and then returned to Russia. Only in 1921 did he come to Palestine permanently. He was a Marxist, and he wrote much of his political poetry under the influence of **Mayakovsky**, whose power and individualism he possessed. He is the sort of poet who, a critic has written, as we read him 'we feel he is the best'. His greatest poems are his more personal ones. With Eliezir Steinman he started an important magazine, *Kethubim*,

in 1925. He translated **Pushkin** and **Shakespeare**, and founded the Worker's Library. The best poems in English translation are to be found in Abraham Birman's *Anthology of Modern Hebrew Poetry* (1968).
▷M Waxman, *A History of Jewish Literature* (1947)

SHOLEM ALEICHEM, or Sholom, or Shalom, pseud of Solomon J Rabinowitz
(1859–1916)

Russian–Jewish author, born in Pereyaslev in the Ukraine, the son of Russian–Jewish shopkeepers. He spent much of his youth in and around the neighbouring town of Voronkov, which was to feature as Krasilevke, the setting of many of his stories. After working for some years as a rabbi, he devoted himself to writing and Yiddish culture, contributing to the Hebrew magazine *Hamelitz* and the first Yiddish newspaper, established in 1883. In 1893 he moved to Kiev, but the pogroms of 1905 drove him to the USA, where he attempted to establish himself as a playwright for the Yiddish theatre, which was flourishing in New York at the time. He travelled widely, giving readings of his work in many European cities, and from 1908 to 1914 spent most of his time in Italy to improve his health. He returned to settle in New York in 1914. His short stories and plays portray Jewish life in Russia in the late 19th century with vividness, humour and sympathy, and were first widely introduced to a non-Jewish public in 1943 in Maurice Samuel's *The World of Sholom Aleichem*; nearly all his work has been translated into English, including *Jewish Children* (Eng trans 1920), *Stories and Satires* (Eng trans 1959) and *Old Country Tales* (Eng trans 1966). The popular musical *Fiddler on the Roof* is based on his stories.

SHOLOKHOV, Mikhail Alexandrovich
(1905–84)

Russian novelist and winner of the Nobel Prize for literature, born in Kruzhilin. He was educated at schools in Moscow, Boguchar and Veshenskaya. From 1920 to 1922 he served in the army, after which he had multifarious occupations: teacher, clerk, tax inspector, labourer, playwright, actor and journalist. During World War II he was a war correspondent. His literary career began with some 30 short stories written between 1923 and 1927. Most focus on the merciless sociopolitical struggle within Don Cossack families and villages during the civil war and early years of Soviet rule. Uneven in quality, they nevertheless demonstrate a rapid development from a sedulous ape into an original craftsman. His masterpiece is *Tikhy Don* (4 vols, 1928–40, rev edn 1953, Eng trans in 2 vols: *And Quiet Flows the Don* and *The Don*

Flows Home to the Sea, 1934–40). Set in the years 1912–22, it is a monument to the Don Cossacks, offering a panoramic view of their life in time of peace and during the turbulent years of war and revolution. The characterization is splendid and the dialogue earthy. Since 1928 his authorship of the novel has been questioned on the grounds that he was too young and had previously shown no indication that he could write such an epic work, but the evidence to support these allegations is thin. *Podnyataya tselina* (1932–60, Eng trans in 2 vols: *Virgin Soil Upturned* and *Harvest on the Don*, 1935–60) is much inferior, attributable to his toeing of the official line, alcoholism and decline of his creative powers. He received the Stalin Prize in 1941 and the 1965 Nobel Prize for literature.
▷ I G Lezhnev, *Mikhail Sholokhov* (1948)

SHORT, Luke
(1908–75)

American writer of Westerns. Without literary merit, but with simple and bold plots, they sold phenomenally well.

SHORTHOUSE, Joseph Henry
(1834–1903)

English novelist, born in Birmingham. He became a chemical manufacturer. In 1881 his romance, *John Inglesant*, revealed a subtle and sympathetic insight into old-world phases of the spiritual mind. It was followed by *The Little Schoolmaster Mark* (1883–4), *Sir Percival* (1886), *A Teacher of the Violin* (1888), *The Countess Eve* (1888) and *Blanche, Lady Falaise* (1891).

SHUSHKIN, Vasily
(1929–74)

Russian writer of fiction and film-scripts, born in Siberia. He was killed in a car crash just after achieving extraordinary success with his novel about a repentant thief, *Kalina krasnaya* (1973, Eng trans *Snowball Berry Red*, 1979), and then with the film he made of it with himself in the leading role. There is much about him in the translation of his most famous work, which contains other stories.

SHUTE, Nevil, pseud of Nevil Shute Norway
(1899–1960)

English novelist, born in Ealing. He served in World War I and immediately afterwards began an aeronautical career. He was chief calculator of the Airship Guarantee Company during the construction of the airship R100, and he flew the Atlantic twice in her. He founded Airspeed Ltd, aircraft constructors, and became its managing director. He emigrated to Australia after World War II. His novels include *The Pied Piper* (1942),

Most Secret (1945), *The Chequerboard* (1947), *No Highway* (1948), *A Town Like Alice* (1949), *Round the Bend* (1951), *Requiem for a Wren* (1955), *Beyond the Black Stump* (1956) and *On The Beach* (1957), about an atomic war catastrophe. His success was largely due to his brisk style and his ability to make technical language and procedure understandable to a lay public.
▷ *Slide Rule* (1954)

SHVARTS, Yevgeny
(1896–1958)

Russian (Jewish) playwright (and novelist and storyteller), for adults and children, born in Kazan. His knowledge of the theatre was gained from his acting experience. He was only moderately well known until after his death, when his reputation suddenly and dramatically rose. His humorous attacks on the Stalinist system—he hardly made a secret of his witty scorn for it—did not escape the attention of the censors, for some of his plays were banned; but for some reason the really important ones, such as *Ten* (1940), *The Shadow* and *Drakon* (1943, Eng trans *The Dragon* in *Three Soviet Plays*, 1966), were not. He wrote for puppets and for live casts. In an age of deceit, treachery and craven foolishness, Shvarts was an exception: an honourable, witty and decent man, he left exactly that mark with his work. His usual method was to adapt a fairy tale, in the style established by **Ludwig Fulda**, and then pillory his Stalinist or Nazi victim. He owed much of his theatrical success to the efforts of N P Akimov, the director of Leningrad's Comic Theatre, who persisted in putting on his plays during his lifetime and then revived them in the 1960s after his death. He has been called 'the only Soviet playwright of status'.

SIDNEY, Sir Philip
(1554–86)

English poet and patron, born in Penshurst Place, Kent. The eldest son of Sir Henry Sidney (Lord Deputy of Ireland), he was educated at Shrewsbury School and Christ Church, Oxford. He may also have been enrolled at Cambridge. From 1572 to 1575 he travelled in France, Germany, Austria and Italy, where he spent a year studying history and ethics, and was painted by Veronese. Returning to England he did not rise politically as anticipated and waited until 1585 for his appointment as governor of Flushing, having been knighted in 1582. Much of his life was reposeful and conducive to composition. None of his work was published in his lifetime. The revised *Arcadia* was published in 1590 in three books, and again in an augmented edition in 1593. *Astrophel and Stella* appeared first, in 1591, with a corrupt text

in a pirated edition, then in the authorized version. *A Defence of Poetry* was published in 1595. The *Arcadia* was probably written while he was lodging with his sister, **Mary, Countess of Pembroke**. It is probable that Penelope Devereux, whose father approved of Sidney and wished him to marry his daughter, is the 'Stella' of the sonnets. However, she married Baron Robert Rich, and Sidney, in 1583, married Frances, daughter of Sir Francis Walsingham. Throughout this time he bestowed patronage on a number of poets as dedications in various works testify, the most notable being that in **Edmund Spenser**'s *The Shepheardes Calendar* in 1579. He spent his last years in the Netherlands, where he successfully plotted an attack on the town of Axel. In September of the same year he led an attack on a Spanish convoy transporting arms to Zutphen, was shot in the thigh and died from the infection. He was buried in St Paul's Cathedral, much loved by contemporary poets and alluded to with affection and respect by **W B Yeats**, **John Ruskin** and others.
▷M Wilson, *Sir Philip Sidney* (1931)

SIDONIUS APOLLINARIS, Gaius Sollius
(c.430–c.483)

Gallo-Roman poet and prelate, born in Lugdunum (Lyons) of a prominent Christian family. He held high civil offices in Rome, and in 472 became Bishop of Clermont-Ferrand in the Auvergne. His letters are modelled on **Pliny**'s; his poems comprise panegyrics on three emperors, and two poems celebrating a marriage. He was canonized as St Sidonius Apollinaris.
▷C E Stevens, *Sidonius and his Age* (1973)

SIENKIEWICZ, Henryk
(1846–1916)

Polish novelist, winner of the Nobel Prize for literature, born near Luków. He lived in the USA from 1876 to 1878, and after a hunting expedition in East Africa (1892) wrote the children's story *W pustyni i w puszczy* (1911, Eng trans *In Desert and Wilderness*, 1912). Most of his works, however, are strongly realistic; many have been translated, among them the trilogy, *Ogniem i mieczem* (1884, Eng trans *With Fire and Sword*, 1890), *Potop* (1886, Eng trans *The Deluge*, 1892) and *Pan Wolodyjowski* (1887–8, Eng trans *Pan Michael*, 1895); also *Rodzina Polanieckich* (1894, Eng trans *Children of the Soil*, 1895) and *Quo Vadis?* (1896, Eng trans 1896). He was awarded the Nobel Prize for literature in 1905.
▷M Gardner, *The Novels of Henryk Sienkiewicz* (1926)

SIGAL, Clancy
(1926–)

American novelist and journalist, resident in the UK since 1957. He was born in Chicago and educated in California. He worked in the union movement, as a story analyst in Hollywood, and as a literary agent. His involvement in the anti-war and civil rights movement led to his removal to Britain. His reputation is based almost entirely on two documentary novels, *Weekend in Dinlock* (1960), an **Orwell**ian study of a small mining village in the Midlands, and the 'report, memoir', *Going Away* (1962), which examines his responses to the country of his birth. A third novel, *Zone of the Interior* (1976), reflected Sigal's interest in radical therapeutic philosophies, but the author was perhaps too close (though not necessarily sympathetic) to the subject to maintain the precise reserve of the earlier books. Since the 1970s, Sigal has continued to write trenchant, often provocative journalism.

SIGOURNEY, Lydia Howard Huntley
(1791–1865)

American poet and essayist, born in Norwich, Connecticut. She began publishing her work anonymously because her husband, a wealthy businessman, feared his reputation would be damaged if it was known that his wife was a writer, especially one supporting such causes as that of the Native Americans. *Traits of the Aborigines of America* (1822) records Native American legend in blank verse. Native American themes recur in *Pocahontas and Other Poems* (1841). Since the early 1830s, as a result of her husband's business collapsing, Sigourney was publishing under her own name. She was also successful: the appearance of *Poems* in 1834 resulted in her being acclaimed as a 'female Milton'. Later books include *Pleasant Memories of Pleasant Lands* (1842), an entertaining record of her travels.
▷G S Haight, *Lydia Sigourney* (1930)

SIGUR-ÐARDÓTTIR, Fríða Á
(1940–)

Icelandic short-story writer and novelist. Born in Hesteyri, in the west of Iceland, she worked as a librarian before concentrating on writing. The short stories in her first book, *Þetta er ekkert alvarlegt* (1980, 'This Isn't Serious'), focus on marital relationships, while her novel *Sólin og skugginn* (1981, 'The Sun and the Shadow') explores feminine powerlessness. *Við gluggann* (1984, 'By the Window') is a book of short stories in which her earlier realism becomes marginalized by a style dependent on metaphor and stream of consciousness. Her novel *Meðan nóttin líður* (1990, 'While the Night is Passing') confronts a modern career woman with memories of six generations of women, all of them less independent than she is but enjoying an affinity with their families and their world that she lacks. The novel won the 1992 Nordic Council Literature Prize.

▷S Hilmarsdóttir, 'Friða Á. Sigurðaróttir', in *Norsk Litterær Årbok* (1992)

SIGUR-ĐARDÓTTIR, Jakobína
(1918–)

Icelandic short-story writer and novelist. Born in the west of Iceland into a working-class family, she subsequently ran a farm with her husband in the north of the country. She writes a realist prose that is at once accessible and innovative, her critique of contemporary Iceland focusing on the swift transition from a traditional way of life to a modern, industrial economy dependent on foreign capital. She published a children's book in 1959, and her first collection of short stories, *Púnktur á skökkum stað* ('Full Stop in the Wrong Place'), in 1964. *Dægurvísa* (1965, 'Twenty-four Hour Tune') introduced the collective novel into Icelandic literature; and the novel *Snaran* (1968, 'The Noose'), written as one long address to a respondent who never replies, strikingly pinpoints the loss of identity brought about by the presence in Iceland this century of politically and economically powerful foreigners, notably Americans.

▷E Skyum Nielsen (ed), 'Indledning', *Tale i røret—moderne islandsk prosa* (1981)

SIGURJÓNSSON, Jóhann
(1880–1919)

Icelandic dramatist and poet, pioneer of Icelandic theatre and the first Icelandic writer in modern times to achieve international recognition. Born in Laxamýri in the north of Iceland, he studied veterinary science in Copenhagen but turned to literature instead. He wrote simultaneously in Danish and Icelandic in order to gain a wider audience, and used Icelandic folk-tale motifs for his most successful plays: *Fjalla-Eyvindur* in 1911 (Eng trans *Eyvind of the Mountains*), which was made into a film as *Berg Eyvind och hans hustru* (1917) by the Swedish director Victor Sjöström, and *Galdra-Loftur* in 1914 (Eng trans *The Wish*, 1967). His other plays were *Dr Rung* (1908), *Bóndeð á Hrauni* (1908, 'The Farmer at Hraun') and *Løgneren* (1917, 'The Liar'), based on a theme from *Njál's Saga*. He also wrote lyric poetry of touching sensitivity.

▷H Toldberg, *Jóhann Sigurjónsson* (1965)

SIKELIANOS, Angelos
(1884–1951)

Greek nature poet, born on Leucas in the Ionian islands. The publication of his *Prologos Sti Zoë* ('Prologue To Life') between 1915 and 1917 instigated a period of Greek mysticism. His work was brought to a wider public with the publication of *Panaghia* (1917), about the death of the dancer Isadora Duncan—his sister Penelope was married to the dancer's brother Raymond. Sikelianos also married an American, Eva Palmer, and with her help he attempted in 1927 to set up a Delphic University dedicated to 'intellectual independence, spiritual redemption and unity beyond the fragmented self'. Together they devised the first Delphic Festival, to promote this university, which resulted in the first staging of ancient Greek tragedy in its home since antiquity, but which was a spectacular financial disaster. Sikelianos turned to writing tragedies, and achieved a respectable critical success with *Sybil* (1940, 'The Sybil').

SILIUS ITALICUS, Tiberius Catius Asconius
(25–101)

Latin poet and politician. He became a prominent orator in the Roman courts, was consul in 68, and then proconsul in Asia (77). He lived thereafter in retirement on his rich estates near Naples, and became a patron of literature and the arts. Having contracted an incurable disease, he starved himself to death. He was the author of the longest surviving Latin poem, *Punica*, an epic in 17 books on the 2nd Punic War.

▷H M Butler, *Post Augustan Poets* (1926)

SILKIN, Jon
(1930–)

English poet, born into a Jewish family in London. He was educated at Dulwich College, and has been editor of the literary magazine *Stand* since 1952 (with a short break in 1957–60). A deeply committed poet, his work can be linguistically and semantically obscure, but his best writing has a powerfully direct, discursive appeal. *The Peaceable Kingdom* (1954) was his first substantial collection. Other important volumes include *Nature With Man* (1965), *The Little Time-Keeper* (1976) and *Autobiographical Stanzas* (1984). He has compiled a number of anthologies, and written a study of the poetry of World War I, *Out of Battle* (1972, rev edn 1987). *Selected Poems* appeared in 1980, and was revised in 1988.

SILKO, Leslie Marmon
(1948–)

American writer, born in Albuquerque, New Mexico. Of mixed Laguna, Mexican and White descent, Silko was brought up on the Laguna Pueblo reservation in New Mexico, and the Laguna cultural traditions and Southwestern desert landscape are central to her work. The poems in *Laguna Woman* (1974), her first publication, display the richly sensuous imagery combined with humour and naturalistic dialogue that characterize her work. Her novel *Ceremony* (1977) describes the spiritual and cultural reconstruction of a young Pueblo war veteran, fighting the destructive power of witchery over his people, while in the autobiographical *Storyteller* (1981), Silko blends personal family history and photography with stories and poems drawing on Laguna oral tradition and contemporary life. Through the publication of *Ceremony*, Silko began a correspondence with the poet **James Wright**, and their letters were published in 1985 as *The Delicacy and Strength of Lace*. The novel *Almanac of the Dead* (1992), published with poetic irony in the year of the Columbus quincentennial, is a dark, millennium-end account of the Native American peoples retaking of their ancestral lands in the face of an Anglo–American society in moral, psychological and ecological collapse.

▷P Seyersted, *Leslie Marmon Silko* (1980)

SILLANPÄÄ, Frans Eemil
(1888–1964)
Finnish novelist, winner of the Nobel Prize for literature, born in Hämeenkyrö. Of humble peasant stock, he became the foremost Finnish writer of his time and his work always reflected his origins. His major works were *Hurskas kurjuus* (1919, 'Meek Heritage'), a novel about the Finnish civil war, and *Nuorena nukkunut* (1931, Eng trans *The Maid Silja*, 1931), about the collapse of traditional values in Finland, and *Ihmiset suviyössä* (1934, 'People in the Summer Night'). He was awarded the 1939 Nobel Prize for literature. In old age he became a much loved radio broadcaster.

▷A Laurila, *F. E. Sillanpään Romaantaide* (1979)

SILLITOE, Alan
(1928–)
English novelist, born in Nottingham. He left school to work in a factory at 14, and served as a wireless operator in the RAF (1946–9). He lived in France and Spain (1952–8), and began writing while convalescing from tuberculosis. He scored a major success with his first novel, *Saturday Night and Sunday Morning* (1958), with its energetic young antihero, Arthur Seaton. The stories in *The Loneliness of the Long Distance Runner* (1959) were equally acclaimed. The outsider struggling in a brutal society is a recurring theme in his subsequent, more overtly political novels and stories, and the best of them echo the Midlands setting and gritty realism of his earlier books. They include *Key to the Door* (1962),

The Widower's Son (1977) and *Lost Loves* (1991). He has written several volumes of poems, plays and children's books. He married **Ruth Fainlight** in 1959.

SILONE, Ignazio, originally Secondo Tranquilli
(1900–78)
Born in the Abruzzi, the son of a tenant-farmer, he was inspired to political and literary activity by the corruption of local officialdom exacerbated by the ascendant fascist regime of the 1920s. His early novels, *Fontamara* (1933), *Pane e Vino* (1937) and *Il seme sotto la neve* (1941), mirror his strength of feeling for the peasant farmer, his growing disenchantment with party politics, and his personal integrity. All three were originally published in Switzerland where the author was in exile until 1944. On returning to Italy, his international reputation as a writer and left-wing intellectual was assured by novels which turned their attention from fascist corruption to communist betrayals, by his journalism, and by his autobiographical work, *Uscita di sicurezza* (1965).

SILVA, Antonio José da
(1705–39)
Portuguese playwright and Offenbachian librettist, born in Rio de Janeiro. He studied law at Coimbra, and was burnt with wife and mother by the Inquisition at Lisbon as a relapsed Jew.

▷T Braga, *O Poete Judeu e a Inquisição* (1901)

SILVA, José Asunción
(1865–95)
Colombian poet and novelist, born in Bogotá, son of the regional writer Ricardo Silva. Silva went to France and came under the influence of **Verlaine** and the French cult for **Poe**. He returned to Colombia, was desperately unhappy, and, persecuted by creditors, shot himself. At his least original he was simply an imitative decadent, but in his few outstanding poems, such as the famous 'Nocturno', written in memory of his beloved sister, who died in 1891, he achieved technical originality and a high degree of modernity. He is still much read, and his fictional autobiography, *De sobremesa* (1887–96, 'Sitting at Table After Eating'), re-written after he had lost the first manuscript at sea, is a key book.

▷A Miramón, *José Asunción Silva* (1957, in Spanish)

SILVERBERG, Robert
(1935–)
American science-fiction writer, born in New York City. He began writing science fiction

while studying at Columbia University, and went through a high-pressure apprenticeship supplying magazine fodder at an incredible rate and under a welter of pseudonyms. He moved away from the stock conventions of the genre with the more stylistically and thematically experimental novel *Thorns* (1967), the beginning of a period of astonishingly intense and sustained creativity which included *Tower of Glass* (1970) and *The Stochastic Man* (1975). After a four-year break, he returned with the whimsical fantasy *Lord Valentine's Castle* (1980). His subsequent work, while polished and inventive, has been less high-powered, and has included historical novels as well as science fiction.

SIMAK, Clifford Donald
(1904–88)

American science-fiction writer, born in Milville, Wisconsin, of an immigrant Czech father and an American mother. During the Depression he entered journalism in Michigan and then joined the Minneapolis *Star*, to which he contributed a weekly science column for the rest of his life. He started publishing science-fiction stories in 1931; his major work was the story sequence *The City* (1952), a chronicle in which dogs and robots take over a world abandoned by men. *Way Station* (1962) and *All Flesh is Grass* (1965) are more subtle.

SIMENON, Georges Joseph Christian
(1903–89)

Belgian-born French novelist, born in Liège. At 16 he began work as a journalist on the *Gazette de Liège*. He moved to Paris in 1922 and became a prolific writer of popular fiction, writing under a plethora of pseudonyms. He also wrote serious psychological novels, much-admired but neglected in favour of almost a hundred short, economical novels featuring Jules Maigret, the pipe-smoking, persistent detective. His prototype is popularly supposed to have been the French detective Marcel Guillaume, though Simenon said he could not remember where the inspiration for him came from. A 'Commissaire Maigret' appeared in three of the *romans populaires* that Simenon produced but he bears little resemblance to the character now known the world over, partly through films and television adaptations. The first two in the series were published in 1931: *M. Gallet décède* (Eng trans *The Death of Monsieur Gallet*, 1932) and *Le Pendu de Saint-Pholien* (Eng trans *The Crime of Inspector Maigret*, 1933). Like **Arthur Conan Doyle** with Sherlock Holmes, Simenon often tried to shake off his sleuth but he reappeared at least once a year until the 1970s, when he finally put the cover on his typewriter. In *Les Mémoires de Maigret* (1960, Eng trans *Maigret's Memoirs*, 1963), in which Maigret is ostensibly the author, he describes his childhood and career, and with laboured humour displays slight resentment at the liberties taken by his creator. Simenon published more than 500 novels and innumerable short stories but told the *New Yorker*, 'I have no imagination; I take everything from life'. Autobiographical writings include *Quand j'étais vieux* (1970, Eng trans *When I Was Old*, 1971) and *Mémoires Intimes* (1981, Eng trans *Intimate Memoirs*, 1984).

▷B de Fallois, *Georges Simenon* (1961, in French)

SIMIC, Charles
(1938–)

Yugoslavian-born American poet, born in Belgrade. He emigrated to the USA in 1954, and became a naturalized American citizen in 1971. He was educated at the University of Chicago and New York University, and worked as a proofreader before taking up an academic career. He has published around 20 books of terse but richly imagistic poems, and was awarded the Pulitzer Prize for Poetry in 1990 for his collection of 'prose poems' *The World Doesn't End* (1989). His other books include *Dismantling the Silence* (1971), the book-length poem *White* (1972, rev edn 1980), and the collections *Weather Forecast for Utopia and Vicinity: Poems 1967–1982* (1983) and *Selected Poems 1963–1983* (1983).

SIMMONS, James
(1933–)

Irish poet, born in Derry. He was the founding editor of the literary magazine *The Honest Ulsterman* (1968), lectured at the New University of Coleraine, and in the 1980s became co-administrator of The Poets' House, a cultural conference centre in Islandmagee. A prolific writer, his poems, ballads and lyrics 'give tongue' to a Protestant/Loyalist tradition that is significant in his thinking. The romanticism of his early work, *Energy to Burn* (1971), gave way to autobiographical detail in *West Strand Visions* (1974), but both styles and themes later came together, in the bitter-sweet *Judy Garland and the Cold War* (1976). He is an important voice in Irish letters.

SIMMS, William Gilmore
(1806–70)

American novelist, born in Charleston. He edited the *City Gazette* in Charleston and published *Lyrical and other Poems* (1827), *The Vision of Cortes* (1829), *The Tricolour* (1830), *Atalantis* (1832). Perhaps his best book, *The Yemassee* (1835), is a sympathetic account of Native Americans, a subject he returned to in the short stories that make up *The Wigwam and the Cabin* (1845–6) and *The Cassique of Kiawah* (1859); *The Partisan* (1835) and its semi-sequel *Katharine Walton* (1851) are both powerful. Despite his liberal sympathies, he was an apologist for slavery and the South.

▷E W Parks, *William Gilmore Simms as Literary Critic* (1962)

SIMON, Claude Eugène Henri
(1913–)

French novelist, winner of the Nobel Prize for literature, born in Tananarive, Madagascar. He was educated at Collège Stanislas, Paris, and briefly at Oxford and Cambridge universities, and studied painting before serving in the French cavalry. In World War II he joined the Resistance in Perpignan. Some align him with practitioners of the *nouveau roman* but he owes more to **Proust**, **Joseph Conrad**, **James Joyce** and **Faulkner** than his contemporary, **Camus**. The absence of story, time and punctuation is his hallmark, his style rich, sensuous and complex. *Le Vent* (1957, Eng trans *The Wind*, 1959) and *La Route des Flandres* (1960, Eng trans *The Flanders Road*, 1962) are his most important novels, both eloquently expressing his innate pessimism. In 1985 he was awarded the Nobel Prize for literature.

▷R Jean, *La littérature et le réel* (1965)

SIMON, (Marvin) Neil
(1927–)

American dramatist, born in New York and educated at New York University, the only living American playwright to have had a Broadway theatre named after him. He began by writing gags for radio and television personalities, and had a New York hit with his first comedy, *Come Blow Your Horn* (1961). His plays include the musical farce *Little Me* (1962); *Barefoot in the Park* (1963); *The Odd Couple* (1965); the musical, *Sweet Charity*, and *The Star-Spangled Girl* (1966); *Plaza Suite*; and the musical *Promises, Promises* (1968). *The Gingerbread Lady*, a play about alcoholism, was not as enthusiastically received, but he persevered with serious themes, as in *The Prisoner of Second Avenue* (1972) and *The Sunshine Boys* (1972). Moving from New York to California he made another hit with *California Suite* (1976). *Chapter Two* opened in 1977, and in 1979, his fourth musical, *They're Playing Our Song*, gave him yet another hit. Later he produced a semi-autobiographical trilogy: *Brighton Beach Memoirs* (1983), *Biloxi Blues* (1984) and *Broadway Bound* (1986).

▷R Johnson, *Neil Simon* (1983)

SIMONIDES OF CEOS
(556–468 BC)

Greek lyric poet, born on the island of Ceos. He travelled extensively, and lived many years in Athens. When Persia invaded Greece he devoted his powers to celebrating the heroes and the battles of that struggle in elegies, epigrams, odes and dirges. He won poetical contests 56 times, and beat **Aeschylus** in a contest with an elegy on the heroes who fell at Marathon in 490 BC. A handful of epigrams in the Greek Anthology are all that survive of his work.

▷B Gentili, *Simonide* (1959)

SIMONIDES, Simon
(1558–1629)

Polish poet, born in Lvov. He was famous for his Latin verse, but is now remembered for his *Sielanki* ('Idylls', 1614, Eng translations of some in *Specimens of Polish Poetry*, 1914), modelled on **Theocritus**, and written in Polish. He is often, but wrongly, called Szymonowicz.

SIMONOV, Konstantin Mikhailovich
(1915–79)

Russian writer, born in Petrograd (St Petersburg). He worked as a metal-cutter as a teenager, studied as an evening student, and became a journalist. He was a war correspondent in Mongolia (1934–8), and much of his best writing came out of his experiences in World War II, including his novel about the defence of Stalingrad, *Dni i nochi* (1945, Eng trans *Days and Nights*, 1945). He achieved a considerable reputation by his historical poem about Alexander Nevski, his poems of World War II, and the play *Russkye liudi* (1943, Eng trans *The Russians*, 1944). He was awarded the Stalin Prize three times.

▷L Lazarev, *Dramaturgiye Konstantin Simonov* (1952)

SIMPSON, Helen de Guerry
(1897–1940)

Australian-born British writer, born in Sydney. Her early books included verse, a play, and a collection of fairy stories. The first to attract notice was *Boomerang* (1932), which despite its title had little Australian content, and *Under Capricorn* (1937), a story of Sydney in the early 1800s, filmed by Hitchcock in 1949 with Ingrid Bergman and Michael Wilding. Nine further novels followed, including another historical novel *Saraband for Dead Lovers* (1935) which was also filmed, and three in collaboration with **Clemence Dane**. *The Woman on the Beast* (1933) comprises three novellas including the futuristic tale of an end-of-20th-century Australia. Other writings include historical biographies, *The Spanish Marriage* (1933) and *Henry VIII* (1934), and a study of the English traveller Mary Kingsley, *A Woman among Wild Men* (1938). She was killed in a London air raid.

SIMPSON, Louis Aston Marantz
(1923–)

American poet, novelist and critic, born in Jamaica, but who emigrated to the USA in 1940. His first collection, *The Arrivistes: Poems 1940–49*, was published in Paris in 1949. Later volumes include *Good News of Death and Other Poems* (1955); *Searching for the Ox* (1976), *At the End of the Open Road* (1963, Pulitzer Prize) and *The Best Hour of the Night* (1983). Much of his poetry has undertones of myth and legend and is noted for its elegant construction. Simpson has also published critical studies of **James Hogg**, **Ezra Pound** and **T S Eliot**, and two important critical works, *An Introduction to Poetry* (1967) and *A Revolution in Taste: Studies of Dylan Thomas, Allen Ginsberg, Sylvia Plath and Robert Lowell* (1978). A novel, *Riverside Drive*, appeared in 1965.

SIMPSON, N(orman) F(rederick)
(1919–)

English playwright, born and educated in London, whose unquantifiable style of surreal comedy and verbal improvization is in the haphazard tradition of **Carroll**, **Lear** and Monty Python. His first play, *A Resounding Tinkle* (1957), was staged at the Royal Court after winning a prize in a competition organized by *The Observer*, and inspired Kenneth Tynan to call him 'the most gifted comic writer the English stage has discovered since the war'. *One Way Pendulum* (1959), which he described as 'an evening of high drung and slarrit', and *The Cresta Run* (1965) established him as an important atonal voice in British theatre. He has written extensively for the stage and television, and has produced one novel, *Harry Bleachbaker* (1976).

SINCLAIR, May
(?1865–1946)

English novelist, born in Rock Ferry, Cheshire. She was educated at Cheltenham College, was an advocate of women's suffrage, and took an interest in psychoanalysis, which is revealed in some of her 24 novels. They include *The Divine Fire* (1904), *The Creators* (1910), *The Three Sisters* (1914) and *The Dark Night* (1924). Her novels *Mary Olivier* (1919) and *The Life and Death of Harriett Frean* (1922) reveal her adoption of the 'stream-of-consciousness' method; *Mary Olivier* contains clear autobiographical echoes. She also wrote books on philosophical idealism.
▷H D Zegge, *May Sinclair* (1976)

SINCLAIR, Upton Beall
(1878–1968)

American novelist and social reformer, born in Baltimore, Maryland. He horrified the world with his exposure of meat-packing conditions in Chicago in his novel *The Jungle* (1906), which resulted in the passing of a Pure Food and Drug Bill by Congress ('I aimed at the public's heart, and by accident I hit it in the stomach'). Later novels such as *Metropolis* (1908), *King Coal* (1917), *Oil!* (1927) and *Boston* (1928) were increasingly moulded by his socialist beliefs. He was for many years prominent in Californian politics and attempted to found a communistic colony in Englewood, New Jersey (1907). He also wrote a monumental 11-volume series about Lanny Budd, starting with *World's End* (1940) and including *Dragon's Teeth* (1942), which won the Pulitzer Prize. He wrote autobiographical works (1932, 1962) and *A World to Win* (1946).
▷L Harris, *Upton Sinclair: American Rebel* (1975)

SINGER, Esther (Mrs Kreitman)
(1892–)

Polish Yiddish novelist, born in Radzymin, sister of **Isaac Bashevis** and **Israel Joshua Singer**. Her *Der sheydim tants* was published in Warsaw in 1936 and translated 10 years later as *Deborah*.

SINGER, Isaac Bashevis
(1904–91)

Polish-born American Yiddish writer, winner of the Nobel Prize for literature, born in Radzymin, the son of a rabbi, brother of **Esther** and **Israel Joshua Singer**. He was educated at the Tachkemoni Rabbinical Seminary in Warsaw (1920–2), and worked for 10 years as a proof-reader and translator. He emigrated to the USA in 1935, where he joined his brother, as a journalist for the *Jewish Daily Forward*. A firm believer in story-telling rather than commentary by the author, he set his novels and short stories among the Jews of Poland, Germany and America, combining a deep psychological insight with dramatic and visual impact. Considered by many to be the last and greatest Yiddish writer, he was awarded the Nobel Prize for literature in 1978. His novels include *The Family Moskat* (1950), *Satan in Goray* (1955), *The Magician of Lublin* (1960), *The Manor* (1967), *The Estate* (1970) and *Enemies: A Love Story* (1972). Among his short stories are *Gimpel* *the Fool and Other Stories* (1957), *The Spinoza of Market Street* (1961), *The Séance* (1968), *A Friend of Kafka* (1970) and *A Crown of Feathers* (1973). He also wrote one play, *Schlemiel the First* (1974), and many stories for children. He wrote his autobiography, *In My Father's Court*, in 1966.

▷C Sinclair, *The Brothers Singer* (1987)

SINGER, Israel Joshua
(1893–1944)

Polish-born American Yiddish writer, born in Bilgorai, the son of a rabbi, brother of **Esther** and **Isaac Bashevis Singer**. He studied at the Rabbinical Yeshivah School in Warsaw, and after World War I became a journalist in Kiev. He became foreign correspondent in Warsaw for the New York *Jewish Daily Forward*, for which he continued to write after emigrating to the USA in 1933. His novels have been widely translated, and include *The Sinner* (*Yoshe Kalt*, 1933), *The Brothers Ashkenazi* (1936), *The River Breaks Up* (1938) and *East of Eden* (1939).

▷C Sinclair, *The Brothers Singer* (1987)

SINGH, Bhai Vir
(1872–1957)

Indian (Punjabi), poet who made the creation of a modern Punjabi literature his life's task. Best remembered today are his lyrical poems, which have been translated into English, if in a rather old-fashioned style, in *Nargas: Songs of a Sikh* (1924). He wrote a verse epic, and also a massive fictional trilogy about the history of Sikhs, which is essential reading for those who want to understand its subject, but is not, unfortunately, a readable work.

SINGH, Kushwant
(1915–90)

Pakistani novelist and major historian of the Sikhs, born in Hadali. His masterpiece is the searing *Train to Pakistan* (1956), certainly the most distinguished and graphic work on the subject of the partition of India; it tells of a Sikh–Muslim conflict in a border town.

SINGH, Nanak
(1897–)

Indian (Punjabi) novelist, author of the important *Ik miyan do talwar* (1961, Eng trans *Two Swords in a Single Scabbard*, 1961). It harks back to a past in which a section of the Sikhs calling themselves the Ghadar Party formed alliances with their traditional enemies in the interests of getting rid of the British. Those wishing to learn the history of India and of the 'Sikh problem' have always been obliged to read this imaginative account.

SINYAVSKY, Andrey
(1925–)

Russian novelist, critic and story writer from Moscow, who became a cause célèbre when, in 1966, with a lesser writer, Yuri Daniel, he was tried and sentenced (to seven years in prison), for publishing books abroad (he had used the name Abram Tertz) that were alleged to be 'slanderous to the Soviet Union'. After his release Sinyavsky went to Paris and became a teacher at the Sorbonne. His notoriety apart, Sinyavsky is and was an important Russian writer, a man who, through his writings, had graduated from a sincere Marxism to a position that has very aptly been defined as being closely akin to that of **Martin Buber**. His most substantial work, the novel *Lyubimov* (1965, Eng trans *The Makepiece Experiment*, 1965), is a profound piece of symbolism which transforms the particular Stalinist terror into one involving the world. His *Chto sotsialicheskiy realizm* (1960, Eng trans *On Socialist Realism*, 1967) says everything about that literary experiment which needs to be said. His art is seen at its most subtle and compelling in *Fantasticheskiye povesti* (1961, Eng trans *Fantastic Stories*, 1963), and in the aphorisms of *Golos iz khora* (1973, Eng trans *A Voice from the Chorus*, 1976). Sinyavsky is the direct descendant of the writers who, in the 1920s, called themselves the Serapion Brothers, and through them has roots in **Gogol** and **Dostoyevsky**.

▷R Lourie, *Letters to the Future* (1975)

SISSMAN, L E
(1928–76)

American poet, born in Detroit, Michigan. By profession he was an advertising executive. He had written poetry as a young man, but gave it up when he failed to find a publisher; then, at 35, started again. In 1964 he began to have his odd, highly original poems published in the *New Yorker*. His first collection was *Dying: An Introduction* (1968). He soon established himself as a much discussed poet who 'compartmentalized his careers': an 'autobiographical poet who treated illness and death with perspective, detachment'. The themes of illness and death became predominant in Sissman's poetry because in 1965 he was diagnosed as having Hodgkin's Disease, which killed him within 11 years. *Hello, Darkness: The Collected Poems* (1978) included much work that he had not published, and sealed his reputation as a courageous man who had left a body of poetry that made sense of his predicament.

▷D Hoffman (ed), *Harvard Guide to Contemporary American Writing* (1979)

SISSON, C(harles) H(ubert)
(1914–)

English poet, born in Bristol. He was educated at Bristol University and in Berlin, Freiburg and Paris. He served in the British Army Intelligence Corps in India (1942–5), and had risen to a high rank in the civil service on his retirement in 1973. He wrote a critical account of it in *The Spirit of British Administration* (1959). His tightly controlled and original poetry has grown more complex and ambiguous with passing volumes, and is somewhat pessimistic in tone, although never despairing. Important collections include *In the Trojan Ditch: Collected Poems and Translations* (1974) and *Collected Poems 1943–1983* (1984), and the later volumes *God Bless Karl Marx!* (1987), *16 Sonnets* (1990) and *Antidotes* (1991). He has also written two novels, several volumes of essays, and translations.
▷ *On the Look Out: A Partial Autobiography* (1989)

SITWELL, Dame Edith Louisa
(1887–1964)

English poet, born in Scarborough, Yorkshire, daughter of an eccentric, Sir George Sitwell, and sister of **Osbert** and **Sacheverell Sitwell**. She had an unhappy, lonely and frustrated childhood in the family home in Renishaw Hall, Derbyshire, until her governess introduced her to music and literature, in particular the poetry of **Swinburne** and the Symbolists. She first attracted notice by her editorship of an anthology of new poetry entitled *Wheels* (1916–21). This was a new type of poetry which repudiated the flaccid quietism of Georgian verse, but her shock tactics were not fully displayed till *Façade* appeared in 1923, with William Walton's music, and was given a stormy public reading in London. It was followed by *Bucolic Comedies* (1923), which is for the most part in the same fantastic vein, but the elegiac romantic style begins to appear and this vein is fully exploited in *The Sleeping Beauty* (1924), and finally worked out in the amazing *Elegy for Dead Fashion* (1926). The short poems of this romantic period, 'Colonel Fantock', 'Daphne', 'The Strawberry' and above all 'The Little Ghost who died for Love' are probably the most beautiful things she ever wrote. At the close of this period she suddenly flamed into indignation over the evil in society—in *Gold Coast Customs* (1929), expressing the horror underlying civilization. In the 1930s she turned to prose work. During World War II she denounced with great vehemence the cruelty of man in the prophetic utterance of *Street Songs* (1942), *Green Song* (1944) and *The Song of the Cold* (1945). She set out to refresh the exhausted rhythms of traditional poetry by introducing the rhythms of jazz and other dance music, and also by free association in expression and the transference of the bodily senses with the result that sense was sacrificed to the evocation of states of feeling. She abandoned this style in her later verse but there is a certain lack of control in her poems on the age of the atom bomb—*The Shadow of Cain* (1947) and *The Canticle of the Rose* (1949). Other works include *The English Eccentrics* (1933), *Victoria of England* (1936), *Fanfare of Elizabeth* (1946), *The Outcasts* (verse; 1962) and *The Queens and the Hive* (1962). Her autobiography, *Taken Care Of*, was published posthumously in 1965.
▷ V Glendinning, *A Lion among the Unicorns* (1981)

SITWELL, Sir (Francis) Osbert
(1892–1969)

English author, born in London, brother of **Edith** and **Sacheverell Sitwell**. He was educated at Eton, and his youth was spent mainly at the family home at Renishaw Hall, Derbyshire with occasional visits to Scarborough, which figures a good deal in his own satiric work, as a symbol of Victorian decrepitude. He served in the Brigade of Guards in World War I, and in 1916 was invalided home. This provided him with the leisure to set up as a satirist of war and the types which ingloriously prosper at home. Many of his satirical poems were published in the *Nation* and collected in *Argonaut and Juggernaut* (1919) and *Out of the Flame* (1923). After the war he narrowed his literary acquaintance to his sister and brother, **Ezra Pound**, **T S Eliot** and **Wyndham Lewis**. The object of the group was the regeneration of arts and letters, and in this pursuit the Sitwells acquired notoriety, Sir Osbert not least by his novel *Before the Bombardment* (1927), which anatomized the grandees of Scarborough and by implication the social orders in general. Neither this nor his other novel, *Miracle on Sinai* (1933), was successful, and his forte was always the short story, especially those, like the collection *Dumb Animal* (1930), where his delicacy of observation and natural compassion are more in evidence than his satire. The paternalism of the aristocracy is expressed in *England Reclaimed, a Book of Eclogues* (1927). His collected works show the contrast between his mordant satire and human kindliness—the satiric sharpness of *Triple Fugue* (1924) with the humanity of the stories in *Dumb Animal* parallels the resentment of the early verse with the acceptance of rural manners in the *Eclogues*. His aristocratic disposition took the form of travel in the grand manner in the 1930s. He had published *Discursions on Travel, Art and Life* in 1925, but then *Winters of Content* (1932) displayed

mature descriptive powers. *Brighton* (1935, in collaboration with Margaret Barton) anticipated the vogue of 18th- and early 19th-century architecture. At the close of the 1930s *Escape with Me*, describing a journey to China, proved his most charming book of travel. All these elements contributed to the great autobiography he was planning. The first volume of *Left Hand: Right Hand* appeared in 1944, to be followed by *The Scarlet Tree* (1946), *Great Morning* (1947) and *Laughter in the Next Room* (1948). *Noble Essences* (1950) completed this work. Other collections of essays and stories include *Penny Foolish* (1935), *Sing High, Sing Low* (1944), *Alive-Alive Oh* (1947) and *Pound Wise* (1963).
▷ J Lehman, *A Nest of Tigers* (1968)

SITWELL, Sacheverell
(1897–1988)

English poet, essayist and biographer, the less flamboyant brother of **Osbert** and **Edith Sitwell**. His poetry was capable and interesting, but has never captured the imagination of readers, and is now hardly read, even though Michael Roberts included it in the most influential of all modern anthologies, *The Faber Book of Modern Verse* (1936). He is now best remembered for his mannered but lively travel books and eccentric cultural commentaries, such as *Monks, Nuns and Monasteries* (1965) and *Spanish Baroque Art* (1924). His reminiscences attracted some attention, but he was the least gifted of his remarkable family.
▷ J Lehmann, *A Nest of Tigers* (1968)

SJÖBERG, Birger
(1885–1929)

Swedish poet and novelist. Born in Vänersborg, he embarked on a career as a journalist. His first collection of poetry, *Fridas bok* (1922, 'Frida's Book'), centres on a young shop-assistant's relationship with his beloved in an idyllic Swedish town, the stylistic versatility opening up for parody and irony. Set to music by the poet, who was an accomplished performer, a number of these poems have become popular songs. The novel *Kvartetten som sprängdes* (1924, 'The Quartet That Was Broken Up') shows a **Dickens**ian breadth in its depiction of contemporary society, the many-faceted style imbued with a rich sense of humour. The modernist poems in *Kriser och kransar* (1926, 'Crises and Wreaths') rely on a wealth of imagery and boldly disjointed rhythms to convey a fragmented, anguished perspective on humankind.
▷ E H Olafson, *Fridas visor och folkets visor. Om parodi hos Birger Sjöberg* (1985)

SKALBE, Karlis
(1876–1945)

Latvian poet and teller of folk tales, born in Vecpiebalga canton. He is renowned for his pure language, which comes across in W K Matthews's translations of his poetry: *Tricolour Sun* (1936) and *Pussy's Water Mill* (1952). He died in exile in Stockholm.

SKALLAGRÍMSSON, Egil(l)
(c.910–990)

Icelandic poet and warrior, born on the farm of Borg in Iceland. His father had emigrated to Iceland after falling foul of King Harald Fine-Hair of Norway, and Egil became a professional Viking and court-poet. He fought in the service of King Athelstan of England at the battle of Brunanburh (937), fell out with King Erik Blood-Axe Haraldsson of Norway, but visited him when he was king in the city of York in 948; there he only escaped execution by composing a eulogy in Erik's honour, the *Höfuðlausn* ('Head Ransom'). In 960 he lost two young sons, and composed the greatest lament in Old Icelandic poetry, *Sonatorrek* ('On the Loss of Sons'). His other major verse-sequence was *Arinbjarnarkviða* ('The Lay of Arinbjörn'), a eulogy to his friend and protector, Arinbjörn. Egil is the eponymous hero of the Icelandic *Egils saga*, probably written by his descendant, **Snorri Sturluson**, which also contains more than 40 occasional verses ascribed to him.
▷ H Palsson and P Edwards, introduction to *Egil's Saga* (1976)

SKARMETA, Antonio
(1940–)

The most outstanding Chilean writer of the later 20th century, Skarmeta is a leading figure in the Post-Boom in Latin America. His novels *Soñe que la nieve ardia* (1975, Eng trans *I Dreamt the Snow was Burning*, 1985) and *La insurrección* (1982, Eng trans *The Insurrection*, 1983) deal with personal involvement in political struggles, while *Ardiente paciencia* (1985, Eng trans *Burning Patience*, 1987) is a humorous commentary on language, fame and love. Skarmeta also writes short stories, screenplays and literary criticism, and has been a visiting professor at various North American universities.

SKELTON, John
(c.1460–1529)

English satirical poet, born in Norfolk. He studied at both Oxford and Cambridge, and was created 'poet laureate' by both. Later he was tutor to Prince Henry (the future Henry VIII), took holy orders in 1498, and became rector of Diss in 1502, but seems to have been suspended in 1511 for having a concubine or wife. He had produced some translations and elegies in 1489, but began to write satirical vernacular poetry, overflowing with grotesque words and images and unrestrained joviality, as in *The Bowge of Courte, Colyn Cloute* and *Why come ye nat to Courte*. Of these, the first is an allegorical poem; the second an unsparing attack on the corruptions of the church; and the last a sustained invective against Wolsey, for which Skelton had to take sanctuary at Westminster, although *The Garlande of Laurell* (1523) is dedicated to him. Other important works include *The Boke of Phyllyp Sparowe*, a eulogy, and the boisterous *The Tunnyng of Elynour Rummynge*.

▷C J Lloyd, *John Skelton* (1938)

SKELTON, Robin
(1925–)

English-born poet and academic, born in Yorkshire but mainly resident in Canada. The founder member of the Peterloo group of poets and painters, he has held several university posts, notably at the University of Victoria, where he was for a long time editor of the influential 'Malahat Review'. He also edited the important anthologies *Poetry of the Thirties* (1964) and *Poetry of the Forties* (1968). In the seventies he published a trilogy of books about the poetic craft: *The Practice of Poetry* (1971), *The Poet's Calling* (1975) and *Poetic Truth* (1978). His own poems are influenced by **David Gascoyne**, whose work he has edited.

SKENDO, Lumo, pseud of Mid'hat Frasheri
(1880–1949)

Albanian story writer and critic, scion of a famous literary family. He resisted fascist rule during World War II, but was driven out of Albania by Hoxha. Nothing has been translated, but his history of Albanian literature (1909) and his tales are still occasionally read.

SKRAM, (Bertha) Amalie, née Alver
(1847–1905)

Norwegian feminist novelist, born in Bergen, whose commercial life was the main setting for her work. After divorcing her first husband in 1878, she worked as a critic and short-story writer. In 1884 she married Erik Skram, a Danish writer, and following this wrote a collection of novels in which she explored women's issues, and sex in particular. Her best-known works include *Constance Ring* (1885, Eng trans 1988), the tetralogy *Hellemyrsfolket* (1887–98, 'The People at Hellemyr'), and *Foraadt* (1892, Eng trans *Betrayed*, 1987). She was divorced from Skram in 1900, and thereafter never recovered her mental health, ironically reflecting

the plight she had fictionalized in *Professor Hieronimus* (1895, Eng trans 1899) and *På St Jørgen* (1895, 'At St Jørgen's').

▷I Engelstad, *Amalie Skram* (1978)

SKVORECKÝ, Josef
(1924–)

Czechoslovakian-born Canadian poet, born in Náchod, who since 1975 has lived in exile in the West, latterly in Toronto. Educated at Prague University, he fell foul of the communist authorities in 1958 with his first novel *Zbabělci* (Eng trans *The Cowards*, 1970). Later attacks on totalitarianism, such as *Smutek poručika Boruvky* (1966, Eng trans *The Mournful Demeanour of Lt Borucha*, 1973) and *Lvíče* (1969, Eng trans *Miss Silver's Past*, 1974) were less overt, but no less powerful. His best-known book, however, is *Bassaxofon* (1967, Eng trans *The Bass Saxophone*, 1977), which recalls the liberating power of jazz in the communist bloc. It is widely acknowledged that Skvorecký's fiction has been less powerful since his move to the West. *Příběh inženýra lidských duší* (1977, Eng trans *The Engineer of Human Souls*, 1984), a phrase associated with Stalin, seems for the first time discursive and polemical. Now a professor of English and film studies in Toronto, Skvorecký continues to write persuasively about movie making and jazz.

SLATER, Francis Carey
(1876–1959)

South African poet, born near Grahamstown. He was a bank manager until, in 1930, he resigned to devote himself to his writing. His greatest achievement, in a verse that seldom really catches fire, even though it is sometimes on the verge of it—in part owing to its author's very conscientiousness—is to give some expression to the feelings of the Xhosa peoples in 'Dark Folk' (1935), a sequence contained in his *Collected Poems* (1957).

SLAUERHOFF, Jan Jacob
(1898–1936)

Major Dutch poet, novelist and translator, regarded as Holland's great 'poète maudit', born in Leeuwarden. He was by profession a ship's doctor. His first collection, *Archipel* (1923, 'Archipelago'), immediately revealed his grand mastery of technique. With *Schuim en asch* (1930, 'Scum and Ashes') he reaches the high point of his inspiration. *Het verboden rijk* (1932, 'The Forbidden Empire') is a novel combining the life of **Camoens** with his own life. Slauerhoff has not yet gained the reputation he deserves outside Holland as a major poet by international standards.

SLAUGHTER, Frank G(ill), pseud **C V Terry**
(1908–)

American physician and novelist, his fiction almost always has a medical background; perhaps because his family name had unfortunate connotations in surgical circles, he also used a pseudonym. Slaughter qualified MD in 1930, wrote a number of technical books on surgery and psychosomatic medicine and then began to write novels. These include *Spencer Brade MD* (1942), *Air Surgeon* (1943), *In a Dark Garden* (1946), *The Stubborn Heart* (1950), *The Healer* (1955) and *Sword and Scalpel* (1957). They are detailed and authentic but never rely simply on technical infilling to support their plots, which are usually sound and satisfyingly rounded out.

SLAVEYKOV, Petko
(1827–95)

Bulgarian poet, diarist and nationalist, who dedicated his life to creating a Bulgarian tradition free of Turkish, Greek and Catholic influences. He became known as 'Grandpa Slavekov', and was a co-founder of the Democratic Party.
▷C Manning and R Smal-Stocki, *The History of Modern Bulgarian Literature* (1960)

SLAVEYKOV, Pencho
(1866–1912)

Bulgarian poet, son of **Petko Slaveykov**—and more distinguished as a literary genius, if not as a patriot. He differed from his father, too, in looking to the wider context of Europe. He was the most notable Bulgarian follower of **Nietzsche**. As a result of an accident in youth he was a lifelong cripple, and saw himself as Bulgaria's crippled 'overman'. His shorter and more lyrical poems are his best, since his longer philosophical ones are ponderous, and now read poorly. There are English translations of his work in V Pinto, *Bulgarian Prose and Verse* (1957).
▷C Manning and R Smal-Stocki, *The History of Modern Bulgarian Literature* (1960)

SLESINGER, Tess
(1900–45)

American novelist, she died before realizing her full potential, which was considerable. She grew up in New York City and became associated with the *Menorah Journal* crowd, about whom she wrote in her one completed novel, *The Unpossessed* (1934). It examines the tension between public and private values and the pressures imposed by marriage. This was also the subtext of a posthumous collection, *On Hearing That Her Second Husband Has Taken His First Lover* (1948). Slesinger went to work in Hollywood and, like **F Scott**

Fitzgerald, left a novel about the movie industry unfinished at the time of her death.

SLESSOR, Kenneth Adolf
(1901–71)

Australian poet and journalist, born in Orange, New South Wales. He worked as reporter and columnist on various Sydney and Melbourne newspapers until he joined *Smith's Weekly* in 1927, later becoming editor-in-chief until 1939. He was appointed an official war correspondent and covered the Battle of Britain and then followed the Australian Imperial Forces through the Near East and North Africa, and on to New Guinea. Slessor had contributed many poems to various periodicals; in 1924 he published *Thief of the Moon*, and in 1926 *Earth-Visitors*. *Darlinghurst Nights and Morning Glories* (1933) celebrates 'The Cross', the bohemian district of Sydney. The title poem in his last collection *Five Bells* (1939) was written for a friend who fell overboard from a Sydney ferry. Although essentially a *bon-viveur* he loved the raffish atmosphere of his city, and his feeling for a romanticized past is shown in his *Five Visions of Captain Cook* (1931). His verse was collected in *One Hundred Poems: 1919–1939* (1944, reissued as *Poems*, 1957) and the best of his prose in *Bread and Wine* (1970). He edited *Australian Poetry* (1945) and co-edited *The Penguin Book of Australian Verse* (1958, rev edn 1961).
▷D Stewart, *A Man of Sydney—An Appreciation of Kenneth Slessor* (1977)

SLONIMSKI, Antoni
(1895–1970)

Polish poet, novelist and dramatist, a leader of the original *Skamander* movement, who escaped from Poland in the aftermath of the Nazi invasion and for many years lived in England. Like his *Skamander* colleagues, Slonimski was conservative but at the same time determinedly modernist—not to say ironic—in spirit, and his poetry has been much valued for its relatively simple statements of humane values. As a playwright he was often compared to **George Bernard Shaw**, as a novelist to **H G Wells**. The best selection from his poetry in translation is in **Czeslaw Milosz**'s *Post-War Polish Poetry* (1965).

SLOWACKI, Juliuz
(1809–49)

Polish poet and dramatist, born in Krzemuniec. He lived mostly abroad, and died in Paris. At first influenced by **Bryon**, he later became a mystic, and his last and best poems reflect this change. His letters, in *Auhelli* (1838, Eng trans 1930) and elsewhere, are remarkable. His collected works have been translated into French. His greatest, unfinished, poem, *Król Duch*, which has the doctrine of metempsychosis as one of its themes, has been claimed as a masterpiece.

▷M Kridl, *The Lyric Poems of Juliusz Slowacki* (1958)

SLUTSKY, Boris
(1919–)

Russian poet from Slavyansk who is mainly distinguished because, without actually offending the authorities, he decisively rejected the mechanical rhetoric of the official Soviet bards. His first collection did not appear until he was almost 40. His famous 'Bog' (Eng trans, 'God', 1974), really about Stalin as monster, was an important piece of *samizdat*.

▷R M Gulland, *Soviet Russian Poets* (1961)

SMART, Christopher
(1722–71)

English poet, born in Shipbourne near Tonbridge. He studied at Pembroke College, Cambridge, and was elected a fellow in 1745. Improvidence, wit and a secret marriage upset his academic career and he settled to a precarious living in London. He died insane. **Samuel Johnson** assisted him in his monthly *Universal Visitor*. Smart's works include sacred poems, epigrams, birthday odes and occasional poems; the *Hilliad* (1753), a satire on a quack doctor; and several translations from the Bible and the classics. His most celebrated work is *A Song to David* (1763). His remarkable *Jubilate Agro* was not published until 1939, but has helped to confirm his modern reputation as an original poetic voice.

SMART, Elizabeth
(1913–86)

Canadian novelist and poet, born in Ottawa. Her long relationship with the poet **George Barker**, by whom she had four children while he was married to another woman, is fictionalized in her condensed and poetic novel *By Grand Central Station I Sat Down and Wept* (1945). She had moved to England in 1943; apart from one two-year spell back in Canada, she remained there until her death, working in copywriting and journalism. The publication in 1977 of *A Bonus* (poetry) and *The Assumption of the Rogues and Rascals* (prose) revived interest in her; *Eleven Poems* followed five years later, in 1983. Her journals are available in two volumes: *Necessary Secrets* (1986) and *Early Writings* (1987).

▷R Sullivan, *By Heart* (1991)

SMILEY, Jane
(1949–)

American novelist, born in Los Angeles and brought up in Saint Louis. She graduated from the University of Iowa with a PhD in creative writing and went on to hold teaching positions both there and at Iowa State University, where she is Distinguished Professor. Her first novel, *At Paradise Gate* (1981), was followed by the short stories and novellas gathered in *The Age of Grief* (1988) and *Ordinary Love and Good Will* (1989). Her most ambitious work to date is the novel *A Thousand Acres* (1991), a remarkable re-working of the *King Lear* story, set in a contemporary farming community in Iowa, which was awarded the Pulitzer Prize in 1992.

SMITH, A J M
(1902–80)

Canadian poet, anthologist and critic, born in Montreal. He was associated with **F R Scott**, and edited the influential *Oxford Book of Canadian Verse* (1960). He was for many years a teacher at the University of Michigan. His own poetry—of which he published little—was graceful, well crafted, sometimes stately, and mainly influenced by that of **W B Yeats**. He was regarded as the leader of 'academic poetry', and as being somewhat passionless—but this was his intention. His best work is in *Poems: New and Collected* (1967).

▷G Woodcock, *Odysseus Ever Returning* (1970)

SMITH, Alexander
(1830–67)

Scottish poet and essayist, born in Kilmarnock, Ayrshire, the son of a lace-pattern designer. He himself became a pattern designer in Glasgow and Paisley, though he was not particularly gifted in this, and was more interested in his own poetry, sending occasional pieces to the *Glasgow Citizen*. His *Life Drama* (1851) was highly successful at first but was satirized by **Aytoun** in *Firmilian, a Spasmodic Tragedy* (1854), and the adjective 'spasmodic' has stuck to Smith's poetry ever since. In 1854 he was appointed Secretary to Edinburgh University, and the following year produced *Sonnets on the War* with **Sydney Dobell**, his brother poet of the 'Spasmodic' school. *City Poems* (1857) and *Edwin of Deira* (1861) were followed by essays, collected under the title *Dreamthorp* (1863), novels, and *A Summer in Skye* (1865), an enthusiastic and vivid evocation of the island.

▷T Brisbane, *The Early Years of Alexander Smith* (1969)

SMITH, Charlotte, née Turner
(1749–1806)

English poet and novelist, born in London into a land-owning family. Her mother died when she was three and she was educated at school in Kensington, but was married at 15 to the spendthrift son of a wealthy West Indian merchant. Her *Elegiac Sonnets* (1784) were written while he was in prison for debt. Financial difficulties and marital problems dogged her life; she separated from her husband in 1788 and relied on writing to support her large family, publishing, among other works, 10 novels in as many years (1788–98). All were cast in the popular sentimental mode, but in *Emmeline* (1788) she combined sentiment with Gothic elements and social comedy, while *Desmond* (1792) reflects the hopes of the French Revolution she then held. *The Emigrants. A Poem* (1793) voices her disillusionment. The melancholy that suffuses her poetry made it influential in establishing the sonnet as a vehicle for romantic feeling.

▷K Ravin, in *Eighteenth-Century British Poets*, pt 2, ed J Sitter, *Dictionary of Literary Biography* 109 (1991); C L Fry, *Charlotte Smith, Popular Novelist* (1980)

SMITH, Cordwainer, pseud of Paul Myron Anthony Linebarger
(1913–66)

American science-fiction writer, born in Milwaukee, Wisconsin. He spent much of his childhood in Europe, Japan and China. He served as a military adviser in Korea and Malaya, and was an expert in 'brainwashing' techniques and psychological warfare. Most of his science fiction (including his first story, 'War No 81-Q', written when he was only 15) falls within an overarching structure known as 'The Instrumentality of Mankind', an invented far-future universe which was never completed. The fragments are powerfully and romantically conceived, and reflect his ideological standpoint as a political right-winger and committed High Anglican. The main collections under this heading include *You Will Never Be The Same* (1963), *Under Old Earth* (1970) and his best book, *Norstrilia* (1975). He also wrote a Chinese fable, *The Ocean War* (1937), and three non science-fiction novels.

SMITH, Dodie, pseud (until 1935) C L Anthony
(1896–1990)

English playwright, novelist and theatre producer. She started as an actress but took up a business career. Her first play, *Autumn Crocus* (1930), was an instant success and enabled her to devote all her time to writing. Other plays include *Dear Octopus* (1938), *Letter from Paris* (adapted from *The Reverberator* by **Henry James**, 1952) and *I Capture the Castle* (adapted from her own novel, 1952).

Other works include the highly popular children's book *The Hundred and One Dalmations* (1956).

▷*Look Back with Love* (1974); *Look Back with Mixed Feelings* (1977); *Look Back with Astonishment* (1979); *Look Back with Gratitude* (1985)

SMITH, E(dward) E(lmer) 'Doc'
(1890–1965)

American science-fiction writer, born in Sheboygan, Wisconsin. He had a PhD in food chemistry, the source of his writing nickname. He was an immensely popular creator of science-fiction space adventure stories in the 'pulp' magazine era before World War II, and is widely regarded as the progenitor of 'space opera'. His work was reprinted in paperback and has been a consistent bestseller. Colourful, racy and exciting, it plays fast and loose with both probability and literary rectitude. His best-known works are the multi-volume sequences *Skylark* (begun 1928) and *Lensman* (begun 1948). The later *Family d'Alembert* series (begun 1964) appeared posthumously, and was completed by other writers.

SMITH, Horace or Horatio *see* SMITH, James

SMITH, Iain Crichton, Gaelic Blain Mac A'Ghobhainn
(1928–)

Scottish poet and novelist, born on the Isle of Lewis. He was educated at the Nicolson Institute, Stornoway, and Aberdeen University. His career as a writer ran in tandem with that of a teacher in Clydebank, Dumbarton and Oban (retired 1977). Bilingual in Gaelic and English, he is an ambidextrous writer, rooted in the native culture but sensible to the wider audience that English admits. His first collection of poems, *The Long River*, appeared in 1955. Five years later came *Burn is Aran*, stories and poems in Gaelic which were highly praised. Since then he has been prolific and, while his output is of varied quality, at his best he is one of the modern masters of Scottish literature. *Consider the Lilies* (1968) is undoubtedly his best-known work. Focusing on the plight of an old woman evicted from her croft and betrayed by the Church (Smith is no lover of the Free Church), it is a powerful indictment of the Clearances and the harsh reality of Highland life. *My Last Duchess* (1971) and *An End to Autumn* (1978) are similarly beautiful but bleak, although it would be wrong to imply that the sensibility behind them is humourless. Particularly since the publication of *Murdo and Other Stories* (1981) there is evidence of a writer hell-bent on mischief, the absurd side of his nature triumphing over a tendency towards introspection. In his poetry, however, Calvinism and the Isle of Lewis fuse to generate love and hate in almost equal measure, producing in the best poems a dramatic grandeur and awesome tension. *Selected Poems* was published in 1982, and *Collected Poems* in 1992. He has been the recipient of many prizes.

▷ A Bold, 'The Parish and the Island', in *Modern Scottish Literature* (1983)

SMITH, James
(1775–1839)
SMITH, Horatio Horace
(1779–1849)

English authors of *The Rejected Addresses*. They were educated at Chigwell, Essex. James succeeded his father as solicitor to the Board of Ordnance; Horace made a fortune as a stockbroker. Both wrote for magazines. When a prize was advertised for an address to be spoken at the opening of the new Drury Lane Theatre in 1812, the brothers produced a series of supposed 'Rejected Addresses', James furnishing imitations of **Wordsworth**, **Robert Southey** and **Coleridge**; Horace those of Sir **Walter Scott**, **Byron**, **Matthew** ('Monk') **Lewis** and **Moore**. James also wrote for the comic actor Charles Mathews and Horace wrote the *Tin Trumpet* (1836) and more than a score of novels. Of Horace's *Poems* (1846) the best known is the 'Ode to an Egyptian Mummy'.

SMITH, Lillian Eugenia
(1897–1966)

American novelist, editor and educator, born in Jasper, Florida. As a young woman she travelled and taught, and in 1925 became manager of a camp for girls at Laurel Falls, Georgia, a post she maintained until 1949, and where she introduced several of her own progressive teaching programmes in the arts. During the 1930s she founded a small magazine, publishing women and black writers, and in 1944 published her first novel, *Strange Fruit*, a tragic, interracial love story. Her anger against racial conflict and segregation is also evident in several of her subsequent books, including *Killers of the Dream* (1949, rev edn 1961) and *Now Is The Time* (1955). In 1964 she published *Our Faces, Our Words*, an impassioned examination of the American non-violent civil rights movement.

▷ F Clay and L Blackwell, *Lillian Smith* (1971)

SMITH, Logan Pearsall
(1865–1946)

American-born British writer, born in Millville, New Jersey, a member of a Philadelphia Quaker family. Educated at Harvard and Oxford, he settled in England and took British nationality in 1913. He produced critical editions of various authors, and *Milton and His Modern Critics* (1941), but is best remembered for his delightful essays, collected in *All Trivia* (1933) and *Reperusals and Recollections* (1936), and for his short stories, and his love of adverbs.

SMITH, Martin Cruz
(1942–)

American novelist, born in Reading, Pennsylvania, best known for his cold-war thriller, *Gorky Park* (1981), which was turned into a successful Hollywood film. A sequel, *Polar Star*, followed in 1990. Of part Hopi descent, Smith has also written two novels dealing with aspects of Southwestern history and culture: *Nightwing* (1977), a gruesome supernatural thriller in which plague-carrying bats terrorize the Navajo and Hopi reservations, and *Stallion Gate* (1986), describing the atomic testing at Los Alamos in the 1940s from the point of view of a young Pueblo GI posted as Oppenheimer's driver. His fantasy *The Indians Won* (1970) describes an alternative present-day US run by Native Americans, who have succeeded in defeating US forces in the 19th century. Smith has also written mystery novels under the pen-names Nick Carter and Simon Quinn.

SMITH, Pauline
(1882–1959)

South African novelist, born in Oudtshorn, Cape. Her output, two story collections and one novel, *The Beadle* (1926), is small but very distinguished, and attracted the admiration and friendship of **Arnold Bennett**. Her stories of Afrikaaner life, in particular 'The Pain' (1925), are evocative, accurate and moving.

▷ G Haresnape, *Pauline Smith* (1970)

SMITH, Seba ('Major Jack Downing')
(1792–1869)

American humorist. Having failed, after graduation from Bowdoin, as a straight journalist and newspaperman, Smith adopted a pen-name and began to compose a series of highly successful letters poking fun at the administration of the day. They were printed all across the country and when collected as *Letters of J. Downing, Major, Downingville Militia* (1834), the book required 10 editions. Besides political satire, Smith published *Way Down East* (1854), containing affectionate portraits of Yankee life. His wife, Elizabeth Oakes Smith, was a well-known editor and columnist.

SMITH, Stevie, pseud of **Florence Margaret Smith**
(1902–71)

English poet and novelist, born in Hull. At the age of three she moved with her family to the house in the London suburb of Palmer's Green where she was to live with her aunt for most of her life. She attended the local High School and the North London Collegiate School for Girls before working for the Newnes publishing company. In 1935 she took a collection of her poems to a publisher, who rejected them and advised her to try a novel. This she did, and the result was *Novel on Yellow Paper*, published in 1936, a largely autobiographical monologue in an amusing conversational style, which proved a success and was followed in 1938 by *Over the Frontier*, in similar style. *The Holiday* (1949) was again to a great extent autobiographical but had a more conventional structure and told the story of a doomed love affair. Meanwhile her reputation as a poet was becoming established. *A Good Time Was Had By All* was published in 1937, the poetry light and child-like in tone, with chatty amusing language and short verses. She developed a more serious tone, with stronger themes, moving towards the concepts and language of Christianity. Loneliness is often her theme, as in *Not Waving but Drowning* (1957), and she is considered to be a comic writer, but one who talks of serious matters in an amusing tone. Her work also includes *Mother, What is Man?* (1942), *Harold's Leap* (1950), *Selected Poems* (1962), *The Frog Prince* (1966) and *Scorpion* (1972). She wrote many reviews and critical articles, and produced a volume of the line-drawings that often accompanied her poems, entitled *Some Are More Human Than Others* (1958). Her *Collected Poems* appeared in 1975.
▷K Dick, *Ivy and Stevie* (1971)

SMITH, Sydney Goodsir
(1915–75)

New Zealand-born Scottish poet, born in Wellington, son of Sir Sydney Alfred Smith. He moved to Edinburgh in 1928 when his father was appointed Regius Professor of Forensic Medicine there. He studied at Edinburgh University and Oriel College, Oxford, and with such works as *Skail Wind* (1941), *The Devil's Waltz* (1946), *Under the Eildon Tree* (1948, a great modern love poem), *Orpheus and Eurydice* (1955), *So Late into the Night* (1952) and *Figs and Thistles* (1959), established a reputation as the best modern Lallans (lowland Scots) poet after **Hugh MacDiarmid**. He published a loving description of Edinburgh in *Kynd Kittock's Land* in 1965. His first play, *The Wallace*, was commissioned for the Edinburgh Festival of 1960.

He also wrote a comic novel, *Carotid Cornucopius* (1947). His *Collected Poems 1941–75* appeared in 1975.
▷H MacDiarmid, *Sydney Goodsir Smith* (1963)

SMITH, Sydney
(1771–1845)

English clergyman, essayist and wit, born in Woodford, Essex. He was educated at Winchester and New College, Oxford, of which he became a fellow. He was ordained (1794) and served at Netheravon near Amesbury, and Edinburgh. In 1802, with Francis Jeffrey, Francis Horner and Lord Brougham, he started the *Edinburgh Review*. He next lived six years in London, and soon made his mark as a preacher, a lecturer at the Royal Institution on moral philosophy (1804–6), and a brilliant talker; but in 1809 was 'transferred' to the living of Foston in Yorkshire. In 1828 Lord Lyndhurst presented him to a prebend of Bristol, and next year enabled him to exchange Foston for Combe-Florey rectory, Somerset. In 1831 Charles Grey, 2nd Earl Grey appointed him a canon of St Paul's. His writings include 65 articles, collected in 1839 from the *Edinburgh Review*; *Peter Plymley's Letters* (1807–8) in favour of Catholic emancipation; *Three Letters on the Ecclesiastical Commission* (1837–9); and other letters and pamphlets on the ballot, American repudiation, the game laws, prison abuses, etc. Chiefly remembered as the creator of 'Mrs Partington', he was a kindly, sensible humorist who stands immeasurably above **Theodore Hook**, if a good way below **Charles Lamb**.
▷H Pearson, *The Smith of Smiths* (1940)

SMITH, Thorne
(1893–1934)

American novelist, born in Maryland. His early work was published in the navy's paper *Broadside*, and this encouraged him to bring out his first novel *Biltmore Oswald* (1918). His period of success began in 1926 with the publication of Topper, a fantastically plotted novel which was made into a film starring Cary Grant (replaced by a dog in the sequel) in the 1930s, and a TV series in the 50s. *Turnabout* (1931), one of Smith's most inventive books, describing a suburban couple who switch bodies but not personalities, is a good example of the author's fetching whackiness.

SMITH, Vivian
(1933–)

Australian lyric poet, born in Hobart, Tasmania, the seascapes and landscapes of which influenced his first collection, *The Other Meaning* (1956). *An Island South* (1967), *Familiar Places* (1978) and the prize-winning *Tide*

Country (1982) comprise a small but powerful corpus of verse in a traditional style. He has also edited the letters of **Vance Palmer** and his wife (1977), which provide fascinating glimpses of Australian literary circles of the day, and critical studies of *Vance and Nettie Palmer* (1975) and *The Poetry of Robert Lowell* (1974).

SMITH, Wilbur Addison
(1933–)

South African novelist, born in Zambia. A traditional, bestselling author, he writes yarns of stiff, upright machismo. He became a full-time writer in 1964; his subsequent success as an adventure novelist has enabled him to finance expeditions in Africa and Alaska among other places; these have, in turn, helped his research. *When the Lion Feeds* (1964) is a tale of gold prospectors in Africa; *Eagle In The Sky* (1974) has as its central characters a jet pilot and his Israeli girlfriend; and *The Eye of the Tiger* (1975) is about a seaborne treasure hunt which leads first to jealous competition, then to zealous violence.

SMITH, William Jay
(1918–)

American poet, author for children, translator and critic, born in Winnfield, Louisiana, who published his first collection, *Poems*, in 1947. Subsequent volumes include *Poems 1947–1957* (1957) and *The Tin Can and Other Poems* (1966). Smith's themes and verse-forms are many and varied, and while this has left critics struggling almost in vain to classify his poetry, many have admiringly likened the effect, particularly of reading *The Tin Can*, to that of watching a splendid literary variety show.

SMITHER, Elizabeth Edwina
(1941–)

New Zealand poet and novelist, born in New Plymouth. Her taut elliptical verse, owing nothing to other schools of New Zealand writing, first appeared as *Here Come the Clouds: Poems* (1975), and she acknowledged an early influence in the collection *You're Very Seductive, William Carlos Williams* (1978). This was followed in 1979 by *Little Poems* (1979) and six further books before *A Pattern of Marching* (1989). She turned to prose with her historical novel *First Blood* (1983), describing the impact on a new colony of its first murder, and a later novel *Brother-love, Sister-love* (1986). She has also written for children.

SMITHYMAN, (William) Kendrick
(1922–)

New Zealand critic and poet, born in Te Kopura, North Auckland, the first of his generation to be influenced by American writing. His first collection was *Seven Sonnets* (1946), but he produced little after *The Blind Mountain* (1950) until *Earthquake Weather* (1972) and *The Seal in the Dolphin Pool* (1974), followed by three further collections and then *Selected Poems* in 1989. He has written a good deal of criticism, and his *A Way of Saying* (1965) looks at the development of New Zealand poetry. He has also edited two early novels of **William Satchell** and the short stories of **Greville Texidor**.

SMOLENSKIN, Peretz
(1842–85)

Russian Jewish novelist and political activist and editor (of the celebrated periodical *Ha-Schachar*, 'The Dawn', which he founded). He was born in Monastyrshchina, Russia. Known mainly as the leader of the National Jewish Progressive Movement, as the opponent of the notion of 'assimilation'— which he regarded as a negative result of the Haskalah ('Enlightenment')—and as the author of learned and influential treatises in favour of a Jewish national identity, he was also a gifted novelist, and never more so than in his last book, *Kevurat Chamor* (1875–6, 'The Burial of an Ass').

▷R Brainin, *Peretz Smolenskin* (1896); C H Freudlich, *Peretz Smolenskin, Life and Thought* (1965)

SMOLLETT, Tobias George
(1721–71)

Scottish novelist, born on the farm of Dalquharn in the Vale of Leven, Dunbartonshire, grandson of Sir James Smollett. He was educated at Dumbarton Grammar School and Glasgow University, where he took a degree in medicine. He moved to London in 1740 to find a producer for his tragedy, *The Regicide* (1749) but, disappointed in his quest, sailed as surgeon's mate in the expedition to Carthagena against the Spanish in 1741. Three years later he settled in London, practising as a surgeon, but literature in the form of novel-writing was his real interest. His first efforts were successes—*Roderick Random* (1748) and *Peregrine Pickle* (1751). The former is modelled on Le Sage's *Gil Blas*, and as well as describing episodes in the life of the unprincipled hero, it made use of Smollett's experiences in the Carthagena expedition. *Peregrine Pickle* pursues the hero's adventures in love and war throughout Europe. *Ferdinand, Count Fathom* (1753) is the story of another heartless villain, whom

an easy repentance saves from the gallows. **Cervantes** was now his model—he translated *Don Quixote* in 1755—but his imitation of the master, *Sir Launcelote Greaves* (1762), is crude work. In 1753 he settled in Chelsea, editing the new *Critical Review*—which led to his imprisonment for libel in 1760—and writing his *History of England* (3 vols, 1757–8). Ordered abroad for his health, he visited France and Italy and saw little that pleased him. His caustic record, *Travels in France and Italy* (1766), earned for him **Sterne**'s nickname of 'Smelfungus'. His next publication was a coarse satire on public affairs, *The Adventures of an Atom* (1769). In 1771 he wrote *Humphrey Clinker* (1771), which is much more kindly in tone and is still a favourite, in the form of a series of letters from and to members of a party touring round England and 'North Britain'. He spent the last years of his life abroad, and died in Livorno, Italy.
▷L Melville, *The Life and Letters of Tobias Smollett* (1976)

SNODGRASS, W(illiam) D(eWitt)
(1926–)

American poet and critic, born in Pennsylvania and educated at Iowa University. His first collection, *Heart's Needle* (1959, Pulitzer Prize), records the breakdown of his marriage, his divorce and separation from his daughter. Some of his later verse, written in traditional, elegant forms, is also autobiographical but occasionally less bitter. Among his subsequent volumes are *Gallows Songs of Christian Morgenstern* (1967) and *After Experience: Poems and Translations* (1968), which includes translations from **Rilke**, and *Six Minnesinger Songs* (1983). He has lectured widely and written extensively on literary theory, some of his critical writing being collected in *In Radical Pursuit* (1975).

SNOILSKY, Count Carl
(1841–1903)

Swedish minor poet with grandiose ambitions, born in Stockholm. Author of graceful verses, a diplomat until he was involved in a divorce, he aspired to become Sweden's national poet, but alienated the liberals who had once been his readers with his latter-day conservatism. His literary achievement and style have been gratefully compared to those of the English poet **Anthony Thwaite**.

SNOW, C(harles) P(ercy), 1st Baron
(1905–80)

English novelist and physicist, born in Leicester. He was educated at Alderman Newton's School, and then studied science at Leicester University College, and Christ's College, Cambridge, and became a fellow of Christ's College (1930–50) and a tutor there (1935–45). During World War II he was chief of scientific personnel for the Ministry of Labour, and was a Civil Service commissioner from 1945 to 1960. As a writer he started with a detective story, *Death Under Sail* (1932), followed by *The Search* (1934), set in the corridors of science and power. This heralded his major sequence of novels, under the general title *Strangers and Brothers*, starting with a novel of that name in 1940. The continuity is maintained by means of the character Lewis Eliot, through whose eyes the dilemmas of the age are focused. It was followed after the war by *The Light and the Dark* (1947) and *Time of Hope* (1949). *The Masters* (1951) stages the conflict aroused by the election of a new master in a Cambridge college. *The New Men* (1954) poses the dilemma of the scientists in the face of the potentials of nuclear fission. Other volumes are *Home-comings* (1956), *The Conscience of the Rich* (1958), *The Affair* (1960), *Corridors of Power* (1964) and *The Sleep of Reason* (1968). Several have been adapted for theatre and television. Though the chief characters of his cycle are rather supine, being manipulated to exhibit the expressed problems, mostly of power and prestige, in all their facets, his work shows a keen appreciation of moral issues in a science-dominated epoch. His controversial *Two Cultures* (Rede lecture, 1959) discussed the dichotomy between science and literature and his belief in closer contact between them. Created a life peer in 1964, he was made Parliamentary Secretary at the Ministry of Technology (1964–6), and Lord Rector of St Andrews University (1961–4). In 1950 he married the novelist, **Pamela Hansford Johnson**.
▷J Thale, *C. P. Snow* (1964)

SNYDER, Gary
(1930–)

American poet, born in San Francisco. He was educated at the University of California. Originally associated with the Beat poets and portrayed as Japhy Ryder in **Jack Kerouac**'s *The Dharma Bums* (1958), he identified from the outset with the natural world and the values of simple living and hard physical work, making his way as a lumberjack and forestry warden. His writing is informed by an interest in Asian religious practices and literary traditions. This is already evident in *Myths and Texts* (1960) and *The Back Country* (1968) and reaches a climax in the **Whit**manesque *Axe Handles* (1984). *Turtle Island* (1974) was awarded a Pulitzer Prize. *Earth House Hold* (1969) was a founding text of the ecology movement.
▷B Almon, *Gary Snyder* (1979)

SOARES DE PASSOS, António de
(1826–69)

Portuguese poet, a disciple of the romantic historian, poet and novelist Alexandre Herculano, who was born in Oporto. His poetry was skilful and sonorous but he has since been seen as over-sentimental and over-opulent; he had a large following in his time.

SÖDERBERG, Hjalmar
(1869–1941)

Swedish novelist and playwright, known as 'the **Anatole France** of Sweden'. He wrote several collections of witty short stories, such as *Historietter* (1898, Eng trans *Selected Short Stories*, 1935), and novels of upper middle-class life in Stockholm like *Förvillelser* (1895, 'Aberrations'), *Martin Bircks ungdom* (1901, Eng trans *Martin Birck's Youth*, 1930) and *Doktor Glas* (1905, Eng trans 1963). His plays included *Gertrud* (1905). In the last period of his life, he gave up fiction and turned to religious scholarship, obsessively researching the historicity of the New Testament.
▷B Bergman, *Hjalmar Söderberg* (1951)

SÖDERGRAN, Edith
(1892–1923)

Finland–Swedish Expressionist poet, the daughter of a peasant who worked in Alfred Nobel's factory. Her family moved to the Karelia peninsula, where the landscape and contact with the people had a profound effect. Following an unhappy love affair, she published *Dikter* (1916, 'Poems'). This was followed by *Septemberlyran* (1918, 'September Lyre') and *Rosenaltaret* (1919, 'The Rose Altar') and the ironically titled *Fremtidens skugga* (1920, 'The Shadow of the Future'), each of which attested to a growing sense of the poet as a prophetic, almost magical figure. Though she died when barely past 30, Södergran now exerts considerable influence on younger Swedish poets, who value her passionate, almost visionary imagery and a robust metre that occasionally suggests the works of **Emily Dickinson**.
▷L de Freyes, *Edith Södergran* (1970); G S Schoolfield, *Edith Södergran* (1984)

SOFFICI, Ardengo
(1879–1964)

Italian poet and painter, born near Florence. He was in Paris in the decade before World War I, and met **Max Jacob**, **Apollinaire** and Picasso; he came back to broadcast his new ideas in the review *Leonardo*, and became a ferocious adherent of the Futurism of **Marinetti**. He embraced fascism with enthusiasm, but survived to take a part in later literary-political activity. His poetry is still read and studied.

SOFRONOV, Anatoli
(1911–)

Russian playwright and editor (of a mass circulation magazine, *Ogonyok*), whose work pleased Communist Party officials. His agreeable *Million za ulybku* (1955) was seen, as the film *A Million for a Smile*, in London in 1967.
▷P Yershov, *Comedy in the Soviet Theatre* (1956)

SOLDATI, Mario
(1906–88)

Italian novelist and film-director from Turin. As a young man he went to the USA, whose mores he analysed in *America, primo amore* (1935, 'America, First Love'). He made a memorable film (1941) of the novel *Picolo mondo antico* by **Fogazzaro**. Educated by Jesuits, he attacked their hypocrisy in the sardonic and scarifying novel *L'amico gesuita* (1943, 'The Jesuit Friend'); *Salmace* (1955, Eng trans *The Confession*, 1958) contains short stories mocking sexual pretensions and various aspects of the Italian male fantasy of *virilità*. He returned to the theme of Catholic education in *La busta arancione* (1966, Eng trans *The Orange Envelope*, 1969).
▷D Heiney, *America in Modern Italian Literature* (1966)

SOLIS Y RIBADENEYRA, Antonio de
(1610–86)

Spanish author. He was private secretary to Philip IV and historiographer of the Indies. He wrote poems and dramas, and *Historia de la Conquista de Mexico* (1684).
▷L Arocene, *Antonio de Solis y Ribadeneyra* (1963)

SOLOGUB, Fedor, pseud of Fedor Kuzmich Teternikov
(1863–1927)

Russian novelist, born in St Petersburg. He was brought up by a wealthy family, and worked as a schoolmaster for 25 years before concentrating on writing from 1907, the year in which he published his best-known book, *Myelki byes* (1907, Eng trans *The Little Demon*, 1916). He also wrote a trilogy of symbolic novels, *Tvorimaya legenda* (1908–12, Eng trans *The Created Legend*, 1916), and many short stories, fables, fairy tales and poems.
▷S Rubinovitz, *Sologub's Literary Children* (1980)

SOLOMOS, Dionysios
(1798–1857)

The greatest of modern Greek poets, described by **Goethe** as 'the Byron of the East'. He was born on Zakynthos—his father was a rich nobleman on the island and controlled its tobacco monopoly—but studied at the university in Cremona and tutored in Italian at the University of Padua from 1815. He wrote his first poems there, in Italian, but returned to Zakynthos in 1818. He was embraced by the Society of Friends, a secret organization supporting Greek independence and a popular uprising against the Turks, and thereafter wrote all his poems in Greek. In 1823 he published *Hymnus is tis Eleftherian* (Eng trans *Hymn to Liberty*, 1957), a series of 158 quatrains personifying liberty as rising from the bones of all Greek heroes who had died in her defence; set to music by Mazaro in 1863, it became the national anthem of Greece. However, he is perhaps most famous for the hymn on the death of **Byron** which he wrote in 1824. He moved to Corfu in 1828, and lived there until his death.

SOLON
(640 or 638–559 BC)

Athenian lawgiver, a merchant and a poet. Archon in 594 (or 591), in a time of economic distress, he was appointed to reform the constitution. He set free all people who had been enslaved for debt (Seisachtheia), reformed the currency, and admitted a fourth class (Thetes) to the Ecclesia, so that they elected the magistrates, and to the Heliaea, so that they judged them. Thus he laid the foundations for the Athenian democracy; but he was a moderate and kept many privileges of the wealthy. After 10 years' voluntary exile, he returned (580) and, in a poem, stirred up the Athenians to capture 'lovely Salamis' (c.569). He died soon after the usurpation of Pisistratus, the story of his connection with Croesus being legendary.
▷I Linforth, *Solon the Athenian* (1919)

SOLOUKHIN, Vladimir
(1924–)

Russian fiction writer, poet, journalist and critic, born in the village of Alepino in Central Russia. He was, like **Shushkin** and others, a member of the 'village school' of writers. This group sought to circumvent the political demands of Party hacks by exercising their wish to 'return to Nature'. In his poetry, the least important part of his output, Soloukhin has been compared to **Yevtushenko**, although he is far less flashy. One of his most suggestive works is *Chornye doski* (1969, Eng trans *Searching for Icons*, 1971), in which he tells the story of how his boy-scouting activities led to his passionate regard for ancient Russian culture.

SOLOVIEV, Vladimir
(1853–1900)

Russian philosopher, theologian and poet, born in Moscow, son of the historian Sergei Mikhailovitch Soloviev. He proposed a universal Christianity which would unite the Catholic and Orthodox churches, and attempted a synthesis of religious philosophy with science. His main works were *The Crisis of Western Philosophy* (1875), *The Philosophical Principles of Integral Knowledge* (1877), *Russia and the Universal Church* (1889) and *The Justificaion of the Good* (1898).

SOLZHENITSYN, Aleksandr Isayevich
(1918–)

Russian writer and winner of the Nobel Prize for literature, born in Kislovodsk. He was brought up in Rostov where he graduated in mathematics and physics in 1941. After distinguished service with the Red Army in World War II, he was imprisoned (1945–53) for unfavourable comment on Stalin's conduct of the war. Rehabilitated in 1956, his first novel, *Odin den' Ivana Denisovicha*, (1962, Eng trans *One Day in the Life of Ivan Denisovich*, 1963), set in a prison camp, was acclaimed both in Khrushchev's Russia and the West, but his denunciation in 1967 of the strict censorship in Russia led to the banning of his later novels, *Rakovy Korpus* (1968, Eng trans, 2 vols, *The Cancer Ward*, 1968–9) and *V Kruge pervom* (1968, Eng trans *The First Circle*, 1968). They are semi-autobiographical, as he himself has suffered from cancer, and expose corruption in Russian society while defending socialism. He was expelled from the Soviet Writers' Union in 1969, and was awarded the Nobel Prize for literature in 1970. After some trouble with the authorities, he accepted it. His novel, *Avgust chetyrnadtsatovo* (1971, Eng trans *August, 1914*, 1972), the first part of a projected trilogy about the emergence of modern Russia, was published in the West in 1971, and *Arkhipelag Gulag* (3 vols, 1973–6, Eng trans *The Gulag Archipelago 1918–56*, 1974–8), a factual account of the Stalinist terror, between 1973 and 1975. In 1974 he was deported to West Germany. He later settled in the USA, but in 1994 returned to Russia. His memoirs, *Bodalsya telyonok s dubom* (1975), were published in translation (1980) as *The Oak and the Calf*. *Avjust chetyrnadtsatovo* was later much revised as 'Knot 1' of a projected mammoth account of the Russian Revolution, *Krasnoe Koleso* (1990, 'The Red Wheel'). He published *Kak Nam Obustroit' Rossiyu?* (Eng trans *Rebuilding Russia*, 1991) in 1990.
▷M Scammell, *Alexander Solzhenitsyn* (1984)

SOMERVILLE, Edith (Anna Oenone)
(1858–1949)

Irish novelist, born in Corfu, the daughter of an army officer and cousin of **Violet Martin**

SOMERVILLE, William

('Martin Ross', 1862–1915). As a baby she returned to the family home of Drishane in Skibbereen, County Cork. Educated at Alexandra College, Dublin, she studied painting in London, Düsseldorf and Paris, and became a magazine illustrator. She met her cousin, Violet Martin, in 1886, with whom she began a lasting literary partnership as 'Somerville and Ross'. Starting with *An Irish Cousin* (1889), they completed 14 works together, including *The Real Charlotte* (1894) and *Some Experiences of an Irish RM* (1899), the success of which led to two sequels, *Further Expenses...* (1908) and *In Mr Knox's Country* (1915). After Violet's death in 1915, Edith continued to write as 'Somerville and Ross', producing *Irish Memoirs* (1917) and *The Big House at Inver* (1925). A forceful character, she became the first woman Master of Foxhounds in 1903, and was Master of the West Carberry pack from 1912 to 1919. She was also a founder-member of the Irish Academy of Letters (1933).

▷ V Powell, *The Irish Cousins* (1970)

SOMERVILLE, William
(1675–1742)

English poet, born in Wolseley in Staffordshire. Educated at Winchester School and New College, Oxford (where he became a fellow), he was the squire of Edstone, Warwickshire. He wrote *The Chase* (1735), a long poem in praise of hunting. He also wrote *Field Sports* (1742), a poem on hawking, and *Hobbinol* (1740), a burlesque on rural May Day games.

▷ E Sanford, *A Life of William Somerville* (1819)

SØNDERBY, Knud
(1909–66)

Danish novelist, born in the provincial town of Esbjerg and brought up in Copenhagen, which also forms the main location of his novels. His first novel, *Midt i en Jazztid* (1931, 'In the Middle of a Jazz Age'), focuses on a young law student, Peter Hasvig, torn between two women and the contrasting social spheres they represent; it reflects the influence of psychoanalytical ideas, and skilfully and unconventionally captures the 'modernity' of the inter-war years. His subsequent novel *To Mennesker mødes* (1932, 'Two People Meet') is a continued investigation of the fatal attraction across social barriers. Distinctive for his Freudian criticism of the burden of culture, Sønderby's perspective becomes more universal in *En Kvinde er overflødig* (1936, 'A Woman is Superfluous'), about the generation gap in a close family, and in *De kolde Flammer* (1940, 'The Cold Flames'), a love story set in Greenland.

▷ P Bager, *Fylde og tomhed. Om Knud Sønderbys forfatterskab* (1984)

SONDHEIM, Stephen Joshua
(1930–)

American composer and lyricist. As a young man he studied lyric-writing with **Oscar Hammerstein II**, and wrote incidental music for *Girls of Summer* (1956), before writing the lyrics for Bernstein's West Side Story (1957). The first shows for which he wrote both the music *and* the lyrics—still rather unusual in musicals—were *A Funny Thing Happened on the Way to the Forum* (1962) and *Anyone Can Whistle* (1964). *Company* (1970), about married life in New York, was followed, among others, by *Follies* (1971), *A Little Night Music* (1973) and *Merrily We Roll Along* (1981). He won a Pulitzer Prize in 1985 with **James Lapine** for *Sunday in the Park with George* (1984).

SONTAG, Susan
(1933–)

American critic, born in New York City. Though she emerged first as an experimental fiction writer, author of *The Benefactor* (1963) and *Death Kit* (1967), her main impact has been as a critic. She was formerly married to the **Freud**ian intellectual Philip Rieff and absorbed significant concerns from him. Her influential books include *Against Interpretation* (1966), *Styles of Radical Will* (1969), *On Photography* (1976) and *Illness as Metaphor* (1978), a study of the mythology of cancer (Sontag was later a sufferer herself), which she revised (1989) to take account of AIDS, another disease whose social and imaginative construction presents an intellectual challenge. Hugely well-read and polymathic, she is a major commentator, not just on the American scene.

SOPHOCLES
(c.496–405 BC)

Athenian tragedian, one of the great figures of Greek drama, born in Colonus, an Athenian suburb. He had to forgo his ambitions for the stage on account of a weak voice. He wrote well over a hundred plays (including conventional satyr plays of which only the *Ichneutae* ('Trackers') survives), as well as seven major plays, still extant, all written after his victory over **Aeschylus** in a dramatic contest in 468 BC. He won first prize at the Great Dionysia 18 times. The problem of burial is prominent in both the *Ajax* and *Antigone* (possibly c.441 BC), in the first as an Olympian directive that hatred should not pursue a noble adversary beyond the grave, in the second as a clash between a sister's duty to bury a dead traitor brother and obedience to the law imposed by the state. Aeschylus, **Euripides** and Sophocles each wrote versions of *Electra*, the gruesome matricide by Orestes in revenge for his father's death at the hands of his mother's paramour. The great Sophoclean masterpiece, however, is *Oedipus Tyrannus* (c.430 BC), on which Aristotle based his aesthetic theory of drama in the *Poetics* and from which **Freud** derived the name and function of the 'Oedipus complex'. King Oedipus proclaims sentence on the unknown murderer of his predecessor, Laius, whose presence is thought to be the cause of a plague at Thebes. By a gradual unfolding of incidents, he learns that he himself was the assassin and that his wife Jocasta is also his mother. He blinds himself and goes into exile, and Jocasta commits suicide. The dramatic characteristics are the gradual reversal in fortune of an estimable, conventionally 'moral' person, through some untoward discovery in personal relationships, but also linked to some seemingly minor defect in character, in Oedipus' case, pride. This combination of a minor defect with the external cruel machinations of *até*, or personal destiny abetted by the gods, constitutes, according to Aristotle, the famous 'tragic flaw' which arouses the tragic emotions of pity and fear in the spectator and allows their purgation in a harmless manner. This is in sharp contrast to Aeschylean tragedy, which is essentially static. There is no development in the plot; the hero is doomed from the beginning. The *Trachiniae* (c.420 BC, 'Women of Trachis') explores the ruinous love of Heracles and Deianira. The *Philoctetes* (produced in 409 BC) and *Oedipus Coloneus* (produced 401 BC) would hardly be called tragic, except for the grave circumstances which attend the achievement of glory.

▷C M Bowra, *Sophocles's Imagination* (1944)

SORDELLO, or SORDEL
(c.1200–c.1270)

Italian poet, Provençal troubadour, born in Goito near Mantua, into a noble family, and most famous as the subject of an impenetrable poem by **Robert Browning**. Little is known of him save that he was a wanderer who carried off women, including wives—and that he had a fine scorn for political and, surprisingly, moral corruption. **Dante** saw him as an exemplary guide for negligent princes in the *Purgatorio*. He left 42 poems in the Provençal language, all of high quality, and is by far the most important of the Italian-born troubadours. Most often quoted is his *planh* (lament) on the death of Lord Blacatz.

SOREL, Charles, Sieur de Souvigny
(1602–74)

French picaresque novelist, satirist, critic and moralist. A perceptive, ingenious and evasive man, he mostly parodied other writers, as in *Le Berger extravagant* (1627), where he mocks the sentimental romance of the *Astrée* of **Honoré d'Urfé**. But in his exceedingly popular *Histoire comique de francion* (1622–33) he is not only a mocker and ridiculer but also a realist of a very high order: this book gives one of the most vivid of all descriptions of early 17th-century French life, particularly low life. The two chief influences upon him were **Rabelais** and **Cervantes**; he in turn may have influenced **Molière**; certainly he affected the course of the French novel. In *Le Roman bourgeois* of Furetière he is characterized as Charosselles.

SØRENSEN, Villy
(1929–)

Danish short-story writer, philosopher and political thinker, born in Copenhagen, who studied at the universities of Copenhagen and Freiburg. A self-taught scholar of formidable learning, he made his literary debut in 1953 with a pioneering collection of stories, *Sære historier* (1953, Eng trans *Strange Stories*, 1956), followed by *Ufarlige historier* (1955, Eng trans *Harmless Tales*, 1991) and *Formynderfortællinger* (1964, Eng trans *Tutelary Tales*, 1988). Sørensen's stories are absurd and ambiguous, simple and subtle, reminiscent of **Hans Christian Andersen** as well as **Franz Kafka**. With the Cold War as their context but only vaguely defined in space and time, they question the validity of a rigid split between us and them, good and evil, reason and emotion. Sørensen's work, whether fiction or philosophy, can be seen as a continuous endeavour to define a political, philosophical and moral middle ground based upon the nature of man. In the 1980s and 1990s Sørensen has presented enlightening re-interpretations of great mythological traditions: *Ragnarok* (1982, Eng trans *The Downfall of the Gods*, 1989) about the Norse mythology; *Apollons Oprør* (1989, 'The Revolt of Apollo') about the Greek mythology; and *Jesus og Kristus* (1992, 'Jesus and Christ') about the Christian tradition. He has been awarded many prizes, most notably the Swedish Academy's Nordic Literature Prize in 1986.

▷J B Jensen, *Litterær arkæologi* (1978)

SORESCU, Marin
(1936–)

Romanian poet, born in Bulzesti, whose verse, distinguished by its black humour and cynicism, became very well known and much discussed in Romania after the publication of his first collection in 1964.

SORGE, Reinhard Johannes
(1892–1916)

German dramatist, born in Berlin, who was killed on the Somme. His (now almost comically) violent play *Der Bettler* (1912, 'The Beggar'), published before, but unproduced until after, his death, was the first Expressionist play; of little intrinsic interest, it showed the influence of **Nietzsche**, and suited the year 1917, when it was produced. After writing it he became a Roman Catholic, and wrote various religious dramas which have failed to withstand the test of time. But in the history of the German theatre he remains a quite important figure.

▷ R H Thomas, *Expressionism in German Life, Literature and the Stage 1919–1924* (1939)

SORLEY, Charles Hamilton
(1895–1915)

Scottish poet, born in Aberdeen, where his father was Professor of Moral Philosophy. Educated at King's College Choir School, in 1908 he won a scholarship to Marlborough College where, impressed by the rolling Wiltshire countryside, he started to write poetry. Just before the outbreak of World War I, and prior to taking his place at University College, Cambridge, he visited Germany, which coloured ambivalently his attitude to the events that followed. One of the first to enlist, he believed in the war as a necessary evil, as his poems show. In 1915 he went with his battalion to France, where he was killed by a sniper at the Battle of Loos. *Marlborough and Other Poems* was published in 1916, thanks to his family, and his best and probably unfinished work is unsentimental, direct and free from cant. *The Collected Poems of Charles Hamilton Sorley* was edited in 1985.

SORRENTINO, Gilbert
(1929–)

American poet, novelist and short-story writer, born and educated in Brooklyn, New York. He did manual work for several years before editing the experimental literary magazine *Neon*, and working for Grove Press. His first novel was *The Sky Changes* (1966), an ingenious set of variations on traditional quest fiction. His next books, *Steelwork* (1970) and *The Imaginative Qualities of Actual Things* (1971), are plotless, literary and very cool. *Splendide-Hôtel* (1973) is a quasi-fictional study of the poet's role which uses the (not quite standard) alphabet and references to **Rimbaud** as structural devices. Sorrentino's wider reputation was secured,

unusually, by the publication of a nostalgic short story, 'The Moon in Its Flight', in *New American Review* (no.13, 1971). Sorrentino's subsequent fiction has tended to sustain the concerns of the earlier books, but often lacks their excitement. The best of his verse is in *Corrosive Sublimate* (1971) and *A Dozen Oranges* (1976).

▷ G Sorrentino issue, *Review of Contemporary Fiction* (Autumn 1981)

SOSEKI Natsume, pseud of Natsume Kinnosuke
(1867–1916)

Major Japanese novelist and poet, born in Tokyo. Soseki was the most translated of the Japanese writers of his generation (which included the equally gifted **Toson**, not translated until later). He has influenced some important English writers, notably **Francis King**. He was himself influenced by **Zola** and naturalism, but brought a humour and considerable psychological subtlety to his work which most of his contemporaries lacked. His last novels, in particular *Kokoro* (1914, Eng trans 1956, another as *Heart*, 1957), are his finest—and so acute in their analysis of character and their investigations of sexual ambiguity that English readers find it hard to credit their early date. Other major novels include *Botchan* (1906, Eng trans *Young Master*, 1918, 1922), *Kusamakura* (1906, Eng trans as *Pillow of Grass*, 1927, as *Unhuman Tour*, also 1927, as *The Three-Cornered World*, 1965) and *Mon* (1910, Eng trans *The Gate*, 1971).

▷ *Monumenta Nipponica*, XIV, 1958–9, XIX (1964)

SOSYURA, Volodymyr
(1898–1965)

Ukrainian poet, born in Debaltesvo in the Donets Basin. A popular poet who tried—unsuccessfully—to keep to the tenets of socialist realism, he was valued for the fervent lyricism of his work, which made few intellectual demands but spoke directly to the heart. Some of his verse is translated in *Poems of Ukraine* (1939, ed W Kirkconnell).

SOTO DE ROJAS, Pedro
(1584–1638)

Spanish poet and priest, born in Granada. He was one of the leading followers, at the Spanish court, of the more important **Góngora**, who became a friend. Soto de Rojas was Canon of San Salvador, and the most distinguished poet of the group which flourished in Granada. His *culterano* garden poem *Paraíso cerrado para muchos, jardinas abiertos para pocos* (1652—poetry was often not published in book form until after its author's death at this time), with its Góngorista title 'Paradise Shut to the Many, Gardens Open to the Few', has been deservedly compared to the 'garden' poetry of **Andrew Marvell**. His works were edited in 1950.

▷A G Morell, *Pedro Soto de Rojas* (1948, in Spanish)

SOUMAGNE, Henri, pseud of **Henri Wagner** (1891–1951)

Belgian playwright, born into a Catholic family in Brussels. His deliberately blasphemous plays shocked audiences all over Europe, but particularly in his own country. His most famous play was *L'Autre Messie* (1923, 'The Other Messiah'), a presentation of a boxing match, before a group of Warsaw Jews in a bar, the result of which is supposed to settle the question of the existence of God (which has been doubted on the grounds that one of the antagonists has failed to discover a firm-breasted woman). Soumagne was a very capable theatrical craftsman who later turned to competent crime novels. He was accused of anti-Semitism, but the charge has been debated.

SOUSÂNDRADE, Joaquim de Sousa (1833–1902)

Brazilian poet, re-discovered in the 1960s. His most important poem was *O Guesa errante* ('The Wandering Guesa'), of which only parts survive. It is about Guesa, a Colombian Native American who wanders the world before he is sacrificed to the gods. Sousândrade lived in New York for a while, and in this poem there is a section called 'The Inferno of Wall Street', written in English and in Portuguese. It is eccentric, but its attack on capitalism anticipates many more modern poets. His works were collected in 1964.

SOUSTER, Raymond (1921–)

Canadian poet, novelist (pseud Raymond Holmes, and John Holmes), and editor. He was by profession the securities custodian of the Canadian Imperial Bank of Commerce. He is a leading representative of the second generation of those poets who reacted against the British influence upon Canadian poetry—the first one having included **F R Scott**. He attempts, as **George Woodcock** has pointed out, a poetry of 'direct experience', so that those used to embellishments such as metre or even rhythm, as well as metaphors, are often disappointed. But his short lyrics are widely admired and read. His *Collected Poems 1940–88* (1980–9) take up six volumes.

▷ *Tamarack Review* (Winter 1965)

SOUTAR, William (1898–1943)

Scottish poet, born in Perth, the son of a joiner. Educated at Perth Academy, he was conscripted into the Royal Navy (1916–19), where he contracted a form of spondylitis (ossification of the vertebrae), which was to confine him to bed for the last 13 years of his life. After demobilization he studied first medicine and then English at Edinburgh, returning to Perth in 1923. As an undergraduate he published his first volume of verse, anonymously, in *Gleanings by an Undergraduate* (1923), followed by *Conflict* (1931). In 1933 he published his first volume of verse in Scots, *Seeds in the Wind*, for children. This was followed by his *Poems in Scots* (1935) and *Riddles in Scots* (1937), which gave him a permanent place in the Scottish literary revival. The best examples of his work in English are *In the Time of Tyrants* (1939) and the collection *The Expectant Silence* (1944). His remarkable *Diaries of a Dying Man*, published in 1954, mark him out as an exceptional diarist. His *Collected Poems* appeared in 1948.

▷A Scott, *Still Life* (1958)

SOUTHALL, Ivan Francis (1921–)

Australian author, born in Melbourne, who has written prolifically for children, including the escapist adventure series featuring airman Simon Black which began with *Meet Simon Black* (1950). His later books turned more to the contemporary concerns of modern youth and have won many awards. They include *Ash Road* (1966) and *The Long Night Watch* (1986). *Let the Balloon Go* (1968) was filmed in 1975. His war experiences, for which he received the DFC, and his interest in flying have resulted in a history of 461 Squadron, Royal Australian Air Force, *They Shall not Pass Unseen* (1956), and biographies of air hero Keith Truscott and aviation pioneer Lawrence Hargrave.

SOUTHERN, Terry (1924–)

American novelist, born in Texas. He was educated at universities in Dallas, Chicago, Evanston and Paris. His free-wheeling, semi-parodic, irreverent and highly scatalogical style earned him a cult following in the 1960s and early 1970s, but he has written only sporadically since then. His first novel was *Flash and Filigree* (1958), followed by *Candy* (1958, USA 1964), which was first published in Paris to evade US obscenity laws. *The Magic Christian* (1960) was a bizarre satire about an immensely rich practical joker, and was followed by *Lollipop* (1962) then *Blue Movie*

(1970), an often hilarious novel about the making of a pornographic film. The stories in *Red-Dirt Marijuana* (1967) are more wide-ranging in their concerns. He has written journalism and a number of screenplays, including *Easy Rider* (1969).

SOUTHERNE, Thomas
(1660–1746)

Irish dramatist, born in Oxmantown, County Dublin. From Trinity College, Dublin, he passed to the Middle Temple, London, and in 1682 began his career with a compliment to the Duke of York in *The Loyal Brother*. **Dryden** wrote the prologue and epilogue, and Southerne finished Dryden's *Cleomenes* (1692). He served a short time under the Duke of Berwick and, at his request, wrote the *Spartan Dame*. His best plays were *The Fatal Marriage* (1694) and *Oroonoko* (before 1696), based on **Aphra Behn**.
▷ J W Dodds, *Thomas Southerne, Dramatist* (1933)

SOUTHEY, Robert
(1774–1843)

English poet and writer, born in Bristol, the son of a linen draper. After his father's death an uncle sent him to Westminster School, but he was expelled in 1792 for his Jacobin sympathies and for denouncing whipping in the school magazine. He went on to Balliol College, Oxford. He met **Coleridge** in Bristol in 1794 and they planned to form a 'pantisocracy' or communist society but this fell through. They wrote a topical drama together, *The Fall of Robespierre* (1794), and Southey published an early volume of *Poems* (1795) and an epic poem, *Joan of Arc* (1795). Also in 1795 he married Edith Fricker, whose elder sister Sara married Coleridge. He made two trips to Lisbon (1795 and 1800), and then, after studying law, settled at Great Hall, Keswick (where Coleridge and his wife and sister-in-law were already); and there he remained. He had only £160 a year from his school friend Charles Wynn on which to live, until the government gave him a similar amount in 1807. By this time his political views had mellowed and Southey had become something of a Tory. He became poet laureate in 1813, and Peel raised his pension by £300 in 1835. He had joined the *Quarterly Review* in 1809 and remained a contributor under William Gifford and **John Lockhart**. Essentially a family man, he sustained a great shock when his wife died insane in 1838; and, though he married Caroline Anne Bowles, the poet, in 1839, she became little more than a nurse for his last years of life. His literary output was prodigious, and many of his short poems are familiar, such as 'Holly Tree', 'After Blenheim', 'The Scholar', 'Inchcape

Rock', 'Old Woman of Berkeley' and 'God's judgement on a wicked Bishop'. His other works include *The Curse of Kehama* (1810), *Roderick* (1814); biographies of *Nelson* (1813), *Wesley* (1820) and *Bunyan* (1830), *A Vision of Judgment* (1821), *Book of the Church* (1824), *Colloquies on Society* (1829), *Naval History* (1833–40), and *The Doctor* (1834–47), a miscellany, in which appears the nursery classic, *The Three Bears*. He also published a *Journal of a Tour of Scotland in 1819* (1929).
▷ J Simmons, *Robert Southey* (1945)

SOUTHWELL, Robert
(?1561–1595)

English poet and Jesuit martyr, born in Horsham, Norwich. He was educated at Douai and Rome, and entered into the Society of Jesus in 1578. He was appointed prefect of the English College, was ordained priest in 1584, and two years later, arriving in England with Henry Garnet, was first sheltered by Lord Vaux, and next became chaplain to the Countess of Arundel, when he wrote his *Consolation for Catholics* and most of his poems. In 1592 he was betrayed, tortured and thrown into the Tower, and finally he was hanged and quartered at Tyburn for high treason. He was beatified in 1929. His longest poem is *Saint Peter's Complaint*; his most famous, *The Burning Babe*.

SOUTHWORTH, E(mma) D(orothy) E(liza) N(evitte)
(1819–99)

American novelist, born in Washington DC. She became a teacher and published *Retribution*, her first novel, in serial form in a Boston magazine in 1849. Over her writing career she wrote more than 40 novels, many of them being serialized before appearing as bound volumes. Mostly domestic melodramas supporting the social and moral conventions of the time, with titles such as *The Missing Bride* (1853) and *The Maiden Widow* (1870), they became enormously popular. *The Hidden Hand* (1859) is perhaps the most outspoken in that its heroine is unusually independent and determined to succeed on her own terms in a man's world.

SOUZA, Madame de, née Adélaïde Marie Emilie Filleul
(1761–1836)

French novelist, born in the Norman château of Longpré. She married the Comte de Flahaut (1727–93). At the outbreak of the French Revolution (1789) she found refuge with her only son in Germany and England, and there learned of her husband's execution at Arras. She turned to writing, and her first book was the delightful *Adèle de Sénange*

(1794). In 1802 she married the Marquis de Souza-Botelho (1758–1825), Portuguese minister in Paris. Later novels include *Émilie et Alphonse* (1799) and *Charles et Marie* (1801).

SOVA, Antonin
(1864–1928)

Czech poet and novelist, born in Pacov, Bohemia. As a poet he was amongst the three or four most influential of his generation. At first an impressionist writing in the shadow of French poets, he later developed his own brand of subjective and melancholy Symbolism. His personal poems, occasioned by his unhappy married life, were always much better than his more immediately popular 'Utopian' poetry. His novels, such as the autobiographical *Vypravy chudých* (1903, 'The Campaigns of the Poor'), are long-winded but never uninteresting.

SŁOWACKI, Juliusz
(1809–49)

Polish poet, born in Krzemieniec. He settled in Paris in 1831. He belonged to the Romantic school, the influence of **Byron**, among others, being perceptible in his work, which includes the historical drama *Marja Stuart* (1830, 'Mary Stuart'), the dramatized legend *Balladyna* (1834, Eng trans 1938), *Lilla Weneda* (1840), perhaps the most famous Polish tragedy, and *Mazeppa* (1839, Eng trans 1930). His letters to his mother from exile are regarded as classic models of Polish prose.

SOYA, Carl Erik Martin
(1896–1981)

Danish playwright and fiction writer, born in Copenhagen. He found recognition late. His candid novel about the problems and realities of puberty, *Sytten* (1953–4, Eng trans *Seventeen*, 1969), shocked many of his older compatriots; *Min Farmors Hus* (1943, Eng trans *Farmor's House*, 1964), another novel, is regarded as a Danish classic of childhood. His drama, influenced by **Freud**, **Pirandello** and **Abell**, is less serious or successful, but has been sporadically popular in Denmark.
▷N M Wamberg, *Soya* (1966, in Danish)

SOYINKA, Wole, pseud of Akinwande Oluwole Soyinka
(1934–)

Nigerian dramatist, poet and novelist, and winner of the Nobel Prize for literature. Born in Western Nigeria, he was educated in Abeokuta and Ibadan before moving to England to do research at Leeds University and study the contemporary theatre. He was for a while attached to the Royal Court Theatre as a play-reader, and it was there that his first play, *The Inventor*, was given a performance

in 1957, his verse-tragedy, *The Swamp Dwellers*, being produced by students in London the following year. He returned to Ibadan in 1959, and productions of *The Swamp Dwellers*, and a contrasting joyously ribald comedy *The Lion and the Jewel*, immediately established him in the forefront of Nigerian literature. In 1960 he founded the Masks amateur theatre company, and four years later, the professional Orisun Repertory. These companies played an essential part in Soyinka's building up of a new Nigerian drama, in English but using the words, music, dance and pantomime of the traditional festivals. His plays, like all his writing, are deeply concerned with the tension between the old and the new in modern Africa; history opposes tradition, and while there is value in many of the old ways, he condemns an uncritical clinging to the past. The richness of his language ranges from high-flown biblical English to the slang of the Lagos slums. His first poems were published while he was still an Ibadan undergraduate, but his first major collection, *Idanre and Other Poems* (1967), turned from his earlier humorous verse to more sombre themes; *A Shuttle in the Crypt* (1972) appeared after his release in 1969 from two years' political detention, and was as powerfully expressive of his ordeal as his play of 1970, *Madmen and Specialists*. His first novel, *The Interpreters* (1970), has been called the first really modern African novel. His other works include the plays *The Trials of Brother Jero* (1961) and *Kongi's Harvest* (1964), the novel *Season of Anomy* (1973), and the mostly prose 'prison notes', *The Man Died* (1973). He is presently Professor of Comparative Literature and head of the department of dramatic arts at Ife University. He was awarded the Nobel Prize for literature in 1986.

SPARK, Dame Muriel Sarah, née Camberg
(1918–)

Scottish novelist, short-story writer, biographer and poet, born in Edinburgh, the daughter of a Jewish engineer. She was educated in Edinburgh at James Gillespie's School for Girls (the model for Marcia Blaine School in *The Prime of Miss Jean Brodie*) where she was 'the school's Poet and Dreamer', and Heriot-Watt College (now University). After her marriage in 1938 she spent a few years in Central Africa. She came back to England in 1944 when her marriage broke down, and worked in the Political Intelligence Department of the Foreign Office, and stayed on in London after the war to become General Secretary of the Poetry Society and Editor of *Poetry Review* (1947–9). Since then she has devoted herself to writing, from the early

SPEAR, Charles

1960s living mainly in New York and Italy. She became a Catholic in 1954, an event of central importance to her life and work. Her early books include biographical studies of **Wordsworth** (1950) and **Emily Brontë** (1953), but she also published a collection of poems, *The Fanfarlo and Other Poems* (1952). She is pre-eminently a novelist and short-story writer. *The Comforters* (1957) was hailed by **Evelyn Waugh** as 'brilliantly original and fascinating' and her reputation grew steadily. She continued with *Memento Mori* (1959), *The Ballad of Peckham Rye* (1960), and *The Bachelors* (1961), but it was only with the publication of her sixth novel, *The Prime of Miss Jean Brodie* (1961), an eerie portrait of a school-teacher with advanced ideas and her influence over her 'crème de la crème' pupils, that she achieved popular success. Her many novels, which are invariably slim, elegant and imbued with bizarre elements, include *The Girls of Slender Means* (1963), set in a Kensington hostel, *The Abbess of Crewe* (1974), an allegorical fantasy set in an abbey but with parallels to the Watergate scandal, and *A Far Cry from Kensington* (1988), an evocative, comic but sinister portrayal of London in the 1950s. Her stories were collected in 1967 and 1985, and the first volume of her autobiography, *Curriculum Vitae*, was published in 1992. In 1993 she was created DBE.
▷A Bold, *Muriel Spark* (1990)

SPEAR, Charles
(1910–)

New Zealand poet whose only collection, *Twopence Coloured* (1951), contains a collection of mannered, polished verse in a style reminiscent of the early 1900s, drawing heavily on a scholarly and well-read mind yet deeply concerned with contemporary life. It was well written of him that 'literature *is* life'.

SPEE, Friedrich von
(1591–1635)

German mystical poet and humane writer, born in Donauworth. He was a Jesuit priest. His *Guldenes Tugendbuch* (1649, written in 1632) is a collection of religious exercises in the tradition of Loyola; but *Cautio criminalis* (1631) is the most eloquent attack on the persecution of witches of his time, and was extremely influential, especially after it had been translated into German (1649). As a poet he initiated a new type of non-**Opitz**ian poetry, expressing his passion for Christ in **Petrarch**an, pastoral terms.
▷W Kosch, *Friedrich von Spee* (1921, in German)

SPEIGHT, Johnny
(1920–)

English comic writer, born in London. A milkman, insurance salesman and member of a jazz band, he began writing after World War II for such comic stars as Frankie Howerd, Arthur Haynes and Morecambe and Wise. He made his mark on television with the play *The Compartment* (1962), and the creation of the loud-mouthed, working-class bigot Alf Garnett in the controversial assault on sacred cows like religion and royalty, *Till Death Do Us Part* (1964–74). The series earned him Screenwriters' Guild Awards in 1966, 1967 and 1968, and the character was revived for *In Sickness and In Health* (1985–). His other television series include *Spooner's Patch* (1979–82) and *The Nineteenth Hole* (1989–). His publications include *It Stands to Reason* (1973), *The Thoughts of Chairman Alf* (1973), and his autobiography, *For Richer, For Poorer* (1991).

SPENCE, Catherine Helen
(1825–1910)

Scottish-born Australian writer and feminist, born near Melrose. She arrived in Adelaide in 1839 with her parents, with the ambition to be 'a teacher first and a great writer afterwards'. While working as a governess she wrote the first novel of Australian life by a woman, published anonymously in London in 1854 as *Clare Morrison: a Tale of South Australia during the Gold Fever*. Her second novel, also anonymous, was *Tender and True: a Colonial Tale* (1856). Under her own name she wrote *Mr Hogarth's Will* (1865) and *The Author's Daughter* (1868). Both of these had previously been serialized in Adelaide newspapers, as was *Gathered In* in 1881, though not published in book form until 1977; her last novel, *Handfasted*, was not published until 1984. A concern with social problems led her into the public arena, and she made lecture tours of Britain and the USA. In *A Plea for Pure Democracy* (1861) she pressed for Proportional Representation, formed the Effective Voting League of South Australia, and stood for the Federal Convention in 1897, thereby becoming Australia's first woman candidate. *Catherine Helen Spence: an Autobiography* was unfinished at her death; it was completed by her companion Jeanne Young in 1910.
▷J Young, *Catherine Helen Spence: a Study and an Appreciation* (1937)

SPENCER, Bernard
(1909–63)

English poet, of 'the just after Auden generation', born in Madras. A diffident, ironic, mocking man (the qualities seeped into his work), he suffered from depression, which pervades his elegant, original poetry somewhat in the manner that it pervades that of **Bacovia**. An employee of the British Council for much of his life, he edited, with **Lawrence Durrell** and Robin Fedden, the wartime Middle East publication *Personal Landscape*. In his lifetime he published three small collections. He died mysteriously while suffering from fever, depression and confusion. His friend Durrell summed up the consensus when he declared that the best of his work would last.

▷ *Collected Poems* (1981)

SPENCER, Elizabeth
(1921–)

American novelist, born in Mississippi. She was initially influenced by **Donald Davidson**, who had been one of the most fiercely conservative of the Fugitive Group. Her early fiction is mostly set in her native Mississippi, and derives from that of **Eudora Welty** and **Faulkner**. But in *The Voice at the Back Door* (1956) she discovered her own procedures, and this story of the corruption of a decent lawyer in pursuit of the 'art of the possible' is reckoned to be her most powerful novel. *The Snare* (1972) is set in New Orleans, and, characteristically of this author, depicts a woman who discovers herself by settling for less than she had originally demanded. She is also an accomplished story writer, as seen in *The Stories of Elizabeth Spencer* (1981).

▷ L D Rubin, *A Bibliographical Guide to the Study of Southern Literature* (1969)

SPENDER, Sir Stephen
(1909–)

English poet and critic, son of the journalist and biographer Edward Harold Spender (1864–1926), born in London. Educated at University College, Oxford, in the 1930s he was one of the 'modern poets', left-wing in outlook, who set themselves the task of recharging the impulses of poetry both in style and subject-matter. In his thought he is essentially a liberal, despite his earlier flirtings with communism. He translated **Schiller**, **Ernst Toller**, **Rainer Rilke** and **Federico García Lorca**, among others, besides writing much penetrating literary criticism. From his beginnings in 1930 with the novella *Twenty Poems* to *Engaged in Writing* (1957), he relived his experiences in his work. *Poems from Spain* (1939) links up with his service in the Spanish Civil War. In World War II he served as a fireman in the London blitz, and volumes of poems, *Runes and Visions* (1941), *Poems of Dedication* (1941) and *The Edge of Darkness* (1949), continue his self-analysis. Alongside these are critical evaluations such as *The Destructive Element* (1936), *Life and the Poet* (1942), *The Creative Element* (1944), and his first autobiography, *World within World* (1951). From 1939 to 1941 he was co-editor, with **Cyril Connolly**, of the brilliant

monthly, *Horizon*, and from 1953 to 1967 was co-editor of *Encounter*. He was Professor of English at University College, London (1970–7). His later work includes *The Struggle of the Modern* (1963), *The Year of the Young Rebels* (1969), *The Thirties and After* (1978) and *Chinese Journal* (with David Hockney, 1982). *Collected Poems 1928–85* was published in 1985, and his *Journals (1939–83)* in 1987. In 1991, he compiled the volume *Character Studies*, with proceeds from sales going to AIDS patients.

▷ H David, *Stephen Spender* (1993)

SPENSER, Edmund
(c.1552–99)

English poet, born in London, the son of a gentleman tradesman who was connected with the Spencers of Althorp. He was educated at Merchant Taylors' School and Pembroke Hall, Cambridge. His early writings, partly written at Cambridge, include translations of the *Visions* of **Petrarch** and some sonnets of **Joachim Du Bellay**. Shortly after leaving Cambridge (1576) he obtained a place in the Earl of Leicester's household and this led to a friendship with Sir **Philip Sidney** and the Areopagus, a society of wits. His first original work, *The Shepheard's Calender* (1579), dedicated to Sydney, heralded the age of Elizabethan poetry and no doubt assisted in his career as a courtier. In 1580 he was appointed secretary to Lord Grey de Wilton, lord deputy in Ireland, whose assignment was to crush Irish rebellion, and Spenser was involved in this. His reward for his work as one of the 'undertakers' for the settlement of Munster was Kilcolman Castle in the county of Cork, where he settled in 1586 and where he hoped to have leisure to write his *Faerie Queene* and other courtly works, written with an eye to the court no less than as a brilliant presentation of the art and thought of the Renaissance. In 1589 he visited London in company with Sir Walter Raleigh, who had seen the first three books of *The Faerie Queene* at Kilcolman and now carried him off to lay them at Queen Elizabeth's feet. Published in 1590, they were an immediate success, but a previous misdemeanour, the attack in *Mother Hubberd's Tale* on the proposed match between Elizabeth and the Duc d'Alençon, was not forgotten and the poet returned to Ireland in 1591 a disappointed man; he later published his wry reflections on his visit in *Colin Clout's Come Home Again* (1595). *Complaints*, published in 1591, contains, beside his early work, the brilliantly coloured but enigmatic *Muiopotmos; Mother Hubberd's Tale*, to which was now added a bitter satire on Court favour; *The Early Tears of the Muses*, which lamented the lack of patronage; and his pastoral elegy for Sir Philip Sydney which is so frigid as to make us question their friendship. In 1594 he married again, celebrating his wooing of Elizabeth Boyle in the sonnet sequence *Amoretti* and his wedding in the supreme marriage poem *Epithalamion*. He revisited London in 1596, with three more books of *The Faerie Queene*, which were published along with the *Four Hymns*. This was a year of uncommon activity. Under the roof of Lord Essex he wrote *Prothalamion*, and his prose *View of the Present State of Ireland*, which, taken with the fifth book of *The Faerie Queene*, is probably the first explicit statement of the imperialism which is now discredited. In 1598 the Irish rose in rebellion and Kilcolman Castle was burned, but the Spensers escaped to Cork and from there to safety in London. He died the following year and was buried in Westminster Abbey.

▷ A C Judson, *The Life of Spenser* (1945)

SPEYER, Leonora
(1872–1956)

American poet, whose *Fiddler's Farewell* (1926) won a Pulitzer Prize and fulfilled the promise of her earlier collection *A Canopic Jar* (1921). At their best Speyer's poems speak with wit and perception about the female condition, but *Naked Heel* (1931) marked a withdrawal into a constrained formalism and halted her growing reputation. Her work has not, as yet, benefited from reappraisal.

SPIELHAGEN, Friedrich
(1829–1911)

German novelist, born in Magdeburg. He was an advocate of scientific objectivity in the novel, and wrote from an overly didactic perspective of middle-class liberalism and social justice. As well as poems, plays, books of travel, his works include *Durch Nacht zum Licht* (1861, 'Through the Night to the Light'), *Die von Hohenstein* (1863, 'The von Hohensteins'), *In Reih und Glied* (1866, 'In Rank and File') and *Susi* (1895). He also worked as an actor.

▷ E Mensch, *Er lebt noch immer* (1929)

SPILLANE, Mickey (Frank Morrison)
(1918–)

American mystery and detective novelist, born in Brooklyn, New York City. The author of almost 30 books, Spillane is a leading exponent of the sensational school of detective fiction, one critic describing his novels as having 'lurid action, lurid characters, lurid plot, lurid finish'. His first book, *I, the Jury* (1947), introduced Mike Hammer, his most famous character, a hard-drinking, hard-fighting, womanizing private investigator. Hammer punches his way with enormous relish through several books, including *Vengeance is Mine!* (1950) and *The Body Lovers* (1967). Spillane treats sex pruriently, and women as well as men become the objects of Hammer's insatiable violence.

▷ B Docherty, *American Crime Fiction* (1988)

SPINRAD, Norman Richard
(1940–)

American science-fiction writer, born in New York City. He began to publish fairly conventional science-fiction adventure stories in 1963, but by the time of *The Men in the Jungle* (1967) and *Bug Jack Baron* (1969), he had become identified with the 'new wave' movement which coalesced around the magazine *New Worlds*. Their priority was the exploration of inner rather than outer space by genre means, as well as a greater literary sophistication. *The Iron Dream* (1972) imagined an alternative world in which Adolf Hitler propagated his hateful ideas as a writer of fiction. *The Void Captain's Tale* (1983) and *Child of Fortune* (1985) are arguably his best science-fiction works. *Little Heroes* (1987) and *Russian Spring* (1991) are near-future dystopian nightmares. He has written a number of other novels, several short-story collections, and essays on science fiction and writing.

SPITTELER, Karl Friedrich Georg
(1845–1924)

Swiss poet and novelist, winner of the Nobel Prize for literature, born in Liestal (Basel). He studied law and theology at Basel, Zürich and Heidelberg, was a tutor in Russia, teacher and journalist in Switzerland, and retired to Lucerne in 1892. *Der Olympische Frühling* (1900–3, 'The Olympic Spring') is a great mythological epic, but perhaps his most mature work is *Prometheus der Dulder* (1924, 'Prometheus the Sufferer'). As well as poetry he wrote tales, (*Konrad der Leutnant*, 'Conrad the Lieutenant'), and others; essays (*Lachende Wahrheiten*, 'Laughing Truths'), and reminiscences. He was awarded the Nobel Prize for literature in 1919.

▷ J Frankel, *Karl Friedrich Spitteler* (1945)

SPONDE, Jean de
(1557–95)

French poet, humanist and translator (of **Homer**, Aristotle), whose predominantly metaphysical poems were rediscovered (by **Marcel Arland**), or at least revaluated in the 20th century; they were little published in his lifetime, and the first collection of them appeared in 1949. He is now taken as an apt representative of French baroque poetry.

SPRAGUE DE CAMP, L *see* **DE CAMP, L Sprague**

SPRING, Howard
(1889–1965)
Welsh novelist, born in Cardiff. From errand boy he became a newspaper reporter and literary critic and established himself as a writer with his bestselling *Oh Absalom* (1938), renamed *My Son, My Son*. Other novels include *Fame is the Spur* (1940), *Dunkerleys* (1946), *These Lovers Fled Away* (1955) and *Time and the Hour* (1957), as well as three autobiographical works (1939, 1942 and 1946).

SQUIRE, Sir John Collings
(1884–1958)
English author, born in Plymouth. He was educated at Blundell's and St John's College, Cambridge, and was literary editor of *The New Statesman* and founder editor of *The London Mercury* (1919–34). His work is composed of light verse and parody, as in *Steps to Parnassus* (1913) and *Tricks of the Trade* (1917); in anthologies he favoured minor poets. His writings also include criticisms and short stories. His *Collected Poems*, edited by **John Betjeman**, appeared in 1959.

ŠRÁMEK, Frána
(1877–1952)
Czech story writer, novelist, poet and dramatist, born in Sobotka. He was an impressionist, known chiefly for his novel *Telo* (1919, 'The Body'), about a young girl and her erotic and other experiences. His play *Léto* (1915, 'Summer'), was successfully produced. He was a close friend to **S K Neumann**. An honest and lyrical anarchist, he was highly influential in the period between the wars, when Czechoslovakia tasted its first independence, but lost himself in his later work when he tried to go outside his limitations. His collected works, published at the end of his life, take up 10 volumes.
▷J Knap, *Frána Šrámek* (1937, in Czech)

SREMEC, Stevan
(1855–1906)
Serbian novelist and story writer, born in Senta. He fought against the Turks in 1876–7. His comic novels and stories became classics, but never found a translator. Essentially they were shrewd but kindly, seeking their inspiration chiefly in **Gogol**.
▷A Barac, *A History of Yugoslav Literature* (1955)

SSU-MA HSIANG-JU
(d.117 BC)
Chinese poet, born in Ch'engtu, Suzechuan province. He wrote the *Tzu Hse Fu*, a series of poems describing and denouncing the pleasures of the hunt, which hold an important place in Chinese literary history.
▷Y Hervouet, *Un poète de cour sous les han* (1964)

STAAL, Marguerite Jeanne, Baronne de
(1684–1750)
French writer of memoirs, born in Paris, the daughter of a poor Parisian painter, Cordier, whose name she dropped for that of her mother, Delaunay. Her devotion to the interests of her employer, the Duchess of Maine, brought her two years in the Bastille, where she had a love affair with the Chevalier de Menil. In 1735 she married the Baron Staal. Her *Mémoires* (1755, Eng trans 1892) describe the world of the regency with intellect, observation and a subtle irony, and are written in a clear, firm and individual style. Her *Œuvres complètes* appeared in 1821.

STACPOOLE, Henry de Vere
(1863–1951)
Irish physician and writer, born in Kingstown (Dun Laoghaire), the son of a Presbyterian minister. Educated at Malvern College and St George's and St Mary's Hospitals in London, he made several voyages as a ship's doctor. He was the author of over 50 popular novels, including *The Blue Lagoon* (1909), *The Pearl Fishers* (1915) and *Green Coral* (1935). He wrote his autobiography in *Men and Mice* (1942 and 1945).

STADLER, Ernst
(1892–1914)
German poet, the most intelligent, stable and perhaps most gifted of all the expressionist poets who arose in Germany just before World War I, in which he quickly perished. He was a Rhodes Scholar at Oxford (1906–8). He was born in Alsace. Ironically, he had been involved, with **René Schickele**, in trying to cement Franco–German relations, and with Schikele had founded the magazine *Der Stürm*. He was influenced in his poetry above all by **Stefan George** and **Whitman**. Only one volume was published in his lifetime—it was immature, but *Der Aufbruch* (1915, 'The Uprising') is one of the most important collections of its time. In subsequent works, he had begun to form his own inimitable, visionary style. He was a coherent and sensible critic, and of him most of all, of all the German writers who died in World War I, it may be said that he would have gone on to become a towering figure. His loss was equal to that

in Great Britain of **Wilfred Owen** and **Ivor Gurney**.

STAËL, Anne Louise Germaine Necker, Madame de (Baronness of Staël-Holstein)
(1766–1817)

French writer, born in Paris, the only child of the financier and statesman, Jacques Necker. In her girlhood she wrote romantic comedies, tragedies, novels, essays and *Lettres sur Rousseau* (1789). She married in 1786 the Baron Eric Magnus of Staël-Holstein (1742–1802), the bankrupt Swedish ambassador in Paris. She bore him two sons (1790 and 1792) and a daughter (1797), but the marriage was unhappy and she had many affairs, most notably with the writer **Constant de Rebecque**. Her vast enthusiasms and the passionate intensity of her affections created an irresistible personality. Her brilliant *salon* became the centre of political discussion, but with the Revolution and her father's fall she felt compelled to leave Paris for Coppet, by Lake Geneva, in 1792. From Coppet she went to England, where at Mickleham in Surrey she was surrounded by Talleyrand and others of the French *émigrés*. She joined her husband at Coppet in May 1793, and published her *Réflexions sur le procès de la reine* ('Reflections on the Queen's Trial') in the vain hope of saving Marie Antoinette. In 1795 she returned to Paris, where her husband had re-established himself as ambassador. She prepared for a political role by her *Réflexions sur la paix intérieure* (1795, 'Reflections on Civil Peace'), but was advised to return to Coppet. Her *Influence des passions* appeared in 1796. Napoleon allowed her to return to Paris in 1797, but received her friendly advances with such studied coldness that admiration soon turned to hatred. In 1800 she published her famous *Littérature et ses rapports avec les institutions sociales* (Eng trans *The Influence of Literature upon Society*, 1812). Returning to Paris in 1802, she published the novel *Delphine* (Eng trans 1903). At length her friendship with disaffected men like Moreau and Bernadotte, and the appearance of Necker's *Dernières vues* ('Last Views'), exhausted the patience of Napoleon, and in the autumn of 1803 she received orders to keep 40 leagues from Paris. Her husband had died, and in December 1803 she set out with her children for Weimar, where she dazzled the court, and met **Schiller** and **Goethe**. In Berlin she made the acquaintance of **August von Schlegel**. She next went to Vienna, but learned of her father's death and returned to Coppet, writing the touching eulogy, *Du caractère de M. Necker* (1818, Eng trans *Memoirs of the Private Life of My Father*, 1818). Then she set out for Italy with Schlegel, Wilhelm von Humboldt, and Bonstetten, but in 1805 returned to Coppet, where once again a brilliant circle assembled, to write *Corinne* (1807, Eng trans 1807), a romance which at once brought her European fame. She visited Germany at the end of 1807, and began to turn for consolation to religion—she was a Protestant. Her famous *De l'Allemagne* (Eng trans *Germany*, 1813) was finished in 1810, passed by the censor, and partly printed, when the whole impression was seized and destroyed, and she herself was ordered from Paris to Coppet. The work was published by John Murray in London in 1813. But her exile had now become a bitter reality; she found herself surrounded by spies. She escaped secretly to Berne, and from there made her way to St Petersburg, Stockholm and (1813) London. In England admiration reached its climax on the publication of *De l'Allemagne*, the most finished of all her works. It revealed Germany to the French and made Romanticism—she was the first to use the word—acceptable to the Latin peoples. Louis XVIII welcomed her to Paris in 1814, and the two million francs which Necker had left in the Treasury was honourably paid to her. The return of Napoleon drove her from Paris, and she spent the winter in Italy for the sake of the health of Albert de Rocca, an Italian officer in the French service, whom she had married secretly in 1816. She returned to Paris, where she died. Her surviving son and daughter published her unfinished *Considérations sur la Révolution française* (1818, Eng trans *Considerations on the Principal Events of the French Revolution*, 1818), considered her masterpiece by **Charles Sainte-Beuve**, the *Dix Années d'exil* (1821, Eng trans *Ten Years' Exile*, 1821), and her complete works (1820–1).

▷G Andrews, *Madame de Staël* (1964)

STAFF, Leopold
(1878–1957)

Polish poet, whose work has remained respected by his successors—many of whom turned to him for help. Originally he was associated with the pre-World War I movement, 'Young Poland', which brought Polish poetry into the 20th century; of later movements, he had most in common with, and most influence upon, the relatively conservative *Skamander* group. His own later poetry is exemplary in its simplicity and humanness. He could be compared to **Jaroslav Seifert** in Czechoslovakia, but was more gifted. There are English translations of his work in *An Empty Room* (1983)

STAFFORD, Jean
(1915–79)

American short-story writer and novelist, born in Covina, California. Her father had an unsuccessful career as a writer of westerns under the pseudonyms Jack Wonder and Ben Delight. Educated at Colorado University, she won a travelling scholarship to Heidelberg, Germany, in 1936. Returning to the USA she met literary establishment figures **Randall Jarrell**, and **Robert Lowell**, whom she married against his family's wishes in 1940. She worked on the *Southern Review* and taught at Flushing College. *Boston Adventure*, her first novel, was published in 1944 to great praise; *The Mountain Lion*, her second, appeared in 1947. But her stormy marriage to Lowell collapsed and she was admitted to psycho-alcoholic clinics. Divorced from Lowell in 1948, she married Oliver Jensen, an editor on *Life*, in 1950. In 1952 *The Catherine Wheel* was published. She was divorced for a second time in 1955 and later married the writer A J Liebling. She taught throughout the 1960s and published diverse books: short stories, children's books and interviews with the mother of Lee Harvey Oswald, *A Mother in History* (1966). She was one of America's most admired short-story writers, and her *Collected Stories* appeared in 1969, winning a Pulitzer Prize.

STAFFORD, William Edgar
(1914–)

American poet and lecturer, born in Hutchinson, Kansas, whose verse has won him many awards. His first collection, *West of Your City*, appeared in 1960, and a major volume, *Roving Across Fields: A Conversation and Uncollected Poems 1942–1982*, in 1983. Stafford is a poet of the western landscape, of rivers and mountains and the natural world. Several critics claim that in attempting to discover an ethical system by which man might live in harmony with himself and his environment, Stafford is reaffirming the original and central values of the American way of life. Among his other books is *Down in My Heart* (1947), which records Stafford's experiences as a conscientious objector during World War II.

▷ *You Must Revise Your Life* (1986); Donald Hall (ed), *Writing the Australian Crawl: Views on the Writer's Vocation* (1978)

STAGNELIUS, Erik Johan
(1793–1823)

Swedish Romantic poet, son of the Bishop of Kalmar. After graduating at Uppsala he became an unsalaried civil servant in Stockholm. He led a solitary life, and suffered ill-health which was exacerbated by alcohol and laudanum. After his death, of unknown causes, his works were collected and published (1824–6). His considerable output, all written within a decade, comprises epics, like *Vladimir den store* (1817, 'Vladimir the

Great'), plays like *Martyrerna* ('The Martyrs') and *Bacchanterna* (1822, 'The Bacchanalians'), but it is above all his lyric poetry, much of it found in *Liljan i Saron* (1821, 'Lilies of Sharon'), which captures the essence of his genius. He was constantly torn between idealism and erotic sensualism. The object of his desire often centred on Amanda—whether she was a factual character is uncertain and perhaps unimportant for in his poems she became a vision of all that is desirable in woman. Influenced by his reading of **Plato**, Schelling, theosophy, gnosticism and Romantic contemporaries, he gradually accepted the view of two warring factions in the universe: God versus the Devil, spiritual versus temporal; in the beginning the soul (*Anima*), Christ and the angels inhabited the perfect world but were tempted by an evil angel (*Achamot*) and plunged into an earthly existence under Demiurgen. Man's spirit is captive but can reach out to its divine origins in dreams, memories, poetry, beauty, nature and, above all, faith in Christ's redeeming sacrifice. Stagnelius contrasts dream and reality in a series of poems like *Endymion*, *Narcissus* and *Till Natten* ('Ode to Night'). In other poems themes from nature symbolize the soul's longing for heaven, as in *Floden*— 'The River'—and *Flyttfåglarna*—'Migrant Birds'. Stagnelius employs a variety of verse forms with consummate skill. His poetry has an in-built tension between eroticism and spiritualism and is imbued with nature symbolism and imagery couched in the most melodic language in Swedish literature. Little-known in his lifetime, he became posthumously the most influential of Swedish Romantics on succeeding generations.

▷ D Andreae, *Erik Stagnelius* (1919)

STAMPA, Gaspara
(c.1523–1554)

Italian poet, born in Padua. Her substantial *Rime* (1554), published after her death by her sister, tell the story of her love (in Venice) for the Count Collitano do Collato, who betrayed her. She was certainly the finest Italian woman poet of the Renaissance, and superior to many of the men. The poems, **Petrarch**an in style, but often subtly mocking male pretensions, are opulent, passionate and challenging to the prevailing ideas of the time. Since their rediscovery in the last century, by romantic critics, they have been much reinterpreted—and she has justly been compared, although she did not share all her predilections, with **Sappho**.

▷ J Tusiani (ed and translator), *Italian Poets of the Renaissance* (1971); *Modern Language Notes*, 90 (1975)

STANDISH, Burt L *see* **PATTEN, William Gilbert**

STANKOVIĆ, Borisav
(1876–1927)

Serbian story writer, novelist and dramatist, born in Vranje. By profession he was a civil servant. His story collection *Iz starog jevandjelja* (1899, 'From the Old Gospel') established him as the finest chronicler of his native region, with its Eastern-influenced traditions and its 'backwardness', of which he saw both sides. His most famous work is the novel *Necista krv* (1911, Eng trans *Sophka*, 1932), which describes the decline of a once great commercial family, but whose main theme is its careful account of a woman who marries a young boy. He is still widely read.

STAPLEDON, (William) Olaf
(1886–1950)

English science-fiction writer and social philosopher. He was born and raised in Wallasey, Cheshire, educated at Balliol College, Oxford, and took a doctorate at Liverpool University. During World War I, he served with the Friends' Ambulance Unit, and much of his writing, fictional and otherwise, is merely a vehicle for ideas about pacifism and social meliorism. Stapledon worked as a teacher, headmaster, shipping clerk with the Merseyside-based Holt Co, and as a Workers' Educational Association lecturer. His first novel, *Last and First Men* (1930), was 'a story of the near and far future', expressing his conviction that human survival depended on disarmament, the maintenance of peace and the rational management of social ills. It was followed by *Last Men in London* (1932) and by the underrated *Odd John* (1935) and *Starmaker* (1937). With **Norman Mailer** and the composer Shostakovitch, Stapledon spoke at the communist-fronted Waldorf Peace Conference in New York in 1946. A more discursive version of his philosophy can be found in *A Modern Theory of Ethics* (1929), which anticipated much of his better-known later work.
▷L A Fiedler, *Olaf Stapledon: A Man Divided* (1988)

STARING, Antonie Christiaan Wynand
(1747–1840)

Dutch poet, born in Gendringen who, living in an age of mostly florid rhetoric, provided a new example. His poetry was at first in the sentimental style of his age; then, under the influence of **Feith** and **Huygens**, he started to write in a new, terse manner. He wrote both narrative poems and a few starkly observed nature lyrics. **Potgieter** wrote illuminatingly about him in his *Kritische Studien* (1875, 'Critical Studies').

STARK, Dame Freya Madeline
(1893–1993)

English writer and traveller, born in Paris. She spent her childhood in England and Italy, and attended Bedford College, London University, under the tutelage of W P Ker, Professor of Literature. She was a nurse on the Italian front during World War I, and afterwards studied Arabic at the School of Oriental and African Studies, London University, and was invited to Baghdad by the Prime Minister. There she worked on the *Baghdad Times*, followed the crusader routes and mapped the Valley of the Assassins in Luristan, described in *Valley of the Assassins* (1934). During World War II she worked for the Ministry of Information in Aden and Cairo, and was personal assistant to Lady Wavell, describing her experiences in *West is East* (1945). She travelled extensively, financed by her writings, in Europe, Asia and the Middle East. She produced more than 30 titles, including *The Southern Gates of Arabia* (1938), *Traveller's Prelude* (1950), *Beyond Euphrates* (1951), *The Coast of Incense* (1953), *Dust in the Lion's Paw* (1961) and *The Journey's Echo* (1963).

STATIUS, Publius Papinius
(c.45–96)

Roman poet, born in Naples, the son of a school-teacher. He won a poetry prize in Naples, and went to Rome, where he flourished as a court poet and a brilliant improviser in the favour of Domitian until 94, when he retired to Naples. His major work was the *Thebaïs*, an epic in 12 books on the struggle between the brothers Eteocles and Polynices of Thebes. Of another epic, the *Achilleïs*, only a fragment remains. His *Silvae*, or occasional verses, have freshness and vigour.
▷H E Butler, *Post Augustan Poetry* (1909)

STEAD, Christina Ellen
(1902–83)

Australian novelist, born in Rockdale, Sydney, the daughter of David George Stead, a leading English naturalist and writer. She trained as a teacher, but in 1928 left Australia for Europe, where she lived in London and Paris, working as a secretary in a Paris bank (1930–5). She went to live in Spain but left at the outbreak of war and, with her banker husband, settled in the USA. From 1943 to 1944 she was an instructor at the Workshop in the Novel at New York University, and in 1943 became a senior writer for M-G-M in Hollywood. *The Salzburg Tales*, her first collection of stories, was published in 1934, but it was *Seven Poor Men of Sydney* (1934) which attracted attention, with its interweaving of dissimilar but casually connected lives. Her own experience was used to good effect in *House of All Nations* (1938), a critical look at the world of big finance, and her autobiographical novel, *The Man Who Loved Children* (1940), describes suffocating family life under an egoistical father. Her later novels of suburban American and European life were less successful. In all she published 11 novels, including *A Little Tea, A Little Chat* (1948), *The People with the Dogs* (1952), *Cotter's England* (1956) and *Miss Herbert (The Suburban Wife)* (1976). The author of several novellas and the contributor of many short stories to the *New Yorker*, she left the USA in 1947 and settled in England, but finally returned to her homeland in 1974, in which year she was the first winner of the **Patrick White** Literary Award. *I'm Dying Laughing*, a novel begun in the 1940s and ridiculing American Hollywood radicals, was published posthumously in 1986.

▷ R G Geering, *Christina Stead* (1969)

STEAD, C(hristian) K(arlson)
(1932–)

New Zealand poet, critic and novelist, probably still better known for his pioneering study of literary modernism, *The New Poetic: Yeats to Eliot* (1964), than for his verse. He was born and educated in Auckland, where he returned as Professor of English in 1969. His poetry appeared in book form relatively late; *Whether the Will is Free* (1964) gathered work from the mid-50s onwards. It was followed by a novel, *Smith's Dream* (1971), and further verse collections: *Crossing the Bar* (1972), *Quesada* (1975) and *Walking Westward* (1979). The last of these introduced her interest in 'Open Form', which draws on some aspects of American Objectivism in an attempt to make the poem experiential rather than iconic, following the internal logic of the events described. In 1984 Stead published a second novel, *All Visitors Ashore*, which explores the psychology of living and writing on the opposite side of the globe from Europe.

STEDMAN, Edmund Clarence
(1833–1908)

American poet, critic and financier, born in Hartford, Connecticut. He studied at Yale, was war correspondent of the *New York World* (1861–3), and then became a New York stockbroker and banker. He published *Poems* (1860), *Victorian Poets* (1875), *Edgar Allan Poe* (1880), *Poets of America* (1886), *Nature of Poetry* (1892), *Victorian Anthology* (1896), and other works. He also co-edited an important *Library of American Literature*, issued in 11 volumes between 1888 and 1890, which was a significant taste-maker and may have affected early modernist writers.

STEELE, Sir Richard
(1672–1729)

Irish essayist, dramatist and politician, born in Dublin. He was educated at Charterhouse, where **Joseph Addison** was a contemporary, and Merton College, Oxford, after which he entered the army as a cadet in the Life Guards. Reacting against military life, he wrote *The Christian Hero* (1701), to show that the gentlemanly virtues can be practised only on a Christian basis. He next wrote three comedies, *The Funeral, or Grief à la mode* (1702), *The Tender Husband* (1703) and *The Lying Lover* (1704). In 1706 he became gentleman waiter to Prince George of Denmark, and in 1707 Robert Harley (Earl of Oxford) appointed him gazetteer. Steele's first venture in periodical literature, *The Tatler*, ran from 1709 to 1711 and was published on Tuesdays, Thursdays and Saturdays to suit the outgoing post-coaches. Its predecessor was **Daniel Defoe**'s *Review*, and like the *Review* included items of current news, but after No. 83 it concentrated on social and moral essays, with occasional articles on literature, usually written by Addison who had joined forces with Steele on issue No. 18. The chief fare, however, was social comedy, which covered the affectations and vices of society. These were exposed by humorous satire, with the aim of putting the Christian at ease in society. Christianity was to become fashionable and to this end—for formal preaching was unpalatable—a wealth of concrete social situations and types was created, including coffee-house politicians, 'pretty fellows', pedants and bores at every level of society. The coffee houses and chocolate houses provided most of these types, but society women and the family were the theme of many of the articles, for Steele's plea in *The Christian Hero* for a more chivalrous attitude to women implied the correction of female frivolity in high places and the insistence on the family as the source of genuine happiness. Steele is perhaps at his best in scenes of domestic felicity (cf Nos 95, 104 and 150), and these contain the intrusion of bourgeois sentiment and morality which was to be the mark of the age, in contrast to the aristocratic ethos of the Restoration. The beginnings of the domestic novel are here, not only in the relations between the pseudonymous editor, Isaac Bickerstaff, and his half-sister Jennie, but in numerous conversation pieces and in the social context provided by the Trumpet Club, forerunner of the more famous Spectator Club which Steele first outlined in No. 2 of that periodical, though Addison wrote most

of the articles. In 1713 Steele entered parliament, but was expelled the following year on account of a pamphlet, *The Crisis*, written in favour of the house of Hanover, a cause to which his periodical *The Englishman* was also devoted. He was rewarded on the succession of George I with the appointment of supervisor of Drury Lane theatre, and a knighthood followed. In 1718 a difference on constitutional procedure led to an estrangement from Addison, who was in the ministry, and loss of his office. In 1722 financial troubles made him retire to Wales, where he lived until his death. His letters to his wife ('dearest Prue'), whom he married in 1707, attest the sincerity of his sermons on married love.
▷R P Bond, *The Tatler* (1972)

STEELE, Wilbur Daniel
(1886–1970)

American short-story writer, novelist and playwright, born in North Carolina. Sometimes derided as a middle-brow writer, his short fiction, most often set in either Carolina or New England, is ingeniously plotted. *How Beautiful with Shoes*, dramatized in association with Anthony Brown in 1935, is the story of a southern beauty kidnapped by a maniac. She persuades her abductor that she is Mary, he is Jesus, and so she is his mother. He goes to sleep at her feet and is captured. *The Best Short Stories of Wilbur Daniel Steele* (1946) drew from four earlier collections.

STEEN, Marguerite
(1894–1975)

English writer, born in Liverpool, who began as a dancer and actress before writing a succession of quite popular, capably written, but essentially superficial novels such as *Gilt Cage* (1927). She wrote a life of William Nicolson (1943), whose companion she had been. Her most successful novel was *The Sun is my Undoing* (1941). Her work is now largely forgotten.

STEFÁNSSON, Daviô
(1895–1964)

Icelandic poet, born in Fagriskógur, Eyjafjörður. Educated in Akureyri and Reykjavík, he worked as a librarian in Akureyri (1925–52). He became the most popular Romantic poet of his time with a series of volumes of lyrical poetry, starting with *Svartar fjaðrir* (1919, 'Black Feathers') and including *Kveðjur* (1924, 'Greetings'), *Í byggðum* (1933, 'In Human Habitations') and *Aðnorðran* (1936, 'From the North'). He also wrote a historical novel, *Sólon Íslandus* (2 vols, 1940), and a successful play, *Gullna Hliðið* (1941, 'The Golden Gate').

▷E Heage, introduction to *The Golden Gate* (1967)

STEFANYK, Vasyl
(1871–1936)

Ukrainian poet and story writer, born in the small village of Rusiv. He is generally taken to have been Ukraine's greatest short-story writer, but the Soviets discouraged praise of him because of what they considered to be his lack of political commitment. His outstanding collection is *Kaminny khrest* (1900, Eng trans *The Stone Cross*, 1971). His style is laconic, often making use of local dialect, and his tales rarely exceed a few pages in length.
▷D S Struk, *A Study of Vasyl Stefanyk* (1973)

STEGNER, Wallace Earle
(1909–93)

American novelist and short-story writer. He was born in Lake Mills, Iowa, and educated there, in Utah and California. He worked on various campuses around the country, publishing his first novel, *Remembering Laughter* (1937), while teaching in Wisconsin. His fiction is largely concerned with life in the rural Mid-West and he has written various nonfiction accounts of American life and landscape; the best known is *Wolf Willow* (1962). Other novels include *On a Darkling Plain* (1940), *The Big Rock Candy Mountain* (1943), *Second Growth* (1947) and *A Shooting Star* (1961). The best of the short stories are in *The Women on the Wall* (1950). Stegner returned to form in the 1970s and won the Pulitzer Prize for *Angle of Repose* (1971).
▷F G and M G Robinson, *Wallace Stegner* (1977)

STEIN, Gertrude
(1874–1946)

American writer, born in Allegheny, Pennsylvania. She spent her early years in Vienna, Paris and San Francisco, and then studied psychology at Radcliffe College under William James, and medicine at Johns Hopkins University, but settled in Paris, where she was absorbed into the world of experimental art and letters. She sometimes attempted to apply the theories of abstract painting to her own writing, which led to a magnified reputation for obscurity and meaningless repetition. From 1907 she shared an apartment with a close friend from San Francisco, Alice B Toklas. Her influence on contemporary artists—particularly Picasso—is probably less than she imagined, though her collection of pictures was representative of the best of its era. Her first book, *Three Lives* (1908), reveals a sensitive ear for speech rhythms, and by far the larger part of her work is immediately comprehensible. The prose of *Tender Buttons* (1914) is repetitive, canonic and extremely musical. *The Making of Americans* (1925) is a vast, virtually unreadable family saga. She took a more ironic stance in the playfully titled *The Autobiography of Alice B. Toklas* (1933) and *Everybody's Autobiography* (1937). *Four Saints in Three Acts* (1934) and *The Mother Of Us All* (1947) were operas with music by Virgil Thomson. She stayed in Germany in the village of Chloz during World War II, and afterwards wrote *Wars I Have Seen* (1945) and the novel, *Brewsie and Willie* (1946), about the liberation by American soldiers.

▷ J Hobhouse, *Everybody Who Was Anybody: a biography of Gertrude Stein* (1975)

STEINARR, Steinn, pseud of Aðalsteinn Kristmundsson
(1908–58)

Icelandic poet, born in Nauteyrarhreppur, north Iceland. A pioneer of Modernist poetry in Iceland, he moved to Reykjavík and joined the Communist Party as a young man. He wrote poetry of tremendous skill and sensibility which became progressively more abstract and metaphysical. His chief works were *Rauður loginn brann* (1934, 'The Red Flame Burned'), *Spor í sandi* (1940, 'Tracks in the Sand'), *Ferð án fyrirheits* (1942, 'Journey without Promise'), and his final masterpiece, *Tíminn og vatnið* (1948, 'Time and Water').

STEINBECK, John Ernest
(1902–68)

American novelist, winner of the Nobel Prize for literature, born in Salinas, California. He studied marine biology at Stanford University and worked as an agricultural labourer and semi-skilled technician, writing steadily. *Tortilla Flat* (1935), his first novel of repute, is a faithful picture of the shifting *paisanos* of California, foreshadowing the solidarity which characterizes his major work, *The Grapes of Wrath* (1939), a study of the poor in the face of disaster and threatened disintegration. His journalistic grasp of significant detail and pictorial essence make this book a powerful plea for consideration of human values and common justice. It led to much-needed reform, and won for Steinbeck the 1940 Pulitzer Prize. His other works include *In Dubious Battle* (1935), *Of Mice and Men* (1937), *The Moon is Down* (1942), *East of Eden* (1952) and *Winter of our Discontent* (1961), as well as the light-hearted and humorous *Cannery Row* (1945), *The Wayward Bus* (1942) and *The Short Reign of Pippin IV* (1957). He won the Nobel Prize for literature in 1962, a testament to his currently undervalued liberal humanism and generous solidarities.

▷ E Steinbeck and R Wallsten (eds), *John Steinbeck: A Life in Letters* (1975); J Parini, *John Steinbeck: A Biography* (1994)

STEINER, Rudolph
(1861–1925)

German thinker who created the movement called Anthroposophy ('wisdom about man'). This, initially inferred from his understanding of the ideas of **Goethe**, but also drawing upon Eastern religions, particularly Indian, is based upon what Steiner called 'supersensible perception'. Anthroposophists believe that human consciousness is in a process of continual evolution. Anthroposophy has been greatly, and on the whole ignorantly, ridiculed. But although some of its precepts—such as reincarnation—are hard for many Western minds to grasp, and it is certainly hard to follow Steiner's own complex and ill-written expositions, it has also been very successfully influential in the realms of music, education (there are many Steiner schools in Great Britain, the USA and other countries) and farming. More to the point here, it has had a subtle effect on 20th-century literature. Not all the writers who have been influenced by it, or by aspects of it, have admitted to it, but two who did are the Russian **Andrei Bely** and the Italian **Arturo Onofri**; both of these, in particular Bely, were influential in their own right. It has many Gnostic features in common with the ideas of **Gurdjieff** and Ouspensky; **Jung** was not unsympathetic to it.

▷ *Knowledge of the Higher Worlds* (1923)

STENDHAL, pseud of Henri Marie Beyle
(1783–1842)

French novelist, born in Grenoble, where he was educated at the École Centrale. During a Bohemian youth he wrote for the theatre but his plays are poorly constructed and stiff. A cousin offered him a post in the Ministry of War, and from 1800 he followed Napoleon's campaigns in Italy, Germany, Russia and Austria. Between wars he spent his time in Paris drawing-rooms and theatres. When Napoleon fell he retired to Italy, adopted his pseudonym, and began to write books on Italian painting (*Histoire de la Peinture en Italie*, 1817), on Haydn and Mozart, and travels in Italy (*Rome, Naples et Florence en 1817*, Eng trans *Rome, Naples and Florence*, 1818), as well as copious journalism. In 1821 the Austrian police expelled him from the country, and on his return to Paris he completed his book *De l'Amour* (1822, Eng trans *On Love*, 1928). After the 1830 revolution he was appointed Consul at Trieste and Civitavecchia, but his health deteriorated and he returned to Paris where he started a biography of Napoleon. His recognized masterpieces, *Le Rouge et le Noir* (1830, Eng trans

Red and Black, 1900; better known as *Scarlet and Black*, the title of a 1938 translation), and *La Chartreuse de Parme* (1839, Eng trans 1895), were published in 1830 and 1839 respectively. The first follows the rise and decline of Julien Sorel, a provincial youth in the France of the Restoration who can be relied on to make a drama out of a crisis. The second details the fortunes of Fabrice del Dongo at an insignificant Italian court during the same period. Though seminal French novels of the 19th century, neither received great understanding during his lifetime. Among his other novels are *Armance* (1822, Eng trans 1895) and *L'Abbesse de Castro* (1839, 'The Abbess of Castro'). *Lucien Leuwen* (1894, Eng trans 1951) and *Lamiel* (1889, Eng trans 1951), both unfinished, were published posthumously. Autobiographical volumes include his *Journal* (1888, selections translated as *Private Diaries*, 1955), *La Vie de Henri Brulard* (1890, Eng trans *The Life of Henry Brulard*, 1925) and *Souvenirs d'égotisme* (1892, Eng trans *Memoirs of an Egotist*, 1949).

STEPHANSSON, Stephan G, originally Stefán Guðmundarson
(1853–1927)

Icelandic-born Canadian poet, born in Kirkjuhóll in Skagafjörður. He emigrated with his family to North America in 1873, and worked as a railroad labourer and farmhand in Wisconsin before settling in Markerville, Alberta, as a farmer in 1889. There he raised a large family, took a prominent part in local affairs, and in the evenings composed several volumes of poetry in Icelandic, including *Úti á víðavangi* (1894, 'Out in the Open'), *Á ferð og flugi* (1900, 'En route'), and his major work, *Andvökur* (6 vols, 1909–38, 'Wakeful Nights'). A lifelong socialist, he expressed his horror of war in a controversial volume, *Vígslóði* (1920, 'The War Trail'). Recognized as one of the finest of Icelandic poets, his works also give a vivid picture of landscapes and conditions in western Canada.
▷S Nordal, *Stephan Stephansson* (1959)

STEPHENS, James
(1882–1950)

Irish poet, born in Dublin. Sent to an orphanage as a child, he found work as a solicitor's clerk. His first published work was a volume of poems, *Insurrections* (1909), followed by his first novel, *The Charwoman's Daughter* (1912). *The Crock of Gold* (1912), a prose fantasy, made him famous, and turned him into a full-time writer. His later volumes were *Songs from the Clay* (1914), *The Demi-Gods* (1914), *Reincarnation* (1917) and *Deirdre* (1923). He moved to London in 1924. His

Collected Poems was first published in 1926, and revised in 1954.
▷H Pyle, *James Stephens, writings and an account of his life* (1968)

STEPHENS, Meic
(1938–)

Welsh poet and editor, born in Treforest, near Pontypridd, Glamorgan and educated at the universities of Wales and Rennes. He founded *Poetry Wales* in 1965; his poetry collections include *Exiles All* (1973). He compiled and edited *The Oxford Companion to the Literature of Wales* in both Welsh and English (1986), edited the second edition of the *Oxford Illustrated Literary Guide to Great Britain and Ireland* (1992), and is co-editor of the *Writers of Wales* series (1970–), which comprises of 80 volumes. He was literature director of the Welsh Arts Council from 1967 to 1990.

STERLING, George
(1869–1926)

American poet, said to be the 'original' for the character of Russ Brissenden in **Jack London**'s *Martin Eden*. Sterling was a noted Bohemian. Born in New York he went out to the West Coast where the arch-stylist **Ambrose Bierce** took him under his wing. Sterling's poems, which he always submitted firstly to Bierce, for the master's approval, were exotic and rhythmical. Collections include *A Wine of Wizardry* (1909) and *The House of Orchids* (1911). Like his fictional counterpart, Sterling committed suicide.

STERLING, John
(1806–44)

Scottish writer, born at Kames Castle on the Island of Bute. Educated at Glasgow University and Trinity College, Cambridge, he turned to writing, and in 1828 bought the literary magazine, *The Athenaeum*, which he edited. He published numerous essays and long poems, and a novel, *Arthur Coningsby* (1833). He is best known as the subject of **Thomas Carlyle**'s *Life of John Sterling* (1851).

STERN, Gladys
(1890–1973)

English novelist, born in London, who was educated at English, German and Swiss schools and the Royal Academy of Dramatic Art. Brought up in the Jewish faith, she converted to Roman Catholicism after World War II. In 1914, at the outbreak of World War I, she published her first novel, *Pantomime*, although she is remembered now for her series of five semi-autobiographical novels tracing the fortunes of the Rakonitz family. The first, *Tents of Israel*, appeared in 1924, and the last, *The Young Matriarch*, 18 years later in 1942. The most memorable character, Toni, is a determined woman with a fierce sense of family tradition and independence, who builds a successful business empire which she refuses to relinquish for marriage, something she sees as ephemeral. Of her five-volume series of autobiography (1941–56), most notable are *All In Good Time* (1954) and *The Way it Worked Out* (1956).

STERN, Richard Gustave
(1928–)

American novelist and short-story writer, born in New York, long-time Professor of English at Chicago University. Stern's fiction is told in a spare, uninvolved fashion. His short stories *are* short, his novels concise. The most memorable of his books remains the first: *Golk* (1960) featured a comic adult character who sits, eats and sleeps in front of the TV. Stern has enjoyed various encounters with other writers. His correspondence with **Flannery O'Connor** appears in *The Habit of Being*, her collected letters, and *Stitch* (1965) resulted from a meeting with **Ezra Pound**.

STERNE, Laurence
(1713–68)

Irish novelist, born in Clonmel, County Tipperary, the son of an impoverished infantry ensign who died when the boy was two. His early youth was a struggle. In 1724 he was sent to Halifax Grammar School in Yorkshire and, seven years later, to Jesus College, Cambridge. In 1738 he was ordained, and appointed to the living of Sutton-on-the-Forest and made a prebendary of York, where his great-grandfather had been archbishop. In 1758 his marriage failed and his wife was committed to a lunatic asylum. In 1759 he wrote *The History of a Good Warm Watchcoat* (not published until after his death), and also the first two volumes of *The Life and Opinions of Tristram Shandy*, first published in York, but published anew in London in 1760. The public welcomed it; and in April **Robert Dodsley** brought out a second edition. This was followed by *Sermons* of the 'Rev. Mr Yorick'. In 1761, vols III and IV of *Tristram* came out, Sterne having meanwhile moved to Coxwold, thenceforward his infrequent home. Between 1761 and 1767 the rest of *Tristram* appeared; Sterne, whose health was now failing, was spending much of his time in France and Italy. *A Sentimental Journey through France and Italy* appeared in 1768; and the author died in London of pleurisy. Few writers have displayed such mastery over every form of humour both in situation and in character, a humour at times coming near to that of his acknowledged master **Cervantes**.

Yet the wild eccentricity of his manner and arrangement—a deliberate and usually successful bid for laughter—was also the convenient cloak for what some, such as **Oliver Goldsmith**, might call a singularly slipshod literary style. His indecencies, less gross than those of **Jonathan Swift** or **François Rabelais**, are all too prurient. He was unscrupulous in his borrowings. His pathos too often takes the form of overstrained sentimentalism. Yet this very sentimentalism was also his strength. For Sterne's great contribution to the development of the novel was to widen its scope and loosen its structure; and in his hands it became the channel for the utterance of the writer's own sentiments. His *Letters from Yorick to Eliza* (1775 9) contained his correspondence with a young married woman to whom he was devoted.

▷ W C Cross, *Life and Times of Laurence Sterne* (1909–25)

STERNHEIM, Carl
(1878–1942)

German playwright and novelist, born in Leipzig. He was enjoying huge popularity during the 1920s, only to have his aggressive, cynical, debunking plays prohibited when the Nazis came to power. Sternheim excelled at satire, poking fun at the bourgeoisie in such plays as *Die Hose* (1911, 'The Knickers'), in which a woman loses her knickers in an embarrassing situation. The 'indelicacy' of the play caused a minor sensation when it was first produced. Other plays include *Burger Schippel* (1913), a caustic farce about a lowly plumber, who becomes a member of a bourgeois singing group and accumulates bourgeois ideals in the process.

STEVENS, Wallace
(1879–1955)

American poet, born in Reading, Pennsylvania. His father, of Dutch descent, was a lawyer for the Reading Hardware Company and wrote poetry. His education began at private schools, then schools attached to Lutheran churches and later Reading Boys' High School. He enrolled at Harvard (1897–1900) and afterwards went to New York where he started out in journalism but was neither successful nor happy. He entered New York Law School in 1901 and at the age of 28 began working for various law firms, ultimately becoming a diligent executive with an insurance company in Hartford, Connecticut. Poetry was a spare-time activity, and his first collection, *Harmonium*, was not published until 1923. His poetic career falls into three phases: 1898–1900, 1907–24 and 1928–55. Most of his early work, both poems and short stories, was published in *The Harvard Advocate*. In 1907 he began composing poems for Elsie Moll, his future wife. It was from the late 1920s to the middle 1950s, however, that he published the work that has established him as one of the century's great poets: *Ideas of Order* (1936), *The Man With the Blue Guitar* (1937), *Parts of a World* (1942), *Transport to Summer* (1947) and *The Auroras of Autumn* (1950). *Collected Poems* was published in 1954. Critics invariably point out the great influence of the French Symbolist movement, but he drew from many sources and his poems range over an extraordinary variety of subjects. His constant theme was the exploration of aesthetic experience as the key to fundamental reality.

▷G Lensing, *Wallace Stevens: a poet's growth* (1986)

STEVENSON, Anne Katherine
(1933–)

English poet, critic and biographer, born in Cambridge. She was educated in the USA, where she lived for several years, resulting in a volume of poetry, *Living in America* (1965). Returning to Britain, she ·published her second collection, *Reversals* (1969). Other volumes include *Travelling Behind Glass* (1974), *Enough of Green* (1977) and *Selected Poems* (1987). Her poetry is personal, elegiac, emotionally honest, and reflects the sense of the landscape of wherever she happens to be living at the time of writing, be it the Sierra Nevada (*Reversals*) or the north-east coast of Scotland (*Enough of Green*). Her authorized biography of **Sylvia Plath**, *Bitter Fame*, was published in 1989.

STEVENSON, Robert Louis Balfour
(1850–94)

Scottish author, born in Edinburgh, grandson of the engineer Robert Stevenson and son of Thomas Stevenson, engineer to the Board of Northern Lighthouses. A constant invalid in childhood, he was educated at The Edinburgh Academy (1861–3) before his ill-health forced the family to travel abroad. He studied engineering at Edinburgh University for a session (1867) with a view to the family calling, but transferred to law, becoming an advocate in 1875. His true inclination, however, was for writing. He collaborated in four mediocre plays, but for the next few years he travelled, mainly in France. His *Inland Voyage* (1878) describes a canoe tour in Belgium and northern France, and his *Travels with a Donkey in the Cevennes* describes a tour undertaken in the same year. In 1876 he was at Fontainebleau (which he made the subject of travel sketches), and it was at the neighbouring Grez that he met Fanny Osbourne, née Vandegrift (1840–1914), an

American separated from her husband. He followed her to America and they married in 1880, after her divorce. His return to Europe with his wife and stepson Lloyd Osbourne marked the beginning of a struggle against tuberculosis which his natural gaiety as a writer conceals. His wife and stepson have described their makeshift homes—Davos, Pitlochry and elsewhere—yet despite difficult circumstances he was 'making himself' as a writer not only of travel sketches but also of essays and short stories which found their way into magazines. *Thrawn Janet*, a story in the vernacular, appeared in *Cornhill Magazine* (1881), although an earlier tale, *An Old Song*, appeared in 1877 and was then lost until it was located and republished in 1982. *The Merry Men* was published serially in 1882, the same year as *The New Arabian Nights*. *Treasure Island*, the perfect romantic thriller, brought him fame in 1883 and his most successful adventure story, *Kidnapped*, appeared in 1886. *Catriona* (1893), introducing the love element, was also very popular. *The Master of Ballantrae* (1889) is a study in evil of a sort not uncommon in Scottish fiction, but also includes the wildest adventures. *The Strange Case of Dr Jekyll and Mr Hyde* (1886) is not a romance, but it further illustrates Stevenson's metaphysical interest in evil. *The Black Arrow* (1888) is of a rather lower quality, but *Weir of Hermiston* (published posthumously in 1896), though unfinished, is acclaimed by some as his masterpiece, its scope larger, and the issues involved more serious. *St Ives*, which was also left unfinished, was completed by Sir **Arthur Quiller Couch** in 1897. Stevenson's work as an essayist is seen at its best in *Virginibus Puerisque* (1881) and *Familiar Studies of Men and Books* (1882). *A Child's Garden of Verses* (1885) is not poetry in the adult sense, but it is one of the best recollections of childhood in verse. *Underwoods* (1887) illustrates his predilection for preaching in prose or verse; here the poetry is of the good talker rather than the singer, and the tone is usually nostalgic. Only occasionally, as in *The Woodman*, does he touch on metaphysical problems, but vernacular poems such as *A Lowden Sabbath Morn* subtly describe the Calvinism he had renounced but which intrigued him to the end. In 1889 Stevenson settled in Samoa and there with his devoted wife and stepson he spent the last five years of his life on his estate of Vailima, which gives its name to the incomparable series of letters, written to his friend Sidney Colvin. His experiences in the South Seas gave rise to two important long stories, 'The Beach of Falesá' (1893) and 'The Ebb-Tide' (1894), both of which indict European colonialism.

▷J C Furnas, *Voyage to Windward* (1950)

STEVENSON, William
(d.1575)

English scholar. He entered Christ's College, Cambridge, in 1546, and became a fellow; he is known to have staged plays there. He was probably the author of the earliest surviving English comedy, *Gammer Gurton's Needle* (1553), sometimes attributed to John Still or John Bridges.

▷F P Wilson, *English Drama, 1485–1585* (1969)

STEWART, Douglas Alexander
(1913–85)

New Zealand-born Australian author, born in Eltham, Taranaki, and educated at the Victoria University College. For 40 years he was at the forefront of Australian writing, first as assistant and then, from 1940 to 1961, as editor of the 'Red Page' in the *Bulletin* magazine. Stewart then became literary editor for the old-established Australian publishing house of Angus & Robertson, a position which he held until his retirement in 1971. His early books of lyric verse—*Green Lions* (1936) and *The White Cry* (1939)—evoke his homeland; his first Australian verse was in *The Dosser in Springtime* (1946) in which he began to use ballad form, later put to dramatic effect in a sequence on the infamous Scottish Massacre at *Glencoe* (1947). His verse drama *Fire in the Snow* (1939), on Scott's ill-fated Antarctic expedition, is a classic of radio drama. *Back of Beyond* (1954) and *The Birdsville Track* (1955) re-create his visual impressions of the life of the rugged interior. His last verse was in *Rutherford* (1962), the title poem addressed to his compatriot the New Zealand atomic scientist. *Selected Poems* was published in 1963 (rev edn 1973) and *Collected Poems 1936–1967* in 1967. He edited a number of anthologies including *Modern Australian Verse* (1964) and, with Nancy Keesing, two collections of bush ballads (1955–7). Biographies include *Norman Lindsay, a Personal Memoir* (1975) and *A Man of Sydney, an Appreciation of Kenneth Slessor* (1977).

▷*Springtime in Taranaki* (1983); J McAuley, in *The Literature of Australia* (1964, ed G Dalton)

STEWART, George R(ippey)
(1895–1980)

American novelist, biographer and historian of the American West. Stewart's *Names on the Land* (1945) is the standard work on American place-names. His study of the westward overland route, *The California Trail* (1962), is a good example of his skill as a popularizer of history and scholarly information. His fiction is orthodox in style. *Doctor's Oral* (1939) tells the nerve-racking story of a graduate having to undergo an oral exam. *Storm* (1941) is a novelistic treatment of a weather system's journey across the States from the West coast to the East. Stewart held academic posts at Columbia, Michigan and Berkeley, and wrote a biography of **Bret Harte** (1931).

STEWART, Harold
(1916–)

Australian poet and orientalist, born in Drummoyne, Sydney, latterly resident in Japan. His first poems in *Phoenix Wings: Poems 1940–46* (1948) and *Orpheus and Other Poems* (1956) showed the considerable influence of Buddhist and Taoist culture. He has published two popular collections of translations of Japanese *haiku*, *A Net of Fireflies* (1960) and *A Chime of Windbells* (1969), but *By the Old Walls of Kyoto: A Yearly Cycle of Landscape Poems* (1979) is a more ambitious essay which, in a long narrative sequence, melds Japanese and western poetical traditions, illuminated by Stewart's own scholarly commentary.

STEWART, J(ohn) I(nnes) M(ackintosh), pseud **Michael Innes**
(1906–)

Scottish novelist and critic, born in Edinburgh. Educated at Edinburgh Academy and Oriel College, Oxford, he subsequently lectured at Leeds University, the University of Adelaide and Queen's University, Belfast. From 1969 to 1973 he was Reader in English Literature, Oxford University. The novels written under his own name are largely set in an academic and artistic milieu among the middle and upper classes. A prolific writer, he is best known in this vein for the so-called 'Pattullo' sequence, located in the sequestered world of the dons. *A Use of Riches* (1957) and *The Last Tresilians* (1963) are generally regarded as his most important works. As Michael Innes he has made an important contribution to the thriller genre. His range is remarkably wide, from intricate, locked-room type murders to large-scale crime intrigues. In his detectives, John Appleby, the gentleman turned policeman, and the formidable Inspector Cadover, he has created two memorable characters. Notable titles include *Hamlet, Revenge!* (1937), *Lament for a Makar* (1938) and *What Happened at Hazelwood?* (1946). He has also written works on **Kipling**, **Hardy**, **Joyce** and **Conrad**.

STEWART, Mary (Florence Elinor, Lady)
(1916–)

English romantic novelist, born in County Durham, and for several years a lecturer in English at Durham University. A popular and prolific novelist, she began writing her exotic love stories when complications during her first pregnancy left her unable to have children, and achieved instant success with *Madam, Will You Talk?* (1954) and such titles as *Nine Coaches Waiting* (1958) and *This Rough Magic* (1964). In the seventies she published a trilogy about Merlin, which began with *The Crystal Cave* (1970); she has also written several books for children, including *A Walk in Wolf Wood* (1980).

STICKNEY, (Joseph) Trumbull
(1874–1904)

American poet, born in Geneva. He spent his childhood in Europe. He was a brilliant scholar who, with **William Vaughn Moody**, tried to resuscitate verse drama in a manner which (the fragments he left suggest) anticipated later developments. His lyrical poetry is better accomplished and more sincerely felt than that of the majority of his contemporaries, but he did not live long enough to fulfil his promise, and high claims made for him by **James Reeves** and Séan Haldane are hardly justified. He died prematurely as a result of a brain tumour.
▷S Haldane and J Reeves (eds), *Homage to Stickney* (1968); S Haldane, *The Fright of Time: Stickney* (1970); A B Whittle (ed), *The Poems* (1973)

STIERNHIELM, Georg, originally Olofsson
(1598–1672)

Swedish poet and linguist, known as the 'father of Swedish poetry'. He was elevated to the peerage with the name of Stiernhielm in 1631, and held various government appointments, including councillor of war (1663) and director of the college of antiquities (1667). He was the first Swedish poet to write in hexameters, in *Hercules* (1658), an epic allegorical poem about a young man at the crossroads of life. He helped to reform and purify the Swedish language by studying Old Norse literature and incorporating the old vocabulary into modern Swedish.
▷B Swartling, *Georg Stiernhielm* (1909)

STIFTER, Adalbert
(1805–68)

Austrian novelist and painter, born in Oberplan, Bohemia. He studied at Vienna, and as private tutor to various aristocratic families had several unhappy love affairs. Deeply disturbed by the Revolution of 1848, he settled in Linz and became an official in the Ministry of Education. Unhappiness and illness terminated in suicide. His humanism, his love of traditional values and his belief in the greatness of life pervade the *Bildungsroman*, *Der Nachsommer* (1857, 'The Indian Summer'),

Witiko (1865–7), a heroic tale set in 12th-century Bohemia, and the short stories *Der Condor* (1840, Eng trans *The Condor*, 1946). He was also a considerable painter of city views. He wrote two collections of stories, *Studien* (1844–50, augmented 1855) and *Bunte Steine* (1853, Eng trans *Rock Crystal*, 1945).
▷A Blackett, *Adalbert Stifter, a critical study* (1948)

STIRLING, William Alexander, 1st Earl of
(c.1567–1640)

Scottish poet and courtier, born in Alva, Clackmannanshire. A tutor of young noblemen, in 1613 he was attached to the household of Prince Charles (Charles I). He had already published a collection of songs and madrigals in *Aurora* (1604); in 1614 he published part one of his huge poem *Doomesday*, (part two, 1637). He received in 1621 the grant of 'Nova Scotia'—a vast tract in North America soon rendered valueless by French expansion. In 1631 he was made sole printer of King James VI and I's version of the Psalms. From 1626 until his death he was Secretary of State for Scotland. He was created Viscount (1630) and Earl of Stirling (1633), also Earl of Dovan (1639), but he died insolvent in London. His tragedies include *Darius* (1603), *Croesus* (1604), *The Alexandrean Tragedy* (1605) and *Julius Caesar* (1607).
▷T H McGrail, *Sir William Alexander Stirling* (1940)

STIVENS, Dal(las George)
(1911–)

Australian writer, painter and amateur naturalist, born in Blayney, New South Wales, primarily known for his short stories which appeared in many anthologies and in eight collected volumes, of which the most representative is *Selected Stories 1936–1968* (1969). Stivens's love of the 'tall story' shows in *The Demon Bowler and other Cricket Stories* (1979). Five diverse novels include *A Horse of Air* (1970), an account of a dreamlike expedition into the central Australian desert in search of the mythical Night Parrot. Stivens received the **Patrick White** Literary Award in 1981.

STOCKTON, Frank R (Francis Richard)
(1834–1902)

American humorist and engraver, born in Philadelphia. He became assistant editor of *St Nicholas*, and first attracted notice by his stories for children. He is best known as author of *Rudder Grange* (1879). Later works include *The Lady, or the Tiger?* (1884), a teasing fairy tale still left unresolved in a sequel,

Mrs Cliff's Yacht (1896); *The Great Stone of Sardis* (1897) and *The Girl at Cobhurst* (1898).

▷M J Griffin, *Frank R Stockton: A Critical Biography* (1939)

STODDARD, Charles
(1843–1909)

American poet and travel writer, born in Rochester, New York. Because he attended college at Oakland he is often referred to as a Californian author. His travel book *South-Sea Idyls* (1873) became popular in Great Britain as well as in America, and influenced **Robert Louis Stevenson**, his friend, as well as starting a craze for Polynesia. His *Poems* (1867) were edited by **Bret Harte**. *A Troubled Heart* (1885) is the touching story of his conversion to Roman Catholicism. He was close to **Mark Twain**, and acted as his assistant.

STODDARD, Richard Henry
(1825–1903)

American poet and critic, born in Hingham, Massachusetts. He wrote literary reviews for New York periodicals from 1860. His poems include *Songs in Summer* (1857), *The Book of the East* (1867) and *Lion's Cub* (1891). *Under the Evening Lamp* (1893) and *Recollections* (1903) contain literary studies. His wife, Elizabeth Drew, née Barstow (1823–1902), was a novelist and poet.

STOKER, Bram, properly Abraham
(1847–1912)

Irish writer, born in Dublin. He was educated at Trinity College, Dublin, and studied law and science. He entered the civil service, but turned to literature, and partnered Henry Irving in running the Lyceum Theatre in London from 1878 to 1905. He wrote *Personal Reminiscences of Henry Irving* (1906). He is best remembered for the classic vampire story *Dracula* (1897), but wrote a number of other novels dealing with futuristic and occult themes, including *The Jewel of the Seven Stars* (1903), *The Lady of the Shroud* (1909) and *The Lair of the White Worm* (1911). *Dracula* has often been filmed, but usually with little accurate reference to the book.

STOLBERG, Christian, Count of
(1748–1821)

German poet, born in Hamburg. He was one of the Göttingen poet band and was in the public service of Holstein (1777–1800). Besides writing poems, he translated **Sophocles**.

▷E Schmidt, *Christian Stolberg* (1893)

STOLBERG, Friedrich Leopold, Count of
(1750–1819)

German poet, brother of **Christian Stolberg**. He was also a member of the Göttingen school, and was in the Danish service (1789–1800). Then turning Catholic, he published a history of Christianity. He produced poems, dramas and translations from the Greek.

ST OMER, Garth
(1931–)

West Indian novelist, born in Castries, St Lucia, who excels in reproducing the *patois* of his native island. His grim novel *J-, Black Bam and Marauders* (1972), set in St Lucia, impressed critics by its 'odour of decay'.

STONE, Irving, originally Irving Tennenbaum
(1903–89)

American popular novelist and playwright, born in San Francisco. He took his stepfather's name when his parents divorced and his mother remarried. He studied political science at the University of California at Berkeley, and worked as a saxophonist in a dance band. He wrote 25 books in all and is sometimes credited with having created the nonfiction novel. *Lust for Life* (1934), based on the life of Van Gogh, became a bestseller and did much to enhance the Dutch painter's reputation in the USA. *The Agony and the Ecstasy* (1961) fictionalizes the life of Michelangelo. He also wrote *Love Is Eternal* (1954), about Abraham Lincoln's wife; *Passions of the Mind* (1971), about **Sigmund Freud**; *The Origin* (1980), about Charles Darwin, and *Depths of Glory* (1985), about Camille Pissarro.

STONE, Louis, originally William Lewis Stone
(1871–1935)

English-born Australian novelist, born in Leicestershire, who migrated to Brisbane with his family in 1884. He is known mainly for his first book, *Jonah* (1911), which became a popular television series in 1982. He was one of the first to write of the town rather than the bush; his hero is the leader of a Sydney street gang who, through the help of Ma Yabsley, becomes a shopowner but fails to find fulfilment. His other novel, *Betty Wayside*, was serialized in 1914 but appeared the next year only in bowdlerized form; the passions of a lady pianist were not considered appropriate for the bookshops of the day.

STONE, Robert Anthony
(1937–)

American novelist, born in Brooklyn. *Dog Soldiers* (1974) has been Stone's most successful book to date. It tells of a Vietnam veteran involving his wife in heroin smuggling. Stone and Judith Rascoe turned it into a screenplay, filmed in the USA as *Who'll Stop The Rain?* (1978). *A Flag for Sunrise* (1982), set in a Latin-American country during a revolution, is a vehicle for political and philosophical views.

STOPPARD, Tom, originally **Thomas Straussler**
(1937–)

British dramatist, born in Zlin, Czechoslovakia. He went to England in 1946 from India, his mother having married a British army officer after being widowed in Singapore during World War II. The family settled in Bristol, and after attending schools in Nottingham and Yorkshire, Stoppard became a journalist in Bristol. In 1960 after his first play, *A Walk on the Water*, he went to London as a freelance journalist and theatre critic and wrote radio plays including *Albert's Bridge* (1967), *The Dissolution of Dominic Boot* and *M is for Moon Among Other Things* (both 1964). He made his name in 1967 with *Rosencrantz and Guildenstern are Dead* at the Edinburgh Festival, which then transferred to the National Theatre, having won the *Evening Standard* Award. Built around the two 'attendant lords' in **Shakespeare**'s *Hamlet*, the play hilariously examines the meaninglessness of life and questions the possibility of free will. His aim is a 'perfect marriage between the play of ideas and farce': *Jumpers*, commissioned in 1972 by the National Theatre, is a farcical satire of logical positivism, and *Travesties* (1974), written for the Royal Shakespeare Company, has **James Joyce**, Lenin and the Dadaist painter Tristan Zara, who all happened to be living in Zürich during World War I, working together on an amateur production of **Oscar Wilde**'s *The Importance of Being Earnest*. His other plays include *The Real Inspector Hound* (1968), *Dirty Linen* (1976), *Professional Foul* (1977, written for television and inspired by Amnesty International's Prisoner of Conscience Year), *Night and Day* (1978), *On the Razzle* (1981) and *The Real Thing* (1982). In 1977 he collaborated with André Previn on a 'play for actors and orchestra', *Every Good Boy Deserves Favour*, performed with the London Symphony Orchestra. He has also written a novel, *Lord Malaquist and Mr Moon* (1966), short stories, screenplays and film scripts, including *The Russian House* and *Billy Bathgate*. He was married for 20 years (until 1992) to Miriam Stoppard (1937–), a doctor and broadcaster specializing in child care and health.
▷M Billington, *Stoppard the Playwright* (1987)

STOREY, David Malcolm
(1933–)

English dramatist and novelist, born in Wakefield. An art student and professional Rugby League player, he made a hit with his novel, *This Sporting Life* (1960). His later novels include *Pasmore* (1972), *Saville* (1976) and *Present Times* (1984). His first play, *The Restoration of Arnold Middleton*, was staged at the Royal Court Theatre, London, in 1966. *In Celebration* (1969) was followed by *The Contractor* (1969), and *Home* (1970), a piece for four elderly characters who, it transpires, are the inmates of an asylum. *The Changing Room* (1971) deals with a rugby football team. Subsequent plays include *Cromwell* and *The Farm* (both 1973), and *Life Class* (1974), based on his experiences as an art student. *Mother's Day* (1976) and *Sisters* (1978) were premièred in Manchester, while *Early Days* (1980) and *The March on Russia* (1989) and *Stages* (1992) were put on at the National Theatre. He published a collection of poems, *Storey's Lives*, in 1992.
▷J R Taylor, *David Storey* (1974)

STORM, Theodor Woldsen
(1817–88)

German poet and story writer, born in Husum in Schleswig-Holstein. He was a magistrate and judge (1864–80), and had a wide circle of literary acquaintances and correspondents. His early writings are lyric poems, culminating in the cycle *Tiefe Schatten* (1865, 'Deep Shadows'), but he is remembered for his tales, characterized by a vivid, often eerie descriptive power.
▷G Storm, *Theodor Storm* (1912)

STORNI, Alfonsina
(1892–1938)

Argentinian feminist and poet, born in Switzerland. Starting young as an actress with a travelling theatrical company, she later became a teacher and journalist. Her poetry is largely concerned with love and sexual passion. Her books include *La inquietud del rosal* (1916, 'The Solicitude of the Rosebush'), *El dulce daño* (1918, 'Sweet Injury'), *Ocre* (1925, 'Ochre') and *Mascarillo y trébol* (1938). She committed suicide on discovering that she was suffering from cancer. An edition of her verse appeared in 1961.

STORY, William Wetmore
(1819–95)

American poet and sculptor, born in Salem, Massachusetts, son of Joseph Story. He practised law in Boston, but in 1856 settled in Rome and devoted himself to poetry and sculpture. His writings include *Poems*

(1847,1856,1886), *Roba di Roma* (1862), *Castle of St Angelo* (1877), *He and She* (1883), *Fiametta* (1885), *Excursions* (1891) and *A Poet's Portfolio* (1894).

▷H James, *William Wetmore Story and His Friends* (1903)

STOUT, Rex Todhunter
(1886–1975)

American detective-story writer, born in Noblesville, Indiana. Before becoming a writer he invented a school banking system that was installed in 400 cities throughout the USA. His great creation is Nero Wolfe, the phenomenally fat private eye who with the help of his confidential assistant, Archie Goodwin, got to the bottom of numerous mysteries, among them *The League of Frightened Men* (1935), *Black Orchids* (1942) and *A Family Affair* (1975).

▷J McAleer, *Rex Stout: a biography* (1977)

STOW, (Julian) Randolph
(1935–)

Australian novelist, poet and librettist. He was born in Geraldton, Western Australia, worked as an anthropologist in Australia and Papua New Guinea—which provided the background to *Visitants* (1979)—and subsequently taught at the universities of Adelaide, Leeds (UK) and Western Australia. His first novel was *A Haunted Land* (1956), followed by *The Bystander* (1957), which suggested his developing interest in the Jungian unconscious and in visionary 'madness'. *Tourmaline* (1963) was an Australian version of T S Eliot's *The Waste Land*. Perhaps his best novel is *The Merry-Go-Round in the Sea* (1965), which links such visions into recent history by contrasting the bitter 'experience' of a former POW with his innocent young cousin. In 1968 and 1969, while living in England, Stow wrote libretti for two music-theatre works by the composer Peter Maxwell Davies: *Eight Songs for a Mad King* and *Miss Donnithorne's Maggot*. Later novels include *The Girl Green as Elderflower* (1980) and *The Suburbs of Hell* (1984). *Midnite* (1967) is a notable book for children; Stow's verse is collected in *A Counterfeit Silence* (1969).

▷R Willbanks, *Randolph Stow* (1978)

STOWE, Harriet Elizabeth, née Beecher
(1811–96)

American novelist, daughter of Lyman Beecher, born in Litchfield, Connecticut. She was brought up with puritanical strictness and joined her sister Catherine Beecher at her Connecticut Female Seminary at Hartford in 1824. In 1836 she married the Rev Calvin Ellis Stowe, a theological professor at Lane

Seminary, with whom she settled at Brunswick, Maine in 1850. She contributed sketches of southern life to *Western Monthly Magazine*, and won a short-story competition with *A New England Sketch* (1834). She became famous for her *Uncle Tom's Cabin* (1852), prompted by the passing of the Fugitive Slave Law, which immediately focused anti-slavery sentiment in the North. Her second anti-slavery novel, *Dred* (1856), had a record sale in Britain, largely thanks to a review by **George Eliot**, but she lost her popularity with *Lady Byron Vindicated* (1870), although the charges made against **Byron** in the book were later proven. She wrote a host of other books, fiction, biography and children's books. Her best books deal with New England life, such as *The Minister's Wooing* (1859) and *Old Town Folks* (1869).

▷F Wilson, *Crusader in Crinoline* (1941)

STRACHEY, (Giles) Lytton
(1880–1932)

English biographer, born in London, the son of an Indian civil engineer and soldier. Educated at Leamington College and Liverpool University, where he read history, and Trinity College, Cambridge, he was a book reviewer for the *Spectator* (1904–14). He began his writing career as a critic with *Landmarks in French Literature* (1912), which shows clearly his affinities with **Charles Sainte-Beuve** and his francophile sympathies. He was a conscientious objector during World War I. *Eminent Victorians* (1918) was a literary bombshell, constituting, as it did, a vigorous, impertinent challenge to Victorian smug self-assurance. The irony, the mordant wit, the ruthless pinpointing of foible that was his method of evoking character, demolished stuffed legendary figures, and this book was a turning-point in the art of biography. After him, mere accumulation of facts (the product of conscientious hacks) could no longer be the accepted thing. Through Strachey, biography had become a literary genre. He followed up his success with *Queen Victoria* (1921), *Books and Characters, French and English* (1922), *Elizabeth and Essex: A Tragic History* (1928), *Portraits and Miniatures* (1931) and *Characters and Commentaries* (1933).

▷M Holroyd, *Lytton Strachey* (2 vols, 1967–8)

STRAMM, August
(1874–1915)

German poet and dramatist, born in Münster. He was by far the most radical, not to say strident, of the Expressionist group, and has even been called a 'Futurist'. He was killed on the Russian front while serving as a captain in the army. He was a leading contributor to the Expressionist magazine *Der Sturm*. His hectic

Schreidramen, 'scream-plays', less lasting and successful than his ceaselessly experimental war poetry, but important in the development of the European theatre, were in the 'telegraphic' style which he made his own. His terse poetry, equally staccato, but composed with great care, is still effective and moving. His play *Erwachen* (1915, 'Awakening') is translated in *Seven Expressionist Plays* (1968).

▷ C Middleton and M Hamburger (eds), *Modern German Poetry 1910–1969* (1962)

STRAND, Mark
(1934–)

Canadian-born American poet and translator (of **Borges**'s *Texas*), born in Summerside, Prince Edward Island; he moved to America at the age of four. His spare verses are clearly mainly inspired from his reading of **Samuel Beckett**—who, however, as one of Strand's critics has declared, 'is of course the master' (of 'withholding information'). In his ambitious long poem 'The Untelling' Strand has, characteristically, written, 'Although I have tried to return, I have always/ended here, where I am now'. He was the United States Poet Laureate 1990–1.

▷ *Selected Poems* (1980); D Kirby, *Mark Strand and the Poet's Place in Contemporary Culture* (1990)

STRAPAROLA, Giovan Francesco
(d.c.1557)

Italian novelist, born in Caravaggio. Between 1550 and 1554 he published *Piacevoli notti* (Eng trans *The Nights of Straparola*, 1894), a collection of 74 stories set on the island of Murano, in the style of the *Decameron*. Although relatively unsophisticated, they were popular throughout the 16th century.

▷ G Boscardi, *Le Novelle di Giovan Francesco Straparola* (1952)

STRASHIMIROV, Anton
(1872–1937)

Bulgarian novelist and playwright. His work has often been characterized as somewhat spoiled by 'unruly' elements, or too 'rough' in style; but his unconventionality, and his tormented prose, are now due for reappraisal as more proto-expressionist than marred by academic improprieties. He has not been liked by all Bulgarians because he openly espoused the Macedonian cause, and even entered politics (1911) to do so. His most famous play is *Vampir* (1902, 'Vampire'). *Tvorchestvo i khivot* (1930, 'Creativity and Life') is one of the most interesting and informative of all Bulgarian biographies.

▷ C Manning and R Smal-Stocki, *The History of Modern Bulgarian Literature* (1960)

STREATFEILD, (Mary) Noel
(1895–1986)

English children's author, born in Amberley, Sussex. She rebelled against her strict upbringing in a Victorian clergyman's family, becoming an actress and novelist and, with the massive success of her first children's book, *Ballet Shoes* (1936), established herself as the long-standing doyenne of children's writers. She followed this delightful backstage story of strong-willed child performers with further 'career' novels such as *Tennis Shoes* (1937), *The Painted Garden* (1949) and *White Boots* (1951). Perhaps her finest book, *The Circus is Coming* (1938), won the Carnegie Medal. Although the later work never surpassed her first successes, she continued to write popular and accomplished novels with sparky, believable characters.

STREUVELS, Stjin, pseud of **Frank Lateur**
(1871–1969)

Belgian (Flemish) novelist from Heule. He began as the baker for his village, but after 15 years took to writing, depicting the Flemish peasantry, it has been said, 'with the plastic power of a Breughel'. One of his novels, *Langs de wegen* (1902), was translated at the behest of **Ford Madox Ford**, as *Old Jan* (1936). **Willem Elsschot** also admired him, and under his real name of Alfons de Ridder wrote a book on him (1908). Streuvels' greatest novel, of major proportions, is the haunting and hallucinatory *Het leven en de dood in den ast* (1926, 'Life and Death in den ast'), in which two men have to keep a fire going in a chickory-drying house while a tramp dies.

▷ A Denedts, *Stijn Streuvels* (1955)

STRIBLING, T(heodore) S(igismund)
(1881–1965)

American novelist, born in Clifton, Tennessee. Despite recent positive revaluation by Southern critics, Stribling is still an underestimated and neglected novelist, even though he gave inspiration to **Faulkner**. Like Faulkner, in his early life he wrote (for money and to attain freedom from wage-slavery) 'morally uplifting' tales for Sunday School readers, and pulp fiction. Although he never evolved a distinguished style—he could be pretentious—it is hard to see how he could have told his masterpiece, the trilogy consisting of *The Forge* (1931), *The Store* (1932) and *Unfinished Cathedral* (1934), the middle novel of which won him a Pulitzer Prize, other than in the way he did. This, which remains one of the most finely observed accounts of the ante-bellum South, tells the story of the rise of Miltaides Vaiden from poor man to rich landowner.

▷ W Eckley, *Stribling* (1975)

STRINDBERG, (Johan) August
(1849–1912)

Swedish dramatist and novelist, born in Stockholm, considered the greatest writer of modern Sweden. After uncompleted studies at Uppsala University, he returned to Stockholm and worked as a private tutor, actor, journalist and librarian while attempting to begin his career as an author. He had a turbulent personal life, including three unsuccessful marriages and periods of severe persecution mania. He had a propensity for involvement in cultural and personal feuds and lived abroad for long periods, mainly in France and Italy. His first major play was *Mäster Olof* (1872), a historical drama—a genre he was to return to prolifically in the years around 1900 with, for instance, *Gustav Vasa* and *Erik XIV* (both 1899). His breakthrough came with a satirical novel about the art circles of Stockholm, *Röda rummet* (1879, 'The Red Room'), which created an uproar, but is regarded as marking both the arrival of the modern realistic novel in Sweden and that of the naturalist movement. His later naturalist novel *Hemsöborna* (1887, 'The People of Hemsö'), his sunniest work, has become a popular classic. Two collections of short stories, *Giftas I* and *II* (1884–6, 'Married'), put forward his ideas on marriage, women and emancipation. A small incident in the first volume led to his trial on a charge of blasphemy, of which he was acquitted. He then published a bitter autobiography, *Tjänstekvinnans son* (1886, 'The Son of a Servant'), to be followed by *Le Plaidoyer d'un fou* (1888, 'Confessions of a Fool'). The battle between the sexes is at the centre of the three major plays that follow: *Fadren* (1887, 'The Father'), *Fröken Julie* (1888, 'Miss Julie') and *Fordringsägare* (1889, 'The Creditors'). In the 1890s he turned for a time to experiments with the occult and pseudo-science, suffered a spiritual crisis verging on madness, and underwent a conversion with elements of Swedenborgian mysticism, all of which he described in his autobiographical *Inferno* (1897), and which is given dramatic expression in the trilogy *Till Damaskus* (1898–1904, 'To Damascus'). His efforts to find a dramatic means of expressing inner reality in those and later plays, like *Ett drömspel* (1902, 'A Dream Play'), make him a forerunner of expressionism and a major influence on modern theatre.

▷ G Brandell, *Strindberg, ett författarliv* (1987); E Sprigge, *The Strange Life of Strindberg* (1949)

STRITTMATTER, Erwin
(1912–)

German novelist and dramatist, born in Spremburg. Initially a communist, he deserted from the Nazi army and later held high offices in East Germany. He then became a journalist. His play *Katzgraben* (1954), a rural comedy in verse, received high praise from, and was produced by, **Bertolt Brecht**. His novels are dutifully socialist realist, but somewhat redeemed from this by their humour and rustic comedy.

STRODE, William
(1602–45)

English poet and clergyman, born in Plympton. He was educated at Westminster School and Christ Church, Oxford, where he became canon and public orator. He is best known for his elegies and lyric verse, which were rediscovered by Bertram Dobell in 1907, and for his tragi-comedy, *The Floating Island*, performed by the students of Christ Church before Charles I in 1636.

STRONG, Leonard Alfred George
(1896–1958)

English novelist and poet, born in Plymouth. He was educated at Brighton College and Wadham College, Oxford. He took up school teaching until he established a reputation as a lyric poet with *Dublin Days* (1921), *The Lowery Road* (1923), and other volumes. He also wrote novels, including *Dewer Rides* (1929), a macabre novel set in Dartmoor, and *Deliverance* (1955). His collection of short stories, *Travellers*, won the James Tait Black Memorial Prize in 1945.

▷ *Green Memory* (1961)

STRUG, Andrzej, pseud of Tadeusz Galecki
(1871–1937)

Polish novelist. He was exiled to Archangel by the Tsarist Russians, whom he opposed. Always a socialist, he took part in the 1905–6 revolution; he had previously supported Pilsudski, but soon joined the opposition to him after the latter's 1926 coup. But his novels transcend the political, even though they depict the dark side of capitalism, and deal for the most part with 'the underground people'. His novels have not yet been translated into English; *Jutro* (1909, 'Tomorrow'), from his earlier period, and the stories in *Klucz otchlani* (1929, 'The Key to the Precipice'), are amongst the most notable.

STRUGATSKY, Boris and Arkady Natanovitch

STRUGATSKY, Boris Natanovitch
(1931–)
STRUGATSKY, Arkady Natanovitch
(1925–91)

Russian science-fiction writers, born in the Soviet Union. As brothers they began to collaborate on science-fiction writing in the early 1950s. Their early works formed a generally optimistic future history on an interplanetary scale, but a change of tone crept in with books like *Trudno byt' bogom* (1964, Eng trans *Hard To be a God*, 1973), which were more ambiguous in their view of utopian political solutions. They began to draw on folklore and fable as well as science fiction, while their growing political and ideological disillusion is evident in invented worlds which reflect the bureaucratic disasters of their homeland, as in *Skazha o troike* (1968, Eng trans *Tale of the Troika*, 1972) or *Piknik na obochine* (1972, Eng trans *Roadside Picnic*, 1977). Subsequent works like *Za milliard let do kontsa sveta* (1976–7, Eng trans *Definitely Maybe: A Manuscript Discovered under Unusual Circumstances*, 1978) and the later *Grad obrechennyi* (1989, 'The Doomed City') were even bleaker in their vision.

STRUTHER, Jan, pseud of Mrs Joyce Anstruther Placzek
(1901–53)

English writer, born in London. Her most successful creation was Mrs Miniver, whose activities, first narrated in articles to *The Times*, became the subject of one of the best films of World War II.

STUART, Donald
(1913–83)

Australian writer, born in Cottesloe, Perth. He was the author of 'outback' novels, mainly set in the north-west of Western Australia, the first of which was *Yandy* (1950). *The Driven* (1961) tells of a long cattle drive and the developing relationships of the drover boss and his aboriginal and white companions. A semi-autobiographical series of six books, *The Conjuror's Years*, began in 1974 with *Prince of My Country* and concluded with *I Think I'll Live* (1981). His *Morning Star, Evening Star: Tales of Outback Australia* (1973) are unaffected yarns of the hardships and rewards, and the interaction of blacks and whites, in this harsh corner of the country.

STUART, Francis
(1902–)

Irish novelist, poet and dramatist, born in Queensland, Australia, of Irish parents. He was imprisoned on the Republican side during the Irish Civil War in the 1920s. During the next decade and a half he made a prolific start to his writing career, producing 10 novels, a collection of poems, two plays, *Things to Love For: Notes For an Autobiography* (1934) and the ever-useful pamphlet *Racing for Pleasure and Profit in Ireland and Elsewhere* (1937). He spent the duration of World War II in Berlin, from where he broadcasted to the neutral Republic of Ireland. Following post-war imprisonment as a collaborator, he published a series of passionately felt 'epiphanies from a ghetto', among them *The Pillar of Cloud* (1948), *Redemption* (1949) and *Victors and Vanquished* (1958). The searingly autobiographical *Black List, Section H* was published in 1972, followed by *Memorial* in 1973. A series of novels produced in the 1980s examines the uneasy relationship of virtue to the victimized, and is explicated most clearly in his essay *The Abandoned Snail Shell* (1987). ▷G Elborn, *Francis Stuart: A Life* (1990)

STUART, Jesse Hilton
(1907–84)

American novelist, short-story writer and poet, born in Kentucky. Stuart, who worked as a farmer, newspaper editor and schoolteacher, began his writing career with short stories and gradually built them up into novel-length narratives. He held on to the short-story writer's technique of beginning *in medias res* and has been called the 'Grandma Moses' of the American novel, because of the primitive qualities of his characterization and plots. *Taps for Private Tussie* (1943) was a bestseller. The lasting legacy of Stuart's prolific career will not be one of his titles, but his placing of the Appalachians and the oral style of the region's characters on the literary map.

STUART, Ruth McEnery
(1849–1917)

American novelist and short-story writer, born in Louisiana and specializing in accurate rendering of Southern dialects. Most of her books were written after she had left the South to live in New York. Her biggest success was with *Sonny* (1896), the story of a poor white, but in other books she demonstrated an acute knowledge of Creoles and Negroes. She is considered better at short narratives than long fiction and *A Golden Wedding and Other Tales* (1893) is a good example of her short-story technique.

STUB, Ambrosius Christofferson
(1705–58)

Danish poet, born in Gummerup. A serious lyrical poet, he became buffoon-poet (drinking-songs, moralizing pieces) to wealthy men, received no recognition in his lifetime,

and died a pauper. His serious poetry, unpublished until some years after his death, has been compared to that of **Robert Herrick**.
▷H Brix, *Ambrosius Stub* (1960, in Danish)

STUCKENBERG, Viggo
(1863–1905)

Danish poet, born in Copenhagen. He was an important figure in the lyrical revival of the 1890s. His works include *Fagre Ord* (1895) and *Flyvende Sommer* (1898).

STURGEON, Theodore, pseud of **Edward Hamilton**
(1918–85)

American science-fiction writer, born in Staten Island, New York. He published his first stories while at sea as a teenager, and his first science fiction in 1939. Most of his work falls into the period 1946–61, with long fallow years on either side. He revealed a willingness to explore areas usually shunned in genre circles, particularly sexuality, and his best works have a satisfying sense of discovery, and a marvellous exuberance in the writing. He wrote many short stories, which have been collected in numerous editions, and several novels. His best-known work is *More Than Human* (1953), three linked novellas in which a half-dozen 'freaks' find themselves empowered through the force of their combined minds. His other works include a western, *The Rare Breed* (1966), and historical and detective fiction.

STURGES, Preston, originally **Edmund Preston Biden**
(1898–1959)

American screenwriter and film director, born in Chicago. Reared by his mother in a bohemian lifestyle that propelled him through Europe and America, he worked in the cosmetics industry, developing a 'kiss-proof' lipstick, before making his mark as a Broadway dramatist with the play *The Guinea Pig* (1929). In Hollywood from 1930, he became renowned for the speed and richness of his screenwriting talent, notably on *The Power And The Glory* (1933) and *The Good Fairy* (1935). He won an Oscar for the screenplay of the political satire *The Great McGinty* (1940), which also marked his directorial debut, and over the next five years created a succession of sharp social comedies that combined sophisticated wit with lowbrow slapstick. His most fondly-recalled work includes *The Lady Eve* (1941), *Sullivan's Travels* (1942) and *The Miracle of Morgan's Creek* (1944). Later films, however, failed to recapture the dizzy creativity of the war years. He received a posthumous Laurel Award for Achievement in 1974 from the Writer's Guild Of America.

STURLUSON, Snorri
(1179–1241)

Icelandic historian, poet and chieftain, the outstanding writer of medieval Scandinavia. He was born at Hvammur in western Iceland and fostered at Oddi, the home of the powerful chieftain, Jón Loptsson. He amassed wealth and property, including the estate of Borg (former home of his ancestor, the saga hero **Egil Skallagrímsson**) and Reykholt, where he lived much of his life, and rapidly rose to prominence in national life, becoming law-speaker (president) of the Althing (parliament) for the first time in 1215. It was a time of great civil unrest in Iceland (the so-called Sturlung Age), with warring factions in the Icelandic republic jockeying for power, aided and abetted by King Haakon IV Haakonsson ('the Old') of Norway. Eventually, Snorri was assassinated at the king's behest at his home at Reykholt. As an author, Snorri Sturluson towers over his contemporaries. He wrote *Heimskringla*, a monumental prose history of the kings of Norway down to the year 1177, and compiled a prose account of Norse mythology in his *Prose* (or *Younger*) *Edda*, which is also a handbook of poesy illustrated with his own poetry. He is also believed to have written *Egils saga*, a prose biographical history of his ancestor, Egill Skallagrimsson.
▷M Ciklamin, *Snorri Sturluson* (1978)

STYRON, William
(1925–)

American novelist, born in Newport News, Virginia. His first novel, *Lie Down in Darkness*, appeared in 1951. *Set This House on Fire* (1960) portrayed Americans in Europe after the war and was hugely successful in France. Concerned with oppression in its myriad forms he has tackled the black–white question in *The Confessions of Nat Turner* (1967) and the fate of Holocaust survivors in *Sophie's Choice* (1979). *The Long March* (1953) was a taut novella about army life, and *This Quiet Dust* (1982) a miscellany of pieces.
▷*Darkness Visible: A Memoir of Madness* (1990)

SU TUNG-P'O, pseud of SU SHIH
(1036–1101)

Chinese painter, calligrapher, poet, philosopher and politician from Meishan, Sichuan province. Of peasant origins, his family had only recently moved into the mandarinate. Su Tung-p'o's father as well as his own son were literati, collectively known as 'the three Su'. Su Tung-p'o is almost unanimously referred to as one of the most prominent men of his time, a 'universal genius'. Excelling in all the fields of a literati, he epitomized the cultural ideal of 11th-century Chinese humanism. In addition, his checkered political career ranged from Prime Ministership to exile. A great part of Chinese aesthetics, now being taken for granted, derives from his writings and his formulation of *wen jen hua* (literati painting). According to him, the spiritual process of pictorial creation had to be the fruit of the identification of the painter with the object of his painting: 'To paint the bamboo, it is necessary to have it entirely within yourself'. Thus, he also saw the forms born out of the brush as revealing the state of mind of the painter, another concept which only appeared in the West during the latter half of the 19th century.

▷L Yutang, *The Gay Genius* (1947)

SUBERCASEAUX, Benjamin
(1902–73)

Chilean novelist, essayist and dramatist, born in Santiago. Subercaseaux studied in France, like **Jung**, under the psychiatrist Pierre Janet, to whose pioneer work so many of the French surrealists were devoted. After studying and rejecting Roman Catholicism in Rome, he joined the Waldenses, a heretical sect that renounced violence. His masterpiece, one still shamefully neglected outside Latin America, is the novel *Jemmy Button* (1950, Eng trans 1955). Based on a historical event, that of Robert Fitzroy's taking to England of four Tierro de Fuegian natives in order to expose them to 'Christian instruction', it contrasts the 'civilized' with the 'natural' world, and explores the strange and introspective character of Fitzroy. His play, *Pasión y èpopeya de Halcón Kigero* (1957), is about an Araucanian chief. In his last years he devoted himself to anthropological studies.

▷A T Rioseco, *Breve historia de la literatura chilena* (1956)

SUCKLING, Sir John
(1609–41)

English poet and playwright, born in Norfolk. The archetypal Cavalier, he appeared more concerned with the dress of his troops, on which he spent prodigious sums, than with their military ability. He fought for King Charles I in the unsuccessful war against the Scots in 1639, and later fled abroad, where he may have committed suicide. His four plays include the tragedy *Aglaura* (1637), which was revised and republished as a comedy the following year. It is on his poetry, however, that his reputation rests. The posthumously published *Fragmenta Aurea* (1646) was reprinted in 1648 and 1659;

it contains what is probably his most famous work, 'Why So Pale and Wan, Fond Lover?' He is credited by John Aubrey with having invented 'the game of Cribbidge' [sic].

SUDERMANN, Hermann
(1857–1928)

German dramatist and novelist, born in Matzicken, East Prussia. He wrote a succession of skilful, if superficial, realist plays, *Die Ehre* (1889, 'Honour'), *Sodoms Ende* (1891, 'The Fall of Sodom'), *Heimat* (1893, Eng trans *Magda*, 1896), and others, and equally successful novels, including *Frau Sorge* (1887, Eng trans *Dame Care*, 1891), *Der Katzensteg* (1890, Eng trans *Regine*, 1894) and *Es war* (1894, Eng trans *The Undying Past*, 1906).

▷I Leux, *Hermann Sudermann* (1931)

SUE, (Marie Joseph) Eugène
(1804–57)

French novelist, born in Paris. He served as a surgeon in Spain (1823) and at Navarino Bay (1827) and wrote a vast number of **Byron**ic novels, many of which were dramatized, idealizing the poor to the point of melodramatic absurdity, but nevertheless highly successful at the time. They had a profound influence on **Victor Hugo**, whose *Les Misérables* has much in common with Sue's *Les Mystères de Paris* (1843). Other novels include *Le Juif errant* (1845, 'The Wandering Jew'), *Les Sept Péchés capitaux* (1849, 'The Seven Deadly Sins') and *Les Mystères du peuple* (1849, 'Mysteries of the People'), the last condemned as immoral and seditious. A republican deputy, he was driven into exile in 1851.

▷E de Mirecourt, *Eugène Sue* (1855)

SUERIO, Daniel
(1931–)

Spanish novelist, story writer and journalist, born in the province of La Coruña. Almost alone amongst contemporary Spanish novelists, he writes in the direct tradition of **Pio Baroja**. His realistic novels such as *Estos son sus hermanos* (1965, 'These Are Your Brothers'), about the brutal aftermath of the Civil War, are more successful than his experimental ones, such as the science-fiction *Corte de corteza* (1969, 'Brain Transplant').

SUETONIUS, Gaius Suetonius Tranquillus
(c.69–c.140)

Roman biographer and antiquarian. He was for a time a member of the Imperial service (119–c.122) and secretary to the Emperor Hadrian. His best-known work is his *Lives of the Caesars* (from Julius to Domitian). There survive also short biographies of **Virgil** and other Roman poets. In addition, Suetonius wrote numerous lost historical and miscellaneous works (in Greek as well as Latin). The *Caesares* (Eng trans *The Twelve Caesars* by **Robert Graves**, 1957) are an important historical source (though not always dependable without corroboration) and benefit from his access to the Imperial archives and his contact with eye-witnesses. His style (like his general approach) is brisk and straightforward, but he evidently enjoyed the numerous scandalous anecdotes he recorded.

SUCKOW, Ruth
(1892–1960)

American story writer and novelist, born in Hawarden, Iowa. When she started to publish, in the 1920s, Ruth Sukow was regarded as a major talent; since then she has fallen into near-oblivion. She was, however, a good if not profound regional writer, whose work (it has been generally agreed) suffered when she decided to move from the form of the story to that of the novel. The long and successful *The Folks* (1934) is readable, but is essentially a series of vignettes rather than a novel proper. But at least *Iowa Interiors* (1926) and *Children and Older People* (1931), collections of stories, are worthy of preservation for their honest realism.
▷ M Omracanin, *Sukow: A Critical Study of Her Fiction* (1972)

SUITS, Gustav
(1883–1956)

Estonian poet and scholar, major in the context of his literature, born in Vônnu. When the Soviets annexed Estonia for the second time, in 1944, he fled to Sweden, where he was made a member of the Nobel Institute. He was too fastidious to produce the poetry of which he was capable, but the poetry he did write had a delicacy and craftsmanship which meant that it inspired others. His criticism of Estonian literature was crucial—he was a major keeper of standards. *Tuli ja tuul* (1950, Eng trans *Flames on the Wind*, 1953) shows him at his always slightly artificial best.
▷ *American Slavic and East European Review*, IX (1955)

SUKENICK, Ronald
(1932–)

American novelist of markedly experimental disposition (though he obstinately refuses the label). He was born in Brooklyn, New York and educated at Cornell and Brandeis universities, returning to the latter as a lecturer. He has taught at campuses throughout New York and in California. His first 'novel' *Up* (1968) is a reflexive anti-narrative about the difficulties of writing fiction; its successor *Out*

(1973)—not to be confused with a similarly disposed work of that name by **Christine Brooke-Rose**—moves the ostensible setting to the West Coast. In *98.6* (1975) and *Long Talking Bad Conditions Blues* (1979) he attempts to engage with a wider reality; however, the essence of Sukenick's work is to be found in the closed forms of his two short-story collections, *The Death of the Novel and Other Stories* (1969), which includes putatively unedited taped conversations, and *The Endless Short Story* (1986). His aesthetic is most cogently formulated, however, in an earlier study of **Wallace Stevens** called *Musing the Obscure* (1967), in which he examines the poet's desire to create self-contained and autotelic language-worlds.

SUKHOVO-KOBYLIN, Aleksandr
(1817–1903)

Russian dramatist, born in Voskresensk, near Moscow. He wrote only three plays, but these are recognized as masterpieces. A friend of **Gogol**, he was in 1850 tried for the murder of his mistress, and, although he was finally acquitted, the case dragged on for seven years. His first play, *Svadba Krechinskogo* (1855, Eng trans with his other two plays in *The Trilogy of Aleksandr Sukhovo-Kobylin*, 1969), was a comedy. *The Case* and *The Death of Tarelkin* are savage satires on Tsarist idiocy, bureaucracy and tyranny—and were banned until revived by Meyerhold, when they became a regular part of Soviet repertory. Harold B Segal's introduction to his translation of the *Trilogy* is exemplary as criticism and biography. Sukhovo-Kobylin's work has been described as a 'mounting diatribe of gorge', and certainly he is the Gogol of the theatre.

SULLY-PRUDHOMME, René François Armand
(1839–1907)

French poet and winner of the first Nobel Prize for literature, born in Paris. He studied science and developed an interest in philosophy which underlies most of his poetical works. His early *Stances et poèmes* (1865, 'Stanzas and Poems') was praised by **Charles Sainte-Beuve**. Later volumes, *Les Épreuves* (1866, 'Proofs'), *Croquis italiens* (1872, 'Sketches of Italy'), *Les Solitudes* (1869), *Impressions de la guerre* (1872, 'Impressions of War'), *Les Destins* (1872, 'Destinies'), *Les Vaines Tendresses* (1875, 'Hollow Tendernesses'), *La France* (1879) and *La Révolte des fleurs* (1874, 'The Flowers' Revolution'), confirmed his fame as a poet. His didactic poems *La Justice* (1878) and *Le Bonheur* (1888, 'Happiness') are masterpieces of subtlety. Other works are a metrical translation of book one of **Lucretius** (new edn 1886); in

prose, *L'Expression dans les beaux arts* (1883, 'Expression in the Fine Arts'), *Réflexions sur l'art des vers* (1892, 'Reflections on Poetic Art'), *Testament poétique* (1901, 'Poetic Testament') and *La Vraie Religion selon Pascal* (1905, 'The True Religion According to Pascal'). His *Oeuvres complètes* ('Complete Works') appeared between 1883 and 1908. He was awarded the Nobel Prize for literature in 1901.
▷P Flottes, *Sully-Prudhomme* (1930)

SUMARAKOV, Aleksandr
(1718–77)

Russian dramatist and poet, born in Finland. With the actor Volkov he established Russia's first permanent theatre, in St Petersburg; he provided most of its repertoire in the form of pseudo-classical tragedies in the French tradition, which (according to one critic) 'lacked taste and permanence'. He adapted *Hamlet*—with a 'respectable and happy ending'.
▷A Berkov, *Aleksandr Sumarakov* (1949, in Russian)

SUMMERS, Essie, properly **Ethel Snelson Flett**
(1912–)

New Zealand journalist and writer of popular romances, born in Christchurch. Her first book, *New Zealand Inheritance*, was published in 1957 but she had been a contributor to New Zealand and British periodicals since the mid-1930s. In over 50 novels she rarely strayed far from a set formula hinging on family history and faithfulness, as in *Bride in Flight* (1964) and *Heir to Windrush Hill* (1966). Her last book was *High-Country Governess* (1987).
▷ *The Essie Summers Story* (1974)

SUNDBERG, Kjell
(1934–78)

Swedish novelist and dramatist in the existentialist tradition—in certain.ways a latter-day Swedish counterpart to Norway's **Stig Dagerman**—born in Östersund. He mercilessly satirized Sweden's Utopian pretentions in his *Den förvirrade medborgaren* (1967, 'The Confused Citizen'); this vein is continued in *Ja må han leva Häng dig om du kan* (1970, 'Many Happy Returns, Or Hang Yourself if You Can'). But Sundberg failed to develop his gifts beyond satire, and critical claims for him made in his lifetime proved to have been exaggerated.

SUNDMAN, Per Olof
(1922–92)

Swedish novelist and short-story writer, born in Vaxhom outside Stockholm. He was an elected member of the Swedish Academy, and politically active as a representative in parliament for the liberal Centre Party. His narratives—whether pure fiction, as in the short-story collection *Jägarna* (1957, 'The Hunters') or part documentary as in the novel *Expeditionen* (1962, 'The Expedition')—typically involve a limited number of characters who set out on a search or mission; his seemingly simple and straightforward prose, free from psychologizing and moralizing, blends the style of the Icelandic sagas with a touch of the detective story. His masterpiece is the documentary novel *Ingenjör Andrées luftfärd* (1967, 'The Flight of the Eagle'), adapted to film by the distinguished Swedish director Jan Troell in 1982, a detailed account of an ill-fated balloon-trip to the North Pole in 1897.
▷L G Warme, *Per Olof Sundman: Writer of the North* (1984)

SUPERVIELLE, Jules
(1884–1960)

Uruguayan-born French writer, born in Montevideo. He wrote many volumes of poems (including the notable *Poèmes de la France malheureuse*, 1939–41, 'Poems of Unfortunate France'), novels, tales (*L'Enfant de la haute mer*, 1931, 'The Child from the High Seas'; *L'Arche de Noè*, 1938, 'Noah's Ark'), plays (*La Belle au bois*, 1932, 'Beauty in the Woods'; *Shéhérazade*, 1949), and the libretto for *Bolivar*, an opera with music by Milhaud (1950).
▷J A Hiddleton, *L'univers de Supervielle* (1965)

SURREY, Henry Howard, Earl of
(c.1517–1547)

English courtier and poet, eldest son of Thomas Howard (who in 1524 succeeded as third Duke of Norfolk). He commanded troops in France but is now better remembered as a poet than a soldier, having helped to introduce the sonnet to England and being a pioneer of blank verse. He made a number of enemies in high places, however, and in 1547 was charged with high treason, on very flimsy evidence, found guilty and executed. Most of his work was first published in 1557, and collected in 1815–16.
▷E Casady, *Henry Howard, Earl of Surrey* (1938)

SURTEES, R(obert) S(mith)
(1805–64)

English journalist and novelist, born in Durham, where he was educated. He practised as a lawyer and later became a Justice of the Peace and High Sheriff of Durham County. He started the *New Sporting Magazine* in 1831 where he introduced John

Jorrocks, a sporting Cockney, in whom there is an appealing blend of the vulgar and the absurd. Later Jorrocks's adventures were contained in the highly popular *Jorrock's Jaunts and Jollities* (1838) and in *Hillingdon Hall* (1845). Their influence on **Dickens**' *Pickwick Papers* is conspicuous. His other great character, Mr Soapy Sponge, appears in *Mr Sponge's Sporting Tour* (1853), by which time he was combining his passion for sport with his literary work.
▷F Watson, *Robert Smith Surtees, a critical study* (1933)

SUSANN, Jacqueline
(?1926–1974)

American popular novelist, born in Philadelphia. After a moderately successful career as an actress she turned to writing, her first novel, *Valley of the Dolls* (1968), becoming an immediate bestseller. *The Love Machine*, published the following year, enjoyed the same success. She made no literary claims for her work but admitted to writing to provide her readers with an escape from their daily lives into the more sensational world of show business, where ruthless ambition leads to frustration and unhappiness.

SUTCLIFF, Rosemary
(1920–92)

English writer of sophisticated historical fiction, mostly for younger readers. She was born at West Clanden, Surrey, and trained at Bideford School of Art. Her gifts as a miniaturist are also evident in her prose, which is sharply detailed and coloured. Her first novel was *The Armourer's House* (1951), but she received greatest praise for *The Eagle of the Ninth* (1954), a story of the Romans in Britain, and for *The Lantern Bearers* (1959). Their vividness was enhanced by line drawings from C Walter Hodges (later illustrators included Charles Keeping and Shirley Felts). Though seriously affected by osteoarthritis, Sutcliff continued to write into the 1980s.
▷M Meek, *Rosemary Sutcliff* (1962)

SUTRO, Alfred
(1863–1933)

English dramatist, born in London. He gave up a successful business, translated **Maeterlinck**, and from 1900 wrote a series of successful plays—*The Foolish Virgins* (1904), *The Walls of Jericho* (1906), *John Glayde's Honour* (1907), *The Perplexed Husband* (1913), and others.

SUTTNER, Bertha, Freifrau von
(1843–1914)

Czech (Austro-Hungarian) novelist of Bohemian descent, daughter of an imperial general, Count Kinsky. She married Baron von Suttner, an engineer, in 1876. In 1915 she won a Nobel Prize, not for Literature, but for Peace (she founded an Austrian pacifist organization)—Alfred Nobel himself had been persuaded to set up his fund by her example. Her novel *Die Waffen nieder* (1889, Eng trans *Lay Down Your Arms, the Autobiography of Martha von Tilling*, 1892) shocked her readers by its pacifism.
▷E Key, *Florence Nightingale und Bertha von Suttner* (1919)

SVENSSON, Jon Stefán
(1857–1944)

Icelandic writer and churchman, born at Möðruvellir. Educated in France, he became a Jesuit scholar and taught at a Catholic school in Denmark. During convalescence in Holland from a severe illness (1911–12) he began to write a series of children's books about a boy called Nonni growing up in the north of Iceland, which made him a bestselling author. The *Nonni* books, originally written in German, have been translated into many languages.
▷H Hannesson, *Nonni Attrægur* (1937)

SVEVO, Italo, pseud of Ettore Schmitz
(1861–1928)

Italian novelist of German–Jewish descent, born in Trieste. Educated primarily in Bavaria, he wrote in Italian, but had to work as a French and German correspondence clerk in a Trieste bank. In 1892 he wrote and published privately his first novel, *Una Vita* (Eng trans, *A Life*, 1963), whose autobiographical hero felt ill at ease in the commercial world. It was followed in 1898 by *Senilità* (Eng trans *As a Man Grows Older*, 1932). Both fell flat largely through Svevo's ineptitude as a publisher, and in dejection he gave up writing and resolved to concentrate on business. His luck changed in 1906 when he went to a teacher of English then living in Trieste, **James Joyce**, who bolstered his confidence and promoted *La coscienza di Zeno* (Eng trans *The Confessions of Zeno*, 1930). Through Joyce a translation was published in Paris and Svevo soon won recognition in France and the rest of Europe, but he died soon afterwards in a car accident. He wrote a fourth novel, *La novella del buon vecchio e della bella fanciulla* (1929, Eng trans *The Nice Old Man and the Pretty Girl*, 1930), and a fifth, *Il vecchione* (pub 1967, Eng trans *The Grand Old Man*, 1968), was incomplete on his death. Critic Renato Poggioli wrote that 'For a cultivated Italian it is very easy to understand, but almost impossible to appreciate, the Italian of Svevo, perhaps the least literary and even the least literate, certainly the least polished Italian ever used by a man of letters in our time.' To **V S Pritchett** he was 'the first of the psychological novelists to be beatified by a spirit of humility'.

▷P N Furbank, *Italo Svevo, man and writer* (1966)

SWADOS, Harvey
(1920–72)

American novelist and short-story writer. He was raised in Buffalo, New York, and educated at the University of Michigan. He was a college lecturer before publishing his first novel, *Out Went the Candle* (1955), a vivid portrayal of an American family dominated by business values; this was also the background to *The Will* (1963), which looks at the divisive impact of inherited wealth. His left-liberal stance was even more evident in his stories of auto-workers, *On the Line* (1957). In *Standing Fast* (1970), published not long before his death, Swados wrote with then unfashionable nostalgia about the Old Left; his own politicization was traced in *A Radical's America* (1962), one of the most direct and intelligent books of its kind to be written by an American and notably free of sentimentality. Other novels include *False Coin* (1959), *Nights in the Gardens of Brooklyn* (1960), *A Story for Teddy* (1965) and the posthumous *Celebration* (1975).

SWAN, Annie S(hepherd)
(1859–1943)

Scottish novelist, born near Coldingham, Berwickshire, and brought up in Edinburgh and at Gorebridge, Midlothian. In 1883 she married a schoolmaster (later doctor), James Burnett Smith, and from 1896 they lived in England; she returned to Scotland in 1927 after her husband's death. She published her first novel, *Ups and Downs*, in 1878, and made her name with a Border romance, *Aldersyde* (1883), followed by *Carlowie* (1884), *A Divided House* (1885) and *The Gates of Eden* (1887). From then on she published a large number of light romantic novels, and stories for women's magazines like *The Woman at Home*. She published her autobiography, *My Life*, in 1934.

SWENSON, May
(1919–89)

American poet, born in Logan, Utah, the daughter of Swedish Mormons. She later moved to New York City, where she began publishing poems in periodicals and anthologies. Her first collection, *A Cage of Spines*, appeared in 1958 and was followed by six more, including *To Mix With Time* (1963), which meditates upon travelling and the passing years; *Iconographs* (1970), a book of sometimes difficult concrete poetry, and

In Other Words: New Poems (1987), which includes the long poem, *Banyan*, a metaphorical reflection upon the world and its ways, narrated by an ape. She has also written an avant-garde play, *The Floor* (1966), and poetry for children in *Poems to Solve* (1966) and *More Poems to Solve* (1971).

▷S Gilbert and S Gubar, *Shakespeare's Sisters: Feminist Essays on Women Poets* (1979)

SWIFT, Graham
(1949–)

English novelist and short-story writer, born in London and educated at Cambridge and York universities. His writing is frequently preoccupied with history, memory, guilt and the natural world. His first novels, *The Sweet Shop Owner* (1980) and *Shuttlecock* (1981), were critically well received, but international acclaim arrived on publication of his third, the hugely successful *Waterland* (1983). Partly a social and natural history, partly a fictitious history of his family as remembered and imagined by Tom Crick, a teacher, this work is considered by some as one of the most important novels of its time. *Out of This World* (1988) looks at the relationship between a father and daughter, while *Ever After* (1992) records the life of Bill Unwin, a meditative academic.

SWIFT, Jonathan
(1667–1745)

Anglo–Irish poet, satirist and clergyman, born in Dublin, the son of English parents. He was educated at Kilkenny Grammar School and Trinity College, Dublin, where he obtained his degree only by 'special grace' in 1685. Family connections helped him to embark on a career as secretary to the renowned diplomat, Sir **William Temple**, then resident at Moor Park, Farnham. He supported his patron on the side of the Ancients in the 'Querelle des Anciens et des Modernes' which had spread to Britain from France. Swift's contribution was the mock-epic *Battle of the Books* which was published along with the much more powerful satire on religious dissension, *A Tale of a Tub*, in 1704. At Moor Park he first met Esther Johnson (1681–1728), then a child of eight, who from then on as pupil and lover or friend was to play an important role in his life and to survive for posterity in Swift's verse tributes and the *Journal to Stella* (1710–13), but it is uncertain if he ever married her. When Swift was presented to the living of Laracor near Dublin, 'Stella' accompanied him. In 1708, during one of his numerous visits to London, he met Esther Vanhomrigh (1690–1723), who insisted on being near him in Ireland with unhappy consequences to herself. She is the Vanessa of Swift's too clever poem *Cadenus* *and Vanessa*, a tribute to the lady but also a manoeuvre of disengagement. His visits to London were largely political, but he also visited the great in the literary and aristocratic circles. For the first time the literary world met on equal terms with statesmen. Having been introduced to the political world by Temple, he supported the Whigs, but, his first care being the English Church, he gradually veered to the Tory party. The friendship of Harley, later Earl of Oxford, assisted the change which was decisively made in 1710 when Harley returned to power. His *Four Last Years of the Queen Anne* described the ferment of intrigue and pamphleteering during that period. The chief aims of the Tory party were to make the Establishment secure and to bring the war with France to a close. The latter object was powerfully aided by his *On the Conduct of the Allies* (1713), one of the greatest pieces of pamphleteering. The death of Queen Anne in 1714 disappointed all the hopes of Swift and his friends of the Scriblerus Club, founded in 1713. Swift accepted his 'exile' to the Deanery of St Patrick's Cathedral, Dublin, and from then on, except for two visits in 1726 and 1727; correspondence alone kept him in touch with London. Despite his loathing for Ireland he threw himself into a strenuous campaign for Irish liberties, denied by the Whig government. The *Drapier's Letters* is the most famous of these activities, which were concerned with England's restrictions on Irish trade, particularly the exclusion of Irish wool and cattle. This campaign, and his charitable efforts for Dublin's poor, greatly enhanced his reputation. On his first visit to London after the Tory debacle of 1714 he published the world-famous satire *Gulliver's Travels* (1726). In 1729 he published his ironical *A Modest Proposal*. His poems in light verse now range from the diverting *The Grand Question Debated* (1729) to the *Verses on His Own Death* (1731), which, with its mixture of pathos and humour, ranks with the great satirical poems in the lighter manner. He himself considered his *On Poetry; a Rhapsody* (1733) to be his best verse satire. The ironical *Directions to Servants* and *A Complete Collection of Genteel and Ingenious Conversation* followed in 1731. The satire in the first part of *Gulliver's Travels* is directed at political parties and religious dissension. The second part can be equally enjoyed for the ingenious adventures and the detailed verisimilitude which is part of the manner. But there is deepening misanthropy culminating in the king's description of mankind as 'the most pernicious race of little odious vermin that Nature ever suffered to crawl upon the surface of the earth'. The third part, a satire on inventors, is good fun though less plausible. The last part, in the country of the Houyhnhnms, a race of horses governed only by reason, is a savage attack on man which points to the author's final mental collapse. Politics apart, Swift's influence, like that of the 'Scriblerus Club' generally and **Pope** in particular, was directed powerfully against the vogue of deistic science and modern invention and in favour of orthodoxy and good manners.

▷I Ehrenpreis, *Jonathan Swift: the man, his works, the age* (2 vols, 1962–7)

SWINBURNE, Algernon Charles
(1837–1909)

English poet and critic, born in London, the eldest son of Admiral Charles Swinburne and Lady Jane Ashburnham. He was educated partly in France and at Eton (where he was savagely beaten and bullied) and Balliol College, Oxford, but left without taking a degree. He travelled on the Continent, where he came under the spell of **Victor Hugo**. He visited **Walter Savage Landor** in Florence (1864), and on his return became associated with **Dante Gabriel Rossetti** and **William Morris**. After a breakdown due to intemperate living, he submitted to the care of his friend **Theodore Watts-Dunton**, in whose house, No. 2, The Pines, he continued to live in semi-seclusion for the rest of his life. His first publication, the two plays *The Queen Mother* and *Rosamond* (1860), attracted little attention, but *Atalanta in Calydon* (1865), a drama in the Greek form but modern in its spirit of revolt against religious acquiescence in the will of Heaven, proved a success. He returned to Greek myth with his noble lyric drama *Erectheus* (1876). It was, however, the first of the series of *Poems and Ballads* (1866) which took the public by storm. The exciting rhythms of 'Hesperia', 'Itylus', 'The Garden of Proserpine' and 'The Triumph of Time' were intoxicating to English ears, but the uninhibited tone of certain passages affronted English puritanism. The second series of *Poems and Ballads* (1878) found it hard to maintain the excitement and the third series (1889) witnessed his waning vogue in this kind. Meanwhile he found scope for his detestation of kings and priests in the struggle for Italian liberty. *Songs before Sunrise* (1871) best expresses his fervent republicanism. He had been working on a trilogy of Mary, Queen of Scots since before 1865, when his *Chastelard* appeared. The second play of the series, *Bothwell, a Tragedy*, appeared in 1874 and *Mary Stuart* completed the trilogy in 1881. The year following, *Tristram of Lyonesse*, an Arthurian romance in rhymed couplets, achieved a real success and must be considered among the best of Victorian dealings with the medieval cycle. He had resented **Tennyson**'s moralistic treatment of

the theme in *The Idylls of the King. Tristram* is intense and passionate and has some great descriptive passages. When he returned to medieval romance in *A Tale of Balen* (1896), there was obvious lack of power. Swinburne represented the last phase of the Romantic movement. His absorption in romantic themes which he treated with a wealth of rhetoric and an excess of neologisms and archaisms has caused his reputation to diminish, but he made a genuine and lasting contribution to the poetic scene. His novel, *Love's Cross Currents* (1877), published under the pseudonym Mrs H Manners, is a curiosity, but his critical works, above all his work on **Shakespeare** and his contemporaries, are stimulating. His *Essays and Studies* (1875) and *Studies in Prose and Poetry* (1894) are his chief contribution to criticism.
▷ G Lafourcade, *Algernon Swinburne* (1932)

SWINNERTON, Frank Arthur
(1884–1982)

English novelist and critic, born in London. Between 1906 and 1926 he was a reader employed by the publishers Chatto and Windus. He himself wrote over 40 novels, beginning with *The Merry Heart* (1909). *Nocturne* (1917) and *Young Felix* (1923) helped establish him as a perceptive observer of atmosphere and character. His activities as publisher's reader, as a literary critic for *The Observer*, and independent author of a score of critical works, brought him into contact with an enormous number of authors, including **Aldous Huxley**, **Lytton Strachey** and **H G Wells**, and put him at the centre of literary London for several decades.

SYLVESTER, Joshua
(1563–1618)

English minor metaphysical poet and translator, born in Kent. He is now chiefly remembered for his translation of the *Divine Days and Weeks* (1605) of **Du Bartas**, which had an extensive influence throughout the 17th century, although few have professed to understand what most of it (or the original) meant. A secretary in the service of the Merchant Adventurers, he died in Holland.
▷ *The Complete Works* (1880, reprinted 1967)

SYMMACHUS, Quintus Aurelius
(c.340–c.402)

Roman orator. He became prefect of Rome in 384 and consul in 391 under the emperor Theodosius I. He was devoted to paganism, and showed the highest nobility of character in his resistance to Christianity. His extant writings consist of letters, three panegyrics on Valentinian I and Gratian, and a *Relatio* ('Report') addressed to Valentinian II in 384, urging the restoration of the Altar of Victory.
▷ T R Glover, *Life and Literature in the Fourth Century* (1941)

SYMONDS, John Addington
(1840–93)

English author, born in Bristol. He was educated at Harrow School and Balliol College, Oxford, where he won the Newdigate Prize for poetry, and was elected a fellow of Magdalen College in 1862. His *Introduction to the Study of Dante* (1872) was followed by *Studies of the Greek Poets* (1873–6), his great *Renaissance in Italy* (6 vols, 1875–86), and *Shakespeare's Predecessors in the English Drama* (1884). He also wrote sketches of travel in Italy and elsewhere and monographs on **Shelley**, Sir **Philip Sidney** and **Ben Jonson**. He translated the *Sonnets of Michelangelo and Campanella* (1878), Benvenuto Cellini's autobiography, and 12th-century students' Latin songs (1884). He wrote a *Life of Michelangelo* (1892), some verse, and an account of his residence (for health reasons) in Davos (1892).
▷ P Grosskurth, *Symonds* (1964)

SYMONS, Alphonse James Albert
(1900–41)

English bibliophile and biographer, born in London, the brother of **Julian Symons**. His greatest success was *The Quest for Corvo* (1934), an extraordinary biography of the writer and novelist **Frederick Rolfe**, Baron Corvo. He was active in founding the First Edition Club and the Wine and Food Society, and worked for years on a bibliography of the 1890s writers. He published brief lives of the explorers H M Stanley and Emin Pasha and also wrote some brilliant impressionistic chapters of a biography of **Oscar Wilde** which, like many other projects, he left uncompleted.

SYMONS, Arthur William
(1865–1945)

Welsh critic and poet, born of Cornish stock in Wales. He did much to familiarize the British with the literature of France and Italy. He translated **Gabriele D'Annunzio** (1902) and **Baudelaire** (1925). He wrote a number of volumes of lyrics in the Decadent manner of the period, including *Days and Nights* (1889) and *London Nights* (1895), and critical works on *The Symbolist Movement in Literature* (1899) and *The Romantic Movement in English Poetry* (1909).
▷ R Lhombreaud, *Arthur Symons* (1963)

SYMONS, Julian Gustave
(1912–)

English crime novelist, historian, critic and biographer, born in London, the brother of **Alphonse Symons**. Recognized for many years as a master of crime fiction, he published his first novel, *The Immaterial Murder Case*, in 1945. This was followed by almost 30 novels and volumes of short stories. *The End of Solomon Grundy* (1964) and *The Players and the Game* (1972), show him using the crime novel as a means of reflecting and commenting upon the hypocrisies and moral laxity of contemporary society. Elsewhere, as in *The Man Who Lost His Wife* (1970), Symons uses satire to make similar points. His *Bloody Murder*, a history of the genre from the detective story to the crime novel, first appeared in 1972 and has been updated several times. It is an indispensible guide to crime fiction.

SYNGE, John Millington
(1871–1909)

Irish dramatist, born near Dublin. He studied at Trinity College, Dublin, and then studied music in Germany before spending several years in Paris on literary pursuits until, on the advice of **W B Yeats**, he settled among the people of the Aran Islands (1899–1902), who provided the material for his plays *In the Shadow of the Glen* (1903), *Riders to the Sea* (1904), *The Well of the Saints* (1905), and his humorous masterpiece *The Playboy of the Western World* (1907) followed by *The Tinker's Wedding* (1909). He published *Poems and Translations* (1909), and completed his last play, *Deirdre of the Sorrows* (1910), while dying from Hodgkin's Disease. He had a profound influence on the next generation of Irish playwrights and was a director of the Abbey Theatre from 1904.

▷ H H Green and E M Stephens, *J. M. Synge* (1959)

SZABÓ, Lörinc
(1900–57)

Hungarian poet and translator (of English, French and Russian poetry), born in Miskolc. He came into early prominence as one of the European-oriented Nyugat group around **Babits**, with whom (together with **Tóth**) he produced a complete and authoritative translation of **Baudelaire**'s *Fleurs du Mal* (1923). His confusions became apparent in the interwar period, when he passed through phases of anarchism, vitalism and, during World War II, admiration for the Nazis. His last works mainly consist of tortured sonnets, many of them erotic, in a few of which he impressively resolved the extremes between which he lived.

SZERB, Antal
(1901–45)

Hungarian Jewish novelist, critic and essayist, who was persecuted throughout his life for his race, being first barred from holding university posts by the Horthy regime, and then murdered by Nazis. His response, now recognized as profound, was to become his country's finest critic after **Mihály Babits**, and to write some of the most interesting of its fiction. He wrote histories of Hungarian and of world literature, and some extraordinary fiction, including *A Pendragon-legenda* (1934, Eng trans *The Pendragon Legend*, 1963), a fantastic detective thriller based on Rosicrucian intrigue.

SZYMONOWICZ, Simon *see* SIMONIDES, Simon

T

TABB, Father John Bannister
(1845–1909)

American Roman Catholic priest and poet. He served on the Confederate side in the Civil War, as a blockade runner, was converted and ordained, and then became suddenly famous with *Poems* (1894). His poetry is well-crafted, in classical, tight forms; although a few compared it with that of the 17th-century English metaphysicals, it was in fact very conventional in content, and is no longer highly regarded.

▷ F A Litz, *Father Tabb: A Study of His Life and Works* (1950)

TACITUS, Publius or Gaius Cornelius
(c.55–after 115)

Roman historian. He studied rhetoric in Rome, rose to eminence as a pleader at the Roman Bar, and in 77 married the daughter of Agricola, the conqueror of Britain. In 88 he was praetor. Next year he left Rome for Germany, and did not return till 93. He was an eye-witness to Domitian's reign of terror, and we have his own testimony as to the relief wrought by the accession of Nerva and Trajan. Under Nerva he became *consul suffectus* in 97. The high reputation he enjoyed is attested by the eulogistic mention of him in **Pliny**'s letters of which there are 11 addressed to him. Tacitus's earliest surviving work is the *Dialogus de oratoribus*, a dialogue on oratory. This was followed by the *De vita Iulii Agricolæ*, a biography of his father-in-law, Agricola, and the *Germania*, a monograph of great value on the ethnography of Germany. Fourth in order comes the *Historiae*, or the history of the empire from the accession of Galba in AD 68 to the assassination of Domitian in 96. Tacitus is at his strongest here, and his material was drawn from contemporary experience. His last and outstanding work, the *Annales*, is a history of the Julian line from Tiberius to Nero (AD 14 to 68); of probably 18 books only eight have come down to us entire, four are fragmentary, and the others lost. His style is vigorous but often epigrammatic to the point of obscurity. He aimed at impartiality, but is often carried away by his scorn for tyrants like Tiberius.

▷ *The Annals of Imperial Rome* (Eng trans M Grant, 1956)

TADIJANOVIĆ, Dragutin
(1905–)

Croatian poet and translator, born near Slavonski Brod. Under Tito he was director of the Institute for Croatian Literature, in Zagreb. He is a controversial poet, because his deceptively simple poems seem to some to be so close to prose as hardly to be poetry. But he is widely admired and read. His poems have a kind of mystical quality, or, as one critic has put it, 'primitive authenticity', which make them hard to refute. He remains untranslated.

TAGGARD, Genevieve
(1894–1948)

American poet, editor, teacher, biographer and critic, born in Waitsburg, Washington State, and reared in Hawaii. She taught at Sarah Lawrence, and influenced a number of writers, such as **Barbara Howes**. Her biography of **Emily Dickinson** (1930) was one of the first serious treatments of the subject. She founded and edited *The Measure, A Journal of Verse* (1920–6). Her own poetry, metaphysical in style, but ardent in its radicalism, has had few readers since her death. A characteristic collection is *Slow Music* (1946).

TAGORE, Sir Rabindranath
(1861–1941)

Indian poet and philosopher, winner of the Nobel Prize for literature, born in Calcutta, the son of a wealthy Hindu religious reformer, Debendranath Tagore (1817–1905). He studied law in England (1878–80) and for 17 years managed his family estates at Shileida, where he collected the legends and tales he later used in his work. His first book was a volume of poetry, *A Poet's Tale*, when he was 17 (1878), followed by a novel, *Karuna*, and a drama, *The Tragedy of Rudachandra*. In 1901 he founded near Bolpur the Santiniketan, a communal school to blend Eastern and Western philosophical and educational systems, which developed into Visva-Bharati University. He received the Nobel Prize for literature in 1913, the first Asiatic to do so, and was knighted in 1915—an honour which he resigned in 1919 as a protest against British policy in the Punjab. He was openly critical of Mahatma Gandhi's non-cooperation as well as of the Government attitude

in Bengal. His major works include *Binodini* (1902, Eng trans 1964, the first truly modern novel by an Indian writer), *The Crescent Moon* (1913, poems about childhood), *Gitanjali* (1912, Eng trans *Song Offerings*, 1912, a volume of spiritual verse), *Chitra* (1914, his first and finest play), *The Religion of Man* (1931) and *Farewell My Friend* (1940). He also wrote *My Reminiscences* (1917), and *My Boyhood Days* (1940).
▷K R Kripklami, *Rabindranath Tagore* (1962)

TAINE, John, pseud of **Eric Temple Bell**
(1883–1960)

British–American science-fiction writer, born in Aberdeen. He moved at the age of 19 to the USA, where he eventually became an academic mathematician. His first book, *Before the Dawn* (1934), about dinosaurs (in whom he maintained a lifelong interest), was published under his own name—the rest, more than a score, appeared under his pseudonym. Again under his own name, he published a number of successful popular books on mathematics, of which the still read *Men of Mathematics* (1937) was the best known. His science fiction was agreeable, well written, and quite popular in its day.

TAKAMURA Kotaro
(1883–1956)

Japanese poet and sculptor. The son of a sculptor, Takamura went to France after his formal education to study art, and there conceived a great admiration for the European way of life, particularly its individualism. He returned to Japan in 1909 to work as a sculptor, but started writing poetry instead. The most important influence on his work was Chieko, a painter, who became his wife and with whom, unable to put his individualistic ideas into practice in Japan, he lived an isolated, decadent existence in Tokyo until her descent into madness and eventual death in 1938. Their life together and his subsequent despair are documented in his verse. His writing is enormously eclectic in its influences, innovative and beautifully crafted. Of all the poets writing at the time, he is perhaps the most accessible to Western readers, and yet his voice remains distinctively Japanese. In English translation is *Chieko and Other Poems of Takamura Kotaro* (1980).

TAKAZI, pseud (the name of the place of his birth) of **Sivasankara Pillai**
(1914–)

Indian (Malayalam) novelist, and author of the famous *Chemmeen* (1956, Eng trans *Prawns*, 1962), a romance with a prawn-fishing setting. Other novels, influenced by **Zola**,

deal with such delicate subjects as the 'untouchables' *The Scavenger's Son* (1947, Eng trans 1967); *Step on the Ladder* (1964–5, Eng trans 1966) deals with the Keralian past.

TALESE, Gay
(1932–)

American journalist, born in Ocean City, New Jersey. **Tom Wolfe**, generally regarded as the pioneer of 'new journalism', has recognized Talese as its true inventor. A reporter for the *New York Times* (1955–65), he wrote his first non-fiction 'short stories' for *Esquire* magazine, beginning in 1963. His new style reached maturity in his bestselling nonfiction 'novels', *The Kingdom and the Power* (1969), about the *New York Times*, and *Honor Thy Father* (1971), about the Mafia. He has been described as 'a reporter who can write and a writer who can report'.

TALEV, Dimitur
(1898–1966)

Bulgarian historical novelist who was born in Macedonia. In the years of socialist realism he was Bulgaria's leading writer of fiction; but his work far transcends this category— and, indeed, implicitly criticizes it. His *Prespanskite kambani* (1954, 'The Bells of Prespa'), the third part of a massive tetralogy dealing with Macedonian history by tracing the fortunes of a single family, is one of his most impressive works.
▷C Manning and R Smal-Stocki, *The History of Modern Bulgarian Literature* (1960)

TALIESIN
(late 6th century)

Ancient British court poet and subsequently mythical figure of supernatural powers. He is mentioned along with **Aneirin** by Nennius in his *Historia Britonum* (c.800) as a great poet of the Old North, but while his only certain association is with King Urien Rheged, which places him in what is now Cumbria, he would seem to have been a visitor, possibly from the p-Celtic kingdom of Strathclyde. The eight poems firmly ascribed to him, amidst many which are either doubtful or spurious in the much later *Book of Taliesin*, are poems in praise of Rheged and his son Owain. These, which seem authentic, describe battles against the Picts as well as the Angles from the east, which puts Taliesin firmly enough as a frontier bard of the Strathclyde as well as Cumbrian region. Although later Welsh opinion credited him with coming from Powys, he clearly thought of Urien as his patron. He also spoke warmly of the king and his son's courage in battle, and provided the basis for their place among leaders of the Brythonic resistance to the Anglo-Saxon invaders and

Pictish predators. He acquired an extraordinary identity of his own in legend, which attributed to him a supernatural birth, vast odysseys of travel, and a collegiality with Myrddin (Merlin). This Welsh tradition may go back to the 9th or 10th century. If all of the work ascribed to him is authentic, he is not only the product of multiple successive births but is alive and will survive us all. Authenticity limits him to the western Scottish borders, and to a poet of dignity, fidelity, patriotism and human affection.

▷ J Morris Jones, *Taliesin* (1918)

TAMÁSI, Áron
(1897–1966)

Hungarian novelist and dramatist, born in Farkaslaka (now in Romania). From 1923 until 1926 he was in the USA. His chief interest throughout his life was in his Transylvanian (Szekler) background. Most of his books deal with the Szekler people in a straightforward and unbiased manner. His 'Abel' trilogy (1932–4), about a young forester who emigrates, was more successful in its first book—translated as *Abel Alone* (1966)—than at its end. Later, a liberal disillusioned with theoretical politics, he turned to an almost mythological interpretation of Szekler people, reaching his peak with *Szülöföldem* (1939, 'My Birthplace').

TAMAYO Y BAUS, Manuel
(1829–98)

Spanish playwright, born into an acting family, whose work was popular in its time. He is now remembered by some for his tragedy in the manner of **Alfieri**, *Virginia* (1853), but by more for his one truly original play, *Un drama nuevo* (1867, Eng trans *A New Drama*, 1916), which is set in **Shakespeare**'s England, and employs a play-within-play technique. A rabid conservative, disappointed with the failure of his last play, he gave up writing for the stage in 1870 and became Director of the National Academy.

TAMMSAARE, A H, pseud of Anton Hansen
(1878–1940)

Estonian novelist and playwright, the counterpart in fiction to **Marie Under** in poetry. Like Under, he was associated with the 1917 expressionist movement named after an Estonian mythical bird, 'Siuru', but, the most important Estonian novelist of his century, he transcended all movements. He translated **George Bernard Shaw**, and was influenced by him, by **Knut Hamsun** and, above all, by **Dostoyevsky**. His five-volume

masterpiece, the epic *Tode ja oigus* ('Truth and Justice'), about Estonian peasant life in the transitional period at the end of the 19th century and the beginning of the 20th, has so far been translated only into French and German.

▷ A Mägi, *Estonian Literature* (1968)

TAMMUZ, Binyamin
(1919–)

Hebrew novelist and literary editor, born in the Ukraine. His work, well respected in Israel, has not yet been translated. He was a member of the extremist but highly influential 'Canaanite circle' around the poet **Ratosh**: the Jew of Israel, it is asserted by many Israeli critics, has no connection with the Jew of the diaspora—the diaspora was just an 'inconsequential period in Jewish history'. Tammuz wrote with these convictions, and, as in *Yaakob* (1971, 'Jacob'), in the tradition of Jewish reproof. He is therefore hard for outsiders to understand; but his tales of characters in flight from themselves are compelling, vivid and psychologically astute.

TAM'SI, Tchicaya U
(1931–88)

Congolese poet, novelist and playwright, born at Npili in what was then the French colony of Moyen Congo and is now the Congolese Republic. He was educated in French Lycées in Orléans and Paris from the age of 15, after his father was elected a deputy to the French National Assembly, and lived in Paris for most of the rest of his life. He published several volumes of Surrealist poetry, notably *Le Mauvais Sang* (1955, 'Bad Blood'), *Le Ventre* (1964, 'The Stomach') and *Feu de Brousse* (1964, 'Bush Fire'); his best-known poems are in *Epitomé* (1962), which records the events surrounding the imprisonment and murder of Patrice Lumumba. The best of his poems were translated into English by Gerald Moore in *Selected Poems* (1970).

TANIZAKI Jun'ichiro
(1886–1965)

Japanese novelist and playwright. He was born and educated in Tokyo, where he studied Japanese literature at the Imperial University. After the earthquake of 1923, he removed to Kyoto-Osaka, which was to be the setting of his greatest work, *Sasameyuki* (1948, Eng trans *The Makioka Sisters*, 1957). Tanizaki's aestheticism greatly influenced the younger **Yukio Mishima**, but takes a gentler form in his own work. It was, indeed, too gentle for pre-war Japanese critics and fellow-

writers, who demanded a more aggressive approach reflecting contemporary realities. From his first work onwards, Tanizaki was concerned with the transformative power of the imagination; *Shisei* (1910, 'Tattoo') is a story about a girl whose personality is changed by bodily decoration. His other great work was *Tade kuu mushi* (1929, Eng trans *Some Prefer Nettles*, 1955), a story that underlined his cultural nationalism. His works were still being translated in the 1980s: *Bushuko hiwa* (1935) and *Yoshino kuzu* (1937) appeared together in 1982 as *The Secret History of the Lord of Musashi* and *Arrowroot* respectively. Tanizaki wrote a number of plays, literary essays and translations.
▷ *Setsugoan yawa* (posthumous, 1968); G B Petersen, *The Moon in the Water* (1979)

TANNAHILL, Robert
(1774–1810)

Scottish poet and songwriter, born in Paisley, the son of a handloom weaver. He composed many of his best songs to the music of his shuttle. He helped to found a **Burns** Club in 1803 for which he composed songs set on traditional airs. His *Poems and Songs* (1807) proved popular, the best known being 'Gloomy Winter's noo awa', 'Jessie the Flower o' Dunblane', 'The Braes o' Gleniffer', 'Loudon's Bonnie Woods and Braes' and 'The Wood o' Craigielea'. But after a publisher declined a revised edition he drowned himself in a canal near Paisley.

TANNHÄUSER, Der
(c.1210–c.1270)

German poet and Minnesinger, probably from Bavaria. He was court poet to the ruler of Austria, and is thought (because of what he says in his poetry) to have travelled a great deal, including taking part in one of the crusades. This is the source of the body of legend (as in Wagner's opera) which has grown up around the historical figure. His literary significance lies in his breaking away from the rigid conventions of previous Minnesang. His verse contains humour, irony and even parody, as well as great sensuality in erotic passages. Several of his songs survive with melodies.

TANSILLO, Luigi
(1510–68)

Prolific Italian courtier poet, born in Venosa. He served the Viceroy of Spain in Naples, Don Pedro di Toledo. His most valued work lies in his **Petrarch**an sonnets and in his long *Le lagrime di San Pietro* (1585, 'The Tears of St Peter'). His quaint *La balia* (1566, Eng trans *The Nurse*, 1800) is a plea to mothers to breastfeed their children themselves.

TARDIEU, Jean
(1903–)

French dramatist, translator (of, amongst others, **Hölderlin**) and poet, now well recognized as an important precursor of the Theatre of the Absurd. He began as poet, and his name was often associated with that of **Ponge** as an experimenter with language. He started writing plays in 1947; his short chamber plays, as he termed them, are often mentioned as resembling those of **Ionesco** and **Genet**, but more often he anticipated or influenced those writers. In one of the plays, *Une Voix Sans Personne* (1956, 'A Voice Without Anyone'), there are no characters. His humour has been compared to that of the composer Erik Satie. Available in English translation is *The Underground Lovers and Other Experimental Plays* (1968).

TARKINGTON, (Newton) Booth
(1869–1946)

American author, born in Indianapolis. Many of his novels have an Indiana setting, but he is best known as the author of *Monsieur Beaucaire* (1900) and his 'Penrod' books—*Penrod* (1914) and *Seventeen* (1916). His other works include a trilogy, *Growth* (1927), including *The Magnificent Ambersons* (1918), which won the Pulitzer Prize and was made into a successful film by Orson Welles, *Alice Adams* (1921, Pulitzer Prize), and a book of reminiscences, *The World does Move* (1928).
▷ A D Dickinson, *Booth Tarkington* (1926)

TÁSAROV-RODINIOV, Aleksandre Ignatiyevich
(1885–1938)

Russian novelist, born in Astrakhan. His novel *Shokolad* (1922, Eng trans *Chocolate*, 1932) prophesied the Stalin 1938 crackdown in which he himself perished. *Linyov* (1924), later called *Trava i krov* ('Grass and Blood'), attacks Lenin. The author was a man who had worked keenly for the communists, but changed his mind. He was 'rehabilitated' comparatively early.

TASSO, Bernardo
(1493–1569)

Italian poet, born in Venice of an illustrious family of Bergamo. After suffering poverty and exile owing to the outlawry by Charles V (1547) of his patron, the Duke of Salerno, he took service with the Duke of Mantua. His romantic epic *Amadigi di Gaula* (1560), an epic on the Amadis of Gaul, is a melodious imitation of **Ludovico Ariosto**'s manner, but exaggerated in sentiment. He began another epic, *Iloridante*, which was finished by his son

TASSO, Torquato

Torquato Tasso (1587), and wrote numerous lyrics (1560).

▷E Williamson, *Bernardo Tasso* (1951)

TASSO, Torquato
(1544–95)

Italian poet, son of **Bernardo Tasso**, born in Sorrento. He shared his exiled father's wandering life, but in 1560 he was sent to study law and philosophy at Padua, where he published his first work, a romantic poem, *Rinaldo* (1562, Eng trans 1792). In the service of Cardinal Luigi d'Este he was introduced to the court of the Duke of Ferrara; and there, encouraged by the sisters of the duke, he began his great epic poem and masterpiece, *Gerusalemme Liberata* (1580, Eng trans *Godfrey of Bouillon: The Recovery of Jerusalem*, 1600), an idealized story of the First Crusade. In 1571 he accompanied Cardinal d'Este to France, and on his return to Italy in 1572 became attached to the service of Duke Alfonso at Ferrara. For the court theatre he wrote his beautiful pastoral play, *Aminta* (1573, Eng trans 1591). Tasso completed his great epic in 1575, and submitted it before publication to the critics of the day. Their fault-finding and Tasso's replies are recorded in his correspondence and in his *Apologia*. In 1576 he showed the first signs of mental disorder; he became suspicious and melancholy, and obsessed with fears of assassination. He was confined at Ferrara, but escaped, and eventually made his way to Naples, Rome and Turin, where he was welcomed by the Duke of Savoy. Returning to Ferrara in 1579 he met with a cold reception, and, wounded by some real or imagined slight, broke into furious invectives against the duke, his courtiers, and all the world. He was confined at Ferrara by order of the duke as insane, not, as is often alleged, for his love for the Princess Leonora, a story on which **Byron** based his *Lament of Tasso*. In his seven years' confinement he wrote many noble verses and philosophical dialogues and a vigorous defence of his *Gerusalemme Liberata*, published without his leave and with many errors. The cruel contrast between his fate and the growing fame of his great poem had excited popular interest, and in July 1586 he was freed on the intercession of Prince Vincenzo Gonzaga. He followed his new patron to Mantua, where he wrote his only tragedy, *Il Re Torrismondo* (1586, 'King Torrismondo'). Broken in health and spirits, he began again his restless wanderings, spending, however, most of these later years in Rome and Naples, helped and protected by many kind friends and patrons. He busied himself in rewriting his great epic, according to the modifications proposed by his numerous critics. The result, a poor semblance of his masterpiece, was published as *Gerusalemme Conquistata* (1593, 'Jerusalem Conquered'). Summoned to Rome by Pope Clement VIII to be crowned on the Capitol as poet laureate, he took ill on arrival and died in the monastery of Sant' Onofrio on the Janiculum.

▷A Solerti, *Vita di Tasso* (3 vols, 1895)

TASSONI, Allessandro
(1565–1635)

Italian poet and critic, born in Modena into a noble family. He was resolutely anti-Spanish throughout his life, and wrote tracts against the Spaniards. His most famous work is the mock epic *La secchia rapita* (1622, Eng trans *The Rape of the Bucket*, 1825), describing a war between Bologna and Modena over a bucket. For those who can read it in context it is still often funny.

▷V G Rossi, *Tassoni* (1931, in Italian)

TATARKA, Dominic
(1913–)

Slovak novelist and translator (from the French), born in Drienové. He wrote conventional and then socialist-realist novels of little interest; but *Farská republika* (1948, 'The Parsons' Republic'), written before he began to pretend to conform to state requirements, is an important account of Slovakia under the Nazis, and of a man's efforts to escape its spiritual oppressiveness. *Démon súhlasu* (1963, 'The Demon of Compliance'), a short work, announced his complete break with socialist realism, and for a long time after 1968 he could not publish in his own country.

▷A J Liehm, *The Politics of Culture* (1970)

TATE, (John Orley) Allen
(1899–1979)

American poet, born in Winchester. He made an abortive start in a business career before entering academe, and became a professor first at Princeton and later at Minnesota University. He was Editor of the influential *Sewanee Review* (1944–5). A metaphysical poet in thrall to **T S Eliot**, his writing career was diverse and encompassed many books, including biographies of Thomas Stonewall Jackson (1928) and Jefferson Davies (1929). Collections of verse include *Mr Pope and Other Poems* (1928), *Poems 1928–31* (1932), *The Mediterranean and Other Poems* (1936) and *Winter Sea* (1945). He converted to Catholicism in 1950. He won the Bollingen Prize in 1956. He was married to the novelist **Caroline Gordon** for 35 years; they divorced in 1959.

▷G Hemphill, *Allen Tate* (1964)

TATE, James
(1943–)

American poet, story writer (*Hottentot Ossuary*, 1974) and (in collaboration) novelist, born in Kansas City, Missouri. By profession he is an academic, but his prolific poetry (nearly 30 volumes) mixes all kinds of non-academic American traditions, crossing the styles of **Berryman**, **Mark Twain**, Surrealism in the style of **Mark Strand**, and Bob Dylan; he even, in the words of one of his admirers, 'hangs up his shingle' (in *Absences: New Poems*, 1972) 'as a nihilist': in these poems he feared 'not the void' but said 'exactly what was expected of' him. Later, in love poems, unexpected subtleties are found: 'Rubberducky that part of woman/that has to be going to the store/... sexual eggs, I touch you': it has been explained that for Tate 'woman' is not 'a woman'. *Lucky Darryl* (1977) is a novel, written with Bill Knott. There is as yet a dearth of critical exegesis.

TATE, Nahum
(1652–1715)

Irish poet and dramatist, born in Dublin. He studied at Trinity College there and saw his first play staged in London in 1678. With **Dr Johnson**'s approval, he wrote a number of 'improved' versions of **Shakespeare**'s tragedies, substituting happy endings to suit the popular taste. With **Dryden**'s help he wrote a second part to the poet's *Absalom and Achitophel* (1682) and with Nicholas Brady compiled a metrical version of the psalms. 'While Shepherds watched their Flocks by Night' is attributed to him, and he wrote the libretto of Purcell's *Dido and Aeneas* (1689). He succeeded **Thomas Shadwell** as poet laureate in 1692. His best-known work is *Panacea or a Poem on Tea* (1700).
▷H F S Thomas, *The Life and Times of Nahum Tate* (1934)

TATHAM, John
(b.1610)

English dramatist and poet, who flourished between about 1632 and 1664. At a young age he had some success with the pastoral *Love Crowns the End* (1632) before seeing military service in the English Civil War under Lord Carnarvon. Between 1657 and 1664 he wrote London's city pageants, which were generally called *London's Triumph(s)* or *London's Glory*. He also wrote verse, often echoing **Abraham Cowley**. His plays show a hatred of strangers, especially the Scots: thus his crude 1652 offering was entitled *The Scots Figgaries, or a Knot of Knaves*. He fades from historical view after about 1664.

TAUNAY, Alfred d'Escagnolle, Vicomte de
(1843–99)

Brazilian novelist of French descent. His *Memórias* (1948), which were published long after his death, are invaluable. Initially he wrote under pseudonyms ('Silvio Dinarte', 'Heitor Malgheiro'), and some early books were first published in French. He took part in the Mato Grosso Expedition. His masterpiece is the novel *Innocência* (1872, rev edn 1884, Eng trans *Innocence*, 1945), which combines beautifully observed regionalism with deep sympathy for the native population.
▷P Serpa, *Vicomte de Taunay* (1952, in Portuguese)

TAYAMA Katai
(1872–1930)

Japanese writer, born into a wealthy, upper middle-class family, and sent abroad (to England) to study. He is credited with inventing the *watakushi shosetsu* (I-novel), the most extreme product of Japanese naturalism, the dominant literary movement in the first half of the 20th century, in which realism is achieved by concentrating solely upon the internal workings of the narrator's mind. *Futon* (1907) is his best and best-known work, and is typical of his style. Nothing very much happens in it, except for the narrator losing his girlfriend; it is, instead, a long, intricately described account of his feelings and states of mind. *Inaka Kyoshi* (1909, 'The Country Teacher') is constructed along similar lines.

TAYLOR, (James) Bayard
(1825–78)

American travel-writer and poet, born in Chester county, Pennsylvania. Apprenticed to a printer, he wrote a volume of poems (1844), visited Europe, published *Views Afoot* (1846), and obtained a post on the *New York Tribune*. As its correspondent he made extensive travels in California and Mexico, up the Nile, in Asia Minor and Syria, across Asia to India, China and Japan, which he recorded in a great number of travel books which he later published. In 1862–3 he was secretary of legation at St Petersburg and in 1878 became ambassador at Berlin, where he died.
▷R C Bently, *Bayard Taylor, laureate of the Gilded Age* (1936)

TAYLOR, Edward
(c.1644–1729)

American Puritan poet, born near Coventry, England. His poems were not published until 1937, when they were fulsomely received by critics specializing in the sombre colonial period. Early in life he emigrated to Boston and went to Harvard. After graduation he became pastor of Westfield, a position he held for the rest of his life. He was married twice and had 13 children. On Taylor's death, his grandson, Ezra Stiles, deposited an unopened package of the poems in the library at Yale. The 1937 publication and a more comprehensive edition of Poems in 1960 have led to Taylor taking his place as foremost Puritan poet, and the only American of his period worthy to be compared with **George Herbert** or **Richard Crashaw**.

▷ N S Grabo, *Edward Taylor* (1962)

TAYLOR, Elizabeth, born **Elizabeth Coles**
(1912–75)

English novelist, born in Reading, Berkshire. The daughter of an insurance inspector, she was educated locally at the Abbey School and worked as a governess and librarian. She married John Taylor, the director of a sweet factory, when she was 24, and wrote her first novel, *At Mrs Lippincote's* (1945), while her husband was in the Royal Air Force. This was followed by such novels as *Palladian* (1946), *A Wreath of Roses* (1949), *A Game of Hide-and-Seek* (1951), *Angel* (1957), *The Wedding Group* (1968), *Mrs Palfrey at the Claremont* (1971) and *Blaming*, published posthumously in 1976. Her hallmark is quiet, shrewd observation of middle-class life in the south-east of England, reminiscent of **Jane Austen** with whom she is quite often compared. Like her, her life was more domestic than literary. Her stories, collected in four volumes (1954–72), are no less admired than her novels.

▷ R Liddell, *Ivy and Elizabeth* (1966)

TAYLOR, Sir Henry
(1800–86)

English poet, born in Bishop in Durham, the son of a gentleman farmer. He was an administrator in the colonial office (1824–72). He wrote four tragedies, *Isaac Comnenus* (1827), a remarkable study in character, *Philip van Artefelde* (1834), *Edwin the Fair* (1842) and *St Clement's Eve* (1862). A romantic comedy, *The Virgin Widow* (1850), was afterwards entitled *A Sicilian Summer*. In 1845 he published a volume of lyrical poetry, and in 1847 *The Eve of the Conquest*. His prose included *The Statesman* (1836) and an *Autobiography* (1885).

▷ J B Bilderbeck, *Sir Henry Taylor and his Drama of Philip van Artevelde* (1877)

TAYLOR, Henry Splawn
(1942–)

American poet, born in Loudoun County, Virginia. He is Professor of Literature at the American University in Washington, DC. His first book of poems was *The Horse Show at*

Midnight (1966), followed by *Breakings* (1971), *An Afternoon of Pocket Billiards* (1974) and *Desperado* (1979). He was awarded the Pulitzer Prize for Poetry in 1986 for his collection *The Flying Change* (1985). His other works include translations and anthologies.

TAYLOR, John
(1580–1653)

English poet and pamphleteer, known as the 'Water-poet', born in Gloucester. He became a Thames waterman, but, pressed into the navy, served at the siege of Cadiz (1625). At the outbreak of the Civil War (1642) he kept a public house in Oxford, but gave it up for another in London, and there wrote his own doggerel poems, full of natural humour and low wit. The chief event of his life was his journey on foot from London to Edinburgh (1618), described in his *Penniless Pilgrimage* (1618); similar books were his *Travels in Germanie* (1617) and *The Praise of Hempseed* (1618), a story of a voyage in a brown paper boat from London to Queensborough.

▷ W Thorp, *John Taylor* (1922)

TAYLOR, Mildred D
(1943–)

American novelist, born in Jackson, Mississippi. Educated at Toledo University, she has worked as an English and history teacher with the Peace Corps in Ethiopia, and as a Peace Corps recruiter. An unusually powerful historical novelist for children, she focuses mainly on the era of the 1930s–1950s and the inequalities and oppression then faced by American blacks. A vivid writer who deals honestly with uncomfortable situations and ethics, her most notable fiction is the series that begins with *Song of the Trees* (1975), in which life is viewed through the courageous eyes of Cassie Logan, a highly intelligent black girl who cannot always make sense of the warped ways of her world.

TAYLOR, Peter Hillsman
(1917–)

American short-story writer, novelist, and playwright, born in Trenton, Tennessee and educated in Nashville, Memphis, and Kenyon College, Ohio. Concerned with the smaller crises and collisions of urban middle-class life in the southern states of America, primarily Tennessee, his vision is an alloy of sentiment and irony. He writes about what he knows and the areas where he grew up in Memphis, St Louis and Nashville. Representative stories are 'The Scoutmaster', 'The Old Forest', 'The Death of a Kinsman' and 'A Long Fourth'. *The Collected Stories of Peter Taylor* was published in 1969. His sole novel, *A Summons* to *Memphis* (1987), is a quiet but powerful tale of family tension and resentment; it won the Pulitzer Prize.

TAYLOR, Robert Lewis
(1912–)

American journalist, biographer and writer of fiction, born in Illinois, whose career began as a reporter on the *St. Louis Post*. Taylor's many years of writing profiles for the *New Yorker* led to full-length biographies, including *W. C. Fields: His Follies and Fortunes* (1949) and *Winston Churchill: An Informal Study in Greatness* (1958). His best work, however, is to be found in his picaresque fiction, especially the Pulitzer Prize-winning *The Travels of Jamie McPheeter* (1958), about a teenage boy travelling to California in the Gold Rush.

TAYLOR, Tom
(1817–80)

Scottish dramatist and editor, born in Sunderland. He studied at Glasgow and Trinity College, Cambridge, and was elected a fellow. Professor of English for two years at University College, London, and called to the Bar in 1845, he was secretary to the Board of Health (1850–72), and then to the Local Government Act Office. From 1846 he wrote or adapted over a hundred pieces for the stage, among them *Still Waters Run Deep* (1855), *Our American Cousin*, (1858), *The Ticket of Leave Man* (1863) and *'Twixt Axe and Crown*. He edited the autobiographies of Benjamin Haydon and Charles Robert Leslie, completed the latter's *Life and Times of Reynolds*, translated *Ballads and Songs of Brittany* (1865), and in 1874 became Editor of *Punch*. He was *The Times* art critic, and appeared as a witness for **John Ruskin** in the libel action brought against him by Whistler in 1878.

TCHERNIKOWSKI, Saul
(1875–1943)

Hebrew poet and master-translator, who was born in Mikhailovka in the Crimea, and did not learn Hebrew until he was seven years old. He was a doctor by profession, and practised as one in Russia and in Palestine (from 1930). He differs from most of his contemporaries in that he was not a conspicuously nationalistic or even religious poet: his work brought into Hebrew poetry a new, and secular note. He was in his youth a noted philanderer, and wrote lushly, candidly and beautifully of his continual state of ongoing and optimistic eroticism. His translations of the *Iliad*, *Odyssey*, *Gilgamesh* and the Finnish epic *Kalevala* are unmatched. Good translations into English are to be found in such anthologies as Birman's *Modern Hebrew*

Poetry (1947), and in J Klausner's *Saul Tchernikowski: Poet of Revolt* (1965).
▷ M Waxman, *A History of Jewish Literature* (1947)

TEASDALE, Sara
(1884–1933)

American poet, born in St Louis, Missouri and educated at the Mary Institute and Hosmer Hall. The first person to receive a Pulitzer Prize for poetry (for her collection *Love Songs*, 1917), Teasdale initially earned a reputation as a writer of 'feminine' love poetry. However, much of her poetry is in fact based on her own sheltered early life and unhappy marriage, and expresses the conflicting needs for independence and freedom, love and security. She wrote nine collections of poetry, two of which were published after her death, a suspected suicide.
▷ C B Schoen, *Sara Teasdale* (1986)

TEBALDEO, Antonio
(1463–1537)

Italian poet, born in Ferrara, who was at one time secretary to Lucrezia Borgia. He enjoyed the patronage of Pope Leo X in Rome, but then suffered after the sack of 1527, spending the rest of his life in poverty. When a cousin issued a collection of his poetry without his permission in 1499, it immediately became popular. But since the vogue for him faded, his poems have been regarded as somewhat feeble imitations of **Petrarch**.

TEGNÉR, Elaias
(1782–1846)

Swedish poet and churchman, born in Kyrkerud in Värmland, the son of a pastor. Educated at Lund, he was appointed lecturer there in 1802. His stirring *Krigssång för Landtvärnet* (1808, 'War-song for the Militia of Scania') made his name as a poet, and *Svea* (1811) made him famous. He was appointed Professor of Greek at Lund (1812–26), and Bishop of Växjö (1824). His best-known works include *Sång till Solen* (1817, 'Song to the Sun'), *Epilog vid magisterpromotionen i Lund 1820* (1820, 'Degree Day at Lund'), his religious idyll *Nattvardsbarn* (1820, 'The Communion Children'), *Axel*, a narrative romance of the days of King Karl XII (1822), and his masterpiece, *Frithjof's Saga* (1825). He also had a keen interest in education.
▷ A Werin, *Elaias Tegnér* (1934)

TEIRLINCK, Herman
(1879–1967)

Major Belgian (Flemish) novelist, playwright and critic, born in Brussels, the son of Isidoor Teirlinck, himself a noted writer and Flemish nationalist. Eventually Herman was chosen by the King of Belgium (Albert) to advise him on cultural and scientific matters, and then by King Baudouin to help him with the problems posed by the coexistence of Flemish and French in Belgium. From early on in his literary career he was as much read in Holland as in his own country, partly perhaps because he had taken his initial inspiration from the Dutchman Lodewijk van Deyssel. He started an epistolary novel with **Karel van de Woestijne**, but they did not complete it. His fictional masterpiece came late in his productive life: *Zelfportret op het Galgemaal* (1956, Eng trans *The Man in the Mirror*, 1963), in which a greedy and sensual old banker—a masterly portrait of the type—addresses himself in the second person. Teirlinck was also an important playwright, whose *De vertraagde film* (1922, 'Slow-Film') inspired *L'Inconnue d'Arras* (1935) of **Armand Salacrou**. Many find his plays superior to those of one who undoubtedly influenced him, **Maurice Maeterlinck**. The expressionistic and allegorical *De Man zonder lif* (1925, 'The Man without a Body'), certainly improves upon, whilst it frankly employs the form of, Maeterlinck's *L'Oiseau bleu* (1908), as well as drawing upon the methods of **Pirandello**. His experiments with theatre groups were important and influential, as were his essays on theatre. He was much loved and respected in Dutch and Flemish literary circles.

▷ T O van de Wal, *Herman Teirlinck* (1965, in Flemish); S Lilar, *The Belgian Theatre Since 1890* (1962)

TEMPLE, Sir William
(1628–99)

English diplomatist and essay writer, born in London. He studied at Emmanuel College, Cambridge. After a successful diplomatic career, during which he helped to cement the Triple Alliance between England, Holland and Sweden against France, and suggested the scheme of a reformed privy council of 30, he decided to concentrate on a literary life and established a considerable reputation as an essayist. His works include *Miscellanea* (1679, 1692) and the famous essay 'Upon the Ancient and Modern Learning'.

▷ C Marburg, *Sir William Temple* (1929)

TENCIN, Claudine Alexandrine Guérin de
(1681–1749)

French writer and courtesan, born in Grenoble. She entered the religious life, but in 1714 moved to Paris, where her wit and beauty attracted a crowd of lovers, among them the regent and Cardinal Dubois. She had much political influence, enriched herself, and helped the fortunes of her brother, Cardinal Pierre Guérin de Tencin (1680–1758). But her importance died with the regent and the cardinal in 1723. In 1726 she was imprisoned for a short time in the Bastille, after one of her lovers had shot himself in her house. Her later life was more decorous, and her *salon* one of the most popular in Paris. **Bernard le Fontenelle** was one of her oldest lovers; d'Alembert one of her children. Her romances include *Mémoires du Comte de Comminges* (1735, 'Memoirs of the Count of Comminges'), *Le Siège de Calais* (1739, 'The Siege of Calais') and *Les Malheurs de l'amour* (1747, 'Misfortunes of Love').

TENNANT, Emma Christina
(1937–)

British novelist, born in London and brought up in Scotland. Her first novel was published under the name 'Catherine Aydy' in 1964. Her fiction has shown a willingness to deal in imaginative and unconventional fashion with themes drawn from genre models, including fantasy, the supernatural, science fiction and detection, as in the apocalyptic *The Time of the Crack* (1973), in which a strange faultline threatens London, or *Hotel de Dream* (1976), in which dream and reality merge. Gothic strains are evident in *The Bad Sister* (1978), arguably her best book, and *Wild Nights* (1980). She draws directly on literary predecessors in *Two Women in London: The Strange Case of Ms Jeykll and Mrs Hyde* (1989) and *Faustine* (1992), while *Sisters and Strangers: A Moral Tale* (1990) is a fable in which Adam and Eve have survived until the present. She writes from a feminist perspective, and founded and edited the radical literary magazine *Bananas* (1975–9).

TENNANT, Kylie
(1912–88)

Australian author, born in Manly, New South Wales, whose novels demonstrate enduring faith in the essential Australian character, which she portrays with affection, sympathy and humour. Her earliest books, from *Tiburon* (1935) to the award-winning *The Battlers* (1941), describe the 1930s Depression as experienced in both city and outback. She spent a week in gaol in search of authenticity for *Tell Morning This* (1978), which pictures the seamy underside of Sydney in wartime; it was originally published in a censored version in 1953 as *The Joyful Condemned*. Her last book, *Tantavallon* (1983), is a surreal story which effectively combines the tragic and comic strands pre-eminent in her writing.

TENNANT, William
(1784–1848)

Scottish poet and scholar, born in Anstruther, Fife. He studied at St Andrews University, and in 1812 published a mock-heroic poem *Anster Fair*, which was the first attempt to naturalize the Italian *ottava rima*. He was a teacher from 1816 at Lasswade, from 1819 at Dollar Academy, and from 1835 Professor of Oriental Languages at St Andrews. His *Synopsis of Chaldaic and Syriac Grammar* (1840) became a standard authority. Other poems were the *Thane of Fife* (1822) and *Papistry Stormed* (1827); dramas were *Cardinal Beaton* (1823) and *John Baliol* (1825).

TENNYSON, Alfred, 1st Baron Tennyson
(1809–92)

English poet, born in Somersby rectory, Lincolnshire, the fourth son of the rector. His elder brothers, Frederick and Charles, also wrote poetry. He was educated at Louth Grammar School, and in 1827 went to Trinity College, Cambridge, where he became a member of an ardent group of young men, including Arthur Hallam, whose early death was to be mourned in that great elegiac poem *In Memoriam* (1850). His early ventures in verse, *Poems Chiefly Lyrical* (1830) and *Poems* (1833), were understandably slighted by the critics as being too sentimental. But the critics ought to have detected the great poet in the first version of 'The Lady of Shalott', 'Oenone', 'The Lotus-eaters' and other poems in the 1833 volume. Nine years of revising these poems and adding fresh material resulted in the volume of *Poems* of 1842, which established his fame. He had been engaged since 1833 in writing the series of loosely connected lyrics or elegies which as *In Memoriam* crowned his fame in 1850, the year he succeeded **Wordsworth** as poet laureate and the year of his marriage to Emily Sarah Sellwood. In 1853 he settled in a house on the Isle of Wight, 'Farringford', and in 1868 built 'Aldworth' in Sussex as a summer home. He was flattered by the homage of the entire nation from Queen Victoria downwards, such was his popularity. With his wife he made short tours but rarely left England. The volume of 1842 and *In Memoriam* contain some of the most finished artistry in English poetry, in which the mood of the poem is perfectly reflected in rhythm and language. After 1850 he devoted himself to the fashionable verse novelette—*Maud; a Monodrama* (1855), *Enoch Arden* (1864) and *Locksley Hall Sixty Years After* (1886). The public, however, was waiting for what was to be the crowning triumph. The first instalment of *Idylls of the King* (1859) seemed to the Victorians to be just that, but in *Geraint and Enid* and *Lancelot and Elaine* and throughout the whole series (completed in 1885) Victorian morality imposed on the old chivalric matter stifles the poetry except in the descriptive passages. In the 1870s he attempted drama. Henry Irving gave *Becket* a considerable run, but *Harold*, *Queen Mary* and others were not successful. He had a late flowering in his seventies when he wrote the perfect poem *To Virgil*, *Tiresias*, and the powerful *Rizpah*, but the conflict between science and the Faith, discussed optimistically in *In Memoriam*, now becomes an obsession. *The Princess* (1847) gave him a chance to make a social comment, but the subject of woman's education is treated in serio-comic fashion, which is trying, and the image of John Bull he projects in the poem is offensive to modern taste. His last poem was a 16-line lyric written in 1889 while crossing from Lymington to the Isle of Wight, *Crossing the Bar*.

▷ T R Lousbury, *The Life and Times of Alfred Lord Tennyson, 1809–1850* (1862); Hallam Tennyson, *Alfred Lord Tennyson, a memoir* (1897)

TENNYSON TURNER, Charles
(1808–79)

English poet, born in Somersby, an elder brother of **Alfred Tennyson**. He graduated from Trinity College, Cambridge, in 1832, and was for many years vicar of Grasby, Lincolnshire. He took the name Turner under the will of a great-uncle. As well as collaborating with his brother in *Poems by Two Brothers* (1827), he wrote 341 sonnets (collected, with introductory essay by Spedding, 1880).

▷ H Nicholson, *Tennyson's Two Brothers* (1947)

TERENCE (Publius Terentius Afer)
(c.195–159 BC)

Roman comedy writer, born in Carthage. He became the slave of the Roman senator P Terentius Lucanus, who brought him to Rome, educated him, and set him free. His first play was the *Andria* (166 BC, 'The Girl from Andros'); its success introduced Terence to the most refined society of Rome. His chief patrons were Laelius and Scipio Æmilianus, the younger. After spending some years in Rome he went to Greece. Six of his comedies are still extant: *Andria* (166 BC), *Eunuchus* (161 BC), *Heauton Timoroumenos* (163 BC, 'Self-Tormentor'), *Phormio* (161 BC), *Hecyra* (165 BC, 'Mother-in-Law') and *Adelphi* (160 BC, 'Brothers'). His plays, Greek in origin and Greek in scene, were mostly based on **Menander**. His excellence lies in the fact that he wrote in singularly pure and perfect Latin. Many of his conventions and plot constructions were later used by **Molière**, **Richard Brinsley Sheridan**, and others.

▷ J Strauss, *Terence and Menander* (1955)

TERESA DE JESÚS, Santa
(1515–82)

Spanish Carmelite mystic and writer, born of a noble family in Ávila, Old Castile. In 1533 she entered a Carmelite convent there. About 1555 her religious exercises reached an extraordinary pitch of asceticism; she experienced ecstasies, and the fame of her sanctity spread widely. In 1562, with papal permission, she founded the Convent of St Joseph to re-establish the ancient Carmelite rule, with additional observances, later extending her reforms, which were adopted by many convents within her lifetime. Although she wrote some poetry, she is remembered mainly for her prose works, primarily her autobiography, *Libro de la vida* (1562) and *Las moradas* (1577, 'The Interior Castle'), in which she discusses her spiritual experiences by comparing the soul to a castle which contains many secret chambers, and her *Libro de las fundaciones* (1610, 'The Book of Foundations'), in which she describes her struggle to found various convents, but which is also a detailed and revealing chronicle of her tempestuous times. She stresses the physical aspects of her experiences and uses erotic imagery to convey a sense of spiritual rapture, but her most endearing feature is undoubtedly her distinctive prose style, which effectively captures the rhythm and intimacy of the spoken language, showing a disregard for conventional syntax and frequently losing its train of thought in mid-sentence. She was canonized in 1622.

▷ H Hatzfeld, *Estudios literarios sobre mistica española* (1968); E A Peers, *The Complete Works of Saint Teresa of Jesus* (1982)

TERHUNE, Mary Virginia
(1830–1922)

American author of more than two dozen highly popular romantic novels. Terhune began writing as Marion Harland and published her first novel, *Alone*, in 1854. She married a clergyman and moved to a parsonage at Newark, New Jersey, which later became the home of her son, Albert Payson Terhune, author of a series of novels about dogs. In middle life Mary Terhune became more noted for her books on etiquette and home economics than for her fiction. At the turn of the century few kitchens in the US lacked a copy of her *American Cookbook* (1896).

TERKEL, Studs (Louis)
(1912–)

American writer and oral historian, born in New York City. He grew up and went to Law School in Chicago. He has acted in radio soap operas, been a disc jockey, a radio commentator and a television host, and has travelled worldwide conducting interviews with the famous and the anonymous. Described by J K Galbraith as 'a national resource', his publications include *Giants of Jazz* (1957), *Division Street: America* (1967), *Hard Times*

(1970), *Working* (1974), about the Depression, *American Dreams: Lost and Found* (1980), and *The Good War: An Oral History of World War Two* (1984), for which he was awarded the Pulitzer Prize .
▷ *Talking to Myself* (1977)

TERSON, Peter, pseud of Peter Patterson
(1932–)

English dramatist, born in Newcastle, who worked as a teacher before his first play, *A Night to Make Angels Weep*, was produced at the Victoria Theatre, Stoke-on-Trent, in 1964. For 18 months he was resident dramatist with the theatre and has subsequently had over 20 plays staged there. He has also had a long association with the National Youth Theatre, for which he wrote *Zigger-Zagger* (1967), a large-scale play about fanatical football fans, and such works as *The Apprentices* (1968), *Good Lads at Heart* (1971) and *Geordie's March* (1979). Terson returned to the adult theatre and his native north-east with *Strippers* (1984), a study of women living in an area of increasing unemployment, who are forced to take jobs stripping in pubs and clubs to support their families.

TERZAKIS, Angelos
(1907–79)

Greek novelist, short-story writer and essayist. Initially influenced by the Symbolists, he found fame with a series of historical novels, notable for their intense realism. The first of these was *He Menexedhenia Politeia* (1937, 'The Violet City'), his third book. *He Prinkipessa Ysabeau* ('Princess Ysabeau'), widely regarded as his masterpiece, was published in 1946: it was set in the Peloponnese in the 13th century, and spawned a host of imitators. Terzakis won an equal reputation as an essayist, especially for his confessional works *Dhichos Theo* (1953, 'Without God') and *Mystiki Zoë* (1957, 'Mystic Life').

TEXIDOR, Greville, originally Margaret Foster
(1902–64)

English-born Australasian writer who, as a teenager after World War I, posed for Augustus John, Mark Gertler and others of that coterie. In 1929 she married Manuel Texidor, a Catalan industrialist, and later married a refugee from Nazi Germany, with whom she emigrated to New Zealand. Welcomed into Auckland's literary circle, Greville began writing and became a close friend of refugee writer **Anna Kavan**; their work was published in *New Zealand Writing*. Greville's short stories and verse appeared in England in 1943 and in Australia in 1944, when the periodical *Angry Penguins* printed her translations of 12 poems by **Lorca**. It also accepted *These Dark Glasses*, but this was not to be published until 1949. She later moved to Australia and then to the Costa Brava, but in 1962 she returned to Sydney, where she committed suicide. A collection of stories *In Fifteen Minutes you can say a Lot*, with an introduction by **Kendrick Smithyman**, was published in 1987.

TEY, Josephine, pseud of **Elizabeth Mackintosh**
(1897–1952)

Scottish crime and mystery writer, who also produced 'straight' fiction under the name of 'Gordion Daviot'. She grew up in Inverness and trained as a PE teacher. Her main invention, police inspector Alan Grant, tended to prefer cerebral rather than physical exercise. The most extreme instance of this—and probably the most notorious—is *The Daughter of Time* (1952), a re-opening of the file on Richard III's alleged murder of the little princes in the Tower of London; Grant conducts this masterpiece of retrospective investigation from his hospital bed. Grant was introduced in Tey's first novel, *The Man in the Queue* (1929, published in the USA as *Killer in the Crowd*, 1954), for which she used the Daviot pseudonym. *Miss Pym Disposes* (1946) and *The Franchise Affair* (1948) were non-Grant mysteries, as was the popular *Brat Farrar* (1949, published in the USA as *Come and Kill Me*, 1951); it dealt with double and demonic 'twins' and unconsciously revealed her essential Scottishness. This also emerged in her plays *Queen of Scots* (1934) and *Leith Sands* (1946), and in an impressive biography of Claverhouse (1937).
▷S Roy, *Josephine Tey* (1980)

THACKERAY, William Makepeace
(1811–63)

English novelist, born in Calcutta, where his father was in the service of the East India Company. His father died in 1816 and his mother remarried, so young Thackeray was sent home. He went to Charterhouse (1822) and Trinity College, Cambridge (1829), but left without taking a degree. His first venture in print was a parody of **Tennyson**'s prize poem *Timbuctoo*. After dissipating much of his patrimony in travelling abroad, he decided to improve his fortune by journalism, though art equally attracted him. A four-year stay in Paris as an art student came to a close through lack of funds in 1836. He had now married Isabella Shawe (1836), but financial worry, due to the bankruptcy of his stepfather, finally made him decide to earn a living in journalism, and he returned to London. He contributed regularly to *The Times*, the *New Monthly* and *Fraser's Magazine*. Domestic trouble now engulfed him. The birth of

his third daughter affected Mrs Thackeray's mind, the home was broken up and the children sent to their grandmother in Paris. His first publications, starting with *The Paris Sketchbook* (1840), and written under various pseudonyms (Wagstaff, Titmarsh, Fitz-Boodle, Yellowplush, Snob, etc) were a comparative failure although they included *The Yellowplush Papers*, *The Great Hoggarty Diamond* and *The Luck of Barry Lyndon*, all contributed to *Fraser's Magazine* (1841–4). It was his work on *Punch* from 1842 onwards which attracted attention by exploiting the view of society as seen by the butler ('Jeames' Diary') and the theme of English snobbery. The great novels that were to follow—*Vanity Fair* (1847–8), *Pendennis* (1848–50), *Henry Esmond* (1852) and *The Newcomes* (1853–5), all monthly serials—established his fame. *Vanity Fair* is the first novel to give a view of London society with its mingling of rich parvenus and decadent upper class, through both of which the social climber, Becky Sharp, threads her way. The great historical novel, *Henry Esmond*, shows Thackeray's consuming love of the 18th century. Its sequel, *The Virginians* (1857–9), is not considered a success. *The Newcomes* shows a young love at the mercy of scheming relatives and mean-spirited rival suitors. Thackeray retired from *Punch* in 1854 and became the Editor of the *Cornhill Magazine*, where much of his later work appeared—ballads, novels, and so on, now largely unreadable. He also undertook lecturing tours at home and in America, the fruit of which, apart from *The Virginians*, was *The English Humorists of the 18th century* (1853) and *The Four Georges* (1860).
▷G N Ray, *William Makepeace Thackeray* (2 vols, 1955–8)

THARAUD, Jérôme
(1874–1953)
THARAUD, Jean
(1877–1952)

French writers, born in Saint-Junien, Limoges, and generally referred to as 'Les Frères Tharaud' in the manner of the Brothers **Goncourt**. They travelled together, and collaborated in a series of novels and essays characterized by a direct and unpretentious style which was more reportorial than novelistic, and revealed an interest in reflecting topical events. *Dingley, l'illustre écrivain*, set during the Boer War, won the Prix Goncourt in 1906; *La Fête arabe* (1911) dealt with the French colonization of North Africa, while *Un royaume de Dieu* (1921) and other novels focused on Jewish life in central Europe, where Jérôme taught at the University of Budapest. Jérôme was elected to the Académie Française in 1940, and Jean in 1946.

THAXTER, Celia
(1835–94)

American poet, born in New Hampshire, the daughter of a lighthouse-keeper who later became proprietor of a hotel much frequented by literary worthies, such as **Lowell**, **Whittier** and **Thoreau**. It was through such connections that Thaxter made lifelong friends of the publisher James T Fields, and his wife Annie, an association which opened the door to her publication in the *Atlantic* and then other national magazines. In her collections—*Poems* (1872) and *Drift-Weed* (1879)—children's and adult verse is mixed together, as are the influences of **Longfellow** and **Bryant**.

THELEMIS, George
(1900–76)

Greek poet, born in Samos. A teacher, he regarded poetry as a 'method of self-knowledge'; at least one English student of modern Greek poetry has called him 'different, original ... misunderstood ... more rewarding than **Ritsos** or **Elytis**'. He wrote one of the most revealing books on the poet **Cavafy**.
▷L Politis, *A History of Modern Greek Literature* (1973)

THEOCRITUS
(c.310–250 BC)

Greek pastoral poet, born probably in Syracuse, Sicily. He was brought up on the island of Cos, but lived for a time at the court of Ptolemy III, Philadelphus in Alexandria, returning later to Cos. The authenticity of some of his 30 extant bucolic poems has been disputed. They fall into three classes—half-epic, mimic and idyllic. Probably the half-epic poems were the earliest. He wrote a series of poems dealing with heroic legend, especially that of Heracles. His famous 15th Idyll, *Syracusii* ('The Ladies of Syracuse'), said to be copied from Sophron, describes delightfully the visit of a Syracusan lady and her friend, both living in Alexandria, to the festival of Adonis. Theocritus raised the rude pastoral poetry of the Doric race in Sicily into a new and perfect form of literature. His short poems dealing with pastoral subjects, and representing a single scene, came to be called Idylls (*eidullia*). He combined realism with romanticism, and every touch is natural. **Virgil** imitates him closely in his *Eclogues*; **Tennyson** was deeply influenced by him, as were the pastoral poets of the Renaissance.
▷A S F Gow, *Theocritus* (1952)

THEOGNIS
(fl.544–541 BC)

Greek elegiac poet, a Dorian noble of Megara on the Isthmus of Corinth. During the confusion which followed the overthrow of the tyrant Theagenes, he was driven from Megara, and visited Euboea and Sicily. Under his name survive 1389 elegiac verses, social, political and gnomic, but perhaps only some of them are his.
▷C M Bowra, *Early Greek Elegists* (1938)

THEOTOKAS, George
(1905–66)

Greek novelist. Born into a wealthy family in Constantinople, he studied in Athens, Paris and London, before returning to Greece. His essay *Elefthero Prefma* ('Free Spirit') was published in 1929 and served as a manifesto for his generation of novelists. His first three novels were not, however, so successful, and it was only with the publication of *Leonis* in 1940 that his reputation was secured; set in the Constantinople of Theotokas's childhood, it tells the story of a man's physical and spiritual growth. After World War II Theotokas turned to the theatre and to travel writing, completing *Asthenis Ke Hodhipori* (1964, 'Sick Persons and Travellers') about the Greco–German War; his later travel books include accounts of his journeys to America and the Middle East.

THEROUX, Paul Edward
(1941–)

American writer, born in Medford, Massachusetts. His literary output reflects his footloose life. *Waldo* (1969), his first novel, was followed by fictions that drew on his experience of three years in Africa. He subsequently taught at Singapore University, a sojourn that produced a collection of short stories, *Sinning with Annie* (1976), and a novel, *Saint Jack* (1973). Others, for example *The Family Arsenal* (1976), *Doctor Slaughter* (1984), which made an unfortunate transition to celluloid, and *The London Embassy* (1982), have been based in London where he lived part of the year. His novels are urbane and paradoxical, sometimes bleak and frequently funny; *Millroy the Magician* (1993) was a quantum step, concentrating themes and ideas that have surfaced throughout his career. The same can be said of his extended rail journeys, recounted in *The Great Railway Bazaar: By Train Through Asia* (1975), and *The Old Patagonian Express: By Train Through the Americas* (1979), in which Theroux emerges as a crusty loner, an intelligent observer with the tolerance of a misanthrope.

THESIGER, Wilfred
(1910–)

English traveller, born in Ethiopia (then Abyssinia), where his father was British Minister in charge of the Legation at Addis Ababa. He remained there till he was nine, when he transferred to Eton. Later he went to Oxford where he acquired—in the boxing ring—his prominent dog-leg nose. Described by Douglas Newbold, his Provincial Governor in the Sudan Service, as 'a misfit owing to excess of virtues and not because of any vices—a brave, awkward, attractive creature', he has won the Gold Medal of the Royal Geographical Society, shot 70 lions in the Sudan, ridden 115 miles on a camel in 24 hours, fought with the Special Air Service (SAS) in North Africa and written a classic of travel literature, *Arabian Sands* (1959). Drawn spiritually to remote parts of the globe—Arabia, Abyssinia, Kenya, Kurdistan, Nuristan, the White Nile and the Marshes of Iraq—he has spent much of his life among nomadic tribesmen with whom he instinctively empathizes. Described by **Eric Newby** as 'the last of the great explorers', he also wrote *The Marsh Arabs* (1964), *Desert, Marsh, Mountain* (1979) and *Visions of a Nomad* (1987). *The Life of My Choice*, his autobiography, was published in 1987.

THESPIS
(6th century BC)

Greek poet from Icaria, the reputed founder of Greek drama. He is said to have won the first prize for tragedy at a festival in Athens in c.534 BC. According to Aristotle, he used single actors to deliver speeches, in addition to the traditional chorus.

▷A W Pichard-Cambridge, *Thespis* (1962)

THEURIET, André
(1833–1907)

French poet and novelist, born in Marly-le-Roi, Seine-et-Oise. In 1857 he received a post under the finance minister. His collections of verse include *Le Chemin des bois* (1867, 'The Way through the Woods'), the so-called epic *Les Paysans de l'Argonne, 1792* (1871, 'The Peasants of Argonne, 1792') and *Le Bleu et le Noir* (1872, 'The Blue and the Black'). He is best known for his novels *Le Mariage de Gérard* (1875, Eng trans *Gerard's Marriage*, 1877), *Raymonde* (1877, Eng trans 1878) and *Sauvageonne* (1880, 'The Little Savage Girl').

THIBAUT (THEOBALD) IV
(1201–53)

French trouvere poet, Count of Champagne and Brie, and King of Navarre. He was more successful as a poet than as a ruler and soldier, though the chief virtues of his verse are its wide range of style and subject-matter—he is the author of pastoral and courtly poems, crusade songs, and religious works—and the fact that so much of it has survived. It is said that he was the lover of Blanche de Castile, Regent of France (he is even said to have poisoned her husband, the king), and that Blanche was the inspiration for many of his songs. This may not be true, but it shows, perhaps, his unpopularity at the time.

THIELE, Colin Milton
(1920–)

Australian writer of children's books, radio drama and poetry, born in Eudunda, South Australia. He is an educationist by profession, and much of his work has been directed to this end. His books for younger readers have been recognized by numerous awards and commendations: *The Sun on the Stubble* (1961), *Blue Fin* (1969, filmed 1978), *The Fire in the Stone* (1973, winner of the **Edgar Allan Poe** Award) and *Storm Boy* (1963, filmed 1976). Some writing evokes his home state of South Australia, for example the adult novel *Labourers in the Vineyard* (1970), set in the wine-growing district of the Barossa Valley.

THIRKELL, Angela Margaret, née Mackail
(1891–1961)

English novelist, daughter of John William Mackail, grand-daughter of Sir Edward Burne-Jones, and cousin of **Rudyard Kipling**. She wrote more than 30 novels set in 'Barsetshire', dealing with the descendants of characters from **Trollope**'s Barsetshire novels, including *Coronation Summer* (1937) and *Growing Up* (1943). Her son was the novelist **Colin MacInnes**.

▷M Strickland, *Angela Thirkell* (1972)

THIRY, Marcel
(1897–1977)

Belgian poet and novelist, born in Charleroi. His most famous work was his earliest: *Toi qui pâlis au nom de Vancouver* (1924, 'You Who Turn Pale at the Name of Vancouver'), based on his experiences as a soldier in World War I. His writing is interesting but haunted by a kind of grandiloquence which he seems unable to escape, and which threatens to engulf him in the commonplace. The main influence upon him has been **Apollinaire**.

THOMAS
(fl.12th century)

Anglo–Norman poet. He was author of the earliest extant text (c.1155–1170) of the legend of Tristan and Iseult, a fragment of 3144 lines covering the final episodes including the death of the lovers. Though he has greater pretensions to a literary style, Thomas lacks the impressive primitive simplicity of Béroul, author of the slightly later and fuller of the two early versions, both of which appear to be based on an earlier poem now lost. He is sometimes confused with **Thomas the Rhymer**.

▷M D Legge, *Anglo Norman Literature* (1963)

THOMAS, Audrey
(1935–)

Canadian short-story writer and novelist, born in Binghamton, New York and educated at Smith College, St Andrews University and the University of British Columbia. She lived in Ghana, England, and the USA before settling in Canada, where she works as a Visiting Professor at Concordia University in Montreal. She won the Atlantic Firsts Award in 1965 and has received numerous Canadian Council and Senior Arts grants. Novels include *Mrs Blood* (1970), *Songs My Mother Taught Me* (1973) and *Real Mothers* (1981). Shorter fiction, however, remains her forte, as seen in her early collection of stories, *Ten Green Bottles* (1967) and *Two in the Bush and Other Stories* (1981). Her work has been described as semi-autobiographical.

▷A Thomas issue of *Room of One's Own*, vol 10, no 3–4 (1985–6)

THOMAS, Brandon
(1849–1914)

English actor and playwright, born in Liverpool. He first appeared as a comedy actor in 1879, and wrote a number of successful light plays, one of which, *Charley's Aunt* (1892), has retained enormous popularity.

THOMAS, D(onald) M(itchell)
(1935–)

English poet and novelist, born in Cornwall. He was educated in England and Australia, and graduated from New College, Oxford, in 1958. He learned Russian while on National Service, and has published numerous translations. His early writings were poems which ranged across science fiction, erotica, and evocations of his native Cornwall, all represented in *Selected Poems* (1983). Later poems became, like those in *The Puberty Tree: New and Selected Poems* (1992), more directly autobiographical. His first novel was *The Flute Player* (1979), followed by *Birthstone* (1980), but his most successful has been the powerful, semi-fantastic meditation on **Freud**ian psychology, *The White Hotel* (1981). His other fiction includes the five 'improvisations' on Cold War themes which make up the *Russian Nights* sequence (1983–9), *Flying in to Love* (1992) and *Pictures at an Exhibition* (1993).

▷ *Memories and Hallucinations* (1988)

THOMAS, Dylan Marlais
(1914–53)

Welsh poet, born in Swansea, the son of a schoolmaster. He worked for a time as a reporter on the *South Wales Evening Post* and established himself with the publication of *Eighteen Poems* in 1934. He married Caitlin Macnamara in 1936, with whom he was to have a stormy marriage, and published *Twenty-Five Poems* the same year. His other works include *The Map of Love* (1939), *Portrait of the Artist as a Young Dog* (1940), *The World I Breathe* (1940), *Deaths and Entrances* (1946) and a scenario, *The Doctor and the Devils* (1966). *Collected Poems, 1934–52*, was published in 1952 and he then turned to larger dramatic works. From 1944 he worked intermittently on a radio script about a Welsh seaside village—in its first form it was called *Quite Early One Morning*, but Thomas expanded it into *Under Milk Wood* (published 1954). Until then his work had been praised by critics, among them **Edith Sitwell**, for his striking rhythms, his original imagery and his technical ingenuity, but he could in no sense have been called a popular writer. *Under Milk Wood* was immediately comprehensible, **Rabelais**ianly funny, with moments of lyric tenderness and fresh yet recognizable similes, it presented most of the non-intellectual English concepts of Welsh thought and behaviour. It had a second success as a stage play, and inspired a jazz suite by Stan Tracey (1965). In 1955 *Adventures in the Skin Trade*, an unfinished novel, was published, and a collection of stories and essays, *A Prospect of the Sea*. An authoritative edition of his *Poems* appeared in 1971. He died of alcoholic abuse on a lecture tour of the USA.

▷C Fitzgibbon, *Dylan Thomas* (1965)

THOMAS, (Philip) Edward
(1878–1917)

English poet and nature writer, born in London of Welsh parents. He was educated at St Paul's School and Lincoln College, Oxford, where he got married. He became a hack writer of reviews, critical studies and topographical works. Not until 1914, encouraged by **Robert Frost**, did he realize his potential as a poet, writing most of his poetry during active service in World War I. *Six Poems* was published in 1916. He died in action at Arras (April 1917) before the publication of *Poems* (1917), under the pseudonym 'Edward Eastaway'. His impressive poetry, though rooted in the English tradition of nature poetry, broke with the Georgian tradition in its lack of rhetoric and formality and in its emphasis on the austerity of Nature and solitariness of man. He also wrote a novel, *The Happy-Go-Lucky Morgans* (1913), and several books about the English countryside.

▷W Cooke, *Edward Thomas, a critical biography* (1930)

THOMAS, Leslie John
(1931–)

English novelist and travel writer, born in Newport, Monmouthshire. The son of a sailor lost at sea in 1943, he described his boyhood life in an orphanage in *This Time Next Week* (1964). His first novel, *The Virgin Soldiers*, published two years later, is a bawdy comedy deriving from his experiences as a national serviceman in Malaya, and became a bestseller, establishing its author as one of the most popular of modern story-tellers. His writing is unaffected, atmospheric, truthful, funny and often poignant. His many other novels include *Onward Virgin Soldiers* (1971), *Tropic of Ruislip* (1974), *The Dearest and the Best* (1984) and *The Loves and Journeys of Revolving Jones* (1991). *Dangerous by Moonlight* (1993) follows the adventures of the hapless London police constable first encountered in *Dangerous Davies* (1976).

THOMAS, R(onald) S(tuart)
(1913–)

Welsh poet and priest, born in Cardiff. Educated at the University College of North Wales, Bangor, he trained for the church at St Michael's College, Llandaff. He was ordained deacon in 1936 and priest in 1937. He was rector of Manafon (1942–54), vicar of Eglwysach (1954–67), and vicar of St Hywyn, Aberdaron (1967–78). He published his first, deceptively simple volume of poetry, *The Stones of the Field*, in 1946, followed by *An Acre of Land* (1952) and *The Minister* (1953). He only came to attention outside Wales with the publication of *Song at the Year's Turning* (1955). His later volumes, such as *Poetry for Supper* (1958), *The Bread of Truth* (1963), *Laboratories of the Spirit* (1976) and *Between Here and Now* (1981), deal with pastoral themes and the nature of God, coupled with an intense love of Wales and its people, evoked by his use of nature imagery. His other works include *Later Poems, 1972–1982* (1983), *Experimenting with an Amen* (1986) and *Counterpoint* (1990).

▷R George Thomas, *R. S. Thomas* (1964)

THOMAS, William
(1832–78)

Welsh poet, born in Ynysddu, Monmouthshire. Originally a land surveyor, he was ordained into the rather Calvinistic Methodist ministry in 1859, by which time he had preached a number of sermons. His attempts to write poetry in English were a failure but the philosophical poem *The Storm*, 9 000 lines long, has been acknowledged the finest Welsh

poem of the century. He also edited the Welsh poetry column in a number of periodicals. Collections of his work were published in 1854, 1867 and 1871 before a complete edition of the poems in Welsh, *Gweithiau Islwyn*, appeared in 1897.

THOMAS OF HAILES, or HALES
(fl.1250)

English friar and author of religious poetry. His *Luue Ron*, ('Love Runes'—a translation of *Amatoria Carmina*) compare human love to the divine, unfavourably, arguing that the sweetest love of all is the love of Christ. Thomas is eclectic in his sources: he makes use of biblical and classical references, and also of references to popular literature.

THOMAS THE RHYMER, or THOMAS RYMOUR OF ERCELDOUNE
(c.1220–c.1297)

Scottish seer and poet. He lived at Erceldoune (now Earlston, Berwickshire), and in 1286 is said to have predicted the death of Alexander III and the Battle of Bannockburn, thus becoming known as 'True Thomas'. Boece calls him Thomas Learmont. Legend relates that he was carried off to Elfland, and after three years allowed to revisit the earth, but ultimately returned to his mistress, the fairy queen. In a charter of Petrus de Haga of Bemersyde c.1260–1270 the Rhymer appears as a witness; and in another of 1294 Thomas of Erceldoune, 'son and heir of Thomas Rymour of Erceldoune', conveys lands to the hospice of Soutra. The Rhymer's 'prophecies' were collected and published in 1603. Sir **Walter Scott** believed him to be the author of the poem of *Sir Tristrem*, which was founded on a 12th-century French poem by another Thomas, a poet of genius, almost certainly an Englishman.

▷H M Flasdieck, *Tom der Reimer* (1934)

THOMPSON, E V (Ernest Victor)
(1931–)

English writer of historical and romantic fiction, especially well-known for the bestselling 'Retallick' saga. He was born in London, spent nine years in the navy, worked as an investigator for BOAC and was Chief Security Officer of the Department of Civil Aviation in (the then) Rhodesia. On his return to England in the seventies he settled in Cornwall, where much of his fiction is set, and won the Best Historical Novelist Award with *Chase The Wind* (1977). Since then his 'supreme readability' has ensured constant sales and success. He has also written a number of West Country guide books.

THOMPSON, Flora (Jane), née **Timms**
(1876–1947)

English social historian, born in Juniper Hill, Oxfordshire. She left school at 14 to work in the local post office. She married young and with her postmaster husband settled in Bournemouth, writing mass-market fiction to help support her increasing family. In her sixties she published the semi-autobiographical trilogy combined as *Lark Rise to Candleford* (1945), its three parts, *Lark Rise* (1939), *Over to Candleford* (1941) and *Candleford Green* (1943), having appeared separately. It is an outstanding feat of observation and memory, showing the erosion of rural society before modern industrialism.

▷M Lane, *Flora Thompson* (1976)

THOMPSON, Francis
(1859–1907)

English poet, born in Preston, Lancashire. He was brought up in the Catholic faith and studied for the priesthood at Ushaw College. By temperament unsuited for this, he turned to medicine at Owens College, Manchester, but failed to graduate. He moved to London, where extreme poverty and ill-health drove him to become an opium addict. From this he was rescued by Wilfrid and **Alice Meynell**, to whom he had sent some poems for the magazine *Merry England*. His health was restored at the monastery of Storrington Priory in Sussex, where he wrote several poems, including the well-known *Hound of Heaven*. From then on the Meynells looked after him until his death from tuberculosis. His works include *Poems* (1893), *Sister Songs* (1895, written for the Meynell girls) and *New Poems* (1897). His notable *Essay on Shelley* (1909) appeared posthumously, as did his *Life of St Ignatius Loyola* (1909). His poems, mainly religious in theme, are rich in imagery and poetic vision.

▷E Meynell, *Francis Thompson* (1913)

THOMPSON, Hunter S(tockton)
(1939–)

American journalist, author, editor and small game hunter, born in Louisville, Kentucky. An adherent of the 'new journalism', he eshews objectivity, his search for a story taking him into 'the middle of whatever I'm writing about'. This has led to bizarre incidents and idiosyncratic reportage, marked by intemperate language and behaviour. He was the first reporter to infiltrate the Hell's Angels and rode with them for a year, an experience which led to his being savagely beaten up and a book, *Hell's Angels: A Strange and Terrible Saga* (1966). The acme of the anti-establishment, he styled his unique brand of journalism 'Gonzo', awarded himself a doctorate

and produced a stream of books as outspoken as they were outrageous, including *Fear and Loathing in Las Vegas* (1972), *Fear and Loathing on the Campaign Trail* (1972), *The Great Shark Hunt* (1972), *The Curse of Lono* (1977) and *Generation of Swine* (1988). Much of his work appeared originally in magazines, particularly *Scanlan's*, *Rolling Stone* and the *National Observer*, and at the end of the 1980s he contributed a weekly column to the *San Francisco Examiner*.

THOMPSON, James (Jim)
(1844–1901)

American novelist and editor, who also wrote poetry, born in Indiana. His historical novel, *Alice of Old Vincennes* (1900), based on George Rogers Clark's famous 1779 expedition, was a popular success. He wrote *Hoosier Mosaics* (1875), a series of sketches in dialect.

THOMSON, Derick, Gaelic **Ruaraidh MacThómais**
(1921–)

Scottish poet, born in Stornoway, Isle of Lewis. He was educated at the Nicolson Institute in Stornoway, and at the universities of Aberdeen, Cambridge and North Wales. He served in the Royal Air Force during World War II. He taught at the universities of Edinburgh, Aberdeen and Glasgow, where he became Professor of Celtic in 1963. In 1952 he founded, and remains the editor of, the Gaelic language quarterly *Gairm*, and helped set up the Gaelic Books Council in 1968. He has written important critical works on Gaelic poetry, notably *An Introduction to Gaelic Poetry* (1974, rev 1989), compiled a *New English-Gaelic Dictionary* (1981), and edited *The Companion to Gaelic Scotland* (1983). His own poetry constitutes one of the most significant bodies of modern Gaelic verse; much of it is collected, in both Gaelic and his own English versions, in *Creachadh na Clàrsaich* (*Plundering the Harp—Collected Poems 1940–1980*, 1982). His poetry tends to focus on his ambivalent relationship with the Outer Hebrides, and on his sometimes impatient sense of nationalism, but, like that of **Sorley MacLean**, continually finds universal truths emerging from the particular. A new collection, *Smeur an doch ais* ('The Bramble of Hope'), appeared in 1991.

THOMSON, James, occasional pseud '**B V**'
(1834–82)

Scottish poet, born in Port Glasgow, the son of a merchant seaman. He was educated in the Royal Caledonian Asylum orphanage and trained as an army schoolmaster at the

Royal Military Asylum, Chelsea, but was dismissed from army service for alcoholism in 1862. A friend of Charles Bradlaugh, editor and owner of the *National Reformer*, between 1862 and 1875 he contributed many of his sombre, sonorous poems to the paper, including *The City of Dreadful Night* (1874), his greatest work. He became a lawyer's clerk in 1862, went into business (1864–9), went to the USA as a mining agent (1872–3), was war correspondent in Spain with the Carlists (1873), and from 1875 onwards depended largely on contributions to a tobacconists' trade monthly. Ill-health and melancholia drove him to narcotics and stimulants. *The City of Dreadful Night and other Poems* (1880) was followed by *Vane's Story* (1881), *Essays and Phantasies* (1881), *A Voice from the Nile* (1884), *Shelley, a Poem* (1885) and *Biographical and Critical Studies* (1896). His pseudonym B V, Bysshe Vanolis, was partly from **Shelley**'s second name, partly from an anagram of Novalis. The poet **Tom Leonard** published a remarkable biographical meditation on his life and work, *Places of the Mind*, in 1993.

▷I Waller, *James Thomson (BV)* (1950); T Leonard, *James B.V. Thomson* (1993)

THOMSON, James
(1700–48)

Scottish poet, born in Ednam, Roxburghshire. He was educated at Jedburgh School and studied at Edinburgh University for the ministry, but he abandoned his studies and went to seek his fortune as a writer in London. He published *Winter* (1726), a short poem in blank verse, *Summer* (1727), *Spring*, (1728), and *Autumn*, which appeared with the other three under the collective title *The Seasons* (1730). It was substantially revised in 1744, and became a source-book for much later bird poetry. In 1729 his *Sophonisba* was produced. His other tragedies were *Agamemnon* (1738), *Edward and Eleonora* (1739), *Tancred and Sigismunda* (1745) and *Coriolanus* (1748). The poem *Liberty* (1735–6) was inspired by the Grand Tour which he undertook as tutor to Charles Talbot's son in 1731, and was dedicated to the Prince of Wales, who awarded him a pension. 'A Poem sacred to the Memory of Isaac Newton' (1727) and 'Britannia' (1729), which criticized Walpole's foreign policy, secured him further patronage and the sinecure of Surveyor-General of the Leeward Isles (1744). *Alfred, a Masque* (1740) contains the song 'Rule Britannia', also claimed by **David Mallet**. The Spenserian *The Castle of Indolence* (1748) is considered his masterpiece.

▷J Grant, *James Thomson* (1957)

THOOR, Jesse, pseud of **Peter Karl Höfler**
(1905–52)

Austrian poet, who went into exile—he became a silversmith in London—on the advent of Hitler. He was originally a communist. He was born in Berlin, but died at Lienz in his native Austria, of a heart ailment, while on a visit. Aloof from movements, still a trifle neglected (though well appreciated by those who know his work), he produced poems of great religious power, in his *Die Sonnete und Lieder* (1956, 'Sonnets and Songs'). He is regarded as one of the greatest sonneteers in the German language since **Andreas Gryphius**. His collected works were edited in German by **Michael Hamburger** (1965), who translated some of the poems in his (and **Christopher Middleton**'s) *Modern German Poetry* (1962).

THORARENSEN, Bjarni Vigfússon
(1786–1841)

Icelandic romantic poet and jurist, born in Brautarholt and brought up at Hlíðarendi. A precociously brilliant student, he went to Copenhagen University at the age of 15 to study law. After government service in Denmark, he was appointed a deputy justice in Reykjavík (1811), and justice of the supreme court (1817). In 1833 he was appointed governor of North and East Iceland. As a lyric poet he celebrated Icelandic nature and nationalism, using the metres of classical heroic poetry; one of his poems, *Eldgamla Ísafold* ('Ancient Iceland'), was regarded as an unofficial national anthem, set to the music of *God Save the Queen*.

▷Þ Gíslason, *Bjarni Thorarensen* (1932)

THOREAU, Henry David
(1817–62)

American essayist and poet, the 'hermit of Walden', born of Jersey stock in Concord, Massachusetts. He graduated from Harvard in 1837, became a teacher in Concord, and lectured. He soon gave up teaching, and joined his father in making lead pencils, but about 1839 began his walks and studies of nature as the serious occupation of his life. In 1839 he made the voyage described in his *Week on the Concord and Merrimack Rivers* (1849). Thoreau made the acquaintance of **Ralph Waldo Emerson**, and between 1841 and 1843 and in 1847 was a member of his household. In 1845 he built himself a shanty in the woods by Walden Pond, where he lived from 1845 to 1847 and wrote much of the *Week*, his essay on **Thomas Carlyle**, and the American classic, *Walden, or Life in the Woods* (1854). After the Walden episode he supported himself by whitewashing, gardening, fence building and land surveying. He also lectured now and then, and wrote for magazines. He made three trips to the Maine woods in 1846, 1853 and 1857, described in papers collected after his death (1864). In 1850 he made a trip to Canada, which produced *A Yankee in Canada* (1866). In 1835 he began to keep a daily journal of his walks and observations, from whose 30 volumes were published *Early Spring in Massachusetts* (1881), *Summer* (1884) and *Winter* (1887). Other publications are *Excursions in Field and Forest*, with memoir by Emerson (1863), *Cape Cod* (1865), *Letters to Various Persons*, with nine poems (1865), *Familiar Letters* (1894) and *Poems of Nature* (1896), and a celebrated essay, *Civil Disobedience* (1849), provoked by his opposition to the Mexican War.

▷ R D Richardson Jnr, *Thoreau: a life of the mind* (1986)

THORLÁKSSON, Jón
(1744–1819)

Icelandic poet and scholar, born in Selárdalur, the son of a parson. He himself became a parson, but was twice defrocked for illegal carnal intercourse. He was eventually rehabilitated and lived in penury in a country parish at Bægisá. He was a prolific writer of poetry and occasional verse, but his most important work was as a translator into Icelandic of **Pope**'s *Essay on Man* (1798), **Milton**'s *Paradise Lost* (1828) and **Friedrich Klopstock**'s *Messiah* (published 1834–8).

▷ R Beck, *Jón Thorláksson* (1957)

THORODDSEN, Jón, originally Thórðarson
(1818–68)

Icelandic novelist and poet, born in Reykhólar. Regarded as the father of the modern Icelandic novel, he studied law at Copenhagen and wrote drinking songs in the style of **Carl Bellmann**. He was an avid reader of Sir **Walter Scott**, and used him as a model for his first book, *Piltur og stúlka* (1850, 'Boy and Girl'), the earliest proper novel produced in Iceland. In 1850 he returned to Iceland and was appointed a district magistrate on the island of Flatey. In addition to a sheaf of lyrics, he also wrote an unfinished sequel to his first novel, *Maður og kona* ('Man and Woman', published posthumously in 1876).

▷ S J Ðorsteinsson, *Thoroddsen og skaldsogur hans* (1943)

THORSTEINSSON, Steingrímur (Bjarnason)
(1831–1913)

Icelandic poet and scholar, born in Arnarstapi on Snæfellsnes. He studied classical philology and modern European literature at Copenhagen (1851–63), and worked in Copenhagen (1863–72), where he wrote patriotic poetry in support of Jón Sigurðsson's independence movement. He returned to Iceland as teacher, later headmaster, at the Latin School in Reykjavík (1872–1913). His major importance was to enrich Icelandic native culture through his fine translations of all the modern European poets, as well as *King Lear*, *The Arabian Nights*, *Robinson Crusoe*, and **Hans Christian Andersen**.

▷ H Petursson, *Steingrimur Thorsteinsson, lif og hanslist* (1964)

THORUP, Kirsten
(1942–)

Danish novelist, poet and writer of short stories and plays for television. Born in Gelsted, on Funen, she published her first book of poetry in 1967, evolving a modernist aesthetics which reflects the alienation and fragmentation of contemporary life. The poetic texts in *Love from Trieste* (1969, Eng trans 1980) and *I dag er det Daisy* (1971, 'It's Daisy Today') show the influence of the thinking of R D Laing, while the highly successful novel *Baby* (1973, Eng trans 1980) is an exploration of individual powerlessness in a context in which cause and effect, and thus a coherent pattern of meaning, are non-existent. She has subsequently enjoyed great success as a realist novelist, notably with *Lille Jonna* (1977, 'Little Jonna') and *Den lange sommer* (1979, 'The Long Summer'). A prolific writer of television drama, she based *Else Kant* (1978) on two novels by **Amalie Skram**.

▷ M-L Paludan, 'Kirsten Thorup', in T Brostrøm and M Winge (eds), *Danske digtere i det 20. århundrede*, vol V (1982)

THUBRON, Colin Gerald Dryden
(1939–)

English novelist and travel writer, born in London, a descendant of **John Dryden**. Thubron abandoned a career in publishing in order to travel, mainly in Asia and northern Africa, and the vivid accounts of his journeys have made him one of the most highly respected of travel writers. His best-known titles include *Among the Russians* (1983) and *Behind the Wall* (1987), an intriguing insight into modern China, in which personal day-to-day lives are set against the political and economic context. Among his novels are *A Cruel Madness* (1984), a study of instability, and *Falling* (1989), a poignant story of love and loss.

THUCYDIDES
(c.460–c.400 BC)

Greek historian of the Peloponnesian war, born near Athens. He suffered in the Athenian plague (c.430) but recovered. He commanded an Athenian squadron of seven ships at Thasos (424), when he failed to relieve Amphipolis; condemned as a traitor, he retired to his Thracian estates. He lived in exile for 20 years (possibly visiting Sicily), writing his eight-book *De Bello Peloponnesiaco*, and probably returned to Athens in 404. He did not live long enough to bring his history down to the end of the war (his account ends in 411 BC). Much of his matter is based on the speeches of leading politicians (reconstructed largely on the testimony of witnesses). He aimed at a lucid and unbiased narrative, and an almost scientific analysis of the reasons for the defeat of Athens. His work is of outstanding importance, both for the detailed information it gives about one of the great conflicts (of ideas as well as of interests) in antiquity and as a model of careful research. The *Hellenica* of **Xenophon** was written to carry Thucydides' narrative down to the end of the war in 404 BC.

▷ *The Peloponnesian War* (Eng trans Rex Warner, 1954)

THURBER, James Grover
(1894–1961)

American humorist and cartoonist, born in Columbus, Ohio. When he was six years old, one of his brothers shot him with an arrow and he lost the sight of his left eye; towards the end of his life, he gradually lost the sight in his good eye. He attended schools in Columbus and went to Ohio State University where, as he stated modestly in his fragmentary autobiography, *My Life and Hard Times* (1933), he passed all his courses save botany. In the early 1920s he reported for various papers in America and Europe but in February 1927 **E B White** introduced him to Harold Ross, Editor of the *New Yorker*, and he was instantly appointed its managing editor. It was not a job to which he was suited and he drifted into writing, before leaving the staff altogether. But he contributed regularly, humorous essays at first, then the inimitable sketches of dogs, barking seals and marital discord. His drawings first appeared in *Is Sex Necessary?* (1929) which he co-authored with White. A plethora of books followed, often combining humorous essays with characteristic doodles, including *The Owl in the Attic and Other Perplexities* (1931), *The Seal in the Bedroom and Other Predicaments* (1932), *The Middle-Aged Man on the Flying Trapeze* (1935), *Men, Women and Dogs* (1943) and *The Wonderful O* (1957). He was also a dramatist and appeared as himself in a brief run of *A Thurber Carnival* in 1960, and wrote a number of notable short stories, of which *The Secret Life of Walter Mitty*, filmed with Danny Kaye (1946), is best known. *The Years With Ross* (1959) is an anecdotal memoir

recounting his experience of the unpredictable *New Yorker* editor.

▷ B Bernstein, *James Thurber, a biography* (1975)

THWAITE, Anthony Simon
(1930–)

English poet, born in Chester and educated at Kingswood School, Bath, and Christ Church, Oxford. He was literary editor of *The Listener* (1962–5) and *The New Statesman* (1968–72), and co-editor of *Encounter* (1973–85). He became poetry editor at Secker and Warburg in 1986. He edited **Philip Larkin**'s *Collected Poems* (1988) and *Letters* (1992). He has published a number of volumes, the most important of which are the Larkin-esque *The Owl in the Trees* (1963); *New Confessions* (1974), which is based on St Augustine and made use of the monologue form; and the lyrics in *Victorian Voices* (1980). His work has been collected in *Poems 1953–88* (1989), and is too varied to permit easy categorization.

THWAITES, F(rederick) J(oseph)
(1908–79)

Australian writer of popular and sentimental novels, born in Balmain, Sydney. Possibly Australia's bestselling author in the inter-war period, he published many of the books himself, starting with his first novel *The Broken Melody* (1930). Typical titles (and locales) are *Fever* (1939), *Whispers in Tahiti* (1940) and *Shadows over Rangoon* (1941). *The Broken Melody* was reprinted steadily between the wars, and in its description of the corrupting effects of cocaine addiction, and its impact on family life, was in advance of its time.

TIBULLUS, Albius
(c.50–19 BC)

Roman elegiac poet, perhaps born in Gabii. He acquired the friendship of the poet-statesman, M Valerius Messalla, and joined his staff, when Augustus commissioned him (30 BC) to crush a revolt in Aquitania. While he distinguished himself in the campaign, he disliked a soldier's life as much as he enjoyed Roman society. When he started with Messalla on a mission to Asia, he became ill on the voyage, and turned back at Corcyra. His sentimental elegiac love poems to his mistresses persuaded Quintilian to place Tibullus at the head of Roman elegiac poets.

▷ G Luck, *The Latin Love Elegy* (1969)

TICKELL, Thomas
(1686–1740)

English poet, born at Bridekirk, Carlisle. He was a fellow of Queen's College, Oxford

(1710–26). His complimentary verses on *Rosamond* (1709) gained him the favour, and his own virtues the friendship, of **Joseph Addison**, who, on becoming in 1717 secretary of state, made him his under-secretary; from 1725 he was secretary to the lords justices of Ireland. He was skilful in occasional poetry, and was favourably reviewed in the *Spectator*. His translation of book one of the *Iliad* appeared in 1715, about the same time as **Pope**'s. Pope professed to believe it the work of Addison himself, designed to eclipse his own version, and wrote the famous satire on Atticus. But though Addison corrected it, the translation was doubtless by Tickell. His longest poem is *Kensington Gardens*; his most popular, *Colin and Lucy*; his finest, the exquisite elegy prefixed to his edition of Addison's *Works* (1721).

▷ R E Tickell, *Thomas Tickell and 18th Century Poetry* (1931)

TIECK, Johann Ludwig
(1773–1853)

German critic and poet of the Romantic school, born in Berlin. He lived the life of a writer, in Berlin, Dresden and near Frankfurt an der Oder. After two or three immature romances, he produced a new line in clever dramatized versions (*Märchendramen*) of *Der gestiefelte Kater* (1797, 'Puss in Boots'), *Ritter Blaubart* (1797, 'Blue Beard'), and others. He followed up this first success by the satire *Anti-Faust, oder Geschichte eines dummen Teufels* (1801, 'Anti-Faust, or the Story of a Dim Devil'), the horror story *Der Runenberg* (1804, 'The Rune Mountain'), and *Phantasus* (1812–17), a collection of traditional lore in story and drama. Besides supervising the completion of **August von Schlegel**'s translation of **Shakespeare**, he edited the doubtful plays and wrote a series of essays (*Shakespeares Vorschule*, 1823–9, 'Shakespeare's Preparatory School'). He translated *Don Quixote* in 1799–1804. He holds an honourable place among Germany's dramatic and literary critics, because of his *Dramaturgische Blätter* (2nd edn 1852, 'Dramaturgical Pages') and *Kritische Schriften* (1848, 'Critical Writings').

▷ E H Zeydel, *Ludwig Tieck, the German Romanticist* (1935)

TIEN HAN
(1898–1968)

Chinese playwright, from Hunan province. Much of his work strikes the western reader as little more than propagandizing—his plays *Uei yu* (1931, 'Flood') and *Lu-kou-chi'iao* (1933, 'Drought') are vehicles for conveying strongly pro-communist messages. There is more literary merit in *Cha-fei-tien chih yeh* (1922, 'A Night in the Café') and *Huo hu chih yeh* (1921, 'The Night the Tiger Escaped') in that, although the political content is unmistakable, some attempt has been made to draw real characters and construct plotlines which do more than provide an opportunity for the downtrodden peasantry to arise and overthrow the evil oppressor.

TIKHONOV, Nikolay
(1896–1971)

Russian poet, born in St Petersburg. He began under the influence of **Gumilev** and the Serapion Brothers, and wrote an independent and affirmative poetry which had much in common with that of the Futurists; but, never strikingly original, he gradually submitted himself to officialdom, and his powers faded. However, he called upon his head the wrath of Zhdanov for his 'dissidence'. All his best poems were written in the 1920s.

▷ G Struve, *Russian Literature Under Lenin and Stalin 1917–1953* (1971)

TIKKANEN, Märta
(1935–)

Finland–Swedish novelist and poet. Born in Helsinki, she completed a degree and then worked as a journalist. Her first novel, *nu imorron* (1970, 'now tomorrow'), uses stylistic experimentation to convey the situation of an over-worked wife and mother, while *Män kan inte våldtas* (1975, Eng trans *Manrape*, 1978), her first major success, is a realist account of a woman who takes revenge on the man who has raped her by raping him. The poems in *Århundradets kärlekssaga* (1978, Eng trans *Love Story of the Century*, 1984) depict the experience of a family in which the husband and father is an alcoholic. One of her other novels, *Rödluvan* (1986, 'Little Red Riding Hood'), employs mythical patterns to draw into focus a marital relationship.

▷ M Mazzarella, 'Märta Tikkanen (1935–). Passion eller jämlikhet?', *Från Fredrika Runeberg till Märta Tikkanen. Frihet och beroende i finlandssvensk kvinnolitteratur* (1985)

TIMON OF PHLIUS
(c.325–c.235 BC)

Greek philosopher and poet from the northern Peloponnese. He was Pyrrho's leading disciple and his biographer, and an enthusiastic exponent of the theories of scepticism. After a period as an itinerant lecturer he retired to Athens where he was a leading member of the local intelligentsia and a versatile author. He wrote satyr-plays, comedies, tragedies, epic poems and a famous series of *Silloi*, satirical mock-heroic poems which parody and insult most earlier Greek philosophers, who are seen as doctrinaire, pretentious and generally aberrant predecessors of the Pyrrhonian enlightenment. Only brief fragments of his work have survived.

TIMROD, Henry
(1828–67)

American poet and critic, 'The Laureate of the Confederacy', born in Charleston, South Carolina, whose classically orientated, severe but fervently felt work is still anthologized for its importance in the development of American poetry. He published only one collection in his lifetime, *Poems* (1860), but the posthumous *Complete Poems* (1899) adds many more. He suffered from tuberculosis, which was aggravated by what he called the 'beggary, starvation, death, bitter grief, utter want of hope' which eventuated when the city of Columbia, where he had worked for a newspaper, was captured and burned in 1865. He is famous for his 'Katie' poems (to the woman he married), and for his elegies for the confederate dead, including the famous 'Ode': 'Sleep sweetly in your humble graves,/Sleep, martyrs of a fallen cause;/Though yet no marble column craves/The pilgrim here to pause'.
▷E W Parks (ed), *The Essays of Henry Timrod* (1942, with an important introduction); Henry T Thompson, *Henry Timrod* (1928)

TING LING
(1907–)

Chinese writer, and *habitué* of literary circles in the run-up to the revolution. Her reputation rests solely on her masterly revolutionary document *T'ai-yang chao tsai Sung-kan-ho shang* (1948, Eng trans *The Sun Shines over the Sangkan River*, 1953), which was written when she had been sent into the country for political re-education. Ostensibly a novel (though large sections of it are obviously closer to *reportage*), it documents the overthrow of the feudal system and the effects of land reform on the peasantry. It won her the Stalin Prize in 1949, though she later fell out of favour with the communist authorities because of her maverick ways and a number of politically imprudent political statements.

TIPTREE, James, pseud of Alice Hastings Bradley Sheldon
(1915–87)

American science-fiction writer, born in Chicago. She spent much of her childhood in Africa and India (her mother was a geographer and travel writer), worked for the US Government until 1955, then trained as a psychologist. She published her first story as 'Alice Sheldon' in 1946, but began to write science fiction as James Tiptree in 1967, and was widely assumed to be a man until her

'exposure' in 1977. Her psychologically complex, death-haunted fiction is found at its best in the short story form, the most important of which are collected in *Ten Thousand Light Years From Home* (1973), *Star Songs of an Old Primate* (1978) and *Crown of Stars* (1988). Two important novellas, 'The Girl Who Was Plugged In' (1973) and 'Houston, Houston, Do Your Read' (1977), were issued together in 1989. *Up The Walls of the World* (1978) is the best of her four longer works, two of which are made up of interlinked stories.

TIRSO DE MOLINA, pseud of Gabriel Téllez
(c.1571–1648)

Spanish playwright, born in Madrid. He was prior of the monastery of Soria. Lacking his great contemporary **Lope de Vega**'s lyrical gifts, he wrote *Comedias* (5 vols, 1627–36), partly Interludes, and *Autos Sacramentales* (originally about 300), excelling in the portrayal of character, particularly of spirited women, and in his treatment of the Don Juan legend in his masterpiece, *El burlador de Sevilla* (1634, Eng trans *The Trickster of Seville*, 1959).
▷K Vosler, *Lecciones sobre Zirso* (1965)

TODI, Jacopone da
(c.1230–1306)

Italian religious poet, born in Todi in the duchy of Spoleto. He practised as an advocate, was converted to an ascetic life in 1268 and became a Franciscan lay brother in 1278. He was imprisoned (1298–1303) for satirizing Pope Boniface VIII. To him is ascribed the authorship of the *Stabat Mater* and other Latin hymns. He also wrote *Laude* ('Hymns of Praise'), which became important in the development of Italian drama.

TODOROV, Petko
(1879–1916)

Bulgarian dramatist and writer of prose idylls, a friend and disciple of **Pencho Slaveykov**. His style, though a little artificial by today's standards, brought a new combination of sophistication and folkloristic elements into the literature.
▷C Manning and R Smal-Stocki, *The History of Modern Bulgarian Literature* (1960)

TOLENTINO DE ALMEIDA, Nicolau
(1741–1811)

Portuguese poet who became rich by dint of cultivating the powers that were, but continued to feign poverty in his verse until his death: his satire could be repressed by 'the gift of a pheasant'. However, his poetry 'sheds a gentle light on the manners of the time', and his satire is interesting, especcially because in it he appeared ironically to adopt the very position he wished to attack.

▷A Bell, *Portuguese Literature* (1922)

TOLKIEN, J(ohn) R(onald) R(euel)
(1892–1973)

South African-born philologist and author, born in Bloemfontein. Educated at King Edward VI School, Birmingham, and Merton College, Oxford, he became Professor of Anglo-Saxon there (1925–45), and of English Language and Literature (1945–59). His scholarly publications include an edition of *Sir Gawain and the Green Knight* (1925), and studies on **Chaucer** (1934) and *Beowulf* (1937). His interest in language and saga and his fascination for the land of Faerie prompted him to write tales of a world of his own invention peopled by strange beings with their own carefully constructed language and mythology. These include *The Hobbit* (1937), a fascinating tale of the perilous journey of Bilbo Baggins and the dwarfs to recover treasure from the sly dragon Smaug, and the more complex sequel, *The Lord of the Rings* (3 vols, 1954–5), in which Bilbo's nephew, Frodo, sets out to destroy a powerful but dangerous ring in Mordor, the land of darkness and evil. Later works include *The Adventure of Tom Bombadil* (1962), *Smith of Wootton Major* (1967) and *The Silmarillion* (posthumous, 1977).

▷C R Stimpson, *J. R. R. Tolkien* (1970)

TOLLENS, Hendrik
(1780–1856)

Dutch poet, born in Rotterdam. He was author of the Dutch national hymn (until the 20th century), *Wien Neerlandsch Bloed*. He also wrote comedies and a tragedy, romances and ballads.

▷G D J Schotch, *Tollens e zijn tid* (1860)

TOLLER, Ernst
(1893–1939)

German–Jewish poet and playwright, born in Samotschin. A political activist, he was imprisoned in Germany as a socialist revolutionary (1919–24). He was elected to the Bavarian diet in 1924, was banished by the Nazis in 1933 and went to the USA, where he committed suicide in New York in 1939. His expressionist plays include *Masse Mensch* (1921, Eng trans *Masses and Man*, 1923), *Die Maschinenstürmer* (1922, Eng trans *The Machine-Wreckers*, 1923), and others. He also wrote poetry and the autobiographical *Eine Jugend in Deutschland* (1933, Eng trans *I Was a German ...*, 1934).

TOLLET, Elizabeth
(1694–1754)

English poet, well educated by her father, Commissioner of the Navy, and a friend of Isaac Newton to whom she addressed one of her poems. She lived with her father in the Tower of London in her early years, later at Stratford and West Ham. Her *Poems on Several Occasions* (anonymous, 1724) show her well read and accomplished in both Latin and English verse. Her tonal range is wide, encompassing philosophical reflection, devout religious feeling, epigrammatic wit and light-hearted satire. The volume includes imaginary epistles by historical women, such as Anne Boleyn and Mary, Queen of Scots; 'Hypatia' pleads eloquently for the education and intellectual development of women.

▷D B Wyrick, in *Eighteenth-Century British Poets*, pt 1, ed J Sitter, *Dictionary of Literary Biography*, 95 (1990)

TOLSON, Melvin
(1900–66)

American poet, known for his stylistic mishmash of the formal and informal. Tolson was born in Missouri, was taught at Langston University and later became mayor of the town. He was a black American who tried to relate his Negro inheritance to the European traditions of his country. As such Tolson was somewhat overlooked by the wave of interest in more radical black writing during the 1960s and 70s, despite the fact that his last book, *Harlem Gallery* (1965), was the first volume in a projected epic about black history.

TOLSTOY, Count Alexey Konstantinovich
(1817–75)

Russian dramatist, lyrical poet and novelist, born in St Petersburg, distantly related to **Leo Tolstoy**. He wrote a historical trilogy in verse (1867, Eng trans *The Death of Ivan the Terrible*, 1869), *Tsar Fyodor Ioannovich* (1868, Eng trans 1874) and *Tsar Boris* (1870), but only the first work was staged in his lifetime. His other works include nonsense verse and a historical novel, *Prince Serebrenni* (1863, Eng trans 1874).

▷M Dalton, *Alexey Konstantinovich Tolstoy* (1972)

TOLSTOY, Count Alexey Nikolayevich
(1882–1945)

Russian writer, born in Nikolayevsk, Samara, distantly related to **Leo Tolstoy**. He joined the White Army after the 1917 Revolution, which he portrayed vividly in *Khozhdenie po mukam* (1920, Eng trans *Darkness and Dawn*, 1935), was an émigré in Paris (1919–23) but returned to Russia as an honoured man of letters. Other novels include *Khromoĭ barin* (1912, Eng trans *The Lame Prince*, 1912).

▷Y Krestinsky, *Alexey Nicolayevich Tolstoy* (1960)

TOLSTOY, Count Leo Nikolayevich
(1828–1910)

Russian writer, aesthetic philosopher, moralist and mystic, born on the family estate of Yasnaya Polyana in Tula province. He was educated privately and at Kazan University, where he read law and oriental languages but did not graduate. He led a dissolute life in town, played the gentleman farmer, and finally, in 1851, accompanied his elder brother Nikolay to the Caucasus, where he joined an artillery regiment and there began his literary career. *Istoria vcherashchnevo dnya* (1851, 'Accounts of Yesterday') was followed by the autobiographical trilogy, *Detstvo* (1852), *Otrochestvo* (1854) and *Yunost'* (1856, collective Eng trans *Childhood, Boyhood, Youth*, 1886). Commissioned at the outbreak of the Crimean War (1854), he commanded a battery during the defence of Sebastopol (1854–5). After the war, the horrors of which inspired *Sevastopolskiye rasskazy* (1855–6, Eng trans *Sebastopol*, 1887), he left the army, was fêted by the literary circle in St Petersburg (1856), travelled abroad, visiting Britain, and in 1862 married Sophie Andreyevna Behrs who bore him 13 children. He settled on his Volga estate and combined the duties of a progressive landlord with the six years' literary toil which produced *Vonya i mir* (1863–9, Eng trans *War and Peace*, 1866), by many considered the greatest novel ever written. This is at the same time a domestic tale, depicting the fortunes of two notable families, the Rostovs and the Bolkonskis, and a national epic of Russia's struggle, defeat and victory over Napoleon. The proud, shy, duty-conscious Prince Andrew and the direct, friendly, pleasure-loving but introspective, morally questing Pierre reflect the dualism in Tolstoy's own character. On his vivid description of military life Tolstoy mounts his conception of history, which demotes 'great men' to mere creatures of circumstance and ascribes victory in battle to the confused chance events which make up the unpredictable fortunes of war. In Pierre's association with freemasonry, Tolstoy expressed his criticism of the established autocratic order. His second great work, *Anna Karenina* (1874–6, Eng trans 1886), carries with it the seeds of Tolstoy's personal crisis between the claims of the creative novelist and the moralizing, 'committed' propagator of his own ethical code, which culminated in *Ispoved'* (1884, Eng trans *A Confession*, 1885) and the dialectical pamphlets and stories such as *A. Smert' Ivana Ilicha* (1886, Eng trans *(The Death of) Ivan Ilyitch*, 1887), *Kreytserova sonata* (1889, Eng trans *The Kreutzer Sonata*,

1890) and *V chom moya vera?* (1884, Eng trans *My Religion*, 1885). Christianity is purged of its mysticism and transformed into a severe asceticism based on the doctrine of non-resistance to evil. *Tsarstvo Bozhye vnutri vas* (2 vols, 1893–4, Eng trans *The Kingdom of God Is within You*, 1894), *Khozyain i rabotnik* (1894, Eng trans *Master and Man*, 1895), the play *Plody prosveshcheniya* (1889, Eng trans *The Fruits of Enlightenment*, 1891) and *Voskreseniye* (1899, Eng trans *Resurrection*, 1899) strayed so far from orthodoxy that the Holy Synod excommunicated him (1901), and he denounced the worship of Jesus as blasphemy. In *Chto takoye iskusstvo?* (1898, Eng trans *What is Art?*, 1898) he argued that only simple works, such as the parables of the Bible, constitute great art. Everything sophisticated, stylized and detailed, such as his own great novels, he condemned as worthless. He handed over his fortune to his wife and lived poorly as a peasant under her roof. Domestic quarrels made him leave home clandestinely one October night, accompanied only by a daughter and his personal physician. He caught a chill and died in a siding of Astapovo railway station, refusing to see his waiting wife to the last. His doctrines founded a sect and Yasnaya Polyana became a place of pilgrimage. Mahatma Gandhi, who had corresponded with him, adopted the doctrine of nonresistance. But he is best known as the consummate master of the 'psychological' novel. **Boris Pasternak**'s father, Leonid, illustrated Tolstoy's works.
▷A Maude, *The Life of Tolstoy* (1910); I Berlin, *The Hedgehog and the Fox* (1953)

TOMLINSON, Charles
(1927–)

English poet and erstwhile critic, born in Stoke-on-Trent. His melancholy and accomplished work, much of it sensitively descriptive of landscape, has failed to gain a wide audience, but is greatly admired in certain quarters. He has been said, by a generally hostile critic, to have 'renounced experience as a poetic source', but to possess a 'hidden acknowledgement' of 'vivid humanity'. He claims to create a 'moral landscape' through 'images' of a 'certain mental climate', and his attempts to achieve this have much intelligence, discernment and appreciation of foreign poetries, to which he is unusually sensitive.
▷ *Poems: a Selection* (1964); *The Flood* (1981)

TOMLINSON, Henry Major
(1873–1958)

English author, born in London. He worked in a shipping office in his native docklands before becoming a journalist, and his love of the sea is reflected in books like *The Sea and*

TOOLE, John Kennedy

the Jungle (1912), *Tidemarks* (1924) and other travel books, as well as novels such as *Waiting for Daylight* (1922) and his two best-known works, *Gallions Reach* (1927) and *All Our Yesterdays* (1930), an anti-war novel about World War I. He also wrote several other novels, the autobiographical reminiscences in *A Mingled Yarn* (1953), and a biography of **Norman Douglas** (1931).

TOOLE, John Kennedy
(1937–69)

American novelist, born in New Orleans. He was educated at Tulane and Columbia universities, and committed suicide without publishing anything in his lifetime. Eleven years after his death, his mother persuaded the novelist **Walker Percy** to read a manuscript he had left. *A Confederacy of Dunces*, a sprawling, blackly comic social satire set in his native New Orleans, was published in 1980, and won a Pulitzer prize and considerable attention. A second brief novel, *The Neon Bible* (1989), is an elegiac evocation of a rural Southern childhood.

TOOMER, Jean, originally Nathan Eugene Toomer
(1894–1967)

American writer of verse and poetic fiction. He grew up in Washington, DC, where his grandfather had been an influential black politician. Toomer showed no particular academic aptitude and became a physical training instructor; he also did manual work. His one major book was *Cane* (1923), an uncategorizable anthology of prose and verse segments which offers a haunting collage of black life in America. Perhaps partly because of his complex racial background, Toomer refused to align himself with the quasi-nationalism of the 'Harlem Renaissance'. His instincts were already metaphysical, as can be seen from the long poem 'Blue Meridian', a passionate **Whitman**esque vision of a racially and socially harmonized America. Like most of his work after *Cane*, it only became widely known after his death, largely through Darwin Turner's edited collection of Toomer's writings, *The Wayward and the Seeking* (1980); the *Collected Poems* appeared as late as 1988. In 1924 Toomer went to study with **Gurdjieff** at Fontainebleau, and later founded Gurdjieff centres in the USA. He largely stopped writing after the 1940s, and *Cane* stands out as his only substantial achievement. Its status as a great American masterpiece is now firmly established.
▷ N Y McKay, *Jean Toomer, Artist: A Study of his Literary Life and Work* (1984)

TOPELIUS, Zacharias Sakari (Zachris)
(1818–98)

Finnish novelist and scholar, born in Unsikaarlepyy. He studied at Helsinki, and became Editor of the *Helsingfors Tidningar* newspaper (1842–78). He was appointed Professor of Finnish history at Helsinki (1854–78) and rector (1875–8). Writing in Swedish, he is regarded as the father of the Finnish historical novel, with stories of life in the 17th and 18th centuries, published as *Fältskärns berättelser* (1853–67, Eng trans *The Surgeon's Stories*, 1883–4). He also published five volumes of lyrical poetry, and wrote several plays.
▷ V Vasenius, *Zacharias Topelius* (6 vols, 1912–56)

TÖPFFER, Rodolphe
(1799–1846)

Swiss cartoonist and writer, born in Geneva. In 1825 he founded a boarding-school (which he ran for the rest of his life), and in 1832 became Professor of Rhetoric at Geneva Academy. He was the author of the humorous short story 'La Bibliothèque du mon oncle' (1832, 'My Uncle's Library'), published in *Nouvelles genevoises* (1841, 'Stories of Geneva'), and *Rosa et Gertrude* (1846), amongst others. His drawings were equally felicitous, especially in his *Voyages en zig-zag* (1843–53, 'Zig-zag Journeys').

TORGA, Miguel, pseud of Alfredo Rocha
(1907–90)

Portuguese poet, dramatist, novelist, essayist and diarist. He was for many years a doctor in Coimbra, and was one of the most widely read and prolific writers of modern Portugal. He was several times nominated for the Nobel Prize. He kept a diary incorporating his poems and essays, and published it at intervals from 1941 onwards. By far his most popular book was *Bichos* (1940, Eng trans *Farruscio the Blackbird*, 1951), a series of animal–human fables which he followed up with others. *Vindima* (1945) is a harrowing novel about the failure of a vineyard on a Douro estate. A pessimistic writer and in his poetry an atheist, he also wrote plays. The publication of each instalment of his diaries was a literary event.

TORRE, Guillermo de
(1900–)

Spanish minor poet, critic, scholar, editor and translator, born in Madrid. An associate of the Chilean poet **Vicente Huidobro**, he was one of the leaders of the so-called *ultraísmo* movement—this propounded an expressionist theory very close to Huidobro's creationism, and was deeply influenced by cubism.

He remained an ardent defender of the avant garde, translated the poems of **Max Jacob** into Spanish, and was one of the early editors of **García Lorca**.

TORRES BODET, Jaime
(1902–74)

Mexican poet, editor and novelist, a member of the *Contemporáneos* group, born in Mexico City. He was by profession a diplomat and at one time served as Minister of Education. He progressed from a too prolific poet in a variety of styles, through Surrealism, to a final Hermeticism. His novels, all experimental and somewhat insubstantial, seem mostly to have been influenced by **Unamuno**; of these, *Margarita de niebla* (1927, 'Margaret the Cloud'), is typical.
▷ *Selected Poems* (1964, bilingual)

TORRES NAHARRO, Bartolomé
(?1485–?1520)

Major Spanish dramatist and poet, born in La Torre de Miguel Sesmero, Badajoz, but who wrote most of his plays in Italy. Little is known of his life, except that he was a priest who probably turned soldier. He was a member of the large Spanish colony in Rome, which he may have come to via imprisonment by Moorish pirates. His most famous play is *Ymenea* (?1516), derived from *La Celestina* by **Fernando de Rojas**; it develops the tradition of Latin comedies by **Plautus** and **Terence**. *Soldadesca* (1517) is a vigorous satire on the brutality and corruption of military life in Italy, characterized—as are most of his other plays—by a candid obscenity, which caused his work to be placed on the Index for a time.
▷ J E Gillet, *Tores Naharro and the Drama of the Renaissance*, vol 4 of Gillet's edition of some of Torres's works (1943–61)

TÓTH, Árpád
(1886–1928)

Hungarian poet, translator (**Keats**, **Flaubert**, **Wilde**, **Shelley**) and man of letters, born in Debrecen. He supported Bela Kun's brief Hungarian Soviet Republic in 1919 with an excited but hardly seriously Marxist poem, 'Hz v Isten' (1919, 'The New God'), for which he was ever after subtly persecuted. He was a close friend to **Babits**, and is one of the leading representatives of the Nyugat generation. Like so many of his compatriots he was deeply influenced by **Ady** and by French poetry, and (with Babits and **Szabó**) translated **Baudelaire**. Lonely, poor and ill (he died of tuberculosis), Tóth graduated to a melancholy grandeur in his last exquisite poems of longing for a different life and for more real experience. Babits edited his works after his death.

▷ J Reményi, *Hungarian Writers and Literature* (1964)

TOULET, Paul-Jean
(1867–1920)

French poet and novelist, born in Pau. His early work reflects his Parisian life as dandy and self-conscious decadent, but it was never superficial, and deepened as he grew older and poorer and more serious. The Fantaisiste group of minor poets (c.1910–12) was formed around his example, and that of **Laforgue**, and this left its mark upon **Apollinaire**. Toulet wrote some interesting fiction, but it is as a minor poet that he is really important. His poems, all in *Contrerimes* (1920, 'Counter-rhymes'), some of them written or revised when he was debilitated by alcohol and opium, are almost paradigmatically 'decadent'; but they are delicate and elegant, and the underlying despair—of ever being able to love or be loved—is genuine.

TOURGÉE, Albion W(inegar)
(1838–1905)

American novelist and carpetbagger, born in Ohio. Tourgée left university to join the Union Army in the Civil War. He led a successful protest against army food but was seriously wounded in action. The wheel of a gun carriage struck him in the back and he was temporarily paralysed from the waist down. After the war he moved to North Carolina and became involved in the politics of Reconstruction. His romantically plotted but realistically presented novels reflect Tourgée's strong Republican viewpoint. *Bricks Without Straw* (1880) shows a New England teacher in the South sympathizing with blacks, and *Hot Plowshares* (1883), set during Reconstruction, was one of the first books to talk about miscegenation.

TOURNEUR, Cyril
(c.1575–1626)

English dramatist. Little is known of his life. In 1600 he published his *Transformed Metamorphosis* (discovered in 1872), a satirical poem; and in 1609 a *Funeral Poem* on Sir Francis Vere. In 1613 he wrote an *Elegy* on Prince Henry. His fame rests on two plays, *The Revenger's Tragedy* (printed in 1607), which some critics believed was written by **Thomas Middleton** or **John Webster**, and the inferior *The Atheist's Tragedy*, printed in 1611.
▷ P B Murray, *A Study of Cyril Tourneur* (1964)

TOURNIER, Michel
(1924–)

French novelist and broadcaster, born in Paris. His critical acclaim has consistently outweighed his sales, although his works are more accessible than those of his more experimental peers. *Vendredi, ou les limbes du Pacifique* (1967, Eng trans *Friday, or the Other Island*, 1969) retells the Robinson Crusoe story from the point of view of the white sailor's 'inferior' assistant. *Le Roi des Aulnes* (1970, Eng trans *The Erl King*, 1972) won the Prix **Goncourt**, while his play *Le Fétichiste* (1974, 'The Fetishist') won the Grand Prix du Roman from the Académie française.

TOURTEL, Mary
(1874–1948)

English writer and illustrator, born in Canterbury and educated at Canterbury Art School. She began her career in the 1890s but found lasting fame with her 'Rupert the Bear' cartoon strip in the *Daily Express* between 1920 and 1935, after which time Rupert was carried on by others. About 50 Rupert books were published. Her hero is usually accompanied in his adventures by such characters as Bill Badger, Algy Pug and Podgy Pig; sometimes we see a pair of magic flying boots or an encounter with smugglers; other occasions involve simply a pleasant trip to the seaside. Unlike the work of **A A Milne** or **Beatrix Potter**, Tourtel's Rupert has insufficient wit or irony to please many older readers.

▷ G Perry, *Rupert, A Bear's Life* (1985)

TOWNE, Robert Burton
(c.1935–)

American screenwriter, born in Los Angeles. A student of English and philosophy at Pomona State College, he later studied acting, served in the United States Army and worked as a commercial fisherman before writing the screenplay of *The Last Woman On Earth* (1960) for film producer Roger Corman. A contributor to such television series as *The Man From UNCLE* (1964–8) and a consultant on *Bonnie And Clyde* (1967), he gained almost legendary renown as a film industry 'script doctor' whose skills could transform the most unpromising material into something filmable and even memorable. He has made uncredited contributions to such screenplays as *The Godfather* (1972), *Marathon Man* (1976) and *Frantic* (1988). As a credited screenwriter, he received the Oscar for *Chinatown* (1974) and further nominations for *The Last Detail* (1973) and *Shampoo* (1975). His best work has focused on isolated individuals bemused by an uncertain and even unwelcoming wider world. He made his directorial debut with *Personal Best* (1982), a sensitive account of a lesbian relationship; he continues to rescue stricken scripts, although his disgust at the final version of his screenplay for *Greystoke* (1984)

led him to relinquish his on-screen credit to P H Vazak: the name of his recently deceased Hungarian sheepdog.

TOWNSEND, Sue
(1945–)

English humorist, novelist and playwright, born in Leicester. She is best known for *The Secret Diary of Adrian Mole Aged 13¾* (1982) and *The Growing Pains of Adrian Mole* (1984). Witty and perceptive works, they are written in the form of a diary from the point of a view of an intellectually ambitious adolescent boy living in the Midlands, who copes with a precarious family life and emotional problems and fantasies (mostly involving the beautiful teenager Pandora Braithwaite). His adventures continue in three further books, including *Adrian Mole: The Wilderness Years* (1993), in which Mole, aged 23¾, battles on in a perplexing world. Of her plays, *The Great Celestial Cow* (1984) looks at the cultural problems of Asian women in Leicester, while her bestselling novel, *The Queen and I* (1992), imagines the demise of the British Royal family.

TOWNSHEND, Aurelian
(c.1583–c.1643)

English poet, about whom few biographical details are known. He was brought up, and possibly born, in Norfolk. He entered the service of Sir Robert Cecil, with whom he travelled extensively in Europe, and left upon Cecil's death in 1612. He wrote lyrics and poetry, a handful of which survives, and later collaborated with the architect and artist Inigo Jones on two spectacular court masques, *Albion's Triumph* and *Tempe Restored*.

TOYNBEE, (Theodore) Philip
(1916–81)

English novelist and journalist, born in Oxford, a son of the historian Arnold Toynbee, and educated at Christ Church, Oxford. He was a journalist on *The Observer* for several years and published his first novel, *The Savage Days*, in 1937. He became highly regarded as an experimental novelist, his most structurally innovative works being the *Pantaloon* sequence, a semi-autobiographical series of four books, written in verse. The first, *Pantaloon, or The Valediction*, appeared in 1961, and the second, *The Fifth Day of the Valediction of Pantaloon*, in 1964. *The Sixth Day ...* and *The Seventh Day ...* followed in 1966 and 1968. Many literary critics were perplexed by the books, although several poets acclaimed them. Toynbee also wrote and edited non-fiction work, of which *The Distant Drum: Reflections on the Spanish Civil*

War (1976), on which he worked with his father, is the finest.

TOZZI, Federigo
(1883–1920)

Italian fiction writer (and, initially, poet) and dramatist, from Siena—one of Italy's greatest writers of his century, although critics were slow to catch up with this fact. **Moravia**, in a scarcely challenged judgement, believed him to be the 'fourth' Italian writer, after **Manzoni**, **Svevo** and **Verga**. Tozzi had a disturbed childhood: his mother was epileptic and died young, and he was at constant odds with his brutal father, an innkeeper; he was expelled from many schools. The events of his unhappy life—cut short by pneumonia—are of the utmost importance in his work, for in the latter he cultivated a gnostic, humorous stoicism which resembled that of **Kafka** and anticipated a mid-century attitude. During 1907, when he left home, and 1908, he worked for the railways. Then he returned to Siena, where he tried to manage two farms. Throughout the rest of his life he struggled against adversity, meanwhile writing his masterpieces: the stories in *Bestie* (1917, 'Animals') and *L'Amore* (1920, 'Love'), and the novels *Tre croci* (1920, Eng trans *Three Crosses*, 1921), *Il podere* (1921, 'The Farm') and *Ricordi di un impiegato* (1920, Eng trans *Journal of a Clerk*, 1964). He had, a critic has noted, an 'abrasive genius', well adapted to triumph over the too-soft Italian admiration for *bello estilo*, smooth, elegant style. **Borgese** praised him, and saw his worth, but it was left to the post-fascist critics to recognize his greatness. The insufficiency of translations of Tozzi—many of whose works were published posthumously—into English is one of the enduring scandals of modern letters. His complete works were published in Italian, in four volumes (1961–70), by Vallecchi of Florence in *Opere*.

▷S Pacifici, *From Verismo to Experimentalism* (1969), *The Italian Novel from Capuana to Tozzi* (1973); *Italian Quarterly*, 14 (1971); F Ulivi, *Federigo Tozzi* (1962, in Italian)

TRABA, Marta
(1930–84)

Argentinian novelist and short-story writer, who also has written extensively on art history. She graduated from the Universidad Nacional in Argentina with a doctorate in literature in 1950, but has spent most of her life in other countries, most notably Colombia. She won the Casa de las Americas Prize in 1966 for her novel *Las ceremonias del verano* ('Ceremonies of Summer'). In the forefront of new Latin-American feminist writing, her

most widely acclaimed novels are *Conversación al sur* (1981, 'Conversation of the South') and *En cualquier lugar* (1984, 'Anywhere'). One of her main themes is the difference between the utterable and the unutterable, the said and the understood.

TRAHERNE, Thomas
(c.1636–1674)

English poet, born in Hereford, the son of a shoemaker. He studied at Brasenose College, Oxford, became rector of Credenhill (1657) and in 1667 became chaplain to the Lord Keeper of the great seal, Sir Orlando Bridgeman. He wrote the anti-Catholic *Roman Forgeries* (1673), and *Christian Ethicks*, published after his death in 1675. His major work, *Centuries of Religious Meditations* in prose, was first published in 1908. He also wrote poetry, which was not published until 1903. A late discovery, *Poems of Felicity*, was published in 1910. His work is full of the strikingly original imagery of the mystic, yet a mystic who as a 'Christian Epicurean' was prepared to give *Thanksgiving for the Body*.

▷K W Salter, *Thomas Traherne* (1964)

TRAKL, Georg
(1887–1914)

Austrian poet, born and educated in Salzburg. He trained and worked as a pharmacist, and his verse—only one volume of which, *Gedichte* (1913, 'Poems'), was published in his lifetime—has an internal balance and precision that suggests every word has been weighed and gauged with almost scientific exactness. Though he has something in common with the French Symbolists, the only poet he closely resembles is **Friedrich Hölderlin**; he clearly also identifies with the *tabula rasa* consciousness of Kaspar Hauser and, in *Sebastian im Traum* (posthumous, 1915), with the martyred saint. The pre-war poems are registered in dark, brooding colours and aural tonalities and with a dense inwardness which displaces conventional semantics. Trakl's first and best English translator was **Michael Hamburger** (1952); since then, he has been tackled by **James Wright** and **Robert Bly** and, notably, by **Christopher Middleton**.

▷F M Sharp, *The Poet's Madness: A Reading of Trakl* (1981)

TRANSTRÖMER, Tomas
(1931–)

Swedish poet and psychologist, born in Stockholm. He graduated there in 1956, since when he has worked as a psychologist, including a spell at Roxtuna institution for young offenders. His first collection of poems, *17 dikter* (1954, '17 Poems'), characterized by a visionary reality couched in precise pictures, aroused attention and he has since become a leading poet of the post-war era. Refusing to be hustled by his activist colleagues demanding political 'commitment', he chose to ponder 'the great mystery of existence'. His poems consider the contrast between man's spiritual and mental existence, his need for solitude and yet social contact; and how history lives on in the present. These tensions are reflected in his poetic style which skilfully juxtaposes movement and stasis, muted language and striking images. His metaphors are often inspired by music, travel and nature. His 10 collections of poems have been translated into English either in part or *in toto* by Robin Fulton in *Three Swedish Poets* (1970), *Selected Poems* (1974) and *Collected Poems* (1987).

▷K Espmark, *Resans Formler* (1983)

TRANTER, John Ernest
(1943–)

Australian poet, editor and critic, born in Cooma, New South Wales. As editor of 'little magazines' such as *Leatherjacket* and *Transit*, he has been a constant proponent of modernism in poetry, as his own work shows. His first book, *Parallax*, was published as the June 1970 edition of *Poetry Australia*. Four later books were followed by *100 Sonnets* (1977), *Selected Poems* (1982) and *Under Berlin—New Poems 1988* (1988). He edited the anthologies *Preface to the 70s* for *Poetry Australia*, *The New Australian Poetry* (1979) and *Tin Wash Dish: Poems from Today's Australians* (1989), and co-edited *The Penguin Book of Modern Australian Poetry* (1991).

TRANTER, Nigel,
(1909–)

Scottish novelist and historian, born in Glasgow. Educated at George Heriot's School in Edinburgh, he trained as an accountant before becoming a full-time writer in 1936. His output has been prodigious, numbering well over a hundred books. His best known novels are those on historical themes, most notably the trilogy on the life of Robert the Bruce, *The Steps to the Empty Throne* (1969), *The Path of the Hero King* (1970) and *The Price of the King's Peace* (1971). His non-fiction works include significant studies of Scottish castles and fortified houses. A writer whose talent lies in careful historical research rather than stylistic graces, in *Nigel Tranter's Scotland* (1981) he gave an account of his lifelong fascination with rural Scotland's history, heritage, and public affairs.

TRASK, Betty (Margaret Elizabeth)
(1895–1983)

English light romantic novelist, who lived reclusively in Frome, Somerset. She is best known today for her bequest, in 1983, of about £400 000 in order to create an annual award for novels of a non-experimental nature (the first winner of which was **Ronald Frame**). She herself published the first of more than 50 novels, *Cotton Glove Country*, in 1928, and continued writing until the late 1950s. Her books tend towards the heartthrob genre, with such florid titles as *Desire Me Not* (1935) and *Thunder Rose* (1952); her characters are decent, middle-class people and her recurring theme is the eventual triumph of true love. After her death, it was noted in *The Times* that although her novels dwelt upon love, there had sadly never been any reported romance in her own life.

TRAVEN, B, pseud of Berick Traven Torsvan, originally Albert Otto Max Feige, also known as Ret Marut
(1890–1969)

Polish-born German novelist of working-class stock, born in Swiebodzin, a Polish town since subsumed into Germany. His first stories emerged in Germany in 1925 as *Die Baumwollpflücker* (Eng trans *The Cotton-pickers*, 1956) and it is thought he was active as a communist there at the end of World War I. *Das Totenschiff* (1932, Eng trans *The Death Ship*, 1934), an anti-capitalist tale of a seaman caught up in a plan by shipowners to sink the Yorikke and cash in on the insurance, was highly popular. In the mid-1920s he went to Mexico and from there, in German, came 12 novels and short stories, the most famous being *Der Schatz der Sierra Madre* (1927, Eng trans *The Treasure of the Sierra Madre*, 1934, and filmed by John Huston in 1947).

▷W Wyatt, *The Man who was Traven* (1980)

TRAVERS, Ben (Benjamin)
(1886–1980)

English dramatist and novelist, born in Hendon. He was educated at Charterhouse, served in the RAF in both World Wars and was awarded the Air Force Cross (1920). A master of light farce, he wrote to suit the highly individual comic talents of Ralph Lynn, Robertson Hare and Tom Walls in such pieces as *A Cuckoo in the Nest* (1925), *Rookery Nook* (1926), *Thark* (1927) and *Plunder* (1928), which played in the Aldwych Theatre, London for many years. His last work was a comedy, *The Bed Before Yesterday* (1976).

TREASE, Geoffrey
(1909–)

English novelist and historian, born in Nottingham and educated at Oxford. A prolific author, Trease has turned his hand to many kinds of writing—history of the popular, romantic sort featuring cavaliers and castles, and novels. He is best known, however, as a children's author, and has written almost 90 books for younger readers, the first being *Bows Against the Barons* (1934), set during the Wars of the Roses. Almost all feature historical settings, and the majority take place in England. *The Popinjay Mystery* (1973) is a rip-roaring thriller about **Samuel Pepys**; *Aunt Augusta's Elephant* (1969) is a charming Edwardian tale. His books are strong on narrative drive and sense of place, and adapt extremely well for radio—many of his readers came to him in the 1950s and 60s via the BBC, though he is less in vogue now.

TREECE, Henry
(1911–66)

English novelist, poet and essayist, born in the West Midlands. His early creative years were devoted to poetry, which he financed by working as an English teacher. In 1938 he became the founder, with J F Hendry, of the 'New Apocalypse', a romantic literary movement of evanescent influence. His first novel, *The Dark Island* (1952), was written for adults, and centres on the struggle of the Welsh chieftain Caractacus against the Romans. He is now best known as a historical novelist for children. His books of that type, most of which have a child as the witness of the action, include *Viking's Dawn* (1955) and *The Dream-Time* (1967, about a Stone Age boy).

TREMAIN, Rose
(1943–)

English novelist, dramatist, historian and short-story writer, born in London and educated at the Sorbonne and East Anglia University. Her first books appeared only in the USA: *The Fight for Freedom for Women* (1973) surveys the suffragette movement in Britain and the US, while her life of Stalin (1975) makes a special study of his upbringing in order to analyse his adult actions. Her first novel, *Sadler's Birthday*, was published in 1976. Others include *The Swimming Pool Season* (1985), and her best-known, *Restoration* (1989), which looks at the reign of Charles II in order to study contemporary Britain. Her books are cerebral, stimulating, and often bleak. She has also written for the stage and radio, *Temporary Shelter* being published in *Best Radio Plays of 1984*.

TREMBLAY, Michel
(1942–)

French–Canadian dramatist, born in Montreal. His best-known play, *Les Belles Soeurs* (1968), originally produced in Montreal, is a broad and sometimes vulgar comedy written in *joual*, partly-Quebecois dialect and partly an anarchic mix of French, English and all kinds of slang. As *The Sisters-in-Law* it has played in many other countries, and as *The Guid Sisters* it has enjoyed great popularity in Scotland. His plays frequently dwell on sexual repression and its imaginative release: examples are *La Duchesse de Langeais* (1969), a monologue by an ageing drag artist, and *Sacrée Sandra (Sandra/Manon)* (1977), a play about sexual identity. Among his later plays, *Le Vrai Monde?* (1987, 'The Real World?') considers the problems of the writer confronting his own family and emotional heritage.

TRENCH, Frederick Herbert
(1865–1923)

Irish poet, dramatist and producer, born in Avoncore, County Cork. Educated at Haileybury and Keble College, Oxford, he wrote volumes of verse such as *Deirdre Wed* (1900) and *New Poems* (1907); his best-known poem is the dramatic metaphysical enquiry 'Apollo and the Seaman' (1907). He was artistic director of the Haymarket Theatre (1909–11), but his own efforts at writing for the stage met with little success.

TRESSELL, Robert
(1870–1911)

Irish novelist, born into a middle-class Dublin family. Having emigrated to South Africa, he returned and settled in England after his wife's death. There he became involved in left-wing politics and worked as a house-painter, both activities feeding into his great novel, *The Ragged Trousered Philanthropist*, an amusing and moving exposé of the moral turpitude and corruption at the heart of the Edwardian social system. Publishers were understandably wary of this 1 700-page manuscript, and at one point Tressell consigned it to the fire. It was eventually published after his death: in an abridged version in 1914, and in full in 1955.

TREVOR, William (William Trevor Cox)
(1928–)

Irish short-story writer, novelist and playwright, born in Mitchelstown, County Cork. Educated at St Columba's College and Trinity College, Dublin, he taught history and art, sculpted and wrote advertising copy before devoting himself to literature. His first book was a novel, *A Standard of Behaviour* (1958), but though he has published 10 subsequently, including *Mrs Eckdorff in O'Neill's Hotel* (1969), *The Children of Dynmouth* (1976) and *Nights at the Alexandra* (1987), he is by inclination a short-story writer. He has lived in England for much of his life, but Ireland is the source of his inspiration. A superlative storyteller, his collections include *The Day We Got Drunk on Cake* (1967), *The Ballroom of Romance* (1972), *Angels at the Ritz* (1975), *The News from Ireland* (1986) and *Family Sins* (1990). *The Stories of William Trevor* appeared in 1983. He has also written a number of plays and screenplays.

▷G Schirmer, *William Trevor* (1990)

TRIANA, José
(1931–)

Cuban dramatist, who began to write under the influence of Cuba's leading playwright of the 1950s, **Virgilio Piñera**, and the European contemporary masters to whom he had turned for his models. His most celebrated play is *La noche de los asesinos* (1965), produced successfully in New York and in London as *The Criminals*. Drawing on *The Maids* of **Jean Genet** and *Les Enfants Terribles* of **Jean Cocteau**, it depicts the antics of three murderous, or perhaps just fantasizing, adolescents.

TRIFONOV, Yuri
(1925–81)

Russian novelist and dramatist, one of the most outstanding to have emerged since World War II. Born into a high-ranking family, his father was one of the Old Bolsheviks who had joined the Communist Party before the Revolution but who disappeared in one of Stalin's purges. Trifonov was never a dissident himself but achieved the delicate balancing act of maintaining both his membership of the Writers' Union and the respect of his more outspoken colleagues. He wrote two plays, *The House on the Embankment* (1980), depicting the privileges of the Soviet ruling class, and *Exchange*, a satirical tragicomedy about the difficulties of the Moscow housing market for ordinary citizens, which was produced in Britain in 1989. At his death, he was completing *Disappearance*, a novel portraying the effects of the purges and World War II upon Russia.

TRILLING, Lionel
(1905–75)

American critic and academic. He was born in New York City and educated there at Columbia University, where he returned as an instructor in 1932, three years after his marriage to fellow-critic Diana (Rubin) Trilling. He was admitted to the professoriat in 1948,

a year after publishing his only novel, *The Middle of the Journey* (1947), a quasi-allegorical but psychologically sophisticated account of political fellow-travelling and its aftermath. Trilling's first critical work was a study of **Matthew Arnold** (1939), still considered a definitive study of the moral imagination, as was its successor, on **E M Forster** (1943). His most important contributions to the recovery of liberalism in the post-war years and its synthesis with psychoanalytic ideas were *The Liberal Imagination* (1950), *The Opposing Self* (1955) and, in particular, *Freud and the Crisis of Our Culture* (1956, rev edn *Beyond Culture*, 1965). In that last year, he was appointed to the Woodberry chair of literature and criticism at Columbia University, which he held until 1970. His interest thereafter focused very largely on Romanticism; he published *Sincerity and Authenticity* in 1972. After his death, Diana Trilling supervised a 12-volume *Complete Works* (1978–80); she also compiled a volume of his short stories, *Of This Time, Of That Place* (1979).

▷M Krupnick, *Lionel Trilling and the Fate of Cultural Criticism* (1986)

TRIPATHI, Govardhanram
(1855–1955)

Indian (Gujurati) novelist, author of the massive realist novel *Sarasvaticandra* (1887–1901), said to be as yet unbettered in the language.

TRIPP, John
(1927–86)

Welsh poet, born in Bargoed, Glamorgan, and brought up, a farrier's son, in Whitchurch, Cardiff. After working as a journalist in London, he returned to Wales in 1969 and worked as a free-lance writer for the rest of his life. He published six volumes of poetry, his principal subjects being the history of Wales and the present condition of its people.

TRISTAN L'HERMITE, pseud of **François l'Hermite**
(c.1601–1655)

French poet and playwright, the chief of those who prepared the way for the perfectly executed classical French drama of **Racine**. His most famous play, a tragedy, is *La Mariane* (1637), presented, as most of his plays were, at the Marais Theatre in Paris. He was a gambler who led an unhappy and difficult life, some of which he recounts in his racy autobiographical novel, *Le Page disgracié* (1643, 'The Disgraced Page').

▷H C Lancaster, *A History of French Dramatic Literature in the XVIIth Century* (1932)

TROLLOPE, Anthony
(1815–82)

English novelist, born in London. His father was an unsuccessful lawyer and barrister and consequently his school days at Harrow and Winchester were miserable. Later, when the family's financial circumstances were at their lowest, they moved to Belgium where his father died. His mother, **Frances Trollope**, a woman of enviable energy, maintained the family by her prolific writing. In 1834 Trollope became a junior clerk in the General Post Office in London where he marked time, professionally speaking, until he was transferred to Ireland in 1841. He left the Civil Service in 1867, an important but idiosyncratic official whose achievements included the introduction in Great Britain of the pillar-box for letters. A year later he stood unsuccessfully for parliament, and from 1867 to 1870 he edited the *St Paul's Magazine*, in which several of his books were serialized. His first novel, *The Macdermots of Ballycloran*, did not appear until 1847, and his second, *The Kellys and the O'Kellys* (1848), shared its lack of success. With *The Warden* (1855), the first of the Barchester novels, came an inkling of Trollope's genius. It is the story of the struggle over Harding's Hospital, and introduced into English fiction some of its most durable and memorable characters— Mr Harding, who recurs constantly throughout the Barchester series, Archdeacon Grantly, and Bishop Proudie who, with his redoubtable wife, dominates *Barchester Towers* (1857). The rest of the series are: *Doctor Thorne* (1858), *Framley Parsonage* (1861), *The Small House at Allington* (1864), and *The Last Chronicle of Barset* (1867). Interconnected by character and unified by their West Country setting in the imaginary town of Barset, the novels are distinguished by their quiet comedy, slow pace and piquant detail. The series format appealed to Trollope's industry and he embarked on a second, more ambitious sequence—known collectively as the 'Palliser' novels, after Plantagenet Palliser, who features in each—with the publication in 1864 of *Can You Forgive Her?* Its sequel was *Phineas Finn* (1869), and others in the series are *The Eustace Diamonds* (1873), *Phineas Redux* (1876), *The Prime Minister* (1876) and *The Duke's Children* (1880). Regarding himself more as a craftsman than an artist, Trollope claims to have begun work every morning at 5.30 and to have generally completed his planned quota of literary work before he dressed for breakfast. His output was consequently prodigious and comprises 47 novels, travel books, biographies of **Thackeray**, **Cicero** and Lord Palmerston, plays, short stories and literary sketches. His two renowned series apart, other novels worthy of note include *The Three Clerks* (1857), *The Bertrams* (1859), *Orley Farm* (1862), *The Vicar of Bullhampton* (1870), *The Way We Live Now* (1875) and *Doctor Wortle's School* (1881). Periodically he falls from fashion but is currently enjoying a resurgence. His *Autobiography* (1883) is an antidote to more romantic accounts of the literary life.

▷A O J Cockshut, *Anthony Trollope* (1955)

TROLLOPE, Frances, née Milton
(1780–1863)

English novelist, born in Stapleton near Bristol, the mother of **Anthony Trollope**. In 1809 she married Thomas Anthony Trollope (1774–1835), a failed barrister and fellow of New College, Oxford. In 1827 she fell into dire financial difficulties, which were not relieved by moving to Cincinnati, Ohio, in 1827. During her three years in the USA, Mrs Trollope amassed the material for her *Domestic Manners of the Americans* (1832), a critical and witty book much resented in America. Left a widow in 1835, she travelled widely on the Continent, writing articles and fiction for her livelihood, and eventually settled in Florence (1843), where she lived until her death. Of her novels, the most successful were *The Vicar of Wrexhill* (1837) and *The Widow Barnaby* (1839), with its sequel, *The Widow Married* (1840). In all she wrote 115 volumes, now mostly forgotten.

▷U Pope-Hennessy, *Three English Women in America* (1929)

TROTZIG, Birgitta
(1929–)

Swedish modernist writer. Born in Gothenburg, she lived in France from 1954 to 1969, becoming a Roman Catholic in 1955. Consistently asserting the integrity of art, she is a major critic of Swedish materialism and secularization. Her texts confront their readers with a world of suffering and degradation in which a total empathy becomes the prerequisite for bridging the gap to others and thus to God. In an early novel such as *De utsatta* (1957, 'The Exposed'), the priest becomes a Christ-figure as well as a helpless human being, while in *Dykungens dotter* (1985, 'The Marsh King's Daughter') elements of fairy-tale and myth focus the fall and the significance of grace. She has published several volumes of prose fragments and essays, including *Ett landskap* (1959, 'A Landscape') and *Jaget och världen* (1977, 'The I and the World').

▷U Olsson, *I det lysande mörkret. En läsning av Birgitta Trotzigs De utsatta* (1988)

TROYAT, Henri, pseud of **Lev Tarasov**
(1911–)
Russian-born French writer, a prolific producer of novels, novel-cycles, and biographies
of Russian writers. Both his individual
novels, such as *L'Araigné* (1938, winner of
the Prix **Goncourt**), and four of the cycles—
for instance, the five-volume *La Lumière des
Justes* (1959–63)—paint a panoramic picture
of Russian life from the mid-19th century.
Now best known in the Anglophone world as
a biographer, his studies in that field include
works on **Pushkin** (1946, Eng trans 1950),
Tolstoy (1965, Eng trans 1967) and **Chekhov**
(1984, Eng trans 1986). He was elected to the
Académie française in 1959.

TRUJILLO, Bernardo Arias
(1904–39)
Colombian novelist, born in Antioquia,
whose 'tragically early death', wrote the historian of the Spanish–American novel Kessel
Schwartz, 'prevented him from becoming one
of the great Colombian novelists'. He wrote
one novel, *Risaralda* (1936), set in Portobello
on the Risaralda river; it is one of the very
few Negro novels of Spanish America, unique
for its time, and, although written in an over-
grandiloquent style, remains a singular
achievement.
▷G R Coulthard, *Race and Colour in Caribbean Literature* (1962)

TRUMBULL, John
(1750–1831)
American lawyer and poet, born in Watertown, Connecticut, first cousin of Jonathan
Trumbull. He practised law in Boston, New
Haven and Hartford, and became a judge of
the Connecticut supreme court (1809–13). He
wrote a satire on educational methods, *The
Progress of Dullness* (1772–3), and a satire
on British blunders in the American War of
Independence, *McFingal* (1775–82), in imitation of **Samuel Butler**'s *Hudibras*.
▷A Cowie, *John Trumbull, Connecticut Wit*
(1936)

TSAO YU, pseud of **Wan Chia-Pao**
(1905–)
Chinese playwright, usually described as
'modern China's first great' one, born in
Chien-Kiang, Hupei. He started out as an
actor, and made a famous appearance as
Nora in **Ibsen**'s *Doll's House*. The play which
made him famous was *Lei Yü* (1934, Eng
trans *Thunderstorm*, in *Three Famous Chinese
Plays*, 1946): an accomplished piece of
drama, it was Western in style, but its characters remained Chinese. The most potent
influence upon it was **Eugene O'Neill**.
▷F Bowers, *Theatre in the East* (1956)

TSO CH'IU MING
(c.6th century BC)
Chinese author, mentioned by Confucius in
his *Analects*. He wrote the *Tso Chuan*, a commentary on the *Ch'un Ch'iu*, one of the five
classics. Scholars also ascribe to him the *Kuo
Yü*, and these two works comprise the most
important historical sources of the period.
The simplicity of his style served as a model
to later writers.

TSUBOUCHI Shoyo
(1859–1935)
Japanese literary theorist and critic, born in
Mino. An academic at Tokyo University, he
produced, in 1886, his seminal *Shoetsu Shin-
zui* ('The Essentials of the Novel'). It was
widely taken up and became a manifesto for
Japanese naturalism, the dominant form of
novel and story writing in Japan for the next
70 years. It holds, simply, that the writer
should concentrate on what he knows, not
speculate or indulge in fantasy, and that what
is important is not what happens but how
characters respond to what happens. The
novels the theory gave rise to (those of **Shimazaki**, **Tanizaki**, **Natsume** and **Shiga**,
amongst many others) are minutely described
and closely narrated; in their most extreme
form they become internal monologues.

TSUSHIMA Yuko
(1947–)
Japanese writer and novelist, born in Tokyo.
The daughter of **Osamu Dazai**, Tsushima is a
prolific and popular writer of short stories,
one of the first of a generation of Japanese
women writers to achieve a degree of popular
success whilst writing about what might
broadly be termed 'women's issues'. She has
also written novels: *Choji* (1978, Eng trans
Child of Fortune, 1983) is the tale of a divorcee
who finds herself pregnant in a society where
there is considerable stigma attached to
unmarried motherhood.

TSVETAYEVA, Marina
(1892–1941)
Major Russian poet, dramatist and memoirist, usually regarded as of similar status to
Akhmatova. Her pallid, romantic early poetry
was technically well accomplished and gained
her a high reputation; but now receives little
attention. Her husband fought against the
Bolsheviks (for her, Satan), and much of the
poetry of her middle period—in particular
Lebediny stan (1917–22, 'The Swans'
Encampment')—is anti-Bolshevik in spirit.
She also wrote a number of historical verse
plays. **Pasternak**, in writing of her *Versty*
(1922, 'Versts'), spoke of the 'intense lyrical
power of her poetic form'. She emigrated in

1922, and became, in Paris, a symbol of Russia-in-exile. Her memoirs of such writers as **Blok**, **Voloshin** and **Kuzmin** are illuminating, although somewhat nervously self-centred. She proved too individualistic to be able to remain in Paris, returned to Russia in 1939, and hanged herself. Her poetry has been outstandingly well translated by **Elaine Feinstein**.

▷E Feinstein, *A Captive Lion* (1987)

TU FU
(712–70)

Greatest Chinese poet of the T'ang Dynasty and one of the foremost lyricists in the language. He was born in Hsiang-yang, and spent much of his youth travelling, during which time he soaked up impressions of his country's sharply juxtaposed cultural riches and social ills. He was largely unsuccessful in his attempts to gain a position in the imperial service, gaining only temporary appointments. He saw his own situation reflected in the corruption, cynicism and waste of a dynasty which had lost its burnish of optimism and moral uprightness. 'The Ballad of Beautiful Women' is a famous example of his passionate good-heartedness; other poems like 'The Newlyweds' Parting' and 'The Chariots' Song' reflect the violent uncertainties of life at the time, but they are also beautifully crafted and full of memorable imagery. In his later years, Tu Fu was supported financially by an old friend, who enabled him to travel once more, in greater comfort than he had experienced in his youth. The best English-language source for Tu Fu is still Florence Ayscough's two-volume *The Autobiography of a Chinese Poet* (1929); a definitive edition of the complete works appeared in Peking in 1979.

▷W Hung, *Tu Fu, China's Greatest Poet* (1952)

TUCCI, Niccolò
(1908–)

Italian-born American novelist, playwright, columnist and contributor to the *New Yorker*. His novels include *Before My Time* (1962) and *Unfinished Funeral* (1964). His short fiction can be found in *The Rain Came Last and Other Stories* (1990).

TUCHOLSKY, Kurt
(1890–1935)

German satirist, dramatist, novelist, pacifist and left-wing cabaret poet—in the tradition of **Ringelnatz** but more specifically political—who killed himself in Switzerland after the Nazis had burned his books and taken away his nationality. His chansons are still sung,

and are still enjoyable for the Berlin atmosphere which they so colourfully evoke. English translations (selections): H Zohn (ed), *The World is a Comedy* (1957); H Zohn and K F Ross, *What If?—Satirical Writings* (1967)

TUCKERMAN, Frederick Goddard
(1821–73)

American poet, one of the most important of his century, born in Boston. He qualified and briefly practised law, but spent the last 25 years of his life as a recluse in Greenfield, Massachusetts, making notes of eclipses and studying local fauna. Like **Hopkins** in England, with whom he has some affinities, he was scarcely known in his own lifetime, although his single collection, *Poems* (1860), was highly regarded by **Tennyson**. After his death his work, much of which consists of irregular sonnets (one of them speaks of the 'spermal odor of the barberry flower'—highly repulsive, like his metrical unconventionalities, to his more regular compatriots), went into oblivion, but was revised in 1831 by **Witter Bynner** with the *Sonnets of Frederick Goddard Tuckerman* (1931). His ode 'The Cricket', not published until 1950, and then in a bad text, is justifiably regarded as a key poem in American literature: occasioned by his wife's death in childbirth, it deals with his mystical refusal to interpret nature 'for the benefit of his readers' ('Then Cricket, sing thy song! or answer mine!/Thine whispers blame, but mine has naught but praises.').

▷N Scott Momaday (ed), *The Complete Poems* (1965); S A Golden, *Tuckerman* (1966)

TUDUR ALED
(c.1465–c.1525)

Welsh poet, born in Denbighshire. Like **Dafydd ap Gwilym** and **Dafydd Nanmor**, he was amongst the greatest of the school of poets known as the *Beirdd yr Uchelwyr* (poets of the gentry). He was a master of the *awdl* and the *cywydd*, many of which survive. He was the last great Welsh poet; during his lifetime, Welsh literature and culture was beginning its great deterioration, as English began to supplant the native language.

TULSĪDĀS
(1532–1623)

Indian Hindi devotional poet, born in Eastern India. Traditionally believed to have lived for 120 years, the time allotted to a sinless human being, he wrote more than a dozen works. His best-known is *Rāmacaritamānas* ('The Holy Lake of Rāma's Deeds'), an immensely popular Eastern Hindi version of the *Rāmāyana* epic, which he began in 1574. His *bhakti* or devotional approach, concern for moral conduct, and idea of salvation through Rāma incarnated as absolute knowledge and love, suggest a Nestorian Christian influence on his work.

▷ W D P Will, *The Holy Lake of the Acts of Ram* (1953)

TUNSTRÖM, Göran
(1937–)

Swedish author, born in Sunne, Värmland. His first work, *Inringning* ('Encircling'), appeared in 1958, since when he has published poems, plays, travel books (he and his wife, the painter Lena Cronquist, are intrepid travellers) and several long novels. His novels have an inventive plot borne by a rich tapestry of vivid, eccentric characters, but the underlying message is that we need more human love and kindness in our lives. Recurring themes are a search for identity, lost childhood and, inter-connected, father-and-son relationships. His own father, a clergyman whom he dearly loved, died when he was 12 and his world fell apart. In his fiction he recaptures his childhood and tries to come to terms with his loss. He also looks at human responsibility and betrayal in both provincial and international settings. His most popular novels to date are the prize-winning *Juloratoriet* (1982, 'The Christmas Oratorio') and *Tjuven* (1986, 'The Thief').

TUPPER, Martin Farquhar
(1810–89)

English writer, born in Marylebone. He studied at Charterhouse and at Christ Church, Oxford. He was called to the Bar (1835), but soon turned to writing. Of his 40 works, only *Proverbial Philosophy* (1838–67), a series of moralizing commonplaces in free verse, achieved huge worldwide popularity. He also published several novels and plays, and an autobiography, none of which are now read.

TURBERVILE, George
(c.1540–c.1610)

English poet, and secretary to Sir **Thomas Randolph**, born in Whitchurch, Dorset. He was educated at Winchester and New College, Oxford. He wrote epigrams, songs, sonnets, *The Booke of Falconrie* (1575), *The Noble Art of Venerie* (1576), and translated **Ovid**, the Italian poets and others. He was a pioneer in the use of blank verse.

TURGENEV, Ivan Sergeevich
(1818–83)

Russian novelist, born in the province of Orel. The child of landed gentry, he had an unsatisfactory childhood through the cruelty of his mother, whose great inherited wealth made her a petty tyrant in the home. After graduating from St Petersburg University he broke away by going to study philosophy in Berlin and there mingled with the radical thinkers of the day. He became firm friends with **Alexander Herzen**. He returned to Russia in 1841 to enter the civil service, but in 1843 abandoned this to take up literature. His mother strongly disapproved and his infatuation for a singer, Paulina Garcia (Mme Viardot), also displeased her. She stopped his allowance and until her death in 1850, when he came into his inheritance, he had to support himself by his writings. He began with verse, *Parasha* (1843), showing the influence of **Alexander Pushkin**, but soon recognized prose as his medium and in 1847 produced *Khor i Khalynich* ('Khor and Khalynich'), his first sketch of peasant life, which appeared again in *Zapiski okhotnika* (1852, Eng trans *Russian Life in the Interior*, 1855). This book, sympathetic studies of the peasantry, made his reputation, but earned governmental displeasure, as it was interpreted as an attack on serfdom. A notice praising **Nikolai Gogol** on his death in 1852 exacerbated the ill-feeling and resulted in a two years' banishment to his country estates. After his exile he spent much time in Europe, writing nostalgically of life in Russia. *Rudin* (Eng trans *Dmitri Roudine*, 1873) appeared in 1856, *Dvoryanskoye gnezdo* (Eng trans *A Nest of Gentlefolk*, 1869) in 1859, *Nakanune* (Eng trans *On the Eve*, 1871) in 1860, all faithful descriptions of Russian liberalism, with its attendant weaknesses and limitations. In his greatest novel, *Ottsy i dety* (1862, Eng trans *Fathers and Sons*, 1867), he portrayed the new generation with its reliance on the practical and materialistic, its faith in science and lack of respect for tradition and authority, in short the Nihilists. But the hero, Bazarov, pleased neither the revolutionaries who thought the portrait a libel nor the reactionaries who thought it a glorification of iconoclasm. Turgenev's popularity slumped in Russia but rose abroad, particularly in Britain, where the book was recognized as a major contribution to literature. Successive novels were *Dym* (1867, Eng trans *Smoke*, 1868) and *Nov'* (1877, Eng trans *Virgin Soil*, 1877). He returned to the short story, producing powerful pieces like *Stepnoy Korol' Lir* (1870, Eng trans *A Lear of the Steppes*, 1874) and tales of the supernatural to which his increasing melancholy drew him.

▷ L Schapiro, *Turgenev, his life and times* (1978)

TURNER, Ethel Mary
(1870–1958)

English-born Australian novelist and children's author, born in Balby, Yorkshire. Her father, Bennett George Burwell, died before she was two, and for her writing she took her step-father's surname. She moved to Australia at the age of nine. With her sister Lilian she started *Iris*, a magazine for schoolgirls, for which Ethel wrote the children's page, later doing the same for the *Illustrated Sydney News* and the *Bulletin*. Her first book, *Seven Little Australians* (1894), is now a classic of Australian literature. It has been in print ever since publication, was filmed as early as 1939 and has been adapted for British and Australian television and as a stage musical. A sequel, *The Family at Misrule*, came out in 1895 and there followed a steady stream of juvenile books, short stories and verse. Her daughter Jean Curlewis (1899–1930) edited the children's column in the Sydney *Daily Telegraph*, wrote a number of books for older children including *The Ship that Never Set Sail* (1921) and collaborated with her mother on such books as *The Sunshine Family: a Book of Nonsense for Girls and Boys* (1923).

TURNER, George
(1916–)

Australian novelist, science-fiction writer and critic, born in Melbourne. *A Young Man of Talent* came out in 1959, and was followed by *A Stranger and Afraid* (1961), the first of five books loosely centred on the fictional town of Treelake. The second 'Treelake' title was *The Cupboard Under the Stairs* (1962), a powerful story of a mental hospital patient and his return to the world. It shared the **Miles Franklin** Award in 1962. In science fiction he has written a trilogy, *Beloved Son* (1978), *Vaneglory* (1981) and *Yesterday's Men* (1982), which, especially in using character and location to provide continuity, often mirrors the 'Treelake' tetralogy. *The Sea and the Summer* (1987) pictures the civilization in a 21st century Melbourne after devastating *tsunamis* or tidal waves.
▷ *In the Heart or in the Head* (1984)

TURNER, Walter James Redfern
(1884–1946)

Australian-born British poet and critic, born in Melbourne. He left Australia in 1907 and served in World War I, during which his first and best collection of verse, *The Hunter and Other Poems* (1916), was published. The patron Edward Marsh included a number of Walter's poems in *Georgian Poetry 1916–17* (1917), as a result of which he was accepted into London literary circles. Later verse included *The Dark Fire* (1918) and *The Landscape of Cytherea* (1923). After the war he was sometime Literary Editor of the *Daily Herald*, drama critic of the *London Mercury* and music critic of the *New Statesman*. He became Literary Editor of the *Spectator* in 1942. His other books of verse, mainly on the

metaphysical concept of love, include *Marigold* (1926), *Pursuit of Psyche* (1931) and *Fossils of a Future Time* (1946). He wrote nearly 20 plays, though only two were both published and performed. An accomplished amateur musician, he wrote a number of serious studies, including *Beethoven: the Search for Reality* (1927) and *Mozart: the Man and His Work* (1937). He will perhaps be remembered best as the creator and General Editor of the Collins' series 'Britain in Pictures' (1941–6).
▷W McKenna, *W J Turner: Poet and Music Critic* (1990)

TUTUOLA, Amos
(1920–)

Nigerian novelist, born in Abeokuta. He was educated at a Salvation Army school and later taught at Lagos High School. *The Palm-Wine Drinkard* (1952), his most popular book, written in a musical pidgin, deals with its hero's adventures among the 'Deads'—the spirits of the departed.
▷G Collins, *Amos Tutuola* (1969)

TUWHARE, Hone
(1922–)

New Zealand Maori poet, a major figure who uses the strength of Maori oral tradition and the passions of working-class roots to drive home his political message. His first book, *No Ordinary Sun* (1964, rev edn 1977), became instantly popular, and was followed by *Come Rain Hail* (1970) and *Sapwood and Milk* (1973). *Selected Poems* was published in 1980, *Mihi: Collected Poems* in 1987, and *Deep River Talk: Collected Poems* in 1993.

TWAIN, Mark, pseud of **Samuel Langhorne Clemens**
(1835–1910)

American writer, born in Florida, Missouri. A printer first (1847–55), and later a Mississippi river-boat pilot (1857–61), he adopted his pen-name from a well-known call of the man sounding the river in shallow places ('mark twain' meaning 'by the mark two fathoms'). In 1861 he went to Carson City, Nevada, as secretary to his brother, who was in the service of the governor, and while there tried goldmining without success. He next edited for two years the Virginia City *Territorial Enterprise* and in 1864 moved to San Francisco as a reporter. His first success was *The Celebrated Jumping Frog of Calaveras County* (1865), published as a book with other sketches in 1867. In 1867 he visited France, Italy and Palestine, gathering material for his *Innocents Abroad* (1869), which established his reputation as a humorist. Later he was editor of a newspaper in Buffalo, where he married the wealthy Olivia Langdon. Later

he moved to Hartford, Connecticut, and joined a publishing firm which failed, but largely recouped his losses by lecturing and writing. *Roughing It* (1872) is a humorous account of his Nevada experiences, while *The Gilded Age* (1873), written with **Charles Dudley Warner**, a novel which was later dramatized, exposes the readjustment period after the Civil War. His two greatest masterpieces, *Tom Sawyer* (1876) and *Huckleberry Finn* (1884), drawn from his own boyhood experiences, are firmly established among the world's classics; other favourites are *A Tramp Abroad* (1880) and *A Connecticut Yankee in King Arthur's Court* (1889). Mark Twain pokes fun at entrenched institutions and traditions, but his 'debunking' is mostly without malice and his satire is free from bitterness, except in later work, such as *The Tragedy of Pudd'nhead Wilson* (1894), when fate had been unkind to him. In places his subject-matter is inclined to date, but his best work is not only classic humorous writing but a graphic picture of the 19th-century American scene.
▷J Kaplan, *Mark Twain, a biography* (1966); E Emerson, *The Authentic Twain, a biography of Clemens* (1984)

TWARDOWSKI, Samuel ze Skrzpny
(c.1600–1661)
Polish Baroque poet, born on the Lutynia River in western Poland. Educated by Jesuits, he acquired the nickname of the 'Polish Virgil' on account of his narrative poems. He wrote an opera, *Daphnis* (1638), and a pastoral romance called *Nadobna Pasqualina* (1655), which he claimed was based on an unknown Spanish original. This complex poem, whose intended symbolic meaning has never been fully ascertained, presents a woman defeating Venus and causing Cupid's suicide.

TYARD, or **THIARD**, **Pontus de**
(1521–1605)
French poet, born in Bissy-sur-Fleys (Saône-et-Loire). He belonged to the group of Lyons poets who took **Petrarch** for their master. Influenced, however, by the work of **Pierre de Ronsard**, his verse bridges the gap between the Petrarchan style and that of the Pléiade poets. Volumes of poetry include *Erreurs amoureuses* (1549–55, 'Mistakes in Love'), *Le Livre des vers lyriques* (1555, 'Book of Lyrical Verses') and *Œuvres poétiques* (1573, 'Poetic Works'). He was Bishop of Châlon-sur-Saône (1578–94) and wrote also theological and philosophical works, including *Discours philosophiques* (1587).
▷K M Hall, *Pontus de Tyard and his Discours philosophiques* (1963)

TYCHNA, Pavel
(1891–1967)
Ukrainian Symbolist poet and translator (mainly from Russian poetry), born in Pisky. Tychna is usually regarded as the greatest of 20th-century Ukrainian poets. *Sonyashni klyarnety* (1918, 'The Clarinets of the Sun') is one of the outstanding first collections in world literature, and has its place alongside the *Heraldos Negros* of **Vallejo**. Like **Blok**, he saw the Revolution of 1917 in religious, even cosmic, terms. Later he adopted socialist realism, was awarded state prizes, and lost all his gifts but his technique and rhetorical effectiveness. The original Tychna has much in common with the Hungarian **Ady**.

TYLER, Anne
(1941–)
American novelist and short-story writer, born in Minneapolis, Minnesota, and raised in Raleigh, North Carolina. She graduated from Duke University at 19, where she twice won the Anne Flexner Award for creative writing, and has been a Russian bibliographer and assistant to the librarian, McGill University Law Library. Writing mainly of life in Baltimore or in Southern small towns, and concerned with the themes of loneliness, isolation and human interactions, she has had a productive career since her debut in 1964 with *If Morning Ever Comes*. Significant subsequent titles include *Morgan's Passing* (1980), *Dinner at the Homesick Restaurant* (1982) and *The Accidental Tourist* (1985).
▷A Petty, *Understanding Anne Tyler* (1990)

TYLER, Royall
(1757–1826)
American dramatist and novelist, born in Boston and educated at Harvard. He enjoyed a long legal career in which he became Chief Justice of the Supreme Court of Vermont and, from 1811 to 1814, Professor of Jurisprudence at the University of Vermont. His claim to fame as a dramatist is based almost exclusively upon his first play, *The Contrast* (1787), a light satire in the style of **Sheridan**'s *The School for Scandal*, and the first comedy written by a native American author to be produced. It was enormously popular, but Tyler failed to match this success. He wrote satires and even a comic opera, farce and a sacred verse drama, but to no avail. His later work did not even find a producer. His best-known novel is *The Algerine Captive* (1797).

TYNAN, Katharine
(1861–1931)
Irish poet and novelist, born in Clondalkin, County Dublin. She was a friend of Parnell, the **Meynell**s and the **Rossetti**s and a leading

author of the Celtic literary revival. She married in 1893 H A Hinkson, who was a resident magistrate in County Mayo from 1914 to 1919. Her journalism established her reputation, but she also wrote some 18 volumes of tender, gentle verse, over a hundred novels, including *Oh! What a Plague is Love* (1896), *She Walks in Beauty* (1899) and *The House in the Forest* (1928), and around 40 other books, including five autobiographical works, the last of which was *Memoires* (1924). Her *Collected Poems* appeared in 1930.

▷M G Rose, *Katharine Tynan* (1974)

TYNNI, Aarlo
(1913–)

Finnish poet and translator, born in Kolppana, Inkeri, and a forerunner of the post-World War II Finnish poetic modernism. Her own well-made poetry could be compared to that of the Australian **Judith Wright**, but she is perhaps best known for her invaluable anthology of translations from foreign poets of all ages and nations, *Tuhat laulujen vuotta* (1957, 'Songs of a Thousand Years').

TYRTAEUS
(fl.c.685–668 BC)

Greek elegiac poet, probably born in Sparta. His warsongs inspired the Spartans during the second Messenian War (650–630 BC).
▷C M Bowra, *Early Greek Elegists* (1938)

TYUTCHEV, Fyodor Ivanovich
(1803–73)

Russian lyric poet, born in Ovstug, Oryol, of a noble landowning family. He spent 20 years abroad in the diplomatic service and then worked in the censorship department. His first collection of poems appeared in 1854 and was hailed with enthusiasm. A metaphysical romantic, he reached full recognition with the advent of Symbolism. The tragic love poems of his later period are outstanding in Russian literature.

▷D D Yazykov, *Fyodor Ivanovich Tyutchev* (1904)

TZARA, Tristan
(1896–1963)

Romanian poet, born in Bucharest, one of the founders of Dadaism and later a Surrealist. The products of his involvement with Dadaism—revolutionary at the time, almost unreadable now—include *Vingt-cinq Poèmes* (1918, '25 Poems') and *Sept Manifestes Dada* (1924, 'Seven Dadaist Manifestos'). A resident of Paris from 1920, he contributed to the Dadaist journal *Litterature*, was an active participant in the movement's 'happenings' (which often degenerated into bunfights), and was responsible for some splendidly splenetic assaults on the bourgeois order. He became a card-carrying Surrealist in 1929, producing *L'homme Approximatif* two years later, but never recaptured the anarchic vitality of his early years.

U

UA BROLCHÁN, Máel Isu
(c.1000–1086)

Irish poet and monk, called 'the doyen and chief sage of all Ireland'. A few well-known religious poems, which can be found in *Early Irish Lyrics* (1956), have been attributed to him.

UDALL, or UVEDALE, Nicholas
(1504–56)

English dramatist, born in Hampshire. He was educated at Winchester and Corpus Christi College, Oxford, and became headmaster of Eton c.1534. He published a selection from **Terence**, *Flowers of Latin Speaking*, for his pupils, who soon learnt of his predilection for corporal punishment. His dismissal in 1541 for indecent offences did not affect his standing at the court. Edward VI appointed him prebendary of Windsor, and despite his great enthusiasm for the Reformation, he survived the reign of Queen Mary I without disfavour. He translated **Erasmus**, selections from the Great Bible and Latin commentaries on the later, but is chiefly remembered as the author of the comedy, *Ralph Roister Doister*, written c.1553 but not published until 1567, which, inspired by his favourite classical writers, **Plautus** and Terence, was to influence later English writers of comedies.
▷C M Saxby, in *Representative English Dramatists* (1903)

UHLAND, Johannn Ludwig
(1787–1862)

German lyric poet, the leader of the 'Swabian School', born in Tübingen, where he studied law. He published poems from an early age and gradually added to his *Gedichte* (1815, 'Poems'), which contain such popular songs as 'Der gute Kamerad' ('The Good Comrade'). He also wrote a number of admirable literary essays. He was a Liberal deputy for Tübingen at the assemblies of Württemberg (1819) and Frankfurt (1848).
▷G Schwarz, *Johann Uhland* (1964)

UHRY, Alfred Fox
(1936–)

American playwright, born in Atlanta, Georgia. He graduated from Brown University in 1958. He wrote lyrics for a number of musicals, including *The Robber Bridegroom*

(1975), and also wrote for television. He scored a major success with his first serious stage drama, *Driving Miss Daisy* (1987), a lightweight but warm-hearted account of the relationship between an aristocratic Southern matron and her black chauffeur. It won him a Pulitzer Prize in 1988, and was successfully filmed in 1989.

UJEVÍC, Tin
(1891–1955)

Croatian poet, prose-poet, translator and critic, born in Vrgorac. He was well known from his youth, both as a promising poet, a political agitator and (later), for being, in the words of a critic, 'solitary, egocentric, disorderly and alcoholic'. Disapproval of Ujevíc's inexcusable lifestyle harmed appreciation of his extraordinary poetry for many years, but critics are now learning to read him more constructively, and to understand that his abundant criticism, much influenced by his Indian studies, may be more profound than chaotic: far from 'having no consistent view of literature', it has been suggested that he learned from Indian aesthetics that this is impossible. It is unfortunate that he should have lacked a translator, for such visionary work as is contained in, for example, *Ojadjeno Zvono* (1933, 'The Aggrieved Bell'), would have been—and still may be—influential in European poetry. Many of his critical insights into Yugoslav and French poetry are invaluable. As it stands he is one of the great untranslated poets of the 20th century.

UKRAINKA, pseud of Larysa Kosach-Kvitka
(1871–1913)

Ukrainian revolutionary poet and dramatist, born in Novohrad Volynsky. She died young of tuberculosis. She was a fine rhetorical poet, fervent and sincere, but her language and her attitudes have now dated. Her best work is in drama.
▷P Cundy, *Spirit of Flame* (1950)

ULFELDT, Leonora Christine
(1621–98)

Danish author, and daughter of the Danish king Christian IV. She was engaged at the age of 10 to Corfitz Ulfeldt, a nobleman who subsequently fell out with King Fredrik III and had to leave the country with his family.

In 1663 Leonora Christine was arrested and interned in the Blue Tower at Copenhagen Castle where she spent 22 years. While imprisoned, she wrote an autobiography in French. More importantly, she began her remarkable *Jammers Minde* ('Misery Remembered') which, although written in Danish, was not published until the mid-19th century. An attempt to gain a perspective on her situation, the text presents her experiences in terms of a biblical drama which encompasses strikingly realistic accounts of prison conditions and her fellow prisoners. Stylistically highly accomplished, the work testifies to her exceptional resilience as well as her profound religious conviction.

▷'Troskab, lidelse og lidenskab. Om Leonora Christine Ulfeldt', in E Møller Jensen (ed), *Nordisk kvindelitteraturhistorie*, vol I, (1993)

ULRICH VON LICHTENSTEIN
(c.1200–c.1275)

Middle High Austrian Minnesinger (Minnesang was the formal love poetry of the chivalric age), born of a noble family. He became Marshal of his native Styria. He assembled his work, deriving and developing from such poets as **Walther von der Vogelweide**, as *Frauendienst*, a collection of love lyrics framed by a connecting first-person tale in verse (about 4000 lines in itself). He was almost the last German-language poet to be devoted to the older notion of courtly love. Opinions differ as to his achievement, and of the degree of his truthfulness—but his account of how he served a mistress and a wife by standards of old-style *amour courtois* is fascinating.

▷O Sayce, *The Poets of the Minnesang* (1967)

UNAMUNO, Miguel de
(1864–1936)

Spanish philosopher and author, born in Bilbao, of Basque parentage. He was Professor of Greek at Salamanca from 1892. He wrote mystic philosophy, historical studies, brilliant essays, books on travel, and austere poetry. Among his most important works are *Vida de Don Quijote y Sancho* (1905, Eng trans *The Life of Don Quixote and Sancho*, 1927), his novel *Niebla* (1914, Eng trans *Mist*, 1928), *Del sentimiento trágico de la vida* (1913, Eng trans *The Tragic Sense of Life in Men and in Peoples*, 1926) and a volume of religious poetry, *El Cristo de Velázquez* (1920, Eng trans *The Christ of Velasquez*, 1951). From 1924 to 1930 he was exiled as a Republican to the island of Fuerteventura, and reinstated at Salamanca on the founding of the republic in 1931. Always a rebel and an individualist though with the deepest faith in and interest of his country at heart, he was soon at variance with the socialist regime. The Civil War for him was a nationalist struggle and he denounced foreign interference.

▷A Barea, *Miguel de Unamuno* (1952)

UNDER, Marie
(1883–1977)

Estonian poet, considered by many as the greatest in her language, who has been compared to **Rilke** and even to **Goethe**. She was the leading poet in the expressionistic and Futurist 'Siuru' Group (named after a fabulous bird in Estonian mythology), which in 1917 ushered in the most colourful and exciting period in this Finno–Ugric literature. Her work developed from a delicately impressionistic love poetry to one of magnificent visionary power: one of the great woman poets of the century in international terms, her work only awaits adequate translation for it to be so recognized. Translations of her poetry are in W K Matthews (ed), *Anthology of Modern Estonian Poetry* (1953).

▷A Mägi, *Estonian Literature* (1968)

UNDERHILL, Evelyn
(1875–1941)

English poet and mystic, born in Wolverhampton. She was educated at King's College, London. In 1907 she married Herbert Stuart Moore, a barrister, and in 1921 became lecturer on the philosophy of religion at Manchester College, Oxford. A friend and disciple of Hügel, she found her way intellectually from agnosticism to Christianity, wrote numerous books on mysticism, including *The Life of the Spirit* (1922), volumes of verse, and four novels. Her *Mysticism* (1911) became a standard work.

UNDSET, Sigrid
(1882–1949)

Norwegian novelist and winner of the Nobel Prize for literature, born in Kalundborg, in Denmark. The daughter of a noted Norwegian archaeologist, she inherited an interest in medieval Norway. From 1899 she worked in an office, and the problems facing young contemporary women formed the basis of her early novels, including *Jenny* (1911). Her masterpiece, *Kristin Lavransdatter* (3 vols, 1920–2), which tells a graphic story of love and religion in 14th-century Norway, was followed by *Olav Audunsson* (4 vols, 1925–7), *Gymadenia* (1929) and *Den trofaste hustru* (1936, Eng trans *The Faithful Spouse*, 1937). She became a Roman Catholic in 1924, after which her work deepened in religious intensity. She was awarded the Nobel Prize for literature in 1928. During World War II she was exiled in the USA, an outspoken opponent of Nazism.

▷ M Brunsdale, *Sigrid Undset* (1988)

UNGARETTI, Giuseppe
(1888–1970)

Italian poet, born in Alexandria. He first visited Italy when he was 26; soon afterwards he joined the army and fought on the Austrian front. From 1912 to 1914 he lived in Paris where he met **Guillaume Apollinaire**. His first collection, *Il porto sepolto* ('The Buried Harbour'), was published in 1916 with a preface by Mussolini, and immediately gained him admission to the ranks of the great Italian poets of the 20th century. Largely defying translation, he is less well known than **Eugenio Montale** or **Salvatore Quasimodo**, but among his distinguished collections is *Vita d'un uomo* (7 vols, 1942–61, 'Life of a Man'), which includes *Il dolore* (1947, 'Grief'). He studied in Paris, and was Professor of Italian Literature at São Paulo, Brazil (1936–42) and at Rome (1942–58). He is the author of 'hermetic' poems characterized by their symbolism, compressed imagery and modern verse structure.

▷ P Piccioni, *Vita di un poeta* (1970)

UNRUH, Fritz von
(1885–1970)

German playwright and novelist, born in Koblenz. He served in World War I as a cavalry officer. He was an ardent pacifist, and the ideal of a new humanity underlies all his Expressionist works, particularly the novel *Opfergang* (1916, Eng trans *The Way of Sacrifice*, 1928), and the two parts of an unfinished dramatic trilogy, *Ein Geschlecht* (1916, 'A Species') and *Platz* (1920, 'Place'). He left Germany in 1932 and went to the USA, where he wrote several works, including *Der nie Verlor* (1948, Eng trans *The End is not Yet*, 1948) and *Die jüngste Nacht* (1948, 'The Youngest Night'). He returned to Germany in 1952.

▷ A Kronacher, *Fritz von Unruh* (1946)

UNSWORTH, Barry (Foster)
(1930–)

English novelist, born in Durham; he was the first of his family not to go down the mines. Educated at Stockton Grammar School and Manchester University, he has travelled widely and held a variety of teaching posts, including some time at the University of Istanbul. His first novel, *The Partnership* (1966), was followed by four more before *Pascali's Island* (1980), which was shortlisted for the Booker Prize, and later filmed. His books often reflect on historical themes, and

are set in locations which mirror his own wanderings, notably Turkey, Greece, and Italy, the setting for *Stone Virgin* (1985). His major work is the novel *Sacred Hunger* (1992), an epic account of the 18th-century Atlantic slave trade, which was jointly awarded the Booker Prize, alongside **Michael Ondaatje**.

UNTERMEYER, Louis
(1886–1977)

American anthologist, critic, poet and (most lastingly of all) parodist (*Collected Parodies*, 1926). He was best known, however, for his anthologies, particularly for *Modern American Poetry* (1919) which, although mocked by such as **Cummings** ('mr u will not be missed/who as an anthologist/sold the many on the few/not excluding'), ran into many editions, and educated mid-market readers into an acceptance of modernism. He also compiled a useful set of brief biographies, *Makers of the Modern World* (1955).

UPDIKE, John Hoyer
(1932–)

American novelist, poet and critic, born in Shillington, Pennsylvania. He studied at Harvard and the Ruskin School of Drawing and Fine Art in Oxford (1954–5), then returned to New York and served for two years on the staff of the *New Yorker* (1955–7), the beginning of a long and fruitful relationship with the magazine to which he has contributed short stories, poems and book reviews. His first book was a collection of verse, *The Carpentered Hen and Other Tame Creatures* (1958), but his status as one of the world's major writers is due largely to his fiction. Beginning with *The Poorhouse Fair* (1959), he has published many novels and many collections of short stories. Sophisticated, linguistically supple, fluent and inventive, his beat is middle-class America, his concerns those that have dominated the 20th century: sex, marriage, adultery, divorce, religion, materialism. Among his best-known books are, *The Centaur* (1963), the Rabbit tetralogy—*Rabbit, Run* (1960), *Rabbit Redux* (1971), *Rabbit is Rich* (1981) and *Rabbit at Rest* (1990)—spanning 40 years in the life of a car salesman, *Couples* (1968), *The Coup* (1978) and *The Witches of Eastwick* (1984). More recent novels are *Memoirs of the Ford Administration* (1993) and *Brazil* (1994). *A Month of Sundays* (1975), *Roger's Version* (1986) and *S.* (1988) collectively represent a reworking of **Hawthorne**'s *The Scarlet Letter*. *Self-Consciousness*, a memoir consisting of six chapters concerning his hometown, his suffering from psoriasis, his stuttering, his thoughts on the Vietnam War, his paternal ancestors, and his attitude towards his religion, was published in 1989.

▷R Detweiler, *John Updike* (1972, rev edn 1984)

UPFIELD, Arthur W(illiam)
(1888–1964)

English-born Australian writer of detective fiction, almost all of it featuring the specialized skills of the half-Aboriginal Inspector Napoleon Bonaparte. Upfield grew up in Hampshire and trained as a surveyor and land agent before emigrating to the Antipodes in 1911. He lived in England again briefly after military service in World War I, but returned to Australia, working at a variety of jobs before turning to writing. His first novel, *The House of Cain*, appeared in 1928, but it was with *The Barrakee Mystery* the following year (published in the USA as *The Lure of the Bush*, 1965) that he made his mark. The novel introduced 'Bony' as a man poised between races and intellectual standpoints: blue-eyed, polished, university-educated, but also profoundly in touch with the tiny clues afforded the investigative detective by the natural environment. Upfield wrote 29 Bonaparte mysteries; an unfinished 30th was completed and published posthumously. The best of them are *Death of a Swagman* (1945), *An Author Bites the Dust* (1948), which takes good-natured revenge on the literary mafia, and *Bony and the Black Virgin* (1959). The later plots tend to plod a little, but they do also document a significant sea-change in Australian attitudes to Aboriginal and mixed-race people, to women and to culture.
▷J Hawke, *Follow My Dust! A Biography of Arthur Upfield* (1957)

UPWARD, Edward Falaise
(1903–)

English novelist, born in Romford, Essex, who met his contemporary, the future novelist **Christopher Isherwood**, while at school. They became lifelong friends. During the 1930s, Upward joined the Communist Party, and several of his books reflect his political hopes and fears. *Journey to the Border* (1938) is an account of a private tutor who becomes a political radical. When Upward began to doubt his commitment, he retreated for 20 years into literary silence, pondering Party dogma and political theory. He emerged in 1962 to publish *In the Thirties. The Rotten Elements* followed in 1969, and *No Home but the Struggle* in 1977. Together, they comprise *The Spiral Ascent* trilogy, a semi-autobiographical work charting the life and political times of Alan Sebrill, schoolteacher and Marxist.

URIS, Leon M(arcus)
(1924–)

American popular author, born in Baltimore. He dropped out of high school and joined the Marine Corps, taking part in battles in the Pacific. *Battle Cry* (1956) uses the experience to telling effect. *Exodus* (1958) remains the book by which he is best known. Depicting the early years of the state of Israel, it was made into a highly successful film though it was not commended by the critics. *QBVII* (1970) concerns a libel trial over a former Nazi war criminal. *The Haj* was published in 1984.

URMUZ, or HURMUZ, pseud of D Demetrescu-Buzău
(1883–1923)

Romanian experimental writer who anticipated such Dadaists as his compatriot **Tristan Tzara**. His work is of little interest except from a historical viewpoint—the 'absurd' being an allegedly Romanian phenomenon (eg **Ionesco**).

URQUHART, Fred
(1912–)

Scottish short-story writer and novelist, born in Edinburgh, the son of a chauffeur. He grew up in Fife, Perth and Wigtown, leaving school at 15 and then working as bookseller's assistant and labourer. He published his first novel, *Time Will Knit*, in 1938. He has published 11 collections of his short stories, many initially broadcast by the BBC, and has edited nine anthologies of short stories. His other novels to date are *The Ferret Was Abraham's Daughter* (1949), *Jezebel's Dust* (1951) and *Palace of Green Days* (1979, the first of a projected series). He has been publisher's reader, and literary editor of *Tribune*. His outstanding achievement is his quite exceptional ability to convey narrative plots through the eyes of female characters, initially in the Scotland of his childhood and adolescence and more recently using ghost stories, historical fiction and other forms.
▷C Affleck, 'Fred Urquhart', in *Dictionary of Literary Biography*, Vol 139 (1994)

URQUHART, Sir Thomas
(c.1611–1660)

Scottish author, born in Cromarty, the son of a land-owner. He studied at King's College, Aberdeen, and travelled in France, Spain and Italy. On his return he took up arms against the Covenanting party in the north but was defeated and forced to flee to England. Becoming attached to the court, he was knighted in 1641. The same year he published his *Epigrams: Divine and Moral*. On succeeding his father in 1642 he returned north. In Cromarty, though much troubled by his creditors, he produced his *Trissotetras; or a most exquisite Table for Resolving Triangles, etc* (1645), a study of trigonometry based on

Napier's invention of logarithms. In 1649 his library was seized and sold. He again took up arms in the royal cause, and was present at the battle at Worcester (1651), where he lost most of his MSS. In London, through Cromwell's influence, he was allowed considerable liberty, and in 1652 he published his *Pantochronochanon* (1652), an exact account of the Urquhart family, in which they are traced back to Adam. He also published *Ekskubalauron* (1652), better known as *The Discoverie of a most Exquisite Jewel*, an attack on the Scottish clergy which contains a ribald account of James Crichton (the 'Admirable Crichton'), but is chiefly a work praising the Scots nation. In 1653 he issued his *Introduction to the Universal Language* and the first two books of that English classic, his brilliant translation of *Rabelais*. The third was not issued till after his death. He is said to have died abroad, in a fit of mirth on hearing of the Restoration. His learning was vast, his scholarship defective.

▷J Willcock, *Sir Thomas Urquhart of Cromartie* (1895)

USAKLIGIL, Halit Ziya
(1866–1945)

Turkish novelist, 'the towering figure in Turkish fiction at the start of the twentieth century', often called the 'Turkish Alphonse Daudet'. His most famous novels were *Mai ve Siyah* (1897, 'The Blue and the Black'), still one of the most moving novels about a writer's struggle for existence and recognition, and *Ask-i Memnu* (1900, 'Forbidden Love'), a love story set in Istanbul high society. He was a bold and lucid stylist, who prepared the way for later realists.

USIGLI, Rodolfo
(1905–)

Mexican dramatist, poet and theatre director, born in Mexico City of an Italian father and a Polish mother. He was Mexico's most important dramatist, his position being analogous to that in the United Kingdom of **Shaw** (who greatly admired his *Corona de Sombra*, 1943, Eng trans *Crown of Shadows*, 1946). He was always highly critical of the Mexican government, and not all his plays have been published or performed. The most original of his many plays is the Pirandellian *El gesticulador* (1937, 'The Gesticulator'), a masterful satirical analysis of Mexico's proneness to lying and the creation of false myths: a mad retired professor impersonates a revolutionary, and dies at the hands of his assassin.

▷E Anderson-Imbert, *Spanish-American Literature: A History* (1963)

USK, Thomas
(d.1388)

English poet, born in London and attached to a clerical order of some kind, judging by the theological knowledge he displays. He became secretary to John de Northampton, the democratic and Wycliffite mayor of London who, after his term, was charged with a number of crimes in office. Usk betrayed his master to save himself, but was later executed after mishandling intrigues at Court. His poem 'The Testament of Love' is a poor and uninventive imitation of **Chaucer** on **Boethius**: while in prison the narrator is visited and inspired by a beautiful lady called 'Love'. **C S Lewis** found the poem 'more interesting than beautiful'.

USLAR PIETRI, Arturo
(1906–)

Venezuelan historical novelist and story writer, born in Caracas. Originally a professor of economics, he has held government posts, and has taught at Columbia University in the USA. He is generally regarded as the leading historical novelist of modern Latin America. His two most important novels are *Las lanzas coloradas* (1931, Eng trans *The Red Lances*, 1963) and *El camino de El Dorado* (1947, 'The Road to El Dorado'). The first is a history of colonial Venezuela, dealing with Bolívar and with creoles and Spaniards. The second is the fictional biography of the tyrant Lope de Aguirre, worthy to be compared with the novel on the same subject by **Ramón Sender**. A much later success was *La visita en el tiempo* (1990), about the enigmatic figure of Don Juan de Austria. Uslar Pietri has been called a 'leading exponent of magic realism', but his writing, although lyrical, is more straightforward, and possibly less subtle, than that of **García Márquez** or **Roa Bastos**.

▷A Flores, *The Literature of Spanish America* (1966–9)

USPENSKI, Gleb Ivanovich
(c.1840–1902)

Russian author, born in Tula. He wrote novels of peasant life, such as *Vlact' zemli* (1882, 'Power of the Soil'), notable for their realism in contrast to the prevalent romantic conception of the agricultural worker. He died insane.

▷N Prutskov, *Gleb Ivanovich Uspenski* (1972)

USTINOV, Sir Peter Alexander
(1921–)

British actor and dramatist, born in London. The son of White Russian parents, Ustinov first appeared on the stage in 1938, and had established himself as an accomplished artist both in revues and legitimate drama by 1942, when four years' army service interrupted his career. His subsequent work for films as actor, writer and producer, and in broadcasting as a satirical comedian, has enhanced his reputation. He is a prolific playwright, and his works— most successful amongst which are *The Love of Four Colonels* (1951) and *Romanoff and Juliet* (1956)—are marked by a serious approach to human problems, often presented with an acute sense of comedy and a mastery of unconventional stagecraft. Among his other plays are *Photo Finish* (1962), *The Unknown Soldier and his Wife* (1967) and *Overheard* (1981). His other works include an autobiography, *Dear Me* (1977), the two novellas collected as *The Disinformer* (1989), and *The Old Man and Mr. Smith* (1990).

UTTLEY, Alison
(1884–1976)

English author of children's stories, born on a farm in Derbyshire. She was widowed in 1930 and turned to writing to support herself and her young son. *The Country Child* (1931) was followed by a flood of books, mainly for children, which revealed her great love for and knowledge of the countryside and country lore. Many of her books were in the **Beatrix Potter** tradition, featuring much-loved characters such as Grey Rabbit and Sam Pig.

▷E Saintsbury, *The World of Alison Uttley* (1980)

UZ, Johann Peter
(1720–96)

German minor poet, born in Ansbach. A lawyer by profession, he helped to translate **Anacreon**, and wrote frivolous if skilful verse in the Anacreontic style; but his best poems, somewhat resembling those of **Klopstock**, were deeper in intention, seeking to fuse Christianity with a superficial hedonism.

V

VAA, Aslaug
(1889–1965)

Norwegian poet and dramatist, born in Telemark, and educated in literature and art history at universities in Paris and Berlin. Best known for her dialect-coloured poetry, distinguished by a strong feeling for nature and traditional life, she seeks fundamental values, often in contrast to the negative aspects of modern life. She made her debut with the poetry collection *Nord i leitet* (1934, 'In the Northern Horizon'), but her best-known work is the collection *Skjenkersveinens visur* (1954, 'The Innkeeper's Songs').

▷L Maehle, 'Det lydde eit bod—Om Aslaug Vaa og diktinga hennar', in *Frå bygda til verda* (1967)

VAFOPOULOS, George
(1903–)

Greek poet, born in the northern city of Thessaloniki and representative of a 'northern' school of writers. He started to publish poems in 1921, but achieved fame a decade later with his first collection, *Rhodhina tou Mytilene* ('Roses of Mytilene'), which displayed an unfashionable Neo-Classical approach, and the influence of **Costas Karyotakis**. After World War II Vafopoulos's poetry changed in tone, becoming more stark and cold, in collections such as *To Dhapedho* (1951, 'The Floor'). Unlike most Greek poets he often writes in the formal *Katharevousa*, and his poems have an ecclesiastical dignity to them.

VAICIULAITIS, Antanas
(1906–)

Lithuanian novelist and story writer, the leading prose writer of his generation. He went into exile in the USA. His reputation rests on his novel *Valentina* (1936), a subtle study of a girl who cannot decide whether to choose the man she loves or the one to whom she is indebted. But his folk-like tales written since then have their own unique delicacy and depth. He wrote (in English) *An Outline History of Lithuanian Literature* (1942).

▷R Silbajoris, *Perfection in Exile: Fourteen Contemporary Lithuanian Writers* (1970)

VAILLAND, Roger
(1907–65)

French novelist, born in Paris. His picaresque bohemian life was reflected in many of his works, among them *La Loi* (1957, Eng trans *The Law*, 1958), which was awarded the Prix **Goncourt**. The debut novel which made his name, however—*Drole de jeu* (1945, Eng trans *Playing With Fire*, 1948)—had as its subject a more serious matter, the French resistance, in which he had fought. A member of the Communist Party from 1952 to 1956, he also wrote plays and essays, such as his study of Choderlos de Laclos (1953).

VAIZGANTAS, pseud of Juozas Tumas
(1869–1933)

Lithuanian novelist and critic, born in Svedasai parish. A priest, educated in Latvia, he returned from abroad to devote himself to the cause of an independent Lithuania. His voluminous and worthy works, which fill 10 volumes, are not of literary importance, but they inspired many more gifted writers.

VAJDA, János
(1827–99)

Hungarian poet, editor and critic—by profession an actor and journalist—born in Pest (not then joined to Buda). Little heed was taken of Vajda in his own time, although he attracted attention as a critic; but he has now been elevated to major status, second only to **Ady**, whom in certain respects he anticipated. He was a close friend to **Petőfi**, to whom he was by no means inferior: It is in his anguished poems to his elusive 'Gina' that he anticipates Ady. Some of his poetry is indifferently translated in *The Magyar Muse* (1933, ed W Kirkconnell) and in *Hungarian Poems and Fables* (1877). His mind was altogether subtler than that of **Jokai** or his more thoroughgoingly romantic contemporaries, and he had to wait for Ady and others to understand and appreciate his 'self-tormenting pessimism'.

▷A Komlós, *Vajda János* (1954, in Hungarian)

VALA, Katri, pseud of Alice Wadenström
(1901–44)

Finnish poet, the leading woman poet of the semi-modernist Tulenkantajat ('Torchbearers') Group, and yet another Finnish victim of the scourge of tuberculosis. She was among the first to write in free verse. She died in exile in Sweden.

VALAORITÍS, Aristotelís
(1824–79)

Greek poet of the so-called 'Heptanesian' school, born in Leucas, but educated in Italy and France. In 1848 he returned to the Ionian islands and became involved in local politics. His second collection, *Elegies*, published in 1857, gained him attention; his lyricism seemed to have more in common with the French Romantics than with his Greek contemporaries, but his subject-matter was the Greek War of Independence, and poems like 'Samuel' and 'He Fyghi' ('The Flight') became songs of resistance. In the last 10 years of his life he gave up politics, retired to the island of Madouri, and dedicated himself to writing, but he never again achieved the popular acclaim of his earlier career.

VALAORITIS, Nanos
(1921–)

Greek poet, born in Lausanne, the great-grandson of the famous 19th-century poet **Aristotelís Valaoritis**. He has lived in London, Paris and Athens. He was friendly with **Bernard Spencer** and also with **Lawrence Durrell**, whom he helped to prepare a volume of translations from **Seferis** into English. His playful Surrealist poetry has a cosmopolitan following.

VALDELOMAR, Abraham
(1888–1918)

Peruvian fiction-writer, editor, critic and poet, born in Ica. He was one of the first *mestizos* to write fiction in Peru. He began as a crude imitator of **D'Annunzio**, but then turned away from romantic decadence to realism with his fictionalized biography of Doña Francisca Zubuiaga (wife of the celebrated General Agustin Gamarra), *La Mariscala* (1915). His best work is in the short story collections: *El Cabellero Caremelo* (1918) and *Los hijos del sol* (1921, 'Sons of the Sun'). The latter contained memorable stories of the Inca period.
▷C A Cabellero, *Vida y obra de Abraham Valdelomar* (1964); E A Aldrich, *The Modern Short Story in Peru* (1966)

VALDÉS, Armando Palacio
(1853–1938)

Spanish novelist, born in Entralgo in Asturias. Some of his psychological and naturalistic novels were *Marta y María* (1886, Eng trans *The Marquis of Peñalta*, 1886), *Maximina* (1887, Eng trans 1888), *La Hermana San Sulpicio* (1889, Eng trans *Sister Saint Sulpice*, 1890), *La Espuma* (1890, Eng trans *Froth*, 1891) and *El Maestrante* (1893, Eng trans *The Grandee*, 1894).

VALDIVIELSO, José de
(1560–1638)

Spanish poet, dramatist and priest, born in Toledo. He was a close friend to **Lope de Vega**. His baroque essays in 'folk poetry' were studied by **Lorca**. He excelled in the ubiquitous Spanish form known as the *auto sacremental*: a one-act allegorical play, played at Corpus Christi, dealing with the Eucharist, which developed into all kinds of allegories, and finally degenerated into vulgar farce.
▷B W Wardropper, *Introducción al teatro religioso del Siglo de Oro* (1967)

VALENTE, José Angel
(1929–)

Spanish poet and translator, born in Orense. He has lived abroad for much of his life, and lectured at Oxford in the 1950s on Spanish literature. He has been called a 'minimalist' poet because he aims at 'the maximum of expression with the minimum of verbal construction'. There are two literal translations of his dignified, intimate poems in J M Cohen's *Penguin Book of Spanish Verse* (1960).

VALENZUELA, Luisa
(1938–)

Argentinian writer and journalist, born in Buenos Aires. She has written seven novels and three collections of stories, and is considered among the most important women writers of Latin America. She moved to the USA in 1979, as a result of the political situation in Argentina, but since the reestablishment of democracy, has returned to Argentina. Most of her work is highly experimental, including such techniques as linguistic distortion, shifting points of view and use of metaphor to communicate an ironic view of gender relations. Titles include the short-story collection *Cabio de armas* (1975, 'Other Weapons'), the narrative collection *El gato eficaz* (1972, 'Cat-o-Nine-Deaths') and *Cola de, lagartija* (1983, 'The Lizard's Tail'). She has won several awards, including Fulbright and Guggenheim fellowships.

VALERA, Don Juan
(1824–1905)

Spanish novelist and critic, born in Cabra in Córdoba. He held diplomatic posts in Europe and the USA, and was a deputy, Minister of Commerce, Minister of Public Instruction and councillor of state senator. His literary studies, *Estudios críticos* (1864), and essays, *Cuentos y Diálogos* (1882) made his reputation but his fame depends on his romances, *Pepita Jiménez* (1874, Eng trans 1891), *Las ilusiones del Doctor Faustino* (1876, 'The Illusions of Dr Faustus'), *El comendador*

VALÉRY, Paul Ambroise

Mendoza (1877, Eng trans *Commander Mendoza*, 1893), *Doña Luz* (1878, Eng trans 1892) and *La buena fama* (1895, 'The Good Reputation'). He was also a noted translator of **Goethe**'s *Faust* and other classics.

▷ A Z Romera, *Don Valera y Alcala Galiano* (1966)

VALÉRY, Paul Ambroise
(1871–1945)

French poet and writer, born in Cette. He settled in Paris in 1892, and after publishing some remarkable verse in the style of **Stéphane Mallarmé**, he relapsed into a 20 years' silence, taken up with mathematics and philosophical speculations. He emerged in 1917 with a new poetic outlook and technique in *La Jeune Parque* (1917, 'The Young Fate'), a poem full of difficult symbolism. This was followed by a significant collection, *Charmes* (1922), containing 'Le Cimetière marin' (Eng trans *The Graveyard by the Sea*, 1946), 'L'Ébauche d'un serpent' ('The Outline of a Snake'), 'Au platane' ('In the Plane Tree'), and others, noted for the poetic shorthand, the compression and conciseness of his imagery and ideas. His prose works include *Soirèe avec M Teste* (1895, Eng trans *An Evening with Mr Teste*, 1925), and several aesthetic studies, such as the dialogue *Eupalinos ou l'architecte* (1924, Eng trans *Eupalinos; or, the Architect*, 1932), in which architecture and music are compared, and *L'Âme et la danse* (1924, Eng trans *Dance and the Soul*, 1951). A late, short play, *Le Solitaire* ('The Solitary Man'), foreshadows **Samuel Beckett**.

▷ F Scarfe, *The Art of Paul Valéry* (1954)

VALLE Y CAVIEDES, Juan del
(c.1652–c.1697)

Peruvian poet and dramatist, born in Porcuna, Andalusia, but taken to Peru when still a small child. A disciple of **Quevedo**, he wrote mystical poetry, lyrics and, above all, satires. His work did not see public light, at least in bulk, until 1873, and only then by courtesy of the great **Ricardo Palma**. His best poetry attacks the medical profession with both wit and point.

▷ D R Reedy, *The Poetic Art of Juan del Valle Caviedes* (1964)

VALLE-INCLÁN, Ramón María del
(1869–1936)

Spanish novelist, dramatist and poet, born in Puebla de Caramiñal. Among his works are four *Sonatas* on the seasons (1902–7), written in fine prose in the form of novels, a graphic but erroneous history *La guerra carlista* (1908, 'The Carlist War'), and the masterly *Águila de blasón* (1907, 'The Eagle of Honour') and *Romance de Lobos* (1908, Eng trans

Wolves! Wolves!, 1957), set in a vivid medieval background. Many of his novels and plays are collected in *Esperpentos*, and among several comedies is his *Cara de Plata* (1923, 'Silver Face').

▷ A Zacharias, *Ramón del Valle-Inclán, an appraisal* (1968)

VALLÈS, Jules
(1832–85)

French writer, born in Le Puy-en-Velay of poor peasants. His fiction, his revolutionary attitude and his bitter manner make him into one of the more important precursors of **Céline**. He was imprisoned and later exiled for his part in the Paris Commune (1871). His works fill eight volumes; outstanding is his trilogy *Jacques Vingtras* (1879–86). He has been said to have hated the rich too extravagantly; this common but not universal judgement perhaps misses his sense of irony and burning hatred of injustice. His books and journalism, in particular his volume about his years of exile in London, *La Rue à Londres* (1883), are racy, vivid, observant and readable.

VALLEJO, César Abraham
(1892–1938)

Peruvian poet, novelist and playwright, born in Santiago de Chuco into a poor family of mixed Spanish and Peruvian Indian descent. He took a law degree and studied medicine in Lima, and held various jobs, including teaching posts. He was imprisoned in 1920–1 for political reasons, and moved to Europe in 1923, living mainly in France and Spain until his death. His first book of poems, *Los heraldos negros* (1919, 'The Dark Messengers'), announced an immensely powerful talent, but only one more volume appeared in his lifetime, *Trilce* (1922, Eng trans *Trilce*, 1973). The great *Poemas humanos* (1939) and *España, aparta de mé este cáliz* (1940, *Spain, Take Thou this Cup from Me*) were both posthumous, and are included in English translation in *The Complete Posthumous Poems* (1978). He also wrote some indifferent novels and several volumes of non-fiction, but his reputation rests on his poetry. English selections are *Neruda and Vallejo: Selected Poems* (1971) and *Selected Poems* (1976). A *Poesia completa* appeared in Spanish in 1978.

VALVERDE, José Maria
(1926–)

Spanish poet and critic, born in Valcia de Alcántara. A dry and intellectual but religious poet, Valverde began as a member of a group calling itself 'Juventud Creadora': he, and his friends, were searching for a means to circumvent the ferocious and philistine censorship imposed by the Franco dictatorship. He gradually became more open and emotional, largely as a result of his study of the great Peruvian **Vallejo**. He spent some time away from Spain, but then returned to Barcelona to teach.

VANBRUGH, Sir John
(1664–1726)

English playwright and baroque architect, born in London, the son of a tradesman and grandson of a Protestant refugee merchant from Ghent. He was educated in France, commissioned into Lord Huntingdon's regiment and suffered imprisonment in the Bastille as a suspected spy (1690–2). A staunch Whig, he became a leading spirit in society life and scored a success with his first comedy, *The Relapse* (1696), followed, again with success, by *The Provok'd Wife* (1697). *The Confederacy* (1705) was put on in the Haymarket, where **William Congreve** and Vanbrugh joined together as theatre managers. His *The Provok'd Husband* was left unfinished, and was completed by Colley Cibber (1728). A natural playwright of the uninhibited Restoration comedy of manners period, he also achieved success as architect of Castle Howard (1702) and in 1705 was commissioned to design Blenheim Palace at Woodstock. The immense baroque structure aroused the ridicule of **Jonathan Swift** and **Pope**, and the Duchess of Marlborough disliked the plans and was so appalled at its enormous cost that she long refused to pay Vanbrugh. He was made comptroller of royal works in 1714, and was Clarencieux king-of-arms (1705–25).

▷L Whistler, *Sir John Vanbrugh* (1938)

VANCE, Jack (John Holbrook)
(1916–)

American science-fiction and fantasy writer, born in San Francisco. His early stories were published in pulp magazines, but he signalled the emergence of a more mature talent with the science fantasy collection *The Dying Earth* (1950), set in a far future world dominated by magic, to which he returned in several later books. The creation of vividly evoked imaginary planets which began with *Big Planet* (1952) became the second principle stream of his fiction, and has produced some of his most significant work, including *The Dragon Masters* (1963) and *Showboat World* (1978). He wrote a number of sequence novels in both fantasy and science-fiction forms, including *Planet of Adventure* (from 1968) and *Cadwal Chronicles* (from 1987). He has also written mystery novels.

VANCURA, Vladislav
(1891–1942)

Czech novelist, murdered by a Nazi firing-squad as one of the reprisals for the death of Heydrich. He was originally a doctor, but devoted himself early to literature. A supporter of the communists, he was an experimental novelist who brought both vernacular and archaic elements into his language. *Pekar Jan Marhoul* (1924, 'The Baker Jan Marhoul') is a portrait of an ideal communist, in which Vancura used expressionistic techniques; only the adventure novel *Konec stárých casu* (1934) was translated into English, as *The End of Old Times* (1965). He has been mentioned as an influence on **Milan Kundera**.

VANDERHAEGE, Guy Clarence
(1951–)

Canadian short-story writer and novelist, born in Esterhazy, Saskatchewan, currently a professor of English at the University of Ottawa. He won a Governor General's Prize for fiction with his first collection of stories, *Man Descending* (1982). This was followed by another collection, *The Trouble with Heroes* (1983), *My Present Age* (1984), a novel about loneliness, and the acclaimed *Homesick* (1989). A writer of dry humour and effortless prose, Vanderhaege has contributed to several British periodicals and won the Geoffrey Faber Memorial Prize in 1987. A third collection of stories, *Things As They Are?*, appeared in 1992.

VANDERLOO, Jos
(1925–)

Belgian (Flemish) novelist, born in Zonhoven. His work draws on **Kafka** and other Flemish, predecessors. *Het Gevaar* (1960, 'The Danger') is characteristic in its depiction of injustice and menace—ostensibly a fantasy, it is in fact closely realistic: three men who have received fatal medical treatment are refused the chance to enter into the 'normal' world.

VAN DER POST, Sir Laurens (Jan)
(1906–)

South African soldier, explorer, writer and philosopher. He served with distinction in World War II in Ethiopia, the Western Desert, Syria and the far east, where he was captured by the Japanese. On his release he joined Mountbatten's staff in Java. He has since worked for the British government on a variety of missions in Africa, and with the Kalahari Bushmen of southern Africa. A sensitive writer of lyrical insight, his books include *The Lost World of the Kalahari* (1958), *The Heart of the Hunter* (1961), *The*

Seed and the Sower (1963, filmed as *Merry Christmas, Mr Lawrence*, 1983), *The Hunter and the Whale* (1967), *A Story Like the Wind* (1972), *A Far Off Place* (1974), *A Mantis Carol* (1975), *Jung and the Story of Our Time* (1976) and *Yet Being Someone Other* (1982).
▷F Carpenter, *Laurens van der Post* (1969)

VAN DOREN, Carl Clinton
(1885–1950)

American critic and biographer, brother of **Mark Albert Van Doren**, born in Hope, Illinois. He studied at the state university and at Columbia, where he lectured in English literature (1911–30). He was literary editor of the *Nation* (1919–22), of the *Century Magazine* (1922–5) and of the *Cambridge History of American Literature* (1917–21). He was also a distinguished biographer of **Thomas Love Peacock** (1911), **James Branch Cabell** (1925), **Jonathan Swift** (1930), **Sinclair Lewis** (1933) and **Benjamin Franklin** (1938, Pulitzer Prize, 1939). He was on the management committee of the *Dictionary of American Biography* (1926–36). He edited Franklin's *Letters and Papers* (1947); his critical studies include *The American Novel* (1921) and, with his brother, *American and British Literature since 1890* (1925). He also wrote *The Ninth Wave* (1926), a novel, and his autobiography, *Three Worlds* (1936).

VAN DOREN, Mark Albert
(1894–1972)

American poet and critic, brother of **Carl Clinton van Doren**, born in Hope, Illinois. He studied at the state university and at Columbia, where he taught from 1920 and became Professor of English in 1942. He served in the army during World War I, followed his brother to the editorship of the *Nation* (1924–8) and was awarded the Pulitzer Prize (1940) for his *Collected Poems* (1939), chosen from such volumes of verse as *Spring Thunder* (1924) and *Now the Sky* (1928). Later volumes include *The Mayfield Deer* (1941), *The Country Year* (1946), *New Poems* (1948) and *Spring Birth* (1953). He collaborated with Carl in *American and British Literature since 1890* (1925), edited the *Oxford Book of American Prose*, wrote critical studies of **Henry Thoreau** (1916), **Dryden** (1920), **Shakespeare** (1939) and **Nathaniel Hawthorne** (1949), and the novels *Transients* (1935) and *Windless Cabins* (1940). Further collections of poetry were published in 1963, 1964 and 1967.

VAN DRUTEN, John William
(1901–57)

American playwright of Dutch extraction, born in London. He is remembered mainly for *I am a Camera*, his stage adaptation of

Christopher Isherwood's Berlin stories, produced in New York in 1951 and London in 1954. He had, however, come to prominence almost 30 years previously with *Young Woodley* (1925), a wry, sentimental piece about growing up. He became the successful author of a string of domestic light comedies, including *After All* (1929), *There's Always Juliet* (1931) and *The Distaff Side* (1933), in which Sybil Thorndike gave an acclaimed performance as the imperious mother. *Bell, Book and Candle* (1950), another comedy, but this time about witchcraft, provided an amiable vehicle for Rex Harrison.

VAN DUYN, Mona Jane
(1921–)

American poet, born in Waterloo, Iowa. She was educated at the University of North Iowa and the University of Iowa, and taught English at a number of universities, including the University of Louisville, Kentucky, and Washington University, St Louis. Her first collection, *Valentines in the Wide World* (1959), was followed by a small but admirable body of skilfully crafted and insightful poems in *A Time of Bees* (1964), *To See, To Take* (1970), *Bedtime Stories* (1972), *Merciful Disguises* (1973) and *Letters from a Father* (1982). A gap of eight years passed before her next volume, *Near Changes* (1990); it won her the Pulitzer Prize for Poetry in 1991.

VAN DYKE, Henry
(1852–1933)

American clergyman and writer, born in Germantown, Pennsylvania. He studied theology at Princeton and Berlin and was a prominent pastor of the Brick Presbyterian Church, New York (1883–99). He was Professor of English literature at Princeton (1899–1923) and, under Woodrow Wilson, American minister to the Netherlands (1913–16). He was awarded the Legion of Honour for his services as naval chaplain in World War I. His many writings include poems, essays and short stories, mostly on religious themes, such as the Christmas tale *The Story of the other Wise Man* (1896), *The Ruling Passion* (1901), *The Blue Flower* (1902), *The Unknown Quantity* (1912) and *Collected Poems* (1911).

VAN LERBERGHE, Charles
(1861–1907)

Belgian poet, born in Ghent into a wealthy family, who early allied himself to the French Symbolists. His poetry evoked, according to one critic, 'the mysterious Eve who gradually takes possession of a world of dreamlike fluidity'.

VAN OSTAIJEN, Paul
(1896–1928)

Belgian (Flemish) poet, critic and editor (of
the magazine *Avontuur*), born in Antwerp.
He died young from tuberculosis. He was
Flanders' pioneer of Modernism, particularly
of Expressionism, Dada and literary Cubism;
and he had intimate contacts with the leading
proponents of the first two of these movements while he was in Germany just after
World War I. The most powerful influence
upon his poetry, **August von Stramm**, had,
however, been killed in the war. Neither his
somewhat strident, but thoughtful and ver-
bally exciting poetry, nor his criticism,
received much attention until the 1950s, when
Dutch and Belgian Flemish poets took him
up as an important precursor. He was also an
art critic of note.
▷E Schoonhaven, *Paul van Ostaijen* (1951,
in French)

VAN SCHENDEL, Arthur
(1874–1946)

Major Dutch novelist, born in Batavia in present-day Indonesia, but who lived in Italy
for many years. His masterpieces, among a
number of well-crafted and deeply interesting
novels, are *Het fregatschip Johanna Maria*
(1930, Eng trans *The Johanna Maria*, 1935),
about a man who, having sailed with his ship
all his life, is cheated by death of his wish to
own her, and *De waterman* (1933, Eng trans
The Waterman, 1963), a similar but more
extended chronicle. Van Schendel's novels
give a marvellously compact and authentic
portrait of Dutchmen of various types, but in
addition are distinguished by a fruitful and
poetic inquisitiveness about the nature of
fate.

VAN VECHTEN, Carl
(1880–1964)

American novelist, photographer and critic.
He was born in Cedar Rapids, Iowa, which
he portrays in his third novel, *The Tattooed
Countess* (1924), and took his degree at the
University of Chicago. His early career was
spent as a composer and music and drama
reviewer in New York. He published three
collections of critical essays, the prescient
Music after the Great War (1915), *Music
and Bad Manners* (1916) and, best of all,
Interpreters and Interpretations (1917); each
showed off his bright, witty intelligence.
Arguably his most widely-known book today
is *Tiger in the House* (1920), an unsentimental
study of domestic cats; one perfectly innocent
picture of a kitten cleaning its hindquarters
was thought to be 'indecent', sparking off a
brief but ludicrous furore. Van Vechten's first
novel was *Peter Whiffle, His Life and Works*

(1922), the imaginary memoirs of a dilettante.
By far his best and most perceptive book is
Nigger Heaven (1926), a hectic but often
thoughtful story about life in Harlem; though
Van Vechten was white, he made a significant
impact on the literature of the 'Harlem
Renaissance'. His desire to make visible the
previously invisible comes through in the portrait photography which made him a star in
the 1930s; a selection was published as *Portraits* in 1978.
▷E Lueders, *Carl Van Vechten* (1965)

VAN VOGT, A(lfred) E(lton)
(1912–)

American science-fiction writer, born in
Manitoba, Canada. He moved to the USA in
1944, by which time he was an established
writer. Fascinated by systematic methods of
mental and physical development, however
eccentric, he converted to Dianetics in 1950,
and wrote little in the ensuing decade, but
still has a prolific output to his name. He is
best known as a writer of elaborate and highly
speculative 'space operas', working on huge
and complex canvases which fall neatly into
genre expectations, but also attempt to push
beyond them in metaphysical reach. His best-
known works are *Slan* (1946, rev edn 1951),
The Weapon Shops of Ishar (1951) and its
sequel *The Weapon Makers* (1946), and the
Null-A sequence of novels (from 1948).
▷ *Reflections of A E Van Vogt* (1975)

VAPTSAROV, Nikolai
(1909–42)

Bulgarian poet, sometimes described as Bulgaria's **Mayakovsky**, who was executed by the
Nazis, and who therefore left a legend behind
him. He was a committed communist, but his
poems to his wife written during his last hours
are, not surprisingly, more personal and moving than his other works.

VARGAS LLOSA, Mario
(1936–)

Peruvian novelist, born in Arequipa. After
studying law and literature in Peru, he spent
many years abroad as a student in Paris and
Madrid, building up a reputation as a writer,
eventually returning to Lima shortly before
the restoration of democratic government in
Peru in 1980. *La ciudad y los perros* (Eng trans
The Time of the Hero, 1966 (US); 1967 (UK)),
his first novel, published in 1962, is a powerful
social satire and so outraged the authorities
that a thousand copies were publicly burned.
In 1965 came *La casa verde* (Eng trans *The
Green House*, 1968 (US); 1969 (UK)), a novel
that brings to life the teeming society of Peru
in the days of the rubber boom. Subsequent
novels are *Conversación en la catedral* (1969,

Eng trans *Conversation in the Cathedral*, 1975 (US)) and *Pantaléon y las visitadoras* (1973, Eng trans *Captain Pantoja and the Special Service*, 1978 (US and UK)). *La tia Julia y el escribidor* (1977, Eng trans *Aunt Julia and the Scriptwriter*, 1982 (US); 1983 (UK)), his masterpiece, is an energetic, inventive comedy which was made into a television series in Colombia. He has also written *La guerra del fin del mundo* (1981, Eng trans *The War of the End of the World*, 1984) and *La Historia de Alejandro Mayta* (1984, Eng trans *The Real Life of Alejandro Mayta*, 1986). *La orgia perpetua* (1975, 'The Perpetual Orgy') is an expression of his obsession with **Flaubert's** *Madame Bovary*. A proponent of 'magic realism', he began on the extreme left, but has gravitated towards the right; he was defeated in his bid for the presidency of Peru—fortunately, many believe, for his considerable future as a writer.

▷C Rossman and A W Friedman (eds), *Mario Vargas Llosa* (1978)

VARNALIS, Kostis
(1883–1974)

Greek poet, a Cretan contemporary of **Sikelianos** and **Kazantzakis**. His early work, heavily influenced by the French Symbolists, was not well received. He studied literature at Athens and from 1908 worked as a teacher there. In 1919 he won a state scholarship to Paris, where he embraced dialectical materialism and Marxist ideology. The first book he wrote on his return, *To Fos Pou Kai* (1922, 'The Light That Burns'), as well as its successor, *Sklabi Poliorkimeni* (1927, 'The Enslaved Beseiged'), reflected these interests. In later years he turned to prose, publishing *He Aleethini Apologia tou Sokrati* (1931, Eng trans *The True Apology of Socrates*, 1955) and *To Heemerologia tis Penelopis* (1946, Eng trans *The Journal of Penelope*), which were influential on a generation of Marxist Greek poets.

VARNHAGEN VON ENSE, Karl August
(1785–1858)

German writer and diplomat, born in Düsseldorf. In 1809 he joined the Austrian army and was wounded at the battle of Wagram. In 1813 he went over to the Russian service, and was sent to Paris as an adjutant. Here he was called to the Prussian diplomatic service, and accompanied Hardenberg to the Congress of Vienna (1814) and to Paris, becoming next resident minister at Karlsruhe (till 1819). In 1814 he married Rahel Levin, who presided over a glittering literary salon in Berlin. He wrote lives of **Goethe** (1823), Marshal Keith (1844), General von Bülow (1853),

and others; *Biographische Denkmäler* (1824–30, 'Biographical Monuments') and *Denkwürdigkeiten* (1843–59, 'Things Worth Remembering'). His Correspondence and Diaries fill 22 volumes (1860–70), and are now considered his most valuable legacy.

▷C Misch, *Varnhagen in Beruf und Politik* (1925)

VARRO, Marcus Terentius
(116–27 BC)

Roman scholar and author, born in Reate. He studied at Athens, saw service under Pompey, and in the Civil War was legate in Spain. He awaited the result of Pharsalus with **Cicero** and Cato at Dyrrachium, and was kindly treated by the conqueror, who appointed him librarian. Under the second triumvirate Mark Antony plundered his villa, burned his books, and placed his name on the list of the proscribed. But he was soon exempted, and Augustus restored his property. His prose writings embraced oratory, history, jurisprudence, grammar, philosophy, geography and husbandry. The chief were *Saturae Menippeae* ('Menippean Satires'), *Antiquitates Rerum Humanarum et Divinarum* ('Antiquities in Matters Human and Divine'), *De Lingua Latina* ('On the Latin Language') and *De Re Rusticae* ('Country Affairs'). His *Disciplinarum Libri IX* was an encyclopaedia of the liberal arts; his *Imagines*, or *Hebdomades*, a series of 700 Greek and Roman biographies.

▷J Collart, *Varron grammairien latin* (1954)

VARRO, Publius Terentius
(c.82–37 BC)

Roman poet, called Atacinus from his birth in the valley of the Atax in Narbonensian Gaul. He wrote satires and an epic poem on Caesar's Gallic wars, called *Bellum Sequanicum*. His *Argonautica* was an adaptation of **Apollonius Rhodius** and his erotic elegies pleased **Propertius**.

VARTHEMA, Ludovico de
(c.1465–c.1510)

Italian traveller and writer, born in Bologna. He was the first European and Christian recorded to have entered, and left alive, the Islamic City of Mecca. He made a six-year journey through Arabia, Persia, India and on across the Pacific to the Spice Islands (1502–7). He published an account of his travels in *Itinerario de Lodovico de Varthema Bolognese* (1510).

VAS, Istvan
(1910–92)

Hungarian poet and essayist, whose graceful minor poems were written in the rational tradition established by **Mihály Babits** in his *Nyugat* magazine.

VASCONCELOS, Carolina Michaëlis De
(1851–1925)

Portuguese scholar and writer, born in Berlin. She studied and wrote on romance philology and literature. An honorary professor of Hamburg University, she lived, after her marriage in 1876, in Oporto, where she did much scholarly research on the Portuguese language, its literature, and especially its folk literature. Most noteworthy is her edition of the late 13th- or early 14th-century *Cancioneiro da Ajuda* ('Book of Songs of Help'). Other writings include *Notas Vicentinas* (1912, 'Vincentian Notes'), an edition of the poetry of **Francisco Sá de Miranda**, and essays, studies and correspondence with other Portuguese scholars.

VASCONCELOS, Jorge Ferreira de
(c.1515–c.1585)

Portuguese author of closet comedies (really novels in dialogue—they were not for theatrical production) and romance-writer. His Arthurian romance is less important than his three 'plays', *Eufrosina* (1555), *Ulissipo* (1618) and *Aulegrafia* (1619). The first of these, partly deriving, but very different, from the *Celestina* of the Spanish **Fernando de Rojas**, is his masterpiece. It is chiefly important for the incomparable picture it gives of Portugal, but also for its discussion of love, considered from a Platonic point of view, and its vivid characterization.
▷A F G Bell, *Portuguese Literature* (1922)

VASILEV, Pavlo
(1910–37)

Russian poet, born in Kazakhstan. A belated member of the peasant movement, he had vast energies and abilities, but seldom fulfilled them. His best poems are in various anthologies, including one in the *Penguin Book of Russian Verse* (1965, ed Dimitry Obolensky). He perished in the Purges through, as **Ehrenburg** put it, 'drinking and chattering too much'.

VASSILIKOS, Vasilis
(1933–)

Greek novelist, short-story writer and filmmaker. He was born in the northern Greek town of Kavala, and began his career as a reporter on the weekly magazine *Tachydromos* and also worked as the director of documentary films. He came to prominence with the publication of a trilogy of protest novels in the early 1960s: *To Fyllo, To Pighadhi* and *To Angeliasma* (Eng trans *The Leaf, The Well, The Message*, 1964). In 1966 he published *Z* (Eng trans, 1968), later made into a hugely popular film. The novel told the story of the murder of the socialist folk hero Lambrakis and was promptly banned by the right-wing government. His other novels include *Photographs* (1973), written, like most of his works, in a difficult style, using stream of consciousness narrative in the manner of **Joyce**.

VAUGHAN, Henry
(1622–95)

Welsh religious poet, born in Newton-by-Usk, Llansantfraed, Powys, twin brother of the alchemist Thomas Vaughan (1622–66). He was called the self-styled 'Silurist' as a native of south Wales, the land of the ancient tribe of Silures. He entered Jesus College, Oxford in 1638, and in 1646 published *Poems, with the tenth Satyre of Juvenal Englished*. He took his MD, and practised as a physician first in Brecon and then in Newton-by-Usk. The collection of poems entitled *Olor Iscanus* was published by his twin brother, without authority, in 1651. In 1650 he printed his *Silex Scintillans* ('Sparkling Flint'), a notable volume of mystical and religious poems, enlarged in 1655. In 1652 he published *The Mount of Olives*, devotions in prose, and the *Flores Solitudinis* ('Flowers of Solitude'), also in prose. *Thalia Rediviva: the Pastimes and Diversions of a Country Muse*, a collection of elegies, translations and religious pieces, was also published without authority (1678) by a friend.
▷R A Dunn, *The Mystical Poetry of Henry Vaughan* (1962)

VAUGHAN, William
(1577–1641)

Welsh poet and colonizer, born in south Wales. He graduated at Jesus College, Oxford (1597), and bought an interest in Newfoundland, where he sent out settlers in 1617. He wrote an allegory, *The Golden Fleece* (1626), and other works.

VAUTHIER, Jean
(1910–)

French avant-garde playwright and essayist, born in Liège. At first a journalist and illustrator, he took to the theatre late. But Gérard Philippe and Jean-Louis Barrault subsequently appeared in his plays, which have been successful. Barrault's production of his near-monodrama *Le Personnage combattant* (1956, 'The Character Against Himself') made him famous. This memorably depicts an old popular writer vainly trying to return

to his youthful integrity—finally he is killed by a homosexual hotel servant. Mainly influenced by **Antonin Artaud**, but also by **Michel de Ghelderode**, Vauthier is a dramatist of great power and unconventionality, whose deeply religious *Les Prodiges* (1958), about a man who finds solace after being left by his evil lover, is probably his best play.
▷L Pronko, *Avant-Garde* (1962)

VAUX, Lord Thomas
(1516–56)

English poet, born at Harvonden and educated at Cambridge University. In 1523 he succeeded to his father's barony, and as a very young man he attended Cardinal Wolsey on diplomatic missions. Belonging to the court culture of Henry VIII and Edward VI, he emulated Sir **Thomas Wyatt** and **Surrey** in his verse. Some of his short, melancholy love lyrics were included in *Tottel's Miscellany* (1557) and then in Puttenham's *Art of English Poesie* (1589). His best work (from the mere 15 poems known to be his) is probably seen in the medieval love allegory *The Assault of Cupid* and *The Aged Lover Renounceth Love*, on bodily deterioration.

VAZOV, Ivan
(1850–1921)

Bulgarian national poet, born in Sopot. He wrote a collection of poems and songs under the title *Pod igoto* (1894, Eng trans *Under the Yoke*, 1896), and other novels. He was twice exiled from his native land for his nationalist sympathies, but became Minister of Education in 1897.
▷N S Derjavin, *Ivan Vazov* (1950)

VEGA, Lope de, in full Lope Félix de Vega Carpio
(1562–1635)

Spanish dramatist and poet, born in Madrid. Orphaned at an early age, he was a student and graduate of Alcalá. He served in the Portuguese campaign of 1580, and in the Spanish Armada (1588). He became secretary to the Duke of Alva, Marquis of Malpica, and Marquis of Sarria. A favourite with the ladies, he had many love affairs, was twice married, and fathered at least six children, three of them illegitimate, was banished from Madrid because of a quarrel, and lived two years in Valencia. He took orders in 1614, and became an officer of the Inquisition. He died poor, for his large income from his dramas and other sources was all but wholly devoted to charity and church. The mere list of Lope's works presents a picture of unparalleled intellectual activity. His first work of any length was a poem, the *Angelica*, written at sea in 1588, but not printed till 1602. The *Arcadia*,

the story, in a pompous, pastoral setting, of the prenuptial vagaries of the Duke of Alva, was written before the duke's marriage, July 1590, but it was kept back till 1598. The *Dragoneta*, celebrating the death of Drake, appeared the same year, and was Lope's first publication under his name. But it was as a ballad-writer that he made his mark. The more notable of his miscellaneous works are the *Rimas* (1604); *Peregrino en su Patria* (1604, Eng trans *The Pilgrim of Casteele*, 1621), a romance; *Jerusalém Conquistada* (1609), an epic; *Pastores de Belén* (1612), a religious pastoral; *Filomena* (1621) and *Circe* (1624), miscellanies in the style of **Cervantes**; *Corona Trágica* (1627, 'Tragic Crown'), an epic on Mary, Queen of Scots; *Laurel de Apolo* (1630); *Rimas de Tomé de Burguillos* (1634), a collection of lighter verse, with the *Gatomaquia* (pub 1807), a mock-heroic. *Dorotea* (1632), in the form a prose drama, is obviously the story of his own early love adventures. Lope was a master of easy, flowing, musical, graceful verse. Though he had written plays, he did not become a writer for the stage until after 1588. He gave the public what it wanted—excitement pure and simple. Lope's plays may be roughly divided into the historical or quasi-historical and those that deal with everyday life. Of the latter the most characteristic are the 'cloak and sword plays'. The *Noche de San Juan* ('The Night of St John'), one of his very last plays; the *Maestro de Danzar*, one of his first; and the *Azero de Madrid*, the source clearly of **Molière**'s *Médecin malgré lui*, are excellent examples. Other plays include *Perro del hortelano* (Eng trans *The Gardener's Dog*, 1936), *Desprecio agradecido* ('Welcomed Contempt'), *Esclava de su Galán* ('Slave of her Gallant'), *Premio del bien hablar* ('The Talking Prize'); and *Alcalde de Zalamea*, a bold vigorous outline which **Calderón de la Barca** improved upon. The number of Lope's plays seems to have been 1500, exclusive of 400 *autos*. Of these the very names of all but between 600 and 700 have been lost, and often nothing but the name survives. There are about 440 plays and 40 *autos* in print or MS.
▷F C Hayes, *Lope de Vega Carpio* (1967)

VEGA, Ventura de la
(1807–65)

Argentinian–Spanish dramatist, poet, librettist and director of Madrid's national theatre. He left Argentina at the age of 11. His poetry is of little account, but he was a skilful playwright whose verse comedy *El hombre de mundo* (1845, 'The Man of the World') anticipated **Benavente**.

VEGETIUS (Flavius Vegetius Renatus)
(4th century)

Roman military writer under the emperor Theodosius I the Great. After AD 375 he produced the *Epitome Institutionum Rei Militaris* on classic legionary operations, mainly extracted from other authors, which during the Middle Ages was a supreme authority on warfare.

▷T R Phillips, *A Collection of Military Classics* (1941)

VELDEKE, Hendrik van (Heinrich von)
(c.1140–c.1205)

Dutch or German poet and knight from the Rhineland. His first work was a biography of St Servatius, which is written in a form of Low German very close to Dutch, and which seems to have been his native language. He is best known, however, for his *Eneit*, a reworking of a French Romance based on parts of **Virgil**'s *Aeneid*. It is in High German, though there are traces of the Dutch influence in it. An epilogue to the poem tells how it was stolen from him, half-finished, in Strasbourg, and returned to him nine years later in Thuringia. It contains fantastical imagery and shows considerable powers of poetic invention.

VELEZ DE GUEVARA, Luis
(1579–1644)

Spanish novelist and playwright. He graduated from the University of Osuna, joined the army and went to Italy. Later he settled in Madrid in the service of Conde Saldana, practising law but also writing. By 1608 he was an established author. His best-known works are *El Diablo Cojuelo* (1641, 'The Devil on Two Sticks'), a 'costumbrista' novel of contemporary manners, and his historical drama *Reinar Después de Morir* (1652, 'To Reign after Death'), about the life of Inés de Castro. He also collaborated with **Calderón de la Barca** and **Rojas Zorilla**. His style is satirical and baroque with a tendency to the unexpected and spectacular (supernatural and miraculous scenes in strange landscapes and dreamlike atmospheres). Despite his fame, Velez de Guevara was constantly plagued by money troubles which he unsuccessfully tried to relieve by four marriages.

VENANTIUS FORTUNATUS
(c.530–600)

Christian Latin poet, born near Treviso in northern Italy and educated at Ravenna. While there he became blind, but later regained his sight, and in 565 he left Italy for Gaul in order to give thanks for his recovery to St Martin of Tours at his shrine. He stayed in Gaul for the rest of his life, eventually becoming Bishop of Poitiers, and was later canonized. Venantius was a voluminous poet, producing 11 books of occasional verse on his life and travels, reminiscences of his friends and memorable meals, hymns (the best-known is 'Vexilla regis prodeunt') and an epic poem on the life of St Martin.

▷H Waddell, *Mediaeval Latin Lyrics* (1929)

VENEZIS, Elias, pen-name of Elias Mellos
(1904–73)

Greek novelist, born in the Turkish town of Ayvalik, opposite Mytilene. In 1922 he was conscripted by the Turks into the compulsory work corps in the interior. The experience furnished his first novel, *Number 31328* (1931), a realistic account of his captivity which was an immediate success. His other novels include *Ghalini* (1939, 'Calm'), an account of the plight of Aeolian people forced to return to Greece, and *Aeolixi Ghi* (1943, Eng trans *Aeolia* 1949) an evocative recreation of his childhood. In later works he moved away from personal experiences, and his reputation went into serious decline, with one critic identifying 'a literary feebleness and an exhaustion of the lyric impulse'.

VERDAGUER, Mosen Jacinto
(1845–1902)

Catalan poet, born in Folgarolas. He became a priest with a vast popular following. He wrote *L'Atlántida* (1877) and *Lo Canigó* (1886), two epic poems of great beauty, and on the first of these Manuel de Falla based his choral work *Atlántida*. His *Idilis y Cants Místichs* (1870, 'Mystical Idylls and Songs'), also set to music, have become part of the music of the Catalan Church.

VERDE, José Joaquim Cesário
(1855–86)

Portuguese poet, who was born and died, prematurely, in Lisbon. His poetry did not become widely known until a friend posthumously edited it, in a volume published a year after his death: *O Livra de Casário Verde* (1887). He had the gift of clarity in an age of overblown rhetoric, and in certain respects anticipated the later fascination with the city which was the hallmark of the early work of **Verhaeren**. He is one of those, like his compatriot **Sá-Carneiro**, who might have developed into a major poet.

▷J Serrão, *Cesário Verde* (1961, in Portuguese)

VERE, Edward de, 17th Earl of Oxford
(1550–1604)

English court poet, who was born near Francis Vere and Sir Horace Vere. He was an Italianate Englishman, violent and a spendthrift, but one of the best of the Elizabethan courtier-poets. Of his lyrics, published in various collections, 'What cunning can expresse' is perhaps the best.

VERGA, Giovanni
(1840–1922)

Italian novelist, born in Catania in Sicily. He wrote numerous violent short stories describing the hopeless, miserable life of Sicilian peasantry, including *La vita dei campi* (1880, Eng trans *Under the Shadow of Etna*, 1896) and *Cavalleria rusticana* (1884, Eng trans *Cavallera Rusticana and Other Tales of Sicilian Life*, 1893), which was made into an opera by Mascagni. The same **Zola**esque theme prevails in his novels, *I Malavoglia* (1881, Eng trans *The House by the Medlar Tree*, 1890), *Mastro Don Gesualdo* (1888, Eng trans *Master Don Gesualdo*, 1893), and others. **D H Lawrence** translated some of his works, including his *Novelle rusticane* (1882, Eng trans *Little Novels of Sicily*, 1925).
▷ L Russo, *Giovanni Verga* (1947)

VERHAEREN, Emile
(1855–1916)

Belgian poet, born in St Armand near Termonde. He studied law, but turned to literature, writing in French. His poetry hovers between powerful sensuality, as in *Les Flamandes* (1883, 'The Flemish Women'), and the harrowing despair of *Les Débâcles* (1888), the affirmation of the life force and the revulsion against modern industrial conditions. His best work is possibly *La Multiple Splendeur* (1906). He died in a train accident.
▷ M Sadleir, *Things Past* (1944)

VERISSIMO, Erico
(1905–)

Brazilian novelist, critic and travel writer, born in Porto Alegre. Of all modern Brazilian novelists, he has been most cosmopolitan and influenced by such fashionable American writers as **Hemingway**. There is some argument, owing to his extreme conservatism, as to whether he is essentially a popular or a serious novelist. His best-known novel is *Caminhos Cruzados* (1935, Eng trans *Crossroads*, 1943), a work owing much to *The Bridge of San Luis Rey*, by **Thornton Wilder**. His best novel, though, is undoubtedly the uncharacteristic *Noite* (1940, Eng trans *Night*, 1956), about an unknown and alienated stranger.

VERLAINE, Paul
(1844–96)

French poet, born in Metz. He was educated at the Lycée Condorcet and entered the civil service. Already an aspiring poet, he mixed with the leading Parnassian poets and writers in the cafés and salons. Under their battle cry 'Art for art's sake', against the formless sentimentalizing of the Romantic school, he gained recognition by contributing articles and poems to their avant garde literary magazines, especially the short-lived *Le Parnasse contemporain*. The youthful morbidity of his first volume of poems, *Poèmes saturniens* (1866, 'Saturnine Poems'), was criticized by **Charles Sainte-Beuve** as trying vainly to outdo **Baudelaire**. The evocation of a past age, the 18th century, provided the theme of his second work, *Fêtes galantes* (1869, Eng trans *Gallant Parties*, 1912), by many considered his finest poetical achievement. His love for the 16-year-old Mathilde Mauté during an engagement prolonged by the doubts of the girl's father was expressed in *La Bonne Chanson* (1870, 'The Pretty Song'). During the Franco–Prussian war Verlaine did guard duty in Paris and then served as press-officer for the Communards. The birth of a son did nothing to heal the incompatibilities of his married life, from which he escaped (1872) on travels in Flanders, Belgium and England in a homosexual affair with the fledgling poet **Arthur Rimbaud**, 10 years his junior. Their friendship ended in Brussels in 1873, when Verlaine, drunk and desolate at Rimbaud's intention to leave him, shot him in the wrist. Verlaine's overpowering remorse made it psychologically impossible for Rimbaud to leave, so he staged an incident in the street and had Verlaine arrested. He did not foresee that the police, searching for a motive, would suspect immorality. Verlaine was convicted and sentenced to two years' hard labour, and his past associations with the Communards disqualified him from any intercession by the French ambassador. *Romances sans paroles* (1874, Eng trans *Romances Without Words*, 1921) were written in Mons prison, where he studied **Shakespeare** in the original, and after his wife had left him, he turned Catholic (1874). He unsuccessfully attempted to enter a monastery on release, taught French at Stickney, Lincolnshire, and St Aloysius' College, Bournemouth (1875), where he completed his second masterpiece *Sagesse* (1880, 'Wisdom'), full of the spirit of penitence and self-confession that appeared again in *Parallèlement* (1889, 'In Parallel'). In 1877 he returned to France to teach English at the Collège of Notre Dame at Rethel. There he adopted a favourite pupil, Lucien Létinois, for whom he acquired a farm at Coulommes and whose death from typhus (1883) occasioned *Amour* (1888, 'Love'). *Poètes maudits* (1884, 'Accursed Poets'), comprising critical studies, was followed by short stories such as *Le Poteau* (1886, 'The Stake'), sacred and profane verse *Liturgies intimes* (1892, 'Intimate Liturgies') and *Élégies* (1893). Verlaine is the consummate master of a poetry

which sacrificed all for sound, in which the commonplace expressions take on a magic freshness. He lived during his last years in Parisian garret poverty, relieved by frequent spells in hospitals and finally by a grand lecture tour in Belgium, Holland and England (1893), the last sponsored in part by William Rothenstein, who drew several portraits of him.
▷C Morire, *Paul Verlaine, poète maudit* (1947)

VERMEYLEN, August
(1872–1945)

Belgian (Flemish) novelist, art historian, critic and statesman, born in Brussels. A Roman Catholic until he lost his faith, he was educated in Germany and Austria. He was a member of the Flemish literary society called 'De Distel' ('The Thistle'). He was one of the leading figures in the revival of Flemish literature which took place in Belgium at the end of the 19th century, and which was marked by the publication of the periodical *Van Nu en Straks*, which he co-founded. His most famous and best work is *De Wanderlende Jood* (1906, 'The Wandering Jew'), more of an allegory than a novel; its purpose is the promotion of an atheist humanism. He was a socialist politician in his last 20 years, and refused—notably—to join the Nazis when they promised a revival of Flemish literature at the expense of French.
▷R Roemens, *Het werk van Prof. Dr. August Vermeylen* (1953)

VERNE, Jules
(1828–1905)

French novelist, born in Nantes. He studied law, and from 1848 wrote opera libretti until in 1863, with the publication of *Cinq Semaines en ballon* (Eng trans *Five Weeks in a Balloon*, 1870), he struck a new vein in fiction—exaggerating and often anticipating the possibilities of science and describing adventures carried out by means of scientific inventions in exotic places, like submarines and space travel. He greatly influenced the early science fiction of **H G Wells**. His best-known books, all of which have been translated, are *Voyage au centre de la terre* (1864, Eng trans *A Journey to the Centre of the Earth*, 1872), *De la Terre á la Lune* (1865, Eng trans *From the Earth to the Moon*, 1873), *Vingt mille lieues sous les mers* (1869, Eng trans *Twenty Thousand Leagues Under the Sea*, 1873) and *Le Tour du monde en quatre-vingts jours* (1873, Eng trans *Around the World in Eighty Days*, 1874). Film versions of the last two achieved an astonishing popularity.
▷M L Allotte de la Frye, *Jules Verne* (1955)

VERRÍSIMO, Érico
(1905–75)

Brazilian popular novelist and travel writer, born in Cruz Alta, in the gaucho state of Rio Grande do Sul. Verrísimo's fiction, somewhat self-consciously influenced by English models such as **Aldous Huxley** and **Ernest Hemingway**, is uneven and often superficial, and his modernism has been found by most critics to be ersatz. But it is readable and seriously intended, and he has been much translated. The success of *Olhai os Lirios do Campo* (1938, Eng trans *Consider the Lilies of the Field*, 1947), an urban novel about a man torn between selfishness and love, was deserved. But his outstanding novel was the pessimistic and driven *Noite* (1940, Eng trans *Night*, 1964), in which the unnamed protagonist is an amnesiac. Verrísimo held lecturing posts in the United States, and wrote books for children.

VERWEY, Albert
(1865–1937)

Dutch poet, critic, dramatist, translator (of **Dante**) and scholar, from Amsterdam. A major figure in his literature, Verwey was one of the founders, with his friend and mentor **Kloos**, of the magazine of the 'Men of the Eighties', *De Nieuwe Gids* ('The New Guide'). This individualistic movement rescued Dutch literature from 'the dead weight of the past' by throwing off old clichés and rhetoric; its chief inspirers were the English poets **Shelley** and **Keats**. His *Persephone en andeare gedichten* (1885, 'Persephone and Other Poems') embodied these ideals. But then, like many Dutch poets, he came under the influence of Spinoza, and rejected sensuality (much advanced by the 'Eighties') in favour of a pantheism based on Spinoza's philosophy; later still he became associated with the circle of **Stefan George** in Germany. Eventually he became a primarily philosophical poet, and as such lost some of his appeal. He is now remembered mainly as a critic who wrote some distinguished but not crucial poetry.
▷R P Meijer, *Literature of the Low Countries* (1971)

VERY, Jones
(1813–80)

American mystic and poet, born in Salem in Massachusetts and educated at the Harvard Divinity School. He lived quietly in Salem with his sisters, writing sonnets and prose pieces of intense religious inspiration. These were published in *Essays and Poems* (1839). So intense was his personality that he was briefly committed to a lunatic asylum; his friend **Emerson** defended him.
▷E Gittleman, *Jones Very, the effective years, 1833–40* (1967)

VESAAS, Tarjei
(1897–1970)

Norwegian novelist and lyric poet, from Telemark. A writer of symbolic and allegorical works, he was the most important novelist using *Landsmål* ('country language', renamed *Nynorsk*, 'New Norwegian') after World War II. His first novel was *Die svarte hestane* (1928, 'The Black Horses'). His best-known books are *Fuglane* (1957, Eng trans *The Birds*, 1968) and *Is-slottet* (1963, 'The Ice Castle'). He published his autobiography, *Båten om kvelden* ('Boat in the Evening') in 1968 but his mature style emerged in *Kimen* (1940, Eng trans *The Seed*, 1964).

▷ R Skrede, *Tarjei Vesaas* (1964)

VESTDIJK, Simon
(1898–1971)

Major Dutch novelist, poet and critic from Harlingen, who wrote, his compatriots declared, 'faster than God can read'. During World War II he was imprisoned for a year by the Nazi occupiers. He is best remembered for his eight-novel roman-fleuve about Anton Wachter, but he wrote many other novels, chief amongst which was his own favourite, *De koperin tuin* (1950, Eng trans *The Garden Where the Brass Band Played*, 1965), in which a tragic love is played out against a musical background. His historical novels, and those based on Greek mythology, were amongst his most popular. He received most of the prizes available to Dutch authors, and was once put forward as the Netherlands' candidate for the Nobel Prize for literature, which he might worthily have won. He wrote much music and literary criticism, including a book about **Albert Verwey**.

VESTLY, Anne-Cath(arina)
(1920–)

Norwegian author of children's books. From her first stories about *Ole Aleksander Filibombom-bom* (from 1953 onwards), she has displayed a unique ability to find a language children will understand. Similarly full of warmth, solidarity and humour is her series about *Mormor og de åtte ungene* ('Grandma and the eight children', from 1957) and *Knerten* (from 1962). In her last two series, about the girls *Aurora* (from 1966) and *Guro* (from 1975), we meet families where the sex roles are reversed, expressing Vestly's wish for children both to learn something from reading her books and to question their environment.

VIAN, Boris
(1920–59)

French playwright, novelist and poet, born in Ville d'Avray. A Bohemian with a bad heart, he dabbled in many things—acting, jazz, engineering, anarchism, pornography—and excelled in fiction. A tragi-comic writer, he won a cult following for such novels as *L'Écume des jours* (1947, Eng trans *Froth on the Daydream*, 1967) and *L'Arrache-coeur* (1953, Eng trans *Heartsnatcher*, 1968).

▷ D Noakes, *Boris Vian* (1964)

VIANA, Javier de
(1871–1925)

Uruguayan story writer, dramatist and novelist, born in Montevideo. Beginning under the influence of **Zola** and naturalism, Viana was amongst the first to write realistically of the too often sentimentalized gaucho, the cowboy. Critics did and do upbraid Viana for his brutality, but the extent of this—for example in his collection *Campo* (1896, 'The Open Spaces')—has been exaggerated. The melodrama of the novel *La gaucha* (1899) is relieved by some fine writing. Viana's later works, written as he became an alcoholic, remain popular, but are not as well observed as the earlier, especially the stories in his finest volume, *Gurí* (1901), in which he developed his technique to its peak.

▷ J F Garganigo, *Javier de Viana* (1972)

VIAU, Théophile de
(1590–1626)

French poet, born in Clairac. He wrote the tragedy *Pyramé et Thisbé* (1621) and love poetry distinguished by its naturalness. He was condemned to the stake (1623) for the impiety and obscenity of the poems he contributed to *Le Parnasse satyrique*, but his sentence was commuted to exile for life.

▷ F Lachevre, *Le procès de Théophile de Viau* (1909)

VIAUD, Louis Marie Julien *see* **LOTI, Pierre**

VICENTE, Gil
(c.1470–c.1537)

Portuguese dramatist, born in Lisbon, considered the father of Portuguese drama. He wrote 44 plays, 16 in Portuguese, 11 in Spanish and 17 using both languages. His early plays were religious, but gradually social criticism was added. His farces *Inês Pereira*, *Juiz da Beira* and the three *Autos das barcas* (*Inferno*, *Purgatório* and *Glória*, collective Eng trans *The Ship of Hell*, 1929) are his best. He displays great psychological insight, superb lyricism and a predominantly comical spirit.

▷ L Keats, *The Court Theatre of Gil Vicente* (1962)

VIDA, Marco Girolamo, the 'Christian Virgil'
(c.1480–1566)

Italian Latin poet, born in Cremona. He was made Bishop of Alba in 1532. He wrote Latin orations and dialogues, a religious epic, *Christias* (1535), *De Arte Poetica* (1537, 'On the Art of Poetry'), and poems on silk-culture and chess (1527).
▷M P de Cesare, *Vida's Christiad and the Vergilian Epic* (1964)

VIDAL, Gore (Eugene Luther, Jr)
(1925–)

American novelist, essayist and polemicist, born at the United States Military Academy in West Point, New York, where his father was an aeronautics instructor. Much of his childhood was spent in Washington under the influence of his scholarly, witty and blind grandfather, Senator Thomas Gore. He was educated at Phillips Exeter Academy, where he began to write an (unfinished) novel about Mussolini. But he was a mediocre student and in 1943, instead of going to Harvard, joined the United States Army Reserve Corps, which gave him the material for his first novel, *Williwaw* (1946), published to some acclaim when he was just 19. However his second novel, *In a Yellow Wood* (1947), was slated and his third, *The City and the Pillar* (1948), a clinical and unsentimental account of a young man coming to terms with his homosexuality, precipitated a decline in his career. His next five novels, among them *Dark Green, Bright Red* (1950), *A Search for the King* (1950) and *The Judgment of Paris* (1952), also had a lukewarm reception. After a period as a TV commentator he returned to the novel in 1964 with *Julian*, his first major book, which purports to be the emperor Julian's autobiographical memoir and journal, followed by a trilogy of books dealing with affairs of state—*Washington, DC* (1967), *Burr* (1973) and *1876* (1976). His taste for camp extravagance reached its apotheosis in the 'apocalyptic' *Myra Breckenridge* (1968) and *Myron* (1974), 'Myra's comeback'. Since then his historical fiction has been dominant. Even his tour de force, *Creation* (1981), was overshadowed by *Lincoln* (1984), an engrossing, meticulously researched, insightful portrait of America's 16th President. In *Empire* (1987), set at the beginning of the American Empire, his fascination with power (he ran for congress in 1960) was again to the fore, and also in 1987 he published *Armageddon: Essays 1983–1987*, 'random pieces' that reflect his ambivalent obsession with what he has called, with characteristic hauteur, 'the land of the dull and the home of the literal'.

VIDRÍC, Vladimir
(1875–1909)

Croatian poet, born in Zagreb. He combined decadence with an elegant lyricism, and his few poems are prized for their technical perfection and their evocative versions of Greek myths.

VIEBIG, Clara, pseud of Clara Viebig Cohn
(1860–1952)

German novelist, born in Trier. Now neglected, Viebig began as a follower of Zola. The background of her fiction is the menacing landscape of her native Eifel. *Das schlafende Heer* (1904, Eng trans *The Sleeping Army*, 1929) depicts Polish peasants under the Germans. Her most famous novel, telling the story of the life of a servant girl, was *Das tägliche Brot* (1900, Eng trans *Our Daily Bread*, 1908).
▷C Scheuffler, *Clara Viebig* (1926)

VIELÉ-GRIFFIN, Francis
(1864–1937)

American-born French Symbolist poet, the son of the American general Egbert Louis Vielé (1825–1902), born in Norfolk, Virginia. He made his home in Touraine, France, and became a leading exponent of *vers libre*. His poems collected under the titles *Cueille d'avril* (1886, 'April Harvest'), *Poèmes et Poésies* (1895, 'Poems and Verses'), *Sapho* (1911), and *La Sagesse d'Ulysse* (1925, 'The Wisdom of Ulysses'), are of high lyrical quality, tending towards musical impressionism, and embody a serene outlook on life. His brother, Herman Knickerbocker Vielé (1856–1908), was a painter and novelist.
▷J de Cours, *Francis Vielé-Griffin* (1970)

VIERECK, Peter
(1916–)

American poet and 'liberal conservative', son of George Sylvester Viereck, an originally German novelist and essayist well known in his day; he was born in New York. His first collection, *Terror and Decorum* (1948), won a Pulitzer Prize, and gained him wide attention, both hostile and otherwise. Wild and exuberant, these poems attempted to deal with his war experiences with a gleeful lyricism described by **William Carlos Williams** as 'sensitive, distinguished in feeling'. Later poetry, though copious, has foundered on Viereck's tendency to oversell himself and his modest technical gifts, and on his rhymes, which have been called 'ludicrous' (for example: 'Barrack/Weimaric/Pyrrhic/Wreck/Viereck'). His *New and Selected Poems 1932–1967* appeared in 1967. *Conservatism Revisited* (1949) is one of many similar studies.
▷M Henault, *Peter Viereck* (1969)

VIGNY, Alfred Victor, Comte de
(1797–1863)

French romantic writer, born in Loches, Indre-et-Loire. He served in the Royal Guards (1814–28), retiring with a captaincy. His experiences provided the material for *Servitude et grandeur militaires* (1835, Eng trans *Military Servitude and Grandeur*, 1919), a candid commentary on the boredom and irresponsibility, yet desire for devotion and self-sacrifice, induced by peace-time soldiering. He married an Englishwoman, Lydia Bunbury (1828). He had already published anonymously a volume of verse (1822) followed by *Eloa* (1824), the fallen angel condemned for self-pity, and *Poèmes antiques et modernes* (1826, 'Ancient and Modern Poems'; expanded edn 1829), which includes his grand poetic conception of Moses as the hopelessly overburdened servant of God. His life, marred by domestic unhappiness and his failure to enter parliament (1848–9), was that of a congenital misfit who bears his loneliness with dignity. This is reflected in his work, especially in that masterpiece of romantic drama, *Chatterton* (1835, Eng trans 1847), written for his love, the actress Marie Dorval, as well as in *Stello* (1832), which describes the tragic fates of the young poets, **Thomas Chatterton**, Gilbert and **Chénier**, and is concluded in the posthumously published sequel *Daphné* (1912). These exemplify Vigny's pessimism, and his exaltation of the poet as a godlike outsider whose knowledge is yet necessary for society. Other notable works include the historical novel *Cinq-Mars* (1826, Eng trans 1847), the plays *Le More de Venise* (1829, based on **Shakespeare**'s *Othello*) and *La Maréchale d'Ancre* (1831, 'The Wife of the Marshal of Ancre'), the philosophical poems glorifying social order and discipline, *Les Destinées* (post 1864), and the biographical notes, *Journal* (1867).
▷A Whitridge, *Alfred Vigny* (1933)

VIITA, Lauri Arvi
(1916–65)

Finnish novelist and poet, born in Pirkkala. His death in a car accident at the age of only 48 was a major loss to Finnish literature. His early vitalist poems in his initial collection *Concreter* (1947) made a strong impression. His novel *Moraine* (1950) was a study of urban life set during the bitter Finnish Civil War.

VIK, Bjørg
(1935–)

Norwegian short-story writer, playwright and novelist. She grew up in Oslo and began her career as a journalist, publishing her first volume of short stories in 1963. Elegant and complex, her short stories focus the situation of the middle-class housewife trapped by family duties and the demands of materialism. The texts in *Kvinneakvariet* (1972, Eng trans *An Aquarium of Women*, 1987), depicting women of different ages at times of crisis, reflect her involvement with 'second-wave' feminism, as does her successful play *To akter for fem kvinner* (1974, 'Two Acts for Five Women'). A leading figure in Norwegian literary life, she has also published a semi-autobiographical novel, *Små nøkler store rom* (1988, 'Small Keys Large Rooms').
▷J Garton, 'Bjørg Vik', in *Norwegian Women's Writing 1850–1990* (1993)

VILDE, Edouard
(1865–1933)

Estonian realist novelist and dramatist, one of the first considerable figures in the modern literature of his country. He ended as a fierce and anti-modernist conservative—yet, after a youthful period which he spent in journalism and purveying light popular fiction, he had contributed to the modernist movement. His (incomplete) collected works ran to 33 volumes, but nothing was translated into English. *Mäeküla piimamees* (1916, 'The Dairyman of Mäelüka') is often mentioned as his best novel.
▷A Mägi, *Estonian Literature* (1968)

VILDRAC, Charles, pseud of Charles Messager
(1882–1971)

French poet, critic, children's writer and dramatist. He was one of the founders of *L'Abbaye*, or unanimist, group (**Duhamel**, Vildrac's brother-in-law, **Romains** and others). His collection *Livre d'Amour* (1910, Eng trans *A Book of Love*) charmingly, and in a minor key, expresses the ideals of the group. He is best known, however, for his plays, and in particular for the successful seaport drama *Le Paquebot Tenacity* (1919, Eng trans *The Steamship Tenacity*, 1921), which was produced by Jacques Coupeau's Vieux Colombier.

VILHJÁLMSSON, Thor
(1925–)

Icelandic novelist and critic, born in Edinburgh, Scotland, but brought up in Reykjavík. He is the foremost Icelandic author writing in the existentialist tradition (he was in Paris just after World War II). Early stories are collected in *Andlit í spegli dropans* (1957, Eng trans *Faces Reflected in a Drop*, 1966). His novels are concerned with such themes as European culture, nuclear warfare, and with the unnatural speed of life in the modern world.

VILJANEN, Lauri Sakari
(1900–)

Finnish poet, translator (of European poetry), critic and academic, born in Kaarina. He was a leading associate of the semi-modernist Tulenkantajat ('Torchbearers') Group of the 1920s. He sought in many ways to be a counterpart in literature to Sibelius in music, and even dedicated a book to the composer's memory. Viljanen eventually came to be regarded by many younger Finns as 'dictatorial' and dated in his literary approach.
▷E Tompuri, *Voice from Finland* (1947)

VILLAESPESA, Francisco
(1877–1936)

Spanish poet, novelist and dramatist, once widely read but now almost forgotten. He followed in the footsteps of **Rubén Darío**, but his poetry was too facile and vulgar to last. However, for a short time **Juan Ramón Jiménez** and **Antonio Machado** admired him as an authentic Spanish *modernista* poet in Darío's style.

VILLAURUTIA, Xavier
(1903–50)

Mexican poet and dramatist, born in Mexico City. His uncle, the *modernista* poet Jésus Valenzuela, a founder of the magazine the *Revista Moderna* (1898–1911), had a decisive influence. **Paz** said of him: 'I discovered that his good manners hid an irritable temperament, and that the epigrams he fired off served to defend an insecure and anguished being, a victim of paralysis of will and depression'—of what the Spanish had called *abulia*. His early poetry was *modernista* in style, showing the influence of his reading of **Jammes** and other French poets, and above all of Mexico's greatest poet after **Sor Juana Inés de la Cruz**, **Ramón López Velarde**, of whose work he became a leading critic. With **Jaime Torres Bodet** and **Novo** he founded the influential magazine *La Falange* (1922–3), and with the latter the even more important *Ulisis* (c.1924), which preceded *Contemporáneos*, Villaurutia becoming a leading member of those involved in the magazine. But when *Contemporáneos* collapsed under the onslaught of a more conventional and 'nationalist' poetic, Villaurutia suffered, and stated to his audience: 'I suffer because I cannot please you'. He moved, with **Alfonso Reyes**, Mexico's keeper of conscience, into the realm of avant-garde theatrical activity: he translated plays by **Pirandello** and others, and contributed his own *En qué piensas?* (1938). Later he wrote *La Hiedra* (1941, 'Ivy'), an ironically commercial play, which was a success, and earned him many enemies amongst his former colleagues. But his poetry is the most important part of his work, and it is likely that he will be considered, with Reyes, as the most substantial of Mexico's 20th-century poets. It has been stated that he killed himself; in fact he died of a heart attack.
▷E L Moretta, *The Poetic Achievement of Xavier Villaurutia* (1971)

VILLAVERDE, Cirilio
(1812–94)

Cuban novelist, born in Pinar del Rio, who was harrassed by the Spanish authorities for his identification with the cause of Cuban independence. He was forced to spend many years in the USA. He published the first part of his major novel, *Cecilia Valdés* (1839–1882, Eng trans 1962), at the age of 27, but could not complete it until he was 67. Its eponymous heroine is a beautiful mulatto, and the book has great importance in the history of the depiction of the racial problem in Cuba—it has a plain anti-slavery thesis. It is also, despite its sensationalist plot, of literary value, containing incomparably vivid descriptions of Cuban 19th-century life, and is worthy of Villaverde's avowed models, Sir **Walter Scott**, **Balzac** and **Manzoni**. He wrote other fiction, and two of his novellas deal with incestuous relationships (which also feature in *Cecilia Valdés*). He died in New York.
▷G Coulthard, *Race and Colour in Caribbean Literature* (1962)

VILLIERS, George, 2nd Duke of Buckingham
(1628–87)

English playwright and politician, brought up in the household of Charles I. Villiers had an early introduction to the vicissitudes of the political life: his father was assassinated in the year of his birth. His marriage to Maria Fairfax in September 1657 cemented his alliance with one of the leading parliamentarian families, and allowed him to reclaim the bulk of the estates which, as a royalist, he had forfeited; **Cowley** celebrated the wedding in a poem addressed to the bridegroom. Villiers ended up by squandering his vast fortune, and in his latter years was roundly reviled as a debauchee. His personal excesses apart, he is best remembered for the witty play *The Rehearsal* (1671), an attack on the pomposity of heroic drama, and, it is thought, on **Dryden** in particular.

VILLIERS DE L'ISLE ADAM, Auguste, Comte de
(1838–89)

French writer, pioneer of the Symbolist movement, born in St Brieuc. He was a Breton count who claimed descent from the

Knights of Malta. He dedicated his *Premières Poésies* (1856–8, 'First Poetic Works') to **de Vigny**, but developed into a considerable stylist in prose. His famous short stories, *Contes cruels* (1883, 'Cruel Stories') and *Nouveaux Contes cruels* (1888, 'New Cruel Stories'), are after the manner of **Edgar Allan Poe**. Hegelian idealism and Wagnerian Romanticism inspire his highly didactic novels and plays. The former include *Isis* (1862) on the Ideal and *L'Ève future* (1886, 'Eve of the Future'), a satire on the materialism of modern science. The latter include his masterpiece, *Axel* (1885). A pronounced Catholic aristocrat, he lived for a while with the monks of Solesmes.
▷H Chapoutout, *Villiers de l'Isle Adam* (1908)

VILLINCH *see* **BIZCARRONDO, Indalecio**

VILLON, François, originally **François de Montcorbier** or **de Logos**
(1431–after 1463)

French poet, born in Paris. He took the surname of his guardian, Guillaume de Villon, a priest and a close relative, who enabled François to study at university, to graduate (1449) and to become MA (1452). While a student he fell into bad company and in 1455 had to flee from Paris after fatally wounding a priest in a street brawl. He joined a criminal organization, the 'Brotherhood of the Coquille', which had its own secret jargon in which Villon was to write some of his ballades. Pardoned in 1456, he returned to Paris and there wrote the *Petit Testament*. He took part in the organized robbery of the funds of the Collège of Navarre, and fled to the court of the Duke of Orléans at Blois. There he was sentenced to death for another unknown crime, but released as an act of grace on a public holiday. The same happened again at Meung-sur-Loire (1461), the year of the *Grand Testament*. In 1462–3 he was in trouble again for theft and brawling. Sentence of death was commuted to banishment in January 1463. He left Paris and nothing further is known of him. The first printed edition of his works was published in 1489. The *Petit Testament* comprises 40 octosyllabic octaves, the *Grand Testament* comprises 172, bridged by 16 ballades and other verse forms. Six of the Coquille jargon ballades have been definitely attributed to him. Collections of his work in translation were published in 1968, 1971, 1973 and 1977.
▷P Champion, *François Villon* (1913, in French)

VIÑAS, David
(1929–)

Argentinian novelist and polemicist, born in Buenos Aires into a partly Jewish family.

Viñas has in his time been Argentina's 'angry young man', belonging to groups with such slogans as 'rebellion, rejection, disorder'. He has attacked **Borges**, **Mallea**, and other leading Argentinian writers, for not 'writing and living as guilty'. His chief work lies in his fiction, in particular the novel *Jauría* (1974), a harsh and uncompromising picture of the *macho* military and of the terrified repressed homosexuality underlying it. After the fall of the military dictatorships he returned from Mexico to his own country. He has been active in films and in the theatre. He now holds the chair of 19th-century Argentine Literature at the University of Buenos Aires. It is generally agreed that he has been unlucky to have escaped the attention of translators.
▷G R McMurray, *Spanish American Writing since 1941* (1987)

VINE, Barbara *see* **RENDELL, Ruth**

VINJE, Aasmund, originally **Olavson**
(1816–70)

Norwegian poet and critic, born in Vinje. He was a leader of the movement to establish the 'country language' called *Landsmål* (later known as *Nynorsk*, 'New Norwegian'), and produced a weekly journal, *Dølen*, from 1858 to 1866. He wrote a book of travel reminiscences on Norway (1861), and visited England in 1862 and published a critical *Norseman's View of Britain and the British* in English in 1863. His poetic works include *En Ballade om Kongen* (1853), his epic cycle *Storegut* (1866) and *Blandkorn* (1867).

VINOKUROV, Yevgeny
(1925–)

Russian poet, born in Bryansk. He fought in World War II, and from the start of his poetic career eschewed rhetoric. A restrained poet, sometimes almost 'minimalist', he gains his effects from understatement. He has received little attention outside Russia, but within it he is perhaps more highly respected than some other poets who have sought public attention. He was poetry editor of *Novy Mir*.

VIRGIL (Publius Vergilius Maro)
(70–19 BC)

Roman poet, born in Andes, near Mantua in Cisalpine Gaul, where his father owned a small property. The boy was sent to school at Cremona and Milan, and at 16 went to Rome and studied rhetoric and philosophy. In 41 BC the victorious triumvirs were settling disbanded soldiers on confiscated lands throughout Italy. Virgil's farm was part of the confiscated territory; but by advice of the governor of the district, Asinius Pollio, he went to Rome, with special recommendations

to Octavian (Augustus); and though his own property was not restored to him, he obtained ample compensation from the government, and became one of the endowed court poets who gathered round the statesman Maecenas. In 37 BC his *Eclogues*, 10 pastorals modelled on those of **Theocritus**, were received with great enthusiasm. Soon afterwards he left Rome and moved to Campania. The generosity of Maecenas had placed him in affluent circumstances. He had a villa at Naples and a country-house near Nola. The *Georgics*, or *Art of Husbandry*, in four books, dealing with tillage and pasturage, the vine and olive, horses, cattle, and bees, appeared in 30 BC, and confirmed his position as the foremost poet of the age. The remaining 11 years of his life were devoted to a larger task, undertaken at the urgent request of the emperor, the composition of a great national epic based on the story of Aeneas the Trojan, legendary founder of the Roman nation and of the Julian family. This covered the hero's life from the fall of Troy to his arrival in Italy, his wars and alliances with the native Italian races, and his final establishment in his new kingdom. By 19 BC the *Aeneid* was practically completed, and in that year Virgil left Italy to travel in Greece and Asia; but in Athens he fell ill, and returned only to die. At his own wish he was buried in Naples, on the road to Pozzuoli; his tomb, for many hundreds of years after, was worshipped as a sacred place. A few juvenile pieces of more or less probable authenticity are extant under his name. These are the *Culex* and the *Moretum*, both in hexameter verse; the *Copa*, a short elegiac piece; and 14 little poems in various metres, some serious, others trivial. The *Ciris* is now agreed to be by a contemporary imitator. The supremacy of Virgil in Latin poetry was immediate and almost unquestioned; his works were established classics even in his lifetime, and soon after his death they had become the textbooks of western Europe. By the 3rd century his poems ranked as sacred books, and were regularly used for purposes of divination. In the Middle Ages his fabled powers as a magician almost eclipsed his real fame as a poet; but with the revival of learning he resumed his old place. His works were translated in three volumes by **Cecil Day-Lewis**, 1940–63.
▷F Klinger, *Vergil* (1967)

VISHNEVSKY, Vsevolod
(1900–51)

Russian dramatist from St Petersburg who wrote the most popular of all Soviet plays, *Optimisticheskaya tragediya* (1933, Eng trans *An Optimistic Tragedy*, in B Blake, *Four Soviet Plays*, 1937). This is agitprop at its most skilful. Later he wrote *Nezabbyvayemyy 1919*

(1919), a distortion of Stalin's part in history—for which he was awarded the Stalin Prize First Class.
▷G Struve, *Soviet Russian Literature 1917–1950* (1951)

VITRAC, Roger
(1899–1952)

French playwright and Surrealist poet. He was associated with **Tzara** in the founding of the Dada movement, and with **Artaud** in that of the Théâtre Alfred Jarry. His most substantial play is *Victor ou les enfants au pouvoir* (1928, 'Victor, or Children in Power'), which was revived in 1962 by **Jean Anouilh**. This is a bitter Surrealist parody of superficial bedroom farce, depicting monstrous children, and will survive as one of the most effective and playable examples of the many assaults made by similar playwrights on the emptiness of bourgeois society. In English translation is *Les Mystères de l'amour* (1927), *Mysteries of Love*, in *Modern French Theatre* (1964).

VITTORINI, Elio
(1908–66)

Sicilian novelist, critic and translator, born in Syracuse. He educated himself despite great obstacles, and he became Italy's most influential writer, helping younger writers. He was founder editor of *Il Politecnico* (1945–7) and *Il Menabò* (1959–66), and translated modern American writers like **Edgar Allan Poe**, **John Steinbeck** and **William Faulkner**. *Conversazione in Sicilia* (1941, Eng trans *Conversation in Sicily*, 1949) is his metaphorical masterpiece.
▷S Pautasso, *Elio Vittorini* (1967)

VIZENOR, Gerald Robert
(1934–)

American writer, born in Minneapolis. A member of the Minnesota Chippewa tribe, whose father was born on the White Earth reservation, much of Vizenor's work draws on his Ojibwe heritage, in particular on the tradition of the trickster hero. *Griever: An American Monkey King in China* reflects his experience of university teaching in China, and combines the Native American trickster tradition with that of the Chinese Monkey King. His best-known work of fiction is the picaresque novel, *Darkness in Saint Louis Bearheart* (1973), a darkly comic account of the travels of his modern-day trickster hero, Proude Cedarfair. Vizenor has published several collections of historical and cultural essays, and numerous volumes of poetry: reworkings of traditional Ojibwe songs in *Summer in the Spring* (1965) and *Anishinabe Nagamon* (1970), and his own haiku in *Seventeen Chirps* (1964), *Empty Swings* (1967) and *Matsushima: Pine Islands* (1984). A reporter for the *Minneapolis Tribune* during the 1970s, Vizenor wrote many newspaper articles on contemporary Native American issues, which have recently been collected in *Crossbloods: Bone Courts, Bingo and Other Reports* (1990). He has also written an award-winning filmscript which was filmed as *Harold of Orange*. His novel *Dead Voices* (1992) is a fantastic cycle of Native American stories, narrated by a bear-woman.

VLAYKOV, Todor
(1865–1943)

Bulgarian story writer who published under the name Venelin, but is now known by his real name. He was from early on influenced by **Tolstoy** and other Russians, and dedicated his life to improvement of the peasantry by means of *narodnik* ideals. For many years he devoted himself to the Radical Party, and was a member of the 1919–23 government, a unique peasant dictatorship, hostile to left and right, eventually overthrown by a military coup owing to its attempts to suppress Macedonian terrorism. His stories of peasant life show far deeper understanding of women than those of **Petko Todorov**.
▷ *Slavonic Review* (1954, 1958)

VODNIK, Valentin
(1758–1819)

Slovene poet and teacher, born in Zgornja Šiška, near Ljubljana. By his writings he helped to revive Slovene nationalism. He wrote poetry, educational and school books in the language of the peasantry, and this became established as the literary language of Yugoslavia.
▷ F Levstik, *Valentin Vodnik* (1935)

VOIGT, Cynthia
(1942–)

American children's author, born in Boston, Massachusetts and educated at Smith College. She has worked as a high school teacher since 1965 and has received the **Newbery** Medal (1983) and the Mystery Writers of America **Edgar Allan Poe** Award (1984). Her novels tend to focus on independent adolescents, 'outsiders', who gradually come to create bonds with family and friends; several of them, including her first, *Homecoming* (1981), centre on one family, the Tillermans. She writes primarily for children and from 1981 has published at least one book a year.

VOINOVICH, Vladimir Nikolaevich
(1932–)

Russian novelist, born in Dushanbe, who emigrated to the West in 1980. After military service, he worked in various manual trades

before moving into radio and then full-time writing. After three early novels, he wrote *Zhizni neobychaynye priklyucheniya Ivana Chonkina*, the first part of a massive comic work-in-progress. Its satirical view of Soviet behaviour during World War II led to its suppression; Voinovich was expelled from the Union of Soviet Writers in 1974 and the novel received its first (Russian) publication in France the following year. It concerns a holy fool—much like **Hašek**'s Svejk/Schweik—who becomes a mirror for the stupidities of ideology and high-echelon politics. The English translation, *The Life and Extraordinary Adventures of Private Ivan Chonkin* (1977), made a big impact, and the second volume, *Pretendent na prestol: Novye priklyucheniya soldata Ivana Chonkina* (1979, Eng trans *Pretender to the Throne: The Further Adventures of Private Ivan Chonkin*, 1981), was equally warmly received. Voinovich's travails at home were documented in the self-mocking (and slyly mythifying) *Ivankiada: Ili rasskaz o vselenii pisatelya Voinovicha v novuyu kvartiru* (1976, Eng trans *The Ivankiad: The Tale of the Writer Voinovich's Installation in His New Apartment*, 1977). The year following his defection he was stripped of his Soviet citizenship.

VOITURE, Vincent
(1598–1648)

French poet and letter-writer, born in Amiens. He was an original member of the Académie française, and enjoyed the favour of Gaston d'Orléans, Richelieu, Mazarin and Louis XIII. His brilliant sonnets and *vers de société* were the delight of the Hôtel Rambouillet, the Marquise de Rambouillet's literary *salon*, but were not published till 1650. His letters, first published in 1654, are an elegant mirror of his age and social milieu.
▷ C A Sainte-Beuve, in *Causeries de lundi* (1867)

VOJNAVĆ, Ivo
(1857–1929)

Croatian poet, story writer and dramatist, born in Dubrovnik. He experienced early hardship when the Austrians arrested him for his advocacy of an independent Yugoslavia. But he became famous despite them, for his powerful drama and affecting tales. He had a profound understanding of European literatures, and adapted many techniques, both in such stories as 'Geranium', influenced by **Flaubert**, and in such dramas as *Ekvinocij* (1902, 'Equinox'), where he exploits Symbolism. Some of his poems are translated in the *Slavonic and East European Review* (I,1, 1922).

VOLNEY, Constantin François Chasse-b'uf, Comte de
(1757–1820)

French scholar and author, born in Craon in Mayenne. He studied medicine, history and oriental languages at Paris, adopted the name of Volney, and travelled in Egypt and Syria (1783–7) before publishing his valuable *Voyage* (1787). A zealous reformer, he was elected to the Constituent Assembly in 1789, but later was thrown into prison until the downfall of Robespierre (1794). His reputation chiefly rests on his famous work *Les Ruines, ou Méditations sur les révolutions des empires* (1791, 'The Ruins; or, Meditations on the Revolutions of the Empires').

VOLODIN, A, pseud of **A Lifshits**
(1919–)

Russian dramatist, whose work initially attracted much attention for its alleged failure to observe socialist-realistic tenets. His *Pyat vechoerov* (1959), a romantic play about youthful love, was translated as *Five Evenings* (1966).

VOLOSHIN, Maximilian, pseud of **Maximilian Kirienko-Voloshin**
(1877–1932)

Russian poet, translator, critic and painter, born in Kiev. He was greatly influenced by the French poetry he read while he was living in Paris as a young man, and he was able to welcome the Revolution in the mystical manner in which so many other non-communist poets (such as **Blok**) did. But he grew disillusioned; there was no room for him in Soviet society, and he stopped writing, and lived in retirement in Koktebel. His poetry was neglected for many years, but is now being read again for its unique blend of mysticism and realism. Two of his poems are included in the *Penguin Book of Russian Verse* (1965, ed Dimitry Obolensky).

VOLPONi, Paolo
(1924–)

Italian novelist and poet, born in Urbino. He worked for the firm of Olivetti from 1950 until 1971. His Gramscian poetry has won some success, but better known is his fiction, sharply critical of modern life and technology; his novels include *Memoriale* (1962, Eng trans *My Troubles Began*, 1964) and the diary of a madman, *La macchina mondiale* (1965, Eng trans *The Worldwide Machine*, 1967).

▷ G C Feretti, *Volpone* (1972, in Italian)

VOLTAIRE, François Marie Arouet de
(1694–1778)

French author, the embodiment of the 18th-century 'Enlightenment', born in Paris. His father, François Arouet, held a post in the chambre des comptes in Paris. He was educated at Collège Louis-le-Grand, the chief French seminary of the Jesuits. Leaving college at the age of 17, he was destined for the Bar, but law disgusted him. Alarmed by the dissipated life which he was leading, his father gladly saw him admitted into the service of his godfather's brother, the Marquis de Châteauneuf, the French ambassador to Holland; but in consequence of an undiplomatic love affair with a French Protestant *émigrée* in The Hague, Voltaire was sent home. He again entered an attorney's office, but his stay there was short, and he soon obtained notoriety as the author of a satire on his successful rival in the poetic competition for an Academy prize. In 1716, on suspicion of satirizing the regent, the Duc d'Orléans, he was banished for several months from Paris; and in 1717–18, a savage attack accusing the regent of all manner of crimes resulted in 11 months' imprisonment in the Bastille, where he re-wrote his tragedy *Œdipe*, began a poem on Henri IV and assumed the name Voltaire. *Œdipe* was performed in 1718, and was triumphantly successful. His next dramatic attempts were almost failures, and he devoted himself to his poem on Henri IV. But the authorities refused to sanction its publication on account of its championship of Protestantism and of religious toleration, so Voltaire had the epic poem surreptitiously printed in Rouen (1723) and smuggled into Paris, as *La Ligue ou Henri le Grand* (Eng trans *Henriade*, 1732). Now famous and a favourite at court, he was denounced by the Chevalier de Rohan-Chabot as a parvenu. Voltaire retorted with spirit, and circulated caustic epigrams on the Chevalier, whose revenge was to have Voltaire beaten up. Voltaire challenged the Chevalier and was once more thrown into the Bastille, and freed only on the condition that he would go at once to England, where he landed in May 1726. Here Bolingbroke introduced him to **Pope** and his circle. He made the acquaintance of Peterborough, Chesterfield, the Herveys and the Duchess of Marlborough, and became friendly with **Edward Young**, the Scottish poet **James Thomson** and **John Gay**. He acquired some knowledge of **Shakespeare** and **Milton**, **Dryden** and **Samuel Butler**, **Joseph Addison**'s *Cato*, and the Restoration dramatists. He was strongly attracted to Locke's philosophy, and he mastered the elements of Newton's astronomical physics. Queen Caroline of Anspach accepted his dedication to her of the *Henri-ade*, the new form of *La Ligue*; and when permitted to return to France in 1729 he took with him his *History of Charles XII* (2 vols, 1731) and the materials for his *Lettres écrites de Londres sur les Anglais* (1734, Eng trans

Letters Concerning the English Nation, 1734). He laid the foundation of his great wealth by purchasing shares in a government lottery and by speculating in the corn trade, ultimately increased by the profits from large army contracts. He formed an intimacy with Madame du Châtelet-Lomont, and went to live with her at her husband's château of Cirey in Champagne (1734). Here he wrote dramas—among them *Mahomet* (1741, Eng trans *Mohamet the Imposter*, 1744) and *Mérope* (1743, Eng trans 1744); poetry, his *Traité de métaphysique* (1784, 'Treatise on Metaphysics'), much of his *Siècle de Louis Quatorze* (1751, Eng trans *The Age of Louis XIV*, 1752) and *Les Mœurs et l'esprit des nations* (1756, rev 1761-3, Eng trans *The General History and State of Europe*, 1756), with his *Eléments de la philosophie de Newton* (1738, Eng trans *The Elements of Newton's Philosophy*, 1738). His correspondence (1740-50) testifies to a love affair with his niece, the widowed Madame Denis. Since the appearance of his *Lettres écrites de Londres sur les Anglais* he had been out of favour at the French court. But his *Princesse de Navarre*, performed on the occasion of the Dauphin's marriage (February 1745), pleased Louis XV by its clever adulation. This and the patronage of Madame de Pompadour won him the appointments of official royal historian and of gentleman-in-ordinary to the king. In 1747 an imprudent speech at a court card-party drove him to take refuge with the Duchess de Maine, for whose amusement he now wrote *Zadig* (1748, Eng trans *Zadig and Other Stories*, 1971) and other oriental tales. When he was allowed to reappear at court, some injudicious flattery of Madame de Pompadour excited the indignation of the queen, and Voltaire had again to migrate. The death (1749) of Madame du Châtelet allowed him at last to accept the repeated invitation of Frederick II, the Great. In July 1750 Voltaire found himself in Berlin as king's chamberlain, with a pension of 20 000 francs and board in one of the royal palaces. But he entered into questionable financial transactions with a Berlin Jew and Frederick was still more gravely offended by his satirical criticisms on Maupertuis in *Micromégas* (1752, Eng trans 1753) and in March 1753 Frederick and Voltaire parted, never to meet again. In Prussia Voltaire had published his *Siècle de Louis Quatorze* (1751). On his way home he was arrested at Frankfurt, through Frederick's representative there, who had been instructed to recover from Voltaire a volume of the king's poems. Voltaire avenged himself by writing a malicious sketch of Frederick's character and account of his habits, first printed after Voltaire's death. He settled in 1755 near Geneva and after 1758 at Ferney, four

miles from Geneva. In 1756-9 appeared his *Mœurs et l'Esprit des nations*, his pessimistic *Poème sur le désastre de Lisbonne* (1756, 'Poem on the Lisbon Earthquake') and that satirical masterpiece, the novel *Candide* (Eng trans *Candid*, 1759), which attacked what Voltaire understood by the Leibnizian optimistic theology that 'all is for the best in this best of all possible worlds'. The suspension of the *Encyclopédie* by the French government, and the condemnation by the parliament of Paris of a harmless poem of his own on natural religion, impelled him to declare war by word and deed against the bigoted, 'L'Infâme'. In 1762 appeared the first of his antireligious writings which were to include didactic tragedies, biased histories, pamphlets and the *Dictionnaire philosophique portatif* (1764, Eng trans *The Philosophical Dictionary for the Pocket*, 1765). The judicial murder (1762) of Jean Calas, falsely accused of having, from Protestant zeal, killed one of his sons to keep him from turning a Catholic, aroused Voltaire to exert himself (successfully) to establish his innocence and to rescue members of the Calas family from punishment. This and similar efforts on behalf of victims of French fanaticism, for whom he provided a refuge at Ferney, won widespread admiration. The Genevan government prevented Voltaire from staging plays and from establishing a theatre in Geneva. **Rousseau**'s support for the Swiss government terminated Voltaire's friendship with the philosopher (1758). In 1778, in his eighty-fourth year, he was given a 'royal' welcome in Paris, when he arrived to put on his last tragedy, *Irène* (1778). The excitement brought on illness and his death. After the Revolution, which his works and ideas helped to foster, his remains were reinterred in the Panthéon, Paris.

▷ S G Tallentyre, *Voltaire* (1903)

VONDEL, Joost van den
(1587–1679)

Dutch poet and dramatist, born in Cologne of Dutch immigrant parents. He became a prosperous hosier in Amsterdam and devoted his leisure to writing satirical verse, himself turning from Anabaptism through Armenianism to Roman Catholicism. Having acquired a wide knowledge of the classics, he turned to Sophoclean drama and produced *Jephtha* (1659) and *Lucifer* (1654), a masterpiece of lyrical religious drama. He greatly influenced the German poetical revival after the Thirty Years War (1618–48).

▷ A J Barouq, *Joost van den Vondel* (1925)

VON KRUSENSTJERNA, Agnes
(1894–1940)

Swedish novelist born in Växjö, into an upper-class family. Her schooling was limited, and the psychiatric problems which were to recur throughout her life surfaced while she was still a child. Her first major work was the trilogy about Tony Hastfehr (1922–6), an *Entwicklungsroman* in which the young girl's discovery of sexual desire becomes a significant element. The seven-volume *Fröknarna von Pahlen* (1930–5), 'The Misses von Pahlen') is a radical exploration of the feminine psyche and women's lives, culminating in the ideal of the maternal family. The sexual explicitness of this work resulted in a wide-ranging public controversy. The four-volume *Fattigadel* (1935–8, 'Petty Nobility') traces the development of an upper-class woman in a perceptively depicted social setting on the verge of change.

▷ B Svanberg, *Sanningen om kvinnorna. En läsning av Agnes von Krusenstjernas romanserie Fröknarna von Pahlen* (1989)

VON LA ROCHE, Sophie
(1730–1807)

German novelist, best-known for her epistolary work in the style of **Richardson**'s *Clarissa, Geschichte des Fräuleins von Sternheim* (1771), claimed as the first German 'woman's novel'. The erotic style was influenced by her cousin, the seraphic poet **C M Wieland**, with whom she had an adolescent affair. She had married, in 1754, the illegitimate son of a count, Georg von La Roche, and began to write as a means of giving her life meaning after her daughters had been sent away to boarding school. One of these daughters later died, leaving 12 orphans. Sophie took charge of the younger grandchildren, including Bettina Brentano, whose childhood correspondence with **Goethe** was later published.

VONNEGUT, Kurt, Jr
(1922–)

American novelist, born in Indianapolis, Indiana. Educated at Cornell University, Chicago University and the Carnegie Institute, Pittsburgh, he served in the US army infantry (1942–5) and was given the Purple Heart. During the 1960s he emerged as one of America's most influential, potent and provocative writers, a ribald commentator of the horrors of the century: holocaustic wars, the desperate state of the environment, and the dehumanization of the individual in a society dominated by science and technology. *Player Piano* (1952) was his first novel and there were another three before *Slaughterhouse-Five* (1969), in which its two main characters—the author himself and the protagonist, Billy Pilgrim—see beneath the tragic realities of human history but make no attempt to effect change. The central event of the novel is the destruction of Dresden during World War II which the author witnessed as a prisoner-of-war. *Breakfast of Champions* (1973) was even more experimental in form, a metafictional duel between Vonnegut and the imaginary science-fiction writer Kilgore Trout, inventor of the planet Tralfamador; Trout recurs in Vonnegut's fiction. Later novels continued to satirize human folly in its various manifestations: *Slapstick* (1973), *Jailbird* (1979) and *Deadeye Dick* (1982).

▷ J Lundquist, *Kurt Vonnegut* (1977)

VON REZZORI, Gregor
(1914–)

Austrian novelist, born in the Bukovina, the remote eastward tip of the old Austrian empire. He was a descendant of an impoverished Sicilian noble family who moved to Vienna in the 18th century. He studied at Vienna University and for a time lived in Bucharest. In Germany after the war he was a film-maker, broadcaster and writer. His most significant books are *Memorien eines Antisemiten* (1979, Eng trans *Memories of an Anti-Semite*, 1984) and *Der Tod Meines Bruders Abel* (1976, Eng trans *The Death of My Brother Abel*, 1986).

VON SCHOULTZ, Solveig
(1907–)

Finland–Swedish poet and short-story writer. Born in Borgå, Finland, she has been influenced by the Finland–Swedish modernists but has developed her own idiom, her style gradually characterized by a simplicity bordering on the laconic. The situation of women is a recurring theme, from books of poetry such as *Eko av ett rop* (1945, 'The Echo of a Cry') and *Nattlig äng* (1949, 'Meadow at Night') to collections of short stories such as *Den blomstertid* (1958, 'Flower Season') and *Somliga mornar* (1976, 'Some Mornings'). *De sju dagarna* (1942, 'The Seven Days') is a subtle account of the development of young children, while *Längs vattenbrynet* ('Along the Water's Edge', 1992) is an autobiographical text.

▷ T Warburton, 'Solveig von Schoultz', in *Åttio år finlandssvensk litteratur* (1984)

VÖRÖSMARTY, Michael
(1800–55)

Hungarian poet and dramatist, born in Szekesfehervar. He was an advocate and, after Kossuth's revolution, a member of the National Assembly in 1848. He wrote the national song, *Szozat* (1840, 'The Call'), lyric and epic poetry and 11 plays, of which the fairy drama *Csongor es Tünde* (1831, 'Csongor and Tünde') is his masterpiece. He also translated **Shakespeare**an tragedies.

▷ D Toth, *Michael Vörösmarty* (1957)

VOSS, Johann Heinrich
(1751–1826)
German poet and philologist, born in Sommersdorf in Mecklenburg. He studied at Göttingen, and in 1778 went from editing the *Musenalmanach* at Wandsbeck to be schoolmaster at Otterndorf. Here he translated the *Odyssey*. In 1782 he became rector of a school at Eutin, and in 1789 he issued his translation of **Virgil**'s *Georgics*. In 1802 he settled in Jena, and in 1805 was appointed professor at Heidelberg, where he translated **Horace**, **Hesiod**, **Theocritus**, Bion, Moschus, **Tibullus** and **Propertius**; other translations were of **Aristophanes** and (with the aid of his two sons) **Shakespeare**. *Luise* (1795), an idyll, is his best original poem, although his lyric poems were popular in his own day.
▷ W Herbst, *Johann Heinrich Voss* (1872–6)

VOVCHOK, Marko, pseud of **Maria Markovych**, originally **Maria Vilinskaya**
(1834–1907)
Ukrainian writer of fiction. She wrote realistic stories in both Ukrainian and Russian, many of them demonstrating the evils of serfdom.
▷ *Ukrainian Quarterly*, III (1947)

VOZNESENSKY, Andrey
(1933–)
Russian poet (and painter), born in Vladimir, originally trained as an architect. For many years, during the 1960s and 1970s, he was regarded in the West as the most gifted poet of his generation. With **Yevtushenko** and **Akhmadulina** he toured the USA and other countries, giving readings. His facile, punning, clever and modernist poetry mesmerized such poets as **W H Auden**, **Stanley Kunitz** and **Robert Lowell**, who over-praised him; but he had real gifts, which led perceptive critics to ask what he might yet do. His long work *Osa* (1962), a mixture of poetry and prose cast in the form of the diary of a girl, Osa, is perhaps his most successful. But much of his ebullient poetry has inevitably dated. English translations (selections): *Antiworlds and the Fifth Ace* (1963); *Story Under Full Sail* (1974).

VRATISLAV z MITROVIC, Václav
(1576–1635)
Czech travel-writer who was imprisoned by the Turks, served on their galleys, and survived to tell the tale in the classic *Prihody* (1599, Eng trans *The Adventures of Baron Wenceslas Wraitslaw of Mitrowisz*, 1862), a vivid account of the Turks of the time.

VRCHLICKY, Jaroslav, pseud of **Emil Frída**
(1853–1912)
Czech poet and translator of the classics of European poetry, born in Laun. He was a pupil of **Victor Hugo**, who inspired the *Fragments of the Epic of Humanity*. His best ballads, *Legenda o sv. Prokopu* (1879, 'Legend of St Procopius') and *Zlomky epopeje* (1886, 'Peasant Ballads'), are on nationalistic and patriotic themes. His early lyric poetry on love and the pleasures of life gave way to reflections upon suffering and misfortune. In 1893 he was appointed Professor of European Literature at Prague.
▷ V Ticly, *Jaroslav Vrchlicky* (1951)

VYNNYCHENKO, Volodymyr
(1880–1941)
Ukrainian playwright and novelist, born in Kherson province. He was one of the leaders of the Revolution of 1917, and in 1919 was obliged to emigrate to France. He made his mark with the novel *Chesnist z soboyu* (1911, 'Honesty With Oneself'). In France he wrote plays which were temporarily successful; but he was forgotten in his own country until quite recently.

VYSHNYA, Ostap, pseud of **Pavlo Hubenko**
(1889–1956)
Ukrainian comic writer, born in Grun, Sumy. After 1943 and a period of imprisonment on a trumped-up charge he was forced, like his Soviet counterpart **Zoschenko** a little later, to conform to socialist realism. He was the greatest humorist of his time. Some of his earthy stories are translated in *25 Stories from the Soviet Republics* (1958).

W

WACE, Robert
(c.1115–c.1183)

Anglo–Norman poet, born in Jersey. He studied in Paris, and was a canon of Bayeux between 1160 and 1170. He wrote several verse lives of the saints, but his main work was *Roman de Brut* (1155), a free Norman–French version of Geoffrey of Monmouth's *Historia Regum Britanniae*, used by **Layamon** and **Robert Mannyng**. He also wrote the *Roman de Rou* (Rollo), an epic of the exploits of the Dukes of Normandy.

▷M Pela, *Influence de Brut de Wace* (1931)

WACKENRODER, Wilhelm Heinrich
(1773–98)

German writer, born in Berlin. He was an early exponent of Romanticism and a close friend of **Johann Tieck**, with whom he collaborated in *Herzensergiessungen eines kunstliebenden Klosterbruders* (1797, 'Outpourings from the Heart of an Art-loving Monk') and *Phantasien über die Kunst* (1799, 'Fantasies about Art').

▷E Gulzow, *Wackenroder* (1930)

WADDINGTON, Miriam
(1917–)

Canadian poet, born in Winnipeg to Yiddish-speaking Russian–Jewish parents. She was a social worker for many years before joining the English department at the University of Toronto. Since her first collection *Green World* (1945), Waddington has been acclaimed as one of the finest lyric poets of her time. Her work is personal and confessional, but highly intelligent; in the collections *Dream Telescope* (1972) and *The Visitants* (1981) she began to use short lines and a truncated syntax reminiscent of **Gertrude Stein**.

WÄGNER, Elin
(1882–1949)

Swedish novelist and journalist, feminist and pacifist. Born in Lund, she attended a girls' high school and embarked on a career as a journalist. Experiences from the Swedish women's suffrage movement are reflected in *Pennskaftet* (1910, 'Pen Woman'), which combines wit and irreverence with poignancy and earnestness. *Åsa-Hanna* (1918) is a many-faceted investigation of the plight of a peasant woman facing the misogyny of society, including the church. Notions of a matriarchal past, translated into subtle mythical patterns, result in increasingly critical perspectives on the present, as in *Dialogen fortsätter* (1932, 'The Dialogue is Continuing'). The remarkable eco-feminist essay *Väckarklocka* (1941, 'Alarm Clock') highlights the need for respect and restraint between human beings and towards Mother Earth.

▷U Isaksson and E H Linder, *Elin Wägner, I–II* (1977–80)

WAGONER, David Russell
(1926–)

American poet and novelist, born in Massilon, Ohio. One of the most decisive influences upon him was that of his teacher at Pennsylvania State University, **Theodore Roethke**. He has been a prolific and much read poet (and novelist), with a penchant for the dramatic lyric, initially in the manner of the *Spoon River* poems of **Edgar Lee Masters**. His poems about Native Americans, *Who Shall be the Sun? Poems Based on the Lore, Legends, and Myths of Northwest Coast and Plateau Indians* (1978), were highly praised. Of his many novels, *Where is My Wandering Boy Tonight?* (1970), about a boy caught up in corrupt adult machinations, and with a destructive mother, is outstanding.

▷R McFarland, *David Wagoner* (1989)

WAHLÖÖ, Per
(1926–75)

Swedish novelist, born in Gothenburg; he worked as a crime reporter before publishing his first novel in 1959. He published seven novels and a collection of short stories under his own name before starting to co-write police procedurals with his wife Maj Sjöwall (1935–). From the outset their ambition was to write a series of 10 novels using the crime genre as a vehicle for depiction and critical analysis of the Swedish welfare state. Starting with *Roseanna* in 1965, the series, now internationally renowned, was completed 10 years later with *Terroristerna* ('The Terrorists'), published shortly after Wahlöö's untimely death in 1975. The novels express an ironic and devastating left-wing criticism of the social and legal system in Social Democratic Sweden. The world of crime is viewed partly through the eyes of a group of detectives of the National Homicide Squad in Stockholm and its liberal-minded head Martin Beck; the detectives are not idealized, and the authors dwell on Beck's stomach aches and marital problems as much as on the procedures and work environment of the police. A joint Danish, German and Swedish film production of six of the novels was begun in 1993, including *Mannen på Balkongen* (1967, 'The Man on the Balcony') and *Brandbilen som försvann* (1969, 'The Fire Engine that Disappeared').

▷ E Søholm, *'Roman om en forbrydelse'— Sjöwall/Wahlöö's vaerk og virkelighet* (1976)

WAIN, John Barrington
(1925–)

English critic and novelist, born in Stoke-on-Trent. He studied at, and was elected fellow of, St John's College, Oxford, and lectured in English literature at Reading University (1947–55) before turning freelance author. His first four novels, *Hurry on Down* (1953), *Living in the Present* (1955), *The Contenders* (1958) and *Travelling Woman* (1959), tilt at post-war British, particularly London, social values as viewed by a provincial. His debunking vigour and humour has affinities with that of **Kingsley Amis**. He has also written poetry such as *Weep Before God* (1961), *Feng* (1975) and *Open Country* (1987); his *Poems 1949–1979* appeared in 1980. His other work includes plays, and critical studies, and he has edited literary magazines. His later novels include *The Young Visitors* (1965), *The Pardoner's Tale* (1978), *Young Shoulders* (1982), *Where The Rivers Meet* (1988), *Comedies* (1990), and the children's book *Lizzie's Floating Shop* (1981). He also wrote a biography of **Samuel Johnson**(1974). He was Professor of Poetry at Oxford (1973–8).

▷ *Sprightly Running* (1962)

WAKEFIELD MASTER, the
(15th century)

English playwright. Nothing whatsoever is known about the person or persons responsible for the Wakefield cycle (also known as the Towneley Cycle) of Miracle plays, written for performance by the townsfolk at their annual pageants. There are 32 plays in all, but six of them, the *First* and *Second Shepherds' Pageants* and four others, are by the same author, known as the Wakefield Master. Rich in humour, in colour and in their use of West Yorkshire dialect, and written in a characteristic nine-line stanza form, they are the best-crafted of all the surviving English Miracle plays.

▷ A C Cauley (ed), *Everyman and the Medieval Miracle Plays* (1956)

WAKOSKI, Diane
(1937–)

American poet. She was born and educated in California and has taught at a number of American campuses. Her first verse was published in *Coins and Coffins* (1962) and the *Four Young Lady Poets* anthology (1962), which was edited by **Amiri Baraka**. These showed her to have a narrative of verbal power, conveying strong feeling about gender, America, violence and capitalism with a vividness of surface that was clearly influenced by **Wallace Stevens**. In 1968, she began to publish a sequence of chapbooks called *Greed*, parts one, two, etc, which were eventually gathered as *The Complete Greed: Parts 1–13* (1984). She also published her best-known collection, *Inside the Blood Factory* (1968), which used Surrealist imagery to portray life in the US and the contradictions of femininity. Other distinctive volumes include *Looking for the King of Spain* (1974) and *Waiting for the King of Spain* (1976), which explore feelings of yearning and loss, and *Looking for Beethoven in Las Vegas* (1983). Wakoski's prose includes *Creating a Personal Mythology* (1975), which offers important insights into her verse.

WALCOTT, Derek Alton
(1930–)

Caribbean poet, playwright, winner of the Nobel Prize for literature. He was born on St Lucia and educated there and at Kingston, Jamaica, to both of which he subsequently returned as a teacher. He worked briefly as a journalist and was founding director (from 1959) of the Trinidad Theatre Workshop. His first poems were published in Trinidad in 1948, followed by *Epitaph for the Young: XII Cantos* (1949). The slight stiffness of the early poems, evidenced throughout *In a Green Night: Poems 1948–1960* (1962), quickly disappeared, revealing a poet with strong ties to English Romanticism and back beyond that to the Elizabethans. From the mid-60s onwards, Walcott was utterly distinctive, writing with a musicality that penetrated down into his imagery. Volumes include *The Castaway* (1965), *The Gulf* (1969), *Another Life* (1973) and *Sea Grapes* (1976). The title of arguably his best book, *The Star-Apple Kingdom* (1979), suggests that the poetry needs to be bitten into and tasted in order to reveal its sometimes fugitive inner make-up. In 1981 Walcott published *The Fortunate Traveller*, a virtuosic reworking in verse of **Thomas Nashe**'s 16th-century novel, *The Unfortunate Traveller*. In 1981 *Omeros*, a brilliant Caribbean Odyssey, confirmed his international stature and in 1993 he was awarded the Nobel Prize for literature.

▷ R D Hamner, *Derek Walcott* (1981)

WALKER, Alice Malsenior
(1944–)

American novelist and poet, born in Eaton-ville, Georgia, into a poor black family. Educated at Spelman College, Atlanta, and Sarah Lawrence College, she has been employed registering voters, as a social worker, and as a teacher and a lecturer. Her essay *In Search of Our Mother's Gardens* (1983) is an important rediscovery of a black female literary and cultural tradition. An accomplished poet, as seen in *Horses Make a Landscape Look More Beautiful* (1984), she is, however, better known for her novels, of which *The Color Purple* (1982) is her third and most popular. The winner of the 1983 Pulitzer Prize for fiction and later made into a successful film, it tells in letters the story of two sisters in the cruel, segregated world of the Deep South between the wars. It was preceded by *The Third Life of Grange Copeland* (1970) and *Meridian* (1976). In 1988 she published the novel *The Temple of My Familiar*.
▷ *Living By the Word* (1989)

WALKER, Kath *see* OODGEROO, Noonuccal Moongalba

WALL, Dorothy
(1894–1942)

New Zealand illustrator and writer of books for younger readers. Born in Wellington, she migrated to Sydney in 1914, and retired to New Zealand in 1937. She is best known for the books which feature her engaging koala hero and gumnut addict who first appeared in *Blinky Bill the Quaint Little Australian* in 1933. The next, *Blinky Bill Grows Up* (1934), was followed by a number of anthropomorphic adventures until, in 1940, real life caught up with him in *Blinky Bill Joins the Army*.

WALLACE, (Richard Horatio) Edgar
(1875–1932)

English writer. He was found abandoned in Greenwich when nine days old and brought up by a Billingsgate fish-porter. He served in the army in South Africa, where he later became a journalist (1899), and in 1905 he published his first success, the adventure story *The Four Just Men*. Another early series in a different vein was set in West Africa and included *Sanders of the River* (1911) and *Bones* (1915). From then on he wrote prolifically—his output numbering over 170 novels and plays—being best remembered for his crime novels, such as *The Clue of the Twisted Candle* (1916) and *The Ringer* (1926). He became a scriptwriter in Hollywood, where he died.
▷ *People* (1926)

WALLACE, Lew(is)
(1827–1905)

American author and soldier, born in Brookville, Indiana. He served in the Mexican War (1846–8) and with distinction as a major-general in the Federal army in the American Civil War (1861–5). Governor of New Mexico (1878–81) and minister to Turkey (1881–5), he was author of several novels, including the remarkably successful religious novel *Ben Hur* (1880), which has twice formed the subject of a spectacular film. He also wrote an *Autobiography* (1906).
▷ I McKee, *'Ben-Hur' Wallace* (1947)

WALLACE-CRABBE, Chris
(1934–)

Australian poet and academic, born in Richmond, Melbourne, brother of painter/printmaker Robin Wallace-Crabbe (1938–). His first published poetry was *The Music of Division* (1959). Four more titles followed, from which was drawn *Selected Poems* (1973). In the same year he recorded a selection of his verse for the University of Queensland Press series *Poets on Record*. From rather formal and uninvolved poetry he turned in later works to the 'new romanticism' of which *Neighbours in a Thicket* (1974) is typical. *The Emotions are not Skilled Workers* (1980) includes his most ambitious work, 'The Shapes of Gallipoli'.

WALLANT, Edward Lewis
(1926–62)

American novelist, who died unseasonably young. He was born in New Haven, Connecticut, and worked in the advertising business, where he also began to write short stories. Revealing his great talent, his first novel, *The Human Season* (1960), was a mature and unsentimental study of loss and grief. The tone deepened markedly in *The Pawnbroker* (1961); its central character is a Polish Jew running a loan shop in Harlem, where poverty compounds racial tension, forcing him to relive the horrors of the concentration camps. The book was subsequently made into an excellent film, starring Rod Steiger. *The Pawnbroker* was the last of Wallant's books published in his lifetime. *The Tenants of Moonbloom* (1963) was prepared for publication by his widow.

WALLER, Edmund
(1606–87)

English poet and politician, born in Coleshill near Amersham, Hertfordshire (now Buckinghamshire), a cousin of John Hampden. He was educated at Eton and King's College, Cambridge. Thought to have represented

Amersham in 1621, he was returned for Il-chester in 1624, Chipping Wycombe in 1625 and Amersham in 1627. In 1631 he married a London heiress, who died in 1634, and from about 1635 to 1638 he unsuccessfully courted Lady Dorothy Sidney, eldest daughter of the Earl of Leicester, whom he commemorated in verse as 'Sacharissa'. Returned to the Long Parliament in 1640, he opened the proceedings in 1641 against the judge, Sir Francis Crawley, impeached for his judgments in the king's favour. In 1643 Waller plunged into a conspiracy ('Waller's plot') against parliament on behalf of Charles I, was arrested, and expelled from the House. He avoided execution, unlike his fellow conspirators, by abject confession and the payment of a £10 000 fine, and was banished from the realm. He lived mostly in France, entertaining impoverished exiles in Paris, his own banishment being revoked in 1651, after which he returned to England. His collected poems, reviving the heroic couplet and including 'Go, lovely Rose', had been published in 1645 and were followed by *A Panegyric to my Lord Protector* (1655) and *To the King upon his Majesty's Happy Return* (1660), addressed to Cromwell and Charles II respectively.

▷ W L Chernaik, *The Poetry of Limitation* (1968)

WALPOLE, Horace, 4th Earl of Orford
(1717–97)

English writer, youngest son of Sir Robert Walpole, born in London. At Eton and at King's College, Cambridge, he had the poet **Thomas Gray** as a friend, and while still at the university was appointed by his father to lucrative government sinecures. Gray and he started on the Grand Tour, but quarrelled and separated at Reggio, where Walpole fell ill. He returned to England (1741) to take his seat for Callington in Cornwall. Although he interested himself in cases like the John Byng trial of 1757, his function in politics was that of the chronicling spectator rather than the earnest actor. He exchanged his Cornish seat in 1754 for the family borough of Castle Rising, which he vacated in 1757 for the other family borough of King's Lynn. In 1745 his father died, leaving him with ample means. In 1747 he purchased, near Twickenham, the former coachman's cottage which he gradually 'gothicized' (1753–76) into the stuccoed and battlemented pseudo-castle of Strawberry Hill, which helped in its way to reverse the fashion for classical and Italianate design. He spent all his time on this transformation, on his correspondence and writings, visits to Paris, and the establishment of a private press on which some of his own works as well as **Lucan**'s *Pharsalia* with Richard Bentley's

notes, and Gray's *Progress of Poesy* and *The Bard*, were printed. He inherited his brother's title in 1791. His essays in **Edward Moore**'s *World* exhibit a light hand, and he had gifts as a verse-writer. In such satires as the *Letter from Xo Ho to his friend Lien Chi at Pekin* (1757) he is at his best. His *Castle of Otranto* (1764) set the fashion for supernatural romance. His tragedy of *The Mysterious Mother* (1768) is strong but gruesome. Other works are *Catalogue of Royal and Noble Authors* (1758), *Fugitive Pieces in Verse and Prose* (1758), *Anecdotes of Painting in England* (1761–71), *Catalogue of Engravers* (1763), *Historic Doubts on Richard III* (1768) and *Essay on Modern Gardening* (1785). His literary reputation rests chiefly upon his letters, which deal, in the most vivacious way, with party politics, foreign affairs, literature, art and gossip. His firsthand accounts in them of such events as the Jacobite trials after the 1745 Rising and the Gordon Riots are invaluable. Two of his chief correspondents were Sir Horace Mann and Madame du Deffand; with the latter he exchanged more than 1600 letters.

▷ A Dobson, *Horace Walpole, a memoir* (1893)

WALPOLE, Sir Hugh Seymour
(1884–1941)

English novelist, born in Auckland, New Zealand, son of the Reverend G H S Walpole who subsequently became Bishop of Edinburgh. He was educated in England at King's School, Canterbury, and graduated from Emmanuel College, Cambridge, in 1906. He was intended for the church but turned schoolmaster at a boys' prep school and then author. Widely read in English literature, he wrote prolifically. His books, which were enormously popular during his lifetime, display a straightforward, easy-flowing style, great descriptive power, and a genius for evoking atmosphere which he unfortunately overworked at times, and which sometimes made his work open to parody. His many novels include *Mr Perrin and Mr Traill* (1911), based on his experience as a school teacher, *Fortitude* (1913), *The Dark Forest* (1916), *The Secret City* (1919, James Tait Black Memorial Prize), *The Cathedral* (1922), which owes much to **Trollope**, one of Walpole's favourite authors, and *The Herries Chronicle* (1930–3).

▷ R Hart-Davis, *Hugh Walpole* (1952)

WALSCHAP, Gerard
(1898–)

Belgian (Flemish) novelist and critic, born in Londerzeel. He began as a rather pallid Catholic poet and dramatist, but soon published novels highly critical of his church, with which he openly broke in 1940. He was by profession an inspector of public libraries. His early, explicitly moralistic but nonetheless naturalistic novels, such as *Adelaide* (1929), have some affinities with **François Mauriac** and **Julien Green**. They present people in conflict with Catholic puritanism, and they were attacked by conservative critics for their candour. His most typical and best novel is *Houtekiet* (1939), a portrait of a Catholic Utopian community. Deps, the settlement founded by the eponymous hero, Jan Houtekiet, is based on principles which attack conventional Catholic morality. He continued the story in a lesser novel, *Nieuwe Deps* (1961, 'The New Deps').

WALSER, Martin
(1927–)

German novelist and playwright from Wasserburg, associated with the literary circle Gruppe '47, and active in broadcasting in the post-war period. His early stories were influenced by **Kafka**, on whom he had written for his PhD at the University of Tübingen. His writing gained substance when he dedicated himself to longer novels, including the trilogy about his character Kristeln: *Halbzeit* (1960, 'Half-time'), *Das Einhorn* (1966, Eng trans *The Unicorn*, 1971), and *Der Sturz* (1973, 'The Fall'), which is his best work. He wrote some thoughtful plays, but then reached out for a far wider audience with *Jensits der Liebe* (1976, 'Beyond Love'); *Das fliehende Pferd* (1978, 'The Horse in Flight') was a runaway bestseller. It has been said that, while he is not a profound writer, he is nevertheless an important social critic.

WALSER, Robert
(1878–1956)

Swiss (German) writer of novels and stories, born in Biel (Berne). From the age of 51 until his death he was in psychiatric hospitals, latterly at Herisau. Walser's name was scarcely known between the 1920s and the 1950s, when it was pointed out that his novels and short, often almost pointilliste, sketches had exercised an undeniable influence on such major writers as **Kafka** and **Musil** (who first noted the influence on Kafka). Attention was then directed to the work itself, and at least *Jakob von Gunten* (1909, Eng trans 1969) and many of his stories—of which there is a good selection in *The Walk* (Eng trans 1957)—were themselves major. *Jakob von Gunten* tells of a school: there is only one lesson, and all the pupils are destined to become valets. Walser, unlike Kafka, resolved his story positively: his unequivocal message is that people can find peace and fulfilment only by loving and serving one another—but he does this without recourse to moral cliché or sentimentality,

and remains one of the world's as yet only half-discovered great writers.
▷ G C Avery, *Enquiry and Testament: A Study of Robert Walser* (1968)

WALSH, William
(1663–1708)

English poet, born in Abberley, Worcestershire. He entered Wadham College, Oxford in 1678 but did not graduate, later becoming Whig MP and Gentleman of the Horse to Queen Anne (1702–8). He published prose dialogues, poems on public occasions, *Letters and Poems Amorous and Gallant* (1692), and a play, *Squire Trelooby* (1704), adapted from *Molière* in collaboration with **Vanbrugh** and **Congreve**. He was admired by **Dryden** and **Pope** as a critic, but his verse, mostly love-songs, epigrams and elegies, is slight: as **Johnson** observed, it has 'more elegance than vigour'. *Works in Prose and Verse* was published in 1736.
▷ Dr S Johnson, *The Lives of the English Poets* (1779–81)

WALTARI, Mika (Toami)
(1908–79)

Finnish novelist. Writing in Finnish, he was the best-known of the pre-war 'Torch-bearers' circle of writers on urban themes, including his novel *Suuri illusioni* (1928, 'The Great Illusion'). After the war he turned to historical novels, as in *Sinuhe, egyptiläinen* (1945, 'Sinuhe, the Egyptian'), *Mikael Hakim* (1949, 'The Wanderer') and *Turms, kuolematen* (1955, 'The Etruscan'). He also wrote detective stories and plays, many of them pseudonymously.
▷ S Musikka, *Mika Waltarin juhlakirje* (1968)

WALTER OF CHATILLON
(d.c.1190)

French poet, who spent most of his life in Rheims, where he held the post of canon. He also worked for Henry II of England for a time. The most famous, and probably the best, Latin poet of his time, he wrote epic classical verse, of which the best-known example is *Alexandreis* (a life of Alexander the Great), but his reputation rests equally on his skill as a satirist. Often writing in Goliardic verse (a measure employed solely for satire), he launched ferocious attacks on the church and the Curia. His *De Clericis* ('On the Priesthood') begins 'Licet eger cum egrotis/Et ignotus cum ignotis/fungar tamen vice cotis/ius usurpans sacerdotis' (which roughly means: 'Ignore the law in any way/A priest's allowed to get away'). It displays a less than reverential attitude. Some of his devotional poetry survives with musical settings.

WALTHER VON DER VOGELWEIDE
(c.1170–c.1230)

Austro–German lyric poet. Little is known of his early life, but he was active in Vienna towards the end of the century, and emerges in palace rolls throughout southern Germany during the next 25 years; his last known poem is from the late 1220s. Walther wrote both love poetry—the highly formalized *Minnesang*—largely influenced by French models, but he also pioneered verse as a vehicle for social and political commentary. Much of it is frankly propagandistic, written to serve the interests of a courtly patron, but it is never sycophantic and is, on the contrary, marked by an almost arrogant self-assurance that is strikingly 'modern'. The most powerful of these patrons was the emperor Frederick II, from whom Walther gained a grant of land near Würzburg in 1212. The most reliable editions of his work are *Die Gedichte* (1965), edited by Lachmann and Kuhn, and the two-volume *Die Lieder* (1967, 1974), edited by Friedrich Laurer. The first English translation was by Edwin Zeydel and Bayard Q Morgan in 1952.
▷G F Jones, *Walther von der Vogelweide* (1968)

WALTON, Izaak
(1593–1683)

English writer, born in Stafford, the son of an alehouse-keeper. In 1621 he was settled in London as an ironmonger or a linen-draper in Fleet Street, where he became friends with **John Donne**, and about 1644 he retired. In 1626 he married a great-grandniece of Cranmer, and in 1647 Ann Ken, a half-sister of the hymn writer Thomas Ken. He spent most of his time 'in the families of the eminent clergymen of England'. His later years were spent in Winchester. His most celebrated work is his *The Compleat Angler, or the Contemplative Man's Recreation*, which first appeared in 1653; the fifth edition, expanded from 13 chapters to 21 in 1676, also contained a treatise by **Charles Cotton**. The description of fishes, of English rivers, of fishponds, and of rods and lines is interspersed with scraps of dialogue, moral reflections, quaint old verses, songs and sayings, and idyllic glimpses of country life. The anonymous *Arte of Angling* (1577), discovered in 1957, has been found to be one of his chief sources. Equally exquisite are his biographies—of Donne (1640), Wotton (1651), Hooker (1665), Richard Herbert (1670) and George Sanderson (1678).
▷J Bevan, *Izaak Walton* (1987)

WANG MENG
(1934–)

Chinese novelist, born in Beijing, the son of a Professor of Philosophy. He joined the communist youth league in 1949 as a schoolboy, and published two novels, *Long Live Youth* (1953) and *The Young New-comer in the Organization Department* (1956). He was denounced as a rightist in the 'Anti-Rightist Campaign' of 1958, and forced to work as a manual labourer for 20 years in the remote provinces. He was then allowed to return to Beijing, and re-emerged with *Young Forever* (1979). Since then he has held various party posts, and published collections of short stories like *A Night in the City* (1980) and *Andante Cantabile* (1981). After the fall of the Gang of Four he was rehabilitated and became Minister of Culture.

WANG WEI
(699–759)

Chinese poet and painter of the T'ang dynasty. An ardent Buddhist, he founded a monochrome school of painting.
▷L C and D B Walmsley, *Wang Wei the Painter Poet* (1968)

WARBURTON, Eliot, in full Bartholomew Elliott George
(1810–52)

Irish novelist, born in Tullamore, County Offaly. Educated at Cambridge, he was called to the Bar in 1837, but soon devoted himself to literature. His eight works include *The Crescent and the Cross* (1844), a collection of travel articles for the *Dublin University Magazine*, *Memoirs of Prince Rupert* (1849), *Memoirs of Horace Walpole* (1852), and two historical novels, *Reginald Hastings* (1850) and *Darien* (1852), describing the horrors of a ship on fire. Sailing to Panama, he was lost in a fire on board the *Amazon* off Land's End on its maiden voyage to Darien.

WARD, Artemus, pseud of Charles Farrar Browne
(1834–67)

American humorist, born in Maine. One of America's most famous comic writers, he began in the newspaper, the Cleveland *Plain Dealer* to contribute a column, 'Artemus Ward's Sayings' (1857); these fictional adventures of a near-illiterate travelling salesman of wax figures made him famous throughout America. Ward is partly based on the Jack Downing of **Seba Smith**, but he has his own robust traits, and the form Browne used, the serious Lyceum 'lecture', which he parodied, was his own—as were his expert 'misspellings'. Browne edited *Vanity Fair*, went to London as a lecturer, contributed to *Punch*, and was acquiring even more fame when he succumbed to consumption. Lincoln was a great admirer of his writing, for all that Browne's views were mainly those of the democratic party. He satirized militant feminism, Mormons, war-profiteers, Shakers, temperance men, and many others. Essentially a comedian, he became one of the best-loved figures of America.

▷A J Nock (ed), *Selected Works* (1924); J C Austin, *Ward* (1964)

WARD, Elizabeth Stuart Phelps
(1844–1911)

American author of a string of emotionally religious novels—*The Gates Ajar* (1868), *Beyond The Gates* (1883), *The Gates Between* (1889), *Within The Gates (1901)*—which enjoyed wide sentimental appeal. The early inspiration of these books about Heaven was the death of her beloved in the Civil War. She vowed never to marry another and threw her energies into writing. In her mid-forties she relented and married the 27-year-old Herbert Dickinson. Feminists have applauded her insistence on women's right to self-fulfilment and *Doctor Zay* (1882) broke new ground in representing women in the medical profession.

▷C F Kessler, *Elizabeth Stuart Phelps Ward* (1982); L D Kelly, *The Life and Works of Elizabeth Stuart Phelps Ward* (1983)

WARD, Mary Augusta, Mrs Humphry, née Arnold
(1851–1920)

English novelist, born in Hobart, Tasmania, a grand-daughter of Dr Thomas Arnold of Rugby, and niece of **Matthew Arnold**. The family returned to Britain in 1856 and, after attending private boarding schools, she joined them in Oxford in 1867. In 1872 she married Thomas Humphry Ward (1845–1926), a fellow and tutor of Brasenose College, Oxford, member of the staff of *The Times*, and editor of *The English Poets* (5 vols, 1880–1918). Mrs Ward contributed to *Macmillan's* and, a student of Spanish literature, biographies of early Spanish ecclesiastics to Sir William Smith's *Dictionary of Christian Biography*. In 1879 she became secretary to Somerville College, Oxford, before moving to London in 1881, where she wrote for various periodicals. A children's story, *Milly and Olly* (1881), *Miss Bretherton* (1884), a slight novel, and a translation (1885) of Amiel's *Journal intime* preceded her greatest success, the bestselling spiritual romance *Robert Elsmere* (1888), which inspired the philanthropist Passmore Edwards to found a settlement for the London poor in 1897 in Tavistock Square. Her later novels, all on social or religious issues, include *Marcella* (1894), *Sir George Tressady* (1896) and *The Case of Richard Meynell* (1911). She was an enthusiastic social worker and anti-suffragette, and became first President of the Anti-Suffrage League in 1908. She published *A Writer's Recollections* in 1918.

▷E M Smith, *Mrs Humphry Ward* (1980)

WARD, Ned (Edward)
(1667–1731)

English poet and miscellaneous writer, born in Oxfordshire of poor parents. He visited Jamaica in his youth, before keeping a public house in London where he entertained customers with wit as well as liquor. A High Church Tory, he was put in the pillory for anti-government satire in his burlesque poem *Hudibras Redivivus* (1705). His huge output of comic and satirical verse and prose was intended for popular reading and was scorned by the literary establishment, but his racy, colloquial style, earthy humour and realism wear well. His most famous work, *The London Spy* (1698–1703), gives a graphic picture of low life in Augustan London.

▷H W Troyer, *Ned Ward of Grubstreet* (1946)

WARNER, Charles Dudley
(1829–1900)

American writer, born in Plainfield, Massachusetts. He practised law in Chicago until 1869, then settled as an editor in Hartford. In 1884 he became co-editor of *Harper's Magazine*, in which his papers on the South, Mexico and the Great West appeared. He published several books of essays, and in 1873 he co-wrote *The Gilded Age* with **Mark Twain**. He also wrote literary criticism, most significantly *The Relation of Literature to Life* (1896).

▷A Fields, *Charles Dudley Warner* (1902)

WARNER, Rex
(1905–86)

English author, born in Birmingham. A specialist in classical literature, he was a teacher before turning to writing. Pre-eminently a novelist of ideas, his distinction lies in the original, imaginative handling of conflicting ideologies. *The Wild Goose Chase* (1937), *The Professor* (1938) and *The Aerodrome* (1941) established his reputation as a writer concerned with the problems of the individual involved with authority. *Men of Stones* (1949) explores the nature of totalitarianism, but it and *Why was I Killed?* (1944) are less successful than his other works. He was perhaps best known for his later historical novels such as *The Young Caesar* (1958), *Imperial Caesar* (1960) and *Pericles the Athenian* (1963). He was a poet of sensuous quality (*Poems*, 1931, and *Poems and Contradictions*, 1945), and also a translator of Greek classics.

WARNER, Susan Bogert

WARNER, Susan Bogert, pseud **Elizabeth Wetherell**
(1819–85)

American novelist, born in New York. She had a huge success with *The Wide, Wide World* (1851), followed by *Queechy* (1852) and other sentimental and emotional tales. She collaborated in many books with her sister Anna Bartlett Warner (1827–1915) who, as Amy Lothrop, wrote popular stories such as *Stories of Vinegar Hill* (6 vols, 1892) and was the author of popular children's hymns like 'Jesus Loves Me, This I Know' and 'Jesus bids us Shine'.

WARNER, Sylvia Townsend
(1893–1978)

English novelist, born in Harrow. A student of music, she researched music in the 15th and 16th centuries and was one of the four editors of the 10-volume *Tudor Church Music* (1923–9). A communist and a lesbian, she lived most of her life with the extraordinary Valentine Ackland, an alcoholic amazon. A writer of great gifts whose novels defy strait-jacketing, Warner published seven novels, four volumes of poetry, essays, and eight volumes of short stories, many of which had previously appeared in the *New Yorker*. Ranging widely in theme, locale and period, significant titles are *Lolly Willowes* (1926), *Mr Fortune's Maggot* (1927), *Summer Will Show* (1936), *After the Death of Don Juan* (1938) and *The Corner That Held Them* (1948).
▷W Mulford, *Sylvia Townsend Warner* (1988)

WARNER, William
(c.1558–1609)

English poet, born in London. Educated at Oxford, he practised as an attorney, wrote *Pan his Syrinx Pipe* (1585), translated **Plautus** (*Menaechmi*, 1595), and gained a high contemporary reputation with his *Albion's England* (1586–1606), a long metrical history in 14-syllable verse.

WARR, Bertram
(1917–43)

Canadian poet, killed in the air force during World War II. His lyrical gifts, originality and his fine technique, were only just becoming markedly apparent when he died. It is thought that he might have become Canada's major poet. His one collection, *Yet a Little Onwards* (1941), evoked the admiration of **Robert Graves**. Three of his poems are included in **A J M Smith**'s *Oxford Book of Canadian Verse* (1960).

WARREN, Robert Penn
(1905–89)

American novelist and poet, born in Guthrie, Kentucky. He was educated at Vanderbilt, Berkeley and Yale universities, and was a Rhodes scholar at Oxford. Professor of English at Louisiana (1934–42) and Minnesota (1942–50), he was Professor of Drama (1951–6) and of English at Yale (1962–73). Recipient of two Pulitzer Prizes (fiction, 1947; poetry, 1958), he established an international reputation by his political novel about the governor of a Southern state, *All the King's Men* (1943; filmed 1949), in which the demagogue Willie Stark closely resembles Governor Huey Long. Other works include *John Brown, the Making of a Martyr* (1929), *Night Rider* (1939), *The Cave* (1959), *Wilderness* (1961), the story of a Jew in the Civil War, and *Meet Me in the Green Glen* (1971). He also published some volumes of short stories, and verse including *Selected Poems, Old and New, 1923–66* (1966), *Or Else* (1974) and *Rumour Verified* (1981).
▷K Snipes, *Robert Penn Warren* (1983)

WASHINGTON, Booker T(aliaferro)
(1856–1915)

Black American social reformer, journalist and autobiographer, born at Hale's Ford, a plantation in Franklin County, Virginia. After various manual jobs, he gained an impressive education, and in 1881 became the founder and first principal of the Tuskegee Normal School in Alabama (the Tuskegee Institute from 1893). His first books were collections of wise apothegms and homely advice. These were given a wider context in *The Future of the American Negro* (1899), but Washington had no natural gift for large-scale discourse. His masterpiece remains *Up From Slavery* (1901), which, with its less well-known predecessor *The Story of My Life and Work* (1900, as *An Autobiography*, 1901), is one of the classic American life-stories, recalling in vivid detail the hardships and racial hatreds of the South. His later books include a sympathetic life of his (rather more radical) fellow-reformer **Frederick Douglass** (1907).
▷L R Harlan, *Washington: The Making of a Black Leader* (1972); *The Wizard of Tuskegee* (1983)

WASSERMAN, Jakob
(1873–1934)

German novelist, born in Fürth in Bavaria. He lived in Vienna and in Syria. His impressive novel *Die Juden von Zirndorf* (1897, Eng trans *The Jews of Zirndorf*, 1933) was followed by a succession of novels culminating in the trilogy completed just before his death: *Der Fall Maurizius* (1928, Eng trans *The*

Maurizius Case, 1930), *Etzel Andergast* (1931, Eng trans 1932) and *Joseph Kerkhovens dritte Existenz* (1934, Eng trans *Joseph Kerkhoven's Third Existence,* 1934). He also wrote short stories, biographies of Columbus and H M Stanley, and an autobiography (1921).
▷J C Blankenagel, *Writings of Jakob Wasserman* (1942)

WASSERSTEIN, Wendy
(1950–)

American playwright, born in Brooklyn, New York City. She was educated at Mount Hoylake College and Yale Drama School. She has written adaptations and screenplays for television, notably **John Cheever**'s *The Sorrows of Gin.* Her plays include the punningly titled *When Dinah Shore Ruled the Earth* (1975) and *Isn't It Romantic* (1981), a topical account of the lives of a group of young women in New York which enjoyed a successful revival in 1983. She won a Pulitzer Prize in 1989 for *The Heidi Chronicles* (1988), a play about an unfulfilled feminist lecturer.

WASSMO, Herbjørg
(1942–)

Norwegian novelist, poet and playwright. Born on Skogsøya, Vesterålen, in the far north of Norway, she worked as a teacher and published a couple of volumes of poetry before making her breakthrough as a novelist. Her widely acclaimed trilogy about Tora, *Huset med den blinde glassveranda* (1981, Eng trans *The House with the Blind Glass Windows,* 1987), *Det stumme rommet* (1983, 'The Silent Room') and *Hudløs himmel* (1986, 'Flayed Heavens'), traces the childhood and adolescence of a girl fathered by a German soldier during the occupation of Norway in World War II. Her sense of alienation is reinforced by the sexual abuse she suffers from her step-father, her mounting psychosis reflected in a world of fantasy that replaces the novel's psychological realism. *Dinas bok* (1989, 'Dina's Book') is a historical novel mixing third- and first-person narrative to highlight an intrepid and brutally powerful female character.
▷J Garton, 'Herbjørg Wassmo', in *Norwegian Women's Writing 1850–1990* (1993)

WAT, Aleksander, pseud of **Aleksander Chwat**
(1900–67)

Polish poet, who began his career in vigorous Futurist opposition to the conservative *Skamander* movement, which was founded at the end of World War I. After that he became a dogmatic, noisy Marxist. He spent World War II as a prisoner in Russia, then fell foul of the communist regime until 1956, when a new collection of poetry—still playful, but now matured, serious and underlyingly humane—was suddenly greeted with acclaim by younger Poles. He lived out his last years in France. There is a substantial selection of his poems in translation in **Czeslaw Milosz**'s *Post-War Polish Poetry* (1965).

WATEN, Judah
(1911–85)

Ukrainian-born Australian novelist and short-story writer, born in Odessa; he settled with his family in Western Australia in 1914. He revisited Europe in the 1930s, was active in the Communist Party, and always maintained close links with writers in the USSR. His childhood reminiscences, *Alien Sun,* appeared in 1952 and depicts a new homeland through the eyes of immigrants. A visit to the Soviet Union was described in *From Odessa to Odessa* (1969). Waten wrote seven novels, from *The Unbending* (1954) to the partly autobiographical *Scenes from Revolutionary Life* (1982), and jointly edited two collections of Australian short stories. Through all his writing runs the fatalism of the dispossessed Jew; the posthumous announcement of his **Patrick White** Literary Award in 1985 would doubtless have been greeted with a wry shrug.

WATERHOUSE, Keith Spencer
(1929–)

English novelist, dramatist, humorist and journalist, born in Leeds. He first came to critical and popular attention with *Billy Liar* (1959), a whimsical and often poignant novel about a north-of-England working-class dreamer. The following year it became the basis of a successful play, on which Waterhouse collaborated with **Willis Hall**. Waterhouse has since pursued an energetic career, writing mordantly humorous novels in which his characters appear both products of, and beleaguered by, the stresses and strains of the modern urban day-to-day grind. Among his best are *Jubb* (1963), *Office Life* (1978) and *Maggie Muggins, or Spring in Earl's Court* (1981). His plays, with Hall, include *Saturday, Sunday, Monday* (1973) and *Filumena* (1977), both adapted from **Eduardo de Filippo**, and, by himself, *Jeffrey Bernard Is Unwell* (1989).

WATERS, Frank Joseph
(1902–)

American author, born in Colorado Springs, with alleged Cheyenne ancestry. In his long career as an author (he began publishing in the 1930s and was still writing in his nineties) Waters has tried to evoke the world of the Native American. *The Man Who Killed the Deer* (1942) was one of the first novels to attempt an understanding of their religion. *Pike's Peak: A Family Saga* (1971) won a Western Heritage Award and Waters has been nominated several times for the Nobel Prize. *Brave Are My People* (1992) continues his portrait of Native American courage and transcendental wisdom.

▷T J Lyon, *Frank Waters* (1973)

WATKINS, Vernon Phillips
(1906–67)

Welsh poet, born in Maesteg, Glamorgan, and educated at Magdalene College, Cambridge. For much of his life he lived at Pennard, Gower, and used the shoreline as illustrative material for his poetry. He published eight collections of verse during his lifetime, including *Ballad of Mari Lwyd* (1941), *Death Bell* (1954) and *Affinities* (1962). Regarded as one of the greatest Welsh poets in English, as well as one of the most unusual, he was long overshadowed by his friend **Dylan Thomas**. A posthumous volume, *Fidelities* (1968), was followed by *The Collected Poems* (1986).

▷L Norris, *Vernon Watkins* (1970)

WATSON, (Elliot Lovegood) Grant
(1885–1970)

English anthropologist, naturalist and novelist, born in Staines, Middlesex, best known for his series of nature books *What to Look For in Winter/Summer/Autumn/Springtime* (1959–60). In 1910 he joined the Radcliffe-Brown scientific expedition with Daisy Bates to the north of Western Australia. Much affected by what he saw of aboriginal culture, he wrote a number of novels which encapsulate his philosophy of the conflict between good and evil. *Where Bonds are Loosed* (1914) is set in a syphilis hospital for aborigines on an Indian Ocean island; in its sequel, *The Mainland* (1918), a boy of the islands escapes to the mainland only to find another form of isolation. His other 'Australian' novels all in some way concern themselves with man's struggle to know himself. In 1968 he wrote a travel book, *Journey under the Southern Stars*, in which he describes the profound impact his visits to Australia made on him and his thinking.

▷*But to What Purpose* (1946)

WATSON, Thomas
(c.1557–1592)

English lyric poet, born in London. He was educated at Oxford, and studied law in London. Coming to **Christopher Marlowe**'s help in a street fight, he killed a man in 1589. He excelled in English 'sonnets' in *Hecatompathia or Passionate Century of Love* (1582) and *The Tears of Fancie* (1593) and

his sonnets were very probably studied by **Shakespeare**. He also translated classics into Latin and English, including **Sophocles**, **Tasso**, and Italian madrigals.

WATSON, Sir (John) William
(1858–1935)

English poet, born in Burley-in-Wharfedale, Yorkshire. He first attracted notice with *Wordsworth's Grave* (1890), and *Lachrymoe musarum* (1892), which contained a eulogy on **Tennyson**, his primary influence. *Odes and Other Poems* followed in 1894, *The Father of the Forest* in 1895, *For England* (1903), *Sable and Purple* (1910), *Heralds of the Dawn* (1912), *The Man who Saw* (1917), *The Superhuman Antagonists* (1919) and *Poems, Brief and New* (1925). His poem 'April, April, Laugh thy Girlish Laughter' appears in many anthologies, but his other work is largely forgotten.

WATTS, Alaric Alexander
(1797–1864)

English journalist and poet, born in London. He founded the *United Services Gazette* (1833) and the annual *Literary Souvenir* (1823–37), and published two volumes of poetry, but is now remembered chiefly for his alliterative alphabetical *jeu d'esprit*, 'An Austrian army awfully arrayed'.

WATTS-DUNTON, Walter Theodore
(1832–1914)

English poet and critic, born in St Ives, Cambridgeshire, the son of a solicitor. He practised law for a time, but in London he became the centre of a remarkable literary and artistic company, and the intimate friend of **Dante Gabriel Rossetti**, **William Morris**, **Swinburne**, **Philip Marston** and afterwards **Tennyson**. He wrote enough to fill many volumes in the *Athenaeum* (1876–98) and elsewhere. In *The Coming of Love* (1897) he gave a selection of his poems. In 1898 appeared his novel of gypsy life, *Aylwin*. *Old Familiar Faces* (1915) contains recollections from the *Athenaeum*. At his home in Putney he looked after Swinburne for the last 30 years of the poet's life.

WAUGH, Alec (Alexander Raban)
(1898–1981)

English novelist and travel writer, born in London, brother of **Evelyn Waugh**. He was educated at Sherborne where he was involved in a homosexual scandal and left in 1915 to become a cadet in the Inns of Court Officers Training Corps. He spent two years in training before being posted to a machine-gun unit in France, just in time for Passchendaele. In seven and a half weeks he wrote his first book, the autobiographical *Loom of Youth* (1917), in which he expressed the bitterness and love he felt for his school. A good novel, it was an immediate success, but it was tainted with notoriety and has overshadowed worthy successors: *Wheels within Wheels* (1933), *Where the Clock Chimes Twice* (1952), and various travel books, the most popular being *Island in the Sun* (1956). He wrote several autobiographical volumes including *The Early Years of Alec Waugh* (1962), *My Brother Evelyn and Other Portraits* (1967) and *The Best Wine Last* (1978).

WAUGH, Auberon Alexander
(1939–)

English journalist and novelist, the eldest son of **Evelyn Waugh**, born in Pixton Park, Dulverton, Somerset. His school days were miserable and left him with a deep detestation of the public school system. He did his National Service in the Royal Horse Guards and was sent to Cyprus where he accidentally shot himself, losing a lung, his spleen, several ribs and a finger. He denied speculation that he had been fired on by his own troops. Completing his education at Oxford, he got a job on *The Daily Telegraph* in 1960, the same year he published his first novel, *The Foxglove Saga*. There followed four novels, each courteously received and, in varying degrees, funny, but he abandoned fiction for lack of financial reward and the government's prevarication over implementing a scheme for public lending right. There are few national papers to which he has not contributed, but his best work has appeared in the *New Statesman*, the *Spectator* and the defunct *Books and Bookmen*. Since 1986 he has been Editor of the *Literary Review*, and sounds forth on the literary evils of the nation in his 'From the Pulpit' column.
▷ *Will This Do?* (1991)

WAUGH, Evelyn Arthur St John
(1903–66)

English novelist, travel writer and biographer, born in Hampstead, London, younger brother of **Alec Waugh**. He was educated at Lancing and Hertford College, Oxford, where he read modern history but with little application. From 1925 to 1927 he was a schoolmaster, an unhappy period during which he attempted suicide, but the experience gave him the material for *Decline and Fall* (1928), his first and immoderately successful novel which had been preceded only by *PRB; an essay on the Pre-Raphaelite Brotherhood* (privately printed in 1926) and a biography of **Dante Gabriel Rossetti**, published earlier in 1928. The novel made him the talk of the town for, its comic genius apart, it was obviously a *roman à clef*. After a brief and unsuccessful marriage, he spent the next few years travelling restlessly. He contributed variously to newspapers, particularly the *Daily Mail*, published the social satire *Vile Bodies* (1930) and two travel books, *Labels* (1930) and *Remote People* (1931). In 1930 he became a Roman Catholic, an event which he regarded as the most important in his life. His itinerant existence continued and between 1932 and 1937 (when he re-married) he visited British Guiana, Brazil, Morocco and Abyssinia, and cruised in the Mediterranean. He published the novels *Black Mischief* (1932), set in Africa, and *A Handful of Dust* (1934). After he married Laura Herbert he settled at Piers Court, Stinchcombe, Gloucestershire, and in 1938 published *Scoop*, a hilarious newspaper farce in which the wrong correspondent is sent to cover the civil war in the African Republic of Ishmaelia. Further travels to Hungary and Mexico followed before the outbreak of the war, which Waugh spent in a variety of postings as a junior officer. He managed to publish in the war years four books, including *Put Out More Flags* (1942) and the enduring *Brideshead Revisited* (1945), a nostalgic, highly-wrought evocation of halcyon days at Oxford. From the war he also mined 'The Sword of Honour' trilogy—*Men at Arms* (1952), *Officers and Gentlemen* (1955) and *Unconditional Surrender* (1961)—in which he described, in parallel to his own experience, the significance to men and women of the ordeal of crisis of civilization which reached its climax in World War II. Other books published during this period include *The Loved One* (1947), *Helena* (1950) and *The Ordeal of Gilbert Pinfold* (1957), a painfully personal but fictionalized account of a middle-aged writer's mental collapse. In 1964 he published *A Little Learning*, intended as the first of several volumes of an autobiography he never completed. He died suddenly in Combe Florey in Somerset, revered as a wit and a stylist and one of the 20th century's greatest comic novelists. *The Diaries of Evelyn Waugh* were published in 1976; his *Letters*, edited by Mark Amory, in 1980.

WAYMAN, Tom
(1945–)

Canadian poet, born in Ontario. Between 1966 and 1968 he was a student at the University of California, where he became active in the radical student movement. Wayman has lost none of his political commitment, but his voice is not a strident one. He projects a comic persona to the world, has been called 'a kind of Schweikian guerilla' and likes to feature himself in the titles of his collections, as in *Waiting for Wayman* (1973) and *Tom Wayman Country* (1980). He has also been industrious as an editor of poetry about labour, the best of his anthologies being *A Government Job at Last: An Anthology of Working Poems* (1976).

WEBB, Harri
(1920–)

Welsh poet, born in Swansea and educated at Magdalen College, Oxford. He has published two collections of verse, *The Green Desert* (1969) and *A Crown for Branwen* (1974), and two collections of Welsh songs and ballads, *Rampage and Revel* (1967) and *Poems and Points* (1983), and has written numerous scripts for television. His work is ingrained with a strong nationalism and a biting wit. A prolific journalist, public speaker and pamphleteer, he has been active since 1959 on behalf of *Plaid Cymru*, the Welsh Nationalist party, mainly in the industrial valleys of south-east Wales.

WEBB, Mary Gladys, née Meredith
(1881–1927)

English writer, born in Keighton, near the Wrekin. In 1912 she married Henry B L Webb and lived mostly in Shropshire, market gardening and novel-writing. *Precious Bane* (1924) won her belated fame as a novelist of the soil, the dialect, and superstition, of Shropshire, expressing 'the continuity of country life'. Her other works include the novels *The Golden Arrow* (1916), *Gone to Earth* (1917, filmed by Michael Powell and Emeric Pressburger in 1950), *The House in Dormer Forest* (1920), *Seven for a Secret* (1922) and the unfinished *Armour Wherein He Trusted* (1929); nature essays, *The Spring of Joy* (1917); and poems.
▷ G M Coles, *The Flower of Light* (1978)

WEBB, Phyllis
(1927–)

Canadian poet and teacher of literature and creative writing, born in Victoria, British Columbia, and educated at the University of British Columbia and McGill, Montreal. The recipient of a Governor General's Award for *The Vision Tree* (1982)—a collection of poetry spanning 30 years—she is recognized as one of Canada's 'leading poets'. Her poetry has been described as 'honed down to an extraordinary intellectual spareness', but this judgement excludes the conversational tone that Webb uses to convey her complex ideas and surreal imagery.
▷ S Scobie, *Signature, Even, Context* (1989)

WEBSTER, John
(c.1580–c.1625)

English dramatist, supposed to have been at one time clerk of St Andrews, Holborn. In *Lady Jane* and *The Two Harpies* (both lost) he was the collaborator of **Thomas Dekker**, **Michael Drayton**, **Henry Chettle** and others. In 1604 he made some additions to *The Malcontent* of **John Marston**. In 1607 were printed the *Famous History of Sir Thomas Wyat*, a tragedy, and two comedies, *Westward Hoe* and *Northward Hoe*, all three the joint work of Webster and Dekker. *The White Devil* (1612) first revealed his powers. *The Duchess of Malfi* (1623) is a yet greater achievement. *Appius and Virginia* (first published 1654) may be **Thomas Heywood**'s (or partly so); *The Devil's Law Case* (1623) is largely disagreeable and sordid. A poem of the death of Prince Henry, and other fragments of verse, survive, with some doubtful works. The tragedy, *A Late Murder of the Son upon the Mother* (1624), unpublished and lost, although licensed, was written by **John Ford** and Webster. Not popular in his own day, Webster's stature was first recognized by **Charles Lamb**.
▷ G M Lagarde, *John Webster* (1968)

WECHSBERG, Joseph
(1907–83)

American journalist and fiction writer, born in Czechoslovakia. Wechsberg travelled to the USA in 1938 and became a US citizen in 1944. *Looking for a Bluebird* (1945), his first book in English, was a collection of sketches which had first appeared in *Esquire* and the *New Yorker*. *Sweet and Sour* (1948) was a similar concoction. His novels include *The Centennial Touch* (1948) and *Avalanche* (1958), but he also wrote widely about food (*Blue Trout and Truffles*, 1953), and music (*Sounds of Vienna*, 1968, *The Opera*, 1972 and *Schubert*, 1977).

WEDDE, Ian Curtis
(1946–)

New Zealand poet, novelist, short-story writer and anthologist, born in Blenheim. His first collection of verse was *Homage to Matise* (1971), followed by *Made Over* (1974). *Driving into the Storm: Selected Poems* was published in 1987. Fiction includes *The Shirt Factory and Other Stories* (1981) in which he closely observes the small details of life, and his novel, *Symmes Hole* (1986), a gently comic revisionist history of 19th-century Pacific voyaging. He has co-edited two major anthologies: the *Penguin Book of New Zealand Verse* (1985) and the *Penguin Book of Contemporary New Zealand Poetry* (1989). To the former he contributed a searching introduction on the identity of New Zealand poetry. In 1993 he published a collection of new poems, *The Drummer*.

WEDEKIND, Frank
(1864–1918)

German dramatist, born in Hanover. The son of a doctor and an actress, he grew up in Switzerland, but returned to Germany, where he was an actor and cabaret singer as well as a writer. He won fame with *Der Erdgeist* (1895, Eng trans *Earth Spirit*, 1914), *Frühlings Erwachen* (1891, first performed 1906, Eng trans *The Awakening of Spring*, 1909; better known as *Spring Awakening*, the title of the 1980 translation), *Die Büchse der Pandora* (1903, first performed 1918, Eng trans *Pandora's Box*, 1918), and other unconventional tragedies, which foreshadowed the emergence of the Expressionist movement both in their themes and performance styles. He was imprisoned in 1899 after publishing satirical poems in *Simplicissimus* in Munich. His work is highly individual, but also seems a forerunner of the Theatre of the Absurd.
▷S Gittelman, *Frank Wedekind* (1969)

WEEMS, Mason Locke
(1759–1825)

American biographer, chapman and clergyman, born in Maryland. After studying theology in London, 'Parson' Weems alienated fellow Episcopalians with his admiration for **Tom Paine**. He became a peddler of chapbooks and is best remembered for his own highly imaginative biography of Washington, *The Life and Memorable Actions of George Washington* (1800), a book which added fresh anecdotes with every new edition, the most lingering being the story of Washington and the cherry tree. Weems's other biographies included a life of Franklyn, but his most earnest work was reserved for moral tracts such as *The Drunkard's Looking-Glass* (1812) and *God's Revenge Against Adultery* (1815).

WEIDMAN, Jerome
(1913–)

American novelist and playwright, born in New York City and educated at City College and the New York University Law School. He was President of the Authors League of America for five years, and in 1960 received three prestigious awards: the Pulitzer Prize for Drama, the New York Drama Critics Circle Award, and the Tony Award. He has written over 20 novels and 10 plays, most of them collaborative musical comedies. His characters frequently struggle with their Jewishness and suffer from anti-Semitism. His first novel, *I Can Get It for You Wholesale* (1937), describes the New York garment industry and is considered a minor classic, but he is best known for his musical *Fiorello!* (1960).
▷D Walden (ed), *Twentieth-Century American-Jewish Fiction Writers* (1984)

WEIL, Simone
(1909–43)

French philosopher and mystic, born and bred in Paris. Although she was not a creative writer per se, Weil's essays reach a singular beauty of creative utterance, and she has influenced countless writers with her quest for purity and justice. After a brilliant career as a student she worked for an anarchist trade union and in a factory, shared her wages with the unemployed, and lived in poverty. She fought against Franco in the Spanish Civil War and then moved to England, where she died, in Ashford, Kent, of 'self-imposed privation and anorexia'. In her profound theological thinking she concluded that God, who certainly existed and exists, withdrew himself from the universe after creating it; man is obliged to withdraw himself likewise, from material considerations, and thus return to God. She is seen at her radiant best in her notebooks, *Cahiers* (1951–6, Eng trans *Notebooks*, 1956), and in *Seventy Letters* (1965). Other influential books include *L'Attente de Dieu* (1949, Eng trans *Waiting for God*, 1959) and *L'Enracinement* (1949–50, Eng trans *The Need for Roots*, 1955). Weil's prose style is important because in it she increasingly and successfully strove to make herself clear to her reader, eschewing all pretension. She has been accused of over-paradoxicality, but, whether that is just or not, she commands wide respect for her ruthless sincerity and lucidity.
▷R Rees, *Simone Weil* (1965); M M Davy, *Simone Weil* (1966)

WEINBAUM, Stanley G(rauman)
(1900–35)

American science-fiction writer, born in Louisville, Kentucky. His career as a living, published writer lasted a mere 18 months, and only hints at what he might have achieved. His debut story, the much-anthologized 'A Martian Odyssey' (1934), is one of the first sympathetic portrayals of aliens in the genre. His ability to empathize with the non-human, coupled with a strong element of humour, gave his stories an instant appeal for the readers (and editors) of pulp magazines. A more considered, carefully-wrought side to his work can be found in his novels—especially *The New Adam* (1939), in which a superman feels isolated in a world of mere humans.

WEINERT, Erich
(1890–1959)

German poet, political activist, orator, speaker of cabaret verse and journalist. He was a communist from 1924, and held office in the educational establishment of the German

Democratic Republic (the former East Germany). His poetry, laconic and effective, is too often politically motivated; but it has a sharpness and pungent edge which makes the best of it memorable.

WEINGARTEN, Romain
(1926–)

French playwright of the 'nouveau-théâtre'. Born in Paris, a cherished only son, he was interested in the arts from a very early age, and wrote his first play, Akara, when he was only 20, appearing himself in its first production in 1948. A Surrealist writer, Weingarten blends the real and the fantastic, producing phantasmagorical series of events through which he demonstrates the unreliability of language as a means of apprehending the world. His plays include Les Nourrices (1961), L'Été (1966), Le Pain Sec (1967) and, most famously, Alice aux Jardins de Luxembourg (1969). Comme la Pierre entered the repertoire of the Comédie-Française in 1970; thereafter his work became more minimalist, with a greater emphasis on the interior drama (as in La Mandore, 1973, and Neige, 1979). He is known also for his edition of the Arthurian cycle, Le Roman de la Table Ronde ou le livre de Blaise (1983).

WEINHEBER, Josef
(1892–1945)

Austrian poet and novelist, born in Kirchstetten. He was a gifted poet when he was not trying to be ambitiously political, and was decisively but not fatally influenced by Hölderlin; the story of his childhood in an orphanage, told in his novel Das Waisenhaus (1925, 'The Orphanage'), is moving and without self-pity. He still awaits a balanced critic: he has been overpraised by conservatives, yet ignored or underestimated by those who cannot stomach his support of the Nazi regime— he had written poetry praising it as early as 1934, and killed himself when he saw that it was collapsing. But the power and self-knowledge expressed in such poems as 'Auf das Unabwendbare' ('To the Inevitable', Eng trans in Twentieth-Century German Verse, 1963, ed Patrick Bridgewater), with its sonorous refrain 'Dies alles ist furchtbar' ('All this is dreadful') is undeniable.

WEISS, Peter Ulrich
(1916–82)

German dramatist, painter, film-maker and novelist, born in Berlin. Known initially as a graphic artist and novelist, he fled Nazi Germany and settled in Sweden in 1939. He became famous with his first play, Die Verfolgung und Ermordung Jean Paul Marats, dargestellt durch die Schanspielgruppe des Hospizes zu Charenton unter Anleitung des Herrn de Sade (1964, Eng trans The Persecution and Assassination of Jean-Paul Marat as Performed by the Inmates of the Asylum of Charenton under the direction of the Marquis de Sade, 1965), known more simply as Marat/Sade. His next play, Die Ermittlung (1965, Eng trans The Investigation, 1966), was a documentary based on transcripts of the Auschwitz trials. Gesang vom Lusitanischen Popanz (1967, Eng trans The Song of the Lusitanian Bogey, 1970) was a more cogent attack on the capitalist system. Among his other works are Diskurs über Viet Nam (1967, Eng trans Vietnam Discourse, 1970), Trotski im Exil (1970, Eng trans Trotsky in Exile, 1971) and Hölderlin (1971). He also wrote the autobiographical novels Abschied von den Eltern (1961, Eng trans The Leavetaking, 1962) and Fluchtpunkt (1962, Eng trans Vanishing Point, 1966).

WELCH, (Maurice) Denton
(1915–48)

English novelist, born in Shanghai. His fiction is almost entirely autobiographical; his flight from Repton School and a subsequent holiday in China are described in Maiden Voyage (1943), and In Youth is Pleasure (1945) also deals frankly with his adolescent angst. His life was disrupted by a road accident in 1935, while he was studying at Goldsmith School of Art; his serious injuries eventually caused his premature death, which prevented the completion of A Voice Through a Cloud (1950), a typically precise, honest and sensitive examination of his accident and its aftermath. His posthumously published Journals (complete edn 1984) display the same blend of almost obsessively detailed observation, interest in antique objects, and homoeroticism. Edith Sitwell described him as a 'born writer'.
▷M De-la-Noy, Denton Welch: The Making of a Writer (1984)

WELCH, James
(1940–)

American writer, born in Browning, Montana. Welch grew up on the Blackfoot and Fort Belknap reservations and graduated from the University of Montana, where he now teaches. Of Blackfoot and Gros Ventre descent, he writes about the Native American culture of the Northwest. His first two novels—Winter in the Blood (1974) and The Death of Jim Loney (1979)—and his poetry collection, Riding the Earthboy 40 (1971), all describe contemporary reservation life. In Fools Crow (1986) he diverged to write a historical novel from the point of view of a band of Pikuni (Blackfoot) people at the time of first contact with Whites; as with all Welch's work, the book is characterized by the striking clarity of his prose and imagery. *The Indian Lawyer* (1990) describes the moral dilemmas faced by a young Blackfoot lawyer and former basketball star, Sylvester Yellow Calf, in the format of a thriller which encompasses the language and culture of prison, basketball and local politics in Montana.

▷P Wild, *James Welch* (1983)

WELDON, Fay
(1931–)

English novelist and author of television screenplays, born in Alvechurch, Worcestershire and educated at St Andrews University. She became a successful advertising copywriter and is credited with creating the slogan: 'Go to work on an Egg'. Her first novel, *The Fat Woman's Joke*, appeared in 1967. It has been followed by many more, in which her recurring themes include the nature of women's sexuality and experience in a patriarchal world. Although her women are usually morally and culturally more sophisticated than the men around them, they can also exert an uncompromising revenge upon the world, as in *The Life and Loves of a She-Devil* (1983), in which an ugly and rejected heroine seeks retribution. Other novels include *Puffball* (1980), which looks at pregnancy and womanhood, and *The Cloning of Joanna May* (1989), which considers genetic engineering.

▷O Kenyon, *Women Novelists Today* (1988)

WELLS, Charles Jeremiah
(c.1800–1879)

English poet, born in London. He was educated at Edmonton, where he met **Keats**. He practised as a solicitor in London (1820–30) and taught English in France. He died in Marseilles. His *Stories after Nature* (1822) were followed in 1824 by the biblical drama, *Joseph and his Brethren*, which remained unknown until **Swinburne** praised it in the *Fortnightly* (1875).

▷H Rischbieter, *Charles Jeremiah Wells* (1967)

WELLS, H(erbert) G(eorge)
(1866–1946)

English novelist, short-story writer and popular historian, born in Bromley, Kent, the third son of an unsuccessful shopkeeper. At 18 he left his job as a draper's apprentice and became a pupil teacher at the Midhurst Grammar School, from where he won a scholarship to the Normal School of Science, South Kensington, and studied biology under T H Huxley. Although distracted by politics, writing and teaching he obtained a BSc in 1890 and then lectured for the Universal Tutorial College until the success of his short stories allowed him to concentrate full-time on writing. Idealistic, impatient and dynamic, he threw himself into contemporary issues—free love, Fabianism, progressive education, scientific theory, 'world government' (he was an early agitator for a League of Nations) and human rights. His private life was no less restless than his public. His first marriage was to his cousin Isabel in 1890, but ended in divorce. His second, to Amy Catherine ('Jane') Robbins, in 1895, suited him domestically but he sought physical solace elsewhere and had numerous affairs, notably with 'new' women, including Amber Reeves, Elizabeth von Arnim, **Rebecca West**, Odette Keun and Moura Budberg, **Maxim Gorky**'s mistress. He wrote over a hundred books and countless articles, achieving unparalleled fame in his lifetime, but by the time of his death his popularity had waned. *The Time Machine* (1895), an allegory set in the year 802701 describing a two-tier society, pioneered English science fiction and was followed by significant contributions to the genre: *The Wonderful Visit* (1895), *The Island of Doctor Moreau* (1896), *The Invisible Man* (1897), *The War of the Worlds* (1898), *When the Sleeper Awakes* (1899), *The First Men in the Moon* (1901) and *Men Like Gods* (1923). A satirical visionary, he was disputatious and fought with Fabian colleagues—**George Bernard Shaw** and the **Webb**s, for instance—as well as with his fellow novelist **Henry James**, who sprinkled condescension on Wells' novels. Wells responded with sarcasm and continued to produce a spate of social satires, drawing heavily on his own varied experience. He wrote some of the best-known English comic novels—*Love and Mr Lewisham* (1900), *Kipps* (1905) and *The History of Mr Polly* (1910)—and books that concentrated on specific contemporary issues: *Ann Veronica* (1909), an early feminist novel, *Tono Bungay* (1909), which charts the decline of the upper classes, and *The New Machiavelli* (1911), about a politician embroiled in a sex scandal. *Mr Britling Sees It Through* (1916) and *The World of William Clissold* (1926) are lesser books but autobiographically illuminating. *The Country of the Blind, and other stories* (1911) is the best of his several collections. In 1920 he published *The Outline of History*, which enjoyed a vast circulation, and among his many other works is *The Shape of Things to Come* (1933), a plea to confront fascism before it was too late, and the despairing *Mind at the End of its Tether* (1945). *Experiment in Autobiography* (1934) includes a striking self-portrait and studies of friends and contemporaries.

▷P Parrinder, *H.G. Wells* (1976)

WELLS, John

WELLS, John
(1936–)

English actor, dramatist, humorist and director. He read French and German at Oxford, and taught both languages at Eton (1961–3), while contributing material for revues at the Edinburgh Festival. He was a co-editor of the satirical magazine, *Private Eye* (1964–7), and has written for the magazine ever since, notably the supposed diary of Mrs Wilson, Harold Wilson's wife, and the Dear Bill letters, the supposed correspondence of Denis Thatcher, husband of Margaret Thatcher. He has written a number of plays for the theatre, starting with *Listen to the Knocking Bird* in 1965. *Mrs Wilson's Diary* (1968) was followed by *Anyone for Denis* (1981), in which he played the title role. (As an actor he made his London debut in the farce *An Italian Straw Hat*, in 1961.) He is also highly regarded as a translator of plays and opera from the French and German. He directed a revival of *The Mikado* in 1989.

WELTY, Eudora
(1909–)

American novelist and short-story writer, born in Jackson, Mississippi. She was educated at the Mississippi State College for Women, the University of Wisconsin and the Columbia University School of Advertizing in New York. After leaving college she was a publicity agent with the Works Progress Administration in Mississippi, which involved extensive travel through the state. She took numerous photographs which were published as *One Time, One Place: Mississippi in the Depression: A Snapshot Album* (1971). During World War II she was on the staff of the *New York Review of Books*. She started writing short stories with 'Death of a Travelling Salesman', and published several collections from 1941 to 1954. She has also written five novels, mostly drawn from Mississippi life: *The Robber Bridegroom* (1942), *Delta Wedding* (1946), *The Ponder Heart* (1954), *Losing Battles* (1970) and *The Optimist's Daughter* (1972). *The Collected Stories of Eudora Welty* was published in 1980. Among her many accolades, she has received two Guggenheim fellowships, three **O Henry** awards, the Pulitzer Prize and the National Medal for Literature. Her autobiography, *One Writer's Beginnings*, was published in 1984.

▷ E Evans, *Eudora Welty* (1980)

WEN I-to
(1899–1946)

Chinese poet and artist, educated in Peking and America. He was the most influential poet of the pre-revolutionary generation, a strict formalist in his approach to writing but able to invest his verse with great emotional power. He was greatly exercised by seeing poverty and oppression in his travels around China, and described these to great effect in his verse, often employing a savage irony. He was natural material for conversion to communism during the revolution but, once converted, stopped writing, throwing all his weight into the struggle. He was killed by nationalist troops in Kunming in 1946.

WENDT, Albert
(1939–)

New Zealand academic and writer, born in Apia, Western Samoa. His first novel was *Sons for the Return Home* (1973), followed by *Pouliuli* (1977) and *Leaves of the Baynan Tree* (1979, 'Wattie' Book of the Year, 1980). He has also published two collections of short stories and some verse, including *Inside Us the Dead; Poems 1961 to 1974* (1976). He was Professor of Pacific Literature at the University of the South Pacific (1980–7), and is now Professor of English at Auckland University.

WENZ, Paul
(1869–1939)

French-born Australian writer, born in Rheims and dubbed 'France's **Henry Lawson**'. He arrived in Australia in 1892 after travelling through Africa and South America. Marrying an Australian woman, he settled down to station life in northern New South Wales, writing graphic and sympathetic stories of Australian bush and station life in *A l'autre bout du monde* (1905) and *Sous la Croix du Sud* (1910). He served with the French army in World War I but returned to write four novels including *L'Homme du soleil couchant* (1923, 'The Sundowner'). His only English-language book was *Diary of a New Chum* (1908). His writings in French were published in France under the name 'Paul Warrego'.

WEÖRES, Sándor
(1913–)

Hungarian poet and translator, born in Szombathely and educated at the University of Pécs. He worked as a librarian during the war years, turning to writing full-time in 1950, by which time he had published nine volumes of verse, including *A teremtés dicsérete* (1938, 'In Praise of the Creation') and three critical books. These reflected the interest in Zen Buddhism and other Eastern philosophies which put Weöres at odds with the post-war communist authorities. A poet of extraordinary variety and stylistic range, he has produced work in almost every conceivable form, from short, almost child-like lyrics, to long, discursive meditations on the great themes of Western culture. He became more widely known in the West with *Selected Poems* (1970), shared with **Ferenc Juhász** and put into English by David Wevill and **Edwin Morgan**. In that year, he was also awarded the prestigious Kossuth Prize, a sign of recognition in his homeland. Perhaps his most profound volume is *Psyché: Egy hajdani költönö* (1972, 'Psyche: Words of an Ancient Poet'), which sees him working back into the far mythological past. Weöres has translated extensively, including Chinese poetry, **Shelley** and **Vasko Popa**.

WERFEL, Franz
(1890–1945)

Austrian author, born in Prague. He lived in Vienna until 1938, when he moved to France, from where he fled from the Nazi occupation in 1940 to the USA. He was associated with the Expressionist movement, and his early poems and plays betray that influence, but he is best known for his novels, including *Das Lied von Bernadette* (1941, 'The Song of Bernadette').
▷L Zahn, *Franz Werfel* (1966)

WERGELAND, Hendrik Arnold
(1808–45)

Norwegian poet and patriot, known as 'Norway's Lord Byron', and brother of the novelist **Camilla Collett**. He championed the cause of Norwegian nationalism in literature. A prolific lyrical poet and playwright, his chief work was a philosophical verse drama, *Skabelsen, mennesket og messias* (1830, 'Creation, Man and Messiah'). His last work, *Den engelske Lods* (1944, 'The English Pilot'), celebrated the liberation of the human mind.
▷H Beyer, *Hendrik Wergeland* (1964)

WERNER, (Friedrich Ludwig) Zacharias
(1768–1823)

German romantic dramatist, born in Königsberg. His chief works are *Die Söhne des Thals* (1803, 'The Sons of the Valley'), *Das Kreuz an der Ostsee* (1804, 'The Cross on the Baltic Sea') and *Martin Luther* (1806), although he later wrote a recantation of his praise of Luther after his conversion to Catholicism. He was ordained a priest in Vienna, and became a fashionable preacher, but his earlier dramas remained his most significant work, and place him among the leading dramatists of the Romantic movement.
▷P Hankhamen, *Zacharias Werner* (1970)

WESCOTT, Glenway
(1901–87)

American novelist, born in Wisconsin. Most of his fiction is set in his native state, although his early life was that of an expatriate. He knew and was initially encouraged by **Gertrude Stein** in Paris (she said of him that he was 'syrup', but 'did not pour'). His best-known book, **James**ian in presentation, is *The Grandmothers* (1927), in which an expatriate youth tells the story of his Wisconsin family. This was well received, as was *Pilgrim Hawk* (1940), about different kinds of love. *Images of Truth* (1962) collected valuable essays about such contemporaries as **Katherine Anne Porter** and **Thomas Mann**. *Goodbye Wisconsin* (1928) is a volume of stories, which many critics have maintained contains his best work.

WESKER, Arnold
(1932–)

English dramatist, born in London's East End, of Jewish immigrant parentage. He left school at 14. His Jewish family background and his varied attempts at earning a living are important ingredients of his plays. The Kahn family trilogy, *Chicken Soup with Barley*, *Roots* and *I'm talking about Jerusalem* (1958–60), echoes the march of events, pre- and post-World War II, in the aspirations and disappointments of the members of a left-wing family. *Roots* is an eloquent manifesto of Wesker's socialism: an aesthetic recipe for all which he attempted to put into practice by taking art to the workers through his Centre-42 (1961–70). Other plays are *The Kitchen* (1959), *Chips with Everything* (1962), *The Four Seasons* (1965) and *Their Very Own and Golden City* (1966), *The Friends* (1970), *The Old Ones* (1972), *The Merchant* (1977) and *Love Letters on Blue Paper* (1978), originally written for television in 1976. He also wrote the essay collection *Fears of Fragmentation* (1970) and *Words—as Definitions of Experience* (1976). No major new Wesker play has been produced in Britain for some time, although a one-woman play, *Annie Wobbler* (1984), was well received. He wrote a libretto for his play *Caritas* (1981) in 1991, and his plays have been collected in five volumes in 1989–90. So far his reputation still rests firmly on his earliest plays.
▷J R Taylor, *Anger and After* (1962)

WESLEY, Mary, pseud of Aline Farmer
(1912–)

English novelist, born in Englefield Green, Berkshire. She wrote two children's books, *Speaking Terms* and *The Sixth Seal* (both 1969), before publishing her first adult novel, *Jumping the Queue*, in 1983, at the age of 70. She has since produced a succession of books dealing with middle class mores, each written with ironic, detached amusement and taking an unblinkered though compassionate look at sexual values. *The Camomile Lawn* (1984) considers sexual and emotional relationships in the turmoil of war, while *Second Fiddle* (1988) deals with the relationship between a middle-aged woman and a young, hopeful male novelist.

WEST, Jessamyn
(1907–84)

American novelist and short-story writer, born in North Vernon, Indiana and educated at Whittier College and the University of California. She worked as a teacher and secretary and led several writers' conferences. In 1976 she received the Janet Kafka Prize. Her novels and short stories concentrate on a blend of western and romance writing: the frontier figures largely in her work, as do depictions of motherhood and relationships between men and women. Her first novel, *The Friendly Persuasion* (1945), focuses on Quaker life in Indiana. Later works include semi-autobiographical books, such as *A Matter of Time* (1966) and *The Woman Said Yes* (1976), about her sister's sickness and her own ill-health as a result of tuberculosis.
▷ A D Farmer, *Jessamyn West* (1982)

WEST, Joyce
(1908–85)

New Zealand children's writer and author of romantic and historical novels. She was a regular contributor of short romances to the *New Zealand Herald* in the mid-1930s, and wrote novels of country life such as *Drover's Road* (1953), the first of three set in the North Island sheep-farming country, and *The Year of the Shining Cuckoo* (1961), centred on the dairy farming districts. With **Mary Scott** she wrote a series of crime novels.

WEST, Morris Langlo
(1916–)

Australian novelist and playwright, born in St Kilda, Victoria, who trained for the priesthood but left before taking vows. After war service his first novel, *Moon in My Pocket* (1945), was published, under the pseudonym 'Julian Morris', and dealt with the conflicts facing a Catholic novitiate. In 1955 he left Australia for Italy, where his fourth novel, *Children of the Sun* (1957), a tale of Neapolitan slum urchins, attracted attention. *The Devil's Advocate* (1959, James Tait Black Memorial Prize, filmed 1977) became an international bestseller, since when his books have been eagerly awaited. Such novels as *The Shoes of the Fisherman* (1963), *Summer of the Red Wolf* (1971), *The Clowns of God* (1981), *Lazarus* (1990) and *The Ringmaster* (1991) have won him many awards. His novels, some of which he has dramatized, deal

with significant religious and political issues in the context of essential humanity.

WEST, Nathanael, pseud of **Nathan Wallenstein Weinstein**
(1903–40)

American novelist, born in New York City. After attending Brown University, Rhode Island, he lived in Paris for a few years, where he wrote *The Dream Life of Balso Snell* (1931), self-consciously avant garde but illuminating in his preoccupation with the hollowness of contemporary life. On his return to New York he mismanaged a hotel and was associate editor with **William Carlos Williams** of the magazine *Contact*. *Miss Lonelyhearts*, the story of a newspaper agony columnist who becomes more involved with his correspondents than is good for him, appeared in 1933. There are parallels in West's own life but he renounced journalism and went to Hollywood in 1935 to write scripts for a minor studio, plundering this experience for *The Day of the Locust* (1939), his surreal masterpiece. His only other novel, *A Cool Million*, was published in 1934. A black humorist and biting satirist, he was killed, along with his wife, Eileen McKenney, when he ignored a traffic signal.
▷ J Martin, *Nathanael West: the art of his life* (1970)

WEST, Dame Rebecca, the adopted name of **Cecily Isabel Fairfield**
(1892–1983)

Irish novelist, biographer, journalist and critic, born in County Kerry. Her father, a journalist, left her mother and the family moved to Edinburgh where they lived in straitened circumstances. She was educated at George Watson's Ladies College, and trained for the stage in London, where in 1912 she adopted the nom de plume Rebecca West, the heroine of **Ibsen**'s *Rosmersholm* which she had once played, and who is characterized by a passionate will. From a formative age she was involved with the suffragettes and in 1911 joined the staff of the *Freewoman*, the following year becoming a political writer on the *Clarion*, a socialist newspaper. Her love affair with **H G Wells** began in 1913 and lasted for 10 turbulent years, during which time she bore him a son and laid the foundations for her career as a writer. Her first published book was a critical study of **Henry James** (1916); her second, a novel, *The Return of the Soldier* (1918), describes the homecoming of a shell-shocked soldier. After the final break with Wells she went to the USA where she lectured and formed a long association with the New York *Herald Tribune*. In 1930 she married Henry Maxwell Andrews, a banker, and they lived in Buckinghamshire until his death in 1968. She published eight novels including *The Judge* (1922), *Harriet Hume* (1929), *The Thinking Reed* (1936) and the largely autobiographical *The Fountain Overflows* (1957). Her last (unfinished) novel was *Cousin Rosamund* (1988). In the mid-1930s she made several trips to the Balkans to gather material for a travel book, but her interest deepened and resulted in her masterful analysis of the origins of World War II, *Black Lamb and Grey Falcon*, published in two volumes in 1941. It is generally considered her magnum opus. During the war she superintended BBC broadcasts to Yugoslavia and in its aftermath she attended the Nuremberg War Crimes Trials. From this and other cases came *The Meaning of Treason* (1949) and *A Train of Powder* (1955). Witty, incisive and combative, she was described by **George Bernard Shaw** as handling a pen 'as brilliantly as ever I could and much more savagely'.

▷V Glendinning, *Rebecca West* (1987)

WESTALL, Robert
(1929–93)

English children's novelist, born and brought up in Tynemouth. At various times a journalist, teacher and antiques dealer, he was 44 before he published a book. *The Machine Gunners* (1975), a Carnegie Medal winner, is one of several works set in his home area during World War II. *The Scarecrow* (1981) also won a Carnegie Medal, while *The Kingdom by the Sea* (1992) was the recipient of the Guardian Fiction Award. Staying in teaching until his fifties enabled him to keep in touch with the eagerness and energy of children; his best works depict characters with a raw hunger for experience, and the self-belief to overcome adversity.

WEXLEY, John
(1907–85)

American playwright, born in New York, a nephew of the Yiddish actor Maurice Schwartz. Wexley is best known for *The Last Mile* (1930), a play about the last hours of a condemned man. The play was also significant for being the first big stage success for Spencer Tracy, who played ring-leader in a group of prisoners who seize a guard and murder him. Other plays include *Steel* (1931), *They Shall Not Die* (1934) and *Running Dogs* (1938).

WEYMAN, Stanley John
(1855–1928)

English novelist, born in Ludlow. He was educated at Christ Church, Oxford, and taught history before turning to law in 1877–

91. He began writing short stories for magazine publication, then his first novel, *The House of the Wolf* (1888–9), but his success as a popular historical novelist dates from *A Gentleman of France* (1893), set in the time of Henry of Navarre, and admired by **R L Stevenson**. He wrote many more in a similar vein, including *Under the Red Robe* (1894), *The Red Cockade* (1895), *Count Hannibal* (1901) and *Chipping* (1906). Several were successfully dramatized.

WHALEN, Philip
(1923–)

American poet, born in Portland, Oregon. He was ordained as a Zen priest in 1973, and lives in a Zen community, One Mountain Temple, San Francisco. Originally associated with the beat poets, he writes some verse in which the typography reinforces the meaning, in a quasi 'concrete' fashion; but most of his work remains discursive and in free rhythms.

▷*The Kindness of Strangers: Poems 1969–1974* (1975)

WHARTON, Edith Newbold, née Jones
(c.1861–1937)

American novelist and short-story writer, born in New York. Her family was wealthy and aristocratic and she was educated at home and in Europe. In 1885 she married Edward Wharton, a friend of the family, and they travelled widely, before settling in Paris in 1907. Her husband, however, was mentally unbalanced and they were divorced in 1913. Socially gregarious, she formed a durable friendship with **Henry James** who did much to encourage and influence her work, and a voluminous correspondence with, among others, the art historian Bernard Berenson. *The Greater Inclination* (1899), her first collection of short stories, was followed by a novella, *The Touchstone* (1900), but it was *The House of Mirth* (1905), a tragedy about a beautiful and sensitive girl who is destroyed by the very society her upbringing has designed her to meet, that established her as a major novelist. Many other works followed, almost 50 in all, including travel books and volumes of verse, but she is known principally as a novelist of manners, a keen observer of society, witty and satirical. Her most uncharacteristic novel is *Ethan Frome* (1911), which deals partly with her unhappy marriage, partly with primitive people in rural America. Important later works are *The Age of Innocence* (1920), *The Mother's Recompense* (1925), *The Children* (1928) and *Hudson River Bracketed* (1929). Her approach to her work is discussed in *The Writing of Fiction* (1925). *A Backwards Glance* (1934) is her revealing autobiography.

▷L Auchincloss, *Edith Wharton* (1961)

WHEATLEY, Denis Yates
(1897–1977)

English novelist, born in London. He inherited the family wine business but sold up in 1931 to concentrate on novel writing. His métier was an alloy of satanism and historical fiction, highly coloured and frequently burdened with undigested research, but enormously popular. Indicative titles in a lurid occult oeuvre are *The Devil Rides Out* (1935), *The Scarlet Impostor* (1942) and *The Sultan's Daughter* (1963). His three-volume autobiography was published posthumously (1978–80).

WHEATLEY, Phillis
(c.1753–1785)

American Negro poet, born in Africa, possibly Senegal. As a child she was shipped to the slave-market in Boston, Massachusetts (1761), and sold as a maidservant to the family of a Boston tailor, John Wheatley, who educated her with the rest of his family. She studied Latin and Greek, and started writing poetry in English at the age of 13. She published *Poems on Various Subjects, Religious and Moral* (1783) and visited England in that year, to huge popular interest, although some cast doubt on her poems' authenticity. In 1778 she married John Peters, a free negro of Boston. A *Collected Works* appeared in 1988.
▷W H Robinson, *Critical Essays on Phillis Wheatley* (1982)

WHEELOCK, John Hall
(1886–1978)

American poet, born in Far Rockway, New York. He joined the publisher Charles Scribner's Sons in 1911, and became a director, and its treasurer. He attracted attention early in his career, when, with his friend **Van Wyck Brooks**, he published *Verses of Two Undergraduates* (1905), while still at Harvard. He was essentially a popular, traditional, somewhat rhetorico-religious poet, whose work is not now included in anthologies such as **Richard Ellmann**'s *New Oxford Book of American Verse* (1976); but he was well respected, and his *The Gardener* (1961) won him the Bollingen Prize.

WHEELWRIGHT, John Brooks
(1897–1940)

American poet. He was born in Boston into an upper-class family, being the descendant of the 17th-century religious writer whose name he shared, and of a 19th-century governor, John Brooks. Despite this lineage and his father's wealth, he embraced communism shortly after leaving Harvard and MIT. He joined the Socialist Party of Massachusetts in 1932 and later became a political activist,

returning to his sumptuous home after a day on the stump and often wearing his famous raccoon coat while lecturing to unemployed dockers or striking longshoremen. He was a founder member in 1937 of the Trotskyist Socialist Workers Party. Wheelwright's verse, of which five volumes were published in his lifetime—*North Atlantic Passage* (1925), *Rock and Shell* (1933), *Masque With Clowns* (1936), *Mirrors of Venus* (1938) and *Political Self-Portrait* (1940)—is dense and highly wrought, incorporating religious symbols and obscure gnostic references alongside scraps of contemporary reality and political theory. It superficially resembles the work of **Hart Crane**, though **T S Eliot** is perhaps the strongest single influence. Wheelwright was killed on a Boston street by a hit-and-run driver. His *Collected Poems* appeared in 1972.
▷A M Wald, *The Revolutionary Imagination: The Poetry and Politics of John Wheelwright and Sherry Mangan* (1983)

WHETSTONE, George
(c.1544–1587)

English hack writer, born in London, who tried to make his fortune at court. A gambler and womanizer, he denounced the shocking depravity of his own city in various pamphlets. He joined the army more than once, serving with distinction; when not thus employed, he turned to writing to support himself, producing plays, poems and treatises, and biographies of distinguished men. Much of this work was mediocre, such as his lines 'In Praise of Gascoigne and his Posies' (1575). His last known work, the sycophantic *Censure Upon Notable Traitors* (1587), goes through a catalogue of plotters against the queen, declaiming on their wickedness and on Divine Providence saving Elizabeth's life.

WHITE, Antonia, pseud of Eirene Botting
(1899–1980)

English novelist and journalist, born in London. By the age of 30 she had married three times, the first two being annulled on the grounds of non-consummation. She also suffered periods of mental breakdown and underwent **Freud**ian analysis for four years. Her first novel, *Frost in May* (1933), is a semi-autobiographical study of a young girl's miserable convent education. *The Lost Traveller* (1950), *The Sugar House* (1952) and *Beyond the Glass* (1954) continue her autobiographical journey through her protagonist's relations with men, reconversion to Roman Catholicism and mental illness. A difficult, colourful, mysterious personality, White also translated extensively from French, including many works by **Colette**.
▷L Hopkinson, *Nothing to Forgive* (1988);

S Chitty, *Antonia White: Diaries 1958–1979* (1992)

WHITE, E(lwyn) B(rooks)
(1899–1985)

American essayist, children's novelist, poet and parodist, born in Mount Vernon, New York, in Westchester County. Long associated with the *New Yorker* from 1925, he did as much to make its name as it did his. His reputation rests on his three bestselling novels for children (*Stuart Little*, 1945; *Charlotte's Web*, 1952; and *The Trumpet of the Swan*, 1970), the essays he wrote in the column 'One Man's Meat', his collaboration with **James Thurber** on *Is Sex Necessary? Or Why You Feel The Way You Do* (1929), *The Elements of Style* (1959, a revision of William Strunk's original), a long article entitled 'Here Is New York', and a peerless parody of **Ernest Hemingway**, 'Across the Street and into the Grill'. Succinct, graceful and witty, his writing prompted Thurber to declare that 'Many of the things he writes seem to me as lovely as a tree'. Inclined towards rusticity, he spent much time in Maine fretting over livestock, retiring to a boathouse to sculpt his pieces. He was married to Katharine Angell, the first fiction editor of the *New Yorker*.

WHITE, Edmund
(1940–)

American novelist, probably the most sensitive writer about the gay scene since **James Baldwin**. White had already written several books, including *Forgetting Elena* (1973) and *Nocturnes for the King of Naples* (1978), before he came to notice with the publication *A Boy's Own Story* (1982). As the title is meant to suggest, it deliberately subverts the action-laden clichés that **Hemingway** attached to the young male adolescent, presenting instead a sensitive portrayal of a youth coming to terms with his sexuality and attempting to find a place for it in a ruthlessly heterosexual power struggle. In the same year, White published the essay *States of Desire: Travels in Gay America* (1980), a pre-AIDS update on **John Rechy**'s fictionalized *City of Night*. Less than a decade later, his novel *The Beautiful Room is Empty* (1988) had to contend with a very different social reality.

WHITE, Henry Kirke
(1785–1806)

English poet, born in Nottingham, the son of a butcher. Articled to a solicitor, in 1803 he published his verse sketch *Clifton Grove*, which brought him the friendship of **Robert Southey** and the Rev Charles Simeon, through whom he became a sizar of St John's College, Cambridge. After his tragically early death, Southey edited his *Remains* (1807).

WHITE, Kenneth
(1936–)

Scottish-born poet, essayist and travel writer, born in Glasgow. He studied at Glasgow University, graduating with a double first in French and German. It could be said that he has made a career as an exile, first by spending many years travelling in Europe, America and elsewhere, and latterly as an academic in France, where he now holds the chair of 20th-century literature at the Sorbonne. For years his work remained out of print in Britain and he was largely unsung in Scotland. In France, however, he is highly acclaimed, both as a poet and as a thinker, his ruminative verse and Zen-influenced philosophy finding like minds. He has received some of France's most prestigious literary awards, including the Prix Medicis Etranger and the Grand Prix du Rayonnement. Early publications included *The Cold Wind of Dawn* (1966) and *The Most Difficult Area* (1968). He has found a new generation of Scots more receptive to him, and recent publications, largely reprinting material unavailable in English, include *The Bird Path: Collected Longer Poems* (1989), *Travels in a Drifting Dawn* (1989), *Handbook for the Diamond Country: Collected Shorter Poems 1960–1990* (1990) and *The Blue Road* (1990).

WHITE, Patrick Victor Martindale
(1912–90)

Australian novelist and winner of the Nobel Prize for literature, born in London into an old Australian pastoralist family. He was educated at Cheltenham College and then worked in Australia for two years before going to King's College, Cambridge. After war service in the RAF he wrote *Happy Valley* (1939), *The Living and the Dead* (1941) and *The Aunt's Story* (1946), and then bought a farm near Sydney and settled in Australia. He achieved international success with *The Tree of Man* (1954). In this symbolic novel about a small community in the Australian bush, he attempts to portray every aspect of human life and to find the secret that makes it bearable. In 1957 appeared *Voss*, an allegorical account, in religious terms, of a gruelling attempt to cross the Australian continent. This was followed by *Riders in the Chariot* (1961), *The Solid Mandala* (1966), *The Eye of the Storm* (1973) and *The Twyborn Affair* (1979). He also published short stories, *The Burnt Ones* (1964) and *The Cockatoos* (1974), and plays, including *Four Plays* (1965) and *Signal Driver* (1981). His own 'self-portrait', *Flaws in the Glass* (1981), describes the background to his supposedly 'ungracious' receipt of the Nobel Prize for literature in 1973. With the proceeds of the prize he established the Patrick White Literary Award, which makes an annual grant to an older Australian writer whose work has not received appropriate critical or financial recognition.

▷D Marr, *Patrick White: a biography* (1991)

WHITE, T(erence) H(anbury)
(1906–64)

English novelist, born in Bombay, India. He was educated at Cheltenham College and Queens' College, Cambridge. Until 1936 he was a master at Stowe and later lived in a gamekeeper's cottage near the school. Always a keen sportsman, he was an ardent falconer and fisherman, and his knowledge and love of nature are imbued in his work. He wrote more than 25 books, but he is best known for his interpretation of the Arthurian legend, a tetralogy known collectively as *The Once and Future King* (1958), the first part of which, *The Sword in the Stone* (1937), is a children's classic. A fifth volume, found among his papers, was published as *The Book of Merlyn* (1977). *Mistress Masham's Repose* (1947) is another notable children's book. His adult works include *The Goshawk* (1951), set at the onset of World War II, a chronicle of the taming and training of one of Germany's noblest birds of prey, *The Master* (1957), a science-fiction parable, and *The Book of Beasts* (1954), translated from a 12th-century Latin bestiary.

▷S T Warner, *T. H. White* (1967)

WHITE, William Hale, pseud Mark Rutherford
(1831–1913)

English novelist and journalist, born in Bedford. Having abandoned his training as an independent religious minister, he worked briefly in the offices of the *Westminster Review*, where he met **George Eliot**, before entering the Civil Service. He continued writing journalism, becoming London correspondent of *The Scotsman*, and during the 1850s began to publish novels and works of philosophy. All take a high moral tone and are somewhat humourless, even depressing, although the novels are atmospherically strong. The best are *The Autobiography of Mark Rutherford, Dissenting Minister* (1881) and *Mark Rutherford's Deliverance* (1885), recounting White's spiritual journey.

WHITEHEAD, Charles
(1804–62)

English poet and novelist, born in London, the son of a wine merchant. He devoted himself to writing after publishing *The Solitary* (1831), a poem of reflection. His *Autobiography of Jack Ketch* (1834) showed humour, but when Chapman & Hall asked him for a popular book in instalments he declined, recommending young **Dickens**, who thus began the *Pickwick Papers*. His novel, *Richard Savage* (1842), earned the praises of Dickens and **Dante Gabriel Rossetti**. Whitehead went out to Melbourne in 1857, but died miserably, leaving unfinished the *Spanish Marriage*, a drama.

▷M Bell, *A Forgotten Genius* (1884)

WHITEHEAD, Paul
(1710–74)

English satirist and minor poet, born in Holborn, a tailor's son. He was apprenticed to a mercer, and later married a short-lived imbecile with a fortune of £10 000. He spent some years in Fleet prison for the nonpayment of a sum for which he had stood security. He became active in politics, was one of the infamous 'monks' of Medmenham Abbey, and became deputy treasurer of the Chamber. Among his satires are *State Dunces* (1733), inscribed to **Pope**, and *Manners* (1739), for which **Robert Dodsley** the publisher was brought before the House of Lords. His *Collected Works* appeared in 1777.

WHITEHEAD, William
(1715–85)

English poet and dramatist, born in Cambridge, the son of a baker. He was educated at Winchester and Clare Hall, Cambridge, and became a fellow in 1742. He travelled as tutor to Lord Jersey's son, became in 1755 secretary of the Order of the Bath, and in 1757 was appointed poet laureate. He defended his acceptance against hostile criticism in *A Charge to the Poets* (1762). He wrote tragedies—*The Roman Father* (1750), in imitation of **Corneille**'s *Horace*, and *Creusa* (1754)—and a comedy, *School for Lovers* (1762). His *Plays and Poems* were collected in 1774, with *Complete Poems* following in 1788.

WHITING, John
(1917–63)

English playwright, born in Salisbury. Educated at Taunton School, he studied at the Royal Academy of Dramatic Art (1935–7). After serving in the Royal Artillery in World War II he resumed his acting career before emerging as a dramatist. *Saint's Day* (1951), depicting the sense of hopelessness, failure and self-destruction of the Southman ménage, gained recognition for his talent although it was not a popular success. It was followed by *A Penny for a Song* (1951), a comedy, and *Marching Song* (1954), a play of ideas with little action or dramatic situation whose plot deals with the decision facing General Rupert Forster: to stand trial as a scapegoat for his country's failure or to commit suicide. After *Gates of Summer* (1956) he was commissioned by the Royal Shakespeare Company to dramatize **Aldous Huxley's** *The Devils of Loudon*, as *The Devils* (1961), which achieved great success, despite harrowing scenes such as the torture of Grandier. His *Collected Plays* (1969) included a number of works which he did not live to see on stage.

WHITMAN, Walt(er)

(1819–92)

American poet, born in West Hills, Long Island, New York, the son of a radical, free-thinking carpenter. He was brought up in Brooklyn from the age of four. He served first in a lawyer's and then in a doctor's office, and finally in a printer's. He next became an itinerant teacher in country schools. He returned to printing, wrote an earnest temperance novel, *Franklin Evans or, The Inebriate* (1842), and in 1846 became Editor of the *Brooklyn Eagle*. This and his other numerous press engagements were only of short duration. In 1848 he travelled with his brothers to New Orleans in search of work on the New Orleans *Crescent*, but came back to Brooklyn as a journalist (1848–54). He seemed unable to find free expression for his emotions until he hit upon the curious, irregular, recitative measures of *Leaves of Grass* (1855). Originally a small folio of 95 pages published anonymously with the author's portrait in work clothes enigmatically facing the title page, it grew in the eight succeeding editions to nearly 440 pages. This, with his prose book, *Specimen Days and Collect* (1882), constitutes his main life-work as a writer. Summoned to tend his brother, wounded in the Civil War, he became a volunteer nurse in the hospitals of the Northern army. The exertion, exposure, and strain of those few years left Whitman a shattered and prematurely aged man. In 1865 he received a government clerkship, but was dismissed by Secretary Harlan as the author of 'an indecent book' (*Leaves of Grass*). Almost immediately he obtained another similar post. In 1873 he was stricken with paralysis and left Washington for Camden, New Jersey, where he spent the remainder of his life. He would have fallen into absolute poverty but for the help of trans-Atlantic admirers. Later on, several wealthy American citizens liberally provided for his simple wants. Whitman set himself the task of uplifting into the sphere of poetry the whole of modern life and man; thus the inclusion of subjects at that time which were tabooed. Many of his poems for *Leaves of Grass* are now considered American classics, such as 'Drum Taps', 'When Lilacs Last in the Courtyard Bloom'd' and 'O Captain! My Captain!'.

▷ G W Allen, *The Solitary Singer* (1955)

WHITTEMORE, (Edward) Reed II

(1919–)

American poet, editor (he co-edited *Furioso*), critic, teacher and biographer, born in New Haven, Connecticut. As a biographer of **William Carlos Williams** (1975) he was mostly influenced by this poet and his free rhythms. One poem of his in particular has been much praised: 'Lines Upon Reading an Announcement by Civil Defence Authorities Recommending That I Build a Bomb Shelter in My Backyard'. His survey, *Little Magazines* (1963), is authoritative, as is *Poets and Anthologists: A Look at the Current Poet-Packaging Process* (1986).

WHITTIER, John Greenleaf

(1807–92)

American Quaker poet and abolitionist, born near Haverhill, Massachusetts, the son of a poor farmer. Largely self-educated, in 1829 he entered journalism, and in 1831 published *Legends of New England*, a collection of poems and stories. In 1840 he settled at Amesbury, a village near his birthplace, and devoted himself to the cause of emancipation. His collection *In War Time* (1864) contains the well-known ballad 'Barbara Frietchie'. *At Sundown* was published in 1892. In his day he was considered second only to **Longfellow**.

▷ E Wagenknecht, *John Greenleaf Whittier* (1967)

WHYTE-MELVILLE, George John

(1821–78)

Scottish novelist and authority on field sports, born at Mount-Melville, St Andrews. Educated at Eton, he became a captain in the Coldstream Guards and served in the Crimean War, commanding a regiment of Turkish cavalry irregulars. For the rest of his life he devoted himself to field-sports, and wrote numerous novels involving fox-hunting and steeplechasing, including *Digby Grand* (1853) and *Tilbury Nego* (1861). He also wrote serious historical novels, including *Market Harborough* (1861), *The Gladiators* (1863) and *The Queen's Maries* (1862), on Mary, Queen of Scots, and published *Songs and Verse* in 1869. He was killed in a hunting accident.

WICKRAM, Georg or Jörg

(1505–before 1562)

German poet and popular novelist, born in Kolmar. The bastard son of a careless but wealthy burgher, he was by profession goldsmith, painter and town clerk of Burgheim, where he died. As a poet he wrote standard but lively poems and plays in the Meistersinger tradition; as a novelist he was outstanding. He wrote two courtly romances, but also, much more notably, the story of a boy's rise to success, *Der Jungen Knaben Spiegel* (1554, 'The Young Boy Spiegel')—often considered to be the first German novel proper—and *Von güten und bösen Nachbarn* (1554, 'The Good and Bad Neighbours'), his finest work. He adapted the *Metamorphoses* of **Ovid**.

▷ G Fauth, *Jörg Wickram* (1916, in German)

WIDDEMER, Margaret
(1884–1978)

American poet and novelist, born in Pennsylvania. She first came to notice with a poem denouncing the employment of children. It was reprinted as the title poem in her first collection, *The Factories and Other Poems* (1915). In the same year her novel, *The Rose-Garden Husband*, which told the story of a young librarian (Widdemer was herself a trained librarian), became a bestseller. Later poetry lost the hard edge of *The Factories*. Her best verse is to be found in *Collected Poems* (1957). In addition to her romantic and historical novels for adults she also wrote the 'Winona' series for girls.

WIDEMAN, John Edgar
(1941–)

Black American novelist, born in Washington, DC, but brought up in the Homewood area of Pittsburgh. He was educated at the University of Pennsylvania, and has taught English and Afro-American Studies in several universities. He is a powerful chronicler of black urban experience, and much of his fiction is set in Homewood. His first novel was *A Glance Away* (1967), about a drug addict. Subsequent titles include *The Lynchers* (1973), which takes a multi-perspective look at black urban life. His Homewood experience is also central to *Sent For You Yesterday* (1983) and *Reuben* (1987), and the stories collected in *Damballah* (1981). A second collection, *Fever* (1989), is more wide-ranging. The novel *Philadelphia Fire* (1990) is based on a police fire-bombing of a radical black commune in 1985.

▷ *Brothers and Keepers* (1984)

WIEBE, Rudy
(1934–)

Canadian novelist and short-story writer, born in Fairholme, Saskatchewan, into the Menonite community. Educated at the universities of Alberta and Tübingen, he edited *The Menonite Brethren Herald* and taught at the University of Alberta. As a Menonite he writes of peace-loving in a violent, macho world and as a prairie writer revises Ottawadominated history. *Peace Shall Destroy Many* (1962) and *The Blue Mountains of China* (1974) deal with the temptations of the Menonite community in the world. His masterpieces, *The Temptations of Big Bear* (1973) and *The Scorched Wood People* (1977), treat 19th-century rebellions against Ottawa led by religious figures. *The Mad Trapper* (1980) is a yarn about another rebel, but one who stands alone against the world, while *My Lovely Enemy* (1983) turns to religious adultery on campus. Wiebe's style is awkward but the depth of his religious and historical imagination generously compensates for that.

▷ W J Keith, *Epic Fiction: the Art of Rudy Wiebe* (1981)

WIECHERT, Ernst
(1887–1950)

German writer, born in Kleinort in East Prussia. He published novels dealing with psychological problems such as post-war readjustment, among them *Der Wald* (1922, 'The Forest'), *Der Totenwolf* (1924, 'The Wolf of Death'), *Der silberne Wagen* (1928, 'The Silver Wagon'), *Die Majorin* (1934, Eng trans *The Baroness*, 1936) and *Das einfache Leben* (1939, Eng trans *The Simple Life*, 1954), the last-named probably his masterpiece. *Wälder und Menschen* (1936, 'Forests and Men') is autobiographical, as is *Der Totenwald* (1946, Eng trans *The Forest of the Dead*, 1947), which describes his six months' confinement in Buchenwald concentration camp.

▷ H Ebling, *Ernst Wiechert* (1947)

WIED, Gustav
(1858–1914)

Danish fiction-writer and dramatist, born on the island of Loland. His masterpiece is generally reckoned to be *Skoerydsler* (1901, 'Skirmishes'), a grotesque play about old people. He was often compared to **Strindberg**, but possessed a much greater degree of humour than the Swede. He wrote ironic and bizarre prose sketches, resisted his tragic sense of life so long as he could, but finally killed himself. One of his best plays, *Ranke Vilje* (1906) was translated as *2 × 2 = 5* in *Contemporary Danish Plays* (1955).

WIELAND, Christoph Martin
(1733–1813)

German writer, born near Biberach, the son of a pietist pastor. In 1752 Bodmer invited him to Zürich, and inspired him to write *Der geprüfte Abraham* (1753, 'The Testing of

Abraham') and other books full of sentimentality and religious mysticism. But Wieland turned away from that particular style of writing, and from 1760 to 1770, as well as making the first German translation of **Shakespeare** (22 plays, 1762–6), he wrote the romances *Agathon* (1766–7, Eng trans 1773) and *Don Silvio von Rosalva* (1764, Eng trans 1785), *Die Grazien* (1768, Eng trans *The Graces*, 1823) and other tales, and the didactic poem *Musarion* (1768). Their elegance, grace and lightness made Wieland popular with fashionable society. After holding for three years a professorship at Erfurt, he was called to Weimar to train the grand-duchess's sons, and there he spent most of the rest of his life, the friend of **Goethe** and **Johann Herder**. The Weimar period produced his heroic poem *Oberon* (1780, Eng trans 1798), by which he is best remembered, and various other works; he also edited several magazines.

▷ D M von Abbe, *Christoph Wieland* (1961)

WIENERS, John
(1934–)

American poet, born in Boston, who claims inspiration from **Edna St Vincent Millay**. After a spell at Black Mountain College, he became associated with the Beats, but wrote in a different vein. The poignant lyricism of the early collection *Hotel Wentley Poems* (1958) was widely admired. It did contain much verbal dexterity, but from 'A poem for cocksuckers' onwards Wieners's unwavering gay perspective and his tumid anguish have restricted his audience.

WIERZYNSKI, Kazimierz
(1894–1969)

Polish poet, born in the Carpathian mountain region, in Drohobycz. He left Poland for the USA in 1940, but died in London. He was a co-founder of the important middle-of-the-road Skamander group. His early poetry was vitalist, and celebrated athletics; later the note deepened, and in the USA he wrote tragic poetry of exile. But **Milosz** has claimed that his last poems, closer in style to the younger poets writing in Poland itself, 'are striking in their generosity and openness to the world ... [they] rank amongst his greatest achievements'. His *Life and Death of Chopin*, one of the best books on the composer, first written as *W garderobie duchów* in 1938, was translated in a revised edition in 1951; *Selected Poems* appeared in 1959. He has also published a collection of stories and much theatre criticism.

WIGGIN, Kate Douglas, née Smith
(1856–1953)

American novelist, born in Philadelphia. She wrote novels for both adults and children, but was more successful with the latter. *Rebecca of Sunnybrook Farm* (1903) is probably her best-known book, although the *Penelope* exploits, *The Birds' Christmas Carol* (1888) and *Mother Carey's Chickens* (1911), were all firm favourites.

▷ *My Garden of Memory* (1923)

WIGGLESWORTH, Michael
(1631–1705)

English-born American poet and clergyman, born in Yorkshire. He was taken to Massachusetts Bay colony at the age of seven. Educated at Harvard, he was married to Mary Reyner (1655), to Martha Mudge (1679), and to Sybil Sparhawk Avery (1691), and eight children resulted. Fellow and tutor at Harvard from 1652 to 1654, and again from 1697 to 1705, he was ordained to the ministry of the Puritan Church in Malden, c.1656. His epic poem, the first American epic, 'Day of Doom' (1662), takes a lengthy and somewhat pessimistic view of the Day of Judgement. He wrote a shorter poem intended for edification in 1669: 'Meat out of the Eater or Meditations Concerning the Necessity, End and Usefulness of Afflictions Unto God's Children'. His *Diary* was published in 1951.

▷ R Crowder, *No Featherbed to Heaven* (1962)

WILBUR, Richard
(1921–)

American poet. He grew up in New York City and was educated at Harvard, joining the faculty around the time his first major collection, *The Beautiful Changes* (1947), was published. It was followed by *Ceremony and Other Poems* (1950) and *Things of This World* (1956), a significant title in view of Wilbur's stylistic hybridization of **William Carlos Williams**'s and **Marianne Moore**'s objectivism with the English Metaphysicals. In 1957 he published the plain-spoken *Poems* and that year began teaching at Wesleyan University. Two years earlier, he had published an acclaimed translation of **Molière** and in 1957 Leonard Bernstein invited him to contribute songs to *Candide*. A collection was published in 1963, at a time when Wilbur's powers appeared to be failing; however, *The Mind Reader* and a prose collection *Responses*, both published in 1976, reawakened interest in his work.

WILCOX, Ella Wheeler
(1850–1919)

American journalist and prolific producer of verse, born in Johnstown Center, Wisconsin. In 1884 she married Robert M Wilson (d.1916). She had completed a novel before she was 10, and later wrote at least two poems a day. The first of her many volumes of verse was *Drops of Water* (1872); the most successful was *Poems of Passion* (1883). She also wrote a great deal of fiction, and contributed essays to many periodicals. Her *Story of a Literary Career* (1905) and *The World and I* (1918) were autobiographical.

WILDE, Lady Jane Francesca, known as 'Speranza'
(1826–96)

Irish poet and hostess, born in Dublin. An ardent nationalist, she contributed poetry and prose to the *Nation* from 1845 under the pen-name of 'Speranza'. In 1851 she married Sir William Wilde; their son was **Oscar Wilde**. Her salon was the most famous in Dublin. After her husband's death she moved to London, and published several works on folklore, including *Ancient Legends of Ireland* (1887) and *Ancient Cures* (1891).

WILDE, Oscar Fingall O'Flahertie Wills
(1854–1900)

Irish playwright, novelist, essayist, poet and wit, born in Dublin. His father was Sir William Wilde; his mother Lady **Jane Francesca Wilde**. From the age of nine to 16 he went to Portora Royal School in Enniskillen, which **Samuel Beckett** later attended. He went on to Trinity College, Dublin, and to Magdalen College, Oxford, where he was dandified, sexually ambiguous, sympathetic towards the Pre-Raphaelites, and contemptuous of conventional morality. He was also an accomplished classicist, and won the Newdigate Prize in 1878 for the poem 'Ravenna', which his biographer, **Richard Ellmann**, described as 'a clever hodgepodge of personal reminiscence, topographical description, political and literary history'. In 1881, the year in which he was ridiculed in **Gilbert** and Sullivan's *Patience* as an adherent of the cult of Art for Art's sake, his first collection of poetry was published. The next year he embarked on a lecture tour of the USA where, apparently, when asked if he had anything to declare he replied, 'Only my genius'. The tour, wrote Ellmann, 'was an advertisement of courage and grace, along with ineptitude and self-advertisement'. Wilde boasted to Whistler, 'I have already civilized America'. He married, in 1884, Constance Lloyd, and had two sons for whom he wrote the classic children's fairy stories *The Happy Prince and Other Tales* (1888). Two years later came *The Picture of Dorian Gray*, modelled on his presumed lover, the poet John Gray. More fairy stories appeared in 1891 in *A House of Pomegranates*. In this year he also published *Lord Arthur Savile's Crime and Other Stories*, and

a second play, *The Duchess of Padua*, an uninspired verse tragedy. But over the next five years he built his dramatic reputation, first with *Lady Windermere's Fan* (1892), followed by *A Woman of No Importance* (1893), *An Ideal Husband* (1895) and, the *pièce de résistance*, *The Importance of Being Earnest* (1895). *Salome*, originally written in French, appeared in 1894 in a translation by Lord **Alfred Douglas**. By now his homosexuality was commonly known, and the Marquis of Queensberry, father of Lord Alfred, left a card at Wilde's club addressed 'To Oscar Wilde posing as a Somdomite' (*sic*). Wilde took it that he meant 'ponce and Sodomite' and sued for libel. He lost the case, and was himself prosecuted and imprisoned for homosexuality. In 1905 his bitter reproach to Lord Alfred was published as *De Profundis*. He was released in 1897 and went to France under the alias Sebastian Melmoth, the name of his favourite martyr linked with the hero of *Melmoth the Wanderer*, the novel written by his great-uncle, **Charles Maturin**. *The Ballad of Reading Gaol* was published in 1898. He also wrote literary essays, and *The Soul of Man Under Socialism* (1891), a riposte to **George Bernard Shaw**. His last years were spent wandering and idling on the continent.
▷ R Ellmann, *Oscar Wilde* (1990)

WILDENBRUCH, Ernst von
(1845–1909)

German romantic novelist, poet and dramatist, born in Beirut. He served in the army and Foreign Office. He wrote a number of short epic poems, but is best known as a playwright. His strongly expressed patriotism made him the national dramatist of Prussia during the empire of the Hohenzollern, to whom he was related. He also wrote short stories.
▷ H M Elster, *Ernst von Wildenbruch* (1934)

WILDENVEY, Herman
(1886–1959)

Norwegian poet, born in Eiker. At first basing himself on the poetry of **Knut Hamsun**, he soon outstripped his mentor. Facile but gifted, he became Norway's most popular lyrical poet. Some of his verse is translated in *Owls to Athens* (1934).

WILDER, Laura Ingalls
(1867–1957)

American children's author, born in Pepin, Wisconsin. A farm woman all her life, it was not until she was in her sixties, when her daughter suggested that she write down her childhood memories, that her evocative 'Little House' series began to appear. *Little House in the Big Woods* (1932) caught on instantly in the USA and was followed by several sequels: *Little House on the Prairie* (1935), *By the Shores of Lake Silver* (1939), *Little Town on the Prairie* (1941), *Farmer Boy* (1933) and *Those Happy Golden Years* (1943). A television series in the 1950s assured their success in Britain.

WILDER, Thornton Niven
(1897–1975)

American author and playwright, born in Madison, Wisconsin. He was educated at Yale and served in both wars, becoming a lieutenant-colonel in 1944. He started his career as a teacher of English at Lawrenceville Academy (1921–8) and the University of Chicago (1930–7). His first novel, *The Cabala*, appeared in 1926. Set in contemporary Rome, it established the cool atmosphere of sophistication and detached irony that was to permeate all his books. These include *The Bridge of San Luis Rey* (1927), a bestseller and winner of the Pulitzer Prize, *The Woman of Andros* (1930), *Heaven's My Destination* (1935) and *The Ides of March* (1948). His first plays—*The Trumpet Shall Sound* (1926), *The Angel That Troubled the Waters* (1928) and *The Long Christmas Dinner* (1931)—were literary rather than dramatic; but in 1938 he produced *Our Town*, a successful play that evokes without scenery or costumes a universal flavour of provincial life. This was followed in 1942 by *The Skin of Our Teeth*, an amusing yet profound fable of humanity's struggle to survive. Both these plays were awarded the Pulitzer Prize. His later plays include *The Matchmaker* (1954), *A Life in the Sun* (1955), *The Eighth Day* (1967), *Theophilus North* (1974) and, in 1964, the musical *Hello Dolly*, based on *The Matchmaker*.
> R Burbank, *Thornton Wilder* (1978)

WILDGANS, Anton
1881–1932)

Austrian poet and dramatist, born in Vienna. He trained as a lawyer, but gave up his practice to concentrate on literature in 1912. His plays include *Dies Irae* (1918, 'Day of Anger') and the biblical tragedy *Kain* (1920). The epic poem *Kirbisch* appeared in 1927, and he published a number of collections of verse. He was twice director of the Vienna Burgtheater, in 1921–2 and 1930–1.

WILHELM, Kate
1928–)

American science-fiction writer, born in Toledo, Ohio. A slowly maturing author, she won a Nebula Award in 1969 for her short story 'The Planners', but did not begin to produce her best work as a novelist until around a decade later. *Where Late The Sweet Birds Sang* (1976), set in a post-holocaust America, won a Hugo Award. *Juniper Time* (1979), which takes place in a drought-stricken US, is one of the most effective of the genre's many works with an ecological theme. She has also written several mainstream novels. One of the most subtle and intelligent voices in modern science fiction, she was married to the science-fiction author and editor **Damon Knight**.

WILLARD, Josiah, pseud Josiah Flynt
(1869–1907)

American author and traveller, born in Wisconsin, the nephew of Frances Willard, a leading temperance activist. He travelled in Europe and America as a hobo, befriending **Arthur Symons** in London, and working on the **Tolstoy** estate in Russia. He expressed solidarity with other vagrants, defending their cause against what he saw as the injustice of the police. His work, published under the name Josiah Flynt, can best be described as autobiographical amateur sociology. Titles include *Tramping with Tramps* (1899) and *The World of Graft* (1901).
> *My Life* (1908)

WILLARD, Nancy
(1936–)

American poet and writer of fiction, born in Michigan. Willard has been described as a 'domestic poet par excellence'. Her young son features in the collection *Household Tales of Moon and Water*. Her cycle of poems for children, *A Visit to William Blake's Inn: Poems for Innocent and Experienced Travellers* (1981) won a **Newbery** Medal. Willard lectures in English at Vassar and is a member of the **Lewis Carroll** and **George MacDonald** societies.

WILLIAMS, Charles Walter Stansby
(1886–1945)

English poet, novelist, biographer and theologian, born in London and educated at University College, London. For many years he was a member of the editorial staff of Oxford University Press. His first volume of poetry, *The Silver Stair* (1912), is considered to be influenced by **Yeats**, while his later work, such as the plays *Thomas Cranmer* (1936) and *Seed of Adam* (1948), echo the currently fashionable and high-minded verse drama written by **T S Eliot**. He wrote several sensational psychological and supernatural thrillers, such as *Many Dimensions* (1931) and *All Hallows Eve* (1944), as well as books meditating upon the Arthurian legend, and theological works including *Descent of the Dove* (1939). Much of his writing, in all its forms, deals with the fundamental conflict between good and evil and the question of individual redemption. His biographies include *James I* (1934) and *Elizabeth* (1936).

WILLIAMS, David John
(1896–1970)

Welsh writer, born in Rhydcymerau, a district in Carmarthenshire which he made famous in his autobiography *Hen Dŷ Ffarm* (1953, Eng trans *The Old Farmhouse*, 1961) and its sequel *Yn chwech ar Hugain Oed* (1959, 'Twenty-Six Years Old'). He worked as a collier but then became a schoolmaster. With **Saunders Lewis**, and as founder member of *Plaid Cymru*, he took part in the protest over the Penyberth bombing-school outrage, and was unjustly jailed as a result. He excelled in characterization, and was deservedly famous for his exemplary understanding of and love for animals.
▷ D Jenkins, *D. J. Williams* (1973)

WILLIAMS, Edward ('Iolo Morganwg')
(1747–1826)

Welsh poet, antiquary and cultural inventor, born in Llancarfan, Glamorgan. He worked there as a stonemason, and became a poet in Welsh and English. He had links with 18th-century Radicalism, mingling its ideas with Romantic exaltation of the Welsh past and established neo-Druidic cults and celebrations in Wales from 1792. He published collected poems purportedly by the 14th-century poet Dafydd ap Gwilym, which in fact were his own work. He co-edited *The Myvyrian Archaeology* (3 vols, 1801–7), and produced posthumously a vast corpus of cultural material from the Welsh past in varying degrees of authenticity. A brilliant forger whose deceptions far outlived his own time, his work prolonged, revived and reinvigorated ancient and modern Welsh culture.
▷ G J Williams, *Iolo Morganwg* (1963)

WILLIAMS, (George) Emlyn
(1905–87)

Welsh playwright and actor, born in Mostyn, Clwyd, the son of a steel-works foreman. He won a scholarship to Oxford, where he entered Christ Church. In 1927, attracted by the stage, he joined J B Fagan's repertory company. His first real success as a dramatist was with *A Murder has been Arranged* (1930). He then adapted a French play by René Fauchois—*The Late Christopher Bean* (1933)—and continued his success with the terrifying psychological thriller *Night Must Fall* (1935). He was not limited to light entertainment, and a seriousness of purpose characterizes most of his other work. Other successes were *The Corn is Green* (1938), *The Light of Heart*

(1940), *The Wind of Heaven* (1945), *Trespass* (1947) and *Accolade* (1951). He generally played the lead in his own and acted in other dramatists' plays, as well as appearing at the Old Vic and at Stratford, and featuring in films. His solo performance as **Charles Dickens** giving his celebrated readings from his works was greeted with acclaim, but a similar endeavour as **Dylan Thomas** did not meet with such success. He wrote the autobiographical *George* (1961) and *Emlyn* (1973), as well as *Beyond Belief* (1967), and a novel, *Headlong* (1980).

WILLIAMS, Francis
(c.1700–c.1770)

Jamaican poet, born of free negro parents but sent to an English grammar school and Cambridge University by the duke of Montagu who wanted to discover if a negro, properly educated, could become 'as capable of literature as a white person'. On return to Jamaica he opened a school in Spanish Town, teaching reading, writing, Latin and mathematics. Of his verse, only one ode in elegant Latin survives. Addressed to George Haldane on his appointment as Governor of Jamaica (1759), it voices conflicting feelings of pride in his British nurture and humility as a black, but pleads that there is no colour distinction ('honesto nullus inest animo, nullus in arte color').
▷ E Long, *The History of Jamaica* (1774)

WILLIAMS, Helen Maria
(c.1761–1827)

British writer, born in London, daughter of a Welsh army officer, but educated by her Scottish mother at Berwick-upon-Tweed after her father's death in 1770. She lived in London from 1781, intimate with radical and feminist intellectuals. An ardent supporter of the French Revolution, she settled in France in 1792, where her Girondist views landed her in prison (1793). From 1782 she published voluminously: poems, novels, history, translations and the much admired series of *Letters from France* (1790–6), giving vivid if inaccurate eye-witness accounts of the revolution. Her poems are mostly sentimental or politically idealistic, condemning slavery and colonialism. Her novel *Julia* (1790), modelled on **Rousseau**'s *Nouvelle Héloïse*, highlights the dangers of excessive sensibility and uncontrolled passion. *Poems on Various Subjects* was published in 1823.
▷ L D Woodward, *Une adhérente anglaise de la Révolution française, Hélène-Maria Williams* (1930)

WILLIAMS, Jesse Lynch
(1871–1929)

American novelist, short-story writer and playwright, born in Sterling, Illinois. He graduated from Princeton University in 1892, and published his first book, *Princeton Stories*, in 1895. He also wrote a number of novels, including *The Married Life of the Frederic Carrolls* (1910), *Not Wanted* (1923) and *She Knew She Was Right* (1930). He is best-known as a dramatist, and won the Pulitzer Prize for Drama in 1918 with the social comedy *Why Marry?* (1917). His first play, *The Stolen Story* (1906), drew on his experiences as a journalist with the New York *Sun*. His other plays include *Why Not?* (1922) and the comedy *Lovely Lady* (1925).

WILLIAMS, John A(lfred)
(1925–)

American novelist and journalist, born in Mississippi. Williams joined the US Navy during World War II and was admitted to the hospital corps. Bitter at the racism he experienced in the navy (he was assigned to a land force because 'black hospital corpsmen were not wanted aboard ship'), all his novels have been about the black plight. *The Angry Ones* (1960) was about black musicians, *!Click Song* (1982) about the ups and downs of a black writer, and *This Is My Country Too* (1965) is a collection of powerfully felt essays.

WILLIAMS, Raymond
(1921–88)

Welsh critic and novelist, born in Pandy, Gwent, the son of a railway signalman. Educated at King Henry VIII Grammar School, Abergavenny and Cambridge, he wrote *Culture and Society* (1958), which required socialists to seek inspiration in such figures as **Edmund Burke**, **Robert Southey** and **Thomas Carlyle**. He opened up questions of mass readership and cultural and ethical values in *The Long Revolution* (1966). He was made a fellow of Jesus College, Cambridge, in 1961, and was Professor of Drama there from 1974 to 1983. He was active in New Left intellectual movements, producing the *May Day Manifesto* (1968), but his novels *Border Country* (1960), *Second Generation* (1964), *The Volunteers* (1978), *The Fight for Manod* (1979) and *Loyalties* (1985) underline the significance of Welsh consciousness for him, and he was later identified with Welsh nationalism. Of his many major works in socio-literary criticism, *The Country and the City* (1973) was perhaps the most inspirational.

WILLIAMS, Tennessee, originally **Thomas Lanier**
(1911–83)

American playwright, born in Columbus, Mississippi, the son of a travelling salesman. Prone to illness as a child, he found writing to be a tonic. He had an itinerant college education, first at Washington University in St Louis, then at the University of Missouri, finally receiving a degree from the University of Iowa in 1938. He worked at various menial jobs, among them as a poet-waiter at a Greenwich Village restaurant and as a cinema usher. Recognition of his literary skill came in 1940, when he received a Rockefeller Fellowship for his first play, *Battle of Angels*. In 1943 he signed a six-month contract with M-G-M, later cancelled when he submitted a script that became *The Glass Menagerie*. This play, which in 1945 earned him the New York Drama Critics' Circle Award, introduced him as an important American playwright. He then wrote *Summer and Smoke* (1948), and in 1948 was awarded the Pulitzer Prize for *A Streetcar Named Desire*. After *The Rose Tattoo* (1951) and *Camino Red* (1953), he won the Pulitzer Prize again in 1955 for *Cat on a Hot Tin Roof*. He continued with *Suddenly Last Summer* (1958), *Sweet Bird of Youth* (1959) and *The Night of the Iguana* (1961). He won the Gold Medal for Literature in 1969 from both the American Academy of Arts & Letters and the National Institute of Arts and Letters. In addition to his plays, he published collections of poetry—*The Summer Belvedere* (1944), *Winter of Cities* (1956); and short stories—*Hard Candy* (1954), *Eight Mortal Ladies Possessed* (1974) and *It Happened the Day the Sun Rose* (1982). He wrote one novel, *The Roman Spring of Mrs Stone* (1950), and wrote the scripts for several films, including *Baby Doll* (1956). *Where I Live: Selected Essays* (1978) is autobiographical.
▷D Spoto, *The Kindness of Strangers* (1985)

WILLIAMS, Waldo
(1904–71)

Welsh poet, born in Haverfordwest. He was educated at Narberth Grammar School and University College, Aberystwyth. Considered by many to be the most astonishingly original poet in the Welsh language, his work, deeply influenced by the Romantic poets, is concerned with universal brotherhood and mankind's relationship with the natural world. A committed pacifist, he supported civil disobedience as advocated by **Henry Thoreau** and Mahatma Gandhi. In 1950 he withheld his income tax in response to the Korean War. He spent six weeks in prison for nonpayment of tax in 1960, and served a second sentence in 1961.
▷B G Owens, *Gwaithacu Waldo Williams* (1972)

WILLIAMS, William Carlos
(1883–1963)

American poet, novelist and also a cultural historian. An 'offshore American', with

French, Jewish, Basque and British ante-cedents, he was born in Rutherford, Con-necticut, and spent most of his life there. After returning from school in Switzerland and Paris, he took his MD at the University of Pennsylvania, Philadelphia. Following an internship in New York City, he went to Leipzig to study paediatrics, returning to Rutherford as a general practitioner and pae-diatrician until his retirement. At Phil-adelphia, he had met both **Ezra Pound** and **Hilda Doolittle** ('HD'), both of whom had a considerable impact on his developing inter-est in poetry. His first volume, *Poems*, had been privately printed in Rutherford in 1909. The second and third, *The Tempers* (1913) and *Al Que Quiere!* (1917), established a dis-tinctive voice and steered him towards the Modernist avant-garde. *Kora in Hell* (1920) was a book of experimental prose impro-visations in the manner of **Rimbaud** and **Bau-delaire**, but it was with *Spring and All* (1923) and his ironic *The Great American Novel* (1923) that he reached full creative maturity. *In the American Grain* (1925) was a brilliant study of American myths, strongly influenced by **D H Lawrence**'s mytho-psychoanalytic *Studies in Classic American Literature* (1923); it provided a critical counterbalance to pre-vailing Puritan explanations of American cul-ture. In 1928, he attempted a real novel for the first time, *A Voyage in Pagany*. His poetic output had slackened considerably and it was not until *Collected Poems, 1921–1931* appeared in 1934 that he seemed to be back on track. Other volumes followed. In 1937 he published *White Mule* (1937), the first in a trilogy of novels completed by *In the Money* (1940) and *The Build-Up* (1952), but it was in 1946 that he published the first book of his poetic masterpiece, *Paterson*, a vast synoptic study of a (real) American town. Parts II (1948), III (1949) and IV (1951) deal with the search for an authentic American language in verse (echoes of **Whitman** are prevalent), mythic destruction and rebirth (akin to elements in Pound's *Cantos*), and the poet-narrator's ageing; a fifth section was added in 1958. Williams's objectivist credo 'No ideas but in things' had become a major tenet of Modernist writing and he remained a rally-ing-point for the New York avant-garde. His main works after *Paterson* were *The Desert Music* (1954), *Journey to Love* (1955) and *Pic-tures from Breughel* (1962), though two retro-spective volumes, *The Collected Later Poems* (1950, rev edn 1963) and *The Collected Earlier Poems* (1951) exerted greater influence on a rising generation. He suffered the first of a series of cerebral episodes in the early 1950s, shortly after completing his *Autobiography* (1951). These steadily incapacitated him, forcing his retiral and severely curtailing his writing. A great, late poem, 'Asphodel', was written on a typewriter, using the tab key to create a staggered, three-line strophe. It is a mysterious, curiously elusive meditation on death, written by a man who, having dealt with mortality all his professional life, found himself facing up to his own extinction.

▷C F Terrell, *Williams: Man and Poet* (1983)

WILLIAMS PANTYCELYN, William
(1717–91)

Welsh hymn-writer, poet, translator and prose writer, born in Cefn-coed in Car-marthenshire. His mother, widowed in 1742, took him to live in Pantycelyn, hence his name. He devoted his life to itinerant preach-ing on behalf of the Methodist movement, and was ultimately regarded as one of the leaders of Welsh Methodism. The most important hymn-writer of Wales, he is seen by some (exaggeratedly) as its most important poet too. His hymns are as good as anyone's have been, possibly even better, and the 5 500-line poem *Golwg ar Deyrnas Crist* (1756, rev edn 1764, 'A View of Christ's Kingdom') is an extraordinary—although flawed—achievement. *Bywyd a Marwolaeth Theo-memphus* (1764, 'The Life and Death of Theo-memphus'), another long (6 000-line) poem, is a dramatic work without precedent in Welsh or any other poetry, which describes the spiritual pilgrimage of its hero in often startling detail. He wrote many theological works (he had produced over 90 volumes by the time of his death), and seriously deserves attention outside his native land as a poet and thinker of the first rank. The study of him by **Saunders Lewis** is in itself a critical classic; its views are attacked in the article quoted below.

▷S Lewis, *Williams Pantycelyn* (1927); *Anglo-Welsh Review*, 15, 35 (1965)

WILLIAMSON, David Keith
(1942–)

Australian playwright, born in Melbourne, Victoria. He graduated in mechanical engin-eering from Monash University, Melbourne, but turned to writing plays and scripts for films and television. His first works to receive recognition were *The Removalists* (1972) and *Don's Party* (1973); other successes include *The Club* (1977) and *The Perfectionist* (1982). Mostly leaning on the male-oriented Aus-tralian 'yuppie' class, his plays are much of a kind, though *What If You Died Tomorrow* (1974) shows the serious–comic side of a wri-ter's life. Some of his stage works have sub-sequently been filmed, and he has also written other film scripts, including those for *Gallipoli* (1981) and *Phar Lap* (1983).

WILLIAMSON, Henry
(1895–1977)

English author, born in Bedfordshire. After service in World War I he became a journalist, but turned to farming in Norfolk and eventually settled in a cottage on Exmoor. He wrote several semi-autobiographical novels, including his long series *A Chronicle of Ancient Sunlight* on the life story of the hero, Phillip Maddison. He is best known, however, for his classic nature stories, staring with *The Peregrine's Saga* (1923) and *The Old Stag* (1926). He achieved enduring fame with *Tarka the Otter* (1927, Hawthornden Prize) and *Salar the Salmon* (1935). His trenchant anti-war novel *A Patriot's Progress* (1930) was much admired, but his support for Mosley and Hitler greatly damaged his reputation. He wrote two autobiographical works, *The Wet Flanders Plain* (1929) and *A Clear Water Stream* (1958), and a biography of his friend T E Lawrence (1941).

▷H F West, *The Dreamer of Devon* (1932)

WILLIAMSON, Thames (Ross)
(1894–)

American novelist and non-fiction writer, born in Ohio. Williamson is astonishingly prolific and has used as many as five pseudonyms, including 'S. S. Smith'. He has one of those classic fly-leaf biographies: ran away from home at 14 to join the circus and became a hobo, etc. His earliest novel was *Run, Sheep, Run* (1925) and he has written a number of textbooks, including an *Introduction to Sociology* (1926). More mature works include *Far North Country* (1944), about Alaska, and *The Gladiators* (1948).

WILLINGHAM, Calder Baynard, Jr
(1922–)

American novelist. He was born in Atlanta, Georgia, and educated in the South at Charleston and Charlottesville. His first novel, *End as a Man* (1947), appeared in a year when a number of the post-war literary lions were making their debut, and he was catapulted into prominence. Throughout his career—later novels include *Geraldine Bradshaw* (1950), *Reach to the Stars* (1951) and his best, *To Eat a Peach* (1955)—Willingham struck a balance between the hard, action-driven dictates of the bestseller list and a more contemplative style that offered striking insights into human motivation. His short stories, *The Gates of Hell* (1951), are rather disappointing and gave warning of the diminishing of his powers that was to set in after *To Eat a Peach*. Like many novelists, Willingham struck a pact with Hollywood, writing screenplays for Stanley Kubrick's *Paths of Glory* (1957), as well as *The Vikings* (1958), *One-Eyed Jacks*

(1961), *The Graduate* (1967) and *Little Big Man* (1970).

WILLIS, Nathaniel Parker
(1806–67)

American editor and writer, born in Portland, Maine. He published several volumes of poetry, founded the *American Monthly Magazine* in Boston (1829) and in 1831 visited Europe, and contributed to the *New York Mirror* his *Pencillings by the Way*. Appointed *attaché* to the American legation at Paris, he visited Greece and Turkey, and returned to England in 1837. He contributed to the London *New Monthly* his *Inklings of Adventure* (collected 1836), and published *Letters from under a Bridge* (1840). In 1844 he engaged in editing the *Daily Mirror*, revisited Europe, and published *Dashes at Life with a Free Pencil* (1845). He returned to New York in 1846, and established the *Home Journal*, in which much of his work first appeared. His sister, Sara Payson Willis, 'Fanny Fern' (1811–72), married to the biographer James Parton, was a popular writer.

▷C P Aulzer, *Nathaniel Willis* (1969)

WILLIS, Sara Payson, pseud Fanny Fern
(1811–72)

American essayist, columnist and children's author, the sister of **N P Willis**. Her *Fern Leaves from Fanny's Portfolio* (1853) which, despite its fey title, was witty and acerbic, sold over 70 000 copies in its first year. The first follow-up appeared in 1854. Sara Willis's talent for satire was put to good effect the following year when, enraged by rumours concerning her rakish brother, she wrote *Ruth Hall*, a novel which does not spare members of her own family.

WILLS, William Gorman
(1828–91)

Irish playwright and poet, born in Kilkenny County. He studied at Trinity College, Dublin, and started as an artist, and was a successful portrait painter. His *Man o'Airlie* (1866) was a huge success on the stage, followed by *Charles I* (1872), *Jane Shore* (1876), *Olivia* (1878) and *Claudian* (1885), as well as a version of *Faust* (1885). He also wrote novels, but considered verse a higher literary form. His poems include a long work, *Melchior* (1885), and his ballads include 'I'll sing thee Songs of Araby'.

WILLUMSEN, Dorrit
(1940–)

Danish novelist, short-story writer and poet, born in Copenhagen. Her first book of short stories (1965) established her as a notable modernist with conspicuous stylistic skills

The novel *Da* (1968, 'Then') explores the gap between a child's perspective on the world and the adult one, while *the krydderi acryl salær græshopper* (1970, 'tea spice acrylic fee grasshoppers') and *Modellen Coppelia* (1973, 'Coppelia the Model') transcend the traditional boundaries between genres, the former raising issues of motherhood by means of a collage technique, and the latter combining poetry and short stories to illuminate the reification of woman. In the novel *Programmeret til kærlighed* (1981, 'Programmed for Love'), the character of a living doll is used to emphasize the conventional concept of woman. *Marie* (1983, Eng trans 1986) is a historical novel about Madame Tussaud.

▷A B Richard, *På sporet af den tabte hverdag. Om Dorrit Willumsens forfatterskab og den moderne virkelighed* (1979)

WILSON, Alexander
(1766–1813)

Scottish-born American ornithologist, born in Paisley, the son of a prosperous weaver, and regarded as the 'father of American ornithology'. He worked as a weaver from the age of 13, and as a travelling pedlar. He also wrote nature poetry and verses about life in the weaving sheds, and published *Poems* (1790) and *Watty and Meg* (1792). He was prosecuted for a libellous poem against the mill-owners, which he denied writing, but was jailed for 18 months. In 1794 he emigrated to the USA, and became a schoolteacher in rural schools in New Jersey and Philadelphia. Encouraged by a neighbour, the naturalist William Bartram (son of the botanist John Bartram), he decided to devote himself to ornithology. He made several journeys across America, collecting species and drawing them, and wrote a poetic account of his first journey, an excursion on foot to Niagara Falls, in *The Foresters, A Poem* (1805). He had a long-running feud with the ornithologist John James Audubon. In 1806 he was employed on the American edition of *Rees's Cyclopaedia*, and prevailed on the publisher to undertake an illustrated *American Ornithology* (7 vols, 1808–14); the 8th and 9th volumes were completed after his death. Wilson's Storm-Petrel and Wilson's Phalarope were named in his honour.

▷J Wilson, *Alexander Wilson, Poet-Novelist* (1906)

WILSON, A(ndrew) N(orman)
(1950–)

English novelist, biographer, critic and journalist, born in Stone, Staffordshire, and educated at Rugby School and Oxford. Since publishing his first novel, *The Sweets of Pimlico* (1977), Wilson has maintained a hugely prolific output. The earlier novels were comedies of manners, but in works such as *The Healing Art* (1980), in which a patient is mistakenly diagnosed as having cancer, and *Wise Virgin* (1982), dealing with the relationship between an academic and his daughter, he looks more closely at specific moral issues. Later works are perceptive, waspish, atmospheric and topical, and include *A Bottle in the Smoke* (1989), in which a young man seeks fame and art in the Soho of the 1950s, and *The Vicar of Sorrows* (1993), in which a disenchanted vicar falls for a young, female New Age traveller. His biographies include *Sir Walter Scott* (1980), *Milton* (1983), *Tolstoy* (1987) and the controversial *Jesus* (1992). He has frequently given the public impression of being a High Church Conservative, and can be a harsh literary and ethical commentator.

WILSON, Sir Angus Frank Johnstone
(1913–91)

English writer, born in Bexhill, Sussex, the son of an English father and a South African mother. He was educated at Westminster School and Merton College, Oxford. He joined the staff of the British Museum library in 1937. He began writing in 1946 and rapidly established a reputation with his brilliant collection of short stories, *The Wrong Set* (1949), satirizing the more aimless sections of prewar middle-class society. *Such Darling Dodos* (1950), *For Whom the Cloche Tolls* (1953) and *A Bit off the Map* (1957) added to his prestige, and in 1955 he gave up his office of deputy-superintendent of the British Museum reading room to devote himself solely to writing. The novels *Hemlock and After* (1952) and *Anglo-Saxon Attitudes* (1956) were both bestsellers, and his later novels, including *The Old Men in the Zoo* (1961), *Late Call* (1965) and *No Laughing Matter* (1967), an ambitious family chronicle of the egocentric Matthews family spanning the 20th century, also received critical acclaim. His later novels include *As If By Magic* (1973) and *Setting the World on Fire* (1980). He also wrote one play, *The Mulberry Bush* (1955). He was Professor of English Literature at the University of East Anglia from 1966 to 1978.

▷J L Halio, *Angus Wilson* (1964)

WILSON, August
(1945–)

American playwright, born in Pittsburgh into a black working-class family. He dropped out of high school, but began to write poetry in his twenties, then turned to drama. His work focuses on black American life in both historical and contemporary settings, and draws on a wide variety of disparate technical and stylistic devices. He has been lionized as an original by some critics, and rejected by others, and has twice been awarded the Pulitzer Prize for Drama, for *Fences* in 1987 and *The Piano Lesson* in 1990. His other works include *Ma Rainey's Black Bottom* (1984) and *Joe Turner's Come and Gone* (1981).

WILSON, Colin Henry
(1931–)

English novelist, critic and commentator, born in Leicester, who held a variety of jobs, from tax collector to hospital porter, before turning full-time to writing. His first book, *The Outsider* (1956), a study of alienation, precisely caught (or was caught by) the literary spirit of the times, for it followed in the wake of **Kingsley Amis**'s *Lucky Jim* and appeared in the same year as **John Osborne**'s *Look Back in Anger*. Nothing Wilson has written since has drawn equal attention, although he has maintained a stream of novels, including violent thrillers of the 'psychological' genre, such as *The Mind Parasites* (1967) and *The Janus Murder Case* (1984). Several of his volumes of non-fiction deal with the paranormal and the occult.
▷H Ritchie, *Success Stories* (1988)

WILSON, Edmund
(1895–1972)

American literary critic, social commentator and novelist, born in Red Bank, New Jersey. He was educated at Princeton, became a journalist with *Vanity Fair* and Editor of the *New Republic* (1926–31), and was chief book reviewer for the *New Yorker*. A lively, waspish critic of other writers, his own fiction, of which *Memoirs of Hecate Country* (1946) is the most notable example, is largely forgotten. But few critics have caused such a stir as he, and he was more listened to than most. *Axel's Castle* (1931), a study of Symbolist literature, is a landmark, but *To the Finland Station* (1940), an account of the origins of the Bolshevik Revolution, and *The Wound and the Bow* (1941), a study of the relation between psychic malaise and creativity, are no less significant. In *Patriotic Gore: Studies in the Literature of the Civil War* (1962) he surveyed in detail the writers of the period. Over a wide-ranging oeuvre and argumentative life he published on many subjects and in a variety of forms, encompassing plays, articles, correspondence (see that with **Nabokov**) and, in *The Scrolls from the Dead Sea* (1955), for which he learned Hebrew, a contentious but illuminating guide to a complex subject. Various memoirs detailing his life have appeared; he married four times, the third marriage being to the novelist **Mary McCarthy**, whose own turbulent career he defended even after their relationship had foundered.
▷D Castronovo, *Edmund Wilson* (1984)

WILSON, Ethel
(1888–1980)

Canadian novelist and short-story writer, born in South Africa: her childhood was spent in England after the death of her mother, and in Vancouver with her grandmother, after the death of her father in 1898. As a novelist, she handles the emotional entanglements of her characters with great skill, focusing on the sacrificial and selfish nature of human love. Her fiction is characterized by a compelling and distinctive Canadian landscape, into which these characters are woven. Her first novel, *Hetty Dorval* (1947), was followed by *The Innocent Traveller* (1949), *The Equations of Love* (1952), *Swamp Angel* (1954) and *Love and Salt Water* (1956), her final novel. She also wrote many short stories, collected as *Mrs Golightly and Other Stories* (1961).
▷ *Papers from the 'Ethel Wilson Symposium'*, University of Ottawa (1981)

WILSON, Harriet
(c.1807–c.1870)

American writer, born in Fredericksburg, Virginia. She was author of the first book by an Afro–American woman—*Our Nig (Sketches from the Life of a Free Black)* (1859). Written in the style of the sentimental 19th-century novel, it tells the story of a mixed marriage. When the book's authorship was first discovered, oversimplistic parallels were drawn between Wilson's own life and the story she told. Since the book's reprinting in 1983 Wilson has been given the credit due for her stylistic intelligence and the cool way in which she handles the power struggles at play in a nominally Christian family.

WILSON, Harry Leon
(1867–1939)

American novelist, humorist and playwright, born in Illinois. Wilson joined the staff of *Puck* in 1892 and became its editor four years later. He left in 1902, and began to produce his best work. He is mainly remembered for *Ruggles of Red Gap* (1915), a comical novel about an English butler in the American West, made into a film starring Charles Laughton in 1935. Wilson became rich when he sold the rights to *Merton of the Movies* (1922), the story of a small-town clerk making it to Hollywood. His most notable stage success was a play written in collaboration with his friend **Booth Tarkington**, *The Man from Home* (1907), which ran for six years.

WILSON, John, pseud Christopher North
(1785–1854)

Scottish critic and essayist, born in Paisley. He studied at Glasgow University and Magdalen College, Oxford, where he won the

WILSON, John Mackay

Newdigate Prize for poetry and gained a reputation as an outstanding athlete. In 1807 he bought an estate at Elleray, Westmorland, and became acquainted with the Lake District circle of poets (**Wordsworth**, **Coleridge**, **De Quincey**, **Southey**). Here he wrote three long poems, *The Isle of Palms* (1812), *The Magic Mirror* (1812, addressed to Sir **Walter Scott**) and *The City of the Plague* (1816). Having lost his estate through an uncle's mismanagement, he settled in Edinburgh as an advocate in 1815. In 1817 he joined **John Gibson Lockhart** and **James Hogg** in launching *Blackwood's Magazine*. Despite lacking any qualification for the post, he was appointed Professor of Moral Philosophy at Edinburgh (1820–51) in succession to Thomas Brown. As contributing editor of *Blackwood's* he wrote several notable series under the pseudonym 'Christopher North', such as *Noctes Ambrosianae* (1822–35), and a series of rural short stories, *Lights and Shadows of Scottish Life* (1822). He also published two novels, *The Trials of Margaret Lyndsay* (1823) and *The Foresters* (1825). His *Works* (1855–8) were edited by his son-in-law, James Frederick Ferrier.
▷E Swan, *Christopher North* (1934)

WILSON, John Mackay
(1804–35)

Scottish writer and editor, born in Tweedmouth. He is known for his *Tales of the Borders* (6 vols, 1834–40), originally issued in weekly numbers, and continued after his death for his widow with Alexander Leighton (1800–74) as editor.

WILSON, Lanford
(1937–)

American playwright, born in Lebanon, Missouri, whose first full-length play, *Balm in Gilead* (1964), is set among the characters haunting a seedy all-night coffee shop. A similar location, that of a down-at-heel city hotel, forms the backdrop for one of his most successful dramas, *The Hot l Baltimore* (sic, 1973). These are sympathetic and shrewdly observed plays; later pieces are sharper, such as *The 5th of July* (1978), in which a group of former student radicals meet at the home of Ken Talley, a crippled Vietnam veteran. The play is the first part of a series including *Talley's Folly* (1979, Pulitzer Prize) and *Talley and Son* (1985), looking at generations of the Talley family. *Burn This* (1987), the most publicized of his more recent plays, is a violent, bravura piece, and deals with a man calling at his dead brother's former home and compulsively falling for his grieving female partner.

WILSON, Robert
(?1553–1600)

English actor and playwright, of whom few biographical details are known. During the early 1570s he became a member of the Earl of Leicester's Men, an acting company, and in 1583 appeared in the company of Queen Elizabeth's Men. Three plays survive which he is known to have written either wholly, or on which he was the dominant collaborator. These are *The Ladies of London* (c.1581), *The Three Lords and Three Ladies of London* (c.1589) and *Prophecy* (c.1594). All are robust dramas with elements of comedy and satire.

WILSON, Sloan
(1920–)

American novelist, born in Connecticut. He is famous for *The Man in the Grey Flannel Suit* (1955), but is usually classed as a merely popular writer; a few have made higher claims for him. *The Man in the Grey Flannel Suit*, about a business executive called Tom Rath, is a kind of plea, sometimes touching, for 'ordinary values'. Books such as *All the Best People* (1970) are readable, untidy, and deliberately unsubtle; a critic thought that in his admiration for the middle classes Wilson created an effect different from the one he intended: 'not without a certain horror'.

WINCHILSEA, Anne Finch, Countess of, née **Kingsmill**
(1661–1720)

English poet, born in Sidmonton, near Southampton. She was daughter of Sir William Kingsmill, and in 1684 she married Heneage Finch, Earl of Winchilsea (from 1712). Her longest poem, a Pindaric ode called *The Spleen*, was printed in 1701; her *Miscellany Poems* in 1713. She was a friend of **Pope**, **Swift** and **Gay**, and her nature poems were admired by **Wordsworth** in his *Lyrical Ballads*.
▷K M Rogers, in S Gilbert and S Gubar, *Shakespeare's Sisters* (1979)

WINKLER, Eugen Gotlob
(1912–36)

German painter, story writer, poet and critic, born in Zürich, son of an engineer. Known only as an essayist and frustrated artist who could not equal the achievements of his admired Van Gogh, he committed suicide in Munich, whereupon his friends discovered his work, which they published in two volumes. He admired **Ernst Jünger**, and offers an example of extreme late decadence and 'art for art's sake' nihilism; unfortunately he was possessed of only a minor talent, and this, together with persecution by Nazi officials and inability to fend for himself in ordinary life, persuaded him to kill himself. The chief influence upon him was **Paul Valéry**.

WINTERS, (Arthur) Yvor
(1900–68)

American critic and poet, born in Chicago. He was educated at Chicago, Colorado, and Stanford universities, and in 1949 was appointed Professor of English at Stanford. His verse was published in *The Immobile Wind* (1921), *The Bare Hills* (1927), *The Proof* (1930), *The Journey* (1931), *Before Disaster* (1934) and *The Giant Weapon* (1943). A *Collected Poems* was published in 1952, winning the Bollingen Prize. However, he is remembered primarily as a quirky, irascible critic, anti the expressionists and with a sharp eye for detail. Significant books are *Maule's Curse* (1938), *In Defence of Reason* (1947), *The Function of Criticism* (1957) and *Uncollected Essays and Reviews* (1976).
▷T Comito, *In Defense of Winters* (1986)

WINTERSON, Jeanette
(1959–)

English novelist, born in Manchester who, after graduating from Oxford, worked in London fringe theatre and publishing. Her first novel, the autobiographical *Oranges Are Not the Only Fruit* (1985), recounts an upbringing as the daughter of fundamentalist Christian parents and the emergence of her lesbian sensibilities. It was critically acclaimed, as was *Sexing the Cherry* (1989), a far more experimental novel set in a fantastical 17th century. *Written On the Body* (1992) was followed in 1994 by *Art and Lies*. A confident, often provocative writer, her work is deliberately challenging.

WISEMAN, Adele
(1928–)

Canadian novelist, born in Winnipeg. Wiseman's parents had fled the Ukraine and her first novel, *The Sacrifice* (1956), was an exploration of the immigrant mentality. Wiseman has not been prolific. *Crackpot* (1974) had as protagonist a strapping whore. *Memoirs of a Book Molesting Childhood and Other Essays* (1987) contains autobiographical material.

WISTER, Owen
(1860–1938)

American author, born in Philadelphia. He took a music degree at Harvard and intended to be a composer, but won fame with his novel of cowboy life in Wyoming, *The Virginian* (1902), and other books, including *Lin McLean* (1898) and *Lady Baltimore* (1906).
▷D Payne, *Owen Wister: chronicler of the West, gentleman of the East* (1985)

WITHEFORD, Hubert
(1921–)

New Zealand poet, a member of the 'Wellington Group' of the 1950s. His early work was included in *New Zealand New Writing* during World War II and later collected in *Shadow of the Flame: Poems 1942–7* (1950), followed by *The Falcon Mask* in 1951. Other books are *The Lightning Makes a Difference* (1962) and *A Native, Perhaps Beautiful* (1967). The best of his verse shows an awareness of his natural environment and relates it to an 'inner landscape'.

WITHER, George
(1588–1667)

English poet and pamphleteer, born in Bentworth, Hampshire. He studied at Magdalen College, Oxford (1604–6), and entered Lincoln's Inn in 1615. For his *Abuses Stript and Whipt* (1613) he was imprisoned. In prison he wrote a book of five pastorals, *The Shepherd's Hunting* (1615), followed by a love elegy, *Fidelia* (1617). It is supposed that his satire addressed to the king (1614), together with the Earl of Pembroke's intercession, procured his release. In 1621 appeared the satirical *Wither's Motto*, a curious piece of self-confession, which landed him in jail again. His finest poem is *Fair Virtue, or the Mistress of Philarete* (1622). There followed his *Hymns and Songs of the Church* (1623), *Psalms of David translated* (1631), *Emblems* (1634) and *Hallelujah* (1641). Now a fiery Puritan, in 1642 he sold his estate to raise a troop of horse for parliament, but was taken prisoner. Later Cromwell made him major-general in Surrey and master of the Statute Office. At the Restoration (1660) he lost his position and property, and, on suspicion of having written the *Vox Vulgi*, a satire on the parliament of 1661, was imprisoned. He was released in 1663. His poetry fell into almost complete oblivion, but the praises of **Robert Southey**, Sir Egerton Brydges, Hallam, and **Charles Lamb** in particular revived interest in his work.
▷C S Hansby, *The Literary Career of George Wither* (1969)

WITKIEWICZ, Stanislaw Ignacy
(1885–1939)

Polish novelist, playwright and painter, born in Cracow, universally known as 'Witkacy'. He was one of the most original minds of his generation, and only now are his novels beginning to be fully appreciated. He killed himself when the Nazis invaded his country. His novel *Nienasycenie* (1930, Eng trans *Insatiability*, 1975), is a dystopia worthy to rank with those of **Zamyatin**, **Orwell** and **Huxley**, but is subtler and more complex. The

English translation is a tour de force. It has been said of him that 'there is a terrible sanity in his self-induced madness'.

▷Introduction to translation, above (1975)

WITTENWEILER, Heinrich

(fl.1420)

Swiss poet, from Wyl. He seems to have been a wealthy burger, and is author of a long, bawdy satire, *Der Ring*. It pokes fun at peasants, their coarseness and crude living, though the gentry do not emerge unscathed either, as a country wedding causes ructions and intrigue in the local community.

WITTIG, Monique

(1935–)

French novelist and critic. A radical lesbian and founder of the group Féministes Révolutionnaires, she gained notoriety in 1978 by claiming that 'Lesbians are not women', by which she meant that the conventional man-/woman opposition is inadequate for the gender analysis feminism should be undertaking. In *The Straight Mind and Other Essays* (1992) she describes her own position as 'Materialist Lesbianism' (despite the idealism), believing that 'it is oppression that creates sex'. Her avant-garde utopian novel *Les guérillères* (1969) intersperses scenes of an all-woman community fighting against men with otherwise blank pages containing series of women's names in capitals.

▷E Ostrovsky, *A Constant Journey: The Fiction of Monique Wittig* (1991)

WODEHOUSE, Sir P(elham) G(renville)

(1881–1975)

English novelist, born in Guildford. He was educated at Dulwich College, and worked for the Hong Kong and Shanghai Bank for two years before beginning to earn a living as a journalist and story writer, writing the 'By the Way' column in the *Globe*. He also contributed to a series of school stories in a magazine for boys, the *Captain*, in which 'Psmith' first made an appearance. Going to America before World War I, he sold a serial to the *Saturday Evening Post* and for a quarter of a century almost all his books appeared first in that magazine. He was co-author and writer of the lyrics to 18 musical comedies, including *Kissing Time*. He married in 1914. World War II blighted his otherwise stainless reputation. Captured by the Germans at Le Touquet, he was interned then released but not allowed to leave Germany. Foolishly he agreed to make broadcasts for the Germans and though they were harmless he was branded as a traitor. Writing in his defence, **Orwell** observed that 'The general upshot of the talks...was that he had not been ill-treated and bore no

malice'. Eventually his name was cleared but he made America his home where the climate allowed him to indulge his passion for golf. He became an American citizen in 1955. His copious oeuvre—he wrote over 100 books—falls into three well-marked periods; the school stories which include *The Pothunters* (1902) and *The Gold Bat* (1904); the American period, during which he wrote *Psmith, Journalist* (1915), *The Indiscretions of Archie* (1921) and *Piccadilly Jim* (1917); and what might be called the country house period in which can be included a plethora of titles set in country mansions, bachelor pads in the metropolis and exclusive golf clubs. It is to this group that characters like Lord Emsworth, Gussie Fink-Nottle, Bertie Wooster and his legendary valet, Jeeves, belong. Of his many felicitous titles, *Right Ho, Jeeves* (1934), *Quick Service* (1940) and *The Mating Season* (1949) stand out. Wodehouse summed up his attitude to writing thus: 'I believe there are two ways of writing novels. One is mine, making a sort of musical comedy without music and ignoring real life altogether; the other is going deep down into life and not caring a damn'.

▷R Usborne, *Wodehouse at Work* (1961)

WOESTIJNE, Karel van de

(1879–1929)

Belgian (Flemish) poet and editor, born in Ghent. He was one of the chief members of the literary movement Van Nu en Straks ('Today and Tomorrow'), an individualistic, internationalistic and liberal tendency to which **Buysse**, **Streuvels** and **Teirlinck** subscribed. Woestijne was its great and most gifted poet, and his work has not yet received full recognition outside Belgium and the Netherlands. He has been authoritatively described as 'the only ... major twentieth-century poet in Dutch besides Achterberg'. Influenced by **Kloos**, **George** and **Rilke**, his poetry explores his own conceit of being both a hazel-nut and the greedy worm within it. There is no good English translation, but *Poèmes choisis* (1964) is a selection in a good French translation. He also wrote symbolic stories important in his literature.

WOIWODE, Larry Alfred

(1941–)

American novelist, story writer and poet, born in Carrington, North Dakota. His first novel, *What I'm Going to Do, I Think* (1970), attracted little attention, but his second, *Beyond the Bedroom Wall: A Family Album* (1975), earned him a high reputation. It is a novel of the midwest, spanning four generations, about the family established by a German immigrant of 1881. *Poppa John* (1981), on a much smaller scale, describes a pathetic old television actor who spouts pious rigmarole. Woiwode collected his poems in *Even Tide* (1977).

WOLCOT, John, pseud Peter Pindar
(1738–1819)

English satirist, born in Dodbrooke, Devon. He studied medicine for seven years in London, took his MD at Aberdeen (1767) and, going to Jamaica, became physiciangeneral of the island. He returned to England to take holy orders, but soon started medical practice at Truro. Here he discovered the talents of the young painter John Opie, and went with him in 1780 to London, to devote himself to writing audacious satires in verse. His 60 or 70 poetical pamphlets (1778–1818) include *The Lousiad, The Apple-dumplings and a King, Whitbread's Brewery visited by their Majesties, Bozzy and Piozzi* and *Lyrical Odes* on the Royal Academy Exhibitions. Although witty and fluent, his works were coarse and ephemeral.
▷T Girton, *Drama with Two Aunts* (1959)

WOLF, Christa
(1929–)

German novelist, whose earlier career was spent in the Eastern bloc, a fact which has significantly restricted her publishing career. She was born in Landsberg, Warthe, and educated at Leipzig and Jena universities. Many of her books received only limited circulation in East Germany. The most important of them, *The Quest for Christa T* (1976), was published in English translation. Her novel/essay *Kassandra: Erzahlung* (1983) appeared in English two years later. The *Mosakuer Novelle* have not so far been translated. Wolf examines the fate of personality in totalitarian situations, by which she means something larger and more universal than the specific political situation in her homeland.

WOLF, Friedrich
1883–1953)

German dramatist from Neuwied, an early communist who emigrated in 1933 and returned to East Germany in 1945. He was for long generally considered to be second only to **Bertolt Brecht** in importance in his chosen country. His first plays were expressionist, but his theatrical successes came with more conventional drama, particularly with *Professor Mamlocks Ausweg* 1935), made into a famous Soviet film, *Professor Mamlock*, the powerful account of a Jewish surgeon driven to suicide by his Nazi oppressors. His final plays are more socialist realist in type, but at the end of his life he publicly reproached himself for 'abandoning the fight against tyranny'.

▷H F Garten, *Modern German Drama* (1964)

WOLFE, Charles
(1791–1823)

Irish poet and clergyman, born in Blackhall, County Kildare. He was educated at Winchester, and Trinity College, Dublin. He took holy orders in 1817 and became curate of Ballyclog, County Tyrone, and Donoughmore, County Down (1818). He is remembered for his poem *The Burial of Sir John Moore at Corunna*, which appeared anonymously in 1817 and at once caught the admiration of the public.

WOLFE, Humbert
(1885–1940)

English poet and critic, born in Milan, Italy. In 1908 he entered the Civil Service, becoming in 1938 deputy secretary to the Ministry of Labour. He published *London Sonnets* (1919), *Lampoons* (1925), *Requiem* (1927), and several other collections of verse, all marked by deep feeling and meticulous craftsmanship. His critical writings included *Notes on English Verse Satire* (1929) and studies of **Tennyson**, **Robert Herrick**, **Shelley** and **George Moore**.

WOLFE, Thomas Clayton
(1900–38)

American novelist, born at Asheville, North Carolina, into a large family in an overcrowed house. His father, an alcoholic, was a skilled stone-cutter who sculpted tombstones for a living. In 1904 his mother decided to open a boarding-house in St Louis during the World's Fair, but her attempt at independence ended with the death of one of her sons. But in 1906 she opened 'The Old Kentucky Home', taking with her her youngest son, leaving the other children with their father. Thomas was educated at the University of North Carolina and at Harvard. His writing career began abortively as a playwright, and in 1925 he embarked on a turbulent affair with Mrs Aline Bernstein, a maternal figure who did much to encourage his writing, particularly his first novel *Look Homeward, Angel* (1929), which was patently autobiographical. The massive, shapeless manuscript of *Of Time and the River* (1935), its sequel, was honed into shape by Max Perkins, his editor at Scribner's. Both these novels feature Eugene Gant, Wolfe's alter ego. He later changed publishers and *The Web and the Rock* (1939) and *You Can't Go Home Again* (1940) were published posthumously. Prolix, careless, bombastic and overambitious, he nevertheless wrote vividly of people and places. Some assert that his best work is to be found in the stories in *From Death to Morning* (1935). His *Letters* were published in 1956.

▷C H Holman, *Thomas Wolfe* (1960)

WOLFE, Tom (Thomas Kennerley)
(1931–)

American journalist, pop-critic and novelist, born in Richmond, Virginia. Graduating from Washington and Lee University, he received his doctorate in American Studies from Yale University. Later he worked as a reporter for the *Springfield Union*, *The Washington Post* and the New York *Herald Tribune*. A proponent of the New Journalism, his style is distinctive, hyper-clever and narcissistic. A fashion-leader and follower, he has written a number of books with eye-catching titles: *The Electric Kool-Aid Acid Test* (1968), about **Ken Kesey** and the Merry Pranksters, *Radical Chic & Mau-Mauing the Flak Catchers* (1970) and *The Kandy-Kolored Tangerine-Flake Streamline Baby* (1965). Much of his work previously appeared in periodicals like *The Rolling Stone*, as did his only novel, *The Bonfire of the Vanities* (1988), which was a bestseller.

WOLFF, Tobias
(1945–)

American short-story writer and novelist, born in Birmingham, Alabama. He signed up for the army while still a schoolboy, and was a paratrooper for four years, part of which time was spent on active service in Vietnam. His first collection of short stories, *In the Garden of the North American Martyrs*, was published in 1981, but it was the publication of his austere, disciplined novella *The Barracks Thief* in 1984 which earned him a place in the front rank of American writers. He has subsequently published a further volume of short stories, *Back in the World* (1985), and an autobiography, *This Boy's Life* (1989).

WOLFF-BEKKER, Elizabeth, originally Betje Dekker
(1739–1804)

Dutch novelist, poet, critic and translator, born in Flushing. In 1759 she married a parson 30 years older than herself, and until his death in 1777 studied literature (of which she had an extensive and profound knowledge), wrote amusing verse, and indulged her admiration for **Rousseau**. Then she set up house with **Agatha Deken**, with whom she wrote epistolary novels in the style of **Richardson**. *Willem Leevend* (1784–5), her masterpiece (for it was she who did most of the real work), has been described as superior even to Richardson, on account of her refusal to resort to melodrama. It has been pronounced to be too

long; but this is to fail to see the significance of its lengthy and often satirical theological passages. In fact *Willem Leevend* is, as has been said, 'a part of world literature', and a translation is seriously overdue: acute psychologically, sardonic, tolerant, humane, it is one of the great novels written by women, and remains to be discovered by English-speaking feminists. In 1788 Wolff-Bekker, who sometimes used the pseudonym 'Sylvania', had to go into exile in France with her friend Deken; when 10 years later they could return, they were forced to do hack translations. They died within a few weeks of each other.

▷H C M Ghijsen, *Boeket voor Betje en Aagje* (1954)

WOLFRAM VON ESCHENBACH
(fl. beginning of 13th century)

German poet, born near Anspach in Bavaria. He lived some time in the Warburg near Eisenach, at the court of the Count of Thuringia. As well as *Parzival* (Eng trans 1894) he left *Die Lyrik*, seven love songs, a short epic, *Willehalm*, and two fragments called *Titurel*. The *Parzival* is an epic, having for its main theme the history of the Grail, and is one of the most notable poems of the Middle Ages. From it Wagner derived the libretto of his opera *Parsifal*.

▷M F Riley, *Medieval German Love Lyrics* (1969)

WOLKER, Jiri
(1900–24)

Czech 'proletarian' poet who was early struck down by tuberculosis. Like **Alexander Blok**, he could combine love of Lenin with love of Christ. But his visionary poems and ballads, imbued with love of the poor and hope for a Utopian future, transcend categories. His work awaits complete translation into English.

▷A French, *The Poets of Prague* (1969)

WOLKERS, Jan Hendrick
(1925–)

Dutch novelist, dramatist (and painter and sculptor) from Oegstgeest, who was a dominant voice in his literature during the 1960s and 1970s. He was notorious amongst conservatives for the apparently 'pornographic' nature of his writing. Many of his novels were translated, including *Een roos van vlees* (1963, Eng trans *A Rose of Flesh*, 1967), about a couple whose negligence leads to their daughter's being scalded, and *Horrible Tango* (1967, Eng trans *The Horrible Tango*, 1970), based on his brother's life and death. He has not yet fully realized his considerable gifts.

WOLOSZYNOWSKI, Julian
(1898–)

Polish novelist, born in Serby, initially a poet. His work, in particular his meticulous novel about the romantic poet **Slowacki** (1928), has been described as 'deplorably underrated in official criticism' by the critic Jerzy Peterkiewicz, but no one has yet responded to this enthusiasm. *Roc 1863* (1931) is an equally meticulous reconstruction of a revolutionary year in Polish history, illustrated with contemporary pictures.

WONGAR, Banumbir or Birimbir,
originally **Sreten Bozic**
(1936–)

Yugoslav-born writer, who emigrated to Australia in 1960. He was originally promoted as an 'aboriginal' author. His early short stories appeared under various names during the 1970s, collected as *The Sinner* (1972) and *The Trackers* (1978). His true origins were disclosed in 1981 but his trilogy of novels, *Karan* (1985), *Walg* (1986) and *Gabo Djara* (1987), show remarkable sympathy and an understanding of a marginal culture.

WOOD, Mrs Henry, née Ellen Price
(1814–87)

English novelist, born in Worcester, the daughter of a manufacturer. A spinal disease confined her to bed or a sofa for most of her life. She married Henry Wood, a ship agent living in France, but returned to England with him in 1860 and settled in Norwood. After his death in 1866 she settled in London, and wrote for magazines. Her second published novel, *East Lynne* (1861), had an immense success. She never rose above the commonplace in her many novels, but showed some power in the analysis of character in her anonymous *Johnny Ludlow* stories (1874–80). In 1867 she bought the monthly *Argosy*, which she edited, and her novels went on appearing in it long after her death.

WOODCOCK, George
1912–)

Canadian critic, biographer, poet, dramatist, sometime anarchist. Woodcock was for many years in England, and edited the periodical *Now*, knew **George Orwell**, about whom he wrote a book (*The Crystal Spirit: George Orwell*, 1966), and was active in left-wing and anarchist circles. He returned to Canada soon after World War II, and became one of its leading interpreters, writing books on all aspects of it. **Julian Symons**, who had known him well, thought that he had written 'charming and poignant poems', but that when the war ended he 'lost his poetic vision'. *Selected Poems* (1967) is his most representative collection. He is now best known as a critic and an interpreter.
▷P Hughes, *George Woodcock* (1974)

WOOLF, (Adeline) Virginia, née Stephen
(1882–1941)

English novelist, critic and essayist, born in London, daughter of Sir Leslie Stephen. She was close to her sister, Vanessa Bell, and was from an early age the family story-teller. She was taught at home, by her parents and governesses, and received an uneven education. In 1891 she started the *Hyde Park Gate News* which was read by grown-ups and appeared weekly until 1895. In it appeared her first efforts at fiction. Her father died in 1904 and the family moved to Bloomsbury where the family formed the nucleus of the Bloomsbury Group, comprising—among others—Keynes, **E M Forster**, Roger Fry, Duncan Grant and **Lytton Strachey**: philosophers, writers and artists. A year later she began her long association with the *Times Literary Supplement*. She married Leonard Woolf in 1912 and her first novel, *The Voyage Out*, was published in 1915. It was greeted cordially and though realistic there were hints of the lyricism which would later become her hallmark. But already her health was poor and she suffered recurring depressions and had attempted suicide in 1913. In 1917, she and Leonard formed the Hogarth Press, partly for therapeutic reasons. Its first publication was *Two Stories*, one by each of the founders. Her second novel, *Night and Day*, appeared in 1919. Again its mode is realistic, focussing on Katherine Hilberry, whose activities in a literary milieu are counterpointed with those of her friend Mary who is involved in the women's movement. Some critics still think it her best work. *Jacob's Room* followed in 1922 and marked a turning point in her fiction, and shows her experimenting with narrative and language. Well-received, it made her a celebrity. In 1924 she went to Cambridge to speak on 'Character in Modern Fiction'; the result was *Mr Bennett and Mrs Brown*, an attack on the 'Georgian novelists' **Arnold Bennett**, **John Galsworthy** and **H G Wells**, and can be read as her own aesthetic manifesto. Regarded now as an archetypal Modernist, she published in six years the three novels that have made her one of the century's great writers; *Mrs Dalloway* (1925), *To the Lighthouse* (1927) and *The Waves* (1931). But her work took its toll on her health and though she wrote prolifically she was beset by deep depressions and debilitating headaches. Throughout the 1930s she worked on *The Years*, which was published in 1937. A year later appeared *Three Guineas*, provisionally titled 'Professions for Women',

intended as a sequel to *A Room of One's Own* (1929), regarded as epochal by feminists. In this she stated that 'A woman must have money and a room of her own if she is to write fiction.' *Between the Acts*, an experimental novel, was published posthumously in 1941, after she had forced a large stone into her pocket and drowned herself in the River Ouse, near her home at Rodmell in Sussex. There are several volumes of essays, letters and diaries, indispensable to literary historians and gossips, as well as offering a remarkable entrée to the creative mind. She is, with **James Joyce** (whose novel, *Ulysses*, the Hogarth Press declined to publish), regarded as one of the great modern innovators of the novel in English.
▷ Q Bell, *Virginia Woolf* (1972)

WOOLNER, Thomas
(1826–92)

English poet and sculptor, born in Hadleigh. He studied at the Royal Academy from 1842. In 1843 his first major painting, *Eleanor sucking the Poison from Prince Edward's Wound*, attracted much attention. As a conspicuous member of the Pre-Raphaelite Brotherhood he contributed poems to *The Germ*, which with others were published in a volume as *My Beautiful Lady* (1863). From 1852 to 1854 he was in Australia. He produced statues or portrait busts of most of his famous contemporaries (his bust of **Tennyson** is in Westminster Abbey). He was Professor of Sculpture at the Academy (1877–9). His other poems include *Pygmalion* (1881).
▷ A Woolner, *A Life of Thomas Woolner* (1917)

WOOLSON, Constance Fenimore
(1840–94)

American short-story writer and novelist, grand-niece (on her mother's side) of **James Fenimore Cooper**. Woolson grew up in Cleveland, Ohio, and in her first novel, *Anne* (1862), described her education at the Cleveland Female Seminary. She moved to Europe with her sister in 1879 and spent much of her time in Italy, where she met and was praised by **Henry James**. Her best-known book is her last, *Horace Chase* (1894), which tells the story of a wife's relationship with her vulgar Southern husband. Woolson died in Venice in the year of this book's publication, apparently by suicide.
▷ C B Torsney, *Constance Fenimore Woolson: The grief of artistry* (1989)

WORDSWORTH, Dorothy
(1771–1855)

English writer, only sister of **William Wordsworth**, born in Cockermouth, Cumberland.

She was his constant companion through life, both before and after his marriage, and on tours to Scotland, the Isle of Man and abroad, the records of which are to be found in her *Journals*. The *Journals* show that Dorothy's keen observation and sensibility provided a good deal of poetic imagery for both her brother and his friend **Coleridge**—more than that, they regarded her as the embodiment of that joy in Nature which it was their object to depict. In 1829 she suffered a breakdown from which she never fully recovered. Her *Recollections of a Tour made in Scotland AD 1803* (1874) is a classic.
▷ E de Selincourt, *Dorothy Wordsworth* (1933)

WORDSWORTH, William
(1770–1850)

English poet, born in Cockermouth, the son of an attorney. Orphaned at an early age, he was sent to Hawkshead in the Lake District for board and education and this was one of the formative periods of his life. His guardian sent him to Cambridge (1787–91), where he was exposed to agnostic and revolutionary ideas. A walking tour through France and Switzerland in 1790 showed him France under the influence of the earlier stage of the revolution before disillusionment had set in. Two immature poems belong to this period— *An Evening Walk* and *Descriptive Sketches*, both published in 1793. Leaving Cambridge without a profession, he stayed for a little over a year at Blois, and there he had an affair with Annette Vallon, the result of which was an illegitimate daughter, Ann Caroline. The incident is reflected in *Vaudracour and Julia*. The declaration of war with France (January 1793) drove the poet back to England, but the depressing poem *Guilt and Sorrow*, which dates from this period, shows that he was not yet cured of his passion for social justice. For a time he fell under the spell of **William Godwin**'s philosophic anarchism, but the unreadable *Borderers* shows that by 1795 he was turning his back both on the revolution and on Godwinism. With the help of his sister **Dorothy Wordsworth**, with whom he set up house at Racedown in Dorset, and of **Coleridge**, who had renounced his revolutionary ardour somewhat earlier, he discovered his true vocation, that of the poet exploring the lives of humble folk living in contact with Divine nature and untouched by the rebellious spirit of the times. When the Wordsworths settled at Alfoxden in Somerset with Coleridge three miles away at Nether Stowey (1797), there began a close association which resulted in *Lyrical Ballads* (1798), the first manifesto of the new poetry, which opened with Coleridge's *Ancient Mariner* and concluded with Wordsworth's *Tintern Abbey*.

The removal of the Wordsworths to Grasmere after a visit to Germany with Coleridge, and the marriage of the poet to Mary Hutchinson (1802), closes this first stormy period, with Wordsworth set on his proper task and modestly provided for by a legacy of £900. Now followed a long spell of routine work and relative happiness broken only by family misfortunes—the death of his sailor brother John (1805), which may have inspired the *Ode to Duty*, and Dorothy's mental breakdown. Meanwhile Napoleon's ambitions had completely discouraged the poet from revolutionary sympathies, as the patriotic sonnets sent to the *Morning Post* at about the time of the Peace of Amiens (1802–3) and after show. Apart from the sonnets, this was his most inspired period. The additions to the third edition of *Lyrical Ballads* (1801) contained the grave pastoral *Michael*, *Ruth* and four of the exquisite *Lucy* poems. The first of his tours in Scotland (1803), of which Dorothy wrote the perfect tour journal, yielded some fine poems, including *The Solitary Reaper*. The great poem he was now contemplating—*The Recluse*—was never finished, but *The Prelude*, the record of the poet's mind, was read to Coleridge in 1805. It remained unpublished till after his death, when it appeared with all the tamperings of a lifetime but substantially in its form of 1805, which fortunately has survived. Two volumes of poems appeared in 1807, the product of five years of intense activity. The ode *Intimations of Immortality* is only the loftiest of a number of masterpieces, including the patriotic sonnets, the *Affliction of Margaret*, the *Memorials of a Tour in Scotland*, the *Ode to Duty*, and many others. He had now reached the peak of his poetic form and the remainder of his work, including *The Excursion* (1814, which incorporated material from 'The Recluse'), the *Ecclesiastical Sonnets* and the *Memorials* of his various tours, do not fully reflect his genius. He succeeded **Robert Southey** as poet laureate in 1843.

>M Moorman, *The Life of William Wordsworth* (1957–65)

NOUK, Herman
(1915–)

American novelist, born in New York City, the son of Jewish immigrants. He attended Columbia University, wrote radio scripts and served in the US navy in the South Pacific in World War II, the experience of which he drew on for his classic war novel, *The Caine Mutiny* (1951). It won the Pulitzer Prize and became a successful play and film. Later books—*Marjorie Morningstar* (1955) and *Youngblood Hawke* (1962)—sold well but did not critically eclipse his earlier success. Other books include *The Winds of War* (1971) and

War and Remembrance (1975), which became popular television serials.

WRAXALL, Sir Nathanael William
(1751–1831)

English writer of memoirs, born in Bristol. He was in the East India Company's service, travelled over Europe (1772–9), and had a confidential mission from Queen Caroline-Matilda of Denmark to her brother George III. He published his *Cursory Remarks made in a Tour* in 1775, his *Memoirs of the Valois Kings* in 1777, entered parliament in 1780 as a follower of Lord North, but went over to Pitt. His next books were the *History of France from Henry III to Louis XIV* (1795); *Memoirs of the Courts of Berlin, Dresden, Warsaw, and Vienna* (1799); and the famous *Historical Memoirs of my own Time, 1772–84* (1815). For a libel on Count Woronzov, Russian envoy to England, he was fined £500 and sentenced to six months' imprisonment. Violent attacks on his veracity were made by the reviews, but Wraxall's *Answers* were accounted on the whole satisfactory. A continuation of *Memoirs* (1784–90) was published in 1836.

WREN, P(ercival) C(hristopher)
(1885–1941)

English novelist, born in Devon. He was successively a teacher, journalist, explorer and soldier before eventually finding fame as a writer with *Beau Geste* (1924). This novel of the French Foreign Legion has often been imitated, to the extent that the book itself now appears far more self-parodic in its repressed stoicism than it did when originally published. The book spawned a thousand sequels, among them one by Wren himself, *Beau Ideal* (1928). Among his many other novels, all of a similar stamp—adventurous subject matter, less-than-exciting prose style —are *Valiant Dust* (1932) and *The Uniform of Glory* (1941). None was able to emulate the success of *Beau Geste*.

WRIGHT, David McKee
(1869–1928)

Irish-born Australian–New Zealand poet, born in Ballynaskeagh, County Down, who migrated to New Zealand in 1887. He was a protestant minister. His ballads of bush life look to his near-contemporary **Henry Lawson**, though his more lyrical verse echoes **Henry Kendall**, and he idealizes the open-air life of itinerant workers in a manner which anticipates **W H Davies**. His first verses were published in New Zealand as *Aorangi* (1896), followed by his best-known collection, *Station Ballads* (1897). Some of these were reissued, with a memoir, by **John A Lee** as

The Station Ballads and Other Verses (1945). In 1910 Wright went to Sydney, where he freelanced on the *Bulletin*, using such pen-names as Mary McCommonwealth and Pat O'Maori, and for some years edited its celebrated literary section, the 'Red Page'. His most ambitious collection of verse was *An Irish Heart* (1918). He won the **Rupert Brooke** Memorial Prize for his poem 'Gallipoli' (1920), and in 1925 edited the *Poetical Works of Henry Lawson*. After a long relationship he married the poet **Zora Cross**.

▷ *The Station Ballads and Other Verses* (1945, with a memoir by J A Lee)

WRIGHT, Frances, or **Fanny**, also known as **Frances Darusmont**
(1795–1852)

Scottish-born American reformer and abolitionist, born in Dundee, the heiress to a large fortune. She emigrated to the USA in 1818 and the following year produced her play *Altorf*, dealing with the Swiss struggle for independence. She toured widely, publishing *Views of Society and Manners in America* in 1821, and, in 1822, a historical novel, *A Few Days in Athens*. In the company of the reformer Marie Joseph Lafayette, she founded a short-lived community for freed slaves at Nashoba in western Tenessee. Settling in New York in 1829, she published with Robert Dale Owen a socialist journal, *Free Enquirer*. One of the early suffragettes, whose courage and perseverance were a significant influence in the development of the women's movement, she campaigned vigorously against religion and for the emancipation of women. In 1838 she contracted an unhappy marriage with a Frenchman, William Philquepal d' Arusmont. They had one daughter and some time later divorced. After her marriage, the issues she championed grew increasingly controversial, such as birth control and the equal division of wealth.

WRIGHT, Harold Bell
(1872–1944)

American novelist, born on a farm in New York state and educated at Hiram College (1894–6). His novels, which he began to write in earnest after moving to the Ozark mountains for his health, were extraordinarily successful, although slammed by critics for their overly wholesome moral tone. Wright was, for 10 years, a pastor in the Church of Disciples, and the chief criticism of his books is that they are vehicles for preaching to a lay audience. *The Winning of Barbara Worth* (1911) eventually notched up sales of one and a half million dollars.

WRIGHT, James Arlington
(1927–80)

American poet, born in St Martin's Ferry, Ohio, and educated at Kenyon College and Washington University. He became a teacher, lecturing at Hunter College, New York City, from 1966 until his death. His first collection, *The Green Wall*, appeared in 1957, and was followed by eight more, including *The Branch Will Not Break* (1963), *Shall We Gather at the River?* (1968), and *To A Blossoming Pear Tree* (1977). His *Collected Poems* appeared in 1971 and won a Pulitzer Prize. Wright's subjects range from politics and social issues to the natural world, and while his writing is both direct and clear, his approach is always that of a compassionate humanitarian.

WRIGHT, Judith
(1915–)

Australian poet, born in Armidale, New South Wales. Her upbringing was on the family sheep farm, Wallamumbi, in pastoral New South Wales. She was educated at Sydney University and travelled in Britain and Europe before returning to Sydney (1938–9) to concentrate on her writing. The war disrupted her plans and lack of work led her back to her rural roots in the Queensland mountains, the source of her inspiration. *The Moving Image* (1946) was her first collection, since when she has been an industrious poet, critic, anthologist, editor and short-story writer. Her main volumes of poetry are *Woman to Man* (1949), *The Gateway* (1953), *The Two Fires* (1955), *Birds* (1962), *City Sunrise* (1964), *The Other Half* (1966), *Alive* (1973) and *Fourth Quarter and Other Poems* (1976). Her *Collected Poems 1942–1970* and *The Double Tree: Selected Poems: 1942–1976* were published in 1971 and 1978 respectively. Her literary criticism was published in *Preoccupations in Australian Poetry* (1965). *The Cry for the Dead* (1981) is an account of the impact of European immigration on the aborigines. A collection of essays on aboriginal culture, *Born of the Conquerors*, was published in 1991. She edited the Oxford anthology *A Book of Australian Verse* in 1956, and has written on **Charles Harpur** and **Henry Lawson**. In *The Generations of Men* (1959) and *The Cry for the Dead* (1981) she recreates from family documents the life of her pioneering pastoralist forebears, and in doing so demonstrates her own abiding affection for the Australian landscape. In 1993 she became the first Australian to receive the Queen's Medal for Poetry, awarded on the recommendation of the Poet Laureate.

▷ A K Thompson, *Critical Essays on Judith Wright* (1968)

WRIGHT, Mehetabel (Hetty), née Wesley
(1697–1750)

English poet, born in Epworth, elder sister of
John and Charles Wesley. Well educated by
her mother, she was reading Greek at the
age of eight. In 1725, after leaving home and
returning pregnant, she was forced to marry.
Her husband ran a prosperous business as a
plumber in London but treated her unkindly,
and their children all died young. In 1744
she was converted to Methodism under her
brother John's influence. Only two poems
were printed in her life, others appeared
posthumously, mainly in Wesleyan sources;
eloquent laments for her children and indignation at the inequities of marriage are the
predominant motifs.
▷R Lonsdale (ed), *Eighteenth-Century
Women Poets* (1989)

WRIGHT, Richard Nathaniel
(1908–60)

American novelist, short-story writer and
critic, born on a plantation in Mississippi.
His father abandoned his family when he was
five, and he was placed in an orphanage. His
mother having had a stroke, he was ill-treated
by relatives, received a poor education and
was exposed to religious fanaticism. In the
Depression he left the South and became a
journalist, as well as joining the progressive
Writers' Project. *Uncle Tom's Children*, a volume of short stories, appeared in 1938; by
this time Wright had been manipulated by
the Communist Party, and he consequently
became a pessimistic humanist. A naturalist
and later in Paris an existentialist who knew
Sartre, he wrote *Native Son* (1940), a novel
about a Negro youth who murders a white
woman and is sent to the electric chair; this
became a central—albeit problematic—work
in the development of a black literary sensibility. *Native Son* was followed by *Black Boy*
(1945), a harrowing autobiographical novel,
and the novel *The Outsider* (1953).
▷A Gayle Jr, *Richard Wright: Ordeal of a
Native Son* (1980)

WRIGHTSON, Patricia
(1921–)

Australian writer of award-winning children's fiction, born in Lismore, New South
Wales. Her first book, *The Crooked Snake*
(1955), marked the arrival of a writer sensitive
to the concerns of youth and was followed by
The Bunyip Hole (1957) with its introduction
of aboriginal lore. *I Own the Racecourse!*
(1968), an engaging study of a subnormal
boy, won the **Hans Andersen** Award. Her trilogy of adventure stories featuring an aboriginal boy, *The Ice is Coming*, *The Dark

Bright Water and *Behind the Wind*, were published as *The Book of Wirrun* in 1983.

WROTH, Lady Mary
(?1587–1651)

English poet, the most accomplished writer
of prose fiction and poetry in her day, according to the *Norton Anthology of English Literature*. A friend of **Jonson** and the niece of **Philip
Sidney** and **Mary, Countess of Pembroke**, in
1621 she published a long prose romance, *The
Countess of Montgomery's Urania* (punctuated with verse eclogues, along the lines
of Sidney's *Arcadia*), causing scandal by
allusions to naughty goings-on at the Jacobean court. The work is, however, dull. More
poetically inspired is her sonnet sequence
Pamphilia to Amphilanthus, which has a
woman speaker and in which the conventional sex roles are reversed.

WU CHENG-EN
(fl.16th century)

Chinese author of the novel *Hsi-yu chi* (1593,
Eng trans *Monkey*, 1942), based on the pilgrimage of Hsuang Tsang.
▷C T Hsia, *The Classic Chinese Novels*
(1968)

WULFSTAN
(d.1023)

Anglo-Saxon prelate and writer. He was
Bishop of London (996–1002) and Archbishop of York from 1002, and also Bishop
of Worcester (1003–16). He was the author
of homilies in the vernacular, including a celebrated address to the English, *Sermo Lupi
ad Anglos*.
▷K Jost, *Wulfstan Studien* (1950)

WURDEMANN, Audrey Mary
(1911–60)

American poet, born in Seattle, Washington.
She graduated from the University of Washington, and lived in New York, where she
married the writer Joseph Auslander (1897–
1965); they collaborated on two books,
including *The Islanders* (1951). She published
her first collection of poems, *The House of
Silk* (1936), when still in her mid-teens, and
became the youngest recipient of the Pulitzer
Prize for Poetry in 1935 for her collection
Bright Ambush (1934). Her other collections
are *The Seven Sins* (1935), *Splendour in the
Grass* (1936) and the sonnet sequence *Testament of Love* (1938).

WURLITZER, Rudolph
(?1938–)

American novelist and screenplay writer. Little is known about Wurlitzer's background and his own enigmatic comments have not been designed to help. He came to attention in 1969, with a strange, apocalyptic novel called *Nog* (published as *The Octopus* in the UK), followed by *Flats* (1970), *Quake* (1972), a **Nathanael West**-like account of a Californian earthquake, and, after a decade working exclusively in Hollywood, *Slow Fade* (1974), which may be his best book. Wurlitzer co-wrote a play, *Two-Lane Blacktop* (1971), with Will Corry. It was subsequently turned into a cult movie by Monte Hellman. His next major movie success was the more mainstream but still modestly surreal *Pat Garrett and Billy the Kid* (1973) for Sam Peckinpah; Wurlitzer also appeared in the film. More recently he wrote and directed his own *Voyager* (1991), starring Sam Shepherd, in which many of the themes of his fiction—alienation, loneliness, societal breakdown—are given a definitive statement.

WYATT, Sir Thomas
(1503–42)

Major English poet and courtier, born in Kent. Wyatt published nothing in his lifetime (nor was that unusual), but has served as an exemplar for English love poets ever since. His best work, in his lyrics and sonnets, has a unique force and economy. He was regarded as the most important of all the English poets who imitated—and then added to—Italian models. The best edition remains Kenneth Muir's (1949, rev edn 1963), and standard life is Muir's *Life and Letters* (1963).

WYCHERLEY, William
(c.1640–1716)

English dramatist, born in Clive near Shrewsbury. In early youth he was sent to France, left Queen's College, Oxford without a degree, and entered the Middle Temple. For some years he lived as a man about town and a courtier, but took early to work as a dramatist. *Love in a Wood, or St James's Park*, a brisk comedy founded on **Charles Sedley**'s *Mulberry Garden*, was acted with much applause in 1671. Buckingham gave him a commission in a regiment, and King Charles II made him a present of £500. He served for a short time in the fleet, and was present at a sea fight—probably one of the drawn battles fought between Prince Rupert and De Ruyter in 1673. *The Gentleman Dancing-master* (1672) was a clever farcical comedy of intrigue; *The Country Wife* (1675), Wycherley's coarsest but strongest play, partly founded on **Molière**'s *École des Femmes*, was followed in 1677 by *The Plain Dealer*, founded partly on Molière's *Misanthrope*. A little after 1679 Wycherley married the young widowed Countess of Drogheda, with whom he lived unhappily. At her death a few years later she left him all her fortune, a bequest which involved him in a lawsuit whereby he was reduced to poverty and cast into the Fleet prison for some years. At last James II, having seen a representation of *The Plain Dealer*, paid his debts and gave him a pension of £200 a year. At 64 Wycherley made the acquaintance of **Pope**, then a youth of 16, to whom he entrusted the revision of a number of his verses, the result being a quarrel. Wycherley's money troubles continued to the end of his days. At the age of 75 he married a young woman in order to balk the hopes of his nephew; and he died 11 days after his marriage; according to Pope, in the Roman Catholic faith. In literary brilliance **William Congreve** infinitely outshines him, but Wycherley is a far more dexterous playwright.
▷ R A Zimbando, *Wycherley's Drama* (1965)

WYLIE, Elinor Hoyt
(1885–1928)

American author, born in Somerville, New Jersey. Her first volume of poetry, *Nets to Catch the Wind*, which won the Julia Elsworth Ford Prize in 1921, was followed by several more collections and by four highly individual novels, *Jennifer Lorn* (1923), *The Venetian Glass Nephew* (1925), *The Orphan Angel* (1927) and *Mr Hodge and Mr Hazard* (1928). The fiction is as fantastic and artificial as the poetry is terse, direct and positive.
▷ T A Gray, *Elinor Wylie* (1969)

WYLIE, Philip Gordon
(1902–71)

American fiction writer and essayist. Born in Beverly, Massachusetts, he co-wrote two apocalyptic science-fiction novels, *When Worlds Collide* (1934) and *After Worlds Collide* (1934), before turning his attention to more worldly matters. In *Generation of Vipers* (1942) he invented the term 'momism' to characterize America's Oedipal fixations. *Essay on Morals* (1947) attacked the religious establishment, while *Opus 21* (1949) looked at American attitudes to sexuality. Like **Olaf Stapledon**, Wylie was more of a crusader than a natural novelist, using fictional narrative or imaginary dialogue to explore pressing social issues.

WYNDHAM, John, pseud of John Wyndham Parkes Lucas Beynon Harris
(1903–69)

English science-fiction writer, born in Knowle, Warwickshire. As a child he was fascinated by the stories of **H G Wells**, and in the late 1920s began to write science-fiction tales for popular magazines, showing a much greater regard for literary style and moral and philosophical values than was common in this field. In 1951 he published his first novel, *The Day of the Triffids*, which describes the fortunes of the blinded survivors of a thermo-nuclear explosion who are threatened by the triffids, intelligent vegetable beings hostile to man. Here, as in his later novels, he is less concerned with the inventive, imaginative aspect of the 'logical fantasies' than with what happens to man's behaviour and moral values when faced with unforeseen and uncon-trollable situations. His other novels are: *The Kraken Wakes* (in the USA, *Out of the Deeps*, 1953), *The Chrysalids* (in the USA, *Rebirth*, 1955), *The Midwych Cuckoos* (1957), *The Trouble With Lichen* (1960) and *Chocky* (1968). *Consider Her Ways* (1961) and *Seeds of Time* (1969) are collections of short stories.

WYNTOUN, Andrew of
(?1350–?1420)

Scottish chronicler. He was a canon regular of St Andrews, and in about 1395 became prior of the monastery of St Serf on Loch Leven. He wrote *The Orygynale Cronykil of Scotland*, written in rhyming couplets. Especially valuable as a specimen of old Scots, the work covers the period from the world's creation up until 1406; of its nine books, the first five give a valuable, though fragmentary, outline of the history and geography of the ancient and medieval Scot-tish world.

WYSPIANSKI, Stanislaw
(1869–1907)

Polish poet and painter, born in Cracow. A leader of the Polish Neo-Romantics, besides portraits and genre pictures he executed win-dow designs for the cathedral and the Fran-ciscan Church at Cracow. The loss of an arm obliged him to abandon art for poetry and drama and he became the father of modern Polish theatre. His plays used themes from mythology and Polish history.
▷S Kolbuszenski, *Stanislaw Wyspianski* (1962)

WYSS, Johann Rudolf
(1781–1830)

Swiss writer, born in Bern. Professor of phil-osophy at Bern from 1805, he was the author of the Swiss national anthem, 'Rufst du mein Vaterland' ('Call You My Fatherland'), and collected Swiss folk-tales. He is best known for his connection with *Der schweizerische Robinson* (4 vols, 1812–27, Eng trans *The Swiss Family Robinson*, 1814–28); he com-pleted and edited the novel originally written by his father, Johann David Wyss (1743–1818).

X

XENOPHON
(c.435–c.354 BC)

Greek historian, essayist, and military commander, the son of Gryllus, an Athenian knight, and disciple of Socrates. He was a skilled soldier and inspirational leader of his armies, and saw action in several campaigns before returning to Scillus, near Olympia, a town taken from Elis. He went there in 391 with his wife Philesia and his two sons, Gryllus and Diodorus; and here he spent the next 20 years of his life, writing his books and indulging in the pursuits of a country gentleman. But the break-up of Spartan ascendancy after the battle of Leuctra (371) drove him from his retreat, when Elis reclaimed Scyllus. The Athenians, who had now joined the Spartans against Thebes, repealed the sentence of banishment against him. But he settled and died in Corinth. His writings give us the idea of having been written with great singleness of purpose, modesty, and love of truth. They may be distributed into four groups: (1) historical—the *Hellenica* (Eng trans *History of My Times*, 1966, the history of Greece for 49 years serving as a continuation of Thucydides), *Anabasis* (Eng trans *The March Upcountry*, 1947, the story of the expedition with Cyrus) and *Encomium of Agesilaus*; (2) technical and didactic—*De Praefectura Equestri* (on horsemanship), the *Hipparchicus* ('guide for a cavalry commander') and the *Cynegeticus* ('guide to hunting'); (3) politico-philosophical—*Respublica Lacedaemoniorum* ('The Spartan Constitution'), *Cyropaedia* ('the education of Cyrus', rather a historical romance) and *The Revenues* (on Athenian finance); (4) ethico-philosophical—*Memorabilia Socratis* (sketches and dialogues illustrating the life and character of his master), *Symposium* (Eng trans 1970), *Oeconomicus* (Eng trans 1970), *Hieron* and *Apologia* (Eng trans *Socrates' Defence Before the Jury*, 1965). The *Respublica Atheniensium*, an anonymous work written about 415 BC, is now known not to be by Xenophon. Xenophon's style and language are unaffected, simple and clear, without any attempt at ornamentation.

▷ F Delebrecque, *Essai sur la vie de Xenophon* (1957)

XENOPOULOS, Gregorios
(1867–1951)

Greek novelist and dramatist, born in Zakynthos. Influenced by **Dickens** and, above all, **Zola**, he was largely responsible for the Greek novel's 'coming of age'. He began as a writer of 'genre stories', in other words, regionalistic fiction. Then he began to produce better and more fully constructed novels and plays: he was a prolific writer, and is still widely read. It has been said that he lacked genius, but, if that is true, he still did much for his literature—and he was the earliest critic to recognize the greatness of **Cavafy**.

Y

YAÑEZ, Agustín
(1904–80)

Major Mexican novelist, story writer, editor and politician, born in Guadalajara, one of the most influential literary figures in modern Mexico. His masterpiece is *Al filo del agua* (1955, Eng trans *On the Edge of the Storm*, 1963), which gives an incomparable picture of Jalisco (where he was governor), and of the background to the 1910 revolution. Many have compared his stultified town of Yahualica to the Southern towns created by **Faulkner**.

YATES, Dornford, pseud of Cecil William Mercer
(1885–1960)

English novelist, born in London. He achieved great popularity with two entertaining series of novels, one of international adventure, such as *Blind Corner* (1927) and one of primarily humorous banter, about his character Berry Pleydell and his rich, indolent circle, such as *Berry and Co* (1920). A prolific author, he was a nephew of **Anthony Hope**, whose work may well have been an influence on his.

YATES, Elizabeth
(1905–)

American author, born in Buffalo, New York State. She wrote *Wind of Spring* (1945) and other books for adults, but her moralistic tales for juveniles, such as *Rainbow Round the World* (1954), were the books which made her reputation in her day. She won the **Newbery** Medal for *Amos Fortune, Free Man* (1950).

YATES, Richard
(1926–92)

American novelist and short-story writer, born in Yonkers, New York, who will be remembered mainly for his first novel, *Revolutionary Road* (1961). The story of Frank Wheeler, a suburban salesman whose professional and emotional life is disintegrating, it is written in relentlessly hard-edged prose, and vividly reflects Yates's life-long theme of mankind's inability to live up to its own ideals.

YAVAROV, Peyo, pseud of Peyo Krachelov
(1879–1914)

Bulgarian poet. He has been called 'the first truly tormented soul in Bulgarian literature', and eventually committed suicide. His earlier poetry is *narodnik* in spirit, but he became disillusioned just after the turn of the century, and turned increasingly to Symbolist procedures. The communists favoured him, and he is still studied and valued.
▷C Manning and R Smal-Stocki, *The History of Modern Bulgarian Literature* (1960)

YEARSLEY, Ann, née Cromartie
(1753–1806)

English poet, born in Bristol to humble parents. She married a labourer in 1774 and brought up a large family in grinding poverty, working as a milkwoman and reading and writing at night. She was taken up by **Hannah More** who organized publication of her *Poems on Several Occasions* (1785) and tried to govern her life. Yearsley fiercely rejected More's patronage and made her way thereafter largely by her own efforts. In 1793 she opened a circulating library, but in her last years she retired to Melksham and became a recluse. She published four more books of verse, a historical play *Earl Goodwin*, performed at Bristol in 1791, and a novel *The Royal Captives* (1795) about the Man in the Iron Mask; but it is in her poetry that her fearless personality, imaginative energy, and radical ideas receive their fullest expression.
▷D Landry, in *Eighteenth-Century British Poets*, pt 2, ed J Sitter, *Dictionary of Literary Biography* 109 (1991)

YEATS, W(illiam) B(utler)
(1865–1939)

Irish poet, winner of the Nobel Prize for literature, born in Sandymount, a Dublin suburb. His father was the artist John Butler Yeats (1839–1922). His mother came from Sligo, a wild and naturally beautiful county where Yeats spent much time as a child. When he was nine the family moved to London, where he attended the Godolphin School, Hammersmith, but the connection with Ireland was always potent, and in 1880 they moved back there and lived in Howth near Dublin where he went to the High School. In 1884 he entered art school but his early enthusiasm for poetry surfaced the following year when his first lyrics were published in *The Dublin University Review*. Preoccupied with mysticism and the occult, with a few friends he founded the Dublin Hermetic Society, and pursued his interest in Irish mythology, the source from which so much of his poetry springs. His first volume of verse was *Mosada: A Dramatic Poem* (1886), which had previously appeared in *The Dublin University Review*. Returning to London the following year with his family he contributed to anthologies of Irish poets and edited *Fairy and Folk Tales of the Irish Peasantry* (1888) to which he was also a contributor. Gradually poems were accepted by English magazines, and two American newspapers appointed him literary correspondent. His circle of friends widened and he knew **William Morris, George Bernard Shaw, Oscar Wilde** and others. In 1889 came *The Wanderings of Oisin and Other Poems*, which was charitably reviewed and established him as a literary figure; but the more accepted he became the more homesick he felt and he returned to Ireland in 1891. A year later he published *John Sherman* and *Dhoya* (1892), two stories on Celtic themes suggested by his father. He toyed with the idea of writing a novel but his meeting with Maud Gonne, an ardent Irish nationalist who ultimately refused to marry him, led him down another road. Inspired by her he began *The Countess Kathleen* (1892), a Celtic drama rich in imagery, and founded the Irish Literary Society. In 1893 he published *The Celtic Twilight*, a collection of stories and anecdotes, whose title haunted him until his death and stalks his reputation with its connotation of romantic vagueness. His best-known drama, *The Land of Heart's Desire* (1894), is slight but potent, telling of a young woman spirited away by a fairy child. He met Olivia Shakespear and worked on *Poems* (1895), which elevated him to the ranks of the major poets. In 1896 came his fateful meeting with Lady Gregory, the mistress of an estate at Coole in Galway, where he set and composed many of his finest poems. He published a plethora of books and his life was a tangled skein of political and cultural involvement and personal upheaval. With the move in 1904 to the Abbey Theatre of the Irish Players, the Irish cultural renaissance had something tangible to show for its agitation and Yeats played an important part in propagandizing. Significant books during these years were *The Wind Among the Reeds* (1899), which concludes with 'The Fiddler of Dooney', *The Shadowy Waters* (1900) and *Cathleen ni Houlihan* (1902), a play with Maud Gonne in the title role, which it is thought may have sparked the Rising of Easter 1916. Yeats went to America in 1903

where he heard that Maud Gonne had married John MacBride, who was executed in the aftermath of the 1916 rising. Yeats remembered him and others in his famous poem, 'Easter 1916'. *The Collected Works in Prose and Verse* in eight volumes were published in 1906 and he wrote *The Player Queen* for the actress Mrs Patrick Campbell. His last attempt to write poetic drama using legends as a source appeared in *The Green Helmet and Other Poems* (1910) and in 1916 he published *Responsibilities*, aimed at philistines. It was highly effective. He was awarded a Civil List pension in 1910 on condition that he remained active in Irish political matters. He married Georgie Hyde-Lees in 1917, having had an earlier proposal turned down, when he was 52 and she 15. Together they shared an interest in psychical research which influenced later work. *A Vision* was published in 1924, and *The Wild Swans at Coole* the same year. *Michael Roberts and the Dancer* (1920) pre-empted the outbreak of the civil war a year later and it was eight years before he published his next collection of poems. But during the intervening years he was engaged in playwriting, politics (he became a member of the Irish senate in 1922), and in 1923 was awarded the Nobel Prize for literature. In 1928 he moved to Rapallo in Italy and in that year published *The Tower*, a dark vision of the future exquisitely expressed. *The Winding Stair* (1933) is more optimistic. The controversial anthology, *The Oxford Book of Modern Verse 1892–1935*, appeared in 1936. He was very much a grand literary and public figure, but his reputation was tainted by his flirtation with fascism. He moved to Cap Martin, Alpes Maritimes, in 1938, where he died. A titan of 20th-century literature, his various volumes of autobiography are collected in *Autobiographies* (1955).
▷ R Ellmann, *The Man and the Masks* (1949) and *The Identity of Yeats* (1953)

YEHOSHUA, Abraham B
(1937–)

Hebrew novelist, who was born in Haifa, began by writing short novels, but finally, with *A Late Divorce* (1982, translated in 1984), produced a full-length novel about comparatively elderly parents conducting a divorce. Many critics have felt shorter and earlier work by Yehoshua, such as the novella *The Lover* (1971, Eng trans 1977), show more subtlety and mastery. Particularly treasured is his *Early in the Summer of 1970* (1971, translated in 1977), the sad tale of a man who cannot help destroying his own son.

YERBY, Frank
(1916–)

American novelist, born in Augusta, Georgia. He studied at Fisk University, Tennessee, and the University of Chicago. His first novel, written during World War II and published in 1946, was *The Foxes of Harrow*. Set in the ante-bellum South, it was a commercial success, and established the tone for the first phase of Yerby's career. Later, he moved to France and then Spain, and turned from quasi-romantic novels of the American past to more sombre, thoughtful historical works. These include *Judas, My Brother* (1968, set at the time of Christ), and *The Dahomean* (1971), which, in its exploration of the author's African ancestry, may be regarded as a forerunner to **Alex Hayley**'s more celebrated work on a similar theme, *Roots*.

YESENIN, Sergey
(1895–1925)

Russian peasant poet, the most distinguished of the 20th century, born in Ryazan province to a peasant family. He became well known when he began to associate with the Surikov circle of peasant-proletarian poets in Moscow. The chief influence upon him was that of his friend **Nikolay Klyuyev**. Although his peasant persona was a very artificial one, Yesenin was nonetheless an inspired poet; the notion that he was one of the dozen or so greatest poets of his century has been hard to resist. But the price he paid was that of an atrocious life, which he himself ended when he hanged himself after writing a suicide note in his own blood. His original view of the Revolution was Klyuyev's: that it was a mystical cataclysm. In his amazing first collection, *Radunitsa* (1915, 'Memorial Service'), there had been nothing antipathetic to Bolshevism, but his second, *Goluben* (1918), and some subsequent ones, tried—fatally to their integrity—to come to terms with it. His greatest poetry was written after he had rejected it, and had become an alcoholic and 'hooligan' (as indeed he was), wandering about Russia and elsewhere in a haze of 'riotous living' which became legendary. He married the dancer Isadora Duncan, with whom he was unable to exchange a word, as she knew no Russian and he knew no English. But in such collections as *Moskva kabatskaya* (1924, 'Moscow Tavern') and *Rus sovetskaya* (1925, 'Soviet Russia'), Yesenin knew himself thoroughly: his disillusion, his disingenuousness in writing odes to Lenin and in posing as the peasant he no longer was. Then his poetry took on new dimensions in its expression of his regrets for the death of his hopes for himself and for Russia. The communists suppressed his work for many years after his death, but in the 1960s it was revived, with great success, and he took his rightful place as one of Russia's most profound and evocative writers.

▷F de Graff, *Sergei Esenin: A Biographical Sketch* (1966)

YEVTUSHENKO, Yevgeny Aleksandrovich
(1933–)

Russian poet, born in Zima in Siberia. He moved permanently to Moscow with his mother in 1944. His work attracted no great attention until the publication of *Trety Sneg* (1955, 'Third Snow'), *Shosse Entuziastov* (1956, 'Highway of the Enthusiasts') and *Obeshchaniye* (1957, 'The Promise') made him a spokesman for the young post-Stalin generation, and he became a well-known and controversial figure. His long poem *Stantsya Zima* ('Zima Junction'), considering issues raised by the death of Stalin, prompted criticism, as did *Babi Yar* (1962), which attacked anti-Semitism in Russia as well as Nazi Germany. In 1960 travel abroad inspired poems such as those published in *Vzmakh ruki* (1962, 'A Wave of the Hand'). He has never been afraid to express his beliefs and opinions even at the risk of official disapproval and in 1974 he publicly supported **Solzhenitsyn** on his arrest. His hatred of hypocrisy has compelled him to speak out clearly for his ideal of a new, post-Stalinist spiritual revolution. His later work includes *Love Poems* (1977), *Ivanovskiye sitsy* (1976, Eng trans *Ivan the Terrible and Ivan the Fool*, 1979) and a novel *Yagodnye mesta* (1982, Eng trans *Wild Berries*, 1984). Shostakovich set five of his poems to music, including *Babi Yar*, as his Thirteenth Symphony. In 1963 he published his *Avtobiografiya* (Eng trans *A Precocious Autobiography*, 1963).

YEZIERSKA, Anzia
(1885–1970)

American novelist and short-story writer, born in Plinsk, Russia, in a mud hut. Yezierska moved to New York at the turn of the century, went to night-school to learn English and worked in sweatshops, the inspiration for her early fiction. She won a scholarship to attend Columbia University and was encouraged by John Dewey in her ambition to become a writer. Her first book, *Hungry Hearts* (1920), a chronicle of Jewish immigrant life, earned her $10 000 in movie rights. *Salome of the Tenements* (1922), *Children of Loneliness* (1923) and *Bread Givers* (1925) maintained her success. Yezierska continued writing and publishing but became less popular from the 1930s onwards.

YONGE, Charlotte Mary
(1823–1901)

English novelist, born in Otterbourne, Hampshire. She achieved great popular success with *The Heir of Redclyffe* (1853) and its successors, publishing some 120 volumes of fiction, high church in tone. Part of the profits of her *Heir of Redclyffe* was devoted to fitting out the missionary schooner *Southern Cross* for Bishop George Selwyn; and the profits of the *Daisy Chain* (£2000) she gave to build a missionary college in New Zealand. She also published historical works, a book on *Christian Names* (1863), a *Life of Bishop Patterson* (1873), and a sketch of *Hannah More* (1888). She edited the girls' magazine *Monthly Packet* from 1851 to 1890.

YOSANO Akiko
(1878–1941)

Japanese poet, born in Sakai. Yosano chose to specialize in the verse form called *tanka*, which had been the standard form since medieval times but which, in the 19th century, had been replaced by *haiku* and *waka*, which were thought more capable of conveying emotional power. Her versions of the form, however, were like none that had gone before and her collection *Midaregami*, on its publication in 1901, caused great controversy because of its attempts to reform the tanka. Exquisitely crafted, her poems combine great emotional depth with an instant appeal which is not common in Japanese poetry. There is an English translation, *Tangled Hair: Selected Tanka from Midaregami* (1971).

YOUNG, Al(bert James)
(1939–)

American poet and novelist, born in Mississippi, at one time a member of the Stanford writing school and a Stegner Fellow in 1966. Young has spent most of his career on the West coast, starting out as a freelance musician and disc jockey. *Snakes* (1970), his first novel, told the story of a black jazz musician. He has called poetry a magic wafer you 'swallow for dear life'. His first collection was *Dancing* (1969). *The Blues Don't Change* (1982) shows the influences of jazz and **Whitman**.

YOUNG, Andrew John
(1885–1971)

Scottish poet and clergyman, born in Elgin, Moray. Educated at the Royal High School, Edinburgh, and at New College, Edinburgh, he became a United Free Church minister in Temple, Midlothian, in 1912. During World War I he was attached to the YMCA in France. After the war he left Scotland and took charge of the English Presbyterian Church at Hove in Sussex (1941–59). Later he joined the Anglican Church and became vicar of Stoneygate, Sussex (1941–59). His early verse—*Songs of Night* (1910), which was paid for by his father, *Boaz and Ruth* (1920)

and *Thirty-One Poems* (1922)—revealed an almost mystical belief in the sanctity of nature and the part it plays in Christian belief, later confirmed by *Winter Harvest* (1933), and his *Collected Poems* (1936). He also wrote an account of the poetry, folklore and natural history of the British Isles in *The Poets and the Landscape* (4 vols, 1962).

YOUNG, Douglas
(1913–73)

Scottish poet, scholar and dramatist, born in Tayport, Fife. He spent his early childhood in India, and was educated at Merchiston Castle School, Edinburgh, and St Andrews University, where he read classics, and New College, Oxford. He was a lecturer in Greek at Aberdeen until 1941. Joining the Scottish National Party, he was jailed for refusing war service except in an independent Scotland's army; his attitude split the Scottish National Party, of which he was controversially elected chairman in 1942. Following the war, he became a Labour parliamentary candidate. After teaching at University College, Dundee, and St Andrews University, he was appointed Professor of Classics at McMaster University in Canada, and Professor of Greek at the University of North Carolina in 1970. His three collections of verse were *Auntran Blads* (1943), *A Braird o'Thristles* (1947) and *Selected Poems* (1950). He is best known for *The Puddocks* (1957) and *The Burdies* (1959), translations into Lallans of **Aristophanes**'s plays.

YOUNG, Edward
(1683–1765)

English poet, born in Upham rectory near Winchester, the son of a future dean of Salisbury. Educated at Winchester and New College and Corpus Christi College, Oxford, in 1708 he received a law fellowship of All Souls, Oxford. His first poetic work was in 1712, an *Epistle* to George Granville on being created Lord Lansdowne. In 1719 he produced a tragedy, *Busiris*, at Drury Lane. His second tragedy, *The Revenge*, was produced in 1721; his third and last, *The Brothers*, in 1753. His satires, *The Love of Fame, the Universal Passion* (1725–8), brought financial reward as well as fame. For *The Instalment* (1726), a poem addressed to Sir Robert Walpole, he received a pension of £200. In 1724 Young took orders and in 1727 he was appointed a royal chaplain. In 1730 he became rector of Welwyn. The following year he married Lady Elizabeth Lee, widowed daughter of the 2nd Earl of Lichfield. *The Complaint, or Night Thoughts on Life, Death and Immortality* (1742–5), usually known as *Night Thoughts*, occasioned by her death and other sorrows, is a remarkable piece of work, and many of its lines have passed into proverbial use.

▷ H C Shelby, *The Life and Letters of Edward Young* (1912)

YOUNG, E H (Emily)
(1880–1949)

English novelist, born in Northumberland. In 1902 she married and moved to Bristol, her husband later dying in World War I. Her novels include *A Corn of Wheat* (1910), *Yonder* (1912) and *Moor Fires* (1916). Generally sensitively-told middle/lower middle-class tales, they reveal her eye for social dilemmas and embarrassments, and tend to lack full-blooded emotion or sensation. *William* (1925) concerns an ordinary father who ends up defending his married daughter for eloping with another man. *Miss Mole* (1930), about a housekeeper with an intense, unrecognized inner life who works in the home of a non-conformist minister, won the James Tait Black Memorial Prize.

YOUNG, Francis Brett
(1884–1954)

English novelist, born in Halesowen, Worcestershire. Established first as a physician, with a period as ship's doctor, he achieved celebrity as a writer with *Portrait of Clare* (1927), which won the James Tait Black Memorial Prize. From then on he wrote a succession of novels of leisurely charm, characterized by a deep love of his native country. Noteworthy titles are *My Brother Jonathan* (1928), *Far Forest* (1936), *Dr. Bradley Remembers* (1935), *A Man about the House* (1942) and *Portrait of a Village* (1951). He also wrote short stories and poetry, including *Poems 1916–1918* (1919) and *The Island* (1944), a verse history of England using historically appropriate forms.

YOURCENAR, Marguerite, pseud of Marguerite de Crayencour
(1903–87)

Belgian-born French novelist and poet, born in Brussels. Educated at home in a wealthy and cultured household, she read Greek authors at the age of eight, and her first poems were privately printed in her teens. She travelled widely, and wrote a series of distinguished novels, plays, poems and essays. Her novels, many of them historical reconstructions, include *La Nouvelle Eurydice* 1931, 'The New Eurydice'), *Le Coup de grâce* 1939, revd 1953, Eng trans 1957), *Les Mémoires d'Hadrien* (1941, Eng trans *Memoirs of Hadrian*, 1954) and *L'oeuvre au noir* (1968, Eng trans *The Abyss*, 1976). She has also written on her religious experiences

in *Préface à Gita-Govinda* (1958), an anthology of American spirituals (*Fleuve profond, sombre rivière*, 1964, 'The Deep Dark River'), a long prose poem (*Feux*, 1939, Eng trans *Fires*, 1981), and an autobiography, *Souvenirs pieux* (1977, 'Pious Memories'). She emigrated to the USA in 1939, but was later given French citizenship by presidential decree, and in 1980 became the first woman writer to be elected to the Académie française.

YOVKOV, Yordan
(1880–1937)

Bulgarian novelist, story writer and dramatist, who worked for the inter-war governments as a diplomat. He was amongst the first to depict the Bulgarian peasant in his enforced role as cannon-fodder for non-Bulgarian interests. His best stories are centred on the region adjoining Romania. He was in favour with the communists and remains one of the most studied of all Bulgarian writers. Nothing has yet been translated from a language from which little has been rendered into English (although there is more in French).

▷ C Manning and R Smal-Stocki, *The History of Modern Bulgarian Literature* (1960)

YURICK, Sol
(1925–)

American novelist, born and educated in New York City. After military service at the end of World War II, he worked as a librarian at New York University, and as a social investigator with the city welfare department, an experience deeply reflected in his sprawling synoptic novels of the metropolis. The first of these was *The Warriors* (1965), a story of gang warfare and truce that takes its form and narrative outline from **Xenophon**'s *Anabasis*—in the 1970s the novel was controversially adapted for the screen, sparking off a (carefully stage-managed) moral panic about the power of the gangs. *Fertig* (1966) is a revenge tragedy: though it initially presents itself as a more realistic portrayal of the Jewish middle-class, it also rests on a similar classical/mythological underpinning. *The Bag* (1968) reintroduced several characters from *The Warriors*, including Ismael, who works for the slum-lord Faust as a rentman and enforcer, and presents Yurick's most complete vision of the city as a network of countervailing forces and economic antagonisms. Later novels, including *An Island Death* (1975) and *Richard A* (1982), have been much less focused. Yurick's short fiction was collected as *Someone Just Like You* (1973).

▷ B Morton, *Dreadful Nights: Images of the American City* (1987)

Z

ZABOLOTSKY, Nikolay
(1903–58)

Russian poet and translator, born near Kazan. He studied to become a teacher, but soon became involved in the founding of the loosely structured avant-garde group OBERIU (acronym of the Russian for Association for Real Art), of which he, with **Daniil Kharms**, was the leading member. Their aim was to link Futurism with Acmeism—both earlier modernist movements. His collection *Stolbsty* (1929, Eng trans of selections, *Scrolls*, 1971), the most original first collection of poems published in Russia in the inter-war period, upset orthodox critics, as did the innocently ironic narrative 'Torzhestvo zemledeliya' ('The Triumph of Agriculture'), much influenced by **Khlebnikov**, published in the journal *Zvezda* (1933). For a time he worked on children's books, with, amongst others, **Shvarts**; but in 1938 he was arrested on a false charge and he was imprisoned until 1946. Released, he worked at his translation of the medieval *Lay of Igor*, but also at his final and greatest poems, in which he disciplined himself to work deliberately within strict conventions, and which released his genius to the full ('peace', he could state, 'is only an illusion of itself'). This much misunderstood poet has only recently been recognized as one of Russia's supreme talents.
▷ *Slavonic Review*, 26, 4 (1967)

ZAKUTO, Moses
(1625–97)

Italian Hebrew liturgical poet and playwright (sometimes called Hebrew's first), born in Amsterdam. He was a cabbalist who served as a rabbi at Venice and Mantua, having been dissuaded from a pilgrimage to the Holy Land. In his youth he was a fellow student of Spinoza. His plays are important in the history of early Hebrew drama. *Yesod Olam* depicts the rescue of the prophet Abraham from a furnace into which he had been thrown after destroying his father's idols; *Tofteh Aruch* is a mystery play about a journey to the next world. The latter was acted by synagogue worshippers in Ferrara not long after the author's death. Zakuto founded a mystical school.
▷ M Waxman, *A History of Jewish Literature* (1947)

ZAMFIRESCU, Duiliu
(1858–1922)

Romanian novelist, and father of the genre in his language. He began as a poet, but failed thus to fulfil himself. A lawyer, and Foreign Minister in the post-World War I government, he rejected French in favour of Russian influences. His five-novel cycle about a Romanian boyar family (1895–1916), one volume of which was translated into English as *Sasha* (1927), broke new ground in Romanian fiction because of its convincing characterization, its overall coherence and its descriptive powers.

ZAMYATIN, Yevgeny Ivanovich
(1884–1937)

Russian writer, born in Lebedyan, Tambov Province. His first published work was *Uyezdnoye* ('A Provincial Tale'), which appeared in 1913. In 1914 he wrote a novella, *Na kulichkakh* ('At the World's End'), satirizing the life of army officers in a remote garrison town, and was tried but ultimately acquitted of 'maligning the officer corps'. A naval architect by training, he spent 18 months in Glasgow and the north of England during World War I, designing and supervising the building of ice-breakers for Russia. He returned to Russia and St Petersburg in 1917 and wrote stories, plays and criticism, lectured on literature and participated in various co-operative literary projects. But while supportive of the revolution, he was also an outspoken critic and he was among the first writers to be hounded by the party *apparatchiks*. Trotsky branded him 'an internal émigré' and he was repeatedly attacked as 'a bourgeois intellectual', but he was a man of incorruptible and uncompromising courage who refused to tailor his art to political dogma. *My* (Eng trans *We*, 1924), a dystopian fantasy set in the 26th century AD and written in 1920, prophesied Stalinism and the failure of the revolution to be revolutionary. Its influence on **Aldous Huxley's** *Brave New World* (1932) is striking and it was read by **George Orwell** before he wrote *Nineteen Eighty-four* (1949). His best stories are contained in *The Dragon*, first published in English in 1966. With **Maxim Gorky's** help he was allowed to leave Russia in 1931 and he settled for exile in Paris, where he died.

▷A Shore, *The Life and Works of Yevgeny Zamyatin* (1968)

ZANGWILL, Israel
(1864–1926)

English writer, born in London. He went to school in Plymouth and Bristol, but was mainly self-taught, and graduated with honours at London University, and, after teaching, became a journalist, as editor of the comic journal *Ariel*, in which he published witty tales collected as *The Bachelors' Club* (1891) and *The Old Maids' Club* (1892). A leading Zionist, he wrote poems, plays and essays, and became widely known for his novels on Jewish themes, including *Children of the Ghetto* (1892) and *Ghetto Tragedies* (1894). Other works are *The Master* (1895), *Without Prejudice* (essays, 1896) and the plays *The Revolted Daughter* (1901), *The Melting Pot* (1908) and *We Moderns* (1925).

ZANZOTTO, Andrea
(1921–)

Italian poet, born in Pieve di Soligo in Treviso; he has lived and worked there (as a teacher) ever since. The chief influences upon him are **Montale**, **Luzi** and **Pasolini** (who praised him), and also the less well acknowledged **Quasimodo**. Not a few Italian critics think of his rather self-conscious modernism as being vital to contemporary Italian poetry. There is a good collection of translations in *Selected Poetry of Andrea Zanzotto* (1975, R Feldman and B Swann eds), in bilingual format.

ZAPOLSKA, Gabriela, pseud of Gabriela Korwin-Piotrowska
(1857–1921)

Polish playwright and novelist, who reacted against her aristocratic background and convent education by first leaving her military husband when she became pregnant by a literary man, and then pursuing a career as an actress in Paris for five years. As a writer she tended to the sensational; but she helped to shatter the Austrian ideals of propriety which had been forced upon the Polish theatre.

ZATURENSKA, Marya
(1902–82)

Russian-born American poet, born in Kiev. She moved to America at the age of eight, and was educated at the University of Wisconsin, where she met and married the poet and critic **Horace Gregory**. They wrote together the influential *A History of American Poetry, 1900–1940* (1946). She also wrote one of the best critical biographies of **Christina Rossetti** (1949). Her second collection, *Cold Morning Sky* (1938), won her a Pulitzer Prize. Her

poetry was mystical, lyrical, and often meditative, but has failed to last owing to its lack of true originality.

ZAVATTINI, Cesare
(1902–89)

Italian author and screenwriter, born in Luzzara Emilia. A student and journalist in Milan, he turned his hand to fiction with such novels as *Parliamo Tanto Di Me* (1931, 'Let's Talk a While About Me') before writing his first screenplay for *Daro Un Milione* (1935, 'I'll Give a Million'). His long association with director Vittorio De Sica began with *Teresa Venerdi* (1941). Together, they became central architects of the Italian neo-realist school of film-making that flourished in the immediate post-war period. Creating drama from the extraordinariness of ordinary lives, he advocated a form of cinema that reflected social reality through the use of non-professional actors and the eschewal of more traditional Hollywood-style techniques of cinematic narrative. Among the many moving human dramas that he wrote were such acknowledged classics as *Sciuscia* (1946, 'Shoeshine'), *Ladri Di Biciclette* (1948, 'Bicycle Thieves'), *Umberto D* (1952) and *La Ciociara* (1961, 'Two Women'). He wrote his last film for De Sica, *Una Breve Vacanza* ('A Brief Vacation'), in 1973, and made his directorial debut with the surreal *La Veritaaa* (1982, 'The Truth').

ZAYDAN, Jurji
(1861–1914)

Egyptian author of partly educative historical novels, born into a Christian family. He was a prolific writer, and all 22 of his novels were serialized in newspapers. They dealt with the Islamic rather than the strictly Egyptian past, and were served up in a popular manner, so that they appeared to have little literary merit—but they made people aware of some of their heritage. He also wrote a guide to Islamic literature.

ZECH, Paul
(1881–1946)

German poet, dramatist, story writer and critic, born in Briesen, who praised his own works under the names of Timm Borah and Paul Robert. He emigrated to Argentina in 1933 and died there. His original and rather underestimated poetry and fiction anticipated modern 'Green' concerns, and warned of the dangers of industrialization, but also celebrated machinery in a Futurist manner. His first work is clearly expressionist, but he always avoided the stridency of his colleagues, and the influence of **Rilke** is also apparent; his irregular magazine *Das neue*

Pathos was eclectic. His autobiographical novel *Ich suchte Schmied und fand Malva* (1941, 'I Sought Schmied and Found Malva'), is a document instructive about him and his times.

▷ W B Lewis, *Poetry and Exile: An Annotated Bibliography of Works and Criticism of Paul Zech* (1975)

ZELAZNY, Roger Joseph
(1937–)

American science-fiction and fantasy writer, born in Cleveland, Ohio. He graduated from Columbia University in 1962, published his first story that year, and became a full-time writer in 1969. His unorthodox approach to genre conventions quickly placed him with the experimental talents of the 'new wave', and his explorations of inner worlds were often conducted within an overtly mythological framework, even if one of his own devising. His most popular books have been the *Amber* series of fantasy novels (from 1970), but his most significant achievements have lain in the science-fiction field. They include *The Dream Master* (1966) and *Lord of Light* (1967). He has continued to write steadily in both genres; later books include several collaborations, with **Philip K Dick** and **Robert Sheckley** among others.

ZEROMSKI, Stefan
(1864–1925)

Polish novelist, born in Strawczyn. He was a tutor and a librarian, and became a respected writer. His early poems were published under the pseudonym 'Zych', to avoid political censorship. He wrote *Ludzie Bezdomni* (1900, 'The Homeless'), *Popioły* (1904, Eng trans *Ashes*, 1928), an epic of life during the Napoleonic Wars, *Wierna rzeka* (1912, Eng trans *The Faithful River*, 1943), about the 1883 national uprising, *Walka z Szatanem* (trilogy, 1916–18, 'The Fight with Satan'), and other books, pessimistic, patriotic, and lyrical in tone.

▷ J Kadziak, *Stefan Zeromski* (1964)

ZESEN, Philipp von
(1619–89)

German poet, translator (eg of **Madeleine de Scudéry**) and novelist, born in Priorau near Dessau. For a long period of his life he lived in Holland, although he ultimately returned to Germany. His convoluted but by no means entirely ridiculous efforts to purify the German language earned him the ridicule of **Rist**, who caricatured his pedantry and apparent pomposity and lack of humour. But he managed to live off money provided by noble patrons, and by undertaking delicate missions; and his lyrical poetry, though hardly warm, is not without interest. His best work is to be found in the epistolary novel, *Die adriatische Rosemund* (1645), which is original and contains many psychological insights, but which is marred (once again) by pedantry and lack of narrative interest. A great favourite with ladies, some of his coinages have remained in the German language.

▷ W Kettler, *Zesen und die barock Empfindsamkeit* (1948)

ZEYER, Julius
(1841–1901)

Czech novelist, poet and dramatist, born in Prague. His greatest achievement was in the novel, and in particular his autobiographical *Jan Maria Plojhar* (1888), an analysis of a Czech writer's temperament. Zeyer was a cosmopolitan neo-romantic, a friend to **Huysmans**, and a mystical decadent, whose visions are expressed in a language so clear that it is surprising that it has not attracted more attention from outside his country. He did lack any understanding of the solid Czech peasant tradition, but he offered quite as much as any other writer whose first language was German.

ZHANG JIE
(1937–)

Chinese short-story writer and novelist, a graduate of the People's University of Beijing and one of the most important writers to emerge from China after the death of Mao. Zhang came to writing in middle age but achieved a measure of success (and official disapprobation) almost immediately, winning literary prizes with her very first published stories. Her writing, which is often satirical in its attitudes to officialdom, marriage and the small-mindedness of ordinary people, is a potent blend of the domestic and the bizarre, which has no real equivalent in the West. She has yet to gain a significant reputation outside China. Some of her work has been translated (*Leaden Wings* and *As Long as Nothing Happens, Nothing Will* are both published in English), but the translations to date are not entirely satisfactory.

ZHUKOVSKY, Vasily
(1783–1852)

Russian poet from Mishenskoye, Tula, the illegitimate son of a squire—who 'did right' by him—and a Turkish serf-girl. He became tutor to the future Alexander II, and was in his own time most famous for his patriotic poems and lays, and for his masterful translation (1802) of the *Elegy* of **Thomas Gray**. He also translated **Homer**'s *Odyssey*. A liberal and a mystic at heart, he helped many writers through his influence at the royal court, but remained a nominal conservative. With his harmonious and perfectly executed lyrics modern Russian poetry has been said to have begun: he was intelligent, learned and generous towards other poets, although without perhaps ever reaching the heights achieved by **Pushkin**—who was influenced by him—or **Lermontov**.

ZIEGLER UND KLIPHAUSEN, Heinrich Anselm von
(1663–96)

German novelist, born in Radmeritz, now remembered solely for his immense Baroque and proto-Gothic oriental novel, *Die Asiatische Banise oder Das blutig—doch muthige Pegu* (1689). Some, such as **Gottsched**, regarded it as the greatest German novel. An energetic mixture of violent source material (amply documented), gallantry, sadism and 'superhuman consistency', it was immensely popular, and Hamann even wrote a sequel to it.

▷M Pistorius, *H.A. von Ziegler, sein Leben und seine Werke* (1928)

ZIHALY, Lajos
(1891–1974)

Hungarian novelist and dramatist, born in Nagyszalonta. Like **Márai**, he left Hungary for the USA after the communists had taken over the government. Between the wars he was one of the best-known Hungarian writers outside his own country: his intelligent narratives, written with intimate knowledge of the aristocracy, made a wide appeal to readers of many cultures. But he was a liberal who, as has been well said, mediated in the interwar period between Horthy's conservative rule and the so-called populists. Most of his books were translated: they include *A Két Fogoly* (1931, Eng trans *Two Prisoners*, 1931) and *The Angry Angel* (1953), which had no Hungarian edition. His light plays were also popular, and some were filmed.

ZIMOROWIC, Józef Bartolomiej
(1597–1677)

Polish (and Latin) Baroque poet, born in—and burgomaster of—Lvov. He wrote Latin works describing the city, but his pastoral and Baroque elegies in Polish (1663) are his main contribution. His younger brother 'Szymon' (1608–29) was also a poet, and Józef published his own work under Szymon's name, so there is a certain amount of confusion as to who wrote the amorous *Roxolanki* (1654), also remarkable; it seems likely, however, that these poems, too, were Józef's.

ZINDEL, Paul
(1936–)

American writer of children's fiction, born in New York City. Such early novels as *The Pigman* (1968) and *My Darling, My Hamburger* (1969) established him as a new kind of writer for teenagers: one who was free of the moralistic authorial overview of much traditional children's fiction, and who was able instead to empathize with the fragile feelings of his adolescent readership. Later volumes, such as *Pardon Me, You're Stepping On My Eyeball* (1976), continue the successful combination of sensitive characterization and zany wit. His penchant for obscure titles reached a peak with his play for adults, *The Effect of Gamma Rays on Man-in-the-Moon Marigolds* (1971), which was subsequently—and successfully—filmed.

ZIVERTS, Martins
(1903–)

Popular Latvian playwright who, like many of his countrymen, went into exile in Sweden. His earliest work is regarded as his best by critics; but audiences always enjoyed his plays.

ZMICHOWSKA, Narcyza
(1819–76)

Polish novelist and poet who wrote under the name 'Gabryella', born in Warsaw. She was imprisoned for three years (1849–52) for her patriotic activities. Her best work is in the erotic and psychologically penetrating novel *Poganka* (1846), and in her voluminous correspondence (1885–90).

ZOLA, Émile
(1840–1902)

French novelist, born in Paris, the son of an Italian engineer. He entered the publishing house of Hachette as a clerk, but soon became an active journalist. His work in criticism, politics and drama was almost uniformly unfortunate. His true forte for short stories showed itself in the charming *Contes à Ninon* (1864, Eng trans *Stories for Ninon*, 1895), *Nouveaux Contes à Ninon* (1874, 'New Stories for Ninon'), the collections entitled *Le Capitaine Burle* (1882) and *Naïs Micoulin* (1884), and the splendid *Attaque de Moulin* (1880, Eng trans *Attack on the Mill*, 1892). In the later years of the Empire he had formed with **Gustave Flaubert, Alphonse Daudet**, the **Goncourts**, and **Ivan Turgenev** a sort of informal society, out of which grew the 'Naturalist school'. In this direction *Thérèse Raquin* (1867, Eng trans 1887) is a very powerful picture of remorse, which he later dramatized (1873, Eng trans *Seeds*, 1966). But it was not until after the war that he began the great series of novels with a purpose called *Les Rougon-Macquart*; it comprises a score of volumes, all connected by the appearance of the same or different members of the family. The two 'mother ideas' of Zola's naturalism were heredity and a certain cerebral infirmity; and in order to apply his theory to the study of *le document humain*, he mastered the technical details of most professions, occupations and crafts, as well as the history of recent events in France. He began with a sort of general sketch called *La Fortune des Rougon* (1871, Eng trans *The Fortune of the Rougons*, 1886). *La Curée* (1872, Eng trans *The Rush for the Spoils*, 1886) and *Son Excellence Eugène Rougon* (1876, Eng trans *Clorinda; or, The Rise and Reign of His Excellency Eugène Rougon*, 1880) deal with the society of the later days of the Second Empire. *La Faute de l'Abbé Mouret* (1875, Eng trans *Abbé Mouret's Transgression*, 1886) is an attack upon celibacy, and is, like *La Conquête de Plassans* (1874, Eng trans *The Conquest of Plassans*, 1887), a vivid study of provincial life. *Le Ventre de Paris* (1873, Eng trans *La Belle Lisa; or, The Paris Market Girls*, 1882) deals with the lowest strata of the Parisian population, *L'Assommoir* (1877, Eng trans 1879) depicts drunkenness; *Pot-Bouille* (1882, Eng trans *Piping Hot!*, 1885) the lower *bourgeoisie* and their servants; *Au Bonheur des Dames* (1883, Eng trans *Shop Girls of Paris*, 1883), *Une Page d'amour* (1878, Eng trans *Hélène: A Love Episode*, 1878) and *La Joie de vivre* (1884, Eng trans *How Jolly Life Is!*, 1886) are more generally human. *Nana* (1880, Eng trans 1884) is devoted to the cult of the goddess Lubricity. *L'Oeuvre* (1886, Eng trans *The Masterpiece*, 1886) deals with art and literature, *La Terre* (1887, Eng trans *The Soil*, 1888) is an appallingly repulsive study of the French peasant, and *Germinal* (1885, Eng trans 1885) of the miner; *La Bête Humaine* (1890, Eng trans *The Human Beast*, 1891) contains minute information as to the working of railways; *Le Rêve* (1888, Eng trans *The Dream*, 1893) displays a remarkable acquaintance with the details of church ritual; *L'Argent* (1891, Eng trans *Money*, 1894) exploits financial crashes, and *La Débâcle* (1892, Eng trans *The Downfall*, 1892) recounts the great disaster of 1870. *Le Docteur Pascal* (1893, Eng trans *Doctor Pascal*, 1893) is a sort of feeble summing-up. *Lourdes* (1894, Eng trans 1894), dealing with faith-healing, is hardly a novel, any more than is *Rome* (1896, Eng trans 1896), a critical study of the Papal Curia, or *Paris* (1898, Eng trans 1898). *Fécondité* (1899, Eng trans *Fruitfulness*, 1900), *Travail* (1901, Eng trans *Work*, 1901) and *Vérité* (1903, Eng trans *Truth*, 1903) form part of 'Les Quatre Évangiles' ('The Four Gospels'). Zola espoused the

cause of Dreyfus, impeached the military authorities, and was sentenced to imprisonment (1898), escaped for a year to England, but was welcomed back as a hero. He died in Paris, accidentally suffocated by charcoal fumes.

▷F W J Hemmings, *The Life and Times of Zola* (1977)

ZOLKIEWSKI, Stanislav
(1547–1620)

Polish soldier and memoirist, born in Turynka. He commanded the Polish army in the war against Russia, and wrote a remarkably vivid account of it in *Poczatek i progres wojny moskiewskiej* (1612, Eng trans *Beginning and Progress of the Muscovy War*, 1959), of which the English version has been much praised. The author models himself on **Caesar** and presents himself in the third person.

ZORRILLA Y MORAL, José
(1817–93)

Spanish poet and dramatist, born in Valladolid. He wrote many plays based on national legends and history. His play *Don Juan Tenorio* (1844), in which Don Juan is presented as a popular hero saved from hell by the pure love of a woman, is performed annually on All Saints' Day in Spanish-speaking countries.

▷A Cortes, *José Zorrilla y Moral, su vita y sus obras* (1947)

ZOSHCHENKO, Mikhail
(1895–1958)

Soviet Russia's foremost humorous writer, born in Poltava in the Ukraine. He fought vainly against socialist-realist suppression of his unique, and exceedingly melancholy, humour, and was finally expelled (1946) from the Union of Soviet Writers when he was criticized by Stalin's 'cultural' thug, Zhdanov, although he was later, after he had published uninteresting work, partly 'rehabilitated'. He fought and was wounded in World War I, then joined the Red Army, and only began writing at the age of 25. He quickly became very popular. He was associated with the Serapion Brothers, the 'fellow-travelling' group who wished to keep literature independent. His early stories more or less openly mocked the solemn excesses of the regime, but were so good-natured that they made everyone laugh. After the crackdown on writers in 1929–30 Zoshchenko had to write ideologically correct works; but he accompanied these with equivocal stories which interested him. His most profound book, the autobiographical *Pered voskhodam solnsta* (1943, Eng trans *Before Sunrise*,

1974), was an attempt to ape Soviet 'self-criticism' and achieve an actual satirical self-analysis; but it aroused furious envy amongst his inferiors, led to his 'disgrace', and he was never able to finish it. Zoshchenko's fate is that of the humorist almost completely crushed by the forces of barbarism, and the best Western essay on him (see below) has the appropriate title 'The Tragedy of a Soviet Satirist'.

▷E J Simmons, *Through the Glass Darkly* (1953)

ZSCHOKKE, Johann Heinrich Daniel
(1771–1848)

Swiss writer, born in Magdeburg. A strolling playwright, then a student at Frankfurt, he lectured there and adapted plays, and finally opened a boarding-school at Reichenau in the Grisons. In 1799 he settled in Aarau, where he became a member of the Great Council. His books include histories of Bavaria and Switzerland, and a long series of tales, including *Der Creole* (1830, Eng trans *The Creole*, 1846), *Jonathan Frock* (1840, Eng trans 1844) and *Meister Jordan* (1845, Eng trans *Labour Stands on Golden Feet*, 1852), and others. The most popular of all was the *Stunden der Andacht* (1809–16, Eng trans *Hours of Meditation*, 1843), a Sunday periodical, expounding rationalism with eloquence and zeal. His collected writings fill 35 volumes (1851–4).

▷P Scheffel, *Heinrich Zschokke* (1949)

ZUCKMAYER, Carl
(1896–1977)

German dramatist, born in Nackenheim, Rhineland. He lived in Austria, but after its annexation in 1939 he emigrated to the USA. He lived in Switzerland from 1946. His best-known plays are *Der Hauptmann von Köpenick* (1931, The Captain of Köpenick') and *Des Teufels General* (1942–5, 'The Devil's General'), both filmed. His work also includes the plays *Das kalte Licht* (1955, 'The Cold Light') and *Die Uhr schlägt eins* (1961, 'The Clock Strikes One'), a novel and some poetry. He wrote his autobiography *Als wärs ein Stück von mir* ('As If It Was a Part of Me')in 1966.

▷P Meinherz, *Carl Zuckmayer* (1960)

ZUGSMITH, Leanne
(1903–69)

American novelist and short-story writer, born in Kentucky. Zugsmith has been called a 'proletarian' author; she rejected this description, but her six novels do reflect the predominant political issues of the Depression years. *Never Enough* (1932) took a cynical look at the dissolute lifestyle of the

1920s and the earlier *All Victories Are Alike* (1929) was about a newspaper columnist. Zugsmith herself had begun adulthood working for mass-market magazines. She married a journalist in 1940 and settled in New York. The title of one of her short-story collections, *Hard Times with Easy Payments* (1941), is further evidence of her sense of solidarity with the hard-up.

ZUKOFSKY, Louis
(1904–78)

American poet, born in New York City. Associated with the 'Objectivist' school, his poetry was first published in *An 'Objectivists' Anthology* (1932), edited by himself. *First Half of 'A'* appeared in 1940 and for the next 38 years he continued to work on it; it was finally completed in the year of his death. Labyrinthine in its explorations, its main themes are the inter-relationship of literature and music, aesthetics, history and philosophy.

▷B Ahearn, *Louis Zukofsky's 'A': an introduction* (1980)

ZUNZUNEGUI, Juan Antonio de
(1901–)

Spanish novelist and story writer. A Basque, he was one of the most widely read novelists of his generation. Essentially he was a good popular realist, who wrote highly readable stories which owe much to **Balzac**, and even more to **Peréz Galdós**; he does not spare his reader unpleasant detail, and does not mean to. He never found an English translator, and had little following amongst critics.

ZWEIG, Arnold
(1887–1968)

German novelist and critic, born in Gross-Glogau, Silesia, into a Jewish family. He began as a fine ironist, impressing with the stories in *Novellen um Claudia* (1917, Eng trans *Claudia*, 1930), which possessed unusual and sensitive insight into women. Later Zweig, who had been forced to live in Palestine during the years of the Third Reich, returned to East Germany, where he was honoured. He became a rather cruder writer, dedicated to communism and Zionism, although his work, including four novels, was never less than capable. *Das Beil von Wandsbeck* (1947, Eng trans before German publication as *The Axe of Wandsbeck*, 1946) is an outstanding novel of the Third Reich. But Zweig wrote one great novel, about which there is no dispute, and which towers over the rest of his work. *Der Sreit um den Sereanten Grischa* (1927, Eng trans *The Case of Sergeant Grischa*, 1927). This is among the best realist novels of the century. It is the

unforgettable story of a Russian sergeant who falls victim to the Prussian war machine and its power-mad bureaucracy, which murders him because it knows of his innocence.
▷G Salamon, *Arnold Zweig* (1975)

ZWEIG, Stefan
(1881–1942)

Austrian writer, born in Vienna of Jewish parentage. He studied in Austria, France and Germany, and settled in Salzburg in 1913. He was first known as poet and translator of **Ben Jonson**, then as biographer of **Honoré de Balzac**, **Dickens**, and Marie Antoinette. He

also wrote short stories such as *Kaleidoskop* (1934, Eng trans *Kaleidoscope*, 1934) and novels, including *Der Zwang* (1927, Eng trans *Passion and Pain*, 1924) and *Ungeduld des Herzens* (1939, Eng trans *Beware of Pity*, 1939). A feature of all his work is its deep psychological insight. From 1934 to 1940 he lived in London, and acquired British nationality. He later went to the USA and Brazil, where he died by his own hand. His autobiographical *Die Welt von Gestern* (Eng trans *The World of Yesterday*, 1943) was published posthumously (1943).
▷A Barrie, *Stefan Zweig* (1969); B Jarnés, *Stefan Zweig* (1942)